SECURITIES REGULATION

SELECTED STATUTES, RULES AND FORMS

2023 Edition

Selected and Edited by

THOMAS LEE HAZEN

Cary C. Boshamer Distinguished Professor of Law
The University of North Carolina at Chapel Hill

WEST ACADEMIC PUBLISHING

COPYRIGHT © 1982, 1985, 1987, 1990, 1992–1998 WEST PUBLISHING CO.

© West, a Thomson business, 1999–2008

© 2009–2013 Thomson Reuters

© 2014–2022 LEG, Inc. d/b/a West Academic

© 2023 LEG, Inc. d/b/a West Academic

    860 Blue Gentian Road, Suite 350

    Eagan, MN 55121

    1-877-888-1330

Printed in the United States of America

ISBN: 978-1-68561-440-9

PREFACE

———

This book, containing the full text of the basic federal securities laws, as well as the principal SEC rules and forms under those laws and other related laws and regulations, is designed as a supplement to the texts used in law school courses in securities regulation. However, it can also serve as a basic reference source for lawyers, securities professionals, corporate officers and others who have occasion to deal with questions of securities law.

This book contains the text of the Securities Act of 1933, the Securities Exchange Act of 1934, the Investment Company Act of 1940, and the Investment Advisers Act of 1940. It also contains the full text of most rules of general applicability and the principal forms under the 1933 and 1934 Acts and selected rules under the 1940 Acts, as well as the SEC's Rules of Practice, Rules on Informal and Other Procedures, Rules Relating to Investigations, and the attorney conduct rules.

In addition to the SEC materials, the book contains the pertinent provisions of some other statutes relevant to securities questions, including the Mail Fraud Statutes, the Foreign Corrupt Practices Act, the Racketeer Influenced and Corrupt Organizations Act (RICO), the Sarbanes-Oxley Act of 2002, and the Bankruptcy Reform Act of 1978. It also contains a comprehensive Index to facilitate its use as a research tool.

This edition incorporates all amendments through October 15, 2022. It is my intention to continue annual updates in the fall, thus making it the most up-to-date reference work for winter and spring term courses in securities regulation.

I hope you will find this volume useful, and I welcome your comments or suggestions for improvement.

THOMAS LEE HAZEN
CHAPEL HILL, N.C.

October, 2022

TABLE OF CONTENTS

SECURITIES REGULATION

SELECTED STATUTES, RULES AND FORMS

2023 Edition

I. FEDERAL SECURITIES LAWS AND REGULATIONS

A. SECURITIES ACT OF 1933, RULES, AND SELECTED FORMS

15 U.S.C.A. § 77a et seq.

TITLE I

SCHEDULE OF INFORMATION REQUIRED IN REGISTRATION STATEMENT (77aa)

TITLE I

Short Title

Sec. 1.   This Act may be cited as the "Securities Act of 1933."

Definitions

Sec. 2.   (a)   When used in this Act, unless the context otherwise requires—

(1)   The term "security" means any note, stock, treasury stock, security future, security-based swap, bond, debenture, evidence of indebtedness, certificate of interest or participation in any profit-sharing agreement, collateral-trust certificate, preorganization certificate or subscription, transferable share, investment contract, voting-trust certificate, certificate of deposit for a security, fractional undivided interest in oil, gas, or other mineral rights, any put, call, straddle, option, or privilege on any security, certificate of deposit, or group or index of securities (including any interest therein or based on the value thereof), or any put, call, straddle, option, or privilege entered into on a national securities exchange relating to foreign currency, or, in general, any interest or instrument commonly known as a "security," or any certificate of interest or participation in, temporary or interim certificate for, receipt for, guarantee of, or warrant or right to subscribe to or purchase, any of the foregoing.

(2)   The term "person" means an individual, a corporation, a partnership, an association, a joint-stock company, a trust, any unincorporated organization, or a government or political subdivision thereof. As used in this paragraph the term "trust" shall include only a trust where the interest or interests of the beneficiary or beneficiaries are evidenced by a security.

(3)   The term "sale" or "sell" shall include every contract of sale or disposition of a security or interest in a security, for value. The term "offer to sell", "offer for sale", or "offer" shall include every attempt or offer to dispose of, or solicitation of an offer to buy, a security or interest in a security, for value. The terms defined in this paragraph and the term "offer to buy" as used in subsection (c) of section 5 shall not include preliminary negotiations or agreements between an issuer (or any person directly or indirectly controlling or controlled by an issuer, or under direct or indirect common control with an issuer) and any underwriter or among underwriters who are or are to be in privity of contract with an issuer (or any person directly or indirectly controlling or controlled by an issuer, or under direct or indirect common control with an issuer). Any security given or delivered with, or as a bonus on account of, any purchase of securities or any other thing, shall be conclusively presumed to constitute a part of the subject of such purchase and to have been offered and sold for value. The issue or transfer of a right or privilege, when originally issued or transferred with a security, giving the holder of such security the right to convert such security into another security of the same issuer or of another person, or giving a right to subscribe to another security of the same issuer or of another person, which right cannot be exercised until some future date, shall not be deemed to be an offer or sale of such other security; but the issue or transfer of such other security upon the exercise of such right of conversion or subscription shall be deemed a sale of such other security. Any offer or sale of a security futures product by or on behalf of the issuer of the securities underlying the security futures product, an affiliate of the issuer, or an underwriter, shall constitute a contract for sale of, sale of, offer for sale, or offer to sell the underlying securities. Any offer or sale of a security-based swap by or on behalf of the issuer of the securities upon which such security-based swap is based or is referenced, an affiliate of the issuer, or an underwriter, shall constitute a contract for sale of, sale of, offer for sale, or offer to sell such securities. The publication or distribution by a broker or dealer of a research report about an emerging growth company that is the subject of a proposed public offering of the common equity securities of such emerging growth company pursuant to a registration statement that the issuer proposes to file, or has filed, or that is effective shall be deemed for purposes of paragraph (10) of this subsection and section 5(c) not to constitute an offer for sale or offer to sell a security, even if the broker or dealer is participating or will participate in the registered offering of the securities of the issuer. As used in this paragraph, the term "research report" means a written, electronic, or oral communication that includes information, opinions, or recommendations with respect to securities of an issuer or an

analysis of a security or an issuer, whether or not it provides information reasonably sufficient upon which to base an investment decision.

(4) The term "issuer" means every person who issues or proposes to issue any security; except that with respect to certificates of deposit, voting-trust certificates, or collateral-trust certificates, or with respect to certificates of interest or shares in an unincorporated investment trust not having a board of directors (or persons performing similar functions) or of the fixed, restricted management, or unit type, the term "issuer" means the person or persons performing the acts and assuming the duties of depositor or manager pursuant to the provisions of the trust or other agreement or instrument under which such securities are issued; except that in the case of an unincorporated association which provides by its articles for limited liability of any or all of its members, or in the case of a trust, committee, or other legal entity, the trustees or members thereof shall not be individually liable as issuers of any security issued by the association, trust, committee, or other legal entity; except that with respect to equipment-trust certificates or like securities, the term "issuer" means the person by whom the equipment or property is or is to be used; and except that with respect to fractional undivided interests in oil, gas, or other mineral rights, the term "issuer" means the owner of any such right or of any interest in such right (whether whole or fractional) who creates fractional interests therein for the purpose of public offering.

(5) The term "Commission" means the Securities and Exchange Commission.

(6) The term "Territory" means Puerto Rico, the Virgin Islands, and the insular possessions of the United States.

(7) The term "interstate commerce" means trade or commerce in securities or any transportation or communication relating thereto among the several States or between the District of Columbia or any Territory of the United States and any State or other Territory, or between any foreign country and any State, Territory, or the District of Columbia, or within the District of Columbia.

(8) The term "registration statement" means the statement provided for in section 6, and includes any amendment thereto and any report, document, or memorandum filed as part of such statement or incorporated therein by reference.

(9) The term "write" or "written" shall include printed, lithographed, or any means of graphic communication.

(10) The term "prospectus" means any prospectus, notice, circular, advertisement, letter, or communication, written or by radio or television, which offers any security for sale or confirms the sale of any security; except that (a) a communication sent or given after the effective date of the registration statement (other than a prospectus permitted under subsection (b) of section 10) shall not be deemed a prospectus if it is proved that prior to or at the same time with such communication a written prospectus meeting the requirements of subsection (a) of section 10 at the time of such communication was sent or given to the person to whom the communication was made, and (b) a notice, circular, advertisement, letter, or communication in respect of a security shall not be deemed to be a prospectus if it states from whom a written prospectus meeting the requirements of section 10 may be obtained and, in addition, does no more than identify the security, state the price thereof, state by whom orders will be executed, and contain such other information as the Commission, by rules or regulations deemed necessary or appropriate in the public interest and for the protection of investors, and subject to such terms and conditions as may be prescribed therein, may permit.

(11) The term "underwriter" means any person who has purchased from an issuer with a view to, or offers or sells for an issuer in connection with, the distribution of any security, or participates or has a direct or indirect participation in any such undertaking, or participates or has a participation in the direct or indirect underwriting of any such undertaking; but such term shall not include a person whose interest is limited to a commission from an underwriter or dealer not in excess of the usual and customary distributors' or sellers' commission. As used in this paragraph the term "issuer" shall include, in addition to an issuer, any person directly or indirectly controlling or controlled by the issuer, or any person under direct or indirect common control with the issuer.

(12) The term "dealer" means any person who engages either for all or part of his time, directly or indirectly, as agent, broker, or principal, in the business of offering, buying, selling, or otherwise dealing or trading in securities issued by another person.

(13) The term "insurance company" means a company which is organized as an insurance company, whose primary and predominant business activity is the writing of insurance or the reinsuring of risks underwritten by insurance companies, and which is subject to supervision by the insurance commissioner, or a similar official or agency of a State or territory or the District of Columbia; or any receiver or similar official or any liquidating agent for such company, in his capacity as such.

(14) The term "separate account" means an account established and maintained by an insurance company pursuant to the laws of any State or territory of the United States, the District of Columbia, or of Canada or any province thereof, under which income, gains and losses, whether or not realized, from assets allocated to such account, are, in accordance with the applicable contract, credited to or charged against such account without regard to other income, gains or losses of the insurance company.

(15) The term "accredited investor" shall mean—

(i) a bank as defined in section 3(a)(2) whether acting in its individual or fiduciary capacity; an insurance company as defined in paragraph 13 of the Act; an investment company registered under the Investment Company Act of 1940 or a business development company as defined in section 2(a)(48) of that Act; a Small Business Investment Company licensed by the Small Business Administration; or an employee benefit plan, including an individual retirement account, which is subject to the provisions of the Employee Retirement Income Security Act of 1974, if the investment decision is made by a plan fiduciary, as defined in section 3(21) of such Act, which is either a bank, insurance company, or registered investment adviser; or

(ii) any person who, on the basis of such factors as financial sophistication, net worth, knowledge, and experience in financial matters, or amount of assets under management qualifies as an accredited investor under rules and regulations which the Commission shall prescribe.

(16) The terms "security future", "narrow-based security index", and "security futures product" have the same meanings as provided in section 3(a)(55) of the Securities Exchange Act of 1934.

(17) The terms "swap" and "security-based swap" have the same meanings as in section 1a of the Commodity Exchange Act (7 U.S.C. § 1a).

(18) The terms "purchase" or "sale" of a security-based swap shall be deemed to mean the execution, termination (prior to its scheduled maturity date), assignment, exchange, or similar transfer or conveyance of, or extinguishing of rights or obligations under, a security-based swap, as the context may require.

(19) The term "emerging growth company" means an issuer that had total annual gross revenues of less than $1,000,000,000 (as such amount is indexed for inflation every 5 years by the Commission to reflect the change in the Consumer Price Index for All Urban Consumers published by the Bureau of Labor Statistics, setting the threshold to the nearest 1,000,000) during its most recently completed fiscal year. An issuer that is an emerging growth company as of the first day of that fiscal year shall continue to be deemed an emerging growth company until the earliest of—

(A) the last day of the fiscal year of the issuer during which it had total annual gross revenues of $1,000,000,000 (as such amount is indexed for inflation every 5 years by the Commission to reflect the change in the Consumer Price Index for All Urban Consumers published by the Bureau of Labor Statistics, setting the threshold to the nearest 1,000,000) or more;

(B) the last day of the fiscal year of the issuer following the fifth anniversary of the date of the first sale of common equity securities of the issuer pursuant to an effective registration statement under this Act;

(C) the date on which such issuer has, during the previous 3-year period, issued more than $1,000,000,000 in non-convertible debt; or

(D) the date on which such issuer is deemed to be a "large accelerated filer", as defined in Rule 12b–2, or any successor thereto.

(b) Consideration of promotion of efficiency, competition, and capital formation—Whenever pursuant to this Act the Commission is engaged in rulemaking and is required to consider or determine whether an action is necessary or appropriate in the public interest, the Commission shall also consider, in addition to the protection of investors, whether the action will promote efficiency, competition, and capital formation.

Swap Agreements

Sec. 2A. (a) [(reserved)]

(b) Security-based swap agreements.—

(1) The definition of "security" in section 2(a)(1) of this Act does not include any security-based swap agreement (as defined in section 3(a)(78) of the Securities Exchange Act of 1934).

(2) The Commission is prohibited from registering, or requiring, recommending, or suggesting, the registration under this Act of any security-based swap agreement (as defined in section 3(a)(78) of the Securities Exchange Act of 1934). If the Commission becomes aware that a registrant has filed a registration statement with respect to such a swap agreement, the Commission shall promptly so notify the registrant. Any such registration statement with respect to such a swap agreement shall be void and of no force or effect.

(3) The Commission is prohibited from—

(A) promulgating, interpreting, or enforcing rules; or

(B) issuing orders of general applicability;

under this Act in a manner that imposes or specifies reporting or recordkeeping requirements, procedures, or standards as prophylactic measures against fraud, manipulation, or insider trading with respect to any security-based swap agreement (as defined in section 3(a)(78) of the Securities Exchange Act of 1934).

(4) References in this Act to the "purchase" or "sale" of a security-based swap agreement shall be deemed to mean the execution, termination (prior to its scheduled maturity date), assignment, exchange, or similar transfer or conveyance of, or extinguishing of rights or obligations under, a security-based swap agreement (as defined in section 3(a)(78) of the Securities Exchange Act of 1934), as the context may require.

Exempted Securities

Sec. 3. (a) Except as hereinafter expressly provided, the provisions of this Act shall not apply to any of the following classes of securities:

(1) [Reserved].

(2) Any security issued or guaranteed by the United States or any territory thereof, or by the District of Columbia, or by any State of the United States, or by any political subdivision of a State or Territory, or by any public instrumentality of one or more States or Territories, or by any person controlled or supervised by and acting as an instrumentality of the Government of the United States pursuant to authority granted by the Congress of the United States; or any certificate of deposit for any of the foregoing; or any security issued or guaranteed by any bank; or any security issued by or representing an interest in or a direct obligation of a Federal Reserve bank; or any interest or participation in any common trust fund or similar fund that is excluded from the definition of the term "investment company" under Section 3(c)(3) of the Investment Company Act of 1940; or any security which is an industrial development bond (as defined in section 103(c)(2) of the Internal Revenue Code of 1954) the interest on which is excludable from gross income under section 103(a)(1) of such Code if, by reason of the application of paragraph (4) or (6) of section 103(c) of such Code (determined as if paragraphs (4)(A), (5), and (7) were not included in such section 103(c)), paragraph (1) of such section 103(c) does not apply to such security; or any interest or participation in a single trust fund, or in a collective trust fund maintained by a bank, or any security arising out of a contract issued by an insurance company, which interest, participation, or security is issued in connection with (A) a stock

bonus, pension, or profit-sharing plan which meets the requirements for qualification under section 401 of the Internal Revenue Code of 1954, (B) an annuity plan which meets the requirements for the deduction of the employer's contributions under section 404(a)(2) of such Code, (C) a governmental plan as defined in section 414(d) of such Code which has been established by an employer for the exclusive benefit of its employees or their beneficiaries for the purpose of distributing to such employees or their beneficiaries the corpus and income of the funds accumulated under such plan, if under such plan it is impossible, prior to the satisfaction of all liabilities with respect to such employees and their beneficiaries, for any part of the corpus or income to be used for, or diverted to, purposes other than the exclusive benefit of such employees or their beneficiaries, or (D) a church plan, company, or account that is excluded from the definition of an investment company under section 3(c)(14) of the Investment Company Act of 1940, other than any plan described in clause (A), (B), (C), or (D) of this paragraph (i) the contributions under which are held in a single trust fund or in a separate account maintained by an insurance company for a single employer and under which an amount in excess of the employer's contribution is allocated to the purchase of securities (other than interests or participations in the trust or separate account itself) issued by the employer or any company directly or indirectly controlling, controlled by, or under common control with the employer, (ii) which covers employees some or all of whom are employees within the meaning of section 401(c)(1) of such Code (other than a person participating in a church plan who is described in section 414(e)(3)(B) of the Internal Revenue Code of 1986), or (iii) which is a plan funded by an annuity contract described in section 403(b) of such Code (other than a retirement income account described in section 403(b)(9) of the Internal Revenue Code of 1986, to the extent that the interest or participation in such single trust fund or collective trust fund is issued to a church, a convention or association of churches, or an organization described in section 414(e)(3)(A) of such Code establishing or maintaining the retirement income account or to a trust established by any such entity in connection with the retirement income account). The Commission, by rules and regulations or order, shall exempt from the provisions of section 5 of this title any interest or participation issued in connection with a stock bonus, pension, profit-sharing, or annuity plan which covers employees some or all of whom are employees within the meaning of section 401(c)(1) of the Internal Revenue Code of 1954, if and to the extent that the Commission determines this to be necessary or appropriate in the public interest and consistent with the protection of investors and the purposes fairly intended by the policy and provisions of this Act. For the purposes of this paragraph, a security issued or guaranteed by a bank shall not include any interest or participation in any collective trust fund maintained by a bank; and the term "bank" means any national bank, or any banking institution organized under the laws of any State, territory, or the District of Columbia, the business of which is substantially confined to banking and is supervised by the State or territorial banking commission or similar official; except that in the case of a common trust fund or similar fund, or a collective trust fund, the term "bank" has the same meaning as in the Investment Company Act of 1940;

(3)   Any note, draft, bill of exchange, or banker's acceptance which arises out of a current transaction or the proceeds of which have been or are to be used for current transactions, and which has a maturity at the time of issuance of not exceeding nine months, exclusive of days of grace, or any renewal thereof the maturity of which is likewise limited;

(4)   Any security issued by a person organized and operated exclusively for religious, educational, benevolent, fraternal, charitable, or reformatory purposes and not for pecuniary profit, and no part of the net earnings of which inures to the benefit of any person, private stockholder, or individual, or any security of a fund that is excluded from the definition of an investment company under section 3(c)(10)(B) of the Investment Company Act of 1940;

(5)   Any security issued (A) by a savings and loan association, building and loan association, cooperative bank, homestead association, or similar institution, which is supervised and examined by State or Federal authority having supervision over any such institution; or (B) by (i) a farmer's cooperative organization exempt from tax under section 521 of the Internal Revenue Code of 1954, (ii) a corporation described in section 501(c)(16) of such Code and exempt from tax under section 501(a) of such Code, or (iii) a corporation described in section 501(c)(2) of such Code which is exempt from tax under section 501(a) of such Code and is organized for the exclusive purpose of holding title to property, collecting income therefrom, and turning over the entire amount thereof, less expenses, to an organization or corporation described in clause (i) or (ii);

(6)   Any interest in a railroad equipment trust. For purposes of this paragraph "interest in a railroad equipment trust" means any interest in an equipment trust, lease, conditional sales contract or other similar arrangement entered into, issued, assumed, guaranteed by, or for the benefit of, a common carrier to finance the acquisition of rolling stock, including motive power;

(7)   Certificates issued by a receiver or by a trustee or debtor in possession in a case under Title 11 of the United States Code, with the approval of the court;

(8)   Any insurance or endowment policy or annuity contract or optional annuity contract, issued by a corporation subject to the supervision of the insurance commissioner, bank commissioner, or any agency or officer performing like functions, of any State or Territory of the United States or the District of Columbia;

(9)   Except with respect to a security exchanged in a case under Title 11 of the United States Code, any security exchanged by the issuer with its existing security holders exclusively where no commission or other remuneration is paid or given directly or indirectly for soliciting such exchange;

(10)   Except with respect to a security exchanged in a case under Title 11 of the United States Code, any security which is issued in exchange for one or more bona fide outstanding securities, claims or property interests, or partly in such exchange and partly for cash, where the terms and conditions of such issuance and exchange are approved, after a hearing upon the fairness of such terms and conditions at which all persons to whom it is proposed to issue securities in such exchange shall have the right to appear, by any court, or by any official or agency of the United States, or by any State or Territorial banking or insurance commission or other governmental authority expressly authorized by law to grant such approval;

(11)   Any security which is a part of an issue offered and sold only to persons resident within a single State or Territory, where the issuer of such security is a person resident and doing business within, or, if a corporation, incorporated by and doing business within, such State or Territory;

(12)   Any equity security issued in connection with the acquisition by a holding company of a bank under section 3(a) of the Bank Holding Company Act of 1956 or a savings association under section 10(e) of the Home Owners' Loan Act, if—

(A)   the acquisition occurs solely as part of a reorganization in which security holders exchange their shares of a bank or savings association for shares of a newly formed holding company with no significant assets other than securities of the bank or savings association and the existing subsidiaries of the bank or savings association;

(B)   the security holders receive, after that reorganization, substantially the same proportional share interests in the holding company as they held in the bank or savings association, except for nominal changes in shareholders' interests resulting from lawful elimination of fractional interests and the exercise of dissenting shareholders' rights under State or Federal law;

(C)   the rights and interests of security holders in the holding company are substantially the same as those in the bank or savings association prior to the transaction, other than as may be required by law; and

(D)   the holding company has substantially the same assets and liabilities, on a consolidated basis, as the bank or savings association had prior to the transaction.

For purposes of this paragraph, the term "savings association" means a savings association (as defined in section 3(b) of the Federal Deposit Insurance Act) the deposits of which are insured by the Federal Deposit Insurance Corporation.

(13)   Any security issued by or any interest or participation in any church plan, company or account that is excluded from the definition of an investment company under section 3(c)(14) of the Investment Company Act of 1940.

(14)   Any security futures product that is—

(A)   cleared by a clearing agency registered under section 17A of the Securities Exchange Act of 1934 or exempt from registration under subsection (b)(7) of such section 17A; and

(B) traded on a national securities exchange or a national securities association registered pursuant to section 15A(a) of the Securities Exchange Act of 1934.

(b) Additional exemptions.—

(1) Small issues exemptive authority.—

The Commission may from time to time by its rules and regulations, and subject to such terms and conditions as may be prescribed therein, add any class of securities to the securities exempted as provided in this section, if it finds that the enforcement of this Act with respect to such securities is not necessary in the public interest and for the protection of investors by reason of the small amount involved or the limited character of the public offering; but no issue of securities shall be exempted under this subsection where the aggregate amount at which such issue is offered to the public exceeds $5,000,000.

(2) Additional issues.—The Commission shall by rule or regulation add a class of securities to the securities exempted pursuant to this section in accordance with the following terms and conditions:

(A) The aggregate offering amount of all securities offered and sold within the prior 12-month period in reliance on the exemption added in accordance with this paragraph shall not exceed $50,000,000.

(B) The securities may be offered and sold publicly.

(C) The securities shall not be restricted securities within the meaning of the Federal securities laws and the regulations promulgated thereunder.

(D) The civil liability provision in section 12(a)(2) shall apply to any person offering or selling such securities.

(E) The issuer may solicit interest in the offering prior to filing any offering statement, on such terms and conditions as the Commission may prescribe in the public interest or for the protection of investors.

(F) The Commission shall require the issuer to file audited financial statements with the Commission annually.

(G) Such other terms, conditions, or requirements as the Commission may determine necessary in the public interest and for the protection of investors, which may include—

(i) a requirement that the issuer prepare and electronically file with the Commission and distribute to prospective investors an offering statement, and any related documents, in such form and with such content as prescribed by the Commission, including audited financial statements, a description of the issuer's business operations, its financial condition, its corporate governance principles, its use of investor funds, and other appropriate matters; and

(ii) disqualification provisions under which the exemption shall not be available to the issuer or its predecessors, affiliates, officers, directors, underwriters, or other related persons, which shall be substantially similar to the disqualification provisions contained in the regulations adopted in accordance with section 926 of the Dodd-Frank Wall Street Reform and Consumer Protection Act.

(3) Limitation.—Only the following types of securities may be exempted under a rule or regulation adopted pursuant to paragraph (2): equity securities, debt securities, and debt securities convertible or exchangeable to equity interests, including any guarantees of such securities.

(4) Periodic disclosures.—Upon such terms and conditions as the Commission determines necessary in the public interest and for the protection of investors, the Commission by rule or regulation may require an issuer of a class of securities exempted under paragraph (2) to make available to investors and file with the Commission periodic disclosures regarding the issuer, its business operations, its financial condition, its corporate governance principles, its use of investor funds, and other appropriate matters, and also may provide for the suspension and termination of such a requirement with respect to that issuer.

(5)   Adjustment.—Not later than 2 years after the date of enactment of the Small Company Capital Formation Act of 2011 and every 2 years thereafter, the Commission shall review the offering amount limitation described in paragraph (2)(A) and shall increase such amount as the Commission determines appropriate. If the Commission determines not to increase such amount, it shall report to the Committee on Financial Services of the House of Representatives and the Committee on Banking, Housing, and Urban Affairs of the Senate on its reasons for not increasing the amount.

(c)   The Commission may from time to time by its rules and regulations and subject to such terms and conditions as may be prescribed therein, add to the securities exempted as provided in this section any class of securities issued by a small business investment company under the Small Business Investment Act of 1958 if it finds, having regard to the purposes of that Act, that the enforcement of this Act with respect to such securities is not necessary in the public interest and for the protection of investors.

Exempted Transactions

Sec. 4.   (a)   The provisions of section 5 shall not apply to—

(1)   transactions by any person other than an issuer, underwriter, or dealer.

(2)   transactions by an issuer not involving any public offering.

(3)   transactions by a dealer (including an underwriter no longer acting as an underwriter in respect of the security involved in such transaction), except—

(A)   transactions taking place prior to the expiration of forty days after the first date upon which the security was bona fide offered to the public by the issuer or by or through an underwriter,

(B)   transactions in a security as to which a registration statement has been filed taking place prior to the expiration of forty days after the effective date of such registration statement or prior to the expiration of forty days after the first date upon which the security was bona fide offered to the public by the issuer or by or through an underwriter after such effective date, whichever is later (excluding in the computation of such forty days any time during which a stop order issued under section 8 is in effect as to the security), or such shorter period as the Commission may specify by rules and regulations or order, and

(C)   transactions as to securities constituting the whole or a part of an unsold allotment to or subscription by such dealer as a participant in the distribution of such securities by the issuer or by or through an underwriter.

With respect to transactions referred to in clause (B), if securities of the issuer have not previously been sold pursuant to an earlier effective registration statement the applicable period, instead of forty days, shall be ninety days, or such shorter period as the Commission may specify by rules and regulations or order.

(4)   brokers' transactions executed upon customers' orders on any exchange or in the over-the-counter market but not the solicitation of such orders.

(5)   transactions involving offers or sales by an issuer solely to one or more accredited investors, if the aggregate offering price of an issue of securities offered in reliance on this paragraph does not exceed the amount allowed under section 3(b) of this Act, if there is no advertising or public solicitation in connection with the transaction by the issuer or anyone acting on the issuer's behalf, and if the issuer files such notice with the Commission as the Commission shall prescribe.

(6)   transactions involving the offer or sale of securities by an issuer (including all entities controlled by or under common control with the issuer), provided that—

(A)   the aggregate amount sold to all investors by the issuer, including any amount sold in reliance on the exemption provided under this paragraph during the 12-month period preceding the date of such transaction, is not more than $1,000,000;

(B)   the aggregate amount sold to any investor by an issuer, including any amount sold in reliance on the exemption provided under this paragraph during the 12-month period preceding the date of such transaction, does not exceed—

(i) the greater of $2,000 or 5 percent of the annual income or net worth of such investor, as applicable, if either the annual income or the net worth of the investor is less than $100,000; and

(ii) 10 percent of the annual income or net worth of such investor, as applicable, not to exceed a maximum aggregate amount sold of $100,000, if either the annual income or net worth of the investor is equal to or more than $100,000;

(C) the transaction is conducted through a broker or funding portal that complies with the requirements of section 4A(a); and

(D) the issuer complies with the requirements of section 4A(b).

(7) transactions meeting the requirements of subsection (d).

(b) Offers and sales exempt under Rule 506 (as revised pursuant to section 201 of the Jumpstart Our Business Startups Act) shall not be deemed public offerings under the Federal securities laws as a result of general advertising or general solicitation.

(c) (1) With respect to securities offered and sold in compliance with Rule 506 of Regulation D under this Act, no person who meets the conditions set forth in paragraph (2) shall be subject to registration as a broker or dealer pursuant to section 15(a)(1) of this Act, solely because—

(A) that person maintains a platform or mechanism that permits the offer, sale, purchase, or negotiation of or with respect to securities, or permits general solicitations, general advertisements, or similar or related activities by issuers of such securities, whether online, in person, or through any other means;

(B) that person or any person associated with that person co-invests in such securities; or

(C) that person or any person associated with that person provides ancillary services with respect to such securities.

(2) The exemption provided in paragraph (1) shall apply to any person described in such paragraph if—

(A) such person and each person associated with that person receives no compensation in connection with the purchase or sale of such security;

(B) such person and each person associated with that person does not have possession of customer funds or securities in connection with the purchase or sale of such security; and

(C) such person is not subject to a statutory disqualification as defined in section 3(a)(39) of this Act and does not have any person associated with that person subject to such a statutory disqualification.

(3) For the purposes of this subsection, the term "ancillary services" means—

(A) the provision of due diligence services, in connection with the offer, sale, purchase, or negotiation of such security, so long as such services do not include, for separate compensation, investment advice or recommendations to issuers or investors; and

(B) the provision of standardized documents to the issuers and investors, so long as such person or entity does not negotiate the terms of the issuance for and on behalf of third parties and issuers are not required to use the standardized documents as a condition of using the service.

(d) Certain accredited investor transactions

The transactions referred to in subsection (a)(7) are transactions meeting the following requirements:

(1) Accredited investor requirement.—Each purchaser is an accredited investor, as that term is defined in section 230.501(a) of title 17, Code of Federal Regulations (or any successor regulation).

(2) Prohibition on general solicitation or advertising.—Neither the seller, nor any person acting on the seller's behalf, offers or sells securities by any form of general solicitation or general advertising.

(3) Information requirement.—In the case of a transaction involving the securities of an issuer that is neither subject to section 13 or 15(d) of the Securities Exchange Act of 1934 (15 U.S.C. 78m; 78o(d)), nor exempt from reporting pursuant to section 240.12g3–2(b) of title 17, Code of Federal Regulations, nor a foreign government (as defined in section 230.405 of title 17, Code of Federal Regulations) eligible to register securities under Schedule B, the seller and a prospective purchaser designated by the seller obtain from the issuer, upon request of the seller, and the seller in all cases makes available to a prospective purchaser, the following information (which shall be reasonably current in relation to the date of resale under this section):

(A) The exact name of the issuer and the issuer's predecessor (if any).

(B) The address of the issuer's principal executive offices.

(C) The exact title and class of the security.

(D) The par or stated value of the security.

(E) The number of shares or total amount of the securities outstanding as of the end of the issuer's most recent fiscal year.

(F) The name and address of the transfer agent, corporate secretary, or other person responsible for transferring shares and stock certificates.

(G) A statement of the nature of the business of the issuer and the products and services it offers, which shall be presumed reasonably current if the statement is as of 12 months before the transaction date.

(H) The names of the officers and directors of the issuer.

(I) The names of any persons registered as a broker, dealer, or agent that shall be paid or given, directly or indirectly, any commission or remuneration for such person's participation in the offer or sale of the securities.

(J) The issuer's most recent balance sheet and profit and loss statement and similar financial statements, which shall-

(i) be for such part of the 2 preceding fiscal years as the issuer has been in operation;

(ii) be prepared in accordance with generally accepted accounting principles or, in the case of a foreign private issuer, be prepared in accordance with generally accepted accounting principles or the International Financial Reporting Standards issued by the International Accounting Standards Board;

(iii) be presumed reasonably current if—

(I) with respect to the balance sheet, the balance sheet is as of a date less than 16 months before the transaction date; and

(II) with respect to the profit and loss statement, such statement is for the 12 months preceding the date of the issuer's balance sheet; and

(iv) if the balance sheet is not as of a date less than 6 months before the transaction date, be accompanied by additional statements of profit and loss for the period from the date of such balance sheet to a date less than 6 months before the transaction date.

(K) To the extent that the seller is a control person with respect to the issuer, a brief statement regarding the nature of the affiliation, and a statement certified by such seller that they have no reasonable grounds to believe that the issuer is in violation of the securities laws or regulations.

(4) Issuers disqualified.—The transaction is not for the sale of a security where the seller is an issuer or a subsidiary, either directly or indirectly, of the issuer.

(5) Bad actor prohibition.—Neither the seller, nor any person that has been or will be paid (directly or indirectly) remuneration or a commission for their participation in the offer or sale of the securities, including solicitation of purchasers for the seller is subject to an event that would disqualify

an issuer or other covered person under Rule 506(d)(1) of Regulation D (17 CFR 230.506(d)(1)) or is subject to a statutory disqualification described under section 78c(a)(39) of this title.

(6) Business requirement.—The issuer is engaged in business, is not in the organizational stage or in bankruptcy or receivership, and is not a blank check, blind pool, or shell company that has no specific business plan or purpose or has indicated that the issuer's primary business plan is to engage in a merger or combination of the business with, or an acquisition of, an unidentified person.

(7) Underwriter prohibition.—The transaction is not with respect to a security that constitutes the whole or part of an unsold allotment to, or a subscription or participation by, a broker or dealer as an underwriter of the security or a redistribution.

(8) Outstanding class requirement.—The transaction is with respect to a security of a class that has been authorized and outstanding for at least 90 days prior to the date of the transaction.

(e) Additional requirements

(1) In general.—With respect to an exempted transaction described under subsection (a)(7):

(A) Securities acquired in such transaction shall be deemed to have been acquired in a transaction not involving any public offering.

(B) Such transaction shall be deemed not to be a distribution for purposes of section 77b(a)(11) of this title.

(C) Securities involved in such transaction shall be deemed to be restricted securities within the meaning of Rule 144 (17 CFR 230.144).

(2) Rule of construction.—The exemption provided by subsection (a)(7) shall not be the exclusive means for establishing an exemption from the registration requirements of section 5.

Requirements With Respect to Certain Small Transactions

Sec. 4A. (a) Requirements on intermediaries.—A person acting as an intermediary in a transaction involving the offer or sale of securities for the account of others pursuant to section 4(a)(6) shall—

(1) register with the Commission as—

(A) a broker; or

(B) a funding portal (as defined in section 3(a)(80) of the Securities Exchange Act of 1934;

(2) register with any applicable self-regulatory organization (as defined in section 3(a)(26) of the Securities Exchange Act of 1934;

(3) provide such disclosures, including disclosures related to risks and other investor education materials, as the Commission shall, by rule, determine appropriate;

(4) ensure that each investor—

(A) reviews investor-education information, in accordance with standards established by the Commission, by rule;

(B) positively affirms that the investor understands that the investor is risking the loss of the entire investment, and that the investor could bear such a loss; and

(C) answers questions demonstrating—

(i) an understanding of the level of risk generally applicable to investments in startups, emerging businesses, and small issuers;

(ii) an understanding of the risk of illiquidity; and

(iii) an understanding of such other matters as the Commission determines appropriate, by rule;

(5) take such measures to reduce the risk of fraud with respect to such transactions, as established by the Commission, by rule, including obtaining a background and securities enforcement

regulatory history check on each officer, director, and person holding more than 20 percent of the outstanding equity of every issuer whose securities are offered by such person;

(6)   not later than 21 days prior to the first day on which securities are sold to any investor (or such other period as the Commission may establish), make available to the Commission and to potential investors any information provided by the issuer pursuant to subsection (b);

(7)   ensure that all offering proceeds are only provided to the issuer when the aggregate capital raised from all investors is equal to or greater than a target offering amount, and allow all investors to cancel their commitments to invest, as the Commission shall, by rule, determine appropriate;

(8)   make such efforts as the Commission determines appropriate, by rule, to ensure that no investor in a 12-month period has purchased securities offered pursuant to section 4(6) that, in the aggregate, from all issuers, exceed the investment limits set forth in section 4(a)(6)(B);

(9)   take such steps to protect the privacy of information collected from investors as the Commission shall, by rule, determine appropriate;

(10) not compensate promoters, finders, or lead generators for providing the broker or funding portal with the personal identifying information of any potential investor;

(11) prohibit its directors, officers, or partners (or any person occupying a similar status or performing a similar function) from having any financial interest in an issuer using its services; and

(12) meet such other requirements as the Commission may, by rule, prescribe, for the protection of investors and in the public interest.

(b)   Requirements for issuers.—For purposes of section 4(a)(6), an issuer who offers or sells securities shall—

(1)   file with the Commission and provide to investors and the relevant broker or funding portal, and make available to potential investors—

(A)   the name, legal status, physical address, and website address of the issuer;

(B)   the names of the directors and officers (and any persons occupying a similar status or performing a similar function), and each person holding more than 20 percent of the shares of the issuer;

(C)   a description of the business of the issuer and the anticipated business plan of the issuer;

(D)   a description of the financial condition of the issuer, including, for offerings that, together with all other offerings of the issuer under section 4(a)(6) within the preceding 12-month period, have, in the aggregate, target offering amounts of—

(i) $100,000 or less—

(I)   the income tax returns filed by the issuer for the most recently completed year (if any); and

(II) financial statements of the issuer, which shall be certified by the principal executive officer of the issuer to be true and complete in all material respects;

(ii)   more than $100,000, but not more than $500,000, financial statements reviewed by a public accountant who is independent of the issuer, using professional standards and procedures for such review or standards and procedures established by the Commission, by rule, for such purpose; and

(iii) more than $500,000 (or such other amount as the Commission may establish, by rule), audited financial statements;

(E)   a description of the stated purpose and intended use of the proceeds of the offering sought by the issuer with respect to the target offering amount;

(F)   the target offering amount, the deadline to reach the target offering amount, and regular updates regarding the progress of the issuer in meeting the target offering amount;

(G) the price to the public of the securities or the method for determining the price, provided that, prior to sale, each investor shall be provided in writing the final price and all required disclosures, with a reasonable opportunity to rescind the commitment to purchase the securities;

(H) a description of the ownership and capital structure of the issuer, including—

(i) terms of the securities of the issuer being offered and each other class of security of the issuer, including how such terms may be modified, and a summary of the differences between such securities, including how the rights of the securities being offered may be materially limited, diluted, or qualified by the rights of any other class of security of the issuer;

(ii) a description of how the exercise of the rights held by the principal shareholders of the issuer could negatively impact the purchasers of the securities being offered;

(iii) the name and ownership level of each existing shareholder who owns more than 20 percent of any class of the securities of the issuer;

(iv) how the securities being offered are being valued, and examples of methods for how such securities may be valued by the issuer in the future, including during subsequent corporate actions; and

(v) the risks to purchasers of the securities relating to minority ownership in the issuer, the risks associated with corporate actions, including additional issuances of shares, a sale of the issuer or of assets of the issuer, or transactions with related parties; and

(I) such other information as the Commission may, by rule, prescribe, for the protection of investors and in the public interest;

(2) not advertise the terms of the offering, except for notices which direct investors to the funding portal or broker;

(3) not compensate or commit to compensate, directly or indirectly, any person to promote its offerings through communication channels provided by a broker or funding portal, without taking such steps as the Commission shall, by rule, require to ensure that such person clearly discloses the receipt, past or prospective, of such compensation, upon each instance of such promotional communication;

(4) not less than annually, file with the Commission and provide to investors reports of the results of operations and financial statements of the issuer, as the Commission shall, by rule, determine appropriate, subject to such exceptions and termination dates as the Commission may establish, by rule; and

(5) comply with such other requirements as the Commission may, by rule, prescribe, for the protection of investors and in the public interest.

(c) Liability for material misstatements and omissions.—

(1) Actions authorized.—

(A) In general.—Subject to paragraph (2), a person who purchases a security in a transaction exempted by the provisions of section 4(a)(6) may bring an action against an issuer described in paragraph (2), either at law or in equity in any court of competent jurisdiction, to recover the consideration paid for such security with interest thereon, less the amount of any income received thereon, upon the tender of such security, or for damages if such person no longer owns the security.

(B) Liability.—An action brought under this paragraph shall be subject to the provisions of section 12(b) and section 13, as if the liability were created under section 12(a)(2).

(2) Applicability.—An issuer shall be liable in an action under paragraph (1), if the issuer—

(A) by the use of any means or instruments of transportation or communication in interstate commerce or of the mails, by any means of any written or oral communication, in the offering or sale of a security in a transaction exempted by the provisions of section 4(a)(6), makes an untrue statement of a material fact or omits to state a material fact required to be stated or necessary in order to make the statements, in the light of the circumstances under which they were made, not misleading, provided that the purchaser did not know of such untruth or omission; and

    (B)   does not sustain the burden of proof that such issuer did not know, and in the exercise of reasonable care could not have known, of such untruth or omission.

    (3)   Definition.—As used in this subsection, the term "issuer" includes any person who is a director or partner of the issuer, and the principal executive officer or officers, principal financial officer, and controller or principal accounting officer of the issuer (and any person occupying a similar status or performing a similar function) that offers or sells a security in a transaction exempted by the provisions of section 4(a)(6), and any person who offers or sells the security in such offering.

    (d)   Information available to States.—The Commission shall make, or shall cause to be made by the relevant broker or funding portal, the information described in subsection (b) and such other information as the Commission, by rule, determines appropriate, available to the securities commission (or any agency or office performing like functions) of each State and territory of the United States and the District of Columbia.

    (e)   Restrictions on sales.—Securities issued pursuant to a transaction described in section 4(a)(6)—

    (1)   may not be transferred by the purchaser of such securities during the 1-year period beginning on the date of purchase, unless such securities are transferred—

    (A)   to the issuer of the securities;

    (B)   to an accredited investor;

    (C)   as part of an offering registered with the Commission; or

    (D)   to a member of the family of the purchaser or the equivalent, or in connection with the death or divorce of the purchaser or other similar circumstance, in the discretion of the Commission; and

    (2)   shall be subject to such other limitations as the Commission shall, by rule, establish.

    (f)   Applicability.—Section 4(a)(6) shall not apply to transactions involving the offer or sale of securities by any issuer that—

    (1)   is not organized under and subject to the laws of a State or territory of the United States or the District of Columbia;

    (2)   is subject to the requirement to file reports pursuant to section 13 or section 15(d) of the Securities Exchange Act of 1934;

    (3)   is an investment company, as defined in section 3 of the Investment Company Act of 1940, or is excluded from the definition of investment company by section 3(b) or section 3(c) of that Act; or

    (4)   the Commission, by rule or regulation, determines appropriate.

    (g)   Rule of construction.—Nothing in this section or section 4(a)(6) shall be construed as preventing an issuer from raising capital through methods not described under section 4(a)(6).

    (h)   Certain calculations.—

    (1)   Dollar amounts.—Dollar amounts in section 4(a)(6) and subsection (b) of this section shall be adjusted by the Commission not less frequently than once every 5 years, by notice published in the Federal Register to reflect any change in the Consumer Price Index for All Urban Consumers published by the Bureau of Labor Statistics.

    (2)   Income and net worth.—The income and net worth of a natural person under section 4(a)(6)(B) shall be calculated in accordance with any rules of the Commission under this title regarding the calculation of the income and net worth, respectively, of an accredited investor.

Prohibitions Relating to Interstate Commerce and the Mails

Sec. 5. (a) Unless a registration statement is in effect as to a security, it shall be unlawful for any person, directly or indirectly—

(1) to make use of any means or instruments of transportation or communication in interstate commerce or of the mails to sell such security through the use or medium of any prospectus or otherwise; or

(2) to carry or cause to be carried through the mails or in interstate commerce, by any means or instruments of transportation, any such security for the purpose of sale or for delivery after sale.

(b) It shall be unlawful for any person, directly or indirectly—

(1) to make use of any means or instruments of transportation or communication in interstate commerce or of the mails to carry or transmit any prospectus relating to any security with respect to which a registration statement has been filed under this Act, unless such prospectus meets the requirements of section 10; or

(2) to carry or cause to be carried through the mails or in interstate commerce any such security for the purpose of sale or for delivery after sale, unless accompanied or preceded by a prospectus that meets the requirements of subsection (a) of section 10.

(c) It shall be unlawful for any person, directly or indirectly, to make use of any means or instruments of transportation or communication in interstate commerce or of the mails to offer to sell or offer to buy through the use or medium of any prospectus or otherwise any security, unless a registration statement has been filed as to such security, or while the registration statement is the subject of a refusal order or stop order or (prior to the effective date of the registration statement) any public proceeding or examination under section 8.

(d) Limitation.—Notwithstanding any other provision of this section, an emerging growth company or any person authorized to act on behalf of an emerging growth company may engage in oral or written communications with potential investors that are qualified institutional buyers or institutions that are accredited investors, as such terms are respectively defined in Rule 144A and Rule 501(a), or any successor thereto, to determine whether such investors might have an interest in a contemplated securities offering, either prior to or following the date of filing of a registration statement with respect to such securities with the Commission, subject to the requirement of subsection (b)(2).

(e) Notwithstanding the provisions of section 3 or 4, unless a registration statement meeting the requirements of section 10(a) is in effect as to a security-based swap, it shall be unlawful for any person, directly or indirectly, to make use of any means or instruments of transportation or communication in interstate commerce or of the mails to offer to sell, offer to buy or purchase or sell a security-based swap to any person who is not an eligible contract participant as defined in section 1a(18) of the Commodity Exchange Act (7 U.S.C. 1a(18)).

Registration of Securities and Signing of Registration Statement

Sec. 6. (a) Any security may be registered with the Commission under the terms and conditions hereinafter provided, by filing a registration statement in triplicate, at least one of which shall be signed by each issuer, its principal executive officer or officers, its principal financial officer, its comptroller or principal accounting officer, and the majority of its board of directors or persons performing similar functions (or, if there is no board of directors or persons performing similar functions, by the majority of the persons or board having the power of management of the issuer), and in case the issuer is a foreign or Territorial person by its duly authorized representative in the United States; except that when such registration statement relates to a security issued by a foreign government, or political subdivision thereof, it need be signed only by the underwriter of such security. Signatures of all such persons when written on the said registration statements shall be presumed to have been so written by authority of the person whose signature is so affixed and the burden of proof, in the event such authority shall be denied, shall be upon the party denying the same. The affixing of any signature without the authority of the purported signer shall constitute a violation of this Act. A registration statement shall be deemed effective only as to the securities specified therein as proposed to be offered.

(b) Registration Fee.—

(1)   Fee payment required.—

At the time of filing a registration statement, the applicant shall pay to the Commission a fee at a rate that shall be equal to $92 per $1,000,000 of the maximum aggregate price at which such securities are proposed to be offered, except that during fiscal year 2003 and any succeeding fiscal year such fee shall be adjusted pursuant to paragraph (2).

(2)   Annual adjustment.—

For each fiscal year, the Commission shall by order adjust the rate required by paragraph (2) for such fiscal year to a rate that, when applied to the baseline estimate of the aggregate maximum offering prices for such fiscal year, is reasonably likely to produce aggregate fee collections under this subsection that are equal to the target fee collection amount for such fiscal year.

(3)   Pro rata application.—

The rates per $1,000,000 required by this subsection shall be applied pro rata to amounts and balances of less than $1,000,000.

(4)   Review and effective date.—

Review and effective date—In exercising its authority under this subsection, the Commission shall not be required to comply with the provisions of section 553 of title 5, United States Code. An adjusted rate prescribed under paragraph (2) and published under paragraph (5) shall not be subject to judicial review. An adjusted rate prescribed under paragraph (2) shall take effect on the first day of the fiscal year to which such rate applies.

(5)   Publication.—

The Commission shall publish in the Federal Register notices of the rate applicable under this subsection . . . for each fiscal year not later than August 31 of the fiscal year preceding the fiscal year to which such rate applies, together with any estimates or projections on which such rate is based.

(6)   Definitions.—

For purposes of this subsection:

(A)   Target fee collection amount.—

The target fee collection amount for each fiscal year is determined according to the following table:

Fiscal year:	Collection amount
2002	$377,000,000
2003	$435,000,000
2004	$467,000,000
2005	$570,000,000
2006	$689,000,000
2007	$214,000,000
2008	$234,000,000
2009	$284,000,000
2010	$334,000,000
2011	$394,000,000
2012	$425,000,000
2013	$455,000,000
2014	$485,000,000

Fiscal year:	Collection amount
2015	$515,000,000
2016	$550,000,000
2017	$585,000,000
2018	$620,000,000
2019	$660,000,000
2020	$705,000,000
2021 and each fiscal year thereafter.	An amount that is equal to the target fee collection amount for the prior fiscal year, adjusted by the rate of inflation.

(B)   Baseline estimate of the aggregate maximum offering prices.—

The baseline estimate of the aggregate maximum offering prices for any fiscal year is the baseline estimate of the aggregate maximum offering price at which securities are proposed to be offered pursuant to registration statements filed with the Commission during such fiscal year as determined by the Commission, after consultation with the Congressional Budget Office and the Office of Management and Budget, using the methodology required for projections pursuant to section 907 of Title 2.

(c)   The filing with the Commission of a registration statement, or of any amendment to a registration statement, shall be deemed to have taken place upon the receipt thereof, but the filing of a registration statement shall not be deemed to have taken place unless it is accompanied by a United States postal money order or a certified bank check or cash for the amount of the fee required under subsection (b).

(d)   The information contained in or filed with any registration statement shall be made available to the public under such regulations as the Commission may prescribe, and copies thereof, photostatic or otherwise, shall be furnished to every applicant at such reasonable charge as the Commission may prescribe.

(e)   Emerging growth companies.—

(1)   In general.—Any emerging growth company, prior to its initial public offering date, may confidentially submit to the Commission a draft registration statement, for confidential nonpublic review by the staff of the Commission prior to public filing, provided that the initial confidential submission and all amendments thereto shall be publicly filed with the Commission not later than 15 days before the date on which the issuer conducts a road show, as such term is defined in Rule 433(h)(4) of title 17, Code of Federal Regulations, or any successor thereto. An issuer that was an emerging growth company at the time it submitted a confidential registration statement or, in lieu thereof, a publicly filed registration statement for review under this subsection but ceases to be an emerging growth company thereafter shall continue to be treated as an emerging market growth company for the purposes of this subsection through the earlier of the date on which the issuer consummates its initial public offering pursuant to such registrations statement or the end of the 1-year period beginning on the date the company ceases to be an emerging growth company.

(2)   Confidentiality.—Notwithstanding any other provision of this Act, the Commission shall not be compelled to disclose any information provided to or obtained by the Commission pursuant to this subsection. For purposes of section 552 of title 5, United States Code, this subsection shall be considered a statute described in subsection (b)(3)(B) of such section 552. Information described in or obtained pursuant to this subsection shall be deemed to constitute confidential information for purposes of section 24(b)(2) of the Securities Exchange Act of 1934.

Information Required in Registration Statement

Sec. 7.   (a)   Information Required in Registration Statement.—

(1)   In general.—

The registration statement, when relating to a security other than a security issued by a foreign government, or political subdivision thereof, shall contain the information, and be accompanied by the documents specified in Schedule A, and when relating to a security issued by a foreign government, or political subdivision thereof, shall contain the information, and be accompanied by the documents, specified in Schedule B; except that the Commission may by rules or regulations provide that any such information or document need not be included in respect of any class of issuers or securities if it finds that the requirement of such information or document is inapplicable to such class and that disclosure fully adequate for the protection of investors is otherwise required to be included within the registration statement. If any accountant, engineer, or appraiser, or any person whose profession gives authority to a statement made by him, is named as having prepared or certified any part of the registration statement, or is named as having prepared or certified a report or valuation for use in connection with the registration statement, the written consent of such person shall be filed with the registration statement. If any such person is named as having prepared or certified a report or valuation (other than a public official document or statement) which is used in connection with the registration statement, but is not named as having prepared or certified such report or valuation for use in connection with the registration statement, the written consent of such person shall be filed with the registration statement unless the Commission dispenses with such filing as impracticable or as involving undue hardship on the person filing the registration statement. Any such registration statement shall contain such other information, and be accompanied by such other documents, as the Commission may by rules or regulations require as being necessary or appropriate in the public interest or for the protection of investors.

(2)   Treatment of emerging growth companies.—An emerging growth company—

(A)   need not present more than 2 years of audited financial statements in order for the registration statement of such emerging growth company with respect to an initial public offering of its common equity securities to be effective, and in any other registration statement to be filed with the Commission, an emerging growth company need not present selected financial data in accordance with section 229.301 of title 17, Code of Federal Regulations, for any period prior to the earliest audited period presented in connection with its initial public offering; and

(B)   may not be required to comply with any new or revised financial accounting standard until such date that a company that is not an issuer (as defined under section 2(a) of the Sarbanes-Oxley Act of 2002 is required to comply with such new or revised accounting standard, if such standard applies to companies that are not issuers.

(b)(1)   The Commission shall prescribe special rules with respect to registration statements filed by any issuer that is a blank check company. Such rules may, as the Commission determines necessary or appropriate in the public interest or for the protection of investors—

(A)   require such issuers to provide timely disclosure, prior to or after such statement becomes effective under section 8, of (i) information regarding the company to be acquired and the specific application of the proceeds of the offering, or (ii) additional information necessary to prevent such statement from being misleading;

(B)   place limitations on the use of such proceeds and the distribution of securities by such issuer until the disclosures required under subparagraph (A) have been made; and

(C)   provide a right of rescission to shareholders of such securities.

(2)   The Commission may, as it determines consistent with the public interest and the protection of investors, by rule or order exempt any issuer or class of issuers from the rules prescribed under paragraph (1).

(3)   For purposes of paragraph (1) of this subsection, the term "blank check company" means any development stage company that is issuing a penny stock (within the meaning of section 3(a)(51) of the Securities Exchange Act of 1934) and that—

(A)   has no specific business plan or purpose; or

(B)   has indicated that its business plan is to merge with an unidentified company or companies.

(c)   Disclosure Requirements.—

(1)   In general.—The Commission shall adopt regulations under this subsection requiring each issuer of an asset-backed security to disclose, for each tranche or class of security, information regarding the assets backing that security.

(2)   Content of regulations—In adopting regulations under this subsection, the Commission shall—

(A)   set standards for the format of the data provided by issuers of an asset-backed security, which shall, to the extent feasible, facilitate comparison of such data across securities in similar types of asset classes; and

(B)   require issuers of asset-backed securities, at a minimum, to disclose asset-level or loan-level data, if such data are necessary for investors to independently perform due diligence, including—

(i)   data having unique identifiers relating to loan brokers or originators;

(ii)   the nature and extent of the compensation of the broker or originator of the assets backing the security; and

(iii)   the amount of risk retention by the originator and the securitizer of such assets.

(d)   Registration Statement for Asset-backed Securities.—Not later than 180 days after the date of enactment of this subsection, the Commission shall issue rules relating to the registration statement required to be filed by any issuer of an asset-backed security (as that term is defined in section 3(a)(77) of the Securities Exchange Act of 1934) that require any issuer of an asset-backed security—

(1)   to perform a review of the assets underlying the asset-backed security; and

(2)   to disclose the nature of the review under paragraph (1).

Taking Effect of Registration Statements and Amendments Thereto

Sec. 8.   (a)   Except as hereinafter provided, the effective date of a registration statement shall be the twentieth day after the filing thereof or such earlier date as the Commission may determine, having due regard to the adequacy of the information respecting the issuer theretofore available to the public, to the facility with which the nature of the securities to be registered, their relationship to the capital structure of the issuer and the rights of holders thereof can be understood, and to the public interest and the protection of investors. If any amendment to any such statement is filed prior to the effective date of such statement, the registration statement shall be deemed to have been filed when such amendment was filed; except that an amendment filed with the consent of the Commission, prior to the effective date of the registration statement, or filed pursuant to an order of the Commission, shall be treated as a part of the registration statement.

(b)   If it appears to the Commission that a registration statement is on its face incomplete or inaccurate in any material respect, the Commission may, after notice by personal service or the sending of confirmed telegraphic notice not later than ten days after the filing of the registration statement, and opportunity for hearing (at a time fixed by the Commission) within ten days after such notice by personal service or the sending of such telegraphic notice, issue an order prior to the effective date of registration refusing to permit such statement to become effective until it has been amended in accordance with such order. When such statement has been amended in accordance with such order the Commission shall so declare and the registration shall become effective at the time provided in subsection (a) or upon the date of such declaration, whichever date is the later.

(c)   An amendment filed after the effective date of the registration statement, if such amendment, upon its face, appears to the Commission not to be incomplete or inaccurate in any material respect, shall become effective on such date as the Commission may determine, having due regard to the public interest and the protection of investors.

(d)   If it appears to the Commission at any time that the registration statement includes any untrue statement of a material fact or omits to state any material fact required to be stated therein or necessary to make the statements therein not misleading, the Commission may, after notice by personal service or the sending of confirmed telegraphic notice, and after opportunity for hearing (at a time fixed by the Commission) within fifteen days after such notice by personal service or the sending of such telegraphic notice, issue a stop order suspending the effectiveness of the registration statement. When such statement has been amended in accordance with such stop order the Commission shall so declare and thereupon the stop order shall cease to be effective.

(e) The Commission is hereby empowered to make an examination in any case in order to determine whether a stop order should issue under subsection (d). In making such examination the Commission or any officer or officers designated by it shall have access to and may demand the production of any books and papers of, and may administer oaths and affirmations to and examine, the issuer, underwriter, or any other person, in respect of any matter relevant to the examination, and may, in its discretion, require the production of a balance sheet exhibiting the assets and liabilities of the issuer, or its income statement, or both, to be certified to by a public or certified accountant approved by the Commission. If the issuer or underwriter shall fail to cooperate, or shall obstruct or refuse to permit the making of an examination, such conduct shall be proper ground for the issuance of a stop order.

(f) Any notice required under this section shall be sent to or served on the issuer, or, in case of a foreign government or political subdivision thereof, to or on the underwriter, or, in the case of a foreign or Territorial person, to or on its duly authorized representative in the United States named in the registration statement, properly directed in each case of telegraphic notice to the address given in such statement.

Cease and Desist Proceedings

Sec. 8A. (a) Authority of the Commission.—

If the Commission finds, after notice and opportunity for hearing, that any person is violating, has violated, or is about to violate any provision of this Act, or any rule or regulation thereunder, the Commission may publish its findings and enter an order requiring such person, and any other person that is, was, or would be a cause of the violation, due to an act or omission the person knew or should have known would contribute to such violation, to cease and desist from committing or causing such violation and any future violation of the same provision, rule, or regulation. Such order may, in addition to requiring a person to cease and desist from committing or causing a violation, require such person to comply, or to take steps to effect compliance, with such provision, rule, or regulation, upon such terms and conditions and within such time as the Commission may specify in such order. Any such order may, as the Commission deems appropriate, require future compliance or steps to effect future compliance, either permanently or for such period of time as the Commission may specify, with such provision, rule, or regulation with respect to any security, any issuer, or any other person.

(b) Hearing.—

The notice instituting proceedings pursuant to subsection (a) shall fix a hearing date not earlier than 30 days nor later than 60 days after service of the notice unless an earlier or a later date is set by the Commission with the consent of any respondent so served.

(c) Temporary Order.—

(1) In general.—

Whenever the Commission determines that the alleged violation or threatened violation specified in the notice instituting proceedings pursuant to subsection (a) or the continuation thereof, is likely to result in significant dissipation or conversion of assets, significant harm to investors, or substantial harm to the public interest, including, but not limited to, losses to the Securities Investor Protection Corporation, prior to the completion of the proceedings, the Commission may enter a temporary order requiring the respondent to cease and desist from the violation or threatened violation and to take such action to prevent the violation or threatened violation and to prevent dissipation or conversion of assets, significant harm to investors, or substantial harm to the public interest as the Commission deems appropriate pending completion of such proceeding. Such an order shall be entered only after notice and opportunity for a hearing, unless the Commission determines that notice and hearing prior to entry would be impracticable or contrary to the public interest. A temporary order shall become effective upon service upon the respondent and, unless set aside, limited, or suspended by the Commission or a court of competent jurisdiction, shall remain effective and enforceable pending the completion of the proceedings.

(2)   Applicability.—

This subsection shall apply only to a respondent that acts, or, at the time of the alleged misconduct acted, as a broker, dealer, investment adviser, investment company, municipal securities dealer, government securities broker, government securities dealer, or transfer agent, or is, or was at the time of the alleged misconduct, an associated person of, or a person seeking to become associated with, any of the foregoing.

(d)   Review of Temporary Orders.—

(1)   Commission review.—

At any time after the respondent has been served with a temporary cease-and-desist order pursuant to subsection (c), the respondent may apply to the Commission to have the order set aside, limited, or suspended. If the respondent has been served with a temporary cease-and-desist order entered without a prior Commission hearing, the respondent may, within 10 days after the date on which the order was served, request a hearing on such application and the Commission shall hold a hearing and render a decision on such application at the earliest possible time.

(2)   Judicial Review. Within—(A) 10 days after the date the respondent was served with a temporary cease-and-desist order entered with a prior Commission hearing, or

(B)   10 days after the Commission renders a decision on an application and hearing under paragraph (1), with respect to any temporary cease-and-desist order entered without a prior Commission hearing, the respondent may apply to the United States district court for the district in which the respondent resides or has its principal place of business, or for the District of Columbia, for an order setting aside, limiting, or suspending the effectiveness or enforcement of the order, and the court shall have jurisdiction to enter such an order. A respondent served with a temporary cease-and-desist order entered without a prior Commission hearing may not apply to the court except after hearing and decision by the Commission on the respondent's application under paragraph (1) of this subsection.

(3)   No automatic stay of temporary order.—

The commencement of proceedings under paragraph (2) of this subsection shall not, unless specifically ordered by the court, operate as a stay of the Commission's order.

(4)   Exclusive review.—

Section 9(a) of this Act shall not apply to a temporary order entered pursuant to this section.

(e)   Authority to Enter An Order Requiring An Accounting and Disgorgement.—

In any cease-and-desist proceeding under subsection (a), the Commission may enter an order requiring accounting and disgorgement, including reasonable interest. The Commission is authorized to adopt rules, regulations, and orders concerning payments to investors, rates of interest, periods of accrual, and such other matters as it deems appropriate to implement this subsection.

(f)   Authority of the Commission to Prohibit Persons From Serving As Officers or Directors.—

In any cease-and-desist proceeding under subsection (a), the Commission may issue an order to prohibit, conditionally or unconditionally, and permanently or for such period of time as it shall determine, any person who has violated section 17(a)(1) or the rules or regulations thereunder, from acting as an officer or director of any issuer that has a class of securities registered pursuant to section 12 of the Securities Exchange Act of 1934, or that is required to file reports pursuant to section 15(d) of that Act, if the conduct of that person demonstrates unfitness to serve as an officer or director of any such issuer.

(g)   Authority to Impose Money Penalties.—

(1)   Grounds.—In any cease-and-desist proceeding under subsection (a), the Commission may impose a civil penalty on a person if the Commission finds, on the record, after notice and opportunity for hearing, that—

(A)   such person—

(i)   is violating or has violated any provision of this title, or any rule or regulation issued under this title; or

(ii)   is or was a cause of the violation of any provision of this title, or any rule or regulation thereunder; and

(B)   such penalty is in the public interest.

(2)   Maximum amount of penalty.—

(A)   First tier—The maximum amount of a penalty for each act or omission described in paragraph (1) shall be $7,500 for a natural person or $75,000 for any other person.

(B)   Second tier—Notwithstanding subparagraph (A), the maximum amount of penalty for each such act or omission shall be $75,000 for a natural person or $375,000 for any other person, if the act or omission described in paragraph (1) involved fraud, deceit, manipulation, or deliberate or reckless disregard of a regulatory requirement.

(C)   Third tier.—Notwithstanding subparagraphs (A) and (B), the maximum amount of penalty for each such act or omission shall be $150,000 for a natural person or $725,000 for any other person, if—

(i)   the act or omission described in paragraph (1) involved fraud, deceit, manipulation, or deliberate or reckless disregard of a regulatory requirement; and

(ii)   such act or omission directly or indirectly resulted in—

(I)   substantial losses or created a significant risk of substantial losses to other persons; or

(II)   substantial pecuniary gain to the person who committed the act or omission.

(3)   Evidence Concerning Ability to Pay.—In any proceeding in which the Commission may impose a penalty under this section, a respondent may present evidence of the ability of the respondent to pay such penalty. The Commission may, in its discretion, consider such evidence in determining whether such penalty is in the public interest. Such evidence may relate to the extent of the ability of the respondent to continue in business and the collectability of a penalty, taking into account any other claims of the United States or third parties upon the assets of the respondent and the amount of the assets of the respondent.

Court Review of Orders

Sec. 9.   (a)   Any person aggrieved by an order of the Commission may obtain a review of such order in the court of appeals of the United States, within any circuit wherein such person resides or has his principal place of business, or in the United States Court of Appeals for the District of Columbia, by filing in such Court, within sixty days after the entry of such order, a written petition praying that the order of the Commission be modified or be set aside in whole or in part. A copy of such petition shall be forthwith transmitted by the clerk of the court to the Commission, and thereupon the Commission shall file in the court the record upon which the order complained of was entered, as provided in Section 2112 of Title 28, United States Code. No objection to the order of the Commission shall be considered by the court unless such objection shall have been urged before the Commission. The finding of the Commission as to the facts, if supported by evidence, shall be conclusive. If either party shall apply to the court for leave to adduce additional evidence, and shall show to the satisfaction of the court that such additional evidence is material and that there were reasonable grounds for failure to adduce such evidence in the hearing before the Commission, the court may order such additional evidence to be taken before the Commission and to be adduced upon the hearing in such manner and upon such terms and conditions as to the court may seem proper. The Commission may modify its findings as to the facts by reason of the additional evidence so taken, and it shall file such modified or new findings, which, if supported by evidence, shall be conclusive, and its recommendation, if any, for the modification or setting aside of the original order. The jurisdiction of the court shall be exclusive and its judgment and decree, affirming, modifying, or setting aside, in whole or in part, any order of the Commission, shall be final, subject to review by the Supreme Court of the United States upon certiorari or certification as provided in Section 1254 of Title 28, United States Code.

(b)   The commencement of proceedings under subsection (a) shall not, unless specifically ordered by the court, operate as a stay of the Commission's order.

Information Required in Prospectus

Sec. 10.   (a)   Except to the extent otherwise permitted or required pursuant to this subsection or subsections (c), (d), or (e)—

(1)   a prospectus relating to a security other than a security issued by a foreign government or political subdivision thereof, shall contain the information contained in the registration statement, but it need not include the documents referred to in paragraphs (28) to (32), inclusive, of Schedule A;

(2)   a prospectus relating to a security issued by a foreign government or political subdivision thereof shall contain the information contained in the registration statement, but it need not include the documents referred to in paragraphs (13) and (14) of Schedule B;

(3)   notwithstanding the provisions of paragraphs (1) and (2) of this subsection (a) when a prospectus is used more than nine months after the effective date of the registration statement, the information contained therein shall be as of a date not more than sixteen months prior to such use, so far as such information is known to the user of such prospectus or can be furnished by such user without unreasonable effort or expense;

(4)   there may be omitted from any prospectus any of the information required under this subsection (a) which the Commission may by rules or regulations designate as not being necessary or appropriate in the public interest or for the protection of investors.

(b)   In addition to the prospectus permitted or required in subsection (a), the Commission shall by rules or regulations deemed necessary or appropriate in the public interest or for the protection of investors permit the use of a prospectus for the purposes of subsection (b)(1) of section 5 which omits in part or summarizes information in the prospectus specified in subsection (a). A prospectus permitted under this subsection shall, except to the extent the Commission by rules or regulations deemed necessary or appropriate in the public interest or for the protection of investors otherwise provides, be filed as part of the registration statement but shall not be deemed a part of such registration statement for the purposes of section 11. The Commission may at any time issue an order preventing or suspending the use of a prospectus permitted under this subsection (b), if it has reason to believe that such prospectus has not been filed (if required to be filed as part of the registration statement) or includes any untrue statement of a material fact or omits to state any material fact required to be stated therein or necessary to make the statements therein, in the light of the circumstances under which such prospectus is or is to be used, not misleading. Upon issuance of an order under this subsection, the Commission shall give notice of the issuance of such order and opportunity for hearing by personal service or the sending of confirmed telegraphic notice. The Commission shall vacate or modify the order at any time for good cause or if such prospectus has been filed or amended in accordance with such order.

(c)   Any prospectus shall contain such other information as the Commission may by rules or regulations require as being necessary or appropriate in the public interest or for the protection of investors.

(d)   In the exercise of its powers under subsections (a), (b), or (c), the Commission shall have authority to classify prospectuses according to the nature and circumstances of their use or the nature of the security, issue, issuer, or otherwise, and, by rules and regulations and subject to such terms and conditions as it shall specify therein, to prescribe as to each class the form and contents which it may find appropriate and consistent with the public interest and the protection of investors.

(e)   The statements or information required to be included in a prospectus by or under authority of subsections (a), (b), (c), or (d), when written, shall be placed in a conspicuous part of the prospectus and, except as otherwise permitted by rules or regulations, in type as large as that used generally in the body of the prospectus.

(f)   In any case where a prospectus consists of a radio or television broadcast, copies thereof shall be filed with the Commission under such rules and regulations as it shall prescribe. The Commission may by rules and regulations require the filing with it of forms and prospectuses used in connection with the offer or sale of securities registered under this Act.

Civil Liabilities on Account of False Registration Statement

Sec. 11. (a) In case any part of the registration statement, when such part became effective, contained an untrue statement of a material fact or omitted to state a material fact required to be stated therein or necessary to make the statements therein not misleading, any person acquiring such security (unless it is proved that at the time of such acquisition he knew of such untruth or omission) may, either at law or in equity, in any court of competent jurisdiction, sue—

(1) every person who signed the registration statement;

(2) every person who was a director of (or person performing similar functions) or partner in, the issuer at the time of the filing of the part of the registration statement with respect to which his liability is asserted;

(3) every person who, with his consent, is named in the registration statement as being or about to become a director, person performing similar functions, or partner;

(4) every accountant, engineer, or appraiser, or any person whose profession gives authority to a statement made by him, who has with his consent been named as having prepared or certified any part of the registration statement, or as having prepared or certified any report or valuation which is used in connection with the registration statement, with respect to the statement in such registration statement, report, or valuation, which purports to have been prepared or certified by him;

(5) every underwriter with respect to such security.

If such person acquired the security after the issuer has made generally available to its security holders an earning statement covering a period of at least twelve months beginning after the effective date of the registration statement, then the right of recovery under this subsection shall be conditioned on proof that such person acquired the security relying upon such untrue statement in the registration statement or relying upon the registration statement and not knowing of such omission, but such reliance may be established without proof of the reading of the registration statement by such person.

(b) Notwithstanding the provisions of subsection (a) no person, other than the issuer, shall be liable as provided therein who shall sustain the burden of proof—

(1) that before the effective date of the part of the registration statement with respect to which his liability is asserted (A) he had resigned from or had taken such steps as are permitted by law to resign from, or ceased or refused to act in, every office, capacity, or relationship in which he was described in the registration statement as acting or agreeing to act, and (B) he had advised the Commission and the issuer in writing that he had taken such action and that he would not be responsible for such part of the registration statement; or

(2) that if such part of the registration statement became effective without his knowledge, upon becoming aware of such fact he forthwith acted and advised the Commission, in accordance with paragraph (1), and, in addition, gave reasonable public notice that such part of the registration statement had become effective without his knowledge; or

(3) that

(A) as regards any part of the registration statement not purporting to be made on the authority of an expert, and not purporting to be a copy of or extract from a report or valuation of an expert, and not purporting to be made on the authority of a public official document or statement, he had, after reasonable investigation, reasonable ground to believe and did believe, at the time such part of the registration statement became effective, that the statements therein were true and that there was no omission to state a material fact required to be stated therein or necessary to make the statements therein not misleading; and

(B) as regards any part of the registration statement purporting to be made upon his authority as an expert or purporting to be a copy of or extract from a report or valuation of himself as an expert,

(i) he had, after reasonable investigation, reasonable ground to believe and did believe, at the time such part of the registration statement became effective, that the statements therein were true and that there was no omission to state a material fact required to be stated therein or necessary to make the statements therein not misleading, or

(ii)   such part of the registration statement did not fairly represent his statement as an expert or was not a fair copy of or extract from his report or valuation as an expert; and

(C)   as regards any part of the registration statement purporting to be made on the authority of an expert (other than himself) or purporting to be a copy of or extract from a report or valuation of an expert (other than himself), he had no reasonable ground to believe and did not believe, at the time such part of the registration statement became effective, that the statements therein were untrue or that there was an omission to state a material fact required to be stated therein or necessary to make the statements therein not misleading, or that such part of the registration statement did not fairly represent the statement of the expert or was not a fair copy of or extract from the report or valuation of the expert; and

(D)   as regards any part of the registration statement purporting to be a statement made by an official person or purporting to be a copy of or extract from a public official document, he had no reasonable ground to believe and did not believe, at the time such part of the registration statement became effective, that the statements therein were untrue, or that there was an omission to state a material fact required to be stated therein or necessary to make the statements therein not misleading, or that such part of the registration statement did not fairly represent the statement made by the official person or was not a fair copy of or extract from the public official document.

(c)   In determining, for the purpose of paragraph (3) of subsection (b) of this section, what constitutes reasonable investigation and reasonable ground for belief, the standard of reasonableness shall be that required of a prudent man in the management of his own property.

(d)   If any person becomes an underwriter with respect to the security after the part of the registration statement with respect to which his liability is asserted has become effective, then for the purposes of paragraph (3) of subsection (b) of this section such part of the registration statement shall be considered as having become effective with respect to such person as of the time when he became an underwriter.

(e)   The suit authorized under subsection (a) may be to recover such damages as shall represent the difference between the amount paid for the security (not exceeding the price at which the security was offered to the public) and (1) the value thereof as of the time such suit was brought, or (2) the price at which such security shall have been disposed of in the market before suit, or (3) the price at which such security shall have been disposed of after suit but before judgment if such damages shall be less than the damages representing the difference between the amount paid for the security (not exceeding the price at which the security was offered to the public) and the value thereof as of the time such suit was brought: Provided, That if the defendant proves that any portion or all of such damages represents other than the depreciation in value of such security resulting from such part of the registration statement, with respect to which his liability is asserted, not being true or omitting to state a material fact required to be stated therein or necessary to make the statements therein not misleading, such portion of or all such damages shall not be recoverable. In no event shall any underwriter (unless such underwriter shall have knowingly received from the issuer for acting as an underwriter some benefit, directly or indirectly, in which all other underwriters similarly situated did not share in proportion to their respective interests in the underwriting) be liable in any suit or as a consequence of suits authorized under subsection (a) for damages in excess of the total price at which the securities underwritten by him and distributed to the public were offered to the public. In any suit under this or any other section of this Act the court may, in its discretion, require an undertaking for the payment of the costs of such suit, including reasonable attorney's fees, and if judgment shall be rendered against a party litigant, upon the motion of the other party litigant, such costs may be assessed in favor of such party litigant (whether or not such undertaking has been required) if the court believes the suit or the defense to have been without merit, in an amount sufficient to reimburse him for the reasonable expenses incurred by him, in connection with such suit, such costs to be taxed in the manner usually provided for taxing of costs in the court in which the suit was heard.

(f)(1)   Except as provided in paragraph (2), all or any one or more of the persons specified in subsection (a) shall be jointly and severally liable, and every person who becomes liable to make any payment under this section may recover contribution as in cases of contract from any person who, if sued separately, would have been liable to make the same payment, unless the person who has become liable was, and the other was not, guilty of fraudulent misrepresentation.

(2)(A) The liability of an outside director under subsection (e) shall be determined in accordance with section 21D(f) of the Securities Exchange Act of 1934.

(B) For purposes of this paragraph, the term "outside director" shall have the meaning given such term by rule or regulation of the Commission.

(g) In no case shall the amount recoverable under this section exceed the price at which the security was offered to the public.

Civil Liabilities Arising in Connection With Prospectuses and Communications

Sec. 12. (a) In general.—

Any person who—

(1) offers or sells a security in violation of section 5, or

(2) offers or sells a security (whether or not exempted by the provisions of section 3, other than paragraphs (2) and (14) of subsection (a) thereof), by the use of any means or instruments of transportation or communication in interstate commerce or of the mails, by means of a prospectus or oral communication, which includes an untrue statement of a material fact or omits to state a material fact necessary in order to make the statements, in the light of the circumstances under which they were made, not misleading (the purchaser not knowing of such untruth or omission), and who shall not sustain the burden of proof that he did not know, and in the exercise of reasonable care could not have known, of such untruth or omission,

shall be liable subject to subsection (b), to the person purchasing such security from him, who may sue either at law or in equity in any court of competent jurisdiction, to recover the consideration paid for such security with interest thereon, less the amount of any income received thereon, upon the tender of such security, or for damages if he no longer owns the security.

(b) Loss Causation.—

In an action described in subsection (a)(2), if the person who offered or sold such security proves that any portion or all of the amount recoverable under subsection (a)(2) represents other than the depreciation in value of the subject security resulting from such part of the prospectus or oral communication, with respect to which the liability of that person is asserted, not being true or omitting to state a material fact required to be stated therein or necessary to make the statement not misleading, then such portion or amount, as the case may be, shall not be recoverable.

Limitation of Actions

Sec. 13. No action shall be maintained to enforce any liability created under section 11 or section 12(a)(2) unless brought within one year after the discovery of the untrue statement or the omission, or after such discovery should have been made by the exercise of reasonable diligence, or, if the action is to enforce a liability created under section 12(a)(1), unless brought within one year after the violation upon which it is based. In no event shall any such action be brought to enforce a liability created under section 11 or section 12(a)(1) more than three years after the security was bona fide offered to the public, or under section 12(a)(2) more than three years after the sale.

Contrary Stipulations Void

Sec. 14. Any condition, stipulation, or provision binding any person acquiring any security to waive compliance with any provision of this Act or of the rules and regulations of the Commission shall be void.

Liability of Controlling Persons

Sec. 15. (a) Controlling Persons.—Every person who, by or through stock ownership, agency, or otherwise, or who, pursuant to or in connection with an agreement or understanding with one or more other persons by or through stock ownership, agency, or otherwise, controls any person liable under section 11 or

12, shall also be liable jointly and severally with and to the same extent as such controlled person to any person to whom such controlled person is liable, unless the controlling person had no knowledge of or reasonable grounds to believe in the existence of the facts by reason of which the liability of the controlled person is alleged to exist.

(b)   Prosecution of Persons Who Aid and Abet Violations—For purposes of any action brought by the Commission under subparagraph (b) or (d) of section 20, any person that knowingly or recklessly provides substantial assistance to another person in violation of a provision of this Act, or of any rule or regulation issued under this Act, shall be deemed to be in violation of such provision to the same extent as the person to whom such assistance is provided.

Additional Remedies; Limitation on Remedies

Sec. 16.   (a)   Remedies Additional.—

Except as provided in subsection (b), the rights and remedies provided by this subchapter shall be in addition to any and all other rights and remedies that may exist at law or in equity.

(b)   Class Action Limitations.—

No covered class action based upon the statutory or common law of any State or subdivision thereof may be maintained in any State or Federal court by any private party alleging—

(1)   an untrue statement or omission of a material fact in connection with the purchase or sale of a covered security; or

(2)   that the defendant used or employed any manipulative or deceptive device or contrivance in connection with the purchase or sale of a covered security.

(c)   Removal of Covered Class Actions.—

Any covered class action brought in any State court involving a covered security, as set forth in subsection (b), shall be removable to the Federal district court for the district in which the action is pending, and shall be subject to subsection (b).

(d)   Preservation of Certain Actions.—

(1)   Actions under State law of State of incorporation.—

(A)   Actions preserved.—

Notwithstanding subsection (b) or (c), a covered class action described in subparagraph (B) of this paragraph that is based upon the statutory or common law of the State in which the issuer is incorporated (in the case of a corporation) or organized (in the case of any other entity) may be maintained in a State or Federal court by a private party.

(B)   Permissible actions.—

A covered class action is described in this subparagraph if it involves—

(i)   the purchase or sale of securities by the issuer or an affiliate of the issuer exclusively from or to holders of equity securities of the issuer; or

(ii)   any recommendation, position, or other communication with respect to the sale of securities of the issuer that—

(I)   is made by or on behalf of the issuer or an affiliate of the issuer to holders of equity securities of the issuer; and

(II)   concerns decisions of those equity holders with respect to voting their securities, acting in response to a tender or exchange offer, or exercising dissenters' or appraisal rights.

(2)   State actions.—

(A)   In General.—

Notwithstanding any other provision of this section, nothing in this section may be construed to preclude a State or political subdivision thereof or a State pension plan from bringing an action involving a covered security on its own behalf, or as a member of a class comprised solely of other States, political subdivisions, or State pension plans that are named plaintiffs, and that have authorized participation, in such action.

(B)   State pension plan defined.—

For purposes of this paragraph, the term "State pension plan" means a pension plan established and maintained for its employees by the government of the State or political subdivision thereof, or by any agency or instrumentality thereof.

(3)   Actions under contractual agreements between issuers and indenture trustees.—

Notwithstanding subsection (b) or (c), a covered class action that seeks to enforce a contractual agreement between an issuer and an indenture trustee may be maintained in a State or Federal court by a party to the agreement or a successor to such party.

(4)   Remand of removed actions.—

In an action that has been removed from a State court pursuant to subsection (c), if the Federal court determines that the action may be maintained in State court pursuant to this subsection, the Federal court shall remand such action to such State court.

(e)   Preservation of State Jurisdiction.—

The securities commission (or any agency or office performing like functions) of any State shall retain jurisdiction under the laws of such State to investigate and bring enforcement actions.

(f)   Definitions.—

For purposes of this section, the following definitions shall apply:

(1)   Affiliate of the issuer.—

The term "affiliate of the issuer" means a person that directly or indirectly, through one or more intermediaries, controls or is controlled by or is under common control with, the issuer.

(2)   Covered class action.—

(A)   In general.—

The term "covered class action" means—

(i)   any single lawsuit in which—

(I)   damages are sought on behalf of more than 50 persons or prospective class members, and questions of law or fact common to those persons or members of the prospective class, without reference to issues of individualized reliance on an alleged misstatement or omission, predominate over any questions affecting only individual persons or members; or

(II)   one or more named parties seek to recover damages on a representative basis on behalf of themselves and other unnamed parties similarly situated, and questions of law or fact common to those persons or members of the prospective class predominate over any questions affecting only individual persons or members; or

(ii)   any group of lawsuits filed in or pending in the same court and involving common questions of law or fact, in which—

(I)   damages are sought on behalf of more than 50 persons; and

(II)   the lawsuits are joined, consolidated, or otherwise proceed as a single action for any purpose.

(B)   Exception for derivative actions.—

Notwithstanding subparagraph (A), the term "covered class action" does not include an exclusively derivative action brought by one or more shareholders on behalf of a corporation.

(C)   Counting of certain class members.—

For purposes of this paragraph, a corporation, investment company, pension plan, partnership, or other entity, shall be treated as one person or prospective class member, but only if the entity is not established for the purpose of participating in the action.

(D)   Rule of construction.—

Nothing in this paragraph shall be construed to affect the discretion of a State court in determining whether actions filed in such court should be joined, consolidated, or otherwise allowed to proceed as a single action.

(3)   Covered security.—

The term "covered security" means a security that satisfies the standards for a covered security specified in paragraph (1) or (2) of section 18(b), at the time during which it is alleged that the misrepresentation, omission, or manipulative or deceptive conduct occurred, except that such term shall not include any debt security that is exempt from registration under this Act pursuant to rules issued by the Commission under section 4[(a)](2) of this Act.

Fraudulent Interstate Transactions

Sec. 17.   (a)   Scope of Exemption.—

It shall be unlawful for any person in the offer or sale of any securities (including security-based swaps) or any security-based swap agreement (as defined in section 3(a)(78) of the Securities Exchange Act) by the use of any means or instruments of transportation or communication in interstate commerce or by use of the mails, directly or indirectly—

(1)   to employ any device, scheme, or artifice to defraud, or

(2)   to obtain money or property by means of any untrue statement of a material fact or any omission to state a material fact necessary in order to make the statements made, in light of the circumstances under which they were made, not misleading; or

(3)   to engage in any transaction, practice, or course of business which operates or would operate as a fraud or deceit upon the purchaser.

(b)   It shall be unlawful for any person, by the use of any means or instruments of transportation or communication in interstate commerce or by the use of the mails, to publish, give publicity to, or circulate any notice, circular, advertisement, newspaper, article, letter, investment service, or communication which, though not purporting to offer a security for sale, describes such security for a consideration received or to be received, directly or indirectly, from an issuer, underwriter, or dealer, without fully disclosing the receipt, whether past or prospective, of such consideration and the amount thereof.

(c)   The exemptions provided in section 3 shall not apply to the provisions of this section.

(d)   The authority of the Commission under this section with respect to security-based swap agreements (as defined in section 3(a)(78) of the Securities Exchange Act of 1934) shall be subject to the restrictions and limitations of section 2A(b) of this Act.

Exemption From State Regulation of Securities Offerings

Sec. 18.   (a)   Except as otherwise provided in this section, no law, rule, regulation, or order, or other administrative action of any State or any political subdivision thereof—

(1)   requiring, or with respect to, registration or qualification of securities, or registration or qualification of securities transactions, shall directly or indirectly apply to a security that—

(A)   is a covered security; or

(B)   will be a covered security upon completion of the transaction;

(2)   shall directly or indirectly prohibit, limit, or impose any conditions upon the use of—

(A)   with respect to a covered security described in subsection (b), any offering document that is prepared by or on behalf of the issuer; or

(B) any proxy statement, report to shareholders, or other disclosure document relating to a covered security or the issuer thereof that is required to be and is filed with the Commission or any national securities organization registered under section 15A of the Securities Exchange Act of 1934, except that this subparagraph does not apply to the laws, rules, regulations, or orders, or other administrative actions of the State of incorporation of the issuer; or

(3) shall directly or indirectly prohibit, limit, or impose conditions, based on the merits of such offering or issuer, upon the offer or sale of any security described in paragraph (1).

(b) Covered Securities.—

For purposes of this section, the following are covered securities:

(1) Exclusive federal registration of nationally traded securities.—

A security is a covered security if such security is—

(A) a security designated as qualified for trading in the national market system pursuant to section 11A(a)(2) of the Securities Exchange Act of 1934 (15 U.S.C. 78k–1(a)(2)) that is listed, or authorized for listing, on a national securities exchange (or tier or segment thereof); or

(B) a security of the same issuer that is equal in seniority or that is a senior security to a security described in subparagraph (A).

(2) Exclusive federal registration of investment companies.—

A security is a covered security if such security is a security issued by an investment company that is registered, or that has filed a registration statement, under the Investment Company Act of 1940.

(3) Sales to qualified purchasers.—

A security is a covered security with respect to the offer or sale of the security to qualified purchasers, as defined by the Commission by rule. In prescribing such rule, the Commission may define the term "qualified purchaser" differently with respect to different categories of securities, consistent with the public interest and the protection of investors.

(4) Exemption in connection with certain exempt offerings.—

A security is a covered security with respect to a transaction that is exempt from registration under this Act pursuant to—

(A) paragraph (1) or (3) of section 4, and the issuer of such security files reports with the Commission pursuant to section 13 or 15(d) of the Securities Exchange Act of 1934;

(B) section 4(a)(4);

(C) section 4(a)(6);

(D) a rule or regulation adopted pursuant to section 3(b)(2) and such security is—

(i) offered or sold on a national securities exchange; or

(ii) offered or sold to a qualified purchaser, as defined by the Commission pursuant to paragraph (3) with respect to that purchase or sale;

(E) section 3(a), other than the offer or sale of a security that is exempt from such registration pursuant to paragraph (4), (10), or (11) of such section, except that a municipal security that is exempt from such registration pursuant to paragraph (2) of such section is not a covered security with respect to the offer or sale of such security in the State in which the issuer of such security is located;

(F) Commission rules or regulations issued under section 4(2), except that this subparagraph does not prohibit a State from imposing notice filing requirements that are substantially similar to those required by rule or regulation under section 4(2) that are in effect on September 1, 1996; or

(G) section 4(a)(7) of this Act.[1]

---

[1] Although the US Code refers to § 78d(a)(7), this was intended to refer to § 77(d)(a)(7).

(c)   Preservation of Authority.—

(1)   Fraud authority.—

Consistent with this section, the securities commission (or any agency or office performing like functions) of any State shall retain jurisdiction under the laws of such State to investigate and bring enforcement actions, in connection with securities or securities transactions.

    (A)   with respect to—

        (i)   fraud or deceit; or

        (ii)   unlawful conduct by a broker, or dealer; and

    (B)   in connection with a transaction described under section 4(a)(6), with respect to—

        (i)   fraud or deceit; or

        (ii)   unlawful conduct by a broker, dealer, funding portal, or issuer.

(2)   Preservation of filing requirements.—

    (A)   Notice of filings permitted.—

Nothing in this section prohibits the securities commission (or any agency or office performing like functions) of any State from requiring the filing of any document filed with the Commission pursuant to this Act, together with annual or periodic reports of the value of securities sold or offered to be sold to persons located in the State (if such sales data is not included in documents filed with the Commission), solely for notice purposes and the assessment of any fee, together with a consent to service of process and any required fee.

    (B)   Preservation of fees.—

        (i)   In general.—

Until otherwise provided by law, rule, regulation, or order, or other administrative action of any State or any political subdivision thereof, adopted after the date of enactment of the National Securities Markets Improvement Act of 1996, filing or registration fees with respect to securities or securities transactions shall continue to be collected in amounts determined pursuant to State law as in effect on the day before such date.

        (ii)   Schedule.—

The fees required by this subparagraph shall be paid, and all necessary supporting data on sales or offers for sales required under subparagraph (A), shall be reported on the same schedule as would have been applicable had the issuer not relied on the exemption provided in subsection (a).

    (C)   Availability of preemption contingent on payment of fees.—

        (i)   In general.—

During the period beginning on the date of enactment of the National Securities Markets Improvement Act of 1996 and ending 3 years after that date of enactment, the securities commission (or any agency or office performing like functions) of any State may require the registration of securities issued by any issuer who refuses to pay the fees required by subparagraph (B).

        (ii)   Delays.—

For purposes of this subparagraph, delays in payment of fees or underpayments of fees that are promptly remedied shall not constitute a refusal to pay fees.

    (D)   Fees not permitted on listed securities.—

Notwithstanding subparagraphs (A), (B), and (C), no filing or fee may be required with respect to any security that is a covered security pursuant to subsection (b)(1), or will be such a covered security upon completion of the transaction, or is a security of the same issuer that is equal in seniority or that is a senior security to a security that is a covered security pursuant to subsection (b)(1).

(F)[2] Fees not permitted on crowdfunded securities.—Notwithstanding subparagraphs (A), (B), and (C), no filing or fee may be required with respect to any security that is a covered security pursuant to subsection (b)(4)(B), or will be such a covered security upon completion of the transaction, except for the securities commission (or any agency or office performing like functions) of the State of the principal place of business of the issuer, or any State in which purchasers of 50 percent or greater of the aggregate amount of the issue are residents, provided that for purposes of this subparagraph, the term "State" includes the District of Columbia and the territories of the United States.

(3) Enforcement of requirements.—

Nothing in this section shall prohibit the securities commission (or any agency or office performing like functions) of any State from suspending the offer or sale of securities within such State as a result of the failure to submit any filing or fee required under law and permitted under this section.

(d) Definitions.—

For purposes of this section, the following definitions shall apply:

(1) Offering document.—

The term "offering document"—

(A) has the meaning given the term "prospectus" in section 2(a)(10), but without regard to the provisions of subparagraphs (a) and (b) of that section; and

(B) includes a communication that is not deemed to offer a security pursuant to a rule of the Commission.

(2) Prepared by or on behalf of the issuer.—

Not later than 6 months after the date of enactment of the National Securities Markets Improvement Act of 1996, the Commission shall, by rule, define the term "prepared by or on behalf of the issuer" for purposes of this section.

(3) State.—

The term "State" has the same meaning as in section 3 of the Securities Exchange Act of 1934.

(4) Senior security.—

The term "senior security" means any bond, debenture, note, or similar obligation or instrument constituting a security and evidencing indebtedness, and any stock of a class having priority over any other class as to distribution of assets or payment of dividends.

Preemption of State Law

Sec. 18A. (a) Authority to purchase, hold, and invest in securities; securities considered as obligations of United States.

(1) Any person, trust, corporation, partnership, association, business trust, or business entity created pursuant to or existing under the laws of the United States or any State shall be authorized to purchase, hold, and invest in securities that are—

(A) offered and sold pursuant to section 4(5) of the Securities Act of 1933,

(B) mortgage related securities (as that term is defined in section 3(a)(41) of the Securities Exchange Act of 1934),

(C) small business related securities (as defined in section 3(a)(53) of the Securities Exchange Act of 1934), or

(D) securities issued or guaranteed by the Federal Home Loan Mortgage Corporation or the Federal National Mortgage Association, to the same extent that such person, trust, corporation,

---

[2] So in original. No subpar. (E) has been enacted.

partnership, association, business trust, or business entity is authorized under any applicable law to purchase, hold or invest in obligations issued by or guaranteed as to principal and interest by the United States or any agency or instrumentality thereof.

(2) Where State law limits the purchase, holding, or investment in obligations issued by the United States by such a person, trust, corporation, partnership, association, business trust, or business entity, such securities that are—

(A) offered and sold pursuant to section 4(5) of the Securities Act of 1933,

(B) mortgage related securities (as that term is defined in section 3(a)(41) of the Securities Exchange Act of 1934),

(C) small business related securities (as defined in section 3(a)(53) of the Securities Exchange Act of 1934), or

(D) securities issued or guaranteed by the Federal Home Loan Mortgage Corporation or the Federal National Mortgage Association, shall be considered to be obligations issued by the United States for purposes of the limitation.

(b) Exception; validity of contracts under prior law. The provisions of subsection (a) of this section shall not apply with respect to a particular person, trust, corporation, partnership, association, business trust, or business entity or class thereof in any State that, prior to the expiration of seven years after October 3, 1984, enacts a statute that specifically refers to this section and either prohibits or provides for a more limited authority to purchase, hold, or invest in such securities by any person, trust, corporation, partnership, association, business trust, or business entity or class thereof than is provided in subsection (a) of this section. The enactment by any State of any statute of the type described in the preceding sentence shall not affect the validity of any contractual commitment to purchase, hold, or invest that was made prior thereto and shall not require the sale or other disposition of any securities acquired prior thereto.

(c) Registration and qualification requirements; exemption; subsequent enactment by State. Any securities that are offered and sold pursuant to section 4(5) of the Securities Act of 1933, that are mortgage related securities (as that term is defined in section 3(a)(41) of the Securities Exchange Act of 1934), or that are small business related securities (as defined in section 3(a)(53) of the Securities Exchange Act of 1934) shall be exempt from any law of any State with respect to or requiring registration or qualification of securities or real estate to the same extent as any obligation issued by or guaranteed as to principal and interest by the United States or any agency or instrumentality thereof. Any State may, prior to the expiration of seven years after October 3, 1984, enact a statute that specifically refers to this section and requires registration or qualification of any such security on terms that differ from those applicable to any obligation issued by the United States.

(d)(1) The provisions of subsections (a) and (b) of this section concerning small business related securities shall not apply with respect to a particular person, trust, corporation, partnership, association, business trust, or business entity or class thereof in any State that, prior to the expiration of 7 years after September 23, 1994, enacts a statute that specifically refers to this section and either prohibits or provides for a more limited authority to purchase, hold, or invest in such small business related securities by any person, trust, corporation, partnership, association, business trust, or business entity or class thereof than is provided in this section. The enactment by any State of any statute of the type described in the preceding sentence shall not affect the validity of any contractual commitment to purchase, hold, or invest that was made prior to such enactment, and shall not require the sale or other disposition of any small business related securities acquired prior to the date of such enactment.

(2) Any State may, not later than 7 years after September 23, 1994, enact a statute that specifically refers to this section and requires registration or qualification of any small business related securities on terms that differ from those applicable to any obligation issued by the United States.

Special Powers of Commission

Sec. 19. (a) The Commission shall have authority from time to time to make, amend, and rescind such rules and regulations as may be necessary to carry out the provisions of this Act, including rules and regulations governing registration statements and prospectuses for various classes of securities and issuers, and defining accounting, technical, and trade terms used in this Act. Among other things, the Commission shall have authority, for the purposes of this Act, to prescribe the form or forms in which required information shall be set forth, the items or details to be shown in the balance sheet and earning statement, and the methods to be followed in the preparation of accounts, in the appraisal or valuation of assets and liabilities, in the determination of depreciation and depletion, in the differentiation of recurring and nonrecurring income, in the differentiation of investment and operating income, and in the preparation, where the Commission deems it necessary or desirable, of consolidated balance sheets or income accounts of any person directly or indirectly controlling or controlled by the issuer, or any person under direct or indirect common control with the issuer. The rules and regulations of the Commission shall be effective upon publication in the manner which the Commission shall prescribe. No provision of this Act imposing any liability shall apply to any act done or omitted in good faith in conformity with any rule or regulation of the Commission, notwithstanding that such rule or regulation may, after such act or omission, be amended or rescinded or be determined by judicial or other authority to be invalid for any reason.

(b)   Recognition of Accounting Standards.—

(1)   In general.—

In carrying out its authority under subsection (a) and under section 13(b) of the Securities Exchange Act of 1934, the Commission may recognize, as "generally accepted" for purposes of the securities laws, any accounting principles established by a standard setting body—

(A)   that—

(i)   is organized as a private entity;

(ii)   has, for administrative and operational purposes, a board of trustees (or equivalent body) serving in the public interest, the majority of whom are not, concurrent with their service on such board, and have not been during the 2-year period preceding such service, associated persons of any registered public accounting firm;

(iii)   is funded as provided in section 109 of the Sarbanes-Oxley Act of 2002;

(iv)   has adopted procedures to ensure prompt consideration, by majority vote of its members, of changes to accounting principles necessary to reflect emerging accounting issues and changing business practices; and

(v)   considers, in adopting accounting principles, the need to keep standards current in order to reflect changes in the business environment, the extent to which international convergence on high quality accounting standards is necessary or appropriate in the public interest and for the protection of investors; and

(B)   that the Commission determines has the capacity to assist the Commission in fulfilling the requirements of subsection (a) and section 13(b) of the Securities Exchange Act of 1934, because, at a minimum, the standard setting body is capable of improving the accuracy and effectiveness of financial reporting and the protection of investors under the securities laws.

(2)   Annual report.—

A standard setting body described in paragraph (1) shall submit an annual report to the Commission and the public, containing audited financial statements of that standard setting body.

(c)   For the purpose of all investigations which, in the opinion of the Commission, are necessary and proper for the enforcement of this Act, any member of the Commission or any officer or officers designated by it are empowered to administer oaths and affirmations, subpoena witnesses, take evidence, and require the production of any books, papers, or other documents which the Commission deems relevant or material to the inquiry. Such attendance of witnesses and the production of such documentary evidence may be required from any place in the United States or any Territory at any designated place of hearing.

(d)(1)   The Commission is authorized to cooperate with any association composed of duly constituted representatives of State governments whose primary assignment is the regulation of the securities business within those States, and which, in the judgment of the Commission, could assist in effectuating greater uniformity in Federal-State securities matters. The Commission shall, at its discretion, cooperate, coordinate, and share information with such an association for the purposes of carrying out the policies and projects set forth in paragraphs (2) and (3).

(2) It is the declared policy of this subsection that there should be greater Federal and State cooperation in securities matters, including—

    (A) maximum effectiveness of regulation,

    (B) maximum uniformity in Federal and State regulatory standards,

    (C) minimum interference with the business of capital formation, and

    (D) a substantial reduction in costs and paperwork to diminish the burdens of raising investment capital (particularly by small business) and to diminish the costs of the administration of the Government programs involved.

(3) The purpose of this subsection is to engender cooperation between the Commission, any such association of State securities officials and other duly constituted securities associations in the following areas:

    (A) the sharing of information regarding the registration or exemption of securities issues applied for in the various States;

    (B) the development and maintenance of uniform securities forms and procedures; and

    (C) the development of a uniform exemption from registration for small issuers which can be agreed upon among several States or between the States and the Federal Government. The Commission shall have the authority to adopt such an exemption as agreed upon for Federal purposes. Nothing in this Act shall be construed as authorizing preemption of State law.

(4) In order to carry out these policies and purposes, the Commission shall conduct an annual conference as well as such other meetings as are deemed necessary, to which representatives from such securities associations, securities self-regulatory organizations, agencies, and private organizations involved in capital formation shall be invited to participate.

(5) For fiscal year 1982, and for each of the three succeeding fiscal years, there are authorized to be appropriated such amounts as may be necessary and appropriate to carry out the policies, provisions, and purposes of this subsection. Any sums so appropriated shall remain available until expended.

(6) Notwithstanding any other provision of law, neither the Commission nor any other person shall be required to establish any procedures not specifically required by the securities laws, as that term is defined in section 3(a)(47) of the Securities Exchange Act of 1934, or by Chapter 5 of Title 5, in connection with cooperation, coordination, or consultation with—

    (A) any association referred to in paragraph (1) or (3) or any conference or meeting referred to in paragraph (4), while such association, conference, or meeting is carrying out activities in furtherance of the provisions of this subsection; or

    (B) any forum, agency, or organization, or group referred to in section 503 of the Small Business Investment Incentive Act of 1980, while such forum, agency, organization, or group is carrying out activities in furtherance of the provisions of such section 503.

As used in this paragraph, the terms "association" "conference", "meeting", "forum", "agency", "organization", and "group" include any committee, subgroup, or representative of such entities.

(e) Evaluation of Rules or Programs.—For the purpose of evaluating any rule or program of the Commission issued or carried out under any provision of the securities laws, as defined in section 3 of the Securities Exchange Act of 1934 (15 U.S.C. 78c), and the purposes of considering, proposing, adopting, or engaging in any such rule or program or developing new rules or programs, the Commission may—

    (1) gather information from and communicate with investors or other members of the public;

    (2) engage in such temporary investor testing programs as the Commission determines are in the public interest or would protect investors; and

    (3) consult with academics and consultants, as necessary to carry out this subsection.

(f) Rule of Construction.—For purposes of the Paperwork Reduction Act (44 U.S.C. 3501 et seq.), any action taken under subsection (e) shall not be construed to be a collection of information.

(g)   Funding for the GASB.—

(1)   In general.—The Commission may, subject to the limitations imposed by section 15B of the Securities Exchange Act of 1934 (15 U.S.C. 78o–4), require a national securities association registered under the Securities Exchange Act of 1934 to establish—

(A)   a reasonable annual accounting support fee to adequately fund the annual budget of the Governmental Accounting Standards Board (referred to in this subsection as the "GASB"); and

(B)   rules and procedures, in consultation with the principal organizations representing State governors, legislators, local elected officials, and State and local finance officers, to provide for the equitable allocation, assessment, and collection of the accounting support fee established under subparagraph (A) from the members of the association, and the remittance of all such accounting support fees to the Financial Accounting Foundation.

(2)   Annual budget.—For purposes of this subsection, the annual budget of the GASB is the annual budget reviewed and approved according to the internal procedures of the Financial Accounting Foundation.

(3)   Use of funds.—Any fees or funds collected under this subsection shall be used to support the efforts of the GASB to establish standards of financial accounting and reporting recognized as generally accepted accounting principles applicable to State and local governments of the United States.

(4)   Limitation on fee.—The annual accounting support fees collected under this subsection for a fiscal year shall not exceed the recoverable annual budgeted expenses of the GASB (which may include operating expenses, capital, and accrued items).

(5)   Rules of construction.—

(A)   Fees not public monies.—Accounting support fees collected under this subsection and other receipts of the GASB shall not be considered public monies of the United States.

(B)   Limitation on authority of the commission.—Nothing in this subsection shall be construed to—

(i)   provide the Commission or any national securities association direct or indirect oversight of the budget or technical agenda of the GASB; or

(ii)   affect the setting of generally accepted accounting principles by the GASB.

(C)   Noninterference with states.—Nothing in this subsection shall be construed to impair or limit the authority of a State or local government to establish accounting and financial reporting standards.

Injunctions and Prosecution of Offenses

Sec. 20.   (a)   Whenever it shall appear to the Commission, either upon complaint or otherwise, that the provisions of this Act, or of any rule or regulation prescribed under authority thereof, have been or are about to be violated, it may, in its discretion, either require or permit such person to file with it a statement in writing, under oath, or otherwise, as to all the facts and circumstances concerning the subject matter which it believes to be in the public interest to investigate, and may investigate such facts.

(b)   Whenever it shall appear to the Commission that any person is engaged or about to engage in any acts or practices which constitute or will constitute a violation of the provisions of this Act, or of any rule or regulation prescribed under authority thereof, the Commission may in its discretion, bring an action in any district court of the United States, or United States court of any Territory, to enjoin such acts or practices, and upon a proper showing a permanent or temporary injunction or restraining order shall be granted without bond. The Commission may transmit such evidence as may be available concerning such acts or practices to the Attorney General who may, in his discretion, institute the necessary criminal proceedings under this Act. Any such criminal proceeding may be brought either in the district wherein the transmittal of the prospectus or security complained of begins, or in the district wherein such prospectus or security is received.

(c)   Upon application of the Commission the district courts of the United States and the United States courts of any Territory shall have jurisdiction to issue writs of mandamus commanding any person to comply with the provisions of this Act or any order of the Commission made in pursuance thereof.

(d)   Money Penalties in Civil Actions.—

(1)   Authority of Commission.—

Whenever it shall appear to the Commission that any person has violated any provision of this Act, the rules or regulations thereunder, or a cease-and-desist order entered by the Commission pursuant to section 8A of this Act, other than by committing a violation subject to a penalty pursuant to section 21A of the Securities Exchange Act of 1934, the Commission may bring an action in a United States district court to seek, and the court shall have jurisdiction to impose, upon a proper showing, a civil penalty to be paid by the person who committed such violation.

(2)   Amount of Penalty.—

(A)   First tier.—

The amount of the penalty shall be determined by the court in light of the facts and circumstances. For each violation, the amount of the penalty shall not exceed the greater of (i) $5,000 for a natural person or $50,000 for any other person, or (ii) the gross amount of pecuniary gain to such defendant as a result of the violation.

(B)   Second tier.—

Notwithstanding subparagraph (A), the amount of penalty for each such violation shall not exceed the greater of (i) $50,000 for a natural person or $250,000 for any other person, or (ii) the gross amount of pecuniary gain to such defendant as a result of the violation, if the violation described in paragraph (1) involved fraud, deceit, manipulation, or deliberate or reckless disregard of a regulatory requirement.

(C)   Third tier.—

Notwithstanding subparagraphs (A) and (B), the amount of penalty for each such violation shall not exceed the greater of (i) $100,000 for a natural person or $500,000 for any other person, or (ii) the gross amount of pecuniary gain to such defendant as a result of the violation, if—

(I)   the violation described in paragraph (1) involved fraud, deceit, manipulation, or deliberate or reckless disregard of a regulatory requirement; and

(II)   such violation directly or indirectly resulted in substantial losses or created a significant risk of substantial losses to other persons.

(3)   Procedures for Collection.—

(A)   Payment of penalty to treasury.—

A penalty imposed under this section shall be payable into the Treasury of the United States, except as otherwise provided in section 308 of the Sarbanes-Oxley Act of 2002, and section 21F of the Securities Exchange Act of 1934.

(B)   Collection of penalties.—

If a person upon whom such a penalty is imposed shall fail to pay such penalty within the time prescribed in the court's order, the Commission may refer the matter to the Attorney General who shall recover such penalty by action in the appropriate United States district court.

(C)   Remedy not exclusive.—

The actions authorized by this subsection may be brought in addition to any other action that the Commission or the Attorney General is entitled to bring.

(D)   Jurisdiction and venue.—

For purposes of Section 22 of this Act actions under this section shall be actions to enforce a liability or a duty created by this title.

(4)   Special Provisions Relating to A Violation of A Cease-And-Desist Order.—

In an action to enforce a cease-and-desist order entered by the Commission pursuant to Section 8A, each separate violation of such order shall be a separate offense, except that in the case of a violation through a continuing failure to comply with such an order, each day of the failure to comply with the order shall be deemed a separate offense.

(e)   Authority of A Court to Prohibit Persons From Serving As Officers and Directors.—

In any proceeding under subsection (b), the court may prohibit, conditionally or unconditionally, and permanently or for such period of time as it shall determine, any person who violated Section 17(a)(1) of this Act from acting as an officer or director of any issuer that has a class of securities registered pursuant to Section 12 of the Securities Exchange Act of 1934 or that is required to file reports pursuant to Section 15(d) of such Act if the person's conduct demonstrates unfitness to serve as an officer or director of any such issuer.

(f)   Prohibition of Attorneys' Fees Paid From Commission Disgorgement Funds.—

Except as otherwise ordered by the court upon motion by the Commission, or, in the case of an administrative action, as otherwise ordered by the Commission, funds disgorged as the result of an action brought by the Commission in Federal court, or as a result of any Commission administrative action, shall not be distributed as payment for attorneys' fees or expenses incurred by private parties seeking distribution of the disgorged funds.

(g)   Authority of a court to prohibit persons from participating in an offering of penny stock.—

(1)   In general.—In any proceeding under subsection (a) of this section against any person participating in, or, at the time of the alleged misconduct, who was participating in, an offering of penny stock, the court may prohibit that person from participating in an offering of penny stock, conditionally or unconditionally, and permanently or for such period of time as the court shall determine.

(2)   Definition.—For purposes of this subsection, the term "person participating in an offering of penny stock" includes any person engaging in activities with a broker, dealer, or issuer for purposes of issuing, trading, or inducing or attempting to induce the purchase or sale of, any penny stock. The Commission may, by rule or regulation, define such term to include other activities, and may, by rule, regulation, or order, exempt any person or class of persons, in whole or in part, conditionally or unconditionally, from inclusion in such term.

Hearings by Commission

Sec. 21.   All hearings shall be public and may be held before the Commission or an officer or officers of the Commission designated by it, and appropriate records thereof shall be kept.

Jurisdiction of Offenses and Suits

Sec. 22.   (a)   The district courts of the United States and the United States courts of any Territory shall have jurisdiction of offenses and violations under this Act and under the rules and regulations promulgated by the Commission in respect thereto, and, concurrent with State and Territorial courts except as provided in Section 16 with respect to covered class actions, of all suits in equity and actions at law brought to enforce any liability or duty created by this Act. Any such suit or action may be brought in the district wherein the defendant is found or is an inhabitant or transacts business, or in the district where the offer or sale took place, if the defendant participated therein, and process in such cases may be served in any other district of which the defendant is an inhabitant or wherever the defendant may be found. In any action or proceeding instituted by the Commission under this title in a United States district court for any judicial district, a subpoena issued to compel the attendance of a witness or the production of documents or tangible things (or both) at a hearing or trial may be served at any place within the United States. Rule 45(c)(3)(A)(ii) of the Federal Rules of Civil Procedure shall not apply to a subpoena issued under the preceding sentence. Judgments and decrees so rendered shall be subject to review as provided in Sections 1254, 1291, 1292 and 1294 of Title 28, United States Code. Except as provided in Section 16(c), no case arising under this Act and brought in any State court of competent jurisdiction shall be removed to any court of the United States. No costs shall be assessed for or against the Commission in any proceeding under this Act brought by or against it in the Supreme Court or such other courts.

(b)   In case of contumacy or refusal to obey a subpena issued to any person, any of the said United States courts, within the jurisdiction of which said person guilty of contumacy or refusal to obey is found or resides, upon application by the Commission may issue to such person an order requiring such person to appear before the Commission, or one of its examiners designated by it, there to produce documentary evidence if so ordered, or there to give evidence touching the matter in question; and any failure to obey such order of the court may be punished by said court as a contempt thereof.

(c)   Extraterritorial Jurisdiction.—The district courts of the United States and the United States courts of any Territory shall have jurisdiction of an action or proceeding brought or instituted by the Commission or the United States alleging a violation of section 17(a) involving—

(1)   conduct within the United States that constitutes significant steps in furtherance of the violation, even if the securities transaction occurs outside the United States and involves only foreign investors; or

(2)   conduct occurring outside the United States that has a foreseeable substantial effect within the United States.

Unlawful Representations

Sec. 23. Neither the fact that the registration statement for a security has been filed or is in effect nor the fact that a stop order is not in effect with respect thereto shall be deemed a finding by the Commission that the registration statement is true and accurate on its face or that it does not contain an untrue statement of fact or omit to state a material fact, or be held to mean that the Commission has in any way passed upon the merits of, or given approval to, such security. It shall be unlawful to make, or cause to be made, to any prospective purchaser any representation contrary to the foregoing provisions of this section.

Penalties

Sec. 24. Any person who willfully violates any of the provisions of this Act, or the rules and regulations promulgated by the Commission under authority thereof, or any person who willfully, in a registration statement filed under this Act, makes any untrue statement of a material fact or omits to state any material fact required to be stated therein or necessary to make the statements therein not misleading, shall upon conviction be fined not more than $10,000 or imprisoned not more than five years, or both.

Jurisdiction of Other Government Agencies Over Securities

Sec. 25. Nothing in this Act shall relieve any person from submitting to the respective supervisory units of the Government of the United States information, reports, or other documents that are now or may hereafter be required by any provision of law.

Separability of Provisions

Sec. 26. If any provision of this Act, or the application of such provision to any person or circumstance, shall be held invalid, the remainder of this Act, or the application of such provision to persons or circumstances other than those as to which it is held invalid, shall not be affected thereby.

Private Securities Litigation

Sec. 27. (a)   Private Class Actions.—

(1)   In general.—

The provisions of this subsection shall apply to each private action arising under this Act that is brought as a plaintiff class action pursuant to the Federal Rules of Civil Procedure.

(2)   Certification filed with complaint.—

(A)   In general.—

Each plaintiff seeking to serve as a representative party on behalf of a class shall provide a sworn certification, which shall be personally signed by such plaintiff and filed with the complaint, that—

(i)   states that the plaintiff has reviewed the complaint and authorized its filing;

(ii)   states that the plaintiff did not purchase the security that is the subject of the complaint at the direction of plaintiff's counsel or in order to participate in any private action arising under this Act;

(iii) states that the plaintiff is willing to serve as a representative party on behalf of a class, including providing testimony at deposition and trial, if necessary;

(iv)   sets forth all of the transactions of the plaintiff in the security that is the subject of the complaint during the class period specified in the complaint;

(v)   identifies any other action under this Act, filed during the 3-year period preceding the date on which the certification is signed by the plaintiff, in which the plaintiff has sought to serve, or served, as a representative party on behalf of a class; and

(vi)   states that the plaintiff will not accept any payment for serving as a representative party on behalf of a class beyond the plaintiff's pro rata share of any recovery, except as ordered or approved by the court in accordance with paragraph (4).

(B)   Nonwaiver of attorney-client privilege.—

The certification filed pursuant to subparagraph (A) shall not be construed to be a waiver of the attorney-client privilege.

(3)   Appointment of lead plaintiff.—

(A)   Early notice to class members.—

(i)   In general.—

Not later than 20 days after the date on which the complaint is filed, the plaintiff or plaintiffs shall cause to be published, in a widely circulated national business-oriented publication or wire service, a notice advising members of the purported plaintiff class—

(I)   of the pendency of the action, the claims asserted therein, and the purported class period; and

(II)   that, not later than 60 days after the date on which the notice is published, any member of the purported class may move the court to serve as lead plaintiff of the purported class.

(ii)   Multiple actions.—

If more than one action on behalf of a class asserting substantially the same claim or claims arising under this Act is filed, only the plaintiff or plaintiffs in the first filed action shall be required to cause notice to be published in accordance with clause (i).

(iii) Additional notices may be required under federal rules.—

Notice required under clause (i) shall be in addition to any notice required pursuant to the Federal Rules of Civil Procedure.

(B)   Appointment of lead plaintiff.—

(i)   In general.—

Not later than 90 days after the date on which a notice is published under subparagraph (A)(i), the court shall consider any motion made by a purported class member in response to the notice, including any motion by a class member who is not individually named as a plaintiff in the complaint or complaints, and shall appoint as lead plaintiff the member or members of the purported plaintiff class that the court determines to be most capable of adequately representing the interests of class members (hereafter in this paragraph referred to as the "most adequate plaintiff") in accordance with this subparagraph.

(ii)   Consolidated actions.—

If more than one action on behalf of a class asserting substantially the same claim or claims arising under this title has been filed, and any party has sought to consolidate those actions for pretrial purposes or for trial, the court shall not make the determination required by clause (i) until after the decision on the motion to consolidate is rendered. As soon as practicable after such decision is rendered, the court shall appoint the most adequate plaintiff as lead plaintiff for the consolidated actions in accordance with this subparagraph.

(iii)   Rebuttable presumption.—

(I)   In general.—

Subject to subclause (II), for purposes of clause (i), the court shall adopt a presumption that the most adequate plaintiff in any private action arising under this Act is the person or group of persons that—

(aa) has either filed the complaint or made a motion in response to a notice under subparagraph (A)(i);

(bb) in the determination of the court, has the largest financial interest in the relief sought by the class; and

(cc) otherwise satisfies the requirements of Rule 23 of the Federal Rules of Civil Procedure.

(II)   Rebuttal evidence.—

The presumption described in subclause (I) may be rebutted only upon proof by a member of the purported plaintiff class that the presumptively most adequate plaintiff—

(aa) will not fairly and adequately protect the interests of the class; or

(bb) is subject to unique defenses that render such plaintiff incapable of adequately representing the class.

(iv)   Discovery.—

For purposes of this subparagraph, discovery relating to whether a member or members of the purported plaintiff class is the most adequate plaintiff may be conducted by a plaintiff only if the plaintiff first demonstrates a reasonable basis for a finding that the presumptively most adequate plaintiff is incapable of adequately representing the class.

(v)   Selection of lead counsel.—

The most adequate plaintiff shall, subject to the approval of the court, select and retain counsel to represent the class.

(vi)   Restrictions on professional plaintiffs.—

Except as the court may otherwise permit, consistent with the purposes of this section, a person may be a lead plaintiff, or an officer, director, or fiduciary of a lead plaintiff, in no more than 5 securities class actions brought as plaintiff class actions pursuant to the Federal Rules of Civil Procedure during any 3-year period.

(4)   Recovery by plaintiffs.—

The share of any final judgment or of any settlement that is awarded to a representative party serving on behalf of a class shall be equal, on a per share basis, to the portion of the final judgment or settlement awarded to all other members of the class. Nothing in this paragraph shall be construed to limit the award of reasonable costs and expenses (including lost wages) directly relating to the representation of the class to any representative party serving on behalf of the class.

(5)   Restrictions on settlements under seal.—

The terms and provisions of any settlement agreement of a class action shall not be filed under seal, except that on motion of any party to the settlement, the court may order filing under seal for those portions of a settlement agreement as to which good cause is shown for such filing under seal. For purposes of this paragraph, good cause shall exist only if publication of a term or provision of a settlement agreement would cause direct and substantial harm to any party.

(6) Restrictions on payment of attorneys' fees and expenses.—

Total attorneys' fees and expenses awarded by the court to counsel for the plaintiff class shall not exceed a reasonable percentage of the amount of any damages and prejudgment interest actually paid to the class.

(7) Disclosure of settlement terms to class members.—

Any proposed or final settlement agreement that is published or otherwise disseminated to the class shall include each of the following statements, along with a cover page summarizing the information contained in such statements:

(A) Statement of plaintiff recovery.—

The amount of the settlement proposed to be distributed to the parties to the action, determined in the aggregate and on an average per share basis.

(B) Statement of potential outcome of case.—

    (i) Agreement on amount of damages.—

    If the settling parties agree on the average amount of damages per share that would be recoverable if the plaintiff prevailed on each claim alleged under this Act, a statement concerning the average amount of such potential damages per share.

    (ii) Disagreement on amount of damages.—

    If the parties do not agree on the average amount of damages per share that would be recoverable if the plaintiff prevailed on each claim alleged under this Act, a statement from each settling party concerning the issue or issues on which the parties disagree.

    (iii) Inadmissibility for certain purposes.—

    A statement made in accordance with clause (i) or (ii) concerning the amount of damages shall not be admissible in any Federal or State judicial action or administrative proceeding, other than an action or proceeding arising out of such statement.

(C) Statement of attorneys' fees or costs sought.—

If any of the settling parties or their counsel intend to apply to the court for an award of attorneys' fees or costs from any fund established as part of the settlement, a statement indicating which parties or counsel intend to make such an application, the amount of fees and costs that will be sought (including the amount of such fees and costs determined on an average per share basis), and a brief explanation supporting the fees and costs sought.

(D) Statement of attorneys' fees or costs sought.—

The name, telephone number, and address of one or more representatives of counsel for the plaintiff class who will be reasonably available to answer questions from class members concerning any matter contained in any notice of settlement published or otherwise disseminated to the class.

(E) Reasons for settlement.—

A brief statement explaining the reasons why the parties are proposing the settlement.

(F) Other information.—

Such other information as may be required by the court.

(8) Attorney conflict of interest.—

If a plaintiff class is represented by an attorney who directly owns or otherwise has a beneficial interest in the securities that are the subject of the litigation, the court shall make a determination of whether such ownership or other interest constitutes a conflict of interest sufficient to disqualify the attorney from representing the plaintiff class.

(b)   Stay of Discovery; Preservation of evidence.—

(1)   In general.—

In any private action arising under this Act, all discovery and other proceedings shall be stayed during the pendency of any motion to dismiss, unless the court finds, upon the motion of any party, that particularized discovery is necessary to preserve evidence or to prevent undue prejudice to that party.

(2)   Preservation of evidence.—

During the pendency of any stay of discovery pursuant to this subsection, unless otherwise ordered by the court, any party to the action with actual notice of the allegations contained in the complaint shall treat all documents, data compilations (including electronically recorded or stored data), and tangible objects that are in the custody or control of such person and that are relevant to the allegations, as if they were the subject of a continuing request for production of documents from an opposing party under the Federal Rules of Civil Procedure.

(3)   Sanction for willful violation.—

A party aggrieved by the willful failure of an opposing party to comply with paragraph (2) may apply to the court for an order awarding appropriate sanctions.

(4)   Circumvention of stay of discovery.—

Upon a proper showing, a court may stay discovery proceedings in any private action in a State court as necessary in aid of its jurisdiction, or to protect or effectuate its judgments, in an action subject to a stay of discovery pursuant to this subsection.

(c)   Sanctions for Abusive Litigation.—

(1)   Mandatory review by court.—

In any private action arising under this Act, upon final adjudication of the action, the court shall include in the record specific findings regarding compliance by each party and each attorney representing any party with each requirement of Rule 11(b) of the Federal Rules of Civil Procedure as to any complaint, responsive pleading, or dispositive motion.

(2)   Mandatory sanctions.—

If the court makes a finding under paragraph (1) that a party or attorney violated any requirement of Rule 11(b) of the Federal Rules of Civil Procedure as to any complaint, responsive pleading, or dispositive motion, the court shall impose sanctions on such party or attorney in accordance with Rule 11 of the Federal Rules of Civil Procedure. Prior to making a finding that any party or attorney has violated Rule 11 of the Federal Rules of Civil Procedure, the court shall give such party or attorney notice and an opportunity to respond.

(3)   Presumption in favor of attorneys' fees and costs.—

(A)   In general.—

Subject to subparagraphs (B) and (C), for purposes of paragraph (2), the court shall adopt a presumption that the appropriate sanction—

(i)   for failure of any responsive pleading or dispositive motion to comply with any requirement of Rule 11(b) of the Federal Rules of Civil Procedure is an award to the opposing party of the reasonable attorneys' fees and other expenses incurred as a direct result of the violation; and

(ii)   for substantial failure of any complaint to comply with any requirement of Rule 11(b) of the Federal Rules of Civil Procedure is an award to the opposing party of the reasonable attorneys' fees and other expenses incurred in the action.

(B)   Rebuttal evidence.—

The presumption described in subparagraph (A) may be rebutted only upon proof by the party or attorney against whom sanctions are to be imposed that—

(i)   the award of attorneys' fees and other expenses will impose an unreasonable burden on that party or attorney and would be unjust, and the failure to make such an award would not impose a greater burden on the party in whose favor sanctions are to be imposed; or

(ii)   the violation of Rule 11(b) of the Federal Rules of Civil Procedure was de minimis.

(C)   Sanctions.—

If the party or attorney against whom sanctions are to be imposed meets its burden under subparagraph (B), the court shall award the sanctions that the court deems appropriate pursuant to Rule 11 of the Federal Rules of Civil Procedure.

(d)   Defendant's Right to Written Interrogatories.—

In any private action arising under this Act in which the plaintiff may recover money damages only on proof that a defendant acted with a particular state of mind, the court shall, when requested by a defendant, submit to the jury a written interrogatory on the issue of each such defendant's state of mind at the time the alleged violation occurred.

Application of Safe Harbor for Forward-Looking Statements

Sec. 27A. (a) Applicability.—

This section shall apply only to a forward-looking statement made by—

(1)   an issuer that, at the time that the statement is made, is subject to the reporting requirements of section 13(a) or section 15(d) of the Securities Exchange Act of 1934;

(2)   a person acting on behalf of such issuer;

(3)   an outside reviewer retained by such issuer making a statement on behalf of such issuer; or

(4)   an underwriter, with respect to information provided by such issuer or information derived from information provided by the issuer.

(b)   Exclusions.—

Except to the extent otherwise specifically provided by rule, regulation, or order of the Commission, this section shall not apply to a forward-looking statement—

(1)   that is made with respect to the business or operations of the issuer, if the issuer—

(A)   during the 3-year period preceding the date on which the statement was first made—

(i)   was convicted of any felony or misdemeanor described in clauses (i) through (iv) of section 15(b)(4)(B) of the Securities Exchange Act of 1934; or

(ii)   has been made the subject of a judicial or administrative decree or order arising out of a governmental action that—

(I)   prohibits future violations of the antifraud provisions of the securities laws;

(II)   requires that the issuer cease and desist from violating the antifraud provisions of the securities laws; or

(III)   determines that the issuer violated the antifraud provisions of the securities laws;

(B)   makes the forward-looking statement in connection with an offering of securities by a blank check company;

(C)   issues penny stock;

(D)   makes the forward-looking statement in connection with a rollup transaction; or

(E)   makes the forward-looking statement in connection with a going private transaction; or

(2)   that is—

(A)   included in a financial statement prepared in accordance with generally accepted accounting principles;

(B)   contained in a registration statement of, or otherwise issued by, an investment company;

(C)   made in connection with a tender offer;

(D)   made in connection with an initial public offering;

(E)   made in connection with an offering by, or relating to the operations of, a partnership, limited liability company, or a direct participation investment program; or

(F)   made in a disclosure of beneficial ownership in a report required to be filed with the Commission pursuant to section 13(d) of the Securities Exchange Act of 1934.

(c)   Safe Harbor.—

(1)   In General.—

Except as provided in subsection (b), in any private action arising under this title that is based on an untrue statement of a material fact or omission of a material fact necessary to make the statement not misleading, a person referred to in subsection (a) shall not be liable with respect to any forward-looking statement, whether written or oral, if and to the extent that—

(A)   the forward-looking statement is—

(i)   identified as a forward-looking statement, and is accompanied by meaningful cautionary statements identifying important factors that could cause actual results to differ materially from those in the forward-looking statement; or

(ii)   immaterial; or

(B)   the plaintiff fails to prove that the forward-looking statement—

(i)   if made by a natural person, was made with actual knowledge by that person that the statement was false or misleading; or

(ii)   if made by a business entity, was—

(I)   made by or with the approval of an executive officer of that entity, and

(II)   made or approved by such officer with actual knowledge by that officer that the statement was false or misleading.

(2)   Oral Forward-Looking Statements.—

In the case of an oral forward-looking statement made by an issuer that is subject to the reporting requirements of section 13(a) or section 15(d) of the Securities Exchange Act of 1934, or by a person acting on behalf of such issuer, the requirement set forth in paragraph (1)(A) shall be deemed to be satisfied—

(A)   if the oral forward-looking statement is accompanied by a cautionary statement—

(i)   that the particular oral statement is a forward-looking statement; and

(ii)   that the actual results could differ materially from those projected in the forward-looking statement; and

(B)   if—

(i)   the oral forward-looking statement is accompanied by an oral statement that additional information concerning factors that could cause actual results to differ materially from those in the forward-looking statement is contained in a readily available written document, or portion thereof;

(ii)   the accompanying oral statement referred to in clause (i) identifies the document, or portion thereof, that contains the additional information about those factors relating to the forward-looking statement; and

(iii) the information contained in that written document is a cautionary statement that satisfies the standard established in paragraph (1)(A).

(3)   Availability.—

Any document filed with the Commission or generally disseminated shall be deemed to be readily available for purposes of paragraph (2).

(4)   Effect on Other Safe Harbors.—

The exemption provided for in paragraph (1) shall be in addition to any exemption that the Commission may establish by rule or regulation under subsection (g).

(d)   Duty to Update.—

Nothing in this section shall impose upon any person a duty to update a forward-looking statement.

(e)   Dispositive Motion.—

On any motion to dismiss based upon subsection (c)(1), the court shall consider any statement cited in the complaint and cautionary statement accompanying the forward-looking statement, which are not subject to material dispute, cited by the defendant.

(f)   Stay Pending Decision on Motion.—

In any private action arising under this Act, the court shall stay discovery (other than discovery that is specifically directed to the applicability of the exemption provided for in this section) during the pendency of any motion by a defendant for summary judgment that is based on the grounds that—

(1)   the statement or omission upon which the complaint is based is a forward-looking statement within the meaning of this section; and

(2)   the exemption provided for in this section precludes a claim for relief.

(g)   Exemption of Authority.—

In addition to the exemptions provided for in this section, the Commission may, by rule or regulation, provide exemptions from or under any provision of this Act, including with respect to liability that is based on a statement or that is based on projections or other forward-looking information, if and to the extent that any such exemption is consistent with the public interest and the protection of investors, as determined by the Commission.

(h)   Effect on Other Authority of Commission.—

Nothing in this section limits, either expressly or by implication, the authority of the Commission to exercise similar authority or to adopt similar rules and regulations with respect to forward-looking statements under any other statute under which the Commission exercises rulemaking authority.

(i)   Definitions.—

For purposes of this section, the following definitions shall apply:

(1)   Forward-looking statement.—

The term "forward-looking statement" means—

(A)   a statement containing a projection of revenues, income (including income loss), earnings (including earnings loss) per share, capital expenditures, dividends, capital structure, or other financial items;

(B)   a statement of the plans and objectives of management for future operations, including plans or objectives relating to the products or services of the issuer;

(C)   a statement of future economic performance, including any such statement contained in a discussion and analysis of financial condition by the management or in the results of operations included pursuant to the rules and regulations of the Commission;

(D)   any statement of the assumptions underlying or relating to any statement described in subparagraph (A), (B), or (C);

(E)   any report issued by an outside reviewer retained by an issuer, to the extent that the report assesses a forward-looking statement made by the issuer; or

(F)   a statement containing a projection or estimate of such other items as may be specified by rule or regulation of the Commission.

(2)   Investment company.—

The term "investment company" has the same meaning as in section 3(a) of the Investment Company Act of 1940.

(3)   Penny stock.—

The term "penny stock" has the same meaning as in section 3(a)(51) of the Securities Exchange Act of 1934, and the rules and regulations, or orders issued pursuant to that section.

(4)   Going private transaction.—

The term "going private transaction" has the meaning given that term under the rules or regulations of the Commission issued pursuant to section 13(e) of the Securities Exchange Act of 1934.

(5)   Securities laws.—

The term "securities laws" has the same meaning as in section 3 of the Securities Exchange Act of 1934.

(6)   Person acting on behalf of an issuer.—

The term "person acting on behalf of an issuer" means an officer, director, or employee of the issuer.

(7)   Other terms.—

The terms "blank check company", "rollup transaction", "partnership", "limited liability company", "executive officer of an entity" and "direct participation investment program", have the meanings given those terms by rule or regulation of the Commission.

Conflicts of Interest Relating to Certain Securitizations

Sec. 27B. (a) In General.—An underwriter, placement agent, initial purchaser, or sponsor, or any affiliate or subsidiary of any such entity, of an asset-backed security (as such term is defined in section 3 of the Securities and Exchange Act of 1934, which for the purposes of this section shall include a synthetic asset-backed security), shall not, at any time for a period ending on the date that is one year after the date of the first closing of the sale of the asset-backed security, engage in any transaction that would involve or result in any material conflict of interest with respect to any investor in a transaction arising out of such activity.

(b)   Rulemaking.—Not later than 270 days after the date of enactment of this section, the Commission shall issue rules for the purpose of implementing subsection (a).

(c)   Exception.—The prohibitions of subsection (a) shall not apply to—

(1)   risk-mitigating hedging activities in connection with positions or holdings arising out of the underwriting, placement, initial purchase, or sponsorship of an asset-backed security, provided that such activities are designed to reduce the specific risks to the underwriter, placement agent, initial purchaser, or sponsor associated with positions or holdings arising out of such underwriting, placement, initial purchase, or sponsorship; or

(2)   purchases or sales of asset-backed securities made pursuant to and consistent with—

(A)   commitments of the underwriter, placement agent, initial purchaser, or sponsor, or any affiliate or subsidiary of any such entity, to provide liquidity for the asset-backed security, or

(B)   bona fide market-making in the asset backed security.

(d)   Rule of Construction.—This subsection shall not otherwise limit the application of section 15G of the Securities Exchange Act of 1934.

General Exemptive Authority

Sec. 28. The Commission, by rule or regulation, may conditionally or unconditionally exempt any person, security, or transaction, or any class or classes of persons, securities, or transactions, from any provision or provisions of this Act or of any rule or regulation issued under this Act, to the extent that such exemption is necessary or appropriate in the public interest, and is consistent with the protection of investors.

SCHEDULE OF INFORMATION REQUIRED
IN REGISTRATION STATEMENT

Schedule A

(1) The name under which the issuer is doing or intends to do business;

(2) the name of the State or other sovereign power under which the issuer is organized;

(3) the location of the issuer's principal business office, and if the issuer is a foreign or territorial person, the name and address of its agent in the United States authorized to receive notice;

(4) the names and addresses of the directors or persons performing similar functions, and the chief executive, financial and accounting officers, chosen or to be chosen if the issuer be a corporation, association, trust, or other entity; of all partners, if the issuer be a partnership; and of the issuer, if the issuer be an individual; and of the promoters in the case of a business to be formed, or formed within two years prior to the filing of the registration statement;

(5) the names and addresses of the underwriters;

(6) the names and addresses of all persons, if any, owning of record or beneficially, if known, more than 10 per centum of any class of stock of the issuer, or more than 10 per centum in the aggregate of the outstanding stock of the issuer as of a date within 20 days prior to the filing of the registration statement;

(7) the amount of securities of the issuer held by any person specified in paragraphs (4), (5), and (6) of this schedule, as of a date within 20 days prior to the filing of the registration statement, and, if possible, as of one year prior thereto, and the amount of the securities, for which the registration statement is filed, to which such persons have indicated their intention to subscribe;

(8) the general character of the business actually transacted or to be transacted by the issuer;

(9) a statement of the capitalization of the issuer, including the authorized and outstanding amounts of its capital stock and the proportion thereof paid up, the number and classes of shares in which such capital stock is divided, par value thereof, or if it has no par value, the stated or assigned value thereof, a description of the respective voting rights, preferences, conversion and exchange rights, rights to dividends, profits, or capital of each class, with respect to each other class, including the retirement and liquidation rights or values thereof;

(10) a statement of the securities, if any, covered by options outstanding or to be created in connection with the security to be offered, together with the names and addresses of all persons, if any, to be allotted more than 10 per centum in the aggregate of such options;

(11) the amount of capital stock of each class issued or included in the shares of stock to be offered;

(12) the amount of the funded debt outstanding and to be created by the security to be offered, with a brief description of the date, maturity, and character of such debt, rate of interest, character of amortization provisions, and the security, if any, therefor. If substitution of any security is permissible, a summarized statement of the conditions under which such substitution is permitted. If substitution is permissible without notice, a specific statement to that effect;

(13) the specific purposes in detail and the approximate amounts to be devoted to such purposes, so far as determinable, for which the security to be offered is to supply funds, and if the funds are to be raised in part from other sources, the amounts thereof and the sources thereof, shall be stated;

(14) the remuneration, paid or estimated to be paid, by the issuer or its predecessor, directly or indirectly, during the past year and ensuing year, to (a) the directors or persons performing similar

functions, and (b) its officers and other persons, naming them wherever such remuneration exceeded $25,000 during any such year;

(15) the estimated net proceeds to be derived from the security to be offered;

(16) the price at which it is proposed that the security shall be offered to the public or the method by which such price is computed and any variation therefrom at which any portion of such security is proposed to be offered to any persons or classes of persons, other than the underwriters, naming them or specifying the class. A variation in price may be proposed prior to the date of the public offering of the security, but the Commission shall immediately be notified of such variation;

(17) all commissions or discounts paid or to be paid, directly or indirectly, by the issuer to the underwriters in respect of the sale of the security to be offered. Commissions shall include all cash, securities, contracts, or anything else of value, paid, to be set aside, disposed of, or understandings with or for the benefit of any other persons in which any underwriter is interested, made, in connection with the sale of such security. A commission paid or to be paid in connection with the sale of such security by a person in which the issuer has an interest or which is controlled or directed by, or under common control with, the issuer shall be deemed to have been paid by the issuer. Where any such commission is paid the amount of such commission paid to each underwriter shall be stated;

(18) the amount or estimated amounts, itemized in reasonable detail, of expenses, other than commissions specified in paragraph (17) of this schedule, incurred or borne by or for the account of the issuer in connection with the sale of the security to be offered or properly chargeable thereto including legal, engineering, certification, authentication, and other charges;

(19) the net proceeds derived from any security sold by the issuer during the two years preceding the filing of the registration statement, the price at which such security was offered to the public, and the names of the principal underwriters of such security;

(20) any amount paid within two years preceding the filing of the registration statement or intended to be paid to any promoter and the consideration for any such payment;

(21) the names and addresses of the vendors and the purchase price of any property, or good will, acquired or to be acquired, not in the ordinary course of business, which is to be defrayed in whole or in part from the proceeds of the security to be offered, the amount of any commission payable to any person in connection with such acquisition, and the name or names of such person or persons, together with any expense incurred or to be incurred in connection with such acquisition, including the cost of borrowing money to finance such acquisition;

(22) full particulars of the nature and extent of the interest, if any, of every director, principal executive officer, and of every stockholder holding more than 10 per centum of any class of stock or more than 10 per centum in the aggregate of the stock of the issuer, in any property acquired, not in the ordinary course of business of the issuer, within two years preceding the filing of the registration statement or proposed to be acquired at such date;

(23) the names and addresses of counsel who have passed on the legality of the issue;

(24) dates of and parties to, and the general effect concisely stated of every material contract made, not in the ordinary course of business, which contract is to be executed in whole or in part at or after the filing of the registration statement or which contract has been made not more than two years before such filing. Any management contract or contract providing for special bonuses or profit-sharing arrangements, and every material patent or contract for a material patent right, and every contract by or with a public utility company or an affiliate thereof, providing for the giving or receiving of technical or financial advice or service (if such contract may involve a charge to any party thereto at a rate in excess of $2,500 per year in cash or securities or anything else of value), shall be deemed a material contract;

(25) a balance sheet as of a date not more than ninety days prior to the date of the filing of the registration statement showing all of the assets of the issuer, the nature and cost thereof, whenever determinable, in such detail and in such form as the Commission shall prescribe (with intangible items segregated), including any loan in excess of $20,000 to any officer, director, stockholder or person directly or indirectly controlling or controlled by the issuer, or person under direct or indirect common control with the issuer. All the liabilities of the issuer in such detail and such form as the Commission shall prescribe, including surplus of the issuer showing how and from what sources such surplus was created, all as of a

date not more than ninety days prior to the filing of the registration statement. If such statement be not certified by an independent public or certified accountant, in addition to the balance sheet required to be submitted under this schedule, a similar detailed balance sheet of the assets and liabilities of the issuer, certified by an independent public or certified accountant, of a date not more than one year prior to the filing of the registration statement, shall be submitted;

(26) a profit and loss statement of the issuer showing earnings and income, the nature and source thereof, and the expenses and fixed charges in such detail and such form as the Commission shall prescribe for the latest fiscal year for which such statement is available and for the two preceding fiscal years, year by year, or, if such issuer has been in actual business for less than three years, then for such time as the issuer has been in actual business, year by year. If the date of the filing of the registration statement is more than six months after the close of the last fiscal year, a statement from such closing date to the latest practicable date. Such statement shall show what the practice of the issuer has been during the three years or lesser period as to the character of the charges, dividends or other distributions made against its various surplus accounts, and as to depreciation, depletion, and maintenance charges, in such detail and form as the Commission shall prescribe, and if stock dividends or avails from the sale of rights have been credited to income, they shall be shown separately with a statement of the basis upon which the credit is computed. Such statement shall also differentiate between any recurring and nonrecurring income and between any investment and operating income. Such statement shall be certified by an independent public or certified accountant;

(27) if the proceeds, or any part of the proceeds, of the security to be issued is to be applied directly or indirectly to the purchase of any business, a profit and loss statement of such business certified by an independent public or certified accountant, meeting the requirements of paragraph (26) of this schedule, for the three preceding fiscal years, together with a balance sheet, similarly certified, of such business, meeting the requirements of paragraph (25) of this schedule of a date not more than ninety days prior to the filing of the registration statement or at the date such business was acquired by the issuer if the business was acquired by the issuer more than ninety days prior to the filing of the registration statement;

(28) a copy of any agreement or agreements (or, if identical agreements are used, the forms thereof) made with any underwriter, including all contracts and agreements referred to in paragraph (17) of this schedule;

(29) a copy of the opinion or opinions of counsel in respect to the legality of the issue, with a translation of such opinion, when necessary, into the English language;

(30) a copy of all material contracts referred to in paragraph (24) of this schedule, but no disclosure shall be required of any portion of any such contract if the Commission determines that disclosure of such portion would impair the value of the contract and would not be necessary for the protection of the investors;

(31) unless previously filed and registered under the provisions of this Act, and brought up to date, (a) a copy of its articles of incorporation, with all amendments thereof and of its existing bylaws or instruments corresponding thereto, whatever the name, if the issuer be a corporation; (b) copy of all instruments by which the trust is created or declared, if the issuer is a trust; (c) a copy of its articles of partnership or association and all other papers pertaining to its organization, if the issuer is a partnership, unincorporated association, joint-stock company, or any other form of organization; and

(32) a copy of the underlying agreements or indentures affecting any stock, bonds, or debentures offered or to be offered.

In case of certificates of deposit, voting trust certificates, collateral trust certificates, certificates of interest or shares in unincorporated investment trusts, equipment trust certificates, interim or other receipts for certificates, and like securities, the Commission shall establish rules and regulations requiring the submission of information of a like character applicable to such cases, together with such other information as it may deem appropriate and necessary regarding the character, financial or otherwise, of the actual issuer of the securities and/or the person performing the acts and assuming the duties of depositor or manager.

RULES AND REGULATIONS UNDER SECURITIES ACT OF 1933

17 C.F.R. § 227.___

CROWDFUNDING

GENERAL

Rule 100. Crowdfunding Exemption and Requirements.

(a) *Exemption.* An issuer may offer or sell securities in reliance on section 4(a)(6) of the Securities Act of 1933 (the "Securities Act"), provided that:

(1) The aggregate amount of securities sold to all investors by the issuer in reliance on section 4(a)(6) of the Securities Act (15 U.S.C. 77d(a)(6)) during the 12-month period preceding the date of such offer or sale, including the securities offered in such transaction, shall not exceed $5,000,000;

(2)   Where the purchaser is not an accredited investor (as defined in Rule 501 (§ 230.501 of this chapter)), the aggregate amount of securities sold to such an investor across all issuers in reliance on section 4(a)(6) of the Securities Act (15 U.S.C. 77d(a)(6)) during the 12-month period preceding the date of such transaction, including the securities sold to such investor in such transaction, shall not exceed:

(i)   The greater of $2,200, or 5 percent of the greater of the investor's annual income or net worth, if either the investor's annual income or net worth is less than $107,000; or

(ii)   Ten percent of the greater of the investor's annual income or net worth, not to exceed an amount sold of $107,000, if both the investor's annual income and net worth are equal to or more than $107,000;

Instruction 1 to paragraph (a)(2). To determine the investment limit for a natural person, the person's annual income and net worth shall be calculated as those values are calculated for purposes of determining accredited investor status in accordance with § 230.501 of this chapter.

Instruction 2 to paragraph (a)(2). A person's annual income and net worth may be calculated jointly with that person's spouse; however, when such a joint calculation is used, the aggregate investment of the investor spouses may not exceed the limit that would apply to an individual investor at that income or net worth level.

Instruction 3 to paragraph (a)(2). An issuer offering and selling securities in reliance on section 4(a)(6) of the Securities Act (15 U.S.C. 77d(a)(6)) may rely on the efforts of an intermediary required by § 227.303(b) to ensure that the aggregate amount of securities purchased by an investor in offerings pursuant to section 4(a)(6) of the Securities Act will not cause the investor to exceed the limit set forth in section 4(a)(6) of the Securities Act and § 227.100(a)(2), *provided that* the issuer does not know that the investor has exceeded the investor limits or would exceed the investor limits as a result of purchasing securities in the issuer's offering.

(3)   The transaction is conducted through an intermediary that complies with the requirements in section 4A(a) of the Act and the related requirements in this part, and the transaction is conducted exclusively through the intermediary's platform; and

Instruction to paragraph (a)(3). An issuer shall not conduct an offering or concurrent offerings in reliance on section 4(a)(6) of the Act using more than one intermediary.

(4)   The issuer complies with the requirements in section 4A(b) of the Act and the related requirements in this part; *provided, however,* that the failure to comply with §§ 227.202, 227.203(a)(3) and 227.203(b) shall not prevent an issuer from relying on the exemption provided by section 4(a)(6) of the Act.

(b)   *Applicability.* The crowdfunding exemption shall not apply to transactions involving the offer or sale of securities by any issuer that:

(1)   Is not organized under, and subject to, the laws of a State or territory of the United States or the District of Columbia;

(2)   Is subject to the requirement to file reports pursuant to section 13 or section 15(d) of the Securities Exchange Act of 1934 (the "Exchange Act");

(3)   Is an investment company, as defined in section 3 of the Investment Company Act of 1940, or is excluded from the definition of investment company by section 3(b) or section 3(c) of that Act;

(4)   Is not eligible to offer or sell securities in reliance on section 4(a)(6) of the Securities Act) as a result of a disqualification as specified in § 227.503(a);

(5)   Has sold securities in reliance on section 4(a)(6) of the Securities Act and has not filed with the Commission and provided to investors, to the extent required, the ongoing annual reports required by this part during the two years immediately preceding the filing of the required offering statement; or

Instruction to paragraph (b)(5). An issuer delinquent in its ongoing reports can again rely on section 4(a)(6) of the Securities Act once it has filed with the Commission and provided to investors both of the annual reports required during the two years immediately preceding the filing of the required offering statement.

(6)   Has no specific business plan or has indicated that its business plan is to engage in a merger or acquisition with an unidentified company or companies.

(7)   Seeks to rely on § 227.201(aa) to conduct an offering on an expedited basis due to circumstances relating to coronavirus disease 2019 (COVID-19), where such offering is initiated between May 4, 2020, and February 28, 2021, or seeks to rely on § 227.201(bb), where such offering is initiated between March 1, 2021, and August 28, 2022, and:

(i)   Was organized and had operations less than six months prior to the commencement of the offering; or

(ii)   Sold securities in reliance on section 4(a)(6) of the Securities Act and has not complied with the requirements in section 4A(b) of the Securities Act) and the related requirements in this part.

(c)   *Issuer.* For purposes of § 227.201(r), calculating aggregate amounts offered and sold in § 227.100(a) and § 227.201(t), and determining whether an issuer has previously sold securities in § 227.201(t)(3), *issuer* includes all entities controlled by or under common control with the issuer and any predecessors of the issuer.

Instruction to paragraph (c). The term *control* means the possession, direct or indirect, of the power to direct or cause the direction of the management and policies of the entity, whether through the ownership of voting securities, by contract or otherwise.

(d)   *Investor.* For purposes of this part, investor means any investor or any potential investor, as the context requires. A crowdfunding vehicle (as defined in § 270.3a–9 of this chapter) is not considered an investor for the purposes of this part.

(e)   *Integration with other offerings.* To determine whether offers and sales should be integrated, please see § 230.152 of this chapter.

REQUIREMENTS FOR ISSUERS

Rule 201.   Disclosure Requirements.

An issuer offering or selling securities in reliance on section 4(a)(6) of the Securities Act and in accordance with section 4A of the Securities Act and this part, and any co-issuer jointly offering or selling securities with such an issuer in reliance on the same, must file with the Commission and provide to investors and the relevant intermediary the following information:

(a)   The name, legal status (including its form of organization, jurisdiction in which it is organized and date of organization), physical address and Web site of the issuer;

(b)   The names of the directors and officers (and any persons occupying a similar status or performing a similar function) of the issuer, all positions and offices with the issuer held by such persons, the period of time in which such persons served in the position or office and their business experience during the past three years, including:

(1)   Each person's principal occupation and employment, including whether any officer is employed by another employer; and

(2)   The name and principal business of any corporation or other organization in which such occupation and employment took place.

Instruction to paragraph (b). For purposes of this paragraph (b), the term *officer* means a president, vice president, secretary, treasurer or principal financial officer, comptroller or principal accounting officer, and any person routinely performing similar functions.

(c)   The name of each person, as of the most recent practicable date but no earlier than 120 days prior to the date the offering statement or report is filed, who is a beneficial owner of 20 percent or more of the issuer's outstanding voting equity securities, calculated on the basis of voting power;

(d)   A description of the business of the issuer and the anticipated business plan of the issuer;

(e)   The current number of employees of the issuer;

(f)   A discussion of the material factors that make an investment in the issuer speculative or risky;

(g)   The target offering amount and the deadline to reach the target offering amount, including a statement that if the sum of the investment commitments does not equal or exceed the target offering amount at the offering deadline, no securities will be sold in the offering, investment commitments will be cancelled and committed funds will be returned;

(h)   Whether the issuer will accept investments in excess of the target offering amount and, if so, the maximum amount that the issuer will accept and how oversubscriptions will be allocated, such as on a pro-rata, first come-first served, or other basis;

(i)   A description of the purpose and intended use of the offering proceeds;

Instruction to paragraph (i). An issuer must provide a reasonably detailed description of any intended use of proceeds, such that investors are provided with enough information to understand how the offering proceeds will be used. If an issuer has identified a range of possible uses, the issuer should identify and describe each probable use and the factors the issuer may consider in allocating proceeds among the potential uses. If the issuer will accept proceeds in excess of the target offering amount, the issuer must describe the purpose, method for allocating oversubscriptions, and intended use of the excess proceeds with similar specificity.

(j)   A description of the process to complete the transaction or cancel an investment commitment, including a statement that:

(1)   Investors may cancel an investment commitment until 48 hours prior to the deadline identified in the issuer's offering materials;

(2)   The intermediary will notify investors when the target offering amount has been met;

(3)   If an issuer reaches the target offering amount prior to the deadline identified in its offering materials, it may close the offering early if it provides notice about the new offering deadline at least five business days prior to such new offering deadline (absent a material change that would require an extension of the offering and reconfirmation of the investment commitment); and

(4)   If an investor does not cancel an investment commitment before the 48-hour period prior to the offering deadline, the funds will be released to the issuer upon closing of the offering and the investor will receive securities in exchange for his or her investment;

(k)   A statement that if an investor does not reconfirm his or her investment commitment after a material change is made to the offering, the investor's investment commitment will be cancelled and the committed funds will be returned;

(*l*)   The price to the public of the securities or the method for determining the price, provided that, prior to any sale of securities, each investor shall be provided in writing the final price and all required disclosures;

(m)   A description of the ownership and capital structure of the issuer, including:

(1)   The terms of the securities being offered and each other class of security of the issuer, including the number of securities being offered and/or outstanding, whether or not such securities have voting rights, any limitations on such voting rights, how the terms of the securities being offered may be modified and a summary of the differences between such securities and each other class of security of the issuer, and how the rights of the securities being offered may be materially limited, diluted or qualified by the rights of any other class of security of the issuer;

(2)   A description of how the exercise of rights held by the principal shareholders of the issuer could affect the purchasers of the securities being offered;

56

(3)   The name and ownership level of each person, as of the most recent practicable date but no earlier than 120 days prior to the date the offering statement or report is filed, who is the beneficial owner of 20 percent or more of the issuer's outstanding voting equity securities, calculated on the basis of voting power;

(4)   How the securities being offered are being valued, and examples of methods for how such securities may be valued by the issuer in the future, including during subsequent corporate actions;

(5)   The risks to purchasers of the securities relating to minority ownership in the issuer and the risks associated with corporate actions including additional issuances of securities, issuer repurchases of securities, a sale of the issuer or of assets of the issuer or transactions with related parties; and

(6)   A description of the restrictions on transfer of the securities, as set forth in § 227.501;

(n)   The name, SEC file number and Central Registration Depository (CRD) number (as applicable) of the intermediary through which the offering is being conducted;

(o)   A description of the intermediary's financial interests in the issuer's transaction and in the issuer, including:

(1)   The amount of compensation to be paid to the intermediary, whether as a dollar amount or a percentage of the offering amount, or a good faith estimate if the exact amount is not available at the time of the filing, for conducting the offering, including the amount of referral and any other fees associated with the offering, and

(2)   Any other direct or indirect interest in the issuer held by the intermediary, or any arrangement for the intermediary to acquire such an interest;

(p)   A description of the material terms of any indebtedness of the issuer, including the amount, interest rate, maturity date and any other material terms;

(q)   A description of exempt offerings conducted within the past three years;

Instruction to paragraph (q). In providing a description of any prior exempt offerings, disclose:

(1)   The date of the offering;

(2)   The offering exemption relied upon;

(3)   The type of securities offered; and

(4)   The amount of securities sold and the use of proceeds;

(r)   A description of any transaction since the beginning of the issuer's last fiscal year, or any currently proposed transaction, to which the issuer was or is to be a party and the amount involved exceeds five percent of the aggregate amount of capital raised by the issuer in reliance on section 4(a)(6) of the Securities Act during the preceding 12-month period, inclusive of the amount the issuer seeks to raise in the current offering under section 4(a)(6) of the Securities Act, in which any of the following persons had or is to have a direct or indirect material interest:

(1)   Any director or officer of the issuer;

(2)   Any person who is, as of the most recent practicable date but no earlier than 120 days prior to the date the offering statement or report is filed, the beneficial owner of 20 percent or more of the issuer's outstanding voting equity securities, calculated on the basis of voting power;

(3)   If the issuer was incorporated or organized within the past three years, any promoter of the issuer; or

(4)   Any member of the family of any of the foregoing persons, which includes a child, stepchild, grandchild, parent, stepparent, grandparent, spouse or spousal equivalent, sibling, mother-in-law, father-in-law, son-in-law, daughter-in-law, brother-in-law, or sister-in-law, and shall include adoptive relationships. The term *spousal equivalent* means a cohabitant occupying a relationship generally equivalent to that of a spouse.

Instruction 1 to paragraph (r). For each transaction identified, disclose the name of the specified person and state his or her relationship to the issuer, and the nature and, where practicable, the approximate amount of his or her interest in the transaction. The amount of such interest shall be computed without regard to the amount of the profit or loss involved in the transaction. Where it is not practicable to state the approximate amount of the interest, the approximate amount involved in the transaction shall be disclosed.

Instruction 2 to paragraph (r). For purposes of paragraph (r), a transaction includes, but is not limited to, any financial transaction, arrangement or relationship (including any indebtedness or guarantee of indebtedness) or any series of similar transactions, arrangements or relationships.

    (s)   A discussion of the issuer's financial condition, including, to the extent material, liquidity, capital resources and historical results of operations;

Instruction 1 to paragraph (s). The discussion must cover each period for which financial statements of the issuer are provided. An issuer also must include a discussion of any material changes or trends known to management in the financial condition and results of operations of the issuer subsequent to the period for which financial statements are provided.

Instruction 2 to paragraph (s). For issuers with no prior operating history, the discussion should focus on financial milestones and operational, liquidity and other challenges. For issuers with an operating history, the discussion should focus on whether historical results and cash flows are representative of what investors should expect in the future. Issuers should take into account the proceeds of the offering and any other known or pending sources of capital. Issuers also should discuss how the proceeds from the offering will affect the issuer's liquidity, whether receiving these funds and any other additional funds is necessary to the viability of the business, and how quickly the issuer anticipates using its available cash. In addition, issuers should describe the other available sources of capital to the business, such as lines of credit or required contributions by shareholders.

Instruction 3 to paragraph (s). References to the issuer in this paragraph and its instructions refer to the issuer and its predecessors, if any.

    (t)   For offerings that, together with all other amounts sold under section 4(a)(6) of the Securities Act within the preceding 12-month period, have, in the aggregate, the following target offering amounts:

    (1) $107,000 or less, the amount of total income, taxable income and total tax, or the equivalent line items, as reported on the federal income tax returns filed by the issuer for the most recently completed year (if any), which shall be certified by the principal executive officer of the issuer to reflect accurately the information reported on the issuer's federal income tax returns, and financial statements of the issuer, which shall be certified by the principal executive officer of the issuer to be true and complete in all material respects. If financial statements of the issuer are available that have either been reviewed or audited by a public accountant that is independent of the issuer, the issuer must provide those financial statements instead and need not include the information reported on the federal income tax returns or the certifications of the principal executive officer;

    (2)   More than $107,000, but not more than $535,000, financial statements of the issuer reviewed by a public accountant that is independent of the issuer. If financial statements of the issuer are available that have been audited by a public accountant that is independent of the issuer, the issuer must provide those financial statements instead and need not include the reviewed financial statements; and

    (3)   More than $535,000, financial statements of the issuer audited by a public accountant that is independent of the issuer; *provided, however,* that for issuers that have not previously sold securities in reliance on section 4(a)(6) of the Securities Act, offerings that have a target offering amount of more than $535,000, but not more than $1,070,000, financial statements of the issuer reviewed by a public accountant that is independent of the issuer. If financial statements of the issuer are available that have been audited by a public accountant that is independent of the issuer, the issuer must provide those financial statements instead and need not include the reviewed financial statements.

Instruction 1 to paragraph (t). To determine the financial statements required under this paragraph (t), an issuer must aggregate amounts sold in reliance on section 4(a)(6) of the Securities Act within the preceding 12-month period and the offering amount in the offering for which disclosure is being provided. If the issuer will accept proceeds in excess of the target offering amount, the issuer must include the maximum offering amount that the issuer will accept in the calculation to determine the financial statements required under this paragraph (t).

Instruction 2 to paragraph (t). An issuer may voluntarily meet the requirements of this paragraph (t) for a higher aggregate target offering amount.

Instruction 3 to paragraph (t). The financial statements must be prepared in accordance with U.S. generally accepted accounting principles and include balance sheets, statements of comprehensive income, statements of cash flows, statements of changes in stockholders' equity and notes to the financial statements. If the financial statements are not audited, they must be labeled as "unaudited." The financial statements must cover the two most recently completed fiscal years or the period(s) since inception, if shorter.

Instruction 4 to paragraph (t). For an offering conducted in the first 120 days of a fiscal year, the financial statements provided may be for the two fiscal years prior to the issuer's most recently completed fiscal year; however, financial statements for the two most recently completed fiscal years must be provided if they are otherwise available. If more than 120 days have passed since the end of the issuer's most recently completed fiscal year, the financial statements provided must be for the issuer's two most recently completed fiscal years. If the 120th day falls on a Saturday, Sunday, or holiday, the next business day shall be considered the 120th day for purposes of determining the age of the financial statements.

Instruction 5 to paragraph (t). An issuer may elect to delay complying with any new or revised financial accounting standard that applies to companies that are not issuers (as defined under section 2(a) of the Sarbanes-Oxley Act of 2002 until the date that such companies are required to comply with such new or revised accounting standard. Issuers electing this accommodation must disclose it at the time the issuer files its offering statement and apply the election to all standards. Issuers electing not to use this accommodation must forgo this accommodation for all financial accounting standards and may not elect to rely on this accommodation in any future filings.

Instruction 6 to paragraph (t). An issuer required to provide information from a tax return under paragraph (t)(1) of this rule before filing a tax return with the U.S. Internal Revenue Service for the most recently completed fiscal year may provide information from its tax return for the prior year (if any), provided that the issuer provides information from the tax return for the most recently completed fiscal year when it is filed with the U.S. Internal Revenue Service (if the tax return is filed during the offering period). An issuer that requested an extension from the U.S. Internal Revenue Service would not be required to provide information from the tax return until the date the return is filed, if filed during the offering period. If an issuer has not yet filed a tax return and is not required to file a tax return before the end of the offering period, then the tax return information does not need to be provided.

Instruction 7 to paragraph (t). An issuer providing financial statements that are not audited or reviewed and tax information as specified under paragraph (t)(1) of this rule must have its principal executive officer provide the following certification:

I, [identify the certifying individual], certify that:

    (1)   the financial statements of [identify the issuer] included in this Form are true and complete in all material respects; and

    (2)   the tax return information of [identify the issuer] included in this Form reflects accurately the information reported on the tax return for [identify the issuer] filed for the fiscal year ended [date of most recent tax return].

[Signature and title].

Instruction 8 to paragraph (t). Financial statement reviews shall be conducted in accordance with the Statements on Standards for Accounting and Review Services issued by the Accounting and Review Services Committee of the American Institute of Certified Public Accountants. A signed review report must accompany the reviewed financial statements, and an issuer must notify the public accountant of the issuer's intended use of the review report in the offering. An issuer will not be in compliance with the requirement to provide reviewed financial statements if the review report includes modifications.

Instruction 9 to paragraph (t). Financial statement audits shall be conducted in accordance with either auditing standards issued by the American Institute of Certified Public Accountants (referred to as U.S. Generally Accepted Auditing Standards) or the standards of the Public Company Accounting Oversight Board. A signed audit report must accompany audited financial statements, and an issuer must notify the public accountant of the issuer's intended use of the audit report in the offering. An issuer will not be in compliance with the requirement to provide audited financial statements if the audit report includes a qualified opinion, an adverse opinion, or a disclaimer of opinion.

Instruction 10 to paragraph (t). To qualify as a public accountant that is independent of the issuer for purposes of this part, the accountant must satisfy the independence standards of either:

(i)   17 CFR 210.2–01 of this chapter, or

(ii)   The American Institute of Certified Public Accountants. The public accountant that audits or reviews the financial statements provided by an issuer must be:

(A)   Duly registered and in good standing as a certified public accountant under the laws of the place of his or her residence or principal office; or

(B)   In good standing and entitled to practice as a public accountant under the laws of his or her place of residence or principal office.

Instruction 11 to paragraph (t). Except as set forth in § 227.100(c), references to the issuer in this paragraph (t) and its instructions (2) through (10) refer to the issuer and its predecessors, if any.

(u)   Any matters that would have triggered disqualification under § 227.503(a) but occurred before May 16, 2016. The failure to provide such disclosure shall not prevent an issuer from continuing to rely on the exemption provided by section 4(a)(6) of the Securities Act if the issuer establishes that it did not know and, in the exercise of reasonable care, could not have known of the existence of the undisclosed matter or matters;

Instruction to paragraph (u). An issuer will not be able to establish that it could not have known of a disqualification unless it has made factual inquiry into whether any disqualifications exist. The nature and scope of the factual inquiry will vary based on the facts and circumstances concerning, among other things, the issuer and the other offering participants.

(v)   Updates regarding the progress of the issuer in meeting the target offering amount, to be provided in accordance with § 227.203;

(w)   Where on the issuer's Web site investors will be able to find the issuer's annual report, and the date by which such report will be available on the issuer's Web site;

(x)   Whether the issuer or any of its predecessors previously failed to comply with the ongoing reporting requirements of § 227.202; and

(y)   Any material information necessary in order to make the statements made, in light of the circumstances under which they were made, not misleading.

Instruction to § 227.201. If disclosure provided pursuant to any paragraph of this rule also satisfies the requirements of one or more other paragraphs of this rule, it is not necessary to repeat the disclosure. Instead of repeating information, an issuer may include a cross-reference to disclosure contained elsewhere in the offering statement or report, including to information in the financial statements.

(z)   Any written communication or broadcast script provided in accordance with Rule 206 or, if within 30 days of the initial filing of the offering statement, § 230.241 of this chapter.

Instruction to § 227.201(a) through (z). If disclosure provided pursuant to any paragraph of this section also satisfies the requirements of one or more other paragraphs of this section, it is not necessary to repeat the disclosure. Instead of repeating information, an issuer may include a cross-reference to disclosure contained elsewhere in the offering statement or report, including to information in the financial statements.

(aa) Between May 4, 2020, and February 28, 2021, an issuer may initiate an offering intended to be conducted on an expedited basis due to circumstances relating to COVID-19. Such issuer:

(1) Must prominently provide the following information:

(i) A statement that the offering is being conducted on an expedited basis due to circumstances relating to COVID-19 and pursuant to the Commission's temporary regulatory COVID-19 relief set out in this part;

(ii) If the issuer is relying on paragraph (aa)(2) of this section to omit the information required by paragraph (t) of this section in the initial Form C: Offering Statement (Form C) (§ 239.900 of this chapter) filed with the Commission and provided to investors and the relevant intermediary in accordance with § 227.203(a)(1), a statement that:

(A) The financial information that has been omitted is not currently available and will be provided by an amendment to the offering materials;

(B) The investor should review the complete set of offering materials, including previously omitted financial information, prior to making an investment decision; and

(C) No investment commitments will be accepted until after such financial information has been provided; and

(iii) If the issuer is relying on paragraph (aa)(3) of this section to provide financial statement information required by paragraph (t)(1) of this section, a statement that financial information certified by the principal executive officer of the issuer has been provided instead of financial statements reviewed by a public accountant that is independent of the issuer; and

(iv) In lieu of the information required by paragraph (j) of this section, a description of the process to complete the transaction or cancel an investment commitment, including a statement that:

(A) Investors may cancel an investment commitment for any reason within 48 hours from the time of his or her investment commitment (or such later period as the issuer may designate);

(B) The intermediary will notify investors when the target offering amount has been met;

(C) The issuer may close the offering at any time after it has aggregate investment commitments for which the right to cancel pursuant to paragraph (aa)(1)(iv)(A) of this section has lapsed that equal or exceed the target offering amount (absent a material change that would require an extension of the offering and reconfirmation of the investment commitment); and

(D) If an investor does not cancel an investment commitment within 48 hours from the time of the initial investment commitment, the funds will be released to the issuer upon closing of the offering and the investor will receive securities in exchange for his or her investment;

(2) May omit the information required by paragraph (t) of this section in the initial Form C: Offering Statement (Form C) (§ 239.900 of this chapter) filed with the Commission and provided to investors and the relevant intermediary in accordance with § 227.203(a)(1) if such information is unavailable at the time of filing, but the intermediary may not accept any investment commitments until complete information required under paragraph (t) of this section is provided through an amendment to the Form C in accordance with § 227.203(a)(2); and

(3) May comply with the requirements of paragraph (t)(1) of this section instead of paragraph (t)(2) of this section for an offering or offerings that, together with all other amounts sold under section 4(a)(6) of the Securities Act (15 U.S.C. 77d(a)(6)) within the preceding 12-month period, have, in the aggregate, a target offering amount of more than $107,000, but not more than

$250,000, and financial statements of the issuer that have either been reviewed or audited by a public accountant that is independent of the issuer are unavailable at the time of filing.

(bb) Between March 1, 2021, and August 28, 2022, an issuer may comply with the requirements of paragraph (t)(1) of this section instead of paragraph (t)(2) of this section for an offering or offerings that, together with all other amounts sold under section 4(a)(6) of the Securities Act (15 U.S.C. 77d(a)(6)) within the preceding 12-month period, have, in the aggregate, a target offering amount of more than $107,000, but not more than $250,000, and financial statements of the issuer that have either been reviewed or audited by a public accountant that is independent of the issuer are unavailable at the time of filing. Such issuer must prominently provide a statement that financial information certified by the principal executive officer of the issuer has been provided instead of financial statements reviewed by a public accountant that is independent of the issuer.

Rule 202.   Ongoing Reporting Requirements.

(a)   An issuer that has offered and sold securities in reliance on section 4(a)(6) of the Securities Act and in accordance with section 4A of the Securities Act and this part must file with the Commission and post on the issuer's Web site an annual report along with the financial statements of the issuer certified by the principal executive officer of the issuer to be true and complete in all material respects and a description of the financial condition of the issuer as described in § 227.201(s). If, however, an issuer has available financial statements that have either been reviewed or audited by a public accountant that is independent of the issuer, those financial statements must be provided and the certification by the principal executive officer will not be required. The annual report also must include the disclosure required by paragraphs (a), (b), (c), (d), (e), (f), (m), (p), (q), (r), and (x) of § 227.201. The report must be filed in accordance with the requirements of § 227.203 and Form C (§ 239.900 of this chapter) and no later than 120 days after the end of the fiscal year covered by the report.

Instruction 1 to paragraph (a). Instructions (3), (8), (9), (10), and (11) to paragraph (t) of Rule 201 shall apply for purposes of this rule.

Instruction 2 to paragraph (a). An issuer providing financial statements that are not audited or reviewed must have its principal executive officer provide the following certification:

I, [identify the certifying individual], certify that the financial statements of [identify the issuer] included in this Form are true and complete in all material respects.

[Signature and title].

(a)   An issuer must continue to comply with the ongoing reporting requirements until one of the following occurs:

(1)   The issuer is required to file reports under section 13(a) or section 15(d) of the Exchange Act;

(2)   The issuer has filed, since its most recent sale of securities pursuant to this part, at least one annual report pursuant to this rule and has fewer than 300 holders of record;

(3)   The issuer has filed, since its most recent sale of securities pursuant to this part, the annual reports required pursuant to this rule for at least the three most recent years and has total assets that do not exceed $10,000,000;

(4)   The issuer or another party repurchases all of the securities issued in reliance on section 4(a)(6) of the Securities Act, including any payment in full of debt securities or any complete redemption of redeemable securities; or

(5)   The issuer liquidates or dissolves its business in accordance with state law.

Rule 203.   Filing Requirements and Form.

(a)   Form C—Offering statement and amendments (§ 239.900 of this chapter).

(1)   *Offering statement.* Except as allowed by § 227.206, an issuer offering or selling securities in reliance on section 4(a)(6) of the Securities Act and in accordance with section 4A of the Securities Act

and this part, and any co-issuer jointly offering or selling securities with such an issuer in reliance on the same, must file with the Commission and provide to investors and the relevant intermediary a Form C: Offering Statement (Form C) (§ 239.900 of this chapter) prior to the commencement of the offering of securities. An issuer that is both offering or selling securities with a co-issuer and separately offering or selling securities on its own must file with the Commission and provide to investors and the relevant intermediary a separate Form C for such offering. Every Form C must include the information required by Rule 201.

(2) *Amendments to offering statement.* An issuer must file with the Commission and provide to investors and the relevant intermediary an amendment to the offering statement filed on Form C (§ 239.900 of this chapter) to disclose any material changes, additions or updates to information that it provides to investors through the intermediary's platform, for any offering that has not yet been completed or terminated. The amendment must be filed on Form C: Amendment (Form C/A) (§ 239.900 of this chapter), and if the amendment reflects material changes, additions or updates, the issuer shall check the box indicating that investors must reconfirm an investment commitment within five business days or the investor's commitment will be considered cancelled.

(3) *Progress updates.* (i) An issuer must file with the Commission and provide to investors and the relevant intermediary a Form C: Progress Update (Form C–U) (§ 239.900 of this chapter) to disclose its progress in meeting the target offering amount no later than five business days after each of the dates when the issuer reaches 50 percent and 100 percent of the target offering amount.

(ii) If the issuer will accept proceeds in excess of the target offering amount, the issuer must file with the Commission and provide to investors and the relevant intermediary, no later than five business days after the offering deadline, a final Form C–U (§ 239.900 of this chapter) to disclose the total amount of securities sold in the offering.

(iii) The requirements of paragraphs (a)(3)(i) and (ii) of this rule shall not apply to an issuer if the relevant intermediary makes publicly available on the intermediary's platform frequent updates regarding the progress of the issuer in meeting the target offering amount; however, the issuer must still file a Form C–U (§ 239.900 of this chapter) to disclose the total amount of securities sold in the offering no later than five business days after the offering deadline.

Instruction to paragraph (a)(3). If multiple Forms C–U (§ 239.900 of this chapter) are triggered within the same five business day period, the issuer may consolidate such progress updates into one Form C–U, so long as the Form C–U discloses the most recent threshold that was met and the Form C–U is filed with the Commission and provided to investors and the relevant intermediary by the day on which the first progress update is due.

Instruction 1 to paragraph (a). An issuer would satisfy the requirement to provide to the relevant intermediary the information required by this paragraph (a) if it provides to the relevant intermediary a copy of the disclosures filed with the Commission.

Instruction 2 to paragraph (a). An issuer would satisfy the requirement to provide to investors the information required by this paragraph (a) if the issuer refers investors to the information on the intermediary's platform by means of a posting on the issuer's Web site or by email.

(a) *Form C: Annual report and termination of reporting* (§ 239.900 of this chapter). (1) *Annual reports.* An issuer that has sold securities in reliance on section 4(a)(6) of the Securities Act and in accordance with section 4A of the Securities Act and this part must file an annual report on Form C: Annual Report (Form C–AR) (§ 239.900 of this chapter) with the Commission no later than 120 days after the end of the fiscal year covered by the report. The annual report shall include the information required by § 227.202(a).

(2) *Amendments to annual report.* An issuer must file with the Commission an amendment to the annual report filed on Form C: Annual Report (Form C–AR) (§ 239.900 of this chapter) to make a material change to the previously filed annual report as soon as practicable after discovery of the need for the material change. The amendment must be filed on Form C: Amendment to Annual Report (Form C–AR/A) (§ 239.900 of this chapter).

(3)   *Termination of reporting.* An issuer eligible to terminate its obligation to file annual reports with the Commission pursuant to § 227.202(b) must file with the Commission, within five business days from the date on which the issuer becomes eligible to terminate its reporting obligation, Form C: Termination of Reporting (Form C–TR) (§ 239.900 of this chapter) to advise investors that the issuer will cease reporting pursuant to this part.

Rule 204.   Advertising.

(a)   An issuer may not, directly or indirectly, advertise the terms of an offering made in reliance on section 4(a)(6) of the Securities Act, except for oral or written communications that meet the requirements of paragraph (b) of this section or of Rule 206.

Instruction to paragraph (a). For purposes of this paragraph (a), issuer includes persons acting on behalf of the issuer.

(b)   A notice may advertise any of the terms of an issuer's offering made in reliance on section 4(a)(6) of the Securities Act if it directs investors to the intermediary's platform and includes no more than the following information:

(1)   A statement that the issuer is conducting an offering pursuant to section 4(a)(6) of the Securities Act, the name of the intermediary through which the offering is being conducted, and information (including a link in any written communications) directing the potential investor to the intermediary's platform.

(2)   The terms of the offering; and

(3)   Factual information about the legal identity and business location of the issuer, limited to the name of the issuer of the security, the address, phone number and Web site of the issuer, the email address of a representative of the issuer and a brief description of the business of the issuer.

(b)   Notwithstanding the prohibition on advertising any of the terms of the offering, an issuer, and persons acting on behalf of the issuer, may communicate with investors and potential investors about the terms of the offering through communication channels provided by the intermediary on the intermediary's platform, provided that an issuer identifies itself as the issuer in all communications. Persons acting on behalf of the issuer must identify their affiliation with the issuer in all communications on the intermediary's platform.

(c)   Notwithstanding the prohibition on advertising any of the terms of the offering, an issuer, and persons acting on behalf of the issuer, may communicate with investors and potential investors about the terms of the offering through communication channels provided by the intermediary on the intermediary's platform, provided that an issuer identifies itself as the issuer in all communications. Persons acting on behalf of the issuer must identify their affiliation with the issuer in all communications on the intermediary's platform.

(d)   Notwithstanding the requirement that a notice advertising any of the terms of an issuer's offering made in reliance on section 4(a)(6) of the Securities Act include no more than the information specified in paragraph (b) of this section, an issuer conducting an offering in reliance on Regulation Crowdfunding concurrently with another offering that discloses the terms of the Regulation Crowdfunding offering in the disclosure document for the other offering will not be deemed to have exceeded these disclosure limitations if the disclosure document for the other offering satisfies all the other requirements of this section. If the disclosure document for the other offering is filed on the Commission's Electronic Data Gathering and Retrieval System (EDGAR), the link required by paragraph (b)(1) may not be a live hyperlink.

Instruction to § 227.204. For purposes of this section, terms of the offering means the amount of securities offered, the nature of the securities, the price of the securities, the closing date of the offering period, the planned use of proceeds and the issuer's progress toward meeting its funding target.

Rule 205.   Promoter Compensation.

(a)   An issuer, or person acting on behalf of the issuer, shall be permitted to compensate or commit to compensate, directly or indirectly, any person to promote the issuer's offerings made in reliance on section

4(a)(6) of the Securities Act through communication channels provided by an intermediary on the intermediary's platform, but only if the issuer or person acting on behalf of the issuer, takes reasonable steps to ensure that the person promoting the offering clearly discloses the receipt, past or prospective, of such compensation with any such communication.

Instruction to paragraph (a). The disclosure required by this paragraph is required, with each communication, for persons engaging in promotional activities on behalf of the issuer through the communication channels provided by the intermediary, regardless of whether or not the compensation they receive is specifically for the promotional activities. This includes persons hired specifically to promote the offering as well as to persons who are otherwise employed by the issuer or who undertake promotional activities on behalf of the issuer.

(b)   Other than as set forth in paragraph (a) of this rule, an issuer or person acting on behalf of the issuer shall not compensate or commit to compensate, directly or indirectly, any person to promote the issuer's offerings made in reliance on section 4(a)(6) of the Securities Act, unless such promotion is limited to notices permitted by, and in compliance with, § 227.204.

Rule 206.   Solicitations of interest and other communications.

(a)   *Solicitation of interest.* At any time before the filing of an offering statement, an issuer may communicate orally or in writing to determine whether there is any interest in a contemplated securities offering. Such communications are deemed to be an offer of a security for sale for purposes of the antifraud provisions of the Federal securities laws. No solicitation or acceptance of money or other consideration, nor of any commitment, binding or otherwise, from any person is permitted until the offering statement is filed.

(b)   *Conditions.* The communications must:

(1)   State that no money or other consideration is being solicited, and if sent in response, will not be accepted;

(2)   State that no offer to buy the securities can be accepted and no part of the purchase price can be received until the offering statement is filed and only through an intermediary's platform; and

(3)   State that a person's indication of interest involves no obligation or commitment of any kind.

(c)   *Indications of interest.* Any written communication under this rule may include a means by which a person may indicate to the issuer that such person is interested in a potential offering. This issuer may require the name, address, telephone number, and/or email address in any response form included pursuant to this paragraph (c).

REQUIREMENTS FOR INTERMEDIARIES

Rule 300.   Intermediaries.

(a)   *Requirements.* A person acting as an intermediary in a transaction involving the offer or sale of securities in reliance on section 4(a)(6) of the Securities Act must:

(1)   Be registered with the Commission as a broker under section 15(b) of the Exchange Act) or as a funding portal in accordance with the requirements of § 227.400; and

(2)   Be a member a national securities association registered under section 15A of the Exchange Act.

(b)   *Financial interests.* Any director, officer or partner of an intermediary, or any person occupying a similar status or performing a similar function, may not have a financial interest in an issuer that is offering or selling securities in reliance on section 4(a)(6) of the Securities Act through the intermediary's platform, or receive a financial interest in an issuer as compensation for the services provided to or for the benefit of the issuer in connection with the offer or sale of such securities. An intermediary may not have a financial interest in an issuer that is offering or selling securities in reliance on section 4(a)(6) of the Securities Act through the intermediary's platform unless:

(1)   The intermediary receives the financial interest from the issuer as compensation for the services provided to, or for the benefit of, the issuer in connection with the offer or sale of the securities

being offered or sold in reliance on section 4(a)(6) of the Securities Act through the intermediary's platform; and

(2)   the financial interest consists of securities of the same class and having the same terms, conditions and rights as the securities being offered or sold in reliance on section 4(a)(6) of the Securities Act through the intermediary's platform. For purposes of this paragraph, a *financial interest in an issuer* means a direct or indirect ownership of, or economic interest in, any class of the issuer's securities.

(c)   *Definitions.* For purposes of this part:

(1)   *Associated person of a funding portal* or *person associated with a funding portal* means any partner, officer, director or manager of a funding portal (or any person occupying a similar status or performing similar functions), any person directly or indirectly controlling or controlled by such funding portal, or any employee of a funding portal, except that any person associated with a funding portal whose functions are solely clerical or ministerial shall not be included in the meaning of such term for purposes of section 15(b) of the Exchange Act (other than paragraphs (4) and (6) of section 15(b) of the Exchange Act).

(2)   *Funding portal* means a broker acting as an intermediary in a transaction involving the offer or sale of securities in reliance on section 4(a)(6) of the Securities Act, that does not:

(i)   Offer investment advice or recommendations;

(ii)   Solicit purchases, sales or offers to buy the securities displayed on its platform;

(iii) Compensate employees, agents, or other persons for such solicitation or based on the sale of securities displayed or referenced on its platform; or

(iv)   Hold, manage, possess, or otherwise handle investor funds or securities.

(3)   *Intermediary* means a broker registered under section 15(b) of the Exchange Act or a funding portal registered under § 227.400 and includes, where relevant, an associated person of the registered broker or registered funding portal.

(4)   *Platform* means a program or application accessible via the Internet or other similar electronic communication medium through which a registered broker or a registered funding portal acts as an intermediary in a transaction involving the offer or sale of securities in reliance on section 4(a)(6) of the Securities Act.

Instruction to paragraph (c)(4). An intermediary through which a crowdfunding transaction is conducted may engage in back office or other administrative functions other than on the intermediary's platform.

Rule 301.   Measures to Reduce Risk of Fraud.

An intermediary in a transaction involving the offer or sale of securities in reliance on section 4(a)(6) of the Securities Act must:

(a)   Have a reasonable basis for believing that an issuer seeking to offer and sell securities in reliance on section 4(a)(6) of the Securities Act through the intermediary's platform complies with the requirements in section 4A(b) of the Act and the related requirements in this part. In satisfying this requirement, an intermediary may rely on the representations of the issuer concerning compliance with these requirements unless the intermediary has reason to question the reliability of those representations;

(b)   Have a reasonable basis for believing that the issuer has established means to keep accurate records of the holders of the securities it would offer and sell through the intermediary's platform, provided that an intermediary may rely on the representations of the issuer concerning its means of recordkeeping unless the intermediary has reason to question the reliability of those representations. An intermediary will be deemed to have satisfied this requirement if the issuer has engaged the services of a transfer agent that is registered under Section 17A of the Exchange Act.

(c)   Deny access to its platform to an issuer if the intermediary:

(1) Has a reasonable basis for believing that the issuer or any of its officers, directors (or any person occupying a similar status or performing a similar function) or beneficial owners of 20 percent or more of the issuer's outstanding voting equity securities, calculated on the basis of voting power, is subject to a disqualification under § 227.503. In satisfying this requirement, an intermediary must, at a minimum, conduct a background and securities enforcement regulatory history check on each issuer whose securities are to be offered by the intermediary and on each officer, director or beneficial owner of 20 percent or more of the issuer's outstanding voting equity securities, calculated on the basis of voting power.

(2) Has a reasonable basis for believing that the issuer or the offering presents the potential for fraud or otherwise raises concerns about investor protection. In satisfying this requirement, an intermediary must deny access if it reasonably believes that it is unable to adequately or effectively assess the risk of fraud of the issuer or its potential offering. In addition, if an intermediary becomes aware of information after it has granted access that causes it to reasonably believe that the issuer or the offering presents the potential for fraud or otherwise raises concerns about investor protection, the intermediary must promptly remove the offering from its platform, cancel the offering, and return (or, for funding portals, direct the return of) any funds that have been committed by investors in the offering.

(d) Have a reasonable basis for believing that an issuer seeking to initiate an offering of securities between May 4, 2020, and August 31, 2020, in reliance on section 4(a)(6) of the Securities Act through the intermediary's platform on an expedited basis due to circumstances relating to COVID-19 that has previously sold securities in reliance on section 4(a)(6) of the Securities Act has complied with the requirements in section 4A(b) of the Act) and the related requirements in this part. In satisfying the requirement in this paragraph (d), an intermediary may rely on the representations of the issuer concerning compliance with the requirements in this paragraph (d) unless the intermediary has reason to question the reliability of those representations.

(e) Have a reasonable basis for believing that an issuer seeking to initiate an offering of securities between March 1, 2021, and August 28, 2022, in reliance on section 4(a)(6) of the Securities Act through the intermediary's platform that is relying on Rule 201(bb) and that has previously sold securities in reliance on section 4(a)(6) of the Securities Act has complied with the requirements in section 4A(b) of the Act and the related requirements in this part. In satisfying the requirement in this paragraph (e), an intermediary may rely on the representations of the issuer concerning compliance with the requirements in this paragraph (e) unless the intermediary has reason to question the reliability of those representations.

Rule 302.   Account Opening.

(a) *Accounts and electronic delivery.*

(1) No intermediary or associated person of an intermediary may accept an investment commitment in a transaction involving the offer or sale of securities in reliance on section 4(a)(6) of the Securities Act until the investor has opened an account with the intermediary and the intermediary has obtained from the investor consent to electronic delivery of materials.

(2) An intermediary must provide all information that is required to be provided by the intermediary under subpart C of this part (§§ 227.300 through 227.305), including, but not limited to, educational materials, notices and confirmations, through electronic means. Unless otherwise indicated in the relevant rule of subpart C of this part, in satisfying this requirement, an intermediary must provide the information through an electronic message that contains the information, through an electronic message that includes a specific link to the information as posted on intermediary's platform, or through an electronic message that provides notice of what the information is and that it is located on the intermediary's platform or on the issuer's Web site. Electronic messages include, but are not limited to, email, social media messages, instant messages or other electronic media messages.

(b) *Educational materials.* (1) In connection with establishing an account for an investor, an intermediary must deliver educational materials to such investor that explain in plain language and are otherwise designed to communicate effectively and accurately:

(i)   The process for the offer, purchase and issuance of securities through the intermediary and the risks associated with purchasing securities offered and sold in reliance on section 4(a)(6) of the Securities Act;

(ii)   The types of securities offered and sold in reliance on section 4(a)(6) of the Securities Act available for purchase on the intermediary's platform and the risks associated with each type of security, including the risk of having limited voting power as a result of dilution;

(iii)   The restrictions on the resale of a security offered and sold in reliance on section 4(a)(6) of the Securities Act;

(iv)   The types of information that an issuer is required to provide under § 227.202, the frequency of the delivery of that information and the possibility that those obligations may terminate in the future;

(v)   The limitations on the amounts an investor may invest pursuant to § 227.100(a)(2);

(vi)   The limitations on an investor's right to cancel an investment commitment and the circumstances in which an investment commitment may be cancelled by the issuer;

(vii) The need for the investor to consider whether investing in a security offered and sold in reliance on section 4(a)(6) of the Securities Act is appropriate for that investor;

(viii) That following completion of an offering conducted through the intermediary, there may or may not be any ongoing relationship between the issuer and intermediary; and

(ix)   That under certain circumstances an issuer may cease to publish annual reports and, therefore, an investor may not continually have current financial information about the issuer.

(2)   An intermediary must make the most current version of its educational material available on its platform at all times and, if at any time, the intermediary makes a material revision to its educational materials, it must make the revised educational materials available to all investors before accepting any additional investment commitments or effecting any further transactions in securities offered and sold in reliance on section 4(a)(6) of the Securities Act.

(c)   *Promoters.* In connection with establishing an account for an investor, an intermediary must inform the investor that any person who promotes an issuer's offering for compensation, whether past or prospective, or who is a founder or an employee of an issuer that engages in promotional activities on behalf of the issuer on the intermediary's platform, must clearly disclose in all communications on the intermediary's platform, respectively, the receipt of the compensation and that he or she is engaging in promotional activities on behalf of the issuer.

(d)   *Compensation disclosure.* When establishing an account for an investor, an intermediary must clearly disclose the manner in which the intermediary is compensated in connection with offerings and sales of securities in reliance on section 4(a)(6) of the Securities Act.

Rule 303.   Requirements with Respect to Transactions.

(a)   *Issuer information.* An intermediary in a transaction involving the offer or sale of securities in reliance on section 4(a)(6) of the Securities Act must make available to the Commission and to investors any information required to be provided by the issuer of the securities under §§ 227.201 and 227.203(a).

(1)   This information must be made publicly available on the intermediary's platform, in a manner that reasonably permits a person accessing the platform to save, download, or otherwise store the information;

(2)   This information must be made publicly available on the intermediary's platform for a minimum of 21 days before any securities are sold in the offering, during which time the intermediary may accept investment commitments;

(3)   This information, including any additional information provided by the issuer, must remain publicly available on the intermediary's platform until the offer and sale of securities in reliance on section 4(a)(6) of the Securities Act is completed or cancelled; and

(4)   An intermediary may not require any person to establish an account with the intermediary to access this information.

(b)   *Investor qualification.* Each time before accepting any investment commitment (including any additional investment commitment from the same person), an intermediary must:

(1)   Have a reasonable basis for believing that the investor satisfies the investment limitations established by section 4(a)(6)(B) of the Act and this part. An intermediary may rely on an investor's representations concerning compliance with the investment limitation requirements concerning the investor's annual income, net worth, and the amount of the investor's other investments made pursuant to section 4(a)(6) of the Securities Act unless the intermediary has reason to question the reliability of the representation.

(2)   Obtain from the investor:

(i)   A representation that the investor has reviewed the intermediary's educational materials delivered pursuant to § 227.302(b), understands that the entire amount of his or her investment may be lost, and is in a financial condition to bear the loss of the investment; and

(ii)   A questionnaire completed by the investor demonstrating the investor's understanding that:

(A)   There are restrictions on the investor's ability to cancel an investment commitment and obtain a return of his or her investment;

(B)   It may be difficult for the investor to resell securities acquired in reliance on section 4(a)(6) of the Securities Act; and

(C)   Investing in securities offered and sold in reliance on section 4(a)(6) of the Securities Act involves risk, and the investor should not invest any funds in an offering made in reliance on section 4(a)(6) of the Securities Act unless he or she can afford to lose the entire amount of his or her investment.

(c)   *Communication channels.* An intermediary must provide on its platform communication channels by which persons can communicate with one another and with representatives of the issuer about offerings made available on the intermediary's platform, provided:

(1)   If the intermediary is a funding portal, it does not participate in these communications other than to establish guidelines for communication and remove abusive or potentially fraudulent communications;

(2)   The intermediary permits public access to view the discussions made in the communication channels;

(3)   The intermediary restricts posting of comments in the communication channels to those persons who have opened an account with the intermediary on its platform; and

(4)   The intermediary requires that any person posting a comment in the communication channels clearly and prominently disclose with each posting whether he or she is a founder or an employee of an issuer engaging in promotional activities on behalf of the issuer, or is otherwise compensated, whether in the past or prospectively, to promote the issuer's offering.

(d)   *Notice of investment commitment.* An intermediary must promptly, upon receipt of an investment commitment from an investor, give or send to the investor a notification disclosing:

(1)   The dollar amount of the investment commitment;

(2)   The price of the securities, if known;

(3)   The name of the issuer; and

(4)   The date and time by which the investor may cancel the investment commitment.

(e)   *Maintenance and transmission of funds.* (1) An intermediary that is a registered broker must comply with the requirements of Exchange Act Rule 15c2–4.

(2)   An intermediary that is a funding portal must direct investors to transmit the money or other consideration directly to a qualified third party that has agreed in writing to hold the funds for the benefit of, and to promptly transmit or return the funds to, the persons entitled thereto in accordance with paragraph (e)(3) of this rule. For purposes of this subpart C (§§ 227.300 through 227.305), a qualified third party means a:

    (i)   Registered broker or dealer that carries customer or broker or dealer accounts and holds funds or securities for those persons; or

    (ii)   Bank or credit union (where such credit union is insured by National Credit Union Administration) that has agreed in writing either to hold the funds in escrow for the persons who have the beneficial interests therein and to transmit or return such funds directly to the persons entitled thereto when so directed by the funding portal as described in paragraph (e)(3) of this rule, or to maintain a bank or credit union account (or accounts) for the exclusive benefit of investors and the issuer.

(3)   A funding portal that is an intermediary in a transaction involving the offer or sale of securities in reliance on section 4(a)(6) of the Securities Act shall promptly direct the qualified third party to:

    (i)   Transmit funds from the qualified third party to the issuer when the aggregate amount of investment commitments from all investors is equal to or greater than the target amount of the offering and the cancellation period as set forth in § 227.304 has elapsed, *provided that* in no event may the funding portal direct this transmission of funds earlier than 21 days after the date on which the intermediary makes publicly available on its platform the information required to be provided by the issuer under §§ 227.201 and 227.203(a);

    (ii)   Return funds to an investor when an investment commitment has been cancelled in accordance with § 227.304 (including for failure to obtain effective reconfirmation as required under § 227.304(c)); and

    (iii)   Return funds to investors when an issuer does not complete the offering.

(f)   *Confirmation of transaction.* (1) An intermediary must, at or before the completion of a transaction in a security in reliance on section 4(a)(6) of the Securities Act, give or send to each investor a notification disclosing:

    (i)   The date of the transaction;

    (ii)   The type of security that the investor is purchasing;

    (iii)   The identity, price, and number of securities purchased by the investor, as well as the number of securities sold by the issuer in the transaction and the price(s) at which the securities were sold;

    (iv)   If a debt security, the interest rate and the yield to maturity calculated from the price paid and the maturity date;

    (v)   If a callable security, the first date that the security can be called by the issuer; and

    (vi)   The source, form and amount of any remuneration received or to be received by the intermediary in connection with the transaction, including any remuneration received or to be received by the intermediary from persons other than the issuer.

(2)   An intermediary satisfying the requirements of paragraph (f)(1) of this rule is exempt from the requirements of § 240.10b–10 of this chapter with respect to a transaction in a security offered and sold in reliance on section 4(a)(6) of the Securities Act.

(g)   *Temporary requirements.* (1) An intermediary in a transaction involving the offer or sale of securities initiated between May 4, 2020, and August 31, 2020, in reliance on section 4(a)(6) of the Securities Act by an issuer that is conducting an offering on an expedited basis due to circumstances relating to COVID-19:

(i)   Shall prominently make publicly available on the intermediary's platform the issuer information required pursuant to § 227.201(aa)(1);

(ii) Shall not be required to comply with paragraph (a)(2) of this rule; and

(iii) Shall make the issuer information described in paragraph (g)(1)(i) of this rule publicly available on the intermediary's platform before any securities are sold in the offering. The intermediary may accept investment commitments during the time such information is made available, but only if the issuer has provided the information required by § 227.201(t) or, if applicable, § 227.201(z)(3) in either the initial Form C: Offering Statement (Form C) (§ 239.900 of this chapter) filed with the Commission and provided to investors and the relevant intermediary in accordance with § 227.203(a)(1) or through an amendment to the Form C in accordance with § 227.203(a)(2); and

(2)   A funding portal that is an intermediary in a transaction involving the offer or sale of securities initiated between May 4, 2020, and August 31, 2020, in reliance on section 4(a)(6) of the Securities Act by an issuer that is conducting an offering on an expedited basis due to circumstances relating to COVID-19 shall not be required to comply with the requirement in paragraph (e)(3)(i) of this rule that a funding portal not direct a transmission of funds earlier than 21 days after the date on which the intermediary makes publicly available on its platform the information required to be provided by the issuer under §§ 227.201 and 227.203(a).

Rule 304.   Completion of offerings, cancellations, and reconfirmations.

(a)   *Generally.* An investor may cancel an investment commitment for any reason until 48 hours prior to the deadline identified in the issuer's offering materials. During the 48 hours prior to such deadline, an investment commitment may not be cancelled except as provided in paragraph (c) of this rule.

(b)   *Early completion of offering.* If an issuer reaches the target offering amount prior to the deadline identified in its offering materials pursuant to § 227.201(g), the issuer may close the offering on a date earlier than the deadline identified in its offering materials pursuant to § 227.201(g), *provided that*

(1)   The offering remains open for a minimum of 21 days pursuant to § 227.303(a);

(2)   The intermediary provides notice to any potential investors, and gives or sends notice to investors that have made investment commitments in the offering, of:

(i)   The new, anticipated deadline of the offering;

(ii) The right of investors to cancel investment commitments for any reason until 48 hours prior to the new offering deadline; and

(iii) Whether the issuer will continue to accept investment commitments during the 48-hour period prior to the new offering deadline.

(3)   The new offering deadline is scheduled for and occurs at least five business days after the notice required in paragraph (b)(2) of this rule is provided; and

(4)   At the time of the new offering deadline, the issuer continues to meet or exceed the target offering amount.

(c)   *Cancellations and reconfirmations based on material changes.* (1) If there is a material change to the terms of an offering or to the information provided by the issuer, the intermediary must give or send to any investor who has made an investment commitment notice of the material change and that the investor's investment commitment will be cancelled unless the investor reconfirms his or her investment commitment within five business days of receipt of the notice. If the investor fails to reconfirm his or her investment within those five business days, the intermediary within five business days thereafter must:

(i)   Give or send the investor a notification disclosing that the commitment was cancelled, the reason for the cancellation and the refund amount that the investor is expected to receive; and

(ii) Direct the refund of investor funds.

(2)   If material changes to the offering or to the information provided by the issuer regarding the offering occur within five business days of the maximum number of days that an offering is to remain open, the offering must be extended to allow for a period of five business days for the investor to reconfirm his or her investment.

(3)   If material changes to the offering or to the information provided by the issuer regarding the offering occur within five business days of the maximum number of days that an offering is to remain open, the offering must be extended to allow for a period of five business days for the investor to reconfirm his or her investment.

(d)   *Return of funds if offering is not completed.* If an issuer does not complete an offering, an intermediary must within five business days:

(1)   Give or send each investor a notification of the cancellation, disclosing the reason for the cancellation, and the refund amount that the investor is expected to receive;

(2)   Direct the refund of investor funds; and

(3)   Prevent investors from making investment commitments with respect to that offering on its platform.

(e)   *Temporary requirements.* The following shall apply in lieu of paragraphs (a) and (b) of this section with respect to an offering initiated between May 4, 2020, and February 28, 2021, that is intended to be conducted on an expedited basis due to circumstances relating to COVID-19:

(1)   An investor may cancel an investment commitment for any reason within 48 hours from the time of his or her investment commitment (or such later period as the issuer may designate). After such 48 hour period, an investment commitment may not be cancelled except as provided in paragraph (c) of this section; and

(2)   If an issuer has received aggregate investment commitments for which the right to cancel pursuant to paragraph (e)(1) has lapsed covering the target offering amount prior to the deadline identified in its offering materials pursuant to § 227.201(g), the issuer may close the offering on a date earlier than the deadline identified in its offering materials pursuant to § 227.201(g), provided that:

(i)   The issuer has complied with § 227.201(z);

(ii)   The intermediary provides notice to any potential investors, and gives or sends notice to investors that have made investment commitments in the offering, that the target offering amount has been met; and

(iii)   At the time of the closing of the offering, the issuer continues to meet or exceed the target offering amount.

Rule 305.   Payment to third parties.

(a)   *Prohibition on payments for personally identifiable information.* An intermediary may not compensate any person for providing the intermediary with the personally identifiable information of any investor or potential investor in securities offered and sold in reliance on section 4(a)(6) of the Securities Act.

(b)   For purposes of this rule, personally identifiable information means information that can be used to distinguish or trace an individual's identity, either alone or when combined with other personal or identifying information that is linked or linkable to a specific individual.

FUNDING PORTAL REGULATION

Rule 400.   Registration of funding portals.

(a)   *Registration.* A funding portal must register with the Commission, by filing a complete Form Funding Portal (§ 249.2000 of this chapter) in accordance with the instructions on the form, and become a member of a national securities association registered under section 15A of the Exchange Act. The registration will be effective the later of:

(1) Thirty calendar days after the date that the registration is received by the Commission; or

(2) The date the funding portal is approved for membership by a national securities association registered under section 15A of the Exchange Act.

(b) *Amendments to registration.* A funding portal must file an amendment to Form Funding Portal (§ 249.2000 of this chapter) within 30 days of any of the information previously submitted on Form Funding Portal becoming inaccurate for any reason.

(c) *Successor registration.* (1) If a funding portal succeeds to and continues the business of a registered funding portal, the registration of the predecessor will remain effective as the registration of the successor if the successor, within 30 days after such succession, files a registration on Form Funding Portal (§ 249.2000 of this chapter) and the predecessor files a withdrawal on Form Funding Portal; *provided, however,* that the registration of the predecessor funding portal will be deemed withdrawn 45 days after registration on Form Funding Portal is filed by the successor.

(2) Notwithstanding paragraph (c)(1) of this rule, if a funding portal succeeds to and continues the business of a registered funding portal and the succession is based solely on a change of the predecessor's date or state of incorporation, form of organization, or composition of a partnership, the successor may, within 30 days after the succession, amend the registration of the predecessor on Form Funding Portal (§ 249.2000 of this chapter) to reflect these changes.

(d) *Withdrawal.* A funding portal must promptly file a withdrawal of registration on Form Funding Portal (§ 249.2000 of this chapter) in accordance with the instructions on the form upon ceasing to operate as a funding portal. Withdrawal will be effective on the later of 30 days after receipt by the Commission (after the funding portal is no longer operational), or within such longer period of time as to which the funding portal consents or which the Commission by order may determine as necessary or appropriate in the public interest or for the protection of investors.

(e) *Applications and reports.* The applications and reports provided for in this rule shall be considered filed when a complete Form Funding Portal (§ 249.2000 of this chapter) is submitted with the Commission. Duplicate originals of the applications and reports provided for in this rule must be filed with surveillance personnel designated by any registered national securities association of which the funding portal is a member.

(f) *Nonresident funding portals.* Registration pursuant to this rule by a nonresident funding portal shall be conditioned upon there being an information sharing arrangement in place between the Commission and the competent regulator in the jurisdiction under the laws of which the nonresident funding portal is organized or where it has its principal place of business, that is applicable to the nonresident funding portal.

(1) *Definition.* For purposes of this rule, the term *nonresident funding portal* shall mean a funding portal incorporated in or organized under the laws of a jurisdiction outside of the United States or its territories, or having its principal place of business in any place not in the United States or its territories.

(2) *Power of attorney.* (i) Each nonresident funding portal registered or applying for registration pursuant to this rule shall obtain a written consent and power of attorney appointing an agent in the United States, other than the Commission or a Commission member, official or employee, upon whom may be served any process, pleadings or other papers in any action under the federal securities laws. This consent and power of attorney must be signed by the nonresident funding portal and the named agent(s) for service of process.

(ii) Each nonresident funding portal registered or applying for registration pursuant to this rule shall, at the time of filing its application on Form Funding Portal (§ 249.2000 of this chapter), furnish to the Commission the name and address of its United States agent for service of process on Schedule C to the Form.

(iii) Any change of a nonresident funding portal's agent for service of process and any change of name or address of a nonresident funding portal's existing agent for service of process shall be communicated promptly to the Commission through amendment of the Schedule C to Form Funding Portal (§ 249.2000 of this chapter).

(iv) Each nonresident funding portal must promptly appoint a successor agent for service of process if the nonresident funding portal discharges its identified agent for service of process or if its agent for service of process is unwilling or unable to accept service on behalf of the nonresident funding portal.

(v) Each nonresident funding portal must maintain, as part of its books and records, the written consent and power of attorney identified in paragraph (f)(2)(i) of this rule for at least three years after the agreement is terminated.

(3) *Access to books and records; inspections and examinations—*(i) *Certification and opinion of counsel.* Any nonresident funding portal applying for registration pursuant to this rule shall:

(A) Certify on Schedule C to Form Funding Portal (§ 249.2000 of this chapter) that the nonresident funding portal can, as a matter of law, and will provide the Commission and any registered national securities association of which it becomes a member with prompt access to the books and records of such nonresident funding portal and can, as a matter of law, and will submit to onsite inspection and examination by the Commission and any registered national securities association of which it becomes a member; and

(B) Provide an opinion of counsel that the nonresident funding portal can, as a matter of law, provide the Commission and any registered national securities association of which it becomes a member with prompt access to the books and records of such nonresident funding portal and can, as a matter of law, submit to onsite inspection and examination by the Commission and any registered national securities association of which it becomes a member.

(ii) *Amendments.* The nonresident funding portal shall re-certify, on Schedule C to Form Funding Portal (§ 249.2000 of this chapter), within 90 days after any changes in the legal or regulatory framework that would impact the nonresident funding portal's ability to provide, or the manner in which it provides, the Commission, or any registered national securities association of which it is a member, with prompt access to its books and records or that would impact the Commission's or such registered national securities association's ability to inspect and examine the nonresident funding portal. The re-certification shall be accompanied by a revised opinion of counsel describing how, as a matter of law, the nonresident funding portal can continue to meet its obligations under paragraphs (f)(3)(i)(A) and (B) of this rule.

Rule 401.   Exemption.

A funding portal that is registered with the Commission pursuant to § 227.400 is exempt from the broker registration requirements of section 15(a)(1) of the Exchange Act in connection with its activities as a funding portal.

Rule 402.   Conditional safe harbor.

(a) *General.* Under section 3(a)(80) of the Exchange Act, a funding portal acting as an intermediary in a transaction involving the offer or sale of securities in reliance on section 4(a)(6) of the Securities Act (15 U.S.C. 77d(a)(6)) may not: offer investment advice or recommendations; solicit purchases, sales, or offers to buy the securities offered or displayed on its platform or portal; compensate employees, agents, or other persons for such solicitation or based on the sale of securities displayed or referenced on its platform or portal; hold, manage, possess, or otherwise handle investor funds or securities; or engage in such other activities as the Commission, by rule, determines appropriate. This rule is intended to provide clarity with respect to the ability of a funding portal to engage in certain activities, consistent with the prohibitions under section 3(a)(80) of the Exchange Act. No presumption shall arise that a funding portal has violated the prohibitions under section 3(a)(80) of the Exchange Act or this part by reason of the funding portal or its associated persons engaging in activities in connection with the offer or sale of securities in reliance on section 4(a)(6) of the Securities Act that do not meet the conditions specified in paragraph (b) of this rule. The antifraud provisions and all other applicable provisions of the federal securities laws continue to apply to the activities described in paragraph (b) of this rule.

(b) *Permitted activities.* A funding portal may, consistent with the prohibitions under section 3(a)(80) of the Exchange Act and this part:

(1) Determine whether and under what terms to allow an issuer to offer and sell securities in reliance on section 4(a)(6) of the Securities Act through its platform; provided that a funding portal otherwise complies with this part;

(2) Apply objective criteria to highlight offerings on the funding portal's platform where:

    (i) The criteria are reasonably designed to highlight a broad selection of issuers offering securities through the funding portal's platform, are applied consistently to all issuers and offerings and are clearly displayed on the funding portal's platform;

    (ii) The criteria may include, among other things, the type of securities being offered (for example, common stock, preferred stock or debt securities); the geographic location of the issuer; the industry or business segment of the issuer; the number or amount of investment commitments made, progress in meeting the issuer's target offering amount or, if applicable, the maximum offering amount; and the minimum or maximum investment amount; provided that the funding portal may not highlight an issuer or offering based on the advisability of investing in the issuer or its offering; and

    (iii) The funding portal does not receive special or additional compensations for highlighting one or more issuers or offerings on its platform;

(3) Provide search functions or other tools that investors can use to search, sort, or categorize the offerings available through the funding portal's platform according to objective criteria where;

    (i) The criteria may include, among other things, the type of securities being offered (for example, common stock, preferred stock or debt securities); the geographic location of the issuer; the industry or business segment of the issuer; the number or amount of investment commitments made, progress in meeting the issuer's target offering amount or, if applicable, the maximum offering amount; and the minimum or maximum investment amount; and

    (ii) The criteria may not include, among other things, the advisability of investing in the issuer or its offering, or an assessment of any characteristic of the issuer, its business plan, its key management or risks associated with an investment.

(4) Provide communication channels by which investors can communicate with one another and with representatives of the issuer through the funding portal's platform about offerings through the platform, so long as the funding portal (and its associated persons):

    (i) Does not participate in these communications, other than to establish guidelines for communication and remove abusive or potentially fraudulent communications;

    (ii) Permits public access to view the discussions made in the communication channels;

    (iii) Restricts posting of comments in the communication channels to those persons who have opened an account on its platform; and

    (iv) Requires that any person posting a comment in the communication channels clearly disclose with each posting whether he or she is a founder or an employee of an issuer engaging in promotional activities on behalf of the issuer, or is otherwise compensated, whether in the past or prospectively, to promote an issuer's offering;

(5) Advise an issuer about the structure or content of the issuer's offering, including assisting the issuer in preparing offering documentation;

(6) Compensate a third party for referring a person to the funding portal, so long as the third party does not provide the funding portal with personally identifiable information of any potential investor, and the compensation, other than that paid to a registered broker or dealer, is not based, directly or indirectly, on the purchase or sale of a security in reliance on section 4(a)(6) of the Securities Act offered on or through the funding portal's platform;

(7)   Pay or offer to pay any compensation to a registered broker or dealer for services, including referrals pursuant to paragraph (b)(6) of this rule, in connection with the offer or sale of securities by the funding portal in reliance on section 4(a)(6) of the Act, provided that:

(i)   Such services are provided pursuant to a written agreement between the funding portal and the registered broker or dealer;

(ii)   Such services and compensation are permitted under this part; and

(iii) Such services and compensation comply with the rules of any registered national securities association of which the funding portal is a member;

(8)   Receive any compensation from a registered broker or dealer for services provided by the funding portal in connection with the offer or sale of securities by the funding portal in reliance on section 4(a)(6) of the Securities Act, provided that:

(i)   Such services are provided pursuant to a written agreement between the funding portal and the registered broker or dealer;

(ii)   Such compensation is permitted under this part; and

(iii) Such compensation complies with the rules of any registered national securities association of which the funding portal is a member;

(9)   Advertise the existence of the funding portal and identify one or more issuers or offerings available on the portal on the basis of objective criteria, as long as:

(i)   The criteria are reasonably designed to identify a broad selection of issuers offering securities through the funding portal's platform, and are applied consistently to all potential issuers and offerings;

(ii)   The criteria may include, among other things, the type of securities being offered (for example, common stock, preferred stock or debt securities); the geographic location of the issuer; the industry or business segment of the issuer; the expressed interest by investors, as measured by number or amount of investment commitments made, progress in meeting the issuer's target offering amount or, if applicable, the maximum offering amount; and the minimum or maximum investment amount; and

(iii) The funding portal does not receive special or additional compensation for identifying the issuer or offering in this manner;

(10) Deny access to its platform to, or cancel an offering of an issuer, pursuant to § 227.301(c)(2), if the funding portal has a reasonable basis for believing that the issuer or the offering presents the potential for fraud or otherwise raises concerns about investor protection;

(11) Accept, on behalf of an issuer, an investment commitment for securities offered in reliance on section 4(a)(6) of the Securities Act by that issuer on the funding portal's platform;

(12) Direct investors where to transmit funds or remit payment in connection with the purchase of securities offered and sold in reliance on section 4(a)(6) of the Securities Act; and

(13) Direct a qualified third party, as required by § 227.303(e), to release proceeds to an issuer upon completion of a crowdfunding offering or to return proceeds to investors in the event an investment commitment or an offering is cancelled.

Rule 403.   Compliance.

(a)   *Policies and procedures.* A funding portal must implement written policies and procedures reasonably designed to achieve compliance with the federal securities laws and the rules and regulations thereunder relating to its business as a funding portal.

(b)   *Privacy.* A funding portal must comply with the requirements of part 248 of this chapter as they apply to brokers.

(c) *Inspections and examinations.* A funding portal shall permit the examination and inspection of all of its business and business operations that relate to its activities as a funding portal, such as its premises, systems, platforms, and records by representatives of the Commission and of the registered national securities association of which it is a member.

Rule 404.   Records to be made and kept by funding portals.

(a) *Generally.* A funding portal shall make and preserve the following records for five years, the first two years in an easily accessible place:

(1) All records related to an investor who purchases or attempts to purchase securities through the funding portal;

(2) All records related to issuers who offer and sell or attempt to offer and sell securities through the funding portal and the control persons of such issuers;

(3) Records of all communications that occur on or through its platform;

(4) All records related to persons that use communication channels provided by a funding portal to promote an issuer's securities or communicate with potential investors;

(5) All records required to demonstrate compliance with the requirements of subparts C (§§ 227.300 through 227.305) and D (§§ 227.400 through 227.404) of this part;

(6) All notices provided by such funding portal to issuers and investors generally through the funding portal's platform or otherwise, including, but not limited to, notices addressing hours of funding portal operations (if any), funding portal malfunctions, changes to funding portal procedures, maintenance of hardware and software, instructions pertaining to access to the funding portal and denials of, or limitations on, access to the funding portal;

(7) All written agreements (or copies thereof) entered into by such funding portal relating to its business as such;

(8) All daily, monthly and quarterly summaries of transactions effected through the funding portal, including:

(i) Issuers for which the target offering amount has been reached and funds distributed; and

(ii) Transaction volume, expressed in:

(A) Number of transactions;

(B) Number of securities involved in a transaction;

(C) Total amounts raised by, and distributed to, issuers; and

(D) Total dollar amounts raised across all issuers, expressed in U.S. dollars; and

(9) A log reflecting the progress of each issuer who offers or sells securities through the funding portal toward meeting the target offering amount.

(b) *Organizational documents.* A funding portal shall make and preserve during the operation of the funding portal and of any successor funding portal, all organizational documents relating to the funding portal, including but not limited to, partnership agreements, articles of incorporation or charter, minute books and stock certificate books (or other similar type documents).

(c) *Format.* The records required to be maintained and preserved pursuant to paragraph (a) of this rule must be produced, reproduced, and maintained in the original, non-alterable format in which they were created or as permitted under § 240.17a–4(f) of this chapter.

(d) *Third parties.* The records required to be made and preserved pursuant to this rule may be prepared or maintained by a third party on behalf of a funding portal. An agreement with a third party shall not relieve a funding portal from the responsibility to prepare and maintain records as specified in this rule. A funding portal must file with the registered national securities association of which it is a member, a written undertaking in a form acceptable to the registered national securities association, signed by a duly authorized person of the third party, stating in effect that such records are the property of the funding portal and will be surrendered promptly on request of the funding portal. The undertaking shall include the following provision:

> With respect to any books and records maintained or preserved on behalf of [name of funding portal], the undersigned hereby acknowledges that the books and records are the property of [name of funding portal], and hereby undertakes to permit examination of such books and records at any time, or from time to time, during business hours by representatives of the Securities and Exchange Commission and the registered national securities association of which the funding portal is a member, and to promptly furnish to the Commission, its representatives, and the registered national securities association of which the funding portal is a member, a true, correct, complete and current hard copy of any, all, or any part of, such books and records.

(e)　*Review of records.* All records of a funding portal are subject at any time, or from time to time, to reasonable periodic, special, or other examination by the representatives of the Commission and the registered national securities association of which a funding portal is a member. Every funding portal shall furnish promptly to the Commission, its representatives, and the registered national securities association of which the funding portal is a member true, correct, complete and current copies of such records of the funding portal that are requested by the representatives of the Commission and the registered national securities association.

(f)　*Financial recordkeeping and reporting of currency and foreign transactions.* A funding portal that is subject to the requirements of the Currency and Foreign Transactions Reporting Act of 1970 shall comply with the reporting, recordkeeping and record retention requirements of 31 CFR chapter X. Where 31 CFR chapter X and § 227.404(a) and (b) require the same records or reports to be preserved for different periods of time, such records or reports shall be preserved for the longer period of time.

MISCELLANEOUS PROVISIONS

Rule 501.　　Restrictions on resales.

(a)　Securities issued in a transaction exempt from registration pursuant to section 4(a)(6) of the Securities Act and in accordance with section 4A of the Securities Act and this part may not be transferred by any purchaser of such securities during the one-year period beginning when the securities were issued in a transaction exempt from registration pursuant to section 4(a)(6) of the Securities Act, unless such securities are transferred:

(1)　To the issuer of the securities;

(2)　To an accredited investor;

(3)　As part of an offering registered with the Commission; or

(4)　To a member of the family of the purchaser or the equivalent, to a trust controlled by the purchaser, to a trust created for the benefit of a member of the family of the purchaser or the equivalent, or in connection with the death or divorce of the purchaser or other similar circumstance.

(b)　For purposes of this § 227.501, the term *accredited investor* shall mean any person who comes within any of the categories set forth in Securities Act Rule 501(a), or who the seller reasonably believes comes within any of such categories, at the time of the sale of the securities to that person.

(c)　For purposes of this rule, the term *member of the family of the purchaser or the equivalent* includes a child, stepchild, grandchild, parent, stepparent, grandparent, spouse or spousal equivalent, sibling, mother-in-law, father-in-law, son-in-law, daughter-in-law, brother-in-law, or sister-in-law of the purchaser, and shall include adoptive relationships. For purposes of this paragraph (c), the term *spousal equivalent* means a cohabitant occupying a relationship generally equivalent to that of a spouse.

Rule 502.   Insignificant deviations from a term, condition or requirement of this part (Regulation Crowdfunding).

(a)   A failure to comply with a term, condition, or requirement of this part will not result in the loss of the exemption from the requirements of Section 5 of the Securities Act for any offer or sale to a particular individual or entity, if the issuer relying on the exemption shows:

(1)   The failure to comply was insignificant with respect to the offering as a whole;

(2)   The issuer made a good faith and reasonable attempt to comply with all applicable terms, conditions and requirements of this part; and

(3)   The issuer did not know of such failure where the failure to comply with a term, condition or requirement of this part was the result of the failure of the intermediary to comply with the requirements of section 4A(a) of the Securities Act and the related rules, or such failure by the intermediary occurred solely in offerings other than the issuer's offering.

(b)   Paragraph (a) of this rule shall not preclude the Commission from bringing an enforcement action seeking any appropriate relief for an issuer's failure to comply with all applicable terms, conditions and requirements of this part.

Rule 503.   Disqualification provisions.

(a)   *Disqualification events.* No exemption under section 4(a)(6) of the Securities Act shall be available for a sale of securities if the issuer; any predecessor of the issuer; any affiliated issuer; any director, officer, general partner or managing member of the issuer; any beneficial owner of 20 percent or more of the issuer's outstanding voting equity securities, calculated on the basis of voting power; any promoter connected with the issuer in any capacity at the time of filing, any offer after filing, or such sale; any person that has been or will be paid (directly or indirectly) remuneration for solicitation of purchasers in connection with such sale of securities; or any general partner, director, officer or managing member of any such solicitor:

(1)   Has been convicted, within 10 years before the filing of the offering statement or such sale (or five years, in the case of issuers, their predecessors and affiliated issuers), of any felony or misdemeanor:

(i)   In connection with the purchase or sale of any security;

(ii)   Involving the making of any false filing with the Commission; or

(iii)   Arising out of the conduct of the business of an underwriter, broker, dealer, municipal securities dealer, investment adviser, funding portal or paid solicitor of purchasers of securities;

(2)   Is subject to any order, judgment or decree of any court of competent jurisdiction, entered within five years before the filing of the information required by section 4A(b) of the Securities Act or such sale that, at the time of such filing or sale, restrains or enjoins such person from engaging or continuing to engage in any conduct or practice:

(i)   In connection with the purchase or sale of any security;

(ii)   Involving the making of any false filing with the Commission; or

(iii)   Arising out of the conduct of the business of an underwriter, broker, dealer, municipal securities dealer, investment adviser, funding portal or paid solicitor of purchasers of securities;

(3)   Is subject to a final order of a State securities commission (or an agency or officer of a State performing like functions); a State authority that supervises or examines banks, savings associations or credit unions; a State insurance commission (or an agency or officer of a state performing like functions); an appropriate Federal banking agency; the U.S. Commodity Futures Trading Commission; or the National Credit Union Administration that:

(i)   At the time of the filing of the information required by section 4A(b) of the Securities Act (15 U.S.C. 77d–1(b)) or such sale, bars the person from:

(A)   Association with an entity regulated by such commission, authority, agency or officer;

(B)   Engaging in the business of securities, insurance or banking; or

(C)   Engaging in savings association or credit union activities; or

(ii)   Constitutes a final order based on a violation of any law or regulation that prohibits fraudulent, manipulative or deceptive conduct entered within ten years before such filing of the offering statement or such sale;

Instruction to paragraph (a)(3). Final order shall mean a written directive or declaratory statement issued by a Federal or State agency, described in Rule 503(a)(3), under applicable statutory authority that provides for notice and an opportunity for hearing, which constitutes a final disposition or action by that Federal or State agency.

(4)   Is subject to an order of the Commission entered pursuant to section 15(b) or 15B(c) of the Exchange Act or Section 203(e) or (f) of the Investment Advisers Act of 1940 that, at the time of the filing of the information required by section 4A(b) of the Securities Act or such sale:

(i)   Suspends or revokes such person's registration as a broker, dealer, municipal securities dealer, investment adviser or funding portal;

(ii)   Places limitations on the activities, functions or operations of such person; or

(iii)   Bars such person from being associated with any entity or from participating in the offering of any penny stock;

(5)   Is subject to any order of the Commission entered within five years before the filing of the information required by section 4A(b) of the Securities Act or such sale that, at the time of such filing or sale, orders the person to cease and desist from committing or causing a violation or future violation of:

(i)   Any scienter-based anti-fraud provision of the Federal securities laws, including without limitation Section 17(a)(1) of the Securities Act, Section 10(b) of the Exchange Act and Rule 10b–5, section 15(c)(1) of the Exchange Act and Section 206(1) of the Investment Advisers Act of 1940 or any other rule or regulation thereunder; or

(ii)   Section 5 of the Securities Act;

(6)   Is suspended or expelled from membership in, or suspended or barred from association with a member of, a registered national securities exchange or a registered national or affiliated securities association for any act or omission to act constituting conduct inconsistent with just and equitable principles of trade;

(7)   Has filed (as a registrant or issuer), or was or was named as an underwriter in, any registration statement or Regulation A (17 CFR 230.251 through 230.263) offering statement filed with the Commission that, within five years before the filing of the information required by section 4A(b) of the Securities Act or such sale, was the subject of a refusal order, stop order, or order suspending the Regulation A exemption, or is, at the time of such filing or sale, the subject of an investigation or proceeding to determine whether a stop order or suspension order should be issued; or

(8)   Is subject to a United States Postal Service false representation order entered within five years before the filing of the information required by section 4A(b) of the Securities Act or such sale, or is, at the time of such filing or sale, subject to a temporary restraining order or preliminary injunction with respect to conduct alleged by the United States Postal Service to constitute a scheme or device for obtaining money or property through the mail by means of false representations.

Instruction to paragraph (a): With respect to any beneficial owner of 20 percent or more of the issuer's outstanding voting equity securities, calculated on the basis of voting power, the issuer is required to determine whether a disqualifying event has occurred only as of the time of filing of the offering statement and not from the time of such sale.

(b)   *Transition, waivers, reasonable care exception.* Paragraph (a) of this rule shall not apply:

(1)   With respect to any conviction, order, judgment, decree, suspension, expulsion or bar that occurred or was issued before May 16, 2016;

(2)   Upon a showing of good cause and without prejudice to any other action by the Commission, if the Commission determines that it is not necessary under the circumstances that an exemption be denied;

(3)   If, before the filing of the information required by section 4A(b) of the Securities Act or such sale, the court or regulatory authority that entered the relevant order, judgment or decree advises in writing (whether contained in the relevant judgment, order or decree or separately to the Commission or its staff) that disqualification under paragraph (a) of this section should not arise as a consequence of such order, judgment or decree; or

(4)   If the issuer establishes that it did not know and, in the exercise of reasonable care, could not have known that a disqualification existed under paragraph (a) of this rule.

Instruction to paragraph (b)(4). An issuer will not be able to establish that it has exercised reasonable care unless it has made, in light of the circumstances, factual inquiry into whether any disqualifications exist. The nature and scope of the factual inquiry will vary based on the facts and circumstances concerning, among other things, the issuer and the other offering participants.

(c)   *Affiliated issuers.* For purposes of paragraph (a) of this rule, events relating to any affiliated issuer that occurred before the affiliation arose will be not considered disqualifying if the affiliated entity is not:

(1)   In control of the issuer; or

(2)   Under common control with the issuer by a third party that was in control of the affiliated entity at the time of such events.

(d)   *Intermediaries.* A person that is subject to a statutory disqualification as defined in section 3(a)(39) of the Exchange Act may not act as, or be an associated person of, an intermediary in a transaction involving the offer or sale of securities in reliance on section 4(a)(6) of the Securities Act unless so permitted pursuant to Commission rule or order.

Instruction to paragraph (d). § 240.17f–2 of this chapter generally requires the fingerprinting of every person who is a partner, director, officer or employee of a broker, subject to certain exceptions.

Rule 504. Definition of "qualified purchaser".

For purposes of Section 18(b)(3) of the Securities Act, a "qualified purchaser" means any person to whom securities are offered or sold pursuant to an offering under Rules 100 through 504 (Regulation Crowdfunding).

1933 ACT RULES

17 C.F.R. § 230.___

GENERAL

1933 ACT RULES

1933 ACT RULES

MISCELLANEOUS EXEMPTIONS

REGULATION A—CONDITIONAL SMALL ISSUES EXEMPTION

REGULATION C—REGISTRATION

GENERAL REQUIREMENTS

FORM AND CONTENT OF PROSPECTUSES

WRITTEN CONSENTS

FILINGS; FEES; EFFECTIVE DATE

AMENDMENTS; WITHDRAWALS

GENERAL

ATTENTION ELECTRONIC FILERS

THIS REGULATION SHOULD BE READ IN CONJUNCTION WITH REGULATION S–T, WHICH GOVERNS THE PREPARATION AND SUBMISSION OF DOCUMENTS IN ELECTRONIC FORMAT. MANY PROVISIONS RELATING TO THE PREPARATION AND SUBMISSION OF DOCUMENTS IN PAPER FORMAT CONTAINED IN THIS REGULATION ARE SUPERSEDED BY THE PROVISIONS OF REGULATION S–T FOR DOCUMENTS REQUIRED TO BE FILED IN ELECTRONIC FORMAT.

Rule 100.   Definitions of Terms Used in the Rules and Regulations

(a) As used in the rules and regulations prescribed by the Securities and Exchange Commission pursuant to the Securities Act of 1933, unless the context otherwise requires—

(1) The term "Commission" means the Securities and Exchange Commission.

(2) The term "Act" means the Securities Act of 1933.

(3) The term "rules and regulations" refers to all rules and regulations adopted by the Commission pursuant to the Act, including the forms and accompanying instructions thereto.

(4) The term "registrant" means the issuer of securities for which a registration statement is filed.

(5) The term "agent for service" means the person authorized in the registration statement to receive notices and communications from the Commission.

(6) The term "electronic filer" means a person or an entity that submits filings electronically pursuant to Rules 101, 901, 902 or 903 of Regulation S–T.

(7) The term "electronic filing" means a document under the federal securities laws that is transmitted or delivered to the Commission in electronic format.

(b) Unless otherwise specifically provided, the terms used in the rules and regulations shall have the meanings defined in the Act.

(c) A rule in the General Rules and Regulations which defines a term without express reference to the Act or to the rules and regulations or to a portion thereof defines such terms for all purposes as used both in the Act and in the rules and regulations, unless the context otherwise requires.

Rule 110.   Business Hours of the Commission

(a) *General.* The principal office of the Commission, at 100 F Street, NE, Washington, D.C. 20549, is open each day, except Saturdays, Sundays and federal holidays, from 9:00 a.m. to 5:30 p.m., Eastern Standard Time or Eastern Daylight Saving Time, whichever is currently in effect, *provided that* hours for the filing of documents pursuant to the Act or the rules and regulations thereunder are as set forth in paragraphs (b), (c) and (d) of this rule.

(b) *Submissions Made in Paper.* Paper documents filed with or otherwise furnished to the Commission may be submitted each day, except Saturdays, Sundays and federal holidays, from 8 a.m. to 5:30 p.m., Eastern Standard Time or Eastern Daylight Saving Time, whichever is currently in effect.

(c) *Filings by Direct Transmission.* Filings made by direct transmission may be submitted to the Commission each day, except Saturdays, Sundays and federal holidays, from 8:00 a.m. to 10:00 p.m., Eastern Standard Time or Eastern Daylight Saving Time, whichever is currently in effect.

(d) *Filings by Facsimile.* Registration statements and post-effective amendments thereto filed by facsimile transmission pursuant to Rule 462(b) and Rule 455 may be filed with the Commission each day, except Saturdays, Sundays and federal holidays, from 5:30 p.m. to 10:00 p.m., Eastern Standard Time or Eastern Daylight Savings Time, whichever is currently in effect.

Rule 111.   Payment of Fees

All payments of fees for registration statements under the Act shall be made by wire transfer, or by certified check, bank cashier's check, United States postal money order, or bank money order payable to the Securities and Exchange Commission, omitting the name or title of any official of the Commission. There will be no refunds. Payment of fees required by this rule shall be made in accordance with the directions set forth in § 202.3a of this chapter.

Rule 120.   Inspection of Registration Statements

Except for material contracts or portions thereof accorded confidential treatment pursuant to Rule 406, all registration statements are available for public inspection, during business hours, at the principal office of the Commission in Washington, D.C. Electronic registration statements made through the Electronic Data Gathering, Analysis, and Retrieval System are publicly available through the Commission's Web site (http://www.sec.gov).

Rule 122.   Nondisclosure of Information Obtained in the Course of Examinations and Investigations

Information or documents obtained by officers or employees of the Commission in the course of any examination or investigation pursuant to section 8(e) or 20(a) shall, unless made a matter of public record, be deemed confidential. Except as provided by 17 CFR 203.2, officers and employees are hereby prohibited from making such confidential information or documents or any other non-public records of the Commission available to anyone other than a member, officer or employee of the Commission, unless the Commission or the General Counsel, pursuant to delegated authority, authorizes the disclosure of such information or the production of such documents as not being contrary to the public interest. Any officer or employee who is served with a subpoena requiring the disclosure of such information or the production of such documents shall appear in court and, unless the authorization described in the preceding sentence shall have been given, shall respectfully decline to disclose the information or produce the documents called for, basing his or her refusal upon this rule. Any officer or employee who is served with such subpoena shall promptly advise the General Counsel of the service of such subpoena, the nature of the information or documents sought, and any circumstances which may bear upon the desirability of making available such information or documents.

Rule 130.   Definition of "Rules and Regulations" as Used in Certain Sections of the Act

The term "rules and regulations" as used in sections 7, 10(a), (c) and (d) and 19(a) of the Act, shall include the forms for registration of securities under the Act and the related instructions thereto.

Rule 131.   Definition of Security Issued Under Governmental Obligations

(a)   Any part of an obligation evidenced by any bond, note, debenture, or other evidence of indebtedness issued by any governmental unit specified in section 3(a)(2) of the Act which is payable from payments to be made in respect of property or money which is or will be used, under a lease, sale, or loan arrangement, by or for industrial or commercial enterprise, shall be deemed to be a separate "security" within the meaning of section 2(1) of the Act, issued by the lessee or obligor under the lease, sale or loan arrangement.

(b)   An obligation shall not be deemed a separate "security" as defined in paragraph (a) hereof if,

(1)   the obligation is payable from the general revenues of a governmental unit, specified in section 3(a)(2) of the Act, having other resources which may be used for the payment of the obligation, or

(2)   the obligation relates to a public project or facility owned and operated by or on behalf of and under the control of a governmental unit specified in such section, or

(3) the obligation relates to a facility which is leased to and under the control of an industrial or commercial enterprise but is a part of a public project which, as a whole, is owned by and under the general control of a governmental unit specified in such section, or an instrumentality thereof.

(c) This rule shall apply to transactions of the character described in paragraph (a) only with respect to bonds, notes, debentures or other evidences of indebtedness sold after December 31, 1968.

Rule 132.   Definition of "Common Trust Fund" as Used in Section 3(a)(2) of the Act

The term "common trust fund" as used in section 3(a)(2) of the Act shall include a common trust fund which is maintained by a bank which is a member of an affiliated group, as defined in section 1504(a) of the Internal Revenue Code of 1954, and which is maintained exclusively for the collective investment and reinvestment of monies contributed thereto by one or more bank members of such affiliated group in the capacity of trustee, executor, administrator, or guardian, *Provided that*:

(a) The common trust fund is operated in compliance with the same state and federal regulatory requirements as would apply if the bank maintaining such fund and any other contributing banks were the same entry; and

(b) The rights of persons for whose benefit a contributing bank acts as trustee, executor, administrator, or guardian would not be diminished by reason of the maintenance of such common trust fund by another bank member of the affiliated group.

Rule 134.   Communications Not Deemed a Prospectus

Except as provided in paragraphs (e) and (g) of this rule, the terms "prospectus" as defined in section 2(a)(10) of the Act or "free writing prospectus" as defined in Rule 405 shall not include a communication limited to the statements required or permitted by this rule, provided that the communication is published or transmitted to any person only after a registration statement relating to the offering that includes a prospectus satisfying the requirements of section 10 of the Act (except as otherwise permitted in paragraph (a) of this rule) has been filed.

(a) Such communication may include any one or more of the following items of information, which need not follow the numerical sequence of this paragraph, provided that, except as to paragraphs (a)(4) through (6) of this rule, the prospectus included in the filed registration statement does not have to include a price range otherwise required by rule:

(1) Factual information about the legal identity and business location of the issuer limited to the following: the name of the issuer of the security, the address, phone number, and e-mail address of the issuer's principal offices and contact for investors, the issuer's country of organization, and the geographic areas in which it conducts business;

(2) The title of the security or securities and the amount or amounts being offered, which title may include a designation as to whether the securities are convertible, exercisable, or exchangeable, and as to the ranking of the securities;

(3) A brief indication of the general type of business of the issuer, limited to the following:

(i) In the case of a manufacturing company, the general type of manufacturing, the principal products or classes of products manufactured, and the segments in which the company conducts business;

(ii) In the case of a public utility company, the general type of services rendered, a brief indication of the area served, and the segments in which the company conducts business;

(iii) In the case of an asset-backed issuer, the identity of key parties, such as sponsor, depositor, issuing entity, servicer or servicers, and trustee, the asset class of the transaction, and the identity of any credit enhancement or other support; and

(iv) In the case of any other type of company, a corresponding statement;

(4)   The price of the security, or if the price is not known, the method of its determination or the bona fide estimate of the price range as specified by the issuer or the managing underwriter or underwriters;

(5)   In the case of a fixed income security, the final maturity and interest rate provisions or, if the final maturity or interest rate provisions are not known, the probable final maturity or interest rate provisions, as specified by the issuer or the managing underwriter or underwriters;

(6)   In the case of a fixed income security with a fixed (non-contingent) interest rate provision, the yield or, if the yield is not known, the probable yield range, as specified by the issuer or the managing underwriter or underwriters and the yield of fixed income securities with comparable maturity and security rating;

(7)   A brief description of the intended use of proceeds of the offering, if then disclosed in the prospectus that is part of the filed registration statement;

(8)   The name, address, phone number, and e-mail address of the sender of the communication and the fact that it is participating, or expects to participate, in the distribution of the security;

(9)   The type of underwriting, if then included in the disclosure in the prospectus that is part of the filed registration statement;

(10)   The names of underwriters participating in the offering of the securities, and their additional roles, if any, within the underwriting syndicate;

(11)   The anticipated schedule for the offering (including the approximate date upon which the proposed sale to the public will begin) and a description of marketing events (including the dates, times, locations, and procedures for attending or otherwise accessing them);

(12)   A description of the procedures by which the underwriters will conduct the offering and the procedures for transactions in connection with the offering with the issuer or an underwriter or participating dealer (including procedures regarding account-opening and submitting indications of interest and conditional offers to buy), and procedures regarding directed share plans and other participation in offerings by officers, directors, and employees of the issuer;

(13)   Whether, in the opinion of counsel, the security is a legal investment for savings banks, fiduciaries, insurance companies, or similar investors under the laws of any State or Territory or the District of Columbia, and the permissibility or status of the investment under the Employee Retirement Income Security Act of 1974;

(14)   Whether, in the opinion of counsel, the security is exempt from specified taxes, or the extent to which the issuer has agreed to pay any tax with respect to the security or measured by the income therefrom;

(15)   Whether the security is being offered through rights issued to security holders, and, if so, the class of securities the holders of which will be entitled to subscribe, the subscription ratio, the actual or proposed record date, the date upon which the rights were issued or are expected to be issued, the actual or anticipated date upon which they will expire, and the approximate subscription price, or any of the foregoing;

(16)   Any statement or legend required by any state law or administrative authority;

(17)   [RESERVED]

(18)   The names of selling security holders, if then disclosed in the prospectus that is part of the filed registration statement;

(19)   The names of securities exchanges or other securities markets where any class of the issuer's securities are, or will be, listed;

(20)   The ticker symbols, or proposed ticker symbols, of the issuer's securities;

(21)   The CUSIP number as defined in Rule 17Ad–19(a)(5) of the Securities Exchange Act of 1934 assigned to the securities being offered; and

(22) Information disclosed in order to correct inaccuracies previously contained in a communication permissibly made pursuant to this rule.

(b)   Except as provided in paragraph (c) of this rule, every communication used pursuant to this rule shall contain the following:

(1)   If the registration statement has not yet become effective, the following statement:

A registration statement relating to these securities has been filed with the Securities and Exchange Commission but has not yet become effective. These securities may not be sold nor may offers to buy be accepted prior to the time the registration statement becomes effective; and

(2)   The name and address of a person or persons from whom a written prospectus for the offering meeting the requirements of section 10 of the Act (other than a free writing prospectus as defined in Rule 405) including as to the identified paragraphs above a price range where required by rule, may be obtained.

(c)   Any of the statements or information specified in paragraph (b) of this rule may, but need not, be contained in a communication which:

(1)   Does no more than state from whom and include the uniform resource locator (URL) where a written prospectus meeting the requirements of section 10 of the Act (other than a free writing prospectus as defined in Rule 405) may be obtained, identify the security, state the price thereof and state by whom orders will be executed; or

(2)   Is accompanied or preceded by a prospectus or a summary prospectus, other than a free writing prospectus as defined in Rule 405, which meets the requirements of section 10 of the Act, including a price range where required by rule, at the date of such preliminary communication.

(d)   A communication sent or delivered to any person pursuant to this rule which is accompanied or preceded by a prospectus which meets the requirements of section 10 of the Act (other than a free writing prospectus as defined in Rule 405), including a price range where required by rule, at the date of such communication, may solicit from the recipient of the communication an offer to buy the security or request the recipient to indicate whether he or she might be interested in the security, if the communication contains substantially the following statement:

No offer to buy the securities can be accepted and no part of the purchase price can be received until the registration statement has become effective, and any such offer may be withdrawn or revoked, without obligation or commitment of any kind, at any time prior to notice of its acceptance given after the effective date.

Provided, that such statement need not be included in such a communication to a dealer.

(e)   A section 10 prospectus included in any communication pursuant to this rule shall remain a prospectus for all purposes under the Act.

(f)   The provision in paragraphs (c)(2) and (d) of this rule that a prospectus that meets the requirements of section 10 of the Act precede or accompany a communication will be satisfied if such communication is an electronic communication containing an active hyperlink to such prospectus.

(g)   This section does not apply to a communication relating to an investment company registered under the Investment Company Act of 1940, other than a registered closed-end investment company.

Rule 134A.   Options Material Not Deemed a Prospectus

Written materials, including advertisements, relating to standardized options, as that term is defined in Rule 9b–1 under the Securities Exchange Act of 1934, shall not be deemed to be a prospectus for the purposes of Section 2(a)(10) of the Securities Act of 1933: *Provided,* That such materials are limited to explanatory information describing the general nature of the standardized options markets or one or more strategies: *And, Provided further,* That:

(a)   The potential risks related to options trading generally and to each strategy addressed are explained;

(b)   No past or projected performance figures, including annualized rates of return are used;

(c)   No recommendation to purchase or sell any option contract is made;

(d)   No specific security is identified other than:

(1)   An option or other security exempt from registration under the Act, or

(2)   An index option, including the component securities of the index; and

(e)   If there is a definitive options disclosure document, as defined in Rule 9b–1 under the Securities Exchange Act of 1934, the materials shall contain the name and address of a person or persons from whom a copy of such document may be obtained.

Rule 134B.   Statements of Additional Information

For the purpose only of Section 5(b) of the Act, the term "prospectus" as defined in Section 2(a)(10) of the Act does not include a Statement of Additional Information filed as part of a registration statement on Form N–1A, Form N–2, Form N–3, Form N–4, or Form N–6 transmitted prior to the effective date of the registration statement if it is accompanied or preceded by a preliminary prospectus meeting with the requirements of Rule 430.

Rule 135.   Notice of Proposed Registered Offerings

(a)   For purposes of section 5 of the Act only, an issuer or a selling security holder (and any person acting on behalf of either of them) that publishes through any medium a notice of a proposed offering to be registered under the Act will not be deemed to offer its securities for sale through that notice if:

(1)   The notice includes a statement to the effect that it does not constitute an offer of any securities for sale; and

(2)   the notice otherwise includes no more than the following information:

(i)   The name of the issuer;

(ii)   The title, amount and basic terms of the securities offered;

(iii)   The amount of the offering, if any, to be made by selling security holders;

(iv)   The anticipated timing of the offering;

(v)   A brief statement of the manner and the purpose of the offering without naming the underwriters;

(vi)   Whether the issuer is directing its offering to only a particular class of purchasers;

(vii)   Any statements or legends required by the laws of any state or foreign country or administrative authority; and

(viii) In the following offerings, the notice may contain additional information, as follows:

(A)   In a rights offering to existing security holders:

(1)   The class of security holders eligible to subscribe;

(2)   The subscription ratio and expected subscription price;

(3)   The proposed record date;

(4)   The anticipated issuance date of the rights; and

(5)   The subscription period or expiration date of the rights offering.

(B)   In an offering to employees of the issuer or an affiliated company:

(1)   The name of the employer;

(2)   The class of employees being offered the securities;

(3)   The offering price; and

(4)   The duration of the offering period.

(C)   In an exchange offer:

(1)   The basic terms of the exchange offer;

(2)   The name of the subject company;

(3)   The subject class of securities sought in the exchange offer.

(D)   In a Rule 145(a) offering:

(1)   The name of the person whose assets are to be sold in exchange for the securities to be offered;

(2)   The names of any other parties to the transaction;

(3)   A brief description of the business of the parties to the transaction;

(4)   The date, time and place of the meeting of security holders to vote on or consent to the transaction; and

(5)   A brief description of the transaction and the basic terms of the transaction.

(b)   A person that publishes a notice in reliance on this rule may issue a notice that contains no more information than is necessary to correct inaccuracies published about the proposed offering.

NOTE to Rule 135. Communications under this rule relating to business combination transactions must be filed as required by Rule 425(b).

Rule 135A.   Generic Advertising

(a)   For the purposes only of section 5 of the Act, a notice, circular, advertisement, letter, sign, or other communication, published or transmitted to any person which does not specifically refer by name to the securities of a particular investment company, to the investment company itself, or to any other securities not exempt under section 3(a) of the Act, will not be deemed to offer any security for sale, provided:

(1)   Such communication is limited to any one or more of the following:

(i)   Explanatory information relating to securities of investment companies generally or to the nature of investment companies, or to services offered in connection with the ownership of such securities,

(ii)   The mention or explanation of investment companies of different generic types or having various investment objectives, such as "balanced funds," "growth funds," "income funds," "leveraged funds," "specialty funds," "variable annuities," "bond funds," and "no-load funds,"

(iii)   Offers, descriptions, and explanations of various products and services not constituting a security subject to registration under the Act: *Provided,* That such offers, descriptions, and explanations do not relate directly to the desirability of owning or purchasing a security issued by a registered investment company,

(iv)   Invitation to inquire for further information, and

(2)   Such communication contains the name and address of a registered broker or dealer or other person sponsoring the communication.

(b)   If such communication contains a solicitation of inquiries and prospectuses for investment company securities are to be sent or delivered in response to such inquiries, the number of such investment companies and, if applicable, the fact that the sponsor of the communication is the principal underwriter or investment adviser in respect to such investment companies shall be stated.

(c)   With respect to any communication describing any type of security, service, or product, the broker, dealer, or other person sponsoring such communication must offer for sale a security, service, or product of the type described in such communication.

Rule 135B.   Materials Not Deemed an Offer to Sell or Offer to Buy nor a Prospectus

Materials meeting the requirements of Rule 9b–1 of the Securities Exchange Act of 1934 shall not be deemed an offer to sell or offer to buy a security for purposes solely of section 5 of this Act, nor shall such materials be deemed a prospectus for purposes of sections 2(a)(10) and 12(a)(2) of this Act, even if such materials are referred to in, deemed to be incorporated by reference into, or otherwise in any manner deemed to be a part of a Form S–20 prospectus.

Rule 135C.   Notice of Certain Proposed Unregistered Offerings

(a)   For the purposes only of section 5 of the Act, a notice given by an issuer required to file reports pursuant to Section 13 or 15(d) of the Securities Exchange Act of 1934 or a foreign issuer that is exempt from registration under the Securities Exchange Act of 1934 pursuant to Rule 12g3–2(b) thereunder that it proposes to make, is making or has made an offering of securities not registered or required to be registered under the Act shall not be deemed to offer any securities for sale if:

(1)   Such notice is not used for the purpose of conditioning the market in the United States for any of the securities offered;

(2)   Such notice states that the securities offered will not be or have not been registered under the Act and may not be offered or sold in the United States absent registration or an applicable exemption from registration requirements; and

(3)   Such notice contains no more than the following additional information:

(i)   The name of the issuer;

(ii)   The title, amount and basic terms of the securities offered, the amount of the offering, if any, made by selling security holders, the time of the offering and a brief statement of the manner and purpose of the offering without naming the underwriters;

(iii)   In the case of a rights offering to security holders of the issuer, the class of securities the holder of which will be or were entitled to subscribe to the securities offered, the subscription ratio, the record date, the date upon which the rights are proposed to be or were issued, the term or expiration date of the rights and the subscription price, or any of the foregoing;

(iv)   In the case of an offering of securities in exchange for other securities of the issuer or of another issuer, the name of the issuer and the title of the securities to be surrendered in exchange for the securities offered, the basis upon which the exchange may be made, or any of the foregoing;

(v)   In the case of an offering to employees of the issuer or to employees of any affiliate of the issuer, the name of the employer and class or classes of employees to whom the securities are offered, the offering price or basis of the offering and the period during which the offering is to be or was made or any of the foregoing; and

(vi)   Any statement or legend required by State or foreign law or administrative authority.

(b)   Any notice contemplated by this rule may take the form of a news release or a written communication directed to security holders or employees, as the case may be, or other published statements.

(c)   Notwithstanding the provisions of paragraphs (a) and (b) of this rule, in the case of a rights offering of a security listed or subject to unlisted trading privileges on a national securities exchange or quoted on the NASDAQ inter-dealer quotation system information with respect to the interest rate, conversion ratio and subscription price may be disseminated through the facilities of the exchange, the consolidated transaction reporting system, the NASDAQ system or the Dow Jones broad tape, provided such information is already disclosed in a Form 8–K on file with the Commission, in a Form 6–K furnished to the Commission or, in the case of an issuer relying on Rule 12g3–2(b), in a submission made pursuant to that rule to the Commission.

(d)   The issuer shall file any notice contemplated by this rule with the Commission under cover of Form 8–K or furnish such notice under Form 6–K, as applicable, and, if relying on Rule 12g3–2(b), shall furnish such notice to the Commission in accordance with the provisions of that exemptive Section.

Rule 135D.   Communications Involving Security-Based Swaps

(a)   For the purposes only of Section 5 of the, the publication or distribution of quotes relating to security-based swaps that may be purchased only by persons who are eligible contract participants (as defined in Section 1a(18) of the Commodity Exchange Act (7 U.S.C. 1a(18))) and are traded or processed on or through a trading system or platform that either is registered as a national securities exchange under Section 6(a) of the Securities Exchange Act of 1934 or as a security-based swap execution facility under Section 3D(a) of the Securities Exchange Act of 1934, or is exempt from registration as a security-based swap execution facility under Section 3D(a) of the Securities Exchange Act of 1934 pursuant to a rule, regulation, or order of the Commission shall not be deemed to constitute an offer, an offer to sell, or a solicitation of an offer to buy or purchase any security-based swap or any guarantee of such security-based swap that is a security; and

(b)   For the purposes only of Section 5 of the Act, a broker, dealer, or security-based swap dealer's publication or distribution of a research report (as defined in § 230.139(d)) that discusses security-based swaps that may be purchased only by persons who are eligible contract participants (as defined in Section 1a(18) of the Commodity Exchange Act (7 U.S.C. 1a(18))) shall not be deemed to constitute an offer, an offer to sell, or a solicitation of an offer to buy or purchase any security-based swap or any guarantee of such security-based swap that is a security, provided that the broker, dealer, or security-based swap dealer publishes or distributes research reports on the issuer underlying the security-based swap or its securities in the regular course of its business and the publication or distribution of the research report does not represent the initiation of publication of research reports about such issuer or its securities or the reinitiation of such publication following discontinuation of publication of such research reports. For purposes of this rule, the term issuer as used in the definition of "research report" means the issuer of any security or loan referenced in the security-based swap, each issuer of a security in a narrow-based security index referenced in the security-based swap, or each issuer referenced in the security-based swap.

Rule 135E.   Offshore Press Conferences, Meetings With Issuer Representatives Conducted Offshore, and Press-Related Materials Released Offshore

(a)   For the purposes only of Section 5 of the Act, an issuer that is a foreign private issuer (as defined in Rule 405) or a foreign government issuer, a selling security holder of the securities of such issuers, or their representatives will not be deemed to offer any security for sale by virtue of providing any journalist with access to its press conferences held outside of the United States, to meetings with issuer or selling security holder representatives conducted outside of the United States, or to written press-related materials released outside the United States, at or in which a present or proposed offering of securities is discussed, if:

(1)   The present or proposed offering is not being, or to be, conducted solely in the United States;

NOTE to paragraph (a)(1). An offering will be considered not to be made solely in the United States under this paragraph (a)(1) only if there is an intent to make a bona fide offering offshore.

(2)   Access is provided to both U.S. and foreign journalists; and

(3)   Any written press-related materials pertaining to transactions in which any of the securities will be or are being offered in the United States satisfy the requirements of paragraph (b) of this rule.

(b)   Any written press-related materials specified in paragraph (a)(3) of this rule must:

(1)   State that the written press-related materials are not an offer of securities for sale in the United States, that securities may not be offered or sold in the United States absent registration or an exemption from registration, that any public offering of securities to be made in the United States will be made by means of a prospectus that may be obtained from the issuer or the selling security holder and that will contain detailed information about the company and management, as well as financial statements;

(2)   If the issuer or selling security holder intends to register any part of the present or proposed offering in the United States, include a statement regarding this intention; and

(3)   Not include any purchase order, or coupon that could be returned indicating interest in the offering, as part of, or attached to, the written press-related materials.

(c)   For the purposes of this rule, "United States" means the United States of America, its territories and possessions, any State of the United States, and the District of Columbia.

Rule 136.   Definition of Certain Terms in Relation to Assessable Stock

(a)   An "offer," "offer to sell" or "offer for sale" of securities shall be deemed to be made to the holders of assessable stock of a corporation when such corporation shall give notice of an assessment to the holders of such assessable stock. A "sale" shall be deemed to occur when a stockholder shall pay or agree to pay all or any part of such an assessment.

(b)   The term "transactions by any person other than an issuer, underwriter or dealer" in section 4(1) of the Act shall not be deemed to include the offering or sale of assessable stock, at public auction or otherwise, upon the failure of the holder of such stock to pay an assessment levied thereon by the issuer, where the offer or sale is made for the purpose of realizing the amount of the assessment and any of the proceeds of such sale are to be received by the issuer. However, any person whose functions are limited to acting as auctioneer at such an auction sale shall not be deemed to be an underwriter of the securities offered or sold at the auction sale. Any person who acquires assessable stock at any such public auction or other sale with a view to the distribution thereof shall be deemed to be an underwriter of such assessable stock.

(c)   The term "assessable stock" means stock which is subject to resale by the issuer pursuant to statute or otherwise in the event of a failure of the holder of such stock to pay any assessment levied thereon.

Rule 137.   Definition of "Offers", "Participates", or "Participation" in Section 2(a)(11) in Relation to Certain Publications by Persons Independent of Participants in a Distribution

Under the following conditions, the terms "offers," "participates," or "participation" in section 2(a)(11) of the Act shall not be deemed to apply to the publication or distribution of research reports with respect to the securities of an issuer which is the subject of an offering pursuant to a registration statement that the issuer proposes to file, or has filed, or that is effective:

(a)   The broker or dealer (and any affiliate) that has distributed the report and, if different, the person (and any affiliate) that has published the report have not participated, are not participating, and do not propose to participate in the distribution of the securities that are or will be the subject of the registered offering.

(b)   In connection with the publication or distribution of the research report, the broker or dealer (and any affiliate) that has distributed the report and, if different, the person (and any affiliate) that has published the report are not receiving and have not received consideration directly or indirectly from, and are not acting under any direct or indirect arrangement or understanding with:

(1)   The issuer of the securities;

(2)   A selling security holder;

(3)   Any participant in the distribution of the securities that are or will be the subject of the registration statement; or

(4)   Any other person interested in the securities that are or will be the subject of the registration statement.

Instruction to Rule 137(b).

This paragraph (b) does not preclude payment of:

1.   The regular price being paid by the broker or dealer for independent research, so long as the conditions of this paragraph (b) are satisfied; or

2.   The regular subscription or purchase price for the research report.

(c)   The broker or dealer publishes or distributes the research report in the regular course of its business.

(d)   The issuer is not and during the past three years neither the issuer nor any of its predecessors was:

   (1)   A blank check company as defined in Rule 419(a)(2);

   (2)   A shell company, other than a business combination related shell company, each as defined in Rule 405; or

   (3)   An issuer for an offering of penny stock as defined in Rule 3a51–1 of the Securities Exchange Act of 1934.

(e)   Definition of research report. For purposes of this rule, research report means a written communication, as defined in Rule 405, that includes information, opinions, or recommendations with respect to securities of an issuer or an analysis of a security or an issuer, whether or not it provides information reasonably sufficient upon which to base an investment decision.

Rule 138.   Definition of "Offer for Sale" and "Offer to Sell" in Sections 2(a)(10) and 5(c) in Relation to Certain Publications

(a)   Registered offerings. Under the following conditions, a broker's or dealer's publication or distribution of research reports about securities of an issuer shall be deemed for purposes of sections 2(a)(10) and 5(c) of the Act not to constitute an offer for sale or offer to sell a security which is the subject of an offering pursuant to a registration statement that the issuer proposes to file, or has filed, or that is effective, even if the broker or dealer is participating or will participate in the registered offering of the issuer's securities:

   (1)(i) The research report relates solely to the issuer's common stock, or debt securities, or preferred stock convertible into its common stock, and the offering involves solely the issuer's non-convertible debt securities or non-convertible, non-participating preferred stock; or

      (ii)   The research report relates solely to the issuer's non-convertible debt securities or non-convertible, non-participating preferred stock, and the offering involves solely the issuer's common stock, or debt securities, or preferred stock convertible into its common stock.

Instruction to paragraph (a)(1): If the issuer has filed a shelf registration statement under Rule 415(a)(1)(x) (§ 230.415(a)(1)(x)) or pursuant to General Instruction I.D. of Form S–3, General Instruction I.C. of Form F–3 (§ 239.13 or § 239.33 of this chapter), or pursuant to General Instructions A.2 and B of Form N–2 (§ 239.14 and § 274.11a–1 of this chapter) with respect to multiple classes of securities, the conditions of paragraph (a)(1) of this section must be satisfied for the offering in which the broker or dealer is participating or will participate.

   (2)   The issuer as of the date of reliance on this section:

      (i)(A)   Is required to file reports, and has filed all periodic reports required during the preceding 12 months (or such shorter time that the issuer was required to file such reports) on Forms 10–K (§ 249.310 of this chapter), 10–Q (§ 249.308a of this chapter), and 20–F (§ 249.220f of this chapter) pursuant to Section 13 or Section 15(d) of the Securities Exchange Act of 1934; or

      (B)(1)   Is a registered closed-end investment company; and (2) Is required to file reports, and has filed all periodic reports required during the preceding 12 months (or such shorter time that the issuer was required to file such reports) on Forms N-CSR (§§ 249.331 and 274.128 of this chapter), N-PORT (§ 274.150 of this chapter), and N-CEN (§§ 249.330 and 274.101 of this chapter) pursuant to Section 30 of the Investment Company Act; or

      (ii)   Is a foreign private issuer that:

      (A)   Meets all of the registrant requirements of Form F–3 other than the reporting history provisions of General Instructions I.A.1. and I.A.2(a) of Form F–3;

      (B)   Either:

        (1)   Satisfies the public float threshold in General Instruction I.B.1. of Form F–3; or

        (2)   Is issuing non-convertible securities, other than common equity, and the issuer meets the provisions of General Instruction I.B.2. of Form F–3; and

      (C)   Either:

        (1)   Has its equity securities trading on a designated offshore securities market as defined in Rule 902(b) and has had them so traded for at least 12 months; or

        (2)   Has a worldwide market value of its outstanding common equity held by non-affiliates of $700 million or more.

        (3)   The broker or dealer publishes or distributes research reports on the types of securities in question in the regular course of its business; and

        (4)   The issuer is not, and during the past three years neither the issuer nor any of its predecessors was:

           (i)   A blank check company as defined in Rule 419(a)(2);

           (ii)   A shell company, other than a business combination related shell company, each as defined in Rule 405; or

           (iii)   An issuer for an offering of penny stock as defined in Rule 3a51–1 of the Securities Exchange Act of 1934.

  (b)   **Rule 144A offerings.**—If the conditions in paragraph (a) of this rule are satisfied, a broker's or dealer's publication or distribution of a research report shall not be considered an offer for sale or an offer to sell a security or general solicitation or general advertising, in connection with an offering relying on Rule 144A.

  (c)   **Regulation S offerings.**—If the conditions in paragraph (a) of this rule are satisfied, a broker's or dealer's publication or distribution of a research report shall not:

        (1)   Constitute directed selling efforts as defined in Rule 902(c) for offerings under Regulation S; or

        (2)   Be inconsistent with the offshore transaction requirement in Rule 902(h) for offerings under Regulation S.

  (d)   **Definition of research report.**—For purposes of this rule, research report means a written communication, as defined in Rule 405, that includes information, opinions, or recommendations with respect to securities of an issuer or an analysis of a security or an issuer, whether or not it provides information reasonably sufficient upon which to base an investment decision.

Rule 139.   Publications or Distributions of Research Reports by Brokers or Dealers Distributing Securities

  (a)   **Registered offerings.** Under the conditions of paragraph (a)(1) or (2) of this rule, a broker's or dealer's publication or distribution of a research report about an issuer or any of its securities shall be deemed for purposes of sections 2(a)(10) and 5(c) of the Act not to constitute an offer for sale or offer to sell a security that is the subject of an offering pursuant to a registration statement that the issuer proposes to file, or has filed, or that is effective, even if the broker or dealer is participating or will participate in the registered offering of the issuer's securities. For purposes of the Fair Access to Investment Research Act of 2017, a safe harbor has been established for covered investment fund research reports, and the specific terms of that safe harbor are set forth in Rule 139B.

    (1)   Issuer-specific research reports.

       (i)   The issuer either:

          (A)(1)   At the later of the time of filing its most recent Form S–3 or Form F–3 or the time of its most recent amendment to such registration statement for purposes of complying with section 10(a)(3) of the Act or, if no Form S–3 or Form F–3 has been filed, at the date of reliance on this rule, meets the registrant requirements of such Form S–3 or Form F–3 and:

(i)   At such date, meets the minimum float provisions of General Instruction I.B.1 of such Forms; or

(ii)   At the date of reliance on this rule, is, or if a registration statement has not been filed, will be, offering non-convertible securities, other than common equity, and meets the requirements for the General Instruction I.B.2. of Form S–3 or Form F–3; or

(iii)   At the date of reliance on this rule is a well-known seasoned issuer as defined in Rule 405, other than a majority-owned subsidiary that is a well-known seasoned issuer by virtue of paragraph (1)(ii) of the definition of well-known seasoned issuer in Rule 405; and

(2)   As of the date of reliance on this rule, has filed all periodic reports required during the preceding 12 months on Forms 10–K, 10–Q, and 20–F pursuant to section 13 or section 15(d) of the Securities Exchange Act of 1934; or

(B)   Is a foreign private issuer that as of the date of reliance on this rule:

(1)   Meets all of the registrant requirements of Form F–3 other than the reporting history provisions of General Instructions I.A.1. and I.A.2(a) of Form F–3;

(2)   Either:

(i)   Satisfies the public float threshold in General Instruction I.B.1. of Form F–3; or

(ii)   Is issuing non-convertible securities, other than common equity, and meets the provisions of General Instruction I.B.2. of Form F–3; and

(3)   Either:

(i)   Has its equity securities trading on a designated offshore securities market as defined in Rule 902(b) and has had them so traded for at least 12 months; or

(ii)   Has a worldwide market value of its outstanding common equity held by non-affiliates of $700 million or more;

(ii)   The issuer is not and during the past three years neither the issuer nor any of its predecessors was:

(A)   A blank check company as defined in Rule 419(a)(2);

(B)   A shell company, other than a business combination related shell company, each as defined in Rule 405; or

(C)   An issuer for an offering of penny stock as defined in Rule 3a51–1 of the Securities Exchange Act of 1934; and

(iii)   The broker or dealer publishes or distributes research reports in the regular course of its business and such publication or distribution does not represent the initiation of publication of research reports about such issuer or its securities or reinitiation of such publication following discontinuation of publication of such research reports.

(2)   Industry reports.—

(i)   The issuer is required to file reports pursuant to section 13 or section 15(d) of the Securities Exchange Act of 1934 or satisfies the conditions in paragraph (a)(1)(i)(B) of this rule;

(ii)   The condition in paragraph (a)(1)(ii) of this rule is satisfied;

(iii)   The research report includes similar information with respect to a substantial number of issuers in the issuer's industry or sub-industry, or contains a comprehensive list of securities currently recommended by the broker or dealer;

(iv) The analysis regarding the issuer or its securities is given no materially greater space or prominence in the publication than that given to other securities or issuers; and

(v) The broker or dealer publishes or distributes research reports in the regular course of its business and, at the time of the publication or distribution of the research report, is including similar information about the issuer or its securities in similar reports.

(b) Rule 144A offerings.—If the conditions in paragraph (a)(1) or (a)(2) of this rule are satisfied, a broker's or dealer's publication or distribution of a research report shall not be considered an offer for sale or an offer to sell a security or general solicitation or general advertising, in connection with an offering relying on Rule 144A.

(c) Regulation S offerings.—If the conditions in paragraph (a)(1) or (a)(2) of this rule are satisfied, a broker's or dealer's publication or distribution of a research report shall not:

(1) Constitute directed selling efforts as defined in Rule 902(c) for offerings under Regulation S; or

(2) Be inconsistent with the offshore transaction requirement in Rule 902(h) for offerings under Regulation S.

(d) Definition of research report. For purposes of this rule, research report means a written communication, as defined in Rule 405, that includes information, opinions, or recommendations with respect to securities of an issuer or an analysis of a security or an issuer, whether or not it provides information reasonably sufficient upon which to base an investment decision.

Instruction to Rule 139.

Projections. A projection constitutes an analysis or information falling within the definition of research report. When a broker or dealer publishes or distributes projections of an issuer's sales or earnings in reliance on paragraph (a)(2) of this rule, it must:

1. Have previously published or distributed projections on a regular basis in order to satisfy the "regular course of its business" condition;

2. At the time of publishing or disseminating a research report, be publishing or distributing projections with respect to that issuer; and

3. For purposes of paragraph (a)(2)(iii) of this rule, include projections covering the same or similar periods with respect to either a substantial number of issuers in the issuer's industry or sub-industry or substantially all issuers represented in the comprehensive list of securities contained in the research report.

Rule 139A. Publications by Brokers or Dealers Distributing Asset-Backed Securities

The publication or distribution by a broker or dealer of information, an opinion or a recommendation with respect to asset-backed securities meeting the criteria of Form SF–3 ("SF–3 ABS") shall not be deemed to constitute an offer for sale or offer to sell SF–3 ABS registered or proposed to be registered for purposes of sections 2(a)(10) and 5(c) of the Act (the "registered securities"), even if such broker or dealer is or will be a participant in the distribution of the registered securities, if the following conditions are met:

(a) The broker or dealer shall have previously published or distributed with reasonable regularity information, opinions or recommendations relating to SF–3 ABS backed directly (or, with respect to securitizations of other securities, indirectly) by substantially similar collateral as that directly or indirectly backing SF–3 ABS that is the subject of the information, opinion or recommendation that is proposed to be published or distributed.

(b) If the registered securities are proposed to be offered, offered or part of an unsold allotment or subscription, the information, opinion or recommendation shall not:

(1) Identify the registered securities;

(2) Give greater prominence to specific structural or collateral-related attributes of the registered securities than it gives to the same attributes of other asset-backed securities that it mentions; or

(3) Contain any ABS informational and computational material (as defined in Item 1101 of Regulation AB) relating to the registered securities.

(c) Sufficient information is available from one or more public sources to provide a reasonable basis for the view expressed by the broker or dealer with respect to the asset-backed securities that are the subject of the information, opinion or recommendation.

(d) If the material published by the broker or dealer identifies asset-backed securities backed directly or indirectly by substantially similar collateral as that directly or indirectly backing the registered securities and specifically recommends that such asset-backed securities be preferred over other asset-backed securities backed by different types of collateral, then the material shall explain in reasonable detail the reasons for such preference.

Rule 139B. Publications or Distributions of Covered Investment Fund Research Reports by Brokers or Dealers Distributing Securities

(a) **Registered offerings.** Under the conditions of paragraph (a)(1) or (2) of this rule, the publication or distribution of a covered investment fund research report by a broker or dealer that is not an investment adviser to the covered investment fund and is not an affiliated person of the investment adviser to the covered investment fund shall be deemed for purposes of sections 2(a)(10) and 5(c) of the Act not to constitute an offer for sale or offer to sell a security that is the subject of an offering pursuant to a registration statement of the covered investment fund that is effective, even if the broker or dealer is participating or may participate in the registered offering of the covered investment fund's securities. This rule does not affect the availability of any other exemption or exclusion from sections 2(a)(10) or 5(c) of the Act available to the broker or dealer.

(1) Issuer-specific research reports. (i) At the date of reliance on this rule:

(A) The covered investment fund:

(1) Has been subject to the reporting requirements of section 30 of the Investment Company Act of 1940 (the "Investment Company Act") for a period of at least 12 calendar months and has filed in a timely manner all of the reports required, as applicable, to be filed for the immediately preceding 12 calendar months on Forms N-CSR, N-Q, N-PORT, N-MFP, and N-CEN pursuant to section 30 of the Investment Company Act; or

(2) If the covered investment fund is not a registered investment company under the Investment Company Act, has been subject to the reporting requirements of section 13 or section 15(d) of the Securities Exchange Act of 1934 (the "Exchange Act") (for a period of at least 12 calendar months and has filed in a timely manner all of the reports required to be filed for the immediately preceding 12 calendar months on Forms 10–K and 10–Q or 20–F pursuant to section 13 or section 15(d) of the Exchange Act; and

(B) At the time of the broker's or dealer's initial publication or distribution of a research report on the covered investment fund (or reinitiation thereof), and at least quarterly thereafter;

(1) If the covered investment fund is of the type defined in paragraph (c)(2)(i) of this rule, the aggregate market value of voting and non-voting common equity held by affiliates and non-affiliates equals or exceeds the aggregate market value specified in General Instruction I.B.1 of Form S–3;

(2) If the covered investment fund is of the type defined in paragraph (c)(2)(ii) of this rule, the aggregate market value of voting and non-voting common equity held by nonaffiliates equals or exceeds the aggregate market value specified in General Instruction I.B.1 of Form S–3; or

(3) If the covered investment fund is a registered open-end investment company (other than an exchange-traded fund) its net asset value (inclusive of shares held by affiliates and nonaffiliates) equals or exceeds the aggregate market value specified in General Instruction I.B.1 of Form S–3; and

(ii)   The broker or dealer publishes or distributes research reports in the regular course of its business and, in the case of a research report regarding a covered investment fund that does not have a class of securities in substantially continuous distribution, such publication or distribution does not represent the initiation of publication of research reports about such covered investment fund or its securities or reinitiation of such publication following discontinuation of publication of such research reports.

(2)   *Industry reports.*

(i)   The covered investment fund is subject to the reporting requirements of section 30 of the Investment Company Act or, if the covered investment fund is not a registered investment company under the Investment Company Act, is subject to the reporting requirements of section 13 or section 15(d) of the Exchange Act;

(ii)   The covered investment fund research report:

(A)   Includes similar information with respect to a substantial number of covered investment fund issuers of the issuer's type (e.g., money market fund, bond fund, balanced fund, etc.), or investment focus (e.g., primarily invested in the same industry or sub-industry, or the same country or geographic region); or

(B)   Contains a comprehensive list of covered investment fund securities currently recommended by the broker or dealer (other than securities of a covered investment fund that is an affiliate of the broker or dealer, or for which the broker or dealer serves as investment adviser (or for which the broker or dealer is an affiliated person of the investment adviser));

(iii)   The analysis regarding the covered investment fund issuer or its securities is given no materially greater space or prominence in the publication than that given to other covered investment fund issuers or securities; and

(iv)   The broker or dealer publishes or distributes research reports in the regular course of its business and, at the time of the publication or distribution of the research report (in the case of a research report regarding a covered investment fund that does not have a class of securities in substantially continuous distribution), is including similar information about the issuer or its securities in similar reports.

(3)   Disclosure of standardized performance. In the case of a research report about a covered investment fund that is a registered open-end management investment company or a trust account (or series or class thereof), any quotation of the issuer's performance must be presented in accordance with the conditions of paragraphs (d), (e), and (g) of Rule 482. In the case of a research report about a covered investment fund that is a registered closed-end investment company, any quotation of the issuer's performance must be presented in a manner that is in accordance with instructions to item 4.1(g) of Form N–2, provided, however, that other historical measures of performance may also be included if any other measurement is set out with no greater prominence than the measurement that is in accordance with the instructions to item 4.1(g) of Form N–2.

(b)   Self-regulatory organization rules. A self-regulatory organization shall not maintain or enforce any rule that would prohibit the ability of a member to publish or distribute a covered investment fund research report solely because the member is also participating in a registered offering or other distribution of any securities of such covered investment fund; or to participate in a registered offering or other distribution of securities of a covered investment fund solely because the member has published or distributed a covered investment fund research report about such covered investment fund or its securities. For purposes of section 19(b) of the Exchange Act, this paragraph (b) shall be deemed a rule under that Act.

(c)   *Definitions.* For purposes of this rule:

(1)   *Affiliated person* has the meaning given the term in section 2(a) of the Investment Company Act.

(2)   *Covered investment fund* means:

    (i)   An investment company (or a series or class thereof) registered under, or that has filed an election to be treated as a business development company under, the Investment Company Act and that has filed a registration statement under the Act for the public offering of a class of its securities, which registration statement has been declared effective by the Commission; or

    (ii)   A trust or other person:

        (A)   Issuing securities in an offering registered under the Act and which class of securities is listed for trading on a national securities exchange;

        (B)   The assets of which consist primarily of commodities, currencies, or derivative instruments that reference commodities or currencies, or interests in the foregoing; and

        (C)   That provides in its registration statement under the Act that a class of its securities are purchased or redeemed, subject to conditions or limitations, for a ratable share of its assets.

    (3)   *Covered investment fund research report* means a research report published or distributed by a broker or dealer about a covered investment fund or any securities issued by the covered investment fund, but does not include a research report to the extent that the research report is published or distributed by the covered investment fund or any affiliate of the covered investment fund, or any research report published or distributed by any broker or dealer that is an investment adviser (or any affiliated person of an investment adviser) for the covered investment fund.

    (4)   *Exchange-traded fund* has the meaning given the term in General Instruction A to Form N–1A.

    (5)   *Investment adviser* has the meaning given the term in section 2(a) of the Investment Company Act.

    (6)   *Research report* means a written communication, as defined in Rule 405 that includes information, opinions, or recommendations with respect to securities of an issuer or an analysis of a security or an issuer, whether or not it provides information reasonably sufficient upon which to base an investment decision.

Rule 140.   Definition of "Distribution" in Section 2(a)(11), for Certain Transactions

A person, the chief part of whose business consists of the purchase of the securities of one issuer, or of two or more affiliated issuers, and the sale of its own securities, including the levying of assessments on its assessable stock and the resale of such stock upon the failure of the holder thereof to pay any assessment levied thereon, to furnish the proceeds with which to acquire the securities of such issuer or affiliated issuers, is to be regarded as engaged in the distribution of the securities of such issuer or affiliated issuers within the meaning of section 2(a)(11) of the Act.

Rule 141.   Definition of "Commission From an Underwriter or Dealer Not in Excess of the Usual and Customary Distributors' or Sellers' Commissions" in Section 2(a)(11), for Certain Transactions

    (a)   The term "commission" in section 2(a)(11) of the Act shall include such remuneration, commonly known as a spread, as may be received by a distributor or dealer as a consequence of reselling securities bought from an underwriter or dealer at a price below the offering price of such securities, where such resales afford the distributor or dealer a margin of profit not in excess of what is usual and customary in such transactions.

    (b)   The term "commission from an underwriter or dealer" in section 2(a)(11) of the Act shall include commissions paid by an underwriter or dealer directly or indirectly controlling or controlled by, or under direct or indirect common control with the issuer.

    (c)   The term "usual and customary distributors' or sellers' commission" in section 2(a)(11) of the Act shall mean a commission or remuneration, commonly known as a spread, paid to or received by any person selling securities either for his own account or for the account of others, which is not in excess of the amount usual and customary in the distribution and sale of issues of similar type and size; and not in excess of the amount allowed to other persons, if any, for comparable service in the distribution of the particular issue; but such term shall not include amounts paid to any person whose function is the management of the distribution of all or a substantial part of the particular issue, or who performs the functions normally performed by an underwriter or underwriting syndicate.

Rule 142.   Definition of "Participates" and "Participation," as Used in Section 2(a)(11), in Relation to Certain Transactions

(a)   The terms "participates" and "participation" in section 2(a)(11) shall not include the interest of a person

(1)   Who is not in privity of contract with the issuer nor directly or indirectly controlling, controlled by, or under common control with, the issuer, and

(2)   Who has no association with any principal underwriter of the securities being distributed, and

(3)   Whose function in the distribution is confined to an undertaking to purchase all or some specified proportion of the securities remaining unsold after the lapse of some specified period of time, and

(4)   Who purchases such securities for investment and not with a view to distribution.

(b)   As used in this rule:

(1)   The term "issuer" shall have the meaning defined in section 2(a)(4) and in the last sentence of section 2(a)(11).

(2)   The term "association" shall include a relationship between two persons under which one:

(i)   Is directly or indirectly controlling, controlled by, or under common control with, the other, or

(ii)   Has, in common with the other, one or more partners, officers, directors, trustees, branch managers, or other persons occupying a similar status or performing similar functions, or

(iii)   Has a participation, direct or indirect, in the profits of the other, or has a financial stake, by debtor-creditor relationship, stock ownership, contract or otherwise, in the income or business of the other.

(3)   The term "principal underwriter" shall have the meaning defined in Rule 405.

Rule 143.   Definition of "Has Purchased", "Sells for", "Participates", and "Participation", as Used in Section 2(a)(11), in Relation to Certain Transactions of Foreign Governments for War Purposes

The terms "has purchased," "sells for," "participates," and "participation," in section 2(a)(11), shall not be deemed to apply to any action of a foreign government in acquiring, for war purposes and by or in anticipation of the exercise of war powers, from any person subject to its jurisdiction securities of a person organized under the laws of the United States or any State or Territory, or in disposing of such securities with a view to their distribution by underwriters in the United States, notwithstanding the fact that the price to be paid to such foreign government upon the disposition of such securities by it may be measured by or may be in direct or indirect relation to such price as may be realized by the underwriters.

Preliminary Note to Rule 144

Certain basic principles are essential to an understanding of the registration requirements in the Securities Act of 1933 and the purposes underlying Rule 144:

1.   If any person sells a non-exempt security to any other person, the sale must be registered unless an exemption can be found for the transaction.

2.   Section 4(1) of the Securities Act provides one such exemption for a transaction "by a person other than an issuer, underwriter, or dealer." Therefore, an understanding of the term "underwriter" is important in determining whether or not the Section 4(1) exemption from registration is available for the sale of the securities.

The term "underwriter" is broadly defined in Section 2(a)(11) of the Securities Act to mean any person who has purchased from an issuer with a view to, or offers or sells for an issuer in connection with, the distribution of any security, or participates, or has a direct or indirect participation in any such undertaking, or participates or has a participation in the direct or indirect underwriting of any such undertaking. The interpretation of this definition traditionally has focused on the words "with a view to" in the phrase "purchased from an issuer with a view to . . . distribution." An investment banking firm which arranges with an issuer for the public sale of its securities is clearly an "underwriter" under that section. However, individual investors who are not professionals in the securities business also may be "underwriters" if they act as links in a chain of transactions through which securities move from an issuer to the public.

Since it is difficult to ascertain the mental state of the purchaser at the time of an acquisition of securities, prior to and since the adoption of Rule 144, subsequent acts and circumstances have been considered to determine whether the purchaser took the securities "with a view to distribution" at the time of the acquisition. Emphasis has been placed on factors such as the length of time the person held the securities and whether there has been an unforeseeable change in circumstances of the holder. Experience has shown, however, that reliance upon such factors alone has led to uncertainty in the application of the registration provisions of the Act.

The Commission adopted Rule 144 to establish specific criteria for determining whether a person is not engaged in a distribution. Rule 144 creates a safe harbor from the Section 2(a)(11) definition of "underwriter." A person satisfying the applicable conditions of the Rule 144 safe harbor is deemed not to be engaged in a distribution of the securities and therefore not an underwriter of the securities for purposes of Section 2(a)(11). Therefore, such a person is deemed not to be an underwriter when determining whether a sale is eligible for the Section 4(1) exemption for "transactions by any person other than an issuer, underwriter, or dealer." If a sale of securities complies with all of the applicable conditions of Rule 144:

1.   Any affiliate or other person who sells restricted securities will be deemed not to be engaged in a distribution and therefore not an underwriter for that transaction;

2.   Any person who sells restricted or other securities on behalf of an affiliate of the issuer will be deemed not to be engaged in a distribution and therefore not an underwriter for that transaction; and

3.   The purchaser in such transaction will receive securities that are not restricted securities.

Rule 144 is not an exclusive safe harbor. A person who does not meet all of the applicable conditions of Rule 144 still may claim any other available exemption under the Act for the sale of the securities. The Rule 144 safe harbor is not available to any person with respect to any transaction or series of transactions that, although in technical compliance with Rule 144, is part of a plan or scheme to evade the registration requirements of the Act.

Rule 144.   Persons Deemed Not to Be Engaged in a Distribution and Therefore Not Underwriters

(a)   *Definitions.* The following definitions shall apply for the purposes of this rule.

(1)   An "affiliate" of an issuer is a person that directly, or indirectly through one or more intermediaries, controls, or is controlled by, or is under common control with, such issuer.

(2)   The term "person" when used with reference to a person for whose account securities are to be sold in reliance upon this rule includes, in addition to such person, all of the following persons:

(i)   Any relative or spouse of such person, or any relative of such spouse, any one of whom has the same home as such person;

(ii)   Any trust or estate in which such person or any of the persons specified in paragraph (a)(2)(i) of this rule collectively own 10 percent or more of the total beneficial interest or of which any of such persons serve as trustee, executor or in any similar capacity; and

(iii)   Any corporation or other organization (other than the issuer) in which such person or any of the persons specified in paragraph (a)(2)(i) of this rule are the beneficial owners collectively of 10 percent or more of any class of equity securities or 10 percent or more of the equity interest.

(3)   The term "restricted securities" means:

(i)   Securities that are acquired directly or indirectly from the issuer, or from an affiliate of the issuer, in a transaction or chain of transactions not involving any public offering;

(ii)   Securities acquired from the issuer that are subject to the resale limitations of Rule 502(d) under Regulation D or Rule 701(c);

(iii)   Securities that are acquired in a transaction or chain of transactions meeting the requirements of Rule 144A;

(iv)   Securities acquired from the issuer in a transaction subject to the conditions of Regulation CE;

(v)   Equity securities of domestic issuers acquired in a transaction or chain of transactions subject to the conditions of Rule 901 or Rule 903 under Regulation S;

(vi)   Securities acquired in a transaction made under Rule 801 to the same extent and proportion that the securities held by the security holder of the class with respect to which the rights offering was made were, as of the record date for the rights offering, "restricted securities" within the meaning of this paragraph (a)(3);

(vii)   Securities acquired in a transaction made under Rule 802 to the same extent and proportion that the securities that were tendered or exchanged in the exchange offer or business combination were "restricted securities" within the meaning of this paragraph (a)(3); and

(viii) Securities acquired from the issuer in a transaction subject to an exemption under section 4(5) of the Act.

(4)   The term "debt securities" means:

(i)   Any security other than an equity security as defined in Rule 405;

(ii)   Non-participatory preferred stock, which is defined as non-convertible capital stock, the holders of which are entitled to a preference in payment of dividends and in distribution of assets on liquidation, dissolution, or winding up of the issuer, but are not entitled to participate in residual earnings or assets of the issuer; and

(iii)   Asset-backed securities, as defined in Item 1101 of Regulation AB.

(b)   *Conditions to be Met.* Subject to paragraph (i) of this rule, the following conditions must be met:

(1)   *Non-Affiliates.*

(i)   If the issuer of the securities is, and has been for a period of at least 90 days immediately before the sale, subject to the reporting requirements of section 13 or 15(d) of the Securities Exchange Act of 1934, any person who is not an affiliate of the issuer at the time of the sale, and has not been an affiliate during the preceding three months, who sells restricted securities of the issuer for his or her own account shall be deemed not to be an underwriter of those securities within the meaning of section 2(a)(11) of the Act if all of the conditions of paragraphs (c)(1) and (d) of this rule are met. The requirements of paragraph (c)(1) of this rule shall not apply to restricted securities sold for the account of a person who is not an affiliate of the issuer at the time of the sale and has not been an affiliate during the preceding three months, provided a period of one year has elapsed since the later of the date the securities were acquired from the issuer or from an affiliate of the issuer.

(ii)   If the issuer of the securities is not, or has not been for a period of at least 90 days immediately before the sale, subject to the reporting requirements of section 13 or 15(d) of the Securities Exchange Act of 1934, any person who is not an affiliate of the issuer at the time of the sale, and has not been an affiliate during the preceding three months, who sells restricted securities of the issuer for his or her own account shall be deemed not to be an underwriter of those securities within the meaning of section 2(a)(11) of the Act if the condition of paragraph (d) of this rule is met.

(2) *Affiliates or persons selling on behalf of affiliates.* Any affiliate of the issuer, or any person who was an affiliate at any time during the 90 days immediately before the sale, who sells restricted securities, or any person who sells restricted or any other securities for the account of an affiliate of the issuer of such securities, or any person who sells restricted or any other securities for the account of a person who was an affiliate at any time during the 90 days immediately before the sale, shall be deemed not to be an underwriter of those securities within the meaning of section 2(a)(11) of the Act if all of the conditions of this rule are met.

(c) *Current Public Information.* Adequate current public information with respect to the issuer of the securities must be available. Such information will be deemed to be available only if the applicable condition set forth in this paragraph is met:

(1) *Reporting Issuers.* The issuer is, and has been for a period of at least 90 days immediately before the sale, subject to the reporting requirements of section 13 or 15(d) of the Securities Exchange Act of 1934 and has:

(i) Filed all required reports under section 13 or 15(d) of the Exchange Act, as applicable, during the 12 months preceding such sale (or for such shorter period that the issuer was required to file such reports), other than Form 8–K reports; and

(ii) Submitted electronically every Interactive Data File (§ 232.11 of this chapter) required to be submitted pursuant to § 232.405 of this chapter, during the 12 months preceding such sale (or for such shorter period that the issuer was required to submit such files); or

(2) *Non-reporting Issuers.* If the issuer is not subject to the reporting requirements of section 13 or 15(d) of the Securities Exchange Act of 1934, there is publicly available the information concerning the issuer specified in paragraphs (a)(5)(i) to (xiv), inclusive, and paragraph (a)(5)(xvi) of Rule 15c2–11 under the Securities Exchange Act of 1934, or, if the issuer is an insurance company, the information specified in section 12(g)(2)(G)(i) of the Securities Exchange Act of 1934.

NOTE to Rule 144(c). With respect to paragraph (c)(1), the person can rely upon:

1. A statement in whichever is the most recent report, quarterly or annual, required to be filed and filed by the issuer that such issuer has:

a. Filed all reports required under section 13 or 15(d) of the Exchange Act, as applicable, during the preceding 12 months (or for such shorter period that the issuer was required to file such reports), other than Form 8–K reports, and has been subject to such filing requirements for the past 90 days; and

b. Submitted electronically every Interactive Data File (§ 232.11 of this chapter) required to be submitted pursuant to § 232.405 of this chapter, during the preceding 12 months (or for such shorter period that the issuer was required to submit such files); or

2. A written statement from the issuer that it has complied with such reporting or submission requirements.

3. Neither type of statement may be relied upon, however, if the person knows or has reason to believe that the issuer has not complied with such requirements.

(d) *Holding Period for Restricted Securities.* If the securities sold are restricted securities, the following provisions apply:

(1) *General Rule.*

(i) If the issuer of the securities is, and has been for a period of at least 90 days immediately before the sale, subject to the reporting requirements of section 13 or 15(d) of the Securities Exchange Act of 1934, a minimum of six months must elapse between the later of the date of the acquisition of the securities from the issuer, or from an affiliate of the issuer, and any resale of such securities in reliance on this rule for the account of either the acquiror or any subsequent holder of those securities.

(ii) If the issuer of the securities is not, or has not been for a period of at least 90 days immediately before the sale, subject to the reporting requirements of section 13 or 15(d) of the

Securities Exchange Act of 1934, a minimum of one year must elapse between the later of the date of the acquisition of the securities from the issuer, or from an affiliate of the issuer, and any resale of such securities in reliance on this rule for the account of either the acquiror or any subsequent holder of those securities.

(iii) If the acquiror takes the securities by purchase, the holding period shall not begin until the full purchase price or other consideration is paid or given by the person acquiring the securities from the issuer or from an affiliate of the issuer.

(2) *Promissory Notes, Other Obligations or Installment Contracts.* Giving the issuer or affiliate of the issuer from whom the securities were purchased a promissory note or other obligation to pay the purchase price, or entering into an installment purchase contract with such seller, shall not be deemed full payment of the purchase price unless the promissory note, obligation or contract:

(i) Provides for full recourse against the purchaser of the securities;

(ii) Is secured by collateral, other than the securities purchased, having a fair market value at least equal to the purchase price of the securities purchased; and

(iii) Shall have been discharged by payment in full prior to the sale of the securities.

(3) *Determination of Holding Period.* The following provisions shall apply for the purpose of determining the period securities have been held:

(i) *Stock Dividends, Splits and Recapitalizations.* Securities acquired from the issuer as a dividend or pursuant to a stock split, reverse split or recapitalization shall be deemed to have been acquired at the same time as the securities on which the dividend or, if more than one, the initial dividend was paid, the securities involved in the split or reverse split, or the securities surrendered in connection with the recapitalization.

(ii) *Conversions and Exchanges.* If the securities sold were acquired from the issuer solely in exchange for other securities of the same issuer, the newly acquired securities shall be deemed to have been acquired at the same time as the securities surrendered for conversion or exchange, even if the securities surrendered were not convertible or exchangeable by their terms.

NOTE to Rule 144(d)(3)(ii). If the surrendered securities originally did not provide for cashless conversion or exchange by their terms and the holder provided consideration, other than solely securities of the same issuer, in connection with the amendment of the surrendered securities to permit cashless conversion or exchange, then the newly acquired securities shall be deemed to have been acquired at the same time as such amendment to the surrendered securities, so long as, in the conversion or exchange, the securities sold were acquired from the issuer solely in exchange for other securities of the same issuer.

(iii) *Contingent Issuance of Securities.* Securities acquired as a contingent payment of the purchase price of an equity interest in a business, or the assets of a business, sold to the issuer or an affiliate of the issuer shall be deemed to have been acquired at the time of such sale if the issuer or affiliate was then committed to issue the securities subject only to conditions other than the payment of further consideration for such securities. An agreement entered into in connection with any such purchase to remain in the employment of, or not to compete with, the issuer or affiliate or the rendering of services pursuant to such agreement shall not be deemed to be the payment of further consideration for such securities.

(iv) *Pledged Securities.* Securities which are bona-fide pledged by an affiliate of the issuer when sold by the pledgee, or by a purchaser, after a default in the obligation secured by the pledge, shall be deemed to have been acquired when they were acquired by the pledgor, except that if the securities were pledged without recourse they shall be deemed to have been acquired by the pledgee at the time of the pledge or by the purchaser at the time of purchase.

(v) *Gifts of Securities.* Securities acquired from an affiliate of the issuer by gift shall be deemed to have been acquired by the donee when they were acquired by the donor.

(vi) *Trusts.* Where a trust settlor is an affiliate of the issuer, securities acquired from the settlor by the trust, or acquired from the trust by the beneficiaries thereof, shall be deemed to have been acquired when such securities were acquired by the settlor.

(vii) *Estates*. Where a deceased person was an affiliate of the issuer, securities held by the estate of such person or acquired from such estate by the estate beneficiaries shall be deemed to have been acquired when they were acquired by the deceased person, except that no holding period is required if the estate is not an affiliate of the issuer or if the securities are sold by a beneficiary of the estate who is not such an affiliate.

NOTE to Rule 144(d)(3)(vii). While there is no holding period or amount limitation for estates and estate beneficiaries which are not affiliates of the issuer, paragraphs (c) and (h) of this rule apply to securities sold by such persons in reliance upon this rule.

(viii) *Rule 145(a) Transactions*. The holding period for securities acquired in a transaction specified in Rule 145(a) shall be deemed to commence on the date the securities were acquired by the purchaser in such transaction, except as otherwise provided in paragraphs (d)(3)(ii) and (ix) of this rule.

(ix) *Holding Company Formations*. Securities acquired from the issuer in a transaction effected solely for the purpose of forming a holding company shall be deemed to have been acquired at the same time as the securities of the predecessor issuer exchanged in the holding company formation where:

(A) The newly formed holding company's securities were issued solely in exchange for the securities of the predecessor company as part of a reorganization of the predecessor company into a holding company structure;

(B) Holders received securities of the same class evidencing the same proportional interest in the holding company as they held in the predecessor, and the rights and interests of the holders of such securities are substantially the same as those they possessed as holders of the predecessor company's securities; and

(C) Immediately following the transaction, the holding company has no significant assets other than securities of the predecessor company and its existing subsidiaries and has substantially the same assets and liabilities on a consolidated basis as the predecessor company had before the transaction.

(x) *Cashless Exercise of Options and Warrants*. If the securities sold were acquired from the issuer solely upon cashless exercise of options or warrants issued by the issuer, the newly acquired securities shall be deemed to have been acquired at the same time as the exercised options or warrants, even if the options or warrants exercised originally did not provide for cashless exercise by their terms.

NOTE 1 to Rule 144(d)(3)(x). If the options or warrants originally did not provide for cashless exercise by their terms and the holder provided consideration, other than solely securities of the same issuer, in connection with the amendment of the options or warrants to permit cashless exercise, then the newly acquired securities shall be deemed to have been acquired at the same time as such amendment to the options or warrants so long as the exercise itself was cashless.

NOTE 2 to Rule 144(d)(3)(x). If the options or warrants are not purchased for cash or property and do not create any investment risk to the holder, as in the case of employee stock options, the newly acquired securities shall be deemed to have been acquired at the time the options or warrants are exercised, so long as the full purchase price or other consideration for the newly acquired securities has been paid or given by the person acquiring the securities from the issuer or from an affiliate of the issuer at the time of exercise.

(e) *Limitation on Amount of Securities Sold*. Except as hereinafter provided, the amount of securities sold for the account of an affiliate of the issuer in reliance upon this rule shall be determined as follows:

(1) If any securities are sold for the account of an affiliate of the issuer, regardless of whether those securities are restricted, the amount of securities sold, together with all sales of securities of the same class sold for the account of such person within the preceding three months, shall not exceed the greatest of:

(i) One percent of the shares or other units of the class outstanding as shown by the most recent report or statement published by the issuer, or

(ii) The average weekly reported volume of trading in such securities on all national securities exchanges and/or reported through the automated quotation system of a registered securities association during the four calendar weeks preceding the filing of notice required by paragraph (h), or if no such notice is required the date of receipt of the order to execute the transaction by the broker or the date of execution of the transaction directly with a market maker, or

(iii) The average weekly volume of trading in such securities reported pursuant to an effective transaction reporting plan or an effective national market system plan as those terms are defined in Item 600 of Regulation NMS during the four-week period specified in paragraph (e)(1)(ii) of this rule.

(2) If the securities sold are debt securities, then the amount of debt securities sold for the account of an affiliate of the issuer, regardless of whether those securities are restricted, shall not exceed the greater of the limitation set forth in paragraph (e)(1) of this rule or, together with all sales of securities of the same tranche (or class when the securities are non-participatory preferred stock) sold for the account of such person within the preceding three months, ten percent of the principal amount of the tranche (or class when the securities are non-participatory preferred stock) attributable to the securities sold.

(3) *Determination of Amount.* For the purpose of determining the amount of securities specified in paragraph (e)(1) of this rule and, as applicable, paragraph (e)(2) of this rule, the following provisions shall apply:

(i) Where both convertible securities and securities of the class into which they are convertible are sold, the amount of convertible securities sold shall be deemed to be the amount of securities of the class into which they are convertible for the purpose of determining the aggregate amount of securities of both classes sold;

(ii) The amount of securities sold for the account of a pledgee of those securities, or for the account of a purchaser of the pledged securities, during any period of three months within six months (or within one year if the issuer of the securities is not, or has not been for a period of at least 90 days immediately before the sale, subject to the reporting requirements of section 13 or 15(d) of the Securities Exchange Act of 1934) after a default in the obligation secured by the pledge, and the amount of securities sold during the same three-month period for the account of the pledgor shall not exceed, in the aggregate, the amount specified in paragraph (e)(1) or (2) of this rule, whichever is applicable;

NOTE to Rule 144(e)(3)(ii). Sales by a pledgee of securities pledged by a borrower will not be aggregated under paragraph (e)(3)(ii) with sales of the securities of the same issuer by other pledgees of such borrower in the absence of concerted action by such pledgees.

(iii) The amount of securities sold for the account of a donee of those securities during any three-month period within six months (or within one year if the issuer of the securities is not, or has not been for a period of at least 90 days immediately before the sale, subject to the reporting requirements of section 13 or 15(d) of the Securities Exchange Act of 1934) after the donation, and the amount of securities sold during the same three-month period for the account of the donor, shall not exceed, in the aggregate, the amount specified in paragraph (e)(1) or (2) of this rule, whichever is applicable;

(iv) Where securities were acquired by a trust from the settlor of the trust, the amount of such securities sold for the account of the trust during any three-month period within six months (or within one year if the issuer of the securities is not, or has not been for a period of at least 90 days immediately before the sale, subject to the reporting requirements of section 13 or 15(d) of the Securities Exchange Act of 1934) after the acquisition of the securities by the trust, and the amount of securities sold during the same three-month period for the account of the settlor, shall not exceed, in the aggregate, the amount specified in paragraph (e)(1) or (2) of this rule, whichever is applicable;

(v) The amount of securities sold for the account of the estate of a deceased person, or for the account of a beneficiary of such estate, during any three-month period and the amount of securities sold during the same three-month period for the account of the deceased person prior to his death shall not exceed, in the aggregate, the amount specified in paragraph (e)(1) or (2) of this rule, whichever is applicable: *Provided*, that no limitation on amount shall apply if the estate or beneficiary of the estate is not an affiliate of the issuer;

(vi) When two or more affiliates or other persons agree to act in concert for the purpose of selling securities of an issuer, all securities of the same class sold for the account of all such persons during any three-month period shall be aggregated for the purpose of determining the limitation on the amount of securities sold;

(vii) The following sales of securities need not be included in determining the amount of securities to be sold in reliance upon this rule:

(A) Securities sold pursuant to an effective registration statement under the Act;

(B) Securities sold pursuant to an exemption provided by Regulation A (Rules 251 through 263) under the Act;

(C) Securities sold in a transaction exempt pursuant to section 4 of the Act and not involving any public offering; and

(D) Securities sold offshore pursuant to Regulation S (17 C.F.R. Rules 901 through 905, and Preliminary Notes) under the Act.

(f) *Manner of Sale.*

(1) The securities shall be sold in one of the following manners:

(i) Brokers' transactions within the meaning of section 4(4) of the Act;

(ii) Transactions directly with a market maker, as that term is defined in section 3(a)(38) of the Securities Exchange Act of 1934; or

(iii) Riskless principal transactions where:

(A) The offsetting trades must be executed at the same price (exclusive of an explicitly disclosed markup or markdown, commission equivalent, or other fee);

(B) The transaction is permitted to be reported as riskless under the rules of a self-regulatory organization; and

(C) The requirements of paragraphs (g)(2) (applicable to any markup or markdown, commission equivalent, or other fee), (g)(3), and (g)(4) of this rule are met.

NOTE to Rule 144(f)(1): For purposes of this paragraph, a riskless principal transaction means a principal transaction where, after having received from a customer an order to buy, a broker or dealer purchases the security as principal in the market to satisfy the order to buy or, after having received from a customer an order to sell, sells the security as principal to the market to satisfy the order to sell.

(2) The person selling the securities shall not:

(i) Solicit or arrange for the solicitation of orders to buy the securities in anticipation of or in connection with such transaction, or

(ii) Make any payment in connection with the offer or sale of the securities to any person other than the broker or dealer who executes the order to sell the securities.

(3) Paragraph (f) of this rule shall not apply to:

(i) Securities sold for the account of the estate of a deceased person or for the account of a beneficiary of such estate provided the estate or estate beneficiary is not an affiliate of the issuer; or

(ii) Debt securities.

(g) *Brokers' Transactions.* The term "brokers' transactions" in section 4(4) of the Act shall for the purposes of this rule be deemed to include transactions by a broker in which such broker:

(1)   Does no more than execute the order or orders to sell the securities as agent for the person for whose account the securities are sold;

(2)   Receives no more than the usual and customary broker's commission;

(3)   Neither solicits nor arranges for the solicitation of customers' orders to buy the securities in anticipation of or in connection with the transaction; *Provided*, that the foregoing shall not preclude:

(i)   Inquiries by the broker of other brokers or dealers who have indicated an interest in the securities within the preceding 60 days;

(ii)   Inquiries by the broker of his customers who have indicated an unsolicited bona fide interest in the securities within the preceding 10 business days;

(iii) The publication by the broker of bid and ask quotations for the security in an inter-dealer quotation system provided that such quotations are incident to the maintenance of a bona fide inter-dealer market for the security for the broker's own account and that the broker has published bona fide bid and ask quotations for the security in an inter-dealer quotation system on each of at least twelve days within the preceding thirty calendar days with no more than four business days in succession without such two-way quotations; or

(iv)   The publication by the broker of bid and ask quotations for the security in an alternative trading system, as defined in Rule 300 of Regulation ATS, provided that the broker has published bona fide bid and ask quotations for the security in the alternative trading system on each of the last twelve business days; and

NOTE to Rule 144(g)(3)(ii): The broker should obtain and retain in his files written evidence of indications of bona fide unsolicited interest by his customers in the securities at the time such indications are received.

(4)   After reasonable inquiry is not aware of circumstances indicating that the person for whose account the securities are sold is an underwriter with respect to the securities or that the transaction is a part of a distribution of securities of the issuer. Without limiting the foregoing, the broker shall be deemed to be aware of any facts or statements contained in the notice required by paragraph (h) of this rule.

NOTES: i. The broker, for his own protection, should obtain and retain in his files a copy of the notice required by paragraph (h) of this rule.

ii.   The reasonable inquiry required by paragraph (g)(3) of this rule should include, but not necessarily be limited to, inquiry as to the following matters:

(a)   The length of time the securities have been held by the person for whose account they are to be sold. If practicable, the inquiry should include physical inspection of the securities;

(b)   The nature of the transaction in which the securities were acquired by such person;

(c)   The amount of securities of the same class sold during the past 3 months by all persons whose sales are required to be taken into consideration pursuant to paragraph (e) of this rule;

(d)   Whether such person intends to sell additional securities of the same class through any other means;

(e)   Whether such person has solicited or made any arrangement for the solicitation of buy orders in connection with the proposed sale of securities;

(f)   Whether such person has made any payment to any other person in connection with the proposed sale of the securities; and

(g)   The number of shares or other units of the class outstanding, or the relevant trading volume.

(h)   *Notice of Proposed Sale.*

(1)   *Reporting issuers.* If the issuer is, and has been for a period of at least 90 days immediately before the sale, subject to the reporting requirements of section 13 or 15(d) of the Exchange Act and the amount of securities to be sold in reliance upon this rule during any period of three months exceeds 5,000 shares or other units or has an aggregate sale price in excess of $50,000, a notice on Form 144 (§ 239.144 of this chapter) shall be filed electronically with the Commission.

(2) *Non-reporting issuers.* If the issuer is not subject to the reporting requirements of section 13 or 15(d) of the Exchange Act, and the amount of securities to be sold in reliance upon this rule during any period of three months exceeds 5,000 shares or other units or has an aggregate sale price in excess of $50,000, three copies of a notice on Form 144 shall be filed with the Commission.

(i) *Unavailability to Securities of Issuers With No or Nominal Operations and No or Nominal Non-Cash Assets.*

(1) This rule is not available for the resale of securities initially issued by an issuer defined below:

(i) An issuer, other than a business combination related shell company, as defined in Rule 405, or an asset-backed issuer, as defined in Item 1101(b) of Regulation AB (Item 1101(b) of Regulation AB), that has:

(A) No or nominal operations; and

(B) Either:

(1) No or nominal assets;

(2) Assets consisting solely of cash and cash equivalents; or

(3) Assets consisting of any amount of cash and cash equivalents and nominal other assets; or

(ii) An issuer that has been at any time previously an issuer described in paragraph (i)(1)(i).

(2) Notwithstanding paragraph (i)(1), if the issuer of the securities previously had been an issuer described in paragraph (i)(1)(i) but has ceased to be an issuer described in paragraph (i)(1)(i); is subject to the reporting requirements of section 13 or 15(d) of the Securities Exchange Act of 1934; has filed all reports and other materials required to be filed by section 13 or 15(d) of the Securities Exchange Act of 1934, as applicable, during the preceding 12 months (or for such shorter period that the issuer was required to file such reports and materials), other than Form 8–K reports; and has filed current "Form 10 information" with the Commission reflecting its status as an entity that is no longer an issuer described in paragraph (i)(1)(i), then those securities may be sold subject to the requirements of this rule after one year has elapsed from the date that the issuer filed "Form 10 information" with the Commission.

(3) The term "Form 10 information" means the information that is required by Form 10 or Form 20–F, as applicable to the issuer of the securities, to register under the Securities Exchange Act of 1934 each class of securities being sold under this rule. The issuer may provide the Form 10 information in any filing of the issuer with the Commission. The Form 10 information is deemed filed when the initial filing is made with the Commission.

Preliminary Notes to Rule 144A

1. This rule relates solely to the application of section 5 of the Act and not to antifraud or other provisions of the federal securities laws.

2. Attempted compliance with this rule does not act as an exclusive election; any seller hereunder may also claim the availability of any other applicable exemption from the registration requirements of the Act.

3. In view of the objective of this rule and the policies underlying the Act, this rule is not available with respect to any transaction or series of transactions that, although in technical compliance with this rule, is part of a plan or scheme to evade the registration provisions of the Act. In such cases, registration under the Act is required.

4. Nothing in this rule obviates the need for any issuer or any other person to comply with the securities registration or broker-dealer registration requirements of the Securities Exchange Act of 1934 (the "Exchange Act"), whenever such requirements are applicable.

5.   Nothing in this rule obviates the need for any person to comply with any applicable state law relating to the offer or sale of securities.

6.   Securities acquired in a transaction made pursuant to the provisions of this rule are deemed to be "restricted securities" within the meaning of Rule 144(a)(3).

7.   The fact that purchasers of securities from the issuer thereof may purchase such securities with a view to reselling such securities pursuant to this rule will not affect the availability to such issuer of an exemption under section 4(a)(2) of the Act, or Regulation D under the Act, from the registration requirements of the Act.

Rule 144A.   Private Resales of Securities to Institutions

(a)   *Definitions.* (1) For purposes of this rule, "qualified institutional buyer" shall mean:

(i)   Any of the following entities, acting for its own account or the accounts of other qualified institutional buyers, that in the aggregate owns and invests on a discretionary basis at least $100 million in securities of issuers that are not affiliated with the entity:

(A)   Any "insurance company" as defined in section 2(a)(13) of the Act;

NOTE: A purchase by an insurance company for one or more of its separate accounts, as defined by Rule 2(a)(37) of the Investment Company Act of 1940 (the "Investment Company Act"), which are neither registered under Rule 8 of the Investment Company Act nor required to be so registered, shall be deemed to be a purchase for the account of such insurance company.

(B)   Any "investment company" registered under the Investment Company Act or any "business development company" as defined in section 2(a)(48) of that Act;

(C)   Any *Small Business Investment Company* licensed by the U.S. Small Business Administration under section 301(c) or (d) of the Small Business Investment Act of 1958 or any *Rural Business Investment Company* as defined in section 384A of the Consolidated Farm and Rural Development Act;

(D)   Any "plan" established and maintained by a state, its political subdivisions, or any agency or instrumentality of a state or its political subdivisions, for the benefit of its employees;

(E)   Any "employee benefit plan" within the meaning of title I of the Employee Retirement Income Security Act of 1974;

(F)   Any trust fund whose trustee is a bank or trust company and whose participants are exclusively plans of the types identified in paragraph (a)(1)(i)(D) or (E) of this rule, except trust funds that include as participants individual retirement accounts or H.R. 10 plans.

(G)   Any "business development company" as defined in section 202(a)(22) of the Investment Advisers Act of 1940;

(H)   Any organization described in section 501(c)(3) of the Internal Revenue Code, corporation (other than a bank as defined in section 3(a)(2) of the Act or a savings and loan association or other institution referenced in section 3(a)(5)(A) of the Act or a foreign bank or savings and loan association or equivalent institution), partnership, limited liability company, or Massachusetts or similar business trust;

(I)   any "investment adviser" registered under the Investment Advisers Act;

(J)   Any institutional accredited investor, as defined in rule 501(a) under the Act (17 CFR 230.501(a)), of a type not listed in paragraphs (a)(1)(i)(A) through (I) or paragraphs (a)(1)(ii) through (vi).

NOTE: An entity seeking qualified institutional buyer status under Rule 144A(a)(1)(i)(J) may be formed for the purpose of acquiring the securities being offered under this section.

(ii)   Any "dealer" registered pursuant to section 15 of the Exchange Act, acting for its own account or the accounts of other qualified institutional buyers, that in the aggregate owns and invests on a discretionary basis at least $10 million of securities of issuers that are not affiliated with the dealer, *Provided,* That securities constituting the whole or a part of an unsold allotment to or subscription by a dealer as a participant in a public offering shall not be deemed to be owned by such dealer;

(iii) Any "dealer" registered pursuant to section 15 of the Exchange Act acting in a riskless principal transaction on behalf of a qualified institutional buyer;

NOTE: A registered dealer may act as agent, on a non-discretionary basis, in a transaction with a qualified institutional buyer without itself having to be a qualified institutional buyer.

(iv) Any investment company registered under the Investment Company Act, acting for its own account or for the accounts of other qualified institutional buyers, that is part of a family of investment companies which own in the aggregate at least $100 million in securities of issuers, other than issuers that are affiliated with the investment company or are part of such family of investment companies. "Family of investment companies" means any two or more investment companies registered under the Investment Company Act, except for a unit investment trust whose assets consist solely of shares of one or more registered investment companies, that have the same investment adviser (or, in the case of unit investment trusts, the same depositor), *Provided That*, for purposes of this rule:

(A) Each series of a series company (as defined in Rule 18f–2 under the Investment Company Act) shall be deemed to be a separate investment company; and

(B) Investment companies shall be deemed to have the same adviser (or depositor) if their advisers (or depositors) are majority-owned subsidiaries of the same parent, or if one investment company's adviser (or depositor) is a majority-owned subsidiary of the other investment company's adviser (or depositor);

(v) Any entity, all of the equity owners of which are qualified institutional buyers, acting for its own account or the accounts of other qualified institutional buyers; and

(vi) Any "bank" as defined in section 3(a)(2) of the Act, any savings and loan association or other institution as referenced in section 3(a)(5)(A) of the Act, or any foreign bank or savings and loan association or equivalent institution, acting for its own account or the accounts of other qualified institutional buyers, that in the aggregate owns and invests on a discretionary basis at least $100 million in securities of issuers that are not affiliated with it and that has an audited net worth of at least $25 million as demonstrated in its latest annual financial statements, as of a date not more than 16 months preceding the date of sale under the rule in the case of a U.S. bank or savings and loan association, and not more than 18 months preceding such date of sale for a foreign bank or savings and loan association or equivalent institution.

(2) In determining the aggregate amount of securities owned and invested on a discretionary basis by an entity, the following instruments and interests shall be excluded: bank deposit notes and certificates of deposit; loan participations; repurchase agreements; securities owned but subject to a repurchase agreement; and currency, interest rate and commodity swaps.

(3) The aggregate value of securities owned and invested on a discretionary basis by an entity shall be the cost of such securities, except where the entity reports its securities holdings in its financial statements on the basis of their market value, and no current information with respect to the cost of those securities has been published. In the latter event, the securities may be valued at market for purposes of this rule.

(4) In determining the aggregate amount of securities owned by an entity and invested on a discretionary basis, securities owned by subsidiaries of the entity that are consolidated with the entity in its financial statements prepared in accordance with generally accepted accounting principles may be included if the investments of such subsidiaries are managed under the direction of the entity, except that, unless the entity is a reporting company under section 13 or 15(d) of the Exchange Act, securities owned by such subsidiaries may not be included if the entity itself is a majority-owned subsidiary that would be included in the consolidated financial statements of another enterprise.

(5) For purposes of this rule, "riskless principal transaction" means a transaction in which a dealer buys a security from any person and makes a simultaneous offsetting sale of such security to a qualified institutional buyer, including another dealer acting as riskless principal for a qualified institutional buyer.

(6) For purposes of this rule, "effective conversion premium" means the amount, expressed as a percentage of the security's conversion value, by which the price at issuance of a convertible security exceeds its conversion value.

(7) For purposes of this rule, "effective exercise premium" means the amount, expressed as a percentage of the warrant's exercise value, by which the sum of the price at issuance and the exercise price of a warrant exceeds its exercise value.

(b) *Sales by Persons Other Than Issuers or Dealers.* Any person, other than the issuer or a dealer, who offers or sells securities in compliance with the conditions set forth in paragraph (d) of this rule shall be deemed not to be engaged in a distribution of such securities and therefore not to be an underwriter of such securities within the meaning of sections 2(a)(11) and 4(a)(1) of the Act.

(c) *Sales by Dealers.* Any dealer who offers or sells securities in compliance with the conditions set forth in paragraph (d) of this rule shall be deemed not to be a participant in a distribution of such securities within the meaning of section 4(a)(3)(A) of the Act and not to be an underwriter of such securities within the meaning of section 2(a)(11) of the Act, and such securities shall be deemed not to have been offered to the public within the meaning of section 4(a)(3)(A) of the Act.

(d) *Conditions to Be Met.* To qualify for exemption under this rule, an offer or sale must meet the following conditions:

(1) The securities are sold only to a qualified institutional buyer or to a purchaser that the seller and any person acting on behalf of the seller reasonably believe is a qualified institutional buyer. In determining whether a prospective purchaser is a qualified institutional buyer, the seller and any person acting on its behalf shall be entitled to rely upon the following non-exclusive methods of establishing the prospective purchaser's ownership and discretionary investments of securities:

(i) The prospective purchaser's most recent publicly available financial statements, *Provided* That such statements present the information as of a date within 16 months preceding the date of sale of securities under this rule in the case of a U.S. purchaser and within 18 months preceding such date of sale for a foreign purchaser;

(ii) The most recent publicly available information appearing in documents filed by the prospective purchaser with the Commission or another United States federal, state, or local governmental agency or self-regulatory organization, or with a foreign governmental agency or self-regulatory organization, *Provided* That any such information is as of a date within 16 months preceding the date of sale of securities under this rule in the case of a U.S. purchaser and within 18 months preceding such date of sale for a foreign purchaser;

(iii) The most recent publicly available information appearing in a recognized securities manual, *Provided* That such information is as of a date within 16 months preceding the date of sale of securities under this rule in the case of a U.S. purchaser and within 18 months preceding such date of sale for a foreign purchaser; or

(iv) A certification by the chief financial officer, a person fulfilling an equivalent function, or other executive officer of the purchaser, specifying the amount of securities owned and invested on a discretionary basis by the purchaser as of a specific date on or since the close of the purchaser's most recent fiscal year, or, in the case of a purchaser that is a member of a family of investment companies, a certification by an executive officer of the investment adviser specifying the amount of securities owned by the family of investment companies as of a specific date on or since the close of the purchaser's most recent fiscal year;

(2) The seller and any person acting on its behalf takes reasonable steps to ensure that the purchaser is aware that the seller may rely on the exemption from the provisions of section 5 of the Act provided by this rule;

(3) The securities offered or sold:

(i) Were not, when issued, of the same class as securities listed on a national securities exchange registered under section 6 of the Exchange Act or quoted in a U.S. automated inter-dealer quotation system; *Provided*, that securities that are convertible or exchangeable into securities so listed or quoted at the time of issuance and that had an effective conversion premium of less than 10 percent, shall be treated as securities of the class into which they are convertible or exchangeable; and that warrants that may be exercised for securities so listed or quoted at the time of issuance, for a period of less than 3 years from the date of issuance, or that had an effective exercise premium of less than 10 percent, shall be treated as securities of the class to be issued upon exercise; and *provided further,* That the Commission may from time to time, taking into account then-existing market practices, designate additional securities and classes of securities that will not be deemed of the same class as securities listed on a national securities exchange or quoted in a U.S. automated inter-dealer quotation system; and

(ii)   Are not securities of an open-end investment company, unit investment trust or face-amount certificate company that is or is required to be registered under section 8 of the Investment Company Act; and

(4)(i)   In the case of securities of an issuer that is neither subject to section 13 or 15(d) of the Exchange Act, nor exempt from reporting pursuant to Rule 12g3–2(b) under the Exchange Act, nor a foreign government as defined in Rule 405 eligible to register securities under Schedule B of the Act, the holder and a prospective purchaser designated by the holder have the right to obtain from the issuer, upon request of the holder, and the prospective purchaser has received from the issuer, the seller, or a person acting on either of their behalf, at or prior to the time of sale, upon such prospective purchaser's request to the holder or the issuer, the following information (which shall be reasonably current in relation to the date of resale under this rule): a very brief statement of the nature of the business of the issuer and the products and services it offers; and the issuer's most recent balance sheet and profit and loss and retained earnings statements, and similar financial statements for such part of the two preceding fiscal years as the issuer has been in operation (the financial statements should be audited to the extent reasonably available).

(ii)   The requirements that the information be "reasonably current" will be presumed to be satisfied if:

(A)   The balance sheet is as of a date less than 16 months before the date of resale, the statements of profit and loss and retained earnings are for the 12 months preceding the date of such balance sheet, and if such balance sheet is not as of a date less than 6 months before the date of resale, it shall be accompanied by additional statements of profit and loss and retained earnings for the period from the date of such balance sheet to a date less than 6 months before the date of resale; and

(B)   The statement of the nature of the issuer's business and its products and services offered is as of a date within 12 months prior to the date of resale; or

(C)   With regard to foreign private issuers, the required information meets the timing requirements of the issuer's home country or principal trading markets.

(e)   Offers and sales of securities pursuant to this rule shall be deemed not to affect the availability of any exemption or safe harbor relating to any previous or subsequent offer or sale of such securities by the issuer or any prior or subsequent holder thereof.

Preliminary Note to Rule 145

Rule 145 is designed to make available the protection provided by registration under the Securities Act of 1933, as amended (Act), to persons who are offered securities in a business combination of the type described in paragraphs (a)(1), (2) and (3) of the rule. The thrust of the rule is that an "offer," "offer to sell," "offer for sale," or "sale" occurs when there is submitted to security holders a plan or agreement pursuant to which such holders are required to elect, on the basis of what is in substance a new investment decision, whether to accept a new or different security in exchange for their existing security. Rule 145 embodies the Commission's determination that such transactions are subject to the registration requirements of the Act, and that the previously existing "no-sale" theory of Rule 133 is no longer consistent with the statutory purposes of the Act. *See* Release No. 33–5316 (October 6, 1972). Securities issued in transactions described in paragraph (a) of Rule 145 may be registered on Form S–4 or F–4 or Form N–14 under the Act.

Transactions for which statutory exemptions under the Act, including those contained in sections 3(a)(9), (10), (11) and 4(2), are otherwise available are not affected by Rule 145. Reference is made to Rule 153a of the Securities Exchange Act of 1933 describing the prospectus delivery required in a transaction of the type referred to in Rule 145. A reclassification of securities covered by Rule 145 would be exempt from registration pursuant to section 3(a)(9) or (11) of the Act if the conditions of either of these sections are satisfied.

Rule 145.   Reclassifications of Securities, Mergers, Consolidations and Acquisitions of Assets

(a) *Transactions Within the Rule.* An "offer", "offer to sell", "offer for sale," or "sale" shall be deemed to be involved, within the meaning of Section 2(a)(3) of the Act, so far as the security holders of a corporation or other person are concerned where, pursuant to statutory provisions of the jurisdiction under which such corporation or other person is organized, or pursuant to provisions contained in its certificate of incorporation or similar controlling instruments, or otherwise, there is submitted for the vote or consent of such security holders a plan or agreement for—

(1) *Reclassifications.* A reclassification of securities of such corporation or other person, other than a stock split, reverse stock split, or change in par value, which involves the substitution of a security for another security;

(2) *Mergers or Consolidations.* A statutory merger or consolidation or similar plan or acquisition in which securities of such corporation or other person held by such security holders will become or be exchanged for securities of any other person, unless the sole purpose of the transaction is to change an issuer's domicile solely within the United States; or

(3) *Transfers of Assets.* A transfer of assets of such corporation or other person, to another person in consideration of the issuance of securities of such other person or any of its affiliates, if:

(i) Such plan or agreement provides for dissolution of the corporation or other person whose security holders are voting or consenting; or

(ii) Such plan or agreement provides for a pro rata or similar distribution of such securities to the security holders voting or consenting; or

(iii) The board of directors or similar representatives of such corporation or other person, adopts resolutions relative to (i) or (ii) above within one year after the taking of such vote or consent; or

(iv) The transfer of assets is a part of a pre-existing plan for distribution of such securities, notwithstanding (i), (ii) or (iii), above.

(b) *Communications Before a Registration Statement is Filed.* Communications made in connection with or relating to a transaction described in paragraph (a) of this rule that will be registered under the Act may be made under Rule 135, Rule 165, or Rule 166.

(c) *Persons and Parties Deemed to be Underwriters.* For purposes of this rule, if any party to a transaction specified in paragraph (a) of this rule is a shell company, other than a business combination related shell company, as those terms are defined in Rule 405, any party to that transaction, other than the issuer, or any person who is an affiliate of such party at the time such transaction is submitted for vote or consent, who publicly offers or sells securities of the issuer acquired in connection with any such transaction, shall be deemed to be engaged in a distribution and therefore to be an underwriter thereof within the meaning of Section 2(a)(11) of the Act.

(d) *Resale Provisions for Persons and Parties Deemed Underwriters.* Notwithstanding the provisions of paragraph (c), a person or party specified in that paragraph shall not be deemed to be engaged in a distribution and therefore not to be an underwriter of securities acquired in a transaction specified in paragraph (a) that was registered under the Act if:

(1) The issuer has met the requirements applicable to an issuer of securities in paragraph (i)(2) of Rule 144; and

(2) One of the following three conditions is met:

(i)   Such securities are sold by such person or party in accordance with the provisions of paragraphs (c), (e), (f), and (g) of Rule 144 and at least 90 days have elapsed since the date the securities were acquired from the issuer in such transaction; or

(ii)   Such person or party is not, and has not been for at least three months, an affiliate of the issuer, and at least six months, as determined in accordance with paragraph (d) of Rule 144, have elapsed since the date the securities were acquired from the issuer in such transaction, and the issuer meets the requirements of paragraph (c) of Rule 144; or

(iii)   Such person or party is not, and has not been for at least three months, an affiliate of the issuer, and at least one year, as determined in accordance with paragraph (d) of Rule 144, has elapsed since the date the securities were acquired from the issuer in such transaction.

NOTE to Rule 145(c) and (d): Paragraph (d) is not available with respect to any transaction or series of transactions that, although in technical compliance with the rule, is part of a plan or scheme to evade the registration requirements of the Act.

(e)   *Definitions.*

(1)   The term "affiliate" as used in paragraphs (c) and (d) of this rule shall have the same meaning as the definition of that term in Rule 144.

(2)   The term "party" as used in paragraphs (c) and (d) of this rule shall mean the corporations, business entities, or other persons, other than the issuer, whose assets or capital structure are affected by the transactions specified in paragraph (a) of this rule.

(3)   The term "person" as used in paragraphs (c) and (d) of this rule, when used in reference to a person for whose account securities are to be sold, shall have the same meaning as the definition of that term in paragraph (a)(2) of Rule 144.

Rule 146.   Definition of "Prepared by or on Behalf of the Issuer" for Purposes of Section 18 of the Act

(a)   *Prepared By or on Behalf of the Issuer.* An offering document (as defined in section 18(d)(1) of the Act) is "prepared by or on behalf of the issuer" for purposes of section 18 of the Act, if the issuer or an agent or representative:

(1)   Authorizes the document's production, and

(2)   Approves the document before its use.

(b)   *Covered Securities for Purposes of Section 18.*

(1)   For purposes of Section 18(b) of the Act, the Commission finds that the following national securities exchanges, or segments or tiers thereof, have listing standards that are substantially similar to those of the New York Stock Exchange ("NYSE"), the NYSE American LLC ('NYSE American"), or the National Market System of the Nasdaq Stock Market ("Nasdaq/NGM"), and that securities listed, or authorized for listing, on such exchanges shall be deemed covered securities:

(i)   Tier I of the NYSE Arca, Inc.;

(ii)   Tier I of the NASDAQ PHLX LLC;

(iii)   The Chicago Board Options Exchange, Incorporated;

(iv)   Options listed on the International Securities Exchange, LLC; and

(v)   The Nasdaq Capital Market.

(vi)   Tier I and Tier II of BATS Exchange, Inc.

(vii)   Investros Exchange LLC.

(2)   The designation of securities in paragraphs (b)(1)(i) through (vii) of this rule as covered securities is conditioned on such exchanges' listing standards (or segments or tiers thereof) continuing to be substantially similar to those of the NYSE, NYSE American, or Nasdaq/NGM.

Rule 147.   Intrastate Offers and Sales

(a)   This rule shall not raise any presumption that the exemption provided by section 3(a)(11) of the Act is not available for transactions by an issuer which do not satisfy all of the provisions of this rule.

(b)   *Manner of offers and sales.* An issuer, or any person acting on behalf of the issuer, shall be deemed to conduct an offering in compliance with section 3(a)(11) of the Act, where offers and sales are made only to persons resident within the same state or territory in which the issuer is resident and doing business, within the meaning of section 3(a)(11) of the Act, so long as the issuer complies with the provisions of paragraphs (c), (d), and (f) through (h) of this rule.

(c)   *Nature of the issuer.* The issuer of the securities shall at the time of any offers and sales be a person resident and doing business within the state or territory in which all of the offers and sales are made.

(1)   The issuer shall be deemed to be a resident of the state or territory in which:

(i)   It is incorporated or organized, and it has its principal place of business, if a corporation, limited partnership, trust or other form of business organization that is organized under state or territorial law. The issuer shall be deemed to have its principal place of business in a state or territory in which the officers, partners or managers of the issuer primarily direct, control and coordinate the activities of the issuer;

(ii)   It has its principal place of business, as defined in paragraph (c)(1)(i) of this rule, if a general partnership or other form of business organization that is not organized under any state or territorial law;

(iii)   Such person's principal residence is located, if an individual.

(2)   The issuer shall be deemed to be doing business within a state or territory if the issuer satisfies at least one of the following requirements:

(i)   The issuer derived at least 80% of its consolidated gross revenues from the operation of a business or of real property located in or from the rendering of services within such state or territory;

(ii)   The issuer had at the end of its most recent semi-annual fiscal period prior to an initial offer of securities in any offering or subsequent offering pursuant to this rule, at least 80% of its assets and those of its subsidiaries on a consolidated basis located within such state or territory;

(iii)   The issuer intends to use and uses at least 80% of the net proceeds to the issuer from sales made pursuant to this rule in connection with the operation of a business or of real property, the purchase of real property located in, or the rendering of services within such state or territory; or

(iv)   A majority of the issuer's employees are based in such state or territory.

Instruction to Paragraph (c)(1): An issuer that has previously conducted an intrastate offering pursuant to this rule or Rule 147A may not conduct another intrastate offering pursuant to this rule in a different state or territory, until the expiration of the time period specified in paragraph (e) of this rule or paragraph (e) of Rule 147A, calculated on the basis of the date of the last sale in such offering.

Instruction to Paragraph (c)(2)(i): Revenues must be calculated based on the issuer's most recent fiscal year, if the first offer of securities pursuant to this rule is made during the first six months of the issuer's current fiscal year, and based on the first six months of the issuer's current fiscal year or during the twelve-month fiscal period ending with such six-month period, if the first offer of securities pursuant to this rule is made during the last six months of the issuer's current fiscal year.

(d)   *Residence of offerees and purchasers.* Offers and sales of securities pursuant to this rule shall be made only to residents of the state or territory in which the issuer is resident, as determined pursuant to paragraph (c) of this rule, or who the issuer reasonably believes, at the time of the offer and sale, are residents of the state or territory in which the issuer is resident. For purposes of determining the residence of offerees and purchasers:

(1) A corporation, partnership, limited liability company, trust or other form of business organization shall be deemed to be a resident of a state or territory if, at the time of the offer and sale to it, it has its principal place of business, as defined in paragraph (c)(1)(i) of this rule, within such state or territory.

(2) Individuals shall be deemed to be residents of a state or territory if such individuals have, at the time of the offer and sale to them, their principal residence in the state or territory.

(3) A corporation, partnership, trust or other form of business organization, which is organized for the specific purpose of acquiring securities offered pursuant to this rule, shall not be a resident of a state or territory unless all of the beneficial owners of such organization are residents of such state or territory.

Instruction to Paragraph (d): Obtaining a written representation from purchasers of in-state residency status will not, without more, be sufficient to establish a reasonable belief that such purchasers are in-state residents.

Instruction to Paragraph (d)(1): A trust that is not deemed by the law of the state or territory of its creation to be a separate legal entity is deemed to be a resident of each state or territory in which its trustee is, or trustees are, resident.

(e) *Limitation on resales.* For a period of six months from the date of the sale by the issuer of a security pursuant to this rule, any resale of such security shall be made only to persons resident within the state or territory in which the issuer was resident, as determined pursuant to paragraph (c) of this rule, at the time of the sale of the security by the issuer.

Instruction to Paragraph (e): In the case of convertible securities, resales of either the convertible security, or if it is converted, the underlying security, could be made during the period described in paragraph (e) only to persons resident within such state or territory. For purposes of this paragraph (e), a conversion in reliance on section 3(a)(9) of the Act does not begin a new period.

(f) *Precautions against interstate sales.* (1) The issuer shall, in connection with any securities sold by it pursuant to this rule:

(i) Place a prominent legend on the certificate or other document evidencing the security stating that: "Offers and sales of these securities were made under an exemption from registration and have not been registered under the Securities Act of 1933. For a period of six months from the date of the sale by the issuer of these securities, any resale of these securities (or the underlying securities in the case of convertible securities) shall be made only to persons resident within the state or territory of [identify the name of the state or territory in which the issuer was resident at the time of the sale of the securities by the issuer].";

(ii) Issue stop transfer instructions to the issuer's transfer agent, if any, with respect to the securities, or, if the issuer transfers its own securities, make a notation in the appropriate records of the issuer; and

(iii) Obtain a written representation from each purchaser as to his or her residence.

(2) The issuer shall, in connection with the issuance of new certificates for any of the securities that are sold pursuant to this rule that are presented for transfer during the time period specified in paragraph (e), take the steps required by paragraphs (f)(1)(i) and (ii) of this rule.

(3) The issuer shall, at the time of any offer or sale by it of a security pursuant to this rule, prominently disclose to each offeree in the manner in which any such offer is communicated and to each purchaser of such security in writing a reasonable period of time before the date of sale, the following: "Sales will be made only to residents of [identify the name of the state or territory in which the issuer was resident at the time of the sale of the securities by the issuer]. Offers and sales of these securities are made under an exemption from registration and have not been registered under the Securities Act of 1933. For a period of six months from the date of the sale by the issuer of the securities, any resale of the securities (or the underlying securities in the case of convertible securities) shall be made only to persons resident within the state or territory of [identify the name of the state or territory in which the issuer was resident at the time of the sale of the securities by the issuer]."

(g)   *Integration with other offerings.* To determine whether offers and sales should be integrated, refer to Rule 152.

Instruction to Paragraph (g): If none of the safe harbors applies, whether subsequent offers and sales of securities will be integrated with any securities offered or sold pursuant to this rule will depend on the particular facts and circumstances.

(h)   *Offerings limited to qualified institutional buyers and institutional accredited investors.*

Where an issuer decides to register an offering under the Act after making offers in reliance on this rule limited only to qualified institutional buyers and institutional accredited investors referenced in section 5(d) of the Act, such offers will not be subject to integration with any subsequent registered offering. If the issuer makes offers in reliance on this rule to persons other than qualified institutional buyers and institutional accredited investors referenced in section 5(d) of the Act, such offers will not be subject to integration if the issuer (and any underwriter, broker, dealer, or agent used by the issuer in connection with the proposed offering) waits at least 30 calendar days between the last such offer made in reliance on this rule and the filing of the registration statement with the Commission.

Rule 147A.   Intrastate Sales Exemption

(a)   *Scope of the exemption.* Offers and sales by or on behalf of an issuer of its securities made in accordance with this rule are exempt from section 5 of the Act. This exemption is not available to an issuer that is an investment company registered or required to be registered under the Investment Company Act of 1940.

(b)   *Manner of offers and sales.* An issuer, or any person acting on behalf of the issuer, may rely on this exemption to make offers and sales using any form of general solicitation and general advertising, so long as the issuer complies with the provisions of paragraphs (c), (d), and (f) through (h) of this rule.

(c)   *Nature of the issuer.* The issuer of the securities shall at the time of any offers and sales be a person resident and doing business within the state or territory in which all of the sales are made.

(1)   The issuer shall be deemed to be a resident of the state or territory in which it has its principal place of business. The issuer shall be deemed to have its principal place of business in a state or territory in which the officers, partners or managers of the issuer primarily direct, control and coordinate the activities of the issuer.

(2)   The issuer shall be deemed to be doing business within a state or territory if the issuer satisfies at least one of the following requirements:

(i)   The issuer derived at least 80% of its consolidated gross revenues from the operation of a business or of real property located in or from the rendering of services within such state or territory;

(ii)   The issuer had at the end of its most recent semi-annual fiscal period prior to an initial offer of securities in any offering or subsequent offering pursuant to this rule, at least 80% of its assets and those of its subsidiaries on a consolidated basis located within such state or territory;

(iii)   The issuer intends to use and uses at least 80% of the net proceeds to the issuer from sales made pursuant to this rule in connection with the operation of a business or of real property, the purchase of real property located in, or the rendering of services within such state or territory; or

(iv)   A majority of the issuer's employees are based in such state or territory.

Instruction to Paragraph (c): An issuer that has previously conducted an intrastate offering pursuant to this rule or Rule 147 may not conduct another intrastate offering pursuant to this rule in a different state or territory, until the expiration of the time period specified in paragraph (e) of rule or paragraph (e) of Rule 147, calculated on the basis of the date of the last sale in such offering.

Instruction to Paragraph (c)(2)(i): Revenues must be calculated based on the issuer's most recent fiscal year, if the first offer of securities pursuant to this rule is made during the first six months of the issuer's current fiscal year, and based on the first six months of the issuer's current fiscal year or during the twelve-month fiscal period ending with such six-month period, if the first offer of securities pursuant to this rule is made during the last six months of the issuer's current fiscal year.

(d) *Residence of purchasers.* Sales of securities pursuant to this rule shall be made only to residents of the state or territory in which the issuer is resident, as determined pursuant to paragraph (c) of this rule, or who the issuer reasonably believes, at the time of sale, are residents of the state or territory in which the issuer is resident. For purposes of determining the residence of purchasers:

(1) A corporation, partnership, limited liability company, trust or other form of business organization shall be deemed to be a resident of a state or territory if, at the time of sale to it, it has its principal place of business, as defined in paragraph (c)(1) of this rule, within such state or territory.

(2) Individuals shall be deemed to be residents of a state or territory if such individuals have, at the time of sale to them, their principal residence in the state or territory.

(3) A corporation, partnership, trust or other form of business organization, which is organized for the specific purpose of acquiring securities offered pursuant to rule, shall not be a resident of a state or territory unless all of the beneficial owners of such organization are residents of such state or territory.

Instruction to Paragraph (d): Obtaining a written representation from purchasers of in-state residency status will not, without more, be sufficient to establish a reasonable belief that such purchasers are in-state residents.

Instruction to Paragraph (d)(1): A trust that is not deemed by the law of the state or territory of its creation to be a separate legal entity is deemed to be a resident of each state or territory in which its trustee is, or trustees are, resident.

(e) *Limitation on resales.* For a period of six months from the date of the sale by the issuer of a security pursuant to this rule, any resale of such security shall be made only to persons resident within the state or territory in which the issuer was resident, as determined pursuant to paragraph (c) of this rule, at the time of the sale of the security by the issuer.

Instruction to Paragraph (e): In the case of convertible securities, resales of either the convertible security, or if it is converted, the underlying security, could be made during the period described in paragraph (e) only to persons resident within such state or territory. For purposes of this paragraph (e), a conversion in reliance on section 3(a)(9) of the does not begin a new period.

(f) *Precautions against interstate sales.* (1) The issuer shall, in connection with any securities sold by it pursuant to this rule:

(i) Place a prominent legend on the certificate or other document evidencing the security stating that: "Offers and sales of these securities were made under an exemption from registration and have not been registered under the Securities Act of 1933. For a period of six months from the date of the sale by the issuer of these securities, any resale of these securities (or the underlying securities in the case of convertible securities) shall be made only to persons resident within the state or territory of [identify the name of the state or territory in which the issuer was resident at the time of the sale of the securities by the issuer].";

(ii) Issue stop transfer instructions to the issuer's transfer agent, if any, with respect to the securities, or, if the issuer transfers its own securities, make a notation in the appropriate records of the issuer; and

(iii) Obtain a written representation from each purchaser as to his or her residence.

(2) The issuer shall, in connection with the issuance of new certificates for any of the securities that are sold pursuant to this rule that are presented for transfer during the time period specified in paragraph (e), take the steps required by paragraphs (f)(1)(i) and (ii) of this rule.

(3) The issuer shall, at the time of any offer or sale by it of a security pursuant to this rule, prominently disclose to each offeree in the manner in which any such offer is communicated and to each purchaser of such security in writing a reasonable period of time before the date of sale, the following: "Sales will be made only to residents of the state or territory of [identify the name of the

state or territory in which the issuer was resident at the time of the sale of the securities by the issuer]. Offers and sales of these securities are made under an exemption from registration and have not been registered under the Securities Act of 1933. For a period of six months from the date of the sale by the issuer of the securities, any resale of the securities (or the underlying securities in the case of convertible securities) shall be made only to persons resident within the state or territory of [identify the name of the state or territory in which the issuer was resident at the time of the sale of the securities by the issuer]."

(g)   *Integration with other offerings.* To determine whether offers and sales should be integrated, refer to Rule 152.

(h)   *Offerings limited to qualified institutional buyers and institutional accredited investors.*

Where an issuer decides to register an offering under the Act after making offers in reliance on this rule limited only to qualified institutional buyers and institutional accredited investors referenced in section 5(d) of the Act, such offers will not be subject to integration with any subsequent registered offering. If the issuer makes offers in reliance on this rule to persons other than qualified institutional buyers and institutional accredited investors referenced in section 5(d) of the Act, such offers will not be subject to integration if the issuer (and any underwriter, broker, dealer, or agent used by the issuer in connection with the proposed offering) waits at least 30 calendar days between the last such offer made in reliance on this rule and the filing of the registration statement with the Commission.

Rule 148.   Exemption from General Solicitation or General Advertising

(a)   A communication will not be deemed to constitute general solicitation or general advertising if made in connection with a seminar or meeting in which more than one issuer participates that is sponsored by a college, university, or other institution of higher education, State or local government or instrumentality thereof, nonprofit organization, or angel investor group, incubator, or accelerator, provided that:

(1)   No advertising for the seminar or meeting references a specific offering of securities by the issuer;

(2)   The sponsor of the seminar or meeting does not:

(i)   Make investment recommendations or provide investment advice to attendees of the event;

(ii)   Engage in any investment negotiations between the issuer and investors attending the event;

(iii)   Charge attendees of the event any fees, other than reasonable administrative fees;

(iv)   Receive any compensation for making introductions between event attendees and issuers or for investment negotiations between such parties; and

(v)   Receive any compensation with respect to the event that would require registration of the sponsor as a broker or a dealer under the Securities Exchange Act of 1934 (15 U.S.C. 78a *et seq.*) or an investment adviser under the Investment Advisers Act of 1940;

(3)   The type of information regarding an offering of securities by the issuer that is communicated or distributed by or on behalf of the issuer in connection with the event is limited to a notification that the issuer is in the process of offering or planning to offer securities, the type and amount of securities being offered, the intended use of proceeds of the offering, and the unsubscribed amount in an offering; and

(2)   If the event allows attendees to participate virtually, rather than in person, online participation in the event is limited to:

(i)   individuals who are members of, or otherwise associated with the sponsor organization;

(ii)   individuals that the sponsor reasonably believes are accredited investors; or

(iii) individuals who have been invited to the event by the sponsor based on industry or investment-related experience reasonably selected by the sponsor in good faith and disclosed in the public communications about the event.

Instruction to paragraph (a): For purposes of this paragraph, the term "angel investor group" means a group of accredited investors that holds regular meetings and has defined processes and procedures for making investment decisions, either individually or among the membership of the group as a whole, and is neither associated nor affiliated with brokers, dealers, or investment advisers.

(b) [Reserved]

Rule 149. Definition of "Exchanged" in Section 3(a)(9), for Certain Transactions

The term "exchanged" in section 3(a)(9) of the Act shall be deemed to include the issuance of a security in consideration of the surrender, by the existing security holders of the issuer, of outstanding securities of the issuer, notwithstanding the fact that the surrender of the outstanding securities may be required by the terms of the plan of exchange to be accompanied by such payment in cash by the security holder as may be necessary to effect an equitable adjustment, in respect of dividends or interest paid or payable on the securities involved in the exchange, as between such security holder and other security holders of the same class accepting the offer of exchange.

Rule 150. Definition of "Commission or Other Remuneration" in Section 3(a)(9), for Certain Transactions

The term "commission or other remuneration" in section 3(a)(9) of the fact shall not include payments made by the issuer, directly or indirectly, to its security holders in connection with an exchange of securities for outstanding securities, when such payments are part of the terms of the offer of exchange.

Rule 151. Safe Harbor Definition of Certain "Annuity Contracts or Optional Annuity Contracts" Within the Meaning of Section 3(a)(8)

(a) Any annuity contract or optional annuity contract (a "contract") shall be deemed to be within the provisions of section 3(a)(8) of the Securities Act of 1933, *Provided,* That

(1) The annuity or optional annuity contract is issued by a corporation (the "insurer") subject to the supervision of the insurance commissioner, bank commissioner, or any agency or officer performing like functions, of any State or Territory of the United States or the District of Columbia;

(2) The insurer assumes the investment risk under the contract as prescribed in paragraph (b) of this rule; and

(3) The contract is not marketed primarily as an investment.

(b) The insurer shall be deemed to assume the investment risk under the contract if:

(1) The value of the contract does not vary according to the investment experience of a separate account;

(2) The insurer for the life of the contract

(i) Guarantees the principal amount of purchase payments and interest credited thereto, less any deduction (without regard to its timing) for sales, administrative or other expenses or charges; and

(ii) Credits a specified rate of interest (as defined in paragraph (c) of this rule) to net purchase payments and interest credited thereto; and

(3) The insurer guarantees that the rate of any interest to be credited in excess of that described in paragraph (b)(2)(ii) of this rule will not be modified more frequently than once per year.

(c) The term "specified rate of interest," as used in paragraph (b)(2)(ii) of this rule, means a rate of interest under the contract that is at least equal to the minimum rate required to be credited by the relevant nonforfeiture law in the jurisdiction in which the contract is issued. If that jurisdiction does not have any applicable nonforfeiture law at the time the contract is issued (or if the minimum rate applicable to an existing contract is no longer mandated in that jurisdiction), the specified rate under the contract must at least be equal to the minimum rate then required for individual annuity contracts by the NAIC Standard Nonforfeiture Law.

Rule 152.   Definition of "Transactions by an Issuer Not Involving Any Public Offering" in Section 4(a)(2), for Certain Transactions

This Rule provides a general principle of integration and non-exclusive safe harbors from integration of registered and exempt offerings. Because of the objectives of this rule and the policies underlying the Act, the provisions of this rule will not have the effect of avoiding integration for any transaction or series of transactions that, although in technical compliance with the rule, is part of a plan or scheme to evade the registration requirements of the Act.

(a)   *General principle of integration.* If the safe harbors in paragraph (b) of this section do not apply, in determining whether two or more offerings are to be treated as one for the purpose of registration or qualifying for an exemption from registration under the Act, offers and sales will not be integrated if, based on the particular facts and circumstances, the issuer can establish that each offering either complies with the registration requirements of the Act, or that an exemption from registration is available for the particular offering. In making this determination:

(1)   For an exempt offering prohibiting general solicitation, the issuer must have a reasonable belief, based on the facts and circumstances, with respect to each purchaser in the exempt offering prohibiting general solicitation, that the issuer (or any person acting on the issuer's behalf) either:

(i)   Did not solicit such purchaser through the use of general solicitation; or

(ii)   Established a substantive relationship with such purchaser prior to the commencement of the exempt offering prohibiting general solicitation; and

(2)   For two or more concurrent exempt offerings permitting general solicitation, in addition to satisfying the requirements of the particular exemption relied on, general solicitation offering materials for one offering that includes information about the material terms of a concurrent offering under another exemption may constitute an offer of securities in such other offering, and therefore the offer must comply with all the requirements for, and restrictions on, offers under the exemption being relied on for such other offering, including any legend requirements and communications restrictions.

(b)   *Safe harbors.* No integration analysis under paragraph (a) of this section is required, if any of the following non-exclusive safe harbors apply:

(1)   Any offering made more than 30 calendar days before the commencement of any other offering, or more than 30 calendar days after the termination or completion of any other offering, will not be integrated with such other offering, *provided that* for an exempt offering for which general solicitation is not permitted that follows by 30 calendar days or more an offering that allows general solicitation, the provisions of § 230.152(a)(1) shall apply.

(2)   Offers and sales made in compliance with § 230.701, pursuant to an employee benefit plan, or in compliance with §§ 230.901 through 230.905 (Regulation S) will not be integrated with other offerings;

(3)   An offering for which a registration statement under the Act has been filed will not be integrated if it is made subsequent to:

(i)   A terminated or completed offering for which general solicitation is not permitted;

(ii)   A terminated or completed offering for which general solicitation is permitted made only to qualified institutional buyers and institutional accredited investors; or

(iii)   An offering for which general solicitation is permitted that terminated or completed more than 30 calendar days prior to the commencement of the registered offering; or

(4)   Offers and sales made in reliance on an exemption for which general solicitation is permitted will not be integrated if made subsequent to any terminated or completed offering.

(c)   *Commencement of an offering.* For purposes of this section, an offering of securities will be deemed to be commenced at the time of the first offer of securities in the offering by the issuer or its agents. The following non-exclusive list of factors should be considered in determining when an offering is deemed to be commenced. Pursuant to the requirements for registered and exempt offerings, an issuer or its agents may commence an offering in reliance on:

    (1)   Rule 241, on the date the issuer first made a generic offer soliciting interest in a contemplated securities offering for which the issuer had not yet determined the exemption under the Act under which the offering of securities would be conducted;

    (2)   Section 4(a)(2) of the Securities Act, Rules 501 through 508 (Regulation D), or Rule147 or Rule 147A, on the date the issuer first made an offer of its securities in reliance on these exemptions;

    (3)   Rules 251 through 263 (Regulation A), on the earlier of the date the issuer first made an offer soliciting interest in a contemplated securities offering in reliance on Rule 255, or the public filing of a Form 1–A offering statement;

    (4)   Rules 100 through 503 (Regulation Crowdfunding), on the earlier of the date the issuer first made an offer soliciting interest in a contemplated securities offering in reliance on Rule 206, or the public filing of a Form C offering statement; and

    (5)   A registration statement filed under the Act, in the case of:

        (i)   A continuous offering that will commence promptly on the date of initial effectiveness, on the date the issuer first filed its registration statement for the offering with the Commission, or

        (ii)   A delayed offering, on the earliest date on which the issuer or its agents commenced public efforts to offer and sell the securities, which could be evidenced by the earlier of:

            (A)   The first filing of a prospectus supplement with the Commission describing the delayed offering, or

            (B)   The issuance of a widely disseminated public disclosure, such as a press release, confirming the commencement of the delayed offering.

Note to paragraph (c)(5): Offers by the issuer, or persons acting on behalf of the issuer, limited exclusively to qualified institutional buyers and institutional accredited investors, including those that would qualify for the safe harbor in Rule 163B, will not be considered the commencement of a registered offering for purposes of this section.

  (d)   *Termination or completion of an offering.* For purposes of this section, the termination or completion of an offering is deemed to have occurred when the issuer and its agents cease efforts to make further offers to sell the issuer's securities under such offering. The following non-exclusive list of factors should be considered in determining when an offering is deemed to be terminated or completed including for offerings made in reliance on:

    (1)   Section 4(a)(2), Regulation D, or Rules 147 or 147A, on the later of the date:

        (i)   The issuer entered into a binding commitment to sell all securities to be sold under the offering (subject only to conditions outside of the investor's control); or

        (ii)   The issuer and its agents ceased efforts to make further offers to sell the issuer's securities under such offering;

    (2)   Regulation A, on:

        (i)   The withdrawal of an offering statement under Rule 259(a);

        (ii)   The filing of a § 239.94 of this chapter (Form 1–Z) with respect to a Tier I offering under § 230.257(a);

        (iii)   The declaration by the Commission that the offering statement has been abandoned under § 230.259(b); or

(iv)   The date, after the third anniversary of the date the offering statement was initially qualified, on which § 230.251(d)(3)(i)(F) prohibits the issuer from continuing to sell securities using the offering statement, or any earlier date on which the offering terminates by its terms;

(3)   Regulation Crowdfunding, on the deadline of the offering identified in the offering materials pursuant to § 227.201(g), or indicated by the Regulation Crowdfunding intermediary in any notice to investors delivered under § 227.304(b); and

(4)   A registration statement filed under the Act:

(i)   On the withdrawal of the registration statement after an application is granted or deemed granted under § 230.477;

(ii)   On the filing of a prospectus supplement or amendment to the registration statement indicating that the offering, or particular delayed offering in the case of a shelf registration statement, has been terminated or completed;

(iii)   On the entry of an order of the Commission declaring that the registration statement has been abandoned under § 230.479;

(iv)   On the date, after the third anniversary of the initial effective date of the registration statement, on which § 230.415(a)(5) prohibits the issuer from continuing to sell securities using the registration statement, or any earlier date on which the offering terminates by its terms; or

(v)   Any other factors that indicate that the issuer has abandoned or ceased its public selling efforts in furtherance of the offering, or particular delayed offering in the case of a shelf registration statement, which could be evidenced by:

(A)   The filing of a Current Report on Form 8–K; or

(B)   The issuance of a widely disseminated public disclosure by the issuer, or its agents, informing the market that the offering, or particular delayed offering, in the case of a shelf registration statement, has been terminated or completed.

Note to Rule 152(d)(4): A particular delayed offering may be deemed terminated or completed, even though the issuer's shelf registration statement may still have an aggregate amount of securities available to offer and sell in a later delayed offering.

Rule 152A.   Offer or Sale of Certain Fractional Interests

Any offer or sale of a security, evidenced by a scrip certificate, order form or similar document which represents a fractional interest in a share of stock or similar security shall be deemed a transaction by a person other than an issuer, underwriter or dealer, within the meaning of section 4(1) of the Act, if the fractional interest

(a)   resulted from a stock dividend, stock split, reverse stock split, conversion, merger or similar transaction, and

(b)   is offered or sold pursuant to arrangements for the purchase and sale of fractional interests among the person entitled to such fractional interests for the purpose of combining such interests into whole shares, and for the sale of such number of whole shares as may be necessary to compensate security holders for any remaining fractional interests not so combined, notwithstanding that the issuer or an affiliate of the issuer may act on behalf of or as agent for the security holders in effecting such transactions.

Rule 153.   Definition of "Preceded by a Prospectus", as Used in Section 5(b)(2), in Relation to Certain Transactions

(a)   Definition of preceded by a prospectus. The term preceded by a prospectus as used in section 5(b)(2) of the Act, regarding any requirement of a broker or dealer to deliver a prospectus to a broker or dealer as a result of a transaction effected between such parties on or through a national securities exchange or facility thereof, trading facility of a national securities association, or an alternative trading system, shall mean the satisfaction of the conditions in paragraph (b) of this rule.

(b) Conditions. Any requirement of a broker or dealer to deliver a prospectus for transactions covered by paragraph (a) of this rule will be satisfied if:

(1) Securities of the same class as the securities that are the subject of the transaction are trading on that national securities exchange or facility thereof, trading facility of a national securities association, or alternative trading system;

(2) The registration statement relating to the offering is effective and is not the subject of any pending proceeding or examination under section 8(d) or 8(e) of the Act;

(3) Neither the issuer, nor any underwriter or participating dealer is the subject of a pending proceeding under section 8A of the Act in connection with the offering; and

(4) The issuer has filed or will file with the Commission a prospectus that satisfies the requirements of section 10(a) of the Act.

(c) Definitions.

(1) The term national securities exchange, as used in this rule, shall mean a securities exchange registered as a national securities exchange under section 6 of the Securities Exchange Act of 1934.

(2) The term trading facility, as used in this rule, shall mean a trading facility sponsored and governed by the rules of a registered securities association or a national securities exchange.

(3) The term alternative trading system, as used in this rule, shall mean an alternative trading system as defined in Rule 300(a) of Regulation ATS under the Securities Exchange Act of 1934 registered with the Commission pursuant to Rule 301 of Regulation ATS under the Securities Exchange Act of 1934.

Rule 153A. Definition of "Preceded by a Prospectus" as Used in Section 5(b)(2) of the Act, in Relation to Certain Transactions Requiring Approval of Security Holders

The term "preceded by a prospectus," as used in section 5(b)(2) of the Act with respect to any requirement for the delivery of a prospectus to security holders of a corporation or other person, in connection with transactions of the character specified in paragraph (a) of Rule 145, shall mean the delivery of a prospectus:

(a) Prior to the vote of security holders on such transactions; or,

(b) With respect to actions taken by consent, prior to the earliest date on which the corporate action may be taken;

to all security holders of record of such corporation or other person, entitled to vote on or consent to the proposed transaction, at their address of record on the transfer records of the corporation or other person.

Rule 153B. Definition of "Preceded by a Prospectus," as Used in Section 5(b)(2), in Connection With Certain Transactions in Standardized Options

The term "preceded by a prospectus", as used in section 5(b)(2) of the Act with respect to any requirement for the delivery of a prospectus relating to standardized options registered on Form S–20, shall mean the delivery, prior to any transactions, of copies of such prospectus to each options market upon which the options are traded, for the purpose of redelivery to options customers upon their request, *Provided* That:

(a) Such options market shall thereto have requested of the issuer, from time to time, such number of copies of such prospectus as may have appeared reasonably necessary to comply with the requests of options customers, and shall have delivered promptly from its supply on hand a copy to any options customer making a request thereof; and

(b) The issuer shall have furnished such options market with such reasonable number of copies of such prospectus as may have been requested by the options market for the purpose stated above.

Rule 154.   Delivery of Prospectuses to Investors at the Same Address

(a)   *Delivery of a Single Prospectus.* If you must deliver a prospectus under the federal securities laws, for purposes of sections 5(b) and 2(a)(10) of the Act or Rule 15c2–8(b) under the Exchange Act, you will be considered to have delivered a prospectus to investors who share an address if:

(1)   You deliver a prospectus to the shared address;

(2)   You address the prospectus to the investors as a group (for example, "ABC Fund [or Corporation] Shareholders," "Jane Doe and Household," "The Smith Family") or to each of the investors individually (for example, "John Doe and Richard Jones"); and

(3)   The investors consent in writing to delivery of one prospectus.

(b)   *Implied Consent.* You do not need to obtain written consent from an investor under paragraph (a)(3) of this rule if all of the following conditions are met:

(1)   The investor has the same last name as the other investors, or you reasonably believe that the investors are members of the same family;

(2)   You have sent the investor a notice at least 60 days before you begin to rely on this rule concerning delivery of prospectuses to that investor. The notice must be a separate written statement and:

(i)   State that only one prospectus will be delivered to the shared address unless you receive contrary instructions;

(ii)   Include a toll-free telephone number or be accompanied by a reply form that is pre-addressed with postage provided, that the issuer can use to notify you that he or she wishes to receive a separate prospectus;

(iii)   State the duration of the consent;

(iv)   Explain how an investor can revoke consent;

(v)   State that you will begin sending individual copies to an investor within 30 days after you receive revocation of the investor's consent; and

(vi)   Contain the following prominent statement, or similar clear and understandable statement, in bold-face type: "Important Notice Regarding Delivery of Shareholder Documents." This statement also must appear on the envelope in which the notice is delivered. Alternatively, if the notice is delivered separately from other communications to investors, this statement may appear either on the notice or on the envelope in which the notice is delivered;

NOTE to paragraph (b)(2). The notice should be written in plain English. See Rule 421(d)(2) for a discussion of plain English principles.

(3)   You have not received the reply form or other notification indicating that the investor wishes to continue to receive an individual copy of the prospectus, within 60 days after you sent the notice; and

(4)   You deliver the prospectus to a post office box or to a residential street address. You can assume a street address is a residence unless you have information that indicates it is a business.

(c)   *Revocation of Consent.* If an investor, orally or in writing, revokes consent to delivery of one prospectus to a shared address (provided under paragraphs (a)(3) or (b) of this rule), you must begin sending individual copies to that investor within 30 days after you receive the revocation. If the individual's consent concerns delivery of the prospectus of a registered open-end management investment company, at least once a year you must explain to the investors who have consented how they can revoke their consent. The explanation must be reasonably designed to reach these investors.

(d)   *Definition of Address.* For purposes of this rule, "address" means a street address, a post office box number, or other similar destination to which paper or electronic documents are delivered, unless otherwise provided in this rule. If you have reason to believe that an address is the street address of a multi-unit building, the address must include the unit number.

Rule 155.   [Removed and reserved]

Rule 156.   Investment Company Sales Literature

(a)   Under the federal securities laws, including section 17(a) of the Securities Act of 1933 and section 10(b) of the Securities Exchange Act of 1934 and Rule 10b–5 thereunder, it is unlawful for any person, directly or indirectly, by the use of any means or instrumentality of interstate commerce of the mails, to use sales literature which is materially misleading in connection with the offer or sale of securities issued by an investment company. Under these provisions, sales literature is materially misleading if it (1) contains an untrue statement of a material fact or (2) omits to state a material fact necessary in order to make a statement made, in the light of the circumstances of its use, not misleading.

(b)   Whether or not a particular description, representation, illustration, or other statement involving a material fact is misleading depends on evaluation of the context in which it is made. In considering whether a particular statement involving a material fact is or might be misleading, weight should be given to all pertinent factors, including, but not limited to, those listed below.

(1)   A statement could be misleading because of:

(i)   Other statements being made in connection with the offer of sale or sale of the securities in question;

(ii)   The absence of explanations, qualifications, limitations or other statements necessary or appropriate to make such statement not misleading; or

(iii)   General economic or financial conditions or circumstances.

(2)   Representations about past or future investment performance could be misleading because of statements or omissions made involving a material fact, including situations where:

(i)   Portrayals of past income, gain, or growth of assets convey an impression of the net investment results achieved by an actual or hypothetical investment which would not be justified under the circumstances, including portrayals that omit explanations, qualifications, limitations, or other statements necessary or appropriate to make the portrayals not misleading; and

(ii)   Representations, whether express or implied, about future investment performance, including:

(A)   Representations, as to security of capital, possible future gains or income, or expenses associated with an investment;

(B)   Representations implying that future gain or income may be inferred from or predicted based on past investment performance; or

(C)   Portrayals of past performance, made in a manner which would imply that gains or income realized in the past would be repeated in the future.

(3)   A statement involving a material fact about the characteristics or attributes of an investment company could be misleading because of:

(i)   Statements about possible benefits connected with or resulting from services to be provided or methods of operation which do not give equal prominence to discussion of any risks or limitations associated therewith;

(ii)   Exaggerated or unsubstantiated claims about management skill or techniques, characteristics of the investment company or an investment in securities issued by such company, services, security of investment or funds, effects of government supervision, or other attributes; and

(iii)   Unwarranted or incompletely explained comparisons to other investment vehicles or to indexes.

(4)   Representations about the fees or expenses associated with an investment in the fund could be misleading because of statements or omissions made involving a material fact, including situations where portrayals of the fees and expenses associated with an investment in the fund omit explanations,

qualifications, limitations, or other statements necessary or appropriate to make the portrayals not misleading.

(c)   For purposes of this rule, the term "sales literature" shall be deemed to include any communication (whether in writing, by radio, or by television) used by any person to offer to sell or induce the sale of securities of any investment company. Communications between issuers, underwriters and dealers are included in this definition of sales literature if such communications, or the information contained therein, can be reasonably expected to be communicated to prospective investors in the offer or sale of securities or are designed to be employed in either written or oral form in the offer or sale of securities.

(d)   Nothing in this section may be construed to prevent a business development company or a registered closed-end investment company, from qualifying for an exemption under Rule 168 of this chapter or Rule169 of this chapter.

Rule 157.   Small Entities for Purposes of the Regulatory Flexibility Act

For purposes of Commission rulemaking in accordance with the provisions of Chapter Six of the Administrative Procedure Act, and unless otherwise defined for purposes of a particular rulemaking proceeding, the term "small business" or "small organization" shall—

(a)   When used with reference to an issuer, other than an investment company, for purposes of the Securities Act of 1933, mean an issuer whose total assets on the last day of its most recent fiscal year were $5,000,000 or less and that is engaged or proposing to engage in small business financing. An issuer is considered to be engaged or proposing to engage in small business financing under this rule if it is conducting or proposes to conduct an offering of securities which does not exceed the dollar limitation prescribed by section 3(b) of the Securities Act.

(b)   When used with reference to an investment company that is an issuer for purposes of the Act, have the meaning ascribed to those terms by Rule 0–10 of the Investment Company Act of 1940.

Rule 158.   Definitions of Certain Terms in the Last Paragraph of Section 11(a)

(a)   An "earning statement" made generally available to security holders of the registrant pursuant to the last paragraph of section 11(a) of the Act shall be sufficient for the purposes of such paragraph if

(1)   There is included the information required for statements of comprehensive income (as defined in item 1–02 of Regulation S–X of this chapter) contained either:

(i)   In Item 8 of Form 10–K, part I, Item 1 of Form 10–Q, or Rule 14a–3(b) under the Securities Exchange Act of 1934,

(ii)   In Item 17 of Form 20–F, if appropriate; or

(iii)   In Form 40F;

(2)   The information specified in the last paragraph of section 11(a) is contained in one report or any combination of reports either:

(i)   On Form 10–K, Form 10–Q, Form 8–K, or in the annual report to security holders pursuant to Rule 14a–3 under the Securities Exchange Act of 1934; or

(ii)   On Form 20–F, Form 40–F, or Form 6–K.

Note 1 to paragraph (a). A subsidiary issuing debt securities guaranteed by its parent will be deemed to have met the requirements of this paragraph (a) if the parent's statements of comprehensive income (as defined in item 1–02 of Regulation S–X) satisfy the criteria of this paragraph and information respecting the subsidiary is included to the same extent as was presented in the registration statement. An "earning statement" not meeting the requirements of this paragraph (a) may otherwise be sufficient for purposes of the last paragraph of section 11(a) of the Act.

(b)   For purposes of the last paragraph of section 11(a) only, the "earning statement" contemplated by paragraph (a) of this rule shall be deemed to be "made generally available to its security holders" if the registrant:

(1) Is required to file reports pursuant to section 13 or 15(d) of the Securities Exchange Act of 1934 and

(2) Has filed its report or reports on Form 10–K, Form 10–Q, Form 8–K, Form 20–F, Form 40–F, or Form 6–K, or has submitted to the Commission in electronic format, in accordance with the EDGAR Filer Manual, its annual report sent to security holders pursuant to Rule 14a–3(c) containing such information. A registrant may use other methods to make an earning statement "generally available to its security holders" for purposes of the last paragraph of section 11(a).

A registrant may use other methods to make an earning statement "generally available to its security holders" for purposes of the last paragraph of section 11(a).

(c) For purposes of the last paragraph of section 11(a) of the Act only, the effective date of the registration statement is deemed to be the date of the latest to occur of:

(1) The effective date of the registration statement;

(2) The effective date of the last post-effective amendment to the registration statement next preceding a particular sale of the issuer's registered securities to the public filed for the purposes of:

(i) Including any prospectus required by section 10(a)(3) of the Act; or

(ii) Reflecting in the prospectus any facts or events arising after the effective date of the registration statement (or the most recent post-effective amendment thereof) which, individually or in the aggregate, represent a fundamental change in the information set forth in the registration statement;

(3) The date of filing of the last report of the issuer incorporated by reference into the prospectus that is part of the registration statement or the date that a form of prospectus filed pursuant to Rule 424(b) or Rule 497(b), (c), (d), or (e) is deemed part of and included in the registration statement, and relied upon in either case in lieu of filing a post-effective amendment for purposes of paragraphs (c)(2)(i) and (ii) of this rule next preceding a particular sale of the issuer's registered securities to the public; or

(4) As to the issuer and any underwriter at that time only, the most recent effective date of the registration statement for purposes of liability under section 11 of the Act of the issuer and any such underwriter only at the time of or next preceding a particular sale of the issuer's registered securities to the public determined pursuant to Rule 430B.

(d) If an earnings statement was made available by "other methods" than those specified in paragraphs (a) and (b) of this rule, the earnings statement must be filed as exhibit 99 to the next periodic report required by section 13 or 15(d) of the Exchange Act covering the period in which the earnings statement was released.

Rule 159.   Information Available to Purchaser at Time of Contract of Sale

(a) For purposes of section 12(a)(2) of the Act only, and without affecting any other rights a purchaser may have, for purposes of determining whether a prospectus or oral statement included an untrue statement of a material fact or omitted to state a material fact necessary in order to make the statements, in the light of the circumstances under which they were made, not misleading at the time of sale (including, without limitation, a contract of sale), any information conveyed to the purchaser only after such time of sale (including such contract of sale) will not be taken into account.

(b) For purposes of section 17(a)(2) of the Act only, and without affecting any other rights the Commission may have to enforce that section, for purposes of determining whether a statement includes or represents any untrue statement of a material fact or any omission to state a material fact necessary in order to make the statements made, in light of the circumstances under which they were made, not misleading at the time of sale (including, without limitation, a contract of sale), any information conveyed to the purchaser only after such time of sale (including such contract of sale) will not be taken into account.

(c) For purposes of section 12(a)(2) of the Act only, knowing of such untruth or omission in respect of a sale (including, without limitation, a contract of sale), means knowing at the time of such sale (including such contract of sale).

Rule 159A.　Certain Definitions for Purposes of Section 12(a)(2) of the Act

(a)　Definition of seller for purposes of section 12(a)(2) of the Act. For purposes of section 12(a)(2) of the Act only, in a primary offering of securities of the issuer, regardless of the underwriting method used to sell the issuer's securities, seller shall include the issuer of the securities sold to a person as part of the initial distribution of such securities, and the issuer shall be considered to offer or sell the securities to such person, if the securities are offered or sold to such person by means of any of the following communications:

(1)　Any preliminary prospectus or prospectus of the issuer relating to the offering required to be filed pursuant to Rule 424 or Rule 497;

(2)　Any free writing prospectus as defined in Rule 405 relating to the offering prepared by or on behalf of the issuer or used or referred to by the issuer and, in the case of an issuer that is an open-end management company registered under the Investment Company Act of 1940, any summary prospectus relating to the offering provided pursuant to Rule 498;

(3)　The portion of any other free writing prospectus (or, in the case of an issuer that is an investment company registered under the Investment Company Act of 1940 or a business development company as defined in section 2(a)(48) of the Investment Company Act of 1940, any advertisement pursuant to Rule 482) relating to the offering containing material information about the issuer or its securities provided by or on behalf of the issuer; and

(4)　Any other communication that is an offer in the offering made by the issuer to such person.

Notes to paragraph (a) of Rule 159A

1.　For purposes of paragraph (a) of this rule, information is provided or a communication is made by or on behalf of an issuer if an issuer or an agent or representative of the issuer authorizes or approves the information or communication before its provision or use. An offering participant other than the issuer shall not be an agent or representative of the issuer solely by virtue of its acting as an offering participant.

2.　Paragraph (a) of this rule shall not affect in any respect the determination of whether any person other than an issuer is a "seller" for purposes of section 12(a)(2) of the Act.

(b)　Definition of by means of for purposes of section 12(a)(2) of the Act.

(1)　For purposes of section 12(a)(2) of the Act only, an offering participant other than the issuer shall not be considered to offer or sell securities that are the subject of a registration statement by means of a free writing prospectus as to a purchaser unless one or more of the following circumstances shall exist:

(i)　The offering participant used or referred to the free writing prospectus in offering or selling the securities to the purchaser;

(ii)　The offering participant offered or sold securities to the purchaser and participated in planning for the use of the free writing prospectus by one or more other offering participants and such free writing prospectus was used or referred to in offering or selling securities to the purchaser by one or more of such other offering participants; or

(iii)　The offering participant was required to file the free writing prospectus pursuant to the conditions to use in Rule 433.

(2)　For purposes of section 12(a)(2) of the Act only, a person will not be considered to offer or sell securities by means of a free writing prospectus solely because another person has used or referred to the free writing prospectus or filed the free writing prospectus with the Commission pursuant to Rule 433.

Rule 160.　Registered Investment Company Exemption From Section 101(c)(1) of the Electronic Signatures in Global and National Commerce Act

A prospectus for an investment company registered under the Investment Company Act of 1940 that is sent or given for the sole purpose of permitting a communication not to be deemed a prospectus under section 2(a)(10)(a) of the Act shall be exempt from the requirements of section 101(c)(1) of the Electronic Signatures in Global and National Commerce Act.

Rule 161.   Amendments to Rules and Regulations Governing Exemptions

The rules and regulations governing the exemption of securities under section 3(b) of the Act, as in effect at the time the securities are first bona fide offered to the public in conformity therewith, shall continue to govern the exemption of such securities notwithstanding the subsequent amendment of such rules and regulations. This rule shall not apply, however, to any new offering of such securities by an issuer or underwriter after the effective date of any such amendment, nor shall it apply to any offering after January 1, 1959, of securities by an issuer or underwriter pursuant to Regulation D or pursuant to Regulation A as in effect at any time prior to July 23, 1956.

Rule 162.   Submission of Tenders in Registered Exchange Offers

(a)   Notwithstanding section 5(a) of the Act, an offeror may solicit tenders of securities in an exchange offer before a registration statement is effective as to the security offered, so long as no securities are purchased until the registration statement is effective and the tender offer has expired in accordance with the tender offer rules, and either:

(1)   The exchange offer is subject to Rule 13e–4 or Rules 240.14d–1 through 14d–11 of this chapter; or

(2)   The offeror provides withdrawal rights to the same extent as would be required if the exchange offer were subject to the requirements of Rule 13e–4 or Rules 14d–1 through 14d–11 of this chapter; and if a material change occurs in the information published, sent or given to security holders, the offeror complies with the provisions of Rule 13e–4(e)(3) or Rule 240.14d–4(b) and (d) of this chapter in disseminating information about the material change to security holders, and including the minimum periods during which the offer must remain open (with withdrawal rights) after notice of the change is provided to security holders.

(b)   Notwithstanding Section 5(b)(2) of the Act, a prospectus that meets the requirements of Section 10(a) of the Act need not be delivered to security holders in an exchange offer that commences before the effectiveness of a registration statement in accordance with the provisions of Rule 162(a), so long as a preliminary prospectus, prospectus supplements and revised prospectuses are delivered to security holders in accordance with Rule 13e–4(e)(2) or Rule 14d–4(b) of this chapter. This applies not only to exchange offers subject to those provisions, but also to exchange offers not subject to those provisions that meet the conditions in Rule 162(a)(2).

Instruction to Rule 162:

Notwithstanding the provisions of Rule 162 of this rule above, for going-private transactions (as defined by Rule 13e–3) and roll-up transactions (as described by Item 901 of Regulation S–K), a registration statement registering the securities to be offered must have become effective and only a prospectus that meets the requirements of Section 10(a) of the Securities Act may be delivered to security holders on the date of commencement.

Rule 163.   Exemption From Section 5(c) of the Act for Certain Communications by or on Behalf of Well-Known Seasoned Issuers

Preliminary Note to Rule 163

Attempted compliance with this rule does not act as an exclusive election and the issuer also may claim the availability of any other applicable exemption or exclusion. Reliance on this rule does not affect the availability of any other exemption or exclusion from the requirements of section 5 of the Act.

(a)   In an offering by or on behalf of a well-known seasoned issuer, as defined in Rule 405, that will be or is at the time intended to be registered under the Act, an offer by or on behalf of such issuer is exempt from the prohibitions in section 5(c) of the Act on offers to sell, offers for sale, or offers to buy its securities before a registration statement has been filed, provided that:

(1)   Any written communication that is an offer made in reliance on this exemption will be a free writing prospectus as defined in Rule 405 and a prospectus under section 2(a)(10) of the Act relating to a public offering of securities to be covered by the registration statement to be filed; and

(2)   The exemption from section 5(c) of the Act provided in this rule for such written communication that is an offer shall be conditioned on satisfying the conditions in paragraph (b) of this rule.

(b)   *Conditions.*

(1)   *Legend.*

(i)   Every written communication that is an offer made in reliance on this exemption shall contain substantially the following legend:

The issuer may file a registration statement (including a prospectus) with the SEC for the offering to which this communication relates. Before you invest, you should read the prospectus in that registration statement and other documents the issuer has filed with the SEC for more complete information about the issuer and this offering. You may get these documents for free by visiting EDGAR on the SEC Web site at www.sec.gov. Alternatively, the company will arrange to send you the prospectus after filing if you request it by calling toll-free 1-8[xx-xxx-xxxx]; or

(ii)   Communications by an issuer that is an investment company registered under the Investment Company Act of 1940, other than a registered closed-end investment company.

(2)   *Filing condition.*

(i)   Subject to paragraph (b)(2)(ii) of this rule, every written communication that is an offer made in reliance on this exemption shall be filed by the issuer with the Commission promptly upon the filing of the registration statement, if one is filed, or an amendment, if one is filed, covering the securities that have been offered in reliance on this exemption.

(ii)   The condition that an issuer shall file a free writing prospectus with the Commission under this rule shall not apply in respect of any communication that has previously been filed with, or furnished to, the Commission or that the issuer would not be required to file with the Commission pursuant to the conditions of Rule 433 if the communication was a free writing prospectus used after the filing of the registration statement. The condition that the issuer shall file a free writing prospectus with the Commission under this rule shall be satisfied if the issuer satisfies the filing conditions (other than timing of filing which is provided in this rule) that would apply under Rule 433 if the communication was a free writing prospectus used after the filing of the registration statement.

(iii)   An immaterial or unintentional failure to file or delay in filing a free writing prospectus to the extent provided in this rule will not result in a violation of section 5(c) of the Act or the loss of the ability to rely on this rule so long as:

(A)   A good faith and reasonable effort was made to comply with the filing condition; and

(B)   The free writing prospectus is filed as soon as practicable after discovery of the failure to file.

(3)   *Ineligible offerings.* The exemption in paragraph (a) of this rule shall not be available to:

(i)   Communications relating to business combination transactions that are subject to Rule 165 or Rule 166;

(ii)   Communications by an issuer that is an investment company registered under the Investment Company Act of 1940; or

(iii)   Communications by an issuer that is a business development company as defined in section 2(a)(48) of the Investment Company Act of 1940.

(c)   For purposes of this rule, a communication is made by or on behalf of an issuer if the issuer or an agent or representative of the issuer, other than an offering participant who is an underwriter or dealer, authorizes or approves the communication before it is made.

(d)   For purposes of this rule, a communication for which disclosure would be required under section 17(b) of the Act as a result of consideration given or to be given, directly or indirectly, by or on behalf of an issuer is deemed to be an offer by the issuer and, if a written communication, is deemed to be a free writing prospectus of the issuer.

(e)   A communication exempt from section 5(c) of the Act pursuant to this rule will not be considered to be in connection with a securities offering registered under the Securities Act for purposes of Rule 100(b)(2)(iv) of Regulation FD under the Securities Exchange Act of 1934.

Rule 163A.   Exemption From Section 5(c) of the Act for Certain Communications Made by or on Behalf of Issuers More Than 30 Days Before a Registration Statement Is Filed

Preliminary Note to Rule 163A

Attempted compliance with this rule does not act as an exclusive election and the issuer also may claim the availability of any other applicable exemption or exclusion. Reliance on this rule does not affect the availability of any other exemption or exclusion from the requirements of section 5 of the Act.

(a)   Except as excluded pursuant to paragraph (b) of this rule, in all registered offerings by issuers, any communication made by or on behalf of an issuer more than 30 days before the date of the filing of the registration statement that does not reference a securities offering that is or will be the subject of a registration statement shall not constitute an offer to sell, offer for sale, or offer to buy the securities being offered under the registration statement for purposes of section 5(c) of the Act, provided that the issuer takes reasonable steps within its control to prevent further distribution or publication of such communication during the 30 days immediately preceding the date of filing the registration statement.

(b)   The exemption in paragraph (a) of this rule shall not be available with respect to the following communications:

(1)   Communications relating to business combination transactions that are subject to Rule 165 or Rule 166;

(2)   Communications made in connection with offerings registered on Form S–8, other than by well-known seasoned issuers;

(3)   Communications in offerings of securities of an issuer that is, or during the past three years was (or any of whose predecessors during the last three years was):

(i)   A blank check company as defined in Rule 419(a)(2);

(ii)   A shell company, other than a business combination related shell company, each as defined in Rule 405; or

(iii)   An issuer for an offering of penny stock as defined in Rule 3a51–1 of the Securities Exchange Act of 1934; or

(4)   Communications made by an issuer that is an investment company registered under the Investment Company Act of 1940, other than a registered closed-end investment company.

(c)   For purposes of this rule, a communication is made by or on behalf of an issuer if the issuer or an agent or representative of the issuer, other than an offering participant who is an underwriter or dealer, authorizes or approves the communication before it is made.

(d)   A communication exempt from section 5(c) of the Act pursuant to this rule will not be considered to be in connection with a securities offering registered under the Securities Act for purposes of Rule 100(b)(2)(iv) of Regulation FD under the Securities Exchange Act of 1934.

Rule 163B.   Exemption From Section 5(b)(1) and Section 5(c) of the Act for Certain Communications to Qualified Institutional Buyers or Institutional Accredited Investors

(a)   Attempted compliance with this rule does not act as an exclusive election, and the issuer also may claim the availability of any other applicable exemption or exclusion. Reliance on this rule does not affect the availability of any other exemption or exclusion from the requirements of section 5 of the Act.

(b)(1)   An issuer, or any person authorized to act on behalf of an issuer, may engage in oral or written communications with potential investors described in paragraph (c) of this rule to determine whether such investors might have an interest in a contemplated registered securities offering, either prior to or following the date of filing of a registration statement with respect to such securities with the Commission. Communications under this rule will be exempt from section 5(b)(1) and section 5(c) of the Act.

(2)   Any oral or written communication by an issuer, or any person authorized to act on behalf of an issuer, made in reliance on this rule will be deemed an "offer" as defined in section 2(a)(3) of the Act.

(3)   Any oral or written communication by an issuer, or any person authorized to act on behalf of an issuer, made in reliance on this rule is not required to be filed with the Commission, including pursuant Rule 424(a) or Rule 497(a) of Regulation C under the Act or section 24(b) of the Investment Company Act of 1940 and the rules and regulations thereunder.

(c)   Communications under this rule may be made with potential investors that are, or that an issuer or person authorized to act on its behalf reasonably believes are:

(1)   Qualified institutional buyers, as defined in Rule 144A; or

(2)   Institutions that are accredited investors, as defined in §§ 230.501(a)(1), (a)(2), (a)(3), (a)(7), (a)(8), (a)(9), (a)(12), or (a)(13).

Note: Though the definition of "family client" from Rule 501(a)(13) includes both natural persons and institutions, only family clients that are institutions may be considered institutional accredited investors.

Rule 164.   Post-filing Free Writing Prospectuses in Connection With Certain Registered Offerings

Preliminary Notes to Rule 164

1.   This rule is not available for any communication that, although in technical compliance with this rule, is part of a plan or scheme to evade the requirements of section 5 of the Act.

2.   Attempted compliance with this rule does not act as an exclusive election and the person relying on this rule also may claim the availability of any other applicable exemption or exclusion. Reliance on this rule does not affect the availability of any other exemption or exclusion from the requirements of section 5 of the Act.

(a)   In connection with a registered offering of an issuer meeting the requirements of this rule, a free writing prospectus, as defined in Rule 405, of the issuer or any other offering participant, including any underwriter or dealer, after the filing of the registration statement will be a section 10(b) prospectus for purposes of section 5(b)(1) of the Act provided that the conditions set forth in Rule 433 are satisfied.

(b)   An immaterial or unintentional failure to file or delay in filing a free writing prospectus as necessary to satisfy the filing conditions contained in Rule 433 will not result in a violation of section 5(b)(1) of the Act or the loss of the ability to rely on this rule so long as:

(1)   A good faith and reasonable effort was made to comply with the filing condition; and

(2)   The free writing prospectus is filed as soon as practicable after discovery of the failure to file.

(c)   An immaterial or unintentional failure to include the specified legend in a free writing prospectus as necessary to satisfy the legend condition contained in Rule 433 will not result in a violation of section 5(b)(1) of the Act or the loss of the ability to rely on this rule so long as:

(1)   A good faith and reasonable effort was made to comply with the legend condition;

(2)   The free writing prospectus is amended to include the specified legend as soon as practicable after discovery of the omitted or incorrect legend; and

(3)   If the free writing prospectus has been transmitted without the specified legend, the free writing prospectus must be retransmitted with the legend by substantially the same means as, and directed to substantially the same prospective purchasers to whom, the free writing prospectus was originally transmitted.

(d)   Solely for purposes of this rule, an immaterial or unintentional failure to retain a free writing prospectus as necessary to satisfy the record retention condition contained in Rule 433 will not result in a violation of section 5(b)(1) of the Act or the loss of the ability to rely on this rule so long as a good faith and reasonable effort was made to comply with the record retention condition. Nothing in this paragraph will affect, however, any other record retention provisions applicable to the issuer or any offering participant.

(e)   *Ineligible issuers.*

(1)   This rule and Rule 433 are available only if at the eligibility determination date for the offering in question, determined pursuant to paragraph (h) of this rule, the issuer is not an ineligible issuer as defined in Rule 405 (or in the case of any offering participant, other than the issuer, the participant has a reasonable belief that the issuer is not an ineligible issuer);

(2)   Notwithstanding paragraph (e)(1) of this rule, this rule and Rule 433 are available to an ineligible issuer with respect to a free writing prospectus that contains only descriptions of the terms of the securities in the offering or the offering (or in the case of an offering of asset-backed securities, contains only information specified in paragraphs (a)(1), (2), (3), (4), (6), (7), and (8) of the definition of ABS informational and computational materials in Item 1101 of Regulation AB, unless the issuer is or during the last three years the issuer or any of its predecessors was):

(i)   A blank check company as defined in Rule 419(a)(2);

(ii)   A shell company, other than a business combination related shell company, as defined in Rule 405; or

(iii)   An issuer for an offering of penny stock as defined in Rule 3a51–1 of the Securities Exchange Act of 1934.

(f)   *Excluded issuers.* This rule and Rule 433 are not available if the issuer is an investment company registered under the Investment Company Act of 1940, other than a registered closed-end investment company.

(g)   *Excluded offerings.* This rule and Rule 433 are not available if the issuer is registering a business combination transaction as defined in Rule 165(f)(1) or the issuer, other than a well-known seasoned issuer, is registering an offering on Form S–8.

(h)   For purposes of this rule and Rule 433, the determination date as to whether an issuer is an ineligible issuer in respect of an offering shall be:

(1)   Except as provided in paragraph (h)(2) of this rule, the time of filing of the registration statement covering the offering; or

(2)   If the offering is being registered pursuant to Rule 415, the earliest time after the filing of the registration statement covering the offering at which the issuer, or in the case of an underwritten offering the issuer or another offering participant, makes a bona fide offer, including without limitation through the use of a free writing prospectus, in the offering.

Rule 165.   Offers Made in Connection With a Business Combination Transaction

Preliminary Note: This rule is available only to communications relating to business combinations. The exemption does not apply to communications that may be in technical compliance with this rule, but have the primary purpose or effect of conditioning the market for another transaction, such as capital-raising or resale transaction.

(a)   *Communications Before a Registration Statement is Filed.* Notwithstanding section 5(c) of the Act, the offeror of securities in a business combination transaction to be registered under the Act may make an offer to sell or solicit an offer to buy those securities from and including the first public announcement until the filing of a registration statement related to the transaction, so long as any written communication (other than non-public communications among participants) made in connection with or relating to the transaction (*i.e.*, prospectus) is filed in accordance with Rule 425 and the conditions in paragraph (c) of this rule are satisfied.

(b)   *Communications After a Registration Statement is Filed.* Notwithstanding section 5(b)(1) of the Act, any written communication (other than non-public communications among participants) made in connection with or relating to a business combination transaction (*i.e.,* prospectus) after the filing of a registration statement related to the transaction need not satisfy the requirements of section 10 of the Act, so long as the prospectus is filed in accordance with Rule 424 or Rule 425 and the conditions in paragraph (c) of this rule are satisfied.

(c)   *Conditions.* To rely on paragraphs (a) and (b) of this rule:

(1)   Each prospectus must contain a prominent legend that urges investors to read the relevant documents filed or to be filed with the Commission because they contain important information. The legend also must explain to investors that they can get the documents for free at the Commission's web site and describe which documents are available free from the offeror; and

(2)   In an exchange offer, the offer must be made in accordance with the applicable tender offer rules (Rules 14d–1 through 14e–8); and, in a transaction involving the vote of security holders, the offer must be made in accordance with the applicable proxy or information statement rules (Rule 14a–1 through 14a–101 and Rules 14c–1 through 14c–101).

(d)   *Applicability.* This rule is applicable not only to the offeror of securities in a business combination transaction, but also to any other participant that may need to rely on and complies with this rule in communicating about the transaction.

(e)   *Failure to File or Delay in Filing.* An immaterial or unintentional failure to file or delay in filing a prospectus described in this rule will not result in a violation of section 5(b)(1) or (c) of the Exchange Act, so long as:

(1)   A good faith and reasonable effort was made to comply with the filing requirement; and

(2)   The prospectus is filed as soon as practicable after discovery of the failure to file.

(f)   *Definitions.* (1) A "business combination transaction" means any transaction specified in Rule 145(a) or exchange offer;

(2)   A "participant" is any person or entity that is a party to the business combination transaction and any persons authorized to act on their behalf; and

(3)   "Public announcement" is any oral or written communication by a participant that is reasonably designed to, or has the effect of, informing the public or security holders in general about the business combination transaction.

Rule 166.   Exemption From Section 5(c) for Certain Communications in Connection With Business Combination Transactions

Preliminary Note: This rule is available only to communications relating to business combinations. The exemption does not apply to communications that may be in technical compliance with this rule, but have the primary purpose or effect of conditioning the market for another primary purpose or effect of conditioning the market for another transaction, such as a capital-raising or resale transaction.

(a)   *Communications.* In a registered offering involving a business combination transaction, any communication made in connection with or relating to the transaction before the first public announcement of the offering will not constitute an offer to sell or a solicitation of an offer to buy the securities offered for purposes of section 5(c) of the Exchange Act, so long as the participants take all reasonable steps within their control to prevent further distribution or publication of the communication until either the first public announcement is made or the registration statement related to the transaction is filed.

(b)   *Definitions.* The terms business combination transaction, participant and public announcement have the same meaning as set forth in Rule 165(f).

Rule 167.   **Communications in Connection With Certain Registered Offerings of Asset-backed Securities**

Preliminary Note: This rule is available only to communications in connection with certain offerings of asset-backed securities. The exemption does not apply to communications that may be in technical compliance with this rule, but have the primary purpose or effect of conditioning the market for another transaction or are part of a plan or scheme to evade the requirements of section 5 of the Act.

(a)   In an offering of asset-backed securities registered on Form SF–3, ABS informational and computational material regarding such securities used after the effective date of the registration statement and before the sending or giving to investors of a final prospectus that meets the requirements of section 10(a) of the Act regarding such offering is exempt from section 5(b)(1) of the Act, if the conditions in paragraph (b) of this rule are met.

(b)   *Conditions.* To rely on paragraph (a) of this rule:

(1)   The communications shall be filed to the extent required pursuant to Rule 426.

(2)   Every communication used pursuant to this rule shall include prominently on the cover page or otherwise at the beginning of such communication:

(i)   The issuing entity's name and the depositor's name, if applicable;

(ii)   The Commission file number for the related registration statement;

(iii)   A statement that such communication is ABS informational and computational material used in reliance on Securities Act Rule 167; and

(iv)   A legend that urges investors to read the relevant documents filed or to be filed with the Commission because they contain important information. The legend also shall explain to investors that they can get the documents for free at the Commission's Web site and describe which documents are available free from the issuer or an underwriter.

(c)   This rule is applicable not only to the offeror of the asset-backed securities, but also to any other participant that may need to rely on and complies with this rule in communicating about the transaction. A participant for purposes of this rule is any person or entity that is a party to the asset-backed securities transaction and any persons authorized to act on their behalf.

(d)   Failure by a particular underwriter to cause the filing of a prospectus described in this rule will not affect the ability of any other underwriter who has complied with the procedures to rely on the exemption.

(e)   An immaterial or unintentional failure to file or delay in filing a prospectus described in this rule will not result in a violation of section 5(b)(1) of the Act, so long as:

(1)   A good faith and reasonable effort was made to comply with the filing requirement; and

(2)   The prospectus is filed as soon as practicable after discovery of the failure to file.

(f)   Terms used in this rule have the same meaning as in Item 1101 of Regulation AB.

Rule 168.   **Exemption From Sections 2(a)(10) and 5(c) of the Act for Certain Communications of Regularly Released Factual Business Information and Forward-Looking Information**

Preliminary Notes to Rule 168

1.   This rule is not available for any communication that, although in technical compliance with this rule, is part of a plan or scheme to evade the requirements of section 5 of the Act.

2.   This rule provides a non-exclusive safe harbor for factual business information and forward-looking information released or disseminated as provided in this rule. Attempted compliance with this rule does not act as an exclusive election and the issuer also may claim the availability of any other applicable exemption or exclusion. Reliance on this rule does not affect the availability of any other exemption or exclusion from the definition of prospectus in section 2(a)(10) or the requirements of section 5 of the Act.

3. The availability of this rule for a release or dissemination of a communication that contains or incorporates factual business information or forward-looking information will not be affected by another release or dissemination of a communication that contains all or a portion of the same factual business information or forward-looking information that does not satisfy the conditions of this rule.

(a) For purposes of sections 2(a)(10) and 5(c) of the Act, the regular release or dissemination by or on behalf of an issuer (and, in the case of an asset-backed issuer, the other persons specified in paragraph (a)(3) of this rule) of communications containing factual business information or forward-looking information shall be deemed not to constitute an offer to sell or offer for sale of a security which is the subject of an offering pursuant to a registration statement that the issuer proposes to file, or has filed, or that is effective, if the conditions of this rule are satisfied by any of the following:

(1) An issuer that is required to file reports pursuant to section 13 or section 15(d) of the Securities Exchange Act of 1934;

(2) A foreign private issuer that:

(i) Meets all of the registrant requirements of Form F–3 other than the reporting history provisions of General Instructions I.A.1. and I.A.2.(a) of Form F–3;

(ii) Either:

(A) Satisfies the public float threshold in General Instruction I.B.1. of Form F–3; or

(B) Is issuing non-convertible securities, other than common equity, and meets the provisions of General Instruction I.B.2. of Form F–3; and

(iii) Either:

(A) Has its equity securities trading on a designated offshore securities market as defined in Rule 902(b) and has had them so traded for at least 12 months; or

(B) Has a worldwide market value of its outstanding common equity held by non-affiliates of $700 million or more; or

(3) An asset-backed issuer or a depositor, sponsor, or servicer (as such terms are defined in Item 1101 of Regulation AB) or an affiliated depositor, whether or not such other person is the issuer.

(b) *Definitions.*

(1) *Factual business information* means some or all of the following information that is released or disseminated under the conditions in paragraph (d) of this section, including, without limitation, such factual business information contained in reports or other materials filed with, furnished to, or submitted to the Commission pursuant to the Securities Exchange Act of 1934 or the Investment Company Act of 1940:

(i) Factual information about the issuer, its business or financial developments, or other aspects of its business;

(ii) Advertisements of, or other information about, the issuer's products or services; and

(iii) Dividend notices.

(2) *Forward-looking information* means some or all of the following information that is released or disseminated under the conditions in paragraph (d) of this section, including, without limitation, such forward-looking information contained in reports or other materials filed with, furnished to, or submitted to the Commission pursuant to the Securities Exchange Act of 1934 or pursuant to the Investment Company Act of 1940:

(i) Projections of the issuer's revenues, income (loss), earnings (loss) per share, capital expenditures, dividends, capital structure, or other financial items;

(ii) Statements about the issuer management's plans and objectives for future operations, including plans or objectives relating to the products or services of the issuer;

(iii) Statements about the issuer's future economic performance, including statements of the type contemplated by the management's discussion and analysis of financial condition and results of operation described in Item 303 of Regulations S–B and S–K or the operating and financial review and prospects described in Item 5 of Form 20–F; and

(iv) Assumptions underlying or relating to any of the information described in paragraphs (b)(2)(i), (b)(2)(ii) and (b)(2)(iii) of this rule.

(3) For purposes of this rule, the release or dissemination of a communication is by or on behalf of the issuer if the issuer or an agent or representative of the issuer, other than an offering participant who is an underwriter or dealer, authorizes or approves such release or dissemination before it is made.

(4) For purposes of this rule, in the case of communications of a person specified in paragraph (a)(3) of this rule other than the asset-backed issuer, the release or dissemination of a communication is by or on behalf of such other person if such other person or its agent or representative, other than an underwriter or dealer, authorizes or approves such release or dissemination before it is made.

(c) *Exclusion.* A communication containing information about the registered offering or released or disseminated as part of the offering activities in the registered offering is excluded from the exemption of this rule.

(d) *Conditions to exemption.* The following conditions must be satisfied:

(1) The issuer (or in the case of an asset-backed issuer, the issuer and the other persons specified in paragraph (a)(3) of this rule, taken together) has previously released or disseminated information of the type described in this rule in the ordinary course of its business;

(2) The timing, manner, and form in which the information is released or disseminated is consistent in material respects with similar past releases or disseminations; and

(3) The issuer is not an investment company registered under the Investment Company Act of 1940, other than a registered closed-end investment company.

Rule 169.   Exemption From Sections 2(a)(10) and 5(c) of the Act for Certain Communications of Regularly Released Factual Business Information

Preliminary Notes to Rule 169

1.   This rule is not available for any communication that, although in technical compliance with this rule, is part of a plan or scheme to evade the requirements of section 5 of the Act.

2.   This rule provides a non-exclusive safe harbor for factual business information released or disseminated as provided in this rule. Attempted compliance with this rule does not act as an exclusive election and the issuer also may claim the availability of any other applicable exemption or exclusion. Reliance on this rule does not affect the availability of any other exemption or exclusion from the definition of prospectus in section 2(a)(10) or the requirements of section 5 of the Act.

3.   The availability of this rule for a release or dissemination of a communication that contains or incorporates factual business information will not be affected by another release or dissemination of a communication that contains all or a portion of the same factual business information that does not satisfy the conditions of this rule.

(a)   For purposes of sections 2(a)(10) and 5(c) of the Act, the regular release or dissemination by or on behalf of an issuer of communications containing factual business information shall be deemed not to constitute an offer to sell or offer for sale of a security by an issuer which is the subject of an offering pursuant to a registration statement that the issuer proposes to file, or has filed, or that is effective, if the conditions of this rule are satisfied.

(b)   *Definitions.*

(1)   Factual business information means some or all of the following information that is released or disseminated under the conditions in paragraph (d) of this rule:

(i)   Factual information about the issuer, its business or financial developments, or other aspects of its business; and

(ii)   Advertisements of, or other information about, the issuer's products or services.

(2)   For purposes of this rule, the release or dissemination of a communication is by or on behalf of the issuer if the issuer or an agent or representative of the issuer, other than an offering participant who is an underwriter or dealer, authorizes or approves such release or dissemination before it is made.

(c)   *Exclusions.* A communication containing information about the registered offering or released or disseminated as part of the offering activities in the registered offering is excluded from the exemption of this rule.

(d)   *Conditions to exemption.* The following conditions must be satisfied:

(1)   The issuer has previously released or disseminated information of the type described in this rule in the ordinary course of its business;

(2)   The timing, manner, and form in which the information is released or disseminated is consistent in material respects with similar past releases or disseminations;

(3)   The information is released or disseminated for intended use by persons, such as customers and suppliers, other than in their capacities as investors or potential investors in the issuer's securities, by the issuer's employees or agents who historically have provided such information; and

(4)   The issuer is not an investment company registered under the Investment Company Act of 1940, other than a registered closed-end investment company.

Rule 170.   Prohibition of Use of Certain Financial Statements

Financial statements which purport to give effect to the receipt and application of any part of the proceeds from the sale of securities for cash shall not be used unless such securities are to be offered through underwriters and the underwriting arrangements are such that the underwriters are or will be committed to take and pay for all of the securities, if any are taken, prior to or within a reasonable time after the commencement of the public offering, or if the securities are not so taken to refund to all subscribers the full amount of all subscription payments made for the securities. The caption of any such financial statement shall clearly set forth the assumptions upon which such statement is based. The caption shall be in type at least as large as that used generally in the body of the statement.

Rule 171.   Disclosure Detrimental to the National Defense or Foreign Policy

(a)   Any requirement to the contrary notwithstanding, no registration statement, prospectus, or other document filed with the Commission or used in connection with the offering or sale of any securities shall contain any document or information which, pursuant to Executive order, has been classified by an appropriate department or agency of the United States for protection in the interests of national defense or foreign policy.

(b)   Where a document or information is omitted pursuant to paragraph (a) of this rule, there shall be filed, in lieu of such document or information, a statement from an appropriate department or agency of the United States to the effect that such document or information has been classified or that the status thereof is awaiting determination. Where a document is omitted pursuant to paragraph (a) of this rule, but information relating to the subject-matter of such document is nevertheless included in material filed with the Commission pursuant to a determination of an appropriate department or agency of the United States that disclosure of such information would not be contrary to the interests of national defense or foreign policy, a statement from such department or agency to that effect shall be submitted for the information of the Commission. A registrant may rely upon any such statement in filing or omitting any document or information to which the statement relates.

(c)   The Commission may protect any information in its possession which may require classification in the interests of national defense or foreign policy pending determination by an appropriate department or agency as to whether such information should be classified.

(d)   It shall be the duty of the registrant to submit the documents or information referred to in paragraph (a) of this rule to the appropriate department or agency of the United States prior to filing them with the Commission and to obtain and submit to the Commission, at the time of filing such documents or information, or in lieu thereof, as the case may be, the statements from such department or agency required by paragraph (b) of this rule All such statements shall be in writing.

Rule 172.   Delivery of Prospectuses

(a)   Sending confirmations and notices of allocations. After the effective date of a registration statement, the following are exempt from the provisions of section 5(b)(1) of the Act if the conditions set forth in paragraph (c) of this rule are satisfied:

(1)   Written confirmations of sales of securities in an offering pursuant to a registration statement that contain information limited to that called for in Rule 10b–10 under the Securities Exchange Act of 1934 and other information customarily included in written confirmations of sales of securities, which may include notices provided pursuant to Rule 173; and

(2)   Notices of allocation of securities sold or to be sold in an offering pursuant to the registration statement that may include information identifying the securities (including the CUSIP number) and otherwise may include only information regarding pricing, allocation and settlement, and information incidental thereto.

(b)   Transfer of the security. Any obligation under section 5(b)(2) of the Act to have a prospectus that satisfies the requirements of section 10(a) of the Act precede or accompany the carrying or delivery of a security in a registered offering is satisfied if the conditions in paragraph (c) of this rule are met.

(c)   *Conditions.*

(1)   The registration statement relating to the offering is effective and is not the subject of any pending proceeding or examination under section 8(d) or 8(e) of the Act;

(2)   Neither the issuer, nor an underwriter or participating dealer is the subject of a pending proceeding under section 8A of the Act in connection with the offering; and

(3)   The issuer has filed with the Commission a prospectus with respect to the offering that satisfies the requirements of section 10(a) of the Act or the issuer will make a good faith and reasonable effort to file such a prospectus within the time required under Rule 424 and, in the event that the issuer fails to file timely such a prospectus, the issuer files the prospectus as soon as practicable thereafter.

(4)   The condition in paragraph (c)(3) of this rule shall not apply to transactions by dealers requiring delivery of a final prospectus pursuant to section 4(3) of the Act.

(d)   *Exclusions.* This rule shall not apply to any:

(1)   Offering of any investment company registered under the Investment Company Act of 1940, other than a registered closed-end investment company;

(2)   Offering of any business development company as defined in section 2(a)(48) of the Investment Company Act of 1940;

(3)   A business combination transaction as defined in Rule 165(f)(1); or

(4)   Offering registered on Form S–8.

Rule 173.   Notice of Registration

(a)   In a transaction that represents a sale by the issuer or an underwriter, or a sale where there is not an exclusion or exemption from the requirement to deliver a final prospectus meeting the requirements of section 10(a) of the Act pursuant to section 4(3) of the Act or Rule 174, each underwriter or dealer selling in such transaction shall provide to each purchaser from it, not later than two business days following the completion of such sale, a copy of the final prospectus or, in lieu of such prospectus, a notice to the effect that the sale was made pursuant to a registration statement or in a transaction in which a final prospectus would have been required to have been delivered in the absence of Rule 172.

(b)   If the sale was by the issuer and was not effected by or through an underwriter or dealer, the responsibility to send a prospectus, or in lieu of such prospectus, such notice as set forth in paragraph (a) of this rule, shall be the issuer's.

(c)   Compliance with the requirements of this rule is not a condition to reliance on Rule 172.

(d)   A purchaser may request from the person responsible for sending a notice a copy of the final prospectus if one has not been sent.

(e)   After the effective date of the registration statement with respect to an offering, notices as set forth in paragraph (a) of this rule, are exempt from the provisions of Rule 5(b)(1) of the Act.

(f)   *Exclusions.* This rule shall not apply to any:

(1)   Transaction solely between brokers or dealers in reliance on Rule 153;

(2)   Offering of an investment company registered under the Investment Company Act of 1940, other than a registered closed-end investment company;

(3)   A business combination transaction as defined in Rule 165(f)(1); or

(4)   Offering registered on Form S–8.

Rule 174.   Delivery of Prospectus by Dealers; Exemptions Under Section 4(3) of the Act

The obligations of a dealer (including an underwriter no longer acting as an underwriter in respect of the security involved in such transactions) to deliver a prospectus in transactions in a security as to which a registration statement has been filed taking place prior to the expiration of the 40- or 90-day period specified in section 4(3) of the Act after the effective date of such registration statement or prior to the expiration of such period after the first date upon which the security was bona fide offered to the public by the issuer or by or through an underwriter after such effective date, whichever is later, shall be subject to the following provisions:

(a)   No prospectus need be delivered if the registration statement is on Form F–6.

(b)   No prospectus need be delivered if the issuer is subject, immediately prior to the time of filing the registration statement, to the reporting requirements of section 13 or 15(d) of the Securities Exchange Act of 1934.

(c)   Where a registration statement relates to offerings to be made from time to time no prospectus need be delivered after the expiration of the initial prospectus delivery period specified in section 4(3) of the Act following the first bona fide offering of securities under such registration statement.

(d)   If (1) the registration statement relates to the security of an issuer that is not subject, immediately prior to the time of filing the registration statement, to the reporting requirements of section 13 or 15(d) of the Securities Exchange Act of 1934, and (2) as of the offering date, the security is listed on a registered national securities exchange or authorized for inclusion in an electronic inter-dealer quotation system sponsored and governed by the rules of a registered securities association, no prospectus need be delivered after the expiration of twenty-five calendar days after the offering date. For purposes of this provision, the term "offering date" refers to the later of the effective date of the registration statement or the first date on which the security was bona fide offered to the public.

(e)   Notwithstanding the foregoing, the period during which a prospectus must be delivered by a dealer shall be:

(1)   As specified in section 4(3) of the Act if the registration statement was the subject of a stop order issued under section 8 of the Act; or

(2)   As the Commission may provide upon application or on its own motion in a particular case.

(f)   Nothing in this rule shall affect the obligation to deliver a prospectus pursuant to the provisions of section 5 of the Act by a dealer who is acting as an underwriter with respect to the securities involved or who is engaged in a transaction as to securities constituting the whole or a part *of an unsold allotment to or subscription by such dealer as a participant in the distribution of such securities by the issuer or by or through an underwriter.*

(g) If the registration statement relates to an offering of securities of a "blank check company," as defined in Rule 419 under the Act, the statutory period for prospectus delivery specified in section 4(3) of the Act shall not terminate until 90 days after the date funds and securities are released from the escrow or trust account pursuant to Rule 419 under the Act.

(h) Any obligation pursuant to Section 4(3) of the Act and this rule to deliver a prospectus, other than pursuant to paragraph (g) of this rule, may be satisfied by compliance with the provisions of Rule 172.

Rule 175.   Liability for Certain Statements by Issuers

(a) A statement within the coverage of paragraph (b) of this rule which is made by or on behalf of an issuer or by an outside reviewer retained by the issuer shall be deemed not to be a fraudulent statement (as defined in paragraph (d) of this rule), unless it is shown that such statement was made or reaffirmed without a reasonable basis or was disclosed other than in good faith.

(b) This rule applies to the following statements:

(1) A forward-looking statement (as defined in paragraph (c) of this rule) made in a document filed with the Commission, in Part I of a quarterly report on Form 10–Q, or in an annual report to security holders meeting the requirements of Rules 14a–3(b) and (c) or 14c–3(a) and (b) under the Securities Exchange Act of 1934, a statement reaffirming such forward-looking statement after the date the document was filed or the annual report was made publicly available, or a forward-looking statement made before the date the document was filed or the date the annual report was publicly available if such statement is reaffirmed in a filed document, in Part I of a quarterly report on Form 10–Q, or in an annual report made publicly available within a reasonable time after the making of such forward-looking statement;

Provided, That

(i) At the time such statements are made or reaffirmed, either the issuer is subject to the reporting requirements of section 13(a) or 15(d) of the Securities Exchange Act of 1934 and has complied with the requirements of Rule 13a–1 or 15d–1 thereunder, if applicable, to file its most recent annual report on Form 10–K, Form 20–F, or Form 40–F; or if the issuer is not subject to the reporting requirements of section 13(a) or 15(d) of the Securities Exchange Act of 1934, the statements are made in a registration statement filed under the Securities Act of 1933, offering statement or solicitation of interest, written document or broadcast script under Regulation A or pursuant to section 12(b) or (g) of the Securities Exchange Act of 1934; and

(ii) The statements are not made by or on behalf of an issuer that is an investment company registered under the Investment Company Act of 1940; and

(2) Information that is disclosed in a document filed with the Commission, in Part I of a quarterly report on Form 10–Q or in an annual report to shareholders meeting the requirements of Rules 14a–3(b) and (c) or 14c–3(a) and (b) under the Securities Exchange Act of 1934 and that relates to:

(i) The effects of changing prices on the business enterprise, presented voluntarily or pursuant to Item 303 of Regulation S–K, "Management's Discussion and Analysis of Financial Condition and Results of Operations," Item 5 of Form 20–F, "Operating and Financial Review and Prospects," Item 302 of Regulation S–K, "Supplementary Financial Information," or Rule 3–20(c) of Regulation S–X; or

(ii) The value of proved oil and gas reserves (such as a standardized measure of discounted future net cash flows relating to proved oil and gas reserves as set forth in FASB ASC paragraph 932–235–50–24 (Extractive Activities—Oil and Gas Topic)) presented voluntarily or pursuant to Item 302 of Regulation S–K.

(c)   For the purpose of this rule the term "forward-looking statement" shall mean and shall be limited to:

(1)   A statement containing a projection of revenues, income (loss), earnings (loss) per share, capital expenditures, dividends, capital structure or other financial items;

(2)   A statement of management's plans and objectives for future operations;

(3)   A statement of future economic performance contained in management's discussion and analysis of financial condition and results of operations included pursuant to Item 303 of Regulation S–K or Item 5 of Form 20–F; or

(4)   Disclosed statements of the assumptions underlying or relating to any of the statements described in paragraphs (c)(1), (2) or (3) above.

(d)   For the purpose of this rule the term "fraudulent statement" shall mean a statement which is an untrue statement of a material fact, a statement false or misleading with respect to any material fact, an omission to state a material fact necessary to make a statement not misleading, or which constitutes the employment of a manipulative, deceptive, or fraudulent device, contrivance, scheme, transaction, act, practice, course of business, or an artifice to defraud, as those terms are used in the Securities Act of 1933 or the rules or regulations promulgated thereunder.

Rule 176.   Circumstances Affecting the Determination of What Constitutes Reasonable Investigation and Reasonable Grounds for Belief Under Section 11 of the Securities Act

In determining whether or not the conduct of a person constitutes a reasonable investigation or a reasonable ground for belief meeting the standard set forth in section 11(c), relevant circumstances include, with respect to a person other than the issuer:

(a)   The type of issuer;

(b)   The type of security;

(c)   The type of person;

(d)   The office held when the person is an officer;

(e)   The presence or absence of another relationship to the issuer when the person is a director or proposed director;

(f)   Reasonable reliance on officers, employees, and others whose duties should have given them knowledge of the particular facts (in the light of the functions and responsibilities of the particular person with respect to the issuer and the filing);

(g)   When the person is an underwriter, the type of underwriting arrangement, the role of the particular person as an underwriter and the availability of information with respect to the registrant; and

(h)   Whether, with respect to a fact or document incorporated by reference, the particular person had any responsibility for the fact or document at the time of the filing from which it was incorporated.

Rule 180.   Exemption From Registration of Interests and Participations Issued in Connection With Certain H.R. 10 Plans

(a)   Any interest or participation in a single trust fund or in a collective trust fund maintained by a bank, or any security arising out of a contract issued by an insurance company, issued to an employee benefit plan shall be exempt from the provisions of section 5 of the Act if the following terms and conditions are met:

(1)   The plan covers employees, some or all of whom are employees within the meaning of section 401(c)(1) of the Internal Revenue Code of 1954, and is either: (i) a pension or profit-sharing plan which meets the requirements for qualification under section 401 of such Code, or (ii) an annuity plan which

meets the requirements for the deduction of the employer's contribution under section 404(a)(2) of such Code;

(2)   The plan covers only employees of a single employer or employees of interrelated partnerships; and

(3)   The issuer of such interest, participation or security shall have reasonable grounds to believe and, after making reasonable inquiry, shall believe immediately prior to any issuance that:

(i)   The employer is a law firm, accounting firm, investment banking firm, pension consulting firm or investment advisory firm that is engaged in furnishing services of a type that involve such knowledge and experience in financial and business matters that the employer is able to represent adequately its interests and those of its employees; or

(ii)   In connection with the plan, the employer prior to adopting the plan obtains the advice of a person or entity that

(A)   is not a financial institution providing any funding vehicle for the plan, and is neither an affiliated person as defined in section 2(a)(3) of the Investment Company Act of 1940 of, nor a person who has a material business relationship with, a financial institution providing a funding vehicle for the plan; and

(B)   is, by virtue of knowledge and experience in financial and business matters, able to represent adequately the interests of the employer and its employees.

(b)   Any interest or participation issued to a participant in either a pension or profit-sharing plan which meets the requirements for qualification under section 401 of the Internal Revenue Code of 1954 or an annuity plan which meets the requirements for the deduction of the employer's contribution under section 404(a)(2) of such Code, and which covers employees, some or all of whom are employees within the meaning of section 401(c)(1) of such Code, shall be exempt from the provisions of section 5 of the Act.

Rule 190.   Registration of Underlying Securities in Asset-backed Securities Transactions

(a)   In an offering of asset-backed securities where the asset pool includes securities of another issuer ("underlying securities"), unless the underlying securities are themselves exempt from registration under section 3 of the Act, the offering of the relevant underlying securities itself must be registered as a primary offering of such securities in accordance with paragraph (b) of this rule unless all of the following are true. Terms used in this rule have the same meaning as in Item 1101 of Regulation AB.

(1)   Neither the issuer of the underlying securities nor any of its affiliates has a direct or indirect agreement, arrangement, relationship or understanding, written or otherwise, relating to the underlying securities and the asset-backed securities transaction;

(2)   Neither the issuer of the underlying securities nor any of its affiliates is an affiliate of the sponsor, depositor, issuing entity or underwriter of the asset-backed securities transaction;

(3)   If the underlying securities are restricted securities, as defined in Rule 144(a)(3), Rule 144 must be available for the sale of the securities, provided however, that notwithstanding any other provision of Rule 144, Rule 144 shall only be so available if at least two years have elapsed since the later of the date the securities were acquired from the issuer of the underlying securities or from an affiliate of the issuer of the underlying securities; and

(4)   The depositor would be free to publicly resell the underlying securities without registration under the Act. For example, the offering of the asset-backed security does not constitute part of a distribution of the underlying securities. An offering of asset-backed securities with an asset pool containing underlying securities that at the time of the purchase for the asset pool are part of a subscription or unsold allotment would be a distribution of the underlying securities. For purposes of this rule, in an offering of asset-backed securities involving a sponsor, depositor or underwriter that was an underwriter or an affiliate of an underwriter in a registered offering of the underlying securities, the distribution of the asset-backed securities will not constitute part of a distribution of the underlying securities if the underlying securities were purchased at arm's length in the secondary

market at least three months after the last sale of any unsold allotment or subscription by the affiliated underwriter that participated in the registered offering of the underlying securities.

(b) If all of the conditions in paragraph (a) of this rule are not met, the offering of the relevant underlying securities itself must be registered as a primary offering of such securities in accordance with the following:

(1) If the offering of asset-backed securities is registered on Form SF–3, the offering of the underlying securities itself must be eligible to be registered under Form SF–3, Form S–3, or F–3 as a primary offering of such securities;

(2) The plan of distribution in the registration statement for the offering of the underlying securities contemplates this type of distribution at the time of the commencement of the offering of the asset-backed securities;

(3) The prospectus for the asset-backed securities offering describes the plan of distribution for both the underlying securities and the asset-backed securities;

(4) The prospectus relating to the offering of the underlying securities is delivered simultaneously with the delivery of the prospectus relating to the offering of the asset-backed securities, and the prospectus for the asset-backed securities includes disclosure that the prospectus for the offering of the underlying securities will be delivered along with, or is combined with, the prospectus for the offering of the asset-backed securities;

(5) The prospectus for the asset-backed securities offering identifies the issuing entity, depositor, sponsor and each underwriter for the offering of the asset-backed securities as an underwriter for the offering of the underlying securities; and

(6) Neither prospectus disclaims or limits responsibility by the issuing entity, sponsor, depositor, trustee or any underwriter for information regarding the underlying securities.

(c) Notwithstanding paragraphs (a) and (b) of this rule, if the asset pool for the asset-backed securities includes a pool asset representing an interest in or the right to the payments or cash flows of another asset pool, then that pool asset is not considered an "underlying security" for purposes of this rule (although its distribution in connection with the asset-backed securities transaction may need to be separately registered) if the following conditions are met:

(1) Both the issuing entity for the asset-backed securities and the entity issuing the pool asset were established under the direction of the same sponsor and depositor;

(2) The pool asset is created solely to satisfy legal requirements or otherwise facilitate the structuring of the asset-backed securities transaction;

(3) The pool asset is not part of a scheme to avoid registration or the requirements of this rule; and

(4) The pool asset is held by the issuing entity and is a part of the asset pool for the asset-backed securities.

(d) Notwithstanding paragraph (c) of this rule (that is, although the pool asset described in paragraph (c) of this rule is an not an "underlying security" for purposes of this rule), if the pool assets for the asset-backed securities are collateral certificates or special units of beneficial interest, those collateral certificates or special units of beneficial interest must be registered concurrently with the registration of the asset-backed securities. However, pursuant to 1933 Act Rule 457(t) no separate registration fee for the certificates or special units of beneficial interest is required to be paid.

Rule 191.   Definition of "Issuer" in Section 2(a)(4) of the Act in Relation to Asset-backed Securities

The following applies with respect to asset-backed securities under the Act. Terms used in this rule have the same meaning as in Item 1101 of Regulation AB.

(a) The depositor for the asset-backed securities acting solely in its capacity as depositor to the issuing entity is the "issuer" for purposes of the asset-backed securities of that issuing entity.

(b)   The person acting in the capacity as the depositor specified in paragraph (a) of this rule is a different "issuer" from that same person acting as a depositor for another issuing entity or for purposes of that person's own securities.

Rule 193. Review of Underlying Assets in Asset-Backed Securities Transactions

An issuer of an "asset-backed security," as that term is defined in Section 3(a)(79) of the Securities Exchange Act of 1934, offering and selling such a security pursuant to a registration statement shall perform a review of the pool assets underlying the asset-backed security. At a minimum, such review must be designed and effected to provide reasonable assurance that the disclosure regarding the pool assets in the form of prospectus filed pursuant to Rule 424 of this chapter is accurate in all material respects. The issuer may conduct the review or an issuer may employ a third party engaged for purposes of performing the review. If the findings and conclusions of the review are attributed to the third party, the third party must be named in the registration statement and consent to being named as an expert in accordance with Rule 436 of this chapter.

Instruction to Rule 193: An issuer of an "asset-backed security" may rely on one or more third parties to fulfill its obligation to perform a review under this rule, provided that the reviews performed by the third parties and the issuer, in the aggregate, comply with the minimum standard in this rule. The issuer must comply with the requirements of this rule for each third party engaged by the issuer to perform the review for purposes of this rule. An issuer may not rely on a review performed by an unaffiliated originator for purposes of performing the review required under this rule.

Rule 194. Definitions of the Terms "Swap" and "Security-Based Swap" as Used in the Act

(a)   The term *swap* as used in section 2(a)(17) of the Act (has the same meaning as provided in section 3(a)(69) of the Securities Exchange Act of 1934 and Exchange Act Rules 3a69–1 through 3a69–3.

(b)   The term *security-based swap* as used in section 2(a)(17) of the Act (has the same meaning as provided in section 3(a)(68) of the Securities Exchange Act of 1934 and Exchange Act Rules 3a68–1a through 3a68–5.

Rule 215. Accredited Investor

The term *accredited investor* as used in section 2(a)(15)(ii) of the Securities Act of 1933 shall have the same meaning as the definition of that term in Rule 501(a) under the Act.

MISCELLANEOUS EXEMPTIONS

Rule 236. Exemption of Shares Offered in Connection With Certain Transactions

Shares of stock or similar security offered to provide funds to be distributed to shareholders of the issuer of such securities in lieu of issuing fractional shares, scrip certificates or order forms, in connection with a stock dividend, stock split, reverse stock split, conversion, merger or similar transaction, shall be exempt from registration under the Act if the following conditions are met:

(a)   The issuer of such shares is required to file and has filed reports with the Commission pursuant to section 13 or 15(d) of the Securities Exchange Act of 1934.

(b)   The aggregate gross proceeds from the sale of all shares offered in connection with the transaction for the purpose of providing such funds does not exceed $300,000.

(c)   At least ten days prior to the offering of the shares, the issuer shall furnish to the Commission in writing the following information: (1) That it proposes to offer shares in reliance upon the exemption provided by this rule; (2) the estimated number of shares to be so offered; (3) the aggregate market value of such shares as of the latest practicable date; and (4) a brief description of the transaction in connection with which the shares are to be offered.

Rule 237.   Exemption for Offers and Sales to Certain Canadian Tax-Deferred Retirement Savings Accounts

(a)   *Definitions.* As used in this rule:

(1)   "Canadian law" means the federal laws of Canada, the laws of any province or territory of Canada, and the rules or regulations of any federal, provincial, or territorial regulatory authority, or any self-regulatory authority, of Canada.

(2)   "Canadian Retirement Account" means a trust or other arrangement, including, but not limited to, a "Registered Retirement Savings Plan" or "Registered Retirement Income Fund" administered under Canadian law, that is managed by the Participant and:

(i)   Operated to provide retirement benefits to a Participant; and

(ii)   Established in Canada, administered under Canadian law, and qualified for tax-deferred treatment under Canadian law.

(3)   "Eligible security" means a security issued by a Qualified Company that:

(i)   Is offered to a Participant, or sold to his or her Canadian Retirement Account, in reliance on this rule; and

(ii)   May also be purchased by Canadians other than Participants.

(4)   "Foreign Government" means the government of any foreign country or of any political subdivision of a foreign country.

(5)   "Foreign Issuer" means any issuer that is a Foreign Government, a national of any foreign country or a corporation or other organization incorporated or organized under the laws of any foreign country, except an issuer meeting the following conditions:

(i)   More than 50 percent of the outstanding voting securities of the issuer are held of record either directly or through voting trust certificates or depositary receipts by residents of the United States; and

(ii)   Any of the following:

(A)   The majority of the executive officers or directors are United States citizens or residents;

(B)   More than 50 percent of the assets of the issuer are located in the United States; or

(C)   The business of the issuer is administered principally in the United States.

(iii)   For purposes of this definition, the term "resident," as applied to security holders, means any person whose address appears on the records of the issuer, the voting trustee, or the depositary as being located in the United States.

(6)   "Participant" means a natural person who is a resident of the United States, or is temporarily present in the United States, and who contributes to, or is or will be entitled to receive the income and assets from, a Canadian Retirement Account.

(7)   "Qualified Company" means a Foreign Issuer whose securities are qualified for investment on a tax-deferred basis by a Canadian Retirement Account under Canadian law.

(8)   "United States" means the United States of American, its territories and possessions, any state of the United States, and the District of Columbia.

(b)   *Exemption.* The offer to a Participant, or the sale to his or her Canadian Retirement Account, of Eligible Securities by any person is exempt from section 5 of the Act if the person:

(1)   Includes in any written offering materials delivered to a Participant, or his or her Canadian Retirement Account, a prominent statement that the Eligible Security is not registered with the U.S. Securities and Exchanges Commission and the Eligible Security is being offered or sold in the United States under an exemption from registration.

(2) Has not asserted that Canadian law, or the jurisdiction of the courts of Canada, does not apply in a proceeding involving an Eligible Security.

Rule 238. Exemption for Standardized Options

(a) *Exemption.* Except as expressly provided in paragraphs (b) and (c) of this rule, the Act does not apply to any standardized option, as that term is defined by Rule 9b–1(a)(4) under the Exchange Act, that is:

(1) Issued by a clearing agency registered under section 17A of the Securities Exchange Act of 1934; and

(2) Traded on a national securities exchange registered pursuant to section 6(a) of the Securities Exchange Act of 1934 or on a national securities association registered pursuant to section 15A(a) of the Securities Exchange Act of 1934.

(b) *Limitation.* The exemption provided in paragraph (a) of this rule does not apply to the provisions of section 17 of the Act.

(c) *Offers and Sales.* Any offer or sale of a standardized option by or on behalf of the issuer of the securities underlying the standardized option, an affiliate of the issuer, or an underwriter, will constitute a contract for sale of, sale of, offer for sale, or offer to sell the underlying securities as defined in section 2(a)(3) of the Act.

Rule 239. Exemption for Offers and Sales of Certain Security-Based Swaps

(a) Provided that the conditions of paragraph (b) of this rule are satisfied and except as expressly provided in paragraph (c) of this rule, the Act does not apply to any offer or sale of a security-based swap that:

(1) Is issued or will be issued by a clearing agency that is either registered as a clearing agency under Section 17A of the Securities Exchange Act of 1934 or exempt from registration under Section 17A of the Securities Exchange Act of 1934 pursuant to a rule, regulation, or order of the Commission ("eligible clearing agency"), and

(2) The Commission has determined is required to be cleared or that is permitted to be cleared pursuant to the eligible clearing agency's rules.

(b) The exemption provided in paragraph (a) of this rule applies only to an offer or sale of a security-based swap described in paragraph (a) of this rule if the following conditions are satisfied:

(1) The security-based swap is offered or sold in a transaction involving the eligible clearing agency in its function as a central counterparty with respect to such security-based swap;

(2) The security-based swap is sold only to an eligible contract participant (as defined in Section 1a(18) of the Commodity Exchange Act; and

(3) The eligible clearing agency posts on its publicly available Web site at a specified Internet address or includes in its agreement covering the security-based swap that the eligible clearing agency provides or makes available to its counterparty the following:

(i) A statement identifying any security, issuer, loan, or narrow-based security index underlying the security-based swap;

(ii) A statement indicating the security or loan to be delivered (or class of securities or loans), or if cash settled, the security, loan, or narrow-based security index (or class of securities or loans) whose value is to be used to determine the amount of the settlement obligation under the security-based swap; and

(iii) A statement of whether the issuer of any security or loan, each issuer of a security in a narrow-based security index, or each referenced issuer underlying the security-based swap is subject to the reporting requirements of Sections 13 or 15(d) of the Securities Exchange Act of

1934 and, if not subject to such reporting requirements, whether public information, including financial information, about any such issuer is available and where the information is available.

(c)   The exemption provided in paragraph (a) of this rule does not apply to the provisions of Section 17(a) of the Act.

Rule 240.   Exemption for Certain Security-Based Swaps

(a)   Except as expressly provided in paragraph (b) of this rule, the Act does not apply to the offer or sale of any security-based swap that is:

(1)   A security-based swap agreement, as defined in Section 2A of the Act as in effect prior to July 16, 2011; and

(2)   Entered into between eligible contract participants (as defined in Section 1a(12) of the Commodity Exchange Act as in effect prior to July 16, 2011, other than a person who is an eligible contract participant under Section 1a(12)(C) of the Commodity Exchange Act as in effect prior to July 16, 2011).

(b)   The exemption provided in paragraph (a) of this rule does not apply to the provisions of Section 17(a) of the Act.

(c)   This rule will expire on February 11, 2017. In such event, the Commission will publish a rule removing this rule from 17 CFR part 230 or modifying it as appropriate.

Rule 241.   Solicitations of Interest

(a)   *Solicitation of interest.* At any time before making a determination as to the exemption from registration under the Act under which an offering of securities will be conducted, an issuer or any person authorized to act on behalf of an issuer may communicate orally or in writing to determine whether there is any interest in a contemplated offering of securities exempt from registration under the Act. Such communications are deemed to be an offer of a security for sale for purposes of the antifraud provisions of the Federal securities laws. No solicitation or acceptance of money or other consideration, nor of any commitment, binding or otherwise, from any person is permitted until the issuer makes a determination as to the exemption to be relied on and the offering, meeting the requirements of the exemption, is commenced.

(b)   *Conditions.* The communications must state that:

(1)   The issuer is considering an offering of securities exempt from registration under the Act, but has not determined a specific exemption from registration the issuer intends to rely on for the subsequent offer and sale of the securities;

(2)   No money or other consideration is being solicited, and if sent in response, will not be accepted;

(3)   No offer to buy the securities can be accepted and no part of the purchase price can be received until the issuer determines the exemption under which the offering is intended to be conducted and, where applicable, the filing, disclosure, or qualification requirements of such exemption are met; and

(4)   A person's indication of interest involves no obligation or commitment of any kind.

(c)   *Indications of interest.* Any written communication under this rule may include a means by which a person may indicate to the issuer that such person is interested in a potential offering. The issuer may require the name, address, telephone number, and/or email address in any response form included pursuant to this paragraph (c).

REGULATION A—CONDITIONAL SMALL ISSUES EXEMPTION

NOTE—Amendments to Regulation A

Until 2018, Regulation A was only available to companies not subject to the 1934 Act's periodic reporting requirements. In 2018, congress enacted and the president signed into law the Economic Growth, Regulatory Relief and Consumer Protection Act (Pub. L. No. 115–174 (S. 2155) § 508, 132 Stat. 1356 (May 24, 2018)), which, among other things, directs the SEC to amend Regulation A to make it available to companies subject to the 1934 Act reporting immediately prior to the Regulation A offering. The Act also mandates that the SEC eliminate Rule 257's Regulation A periodic and current reporting requirements that otherwise would be required for an issuer completing a Tier 2 offering under Regulation A, for any issuer that is subject to the reporting requirements of the Exchange Act if the issuer is in compliance with its obligations thereunder. The rules had not been adopted as this supplement went to press.

Rule 251.   Scope of Exemption

(a)   *Tier 1 and Tier 2.* A public offer or sale of eligible securities, as defined in Rule 261, pursuant to Regulation A shall be exempt under section 3(b) from the registration requirements of the Securities Act of 1933 (the "Securities Act").

    (1)   *Tier 1.* Offerings pursuant to Regulation A in which the sum of all cash and other consideration to be received for the securities being offered ("aggregate offering price") plus the gross proceeds for all securities sold pursuant to other offering statements within the 12 months before the start of and during the current offering of securities ("aggregate sales") does not exceed $20,000,000, including not more than $6,000,000 offered by all selling securityholders that are affiliates of the issuer ("Tier 1 offerings").

    (2)   *Tier 2.* Offerings pursuant to Rules 251 through 263 (Regulation A) in which the sum of the aggregate offering price and aggregate sales does not exceed $75,000,000, including not more than $22,500,000 offered by all selling securityholders that are affiliates of the issuer ("Tier 2 offerings").

    (3)   *Additional limitation on secondary sales in first year.* The portion of the aggregate offering price attributable to the securities of selling securityholders shall not exceed 30% of the aggregate offering price of a particular offering in:

        (i)   The issuer's first offering pursuant to Regulation A; or

        (ii)   Any subsequent Regulation A offering that is qualified within one year of the qualification date of the issuer's first offering.

NOTE to paragraph (a). Where a mixture of cash and non-cash consideration is to be received, the aggregate offering price must be based on the price at which the securities are offered for cash. Any portion of the aggregate offering price or aggregate sales attributable to cash received in a foreign currency must be translated into United States currency at a currency exchange rate in effect on, or at a reasonable time before, the date of the sale of the securities. If securities are not offered for cash, the aggregate offering price or aggregate sales must be based on the value of the consideration as established by bona fide sales of that consideration made within a reasonable time, or, in the absence of sales, on the fair value as determined by an accepted standard. Valuations of non-cash consideration must be reasonable at the time made. If convertible securities or warrants are being offered and such securities are convertible, exercisable, or exchangeable within one year of the offering statement's qualification or at the discretion of the issuer, the underlying securities must also be qualified and the aggregate offering price must include the actual or maximum estimated conversion, exercise, or exchange price of such securities.

(b)   *Issuer.* The issuer of the securities:

    (1)   Is an entity organized under the laws of the United States or Canada, or any State, Province, Territory or possession thereof, or the District of Columbia, with its principal place of business in the United States or Canada;

    (2)   [Reserved];

    (3)   Is not a development stage company that either has no specific business plan or purpose, or has indicated that its business plan is to merge with or acquire an unidentified company or companies;

    (4)   Is not an investment company registered or required to be registered under the Investment Company Act of 1940 or a business development company as defined in section 2(a)(48) of the Investment Company Act of 1940;

    (5)   Is not issuing fractional undivided interests in oil or gas rights, or a similar interest in other mineral rights;

(6)   Is not, and has not been, subject to any order of the Commission entered pursuant to Section 12(j) of the Securities Exchange Act of 1934 (the "Exchange Act") within five years before the filing of the offering statement;

(7)   Has filed with the Commission all reports required to be filed, if any, pursuant to Rule 257 during the two years before the filing of the offering statement (or for such shorter period that the issuer was required to file such reports); and

(8)   Is not disqualified under Rule 262.

(c)   *Integration with other offerings.* Offers or sales made in reliance on this Regulation A will not be integrated with:

(1)   Prior offers or sales of securities; or

(2)   Subsequent offers or sales of securities that are:

(i)   Registered under the Securities Act, except as provided in Rule 255(e);

(ii)   Exempt from registration under Rule 701;

(iii)   Made pursuant to an employee benefit plan;

(iv)   Exempt from registration under Regulation S;

(v)   Made more than six months after the completion of the Regulation A offering; or

(vi)   Exempt from registration under Section 4(a)(6) of the Securities Act.

NOTE to paragraph (c). If these safe harbors do not apply, whether subsequent offers and sales of securities will be integrated with the Regulation A offering will depend on the particular facts and circumstances.

(d)   *Offering conditions*—(1) *Offers.* (i) Except as allowed by Rule 255, no offer of securities may be made unless an offering statement has been filed with the Commission.

(ii)   After the offering statement has been filed, but before it is qualified:

(A)   Oral offers may be made;

(B)   Written offers pursuant to Rule 254 may be made; and

(C)   Solicitations of interest and other communications pursuant to Rule 255 may be made.

(iii)   Offers may be made after the offering statement has been qualified, but any written offers must be accompanied with or preceded by the most recent offering circular filed with the Commission for such offering.

(2)   *Sales.* (i) No sale of securities may be made:

(A)   Until the offering statement has been qualified;

(B)   By issuers that are not currently required to file reports pursuant to Rule 257(b), until a Preliminary Offering Circular is delivered at least 48 hours before the sale to any person that before qualification of the offering statement had indicated an interest in purchasing securities in the offering, including those persons that responded to an issuer's solicitation of interest materials; and

(C)   In a Tier 2 offering of securities that are not listed on a registered national securities exchange upon qualification, unless the purchaser is either an accredited investor (as defined in Rule 501) or the aggregate purchase price to be paid by the purchaser for the securities (including the actual or maximum estimated conversion, exercise, or exchange price for any underlying securities that have been qualified) is no more than ten percent (10%) of the greater of such purchaser's:

(1)   Annual income or net worth if a natural person (with annual income and net worth for such natural person purchasers determined as provided in Rule 501; or

(2) Revenue or net assets for such purchaser's most recently completed fiscal year end if a non-natural person.

NOTE to paragraph (d)(2)(i)(C). When securities underlying warrants or convertible securities are being qualified pursuant to Tier 2 of Regulation A one year or more after the qualification of an offering for which investment limitations previously applied, purchasers of the underlying securities for which investment limitations would apply at that later date may determine compliance with the ten percent (10%) investment limitation using the conversion, exercise, or exchange price to acquire the underlying securities at that later time without aggregating such price with the price of the overlying warrants or convertible securities.

(D) The issuer may rely on a representation of the purchaser when determining compliance with the ten percent (10%) investment limitation in this paragraph (d)(2)(i)(C), provided that the issuer does not know at the time of sale that any such representation is untrue.

(ii) In a transaction that represents a sale by the issuer or an underwriter, or a sale by a dealer within 90 calendar days after qualification of the offering statement, each underwriter or dealer selling in such transaction must deliver to each purchaser from it, not later than two business days following the completion of such sale, a copy of the Final Offering Circular, subject to the following provisions:

(A) If the sale was by the issuer and was not effected by or through an underwriter or dealer, the issuer is responsible for delivering the Final Offering Circular as if the issuer were an underwriter;

(B) For continuous or delayed offerings pursuant to paragraph (d)(3) of this rule, the 90 calendar day period for dealers shall commence on the day of the first bona fide offering of securities under such offering statement;

(C) If the security is listed on a registered national securities exchange, no offering circular need be delivered by a dealer more than 25 calendar days after the later of the qualification date of the offering statement or the first date on which the security was bona fide offered to the public;

(D) No offering circular need be delivered by a dealer if the issuer is subject, immediately prior to the time of the filing of the offering statement, to the reporting requirements of Rule 257(b); and

(E) The Final Offering Circular delivery requirements set forth in paragraph (d)(2)(ii) of this rule may be satisfied by delivering a notice to the effect that the sale was made pursuant to a qualified offering statement that includes the uniform resource locator ("URL"), which, in the case of an electronic-only offering, must be an active hyperlink, where the Final Offering Circular, or the offering statement of which such Final Offering Circular is part, may be obtained on the Commission's Electronic Data Gathering, Analysis and Retrieval System ("EDGAR") and contact information sufficient to notify a purchaser where a request for a Final Offering Circular can be sent and received in response.

(3) *Continuous or delayed offerings.* (i) Continuous or delayed offerings may be made under this Regulation A, so long as the offering statement pertains only to:

(A) Securities that are to be offered or sold solely by or on behalf of a person or persons other than the issuer, a subsidiary of the issuer, or a person of which the issuer is a subsidiary;

(B) Securities that are to be offered and sold pursuant to a dividend or interest reinvestment plan or an employee benefit plan of the issuer;

(C) Securities that are to be issued upon the exercise of outstanding options, warrants, or rights;

(D) Securities that are to be issued upon conversion of other outstanding securities;

(E) Securities that are pledged as collateral; or

(F)   Securities the offering of which will be commenced within two calendar days after the qualification date, will be made on a continuous basis, may continue for a period in excess of 30 calendar days from the date of initial qualification, and will be offered in an amount that, at the time the offering statement is qualified, is reasonably expected to be offered and sold within two years from the initial qualification date. These securities may be offered and sold only if not more than three years have elapsed since the initial qualification date of the offering statement under which they are being offered and sold; provided, however, that if a new offering statement has been filed pursuant to this paragraph (d)(3)(i)(F), securities covered by the prior offering statement may continue to be offered and sold until the earlier of the qualification date of the new offering statement or 180 calendar days after the third anniversary of the initial qualification date of the prior offering statement. Before the end of such three-year period, an issuer may file a new offering statement covering the securities. The new offering statement must include all the information that would be required at that time in an offering statement relating to all offerings that it covers. Before the qualification date of the new offering statement, the issuer may include as part of such new offering statement any unsold securities covered by the earlier offering statement by identifying on the cover page of the new offering circular, or the latest amendment, the amount of such unsold securities being included. The offering of securities on the earlier offering statement will be deemed terminated as of the date of qualification of the new offering statement. Securities may be sold pursuant to this paragraph (d)(3)(i)(F) only if the issuer is current in its annual and semiannual filings pursuant to Rule 257(b), at the time of such sale.

(ii)   At the market offerings, by or on behalf of the issuer or otherwise, are not permitted under this Regulation A. As used in this paragraph (d)(3)(ii), the term *at the market offering* means an offering of equity securities into an existing trading market for outstanding shares of the same class at other than a fixed price.

(e)   *Confidential treatment.* A request for confidential treatment may be made under Rule 406 for information required to be filed, and Rule 83 for information not required to be filed.

(f)   *Electronic filing.* Documents filed or otherwise provided to the Commission pursuant to this Regulation A must be submitted in electronic format by means of EDGAR in accordance with the EDGAR rules set forth in Regulation S–T.

Rule 252.   Offering Statement

(a)   *Documents to be included.* The offering statement consists of the contents required by Form 1–A and any other material information necessary to make the required statements, in light of the circumstances under which they are made, not misleading.

(b)   *Paper, printing, language and pagination.* Except as otherwise specified in this rule, the requirements for offering statements are the same as those specified in Rule 403 for registration statements under the Act. No fee is payable to the Commission upon either the submission or filing of an offering statement on Form 1–A, or any amendment to an offering statement.

(c)   *Signatures.* The issuer, its principal executive officer, principal financial officer, principal accounting officer, and a majority of the members of its board of directors or other governing body, must sign the offering statement in the manner prescribed by Form 1–A. If a signature is by a person on behalf of any other person, evidence of authority to sign must be filed, except where an executive officer signs for the issuer.

(d)   *Non-public submission.* An issuer whose securities have not been previously sold pursuant to a qualified offering statement under this Regulation A or an effective registration statement under the Securities Act may submit a draft offering statement to the Commission for non-public review by the staff of the Commission before public filing, provided that the offering statement shall not be qualified less than 21 calendar days after the public filing with the Commission of:

(1)   The initial non-public submission;

(2)   All non-public amendments; and

(3) All non-public correspondence submitted by or on behalf of the issuer to the Commission staff regarding such submissions (subject to any separately approved confidential treatment request under Rule 251(e).

(e) *Qualification.* An offering statement and any amendment thereto can be qualified only at such date and time as the Commission may determine.

(f) *Amendments.* (1)(i) Amendments to an offering statement must be signed and filed with the Commission in the same manner as the initial filing. Amendments to an offering statement must be filed under cover of Form 1–A and must be numbered consecutively in the order in which filed.

(ii) Every amendment that includes amended audited financial statements must include the consent of the certifying accountant to the use of such accountant's certification in connection with the amended financial statements in the offering statement or offering circular and to being named as having audited such financial statements.

(iii) Amendments solely relating to Part III of Form 1–A must comply with the requirements of paragraph (f)(1)(i) of this rule, except that such amendments may be limited to Part I of Form 1–A, an explanatory note, and all of the information required by Part III of Form 1–A.

(2) Post-qualification amendments must be filed in the following circumstances for ongoing offerings:

(i) At least every 12 months after the qualification date to include the financial statements that would be required by Form 1–A as of such date; or

(ii) To reflect any facts or events arising after the qualification date of the offering statement (or the most recent post-qualification amendment thereof) which, individually or in the aggregate, represent a fundamental change in the information set forth in the offering statement.

Rule 253.   Offering Circular

(a) *Contents.* An offering circular must include the information required by Form 1–A for offering circulars.

(b) *Information that may be omitted.* Notwithstanding paragraph (a) of this rule, a qualified offering circular may omit information with respect to the public offering price, underwriting syndicate (including any material relationships between the issuer or selling securityholders and the unnamed underwriters, brokers or dealers), underwriting discounts or commissions, discounts or commissions to dealers, amount of proceeds, conversion rates, call prices and other items dependent upon the offering price, delivery dates, and terms of the securities dependent upon the offering date; provided, that the following conditions are met:

(1) The securities to be qualified are offered for cash.

(2) The outside front cover page of the offering circular includes a bona fide estimate of the range of the maximum offering price and the maximum number of shares or other units of securities to be offered or a bona fide estimate of the principal amount of debt securities offered, subject to the following conditions:

(i) The range must not exceed $2 for offerings where the upper end of the range is $10 or less or 20% if the upper end of the price range is over $10; and

(ii) The upper end of the range must be used in determining the aggregate offering price under Rule 251(a).

(3) The offering statement does not relate to securities to be offered by competitive bidding.

(4) The volume of securities (the number of equity securities or aggregate principal amount of debt securities) to be offered may not be omitted in reliance on this paragraph (b).

NOTE to paragraph (b). A decrease in the volume of securities offered or a change in the bona fide estimate of the offering price range from that indicated in the offering circular filed as part of a qualified offering statement may be disclosed in the offering circular filed with the Commission pursuant to Rule 253(g), so long as the decrease in the volume of securities offered or change in the price range would not materially change the disclosure contained in the offering statement at qualification. Notwithstanding the foregoing, any decrease in the volume of securities offered and any deviation from the low or high end of the price range may be reflected in the offering circular supplement filed with the Commission pursuant to Rule 253(g)(1) or (3) if, in the aggregate, the decrease in volume and/or change in price represent no more than a 20% change from the maximum aggregate offering price calculable using the information in the qualified offering statement. In no circumstances may this paragraph be used to offer securities where the maximum aggregate offering price would result in the offering exceeding the limit set forth in Rule 251(a) or if the change would result in a Tier 1 offering becoming a Tier 2 offering. An offering circular supplement may not be used to increase the volume of securities being offered. Additional securities may only be offered pursuant to a new offering statement or post-qualification amendment qualified by the Commission.

(c) *Filing of omitted information.* The information omitted from the offering circular in reliance upon paragraph (b) of this rule must be contained in an offering circular filed with the Commission pursuant to paragraph (g) of this rule; except that if such offering circular is not so filed by the later of 15 business days after the qualification date of the offering statement or 15 business days after the qualification of a post-qualification amendment thereto that contains an offering circular, the information omitted in reliance upon paragraph (b) of this rule must be contained in a qualified post-qualification amendment to the offering statement.

(d) *Presentation of information.* (1) Information in the offering circular must be presented in a clear, concise and understandable manner and in a type size that is easily readable. Repetition of information should be avoided; cross-referencing of information within the document is permitted.

(2)   Where an offering circular is distributed through an electronic medium, issuers may satisfy legibility requirements applicable to printed documents by presenting all required information in a format readily communicated to investors.

(e) *Date.* An offering circular must be dated approximately as of the date it was filed with the Commission.

(f) *Cover page legend.* The cover page of every offering circular must display the following statement highlighted by prominent type or in another manner:

The United States Securities and Exchange Commission does not pass upon the merits of or give its approval to any securities offered or the terms of the offering, nor does it pass upon the accuracy or completeness of any offering circular or other solicitation materials. These securities are offered pursuant to an exemption from registration with the Commission; however, the Commission has not made an independent determination that the securities offered are exempt from registration.

(g) *Offering circular supplements.* (1) An offering circular that discloses information previously omitted from the offering circular in reliance upon Rule 253(b) must be filed with the Commission no later than two business days following the earlier of the date of determination of the offering price or the date such offering circular is first used after qualification in connection with a public offering or sale.

(2)   An offering circular that reflects information other than that covered in paragraph (g)(1) of this rule that constitutes a substantive change from or addition to the information set forth in the last offering circular filed with the Commission must be filed with the Commission no later than five business days after the date it is first used after qualification in connection with a public offering or sale. If an offering circular filed pursuant to this paragraph (g)(2) consists of an offering circular supplement attached to an offering circular that previously had been filed or was not required to be filed pursuant to paragraph (g) of this rule because it did not contain substantive changes from an offering circular that previously was filed, only the offering circular supplement need be filed under paragraph (g) of this rule, provided that the cover page of the offering circular supplement identifies the date(s) of the related offering circular and any offering circular supplements thereto that together constitute the offering circular with respect to the securities currently being offered or sold.

(3)   An offering circular that discloses information, facts or events covered in both paragraphs (g)(1) and (2) of this rule must be filed with the Commission no later than two business days following the earlier of the date of the determination of the offering price or the date it is first used after qualification in connection with a public offering or sale.

(4)   An offering circular required to be filed pursuant to paragraph (g) of this rule that is not filed within the time frames specified in paragraphs (g)(1) through (3) of this rule, as applicable, must be filed pursuant to this paragraph (g)(4) as soon as practicable after the discovery of such failure to file.

(5)   Each offering circular filed under this rule must contain in the upper right corner of the cover page the paragraphs of paragraphs (g)(1) through (4) of this rule under which the filing is made, and the file number of the offering statement to which the offering circular relates.

Rule 254.   Preliminary Offering Circular

After the filing of an offering statement, but before its qualification, written offers of securities may be made if they meet the following requirements:

(a)   *Outside front cover page.* The outside front cover page of the material bears the caption *Preliminary Offering Circular,* the date of issuance, and the following legend, which must be highlighted by prominent type or in another manner:

An offering statement pursuant to Regulation A relating to these securities has been filed with the Securities and Exchange Commission. Information contained in this Preliminary Offering Circular is subject to completion or amendment. These securities may not be sold nor may offers to buy be accepted before the offering statement filed with the Commission is qualified. This Preliminary Offering Circular shall not constitute an offer to sell or the solicitation of an offer to buy nor may there be any sales of these securities in any state in which such offer, solicitation or sale would be unlawful before registration or qualification under the laws of any such state. We may elect to satisfy our obligation to deliver a Final Offering Circular by sending you a notice within two business days after the completion of our sale to you that contains the URL where the Final Offering Circular or the offering statement in which such Final Offering Circular was filed may be obtained.

(b)   *Other contents.* The Preliminary Offering Circular contains substantially the information required to be in an offering circular by Form 1–A, except that certain information may be omitted under Rule 253(b) subject to the conditions set forth in such rule.

(c)   *Filing.* The Preliminary Offering Circular is filed as a part of the offering statement.

Rule 255.   Solicitations of Interest and Other Communications

(a)   *Solicitation of interest.* At any time before the qualification of an offering statement, including before the non-public submission or public filing of such offering statement, an issuer or any person authorized to act on behalf of an issuer may communicate orally or in writing to determine whether there is any interest in a contemplated securities offering. Such communications are deemed to be an offer of a security for sale for purposes of the antifraud provisions of the federal securities laws. No solicitation or acceptance of money or other consideration, nor of any commitment, binding or otherwise, from any person is permitted until qualification of the offering statement.

(b)   *Conditions.* The communications must:

(1)   State that no money or other consideration is being solicited, and if sent in response, will not be accepted;

(2)   State that no offer to buy the securities can be accepted and no part of the purchase price can be received until the offering statement is qualified, and any such offer may be withdrawn or revoked, without obligation or commitment of any kind, at any time before notice of its acceptance given after the qualification date;

(3)   State that a person's indication of interest involves no obligation or commitment of any kind; and

(4)   After the public filing of the offering statement:

(i)   State from whom a copy of the most recent version of the Preliminary Offering Circular may be obtained, including a phone number and address of such person;

(ii)   Provide the URL where such Preliminary Offering Circular, or the offering statement in which such Preliminary Offering Circular was filed, may be obtained; or

(iii) Include a complete copy of the Preliminary Offering Circular.

(c)   *Indications of interest.* Any written communication under this rule may include a means by which a person may indicate to the issuer that such person is interested in a potential offering. This issuer may require the name, address, telephone number, and/or email address in any response form included pursuant to this paragraph (c).

(d)   *Revised solicitations of interest.* If solicitation of interest materials are used after the public filing of the offering statement and such solicitation of interest materials contain information that is inaccurate or inadequate in any material respect, revised solicitation of interest materials must be redistributed in a substantially similar manner as such materials were originally distributed. Notwithstanding the foregoing in this paragraph (d), if the only information that is inaccurate or inadequate is contained in a Preliminary Offering Circular provided with the solicitation of interest materials pursuant to paragraphs (b)(4)(i) or (ii) of this rule, no such redistribution is required in the following circumstances:

(1)   in the case of paragraph (b)(4)(i) of this rule, the revised Preliminary Offering Circular will be provided to any persons making new inquiries and will be recirculated to any persons making any previous inquiries; or

(2)   in the case of paragraph (b)(4)(ii) of this rule, the URL continues to link directly to the most recent Preliminary Offering Circular or to the offering statement in which such revised Preliminary Offering Circular was filed.

(e)   *Abandoned offerings.* Where an issuer decides to register an offering under the Securities Act after soliciting interest in a contemplated, but subsequently abandoned, Regulation A offering, the abandoned Regulation A offering would not be subject to integration with the registered offering if the issuer engaged in solicitations of interest pursuant to this rule only to qualified institutional buyers and institutional accredited investors permitted by Section 5(d) of the Securities Act. If the issuer engaged in solicitations of interest to persons other than qualified institutional buyers and institutional accredited investors, an abandoned Regulation A offering would not be subject to integration if the issuer (and any underwriter, broker, dealer, or agent used by the issuer in connection with the proposed offering) waits at least 30 calendar days between the last such solicitation of interest in the Regulation A offering and the filing of the registration statement with the Commission.

Rule 256.   Definition of "Qualified Purchaser"

For purposes of Section 18(b)(3) of the Securities Act, a "qualified purchaser" means any person to whom securities are offered or sold pursuant to a Tier 2 offering of this Regulation A.

Rule 257.   Periodic and Current Reporting; Exit Report

(a)   *Tier 1: Exit report.* Each issuer that has filed an offering statement for a Tier 1 offering that has been qualified pursuant to this Regulation A must file an exit report on Form 1–Z not later than 30 calendar days after the termination or completion of the offering.

(b)   *Tier 2: Periodic and current reporting.* Each issuer that has filed an offering statement for a Tier 2 offering that has been qualified pursuant to this Regulation A must file with the Commission the following periodic and current reports:

(1)   *Annual reports.* An annual report on Form 1–K for the fiscal year in which the offering statement became qualified and for any fiscal year thereafter, unless the issuer's obligation to file such annual report is suspended under paragraph (d) of this rule. Annual reports must be filed within the period specified in Form 1–K.

(2)   *Special financial report.* (i) A special financial report on Form 1–K or Form 1–SA if the offering statement did not contain the following:

(A)   Audited financial statements for the issuer's most recent fiscal year (or for the life of the issuer if less than a full fiscal year) preceding the fiscal year in which the issuer's offering statement became qualified; or

(B)   unaudited financial statements covering the first six months of the issuer's current fiscal year if the offering statement was qualified during the last six months of that fiscal year.

(ii)   The special financial report described in paragraph (b)(2)(i)(A) of this rule must be filed under cover of Form 1–K within 120 calendar days after the qualification date of the offering statement and must include audited financial statements for such fiscal year or other period specified in that paragraph, as the case may be. The special financial report described in paragraph (b)(2)(i)(B) of this rule must be filed under cover of Form 1–SA within 90 calendar days after the qualification date of the offering statement and must include the semiannual financial statements for the first six months of the issuer's fiscal year, which may be unaudited.

(iii)   A special financial report must be signed in accordance with the requirements of the form on which it is filed.

(3)   *Semiannual report.* A semiannual report on Form 1–SA within the period specified in Form 1–SA. Semiannual reports must cover the first six months of each fiscal year of the issuer, commencing with the first six months of the fiscal year immediately following the most recent fiscal year for which full financial statements were included in the offering statement, or, if the offering statement included financial statements for the first six months of the fiscal year following the most recent full fiscal year, for the first six months of the following fiscal year.

(4)   *Current reports.* Current reports on Form 1–U with respect to the matters and within the period specified in that form, unless substantially the same information has been previously reported to the Commission by the issuer under cover of Form 1–K or Form 1–SA.

(5)   *Reporting by successor issuers.* Where in connection with a succession by merger, consolidation, exchange of securities, acquisition of assets or otherwise, securities of any issuer that is not required to file reports pursuant to paragraph (b) of this rule are issued to the holders of any class of securities of another issuer that is required to file such reports, the duty to file reports pursuant to paragraph (b) of this rule shall be deemed to have been assumed by the issuer of the class of securities so issued. The successor issuer must, after the consummation of the succession, file reports in accordance with paragraph (b) of this rule, unless that issuer is exempt from filing such reports or the duty to file such reports is terminated or suspended under paragraph (d) of this rule.

(6)   *Exchange Act reporting requirements.* The duty to file reports under this rule shall be deemed to have been met if the issuer is subject to the reporting requirements of Section 13 or 15(d) of the Exchange Act and, as of each Form 1–K and Form 1–SA due date, has filed all reports required to be filed by Section 13 or 15(d) of the Exchange Act during the 12 months (or such shorter period that the registrant was required to file such reports) preceding such due date.

(c)   *Amendments.* All amendments to the reports described in paragraphs (a) and (b) of this rule must be filed under cover of the form amended, marked with the letter *A* to designate the document as an amendment, *e.g.,*"1–K/A," and in compliance with pertinent requirements applicable to such reports. Amendments filed pursuant to this paragraph (c) must set forth the complete text of each item as amended, but need not include any items that were not amended. Amendments must be numbered sequentially and be filed separately for each report amended. Amendments must be signed on behalf of the issuer by a duly authorized representative of the issuer. An amendment to any report required to include certifications as specified in the applicable form must include new certifications by the appropriate persons.

(d)   *Suspension of duty to file reports.* (1) [Reserved];

(2)   The duty to file reports under paragraph (b) of this rule with respect to a class of securities held of record (as defined in Rule 12g5–1 of the Securities Exchange Act of 1934) by less than 300 persons, or less than 1,200 persons for a bank (as defined in Section 3(a)(6) of the Exchange Act), or a bank holding company (as defined in section 2 of the Bank Holding Company Act of 1956, shall be suspended for such class of securities immediately upon filing with the Commission an exit report on

Form 1–Z if the issuer of such class has filed all reports due pursuant to this rule before the date of such Form 1–Z filing for the shorter of:

(i)   The period since the issuer became subject to such reporting obligation; or

(ii)   Its most recent three fiscal years and the portion of the current year preceding the date of filing Form 1–Z.

(3)   For the purposes of paragraph (d)(2) of this rule, the term *class* shall be construed to include all securities of an issuer that are of substantially similar character and the holders of which enjoy substantially similar rights and privileges. If the Form 1–Z is subsequently withdrawn or if it is denied because the issuer was ineligible to use the form, the issuer must, within 60 calendar days, file with the Commission all reports which would have been required if such exit report had not been filed. If the suspension resulted from the issuer's merger into, or consolidation with, another issuer or issuers, the notice must be filed by the successor issuer.

(4)   The ability to suspend reporting, as described in paragraph (d)(2) of this rule, is not available for any class of securities if:

(i)   During that fiscal year a Tier 2 offering statement was qualified;

(ii)   The issuer has not filed an annual report under this rule or the Exchange Act for the fiscal year in which a Tier 2 offering statement was qualified; or

(iii) Offers or sales of securities of that class are being made pursuant to a Tier 2 Regulation A offering.

(e)   *Termination of duty to file reports.* If the duty to file reports is deemed to have been met pursuant to paragraph (b)(6) of this rule and such status ends because the issuer terminates or suspends its duty to file reports under the Exchange Act, the issuer's obligation to file reports under paragraph (b) of this rule shall:

(1)   Automatically terminate if the issuer is eligible to suspend its duty to file reports under paragraphs (d)(2) and (3) of this rule; or

(2)   Recommence with the report covering the most recent financial period after that included in any effective registration statement or filed Exchange Act report.

Rule 258.   Suspension of the Exemption

(a)   *Suspension.* The Commission may at any time enter an order temporarily suspending a Regulation A exemption if it has reason to believe that:

(1)   No exemption is available or any of the terms, conditions or requirements of Regulation A have not been complied with;

(2)   The offering statement, any sales or solicitation of interest material, or any report filed pursuant to Rule 257 contains any untrue statement of a material fact or omits to state a material fact necessary in order to make the statements made, in light of the circumstances under which they are made, not misleading;

(3)   The offering is being made or would be made in violation of section 17 of the Securities Act;

(4)   An event has occurred after the filing of the offering statement that would have rendered the exemption hereunder unavailable if it had occurred before such filing;

(5)   Any person specified in Rule 262(a) has been indicted for any crime or offense of the character specified in Rule 262(a)(1), or any proceeding has been initiated for the purpose of enjoining any such person from engaging in or continuing any conduct or practice of the character specified in Rule 262(a)(2), or any proceeding has been initiated for the purposes of Rule 262(a)(3)–(8); or

(6)   The issuer or any promoter, officer, director, or underwriter has failed to cooperate, or has obstructed or refused to permit the making of an investigation by the Commission in connection with any offering made or proposed to be made in reliance on Regulation A.

(b) *Notice and hearing.* Upon the entry of an order under paragraph (a) of this rule, the Commission will promptly give notice to the issuer, any underwriter, and any selling securityholder:

(1) That such order has been entered, together with a brief statement of the reasons for the entry of the order; and

(2) That the Commission, upon receipt of a written request within 30 calendar days after the entry of the order, will, within 20 calendar days after receiving the request, order a hearing at a place to be designated by the Commission.

(c) *Suspension order.* If no hearing is requested and none is ordered by the Commission, an order entered under paragraph (a) of this rule shall become permanent on the 30th calendar day after its entry and shall remain in effect unless or until it is modified or vacated by the Commission. Where a hearing is requested or is ordered by the Commission, the Commission will, after notice of and opportunity for such hearing, either vacate the order or enter an order permanently suspending the exemption.

(d) *Permanent suspension.* The Commission may, at any time after notice of and opportunity for hearing, enter an order permanently suspending the exemption for any reason upon which it could have entered a temporary suspension order under paragraph (a) of this rule. Any such order shall remain in effect until vacated by the Commission.

(e) *Notice procedures.* All notices required by this rule must be given by personal service, registered or certified mail to the addresses given by the issuer, any underwriter and any selling securityholder in the offering statement.

Rule 259. Withdrawal or Abandonment of Offering Statements

(a) *Withdrawal.* If none of the securities that are the subject of an offering statement has been sold and such offering statement is not the subject of a proceeding under Rule 258, the offering statement may be withdrawn with the Commission's consent. The application for withdrawal must state the reason the offering statement is to be withdrawn and must be signed by an authorized representative of the issuer. Any withdrawn document will remain in the Commission's files, as well as the related request for withdrawal.

(b) *Abandonment.* When an offering statement, or a post-qualification amendment to such statement, has been on file with the Commission for nine months without amendment and has not become qualified, the Commission may, in its discretion, declare the offering statement or post-qualification amendment abandoned. If the offering statement has been amended, or if the post-qualification amendment has been amended, the nine-month period shall be computed from the date of the latest amendment.

Rule 260. Insignificant Deviations From a Term, Condition or Requirement of Regulation A

(a) *Failure to comply.* A failure to comply with a term, condition or requirement of Regulation A will not result in the loss of the exemption from the requirements of section 5 of the Securities Act for any offer or sale to a particular individual or entity, if the person relying on the exemption establishes that:

(1) The failure to comply did not pertain to a term, condition or requirement directly intended to protect that particular individual or entity;

(2) The failure to comply was insignificant with respect to the offering as a whole, provided that any failure to comply with Rule 251(a), (b), and (d)(1) and (3) shall be deemed to be significant to the offering as a whole; and

(3) A good faith and reasonable attempt was made to comply with all applicable terms, conditions and requirements of Regulation A.

(b) *Action by Commission.* A transaction made in reliance upon Regulation A must comply with all applicable terms, conditions and requirements of the regulation. Where an exemption is established only through reliance upon paragraph (a) of this rule, the failure to comply shall nonetheless be actionable by the Commission under section 20 of the Securities Act.

(c) *Suspension.* This provision provides no relief or protection from a proceeding under Rule 258.

Rule 261.   Definitions

As used in this Regulation A, all terms have the same meanings as in Rule 405, except that all references to *registrant* in those definitions shall refer to the issuer of the securities to be offered and sold under Regulation A. In addition, these terms have the following meanings:

(a) *Affiliated issuer.* An affiliate (as defined in Rule 501) of the issuer that is issuing securities in the same offering.

(b) *Business day.* Any day except Saturdays, Sundays or United States federal holidays.

(c) *Eligible securities.* Equity securities, debt securities, and securities convertible or exchangeable to equity interests, including any guarantees of such securities, but not including asset-backed securities as such term is defined in Item 1101(c) of Regulation AB.

(d) *Final order.* A written directive or declaratory statement issued by a federal or state agency described in Rule 262(a)(3) under applicable statutory authority that provides for notice and an opportunity for hearing, which constitutes a final disposition or action by that federal or state agency.

(e) *Final offering circular.* The more recent of: the current offering circular contained in a qualified offering statement; and any offering circular filed pursuant to Rule 253(g). If, however, the issuer is relying on Rule 253(b), the Final Offering Circular is the most recent of the offering circular filed pursuant to Rule 253(g)(1) or (3) and any subsequent offering circular filed pursuant to Rule 253(g).

(f) *Offering statement.* An offering statement prepared pursuant to Regulation A.

(g) *Preliminary offering circular.* The offering circular described in Rule 254.

Rule 262.   Disqualification Provisions

(a) *Disqualification events.* No exemption under §§ 230.251 through 230.263 (Regulation A) shall be available for a sale of securities if the issuer; any predecessor of the issuer; any affiliated issuer; any director, executive officer, other officer participating in the offering, general partner or managing member of the issuer; any beneficial owner of 20 percent or more of the issuer's outstanding voting equity securities, calculated on the basis of voting power; any promoter connected with the issuer in any capacity at the time of filing, any offer after qualification, or such sale; any person that has been or will be paid (directly or indirectly) remuneration for solicitation of purchasers in connection with such sale of securities; any general partner or managing member of any such solicitor; or any director, executive officer or other officer participating in the offering of any such solicitor or general partner or managing member of such solicitor:

(1) Has been convicted, within 10 years before the filing of the offering statement or such sale (or five years, in the case of issuers, their predecessors and affiliated issuers), of any felony or misdemeanor:

(i) In connection with the purchase or sale of any security;

(ii) Involving the making of any false filing with the Commission; or

(iii) Arising out of the conduct of the business of an underwriter, broker, dealer, municipal securities dealer, investment adviser or paid solicitor of purchasers of securities;

(2) Is subject to any order, judgment or decree of any court of competent jurisdiction, entered within five years before the filing of the offering statement or such sale that, at the time of such filing or such sale, restrains or enjoins such person from engaging or continuing to engage in any conduct or practice:

(i) In connection with the purchase or sale of any security;

(ii) Involving the making of any false filing with the Commission; or

(iii) Arising out of the conduct of the business of an underwriter, broker, dealer, municipal securities dealer, investment adviser or paid solicitor of purchasers of securities;

(3)   Is subject to a final order (as defined in § 230.261) of a State securities commission (or an agency or officer of a State performing like functions); a State authority that supervises or examines banks, savings associations, or credit unions; a State insurance commission (or an agency or officer of a State performing like functions); an appropriate Federal banking agency; the U.S. Commodity Futures Trading Commission; or the National Credit Union Administration that:

    (i)   At the time of the filing of the offering statement or such sale, bars the person from:

        (A)   Association with an entity regulated by such commission, authority, agency, or officer;

        (B)   Engaging in the business of securities, insurance or banking; or

        (C)   Engaging in savings association or credit union activities; or

    (ii)   Constitutes a final order based on a violation of any law or regulation that prohibits fraudulent, manipulative, or deceptive conduct entered within ten years before such filing of the offering statement or such sale;

(4)   Is subject to an order of the Commission entered pursuant to section 15(b) or 15B(c) of the Securities Exchange Act of 1934 or section 203(e) or (f) of the Investment Advisers Act of 1940 that, at the time of the filing of the offering statement or such sale:

    (i)   Suspends or revokes such person's registration as a broker, dealer, municipal securities dealer or investment adviser;

    (ii)   Places limitations on the activities, functions or operations of such person; or

    (iii)   Bars such person from being associated with any entity or from participating in the offering of any penny stock;

(5)   Is subject to any order of the Commission entered within five years before the filing of the offering statement or such sale that, at the time of such filing or sale, orders the person to cease and desist from committing or causing a violation or future violation of:

    (i)   Any scienter-based anti-fraud provision of the Federal securities laws, including without limitation section 17(a)(1) of the Securities Act of 1933, section 10(b) of the Securities Exchange Act of 1934 and Rule 10b–5, section 15(c)(1) of the Securities Exchange Act of 1934) and section 206(1) of the Investment Advisers Act of 1940, or any other rule or regulation thereunder; or

    (ii)   Section 5 of the Securities Act of 1933.

(6)   Is suspended or expelled from membership in, or suspended or barred from association with a member of, a registered national securities exchange or a registered national or affiliated securities association for any act or omission to act constituting conduct inconsistent with just and equitable principles of trade;

(7)   Has filed (as a registrant or issuer), or was or was named as an underwriter in, any registration statement or offering statement filed with the Commission that, within five years before the filing of the offering statement or such sale, was the subject of a refusal order, stop order, or order suspending the Regulation A exemption, or is, at the time of such filing or such sale, the subject of an investigation or proceeding to determine whether a stop order or suspension order should be issued; or

(8)   Is subject to a United States Postal Service false representation order entered within five years before the filing of the offering statement or such sale, or is, at the time of such filing or such sale, subject to a temporary restraining order or preliminary injunction with respect to conduct alleged by the United States Postal Service to constitute a scheme or device for obtaining money or property through the mail by means of false representations.

Instruction to paragraph (a): With respect to any beneficial owner of 20 percent or more of the issuer's outstanding voting equity securities, calculated on the basis of voting power, the issuer is required to determine whether a disqualifying event has occurred only as of the time of filing of the offering statement and not from the time of such sale.

(b)   *Transition, waivers, reasonable care exception.* Paragraph (a) of this rule shall not apply:

(1)   With respect to any order under Rule 262(a)(3) or (5) that occurred or was issued before June 19, 2015;

(2)   Upon a showing of good cause and without prejudice to any other action by the Commission, if the Commission determines that it is not necessary under the circumstances that an exemption be denied;

(3)   If, before the filing of the offering statement or the relevant sale, the court or regulatory authority that entered the relevant order, judgment or decree advises in writing (whether contained in the relevant judgment, order or decree or separately to the Commission or its staff) that disqualification under paragraph (a) of this section should not arise as a consequence of such order, judgment or decree; or

(4)   If the issuer establishes that it did not know and, in the exercise of reasonable care, could not have known that a disqualification existed under paragraph (a) of this rule.

NOTE to paragraph (b)(4). An issuer will not be able to establish that it has exercised reasonable care unless it has made, in light of the circumstances, factual inquiry into whether any disqualifications exist. The nature and scope of the factual inquiry will vary based on the facts and circumstances concerning, among other things, the issuer and the other offering participants.

(c)   *Affiliated issuers.* For purposes of paragraph (a) of this rule, events relating to any affiliated issuer that occurred before the affiliation arose will be not considered disqualifying if the affiliated entity is not:

(1)   In control of the issuer; or

(2)   Under common control with the issuer by a third party that was in control of the affiliated entity at the time of such events.

(d)   *Disclosure of prior "bad actor" events.* The issuer must include in the offering circular a description of any matters that would have triggered disqualification under paragraphs (a)(3) and (5) of this rule but occurred before June 19, 2015. The failure to provide such information shall not prevent an issuer from relying on Regulation A if the issuer establishes that it did not know and, in the exercise of reasonable care, could not have known of the existence of the undisclosed matter or matters.

Rule 263.   Consent to Service of Process

(a)   If the issuer is not organized under the laws of any of the states or territories of the United States of America, it shall furnish to the Commission a written irrevocable consent and power of attorney on Form F–X at the time of filing the offering statement required by Rule 252.

(b)   Any change to the name or address of the agent for service of the issuer shall be communicated promptly to the Commission through amendment of the requisite form and referencing the file number of the relevant offering statement.

REGULATION C—REGISTRATION

Rule 400.   Application of Rules 400 to 494, Inclusive

Rules 400 to 494 shall govern every registration of securities under the Act, except that any provision in a form, or an item of Regulation S–K referred to in such form, covering the same subject matter as any such rule shall be controlling unless otherwise specifically provided in Rules 400 to 494.

GENERAL REQUIREMENTS

Rule 401.   Requirements as to Proper Form

(a)   The form and contents of a registration statement and prospectus shall conform to the applicable rules and forms as in effect on the initial filing date of such registration statement and prospectus.

(b) If an amendment to a registration statement and prospectus is filed for the purpose of meeting the requirements of section 10(a)(3) of the Act or pursuant to the provisions of section 24(e) or 24(f) of the Investment Company Act of 1940, the form and contents of such an amendment shall conform to the applicable rules and forms as in effect on the filing date of such amendment.

(c) An amendment to a registration statement and prospectus, other than an amendment described in paragraph (b) of this rule, may be filed on any shorter Securities Act registration form for which it is eligible on the filing date of the amendment. At the issuer's option, the amendment also may be filed on the same Securities Act registration form used for the most recent amendment described in paragraph (b) of this rule or, if no such amendment has been filed, the initial registration statement and prospectus.

(d) The form and contents of a prospectus forming part of a registration statement which is the subject of a stop order entered under section 8(d) of the Act, if used after the date such stop order ceases to be effective, shall conform to the applicable rules and forms as in effect on the date such stop order ceases to be effective.

(e) A prospectus filed as part of an amendment to an effective registration statement, or other amendment to such registration statement, on any form may be prepared in accordance with the requirements of any other form which would then be appropriate for the registration of securities to which the prospectus or other amendment relates, provided that all of the other requirements of such other form and applicable rules (including any required undertakings) are met.

(f) Notwithstanding the provisions of this rule, a registrant (1) shall comply with the rules and forms as in effect at a date different from those specified in paragraphs (a), (b), (c) and (d) of this rule if the rules or forms or amendments thereto specifically so provide; and (2) may comply voluntarily with the rules and forms as in effect at dates subsequent to those specified in paragraphs (a), (b), (c) and (d) of this rule, provided that all of the requirements of the particular rules and forms in effect at such dates (including any required undertakings) are met.

(g)(1) Subject to paragraphs (g)(2), (g)(3), and (g)(4) of this rule, except for registration statements and post-effective amendments that become effective immediately pursuant to Rule 462 and Rule 464, a registration statement or any amendment thereto is deemed filed on the proper registration form unless the Commission objects to the registration form before the effective date.

(2) An automatic shelf registration statement as defined in Rule 405 and any post-effective amendment thereto are deemed filed on the proper registration form unless and until the Commission notifies the issuer of its objection to the use of such form. Following any such notification, the issuer must amend its automatic shelf registration statement onto the registration form it is then eligible to use, provided, however, that any continuous offering of securities pursuant to Rule 415 that the issuer has commenced pursuant to the registration statement before the Commission has notified the issuer of its objection to the use of such form may continue until the effective date of a new registration statement or post-effective amendment to the registration statement that the issuer has filed on the proper registration form, if the issuer files promptly after notification the new registration statement or post-effective amendment and if the offering is permitted to be made under the new registration statement or post-effective amendment.

(3) Violations of General Instruction I.B.6. of Form S–3 or General Instruction I.B.5. of Form F–3 will also violate the requirements as to proper form under this rule notwithstanding that the registration statement may have been declared effective previously.

(4) Notwithstanding that the registration statement may have become effective previously, requirements as to proper form under this rule will have been violated for any offering of securities where the requirements of General Instruction I.A. of Form SF–3 have not been met as of ninety days after the end of the depositor's fiscal year end prior to such offering.

Rule 402.   Number of Copies; Binding; Signatures

(a) Three copies of the complete registration statement, including exhibits and all other papers and documents filed as a part of the statement, shall be filed with the Commission. Each copy shall be bound, in one or more parts, without stiff covers. The binding shall be made on the side or stitching margin in such manner as to leave the reading matter legible. At least one such copy of every registration shall be signed by the persons specified in section 6(a) of the Act. Unsigned copies shall be conformed.

(b)   Ten additional copies of the registration statement, similarly bound, shall be furnished for use in the examination of the registration statement, public inspection, copying and other purposes. Where a registration statement incorporates into the prospectus documents which are required to be delivered with the prospectus in lieu of prospectus presentation, the ten additional copies of the registration statement shall be accompanied by ten copies of such documents. No other exhibits are required to accompany such additional copies.

(c)   Notwithstanding any other provision of this rule, if a registration statement is filed on Form S-8, three copies of the complete registration statement, including exhibits and all other papers and documents filed as a part of the statement, shall be filed with the Commission. Each copy shall be bound, in one or more parts, without stiff covers. The binding shall be made on the side or stitching margin in such manner as to leave the reading matter legible. At least one such copy shall be signed by the persons specified in section 6(a) of the Act. Unsigned copies shall be conformed. Three additional copies of the registration statement, similarly bound, also shall be furnished to the Commission for use in the examination of the registration statement, public inspection, copying and other purposes. No exhibits are required to accompany the additional copies of registration statements filed on Form S-8.

(d)   Notwithstanding any other provision of this rule, if a registration statement is filed pursuant to Rule 462(b) and Rule 110(d), one copy of the complete registration statement, including exhibits and all other papers and documents filed as a part thereof shall be filed with the Commission. Such copy should not be bound and may contain facsimile versions of manual signatures in accordance with paragraph (e) of this rule.

(e)   *Signatures.* Where the Act or the rules thereunder, including paragraphs (a) and (c) of this rule, require a document filed with or furnished to the Commission to be signed, such document shall be manually signed, or signed using either typed signatures or duplicated or facsimile versions of manual signatures. Where typed, duplicated or facsimile signatures are used, each signatory to the filing shall manually sign a signature page or other document authenticating, acknowledging or otherwise adopting his or her signature that appears in the filing. Such document shall be executed before or at the time the filing is made and shall be retained by the registrant for a period of five years. Upon request, the registrant shall furnish to the Commission or its staff a copy of any or all documents retained pursuant to this rule.

Rule 403.   Requirements as to Paper, Printing, Language and Pagination

(a)   Registration statements, applications and reports shall be filed on good quality, unglazed, white paper no larger than $8^{1}/_{2} \times 11$ inches in size, insofar as practicable. To the extent that the reduction of larger documents would render them illegible, such documents may be filed on paper larger than $8^{1}/_{2} \times 11$ inches in size.

(b)   The registration statement and, insofar as practicable, all papers and documents filed as a part thereof shall be printed, lithographed, mimeographed or typewritten. However, the statement or any portion thereof may be prepared by any similar process which, in the opinion of the Commission, produces copies suitable for a permanent record. Irrespective of the process used, all copies of any such material shall be clear, easily readable and suitable for repeated photocopying. Debits in credit categories and credits in debit categories shall be designated so as to be clearly distinguishable as such on photocopies.

(c)(1)   All Securities Act filings and submissions must be in the English language, except as otherwise provided by this rule. If a registration statement or other filing requires the inclusion of a document that is in a foreign language, the filer must submit instead a fair and accurate English translation of the entire foreign language document, except as provided by paragraph (c)(3) of this rule.

(2)   If a registration statement or other filing or submission subject to review by the Division of Corporation Finance requires the inclusion of a foreign language document as an exhibit or attachment, the filer must submit a fair and accurate English translation of the foreign language document if consisting of any of the following, or an amendment of any of the following:

(i) Articles of incorporation, memoranda of association, bylaws, and other comparable documents, whether original or restated;

(ii) Instruments defining the rights of security holders, including indentures qualified or to be qualified under the Trust Indenture Act of 1939;

(iii) Voting agreements, including voting trust agreements;

(iv) Contracts to which directors, officers, promoters, voting trustees or security holders named in a registration statement are parties;

(v) Contracts upon which a filer's business is substantially dependent;

(vi) Audited annual and interim consolidated financial information; and

(vii) Any document that is or will be the subject of a confidential treatment request under Rule 406 of this Act or Rule 24b–2 under the Securities Exchange Act of 1934.

(3)(i) A filer may submit an English summary instead of an English translation of a foreign language document as an exhibit or attachment to a filing subject to review by the Division of Corporation Finance as long as:

(A) The foreign language document does not consist of any of the subject matter enumerated in paragraph (c)(2) of this rule; or

(B) The applicable form permits the use of an English summary.

(ii) Any English summary submitted under paragraph (c)(3) of this rule must:

(A) Fairly and accurately summarize the terms of each material provision of the foreign language document; and

(B) Fairly and accurately describe the terms that have been omitted or abridged.

(4) When submitting an English summary or English translation of a foreign language document under this rule, a filer must identify the submission as either an English summary or an English translation. A filer may submit a copy of the unabridged foreign language document when including an English summary or English translation of a foreign language document in a filing. A filer must provide a copy of any foreign language document upon the request of Commission staff.

(5) A Canadian issuer may file an exhibit or other part of a registration statement on Form F–7, F–8, F–9, F–10, or F–80, that contains text in both French and English if the issuer included the French text to comply with the requirements of the Canadian securities administrator or other Canadian authority and, for an electronic filing, if the filing is an HTML document, as defined in Regulation S–T Rule 11.

(d) The manually signed original (or in the case of duplicate originals, one duplicate original) of all registrations, applications, statements, reports or other documents filed under the Act shall be numbered sequentially (in addition to any internal numbering which otherwise may be present) by handwritten, typed, printed or other legible form of notation from the first page of the document through the last page of that document and any exhibits or attachments thereto. Further, the total number of pages contained in a numbered original shall be set forth on the first page of the document.

Rule 404.   Preparation of Registration Statement

(a) A registration statement shall consist of the facing sheet of the applicable form; a prospectus containing the information called for by Part I of such form; the information, list of exhibits, undertakings and signatures required to be set forth in Part II of such form; financial statements and schedules; exhibits; any other information or documents filed as part of the registration statement; and all documents or information incorporated by reference in the foregoing (whether or not required to be filed).

(b) All general instructions, instructions to items of the form, and instructions as to financial statements, exhibits, or prospectuses are to be omitted from the registration statement in all cases.

(c)   The prospectus shall contain the information called for by all of the items of Part I of the applicable form, except that unless otherwise specified, no reference need be made to inapplicable items, and negative answers to any item in Part I may be omitted. A copy of the prospectus may be filed as a part of the registration statement in lieu of furnishing the information in item-and-answer form. Wherever a copy of the prospectus is filed in lieu of information in item-and-answer form, the text of the items of the form is to be omitted from the registration statement, as well as from the prospectus, except to the extent provided in paragraph (d) of this rule.

(d)   Where any items of a form call for information not required to be included in the prospectus, generally Part II of such form, the text of such items, including the numbers and captions thereof, together with the answers thereto shall be filed with the prospectus under cover of the facing sheet of the form as a part of the registration statement. However, the text of such items may be omitted provided the answers are so prepared as to indicate the coverage of the item without the necessity of reference to the text of the item. If any such item is inapplicable, or the answer thereto is in the negative, a statement to that effect shall be made. Any financial statements not required to be included in the prospectus shall also be filed as a part of the registration statement proper, unless incorporated by reference pursuant to Rule 411.

Rule 405.   Definitions of Terms

Unless the context otherwise requires, all terms used in Rules 400 to 494, inclusive, or in the forms for registration have the same meanings as in the Act and in the general rules and regulations. In addition, the following definitions apply, unless the context otherwise requires:

Affiliate. An "affiliate" of, or person "affiliated" with, a specified person, is a person that directly, or indirectly through one or more intermediaries, controls or is controlled by, or is under common control with, the person specified.

Amount. The term "amount," when used in regard to securities, means the principal amount if relating to evidences of indebtedness, the number of shares if relating to shares, and the number of units if relating to any other kind of security.

Associate. The term "associate," when used to indicate a relationship with any person, means (1) a corporation or organization (other than the registrant or a majority-owned subsidiary of the registrant) of which such person is an officer or partner or is, directly or indirectly, the beneficial owner of 10 percent or more of any class of equity securities, (2) any trust or other estate in which such person has a substantial beneficial interest or as to which such person serves as trustee or in a similar capacity, and (3) any relative or spouse of such person, or any relative of such spouse, who has the same home as such person or who is a director or officer of the registrant or any of its parents or subsidiaries.

Automatic shelf registration statement. The term automatic shelf registration statement means a registration statement filed on Form S-3, Form F-3, or Form N-2 by a well-known seasoned issuer pursuant to General Instruction I.D. of Form S-3, General Instruction I.C. of Form F-3, or General Instruction B of Form N-2.

Business combination related shell company. The term business combination related shell company means a shell company (as defined in Rule 405) that is:

(1)   Formed by an entity that is not a shell company solely for the purpose of changing the corporate domicile of that entity solely within the United States; or

(2)   Formed by an entity that is not a shell company solely for the purpose of completing a business combination transaction (as defined in Rule 165(f)) among one or more entities other than the shell company, none of which is a shell company.

Business development company. The term "business development company" refers to a company which has elected to be regulated as a business development company under sections 55 through 65 of the Investment Company Act of 1940.

Certified. The term "certified," when used in regard to financial statements, means examined and reported upon with an opinion expressed by an independent public or certified public accountant.

Charter. The term "charter" includes articles of incorporation, declarations of trust, articles of association or partnership, or any similar instrument, as amended, affecting (either with or without filing with any governmental agency) the organization or creation of an incorporated or unincorporated person.

Common equity. The term "common equity" means any class of common stock or an equivalent interest, including but not limited to a unit of beneficial interest in a trust or a limited partnership interest.

Commission. The term "Commission" means the Securities and Exchange Commission.

Control. The term "control" (including the terms "controlling," "controlled by" and "under common control with") means the possession, direct or indirect, of the power to direct or cause the direction of the management and policies of a person, whether through the ownership of voting securities, by contract, or otherwise.

Depositary share. The term "depositary share" means a security, evidenced by an American Depositary Receipt, that represents a foreign security or a multiple of or fraction thereof deposited with a depositary.

Director. The term "director" means any director of a corporation or any person performing similar functions with respect to any organization whether incorporated or unincorporated.

Dividend or interest reinvestment plan. The term "dividend or interest reinvestment plan" means a plan which is offered solely to the existing security holders of the registrant, which allows such persons to reinvest dividends or interest paid to them on securities issued by the registrant, and also may allow additional cash amounts to be contributed by the participants in the plan, provided the securities to be registered are newly issued, or are purchased for the account of plan participants, at prices not in excess of current market prices at the time of purchase, or at prices not in excess of an amount determined in accordance with a pricing formula specified in the plan and based upon average or current market prices at the time of purchase.

Electronic filer. The term "electronic filer" means a person or an entity that submits filings electronically pursuant to Rules 100 and 101 of Regulation S–T.

Electronic filing. The term "electronic filing" means a document under the federal securities laws that is transmitted or delivered to the Commission in electronic format.

Emerging Growth Company. (1) The term *emerging growth company* means an issuer that had total annual gross revenues of less than $1,070,000,000 during its most recently completed fiscal year.

(2)   An issuer that is an emerging growth company as of the first day of that fiscal year shall continue to be deemed an emerging growth company until the earliest of:

    (i)   the last day of the fiscal year of the issuer during which it had total annual gross revenues of $1,070,000,000 or more;

    (ii)   the last day of the fiscal year of the issuer following the fifth anniversary of the date of the first sale of common equity securities of the issuer pursuant to an effective registration statement under the Securities Act of 1933;

    (iii)   the date on which such issuer has, during the previous three year period, issued more than $1,000,000,000 in non-convertible debt; or

    (iv)   the date on which such issuer is deemed to be a large accelerated filer, as defined in Rule 12b–2 of the Exchange Act, or any successor thereto.

Employee. The term "employee" does not include a director, trustee, or officer.

Employee benefit plan. The term "employee benefit plan" means any written purchase, savings, option, bonus, appreciation, profit sharing, thrift, incentive, pension or similar plan or written compensation contract solely for employees, directors, general partners, trustees (where the registrant is a business trust), officers, or consultants or advisors. However, consultants or advisors may participate in an employee benefit plan only if:

    (1)   They are natural persons;

    (2)   They provide bona fide services to the registrant; and

(3) The services are not in connection with the offer or sale of securities in a capital-raising transaction, and do not directly or indirectly promote or maintain a market for the registrant's securities.

Equity security. The term "equity security" means any stock or similar security, certificate of interest or participation in any profit sharing agreement, preorganization certificate or subscription, transferable share, voting trust certificate or certificate of deposit for an equity security, limited partnership interest, interest in a joint venture, or certificate of interest in a business trust; any security future on any such security; or any security convertible, with or without consideration into such a security, or carrying any warrant or right to subscribe to or purchase such a security; or any such warrant or right; or any put, call, straddle, or other option or privilege of buying such a security from or selling such a security to another without being bound to do so.

Executive officer. The term "executive officer," when used with reference to a registrant, means its president, any vice president of the registrant in charge of a principal business unit, division or function (such as sales, administration or finance), any other officer who performs a policy making function or any other person who performs similar policy making functions for the registrant. Executive officers of subsidiaries may be deemed executive officers of the registrant if they perform such policy making functions for the registrant.

Exchange-traded vehicle security. The term "exchange-traded vehicle security" means a security (A) of an issuer (i) that is not a registered investment company under the Investment Company Act of 1940 and (ii) the assets of which consist primarily of commodities, currencies, or derivative instruments that reference commodities or currencies, or interests in the foregoing, (B) offered or sold in a registered offering on a continuous basis pursuant to Rule 415 by or on behalf of the issuer, (C) of a class of securities that is listed for trading on a national securities exchange at or immediately after the time of effectiveness of the registration statement, and (D) which is able to be purchased or redeemed, subject to conditions or limitations as described in the registration statement for the offering of such security, by the issuer for a ratable share of the issuer's assets (or the cash equivalent thereof) at their net asset value each business day.

Fiscal year. The term "fiscal year" means the annual accounting period or, if no closing date has been adopted, the calendar year ending on December 31.

Foreign government. The term "foreign government" means the government of any foreign country or of any political subdivision of a foreign country.

Foreign issuer. The term "foreign issuer" means any issuer which is a foreign government, a national of any foreign country or a corporation or other organization incorporated or organized under the laws of any foreign country.

Foreign private issuer. (1) The term foreign private issuer means any foreign issuer other than a foreign government except an issuer meeting the following conditions as of the last business day of its most recently completed second fiscal quarter:

(i) More than 50 percent of the outstanding voting securities of such issuer are directly or indirectly owned of record by residents of the United States; and

(ii) Any of the following:

(A) The majority of the executive officers or directors are United States citizens or residents;

(B) More than 50 percent of the assets of the issuer are located in the United States; or

(C) The business of the issuer is administered principally in the United States.

(2) In the case of a new registrant with the Commission, the determination of whether an issuer is a foreign private issuer shall be made as of a date within 30 days prior to the issuer's filing of an initial registration statement under either the Act or the Securities Exchange Act of 1934.

(3) Once an issuer qualifies as a foreign private issuer, it will immediately be able to use the forms and rules designated for foreign private issuers until it fails to qualify for this status at the end of its most

recently completed second fiscal quarter. An issuer's determination that it fails to qualify as a foreign private issuer governs its eligibility to use the forms and rules designated for foreign private issuers beginning on the first day of the fiscal year following the determination date. Once an issuer fails to qualify for foreign private issuer status, it will remain unqualified unless it meets the requirements for foreign private issuer status as of the last business day of its second fiscal quarter.

Note to paragraph (1) of the definition of *Foreign private issuer:* To determine the percentage of outstanding voting securities held by U.S. residents:

A.   Use the method of calculating record ownership in § 240.12g3–2(a) of this chapter, except that:

(1)   The inquiry as to the amount of shares represented by accounts of customers resident in the United States may be limited to brokers, dealers, banks and other nominees located in:

(i)   The United States,

(ii)   The issuer's jurisdiction of incorporation, and

(iii)   The jurisdiction that is the primary trading market for the issuer's voting securities, if different than the issuer's jurisdiction of incorporation; and

(2)   Notwithstanding § 240.12g5–1(a)(8) of this chapter, the issuer shall not exclude securities held by persons who received the securities pursuant to an employee compensation plan.

B.   If, after reasonable inquiry, the issuer is unable to obtain information about the amount of shares represented by accounts of customers resident in the United States, the issuer may assume, for purposes of this definition, that the customers are residents of the jurisdiction in which the nominee has its principal place of business.

C.   Count shares of voting securities beneficially owned by residents of the United States as reported on reports of beneficial ownership provided to the issuer or filed publicly and based on information otherwise provided to the issuer.

Free writing prospectus. Except as otherwise specifically provided or the context otherwise requires, a free writing prospectus is any written communication as defined in this rule that constitutes an offer to sell or a solicitation of an offer to buy the securities relating to a registered offering that is used after the registration statement in respect of the offering is filed (or, in the case of a well-known seasoned issuer, whether or not such registration statement is filed) and is made by means other than:

(1)   A prospectus satisfying the requirements of section 10(a) of the Act, Rule 430, Rule 430A, Rule 430B, Rule 430C, Rule 430D, or Rule 431;

(2)   A written communication used in reliance on Rule 167 and Rule 426

(3)   A written communication that constitutes an offer to sell or solicitation of an offer to buy such securities that falls within the exception from the definition of prospectus in clause (a) of section 2(a)(10) of the Act; or

(4)   A written communication used in reliance on Rule 163B or on section 5(d) of the Act.

Graphic communication. The term graphic communication, which appears in the definition of "write, written" in section 2(a)(9) of the Act and in the definition of written communication in this rule, shall include all forms of electronic media, including, but not limited to, audiotapes, videotapes, facsimiles, CD-ROM, electronic mail, Internet Web sites, substantially similar messages widely distributed (rather than individually distributed) on telephone answering or voice mail systems, computers, computer networks and other forms of computer data compilation. Graphic communication shall not include a communication that, at the time of the communication, originates live, in real-time to a live audience and does not originate in recorded form or otherwise as a graphic communication, although it is transmitted through graphic means.

Ineligible issuer. (1) An ineligible issuer is an issuer with respect to which any of the following is true as of the relevant date of determination:

(i)   Any issuer that is required to file reports pursuant to section 13 or 15(d) of the Securities Exchange Act of 1934 or section 30 of the Investment Company Act of 1940 that has not filed all reports and other materials required to be filed during the preceding 12 months (or for such shorter period that the issuer was required to file such reports pursuant to sections 13 or 15(d) of the Securities

Exchange Act of 1934 or section 30 of the Investment Company Act of 1940), other than reports on Form 8–K required solely pursuant to an item specified in General Instruction I.A.3(b) of Form S–3) or General Instruction A.2.a of Form N–2 (or in the case of an asset-backed issuer, to the extent the depositor or any issuing entity previously established, directly or indirectly, by the depositor,(as such terms are defined in Item 1101 of Regulation AB are or were at any time during the preceding 12 calendar months required to file reports pursuant to section 13 or 15(d) of the Securities Exchange Act of 1934 with respect to a class of assetbacked securities involving the same asset class, such depositor and each such issuing entity must have filed all reports and other material required to be filed for such period (or such shorter period that each such entity was required to file such reports), other than reports on Form 8–K required solely pursuant to an item specified in General Instruction I.A.2 of Form SF–3);

(ii)   The issuer is, or during the past three years the issuer or any of its predecessors was:

(A)   A blank check company as defined in Rule 419(a)(2);

(B)   A shell company, other than a business combination related shell company, each as defined in this rule;

(C)   An issuer in an offering of penny stock as defined in Rule 3a51–1 of the Securities Exchange Act of 1934;

(iii)   The issuer is a limited partnership that is offering and selling its securities other than through a firm commitment underwriting;

(iv)   Within the past three years, a petition under the federal bankruptcy laws or any state insolvency law was filed by or against the issuer, or a court appointed a receiver, fiscal agent or similar officer with respect to the business or property of the issuer subject to the following:

(A)   In the case of an involuntary bankruptcy in which a petition was filed against the issuer, ineligibility will occur upon the earlier to occur of:

(1)   90 days following the date of the filing of the involuntary petition (if the case has not been earlier dismissed); or

(2)   The conversion of the case to a voluntary proceeding under federal bankruptcy or state insolvency laws; and

(B)   Ineligibility will terminate under this paragraph (1)(iv) if an issuer has filed an annual report with audited financial statements subsequent to its emergence from that bankruptcy, insolvency, or receivership process;

(v)   Within the past three years, the issuer or any entity that at the time was a subsidiary of the issuer was convicted of any felony or misdemeanor described in paragraphs (i) through (iv) of section 15(b)(4)(B) of the Securities Exchange Act of 1934;

(vi)   Within the past three years (but in the case of a decree or order agreed to in a settlement, not before December 1, 2005), the issuer or any entity that at the time was a subsidiary of the issuer was made the subject of any judicial or administrative decree or order arising out of a governmental action that:

(A)   Prohibits certain conduct or activities regarding, including future violations of, the anti-fraud provisions of the federal securities laws;

(B)   Requires that the person cease and desist from violating the anti-fraud provisions of the federal securities laws; or

(C)   Determines that the person violated the anti-fraud provisions of the federal securities laws;

(vii)   The issuer has filed a registration statement that is the subject of any pending proceeding or examination under section 8 of the Act or has been the subject of any refusal order or stop order under section 8 of the Act within the past three years; or

(viii) The issuer is the subject of any pending proceeding under section 8A of the Act in connection with an offering.

(ix) In the case of an issuer that is a registered closed-end investment company or a business development company, within the past three years any person or entity that at the time was an investment adviser to the issuer, including any sub-adviser, was made the subject of any judicial or administrative decree or order arising out of a governmental action that determines that the investment adviser aided, abetted or caused the issuer to have violated the anti-fraud provisions of the federal securities laws.

(2) An issuer shall not be an ineligible issuer if the Commission determines, upon a showing of good cause, that it is not necessary under the circumstances that the issuer be considered an ineligible issuer. Any such determination shall be without prejudice to any other action by the Commission in any other proceeding or matter with respect to the issuer or any other person.

(3) The date of determination of whether an issuer is an ineligible issuer is as follows:

(i) For purposes of determining whether an issuer is a well-known seasoned issuer, at the date specified for purposes of such determination in paragraph (2) of the definition of well-known seasoned issuer in this rule; and

(ii) For purposes of determining whether an issuer or offering participant may use free writing prospectuses in respect of an offering in accordance with the provisions of Rules 164 and 433, at the date in respect of the offering specified in paragraph (h) of Rule 164.

Majority-owned subsidiary. The term "majority-owned subsidiary" means a subsidiary more than 50 percent of whose outstanding securities representing the right, other than as affected by events of default, to vote for the election of directors, is owned by the subsidiary's parent and/or one or more of the parent's other majority-owned subsidiaries.

Material. The term "material," when used to qualify a requirement for the furnishing of information as to any subject, limits the information required to those matters to which there is a substantial likelihood that a reasonable investor would attach importance in determining whether to purchase the security registered.

Officer. The term "officer" means a president, vice president, secretary, treasurer or principal financial officer, comptroller or principal accounting officer, and any person routinely performing corresponding functions with respect to any organization whether incorporated or unincorporated.

Parent. A "parent" of a specified person is an affiliate controlling such person directly, or indirectly through one or more intermediaries.

Predecessor. The term "predecessor" means a person the major portion of the business and assets of which another person acquired in a single succession, or in a series of related successions in each of which the acquiring person acquired the major portion of the business and assets of the acquired person.

Principal underwriter. The term "principal underwriter" means an underwriter in privity of contract with the issuer of the securities as to which he is underwriter, the term "issuer" having the meaning given in sections 2(4) and 2(11) of the Act.

Promoter. (1) The term "promoter" includes:

(i) Any person who, acting alone or in conjunction with one or more other persons, directly or indirectly takes initiative in founding and organizing the business or enterprise of an issuer; or

(ii) Any person who, in connection with the founding and organizing of the business or enterprise of an issuer, directly or indirectly receives in consideration of services or property, or both services and property, 10 percent or more of any class of securities of the issuer or 10 percent or more of the proceeds from the sale of any class of such securities. However, a person who receives such securities or proceeds either solely as underwriting commissions or solely in consideration of property shall not be deemed a promoter within the meaning of this paragraph if such person does not otherwise take part in founding and organizing the enterprise.

(2)   All persons coming within the definition of "promoter" in paragraph (1) of this definition may be referred to as "founders" or "organizers" or by another term provided that such term is reasonably descriptive of those persons' activities with respect to the issuer.

Prospectus. Unless otherwise specified or the context otherwise requires, the term "prospectus" means a prospectus meeting the requirements of section 10(a) of the Act.

Registered closed-end investment company. The term registered closed-end investment company means a closed-end company, as defined in section 5(a)(2) of the Investment Company Act of 1940, that is registered under the Investment Company Act.

Registrant. The term "registrant" means the issuer of the securities for which the registration statement is filed.

Share. The term "share" means a share of stock in a corporation or unit of interest in an unincorporated person.

Shell company. The term shell company means a registrant, other than an asset-backed issuer as defined in Item 1101(b) of Regulation AB, that has:

(1)   No or nominal operations; and

(2)   Either:

(i)   No or nominal assets;

(ii)   Assets consisting solely of cash and cash equivalents; or

(iii)   Assets consisting of any amount of cash and cash equivalents and nominal other assets.

Note: For purposes of this definition, the determination of a registrant's assets (including cash and cash equivalents) is based solely on the amount of assets that would be reflected on the registrant's balance sheet prepared in accordance with generally accepted accounting principles on the date of that determination.

Significant subsidiary. The term "significant subsidiary" means a subsidiary, including its subsidiaries, which meets any of the following conditions.

(1)   The registrant's and its other subsidiaries' investments in and advances to the subsidiary exceed 10 percent of the total assets of the registrant and its subsidiaries consolidated as of the end of the most recently completed fiscal year (for a proposed combination between entities under common control, this condition is also met when the number of common shares exchanged or to be exchanged by the registrant exceeds 10 percent of its total common shares outstanding at the date the combination is initiated); or

(2)   The registrant's and its other subsidiaries' proportionate share of the total assets (after intercompany eliminations) of the subsidiary exceeds 10 percent of the total assets of the registrants and its subsidiaries consolidated as of the end of the most recently completed fiscal year; or

(3)   The registrant's and its other subsidiaries' equity in the income from continuing operations before income taxes of the subsidiary exclusive of amounts attributable to any noncontrolling interests exceeds 10 percent of such income of the registrant and its subsidiaries consolidated for the most recently completed fiscal year.

NOTE 1: A registrant that files its financial statements in accordance with or provides a reconciliation to U.S. Generally Accepted Accounting Principles shall make the prescribed tests using amounts determined under U.S. Generally Accepted Accounting Principles. A foreign private issuer that files its financial statements in accordance with IFRS as issued by the IASB shall make the prescribed tests using amounts determined under IFRS as issued by the IASB.

COMPUTATIONAL NOTE 1 TO PARAGRAPH (3): For purposes of making the prescribed income test the following guidance should be applied:

1.   When a loss exclusive of amounts attributable to any noncontrolling interests has been incurred by either the parent and its subsidiaries consolidated or the tested subsidiary, but not both, the equity in the income or loss of the tested subsidiary exclusive of amounts attributable to any noncontrolling interests

should be excluded from such income of the registrant and its subsidiaries consolidated for purposes of the computation.

2. If income of the registrant and its subsidiaries consolidated exclusive of amounts attributable to any noncontrolling interests for the most recent fiscal year is at least 10 percent lower than the average of the income for the last five fiscal years, such average income should be substituted for purposes of the computation. Any loss years should be omitted for purposes of computing average income.

Smaller reporting company. As used in this part, the term *smaller reporting company* means an issuer that is not an investment company, an asset-backed issuer (as defined in § 229.1101 of this chapter), or a majority-owned subsidiary of a parent that is not a smaller reporting company and that:

(1) Had a public float of less than $250 million; or

(2) Had annual revenues of less than $100 million and either:

(i) No public float; or

(ii) A public float of less than $700 million.

(3) *Determination.* Whether an issuer is a smaller reporting company is determined on an annual basis.

(i) For issuers that are required to file reports under section 13(a) or 15(d) of the Exchange Act:

(A) Public float is measured as of the last business day of the issuer's most recently completed second fiscal quarter and computed by multiplying the aggregate worldwide number of shares of its voting and non-voting common equity held by non-affiliates by the price at which the common equity was last sold, or the average of the bid and asked prices of common equity, in the principal market for the common equity;

(B) Annual revenues are as of the most recently completed fiscal year for which audited financial statements are available; and

(C) An issuer must reflect the determination of whether it came within the definition of smaller reporting company in its quarterly report on Form 10–Q for the first fiscal quarter of the next year, indicating on the cover page of that filing, and in subsequent filings for that fiscal year, whether it is a smaller reporting company, except that, if a determination based on public float indicates that the issuer is newly eligible to be a smaller reporting company, the issuer may choose to reflect this determination beginning with its first quarterly report on Form 10–Q following the determination, rather than waiting until the first fiscal quarter of the next year.

(ii) For determinations based on an initial registration statement under the Securities Act or Exchange Act for shares of its common equity:

(A) Public float is measured as of a date within 30 days of the date of the filing of the registration statement and computed by multiplying the aggregate worldwide number of shares of its voting and non-voting common equity held by non-affiliates before the registration plus, in the case of a Securities Act registration statement, the number of shares of its voting and non-voting common equity included in the registration statement by the estimated public offering price of the shares;

(B) Annual revenues are as of the most recently completed fiscal year for which audited financial statements are available; and

(C) The issuer must reflect the determination of whether it came within the definition of smaller reporting company in the registration statement and must appropriately indicate on the cover page of the filing, and subsequent filings for the fiscal year in which the filing is made, whether it is a smaller reporting company. The issuer must re-determine its status at the end of its second fiscal quarter and then reflect any change in status as provided in paragraph (3)(i)(C) of this rule. In the case of a determination based on an initial Securities Act registration statement, an issuer that was not determined to be a smaller reporting company has the option to re-determine its status at the conclusion of the offering covered by the registration statement based on the actual offering price and number of shares sold.

(iii)   Once an issuer determines that it does not qualify for smaller reporting company status because it exceeded one or more of the current thresholds, it will remain unqualified unless when making its annual determination either:

(A)   It determines that its public float was less than $200 million; or

(B)   It determines that its public float and its annual revenues meet the requirements for subsequent qualification included in the chart below:

	Prior Public Float	
Prior Annual Revenues	**None or less than $700 million**	**$700 million or more**
Less than $100 million	Neither threshold exceeded	**Public float** Less than $560 million; and
		Revenues Less than $100 million.
$100 million or more	**Public float** None or less than $700 million; and	**Public float** Less than $560 million; and
	Revenues Less than $80 million.	**Revenues** Less than $80 million.

Instruction to definition of "smaller reporting company": A registrant that qualifies as a smaller reporting company under the public float thresholds identified in paragraphs (1) and (3)(iii)(A) of this rule will qualify as a smaller reporting company regardless of its revenues.

Instruction 2 to definition of "smaller reporting company": A foreign private issuer is not eligible to use the requirements for smaller reporting companies unless it uses the forms and rules designated for domestic issuers and provides financial statements prepared in accordance with U.S. Generally Accepted Accounting Principles.

Subsidiary. A "subsidiary" of a specified person is an affiliate controlled by such person directly, or indirectly through one or more intermediaries. (See also "majority owned subsidiary," "significant subsidiary," "totally held subsidiary," and "wholly owned subsidiary.")

Succession. The term "succession" means the direct acquisition of the assets comprising a going business, whether by merger, consolidation, purchase, or other direct transfer. The term does not include the acquisition of control of a business unless followed by the direct acquisition of its assets. The terms "succeed" and "successor" have meanings correlative to the foregoing.

Totally held subsidiary. The term "totally held subsidiary" means a subsidiary (1) substantially all of whose outstanding securities are owned by its parent and/or the parent's other totally held subsidiaries, and (2) which is not indebted to any person other than its parent and/or the parent's other totally held subsidiaries in an amount which is material in relation to the particular subsidiary, excepting indebtedness incurred in the ordinary course of business which is not overdue and which matures within one year from the date of its creation, whether evidenced by securities or not.

Voting securities. The term "voting securities" means securities the holders of which are presently entitled to vote for the election of directors.

Well-known seasoned issuer. A well-known seasoned issuer is an issuer that, as of the most recent determination date determined pursuant to paragraph (2) of this definition:

(1)(i)   Meets all the registrant requirements of General Instruction I.A. of Form S–3 or Form F–3 or General Instructions A.2.a and A.2.b of Form N–2 and either:

(A)   As of a date within 60 days of the determination date, has a worldwide market value of its outstanding voting and non-voting common equity held by nonaffiliates of $700 million or more; or

(B)(1)   As of a date within 60 days of the determination date, has issued in the last three years at least $1 billion aggregate principal amount of non-convertible securities, other than common equity, in primary offerings for cash, not exchange, registered under the Act; and

(2)   Will register only non-convertible securities, other than common equity, and full and unconditional guarantees permitted pursuant to paragraph (1)(ii) of this definition unless, at the determination date, the issuer also is eligible to register a primary offering of its securities relying on General Instruction I.B.1. of Form S–3 or Form F–3.

(3)   Provided that as to a parent issuer only, for purposes of calculating the aggregate principal amount of outstanding non-convertible securities under paragraph (1)(i)(B)(1) of this definition, the parent issuer may include the aggregate principal amount of non-convertible securities, other than common equity, of its majority-owned subsidiaries issued in registered primary offerings for cash, not exchange, that it has fully and unconditionally guaranteed, within the meaning of Rule 3–10 of Regulation S–X in the last three years; or

(ii)   Is a majority-owned subsidiary of a parent that is a well-known seasoned issuer pursuant to paragraph (1)(i) of this definition and, as to the subsidiaries' securities that are being or may be offered on that parent's registration statement:

(A)   The parent has provided a full and unconditional guarantee, as defined in Rule 3–10 of Regulation S–X, of the payment obligations on the subsidiary's securities and the securities are non-convertible securities, other than common equity;

(B)   The securities are guarantees of:

(1)   Non-convertible securities, other than common equity, of its parent being registered; or

(2)   Will register only non-convertible securities, other than common equity, and full and unconditional guarantees permitted pursuant to paragraph (1)(ii) of this definition unless, at the determination date, the issuer also is eligible to register a primary offering of its securities relying on General Instruction I.B.1. of Form S–3 or Form F–3 or is eligible to register a primary offering described in General Instruction I.B.1. of Form S–3 relying on General Instruction A.2 of Form N–2.

(C)   The securities of the majority-owned subsidiary meet the conditions of General Instruction I.B.2 of Form S–3 or Form F–3.

(iii)   Is not an ineligible issuer as defined in this rule.

(iv)   Is not an asset-backed issuer as defined in Item 1101 of Regulation AB.

(v)   Is not an investment company registered under the Investment Company Act of 1940, other than a registered closed-end investment company.

(2)   For purposes of this definition, the determination date as to whether an issuer is a well-known seasoned issuer shall be the latest of:

(i)   The time of filing of its most recent shelf registration statement; or

(ii)   The time of its most recent amendment (by post-effective amendment, incorporated report filed pursuant to section 13 or 15(d) of the Securities Exchange Act of 1934 or form of prospectus) to a shelf registration statement for purposes of complying with section 10(a)(3) of the Act (or if such amendment has not been made within the time period required by section 10(a)(3) of the Act, the date on which such amendment is required); or

(iii)   In the event that the issuer has not filed a shelf registration statement or amended a shelf registration statement for purposes of complying with section 10(a)(3) of the Act for sixteen months, the time of filing of the issuer's most recent annual report on Form 10–K or Form 20–F (or if such report has not been filed by its due date, such due date).

Wholly owned subsidiary. The term "wholly owned subsidiary" means a subsidiary substantially all of whose outstanding voting securities are owned by its parent and/or the parent's other wholly owned subsidiaries.

Written communication. Except as otherwise specifically provided or the context otherwise requires, a written communication is any communication that is written, printed, a radio or television broadcast, or a graphic communication as defined in this rule.

Note to definition of "written communication."

A communication that is a radio or television broadcast is a written communication regardless of the means of transmission of the broadcast.

Rule 406.   Confidential Treatment of Information Filed With the Commission

Preliminary Notes: (1) Confidential treatment of supplemental information or other information not required to be filed under the Act should be requested under 17 CFR section 200.83 and not under this rule.

(2)   All confidential treatment requests shall be submitted in paper format only, whether or not the filer is an electronic filer. *See* Rule 101(c)(1)(i) of Regulation S–T.

(a)   Any person submitting any information in a document required to be filed under the Act may make written objection to its public disclosure by following the procedure in paragraph (b) of this rule, which shall be the exclusive means of requesting confidential treatment of information included in any document (hereinafter referred to as the "material filed") required to be filed under the Act, *except* that if the material filed is a registration statement on Form S–8 or on Form S–3, F–2, F–3 relating to a dividend or interest reinvestment plan, or on Form S–4 complying with General Instruction G of that Form, or if the material filed is a registration statement that does not contain a delaying amendment pursuant to Rule 473, the person shall comply with the procedure in paragraph (b) *prior* to the filing of a registration statement.

(b)   The person shall omit from the material filed the portion thereof which it desires to keep undisclosed (hereinafter called the "confidential portion"). In lieu thereof, the person shall indicate at the appropriate place in the material filed that the confidential portion has been so omitted and filed separately with the Commission. The person shall file with the material filed:

(1)   One copy of the confidential portion, marked "Confidential Treatment," of the material filed with the Commission. The copy shall contain an appropriate identification of the item or other requirement involved and, notwithstanding that the confidential portion does not constitute the whole of the answer or required disclosure, the entire answer or required disclosure, except that in the case where the confidential portion is part of a financial statement or schedule, only the particular financial statement or schedule need be included. The copy of the confidential portion shall be in the same form as the remainder of the material filed;

(2)   An application making objection to the disclosure of the confidential portion. Such application shall be on a sheet or sheets separate from the confidential portion, and shall contain:

(i)   An identification of the portion;

(ii)   A statement of the grounds of the objection referring to and analyzing the applicable exemption(s) from disclosure under section 200.80 of this chapter, the Commission's rule adopted under the Freedom of Information Act, and a justification of the period of time for which confidential treatment is sought;

(iii)   A detailed explanation of why, based on the facts and circumstances of the particular case, disclosure of the information is unnecessary for the protection of investors;

(iv)   A written consent to the furnishing of the confidential portion to other government agencies, offices, or bodies and to the Congress; and

(v)   The name, address and telephone number of the person to whom all notices and orders issued under this rule at any time should be directed;

(3)   The copy of the confidential portion and the application filed in accordance with this paragraph (b) shall be enclosed in a separate envelope marked "Confidential Treatment" and addressed to The Secretary, Securities and Exchange Commission, Washington, D.C. 20549.

(c)   Pending a determination as to the objection, the material for which confidential treatment has been applied will not be made available to the public.

(d)   If it is determined by the Division, acting pursuant to delegated authority, that the application should be granted, an order to that effect will be entered, and a notation to that effect will be made at the appropriate place in the material filed. Such a determination will not preclude reconsideration whenever appropriate, such as upon receipt of any subsequent request under the Freedom of Information Act and, if appropriate, revocation of the confidential status of all or a portion of the information in question.

(e)   If the Commission denies the application, or the Division, acting pursuant to delegated authority, denies the application and Commission review is not sought pursuant to Rule 26 of the Rules of Practice, confirmed telegraphic notice of the order of denial will be sent to the person named in the application pursuant to paragraph (b)(2)(v) of this rule. In such case, if the material filed may be withdrawn pursuant to an applicable statute, rule, or regulation, the registrant shall have the right to withdraw the material filed in accordance with the terms of the applicable statute, rule, or regulation, but without the necessity of stating any grounds for the withdrawal or of obtaining the further assent of the Commission. In the event of such withdrawal, the confidential portion will be returned to the registrant. If the material filed may not be so withdrawn, the confidential portion will be made available for public inspection in the same manner as if confidential treatment had been revoked under paragraph (h) of this rule.

(f)   If a right of withdrawal pursuant to paragraph (e) of this rule is not exercised, the confidential portion will be made available for public inspection as part of the material filed, and the registrant shall amend the material filed to include all information required to be set forth in regard to such confidential portion.

(g)   In any case where a prior grant of confidential treatment has been revoked, the person named in the application pursuant to paragraph (b)(2)(v) of this rule will be so informed by registered or certified mail. Pursuant to Rule 431 of the Rules of Practice, persons making objection to disclosure may petition the Commission for review of a determination by the Division revoking confidential treatment.

(h)   Upon revocation of confidential treatment, the confidential portion shall be made available to the public at the time and according to the conditions specified in paragraphs (h)(1)–(2):

(1)   Upon the lapse of five days after the dispatch of notice by registered or certified mail of a determination disallowing an objection, if prior to the lapse of such five days the person shall not have communicated to the Secretary of the Commission his intention to seek review by the Commission under Rule 26 of the Rules of Practice of the determination made by the Division; or

(2)   If such a petition for review shall have been filed under Rule 431 of the Rules of Practice, upon final disposition adverse to the petitioner.

(i)   If the confidential portion is made available to the public, one copy thereof shall be attached to each copy of the material filed with the Commission.

Rule 408.   Additional Information

(a)   In addition to the information expressly required to be included in a registration statement, there shall be added such further material information, if any, as may be necessary to make the required statements, in the light of the circumstances under which they are made, not misleading.

(b)   Notwithstanding paragraph (a) of this rule, unless otherwise required to be included in the registration statement, the failure to include in a registration statement information included in a free writing prospectus will not, solely by virtue of inclusion of the information in a free writing prospectus as defined in Rule 405, be considered an omission of material information required to be included in the registration statement.

Rule 409.   Information Unknown or Not Reasonably Available

Information required need be given only insofar as it is known or reasonably available to the registrant. If any required information is unknown and not reasonably available to the registrant, either because the obtaining thereof would involve unreasonable effort or expense, or because it rests peculiarly within the knowledge of another person not affiliated with the registrant, the information may be omitted, subject to the following conditions:

(a)   The registrant shall give such information on the subject as it possesses or can acquire without unreasonable effort or expense, together with the sources thereof.

(b)   The registrant shall include a statement either showing that unreasonable effort or expense would be involved or indicating the absence of any affiliation with the person within whose knowledge the information rests and stating the result of a request made to such persons for the information.

Rule 410.   Disclaimer of Control

If the existence of control is open to reasonable doubt in any instance, the registrant may disclaim the existence of control and any admission thereof; in such case, however, the registrant shall state the material facts pertinent to the possible existence of control.

Rule 411.   Incorporation by Reference

(a)   *Prospectuses.* Except as provided by this rule, Item 1100(c) of Regulation AB for registered offerings of asset-backed securities, or unless otherwise provided in the appropriate form, information shall not be incorporated by reference in a prospectus. Where a summary or outline of the provisions of any document is required in the prospectus, the summary or outline may incorporate by reference particular items, sections or paragraphs of any exhibit and may be qualified in its entirety by such reference.

(b)   *Information Not Required in a Prospectus.* Except for exhibits covered by Paragraph (c) of this rule, information may be incorporated by reference in answer, or partial answer, to any item that calls for information not required to be included in a prospectus subject to the following provisions:

(1)   Non-financial information may be incorporated by reference to any document;

(2)   Financial information may be incorporated by reference to any document, provided any financial statement so incorporated meets the requirements of the forms on which the statement is filed. Financial statements or other financial data required to be given in comparative form for two or more fiscal years or periods shall not be incorporated by reference unless the information incorporated by reference includes the entire period for which the comparative data is given;

(3)   Information contained in any part of the registration statement, including the prospectus, may be incorporated by reference in answer, or partial answer, to any item that calls for information not required to be included in the prospectus; and

(4)   Unless the information is incorporated by reference to a document which complies with the time limitations of Rule 24 of the Commission's Rules of Practice, then the document, or part thereof, containing the incorporated information is required to be filed as an exhibit.

(c)   *Exhibits.* Any document or part thereof filed with the Commission pursuant to any Act administered by the Commission may, subject to the limitations of Rule 24 of the Commission's Rules of Practice, be incorporated by reference as an exhibit to any registration statement. If any modification has occurred in the text of any document incorporated by reference since the filing thereof, the registrant shall file with the reference a statement containing the text of such modification and the date thereof.

(d)   *General.* Any incorporation by reference of information pursuant to this rule shall be subject to the provisions of Rule 24 of the Commission's Rules of Practice restricting incorporation by reference of documents which incorporate by reference other information. Information incorporated by reference shall be clearly identified in the reference by page, paragraph, caption or otherwise. If the information is incorporated by reference to a previously filed document, the file number of such document shall be included. Where only certain pages of a document are incorporated by reference and filed with the statement, the document from which the information is taken shall be clearly identified in the reference. An express statement that the specified matter is incorporated by reference shall be made at the particular place in the registration statement where the information is required. Information shall not be incorporated by reference in any case where such incorporation would render the statement incomplete, unclear or confusing.

Rule 412. Modified or Superseded Documents

(a) Any statement contained in a document incorporated or deemed to be incorporated by reference or deemed to be part of a registration statement or the prospectus that is part of the registration statement shall be deemed to be modified or superseded for purposes of the registration statement or the prospectus that is part of the registration statement to the extent that a statement contained in the prospectus that is part of the registration statement or in any other subsequently filed document which also is or is deemed to be incorporated by reference or deemed to be part of the registration statement or prospectus that is part of the registration statement modifies or replaces such statement. Any statement contained in a document that is deemed to be incorporated by reference or deemed to be part of a registration statement or the prospectus that is part of the registration statement after the most recent effective date or after the date of the most recent prospectus that is part of the registration statement may modify or replace existing statements contained in the registration statement or the prospectus that is part of the registration statement.

(b) The modifying or superseding statement may, but need not, state that it has modified or superseded a prior statement or include any other information set forth in the document which is not so modified or superseded. The making of a modifying or superseding statement shall not be deemed an admission that the modified or superseded statement, when made, constituted an untrue statement of a material fact, an omission to state a material fact necessary to make a statement not misleading, or the employment of a manipulative, deceptive, or fraudulent device, contrivance, scheme, transaction, act, practice, course of business or artifice to defraud, as those terms are used in the Act, the Securities Exchange Act of 1934, the Public Utility Holding Company Act of 1935, the Investment Company Act of 1940, or the rules and regulations thereunder.

(c) Any statement so modified shall not be deemed in its unmodified form to constitute part of the registration statement or prospectus for purpose of the Act. Any statement so superseded shall not be deemed to constitute a part of the registration statement or the prospectus for purposes of the Act.

Rule 413. Registration of Additional Securities and Additional Classes of Securities

(a) Except as provided in section 24(f) of the Investment Company Act of 1940 and in paragraph (b) of this rule, where a registration statement is already in effect, the registration of additional securities shall only be effected through a separate registration statement relating to the additional securities.

(b) Notwithstanding paragraph (a) of this rule, the following additional securities or additional classes of securities may be added to an automatic shelf registration statement already in effect by filing a post-effective amendment to that automatic shelf registration statement:

(1) Securities of a class different than those registered on the effective automatic shelf registration statement identified as provided in Rule 430B(a); or

(2) Securities of a majority-owned subsidiary that are permitted to be included in an automatic shelf registration statement, provided that the subsidiary and the securities are identified as provided in Rule 430B and the subsidiary satisfies the signature requirements of an issuer in the post-effective amendment.

Rule 414. Registration by Certain Successor Issuers

If any issuer, except a foreign issuer exempted by Rule 3a12–3 under the Securities Exchange Act of 1934, incorporated under the laws of any State or foreign government and having securities registered under the Act has been succeeded by an issuer incorporated under the laws of another State or foreign government for the purpose of changing the State or country of incorporation of the enterprises, or if any issuer has been succeeded by an issuer for the purpose of changing its form of organization, the registration statement of the predecessor issuer shall be deemed the registration statement of the successor issuer for the purpose of continuing the offering provided:

(a)   Immediately prior to the succession the successor issuer had no assets or liabilities other than nominal assets or liabilities;

(b)   The succession was effected by a merger or similar succession pursuant to statutory provisions or the terms of the organic instruments under which the successor issuer acquired all of the assets and assumed all of the liabilities and obligations of the predecessor issuer;

(c)   The succession was approved by security holders of the predecessor issuer at a meeting for which proxies were solicited pursuant to section 14(a) of the Securities Exchange Act of 1934 or section 20(a) of the Investment Company Act of 1940 or information was furnished to security holders pursuant to section 14(c) of the Securities Exchange Act of 1934; and

(d)   The successor issuer has filed an amendment to the registration statement of the predecessor issuer expressly adopting such statements as its own registration statement for all purposes of the Act and the Securities Exchange Act of 1934 and setting forth any additional information necessary to reflect any material changes made in connection with or resulting from the succession, or necessary to keep the registration statement from being misleading in any material respect, and such amendment has become effective.

Rule 415.   Delayed or Continuous Offering and Sale of Securities

(a)   Securities may be registered for an offering to be made on a continuous or delayed basis in the future. *Provided,* That:

(1)   The registration statement pertains only to:

(i)   Securities which are to be offered or sold solely by or on behalf of a person or persons other than the registrant, a subsidiary of the registrant or a person of which the registrant is a subsidiary;

(ii)   Securities which are to be offered and sold pursuant to a dividend or interest reinvestment plan or an employee benefit plan of the registrant;

(iii)   Securities which are to be issued upon the exercise of outstanding options, warrants or rights;

(iv)   Securities which are to be issued upon conversion of other outstanding securities;

(v)   Securities which are pledged as collateral;

(vi)   Securities which are registered on Form F–6;

(vii)   Asset-backed securities (as defined in Item 1101(c) of Regulation AB) registered (or qualified to be registered) on Form SF–3 which are to be offered and sold on an immediate or delayed basis by or on behalf of the registrant;

Instruction to paragraph (a)(1)(vii): The requirements of General Instruction I.B.1 of Form SF–3 must be met for any offerings of an asset-backed security (as defined in Item 1101(c) of Regulation AB) registered in reliance on this paragraph (a)(1)(vii).

(viii)   Securities which are to be issued in connection with business combination transactions;

(ix)   Securities, other than asset-backed securities (as defined in Item 1101(c) of Regulation AB), the offering of which will be commenced promptly, will be made on a continuous basis and may continue for a period in excess of 30 days from the date of initial effectiveness;

(x)   Securities registered (or qualified to be registered) on Form S–3 or Form F–3, or on Form N–2 pursuant to General Instruction A.2 of that form, which are to be offered and sold on an immediate, continuous or delayed basis by or on behalf of the registrant, a majority-owned subsidiary of the registrant or a person of which the registrant is a majority-owned subsidiary; or

(xi)   Shares of common stock which are to be offered and sold on a delayed or continuous basis by or on behalf of a registered closed-end investment company or business development company that makes periodic repurchase offers pursuant to Rule 23c–3 of the Investment Company Act.

(xii) Asset-backed securities (as defined in Item 1101(c) of Regulation AB) that are to be offered and sold on a continuous basis if the offering is commenced promptly and being conducted on the condition that the consideration paid for such securities will be promptly refunded to the purchaser unless:

    (A)   All of the securities being offered are sold at a specified price within a specified time; and

    (B)   The total amount due to the seller is received by him by a specified date.

(xiii) Exchange-traded vehicle securities which are to be offered and sold on a continuous basis by or on behalf of the registrant in accordance with Rule 456(d).

(2)   Securities in paragraph (a)(1)(viii) of this section and securities in paragraph (a)(1)(ix) of this section that are not registered on Form S–3 or Form F–3 (§ 239.13 or § 239.33 of this chapter), or on Form N–2 (§ 239.14 and § 274.11a–1 of this chapter) pursuant to General Instruction A.2 of that form, may only be registered in an amount which, at the time the registration statement becomes effective, is reasonably expected to be offered and sold within two years from the initial effective date of the registration.

(3)   The registrant furnishes the undertakings required by Item 512(a) of Regulation S–K or Item 512(a), except that a registrant that is an investment company filing on Form N–2 must furnish the undertakings required by Item 34.4 of Form N–2.

(4)   In the case of a registration statement pertaining to an at the market offering of equity securities by or on behalf of the registrant, the offering must come within paragraph (a)(1)(x) of this rule. As used in this paragraph, the term "at the market offering" means an offering of equity securities into an existing trading market for outstanding shares of the same class at other than a fixed price.

(5)   Securities registered on an automatic shelf registration statement and securities described in paragraphs (a)(1)(vii), (ix), and (x) of this rule may be offered and sold only if not more than three years have elapsed since the initial effective date of the registration statement under which they are being offered and sold, provided, however, that if a new registration statement has been filed pursuant to paragraph (a)(6) of this rule:

    (i)   If the new registration statement is an automatic shelf registration statement, it shall be immediately effective pursuant to Rule 462(e); or

    (ii)   If the new registration statement is not an automatic shelf registration statement:

        (A)   Securities covered by the prior registration statement may continue to be offered and sold until the earlier of the effective date of the new registration statement or 180 days after the third anniversary of the initial effective date of the prior registration statement; and

        (B)   A continuous offering of securities covered by the prior registration statement that commenced within three years of the initial effective date may continue until the effective date of the new registration statement if such offering is permitted under the new registration statement.

(6)   Prior to the end of the three-year period described in paragraph (a)(5) of this rule, an issuer may file a new registration statement covering securities described in such paragraph (a)(5) of this rule, which may, if permitted, be an automatic shelf registration statement. The new registration statement and prospectus included therein must include all the information that would be required at that time in a prospectus relating to all offering(s) that it covers. Prior to the effective date of the new registration statement (including at the time of filing in the case of an automatic shelf registration statement), the issuer may include on such new registration statement any unsold securities covered by the earlier registration statement by identifying on the bottom of the facing page of the new registration statement or latest amendment thereto the amount of such unsold securities being included and any filing fee paid in connection with such unsold securities, which will continue to be applied to such unsold securities. The offering of securities on the earlier registration statement will be deemed terminated as of the date of effectiveness of the new registration statement.

(b)   This rule shall not apply to any registration statement pertaining to securities issued by a face-amount certificate company or redeemable securities issued by an open-end management company or unit investment trust under the Investment Company Act of 1940 or any registration statement filed by any foreign government or political subdivision thereof.

Rule 416.   Securities to Be Issued as a Result of Stock Splits, Stock Dividends and Anti-Dilution Provisions and Interests to Be Issued Pursuant to Certain Employee Benefit Plans

(a)   If a registration statement purports to register securities to be offered pursuant to terms which provide for a change in the amount of securities being offered or issued to prevent dilution resulting from stock splits, stock dividends or similar transactions, such registration statement shall, unless otherwise expressly provided, be deemed to cover the additional securities to be offered or issued in connection with any such provision.

(b)   If prior to completion of the distribution of the securities covered by a registration statement, additional securities of the same class are issued or issuable as a result of a stock split or stock dividend, the registration statement shall, unless otherwise expressly provided therein, be deemed to cover such additional securities resulting from the split of, or the stock dividend on, the registered securities. If prior to completion of the distribution of the securities covered by a registration statement, all the securities of a class which includes the registered securities are combined by a reverse split into a lesser amount of securities of the same class, the amount of undistributed securities of such class deemed to be covered by the registration statement shall be proportionately reduced. If paragraph (a) of this rule is not applicable, the registration statement shall be amended prior to the offering of such additional or lesser amount of securities to reflect the change in the amount of securities registered.

(c)   Where a registration statement on Form S–8 relates to securities to be offered pursuant to an employee benefit plan, including interests in such plan that constitute separate securities required to be registered under the Act, such registration statement shall be deemed to register an indeterminate amount of such plan interests.

Rule 417.   Date of Financial Statements

Whenever financial statements of any person are required to be furnished as of a date within a specified period prior to the date of filing the registration statement and the last day of such period falls on a Saturday, Sunday or holiday, such registration statement may be filed on the first business day following the last day of the specified period.

Rule 418.   Supplemental Information

(a)   The Commission or its staff may, where it is deemed appropriate, request supplemental information concerning the registrant, the registration statement, the distribution of the securities, market activities and underwriters' activities. Such information includes, but is not limited to, the following items which the registrant should be prepared to furnish promptly upon request:

(1)(i)   Any reports or memoranda which have been prepared for external use by the registrant or a principal underwriter, as defined in Rule 405, in connection with the proposed offering;

(ii)   A statement as to the actual or proposed use and distribution of the reports or memoranda specified in paragraph (a)(1)(i) of this rule, identifying each class of persons who have received or will receive such reports or memoranda and the number of copies distributed to each such class;

(2)   In the case of a registration statement relating to a business combination as defined in Rule 145(a), exchange offer, tender offer or similar transaction, any feasibility studies, management analyses, fairness opinions or similar reports prepared by or for any of the parties to the subject transaction in connection with such transaction;

(3)   Except in the case of a registrant eligible to use Form S–3 or Form N–2 under General Instruction A.2 of that form, any engineering, management or similar reports or memoranda relating to broad aspects of the business, operations or products of the registrant, which have been prepared

within the past twelve months for or by the registrant and any affiliate of the registrant or any principal underwriter, as defined in Rule 405 (§ 230.405), of the securities being registered except for:

(i)   Reports solely comprised of recommendations to buy, sell or hold the securities of the registrant, unless such recommendations have changed within the past six months; and

(ii)   Any information contained in documents already filed with the Commission.

(4)   Where there is a registration of an at-the-market offering as defined in Rule 100 of Regulation M under the Securities Exchange Act of 1934, of more than 10 percent of the securities outstanding, where the offering includes securities owned by officers, directors or affiliates of the registrant and where there is no underwriting agreement, information (i) concerning contractual arrangements between selling security holders of a limited group or of several groups of related shareholders to comply with the anti-manipulation rules until the offering by all members of the group is completed and to inform the exchange, brokers and selling security holders when the distribution by the members of the group is over; or (ii) concerning the registrant's efforts to notify members of a large group of unrelated sellers of the applicable Commission rules and regulations;

(5)   Where the registrant recently has introduced a new product or has begun to do business in a new industry segment or has made public its intentions to introduce a new product or to do business in a new industry segment, and this action requires the investment of a material amount of the assets of the registrant or otherwise is material, copies of any studies prepared for the registrant by outside persons or any internal studies, documents, reports or memoranda the contents of which were material to the decision to develop the product or to do business in the new segment including, but not limited to, documents relating to financial requirements and engineering, competitive, environmental and other considerations, but excluding technical documents;

(6)   Where reserve estimates are referred to in a document, a copy of the full report of the engineer or other expert who estimated the reserves;

(7)   With respect to the extent of the distribution of a preliminary prospectus, information concerning:

(i)   The date of the preliminary prospectus distributed;

(ii)   The dates or approximate dates of distribution;

(iii)   The number of prospective underwriters and dealers to whom the preliminary prospectus was furnished;

(iv)   The number of prospectuses so distributed;

(v)   The number of prospectuses distributed to others, identifying them in general terms; and

(vi)   The steps taken by such underwriters and dealers to comply with the provisions of Rule 15c2–8 under the Securities Exchange Act of 1934; and

(8)   Any free writing prospectuses used in connection with the offering.

(b)   Supplemental information described in paragraph (a) of this rule shall not be required to be filed with or deemed part of and included in the registration statement unless otherwise required. The information shall be returned to the registrant upon request, provided that:

(1)   Such request is made at the time such information is furnished to the staff;

(2)   The return of such information is consistent with the protection of investors;

(3)   The return of such information is consistent with the provisions of the Freedom of Information Act; and

(4)   The information was not filed in electronic format.

Rule 419.   Offerings by Blank Check Companies

(a)   *Scope of the Rule and Definitions.*

(1)   The provisions of this rule shall apply to every registration statement filed under the Act relating to an offering by a blank check company.

(2)   For purposes of this rule, the term "blank check company" shall mean a company that:

(i)   Is a development stage company that has no specific business plan or purpose or has indicated that its business plan is to engage in a merger or acquisition with an unidentified company or companies, or other entity or person; and

(ii)   Is issuing "penny stock," as defined in Rule 3a51–1 under the Securities Exchange Act of 1934 ("Exchange Act").

(3)   For purposes of this rule, the term "purchaser" shall mean any person acquiring securities directly or indirectly in the offering, for cash or otherwise, including promoters or others receiving securities as compensation in connection with the offering.

(b)   *Deposit of Securities and Proceeds in Escrow or Trust Account.—*

(1)   *General.*

(i)   Except as otherwise provided in this rule or prohibited by other applicable law, all securities issued in connection with an offering by a blank check company and the gross proceeds from the offering shall be deposited promptly into:

(A)   An escrow account maintained by an "insured depository institution," as that term is defined in Section 3(c)(2) of the Federal Deposit Insurance Act; or

(B)   A separate bank account established by a broker or dealer registered under the Exchange Act maintaining net capital equal to or exceeding $25,000 (as calculated pursuant to Exchange Act Rule 15c3–1), in which the broker or dealer acts as trustee for persons having the beneficial interests in the account.

(ii)   If funds and securities are deposited into an escrow account maintained by an insured depository institution, the deposit account records of the insured depository institution must provide that funds in the escrow account are held for the benefit of the purchasers named and identified in accordance with section 330.1 of the regulations of the Federal Deposit Insurance Corporation, and the records of the escrow agent, maintained in good faith and in the regular course of business, must show the name and interest of each party to the account. If funds and securities are deposited in a separate bank account established by a broker or dealer acting as a trustee, the books and records of the broker-dealer must indicate the name, address, and interest of each person for whom the account is held.

(2)   *Deposit and Investment of Proceeds.*

(i)   All offering proceeds, after deduction of cash paid for underwriting commissions, underwriting expenses and dealer allowances, and amounts permitted to be released to the registrant pursuant to paragraph (b)(2)(vi) of this rule, shall be deposited promptly into the escrow or trust account; *provided, however,* that no deduction may be made for underwriting commissions, underwriting expenses or dealer allowances payable to an affiliate of the registrant.

(ii)   Deposited proceeds shall be in the form of checks, drafts, or money orders payable to the order of the escrow agent or trustee.

(iii)   Deposited proceeds and interest or dividends thereon, if any, shall be held for the sole benefit of the purchasers of the securities.

(iv)   Deposited proceeds shall be invested in one of the following:

(A)   An obligation that constitutes a "deposit," as that term is defined in section 3(*1*) of the Federal Deposit Insurance Act;

(B)   Securities of any open-end investment company registered under the Investment Company Act of 1940 that holds itself out as a money market fund meeting the conditions of paragraph (d) of Rule 2a–7 under the Investment Company Act; or

(C)   Securities that are direct obligations of, or obligations guaranteed as to principal or interest by, the United States.

NOTE to Rule 419(b)(2)(iv): Issuers are cautioned that investments in government securities are inappropriate unless such securities can be readily sold or otherwise disposed of for cash at the time required without any dissipation of offering proceeds invested.

(v)   Interest or dividends earned on the funds, if any, shall be held in the escrow or trust account until the funds are released in accordance with the provisions of this rule. If funds held in the escrow or trust account are released to a purchaser of the securities, the purchasers shall receive interest or dividends earned, if any, on such funds up to the date of release. If funds held in the escrow or trust account are released to the registrant, interest or dividends earned on such funds up to the date of release may be released to the registrant.

(vi)   The registrant may receive up to 10 percent of the proceeds remaining after payment of underwriting commissions, underwriting expenses and dealer allowances permitted by paragraph (b)(2)(i) of this rule, exclusive of interest or dividends, as those proceeds are deposited into the escrow or trust account.

(3)   *Deposit of Securities.*

(i)   All securities issued in connection with the offering, whether or not for cash consideration, and any other securities issued with respect to such securities, including securities issued with respect to stock splits, stock dividends, or similar rights, shall be deposited directly into the escrow or trust account promptly upon issuance. The identity of the purchaser of the securities shall be included on the stock certificates or other documents evidencing such securities. *See also* Exchange Act Rule 15g–8 regarding restrictions on sales of, or offers to sell, securities deposited in the escrow or trust account.

(ii)   Securities held in the escrow or trust account are to remain as issued and deposited and shall be held for the sole benefit of the purchasers, who shall have voting rights, if any, with respect to securities held in their names, as provided by applicable state law. No transfer or other disposition of securities held in the escrow or trust account or any interest related to such securities shall be permitted other than by will or the laws of descent and distribution, or pursuant to a qualified domestic relations order as defined by the Internal Revenue Code of 1986 as amended, or Title 1 of the Employee Retirement Income Security Act, or the rules thereunder.

(iii)   Warrants, convertible securities or other derivative securities relating to securities held in the escrow or trust account may be exercised or converted in accordance with their terms; *provided, however,* that securities received upon exercise or conversion, together with any cash or other consideration paid in connection with the exercise or conversion, are promptly deposited into the escrow or trust account.

(4)   *Escrow or Trust Agreement.* A copy of the executed escrow or trust agreement shall be filed as an exhibit to the registration statement and shall contain the provisions of paragraphs (b)(2), (b)(3), and (e)(3) of this rule.

(5)   *Request for Supplemental Information.* Upon request by the Commission or the staff, the registrant shall furnish as supplemental information the names and addresses of persons for whom securities are held in the escrow or trust account.

NOTE to Rule 419(b): With respect to a blank check offering subject to both Rule 419 and Exchange Act Rule 15c2–4, the requirements of Rule 15c2–4 are applicable only until the conditions of the offering governed by that rule are met (*e.g.*, reaching the minimum in a "part-or-none" offering). When those conditions are satisfied, Rule 419 continues to govern the use of offering proceeds.

(c)   *Disclosure of Offering Terms.*

The initial registration statement shall disclose the specific terms of the offering, including, but not limited to:

(1)   The terms and provisions of the escrow or trust agreement and the effect thereof upon the registrant's right to receive funds and the effect of the escrow or trust agreement upon the purchaser's

funds and securities required to be deposited into the escrow or trust account, including, if applicable, any material risk of non-insurance of purchasers' funds resulting from deposits in excess of the insured amounts; and

(2)   The obligation of the registrant to provide, and the right of the purchaser to receive, information regarding an acquisition, including the requirement that pursuant to this rule, purchasers confirm in writing their investment in the registrant's securities as specified in paragraph (e) of this rule.

(d)   *Probable Acquisition Post-Effective Amendment Requirement.* If, during any period in which offers or sales are being made, a significant acquisition becomes probable, the registrant shall file promptly a post-effective amendment disclosing the information specified by the applicable registration statement form and Industry Guides, including financial statements of the registrant and the company to be acquired as well as pro forma financial information required by the form and applicable rules and regulations. Where warrants, rights or other derivative securities issued in the initial offering are exercisable, there is a continuous offering of the underlying security.

(e)   *Release of Deposited and Funds Securities.—*

(1)   *Post-Effective Amendment for Acquisition Agreement.* Upon execution of an agreement(s) for the acquisition(s) of a business(es) or assets that will constitute the business (or a line of business) of the registrant and for which the fair value of the business(es) or net assets to be acquired represents at least 80 percent of the maximum offering proceeds, including proceeds received or to be received upon the exercise or conversion of any securities offered, but excluding amounts payable to non-affiliates for underwriting commissions, underwriting expenses, and dealer allowances, the registrant shall file a post-effective amendment that:

(i)   Discloses the information specified by the applicable registration statement form and Industry Guides, including financial statements of the registrant and the company acquired or to be acquired and pro forma financial information required by the form and applicable rules and regulations;

(ii)   Discloses the results of the initial offering, including but not limited to:

(A)   The gross offering proceeds received to date, specifying the amounts paid for underwriter commissions, underwriting expenses and dealer allowances, amounts disbursed to the registrant, and amounts remaining in the escrow or trust account; and

(B)   The specific amount, use and application of funds disbursed to the registrant to date, including, but not limited to, the amounts paid to officers, directors, promoters, controlling shareholders or affiliates, either directly or indirectly, specifying the amounts and purposes of such payments; and

(iii)   Discloses the terms of the offering as described pursuant to paragraph (e)(2) of this rule.

(2)   *Terms of the Offering.* The terms of the offering must provide, and the registrant must satisfy, the following conditions:

(i)   Within five business days after the effective date of the post-effective amendment(s), the registrant shall send by first class mail or other equally prompt means, to each purchaser of securities held in escrow or trust, a copy of the prospectus contained in the post-effective amendment and any amendment or supplement thereto;

(ii)   Each purchaser shall have no fewer than 20 business days and no more than 45 business days from the effective date of the post-effective amendment to notify the registrant in writing that the purchaser elects to remain an investor. If the registrant has not received such written notification by the 45th business day following the effective date of the post-effective amendment, funds and interest or dividends, if any, held in the escrow or trust account shall be sent by first class mail or other equally prompt means to the purchaser within five business days;

(iii)   The acquisition(s) meeting the criteria set forth in paragraph (e)(1) of this rule will be consummated if a sufficient number of purchasers confirm their investments; and

(iv)   If a consummated acquisition(s) meeting the requirements of this rule has not occurred by a date 18 months after the effective date of the initial registration statement, funds held in the escrow or trust account shall be returned by first class mail or equally prompt means to the purchaser within five business days following that date.

(3)   *Conditions for Release of Deposited Securities and Funds.* Funds held in the escrow or trust account may be released to the registrant and securities may be delivered to the purchaser or other registered holder identified on the deposited securities only at the same time as or after:

(i)   The escrow agent or trustee has received a signed representation from the registrant, together with other evidence acceptable to the escrow agent or trustee, that the requirements of paragraphs (e)(1) and (e)(2) of this rule have been met; and

(ii)   Consummation of an acquisition(s) meeting the requirements of paragraph (e)(2)(iii) of this rule.

(4)   *Prospectus Supplement.* If funds and securities are released from the escrow or trust account to the registrant pursuant to this paragraph, the prospectus shall be supplemented to indicate the amount of funds and securities released and the date of release.

NOTES to Rule 419(e):

1.   With respect to a blank check offering subject to both Rule 419 and Exchange Act Rule 10b–9, the requirements of Rule 10b–9 are applicable only until the conditions of the offering governed by that rule are met (*e.g.,* reaching the minimum in a "part-or-none" offering). When those conditions are satisfied, Rule 419 continues to govern the use of offering proceeds.

2.   If the business(es) or assets are acquired for cash, the fair value shall be presumed to be equal to the cash paid. If all or part of the consideration paid consists of securities or other non-cash consideration, the fair value shall be determined by an accepted standard, such as bona fide sales of the assets or similar assets made within a reasonable time, forecasts of expected cash flows, independent appraisals, etc. Such valuation must be reasonable at the time made.

(f)   *Financial Statements.* The registrant shall:

(1)   Furnish to security holders audited financial statements for the first full fiscal year of operations following consummation of an acquisition pursuant to paragraph (e) of this rule, together with the information required by Item 303(a) of Regulation S–K, no later than 90 days after the end of such fiscal year; and

(2)   File the financial statements and additional information with the Commission under cover of Form 8–K; *provided, however,* that such financial statements and related information need not be filed separately if the registrant is filing reports pursuant to Section 13(a) or 15(d) of the Exchange Act.

FORM AND CONTENT OF PROSPECTUSES

Rule 420.   Legibility of Prospectus

(a)   The body of all printed prospectuses and all notes to financial statements and other tabular data included therein shall be in roman type at least as large and as legible as 10-point modern type. However, (a) to the extent necessary for convenient presentation, financial statements and other tabular data, including tabular data in notes, and (b) prospectuses deemed to be omitting prospectuses under Rule 482 may be in roman type at least as large and as legible as 8-point modern type. All such type shall be leaded at least 2-points.

(b)   Where a prospectus is distributed through an electronic medium, issuers may satisfy legibility requirements applicable to printed documents, such as paper size, type size and font, bold-face type, italics and red ink, by presenting all required information in a format readily communicated to investors, and where indicated, in a manner reasonably calculated to draw investor attention to specific information.

Rule 421.   Presentation of Information in Prospectuses

(a)   The information required in a prospectus need not follow the order of the items or other requirements in the form. Such information shall not, however, be set forth in such fashion as to obscure any of the required information or any information necessary to keep the required information from being incomplete or misleading. Where an item requires information to be given in a prospectus in tabular form it shall be given in substantially the tabular form specified in the item.

(b)   You must present the information in a prospectus in a clear, concise and understandable manner. You must prepare the prospectus using the following standards:

(1)   Present information in clear, concise sections, paragraphs, and sentences. Whenever possible, use short, explanatory sentences and bullet lists;

(2)   Use descriptive headings and subheadings;

(3)   Avoid frequent reliance on glossaries or defined terms as the primary means of explaining information in the prospectus. Define terms in a glossary or other section of the document only if the meaning is unclear from the context. Use a glossary only if it facilitates understanding of the disclosure; and

(4)   Avoid legal and highly technical business terminology.

NOTE to Rule 421(b):

In drafting the disclosure to comply with this rule, you should avoid the following:

1.   Legalistic or overly complex presentations that make the substance of the disclosure difficult to understand;

2.   Vague "boilerplate" explanations that are imprecise and readily subject to different interpretations;

3.   Complex information copied directly from legal documents without any clear and concise explanation of the provision(s); and

4.   Disclosure repeated in different sections of the document that increases the size of the document but does not enhance the quality of the information.

(c)   All information required to be included in a prospectus shall be clearly understandable without the necessity of referring to the particular form or to the general rules and regulations. Except as to financial statements and information required in a tabular form, the information set forth in a prospectus may be expressed in condensed or summarized form. In lieu of repeating information in the form of notes to financial statements, references may be made to other parts of the prospectus where such information is set forth.

(d)(1)   To enhance the readability of the prospectus, you must use plain English principles in the organization, language, and design of the front and back cover pages, the summary, and the risk factors section.

(2)   You must draft the language in these sections so that at a minimum it substantially complies with each of the following plain English writing principles:

(i)   Short sentences;

(ii)   Definite, concrete, everyday words;

(iii)   Active voice;

(iv)   Tabular presentation or bullet lists for complex material, whenever possible;

(v)   No legal jargon or highly technical business terms; and

(vi)   No multiple negatives.

(3)   In designing these sections or other sections of the prospectus, you may include pictures, logos, charts, graphs, or other design elements so long as the design is not misleading and the required information is clear. You are encouraged to use tables, schedules, charts and graphic illustrations of the results of operations, balance sheet, or other financial data that present the data in an understandable manner. Any presentation must be consistent with the financial statements and non-financial information in the

prospectus. You must draw the graphs and charts to scale. Any information you provide must not be misleading.

Instructions to Rule 421:

You should read Securities Act Release No. 33–7497 (January 28, 1998) for information on plain English principles.

Rule 423.   Date of Prospectuses

Except for a form of prospectus used after the effective date of the registration statement and before the determination of the offering price as permitted by Rule 430A(c) under the Securities Act or before the opening of bids as permitted by Rule 445(c) under the Securities Act, each prospectus used after the effective date of the registration statement shall be dated approximately as of such effective date; provided, however, that a revised or amended prospectus used thereafter need only bear the approximate date of its issuance. Each supplement to a prospectus shall be dated separately the approximate date of its issuance.

Rule 424.   Filing of Prospectuses—Number of Copies

(a)   Except as provided in paragraph (f) of this rule, five copies of every form of prospectus sent or given to any person prior to the effective date of the registration statement which varies from the form or forms of prospectus included in the registration statement as filed pursuant to Rule 402(a) under the Securities Act shall be filed as a part of the registration statement not later than the date such form of prospectus is first sent or given to any person: *Provided, however,* that only a form of prospectus that contains substantive changes from or additions to a prospectus previously filed with the Commission as part of a registration statement need be filed pursuant to this paragraph (a).

(b)   Ten copies of each form of prospectus purporting to comply with section 10 of the Act, except for documents constituting a prospectus pursuant to Rule 428(a) or free writing prospectuses pursuant to Rule 164 and Rule 433, shall be filed with the Commission in the form in which it is used after the effectiveness of the registration statement and identified as required by paragraph (e) of this rule; provided, however, that only a form of prospectus that contains substantive changes from or additions to a previously filed prospectus is required to be filed; Provided, further, that this paragraph (b) shall not apply in respect of a form of prospectus contained in a registration statement and relating solely to securities offered at competitive bidding, which prospectus is intended for use prior to the opening of bids. Ten copies of the form of prospectus shall be filed or transmitted for filing as follows:

(1)   A form of prospectus that discloses information previously omitted from the prospectus filed as part of an effective registration statement in reliance upon Rule 430A under the Securities Act shall be filed with the commission no later than the second business day following the earlier of the date of determination of the offering price or the date it is first used after effectiveness in connection with a public offering or sales, or transmitted by a means reasonably calculated to result in filing with the Commission by that date.

(2)   A form of prospectus that is used in connection with a primary offering of securities pursuant to Rule 415(a)(1)(x) or a primary offering of securities registered for issuance on a delayed basis pursuant to Rule 415(a)(1)(vii) or (viii) and that, in the case of Rule 415(a)(1)(viii) discloses the public offering price, description of securities or similar matters, and in the case of Rule 415(a)(1)(vii) and (x) discloses information previously omitted from the prospectus filed as part of an effective registration statement in reliance on Rule 430B or, in the case of asset-backed securities, Rule 430D, shall be filed with the Commission no later than the second business day following the earlier of the date of the determination of the offering price or the date it is first used after effectiveness in connection with a public offering or sales, or transmitted by a means reasonably calculated to result in filing with the Commission by that date.

(3)   A form of prospectus that reflects facts or events other than those covered in paragraphs (b)(1), (2) and (6) of this rule that constitute a substantive change from or addition to the information set forth in the last form of prospectus filed with the Commission under this rule or as part of a registration statement under the Securities Act shall be filed with the Commission no later than the fifth business day after the date it is first used after effectiveness in connection with a public offering

or sales, or transmitted by a means reasonably calculated to result in filing with the Commission by that date.

(4) A form of prospectus that discloses information, facts or events covered in both paragraphs (b)(1) and (3) shall be filed with the Commission no later than the second business day following the earlier of the date of the determination of the offering price or the date it is first used after effectiveness in connection with a public offering or sales, or transmitted by a means reasonably calculated to result in filing with the Commission by that date.

(5) A form of prospectus that discloses information, facts or events covered in both paragraphs (b)(2) and (3) shall be filed with the Commission no later than the second business day following the earlier of the date of the determination of the offering price or the date it is first used after effectiveness in connection with a public offering or sales, or transmitted by a means reasonably calculated to result in filing with the Commission by that date.

(6) A form of prospectus used in connection with an offering of securities under Canada's National Policy Statement No. 45 pursuant to Rule 415 under the Securities Act that is not made in the United States shall be filed with the Commission no later than the date it is first used in Canada, or transmitted by a means reasonably calculated to result in filing with the Commission by that date.

(7) A form of prospectus that identifies selling security holders and the amounts to be sold by them that was previously omitted from the registration statement and the prospectus in reliance upon Rule 430B shall be filed with the Commission no later than the second business day following the earlier of the date of sale or the date of first use or transmitted by a means reasonably calculated to result in filing with the Commission by that date.

(8) A form of prospectus otherwise required to be filed pursuant to paragraph (b) of this rule that is not filed within the time frames specified in paragraph (b) of this rule must be filed pursuant to this paragraph as soon as practicable after the discovery of such failure to file.

Note to paragraph (b)(8) of Rule 424:

A form of prospectus required to be filed pursuant to another paragraph of Rule 424(b) that is filed under Rule 424(b)(8) shall nonetheless be "required to be filed" under such other paragraph.

Instruction to paragraph (b): Notwithstanding Rule 424(b)(2) and (b)(5) above, a form of prospectus or prospectus supplement relating to an offering of asset-backed securities under Rule 415(a)(1)(vii) or 415(a)(1)(xii) that is required to be filed pursuant to paragraph (b) of this rule shall be filed with the Commission no later than the second business day following the date it is first used after effectiveness in connection with a public offering or sales, or transmitted by a means reasonably calculated to result in filing with the Commission by that date.

(c) If a form of prospectus, other than one filed pursuant to paragraph (b)(1) or (b)(4) of this rule, consists of a prospectus supplement attached to a form of prospectus that (1) previously has been filed or (2) was not required to be filed pursuant to paragraph (b) because it did not contain substantive changes from a prospectus that previously was filed, only the prospectus supplement need be filed under paragraph (b) of this rule, provided that the first page of each prospectus supplement includes a cross reference to the date(s) of the related prospectus and any prospectus supplements thereto that together constitute the prospectus required to be delivered by section 5(b) of the Securities Act with respect to the securities currently being offered or sold. The cross reference may be set forth in longhand, provided it is legible.

NOTE: Any prospectus supplement being filed separately that is smaller than a prospectus page should be attached to an $8^{1}/_{2}'' \times 11''$ sheet of paper.

(d) Every prospectus consisting of a radio or television broadcast shall be reduced to writing. Five copies of every such prospectus shall be filed with the Commission in accordance with the requirements of this rule.

(e) Each copy of a form of prospectus filed under this rule shall contain in the upper right corner of the cover page the paragraph of this rule, including the subparagraph if applicable, under which the filing is made, and the file number of the registration statement to which the prospectus relates. The information required by this paragraph may be set forth in longhand, provided it is legible.

(f)   This rule shall not apply with respect to prospectuses of an investment company registered under the Investment Company Act of 1940, other than a registered closed-end investment company. References to "form of prospectus" in paragraphs (a), (b), and (c) of this rule shall be deemed also to refer to the form of Statement of Additional Information.

(g)   A form of prospectus filed pursuant to this rule that operates to reflect the payment of filing fees for an offering or offerings pursuant to Rule 456(b) must include on its cover page the calculation of registration fee table reflecting the payment of such filing fees for the securities that are the subject of the payment.

(h)(1)   Three copies of a form of prospectus relating to an offering of asset-backed securities pursuant Rule 15(a)(1)(vii) or 415(a)(1)(xii) disclosing information previously omitted from the prospectus filed as part of an effective registration statement in reliance on Rule 430D shall be filed with the Commission at least three business days before the date of the first sale in the offering, or if used earlier, the earlier of:

    (i)   The applicable number of business days before the date of the first sale; or

    (ii)   The second business day after first use.

(2)   Three copies of a prospectus supplement relating to an offering of asset-backed securities pursuant to Rule 415(a)(vii) or 415(a)(1)(xii) that reflects any material change from the information contained in a prospectus filed in accordance with Rule 424(h)(1) shall be filed with the Commission at least forty-eight hours before the date and time of the first sale in the offering. The prospectus supplement must clearly delineate what material information has changed and how the information has changed from the prospectus filed in accordance with Rule 424(h)(1).

Instruction to paragraph (h): The filing requirements of this paragraph (h) do not apply if a filing is made solely to add fees pursuant to Rule 457 and for no other purpose.

(i)(1) A form of prospectus filed pursuant to this section that operates to reflect the payment of filing fees for an offering of an indeterminate amount of exchange-traded vehicle securities pursuant to Rule 456(d) and Rule 457(u) (§ 230.456(d) and § 230.457(u)) shall be filed with the Commission within the time period set forth in Rule 456(d). The form of prospectus must be accompanied by the appropriate registration fee.

(2)   The form of prospectus must include the following information:

    (i)   The name and address of issuer;

    (ii)   The name of the securities for which the prospectus is filed;

    (iii)   The Securities Act file number(s) of the registration statement(s) associated with the offering;

    (iv)   The last day of the fiscal year for the issuer for which the prospectus is filed;

    (v)   The calculation of registration fee information calculated pursuant to Rule 457(u); and

    (vi)   The total interest due pursuant to Rule 456(d)(5) and the total amount of registration fee due including any such interest, if the prospectus is being filed more than 90 days after the end of the issuer's fiscal year.

Rule 425.   Filing of Certain Prospectuses and Communications Under Rule 135 in Connection With Business Combination Transactions

(a)   All written communications made in reliance on Rule 165 are prospectuses that must be filed with the Commission under this rule on the date of first use.

(b)   All written communications that contain no more information than that specified in Rule 135 must be filed with the Commission on or before the date of first use except as provided in paragraph (d)(1) of this rule. A communication limited to the information specified in Rule 135 will not be deemed an offer in accordance with Rule 135 even though it is filed under this rule.

(c)   Each prospectus or Rule 135 communication filed under this rule must identify the filer, the company that is the subject of the offering and the Commission file number for the related registration statement or, if that file number is unknown, the subject company's Exchange Act or Investment Company Act file number, in the upper right corner of the cover page.

    (d)   Notwithstanding paragraph (a) of this rule, the following need not be filed under this rule:

        (1)   Any written communication that is limited to the information specified in Rule 135 and does not contain new or different information from that which was previously disclosed and filed under this rule;

        (2)   Any research report used in reliance on Rule 137, Rule 138 and Rule 139;

        (3)   Any confirmation described in Rule 10b–10 under the Exchange Act; and

        (4)   Any prospectus filed under Rule 424.

    NOTE to Rule 425: 1. File five copies of the prospectus or Rule 135 communication if paper filing is permitted.

    2.   No filing is required under Rule 13e–4(c), Rule 14a–12(b), Rule 14d–2(b), or Rule 14d–9(a) under the Exchange Act, if the communication is filed under this rule. Communications filed under this rule also are deemed filed under the other applicable rules.

Rule 426.   Filing of Certain Prospectuses Under Rule 167 in Connection With Certain Offerings of Asset-Backed Securities

    (a)   All written communications made in reliance on Rule 167 are prospectuses that must be filed with the Commission in accordance with paragraphs (b) and (c) of this rule on Form 8–K and incorporated by reference to the related registration statement for the offering of asset-backed securities. Each prospectus filed under this rule must identify the Commission file number of the related registration statement on the cover page of the related Form 8–K in addition to any other information required by that form. The information contained in any such prospectus shall be deemed to be a part of the registration statement as of the earlier of the time of filing of such information or the time of the filing of the final prospectus that meets the requirements of section 10(a) of the Act relating to such offering pursuant to Rule 424(b).

    (b)   Except as specified in paragraph (c) of this rule, ABS informational and computational material made in reliance on Rule 167 that meet the conditions in paragraph (b)(1) of this rule must be filed within the time frame specified in paragraph (b)(2) of this rule.

        (1)   Conditions for which materials must be filed. The materials are provided to prospective investors under the following conditions:

            (i)   If a prospective investor has indicated to the issuer or an underwriter that it will purchase all or a portion of the class of asset-backed securities to which such materials relate, all materials relating to such class that are or have been provided to such prospective investor; and

            (ii)   For any other prospective investor, all materials provided to such prospective investor after the final terms have been established for all classes of the offering.

        (2)   Time frame to file the materials. The materials must be filed by the later of:

            (i)   The due date for filing the final prospectus relating to such offering that meets the requirements of section 10(a) of the Act pursuant to Rule 424(b); or

            (ii)   Two business days after first use.

    (c)   Notwithstanding paragraphs (a) and (b) of this rule, the following need not be filed under this rule:

        (1)   ABS informational and computational material that relate to abandoned structures or that are furnished to a prospective investor prior to the time the final terms have been established for all classes of the offering where such prospective investor has not indicated to the issuer or an underwriter its intention to purchase the asset-backed securities.

        (2)   Any ABS informational and computational material if a prospectus that meets the requirements of section 10(a) of the Act relating to the offering of such asset-backed securities accompanies or precedes the use of such material.

(3)   Any ABS informational and computational material that does not contain new or different information from that which was previously disclosed and filed under this rule.

(4)   Any written communication that is limited to the information specified in Rule 134, Rule 135 or Rule 135c.

(5)   Any research report used in reliance on Rule 137, Rule 138, Rule 139 or Rule 139a.

(6)   Any confirmation described in Rule 10b–10 of this chapter.

(7)   Any prospectus filed under Rule 424.

(8)   Any free writing prospectus used in reliance on Rule 164 and Rule 433.

(d)   Terms used in this rule have the same meaning as in Item 1101 of Regulation AB.

Instruction: The issuer may aggregate data presented in ABS informational and computational material that are to be filed and file such data in consolidated form. Any such aggregation, however, must not result in either the omission of any information contained in such material otherwise to be filed, or a presentation that makes the information misleading.

Rule 427.   Contents of Prospectus Used After Nine Months

There may be omitted from any prospectus used more than 9 months after the effective date of the registration statement any information previously required to be contained in the prospectus insofar as later information covering the same subjects, including the latest available certified financial statement, as of a date not more than 16 months prior to the use of the prospectus is contained therein.

Rule 428.   Documents Constituting a Section 10(a) Prospectus for Form S–8 Registration Statement; Requirements Relating to Offerings of Securities Registered on Form S–8

(a)(1)   Where securities are to be offered pursuant to a registration statement on Form S–8, the following, taken together, shall constitute a prospectus that meets the requirements of section 10(a) of the Act:

(i)   The document(s), or portions thereof as permitted by paragraph (b)(1)(ii) of this rule, containing the employee benefit plan information required by Item 1 of the Form;

(ii)   The statement of availability of registrant information, employee benefit plan annual reports and other information required by Item 2; and

(iii)   The documents containing registrant information and employee benefit plan annual reports that are incorporated by reference in the registration statement pursuant to Item 3.

(2)   The registrant shall maintain a file of the documents that, pursuant to paragraph (a) of this rule, at any time are part of the section 10(a) prospectus, except for documents required to be incorporated by reference in the registration statement pursuant to Item 3 of Form S–8. Each such document shall be included in the file until five years after it is last used as part of the section 10(a) prospectus to offer or sell securities pursuant to the plan. With respect to documents containing specifically designated portions that constitute part of the section 10(a) prospectus pursuant to paragraph (b)(1)(ii) of this rule, the entire document shall be maintained in the file. Upon request, the registrant shall furnish to the Commission or its staff a copy of any or all of the documents included in the file.

(b)   Where securities are offered pursuant to a registration statement on Form S–8:

(1)(i) The registrant shall deliver or cause to be delivered, to each employee who is eligible to participate (or selected by the registrant to participate, in the case of a stock option or other plan with selective participation) in an employee benefit plan to which the registration statement relates, the information required by Part I of Form S–8. The information shall be in written form and shall be updated in writing in a timely manner to reflect any material changes during any period in which offers or sales are being made. When updating information is furnished, documents previously furnished need not be re-delivered, but the registrant shall furnish promptly without charge to each employee, upon written or oral request, a copy of all documents containing the plan information required by Part I that then constitute part of the section 10(a) prospectus.

(ii)   The registrant may designate an entire document or only portions of a document as constituting part of the section 10(a) prospectus. If the registrant designates only portions of a document as constituting part of the prospectus, rather than the entire document, a statement clearly identifying such portions, for example, by reference to section headings, section numbers, paragraphs or page numbers within the document must be included in a conspicuous place in the forepart of the document, or such portions must be specifically designated throughout the text of the document. Registrants shall not designate only words or sentences within a paragraph as part of a prospectus. Unless the portions of a document constituting part of the section 10(a) prospectus are clearly identified, the entire document shall constitute part of the prospectus.

(iii)   The registrant shall date any document constituting part of the section 10(a) prospectus or containing portions constituting part of the prospectus and shall include the following printed, stamped or typed legend in a conspicuous place in the forepart of the document, substituting the bracketed language as appropriate: "This document [Specifically designated portions of this document] constitutes [constitute] part of a prospectus covering securities that have been registered under the Securities Act of 1933."

(iv)   The registrant shall revise the document(s) containing the plan information sent or given to newly eligible participants pursuant to paragraph (b)(1)(i) of this rule, if documents containing updating information would obscure the readability of the plan information.

(2)   The registrant shall deliver or cause to be delivered with the document(s) containing the information required by Part I of Form S–8, to each employee to whom such information is sent or given, a copy of any one of the following:

(i)   The registrant's annual report to security holders containing the information required by Rule 14a–3(b) under the Securities Exchange Act of 1934 ("Exchange Act") for its latest fiscal year;

(ii)   The registrant's annual report on Form 10–K, 20–F or, in the case of registrants described in General Instruction A(2) of Form 40–F for its latest fiscal year;

(iii)   The latest prospectus filed pursuant to Rule 424(b) under the Act that contains audited financial statements for the registrant's latest fiscal year, *Provided that* the financial statements are not incorporated by reference from another filing, and *Provided further* that such prospectus contains substantially the information required by Rule 14a–3(b) or the registration statement was on Form S–1 or F–1; or

(iv)   The registrant's effective Exchange Act registration statement on Form 10, 20–F or, in the case of registrants described in General Instruction A(2) of Form 40–F, containing audited financial statements for the registrants latest fiscal year.

Instructions. 1. If a registrant has previously sent or given an employee a copy of any document specified in clauses (i)–(iv) of paragraph (b)(2) for the latest fiscal year, it need not be redelivered, but the registrant shall furnish promptly, without charge, a copy of such document upon written or oral request of the employee.

2.   If the latest fiscal year of the registrant has ended within 120 days (or 190 days with respect to foreign private issuers) prior to the delivery of the documents containing the information specified by Part I of Form S–8, the registrant may deliver a document containing financial statements for the fiscal year preceding the latest fiscal year, *provided that* within the 120 or 190 day period a document containing financial statements for the latest fiscal year is furnished to each employee.

(3)   The registrant shall deliver or cause to be delivered promptly, without charge, to each employee to whom information is required to be delivered, upon written or oral request, a copy of the information that has been incorporated by reference pursuant to Item 3 of Form S–8 (not including exhibits to the information that is incorporated by reference unless such exhibits are specifically incorporated by reference into the information that the registration statement incorporates).

(4)   Where interests in a plan are registered, the registrant shall deliver or cause to be delivered promptly, without charge, to each employee to whom information is required to be delivered, upon written or oral request, a copy of the then latest annual report of the plan filed pursuant to Section 15(d) of the Exchange Act, whether on Form 11–K or included as part of the registrant's annual report on Form 10–K.

(5)   The registrant shall deliver or cause to be delivered to all employees participating in a stock option plan or plan fund that invests in registrant securities (and other plan participants who request such information orally or in writing) who do not otherwise receive such material, copies of all reports, proxy statements and other communications distributed to its security holders generally, provided that such material is sent or delivered no later than the time it is sent to security holders.

(c)   As used in this rule, the term "employee benefit plan" is defined in Rule 405 of Regulation C and the term "employee" is defined in General Instruction A.1 of Form S–8.

Rule 429.   Prospectus Relating to Several Registration Statements

(a)   Where a registrant has filed two or more registration statements, it may file a single prospectus in the latest registration statement in order to satisfy the requirements of the Act and the rules and regulations thereunder for that offering and any other offering(s) registered on the earlier registration statement(s). The combined prospectus in the latest registration statement must include all of the information that currently would be required in a prospectus relating to all offering(s) that it covers. The combined prospectus may be filed as part of the initial filing of the latest registration statement, in a pre-effective amendment to it or in a post-effective amendment to it.

(b)   Where a registrant relies on paragraph (a) of this rule, the registration statement containing the combined prospectus shall act, upon effectiveness, as a post-effective amendment to any earlier registration statement whose prospectus has been combined in the latest registration statement. The registrant must identify any earlier registration statement to which the combined prospectus relates by setting forth the Commission file number at the bottom of the facing page of the latest registration statement.

Rule 430.   Prospectus for Use Prior to Effective Date

(a)   A form of prospectus filed as a part of the registration statement shall be deemed to meet the requirements of section 10 of the Act for the purpose of section 5(b)(1) thereof prior to the effective date of the registration statement, provided such form of prospectus contains substantially the information required by the Act and the rules and regulations thereunder to be included in a prospectus meeting the requirements of section 10(a) of the Act for the securities being registered, or contains substantially that information except for the omission of information with respect to the offering price, underwriting discounts or commissions, discounts or commissions to dealers, amount of proceeds, conversion rates, call prices, or other matters dependent upon the offering price. Every such form of prospectus shall be deemed to have been filed as a part of the registration statement for the purpose of section 7 of the Act.

(b)   A form of prospectus filed as part of a registration statement on Form N–1A, Form N–2, Form N–3, Form N–4, or Form N–6 shall be deemed to meet the requirements of section 10 of the Act for the purpose of section 5(b)(1) thereof prior to the effective date of the registration statement, provided that:

(1)   Such form of prospectus meets the requirements of paragraph (a) of this rule; and

(2)   Such registration statement contains a form of Statement of Additional Information that is made available to persons receiving such prospectus upon written or oral request, and without charge, unless the form of prospectus contains the information otherwise required to be disclosed in the form of Statement of Additional Information. Every such form of prospectus shall be deemed to have been filed as part of the registration statement for the purpose of section 7 of the Act.

Rule 430A.   Prospectus in a Registration Statement at the Time of Effectiveness

(a)   The form of prospectus filed as part of a registration statement that is declared effective may omit information with respect to the public offering price, underwriting syndicate (including any material relationships between the registrant and underwriters not named therein), underwriting discounts or commissions, discounts or commissions to dealers, amount of proceeds, conversion rates, call prices and other items dependent upon the offering price, delivery dates, and terms of the securities dependent upon the offering date; and such form of prospectus need not contain such information in order for the registration statement to meet the requirements of section 7 of the Securities Act for the purposes of section 5 thereof, *Provided,* That:

(1)   The securities to be registered are offered for cash;

(2)   The registrant furnishes the undertakings required by Item 512(i) of Regulation S–K Item 512, or the undertakings required by Item 34.4 of Form N–2; and

(3)   The information omitted in reliance upon paragraph (a) from the form of prospectus filed as part of a registration statement that is declared effective is contained in a form of prospectus filed with the Commission pursuant to Rule 424(b) or Rule 497(h) under the Securities Act; except that if such form of prospectus is not so filed by the later of fifteen business days after the effective date of the registration statement or fifteen business days after the effectiveness of a post-effective amendment thereto that contains a form of prospectus, or transmitted by a means reasonably calculated to result in filing with the Commission by that date, the information omitted in reliance upon paragraph (a) must be contained in an effective post-effective amendment to the registration statement.

Instruction to paragraph (a): A decrease in the volume of securities offered or change in the bona fide estimate of the maximum offering price range from that indicated in the form of prospectus filed as part of a registration statement that is declared effective may be disclosed in the form of prospectus filed with the Commission pursuant to Rule 424(b) or Rule 497(h) so long as the decrease in the volume or change in the price range would not materially change the disclosure contained in the registration statement at effectiveness. Notwithstanding the foregoing, any increase or decrease in volume (if the total dollar value of securities offered would not exceed that which was registered) and any deviation from the low or high end of the range may be reflected in the form of prospectus filed with the Commission pursuant to Rule 424(b)(1) or Rule 497(h) if, in the aggregate, the changes in volume and price represent no more than a 20% change in the maximum aggregate offering price set forth in the "Calculation of Registration Fee" table in the effective registration statement.

(b)   The information omitted in reliance upon paragraph (a) from the form of prospectus filed as part of an effective registration statement, and contained in the form of prospectus filed with the Commission pursuant to Rule 424(b) or Rule 497(h), shall be deemed to be a part of the registration statement as of the time it was declared effective.

(c)   When used prior to determination of the offering price of the securities, a form of prospectus relating to the securities offered pursuant to a registration statement that is declared effective with information omitted from the form of prospectus filed as part of such effective registration statement in reliance upon this Rule 430A need not contain information omitted pursuant to paragraph (a), in order to meet the requirements of section 10 of the Securities Act for the purpose of section 5(b)(1) thereof. This provision shall not limit the information required to be contained in a form of prospectus meeting the requirements of section 10(a) of the Act for the purposes of section 5(b)(2) thereof or exception (a) of section 2(a)(10) thereof.

(d)   This rule shall not apply to registration statements for securities to be offered by competitive bidding.

(e)   In the case of a registration statement filed on Form N–1A, Form N–2, Form N–3, Form N–4, or Form N–6, the references to "form of prospectus" in paragraphs (a) and (b) of this rule and the accompanying Note shall be deemed also to refer to the form of Statement of Additional Information filed as part of such a registration statement.

(f)   This rule may apply to registration statements that are immediately effective pursuant to Rule 462(e) and (f).

NOTE: If information is omitted in reliance upon paragraph (a) from the form of prospectus filed as part of an effective registration statement, or effective post-effective amendment thereto, the registrant must ascertain promptly whether a form of prospectus transmitted for filing under Rule 424(b) of Rule 497(h) under the Securities Act actually was received for filing by the Commission and, in the event that it was not, promptly file such prospectus.

Rule 430B.   Prospectus in a Registration Statement After Effective Date

(a)   A form of prospectus filed as part of a registration statement for offerings pursuant to Rule 415(a)(1)(x) may omit from the information required by the form to be in the prospectus information that is unknown or not reasonably available to the issuer pursuant to Rule 409. In addition, a form of prospectus filed as part of an automatic shelf registration statement for offerings pursuant to Rule 415(a), other than

Rule 415(a)(1)(viii), also may omit information as to whether the offering is a primary offering or an offering on behalf of persons other than the issuer, or a combination thereof, the plan of distribution for the securities, a description of the securities registered other than an identification of the name or class of such securities, and the identification of other issuers. Each such form of prospectus shall be deemed to have been filed as part of the registration statement for the purpose of section 7 of the Act.

(b) A form of prospectus filed as part of a registration statement for offerings pursuant to Rule 415(a)(1)(i) by an issuer eligible to use Form S–3 or Form F–3 (§ 239.13 or § 239.33 of this chapter) for primary offerings pursuant to General Instruction I.B.1 of such forms, or an issuer eligible to register such a primary offering under General Instruction A.2 of Form N–2, may omit the information specified in paragraph (a) of this rule, and may also omit the identities of selling security holders and amounts of securities to be registered on their behalf if:

(1) The registration statement is an automatic shelf registration statement as defined in Rule 405; or

(2) All of the following conditions are satisfied:

(i) The initial offering transaction of the securities (or securities convertible into such securities) the resale of which are being registered on behalf of each of the selling security holders, was completed;

(ii) The securities (or securities convertible into such securities) were issued and outstanding prior to the original date of filing the registration statement covering the resale of the securities;

(iii) The registration statement refers to any unnamed selling security holders in a generic manner by identifying the initial offering transaction in which the securities were sold; and

(iv) The issuer is not and during the past three years neither the issuer nor any of its predecessors was:

(A) A blank check company as defined in Rule 419(a)(2);

(B) A shell company, other than a business combination related shell company, each as defined in Rule 405; or

(C) An issuer in an offering of penny stock as defined in Rule 3a51–1 of the Securities Exchange Act of 1934.

(c) A form of prospectus that is part of a registration statement that omits information in reliance upon paragraph (a) or (b) of this rule meets the requirements of section 10 of the Act for the purpose of section 5(b)(1) thereof. This provision shall not limit the information required to be contained in a form of prospectus in order to meet the requirements of section 10(a) of the Act for the purposes of section 5(b)(2) thereof or exception (a) of section 2(a)(10) thereof.

(d) Information omitted from a form of prospectus that is part of an effective registration statement in reliance on paragraph (a) or (b) of this rule may be included subsequently in the prospectus that is part of a registration statement by:

(1) A post-effective amendment to the registration statement;

(2) A prospectus filed pursuant to Rule 424(b); or

(3) If the applicable form permits, including the information in the issuer's periodic or current reports filed pursuant to section 13 or 15(d) of the Securities Exchange Act of 1934 that are incorporated or deemed incorporated by reference into the prospectus that is part of the registration statement in accordance with applicable requirements, subject to the provisions of paragraph (h) of this rule.

(e) Information omitted from a form of prospectus that is part of an effective registration statement in reliance on paragraph (a) or (b) of this rule and contained in a form of prospectus required to be filed with the Commission pursuant to Rule 424(b), other than as provided in paragraph (f) of this rule, shall be deemed part of and included in the registration statement as of the date such form of filed prospectus is first used after effectiveness.

(f)(1)   Information omitted from a form of prospectus that is part of an effective registration statement in reliance on paragraph (a) or (b) of this rule and is contained in a form of prospectus required to be filed with the Commission pursuant to Rule 424(b)(2), (b)(5), or (b)(7), shall be deemed to be part of and included in the registration statement on the earlier of the date such subsequent form of prospectus is first used or the date and time of the first contract of sale of securities in the offering to which such subsequent form of prospectus relates.

(2)   The date on which a form of prospectus is deemed to be part of and included in the registration statement pursuant to paragraph (f)(1) of this rule shall be deemed, for purposes of liability under section 11 of the Act of the issuer and any underwriter at the time only, to be a new effective date of the part of such registration statement relating to the securities to which such form of prospectus relates, such part of the registration statement consisting of all information included in the registration statement and any prospectus relating to the offering of such securities (including information relating to the offering in a prospectus already included in the registration statement) as of such date and all information relating to the offering included in reports and materials incorporated by reference into such registration statement and prospectus as of such date, and in each case not modified or superseded pursuant to Rule 412. The offering of such securities at that time shall be deemed to be the initial bona fide offering thereof.

(3)   If a registration statement is amended to include or is deemed to include, through incorporation by reference or otherwise, except as otherwise provided in Rule 436, a report or opinion of any person made on such person's authority as an expert whose consent would be required under section 7 of the Act because of being named as having prepared or certified part of the registration statement, then for purposes of this rule and for liability purposes under section 11 of the Act, the part of the registration statement for which liability against such person is asserted shall be considered as having become effective with respect to such person as of the time the report or opinion is deemed to be part of the registration statement and a consent required pursuant to section 7 of the Act has been provided as contemplated by section 11 of the Act.

(4)   Except for an effective date resulting from the filing of a form of prospectus filed for purposes of including information required by section 10(a)(3) of the Act or pursuant to Item 512(a)(1)(ii) of Regulation S–K or Item 34.3.a(2) of Form N–2, the date a form of prospectus is deemed part of and included in the registration statement pursuant to this paragraph shall not be an effective date established pursuant to paragraph (f)(2) of this rule as to:

(i)   Any director (or person acting in such capacity) of the issuer;

(ii)   Any person signing any report or document incorporated by reference into the registration statement, except for such a report or document incorporated by reference for purposes of including information required by section 10(a)(3) of the Act or pursuant to Item 512(a)(1)(ii) of Regulation S–K or Item 34.3.a(2) of Form N–2 (such person except for such reports being deemed not to be a person who signed the registration statement within the meaning of section 11(a) of the Act).

(5)   The date a form of prospectus is deemed part of and included in the registration statement pursuant to paragraph (f)(2) of this rule shall not be an effective date established pursuant to paragraph (f)(2) of this rule as to:

(i)   Any accountant with respect to financial statements or other financial information contained in the registration statement as of a prior effective date and for which the accountant previously provided a consent to be named as required by section 7 of the Act, unless the form of prospectus contains new audited financial statements or other financial information as to which the accountant is an expert and for which a new consent is required pursuant to section 7 of the Act or Rule 436; and

(ii)   Any other person whose report or opinion as an expert or counsel has, with their consent, previously been included in the registration statement as of a prior effective date, unless the form of prospectus contains a new report or opinion for which a new consent is required pursuant to section 7 of the Act or Rule 436.

(g) Notwithstanding paragraph (e) or (f) of this rule or paragraph (a) of Rule 412, no statement made in a registration statement or prospectus that is part of the registration statement or made in a document incorporated or deemed incorporated by reference into the registration statement or prospectus that is part of the registration statement after the effective date of such registration statement or portion thereof in respect of an offering determined pursuant to this rule will, as to a purchaser with a time of contract of sale prior to such effective date, supersede or modify any statement that was made in the registration statement or prospectus that was part of the registration statement or made in any such document immediately prior to such effective date.

(h) Where a form of prospectus filed pursuant to Rule 424(b) relating to an offering does not include disclosure of omitted information regarding the terms of the offering, the securities, or the plan of distribution, or selling security holders for the securities that are the subject of the form of prospectus, because such omitted information has been included in periodic or current reports filed pursuant to section 13 or 15(d) of the Securities Exchange Act of 1934 incorporated or deemed incorporated by reference into the prospectus, the issuer shall file a form of prospectus identifying the periodic or current reports that are incorporated or deemed incorporated by reference into the prospectus that is part of the registration statement that contain such omitted information. Such form of prospectus shall be required to be filed, depending on the nature of the incorporated information, pursuant to Rule 424(b)(2), (b)(5), or (b)(7).

(i) Issuers relying on this section shall furnish the undertakings required by Item 512(a) of Regulation S–K or Item 34.3 of Form N–2 as applicable.

Note to Rule 430B:

The provisions of paragraph (b) of Rule 401 shall apply to any prospectus filed for purposes of including information required by section 10(a)(3) of the Act.

Rule 430C. Prospectus in a Registration Statement Pertaining to an Offering Other Than Pursuant to Rule 430A or Rule 430B After the Effective Date

(a) In offerings made other than in reliance on Rule 430B or Rule 430D and other than for prospectuses filed in reliance on Rule 430A, information contained in a form of prospectus required to be filed with the Commission pursuant to Rule 424(b) or Rule 497(b), (c), (d), or (e), shall be deemed to be part of and included in the registration statement on the date it is first used after effectiveness.

(b) Notwithstanding paragraph (a) of this rule or paragraph (a) of Rule 412, no statement made in a registration statement or prospectus that is part of the registration statement or made in a document incorporated or deemed incorporated by reference into the registration statement or prospectus that is part of the registration statement will, as to a purchaser with a time of contract of sale prior to such first use, supersede or modify any statement that was made in the registration statement or prospectus that was part of the registration statement or made in any such document immediately prior to such date of first use.

(c) Nothing in this rule shall affect the information required to be included in an issuer's registration statement and prospectus.

(d) Issuers subject to paragraph (a) of this rule shall furnish the undertakings required by Item 512(a) of Regulation S–K or Item 34.4 of Form N–2, as applicable.

Rule 430D. Prospectus in a Registration Statement after Effective Date for Asset-Backed Securities Offerings

(a) A form of prospectus filed as part of a registration statement for primary offerings of asset-backed securities pursuant to Rule 415(a)(1)(vii) or 415(a)(1)(xii) may omit from the information required by the form to be in the prospectus information that is unknown or not reasonably available to the issuer pursuant to Rule 409.

(b) Information omitted from a form of prospectus that is part of an effective registration statement in reliance on paragraph (a) of this rule (other than information with respect to offering price, underwriting syndicate (including any material relationships between the registrant and underwriters not named therein), underwriting discounts or commissions, discounts or commissions to dealers, amount of proceeds or other maters dependent upon the offering price to the extent such information is unknown or not reasonably available to the issuer pursuant to Rule 409) shall be disclosed in a form of prospectus required to be filed with the Commission pursuant to Rule 424(h). Each such form of prospectus shall be deemed to have been filed as part of the registration statement for the purpose of section 7 of the Act.

(c)   A form of prospectus filed as part of a registration statement that omits information in reliance upon paragraph (a) of this rule meets the requirements of section 10 of the Act for the purpose of section 5(b)(1) of the Act. This provision shall not limit the information required to be contained in a form of prospectus in order to meet the requirements of section 10(a) of the Act for the purposes of section 5(b)(2) or exception (a) of section 2(a)(10) of the Act.

(d)(1)   Except as provided in paragraph (b) or (d)(2) of this rule, information omitted from a form of prospectus that is part of an effective registration statement in reliance on paragraph (a) of this rule may be included subsequently in the prospectus that is part of a registration statement by:

    (i)   A post-effective amendment to the registration statement;

    (ii)   A prospectus filed pursuant to Rule 424(b); or

    (iii)   If the applicable form permits, including the information in the issuer's periodic or current reports filed pursuant to section 13 or 15(d) of the Securities Exchange Act of 1934 that are incorporated or deemed incorporated by reference into the prospectus that is part of the registration statement in accordance with the applicable requirements, subject to the provisions of paragraph (h) of this rule.

(2)   Information omitted from a form of prospectus that is part of an effective registration statement in reliance on paragraph (a) of this rule that adds a new structural feature or credit enhancement must be included subsequently in the prospectus that is part of a registration statement by a post-effective amendment to the registration statement.

(e)(1)   Information omitted from a form of prospectus that is part of an effective registration statement in reliance on paragraph (a) of this rule and contained in a form of prospectus required to be filed with the Commission pursuant to Rule 424(b), other than as provided in paragraph (f) of this rule, shall be deemed part of and included in the registration statement as of the date such form of filed prospectus is first used after effectiveness.

(2)   Information omitted from a form of prospectus that is part of an effective registration statement in reliance on paragraph (a) of this rule and contained in a form of prospectus required to be filed with the Commission pursuant to Rule 424(h) shall be deemed part of and included in the registration statement the earlier of the date such form of filed prospectus is filed with the Commission pursuant to Rule 424(h) or, if used earlier than the date of filing, the date it is first used after effectiveness.

(f)(1)   Information omitted from a form of prospectus that is part of an effective registration statement in reliance on paragraph (a) of this rule, and is contained in a form of prospectus required to be filed with the Commission pursuant to Rule 424(b)(2) or (b)(5), shall be deemed to be part of and included in the registration statement on the earlier of the date such subsequent form of prospectus is first used or the date and time of the first contract of sale of securities in the offering to which such subsequent form of prospectus relates.

(2)   The date on which a form of prospectus is deemed to be part of and included in the registration statement pursuant to paragraph (f)(1) of this rule shall be deemed, for purposes of liability under section 11 of the Act of the issuer and any underwriter at the time only, to be a new effective date of the part of such registration statement relating to the securities to which such form of prospectus relates, such part of the registration statement consisting of all information included in the registration statement and any prospectus relating to the offering of such securities (including information relating to the offering in a prospectus already included in the registration statement) as of such date and all information relating to the offering included in reports and materials incorporated by reference into such registration statement and prospectus as of such date, and in each case not

modified or superseded pursuant to Rule 412. The offering of such securities at that time shall be deemed to be the initial bona fide offering thereof.

(3) If a registration statement is amended to include or is deemed to include, through incorporation by reference or otherwise, except as otherwise provided in Rule 436, a report or opinion of any person made on such person's authority as an expert whose consent would be required under section 7 of the Act because of being named as having prepared or certified part of the registration statement, then for purposes of this rule and for liability purposes under section 11 of the Act, the part of the registration statement for which liability against such person is asserted shall be considered as having become effective with respect to such person as of the time the report or opinion is deemed to be part of the registration statement and a consent required pursuant to section 7 of the Act has been provided as contemplated by section 11 of the Act.

(4) Except for an effective date resulting from the filing of a form of prospectus filed for purposes of including information required by section 10(a)(3) of the Act or pursuant to Item 512(a)(1)(ii) of Regulation S–K, the date a form of prospectus is deemed part of and included in the registration statement pursuant to this paragraph shall not be an effective date established pursuant to paragraph (f)(2) of this rule as to:

(i) Any director (or person acting in such capacity) of the issuer;

(ii) Any person signing any report or document incorporated by reference into the registration statement, except for such a report or document incorporated by reference for purposes of including information required by section 10(a)(3) of the Act or pursuant to Item 512(a)(1)(ii) of Regulation S–K (such person except for such reports being deemed not to be a person who signed the registration statement within the meaning of section 11(a) of the Act).

(5) The date a form of prospectus is deemed part of and included in the registration statement pursuant to paragraph (f)(2) of this rule shall not be an effective date established pursuant to paragraph (f)(2) of this rule as to:

(i) Any accountant with respect to financial statements or other financial information contained in the registration statement as of a prior effective date and for which the accountant previously provided a consent to be named as required by section 7 of the Act, unless the form of prospectus contains new audited financial statements or other financial information as to which the accountant is an expert and for which a new consent is required pursuant to section 7 of the Act or Rule 436; and

(ii) Any other person whose report or opinion as an expert or counsel has, with their consent, previously been included in the registration statement as of a prior effective date, unless the form of prospectus contains a new report or opinion for which a new consent is required pursuant to section 7 of the Act or Rule 436.

(g) Notwithstanding paragraph (e) or (f) of this rule or Rule 412(a), no statement made in a registration statement or prospectus that is part of the registration statement or made in a document incorporated or deemed incorporated by reference into the registration statement or prospectus that is part of the registration statement after the effective date of such registration statement or portion thereof in respect of an offering determined pursuant to this rule will, as to a purchaser with a time of contract of sale prior to such effective date, supersede or modify any statement that was made in the registration statement or prospectus that was part of the registration statement or made in any such document immediately prior to such effective date.

(h) Where a form of prospectus filed pursuant to Rule 424(b) relating to an offering does not include disclosure of omitted information regarding the terms of the offering, the securities or the plan of distribution for the securities that are the subject of the form of prospectus, because such omitted information has been included in periodic or current reports filed pursuant to section 13 or 15(d) of the Securities Exchange Act of 1934 incorporated or deemed incorporated by reference into the prospectus, the issuer shall file a form of prospectus identifying the periodic or current reports that are incorporated or deemed incorporated by reference into the prospectus that is part of the registration statement that contain such omitted information. Such form of prospectus shall be required to be filed, depending on the nature of the incorporated information, pursuant to Rule 424(b)(2) or (b)(5).

(i)   Issuers relying on this rule shall furnish the undertakings required by Item 512(a) of Regulation S–K.

Rule 431.   Summary Prospectuses

(a)   A summary prospectus prepared and filed (except a summary prospectus filed by an open-end management investment company registered under the Investment Company Act of 1940) as part of a registration statement in accordance with this rule shall be deemed to be a prospectus permitted under section 10(b) of the Act for the purposes of section 5(b)(1) of the Act if the form used for registration of the securities to be offered provides for the use of a summary prospectus and the following conditions are met:

(1)(i) The registrant is organized under the laws of the United States or any State or Territory or the District of Columbia and has its principal business operations in the United States or its territories; or

(ii)   The registrant is a foreign private issuer eligible to use Form F–2;

(2)   The registrant has a class of securities registered pursuant to section 12(b) of the Securities Exchange Act of 1934 or has a class of equity securities registered pursuant to section 12(g) of that Act or is required to file reports pursuant to section 15(d) of that Act;

(3)   The registrant: (i) Has been subject to the requirements of section 12 or 15(d) of the Securities Exchange Act of 1934 and has filed all the material required to be filed pursuant to sections 13, 14 or 15(d) of that Act for a period of at least thirty-six calendar months immediately preceding the filing of the registration statement; and (ii) has filed in a timely manner all reports required to be filed during the twelve calendar months and any portion of a month immediately preceding the filing of the registration statement and, if the registrant has used (during the twelve calendar months and any portion of a month immediately preceding the filing of the registration statement) Rule 12b–25(b) under the Securities Exchange Act of 1934 with respect to a report or portion of a report, that report or portion thereof has actually been filed within the time period prescribed by that rule; and

(4)   Neither the registrant nor any of its consolidated or unconsolidated subsidiaries has, since the end of its last fiscal year for which certified financial statements of the registrant and its consolidated subsidiaries were included in a report filed pursuant to section 13(a) or 15(d) of the Securities Exchange Act of 1934: (i) failed to pay any dividend or sinking fund installment on preferred stock; or (ii) defaulted on any installment or installments on indebtedness for borrowed money, or on any rental on one or more long term leases, which defaults in the aggregate are material to the financial position of the registrant and its consolidated and unconsolidated subsidiaries, taken as a whole.

(b)   A summary prospectus shall contain the information specified in the instructions as to summary prospectuses in the form used for registration of the securities to be offered. Such prospectus may include any other information the substance of which is contained in the registration statement except as otherwise specifically provided in the instructions as to summary prospectuses in the form used for registration. It shall not include any information the substance of which is not contained in the registration statement except that a summary prospectus may contain any information specified in Rule 134(a). No reference need be made to inapplicable terms and negative answers to any item of the form may be omitted.

(c)   All information included in a summary prospectus, other than the statement required by paragraph (e) of this rule, may be expressed in such condensed or summarized form as may be appropriate in the light of the circumstances under which the prospectus is to be used. The information need not follow the numerical sequence of the items of the form used for registration. Every summary prospectus shall be dated approximately as of the date of its first use.

(d)   When used prior to the effective date of the registration statement, a summary prospectus shall be captioned a "Preliminary Summary Prospectus" and shall comply with the applicable requirements relating to a preliminary prospectus.

(e)   A statement to the following effect shall be prominently set forth in conspicuous print at the beginning or at the end of every summary prospectus:

"Copies of a more complete prospectus may be obtained from" (Insert name(s), address(es) and telephone number(s)).

Copies of a summary prospectus filed with the Commission pursuant to paragraph (g) of this rule may omit the names of persons from whom the complete prospectus may be obtained.

(f)   Any summary prospectus published in a newspaper, magazine or other periodical need only be set in type at least as large as 7 point modern type. Nothing in this rule shall prevent the use of reprints of a summary prospectus published in a newspaper, magazine, or other periodical, if such reprints are clearly legible.

(g)   Eight copies of every proposed summary prospectus shall be filed as a part of the registration statement, or as an amendment thereto, at least 5 days (exclusive of Saturdays, Sundays and holidays) prior to the use thereof, or prior to the release for publication by any newspaper, magazine or other person, whichever is earlier. The Commission may, however, in its discretion, authorize such use or publication prior to the expiration of the 5-day period upon a written request for such authorization. Within 7 days after the first use or publication thereof, 5 additional copies shall be filed in the exact form in which it was used or published.

Rule 432.   Additional Information Required to Be Included in Prospectuses Relating to Tender Offers

Notwithstanding the provisions of any form for the registration of securities under the Act, any prospectus relating to securities to be offered in connection with a tender offer for, or a request or invitation for tenders of, securities which is subject to . . . either Rule 13e–4 or section 14(d) of the Securities Exchange Act of 1934 must include the information required by Rule 13e–4(d)(1) or Rule 14d–6(d)(1) under the Securities Exchange Act of 1934, as applicable, in all tender offers, requests or invitations that are published, sent or given to security holders.

Rule 433.   Conditions to Permissible Post-Filing Free Writing Prospectuses

(a)   Scope of section. This rule applies to any free writing prospectus with respect to securities of any issuer (except as set forth in Rule 164) that are the subject of a registration statement that has been filed under the Act. Such a free writing prospectus that satisfies the conditions of this rule may include information the substance of which is not included in the registration statement. Such a free writing prospectus that satisfies the conditions of this rule will be a prospectus permitted under section 10(b) of the Act for purposes of sections 2(a)(10), 5(b)(1), and 5(b)(2) of the Act and will, for purposes of considering it a prospectus, be deemed to be public, without regard to its method of use or distribution, because it is related to the public offering of securities that are the subject of a filed registration statement.

(b)   Permitted use of free writing prospectus. Subject to the conditions of this paragraph (b) and satisfaction of the conditions set forth in paragraphs (c) through (g) of this rule, a free writing prospectus may be used under this rule and Rule 164 in connection with a registered offering of securities:

(1)   Eligibility and prospectus conditions for seasoned issuers and well-known seasoned issuers. Subject to the provisions of Rule 164(e), (f), and (g), the issuer or any other offering participant may use a free writing prospectus in the following offerings after a registration statement relating to the offering has been filed that includes a prospectus that, other than by reason of this rule or Rule 431, satisfies the requirements of section 10 of the Act:

(i)   Offerings of securities registered on Form S–3 pursuant to General Instruction I.B.1, I.B.2, I.C., or I.D. thereof or on Form SF–3 or on Form N–2 pursuant to General Instruction A.2 with respect to the same transactions;

(ii)   Offerings of securities registered on Form F–3 pursuant to General Instruction I.A.5, I.B.1, I.B.2, or I.C. thereof;

(iii)   Any other offering not excluded from reliance on this rule and Rule 164 of securities of a well-known seasoned issuer; and

(iv) Any other offering not excluded from reliance on this section and Rule 164 of securities of an issuer eligible to use Form S–3 or Form F–3 for primary offerings pursuant to General Instruction I.B.1 of such Forms or an issuer eligible to use General Instruction A.2 of Form N–2 to register a primary offering described in General Instruction I.B.1 of Form S–3.

(2) Eligibility and prospectus conditions for non-reporting and unseasoned issuers. If the issuer does not fall within the provisions of paragraph (b)(1) of this rule, then, subject to the provisions of Rule 164(e), (f), and (g), any person participating in the offer or sale of the securities may use a free writing prospectus as follows:

(i) If the free writing prospectus is or was prepared by or on behalf of or used or referred to by an issuer or any other offering participant, if consideration has been or will be given by the issuer or other offering participant for the dissemination (in any format) of any free writing prospectus (including any published article, publication, or advertisement), or if section 17(b) of the Act requires disclosure that consideration has been or will be given by the issuer or other offering participant for any activity described therein in connection with the free writing prospectus, then a registration statement relating to the offering must have been filed that includes a prospectus that, other than by reason of this rule or Rule 431, satisfies the requirements of section 10 of the Act, including a price range where required by rule, and the free writing prospectus shall be accompanied or preceded by the most recent such prospectus; provided, however, that use of the free writing prospectus is not conditioned on providing the most recent such prospectus if a prior such prospectus has been provided and there is no material change from the prior prospectus reflected in the most recent prospectus; provided, further that after effectiveness and availability of a final prospectus meeting the requirements of section 10(a) of the Act, no such earlier prospectus may be provided in satisfaction of this condition, and such final prospectus must precede or accompany any free writing prospectus provided after such availability, whether or not an earlier prospectus had been previously provided.

Notes to paragraph (b)(2)(i) of Rule 433:

1. The condition that a free writing prospectus shall be accompanied or preceded by the most recent prospectus satisfying the requirements of section 10 of the Act would be satisfied if a free writing prospectus that is an electronic communication contained an active hyperlink to such most recent prospectus; and

2. A communication for which disclosure would be required under section 17(b) of the Act as a result of consideration given or to be given, directly or indirectly, by or on behalf of an issuer or other offering participant is an offer by the issuer or such other offering participant as the case may be and is, if written, a free writing prospectus of the issuer or other offering participant.

(ii) Where paragraph (b)(2)(i) of this rule does not apply, a registration statement relating to the offering has been filed that includes a prospectus that, other than by reason of this rule or Rule 431 satisfies the requirements of section 10 of the Act, including a price range where required by rule. * * * For purposes of paragraph (f) of this rule, the prospectus included in the registration statement relating to the offering that has been filed does not have to include a price range otherwise required by rule.

(3) Successors. A successor issuer will be considered to satisfy the applicable provisions of this paragraph (b) if:

(i) Its predecessor and it, taken together, satisfy the conditions, provided that the succession was primarily for the purpose of changing the state or other jurisdiction of incorporation of the predecessor or forming a holding company and the assets and liabilities of the successor at the time of succession were substantially the same as those of the predecessor; or

(ii) All predecessors met the conditions at the time of succession and the issuer has continued to do so since the succession.

(c) Information in a free writing prospectus.—

(1) A free writing prospectus used in reliance on this rule may include information the substance of which is not included in the registration statement but such information shall not conflict with:

(i) Information contained in the filed registration statement, including any prospectus or prospectus supplement that is part of the registration statement (including pursuant to Rule 430B, Rule 430C or Rule 430D) and not superseded or modified; or

(ii) Information contained in the issuer's periodic and current reports filed or furnished to the Commission pursuant to section 13 or 15(d) of the Securities Exchange Act of 1934 that are incorporated by reference into the registration statement and not superseded or modified, or pursuant to section 30 of the Investment Company Act of 1940.

(2)(i) A free writing prospectus used in reliance on this rule shall contain substantially the following legend:

The issuer has filed a registration statement (including a prospectus) with the SEC for the offering to which this communication relates. Before you invest, you should read the prospectus in that registration statement and other documents the issuer has filed with the SEC for more complete information about the issuer and this offering. You may get these documents for free by visiting EDGAR on the SEC Web site at www.sec.gov. Alternatively, the issuer, any underwriter or any dealer participating in the offering will arrange to send you the prospectus if you request it by calling toll-free 1-8[xx-xxx-xxxx].

(ii) The legend also may provide an e-mail address at which the documents can be requested and may indicate that the documents also are available by accessing the issuer's Web site and provide the Internet address and the particular location of the documents on the Web site.

(3) A free writing prospectus with respect to securities of a registered closed-end investment company or a business development company that includes fee or expense information must comply with paragraphs (i) and (j) of § 230.482 (Rule 482), as applicable.

(d) Filing conditions.

(1) Except as provided in paragraphs (d)(3), (d)(4), (d)(5), (d)(6), (d)(7), (d)(8), and (f) of this rule, the following shall be filed with the Commission under this rule by a means reasonably calculated to result in filing no later than the date of first use. The free writing prospectus filed for purposes of this rule will not be filed as part of the registration statement:

(i) The issuer shall file:

(A) Any issuer free writing prospectus, as defined in paragraph (h) of this rule;

(B) Any issuer information that is contained in a free writing prospectus prepared by or on behalf of or used by any other offering participant (but not information prepared by or on behalf of a person other than the issuer on the basis of or derived from that issuer information); and

(C) A description of the final terms of the issuer's securities in the offering or of the offering contained in a free writing prospectus or portion thereof prepared by or on behalf of the issuer or any offering participant, after such terms have been established for all classes in the offering; and

(ii) Any offering participant, other than the issuer, shall file any free writing prospectus that is used or referred to by such offering participant and distributed by or on behalf of such person in a manner reasonably designed to lead to its broad unrestricted dissemination.

(2) Each free writing prospectus or issuer information contained in a free writing prospectus filed under this rule shall identify in the filing the Commission file number for the related registration statement or, if that file number is unknown, a description sufficient to identify the related registration statement.

(3)   The condition to file a free writing prospectus under paragraph (d)(1) of this rule shall not apply if the free writing prospectus does not contain substantive changes from or additions to a free writing prospectus previously filed with the Commission.

(4)   The condition to file issuer information contained in a free writing prospectus of an offering participant other than the issuer shall not apply if such information is included (including through incorporation by reference) in a prospectus or free writing prospectus previously filed that relates to the offering.

(5)   Notwithstanding the provisions of paragraph (d)(1) of this rule:

(i)   To the extent a free writing prospectus or portion thereof otherwise required to be filed contains a description of terms of the issuer's securities in the offering or of the offering that does not reflect the final terms, such free writing prospectus or portion thereof is not required to be filed; and

(ii)   A free writing prospectus or portion thereof that contains only a description of the final terms of the issuer's securities in the offering or of the offerings shall be filed by the issuer within two days of the later of the date such final terms have been established for all classes of the offering and the date of first use.

(6)(i)   Notwithstanding the provisions of paragraph (d) of this rule, in an offering of asset-backed securities, a free writing prospectus or portion thereof required to be filed that contains only ABS informational and computational materials as defined in Item 1101(a) of Regulation AB, may be filed under this rule within the timeframe permitted by Rule 426(b) and such filing will satisfy the filing conditions under this rule.

(ii)   In the event that a free writing prospectus is used in reliance on this rule and Rule 164 and the conditions of this rule and Rule 164 (which may include the conditions of paragraph (d)(6)(i) of this rule) are satisfied with respect thereto, then the use of that free writing prospectus shall not be conditioned on satisfaction of the provisions, including without limitation the filing conditions, of Rule 167 and Rule 426. In the event that ABS informational and computational materials are used in reliance on Rule 167 and Rule 426 and the conditions of those rules are satisfied with respect thereto, then the use of those materials shall not be conditioned on the satisfaction of the conditions of Rule 164 and this rule.

(7)   The condition to file a free writing prospectus or issuer information pursuant to this paragraph (d) for a free writing prospectus used at the same time as a communication in a business combination transaction subject to Rule 425 shall be satisfied if:

(i)   The free writing prospectus or issuer information is filed in accordance with the provisions of Rule 425, including the filing timeframe of Rule 425;

(ii)   The filed material pursuant to Rule 425 indicates on the cover page that it also is being filed pursuant to Rule 433; and

(iii)   The filed material pursuant to Rule 425 contains the information specified in paragraph (c)(2) of this rule.

(8)   Notwithstanding any other provision of this paragraph (d):

(i)   A road show for an offering that is a written communication is a free writing prospectus, provided that, except as provided in paragraph (d)(8)(ii) of this rule, a written communication that is a road show shall not be required to be filed; and

(ii)   In the case of a road show that is a written communication for an offering of common equity or convertible equity securities by an issuer that is, at the time of the filing of the registration statement for the offering, not required to file reports with the Commission pursuant to section 13 or section 15(d) of the Securities Exchange Act of 1934, such a road show is required to be filed pursuant to this rule unless the issuer of the securities makes at least one version of a bona fide electronic road show available without restriction by means of graphic communication to any person, including any potential investor in the securities (and if there is more than one version of a road show for the offering that is a written communication, the version available without restriction is made available no later than the other versions).

Note to paragraph (d)(8): A communication that is provided or transmitted simultaneously with a road show and is provided or transmitted in a manner designed to make the communication available only as part of the road show and not separately is deemed to be part of the road show. Therefore, if the road show is not a written communication, such a simultaneous communication (even if it would otherwise be a graphic communication or other written communication) is also deemed not to be written. If the road show is written and not required to be filed, such a simultaneous communication is also not required to be filed. Otherwise, a written communication that is an offer contained in a separate file from a road show, whether or not the road show is a written communication, or otherwise transmitted separately from a road show, will be a free writing prospectus subject to any applicable filing conditions of paragraph (d) of this rule.

(e)   Treatment of information on, or hyperlinked from, an issuer's Web site.

(1)   An offer of an issuer's securities that is contained on an issuer's Web site or hyperlinked by the issuer from the issuer's Web site to a third party's Web site is a written offer of such securities by the issuer and, unless otherwise exempt or excluded from the requirements of section 5(b)(1) of the Act, the filing conditions of paragraph (d) of this rule apply to such offer.

(2)   Notwithstanding paragraph (e)(1) of this rule, historical issuer information that is identified as such and located in a separate section of the issuer's Web site containing historical issuer information, that has not been incorporated by reference into or otherwise included in a prospectus of the issuer for the offering and that has not otherwise been used or referred to in connection with the offering, will not be considered a current offer of the issuer's securities and therefore will not be a free writing prospectus.

(f)   Free writing prospectuses published or distributed by media. Any written offer for which an issuer or any other offering participant or any person acting on its behalf provided, authorized, or approved information that is prepared and published or disseminated by a person unaffiliated with the issuer or any other offering participant that is in the business of publishing, radio or television broadcasting or otherwise disseminating written communications would be considered at the time of publication or dissemination to be a free writing prospectus prepared by or on behalf of the issuer or such other offering participant for purposes of this rule subject to the following:

(1)   The conditions of paragraph (b)(2)(i) of this rule will not apply and the conditions of paragraphs (c)(2) and (d) of this rule will be deemed to be satisfied if:

(i)   No payment is made or consideration given by or on behalf of the issuer or other offering participant for the written communication or its dissemination; and

(ii)   The issuer or other offering participant in question files the written communication with the Commission, and includes in the filing the legend required by paragraph (c)(2) of this rule, within four business days after the issuer or other offering participant becomes aware of the publication, radio or television broadcast, or other dissemination of the written communication.

(2)   The filing obligation under paragraph (f)(1)(ii) of this rule shall be subject to the following:

(i)   The issuer or other offering participant shall not be required to file a free writing prospectus if the substance of that free writing prospectus has previously been filed with the Commission;

(ii)   Any filing made pursuant to paragraph (f)(1)(ii) of this rule may include information that the issuer or offering participant in question reasonably believes is necessary or appropriate to correct information included in the communication; and

(iii)   In lieu of filing the actual written communication as published or disseminated as required by paragraph (f)(1)(ii) of this rule, the issuer or offering participant in question may file a copy of the materials provided to the media, including transcripts of interviews or similar materials, provided the copy or transcripts contain all the information provided to the media.

(3)   For purposes of this paragraph (f) of this rule, an issuer that is in the business of publishing or radio or television broadcasting may rely on this paragraph (f) as to any publication or radio or

television broadcast that is a free writing prospectus in respect of an offering of securities of the issuer if the issuer or an affiliate:

(i)   Is the publisher of a bona fide newspaper, magazine, or business or financial publication of general and regular circulation or bona fide broadcaster of news including business and financial news;

(ii)   Has established policies and procedures for the independence of the content of the publications or broadcasts from the offering activities of the issuer; and

(iii)   Publishes or broadcasts the communication in the ordinary course.

(g)   Record retention. Issuers and offering participants shall retain all free writing prospectuses they have used, and that have not been filed pursuant to paragraph (d) or (f) of this rule, for three years following the initial bona fide offering of the securities in question.

Note to paragraph (g) of Rule 433.

To the extent that the record retention requirements of Rule 17a–4 of the Securities Exchange Act of 1934 apply to free writing prospectuses required to be retained by a broker-dealer under this rule, such free writing prospectuses are required to be retained in accordance with such requirements.

(h)   Definitions. For purposes of this rule:

(1)   An issuer free writing prospectus means a free writing prospectus prepared by or on behalf of the issuer or used or referred to by the issuer and, in the case of an asset-backed issuer, prepared by or on behalf of a depositor, sponsor, or servicer (as defined in Item 1101 of Regulation AB) or affiliated depositor or used or referred to by any such person.

(2)   Issuer information means material information about the issuer or its securities that has been provided by or on behalf of the issuer.

(3)   A written communication or information is prepared or provided by or on behalf of a person if the person or an agent or representative of the person authorizes the communication or information or approves the communication or information before it is used. An offering participant other than the issuer shall not be an agent or representative of the issuer solely by virtue of its acting as an offering participant.

(4)   A road show means an offer (other than a statutory prospectus or a portion of a statutory prospectus filed as part of a registration statement) that contains a presentation regarding an offering by one or more members of the issuer's management (and in the case of an offering of asset-backed securities, management involved in the securitization or servicing function of one or more of the depositors, sponsors, or servicers (as such terms are defined in Item 1101 of Regulation AB) or an affiliated depositor) and includes discussion of one or more of the issuer, such management, and the securities being offered; and

(5)   A bona fide electronic road show means a road show that is a written communication transmitted by graphic means that contains a presentation by one or more officers of an issuer or other persons in an issuer's management (and in the case of an offering of asset-backed securities, management involved in the securitization or servicing function of one or more of the depositors, sponsors, or servicers (as such terms are defined in Item 1101 of Regulation AB) or an affiliated depositor) and, if more than one road show that is a written communication is being used, includes discussion of the same general areas of information regarding the issuer, such management, and the securities being offered as such other issuer road show or shows for the same offering that are written communications.

Note to Rule 433.

This rule does not affect the operation of the provisions of clause (a) of section 2(a)(10) of the Act providing an exception from the definition of "prospectus."

WRITTEN CONSENTS

Rule 436.   Consents Required in Special Cases

(a) If any portion of the report or opinion of an expert or counsel is quoted or summarized as such in the registration statement or in a prospectus, the written consent of the expert or counsel shall be filed as an exhibit to the registration statement and shall expressly state that the expert or counsel consents to such quotation or summarization.

(b) If it is stated that any information contained in the registration statement has been reviewed or passed upon by any persons and that such information is set forth in the registration statement upon the authority of or in reliance upon such persons as experts, the written consents of such persons shall be filed as exhibits to the registration statement.

(c) Notwithstanding the provisions of paragraph (b) of this rule, a report on unaudited interim financial information (as defined in paragraph (d) of this rule) by an independent accountant who has conducted a review of such interim financial information shall not be considered a part of a registration statement prepared or certified by an accountant or a report prepared or certified by an accountant within the meaning of sections 7 and 11 of the Act.

(d) The term "report on unaudited interim financial information" shall mean a report which consists of the following:

   (1) A statement that the review of interim financial information was made in accordance with established professional standards for such reviews;

   (2) An identification of the interim financial information reviewed;

   (3) A description of the procedures for a review of interim financial information;

   (4) A statement that a review of interim financial information is substantially less in scope than an audit conducted in accordance with the standards of the Public Company Accounting Oversight Board (United States) ("PCAOB"), the objective of which is an expression of an opinion regarding the financial statements taken as a whole, and, accordingly, no such opinion is expressed; and

   (5) A statement about whether the accountant is aware of any material modifications that should be made to the accompanying financial information so that it conforms with generally accepted accounting principles.

(e) Where a counsel is named as having acted for the underwriters or selling security holders, no consent will be required by reason of his being named as having acted in such capacity.

(f) Where the opinion of one counsel relies upon the opinion of another counsel, the consent of the counsel whose prepared opinion is relied upon need not be furnished.

(g)(1) Notwithstanding the provisions of paragraphs (a) and (b) of this section, the security rating assigned to a class of debt securities, a class of convertible debt securities, or a class of preferred stock by a nationally recognized statistical rating organization, or with respect to registration statements on 1933 Act Form F–9 (§ 239.39 of this chapter) by any other rating organization specified in the Instruction to paragraph (a)(2) of General Instruction I of Form F–9, shall not be considered a part of the registration statement prepared or certified by a person within the meaning of sections 7 and 11 of the Act.

   (2) For the purpose of paragraph (g)(1) of this section, the term nationally recognized statistical rating organization shall have the same meaning as used in 1934 Act Rule 15c3–1(c)(2)(vi)(F) (17 CFR 240.15c3–1(c)(2)(vi)(F)).

(h) Notwithstanding the provisions of paragraphs (a) and (b) of this rule, any description about matters identified by a qualified person pursuant to Rule 1302(f) of this chapter shall not be considered a part of the registration statement prepared or certified by the qualified person within the meaning of Sections 7 and 11 of the Securities Act.

Rule 437.   Application to Dispense With Consent

An application to the Commission to dispense with any written consent of an expert pursuant to section 7 of the Act shall be made by the registrant and shall be supported by an affidavit or affidavits establishing that the obtaining of such consent is impracticable or involves undue hardships on the registrant. Such application shall be filed and the consent of the Commission shall be obtained prior to the effective date of the registration statement.

Rule 438.   Consents of Persons About to Become Directors

If any person who has not signed the registration statement is named therein as about to become a director, the written consent of such person shall be filed with the registration statement. Any such consent, however, may be omitted if there is filed with the registration statement a statement by the registrant, supported by an affidavit or affidavits, setting forth the reasons for such omission and establishing that the obtaining of such consent is impracticable or involves undue hardship on the registrant.

Rule 439.   Consent to Use of Material Incorporated by Reference

(a)   If the Act or the rules and regulations of the Commission require the filing of a written consent to the use of any material in connection with the registration statement, such consent shall be filed as an exhibit to the registration statement even though the material is incorporated therein by reference. Where the filing of a written consent is required with respect to material incorporated in the registration statement by reference, which is to be filed subsequent to the effective date of the registration statement, such consent shall be filed as an amendment to the registration statement no later than the date on which such material is filed with the Commission, unless express consent to incorporation by reference is contained in the material to be incorporated by reference.

(b)   Notwithstanding paragraph (a) of this rule, any required consent may be incorporated by reference into a registration statement filed pursuant to Rule 462(b) or a post-effective amendment filed pursuant to Rule 462(e) from a previously filed registration statement relating to that offering, provided that the consent contained in the previously filed registration statement expressly provides for such incorporation.

FILINGS; FEES; EFFECTIVE DATE

Rule 455.   Place of Filing

All registration statements and other papers filed with the Commission shall be filed at its principal office. Such material may be filed by delivery to the Commission; provided, however, that only registration statements and post-effective amendments thereto filed pursuant to Rule 462(b) and Rule 110(d) may be filed by means of facsimile transmission.

Rule 456.   Date of Filing; Timing of Fee Payment

(a)   The date on which any papers are actually received by the Commission shall be the date of filing thereof, if all the requirements of the Act and the rules with respect to such filing have been complied with and the required fee paid. The failure to pay an insignificant amount of the required fee at the time of filing, as the result of a bona fide error, shall not be deemed to affect the date of filing.

(b)(1)   Notwithstanding paragraph (a) of this rule, a well-known seasoned issuer that registers securities offerings on an automatic shelf registration statement, or registers additional securities or classes of securities thereon pursuant to Rule 413(b), may, but is not required to, defer payment of all or any part of the registration fee to the Commission required by section 6(b)(2) of the Act on the following conditions:

(i)   If the issuer elects to defer payment of the registration fee, it shall pay the registration fees (pay-as-you-go registration fees) calculated in accordance with Rule 457(r) in advance of or in connection with an offering of securities from the registration statement within the time required to file the prospectus supplement pursuant to Rule 424(b) for the offering, provided, however, that if the issuer fails, after a good faith effort to pay the filing fee within the time required by this rule, the issuer may still be considered to have paid the fee in a timely manner if it is paid within four business days of its original due date; and

(ii)   The issuer reflects the amount of the pay-as-you-go registration fee paid or to be paid in accordance with paragraph (b)(1)(i) of this rule by updating the "Calculation of Registration Fee" table to indicate the class and aggregate offering price of securities offered and the amount of registration fee paid or to be paid in connection with the offering or offerings either in a post-effective amendment filed at the time of the fee payment or on the cover page of a prospectus filed pursuant to Rule 424(b).

(2)   A registration statement filed relying on the pay-as-you-go registration fee payment provisions of paragraph (b)(1) of this rule will be considered filed as to the securities or classes of securities identified in the registration statement for purposes of this rule and section 5 of the Act when it is received by the Commission, if it complies with all other requirements of the Act and the rules with respect to it.

(3)   The securities sold pursuant to a registration statement will be considered registered, for purposes of section 6(a) of the Act, if the pay-as-you-go registration fee has been paid and the post-effective amendment or prospectus including the amended "Calculation of Registration Fee" table is filed pursuant to paragraph (b)(1) of this rule.

(c)(1)   Notwithstanding paragraph (a) of this rule, an asset-backed issuer that registers asset-backed securities offerings on Form SF–3, may, but is not required to, defer payment of all or any part of the registration fee to the Commission required by section 6(b)(1) of the Act on the following conditions:

(i)   If the issuer elects to defer payment of the registration fee, it shall pay the registration fees (pay-as-you-go registration fees) calculated in accordance with Rule 457(s) in advance of or in connection with an offering of securities from the registration statement at the time of filing the prospectus pursuant to Rule 424(h) for the offering; and

(ii)   The issuer reflects the amount of the pay-as-you-go registration fee paid or to be paid in accordance with paragraph (c)(1)(i) of this rule by updating the "Calculation of Registration Fee" table to indicate the class and aggregate offering price of securities offered and the amount of registration fee paid or to be paid in connection with the offering or offerings on the cover page of a prospectus filed pursuant to Rule 424(h).

(2)   A registration statement filed relying on the pay-as-you-go registration fee payment provisions of paragraph (c)(1) of this rule will be considered filed as to the securities or classes of securities identified in the registration statement for purposes of this rule and section 5 of the Act when it is received by the Commission, if it complies with all other requirements of the Act and the rules with respect to it.

(3)   The securities sold pursuant to a registration statement will be considered registered, for purpose of section 6(a) of the Act, if the pay-as-you-go registration fee has been paid and the prospectus including the amended "Calculation of Registration Fee" table is filed pursuant to paragraph (c)(1) of this rule.

(d)(1) Notwithstanding paragraph (a) of this rule, where a registration statement relates to an offering of exchange-traded vehicle securities, an issuer may elect to register an offering of an indeterminate amount of such securities if it meets the following conditions:

(i)   The issuer must state in the "Calculation of Registration Fee" table that it is offering an indeterminate amount of such securities; and

(ii)   The issuer must, not later than 90 days after the end of any fiscal year during which it has publicly offered such securities, pay a registration fee to the Commission calculated in accordance with Rule 457(u) and file a prospectus in accordance with Rule 424(i).

Instruction to paragraph (d)(1)(ii): To determine the date on which the registration fee must be paid, the first day of the 90-day period is the first calendar day of the fiscal year following the fiscal year for which the registration fee is to be paid. If the last day of the 90-day period falls on a Saturday, Sunday, or federal holiday, the registration fee is due on the first business day thereafter.

(2)   If a registrant elects to register an offering of an indeterminate amount of exchange traded vehicle securities pursuant to paragraph (d)(1), the securities sold will be considered registered, for purposes of section 6(a) of the Act, if the registration fee has been paid and a prospectus is filed pursuant to paragraph (d)(1) of this section not later than the end of the 90-day period.

(3)   A registration statement filed relying on the registration fee payment provisions of paragraph (d)(1) of this rule will be considered filed as to the securities identified in the registration statement for purposes of this section and section 5 of the Act when it is received by the Commission, if it complies with all other requirements of the Act and the rules with respect to it.

(4)   Issuer ceasing operations; mergers and other transactions. For purposes of this rule, if an issuer ceases operations, the date the issuer ceases operations will be deemed to be the end of its fiscal year. In the case of a liquidation, merger, or sale of all or substantially all of the assets ("merger") of the issuer, the issuer will be deemed to have ceased operations for the purposes of this rule on the date the merger is consummated; provided, however, that in the case of a merger of an issuer or a series of an issuer ("Predecessor Issuer") with another issuer or a series of an issuer ("Successor Issuer"), the Predecessor Issuer will not be deemed to have ceased operations and the Successor Issuer will assume the obligations, fees, and redemption credits of the Predecessor Issuer incurred pursuant to this rule if the Successor Issuer:

(i)   Had no assets or liabilities, other than nominal assets or liabilities, and no operating history immediately prior to the merger;

(ii)   Acquired substantially all of the assets and assumed substantially all of the liabilities and obligations of the Predecessor Issuer; and registered, for purposes of section 6(a) of the Act, if the registration fee has been paid and a prospectus is filed pursuant to paragraph (d)(1) of this rule not later than the end of the 90-day period.

(iii)   The merger is not designed to result in the Predecessor Issuer merging with, or substantially all of its assets being acquired by, an issuer (or a series of an issuer) that would not meet the conditions of paragraph (d)(4)(i) of this rule.

(5)   An issuer paying the fee required by paragraph (d)(1) or any portion thereof more than 90 days after the end of the fiscal year of the issuer shall pay to the Commission interest on unpaid amounts, calculated based on the interest rate in effect at the time of the interest payment by reference to the "current value of funds rate" on the Treasury Department's Financial Management Service Internet site at http://www.fms.treas.gov, or by calling (202) 874-6995, and using the following formula: $I = (X)\ (Y)\ (Z/365)$, where: I = Amount of interest due; X = Amount of registration fee due; Y = Applicable interest rate, expressed as a fraction; Z = Number of days by which the registration fee payment is late. The payment of interest pursuant to this paragraph shall not preclude the Commission from bringing an action to enforce the requirements of this paragraph (d).

(6)   Failure to comply. An immaterial or unintentional failure to comply with a requirement of Rule 456(d) will not result in a violation of section 6(a) of the Act, so long as:

(i)   A good faith and reasonable effort was made to comply with the requirement; and

(ii)   In the case of a late payment of a registration fee, the issuer pays the registration fee and any interest due thereon as soon as practicable after discovery of the failure to pay the registration fee.

Rule 457.   Computation of Fee

(a)   If a filing fee based on a bona fide estimate of the maximum offering price, computed in accordance with this rule where applicable, has been paid, no additional filing fee shall be required as a result of changes in the proposed offering price. If the number of shares or other units of securities, or the principal amount of debt securities to be offered is increased by an amendment filed prior to the effective date of the registration statement, an additional filing fee, computed on the basis of the offering price of the additional securities, shall be paid. There will be no refund once the statement is filed.

(b)   A required fee shall be reduced in an amount equal to any fee paid with respect to such transaction pursuant to sections 13(e) and 14(g) of the Securities Exchange Act of 1934 or any applicable provision of this rule; the fee requirements under sections 13(e) and 14(g) shall be reduced in an amount equal to the fee paid the Commission with respect to a transaction under this rule. No part of a filing fee is refundable.

(c)   Where securities are to be offered at prices computed upon the basis of fluctuating market prices, the registration fee is to be calculated upon the basis of the price of securities of the same class, as follows: either the average of the high and low prices reported in the consolidated reporting system (for exchange traded securities and last sale reported over-the-counter securities) or the average of the bid and asked price (for other over-the-counter securities) as of a specified date within 5 business days prior to the date of filing the registration statement.

(d)   Where securities are to be offered at varying prices based upon fluctuating values of underlying assets, the registration fee is to be calculated upon the basis of the market value of such assets as of a specified date within fifteen days prior to the date of filing, in accordance with the method to be used in calculating the daily offering price.

(e)   Where securities are to be offered to existing security holders and the portion, if any, not taken by such security holders is to be reoffered to the general public, the registration fee is to be calculated upon the basis of the proposed offering price to such security holders or the proposed reoffering price to the general public, whichever is higher.

(f)   Where securities are to be offered in exchange for other securities (except where such exchange results from the exercise of a conversion privilege) or in a reclassification or recapitalization which involves the substitution of a security for another security, a merger, a consolidation, or a similar plan of acquisition, the registration fee is to be calculated as follows:

(1)   Upon the basis of the market value of the securities to be received by the registrant or cancelled in the exchange or transaction as established by the price of securities of the same class, as determined in accordance with paragraph (c) of this rule.

(2)   If there is no market for the securities to be received by the registrant or cancelled in the exchange or transaction, the book value of such securities computed as of the latest practicable date prior to the date of filing the registration statement shall be used, unless the issuer of such securities is in bankruptcy or receivership or has an accumulated capital deficit, in which case one-third of the principal amount, par value or stated value of such securities shall be used.

(3)   If any cash is to be received by the registrant in connection with the exchange or transaction, the amount thereof shall be added to the value of the securities to be received by the registrant or cancelled as computed in accordance with (e)(1) or (2) of this rule. If any cash is to be paid by the registrant in connection with the exchange or transaction, the amount thereof shall be deducted from the value of the securities to be received by the registrant in exchange as computed in accordance with (e)(1) or (2) of this rule.

(4)   Securities to be offered directly or indirectly for certificates of deposit shall be deemed to be offered for the securities represented by the certificates of deposit.

(5)   If a filing fee is paid under this paragraph for the registration of an offering and the registration statement also covers the resale of such securities, no additional filing fee is required to be paid for the resale transaction.

(g)   Where securities are to be offered pursuant to warrants or other rights to purchase such securities and the holders of such warrants or rights may be deemed to be underwriters, as defined in section 2(11) of the Act, with respect to the warrants or rights or the securities subject thereto, the registration fee is to be calculated upon the basis of the price at which the warrants or rights or securities subject thereto are to be offered to the public. If such offering price cannot be determined at the time of filing the registration statement, the registration fee is to be calculated upon the basis of the highest of the following: (1) the price at which the warrants or rights may be exercised, if known at the time of filing the registration statement; (2) the offering price of securities of the same class included in the registration statement; or (3) the price of securities of the same class, as determined in accordance with paragraph (c) of this rule. If the fee is to be calculated upon the basis of the price at which the warrants or rights may be exercised and they are exercisable over a period of time at progressively higher prices, the fee shall be calculated on the basis of the highest price at which they may be exercised. If the warrants or rights are to be registered for distribution in the same registration statement as the securities to be offered pursuant thereto, no separate registration fee shall be required.

(h)(1) Where securities are to be offered pursuant to an employee benefit plan, the aggregate offering price and the amount of the registration fee shall be computed with respect to the maximum number of the registrant's securities issuable under the plan that are covered by the registration statement. If the offering price is not known, the fee shall be computed upon the basis of the price of securities of the same class, as determined in accordance with paragraph (c) of this rule. In the case of an employee stock option plan, the aggregate offering price and the fee shall be computed upon the basis of the price at which the options may be exercised, or, if such price is not known, upon the basis of the price of securities of the same class, as determined in accordance with paragraph (c) of this rule. If there is no market for the securities to be offered, the book value of such securities computed as of the latest practicable date prior to the date of filing the registration statement shall be used.

(2) If the registration statement registers securities of the registrant and also registers interests in the plan constituting separate securities, no separate fee is required with respect to the plan interests.

(3) Where a registration statement includes securities to be offered pursuant to an employee benefit plan and covers the resale of the same securities, no additional filing fee shall be paid with respect to the securities to be offered for resale. A filing fee determined in accordance with paragraph (c) of this rule shall be paid with respect to any additional securities to be offered for resale.

(i) Where convertible securities and the securities into which conversion is offered are registered at the same time, the registration fee is to be calculated on the basis of the proposed offering price of the convertible securities alone, except that if any additional consideration is to be received in connection with the exercise of the conversion privilege the maximum amount which may be received shall be added to the proposed offering price of the convertible securities.

(j) Where securities are sold prior to the registration thereof and are subsequently registered for the purpose of making an offer of rescission of such sale or sales, the registration fee is to be calculated on the basis of the amount at which such securities were sold, except that where securities repurchased pursuant to such offer of rescission are to be reoffered to the general public at a price in excess of such amount the registration fee is to be calculated on the basis of the proposed reoffering price.

(k) Notwithstanding the other provisions of this rule, the proposed maximum aggregate offering price of Depositary Shares evidenced by American Depositary Receipts shall, only for the purpose of calculating the registration fee, be computed upon the basis of the maximum aggregate fees or charges to be imposed in connection with the issuance of such receipts.

(*l*) Notwithstanding the other provisions of this rule, the proposed maximum aggregate offering price of any put or call option which is traded on an exchange and registered by such exchange or a facility thereof which is traded over the counter shall, for the purpose of calculating the registration fee, be computed upon the basis of the maximum aggregate fees or charges to be imposed by such registrant in connection with the issuance of such option.

(m) Notwithstanding the other provisions of this rule, where the securities to be registered include (1) any note, draft, bill of exchange, or bankers' acceptance which meets all the conditions of section 3(a)(3) hereof, and (2) any note, draft, bill of exchange or bankers' acceptance which has a maturity at the time of issuance of not exceeding nine months exclusive of days of grace, or any renewal thereof the maturity date of which is likewise limited, but which otherwise does not meet the conditions of section (a)(3), the registration fee shall be calculated by taking one-fiftieth of 1 per centum of the maximum principal amount of only those securities not meeting the conditions of section 3(a)(3).

(n) Where the securities to be offered are guarantees of other securities which are being registered concurrently, no separate fee for the guarantees shall be payable.

(o) Where an issuer registers an offering of securities, the registration fee may be calculated on the basis of the maximum aggregate offering price of all the securities listed in the "Calculation of Registration

Fee" table. The number of shares or units of securities need not be included in the "Calculation of Registration Fee" Table. If the maximum aggregate offering price increases prior to the effective date of the registration statement, a pre-effective amendment must be filed to increase the maximum dollar value being registered and the additional filing fee shall be paid.

(p) Where all or a portion of the securities offered under a registration statement remain unsold after the offering's completion or termination, or withdrawal of the registration statement, the aggregate total dollar amount of the filing fee associated with those unsold securities (whether computed under Rule 457(a) or (o)) may be offset against the total filing fee due for a subsequent registration statement or registration statements. The subsequent registration statement(s) must be filed within five years of the initial filing date of the earlier registration statement, and must be filed by the same registrant (including a successor within the meaning of Rule 405), a majority-owned subsidiary of that registrant, or a parent that owns more than 50 percent of the registrant's outstanding voting securities. A note should be added to the "Calculation of Registration Fee" table in the subsequent registration statement(s) stating the dollar amount of the filing fee previously paid that is offset against the currently due filing fee, the file number of the earlier registration statement from which the filing fee is offset, and the name of the registrant and the initial filing date of that earlier registration statement.

(q) Notwithstanding any other provisions of this rule, no filing fee is required for the registration of an indeterminate amount of securities to be offered solely for market-making purposes by an affiliate of the registrant.

(r) Where securities are to be offered pursuant to an automatic shelf registration statement, the registration fee is to be calculated in accordance with this rule. When the issuer elects to defer payment of the fees pursuant to Rule 456(b), the "Calculation of Registration Fee" table in the registration statement must indicate that the issuer is relying on Rule 456(b) but does not need to include the number of shares or units of securities or the maximum aggregate offering price of any securities until the issuer updates the "Calculation of Registration Fee" table to reflect payment of the registration fee, including a pay-as-you-go registration fee in accordance with Rule 456(b). The registration fee shall be calculated based on the fee payment rate in effect on the date of the fee payment.

(s) Where securities are asset-backed securities being offered pursuant to a registration statement on Form SF–3, the registration fee is to be calculated in accordance with this rule. When the issuer elects to defer payment of the fees pursuant to Rule 456(c), the "Calculation of Registration Fee" table in the registration statement must indicate that the issuer is relying on Rule 456(c) but does not need to include the number of units of securities or the maximum aggregate offering price of any securities until the issuer updates the "Calculation of Registration Fee" table to reflect payment of the registration fee, including a pay-as-you-go registration fee in accordance with Rule 456(c). The registration fee shall be calculated based on the fee payment rate in effect on the date of the fee payment.

(t) Where the security to be offered is a collateral certificate or is a special unit of beneficial interest, underlying asset-backed securities (as defined in Item 1101(c) of Regulation AB) which are being registered concurrently, no separate fee for the certificate or the special unit of beneficial interest shall be payable.

(u) Where an issuer elects to register an offering of an indeterminate amount of exchange-traded vehicle securities in accordance with Rule 456(d), the registration fee is to be calculated in the following manner:

(1) Determine the aggregate sale price of securities sold during the fiscal year.

(2) Determine the sum of (i) the aggregate redemption or repurchase price of securities redeemed or repurchased during the fiscal year and (ii) the aggregate redemption or repurchase price of securities redeemed or repurchased during any prior fiscal year ending no earlier than August 1, 2021, that were not used previously to reduce registration fees payable to the Commission.

(3) Subtract (2) from (1). If (2) is less than (1), the amount is the net sales amount. If (2) is greater than (1), the resulting negative amount is the amount of redemption credits available for use in future years to offset sales. (4) The registration fee is calculated by multiplying the net sales amount by the fee payment rate in effect on the date of the fee payment. If the issuer determines that it had net redemptions or repurchases for the fiscal year, no registration fee is due.

Rule 459.   Calculation of Effective Date

Saturdays, Sundays, and holidays shall be counted in computing the effective date of registration statements under section 8(a) of the Act. In the case of statements which become effective on the twentieth day after filing, the twentieth day shall be deemed to begin at the expiration of nineteen periods of 24 hours each from 5:30 p.m. Eastern Standard Time or Eastern Daylight-Saving Time, whichever is in effect at the principal office of the Commission on the date of filing.

Rule 460.   Distribution of Preliminary Prospectus

(a)   Pursuant to the statutory requirement that the Commission in ruling upon requests for acceleration of the effective date of a registration statement shall have due regard to the adequacy of the information respecting the issuer theretofore available to the public, the Commission may consider whether the persons making the offering have taken reasonable steps to make the information contained in the registration statement conveniently available to underwriters and dealers who it is reasonably anticipated will be invited to participate in the distribution of the security to be offered or sold.

(b)(1)   As a minimum, reasonable steps to make the information conveniently available would involve the distribution, to each underwriter and dealer who it is reasonably anticipated will be invited to participate in the distribution of the security, a reasonable time in advance of the anticipated effective date of the registration statement, of as many copies of the proposed form of preliminary prospectus permitted by Rule 430 as appears to be reasonable to secure adequate distribution of the preliminary prospectus.

(2)   In the case of a registration statement filed by a closed-end investment company on Form N–2, reasonable steps to make information conveniently available would involve distribution of a sufficient number of as many copies of the Statement of Additional Information required by Rule 430(b) as it appears to be reasonable to secure their adequate distribution either to each underwriter or dealer who it is reasonably anticipated will be invited to participate in the distribution of the security, or to the underwriter, dealer or other source named on the cover page of the preliminary prospectus as being the person investors should contact in order to obtain the Statement of Additional Information.

(c)   The granting of acceleration will not be conditioned upon

(1)   The distribution of a preliminary prospectus in any state where such distribution would be illegal; or

(2)   The distribution of a preliminary prospectus

(i)   In the case of a registration statement relating solely to securities to be offered at competitive bidding, provided the undertaking in Item 512(d)(1) of Regulation S–K is included in the registration statement and distribution of prospectuses pursuant to such undertaking is made prior to the publication or distribution of the invitation for bids, or

(ii)   In the case of a registration statement relating to a security issued by a face-amount certificate company or a redeemable security issued by an open-end management company or unit investment trust if any other security of the same class is currently being offered or sold, pursuant to an effective registration statement by the issuer or by or through an underwriter, or

(iii)   In the case of an offering of subscription rights unless it is contemplated that the distribution will be made through dealers and the underwriters intend to make the offering during the stockholders' subscription period, in which case copies of the preliminary prospectus must be distributed to dealers prior to the effective date of the registration statement in the same fashion as is required in the case of other offerings through underwriters, or

(iv)   In the case of a registration statement pertaining to a security to be offered pursuant to an exchange offer or transaction described in Rule 145.

Rule 461.   Acceleration of Effective Date

(a)   Requests for acceleration of the effective date of a registration statement shall be made by the registrant and the managing underwriters of the proposed issue, or, if there are no managing underwriters, by the principal underwriters of the proposed issue, and shall state the date upon which it is desired that the registration statement shall become effective. Such requests may be made in writing or orally, provided that, if an oral request is to be made, a letter indicating that fact and stating that the registrant and the managing or principal underwriters are aware of their obligations under the Act must accompany the registration statement (or a pre-effective amendment thereto) at the time of filing with the Commission. Written requests may be sent to the Commission by facsimile transmission. If, by reason of the expected arrangement in connection with the offering, it is to be requested that the registration statement shall become effective at a particular hour of the day, the Commission must be advised to that effect not later than the second business day before the day which it is desired that the registration statement shall become effective. A person's request for acceleration will be considered confirmation of such person's awareness of the person's obligations under the Act. Not later than the time of filing the last amendment prior to the effective date of the registration statement, the registrant shall inform the Commission as to whether or not the amount of compensation to be allowed or paid to the underwriters and any other arrangements among the registrant, the underwriters and other broker dealers participating in the distribution, as described in the registration statement, have been reviewed to the extent required by the National Association of Securities Dealers, Inc. and such Association has issued a statement expressing no objections to the compensation and other arrangements.

(b) Having due regard to the adequacy of information respecting the registrant theretofore available to the public, to the facility with which the nature of the securities to be registered, their relationship to the capital structure of the registrant issuer and the rights of holders thereof can be understood, and to the public interest and the protection of investors, as provided in section 8(a) of the Act, it is the general policy of the Commission, upon request, as provided in paragraph (a) of this rule, to permit acceleration of the effective date of the registration statement as soon as possible after the filing of appropriate amendments, if any. In determining the date on which a registration statement shall become effective, the following are included in the situations in which the Commission considers that the statutory standards of section 8(a) may not be met and may refuse to accelerate the effective date:

(1) Where there has not been a bona fide effort to make the prospectus reasonably concise, readable, and in compliance with the plain English requirements of Rule 421(d) of Regulation C, in order to facilitate an understanding of the information in the prospectus.

(2) Where the form of preliminary prospectus, which has been distributed by the issuer or underwriter, is found to be inaccurate or inadequate in any material respect, until the Commission has received satisfactory assurance that appropriate correcting material has been sent to all underwriters and dealers who received such preliminary prospectus or prospectuses in quantity sufficient for their information and the information of others to whom the inaccurate or inadequate material was sent.

(3) Where the Commission is currently making an investigation of the issuer, a person controlling the issuer, or one of the underwriters, if any, of the securities to be offered, pursuant to any of the Acts administered by the Commission.

(4) Where one or more of the underwriters, although firmly committed to purchase securities covered by the registration statement, is subject to and does not meet the financial responsibility requirements of Rule 15c3–1 under the Securities Exchange Act of 1934. For the purposes of this paragraph underwriters will be deemed to be firmly committed even though the obligation to purchase is subject to the usual conditions as to receipt of opinions of counsel, accountants, etc., the accuracy of warranties or representations, the happening of calamities or the occurrence of other events the determination of which is not expressed to be in the sole or absolute discretion of the underwriters.

(5) Where there have been transactions in securities of the registrant by persons connected with or proposed to be connected with the offering which may have artificially affected or may artificially affect the market price of the security being offered.

(6) Where the amount of compensation to be allowed or paid to the underwriters and any other arrangements among the registrant, the underwriters and other broker dealers participating in the distribution, as described in the registration statement, if required to be reviewed by the National Association of Securities Dealers, Inc. (NASD), have been reviewed by the NASD and the NASD has not issued a statement expressing no objections to the compensation and other arrangements.

(7)   Where, in the case of a significant secondary offering at the market, the registrant, selling security holders and underwriters have not taken sufficient measures to insure compliance with Regulation M.

(c)   Insurance against liabilities arising under the Act, whether the cost of insurance is borne by the registrant, the insured or some other person, will not be considered a bar to acceleration, unless the registrant is a registered investment company or a business development company and the cost of such insurance is borne by other than an insured officer or director of the registrant. In the case of such a registrant, the Commission may refuse to accelerate the effective date of the registration statement when the registrant is organized or administered pursuant to any instrument (including a contract for insurance against liabilities arising under the Act) that protects or purports to protect any director or officer of the company against any liability to the company or its security holders to which he or she would otherwise be subject by reason of willful misfeasance, bad faith, gross negligence or reckless disregard of the duties involved in the conduct of his or her office.

Rule 462.   Immediate Effectiveness of Certain Registration Statements and Post-Effective Amendments

(a)   A registration statement on Form S–8 and a registration statement on Form S–3 or on Form F–3 for a dividend or interest reinvestment plan shall become effective upon filing with the Commission.

(b)   A registration statement and any post-effective amendment thereto shall become effective upon filing with the Commission if:

(1)   The registration statement is for registering additional securities of the same class(es) as were included in an earlier registration statement for the same offering and declared effective by the Commission;

(2)   The new registration statement is filed prior to the time confirmations are sent or given; and

(3)   The new registration statement registers additional securities in an amount and at a price that together represent no more than 20% of the maximum aggregate offering price set forth for each class of securities in the "Calculation of Registration Fee" table contained in such earlier registration statement.

(c)   If the prospectus contained in a post-effective amendment filed prior to the time confirmations are sent or given contains no substantive changes from or additions to the prospectus previously filed as part of the effective registration statement, other than price-related information omitted from the registration statement in reliance on Rule 430A of the Act, such post-effective amendment shall become effective upon filing with the Commission.

(d)   A post-effective amendment filed solely to add exhibits to a registration statement shall become effective upon filing with the Commission.

(e)   An automatic shelf registration statement, including an automatic shelf registration statement filed in accordance with Rule 415(a)(6), and any post-effective amendment thereto, including a post-effective amendment filed to register additional classes of securities pursuant to Rule 413(b), shall become effective upon filing with the Commission.

(f)   A post-effective amendment filed pursuant to paragraph (e) of this section for purposes of adding a new issuer and its securities as permitted by Rule 413(b) (§ 230.413(b)) that satisfies the requirements of Form S–3, Form F–3, or General Instruction A.2 of Form N–2, as applicable, including the signatures required by Rule 402(e), and contains a prospectus satisfying the requirements of Rule 430B, shall become effective upon filing with the Commission.

Rule 463.   Report of Offering of Securities and Use of Proceeds Therefrom

(a)   Except as provided in this rule, following the effective date of the first registration statement filed under the Act by an issuer, the issuer or successor issuer shall report the use of proceeds pursuant to Item 701 of Regulation S–B or S–K or Item 14(e) of Form 20–F, as applicable, on its first periodic report filed pursuant to sections 13(a) and 15(d) of the Securities Exchange Act of 1934 after effectiveness, and thereafter on each of its subsequent periodic reports filed pursuant to sections 13(a) and 15(d) of the Securities Exchange Act of 1934 through the later of disclosure of the application of all the offering proceeds or disclosure of the termination of the offering.

(b) A successor issuer shall comply with paragraph (a) of this rule only if a report of the use of proceeds is required with respect to the first effective registration statement of the predecessor issuer.

(c) For purposes of this rule:

(1) The term "offering proceeds" shall not include any amount(s) received for the account(s) of any selling security holder(s).

(2) The term "application" shall not include the temporary investment of proceeds by the issuer pending final application.

(d) This rule shall not apply to any effective registration statement for securities to be issued:

(1) In a business combination described in Rule 145(a);

(2) By an issuer which pursuant to a business combination described in Rule 145(a) has succeeded to another issuer that prior to such business combination had a registration statement become effective under the Act and on the date of such business combination was not subject to paragraph (a) of this rule;

(3) Pursuant to an employee benefit plan;

(4) Pursuant to a dividend or interest reinvestment plan;

(5) As American depository receipts for foreign securities;

(6) By any investment company registered under the Investment Company Act of 1940 and any issuer that has elected to be regulated as a business development company under sections 54 through 65 of the Investment Company Act of 1940; or

(7) By any public utility company or public utility holding company required to file reports with any State or Federal authority.

(8) In a merger in which a vote or consent of the security holders of the company being acquired is not required pursuant to applicable state law; or

(9) In an exchange offer for the securities of the issuer or another entity.

Rule 464. Effective Date of Post-Effective Amendments to Registration Statements Filed on Form S–8 and on Certain Forms S–3, S–4, F–2, and F–3

Provided. That, at the time of filing of each post-effective amendment with the Commission, the issuer continues to meet the requirements of filing on Form S–8; or on Form S–3, F–2 or F–3 for a registration statement relating to a dividend or interest reinvestment plan; or in the case of a registration statement on Form S–4 that there is continued compliance with General Instruction G of that Form:

(a) The post-effective amendment shall become effective upon filing with the Commission: and

(b) With respect to securities sold on or after the filing date pursuant to a prospectus which forms a part of a Form S–8 registration statement; or a Form S–3, F–2, or F–3 registration statement relating to a dividend or interest reinvestment plan; or a Form S–4 registration statement complying with General Instruction G of that Form and which has been amended to include or incorporate new full year financial statements or to comply with the provisions of section 10(a)(3) of the Act, the effective date of the registration statement shall be deemed to be the filing date of the post-effective amendment.

Rule 466. Effective Date of Certain Registration Statements on Form F–6

(a) A depositary that previously has filed a registration statement on Form F–6 may designate a date and time for a registration statement (including post-effective amendments) on Form F–6 to become effective and such registration statement shall become effective in accordance with such designation if the following conditions are met:

(1)   The depositary previously has filed a registration statement on Form F–6, which the Commission has declared effective, with identical terms of deposit, except for the number of foreign securities a Depositary Share represents, and the depositary so certifies; and

(2)   The designation of the effective date and time is set forth on the facing-page of the registration statement, or in any pre-effective amendment thereto. A pre-effective amendment containing such a designation properly made shall be deemed to have been filed with the consent of the Commission.

(b)(1)   The Commission may, in the manner and under the circumstances set forth in paragraph (b)(2) of this rule, suspend the ability of a depositary to designate the date and time of effectiveness of a registration statement, and such suspension shall remain in effect until the Commission furnishes written notice to the depositary that the suspension has been terminated. Any suspension, so long as it is in effect, shall apply to any registration statement that has been filed but has not, at the time of such suspension, become effective and to any registration statement the depositary files after such suspension. Any such suspension applies only to the ability to designate the date and time of effectiveness under paragraph (a) of this rule and does not otherwise affect the registration statement.

(2)   Any suspension under paragraph (b)(1) of this rule becomes effective when the Commission furnishes written notice thereof to the depositary. The Commission may issue a suspension if it appears to the Commission:

(i)   That any registration statement containing a designation under this rule is incomplete or inaccurate in any material respect, whether or not such registration has become effective, or

(ii)   That the depositary has not complied with any of the conditions of this rule. The depositary may petition the Commission to review the suspension. The Commission will order a hearing on the matter if a request for such a hearing is included in the petition.

Rule 467.   Effectiveness of Registration Statements and Post-Effective Amendments Thereto Made on Forms F–7, F–8, F–9, F–10 and F–80

(a)   A registration statement on Form F–7, Form F–8 or Form F–80, and any amendment thereto, shall become effective upon filing with the Commission. A registration statement on Form F–10, and any amendment thereto, relating to an offering being made contemporaneously in the United States and Canada shall become effective upon filing with the Commission, unless designated as preliminary material on the Form.

(b)   Where no contemporaneous offering is being made in Canada, a registrant filing on Form F–10 may designate on the facing page of the registration statement, or any amendment thereto, a date and time for such filing to become effective that is not earlier than seven calendar days after the date of filing with the Commission, and such registration statement or amendment shall become effective in accordance with such designation; provided, however, That such registration statement or amendment may become effective prior to seven calendar days after the date of filing with the Commission if the securities regulatory authority in the review jurisdiction issues a receipt or notification of clearance with respect thereto before such time elapses, in which case the registration statement or amendment shall become effective by order of the Commission as soon as practicable after receipt of written notification by the Commission from the registrant or the applicable Canadian securities regulatory authority of the issuance of such receipt or notification of clearance.

AMENDMENTS; WITHDRAWALS

Rule 470.   Formal Requirements for Amendments

Except for telegraphic amendments filed pursuant to Rule 473, amendments to a registration statement shall be filed under cover of an appropriate facing sheet, shall be numbered consecutively in the order in which filed, and shall indicate on the facing sheet the applicable registration form on which the amendment is prepared and the file number of the registration statement.

Rule 471.   Signatures to Amendments

(a)   Except as provided in Rule 447 and in Rule 478, every amendment to a registration statement shall be signed by the persons specified in section 6(a) of the Act. At least one copy of every amendment filed with the Commission shall be signed. Unsigned copies shall be conformed.

(b)   Where the Act or the rules thereunder require a document filed with or furnished to the Commission to be signed, such document shall be manually signed, or signed using either typed signatures or duplicated or facsimile versions of manual signatures. Where typed, duplicated or facsimile signatures are used, each signatory to the filing shall manually sign a signature page or other document authenticating, acknowledging or otherwise adopting his or her signature that appears in the filing. Such document shall be executed before or at the time the filing is made and shall be retained by the registrant for a period of five years. Upon request, the registrant shall furnish to the Commission or its staff a copy of any or all documents retained pursuant to this rule.

Rule 472.   Filing of Amendments; Number of Copies

(a)   Except for telegraphic amendments filed pursuant to Rule 473, there shall be filed with the Commission three complete, unmarked copies of every amendment, including exhibits and all other papers and documents filed as part of the amendment, and eight additional copies of such amendment at least five of which shall be marked to indicate clearly and precisely, by underlining or in some other appropriate manner, the changes effected in the registration statement by the amendment. Where the amendment to the registration statement incorporates into the prospectus documents which are required to be delivered with the prospectus in lieu of prospectus presentation, the eight additional copies shall be accompanied by eight copies of such documents. No other exhibits are required to accompany such additional copies.

(b)   Every amendment which relates to a prospectus shall include copies of the prospectus as amended. Each such copy of the amended prospectus shall be accompanied by a copy of the cross reference sheet required by Rule 481(a), where applicable, if the amendment of the prospectus resulted in any change in the accuracy of the cross reference sheet previously filed. Notwithstanding the foregoing provisions of this paragraph, only copies of the changed pages of the prospectus, and the cross reference sheet if amended, need be included in an amendment filed pursuant to an undertaking referred to in Item 512(d) of Regulation S–K.

(c)   Every amendment of a financial statement which is not included in the prospectus shall include copies of the financial statement as amended. Every amendment relating to a certified financial statement shall include the consent of the certifying accountant to the use of his certificate in connection with the amended financial statement in the registration statement or prospectus and to being named as having certified such financial statement.

(d)   Notwithstanding any other provision of this rule, if a registration statement filed on Form S–8 is amended, there shall be filed with the Commission three complete, unmarked copies of every amendment, including exhibits and all other papers and documents filed as part of the amendment. Three additional, unmarked copies of such amendments shall be furnished to the Commission. No exhibits are required to accompany the additional copies of amendments to registration statements filed on Form S–8.

(e)   Notwithstanding any other provision of this rule, if a post-effective amendment is filed pursuant to Rule 462(b) and Rule 110(d), one copy of the complete post-effective amendment, including exhibits and all other papers and documents filed as a part thereof shall be filed with the Commission. Such copy should not be bound and may contain facsimile versions of manual signatures in accordance with Rule 402(e).

Rule 473.   Delaying Amendments

(a)   An amendment in the following form filed with a registration statement, or as an amendment to a registration statement which has not become effective, shall be deemed, for the purpose of section 8(a) of the Act, to be filed on such date or dates as may be necessary to delay the effective date of such registration statement (1) until the registrant shall file a further amendment which specifically states as provided in paragraph (b) of this rule that such registration statement shall thereafter become effective in accordance with section 8(a) of the Act, or (2) until the registration statement shall become effective on such date as the Commission, acting pursuant to section 8(a), may determine:

The registrant hereby amends this registration statement on such date or dates as may be necessary to delay its effective date until the registrant shall file a further amendment which specifically states that this registration statement shall thereafter become effective in accordance with section 8(a) of the Securities Act of 1933 or until the registration statement shall become effective on such date as the Commission acting pursuant to said section 8(a), may determine.

(b)   An amendment which for the purpose of paragraph (a)(1) of this rule specifically states that a registration statement shall thereafter become effective in accordance with section 8(a) of the Act, shall be in the following form:

This registration statement shall hereafter become effective in accordance with the provisions of section 8(a) of the Securities Act of 1933.

(c)   An amendment pursuant to paragraph (a) of this rule which is filed with a registration statement shall be set forth on the facing page thereof following the calculation of the registration fee. Any such amendment filed after the filing of the registration statement, any amendment altering the proposed date of public sale of the securities being registered, or any amendment filed pursuant to paragraph (b) of this rule may be made by telegram, letter or facsimile transmission. Each such telegraphic amendment shall be confirmed in writing within a reasonable time by the filing of a signed copy of the amendment. Such confirmation shall not be deemed an amendment.

(d)   No amendments pursuant to paragraph (a) of this rule may be filed with a registration statement on Form F–7, F–8 or F–80; on F–10 relating to an offering being made contemporaneously in the United States and the issuer's home jurisdiction; on Form S–8; on Form S–3 or F–3 relating to a dividend or interest reinvestment plan; on Form S–3 or Form F–3 relating to an automatic shelf registration statement; or on Form S–4 complying with General Instruction G of that Form.

Rule 474.   Date of Filing of Amendments

The date on which amendments are actually received by the Commission shall be the date of filing thereof, if all the requirements of the Act and the rules with respect to such filing have been complied with.

Rule 475.   Amendment Filed With Consent of Commission

An application for the Commission's consent to the filing of an amendment with the effect provided in section 8(a) of the Act may be filed before or after or concurrently with the filing of the amendment. The application shall be signed and shall state fully the grounds upon which it is made. The Commission's consent shall be deemed to have been given and the amendment shall be treated as a part of the registration statement only when the Commission shall after the filing of such amendment enter an order to that effect.

Rule 475A.   Certain Pre-Effective Amendments Deemed Filed With the Consent of Commission

Amendments to a registration statement on Form F–2 relating to a dividend or interest reinvestment plan, or on Form S–4 complying with General Instruction G of that Form, filed prior to the effectiveness of such registration statement shall be deemed to have been filed with a consent of the Commission and shall accordingly be treated as part of the registration statement.

Rule 476.   Amendment Filed Pursuant to Order of Commission

An amendment filed prior to the effective date of a registration statement shall be deemed to have been filed pursuant to an order of the Commission within the meaning of section 8(a) of the Act so as to be treated as a part of the registration statement only when the Commission shall after the filing of such amendment enter an order declaring that it has been filed pursuant to the Commission's previous order.

Rule 477.   Withdrawal of Registration Statement or Amendment

(a)   Except as provided in paragraph (b) of this rule, any registration statement or any amendment or exhibit thereto may be withdrawn upon application if the Commission, finding such withdrawal consistent with the public interest and the protection of investors, consents thereto.

(b)   Any application for withdrawal of a registration statement filed on Form F–2 relating to a dividend or interest reinvestment plan; or on Form S–4 complying with General Instruction G of that Form, and/or any pre-effective amendment thereto, will be deemed granted upon filing if such filing is made prior to the effective date. Any other application for withdrawal of an entire registration statement made before the effective date of the registration statement will be deemed granted at the time the application is filed with the Commission unless, within 15 calendar days after the registrant files the application, the Commission notifies the registrant that the application for withdrawal will not be granted.

(c)   The registrant must sign any application for withdrawal and must state fully in it the grounds on which the registrant makes the application. The fee paid upon the filing of the registration statement will not be refunded to the registrant. The registrant must state in the application that no securities were sold in connection with the offering. If the registrant applies for withdrawal in anticipation of reliance on Rule 155(c), the registrant must, without discussing any terms of the private offering, state in the application that the registrant may undertake a subsequent private offering in reliance on Rule 155(c).

(d)   Any withdrawn document will remain in the Commission's public files, as well as the related request for withdrawal.

Rule 478.   Powers to Amend or Withdraw Registration Statement

All persons signing a registration statement shall be deemed, in the absence of a statement to the contrary, to confer upon the registrant, and upon the agent for service named in the registration statement, the following powers:

(a)   A power to amend the registration statement (1) by the filing of an amendment as provided in Rule 473; (2) by filing any written consent; (3) by correcting typographical errors; (4) by reducing the amount of securities registered, pursuant to an undertaking contained in the registration statement.

(b)   A power to make application pursuant to Rule 475 for the Commission's consent to the filing of an amendment.

(c)   A power to withdraw the registration statement or any amendment or exhibit thereto.

(d)   A power to consent to the entry of an order under section 8(b) of the Act, waiving notice and hearing, such order being entered without prejudice to the right of the registrant thereafter to have the order vacated upon a showing to the Commission that the registration statement as amended is no longer incomplete or inaccurate on its face in any material respect.

Rule 479.   Procedure With Respect to Abandoned Registration Statements and Post-Effective Amendments

When a registration statement, or a post-effective amendment to such a statement, has been on file with the Commission for a period of nine months and has not become effective the Commission may, in its discretion, proceed in the following manner to determine whether such registration statement or amendment has been abandoned by the registrant. If the registration statement has been amended, otherwise than for the purpose of delaying the effective date thereof, or if the post-effective amendment has been amended, the nine-month period shall be computed from the date of the latest such amendment.

(a)   A notice will be sent to the registrant, and to the agent for service named in the registration statement, by registered or certified mail, return receipt requested, addressed to the most recent addresses for the registrant and the agent for service reflected in the registration statement. Such notice will inform the registrant and the agent for service that the registration statement or amendment is out of date and must be either amended to comply with the applicable requirements of the Act and the rules and regulations thereunder or be withdrawn within 30 days after the date of such notice.

(b)   If the registrant or the agent for service fails to respond to such notice by filing a substantive amendment or withdrawing the registration statement and does not furnish a satisfactory explanation as to why it has not done so within such 30 days, the Commission may, where consistent with the public interest and the protection of investors, enter an order declaring the registration statement or amendment abandoned.

(c)   When such an order is entered by the Commission the papers comprising the registration statement or amendment will not be removed from the files of the Commission but an order shall be included in the file for the registration statement in the following manner: "Declared abandoned by order dated _____."

Rule 480.   Title of Securities

If a registration statement is prepared on a form available solely to investment companies registered under the Investment Company Act of 1940, or a business development company which is selling or proposing to sell its securities pursuant to a registration statement which has been filed under the Act, wherever the title of securities is required to be stated there shall be given such information as will indicate the type and general character of the securities, including the following:

(a)   In the case of shares, the par or stated value, if any; the rate of dividends, if fixed, and whether cumulative or non-cumulative; a brief indication of the preference, if any; and, if convertible, a statement to that effect.

(b)   In the case of funded debt, the rate of interest; the date of maturity, or, if the issue matures serially, a brief indication of the serial maturities, such as "maturing serially from 1950 to 1960"; if the payment of principal or interest is contingent, an appropriate indication of such contingency; a brief indication of the priority of the issue; and, if convertible, a statement to that effect.

(c)   In the case of any other kind of security, appropriate information of comparable character.

Rule 481.   Information Required in Prospectus

Disclose the following in registration statements prepared on a form available solely to investment companies registered under the Investment Company Act of 1940 or in registration statements filed under the Act for a company that has elected to be regulated as a business development company under Sections 55 through 65 of the Investment Company Act:

(a)   *Facing page.* Indicate the approximate date of the proposed sale of the securities to the public.

(b)   *Outside front cover page.* If applicable, include the following in plain English as required by Rule 421(d):

(1)   *Commission legend.* Provide a legend that indicates that the Securities and Exchange Commission has not approved or disapproved of the securities or passed upon the accuracy or adequacy of the disclosure in the prospectus and that any contrary representation is a criminal offense. The legend may be in one of the following or other clear and concise language:

Example A: The Securities and Exchange Commission has not approved or disapproved these securities or passed upon the adequacy of this prospectus. Any representation to the contrary is a criminal offense.

Example B: The Securities and Exchange Commission has not approved or disapproved these securities or determined if this prospectus is truthful or complete. Any representation to the contrary is a criminal offense.

(2)   *"Subject to Completion" legend.*

(i)   If a prospectus or Statement of Additional Information will be used before the effective date of the registration statement, include on the outside front cover page of the prospectus or Statement of Additional Information, a prominent statement that:

(A)   The information in the prospectus or Statement of Additional Information will be amended or completed;

(B)   A registration statement relating to these securities has been filed with the Securities and Exchange Commission;

(C)   The securities may not be sold until the registration statement becomes effective; and

230

(D) In a prospectus, that the prospectus is not an offer to sell the securities and it is not soliciting an offer to buy the securities in any state where offers or sales are not permitted, or in a Statement of Additional Information, that the Statement of Additional Information is not a prospectus.

(ii) The legend may be in the following language or other clear and understandable language:

> The information in this prospectus (or Statement of Additional Information) is not complete and may be changed. We may not sell these securities until the registration statement filed with the Securities and Exchange Commission is effective. This prospectus (or Statement of Additional Information) is not an offer to sell these securities and is not soliciting an offer to buy these securities in any state where the offer or sale is not permitted.

(iii) In the case of a prospectus that omits pricing information under Rule 430A, provide the information and legend in paragraph (b)(2) of this rule if the prospectus or Statement of Additional Information is used before the initial public offering price is determined.

(c) *Table of contents.* Include on either the outside front, inside front, or outside back cover page of the prospectus, a reasonably detailed table of contents. It must show the page number of the various sections or subdivisions of the prospectus. Include this table of contents immediately following the cover page in any prospectus delivered electronically.

(d) *Stabilization and Other Transactions.*

(1) Indicate on the front cover page of the prospectus if the underwriter has any arrangement with the issuer, such as an over-allotment option, under which the underwriter may purchase additional shares in connection with the offering, and state the amount of additional shares the underwriter may purchase under the arrangement. Provide disclosure in the prospectus that briefly describes any transaction that the underwriter intends to conduct during the offering that stabilizes, maintains, or otherwise affects the market price of the offered securities. Include information on stabilizing transactions, syndicate short covering transactions, penalty bids, or any other transactions that affect the offered security's price. Describe the nature of the transactions clearly and explain how the transactions affect the offered security's price. Identify the exchange or other market on which these transactions may occur. If true, disclose that the underwriter may discontinue these transactions at any time;

(2) If the stabilizing began before the effective date of the registration statement, disclose in the prospectus the amount of securities bought, the prices at which they were bought and the period within which they were bought. In the event that Rule 430A of this chapter is used, the prospectus filed under Rule 497(h) or included in a post-effective amendment must contain information on the stabilizing transactions that took place before the determination of the public offering price shown in the prospectus; and

(3) If you are making a warrant or rights offering of securities to existing security holders and the securities not purchased by existing security holders are to be reoffered to the public, disclose in the prospectus used in connection with the reoffering:

(i) The amount of securities bought in stabilization activities during the offering period and the price or range of prices at which the securities were bought;

(ii) The amount of the offered securities subscribed for during the offering period;

(iii) The amount of the offered securities subscribed for by the underwriters during the offering period;

(iv) The amount of the offered securities sold during the offering period by the underwriters and the price or range of prices at which the securities were sold; and

(v) The amount of the offered securities to be reoffered to the public and the public offering price.

(e) *Dealer prospectus delivery obligations.* On the outside back cover page of the prospectus, advise dealers of their prospectus delivery obligation, including the expiration date specified by Section 4(3) of the Act and Rule 174. If the expiration date is not known on the effective date of the registration statement, include the expiration date in the copy of the prospectus filed under Rule 497. This information need not be included if dealers are not required to deliver a prospectus under Rule 174 or Section 24(d) of the Investment Company Act of 1940. Use the following or other clear, plain language:

Dealer Prospectus Delivery Obligation

Until (insert date), all dealers that effect transactions in these securities, whether or not participating in this offering, may be required to deliver a prospectus. This is in addition to the dealers' obligation to deliver a prospectus when acting as underwriters and with respect to their unsold allotments or subscriptions.

(f) *Electronic distribution.* Where a prospectus is distributed through an electronic medium, issuers may satisfy legibility requirements applicable to printed documents, such as paper size, type size and font, bold-face type, italics and red ink, by presenting all required information in a format readily communicated to investors, and where indicated, in a manner reasonably calculated to draw investor attention to specific information.

Rule 482.   Advertising by an Investment Company as Satisfying Requirements of Section 10

(a) *Scope of Rule.* This rule applies to an advertisement or other sales material (advertisement) with respect to securities of an investment company registered under the Investment Company Act of 1940 (1940 Act), or a business development company, that is selling or proposing to sell its securities pursuant to a registration statement that has been filed under the Act. This rule does not apply to an advertisement that is excepted from the definition of prospectus by section 2(a)(10) of the Act or to a summary prospectus under Rule 498. An advertisement that complies with this rule, which may include information the substance of which is not included in the prospectus specified in section 10(a) of the Act, will be deemed to be a prospectus under section 10(b) of the Act for the purposes of section 5(b)(1) of the Act.

NOTE to Paragraph (a). The fact that an advertisement complies with this rule does not relieve the investment company, underwriter, or dealer of any obligations with respect to the advertisement under the antifraud provisions of the federal securities laws. For guidance about factors to be weighed in determining whether statements, representations, illustrations, and descriptions contained in investment company advertisements are misleading, *see* Rule 156. In addition, an advertisement that complies with this rule is subject to the legibility requirements of Rule 420.

(b) *Required Disclosure.* This paragraph describes information that is required to be included in an advertisement in order to comply with this rule.

(1) *Availability of Additional Information.* An advertisement must include a statement that:

(i)   Advises an investor to consider the investment objectives, risks, and charges and expenses of the investment company carefully before investing; explains that the prospectus and, if available, the summary prospectus contains this and other information about the investment company; identifies a source from which an investor may obtain a prospectus and, if available, a summary prospectus; and states that the prospectus and, if available, the summary prospectus should be read carefully before investing; or

(ii) If used with a Profile, advises an investor to consider the investment objectives, risks, and charges and expenses of the investment company carefully before investing; explains that the accompanying Profile contains this and other information about the investment company; describes the procedures for investing in the investment company; and indicates the availability of the investment company's prospectus.

(2) *Advertisements Used Prior to Effectiveness of Registration Statement.* An advertisement that is used prior to effectiveness of the investment company's registration statement or the determination of the public offering price (in the case of a registration statement that becomes effective omitting

information from the prospectus contained in the registration statement in reliance upon Rule 430A) must include the "Subject to Completion" legend required by Rule 481(b)(2).

(3) *Advertisements Including Performance Data.* An advertisement that includes performance data of an open-end management investment company or a separate account registered under the 1940 Act as a unit investment trust offering variable annuity contracts (trust account) must include the following:

(i) A legend disclosing that the performance data quoted represents past performance; that past performance does not guarantee future results; that the investment return and principal value of an investment will fluctuate so that an investor's shares, when redeemed, may be worth more or less than their original cost; and that current performance may be lower or higher than the performance data quoted. The legend should also identify either a toll-free (or collect) telephone number or a Web site where an investor may obtain performance data current to the most recent month-end unless the advertisement includes total return quotations current to the most recent month ended seven business days prior to the date of use. An advertisement for a money market fund that is a government money market fund, as defined in Investment Company Act 2a–7(a)(16), or a retail money market fund, as defined in Investment Company Act Rule 2a–7(a)(25) may omit the disclosure about principal value fluctuation; and

NOTE to Paragraph (b)(3)(i). The date of use refers to the date or dates when an advertisement is used by investors, not the date on which an advertisement is published or submitted for publication. The date of use refers to the entire period of use by investors and not simply the first date on which an advertisement is used.

(ii) If a sales load or any other nonrecurring fee is charged, the maximum amount of the load or fee, and if the sales load or fee is not reflected, a statement that the performance data does not reflect the deduction of the sales load or fee, and that, if reflected, the load or fee would reduce the performance quoted.

(4) *Money market funds.* (i) An advertisement for an investment company that holds itself out to be a money market fund, that is not a government money market fund, as defined in Investment Company Act Rule 2a–7(a)(16), or a retail money market fund, as defined in Investment Company Act Rule 2a–7(a)(25), must include the following statement:

> You could lose money by investing in the Fund. Because the share price of the Fund will fluctuate, when you sell your shares they may be worth more or less than what you originally paid for them. The Fund may impose a fee upon sale of your shares or may temporarily suspend your ability to sell shares if the Fund's liquidity falls below required minimums because of market conditions or other factors. An investment in the Fund is not insured or guaranteed by the Federal Deposit Insurance Corporation or any other government agency. The Fund's sponsor has no legal obligation to provide financial support to the Fund, and you should not expect that the sponsor will provide financial support to the Fund at any time.

(ii) An advertisement for an investment company that holds itself out to be a money market fund, that is a government money market fund, as defined in Investment Company Act Rule 2a–7(a)(16) or a retail money market fund, as defined in Investment Company Act Rule 2a–7(a)(25), and that is subject to the requirements of Investment Company Act Rule 2a–7(c)(2)(i) and/or (ii) (or is not subject to the requirements of Rule 2a–7(c)(2)(i) and/or (ii) pursuant to Rule 2a–7(c)(2)(iii) but has chosen to rely on the ability to impose liquidity fees and suspend redemptions consistent with the requirements of Rule 2a–7(c)(2)(i) and/or (ii), must include the following statement:

> You could lose money by investing in the Fund. Although the Fund seeks to preserve the value of your investment at $1.00 per share, it cannot guarantee it will do so. The Fund may impose a fee upon sale of your shares or may temporarily suspend your ability to sell shares if the Fund's liquidity falls below required minimums because of market conditions or other factors. An investment in the Fund is not insured or guaranteed by the Federal Deposit Insurance Corporation or any other government agency. The Fund's sponsor has no legal

obligation to provide financial support to the Fund, and you should not expect that the sponsor will provide financial support to the Fund at any time.

(iii) An advertisement for an investment company that holds itself out to be a money market fund, that is a government money market fund, as defined in Investment Company Act Rule 2a–7(a)(16) that is not subject to the requirements of Investment Company Act Rule 2a–7(c)(2)(i) and/or (ii) pursuant to Investment Company Act Rule 2a–7(c)(2)(iii) and that has not chosen to rely on the ability to impose liquidity fees and suspend redemptions consistent with the requirements of Investment Company Act Rule 2a–7(c)(2)(i) and/or (ii)), must include the following statement:

You could lose money by investing in the Fund. Although the Fund seeks to preserve the value of your investment at $1.00 per share, it cannot guarantee it will do so. An investment in the Fund is not insured or guaranteed by the Federal Deposit Insurance Corporation or any other government agency. The Fund's sponsor has no legal obligation to provide financial support to the Fund, and you should not expect that the sponsor will provide financial support to the Fund at any time.

Note to paragraph (b)(4). If an affiliated person, promoter, or principal underwriter of the Fund, or an affiliated person of such a person, has contractually committed to provide financial support to the Fund, the statement may omit the last sentence ("The Fund's sponsor has no legal obligation to provide financial support to the Fund, and you should not expect that the sponsor will provide financial support to the Fund at any time.") for the term of the agreement. For purposes of this Note, the term "financial support" includes any capital contribution, purchase of a security from the Fund in reliance on Investment Company Act Rule 17a–9, purchase of any defaulted or devalued security at par, execution of letter of credit or letter of indemnity, capital support agreement (whether or not the Fund ultimately received support), performance guarantee, or any other similar action reasonably intended to increase or stabilize the value or liquidity of the fund's portfolio; however, the term "financial support" excludes any routine waiver of fees or reimbursement of fund expenses, routine inter-fund lending, routine inter-fund purchases of fund shares, or any action that would qualify as financial support as defined above, that the board of directors has otherwise determined not to be reasonably intended to increase or stabilize the value or liquidity of the fund's portfolio.

(5) *Presentation.* In a print advertisement, the statements required by paragraphs (b)(1) through (b)(4) of this rule must be presented in a type size at least as large as and of a style different from, but at least as prominent as, that used in the major portion of the advertisement, provided that when performance data is presented in a type size smaller than that of the major portion of the advertisement, the statements required by paragraph (b)(3) of this rule may appear in a type size no smaller than that of the performance data. If an advertisement is delivered through an electronic medium, the legibility requirements for the statements required by paragraph (b)(1) through (b)(4) of this rule relating to type size and style may be satisfied by presenting the statements in any manner reasonably calculated to draw investor attention to them. In a radio or television advertisement, the statements required by paragraph (b)(1) through (b)(4) of this rule must be given emphasis equal to that used in the major portion of the advertisement. The statements required by paragraph (b)(3) of this rule must be presented in close proximity to the performance data, and, in a print advertisement, must be presented in the body of the advertisement and not in a footnote.

(6) *Commission Legend.* An advertisement that complies with this rule need not contain the Commission legend required by Rule 481(b)(1).

(c) *Use of Applications.* An advertisement that complies with this rule may not contain or be accompanied by any application by which a prospective investor may invest in the investment company, except that a prospectus meeting the requirements of section 10(a) of the Act by which a unit investment trust offers variable annuity or variable life insurance contracts may contain a contract application although the prospectus includes, or is accompanied by, information about an investment company in which the unit investment trust invests that, pursuant to this rule, is deemed a prospectus under section 10(b) of the Act.

(d) *Performance Data for Non-Money Market Funds.* In the case of an open-end management investment company or a trust account (other than a money market fund referred to in paragraph (e) of this rule), any quotation of the company's performance contained in an advertisement shall be limited to quotations of:

(1) *Current Yield.* A current yield that:

    (i) Is based on the methods of computation prescribed in Form N–1A, N–3, or N–4;

    (ii) Is accompanied by quotations of total return as provided for in paragraph (d)(3) of this rule;

    (iii) Is set out in no greater prominence than the required quotations of total return; and

    (iv) Adjacent to the quotation and with no less prominence than the quotation, identifies the length of and the date of the last day in the base period used in computing the quotation.

(2) *Tax-equivalent Yield.* A tax-equivalent yield that:

    (i) Is based on the methods of computation prescribed in Form N–1A, N–3, or N–4;

    (ii) Is accompanied by quotations of yield as provided for in paragraph (d)(1) of this rule and total return as provided for in paragraph (d)(3) of this rule;

    (iii) Is set out in no greater prominence than the required quotations of yield and total return;

    (iv) Relates to the same base period as the required quotation of yield; and

    (v) Adjacent to the quotation and with no less prominence than the quotation, identifies the length of and the date of the last day in the base period used in computing the quotation.

(3) *Average Annual Total Return.* Average annual total return for one, five, and ten year periods, except that if the company's registration statement under the Act has been in effect for less than one, five, or ten years, the time period during which the registration statement was in effect is substituted for the period(s) otherwise prescribed. The quotations must:

    (i) Be based on the methods of computation prescribed in Form N–1A, N–3, or N–4;

    (ii) Be current to the most recent calendar quarter ended prior to the submission of the advertisement for publication;

    (iii) Be set out with equal prominence; and

    (iv) Adjacent to the quotation and with no less prominence than the quotation, identify the length of and the last day of the one, five, and ten year periods.

(4) *After-tax Return.* For an open-end management investment company, average annual total return (after taxes on distributions) and average annual total return (after taxes on distributions and redemption) for one, five, and ten year periods, except that if the company's registration statement under the Act has been in effect for less than one, five, or ten years, the time period during which the registration statement was in effect is substituted for the period(s) otherwise prescribed. The quotations must:

    (i) Be based on the methods of computation prescribed in Form N–1A;

    (ii) Be current to the most recent calendar quarter ended prior to the submission of the advertisement for publication;

    (iii) Be accompanied by quotations of total return as provided for in paragraph (d)(3) of this rule;

    (iv) Include both average annual total return (after taxes on distributions) and average annual total return (after taxes on distributions and redemption);

    (v) Be set out with equal prominence and be set out in no greater prominence than the required quotations of total return; and

(vi) Adjacent to the quotations and with no less prominence than the quotations, identify the length of and the last day of the one, five, and ten year periods.

(5) *Other Performance Measures.* Any other historical measure of company performance (not subject to any prescribed method of computation) if such measurement:

(i) Reflects all elements of return;

(ii) Is accompanied by quotations of total return as provided for in paragraph (d)(3) of this rule;

(iii) In the case of any measure of performance adjusted to reflect the effect of taxes, is accompanied by quotations of total return as provided for in paragraph (d)(4) of this rule;

(iv) Is set out in no greater prominence than the required quotations of total return; and

(v) Adjacent to the measurement and with no less prominence than the measurement, identifies the length of and the last day of the period for which performance is measured.

(e) *Performance Data for Money Market Funds.* In the case of a money market fund:

(1) *Yield.* Any quotation of the money market fund's yield in an advertisement shall be based on the methods of computation prescribed in Form N–1A, N–3, or N–4 and may include:

(i) A quotation of current yield that, adjacent to the quotation and with no less prominence than the quotation, identifies the length of and the date of the last day in the base period used in computing that quotation;

(ii) A quotation of effective yield if it appears in the same advertisement as a quotation of current yield and each quotation relates to an identical base period and is presented with equal prominence; or

(iii) A quotation or quotations of tax-equivalent yield or tax-equivalent effective yield if it appears in the same advertisement as a quotation of current yield and each quotation relates to the same base period as the quotation of current yield, is presented with equal prominence, and states the income tax rate used in the calculation.

(2) *Total Return.* Accompany any quotation of the money market fund's total return in an advertisement with a quotation of the money market fund's current yield under paragraph (e)(1)(i) of this rule. Place the quotations of total return and current yield next to each other, in the same size print, and if there is a material difference between the quoted total return and the quoted current yield, include a statement that the yield quotation more closely reflects the current earnings of the money market fund than the total return quotation.

(f) *Advertisements That Make Tax Representations.* An advertisement for an open-end management investment company (other than a company that is permitted under Rule 35d–1(a)(4) under the Investment Company Act of 1940 to use a name suggesting that the company's distributions are exempt from federal income tax or from both federal and state income tax) that represents or implies that the company is managed to limit or control the effect of taxes on company performance must accompany any quotation of the company's performance permitted by paragraph (d) of this rule with quotations of total return as provided for in paragraph (d)(4) of this rule.

(g) *Timeliness of Performance Data.* All performance data contained in any advertisement must be as of the most recent practicable date considering the type of investment company and the media through which the data will be conveyed, except that any advertisement containing total return quotations will be considered to have complied with this paragraph provided that:

(1)(i) The total return quotations are current to the most recent calendar quarter ended prior to the submission of the advertisement for publication; and

(ii) Total return quotations current to the most recent month ended seven business days prior to the date of use are provided at the toll-free (or collect) telephone number or Web site identified pursuant to paragraph (b)(3)(i) of this rule; or

(2)   The total return quotations are current to the most recent month ended seven business days prior to the date of use of the advertisement.

NOTE to Paragraph (g). The date of use refers to the date or dates when an advertisement is used by investors, not the date on which an advertisement is published or submitted for publication. The date of use refers to the entire period of use by investors and not simply the first date on which an advertisement is used.

(h)   *Filing.* An advertisement that complies with this rule need not be filed as part of the registration statement filed under the Act.

NOTE to Paragraph (h). These advertisements, unless filed with NASD Regulation, Inc., are required to be filed in accordance with the requirements of Rule 497.

(i)   *Advertisements including fee or expense figures.* An advertisement that provides fee or expense figures for an investment company must include the following:

(1)   The maximum amount of any sales load, or any other nonrecurring fee, and the total annual expenses without any fee waiver or expense reimbursement arrangement, based on the methods of computation prescribed by the investment company's registration statement or form under the 1940 Act or under the Act for a prospectus and presented at least as prominently as any other fee or expense figure included in the advertisement; and

(2)   The expected termination date of a fee waiver or expense reimbursement arrangement, if the advertisement provides total annual expenses net of fee waiver or expense reimbursement arrangement amounts.

(j)   *Timeliness of fee and expense information.* Fee and expense information contained in an advertisement must be as of the date of the investment company's most recent prospectus or, if the company no longer has an effective registration statement under the Act, as of the date of its most recent annual shareholder report, except that a company may provide more current information if available.

[Rules 483 through 498 are omitted]

REGULATION D—LIMITED OFFERINGS

Rule 500.   Use of Regulation D

Users of Regulation D should note the following:

(a)   Regulation D relates to transactions exempted from the registration requirements of section 5 of the Securities Act of 1933 (the Act). Such transactions are not exempt from the antifraud, civil liability, or other provisions of the federal securities laws. Issuers are reminded of their obligation to provide such further material information, if any, as may be necessary to make the information required under Regulation D, in light of the circumstances under which it is furnished, not misleading.

(b)   Nothing in Regulation D obviates the need to comply with any applicable state law relating to the offer and sale of securities. Regulation D is intended to be a basic element in a uniform system of federal-state limited offering exemptions consistent with the provisions of sections 18 and 19(c) of the Act. In those states that have adopted Regulation D, or any version of Regulation D, special attention should be directed to the applicable state laws and regulations, including those relating to registration of persons who receive remuneration in connection with the offer and sale of securities, to disqualification of issuers and other persons associated with offerings based on state administrative orders or judgments, and to requirements for filings of notices of sales.

(c)   Attempted compliance with any rule in Regulation D does not act as an exclusive election; the issuer can also claim the availability of any other applicable exemption. For instance, an issuer's failure to satisfy all the terms and conditions of Rule 506(b) shall not raise any presumption that the exemption provided by section 4(a)(2) of the Act is not available.

(d)   Regulation D is available only to the issuer of the securities and not to any affiliate of that issuer or to any other person for resales of the issuer's securities. Regulation D provides an exemption only for the transactions in which the securities are offered or sold by the issuer, not for the securities themselves.

(e)   Regulation D may be used for business combinations that involve sales by virtue of Rule 145(a) or otherwise.

(f)   In view of the objectives of Regulation D and the policies underlying the Act, Regulation D is not available to any issuer for any transaction or chain of transactions that, although in technical compliance with Regulation D, is part of a plan or scheme to evade the registration provisions of the Act. In such cases, registration under the Act is required.

(g)   Securities offered and sold outside the United States in accordance with Rules 901 through 905 (Regulation S) need not be registered under the Act. See Release No. 33–6863. Regulation S may be relied on for such offers and sales even if coincident offers and sales are made in accordance with Regulation D inside the United States. See Rule 152(b)(2). Thus, for example, persons who are offered and sold securities in accordance with Regulation S would not be counted in the calculation of the number of purchasers under Regulation D. Similarly, proceeds from such sales would not be included in the aggregate offering price. The provisions of this paragraph (g), however, do not apply if the issuer elects to rely solely on Regulation D for offers or sales to persons made outside the United States. See Rules 502(a) and 152.

Rule 501.   Definitions and Terms Used in Regulation D

As used in Regulation D (Rule 500 of this Act), the following terms shall have the meaning indicated:

(a)   *Accredited investor.* "Accredited investor" shall mean any person who comes within any of the following categories, or who the issuer reasonably believes comes within any of the following categories, at the time of the sale of the securities to that person:

(1)   Any bank as defined in section 3(a)(2) of the Act, or any savings and loan association or other institution as defined in section 3(a)(5)(A) of the Act whether acting in its individual or fiduciary capacity; any broker or dealer registered pursuant to section 15 of the Securities Exchange Act of 1934; any investment adviser registered pursuant to section 203 of the Investment Advisers Act of 1940 or registered pursuant to the laws of a state; any investment adviser relying on the exemption from registering with the Commission under section 203(*l*) or (m) of the Investment Advisers Act of 1940; any insurance company as defined in section 2(a)(13) of the Act; any investment company registered under the Investment Company Act of 1940 or a business development company as defined in section 2(a)(48) of that act; any Small Business Investment Company licensed by the U.S. Small Business Administration under section 301(c) or (d) of the Small Business Investment Act of 1958; any Rural Business Investment Company as defined in section 384A of the Consolidated Farm and Rural Development Act; any plan established and maintained by a state, its political subdivisions, or any agency or instrumentality of a state or its political subdivisions, for the benefit of its employees, if such plan has total assets in excess of $5,000,000; any employee benefit plan within the meaning of the Employee Retirement Income Security Act of 1974 if the investment decision is made by a plan fiduciary, as defined in section 3(21) of such act, which is either a bank, savings and loan association, insurance company, or registered investment adviser, or if the employee benefit plan has total assets in excess of $5,000,000 or, if a self-directed plan, with investment decisions made solely by persons that are accredited investors;

(2)   Any private business development company as defined in section 202(a)(22) of the Investment Advisers Act of 1940;

(3)   Any organization described in section 501(c)(3) of the Internal Revenue Code, corporation, Massachusetts or similar business trust, partnership, or limited liability company, not formed for the specific purpose of acquiring the securities offered, with total assets in excess of $5,000,000;

(4)   Any director, executive officer, or general partner of the issuer of the securities being offered or sold, or any director, executive officer, or general partner of a general partner of that issuer;

(5)   Any natural person whose individual net worth, or joint net worth with that person's spouse or spousal equivalent, exceeds $1,000,000;

(i)   Except as provided in paragraph (a)(5)(ii) of this rule, for purposes of calculating net worth under this paragraph (a)(5):

(A) The person's primary residence shall not be included as an asset;

(B) Indebtedness that is secured by the person's primary residence, up to the estimated fair market value of the primary residence at the time of the sale of securities, shall not be included as a liability (except that if the amount of such indebtedness outstanding at the time of sale of securities exceeds the amount outstanding 60 days before such time, other than as a result of the acquisition of the primary residence, the amount of such excess shall be included as a liability); and

(C) Indebtedness that is secured by the person's primary residence in excess of the estimated fair market value of the primary residence at the time of the sale of securities shall be included as a liability;

(ii) Paragraph (a)(5)(i) of this rule will not apply to any calculation of a person's net worth made in connection with a purchase of securities in accordance with a right to purchase such securities, provided that:

(A) Such right was held by the person on July 20, 2010;

(B) The person qualified as an accredited investor on the basis of net worth at the time the person acquired such right; and

(C) The person held securities of the same issuer, other than such right, on July 20, 2010.

Note 1 to paragraph (a)(5): For the purposes of calculating joint net worth in this paragraph (a)(5): joint net worth can be the aggregate net worth of the investor and spouse or spousal equivalent; assets need not be held jointly to be included in the calculation. Reliance on the joint net worth standard of this paragraph (a)(5) does not require that the securities be purchased jointly.

(6) Any natural person who had an individual income in excess of $200,000 in each of the two most recent years or joint income with that person's spouse or spousal equivalent in excess of $300,000 in each of those years and has a reasonable expectation of reaching the same income level in the current year;

(7) Any trust, with total assets in excess of $5,000,000, not formed for the specific purpose of acquiring the securities offered, whose purchase is directed by a sophisticated person as described in Rule 506(b)(2)(ii); and

(8) Any entity in which all of the equity owners are accredited investors.

Note 1 to paragraph (a)(8): It is permissible to look through various forms of equity ownership to natural persons in determining the accredited investor status of entities under this paragraph (a)(8). If those natural persons are themselves accredited investors, and if all other equity owners of the entity seeking accredited investor status are accredited investors, then this paragraph (a)(8) may be available.

(9) Any entity, of a type not listed in paragraphs (a)(1), (a)(2), (a)(3), (a)(7), or (a)(8), not formed for the specific purpose of acquiring the securities offered, owning investments in excess of $5,000,000;

Note 1 to paragraph (a)(9): For the purposes this paragraph (a)(9), "investments" is defined in rule 2a51–1(b) under the Investment Company Act of 1940 (17 CFR 270.2a51–1(b)).

(10) Any natural person holding in good standing one or more professional certifications or designations or credentials from an accredited educational institution that the Commission has designated as qualifying an individual for accredited investor status. In determining whether to designate a professional certification or designation or credential from an accredited educational institution for purposes of this paragraph (a)(10), the Commission will consider, among others, the following attributes:

(i) The certification, designation, or credential arises out of an examination or series of examinations administered by a self-regulatory organization or other industry body or is issued by an accredited educational institution;

(ii)   The examination or series of examinations is designed to reliably and validly demonstrate an individual's comprehension and sophistication in the areas of securities and investing;

(iii)   Persons obtaining such certification, designation, or credential can reasonably be expected to have sufficient knowledge and experience in financial and business matters to evaluate the merits and risks of a prospective investment; and

(iv)   An indication that an individual holds the certification or designation is either made publicly available by the relevant self-regulatory organization or other industry body or is otherwise independently verifiable;

Note 1 to paragraph (a)(10): The Commission will designate professional certifications or designations or credentials for purposes of this paragraph (a)(10), by order, after notice and an opportunity for public comment. The professional certifications or designations or credentials currently recognized by the Commission as satisfying the above criteria will be posted on the Commission's website.

(11)   Any natural person who is a "knowledgeable employee," as defined in rule 3c–5(a)(4) under the Investment Company Act of 1940 (17 CFR 270.3c–5(a)(4)), of the issuer of the securities being offered or sold where the issuer would be an investment company, as defined in section 3 of such act, but for the exclusion provided by either section 3(c)(1) or section 3(c)(7) of such act;

(12)   Any "family office," as defined in rule 202(a)(11)(G)–1 under the Investment Advisers Act of 1940 (17 CFR 275.202(a)(11)(G)–1):

(i)   With assets under management in excess of $5,000,000,

(ii)   That is not formed for the specific purpose of acquiring the securities offered, and

(iii)   Whose prospective investment is directed by a person who has such knowledge and experience in financial and business matters that such family office is capable of evaluating the merits and risks of the prospective investment; and

(13)   Any "family client," as defined in rule 202(a)(11)(G)–1 under the Investment Advisers Act of 1940 (17 CFR 275.202(a)(11)(G)–1)), of a family office meeting the requirements in paragraph (a)(12) of this section and whose prospective investment in the issuer is directed by such family office pursuant to paragraph (a)(12)(iii).

(b)   *Affiliate.* An "affiliate" of, or person "affiliated" with, a specified person shall mean a person that directly, or indirectly through one or more intermediaries, controls or is controlled by, or is under common control with, the person specified.

(c)   *Aggregate offering price.* "Aggregate offering price" shall mean the sum of all cash, services, property, notes, cancellation of debt, or other consideration to be received by an issuer for issuance of its securities. Where securities are being offered for both cash and non-cash consideration, the aggregate offering price shall be based on the price at which the securities are offered for cash. Any portion of the aggregate offering price attributable to cash received in a foreign currency shall be translated into United States currency at the currency exchange rate in effect at a reasonable time prior to or on the date of the sale of the securities. If securities are not offered for cash, the aggregate offering price shall be based on the value of the consideration as established by bona fide sales of that consideration made within a reasonable time, or, in the absence of sales, on the fair value as determined by an accepted standard. Such valuations of non-cash consideration must be reasonable at the time made.

(d)   *Business combination.* "Business combination" shall mean any transaction of the type specified in paragraph (a) of Rule 145 under the Act and any transaction involving the acquisition by one issuer, in exchange for all or a part of its own or its parent's stock, of stock of another issuer if, immediately after the acquisition, the acquiring issuer has control of the other issuer (whether or not it had control before the acquisition).

(e)   *Calculation of number of purchasers.* For purposes of calculating the number of purchasers under Rule 506(b) only, the following shall apply:

(1)   The following purchasers shall be excluded:

(i)   Any relative, spouse or relative of the spouse of a purchaser who has the same principal residence as the purchaser;

(ii)   Any trust or estate in which a purchaser and any of the persons related to him as specified in paragraph (e)(1)(i) or (e)(1)(iii) of this rule collectively have more than 50 percent of the beneficial interest (excluding contingent interests);

(iii)   Any corporation or other organization of which a purchaser and any of the persons related to him as specified in paragraph (e)(1)(i) or (e)(1)(ii) of this rule collectively are beneficial owners of more than 50 percent of the equity securities (excluding directors' qualifying shares) or equity interests; and

(iv)   Any accredited investor.

(2)   A corporation, partnership or other entity shall be counted as one purchaser. If, however, that entity is organized for the specific purpose of acquiring the securities offered and is not an accredited investor under paragraph (a)(8) of this rule, then each beneficial owner of equity securities or equity interests in the entity shall count as a separate purchaser for all provisions of Regulation D, except to the extent provided in paragraph (e)(1) of this rule.

(3)   A non-contributory employee benefit plan within the meaning of Title I of the Employee Retirement Income Security Act of 1974 shall be counted as one purchaser where the trustee makes all investment decisions for the plan.

NOTE: The issuer must satisfy all the other provisions of Regulation D for all purchasers whether or not they are included in calculating the number of purchasers. Clients of an investment adviser or customers of a broker or dealer shall be considered the "purchasers" under Regulation D regardless of the amount of discretion given to the investment adviser or broker or dealer to act on behalf of the client or customer.

(f)   *Executive officer.* "Executive officer" shall mean the president, any vice president in charge of a principal business unit, division or function (such as sales, administration or finance), any other officer who performs a policy making function, or any other person who performs similar policy making functions for the issuer. Executive officers of subsidiaries may be deemed executive officers of the issuer if they perform such policy making functions for the issuer.

(g)   *Final order. Final order* shall mean a written directive or declaratory statement issued by a federal or state agency described in Rule 506(d)(1)(iii) under applicable statutory authority that provides for notice and an opportunity for hearing, which constitutes a final disposition or action by that federal or state agency.

(h)   *Issuer.* The definition of the term "issuer" in section 2(a)(4) of the Act shall apply, except that in the case of a proceeding under the Federal Bankruptcy Code, the trustee or debtor in possession shall be considered the issuer in an offering under a plan or reorganization, if the securities are to be issued under the plan.

(i)   *Purchaser representative.* "Purchaser representative" shall mean any person who satisfies all of the following conditions or who the issuer reasonably believes satisfies all of the following conditions:

(1)   Is not an affiliate, director, officer or other employee of the issuer, or beneficial owner of 10 percent or more of any class of the equity securities or 10 percent or more of the equity interest in the issuer, except where the purchaser is:

(i)   A relative of the purchaser representative by blood, marriage or adoption and not more remote than a first cousin;

(ii)   A trust or estate in which the purchaser representative and any persons related to him as specified in paragraph (h)(1)(i) or (h)(1)(iii) of this rule collectively have more than 50 percent of the beneficial interest (excluding contingent interest) or of which the purchaser representative serves as trustee, executor, or in any similar capacity; or

(iii)   A corporation or other organization of which the purchaser representative and any persons related to him as specified in paragraph (h)(1)(i) or (h)(1)(ii) of this rule collectively are the beneficial owners of more than 50 percent of the equity securities (excluding directors' qualifying shares) or equity interests;

(2)   Has such knowledge and experience in financial and business matters that he is capable of evaluating, alone, or together with other purchaser representatives of the purchaser, or together with the purchaser, the merits and risks of the prospective investment;

(3)   Is acknowledged by the purchaser in writing, during the course of the transaction, to be his purchaser representative in connection with evaluating the merits and risks of the prospective investment; and

(4)   Discloses to the purchaser in writing a reasonable time prior to the sale of securities to that purchaser any material relationship between himself or his affiliates and the issuer or its affiliates that then exists, that is mutually understood to be contemplated, or that has existed at any time during the previous two years, and any compensation received or to be received as a result of such relationship.

NOTE 1: A person acting as a purchaser representative should consider the applicability of the registration and antifraud provisions relating to brokers and dealers under the Securities Exchange Act of 1934 ("Exchange Act") and relating to investment advisers under the Investment Advisers Act of 1940.

NOTE 2: The acknowledgement required by paragraph (h)(3) and the disclosure required by paragraph (h)(4) of this rule 501 must be made with specific reference to each prospective investment. Advance blanket acknowledgment, such as for "all securities transactions" or "all private placements," is not sufficient.

NOTE 3: Disclosure of any material relationships between the purchaser representative or his affiliates and the issuer or its affiliates does not relieve the purchaser representative of his obligation to act in the interest of the purchaser.

(j)   *Spousal equivalent.* The term *spousal equivalent* shall mean a cohabitant occupying a relationship generally equivalent to that of a spouse.

Rule 502.   General Conditions to Be Met

The following conditions shall be applicable to offers and sales made under Regulation D:

(a)   *Integration.* To determine whether offers and sales should be integrated, please see Rule 152.

(b)   *Information requirements.*—

(1)   *When information must be furnished.* If the issuer sells securities under Rule 506(b) to any purchaser that is not an accredited investor, the issuer shall furnish the information specified in paragraph (b)(2) of this rule to such purchaser a reasonable time prior to sale. The issuer is not required to furnish the specified information to purchasers when it sells securities under Rule 504, or to any accredited investor.

NOTE: When an issuer provides information to investors pursuant to paragraph (b)(1), it should consider providing such information to accredited investors as well, in view of the antifraud provisions of the federal securities laws.

(2)   *Type of information to be furnished.*

(i)   If the issuer is not subject to the reporting requirements of section 13 or 15(d) of the Exchange Act, at a reasonable time prior to the sale of securities the issuer shall furnish to the purchaser, to the extent material to an understanding of the issuer, its business, and the securities being offered:

(A)   *Non-financial statement information.* If the issuer is eligible to use Regulation A, the same kind of information as would be required in Part II of Form 1–A. If the issuer is not eligible to use Regulation A, the same kind of information as required in Part I of a registration statement filed under the Securities Act on the form that the issuer would be entitled to use.

(B)   *Financial statement information.* (1) *Offerings up to $20,000,000.* The financial statement information required by paragraph (b) of Part F/S of Form 1–A. Such financial statement information must be prepared in accordance with generally accepted accounting principles in the United States (US GAAP). If the issuer is a foreign private issuer, such financial statements must be prepared in accordance with either US GAAP or International Financial Reporting Standards (IFRS) as issued by the International Accounting Standards Board (IASB). If the financial statements comply with IFRS, such compliance must be explicitly and unreservedly stated in the notes to the financial statements and if the financial statements are audited, the auditor's report must include an opinion on whether the financial statements comply with IFRS as issued by the IASB.

(1) *Offerings over $20,000,000.* The financial statement information required by paragraph (c) of Part F/S of Form 1–A (referenced in § 239.90 of this chapter). If the issuer is a foreign private issuer, such financial statements must be prepared in accordance with either US GAAP or IFRS as issued by the IASB. If the financial statements comply with IFRS, such compliance must be explicitly and unreservedly stated in the notes to the financial statements and the auditor's report must include an opinion on whether the financial statements comply with IFRS as issued by the IASB.

(2) *Offerings up to $7,500,000.* The financial statement information required in Form S–1 for smaller reporting companies. If an issuer, other than a limited partnership, cannot obtain audited financial statements without unreasonable effort or expense, then only the issuer's balance sheet, which shall be dated within 120 days of the start of the offering, must be audited. If the issuer is a limited partnership and cannot obtain the required financial statements without unreasonable effort or expense, it may furnish financial statements that have been prepared on the basis of Federal income tax requirements and examined and reported on in accordance with generally accepted auditing standards by an independent public or certified accountant.

(3) *Offerings over $7,500,000.* The financial statement as would be required in a registration statement filed under the Act on the form that the issuer would be entitled to use. If an issuer, other than a limited partnership, cannot obtain audited financial statements without unreasonable effort or expense, then only the issuer's balance sheet, which shall be dated within 120 days of the start of the offering, must be audited. If the issuer is a limited partnership and cannot obtain the required financial statements without unreasonable effort or expense, it may furnish financial statements that have been prepared on the basis of Federal income tax requirements and examined and reported on in accordance with generally accepted auditing standards by an independent public or certified accountant.

(C) If the issuer is a foreign private issuer eligible to use Form 20–F, the issuer shall disclose the same kind of information required to be included in a registration statement filed under the Act on the form that the issuer would be entitled to use. The financial statements need be certified only to the extent required by paragraph (b)(2)(i)(B)(*1*), (*2*) or (*3*) of this rule, as appropriate.

(ii) If the issuer is subject to the reporting requirements of section 13 or 15(d) of the Exchange Act, at a reasonable time prior to the sale of securities the issuer shall furnish to the purchaser the information specified in paragraph (b)(2)(ii)(A) or (B) of this rule, and in either event the information specified in paragraph (b)(2)(ii)(C) of this rule:

(A) The issuer's annual report to shareholders for the most recent fiscal year, if such annual report meets the requirements of Rule 14a–3 or Rule 14c–3 under the Exchange Act, the definitive proxy statement filed in connection with that annual report, and, if requested by the purchaser in writing, a copy of the issuer's most recent Form 10–K.

(B) The information contained in an annual report on Form 10–K under the Exchange Act or in a registration statement on Form S–1 or S–11 under the Act or on Form 10 under the Exchange Act, whichever filing is the most recent required to be filed.

(C)   The information contained in any reports or documents required to be filed by the issuer under sections 13(a), 14(a), 14(c), and 15(d) of the Exchange Act since the distribution or filing of the report or registration statement specified in paragraph (b)(2)(ii)(A) or (B), and a brief description of the securities being offered, the use of the proceeds from the offering, and any material changes in the issuer's affairs that are not disclosed in the documents furnished.

(D)   If the issuer is a foreign private issuer, the issuer may provide in lieu of the information specified in paragraph (b)(2)(ii)(A) or (B) of this rule, the information contained in its most recent filing on Form 20–F or Form F–1.

(iii)   Exhibits required to be filed with the Commission as part of a registration statement or report, other than an annual report to shareholders or parts of that report incorporated by reference in a Form 10–K report, need not be furnished to each purchaser that is not an accredited investor if the contents of material exhibits are identified and such exhibits are made available to a purchaser, upon his written request, a reasonable time prior to his purchase.

(iv)   At a reasonable time prior to the sale of securities to any purchaser that is not an accredited investor in a transaction under Rule 506(b), the issuer shall furnish to the purchaser a brief description in writing of any material written information concerning the offering that has been provided by the issuer to any accredited investor but not previously delivered to such unaccredited purchaser. The issuer shall furnish any portion or all of this information to the purchaser, upon his written request a reasonable time prior to his purchase.

(v)   The issuer shall also make available to each purchaser at a reasonable time prior to his purchase of securities in a transaction under Rule 506(b) the opportunity to ask questions and receive answers concerning the terms and conditions of the offering and to obtain any additional information which the issuer possesses or can acquire without unreasonable effort or expense that is necessary to verify the accuracy of information furnished under paragraph (b)(2)(i) or (ii) of this rule.

(vi)   For business combinations or exchange offers, in addition to information required by Form S–4, the issuer shall provide to each purchaser at the time the plan is submitted to security holders, or, with an exchange, during the course of the transaction and prior to sale, written information about any terms or arrangements of the proposed transactions that are materially different from those for all other security holders. For purposes of this paragraph, an issuer which is not subject to the reporting requirements of section 13 or 15(d) of the Exchange Act may satisfy the requirements of Part I.B. or C. of Form S–4 by compliance with paragraph (b)(2)(i) of this rule.

(vii)   At a reasonable time prior to the sale of securities to any purchaser that is not an accredited investor in a transaction under Rule 506(b), the issuer shall advise the purchaser of the limitations on resale in the manner contained in paragraph (d)(2) of this rule. Such disclosure may be contained in other materials required to be provided by this paragraph.

(viii)   At a reasonable time prior to the sale of securities to any purchaser that is not an accredited investor in a transaction under § 230.506(b), the issuer shall provide the purchaser with any written communication or broadcast script used under the authorization of Rule 241 within 30 days prior to such sale.

(c)   *Limitation on manner of offering.* Except as provided in Rule 504(b)(1) or Rule 506(c), neither the issuer nor any person acting on its behalf shall offer or sell the securities by any form of general solicitation or general advertising, including, but not limited to, the following:

(1)   Any advertisement, article, notice or other communication published in any newspaper, magazine, or similar media or broadcast over television or radio; and

(2)   Any seminar or meeting whose attendees have been invited by any general solicitation or general advertising; *Provided, however,* that publication by an issuer of a notice in accordance with Rule 135c shall not be deemed to constitute general solicitation or general advertising for purposes of this rule; *Provided further,* that, if the requirements of Rule 135e are satisfied, providing any journalist

with access to press conferences held outside of the United States, to meetings with issuer or selling security holder representative conducted outside of the United States, or to written press-related materials released outside of the United States, at or in which a present or proposed offering of securities is discussed, will not be deemed to constitute general solicitation or general advertising for purposes of this rule.

(d) *Limitations on resale.* Except as provided in Rule 504(b)(1), securities acquired in a transaction under Regulation D shall have the status of securities acquired in a transaction under section 4(a)(2) of the Act and cannot be resold without registration under the Act or an exemption therefrom. The issuer shall exercise reasonable care to assure that the purchasers of the securities are not underwriters within the meaning of section 2(a)(11) of the Act, which reasonable care may be demonstrated by the following:

(1) Reasonable inquiry to determine if the purchaser is acquiring the securities for himself or for other persons;

(2) Written disclosure to each purchaser prior to sale that the securities have not been registered under the Act and, therefore, cannot be resold unless they are registered under the Act or unless an exemption from registration is available; and

(3) Placement of a legend on the certificate or other document that evidences the securities stating that the securities have not been registered under the Act and setting forth or referring to the restrictions on transferability and sale of the securities.

While taking these actions will establish the requisite reasonable care, it is not the exclusive method to demonstrate such care. Other actions by the issuer may satisfy this provision. In addition, Rule 502(b)(2)(vii) requires the delivery of written disclosure of the limitations on resale to investors in certain instances.

Rule 503.   Filing of Notice of Sales

(a) *When notice of sales on Form D is required and permitted to be filed.*

(1) An issuer offering or selling securities in reliance on Rule 504 or Rule 506 must file with the Commission a notice of sales containing the information required by Form D for each new offering of securities no later than 15 calendar days after the first sale of securities in the offering, unless the end of that period falls on a Saturday, Sunday or holiday, in which case the due date would be the first business day following.

(2) An issuer may file an amendment to a previously filed notice of sales on Form D at any time.

(3) An issuer must file an amendment to a previously filed notice of sales on Form D for an offering:

(i) To correct a material mistake of fact or error in the previously filed notice of sales on Form D, as soon as practicable after discovery of the mistake or error;

(ii) To reflect a change in the information provided in the previously filed notice of sales on Form D, as soon as practicable after the change, except that no amendment is required to reflect a change that occurs after the offering terminates or a change that occurs solely in the following information:

(A) The address or relationship to the issuer of a related person identified in response to Item 3 of the notice of sales on Form D;

(B) An issuer's revenues or aggregate net asset value;

(C) The minimum investment amount, if the change is an increase, or if the change, together with all other changes in that amount since the previously filed notice of sales on Form D, does not result in a decrease of more than 10%;

(D) Any address or state(s) of solicitation shown in response to Item 12 of the notice of sales on Form D;

(E)   The total offering amount, if the change is a decrease, or if the change, together with all other changes in that amount since the previously filed notice of sales on Form D, does not result in an increase of more than 10%;

(F)   The amount of securities sold in the offering or the amount remaining to be sold;

(G)   The number of non-accredited investors who have invested in the offering, as long as the change does not increase the number to more than 35;

(H)   The total number of investors who have invested in the offering; or

(I)   The amount of sales commissions, finders' fees or use of proceeds for payments to executive officers, directors or promoters, if the change is a decrease, or if the change, together with all other changes in that amount since the previously filed notice of sales on Form D, does not result in an increase of more than 10%; and

(iii)   Annually, on or before the first anniversary of the filing of the notice of sales on Form D or the filing of the most recent amendment to the notice of sales on Form D, if the offering is continuing at that time.

(4)   An issuer that files an amendment to a previously filed notice of sales on Form D must provide current information in response to all requirements of the notice of sales on Form D regardless of why the amendment is filed.

(b)   *How notice of sales on Form D must be filed and signed.*

(1)   A notice of sales on Form D must be filed with the Commission in electronic format by means of the Commission's Electronic Data Gathering, Analysis, and Retrieval System (EDGAR) in accordance with EDGAR rules set forth in Regulation S–T (17 CFR Part 232).

(2)   Every notice of sales on Form D must be signed by a person duly authorized by the issuer.

Rule 504.   Exemption for Limited Offerings and Sales of Securities Not Exceeding $10,000,000

(a)   *Exemption.* Offers and sales of securities that satisfy the conditions in paragraph (b) of this rule by an issuer that is not:

(1)   Subject to the reporting requirements of section 13 or 15(d) of the Exchange Act;

(2)   An investment company; or

(3)   A development stage company that either has no specific business plan or purpose or has indicated that its business plan is to engage in a merger or acquisition with an unidentified company or companies, or other entity or person, shall be exempt from the provision of section 5 of the Act under section 3(b) of the Act.

(b)   *Conditions to be met.* (1) *General conditions.* To qualify for exemption under this rule, offers and sales must satisfy the terms and conditions of Rule 501 and Rule 502(a), (c) and (d), except that the provisions of Rule 502(c) and (d) will not apply to offers and sales of securities under this Rule 504 that are made:

(i)   Exclusively in one or more states that provide for the registration of the securities, and require the public filing and delivery to investors of a substantive disclosure document before sale, and are made in accordance with those state provisions;

(ii)   In one or more states that have no provision for the registration of the securities or the public filing or delivery of a disclosure document before sale, if the securities have been registered in at least one state that provides for such registration, public filing and delivery before sale, offers and sales are made in that state in accordance with such provisions, and the disclosure document is delivered before sale to all purchasers (including those in the states that have no such procedure); or

(iii)   Exclusively according to state law exemptions from registration that permit general solicitation and general advertising so long as sales are made only to "accredited investors" as defined in Rule 501(a).

(2) *Offering limit.* The aggregate offering price for an offering of securities under this Rule 504, as defined in Rule 501(c), shall not exceed $10,000,000, less the aggregate offering price for all securities sold within the 12 months before the start of and during the offering of securities under this § 230.504 or in violation of section 5(a) of the Securities Act.

Instruction to paragraph (b)(2): If a transaction under § 230.504 fails to meet the limitation on the aggregate offering price, it does not affect the availability of this § 230.504 for the other transactions considered in applying such limitation. For example, if an issuer sold $10,000,000 of its securities on June 1, 2021, under this Rule 504 and an additional $500,000 of its securities on December 1, 2021, this § 230.504 would not be available for the later sale, but would still be applicable to the June 1, 2021, sale.

(3) *Disqualifications.* No exemption under this rule shall be available for the securities of any issuer if such issuer would be subject to disqualification under Rule 506(d) on or after January 20, 2017; provided that disclosure of prior "bad actor" events shall be required in accordance with Rule 506(e).

Instruction to Paragraph (b)(3): For purposes of disclosure of prior "bad actor" events pursuant to Rule 506(e), an issuer shall furnish to each purchaser, a reasonable time prior to sale, a description in writing of any matters that would have triggered disqualification under this paragraph (b)(3) but occurred before January 20, 2017.

Rule 505.   [removed and reserved]

Rule 506.   Exemption for Limited Offers and Sales Without Regard to Dollar Amount of Offering

(a) *Exemption.* Offers and sales of securities by an issuer that satisfy the conditions in paragraph (b) or (c) of this rule shall be deemed to be transactions not involving any public offering within the meaning of section 4(a)(2) of the Act.

(b) *Conditions to be met in offerings subject to limitation on manner of offering.—*

(1) *General conditions.* To qualify for exemption under this rule, offers and sales must satisfy all the terms and conditions of Rules 501 and 502.

(2) *Specific conditions.—*

(i) *Limitation on number of purchasers.* There are no more than, or the issuer reasonably believes that there are no more than, 35 purchasers of securities from the issuer in offerings under this section in any 90-calendar-day period.

NOTE: See Rule 501(e) for the calculation of the number of purchasers and Rule 502(a) for what may or may not constitute an offering under Rule 506(b).

(ii) *Nature of purchasers.* Each purchaser who is not an accredited investor either alone or with his purchaser representative(s) has such knowledge and experience in financial and business matters that he is capable of evaluating the merits and risks of the prospective investment, or the issuer reasonably believes immediately prior to making any sale that such purchaser comes within this description.

(c) *Conditions to be met in offerings not subject to limitation on manner of offering—*

(1) General conditions. To qualify for exemption under this rule, sales must satisfy all the terms and conditions of Rules 501 and 502(a) and (d).

(2) Specific conditions

(i) Nature of purchasers. All purchasers of securities sold in any offering under paragraph (c) of this rule are accredited investors.

(ii) Verification of accredited investor status. The issuer shall take reasonable steps to verify that purchasers of securities sold in any offering under paragraph (c) of this rule are accredited investors. The issuer shall be deemed to take reasonable steps to verify if the issuer uses, at its option, one of the following non-exclusive and non-mandatory methods of verifying that a natural person who purchases securities in such offering is an accredited investor;

provided, however, that the issuer does not have knowledge that such person is not an accredited investor:

(A) In regard to whether the purchaser is an accredited investor on the basis of income, reviewing any Internal Revenue Service form that reports the purchaser's income for the two most recent years (including, but not limited to, Form W–2, Form 1099, Schedule K–1 to Form 1065, and Form 1040) and obtaining a written representation from the purchaser that he or she has a reasonable expectation of reaching the income level necessary to qualify as an accredited investor during the current year;

(B) In regard to whether the purchaser is an accredited investor on the basis of net worth, reviewing one or more of the following types of documentation dated within the prior three months and obtaining a written representation from the purchaser that all liabilities necessary to make a determination of net worth have been disclosed:

(1) With respect to assets: bank statements, brokerage statements and other statements of securities holdings, certificates of deposit, tax assessments, and appraisal reports issued by independent third parties; and

(2) With respect to liabilities: a consumer report from at least one of the nationwide consumer reporting agencies; or

(C) Obtaining a written confirmation from one of the following persons or entities that such person or entity has taken reasonable steps to verify that the purchaser is an accredited investor within the prior three months and has determined that such purchaser is an accredited investor:

(1) A registered broker-dealer;

(2) An investment adviser registered with the Securities and Exchange Commission;

(3) A licensed attorney who is in good standing under the laws of the jurisdictions in which he or she is admitted to practice law; or

(4) A certified public accountant who is duly registered and in good standing under the laws of the place of his or her residence or principal office.

(D) In regard to any person who purchased securities in an issuer's Rule 506(b) offering as an accredited investor prior to the effective date of paragraph (c) of this rule and continues to hold such securities, for the same issuer's Rule 506(c) offering, obtaining a certification by such person at the time of sale that he or she qualifies as an accredited investor.

(E) In regard to any person that the issuer previously took reasonable steps to verify as an accredited investor in accordance with this paragraph (c)(2)(ii), so long as the issuer is not aware of information to the contrary, obtaining a written representation from such person at the time of sale that he or she qualifies as an accredited investor. A written representation under this method of verification will satisfy the issuer's obligation to verify the person's accredited investor status for a period of five years from the date the person was previously verified as an accredited investor.

Instructions to paragraph (c)(2)(ii)(A) through (D) of this rule:

1. The issuer is not required to use any of these methods in verifying the accredited investor status of natural persons who are purchasers. These methods are examples of the types of non-exclusive and non-mandatory methods that satisfy the verification requirement in Rule 506(c)(2)(ii).

2. In the case of a person who qualifies as an accredited investor based on joint income with that person's spouse, the issuer would be deemed to satisfy the verification requirement in Rule 506(c)(2)(ii)(A) by reviewing copies of Internal Revenue Service forms that report income for

the two most recent years in regard to, and obtaining written representations from, both the person and the spouse.

3.   In the case of a person who qualifies as an accredited investor based on joint net worth with that person's spouse, the issuer would be deemed to satisfy the verification requirement in Rule 506(c)(2)(ii)(B) by reviewing such documentation in regard to, and obtaining written representations from, both the person and the spouse.

(d)   *"Bad Actor" disqualification.* (1) No exemption under this rule shall be available for a sale of securities if the issuer; any predecessor of the issuer; any affiliated issuer; any director, executive officer, other officer participating in the offering, general partner or managing member of the issuer; any beneficial owner of 20% or more of the issuer's outstanding voting equity securities, calculated on the basis of voting power; any promoter connected with the issuer in any capacity at the time of such sale; any investment manager of an issuer that is a pooled investment fund; any person that has been or will be paid (directly or indirectly) remuneration for solicitation of purchasers in connection with such sale of securities; any general partner or managing member of any such investment manager or solicitor; or any director, executive officer or other officer participating in the offering of any such investment manager or solicitor or general partner or managing member of such investment manager or solicitor:

(i)   Has been convicted, within ten years before such sale (or five years, in the case of issuers, their predecessors and affiliated issuers), of any felony or misdemeanor:

(A)   In connection with the purchase or sale of any security;

(B)   Involving the making of any false filing with the Commission; or

(C)   Arising out of the conduct of the business of an underwriter, broker, dealer, municipal securities dealer, investment adviser or paid solicitor of purchasers of securities;

(ii)   Is subject to any order, judgment or decree of any court of competent jurisdiction, entered within five years before such sale, that, at the time of such sale, restrains or enjoins such person from engaging or continuing to engage in any conduct or practice:

(A)   In connection with the purchase or sale of any security;

(B)   Involving the making of any false filing with the Commission; or

(C)   Arising out of the conduct of the business of an underwriter, broker, dealer, municipal securities dealer, investment adviser or paid solicitor of purchasers of securities;

(iii)   Is subject to a final order of a state securities commission (or an agency or officer of a state performing like functions); a state authority that supervises or examines banks, savings associations, or credit unions; a state insurance commission (or an agency or officer of a state performing like functions); an appropriate federal banking agency; the U.S. Commodity Futures Trading Commission; or the National Credit Union Administration that:

(A)   At the time of such sale, bars the person from:

(1)   Association with an entity regulated by such commission, authority, agency, or officer;

(2)   Engaging in the business of securities, insurance or banking; or

(3)   Engaging in savings association or credit union activities; or

(B)   Constitutes a final order based on a violation of any law or regulation that prohibits fraudulent, manipulative, or deceptive conduct entered within ten years before such sale;

(iv)   Is subject to an order of the Commission entered pursuant to section 15(b) or 15B(c) of the Securities Exchange Act of 1934 (15 U.S.C. 78*o*(b) or 78*o*–4(c)) or section 203(e) or (f) of the Investment Advisers Act of 1940 (15 U.S.C. 80b–3(e) or (f)) that, at the time of such sale:

(A)   Suspends or revokes such person's registration as a broker, dealer, municipal securities dealer or investment adviser;

(B)   Places limitations on the activities, functions or operations of such person; or

(C)   Bars such person from being associated with any entity or from participating in the offering of any penny stock;

(v)   Is subject to any order of the Commission entered within five years before such sale that, at the time of such sale, orders the person to cease and desist from committing or causing a violation or future violation of:

(A)   Any scienter-based anti-fraud provision of the federal securities laws, including without limitation section 17(a)(1) of the Securities Act of 1933, (15 U.S.C. 77q(a)(1)), section 10(b) of the Securities Exchange Act of 1934 (15 U.S.C. 78j(b)) and 17 CFR 240.10b–5, section 15(c)(1) of the Securities Exchange Act of 1934 (15 U.S.C. 78o(c)(1)) and section 206(1) of the Investment Advisers Act of 1940 (15 U.S.C. 80b–6(1)), or any other rule or regulation thereunder; or

(B)   Section 5 of the Securities Act of 1933. (15 U.S.C. 77e).

(vi)   Is suspended or expelled from membership in, or suspended or barred from association with a member of, a registered national securities exchange or a registered national or affiliated securities association for any act or omission to act constituting conduct inconsistent with just and equitable principles of trade;

(vii)   Has filed (as a registrant or issuer), or was or was named as an underwriter in, any registration statement or Regulation A offering statement filed with the Commission that, within five years before such sale, was the subject of a refusal order, stop order, or order suspending the Regulation A exemption, or is, at the time of such sale, the subject of an investigation or proceeding to determine whether a stop order or suspension order should be issued; or

(viii)   Is subject to a United States Postal Service false representation order entered within five years before such sale, or is, at the time of such sale, subject to a temporary restraining order or preliminary injunction with respect to conduct alleged by the United States Postal Service to constitute a scheme or device for obtaining money or property through the mail by means of false representations.

(2)   Paragraph (d)(1) of this rule shall not apply:

(i)   With respect to any conviction, order, judgment, decree, suspension, expulsion or bar that occurred or was issued before September 23, 2013;

(ii)   Upon a showing of good cause and without prejudice to any other action by the Commission, if the Commission determines that it is not necessary under the circumstances that an exemption be denied;

(iii)   If, before the relevant sale, the court or regulatory authority that entered the relevant order, judgment or decree advises in writing (whether contained in the relevant judgment, order or decree or separately to the Commission or its staff) that disqualification under paragraph (d)(1) of this rule should not arise as a consequence of such order, judgment or decree; or

(iv)   If the issuer establishes that it did not know and, in the exercise of reasonable care, could not have known that a disqualification existed under paragraph (d)(1) of this rule.

Instruction to paragraph (d)(2)(iv). An issuer will not be able to establish that it has exercised reasonable care unless it has made, in light of the circumstances, factual inquiry into whether any disqualifications exist. The nature and scope of the factual inquiry will vary based on the facts and circumstances concerning, among other things, the issuer and the other offering participants.

(3)   For purposes of paragraph (d)(1) of this rule, events relating to any affiliated issuer that occurred before the affiliation arose will be not considered disqualifying if the affiliated entity is not:

(i)   In control of the issuer; or

(ii)   Under common control with the issuer by a third party that was in control of the affiliated entity at the time of such events.

(e)   *Disclosure of prior "bad actor" events.* The issuer shall furnish to each purchaser, a reasonable time prior to sale, a description in writing of any matters that would have triggered disqualification under paragraph (d)(1) of this rule but occurred before September 23, 2013. The failure to furnish such information timely shall not prevent an issuer from relying on this rule if the issuer establishes that it did not know and, in the exercise of reasonable care, could not have known of the existence of the undisclosed matter or matters.

Instruction to paragraph (e). An issuer will not be able to establish that it has exercised reasonable care unless it has made, in light of the circumstances, factual inquiry into whether any disqualifications exist. The nature and scope of the factual inquiry will vary based on the facts and circumstances concerning, among other things, the issuer and the other offering participants.

Rule 507.   Disqualifying Provision Relating to Exemptions Under Rules 504 and 506

(a)   No exemption under Rule 504 or Rule 506 shall be available for an issuer if such issuer, any of its predecessors or affiliates have been subject to any order, judgment, or decree of any court of competent jurisdiction temporarily, preliminarily or permanently enjoining such person for failure to comply with Rule 503.

(b)   Paragraph (a) of this rule shall not apply if the Commission determines, upon a showing of good cause, that it is not necessary under the circumstances that exemption be denied.

Rule 508.   Insignificant Deviations From a Term, Condition or Requirement of Regulation D

(a)   A failure to comply with a term, condition or requirement of Rule 504 or 506 will not result in the loss of the exemption from the requirements of section 5 of the Act for any offer or sale to a particular individual or entity, if the person relying on the exemption shows:

(1)   The failure to comply did not pertain to a term, condition or requirement directly intended to protect that particular individual or entity; and

(2)   The failure to comply was insignificant with respect to the offering as a whole, provided that any failure to comply with paragraph (c) of Rule 502, paragraph (b)(2) of Rule 504 and paragraph (b)(2)(i) of Rule 506 shall be deemed to be significant to the offering as a whole; and

(3)   A good faith and reasonable attempt was made to comply with all applicable terms, conditions and requirements of Rule 504 or 506.

(b)   A transaction made in reliance on Rule 504 or 506 shall comply with all applicable terms, conditions and requirements of Regulation D. Where an exemption is established only through reliance upon paragraph (a) of this rule, the failure to comply shall nonetheless be actionable by the Commission under section 20 of the Act.

* * *

REGULATION E—EXEMPTION FOR SECURITIES OF SMALL BUSINESS INVESTMENT COMPANIES [OMITTED]

COMPENSATORY BENEFIT PLANS

Rule 701.   Exemption for Offers and Sales of Securities Pursuant to Certain Compensatory Benefit Plans and Contracts Relating to Compensation

Preliminary Notes

1.   This rule relates to transactions exempted from the registration requirements of section 5 of the Securities Act of 1933. These transactions are not exempt from the antifraud, civil liability, or other provisions of the federal securities laws. Issuers and persons acting on their behalf have an obligation to provide investors with disclosure adequate to satisfy the antifraud provisions of the federal securities laws.

2.   In addition to complying with this rule, the issuer also must comply with any applicable state law relating to the offer and sale of securities.

3.   An issuer that attempts to comply with this rule, but fails to do so, may claim any other exemption that is available.

4.   This rule is available only to the issuer of the securities. Affiliates of the issuer may not use this rule to offer or sell securities. This rule also does not cover resales of securities by any person. This rule provides an exemption only for the transactions in which the securities are offered or sold by the issuer, not for the securities themselves.

5.   The purpose of this rule is to provide an exemption from the registration requirements of the Act for securities issued in compensatory circumstances. This rule is not available for plans or schemes to circumvent this purpose, such as to raise capital. This rule also is not available to exempt any transaction that is in technical compliance with this rule but is part of a plan or scheme to evade the registration provisions of the Act. In any of these cases, registration under the Act is required unless another exemption is available.

(a)   *Exemption.* Offers and sales made in compliance with all of the conditions of this rule are exempt from section 5 of the Securities Act of 1933.

(b)   *Issuers Eligible to Use this rule.*

(1)   *General.* This rule is available to any issuer that is not subject to the reporting requirements of section 13 or 15(d) of the Securities Exchange Act of 1934 (the "Exchange Act") and is not an investment company registered or required to be registered under the Investment Company Act of 1940.

(2)   *Issuers that Become Subject to Reporting.* If an issuer becomes subject to the reporting requirements of section 13 or 15(d) of the Exchange Act after it has made offers complying with this rule, the issuer may nevertheless rely on this rule to sell the securities previously offered to the persons to whom those offers were made.

(3)   *Guarantees by Reporting Companies.* An issuer subject to the reporting requirements of section 13 or 15(d) of the Exchange Act may rely on this rule if it is merely guaranteeing the payment of a subsidiary's securities that are sold under this rule.

(c)   *Transactions Exempted by this Rule.* This rule exempts offers and sales of securities (including plan interests and guarantees pursuant to paragraph (d)(2)(ii) of this rule) under a written compensatory benefit plan (or written compensation contract) established by the issuer, its parents, its majority-owned subsidiaries or majority-owned subsidiaries of the issuer's parent, for the participation of their employees, directors, general partners, trustees (where the issuer is a business trust), officers, or consultants and advisors, and their family members who acquire such securities from such persons through gifts or domestic relations orders. This rule exempts offers and sales to former employees, directors, general partners, trustees, officers, consultants and advisors only if such persons were employed by or providing services to the issuer at the time the securities were offered. In addition, the term "employee" includes insurance agents who are exclusive agents of the issuer, its subsidiaries or parents, or derive more than 50% of their annual income from those entities.

(1)   *Special Requirements for Consultants and Advisors.* This rule is available to consultants and advisors only if:

(i)   They are natural persons;

(ii)   They provide bona fide services to the issuer, its parents, its majority-owned subsidiaries or majority-owned subsidiaries of the issuer's parent; and

(iii)   The services are not in connection with the offer or sale of securities in a capital-raising transaction, and do not directly or indirectly promote or maintain a market for the issuer's securities.

(2)   *Definition of "Compensatory Benefit Plan."* For purposes of this rule, a "compensatory benefit plan" is any purchase, savings, option, bonus, stock appreciation, profit sharing, thrift, incentive, deferred compensation, pension or similar plan.

(3)   *Definition of "Family Member."* For purposes of this rule, "family member" includes any child, stepchild, grandchild, parent, stepparent, grandparent, spouse, former spouse, sibling, niece, nephew, mother-in-law, father-in-law, son-in-law, daughter-in-law, brother-in-law, or sister-in-law, including adoptive relationships, any person sharing the employee's household (other than a tenant or employee), a trust in which these persons have more than fifty percent of the beneficial interest, a foundation in which these persons (or the employee) control the management of assets, and any other entity in which these persons (or the employee) own more than fifty percent of the voting interests.

(d) *Amounts that May be Sold.*

(1) *Offers.* Any amount of securities may be offered in reliance on this rule. However, for purposes of this rule, sales of securities underlying options must be counted as sales on the date of the option grant.

(2) *Sales.* The aggregate sales price or amount of securities sold in reliance on this rule during any consecutive 12-month period must not exceed the greatest of the following:

(i) $1,000,000;

(ii) 15% of the total assets of the issuer (or of the issuer's parent if the issuer is a wholly-owned subsidiary and the securities represent obligations that the parent fully and unconditionally guarantees), measured at the issuer's most recent balance sheet date (if no older than its last fiscal year end); or

(iii) 15% of the outstanding amount of the class of securities being offered and sold in reliance on this rule, measured at the issuer's most recent balance sheet date (if no older than its last fiscal year end).

(3) *Rules for Calculating Prices and Amounts.*

(i) *Aggregate Sales Price.* The term "aggregate sales price" means the sum of all cash, property, notes, cancellation of debt or other consideration received or to be received by the issuer for the sale of the securities. Non-cash consideration must be valued by reference to bona fide sales of that consideration made within a reasonable time or, in the absence of such sales, on the fair value as determined by an accepted standard. The value of services exchanged for securities issued must be measured by reference to the value of the securities issued. Options must be valued based on the exercise price of the option.

(ii) *Time of the Calculation.* With respect to options to purchase securities, the aggregate sales price is determined when an option grant is made (without regard to when the option becomes exercisable). With respect to other securities, the calculation is made on the date of sale. With respect to deferred compensation or similar plans, the calculation is made when the irrevocable election to defer is made.

(iii) *Derivative Securities.* In calculating outstanding securities for purposes of paragraph (d)(2)(iii) of this rule, treat the securities underlying all currently exercisable or convertible options, warrants, rights or other securities, other than those issued under this exemption, as outstanding. In calculating the amount of securities sold for other purposes of paragraph (d)(2) of this rule, count the amount of securities that would be acquired upon exercise or conversion in connection with sales of options, warrants, rights or other exercisable or convertible securities, including those to be issued under this exemption.

(iv) *Other Exemptions.* Amounts of securities sold in reliance on this rule do not affect "aggregate offering prices" in other exemptions, and amounts of securities sold in reliance on other exemptions do not affect the amount that may be sold in reliance on this rule.

(e) *Disclosure that Must be Provided.* The issuer must deliver to investors a copy of the compensatory benefit plan or the contract, as applicable. In addition, if the aggregate sales price or amount of securities sold during any consecutive 12-month period exceeds $10 million, the issuer must deliver the following disclosure to investors a reasonable period of time before the date of sale:

(1) If the plan is subject to the Employee Retirement Income Security Act of 1974 ("ERISA"), a copy of the summary plan description required by ERISA;

(2) If the plan is not subject to ERISA, a summary of the material terms of the plan;

(3) Information about the risks associated with investment in the securities sold pursuant to the compensatory benefit plan or compensation contract; and

(4) Financial statements required to be furnished by Part F/S of Form 1–A (Regulation A Offering Statement) under Regulation A. Foreign private issuers as defined in Rule 405 under the Act must provide a reconciliation to generally accepted accounting principles in the United States (U.S. GAAP) if their financial statements are not prepared in accordance with U.S. GAAP or International Financial Reporting

Standards as issued by the International Accounting Standards Board (Item 17 of Form 20–F). The financial statements required by this rule must be as of a date no more than 180 days before the sale of securities in reliance on this exemption.

(5)   If the issuer is relying on paragraph (d)(2)(ii) of this rule to use its parent's total assets to determine the amount of securities that may be sold, the parent's financial statements must be delivered. If the parent is subject to the reporting requirements of section 13 or 15(d) of the Exchange Act, the financial statements of the parent required by Rule 10–01 of Regulation S–X and Item 310 of Regulation S–B, as applicable, must be delivered.

(6)   If the sale involves a stock option or other derivative security, the issuer must deliver disclosure a reasonable period of time before the date of exercise or conversion. For deferred compensation or similar plans, the issuer must deliver disclosure to investors a reasonable period of time before the date the irrevocable election to defer is made.

(f)   *No integration with other offerings.* Offers and sales exempt under this rule are deemed to be a part of a single, discrete offering and are not subject to integration with any other offers or sales, whether registered under the Act or otherwise exempt from the registration requirements of the Act.

(g)   *Resale limitations.*

(1)   Securities issued under this rule are deemed to be "restricted securities" as defined in Rule 144 under the Act.

(2)   Resales of securities issued pursuant to this rule must be in compliance with the registration requirements of the Act or an exemption from those requirements.

(3)   Ninety days after the issuer becomes subject to the reporting requirements of section 13 or 15(d) of the Exchange Act, securities issued under this rule may be resold by persons who are not affiliates (as defined in Rule 144 under the Act) in reliance on Rule 144, without compliance with paragraphs (c) and (d) of Rule 144, and by affiliates without compliance with paragraph (d) of Rule 144.

EXEMPTIONS FOR CROSS-BORDER RIGHTS OFFERINGS, EXCHANGE OFFERINGS AND BUSINESS COMBINATIONS

General Notes Rules 800, 801 and 802

1.   Rules 801 and 802 relate only to the applicability of the registration provisions of the Act and not to the applicability of the anti-fraud, civil liability or other provisions of the federal securities laws.

2.   The exemptions provided in Rule 801 and Rule 802 are not available for any securities transaction or series of transactions that technically complies with Rule 801 and Rule 802 but are part of a plan or scheme to evade the registration provision of the Act.

3.   An issuer who relies on Rule 801 or an offeror who relies on Rule 802 must still comply with the securities registration or broker-dealer registration requirements of the Securities Exchange Act of 1934 and any other applicable provisions of the federal securities laws.

4.   An issuer who relies on Rule 801 or an offeror who relies on Rule 802 must still comply with any applicable state laws relating to the offer and sale of securities.

5.   Attempted compliance with Rule 801 or Rule 802 does not act as an exclusive election; an issuer making an offer or sale of securities in reliance of Rule 801 or Rule 802 may also rely on any other applicable exemption from the registration requirements of the Act.

6.   Rule 801 and Rule 802 provide exemptions only for the issuer of the securities and not for any affiliate of that issuer or for any other person for resales of the issuer's securities. These rules provide exemptions only for the transaction in which the issuer or other person offers or sells the securities, not for the securities themselves. Securities acquired in a Rule 801 or Rule 802 transaction may be resold in the United States only if they are registered under the Act or an exemption from registration is available.

7.   Unregistered offers and sales made outside the United States will not affect contemporaneous offers and sales made in compliance with Rule 801 and Rule 802. A transaction that complies with Rule 801 or Rule 802 will not be integrated with offerings exempt under other provisions of the Act, even if both transactions occur at the same time.

8.   Securities acquired in a rights offering under Rule 801 are "restricted securities" within the meaning of Rule 144(a)(3) to the same extent and proportion that the securities held by the security holder as of the record date for the rights offering were restricted securities. Likewise, securities acquired in an exchange offer or business combination subject to Rule 802 are "restricted securities" within the meaning of Rule 144(a)(3) to the same extent and proportion that the securities tendered or exchanged by the security holder in that transaction were restricted securities.

9.   Rule 801 does not apply to a rights offering by an investment company registered or required to be registered under the Investment Company Act of 1940, other than a registered closed-end investment company. Rule 802 does not apply to exchanges offers or business combinations by an investment company registered or required to be registered under the Investment Company Act of 1940, other than a registered closed-end investment company.

Rule 800.   Definitions

(a)   *Business Combination.* "Business Combination" means a statutory amalgamation, merger, arrangement or other reorganization requiring the vote of security holders of one or more participating companies. It also includes a statutory short form merger that does not require a vote of security holders.

(b)   *Equity Security.* "Equity Security" means the same as in Rule 3a11–1 of the Securities Exchange Act of 1934, but for purposes of this rule only does not include:

(1)   Any debt security that is convertible into an equity security, with or without consideration;

(2)   Any debt security that includes a warrant or right to subscribe to or purchase an equity security;

(3)   Any such warrant or right; or

(4)   Any put, call, straddle, or other option or privilege that gives the holder the option of buying or selling a security but does not require the holder to do so.

(c)   *Exchange offer.* "Exchange offer" means a tender offer in which securities are issued as consideration.

(d)   *Foreign private issuer.* "Foreign private issuer" means the same as in Rule 405 of Regulation C.

(e)   *Foreign subject company.* "Foreign subject company" means any foreign private issuer whose securities are the subject of the exchange offer or business combination.

(f)   *Home jurisdiction.* "Home jurisdiction" means both the jurisdiction of the foreign subject company's (or in the case of a rights offering, the foreign private issuer's) incorporation, organization or chartering and the principal foreign market where the foreign subject company's (or in the case of a rights offering, the issuer's) securities are listed or quoted.

(g)   *Rights offering.* "Rights offering" means offers and sales for cash of equity securities where:

(1)   The issuer grants the existing security holders of a particular class of equity securities (including holders of depositary receipts evidencing those securities) the right to purchase or subscribe for additional securities of that class; and

(2)   The number of additional shares an existing security holder may purchase initially is in proportion to the number of securities he or she holds of record on the record date for the rights offering. If an existing security holder holds depositary receipts, the proportion must be calculated as if the underlying securities were held directly.

(h)   *U.S. holder.* "U.S. holder" means any security holder resident in the United States. To determine the percentage of outstanding securities held by U.S. holders:

(1)   Calculate the percentage of outstanding securities held by U.S. holders as of a date no more than 60 days before or 30 days after the public announcement of a business combination conducted under Rule 802 under the Act or of the record date in a rights offering conducted under Rule 801 under the Act. For a business combination conducted under Rule 802, if you are unable to calculate as of a date within these time frames, the calculation may be made as of the most recent practicable date before public announcement, but in no event earlier than 120 days before public announcement.

(2)   Include securities underlying American Depository Shares convertible or exchangeable into the securities that are the subject of the tender offer when calculating the number of subject securities outstanding, as well as the number held by U.S. holders. Exclude from the calculation other types of securities that are convertible or exchangeable into the securities that are the subject of the tender offer, such as warrants, options and convertible securities. Exclude from those calculations securities held by the acquiror in an exchange offer or business combination;

(3)   Use the method of calculating record ownership in Rule 12g3–2(a) under the Exchange Act, except that your inquiry as to the amount of securities represented by accounts of customers resident in the United States may be limited to brokers, dealers, banks and other nominees located in the United States, the subject company's jurisdiction of incorporation or that of each participant in a business combination, and the jurisdiction that is the primary trading market for the subject securities, if different from the subject company's jurisdiction of incorporation;

(4)   If, after reasonable inquiry, you are unable to obtain information about the amount of securities represented by accounts of customers resident in the United States, you may assume, for purposes of this provision, that the customers are residents of the jurisdiction in which the nominee has its principle place of business.

(5)   Count securities owned by U.S. holders when publicly filed reports of beneficial ownership or information that is otherwise provided to you indicates that the securities are held by U.S. residents.

(6)   For exchange offers conducted pursuant to Rule 802 under the Act by persons other than the issuer of the subject securities or its affiliates that are not made pursuant to an agreement with the issuer of the subject securities, the issuer of the subject securities will be presumed to be a foreign private issuer and U.S. holders will be presumed to hold 10 percent or less of the outstanding subject securities, unless paragraphs (h)(7)(i), (ii) or (iii) of this rule indicate otherwise.

(7)   For rights offerings and business combinations, including exchange offers conducted pursuant to Rule 802 under the Act, where the offeror is unable to conduct the analysis of U.S. ownership set forth in paragraph (h)(3) of this rule, the issuer of the subject securities will be presumed to be a foreign private issuer and U.S. holders will be presumed to hold 10 percent or less of the outstanding subject securities so long as there is a primary trading market for the subject securities outside the United States, as defined in Rule 12h–6(f)(5), unless:

(i)   Average daily trading volume of the subject securities in the United States for a recent twelve-month period ending on a date no more than 60 days before the public announcement of the business combination or of the record date for a rights offering exceeds 10 percent of the average daily trading volume of that class of securities on a worldwide basis for the same period; or

(ii)   The most recent annual report or annual information filed or submitted by the issuer with securities regulators of the home jurisdiction or with the Commission or any jurisdiction in which the subject securities trade before the public announcement of the offer indicates that U.S. holders hold more than 10 percent of the outstanding subject class of securities; or

(iii)   The acquiror or issuer knows or has reason to know, before the public announcement of the offer, that the level of U.S. ownership exceeds 10 percent of such securities. As an example, an acquiror or issuer is deemed to know information about U.S. ownership of the subject class of securities that is publicly available and that appears in any filing with the Commission or any regulatory body in the issuer's jurisdiction of incorporation or (if different) the non-U.S. jurisdiction in which the primary trading market for the subject securities is located. The acquiror in a business combination is deemed to know information about U.S. ownership available from the issuer. The acquiror or issuer is deemed to know information obtained or readily available from any other source that is reasonably reliable, including from persons it has retained to advise it about the transaction, as well as from third-party information providers. These examples are not intended to be exclusive.

(i)   *United States.* "United States" means the United States of American, its territories and possessions, any State of the United States, and the District of Columbia.

Rule 801.   Exemption in Connection With a Rights Offering

A rights offering is exempt from the provisions of section 5 of the Act, so long as the following conditions are satisfied:

(a)   *Conditions.* (1) *Eligibility of issuer.* The issuer is a foreign private issuer on the date the securities are first offered to U.S. holders.

(2)   *Limitation on U.S. ownership.* U.S. holders hold no more than 10 percent of the outstanding class of securities that is the subject of the rights offering (as determined under the definition of "U.S. holder" in Rule 800(h)).

(3)   *Equal treatment.* The issuer permits U.S. holders to participate in the rights offering on terms at least as favorable as those offered the other holders of the securities that are the subject of the offer. The issuer need not, however, extend the rights offering to security holders in those states or jurisdictions that require registration or qualification.

(4)   *Informational documents.* (i) If the issuer publishes or otherwise disseminates an informational document to the holders of the securities in connection with the rights offering, the issuer must furnish that informational document, including any amendments thereto, in English, to the Commission on Form CB by the first business day after publication or dissemination. If the issuer is a foreign company, it must also file a Form F–X with the Commission at the same time as the submission of Form CB to appoint an agent for service in the United States.

(ii)   The issuer must disseminate the informational document to U.S. holders, including any amendments thereto, in English, on a comparable basis to that provided to security holders in the home jurisdiction.

(iii)   If the issuer disseminates by publication in its home jurisdiction, the issuer must publish the information in the United States in a manner reasonably calculated to inform U.S. holders of the offer.

(5)   *Eligibility of securities.* The securities offered in the rights offering are equity securities of the same class as the securities held by the offerees in the United States directly or through American Depositary Receipts.

(6)   *Limitation on transferability of rights.* The terms of the rights prohibit transfers of the rights by U.S. holders except in accordance with Regulation S.

(b)   *Legends.* The following legend or equivalent statement in clear, plain language, to the extent applicable, appears on the cover page or other prominent portion of any information document the issuer disseminates to U.S. holders:

This rights offering is made for the securities of a foreign company. The offer is subject to the disclosure requirements of a foreign country that are different from those of the United States. Financial Statements included in the document, if any, have been prepared in accordance with foreign accounting standards that may not be comparable to the financial statements of United States companies.

It may be difficult for you to enforce your rights and any claim you may have arising under the federal securities laws, since the issuer is located in a foreign country, and some or all of its officers and directors may be residents of a foreign country. You may not be able to sue the foreign company or its officers or directors in a foreign court for violations of the U.S. securities laws. It may be difficult to compel a foreign company and its affiliates to subject themselves to a U.S. court's judgement.

Rule 802.   Exemption for Offerings in Connection With an Exchange Offer or Business Combination for the Securities of Foreign Private Issuers

Offers and sales in any exchange offers for a class of securities of a foreign private issuer, or in any exchange of securities for the securities of a foreign private issuer in any business combination, are exempt from the provisions of section 5 of the Exchange Act, if they satisfy the following conditions:

(a) *Conditions.* (1) *Limitation on U.S. ownership.* Except in the case of an exchange offer or business combination that is commenced during the pendency of a prior exchange offer or business combination made in reliance on this paragraph, U.S. holders of the foreign subject company must hold no more than 10 percent of the securities that are the subject of the exchange offer or business combination (as determined under the definition of "U.S. holder" in Rule 800(h)). In the case of a business combination in which the securities are to be issued by a successor registrant, U.S. holders may hold no more than 10 percent of the class of securities of the successor registrant, as if measured immediately after completion of the business combination.

(2) *Equal treatment.* The offeror must permit U.S. holders to participate in the exchange offer or business combination on terms at least as favorable as those offered any other holder of the subject securities. The offeror, however, need not extend the offer to security holders in those states or jurisdictions that require registration or qualification, except that the offeror must offer the same cash alternative to security holders in any such state that it has offered to security holders in any other state or jurisdiction.

(3) *Informational documents.* (i) If the offeror publishes or otherwise disseminates an informational document to the holders of the subject securities in connection with the exchange offer or business combination, the offeror must furnish that informational document, including any amendments thereto, in English, to the Commission on Form CB by the first business day after publication or dissemination. If the offeror is a foreign company, it must also file a Form F–X with the Commission at the same time as the submission of the Form CB to appoint an agent for service of process in the United States.

(ii) The offeror must disseminate any informational document to U.S. holders, including any amendments thereto, in English, on a comparable basis to that provided to security holders in the foreign subject company's home jurisdiction.

(iii) If the offeror disseminates by publication in its home jurisdiction, the offeror must publish the information in the United States in a manner reasonably calculated to inform U.S. holders of the offer.

(b) *Legends.* The following legend or an equivalent statement in clear, plain language, to the extent applicable, must be included on the cover page or other prominent portion of any informational document the offeror publishes or disseminates to U.S. holders:

This exchange offer or business combination is made for the securities of a foreign company. The offer is subject to disclosure requirements of a foreign country that are different from those of the United States. Financial statements included in the document, if any, have been prepared in accordance with foreign accounting standards that may not be comparable to the financial statements of United States companies.

It may be difficult for you to enforce your rights and any claim you may have arising under the federal securities laws, since the issuer is located in a foreign country, and some or all of its officers and directors may be residents of a foreign country. You may not be able to sue a foreign company or its officers or directors in a foreign court for violations of U.S. securities laws. It may be difficult to compel a foreign company and its affiliates to subject themselves to a U.S. court's judgment.

You should be aware that the issuer may purchase securities otherwise than under the exchange offer, such as in open market or privately negotiated purchases.

REGULATION S—RULES GOVERNING OFFERS AND SALES MADE OUTSIDE THE UNITED STATES WITHOUT REGISTRATION UNDER THE SECURITIES ACT OF 1933

Preliminary Notes

1. The following rules relate solely to the application of section 5 of the Securities Act of 1933 (the "Act") and not to antifraud or other provisions of the federal securities laws.

2. In view of the objective of these rules and the policies underlying the Act, Regulation S is not available with respect to any transaction or series of transactions that, although in technical compliance with these rules,

is part of a plan or scheme to evade the registration provisions of the Act. In such cases, registration under the Act is required.

3.   Nothing in these rules obviates the need for any issuer or any other person to comply with the securities registration or broker-dealer registration requirements of the Securities Exchange Act (the "Exchange Act"), whenever such requirements are applicable.

4.   Nothing in these rules obviates the need to comply with any applicable state law relating to the offer and sale of securities.

Attempted compliance with any rule in Regulation S does not act as an exclusive election; a person making an offer or sale of securities may also claim the availability of any applicable exemption from the registration requirements of the Act.

5.   The availability of the Regulation S safe harbor to offers and sales that occur outside of the United States will not be affected by the subsequent offer and sale of these securities into the United States or to U.S. persons during the distribution compliance period, as long as the subsequent offer and sale are made pursuant to registration or an exemption therefrom under the Act.

6.   Regulation S is available only for offers and sales of securities outside the United States. Securities acquired overseas, whether or not pursuant to Regulation S, may be resold in the United States only if they are registered under the Act or an exemption from registration is available.

7.   Nothing in these rules precludes access by journalists for publications with a general circulation in the United States to offshore press conferences, press releases and meetings with company press spokespersons in which an offshore offering or tender offer is discussed, provided that the information is made available to the foreign and United States press generally and is not intended to induce purchases of securities by persons in the United States or tenders of securities by United States holders in the case of exchange offers. Where applicable, issuers and bidders may also look to Rule 135e and Rule 14d–1(c) under the Exchange Act.

8.   The provisions of this Regulation S shall not apply to offers and sales of securities issued by open-end investment companies or unit investment trusts registered or required to be registered or closed-end investment companies required to be registered, but not registered, under the Investment Company Act of 1940 (the "1940 Act").

Rule 901.   General Statement

For the purposes only of section 5 of the Act, the terms "offer," "offer to sell," "sell," "sale," and "offer to buy" shall be deemed to include offers and sales that occur within the United States and shall be deemed not to include offers and sales that occur outside the United States.

Rule 902.   Definitions

As used in Regulation S, the following terms shall have the meanings indicated.

(a)   *Debt Securities.* "Debt securities" of an issuer is defined to mean any security other than an equity security as defined in Rule 405, as well as the following:

(1)   Non-participatory preferred stock, which is defined as non-convertible capital stock, the holders of which are entitled to a preference in payment of dividends and in distribution of assets on liquidation, dissolution, or winding up of the issuer, but are not entitled to participate in residual earnings or assets of the issuer; and

(2)   Asset-backed securities, which are securities of a type that either:

(i)   Represent an ownership interest in a pool of discrete assets, or certificates of interest or participation in such assets (including any rights designed to assure servicing, or the receipt or timeliness of receipt by holders of such assets, or certificates of interest or participation in such assets, of amounts payable thereunder), provided that the assets are not generated or originated between the issuer of the security and its affiliates; or

(ii)   Are secured by one or more assets or certificates of interest or participation in such assets, and the securities, by their terms, provide for payments of principal and interest (if any) in relation to payments or reasonable projections of payments on assets meeting the requirements

259

of paragraph (a)(2)(i) of this rule, or certificates of interest or participations in assets meeting such requirements.

        (iii) For purposes of paragraph (a)(2)of this rule, the term "assets" means securities, installment sales, accounts receivable, notes, leases or other contracts, or other assets that by their terms convert into cash over a finite period of time.

(b) *Designated Offshore Securities Market.* "Designated offshore securities market" means:

    (1)   The Eurobond market, as regulated by the International Securities Market Association; the Alberta Stock Exchange; the Amsterdam Stock Exchange; the Australian Stock Exchange Limited; the Bermuda Stock Exchange; the Bourse de Bruxelles; the Copenhagen Stock Exchange; the European Association of Securities Dealers Automated Quotation; the Frankfurt Stock Exchange; the Helsinki Stock Exchange; The Stock Exchange of Hong Kong Limited; the Irish Stock Exchange; the Istanbul Stock Exchange; the Johannesburg Stock Exchange; the London Stock Exchange; the Bourse de Luxembourg; the Mexico Stock Exchange; the Borsa Valori di Milan; the Montreal Stock Exchange; the Oslo Stock Exchange; the Bourse de Paris; the Stock Exchange of Singapore Ltd.; the Stockholm Stock Exchange; the Tokyo Stock Exchange; the Toronto Stock Exchange; the Vancouver Stock Exchange; the Warsaw Stock Exchange and the Zurich Stock Exchange; and

    (2)   Any foreign securities exchange or non-exchange market designated by the Commission. Attributes to be considered in determining whether to designate an offshore securities market, among others, include:

        (i)   Organization under foreign law;

        (ii)   Association with a generally recognized community of brokers, dealers, banks, or other professional intermediaries with an established operating history;

        (iii) Oversight by a governmental or self-regulatory body;

        (iv) Oversight standards set by an existing body of law;

        (v)   Reporting of securities transactions on a regular basis to a governmental or self-regulatory body;

        (vi) A system for exchange of price quotations through common communications media; and

        (vii) An organized clearance and settlement system.

(c) *Directed Selling Efforts.*

    (1)   "Directed selling efforts" means any activity undertaken for the purpose of, or that could reasonably be expected to have the effect of, conditioning the market in the United States for any of the securities being offered in reliance on this Regulation S. Such activity includes placing an advertisement in a publication "with a general circulation in the United States" that refers to the offering of securities being made in reliance upon this Regulation S.

    (2)   Publication "with a general circulation in the United States":

        (i)   Is defined as any publication that is printed primarily for distribution in the United States, or has had, during the preceding twelve months, an average circulation in the United States of 15,000 or more copies per issue; and

        (ii)   Will encompass only the U.S. edition of any publication printing a separate U.S. edition if the publication, without considering its U.S. edition, would not constitute a publication with a general circulation in the United States.

    (3)   The following are not "directed selling efforts":

        (i)   Placing an advertisement required to be published under U.S. or foreign law, or under rules or regulations of a U.S. or foreign regulatory or self-regulatory authority, provided the advertisement contains no more information than legally required and includes a statement to the effect that the securities have not been registered under the Act and may not be offered or sold in the United States (or to a U.S. person, if the advertisement relates to an offering under Category 2 or 3 (paragraph (b)(2) or (b)(3)) in Rule 903) absent registration or an applicable exemption from the registration requirements;

(ii)   Contact with persons excluded from the definition of "U.S. person" pursuant to paragraph (k)(2)(vi) of this rule or persons holding accounts excluded from the definition of "U.S. person" pursuant to paragraph (k)(2)(i) of this rule, solely in their capacities as holders of such accounts;

(iii)   A tombstone advertisement in any publication with a general circulation in the United States, provided:

(A)   The publication has less than 20% of its circulation, calculated by aggregating the circulation of its U.S. and comparable non-U.S. editions, in the United States;

(B)   Such advertisement contains a legend to the effect that the securities have not been registered under the Act and may not be offered or sold in the United States (or to a U.S. person, if the advertisement relates to an offering under Category 2 or 3 (paragraph (b)(2) or (b)(3)) in Rule 903) absent registration or an applicable exemption from the registration requirements; and

(C)   Such advertisement contains no more information than:

(1)   The issuer's name;

(2)   The amount and title of the securities being sold;

(3)   A brief indication of the issuer's general type of business;

(4)   The price of the securities;

(5)   The yield of the securities, if debt securities with a fixed (non-contingent) interest provision;

(6)   The name and address of the person placing the advertisement, and whether such person is participating in the distribution;

(7)   The names of the managing underwriters;

(8)   The dates, if any, upon which the sales commenced and concluded;

(9)   Whether the securities are offered or were offered by rights issued to security holders and, if so, the class of securities that are entitled or were entitled to subscribe, the subscription ratio, the record date, the dates (if any) upon which the rights were issued and expired, and the subscription price; and

(10)   Any legend required by law or any foreign or U.S. regulatory or self-regulatory authority;

(iv)   Bona fide visits to real estate, plants or other facilities located in the United States and tours thereof conducted for a prospective investor by an issuer, a distributor, any of their respective affiliates or a person acting on behalf of any of the foregoing;

(v)   Distribution in the United States of a foreign broker-dealer's quotations by a third-party system that distributes such quotations primarily in foreign countries if:

(A)   Securities transactions cannot be executed between foreign broker-dealers and persons in the United States through the system; and

(B)   The issuer, distributors, their respective affiliates, persons acting on behalf of any of the foregoing, foreign broker-dealers and other participants in the system do not initiate contacts with U.S. persons or persons within the United States, beyond those contacts exempted under Rule 15a–6 of the Exchange Act;

(vi)   Publication by an issuer of a notice in accordance with Rule135 or Rule 135c;

(vii) Providing any journalist with access to press conferences held outside of the United States, to meetings with the issuer or selling security holder representatives conducted outside the United States, or to written press-related materials released outside the United States, at or in which a present or proposed offering of securities is discussed, if the requirements of Rule 135e are satisfied; and

(viii) Publication or distribution of a research report by a broker or dealer in accordance with Rule 138(c) or Rule 139(b).

(d) *Distributor.* "Distributor" means any underwriter, dealer, or other person who participates, pursuant to a contractual arrangement, in the distribution of the securities offered or sold in reliance on this Regulation S.

(e) *Domestic Issuer/Foreign Issuer.* "Domestic issuer" means any issuer other than a "foreign government" or "foreign private issuer" (both as defined in Rule 405). "Foreign issuer" means any issuer other than a "domestic issuer."

(f) *Distribution Compliance Period.* "Distribution compliance period" means a period that begins when the securities were first offered to persons other than distributors in reliance upon this Regulation S or the date of closing of the offering, whichever is later, and continues until the end of the period of time specified in the relevant provision of Rule 903, except that:

(1)   All offers and sales by a distributor of an unsold allotment or subscription shall be deemed to be made during the distribution compliance period;

(2)   In a continuous offering, the distribution compliance period shall commence upon completion of the distribution, as determined and certified by the managing underwriter or person performing similar functions;

(3)   In a continuous offering of non-convertible debt securities offered and sold in identifiable tranches, the distribution compliance period for securities in a tranche shall commence upon completion of the distribution of such tranche, as determined and certified by the managing underwriter or person performing similar functions; and

(4)   That in a continuous offering of securities to be acquired upon the exercise of warrants, the distribution compliance period shall commence upon completion of the distribution of the warrants, as determined and certified by the managing underwriter or person performing similar functions, if requirements of Rule 903(b)(5) are satisfied.

(g)   *Offering Restrictions.* "Offering restrictions" means:

(1)   Each distributor agrees in writing:

(i)   That all offers and sales of the securities prior to the expiration of the distribution compliance period specified in Category 2 or 3 (paragraph (b)(2) or (b)(3)) in Rule 903, as applicable, shall be made only in accordance with the provisions of Rule 903 or Rule 904; pursuant to registration of the securities under the Act; or pursuant to an available exemption from the registration requirements of the Act; and

(ii)   For offers and sales of equity securities of domestic issuers, not to engage in hedging transactions with regard to such securities prior to the expiration of the distribution compliance period specified in Category 2 or 3 (paragraph (b)(2) or (b)(3)) in Rule 903, as applicable, unless in compliance with the Act; and

(2)   All offering materials and documents (other than press releases) used in connection with offers and sales of the securities prior to the expiration of the distribution compliance period specified in Category 2 or 3 (paragraph (b)(2) or (b)(3)) in Rule 903, as applicable, shall include statements to the effect that the securities have not been registered under the Act and may not be offered or sold in the United States or to U.S. persons (other than distributors) unless the securities are registered under the Act, or an exemption from the registration requirements of the Act is available. For offers and sales of equity securities of domestic issuers, such offering materials and documents also must state that hedging transactions involving those securities may not be conducted unless in compliance with the Act. Such statements shall appear:

(i)   On the cover or inside cover page of any prospectus or offering circular used in connection with the offer or sale of the securities;

(ii)   In the underwriting section of any prospectus or offering circular used in connection with the offer or sale of the securities; and

(iii) In any advertisement made or issued by the issuer, any distributor, any of their respective affiliates, or any person acting on behalf of any of the foregoing. Such statements may appear in summary form on prospectus cover pages and in advertisements.

(h)   *Offshore Transaction.* (1) An offer or sale of securities is made in an "offshore transaction" if:

(i)   The offer is not made to a person in the United States; and

(ii)   Either:

(A)   At the time the buy order is originated, the buyer is outside the United States, or the seller and any person acting on its behalf reasonably believe that the buyer is outside the United States; or

(B)   For purposes of:

(1)   Rule 903, the transaction is executed in, on or through a physical trading floor of an established foreign securities exchange that is located outside the United States; or

(2)   Rule 904, the transaction is executed in, on or through the facilities of a designated offshore securities market described in paragraph (b) of this rule, and neither the seller nor any person acting on its behalf knows that the transaction has been pre-arranged with a buyer in the United States.

(2)   Notwithstanding paragraph (h)(1) of this rule, offers and sales of securities specifically targeted at identifiable groups of U.S. citizens abroad, such as members of the U.S. armed forces serving overseas, shall not be deemed to be made in "offshore transactions."

(3)   Notwithstanding paragraph (h)(1) of this rule, offers and sales of securities to persons excluded from the definition of "U.S. person" pursuant to paragraph (k)(2)(vi) of this rule or persons holding accounts excluded from the definition of "U.S. person" pursuant to paragraph (k)(2)(i) of this rule, solely in their capacities as holders of such accounts, shall be deemed to be made in "offshore transactions."

(4)   Notwithstanding paragraph (h)(1) of this rule, publication or distribution of a research report in accordance with Rule 138(c) or Rule 139(b) by a broker or dealer at or around the time of an offering in reliance on Regulation S will not cause the transaction to fail to be an offshore transaction as defined in this rule.

(i)   *Reporting Issuer.* "Reporting issuer" means an issuer other than an investment company registered or required to register under the 1940 Act that:

(1)   Has a class of securities registered pursuant to Section 12(b) or 12(g) of the Exchange Act or is required to file reports pursuant to Section 15(d) of the Exchange Act; and

(2)   Has filed all the material required to be filed pursuant to Section 13(a) or 15(d) of the Exchange Act for a period of at least twelve months immediately preceding the offer or sale of securities made in reliance upon this Regulation S (or for such shorter period that the issuer was required to file such material).

(j)   *Substantial U.S. Market Interest.*

(1)   "Substantial U.S. market interest" with respect to a class of an issuer's equity securities means:

(i)   The securities exchanges and inter-dealer quotation systems in the United States in the aggregate constituted the single largest market for such class of securities in the shorter of the issuer's prior fiscal year or the period since the issuer's incorporation; or

(ii)   20 percent or more of all trading in such class of securities took place in, on or through the facilities of securities exchanges and inter-dealer quotation systems in the United States and less than 55 percent of such trading took place in, on or through the facilities of securities markets of a single foreign country in the shorter of the issuer's prior fiscal year or the period since the issuer's incorporation.

(2)   "Substantial U.S. market interest" with respect to an issuer's debt securities means:

(i)   Its debt securities, in the aggregate, are held of record (as that term is defined in Rule 12g5–1 of the Exchange Act and used for purposes of paragraph (j)(2) of this rule) by 300 or more U.S. persons;

(ii) $1 billion or more of: The principal amount outstanding of its debt securities, the greater of liquidation preference or par value of its securities described in Rule 902(a)(1), and the principal amount or principal balance of its securities described in Rule 902(a)(2), in the aggregate, is held of record by U.S. persons; and

(iii)   20 percent or more of: The principal amount outstanding of its debt securities, the greater of liquidation preference or par value of its securities described in Rule 902(a)(1), and the principal amount or principal balance of its securities described in Rule 902(a)(2), in the aggregate, is held of record by U.S. persons.

(3)   Notwithstanding paragraph (j)(2) of this rule, substantial U.S. market interest with respect to an issuer's debt securities is calculated without reference to securities that qualify for the exemption provided by Section 3(a)(3) of the Act.

(k)   *U.S. person.* (1) "U.S. person" means:

(i)   Any natural person resident in the United States;

(ii)   Any partnership or corporation organized or incorporated under the laws of the United States;

(iii)   Any estate of which any executor or administrator is a U.S. person;

(iv)   Any trust of which any trustee is a U.S. person;

(v)   Any agency or branch of a foreign entity located in the United States;

(vi)   Any non-discretionary account or similar account (other than an estate or trust) held by a dealer or other fiduciary for the benefit or account of a U.S. person;

(vii)   Any discretionary account or similar account (other than an estate or trust) held by a dealer or other fiduciary organized, incorporated, or (if an individual) resident in the United States; and

(viii) Any partnership or corporation if:

(A)   Organized or incorporated under the laws of any foreign jurisdiction; and

(B)   Formed by a U.S. person principally for the purpose of investing in securities not registered under the Act, unless it is organized or incorporated, and owned, by accredited investors (as defined in Rule 501(a)) who are not natural persons, estates or trusts.

(2)   The following are not "U.S. persons":

(i)   Any discretionary account or similar account (other than an estate or trust) held for the benefit or account of a non-U.S. person by a dealer or other professional fiduciary organized, incorporated, or (if an individual) resident in the United States;

(ii)   Any estate of which any professional fiduciary acting as executor or administrator is a U.S. person if:

(A)   An executor or administrator of the estate who is not a U.S. person has sole or shared investment discretion with respect to the assets of the estate; and

(B)   The estate is governed by foreign law;

(iii) Any trust of which any professional fiduciary acting as trustee is a U.S. person, if a trustee who is not a U.S. person has sole or shared investment discretion with respect to the trust assets, and no beneficiary of the trust (and no settlor if the trust is revocable) is a U.S. person;

(iv) An employee benefit plan established and administered in accordance with the law of a country other than the United States and customary practices and documentation of such country;

(v) Any agency or branch of a U.S. person located outside the United States if:

(A) The agency or branch operates for valid business reasons; and

(B) The agency or branch is engaged in the business of insurance or banking and is subject to substantive insurance or banking regulation, respectively, in the jurisdiction where located; and

(vi) The International Monetary Fund, the International Bank for Reconstruction and Development, the Inter-American Development Bank, the Asian Development Bank, the African Development Bank, the United Nations, and their agencies, affiliates and pension plans, and any other similar international organizations, their agencies, affiliates and pension plans.

(*l*) *United States.* "United States" means the United States of America, its territories and possessions, any State of the United States, and the District of Columbia.

Rule 903. Offers or Sales of Securities by the Issuer, a Distributor, Any of Their Respective Affiliates, or Any Person Acting on Behalf of Any of the Foregoing; Conditions Relating to Specific Securities

(a) An offer or sale of securities by the issuer, a distributor, any of their respective affiliates, or any person acting on behalf of any of the foregoing, shall be deemed to occur outside the United States within the meaning of Rule 901 if:

(1) The offer or sale is made in an offshore transaction;

(2) No directed selling efforts are made in the United States by the issuer, a distributor, any of their respective affiliates, or any person acting on behalf of any of the foregoing; and

(3) The conditions of paragraph (b) of this rule, as applicable, are satisfied.

(b) *Additional Conditions.*

(1) *Category 1.* No conditions other than those set forth in Rule 903(a) apply to securities in this category. Securities are eligible for this category if:

(i) The securities are issued by a foreign issuer that reasonably believes at the commencement of the offering that:

(A) There is no substantial U.S. market interest in the class of securities to be offered or sold (if equity securities are offered or sold);

(B) There is no substantial U.S. market interest in its debt securities (if debt securities are offered or sold);

(C) There is no substantial U.S. market interest in the securities to be purchased upon exercise (if warrants are offered or sold); and

(D) There is no substantial U.S. market interest in either the convertible securities or the underlying securities (if convertible securities are offered or sold);

(ii) The securities are offered and sold in an overseas directed offering, which means:

(A) An offering of securities of a foreign issuer that is directed into a single country other than the United States to the residents thereof and that is made in accordance with the local laws and customary practices and documentation of such country; or

(B) An offering of non-convertible debt securities of a domestic issuer that is directed into a single country other than the United States to the residents thereof and that is made

265

in accordance with the local laws and customary practices and documentation of such country, provided that the principal and interest of the securities (or par value, as applicable) are denominated in a currency other than U.S. dollars and such securities are neither convertible into U.S. dollar-denominated securities nor linked to U.S. dollars (other than through related currency or interest rate swap transactions that are commercial in nature) in a manner that in effect converts the securities to U.S. dollar-denominated securities.

(iii) The securities are backed by the full faith and credit of a foreign government; or

(iv) The securities are offered and sold to employees of the issuer or its affiliates pursuant to an employee benefit plan established and administered in accordance with the law of a country other than the United States, and customary practices and documentation of such country, provided that:

(A) The securities are issued in compensatory circumstances for bona fide services rendered to the issuer or its affiliates in connection with their businesses and such services are not rendered in connection with the offer or sale of securities in a capital-raising transaction;

(B) Any interests in the plan are not transferable other than by will or the laws of descent or distribution;

(C) The issuer takes reasonable steps to preclude the offer and sale of interests in the plan or securities under the plan to U.S. residents other than employees on temporary assignment in the United States; and

(D) Documentation used in connection with any offer pursuant to the plan contains a statement that the securities have not been registered under the Act and may not be offered or sold in the United States unless registered or an exemption from registration is available.

(2) *Category 2.* The following conditions apply to securities that are not eligible for Category 1 (paragraph (b)(1)) of this rule and that are equity securities of a reporting foreign issuer, or debt securities of a reporting issuer or of a non-reporting foreign issuer.

(i) Offering restrictions are implemented;

(ii) The offer or sale, if made prior to the expiration of a 40-day distribution compliance period, is not made to a U.S. person or for the account or benefit of a U.S. person (other than a distributor); and

(iii) Each distributor selling securities to a distributor, a dealer, as defined in section 2(a)(12) of the Act, or a person receiving a selling concession, fee or other remuneration in respect of the securities sold, prior to the expiration of a 40-day distribution compliance period, sends a confirmation or other notice to the purchaser stating that the purchaser is subject to the same restrictions on offers and sales that apply to a distributor.

(3) *Category 3.* The following conditions apply to securities that are not eligible for Category 1 or 2 (paragraph (b)(1) or (b)(2)) of this rule:

(i) Offering restrictions are implemented;

(ii) In the case of debt securities:

(A) The offer or sale, if made prior to the expiration of a 40-day distribution compliance period, is not made to a U.S. person or for the account or benefit of a U.S. person (other than a distributor); and

(B) The securities are represented upon issuance by a temporary global security which is not exchangeable for definitive securities until the expiration of the 40-day distribution compliance period and, for persons other than distributors, until certification of beneficial ownership of the securities by a non-U.S. person or a U.S. person who purchased securities in a transaction that did not require registration under the Act;

(iii) In the case of equity securities:

(A) The offer or sale, if made prior to the expiration of a one-year distribution compliance period (or six-month distribution compliance period if the issuer is a reporting issuer) is not made to a U.S. person or for the account or benefit of a U.S. person (other than a distributor); and

(B) The offer or sale, if made prior to the expiration of a one-year distribution compliance period (or six-month distribution compliance period if the issuer is a reporting issuer) is made pursuant to the following conditions:

(1) The purchaser of the securities (other than a distributor) certifies that it is not a U.S. person and is not acquiring the securities for the account or benefit of any U.S. person or is a U.S. person who purchased securities in a transaction that did not require registration under the Act;

(2) The purchaser of the securities agrees to resell such securities only in accordance with the provisions of this Regulation S (Rule 901 through Rule 905, and Preliminary Notes), pursuant to registration under the Act, or pursuant to an available exemption from registration; and agrees not to engage in hedging transactions with regard to such securities unless in compliance with the Act;

(3) The securities of a domestic issuer contain a legend to the effect that transfer is prohibited except in accordance with the provisions of this Regulation S (Rule 901 through Rule 905, and Preliminary Notes), pursuant to registration under the Act, or pursuant to an available exemption from registration; and that hedging transactions involving those securities may not be conducted unless in compliance with the Act;

(4) The issuer is required, either by contract or a provision in its bylaws, articles, charter or comparable document, to refuse to register any transfer of the securities not made in accordance with the provisions of this Regulation S (Rule 901 through Rule 905, and Preliminary Notes), pursuant to registration under the Act, or pursuant to an available exemption from registration; *provided, however,* that if the securities are in bearer form or foreign law prevents the issuer of the securities from refusing to register securities transfers, other reasonable procedures (such as a legend described in paragraph (b)(3)(iii)(B)(3) of this rule) are implemented to prevent any transfer of the securities not made in accordance with the provisions of this Regulation S; and

(iv) Each distributor selling securities to a distributor, a dealer (as defined in section 2(a)(12) of the Securities Act of 1933), or a person receiving a selling concession, fee or other remuneration, prior to the expiration of a 40-day distribution compliance period in the case of debt securities, or a one-year distribution compliance period (or six-month distribution compliance period if the issuer is a reporting issuer) in the case of equity securities, sends a confirmation or other notice to the purchaser stating that the purchaser is subject to the same restrictions on offers and sales that apply to a distributor.

(4) *Guaranteed securities.* Notwithstanding paragraphs (b)(1) through (b)(3) of this rule, in offerings of debt securities fully and unconditionally guaranteed as to principal and interest by the parent of the issuer of the debt securities, only the requirements of paragraph (b) of this rule that are applicable to the offer and sale of the guarantee must be satisfied with respect t to the offer and sale of the guaranteed debt securities.

(5) *Warrants.* An offer or sale of warrants under Category 2 or 3 (paragraph (b)(2) or (b)(3)) of this rule also must comply with the following requirements:

(i) Each warrant must bear a legend stating that the warrant and the securities to be issued upon its exercise have not been registered under the Act and that the warrant may not be exercised by or on behalf of any U.S. person unless registered under the Act or an exemption from such registration is available;

(ii) Each person exercising a warrant is required to give:

(A) Written certification that it is not a U.S. person and the warrant is not being exercised on behalf of a U.S. person; or

(B) A written opinion of counsel to the effect that the warrant and the securities delivered upon exercise thereof have been registered under the Act or are exempt from registration thereunder; and

(iii) Procedures are implemented to ensure that the warrant may not be exercised within the United States, and that the securities may not be delivered within the United States upon exercise, other than in offerings deemed to meet the definition of "offshore transaction" pursuant to Rule 902(h), unless registered under the Act or an exemption from such registration is available.

Rule 904.   Offshore Resales

(a) An offer or sale of securities by any person other than the issuer, a distributor, any of their respective affiliates (except any officer or director who is an affiliate solely by virtue of holding such position), or any person acting on behalf of any of the foregoing, shall be deemed to occur outside the United States within the meaning of Rule 901 if:

(1) The offer or sale are made in an offshore transaction;

(2) No directed selling efforts are made in the United States by the seller, an affiliate, or any person acting on their behalf; and

(3) The conditions of paragraph (b) of this rule, if applicable, are satisfied.

(b) *Additional conditions.*

(1) *Resales by dealers and persons receiving selling concessions.* In the case of an offer or sale of securities prior to the expiration of the distribution compliance period specified in Category 2 or 3 (paragraph (b)(2) or (b)(3)) of Rule 903, as applicable, by a dealer, as defined in Section 2(a)(12) of the Act, or a person receiving a selling concession, fee or other remuneration in respect of the securities offered or sold:

(i) Neither the seller nor any person acting on its behalf knows that the offeree or buyer of the securities is a U.S. person; and

(ii) If the seller or any person acting on the seller's behalf knows that the purchaser is a dealer, as defined in Section 2(a)(12) of the Act, or is a person receiving a selling concession, fee or other remuneration in respect of the securities sold, the seller or a person acting on the seller's behalf sends to the purchaser a confirmation or other notice stating that the securities may be offered and sold during the distribution compliance period only in accordance with the provisions of this Regulation S (Rule 901 through Rule 905, and Preliminary Notes); pursuant to registration of the securities under the Act; or pursuant to an available exemption from the registration requirements of the Act.

(2) *Resales by certain affiliates.* In the case of an offer or sale of securities by an officer or director of the issuer or a distributor, who is an affiliate of the issuer or distributor solely by virtue of holding such position, no selling concession, fee or other remuneration is paid in connection with such offer or sale other than the usual and customary broker's commission that would be received by a person executing such transaction as agent.

Rule 905.   Resale Limitations

Equity securities of domestic issuers acquired from the issuer, a distributor, or any of their respective affiliates in a transaction subject to the conditions of Rule 901 or Rule 903 are deemed to be "restricted securities" as defined in Rule 144. Resales of any of such restricted securities by the offshore purchaser must be made in accordance with this Regulation S (Rule 901 through Rule 905, and Preliminary Notes), the registration requirements of the Act or an exemption therefrom. Any "restricted securities," as defined in Rule 144, that are equity securities of a domestic issuer will continue to be deemed to be restricted securities, notwithstanding that they were acquired in a resale transaction made pursuant to Rule 901 or Rule 904.

REGULATION CE—COORDINATED EXEMPTIONS FOR CERTAIN ISSUES OF SECURITIES EXEMPT UNDER STATE LAW

Rule 1001. Exemption for Transactions Exempt From Qualification Under Sec. 25102(n) of the California Corporations Code

Preliminary Notes: (1) Nothing in this rule is intended to be or should be construed as in any way relieving issuers or persons acting on behalf of issuers from providing disclosure to prospective investors necessary to satisfy the antifraud provisions of the federal securities laws. This rule only provides an exemption from the registration requirements of the Securities Act of 1933 ("the Act").

(2) Nothing in this rule obviates the need to comply with any applicable state law relating to the offer and sales of securities.

(3) Attempted compliance with this rule does not act as an exclusive election; the issuer also can claim the availability of any other applicable exemption.

(4) This exemption is not available to any issuer for any transaction which, while in technical compliance with the provision of this rule, is part of a plan or scheme to evade the registration provisions of the Act. In such cases, registration under the Act is required.

(a) *Exemption.* Offers and sales of securities that satisfy the conditions of paragraph (n) of Sec. 25102 of the California Corporations Code, and paragraph (b) of this rule, shall be exempt from the provisions of Section 5 of the Securities Act of 1933 by virtue of section 3(b) of that Act.

(b) *Limitation on and computation of offering price.* The sum of all cash and other consideration to be received for the securities shall not exceed $5,000,000, less the aggregate offering price for all other securities sold in the same offering of securities, whether pursuant to this or another exemption.

(c) *Resale limitations.* Securities issued pursuant to this Rule 1001 are deemed to be "restricted securities" as defined in Securities Act Rule 144. Resales of such securities must be made in compliance with the registration requirements of the Act or an exemption therefrom.

SELECTED FORMS UNDER
SECURITIES ACT OF 1933

17 C.F.R. § 239.__

FORM S–1

17 C.F.R. § 239.11

SECURITIES AND EXCHANGE COMMISSION

REGISTRATION STATEMENT UNDER THE SECURITIES ACT OF 1933

_____

(Exact name of registrant as specified in its charter)

_____

(State or other jurisdiction of incorporation or organization)

_____

(Primary Standard Industrial Classification Code Number)

_____

(I.R.S. Employer Identification No.)

_____

(Address, including zip code, and telephone number, including
area code, of registrant's principal executive offices)

_____

(Name, address, including zip code, and telephone number,
including area code, of agent for service)

_____

Approximate date of commencement of proposed sale to the public _____

If any of the securities being registered on this Form are to be offered on a delayed or continuous basis pursuant to Rule 415 under the Securities Act of 1933 check the following box. ☐

If this Form is filed to register additional securities for an offering pursuant to Rule 462(b) under the Securities Act, please check the following box and list the Securities Act registration statement number of the earlier effective registration statement for the same offering. ☐

If this Form is a post-effective amendment filed pursuant to Rule 462(c) under the Securities Act, check the following box and list the Securities Act registration statement number of the earlier effective registration statement for the same offering. ☐

If this Form is a post-effective amendment filed pursuant to Rule 462(d) under the Securities Act, check the following box and list the Securities Act registration statement number of the earlier effective registration statement for the same offering. ☐

Indicate by check mark whether the registrant is a large accelerated filer, an accelerated filer, a non-accelerated filer, smaller reporting company, or an emerging growth company. See the definitions of "large accelerated filer," "accelerated filer," "smaller reporting company," and "emerging growth company" in Rule 12b–2 of the Exchange Act.

Large accelerated filer ☐   Accelerated filer ☐

Non-accelerated filer ☐   Smaller reporting company ☐

(Do not check if an emerging growth company)

                                              Emerging growth company ☐

1933 ACT FORMS

Indicate by check mark whether the registrant is a large accelerated filer, an accelerated filer, a non-accelerated filer, a smaller reporting company, or an emerging growth company. See the definitions of "large accelerated filer," "accelerated filer," "smaller reporting company," and "emerging growth company" in Rule 12b–2 of the Exchange Act.

Large accelerated filer ☐

Non-accelerated filer ☐

Accelerated filer ☐

Smaller reporting company ☐

Emerging growth company ☐

Note: Specific details relating to the fee calculation shall be furnished in notes to the table, including references to provisions of Rule 457 relied upon, if the basis of the calculation is not otherwise evident from the information presented in the table.

If the filing fee is calculated pursuant to Rule 457(o) under the Securities Act, only the title of the class of securities to be registered, the proposed maximum aggregate offering price for that class of securities and the amount of registration fee need to appear in the Calculation of Registration Fee table. Any difference between the dollar amount of securities registered for such offerings and the dollar amount of securities sold may be carried forward on a future registration statement pursuant to Rule 429 under the Securities Act.

GENERAL INSTRUCTIONS

I. Eligibility Requirements for Use of Form S–1

This Form shall be used for the registration under the Securities Act of 1933 ("Securities Act") of securities of all registrants for which no other form is authorized or prescribed, except that this Form shall not be used for securities of foreign governments or political sub-divisions thereof or asset-backed securities, as defined in Item 1101(c) of Regulation AB.

II. Application of General Rules and Regulations

A. Attention is directed to the General Rules and Regulations under the Securities Act, particularly those comprising Regulation C thereunder. That Regulation contains general requirements regarding the preparation and filing of the registration statement.

B. Attention is directed to Regulation S–K for the requirements applicable to the content of the nonfinancial statement portions of registration statements under the Securities Act. Where this Form directs the registrant to furnish information required by Regulation S–K and the item of Regulation S–K so provides, information need only be furnished to the extent appropriate.

C. A registration statement filed (or submitted for confidential review) under Section 6 of the Securities Act (15 U.S.C. 77f) by an emerging growth company, defined in Section 2(a)(19) of the Securities Act (15 U.S.C. 77b(a)(19)), prior to an initial public offering may omit financial information for historical periods otherwise required by Regulation S–X (17 CFR Part 210) as of the time of filing (or confidential submission) of the registration statement, provided that:

1. The omitted financial information relates to a historical period that the registrant reasonably believes will not be required to be included in this Form at the time of the contemplated offering; and

2. Prior to the registrant distributing a preliminary prospectus to investors, the registration statement is amended to include all financial information required by Regulation S–X at the date of the amendment.

III. Exchange Offers

If any of the securities being registered are to be offered in exchange for securities of any other issuer the prospectus shall also include the information which would be required by Item 11 if the securities of such other issuer were registered on this Form. There shall also be included the information concerning such securities of such other issuer which would be called for by Item 9 if such securities were being registered. In connection with this instruction, reference is made to Rule 409.

IV. Roll-up Transactions

If the securities to be registered on this Form will be issued in a roll-up transaction as defined in Item 901(c) of Regulation S–K, attention is directed to the requirements of Form S–4 applicable to roll-up transactions, including, but not limited to, General Instruction I.

V. Registration of Additional Securities

With respect to the registration of additional securities for an offering pursuant to Rule 462(b) under the Securities Act, the registrant may file a registration statement consisting only of the following: the facing page; a statement that the contents of the earlier registration statement, identified by file number, are incorporated by reference; required opinions and consents; the signature page; and any price-related information omitted from the earlier registration statement in reliance on Rule 430A that the registrant chooses to include in the new registration statement. The information contained in such a Rule 462(b) registration statement shall be deemed to be a part of the earlier registration statement as of the date of effectiveness of the Rule 462(b) registration statement. Any opinion or consent required in the Rule 462(b) registration statement may be incorporated by reference from the earlier registration statement with respect to the offering, if:

(i) such opinion or consent expressly provides for such incorporation; and

(ii) such opinion relates to the securities registered pursuant to Rule 462(b). *See* Rule 439(b) under the Securities Act.

VI. Offerings of Asset-Backed Securities

The following applies if a registration statement on this Form S–1 is being used to register an offering of asset-backed securities. Terms used in this General Instruction VI. have the same meaning as in Item 1101 of Regulation AB.

A. Items That May Be Omitted.

Such registrants may omit the information called for by Item 11, Information with Respect to the Registrant.

B. Substitute Information To Be Included.

In addition to the Items that are otherwise required by this Form, the registrant must furnish in the prospectus the information required by Items 1102 through 1120 of Regulation AB.

C. Signatures.

The registration statement must be signed by the depositor, the depositor's principal executive officer or officers, principal financial officer and controller or principal accounting officer, and by at least a majority of the depositor's board of directors or persons performing similar functions.

VII. Eligibility to Use Incorporation by Reference

If a registrant meets the following requirements in paragraphs A-F immediately prior to the time of filing a registration statement on this Form, it may elect to provide information required by Items 3 through 11 of this Form in accordance with Item 11A and Item 12 of this Form. Notwithstanding the foregoing, in the financial statements, incorporating by reference or crossreferencing to information outside of the financial statements is not permitted unless otherwise specifically permitted or required by the Commission's rules or by U.S. Generally Accepted Accounting Principles or International Financial Reporting Standards as issued by the International Accounting Standards Board, whichever is applicable.

A. The registrant is subject to the requirement to file reports pursuant to Section 13 or Section 15(d) of the Securities Exchange Act of 1934 ("Exchange Act").

B. The registrant has filed all reports and other materials required to be filed by Sections 13(a), 14, or 15(d) of the Exchange Act during the preceding 12 months (or for such shorter period that the registrant was required to file such reports and materials).

C.   The registrant has filed an annual report required under Section 13(a) or Section 15(d) of the Exchange Act for its most recently completed fiscal year.

D.   The registrant is not:

1.   And during the past three years neither the registrant nor any of its predecessors was:

(a)   A blank check company as defined in Rule 419(a)(2);

(b)   A shell company, other than a business combination related shell company, each as defined in Rule 405; or

(c)   A registrant for an offering of penny stock as defined in Rule 3a51–1 of the Exchange Act.

2.   Registering an offering that effectuates a business combination transaction as defined in Rule 165(f)(1).

E.   If a registrant is a successor registrant it shall be deemed to have satisfied conditions A., B., C., and D.2 above if:

1.   Its predecessor and it, taken together, do so, provided that the succession was primarily for the purpose of changing the state of incorporation of the predecessor or forming a holding company and that the assets and liabilities of the successor at the time of succession were substantially the same as those of the predecessor; or

2.   All predecessors met the conditions at the time of succession and the registrant has continued to do so since the succession.

F.   The registrant makes its periodic and current reports filed pursuant to Section 13 or Section 15(d) of the Exchange Act that are incorporated by reference pursuant to Item 11A or Item 12 of this Form readily available and accessible on a Web site maintained by or for the registrant and containing information about the registrant.

PART I. INFORMATION REQUIRED IN PROSPECTUS

Item 1.   Forepart of the Registration Statement and Outside Front Cover Page of Prospectus

Set forth in the forepart of the registration statement and on the outside front cover page of the prospectus the information required by Item 501 of Regulation S–K.

Item 2.   Inside Front and Outside Back Cover Pages of Prospectus

Set forth on the inside front cover page of the prospectus or, where permitted, on the outside back cover page, the information required by Item 502 of Regulation S–K.

Item 3.   Summary Information and Risk Factors

Furnish the information required by Items 105 and 503 of Regulation S–K.

Item 4.   Use of Proceeds

Furnish the information required by Item 504 of Regulation S–K.

Item 5.   Determination of Offering Price

Furnish the information required by Item 505 of Regulation S–K.

Item 6.   Dilution

Furnish the information required by Item 506 of Regulation S–K.

Item 7. Selling Security Holders

Furnish the information required by Item 507 of Regulation S–K.

Item 8. Plan of Distribution

Furnish the information required by Item 508 of Regulation S–K.

Item 9. Description of Securities to Be Registered

Furnish the information required by Item 202 of Regulation S–K.

Item 10. Interests of Named Experts and Counsel

Furnish the information required by Item 509 of Regulation S–K.

Item 11. Information With Respect to the Registrant

Furnish the following information with respect to the registrant:

(a) Information required by Item 101 of Regulation S–K, description of business;

(b) Information required by Item 102 of Regulation S–K, description of property;

(c) Information required by Item 103 of Regulation S–K, legal proceedings;

(d) Where common equity securities are being offered, information required by Item 201 of Regulation S–K, market price of and dividends on the registrant's common equity and related stockholder matters;

(e) Financial statements meeting the requirements of Regulation S–X (Schedules required under Regulation S–X shall be filed as "Financial Statements Schedules" pursuant to Item 15, Exhibits and Financial Statement Schedules, of this form), as well as any financial information required by Rule 3–05 and Article 11 of Regulations S–X. A smaller reporting company may provide the information in Rule 8–04 and 8–05 of Regulation S–X in lieu of the financial information required by Rule 3–05 and Article 11 of Regulation S–X;

(f) Information required by Item 301 of Regulation S–K, selected financial data;

(g) Information required by Item 302 of Regulation S–K, supplementary financial information;

(h) Information required by Item 303 of Regulation S–K, management's discussion and analysis of financial condition and results of operations;

(i) Information required by Item 304 of Regulation S–K, changes in and disagreements with accountants on accounting and financial disclosure;

(j) Information required by Item 305 of Regulation S–K, quantitative and qualitative disclosures about market risk;

(k) Information required by Item 401 of Regulation S–K, directors and executive officers;

(l) Information required by Item 402 of Regulation S–K, executive compensation, and information required by paragraph (e)(4) of Item 407 of Regulation S–K, corporate governance;

(m) Information required by Item 403 of Regulation S–K, security ownership of certain beneficial owners and management; and

(n) Information required by Item 404 of Regulation S–K, transactions with related persons, promoters and certain control persons, and Item 407(a) of Regulation S–K, corporate governance.

Item 11A. Material Changes

If the registrant elects to incorporate information by reference pursuant to General Instruction VII., describe any and all material changes in the registrant's affairs which have occurred since the end of the latest fiscal year for which audited financial statements were included in the latest Form 10–K and which have not been described in a Form 10–Q or Form 8–K filed under the Exchange Act.

Item 12. Incorporation of Certain Information by Reference

If the registrant elects to incorporate information by reference pursuant to General Instruction VII.:

(a)   It must specifically incorporate by reference into the prospectus contained in the registration statement the following documents by means of a statement to that effect in the prospectus listing all such documents:

(1)   The registrant's latest annual report on Form 10–K filed pursuant to Section 13(a) or Section 15(d) of the Exchange Act which contains financial statements for the registrant's latest fiscal year for which a Form 10–K was required to have been filed; and

(2)   All other reports filed pursuant to Section 13(a) or 15(d) of the Exchange Act or proxy or information statements filed pursuant to Section 14 of the Exchange Act since the end of the fiscal year covered by the annual report referred to in paragraph (a)(1) above.

Note to Item 12(a). Attention is directed to Rule 439 regarding consent to use of material incorporated by reference.

(b)   In addition to the incorporation by reference permitted pursuant to paragraph (a) of this Item, a smaller reporting company, as defined in Rule 405 (17 CFR 230.405), may elect to incorporate by reference information filed after the effective date of the registration statement. A smaller reporting company making this election must state in the prospectus contained in the registration statement that all documents subsequently filed by the registrant pursuant to Sections 13(a), 13(c), 14 or 15(d) of the Exchange Act, prior to the termination of the offering shall be deemed to be incorporated by reference into the prospectus.

(c)(1)   The registrant must state:

(i)   That it will provide to each person, including any beneficial owner, to whom a prospectus is delivered, a copy of any or all of the reports or documents that have been incorporated by reference in the prospectus contained in the registration statement but not delivered with the prospectus;

(ii)   That it will provide these reports or documents upon written or oral request;

(iii)   That it will provide these reports or documents at no cost to the requester;

(iv)   The name, address, telephone number, and e-mail address, if any, to which the request for these reports or documents must be made; and

(v)   The registrant's Web site address, including the uniform resource locator (URL) where the incorporated reports and other documents may be accessed.

Note to Item 12(c)(1). If the registrant sends any of the information that is incorporated by reference in the prospectus contained in the registration statement to security holders, it also must send any exhibits that are specifically incorporated by reference in that information.

(2)   The registrant must:

(i)   Identify the reports and other information that it files with the SEC; and

(ii)   State that the SEC maintains an Internet site that contains reports, proxy and information statements, and other information regarding issuers that file electronically with the SEC and state the address of that site (http://www.sec.gov).

Item 12A. Disclosure of Commission Position on Indemnification for Securities Act Liabilities

Furnish the information required by Item 510 of Regulation S–K.

PART II. INFORMATION NOT REQUIRED IN PROSPECTUS

Item 13. Other Expenses of Issuance and Distribution

Furnish the information required by Item 511 of Regulation S–K.

Item 14. Indemnification of Directors and Officers

Furnish the information required by Item 702 of Regulation S–X.

Item 15. Recent Sales of Unregistered Securities

Furnish the information required by Item 701 of Regulation S–K.

Item 16. Exhibits and Financial Statement Schedules

(a)   Subject to the rules regarding incorporation by reference, furnish the exhibits as required by Item 601 of Regulation S–K.

(b)   Furnish the financial statement schedules required by Regulation S–X and Item 11(e) of this Form. These schedules shall be lettered or numbered in the manner described for exhibits in paragraph (a).

Item 17. Undertakings

Furnish the undertakings required by Item 512 of Regulation S–K.

SIGNATURES

Pursuant to the requirements of the Securities Act of 1933, the registrant has duly caused this registration statement to be signed on its behalf by the undersigned, thereunto duly authorized, in the City of _____, State of _____, on _____, 20__.

_____
(Registrant)

_____
By (Signature and Title)

Pursuant to the requirements of the Securities Act of 1933, this registration statement has been signed by the following persons in the capacities and on the dates indicated.

_____
(Signature)

_____
(Title)

_____
(Date)

Instructions. 1. The registration statement shall be signed by the registrant, its principal executive officer or officers, its principal financial officer, its controller or principal accounting officer and by at least a majority of the board of directors or persons performing similar functions. If the registrant is a foreign person, the registration statement shall also be signed by its authorized representative in the United States. Where the registrant is a limited partnership, the registration statement shall be signed by a majority of the board of directors of any corporate general partner signing the registration statement.

2.   The name of each person who signs the registration statement shall be typed or printed beneath his signature. Any person who occupies more than one of the specified positions shall indicate each capacity in which he signs the registration statement. Attention is directed to Rule 402 concerning manual signatures and to Item 601 of Regulation S–K concerning signatures pursuant to powers of attorney.

INSTRUCTIONS AS TO SUMMARY PROSPECTUSES

1.   A summary prospectus used pursuant to Rule 431 shall at the time of its use contain such of the information specified below as is then included in the registration statement. All other information and documents contained in the registration statement may be omitted.

(a)   As to Item 1, the aggregate offering price to the public, the aggregate underwriting discounts and commissions and the offering price per unit to the public;

(b)   As to Item 4, a brief statement of the principal purposes for which the proceeds are to be used;

(c)   As to Item 7, a statement as to the amount of the offering, if any, to be made for the account of security holders;

(d)   As to Item 8, the name of the managing underwriter or underwriters and a brief statement as to the nature of the underwriter's obligation to take the securities; if any securities to be registered are to be offered otherwise than through underwriters, a brief statement as to the manner of distribution; and, if securities are to be offered otherwise than for cash, a brief statement as to the general purposes of the distribution, the basis upon which the securities are to be offered, the amount of compensation and other expenses of distribution, and by whom they are to be borne;

(e)   As to Item 9, a brief statement as to dividend rights, voting rights, conversion rights, interest, maturity;

(f)   As to Item 11, a brief statement of the general character of the business done and intended to be done, the selected financial data (Item 301 of Regulation S–K) and a brief statement of the nature and present status of any material pending legal proceedings; and

(g)   A tabular presentation of notes payable, long term debt, deferred credits, minority interests, if material, and the equity section of the latest balance sheet filed, as may be appropriate.

2.   The summary prospectus shall not contain a summary or condensation of any other required financial information except as provided above.

3.   Where securities being registered are to be offered in exchange for securities of any other issuer, the summary prospectus also shall contain that information as to Items 9 and 11 specified in paragraphs (e) and (f) above which would be required if the securities of such other issuer were registered on this Form.

4.   The Commission may, upon the request of the registrant, and where consistent with the protection of investors, permit the omission of any of the information herein required or the furnishing in substitution therefor of appropriate information of comparable character. The Commission may also require the inclusion of other information in addition to, or in substitution for, the information herein required in any case where such information is necessary or appropriate for the protection of investors.

FORM S–3

17 C.F.R. § 239.13

SECURITIES AND EXCHANGE COMMISSION

REGISTRATION STATEMENT UNDER THE SECURITIES ACT OF 1933

_____
(Exact name of registrant as specified in its charter)

_____
(State or other jurisdiction of incorporation or organization)

_____
(I.R.S. Employer Identification No.)

_____
(Address, including zip code, and telephone number, including
area code, of registrant's principal executive offices)

_____
(Name, address, including zip code, and telephone number,
including area code, of agent for service)

Approximate date of commencement of proposed sale to the public _____

If the only securities being registered on this Form are being offered pursuant to dividend or interest reinvestment plans, please check the following box. ☐

If any of the securities being registered on this Form are to be offered on a delayed or continuous basis pursuant to Rule 415 under the Securities Act of 1933, other than securities offered only in connection with dividend or interest reinvestment plans, check the following box. ☐

If this Form is filed to register additional securities for an offering pursuant to Rule 462(b) under the Securities Act, please check the following box and list the Securities Act registration statement number of the earlier effective registration statement for the same offering. ☐

If this Form is a post-effective amendment filed pursuant to Rule 462(c) under the Securities Act, check the following box and list the Securities Act registration statement number of the earlier effective registration statement for the same offering. ☐

If this Form is a registration statement pursuant to General Instruction I.D. or a post-effective amendment thereto that shall become effective upon filing with the Commission pursuant to Rule 462(e) under the Securities Act, check the following box. ☐

If this Form is a post-effective amendment to a registration statement filed pursuant to General Instruction I.D. filed to register additional securities or additional classes of securities pursuant to Rule 413(b) under the Securities Act, check the following box. ☐

Indicate by check mark whether the registrant is a large accelerated filer, an accelerated filer, a non-accelerated filer, a smaller reporting company, or an emerging growth company. See the definitions of "large accelerated filer," "accelerated filer," "smaller reporting company," and "emerging growth company" in Rule 12b–2 of the Exchange Act.

1933 ACT FORMS

Large accelerated filer ☐

Non-accelerated filer ☐

Accelerated filer ☐

Smaller reporting company ☐

Emerging growth company ☐

If an emerging growth company, indicate by check mark if the registrant has elected not to use the extended transition period for complying with any new or revised financial accounting standards provided pursuant to Rule 7(a)(2)(B) of the Securities Act. ☐

Calculation of Registration Fee

Title of each class of securities to be registered	Amount to be registered	Proposed maximum offering price per unit	Proposed maximum aggregate offering price	Amount of registration fee

Notes to the "Calculation of Registration Fee" Table ("Fee Table"):

1. Specific details relating to the fee calculation shall be furnished in notes to the Fee Table, including references to provisions of Rule 457 relied upon, if the basis of the calculation is not otherwise evident from the information presented in the Fee Table.

2. If the filing fee is calculated pursuant to Rule 457(*o*) under the Securities Act, only the title of the class of securities to be registered, the proposed maximum aggregate offering price for that class of securities, and the amount of registration fee need to appear in the Fee Table. Where two or more classes of securities are being registered pursuant to General Instruction II.D., however, the Fee Table need only specify the maximum aggregate offering price for all classes; the Fee Table need not specify by each class the proposed maximum aggregate offering price (see General Instruction II.D.).

3. If the filing fee is calculated pursuant to Rule 457(r) under the Securities Act, the Fee Table must state that it registers an unspecified amount of securities of each identified class of securities and must provide that the issuer is relying on Rule 456(b) and Rule 457(r). If the Fee Table is amended in a post-effective amendment to the registration statement or in a prospectus filed in accordance with Rule 456(b)(1)(ii), the Fee Table must specify the aggregate offering price for all classes of securities in the referenced offering or offerings and the applicable registration fee.

4. Any difference between the dollar amount of securities registered for such offerings and the dollar amount of securities sold may be carried forward on a future registration statement pursuant to Rule 457 under the Securities Act.

GENERAL INSTRUCTIONS

I. Eligibility Requirements for Use of Form S–3

This instruction sets forth registrant requirements and transaction requirements for the use of Form S–3. Any registrant which meets the Requirements of I.A. below ("Registrant Requirements") may use this Form for the registration of securities under the Securities Act of 1933 ("Securities Act") which are offered in any transaction specified in I.B. below ("Transaction Requirement") provided that the requirements applicable to the specified transaction are met. With respect to majority-owned subsidiaries, see Instruction I.C. below. With respect to well-known seasoned issuers and majority-owned subsidiaries of well-known seasoned issuers, see Instruction I.D. below.

A. Registrant Requirements

Registrants must meet the following conditions in order to use this Form for registration under the Securities Act of securities offered in the transactions specified in I.B. below:

1. The registrant is organized under the laws of the United States or any State or Territory or the District of Columbia and has its principal business operations in the United States or its territories.

2.   The registrant has a class of securities registered pursuant to Section 12(b) of the Securities Exchange Act of 1934 ("Exchange Act") or a class of equity securities registered pursuant to Section 12(g) of the Exchange Act or is required to file reports pursuant to Section 15(d) of the Exchange Act.

3.   The registrant:

(a)   has been subject to the requirements of Section 12 or 15(d) of the Exchange Act and has filed all the material required to be filed pursuant to Section 13, 14 or 15(d) for a period of at least twelve calendar months immediately preceding the filing of the registration statement on this Form; and

(b)   has filed in a timely manner all reports required to be filed during the twelve calendar months and any portion of a month immediately preceding the filing of the registration statement, other than a report that is required solely pursuant to Item 1.01, 1.02, 2.03, 2.04, 2.05, 2.06, 4.02(a), or 502(e) of Form 8–K. If the registrant has used (during the twelve calendar months and any portion of a month immediately preceding the filing of the registration statement) Rule 12b–25(b) under the Exchange Act with respect to a report or a portion of a report, that report or portion thereof has actually been filed within the time period prescribed by that rule.

4.   Neither the registrant nor any of its consolidated or unconsolidated subsidiaries have, since the end of the last fiscal year for which certified financial statements of the registrant and its consolidated subsidiaries were included in a report filed pursuant to Section 13(a) or 15(d) of the Exchange Act:

(a)   failed to pay any dividend or sinking fund installment on preferred stock; or

(b)   defaulted (i) on any installment or installments on indebtedness for borrowed money, or (ii) on any rental on one or more long term leases, which defaults in the aggregate are material to the financial position of the registrant and its consolidated and unconsolidated subsidiaries, taken as a whole.

5.   A foreign issuer, other than a foreign government, which satisfies all of the above provisions of these registrant eligibility requirements except the provisions in I.A.1. relating to organization and principal business shall be deemed to have met these registrant eligibility requirements provided that such foreign issuer files the same reports with the Commission under Section 13(a) or 15(d) of the Exchange Act as a domestic registrant pursuant to I.A.3. above.

6.   If the registrant is a successor registrant, it shall be deemed to have met conditions 1., 2., 3., and 5., above if:

(a)   its predecessor and it, taken together, do so, provided that the succession was primarily for the purpose of changing the state of incorporation of the predecessor or forming a holding company and that the assets and liabilities of the successor at the time of succession were substantially the same as those of the predecessor, or

(b)   if all predecessors met the conditions at the time of succession and the registrant has continued to do so since the succession.

7.   Electronic filings. In addition to satisfying the foregoing conditions, a registrant subject to the electronic filing requirements of Rule 101 of Regulation S–T shall have:

(a)   Filed with the Commission all required electronic filings, including electronic copies of documents submitted in paper pursuant to a hardship exemption as provided by Rule 201 or Rule 202(d) of Regulation S–T; and

(b)   Submitted electronically to the Commission all Interactive Data Files required to be submitted pursuant to Rule 405 of Regulation S–T (§ 232.405 of this chapter) during the twelve calendar months and any portion of a month immediately preceding the filing of the registration statement on this Form (or for such shorter period of time that the registrant was required to submit and post such files).

B.   Transaction Requirements

Security offerings meeting any of the following conditions and made by registrants meeting the Registrant Requirements above may be registered on this Form:

1933 ACT FORMS

1. *Primary Offerings by Certain Registrants.* Securities to be offered for cash by or on behalf of a registrant, or outstanding securities to be offered for cash for the account of any person other than the registrant, including securities acquired by standby underwriters in connection with the call or redemption by the registrant of warrants or a class of convertible securities; *provided* that the aggregate market value of the voting and non-voting common equity held by non-affiliates of the registrant is $75 million or more.

Instruction. For the purposes of this Form, "common equity" is as defined in Securities Act Rule 405. The aggregate market value of the registrant's outstanding voting and non-voting common equity shall be computed by use of the price at which the common equity was last sold, or the average of the bid and asked prices of such common equity, in the principal market for such common equity as of a date within 60 days prior to the date of filing. See the definition of "affiliate" in Securities Act Rule 405.

2. *Primary Offerings of Non-Convertible Securities Other than Common Equity.* Nonconvertible securities, other than common equity, to be offered for cash by or on behalf of a registrant, provided the registrant:

    (i)   has issued (as of a date within 60 days prior to the filing of the registration statement) at least $1 billion in non-convertible securities, other than common equity, in primary offerings for cash, not exchange, registered under the Securities Act, over the prior three years; or

    (ii)   has outstanding (as of a date within 60 days prior to the filing of the registration statement) at least $750 million of non-convertible securities, other than common equity, issued in primary offerings for cash, not exchange, registered under the Securities Act; or

    (iii)   is a wholly-owned subsidiary of a well-known seasoned issuer (as defined in Securities Act Rule 405); or

    (iv)   is a majority-owned operating partnership of a real estate investment trust that qualifies as a well-known seasoned issuer (as defined in Securities Act Rule 405).

Instruction. For purposes of Instruction I.B.2(i) above, an insurance company, as defined in Section 2(a)(13) of the Securities Act, when using this Form to register offerings of securities subject to regulation under the insurance laws of any State or Territory of the United States or the District of Columbia ("insurance contracts"), may include purchase payments or premium payments for insurance contracts, including purchase payments or premium payments for variable insurance contracts (not including purchase payments or premium payments initially allocated to investment options that are not registered under the Securities Act), issued in offerings registered under the Securities Act over the prior three years. For purposes of Instruction I.B.2(ii) above, an insurance company, as defined in Section 2(a)(13) of the Securities Act, when using this Form to register offerings of insurance contracts, may include the contract value, as of the measurement date, of any outstanding insurance contracts, including variable insurance contracts (not including the value allocated as of the measurement date to investment options that are not registered under the Securities Act), issued in offerings registered under the Securities Act.

3. *Transactions Involving Secondary Offerings.* Outstanding securities to be offered for the account of any person other than the issuer, including securities acquired by standby underwriters in connection with the call or redemption by the issuer of warrants or a class of convertible securities, if securities of the same class are listed and registered on a national securities exchange or are quoted on the automated quotation system of a national securities association. (In addition, attention is directed to General Instruction C to Form S–8 for the registration of employee benefit plan securities for resale.)

4. *Rights offerings, dividend or interest reinvestment plans, and conversions, warrants and options.*

    (a)   Securities to be offered:

        (1)   Upon the exercise of outstanding rights granted by the issuer of the securities to be offered, if such rights are granted on a pro rata basis to all existing security holders of the class of securities to which the rights attach;

        (2)   Under a dividend or interest reinvestment plan; or

        (3)   Upon the conversion of outstanding convertible securities or the exercise of outstanding warrants or options issued by the issuer of the securities to be offered, or an affiliate of that issuer.

FORM S-3

(b)   However, Form S–3 is available for registering these securities only if the issuer has sent, within the twelve calendar months immediately before the registration statement is filed, material containing the information required by Rule 14a–3(b) under the Securities Exchange Act of 1934 to:

(1)   All record holders of the rights;

(2)   All participants in the plans; or

(3)   All record holders of the convertible securities, warrants or options, respectively.

(c)   The issuer also must have provided, within the twelve calendar months immediately before the Form S–3 registration statement is filed, the information required by Items 401, 402, 403 and 407(c)(3), (d)(4), (d)(5) and (e)(4) of Regulation S–K to:

(1)   Holders of rights exercisable for common stock;

(2)   Holders of securities convertible into common stock; and

(3)   Participants in plans that may invest in common stock, securities convertible into common stock, or warrants or options exercisable for common stock, respectively.

5.   *Offerings of Investment grade Asset-backed Securities.* This Form shall not be used to register offerings of asset-backed securities, as defined in 17 CFR 229.1101(c).

6.   *Limited Primary Offerings by Certain Other Registrants.* Securities to be offered for cash by or on behalf of a registrant; *provided that*:

(a)   the aggregate market value of securities sold by or on behalf of the registrant pursuant to this Instruction I.B.6. during the period of 12 calendar months immediately prior to, and including, the sale is no more than one-third of the aggregate market value of the voting and non-voting common equity held by non-affiliates of the registrant;

(b)   the registrant is not a shell company (as defined in Rule 405) and has not been a shell company for at least 12 calendar months previously and if it has been a shell company at any time previously, has filed current Form 10 information with the Commission at least 12 calendar months previously reflecting its status as an entity that is not a shell company; and

(c)   the registrant has at least one class of common equity securities listed and registered on a national securities exchange.

Instructions.

1.   "Common equity" is as defined in Rule 405. For purposes of computing the aggregate market value of the registrant's outstanding voting and non-voting common equity pursuant to General Instruction I.B.6., registrants shall use the price at which the common equity was last sold, or the average of the bid and asked prices of such common equity, in the principal market for such common equity as of a date within 60 days prior to the date of sale. *See* the definition of "affiliate" in Rule 405.

2.   For purposes of computing the aggregate market value of all securities sold by or on behalf of the registrant in offerings pursuant to General Instruction I.B.6. during any period of 12 calendar months, registrants shall aggregate the gross proceeds of such sales; *provided*, that, in the case of derivative securities convertible into or exercisable for shares of the registrant's common equity, registrants shall calculate the aggregate market value of any underlying equity shares in lieu of the market value of the derivative securities. The aggregate market value of the underlying equity shall be calculated by multiplying the maximum number of common equity shares into which the derivative securities are convertible or for which they are exercisable as of a date within 60 days prior to the date of sale, by the same per share market price of the registrant's equity used for purposes of calculating the aggregate market value of the registrant's outstanding voting and non-voting common equity pursuant to Instruction 1 to General Instruction I.B.6. If the derivative securities have been converted or exercised, the aggregate market value of the underlying equity shall be calculated by multiplying the actual number of shares into which the securities were converted or received upon exercise, by the market price of such shares on the date of conversion or exercise.

3.   If the aggregate market value of the registrant's outstanding voting and nonvoting common equity computed pursuant to General Instruction I.B.6. equals or exceeds $75 million subsequent to the effective date of this registration statement, then the one-third limitation on sales specified in General Instruction I.B.6(a) shall

not apply to additional sales made pursuant to this registration statement on or subsequent to such date and instead the registration statement shall be considered filed pursuant to General Instruction I.B.1.

4.   The term "Form 10 information" means the information that is required by Form 10 or Form 20–F, as applicable to the registrant, to register under the Securities Exchange Act of 1934 each class of securities being registered using this form. A registrant may provide the Form 10 information in another Commission filing with respect to the registrant.

5.   The date used in Instruction 2 to General Instruction I.B.6. shall be the same date used in Instruction 1 to General Instruction I.B.6.

6.   A registrant's eligibility to register a primary offering on Form S–3 pursuant to General Instruction I.B.6. does not mean that the registrant meets the requirements of Form S–3 for purposes of any other rule or regulation of the Commission apart from Rule 415(a)(1)(x).

7.   Registrants must set forth on the outside front cover of the prospectus the calculation of the aggregate market value of the registrant's outstanding voting and nonvoting common equity pursuant to General Instruction I.B.6. and the amount of all securities offered pursuant to General Instruction I.B.6. during the prior 12 calendar month period that ends on, and includes, the date of the prospectus.

8.   For purposes of General Instruction I.B.6(c), a "national securities exchange" shall mean an exchange registered as such under Section 6(a) of the Securities Exchange Act of 1934.

C.   Majority-Owned Subsidiaries

If a registrant is a majority-owned subsidiary, security offerings may be registered on this Form if:

1.   The registrant-subsidiary itself meets the Registrant Requirements and the applicable Transaction Requirement;

2.   The parent of the registrant-subsidiary meets the Registrant Requirements and the conditions of Transaction Requirement B.2. (Primary Offerings of Non-Convertible Securities Other than Common Equity) are met;

3.   The parent of the registrant-subsidiary meets the Registrant Requirements and the applicable Transaction Requirement, and provides a full and unconditional guarantee, as defined in Rule 3–10 of Regulation S–X, of the payment obligations on the securities being registered, and the securities being registered are non-convertible securities, other than common equity;

4.   The parent of the registrant-subsidiary meets the Registrant Requirements and the applicable Transaction Requirement, and the securities of the registrant subsidiary being registered are full and unconditional guarantees, as defined in Rule 3–10 of Regulation S–X, of the payment obligations on the parent's non-convertible securities, other than common equity, being registered; or

5.   The parent of the registrant-subsidiary meets the Registrant Requirements and the applicable Transaction Requirement, and the securities of the registrant-subsidiary being registered are guarantees of the payment obligations on the nonconvertible securities, other than common equity, being registered by another majority-owned subsidiary of the parent, where the parent provides a full and unconditional guarantee, as defined in Rule 3–10 of Regulation S–X, of such non-convertible securities.

Note to paragraph (c): With regard to paragraphs (c)(3), (c)(4), and (c)(5) of this rule, the guarantor is the issuer of a separate security consisting of the guarantee, which must be concurrently registered, but may be registered on the same registration statement as are the guaranteed non-convertible securities.

D.   Automatic shelf offerings by well-known seasoned issuers

Any registrant that is a well-known seasoned issuer as defined in Rule 405 at the most recent eligibility determination date specified in paragraph (2) of that definition may use this Form for registration under the Securities Act of securities offerings, other than pursuant to Rule 415(a)(1)(vii) or (viii), as follows:

(1)   The securities to be offered are:

(a)   Any securities to be offered pursuant to Rule 415, Rule 430A, or Rule 430B by:

(i)   A registrant that is a well-known seasoned issuer by reason of paragraph (1)(i)(A) of the definition in Rule 405; or

(ii)   A registrant that is a well-known seasoned issuer only by reason of paragraph (1)(i)(B) of the definition in Rule 405 if the registrant also is eligible to register a primary offering of its securities pursuant to paragraph (b)(1) of this rule;

(b)   Non-convertible securities, other than common equity, to be offered pursuant to Rule 415, Rule 430A, or Rule 430B by a registrant that is a well-known seasoned issuer only by reason of paragraph (1)(i)(B) of the definition in Rule 405 and does not fall within paragraph (b)(1) of this rule;

(c)   Securities of majority-owned subsidiaries of the parent registrant to be offered pursuant to Rule 415, Rule 430A, or Rule 430B if the parent registrant is a well-known seasoned issuer and the securities of the majority-owned subsidiary being registered meet the following requirements:

(i)   Securities of a majority-owned subsidiary that is a well-known seasoned issuer at the time it becomes a registrant, other than by virtue of paragraph (1)(ii) of the definition of well-known seasoned issuer in Rule 405;

(ii)   Securities of a majority-owned subsidiary that are non-convertible securities, other than common equity, and the parent registration provides a full and unconditional guarantee, as defined in Rule 3–10 of Regulation S–X, of the payment obligations on the non-convertible securities;

(iii)   Securities of a majority-owned subsidiary that are a guarantee of:

(A)   Non-convertible securities, other than common equity, of the parent registrant being registered;

(B)   Non-convertible securities, other than common equity, of another majority-owned subsidiary being registered and the parent has provided a full and unconditional guarantee, as defined in Rule 3–10 of Regulation S–X, of the payment obligations on such non-convertible securities; or

(iv)   Securities of a majority-owned subsidiary that meet the conditions of the Transaction Requirement set forth in paragraph (b)(2) of this Form (Primary Offerings of Non-Convertible Securities Other than Common Equity).

(d)   Securities to be offered for the account of any person other than the issuer ("selling security holders"), provided that the registration statement and the prospectus are not required to separately identify the selling security holders or the securities to be sold by such persons until the filing of a prospectus, prospectus supplement, post-effective amendment to the registration statement, or periodic or current report under the Exchange Act that is incorporated by reference into the registration statement and prospectus, identifying the selling security holders and the amount of securities to be sold by each of them and, if included in a periodic or current report, a prospectus or prospectus supplement is filed, as required by Rule 430B, pursuant to Rule 424(b)(7);

(2)   The registrant pays the registration fee pursuant to Rule 456(b) and Rule 457(r) or in accordance with Rule 456(a);

(3)   If the registrant is a majority-owned subsidiary, it is required to file and has filed reports pursuant to section 13 or section 15(d) of the Exchange Act and satisfies the requirements of this Form with regard to incorporation by reference or information about the majority-owned subsidiary is included in the registration statement (or a post-effective amendment to the registration statement);

(4)   The registrant may register additional securities or classes of its or its majority-owned subsidiaries' securities on a post-effective amendment pursuant to Rule 413(b); and

(5)   An automatic shelf registration statement and post-effective amendment will become effective immediately pursuant to Rule 462(e) and (f) upon filing. All filings made on or in connection with automatic shelf registration statements on this Form become public upon filing with the Commission.

E.   Rights offerings by foreign private issuers

A Foreign private issuer meeting eligibility requirements in paragraphs (a)(2) and (a)(3) of this rule may use Form S–3 to register securities to be offered upon the exercise of outstanding rights granted by the issuer of the securities to be offered if such rights are granted pro rata to all existing security holders of the class of securities to which the rights attach. In complying with Item 11 of this Form, the registrant shall describe those material changes that have occurred since the end of the latest fiscal year for which certified financial statements were included in the registrant's latest filing on Form 20–F (17 CFR 249.220f). In complying with Item 12 of this Form, the registrant shall incorporate by reference its latest filing on Form 20–F. The registrant also shall:

(1)   Furnish with the prospectus (or have furnished previously) to all its shareholders resident in the United States, including those holding under American Depository Receipts or similar arrangements, a copy of its latest annual report to security holders, if in the English language. Such annual reports or prospectus shall contain the registrant's undertaking to send promptly to any such United States holder, upon written request, a copy of the registrant's latest filing on Form 20–F; or

(2)   Furnish with the prospectus a copy of its latest filing on Form 20–F.

II.   Application of General Rules and Regulations

A.   Attention is directed to the General Rules and Regulations under the Securities Act, particularly Regulation C thereunder. That Regulations contains general requirements regarding the preparation and filing of registration statements.

B.   Attention is directed to Regulation S–K for the requirements applicable to the content of the non-financial statement portions of registration statements under the Securities Act. Where this Form directs the registrant to furnish information required by Regulation S–K and the item of Regulation S–K so provides, information need only be furnished to the extent appropriate. Notwithstanding Item 501 and 502 of Regulation S–K, no table of contents is required to be included in the prospectus or registration statement prepared on this form. In addition to the information expressly required to be included in a registration statement on this Form S–3, registrants also may provide such other information as they may deem appropriate.

C.   A smaller reporting company, defined in Rule 405, that is eligible to use Form S–3 shall use the disclosure items in Regulation S–K with specific attention to the scaled disclosure provided for smaller reporting companies, if any. Smaller reporting companies may provide the financial information called for by Article 8 of Regulation S–X in lieu of the financial information called for by Item 11 in this form.

D.   Non-Automatic Shelf Registration Statements. Where two or more classes of securities being registered on this Form pursuant to General Instruction I.B.1. or I.B.2. are to be offered pursuant to Rule 415(a)(1)(x), and where this Form is not an automatic shelf registration statement, Rule 457(o) permits the registration fee to be calculated on the basis of the maximum offering price of all the securities listed in the Fee Table. In this event, while the Fee Table would list each of the classes of securities being registered and the aggregate proceeds to be raised, the Fee Table need not specify by each class information as to the amount to be registered, proposed maximum offering price per unit, and proposed maximum aggregate offering price.

E.   Automatic Shelf Registration Statements. Where securities are being registered on this Form pursuant to General Instruction I.D., Rule 456(b) permits, but does not require, the registrant to pay the registration fee on a pay-as-you-go basis and Rule 457(r) permits, but does not require, the registration fee to be calculated on the basis of the aggregate offering price of the securities to be offered in an offering or offerings off the registration statement. If a registrant elects to pay all or a portion of the registration fee on a deferred basis, the Fee Table in the initial filing must identify the classes of securities being registered and provide that the registrant elects to rely on Rule 456(b) and Rule 457(r), but the Fee Table does not need to specify any other information. When the registrant amends the Fee Table in accordance with Rule 456(b)(1)(ii), the amended Fee Table must include either the dollar amount of securities being registered if paid in advance of or in connection with an offering or offerings or the aggregate offering price for all classes of securities referenced in the offerings and the applicable registration fee.

F.   Information in Automatic and Non-Automatic Shelf Registration Statements. Where securities are being registered on this Form pursuant to General Instruction I.B.1, I.B.2, I.C., or I.D., information is only required to be furnished as of the date of initial effectiveness of the registration statement to the extent required by Rule 430A or Rule 430B. Required information about a specific transaction must be included in the prospectus in the registration statement by means of a prospectus that is deemed to be part of and included in the registration statement pursuant to Rule 430A or Rule 430B, a post-effective amendment to the registration statement, or a periodic or current report under the Exchange Act incorporated by reference into the registration statement and the prospectus and identified in a prospectus filed, as required by Rule 430B, pursuant to Rule 424(b).

G.   Selling Security Holder Offerings. Where a registrant eligible to register primary offerings on this Form pursuant to General Instruction I.B.1 registers securities offerings on this Form pursuant to General Instruction I.B.1 or I.B.3 for the account of persons other than the registrant, if the offering of the securities, or securities convertible into such securities, that are being registered on behalf of the selling security holders was completed and the securities, or securities convertible into such securities, were issued and outstanding prior to the original date of filing the registration statement covering the resale of the securities, the registrant may, as permitted by Rule 430B(b), in lieu of identifying selling security holders prior to effectiveness of the resale registration statement, refer to unnamed selling security holders in a generic manner by identifying the initial transaction in which the securities were sold. Following effectiveness, the registrant must include in a prospectus filed pursuant to Rule 424(b)(7), a post-effective amendment to the registration statement, or an Exchange Act report incorporated by reference into the prospectus that is part of the registration statement (which Exchange Act report is identified in a prospectus filed, as required by Rule 430B, pursuant to Rule 424(b)(7) the names of previously unidentified selling security holders and amounts of securities that they intend to sell. If this Form is being filed pursuant to General Instruction I.D. by a well-known seasoned issuer to register securities being offered for the account of persons other than the issuer, the registration statement and the prospectus included in the registration statement do not need to designate the securities that will be offered for the account of such persons, identify them, or identify the initial transaction in which the securities, or securities convertible into such securities, were sold until the registrant files a post-effective amendment to the registration statement, a prospectus pursuant to Rule 424(b), or an Exchange Act report (and prospectus filed, as required by Rule 430B, pursuant to Rule 424(b)(7)) containing information for the offering on behalf of such persons.

III. Dividend or Interest Reinvestment Plans: Filing and Effectiveness of Registration Statement; Requests for Confidential Treatment

A registration statement on this Form S–3 relating solely to securities offered pursuant to a dividend or interest reinvestment plan will become effective automatically (Rule 462) upon filing (Rule 456). Post-effective amendments of such a registration statement on this Form shall become effective upon filing (Rule 464). All filings made on or in connection with this Form become public upon filing with the Commission. As a result, requests for confidential treatment made under Rule 406 must be processed with the Commission staff prior to the filing of such a registration statement. The number of copies of the registration statement and of each amendment required by Rules 402 and 472 shall be filed with the Commission: *Provided, however,* That the number of additional copies referred to in Rule 402(b) may be reduced from ten to three and the number of additional copies referred to in Rule 472(a) may be reduced from eight to three, one of which shall be marked clearly and precisely to indicate changes.

IV. Registration of Additional Securities and Additional Classes of Securities

A.   **Registration of Additional Securities Pursuant to Rule 462(b).** With respect to the registration of additional securities for an offering pursuant to Rule 462(b) under the Securities Act, the registrant may file a registration statement consisting only of the following: the facing page; a statement that the contents of the earlier registration statement, identified by file number, are incorporated by reference; required opinions and consents; the signature page; and any price-related information omitted from the earlier registration statement in reliance on Rule 430A that the registrant chooses to include in the new registration statement. The information contained in such a Rule 462(b) registration statement shall be deemed to be a part of the earlier registration statement as of the date of effectiveness of the Rule 462(b) registration statement. Any opinion or consent required in the Rule 462(b) registration statement may be incorporated by reference from the earlier registration statement with respect to the offering, if: (i) such opinion or consent expressly provides for such incorporation; and (ii) such opinion relates to the securities registered pursuant to Rule 462(b). *See* Rule 439(b) under the Securities Act.

B.   **Registration of Additional Securities or Classes of Securities or Additional Registrants After Effectiveness.** A well known seasoned issuer relying on General Instruction I.D. of this Form may register additional securities or classes of securities, pursuant to Rule 413(b) by filing a post-effective amendment to the effective registration statement. The well-known seasoned issuer may add majority-owned subsidiaries as additional registrants whose securities are eligible to be sold as part of the automatic shelf registration statement by filing a post-effective amendment identifying the additional registrants, and the registrant and the additional registrants and other persons required to sign the registration statement must sign the post-effective amendment. The post-effective amendment must consist of the facing page; any disclosure required by this Form that is necessary to update the registration statement to reflect the additional securities, additional classes of securities, or additional registrants; any required opinions and consents; and the signature page. Required information, consents, or opinions may be included in the prospectus and the registration statement through a post-effective amendment or may be provided through a document incorporated or deemed incorporated by reference into the registration statement and the prospectus that is part of the registration statement, or, as to the required information only, contained in a prospectus filed pursuant to Rule 424(b) that is deemed part of and included in the registration statement and prospectus that is part of the registration statement.

PART I. INFORMATION REQUIRED IN PROSPECTUS

Item 1. Forepart of the Registration Statement and Outside Front Cover Page of Prospectus

Set forth in the forepart of the registration statement and on the outside front cover page of the prospectus the information required by Item 501 of Regulation S–K.

Item 2. Inside Front and Outside Back Cover Pages of Prospectus

Set forth on the inside front cover page of the prospectus or, where permitted, on the outside back cover page, the information required by Item 502 of Regulation S–K.

Item 3. Summary Information and Risk Factors

Furnish the information required by Items 105 and 503 of Regulation S–K.

Item 4. Use of Proceeds

Furnish the information required by Item 504 of Regulation S–K.

Item 5. Determination of Offering Price

Furnish the information required by Item 505 of Regulation S–K.

Item 6. Dilution

Furnish the information required by Item 506 of Regulation S–K.

Item 7. Selling Security Holders

Furnish the information required by Item 507 of Regulation S–K.

Item 8. Plan of Distribution

Furnish the information required by Item 508 of Regulation S–K.

Item 9. Description of Securities to Be Registered

Furnish the information required by Item 202 of Regulation S–K unless capital stock is to be registered and securities of the same class are registered pursuant to Section 12 of the Exchange Act.

Item 10. Interests of Named Experts and Counsel

Furnish the information required by Item 509 of Regulation S–K.

Item 11. Material Changes

(a)   Describe any and all material changes in the registrant's affairs that have occurred since the end of the latest fiscal year for which certified financial statements were included in the latest annual report to security holders and that have not been described in a report on Form 10–Q or Form 8–K filed under the Exchange Act.

(b)   Include in the prospectus, if not incorporated by reference therein from the reports filed under the Exchange Act specified in Item 12(a), a proxy or information statement filed pursuant to Section 14 of the Exchange Act, or a prospectus previously filed pursuant to Rule 424(b) or (c) under the Securities Act or, where no prospectus is required to be filed pursuant to Rule 424(b), the prospectus included in the registration statement at effectiveness or a Form 8–K filed during either of the two preceding fiscal years;

(i)   information required by Rule 3.05 and Article 11 of Regulation S–X;

(ii)   restated financial statements prepared in accordance with Regulation S–X if there has been a change in accounting principles or a correction of an error where such change or correction requires a material retroactive restatement of financial statements;

(iii)   restated financial statements prepared in accordance with Regulation S–X where a combination of entities under common control has been consummated subsequent to the most recent fiscal year and the transferred businesses, considered in the aggregate, are significant pursuant to Rule 11–01(b);

(iv)   any financial information required because of a material disposition of assets outside the normal course of business.

Item 12. Incorporation of Certain Information by Reference

(a)   The documents listed in (1) and (2) below shall be specifically incorporated by reference into the prospectus by means of a statement to that effect in the prospectus listing all such documents:

(1)   the registrant's latest annual report on Form 10–K filed pursuant to Section 13(a) or 15(d) of the Exchange Act which contains financial statements for the registrant's latest fiscal year for which a Form 10–K was required to have been filed; and

(2)   all other reports filed pursuant to Section 13(a) or 15(d) of the Exchange Act since the end of the fiscal year covered by the annual report referred to in (1) above; and

(3)   if capital stock is to be registered and securities of the same class are registered under Section 12, of the Exchange Act, the description of such class of securities which is contained in a registration statement filed under the Exchange Act, including any amendment or reports filed for the purpose of updating such description.

(b)   The prospectus shall also state that all documents subsequently filed by the registrant pursuant to Sections 13(a), 13(c), 14 or 15(d) of the Exchange Act, prior to the termination of the offering, shall be deemed to be incorporated by reference into the prospectus.

Instruction. Attention is directed to Rule 439 regarding consent to use of material incorporated by reference.

(c)(1)   You must state (i) that you will provide to each person, including any beneficial owner, to whom a prospectus is delivered, a copy of any or all of the information that has been incorporated by reference in the prospectus but not delivered with the prospectus;

(ii)   that you will provide this information upon written or oral request;

(iii)   that you will provide this information at no cost to the requester; and

(iv)   the name, address, and telephone number to which the request for this information must be made.

NOTE to Item 12(c)(1)

If you send any of the information that is incorporated by reference in the prospectus to security holders, you also must send any exhibits that are specifically incorporated by reference in that information.

(2)   You must (i) identify the reports and other information that you file with the SEC; and

(ii)   State that the SEC maintains an Internet site that contains reports, proxy and information statements, and other information regarding issuers that file electronically with the SEC and state the address of that site (http://www.sec.gov). Disclose your Internet address, if available.

(d)   Any information required in the prospectus in response to Item 3 through Item 11 of this Form may be included in the prospectus through documents filed pursuant to Rule 13(a), 14, or 15(d) of the Exchange Act that are incorporated or deemed incorporated by reference into the prospectus that is part of the registration statement. Notwithstanding the foregoing, in the financial statements, incorporating by reference or cross-referencing to information outside of the financial statements is not permitted unless otherwise specifically permitted or required by the Commission's rules or by U.S. Generally Accepted Accounting Principles or International Financial Reporting Standards as issued by the International Accounting Standards Board, whichever is applicable.

Item 13. Disclosure of Commission Position on Indemnification for Securities Act Liabilities

Furnish the information required by Item 510 of Regulation S–K.

PART II. INFORMATION NOT REQUIRED IN PROSPECTUS

Item 14. Other Expenses of Issuance and Distribution

Furnish the information required by Item 511 of Regulation S–K.

Item 15. Indemnification of Directors and Officers

Furnish the information required by Item 702 of Regulation S–K.

Item 16. Exhibits

Subject to the rules regarding incorporation by reference, furnish the exhibits required by Item 601 of Regulation S–K.

Item 17. Undertakings

Furnish the undertakings required by Item 512 of Regulation S–K.

SIGNATURES

Pursuant to the requirements of the Securities Act of 1933, the registrant certifies that it has reasonable grounds to believe that it meets all of the requirements for filing on Form S–3 and has duly caused this registration statement to be signed on its behalf by the undersigned, thereunto duly authorized, in the City of _____, State of _____, on _____, 20__.

(Registrant)

By (Signature and Title)
_____

Pursuant to the requirements of the Securities Act of 1933, this registration statement has been signed by the following persons in the capacities and on the dates indicated.

(Signature)

(Title)

(Date)
_____

Instructions.   1. The registration statement shall be signed by the registrant, its principal executive officer or officers, its principal financial officer, its controller or principal accounting officer, and by at least a majority of the board of directors or persons performing similar functions. If the registrant is a foreign person, the registration statement shall also be signed by its authorized representative in the United States. Where the registrant is a limited partnership, the registration statement shall be signed by a majority of the board of directors of any corporate general partner signing the registration statement.

2.   The name of each person who signs the registration statement shall be typed or printed beneath his signature. Any person who occupies more than one of the specified positions shall indicate each capacity in which he signs the registration statement. Attention is directed to Rule 402 concerning manual signatures and Item 601 of Regulation S–K concerning signatures pursuant to powers of attorney.

FORM S–4

17 C.F.R. § 239.25

SECURITIES AND EXCHANGE COMMISSION
REGISTRATION STATEMENT UNDER THE SECURITIES ACT OF 1933

_____
(Exact name of registrant as specified in its charter)

_____
(State or other jurisdiction of incorporation or organization)

_____
(Primary Standard Industrial Classification Code Number)

_____
(I.R.S. Employer Identification No.)

_____
(Address, including ZIP Code, and telephone number, including
area code, of registrant's principal executive officers)

_____
(Name, address, including ZIP Code, and telephone number,
including area code, of agent for service)

Approximate date of commencement of proposed sale of the securities to the public _____

_____

If the securities being registered on this Form are being offered in connection with the formation of a holding company and there is compliance with General Instruction G, check the following box. ☐

If this Form is filed to register additional securities for an offering pursuant to Rule 462(b) under the Securities Act, check the following box and list the Securities Act registration statement number of the earlier effective registration statement for the same offering. ☐

If this Form is a post-effective amendment filed pursuant to Rule 462(d) under the Securities Act, check the following box and list the Securities Act registration statement number of the earlier effective registration statement for the same offering. ☐

_____

Indicate by check mark whether the registrant is a large accelerated filer, an accelerated filer, a non-accelerated filer, a smaller reporting company, or an emerging growth company. See the definitions of "large accelerated filer," "accelerated filer," "smaller reporting company," and "emerging growth company" in Rule 12b–2 of the Exchange Act.

Large accelerated filer ☐

Non-accelerated filer ☐

Accelerated filer ☐

Smaller reporting company ☐

Emerging growth company ☐

If an emerging growth company, indicate by check mark if the registrant has elected not to use the extended transition period for complying with any new or revised financial accounting standards provided pursuant to Rule 7(a)(2)(B) of the Securities Act. ☐

If applicable, place an X in the box to designate the appropriate rule provision relied upon in conducting this transaction:

Exchange Act Rule 13e–4(i) (Cross-Border Issuer Tender Offer) ☐

Exchange Act Rule 14d–1(d) (Cross-Border Third-Party Tender Offer) ☐

Note—The text of Form F–4 does not and this amendment will not appear in the Code of Federal Regulations.

Calculation of Registration Fee

Title of each class of securities to be registered	Amount to be registered	Proposed maximum offering price per unit	Proposed maximum aggregate offering price	Amount of registration fee

NOTE: Specific details relating to the fee calculation shall be furnished in notes to the table, including references to provisions of Rule 457 relied upon, if the basis of the calculation is not otherwise evident from the information presented in the table.

GENERAL INSTRUCTIONS

A.   Rule as to Use of Form S–4

1.   This Form may be used for registration under the Securities Act of 1933 ("Securities Act") of securities to be issued (1) in a transaction of the type specified in paragraph (a) of Rule 145; (2) in a merger in which the applicable state law would not require the solicitation of the votes or consents of all of the security holders of the company being acquired; (3) in an exchange offer for securities of the issuer or another entity; (4) in a public reoffering or resale of any such securities acquired pursuant to this registration statement; or (5) in more than one of the kinds of transaction listed in (1) through (4) registered on one registration statement.

2.   If the registrant meets the requirements of and elects to comply with the provisions in any item of this Form or Form F–4 that provides for incorporation by reference of information about the registrant or the company being acquired, the prospectus must be sent to the security holders no later than 20 business days prior to the date on which the meeting of such security holders is held or, if no meeting is held, at least 20 business days prior to either (1) the date the votes, consents or authorizations may be used to effect the corporate action or, (2) if votes, consents or authorizations are not used, the date the transaction is consummated. Attention is directed to Sections 13(e), 14(d) and 14(e) of the Securities Exchange Act of 1934 ("Exchange Act") the rules and regulations thereunder regarding other time periods in connection with exchange offers and going private transactions.

3.   This Form shall not be used if the registrant is a registered investment company or a business development company as defined in Section 2(a)(48) of the Investment Company Act of 1940.

FORM S-4

B. Information With Respect to the Registrant

1. Information with respect to the registrant shall be provided in accordance with the items referenced in one of the following subparagraphs:

    a. Items 10 and 11 of this Form, if the registrant elects this alternative and meets the following requirements of Form S–3 (hereinafter, with respect to the registrant, "meets the requirements for use of Form S–3") for this offering of securities:

        (i) the registrant meets the requirements of General Instruction I.A. of Form S–3; and

        (ii) one of the following is met

            A. The registrant meets the aggregate market value requirement of General Instruction I.B.1. of Form S–3; or

            B. Non-convertible debt or preferred securities are to be offered pursuant to this registration statement and the requirements of General Instruction I.B.2. of Form S–3 have been met for the securities to be registered on this registration statement; or

            C. The registrant is a majority-owned subsidiary and one of the conditions of General Instruction I.C. of Form S–3 is met.

    b. Items 12 and 13 of this Form, if the registrant meets the requirements for use of Form S–3 and elects this alternative; or

    c. Item 14 of this Form, if the registrant does not meet the requirements for use of Form S–3, or if it otherwise elects this alternative.

2. If the registrant is a real estate entity of the type described in General Instruction A to Form S–11, the information prescribed by Items 12, 13, 14, 15 and 16 of Form S–11 shall be furnished about the registrant in addition to the information provided pursuant to Items 10 through 14 of this Form. The information prescribed by such Items of Form S–11 may be incorporated by reference into the prospectus if (a) a registrant qualifies for and elects to provide information pursuant to alternative 1.a. or 1.b. of this instruction and (b) the documents incorporated by reference pursuant to such elected alternative contain such information.

C. Information With Respect to the Company Being Acquired

1. Information with respect to the company whose securities are being acquired (hereinafter including, where securities of the registrant are being offered in exchange for securities of another company, such other company) shall be provided in accordance with the items referenced in one of the following subparagraphs:

    a. Item 15 of this Form, if the company being acquired meets the requirements of General Instructions I.A. and I.B.1. of Form S–3 (hereinafter, with respect to the company being acquired, "meets the requirements for use of Form S–3") of Form S–3 and this alternative is elected;

    b. Item 16 of this Form, if the company being acquired meets the requirements for use of S–3 and this alternative is elected; or

    c. Item 17 of this Form, if the company being acquired does not meet the requirements for use of S–3 or if this alternative is otherwise elected.

2. If the company being acquired is a real estate entity of the type described in General Instruction A to Form S–11, the information that would be required by Items 13, 14, 15 and 16(a) of Form S–11 if securities of such company were being registered shall be furnished about such company being acquired in addition to the information provided pursuant to this Form. The information prescribed by such Items of Form S–11 may be incorporated by reference into the prospectus if (a) the company being acquired would qualify for use of the level of disclosure prescribed by alternative 1.a. or 1.b. of this instruction and such alternative is elected and (b) the documents incorporated by reference pursuant to such elected alternative contain such information.

D. Application of General Rules and Regulations

1. Attention is directed to the General Rules and Regulations under the Securities Act, particularly those comprising Regulation C thereunder. That Regulation contains general requirements regarding the preparation and filing of registration statements.

2. Attention is directed to Regulation S–K for the requirements applicable to the content of non-financial statement portions of registration statements under the Securities Act. Where this Form directs the registrant to furnish information required by Regulation S–K and the item of Regulation S–K so provides, information need only be furnished to the extent appropriate.

3. A "small business issuer," defined in Rule 405, shall refer to the disclosure items in Regulation S–B and not Regulation S–K except with respect to disclosure called for by subpart 900 of Regulation S–K. Small business issuers shall provide or incorporate by reference the information called for by Item 310 of Regulation S–B.

E. Compliance With Exchange Act Rules

1. If a corporation or other person submits a proposal to its security holders entitled to vote on, or consent to, the transaction which the securities being registered are to be issued, and such person's submission to its security holders is subject to Regulation 14A or 14C under the Exchange Act, then the provisions of such Regulations shall apply in all respects to such person's submission, except that

(a) the prospectus may be in the form of a proxy or information statement and may contain the information required by this Form in lieu of that required by Schedule 14A or 14C of Regulation 14A or 14C under the Exchange Act; and

(b) copies of the preliminary and definitive proxy or information statement, form of proxy or other material filed as a part of the registration statement shall be deemed filed pursuant to such person's obligations under such Regulations.

2. If the proxy or information material sent to security holders is not subject to Regulation 14A or 14C, all such material shall be filed as a part of the registration statement at the time the statement is filed or as an amendment thereto prior to the use of such material.

3. If the transaction in which the securities being registered are to be issued is subject to Section 13(e), 14(d) or 14(e) of the Exchange Act, the provisions of those sections and the rules and regulations thereunder shall apply to the transaction in addition to the provisions of this Form.

F. Transactions Involving Foreign Private Issuers

If a U.S. registrant is acquiring a foreign private issuer, as defined by Rule 405, such registrant may use this Form and may present information about the foreign private issuer pursuant to Form F–4. If the registrant is a foreign private issuer, such registrant may use Form F–4 and

(1) if the company being acquired is a foreign private issuer, may present information about such foreign company pursuant to Form F–4 or

(2) if the company being acquired is a U.S. company, may present information about such company pursuant to this Form.

G. Filing and Effectiveness of Registration Statement Involving Formation of Holding Companies; Requests for Confidential Treatment; Number of Copies

Original registration statements on this Form S–4 will become effective automatically on the twentieth day after the date of filing, pursuant to the provisions of Section 8(a) of the Act provided:

1. The transaction in connection with which securities are being registered involves the organization of a bank or savings and loan holding company for the sole purpose of issuing common stock to acquire all of the common stock of the company that is organizing the holding company; and

2. The following conditions are met:

a. the financial institution furnishes its security holders with an annual report that includes financial statements prepared on the basis of generally accepted accounting principles;

b. there are no anticipated changes in the security holders' relative equity ownership interest in the underlying company's assets except for redemption of no more than a nominal number of shares of unaffiliated persons who dissent;

c. in the aggregate, only nominal borrowings are to be incurred for such purposes as organizing the holding company to pay non-affiliated persons who dissent, or to meet minimum capital requirements;

d. there are no new classes of stock authorized other than those corresponding to the stock of the company being acquired immediately prior to the reorganization;

e. there are no plans or arrangements to issue any additional shares to acquire any business other than the company being acquired; and

f. there has been no material adverse change in the financial condition of the company being acquired since the latest fiscal year end included in the annual report to security holders.

Pre-effective amendments with respect to such a registration statement may be filed prior to effectiveness, and such amendments will be deemed to have been filed with the consent of the Commission. Accordingly, the filing of a pre-effective amendment to such a registration statement will not commence a new twenty-day period. Post-effective amendments to such a registration statement on this Form shall become effective upon the date of filing. Delaying amendments are not permitted in connection with either original filings or amendments on such a registration statement, and any attempt to interpose a delaying amendment of any kind will be ineffective. All filings made on or in connection with this Form pursuant to this instruction become public upon filing with the Commission. As a result, requests for confidential treatment made under Rule 406 must be processed by the Commissions staff prior to the filing of such a registration statement. The number of copies of such a registration statement and of each amendment required by Rules 402 and 472 shall be filed with the Commission; *provided, however,* that the number of additional copies referred to in Rule 402(b) may be reduced from ten to three and the number of additional copies referred to in Rule 472(a) may be reduced from eight to three, one of which shall be marked to clearly and precisely indicate changes.

H. Registration Statements Subject to Rule 415(a)(1)(viii)

If the registration statement relates to offerings of securities pursuant to Rule 415(a)(1)(viii), required information about the type of contemplated transaction or the company to be acquired only need be furnished as of the date of initial effectiveness of the registration statement to the extent practicable. The required information about the specific transaction and the particular company being acquired, however, must be included in the prospectus by means of a post-effective amendment; *Provided, however,* that where the transaction in which the securities are being offered pursuant to a registration statement under the Securities Act of 1933 would itself qualify for an exemption from Section 5 of the Act, absent the existence of other similar (prior or subsequent) transactions, a prospectus supplement could be used to furnish the information necessary in connection with such transaction.

I. Roll-up Transactions

1. If securities to be registered on this Form will be issued in a roll-up transaction as defined in Item 901(c) of Regulation S-K, then the disclosure provisions of Subpart 9 of Regulation S-K shall apply to the transaction in addition to the provisions of this Form. A smaller reporting company, defined in Rule 405, that is engaged in a roll-up transaction shall refer to the disclosure items in Subpart 9 of Regulation S-K. To the extent that the disclosure requirements of Subpart 9 are inconsistent with the disclosure requirements of any other applicable forms or schedules, the requirements of Subpart 9 are controlling.

2. If securities to be registered on this Form will be issued in a roll-up transaction as defined in Item 901(c) of Regulation S-K, the prospectus must be distributed to security holders no later than the lesser of 60 calendar days prior to the date on which action is to be taken or the maximum number of days permitted for giving notice under applicable state law.

3. Attention is directed to the proxy rules and Rule 14e-7 of the tender offer rules if securities to be registered on this Form will be issued in a roll-up transaction. Such rules contain provisions specifically applicable to roll-up transactions, whether or not the entities involved have securities registered pursuant to Section 12 of the Exchange Act.

J.   Calculation of Fee

Where two or more classes of securities being registered on the form are to be offered on a delayed or continuous basis pursuant to Rule 415(a)(1)(viii), Rule 457(*o*) under the Securities Act permits the registration fee to be calculated on the basis of the maximum offering price of all the securities listed in the "Calculation of Registration Fee" Table ("Fee Table"). In this event, while the Fee Table would list each of the classes of securities being registered and the aggregate proceeds to be raised, the Fee Table need not specify by each class information as to the amount to be registered, proposed maximum offering price per unit, and proposed maximum aggregate offering price.

K.   Registration of Additional Securities

With respect to the registration of additional securities for an offering pursuant to Rule 462(b) under the Securities Act, the registrant may file a registration statement consisting only of the following: the facing page; a statement that the contents of the earlier registration statement, identified by file number, are incorporated by reference; required opinions and consents; the signature page; and any price-related information omitted from the earlier registration statement in reliance on Rule 430A that the registrant chooses to include in the new registration statement. The information contained in such a Rule 462(b) registration statement shall be deemed to be a part of the earlier registration statement as of the date of effectiveness of the Rule 462(b) registration statement. Any opinion or consent required in the Rule 462(b) registration statement may be incorporated by reference from the earlier registration statement with respect to the offering, if: (i) such opinion or consent expressly provides for such incorporation; and (ii) such opinion relates to the securities registered pursuant to Rule 462(b). *See* Rule 439(b) under the Securities Act.

PART I. INFORMATION REQUIRED IN THE PROSPECTUS

A.   Information About the Transaction

Item 1.   Forepart of Registration Statement and Outside Front Cover Page of Prospectus

Set forth in the forepart of the registration statement and on the outside front cover page of the prospectus the information required by Item 501 of Regulation S–K.

Item 2.   Inside Front and Outside Back Cover Pages of Prospectus

Provide the information required by Item 502 of Regulation S–K. In addition, on the inside front cover page, you must state (1) that the prospectus incorporates important business and financial information about the company that is not included in or delivered with the document; and

(2)   that this information is available without charge to security holders upon written or oral request. Give the name, address, and telephone number to which security holders must make this request. In addition, you must state that to obtain timely delivery, security holders must request the information no later than five business days before the date they must make their investment decision. Specify the date by which security holders must request this information. You must highlight this statement by print type or otherwise.

NOTE to Item 2.

If you send any of the information that is incorporated by reference in the prospectus to security holders, you also must send any exhibits that are specifically incorporated by reference in that information.

Item 3.   Risk Factors, Ratio of Earnings to Fixed Charges and Other Information

Provide in the forepart of the prospectus a summary containing the information required by Items 105 and 503 of Regulation S–K and the following:

(a)   The name, complete mailing address (including the Zip Code), and telephone number (including the area code) of the principal executive offices of the registrant and the company being acquired;

(b)   A brief description of the general nature of the business conducted by the registrant and by the company being acquired;

(c)   A brief description of the transaction in which the securities being registered are to be offered;

(d)   The information required by Item 301 of Regulation S–K (selected financial data) for (i) the registrant; (ii) the company being acquired; and (iii) if material, the registrant, on a pro forma basis, giving effect to the transaction. To the extent the information is required to be presented in the prospectus pursuant to Items 12, 14, 16, or 17, it need not be repeated pursuant to this Item;

(e)   If material, the information required by Item 301 of Regulation S–K for the registrant on a pro forma basis, giving effect to the transaction. To the extent the information is required to be presented in the prospectus pursuant to Items 12 or 14, it need not be repeated pursuant to this Item;

(f)   In comparative columnar form, historical and pro forma per share data of the registrant and historical and equivalent pro forma per share data of the company being acquired for the following items:

    (1)   Book value per share as of the date financial data is presented pursuant to Item 301 of Regulation S–K (selected financial data);

    (2)   Cash dividends declared per share for the periods for which financial data is presented pursuant to Item 301 of Regulation S–K (selected financial data);

    (3)   Income (loss) per share from continuing operations for the periods for which financial data is presented pursuant to Item 301 of Regulation S–K (selected financial data).

Instruction to paragraph (e) and (f). For a business combination, the financial information required by paragraphs (e) and (f) shall be presented only for the most recent fiscal year and interim period. For a combination between entities under common control, the financial information required by paragraphs (e) and (f) (except for information with regard to book value) shall be presented for the most recent three fiscal years and interim period. For a combination between entities under common control, information with regard to book value shall be presented as of the end of the most recent fiscal year and interim period. Equivalent pro forma per share amounts shall be calculated by multiplying the pro forma income (loss) per share before non-recurring charges or credits directly attributable to the transaction, pro forma book value per share, and the pro forma dividends per share of the registrant by the exchange ratio so that the per share amounts are equated to the respective values for one share of the company being acquired.

(g)   In comparative columnar form, the market value of securities of the company being acquired (on an historical and equivalent per share basis) and the market value of the securities of the registrant (on an historical basis) as of the date preceding public announcement of the proposed transaction, or, if no such public announcement was made, as of the day preceding the day the agreement with respect to the transaction was entered into;

(h)   With respect to the registrant and the company being acquired, a brief statement comparing the percentage of outstanding shares entitled to vote held by directors, executive officers and their affiliates and the vote required for approval of the proposed transaction;

(i)   A statement as to whether any federal or state regulatory requirements must be complied with or approval must be obtained in connection with the transaction, and if so, the status of such compliance or approval;

(j)   A statement about whether or not dissenters' rights of appraisal exist, including a cross-reference to the information provided pursuant to Item 18 or 19 of this Form; and

(k)   A brief statement about the tax consequences of the transaction, or if appropriate, consisting of a cross-reference to the information provided pursuant to Item 4 of this Form.

Item 4. Terms of the Transaction

(a)   Furnish a summary of the material features of the proposed transaction. The summary shall include, where applicable:

    (1)   A brief summary of the terms of the acquisition agreement;

    (2)   The reasons of the registrant and of the company being acquired for engaging in the transaction;

(3)   The information required by Item 202 of Regulation S–K, description of registrant's securities, unless: (i) the registrant would meet the requirements for use of Form S–3, (ii) capital stock is to be registered and (iii) securities of the same class are registered under Section 12 of the Exchange Act and (i) listed for trading or admitted to unlisted trading privileges on a national securities exchange; or (ii) are securities for which bid and offer quotations are reported in an automated quotations system operated by a national securities association;

(4)   An explanation of any material differences between the rights of security holders of the company being acquired and the rights of holders of the securities being offered;

(5)   A brief statement as to the accounting treatment of the transaction; and

(6)   The federal income tax consequences of the transaction.

(b)   If a report, opinion or appraisal materially relating to the transaction has been received from an outside party, and such report, opinion or appraisal is referred to in the prospectus, furnish the same information as would be required by Item 1015(b) of Regulation M–A.

(c)   Incorporate the acquisition agreement by reference into the prospectus by means of a statement to that effect.

Item 5.   Pro Forma Financial Information

Furnish financial information required by Article 11 of Regulation S–X with respect to this transaction. A smaller reporting company may provide the information in Rule 8–05 of Regulation S–X in lieu of the financial information required by Article 11 of Regulation S–X.

Instructions. 1. Any other Article 11 information that is presented (rather than incorporated by reference) pursuant to other Items of this Form shall be presented together with the information provided pursuant to Item 5, but the presentation shall clearly distinguish between this transaction and any other.

2.   If pro forma financial information with respect to all other transactions is incorporated by reference pursuant to Item 11 or 15 of this Form only the pro forma results need be presented as part of the pro forma financial information required by this Item.

Item 6.   Material Contacts With the Company Being Acquired

Describe any past, present or proposed material contracts, arrangements, understandings, relationships, negotiations or transactions during the periods for which financial statements are presented or incorporated by reference pursuant to Part I.B. or C. of this Form between the company being acquired or its affiliates and the registrant or its affiliates, such as those concerning: a merger, consolidation or acquisition; a tender offer or other acquisition of securities; an election of directors; or a sale or other transfer of a material amount of assets.

Item 7.   Additional Information Required for Reoffering by Persons and Parties Deemed to Be Underwriters

If any of the securities are to be reoffered to the public by any person or party who is deemed to be an underwriter thereof, furnish the following information in the prospectus, at the time it is being used for the reoffer of the securities to the extent it is not already furnished therein:

(a)   The information required by Item 507 of Regulation S–K, selling security holders; and

(b)   Information with respect to the consummation of the transaction pursuant to which the securities were acquired and any material change in the registrant's affairs subsequent to the transaction.

Item 8.   Interests of Named Experts and Counsel

Furnish the information required by Item 509 of Regulation S–K.

Item 9. Disclosure of Commission Position on Indemnification for Securities Act Liabilities

Furnish the information required by Item 510 of Regulation S–K.

B. Information About the Registrant

Item 10. Information With Respect to S–3 Registrants

If the registrant meets the requirements for use of Form S–3 and elects to furnish information in accordance with the provisions of this Item, furnish information as required below:

(a) Describe any and all material changes in the registrant's affairs that have occurred since the end of the latest fiscal year for which audited financial statements were included in the latest annual report to security holders and that have not been described in a report on Form 10–Q or Form 8–K filed under the Exchange Act.

(b) Include in the prospectus, if not incorporated by reference from the reports filed under the Exchange Act specified in Item 11 of this Form, a proxy or information statement filed pursuant to section 14 of the Exchange Act, a prospectus previously filed pursuant to Rule 424 under the Securities Act, or a Form 8–K filed during either of the two preceding fiscal years:

(1) Financial information required by Rule 3–05 and Article 11 of Regulation S–X with respect to transactions other than that pursuant to which the securities being registered are to be issued;

(2) Restated financial statements prepared in accordance with Regulation S–X, if there has been a change in accounting principles or a correction of an error where such change or correction requires a material retroactive restatement of financial statements;

(3) Restated financial statements prepared in accordance with Regulation S–X where a combination under common control has been consummated subsequent to the most recent fiscal year and the acquired businesses, considered in the aggregate, are significant pursuant to Rule 11–01(b) of Regulation S–X; or

(4) Any financial information required because of a material disposition of assets outside the normal course of business.

Item 11. Incorporation of Certain Information by Reference

If the registrant meets the requirements of Form S–3 and elects to furnish information in accordance with the provisions of Item 10 of this Form:

(a) Incorporate by reference into the prospectus, by means of a statement to that effect listing all documents so incorporated, the documents listed in paragraphs (1), (2) and, if applicable, (3) below.

(1) The registrant's latest annual report on Form 10–K filed pursuant to Section 13(a) or 15(d) of the Exchange Act which contains financial statements for the registrant's latest fiscal year for which a Form 10–K was required to be filed;

(2) All other reports filed pursuant to Section 13(a) or 15(d) of the Exchange Act since the end of the fiscal year covered by the annual report referred to in Item 11(a)(1) of this Form; and

(3) If capital stock is to be registered and securities of the same class are registered under Section 12 of the Exchange Act and:

(i) listed for trading or admitted to unlisted trading privileges on a national securities exchange; or

(ii) are securities for which bid and offer quotations are reported in an automated quotations system operated by a national securities association, the description of such class of securities which is contained in a registration statement filed under the Exchange Act, including any amendment or reports filed for the purpose of updating such description.

(b)   The prospectus also shall state that all documents subsequently filed by the registrant pursuant to Sections 13(a), 13(c), 14 or 15(d) of the Exchange Act, prior to one of the following dates, whichever is applicable, shall be deemed to be incorporated by reference into the prospectus:

(1)   If a meeting of security holders is to be held, the date on which such meeting is held;

(2)   If a meeting of security holders is not to be held, the date on which the transaction is consummated;

(3)   If securities of the registrant are being offered in exchange for securities of any other issuer, the date the offering is terminated; or

(4)   If securities are being offered in a reoffering or resale of securities acquired pursuant to this registration statement, the date the reoffering is terminated.

(c)   You must

(1)   identify the reports and other information that you file with the SEC; and

(2)   State that the SEC maintains an Internet site that contains reports, proxy and information statements, and other information regarding issuers that file electronically with the SEC and state the address of that site (http://www.sec.gov). Disclose your Internet address, if available

Instruction. Attention is directed to Rule 439 regarding consent to the use of material incorporated by reference.

Item 12. Information With Respect to S–3 Registrants

If the registrant meets the requirements for use of Form S–3 and elects to comply with this Item, furnish the information required by either paragraph (a) or (b) of this Item. The information required by paragraph (b) shall be furnished if the registrant satisfies the conditions of paragraph (c) of this Item.

(a)   If the registrant elects to deliver this prospectus together with a copy of either its latest Form 10–K filed pursuant to Sections 13(a) or 15(d) of the Exchange Act or its latest annual report to security holders, which at the time of original preparation met the requirements of either Rule 14a–3 or Rule 14c–3:

(1)   Indicate that the prospectus is accompanied by either a copy of the registrant's latest Form 10–K or a copy of its latest annual report to security holders, whichever the registrant elects to deliver pursuant to paragraph (a) of this Item.

(2)   Provide financial and other information with respect to the registrant in the form required by Part I of Form 10–Q as of the end of the most recent fiscal quarter which ended after the end of the latest fiscal year for which certified financial statements were included in the latest Form 10–K or the latest report to security holders (whichever the registrant elects to deliver pursuant to paragraph (a) of this Item), and more than forty-five days prior to the effective date of this registration statement (or as of a more recent date) by one of the following means:

(i)   including such information in the prospectus;

(ii)   providing without charge to each person to whom a prospectus is delivered a copy of the registrant's latest Form 10–Q; or

(iii)   providing without charge to each person to whom a prospectus is delivered a copy of the registrant's latest quarterly report that was delivered to security holders and that included the required financial information.

(3)   Furnish the information required by the following:

(i)   Item 101(c)(1)(i) of Regulation S–K (§ 229.101(c)(1)(i) of this chapter), industry segments, key products or services;

(4)   Describe any and all material changes in the registrant's affairs which have occurred since the end of the latest fiscal year for which audited financial statements were included in the latest Form 10–K or the latest annual report to security holders (whichever the registrant elects to deliver pursuant

to paragraph (a) of this Item) and that were not described in a Form 10–Q or quarterly report delivered with the prospectus in accordance with paragraphs (a)(2)(ii) or (iii) of this Item.

Instruction. Where the registrant elects to deliver the documents identified in paragraph (a) with a preliminary prospectus, such documents need not be redelivered with the final prospectus.

(b)   If the registrant does not elect to deliver its latest Form 10–K or its latest annual report to security holders:

    (1)   Furnish a brief description of the business done by the registrant and its subsidiaries during the most recent fiscal year as required by Rule 14a–3 to be included in an annual report to security holders. The description also should take into account changes in the registrant's business that have occurred between the end of the latest fiscal year and the effective date of the registration statement.

    (2)   Include financial statements and information as required by Rule 14a–3(b)(1) to be included in an annual report to security holders. In addition, provide:

        (i)   the interim financial information required by Rule 10–01 of Regulation S–X for a filing on Form 10–Q.

        (ii)   financial information required by Rule 3–05 and Article 11 of Regulation S–X with respect to transactions other than that pursuant to which the securities being registered are to be issued;

        (iii)   restated financial statements prepared in accordance with Regulation S–X if there has been a change in accounting principles or a correction of an error where such change or correction requires a material retroactive restatement of financial statements;

        (iv)   restated financial statements prepared in accordance with Regulation S–X where a combination under common control has been consummated subsequent to the most recent fiscal year and the businesses transferred, considered in the aggregate, are significant pursuant to Rule 11–01(b) of Regulation S–X;

        (v)   any financial information required because of a material disposition of assets outside of the normal course of business.

    (3)   Furnish the information required by the following:

        (i)   Item 101(b), (c)(1)(i) and (d) of Regulation S–K, industry segments, classes of similar products or services, foreign and domestic operations and export sales;

        (ii)   Where common equity securities are being offered, Item 201 of Regulation S–K, market price of and dividends on the registrant's common equity and related stockholder matters;

        (iii)   Item 301 or Regulation S–K, selected financial data;

        (iv)   Item 302 of Regulation S–K, supplementary financial information;

        (v)   Item 303 of Regulation S–K, management's discussion and analysis of financial condition and results of operations;

        (vi)   Item 304 of Regulation S–K, changes in and disagreements with accountants on accounting and financial disclosure; and

        (vii)   Item 305 of Regulation S–K, quantitative and qualitative disclosures about market risk.

(c)   The registrant shall furnish the information required by paragraph (b) of this Item if:

    (1)   the registrant was required to make a material retroactive restatement of financial statements because of

        (i)   a change in accounting principles; or

        (ii)   a correction of an error; or

       (iii) a combination under common control was effected subsequent to the most recent fiscal year and the acquired businesses considered in the aggregate meet the test of a significant subsidiary;

       OR

       (2) the registrant engaged in a material disposition of assets outside the normal course of business;

       AND

       (3) such restatement of financial statements or disposition of assets was not reflected in the registrant's latest annual report to security holders and/or its latest Form 10–K filed pursuant to Sections 13(a) or 15(d) of the Exchange Act.

Item 13. Incorporation of Certain Information by Reference

If the registrant meets the requirements of Form S–3 and elects to furnish information in accordance with the provisions of Item 12 of this Form:

(a) Incorporate by reference into the prospectus, by means of a statement to that effect in the prospectus listing all documents so incorporated, the documents listed in paragraphs (1) and (2) of this Item and, if applicable, the portions of the documents listed in paragraphs (3) and (4) thereof.

       (1) The registrant's latest annual report on Form 10–K filed pursuant to Section 13(a) or 15(d) of the Exchange Act which contains audited financial statements for the registrant's latest fiscal year for which a Form 10–K was required to be filed.

       (2) All other reports filed pursuant to Section 13(a) or 15(d) of the Exchange Act since the end of the fiscal year covered by the annual report referred to in paragraph (a)(1) of this Item.

       (3) If the registrant elects to deliver its latest annual report to security holders pursuant to Item 12 of this Form, the information furnished in accordance with the following:

          (i) Item 101(b), (c)(1)(i) and (d) of Regulation S–K, segments, classes of similar products or services, foreign and domestic operations and export sales;

          (ii) Where common equity securities are being issued, Item 201 of Regulation S–K, market price of and dividends on the registrant's common equity and related stockholder matters;

          (iii) Item 301 of Regulation S–K, selected financial data;

          (iv) Item 302 of Regulation S–K, supplementary financial information;

          (v) Item 303 of Regulation S–K, management's discussion and analysis of financial condition and results of operations;

          (vi) Item 304 of Regulation S–K, changes in and disagreements with accountants on accounting and financial disclosure; and

          (vii) Item 305 of Regulation S–K, quantitative and qualitative disclosure about market risk.

       (4) If the registrant elects, pursuant to Item 12(a)(2)(iii) of this Form, to provide a copy of its latest quarterly report which was delivered to security holders, financial information equivalent to that required to be presented in Part I of Form 10–Q.

Instruction. Attention is directed to Rule 439 regarding consent to the use of material incorporated by reference.

(b) The registrant also may state, if it so chooses, that specifically described portions of its annual or quarterly report to security holders, other than those portions required to be incorporated by reference pursuant to paragraphs (a)(3) and (4) of this Item, are not part of the registration statement. In such case, the description of portions that are not incorporated by reference or that are excluded shall be made with clarity and in reasonable detail.

(c) *Electronic filings.* Electronic filers electing to deliver and incorporate by reference all, or any portion, of the quarterly or annual report to security holders pursuant to this Item shall file as an exhibit such quarterly or annual report to security holders, or such portion thereof that is incorporated by reference, in electronic format.

    (d)   You must

        (1)   identify the reports and other information that you file with the SEC; and

        (2)   state that the SEC maintains an Internet site that contains reports, proxy and information statements, and other information regarding issuers that file electronically with the SEC and state the address of that site (http://www.sec.gov). Disclose your Internet address, if available.

Item 14. Information With Respect to Registrants Other Than S–3 Registrants

If the registrant does not meet the requirements for use of Form S–3, or otherwise elects to comply with this Item in lieu of Item 10 or 12, furnish the information required by:

    (a)   Item 101 of Regulation S–K, description of business;

    (b)   Item 102 of Regulation S–K, description of property;

    (c)   Item 103 of Regulation S–K, legal proceedings;

    (d)   Where common equity securities are being issued, Item 201 of Regulation S–K, market price of and dividends on the registrant's common equity and related stockholder matters;

    (e)   Financial statements meeting the requirements of Regulation S–X, (schedules required by Regulation S–X shall be filed as "Financial Statement Schedules" pursuant to Item 21 of this Form), as well as financial information required by Rule 3–05 and Article 11 of Regulation S–X with respect to transactions other than that pursuant to which the securities being registered are to be issued;

    (f)   Item 301 of Regulation S–K, selected financial data;

    (g)   Item 302 of Regulation S–K, supplementary financial information;

    (h)   Item 303 of Regulation S–K, management's discussion and analysis of financial condition and results of operations; and

    (i)   Item 304 of Regulation S–K, disagreements with accountants on accounting and financial disclosure.

    (j)   Item 305 of Regulation S–K, quantitative and qualitative disclosure of market risk.

C.   Information About the Company Being Acquired

Item 15. Information With Respect to S–3 Companies

If the company being acquired meets the requirements for use of Form S–3 and compliance with this Item is elected, furnish the information that would be required by Items 10 and 11 of this Form if securities of such company were being registered.

Item 16. Information With Respect to S–3 Companies

    (a)   If the company being acquired meets the requirements for use of Form S–3 and compliance with this Item is elected, furnish the information that would be required by Items 12 and 13 of this Form if securities of such company were being registered.

    (b)   *Electronic filings.* In addition to satisfying the requirements of paragraph (a) of this Item, electronic filers that elect to deliver and incorporate by reference all, or any portion, of the quarterly or annual report to security holders of a company being acquired pursuant to this Item shall file as an exhibit such quarterly or annual report to security holders, or such portion thereof that is incorporated by reference, in electronic format.

Item 17. Information With Respect to Companies Other Than S–3 Companies

If the company being acquired does not meet the requirements for use of Form S–3, or compliance with this Item is otherwise elected in lieu of Item 15 or 16, furnish the information required by paragraph (a) or (b) of this Item, whichever is applicable.

(a)   If the company being acquired is subject to the reporting requirements of Section 13(a) or 15(d) of the Exchange Act, or compliance with this subparagraph in lieu of subparagraph (b) of this Item is selected, furnish the information that would be required by Item 14 of this Form if the securities of such company were being registered; *however,* only those schedules required by Rules 12–15, 28 and 29 of Regulation S–X need be provided with respect to the company being acquired.

(b)   If the company being acquired is not subject to the reporting requirements of either Section 13(a) or 15(d) of the Exchange Act; or, because of Section 12(i) of the Exchange Act, has not furnished an annual report to security holders pursuant to Rule 14a–3 or Rule 14c–3 for its latest fiscal year; furnish the information that would be required by the following if securities of such company were being registered:

(1)   a brief description of the business done by the company which indicates the general nature and scope of the business;

(2)   Item 201 of Regulation S–K, market price of and dividends on the registrant's common equity and related stockholder matters;

(3)   Item 301 of Regulation S–K, selected financial data;

(4)   Item 302 of Regulation S–K, supplementary financial information;

(5)   Item 303 of Regulation S–K, management's discussion and analysis of financial condition and results of operations;

(6)   Item 304(b) of Regulation S–K, changes in and disagreements with accountants on accounting and financial disclosure;

(7)   financial statements that would be required in an annual report sent to security holders under Rules 14a–3(b)(1) and (b)(2), if an annual report was required. If the registrant's security holders are not voting, the transaction is not a roll-up transaction (as described by Item 901 of Regulation S–K), and:

(i)   The company being acquired is significant to the registrant in excess of the 20% level as determined under Rule 3–05(b)(2), provide financial statements of the company being acquired for the latest fiscal year in conformity with GAAP. In addition, if the company being acquired has provided its security holders with financial statements prepared in conformity with GAAP for either or both of the two fiscal years before the latest fiscal year, provide the financial statements for those years; or

(ii)   The company being acquired is significant to the registrant at or below the 20% level, no financial information (including pro forma and comparative per share information) for the company being acquired need be provided.

Instructions:

(1)   The financial statements required by this paragraph for the latest fiscal year need be audited only to the extent practicable. The financial statements for the fiscal years before the latest fiscal year need not be audited if they were not previously audited.

(2)   If the financial statements required by this paragraph are prepared on the basis of a comprehensive body of accounting principles other than U.S. GAAP or International Financial Reporting Standards as issued by the International Accounting Standards Board, provide a reconciliation to U.S. GAAP in accordance with Item 17 of Form 20–F unless a reconciliation is unavailable or not obtainable without unreasonable cost or expense. At a minimum, provide a narrative description of all material variations in accounting principles, practices and methods used in preparing the non-U.S. GAAP financial statements from those accepted in the U.S. when the financial statements are prepared on a basis other than U.S. GAAP.

(3)   If this Form is used to register resales to the public by any person who is deemed an underwriter within the meaning of Rule 145(c) with respect to the securities being reoffered, the financial statements must be audited for the fiscal years required to be presented under paragraph (b)(2) of Rule 3–05 of Regulation S–X.

(4)   In determining the significance of an acquisition for purposes of this paragraph, apply the tests prescribed in Rule 1–02(w).

(8)   the quarterly financial and other information as would have been required had the company being acquired been required to file Part I of Form 10–Q for the most recent quarter for which such a report would have been on file at the time the registration statement becomes effective or for a period ending as of a more recent date;

(9)   schedules required by Rules 12–15, 28 and 29 of Regulation S–X.

(10) Item 305 of Regulation S–K, quantitative and qualitative disclosures about market risk.

D.   Voting and Management Information

Item 18. Information if Proxies, Consents or Authorizations Are to Be Solicited

(a)   If proxies, consents or authorizations are to be solicited, furnish the following information, except as provided by paragraph (b) of this Item:

(1)   The information required by Item 1 of Schedule 14A, date, time and place information;

(2)   The information required by Item 2 of Schedule 14A, revocability of proxy;

(3)   The information required by Item 3 of Schedule 14A, dissenters' rights of appraisal;

(4)   The information required by Item 4 of Schedule 14A, persons making the solicitation;

(5)   With respect to both the registrant and the company being acquired, the information required by:

(i)   Item 5 of Schedule 14A, interest of certain persons in matters to be acted upon; and

(ii) Item 6 of Schedule 14A, voting securities and principal holders thereof;

(6)   The information required by Item 21 of Schedule 14A, vote required for approval; and

(7)   With respect to each person who will serve as a director or an executive officer of the surviving or acquiring company, the information required by:

(i)   Item 401 of Regulation S–K, directors and executive officers;

(ii) Item 402 of Regulation S–K, executive compensation, and paragraph (e)(4) of Item 407 of Regulation S–K, corporate governance; and

(iii) Item 404 of Regulation S–K, transactions with related persons, promoters and certain control persons, and Item 407(a) of Regulation S–K, corporate governance.

(b)   If the registrant or the company being acquired meets the requirements for use of Form S–3, any information required by paragraphs (a)(5)(ii) and (7) of this Item with respect to such company may be incorporated by reference from its latest annual report on Form 10–K.

Item 19. Information if Proxies, Consents or Authorizations Are Not to Be Solicited or in an Exchange Offer

(a)   If the transaction is an exchange offer or if proxies, consents or authorizations are not to be solicited, furnish the following information, except as provided by paragraph (c) of this Item:

(1)   The information required by Item 2 of Schedule 14C, statement that proxies are not to be solicited;

(2)   The date, time and place of the meeting of security holders, unless such information is otherwise disclosed in material furnished to security holders with the prospectus;

(3)   The information required by Item 3 of Schedule 14A, dissenters' rights of appraisal;

(4) With respect to both the registrant and the company being acquired, a brief description of any material interest, direct or indirect, by security holdings or otherwise, of affiliates of the registrant and of the company being acquired, in the proposed transactions;

Instruction. This subparagraph shall not apply to any interest arising from the ownership of securities of the registrant where the security holder receives no extra or special benefit not shared on a pro rata basis by all other holders of the same class.

(5) With respect to both the registrant and the company being acquired, the information required by Item 6 of Schedule 14A, voting securities and principal holders thereof;

(6) The information required by Item 21 of Schedule 14A, vote required for approval;

(7) With respect to each person who will serve as a director or an executive officer of the surviving or acquiring company, the information required by:

    (i) Item 401 of Regulation S–K, directors and executive officers;

    (ii) Item 402 of Regulation S–K, executive compensation, and paragraph (e)(4) of Item 407 of Regulation S–K, corporate governance; and

    (iii) Item 404 of Regulation S–K, transactions with related persons, promoters and certain controls persons, and Item 407(a) of Regulation S–K, corporate governance.

(b) If the transaction is an exchange offer, furnish the information required by paragraphs (a)(4), (a)(5), and (a)(7) of this Item, except as provided by paragraph (c) of this Item.

(c) If the registrant or the company being acquired meets the requirements for use of Form S–3, any information required by paragraphs (a)(5) and (7) of this Item with respect to such company may be incorporated by reference from its latest annual report on Form 10–K.

PART II. INFORMATION NOT REQUIRED IN PROSPECTUS

Item 20. Indemnification of Directors and Officers

Furnish the information required by Item 702 of Regulation S–K.

Item 21. Exhibits and Financial Statement Schedules

(a) Subject to the rules regarding incorporation by reference, furnish the exhibits as required by Item 601 of Regulation S–K.

(b) Furnish the financial statement schedules required by Regulation S–X and Item 14(e), Item 17(a) or Item 17(b)(9) of this Form. These schedules should be lettered or numbered in the manner described for exhibits in paragraph (a) of this Item.

(c) If information is provided pursuant to Item 4(b) of this Form, furnish the report, opinion or appraisal as an exhibit hereto, unless it is furnished as part of the prospectus.

Item 22. Undertakings

(a) Furnish the undertakings required by Item 512 of Regulation S–K.

(b) Furnish the following undertaking:

The undersigned registrant hereby undertakes to respond to requests for information that is incorporated by reference into the prospectus pursuant to Items 4, 10(b), 11, or 13 of this Form, within one business day of receipt of such request, and to send the incorporated documents by first class mail or other equally prompt means. This includes information contained in documents filed subsequent to the effective date of the registration statement through the date of responding to the request.

(c) Furnish the following undertaking:

The undersigned registrant hereby undertakes to supply by means of a post-effective amendment all information concerning a transaction, and the company being acquired involved therein, that was not the subject of and included in the registration statement when it became effective.

SIGNATURES

Pursuant to the requirements of the Securities Act, the registrant has duly caused this registration statement to be signed on its behalf by the undersigned, thereunto duly authorized, in the City of _____ State of _____, on _____, 20__.

(Registrant)

By (Signature and Title) _____

Pursuant to the requirements of the Securities Act of 1933, this registration statement has been signed by the following persons in the capacities and on the dates indicated.

(Signature)

(Title)

(Date) _____

Instructions. 1. The registration statement shall be signed by the registrant, its principal executive officer or officers, its principal financial officer, its controller or principal accounting officer, and by at least a majority of the board of directors or persons performing similar functions. If the registrant is a foreign person, the registration statement shall also be signed by its authorized representative in the United States. Where the registrant is a limited partnership, the registration statement shall be signed by a majority of the board of directors of any corporate general partner signing the registration statement.

2.   The name of each person who signs the registration statement shall be typed or printed beneath his signature. Any person who occupies more than one of the specified positions shall indicate each capacity in which he signs the registration statement. Attention is directed to Rule 402 concerning manual signatures and Item 601 concerning signatures pursuant to powers of attorney.

3.   If the securities to be offered are those of a corporation not yet in existence at the time the registration statement is filed which will be a party to a consolidation involving two or more existing corporations, then each such existing corporation shall be deemed a registrant and shall be so designated on the cover page of this Form, and the registration statement shall be signed by each such existing corporation and by the officers and directors of each such existing corporation as if each such existing corporation were the registrant.

FORM S–8

17 C.F.R. § 239.16b

SECURITIES AND EXCHANGE COMMISSION

REGISTRATION STATEMENT UNDER THE SECURITIES ACT OF 1933

_____

(Exact name of issuer as specified in its charter)
_____

| (State or other jurisdiction of incorporation or organization) | (I.R.S. Employer Identification No.) |

_____

| (Address of Principal Executive Offices) | (Zip Code) |

_____

(Full title of the plan)
_____

(Name and address of agent for service)
_____

(Telephone number, including area code, of agent for service)

Indicate by check mark whether the registrant is a large accelerated filer, an accelerated filer, a non-accelerated filer, a smaller reporting company, or an emerging growth company. See the definitions of "large accelerated filer," "accelerated filer," "smaller reporting company," and "emerging growth company" in Rule 12b–2 of the Exchange Act.

Large accelerated filer ☐

Non-accelerated filer ☐

Accelerated filer ☐

Smaller reporting company ☐

Emerging growth company ☐

If an emerging growth company, indicate by check mark if the registrant has elected not to use the extended transition period for complying with any new or revised financial accounting standards provided pursuant to Rule 7(a)(2)(B) of the Securities Act. ☐

Calculation of Registration Fee

Title of securities to be registered	Amount to be registered	Proposed maximum offering price per unit	Proposed maximum aggregate offering price	Amount of registration fee

NOTES: 1. If plan interests are being registered, include the following: In addition, pursuant to Rule 416(c) under the Securities Act of 1933, this registration statement also covers an indeterminate amount of interests to be offered or sold pursuant to the employee benefit plan(s) described herein.

2. Specific details relating to the fee calculation shall be furnished in notes to the table, including references to provisions of Rule 457 relied upon, if the basis of the calculation is not otherwise evident from the information presented in the table.

1933 ACT FORMS

GENERAL INSTRUCTIONS

A. Rule as to Use of Form S–8

1.   Any registrant that, immediately prior to the time of filing a registration statement on this Form, is subject to the requirement to file reports pursuant to Section 13 or 15(d) of the Securities Exchange Act of 1934 ("Exchange Act"); has filed all reports and other materials required to be filed by such requirements during the preceding 12 months (or for such shorter period that the registrant was required to file such reports and materials); is not a shell company (as defined in § 405) and has not been a shell company for at least 60 calendar days previously (subject to the exception in paragraph (a)(7) of this Instruction A.1.); and if it has been a shell company at any time previously, has filed current Form 10 information with the Commission at least 60 calendar days previously reflecting its status as an entity that is not a shell company (subject to the exception in paragraph (a)(7) of this Instruction A.1.), may use this Form for registration under the Securities Act of 1933 ("Act") of the following securities:

(a)   Securities of the registrant to be offered under any employee benefit plan to its employees or employees of its subsidiaries or parents. For purposes of this form, the term "employee benefit plan" is defined in Rule 405 of Regulation C.

(1)   For purposes of this form, the term "employee" is defined as any employee, director, general partner, trustee (where the registrant is a business trust), officer, or consultant or advisor. Form S–8 is available for the issuance of securities to consultants or advisors only if:

(i)   They are natural persons;

(ii)   They provide bona fide services to the registrant; and

(iii)   The services are not in connection with the offer or sale of securities in a capital-raising transaction, and do not directly or indirectly promote or maintain a market for the registrant's securities.

(2)   In addition, the term "employee" includes insurance agents who are exclusive agents of the registrant, its subsidiaries or parents, or derive more than 50% of their annual income from those entities.

(3)   The term "employees" also includes former employees as well as executors, administrators or beneficiaries of the estates of deceased employees, guardians or members of a committee for incompetent former employees, or similar persons duly authorized by law to administer the estate or assets of former employees. The inclusion of all individuals described in the preceding sentence in the term "employee" is only to permit registration on Form S–8 of:

(i)   The exercise of employee benefit plan stock options and the subsequent sale of the securities, if these exercises and sales are permitted under the terms of the plan; and

(ii)   The acquisition of registrant securities pursuant to intra-plan transfers among plan funds, if these transfers are permitted under the terms of the plan.

(4)   The term "registrant" as used in this Form means the company whose securities are to be offered pursuant to the plan, and also may mean the plan itself.

(5)   The form also is available for the exercise of employee benefit plan options and the subsequent resale of the underlying securities by an employee's family member who has acquired the options from the employee through a gift or a domestic relations order. For purposes of this form, "family member" includes any child, stepchild, grandchild, parent, stepparent, grandparent, spouse, former spouse, sibling, niece, nephew, mother-in-law, father-in-law, son-in-law, daughter-in-law, brother-in-law, or sister-in-law, including adoptive relationships, any person sharing the employee's household (other than a tenant or employee), a trust in which these persons have more than fifty percent of the beneficial interest, a foundation in which these persons (or the employee) control the management of assets, and any other entity in which these persons (or the employee) own more than fifty percent of the voting interests. Form S–8 is not available for the exercise of options transferred for value. The following transactions are not prohibited transfers for value:

(i)   A transfer under a domestic relations order in settlement of marital property rights; and

(ii) A transfer to an entity in which more than fifty percent of the voting interests are owned by family members (or the employee) in exchange for an interest in that entity.

(6) The term "Form 10 information" means the information that is required by Form 10 or Form 20–F, as applicable to the registrant, to register under the Securities Exchange Act of 1934 each class of securities being registered using this form. A registrant may provide the Form 10 information in another Commission filing with respect to the registrant.

(7) Notwithstanding the last two clauses of the first paragraph of this Instruction A.1., a business combination related shell company may use this form immediately after it:

(i) Ceases to be a shell company; and

(ii) Files current Form 10 information with the Commission reflecting its status as an entity that is not a shell company.

(b) Interests in the above plans, if such interests constitute securities and are required to be registered under the Act. (*See* Release No. 33–6188 (February 1, 1980) and Section 3(a)(2) of the Act.)

2. Where interests in a plan are being registered and the plan's latest annual report filed pursuant to Section 15(d) of the Exchange Act is to be incorporated by reference pursuant to the requirements of Form S–8, the plan shall either:

(i) have been subject to the requirement to file reports pursuant to Section 15(d) and shall have filed all reports required to be filed by such requirements during the preceding 12 months (or for such shorter period that the plan was required to file such reports); or

(ii) if the plan has not previously been subject to the reporting requirements of Section 15(d), concurrently with the filing of the registration statement on Form S–8, the plan shall file an annual report for its latest fiscal year (or if the plan has not yet completed its first fiscal year, then for a period ending not more than 90 days prior to the filing of this registration statement), *provided that* if the plan has not been in existence for at least 90 days prior to the filing date, the requirement to file an employee plan annual report concurrently with the Form S–8 registration statement shall not apply.

3. *Electronic filings.* In addition to satisfying the foregoing conditions, a registrant subject to the electronic filing requirements of Rule 101 of Regulation S–T shall have:

(a) Filed with the Commission all required electronic filings, including electronic copies of documents submitted in paper pursuant to a hardship exemption as provided by Rule 201 or Rule 202(d) of Regulation S–T; and

(b) Submitted electronically to the Commission all Interactive Data Files required to be submitted pursuant to Rule 405 of Regulation S–T (§ 232.405 of this chapter) during the twelve calendar months and any portion of a month immediately preceding the filing of the registration statement on this Form (or for such shorter period of time that the registrant was required to submit such files).

B. Application of General Rules and Regulations

1. Attention is directed to the General Rules and Regulations under the Act, particularly those comprising Regulation C thereunder. That Regulation contains general requirements regarding the preparation and filing of registration statements. However, any provision in this form covering the same subject matter as any such requirement shall be controlling unless otherwise specifically provided in Regulation C.

2. Attention is directed to Regulation S–K for the requirements applicable to the content of the non-financial portions of registration statements under the Act. Where this form directs the registrant to furnish information required by any item of Regulation S–K, information need only be furnished to the extent appropriate.

3. A "smaller reporting company," defined in Rule 405, shall use the disclosure items in Regulation S–K with specific attention to the scaled disclosure provided for smaller reporting companies, if any.

C. Reoffers and Resales

1.   *Securities.* Reoffers and resales of the following securities may be made on a continuous and delayed basis in the future, as provided by Rule 415, pursuant to a registration statement on this form by means of a separate prospectus ("reoffer prospectus"), which is prepared in accordance with the requirements of Part I of Form S–3 (or, if the registrant is a foreign private issuer, in accordance with Part I of Form F–3), and filed with the registration statement on Form S–8 or, in the case of control securities, a post-effective amendment thereto:

(a)   *Control securities,* which are defined for purposes of this General Instruction C as securities acquired under a Securities Act registration statement held by affiliates of the registrant as defined in Rule 405. Control securities may be included in a reoffer prospectus only if they have been or will be acquired by the selling security holder pursuant to an employee benefit plan; or

(b)   *Restricted securities,* which are defined for purposes of this General Instruction C as securities issued under any employee benefit plan of the registrant meeting the definition of "restricted securities" in Rule 144(a)(3), whether or not held by affiliates of the registrant. Restricted securities may be included in a reoffer prospectus only if they have been acquired by the selling security holder prior to the filing of the registration statement.

2.   *Limitations.* The reoffer prospectus may be used as follows:

(a)   If the registrant, at the time of filing such prospectus, satisfies the registrant requirements for use of Form S–3 (or if the registrant is a foreign private issuer eligible to file on Form 20–F, the registrant requirements for use of Form F–3), then control and restricted securities may be registered for reoffer and resale without any limitations.

(b)   If the registrant, at the time of filing such prospectus, does not satisfy the registrant requirements for use of Form S–3 or F–3, as appropriate, then the following limitation shall apply with respect to both control securities and restricted securities: the amount of securities to be reoffered or resold by means of the reoffer prospectus, by each person, and any other person with whom he or she is acting in concert for the purpose of selling securities of the registrant, may not exceed, during any three month period, the amount specified in Rule 144(e).

3.   *Selling Security Holders.*

(a)   *Control Securities.* If the names of the security holders who intend to resell are not known by the registrant at the time of filing the Form S–8 registration statement, the registrant may either: (1) refer to the selling security holders in a generic manner in the reoffer prospectus; later, as their names and the amounts of securities to be reoffered become known, the registrant must supplement the reoffer prospectus with that information; or (2) name in the reoffer prospectus all persons eligible to resell and the amounts of securities available to be resold, whether or not they have a present intent to do so; any additional persons must be added by prospectus supplement. Prospectus supplements must be filed with the Commission as required by Rule 424(b). The registrant may file a reoffer prospectus covering control securities as part of the initial registration statement or by means of a post-effective amendment to the Form S–8 registration statement.

(b)   *Restricted Securities.* All persons (including non-affiliates) holding restricted securities registered for reoffer or resale pursuant to a reoffer prospectus are to be named as selling shareholders in the reoffer prospectus; *provided, however,* that any non-affiliate who holds less than the lesser of 1000 shares or 1% of the shares issuable under the plan to which the Form S–8 registration statement relates need not be named if the reoffer prospectus indicates that certain unnamed non-affiliates, each of whom may sell up to that amount, may use the reoffer prospectus for reoffers and resales. The reoffer prospectus covering restricted securities must be filed with the initial registration statement, not a post-effective amendment thereto.

NOTES to General Instruction C

1.   The term "person" as used in this General Instruction C shall be the same as set forth in Rule 144(a)(2).

2.   If the conditions of this General Instruction C are not satisfied, registration of reoffers or resales must be made by means of a separate registration statement using whichever form is applicable.

D. Filing and Effectiveness of Registration Statement; Requests for Confidential Treatment; Number of Copies

A registration statement on this Form S-8 will become effective automatically (Rule 462) upon filing (Rule 456). In addition, post-effective amendments on this form shall become effective upon filing (Rules 464 and 456). Delaying amendments are not permitted in connection with any registration statement on this form (Rule 473(d)), and any attempt to interpose a delaying amendment of any kind will be ineffective. All filings made on or in connection with this form become public upon filing with the Commission. As a result, requests for confidential treatment made under either Rule 406 or Exchange Act Rule 24b-2 in connection with documents incorporated by reference, must be acted upon, *i.e.*, granted or denied, by the Commission staff prior to the filing of the registration statement. The number of copies of the filing required by Rules 402(c) and 472(d) shall be filed with the Commission.

E. Registration of Additional Securities

With respect to the registration of additional securities of the same class as other securities for which a registration statement filed on this form relating to an employee benefit plan is effective, the registrant may file a registration statement consisting only of the following: the facing page; a statement that the contents of the earlier registration statement, identified by file number, are incorporated by reference; required opinions and consents; the signature page; and any information required in the new registration statement that is not in the earlier registration statement. If the new registration statement covers restricted securities being offered for resale, it shall include the required reoffer prospectus. If the earlier registration statement included a reoffer prospectus, the new registration statement shall be deemed to include that reoffer prospectus; *provided, however,* that a revised reoffer prospectus shall be filed, if the reoffer prospectus is substantively different from that filed in the earlier registration statement. The filing fee required by the Act and Rule 457 shall be paid with respect to the additional securities only.

F. Registration of Plan Interests

Where a registration statement on this form relates to securities to be offered pursuant to an employee stock purchase, savings, or similar plan, the registration statement is deemed to register an indeterminate amount of interests in such plan that are separate securities and required to be registered under the Securities Act. *See* Rule 416(c).

G. Updating

Updating of information constituting the Section 10(a) prospectus pursuant to Rule 428(a) during the offering of the securities shall be accomplished as follows:

(1) Plan information specified by Item 1 of Form S-8 required to be sent or given to employees shall be updated as specified in Rule 428(b)(1). Such information need not be filed with the Commission.

(2) Registrant information shall be updated by the filing of Exchange Act reports, which are incorporated by reference in the registration statement and the Section 10(a) prospectus. Any material changes in the registrant's affairs required to be disclosed in the registration statement but not required to be included in a specific Exchange Act report shall be reported on Form 8-K pursuant to Item 5 thereof (or, if the registrant is a foreign private issuer, on Form 6-K).

(3) An employee plan annual report incorporated by reference in the registration statement from Form 11-K (or Form 10-K and 10-KSB, as permitted by Rule 15d-21) shall be updated by the filing of a subsequent plan annual report on Form 11-K or 10-K.

PART I—INFORMATION REQUIRED IN THE SECTION 10(a) PROSPECTUS

NOTE: The document(s) containing the information specified in this Part I will be sent or given to employees as specified by Rule 428(b)(1). Such documents need not be filed with the Commission either as part of this registration statement or as prospectuses or prospectus supplements pursuant to Rule 424. These documents and the documents incorporated by reference in the registration statement pursuant to Item 3 or Part II of this form, taken together, constitute a prospectus that meets the requirements of Section 10(a) of the Securities Act. *See* Rule 428(a)(1).

Item 1.   Plan Information

The registrant shall deliver or cause to be delivered to each participant material information regarding the plan and its operations that will enable participants to make an informed decision regarding investment in the plan. This information shall include, to the extent material to the particular plan being described, but not be limited to, the disclosure specified in (a) through (j) below. Any unusual risks associated with participation in the plan not described pursuant to a specified item shall be prominently disclosed, as, for example, when the plan imposes a substantial restriction on the ability of a participant to withdraw contributions, or when plan participation may obligate the participant's general credit in connection with purchases on a margin basis. The information may be in one or several documents, provided that it is presented in a clear, concise and understandable manner. *See* Rule 421.

(a)   *General Plan Information*

(1)   Give the title of the plan and the name of the registrant whose securities are to be offered pursuant to the plan.

(2)   Briefly state the general nature and purpose of the plan, its duration, and any provisions for its modification, earlier termination or extension to the extent that they affect the participants.

(3)   Indicate whether the plan is subject to any provisions of the Employee Retirement Income Security Act of 1974 ("ERISA"), and if so, the general nature of those provisions to which it is subject.

(4)   Give an address and a telephone number, including area code, which participants may use to obtain additional information about the plan and its administrators. State the capacity in which the plan administrators act (*e.g.,* trustees or managers) and the functions that they perform. If any person other than a participating employee has discretion with respect to the investment of all or any part of the assets of the plan in one or more investment media, name such person and describe the policies followed and to be followed with respect to the type and proportion of securities or other property in which funds of the plan may be invested. If the plan is not subject to ERISA: (i) state the nature of any material relationship between the administrators and the employees, the registrant or its affiliates; and (ii) describe the manner in which the plan administrators are selected, their term of office, and the manner in which they may be removed from office.

(b)   *Securities to be Offered*

(1)   State the title and total amount of securities to be offered pursuant to the plan.

(2)   Furnish the information required by Item 202 of Regulation S–K, except that if common stock registered under Section 12 of the Exchange Act is offered, such information is unnecessary. If plan interests are being registered, they need not be described pursuant to this item.

(c)   *Employees Who May Participate in the Plan*

Indicate each class or group of employees that may participate in the plan and the basis upon which the eligibility of employees to participate therein is to be determined.

(d)   *Purchase of Securities Pursuant to the Plan and Payment for Securities Offered*

(1)   State the period of time within which employees may elect to participate in the plan, the price at which the securities may be purchased or the basis upon which such price is to be determined, and any terms regarding the amount of securities that an eligible employee can purchase.

(2)   State when and the manner in which employees are to pay for the securities purchased pursuant to the plan. If payment is to be made by payroll deductions or other installment payments, state the percentage of wages or salaries or other basis for computing such payments, and the time and manner in which an employee may alter the amount of such deduction or payment.

(3)   State the amount each employee is required or permitted to contribute or, if not a fixed amount, the percentage of wages or salaries or other basis of computing contributions.

(4)   If contributions are to be made under the plan by the registrant or any employer, state who is to make such contributions, when they are to be made and the nature and amount of each contribution. If such contributions are not a fixed amount, state the basis for computing contributions.

(5)   State the nature and frequency of any reports to be made to participating employees as to the amount and status of their accounts.

(6)   If the plan is not subject to ERISA, state whether securities are to be purchased in the open market or otherwise. If they are not to be purchased in the open market, then state from whom they are to be purchased and describe the fees, commissions or other charges paid. If the employer or any of its affiliates, or any person having a material relationship with the employer or any of its affiliates, directly or indirectly, receives any part of the aggregate purchase price (including fees, commissions or other charges), explain the basis for compensation.

NOTE: If the plan is one under which credit is extended to finance the acquisition of securities, consideration should be given to the applicability of Regulation G or T.

(e)   *Resale Restrictions*

Describe briefly any restriction on resale of the securities purchased under the plan which may be imposed upon the employee purchaser.

(f)   *Tax Effects of Plan Participation*

Describe briefly the tax effects that may accrue to employees as a result of plan participation as well as the tax effects, if any, upon the registrant and whether or not the plan is qualified under Section 401(a) of the Internal Revenue Code.

NOTE: If the plan is not qualified under Section 401 of the Internal Revenue Code of 1986, as amended, consideration should be given to the applicability of the Investment Company Act of 1940. *See* Securities Act Release No. 4790 (July 13, 1965).

(g)   *Investment of Funds*

If participating employees may direct all or any part of the assets under the plan to two or more investment media, furnish a brief description of the provisions of the plan with respect to the alternative investment media; and provide a tabular or other meaningful presentation of financial data for each of the past three fiscal years (or such lesser period for which the data is available with respect to each investment medium) that, in the opinion of the registrant, will apprise employees of material trends and significant changes in the performance of alternative investment media and enable them to make informed investment decisions. Financial data shall be presented for any additional fiscal years necessary to keep the information from being misleading or that the registrant deems appropriate, but the total period presented need not exceed five years.

(h)   *Withdrawal from the Plan; Assignment of Interest*

(1)   Describe the terms and conditions under which a participating employee may (i) withdraw from the plan and terminate his or her interest therein; or (ii) withdraw funds or investments held for the employee's account without terminating his or her interest in the plan.

(2)   State whether, and the terms and conditions upon which, the plan permits an employee to assign or hypothecate his or her interest in the plan.

(3)   No information need be provided as to the effect of a qualified domestic relations order as defined in ERISA Section 206(d) (29 U.S.C. 1056(d)).

(i)   *Forfeitures and Penalties*

Describe briefly every event which could, under the plan, result in a forfeiture by, or a penalty to, a participant, and the consequences thereof.

(j)   *Charges and Deductions and Liens Therefor*

(1)   Describe all charges and deductions (other than deductions described in paragraph (d) and taxes) that may be made against employees participating in the plan or against funds, securities or other property held under the plan and indicate who will receive, directly or indirectly, any part thereof. Such description should include charges and deductions that may be made upon the termination of an employee's interest in the plan, or upon partial withdrawals from the employee's account thereunder.

(2)   State whether or not under the plan, or pursuant to any contract in connection therewith, any person has or may create a lien on any funds, securities, or other property held under the plan. If so, describe fully the circumstances under which the lien was or may be created.

(3)   No information need be provided as to the effect of a qualified domestic relations order as defined in ERISA Section 206(d) (29 U.S.C. 1056(d)).

Item 2.   Registrant Information and Employee Plan Annual Information

The registrant shall provide a written statement to participants advising them of the availability without charge, upon written or oral request, of the documents incorporated by reference in Item 3 of Part II of the registration statement, and stating that these documents are incorporated by reference in the Section 10(a) prospectus. The statement also shall indicate the availability without charge, upon written or oral request, of other documents required to be delivered to employees pursuant to Rule 428(b). The statement shall include the address (giving title or department) and telephone number to which the request is to be directed.

PART II—INFORMATION REQUIRED IN
THE REGISTRATION STATEMENT

Item 3.   Incorporation of Documents by Reference

The registrant, and where interests in the plan are being registered, the plan, shall state that the documents listed in (a) through (c) below are incorporated by reference in the registration statement; and shall state that all documents subsequently filed by it pursuant to Sections 13(a), 13(c), 14 and 15(d) of the Securities Exchange Act of 1934, prior to the filing of a post-effective amendment which indicates that all securities offered have been sold or which deregisters all securities then remaining unsold, shall be deemed to be incorporated by reference in the registration statement and to be part thereof from the date of filing of such documents. Copies of these documents are not required to be filed with the registration statement.

(a)   The registrant's latest annual report, and where interests in the plan are being registered, the plan's latest annual report, filed pursuant to Sections 13(a) or 15(d) of the Exchange Act, or in the case of the registrant either:

(1)   the latest prospectus filed pursuant to Rule 424(b) under the Act that contains audited financial statements for the registrant's latest fiscal year for which such statements have been filed, or

(2)   the registrant's effective registration statement on Form 10, Form 20–F or, in the case of registrants described in General Instruction A.(2) of Form 40–F, on Form 40–F under the Exchange Act containing audited financial statements for the registrant's latest fiscal year.

(b)   All other reports filed pursuant to Section 13(a) or 15(d) of the Exchange Act since the end of the fiscal year covered by the registrant document referred to in (a) above.

(c)   If the class of securities to be offered is registered under Section 12 of the Exchange Act, the description of such class of securities contained in a registration statement filed under such Act, including any amendment or report filed for the purpose of updating such description.

Item 4.   Description of Securities

If the class of securities to be offered is not registered under Section 12 of the Exchange Act, set forth the information required by Item 202 of Regulation S–K. If plan interests are being registered, they need not be described pursuant to this item.

Item 5.   Interests of Named Experts and Counsel

Furnish the information required by Item 509 of Regulation S–K.

Item 6.   Indemnification of Directors and Officers

Furnish the information required by Item 702 of Regulation S–K.

Item 7. Exemption From Registration Claimed

With respect to restricted securities to be reoffered or resold pursuant to this registration statement, the registrant shall indicate the section of the Act or Rule of the Commission under which exemption from registration was claimed and set forth briefly the facts relied upon to make the exemption available.

Item 8. Exhibits

Furnish the exhibits required by Item 601 of Regulation S–K, except that, with respect to Item 601(b)(5):

(a) An opinion of counsel as to the legality of the securities being registered is required only with respect to original issuance securities.

(b) Neither an opinion of counsel concerning compliance with the requirements of ERISA nor an Internal Revenue Service determination letter that the plan is qualified under Section 401 of the Internal Revenue Code shall be required if, in lieu thereof, the response to this Item 8 includes an undertaking that the registrant will submit or has submitted the plan and any amendment thereto to the Internal Revenue Service ("IRS") in a timely manner and has made or will make all changes required by the IRS in order to qualify the plan.

Item 9. Undertakings

Furnish the undertakings required by Item 512(a), (b) and (h) of Regulation S–K, as well as any other applicable undertakings in Item 512.

NOTES to Item 9: (1) The Regulation S–K Item 512(a) undertakings are usually required pursuant to this item since most registration statements on Form S–8 involve the continuous offering and sale of securities under Rule 415.

(2) With respect to registration statements filed on this form, foreign private issuers are not required to furnish the Item 512(a)(4) undertaking.

SIGNATURES

The Registrant. Pursuant to the requirements of the Securities Act of 1933, the registrant certifies that it has reasonable grounds to believe that it meets all of the requirements for filing on Form S–8 and has duly caused this registration statement to be signed on its behalf by the undersigned, thereunto duly authorized, in the City of, _____

State of, _____

on, _____

20___.

(Registrant) _____

By (Signature and Title) _____

Pursuant to the requirements of the Securities Act of 1933, this registration statement has been signed by the following persons in the capacities and on the date indicated. _____

(Signature) _____

(Title) _____

(Date) _____

The Plan. Pursuant to the requirements of the Securities Act of 1933, the trustees (or other persons who administer the employee benefit plan) have duly caused this registration statement to be signed on its behalf by the undersigned, thereunto duly authorized, in the City of, State of, on, 20 _____

(Plan) _____

By (Signature and Title) _____

Instructions. 1. The registration statement shall be signed by the registrant, its principal executive officer or officers, its principal financial officer, its controller or principal accounting officer, and at least a majority of the board of directors or persons performing similar functions. Where interests in the plan are being registered, the registration statement shall be signed by the plan. If the signing person is a foreign person, the registration statement also shall be signed by its authorized representative in the United States. Where the signing person is a limited partnership, the registration statement shall be signed by a majority of the board of directors of any corporate general partner signing the registration statement.

2. The name of each person who signs the registration statement shall be typed or printed beneath the signature. Any person who occupies more than one of the specified positions shall indicate each capacity in which he or she signs the registration statement. Attention is directed to Rule 402 concerning manual signatures and Item 601 of Regulation S–K concerning signatures pursuant to powers of attorney.

FORM 1–A

17 C.F.R. § 239.90

SECURITIES AND EXCHANGE COMMISSION

REGULATION A OFFERING STATEMENT
UNDER THE SECURITIES ACT OF 1933

(Exact name of issuer as specified in its charter)

(State or other jurisdiction of incorporation or organization)

(Address, including zip code, and telephone number,
including area code of issuer's principal executive offices)

(Name, address, including zip code, and telephone number,
including area code, of agent for service)

(Primary Standard Industrial Classification Code Number)

(I.R.S. Employer Identification Number)

The following delaying notation is optional, but see Rule 252(g) before omitting it:

This offering statement shall only be qualified upon order of the Commission, unless a subsequent amendment is filed indicating the intention to become qualified by operation of the terms of Regulation A.

GENERAL INSTRUCTIONS

I. Eligibility Requirements for Use of Form 1–A

This Form is to be used for securities offerings made pursuant to Regulation A. Careful attention should be directed to the terms, conditions and requirements of Regulation A, especially Rule 251, because the exemption is not available to all issuers or for every type of securities transaction. Further, the aggregate offering price and aggregate sales of securities in any 12-month period is strictly limited to $20 million for Tier 1 offerings and $75 million for Tier 2 offerings, including no more than $6 million offered by all selling securityholders that are affiliates of the issuer for Tier 1 offerings and $22.5 million by all selling securityholders that are affiliates of the issuer for Tier 2 offerings. Please refer to Rule 251 of Regulation A for more details.

II. Preparation, Submission and Filing of the Offering Statement

An offering statement must be prepared by all persons seeking exemption under the provisions of Regulation A. Parts I, II and III must be addressed by all issuers. Part II, which relates to the content of the required offering circular, provides alternative formats, of which the issuer must choose one. General information regarding the preparation, format, content, and submission or filing of the offering statement is contained in Rule 252. Information regarding non-public submission of the offering statement is contained in Rule 252(d). Requirements relating to the offering circular are contained in Rules 253 and 254. The offering statement must be submitted or filed with the Securities and Exchange Commission in electronic format by means of the Commission's Electronic Data Gathering, Analysis and Retrieval System (EDGAR) in accordance with the EDGAR rules set forth in Regulation S–T for such submission or filing.

III. Incorporation by Reference and Cross-Referencing

An issuer may incorporate by reference to other documents previously submitted or filed on EDGAR. Cross-referencing within the offering statement is also encouraged to avoid repetition of information. For example, you may respond to an item of this Form by providing a cross-reference to the location of the

1933 ACT FORMS

information in the financial statements, instead of repeating such information. Incorporation by reference and cross-referencing are subject to the following additional conditions:

(a) The use of incorporation by reference and cross-referencing in Part II of this Form:

(1) Is limited to the following items:

(A) Items 2–14 of Part II and Part F/S if following the Offering Circular format;

(B) Items 3–11 of Form S–1 if following the Part I of Form S–1 format; or

(C) Items 3–28, and 30 of Form S–11 if following the Part I of Form S–11 format;

(2) May only incorporate by reference previously submitted or filed financial statements if the issuer meets the following requirements:

(A) the issuer has filed with the Commission all reports and other materials required to be filed, if any, pursuant to Rule 257 or by Sections 13(a), 14 or 15(d) of the Securities Exchange Act of 1934 during the preceding 12 months (or for such shorter period that the issuer was required to file such reports and other materials);

(B) the issuer makes the financial statement information that is incorporated by reference pursuant to this item readily available and accessible on a website maintained by or for the issuer; and the issuer must state that it will provide to each holder of securities, including any beneficial owner, a copy of the financial statement information that have been incorporated by reference in the offering statement upon written or oral request, at no cost to the requester, and provide the issuer's website address, including the uniform resource locator (URL) where the incorporated financial statements may be accessed.

(b) Descriptions of where the information incorporated by reference or cross-referenced can be found must be specific and must clearly identify the relevant document and portion thereof where such information can be found. For exhibits incorporated by reference, this description must be noted in the exhibits index for each relevant exhibit. All descriptions of where information incorporated by reference can be found must be accompanied by a hyperlink to the incorporated document on EDGAR, which hyperlink need not remain active after the filing of the offering statement. Inactive hyperlinks must be updated in any amendment to the offering statement otherwise required.

(c) Reference may not be made to any document if the portion of such document containing the pertinent information includes an incorporation by reference to another document. Incorporation by reference to documents not available on EDGAR is not permitted. Incorporating information into the financial statements from elsewhere is not permitted. Information shall not be incorporated by reference or cross-referenced in any case where such incorporation would render the statement or report incomplete, unclear, or confusing.

(d) If any substantive modification has occurred in the text of any document incorporated by reference since such document was filed, the issuer must file with the reference a statement containing the text and date of such modification.

IV. Supplemental Information

The information specified below must be furnished to the Commission as supplemental information, if applicable. Supplemental information shall not be required to be filed with or deemed part of the offering statement, unless otherwise required. The information shall be returned to the issuer upon request made in writing at the time of submission, provided that the return of such information is consistent with the protection of investors and the provisions of the Freedom of Information Act and the information was not filed in electronic format.

(a) A statement as to whether or not the amount of compensation to be allowed or paid to the underwriter has been cleared with the Financial Industry Regulatory Authority (FINRA).

(b) Any engineering, management, market, or similar report referenced in the offering circular or provided for external use by the issuer or by a principal underwriter in connection with the proposed offering. There must also be furnished at the same time a statement as to the actual or proposed use and distribution of such report or memorandum. Such statement must identify each class of persons who have received or will receive the report or memorandum, and state the number of copies distributed to each such class along with a statement as to the actual or proposed use and distribution of such report or memorandum.

(c)   Such other information as requested by the staff in support of statements, representations and other assertions contained in the offering statement or any correspondence to the staff.

Correspondence appropriately responding to any staff comments made on the offering statement must also be furnished electronically. When applicable, such correspondence must clearly indicate where changes responsive to the staff's comments may be found in the offering statement.

PART I—NOTIFICATION

The following information must be provided in the XML-based portion of Form 1–A available through the EDGAR portal and must be completed or updated before uploading each offering statement or amendment thereto. The format of Part I shown below may differ from the electronic version available on EDGAR. The electronic version of Part I will allow issuers to attach Part II and Part III for filing by means of EDGAR. All items must be addressed, unless otherwise indicated.

* * *

☐ No changes to the information required by Part I have occurred since the last filing of this offering statement.

Item 1.   Issuer Information

Exact name of issuer as specified in the issuer's charter: _____

Jurisdiction of incorporation/organization: _____

Year of incorporation: _____

CIK: _____

Primary Standard Industrial Classification Code: _____

I.R.S. Employer Identification Number: _____

Total number of full-time employees: _____

Total number of part-time employees: _____

Contact Information: _____

Address of Principal Executive Offices: _____

Telephone: (_____)

Provide the following information for the person the Securities and Exchange Commission's staff should call in connection with any pre-qualification review of the offering statement: _____

Name: _____

Address: _____

Telephone: (_____)

Provide up to two email addresses to which the Securities and Exchange Commission's staff may send any comment letters relating to the offering statement. After qualification of the offering statement, such email addresses are not required to remain active:

Financial Statements

Industry Group (select one): ☐ Banking ☐ Insurance ☐ Other

Use the financial statements for the most recent fiscal period contained in this offering statement to provide the following information about the issuer. The following table does not include all of the line items from the financial statements. Long Term Debt would include notes payable, bonds, mortgages, and similar obligations. To determine "Total Revenues" for all companies selecting "Other" for their industry group, refer to Article 5–03(b)(1) of Regulation S–X. For companies selecting "Insurance," refer to Article 7–04 of

Regulation S–X for calculation of "Total Revenues" and paragraphs 5 and 7(a) for "Costs and Expenses Applicable to Revenues".

[If "Other" is selected, display the following options in the Financial Statements table:]

Balance Sheet Information

Cash and Cash Equivalents: _____

Investment Securities: _____

Accounts and Notes Receivable: _____

Property, Plant and Equipment (PP&E): _____

Total Assets: _____

Accounts Payable and Accrued Liabilities: _____

Long Term Debt: _____

Total Liabilities: _____

Total Stockholders' Equity: _____

Total Liabilities and Equity: _____

Statement of Comprehensive Income Information

Total Revenues: _____

Costs and Expenses Applicable to Revenues: _____

Depreciation and Amortization: _____

Net Income: _____

Earnings Per Share—Basic: _____

Earnings Per Share—Diluted: _____

[If "Banking" is selected, display the following options in the Financial Statements table:]

Balance Sheet Information

Cash and Cash Equivalents: _____

Investment Securities: _____

Loans: _____

Property and Equipment: _____

Total Assets: _____

Accounts Payable and Accrued Liabilities: _____

Deposits: _____

Long Term Debt: _____

Total Liabilities: _____

Total Stockholders' Equity: _____

Total Liabilities and Equity: _____

Statement of Comprehensive Income Information

Total Interest Income: _____

Total Interest Expense: _____

Depreciation and Amortization: _____

Net Income: _____

Earnings Per Share—Basic: _____

Earnings Per Share—Diluted: _____

[If "Insurance" is selected, display the following options in the Financial Statements table:]

Balance Sheet Information

Cash and Cash Equivalents: _____

Total Investments: _____

Accounts and Notes Receivable: _____

Property and Equipment: _____

Total Assets: _____

Accounts Payable and Accrued Liabilities: _____

Policy Liabilities and Accruals: _____

Long Term Debt: _____

Total Liabilities: _____

Total Stockholders' Equity: _____

Total Liabilities and Equity: _____

Statement of Comprehensive Income Information

Total Revenues: _____

Costs and Expenses Applicable to Revenues: _____

Depreciation and Amortization: _____

Net Income: _____

Earnings Per Share—Basic: _____

Earnings Per Share—Diluted: _____

[End of section that varies based on the selection of Industry Group]

Name of Auditor (if any): _____

Outstanding Securities

	Name of class (if any)	Units outstanding	CUSIP (if any)	Name of trading center or quotation medium (if any)
Common Equity				
Preferred Equity				
Debt Securities				

Item 2. Issuer Eligibility

☐   Check this box to certify that all of the following statements are true for the issuer(s):

     ☐   Organized under the laws of the United States or Canada, or any State, Province, Territory or possession thereof, or the District of Columbia.

     ☐   Principal place of business is in the United States or Canada.

     ☐   Not a development stage company that either (a) has no specific business plan or purpose, or (b) has indicated that its business plan is to merge with an unidentified company or companies.

☐   Not an investment company registered or required to be registered under the Investment Company Act of 1940.

☐   Not issuing fractional undivided interests in oil or gas rights, or a similar interest in other mineral rights.

☐   Not issuing asset-backed securities as defined in Item 1101(c) of Regulation AB.

☐   Not, and has not been, subject to any order of the Commission entered pursuant to Section 12(j) of the Exchange Act (15 U.S.C. 78*l*(j)) within five years before the filing of this offering statement.

☐   Has filed with the Commission all the reports it was required to file, if any, pursuant to Rule 257 during the two years immediately before the filing of the offering statement (or for such shorter period that the issuer was required to file such reports).

Item 3.   Application of Rule 262

☐   Check this box to certify that, as of the time of this filing, each person described in Rule 262 of Regulation A is either not disqualified under that rule or is disqualified but has received a waiver of such disqualification.

☐   Check this box if "bad actor" disclosure under Rule 262(d) is provided in Part II of the offering statement.

Item 4.   Summary Information Regarding the Offering and Other Current or Proposed Offerings

Check the appropriate box to indicate whether you are conducting a Tier 1 or Tier 2 offering:

☐ Tier 1 ☐ Tier 2

Check the appropriate box to indicate whether the annual financial statements have been audited:

☐ Unaudited ☐ Audited

Types of Securities Offered in this Offering Statement (select all that apply):

☐ Equity (common or preferred stock)

☐ Debt

☐ Option, warrant or other right to acquire another security

☐ Security to be acquired upon exercise of option, warrant or other right to acquire security

☐ Tenant-in-common securities

☐ Other (describe) _____

Does the issuer intend to offer the securities on a delayed or continuous basis pursuant to Rule 251(d)(3)?

Yes ☐ No ☐

Does the issuer intend this offering to last more than one year?

Yes ☐ No ☐

Does the issuer intend to price this offering after qualification pursuant to Rule 253(b)?

Yes ☐ No ☐

Will the issuer be conducting a best efforts offering?

Yes ☐ No ☐

Has the issuer used solicitation of interest communications in connection with the proposed offering?

Yes ☐ No ☐

Does the proposed offering involve the resale of securities by affiliates of the issuer?

Yes ☐ No ☐

Number of securities offered: _____

Number of securities of that class already outstanding: _____

The information called for by this item below may be omitted if undetermined at the time of filing or submission, except that if a price range has been included in the offering statement, the midpoint of that range must be used to respond. Please refer to Rule 251(a) for the definition of "aggregate offering price" or "aggregate sales" as used in this item. Please leave the field blank if undetermined at this time and include a zero if a particular item is not applicable to the offering.

Price per security: $_____

The portion of the aggregate offering price attributable to securities being offered on behalf of the issuer:

$_____

The portion of the aggregate offering price attributable to securities being offered on behalf of selling securityholders:

$_____

The portion of aggregate offering attributable to all the securities of the issuer sold pursuant to a qualified offering statement within the 12 months before the qualification of this offering statement:

$_____

The estimated portion of aggregate sales attributable to securities that may be sold pursuant to any other qualified offering statement concurrently with securities being sold under this offering statement:

$_____

Total: $_____ (the sum of the aggregate offering price and aggregate sales in the four preceding paragraphs).

Anticipated fees in connection with this offering and names of service providers:

	Name of Service Provider	*Fees*
Underwriters:	_____	$_____
Sales Commissions:	_____	$_____
Finders' Fees:	_____	$_____
Audit:	_____	$_____
Legal:	_____	$_____
Promoters:	_____	$_____
Blue Sky Compliance:	_____	$_____

CRD Number of any broker or dealer listed:_____

Estimated net proceeds to the issuer: $_____

Clarification of responses (if necessary):_____

Item 5. Jurisdictions in Which Securities are to be Offered

Using the list below, select the jurisdictions in which the issuer intends to offer the securities:

[List will include all U.S. and Canadian jurisdictions, with an option to add and remove them individually, add all and remove all.]

Using the list below, select the jurisdictions in which the securities are to be offered by underwriters, dealers or sales persons or check the appropriate box:

☐ None

☐ Same as the jurisdictions in which the issuer intends to offer the securities.

[List will include all U.S. and Canadian jurisdictions, with an option to add and remove them individually, add all and remove all.]

Item 6. Unregistered Securities Issued or Sold Within One Year

☐ None

As to any unregistered securities issued by the issuer or any of its predecessors or affiliated issuers within one year before the filing of this Form 1–A, state:

(a)   Name of such issuer

(b)(1)   Title of securities issued

(2)   Total amount of such securities issued

(3)   Amount of such securities sold by or for the account of any person who at the time was a director, officer, promoter or principal securityholder of the issuer of such securities, or was an underwriter of any securities of such issuer

(c)(1)   Aggregate consideration for which the securities were issued and basis for computing the amount thereof.

(2)   Aggregate consideration for which the securities listed in (b)(3) of this item (if any) were issued and the basis for computing the amount thereof (if different from the basis described in (c)(1)).

(d)   Indicate the section of the Securities Act or Commission rule or regulation relied upon for exemption from the registration requirements of such Act and state briefly the facts relied upon for such exemption: _____

PART II—INFORMATION REQUIRED IN OFFERING CIRCULAR

(a)   Financial statement requirements regardless of the applicable disclosure format are specified in Part F/S of this Form 1–A. The narrative disclosure contents of offering circulars are specified as follows:

(1)   The information required by:

(i)   the Offering Circular format described below; or

(ii)   The information required by Part I of Form S–1 or Part I of Form S–11, except for the financial statements, selected financial data, and supplementary financial information called for by those forms. An issuer choosing to follow the Form S–1 or Form S–11 format may follow the requirements for smaller reporting companies if it meets the definition of that term in Rule 405. An issuer may only use the Form S–11 format if the offering is eligible to be registered on that form;

The cover page of the offering circular must identify which disclosure format is being followed.

(2)   The offering circular must describe any matters that would have triggered disqualification under Rule 262(a)(3) or (a)(5) but for the provisions set forth in Rule 262(b)(1);

(3)   The legend required by Rule 253(f) of Regulation A must be included on the offering circular cover page (for issuers following the S–1 or S–11 disclosure models this legend must be included instead of the legend required by Item 501(b)(7) of Regulation S–K);

(4)   For preliminary offering circulars, the legend required by Rule 254(a) must be included on the offering circular cover page (for issuers following the S–1 or S–11 disclosure models, this legend must be included instead of the legend required by Item 501(b)(10) of Regulation S–K); and

(5)   For Tier 2 offerings where the securities will not be listed on a registered national securities exchange upon qualification, the offering circular cover page must include the following legend highlighted by prominent type or in another manner:

Generally, no sale may be made to you in this offering if the aggregate purchase price you pay is more than 10% of the greater of your annual income or net worth. Different rules apply to accredited investors and non-natural persons. Before making any representation that your investment does not exceed applicable thresholds, we encourage you to review Rule 251(d)(2)(i)(C) of Regulation A. For general information on investing, we encourage you to refer to *www.investor.gov.*

(b)   The Commission encourages the use of management's projections of future economic performance that have a reasonable basis and are presented in an appropriate format. See Rule 175.

(c)   Offering circulars need not follow the order of the items or the order of other requirements of the disclosure form except to the extent otherwise specifically provided. Such information may not, however, be set forth in such a fashion as to obscure any of the required information or any information necessary to keep the required information from being incomplete or misleading. Information requested to be presented in a specified tabular format must be given in substantially the tabular format specified. For incorporation by reference, please refer to General Instruction III of this Form.

OFFERING CIRCULAR

Item 1.   Cover Page of Offering Circular

The cover page of the offering circular must be limited to one page and must include the information specified in this item.

(a)   Name of the issuer.

Instruction to Item 1(a):

If your name is the same as, or confusingly similar to, that of a company that is well known, include information to eliminate any possible confusion with the other company. If your name indicates a line of business in which you are not engaged or you are engaged only to a limited extent, include information to eliminate any misleading inference as to your business. In some circumstances, disclosure may not be sufficient and you may be required to change your name. You will not be required to change your name if you are an established company, the character of your business has changed, and the investing public is generally aware of the change and the character of your current business.

(b)   Full mailing address of the issuer's principal executive offices and the issuer's telephone number (including the area code) and, if applicable, Web site address.

(c)   Date of the offering circular.

(d)   Title and amount of securities offered. Separately state the amount of securities offered by selling securityholders, if any. Include a cross-reference to the section where the disclosure required by Item 14 of Part II of this Form 1–A has been provided;

(e)   The information called for by the applicable table below as to all the securities being offered, in substantially the tabular format indicated. If necessary, you may estimate any underwriting discounts and commissions and the proceeds to the issuer or other persons.

	Price to public	Underwriting discount and commissions	Proceeds to issuer	Proceeds to other persons
Per share/unit:	_____	_____	_____	_____
Total:	_____	_____	_____	_____

If the securities are to be offered on a best efforts basis, the cover page must set forth the termination date, if any, of the offering, any minimum required sale and any arrangements to place the funds received in an escrow, trust, or similar arrangement. The following table must be used instead of the preceding table.

	Price to public	Underwriting discount and commissions	Proceeds to issuer	Proceeds to other persons
Per share/unit:				
Total Minimum:				
Total Maximum:				

Instructions to Item 1(e):

1. *The term "commissions" includes all cash, securities, contracts, or anything else of value, paid, to be set aside, disposed of, or understandings with or for the benefit of any other persons in which any underwriter is interested, made in connection with the sale of such security.*

2. *Only commissions paid by the issuer in cash are to be indicated in the table. Commissions paid by other persons or any form of non-cash compensation must be briefly identified in a footnote to the table with a cross-reference to a more complete description elsewhere in the offering circular.*

3. *Before the commencement of sales pursuant to Regulation A, the issuer must inform the Commission whether or not the amount of compensation to be allowed or paid to the underwriters, as described in the offering statement, has been cleared with FINRA.*

4. *If the securities are not to be offered for cash, state the basis upon which the offering is to be made.*

5. *Any finder's fees or similar payments must be disclosed on the cover page with a reference to a more complete discussion in the offering circular. Such disclosure must identify the finder, the nature of the services rendered and the nature of any relationship between the finder and the issuer, its officers, directors, promoters, principal stockholders and underwriters (including any affiliates of such persons).*

6. *The amount of the expenses of the offering borne by the issuer, including underwriting expenses to be borne by the issuer, must be disclosed in a footnote to the table.*

(f)   The name of the underwriter or underwriters.

(g)   Any legend or information required by the law of any state in which the securities are to be offered.

(h)   A cross-reference to the risk factors section, including the page number where it appears in the offering circular. Highlight this cross-reference by prominent type or in another manner.

(i)   Approximate date of commencement of proposed sale to the public.

(j)   If the issuer intends to rely on Rule 253(b) and a preliminary offering circular is circulated, provide (1) a bona fide estimate of the range of the maximum offering price and the maximum number of securities offered or (2) a bona fide estimate of the principal amount of the debt securities offered. The range must not exceed $2 for offerings where the upper end of the range is $10 or less and 20% if the upper end of the price range is over $10.

Instruction to Item 1(j):

The upper limit of the price range must be used in determining the aggregate offering price for purposes of Rule 251(a).

Item 2.   Table of Contents

On the page immediately following the cover page of the offering circular, provide a reasonably detailed table of contents. It must show the page numbers of the various sections or subdivisions of the offering circular. Include a specific listing of the risk factors section required by Item 3 of Part II of this Form 1–A.

Item 3. Summary and Risk Factors

(a)   An issuer may provide a summary of the information in the offering circular where the length or complexity of the offering circular makes a summary useful. The summary should be brief and must not contain all of the detailed information in the offering circular.

(b)   Immediately following the Table of Contents required by Item 2 or the Summary, there must be set forth under an appropriate caption, a carefully organized series of short, concise paragraphs, summarizing the most significant factors that make the offering speculative or substantially risky. Issuers should avoid generalized statements and include only factors that are specific to the issuer.

Item 4. Dilution

Where there is a material disparity between the public offering price and the effective cash cost to officers, directors, promoters and affiliated persons for shares acquired by them in a transaction during the past year, or that they have a right to acquire, there must be included a comparison of the public contribution under the proposed public offering and the average effective cash contribution of such persons.

Item 5. Plan of Distribution and Selling Securityholders

(a)   If the securities are to be offered through underwriters, give the names of the principal underwriters, and state the respective amounts underwritten. Identify each such underwriter having a material relationship to the issuer and state the nature of the relationship. State briefly the nature of the underwriters' obligation to take the securities.

Instructions to Item 5(a):

1.   All that is required as to the nature of the underwriters' obligation is whether the underwriters are or will be committed to take and to pay for all of the securities if any are taken, or whether it is merely an agency or the type of best efforts arrangement under which the underwriters are required to take and to pay for only such securities as they may sell to the public. Conditions precedent to the underwriters' taking the securities, including market outs, need not be described except in the case of an agency or best efforts arrangement.

2.   It is not necessary to disclose each member of a selling group. Disclosure may be limited to those underwriters who are in privity of contract with the issuer with respect to the offering.

(b)   State briefly the discounts and commissions to be allowed or paid to dealers, including all cash, securities, contracts or other consideration to be received by any dealer in connection with the sale of the securities.

(c)   Outline briefly the plan of distribution of any securities being issued that are to be offered through the selling efforts of brokers or dealers or otherwise than through underwriters.

(d)   If any of the securities are to be offered for the account of securityholders, identify each selling securityholder, state the amount owned by the securityholder prior to the offering, the amount offered for his or her account and the amount to be owned after the offering. Provide such disclosure in a tabular format. At the bottom of the table, provide the total number of securities being offered for the account of all securityholders and describe what percent of the pre-offering outstanding securities of such class the offering represents.

Instruction to Item 5(d):

The term "securityholder" in this paragraph refers to beneficial holders, not nominee holders or other such holders of record. If the selling securityholder is an entity, disclosure of the persons who have sole or shared voting or investment power must be included.

(e)   Describe any arrangements for the return of funds to subscribers if all of the securities to be offered are not sold. If there are no such arrangements, so state.

(f)   If there will be a material delay in the payment of the proceeds of the offering by the underwriter to the issuer, the salient provisions in this regard and the effects on the issuer must be stated.

(g)   Describe any arrangement to (1) limit or restrict the sale of other securities of the same class as those to be offered for the period of distribution, (2) stabilize the market for any of the securities to be offered, or

(3) withhold commissions, or otherwise to hold each underwriter or dealer responsible for the distribution of its participation.

(h)   Identify any underwriter that intends to confirm sales to any accounts over which it exercises discretionary authority and include an estimate of the amount of securities so intended to be confirmed.

Instruction to Item 5:

Attention is directed to the provisions of Rules 10b 9 and 15c2–4 under the Securities Exchange Act of 1934. These rules outline, among other things, antifraud provisions concerning the return of funds to subscribers and the transmission of proceeds of an offering to a seller.

Item 6.   Use of Proceeds to Issuer

State the principal purposes for which the net proceeds to the issuer from the securities to be offered are intended to be used and the approximate amount intended to be used for each such purpose. If the issuer will not receive any of proceeds from the offering, so state.

Instructions to Item 6:

1.   If any substantial portion of the proceeds has not been allocated for particular purposes, a statement to that effect must be made together with a statement of the amount of proceeds not so allocated.

2.   State whether or not the proceeds will be used to compensate or otherwise make payments to officers or directors of the issuer or any of its subsidiaries.

3.   For best efforts offerings, describe any anticipated material changes in the use of proceeds if all of the securities being qualified on the offering statement are not sold.

4.   If an issuer must provide the disclosure described in Item 9(c) the use of proceeds and plan of operations should be consistent.

5.   If any material amounts of other funds are to be used in conjunction with the proceeds, state the amounts and sources of such other funds and whether such funds are firm or contingent.

6.   If any material part of the proceeds is to be used to discharge indebtedness, describe the material terms of such indebtedness. If the indebtedness to be discharged was incurred within one year, describe the use of the proceeds arising from such indebtedness.

7.   If any material amount of the proceeds is to be used to acquire assets, otherwise than in the ordinary course of business, briefly describe and state the cost of the assets. If the assets are to be acquired from affiliates of the issuer or their associates, give the names of the persons from whom they are to be acquired and set forth the basis used in determining the purchase price to the issuer.

8.   The issuer may reserve the right to change the use of proceeds, so long as the reservation is prominently disclosed in the section where the use of proceeds is discussed. It is not necessary to describe the possible alternative uses of proceeds unless the issuer believes that a change in circumstances leading to an alternative use of proceeds is likely to occur.

Item 7.   Description of Business

(a)   Narrative description of business.

(1)   Describe the business done and intended to be done by the issuer and its subsidiaries and the general development of the business during the past three years or such shorter period as the issuer may have been in business. Such description must include, but not be limited to, a discussion of the following factors if such factors are material to an understanding of the issuer's business:

(i)   The principal products and services of the issuer and the principal market for and method of distribution of such products and services.

(ii)   The status of a product or service if the issuer has made public information about a new product or service that would require the investment of a material amount of the assets of the issuer or is otherwise material.

(iii)   [Removed and Reserved].

(iv)   The total number of persons employed by the issuer, indicating the number employed full time.

(v)   Any bankruptcy, receivership or similar proceeding.

(vi)   Any legal proceedings material to the business or financial condition of the issuer.

(vii) Any material reclassification, merger, consolidation, or purchase or sale of a significant amount of assets not in the ordinary course of business.

(2)   The issuer must also describe those distinctive or special characteristics of the issuer's operation or industry that are reasonably likely to have a material impact upon the issuer's future financial performance. Examples of factors that might be discussed include dependence on one or a few major customers or suppliers (including suppliers of raw materials or financing), effect of existing or probable governmental regulation (including environmental regulation), material terms of and/or expiration of material labor contracts or patents, trademarks, licenses, franchises, concessions or royalty agreements, unusual competitive conditions in the industry, cyclicality of the industry and anticipated raw material or energy shortages to the extent management may not be able to secure a continuing source of supply.

(b)   [Removed and Reserved].

(c)   Industry Guides. The disclosure guidelines in all Securities Act Industry Guides must be followed. To the extent that the industry guides are codified into Regulation S–K, the Regulation S–K industry disclosure items must be followed.

(d)   For offerings of limited partnership or limited liability company interests, an issuer must comply with the Commission's interpretive views on substantive disclosure requirements set forth in Securities Act Release No. 6900 (June 17, 1991).

Item 8. Description of Property

(a)   State briefly the location and general character of any principal plants or other material physical properties of the issuer and its subsidiaries. If any such property is not held in fee or is held subject to any major encumbrance, so state and briefly describe how held. Include information regarding the suitability, adequacy, productive capacity and extent of utilization of the properties and facilities used in the issuer's business.

(b)   Issuers engaged in mining operations must refer to and, if required, provide the disclosure under subpart 1300 of Regulation S–K, in addition to any disclosure required by this Item. Instruction to Item 8: Except as required by paragraph (b) of this Item, detailed descriptions of the physical characteristics of individual properties or legal descriptions by metes and bounds are not required and should not be given.

Instruction to Item 8:

Except as required by paragraph (b) of this Item, detailed descriptions of the physical characteristics of individual properties or legal descriptions by metes and bounds are not required and should not be given.

Item 9. Management's Discussion and Analysis of Financial Condition and Results of Operations

Discuss the issuer's financial condition, changes in financial condition and results of operations for each year and interim period for which financial statements are required, including the causes of material changes from year to year or period to period in financial statement line items, to the extent necessary for an understanding of the issuer's business as a whole. Information provided also must relate to the segment information of the issuer. Provide the information specified below as well as such other information that is necessary for an investor's understanding of the issuer's financial condition, changes in financial condition and results of operations.

(a)   Operating results. Provide information regarding significant factors, including unusual or infrequent events or transactions or new developments, materially affecting the issuer's income from operations, and, in each case, indicating the extent to which income was so affected. Describe any other significant component of revenue or expenses necessary to understand the issuer's results of operations. To the extent that the financial statements disclose material changes in net sales or revenues, provide a narrative discussion of the extent to which such changes are attributable to changes in prices or to changes in the volume or amount of products or services being sold or to the introduction of new products or services.

Instruction to Item 9(a):

1.   *The discussion and analysis shall focus specifically on material events and uncertainties known to management that would cause reported financial information not to be necessarily indicative of future operating results or of future financial condition. This would include descriptions and amounts of (A) matters that would have an impact on future operations that have not had an impact in the past, and (B) matters that have had an impact on reported operations that are not expected to have an impact upon future operations.*

2.   *Where the consolidated financial statements reveal material changes from year to year in one or more line items, the causes for the changes shall be described to the extent necessary to an understanding of the issuer's businesses as a whole. If the causes for a change in one line item also relate to other line items, no repetition is required and a line-by-line analysis of the financial statements as a whole is not required or generally appropriate. Issuers need not recite the amounts of changes from year to year which are readily computable from the financial statements. The discussion must not merely repeat numerical data contained in the consolidated financial statements.*

3.   *When interim period financial statements are included, discuss any material changes in financial condition from the end of the preceding fiscal year to the date of the most recent interim balance sheet provided. Discuss any material changes in the issuer's results of operations with respect to the most recent fiscal year-to-date period for which a statement of comprehensive income (or statement of net income if comprehensive income is presented in two separate but consecutive financial statements or if no other comprehensive income) is provided and the corresponding year-to-date period of the preceding fiscal year.*

(b)   Liquidity and capital resources. Provide information regarding the following:

(1)   the issuer's liquidity (both short and long term), including a description and evaluation of the internal and external sources of liquidity and a brief discussion of any material unused sources of liquidity. If a material deficiency in liquidity is identified, indicate the course of action that the issuer has taken or proposes to take to remedy the deficiency.

(2)   the issuer's material commitments for capital expenditures as of the end of the latest fiscal year and any subsequent interim period and an indication of the general purpose of such commitments and the anticipated sources of funds needed to fulfill such commitments.

(c)   Plan of Operations. Issuers (including predecessors) that have not received revenue from operations during each of the three fiscal years immediately before the filing of the offering statement (or since inception, whichever is shorter) must describe, if formulated, their plan of operation for the 12 months following the commencement of the proposed offering. If such information is not available, the reasons for its unavailability must be stated. Disclosure relating to any plan must include, among other things, a statement indicating whether, in the issuer's opinion, the proceeds from the offering will satisfy its cash requirements or whether it anticipates it will be necessary to raise additional funds in the next six months to implement the plan of operations.

(d)   Trend information. The issuer must identify the most significant recent trends in production, sales and inventory, the state of the order book and costs and selling prices since the latest financial year. The issuer also must discuss, for at least the current financial year, any known trends, uncertainties, demands, commitments or events that are reasonably likely to have a material effect on the issuer's net sales or revenues, income from continuing operations, profitability, liquidity or capital resources, or that would cause reported financial information not necessarily to be indicative of future operating results or financial condition.

Item 10. Directors, Executive Officers and Significant Employees

(a)   For each of the directors, persons nominated or chosen to become directors, executive officers, persons chosen to become executive officers, and significant employees, provide the information specified below in substantially the following tabular format:

Name	Position	Age	Term of Office*	Approximate hours per week for part-time employees**
Executive Officers:				
Directors:				
Significant Employees:				

*Provide the month and year of the start date and, if applicable, the end date. To the extent you are unable to provide specific dates, provide such other description in the table or in an appropriate footnote clarifying the term of office. If the person is a nominee or chosen to become a director or executive officer, it must be indicated in this column or by footnote.

**For executive officers and significant employees that are working part-time, indicate approximately the average number of hours per week or month such person works or is anticipated to work. This column may be left blank for directors. The entire column may be omitted if all those listed in the table work full time for the issuer.

In a footnote to the table, briefly describe any arrangement or understanding between the persons described above and any other persons (naming such persons) pursuant to which the person was or is to be selected to his or her office or position.

Instructions to Item 10(a):

1.   No nominee or person chosen to become a director or person chosen to be an executive officer who has not consented to act as such may be named in response to this item.

2.   The term "executive officer" means the president, secretary, treasurer, any vice president in charge of a principal business function (such as sales, administration, or finance) and any other person who performs similar policy making functions for the issuer.

3.   The term "significant employee" means persons such as production managers, sales managers, or research scientists, who are not executive officers, but who make or are expected to make significant contributions to the business of the issuer.

(b)   Family relationships. State the nature of any family relationship between any director, executive officer, person nominated or chosen by the issuer to become a director or executive officer or any significant employee.

Instruction to Item 10(b):

The term "family relationship" means any relationship by blood, marriage, or adoption, not more remote than first cousin.

(c)   Business experience. Give a brief account of the business experience during the past five years of each director, executive officer, person nominated or chosen to become a director or executive officer, and each significant employee, including his or her principal occupations and employment during that period and the name and principal business of any corporation or other organization in which such occupations and employment were carried on. When an executive officer or significant employee has been employed by the issuer for less than five years, a brief explanation must be included as to the nature of the responsibilities undertaken by the individual in prior positions to provide adequate disclosure of this prior business experience. What is required is information relating to the level of the employee's professional competence, which may include, depending upon the circumstances, such specific information as the size of the operation supervised.

(d)   Involvement in certain legal proceedings. Describe any of the following events which occurred during the past five years and which are material to an evaluation of the ability or integrity of any director, person nominated to become a director or executive officer of the issuer:

(1)   A petition under the federal bankruptcy laws or any state insolvency law was filed by or against, or a receiver, fiscal agent or similar officer was appointed by a court for the business or property of such person, or any partnership in which he was general partner at or within two years before the time of such filing, or

any corporation or business association of which he was an executive officer at or within two years before the time of such filing; or

(2)   Such person was convicted in a criminal proceeding (excluding traffic violations and other minor offenses).

Item 11. Compensation of Directors and Executive Officers

(a)   Provide, in substantially the tabular format indicated, the annual compensation of each of the three highest paid persons who were executive officers or directors during the issuer's last completed fiscal year.

Name	Capacities in which compensation was received (e.g., Chief Executive Officer, director, etc.)	Cash compensation ($)	Other compensation ($)	Total compensation ($)

(b)   Provide the aggregate annual compensation of the issuer's directors as a group for the issuer's last completed fiscal year. Specify the total number of directors in the group.

(c)   For Tier 1 offerings, the annual compensation of the three highest paid persons who were executive officers or directors and the aggregate annual compensation of the issuer's directors may be provided as a group, rather than as specified in paragraphs (a) and (b) of this item. In such case, issuers must specify the total number of persons in the group.

(d)   Briefly describe all proposed compensation to be made in the future pursuant to any ongoing plan or arrangement to the individuals specified in paragraphs (a) and (b) of this item. The description must include a summary of how each plan operates, any performance formula or measure in effect (or the criteria used to determine payment amounts), the time periods over which the measurements of benefits will be determined, payment schedules, and any recent material amendments to the plan. Information need not be included with respect to any group life, health, hospitalization, or medical reimbursement plans that do not discriminate in scope, terms or operation in favor of executive officers or directors of the issuer and that are available generally to all salaried employees.

Instructions to Item 11:

1.   In case of compensation paid or to be paid otherwise than in cash, if it is impracticable to determine the cash value thereof, state in a note to the table the nature and amount thereof.

2.   This item is to be answered on an accrual basis if practicable; if not so answered, state the basis used.

Item 12. Security Ownership of Management and Certain Securityholders

(a)   Include the information specified in paragraph (b) of this item as of the most recent practicable date (stating the date used), in substantially the tabular format indicated, with respect to voting securities beneficially owned by:

(1)   all executive officers and directors as a group, individually naming each director or executive officer who beneficially owns more than 10% of any class of the issuer's voting securities;

(2)   any other securityholder who beneficially owns more than 10% of any class of the issuer's voting securities as such beneficial ownership would be calculated if the issuer were subject to Rule 13d–3(d)(1) of the Securities Exchange Act of 1934.

(b)   Beneficial Ownership Table:

Title of class	Name and address of beneficial owner[1]	Amount and nature of beneficial ownership	Amount and nature of beneficial ownership acquirable[2]	Percent of class[3]

(1)   The address given in this column may be a business, mailing, or residential address. The address may be included in an appropriate footnote to the table rather than in this column.

(2)   This column must include the amount of equity securities each beneficial owner has the right to acquire using the manner specified in Rule 13d–3(d)(1) of the Securities Exchange Act of 1934. An appropriate footnote must be included if the column heading does not sufficiently describe the circumstances upon which such securities could be acquired.

(3)   This column must use the amounts contained in the two preceding columns to calculate the percent of class owned by such beneficial owner.

Item 13. Interest of Management and Others in Certain Transactions

(a)   Describe briefly any transactions or any currently proposed transactions during the issuer's last two completed fiscal years and the current fiscal year, to which the issuer or any of its subsidiaries was or is to be a participant and the amount involved exceeds $50,000 for Tier 1 or the lesser of $120,000 and one percent of the average of the issuer's total assets at year end for the last two completed fiscal years for Tier 2, and in which any of the following persons had or is to have a direct or indirect material interest, naming the person and stating his or her relationship to the issuer, the nature of the person's interest in the transaction and, where practicable, the amount of such interest:

(1)   Any director or executive officer of the issuer;

(2)   Any nominee for election as a director;

(3)   Any securityholder named in answer to Item 12(a)(2);

(4)   If the issuer was incorporated or organized within the past three years, any promoter of the issuer; or

(5)   Any immediate family member of the above persons. An "immediate family member" of a person means such person's child, stepchild, parent, stepparent, spouse, sibling, mother-in-law, father-in-law, son-in-law, daughter-in-law, brother-in-law, sister-in-law, or any person (other than a tenant or employee) sharing such person's household.

Instructions to Item 13(a):

1.   For purposes of calculating the amount of the transaction described above, all periodic installments in the case of any lease or other agreement providing for periodic payments must be aggregated to the extent they occurred within the time period described in this item.

2.   No information need be given in answer to this item as to any transaction where:

(a)   The rates of charges involved in the transaction are determined by competitive bids, or the transaction involves the rendering of services as a common or contract carrier at rates or charges fixed in conformity with law or governmental authority;

(b)   The transaction involves services as a bank depositary of funds, transfer agent, registrar, trustee under a trust indenture, or similar services;

(c)   The interest of the specified person arises solely from the ownership of securities of the issuer and the specified person receives no extra or special benefit not shared on a pro-rata basis by all of the holders of securities of the class.

3.   This item calls for disclosure of indirect as well as direct material interests in transactions. A person who has a position or relationship with a firm, corporation, or other entity which engages in a transaction with the issuer or its subsidiaries may have an indirect interest in such transaction by reason of the position or relationship. However, a person is deemed not to have a material indirect interest in a transaction within the meaning of this item where:

(a)   the interest arises only (i) from the person's position as a director of another corporation or organization (other than a partnership) that is a party to the transaction, or (ii) from the direct or indirect ownership by the person and all other persons specified in paragraphs (1) through (5) of this item, in the aggregate, of less than a 10 percent equity interest in another person (other than a partnership) that is a party to the transaction, or (iii) from both such position and ownership;

(b)   the interest arises only from the person's position as a limited partner in a partnership in which the person and all other persons specified in paragraphs (1) through (5) of this item had an interest of less than 10 percent; or

(c)   the interest of the person arises solely from the holding of an equity interest (unless the equity interest confers management rights similar to a general partner interest) or a creditor interest in another person that is a party to the transaction with the issuer or any of its subsidiaries and the transaction is not material to the other person.

4.   Include the name of each person whose interest in any transaction is described and the nature of the relationships by reason of which such interest is required to be described. The amount of the interest of any specified person must be computed without regard to the amount of the profit or loss involved in the transaction. Where it is not practicable to state the approximate amount of the interest, the approximate amount involved in the transaction must be disclosed.

5.   Information must be included as to any material underwriting discounts and commissions upon the sale of securities by the issuer where any of the specified persons was or is to be a principal underwriter or is a controlling person, or member, of a firm which was or is to be a principal underwriter. Information need not be given concerning ordinary management fees paid by underwriters to a managing underwriter pursuant to an agreement among underwriters, the parties to which do not include the issuer or its subsidiaries.

6.   As to any transaction involving the purchase or sale of assets by or to any issuer or any subsidiary, otherwise than in the ordinary course of business, state the cost of the assets to the purchaser and, if acquired by the seller within two years before the transaction, the cost to the seller.

7.   Information must be included in answer to this item with respect to transactions not excluded above which involve compensation from the issuer or its subsidiaries, directly or indirectly, to any of the specified persons for services in any capacity unless the interest of such persons arises solely from the ownership individually and in the aggregate of less than 10 percent of any class of equity securities of another corporation furnishing the services to the issuer or its subsidiaries.

(b)   If any expert named in the offering statement as having prepared or certified any part of the offering statement was employed for such purpose on a contingent basis or, at the time of such preparation or certification or at any time thereafter, had a material interest in the issuer or any of its parents or subsidiaries or was connected with the issuer or any of its subsidiaries as a promoter, underwriter, voting trustee, director, officer or employee, describe the nature of such contingent basis, interest or connection.

Item 14. Securities Being Offered

(a)   If capital stock is being offered, state the title of the class and furnish the following information regarding all classes of capital stock outstanding:

(1)   Outline briefly: (i) dividend rights; (ii) voting rights; (iii) liquidation rights; (iv) preemptive rights; (v) conversion rights; (vi) redemption provisions; (vii) sinking fund provisions; (viii) liability to further calls or to assessment by the issuer; (ix) any classification of the Board of Directors, and the impact of classification where cumulative voting is permitted or required; (x) restrictions on alienability of the securities being offered; (xi) any provision discriminating against any existing or prospective holder of such securities as a result of such securityholder owning a substantial amount of securities; and (xii) any rights of holders that may be modified otherwise than by a vote of a majority or more of the shares outstanding, voting as a class.

(2)   Briefly describe potential liabilities imposed on securityholders under state statutes or foreign law, for example, to employees of the issuer, unless such disclosure would be immaterial because the financial resources of the issuer or other factors are such as to make it unlikely that the liability will ever be imposed.

(3)   If preferred stock is to be offered or is outstanding, describe briefly any restriction on the repurchase or redemption of shares by the issuer while there is any arrearage in the payment of dividends or sinking fund installments. If there is no such restriction, so state.

(b)   If debt securities are being offered, outline briefly the following:

(1)   Provisions with respect to interest, conversion, maturity, redemption, amortization, sinking fund or retirement.

(2)   Provisions with respect to the kind and priority of any lien securing the issue, together with a brief identification of the principal properties subject to such lien.

(3)   Material affirmative and negative covenants.

Instruction to Item 14(b):

In the case of secured debt there must be stated: (i) the approximate amount of unbonded property available for use against the issuance of bonds, as of the most recent practicable date, and (ii) whether the securities being issued are to be issued against such property, against the deposit of cash, or otherwise.

(c)   If securities described are to be offered pursuant to warrants, rights, or convertible securities, state briefly:

(1)   the amount of securities issuable upon the exercise or conversion of such warrants, convertible securities or rights;

(2)   the period during which and the price at which the warrants, convertible securities or rights are exercisable;

(3)   the amounts of warrants, convertible securities or rights outstanding; and

(4)   any other material terms of such securities.

(d)   In the case of any other kind of securities, include a brief description with comparable information to that required in (a), (b) and (c) of Item 14.

Part F/S

(a)   General Rules

(1)   The appropriate financial statements set forth below of the issuer, or the issuer and its predecessors or any businesses to which the issuer is a successor must be filed as part of the offering statement and included in the offering circular that is distributed to investors.

(2)   Unless the issuer is a Canadian company, financial statements must be prepared in accordance with generally accepted accounting principles in the United States (US GAAP). If the issuer is a Canadian company, such financial statements must be prepared in accordance with either US GAAP or International Financial Reporting Standards (IFRS) as issued by the International Accounting Standards Board (IASB). If the financial statements comply with IFRS, such compliance must be explicitly and unreservedly stated in the notes to the financial statements and if the financial statements are audited, the auditor's report must include an opinion on whether the financial statements comply with IFRS as issued by the IASB.

(3)   The issuer may elect to delay complying with any new or revised financial accounting standard until the date that a company that is not an issuer (as defined under section 2(a) of the Sarbanes-Oxley Act of 2002) is required to comply with such new or revised accounting standard, if such standard also applies to companies that are not issuers. Issuers electing such extension of time accommodation must disclose it at the time the issuer files its offering statement and apply the election to all standards. Issuers electing not to use this accommodation must forgo this accommodation for all financial accounting standards and may not elect to rely on this accommodation in any future filings.

(b)   Financial Statements for Tier 1 Offerings

(1)   The financial statements prepared pursuant to this paragraph (b), including (b)(7), need not be prepared in accordance with Regulation S–X.

(2)   The financial statements prepared pursuant to paragraph (b), including (b)(7), need not be audited. If the financial statements are not audited, they shall be labeled as "unaudited". However, if an audit of these financial statements is obtained for other purposes and that audit was performed in accordance with either U.S. generally accepted auditing standards or the Standards of the Public Company Accounting Oversight Board by an auditor that is independent pursuant to either the independence standards of the American Institute of Certified Public Accountants (AICPA) or Rule 2–01 of Regulation S–X, those audited financial statements must be filed, and an audit opinion complying with Rule 2–02 of Regulation S–X must be filed along with such financial statements. The auditor may, but need not, be registered with the Public Company Accounting Oversight Board.

(3)   *Consolidated Balance Sheets.* Age of balance sheets at filing and at qualification:

(A)   If the filing is made, or the offering statement is qualified, more than three months but no more than nine months after the most recently completed fiscal year end, include a balance sheet as of the two most recently completed fiscal year ends.

(B)   If the filing is made, or the offering statement is qualified, more than nine months after the most recently completed fiscal year end, include a balance sheet as of the two most recently completed fiscal year ends and an interim balance sheet as of a date no earlier than six months after the most recently completed fiscal year end.

(C)   If the filing is made, or the offering statement is qualified, within three months after the most recently completed fiscal year end, include a balance sheet as of the two fiscal year ends preceding the most recently completed fiscal year end and an interim balance sheet as of a date no earlier than six months after the date of the most recent fiscal year end balance sheet that is required.

(D)   If the filing is made, or the offering statement is qualified, during the period from inception until three months after reaching the annual balance sheet date for the first time, include a balance sheet as of a date within nine months of filing or qualification.

(4)   Statements of comprehensive income, cash flows, and changes in stockholders' equity. File consolidated statements of comprehensive income (either in a single continuous financial statement or in two separate but consecutive financial statements; or a statement of net income if there was no other comprehensive income), cash flows, and changes in stockholders' equity for each of the two fiscal years preceding the date of the most recent balance sheet being filed or such shorter period as the issuer has been in existence.

(5)   *Interim financial statements.*

(i)   If a consolidated interim balance sheet is required by (b)(3) of Part F/S, consolidated interim statements of comprehensive income (either in a single continuous financial statement or in two separate but consecutive financial statements; or a statement of net income if there was no other comprehensive income) and cash flows shall be provided and must cover at least the first six months of the issuer's fiscal year and the corresponding period of the preceding fiscal year. An analysis of the changes in each caption of stockholders' equity presented in the balance sheets must be provided in a note or separate statement. This analysis shall be presented in the form of a reconciliation of the beginning balance to the ending balance for each period for which a statement of comprehensive income is required to be filed with all significant reconciling items described by appropriate captions with contributions from and distributions to owners shown separately. Dividends per share for each class of shares shall also be provided.

(ii)   Interim financial statements of issuers that report under U.S. GAAP may be condensed as described in Rule 8–03(a) of Regulation S–X.

(iii)   The interim statements of comprehensive income for all issuers must be accompanied by a statement that in the opinion of management all adjustments necessary in order to make the interim financial statements not misleading have been included.

(6)   *Oil and Gas Producing Activities.* Issuers engaged in oil and gas producing activities must follow the financial accounting and reporting standards specified in Rule 4–10 of Regulation S–X.

(7)   *Financial Statements of Other Entities.* The circumstances described below may require you to file financial statements of other entities in the offering statement. The financial statements of other entities must be presented for the same periods as if the other entity was the issuer as described above in paragraphs

(b)(3) and (b)(4) unless a shorter period is specified by the rules below. The financial statement of other entities shall follow the same audit requirement as paragraph (b)(2) of this Part F/S.

(i)   *Financial Statements of Guarantors and Issuers of Guaranteed Securities.* Financial statements of a subsidiary that issues securities guaranteed by the parent or guarantees securities issued by the parent must be presented as required by Rule 3–10 of Regulation S–X.

(ii)   *Financial Statements of Affiliates Whose Securities Collateralize an Issuance.* Financial statements for an issuer's affiliates whose securities constitute a substantial portion of the collateral for any class of securities being offered must be presented as required by Rule 3–16 of Regulation S–X.

(iii) *Financial Statements of Businesses Acquired or to be Acquired.* File the financial statements required by Rule 8–04 of Regulation S–X.

(iv)   *Pro Forma Financial Information.* If financial statements are presented under paragraph (b)(7)(iii) above, file pro forma information showing the effects of the acquisition as described in Rule 8–05 of Regulation S–X.

(v)   *Real Estate Operations Acquired or to be Acquired.* File the financial information required by Rule 8–06 of Regulation S–X.

Instructions to paragraph (b) in Part F/S:

1.   *Issuers should refer to Rule 257(b)(2) to determine whether a special financial report will be required after qualification of the offering statement.*

2.   *If the last day that the financial statements included in the offering statement can be accepted, according to the age requirements of this item falls on a Saturday, Sunday, or holiday, such offering statement may be filed on the first business day following the last day of the specified period.*

3.   *As an alternative, an issuer may—but need not—elect to comply with the provisions of paragraph (c).*

(c) **Financial Statement Requirements for Tier 2 Offerings**

(1) In addition to the general rules in paragraph (a), provide the financial statements required by paragraph (b) of this Part F/S, except the following rules should be followed in the preparation of the financial statements:

(i)   Issuers that report under U.S. GAAP and, when applicable, other entities for which financial statements are required, must comply with Article 8 of Regulation S–X, as if they were conducting a registered offering on Form S–1, except the age of financial statements may follow paragraphs (b)(3)–(4) of this Part F/S.

(ii)   Audited financial statements are required for Tier 2 offerings for the issuer and, when applicable, for financial statements of other entities. However, interim financial statements may be unaudited.

(iii) The audit must be conducted in accordance with either U.S. Generally Accepted Auditing Standards or the standards of the Public Company Accounting Oversight Board (United States) and the report and qualifications of the independent accountant shall comply with the requirements of Article 2 of Regulation S–X. Accounting firms conducting audits for the financial statements included in the offering circular may, but need not, be registered with the Public Company Accounting Oversight Board.

PART III—EXHIBITS

Item 16. Index to Exhibits

(a)   An exhibits index must be presented at the beginning of Part III.

(b)   Each exhibit must be listed in the exhibit index according to the number assigned to it under Item 17 below.

(c)   For incorporation by reference, please refer to General Instruction III of this Form.

Item 17. Description of Exhibits

As appropriate, the following documents must be filed as exhibits to the offering statement.

1. *Underwriting agreement*—Each underwriting contract or agreement with a principal underwriter or letter pursuant to which the securities are to be distributed; where the terms have yet to be finalized, proposed formats may be provided.

2. *Charter and bylaws*—The charter and bylaws of the issuer or instruments corresponding thereto as currently in effect and any amendments thereto.

3. *Instruments defining the rights of securityholders*—

(a) All instruments defining the rights of any holder of the issuer's securities, including but not limited to (i) holders of equity or debt securities being issued; (ii) holders of long-term debt of the issuer, and of all subsidiaries for which consolidated or unconsolidated financial statements are required to be filed.

(b) The following instruments need not be filed if the issuer agrees to file them with the Commission upon request: (i) instruments defining the rights of holders of long-term debt of the issuer and all of its subsidiaries for which consolidated financial statements are required to be filed if such debt is not being issued pursuant to this Regulation A offering and the total amount of such authorized issuance does not exceed 5% of the total assets of the issuer and its subsidiaries on a consolidated basis; (ii) any instrument with respect to a class of securities that is to be retired or redeemed before the issuance or upon delivery of the securities being issued pursuant to this Regulation A offering and appropriate steps have been taken to assure such retirement or redemption; and (iii) copies of instruments evidencing scrip certificates or fractions of shares.

4. *Subscription agreement*—The form of any subscription agreement to be used in connection with the purchase of securities in this offering.

5. *Voting trust agreement*—Any voting trust agreements and amendments.

6. *Material contracts*

(a) Every contract not made in the ordinary course of business that is material to the issuer and is to be performed in whole or in part at or after the filing of the offering statement or was entered into not more than two years before such filing. Only contracts need be filed as to which the issuer or subsidiary of the issuer is a party or has succeeded to a party by assumption or assignment or in which the issuer or such subsidiary has a beneficial interest. Schedules (or similar attachments) to material contracts may be excluded if not material to an investment decision or if the material information contained in such schedules is otherwise disclosed in the agreement or the offering statement. The material contract filed must contain a list briefly identifying the contents of all omitted schedules, together with an agreement to furnish supplementally a copy of any omitted schedule to the Commission upon request.

(b) If the contract is such as ordinarily accompanies the kind of business conducted by the issuer and its subsidiaries, it is made in the ordinary course of business and need not be filed unless it falls within one or more of the following categories, in which case it must be filed except where immaterial in amount or significance: (i) any contract to which directors, officers, promoters, voting trustees, securityholders named in the offering statement, or underwriters are parties, except where the contract merely involves the purchase or sale of current assets having a determinable market price, at such market price; (ii) any contract upon which the issuer's business is substantially dependent, as in the case of continuing contracts to sell the major part of the issuer's products or services or to purchase the major part of the issuer's requirements of goods, services or raw materials or any franchise or license or other agreement to use a patent, formula, trade secret, process or trade name upon which the issuer's business depends to a material extent; (iii) any contract calling for the acquisition or sale of any property, plant or equipment for a consideration exceeding 15% of such fixed assets of the issuer on a consolidated basis; or (iv) any material lease under which a part of the property described in the offering statement is held by the issuer.

(c) Any management contract or any compensatory plan, contract or arrangement including, but not limited to, plans relating to options, warrants or rights, pension, retirement or deferred compensation or bonus, incentive or profit sharing (or if not set forth in any formal document, a written description) is deemed material and must be filed except for the following: (i) ordinary purchase and sales agency agreements; (ii) agreements with managers of stores in a chain organization or similar organization; (iii) contracts providing for labor or salesperson's bonuses or payments to a class of securityholders, as such; (iv) any compensatory plan, contract or arrangement that pursuant to its terms is available to employees generally and that in operation provides for the same method of allocation of benefits between management and non-management participants.

7. *Plan of acquisition, reorganization, arrangement, liquidation, or succession*—Any material plan of acquisition, disposition, reorganization, readjustment, succession, liquidation or arrangement and any amendments thereto described in the offering statement. Schedules (or similar attachments) to these exhibits must not be filed unless such schedules contain information that is material to an investment decision and that is not otherwise disclosed in the agreement or the offering statement. The plan filed must contain a list briefly identifying the contents of all omitted schedules, together with an agreement to furnish supplementally a copy of any omitted schedule to the Commission upon request.

8. *Escrow agreements*—Any escrow agreement or similar arrangement which has been executed in connection with the Regulation A offering.

9. *Letter re change in certifying accountant*—A letter from the issuer's former independent accountant regarding its concurrence or disagreement with the statements made by the issuer in the current report concerning the resignation or dismissal as the issuer's principal accountant.

10. *Power of attorney*—If any name is signed to the offering statement pursuant to a power of attorney, signed copies of the power of attorney must be filed. Where the power of attorney is contained elsewhere in the offering statement or documents filed therewith, a reference must be made in the index to the part of the offering statement or document containing such power of attorney. In addition, if the name of any officer signing on behalf of the issuer is signed pursuant to a power of attorney, certified copies of a resolution of the issuer's board of directors authorizing such signature must also be filed. A power of attorney that is filed with the Commission must relate to a specific filing or an amendment thereto. A power of attorney that confers general authority may not be filed with the Commission.

11. *Consents*—

(a) Experts: The written consent of (i) any accountant, counsel, engineer, geologist, appraiser or any persons whose profession gives authority to a statement made by them and who is named in the offering statement as having prepared or certified any part of the document or is named as having prepared or certified a report or evaluation whether or not for use in connection with the offering statement; (ii) the expert that authored any portion of a report quoted or summarized as such in the offering statement, expressly stating their consent to the use of such quotation or summary; (iii) any persons who are referenced as having reviewed or passed upon any information in the offering statement, and that such information is being included on the basis of their authority or in reliance upon their status as experts.

(b) All written consents must be dated and signed.

12. *Opinion re legality*—An opinion of counsel as to the legality of the securities covered by the Offering Statement, indicating whether they will when sold, be legally issued, fully paid and non-assessable, and if debt securities, whether they will be binding obligations of the issuer.

13. *"Testing the waters" materials*—Any written communication or broadcast script used under the authorization of Rule 241 within 30 days of the initial filing of the offering statement, and any written communication or broadcast script used under the authorization of Rule 255. Materials used under the authorization of Rule 255 need not be filed if they are substantively the same as materials previously filed with the offering statement.

14. *Appointment of agent for service of process*—A Canadian issuer must file Form F–X.

15. The technical report summary under Item 601(b)(96) of Regulation S–K—An issuer that is required to file a technical report summary pursuant to Item 1302(b)(2) of Regulation S–K must provide the information specified in Item 601(b)(96) of Regulation S–K as an exhibit to Form 1–A.

16. [Reserved].

SIGNATURES

Pursuant to the requirements of Regulation A, the issuer certifies that it has reasonable grounds to believe that it meets all of the requirements for filing on Form 1–A and has duly caused this offering statement to be signed on its behalf by the undersigned, thereunto duly authorized, in the City of ____, State of ____, on ____(date).

(Exact name of issuer as specified in its charter) _____

By (Signature and Title) _____

This offering statement has been signed by the following persons in the capacities and on the dates indicated.

(Signature) _____

(Title) _____

(Date) _____

Instructions to Signatures:

1.   *The offering statement must be signed by the issuer, its principal executive officer, principal financial officer, principal accounting officer, and a majority of the members of its board of directors or other governing body. If a signature is by a person on behalf of any other person, evidence of authority to sign must be filed with the offering statement, except where an executive officer signs on behalf of the issuer.*

2.   *The offering statement must be signed using a typed signature. Each signatory to the filing must also manually sign a signature page or other document authenticating, acknowledging or otherwise adopting his or her signature that appears in the filing. Such document must be executed before or at the time the filing is made and must be retained by the issuer for a period of five years. Upon request, the issuer must furnish to the Commission or its staff a copy of any or all documents retained pursuant to this rule.*

3.   *The name and title of each person signing the offering statement must be typed or printed beneath the signature.*

FORM 2-A

17 C.F.R. § 239.91

SECURITIES AND EXCHANGE COMMISSION

REPORT OF SALES AND USES OF PROCEEDS
PURSUANT TO RULE 257 OF REGULATION A
FILE NO. 24-_____-__

For period ending __/__/__

      Indicate whether the report is an   initial report   [   ]

                                      amendment   [   ]

                                or final report   [   ]

      If the report is an amendment, indicate the number of such amendment. __/__/__/

        If the offering has terminated, indicate the date of termination __/__/__

General Instructions:

      The report shall be filed in accordance with the provisions of Rule 257 of Regulation A.

      Answer each item in the box(es) or spaces provided. If additional space is required for any response, continue the response on an attached sheet.

      If the issuer is required to file any report(s) on this form subsequent to its initial filing, each subsequent filing shall be deemed to be an amendment to the initial filing. Do not report in any amendment responses to Items 3–11 unless the information has changed.

      No fee is required to accompany this filing.

      Seven copies of the form shall be filed with the Commission in Washington, D.C. At least one copy of the form shall be manually signed; other copies may bear typed or printed signatures.

1.   _____

           Exact name of issuer as specified in its charter.

2.   Date of qualification of the offering statement:

             □□   □□   □□

3.   Has the offering commenced?   [ ] Yes [ ] No.

     If yes, date of commencement: □□   □□   □□

     If no, explain briefly:

_____

_____

_____

4.   Did the offering terminate before any securities were sold?   [   ] Yes [   ] No.

     If yes, explain briefly:

_____

_____

If "yes", do not answer Items 5–11.

5. Did the offering terminate prior to the sale of all the securities qualified under Regulation A?
   [   ] Yes [   ] No.

   If yes, explain briefly:

   ---

6. Indicate the total number of shares or other units offered and sold to date:

   _____ (issuer's account) _____ (selling securityholders)

   Indicate the number of shares or other units still being offered:

   _____ (issuer's account) _____ (selling securityholders)

7. Total amount of dollars received from the public to date: $_____

   Total amount allocable to selling securityholders: $_____

Underwriting discount or commission allowed	$_____
Underwriting expenses paid	$_____
Finders' fees	$_____
Other expenses paid to date by or for issuer:	
Legal (including organization)	$_____
Accounting	$_____
Engineering	$_____
Printing and advertising	$_____
Other (specify) _____	$_____
_____	$_____
_____	$_____
_____	$_____
Total costs and expenses	$_____
Total net proceeds remaining.	$_____

8. Uses of net proceeds to date:

   Instructions:

   1. Do not include any amount in "working capital" to which a more specific category is applicable.

   2. Round all amounts to the nearest dollar.

   3. Specify under "other purposes" any purpose for which at least 5% of the issuer's proceeds or $50,000, whichever is less, has been used.

Salaries and fees	$_____
Construction of plant, building and facilities	$_____

Purchases and installation of machinery and equipment $ _____

Purchase of real estate $ _____

Acquisition of other business(es) $ _____

Repayment of indebtedness $ _____

Working capital $ _____

Development expense (product development, research, patent costs, etc.) $ _____

Temporary investment (specify) _____ $ _____

_____ $ _____

_____ $ _____

Other purposes (specify)

_____ $ _____

_____ $ _____

_____ $ _____

_____ $ _____

_____ $ _____

_____ $ _____

_____ $ _____

_____ $ _____

9.   Do the use(s) of proceeds in Item 8 represent a material change in the use(s) of proceeds described in the offering circular?   [   ]   Yes [   ]   No.

If yes, explain briefly:

_____

_____

10.   State the number of shares held by each promoter, director, officer or controlling person of the issuer, if different from the amount stated in the offering circular.

_____

_____

11.   List the names and addresses of all brokers and dealers who have, to the knowledge of the issuer or underwriters, participated in the distribution of the securities during the period covered by this report.

_____

_____

SIGNATURE

Pursuant to the requirements of Rule 257 and Regulation A, _____ _____ has caused this report to be signed on its behalf by the undersigned thereunto duly authorized.

1933 ACT FORMS

_____

Issuer

By_____

_____

Date

Signature

Instruction:

The report shall be signed by an executive officer, general partner or counsel of the issuer or by any other duly authorized person. The name and any title of the person who signs the report shall be typed or printed beneath the signature.

FORM 144

NOTICE OF PROPOSED SALE OF SECURITIES
PURSUANT TO RULE 144

(a)   Except as indicated in paragraph (b) of this rule, this form shall be filed in triplicate with the Commission at its principal office in Washington, DC, by each person who intends to sell securities in reliance upon Rule 144 of this Act and shall be transmitted for filing concurrently with either the placing with a broker of an order to execute a sale of securities or the execution directly with a market maker of a sale of securities.

(b)   This form need not be filed if the amount of securities to be sold during any period of three months does not exceed 5,000 shares or other units and the aggregate sale price does not exceed $50,000.

(c)   Under sections 2(11), 4(1), 4(2), 4(4) and 19(a) of the Securities Act of 1933 and Rule 144 thereunder, the Commission is authorized to solicit the information required to be supplied by this form by persons desiring to sell unregistered securities. Disclosure of the information specified in this form is mandatory before processing notices of proposed sale of securities under Rule 144 of this Act. The information will be used for the primary purpose of disclosing the proposed sale of unregistered securities by persons deemed not to be engaged in the distribution of securities. This notice will be made a matter of public record. Therefore, any information given will be available for inspection by any member of the public. Because of the public nature of the information, the Commission can utilize it for a variety of purposes, including referral to other governmental authorities or securities self-regulatory organizations for investigatory purposes or in connection with litigation involving the Federal securities laws or other civil, criminal or regulatory statutes or provisions. Failure to disclose the information requested by Form 144 would make an exception under Rule 144 of this Act unavailable and may result in civil or criminal action for violations of the Federal securities laws.

OMB APPROVAL

OMB Number: 3235-0101
Expires: December 31, 2009
Estimated average burden hours per response 2.00

SEC USE ONLY

DOCUMENT SEQUENCE NO.

CUSIP NUMBER

WORK LOCATION

UNITED STATES
SECURITIES AND EXCHANGE COMMISSION
Washington, D.C. 20549

FORM 144

NOTICE OF PROPOSED SALE OF SECURITIES
PURSUANT TO RULE 144 UNDER THE SECURITIES ACT OF 1933

ATTENTION: *Transmit for filing 3 copies of this form concurrently with either placing an order with a broker to execute sale or executing a sale directly with a market maker.*

1 (a) NAME OF ISSUER *(Please type or print)*	(b) IRS IDENT. NO.	(c) S.E.C. FILE NO.

1 (d) ADDRESS OF ISSUER	STREET	CITY	STATE	ZIP CODE

2 (a) NAME OF PERSON FOR WHOSE ACCOUNT THE SECURITIES ARE TO BE SOLD	(b) RELATIONSHIP TO ISSUER	ADDRESS STREET	CITY	STATE	ZIP CODE
				(e) TELEPHONE NO. AREA CODE NUMBER	

INSTRUCTION: *The person filing this notice should contact the issuer to obtain the I.R.S. Identification Number and the S.E.C. File Number.*

3 (a) Title of the Class of Securities To Be Sold	(b) Name and Address of Each Broker Through Whom the Securities are to be Offered or Each Market Maker who is Acquiring the Securities	(c) Number of Shares or Other Units To Be Sold *(See instr. 3(b))*		(d) Aggregate Market Value *(See instr. 3(d))*	(e) Number of Shares or Other Units Outstanding *(See instr. 3(d))*	(f) Approximate Date of Sale *(See instr. 3(f))* (MO. DAY. YR.)	Name of Each Securities Exchange *(See instr. 3(g))*
		SEC USE ONLY					
		Broker-Dealer File Number					

3. (a) Title of the class of securities to be sold
   (b) Name and address of each broker through whom the securities are intended to be sold
   (c) Number of shares or other units to be sold (if debt securities, give the aggregate face amount)
   (d) Aggregate market value of the securities to be sold as of a specified date within 10 days prior to the filing of this notice
   (e) Number of shares or other units of the class outstanding, or if debt securities the face amount thereof outstanding, as shown by the most recent report or statement published by the issuer
   (f) Approximate date on which the securities are to be sold
   (g) Name of each securities exchange, if any, on which the securities are intended to be sold

INSTRUCTIONS:

1. (a) Name of issuer
   (b) Issuer's I.R.S. Identification Number
   (c) Issuer's S.E.C. file number, if any
   (d) Issuer's address, including zip code
   (e) Issuer's telephone number, including area code

2. (a) Name of person for whose account the securities are to be sold
   (b) Such person's relationship to the issuer (e.g., officer, director, 10% stockholder, or member of immediate family of any of the foregoing)
   (c) Such person's address, including zip code

SEC 1147 (08-07)

FORM 144

TABLE I — SECURITIES TO BE SOLD

Furnish the following information with respect to the acquisition of the securities to be sold and with respect to the payment of all or any part of the purchase price or other consideration therefor:

Title of the Class	Date you Acquired	Nature of Acquisition Transaction	Name of Person from Whom Acquired (If gift, also give date donor acquired)	Amount of Securities Acquired	Date of Payment	Nature of Payment

INSTRUCTIONS: If the securities were purchased and full payment therefor was not made in cash at the time of purchase, explain in the table or in a note thereto the nature of the consideration given. If the consideration consisted of any note or other obligation, or if payment was made in installments describe the arrangement and state when the note or other obligation was discharged in full or the last installment paid.

TABLE II — SECURITIES SOLD DURING THE PAST 3 MONTHS

Furnish the following information as to all securities of the issuer sold during the past 3 months by the person for whose account the securities are to be sold.

Name and Address of Seller	Title of Securities Sold	Date of Sale	Amount of Securities Sold	Gross Proceeds

REMARKS:

INSTRUCTIONS:
See the definition of "person" in paragraph (a) of Rule 144. Information is to be given not only as to the person for whose account the securities are to be sold but also as to all other persons included in that definition. In addition, information shall be given as to sales by all persons whose sales are required by paragraph (e) of Rule 144 to be aggregated with sales for the account of the person filing this notice.

ATTENTION:
The person for whose account the securities to which this notice relates are to be sold hereby represents by signing this notice that he does not know any material adverse information in regard to the current and prospective operations of the Issuer of the securities to be sold which has not been publicly disclosed. If such person has adopted a written trading plan or given trading instructions to satisfy Rule 10b5-1 under the Exchange Act, by signing the form and indicating the date that the plan was adopted or the instruction given, that person makes such representation as of the plan adoption or instruction date.

_____
(SIGNATURE)

_____
DATE OF NOTICE

_____
DATE OF PLAN ADOPTION OR GIVING OF INSTRUCTION,
IF RELYING ON RULE 10B5-1

The notice shall be signed by the person for whose account the securities are to be sold. At least one copy of the notice shall be manually signed. Any copies not manually signed shall bear typed or printed signatures.

ATTENTION: Intentional misstatements or omission of facts constitute Federal Criminal Violations (See 18 U.S.C. 1001)

SEC 1147 (04-07)

353

FORM C

17 C.F.R. § 239.900

FILING UNDER REGULATION CROWDFUNDING
UNDER THE SECURITIES ACT OF 1933

(Mark one.)

- ☐ **Form C: Offering Statement**
- ☐ **Form C–U: Progress Update:** _____
- ☐ **Form C/A: Amendment to Offering Statement:** _____
  - ☐ **Check box if Amendment is material and investors must reconfirm within five business days.**
- ☐ **Form C–AR: Annual Report**
- ☐ **Form C–AR/A: Amendment to Annual Report**
- ☐ **Form C–TR: Termination of Reporting**

Name of issuer:

Legal status of issuer:

Form: _____

Jurisdiction of Incorporation/Organization: _____

Date of organization):

Physical address of issuer: _____ Website of issuer: _____

Name of intermediary through which the offering will be conducted: _____

CIK number of intermediary: _____ SEC file number of intermediary: _____

CRD number, if applicable, of intermediary: _____

Amount of compensation to be paid to the intermediary, whether as a dollar amount or a percentage of the offering amount, or a good faith estimate if the exact amount is not available at the time of the filing, for conducting the offering, including the amount of referral and any other fees associated with the offering:

_____

Any other direct or indirect interest in the issuer held by the intermediary, or any arrangement for the intermediary to acquire such an interest:

_____

Type of security offered: _____ Target number of securities to be offered: _____

Price (or method for determining price): _____

Target offering amount:

Oversubscriptions accepted: ☐ Yes   ☐ No

If yes, disclose how oversubscriptions will be allocated: ☐ Pro-rata basis   ☐ First-come, first-served basis
☐ Other—provide a description: _____

Maximum offering amount (if different from target offering amount): _____

Deadline to reach the target offering amount: _____

NOTE: If the sum of the investment commitments does not equal or exceed the target offering amount at the offering deadline, no securities will be sold in the offering, investment commitments will be cancelled and committed funds will be returned.

355

Current number of employees: _____

Total Assets: Most recent fiscal year-end: ___ Prior fiscal year-end: ___ Cash & Cash Equivalents: ___ Most recent fiscal year-end: ___ Prior fiscal year-end: ___ Accounts Receivable: ___ Most recent fiscal year-end: ___ Prior fiscal year-end: ___ Short-term Debt: ___ Most recent fiscal year-end: ___ Prior fiscal year-end: ___ Long-term Debt: ___ Most recent fiscal year-end: ___ Prior fiscal year-end: Revenues/Sales: ___ Most recent fiscal year-end: ___ Prior fiscal year-end: ___ Cost of Goods Sold: ___ Most recent fiscal year-end: ___ Prior fiscal year-end: ___ Taxes Paid: ___ Most recent fiscal year-end: ___ Prior fiscal year-end: ___ Net Income: ___ Most recent fiscal year-end: ___ Prior fiscal year-end: ___

Using the list below, select the jurisdictions in which the issuer intends to offer the securities:

[List will include all U.S. jurisdictions, with an option to add and remove them individually, add all and remove all.]

Is there a co-issuer? _____ yes _____ no. If yes,

Name of co-issuer: _____

Legal status of co-issuer: _____

Form: _____

Jurisdiction of Incorporation/Organization: _____

Date of organization: _____

Physical address of co-issuer: _____

Website of co-issuer: _____

GENERAL INSTRUCTIONS

I. Eligibility Requirements for Use of Form C

This Form shall be used for the offering statement, and any related amendments and progress reports, required to be filed by any issuer offering or selling securities in reliance on the exemption in Securities Act Section 4(a)(6) and in accordance with Section 4A and Regulation Crowdfunding (§ 227.100 *et seq.*). The term "issuer" includes any co-issuer jointly offering or selling securities with an issuer in reliance on the exemption in Securities Act Section 4(a)(6) and in accordance with Securities Act Section 4A and Regulation Crowdfunding (§ 227.100 *et seq.*) This Form also shall be used for an annual report required pursuant to Rule 202 of Regulation Crowdfunding and for the termination of reporting required pursuant to Rule 203(b)(2) of Regulation Crowdfunding. Careful attention should be directed to the terms, conditions and requirements of the exemption.

II. Preparation and Filing of Form C

Information on the cover page will be generated based on the information provided in XML format. Other than the cover page, this Form is not to be used as a blank form to be filled in, but only as a guide in the preparation of Form C. General information regarding the preparation, format and how to file this Form is contained in Regulation S–T (§ 232 *et seq.*).

III. Information to be Included in the Form

Item 1. Offering Statement Disclosure Requirements

An issuer filing this Form for an offering in reliance on Section 4(a)(6) of the Securities Act and pursuant to Regulation Crowdfunding (§ 227.100 *et seq.*) must file the Form prior to the commencement of the offering and include the information required by Rule 201 of Regulation Crowdfunding (§ 227.201).

An issuer must include in the XML-based portion of this Form: the information required by paragraphs (a), (e), (g), (h), (*l*), (n), and (o) of Rule 201 of Regulation Crowdfunding (§ 227.201(a), (e), (g), (h), (*l*), (n), and (o)); selected financial data for the prior two fiscal years (including total assets, cash and cash equivalents, accounts receivable, short-term debt, long-term debt, revenues/sales, cost of goods sold, taxes paid and net income); the jurisdictions in which the issuer intends to offer the securities; and any information required by Rule 203(a)(3) of Regulation Crowdfunding (§ 227.203(a)(3)).

FORM C

Other than the information required to be provided in XML format, an issuer may provide the required information in the optional Question and Answer format included herein or in any other format included on the intermediary's platform, by filing such information as an exhibit to this Form, including copies of screen shots of the relevant information, as appropriate and necessary.

If disclosure in response to any paragraph of Rule 201 of Regulation Crowdfunding (§ 227.201) or

Rule 203(a)(3) is responsive to one or more other paragraphs of Rule 201 of Regulation Crowdfunding (§ 227.201) or to Rule 203(a)(3) of Regulation Crowdfunding (§ 227.203(a)(3)), issuers are not required to make duplicate disclosures.

Item 2. Legends

(a)   An issuer filing this Form for an offering in reliance on Section 4(a)(6) of the Securities Act and pursuant to Regulation Crowdfunding (§ 227.100 *et seq.*) must include the following legends:

A crowdfunding investment involves risk. You should not invest any funds in this offering unless you can afford to lose your entire investment.

In making an investment decision, investors must rely on their own examination of the issuer and the terms of the offering, including the merits and risks involved. These securities have not been recommended or approved by any federal or state securities commission or regulatory authority. Furthermore, these authorities have not passed upon the accuracy or adequacy of this document.

The U.S. Securities and Exchange Commission does not pass upon the merits of any securities offered or the terms of the offering, nor does it pass upon the accuracy or completeness of any offering document or literature.

These securities are offered under an exemption from registration; however, the U.S. Securities and Exchange Commission has not made an independent determination that these securities are exempt from registration.

(b)   An issuer filing this Form for an offering in reliance on Section 4(a)(6) of the Securities Act and pursuant to Regulation Crowdfunding (§ 227.100 *et seq.*) must disclose in the offering statement that it will file a report with the Commission annually and post the report on its website, no later than 120 days after the end of each fiscal year covered by the report. The issuer must also disclose how an issuer may terminate its reporting obligations in the future in accordance with Rule 202(b) of Regulation Crowdfunding (§ 227.202(b)).

Item 3. Annual Report Disclosure Requirements

An issuer filing this Form for an annual report, as required by Regulation Crowdfunding (§ 227.100 *et seq.*), must file the Form no later than 120 days after the issuer's fiscal year end covered by the report and include the information required by Rule 201(a), (b), (c), (d), (e), (f), (m), (p), (q), (r), (s), (t), (x) and (y) of Regulation Crowdfunding (§§ 227.201(a), (b), (c), (d), (e), (f), (m), (p), (q), (r), (s), (t), (x) and (y)). For purposes of paragraph (t), the issuer shall provide financial statements certified by the principal executive officer of the issuer to be true and complete in all material respects. If, however, the issuer has available financial statements prepared in accordance with U.S. generally accepted accounting principles (U.S. GAAP) that have been reviewed or audited by an independent certified public accountant, those financial statements must be provided and the principal executive officer certification will not be required.

An issuer must include in the XML-based portion of this Form: the information required by paragraphs (a), and (e) of Rule 201 of Regulation Crowdfunding (§ 227.201(a) and (e)); and selected financial data for the prior two fiscal years (including total assets, cash and cash equivalents, accounts receivable, short-term debt, long-term debt, revenues/sales, cost of goods sold, taxes paid and net income).

SIGNATURE

Pursuant to the requirements of Sections 4(a)(6) and 4A of the Securities Act of 1933 and Regulation Crowdfunding (§ 227.100 *et seq.*), the issuer certifies that it has reasonable grounds to believe that it meets all of the requirements for filing on Form C and has duly caused this Form to be signed on its behalf by the duly authorized undersigned.

1933 ACT FORMS

(Issuer)

By

(Signature and Title)

Pursuant to the requirements of Sections 4(a)(6) and 4A of the Securities Act of 1933 and Regulation Crowdfunding (§ 227.100 *et seq.*), this Form C has been signed by the following persons in the capacities and on the dates indicated.

(Signature)

(Title)

(Date)

Instructions.

1. The form shall be signed by the issuer, its principal executive officer or officers, its principal financial officer, its controller or principal accounting officer and at least a majority of the board of directors or persons performing similar functions. If there is a co-issuer, the form shall also be signed by the co-issuer, its principal executive officer or officers, its principal financial officer, its controller or principal accounting officer and at least a majority of the board of directors or persons performing similar functions.

2. The name of each person signing the form shall be typed or printed beneath the signature.

Intentional misstatements or omissions of facts constitute federal criminal violations. *See* 18 U.S.C. 1001.

OPTIONAL QUESTION & ANSWER FORMAT FOR AN OFFERING STATEMENT

Respond to each question in each paragraph of this part. Set forth each question and any notes, but not any instructions thereto, in their entirety. If disclosure in response to any question is responsive to one or more other questions, it is not necessary to repeat the disclosure. If a question or series of questions is inapplicable or the response is available elsewhere in the Form, either State that it is inapplicable, include a cross-reference to the responsive disclosure, or omit the question or series of questions. The term "issuer" in these questions and answers includes any "co-issuer" jointly offering or selling securities with the issuer in reliance on the exemption in Securities Act Section 4(a)(6) and in accordance with Securities Act Section 4A and Regulation Crowdfunding (§ 227.100 *et seq.*). Any information provided with respect to the issuer should also be separately provided with respect to any co-issuer.

If you are seeking to rely on the Commission's temporary rules to initiate an offering between May 4, 2020, and February 28, 2021 intended to be conducted on an expedited basis due to circumstances relating to coronavirus disease 2019 (COVID-19), you will likely need to provide additional or different information than described in questions 2, 12, and 29. If you are seeking to rely on the Commission's temporary Rule 201(bb) for an offering initiated between March 1, 2021, and August 28, 2022, you will likely need to provide additional or different information than described in questions 2 and 29. When preparing responses to such questions, please carefully review temporary Rules 100(b)(7), 201(aa), 201(bb), and 304(e) and tailor your responses to those requirements as applicable.

Be very careful and precise in answering all questions. Give full and complete answers so that they are not misleading under the circumstances involved. Do not discuss any future performance or other anticipated event unless you have a reasonable basis to believe that it will actually occur within the foreseeable future. If any answer requiring significant information is materially inaccurate, incomplete or

FORM C

misleading, the Company, its management and principal shareholders may be liable to investors based on that information.

THE COMPANY

1. Name of issuer: _____

ELIGIBILITY

2. ☐ Check this box to certify that all of the following statements are true for the issuer:

   - Organized under, and subject to, the laws of a State or territory of the United States or the District of Columbia.

   - Not subject to the requirement to file reports pursuant to Section 13 or Section 15(d) of the Securities Exchange Act of 1934.

   - Not an investment company registered or required to be registered under the Investment Company Act of 1940.

   - Not ineligible to rely on this exemption under Section 4(a)(6) of the Securities Act as a result of a disqualification specified in Rule 503(a) of Regulation Crowdfunding. (For more information about these disqualifications, see Question 30 of this Question and Answer format).

   - Has filed with the Commission and provided to investors, to the extent required, the ongoing annual reports required by Regulation Crowdfunding during the two years immediately preceding the filing of this offering statement (or for such shorter period that the issuer was required to file such reports).

   - Not a development stage company that (a) has no specific business plan or (b) has indicated that its business plan is to engage in a merger or acquisition with an unidentified company or companies.

INSTRUCTION TO QUESTION 2: If any of these statements is not true, then you are NOT eligible to rely on this exemption under Section 4(a)(6) of the Securities Act.

3. Has the issuer or any of its predecessors previously failed to comply with the ongoing reporting requirements of Rule 202 of Regulation Crowdfunding? ☐ Yes   ☐ No

   Explain: _____

DIRECTORS OF THE COMPANY

4. Provide the following information about each director (and any persons occupying a similar status or performing a similar function) of the issuer:

   Name: _____ Dates of Board Service:_____

   Principal Occupation: _____

   Employer: _____ Dates of Service:_____

   Employer's principal business: _____

List all positions and offices with the issuer held and the period of time in which the director served in the position or office:

   Position: _____ Dates of Service: _____

   Position: _____ Dates of Service: _____

   Position: _____ Dates of Service: _____

Business Experience: List the employers, titles and dates of positions held during past three years with an indication of job responsibilities:

   Employer: _____

   Employer's principal business: _____

1933 ACT FORMS

Title: _____ Dates of Service: _____

Responsibilities: _____

Employer: _____

Employer's principal business: _____

Title: _____ Dates of Service: _____

Responsibilities: _____

Employer: _____

Employer's principal business: _____

Title: _____ Dates of Service: _____

Responsibilities: _____

OFFICERS OF THE COMPANY

5. Provide the following information about each officer (and any persons occupying a similar status or performing a similar function) of the issuer:

Name: _____

Title: _____ Dates of Service: _____

Responsibilities: _____

List any prior positions and offices with the issuer and the period of time in which the officer served in the position or office:

Position: _____ Dates of Service: _____

Responsibilities: _____

Position: _____ Dates of Service: _____

Responsibilities: _____

Position: _____ Dates of Service: _____

Responsibilities: _____

Business Experience: List any other employers, titles and dates of positions held during past three years with an indication of job responsibilities:

Employer: _____

Employer's principal business: _____

Title: _____ Dates of Service: _____

Responsibilities: _____

Employer: _____

Employer's principal business: _____

Title: _____ Dates of Service: _____

Responsibilities: _____

FORM C

Employer: _____

Employer's principal business: _____

Title: _____ Dates of Service: _____

Responsibilities: _____

INSTRUCTION TO QUESTION 5: For purposes of this Question 5, the term officer means a president, vice president, secretary, treasurer or principal financial officer, comptroller or principal accounting officer, and any person routinely performing similar functions.

PRINCIPAL SECURITY HOLDERS

6. Provide the name and ownership level of each person, as of the most recent practicable date, who is the beneficial owner of 20 percent or more of the issuer's outstanding voting equity securities, calculated on the basis of voting power.

Name of Holder Securities Now	No. and Class of Power	Prior to Offering	% of Voting
			0%
_____	_____	_____	0%
_____	_____	_____	0%
_____	_____	_____	0%

INSTRUCTION TO QUESTION 6: The above information must be provided as of a date that is no more than 120 days prior to the date of filing of this offering statement.

To calculate total voting power, include all securities for which the person directly or indirectly has or shares the voting power, which includes the power to vote or to direct the voting of such securities. If the person has the right to acquire voting power of such securities within 60 days, including through the exercise of any option, warrant or right, the conversion of a security, or other arrangement, or if securities are held by a member of the family, through corporations or partnerships, or otherwise in a manner that would allow a person to direct or control the voting of the securities (or share in such direction or control—as, for example, a co-trustee) they should be included as being "beneficially owned." You should include an explanation of these circumstances in a footnote to the "Number of and Class of Securities Now Held." To calculate outstanding voting equity securities, assume all outstanding options are exercised and all outstanding convertible securities converted.

BUSINESS AND ANTICIPATED BUSINESS PLAN

7. Describe in detail the business of the issuer and the anticipated business plan of the issuer.

RISK FACTORS

A crowdfunding investment involves risk. You should not invest any funds in this offering unless you can afford to lose your entire investment.

In making an investment decision, investors must rely on their own examination of the issuer and the terms of the offering, including the merits and risks involved. These securities have not been recommended or approved by any federal or state securities commission or regulatory authority. Furthermore, these authorities have not passed upon the accuracy or adequacy of this document.

The U.S. Securities and Exchange Commission does not pass upon the merits of any securities offered or the terms of the offering, nor does it pass upon the accuracy or completeness of any offering document or literature.

1933 ACT FORMS

These securities are offered under an exemption from registration; however, the U.S. Securities and Exchange Commission has not made an independent determination that these securities are exempt from registration.

8. Discuss the material factors that make an investment in the issuer speculative or risky:

(1) _____

(2) _____

(3) _____

(4) _____

(5) _____

(6) _____

(7) _____

(8) _____

(9) _____

(10) _____

INSTRUCTION TO QUESTION 8: Avoid generalized statements and include only those factors that are unique to the issuer. Discussion should be tailored to the issuer's business and the offering and should not repeat the factors addressed in the legends set forth above. No specific number of risk factors is required to be identified. Add additional lines and number as appropriate.

THE OFFERING

9. What is the purpose of this offering?

10. How does the issuer intend to use the proceeds of this offering?

	If Target Offering Amount Sold	If Maximum Amount Sold
Total Proceeds	$	$
Less: Offering Expenses		
(A)		
(B)		
(C)		
Net Proceeds	$	$
Use of Net Proceeds		
(A)		
(B)		
(C)		
Total Use of Net Proceeds	$	$

362

FORM C

INSTRUCTION TO QUESTION 10: An issuer must provide a reasonably detailed description of any intended use of proceeds, such that investors are provided with an adequate amount of information to understand how the offering proceeds will be used. If an issuer has identified a range of possible uses, the issuer should identify and describe each probable use and the factors the issuer may consider in allocating proceeds among the potential uses. If the issuer will accept proceeds in excess of the target offering amount, the issuer must describe the purpose, method for allocating oversubscriptions, and intended use of the excess proceeds with similar specificity.

11. (a) Did the issuer make use of any written communication or broadcast script for testing the waters either (i) under the authorization of Rule 241 within 30 days of the initial filing of the offering statement, or (ii) under the authorization of Rule 206? If so, provide copies of the materials used.

    (b) How will the issuer complete the transaction and deliver securities to the investors?

12. How can an investor cancel an investment commitment?

NOTE: Investors may cancel an investment commitment until 48 hours prior to the deadline identified in these offering materials.

The intermediary will notify investors when the target offering amount has been met.

If the issuer reaches the target offering amount prior to the deadline identified in the offering materials, it may close the offering early if it provides notice about the new offering deadline at least five business days prior to such new offering deadline (absent a material change that would require an extension of the offering and reconfirmation of the investment commitment).

If an investor does not cancel an investment commitment before the 48-hour period prior to the offering deadline, the funds will be released to the issuer upon closing of the offering and the investor will receive securities in exchange for his or her investment.

If an investor does not reconfirm his or her investment commitment after a material change is made to the offering, the investor's investment commitment will be cancelled and the committed funds will be returned.

OWNERSHIP AND CAPITAL STRUCTURE

The Offering

13. Describe the terms of the securities being offered.

14. Do the securities offered have voting rights? ☐ Yes   ☐ No

15. Are there any limitations on any voting or other rights identified above? ☐ Yes   ☐ No

    Explain: _____

16. How may the terms of the securities being offered be modified?

Restrictions on Transfer of the Securities Being Offered

The securities being offered may not be transferred by any purchaser of such securities during the one year period beginning when the securities were issued, unless such securities are transferred:

    (1) to the issuer;

    (2) to an accredited investor;

    (3) as part of an offering registered with the U.S. Securities and Exchange Commission; or

    (4) to a member of the family of the purchaser or the equivalent, to a trust controlled by the purchaser, to a trust created for the benefit of a member of the family of the purchaser or the equivalent, or in connection with the death or divorce of the purchaser or other similar circumstance.

NOTE: The term "accredited investor" means any person who comes within any of the categories set forth in Rule 501(a) of Regulation D, or who the seller reasonably believes comes within any of such categories, at the time of the sale of the securities to that person.

The term "member of the family of the purchaser or the equivalent" includes a child, stepchild, grandchild, parent, stepparent, grandparent, spouse or spousal equivalent, sibling, mother-in-law, father-in-law, son-in-law, daughter-in-law, brother-in-law, or sister-in-law of the purchaser, and includes adoptive relationships. The term "spousal equivalent" means a cohabitant occupying a relationship generally equivalent to that of a spouse.

Description of Issuer's Securities

17. What other securities or classes of securities of the issuer are outstanding? Describe the material terms of any other outstanding securities or classes of securities of the issuer.

Class of Security	Securities (or Amount) Authorized	Securities (or Amount) Outstanding	Voting Rights	Other Rights
Preferred Stock (list each class in order of preference):				
_____			☐ Yes ☐ No	☐ Yes ☐ No Specify: _____
_____			☐ Yes ☐ No	☐ Yes ☐ No Specify: _____
Common Stock:			☐ Yes ☐ No	☐ Yes ☐ No Specify: _____
Debt Securities:			☐ Yes ☐ No	☐ Yes ☐ No Specify: _____
Other:				
_____			☐ Yes ☐ No	☐ Yes ☐ No Specify: _____
_____			☐ Yes ☐ No	☐ Yes ☐ No Specify: _____

FORM C

Class of Security	Securities Reserved for Issuance upon Exercise or Conversion
Warrants:	
Options:	
Other Right:	
_____	

_____

18. How may the rights of the securities being offered be materially limited, diluted or qualified by the rights of any other class of security identified above?

19. Are there any differences not reflected above between the securities being offered and each other class of security of the issuer? ☐ Yes ☐ No

   Explain: _____

20. How could the exercise of rights held by the principal shareholders identified in Question 6 above affect the purchasers of the securities being offered?

21. How are the securities being offered being valued? Include examples of methods for how such securities may be valued by the issuer in the future, including during subsequent corporate actions.

22. What are the risks to purchasers of the securities relating to minority ownership in the issuer?

23. What are the risks to purchasers associated with corporate actions including:

   • additional issuances of securities,
   • issuer repurchases of securities,
   • a sale of the issuer or of assets of the issuer or
   • transactions with related parties?

24. Describe the material terms of any indebtedness of the issuer:

Creditor(s)	Amount Outstanding	Interest Rate	Maturity Date	Other Material Terms
	$_____	_____%		
	$_____	_____%		
	$_____	_____%		

25. What other exempt offerings has the issuer conducted within the past three years?

Date of Offering	Exemption Relied Upon	Securities Offered	Amount Sold	Use of Proceeds
			$_____	
			$_____	
			$_____	

26. Was or is the issuer or any entities controlled by or under common control with the issuer a party to any transaction since the beginning of the issuer's last fiscal year, or any currently proposed transaction, where the amount involved exceeds five percent of the aggregate amount of capital raised

365

by the issuer in reliance on Section 4(a)(6) of the Securities Act during the preceding 12-month period, including the amount the issuer seeks to raise in the current offering, in which any of the following persons had or is to have a direct or indirect material interest:

(1) any director or officer of the issuer;

(2) any person who is, as of the most recent practicable date, the beneficial owner of 20 percent or more of the issuer's outstanding voting equity securities, calculated on the basis of voting power;

(3) if the issuer was incorporated or organized within the past three years, any promoter of the issuer; or

(4) any immediate family member of any of the foregoing persons.

If yes, for each such transaction, disclose the following:

Issuer	Relationship to	Nature of Interest in Transaction	Amount of Interest	Specified Person
			$_____	
			$_____	
			$_____	

INSTRUCTIONS TO QUESTION 26:

The term transaction includes, but is not limited to, any financial transaction, arrangement or relationship (including any indebtedness or guarantee of indebtedness) or any series of similar transactions, arrangements or relationships.

Beneficial ownership for purposes of paragraph (2) shall be determined as of a date that is no more than 120 days prior to the date of filing of this offering statement and using the same calculation described in Question 6 of this Question and Answer format.

The term "member of the family" includes any child, stepchild, grandchild, parent, stepparent, grandparent, spouse or spousal equivalent, sibling, mother-in-law, father-in-law, son-in-law, daughter-in-law, brother-in-law, or sister-in-law of the person, and includes adoptive relationships. The term "spousal equivalent" means a cohabitant occupying a relationship generally equivalent to that of a spouse.

Compute the amount of a related party's interest in any transaction without regard to the amount of the profit or loss involved in the transaction. Where it is not practicable to state the approximate amount of the interest, disclose the approximate amount involved in the transaction.

FINANCIAL CONDITION OF THE ISSUER

27. Does the issuer have an operating history? ☐ Yes   ☐ No

Describe the financial condition of the issuer, including, to the extent material, liquidity, capital resources and historical results of operations.

INSTRUCTIONS TO QUESTION 28:

The discussion must cover each year for which financial statements are provided. Include a discussion of any known material changes or trends in the financial condition and results of operations of the issuer during any time period subsequent to the period for which financial statements are provided.

For issuers with no prior operating history, the discussion should focus on financial milestones and operational, liquidity and other challenges.

For issuers with an operating history, the discussion should focus on whether historical results and cash flows are representative of what investors should expect in the future.

Take into account the proceeds of the offering and any other known or pending sources of capital. Discuss how the proceeds from the offering will affect liquidity, whether receiving these funds and any other additional funds is necessary to the viability of the business, and how quickly the issuer anticipates using

FORM C

its available cash. Describe the other available sources of capital to the business, such as lines of credit or required contributions by shareholders.

References to the issuer in this Question 28 and these instructions refer to the issuer and its predecessors, if any.

FINANCIAL INFORMATION

29. Include the financial information specified below covering the two most recently completed fiscal years or the period(s) since inception, if shorter:

Aggregate Offering Amount (defined below):	Financial Statement Requirements:	Financial Statement Requirements:
(a) $107,000 or less:		
(b) More than $107,000, but not more than $535,000:		
(c) More than $535,000:		

INSTRUCTIONS TO QUESTION 29: To determine the financial statements required, the Aggregate Offering Amount for purposes of this Question 29 means the aggregate amounts offered and sold by the issuer, all entities controlled by or under common control with the issuer, and all predecessors of the issuer in reliance on Section 4(a)(6) of the Securities Act within the preceding 12-month period plus the current maximum offering amount provided on the cover of this Form.

To determine whether the issuer has previously sold securities in reliance on Regulation Crowdfunding for purposes of paragraph (c) of this Question 29, "issuer" means the issuer, all entities controlled by or under common control with the issuer, and all predecessors of the issuer.

Financial statements must be prepared in accordance with U.S. generally accepted accounting principles and must include balance sheets, statements of comprehensive income, statements of cash flows, statements of changes in stockholders' equity and notes to the financial statements. If the financial statements are not audited, they shall be labeled as "unaudited."

Issuers offering securities and required to provide the information set forth in row (a) before filing a tax return for the most recently completed fiscal year may provide information from the tax return filed for the prior year (if any), provided that the issuer provides information from the tax return for the most recently completed fiscal year when it is filed, if filed during the offering period. An issuer that requested an extension of the time to file would not be required to provide information from the tax return until the date when the return is filed, if filed during the offering period.

A principal executive officer certifying financial statements as described above must provide the following certification:

I, [identify the certifying individual], certify that:

(1) the financial statements of [identify the issuer] included in this Form are true and complete in all material respects; and

(2) the tax return information of [identify the issuer] included in this Form reflects accurately the information reported on the tax return for [identify the issuer] filed for the fiscal year ended [date of most recent tax return].

[Signature] [Title]

To qualify as a public accountant that is independent of the issuer for purposes of this Question 29, the accountant must satisfy the independence standards of either:

(i) Rule 2–01 of Regulation S–X or

(ii) the AICPA.

1933 ACT FORMS

The public accountant that audits or reviews the financial statements provided by an issuer must be (1) duly registered and in good standing as a certified public accountant under the laws of the place of his or her residence or principal office or (2) in good standing and entitled to practice as a public accountant under the laws of his or her place of residence or principal office.

An issuer will not be in compliance with the requirement to provide reviewed financial statement if the issuer received a review report that includes modifications. An issuer will not be in compliance with the requirement to provide audited financial statements if the issuer received a qualified opinion, an adverse opinion, or a disclaimer of opinion.

The issuer must notify the public accountant of the issuer's intended use of the public accountant's audit or review report in the offering.

For an offering conducted in the first 120 days of a fiscal year, the financial statements provided may be for the two fiscal years prior to the issuer's most recently completed fiscal year; however, financial statements for the two most recently completed fiscal years must be provided if they are otherwise available. If more than 120 days have passed since the end of the issuer's most recently completed fiscal year, the financial statements provided must be for the issuer's two most recently completed fiscal years.

If the 120th day falls on a Saturday, Sunday, or holiday, the next business day shall be considered the 120th day for purposes of determining the age of the financial statements.

An issuer may elect to delay complying with any new or revised financial accounting standard until the date that a company that is not an issuer (as defined under section 2(a) of the Sarbanes-Oxley Act of 2002 is required to comply with such new or revised accounting standard, if such standard also applies to companies that are not issuers. Issuers electing such extension of time accommodation must disclose it at the time the issuer files its offering statement and apply the election to all standards. Issuers electing not to use this accommodation must forgo this accommodation for all financial accounting standards and may not elect to rely on this accommodation in any future filings

30. With respect to the issuer, any predecessor of the issuer, any affiliated issuer, any director, officer, general partner or managing member of the issuer, any beneficial owner of 20 percent or more of the issuer's outstanding voting equity securities, calculated in the same form as described in Question 6 of this Question and Answer format, any promoter connected with the issuer in any capacity at the time of such sale, any person that has been or will be paid (directly or indirectly) remuneration for solicitation of purchasers in connection with such sale of securities, or any general partner, director, officer or managing member of any such solicitor, prior to May 16, 2016:

    (1) Has any such person been convicted, within 10 years (or five years, in the case of issuers, their predecessors and affiliated issuers) before the filing of this offering statement, of any felony or misdemeanor:

        (i) in connection with the purchase or sale of any security? ☐ Yes ☐ No

        (ii) involving the making of any false filing with the Commission? ☐ Yes ☐ No

        (iii) arising out of the conduct of the business of an underwriter, broker, dealer, municipal securities dealer, investment adviser, funding portal or paid solicitor of purchasers of securities? ☐ Yes ☐ No

        If Yes to any of the above, explain: _____

    (2) Is any such person subject to any order, judgment or decree of any court of competent jurisdiction, entered within five years before the filing of the information required by Section 4A(b) of the Securities Act that, at the time of filing of this offering statement, restrains or enjoins such person from engaging or continuing to engage in any conduct or practice:

        (i) in connection with the purchase or sale of any security? ☐ Yes ☐ No;

        (ii) involving the making of any false filing with the Commission? ☐ Yes ☐ No

        (iii) arising out of the conduct of the business of an underwriter, broker, dealer, municipal securities dealer, investment adviser, funding portal or paid solicitor of purchasers of securities? ☐ Yes ☐ No

368

FORM C

If Yes to any of the above, explain: _____

(3) Is any such person subject to a final order of a state securities commission (or an agency or officer of a state performing like functions); a state authority that supervises or examines banks, savings associations or credit unions; a state insurance commission (or an agency or officer of a state performing like functions); an appropriate federal banking agency; the U.S. Commodity Futures Trading Commission; or the National Credit Union Administration that:

    (i) at the time of the filing of this offering statement bars the person from:

        (A) association with an entity regulated by such commission, authority, agency or officer? ☐ Yes ☐ No

        (B) engaging in the business of securities, insurance or banking? ☐ Yes ☐ No

        (C) engaging in savings association or credit union activities? ☐ Yes ☐ No

    (ii) constitutes a final order based on a violation of any law or regulation that prohibits fraudulent, manipulative or deceptive conduct and for which the order was entered within the 10-year period ending on the date of the filing of this offering statement? ☐ Yes ☐ No

    If Yes to any of the above, explain: _____

(4) Is any such person subject to an order of the Commission entered pursuant to Section 15(b) or 15B(c) of the Exchange Act or Section 203(e) or (f) of the Investment Advisers Act of 1940 that, at the time of the filing of this offering statement:

    (i) suspends or revokes such person's registration as a broker, dealer, municipal securities dealer, investment adviser or funding portal? ☐ Yes ☐ No

    (ii) places limitations on the activities, functions or operations of such person? ☐ Yes ☐ No

    (iii) bars such person from being associated with any entity or from participating in the offering of any penny stock? ☐ Yes ☐ No

    If Yes to any of the above, explain: _____

(5) Is any such person subject to any order of the Commission entered within five years before the filing of this offering statement that, at the time of the filing of this offering statement, orders the person to cease and desist from committing or causing a violation or future violation of:

    (i) any scienter-based anti-fraud provision of the federal securities laws, including without limitation Section 17(a)(1) of the Securities Act, Section 10(b) of the Exchange Act, Section 15(c)(1) of the Exchange Act and Section 206(1) of the Investment Advisers Act of 1940 or any other rule or regulation thereunder? ☐ Yes ☐ No

    (ii) Section 5 of the Securities Act? ☐ Yes ☐ No

    If Yes to either of the above, explain: _____

(6) Is any such person suspended or expelled from membership in, or suspended or barred from association with a member of, a registered national securities exchange or a registered national or affiliated securities association for any act or omission to act constituting conduct inconsistent with just and equitable principles of trade? ☐ Yes ☐ No

    If Yes, explain: _____

(7) Has any such person filed (as a registrant or issuer), or was any such person or was any such person named as an underwriter in, any registration statement or Regulation A offering statement filed with the Commission that, within five years before the filing of this offering statement, was the subject of a refusal order, stop order, or order suspending the Regulation

369

1933 ACT FORMS

A exemption, or is any such person, at the time of such filing, the subject of an investigation or proceeding to determine whether a stop order or suspension order should be issued? ☐ Yes ☐ No

If Yes, explain: _____

(8)   Is any such person subject to a United States Postal Service false representation order entered within five years before the filing of the information required by Section 4A(b) of the Securities Act, or is any such person, at the time of filing of this offering statement, subject to a temporary restraining order or preliminary injunction with respect to conduct alleged by the United States Postal Service to constitute a scheme or device for obtaining money or property through the mail by means of false representations? ☐ Yes   ☐ No

If Yes, explain: _____

If you would have answered "Yes" to any of these questions had the conviction, order, judgment, decree, suspension, expulsion or bar occurred or been issued after May 16, 2016, then you are NOT eligible to rely on this exemption under Section 4(a)(6) of the Securities Act.

INSTRUCTIONS TO QUESTION 30: Final order means a written directive or declaratory statement issued by a federal or state agency, described in Rule 503(a)(3) of Regulation Crowdfunding, under applicable statutory authority that provides for notice and an opportunity for hearing, which constitutes a final disposition or action by that federal or state agency.

No matters are required to be disclosed with respect to events relating to any affiliated issuer that occurred before the affiliation arose if the affiliated entity is not (i) in control of the issuer or (ii) under common control with the issuer by a third party that was in control of the affiliated entity at the time of such events.

OTHER MATERIAL INFORMATION

31.   In addition to the information expressly required to be included in this Form, include:

(1)   any other material information presented to investors; and

(2)   such further material information, if any, as may be necessary to make the required statements, in the light of the circumstances under which they are made, not misleading.

INSTRUCTIONS TO QUESTION 31: If information is presented to investors in a format, media or other means not able to be reflected in text or portable document format, the issuer should include

(a)   a description of the material content of such information;

(b)   a description of the format in which such disclosure is presented; and

(c)   in the case of disclosure in video, audio or other dynamic media or format, a transcript or description of such disclosure.

ONGOING REPORTING

The issuer will file a report electronically with the Securities & Exchange Commission annually and post the report on its website, no later than:

_____

(120 days after the end of each fiscal year covered by the report).

Once posted, the annual report may be found on the issuer's website at:

_____

The issuer must continue to comply with the ongoing reporting requirements until:

(1)   the issuer is required to file reports under Section 13(a) or Section 15(d) of the Exchange Act;

(2)   the issuer has filed at least one annual report pursuant to Regulation Crowdfunding and has fewer than

FORM C

(3) 300 holders of record and has total assets that do not exceed $10,000,000;

(4) the issuer has filed at least three annual reports pursuant to Regulation Crowdfunding; the issuer or another party repurchases all of the securities issued in reliance on Section 4(a)(6) of the Securities Act, including any payment in full of debt securities or any complete redemption of redeemable securities; or

(5) the issuer liquidates or dissolves its business in accordance with state law.

FORM D

17 C.F.R. § 239.500

NOTICE OF EXEMPT OFFERING OF SECURITIES

(a)   When notice of sales on Form D must be filed.

(1)   An issuer offering or selling securities in reliance on Rule 504 or Rule 506 of this Act or section 4(a)(5) of the Securities Act of 1933 must file with the Commission a notice of sales containing the information required by this form for each new offering of securities no later than 15 calendar days after the first sale of securities in the offering, unless the end of that period falls on a Saturday, Sunday or holiday, in which case the due date would be the first business day following.

(2)   An issuer may file an amendment to a previously filed notice of sales on Form D at any time.

(3)   An issuer must file an amendment to a previously filed notice of sales on Form D for an offering:

(i)   To correct a material mistake of fact or error in the previously filed notice of sales on Form D, as soon as practicable after discovery of the mistake or error;

(ii)   To reflect a change in the information provided in the previously filed notice of sales on Form D, as soon as practicable after the change, except that no amendment is required to reflect a change that occurs after the offering terminates or a change that occurs solely in the following information:

(A)   The address or relationship to the issuer of a related person identified in response to Item 3 of the notice of sales on Form D;

(B)   An issuer's revenues or aggregate net asset value;

(C)   The minimum investment amount, if the change is an increase, or if the change, together with all other changes in that amount since the previously filed notice of sales on Form D, does not result in a decrease of more than 10%;

(D)   Any address or state(s) of solicitation shown in response to Item 12 of the notice of sales on Form D;

(E)   The total offering amount, if the change is a decrease, or if the change, together with all other changes in that amount since the previously filed notice of sales on Form D, does not result in an increase of more than 10%;

(F)   The amount of securities sold in the offering or the amount remaining to be sold;

(G)   The number of non-accredited investors who have invested in the offering, as long as the change does not increase the number to more than 35;

(H)   The total number of investors who have invested in the offering;

(I)   The amount of sales commissions, finders' fees or use of proceeds for payments to executive officers, directors or promoters, if the change is a decrease, or if the change, together with all other changes in that amount since the previously filed notice of sales on Form D, does not result in an increase of more than 10%; and

(iii)   Annually, on or before the first anniversary of the filing of the notice of sales on Form D or the filing of the most recent amendment to the notice of sales on Form D, if the offering is continuing at that time.

(4)   An issuer that files an amendment to a previously filed notice of sales on Form D must provide current information in response to all requirements of the notice of sales on Form D regardless of why the amendment is filed.

(b)   How notice of sales on Form D must be filed and signed.

1933 ACT FORMS

(1)   A notice of sales on Form D must be filed with the Commission in electronic format by means of the Commission's Electronic Data Gathering, Analysis, and Retrieval System (EDGAR) in accordance with EDGAR rules set forth in Regulation S–T.

(2)   Every notice of sales on Form D must be signed by a person duly authorized by the issuer.

UNITED STATES
SECURITIES AND EXCHANGE COMMISSION
Washington, D.C. 20549

FORM D

FORM D
Notice of Exempt Offering of Securities

U.S. Securities and Exchange Commission
Washington, DC 20549

(See instructions beginning on page 5)

Intentional misstatements or omissions of fact constitute federal criminal violations. See 18 U.S.C. 1001.

OMB APPROVAL
OMB Number: 3235-0076
Expires: September 30, 2016
Estimated average burden hours per response: 4.00

Item 1. Issuer's Identity

Name of Issuer

Previous Name(s)   ☐ None

Entity Type (Select one)
☐ Corporation
☐ Limited Partnership
☐ Limited Liability Company
☐ General Partnership
☐ Business Trust
☐ Other (Specify)

Jurisdiction of Incorporation/Organization

Year of Incorporation/Organization
(Select one)
○ Over Five Years Ago   ○ Within Last Five Years (specify year)   ○ Yet to Be Formed

(If more than one issuer is filing this notice, check this box ☐ and identify additional issuer(s) by attaching Items 1 and 2 Continuation Page(s).)

Item 2. Principal Place of Business and Contact Information

Street Address 1

Street Address 2

City

State/Province/Country

ZIP/Postal Code

Phone No.

Item 3. Related Persons

Last Name

First Name

Middle Name

Street Address 1

Street Address 2

City

State/Province/Country

ZIP/Postal Code

Relationship(s):   ☐ Executive Officer   ☐ Director   ☐ Promoter

Clarification of Response (if necessary)

(Identify additional related persons by checking this box ☐ and attaching Item 3 Continuation Page(s).)

Item 4. Industry Group   (Select one)

○ **Agriculture**
Banking and Financial Services
○ Commercial Banking
○ Insurance
○ Investing
○ Investment Banking
○ Pooled Investment Fund

If selecting this industry group, also select one fund type below and answer the question below:
○ Hedge Fund
○ Private Equity Fund
○ Venture Capital Fund
○ Other Investment Fund

Is the issuer registered as an investment company under the Investment Company Act of 1940? ○ Yes   ○ No

○ Other Banking & Financial Services

○ **Business Services**
Energy
○ Electric Utilities
○ Energy Conservation
○ Coal Mining
○ Environmental Services
○ Oil & Gas
○ Other Energy

Health Care
○ Biotechnology
○ Health Insurance
○ Hospitals & Physicians
○ Pharmaceuticals
○ Other Health Care

○ **Manufacturing**
Real Estate
○ Commercial

○ Construction
○ REITS & Finance
○ Residential
○ Other Real Estate

○ **Retailing**
○ **Restaurants**
Technology
○ Computers
○ Telecommunications
○ Other Technology

Travel
○ Airlines & Airports
○ Lodging & Conventions
○ Tourism & Travel Services
○ Other Travel

○ **Other**

SEC1972 (9/13)

Form D 1

1933 ACT FORMS

FORM D

U.S. Securities and Exchange Commission
Washington, DC 20549

Item 5. Issuer Size   (Select one)

Revenue Range (for issuer not specifying "hedge" or "other investment" fund in Item 4 above)

- ○ No Revenues
- ○ $1 - $1,000,000
- ○ $1,000,001 - $5,000,000
- ○ $5,000,001 - $25,000,000
- ○ $25,000,001 - $100,000,000
- ○ Over $100,000,000
- ○ Decline to Disclose
- ○ Not Applicable

OR

Aggregate Net Asset Value Range (for issuer specifying "hedge" or "other investment" fund in Item 4 above)

- ○ No Aggregate Net Asset Value
- ○ $1 - $5,000,000
- ○ $5,000,001 - $25,000,000
- ○ $25,000,001 - $50,000,000
- ○ $50,000,001 - $100,000,000
- ○ Over $100,000,000
- ○ Decline to Disclose
- ○ Not Applicable

Item 6. Federal Exemptions and Exclusions Claimed   (Select all that apply)

- ☐ Rule 504(b)(1) (not (i), (ii) or (iii))
- ☐ Rule 504(b)(1)(i)
- ☐ Rule 504(b)(1)(ii)
- ☐ Rule 504(b)(1)(iii)
- ☐ Rule 505
- ☐ Rule 506(b)
- ☐ Rule 506(c)
- ☐ Securities Act Section 4(a)(5)

Investment Company Act Section 3(c)

- ☐ Section 3(c)(1)
- ☐ Section 3(c)(2)
- ☐ Section 3(c)(3)
- ☐ Section 3(c)(4)
- ☐ Section 3(c)(5)
- ☐ Section 3(c)(6)
- ☐ Section 3(c)(7)

- ☐ Section 3(c)(9)
- ☐ Section 3(c)(10)
- ☐ Section 3(c)(11)
- ☐ Section 3(c)(12)
- ☐ Section 3(c)(13)
- ☐ Section 3(c)(14)

Item 7. Type of Filing

○ New Notice   **OR**   ○ Amendment

Date of First Sale in this Offering: [　　　　　　]   **OR**   ☐ First Sale Yet to Occur

Item 8. Duration of Offering

Does the issuer intend this offering to last more than one year?   ☐ Yes   ☐ No

Item 9. Type(s) of Securities Offered   (Select all that apply)

- ☐ Equity
- ☐ Debt
- ☐ Option, Warrant or Other Right to Acquire Another Security
- ☐ Security to be Acquired Upon Exercise of Option, Warrant or Other Right to Acquire Security

- ☐ Pooled Investment Fund Interests
- ☐ Tenant-in-Common Securities
- ☐ Mineral Property Securities
- ☐ Other (describe)

Item 10. Business Combination Transaction

Is this offering being made in connection with a business combination transaction, such as a merger, acquisition or exchange offer?   ☐ Yes   ☐ No

Clarification of Response (if necessary)

Form D   2

FORM D

FORM D   U.S. Securities and Exchange Commission
Washington, DC 20549

Item 11. Minimum Investment

Minimum investment accepted from any outside investor $ [_____]

Item 12. Sales Compensation

Recipient
[_____]

Recipient CRD Number
[_____]   ☐ No CRD Number

(Associated) Broker or Dealer   ☐ None
[_____]

(Associated) Broker or Dealer CRD Number
[_____]   ☐ No CRD Number

Street Address 1
[_____]

Street Address 2
[_____]

City
[_____]

State/Province/Country
[_____]

ZIP/Postal Code
[_____]

States of Solicitation   ☐ All States

☐ AL	☐ AK	☐ AZ	☐ AR	☐ CA	☐ CO	☐ CT	☐ DE	☐ DC	☐ FL	☐ GA	☐ HI	☐ ID
☐ IL	☐ IN	☐ IA	☐ KS	☐ KY	☐ LA	☐ ME	☐ MD	☐ MA	☐ MI	☐ MN	☐ MS	☐ MO
☐ MT	☐ NE	☐ NV	☐ NH	☐ NJ	☐ NM	☐ NY	☐ NC	☐ ND	☐ OH	☐ OK	☐ OR	☐ PA
☐ RI	☐ SC	☐ SD	☐ TN	☐ TX	☐ UT	☐ VT	☐ VA	☐ WA	☐ WV	☐ WI	☐ WY	☐ PR

(Identify additional person(s) being paid compensation by checking this box ☐ and attaching Item 12 Continuation Page(s).)

Item 13. Offering and Sales Amounts

(a) Total Offering Amount $ [_____]   **OR**   ☐ Indefinite

(b) Total Amount Sold $ [_____]

(c) Total Remaining to be Sold $ [_____]   **OR**   ☐ Indefinite
(Subtract (a) from (b))

Clarification of Response (if necessary)
[_____]

Item 14. Investors

Check this box ☐ if securities in the offering have been or may be sold to persons who do not qualify as accredited investors, and enter the number of such non-accredited investors who already have invested in the offering: [_____]

Enter the total number of investors who already have invested in the offering: [_____]

Item 15. Sales Commissions and Finders' Fees Expenses

Provide separately the amounts of sales commissions and finders' fees expenses, if any. If an amount is not known, provide an estimate and check the box next to the amount.

Sales Commissions $ [_____]   ☐ Estimate

Finders' Fees $ [_____]   ☐ Estimate

Clarification of Response (if necessary)
[_____]

Form D 3

1933 ACT FORMS

FORM D

U.S. Securities and Exchange Commission
Washington, DC 20549

Item 16. Use of Proceeds

Provide the amount of the gross proceeds of the offering that has been or is proposed to be used for payments to any of the persons required to be named as executive officers, directors or promoters in response to Item 3 above. If the amount is unknown, provide an estimate and check the box next to the amount.

$ [   ]   ☐ Estimate

Clarification of Response (if necessary)

[   ]

Signature and Submission

Please verify the information you have entered and review the Terms of Submission below before signing and submitting this notice.

Terms of Submission. In Submitting this notice, each identified issuer is:

Notifying the SEC and/or each State in which this notice is filed of the offering of securities described and undertaking to furnish them, upon written request, in accordance with applicable law, the information furnished to offerees.[*]

Irrevocably appointing each of the Secretary of the SEC and the Securities Administrator or other legally designated officer of the State in which the issuer maintains its principal place of business and any State in which this notice is filed, as its agents for service of process, and agreeing that these persons may accept service on its behalf, of any notice, process or pleading, and further agreeing that such service may be made by registered or certified mail, in any Federal or state action, administrative proceeding, or arbitration brought against the issuer in any place subject to the jurisdiction of the United States, if the action, proceeding or arbitration (a) arises out of any activity in connection with the offering of securities that is the subject of this notice, and (b) is founded, directly or indirectly, upon the provisions of: (i) the Securities Act of 1933, the Securities Exchange Act of 1934, the Trust Indenture Act of 1939, the Investment Company Act of 1940, or the Investment Advisers Act of 1940, or any rule or regulation under any of these statutes; or (ii) the laws of the State in which the issuer maintains its principal place of business or any State in which this notice is filed.

Certifying that, if the issuer is claiming a Regulation D exemption for the offering, the issuer is not disqualified from relying on Regulation D for one of the reasons stated in Rule 505(b)(2)(iii) or Rule 506(d).

---

[*] This undertaking does not affect any limits Section 102(a) of the National Securities Markets Improvement Act of 1996 ("NSMIA") [Pub. L. No. 104-290, 110 Stat. 3416 (Oct. 11, 1996)] imposes on the ability of States to require information. As a result, if the securities that are the subject of this Form D are "covered securities" for purposes of NSMIA, whether in all instances or due to the nature of the offering that is the subject of this Form D, States cannot routinely require offering materials under this undertaking or otherwise and can require offering materials only to the extent NSMIA permits them to do so under NSMIA's preservation of their anti-fraud authority.

Each identified issuer has read this notice, knows the contents to be true, and has duly caused this notice to be signed on its behalf by the undersigned duly authorized person. (Check this box ☐ and attach Signature Continuation Pages for signatures of issuers identified in Item 1 above but not represented by signer below.)

Issuer(s)   Name of Signer
[   ]   [   ]

Signature   Title
[   ]   [   ]

                                             Date
Number of continuation pages attached: [   ]

Persons who respond to the collection of information contained in this form are not required to respond unless the form displays a currently valid OMB number.

Form D   4

FORM D

FORM D

U.S. Securities and Exchange Commission
Washington, DC 20549

Instructions for Submitting a Form D Notice

General Instructions

Who must file: Each issuer of securities that sells its securities in reliance on an exemption provided in Regulation D or Section 4(a)(5) of the Securities Act of 1933 must file this notice containing the information requested with the U.S. Securities and Exchange Commission (SEC) and with the state(s) requiring it. If more than one issuer has sold its securitie in the same transaction, all issuers should be identified in one filing with the SEC, but some states may require a separate filing for each issuer or security sold.

When to file:

o An issuer must file a new notice with the SEC for each new offering of securities no later than 15 calendar days after the "date of first sale" of securities in the offering as explained in the Instruction to Item 7. For this purpose, the date of first sale is the date on which the first investor is irrevocably contractually committed to invest, which, depending on the terms and conditions of the contract, could be the date on which the issuer receives the investor's subscription agreement or check. An issuer may file the notice at any time before that if it has determined to make the offering. An issuer must file a new notice with each state that requires it at the time set by the state. For state filing information, go to www.NASAA.org. A mandatory capital commitment call does not constitute a new offering, but is made under the original offering, so no new Form D filing is required.

o An issuer may file an amendment to a previously filed notice at any time.

o An issuer must file an amendment to a previously filed notice for an offering:

- to correct a material mistake of fact or error in the previously filed notice, as soon as practicable after discovery of the mistake or error;

- to reflect a change in the information provided in the previously filed notice, except as provided below, as soon as practicable after the change; and

- annually, on or before the first anniversary of the most recent previously filed notice, if the offering is continuing at that time.

When amendment is not required: An issuer is not required to file an amendment to a previously filed notice to reflect a change that occurs after the offering terminates or a change that occurs solely in the following information:

- the address or relationship to the issuer of a related person identified in response to Item 3;

- an issuer's revenues or aggregate net asset value;

- the minimum investment amount, if the change is an increase, or if the change, together with all other changes in that amount since the previously filed notice, does not result in a decrease of more than 10%;

- any address or state(s) of solicitation shown in response to Item 12;

- the total offering amount, if the change is a decrease, or if the change, together with all other changes in that amount since the previously filed notice, does not result in an increase of more than 10%;

- the amount of securities sold in the offering or the amount remaining to be sold;

- the number of non-accredited investors who have invested in the offering, as long as the change does not increase the number to more than 35;

- the total number of investors who have invested in the offering; and

- the amount of sales commissions, finders' fees or use of proceeds for payments to executive officers, directors or promoters, if the change is a decrease, or if the change, together with all other changes in that amount since the previously filed notice, does not result in an increase of more than 10%.

Saturdays, Sundays and holidays: If the date on which a notice or an amendment to a previously filed notice is required to be filed falls on a Saturday, Sunday or holiday, the due date is the first business day following.

Amendment content: An issuer that files an amendment to a previously filed notice must provide current information in response to all items of this Form D, regardless of why the amendment is filed.

How to file: Issuers must file this notice with the SEC in electronic format. For state filing information, go to www.NASAA.org.

Filing fee: There is no federal filing fee. For information on state filing fees, go to www. NASAA.org.

Definitions of terms: Terms used but not defined in this form that are defined in Rule 405 and Rule 501 under the Securities Act of 1933, 17 CFR 230.405 and 230.501, have the meanings given to them in those rules.

Form D 5

379

1933 ACT FORMS

FORM D

Item-by-Item Instructions

Item 1. Issuer's Identity. Identify each legal entity issuing any securities being reported as being offered by entering its full name; any previous name used within the past five years; and its jurisdiction of incorporation or organization, type of legal entity, and year of incorporation or organization within the past five years or status as formed over five years ago or not yet formed. If more than one entity is issuing the securities, identify a primary issuer in the first fields shown on the first page of the form, checking the box provided, and identify additional issuers by attaching Items 1 and 2 continuation page(s).

Item 2. Principal Place of Business and Contact Information. Enter a full street address of the issuer's principal place of business. Post office box numbers and "In care of" addresses are not acceptable. Enter a contact telephone number for the issuer. If you identified more than one issuer in response to Item 1, enter the requested information for the primary issuer you identified in response to that item and, at your option, for any or all of the other issuers you identified on your Item 1 and 2 continuation page(s).

Item 3. Related Persons. Enter the full name and address of each person having the specified relationships with any issuer and identify each relationship:

> • Each executive officer and director of the issuer and person performing similar functions (title alone is not determinative) for the issuer, such as the general and managing partners of partnerships and managing members of limited liability companies; and

> • Each person who has functioned directly or indirectly as a promoter of the issuer within the past five years of the later of the first sale of securities or the date upon which the Form D filing was required to be made.

If necessary to prevent the information supplied from being misleading, also provide a clarification in the space provided.

Identify additional persons having the specified relationships by checking the box provided and attaching Item 3 continuation page(s).

Item 4. Industry Group. Select the issuer's industry group. If the issuer or issuers can be categorized in more than one industry group, select the industry group that most accurately reflects the use of the bulk of the proceeds of the offering. For purposes of this filing, use the ordinary dictionary and commonly understood meanings of the terms identifying the industry group.

Item 5. Issuer Size.

• **Revenue Range** (for issuers that do not specify "Hedge Fund" or "Other Investment Fund" in response to Item 4): Enter the revenue range of the issuer or of all the issuers together for the most recently completed fiscal year available, or, if not in existence for a fiscal year, revenue range to date. Domestic SEC reporting companies should state revenues in accordance with Regulation S-X under the Securities Exchange Act of 1934. Domestic non-reporting companies should state revenues in accordance with U.S. Generally Accepted Accounting Principles (GAAP). Foreign issuers should calculate revenues in U.S. dollars and state them in accordance with U.S. GAAP, home country GAAP or International Financial Reporting Standards. If the issuer(s) declines to disclose its revenue range, enter "Decline to Disclose." If the issuer's(s') business is intended to produce revenue but did not, enter "No Revenues." If the business is not intended to produce revenue (for example, the business seeks asset appreciation only), enter "Not Applicable."

• **Aggregate Net Asset Value** (for issuers that specify "Hedge Fund" or "Other Investment Fund" in response to Item 4): Enter the aggregate net asset value range of the issuer or of all the issuers together as of the most recent practicable date. If the issuer(s) declines to disclose its aggregate net asset value range, enter "Decline to Disclose."

Item 6. Federal Exemption(s) and Exclusion(s) Claimed. Select the provision(s) being claimed to exempt the offering and resulting sales from the federal registration requirements under the Securities Act of 1933 and, if applicable, to exclude the issuer from the definition of "investment company" under the Investment Company Act of 1940. Select "Rule 504(b)(1) (not (i), (ii) or (iii))" only if the issuer is relying on the exemption in the introductory sentence of Rule 504 for offers and sales that satisfy all the terms and conditions of Rules 501 and 502(a), (c) and (d).

Item 7. Type of Filing. Indicate whether the issuer is filing a new notice or an amendment to a notice that was filed previously. If this is a new notice, enter the date of the first sale of securities in the offering or indicate that the first sale has "Yet to Occur." For this purpose, the date of first sale is the date on which the first investor is irrevocably contractually committed to invest, which, depending on the terms and conditions of the contract, could be the date on which the issuer receives the investor's subscription agreement or check.

Item 8. Duration of Offering. Indicate whether the issuer intends the offering to last for more than one year.

Form D 6

FORM D

FORM D
Item-by-Item Instructions (Continued)

Item 9. Type(s) of Securities Offered. Select the appropriate type or types of securities offered as to which this notice is filed. If the securities are debt convertible into other securities, however, select "Debt" and any other appropriate types of securities except for "Equity." For purposes of this filing, use the ordinary dictionary and commonly understood meanings of these categories. For instance, equity securities would be securities that represent proportional ownership in an issuer, such as ordinary common and preferred stock of corporations and partnership and limited liability company interests; debt securities would be securities representing money loaned to an issuer that must be repaid to the investor at a later date; pooled investment fund interests would be securities that represent ownership interests in a pooled or collective investment vehicle; tenant-in-common securities would be securities that include an undivided fractional interest in real property other than a mineral property; and mineral property securities would be securities that include an undivided interest in an oil, gas or other mineral property.

Item 10. Business Combination Transaction. Indicate whether or not the offering is being made in connection with a business combination, such as an exchange (tender) offer or a merger, acquisition, or other transaction of the type described in paragraph (a)(1), (2) or (3) of Rule 145 under the Securities Act of 1933. Do not include an exchange (tender) offer for a class of the issuer's own securities. If necessary to prevent the information supplied from being misleading, also provide a clarification in the space provided.

Item 11. Minimum Investment. Enter the minimum dollar amount of investment that will be accepted from any outside investor. If the offering provides a minimum investment amount for outside investors that can be waived, provide the lowest amount below which a waiver will not be granted. If there is no minimum investment amount, enter "0." Investors will be considered outside investors if they are not employees, officers, directors, general partners, trustees (where the issuer is a business trust), consultants, advisors or vendors of the issuer, its parents, its majority owned subsidiaries, or majority owned subsidiaries of the issuer's parent.

Item 12. Sales Compensation. Enter the requested information for each person that has been or will be paid directly or indirectly any commission or other similar compensation in cash or other consideration in connection with sales of securities in the offering, including finders. Enter the CRD number for every person identified and any broker and dealer listed that has a CRD number. CRD numbers can be found at http://brokercheck.finra.org. A person that does not have a CRD number need not obtain one in order to be listed, and must be listed when required regardless of whether the person has a CRD number. In addition, check the State(s) in which the named person has solicited or intends to solicit investors. If more than five persons to be listed are associated persons of the same broker or dealer, enter only the name of the broker or dealer, its CRD number and street address, and the State(s) in which the named person has solicited or intends to solicit investors.

Item 13. Offering and Sales Amounts. Enter the dollar amount of securities being offered under a claim of federal exemption identified in Item 6 above. Also enter the dollar amount of securities sold in the offering as of the filing date. Select the "Indefinite" box if the amount being offered is undetermined or cannot be calculated at the present time, such as if the offering includes securities to be acquired upon the exercise or exchange of other securities or property and the exercise price or exchange value is not currently known or knowable. If an amount is definite but difficult to calculate without unreasonable effort or expense, provide a good faith estimate. The total offering and sold amounts should include all cash and other consideration to be received for the securities, including cash to be paid in the future under mandatory capital commitments. In offerings for consideration other than cash, the amounts entered should be based on the issuer's good faith valuation of the consideration. If necessary to prevent the information supplied from being misleading, also provide a clarification in the space provided.

Item 14. Investors. Indicate whether securities in the offering have been or may be sold to persons who do not qualify as accredited investors as defined in Rule 501(a), 17 CFR 230.501(a), and provide the number of such investors who have already invested in the offering. In addition, regardless of whether securities in the offering have been or may be sold to persons who do not qualify as accredited investors, specify the total number of investors who already have invested.

Item 15. Sales Commission and Finders' Fees Expenses. The information on sales commissions and finders' fees expenses may be given as subject to future contingencies.

Item 16. Use of Proceeds. No additional instructions.

Signature and Submission. An individual who is a duly authorized representative of each issuer identified must sign, date and submit this notice for the issuer. The capacity in which the individual is signing should be set forth in the "Title" field underneath the individual's name.

The name of the issuer(s) on whose behalf the notice is being submitted should be set forth in the "Issuer" field beside the individual's name; if the individual is signing on behalf of all issuers submitting the notice, the word "All" may be set forth in the "Issuer" field. Attach signature continuation page(s) to have different individuals sign on behalf of different issuer(s). Enter the number of continuation pages attached and included in the filing. If no continuation pages are attached, enter "0".

FORM D

U.S. Securities and Exchange Commission
Washington, DC 20549
Items 1 and 2 Continuation Page

Item 1 and 2. Issuer's Identity and Contact Information (Continued)

Name of Issuer

Previous Name(s) ☐ None

Entity Type (Select one)
- ○ Corporation
- ○ Limited Partnership
- ○ Limited Liability Company
- ○ General Partnership
- ○ Business Trust
- ○ Other (Specify)

Jurisdiction of Incorporation/Organization

Year of Incorporation/Organization
(Select one)
- ○ Over Five Years Ago
- ○ Within Last Five Years (specify year)
- ○ Yet to Be Formed

At your option, supply separate contact information for this issuer:

Street Address 1

Street Address 2

City

State/Province/Country

ZIP/Postal Code

Phone No.

Name of Issuer

Previous Name(s) ☐ None

Entity Type (Select one)
- ○ Corporation
- ○ Limited Partnership
- ○ Limited Liability Company
- ○ General Partnership
- ○ Business Trust
- ○ Other (Specify)

Jurisdiction of Incorporation/Organization

Year of Incorporation/Organization
(Select one)
- ○ Over Five Years Ago
- ○ Within Last Five Years (specify year)
- ○ Yet to Be Formed

At your option, supply separate contact information for this issuer:

Street Address 1

Street Address 2

City

State/Province/Country

ZIP/Postal Code

Phone No.

Name of Issuer

Previous Name(s) ☐ None

Entity Type (Select one)
- ○ Corporation
- ○ Limited Partnership
- ○ Limited Liability Company
- ○ General Partnership
- ○ Business Trust
- ○ Other (Specify)

Jurisdiction of Incorporation/Organization

Year of Incorporation/Organization
(Select one)
- ○ Over Five Years Ago
- ○ Within Last Five Years (specify year)
- ○ Yet to Be Formed

At your option, supply separate contact information for this issuer:

Street Address 1

Street Address 2

City

State/Province/Country

ZIP/Postal Code

Phone No.

(Copy and use additional copies of this page as necessary.)

Form D 8

FORM D

FORM D

U.S. Securities and Exchange Commission
Washington, DC 20549

Item 3 Continuation Page

Item 3. Related Persons (Continued)

Last Name	First Name	Middle Name

Street Address 1	Street Address 2

City	State/Province/Country	ZIP/Postal Code

Relationship(s): ☐ Executive Officer ☐ Director ☐ Promoter

Clarification of Response (if necessary)

Last Name	First Name	Middle Name

Street Address 1	Street Address 2

City	State/Province/Country	ZIP/Postal Code

Relationship(s): ☐ Executive Officer ☐ Director ☐ Promoter

Clarification of Response (if necessary)

Last Name	First Name	Middle Name

Street Address 1	Street Address 2

City	State/Province/Country	ZIP/Postal Code

Relationship(s): ☐ Executive Officer ☐ Director ☐ Promoter

Clarification of Response (if necessary)

Last Name	First Name	Middle Name

Street Address 1	Street Address 2

City	State/Province/Country	ZIP/Postal Code

Relationship(s): ☐ Executive Officer ☐ Director ☐ Promoter

Clarification of Response (if necessary)

(Copy and use additional copies of this page as necessary.)

Form D 9

FORM D

U.S. Securities and Exchange Commission
Washington, DC 20549

Item 12 Continuation Page

Item 12. Sales Compensation (Continued)

Recipient

Recipient CRD Number

☐ No CRD Number

(Associated) Broker or Dealer   ☐ None

(Associated) Broker or Dealer CRD Number

☐ No CRD Number

Street Address 1

Street Address 2

City

State/Province/Country

ZIP/Postal Code

States of Solicitation   ☐ All States

☐ AL	☐ AK	☐ AZ	☐ AR	☐ CA	☐ CO	☐ CT	☐ DE	☐ DC	☐ FL	☐ GA	☐ HI	☐ ID
☐ IL	☐ IN	☐ IA	☐ KS	☐ KY	☐ LA	☐ ME	☐ MD	☐ MA	☐ MI	☐ MN	☐ MS	☐ MO
☐ MT	☐ NE	☐ NV	☐ NH	☐ NJ	☐ NM	☐ NY	☐ NC	☐ ND	☐ OH	☐ OK	☐ OR	☐ PA
☐ RI	☐ SC	☐ SD	☐ TN	☐ TX	☐ UT	☐ VT	☐ VA	☐ WA	☐ WV	☐ WI	☐ WY	☐ PR

- -

Recipient

Recipient CRD Number

☐ No CRD Number

(Associated) Broker or Dealer   ☐ None

(Associated) Broker or Dealer CRD Number

☐ No CRD Number

Street Address 1

Street Address 2

City

State/Province/Country

ZIP/Postal Code

States of Solicitation   ☐ All States

☐ AL	☐ AK	☐ AZ	☐ AR	☐ CA	☐ CO	☐ CT	☐ DE	☐ DC	☐ FL	☐ GA	☐ HI	☐ ID
☐ IL	☐ IN	☐ IA	☐ KS	☐ KY	☐ LA	☐ ME	☐ MD	☐ MA	☐ MI	☐ MN	☐ MS	☐ MO
☐ MT	☐ NE	☐ NV	☐ NH	☐ NJ	☐ NM	☐ NY	☐ NC	☐ ND	☐ OH	☐ OK	☐ OR	☐ PA
☐ RI	☐ SC	☐ SD	☐ TN	☐ TX	☐ UT	☐ VT	☐ VA	☐ WA	☐ WV	☐ WI	☐ WY	☐ PR

- -

(Copy and use additional copies of this page as necessary.)

Form D 10

FORM D

FORM D

U.S. Securities and Exchange Commission
Washington, DC 20549

Signature Continuation Page

Signature and Submission

The undersigned is the duly authorized representative of the issuer(s), identied in the field beside the individual's name below.

Issuer

Name of Signer

Signature

Title

Date

Issuer

Name of Signer

Signature

Title

Date

Issuer

Name of Signer

Signature

Title

Date

Issuer

Name of Signer

Signature

Title

Date

(Copy and use additional copies of this page as necessary.)
Form D 11

B. DISCLOSURE GUIDES

REGULATION S–K

GENERAL RULES

General Rules Regarding Disclosures: Regulation S–K—Standard Instructions for Filing Forms Under Securities Act of 1933 and the Securities Exchange Act of 1934

17 C.F.R. § 229.___

REGULATION S-K

Subpart 1—General

Item 10. General

(a) *Application of Regulation S–K.* This part (together with the General Rules and Regulations under the Securities Act of 1933, as amended ("Securities Act"), and the Securities Exchange Act of 1934, as amended ("Exchange Act") the Interpretative Releases under these Acts and the forms under these Acts) states the requirements applicable to the content of the non-financial statement portions of:

(1) Registration statements under the Securities Act to the extent provided in the forms to be used for registration under such Act; and

(2) Registration statements under section 12, annual or other reports under sections 13 and 15(d), annual reports to security holders and proxy and information statements under section 14 of the Exchange Act, and any other documents required to be filed under the Exchange Act, to the extent provided in the forms and rules under such Act.

(b) *Commission Policy on Projections.* The Commission encourages the use in documents specified in Rule 175 under the Securities Act and Rule 3b–6 under the Exchange Act of management's projections of future economic performance that have a reasonable basis and are presented in an appropriate format. The guidelines set forth herein represent the Commission's views on important factors to be considered in formulating and disclosing such projections.

(1) *Basis for Projections.* The Commission believes that management must have the option to present in Commission filings its good faith assessment of a registrant's future performance. Management, however, must have a reasonable basis for such an assessment. Although a history of operations or experience in projecting may be among the factors providing a basis for management's assessment, the Commission does not believe that a registrant always must have had such a history or experience in order to formulate projections with a reasonable basis. An outside review of management's projections may furnish additional support for having a reasonable basis for a projection. If management decides to include a report of such a review in a Commission filing, there also should be disclosure of the qualifications of the reviewer, the extent of the review, the relationship between the reviewer and the registrant, and other material factors concerning the process by which any outside review was sought or obtained. Moreover, in the case of a registration statement under the Securities Act, the reviewer would be deemed an expert and an appropriate consent must be filed with the registration statement.

(2) *Format for projections.* In determining the appropriate format for projections included in Commission filings, consideration must be given to, among other things, the financial items to be projected, the period to be covered, and the manner of presentation to be used. Although traditionally projections have been given for three financial items generally considered to be of primary importance

to investors (revenues, net income (loss) and earnings (loss) per share), projection information need not necessarily be limited to these three items. However, management should take care to assure that the choice of items projected is not susceptible of misleading inferences through selective projection of only favorable items. Revenues, net income (loss) and earnings (loss) per share usually are presented together in order to avoid any misleading inferences that may arise when the individual items reflect contradictory trends. There may be instances, however, when it is appropriate to present earnings (loss) from continuing operations in addition to or in lieu of net income (loss). It generally would be misleading to present sales or revenue projections without one of the foregoing measures of income. The period that appropriately may be covered by a projection depends to a large extent on the particular circumstances of the company involved. For certain companies in certain industries, a projection covering a two or three year period may be entirely reasonable. Other companies may not have a reasonable basis for projections beyond the current year. Accordingly, management should select the period most appropriate in the circumstances. In addition, management, in making a projection, should disclose what, in its opinion, is the most probable specific amount or the most reasonable range for each financial item projected based on the selected assumptions. Ranges, however, should not be so wide as to make the disclosures meaningless. Moreover, several projections based on varying assumptions may be judged by management to be more meaningful than a single number or range and would be permitted.

(3) *Investor Understanding.*

(i) When management chooses to include its projections in a Commission filing, the disclosures accompanying the projections should facilitate investor understanding of the basis for and limitations of projections. In this regard investors should be cautioned against attributing undue certainty to management's assessment, and the Commission believes that investors would be aided by a statement indicating management's intention regarding the furnishing of updated projections. The Commission also believes that investor understanding would be enhanced by disclosure of the assumptions which in management's opinion are most significant to the projections or are the key factors upon which the financial results of the enterprise depend and encourages disclosure of assumptions in a manner that will provide a framework for analysis of the projection.

(ii) Management also should consider whether disclosure of the accuracy or inaccuracy of previous projections would provide investors with important insights into the limitations of projections. In this regard, consideration should be given to presenting the projections in a format that will facilitate subsequent analysis of the reasons for differences between actual and forecast results. An important benefit may arise from the systematic analysis of variances between projected and actual results on a continuing basis, since such disclosure may highlight for investors the most significant risk and profit-sensitive areas in a business operation.

(iii) With respect to previously issued projections, registrants are reminded of their responsibility to make full and prompt disclosure of material facts, both favorable and unfavorable, regarding their financial condition. This responsibility may extend to situations where management knows or has reason to know that its previously disclosed projects no longer have a reasonable basis.

(iv) Since a registrant's ability to make projections with relative confidence may vary with all the facts and circumstances, the responsibility for determining whether to discontinue or to resume making projections is best left to management. However, the Commission encourages registrants not to discontinue or to resume projections in Commission filings without a reasonable basis.

(c) *Commission Policy on Security Ratings.* In view of the importance of security ratings ("ratings") to investors and the marketplace, the Commission permits registrants to disclose, on a voluntary basis, ratings assigned by rating organizations to classes of debt securities, convertible debt securities and preferred stock in registration statements and periodic reports. Set forth herein are the Commission's views on important matters to be considered in disclosing security ratings.

(1) *Securities Act Filings.*

(i) If a registrant includes in a registration statement filed under the Securities Act any rating(s) assigned to a class of securities, it should consider including:

(A) Any other rating intended for public dissemination assigned to such class by a nationally recognized statistical rating organization (NRSRO) ("additional NRSRO rating") that is available on the date of the initial filing of the document and that is materially different from any rating disclosed; and

(B) The name of each rating organization whose rating is disclosed; each such rating organization's definition or description of the category in which it rated the class of securities; the relative rank of each rating within the assigning rating organization's overall classification system; and a statement informing investors that a security rating is not a recommendation to buy, sell or hold securities, that it may be subject to revision or withdrawal at any time by the assigning rating organization, and that each rating should be evaluated independently of any other rating. The registrant also should include the written consent of any rating organization that is not a NRSRO whose rating is included. With respect to the written consent of any rating organization that is not a NRSRO whose rating is included, see Rule 436(g) under the securities Act. When the registrant has filed a registration statement on Form F–9, see Rule 436(g) under the Securities Act with respect to the written consent of any rating organization specified in the Instruction to paragraph (a)(2) of General Instruction I of Form F–9.

(ii) If a change in a rating already included is available subsequent to the filing of the registration statement, but prior to its effectiveness, the registrant should consider including such rating change in the final prospectus. If the rating change is material or if a materially different rating from any disclosed becomes available during this period, the registrant should consider amending the registration statement to include the rating change or additional rating and recirculating the preliminary prospectus.

(iii) If a materially different additional NRSRO rating or a material change in a rating already included becomes available during any period in which offers or sales are being made, the registrant should consider disclosing such additional rating or rating change by means of post-effective amendment or sticker to the prospectus pursuant to Rule 424(b) under the Securities Act, unless, in the case of a registration statement on Form S–3, it has been disclosed in a document incorporated by reference into the registration statement subsequent to its effectiveness and prior to the termination of the offering.

(2) *Exchange Act Filings.* (i) If a registrant includes in a registration statement or periodic report filed under the Exchange Act any rating(s) assigned to a class of securities, it should consider including the information specified in paragraphs (c)(1)(i)(A) and (B) of this Item.

(ii) If there is a material change in the rating(s) assigned by any NRSRO(s) to any outstanding class(es) of securities of a registrant subject to the reporting requirements of section 13(a) or 15(d) of the Exchange Act, the registrant should consider filing a report on Form 8–K or other appropriate report under the Exchange Act disclosing such rating change.

(d) [Removed and Reserved].

(e) *Use of Non-GAAP Financial Measures in Commission Filings.*

(1) Whenever one or more non-GAAP financial measures are included in a filing with the Commission:

(i) The registrant must include the following in the filing:

(A) A presentation, with equal or greater prominence, of the most directly comparable financial measure or measures calculated and presented in accordance with Generally Accepted Accounting Principles (GAAP);

(B) A reconciliation (by schedule or other clearly understandable method), which shall be quantitative for historical non-GAAP measures presented, and quantitative, to the extent available without unreasonable efforts, for forward-looking information, of the differences between the non-GAAP financial measure disclosed or released with the most directly comparable financial measure or measures calculated and presented in accordance with GAAP identified in paragraph (e)(1)(i)(A) of this Item;

(C) A statement disclosing the reasons why the registrant's management believes that presentation of the non-GAAP financial measure provides useful information to investors regarding the registrant's financial condition and results of operations; and

(D) To the extent material, a statement disclosing the additional purposes, if any, for which the registrant's management uses the non-GAAP financial measure that are not disclosed pursuant to paragraph (e)(1)(i)(C) of this Item; and

(ii) A registrant must not:

(A) Exclude charges or liabilities that required, or will require, cash settlement, or would have required cash settlement absent an ability to settle in another manner, from non-GAAP liquidity measures, other than the measures earnings before interest and taxes (EBIT) and earnings before interest, taxes, depreciation, and amortization (EBITDA);

(B) Adjust a non-GAAP performance measure to eliminate or smooth items identified as non-recurring, infrequent or unusual, when the nature of the charge or gain is such that it is reasonably likely to recur within two years or there was a similar charge or gain within the prior two years;

(C) Present non-GAAP financial measures on the face of the registrant's financial statements prepared in accordance with GAAP or in the accompanying notes;

(D) Present non-GAAP financial measures on the face of any pro forma financial information required to be disclosed by Article 11 of Regulation S–X (Items 11–01 through 11–03); or

(E) Use titles or descriptions of non-GAAP financial measures that are the same as, or confusingly similar to, titles or descriptions used for GAAP financial measures; and

(iii) If the filing is not an annual report on Form 10–K or Form 20–F, a registrant need not include the information required by paragraphs (e)(1)(i)(C) and (e)(1)(i)(D) of this Item if that information was included in its most recent annual report on Form 10–K or Form 20–F or a more recent filing, provided that the required information is updated to the extent necessary to meet the requirements of paragraphs (e)(1)(i)(C) and (e)(1)(i)(D) of this Item at the time of the registrant's current filing.

(2) For purposes of this paragraph (e), a non-GAAP financial measure is a numerical measure of a registrant's historical or future financial performance, financial position or cash flows that:

(i) Excludes amounts, or is subject to adjustments that have the effect of excluding amounts, that are included in the most directly comparable measure calculated and presented in accordance with GAAP in the statement of income, balance sheet or statement of cash flows (or equivalent statements) of the issuer; or

(ii) Includes amounts, or is subject to adjustments that have the effect of including amounts, that are excluded from the most directly comparable measure so calculated and presented.

(3) For purposes of this paragraph (e), GAAP refers to generally accepted accounting principles in the United States, except that:

(i) In the case of foreign private issuers whose primary financial statements are prepared in accordance with non-U.S. generally accepted accounting principles, GAAP refers to the principles under which those primary financial statements are prepared; and

(ii) In the case of foreign private issuers that include a non-GAAP financial measure derived from or based on a measure calculated in accordance with U.S. generally accepted accounting principles, GAAP refers to U.S. generally accepted accounting principles for purposes of the application of the requirements of this paragraph (e) to the disclosure of that measure.

(4) For purposes of this paragraph (e), non-GAAP financial measures exclude:

(i) Operating and other statistical measures; and

(ii) Ratios or statistical measures calculated using exclusively one or both of:

    (A) Financial measures calculated in accordance with GAAP; and

    (B) Operating measures or other measures that are not non-GAAP financial measures.

    (5) For purposes of this paragraph (e), non-GAAP financial measures exclude financial measures required to be disclosed by GAAP, Commission rules, or a system of regulation of a government or governmental authority or self-regulatory organization that is applicable to the registrant. However, the financial measure should be presented outside of the financial statements unless the financial measure is required or expressly permitted by the standard-setter that is responsible for establishing the GAAP used in such financial statements.

    (6) The requirements of paragraph (e) of this rule shall not apply to a non-GAAP financial measure included in disclosure relating to a proposed business combination, the entity resulting therefrom or an entity that is a party thereto, if the disclosure is contained in a communication that is subject to Rule 425 under the Securities Act, Rule 14a–12 or Rule 14d–2(b)(2) under the Exchange Act or Item 1015 of Regulation S–K.

    (7) The requirements of paragraph (e) of this Item shall not apply to investment companies registered under section 8 of the Investment Company Act of 1940.

    NOTE to paragraph (e). A non-GAAP financial measure that would otherwise be prohibited by paragraph (e)(1)(ii) of this Item is permitted in a filing of a foreign private issuer if:

    1. The non-GAAP financial measure relates to the GAAP used in the registrant's primary financial statements included in its filing with the Commission;

    2. The non-GAAP financial measure is required or expressly permitted by the standard-setter that is responsible for establishing the GAAP used in such financial statements; and

    3. The non-GAAP financial measure is included in the annual report prepared by the registrant for use in the jurisdiction in which it is domiciled, incorporated or organized or for distribution to its security holders.

    (f) *Smaller Reporting Companies.* The requirements of this part apply to smaller reporting companies. A smaller reporting company may comply with either the requirements applicable to smaller reporting companies or the requirements applicable to other companies for each item, unless the requirements for smaller reporting companies specify that smaller reporting companies must comply with the smaller reporting company requirements. The following items of this part set forth requirements for smaller reporting companies that are different from requirements applicable to other companies:

Item 101	Description of business
Item 201	Market price of and dividends on registrant's common equity and related stockholder matters
Item 301	Selected Financial Data
Item 302	Supplementary Financial Information
Item 303	Management's discussion and analysis of financial condition and results of operations
Item 305	Quantitative and qualitative disclosures about market risk
Item 402	Executive compensation
Item 404	Transactions with related persons, promoters and certain control persons
Item 407	Corporate governance
Item 503	Prospectus summary
Item 504	Use of proceeds
Item 601	Exhibits

    (1) *Definition of smaller reporting company.* As used in this part, the term *smaller reporting company* means an issuer that is not an investment company, an asset-backed issuer (as defined in

§ 229.1101), or a majority-owned subsidiary of a parent that is not a smaller reporting company and that:

   (i)   Had a public float of less than $250 million; or

   (ii)   Had annual revenues of less than $100 million and either:

      (A)   No public float; or

      (B)   A public float of less than $700 million.

  (2)   *Determination.* Whether an issuer is a smaller reporting company is determined on an annual basis.

   (i)   For issuers that are required to file reports under section 13(a) or 15(d) of the Exchange Act:

      (A)   Public float is measured as of the last business day of the issuer's most recently completed second fiscal quarter and computed by multiplying the aggregate worldwide number of shares of its voting and non-voting common equity held by non-affiliates by the price at which the common equity was last sold, or the average of the bid and asked prices of common equity, in the principal market for the common equity;

      (B)   Annual revenues are as of the most recently completed fiscal year for which audited financial statements are available; and

      (C)   An issuer must reflect the determination of whether it came within the definition of smaller reporting company in its quarterly report on Form 10–Q for the first fiscal quarter of the next year, indicating on the cover page of that filing, and in subsequent filings for that fiscal year, whether it is a smaller reporting company, except that, if a determination based on public float indicates that the issuer is newly eligible to be a smaller reporting company, the issuer may choose to reflect this determination beginning with its first quarterly report on Form 10–Q following the determination, rather than waiting until the first fiscal quarter of the next year.

   (ii)   For determinations based on an initial registration statement under the Securities Act or Exchange Act for shares of its common equity:

      (A)   Public float is measured as of a date within 30 days of the date of the filing of the registration statement and computed by multiplying the aggregate worldwide number of shares of its voting and non-voting common equity held by non-affiliates before the registration plus, in the case of a Securities Act registration statement, the number of shares of its voting and non-voting common equity included in the registration statement by the estimated public offering price of the shares;

      (B)   Annual revenues are as of the most recently completed fiscal year for which audited financial statements are available; and

      (C)   The issuer must reflect the determination of whether it came within the definition of smaller reporting company in the registration statement and must appropriately indicate on the cover page of the filing, and subsequent filings for the fiscal year in which the filing is made, whether it is a smaller reporting company. The issuer must re-determine its status at the end of its second fiscal quarter and then reflect any change in status as provided in paragraph (f)(2)(i)(C) of this item. In the case of a determination based on an initial Securities Act registration statement, an issuer that was not determined to be a smaller reporting company has the option to re-determine its status at the conclusion of the offering covered by the registration statement based on the actual offering price and number of shares sold.

   (iii)   Once an issuer determines that it does not qualify for smaller reporting company status because it exceeded one or more of the current thresholds, it will remain unqualified unless when making its annual determination either:

      (A)   It determines that its public float was less than $200 million; or

(B) It determines that its public float and its annual revenues meet the requirements for subsequent qualification included in the chart below:

Prior Annual Revenues	Prior Public Float	
	None or less than $700 million	**$700 million or more**
Less than $100 million	Neither threshold exceeded	**Public float** Less than $560 million; and **Revenues** Less than $100 million.
$100 million or more	**Public float** None or less than $700 million; and **Revenues** Less than $80 million.	**Public float** Less than $560 million; and **Revenues** Less than $80 million.

Instruction to Paragraph (f): A registrant that qualifies as a smaller reporting company under the public float thresholds identified in paragraphs (f)(1)(i) and (f)(2)(iii)(A) of this item will qualify as a smaller reporting company regardless of its revenues.

Instruction 2 to paragraph (f): A foreign private issuer is not eligible to use the requirements for smaller reporting companies unless it uses the forms and rules designated for domestic issuers and provides financial statements prepared in accordance with U.S. Generally Accepted Accounting Principles.

Subpart 100—Business

Item 101.   Description of Business

(a) *General Development of Business.* Describe the general development of the business of the registrant, its subsidiaries, and any predecessor(s).

(1) In describing developments, only information material to an understanding of the general development of the business is required. Disclosure may include, but should not be limited to, the following topics:

(i) Any material changes to a previously disclosed business strategy;

(ii) The nature and effects of any material bankruptcy, receivership, or any similar proceeding with respect to the registrant or any of its significant subsidiaries;

(iii) The nature and effects of any material reclassification, merger or consolidation of the registrant or any of its significant subsidiaries; and

(iv) The acquisition or disposition of any material amount of assets otherwise than in the ordinary course of business.

(2) Notwithstanding the provisions of Rule 411(b) or Rule 12b–23(a) of this chapter, as applicable, a registrant may only forgo providing a full discussion of the general development of its business for a filing other than an initial registration statement if it provides an update to the general development of its business, disclosing all of the material developments that have occurred since the most recent registration statement or report that includes a full discussion of the general development of its business. In addition, the registrant must incorporate by reference, and include one active hyperlink to one registration statement or report that includes, the full discussion of the general development of the registrant's business.

(b) [Removed and Reserved]

(c) *Narrative Description of Business.*

(1) Describe the business done and intended to be done by the registrant and its subsidiaries, focusing upon the registrant's dominant segment or each reportable segment about which financial information is presented in the financial statements. When describing each segment, only information material to an understanding of the business taken as a whole is required. Disclosure may include, but should not be limited to, the information specified in paragraphs (c)(1)(i) through (v) of this item.

(i) Revenue-generating activities, products and/or services, and any dependence on revenue-generating activities, key products, services, product families or customers, including governmental customers;

(ii) Status of development efforts for new or enhanced products, trends in market demand and competitive conditions;

(iii) Resources material to a registrant's business, such as:

    (A) Sources and availability of raw materials; and

    (B) The duration and effect of all patents, trademarks, licenses, franchises, and concessions held;

(iv) A description of any material portion of the business that may be subject to renegotiation of profits or termination of contracts or subcontracts at the election of the Government; and

(v) The extent to which the business is or may be seasonal.

(2) Discuss the information specified in paragraphs (c)(2)(i) and (ii) of this section with respect to, and to the extent material to an understanding of, the registrant's business taken as a whole, except that, if the information is material to a particular segment, you should additionally identify that segment.

(i) The material effects that compliance with government regulations, including environmental regulations, may have upon the capital expenditures, earnings and competitive position of the registrant and its subsidiaries, including the estimated capital expenditures for environmental control facilities for the current fiscal year and any other material subsequent period; and

(ii) A description of the registrant's human capital resources, including the number of persons employed by the registrant, and any human capital measures or objectives that the registrant focuses on in managing the business (such as, depending on the nature of the registrant's business and workforce, measures or objectives that address the development, attraction and retention of personnel).

(d) [Removed and Reserved].

(e) *Available information.* Disclose the information in paragraphs (e)(1), (e)(2) and (e)(3) of this item in any registration statement you file under the Securities Act (15 U.S.C. 77a et seq.), and disclose the information in paragraph (e)(3) of this item in your annual report on Form 10-K. Further disclose the information in paragraph (e)(4) of this item if you are an accelerated filer or a large accelerated filer (as defined in Exchange Act Rule 12b-2) filing an annual report on Form 10-K:

(1) Whether you file reports with the Securities and Exchange Commission. If you are reporting company, identify the reports and other information you file with the SEC.

(2) State that the SEC maintains an Internet site that contains reports, proxy and information statements, and other information regarding issuers that file electronically with the SEC and state the address of that site (http://www.sec.gov).

(3) Disclose your Internet address, if you have one.

(4)(i) Whether you make available free of charge on or through your Internet website, if you have one, your annual report on Form 10-K, quarterly reports on Form 10-Q, current reports on Form 8-K, and amendments to those reports filed or furnished pursuant to Section 13(a) or 15(d) of the Exchange Act as soon as reasonably practicable after you electronically file such material with, or furnish it to, the SEC;

(ii) If you do not make your filings available in this manner, the reasons you do not do so (including, where applicable, that you do not have an Internet website); and

(iii) If you do not make your filings available in this manner, whether you voluntarily will provide electronic or paper copies of your filings free of charge upon request.

(f) *Reports to Security Holders.* Disclose the following information in any registration statement you file under the Securities Act:

(1) If the SEC's proxy rules or regulations, or stock exchange requirements, do not require you to send an annual report to security holders or to holders of American depository receipts, describe briefly the nature and frequency of reports that you will give to security holders. Specify whether the reports that you give will contain financial information that has been examined and reported on, with an opinion expressed "by" an independent public or certified public accountant.

(2) For a foreign private issuer, if the report will not contain financial information prepared in accordance with U.S. generally accepted accounting principles, you must state whether the report will include a reconciliation of this information with U.S. generally accepted accounting principles.

(g) *Enforceability of Civil Liabilities Against Foreign Persons.* Disclose the following if you are a foreign private issuer filing a registration statement under the Securities Act:

(1) Whether or not investors may bring actions under the civil liability provisions of the U.S. federal securities laws against the foreign private issuer, any of its officers and directors who are residents of a foreign country, any underwriters or experts named in the registration statement that are residents of a foreign country, and whether investors may enforce these civil liability provisions when the assets of the issuer or these other persons are located outside of the United States. The disclosure must address the following matters:

(i) The investor's ability to effect service of process within the United States on the foreign private issuer or any person;

(ii) The investor's ability to enforce judgments obtained in U.S. courts against foreign persons based upon the civil liability provisions of the U.S. federal securities laws;

(iii) The investor's ability to enforce, in an appropriate foreign court, judgments of U.S. courts based upon the civil liability provisions of the U.S. federal securities laws; and

(iv) The investor's ability to bring an original action in an appropriate foreign court to enforce liabilities against the foreign private issuer or any person based upon the U.S. federal securities laws.

(2) If you provide this disclosure based on an opinion of counsel, name counsel in the prospectus and file as an exhibit to the registration statement a signed consent of counsel to the use of its name and opinion.

(h) *Smaller Reporting Companies.* A smaller reporting company, as defined by Item 10(f)(1), may satisfy its obligations under this Item by describing the development of its business pursuant to this paragraph (h). In describing developments under paragraphs (h)(1) through (3), information should be provided for the period of time that is material to an understanding of the general development of the business. Notwithstanding the provisions of Rule 411(b) or Rule12b–23(a) of this chapter as applicable, a smaller reporting company may only forgo providing a full discussion of the general development of its business for a filing other than an initial registration statement if it provides an update to the general development of its business disclosing all of the material developments that have occurred since the most recent registration statement or report that includes a full discussion of the general development of its business. In addition, the smaller reporting company must incorporate by reference, and include one active hyperlink to one registration statement or report that includes, the full discussion of the general development of the registrant's business. If the smaller reporting company has not been in business for three years, provide the same information for predecessor(s) of the smaller reporting company if there are any. This business development description should include:

(1) Form and year of organization;

(2) Any bankruptcy, receivership or similar proceeding; and

(3) Any material reclassification, merger, consolidation, or purchase or sale of a significant amount of assets not in the ordinary course of business.

(4) *Business of the smaller reporting company.* Briefly describe the business and include, to the extent material to an understanding of the smaller reporting company:

(i) Principal products or services and their markets;

(ii) Distribution methods of the products or services;

(iii) Status of any publicly announced new product or service;

(iv) Competitive business conditions and the smaller reporting company's competitive position in the industry and methods of competition;

(v) Sources and availability of raw materials and the names of principal suppliers;

(vi) Dependence on one or a few major customers;

(vii) Patents, trademarks, licenses, franchises, concessions, royalty agreements or labor contracts, including duration;

(viii) Need for any government approval of principal products or services. If government approval is necessary and the smaller reporting company has not yet received that approval, discuss the status of the approval within the government approval process;

(ix) Effect of existing or probable governmental regulations on the business;

(x) [Removed and Reserved].

(xi) Costs and effects of compliance with environmental laws (federal, state and local); and

(xii) Number of total employees and number of full-time employees.

(5) *Reports to security holders.* Disclose the following in any registration statement you file under the Securities Act of 1933:

(i) If you are not required to deliver an annual report to security holders, whether you will voluntarily send an annual report and whether the report will include audited financial statements;

(ii) Whether you file reports with the Securities and Exchange Commission. If you are a reporting company, identify the reports and other information you file with the Commission; and

(iii) State that the Commission maintains an Internet site that contains reports, proxy and information statements, and other information regarding issuers that file electronically with the Commission and state the address of that site (http://www.sec.gov). Disclose your Internet address, if available.

(6) *Foreign issuers.* Provide the information required by Item 101(g).

Instructions to Item 101. 1. In determining what information about the segments is material to an understanding of the registrant's business taken as a whole and therefore required to be disclosed, pursuant to paragraph (c) of this Item, the registrant should take into account both quantitative and qualitative factors such as the significance of the matter to the registrant (e.g., whether a matter with a relatively minor impact on the registrant's business is represented by management to be important to its future profitability), the pervasiveness of the matter (e.g., whether it affects or may affect numerous items in the segment information), and the impact of the matter (e.g., whether it distorts the trends reflected in the segment information). Situations may arise when information should be disclosed about a segment, although the information in quantitative terms may not appear significant to the registrant's business taken as a whole.

2. Base the determination of whether information about segments is required for a particular year upon an evaluation of interperiod comparability. For instance, interperiod comparability would require a registrant to report segment information in the current period even if not material under the criteria for reportability of FASB ASC Topic 280, *Segment Reporting* if a segment has been significant in the immediately preceding period and the registrant expects it to be significant in the future.

3. The Commission, upon written request of the registrant and where consistent with the protection of investors, may permit the omission of any of the information required by this Item or the furnishing in substitution thereof of appropriate information of comparable character.

Item 102.   Description of Property

To the extent material, disclose the location and general character of the registrant's principal physical properties. In addition, identify the segment(s), as reported in the financial statements, that use the properties described. If any such property is not held in fee or is held subject to an encumbrance that is material to the registrant, so state and describe briefly how held.

Instruction 1 to Item 102. This item requires information that will reasonably inform investors as to the suitability, adequacy, productive capacity, and extent of utilization of the principal physical properties of the registrant and its subsidiaries, to the extent the described properties are material. A registrant should engage in a comprehensive consideration of the materiality of its properties. If appropriate, descriptions may be provided on a collective basis; detailed descriptions of the physical characteristics of individual properties or legal descriptions by metes and bounds are not required and shall not be given.

Instruction 2 to Item 102. In determining materiality under this Item, the registrant should take into account both quantitative and qualitative factors. See Instruction 1 to Item 101 of Regulation S–K.

Instruction 3 to Item 102. Registrants engaged in mining operations must refer to and, if required, provide the disclosure under Item 1300 through Item 1305 (subpart 1300 of Regulation S–K), in addition to any disclosure required by this item.

Instruction 4 to Item 102. A registrant engaged in oil and gas producing activities shall provide the information required by Subpart 1200 of Regulation S–K.

     A.   If the estimates of reserves, or any estimated valuation thereof, are represented as being based on estimates prepared or reviewed by independent consultants, those independent consultants shall be named in the document.

Instruction 5 to Item 102. The definitions in Item 4–10(a) of Regulation S–X shall apply to this Item with respect to oil and gas operations.

Instruction 6 to Item 102. The attention of certain issuers engaged in oil and gas producing activities is directed to the information called for in Securities Act Industry Guide 4.

Instruction 7 to Item 102. The attention of issuers engaged in real estate activities is directed to the information called for in Guide 5 (Item 801(e)).

Item 103.   Legal Proceedings

(a)   Describe briefly any material pending legal proceedings, other than ordinary routine litigation incidental to the business, to which the registrant or any of its subsidiaries is a party or of which any of their property is the subject. Include the name of the court or agency in which the proceedings are pending, the date instituted, the principal parties thereto, a description of the factual basis alleged to underlie the proceedings and the relief sought. Include similar information as to any such proceedings known to be contemplated by governmental authorities. Information may be provided by hyperlink or cross-reference to legal proceedings disclosure elsewhere in the document, such as in Management's Discussion & Analysis (MD&A), Risk Factors and notes to the financial statements.

(b)   No information need be given under this section for proceedings:

    (1)   That involve negligence or other claims or actions if the business ordinarily results in such claims or actions, unless the claim or action departs from the normal kind of such claims or actions; or

    (2)   That involve primarily a claim for damages if the amount involved, exclusive of interest and costs, does not exceed 10 percent of the current assets of the registrant and its subsidiaries on a consolidated basis. However, if any proceeding presents in large degree the same legal or factual issues as other proceedings pending or known to be contemplated, the amount involved in such other proceedings shall be included in computing such percentage.

(c)   Notwithstanding paragraph (b) of this section, disclosure under this section shall include, but shall not be limited to:

    (1)   Any material bankruptcy, receivership, or similar proceeding with respect to the registrant or any of its significant subsidiaries;

(2) Any material proceedings to which any director, officer or affiliate of the registrant, any owner of record or beneficially of more than five percent of any class of voting securities of the registrant, or any associate of any such director, officer, affiliate of the registrant, or security holder is a party adverse to the registrant or any of its subsidiaries or has a material interest adverse to the registrant or any of its subsidiaries;

(3) Administrative or judicial proceedings (including proceedings which present in large degree the same issues) arising under any Federal, State, or local provisions that have been enacted or adopted regulating the discharge of materials into the environment or primarily for the purpose of protecting the environment. Such proceedings shall not be deemed "ordinary routine litigation incidental to the business" and shall be described if:

(i) Such proceeding is material to the business or financial condition of the registrant;

(ii) Such proceeding involves primarily a claim for damages, or involves potential monetary sanctions, capital expenditures, deferred charges or charges to income and the amount involved, exclusive of interest and costs, exceeds 10 percent of the current assets of the registrant and its subsidiaries on a consolidated basis; or

(iii) A governmental authority is a party to such proceeding and such proceeding involves potential monetary sanctions, unless the registrant reasonably believes that such proceeding will result in no monetary sanctions, or in monetary sanctions, exclusive of interest and costs, of less than $300,000 or, at the election of the registrant, such other threshold that (A) the registrant determines is reasonably designed to result in disclosure of any such proceeding that is material to the business or financial condition is disclosed, (B) the registrant discloses (including any change thereto) in each annual and quarterly report, and (C) does not exceed the lesser of $1 million or one percent of the current assets of the registrant and its subsidiaries on a consolidated basis; provided, however, that such proceedings that are similar in nature may be grouped and described generically.

Item 104.   Mine Safety Disclosure

(a) A registrant that is the operator, or that has a subsidiary that is an operator, of a coal or other mine shall provide the information specified below for the time period covered by the report:

(1) For each coal or other mine of which the registrant or a subsidiary of the registrant is an operator, identify the mine and disclose:

(i) The total number of violations of mandatory health or safety standards that could significantly and substantially contribute to the cause and effect of a coal or other mine safety or health hazard under section 104 of the Federal Mine Safety and Health Act of 1977 for which the operator received a citation from the Mine Safety and Health Administration.

(ii) The total number of orders issued under section 104(b) of such Act.

(iii) The total number of citations and orders for unwarrantable failure of the mine operator to comply with mandatory health or safety standards under section 104(d) of such Act.

(iv) The total number of flagrant violations under section 110(b)(2) of such Act.

(v) The total number of imminent danger orders issued under section 107(a) of such Act.

(vi) The total dollar value of proposed assessments from the Mine Safety and Health Administration under such Act. Instruction to Item 104(a)(1)(vi): Registrants must provide the total dollar value of assessments proposed by MSHA relating to any type of violation during the period covered by the report, regardless of whether the registrant has challenged or appealed the assessment.

(vii) The total number of mining-related fatalities. Instruction to Item 104(a)(1)(vii): Registrants must report all fatalities occurring at a coal or other mine during the period covered by the report unless the fatality has been determined by MSHA to be unrelated to mining activity.

(2) A list of coal or other mines, of which the registrant or a subsidiary of the registrant is an operator, that receive written notice from the Mine Safety and Health Administration of:

(i)   A pattern of violations of mandatory health or safety standards that are of such nature as could have significantly and substantially contributed to the cause and effect of coal or other mine health or safety hazards under section 104(e) of such Act; or

(ii)   The potential to have such a pattern.

(3)   Any pending legal action before the Federal Mine Safety and Health Review Commission involving such coal or other mine. Instruction to Item 104(a)(3): The registrant must report the total number of legal actions that were pending before the Federal Mine Safety and Health Review Commission as of the last day of the time period covered by the report, as well as the aggregate number of legal actions instituted and the aggregate number of legal actions resolved during the reporting period. With respect to the total number of legal actions that were pending before the Federal Mine Safety and Health Review Commission as of the last day of the time period covered by the report, the registrant must also report the number of such legal actions that are:

1.   Contests of citations and orders referenced in Subpart B of 29 CFR part 2700;

2.   Contests of proposed penalties referenced in Subpart C of 29 CFR part 2700;

3.   Complaints for compensation referenced in Subpart D of 29 CFR part 2700;

4.   Complaints of discharge, discrimination or interference referenced in Subpart E of 29 CFR part 2700;

5.   Applications for temporary relief referenced in Subpart F of 29 CFR part 2700; and

6.   Appeals of judges' decisions or orders to the Federal Mine Safety and Health Review Commission referenced in Subpart H of 29 CFR part 2700.

(b)   Definitions. For purposes of this Item:

(1)   The term coal or other mine means a coal or other mine, as defined in section 3 of the Federal Mine Safety and Health Act of 1977, that is subject to the provisions of such Act.

(2)   The term operator has the meaning given the term in section 3 of the Federal Mine Safety and Health Act of 1977.

(3)   The term subsidiary has the meaning given the term in Exchange Act Rule 12b-2. Instructions to Item 104:

1.   The registrant must provide the information required by this Item as specified by Item 601(b)(95) of this Act. In addition, the registrant must provide a statement, in an appropriately captioned section of the periodic report, that the information concerning mine safety violations or other regulatory matters required by Section 1503(a) of the Dodd-Frank Wall Street Reform and Consumer Protection Act and this Item is included in exhibit 95 to the periodic report.

2.   When the disclosure required by this item is included in an exhibit to an annual report on Form 10-K, the information is to be provided for the registrant's fiscal year.

Item 105.   Risk Factors

(a)   Where appropriate, provide under the caption "Risk Factors" a discussion of the material factors that make an investment in the registrant or offering speculative or risky. This discussion must be organized logically with relevant headings and each risk factor should be set forth under a subcaption that adequately describes the risk. The presentation of risks that could apply generically to any registrant or any offering is discouraged, but to the extent generic risk factors are presented, disclose them at the end of the risk factor section under the caption "General Risk Factors."

(b)   Concisely explain how each risk affects the registrant or the securities being offered. If the discussion is longer than 15 pages, include in the forepart of the prospectus or annual report, as applicable, a series of concise, bulleted or numbered statements that is no more than two pages summarizing the principal factors that make an investment in the registrant or offering speculative or risky. If the risk factor discussion is included in a registration statement, it must immediately follow the summary section required by Item 503 of Regulation S-K. If you do not include a summary section, the risk factor section must immediately follow the cover page of the prospectus or the pricing information section that immediately follows the cover page. Pricing information means price and price-related information that you may omit from the prospectus in an effective registration statement based on Rule 430A. The registrant must furnish this information in plain English. See Rule 421(d) of Regulation C of this chapter.

Subpart 200—Securities of the Registrant

Item 201.   Market Price of and Dividends on the Registrant's Common Equity and Related Stockholder Matters

   (a)   *Market Information.*

     (1)(i)   Identify the principal United States market(s) and the corresponding trading symbol(s) for each class of the registrant's common equity. In the case of foreign registrants, also identify the principal foreign public trading market(s), if any, and the corresponding trading symbol(s) for each class of the registrant's common equity.

       (ii)   If the principal United States market for such common equity is not an exchange, indicate, as applicable, that any over-the-counter market quotations reflect inter-dealer prices, without retail mark-up, mark-down or commission and may not necessarily represent actual transactions.

       (iii)   Where there is no established public trading market for a class of common equity, furnish a statement to that effect and, if applicable, state the range of high and low bid information for each full quarterly period within the two most recent fiscal years and any subsequent interim period for which financial statements are included, or are required to be included by Item 3–01 through Item 3–20 of Regulation S–X, indicating the source of such quotations. Reference to quotations shall be qualified by appropriate explanation. For purposes of this Item the existence of limited or sporadic quotations should not of itself be deemed to constitute an "established public trading market."

       (iv)   Where a foreign registrant has identified a principal established foreign trading market for its common equity pursuant to paragraph (a)(1) of this Item, also provide market price information comparable, to the extent practicable, to that required for the principal United States market, including the source of such information. Such prices shall be stated in the currency in which they are quoted. The registrant may translate such prices into United States currency at the currency exchange rate in effect on the date the price disclosed was reported on the foreign exchange. If the primary United States market for the registrant's common equity trades using American Depositary Receipts, the United States prices disclosed shall be on that basis.

       (v)   If the information called for by this Item is being presented in a registration statement filed pursuant to the Securities Act or a proxy or information statement filed pursuant to the Exchange Act, the document also shall include price information as of the latest practicable date, and, in the case of securities to be issued in connection with an acquisition, business combination or other reorganization, as of the date immediately prior to the public announcement of such transaction.

     (2)   If the information called for by this paragraph (a) is being presented in a registration statement on Form S–1 under the Securities Act or on Form 10 under the Exchange Act relating to a class of common equity for which at the time of filing there is no established United States public trading market, indicate the amount(s) of common equity:

       (i)   [Removed and Reserved].

       (ii)   That could be sold pursuant to Rule 144 under the Securities Act or that the registrant has agreed to register under the Securities Act for sale by security holders; or

       (iii)   That is being, or has been publicly proposed to be, publicly offered by the registrant (unless such common equity is being offered pursuant to an employee benefit plan or dividend reinvestment plan), the offering of which could have a material effect on the market price of the registrant's common equity.

   (b)   *Holders.*

(1)   Set forth the approximate number of holders of each class of common equity of the registrant as of the latest practicable date.

(2)   If the information called for by this paragraph is being presented in a registration statement filed pursuant to the Securities Act or a proxy statement or information statement filed pursuant to the Exchange Act that relates to an acquisition, business combination or other reorganization, indicate the effect of such transaction on the amount and percentage of present holdings of the registrant's common equity owned beneficially by

(i)   Any person (including any group as that term is used in section 13(d)(3) of the Exchange Act) who is known to the registrant to be the beneficial owner of more than five percent of any class of the registrant's common equity and

(ii)   Each director and nominee and

(iii)   All directors and officers as a group, and the registrant's present commitments to such persons with respect to the issuance of shares of any class of its common equity.

(c)   [Removed and Reserved].

(d)   *Securities authorized for issuance under equity compensation plans.*

(1)   In the following tabular format, provide the information specified in paragraph (d)(2) of this Item as of the end of the most recently completed fiscal year with respect to compensation plans (including individual compensation arrangements) under which equity securities of the registrant are authorized for issuance, aggregated as follows:

(i)   All compensation plans previously approved by security holders; and

(ii)   All compensation plans not previously approved by security holders.

Plan category	Number of securities to be issued upon exercise of outstanding options, warrants and rights	Weighted-average exercise price of outstanding options, warrants and rights	Number of securities remaining available for future issuance under equity compensation plans (excluding securities reflected in column (a))
	(a)	(b)	(c)
Equity compensation plans approved by security holders			
Equity compensation plans not approved by security holders			
Total			

(2)   The table shall include the following information as of the end of the most recently completed fiscal year for each category of equity compensation plan described in paragraph (d)(1) of this Item:

(i)   The number of securities to be issued upon the exercise of outstanding options, warrants and rights (column (a));

(ii)   The weighted-average exercise price of the outstanding options, warrants and rights disclosed pursuant to paragraph (d)(2)(i) of this Item (column (b)); and

(iii)   Other than securities to be issued upon the exercise of the outstanding options, warrants and rights disclosed in paragraph (d)(2)(i) of this Item, the number of securities remaining available for future issuance under the plan (column (c)).

(3) For each compensation plan under which equity securities of the registrant are authorized for issuance that was adopted without the approval of security holders, describe briefly, in narrative form, the material features of the plan.

Instructions to Paragraph (d). 1. Disclosure shall be provided with respect to any compensation plan and individual compensation arrangement of the registrant (or parent, subsidiary or affiliate of the registrant) under which equity securities of the registrant are authorized for issuance to employees or non-employees (such as directors, consultants, advisors, vendors, customers, suppliers or lenders) in exchange for consideration in the form of goods or services as described in FASB ASC Topic 718, *Compensation—Stock Compensation,* and FASB ASC Subtopic 505–50, *Equity—Equity-Based Payments to Non-Employees.* No disclosure is required with respect to:

    a.   Any plan, contract or arrangement for the issuance of warrants or rights to all security holders of the registrant as such on a pro rata basis (such as a stock rights offering) or

    b.   Any employee benefit plan that is intended to meet the qualification requirements of Section 401(a) of the Internal Revenue Code.

2.   For purposes of this paragraph, an "individual compensation arrangement" includes, but is not limited to, the following: a written compensation contract within the meaning of "employee benefit plan" under Rule 405 of the Securities Act of 1933 and a plan (whether or not set forth in any formal document) applicable to one person as provided under Item 402(a)(6)(ii) of Regulation S–K.

3.   If more than one class of equity security is issued under its equity compensation plans, a registrant should aggregate plan information for each class of security.

4.   A registrant may aggregate information regarding individual compensation arrangements with the plan information required under paragraph (d)(1)(i) and (ii) of this Item, as applicable.

5.   A registrant may aggregate information regarding a compensation plan assumed in connection with a merger, consolidation or other acquisition transaction pursuant to which the registrant may make subsequent grants or awards of its equity securities with the plan information required under paragraph (d)(1)(i) and (ii) of this Item, as applicable. A registrant shall disclose on an aggregated basis in a footnote to the table the information required under paragraph (d)(2)(i) and (ii) of this Item with respect to any individual options, warrants or rights assumed in connection with a merger, consolidation or other acquisition transaction.

6.   To the extent that the number of securities remaining available for future issuance disclosed in column (c) includes securities available for future issuance under any compensation plan or individual compensation arrangement other than upon the exercise of an option, warrant or right, disclose the number of securities and type of plan separately for each such plan in a footnote to the table.

7.   If the description of an equity compensation plan set forth in a registrant's financial statements contains the disclosure required by paragraph (d)(3) of this Item, a cross-reference to such description will satisfy the requirements of paragraph (d)(3) of this Item.

8.   If an equity compensation plan contains a formula for calculating the number of securities available for issuance under the plan, including, without limitation, a formula that automatically increases the number of securities available for issuance by a percentage of the number of outstanding securities of the registrant, a description of this formula shall be disclosed in a footnote to the table.

9.   Except where it is part of a document that is incorporated by reference into a prospectus, the information required by this paragraph need not be provided in any registration statement filed under the Securities Act.

(e)   *Performance graph.* (1) Provide a line graph comparing the yearly percentage change in the registrant's cumulative total shareholder return on a class of common stock registered under section 12 of the Exchange Act (as measured by dividing (i) the sum of (A) the cumulative amount of dividends for the measurement period, assuming dividend reinvestment, and (B) the difference between the registrant's share price at the end and the beginning of the measurement period; by (ii) the share price at the beginning of the measurement period) with:

    (i)   The cumulative total return of a broad equity market index assuming reinvestment of dividends, that includes companies whose equity securities are traded on the same exchange or are of comparable market capitalization; provided, however, that if the registrant is a company within the Standard & Poor's 500 Stock Index, the registrant must use that index; and

(ii)   The cumulative total return, assuming reinvestment of dividends, of:

(A)   A published industry or line-of-business index;

(B)   Peer issuer(s) selected in good faith. If the registrant does not select its peer issuer(s) on an industry or line-of-business basis, the registrant shall disclose the basis for its selection; or

(C)   Issuer(s) with similar market capitalization(s), but only if the registrant does not use a published industry or line-of-business index and does not believe it can reasonably identify a peer group. If the registrant uses this alternative, the graph shall be accompanied by a statement of the reasons for this selection.

(2)   For purposes of paragraph (e)(1) of this Item, the term "measurement period" shall be the period beginning at the "measurement point" established by the market close on the last trading day before the beginning of the registrant's fifth preceding fiscal year, through and including the end of the registrant's last completed fiscal year. If the class of securities has been registered under section 12 of the Exchange Act for a shorter period of time, the period covered by the comparison may correspond to that time period.

(3)   For purposes of paragraph (e)(1)(ii)(A) of this Item, the term "published industry or line-of-business index" means any index that is prepared by a party other than the registrant or an affiliate and is accessible to the registrant's security holders; provided, however, that registrants may use an index prepared by the registrant or affiliate if such index is widely recognized and used.

(4)   If the registrant selects a different index from an index used for the immediately preceding fiscal year, explain the reason(s) for this change and also compare the registrant's total return with that of both the newly selected index and the index used in the immediately preceding fiscal year.

Instructions to Item 201(e):

1.   In preparing the required graphic comparisons, the registrant should:

a.   Use, to the extent feasible, comparable methods of presentation and assumptions for the total return calculations required by paragraph (e)(1) of this Item; *provided, however*, that if the registrant constructs its own peer group index under paragraph (e)(1)(ii)(B), the same methodology must be used in calculating both the registrant's total return and that on the peer group index; and

b.   Assume the reinvestment of dividends into additional shares of the same class of equity securities at the frequency with which dividends are paid on such securities during the applicable fiscal year.

2.   In constructing the graph:

a.   The closing price at the measurement point must be converted into a fixed investment, stated in dollars, in the registrant's stock (or in the stocks represented by a given index) with cumulative returns for each subsequent fiscal year measured as a change from that investment; and

b.   Each fiscal year should be plotted with points showing the cumulative total return as of that point. The value of the investment as of each point plotted on a given return line is the number of shares held at that point multiplied by the then-prevailing share price.

3.   The registrant is required to present information for the registrant's last five fiscal years, and may choose to graph a longer period; but the measurement point, however, shall remain the same.

4.   Registrants may include comparisons using performance measures in addition to total return, such as return on average common shareholders' equity.

5.   If the registrant uses a peer issuer(s) comparison or comparison with issuer(s) with similar market capitalizations, the identity of those issuers must be disclosed and the returns of each component issuer of the group must be weighted according to the respective issuer's stock market capitalization at the beginning of each period for which a return is indicated.

6.   *Smaller reporting companies.* A registrant that qualifies as a smaller reporting company, as defined by Item 10(f)(1), is not required to provide the information required by paragraph (e) of this Item.

7.   The information required by paragraph (e) of this Item need not be provided in any filings other than an annual report to security holders required by Exchange Act Rule 14a–3 or Exchange Act Rule 14c–3 that precedes or accompanies a registrant's proxy or information statement relating to an annual meeting of security

holders at which directors are to be elected (or special meeting or written consents in lieu of such meeting). Such information will not be deemed to be incorporated by reference into any filing under the Securities Act or the Exchange Act, except to the extent that the registrant specifically incorporates it by reference.

8.   The information required by paragraph (e) of this Item shall not be deemed to be "soliciting material" or to be "filed" with the Commission or subject to Regulation 14A or 14C, other than as provided in this item, or to the liabilities of section 18 of the Exchange Act, except to the extent that the registrant specifically requests that such information be treated as soliciting material or specifically incorporates it by reference into a filing under the Securities Act or the Exchange Act.

Instructions to Item 201.

Instruction 1 to Item 201: [Removed and Reserved].

Instruction 2 to Item 201: Bid information reported pursuant to this Item shall be adjusted to give retroactive effect to material changes resulting from stock dividends, stock splits and reverse stock splits.

Instruction 3 to Item 201: The computation of the approximate number of holders of registrant's common equity may be based upon the number of record holders or also may include individual participants in security position listings. See Rule 17Ad–8 under the Exchange Act. The method of computation that is chosen shall be indicated.

Instruction 4 to Item 201: If the registrant is a foreign issuer, describe briefly:

    A.   Any governmental laws, decrees or regulations in the country in which the registrant is organized that restrict the export or import of capital, including, but not limited to, foreign exchange controls, or that affect the remittance of dividends or other payments to nonresident holders of the registrant's common equity; and

    B.   All taxes, including withholding provisions, to which United States common equity holders are subject under existing laws and regulations of the foreign country in which the registrant is organized. Include a brief description of pertinent provisions of any reciprocal tax treaty between such foreign country and the United States regarding withholding. If there is no such treaty, so state.

Instruction 5 to Item 201: If the registrant is a foreign private issuer whose common equity of the class being registered is wholly or partially in bearer form, the response to this Item shall so indicate together with as much information as the registrant is able to provide with respect to security holdings in the United States. If the securities being registered trade in the United States in the form of American Depositary Receipts or similar certificates, the response to this Item shall so indicate together with the name of the depositary issuing such receipts and the number of shares or other units of the underlying security representing the trading units in such receipts.

Item 202.   Description of Registrant's Securities

(a)   *Capital Stock.* If capital stock is to be registered, state the title of the class and describe such of the matters listed in paragraphs (a)(1) through (5) as are relevant. A complete legal description of the securities need not be given.

    (1)   Outline briefly:

        (i)   Dividend rights;

        (ii)   Terms of conversion;

        (iii)   Sinking fund provisions;

        (iv)   Redemption provisions;

        (v)   Voting rights, including any provisions specifying the vote required by security holders to take action;

        (vi)   Any classification of the Board of Directors, and the impact of such classification where cumulative voting is permitted or required;

        (vii)   Liquidation rights;

        (viii)   Preemption rights; and

(ix) Liability to further calls or to assessment by the registrant and for liabilities of the registrant imposed on its stockholders under state statutes (e.g., to laborers, servants or employees of the registrant), unless such disclosure would be immaterial because of the financial resources of the registrant or other factors make it improbable that liability under such state statutes would be imposed;

(x) Any restriction on alienability of the securities to be registered; and

(xi) Any provision discriminating against any existing or prospective holder of such securities as a result of such security holder owning a substantial amount of securities.

(2) If the rights of holders of such stock may be modified otherwise than by a vote of a majority or more of the shares outstanding, voting as a class, so state and explain briefly.

(3) If preferred stock is to be registered, describe briefly any restriction on the repurchase or redemption of shares by the registrant while there is any arrearage in the payment of dividends or sinking fund installments. If there is no such restriction, so state.

(4) If the rights evidenced by, or amounts payable with respect to, the shares to be registered are, or may be, materially limited or qualified by the rights of any other authorized class of securities, include the information regarding such other securities as will enable investors to understand such limitations or qualifications. No information need be given, however, as to any class of securities all of which will be retired, provided appropriate steps to ensure such retirement will be completed prior to or upon delivery by the registrant of the shares.

(5) Describe briefly or cross-reference to a description in another part of the document, any provision of the registrant's charter or by-laws that would have an effect of delaying, deferring or preventing a change in control of the registrant and that would operate only with respect to an extraordinary corporate transaction involving the registrant (or any of its subsidiaries), such as a merger, reorganization, tender offer, sale or transfer of substantially all of its assets, or liquidation. Provisions and arrangements required by law or imposed by governmental or judicial authority need not be described or discussed pursuant to this paragraph (a)(5). Provisions or arrangements adopted by the registrant to effect, or further, compliance with laws or governmental or judicial mandate are not subject to the immediately preceding sentence where such compliance did not require the specific provisions or arrangements adopted.

(b) *Debt Securities.* If debt securities are to be registered, state the title of such securities, the principal amount being offered, and, if a series, the total amount authorized and the total amount outstanding as of the most recent practicable date; and describe such of the matter listed in paragraphs (b)(1) through (10) as are relevant. A complete legal description of the securities need not be given. For purposes solely of this Item, debt securities that differ from one another only as to the interest rate or maturity shall be regarded as securities of the same class. Outline briefly:

(1) Provisions with respect to maturity, interest, conversion, redemption, amortization, sinking fund, or retirement;

(2) Provisions with respect to the kind and priority of any lien securing the securities, together with a brief identification of the principal properties subject to such lien;

(3) Provisions with respect to the subordination of the rights of holders of the securities to other security holders or creditors of the registrant; where debt securities are designated as subordinated in accordance with Instruction 1 to this Item, set forth the aggregate amount of outstanding indebtedness as of the most recent practicable date that by the terms of such debt securities would be senior to such subordinated debt and describe briefly any limitation on the issuance of such additional senior indebtedness or state that there is no such limitation;

(4) Provisions restricting the declaration of dividends or requiring the maintenance of any asset ratio or the creation or maintenance of reserves;

(5) Provisions restricting the incurrence of additional debt or the issuance of additional securities; in the case of secured debt, whether the securities being registered are to be issued on the basis of unbonded bondable property, the deposit of cash or otherwise; as of the most recent practicable date, the approximate amount of unbonded bondable property available as a basis for the issuance of

bonds; provisions permitting the withdrawal of cash deposited as a basis for the issuance of bonds; and provisions permitting the release or substitution of assets securing the issue; *Provided, however,* That provisions permitting the release of assets upon the deposit of equivalent funds or the pledge of equivalent property, the release of property no longer required in the business, obsolete property, or property taken by eminent domain or the application of insurance moneys, and other similar provisions need not be described;

(6)   The general type of event that constitutes a default and whether or not any periodic evidence is required to be furnished as to the absence of default or as to compliance with the terms of the indenture;

(7)   Provisions relating to modification of the terms of the security or the rights of security holders;

(8)   If the rights evidenced by the securities to be registered are, or may be, materially limited or qualified by the rights of any other authorized class of securities, the information regarding such other securities as will enable investors to understand the rights evidenced by the securities; to the extent not otherwise disclosed pursuant to this Item; no information need be given, however, as to any class of securities all of which will be retired, provided appropriate steps to ensure such retirement will be completed prior to or upon delivery by the registrant of the securities;

(9)   If debt securities are to be offered at a price such that they will be deemed to be offered at an "original issue discount" as defined in paragraph (a) of Section 1273 of the Internal Revenue Code, or if a debt security is sold in a package with another security and the allocation of the offering price between the two securities may have the effect of offering the debt security at such an original issue discount, the tax effects thereof pursuant to sections 1271–1278;

(10)   The name of the trustee(s) and the nature of any material relationship with the registrant or with any of its affiliates; the percentage of securities of the class necessary to require the trustee to take action; and what indemnification the trustee may require before proceeding to enforce the lien.

(c)   *Warrants and Rights.* If the securities described are to be offered pursuant to warrants or rights state:

(1)   The amount of securities called for by such warrants or rights;

(2)   The period during which and the price at which the warrants or rights are exercisable;

(3)   The amount of warrants or rights outstanding;

(4)   Provisions for changes to or adjustments in the exercise price; and

(5)   Any other material terms of such rights on warrants.

(d)   *Other Securities.* If securities other than capital stock, debt, warrants or rights are to be registered, include a brief description (comparable to that required in paragraphs (a), (b) and (c) of Item 202) of the rights evidenced thereby.

(e)   *Market Information for Securities Other Than Common Equity.* If securities other than common equity are to be registered and there is an established public trading market for such securities (as that term is used in Item 201 of Regulation S–K) provide market information with respect to such securities comparable to that required by paragraph (a) of Item 201 of Regulation S–K.

(f)   *American Depositary Receipts.* If Depositary Shares represented by American Depositary Receipts are being registered, furnish the following information:

(1)   The name of the depositary and the address of its principal executive office.

(2)   State the title of the American Depositary Receipts and identify the deposited security. Describe briefly the terms of deposit, including the provisions, if any, with respect to:

(i)   The amount of deposited securities represented by one unit of American Depositary Receipts;

(ii)   The procedure for voting, if any, the deposited securities;

(iii)   The collection and distribution of dividends;

(iv)   The transmission of notices, reports and proxy soliciting material;

(v)   The sale or exercise of rights;

(vi)   The deposit or sale of securities resulting from dividends, splits or plans of reorganization;

(vii) Amendment, extension or termination of the deposit;

(viii) Rights of holders of receipts to inspect the transfer books of the depositary and the list of holders of receipts;

(ix)   Restrictions upon the right to deposit or withdraw the underlying securities;

(x)   Limitation upon the liability of the depositary.

(3)   Describe all fees and charges which may be imposed directly or indirectly against the holder of the American Depositary Receipts, indicating the type of service, the amount of fee or charges and to whom paid.

Instructions to Item 202. 1. Wherever the title of securities is required to be stated, there shall be given such information as will indicate the type and general character of the securities, including the following:

A.   In the case of shares, the par or stated value, if any; the rate of dividends, if fixed, and whether cumulative or noncumulative; a brief indication of the preference, if any; and if convertible or redeemable, a statement to that effect;

B.   In the case of debt, the rate of interest; the date of maturity or, if the issue matures serially, a brief indication of the serial maturities, such as "maturing serially from 1955 to 1960"; if the payment of principal or interest is contingent, an appropriate indication of such contingency; a brief indication of the priority of the issue; and, if convertible or callable, a statement to that effect; or

C.   In the case of any other kind of security, appropriate information of comparable character.

2.   If the registrant is a foreign registrant, include (to the extent not disclosed in the document pursuant to Item 201 of Regulation S–K or otherwise) in the description of the securities:

A.   A brief description of any limitations on the right of nonresident or foreign owners to hold or vote such securities imposed by foreign law or by the charter or other constituent document of the registrant, or if no such limitations are applicable, so state;

B.   A brief description of any governmental laws, decrees or regulations in the country in which the registrant is organized affecting the remittance of dividends, interest and other payments to nonresident holders of the securities being registered;

C.   A brief outline of all taxes, including withholding provisions, to which United States security holders are subject under existing laws and regulations of the foreign country in which the registrant is organized; and

D.   A brief description of pertinent provisions of any reciprocal tax treaty between such foreign country and the United States regarding withholding or, if there is no such treaty, so state.

3.   Section 305(a)(2) of the Trust Indenture Act of 1939, U.S.C. 77aaa et seq., as amended ("Trust Indenture Act"), shall not be deemed to require the inclusion in a registration statement, prospectus, or annual report on Form 10–K of any information not required by this Item or Item 601(b)(4)(vi) of this chapter.

4.   Where convertible securities or stock purchase warrants are being registered that are subject to redemption or call, the description of the conversion terms of the securities or material terms of the warrants shall disclose:

A.   Whether the right to convert or purchase the securities will be forfeited unless it is exercised before the date specified in a notice of the redemption or call;

B.   The expiration or termination date of the warrants;

C.   The kinds, frequency and timing of notice of the redemption or call, including the cities or newspapers in which notice will be published (where the securities provide for a class of newspapers or group of cities in which the publication may be made at the discretion of the registrant, the registrant should describe such provision); and

D.   In the case of bearer securities, that investors are responsible for making arrangements to prevent loss of the right to convert or purchase in the event of redemption of call, for example, by reading the newspapers in which the notice of redemption or call may be published.

5.   The response to paragraph (f) shall include information with respect to fees and charges in connection with (A) the deposit or substitution of the underlying securities; (B) receipt and distribution of dividends; (C) the sale or exercise of rights; (D) the withdrawal of the underlying security; and (E) the transferring, splitting or grouping of receipts. Information with respect to the right to collect the fees and charges against dividends received and deposited securities shall be included in response to this Item.

6.   For asset-backed securities, see also Item 1113 of Regulation AB.

NOTE to Item 202: If the securities being described have been accepted for listing on an exchange, the exchange may be identified. The document should not, however, convey the impression that the registrant may apply successfully for listing of the securities on an exchange or that, in the case of an underwritten offering, the underwriters may request the registrant to apply for such listing, unless there is reasonable assurance that the securities to be offered will be acceptable to a securities exchange for listing.

Subpart 300—Financial Information

Item 301.   Selected Financial Data

Furnish in comparative columnar form the selected financial data for the registrant referred to below, for

(a)   Each of the last five fiscal years of the registrant (or for the life of the registrant and its predecessors, if less), and

(b)   Any additional fiscal years necessary to keep the information from being misleading.

(c)   *Smaller reporting companies.* A registrant that qualifies as a smaller reporting company, as defined by Item 10(f)(1), is not required to provide the information required by this Item.

(d)   *Emerging Growth Company.* An emerging growth company, as defined in Rule 405 of the Securities Act of 1933 or Rule 12b–2 of the Securities Exchange Act of 1934, that is providing the information called for by this Item in: (1) a Securities Act registration statement, need not present selected financial data for any period prior to the earliest audited financial statements presented in connection with the registrant's initial public offering of its common equity securities; or (2) a registration statement, periodic report, or other report filed under the Exchange Act, need not present selected financial data for any period prior to the earliest audited financial statements presented in connection with its first registration statement that became effective under the Exchange Act or the Securities Act.

Instructions to Item 301.   1. The purpose of the selected financial data shall be to supply in a convenient and readable format selected financial data which highlight certain significant trends in the registrant's financial condition and results of operations.

2.   Subject to appropriate variation to conform to the nature of the registrant's business, the following items shall be included in the table of financial data: net sales or operating revenues; income (loss) from continuing operations; income (loss) from continuing operations per common share; total assets; long-term obligations and redeemable preferred stock (including long-term debt, capital leases, and redeemable preferred stock as defined in Rule 5–02.27(a) of Regulation S–X); and cash dividends declared per common share. Registrants may include additional items which they believe would enhance an understanding of and would highlight other trends in their financial condition and results of operations.

Briefly describe, or cross-reference to a discussion thereof, factors such as accounting changes, business combinations or dispositions of business operations, that materially affect the comparability of the information reflected in selected financial data. Discussion of, or reference to, any material uncertainties should also be included where such matters might cause the data reflected herein not to be indicative of the registrant's future financial condition or results of operations.

3.   All references to the registrant in the table of selected financial data and in this Item shall mean the registrant and its subsidiaries consolidated.

4.   If interim period financial statements are included, or are required to be included, by Article 3 of Regulation S–X, registrants should consider whether any or all of the selected financial data need to be updated for such interim periods to reflect a material change in the trends indicated; where such updating information is

necessary, registrants shall provide the information on a comparative basis unless not necessary to an understanding of such updating information.

5.   A foreign private issuer shall disclose also the following information in all filings containing financial statements:

A.   In the forepart of the document and as of the latest practicable date, the exchange rate into U.S. currency of the foreign currency in which the financial statements are denominated;

B.   A history of exchange rates for the five most recent years and any subsequent interim period for which financial statements are presented setting forth the rates for period end, the average rates, and the range of high and low rates for each year; and

C.   If equity securities are being registered, a five year summary of dividends per share stated in both the currency in which the financial statements are denominated and United States currency based on the exchange rates at each respective payment date.

6.   A foreign private issuer shall present the selected financial data in the same currency as its financial statements. The issuer may present the selected financial data on the basis of the accounting principles used in its primary financial statements but in such case shall present this data also on the basis of any reconciliations of such data to United States generally accepted accounting principles and Regulation S–X made pursuant to Rule 4–01 of Regulation S–X.

7.   For purposes of this rule, the rate of exchange means the noon buying rate in New York City for cable transfers in foreign currencies as certified for customs purposes by the Federal Reserve Bank of New York. The average rate means the average of the exchange rates on the last day of each month during a year.

Item 302.   Supplementary Financial Information

(a)   *Selected Quarterly Financial Data.* Registrants specified in paragraph (a)(5) of this Item shall provide the information specified below.

(1)   Disclosure shall be made of net sales, gross profit (net sales less costs and expenses associated directly with or allocated to products sold or services rendered), income (loss) from continuing operations, per share data based upon income (loss) from continuing operations, net income (loss), per share data based upon net income (loss) and net income (loss) attributable to the registrant, for each full quarter within the two most recent fiscal years and any subsequent interim period for which financial statements are included or are required to be included by Item 3–01 through Item 3–20 of Regulation S–X.

(2)   When the data supplied pursuant to paragraph (a) of this rule vary from the amounts previously reported on the Form 10–Q and filed for any quarter, such as would be the case when a combination between entities under common control occurs or where an error is corrected, reconcile the amounts given with those previously reported and describe the reason for the difference.

(3)   Describe the effect of any discontinued operations and unusual or infrequently occurring items recognized in each full quarter within the two most recent fiscal years and any subsequent interim period for which financial statements are included or are required to be included by Item 3–01 through Item 3–20 of Regulation S–X, as well as the aggregate effect and the nature of year-end or other adjustments which are material to the results of that quarter.

(4)   If the financial statements to which this information relates have been reported on by an accountant, appropriate professional standards and procedures, as enumerated in the Statements of Auditing Standards issued by the Auditing Standards Board of the American Institute of Certified Public Accountants, shall be followed by the reporting accountant with regard to the data required by this paragraph (a).

(5)   This paragraph (a) applies to any registrant, except a foreign private issuer, that has securities registered pursuant to section 12(b) (other than mutual life insurance companies) or 12(g) of the Exchange Act.

(b)   *Information About Oil and Gas Producing Activities.* Registrants engaged in oil and gas producing activities shall present the information about oil and gas producing activities (as those activities are defined in Regulation S–X, specified in FASB ASC Topic 932, *Extractive Activities—Oil and Gas,* if such oil and gas producing activities are regarded as significant under one or more of the tests set forth in FASB ASC Subtopic 932–235, *Extractive Activities—Oil and Gas—Notes to Financial Statements,* for Significant Activities.

Instructions to Paragraph (b).

Instruction 1 to Paragraph (b): (a) FASB ASC Subtopic 932–235 disclosures that relate to annual periods shall be presented for each annual period for which a statement of comprehensive income (as defined in Item 1–02 of Regulation S–X) is required, (b) FASB ASC Subtopic 932–235 disclosures required as of the end of an annual period shall be presented as of the date of each audited balance sheet required, and (c) FASB ASC Subtopic 932–235 disclosures required as of the beginning of an annual period shall be presented as of the beginning of each annual period for which a statement of comprehensive income (as defined in Item 1–02 of Regulation S–X) is required.

Instruction 2 to Paragraph (b): This paragraph, together with Item 4–10 of Regulation S–X, prescribes financial reporting standards for the preparation of accounts by persons engaged, in whole or in part, in the production of crude oil or natural gas in the United States, pursuant to section 503 of the Energy Policy and Conservation Act of 1975 ("EPCA") and Section 11(c) of the Energy Supply and Environmental Coordination Act of 1974 ("ESECA") as amended by Section 506 of EPCA. The application of this paragraph to those oil and gas producing operations of companies regulated for ratemaking purposes on an individual-company-cost-of-service basis may, however, give appropriate recognition to differences arising because of the effect of the ratemaking process.

Instruction 3 to Paragraph (b): Any person exempted by the Department of Energy from any record-keeping or reporting requirements pursuant to Section 11(c) of ESECA, as amended, is similarly exempted from the related provisions of this paragraph in the preparation of accounts pursuant to EPCA. This exemption does not affect the applicability of this paragraph to filings pursuant to the federal securities laws.

(c) *Smaller reporting companies.* A registrant that qualifies as a smaller reporting company, as defined by Item 10(f)(1), is not required to provide the information required by this Item.

Item 303. Management's Discussion and Analysis of Financial Condition and Results of Operations

(a) *Full Fiscal Years.* Discuss registrant's financial condition, changes in financial condition and results of operations. The discussion shall provide information as specified in paragraphs (a)(1) through (5) of this Item and also shall provide such other information that the registrant believes to be necessary to an understanding of its financial condition, changes in financial condition and results of operations. Discussions of liquidity and capital resources may be combined whenever the two topics are interrelated. Where in the registrant's judgment a discussion of segment information and/or of other subdivisions (e.g., geographic areas) of the registrant's business would be appropriate to an understanding of such business, the discussion shall focus on each relevant, reportable segment and/or other subdivision of the business and on the registrant as a whole.

(1) *Liquidity.* Identify any known trends or any known demands, commitments, events or uncertainties that will result in or that are reasonably likely to result in the registrant's liquidity increasing or decreasing in any material way. If a material deficiency is identified, indicate the course of action that the registrant has taken or proposes to take to remedy the deficiency. Also identify and separately describe internal and external sources of liquidity, and briefly discuss any material unused sources of liquid assets.

(2) *Capital Resources.*

(i) Describe the registrant's material commitments for capital expenditures as of the end of the latest fiscal period, and indicate the general purpose of such commitments and the anticipated source of funds needed to fulfill such commitments.

(ii) Describe any known material trends, favorable or unfavorable, in the registrant's capital resources. Indicate any expected material changes in the mix and relative cost of such resources. The discussion shall consider changes between equity, debt and any off-balance sheet financing arrangements.

(3) *Results of Operations.*

(i)   Describe any unusual or infrequent events or transactions or any significant economic changes that materially affected the amount of reported income from continuing operations and, in each case, indicate the extent to which income was so affected. In addition, describe any other significant components of revenues or expenses that, in the registrant's judgment, should be described in order to understand the registrant's results of operations.

(ii)   Describe any known trends or uncertainties that have had or that the registrant reasonably expects will have a material favorable or unfavorable impact on net sales or revenues or income from continuing operations. If the registrant knows of events that will cause a material change in the relationship between costs and revenues (such as known future increases in costs of labor or materials or price increases or inventory adjustments), the change in the relationship shall be disclosed.

(iii)   To the extent that the financial statements disclose material increases in net sales or revenues, provide a narrative discussion of the extent to which such increases are attributable to increases in prices or to increases in the volume or amount of goods or services being sold or to the introduction of new products or services.

(iv)   For the three most recent fiscal years of the registrant, or for those fiscal years in which the registrant has been engaged in business, whichever period is shortest, discuss the impact of inflation and changing prices on the registrant's net sales and revenues and on income from continuing operations.

(4)   *Off-Balance Sheet Arrangements.*

(i)   In a separately-captioned section, discuss the registrant's off-balance sheet arrangements that have or are reasonably likely to have a current or future effect on the registrant's financial condition, changes in financial condition, revenues or expenses, results of operations, liquidity, capital expenditures or capital resources that is material to investors. The disclosure shall include the items specified in paragraphs (a)(4)(i)(A), (B), (C) and (D) of this Item to the extent necessary to an understanding of such arrangements and effect and shall also include such other information that the registrant believes is necessary for such an understanding.

(A)   The nature and business purpose to the registrant of such off-balance sheet arrangements;

(B)   The importance to the registrant of such off-balance sheet arrangements in respect of its liquidity, capital resources, market risk support, credit risk support or other benefits;

(C)   The amounts of revenues, expenses and cash flows of the registrant arising from such arrangements; the nature and amounts of any interests retained, securities issued and other indebtedness incurred by the registrant in connection with such arrangements; and the nature and amounts of any other obligations or liabilities (including contingent obligations or liabilities) of the registrant arising from such arrangements that are or are reasonably likely to become material and the triggering events or circumstances that could cause them to arise; and

(D)   Any known event, demand, commitment, trend or uncertainty that will result in or is reasonably likely to result in the termination, or material reduction in availability to the registrant, of its off-balance sheet arrangements that provide material benefits to it, and the course of action that the registrant has taken or proposes to take in response to any such circumstances.

(ii)   As used in this paragraph (a)(4), the term off-balance sheet arrangement means any transaction, agreement or other contractual arrangement to which an entity unconsolidated with the registrant is a party, under which the registrant has:

(A)   Any obligation under a guarantee contract that has any of the characteristics identified in FASB ASC paragraph 460–10–15–4 (Guarantees Topic), as may be modified or supplemented, and that is not excluded from the initial recognition and measurement provisions of FASB ASC paragraphs 460–10–15–7, 460–10–25–1, and 460–10–30–1;

(B)   A retained or contingent interest in assets transferred to an unconsolidated entity or similar arrangement that serves as credit, liquidity or market risk support to such entity for such assets;

(C)   Any obligation, including a contingent obligation, under a contract that would be accounted for as a derivative instrument, except that it is both indexed to the registrant's own stock and classified in stockholders' equity in the registrant's statement of financial position, and therefore excluded from the scope of FASB ASC Topic 815, *Derivatives and Hedging,* pursuant to FASB ASC subparagraph 815–10–15–74(a), as may be modified or supplemented; or

(D)   Any obligation, including a contingent obligation, arising out of a variable interest (as defined in the FASB ASC Master Glossary, as may be modified or supplemented) in an unconsolidated entity that is held by, and material to, the registrant, where such entity provides financing, liquidity, market risk or credit risk support to, or engages in leasing, hedging or research and development services with, the registrant.

(5)   *Tabular Disclosure of Contractual Obligations.*

(i)   In a tabular format, provide the information specified in this paragraph (a)(5) as of the latest fiscal year end balance sheet date with respect to the registrant's known contractual obligations specified in the table that follows this paragraph (a)(5)(i). The registrant shall provide amounts, aggregated by type of contractual obligation. The registrant may disaggregate the specified categories of contractual obligations using other categories suitable to its business, but the presentation must include all of the obligations of the registrant that fall within the specified categories. A presentation covering at least the periods specified shall be included. The tabular presentation may be accompanied by footnotes to describe provisions that create, increase or accelerate obligations, or other pertinent data to the extent necessary for an understanding of the timing and amount of the registrant's specified contractual obligations.

Contractual obligations	Payments due by period				
	Total	Less than 1	1–3 years	3–5 years	More than 5 years
[Long-Term Debt Obligations]	....	....	....	....	....
[Capital Lease Obligations]	....	....	....	....	....
[Operating Lease Obligations]	....	....	....	....	....
[Purchase Obligations]	....	....	....	....	....
[Other Long-Term Liabilities	....	....	....	....	....
Reflected on the Registrant's............	....	....	....	....	....
Balance Sheet under GAAP]	....	....	....	....	....
Total	....	....	....	....	....

(ii)   Definitions: The following definitions apply to this paragraph (a)(5):

(A)   Long-Term Debt Obligation means a payment obligation under long-term borrowings referenced in FASB ASC paragraph 470–10–50–1 (Debt Topic), as may be modified or supplemented.

(B)   Capital Lease Obligation means a payment obligation under a lease classified as a capital lease pursuant to FASB ASC Topic 840, Leases, as may be modified or supplemented.

(C)   Operating Lease Obligation means a payment obligation under a lease classified as an operating lease and disclosed pursuant to FASB ASC Topic 840, as may be modified or supplemented.

(D) Purchase Obligation means an agreement to purchase goods or services that is enforceable and legally binding on the registrant that specifies all significant terms, including: fixed or minimum quantities to be purchased; fixed, minimum or variable price provisions; and the approximate timing of the transaction.

Instructions to Paragraph 303(a). 1. The registrant's discussion and analysis shall be of the financial statements and other statistical data that the registrant believes will enhance a reader's understanding of its financial condition, changes in financial condition, and results of operations. Generally, the discussion shall cover the periods covered by the financial statements included in the filing and the registrant may use any presentation that in the registrant's judgment enhances a reader's understanding. A smaller reporting company's discussion shall cover the two-year period required in Article 8 of Regulation S–X and may use any presentation that in the registrant's judgment enhances a reader's understanding. For registrants providing financial statements covering three years in a filing, discussion about the earliest of the three years may be omitted if such discussion was already included in the registrant's prior filings on EDGAR that required disclosure in compliance with Item 303 of Regulation S–K, provided that registrants electing not to include a discussion of the earliest year must include a statement that identifies the location in the prior filing where the omitted discussion may be found. An emerging growth company, as defined in Rule 405 of the Securities Act or Rule 12b–2 of the Exchange Act, may provide the discussion required in paragraph (a) of this Item for its two most recent fiscal years if, pursuant to Section 7(a) of the Securities Act of 1933 (15 U.S.C. 77g(a)), it provides audited financial statements for two years in a Securities Act registration statement for the initial public offering of the emerging growth company's common equity securities.

2. The purpose of the discussion and analysis shall be to provide to investors and other users information relevant to an assessment of the financial condition and results of operations of the registrant as determined by evaluating the amounts and certainty of cash flows from operations and from outside sources.

3. The discussion and analysis shall focus specifically on material events and uncertainties known to management that would cause reported financial information not to be necessarily indicative of future operating results or of future financial condition. This would include descriptions and amounts of (A) matters that would have an impact on future operations and have not had an impact in the past, and (B) matters that have had an impact on reported operations and are not expected to have an impact upon future operations.

4. Where the consolidated financial statements reveal material changes from year to year in one or more line items, the causes for the changes shall be described to the extent necessary to an understanding of the registrant's businesses as a whole; *Provided, however,* That if the causes for a change in one line item also relate to other line items, no repetition is required and a line-by-line analysis of the financial statements as a whole is not required or generally appropriate. Registrants need not recite the amounts of changes from year to year which are readily computable from the financial statements. The discussion shall not merely repeat numerical data contained in the consolidated financial statements.

5. The term "liquidity" as used in this Item refers to the ability of an enterprise to generate adequate amounts of cash to meet the enterprise's needs for cash. Except where it is otherwise clear from the discussion, the registrant shall indicate those balance sheet conditions or income or cash flow items which the registrant believes may be indicators of its liquidity condition. Liquidity generally shall be discussed on both a long-term and short-term basis. The issue of liquidity shall be discussed in the context of the registrant's own business or businesses. For example a discussion of working capital may be appropriate for certain manufacturing, industrial or related operations but might be inappropriate for a bank or public utility.

6. Where financial statements presented or incorporated by reference in the registration statement are required by Item 4–08(e)(3) of Regulation S–X to include disclosure of restrictions on the ability of both consolidated and unconsolidated subsidiaries to transfer funds to the registrant in the form of cash dividends, loans or advances, the discussion of liquidity shall include a discussion of the nature and extent of such restrictions and the impact such restrictions have had and are expected to have on the ability of the parent company to meet its cash obligations.

7. Any forward-looking information supplied is expressly covered by the safe harbor rule for projections. See Rule 175 under the Securities Act, Rule 3b–6 under the Exchange Act and Securities Act Release No. 6084 (June 25, 1979).

8. Registrants are only required to discuss the effects of inflation and other changes in prices when considered material. This discussion may be made in whatever manner appears appropriate under the circumstances. All that is required is a brief textual presentation of management's views. No specific numerical financial data need be presented except as Rule 3–20(c) of Regulation S–X otherwise requires. However,

registrants may elect to voluntarily disclose supplemental information on the effects of changing prices as provided for in FASB ASC Topic, 255, *Changing Prices,* or through other supplemental disclosures. The Commission encourages experimentation with these disclosures in order to provide the most meaningful presentation of the impact of price changes on the registrant's financial statements.

9.   Registrants that elect to disclose supplementary information on the effects of changing prices as specified by FASB ASC Topic 255, may combine such explanations with the discussion and analysis required pursuant to this Item or may supply such information separately with appropriate cross reference.

10.   All references to the registrant in the discussion and in this Item shall mean the registrant and its subsidiaries consolidated.

11.   Foreign private registrants also shall discuss briefly any pertinent governmental economic, fiscal, monetary, or political policies or factors that have materially affected or could materially affect, directly or indirectly, their operations or investments by United States nationals.

12.   If the registrant is a foreign private issuer, the discussion shall focus on the primary financial statements presented in the registration statement or report. There shall be a reference to the reconciliation to United States generally accepted accounting principles, and a discussion of any aspects of the difference between foreign and United States generally accepted accounting principles, not discussed in the reconciliation, that the registrant believes is necessary for an understanding of the financial statements as a whole.

13.   The attention of bank holding companies is directed to the information called for in Guide 3 (Item 801(c) and Item 802(c)).

14.   The attention of property-casualty insurance companies is directed to the information called for in Guide 6 (Item 801(f)).

Instructions to Paragraph 303(a)(4):

1.   No obligation to make disclosure under paragraph (a)(4) of this Item shall arise in respect of an off-balance sheet arrangement until a definitive agreement that is unconditionally binding or subject only to customary closing conditions exists or, if there is no such agreement, when settlement of the transaction occurs.

2.   Registrants should aggregate off-balance sheet arrangements in groups or categories that provide material information in an efficient and understandable manner and should avoid repetition and disclosure of immaterial information. Effects that are common or similar with respect to a number of off-balance sheet arrangements must be analyzed in the aggregate to the extent the aggregation increases understanding. Distinctions in arrangements and their effects must be discussed to the extent the information is material, but the discussion should avoid repetition and disclosure of immaterial information.

3.   For purposes of paragraph (a)(4) of this Item only, contingent liabilities arising out of litigation, arbitration or regulatory actions are not considered to be off-balance sheet arrangements.

4.   Generally, the disclosure required by paragraph (a)(4) shall cover the most recent fiscal year. However, the discussion should address changes from the previous year where such discussion is necessary to an understanding of the disclosure.

5.   In satisfying the requirements of paragraph (a)(4) of this Item, the discussion of off-balance sheet arrangements need not repeat information provided in the footnotes to the financial statements, provided that such discussion clearly cross-references to specific information in the relevant footnotes and integrates the substance of the footnotes into such discussion in a manner designed to inform readers of the significance of the information that is not included within the body of such discussion.

(b)   *Interim Periods.* If interim period financial statements are included or are required to be included by Article 3 of Regulation S–X, a management's discussion and analysis of the financial condition and results of operations shall be provided so as to enable the reader to assess material changes in financial condition and results of operations between the periods specified in paragraphs (b)(1) and (2) of this Item. The discussion and analysis shall include a discussion of material changes in those items specifically listed in paragraph (a) of this Item, except that the impact of inflation and changing prices on operations for interim periods need not be addressed.

(1)   *Material Changes in Financial Condition.* Discuss any material changes in financial condition from the end of the preceding fiscal year to the date of the most recent interim balance sheet provided. If the interim financial statements include an interim balance sheet as of the corresponding interim date of the preceding fiscal year, any material changes in financial condition from that date to

the date of the most recent interim balance sheet provided also shall be discussed. If discussions of changes from both the end and the corresponding interim date of the preceding fiscal year are required, the discussions may be combined at the discretion of the registrant.

(2)   *Material Changes in Results of Operations.* Discuss any material changes in the registrant's results of operations with respect to the most recent fiscal year-to-date period for which a statement of comprehensive income (or statement of operations if comprehensive income is presented in two separate but consecutive financial statements or if no other comprehensive income) is provided and the corresponding year-to-date period of the preceding fiscal year. If the registrant is required to or has elected to provide a statement of comprehensive income (or statement of operations if comprehensive income is presented in two separate but consecutive financial statements or if no other comprehensive income) for the most recent fiscal quarter, such discussion also shall cover material changes with respect to that fiscal quarter and the corresponding fiscal quarter in the preceding fiscal year. In addition, if the registrant has elected to provide a statement of comprehensive income (or statement of operations if comprehensive income is presented in two separate but consecutive financial statements or if no other comprehensive income) for the twelve-month period ended as of the date of the most recent interim balance sheet provided, the discussion also shall cover material changes with respect to that twelve-month period and the twelve-month period ended as of the corresponding interim balance sheet date of the preceding fiscal year. Notwithstanding the above, if for purposes of a registration statement a registrant subject to Item 3–03(b) of Regulation S–X of this chapter provides a statement of comprehensive income (or statement of operations if comprehensive income is presented in two separate but consecutive financial statements or if no other comprehensive income) for the twelve-month period ended as of the date of the most recent interim balance sheet provided in lieu of the interim statements of comprehensive income (or statement of operations if comprehensive income is presented in two separate but consecutive financial statements or if no other comprehensive income) otherwise required, the discussion of material changes in that twelve-month period will be in respect to the preceding fiscal year rather than the corresponding preceding period.

Instructions to Paragraph (b) of Item 303.

Instruction 1 to Paragraph (b): If interim financial statements are presented together with financial statements for full fiscal years, the discussion of the interim financial information shall be prepared pursuant to this paragraph (b) and the discussion of the full fiscal year's information shall be prepared pursuant to paragraph (a) of this Item. Such discussions may be combined.

Instruction 2 to Paragraph (b): In preparing the discussion and analysis required by this paragraph (b), the registrant may presume that users of the interim financial information have read or have access to the discussion and analysis required by paragraph (a) for the preceding fiscal year.

Instruction 3 to Paragraph (b): The discussion and analysis required by this paragraph (b) is required to focus only on material changes. Where the interim financial statements reveal material changes from period to period in one or more significant line items, the causes for the changes shall be described if they have not already been disclosed: *Provided, however,* That if the causes for a change in one line item also relate to other line items, no repetition is required. Registrants need not recite the amounts of changes from period to period which are readily computable from the financial statements. The discussion shall not merely repeat numerical data contained in the financial statements. The information provided shall include that which is available to the registrant without undue effort or expense and which does not clearly appear in the registrant's condensed interim financial statements.

Instruction 4 to Paragraph (b): The registrant's discussion of material changes in results of operations shall identify any significant elements of the registrant's income or loss from continuing operations which do not arise from or are not necessarily representative of the registrant's ongoing business.

Instruction 5 to Paragraph (b): [Removed and Reserved].

Instruction 6 to Paragraph (b): Any forward-looking information supplied is expressly covered by the safe harbor rule for projections. See Rule 175 under the Securities Act, Rule 3b–6 under the Exchange Act and Securities Act Release No. 6084 (June 25, 1979).

Instruction 7 to Paragraph (b): The registrant is not required to include the table required by paragraph (a)(5) of this Item for interim periods. Instead, the registrant should disclose material changes outside the ordinary course of the registrant's business in the specified contractual obligations during the interim period.

Instruction 8 to Paragraph (b): The term statement of comprehensive income shall mean a statement of comprehensive income as defined in Item 1–02 of Regulation S–X.

(c)   *Safe Harbor.*

(1)   The safe harbor provided in section 27A of the Securities Act of 1933 and section 21E of the Securities Exchange Act of 1934 ("statutory safe harbors") shall apply to forward-looking information provided pursuant to paragraphs (a)(4) and (5) of this Item, provided that the disclosure is made by: an issuer; a person acting on behalf of the issuer; an outside reviewer retained by the issuer making a statement on behalf of the issuer; or an underwriter, with respect to information provided by the issuer or information derived from information provided by the issuer.

(2)   For purposes of paragraph (c) of this Item only:

(i)   All information required by paragraphs (a)(4) and (5) of this Item is deemed to be a forward looking statement as that term is defined in the statutory safe harbors, except for historical facts.

(ii)   With respect to paragraph (a)(4) of this Item, the meaningful cautionary statements element of the statutory safe harbors will be satisfied if a registrant satisfies all requirements of that same paragraph (a)(4) of this Item.

(d)   *Smaller Reporting Companies.* A smaller reporting company, as defined in Item 10(f)(1), may provide the information required in paragraph (a)(3)(iv) of this Item for the last two most recent fiscal years of the registrant if it provides financial information on net sales and revenues and on income from continuing operations for only two years. A smaller reporting company is not required to provide the information required by paragraph (a)(5) of this Item.

Item 304.   Changes in and Disagreements With Accountants on Accounting and Financial Disclosure

(a)(1)   If during the registrant's two most recent fiscal years or any subsequent interim period, an independent accountant who was previously engaged as the principal accountant to audit the registrant's financial statements, or an independent accountant who was previously engaged to audit a significant subsidiary and on whom the principal accountant expressed reliance in its report, has resigned (or indicated it has declined to stand for re-election after the completion of the current audit) or was dismissed, then the registrant shall:

(i)   State whether the former accountant resigned, declined to stand for re-election or was dismissed and the date thereof.

(ii)   State whether the principal accountant's report on the financial statements for either of the past two years contained an adverse opinion or a disclaimer of opinion, or was qualified or modified as to uncertainty, audit scope, or accounting principles; and also describe the nature of each such adverse opinion, disclaimer of opinion, modification or qualification.

(iii)   State whether the decision to change accountants was recommended or approved by:

(A)   Any audit or similar committee of the board of directors, if the issuer has such a committee; or

(B)   The board of directors, if the issuer has no such committee.

(iv)   State whether during the registrant's two most recent fiscal years and any subsequent interim period preceding such resignation, declination or dismissal there were any disagreements with the former accountant on any matter of accounting principles or practices, financial statement disclosure, or auditing scope or procedure, which disagreement(s), if not resolved to the satisfaction of the former accountant, would have caused it to make a reference to the subject matter of the disagreement(s) in connection with its report. Also,

(A)   describe each such disagreement;

(B)   state whether any audit or similar committee of the board of directors, or the board of directors, discussed the subject matter of each of such disagreements with the former accountant; and

(C) state whether the registrant has authorized the former accountant to respond fully to the inquiries of the successor accountant concerning the subject matter of each of such disagreement and, if not, describe the nature of any limitation thereon and the reason therefore. The disagreements required to be reported in response to this Item include both those resolved to the former accountant's satisfaction and those not resolved to the former accountant's satisfaction. Disagreements contemplated by this Item are those that occur at the decision-making level, i.e., between personnel of the registrant responsible for presentation of its financial statements and personnel of the accounting firm responsible for rendering its report.

(v) Provide the information required by paragraph (a)(1)(iv) of this Item for each of the kinds of events (even though the registrant and the former accountant did not express a difference of opinion regarding the event) listed in paragraphs (a)(1)(v)(A) through (D) of this Item, that occurred within the registrant's two most recent fiscal years and any subsequent interim period preceding the former accountant's resignation, declination to stand for re-election, or dismissal ("reportable events"). If the event led to a disagreement or difference of opinion, then the event should be reported as a disagreement under paragraph (a)(1)(iv) and need not be repeated under this paragraph.

(A) The accountant's having advised the registrant that the internal controls necessary for the registrant to develop reliable financial statements do not exist;

(B) The accountant's having advised the registrant that information has come to the accountant's attention that has led it to no longer be able to rely on management's representations, or that has made it unwilling to be associated with the financial statements prepared by management;

(C)(1) the accountant's having advised the registrant of the need to expand significantly the scope of its audit, or that information has come to the accountant's attention during the time period covered by Item 304(a)(1)(iv), that if further investigated may

(i) Materially impact the fairness or reliability of either: a previously issued audit report or the underlying financial statements; or the financial statements issued or to be issued covering the fiscal period(s) subsequent to the date of the most recent financial statements covered by an audit report (including information that may prevent it from rendering an unqualified audit report on those financial statements), or

(ii) Cause it to be unwilling to rely on management's representations or be associated with the registrant's financial statements, and

(2) Due to the accountant's resignation (due to audit scope limitations or otherwise) or dismissal, or for any other reason, the accountant did not so expand the scope of its audit or conduct such further investigation; or

(D)(1) the accountant's having advised the registrant that information has come to the accountant's attention that it has concluded materially impacts the fairness or reliability of either (i) a previously issued audit report or the underlying financial statements, or (ii) the financial statements issued or to be issued covering the fiscal period(s) subsequent to the date of the most recent financial statements covered by an audit report (including information that, unless resolved to the accountant's satisfaction, would prevent it from rendering an unqualified audit report on those financial statements), and

(2) Due to the accountant's resignation, dismissal or declination to stand for re-election, or for any other reason, the issue has not been resolved to the accountant's satisfaction prior to its resignation, dismissal or declination to stand for re-election.

(2) If during the registrant's two most recent fiscal years or any subsequent interim period, a new independent accountant has been engaged as either the principal accountant to audit the registrant's financial statements, or as an independent accountant to audit a significant subsidiary and on whom the principal accountant is expected to express reliance in its report, then the registrant shall identify the newly engaged accountant and indicate the date of such accountant's engagement. In addition, if during the registrant's two most recent fiscal years, and any subsequent interim period prior to engaging that accountant, the registrant (or someone on its behalf) consulted the newly engaged accountant regarding (i) either: the application of accounting principles to a specified transaction, either completed or proposed; or

the type of audit opinion that might be rendered on the registrant's financial statements, and either a written report was provided to the registrant or oral advice was provided that the new accountant concluded was an important factor considered by the registrant in reaching a decision as to the accounting, auditing or financial reporting issue; or (ii) any matter that was either the subject of a disagreement (as defined in paragraph 304(a)(1)(iv) and the related instructions to this item) or a reportable event (as described in paragraph 304(a)(1)(v)), then the registrant shall:

(A) So state and identify the issues that were the subjects of those consultations;

(B) Briefly describe the views of the newly engaged accountant as expressed orally or in writing to the registrant on each such issue and, if written views were received by the registrant, file them as an exhibit to the report or registration statement requiring compliance with this Item 304(a);

(C) State whether the former accountant was consulted by the registrant regarding any such issues, and if so, provide a summary of the former accountant's views; and

(D) Request the newly engaged accountant to review the disclosure required by this paragraph (a) before it is filed with the Commission and provide the new accountant the opportunity to furnish the registrant with a letter addressed to the Commission containing any new information, clarification of the registrant's expression of its views, or the respects in which it does not agree with the statements made by the registrant in response to Item 304(a). The registrant shall file any such letter as an exhibit to the report or registration statement containing the disclosure required by this Item.

(3) The registrant shall provide the former accountant with a copy of the disclosures it is making in response to this paragraph (a) that the former accountant shall receive no later than the day that the disclosures are filed with the Commission. The registrant shall request the former accountant to furnish the registrant with a letter addressed to the Commission stating whether it agrees with the statements made by the registrant in response to this paragraph (a) and, if not, stating the respects in which it does not agree. The registrant shall file the former accountant's letter as an exhibit to the report or registration statement containing this disclosure. If the former accountant's letter is unavailable at the time of filing such report or registration statement, then the registrant shall request the former accountant to provide the letter as promptly as possible so that the registrant can file the letter with the Commission within ten business days after the filing of the report or registration statement. Notwithstanding the ten business day period, the registrant shall file the letter by amendment within two business days of receipt; if the letter is received on a Saturday, Sunday or holiday on which the Commission is not open for business, then the two business day period shall begin to run on and shall include the first business day thereafter. The former accountant may provide the registrant with an interim letter highlighting specific areas of concern and indicating a subsequent, more detailed letter will be forthcoming within the ten business day period noted above. If not filed with the report or registration statement containing the registrant's disclosure under this paragraph (a), then the interim letter, if any, shall be filed by the registrant by amendment within two business days of receipt.

(b) If,

(1) In connection with a change in accountants subject to paragraph (a) of this Item, there was any disagreement of the type described in paragraph (a)(1)(iv) or any reportable event as described in paragraph (a)(1)(v) of this Item,

(2) During the fiscal year in which the change in accountants took place or during the subsequent fiscal year, there have been any transactions or events similar to those which involved such disagreement or reportable event and

(3) Such transactions or events were material and were accounted for or disclosed in a manner different from that which the former accountants apparently would have concluded was required, the registrant shall state the existence and nature of the disagreement or reportable event and also state the effect on the financial statements if the method had been followed which the former accountants apparently would have concluded was required. These disclosures need not be made if the method asserted by the former accountants ceases to be generally accepted because of authoritative standards or interpretations subsequently issued.

Instructions to Item 304: 1. The disclosure called for by paragraph (a) of this Item need not be provided if it has been previously reported (as that term is defined in Rule 12b–2 under the Exchange Act); the disclosure called for by paragraph (a) must be provided, however, notwithstanding prior disclosure, if required pursuant to Item 9 of Schedule 14A. The disclosure called for by paragraph (b) of this rule must be furnished, where required, notwithstanding any prior disclosure about accountant changes or disagreements.

2.   When disclosure is required by paragraph (a) of this rule in an annual report to security holders pursuant to Rule 14a–3 or Rule 14c–3 or in a proxy or information statement filed pursuant to the requirements of Schedule 14A or 14C in lieu of a letter pursuant to paragraph (a)(2)(D) or (a)(3), prior to filing such materials with or furnishing such materials to the Commission, the registrant shall furnish the disclosure required by paragraph (a) of this rule to any former accountant engaged by the registrant during the period set forth in paragraph (a) of this rule and to the newly engaged accountant. If any such accountant believes that the statements made in response to paragraph (a) of this rule are incorrect or incomplete, it may present its views in a brief statement, ordinarily expected not to exceed 200 words, to be included in the annual report or proxy or information statement. This statement shall be submitted to the registrant within ten business days of the date the accountant receives the registrant's disclosure. Further, unless the written views of the newly engaged accountant required to be filed as an exhibit by paragraph (a)(2)(B) of this Item have been previously filed with the Commission the registrant shall file a Form 8–K concurrently with the annual report or proxy or information statement for the purpose of filing the written views as exhibits thereto.

3.   The information required by Item 304(a) need not be provided for a company being acquired by the registrant that is not subject to the filing requirements of either section 13(a) or 15(d) of the Exchange Act, or, because of section 12(i) of the Exchange Act, has not furnished an annual report to security holders pursuant to Rule 14a–3 or Rule 14c–3 for its latest fiscal year.

4.   The term "disagreements" as used in this Item shall be interpreted broadly, to include any difference of opinion concerning any matter of accounting principles or practices, financial statement disclosure, or auditing scope or procedure which (if not resolved to the satisfaction of the former accountant) would have caused it to make reference to the subject matter of the disagreement in connection with its report. It is not necessary for there to have been an argument to have had a disagreement, merely a difference of opinion. For purposes of this Item, however, the term disagreements does not include initial differences of opinion based on incomplete facts or preliminary information that were later resolved to the former accountant's satisfaction by, and providing the registrant and the accountant do not continue to have a difference of opinion upon, obtaining additional relevant facts or information.

5.   In determining whether any disagreement or reportable event has occurred, an oral communication from the engagement partner or another person responsible for rendering the accounting firm's opinion (or their designee) will generally suffice as the accountant advising the registrant of a reportable event or as a statement of a disagreement at the "decision-making-level" within the accounting firm and require disclosure under this Item.

Item 305.   Quantitative and Qualitative Disclosures About Market Risk

(a)   *Quantitative information about market risk.*

(1)   Registrants shall provide, in their reporting currency, quantitative information about market risk as of the end of the latest fiscal year, in accordance with one of the following three disclosure alternatives. In preparing this quantitative information, registrants shall categorize market risk sensitive instruments into instruments entered into for trading purposes and instruments entered into for purposes other than trading purposes. Within both the trading and other than trading portfolios, separate quantitative information shall be presented, to the extent material, for each market risk exposure category (i.e., interest rate risk, foreign currency exchange rate risk, commodity price risk, and other relevant market risks, such as equity price risk). A registrant may use one of the three alternatives set forth below for all of the required quantitative disclosures about market risk. A registrant also may choose, from among the three alternatives, one disclosure alternative for market risk sensitive instruments entered into for trading purposes and another disclosure alternative for market risk sensitive instruments entered into for other than trading purposes. Alternatively, a registrant may choose any disclosure alternative, from among the three alternatives, for each risk exposure category within the trading and other than trading portfolios. The three disclosure alternatives are:

(i)(A)(1)   Tabular presentation of information related to market risk sensitive instruments; such information shall include fair values of the market risk sensitive instruments and contract terms sufficient to determine future cash flows from those instruments, categorized by expected maturity dates.

(2) Tabular information relating to contract terms shall allow readers of the table to determine expected cash flows from the market risk sensitive instruments for each of the next five years. Comparable tabular information for any remaining years shall be displayed as an aggregate amount.

(3) Within each risk exposure category, the market risk sensitive instruments shall be grouped based on common characteristics. Within the foreign currency exchange rate risk category, the market risk sensitive instruments shall be grouped by functional currency and within the commodity price risk category, the market risk sensitive instruments shall be grouped by type of commodity.

(4) See the Appendix to this Item for a suggested format for presentation of this information; and

(B) Registrants shall provide a description of the contents of the table and any related assumptions necessary to understand the disclosures required under paragraph (a)(1)(i)(A) of this Item; or

(ii)(A) Sensitivity analysis disclosures that express the potential loss in future earnings, fair values, or cash flows of market risk sensitive instruments resulting from one or more selected hypothetical changes in interest rates, foreign currency exchange rates, commodity prices, and other relevant market rates or prices over a selected period of time. The magnitude of selected hypothetical changes in rates or prices may differ among and within market risk exposure categories; and

(B) Registrants shall provide a description of the model, assumptions, and parameters, which are necessary to understand the disclosures required under paragraph (a)(1)(ii)(A) of this Item; or

(iii)(A) Value at risk disclosures that express the potential loss in future earnings, fair values, or cash flows of market risk sensitive instruments over a selected period of time, with a selected likelihood of occurrence, from changes in interest rates, foreign currency exchange rates, commodity prices, and other relevant market rates or prices;

(B)(1) For each category for which value at risk disclosures are required under paragraph (a)(1)(iii)(A) of this Item, provide either:

(i) The average, high and low amounts, or the distribution of the value at risk amounts for the reporting period; or

(ii) The average, high and low amounts, or the distribution of actual changes in fair values, earnings, or cash flows from the market risk sensitive instruments occurring during the reporting period; or

(iii) The percentage or number of times the actual changes in fair values, earnings, or cash flows from the market risk sensitive instruments exceeded the value at risk amounts during the reporting period;

(2) Information required under paragraph (a)(1)(iii)(B)(1) of this Item 305 is not required for the first fiscal year end in which a registrant must present this Item's information; and

(C) Registrants shall provide a description of the model, assumptions, and parameters, which are necessary to understand the disclosures required under paragraphs (a)(1)(iii)(A) and (B) of this Item.

(2) Registrants shall discuss material limitations that cause the information required under paragraph (a)(1) of this Item not to reflect fully the net market risk exposures of the entity. This discussion shall include summarized descriptions of instruments, positions, and transactions omitted from the quantitative market risk disclosure information or the features of instruments, positions, and

transactions that are included, but not reflected fully in the quantitative market risk disclosure information.

(3)   Registrants shall present summarized market risk information for the preceding fiscal year. In addition, registrants shall discuss the reasons for material quantitative changes in market risk exposures between the current and preceding fiscal years. Information required by this paragraph (a)(3), however, is not required if disclosure is not required under paragraph (a)(1) of this Item for the current fiscal year. Information required by this paragraph (a)(3) is not required for the first fiscal year end in which a registrant must present Item information.

(4)   If registrants change disclosure alternatives or key model characteristics, assumptions, and parameters used in providing quantitative information about market risk (e.g., changing from tabular presentation to value at risk, changing the scope of instruments included in the model, or changing the definition of loss from fair values to earnings), and if the effects of any such change is material, the registrant shall:

(i)   Explain the reasons for the change; and

(ii)   Either provide summarized comparable information, under the new disclosure method, for the year preceding the current year or, in addition to providing disclosure for the current year under the new method, provide disclosures for the current year and preceding fiscal year under the method used in the preceding year.

Instructions to Paragraph 305(a): 1. Under paragraph 305(a)(1):

A.   For each market risk exposure category within the trading and other than trading portfolios, registrants may report the average, high, and low sensitivity analysis or value at risk amounts for the reporting period, as an alternative to reporting year-end amounts.

B.   In determining the average, high, and low amounts for the fiscal year under instruction 1.A. of the Instructions to Paragraph 305(a), registrants should use sensitivity analysis or value at risk amounts relating to at least four equal time periods throughout the reporting period (e.g., four quarter-end amounts, 12 month-end amounts, or 52 week-end amounts).

C.   Functional currency means functional currency as defined by generally accepted accounting principles (see, e.g., FASB ASC Master Glossary).

D.   Registrants using the sensitivity analysis and value at risk disclosure alternatives are encouraged, but not required, to provide quantitative amounts that reflect the aggregate market risk inherent in the trading and other than trading portfolios.

2.   Under paragraph 305(a)(1)(i):

A.   Examples of contract terms sufficient to determine future cash flows from market risk sensitive instruments include, but are not limited to:

i.   Debt instruments—principal amounts and weighted average effective interest rates;

ii.   Forwards and futures—contract amounts and weighted average settlement prices;

iii.   Options—contract amounts and weighted average strike prices;

iv.   Swaps—notional amounts, weighted average pay rates or prices, and weighted average receive rates or prices; and

v.   Complex instruments—likely to be a combination of the contract terms presented in 2.A.i. through iv. of this Instruction;

B.   When grouping based on common characteristics, instruments should be categorized, at a minimum, by the following characteristics, when material:

i.   Fixed rate or variable rate assets or liabilities;

ii.   Long or short forwards and futures;

iii.   Written or purchased put or call options with similar strike prices;

iv.   Receive fixed and pay variable swaps, receive variable and pay fixed swaps, and receive variable and pay variable swaps;

v.   The currency in which the instruments' cash flows are denominated;

vi.   Financial instruments for which foreign currency transaction gains and losses are reported in the same manner as translation adjustments under generally accepted accounting principles (see, e.g., FASB ASC paragraph 830–20–35–3 (Foreign Currency Matters Topic)); and

vii.   Derivatives used to manage risks inherent in anticipated transactions;

C.   Registrants may aggregate information regarding functional currencies that are economically related, managed together for internal risk management purposes, and have statistical correlations of greater than 75% over each of the past three years;

D.   Market risk sensitive instruments that are exposed to rate or price changes in more than one market risk exposure category should be presented within the tabular information for each of the risk exposure categories to which those instruments are exposed;

E.   If a currency swap eliminates all foreign currency exposures in the cash flows of a foreign currency denominated debt instrument, neither the currency swap nor the foreign currency denominated debt instrument are required to be disclosed in the foreign currency risk exposure category. However, both the currency swap and the foreign currency denominated debt instrument should be disclosed in the interest rate risk exposure category; and

F.   The contents of the table and related assumptions that should be described include, but are not limited to:

i.   The different amounts reported in the table for various categories of the market risk sensitive instruments (e.g., principal amounts for debt, notional amounts for swaps, and contract amounts for options and futures);

ii.   The different types of reported market rates or prices (e.g., contractual rates or prices, spot rates or prices, forward rates or prices); and

iii.   Key prepayment or reinvestment assumptions relating to the timing of reported amounts.

3.   Under paragraph 305(a)(1)(ii):

A.   Registrants should select hypothetical changes in market rates or prices that are expected to reflect reasonably possible near-term changes in those rates and prices. In this regard, absent economic justification for the selection of a different amount, registrants should use changes that are not less than 10 percent of end of period market rates or prices;

B.   For purposes of instruction 3.A. of the Instructions to Paragraph 305(a), the term reasonably possible has the same meaning as defined by generally accepted accounting principles (see, e.g., FASB ASC Master Glossary);

C.   For purposes of instruction 3.A. of the Instructions to Paragraph 305(a), the term near term means a period of time going forward up to one year from the date of the financial statements (see FASB ASC Master Glossary);

D.   Market risk sensitive instruments that are exposed to rate or price changes in more than one market risk exposure category should be included in the sensitivity analysis disclosures for each market risk category to which those instruments are exposed;

E.   Registrants with multiple foreign currency exchange rate exposures should prepare foreign currency sensitivity analysis disclosures that measure the aggregate sensitivity to changes in all foreign currency exchange rate exposures, including the effects of changes in both transactional currency/functional currency exchange rate exposures and functional currency/reporting currency exchange rate exposures. For example, assume a French division of a registrant presenting its financial statements in U.S. dollars ($US) invests in a deutschmark (DM)-denominated debt security. In these circumstances, the $US is the reporting currency and the DM is the transactional currency. In addition, assume this division determines that the French franc (FF) is its functional currency according to FASB ASC Topic 830, *Foreign Currency Matters*. In preparing the foreign currency sensitivity analysis disclosures, this registrant should report the aggregate potential loss from hypothetical changes in both the DM/FF exchange rate exposure and the FF/$US exchange rate exposure; and

F.   Model, assumptions, and parameters that should be described include, but are not limited to, how loss is defined by the model (e.g., loss in earnings, fair values, or cash flows), a general description of the modeling technique (e.g., duration modeling, modeling that measures the change in net present values arising from selected hypothetical changes in market rates or prices, and a description as to how optionality is addressed by the model), the types of instruments covered by the model (e.g., derivative financial instruments, other financial instruments, derivative commodity instruments, and whether other instruments are included voluntarily, such as certain commodity instruments and positions, cash flows from anticipated transactions, and certain financial instruments excluded under instruction 3.C.ii. of the General Instructions to Paragraphs 305(a) and 305(b)), and other relevant information about the model's assumptions and parameters, (e.g., the magnitude and timing of selected hypothetical changes in market rates or prices used, the method by which discount rates are determined, and key prepayment or reinvestment assumptions).

4.   Under paragraph 305(a)(1)(iii):

A.   The confidence intervals selected should reflect reasonably possible near-term changes in market rates and prices. In this regard, absent economic justification for the selection of different confidence intervals, registrants should use intervals that are 95 percent or higher;

B.   For purposes of instruction 4.A. of the Instructions to Paragraph 305(a), the term reasonably possible has the same meaning as defined by generally accepted accounting principles (see, e.g., FASB ASC Master Glossary);

C.   For purposes of instruction 4.A. of the Instructions to Paragraphs 305(a), the term near term means a period of time going forward up to one year from the date of the financial statements (see generally SOP 94–6, at paragraph 7 (December 30, 1994));

D.   Registrants with multiple foreign currency exchange rate exposures should prepare foreign currency value at risk analysis disclosures that measure the aggregate sensitivity to changes in all foreign currency exchange rate exposures, including the aggregate effects of changes in both transactional currency/ functional currency exchange rate exposures and functional currency/reporting currency exchange rate exposures. For example, assume a French division of a registrant presenting its financial statements in U.S. dollars ($US) invests in a deutschmark (DM)-denominated debt security. In these circumstances, the $US is the reporting currency and the DM is the transactional currency. In addition, assume this division determines that the French franc (FF) is its functional currency according to FASB ASC Topic 830, *Foreign Currency Matters*. In preparing the foreign currency value at risk disclosures, this registrant should report the aggregate potential loss from hypothetical changes in both the DM/FF exchange rate exposure and the FF/$US exchange rate exposure; and

E.   Model, assumptions, and parameters that should be described include, but are not limited to, how loss is defined by the model (e.g., loss in earnings, fair values, or cash flows), the type of model used (e.g., variance/covariance, historical simulation, or Monte Carlo simulation and a description as to how optionality is addressed by the model), the types of instruments covered by the model (e.g., derivative financial instruments, other financial instruments, derivative commodity instruments, and whether other instruments are included voluntarily, such as certain commodity instruments and positions, cash flows from anticipated transactions, and certain financial instruments excluded under instruction 3.C.ii. of the General Instructions to Paragraphs 305(a) and 305(b)), and other relevant information about the model's assumptions and parameters, (e.g., holding periods, confidence intervals, and, when appropriate, the methods used for aggregating value at risk amounts across market risk exposure categories, such as by assuming perfect positive correlation, independence, or actual observed correlation).

5.   Under paragraph 305(a)(2), limitations that should be considered include, but are not limited to:

A.   The exclusion of certain market risk sensitive instruments, positions, and transactions from the disclosures required under paragraph 305(a)(1) (e.g., derivative commodity instruments not permitted by contract or business custom to be settled in cash or with another financial instrument, commodity positions, cash flows from anticipated transactions, and certain financial instruments excluded under instruction 3.C.ii. of the General Instructions to Paragraphs 305(a) and 305(b)). Failure to include such instruments, positions, and transactions in preparing the disclosures under paragraph 305(a)(1) may be a limitation because the resulting disclosures may not fully reflect the net market risk of a registrant; and

B.   The ability of disclosures required under paragraph 305(a)(1) to reflect fully the market risk that may be inherent in instruments with leverage, option, or prepayment features (e.g., options, including written options, structured notes, collateralized mortgage obligations, leveraged swaps, and options embedded in swaps).

(b)   *Qualitative information about market risk.*

(1)   To the extent material, describe:

(i)   The registrant's primary market risk exposures;

(ii)   How those exposures are managed. Such descriptions shall include, but not be limited to, a discussion of the objectives, general strategies, and instruments, if any, used to manage those exposures; and

(iii)   Changes in either the registrant's primary market risk exposures or how those exposures are managed, when compared to what was in effect during the most recently completed fiscal year and what is known or expected to be in effect in future reporting periods.

(2)   Qualitative information about market risk shall be presented separately for market risk sensitive instruments entered into for trading purposes and those entered into for purposes other than trading.

Instructions to Paragraph 305(b).

1.   For purposes of disclosure under paragraph 305(b), primary market risk exposures means:

A.   The following categories of market risk: interest rate risk, foreign currency exchange rate risk, commodity price risk, and other relevant market rate or price risks (e.g., equity price risk); and

B.   Within each of these categories, the particular markets that present the primary risk of loss to the registrant. For example, if a registrant has a material exposure to foreign currency exchange rate risk and, within this category of market risk, is most vulnerable to changes in dollar/yen, dollar/pound, and dollar/peso exchange rates, the registrant should disclose those exposures. Similarly, if a registrant has a material exposure to interest rate risk and, within this category of market risk, is most vulnerable to changes in short-term U.S. prime interest rates, it should disclose the existence of that exposure.

2.   For purposes of disclosure under paragraph 305(b), registrants should describe primary market risk exposures that exist as of the end of the latest fiscal year, and how those exposures are managed.

General Instructions to Paragraphs 305(a) and 305(b).

1.   The disclosures called for by paragraphs 305(a) and 305(b) are intended to clarify the registrant's exposures to market risk associated with activities in derivative financial instruments, other financial instruments, and derivative commodity instruments.

2.   In preparing the disclosures under paragraphs 305(a) and 305(b), registrants are required to include derivative financial instruments, other financial instruments, and derivative commodity instruments.

3.   For purposes of paragraphs 305(a) and 305(b), derivative financial instruments, other financial instruments, and derivative commodity instruments (collectively referred to as "market risk sensitive instruments") are defined as follows:

A.   Derivative financial instruments has the same meaning as defined by generally accepted accounting principles (see, e.g., FASB ASC Master Glossary), and includes futures, forwards, swaps, options, and other financial instruments with similar characteristics;

B.   Other financial instruments means all financial instruments as defined by generally accepted accounting principles for which fair value disclosures are required (see, e.g., FASB ASC paragraph 825–10–50–8 (Financial Instruments Topic)), except for derivative financial instruments, as defined above;

C.i.   Other financial instruments include, but are not limited to, trade accounts receivable, investments, loans, structured notes, mortgage-backed securities, trade accounts payable, indexed debt instruments, interest-only and principal-only obligations, deposits, and other debt obligations;

ii.   Other financial instruments exclude employers and plans obligations for pension and other post-retirement benefits, substantively extinguished debt, insurance contracts, lease contracts, warranty obligations and rights, unconditional purchase obligations, investments accounted for under the equity method, minority interests in consolidated enterprises, and equity instruments issued by the registrant and classified in stockholders' equity in the statement of financial position (see, e.g., FASB ASC paragraph 825–10–50–8). For purposes of this item, trade accounts receivable and trade accounts payable need not be considered other financial instruments when their carrying amounts approximate fair value; and

D.   Derivative commodity instruments include, to the extent such instruments are not derivative financial instruments, commodity futures, commodity forwards, commodity swaps, commodity options, and other commodity instruments with similar characteristics that are permitted by contract or business custom to be settled in cash or with another financial instrument. For purposes of this paragraph, settlement in cash includes settlement in cash of the net change in value of the derivative commodity instrument (e.g., net cash settlement based on changes in the price of the underlying commodity).

4.A. In addition to providing required disclosures for the market risk sensitive instruments defined in instruction 2. of the General Instructions to Paragraphs 305(a) and 305(b), registrants are encouraged to include other market risk sensitive instruments, positions, and transactions within the disclosures required under paragraphs 305(a) and 305(b). Such instruments, positions, and transactions might include commodity positions, derivative commodity instruments that are not permitted by contract or business custom to be settled in cash or with another financial instrument, cash flows from anticipated transactions, and certain financial instruments excluded under instruction 3.C.ii. of the General Instructions to Paragraphs 305(a) and 305(b).

B. Registrants that voluntarily include other market risk sensitive instruments, positions and transactions within their quantitative disclosures about market risk under the sensitivity analysis or value at risk disclosure alternatives are not required to provide separate market risk disclosures for any voluntarily selected instruments, positions, or transactions. Instead, registrants selecting the sensitivity analysis and value at risk disclosure alternatives are permitted to present comprehensive market risk disclosures, which reflect the combined market risk exposures inherent in both the required and any voluntarily selected instruments, position, or transactions. Registrants that choose the tabular presentation disclosure alternative should present voluntarily selected instruments, positions, or transactions in a manner consistent with the requirements in Item 305(a) for market risk sensitive instruments.

C. If a registrant elects to include voluntarily a particular type of instrument, position, or transaction in their quantitative disclosures about market risk, that registrant should include all, rather than some, of those instruments, positions, or transactions within those disclosures. For example, if a registrant holds in inventory a particular type of commodity position and elects to include that commodity position within their market risk disclosures, the registrant should include the entire commodity position, rather than only a portion thereof, in their quantitative disclosures about market risk.

5.A. Under paragraphs 305(a) and 305(b), a materiality assessment should be made for each market risk exposure category within the trading and other than trading portfolios.

B. For purposes of making the materiality assessment under instruction 5.A. of the General Instructions to Paragraphs 305(a) and 305(b), registrants should evaluate both:

i. The materiality of the fair values of derivative financial instruments, other financial instruments, and derivative commodity instruments outstanding as of the end of the latest fiscal year; and

ii. The materiality of potential, near-term losses in future earnings, fair values, and/or cash flows from reasonably possible near-term changes in market rates or prices.

iii. If either paragraphs B.i. or B.ii. in this instruction of the General Instructions to Paragraphs 305(a) and 305(b) are material, the registrant should disclose quantitative and qualitative information about market risk, if such market risk for the particular market risk exposure category is material.

C. For purposes of instruction 5.B.i. of the General Instructions to Paragraphs 305(a) and 305(b), registrants generally should not net fair values, except to the extent allowed under generally accepted accounting principles (see, e.g., FASB A ASC Subtopic 210–20, *Balance Sheet—Offsetting*). For example, under this instruction, the fair value of assets generally should not be netted with the fair value of liabilities.

D. For purposes of instruction 5.B.ii. of the General Instructions to Paragraphs 305(a) and 305(b), registrants should consider, among other things, the magnitude of:

i. Past market movements;

ii. Reasonably possible, near-term market movements; and

iii. Potential losses that may arise from leverage, option, and multiplier features.

E. For purposes of instructions 5.B.ii and 5.D.ii of the General Instructions to Paragraphs 305(a) and 305(b), the term near term means a period of time going forward up to one year from the date of the financial statements (see FASB ASC Master Glossary).

F. For the purpose of instructions 5.B.ii. and 5.D.ii. of the General Instructions to Paragraphs 305(a) and 305(b), the term reasonably possible has the same meaning as defined by generally accepted accounting principles (see, e.g., FASB ASC Master Glossary).

6.   For purposes of paragraphs 305(a) and 305(b), registrants should present the information outside of, and not incorporate the information into, the financial statements (including the footnotes to the financial statements). In addition, registrants are encouraged to provide the required information in one location. However, alternative presentation, such as inclusion of all or part of the information in Management's Discussion and Analysis, may be used at the discretion of the registrant. If information is disclosed in more than one location, registrants should provide cross-references to the locations of the related disclosures.

7.   For purposes of the instructions to paragraphs 305(a) and 305(b), trading purposes means dealing and other trading activities measured at fair value with gains and losses recognized in earnings). In addition, anticipated transactions means transactions (other than transactions involving existing assets or liabilities or transactions necessitated by existing firm commitments) an enterprise expects, but is not obligated, to carry out in the normal course of business.

(c)   *Interim periods.* If interim period financial statements are included or are required to be included by Article 3 of Regulation S–X, discussion and analysis shall be provided so as to enable the reader to assess the sources and effects of material changes in information that would be provided under Item 305 of Regulation S–K from the end of the preceding fiscal year to the date of the most recent interim balance sheet.

Instructions to Paragraph 305(c).

1.   Information required under paragraph (c) of this Item is not required until after the first fiscal year end in which this Item 305 is applicable.

(d)   *Safe Harbor.* (1) The safe harbor provided in section 27A of the Securities Act of 1933 and Section 21E of the Securities Exchange Act of 1934 ("statutory safe harbors") shall apply, with respect to all types of issuers and transactions, to information provided pursuant to paragraphs (a), (b), and (c) of this Item, provided that the disclosure is made by: an issuer; a person acting on behalf of the issuer; an outside reviewer retained by the issuer making a statement on behalf of the issuer; or an underwriter, with respect to information provided by the issuer or information derived from information provided by the issuer.

(2)   For purposes of paragraph (d) of this Item only:

(i)   All information required by paragraphs (a), (b)(1)(i), (b)(1)(iii), and (c) of this Item is considered forward looking statements for purposes of the statutory safe harbors, except for historical facts such as the terms of particular contracts and the number of market risk sensitive instruments held during or at the end of the reporting period; and

(ii)   With respect to paragraph (a) of this Item, the meaningful cautionary statements prong of the statutory safe harbors will be satisfied if a registrant satisfies all requirements of that same paragraph (a) of this Item.

(e)   *Smaller Reporting Companies.* A smaller reporting company, as defined by Item 10(f)(1), is not required to provide the information required by this Item.

General Instructions to Paragraphs 305(a), 305(b), 305(c), 305(d), and 305(e).

1.   Bank registrants, thrift registrants, and non-bank and non-thrift registrants with market capitalizations on January 28, 1997 in excess of $2.5 billion should provide Item 305 disclosures in filings with the Commission that include annual financial statements for fiscal years ending after June 15, 1997. Non-bank and non-thrift registrants with market capitalizations on January 28, 1997 of $2.5 billion or less should provide Item 305 disclosures in filings with the Commission that include financial statements for fiscal years ending after June 15, 1998.

2.A.   For purposes of instruction 1. of the General Instructions to Paragraphs 305(a), 305(b), 305(c), 305(d), and 305(e), bank registrants and thrift registrants include any registrant which has control over a depository institution.

B.   For purposes of instruction 2.A. of the General Instructions to Paragraphs 305(a), 305(b), 305(c), 305(d), and 305(e), a registrant has control over a depository institution if:

i.   The registrant directly or indirectly or acting through one or more other persons owns, controls, or has power to vote 25% or more of any class of voting securities of the depository institution;

ii.   The registrant controls in any manner the election of a majority of the directors or trustees of the depository institution; or

iii.   The Federal Reserve Board or Office of Thrift Supervision determines, after notice and opportunity for hearing, that the registrant directly or indirectly exercises a controlling influence over the management or policies of the depository institution.

C.   For purposes of instruction 2.B. of the General Instructions to Paragraphs 305(a), 305(b), 305(c), 305(d), and 305(e), a depository institution means any of the following:

i.   An insured depository institution as defined in section 3(c)(2) of the Federal Deposit Insurance Act;

ii.   An institution organized under the laws of the United States, any State of the United States, the District of Columbia, any territory of the United States, Puerto Rico, Guam, American Somoa, or the Virgin Islands, which both accepts demand deposits or deposits that the depositor may withdraw by check or similar means for payment to third parties or others and is engaged in the business of making commercial loans.

D.   For purposes of instruction 1. of the General Instructions to Paragraphs 305(a), 305(b), 305(c), 305(d) and 305(e), market capitalization is the aggregate market value of common equity as set forth in General Instruction I.B.1. of Form S–3; provided however, that common equity held by affiliates is included in the calculation of market capitalization; and provided further that instead of using the 60 day period prior to filing referenced in General Instruction I.B.1. of Form S–3, the measurement date is January 28, 1997.

Appendix to Item 305—Tabular Disclosures

The tables set forth below are illustrative of the format that might be used when a registrant elects to present the information required by paragraph (a)(1)(i)(A) of Item 305 regarding terms and information about derivative financial instruments, other financial instruments, and derivative commodity instruments. These examples are for illustrative purposes only. Registrants are not required to display the information in the specific format illustrated below. Alternative methods of display are permissible as long as the disclosure requirements of the section are satisfied. Furthermore, these examples were designed primarily to illustrate possible formats for presentation of the information required by the disclosure item and do not purport to illustrate the broad range of derivative financial instruments, other financial instruments, and derivative commodity instruments utilized by registrants.

Interest Rate Sensitivity

The table below provides information about the Company's derivative financial instruments and other financial instruments that are sensitive to changes in interest rates, including interest rate swaps and debt obligations. For debt obligations, the table presents principal cash flows and related weighted average interest rates by expected maturity dates. For interest rate swaps, the table presents notional amounts and weighted average interest rates by expected (contractual) maturity dates. Notional amounts are used to calculate the contractual payments to be exchanged under the contract. Weighted average variable rates are based on implied forward rates in the yield curve at the reporting date. The information is presented in U.S. dollar equivalents, which is the Company's reporting currency. The instrument's actual cash flows are denominated in both U.S. dollars ($US) and German deutschmarks (DM), as indicated in parentheses.

December 31, 19X1

Liabilities	Expected maturity date							
	19X2	19X3	19X4	19X5	19X6	Thereafter	Total	Fair value
(7) (US$ Equivalent in millions)								
Long-term Debt:								
Fixed Rate ($US)	$XXX	$XXX	$XXX	$XXX	$XXX	$XXX	$XXX	$X
Average interest rate	X.X %	X.X %	X.X %	X.X %	X.X %	X.X %	X.X %	
Fixed Rate (DM)	XXX	XXX	XXX	XXX	XXX	XXX	XXX	
Average interest rate	X.X %	X.X %	X.X %	X.X %	X.X %	X.X %	X.X %	
Variable Rate ($US)	XXX	XXX	XXX	XXX	XXX	XXX	XXX	X
Average interest rate	X.X %	X.X %	X.X %	X.X %	X.X %	X.X %	X.X %	
Interest Rate Derivatives								
(7) (In millions)								
Interest Rate Swaps:								
Variable to Fixed ($US)	$XXX	$XXX	$XXX	$XXX	$XXX	$XXX	$XXX	$X
Average pay rate	X.X %	X.X %	X.X %	X.X %	X.X %	X.X %	X.X %	
Average receive rate	X.X %	X.X %	X.X %	X.X %	X.X %	X.X %	X.X %	
Fixed to Variable ($US)	XXX	XXX	XXX	XXX	XXX	XXX	XXX	X
Average pay rate	X.X %	X.X %	X.X %	X.X %	X.X %	X.X %	X.X %	
Average receive rate	X.X %	X.X %	X.X %	X.X %	X.X %	X.X %	X.X %	

Exchange Rate Sensitivity

The table below provides information about the Company's derivative financial instruments, other financial instruments, and firmly committed sales transactions by functional currency and presents such information in U.S. dollar equivalents. The table summarizes information on instruments and transactions that are sensitive to foreign currency exchange rates, including foreign currency forward exchange agreements, deutschmark (DM)-denominated debt obligations, and firmly committed DM sales transactions. For debt obligations, the table presents principal cash flows and related weighted average interest rates by expected maturity dates. For firmly committed DM-sales transactions, sales amounts are presented by the expected transaction date, which are not expected to exceed two years. For foreign currency forward exchange agreements, the table presents the notional amounts and weighted average exchange rates by expected (contractual) maturity dates. These notional amounts generally are used to calculate the contractual payments to be exchanged under the contract.

December 31, 19X1

				Expected maturity date				
On-Balance Sheet Financial Instruments	19X2	19X3	19X4	19X5	19X6	Thereafter	Total	Fair value
(7) (US$ Equivalent in millions)								
$US Functional Currency[2]:								
Liabilities								
Long-Term Debt:								
Fixed Rate (DM)	$XXX	$XXX	$XXX	$XXX	$XXX	$XXX	$XXX	$X
Average interest rate	X.X	X.X	X.X	X.X	X.X	X.X	X.X	
(7) Expected maturity or transaction date								
Anticipated Transactions and Related Derivatives[3]								
(7) (US$ Equivalent in millions)								
$US Functional Currency:								
Firmly committed Sales Contracts (DM)	$XXX	$XXX					$XXX	$X
Forward Exchange Agreements								
(Receive $US/Pay DM):								
Contract Amount	XXX	XXX	—	—	—	—	XXX	X
Average Contractual Exchange Rate	X.X	X.X	—	—	—	—	X.X	—

[2] Similar tabular information would be provided for other functional currencies.

[3] Pursuant to General Instruction 4. to Items 305(a) and 305(b) of Regulation S-K, registrants may include cash flows from anticipated transactions and operating cash flows resulting from non-financial and non-commodity instruments.

Commodity Price Sensitivity

The table below provides information about the Company's corn inventory and futures contracts that are sensitive to changes in commodity prices, specifically corn prices. For inventory, the table presents the carrying amount and fair value at December 31, 19x1. For the futures contracts the table presents the notional amounts in bushels, the weighted average contract prices, and the total dollar contract amount by expected maturity dates, the latest of which occurs one year from the reporting date. Contract amounts are used to calculate the contractual payments and quantity of corn to be exchanged under the futures contracts.

December 31, 19X1

	Carrying amount	Fair value
(1) (In millions)		
On Balance Sheet Commodity Position and Related Derivatives..........		
Corn Inventory[4]	$XXX	$XXX

	Expected maturity 1992	Fair value
Related Derivatives		
Futures Contracts (Short):		
Contract Volumes (100,000 bushels)............	XXX	—
Weighted Average Price (Per 100,000 bushels)	$X.XX	—

December 31, 19X1

	Carrying amount	Fair value
Contract Amount ($US in millions)..	$XXX	$XXX

[4] Pursuant to General Instruction 4. to Items 305(a) and 305(b) of Regulation S–K, registrants may include information on commodity positions, such as corn inventory.

Item 306.   [Reserved]

Item 307.   Disclosure Controls and Procedures

Disclose the conclusions of the registrant's principal executive and principal financial officers, or persons performing similar functions, regarding the effectiveness of the registrant's disclosure controls and procedures (as defined in Rule 13a–15(e) or 15d–15(e) under the Exchange Act) as of the end of the period covered by the report, based on the evaluation of these controls and procedures required by paragraph (b) of Rule 13a–15 or 15d–15 under the Exchange Act.

Item 308.   Internal Control Over Financial Reporting

(a)   *Management's Annual Report on Internal Control Over Financial Reporting.* Provide a report of management on the registrant's internal control over financial reporting (as defined in Rule 13a–15(f) or Rule 15d–15(f) under the Exchange Act) that contains:

(1)   A statement of management's responsibility for establishing and maintaining adequate internal control over financial reporting for the registrant;

(2)   A statement identifying the framework used by management to evaluate the effectiveness of the registrant's internal control over financial reporting as required by paragraph (c) of Rule 13a–15 or 15d–15 under the Exchange Act;

(3)   Management's assessment of the effectiveness of the registrant's internal control over financial reporting as of the end of the registrant's most recent fiscal year, including a statement as to whether or not internal control over financial reporting is effective. This discussion must include disclosure of any material weakness in the registrant's internal control over financial reporting identified by management. Management is not permitted to conclude that the registrant's internal control over financial reporting is effective if there are one or more material weaknesses in the registrant's internal control over financial reporting; and

(4)   If the registrant is an accelerated filer or a large accelerated filer (as defined in 1934 Act Rule 12b–2 of this Act), or otherwise includes in its annual report a registered public accounting firm's attestation report on internal control over financial reporting, a statement that the registered public accounting firm that audited the financial statements included in the annual report containing the disclosure required by this Item has issued an attestation report on the registrant's internal control over financial reporting.

(b)   *Attestation report of the registered public accounting firm.* If the registrant, other than a registrant that is an emerging growth company, as defined in Rule 405 of the Securities Act of 1933 or Rule 12b–2 of the Securities Exchange Act of 1934, is an accelerated filer or a large accelerated filer (as defined in 1934 Act Rule 12b–2 of this chapter), provide the registered public accounting firm's attestation report on the registrant's internal control over financial reporting in the registrant's annual report containing the disclosure required by this Item.

(c)   *Changes in Internal Control Over Financial Reporting.* Disclose any change in the registrant's internal control over financial reporting identified in connection with the evaluation required by paragraph (d) of Rule 13a–15 or 15d–15 under the Exchange Act that occurred during the registrant's last fiscal quarter (the registrant's fourth fiscal quarter in the case of an annual report) that has materially affected, or is reasonably likely to materially affect, the registrant's internal control over financial reporting.

Instructions to Item 308

1.   A registrant need not comply with paragraphs (a) and (b) of this Item until it either had been required to file an annual report pursuant to section 13(a) or 15(d) of the Exchange Act for the prior fiscal year or had filed

an annual report with the Commission for the prior fiscal year. A registrant that does not comply shall include a statement in the first annual report that it files in substantially the following form: "This annual report does not include a report of management's assessment regarding internal control over financial reporting or an attestation report of the company's registered public accounting firm due to a transition period established by rules of the Securities and Exchange Commission for newly public companies."

2.   The registrant must maintain evidential matter, including documentation, to provide reasonable support for management's assessment of the effectiveness of the registrant's internal control over financial reporting.

Subpart 400—Management and Certain Security Holders

Item 401.   Directors, Executive Officers, Promoters, and Control Persons

(a)   *Identification of Directors.* List the names and ages of all directors of the registrant and all persons nominated or chosen to become directors; indicate all positions and offices with the registrant held by each such person; state his term of office as director and any period(s) during which he has served as such; describe briefly any arrangement or understanding between him and any other person(s) (naming such person(s)) pursuant to which he was or is to be selected as a director or nominee.

Instructions to Paragraph (a) of Item 401. 1.Do not include arrangements or understandings with directors or officers of the registrant acting solely in their capacities as such.

2.   No nominee or person chosen to become a director who has not consented to act as such shall be named in response to this Item. In this regard, with respect to proxy statements, see Rule 14a–4(d) under the Exchange Act.

3.   If the information called for by this paragraph (a) is being presented in a proxy or information statement, no information need be given respecting any director whose term of office as a director will not continue after the meeting to which the statement relates.

4.   With regard to proxy statements in connection with action to be taken concerning the election of directors, if fewer nominees are named than the number fixed by or pursuant to the governing instruments, state the reasons for this procedure and that the proxies cannot be voted for a greater number of persons than the number of nominees named.

5.   With regard to proxy statements in connection with action to be taken concerning the election of directors, if the solicitation is made by persons other than management, information shall be given as to nominees of the persons making the solicitation. In all other instances, information shall be given as to directors and persons nominated for election or chosen by management to become directors.

(b)   *Identification of Executive Officers.* List the names and ages of all executive officers of the registrant and all persons chosen to become executive officers; indicate all positions and offices with the registrant held by each such person; state his term of office as officer and the period during which he has served as such and describe briefly any arrangement or understanding between him and any other person(s) (naming such person) pursuant to which he was or is to be selected as an officer.

Instructions to Paragraph (b) of Item 401. 1. Do not include arrangements or understandings with directors or officers of the registrant acting solely in their capacities as such.

2.   No person chosen to become an executive officer who has not consented to act as such shall be named in response to this Item.

3.   The information regarding executive officers called for by this Item need not be furnished in proxy or information statements prepared in accordance with Schedule 14A under the Exchange Act by registrants relying on General Instruction G of Form 10–K under the Exchange Act, *Provided,* that such information is furnished in a separate item captioned "Executive officers of the registrant" and included in Part I of the registrant's annual report on Form 10–K.

(c)   *Identification of Certain Significant Employees.* Where the registrant employs persons such as production managers, sales managers, or research scientists who are not executive officers but who make or are expected to make significant contributions to the business of the registrant, such persons shall be identified and their background disclosed to the same extent as in the case of executive officers. Such disclosure need not be made if the registrant was subject to section 13(a) or 15(d) of the Exchange Act or was exempt from section 13(a) by section 12(g)(2)(G) of such Act immediately prior to the filing of the registration statement, report, or statement to which this Item is applicable.

(d) *Family Relationships.* State the nature of any family relationship between any director, executive officer, or person nominated or chosen by the registrant to become a director or executive officer.

Instruction to Paragraph 401(d). The term "family relationship" means any relationship by blood, marriage, or adoption, not more remote than first cousin.

(e) *Business Experience.*

(1) *Background.* Briefly describe the business experience during the past five years of each director, executive officer, person nominated or chosen to become a director or executive officer, and each person named in answer to paragraph (c) of Item 401, including: each person's principal occupations and employment during the past five years; the name and principal business of any corporation or other organization in which such occupations and employment were carried on; and whether such corporation or organization is a parent, subsidiary or other affiliate of the registrant. In addition, for each director or person nominated or chosen to become a director, briefly discuss the specific experience, qualifications, attributes or skills that led to the conclusion that the person should serve as a director for the registrant at the time that the disclosure is made, in light of the registrant's business and structure. If material, this disclosure should cover more than the past five years, including information about the person's particular areas of expertise or other relevant qualifications. When an executive officer or person named in response to paragraph (c) of Item 401 has been employed by the registrant or a subsidiary of the registrant for less than five years, a brief explanation shall be included as to the nature of the responsibility undertaken by the individual in prior positions to provide adequate disclosure of his or her prior business experience. What is required is information relating to the level of his or her professional competence, which may include, depending upon the circumstances, such specific information as the size of the operation supervised.

(2) *Directorships.* Indicate any other directorships held, including any other directorships held during the past five years, held by each director or person nominated or chosen to become a director in any company with a class of securities registered pursuant to section 12 of the Exchange Act or subject to the requirements of section 15(d) of such Act or any company registered as an investment company under the Investment Company Act of 1940, as amended, naming such company.

Instruction to Paragraph (e) of Item 401

For the purposes of paragraph (e)(2), where the other directorships of each director or person nominated or chosen to become a director include directorships of two or more registered investment companies that are part of a "fund complex" as that term is defined in Item 22(a) of Schedule 14A under Exchange Act, the registrant may, rather than listing each such investment company, identify the fund complex and provide the number of investment company directorships held by the director or nominee in such fund complex.

(f) *Involvement in Certain Legal Proceedings.* Describe any of the following events that occurred during the past ten years and that are material to an evaluation of the ability or integrity of any director, person nominated to become a director or executive officer of the registrant:

(1) A petition under the Federal bankruptcy laws or any state insolvency law was filed by or against, or a receiver, fiscal agent or similar officer was appointed by a court for the business or property of such person, or any partnership in which he was a general partner at or within two years before the time of such filing, or any corporation or business association of which he was an executive officer at or within two years before the time of such filing;

(2) Such person was convicted in a criminal proceeding or is a named subject of a pending criminal proceeding (excluding traffic violations and other minor offenses);

(3) Such person was the subject of any order, judgment, or decree, not subsequently reversed, suspended or vacated, of any court of competent jurisdiction, permanently or temporarily enjoining him from, or otherwise limiting, the following activities:

(i) Acting as a futures commission merchant, introducing broker, commodity trading advisor, commodity pool operator, floor broker, leverage transaction merchant, any other person regulated by the Commodity Futures Trading Commission, or an associated person of any of the foregoing, or as an investment adviser, underwriter, broker or dealer in securities, or as an affiliated person, director or employee of any investment company, bank, savings and loan association or insurance company, or engaging in or continuing any conduct or practice in connection with such activity;

(ii)   Engaging in any type of business practice; or

(iii)   Engaging in any activity in connection with the purchase or sale of any security or commodity or in connection with any violation of Federal or State securities laws or Federal commodities laws;

(4)   Such person was the subject of any order, judgment or decree, not subsequently reversed, suspended or vacated, of any Federal or State authority barring, suspending or otherwise limiting for more than 60 days the right of such person to engage in any activity described in paragraph (f)(3)(i) of this Item, or to be associated with persons engaged in any such activity;

(5)   Such person was found by a court of competent jurisdiction in a civil action or by the Commission to have violated any Federal or State securities law, and the judgment in such civil action or finding by the Commission has not been subsequently reversed, suspended, or vacated;

(6)   Such person was found by a court of competent jurisdiction in a civil action or by the Commodities Futures Trading Commission to have violated any Federal commodities law, and the judgment in such civil action or finding by the Commodities Futures Trading Commission has not been subsequently reversed, suspended or vacated;

(7)   Such person was the subject of, or a party to, any Federal or State judicial or administrative order, judgment, decree, or finding, not subsequently reversed, suspended or vacated, relating to an alleged violation of:

(i)   Any Federal or State securities or commodities law or regulation; or

(ii)   Any law or regulation respecting financial institutions or insurance companies including, but not limited to, a temporary or permanent injunction, order of disgorgement or restitution, civil money penalty or temporary or permanent cease-and-desist order, or removal or prohibition order; or

(iii)   Any law or regulation prohibiting mail or wire fraud or fraud in connection with any business entity; or

(8)   Such person was the subject of, or a party to, any sanction or order, not subsequently reversed, suspended or vacated, of any self-regulatory organization (as defined in Section 3(a)(26) of the Exchange Act (15 U.S.C. 78c(a)(26))), any registered entity (as defined in Section 1(a)(29) of the Commodity Exchange Act (7 U.S.C. 1(a)(29))), or any equivalent exchange, association, entity or organization that has disciplinary authority over its members or persons associated with a member.

Instructions to Paragraph (f) of Item 401. 1. For purposes of computing the ten year period referred to in this paragraph, the date of a reportable event shall be deemed the date on which the final order, judgment or decree was entered, or the date on which any rights of appeal from preliminary orders, judgments, or decrees have lapsed. With respect to bankruptcy petitions, the computation date shall be the date of filing for uncontested petitions or the date upon which approval of a contested petition became final.

2.   If any event specified in this paragraph (f) has occurred and information in regard thereto is omitted on the grounds that it is not material, the registrant may furnish to the Commission, at time of filing (or at the time preliminary materials are filed, or ten days before definitive materials are filed if preliminary filing is not required, pursuant to Rule 14a–6 or 14c–5 under the Exchange Act), as supplemental information and not as part of the registration statement, report, or proxy or information statement, materials to which the omission relates, a description of the event and a statement of the reasons for the omission of information in regard thereto.

3.   The registrant is permitted to explain any mitigating circumstances associated with events reported pursuant to this paragraph.

4.   If the information called for by this paragraph (f) is being presented in a proxy or information statement, no information need be given respecting any director whose term of office as a director will not continue after the meeting to which the statement relates.

5.   This paragraph (f)(7) shall not apply to any settlement of a civil proceeding among private litigants.

(g)   *Promoters and control persons.*

(1)   Registrants, which have not been subject to the reporting requirements of section 13(a) or 15(d) of the Exchange Act for the twelve months immediately prior to the filing of the registration statement, report, or statement to which this Item is applicable, and which had a promoter at any time during the past five fiscal years, shall describe with respect to any promoter, any of the events enumerated in paragraphs (f)(1) through (f)(6) of this Item that occurred during the past five years and that are material to a voting or investment decision.

(2)   Registrants, which have not been subject to the reporting requirements of Section 13(a) or 15(d) of the Exchange Act for the twelve months immediately prior to the filing of the registration statement, report, or statement to which this Item is applicable, shall describe with respect to any control person, any of the events enumerated in paragraphs (f)(1) through (f)(6) of this rule that occurred during the past five years and that are material to a voting or investment decision.

Instructions to Paragraph (g) of Item 401.

1.   Instructions 1. through 3. to paragraph (f) shall apply to this paragraph (g).

2.   Paragraph (g) shall not apply to any subsidiary of a registrant which has been reporting pursuant to Section 13(a) or 15(d) of the Exchange Act for the twelve months immediately prior to the filing of the registration statement, report or statement.

Instruction to Item 401. The information regarding executive officers called for by this Item need not be furnished in proxy or information statements prepared in accordance with Schedule 14A or Schedule 14C under the Exchange Act if you are relying on General Instruction G of Form 10–K under the Exchange Act, such information is furnished in a separate section captioned "Information about our Executive Officers," and is included in Part I of your annual report on Form 10–K.

Item 402.   Executive Compensation

(a)   *General.*

(1)   *Treatment of foreign private issuers.* A foreign private issuer will be deemed to comply with this Item if it provides the information required by Items 6.B, 6.E.2, and 6.F of Form 20–F (17 CFR 249.220f), with more detailed information provided if otherwise made publicly available or required to be disclosed by the issuer's home jurisdiction or a market in which its securities are listed or traded, or paragraph (19) of General Instruction B of Form 40–F (17 CFR 249.240f), as applicable. A foreign private issuer that elects to provide domestic Item 402 disclosure must provide the disclosure required by Item 402(w) in its annual report or registration statement, as applicable.

(2)   *All compensation covered.* This Item requires clear, concise and understandable disclosure of all plan and non-plan compensation awarded to, earned by, or paid to the named executive officers designated under paragraph (a)(3) of this Item, and directors covered by paragraph (k) of this Item, by any person for all services rendered in all capacities to the registrant and its subsidiaries, unless otherwise specifically excluded from disclosure in this Item. All such compensation shall be reported pursuant to this Item, even if also called for by another requirement, including transactions between the registrant and a third party where a purpose of the transaction is to furnish compensation to any such named executive officer or director. No amount reported as compensation for one fiscal year need be reported in the same manner as compensation for a subsequent fiscal year; amounts reported as compensation for one fiscal year may be required to be reported in a different manner pursuant to this Item.

(3)   *Persons covered.* Disclosure shall be provided pursuant to this Item for each of the following (the "named executive officers"):

(i)   All individuals serving as the registrant's principal executive officer or acting in a similar capacity during the last completed fiscal year ("PEO"), regardless of compensation level;

(ii)   All individuals serving as the registrant's principal financial officer or acting in a similar capacity during the last completed fiscal year ("PFO"), regardless of compensation level;

(iii) The registrant's three most highly compensated executive officers other than the PEO and PFO who were serving as executive officers at the end of the last completed fiscal year; and

(iv) Up to two additional individuals for whom disclosure would have been provided pursuant to paragraph (a)(3)(iii) of this Item but for the fact that the individual was not serving as an executive officer of the registrant at the end of the last completed fiscal year.

Instructions to Item 402(a)(3).

1. *Determination of most highly compensated executive officers.* The determination as to which executive officers are most highly compensated shall be made by reference to total compensation for the last completed fiscal year (as required to be disclosed pursuant to paragraph (c)(2)(x) of this Item) reduced by the amount required to be disclosed pursuant to paragraph (c)(2)(viii) of this Item, *provided, however,* that no disclosure need be provided for any executive officer, other than the PEO and PFO, whose total compensation, as so reduced, does not exceed $100,000.

2. *Inclusion of executive officer of subsidiary.* It may be appropriate for a registrant to include as named executive officers one or more executive officers or other employees of subsidiaries in the disclosure required by this Item. See Rule 3b–7 under the Exchange Act.

3. *Exclusion of executive officer due to overseas compensation.* It may be appropriate in limited circumstances for a registrant not to include in the disclosure required by this Item an individual, other than its PEO or PFO, who is one of the registrant's most highly compensated executive officers due to the payment of amounts of cash compensation relating to overseas assignments attributed predominantly to such assignments.

(4) *Information for full fiscal year.* If the PEO or PFO served in that capacity during any part of a fiscal year with respect to which information is required, information should be provided as to all of his or her compensation for the full fiscal year. If a named executive officer (other than the PEO or PFO) served as an executive officer of the registrant (whether or not in the same position) during any part of the fiscal year with respect to which information is required, information shall be provided as to all compensation of that individual for the full fiscal year.

(5) *Omission of table or column.* A table or column may be omitted if there has been no compensation awarded to, earned by, or paid to any of the named executive officers or directors required to be reported in that table or column in any fiscal year covered by that table.

(6) *Definitions.* For purposes of this Item:

(i) The term *stock* means instruments such as common stock, restricted stock, restricted stock units, phantom stock, phantom stock units, common stock equivalent units or any similar instruments that do not have option-like features, and the term option means instruments such as stock options, *stock appreciation rights* and similar instruments with option-like features. The term stock appreciation rights ("SARs") refers to SARs payable in cash or stock, including SARs payable in cash or stock at the election of the registrant or a named executive officer. The term *equity* is used to refer generally to stock and/or options.

(ii) The term *plan* includes, but is not limited to, the following: Any plan, contract, authorization or arrangement, whether or not set forth in any formal document, pursuant to which cash, securities, similar instruments, or any other property may be received. A plan may be applicable to one person.

(iii) The term *incentive plan* means any plan providing compensation intended to serve as incentive for performance to occur over a specified period, whether such performance is measured by reference to financial performance of the registrant or an affiliate, the registrant's stock price, or any other performance measure. An *equity incentive plan* is an incentive plan or portion of an incentive plan under which awards are granted that fall within the scope of FASB ASC Topic 718, *Compensation—Stock Compensation.* A *non-equity incentive plan* is an incentive plan or portion of an incentive plan that is not an equity *incentive plan.* The term *incentive plan award* means an award provided under an incentive plan.

(iv) The terms *date of grant* or *grant date* refer to the grant date determined for financial statement reporting purposes pursuant to FASB ASC Topic 718.

(v)   *Closing market price* is defined as the price at which the registrant's security was last sold in the principal United States market for such security as of the date for which the closing market price is determined.

(b)   *Compensation discussion and analysis.*

(1)   Discuss the compensation awarded to, earned by, or paid to the named executive officers. The discussion shall explain all material elements of the registrant's compensation of the named executive officers. The discussion shall describe the following:

(i)   The objectives of the registrant's compensation programs;

(ii)   What the compensation program is designed to reward;

(iii)   Each element of compensation;

(iv)   Why the registrant chooses to pay each element;

(v)   How the registrant determines the amount (and, where applicable, the formula) for each element to pay;

(vi)   How each compensation element and the registrant's decisions regarding that element fit into the registrant's overall compensation objectives and affect decisions regarding other elements; and

(vii)   Whether and, if so, how the registrant has considered the results of the most recent shareholder advisory vote on executive compensation required by section 14A of the Securities Exchange Act of 1934 or Rule 14a–20 under the Exchange Act of 1934 in determining compensation policies and decisions and, if so, how that consideration has affected the registrant's executive compensation decisions and policies.

(2)   While the material information to be disclosed under Compensation Discussion and Analysis will vary depending upon the facts and circumstances, examples of such information may include, in a given case, among other things, the following:

(i)   The policies for allocating between long-term and currently paid out compensation;

(ii)   The policies for allocating between cash and non-cash compensation, and among different forms of non-cash compensation;

(iii)   For long-term compensation, the basis for allocating compensation to each different form of award (such as relationship of the award to the achievement of the registrant's long-term goals, management's exposure to downside equity performance risk, correlation between cost to registrant and expected benefits to the registrant);

(iv)   How the determination is made as to when awards are granted, including awards of equity-based compensation such as options;

(v)   What specific items of corporate performance are taken into account in setting compensation policies and making compensation decisions;

(vi)   How specific forms of compensation are structured and implemented to reflect these items of the registrant's performance, including whether discretion can be or has been exercised (either to award compensation absent attainment of the relevant performance goal(s) or to reduce or increase the size of any award or payout), identifying any particular exercise of discretion, and stating whether it applied to one or more specified named executive officers or to all compensation subject to the relevant performance goal(s);

(vii)   How specific forms of compensation are structured and implemented to reflect the named executive officer's individual performance and/or individual contribution to these items of the registrant's performance, describing the elements of individual performance and/or contribution that are taken into account;

(viii) Registrant policies and decisions regarding the adjustment or recovery of awards or payments if the relevant registrant performance measures upon which they are based are restated or otherwise adjusted in a manner that would reduce the size of an award or payment;

(ix) The factors considered in decisions to increase or decrease compensation materially;

(x) How compensation or amounts realizable from prior compensation are considered in setting other elements of compensation (e.g., how gains from prior option or stock awards are considered in setting retirement benefits);

(xi) With respect to any contract, agreement, plan or arrangement, whether written or unwritten, that provides for payment(s) at, following, or in connection with any termination or change-in-control, the basis for selecting particular events as triggering payment (e.g., the rationale for providing a single trigger for payment in the event of a change-in-control);

(xii) The impact of the accounting and tax treatments of the particular form of compensation;

(xiii) The registrant's equity or other security ownership requirements or guidelines (specifying applicable amounts and forms of ownership), and any registrant policies regarding hedging the economic risk of such ownership;

(xiv) Whether the registrant engaged in any benchmarking of total compensation, or any material element of compensation, identifying the benchmark and, if applicable, its components (including component companies); and

(xv) The role of executive officers in determining executive compensation.

Instructions to Item 402(b).

1. The purpose of the Compensation Discussion and Analysis is to provide to investors material information that is necessary to an understanding of the registrant's compensation policies and decisions regarding the named executive officers.

2. The Compensation Discussion and Analysis should be of the information contained in the tables and otherwise disclosed pursuant to this Item. The Compensation Discussion and Analysis should also cover actions regarding executive compensation that were taken after the registrant's last fiscal year's end. Actions that should be addressed might include, as examples only, the adoption or implementation of new or modified programs and policies or specific decisions that were made or steps that were taken that could affect a fair understanding of the named executive officer's compensation for the last fiscal year. Moreover, in some situations it may be necessary to discuss prior years in order to give context to the disclosure provided.

3. The Compensation Discussion and Analysis should focus on the material principles underlying the registrant's executive compensation policies and decisions and the most important factors relevant to analysis of those policies and decisions. The Compensation Discussion and Analysis shall reflect the individual circumstances of the registrant and shall avoid boilerplate language and repetition of the more detailed information set forth in the tables and narrative disclosures that follow.

4. Registrants are not required to disclose target levels with respect to specific quantitative or qualitative performance-related factors considered by the compensation committee or the board of directors, or any other factors or criteria involving confidential trade secrets or confidential commercial or financial information, the disclosure of which would result in competitive harm for the registrant. The standard to use when determining whether disclosure would cause competitive harm for the registrant is the same standard that would apply when a registrant requests confidential treatment of confidential trade secrets or confidential commercial or financial information pursuant to Securities Act Rule 406 and Exchange Act Rule 24b–2, each of which incorporates the criteria for non-disclosure when relying upon Exemption 4 of the Freedom of Information Act and Rule 80(b)(4) (17 CFR 200.80(b)(4)) thereunder. A registrant is not required to seek confidential treatment under the procedures in Securities Act Rule 406 and Exchange Act Rule 24b–2 if it determines that the disclosure would cause competitive harm in reliance on this instruction; however, in that case, the registrant must discuss how difficult it will be for the executive or how likely it will be for the registrant to achieve the undisclosed target levels or other factors.

5. Disclosure of target levels that are non-GAAP financial measures will not be subject to Regulation G (17 CFR 244.100–102) and Item 10(e); however, disclosure must be provided as to how the number is calculated from the registrant's audited financial statements.

6. In proxy or information statements with respect to the election of directors, if the information disclosed pursuant to Item 407(i) would satisfy paragraph (b)(2)(xiii) of this Item, a registrant may refer to the information disclosed pursuant to Item 407(i).

(c) *Summary compensation table.*

(1) General. Provide the information specified in paragraph (c)(2) of this Item, concerning the compensation of the named executive officers for each of the registrant's last three completed fiscal years, in a Summary Compensation Table in the tabular format specified below.

SUMMARY COMPENSATION TABLE

[Note: The following TABLE/FORM is too wide to be displayed on one screen. You must print it for a meaningful review of its contents. The table has been divided into multiple pieces with each piece containing information to help you assemble a printout of the table. The information for each piece includes: (1) a three line message preceding the tabular data showing by line # and character # the position of the upper left-hand corner of the piece and the position of the piece within the entire table; and (2) a numeric scale following the tabular data displaying the character positions.]

Name and Principal Position	Year	Salary ($)	Bonus ($)	Stock Awards ($)	Option Awards ($)	Non-Equity Incentive Plan Compensation ($)	Change in Pension Value and Nonqualified Deferred Compensation Earnings ($)	All Other Compensation ($)	Total ($)
(a)	(b)	(c)	(d)	(e)	(f)	(g)	(h)	(i)	(j)
PEO									
PFO									
A									
B									
C									

(2) The Table shall include:

(i) The name and principal position of the named executive officer (column (a));

(ii) The fiscal year covered (column (b));

(iii) The dollar value of base salary (cash and non-cash) earned by the named executive officer during the fiscal year covered (column (c));

(iv) The dollar value of bonus (cash and non-cash) earned by the named executive officer during the fiscal year covered (column (d));

Instructions to Item 402(c)(2)(iii) and (iv).

1. If the amount of salary or bonus earned in a given fiscal year is not calculable through the latest practicable date, a footnote shall be included disclosing that the amount of salary or bonus is not calculable through the latest practicable date and providing the date that the amount of salary or bonus is expected to be determined, and such amount must then be disclosed in a filing under Item 5.02(f) of Form 8–K.

2. Registrants shall include in the salary column (column (c)) or bonus column (column (d)) any amount of salary or bonus forgone at the election of a named executive officer under which stock, equity-based or other forms of non-cash compensation instead have been received by the named executive officer. However, the receipt of any such form of non-cash compensation instead of salary or bonus must be disclosed in a footnote added to the salary or bonus column and, where applicable, referring to the Grants of Plan-Based Awards Table (required by

paragraph (d) of this Item) where the stock, option or non-equity incentive plan award elected by the named executive officer is reported.

  (v) For awards of stock, the aggregate grant date fair value computed in accordance with FASB ASC Topic 718 (column (e));

  (vi) For awards of options, with or without tandem SARs (including awards that subsequently have been transferred), the aggregate grant date fair value computed in accordance with FASB ASC Topic 718 (column (f));

Instruction 1 to Item 402(c)(2)(v) and (vi). For awards reported in columns (e) and (f), include a footnote disclosing all assumptions made in the valuation by reference to a discussion of those assumptions in the registrant's financial statements, footnotes to the financial statements, or discussion in the Management's Discussion and Analysis. The sections so referenced are deemed part of the disclosure provided pursuant to this Item.

Instruction 2 to Item 402(c)(2)(v) and (vi). If at any time during the last completed fiscal year, the registrant has adjusted or amended the exercise price of options or SARs previously awarded to a named executive officer, whether through amendment, cancellation or replacement grants, or any other means ("repriced"), or otherwise has materially modified such awards, the registrant shall include, as awards required to be reported in column (f), the incremental fair value, computed as of the repricing or modification date in accordance with FASB ASC Topic 718, with respect to that repriced or modified award.

Instruction 3 to Item 402(c)(2)(v) and (vi). For any awards that are subject to performance conditions, report the value at the grant date based upon the probable outcome of such conditions. This amount should be consistent with the estimate of aggregate compensation cost to be recognized over the service period determined as of the grant date under FASB ASC Topic 718, excluding the effect of estimated forfeitures. In a footnote to the table, disclose the value of the award at the grant date assuming that the highest level of performance conditions will be achieved if an amount less than the maximum was included in the table.

  (vii) The dollar value of all earnings for services performed during the fiscal year pursuant to awards under non-equity incentive plans as defined in paragraph (a)(6)(iii) of this Item, and all earnings on any outstanding awards (column (g));

Instructions to Item 402(c)(2)(vii).

1. If the relevant performance measure is satisfied during the fiscal year (including for a single year in a plan with a multi-year performance measure), the earnings are reportable for that fiscal year, even if not payable until a later date, and are not reportable again in the fiscal year when amounts are paid to the named executive officer.

2. All earnings on non-equity incentive plan compensation must be identified and quantified in a footnote to column (g), whether the earnings were paid during the fiscal year, payable during the period but deferred at the election of the named executive officer, or payable by their terms at a later date.

  (viii) The sum of the amounts specified in paragraphs (c)(2)(viii)(A) and (B) of this Item (column (h)) as follows:

  (A) The aggregate change in the actuarial present value of the named executive officer's accumulated benefit under all defined benefit and actuarial pension plans (including supplemental plans) from the pension plan measurement date used for financial statement reporting purposes with respect to the registrant's audited financial statements for the prior completed fiscal year to the pension plan measurement date used for financial statement reporting purposes with respect to the registrant's audited financial statements for the covered fiscal year; and

  (B) Above-market or preferential earnings on compensation that is deferred on a basis that is not tax-qualified, including such earnings on nonqualified defined contribution plans;

Instructions to Item 402(c)(2)(viii).

1. The disclosure required pursuant to paragraph (c)(2)(viii)(A) of this Item applies to each plan that provides for the payment of retirement benefits, or benefits that will be paid primarily following retirement, including but not limited to tax-qualified defined benefit plans and supplemental executive retirement plans, but excluding tax-qualified defined contribution plans and nonqualified defined contribution plans. For purposes of this disclosure, the registrant should use the same amounts required to be disclosed pursuant to paragraph

(h)(2)(iv) of this Item for the covered fiscal year and the amounts that were or would have been required to be reported for the executive officer pursuant to paragraph (h)(2)(iv) of this Item for the prior completed fiscal year.

2. Regarding paragraph (c)(2)(viii)(B) of this Item, interest on deferred compensation is above-market only if the rate of interest exceeds 120% of the applicable federal long-term rate, with compounding (as prescribed under section 1274(d) of the Internal Revenue Code) at the rate that corresponds most closely to the rate under the registrant's plan at the time the interest rate or formula is set. In the event of a discretionary reset of the interest rate, the requisite calculation must be made on the basis of the interest rate at the time of such reset, rather than when originally established. Only the above-market portion of the interest must be included. If the applicable interest rates vary depending upon conditions such as a minimum period of continued service, the reported amount should be calculated assuming satisfaction of all conditions to receiving interest at the highest rate. Dividends (and dividend equivalents) on deferred compensation denominated in the registrant's stock ("deferred stock") are preferential only if earned at a rate higher than dividends on the registrant's common stock. Only the preferential portion of the dividends or equivalents must be included. Footnote or narrative disclosure may be provided explaining the registrant's criteria for determining any portion considered to be above-market.

3. The registrant shall identify and quantify by footnote the separate amounts attributable to each of paragraphs (c)(2)(viii)(A) and (B) of this Item. Where such amount pursuant to paragraph (c)(2)(viii)(A) is negative, it should be disclosed by footnote but should not be reflected in the sum reported in column (h).

(ix) All other compensation for the covered fiscal year that the registrant could not properly report in any other column of the Summary Compensation Table (column (i)). Each compensation item that is not properly reportable in columns (c)–(h), regardless of the amount of the compensation item, must be included in column (i). Such compensation must include, but is not limited to:

(A) Perquisites and other personal benefits, or property, unless the aggregate amount of such compensation is less than $10,000;

(B) All "gross-ups" or other amounts reimbursed during the fiscal year for the payment of taxes;

(C) For any security of the registrant or its subsidiaries purchased from the registrant or its subsidiaries (through deferral of salary or bonus, or otherwise) at a discount from the market price of such security at the date of purchase, unless that discount is available generally, either to all security holders or to all salaried employees of the registrant, the compensation cost, if any, computed in accordance with FASB ASC Topic 718;

(D) The amount paid or accrued to any named executive officer pursuant to a plan or arrangement in connection with:

(1) Any termination, including without limitation through retirement, resignation, severance or constructive termination (including a change in responsibilities) of such executive officer's employment with the registrant and its subsidiaries; or

(2) A change in control of the registrant;

(E) Registrant contributions or other allocations to vested and unvested defined contribution plans;

(F) The dollar value of any insurance premiums paid by, or on behalf of, the registrant during the covered fiscal year with respect to life insurance for the benefit of a named executive officer; and

(G) The dollar value of any dividends or other earnings paid on stock or option awards, when those amounts were not factored into the grant date fair value required to be reported for the stock or option award in column (e) or (f); and

Instructions to Item 402(c)(2)(ix).

1. Non-equity incentive plan awards and earnings and earnings on stock and options, except as specified in paragraph (c)(2)(ix)(G) of this Item, are required to be reported elsewhere as provided in this Item and are not reportable as All Other Compensation in column (i).

2. Benefits paid pursuant to defined benefit and actuarial plans are not reportable as All Other Compensation in column (i) unless accelerated pursuant to a change in control; information concerning these plans is reportable pursuant to paragraphs (c)(2)(viii)(A) and (h) of this Item.

3. Any item reported for a named executive officer pursuant to paragraph (c)(2)(ix) of this Item that is not a perquisite or personal benefit and whose value exceeds $10,000 must be identified and quantified in a footnote to column (i). This requirement applies only to compensation for the last fiscal year. All items of compensation are required to be included in the Summary Compensation Table without regard to whether such items are required to be identified other than as specifically noted in this Item.

4. Perquisites and personal benefits may be excluded as long as the total value of all perquisites and personal benefits for a named executive officer is less than $10,000. If the total value of all perquisites and personal benefits is $10,000 or more for any named executive officer, then each perquisite or personal benefit, regardless of its amount, must be identified by type. If perquisites and personal benefits are required to be reported for a named executive officer pursuant to this rule, then each perquisite or personal benefit that exceeds the greater of $25,000 or 10% of the total amount of perquisites and personal benefits for that officer must be quantified and disclosed in a footnote. The requirements for identification and quantification apply only to compensation for the last fiscal year. Perquisites and other personal benefits shall be valued on the basis of the aggregate incremental cost to the registrant. With respect to the perquisite or other personal benefit for which footnote quantification is required, the registrant shall describe in the footnote its methodology for computing the aggregate incremental cost. Reimbursements of taxes owed with respect to perquisites or other personal benefits must be included in column (i) and are subject to separate quantification and identification as tax reimbursements (paragraph (c)(2)(ix)(B) of this Item) even if the associated perquisites or other personal benefits are not required to be included because the total amount of all perquisites or personal benefits for an individual named executive officer is less than $10,000 or are required to be identified but are not required to be separately quantified.

5. For purposes of paragraph (c)(2)(ix)(D) of this Item, an accrued amount is an amount for which payment has become due.

         (x) The dollar value of total compensation for the covered fiscal year (column (j)). With respect to each named executive officer, disclose the sum of all amounts reported in columns (c) through (i).

Instructions to Item 402(c).

1. Information with respect to fiscal years prior to the last completed fiscal year will not be required if the registrant was not a reporting company pursuant to section 13(a) or 15(d) of the Exchange Act at any time during that year, except that the registrant will be required to provide information for any such year if that information previously was required to be provided in response to a Commission filing requirement.

2. All compensation values reported in the Summary Compensation Table must be reported in dollars and rounded to the nearest dollar. Reported compensation values must be reported numerically, providing a single numerical value for each grid in the table. Where compensation was paid to or received by a named executive officer in a different currency, a footnote must be provided to identify that currency and describe the rate and methodology used to convert the payment amounts to dollars.

3. If a named executive officer is also a director who receives compensation for his or her services as a director, reflect that compensation in the Summary Compensation Table and provide a footnote identifying and itemizing such compensation and amounts. Use the categories in the Director Compensation Table required pursuant to paragraph (k) of this Item.

4. Any amounts deferred, whether pursuant to a plan established under section 401(k) of the Internal Revenue Code, or otherwise, shall be included in the appropriate column for the fiscal year in which earned.

5. Reduce the amount reported in the applicable Summary Compensation Table column for the fiscal year in which the amount recovered initially was reported as compensation by any amounts recovered pursuant to a registrant's compensation recovery policy required by the listing standards adopted pursuant to 17 CFR 240.10D–1 and identify such amounts by footnote.

         (d) *Grants of plan-based awards table.* (1) Provide the information specified in paragraph (d)(2) of this Item, concerning each grant of an award made to a named executive officer in the last completed fiscal year under any plan, including awards that subsequently have been transferred, in the following tabular format:

GRANTS OF PLAN-BASED AWARDS

Name	Grant Date	Estimated Future Payouts Under Non-Equity Incentive Plan Awards			Estimated Future Payouts Under Equity Incentive Plan Awards			All Other Stock Awards: Number of Shares of Stock or Units (#)	All Other Option Awards: Number of Securities Underlying Options (#)	Exercise or Base Price of Option Awards ($/Sh)	Grant Date Fair Value of Stock and Option Awards
		Threshold ($)	Target ($)	Maximum ($)	Threshold (#)	Target (#)	Maximum (#)				
(a)	(b)	(c)	(d)	(e)	(f)	(g)	(h)	(i)	(j)	(k)	(l)
PEO											
PFO											
A											
B											
C											

(2)   The Table shall include:

(i)   The name of the named executive officer (column (a));

(ii)   The grant date for equity-based awards reported in the table (column (b)). If such grant date is different than the date on which the compensation committee (or a committee of the board of directors performing a similar function or the full board of directors) takes action or is deemed to take action to grant such awards, a separate, adjoining column shall be added between columns (b) and (c) showing such date;

(iii)   The dollar value of the estimated future payout upon satisfaction of the conditions in question under non-equity incentive plan awards granted in the fiscal year, or the applicable range of estimated payouts denominated in dollars (threshold, target and maximum amount) (columns (c) through (e));

(iv)   The number of shares of stock, or the number of shares underlying options to be paid out or vested upon satisfaction of the conditions in question under equity incentive plan awards granted in the fiscal year, or the applicable range of estimated payouts denominated in the number of shares of stock, or the number of shares underlying options under the award (threshold, target and maximum amount) (columns (f) through (h));

(v)   The number of shares of stock granted in the fiscal year that are not required to be disclosed in columns (f) through (h) (column (i));

(vi)   The number of securities underlying options granted in the fiscal year that are not required to be disclosed in columns (f) through (h) (column (j));

(vii)   The per-share exercise or base price of the options granted in the fiscal year (column (k)). If such exercise or base price is less than the closing market price of the underlying security on the date of the grant, a separate, adjoining column showing the closing market price on the date of the grant shall be added after column (k); and

(viii)   The grant date fair value of each equity award computed in accordance with FASB ASC Topic 718 (column (l)). If at any time during the last completed fiscal year, the registrant has adjusted or amended the exercise or base price of options, SARs or similar option-like instruments previously awarded to a named executive officer, whether through amendment, cancellation or replacement grants, or any other means ("repriced"), or otherwise has materially modified such awards, the incremental fair value, computed as of the repricing or modification date in accordance with FASB ASC Topic 718, with respect to that repriced or modified award, shall be reported.

Instructions to Item 402(d).

1.   Disclosure on a separate line shall be provided in the Table for each grant of an award made to a named executive officer during the fiscal year. If grants of awards were made to a named executive officer during the fiscal year under more than one plan, identify the particular plan under which each such grant was made.

2.   For grants of incentive plan awards, provide the information called for by columns (c), (d) and (e), or (f), (g) and (h), as applicable. For columns (c) and (f), threshold refers to the minimum amount payable for a certain level of performance under the plan. For columns (d) and (g), target refers to the amount payable if the specified performance target(s) are reached. For columns (e) and (h), maximum refers to the maximum payout possible under the plan. If the award provides only for a single estimated payout, that amount must be reported as the target in columns (d) and (g). In columns (d) and (g), registrants must provide a representative amount based on the previous fiscal year's performance if the target amount is not determinable.

3.   In determining if the exercise or base price of an option is less than the closing market price of the underlying security on the date of the grant, the registrant may use either the closing market price as specified in paragraph (a)(6)(v) of this Item, or if no market exists, any other formula prescribed for the security. Whenever the exercise or base price reported in column (k) is not the closing market price, describe the methodology for determining the exercise or base price either by a footnote or accompanying textual narrative.

4.   A tandem grant of two instruments, only one of which is granted under an incentive plan, such as an option granted in tandem with a performance share, need be reported only in column (i) or (j), as applicable. For example, an option granted in tandem with a performance share would be reported only as an option grant in column (j), with the tandem feature noted either by a footnote or accompanying textual narrative.

5.   Disclose the dollar amount of consideration, if any, paid by the executive officer for the award in a footnote to the appropriate column.

6.   If non-equity incentive plan awards are denominated in units or other rights, a separate, adjoining column between columns (b) and (c) shall be added quantifying the units or other rights awarded.

7.   Options, SARs and similar option-like instruments granted in connection with a repricing transaction or other material modification shall be reported in this Table. However, the disclosure required by this Table does not apply to any repricing that occurs through a pre-existing formula or mechanism in the plan or award that results in the periodic adjustment of the option or SAR exercise or base price, an antidilution provision in a plan or award, or a recapitalization or similar transaction equally affecting all holders of the class of securities underlying the options or SARs.

8.   For any equity awards that are subject to performance conditions, report in column (*l*) the value at the grant date based upon the probable outcome of such conditions. This amount should be consistent with the estimate of aggregate compensation cost to be recognized over the service period determined as of the grant date under FASB ASC Topic 718, excluding the effect of estimated forfeitures.

(e)   *Narrative disclosure to summary compensation table and grants of plan-based awards table.*

(1)   Provide a narrative description of any material factors necessary to an understanding of the information disclosed in the tables required by paragraphs (c) and (d) of this Item. Examples of such factors may include, in given cases, among other things:

(i)   The material terms of each named executive officer's employment agreement or arrangement, whether written or unwritten;

(ii)   If at any time during the last fiscal year, any outstanding option or other equity-based award was repriced or otherwise materially modified (such as by extension of exercise periods, the change of vesting or forfeiture conditions, the change or elimination of applicable performance criteria, or the change of the bases upon which returns are determined), a description of each such repricing or other material modification;

(iii)   The material terms of any award reported in response to paragraph (d) of this Item, including a general description of the formula or criteria to be applied in determining the amounts payable, and the vesting schedule. For example, state where applicable that dividends will be paid on stock, and if so, the applicable dividend rate and whether that rate is preferential. Describe any performance-based conditions, and any other material conditions, that are applicable to the award. For purposes of the Table required by paragraph (d) of this Item and the narrative disclosure required by paragraph (e) of this Item, performance-based conditions include both performance conditions and market conditions, as those terms are defined in FASB ASC Topic 718; and

    (iv) An explanation of the amount of salary and bonus in proportion to total compensation.

Instructions to Item 402(e)(1).

    1.   The disclosure required by paragraph (e)(1)(ii) of this Item would not apply to any repricing that occurs through a pre-existing formula or mechanism in the plan or award that results in the periodic adjustment of the option or SAR exercise or base price, an antidilution provision in a plan or award, or a recapitalization or similar transaction equally affecting all holders of the class of securities underlying the options or SARs.

    2.   Instructions 4 and 5 to Item 402(b) apply regarding disclosure pursuant to paragraph (e)(1) of target levels with respect to specific quantitative or qualitative performance-related factors considered by the compensation committee or the board of directors, or any other factors or criteria involving confidential trade secrets or confidential commercial or financial information, the disclosure of which would result in competitive harm for the registrant.

    (2)   [Reserved.]

    (f)   *Outstanding equity awards at fiscal year-end table.* (1) Provide the information specified in paragraph (f)(2) of this Item, concerning unexercised options; stock that has not vested; and equity incentive plan awards for each named executive officer outstanding as of the end of the registrant's last completed fiscal year in the following tabular format:

OUTSTANDING EQUITY AWARDS AT FISCAL YEAR-END

[Note: The following TABLE/FORM is too wide to be displayed on one screen. You must print it for a meaningful review of its contents. The table has been divided into multiple pieces with each piece containing information to help you assemble a printout of the table. The information for each piece includes: (1) a three line message preceding the tabular data showing by line # and character # the position of the upper left-hand corner of the piece and the position of the piece within the entire table; and (2) a numeric scale following the tabular data displaying the character positions.]

	Option Awards					Stock Awards			
Name	Number of Securities Underlying Unexercised Options (#) Exercisable	Number of Securities Underlying Unexercised Options (#) Unexercisable	Equity Incentive Plan Awards: Number of Securities Underlying Unexercised Unearned Options (#)	Option Exercise Price ($)	Option Expiration Date	Number of Shares or Units of Stock That Have Not Vested (#)	Market Value of shares or Units of Stock That Have Not Vested (#)	Equity Incentive Plan Awards: Number of Unearned Shares, Units or Other Rights That Have Not Vested (#)	Equity Incentive Plan Awards: Market or Payout Value of Unearned Shares, Units or Other Rights That Have Not Vested ($)
(a)	(b)	(c)	(d)	(e)	(f)	(g)	(h)	(i)	(j)
PEO									
PFO									
A									

B

C

(2)   The Table shall include:

(i)   The name of the named executive officer (column (a));

(ii)   On an award-by-award basis, the number of securities underlying unexercised options, including awards that have been transferred other than for value, that are exercisable and that are not reported in column (d) (column (b));

(iii)   On an award-by-award basis, the number of securities underlying unexercised options, including awards that have been transferred other than for value, that are unexercisable and that are not reported in column (d) (column (c));

(iv)   On an award-by-award basis, the total number of shares underlying unexercised options awarded under any equity incentive plan that have not been earned (column (d));

(v)   For each instrument reported in columns (b), (c) and (d), as applicable, the exercise or base price (column (e));

(vi)   For each instrument reported in columns (b), (c) and (d), as applicable, the expiration date (column (f));

(vii)   The total number of shares of stock that have not vested and that are not reported in column (i) (column (g));

(viii)   The aggregate market value of shares of stock that have not vested and that are not reported in column (j) (column (h));

(ix)   The total number of shares of stock, units or other rights awarded under any equity incentive plan that have not vested and that have not been earned, and, if applicable the number of shares underlying any such unit or right (column (i)); and

(x)   The aggregate market or payout value of shares of stock, units or other rights awarded under any equity incentive plan that have not vested and that have not been earned (column (j)).

Instructions to Item 402(f)(2).

1.   Identify by footnote any award that has been transferred other than for value, disclosing the nature of the transfer.

2.   The vesting dates of options, shares of stock and equity incentive plan awards held at fiscal-year end must be disclosed by footnote to the applicable column where the outstanding award is reported.

3.   Compute the market value of stock reported in column (h) and equity incentive plan awards of stock reported in column (j) by multiplying the closing market price of the registrant's stock at the end of the last completed fiscal year by the number of shares or units of stock or the amount of equity incentive plan awards, respectively. The number of shares or units reported in columns (d) or (i), and the payout value reported in column (j), shall be based on achieving threshold performance goals, except that if the previous fiscal year's performance has exceeded the threshold, the disclosure shall be based on the next higher performance measure (target or maximum) that exceeds the previous fiscal year's performance. If the award provides only for a single estimated payout, that amount should be reported. If the target amount is not determinable, registrants must provide a representative amount based on the previous fiscal year's performance.

4.   Multiple awards may be aggregated where the expiration date and the exercise and/or base price of the instruments is identical. A single award consisting of a combination of options, SARs and/or similar option-like instruments shall be reported as separate awards with respect to each tranche with a different exercise and/or base price or expiration date.

5.   Options or stock awarded under an equity incentive plan are reported in columns (d) or (i) and (j), respectively, until the relevant performance condition has been satisfied. Once the relevant performance condition has been satisfied, even if the option or stock award is subject to forfeiture conditions, options are reported in

column (b) or (c), as appropriate, until they are exercised or expire, or stock is reported in columns (g) and (h) until it vests.

    (g)   *Option exercises and stock vested table.* (1) Provide the information specified in paragraph (g)(2) of this Item, concerning each exercise of stock options, SARs and similar instruments, and each vesting of stock, including restricted stock, restricted stock units and similar instruments, during the last completed fiscal year for each of the named executive officers on an aggregated basis in the following tabular format:

OPTION EXERCISES AND STOCK VESTED

	Option Awards		Stock Awards	
Name	Number of Shares Acquired on Exercise (#)	Value Realized on Exercise ($)	Number of Shares Acquired on Vesting (#)	Value Realized on Vesting ($)
(a)	(b)	(c)	(d)	(e)
PEO				
PFO				
A				
B				
C				

    (3)   The Table shall include:

        (i)   The name of the executive officer (column (a));

        (ii)   The number of securities for which the options were exercised (column (b));

        (iii)   The aggregate dollar value realized upon exercise of options, or upon the transfer of an award for value (column (c));

        (iv)   The number of shares of stock that have vested (column (d)); and

        (v)   The aggregate dollar value realized upon vesting of stock, or upon the transfer of an award for value (column (e)).

    Instruction to Item 402(g)(2).

    Report in column (c) the aggregate dollar amount realized by the named executive officer upon exercise of the options or upon the transfer of such instruments for value. Compute the dollar amount realized upon exercise by determining the difference between the market price of the underlying securities at exercise and the exercise or base price of the options. Do not include the value of any related payment or other consideration provided (or to be provided) by the registrant to or on behalf of a named executive officer, whether in payment of the exercise price or related taxes. (Any such payment or other consideration provided by the registrant is required to be disclosed in accordance with paragraph (c)(2)(ix) of this Item.) Report in column (e) the aggregate dollar amount realized by the named executive officer upon the vesting of stock or the transfer of such instruments for value. Compute the aggregate dollar amount realized upon vesting by multiplying the number of shares of stock or units by the market value of the underlying shares on the vesting date. For any amount realized upon exercise or vesting for which receipt has been deferred, provide a footnote quantifying the amount and disclosing the terms of the deferral.

(h)   *Pension benefits.*

(1)   Provide the information specified in paragraph (h)(2) of this Item with respect to each plan that provides for payments or other benefits at, following, or in connection with retirement, in the following tabular format:

PENSION BENEFITS

Name	Plan Name	Number of Years Credited Service (#)	Present Value of Accumulated Benefit ($)	Payments During Last Fiscal Year ($)
(a)	(b)	(c)	(d)	(e)
PEO				
PFO				
A				
B				
C				

(2)   The Table shall include:

(i)   The name of the executive officer (column (a));

(ii)   The name of the plan (column (b));

(iii)   The number of years of service credited to the named executive officer under the plan, computed as of the same pension plan measurement date used for financial statement reporting purposes with respect to the registrant's audited financial statements for the last completed fiscal year (column (c));

(iv)   The actuarial present value of the named executive officer's accumulated benefit under the plan, computed as of the same pension plan measurement date used for financial statement reporting purposes with respect to the registrant's audited financial statements for the last completed fiscal year (column (d)); and

(v)   The dollar amount of any payments and benefits paid to the named executive officer during the registrant's last completed fiscal year (column (e)).

Instructions to Item 402(h)(2).

1.   The disclosure required pursuant to this Table applies to each plan that provides for specified retirement payments and benefits, or payments and benefits that will be provided primarily following retirement, including but not limited to tax-qualified defined benefit plans and supplemental executive retirement plans, but excluding tax-qualified defined contribution plans and nonqualified defined contribution plans. Provide a separate row for each such plan in which the named executive officer participates.

2.   For purposes of the amount(s) reported in column (d), the registrant must use the same assumptions used for financial reporting purposes under generally accepted accounting principles, except that retirement age shall be assumed to be the normal retirement age as defined in the plan, or if not so defined, the earliest time at which a participant may retire under the plan without any benefit reduction due to age. The registrant must disclose in the accompanying textual narrative the valuation method and all material assumptions applied in

quantifying the present value of the current accrued benefit. A benefit specified in the plan document or the executive's contract itself is not an assumption. Registrants may satisfy all or part of this disclosure by reference to a discussion of those assumptions in the registrant's financial statements, footnotes to the financial statements, or discussion in the Management's Discussion and Analysis. The sections so referenced are deemed part of the disclosure provided pursuant to this Item.

3. For purposes of allocating the current accrued benefit between tax qualified defined benefit plans and related supplemental plans, apply the limitations applicable to tax qualified defined benefit plans established by the Internal Revenue Code and the regulations thereunder that applied as of the pension plan measurement date.

4. If a named executive officer's number of years of credited service with respect to any plan is different from the named executive officer's number of actual years of service with the registrant, provide footnote disclosure quantifying the difference and any resulting benefit augmentation.

(3) Provide a succinct narrative description of any material factors necessary to an understanding of each plan covered by the tabular disclosure required by this paragraph. While material factors will vary depending upon the facts, examples of such factors may include, in given cases, among other things:

(i) The material terms and conditions of payments and benefits available under the plan, including the plan's normal retirement payment and benefit formula and eligibility standards, and the effect of the form of benefit elected on the amount of annual benefits. For this purpose, normal retirement means retirement at the normal retirement age as defined in the plan, or if not so defined, the earliest time at which a participant may retire under the plan without any benefit reduction due to age;

(ii) If any named executive officer is currently eligible for early retirement under any plan, identify that named executive officer and the plan, and describe the plan's early retirement payment and benefit formula and eligibility standards. For this purpose, early retirement means retirement at the early retirement age as defined in the plan, or otherwise available to the executive under the plan;

(iii) The specific elements of compensation (e.g., salary, bonus, etc.) included in applying the payment and benefit formula, identifying each such element;

(iv) With respect to named executive officers' participation in multiple plans, the different purposes for each plan; and

(v) Registrant policies with regard to such matters as granting extra years of credited service.

(i) *Nonqualified defined contribution and other nonqualified deferred compensation plans.*

(1) Provide the information specified in paragraph (i)(2) of this Item with respect to each defined contribution or other plan that provides for the deferral of compensation on a basis that is not tax-qualified in the following tabular format:

NONQUALIFIED DEFERRED COMPENSATION

Name	Executive Contributions in the Last FY ($)	Registrant Contributions in Last FY ($)	Aggregate Earnings in Last FY ($)	Aggregate Withdrawals/ Distributions ($)	Aggregate Balance at Last FYE ($)
(a)	(b)	(c)	(d)	(e)	(f)
PEO					
PFO					

Name	Executive Contributions in the Last FY ($)	Registrant Contributions in Last FY ($)	Aggregate Earnings in Last FY ($)	Aggregate Withdrawals/ Distributions ($)	Aggregate Balance at Last FYE ($)
A					
B					
C					

(2) The Table shall include:

(i) The name of the executive officer (column (a));

(ii) The dollar amount of aggregate executive contributions during the registrant's last fiscal year (column (b));

(iii) The dollar amount of aggregate registrant contributions during the registrant's last fiscal year (column (c));

(iv) The dollar amount of aggregate interest or other earnings accrued during the registrant's last fiscal year (column (d));

(v) The aggregate dollar amount of all withdrawals by and distributions to the executive during the registrant's last fiscal year (column (e)); and

(vi) The dollar amount of total balance of the executive's account as of the end of the registrant's last fiscal year (column (f)).

Instruction to Item 402(i)(2).

Provide a footnote quantifying the extent to which amounts reported in the contributions and earnings columns are reported as compensation in the last completed fiscal year in the registrant's Summary Compensation Table and amounts reported in the aggregate balance at last fiscal year end (column (f)) previously were reported as compensation to the named executive officer in the registrant's Summary Compensation Table for previous years.

(3) Provide a succinct narrative description of any material factors necessary to an understanding of each plan covered by tabular disclosure required by this paragraph. While material factors will vary depending upon the facts, examples of such factors may include, in given cases, among other things:

(i) The type(s) of compensation permitted to be deferred, and any limitations (by percentage of compensation or otherwise) on the extent to which deferral is permitted;

(ii) The measures for calculating interest or other plan earnings (including whether such measure(s) are selected by the executive or the registrant and the frequency and manner in which selections may be changed), quantifying interest rates and other earnings measures applicable during the registrant's last fiscal year; and

(iii) Material terms with respect to payouts, withdrawals and other distributions.

(j) *Potential payments upon termination or change-in-control.* Regarding each contract, agreement, plan or arrangement, whether written or unwritten, that provides for payment(s) to a named executive officer at, following, or in connection with any termination, including without limitation resignation, severance, retirement or a constructive termination of a named executive officer, or a change in control of the registrant or a change in the named executive officer's responsibilities, with respect to each named executive officer:

(1)   Describe and explain the specific circumstances that would trigger payment(s) or the provision of other benefits, including perquisites and health care benefits;

(2)   Describe and quantify the estimated payments and benefits that would be provided in each covered circumstance, whether they would or could be lump sum, or annual, disclosing the duration, and by whom they would be provided;

(3)   Describe and explain how the appropriate payment and benefit levels are determined under the various circumstances that trigger payments or provision of benefits;

(4)   Describe and explain any material conditions or obligations applicable to the receipt of payments or benefits, including but not limited to non-compete, non-solicitation, non-disparagement or confidentiality agreements, including the duration of such agreements and provisions regarding waiver of breach of such agreements; and

(5)   Describe any other material factors regarding each such contract, agreement, plan or arrangement.

Instructions to Item 402(j).

1.   The registrant must provide quantitative disclosure under these requirements, applying the assumptions that the triggering event took place on the last business day of the registrant's last completed fiscal year, and the price per share of the registrant's securities is the closing market price as of that date. In the event that uncertainties exist as to the provision of payments and benefits or the amounts involved, the registrant is required to make a reasonable estimate (or a reasonable estimated range of amounts) applicable to the payment or benefit and disclose material assumptions underlying such estimates or estimated ranges in its disclosure. In such event, the disclosure would require forward-looking information as appropriate.

2.   Perquisites and other personal benefits or property may be excluded only if the aggregate amount of such compensation will be less than $10,000. Individual perquisites and personal benefits shall be identified and quantified as required by Instruction 4 to paragraph (c)(2)(ix) of this Item. For purposes of quantifying health care benefits, the registrant must use the assumptions used for financial reporting purposes under generally accepted accounting principles.

3.   To the extent that the form and amount of any payment or benefit that would be provided in connection with any triggering event is fully disclosed pursuant to paragraph (h) or (i) of this Item, reference may be made to that disclosure. However, to the extent that the form or amount of any such payment or benefit would be enhanced or its vesting or other provisions accelerated in connection with any triggering event, such enhancement or acceleration must be disclosed pursuant to this paragraph.

4.   Where a triggering event has actually occurred for a named executive officer and that individual was not serving as a named executive officer of the registrant at the end of the last completed fiscal year, the disclosure required by this paragraph for that named executive officer shall apply only to that triggering event.

5.   The registrant need not provide information with respect to contracts, agreements, plans or arrangements to the extent they do not discriminate in scope, terms or operation, in favor of executive officers of the registrant and that are available generally to all salaried employees.

(k)   *Compensation of directors.*

(1)   Provide the information specified in paragraph (k)(2) of this Item, concerning the compensation of the directors for the registrant's last completed fiscal year, in the following tabular format:

DIRECTOR COMPENSATION

Name (a)	Fees Earned or Paid in Cash ($) (b)	Stock Awards ($) (c)	Option Awards ($) (d)	Non-Equity Incentive Plan Compensation ($) (e)	Change in Pension Value and Nonqualified Deferred Compensation Earnings (f)	All Other Compensation ($) (g)	Total ($) (h)

A _____

B _____

C _____

D _____

E _____

_____

(2)   The Table shall include:

(i)   The name of each director unless such director is also a named executive officer under paragraph (a) of this Item and his or her compensation for service as a director is fully reflected in the Summary Compensation Table pursuant to paragraph (c) of this Item and otherwise as required pursuant to paragraphs (d) through (j) of this Item (column (a));

(ii)   The aggregate dollar amount of all fees earned or paid in cash for services as a director, including annual retainer fees, committee and/or chairmanship fees, and meeting fees (column (b));

(iii)   For awards of stock, the aggregate grant date fair value computed in accordance with FASB ASC Topic 718 (column (c));

(iv)   For awards of options, with or without tandem SARs (including awards that subsequently have been transferred), the aggregate grant date fair value computed in accordance with FASB ASC Topic 718 (column (d));

Instruction to Item 402(k)(2)(iii) and (iv).

For each director, disclose by footnote to the appropriate column: the grant date fair value of each equity award computed in accordance with FASB ASC Topic 718; for each option, SAR or similar option like instrument for which the registrant has adjusted or amended the exercise or base price during the last completed fiscal year, whether through amendment, cancellation or replacement grants, or any other means ("repriced"), or otherwise has materially modified such awards, the incremental fair value, computed as of the repricing or modification date in accordance with FASB ASC Topic 718; and the aggregate number of stock awards and the aggregate number of option awards outstanding at fiscal year end. However, the disclosure required by this Instruction does not apply to any repricing that occurs through a pre-existing formula or mechanism in the plan or award that results in the periodic adjustment of the option or SAR exercise or base price, an antidilution provision in a plan or award, or a recapitalization or similar transaction equally affecting all holders of the class of securities underlying the options or SARs.

(v)   The dollar value of all earnings for services performed during the fiscal year pursuant to non-equity incentive plans as defined in paragraph (a)(6)(iii) of this Item, and all earnings on any outstanding awards (column (e));

(vi)   The sum of the amounts specified in paragraphs (k)(2)(vi)(A) and (B) of this Item (column (f)) as follows:

(A)   The aggregate change in the actuarial present value of the director's accumulated benefit under all defined benefit and actuarial pension plans (including supplemental plans) from the pension plan measurement date used for financial statement reporting purposes with respect to the registrant's audited financial statements for the prior completed fiscal year to the pension plan measurement date used for financial statement reporting purposes with respect to the registrant's audited financial statements for the covered fiscal year; and

    (B)   Above-market or preferential earnings on compensation that is deferred on a basis that is not tax-qualified, including such earnings on nonqualified defined contribution plans;

    (vii) All other compensation for the covered fiscal year that the registrant could not properly report in any other column of the Director Compensation Table (column (g)). Each compensation item that is not properly reportable in columns (b)—(f), regardless of the amount of the compensation item, must be included in column (g). Such compensation must include, but is not limited to:

        (A)   Perquisites and other personal benefits, or property, unless the aggregate amount of such compensation is less than $10,000;

        (B)   All "gross-ups" or other amounts reimbursed during the fiscal year for the payment of taxes;

        (C)   For any security of the registrant or its subsidiaries purchased from the registrant or its subsidiaries (through deferral of salary or bonus, or otherwise) at a discount from the market price of such security at the date of purchase, unless that discount is available generally, either to all security holders or to all salaried employees of the registrant, the compensation cost, if any, computed in accordance with FASB ASC Topic 718;

        (D)   The amount paid or accrued to any director pursuant to a plan or arrangement in connection with:

            (1)   The resignation, retirement or any other termination of such director; or

            (2)   A change in control of the registrant;

        (E)   Registrant contributions or other allocations to vested and unvested defined contribution plans;

        (F)   Consulting fees earned from, or paid or payable by the registrant and/or its subsidiaries (including joint ventures);

        (G)   The annual costs of payments and promises of payments pursuant to director legacy programs and similar charitable award programs;

        (H)   The dollar value of any insurance premiums paid by, or on behalf of, the registrant during the covered fiscal year with respect to life insurance for the benefit of a director; and

        (I)   The dollar value of any dividends or other earnings paid on stock or option awards, when those amounts were not factored into the grant date fair value required to be reported for the stock or option award in column (c) or (d); and

Instructions to Item 402(k)(2)(vii).

    1.   Programs in which registrants agree to make donations to one or more charitable institutions in a director's name, payable by the registrant currently or upon a designated event, such as the retirement or death of the director, are charitable awards programs or director legacy programs for purposes of the disclosure required by paragraph (k)(2)(vii)(G) of this Item. Provide footnote disclosure of the total dollar amount payable under the program and other material terms of each such program for which tabular disclosure is provided.

    2.   Any item reported for a director pursuant to paragraph (k)(2)(vii) of this Item that is not a perquisite or personal benefit and whose value exceeds $10,000 must be identified and quantified in a footnote to column (g). All items of compensation are required to be included in the Director Compensation Table without regard to whether such items are required to be identified other than as specifically noted in this Item.

    3.   Perquisites and personal benefits may be excluded as long as the total value of all perquisites and personal benefits for a director is less than $10,000. If the total value of all perquisites and personal benefits is $10,000 or more for any director, then each perquisite or personal benefit, regardless of its amount, must be identified by type. If perquisites and personal benefits are required to be reported for a director pursuant to this rule, then each perquisite or personal benefit that exceeds the greater of $25,000 or 10% of the total amount of perquisites and personal benefits for that director must be quantified and disclosed in a footnote. Perquisites and other personal benefits shall be valued on the basis of the aggregate incremental cost to the registrant. With respect to the perquisite or other personal benefit for which footnote quantification is required, the registrant shall describe in the footnote its methodology for computing the aggregate incremental cost. Reimbursements of taxes

owed with respect to perquisites or other personal benefits must be included in column (g) and are subject to separate quantification and identification as tax reimbursements (paragraph (k)(2)(vii)(B) of this Item) even if the associated perquisites or other personal benefits are not required to be included because the total amount of all perquisites or personal benefits for an individual director is less than $10,000 or are required to be identified but are not required to be separately quantified.

(viii) The dollar value of total compensation for the covered fiscal year (column (h)). With respect to each director, disclose the sum of all amounts reported in columns (b) through (g).

Instruction to Item 402(k)(2)

Two or more directors may be grouped in a single row in the Table if all elements of their compensation are identical. The names of the directors for whom disclosure is presented on a group basis should be clear from the Table.

(3)   *Narrative to director compensation table.*

Provide a narrative description of any material factors necessary to an understanding of the director compensation disclosed in this Table. While material factors will vary depending upon the facts, examples of such factors may include, in given cases, among other things:

(i)   A description of standard compensation arrangements (such as fees for retainer, committee service, service as chairman of the board or a committee, and meeting attendance); and

(ii)   Whether any director has a different compensation arrangement, identifying that director and describing the terms of that arrangement.

Instruction to Item 402(k). In addition to the Instruction to paragraphs (k)(2)(iii) and (iv) and the Instructions to paragraph (k)(2)(vii) of this Item, the following apply equally to paragraph (k) of this Item: Instructions 2 and 4 to paragraph (c) of this Item; Instructions to paragraphs (c)(2)(iii) and (iv) of this Item; Instructions to paragraphs (c)(2)(v) and (vi) of this Item; Instructions to paragraph (c)(2)(vii) of this Item; Instructions to paragraph (c)(2)(viii) of this Item; and Instructions 1 and 5 to paragraph (c)(2)(ix) of this Item. These Instructions apply to the columns in the Director Compensation Table that are analogous to the columns in the Summary Compensation Table to which they refer and to disclosures under paragraph (k) of this Item that correspond to analogous disclosures provided for in paragraph (c) of this Item to which they refer.

(*l*)   *Smaller reporting companies and emerging growth companies.* A registrant that qualifies as a "smaller reporting company," as defined by Item 10(f)(1), or is an "emerging growth company," as defined in Rule 405 of the Securities Act or Rule 12b–2 of the Exchange Act, may provide the scaled disclosure in paragraphs (m) through (r) instead of paragraphs (a) through (k), (s), and (u) of this Item.

(m)   *Smaller reporting companies—General—*

(1)   *All compensation covered.* This Item requires clear, concise and understandable disclosure of all plan and non-plan compensation awarded to, earned by, or paid to the named executive officers designated under paragraph (m)(2) of this Item, and directors covered by paragraph (r) of this Item, by any person for all services rendered in all capacities to the smaller reporting company and its subsidiaries, unless otherwise specifically excluded from disclosure in this Item. All such compensation shall be reported pursuant to this Item, even if also called for by another requirement, including transactions between the smaller reporting company and a third party where a purpose of the transaction is to furnish compensation to any such named executive officer or director. No amount reported as compensation for one fiscal year need be reported in the same manner as compensation for a subsequent fiscal year; amounts reported as compensation for one fiscal year may be required to be reported in a different manner pursuant to this Item.

(2)   *Persons covered.* Disclosure shall be provided pursuant to this Item for each of the following (the "named executive officers"):

(i)   All individuals serving as the smaller reporting company's principal executive officer or acting in a similar capacity during the last completed fiscal year ("PEO"), regardless of compensation level;

(ii)   The smaller reporting company's two most highly compensated executive officers other than the PEO who were serving as executive officers at the end of the last completed fiscal year; and

(iii)   Up to two additional individuals for whom disclosure would have been provided pursuant to paragraph (m)(2)(ii) of this Item but for the fact that the individual was not serving as an executive officer of the smaller reporting company at the end of the last completed fiscal year.

Instructions to Item 402(m)(2).

1.   *Determination of most highly compensated executive officers.* The determination as to which executive officers are most highly compensated shall be made by reference to total compensation for the last completed fiscal year (as required to be disclosed pursuant to paragraph (n)(2)(x) of this Item) reduced by the amount required to be disclosed pursuant to paragraph (n)(2)(viii) of this Item, *provided, however,* that no disclosure need be provided for any executive officer, other than the PEO, whose total compensation, as so reduced, does not exceed $100,000.

2.   *Inclusion of executive officer of a subsidiary.* It may be appropriate for a smaller reporting company to include as named executive officers one or more executive officers or other employees of subsidiaries in the disclosure required by this Item. See Rule 3b–7 under the Exchange Act.

3.   *Exclusion of executive officer due to overseas compensation.* It may be appropriate in limited circumstances for a smaller reporting company not to include in the disclosure required by this Item an individual, other than its PEO, who is one of the smaller reporting company's most highly compensated executive officers due to the payment of amounts of cash compensation relating to overseas assignments attributed predominantly to such assignments.

(3)   *Information for full fiscal year.* If the PEO served in that capacity during any part of a fiscal year with respect to which information is required, information should be provided as to all of his or her compensation for the full fiscal year. If a named executive officer (other than the PEO) served as an executive officer of the smaller reporting company (whether or not in the same position) during any part of the fiscal year with respect to which information is required, information shall be provided as to all compensation of that individual for the full fiscal year.

(4)   *Omission of table or column.* A table or column may be omitted if there has been no compensation awarded to, earned by, or paid to any of the named executive officers or directors required to be reported in that table or column in any fiscal year covered by that table.

(5)   *Definitions.* For purposes of this Item:

(i)   The term *stock* means instruments such as common stock, restricted stock, restricted stock units, phantom stock, phantom stock units, common stock equivalent units or any similar instruments that do not have option-like features, and the term option means instruments such as stock options, stock appreciation rights and similar instruments with option-like features. The term *stock appreciation rights* ("*SARs*") refers to SARs payable in cash or stock, including SARs payable in cash or stock at the election of the smaller reporting company or a named executive officer. The term *equity* is used to refer generally to stock and/or options.

(ii)   The term plan includes, but is not limited to, the following: Any plan, contract, authorization or arrangement, whether or not set forth in any formal document, pursuant to which cash, securities, similar instruments, or any other property may be received. A plan may be applicable to one person. Except with respect to disclosure required by paragraph (t) of this Item, smaller reporting companies may omit information regarding group life, health, hospitalization, or medical reimbursement plans that do not discriminate in scope, terms or operation, in favor of executive officers or directors of the smaller reporting company and that are available generally to all salaried employees.

(iii)   The term *incentive plan* means any plan providing compensation intended to serve as incentive for performance to occur over a specified period, whether such performance is measured by reference to financial performance of the smaller reporting company or an affiliate, the smaller reporting company's stock price, or any other performance measure. An *equity incentive plan* is an incentive plan or portion of an incentive plan under which awards are granted that fall within the scope of FASB ASC Topic 718. A *non-equity incentive plan* is an incentive plan or portion of an incentive plan that is not an equity incentive plan. The term *incentive plan award* means an award provided under an incentive plan.

(iv) The terms *date of grant* or *grant date* refer to the grant date determined for financial statement reporting purposes pursuant to FASB ASC Topic 718.

(v) *Closing market price* is defined as the price at which the smaller reporting company's security was last sold in the principal United States market for such security as of the date for which the closing market price is determined.

(n) *Smaller reporting companies—Summary compensation table—*

(1) *General.* Provide the information specified in paragraph (n)(2) of this Item, concerning the compensation of the named executive officers for each of the smaller reporting company's last two completed fiscal years, in a Summary Compensation Table in the tabular format specified below.

Name and principal position (a)	Year (b)	Salary ($) (c)	Bonus ($) (d)	Stock awards ($) (e)	Option awards ($) (f)	Nonequity incentive plan compensation ($) (g)	Non-qualified deferred compensation earnings ($) (h)	All other compensation ($) (i)	Total ($) (j)
PEO									
A									
B									

(2) The Table shall include:

(i) The name and principal position of the named executive officer (column (a));

(ii) The fiscal year covered (column (b));

(iii) The dollar value of base salary (cash and non-cash) earned by the named executive officer during the fiscal year covered (column (c));

(iv) The dollar value of bonus (cash and non-cash) earned by the named executive officer during the fiscal year covered (column (d));

Instructions to Item 402(n)(2)(iii) and (iv).

1. If the amount of salary or bonus earned in a given fiscal year is not calculable through the latest practicable date, a footnote shall be included disclosing that the amount of salary or bonus is not calculable through the latest practicable date and providing the date that the amount of salary or bonus is expected to be determined, and such amount must then be disclosed in a filing under Item 5.02(f) of Form 8–K.

2. Smaller reporting companies shall include in the salary column (column (c)) or bonus column (column (d)) any amount of salary or bonus forgone at the election of a named executive officer under which stock, equity-based or other forms of non-cash compensation instead have been received by the named executive officer. However, the receipt of any such form of non-cash compensation instead of salary or bonus must be disclosed in a footnote added to the salary or bonus column and, where applicable, referring to the narrative disclosure to the Summary Compensation Table (required by paragraph (o) of this Item) where the material terms of the stock, option or non-equity incentive plan award elected by the named executive officer are reported.

(v) For awards of stock, the aggregate grant date fair value computed in accordance with FASB ASC Topic 718 (column (e));

(vi) For awards of options, with or without tandem SARs (including awards that subsequently have been transferred), the aggregate grant date fair value computed in accordance with FASB ASC Topic 718 (column (f));

Instruction 1 to Item 402(n)(2)(v) and (n)(2)(vi). For awards reported in columns (e) and (f), include a footnote disclosing all assumptions made in the valuation by reference to a discussion of those assumptions in the smaller reporting company's financial statements, footnotes to the financial statements, or discussion in the Management's Discussion and Analysis. The sections so referenced are deemed part of the disclosure provided pursuant to this Item.

Instruction 2 to Item 402(n)(2)(v) and (n)(2)(vi). If at any time during the last completed fiscal year, the smaller reporting company has adjusted or amended the exercise price of options or SARs previously awarded to a named executive officer, whether through amendment, cancellation or replacement grants, or any other means ("repriced"), or otherwise has materially modified such awards, the smaller reporting company shall include, as awards required to be reported in column (f), the incremental fair value, computed as of the repricing or modification date in accordance with FASB ASC Topic 718, with respect to that repriced or modified award.

Instruction 3 to Item 402(n)(2)(v) and (vi). For any awards that are subject to performance conditions, report the value at the grant date based upon the probable outcome of such conditions. This amount should be consistent with the estimate of aggregate compensation cost to be recognized over the service period determined as of the grant date under FASB ASC Topic 718, excluding the effect of estimated forfeitures. In a footnote to the table, disclose the value of the award at the grant date assuming that the highest level of performance conditions will be achieved if an amount less than the maximum was included in the table.

(vii) The dollar value of all earnings for services performed during the fiscal year pursuant to awards under non-equity incentive plans as defined in paragraph (m)(5)(iii) of this Item, and all earnings on any outstanding awards (column (g));

Instructions to Item 402(n)(2)(vii).

1.   If the relevant performance measure is satisfied during the fiscal year (including for a single year in a plan with a multi-year performance measure), the earnings are reportable for that fiscal year, even if not payable until a later date, and are not reportable again in the fiscal year when amounts are paid to the named executive officer.

2.   All earnings on non-equity incentive plan compensation must be identified and quantified in a footnote to column (g), whether the earnings were paid during the fiscal year, payable during the period but deferred at the election of the named executive officer, or payable by their terms at a later date.

(viii) Above-market or preferential earnings on compensation that is deferred on a basis that is not tax-qualified, including such earnings on nonqualified defined contribution plans (column (h));

Instruction to Item 402(n)(2)(viii). Interest on deferred compensation is above-market only if the rate of interest exceeds 120% of the applicable federal long-term rate, with compounding (as prescribed under section 1274(d) of the Internal Revenue Code, (26 U.S.C. 1274(d))) at the rate that corresponds most closely to the rate under the smaller reporting company's plan at the time the interest rate or formula is set. In the event of a discretionary reset of the interest rate, the requisite calculation must be made on the basis of the interest rate at the time of such reset, rather than when originally established. Only the above-market portion of the interest must be included. If the applicable interest rates vary depending upon conditions such as a minimum period of continued service, the reported amount should be calculated assuming satisfaction of all conditions to receiving interest at the highest rate. Dividends (and dividend equivalents) on deferred compensation denominated in the smaller reporting company's stock ("deferred stock") are preferential only if earned at a rate higher than dividends on the smaller reporting company's common stock. Only the preferential portion of the dividends or equivalents must be included. Footnote or narrative disclosure may be provided explaining the smaller reporting company's criteria for determining any portion considered to be above-market.

(ix) All other compensation for the covered fiscal year that the smaller reporting company could not properly report in any other column of the Summary Compensation Table (column (i)). Each compensation item that is not properly reportable in columns (c) through (h), regardless of the amount of the compensation item, must be included in column (i). Such compensation must include, but is not limited to:

(A)   Perquisites and other personal benefits, or property, unless the aggregate amount of such compensation is less than $10,000;

(B)   All "gross-ups" or other amounts reimbursed during the fiscal year for the payment of taxes;

(C)   For any security of the smaller reporting company or its subsidiaries purchased from the smaller reporting company or its subsidiaries (through deferral of salary or bonus, or otherwise) at a discount from the market price of such security at the date of purchase, unless that discount is available generally, either to all security holders or to all salaried employees of the smaller reporting company, the compensation cost, if any, computed in accordance with FASB ASC Topic 718;

(D)   The amount paid or accrued to any named executive officer pursuant to a plan or arrangement in connection with:

(1)   Any termination, including without limitation through retirement, resignation, severance or constructive termination (including a change in responsibilities) of such executive officer's employment with the smaller reporting company and its subsidiaries; or

(2)   A change in control of the smaller reporting company;

(E)   Smaller reporting company contributions or other allocations to vested and unvested defined contribution plans;

(F)   The dollar value of any insurance premiums paid by, or on behalf of, the smaller reporting company during the covered fiscal year with respect to life insurance for the benefit of a named executive officer; and

(G)   The dollar value of any dividends or other earnings paid on stock or option awards, when those amounts were not factored into the grant date fair value required to be reported for the stock or option award in column (e) or (f); and

Instructions to Item 402(n)(2)(ix).

1.   Non-equity incentive plan awards and earnings and earnings on stock or options, except as specified in paragraph (n)(2)(ix)(G) of this Item, are required to be reported elsewhere as provided in this Item and are not reportable as All Other Compensation in column (i).

2.   Benefits paid pursuant to defined benefit and actuarial plans are not reportable as All Other Compensation in column (i) unless accelerated pursuant to a change in control; information concerning these plans is reportable pursuant to paragraph (q)(1) of this Item.

3.   Reimbursements of taxes owed with respect to perquisites or other personal benefits must be included in the columns as tax reimbursements (paragraph (n)(2)(ix)(B) of this Item) even if the associated perquisites or other personal benefits are not required to be included because the aggregate amount of such compensation is less than $10,000.

4.   Perquisites and other personal benefits shall be valued on the basis of the aggregate incremental cost to the smaller reporting company.

5.   For purposes of paragraph (n)(2)(ix)(D) of this Item, an accrued amount is an amount for which payment has become due.

(x)   The dollar value of total compensation for the covered fiscal year (column (j)). With respect to each named executive officer, disclose the sum of all amounts reported in columns (c) through (i).

Instructions to Item 402(n).

1.   Information with respect to the fiscal year prior to the last completed fiscal year will not be required if the smaller reporting company was not a reporting company pursuant to section 13(a) or 15(d) of the Exchange Act at any time during that year, except that the smaller reporting company will be required to provide information for any such year if that information previously was required to be provided in response to a Commission filing requirement.

2. All compensation values reported in the Summary Compensation Table must be reported in dollars and rounded to the nearest dollar. Reported compensation values must be reported numerically, providing a single numerical value for each grid in the table. Where compensation was paid to or received by a named executive officer in a different currency, a footnote must be provided to identify that currency and describe the rate and methodology used to convert the payment amounts to dollars.

3. If a named executive officer is also a director who receives compensation for his or her services as a director, reflect that compensation in the Summary Compensation Table and provide a footnote identifying and itemizing such compensation and amounts. Use the categories in the Director Compensation Table required pursuant to paragraph (r) of this Item.

4. Any amounts deferred, whether pursuant to a plan established under section 401(k) of the Internal Revenue Code (26 U.S.C. 401(k)), or otherwise, shall be included in the appropriate column for the fiscal year in which earned.

5. Reduce the amount reported in the applicable Summary Compensation Table column for the fiscal year in which the amount recovered initially was reported as compensation by any amounts recovered pursuant to the compensation recovery policy required by the listing standards adopted pursuant to Rule 10D–1 and identify such amounts by footnote.

(o) *Smaller reporting companies—Narrative disclosure to summary compensation table.* Provide a narrative description of any material factors necessary to an understanding of the information disclosed in the Table required by paragraph (n) of this Item. Examples of such factors may include, in given cases, among other things:

(1) The material terms of each named executive officer's employment agreement or arrangement, whether written or unwritten;

(2) If at any time during the last fiscal year, any outstanding option or other equity-based award was repriced or otherwise materially modified (such as by extension of exercise periods, the change of vesting or forfeiture conditions, the change or elimination of applicable performance criteria, or the change of the bases upon which returns are determined), a description of each such repricing or other material modification;

(3) The waiver or modification of any specified performance target, goal or condition to payout with respect to any amount included in non-stock incentive plan compensation or payouts reported in column (g) to the Summary Compensation Table required by paragraph (n) of this Item, stating whether the waiver or modification applied to one or more specified named executive officers or to all compensation subject to the target, goal or condition;

(4) The material terms of each grant, including but not limited to the date of exercisability, any conditions to exercisability, any tandem feature, any reload feature, any tax-reimbursement feature, and any provision that could cause the exercise price to be lowered;

(5) The material terms of any non-equity incentive plan award made to a named executive officer during the last completed fiscal year, including a general description of the formula or criteria to be applied in determining the amounts payable and vesting schedule;

(6) The method of calculating earnings on nonqualified deferred compensation plans including nonqualified defined contribution plans; and

(7) An identification to the extent material of any item included under All Other Compensation (column (i)) in the Summary Compensation Table. Identification of an item shall not be considered material if it does not exceed the greater of $25,000 or 10% of all items included in the specified category in question set forth in paragraph (n)(2)(ix) of this Item. All items of compensation are required to be included in the Summary Compensation Table without regard to whether such items are required to be identified.

Instruction to Item 402(o). The disclosure required by paragraph (o)(2) of this Item would not apply to any repricing that occurs through a pre-existing formula or mechanism in the plan or award that results in the periodic adjustment of the option or SAR exercise or base price, an antidilution provision in a plan or award, or a recapitalization or similar transaction equally affecting all holders of the class of securities underlying the options or SARs.

(p) *Smaller reporting companies—Outstanding equity awards at fiscal year-end table.*

(1) Provide the information specified in paragraph (p)(2) of this Item, concerning unexercised options; stock that has not vested; and equity incentive plan awards for each named executive officer outstanding as of the end of the smaller reporting company's last completed fiscal year in the following tabular format:

Name (a)	Option awards					Stock awards			
	Number of securities underlying unexercised options (#) exercisable	Number of securities underlying unexercised options (#) unexercisable	Equity incentive plan awards: Number of securities underlying unexercised unearned options (#)	Option exercise price ($)	Option expiration date	Number of shares or units of stock that have not vested (#)	Market value of shares of units of stock that have not vested ($)	Equity incentive plan awards: Number of unearned shares, units or other rights that have not vested (#)	Equity incentive plan awards: Market or payout value of unearned shares, units or other rights that have not vested ($)
	(b)	(c)	(d)	(e)	(f)	(g)	(h)	(i)	(j)
PEO									
A									
B									

(2) The Table shall include:

(i) The name of the named executive officer (column (a));

(ii) On an award-by-award basis, the number of securities underlying unexercised options, including awards that have been transferred other than for value, that are exercisable and that are not reported in column (d) (column (b));

(iii) On an award-by-award basis, the number of securities underlying unexercised options, including awards that have been transferred other than for value, that are unexercisable and that are not reported in column (d) (column (c));

(iv) On an award-by-award basis, the total number of shares underlying unexercised options awarded under any equity incentive plan that have not been earned (column (d));

(v) For each instrument reported in columns (b), (c) and (d), as applicable, the exercise or base price (column (e));

(vi) For each instrument reported in columns (b), (c) and (d), as applicable, the expiration date (column (f));

(vii) The total number of shares of stock that have not vested and that are not reported in column (i) (column (g));

(viii) The aggregate market value of shares of stock that have not vested and that are not reported in column (j) (column (h));

(ix) The total number of shares of stock, units or other rights awarded under any equity incentive plan that have not vested and that have not been earned, and, if applicable the number of shares underlying any such unit or right (column (i)); and

(x) The aggregate market or payout value of shares of stock, units or other rights awarded under any equity incentive plan that have not vested and that have not been earned (column (j)).

Instructions to Item 402(p)(2).

1.   Identify by footnote any award that has been transferred other than for value, disclosing the nature of the transfer.

2.   The vesting dates of options, shares of stock and equity incentive plan awards held at fiscal-year end must be disclosed by footnote to the applicable column where the outstanding award is reported.

3.   Compute the market value of stock reported in column (h) and equity incentive plan awards of stock reported in column (j) by multiplying the closing market price of the smaller reporting company's stock at the end of the last completed fiscal year by the number of shares or units of stock or the amount of equity incentive plan awards, respectively. The number of shares or units reported in column (d) or (i), and the payout value reported in column (j), shall be based on achieving threshold performance goals, except that if the previous fiscal year's performance has exceeded the threshold, the disclosure shall be based on the next higher performance measure (target or maximum) that exceeds the previous fiscal year's performance. If the award provides only for a single estimated payout, that amount should be reported. If the target amount is not determinable, smaller reporting companies must provide a representative amount based on the previous fiscal year's performance.

4.   Multiple awards may be aggregated where the expiration date and the exercise and/or base price of the instruments is identical. A single award consisting of a combination of options, SARs and/or similar option-like instruments shall be reported as separate awards with respect to each tranche with a different exercise and/or base price or expiration date.

5.   Options or stock awarded under an equity incentive plan are reported in columns (d) or (i) and (j), respectively, until the relevant performance condition has been satisfied. Once the relevant performance condition has been satisfied, even if the option or stock award is subject to forfeiture conditions, options are reported in column (b) or (c), as appropriate, until they are exercised or expire, or stock is reported in columns (g) and (h) until it vests.

(q)   *Smaller reporting companies—Additional narrative disclosure.* Provide a narrative description of the following to the extent material:

(1)   The material terms of each plan that provides for the payment of retirement benefits, or benefits that will be paid primarily following retirement, including but not limited to tax-qualified defined benefit plans, supplemental executive retirement plans, tax-qualified defined contribution plans and nonqualified defined contribution plans.

(2)   The material terms of each contract, agreement, plan or arrangement, whether written or unwritten, that provides for payment(s) to a named executive officer at, following, or in connection with the resignation, retirement or other termination of a named executive officer, or a change in control of the smaller reporting company or a change in the named executive officer's responsibilities following a change in control, with respect to each named executive officer.

(r)   *Smaller reporting companies—Compensation of directors.*

(1)   Provide the information specified in paragraph (r)(2) of this Item, concerning the compensation of the directors for the smaller reporting company's last completed fiscal year, in the following tabular format:

Name (a)	Fees earned or paid in cash ($) (b)	Stock awards ($) (c)	Option awards ($) (d)	Non-equity incentive plan compensation ($) (e)	Nonqualified deferred compensation earnings ($) (f)	All other compen- sation ($) (g)	Total ($) (h)
A							
B							
C							
D							
E							

(2)   The Table shall include:

(i)   The name of each director unless such director is also a named executive officer under paragraph (m) of this Item and his or her compensation for service as a director is fully reflected in the Summary Compensation Table pursuant to paragraph (n) of this Item and otherwise as required pursuant to paragraphs (o) through (q) of this Item (column (a));

(ii)   The aggregate dollar amount of all fees earned or paid in cash for services as a director, including annual retainer fees, committee and/or chairmanship fees, and meeting fees (column (b));

(iii)   For awards of stock, the aggregate grant date fair value computed in accordance with FASB ASC Topic 718 (column (c)); (iv) For awards of options, with or without tandem SARs (including awards that subsequently have been transferred), the aggregate grant date fair value computed in accordance with FASB ASC Topic 718 (column (d));

(iv)   For awards of stock options, with or without tandem SARs, the dollar amount recognized for financial statement reporting purposes with respect to the fiscal year in accordance with FAS 123R (column (d));

Instruction to Item 402(r)(2)(iii) and (iv). For each director, disclose by footnote to the appropriate column, the aggregate number of stock awards and the aggregate number of option awards outstanding at fiscal year end.

(v)   The dollar value of all earnings for services performed during the fiscal year pursuant to non-equity incentive plans as defined in paragraph (m)(5)(iii) of this Item, and all earnings on any outstanding awards (column (e));

(vi)   Above-market or preferential earnings on compensation that is deferred on a basis that is not tax-qualified, including such earnings on nonqualified defined contribution plans (column (f));

(vii)   All other compensation for the covered fiscal year that the smaller reporting company could not properly report in any other column of the Director Compensation Table (column (g)). Each compensation item that is not properly reportable in columns (b) through (f), regardless of the amount of the compensation item, must be included in column (g) and must be identified and quantified in a footnote if it is deemed material in accordance with paragraph (o)(7) of this Item. Such compensation must include, but is not limited to:

(A) Perquisites and other personal benefits, or property, unless the aggregate amount of such compensation is less than $10,000;

(B) All "gross-ups" or other amounts reimbursed during the fiscal year for the payment of taxes;

(C) For any security of the smaller reporting company or its subsidiaries purchased from the smaller reporting company or its subsidiaries (through deferral of salary or bonus, or otherwise) at a discount from the market price of such security at the date of purchase, unless that discount is available generally, either to all security holders or to all salaried employees of the smaller reporting company, the compensation cost, if any, computed in accordance with FASB ASC Topic 718;

(D) The amount paid or accrued to any director pursuant to a plan or arrangement in connection with:

(1) The resignation, retirement or any other termination of such director; or

(2) A change in control of the smaller reporting company;

(E) Smaller reporting company contributions or other allocations to vested and unvested defined contribution plans;

(F) Consulting fees earned from, or paid or payable by the smaller reporting company and/or its subsidiaries (including joint ventures);

(G) The annual costs of payments and promises of payments pursuant to director legacy programs and similar charitable award programs;

(H) The dollar value of any insurance premiums paid by, or on behalf of, the smaller reporting company during the covered fiscal year with respect to life insurance for the benefit of a director; and

(I) The dollar value of any dividends or other earnings paid on stock or option awards, when those amounts were not factored into the grant date fair value required to be reported for the stock or option award in column (c) or (d); and

Instruction to Item 402(r)(2)(vii). Programs in which smaller reporting companies agree to make donations to one or more charitable institutions in a director's name, payable by the smaller reporting company currently or upon a designated event, such as the retirement or death of the director, are charitable awards programs or director legacy programs for purposes of the disclosure required by paragraph (r)(2)(vii)(G) of this Item. Provide footnote disclosure of the total dollar amount payable under the program and other material terms of each such program for which tabular disclosure is provided.

(viii) The dollar value of total compensation for the covered fiscal year (column (h)). With respect to each director, disclose the sum of all amounts reported in columns (b) through (g).

Instruction to Item 402(r)(2). Two or more directors may be grouped in a single row in the Table if all elements of their compensation are identical. The names of the directors for whom disclosure is presented on a group basis should be clear from the Table.

(3) *Narrative to director compensation table.* Provide a narrative description of any material factors necessary to an understanding of the director compensation disclosed in this Table. While material factors will vary depending upon the facts, examples of such factors may include, in given cases, among other things:

(i) A description of standard compensation arrangements (such as fees for retainer, committee service, service as chairman of the board or a committee, and meeting attendance); and

(ii) Whether any director has a different compensation arrangement, identifying that director and describing the terms of that arrangement.

Instruction to Item 402(r). In addition to the Instruction to paragraph (r)(2)(vii) of this Item, the following apply equally to paragraph (r) of this Item: Instructions 2 and 4 to paragraph (n) of this Item; the Instructions to paragraphs (n)(2)(iii) and (iv) of this Item; the Instructions to paragraphs (n)(2)(v) and (vi) of this Item; the Instructions to paragraph (n)(2)(vii) of this Item; the Instruction to paragraph (n)(2)(viii) of this Item; the Instructions to paragraph (n)(2)(ix) of this Item; and paragraph (o)(7) of this Item. These Instructions apply to the columns in the Director Compensation Table that are analogous to the columns in the Summary Compensation Table to which they refer and to disclosures under paragraph (r) of this Item that correspond to analogous disclosures provided for in paragraph (n) of this Item to which they refer.

(s)   *Narrative disclosure of the registrant's compensation policies and practices as they relate to the registrant's risk management.* To the extent that risks arising from the registrant's compensation policies and practices for its employees are reasonably likely to have a material adverse effect on the registrant, discuss the registrant's policies and practices of compensating its employees, including non-executive officers, as they relate to risk management practices and risk-taking incentives. While the situations requiring disclosure will vary depending on the particular registrant and compensation policies and practices, situations that may trigger disclosure include, among others, compensation policies and practices: at a business unit of the company that carries a significant portion of the registrant's risk profile; at a business unit with compensation structured significantly differently than other units within the registrant; at a business unit that is significantly more profitable than others within the registrant; at a business unit where compensation expense is a significant percentage of the unit's revenues; and that vary significantly from the overall risk and reward structure of the registrant, such as when bonuses are awarded upon accomplishment of a task, while the income and risk to the registrant from the task extend over a significantly longer period of time. The purpose of this paragraph (s) is to provide investors material information concerning how the registrant compensates and incentivizes its employees that may create risks that are reasonably likely to have a material adverse effect on the registrant. While the information to be disclosed pursuant to this paragraph (s) will vary depending upon the nature of the registrant's business and the compensation approach, the following are examples of the issues that the registrant may need to address for the business units or employees discussed:

(1)   The general design philosophy of the registrant's compensation policies and practices for employees whose behavior would be most affected by the incentives established by the policies and practices, as such policies and practices relate to or affect risk taking by employees on behalf of the registrant, and the manner of their implementation;

(2)   The registrant's risk assessment or incentive considerations, if any, in structuring its compensation policies and practices or in awarding and paying compensation;

(3)   How the registrant's compensation policies and practices relate to the realization of risks resulting from the actions of employees in both the short term and the long term, such as through policies requiring claw backs or imposing holding periods;

(4)   The registrant's policies regarding adjustments to its compensation policies and practices to address changes in its risk profile;

(5)   Material adjustments the registrant has made to its compensation policies and practices as a result of changes in its risk profile; and

(6)   The extent to which the registrant monitors its compensation policies and practices to determine whether its risk management objectives are being met with respect to incentivizing its employees

(t)   *Golden Parachute Compensation.*

(1)   In connection with any proxy or consent solicitation material providing the disclosure required by section 14A(b)(1) of the Securities Exchange Act of 1934 or any proxy or consent solicitation that includes disclosure under Item 14 of Schedule 14A pursuant to Note A of Schedule 14A (excluding any proxy or consent solicitation of an "emerging growth company," as defined in Rule 405 of the Securities Act or Rule 12b–2 of the Exchange Act), with respect to each named executive officer of the acquiring company and the target company, provide the information specified in paragraphs (t)(2) and (3) of this rule regarding any agreement or understanding, whether written or unwritten, between such named executive officer and the acquiring company or target company, concerning any type of compensation, whether present, deferred or contingent, that is based on or otherwise relates to an

acquisition, merger, consolidation, sale or other disposition of all or substantially all assets of the issuer, as follows:

Golden Parachute Compensation

Name	Cash	Equity	Pension/ NQDC	Perquisites/ benefits	Tax reimbursement	Other	Total
	($)	($)	($)	($)	($)	($)	($)
(a)	(b)	(c)	(d)	(e)	(f)	(g)	(h)
PEO							
PFO							
A							
B							
C							

    (2) The table shall include, for each named executive officer:

        (i) The name of the named executive officer (column (a));

        (ii) The aggregate dollar value of any cash severance payments, including but not limited to payments of base salary, bonus, and pro-rated non-equity incentive compensation plan payments (column (b));

        (iii) The aggregate dollar value of:

            (A) Stock awards for which vesting would be accelerated;

            (B) In-the-money option awards for which vesting would be accelerated; and

            (C) Payments in cancellation of stock and option awards (column (c));

        (iv) The aggregate dollar value of pension and nonqualified deferred compensation benefit enhancements (column (d));

        (v) The aggregate dollar value of perquisites and other personal benefits or property, and health care and welfare benefits (column (e));

        (vi) The aggregate dollar value of any tax reimbursements (column (f));

        (vii) The aggregate dollar value of any other compensation that is based on or otherwise relates to the transaction not properly reported in columns (b) through (f) (column (g)); and

        (viii) The aggregate dollar value of the sum of all amounts reported in columns (b) through (g) (column (h)).

Instructions to Item 402(t)(2).

    1. If this disclosure is included in a proxy or consent solicitation seeking approval of an acquisition, merger, consolidation, or proposed sale or other disposition of all or substantially all the assets of the registrant, or in a proxy or consent solicitation that includes disclosure under Item 14 of Schedule 14A pursuant to Note A of Schedule 14A, the disclosure provided by this table shall be quantified assuming that the triggering event took place on the latest practicable date, and that the price per share of the registrant's securities shall be determined as follows: If the shareholders are to receive a fixed dollar amount, the price per share shall be that fixed dollar amount, and if such value is not a fixed dollar amount, the price per share shall be the average closing market

price of the registrant's securities over the first five business days following the first public announcement of the transaction. Compute the dollar value of in-the-money option awards for which vesting would be accelerated by determining the difference between this price and the exercise or base price of the options. Include only compensation that is based on or otherwise relates to the subject transaction. Apply Instruction 1 to Item 402(t) with respect to those executive officers for whom disclosure was required in the issuer's most recent filing with the Commission under the Securities Act of 1933 or Securities Exchange Act of 1934 that required disclosure pursuant to Item 402(c).

2.   If this disclosure is included in a proxy solicitation for the annual meeting at which directors are elected for purposes of subjecting the disclosed agreements or understandings to a shareholder vote under section 14A(a)(1) of the Securities Exchange Act of 1934, the disclosure provided by this table shall be quantified assuming that the triggering event took place on the last business day of the registrant's last completed fiscal year, and the price per share of the registrant's securities is the closing market price as of that date. Compute the dollar value of in-the-money option awards for which vesting would be accelerated by determining the difference between this price and the exercise or base price of the options.

3.   In the event that uncertainties exist as to the provision of payments and benefits or the amounts involved, the registrant is required to make a reasonable estimate applicable to the payment or benefit and disclose material assumptions underlying such estimates in its disclosure. In such event, the disclosure would require forward-looking information as appropriate.

4.   For each of columns (b) through (g), include a footnote quantifying each separate form of compensation included in the aggregate total reported. Include the value of all perquisites and other personal benefits or property. Individual perquisites and personal benefits shall be identified and quantified as required by Instruction 4 to Item 402(c)(2)(ix) of this rule. For purposes of quantifying health care benefits, the registrant must use the assumptions used for financial reporting purposes under generally accepted accounting principles.

5.   For each of columns (b) through (h), include a footnote quantifying the amount payable attributable to a double-trigger arrangement (i.e., amounts triggered by a change-in-control for which payment is conditioned upon the executive officer's termination without cause or resignation for good reason within a limited time period following the change-in-control), specifying the time-frame in which such termination or resignation must occur in order for the amount to become payable, and the amount payable attributable to a single-trigger arrangement (i.e., amounts triggered by a change-in-control for which payment is not conditioned upon such a termination or resignation of the executive officer).

6.   A registrant conducting a shareholder advisory vote pursuant to Rule 14a–21(c) under the Exchange Act of 1934 to cover new arrangements and understandings, and/or revised terms of agreements and understandings that were previously subject to a shareholder advisory vote pursuant to Rule 14a–21(a) under the Exchange Act of 1934, shall provide two separate tables. One table shall disclose all golden parachute compensation, including both the arrangements and amounts previously disclosed and subject to a shareholder advisory vote under section 14A(a)(1) of the Securities Exchange Act of 1934 and Rule 14a–21(a) under the Exchange Act of 1934 and the new arrangements and understandings and/or revised terms of agreements and understandings that were previously subject to a shareholder advisory vote. The second table shall disclose only the new arrangements and/or revised terms subject to the separate shareholder vote under section 14A(b)(2) of the Securities Exchange Act of 1934 and Rule 14a–21(c) under the Exchange Act of 1934.

7.   In cases where this Item 402(t)(2) requires disclosure of arrangements between an acquiring company and the named executive officers of the soliciting target company, the registrant shall clarify whether these agreements are included in the separate shareholder advisory vote pursuant to Rule 14a–21(c) under the Exchange Act of 1934 by providing a separate table of all agreements and understandings subject to the shareholder advisory vote required by section 14A(b)(2) of the Securities Exchange Act of 1934 and Rule 14a–21(c) under the Exchange Act of 1934, if different from the full scope of golden parachute compensation subject to Item 402(t) disclosure.

(3)   Provide a succinct narrative description of any material factors necessary to an understanding of each such contract, agreement, plan or arrangement and the payments quantified in the tabular disclosure required by this paragraph. Such factors shall include, but not be limited to a description of:

(i)   The specific circumstances that would trigger payment(s);

(ii)   Whether the payments would or could be lump sum, or annual, disclosing the duration, and by whom they would be provided; and

(iii)   Any material conditions or obligations applicable to the receipt of payment or benefits, including but not limited to non-compete, non-solicitation, non-disparagement or confidentiality agreements, including the duration of such agreements and provisions regarding waiver or breach of such agreements.

Instructions to Item 402(t).

1.   A registrant that does not qualify as a "smaller reporting company," as defined by Item 10(f)(1) of Regulation S–K, must provide the information required by this Item 402(t) with respect to the individuals covered by Items 402(a)(3)(i), (ii) and (iii) of this rule. A registrant that qualifies as a "smaller reporting company," as defined by Item10(f)(1) of Regulation S–K, must provide the information required by this Item 402(t) with respect to the individuals covered by Items 402(m)(2)(i) and (ii) of this rule.

2.   The obligation to provide the information in this Item 402(t) shall not apply to agreements and understandings described in paragraph (t)(1) of this rule with senior management of foreign private issuers, as defined in Rule 3b–4 under the Exchange Act of 1934.

Instruction to Item 402. Specify the applicable fiscal year in the title to each table required under this Item which calls for disclosure as of or for a completed fiscal year.

(u)   *Pay ratio disclosure.*

(1)   Disclose:

(i)   The median of the annual total compensation of all employees of the registrant, except the PEO of the registrant;

(ii)   The annual total compensation of the PEO of the registrant; and

(iii)   The ratio of the amount in paragraph (u)(1)(i) of this Item to the amount in paragraph (u)(1)(ii) of this Item. For purposes of the ratio required by this paragraph (u)(1)(iii), the amount 283 in paragraph (u)(1)(i) of this Item shall equal one, or, alternatively, the ratio may be expressed narratively as the multiple that the amount in paragraph (u)(1)(ii) of this Item bears to the amount in paragraph (u)(1)(i) of this Item.

(2)   For purposes of this paragraph (u):

(i)   *Total compensation* for the median of annual total compensation of all employees of the registrant and the PEO of the registrant shall be determined in accordance with paragraph (c)(2)(x) of this Item. In determining the total compensation, all references to "named executive officer" in this Item and the instructions thereto may be deemed to refer instead, as applicable, to "employee" and, for non-salaried employees, references to "base salary" and "salary" in this Item and the instructions thereto may be deemed to refer instead, as applicable, to "wages plus overtime";

(ii)   *Annual total* compensation means total compensation for the registrant's last completed fiscal year; and

(iii)   *Registrant* means the registrant and its consolidated subsidiaries.

(3)   For purposes of this paragraph (u), *employee* or *employee of the registrant* means an individual employed by the registrant or any of its consolidated subsidiaries, whether as a full-time, part-time, seasonal, or temporary worker, as of a date chosen by the registrant within the last three months of the registrant's last completed fiscal year. The definition of employee or employee of the registrant does not include those workers who are employed, and whose compensation is determined, by an unaffiliated third party but who provide services to the registrant or its consolidated subsidiaries as independent contractors or "leased" workers.

(4)   For purposes of this paragraph (u), an employee located in a jurisdiction outside the United States (a "non-U.S. employee") may be exempt from the definition of employee or employee of the registrant under either of the following conditions:

(i)   The employee is employed in a foreign jurisdiction in which the laws or regulations governing data privacy are such that, despite its reasonable efforts to obtain or process the information necessary for compliance with this paragraph (u), the registrant is unable to do so without violating such data privacy laws or regulations. The registrant's reasonable efforts shall include, at a minimum, using or seeking an exemption or other relief under any governing data privacy laws or regulations. If the registrant chooses to exclude any employees using this exemption, it shall list the excluded jurisdictions, identify the specific data privacy law or regulation, explain how complying with this paragraph (u) violates such data privacy law or regulation (including the efforts made by the registrant to use or seek an exemption or other relief under such law or regulation), and provide the approximate number of employees exempted from each jurisdiction based on this exemption. In addition, if a registrant excludes any non-U.S. employees in a particular jurisdiction under this exemption, it must exclude all non-U.S. employees in that jurisdiction. Further, the registrant shall obtain a legal opinion from counsel that opines on the inability of the registrant to obtain or process the information necessary for compliance with this paragraph (u) without violating the jurisdiction's laws or regulations governing data privacy, including the registrant's inability to obtain an exemption or other relief under any governing laws or regulations. The registrant shall file the legal opinion as an exhibit to the filing in which the pay ratio disclosure is included.

(ii)   The registrant's non-U.S. employees account for 5% or less of the registrant's total employees. In that circumstance, if the registrant chooses to exclude any non-U.S. employees under this exemption, it must exclude all non-U.S. employees. Additionally, if a registrant's non-U.S. employees exceed 5% of the registrant's total U.S. and non-U.S. employees, it may exclude up to 5% of its total employees who are non-U.S. employees; provided, however, if a registrant excludes any non-U.S. employees in a particular jurisdiction, it must exclude all non-U.S. employees in that jurisdiction. If more than 5% of a registrant's employees are located in any one non-U.S. jurisdiction, the registrant may not exclude any employees in that jurisdiction under this exemption.

(A)   In calculating the number of non-U.S. employees that may be excluded under this Item 402(u)(4)(ii) ("*de minimis*" exemption), a registrant shall count against the total any non-U.S. employee exempted under the data privacy law exemption under Item 402(u)(4)(i) ("data privacy" exemption). A registrant may exclude any non-U.S. employee from a jurisdiction that meets the data privacy exemption, even if the number of excluded employees exceeds 5% of the registrant's total employees. If, however, the number of employees excluded under the data privacy exemption equals or exceeds 5% of the registrant's total employees, the registrant may not use the *de minimis* exemption. Additionally, if the number of employees excluded under the data privacy exemption is less than 5% of the registrant's total employees, the registrant may use the *de minimis* exemption to exclude no more than the number of non-U.S. employees that, combined with the data privacy exemption, does not exceed 5% of the registrant's total employees.

(B)   If a registrant excludes non-U.S. employees under the *de minimis* exemption, it must disclose the jurisdiction or jurisdictions from which those employees are being excluded, the approximate number of employees excluded from each jurisdiction under the *de minimis* exemption, the total number of its U.S. and non-U.S. employees irrespective of any exemption (data privacy or *de minimis*), and the total number of its U.S. and non-U.S. employees used for its *de minimis* calculation.

Instruction 1 to Item 402(u)—Disclosing the date chosen for identifying the median employee. A registrant shall disclose the date within the last three months of its last completed fiscal year that it selected pursuant to paragraph (u)(3) of this Item to identify its median employee. If the registrant changes the date it uses to identify the median employee from the prior year, the registrant shall disclose this change and provide a brief explanation about the reason or reasons for the change.

Instruction 2 to Item 402(u)—Identifying the median employee. A registrant is required to identify its median employee only once every three years and calculate total compensation for that employee each year; *provided that,* during a registrant's last completed fiscal year there has been no change in its employee population or employee compensation arrangements that it reasonably believes would result in a significant change to its pay ratio disclosure. If there have been no changes that the registrant reasonably believes would significantly affect its pay ratio disclosure, the registrant shall disclose that it is using the same median employee in its pay ratio calculation and describe briefly the basis for its reasonable belief. For example, the registrant could disclose that there has been no change in its employee population or employee compensation arrangements that it believes would significantly impact the pay ratio disclosure. If there has been a change in the registrant's employee population or employee compensation arrangements that the registrant reasonably believes would result in a significant change in its pay ratio disclosure, the registrant shall re-identify the median employee for that fiscal year. If it is no longer appropriate for the registrant to use the median employee identified in year one as the median employee in years two or three because of a change in the original median employee's circumstances that the registrant reasonably believes would result in a significant change in its pay ratio disclosure, the registrant may use another employee whose compensation is substantially similar to the original median employee based on the compensation measure used to select the original median employee.

Instruction 3 to Item 402(u)—Updating for the last completed fiscal year. Pay ratio information (*i.e.,* the disclosure called for by paragraph (u)(1) of this Item) with respect to the registrant's last completed fiscal year is not required to be disclosed until the filing of its annual report on Form 10–K for that last completed fiscal year or, if later, the filing of a definitive proxy or information statement relating to its next annual meeting of shareholders (or written consents in lieu of such a meeting) following the end of such fiscal year; *provided that,* the required pay ratio information must, in any event, be filed as provided in General Instruction G(3) of Form 10–K (17 CFR 249.310) not later than 120 days after the end of such fiscal year.

Instruction 4 to Item 402(u)—Methodology and use of estimates. 1. Registrants may use reasonable estimates both in the methodology used to identify the median employee and in calculating the annual total compensation or any elements of total compensation for employees other than the PEO.

2.   In determining the employees from which the median employee is identified, a registrant may use its employee population or statistical sampling and/or other reasonable methods.

3.   A registrant may identify the median employee using annual total compensation or any other compensation measure that is consistently applied to all employees included in the calculation, such as information derived from the registrant's tax and/or payroll records. In using a compensation measure other than annual total compensation to identify the median employee, if that measure is recorded on a basis other than the registrant's fiscal year (such as information derived from tax and/or payroll records), the registrant may use the same annual period that is used to derive those amounts. Where a compensation measure other than annual total compensation is used to identify the median employee, the registrant must disclose the compensation measure used.

4.   In identifying the median employee, whether using annual total compensation or any other compensation measure that is consistently applied to all employees included in the calculation, the registrant may make cost-of-living adjustments to the compensation of employees in jurisdictions other than the jurisdiction in which the PEO resides so that the compensation is adjusted to the cost of living in the jurisdiction in which the PEO resides. If the registrant uses a cost-of-living adjustment to identify the median employee, and the median employee identified is an employee in a jurisdiction other than the jurisdiction in which the PEO resides, the registrant must use the same cost-of-living adjustment in calculating the median employee's annual total compensation and disclose the median employee's jurisdiction. The registrant also shall briefly describe the cost-of-living adjustments it used to identify the median employee and briefly describe the cost-of-living adjustments it used to calculate the median employee's annual total compensation, including the measure used as the basis for the cost-of-living adjustment. A registrant electing to present the pay ratio in this manner also shall disclose the median employee's annual total compensation and pay ratio without the cost-of-living adjustment. To calculate this pay ratio, the registrant will need to identify the median employee without using any cost-of-living adjustments.

5.   The registrant shall briefly describe the methodology it used to identify the median employee. It shall also briefly describe any material assumptions, adjustments (including any cost-of-living adjustments), or estimates it used to identify the median employee or to determine total compensation or any elements of total compensation, which shall be consistently applied. The registrant shall clearly identify any estimates used. The required descriptions should be a brief overview; it is not necessary for the registrant to provide technical analyses or formulas. If a registrant changes its methodology or its material assumptions, adjustments, or estimates from those used in its pay ratio disclosure for the prior fiscal year, and if the effects of any such change are significant, the registrant shall briefly describe the change and the reasons for the change. Registrants must also disclose if they changed from using the cost-of-living adjustment to not using that adjustment and if they changed from not using the cost-of-living adjustment to using it.

6.   Registrants may, at their discretion, include personal benefits that aggregate less than $10,000 and compensation under non-discriminatory benefit plans in calculating the annual total compensation of the median employee as long as these items are also included in calculating the PEO's annual total compensation. The registrant shall also explain any difference between the PEO's annual total compensation used in the pay ratio disclosure and the total compensation amounts reflected in the Summary Compensation Table, if material.

Instruction 5 to Item 402(u)—Permitted annualizing adjustments. A registrant may annualize the total compensation for all permanent employees (full-time or part-time) that were employed by the registrant for less than the full fiscal year (such as newly hired employees or permanent employees on an unpaid leave of absence during the period). A registrant may not annualize the total compensation for employees in temporary or seasonal positions. A registrant may not make a full-time equivalent adjustment for any employee.

Instruction 6 to Item 402(u)—PEO compensation not available. A registrant that is relying on Instruction 1 to Item 402(c)(2)(iii) and (iv) in connection with the salary or bonus of the PEO for the last completed fiscal year, shall disclose that the pay ratio required by paragraph (u) of this Item is not calculable until the PEO salary or bonus, as applicable, is determined and shall disclose the date that the PEO's actual total compensation is expected to be determined. The disclosure required by paragraph (u) of this Item shall then be disclosed in the filing under Item 5.02(f) of Form 8–K (17 CFR 249.308) that discloses the PEO's salary or bonus in accordance with Instruction 1 to Item 402(c)(2)(iii) and (iv).

Instruction 7 to Item 402(u)—Transition periods for registrants. 1. Upon becoming subject to the requirements of Section 13(a) or 15(d) of the Exchange Act (15 U.S.C. 78m or 78o(d)), a registrant shall comply with paragraph (u) of this Item with respect to compensation for the first fiscal year following the year in which it became subject to such requirements, but not for any fiscal year commencing before January 1, 2017. The registrant may omit the disclosure required by paragraph (u) of this Item from any filing until the filing of its annual report on Form 10–K (17 CFR 249.310) for such fiscal year or, if later, the filing of a proxy or information statement relating to its next annual meeting of shareholders (or written consents in lieu of such a meeting) following the end of such year; *provided that,* such disclosure shall, in any event, be filed as provided in General Instruction G(3) of Form 10–K not later than 120 days after the end of such fiscal year.

2. A registrant may omit any employees that became its employees as the result of the business combination or acquisition of a business for the fiscal year in which the transaction becomes effective, but the registrant must disclose the approximate number of employees it is omitting. Those employees shall be included in the total employee count for the triennial calculations of the median employee in the year following the transaction for purposes of evaluating whether a significant change had occurred. The registrant shall identify the acquired business excluded for the fiscal year in which the business combination or acquisition becomes effective.

3. A registrant shall comply with paragraph (u) of this Item with respect to compensation for the first fiscal year commencing on or after the date the registrant ceases to be a smaller reporting company, but not for any fiscal year commencing before January 1, 2017.

Instruction 8 to Item 402(u)—Emerging growth companies. A registrant is not required to comply with paragraph (u) of this Item if it is an emerging growth company as defined in Section 2(a)(19) of the Securities Act (15 U.S.C. 77b(a)(19)) or Section 3(a)(80) of the Exchange Act (15 U.S.C. 78c(a)(80)). A registrant shall comply with paragraph (u) of this Item with respect to compensation for the first fiscal year commencing on or after the date the registrant ceases to be an emerging growth company, but not for any fiscal year commencing before January 1, 2017.

Instruction 9 to Item 402(u)—Additional information. Registrants may present additional information, including additional ratios, to supplement the required ratio, but are not required to do so. Any additional information shall be clearly identified, not misleading, and not presented with greater prominence than the required ratio.

Instruction 10 to Item 402(u)—Multiple PEOs during the year. A registrant with more than one non-concurrent PEO serving during its fiscal year may calculate the annual total compensation for its PEO in either of the following manners:

1. The registrant may calculate the compensation provided to each person who served as PEO during the year for the time he or she served as PEO and combine those figures; or

2. The registrant may look to the PEO serving in that position on the date it selects to identify the median employee and annualize that PEO's compensation.

Regardless of the alternative selected, the registrant shall disclose which option it chose and how it calculated its PEO's annual total compensation.

Instruction 11 to Item 402(u)—Employees' personally identifiable information. Registrants are not required to, and should not, disclose any personally identifiable information about that employee other than his or her compensation. Registrants may choose to generally identify an employee's position to put the employee's compensation in context, but registrants are not required to provide this information and should not do so if providing the information could identify any specific individual.

Instruction to Item 402. Specify the applicable fiscal year in the title to each table required under this Item which calls for disclosure as of or for a completed fiscal year.

(w)   *Disclosure of a registrant's action to recover erroneously awarded compensation.*

(1)   If at any time during or after the last completed fiscal year the registrant was required to prepare an accounting restatement that required recovery of erroneously awarded compensation pursuant to the registrant's compensation recovery policy required by the listing standards adopted pursuant to 17 CFR 240.10D–1, or there was an outstanding balance as of the end of the last completed fiscal year of erroneously awarded compensation to be recovered from the application of the policy to a prior restatement, the registrant must provide the following information:

(i)   For each restatement:

(A)   The date on which the registrant was required to prepare an accounting restatement;

(B)   The aggregate dollar amount of erroneously awarded compensation attributable to such accounting restatement, including an analysis of how the amount was calculated;

(C)   the financial reporting measure as defined in 17 CFR 240.10D–1(d) related to a stock price or total shareholder return metric, the estimates that were used in determining the erroneously awarded compensation attributable to such accounting restatement and an explanation of the methodology used for such estimates;

(D)   The aggregate dollar amount of erroneously awarded compensation that remains outstanding at the end of the last completed fiscal year; and

(E)   If the aggregate dollar amount of erroneously awarded compensation has not yet been determined, disclose this fact, explain the reason(s) and disclose the information required in (B) through (D) in the next filing that is required to include disclosure pursuant to Item 402 of Regulation S–K;

(i)   If recovery would be impracticable pursuant to 17 CFR 240.10D–1(b)(1)(iv), for each current and former named executive officer and for all other current and former executive officers as a group, disclose the amount of recovery forgone and a brief description of the reason the listed registrant decided in each case not to pursue recovery; and

(ii)   For each current and former named executive officer from whom, as of the end of the last completed fiscal year, erroneously awarded compensation had been outstanding for 180 days or longer since the date the registrant determined the amount the individual owed, disclose the dollar amount of outstanding erroneously awarded compensation due from each such individual.

(2)   If at any time during or after its last completed fiscal year the registrant was required to prepare an accounting restatement, and the registrant concluded that recovery of erroneously awarded compensation was not required pursuant to the registrant's compensation recovery policy required by the listing standards adopted pursuant to 17 CFR 240.10D–1, briefly explain why application of the recovery policy resulted in this conclusion.

(3)   The information must appear with, and in the same format as, the rest of the disclosure required to be provided pursuant to this Item 402. The information is required only in proxy or information statements that call for Item 402 disclosure and the registrant's annual report on Form 10–K, and will not be deemed to be incorporated by reference into any filing under the Securities Act, except to the extent that the listed registrant specifically incorporates it by reference.

(4)   The disclosure must be provided in an Interactive Data File in accordance with Rule 405 of Regulation S–T and the EDGAR Filer Manual.

Item 403.   Security Ownership of Certain Beneficial Owners and Management

(a)   *Security Ownership of Certain Beneficial Owners.* Furnish the following information, as of the most recent practicable date, in substantially the tabular form indicated, with respect to any person (including any "group" as that term is used in section 13(d)(3) of the Exchange Act) who is known to the registrant to be the beneficial owner of more than five percent of any class of the registrant's voting securities. The address given in column (2) may be a business, mailing, or residence. Show in column (3) the total number of shares beneficially owned and in column (4) the percentage of class so owned. Of the number of shares shown in column (3), indicate by footnote or otherwise the amount known to be shares with respect to which such listed beneficial owner has the right to acquire beneficial ownership, as specified in Rule 13d–3(d)(1) under the Exchange Act.

(1) Title of Class	(2) Name and address of beneficial owner	(3) Amount and nature of beneficial ownership	(4) Percent of class

(b) *Security Ownership of Management.* Furnish the following information, as of the most recent practicable date, in substantially the tabular form indicated, as to each class of equity securities of the registrant or any of its parents or subsidiaries, including directors' qualifying shares, beneficially owned by all directors and nominees, naming them, each of the named executive officers as defined in Item 402(a)(3), and directors and executive officers of the registrant as a group, without naming them. Show in column (3) the total number of shares beneficially owned and in column (4) the percent of the class so owned. Of the number of shares shown in column (3), indicate, by footnote or otherwise, the amount of shares that are pledged as securities and the amount of shares with respect to which such persons have the right to acquire beneficial ownership as specified in Rule 13d–3(d)(1) under the Exchange Act.

(1) Title of Class	(2) Name of beneficial owner	(3) Amount and nature of beneficial ownership	(4) Percent of class

(c) *Changes in Control.* Describe any arrangements, known to the registrant, including any pledge by any person of securities of the registrant or any of its parents, the operation of which may at a subsequent date result in a change in control of the registrant.

Instructions to Item 403. 1. The percentages are to be calculated on the basis of the amount of outstanding securities, excluding securities held by or for the account of the registrant or its subsidiaries, plus securities deemed outstanding pursuant to Rule 13d–3(d)(1) under the Exchange Act. For purposes of paragraph (b), if the percentage of shares beneficially owned by any director or nominee, or by all directors and officers of the registrant as a group, does not exceed one percent of the class so owned, the registrant may, in lieu of furnishing a precise percentage, indicate this fact by means of an asterisk and explanatory footnote or other similar means.

2. For the purposes of this Item, beneficial ownership shall be determined in accordance with Rule 13d–3 under the Exchange Act. Include such additional subcolumns or other appropriate explanation of column (3) necessary to reflect amounts as to which the beneficial owner has (A) sole voting power, (B) shared voting power, (C) sole investment power, or (D) shared investment power.

3. The registrant shall be deemed to know the contents of any statements filed with the Commission pursuant to section 13(d) or 13(g) of the Exchange Act. When applicable, a registrant may rely upon information set forth in such statements unless the registrant knows or has reason to believe that such information is not complete or accurate or that a statement or amendment should have been filed and was not.

4. For purposes of furnishing information pursuant to paragraph (a) of this Item, the registrant may indicate the source and date of such information.

5. Where more than one beneficial owner is known to be listed for the same securities, appropriate disclosure should be made to avoid confusion. For purposes of paragraph (b), in computing the aggregate number of shares owned by directors and officers of the registrant as a group, the same shares shall not be counted more than once.

6. Paragraph (c) of this Item does not require a description of ordinary default provisions contained in the charter, trust indentures or other governing instruments relating to securities of the registrant.

7.   Where the holder(s) of voting securities reported pursuant to paragraph (a) hold more than five percent of any class of voting securities of the registrant pursuant to any voting trust or similar agreement, state the title of such securities, the amount held or to be held pursuant to the trust or agreement (if not clear from the table) and the duration of the agreement. Give the names and addresses of the voting trustees and outline briefly their voting rights and other powers under the trust or agreement.

Item 404.   Transactions With Related Persons, Promoters and Certain Control Persons

(a)   *Transactions with related persons.* Describe any transaction, since the beginning of the registrant's last fiscal year, or any currently proposed transaction, in which the registrant was or is to be a participant and the amount involved exceeds $120,000, and in which any related person had or will have a direct or indirect material interest. Disclose the following information regarding the transaction:

(1)   The name of the related person and the basis on which the person is a related person.

(2)   The related person's interest in the transaction with the registrant, including the related person's position(s) or relationship(s) with, or ownership in, a firm, corporation, or other entity that is a party to, or has an interest in, the transaction.

(3)   The approximate dollar value of the amount involved in the transaction.

(4)   The approximate dollar value of the amount of the related person's interest in the transaction, which shall be computed without regard to the amount of profit or loss.

(5)   In the case of indebtedness, disclosure of the amount involved in the transaction shall include the largest aggregate amount of principal outstanding during the period for which disclosure is provided, the amount thereof outstanding as of the latest practicable date, the amount of principal paid during the periods for which disclosure is provided, the amount of interest paid during the period for which disclosure is provided, and the rate or amount of interest payable on the indebtedness.

(6)   Any other information regarding the transaction or the related person in the context of the transaction that is material to investors in light of the circumstances of the particular transaction.

Instructions to Item 404(a).

1.   For the purposes of paragraph (a) of this Item, the term related person means:

a.   Any person who was in any of the following categories at any time during the specified period for which disclosure under paragraph (a) of this Item is required:

i.   Any director or executive officer of the registrant;

ii.   Any nominee for director, when the information called for by paragraph (a) of this Item is being presented in a proxy or information statement relating to the election of that nominee for director; or

iii.   Any immediate family member of a director or executive officer of the registrant, or of any nominee for director when the information called for by paragraph (a) of this Item is being presented in a proxy or information statement relating to the election of that nominee for director, which means any child, stepchild, parent, stepparent, spouse, sibling, mother-in-law, father-in-law, son-in-law, daughter-in-law, brother-in-law, or sister-in-law of such director, executive officer or nominee for director, and any person (other than a tenant or employee) sharing the household of such director, executive officer or nominee for director; and

b.   Any person who was in any of the following categories when a transaction in which such person had a direct or indirect material interest occurred or existed:

i.   A security holder covered by Item 403(a); or

ii.   Any immediate family member of any such security holder, which means any child, stepchild, parent, stepparent, spouse, sibling, mother-in-law, father-in-law, son-in-law, daughter-in-law, brother-in-law, or sister-in-law of such security holder, and any person (other than a tenant or employee) sharing the household of such security holder.

2.   For purposes of paragraph (a) of this Item, a transaction includes, but is not limited to, any financial transaction, arrangement or relationship (including any indebtedness or guarantee of indebtedness) or any series of similar transactions, arrangements or relationships.

3.   The amount involved in the transaction shall be computed by determining the dollar value of the amount involved in the transaction in question, which shall include:

a.   In the case of any lease or other transaction providing for periodic payments or installments, the aggregate amount of all periodic payments or installments due on or after the beginning of the registrant's last fiscal year, including any required or optional payments due during or at the conclusion of the lease or other transaction providing for periodic payments or installments; and

b.   In the case of indebtedness, the largest aggregate amount of all indebtedness outstanding at any time since the beginning of the registrant's last fiscal year and all amounts of interest payable on it during the last fiscal year.

4.   In the case of a transaction involving indebtedness:

a.   The following items of indebtedness may be excluded from the calculation of the amount of indebtedness and need not be disclosed: amounts due from the related person for purchases of goods and services subject to usual trade terms, for ordinary business travel and expense payments and for other transactions in the ordinary course of business;

b.   Disclosure need not be provided of any indebtedness transaction for the related persons specified in Instruction 1.b. to paragraph (a) of this Item; and

c.   If the lender is a bank, savings and loan association, or broker-dealer extending credit under Federal Reserve Regulation T (12 CFR part 220) and the loans are not disclosed as nonaccrual, past due, restructured or potential problems (see Item III.C.1. and 2. of Industry Guide 3, Statistical Disclosure by Bank Holding Companies (17 CFR 229.802(c))), disclosure under paragraph (a) of this Item may consist of a statement, if such is the case, that the loans to such persons:

i.   Were made in the ordinary course of business;

ii.   Were made on substantially the same terms, including interest rates and collateral, as those prevailing at the time for comparable loans with persons not related to the lender; and

iii.   Did not involve more than the normal risk of collectibility or present other unfavorable features.

5.a.   Disclosure of an employment relationship or transaction involving an executive officer and any related compensation solely resulting from that employment relationship or transaction need not be provided pursuant to paragraph (a) of this Item if:

i.   The compensation arising from the relationship or transaction is reported pursuant to Item 402; or

ii.   The executive officer is not an immediate family member (as specified in Instruction 1 to paragraph (a) of this Item) and such compensation would have been reported under Item 402 as compensation earned for services to the registrant if the executive officer was a named executive officer as that term is defined in Item 402(a)(3), and such compensation had been approved, or recommended to the board of directors of the registrant for approval, by the compensation committee of the board of directors (or group of independent directors performing a similar function) of the registrant.

iii.   The transaction involves the recovery of erroneously awarded compensation computed as provided in 17 CFR 240.10D–1(b)(1)(iii) and the applicable listing standards for the registrant's securities, that is disclosed pursuant to Item 402(w) (§ 229.402(w)).

b.   Disclosure of compensation to a director need not be provided pursuant to paragraph (a) of this Item if the compensation is reported pursuant to Item 402(k).

6.   A person who has a position or relationship with a firm, corporation, or other entity that engages in a transaction with the registrant shall not be deemed to have an indirect material interest within the meaning of paragraph (a) of this Item where:

a.   The interest arises only:

i.   From such person's position as a director of another corporation or organization that is a party to the transaction; or

ii.   From the direct or indirect ownership by such person and all other persons specified in Instruction 1 to paragraph (a) of this Item, in the aggregate, of less than a ten percent equity interest in another person (other than a partnership) which is a party to the transaction; or

iii.   From both such position and ownership; or

b.   The interest arises only from such person's position as a limited partner in a partnership in which the person and all other persons specified in Instruction 1 to paragraph (a) of this Item, have an interest of less than ten percent, and the person is not a general partner of and does not hold another position in the partnership.

7.   Disclosure need not be provided pursuant to paragraph (a) of this Item if:

a.   The transaction is one where the rates or charges involved in the transaction are determined by competitive bids, or the transaction involves the rendering of services as a common or contract carrier, or public utility, at rates or charges fixed in conformity with law or governmental authority;

b.   The transaction involves services as a bank depositary of funds, transfer agent, registrar, trustee under a trust indenture, or similar services; or

c.   The interest of the related person arises solely from the ownership of a class of equity securities of the registrant and all holders of that class of equity securities of the registrant received the same benefit on a pro rata basis.

(b)   *Review, approval or ratification of transactions with related persons.*

(1)   Describe the registrant's policies and procedures for the review, approval, or ratification of any transaction required to be reported under paragraph (a) of this Item. While the material features of such policies and procedures will vary depending on the particular circumstances, examples of such features may include, in given cases, among other things:

(i)   The types of transactions that are covered by such policies and procedures;

(ii)   The standards to be applied pursuant to such policies and procedures;

(iii)   The persons or groups of persons on the board of directors or otherwise who are responsible for applying such policies and procedures; and

(iv)   A statement of whether such policies and procedures are in writing and, if not, how such policies and procedures are evidenced.

(2)   Identify any transaction required to be reported under paragraph (a) of this Item since the beginning of the registrant's last fiscal year where such policies and procedures did not require review, approval or ratification or where such policies and procedures were not followed.

Instruction to Item 404(b).

Disclosure need not be provided pursuant to this paragraph regarding any transaction that occurred at a time before the related person became one of the enumerated persons in Instruction 1.a.i., ii., or iii. to Item 404(a) if such transaction did not continue after the related person became one of the enumerated persons in Instruction 1.a.i., ii., or iii. to Item 404(a).

(c)   *Promoters and certain control persons.*

(1)   Registrants that are filing a registration statement on Form S-1 under the Securities Act or on Form 10 under the Exchange Act and that had a promoter at any time during the past five fiscal years shall:

(i)   State the names of the promoter(s), the nature and amount of anything of value (including money, property, contracts, options or rights of any kind) received or to be received by each promoter, directly or indirectly, from the registrant and the nature and amount of any assets, services or other consideration therefore received or to be received by the registrant; and

(ii)   As to any assets acquired or to be acquired by the registrant from a promoter, state the amount at which the assets were acquired or are to be acquired and the principle followed or to be followed in determining such amount, and identify the persons making the determination and their relationship, if any, with the registrant or any promoter. If the assets were acquired by the promoter within two years prior to their transfer to the registrant, also state the cost thereof to the promoter.

(2)   Registrants shall provide the disclosure required by paragraphs (c)(1)(i) and (c)(1)(ii) of this Item as to any person who acquired control of a registrant that is a shell company, or any person that

is part of a group, consisting of two or more persons that agree to act together for the purpose of acquiring, holding, voting or disposing of equity securities of a registrant, that acquired control of a registrant that is a shell company. For purposes of this Item, shell company has the same meaning as in Rule 405 under the Securities Act and Rule 12b–2 under the Exchange Act.

(d)   *Smaller reporting companies.* A registrant that qualifies as a "smaller reporting company," as defined by Item 10(f)(1), must provide the following information in order to comply with this Item:

(1)   The information required by paragraph (a) of this Item for the period specified there for a transaction in which the amount involved exceeds the lesser of $120,000 or one percent of the average of the smaller reporting company's total assets at year end for the last two completed fiscal years;

(2)   The information required by paragraph (c) of this Item; and

(3)   A list of all parents of the smaller reporting company showing the basis of control and as to each parent, the percentage of voting securities owned or other basis of control by its immediate parent, if any.

Instruction to Item 404(d).

1.   Include information for any material underwriting discounts and commissions upon the sale of securities by the smaller reporting company where any of the persons specified in paragraph (a) of this Item was or is to be a principal underwriter or is a controlling person or member of a firm that was or is to be a principal underwriter.

2.   For smaller reporting companies information shall be given for the period specified in paragraph (a) of this Item and, in addition, for the fiscal year preceding the small reporting company's last fiscal year.

Instructions to Item 404.

1.   If the information called for by this Item is being presented in a registration statement filed pursuant to the Securities Act or the Exchange Act, information shall be given for the periods specified in the Item and, in addition, for the two fiscal years preceding the registrant's last fiscal year, unless the information is being incorporated by reference into a registration statement on Form S–4, in which case, information shall be given for the periods specified in the Item.

2.   A foreign private issuer will be deemed to comply with this Item if it provides the information required by Item 7.B. of Form 20–F with more detailed information provided if otherwise made publicly available or required to be disclosed by the issuer's home jurisdiction or a market in which its securities are listed or traded.

Item 405.   Compliance With Section 16(a) of the Exchange Act

(a)   *Reporting obligation.* Every registrant having a class of equity securities registered pursuant to Section 12 of the Exchange Act (15 U.S.C. 78*l*) and every closed-end investment company registered under the Investment Company Act of 1940 (15 U.S.C. 80a–1 et seq.) must:

(1)   Under the caption "Delinquent Section 16(a) Reports," identify each person who, at any time during the fiscal year, was a director, officer, beneficial owner of more than ten percent of any class of equity securities of the registrant registered pursuant to Section 12 of the Exchange Act, or any other person subject to Section 16 of the Exchange Act with respect to the registrant because of the requirements of Section 30 of the Investment Company Act ("reporting person") that failed to file on a timely basis reports required by Section 16(a) of the Exchange Act during the most recent fiscal year or prior fiscal years.

(2)   For each such person, set forth the number of late reports, the number of transactions that were not reported on a timely basis, and any known failure to file a required form. A known failure to file would include, but not be limited to, a failure to file a Form 3, which is required of all reporting persons, and a failure to file a Form 5 in the absence of the written representation referred to in paragraph (b)(3) of this item, unless the registrant otherwise knows that no Form 5 is required.

Instruction 1 to paragraph (a) of Item 405. If no disclosure is required, registrants are encouraged to exclude the caption "Delinquent Section 16(a) Reports."

Instruction 2 to paragraph (a) of Item 405. The registrant is only required to disclose a failure to file timely once. For example, if in the most recently concluded fiscal year a reporting person filed a Form 4 disclosing a transaction that took place in the prior fiscal year, and should have been reported in that year, the registrant should disclose that late filing and transaction pursuant to this Item 405 with respect to the most recently concluded fiscal year, but not in material filed with respect to subsequent years.

(b) *Scope of the Inquiry.* In determining whether disclosure is required pursuant to paragraph (a) of this item, the registrant may rely only on the following:

(1) A review of Forms 3 and 4 and amendments thereto filed electronically with the Commission during the registrant's most recent fiscal year;

(2) A review of Forms 5 and amendments thereto filed electronically with the Commission with respect to the registrant's most recent fiscal year; and (3) Any written representation from the reporting person that no Form 5 is required. The registrant must maintain the representation in its records for two years, making a copy available to the Commission or its staff upon request.

Item 406.   Code of Ethics

(a) Disclose whether the registrant has adopted a code of ethics that applies to the registrant's principal executive officer, principal financial officer, principal accounting officer or controller, or persons performing similar functions. If the registrant has not adopted such a code of ethics, explain why it has not done so.

(b) For purposes of this Item 406, the term code of ethics means written standards that are reasonably designed to deter wrongdoing and to promote:

(1) Honest and ethical conduct, including the ethical handling of actual or apparent conflicts of interest between personal and professional relationships;

(2) Full, fair, accurate, timely, and understandable disclosure in reports and documents that a registrant files with, or submits to, the Commission and in other public communications made by the registrant;

(3) Compliance with applicable governmental laws, rules and regulations;

(4) The prompt internal reporting of violations of the code to an appropriate person or persons identified in the code; and

(5) Accountability for adherence to the code.

(c) The registrant must:

(1) File with the Commission a copy of its code of ethics that applies to the registrant's principal executive officer, principal financial officer, principal accounting officer or controller, or persons performing similar functions, as an exhibit to its annual report;

(2) Post the text of such code of ethics on its Internet website and disclose, in its annual report, its Internet address and the fact that it has posted such code of ethics on its Internet Web site; or

(3) Undertake in its annual report filed with the Commission to provide to any person without charge, upon request, a copy of such code of ethics and explain the manner in which such request may be made.

(d) If the registrant intends to satisfy the disclosure requirement under Item 5.05 of Form 8–K regarding an amendment to, or a waiver from, a provision of its code of ethics that applies to the registrant's principal executive officer, principal financial officer, principal accounting officer or controller, or persons performing similar functions and that relates to any element of the code of ethics definition enumerated in paragraph (b) of this Item by posting such information on its Internet website, disclose the registrant's Internet address and such intention.

Instructions to Item 406. 1. A registrant may have separate codes of ethics for different types of officers. Furthermore, a code of ethics within the meaning of paragraph (b) of this Item may be a portion of a broader document that addresses additional topics or that applies to more persons than those specified in paragraph (a). In satisfying the requirements of paragraph (c), a registrant need only file, post or provide the portions of a broader document that constitutes a code of ethics as defined in paragraph (b) and that apply to the persons specified in paragraph (a).

2. If a registrant elects to satisfy paragraph (c) of this Item by posting its code of ethics on its website pursuant to paragraph (c)(2), the code of ethics must remain accessible on its Web site for as long as the registrant remains subject to the requirements of this Item and chooses to comply with this Item by posting its code on its Web site pursuant to paragraph (c)(2).

Item 407.   **Corporate Governance**

(a)   *Director independence.* Identify each director and, when the disclosure called for by this paragraph is being presented in a proxy or information statement relating to the election of directors, each nominee for director, that is independent under the independence standards applicable to the registrant under paragraph (a)(1) of this Item. In addition, if such independence standards contain independence requirements for committees of the board of directors, identify each director that is a member of the compensation, nominating or audit committee that is not independent under such committee independence standards. If the registrant does not have a separately designated audit, nominating or compensation committee or committee performing similar functions, the registrant must provide the disclosure of directors that are not independent with respect to all members of the board of directors applying such committee independence standards.

(1)   In determining whether or not the director or nominee for director is independent for the purposes of paragraph (a) of this Item, the registrant shall use the applicable definition of independence, as follows:

(i)   If the registrant is a listed issuer whose securities are listed on a national securities exchange or in an inter-dealer quotation system which has requirements that a majority of the board of directors be independent, the registrant's definition of independence that it uses for determining if a majority of the board of directors is independent in compliance with the listing standards applicable to the registrant. When determining whether the members of a committee of the board of directors are independent, the registrant's definition of independence that it uses for determining if the members of that specific committee are independent in compliance with the independence standards applicable for the members of the specific committee in the listing standards of the national securities exchange or inter-dealer quotation system that the registrant uses for determining if a majority of the board of directors are independent. If the registrant does not have independence standards for a committee, the independence standards for that specific committee in the listing standards of the national securities exchange or inter-dealer quotation system that the registrant uses for determining if a majority of the board of directors are independent.

(ii)   If the registrant is not a listed issuer, a definition of independence of a national securities exchange or of an inter-dealer quotation system which has requirements that a majority of the board of directors be independent, and state which definition is used. Whatever such definition the registrant chooses, it must use the same definition with respect to all directors and nominees for director. When determining whether the members of a specific committee of the board of directors are independent, if the national securities exchange or national securities association whose standards are used has independence standards for the members of a specific committee, use those committee specific standards.

(iii)   If the information called for by paragraph (a) of this Item is being presented in a registration statement on Form S–1 under the Securities Act or on a Form 10 under the Exchange Act where the registrant has applied for listing with a national securities exchange or in an inter-dealer quotation system that has requirements that a majority of the board of directors be independent, the definition of independence that the registrant uses for determining if a majority of the board of directors is independent, and the definition of independence that the registrant uses for determining if members of the specific committee of the board of directors are independent, that is in compliance with the independence listing standards of the national securities exchange or inter-dealer quotation system on which it has applied for listing, or if the registrant has not adopted such definitions, the independence standards for determining if the majority of the board of directors is independent and if members of the committee of the board of directors are independent of that national securities exchange or inter-dealer quotation system.

(2)   If the registrant uses its own definitions for determining whether its directors and nominees for director, and members of specific committees of the board of directors, are independent, disclose whether these definitions are available to security holders on the registrant's Web site. If so, provide the registrant's Web site address. If not, include a copy of these policies in an appendix to the registrant's proxy statement or information statement that is provided to security holders at least once every three fiscal years or if the policies have been materially amended since the beginning of the registrant's last fiscal year. If a current copy of the policies is not available to security holders on the registrant's Web site, and is not included as an appendix to the registrant's proxy statement or information statement, identify the most recent fiscal year in which the policies were so included in satisfaction of this requirement.

(3)   For each director and nominee for director that is identified as independent, describe, by specific category or type, any transactions, relationships or arrangements not disclosed pursuant to Item 404(a), or for investment companies, Item 22(b) of Schedule 14A, that were considered by the board of directors under the applicable independence definitions in determining that the director is independent.

Instructions to Item 407(a).

1.   If the registrant is a listed issuer whose securities are listed on a national securities exchange or in an inter-dealer quotation system which has requirements that a majority of the board of directors be independent, and also has exemptions to those requirements (for independence of a majority of the board of directors or committee member independence) upon which the registrant relied, disclose the exemption relied upon and explain the basis for the registrant's conclusion that such exemption is applicable. The same disclosure should be provided if the registrant is not a listed issuer and the national securities exchange or inter-dealer quotation system selected by the registrant has exemptions that are applicable to the registrant. Any national securities exchange or inter-dealer quotation system which has requirements that at least 50 percent of the members of a small business issuer's board of directors must be independent shall be considered a national securities exchange or inter-dealer quotation system which has requirements that a majority of the board of directors be independent for the purposes of the disclosure required by paragraph (a) of this Item.

2.   Registrants shall provide the disclosure required by paragraph (a) of this Item for any person who served as a director during any part of the last completed fiscal year, except that no information called for by paragraph (a) of this Item need be given in a registration statement filed at a time when the registrant is not subject to the reporting requirements of section 13(a) or 15(d) of the Exchange Act respecting any director who is no longer a director at the time of effectiveness of the registration statement.

3.   The description of the specific categories or types of transactions, relationships or arrangements required by paragraph (a)(3) of this Item must be provided in such detail as is necessary to fully describe the nature of the transactions, relationships or arrangements.

(b)   *Board meetings and committees; annual meeting attendance.*

(1)   State the total number of meetings of the board of directors (including regularly scheduled and special meetings) which were held during the last full fiscal year. Name each incumbent director who during the last full fiscal year attended fewer than 75 percent of the aggregate of:

(i)   The total number of meetings of the board of directors (held during the period for which he has been a director); and

(ii)   The total number of meetings held by all committees of the board on which he served (during the periods that he served).

(2)   Describe the registrant's policy, if any, with regard to board members' attendance at annual meetings of security holders and state the number of board members who attended the prior year's annual meeting.

Instruction to Item 407(b)(2).

In lieu of providing the information required by paragraph (b)(2) of this Item in the proxy statement, the registrant may instead provide the registrant's Web site address where such information appears.

(3)   State whether or not the registrant has standing audit, nominating and compensation committees of the board of directors, or committees performing similar functions. If the registrant has such committees, however designated, identify each committee member, state the number of

committee meetings held by each such committee during the last fiscal year and describe briefly the functions performed by each such committee. Such disclosure need not be provided to the extent it is duplicative of disclosure provided in accordance with paragraph (c), (d) or (e) of this Item.

(c)   *Nominating committee.* (1) If the registrant does not have a standing nominating committee or committee performing similar functions, state the basis for the view of the board of directors that it is appropriate for the registrant not to have such a committee and identify each director who participates in the consideration of director nominees.

(2)   Provide the following information regarding the registrant's director nomination process:

(i)   State whether or not the nominating committee has a charter. If the nominating committee has a charter, provide the disclosure required by Instruction 2 to this Item regarding the nominating committee charter;

(ii)   If the nominating committee has a policy with regard to the consideration of any director candidates recommended by security holders, provide a description of the material elements of that policy, which shall include, but need not be limited to, a statement as to whether the committee will consider director candidates recommended by security holders;

(iii)   If the nominating committee does not have a policy with regard to the consideration of any director candidates recommended by security holders, state that fact and state the basis for the view of the board of directors that it is appropriate for the registrant not to have such a policy;

(iv)   If the nominating committee will consider candidates recommended by security holders, describe the procedures to be followed by security holders in submitting such recommendations;

(v)   Describe any specific minimum qualifications that the nominating committee believes must be met by a nominating committee-recommended nominee for a position on the registrant's board of directors, and describe any specific qualities or skills that the nominating committee believes are necessary for one or more of the registrant's directors to possess;

(vi)   Describe the nominating committee's process for identifying and evaluating nominees for director, including nominees recommended by security holders, and any differences in the manner in which the nominating committee evaluates nominees for director based on whether the nominee is recommended by a security holder, and whether, and if so how, the nominating committee (or the board) considers diversity in identifying nominees for director. If the nominating committee (or the board) has a policy with regard to the consideration of diversity in identifying director nominees, describe how this policy is implemented, as well as how the nominating committee (or the board) assesses the effectiveness of its policy;

(vii)   With regard to each nominee approved by the nominating committee for inclusion on the registrant's proxy card (other than nominees who are executive officers or who are directors standing for re-election), state which one or more of the following categories of persons or entities recommended that nominee: security holder, non-management director, chief executive officer, other executive officer, third-party search firm, or other specified source. With regard to each such nominee approved by a nominating committee of an investment company, state which one or more of the following additional categories of persons or entities recommended that nominee: security holder, director, chief executive officer, other executive officer, or employee of the investment company's investment adviser, principal underwriter, or any affiliated person of the investment adviser or principal underwriter;

(viii)   If the registrant pays a fee to any third party or parties to identify or evaluate or assist in identifying or evaluating potential nominees, disclose the function performed by each such third party; and

(ix)   If the registrant's nominating committee received, by a date not later than the 120th calendar day before the date of the registrant's proxy statement released to security holders in connection with the previous year's annual meeting, a recommended nominee from a security holder that beneficially owned more than 5% of the registrant's voting common stock for at least one year as of the date the recommendation was made, or from a group of security holders that beneficially owned, in the aggregate, more than 5% of the registrant's voting common stock, with each of the securities used to calculate that ownership held for at least one year as of the date the recommendation was made, identify the candidate and the security holder or security holder group that recommended the candidate and disclose whether the nominating committee chose to nominate the candidate, provided, however, that no such identification or disclosure is required without the written consent of both the security holder or security holder group and the candidate to be so identified.

Instructions to Item 407(c)(2)(ix).

1.   For purposes of paragraph (c)(2)(ix) of this Item, the percentage of securities held by a nominating security holder may be determined using information set forth in the registrant's most recent quarterly or annual report, and any current report subsequent thereto, filed with the Commission pursuant to the Exchange Act (or), in the case of a registrant that is an investment company registered under the Investment Company Act of 1940, the registrant's most recent report on Form N–CSR, unless the party relying on such report knows or has reason to believe that the information contained therein is inaccurate.

2.   For purposes of the registrant's obligation to provide the disclosure specified in paragraph (c)(2)(ix) of this Item, where the date of the annual meeting has been changed by more than 30 days from the date of the previous year's meeting, the obligation under that Item will arise where the registrant receives the security holder recommendation a reasonable time before the registrant begins to print and mail its proxy materials.

3.   For purposes of paragraph (c)(2)(ix) of this Item, the percentage of securities held by a recommending security holder, as well as the holding period of those securities, may be determined by the registrant if the security holder is the registered holder of the securities. If the security holder is not the registered owner of the securities, he or she can submit one of the following to the registrant to evidence the required ownership percentage and holding period:

a.   A written statement from the "record" holder of the securities (usually a broker or bank) verifying that, at the time the security holder made the recommendation, he or she had held the required securities for at least one year; or

b.   If the security holder has filed a Schedule 13D, Schedule 13G, Form 3, Form 4, and/or Form 5, or amendments to those documents or updated forms, reflecting ownership of the securities as of or before the date of the recommendation, a copy of the schedule and/or form, and any subsequent amendments reporting a change in ownership level, as well as a written statement that the security holder continuously held the securities for the one-year period as of the date of the recommendation.

4.   For purposes of the registrant's obligation to provide the disclosure specified in paragraph (c)(2)(ix) of this Item, the security holder or group must have provided to the registrant, at the time of the recommendation, the written consent of all parties to be identified and, where the security holder or group members are not registered holders, proof that the security holder or group satisfied the required ownership percentage and holding period as of the date of the recommendation.

Instruction to Item 407(c)(2).

For purposes of paragraph (c)(2) of this Item, the term nominating committee refers not only to nominating committees and committees performing similar functions, but also to groups of directors fulfilling the role of a nominating committee, including the entire board of directors.

(3)   Describe any material changes to the procedures by which security holders may recommend nominees to the registrant's board of directors, where those changes were implemented after the registrant last provided disclosure in response to the requirements of paragraph (c)(2)(iv) of this Item, or paragraph (c)(3) of this Item.

Instructions to Item 407(c)(3).

1.   The disclosure required in paragraph (c)(3) of this Item need only be provided in a registrant's quarterly or annual reports.

2.   For purposes of paragraph (c)(3) of this Item, adoption of procedures by which security holders may recommend nominees to the registrant's board of directors, where the registrant's most recent disclosure in response to the requirements of paragraph (c)(2)(iv) of this Item, or paragraph (c)(3) of this Item, indicated that the registrant did not have in place such procedures, will constitute a material change.

(d)   *Audit committee.*

(1)   State whether or not the audit committee has a charter. If the audit committee has a charter, provide the disclosure required by Instruction 2 to this Item regarding the audit committee charter.

(2)   If a listed issuer's board of directors determines, in accordance with the listing standards applicable to the issuer, to appoint a director to the audit committee who is not independent (apart from the requirements in Rule 10A–3) including as a result of exceptional or limited or similar circumstances, disclose the nature of the relationship that makes that individual not independent and the reasons for the board of directors' determination.

(3)(i)   The audit committee must state whether:

(A)   The audit committee has reviewed and discussed the audited financial statements with management;

(B)   The audit committee has discussed with the independent auditors the matters required to be discussed by the applicable requirements of the Public Company Accounting Oversight Board ("PCAOB") and the Commission;

(C)   The audit committee has received the written disclosures and the letter from the independent accountant required by applicable requirements of the Public Company Accounting Oversight Board regarding the independent accountant's communications with the audit committee concerning independence, and has discussed with the independent accountant the independent accountant's independence; and

(D)   Based on the review and discussions referred to in paragraphs (d)(3)(i)(A) through (d)(3)(i)(C) of this Item, the audit committee recommended to the board of directors that the audited financial statements be included in the company's annual report on Form 10–K (or, for closed-end investment companies registered under the Investment Company Act of 1940, the annual report to shareholders required by section 30(e) of the Investment Company Act of 1940 and Rule 30d–1 thereunder) for the last fiscal year for filing with the Commission.

(ii)   The name of each member of the company's audit committee (or, in the absence of an audit committee, the board committee performing equivalent functions or the entire board of directors) must appear below the disclosure required by paragraph (d)(3)(i) of this Item.

(4)(i)   If the registrant meets the following requirements, provide the disclosure in paragraph (d)(4)(ii) of this Item:

(A)   The registrant is a listed issuer, as defined in Rule 10A–3;

(B)   The registrant is filing either an annual report on Form 10–K or a proxy statement or information statement pursuant to the Exchange Act if action is to be taken with respect to the election of directors; and

(C)   The registrant is neither:

(1)   A subsidiary of another listed issuer that is relying on the exemption in Rule 10A–3(c)(2); nor

(2)   Relying on any of the exemptions in Rule 10A–3(c)(4) through (c)(7).

(ii)(A)   State whether or not the registrant has a separately-designated standing audit committee established in accordance with section 3(a)(58)(A) of the Exchange Act, or a committee performing similar functions. If the registrant has such a committee, however designated, identify each committee member. If the entire board of directors is acting as the registrant's audit committee as specified in section 3(a)(58)(B) of the Exchange Act, so state.

(B)   If applicable, provide the disclosure required by Rule 10A–3(d) regarding an exemption from the listing standards for audit committees.

(5)   *Audit committee financial expert.*

(i)(A)   Disclose that the registrant's board of directors has determined that the registrant either:

(1) Has at least one audit committee financial expert serving on its audit committee; or

(2) Does not have an audit committee financial expert serving on its audit committee.

(B) If the registrant provides the disclosure required by paragraph (d)(5)(i)(A)(1) of this Item, it must disclose the name of the audit committee financial expert and whether that person is *independent*, as independence for audit committee members is defined in the listing standards applicable to the listed issuer.

(C) If the registrant provides the disclosure required by paragraph (d)(5)(i)(A)(2) of this Item, it must explain why it does not have an audit committee financial expert.

Instruction to Item 407(d)(5)(i).

If the registrant's board of directors has determined that the registrant has more than one audit committee financial expert serving on its audit committee, the registrant may, but is not required to, disclose the names of those additional persons. A registrant choosing to identify such persons must indicate whether they are independent pursuant to paragraph (d)(5)(i)(B) of this Item.

(ii) For purposes of this Item, an *audit committee financial expert* means a person who has the following attributes:

(A) An understanding of generally accepted accounting principles and financial statements;

(B) The ability to assess the general application of such principles in connection with the accounting for estimates, accruals and reserves;

(C) Experience preparing, auditing, analyzing or evaluating financial statements that present a breadth and level of complexity of accounting issues that are generally comparable to the breadth and complexity of issues that can reasonably be expected to be raised by the registrant's financial statements, or experience actively supervising one or more persons engaged in such activities;

(D) An understanding of internal control over financial reporting; and

(E) An understanding of audit committee functions.

(iii) A person shall have acquired such attributes through:

(A) Education and experience as a principal financial officer, principal accounting officer, controller, public accountant or auditor or experience in one or more positions that involve the performance of similar functions;

(B) Experience actively supervising a principal financial officer, principal accounting officer, controller, public accountant, auditor or person performing similar functions;

(C) Experience overseeing or assessing the performance of companies or public accountants with respect to the preparation, auditing or evaluation of financial statements; or

(D) Other relevant experience.

(iv) *Safe harbor.*

(A) A person who is determined to be an audit committee financial expert will not be deemed an expert for any purpose, including without limitation for purposes of section 11 of the Securities Act, as a result of being designated or identified as an audit committee financial expert pursuant to this Item 407.

(B) The designation or identification of a person as an audit committee financial expert pursuant to this Item 407 does not impose on such person any duties, obligations or liability that are greater than the duties, obligations and liability imposed on such person as a member of the audit committee and board of directors in the absence of such designation or identification.

(C) The designation or identification of a person as an audit committee financial expert pursuant to this Item does not affect the duties, obligations or liability of any other member of the audit committee or board of directors.

Instructions to Item 407(d)(5).

1. The disclosure under paragraph (d)(5) of this Item is required only in a registrant's annual report. The registrant need not provide the disclosure required by paragraph (d)(5) of this Item in a proxy or information statement unless that registrant is electing to incorporate this information by reference from the proxy or information statement into its annual report pursuant to General Instruction G(3) to Form 10–K.

2. If a person qualifies as an audit committee financial expert by means of having held a position described in paragraph (d)(5)(iii)(D) of this Item, the registrant shall provide a brief listing of that person's relevant experience. Such disclosure may be made by reference to disclosures required under Item 401(e).

3. In the case of a foreign private issuer with a two-tier board of directors, for purposes of paragraph (d)(5) of this Item, the term board of directors means the supervisory or non-management board. In the case of a foreign private issuer meeting the requirements of Rule 10A–3(c)(3), for purposes of paragraph (d)(5) of this Item, the term board of directors means the issuer's board of auditors (or similar body) or statutory auditors, as applicable. Also, in the case of a foreign private issuer, the term generally accepted accounting principles in paragraph (d)(5)(ii)(A) of this Item means the body of generally accepted accounting principles used by that issuer in its primary financial statements filed with the Commission.

4. A registrant that is an Asset-Backed Issuer (as defined in Item 1101) is not required to disclose the information required by paragraph (d)(5) of this Item.

Instructions to Item 407(d).

1. The information required by paragraphs (d)(1)–(3) of this Item shall not be deemed to be "soliciting material," or to be "filed" with the Commission or subject to Regulation 14A or 14C, other than as provided in this Item, or to the liabilities of section 18 of the Exchange Act, except to the extent that the registrant specifically requests that the information be treated as soliciting material or specifically incorporates it by reference into a document filed under the Securities Act or the Exchange Act. Such information will not be deemed to be incorporated by reference into any filing under the Securities Act or the Exchange Act, except to the extent that the registrant specifically incorporates it by reference.

2. The disclosure required by paragraphs (d)(1)–(3) of this Item need only be provided one time during any fiscal year.

3. The disclosure required by paragraph (d)(3) of this Item need not be provided in any filings other than a registrant's proxy or information statement relating to an annual meeting of security holders at which directors are to be elected (or special meeting or written consents in lieu of such meeting).

(e) *Compensation committee.*

(1) If the registrant does not have a standing compensation committee or committee performing similar functions, state the basis for the view of the board of directors that it is appropriate for the registrant not to have such a committee and identify each director who participates in the consideration of executive officer and director compensation.

(2) State whether or not the compensation committee has a charter. If the compensation committee has a charter, provide the disclosure required by Instruction 2 to this Item regarding the compensation committee charter.

(3) Provide a narrative description of the registrant's processes and procedures for the consideration and determination of executive and director compensation, including:

(i)(A) The scope of authority of the compensation committee (or persons performing the equivalent functions); and

(B) The extent to which the compensation committee (or persons performing the equivalent functions) may delegate any authority described in paragraph (e)(3)(i)(A) of this Item to other persons, specifying what authority may be so delegated and to whom;

(ii) Any role of executive officers in determining or recommending the amount or form of executive and director compensation; and

(iii) Any role of compensation consultants in determining or recommending the amount or form of executive and director compensation (other than any role limited to consulting on any broad-based plan that does not discriminate in scope, terms, or operation, in favor of executive officers or directors of the registrant, and that is available generally to all salaried employees; or providing information that either is not customized for a particular registrant or that is customized based on parameters that are not developed by the compensation consultant, and about which the compensation consultant does not provide advice) during the registrant's last completed fiscal year, identifying such consultants, stating whether such consultants were engaged directly by the compensation committee (or persons performing the equivalent functions) or any other person, describing the nature and scope of their assignment, and the material elements of the instructions or directions given to the consultants with respect to the performance of their duties under the engagement:

(A) If such compensation consultant was engaged by the compensation committee (or persons performing the equivalent functions) to provide advice or recommendations on the amount or form of executive and director compensation (other than any role limited to consulting on any broad-based plan that does not discriminate in scope, terms, or operation, in favor of executive officers or directors of the registrant, and that is available generally to all salaried employees; or providing information that either is not customized for a particular registrant or that is customized based on parameters that are not developed by the compensation consultant, and about which the compensation consultant does not provide advice) and the compensation consultant or its affiliates also provided additional services to the registrant or its affiliates in an amount in excess of $120,000 during the registrant's last completed fiscal year, then disclose the aggregate fees for determining or recommending the amount or form of executive and director compensation and the aggregate fees for such additional services. Disclose whether the decision to engage the compensation consultant or its affiliates for these other services was made, or recommended, by management, and whether the compensation committee or the board approved such other services of the compensation consultant or its affiliates.

(B) If the compensation committee (or persons performing the equivalent functions) has not engaged a compensation consultant, but management has engaged a compensation consultant to provide advice or recommendations on the amount or form of executive and director compensation (other than any role limited to consulting on any broad-based plan that does not discriminate in scope, terms, or operation, in favor of executive officers or directors of the registrant, and that is available generally to all salaried employees; or providing information that either is not customized for a particular registrant or that is customized based on parameters that are not developed by the compensation consultant, and about which the compensation consultant does not provide advice) and such compensation consultant or its affiliates has provided additional services to the registrant in an amount in excess of $120,000 during the registrant's last completed fiscal year, then disclose the aggregate fees for determining or recommending the amount or form of executive and director compensation and the aggregate fees for any additional services provided by the compensation consultant or its affiliates.

(iv) With regard to any compensation consultant identified in response to Item 407(e)(3)(iii) whose work has raised any conflict of interest, disclose the nature of the conflict and how the conflict is being addressed.

Instruction to Item 407(e)(3)(iv).

For purposes of this paragraph, the factors listed in Rules 10C–1(b)(4)(i) through (vi) of the Securities Exchange Act of 1934 are among the factors that should be considered in determining whether a conflict of interest exists.

(4) Under the caption "Compensation Committee Interlocks and Insider Participation":

(i) Identify each person who served as a member of the compensation committee of the registrant's board of directors (or board committee performing equivalent functions) during the last completed fiscal year, indicating each committee member who:

Item 407 **REGULATION S–K**

(A) Was, during the fiscal year, an officer or employee of the registrant;

(B) Was formerly an officer of the registrant; or

(C) Had any relationship requiring disclosure by the registrant under any paragraph of Item 404. In this event, the disclosure required by Item 404 shall accompany such identification.

(ii) If the registrant has no compensation committee (or other board committee performing equivalent functions), the registrant shall identify each officer and employee of the registrant, and any former officer of the registrant, who, during the last completed fiscal year, participated in deliberations of the registrant's board of directors concerning executive officer compensation.

(iii) Describe any of the following relationships that existed during the last completed fiscal year:

(A) An executive officer of the registrant served as a member of the compensation committee (or other board committee performing equivalent functions or, in the absence of any such committee, the entire board of directors) of another entity, one of whose executive officers served on the compensation committee (or other board committee performing equivalent functions or, in the absence of any such committee, the entire board of directors) of the registrant;

(B) An executive officer of the registrant served as a director of another entity, one of whose executive officers served on the compensation committee (or other board committee performing equivalent functions or, in the absence of any such committee, the entire board of directors) of the registrant; and

(C) An executive officer of the registrant served as a member of the compensation committee (or other board committee performing equivalent functions or, in the absence of any such committee, the entire board of directors) of another entity, one of whose executive officers served as a director of the registrant.

(iv) Disclosure required under paragraph (e)(4)(iii) of this Item regarding a compensation committee member or other director of the registrant who also served as an executive officer of another entity shall be accompanied by the disclosure called for by Item 404 with respect to that person.

Instruction to Item 407(e)(4).

For purposes of paragraph (e)(4) of this Item, the term entity shall not include an entity exempt from tax under section 501(c)(3) of the Internal Revenue Code.

(5) Under the caption "Compensation Committee Report:"

(i) The compensation committee (or other board committee performing equivalent functions or, in the absence of any such committee, the entire board of directors) must state whether:

(A) The compensation committee has reviewed and discussed the Compensation Discussion and Analysis required by Item 402(b) with management; and

(B) Based on the review and discussions referred to in paragraph (e)(5)(i)(A) of this Item, the compensation committee recommended to the board of directors that the Compensation Discussion and Analysis be included in the registrant's annual report on Form 10–K, proxy statement on Schedule 14A or information statement on Schedule 14C.

(ii) The name of each member of the registrant's compensation committee (or other board committee performing equivalent functions or, in the absence of any such committee, the entire board of directors) must appear below the disclosure required by paragraph (e)(5)(i) of this Item.

Instructions to Item 407(e)(5).

1. The information required by paragraph (e)(5) of this Item shall not be deemed to be "soliciting material," or to be "filed" with the Commission or subject to Regulation 14A or 14C, other than as provided in this Item, or to the liabilities of section 18 of the Exchange Act, except to the extent that the registrant specifically requests

that the information be treated as soliciting material or specifically incorporates it by reference into a document filed under the Securities Act or the Exchange Act.

2. The disclosure required by paragraph (e)(5) of this Item need not be provided in any filings other than an annual report on Form 10–K, a proxy statement on Schedule 14A or an information statement on Schedule 14C. Such information will not be deemed to be incorporated by reference into any filing under the Securities Act or the Exchange Act, except to the extent that the registrant specifically incorporates it by reference. If the registrant elects to incorporate this information by reference from the proxy or information statement into its annual report on Form 10–K pursuant to General Instruction G(3) to Form 10–K, the disclosure required by paragraph (e)(5) of this Item will be deemed furnished in the annual report on Form 10–K and will not be deemed incorporated by reference into any filing under the Securities Act or the Exchange Act as a result as a result of furnishing the disclosure in this manner.

3. The disclosure required by paragraph (e)(5) of this Item need only be provided one time during any fiscal year.

(f) *Shareholder communications.*

(1) State whether or not the registrant's board of directors provides a process for security holders to send communications to the board of directors and, if the registrant does not have such a process for security holders to send communications to the board of directors, state the basis for the view of the board of directors that it is appropriate for the registrant not to have such a process.

(2) If the registrant has a process for security holders to send communications to the board of directors:

(i) Describe the manner in which security holders can send communications to the board and, if applicable, to specified individual directors; and

(ii) If all security holder communications are not sent directly to board members, describe the registrant's process for determining which communications will be relayed to board members.

Instructions to Item 407(f).

1. In lieu of providing the information required by paragraph (f)(2) of this Item in the proxy statement, the registrant may instead provide the registrant's Web site address where such information appears.

2. For purposes of the disclosure required by paragraph (f)(2)(ii) of this Item, a registrant's process for collecting and organizing security holder communications, as well as similar or related activities, need not be disclosed provided that the registrant's process is approved by a majority of the independent directors or, in the case of a registrant that is an investment company, a majority of the directors who are not "interested persons" of the investment company as defined in section 2(a)(19) of the Investment Company Act of 1940.

3. For purposes of this paragraph, communications from an officer or director of the registrant will not be viewed as "security holder communications." Communications from an employee or agent of the registrant will be viewed as "security holder communications" for purposes of this paragraph only if those communications are made solely in such employee's or agent's capacity as a security holder.

4. For purposes of this paragraph, security holder proposals submitted pursuant to Rule 14a–8, and communications made in connection with such proposals, will not be viewed as "security holder communications."

(g) *Smaller reporting companies and emerging growth companies.* (1) A registrant that qualifies as a "smaller reporting company," as defined by Item 10(f)(1), is not required to provide:

(i) The disclosure required in paragraph (d)(5) of this Item in its first annual report filed pursuant to Section 13(a) or 15(d) of the Exchange Act (15 U.S.C. 78m(a) or 78o(d)) following the effective date of its first registration statement filed under the Securities Act (15 U.S.C. 77a et seq.) or Exchange Act (15 U.S.C. 78a et seq.); and

(ii) The disclosure required by paragraphs (e)(4) and (e)(5) of this Item. (2) A registrant that qualifies as an "emerging growth company," as defined in Rule 405 of the Securities Act or Rule 12b–2 of the Exchange Act, is not required to provide the disclosure required by paragraph (e)(5) of this Item.

(h) *Board leadership structure and role in risk oversight.* Briefly describe the leadership structure of the registrant's board, such as whether the same person serves as both principal executive officer and chairman of the board, or whether two individuals serve in those positions, and, in the case of a registrant that is an investment company, whether the chairman of the board is an "interested person" of the registrant as defined in section 2(a)(19) of the Investment Company Act (15 U.S.C. 80a–2(a)(19)). If one person serves as both principal executive officer and chairman of the board, or if the chairman of the board of a registrant that is an investment company is an "interested person" of the registrant, disclose whether the registrant has a lead independent director and what specific role the lead independent director plays in the leadership of the board. This disclosure should indicate why the registrant has determined that its leadership structure is appropriate given the specific characteristics or circumstances of the registrant. In addition, disclose the extent of the board's role in the risk oversight of the registrant, such as how the board administers its oversight function, and the effect that this has on the board's leadership structure.

(i)   *Employee, officer and director hedging.* In proxy or information statements with respect to the election of directors:

(1)   Describe any practices or policies that the registrant has adopted regarding the ability of employees (including officers) or directors of the registrant, or any of their designees, to purchase financial instruments (including prepaid variable forward contracts, equity swaps, collars, and exchange funds), or otherwise engage in transactions, that hedge or offset, or are designed to hedge or offset, any decrease in the market value of registrant equity securities—

(i)   Granted to the employee or director by the registrant as part of the compensation of the employee or director; or

(ii)   Held, directly or indirectly, by the employee or director.

(2)   A description provided pursuant to paragraph (1) shall provide a fair and accurate summary of the practices or policies that apply, including the categories of persons covered, or disclose the practices or policies in full.

(3)   A description provided pursuant to paragraph (1) shall also describe any categories of hedging transactions that are specifically permitted and any categories of such transactions specifically disallowed.

(4)   If the registrant does not have any such practices or policies regarding hedging, the registrant shall disclose that fact or state that the transactions described in paragraph (1) above are generally permitted.

Instructions to Item 407(i).

1.   For purposes of this Item 407(i), "registrant equity securities" means those equity securities as defined in section 3(a)(11) of the Exchange Act (15 U.S.C. 78c(a)(11)) and Rule 3a11–1 of this Act) that are issued by the registrant or by any parent or subsidiary of the registrant or any subsidiary of any parent of the registrant.

2.   The information required by this Item 407(i) will not be deemed to be incorporated by reference into any filing under the Securities Act or the Exchange Act, except to the extent that the registrant specifically incorporates it by reference.

Instructions to Item 407.

1.   For purposes of this Item:

a.   *Listed issuer* means a listed issuer as defined in Rule 10A–3;

b.   *National securities exchange* means a national securities exchange registered pursuant to section 6(a) of the Exchange Act;

c.   *Inter-dealer quotation system* means an automated inter-dealer quotation system of a national securities association registered pursuant to section 15A(a) of the Exchange Act; and

d.   *National securities association* means a national securities association registered pursuant to section 15A(a) of the Exchange Act that has been approved by the Commission (as that definition may be modified or supplemented).

2.   With respect to paragraphs (c)(2)(i), (d)(1) and (e)(2) of this Item, disclose whether a current copy of the applicable committee charter is available to security holders on the registrant's Web site, and if so, provide the registrant's Web site address. If a current copy of the charter is not available to security holders on the registrant's Web site, include a copy of the charter in an appendix to the registrant's proxy or information statement that is provided to security holders at least once every three fiscal years, or if the charter has been materially amended

since the beginning of the registrant's last fiscal year. If a current copy of the charter is not available to security holders on the registrant's Web site, and is not included as an appendix to the registrant's proxy or information statement, identify in which of the prior fiscal years the charter was so included in satisfaction of this requirement.

Subpart 500—Registration Statement and Prospectus Provisions

Item 501.   **Forepart of Registration Statement and Outside Front Cover Page of Prospectus**

The registrant must furnish the following information in plain English. See Rule 421(d) of Regulation C of the Securities Act.

(a) *Front Cover Page of the Registration Statement.* Where appropriate, include the delaying amendment legend from Rule 473 of Regulation C of the Securities Act.

(b) *Outside Front Cover Page of the Prospectus.* Limit the outside cover page to one page. If the following information applies to your offering, disclose it on the outside cover page of the prospectus.

(1) *Name.* The registrant's name. A foreign registrant must give the English translation of its name.

Instruction to paragraph 501(b)(1).

If your name is the same as that of a company that is well known, include information to eliminate any possible confusion with the other company. If your name indicates a line of business in which you are not engaged or in which you are engaged only to a limited extent, include information to eliminate any misleading inference as to your business.

(2) *Title and amount of securities.* The title and amount of securities offered. Separately state the amount of securities offered by selling security holders, if any. If the underwriter has any arrangement with the issuer, such as an over-allotment option, under which the underwriter may purchase additional shares in connection with the offering, indicate that this arrangement exists and state the amount of additional shares that the underwriter may purchase under the arrangement. Give a brief description of the securities except where the information is clear from the title of the security. For example, you are not required to describe common stock that has full voting, dividend and liquidation rights usually associated with common stock.

(3) *Offering price of the securities.* Where you offer securities for cash, the price to the public of the securities, the underwriter's discounts and commissions, the net proceeds you receive, and any selling shareholder's net proceeds. Show this information on both a per share or unit basis and for the total amount of the offering. If you make the offering on a minimum/maximum basis, show this information based on the total minimum and total maximum amount of the offering. You may present the information in a table, term sheet format, or other clear presentation. You may present the information in any format that fits the design of the cover page so long as the information can be easily read and is not misleading.

Instructions to paragraph 501(b)(3).

1. If a preliminary prospectus is circulated and you are not subject to the reporting requirements of section 13(a) or 15(d) of the Exchange Act, provide, as applicable:

(A) A bona fide estimate of the range of the maximum offering price and the maximum number of securities offered; or

(B) A bona fide estimate of the principal amount of the debt securities offered.

2. If it is impracticable to state the price to the public, explain the method by which the price is to be determined. Instead of explaining the method on the outside front cover page of the prospectus, you may state that the offering price will be determined by a particular method or formula that is described in the prospectus and include a cross-reference to the location of such disclosure in the prospectus, including the page number. Highlight the cross-reference by prominent type or in another manner. If the securities are to be offered at the market price, or if the offering price is to be determined by a formula related to the market price, indicate the market and market price of the securities as of the latest practicable date.

3. If you file a registration statement on Form S–8, you are not required to comply with this paragraph (b)(3).

(4) *Market for the securities*. The national securities exchange(s) where the securities being offered are listed. If the securities being offered are not listed on a national securities exchange, the principal United States market(s) where the registrant, through the engagement of a registered broker-dealer, has actively sought and achieved quotation. In each case, also disclose the corresponding trading symbol(s) for the securities on such market(s).

(5) *Risk factors*. A cross-reference to the risk factors section, including the page number where it appears in the prospectus. Highlight this cross-reference by prominent type or in another manner;

(6) *State legend*. Any legend or statement required by the law of any state in which the securities are to be offered. You may combine this with any legend required by the SEC, if appropriate;

(7) *Commission legend*. A legend that indicates that neither the Securities and Exchange Commission nor any state securities commission has approved or disapproved of the securities or passed upon the accuracy or adequacy of the disclosures in the prospectus and that any contrary representation is a criminal offense. You may use one of the following or other clear, plain language:

Example A: Neither the Securities and Exchange Commission nor any state securities commission has approved or disapproved of these securities or passed upon the adequacy or accuracy of this prospectus. Any representation to the contrary is a criminal offense.

Example B: Neither the Securities and Exchange Commission nor any state securities commission has approved or disapproved of these securities or determined if this prospectus is truthful or complete. Any representation to the contrary is a criminal offense.

(8) *Underwriting*. (i) Name(s) of the lead or managing underwriter(s) and an identification of the nature of the underwriting arrangements;

(ii) If the offering is not made on a firm commitment basis, a brief description of the underwriting arrangements. You may use any clear, concise, and accurate description of the underwriting arrangements. You may use the following descriptions of underwriting arrangements where appropriate:

Example A: Best efforts offering. The underwriters are not required to sell any specific number or dollar amount of securities but will use their best efforts to sell the securities offered.

Example B: Best efforts, minimum-maximum offering. The underwriters must sell the minimum number of securities offered (insert number) if any are sold. The underwriters are required to use only their best efforts to sell the maximum number of securities offered (insert number).

(iii) If you offer the securities on a best efforts or best efforts minimum/maximum basis, the date the offering will end, any minimum purchase requirements, and any arrangements to place the funds in an escrow, trust, or similar account. If you have not made any of these arrangements, state this fact and describe the effect on investors;

(9) *Date of prospectus*. The date of the prospectus;

(10) *Prospectus "Subject to Completion" legend*. (i) If you use the prospectus before the effective date of the registration statement or if you use Securities Act Rule 430A to omit pricing information and the prospectus is used before you determine the public offering price, include a prominent statement that:

(A) The information in the prospectus will be amended or completed;

(B) A registration statement relating to these securities has been filed with the Securities and Exchange Commission;

(C) The securities may not be sold until the registration statement becomes effective; and

(D) The prospectus is not an offer to sell the securities, and it is not soliciting an offer to buy the securities, in any state where offers or sales are not permitted.

(ii) The legend called for by paragraph (b)(10)(i) of this Item may be in the following or other clear, plain language: The information in this prospectus is not complete and may be changed. We may not sell these securities until the registration statement filed with the

Securities and Exchange Commission is effective. This prospectus is not an offer to sell these securities and it is not soliciting an offer to buy these securities in any state where the offer or sale is not permitted.

    (iii) Registrants may exclude the statement in paragraph (b)(10)(i)(D) of this Item if the offering is not prohibited by state law.

    (11) If you use Rule 430A of the Securities Act to omit pricing information and the prospectus is used before you determine the public offering price, the information and legend in paragraph (b)(10) of this Item.

Instruction to Item 501

    For asset-backed securities, see also Item 1102 of Regulation AB.

Item 502.   Inside Front and Outside Back Cover Pages of Prospectus

    The registrant must furnish this information in plain English. See Rule 421(d) of Regulation C of the Securities Act.

    (a) *Table of Contents.* On either the inside front or outside back cover page of the prospectus, provide a reasonably detailed table of contents. It must show the page number of the various sections or subdivisions of the prospectus. Include a specific listing of the risk factors section required by Item 105 of this Regulation S–K. You must include the table of contents immediately following the cover page in any prospectus you deliver electronically.

    (b) *Dealer Prospectus Delivery Obligation.* On the outside back cover page of the prospectus, advise dealers of their prospectus delivery obligation, including the expiration date specified by section 4(3) of the Securities Act and Rule 174. If you do not know the expiration date on the effective date of the registration statement, include the expiration date in the copy of the prospectus you file under Rule 424(b). You do not have to include this information if dealers are not required to deliver a prospectus under Rule 174 of this chapter or section 24(d) of the Investment Company Act. You may use the following or other clear, plain language:

Dealer Prospectus Delivery Obligation

    Until (insert date), all dealers that effect transactions in these securities, whether or not participating in this offering, may be required to deliver a prospectus. This is in addition to the dealers' obligation to deliver a prospectus when acting as underwriters and with respect to their unsold allotments or subscriptions.

Item 503.   Prospectus Summary

    The registrant must furnish this information in plain English. See Rule 421(d) of Regulation C of the Securities Act.

    (a) *Prospectus Summary.* Provide a summary of the information in the prospectus where the length or complexity of the prospectus makes a summary useful. The summary should be brief. The summary should not contain, and is not required to contain, all of the detailed information in the prospectus. If you provide summary business or financial information, even if you do not caption it as a summary, you still must provide that information in plain English.

    Instruction to paragraph 503(a).

    The summary should not merely repeat the text of the prospectus but should provide a brief overview of the key aspects of the offering. Carefully consider and identify those aspects of the offering that are the most significant and determine how best to highlight those points in clear, plain language.

    (b) *Address and Telephone Number.* Include, either on the cover page or in the summary section of the prospectus, the complete mailing address and telephone number of your principal executive offices.

    (c) [Removed and Reserved].

Instruction to Item 503

    For asset-backed securities, see also Item 1103 of Regulation AB.

Item 504.   Use of Proceeds

State the principal purposes for which the net proceeds to the registrant from the securities to be offered are intended to be used and the approximate amount intended to be used for each such purpose. Where registrant has no current specific plan for the proceeds, or a significant portion thereof, the registrant shall so state and discuss the principal reasons for the offering.

Instructions to Item 504. 1. Where less than all the securities to be offered may be sold and more than one use is listed for the proceeds, indicate the order of priority of such purposes and discuss the registrant's plans if substantially less than the maximum proceeds are obtained. Such discussion need not be included if underwriting arrangements with respect to such securities are such that, if any securities are sold to the public, it reasonably can be expected that the actual proceeds will not be substantially less than the aggregate proceeds to the registrant shown pursuant to Item 501 of Regulation S–K.

2. Details of proposed expenditures need not be given; for example, there need be furnished only a brief outline of any program of construction or addition of equipment. Consideration should be given as to the need to include a discussion of certain matters addressed in the discussion and analysis of registrant's financial condition and results of operations, such as liquidity and capital expenditures.

3. If any material amounts of other funds are necessary to accomplish the specified purposes for which the proceeds are to be obtained, state the amounts of such other funds needed for each such specified purpose and the sources thereof.

4. If any material part of the proceeds is to be used to discharge indebtedness, set forth the interest rate and maturity of such indebtedness. If the indebtedness to be discharged was incurred within one year, describe the use of the proceeds of such indebtedness other than short-term borrowings used for working capital.

5. If any material amount of the proceeds is to be used to acquire assets, otherwise than in the ordinary course of business, describe briefly and state the cost of the assets and, where such assets are to be acquired from affiliates of the registrant or their associates, give the names of the persons from whom they are to be acquired and set forth the principle followed in determining the cost to the registrant.

6. Where the registrant indicates that the proceeds may, or will, be used to finance acquisitions of other businesses, the identity of such businesses, if known, or, if not known, the nature of the businesses to be sought, the status of any negotiations with respect to the acquisition, and a brief description of such business shall be included. Where, however, pro forma financial statements reflecting such acquisition are not required by Regulation S–X, including Rule 8–05 for smaller reporting companies, to be included in the registration statement, the possible terms of any transaction, the identification of the parties thereto or the nature of the business sought need not be disclosed, to the extent that the registrant reasonably determines that public disclosure of such information would jeopardize the acquisition. Where Regulation S–X, including Rule 8–04 for smaller reporting companies, as applicable, would require financial statements of the business to be acquired to be included, the description of the business to be acquired shall be more detailed.

7. The registrant may reserve the right to change the use of proceeds, provided that such reservation is due to certain contingencies that are discussed specifically and the alternatives to such use in that event are indicated.

Item 505.   Determination of Offering Price

(a) *Common Equity.* Where common equity is being registered for which there is no established public trading market for purposes of paragraph (a) of Item 201 of Regulation S–K or where there is a material disparity between the offering price of the common equity being registered and the market price of outstanding shares of the same class, describe the various factors considered in determining such offering price.

(b) *Warrants, Rights and Convertible Securities.* Where warrants, rights or convertible securities exercisable for common equity for which there is no established public trading market for purposes of paragraph (a) of Item 201 of Regulation S–K are being registered, describe the various factors considered in determining their exercise or conversion price.

Item 506.   Dilution

Where common equity securities are being registered and there is substantial disparity between the public offering price and the effective cash cost to officers, directors, promoters and affiliated persons of common equity acquired by them in transactions during the past five years, or which they have the right to acquire, and the registrant is not subject to the reporting requirements of section 13(a) or 15(d) of the Exchange Act immediately prior to filing of the registration statement, there shall be included a comparison of the public contribution under the proposed public offering and the effective cash contribution of such persons. In such cases, and in other instances where common equity securities are being registered by a registrant that has had losses in each of its last three fiscal years and there is a material dilution of the purchasers' equity interest, the following shall be disclosed:

(a)   The net tangible book value per share before and after the distribution;

(b)   The amount of the increase in such net tangible book value per share attributable to the cash payments made by purchasers of the shares being offered; and

(c)   The amount of the immediate dilution from the public offering price which will be absorbed by such purchasers.

Item 507.   Selling Security Holders

If any of the securities to be registered are to be offered for the account of security holders, name each such security holder, indicate the nature of any position, office, or other material relationship which the selling security holder has had within the past three years with the registrant or any of its predecessors or affiliates, and state the amount of securities of the class owned by such security holder prior to the offering, the amount to be offered for the security holder's account, the amount and (if one percent or more) the percentage of the class to be owned by such security holder after completion of the offering.

Item 508.   Plan of Distribution

(a)   *Underwriters and Underwriting Obligation.* If the securities are to be offered through underwriters, name the principal underwriters, and state the respective amounts underwritten. Identify each such underwriter having a material relationship with the registrant and state the nature of the relationship. State briefly the nature of the obligation of the underwriter(s) to take the securities.

Instruction to Paragraph 508(a). All that is required as to the nature of the underwriters' obligation is whether the underwriters are or will be committed to take and to pay for all of the securities if any are taken, or whether it is merely an agency or the type of "best efforts" arrangement under which the underwriters are required to take and to pay for only such securities as they may sell to the public. Conditions precedent to the underwriters' taking the securities, including "market-outs," need not be described except in the case of an agency or "best efforts" arrangement.

(b)   *New Underwriters.* Where securities being registered are those of a registrant that has not previously been required to file reports pursuant to section 13(a) or 15(d) of the Exchange Act, or where a prospectus is required to include reference on its cover page to material risks pursuant to Item 501 of Regulation S–K and any one or more of the managing underwriter(s) (or where there are no managing underwriters, a majority of the principal underwriters) has been organized, reactivated, or first registered as a broker-dealer within the past three years, these facts concerning such underwriter(s) shall be disclosed in the prospectus together with, where applicable, the disclosures that the principal business function of such underwriter(s) will be to sell the securities to be registered, or that the promoters of the registrant have a material relationship with such underwriter(s). Sufficient details shall be given to allow full appreciation of such underwriter(s) experience and its relationship with the registrant, promoters and their controlling persons.

(c)   *Other Distributions.* Outline briefly the plan of distribution of any securities to be registered that are to be offered otherwise than through underwriters.

(1)   If any securities are to be offered pursuant to a dividend or interest reinvestment plan the terms of which provide for the purchase of some securities on the market, state whether the registrant or the participant pays fees, commissions, and expenses incurred in connection with the plan. If the participant will pay such fees, commissions and expenses, state the anticipated cost to participants by transaction or other convenient reference.

(2)   If the securities are to be offered through the selling efforts of brokers or dealers, describe the plan of distribution and the terms of any agreement, arrangement, or understanding entered into

with broker(s) or dealer(s) prior to the effective date of the registration statement, including volume limitations on sales, parties to the agreement and the conditions under which the agreement may be terminated. If known, identify the broker(s) or dealer(s) which will participate in the offering and state the amount to be offered through each.

(3)   If any of the securities being registered are to be offered otherwise than for cash, state briefly the general purposes of the distribution, the basis, upon which the securities are to be offered, the amount of compensation and other expenses of distribution, and by whom they are to be borne. If the distribution is to be made pursuant to a plan of acquisition, reorganization, readjustment or succession, describe briefly the general effect of the plan and state when it became or is to become operative. As to any material amount of assets to be acquired under the plan, furnish information corresponding to that required by Instruction 5 of Item 504 of Regulation S–K.

(d)   *Offerings on Exchange.* If the securities are to be offered on an exchange, indicate the exchange. If the registered securities are to be offered in connection with the writing of exchange-traded call options, describe briefly such transactions.

(e)   *Underwriter's Compensation.* Provide a table that sets out the nature of the compensation and the amount of discounts and commissions to be paid to the underwriter for each security and in total. The table must show the separate amounts to be paid by the company and the selling shareholders. In addition, include in the table all other items considered by the Financial Industry Regulatory Authority ("FINRA") to be underwriting compensation for purposes of FINRA rules.

Instructions to paragraph 508(e)

1.   The term "commissions" is defined in paragraph (17) of Schedule A of the Securities Act. Show separately in the table the cash commissions paid by the registrant and selling security holders. Also show in the table commissions paid by other persons. Disclose any finder's fee or similar payments in the table.

2.   Disclose the offering expenses specified in Item 511 of Regulation S–K.

3.   If the underwriter has any arrangement with the issuer, such as an over-allotment option, under which the underwriter may purchase additional shares in connection with the offering, indicate that this arrangement exists and state the amount of additional shares that the underwriter may purchase under the arrangement. Where the underwriter has such an arrangement, present maximum-minimum information in a separate column to the table, based on the purchase of all or none of the shares subject to the arrangement. Describe the key terms of the arrangement in the narrative.

(f)   *Underwriter's Representative on Board of Directors.* Describe any arrangement whereby the underwriter has the right to designate or nominate a member or members of the board of directors of the registrant. The registrant shall disclose the identity of any director so designated or nominated, and indicate whether or not a person so designated or nominated, or allowed to be designated or nominated by the underwriter is or may be a director, officer, partner, employee or affiliate of the underwriter.

(g)   *Indemnification of Underwriters.* If the underwriting agreement provides for indemnification by the registrant of the underwriters or their controlling persons against any liability arising under the Securities Act, furnish a brief description of such indemnification provisions.

(h)   *Dealers' Compensation.* State briefly the discounts and commissions to be allowed or paid to dealers, including all cash, securities, contracts or other considerations to be received by any dealer in connection with the sale of the securities. If any dealers are to act in the capacity of subunderwriters and are to be allowed or paid any additional discounts or commissions for acting in such capacity, a general statement to that effect will suffice without giving the additional amounts to be sold.

(i)   *Finders.* Identify any finder and, if applicable, describe the nature of any material relationship between such finder and the registrant, its officers, directors, principal stockholders, finders or promoters or the principal underwriter(s), or if there is a managing underwriter(s), the managing underwriter(s), (including, in each case, affiliates or associates thereof).

(j)   *Discretionary Accounts.* If the registrant was not, immediately prior to the filing of the registration statement, subject to the requirements of section 13(a) or 15(d) of the Exchange Act, identify any principal underwriter that intends to sell to any accounts over which it exercises discretionary authority and include an estimate of the amount of securities so intended to be sold. The response to this paragraph shall be contained in a pre-effective amendment which shall be circulated if the information is not available when the registration statement is filed.

(k) *Passive Market Making.* If the underwriters or any selling group members intend to engage in passive market making transactions as permitted by Rule 103 of Regulation M, indicate such intention and briefly describe passive market making.

(l) *Stabilization and Other Transactions.*

    (1) Briefly describe any transaction that the underwriter intends to conduct during the offering that stabilizes, maintains, or otherwise affects the market price of the offered securities. Include information on stabilizing transactions, syndicate short covering transactions, penalty bids, or any other transaction that affects the offered security's price. Describe the nature of the transactions clearly and explain how the transactions affect the offered security's price. Identify the exchange or other market on which these transactions may occur. If true, disclose that the underwriter may discontinue these transactions at any time;

    (2) If the stabilizing began before the effective date of the registration statement, disclose the amount of securities bought, the prices at which they were bought and the period within which they were bought. If you use Rule 430A of the Securities Act, the prospectus you file under Rule 424(b) of the Securities Act or include in a post-effective amendment must contain information on the stabilizing transactions that took place before the determination of the public offering price; and

    (3) If you are making a warrants or rights offering of securities to existing security holders and any securities not purchased by existing security holders are to be reoffered to the public, disclose in a supplement to the prospectus or in the prospectus used in connection with the reoffering:

        (i) The amount of securities bought in stabilization activities during the offering period and the price or range of prices at which the securities were bought;

        (ii) The amount of the offered securities subscribed for during the offering period;

        (iii) The amount of the offered securities subscribed for by the underwriter during the offering period;

        (iv) The amount of the offered securities sold during the offering period by the underwriter and the price or price ranges at which the securities were sold; and

        (v) The amount of the offered securities that will be reoffered to the public and the public offering price.

Item 509. Interests of Named Experts and Counsel

If (a) any expert named in the registration statement as having prepared or certified any part thereof (or is named as having prepared or certified a report or valuation for use in connection with the registration statement), or (b) counsel for the registrant, underwriters or selling security holders named in the prospectus as having given an opinion upon the validity of the securities being registered or upon other legal matters in connection with the registration or offering of such securities, was employed for such purpose on a contingent basis, or at the time of such preparation, certification or opinion or at any time thereafter, through the date of effectiveness of the registration statement or that part of the registration statement to which such preparation, certification or opinion relates, had, or is to receive in connection with the offering, a substantial interest, direct or indirect, in the registrant or any of its parents or subsidiaries or was connected with the registrant or any of its parents or subsidiaries as a promoter, managing underwriter (or any principal underwriter, if there are no managing underwriters) voting trustee, director, officer, or employee, furnish a brief statement of the nature of such contingent basis, interest, or connection.

Instructions to Item 509. 1. The interest of an expert (other than an accountant) or counsel will not be deemed substantial and need not be disclosed if the interest, including the fair market value of all securities of the registrant owned, received and to be received, or subject to options, warrants or rights received or to be received by the expert or counsel does not exceed $50,000. For the purpose of this Instruction, the term "expert" or "counsel" includes the firm, corporation, partnership or other entity, if any, by which such expert or counsel is employed or of which he is a member or of counsel to and all attorneys in the case of counsel, and all nonclerical personnel in the case of named experts, participating in such matter on behalf of such firm, corporation, partnership or entity.

2.   Accountants, providing a report on the financial statements, presented or incorporated by reference in the registration statement, should note Item 2–01 of Regulation S–X for the Commission's requirements regarding "Qualification of Accountants" which discusses disqualifying interests.

Item 510.   Disclosure of Commission Position on Indemnification for Securities Act Liabilities

In addition to the disclosure prescribed by Item 702 of Regulation S–K, if the undertaking required by paragraph (i) of Item 512 of Regulation S–K is not required to be included in the registration statement because acceleration of the effective date of the registration statement is not being requested, and if waivers have not been obtained comparable to those specified in paragraph (i), a brief description of the indemnification provisions relating to directors, officers and controlling persons of the registrant against liability arising under the Securities Act (including any provision of the underwriting agreement which relates to indemnification of the underwriter or its controlling persons by the registrant against such liabilities where a director, officer or controlling person of the registrant if such an underwriter or controlling person thereof or a member of any firm which is such an underwriter) shall be included in the prospectus, together with a statement in substantially the following form:

Insofar as indemnification for liabilities arising under the Securities Act of 1933 may be permitted to directors, officers or persons controlling the registrant pursuant to the foregoing provisions, the registrant has been informed that in the opinion of the Securities and Exchange Commission such indemnification is against public policy as expressed in the Act and is therefore unenforceable.

Item 511.   Other Expenses of Issuance and Distribution

Furnish a reasonably itemized statement of all expenses in connection with the issuance and distribution of the securities to be registered, other than underwriting discounts and commissions. If any of the securities to be registered are to be offered for the account of security holders, indicate the portion of such expenses to be borne by such security holder.

Instruction to Item 511.   Insofar as practicable, registration fees, Federal taxes, State taxes and fees, trustees' and transfer agent's fees, costs of printing and engraving, and legal, accounting, and engineering fees shall be itemized separately. Include as a separate item any premium paid by the registrant or any selling security holder on any policy obtained in connection with the offering and sale of the securities being registered which insures or indemnifies directors or officers against any liabilities they may incur in connection with the registration, offering, or sale of such securities. The information may be given as subject to future contingencies. If the amounts of any items are not known, estimates, identified as such, shall be given.

Item 512.   Undertakings

Include each of the following undertakings that is applicable to the offering being registered.

(a)   *Rule 415 Offering.* Include the following if the securities are registered pursuant to Rule 415 under the Securities Act:

The undersigned registrant hereby undertakes:

(1)   To file, during any period in which offers or sales are being made, a post-effective amendment to this registration statement:

(i)   To include any prospectus required by section 10(a)(3) of the Securities Act of 1933;

(ii)   To reflect in the prospectus any facts or events arising after the effective date of the registration statement (or the most recent post-effective amendment thereof) which, individually or in the aggregate, represent a fundamental change in the information set forth in the registration statement. Notwithstanding the foregoing, any increase or decrease in volume of securities offered (if the total dollar value of securities offered would not exceed that which was registered) and any deviation from the low or high end of the estimated maximum offering range may be reflected in the form of prospectus filed with the Commission pursuant to Rule 424(b) if, in the aggregate, the changes in volume and price represent no more than a 20% change in the maximum aggregate offering price set forth in the "Calculation of Registration Fee" table in the effective registration statement.

(iii) To include any material information with respect to the plan of distribution not previously disclosed in the registration statement or any material change to such information in the registration statement;

Provided, however, that:

(A) paragraphs (a)(1)(i) and (a)(1)(ii) of this rule do not apply if the registration statement is on Form S–8, and the information required to be included in a post-effective amendment by those paragraphs is contained in reports filed with or furnished to the Commission by the registrant pursuant to section 13 or section 15(d) of the Securities Exchange Act of 1934 that are incorporated by reference in the registration statement; and

(B) [Interim Rule] Paragraphs (a)(1)(i), (ii), and (iii) of this Item do not apply if the registration statement is on Form S–1 (§ 239.11 of this chapter), Form S–3 (§ 239.13 of this chapter), Form SF–3 (§ 239.45 of this chapter) or Form F–3 (§ 239.33 of this chapter) and the information required to be included in a post-effective amendment by those paragraphs is contained in reports filed with or furnished to the Commission by the registrant pursuant to section 13 or section 15(d) of the Securities Exchange Act of 1934 (15 U.S.C. 78m or 78o(d)) that are incorporated by reference in the registration statement, or, as to a registration statement on Form S–3, Form SF–3 or Form F–3, is contained in a form of prospectus filed pursuant to § 230.424(b) of this chapter that is part of the registration statement.

(C) *Provided further, however,* that paragraphs (a)(1)(i) and (a)(1)(ii) do not apply if the registration statement is for an offering of asset-backed securities on Form S–1 or Form S–3, and the information required to be included in a post-effective amendment is provided pursuant to Item 1100(c) of Regulation AB.

(2) That, for the purpose of determining any liability under the Securities Act of 1933, each such post-effective amendment shall be deemed to be a new registration statement relating to the securities offered therein, and the offering of such securities at that time shall be deemed to be the initial bona fide offering thereof.

(3) To remove from registration by means of a post-effective amendment any of the securities being registered which remain unsold at the termination of the offering.

(4) If the registrant is a foreign private issuer, to file a post-effective amendment to the registration statement to include any financial statements required by Item 8.A of Form 20–F at the start of any delayed offering or throughout a continuous offering. Financial statements and information otherwise required by Section 10(a)(3) of the Act (15 U.S.C. 77j(a)(3)) need not be furnished, provided that the registrant includes in the prospectus, by means of a post-effective amendment, financial statements required pursuant to this paragraph (a)(4) and other information necessary to ensure that all other information in the prospectus is at least as current as the date of those financial statements. Notwithstanding the foregoing, with respect to registration statements on Form F–3, a post-effective amendment need not be filed to include financial statements and information required by Section 10(a)(3) of the Act or Item 8.A of Form 20–F if such financial statements and information are contained in periodic reports filed with or furnished to the Commission by the registrant pursuant to section 13 or section 15(d) of the Securities Exchange Act of 1934 that are incorporated by reference in the Form F–3.

(5) That, for the purpose of determining liability under the Securities Act of 1933 to any purchaser:

(i) If the registrant is relying on Rule 430B:

(A) Each prospectus filed by the registrant pursuant to Rule 424(b)(3) shall be deemed to be part of the registration statement as of the date the filed prospectus was deemed part of and included in the registration statement; and

(B) Each prospectus required to be filed pursuant to Rule 424(b)(2), (b)(5), or (b)(7) as part of a registration statement in reliance on Rule 430B relating to an offering made pursuant to Rule 415(a)(1)(i), (vii), or (x) for the purpose of providing the information required by section 10(a) of the Securities Act of 1933 shall be deemed to be part of and included in the registration statement as of the earlier of the date such form of prospectus is first used after effectiveness or the date of the first contract of sale of securities in the offering described in the prospectus. As provided in Rule 430B, for liability purposes of the issuer and any person that is at that date an underwriter, such date shall be deemed to be a new effective date of the registration statement relating to the securities in the registration statement to which that prospectus relates, and the offering of such securities at that time shall be deemed to be the initial bona fide offering thereof. Provided, however, that no statement made in a registration statement or prospectus that is part of the registration statement or made in a document incorporated or deemed incorporated by reference into the registration statement or prospectus that is part of the registration statement will, as to a purchaser with a time of contract of sale prior to such effective date, supersede or modify any statement that was made in the registration statement or prospectus that was part of the registration statement or made in any such document immediately prior to such effective date; or

(ii)   If the registrant is subject to Rule 430C, each prospectus filed pursuant to Rule 424(b) as part of a registration statement relating to an offering, other than registration statements relying on Rule 430B or other than prospectuses filed in reliance on Rule 430A, shall be deemed to be part of and included in the registration statement as of the date it is first used after effectiveness. Provided, however, that no statement made in a registration statement or prospectus that is part of the registration statement or made in a document incorporated or deemed incorporated by reference into the registration statement or prospectus that is part of the registration statement will, as to a purchaser with a time of contract of sale prior to such first use, supersede or modify any statement that was made in the registration statement or prospectus that was part of the registration statement or made in any such document immediately prior to such date of first use.

(iii)   If the registrant is relying on Rule 430D of the Securities Act of 1933:

(A)   Each prospectus filed by the registrant pursuant to Rules 424(b)(3) and (h) of the Securities Act of 1933 shall be deemed to be part of the registration statement as of the date the filed prospectus was deemed part of and included in the registration statement; and

(B)   Each prospectus required to be filed pursuant to Rules 424(b)(2), (b)(5), or (b)(7) of the Securities Act of 1933 as part of a registration statement in reliance on Rule 430D of the Securities Act of 1933 relating to an offering made pursuant to Rules 415(a)(1)(vii) or (a)(1)(xii) of the Securities Act of 1933 for the purpose of providing the information required by section 10(a) of the Securities Act of 1933 shall be deemed to be part of and included in the registration statement as of the earlier of the date such form of prospectus is first used after effectiveness or the date of the first contract of sale of securities in the offering described in the prospectus. As provided in Rule 430D of the Securities Act of 1933, for liability purposes of the issuer and any person that is at that date an underwriter, such date shall be deemed to be a new effective date of the registration statement relating to the securities in the registration statement to which that prospectus relates, and the offering of such securities at that time shall be deemed to be the initial bona fide offering thereof. Provided, however, that no statement made in a registration statement or prospectus that is part of the registration statement or made in a document incorporated or deemed incorporated by reference into the registration statement or prospectus that is part of the registration statement will, as to a purchaser with a time of contract of sale prior to such effective date, supersede or modify any statement that was made in the registration statement or prospectus that was part of the registration statement or made in any such document immediately prior to such effective date; or

(6)   That, for the purpose of determining liability of the registrant under the Securities Act of 1933 to any purchaser in the initial distribution of the securities:

The undersigned registrant undertakes that in a primary offering of securities of the undersigned registrant pursuant to this registration statement, regardless of the underwriting method used to sell the securities to the purchaser, if the securities are offered or sold to such purchaser by means of any of the following communications, the undersigned registrant will be a seller to the purchaser and will be considered to offer or sell such securities to such purchaser:

(i) Any preliminary prospectus or prospectus of the undersigned registrant relating to the offering required to be filed pursuant to Rule 424;

(ii) Any free writing prospectus relating to the offering prepared by or on behalf of the undersigned registrant or used or referred to by the undersigned registrant;

(iii) The portion of any other free writing prospectus relating to the offering containing material information about the undersigned registrant or its securities provided by or on behalf of the undersigned registrant; and

(iv) Any other communication that is an offer in the offering made by the undersigned registrant to the purchaser.

(7) If the registrant is relying on Rule 430D of the Securities Act of 1933, with respect to any offering of securities registered on Form SF–3, to file the information previously omitted from the prospectus filed as part of an effective registration statement in accordance with Rules 424(h) and 430D of the Securities Act of 1933.

(b) *Filings Incorporating Subsequent Exchange Act Documents by Reference.* Include the following if the registration statement incorporates by reference any Exchange Act document filed subsequent to the effective date of the registration statement:

The undersigned registrant hereby undertakes that, for purposes of determining any liability under the Securities Act of 1933, each filing of the registrant's annual report pursuant to section 13(a) or section 15(d) of the Securities Exchange Act of 1934 (and, where applicable, each filing of an employee benefit plan's annual report pursuant to section 15(d) of the Securities Exchange Act of 1934) that is incorporated by reference in the registration statement shall be deemed to be a new registration statement relating to the securities offered therein, and the offering of such securities at that time shall be deemed to be the initial bona fide offering thereof.

(c) [Removed and Reserved].

(d) [Removed and Reserved].

(e) [Removed and Reserved].

(f) [Removed and Reserved].

(g) *Registration on Form S–4 or F–4 of Securities Offered for Resale.* Include the following if the securities are being registered on Form S–4 or F–4 in connection with a transaction specified in paragraph (a) of Rule 145.

(1) The undersigned registrant hereby undertakes as follows: that prior to any public reoffering of the securities registered hereunder through use of a prospectus which is a part of this registration statement, by any person or party who is deemed to be an underwriter within the meaning of Rule 145(c) the issuer undertakes that such reoffering prospectus will contain the information called for by the applicable registration form with respect to reofferings by persons who may be deemed underwriters, in addition to the information called for by the other Items of the applicable form.

(2) The registrant undertakes that every prospectus (i) that is filed pursuant to paragraph (1) immediately preceding, or (ii) that purports to meet the requirements of section 10(a)(3) of the Act and is used in connection with an offering of securities subject to Rule 415, will be filed as a part of an amendment to the registration statement and will not be used until such amendment is effective, and that, for purposes of determining any liability under the Securities Act of 1933, each such post-effective amendment shall be deemed to be a new registration statement relating to the securities offered therein, and the offering of such securities at that time shall be deemed to be the initial bona fide offering thereof.

(h) *Request for acceleration of effective date or filing of registration statement becoming effective upon filing.* Include the following if acceleration is requested of the effective date of the registration statement pursuant to Rule 461 under the Securities Act, if a Form S–3 or Form F–3 will become effective upon filing with the Commission pursuant to Rule 462(e) or (f) under the Securities Act, or if the registration statement is filed on Form S–8, and:

(1) Any provision or arrangement exists whereby the registrant may indemnify a director, officer or controlling person of the registrant against liabilities arising under the Securities Act, or

(2) The underwriting agreement contains a provision whereby the registrant indemnifies the underwriter or controlling persons of the underwriter against such liabilities and a director, officer or controlling person of the registrant is such an underwriter or controlling person thereof or a member of any firm which is such an underwriter, and

(3) The benefits of such indemnification are not waived by such persons:

Insofar as indemnification for liabilities arising under the Securities Act of 1933 may be permitted to directors, officers and controlling persons of the registrant pursuant to the foregoing provisions, or otherwise, the registrant has been advised that in the opinion of the Securities and Exchange Commission such indemnification is against public policy as expressed in the Act and is, therefore, unenforceable. In the event that a claim for indemnification against such liabilities (other than the payment by the registrant of expenses incurred or paid by a director, officer or controlling person of the registrant in the successful defense of any action, suit or proceeding) is asserted by such director, officer or controlling person in connection with the securities being registered, the registrant will, unless in the opinion of its counsel the matter has been settled by controlling precedent, submit to a court of appropriate jurisdiction the question whether such indemnification by it is against public policy as expressed in the Act and will be governed by the final adjudication of such issue.

(i) Include the following in a registration statement permitted by Rule 430A under the Securities Act of 1933.

The undersigned registrant hereby undertakes that:

(1) For purposes of determining any liability under the Securities Act of 1933, the information omitted from the form of prospectus filed as part of this registration statement in reliance upon Rule 430A and contained in a form of prospectus filed by the registrant pursuant to Rule 424(b)(1) or (4) or 497(h) under the Securities Act shall be deemed to be part of this registration statement as of the time it was declared effective.

(2) For the purpose of determining any liability under the Securities Act of 1933, each post-effective amendment that contains a form of prospectus shall be deemed to be a new registration statement relating to the securities offered therein, and the offering of such securities at that time shall be deemed to be the initial bona fide offering thereof.

(j) *Qualification of Trust Indentures Under the Trust Indenture Act of 1939 for Delayed Offerings.* Include the following if the registrant intends to rely on section 305(b)(2) of the Trust Indenture Act of 1939 for determining the eligibility of the trustee under indentures for securities to be used, offered, or sold on a delayed basis by or on behalf of the registrant:

The undersigned registrant hereby undertakes to file an application for the purpose of determining the eligibility of the trustee to act under subsection (a) of section 310 of the Trust Indenture Act ("Act") in accordance with the rules and regulations prescribed by the Commission under section 305(b)(2) of the Act.

(k) *Filings regarding asset-backed securities incorporating by reference subsequent Exchange Act documents by third parties.* Include the following if the registration statement incorporates by reference any Exchange Act document filed subsequent to the effective date of the registration statement pursuant to Item 1100(c) of Regulation AB:

The undersigned registrant hereby undertakes that, for purposes of determining any liability under the Securities Act of 1933, each filing of the annual report pursuant to section 13(a) or section 15(d) of the Securities Exchange Act of 1934 of a third party that is incorporated by reference in the registration statement in accordance with Item 1100(c)(1) of Regulation AB shall be deemed to be a new registration statement relating to the securities offered therein, and the offering of such securities at that time shall be deemed to be the initial bona fide offering thereof.

The undersigned registrant hereby undertakes that, except as otherwise provided by Item 1105 of Regulation AB, information provided in response to that Item pursuant to Rule 312 of Regulation S–T through the specified Internet address in the prospectus is deemed to be a part of the prospectus included in the registration statement. In addition, the undersigned registrant hereby undertakes to provide to any person without charge, upon request, a copy of the information provided in response to Item 1105 of Regulation AB pursuant to Rule 312 of Regulation S–T through the specified Internet address as of the date of the prospectus included in the registration statement if a subsequent update or change is made to the information.

Subpart 600—Exhibits

Item 601.   **Exhibits**

(a)   *Exhibits and Index Required.* (1) Subject to Rule 411(c) of the Securities Act of 1933 and Rule 12b–23(c) of the Exchange Act of 1934 regarding incorporation of exhibits by reference, the exhibits required in the exhibit table must be filed as indicated, as part of the registration statement or report.

(2)   Each registration statement or report shall contain an exhibit index, which must appear before the required signatures in the registration statement or report. For convenient reference, each exhibit shall be listed in the exhibit index according to the number assigned to it in the exhibit table. If an exhibit is incorporated by reference, this must be noted in the exhibit index. Each exhibit identified in the exhibit index (other than an exhibit filed in eXtensible Business Reporting Language or an exhibit that is filed with Form ABS–EE) must include an active link to an exhibit that is filed with the registration statement or report or, if the exhibit is incorporated by reference, an active hyperlink to the exhibit separately filed on EDGAR. If a registration statement or report is amended, each amendment must include hyperlinks to the exhibits required with the amendment. For a description of each of the exhibits included in the exhibit table, see paragraph (b) of this rule.

(3)   This Item applies only to the forms specified in the exhibit table. With regard to forms not listed in that table, reference shall be made to the appropriate form for the specific exhibit filing requirements applicable thereto.

(4)   If a material contract or plan of acquisition, reorganization, arrangement, liquidation or succession is executed or becomes effective during the reporting period reflected by a Form 10–Q or Form 10–K, it shall be filed as an exhibit to the Form 10–Q or Form 10–K filed for the corresponding period. Any amendment or modification to a previously filed exhibit to a Form 10, 10–K or 10–Q document shall be filed as an exhibit to a Form 10–Q and Form 10–K. Such amendment or modification need not be filed where such previously filed exhibit would not be currently required.

(5)   Schedules (or similar attachments) to the exhibits required by this Item are not required to be filed provided that they do not contain information material to an investment or voting decision and that information is not otherwise disclosed in the exhibit or the disclosure document. Each exhibit filed must contain a list briefly identifying the contents of all omitted schedules. Registrants need not prepare a separate list of omitted information if such information is already included within the exhibit in a manner that conveys the subject matter of the omitted schedules and attachments. In addition, the registrant must provide a copy of any omitted schedule to the Commission or its staff upon request.

(6)   The registrant may redact information from exhibits required to be filed by this Item if disclosure of such information would constitute a clearly unwarranted invasion of personal privacy (e.g., disclosure of bank account numbers, social security numbers, home addresses, and similar information).

Instructions to Item 601. 1. If an exhibit to a registration statement (other than an opinion or consent), filed in preliminary form, has been changed only (A) to insert information as to interest, dividend or conversion rates, redemption or conversion prices, purchase or offering prices, underwriters' or dealers' commission, names, addresses or participation of underwriters or similar matters, which information appears elsewhere in an amendment to the registration statement or a prospectus filed pursuant to Rule 424(b) under the Securities Act or (B) to correct typographical errors, insert signatures or make other similar immaterial changes, then, notwithstanding any contrary requirement of any rule or form, the registrant need not refile such exhibit as so amended. Any such incomplete exhibit may not, however, be incorporated by reference in any subsequent filing under any Act administered by the Commission.

2.   In any case where two or more indentures, contracts, franchises, or other documents required to be filed as exhibits are substantially identical in all material respects except as to the parties thereto, the dates of execution, or other details, the registrant need file a copy of only one of such documents, with a schedule identifying

the other documents omitted and setting forth the material details in which such documents differ from the document a copy of which is filed. The Commission may at any time in its discretion require filing of copies of any documents so omitted.

     3.   Only copies, rather than originals, need be filed of each exhibit required except as otherwise specifically noted.

     4.   Electronic filings. Whenever an exhibit is filed in paper pursuant to a hardship exemption (Rule 201 or 202d), the letter "p" (paper) shall be placed next to the listed exhibit in the list of exhibits required by Item 601(a)(2) of this rule. Whenever an electronic confirming copy of an exhibit is filed pursuant to a hardship exemption Rule 201 or Rule 202(d), the exhibit index should specify where the confirming electronic copy can be located; in addition, the designation "CE" (confirming electronic) should be placed next to the listed exhibit in the exhibit index.

Exhibit Table

Instructions to the Exhibit Table. 1. The exhibit table indicates those documents that must be filed as exhibits to the respective forms listed.

     2.   The "X" designation indicates the documents which are required to be filed with each form even if filed previously with another document, *Provided, however,* that such previously filed documents may be incorporated by reference to satisfy the filing requirements.

     3.   The number used in the far left column of the table refers to the appropriate subsection in paragraph (b) where a description of the exhibit can be found. Whenever necessary, alphabetical or numerical subparts may be used.

Exhibit Table

	Securities act forms										Exchange act forms					
	S–1	S–3	SF–1	SF–3	S–4[1]	S–8	S–11	F–1	F–3	F–4[1]	10	8–K[2]	10–D	10–Q	10–K	ABS–EE
(1) Underwriting agreement	X	X	X	X	X		X	X	X	X		X				
(2) Plan of acquisition, reorganization, arrangement, liquidation or succession	X	X	X	X	X		X	X	X	X	X	X		X	X	
(3)(i) Articles of incorporation	X		X	X	X		X	X		X	X	X	X	X	X	
(ii) Bylaws	X		X	X	X		X	X		X	X	X	X	X	X	
(4) Instruments defining the rights of securities holders, including indentures, (i) through (v)	X	X	X	X	X	X	X	X	X	X	X	X	X	X	X	
(vi) Description of registrant's securities															X	
(5) Opinion re legality	X	X	X	X	X	X	X	X	X	X						
(6) [Reserved]	N/A	N/A	N/A	N/A	N/A	N/A	N/A	N/A	N/A	N/A	N/A	N/A	N/A	N/A	N/A	N/A

(7) Correspondence from an independent accountant regarding non-reliance on a previously issued audit report or completed interim review											X				
(8) Opinion re tax matters	X	X	X	X	X		X	X	X	X					
(9) Voting trust agreement	X				X		X	X		X	X			X	
(10) Material contracts	X		X	X	X		X	X		X	X		X	X	X
(11) [Removed and Reserved]															
(12) [Removed and Reserved]															
(13) Annual report to security holders, Form 10–Q or quarterly report to security holders[3]					X								X	X	
(14) Code of Ethics											X			X	
(15) Letter re unaudited interim financial information	X	X			X	X	X	X	X	X			X		
(16) Letter re change in certifying accountant[4]	X				X		X			X	X			X	
(17) Correspondence on departure of director											X				
(18) Letter re change in accounting principles													X	X	
(19) [Removed and Reserved]															
(20) Other documents or statements to security holders											X				

	1	2	3	4	5	6	7	8	9	10	11	12	13	14	15	16	17
(21) Subsidiaries of the registrant	X		X	X	X		X	X		X	X					X	
(22) [Removed and Reserved]																	
(23) Consents of experts and counsel	X	X	X	X	X	X	X	X	X	X			5X	5X	5X	5X	
(24) Power of attorney	X	X	X	X	X	X	X	X	X	X	X	X			X	X	
(25) Statement of eligibility of trustee	X	X	X	X	X			X	X	X							
(26) [Removed and Reserved]																	
(27) through (30) [Reserved]																	
(31)(i) Rule 13a–14(a)/15d–14(a) Certifications																X	
(ii) Rule 13a–14/15d–14 Certifications																X	
(32) Section 1350 Certifications[6]															X	X	
(33) Report on assessment of compliance with servicing criteria for asset-backed issuers																X	
(34) Attestation report on assessment of compliance with servicing criteria for asset-backed securities																X	
(35) Servicer compliance statement																X	
(36) Depositor Certification for shelf offerings of asset-backed securities				X													
(37) through (94) [Reserved]	N/A	N/A	N/A	N/A	N/A	N/A	N/A	N/A	N/A	N/A	N/A	N/A	N/A	N/A	N/A	N/A	N/A
(95) Mine Safety Disclosure Exhibit															X	X	

(96) Technical Report Summary[7]	X	X			X		X	X	X	X				X		
(97) Policy Relating to Recovery of Erroneously Awarded Compensation															X	
(99) Additional exhibits	X	X	X	X	X	X	X	X	X	X	X	X	X	X	X	
[reserved]																
(101) Interactive Data File	X	X			X		X	X	X			X		X	X	
(102) Asset Data File			X	X								X				X
(103) Asset Related Documents			X	X								X				X
(104) Cover Page Interactive Data File												X		X	X	
(105) [Reserved]																
(106) Static Pool PDF			X	X								X				

[1] An exhibit need not be provided about a company if: (1) With respect to such company an election has been made under Form S–4 or F–4 to provide information about such company at a level prescribed by Form S–3 or F–3; and (2) the form, the level of which has been elected under Form S–4 or F–4, would not require such company to provide such exhibit if it were registering a primary offering.

[2] A Form 8–K exhibit is required only if relevant to the subject matter reported on the Form 8–K report. For example, if the Form 8–K pertains to the departure of a director, only the exhibit described in paragraph (b)(17) of this item need be filed. A required exhibit may be incorporated by reference from a previous filing.

[3] Where incorporated by reference into the text of the prospectus and delivered to security holders along with the prospectus as permitted by the registration statement; or, in the case of the Form 10–K, where the annual report to security holders is incorporated by reference into the text of the Form 10–K.

[4] If required pursuant to Item 304 of Regulation S–K.

[5] Where the opinion of the expert or counsel has been incorporated by reference into a previously filed Securities Act registration statement.

[6] Pursuant to Rules 3a–13(b)(3) and 15d–13(b)(3) of the Securities Exchange Act of 1934, asset-backed issuers are not required to file reports on Form 10–Q.

[7] If required pursuant to Item 1302 of Regulation S–K.

(b) *Description of Exhibits.* Set forth below is a description of each document listed in the exhibit tables.

(1) *Underwriting Agreement.* Each underwriting contract or agreement with a principal underwriter pursuant to which the securities being registered are to be distributed; if the terms of such documents have not been determined, the proposed forms thereof. Such agreement may be filed as an exhibit to a report on Form 8–K which is incorporated by reference into a registration statement subsequent to its effectiveness.

(2) *Plan of acquisition, reorganization, arrangement, liquidation, or succession.*

(i)   Any material plan of acquisition, disposition, reorganization, readjustment, succession, liquidation, or arrangement and any amendments thereto described in the statement or report.

(ii)   The registrant may redact specific provisions or terms of exhibits required to be filed by paragraph (b)(2) of this section if the registrant customarily and actually treats that information as private or confidential and if the omitted information is not material. If it does so, the registrant should mark the exhibit index to indicate that portions of the exhibit or exhibits have been omitted and include a prominent statement on the first page of the redacted exhibit that certain identified information has been excluded from the exhibit because it is both not material and is the type that the registrant treats as private or confidential. The registrant also must include brackets indicating where the information is omitted from the filed version of the exhibit. If requested by the Commission or its staff, the registrant must promptly provide on a supplemental basis an unredacted copy of the exhibit and its materiality and privacy or confidentiality analyses. Upon evaluation of the registrant's supplemental materials, the Commission or its staff may require the registrant to amend its filing to include in the exhibit any previously redacted information that is not adequately supported by the registrant's analyses. The registrant may request confidential treatment of the supplemental material submitted under this paragraph (b)(2)(ii) pursuant to § 200.83 of this chapter while it is in the possession of the Commission or its staff. After completing its review of the supplemental information, the Commission or its staff will return or destroy it if the registrant complies with the procedures outlined in Rule 418 of the Securities Act or Rule 2b–4 of the Exchange Act.

(3)(i)   *Articles of Incorporation.* The articles of incorporation of the registrant or instruments corresponding thereto as currently in effect and any amendments thereto. Whenever the registrant files an amendment to its articles of incorporation, it must file a complete copy of the articles as amended. However, if such amendment is being reported on Form 8–K, the registrant is required to file only the text of the amendment as a Form 8–K exhibit. In such case, a complete copy of the articles of incorporation as amended must be filed as an exhibit to the next Securities Act registration statement or periodic report filed by the registrant to which this exhibit requirement applies. Where it is impracticable for the registrant to file a charter amendment authorizing new securities with the appropriate state authority prior to the effective date of the registration statement registering such securities, the registrant may file as an exhibit to the registration statement the form of amendment to be filed with the state authority. In such a case, if material changes are made after the copy is filed, the registrant must also file the changed copy.

(ii)   *Bylaws.* The bylaws of the registrant or instruments corresponding thereto as currently in effect and any amendments thereto. Whenever the registrant files an amendment to the bylaws, it must file a complete copy of the amended bylaws. However, if such amendment is being reported on Form 8–K, the registrant is required to file only the text of the amendment as a Form 8–K exhibit. In such case, a complete copy of the bylaws as amended must be filed as an exhibit to the next Securities Act registration statement or periodic report filed by the registrant to which this exhibit requirement applies.

(4)   *Instruments Defining the Rights of Security Holders, Including Indentures.* (i) All instruments defining the rights of holders of the equity or debt securities being registered including, where applicable, the relevant portion of the articles of incorporation or by-laws of the registrant.

(ii)   Except as set forth in paragraph (b)(4)(iii) of this Item for filings on Forms S–1, S–4, S–11, N–14, and F–4 under the Securities Act and Forms 10 and 10–K under the Exchange Act all instruments defining the rights of holders of long-term debt of the registrant and its consolidated subsidiaries and for any of its unconsolidated subsidiaries for which financial statements are required to be filed.

(iii)   Where the instrument defines the rights of holders of long-term debt of the registrant and its consolidated subsidiaries and for any of its unconsolidated subsidiaries for which financial statements are required to be filed, there need not be filed (A) any instrument with respect to long-term debt not being registered if the total amount of securities authorized thereunder does not exceed 10 percent of the total assets of the registrant and its subsidiaries on a consolidated basis and if there is filed an agreement to furnish a copy of such agreement to the Commission upon request; (B) any instrument with respect to any class of securities if appropriate steps to assure the redemption or retirement of such class will be taken prior to or upon delivery by the registrant of the securities being registered; or (C) copies of instruments evidencing scrip certificates for fractions of shares.

(iv) If any of the securities being registered are, or will be, issued under an indenture to be qualified under the Trust Indenture Act, the copy of such indenture which is filed as an exhibit shall include or be accompanied by (A) a reasonably itemized and informative table of contents; and (B) a cross-reference sheet showing the location in the indenture of the provisions inserted pursuant to sections 310 through 318(a) inclusive of the Trust Indenture Act of 1939.

(v) With respect to Forms 8–K and 10–Q under the Exchange Act that are filed and that disclose, in the text of the Form 10–Q, the interim financial statements, or the footnotes thereto the creation of a new class of securities or indebtedness or the modification of existing rights of security holders, file all instruments defining the rights of holders of these securities or indebtedness. However, there need not be filed any instrument with respect to long-term debt not being registered which meets the exclusion set forth in paragraph (b)(4)(iii)(A) of this Item.

Instruction 1 to paragraph (b)(4). There need not be filed any instrument which defines the rights of participants (not as security holders) pursuant to an employee benefit plan.

Instruction 2 to paragraph (b)(4) (for electronic filings). If the instrument defining the rights of security holders is in the form of a certificate, the text appearing on the certificate shall be reproduced in an electronic filing together with a description of any other graphic and image material appearing on the certificate, as provided in Rule 304 of Regulation S–T.

(vi) For each class of securities that is registered under Section 12 of the Exchange Act, provide the information required by Item 202(a) through (d) and (f) of Regulation S–K.

Instruction 1 to paragraph (b)(4)(vi). A registrant is only required to provide the information called for by Item 601(b)(4)(vi) if it is filing an annual report under Exchange Act Section 13(a) or 15(d).

Instruction 2 to paragraph (b)(4)(vi). For purposes of Item 601(b)(4)(vi), all references in Item 202 to securities to be or being registered, offered, or sold will mean securities that are registered as of the end of the period covered by the report with which the exhibit is filed. In addition, for purposes of this Item, the disclosure will be required for classes of securities that have not been retired by the end of the period covered by the report.

Instruction 3 to paragraph (b)(4)(vi). The registrant may incorporate by reference to an exhibit previously filed in satisfaction of Item 601(b)(4)(vi) of Regulation S–K, as applicable, so long as there has not been any change to the information called for by Item 202 since the filing date of the linked filing. Such hyperlink will be deemed to satisfy the requirements of Item 601(b)(4)(vi) for the current filing.

(5) *Opinion re Legality.* (i) An opinion of counsel as to the legality of the securities being registered, indicating whether they will, when sold, be legally issued, fully paid and non-assessable, and, if debt securities, whether they will be binding obligations of the registrant.

(ii) If the securities being registered are issued under a plan and the plan is subject to the requirements of ERISA furnish either:

(A) An opinion of counsel which confirms compliance of the provisions of the written documents constituting the plan with the requirements of ERISA pertaining to such provisions; or

(B) A copy of the Internal Revenue Service determination letter that the plan is qualified under section 401 of the Internal Revenue Code; or

(iii) If the securities being registered are issued under a plan which is subject to the requirements of ERISA and the plan has been amended subsequent to the filing of (ii)(A) or (B) above, furnish either:

(A) An opinion of counsel which confirms compliance of the amended provisions of the plan with the requirements of ERISA pertaining to such provisions; or

(B) A copy of the Internal Revenue Service determination letter that the amended plan is qualified under section 401 of the Internal Revenue Code.

NOTE: Attention is directed to Item 8 of Form S–8 for exemptions to this exhibit requirement applicable to that Form.

(6)   Removed and reserved.

(7)   *Correspondence from an Independent Accountant Regarding Non-reliance on a Previously Issued Audit Report or Completed Interim Review.* Any written notice from the registrant's current or previously engaged independent accountant that the independent accountant is withdrawing a previously issued audit report or that a previously issued audit report or completed interim review, covering one or more years or interim periods for which the registrant is required to provide financial statements under Regulation S–X, should no longer be relied upon. In addition, any letter, pursuant to Item 4.02(c) of Form 8–K, from the independent accountant to the Commission stating whether the independent accountant agrees with the statements made by the registrant describing the events giving rise to the notice.

(8)   *Opinion re Tax Matters.* For filings on Form S–11 under the Securities Act or those to which Securities Act Industry Guide 5 applies, an opinion of counsel or of an independent public or certified public accountant or, in lieu thereof, a revenue ruling from the Internal Revenue Service, supporting the tax matters and consequences to the shareholder as described in the filing when such tax matters are material to the transaction for which the registration statement is being filed. This exhibit otherwise need only be filed with the other applicable registration forms where the tax consequences are material to an investor and a representation as to tax consequences is set forth in the filing. If a tax opinion is set forth in full in the filing, an indication that such is the case may be made in lieu of filing the otherwise required exhibit. Such tax opinions may be conditioned or may be qualified, so long as such conditions and qualifications are adequately described in the filing.

(9)   *Voting Trust Agreement.* Any voting trust agreements and amendments thereto.

(10)   *Material contracts.* (i)(A) Every contract not made in the ordinary course of business that is material to the registrant and is to be performed in whole or in part at or after the filing of the registration statement or report. In addition, for newly reporting registrants, every contract not made in the ordinary course of business that is material to the registrant and that was entered into not more than two years before the date on which such registrant:

        (1)   First files a registration statement or report; or

        (2)   Completes a transaction that had the effect of causing it to cease being a public shell company.

        (B)   The only contracts that need to be filed are those to which the registrant or a subsidiary of the registrant is a party or has succeeded to a party by assumption or assignment or in which the registrant or such subsidiary has a beneficial interest.

    (ii)   If the contract is such as ordinarily accompanies the kind of business conducted by the registrant and its subsidiaries, it will be deemed to have been made in the ordinary course of business and need not be filed unless it falls within one or more of the following categories, in which case it shall be filed except where immaterial in amount or significance:

        (A)   Any contract to which directors, officers, promoters, voting trustees, security holders named in the registration statement or report, or underwriters are parties other than contracts involving only the purchase or sale of current assets having a determinable market price, at such market price;

        (B)   Any contract upon which the registrant's business is substantially dependent, as in the case of continuing contracts to sell the major part of registrant's products or services or to purchase the major part of registrant's requirements of goods, services or raw materials or any franchise or license or other agreement to use a patent, formula, trade secret, process or trade name upon which registrant's business depends to a material extent;

        (C)   Any contract calling for the acquisition or sale of any property, plant or equipment for a consideration exceeding 15 percent of such fixed assets of the registrant on a consolidated basis; or

        (D)   Any material lease under which a part of the property described in the registration statement or report is held by the registrant.

(iii)(A)   Any management contract or any compensatory plan, contract or arrangement, including but not limited to plans relating to options, warrants or rights, pension, retirement or deferred compensation or bonus, incentive or profit sharing (or if not set forth in any formal document, a written description thereof) in which any director or any of the named executive officers of the registrant, as defined by Item 402(a)(3), participates shall be deemed material and shall be filed; and any other management contract or any compensatory plan, contract, or arrangement in which any other executive officer of the registrant participates shall be filed unless immaterial in amount or significance.

(B)   Any compensatory plan, contract or arrangement adopted without the approval of security holders pursuant to which equity may be awarded, including, but not limited to, options, warrants or rights (or if not set forth in any formal document, a written description thereof), in which any employee (whether or not an executive officer of the registrant) participates shall be filed unless immaterial in amount or significance. A compensation plan assumed by a registrant in connection with a merger, consolidation or other acquisition transaction pursuant to which the registrant may make further grants or awards of its equity securities shall be considered a compensation plan of the registrant for purposes of the preceding sentence.

(C)   Notwithstanding paragraph (iii)(A) above, the following management contracts or compensatory plans, contracts or arrangements need not be filed:

(1)   Ordinary purchase and sales agency agreements.

(2)   Agreements with managers of stores in a chain organization or similar organization.

(3)   Contracts providing for labor or salesmen's bonuses or payments to a class of security holders, as such.

(4)   Any compensatory plan, contract or arrangement which pursuant to its terms is available to employees, officers or directors generally and which in operation provides for the same method of allocation of benefits between management and non-management participants.

(5)   Any compensatory plan, contract or arrangement if the registrant is a foreign private issuer that furnishes compensatory information under Item 402(a)(1) and the public filing of the plan, contract or arrangement, or portion thereof, is not required in the registrant's home country and is not otherwise publicly disclosed by the registrant.

(6)   Any compensatory plan, contract, or arrangement if the registrant is a wholly owned subsidiary of a company that has a class of securities registered pursuant to section 12 or files reports pursuant to section 15(d) of the Exchange Act and is filing a report on Form 10–K or registering debt instruments or preferred stock which are not voting securities on Form S–1.

(iv)   The registrant may redact specific provisions or terms of exhibits required to be filed by this paragraph (b)(10) if the registrant customarily and actually treats that information as private or confidential and if the omitted information is not material. If it does so, the registrant should mark the exhibit index to indicate that portions of the exhibit or exhibits have been omitted and include a prominent statement on the first page of the redacted exhibit that certain identified information has been excluded from the exhibit because it is both not material and is the type that the registrant treats as private or confidential. The registrant also must include brackets indicating where the information is omitted from the filed version of the exhibit. If requested by the Commission or its staff, the registrant must promptly provide on a supplemental basis an unredacted copy of the exhibit and its materiality and privacy or confidentiality analyses. Upon evaluation of the registrant's supplemental materials, the Commission or its staff may require the registrant to amend its filing to include in the exhibit any previously redacted information that is not adequately supported by the registrant's analyses. The registrant may request confidential treatment of the supplemental material submitted under this paragraph (b)(10)(iv) pursuant to § 200.83 of this chapter while it is in the possession of the Commission or its staff. After completing its review of the supplemental information, the Commission or its staff will return or destroy it if the registrant complies with the procedures outlined in Rule 418 of the Securities Act or Rule 12b–4 of the Exchange Act.

Instruction 1 to paragraph (b)(10) of Item 601: For purposes of paragraph (b)(10)(i) of this Item, a "newly reporting registrant" is:

1.   Any registrant filing a registration statement that, at the time of such filing, is not subject to the reporting requirements of Section 13(a) or 15(d) of the Exchange Act, whether or not such registrant has ever previously been subject to the reporting requirements of Section 13(a) or 15(d),

2.   Any registrant that has not filed an annual report since the revival of a previously suspended reporting obligation, and

3.   Any registrant that: a. Was a shell company, other than a business combination related shell company, as defined in Rule 12b–2 of the Exchange Act, immediately before completing a transaction that has the effect of causing it to cease being a shell company and b. Has not filed a registration statement or Form 8–K as required by Items 2.01 and 5.06 of that form, since the completion of such transaction.

4.   For example, newly reporting registrants would include a registrant that is filing its first registration statement under the Securities Act or the Exchange Act, and a registrant that was a public shell company, other than a business combination related shell company, and completes a reverse merger transaction causing it to cease being a shell company.

Instruction 2 to paragraph (b)(10): With the exception of management contracts, in order to comply with paragraph (b)(10)(iii) of this item, registrants need only file copies of the various compensatory plans and need not file each individual director's or executive officer's personal agreement under the plans unless there are particular provisions in such personal agreements whose disclosure in an exhibit is necessary to an investor's understanding of that individual's compensation under the plan.

Instruction 3 to paragraph (b)(10): If a material contract is executed or becomes effective during the reporting period reflected by a Form 10–Q or Form 10–K, it must be filed as an exhibit to the Form 10–Q or Form 10–K filed for the corresponding period. See paragraph (a)(4) of this Item. With respect to quarterly reports on Form 10–Q, only those contracts executed or becoming effective during the most recent period reflected in the report must be filed.

(11)   [Removed and Reserved].

(12)   [Removed and Reserved].

(13)   *Annual or quarterly report to security holders.* (i) The registrant's annual report to security holders for its last fiscal year or its quarterly report to security holders, if all or a portion thereof is incorporated by reference in the filing. Such report, except for those portions thereof that are expressly incorporated by reference in the filing, is to be furnished for the information of the Commission and is not to be deemed "filed" as part of the filing. If the financial statements in the report have been incorporated by reference in the filing, the accountant's certificate must be manually signed in one copy. See Rule 439 of the Securities Act.

(ii)   Electronic filings. If all, or any portion, of the annual or quarterly to security holders is incorporated by reference into any electronic filing, all, or such portion of the annual or quarterly report to security holders so incorporated, must be filed in electronic format as an exhibit to the filing.

(14)   *Code of Ethics.* Any code of ethics, or amendment thereto, that is the subject of the disclosure required by Item 406 of Regulation S–K or Item 5.05 of Form 8–K, to the extent that the registrant intends to satisfy the Item 406 or Item 5.05 requirements through filing of an exhibit.

(15)   *Letter re Unaudited Interim Financial Information.* A letter, where applicable, from the independent accountant that acknowledges awareness of the use in a registration statement of a report on unaudited interim financial information that pursuant to Rule 436(c) under the Securities Act is not considered a part of a registration statement prepared or certified by an accountant or a report prepared or certified by an accountant within the meaning of sections 7 and 11 of that Act. Such letter

may be filed with the registration statement, an amendment thereto, or a report on Form 10–Q which is incorporated by reference into the registration statement.

(16) *Letter re Change in Certifying Accountant.* A letter from the registrant's former independent accountant regarding its concurrence or disagreement with the statements made by the registrant in the current report concerning the resignation or dismissal as the registrant's principal accountant.

(17) *Correspondence on Departure of Director.* Any written correspondence from a former director concerning the circumstances surrounding the former director's retirement, resignation, refusal to stand for re-election or removal, including any letter from the former director to the registrant stating whether the former director agrees with statements made by the registrant describing the former director's departure.

(18) *Letter re Change in Accounting Principles.* Unless previously filed, a letter from the registrant's independent accountant indicating whether any change in accounting principles or practices followed by the registrant, or any change in the method of applying any such accounting principles or practices, which affected the financial statements being filed with the Commission in the report or which is reasonably certain to affect the financial statements of future fiscal years is to an alternative principle which in his judgment is preferable under the circumstances. No such letter need be filed when such change is made in response to a standard adopted by the Financial Accounting Standards Board that creates a new accounting principle, that expresses a preference for an accounting principle, or that rejects a specific accounting principle.

(19) *Report Furnished to Security Holders.* If the registrant makes available to its security holders or otherwise publishes, within the period prescribed for filing the report, a document or statement containing information meeting some or all of the requirements of Part I of Form 10–Q, the information called for may be incorporated by reference to such published document or statement, provided copies thereof are included as an exhibit to the registration statement or to Part I of the Form 10–Q report.

(20) *Other Documents or Statements to Security Holders.* If the registrant makes available to its stockholders or otherwise publishes, within the period prescribed for filing the report, a document or statement containing information meeting some or all of the requirements of this form the information called for may be incorporated by reference to such published document or statement provided copies thereof are filed as an exhibit to the report on this form.

(21) *Subsidiaries of the Registrant.*

    (i)   List all subsidiaries of the registrant, the state or other jurisdiction of incorporation or organization of each, and the names under which such subsidiaries do business. This list may be incorporated by reference from a document which includes a complete and accurate list.

    (ii)   The names of particular subsidiaries may be omitted if the unnamed subsidiaries, considered in the aggregate as a single subsidiary, would not constitute a significant subsidiary as of the end of the year covered by this report. (See the definition of "significant subsidiary" in Item 1–02(w) of Regulation S–X.) The names of consolidated wholly-owned multiple subsidiaries carrying on the same line of business, such as chain stores or small loan companies, may be omitted, provided the name of the immediate parent, the line of business, the number of omitted subsidiaries operating in the United States and the number operating in foreign countries are given. This instruction shall not apply, however, to banks, insurance companies, savings and loan associations or to any subsidiary subject to regulation by another Federal agency.

(22) *Published Report Regarding Matters Submitted to Vote of Security Holders.* Published reports containing all of the information called for by Item 4 of Part II of Form 10–Q or Item 4 of Part I of Form 10–K that is referred to therein in lieu of providing disclosure in Form 10–Q or 10–K, that are required to be filed as exhibits by Rule 12b–23(a)(3) under the Exchange Act.

(23) *Consents of Experts and Counsel.* (i) *Securities Act Filings.* All written consents required to be filed shall be dated and manually signed. Where the consent of an expert or counsel is contained in his report or opinion or elsewhere in the registration statement or document filed therewith, a reference shall be made in the index to the report, the part of the registration statement or document or opinion, containing the consent.

(ii) *Exchange Act Reports.* Where the filing of a written consent is required with respect to material incorporated by reference in a previously filed registration statement under the Securities Act, such consent may be filed as an exhibit to the material incorporated by reference. Such consents shall be dated and manually signed.

(24) *Power of Attorney.* If any name is signed to the registration statement or report pursuant to a power of attorney, manually signed copies of such power of attorney shall be filed. Where the power of attorney is contained elsewhere in the registration statement or documents filed therewith a reference shall be made in the index to the part of the registration statement or document containing such power of attorney. In addition, if the name of any officer signing on behalf of the registrant is signed pursuant to a power of attorney, certified copies of a resolution of the registrant's board of directors authorizing such signature shall also be filed. A power of attorney that is filed with the Commission shall relate to a specific filing or an amendment thereto, provided, however, that a power of attorney relating to a registration statement under the Securities Act or an amendment thereto also may relate to any registration statement for the same offering that is to be effective upon filing pursuant to Rule 462(b) under the Securities Act. A power of attorney that confers general authority shall not be filed with the Commission.

(25) *Statement of Eligibility of Trustee.* (i) A statement of eligibility and qualification of each person designated to act as trustee under an indenture to be qualified under the Trust Indenture Act of 1939. Such statement of eligibility shall be bound separately from the other exhibits.

(ii) *Electronic filings.* The requirement to bind separately the statement of eligibility and qualification of each person designated to act as a trustee under the Trust Indenture Act of 1939 from other exhibits shall not apply to statements submitted in electronic format. Rather, such statements shall be submitted as exhibits in the same electronic submission as the subject registration statement to which it relates or an amendment thereto, *except that* electronic filers that rely on Trust Indenture Act section 305(b)(2) for determining the eligibility of the trustee under indenture for securities to be issued, offered or sold on a delayed basis by or on behalf of the registrant shall file such statements separately in the manner prescribed by Rules 5b–1 through 5b–3 under the Trust Indenture Act and by the EDGAR Filer Manual.

(26) *Invitations for Competitive Bids.* If the registration statement covers securities to be offered at competitive bidding, any form of communication which is an invitation for competitive bid which will be sent or given to any person shall be filed.

(27) through (30) [Reserved]

(31) *Rule 13a–14(a)/15d–14(a) Certifications.*

(i)   The certifications required by Rule 13a–14(a) or Rule 15d–14(a) exactly as set forth below:

Certifications* I, [identify the certifying individual], certify that:

1.   I have reviewed this [specify report] of [identify registrant];

2.   Based on my knowledge, this report does not contain any untrue statement of a material fact or omit to state a material fact necessary to make the statements made, in light of the circumstances under which such statements were made, not misleading with respect to the period covered by this report;

3.   Based on my knowledge, the financial statements, and other financial information included in this report, fairly present in all material respects the financial condition, results of operations and cash flows of the registrant as of, and for, the periods presented in this report;

4.   The registrant's other certifying officer(s) and I are responsible for establishing and maintaining disclosure controls and procedures (as defined in Exchange Act Rules 13a–

---

*   Provide a separate certification for each principal executive officer and principal financial officer of the registrant. See Rules 13a–14(a) and 15d–14(a).

15(e) and 15d–15(e)) and internal control over financial reporting (as defined in Exchange Act Rules 13a–15(f) and 15d–15(f)) for the registrant and have:

(a)   Designed such disclosure controls and procedures, or caused such disclosure controls and procedures to be designed under our supervision, to ensure that material information relating to the registrant, including its consolidated subsidiaries, is made known to us by others within those entities, particularly during the period in which this report is being prepared;

(b)   Designed such internal control over financial reporting, or caused such internal control over financial reporting to be designed under our supervision, to provide reasonable assurance regarding the reliability of financial reporting and the preparation of financial statements for external purposes in accordance with generally accepted accounting principles;

(c)   Evaluated the effectiveness of the registrant's disclosure controls and procedures and presented in this report our conclusions about the effectiveness of the disclosure controls and procedures, as of the end of the period covered by this report based on such evaluation; and

(d)   Disclosed in this report any change in the registrant's internal control over financial reporting that occurred during the registrant's most recent fiscal quarter (the registrant's fourth fiscal quarter in the case of an annual report) that has materially affected, or is reasonably likely to materially affect, the registrant's internal control over financial reporting; and

5.   The registrant's other certifying officer(s) and I have disclosed, based on our most recent evaluation of internal control over financial reporting, to the registrant's auditors and the audit committee of the registrant's board of directors (or persons performing the equivalent functions):

(a)   All significant deficiencies and material weaknesses in the design or operation of internal control over financial reporting which are reasonably likely to adversely affect the registrant's ability to record, process, summarize and report financial information; and

(b)   Any fraud, whether or not material, that involves management or other employees who have a significant role in the registrant's internal control over financial reporting.

Date:

_____

[Signature]

[Title]

(ii)   Rule 13a–14(d)/15d–14(d) Certifications. If an asset-backed issuer (as defined in 229.1101), the certifications required by Rule 13a–14(d) or Rule 15d–14(d) exactly as set forth below:

Certifications: I, [identify the certifying individual], certify that:

1.   I have reviewed this report on Form 10–K and all reports on Form 10–D required to be filed in respect of the period covered by this report on Form 10–K of [identify the issuing entity] (the "Exchange Act periodic reports");

2.   Based on my knowledge, the Exchange Act periodic reports, taken as a whole, do not contain any untrue statement of a material fact or omit to state a material fact necessary to make the statements made, in light of the circumstances under which such statements were made, not misleading with respect to the period covered by this report;

3.   Based on my knowledge, all of the distribution, servicing and other information required to be provided under Form 10–D for the period covered by this report is included in the Exchange Act periodic reports;

4.   [I am responsible for reviewing the activities performed by the servicer(s) and based on my knowledge and the compliance review(s) conducted in preparing the servicer compliance statement(s) required in this report under Item 1123 of Regulation AB, and except as disclosed in the Exchange Act periodic reports, the servicer(s) [has/have] fulfilled [its/their] obligations under the servicing agreement(s) in all material respects; and]

[Based on my knowledge and the servicer compliance statement(s) required in this report under Item 1123 of Regulation AB, and except as disclosed in the Exchange Act periodic reports, the servicer(s) [has/have] fulfilled [its/their] obligations under the servicing agreement(s) in all material respects; and]

5.   All of the reports on assessment of compliance with servicing criteria for asset-backed securities and their related attestation reports on assessment of compliance with servicing criteria for asset-backed securities required to be included in this report in accordance with Item 1122 of Regulation AB and Exchange Act Rules 13a–18 and 15d–18 have been included as an exhibit to this report, except as otherwise disclosed in this report. Any material instances of noncompliance described in such reports have been disclosed in this report on Form 10–K.

[In giving the certifications above, I have reasonably relied on information provided to me by the following unaffiliated parties [name of servicer, sub-servicer, co-servicer, depositor or trustee].]

Date:

_____

[Signature]

[Title]

Note to paragraph (ii). With respect to asset-backed issuers, the certification must be signed by either: (1) The senior officer in charge of securitization of the depositor if the depositor is signing the report on Form 10–K; or (2) The senior officer in charge of the servicing function of the servicer if the servicer is signing the report on Form 10–K on behalf of the issuing entity. See Rules 13a–14(e) and 15d–14(e). If multiple servicers are involved in servicing the pool assets, the senior officer in charge of the servicing function of the master servicer (or entity performing the equivalent function) must sign if a representative of the servicer is to sign the certification. If there is a master servicer and one or more underlying servicers, the references in the certification relate to the master servicer. A natural person must sign the certification in his or her individual capacity, although the title of that person in the organization of which he or she is an officer may be included under the signature.

Note to paragraph (ii)(4). The first version of paragraph 4 is to be used when the servicer is signing the report on behalf of the issuing entity. The second version of paragraph 4 is to be used when the depositor is signing the report.

Note to paragraph (ii)(5). The certification refers to the reports prepared by parties participating in the servicing function that are required to be included as an exhibit to the Form 10–K. See Item 1122 of Regulation AB and Rules 13a–18 and 15d–18. If a report that is otherwise required to be included is not attached, disclosure that the report is not included and an associated explanation must be provided in the Form 10–K report.

Note to paragraph (ii)(5). Because the signer of the certification must rely in certain circumstances on information provided by unaffiliated parties outside of the signer's control, this paragraph must be included if the signer is reasonably relying on information that unaffiliated trustees, depositors, servicers, sub-servicers or co-servicers have provided.

(32) *Section 1350 Certifications.*

(i)   The certifications required by Rule 13a–14(b) or Rule 15d–14(b) and Section 1350 of Chapter 63 of Title 18 of the United States Code.

(ii) A certification furnished pursuant to this item will not be deemed "filed" for purposes of Section 18 of the Exchange Act, or otherwise subject to the liability of that section. Such certification will not be deemed to be incorporated by reference into any filing under the Securities Act or the Exchange Act, except to the extent that the registrant specifically incorporates it by reference.

(33) *Report on assessment of compliance with servicing criteria for asset-backed securities.* Each report on assessment of compliance with servicing criteria required by Rule 1122(a).

(34) *Attestation report on assessment of compliance with servicing criteria for asset-backed securities.* Each attestation report on assessment of compliance with servicing criteria for asset-backed securities required by Item 1122(b) of Regulation S–K.

(35) *Servicer compliance statement.* Each servicer compliance statement required by Rule 1123.

(36) *Certification for shelf offerings of asset-backed securities.* Provide the certification required by General Instruction I.B.1.(a) of Form SF–3 exactly as set forth below:

Certification

I [identify the certifying individual] certify as of [the date of the final prospectus under Rule 424 of the Securities Act of 1933 that:

1. I have reviewed the prospectus relating to [title of all securities, the offer and sale of which are registered] (the "securities") and am familiar with, in all material respects, the following: The characteristics of the securitized assets underlying the offering (the "securitized assets"), the structure of the securitization, and all material underlying transaction agreements as described in the prospectus;

2. Based on my knowledge, the prospectus does not contain any untrue statement of a material fact or omit to state a material fact necessary to make the statements made, in light of the circumstances under which such statements were made, not misleading;

3. Based on my knowledge, the prospectus and other information included in the registration statement of which it is a part fairly present, in all material respects, the characteristics of the securitized assets, the structure of the securitization and the risks of ownership of the securities, including the risks relating to the securitized assets that would affect the cash flows available to service payments or distributions on the securities in accordance with their terms; and

4. Based on my knowledge, taking into account all material aspects of the characteristics of the securitized assets, the structure of the securitization, and the related risks as described in the prospectus, there is a reasonable basis to conclude that the securitization is structured to produce, but is not guaranteed by this certification to produce, expected cash flows at times and in amounts to service scheduled payments of interest and the ultimate repayment of principal on the securities (or other scheduled or required distributions on the securities, however denominated) in accordance with their terms as described in the prospectus.

5. The foregoing certifications are given subject to any and all defenses available to me under the federal securities laws, including any and all defenses available to an executive officer that signed the registration statement of which the prospectus referred to in this certification is part.

The certification must be signed by the chief executive officer of the depositor, as required by General Instruction I.B.1.(a) of Form SF–3.

(37) to (94) [Reserved]

(95) *Mine Safety Disclosure Exhibit.* A registrant that is an operator, or that has a subsidiary that is an operator, of a coal or other mine must provide the information required by Item 104 of Regulation S–K (Item 104 of this Act) in an exhibit to its Exchange Act annual or quarterly report. For purposes of this Item:

(1) The term *coal or other mine* means a coal or other mine, as defined in section 3 of the Federal Mine Safety and Health Act of 1977, that is subject to the provisions of such Act.

(2)   The term *operator* has the meaning given the term in section 3 of the Federal Mine Safety and Health Act of 1977.

(3)   The term *subsidiary* has the meaning given the term in Exchange Act Rule 12b–2.

(96)   *Technical report summary.* (i) A registrant that, pursuant to Item 1300 through Item 1305 of Regulation S–K, discloses information concerning its mineral resources or mineral reserves must file a technical report summary by one or more qualified persons that, for each material property, identifies and summarizes the scientific and technical information and conclusions reached concerning an initial assessment used to support disclosure of mineral resources, or concerning a preliminary or final feasibility study used to support disclosure of mineral reserves. At its election, a registrant may also file a technical report summary from a qualified person that identifies and summarizes the information reviewed and conclusions reached by the qualified person about the registrant's exploration results. Please refer to Item 1302(b) of Regulation S–K for when a registrant must file the technical report summary as an exhibit to its Securities Act registration statement or Exchange Act registration statement or report.

(ii)   The technical report summary must not include large amounts of technical or other project data, either in the report or as appendices to the report. The qualified person must draft the summary to conform, to the extent practicable, with the plain English principles set forth in Rule 421 of the Securities Act or 13a–20 of the Exchange Act.

(iii)(A)   A technical report summary that reports the results of a preliminary or final feasibility study must provide all of the information specified in paragraph (b)(96)(iii)(B) of this item. A technical report summary that reports the results of an initial assessment must, at a minimum, provide the information specified in paragraphs (b)(96)(iii)(B)(1) through (11) and (20) through (25) of this item, and may also include the information specified in paragraph (b)(96)(iii)(B)(19) of this item. A technical report summary that reports exploration results must, at a minimum, provide the information specified in paragraphs (b)(96)(iii)(B)(1) through (9) and (20) through (25) of this item.

(B)   A qualified person must include the following information in the technical report summary, as required by paragraph (b)(96)(iii)(A) of this item, to the extent the information is material.

(1)   Executive summary. Briefly summarize the most significant information in the technical report summary, including property description (including mineral rights) and ownership, geology and mineralization, the status of exploration, development and operations, mineral resource and mineral reserve estimates, summary capital and operating cost estimates, permitting requirements, and the qualified person's conclusions and recommendations. The executive summary must be brief and should not contain all of the detailed information in the technical support summary.

(2)   Introduction. Disclose:

(i)   The registrant for whom the technical report summary was prepared;

(ii)   The terms of reference and purpose for which the technical report summary was prepared, including whether the technical report summary's purpose was to report mineral resources, mineral reserves, or exploration results;

(iii)   The sources of information and data contained in the technical report summary or used in its preparation, with citations if applicable;

(iv)   The details of the personal inspection on the property by each qualified person or, if applicable, the reason why a personal inspection has not been completed; and

(v)   That the technical report summary updates a previously filed technical report summary, identified by name and date, when applicable.

(3)   Property description. (i) Describe the location of the property, accurate to within one mile, using an easily recognizable coordinate system. The qualified person must provide appropriate maps, with proper engineering detail (such as scale, orientation, and titles) to portray the location of the property. Such maps must be legible on the page when printed.

(ii)   Disclose the area of the property.

(iii)   Disclose the name or number of each title, claim, mineral right, lease, or option under which the registrant and its subsidiaries have or will have the right to hold or operate the property. If held by leases or options, the registrant must provide the expiration dates of such leases or options and associated payments.

(iv)   Describe the mineral rights, and how such rights have been obtained at this location, indicating any conditions that the registrant must meet in order to obtain or retain the property.

(v)   Describe any significant encumbrances to the property, including current and future permitting requirements and associated timelines, permit conditions, and violations and fines.

(vi)   Disclose any other significant factors and risks that may affect access, title, or the right or ability to perform work on the property.

(vii)   If the registrant holds a royalty or similar interest in the property, except as provided under Item 1303(a)(3) and Item 1304(a)(2), the information in paragraph (b)(96)(iii)(B)(3) of this item must be provided for the property that is owned or operated by a party other than the registrant. In this event, for example, the report must address the documents under which the owner or operator holds or operates the property, the mineral rights held by the owner or operator, conditions required to be met by the owner or operator, significant encumbrances, and significant factors and risks relating to the property or work on the property.

(4)   Accessibility, climate, local resources, infrastructure and physiography. Describe:

(i)   The topography, elevation, and vegetation;

(ii)   The means of access to the property, including highways, towns, rivers, railroads, and airports;

(iii)   The climate and the length of the operating season, as applicable; and

(iv)   The availability of and required infrastructure, including sources of water, electricity, personnel, and supplies.

(5)   History. Describe:

(i)   Previous operations, including the names of previous operators, insofar as known; and

(ii)   The type, amount, quantity, and general results of exploration and development work undertaken by any previous owners or operators.

(6)   Geological setting, mineralization, and deposit. (i) Describe briefly the regional, local, and property geology and the significant mineralized zones encountered on the property, including a summary of the surrounding rock types, relevant geological controls, and the length, width, depth, and continuity of the mineralization, together with a description of the type, character, and distribution of the mineralization.

(ii)   Each mineral deposit type that is the subject of investigation or exploration together with the geological model or concepts being applied in the investigation or forming the basis of the exploration program.

(iii)   The qualified person must include at least one stratigraphic column and one cross-section of the local geology to meet the requirements of paragraph (b)(96)(iii)(B)(6) of this item.

(7)   Exploration. Describe the nature and extent of all relevant exploration work, conducted by or on behalf of, the registrant.

(i)   For all exploration work other than drilling, describe: the procedures and parameters relating to the surveys and investigations; the sampling methods and sample quality, including whether the samples are representative, and any factors that may have resulted in sample biases; the location, number, type, nature, and spacing or density of samples collected, and the size of the area covered; and the significant results of and the qualified person's interpretation of the exploration information.

(ii)   For drilling, describe: the type and extent of drilling including the procedures followed; any drilling, sampling, or recovery factors that could materially affect the accuracy and reliability of the results; and the material results and interpretation of the drilling results. For a technical report summary to support disclosure of exploration results, the qualified person must provide information on all samples or drill holes to meet the requirements of this paragraph. If some information is excluded, the qualified person must identify the omitted information and explain why that information is not material.

(iii)   For characterization of hydrogeology, describe: the nature and quality of the sampling methods used to acquire data on surface and groundwater parameters; the type and appropriateness of laboratory techniques used to test for groundwater flow parameters such as permeability, and include discussions of the quality control and quality assurance procedures; results of laboratory testing and the qualified person's interpretation, including any material assumptions, which must include descriptions of permeable zones or aquifers, flow rates, in-situ saturation, recharge rates and water balance; and the groundwater models used to characterize aquifers, including material assumptions used in the modeling.

(iv)   For geotechnical data, testing and analysis, describe: the nature and quality of the sampling methods used to acquire geotechnical data; the type and appropriateness of laboratory techniques used to test for soil and rock strength parameters, including discussions of the quality control and quality assurance procedures; and results of laboratory testing and the qualified person's interpretation, including any material assumptions.

(v)   Reports must include a plan view of the property showing locations of all drill holes and other samples.

(vi)   The technical report summary must include a description of data concerning drilling, hydrogeology, or geotechnical data only to the extent such data is relevant and available.

Instruction 1 to paragraph (b)(96)(iii)(B)(7): The technical report summary must comply with all disclosure standards for exploration results under Item 1300 through Item 1305 of Regulation S–K.

Instruction 2 to paragraph (b)(96)(iii)(B)(7): For a technical report summary to support disclosure of mineral resources or mineral reserves, the qualified person can meet the requirements of paragraph (b)(96)(iii)(B)(7)(ii) of this item by providing sampling (including drilling) plans, representative plans, and cross-sections of results.

Instruction 3 to paragraph (b)(96)(iii)(B)(7): If disclosing an exploration target, provide such disclosure in a subsection of the Exploration section of the technical report summary that is clearly captioned as a discussion of an exploration target. That section must include all of the disclosure required under Item 1302(c).

(8)   Sample preparation, analyses, and security. Describe:

(i)   Sample preparation methods and quality control measures employed prior to sending samples to an analytical or testing laboratory, sample splitting and reduction methods, and the security measures taken to ensure the validity and integrity of samples;

(ii)   Sample preparation, assaying and analytical procedures used, the name and location of the analytical or testing laboratories, the relationship of the laboratory to the registrant, and whether the laboratories are certified by any standards association and the particulars of such certification;

(iii)   The nature, extent, and results of quality control procedures and quality assurance actions taken or recommended to provide adequate confidence in the data collection and estimation process;

(iv)   The adequacy of sample preparation, security, and analytical procedures, in the opinion of the qualified person; and

(v)   If the analytical procedures used are not part of conventional industry practice, a justification by the qualified person for why he or she believes the procedure is appropriate in this instance.

(9)   Data verification. Describe the steps taken by the qualified person to verify the data being reported on or which is the basis of this technical report summary, including:

(i) Data verification procedures applied by the qualified person;

(ii) Any limitations on or failure to conduct such verification, and the reasons for any such limitations or failure; and

(iii) The qualified person's opinion on the adequacy of the data for the purposes used in the technical report summary.

(10) *Mineral processing and metallurgical testing.* Describe:

(i) The nature and extent of the mineral processing or metallurgical testing and analytical procedures;

(ii) The degree to which the test samples are representative of the various types and styles of mineralization and the mineral deposit as a whole;

(iii) The name and location of the analytical or testing laboratories, the relationship of the laboratory to the registrant, whether the laboratories are certified by any standards association and the particulars of such certification;

(iv) The relevant results including the basis for any assumptions or predictions about recovery estimates. Discuss any processing factors or deleterious elements that could have a significant effect on potential economic extraction; and

(v) The adequacy of the data for the purposes used in the technical report summary, in the opinion of the qualified person. If the analytical procedures used in the analysis are not part of conventional industry practice, the qualified person must state so and provide a justification for why he or she believes the procedure is appropriate in this instance.

(11) *Mineral resource estimates.* If this item is included, the technical report summary must:

(i) Describe the key assumptions, parameters, and methods used to estimate the mineral resources, in sufficient detail for a reasonably informed person to understand the basis for and how the qualified person estimated the mineral resources. The technical report summary must include mineral resource estimates at a specific point of reference selected by the qualified person. The selected point of reference must be disclosed in the technical report summary;

(ii) Provide the qualified person's estimates of mineral resources for all commodities, including estimates of quantities, grade or quality, cut-off grades, and metallurgical or processing recoveries. Unless otherwise stated, cut-off grades also refer to net smelter returns, pay limits, and other similar terms. The qualified person preparing the mineral resource estimates must round off, to appropriate significant figures chosen to reflect order of accuracy, any estimates of quantity and grade or quality. If the qualified person chooses to disclose mineral resources inclusive of mineral reserves, he or she must also clearly state the mineral resources exclusive of mineral reserves in the technical report summary;

(iii) Include the qualified person's estimates of cut-off grades based on assumed costs for surface or underground operations and commodity prices that provide a reasonable basis for establishing the prospects of economic extraction for mineral resources. The qualified person must disclose the price used for each commodity and explain, with particularity, his or her reasons for using the selected price, including the material assumptions underlying the selection. This explanation must include disclosure of the time frame used to estimate the commodity price and unit costs for cut-off grade estimation and the reasons justifying the selection of that time frame. The qualified person may use a price set by contractual arrangement, provided that such price is reasonable, and the qualified person discloses that he or she is using a contractual price when disclosing the price used;

(iv) Provide the qualified person's classification of mineral resources into inferred, indicated, and measured mineral resources in accordance with Item 1302(d)(1)(iii)(A) of Regulation S–K. The qualified person must disclose the criteria used to classify a resource as inferred, indicated, or measured and must justify the classification;

(v) Discuss the uncertainty in the estimates of inferred, indicated, and measured mineral resources, and explain the sources of uncertainty and how they were considered in the uncertainty estimates. The qualified person must consider all sources of uncertainty associated with each class of mineral resources. Sources of uncertainty that affect such reporting of uncertainty include sampling or drilling methods, data processing and handling, geologic modeling, and estimation. The qualified person must support the disclosure of uncertainty associated with each class of mineral resources with a list of all factors considered and explain how those factors contributed to the final conclusion about the level of uncertainty underlying the resource estimates. The qualified person is not required to use estimates of confidence limits derived from geostatistics or other numerical methods to support the disclosure of uncertainty surrounding mineral resource classification. If the qualified person chooses to use confidence limit estimates from geostatistics or other numerical methods, he or she should consider the limitations of these methods and adjust the estimates appropriately to reflect sources of uncertainty that are not accounted for by these methods;

(vi)   When reporting the grade or quality for a multiple commodity mineral resource as metal or mineral equivalent, disclose the individual grade of each metal or mineral and the commodity prices, recoveries, and any other relevant conversion factors used to estimate the metal or mineral equivalent grade; and

(vii)   Provide the qualified person's opinion on whether all issues relating to all relevant technical and economic factors likely to influence the prospect of economic extraction can be resolved with further work.

Instruction 1 to paragraph (b)(96)(iii)(B)(11): The technical report summary must comply with all disclosure standards for mineral resources under Item 1300 through Item 1305 of Regulation S–K.

Instruction 2 to paragraph(b)(96)(iii)(B)(11): Items 1303 and 1304 of Regulation S–K notwithstanding, in this technical report summary, mineral resource estimates may be inclusive of mineral reserves so long as this is clearly stated with equal prominence to the rest of the item.

(12)   Mineral reserve estimates. If this item is included, the technical report summary must:

(i)   Describe the key assumptions, parameters, and methods used to estimate the mineral reserves, in sufficient detail for a reasonably informed person to understand the basis for converting, and how the qualified person converted, indicated and measured mineral resources into the mineral reserves. The technical report summary must include mineral reserve estimates at a specific point of reference selected by the qualified person. The qualified person must disclose the selected point of reference in the technical report summary;

(ii)   Provide the qualified person's estimates of mineral reserves for all commodities, including estimates of quantities, grade or quality, cut-off grades, and metallurgical or processing recoveries. The qualified person preparing the mineral resource estimates must round off, to appropriate significant figures chosen to reflect order of accuracy, any estimates of quantity and grade or quality;

(iii)   Include the qualified person's estimates of cut-off grades based on detailed cut-off grade analysis that includes a long term price that provides a reasonable basis for establishing that the project is economically viable. The qualified person must disclose the price used for each commodity and explain, with particularity, his or her reasons for using the selected price, including the material assumptions underlying the selection. This explanation must include disclosure of the time frame used to estimate the price and costs and the reasons justifying the selection of that time frame. The qualified person may use a price set by contractual arrangement, provided that such price is reasonable, and the qualified person discloses that he or she is using a contractual price when disclosing the price used;

(iv)   Provide the qualified person's classification of mineral reserves into probable and proven mineral reserves in accordance with Item 1302(e)(2) of Regulation S–K;

(v)   When reporting the grade or quality for a multiple commodity mineral reserve as metal or mineral equivalent, disclose the individual grade of each metal or mineral and the commodity prices, recoveries, and any other relevant conversion factors used to estimate the metal or mineral equivalent grade; and

(vi) Provide the qualified person's opinion on how the mineral reserve estimates could be materially affected by risk factors associated with or changes to any aspect of the modifying factors.

Instruction 1 to paragraph (b)(96)(iii)(B)(12): The technical report summary must comply with all disclosure standards for mineral reserves under Item 1300 through Item 1305 of Regulation S–K.

(13) Mining methods. Describe the current or proposed mining methods and the reasons for selecting these methods as the most suitable for the mineral reserves under consideration. Include:

(i) Geotechnical and hydrological models, and other parameters relevant to mine designs and plans;

(ii) Production rates, expected mine life, mining unit dimensions, and mining dilution and recovery factors;

(iii) Requirements for stripping, underground development, and backfilling;

(iv) Required mining equipment fleet and machinery, and personnel; and

(v) At least one map of the final mine outline.

(14) Processing and recovery methods. Describe the current or proposed mineral processing methods and the reasons for selecting these methods as the most suitable for extracting the valuable products from the mineralization under consideration. Include:

(i) A description or flow sheet of any current or proposed process plant;

(ii) Plant throughput and design, equipment characteristics and specifications;

(iii) Current or projected requirements for energy, water, process materials, and personnel; and

(iv) If the processing method, plant design, or other parameter has never been used to commercially extract the valuable product from such mineralization, a justification by the qualified person for why he or she believes the approach will be successful in this instance.

Instruction 1 to paragraph (b)(96)(iii)(B)(14): If the processing method, plant design, or other parameter has never been used to commercially extract the valuable product from such mineralization and is still under development, then no mineral resources or reserves can be disclosed on the basis of that method, design, or other parameter.

(15) Infrastructure. Describe the required infrastructure for the project, including roads, rail, port facilities, dams, dumps and leach pads, tailings disposal, power, water, and pipelines, as applicable. Include at least one map showing the layout of the infrastructure.

(16) Market studies. Describe the market for the products of the mine, including justification for demand or sales over the life of the mine (or length of cash flow projections). Include:

(i) Information concerning markets for the property's production, including the nature and material terms of any agency relationships and the results of any relevant market studies, commodity price projections, product valuation, market entry strategies, and product specification requirements; and

(ii) Descriptions of all material contracts required for the issuer to develop the property, including mining, concentrating, smelting, refining, transportation, handling, hedging arrangements, and forward sales contracts. State which contracts have been executed and which are still under negotiation. For all contracts with affiliated parties, discuss whether the registrant obtained the same terms, rates or charges as could be obtained had the contract been negotiated at arm's length with an unaffiliated third party.

(17) Environmental studies, permitting, and plans, negotiations, or agreements with local individuals or groups. Describe the factors pertaining to environmental compliance, permitting, and local individuals or groups, which are related to the project. Include:

(i) The results of environmental studies (e.g., environmental baseline studies or impact assessments);

(ii)   Requirements and plans for waste and tailings disposal, site monitoring, and water management during operations and after mine closure;

(iii)   Project permitting requirements, the status of any permit applications, and any known requirements to post performance or reclamation bonds;

(iv)   Plans, negotiations, or agreements with local individuals or groups;

(v)   Mine closure plans, including remediation and reclamation plans, and the associated costs;

(vi)   The qualified person's opinion on the adequacy of current plans to address any issues related to environmental compliance, permitting, and local individuals or groups; and

(vii)   Descriptions of any commitments to ensure local procurement and hiring.

(18)   Capital and operating costs. (i) Provide estimates of capital and operating costs, with the major components set out in tabular form. Explain and justify the basis for the cost estimates including any contingency budget estimates. State the accuracy level of the capital and operating cost estimates.

(ii)   To assess the accuracy of the capital and operating cost estimates, the qualified person must take into account the risks associated with the specific engineering estimation methods used to arrive at the estimates. As part of this analysis, the qualified person must take into consideration the accuracy of the estimation methods in prior similar environments. The accuracy of capital and operating cost estimates must comply with Item 1302 of Regulation S–K.

(19)   Economic analysis. (i) Describe the key assumptions, parameters, and methods used to demonstrate economic viability, and provide all material assumptions including discount rates, exchange rates, commodity prices, and taxes, royalties, and other government levies or interests applicable to the mineral project or to production, and to revenues or income from the mineral project.

(ii)   Disclose the results of the economic analysis, including annual cash flow forecasts based on an annual production schedule for the life of project, and measures of economic viability such as net present value (NPV), internal rate of return (IRR), and payback period of capital.

(iii)   Include sensitivity analysis results using variants in commodity price, grade, capital and operating costs, or other significant input parameters, as appropriate, and discuss the impact on the results of the economic analysis.

(iv)   The qualified person may, but is not required to, include an economic analysis in an initial assessment. If the qualified person includes an economic analysis in an initial assessment, the qualified person must also include a statement, of equal prominence to the rest of this item, that, unlike mineral reserves, mineral resources do not have demonstrated economic viability. The qualified person may include inferred mineral resources in the economic analysis only if he or she satisfies the conditions set forth in Item 1302(d)(4)(ii) of Regulation S–K.

(20)   Adjacent properties. Where applicable, a qualified person may include relevant information concerning an adjacent property if:

(i)   Such information was publicly disclosed by the owner or operator of the adjacent property;

(ii)   The source of the information is identified;

(iii)   The qualified person states that he or she has been unable to verify the information and that the information is not necessarily indicative of the mineralization on the property that is the subject of the technical report summary; and

(iv)   The technical report summary clearly distinguishes between the information from the adjacent property and the information from the property that is the subject of the technical report summary.

(21)   Other relevant data and information. Include any additional information or explanation necessary to provide a complete and balanced presentation of the value of the property to the registrant. Information included in this item must comply with Item 1300 through Item 1305 of Regulation S–K.

(22) *Interpretation and conclusions.* The qualified person must summarize the interpretations of and conclusions based on the data and analysis in the technical report summary. He or she must also discuss any significant risks and uncertainties that could reasonably be expected to affect the reliability or confidence in the exploration results, mineral resource or mineral reserve estimates, or projected economic outcomes.

(23) *Recommendations.* If applicable, the qualified person must describe the recommendations for additional work with associated costs. If the additional work program is divided into phases, the costs for each phase must be provided along with decision points at the end of each phase.

(24) *References.* Include a list of all references cited in the technical report summary in sufficient detail so that a reader can locate each reference.

(25) *Reliance on information provided by the registrant.* If relying on information provided by the registrant for matters discussed in the technical report summary, as permitted under Item 1302(f) of Regulation S–K, provide the disclosure required pursuant to Item 1302(f)(2).

* * *

(97) *Policy Relating to Recovery of Erroneously Awarded Compensation.* A registrant that at any time during its last completed fiscal year had a class of securities listed on a national securities exchange registered pursuant to section 6 of the Exchange Act (15 U.S.C. 78f) or a national securities association registered pursuant to section 15A of the Exchange Act (15 U.S.C. 78o–3) must file as an exhibit to its annual report the compensation recovery policy required by the applicable listing standards adopted pursuant to 17 CFR 240.10D–1.

(99) *Additional exhibits.* (i) Any additional exhibits that the registrant may wish to file must be so marked as to indicate clearly the subject matters to which they refer.

(ii)   If pursuant to Section 11(a) of the Securities Act (15 U.S.C. 77k(a)) an issuer makes generally available to its security holders an earnings statement covering a period of at least 12 months beginning after the effective date of the registration statement, and if such earnings statement is made available by "other methods" than those specified in paragraphs (a) or (b) of Rule 158 of the Securities Act, it must be filed as an exhibit to the Form 10–Q or the Form 10–K, as appropriate, covering the period in which the earnings statement was released.

(100) Removed and reserved.

(101) *Interactive Data File.* Where a registrant prepares its financial statements in accordance with either generally accepted accounting principles as used in the United States or International Financial Reporting Standards as issued by the International Accounting Standards Board, an Interactive Data File (§ 232.11 of this chapter) is:

(i)   *Required to be submitted.* Required to be submitted to the Commission in the manner provided by § 232.405 of this chapter if the registrant does not prepare its financial statements in accordance with Article 6 of Regulation S–X (17 CFR 210.6–01 *et seq.*), except that an Interactive Data File:

(A)   First is required for a periodic report on Form 10–Q (§ 249.308a of this chapter), Form 20–F (§ 249.220f of this chapter), or Form 40–F (§ 249.240f of this chapter), as applicable;

(B)   Is required for a registration statement under the Securities Act only if the registration statement contains a price or price range; and

(C)   Is required for a Form 8–K (§ 249.308 of this chapter):

(1)   only when the Form 8–K contains audited annual financial statements that are a revised version of financial statements that previously were filed with the Commission and that have been revised pursuant to applicable accounting standards to reflect the effects of certain subsequent events, including a discontinued operation, a change in reportable segments or a change in accounting principle. In such case, the Interactive Data File will be required only as to such revised financial statements regardless of whether the Form 8–K contains other financial statements;

(2) except that a business development company as defined in Section 2(a)(48) of the Investment Company Act of 1940 (15 U.S.C. 80a–2(a)(48)) also is required to submit an Interactive Data File to the extent required by § 232.405(b)(3)(iii) of this chapter.

(ii) *Permitted to be submitted.* Permitted to be submitted to the Commission in the manner provided by § 232.405 of this chapter if the:

(A) Registrant is not registered under the Investment Company Act of 1940 (15 U.S.C. 80a–1 et seq.); and

(B) Interactive Data File is not required to be submitted to the Commission under paragraph (b)(101)(i) of this item.

(iii) Not permitted to be submitted to the Commission if the registrant is registered under the Investment Company Act of 1940 (15 U.S.C. 80a–1 et seq.).

Instruction to paragraphs (b)(101)(i) and (ii): When an Interactive Data File is submitted as provided by § 232.405(a)(3)(i) of this chapter, the exhibit index must include the word "Inline" within the title description for any eXtensible Business Reporting Language (XBRL)-related exhibit.

(c) *Smaller Reporting Companies.* A smaller reporting company need not provide the disclosure required in paragraph (b)(12) of this Item, Statements re computation of ratios.

(102) *Asset Data File.* An Asset Data File (as defined in Rule 11 of Regulation S–T) filed pursuant to Item 1111(h)(3) of Regulation AB (Rule 1111(h)(3)).

(103) *Asset Related Document.* Additional asset-level information or explanatory language pursuant to Item 1111(h)(4) and (5) of Regulation AB (Rule 1111(h)(4) and (h)(5)).

(104) *Cover Page Interactive Data File.* A Cover Page Interactive Data File as required by Rule 406 of Regulation S–T and in the manner provided by the EDGAR Filer Manual.

(105) [Reserved].

(106) *Static pool.* If not included in the prospectus filed in accordance with Rule 424(b)(2) of the Securities Act of 1933 or (5) and (h) of this chapter, static pool disclosure as required by Rule 1105.

Subpart 700—Miscellaneous

Item 701.   Recent Sales of Unregistered Securities; Use of Proceeds From Unregistered Securities

Furnish the following information as to all securities of the registrant sold by the registrant within the past three years which were not registered under the Securities Act. Include sales of reacquired securities, as well as new issues, securities issued in exchange for property, services, or other securities, and new securities resulting from the modification of outstanding securities.

(a) *Securities Sold.* Give the date of sale and the title and amount of securities sold.

(b) *Underwriters and Other Purchasers.* Give the names of the principal underwriters, if any. As to any such securities not publicly offered, name the persons or identify the class of persons to whom the securities were sold.

(c) *Consideration.* As to securities sold for cash, state the aggregate offering price and the aggregate underwriting discounts or commissions. As to any securities sold otherwise than for cash, state the nature of the transaction and the nature and aggregate amount of consideration received by the registrant.

(d) *Exemption from Registration Claimed.* Indicate the section of the Securities Act or the rule of the Commission under which exemption from registration was claimed and state briefly the facts relied upon to make the exemption available.

(e) *Terms of Conversion or Exercise.* If the information called for by this paragraph (e) is being presented on Form 8–K, Form 10–Q, Form 10–K or Form 10–D under the Exchange Act, and where the securities sold by the registrant are convertible or exchangeable into equity securities, or are warrants or options representing equity securities, disclose the terms of conversion or exercise the securities.

(f) *Use of Proceeds*. As required by Rule 463 of the Securities Act, following the effective date of the first registration statement filed under the Securities Act by an issuer, the issuer or successor issuer shall report the use of proceeds on its first periodic report filed pursuant to sections 13(a) and 15(d) of the Exchange Act after effectiveness of its Securities Act registration statement, and thereafter on each of its subsequent periodic reports filed pursuant to sections 13(a) and 15(d) of the Exchange Act through the later of disclosure of the application of all the offering proceeds, or disclosure of the termination of the offering. If a report of the use of proceeds is required with respect to the first effective registration statement of the predecessor issuer, the successor issuer shall provide such a report. The information provided pursuant to paragraphs (f)(2) through (f)(4) of this Item need only be provided with respect to the first periodic report filed pursuant to sections 13(a) and 15(d) of the Exchange Act after effectiveness of the registration statement filed under the Securities Act. Subsequent periodic reports filed pursuant to sections 13(a) and 15(d) of the Exchange Act need only provide the information required in paragraphs (f)(2) through (f)(4) of this Item if any of such required information has changed since the last periodic report filed. In disclosing the use of proceeds in the first periodic report filed pursuant to the Exchange Act, the issuer or successor issuer should include the following information:

(1) The effective date of the Securities Act registration statement for which the use of proceeds information is being disclosed and the Commission file number assigned to the registration statement;

(2) If the offering has commenced, the offering date, and if the offering has not commenced, an explanation why it has not;

(3) If the offering terminated before any securities were sold, an explanation for such termination; and

(4) If the offering did not terminate before any securities were sold, disclose:

(i) Whether the offering has terminated and, if so, whether it terminated before the sale of all securities registered;

(ii) The name(s) of the managing underwriter(s), if any;

(iii) The title of each class of securities registered and, where a class of convertible securities is being registered, the title of any class of securities into which such securities may be converted;

(iv) For each class of securities (other than a class of securities into which a class of convertible securities registered may be converted without additional payment to the issuer) the following information, provided for both the account of the issuer and the account(s) of any selling security holder(s): the amount registered, the aggregate price of the offering amount registered, the amount sold and the aggregate offering price of the amount sold to date;

(v) From the effective date of the Securities Act registration statement to the ending date of the reporting period, the amount of expenses incurred for the issuer's account in connection with the issuance and distribution of the securities registered for underwriting discounts and commissions, finders' fees, expenses paid to or for underwriters, other expenses and total expenses. Indicate if a reasonable estimate for the amount of expenses incurred is provided instead of the actual amount of expense. Indicate whether such payments were:

(A) Direct or indirect payments to directors, officers, general partners of the issuer or their associates; to persons owning ten (10) percent or more of any class of equity securities of the issuer; and to affiliates of the issuer; or

(B) Direct or indirect payments to others;

(vi) The net offering proceeds to the issuer after deducting the total expenses described in paragraph (f)(4)(v) of this Item;

(vii) From the effective date of the Securities Act registration statement to the ending date of the reporting period, the amount of net offering proceeds to the issuer used for construction of plant, building and facilities; purchase and installation of machinery and equipment; purchases of real estate; acquisition of other business(es); repayment of indebtedness; working capital; temporary investments (which should be specified); and any other purposes for which at least five (5) percent of the issuer's total offering proceeds or $100,000 (whichever is less) has been used (which should be specified). Indicate if a reasonable estimate for the amount of net offering proceeds applied is provided instead of the actual amount of net offering proceeds used. Indicate whether such payments were:

(A) Direct or indirect payments to directors, officers, general partners of the issuer or their associates; to persons owning ten (10) percent or more of any class of equity securities of the issuer; and to affiliates of the issuer; or

(B) Direct or indirect payments to others; and

(viii) If the use of proceeds in paragraph (f)(4)(vii) of this Item represents a material change in the use of proceeds described in the prospectus, the issuer should describe briefly the material change.

Instructions. 1. Information required by this Item 701 need not be set forth as to notes, drafts, bills of exchange, or bankers' acceptances which mature not later than one year from the date of issuance.

2. If the sales were made in a series of transactions, the information may be given by such totals and periods as will reasonably convey the information required.

Item 702.   Indemnification of Directors and Officers

State the general effect of any statute, charter provisions, by-laws, contract or other arrangements under which any controlling persons, director or officer of the registrant is insured or indemnified in any manner against liability which he may incur in his capacity as such.

Item 703.   Purchases of Equity Securities by the Issuer and Affiliated Purchasers

(a) In the following tabular format, provide the information specified in paragraph (b) of this Item with respect to any purchase made by or on behalf of the issuer or any "affiliated purchaser," as defined in Rule 10b–18(a)(3) under the Securities Exchange Act of 1934, of shares or other units of any class of the issuer's equity securities that is registered by the issuer pursuant to section 12 of the Exchange Act.

Issuer Purchases of Equity Securities

Period	(a) Total number of shares (or units) purchased	(b) Average price paid per share (or unit)	(c) Total number of shares (or units) purchased as part of publicly announced plans or programs	(d) Maximum number (or approximate dollar value) of shares (or units) that may yet be purchased under the plans or programs
Month #1 (identify beginning and ending dates)				
Month #2 (identify beginning and ending dates)				
Month #3 (identify beginning and ending dates)				
Total				

(b)   The table shall include the following information for each class or series of securities for each month included in the period covered by the report:

(1)   The total number of shares (or units) purchased (column (a));

Instruction to Paragraph (b)(1) of Item 703. Include in this column all issuer repurchases, including those made pursuant to publicly announced plans or programs and those not made pursuant to publicly announced plans or programs. Briefly disclose, by footnote to the table, the number of shares purchased other than through a publicly announced plan or program and the nature of the transaction (e.g., whether the purchases were made in open-market transactions, tender offers, in satisfaction of the company's obligations upon exercise of outstanding put options issued by the company, or other transactions).

(2)   The average price paid per share (or unit) (column (b));

(3)   The total number of shares (or units) purchased as part of publicly announced repurchase plans or programs (column (c)); and

(4)   The maximum number (or approximate dollar value) of shares (or units) that may yet be purchased under the plans or programs (column (d)).

Instructions to Paragraphs (b)(3) and (b)(4) of Item 703. 1. In the table, disclose this information in the aggregate for all plans or programs publicly announced.

2.   By footnote to the table, indicate:

a.   The date each plan or program was announced;

b.   The dollar amount (or share or unit amount) approved;

c.   The expiration date (if any) of each plan or program;

d.   Each plan or program that has expired during the period covered by the table; and

e.   Each plan or program the issuer has determined to terminate prior to expiration, or under which the issuer does not intend to make further purchases.

Instruction to Item 703. Disclose all purchases covered by this Item, including purchases that do not satisfy the conditions of the safe harbor of Rule 10b–18(a)(3) under the Securities Exchange Act of 1934.

Subpart 800—List of Industry Guides

Item 801.   Securities Act Industry Guides

(a)   *Guide 1*. Removed and reserved.

(b)   "Removed and reserved."

(c)   *Guide 3*. Statistical disclosure by bank holding companies.

(d)   *Guide 4*. Prospectuses relating to interests in oil and gas programs.

(e)   *Guide 5*. Preparation of registration statements relating to interests in real estate limited partnerships.

(f)   *Guide 6*. Disclosures concerning unpaid claims and claim adjustment expenses of property-casualty underwriters.

Item 802.   Exchange Act Industry Guides

(a)   *Guide 1*. Removed and reserved.

(b)   "Removed and reserved."

(c)   *Guide 3*. Statistical disclosure by bank holding companies.

(d)   *Guide 4*. Disclosures concerning unpaid claims and claim adjustment expenses of property-casualty underwriters.

Subpart 900—Roll-up Transactions

Item 901.   Definitions

For the purposes of this subpart 229.900:

(a)   *General partner* means the person or persons responsible under state law for managing or directing the management of the business and affairs of a partnership that is the subject of a roll-up transaction including, but not limited to, the general partner(s), board of directors, board of trustees, or other person(s) having a fiduciary duty to such partnership.

(b)(1)   *Partnership* means any:

     (i)   Finite-life limited partnership; or

     (ii)   Other finite-life entity.

(2)(i)   Except as provided in paragraph (b)(2)(ii) of this Item, a limited partnership or other entity is "finite-life" if:

     (A)   It operates as a conduit vehicle for investors to participate in the ownership of assets for a limited period of time; and

     (B)   It has as a policy or purpose distributing to investors proceeds from the sale, financing or refinancing of assets or cash from operations, rather than reinvesting such proceeds or cash in the business (whether for the term of the entity or after an initial period of time following commencement of operations).

     (ii)   A real estate investment trust as defined in I.R.C. section 856 is not finite-life solely because of the distribution to investors of net income as provided by the I.R.C. if its policies or purposes do not include the distribution to investors of proceeds from the sale, financing or refinancing of assets, rather than the reinvestment of such proceeds in the business.

(3)   *Partnership* does not include any entity registered under the Investment Company Act of 1940 or any Business Development Company as defined in section 2(a)(48) of that Act.

(c)(1)   Except as provided in paragraph (c)(2) or (c)(3) of this Item, roll-up transaction means a transaction involving the combination or reorganization of one or more partnerships, directly or indirectly,

528

in which some or all of the investors in any of such partnerships will receive new securities, or securities in another entity.

(2)   Notwithstanding paragraph (c)(1) of this Item, *roll-up transaction* shall not include:

(i)   A transaction wherein the interests of all of the investors in each of the partnerships are repurchased, recalled, or exchanged in accordance with the terms of the preexisting partnership agreement for securities in an operating company specifically identified at the time of the formation of the original partnership;

(ii)   A transaction in which the securities to be issued or exchanged are not required to be and are not registered under the Securities Act of 1933;

(iii)   A transaction that involves only issuers that are not required to register or report under section 12 of the Securities Exchange Act of 1934, both before and after the transaction;

(iv)   A transaction that involves the combination or reorganization of one or more partnerships in which a non-affiliated party succeeds to the interests of a general partner or sponsor, if:

(A)   Such action is approved by not less than 66 2/3% of the outstanding units of each of the participating partnerships; and

(B)   As a result of the transaction, the existing general partners will receive only compensation to which they are entitled as expressly provided for in the preexisting partnership agreements;

(v)   A transaction in which the securities offered to investors are securities of another entity that are reported under a transaction reporting plan declared effective before December 17, 1993 by the Commission under section 11A of the Securities Exchange Act of 1934, if:

(A)   Such other entity was formed, and such class of securities was reported and regularly traded, not less than 12 months before the date on which soliciting material is mailed to investors; and

(B)   The securities of that entity issued to investors in the transaction do not exceed 20% of the total outstanding securities of the entity, exclusive of any securities of such class held by or for the account of the entity or a subsidiary of the entity; and

(C)   For purposes of paragraph (c)(2)(v) of this Item, a regularly traded security means any security with a minimum closing price of $2.00 or more for a majority of the business days during the preceding three-month period and a six-month minimum average daily trading volume of 1,000 shares;

(vi)   A transaction in which all of the investors' partnership securities are reported under a transaction reporting plan declared effective before December 17, 1993 by the Commission under section 11A of the Securities Exchange Act of 1934 and such investors receive new securities or securities in another entity that are reported under a transaction reporting plan declared effective before December 17, 1993 by the Commission under section 11A of the Securities Exchange Act of 1934, except that, for purposes of this paragraph, securities that are reported under a transaction reporting plan declared effective before December 17, 1993 by the Commission under section 11A of the Securities Exchange Act of 1934 shall not include securities listed on the American Stock Exchange's Emerging Company Marketplace;

(vii)   A transaction in which the investors in any of the partnerships involved in the transaction are not subject to a significant adverse change with respect to voting rights, the terms of existence of the entity, management compensation or investment objectives; or

(viii)   A transaction in which all investors are provided an option to receive or retain a security under substantially the same terms and conditions as the original issue.

(3)   The Commission, upon written request or upon its own motion, may exempt by rule or order any security or class of securities, any transaction or class of transactions, or any person or class of persons, in whole or in part, conditionally or unconditionally, from the definition of roll-up transaction

or the requirements imposed on roll-up transactions by Items 902–915 of Regulation S–K, if it finds such action to be consistent with the public interest and the protection of investors.

(d)   *Sponsor* means the person proposing the roll-up transaction.

(e)   *Successor* means the surviving entity after completion of the roll-up transaction or the entity whose securities are being offered or sold to, or acquired by, limited partners of the partnerships or the limited partnerships to be combined or reorganized.

Instruction to Item 901. If a transaction is a roll-up transaction as defined in Item 901(c) of this subpart, the requirements of this subpart apply to each entity proposed to be included in the roll-up transaction, whether or not the entity is a "partnership" as defined in Item 901(b) of this subpart.

Item 902.   Individual Partnership Supplements

(a)   If two or more entities are proposed to be included in the roll-up transaction, provide the information specified in this Item in a separate supplement to the disclosure document for each entity.

(b)   The separate supplement required by paragraph (a) of this Item shall be filed as part of the registration statement, shall be delivered with the prospectus to investors in the partnership covered thereby, and shall include:

(1)   A statement in the forepart of the supplement to the effect that:

(i)   Supplements have been prepared for each partnership;

(ii)   The effects of the roll-up transaction may be different for investors in the various partnerships; and

(iii)   Upon receipt of a written request by an investor or his representative who has been so designated in writing, a copy of any supplement will be transmitted promptly, without charge, by the general partner or sponsor.

This statement must include the name and address of the person to whom investors should make their request.

(2)   A brief description of each material risk and effect of the roll-up transaction, including, but not limited to, federal income tax consequences, for investors in the partnership, with appropriate cross references to the discussions of the risks, effects and tax consequences of the roll-up transaction required in the principal disclosure document pursuant to Items 904 and 915 of this subpart. Such discussion shall address the effect of the roll-up transaction on the partnership's financial condition and results of operations.

(3)   A statement concerning whether the general partner reasonably believes that the roll-up transaction is fair or unfair to investors in the partnership, together with a brief discussion of the bases for such belief, with appropriate cross references to the discussion of the fairness of the roll-up transaction required in the principal disclosure document pursuant to Item 910 of this subpart. If there are material differences between the fairness analysis for the partnership and for the other partnerships, such differences shall be described briefly in the supplement.

(4)   A brief, narrative description of the method of calculating the value of the partnership and allocating interests in the successor to the partnership, and a table showing such calculation and allocation. Such table shall include the following information (or other information of a comparable character necessary to a thorough understanding of the calculation and allocation):

(i)   The appraised value of each separately appraised significant asset (as defined in Item 911(c)(5)) held by the partnership, or, if appraisals have not been obtained for each significant asset, the value assigned for purposes of the valuation of the partnership to each significant asset for which an appraisal has not been obtained;

(ii)   The dollar amount of any mortgages or other similar liabilities to which each of such assets is subject;

(iii)   Cash and cash equivalent assets held by the partnership;

(iv)   Other assets held by the partnership;

(v)   Other liabilities of the partnership;

(vi)   The value assigned to the partnership;

(vii)   The value assigned to the partnership per interest held by investors in the partnership (on an equivalent interest basis, such as per $1,000 original investment);

(viii) The aggregate number of interests in the successor to be allocated to the partnership and the percentage of the total interests of the successor;

(ix)   The number of interests in the successor to be allocated to investors in the partnership for each interest held by such investors (on an equivalent interest basis, such as per $1,000 original investment); and

(x)   The value assigned to the general partner's interest in the partnership, and the number of interests in the successor or other consideration to be allocated in the roll-up transaction to the general partner for such general partnership interest or otherwise as compensation or reimbursement for claims against or interests in the partnership, such as foregone fees, unearned fees and for fees to be earned on the sale or refinancing of an asset.

(5)   The amounts of compensation paid, and cash distributions made, to the general partner and its affiliates by the partnership for the last three fiscal years and the most recently completed interim period and the amounts that would have been paid if the compensation and distributions structure to be in effect after the roll-up transaction had been in effect during such period. If any proposed change(s) in the business or operations of the successor after the roll-up transaction would change materially the compensation and distributions that would have been paid by the successor (e.g., if properties will be sold or purchased after the roll-up transaction and no properties were sold or purchased during the period covered by the table), describe such changes and the effects thereof on the compensation and distributions to be paid by the successor.

(6)   Cash distributions made to investors during each of the last five fiscal years and most recently completed interim period, identifying any such distributions which represent a return of capital.

(7)   An appropriate cross reference to selected financial information concerning the partnership and the pro forma financial statements included in the principal disclosure document in response to Item 914(b)(2).

Item 903.   Summary

(a)   Provide in the forepart of the disclosure document a clear, concise and comprehensible summary of the roll-up transaction.

(b)   The summary required by paragraph (a) of this Item shall include a summary description of each of the following items, as well as any other material terms or consequences of the roll-up transaction necessary to an understanding of such transaction:

(1)   Each material risk and effect on investors, including, but not limited to:

(i)   Changes in the business plan, voting rights, cash distribution policies, form of ownership interest or management compensation;

(ii)   The general partner's conflicts of interest in connection with the roll-up transaction and in connection with the successor's future operations; and

(iii)   The likelihood that securities received by investors in the roll-up transaction will trade at prices substantially below the value assigned to such securities in the roll-up transaction and/or the value of the successor's assets;

(2)   The material terms of the roll-up transaction, including the valuation method used to allocate securities in the successor to investors in the partnerships;

(3)   Whether the general partner reasonably believes that the roll-up transaction is fair or unfair to investors in each partnership, including a brief discussion of the bases for such belief;

(4)   Any opinion from an outside party concerning the fairness of the roll-up transaction, including whether the opinion addresses the fairness of all possible combinations of partnerships or portions of partnerships, and contacts with any outside party concerning fairness opinions, valuations or reports in connection with the roll-up transaction required to be disclosed pursuant to Item 911(a)(5);

(5)   The background of and reasons for the roll-up transaction, as well as alternatives to the roll-up transaction described in response to Item 908(b);

(6)   Rights of investors to exercise dissenters' or appraisal rights or similar rights and to obtain a list of investors in the partnership in which the investor holds an interest; and

(7)   If any affiliates of the general partner or the sponsor may participate in the business of the successor or receive compensation from the successor, an organizational chart showing the relationships between the general partner, the sponsor and their affiliates.

Instruction to Item 903. The description of the material risks and effects of the roll-up transaction required by paragraph (b)(1) of this Item must be presented prominently in the forepart of the summary.

Item 904.   Risk Factors and Other Considerations

(a)   Immediately following the summary required by Item 903, describe in reasonable detail each material risk and effect of the roll-up transaction on investors in each partnership, including, but not limited to:

(1)   The potential risks, adverse effects and benefits of the roll-up transaction for investors and for the general partner, including those which result from each matter described in response to Item 905 of this subpart, with appropriate cross references to the comparative information required by Item 905;

(2)   The material risks arising from an investment in the successor; and

(3)   The likelihood that securities of the successor received by investors in the roll-up transaction will trade in the securities markets at a price substantially below the value assigned to such securities in the roll-up transaction and/or the value of the assets of the successor, and the effects on investors of such a trading market discount.

(b)   Quantify each risk or effect to the extent practicable.

(c)   State whether any of such risks or effects may be different for investors in any partnership and, if so, identify such partnership(s) and describe such difference(s).

Instruction to Item 904. The requirement to quantify the effects of the roll-up transaction shall include, but not be limited to:

(i)   If cost savings resulting from combined administration of the partnerships is identified as a potential benefit of the roll-up transaction, the amount of cost savings and a comparison of such amount to the costs of the roll-up transaction; and

(ii)   If there may be a material conflict of interest of the sponsor or general partner arising from its receipt of payments or other consideration as a result of the roll-up transaction, the amount of such payments and other consideration to be obtained in the roll-up transaction and a comparison of such amounts to the amounts to which the sponsor or general partner would be entitled without the roll-up transaction.

Item 905.   Comparative Information

(a)(1)   Describe the voting and other rights of investors in the successor under the successor's governing instruments and under applicable law. Compare such rights to the voting and other rights of investors in each partnership subject to the transaction under the partnerships' governing instruments and under applicable law. Describe the effects of the change(s) in such rights.

(2)   Describe the duties owed by the general partner of the successor to investors in the successor under the successor's governing instruments and under applicable law. Compare such duties to the duties owed by the general partner of each partnership to investors in the partnership under the partnership's governing instruments and under applicable law. Describe the effects of the change(s) in such duties.

(b)(1) Describe each item of compensation (including reimbursement of expenses) payable by the successor after the roll-up transaction to the general partner and its affiliates or to any affiliate of the successor. Compare such compensation to the compensation currently payable to the general partner and its affiliates by each partnership. Describe the effects of the change(s) in compensation arrangements.

(2) Describe each instance in which cash or other distributions may be made by the successor to the general partner and its affiliates or to any affiliate of the successor. Compare such distributions to the distributions currently paid or payable to the general partner and its affiliates by each partnership. Describe the effects of the change(s) in distribution arrangements. If distributions similar to those currently paid or payable by any partnership to the general partner or its affiliates will not be made by the successor, state whether or not other compensation arrangements with the successor described in response to paragraph (b)(1) of this Item (e.g., incentive fees payable upon sale of a property) will, in effect, replace such distributions.

(3) Provide a table demonstrating the changes in such compensation and distributions setting forth among other things:

(i) The actual amounts of compensation and distributions, separately identified, paid by the partnerships on a combined basis to the general partner and its affiliates for the partnerships' last three fiscal years and most recently ended interim periods; and

(ii) The amounts of compensation and distributions that would have been paid if the compensation and distributions structure to be in effect after the roll-up transaction had been in effect during such period.

(4) If any proposed change(s) in the business or operations of the successor after the roll-up transaction would change materially the compensation and distributions that would have been paid by the successor from that shown in the table provided in response to paragraph (b)(3)(ii) of this Item (e.g., if properties will be sold or purchased after the roll-up transaction and no properties were sold or purchased during the period covered by the table), describe such changes and the effects thereof on the compensation and distributions to be paid by the successor.

(5) Describe the material conflicts that may arise between the interests of the sponsor or general partner and the interests of investors in the successor as a result of the compensation and distribution arrangements described in response to paragraphs (b)(1) and (2) of this Item and describe any steps that will be taken to resolve any such conflicts.

(c) Describe any provisions in the governing instruments of the successor and any policies of the general partner of the successor relating to distributions to investors of cash from operations, proceeds from the sale, financing or refinancing of assets, and any other distributions. Compare such provisions and policies to those of each of the partnerships. Describe the effects of any change(s) in such provisions or policies.

(d)(1) Describe each material investment policy of the successor, including, without limitation, policies with respect to borrowings by the successor. Compare such investment policies to the investment policies of each of the partnerships. Describe the effects of any change(s) in such policies.

(2) Describe any plans of the general partner, sponsor or of any person who will be an affiliate of the successor with respect to:

(i) A sale of any material assets of the partnerships;

(ii) A purchase of any material assets; and

(iii) Borrowings.

(3)(i) State whether or not specific assets have been identified for sale, financing, refinancing or purchase following the roll-up transaction.

(ii) If specific assets have been so identified, describe the assets and the proposed transaction.

(e) Describe any other similar terms or policies of the successor that are material to an investment in the successor. Compare any such terms or policies to those of each of the partnerships. Describe the effects of any change(s) in any such terms or policies.

Instructions to Item 905. (1) The information provided in response to this Item should be illustrated in tables or other readily understandable formats, which should be included together with the disclosures required by this Item.

(2)   The information required by this Item shall be set forth in appropriate separate sections of the principal disclosure document.

Item 906.   Allocation of Roll-up Consideration

(a)   Describe in reasonable detail the method used to allocate interests in the successor to investors in the partnerships and the reasons why such method was used.

(b)   Provide a table showing the calculation of the valuation of each partnership and the allocation of interests in the successor to investors. Such table shall include for each partnership the following information (or other information of a comparable character necessary to an understanding of the calculation and allocation):

(1)   The value assigned to each significant category of assets of the partnership and the total value assigned to the partnership;

(2)   The total value assigned to all partnerships;

(3)   The aggregate amount of interests in the successor to be allocated to each partnership and the percentage of the total amount of all such interests represented thereby; and

(4)   The amount of interests of the successor to be issued to investors per interest held in each partnership (on an equivalent interest basis, such as per $1,000 invested).

(c)   If interests in the successor will be allocated to the general partner in exchange for its general partner interest or otherwise or if the general partner will receive other consideration in connection with the roll-up transaction:

(1)   Describe in reasonable detail the method used to allocate interests in the successor to the general partner or to determine the amount of consideration payable to the general partner and the reasons such method(s) was used; and

(2)   Identify the consideration paid by the general partner for interests in the partnerships that will be exchanged in the roll-up transaction.

Item 907.   Background of the Roll-up Transaction

(a)(1)   Furnish a summary of the background of the transaction. Such summary shall include, but not be limited to, a description of any contacts, negotiations or transactions concerning any of the following matters:

(i)   A merger, consolidation, or combination of any of the partnerships;

(ii)   An acquisition of any of the partnerships or a material amount of any of their assets;

(iii)   A tender offer for or other acquisition of securities of any class issued by any of the partnerships; or

(iv)   A change in control of any of the partnerships.

(2)   The summary required by paragraph (a)(1) of this Item shall:

(i)   Cover the period beginning with each partnership's second full fiscal year preceding the date of the filing of the roll-up transaction;

(ii)   Include contacts, negotiations or transactions between the general partner or its affiliates and any person who would have a direct interest in the matters listed in paragraphs (a)(1)(i)–(iv) of this Item; and

(iii)   Identify the person who initiated such contacts, negotiations or transactions.

(b)   Briefly describe the background of each partnership, including, but not limited to:

(1)   The amount of capital raised from investors, the extent to which net proceeds from the original offering of interests have been invested, the extent to which funds have been invested as planned and the amount not yet invested; and

(2)   The partnership's investment objectives and the extent to which the partnership has achieved its investment objectives.

(c)   Discuss whether the general partner (including any affiliated person materially dependent on the general partner's compensation arrangement with the partnership) or any partnership has experienced since the commencement of the most recently completed fiscal year or is likely to experience any material adverse financial developments. If so, describe such developments and the effect of the transaction on such matters.

Item 908.   Reasons for and Alternatives to the Roll-up Transaction

(a)   Describe the reason(s) for the roll-up transaction.

(b)(1)   If the general partner or sponsor considered alternatives to the roll-up transaction being proposed, describe such alternative(s) and state the reason(s) for their rejection.

(2)   Whether or not described in response to paragraph (b)(1) of this Item, describe in reasonable detail the potential alternative of continuation of the partnerships in accordance with their existing business plans, including the effects of such continuation and the material risks and benefits that likely would arise in connection therewith, and, if applicable, the general partner's reasons for not considering such alternative.

(3)   Whether or not described in response to paragraph (b)(1) of this Item, describe in reasonable detail the potential alternative of liquidation of the partnerships, the procedures required to accomplish liquidation, the effects of liquidation, the material risks and benefits that likely would arise in connection with liquidation, and, if applicable, the general partner's reasons for not considering such alternative.

(c)   State the reasons for the structure of the roll-up transaction and for undertaking such transaction at this time.

(d)   State whether the general partner initiated the roll-up transaction and, if not, whether the general partner participated in the structuring of the transaction.

(e)   State whether the general partner recommends the roll-up transaction and briefly describe the reasons for such recommendation.

Item 909.   Conflicts of Interest

(a)   Briefly describe the general partner's fiduciary duties to each partnership subject to the roll-up transaction and each actual or potential material conflict of interest between the general partner and the investors relating to the roll-up transaction.

(b)(1)   State whether or not the general partner has retained an unaffiliated representative to act on behalf of investors for purposes of negotiating the terms of the roll-up transaction. If no such representative has been retained, describe the reasons therefor and the risks arising from the absence of separate representation.

(2)   If an unaffiliated representative has been retained to represent investors:

(i)   Identify such unaffiliated representative;

(ii)   Briefly describe the representative's qualifications, including a brief description of any other transaction similar to the roll-up transaction in which the representative has served in a similar capacity within the past five years;

(iii)   Describe the method of selection of such representative, including a statement as to whether or not any investors were consulted in the selection of the representative and, if so, the names of such investors;

(iv) Describe the scope and terms of the engagement of the representative, including, but not limited to, what party will be responsible for paying the representative's fees and whether such fees are contingent upon the outcome of the roll-up transaction;

(v) Describe any material relationship between the representative or its affiliates and:

(A) The general partner, sponsor, any affiliate of the general partner or sponsor; or

(B) Any other person having a material interest in the roll-up transaction,

which existed during the past two years or is mutually understood to be contemplated and any compensation received or to be received as a result of such relationship;

(vi) Describe in reasonable detail the actions taken by the representative on behalf of investors; and

(vii) Describe the fiduciary duties or other legal obligations of the representative to investors in each of the partnerships.

Item 910.   Fairness of the Transaction

(a) State whether the general partner reasonably believes that the roll-up transaction is fair or unfair to investors and the reasons for such belief. Such discussion must address the fairness of the roll-up transaction to investors in each of the partnerships and as a whole. If the roll-up transaction may be completed with a combination of partnerships consisting of less than all partnerships, or with portions of partnerships, the belief stated must address each possible combination.

(b) Discuss in reasonable detail the material factors upon which the belief stated in paragraph (a) of this Item is based and, to the extent practicable, the weight assigned to each such factor. Such discussion should include an analysis of the extent, if any, to which such belief is based on the factors set forth in Instructions (2) and (3) to this Item, paragraph (b)(1) of Item 909 and Item 911. This discussion also must:

(1) Compare the value of the consideration to be received in the roll-up transaction to the value of the consideration that would be received pursuant to each of the alternatives discussed in response to Item 908(b); and

(2) Describe any material differences among the partnerships (e.g., different types of assets or different investment objectives) relating to the fairness of the transaction.

(c) If any offer of the type described in Instruction (2)(viii) to this Item has been received, describe such offer and state the reason(s) for its rejection.

(d) Describe any factors known to the general partner that may affect materially the value of the consideration to be received by investors in the roll-up transaction, the values assigned to the partnerships for purposes of the comparisons to alternatives required by paragraph (b) of this Item and the fairness of the transaction to investors.

(e) State whether the general partner's statements in response to paragraphs (a) and (b) of this Item are based, in whole or in part, on any report, opinion or appraisal described in response to Item 911. If so, describe any material uncertainties known to the general partner that relate to the conclusions in any such report, opinion or appraisal including, but not limited to, developments or trends that have affected or are reasonably likely to affect materially such conclusions.

Instructions to Item 910. (1) A statement that the general partner has no reasonable belief as to the fairness of the roll-up transaction to investors will not be considered sufficient disclosure in response to paragraph (a) of this Item.

(2) The factors which are important in determining the fairness of a roll-up transaction to investors and the weight, if any, which should be given to them in a particular context will vary. Normally such factors will include, among others, those referred to in paragraph (b)(1) of Item 909 and whether the consideration offered to investors constitutes fair value in relation to:

(i) Current market prices, if any;

(ii) Historic market prices, if any;

(iii) Net book value;

(iv)   Going concern value;

(v)   Liquidation value;

(vi)   Purchases of limited partnership interests by the general partner or sponsor or their affiliates since the commencement of the partnership's second full fiscal year preceding the date of filing of the disclosure document for the roll-up transaction;

(vii)   Any report, opinion, or appraisal described in Item 911; and

(viii)   Offers of which the general partner or sponsor is aware made during the preceding eighteen months for a merger, consolidation, or combination of any of the partnerships; an acquisition of any of the partnerships or a material amount of their assets; a tender offer for or other acquisition of securities of any class issued by any of the partnerships; or a change in control of any of the partnerships.

(3)   The discussion concerning fairness should specifically address material terms of the transaction including whether the consideration offered to investors constitutes fair value in relation to:

(i)   The form and amount of consideration to be received by investors and the sponsor in the roll-up transaction;

(ii)   The methods used to determine such consideration; and

(iii)   The compensation to be paid to the sponsor in the future.

(4)   Conclusory statements, such as "The roll-up transaction is fair to investors in relation to net book value, going concern value, liquidation value and future prospects of the partnership," will not be considered sufficient disclosure in response to paragraph (b) of this Item.

(5)   Consideration should be given to presenting the comparative numerical data as to the value of the consideration being received by investors, liquidation value and other values in a tabular format. Financial and other information concerning the partnerships should be prepared based upon the most recent available information, such as, in the case of financial information, the periods covered by interim selected financial information included in the prospectus in accordance with Item 914.

Item 911.   Reports, Opinions and Appraisals

(a)(1)   *All material reports, opinions or appraisals.* State whether or not the general partner or sponsor has received any report, opinion (other than an opinion of counsel) or appraisal from an outside party which is materially related to the roll-up transaction including, but not limited to, any such report, opinion or appraisal relating to the consideration or the fairness of the consideration to be offered to investors in connection with the roll-up transaction or the fairness of such transaction to the general partner or investors.

(2)   With respect to any report, opinion or appraisal described in paragraph (a)(1) of this Item;

(i)   Identify such outside party;

(ii)   Briefly describe the qualifications of such outside party;

(iii)   Describe the method of selection of such outside party;

(iv)   Describe any material relationship between:

(A)   The outside party or its affiliates; and

(B)   The general partner, sponsor, the successor or any of their affiliates,

which existed during the past two years or is mutually understood to be contemplated and any compensation received or to be received as a result of such relationship;

(v)   If such report, opinion or appraisal relates to the fairness of the consideration, state whether the general partner, sponsor or affiliate determined the amount of consideration to be paid or whether the outside party recommended the amount of consideration to be paid.

(vi)   Furnish a summary concerning such report, opinion or appraisal which shall include, but not be limited to, the procedures followed; the findings and recommendations; the bases for and methods of arriving at such findings and recommendations; instructions received from the general partner, sponsor or its affiliates; and any limitation imposed by the general partner, sponsor or affiliate on the scope of the investigation. If any limitation was imposed by the general partner, sponsor or affiliate on the scope of the investigation, including, but not limited to, access to its personnel, premises, and relevant books and records, state the reasons therefor.

(vii) State whether any compensation paid to such outside party is contingent on the approval or completion of the roll-up transaction and, if so, the reasons for compensating such parties on a contingent basis.

(3)   Furnish a statement to the effect that upon written request by an investor or his representative who has been so designated in writing, a copy of any such report, opinion or appraisal shall be transmitted promptly, without charge, by the general partner or sponsor. The statement also must include the name and address of the person to whom investors or their representatives should make their request.

(4)   All reports, opinions or appraisals referred to in paragraph (a)(1) of this Item shall be filed as exhibits to the registration statement.

(5)(i)   Describe any contacts in connection with the roll-up transaction between the sponsor or the general partner and any outside party with respect to the preparation by such party of an opinion concerning the fairness of the roll-up transaction, a valuation of a partnership or its assets, or any other report with respect to the roll-up transaction. No description is required, however, of contacts with respect to reports, opinions or appraisals filed as exhibits pursuant to paragraph (a)(4) of this Item.

(ii)   The description of contacts with any outside party required by paragraph (a)(5)(i) of this Item shall include the following:

(A)   The identity of each such party;

(B)   The nature of the contact;

(C)   The actions taken by such party;

(D)   Any views, preliminary or final, expressed on the proposed subject matter of the report, opinion or appraisal; and

(E)   Any reasons such party did not provide a report, opinion or appraisal.

(b)   *Fairness opinions:*

(1)   If any report, opinion or appraisal relates to the fairness of the roll-up transaction to investors in the partnerships, state whether or not the report, opinion or appraisal addresses the fairness of:

(i)   The roll-up transaction as a whole and to investors in each partnership; and

(ii)   All possible combinations of partnerships in the roll-up transaction (including portions of partnerships if the transaction is structured to permit portions of partnerships to participate). If all possible combinations are not addressed:

(A)   Identify the combinations that are addressed;

(B)   Identify the person(s) that determined which combinations would be addressed and state the reasons for the selection of the combinations; and

(C)   State that if the roll-up transaction is completed with a combination of partnerships not addressed, no report, opinion or appraisal concerning the fairness of the roll-up transaction will have been obtained.

(2)   If the sponsor or the general partner has not obtained any opinion on the fairness of the proposed roll-up transaction to investors in each of the affected partnerships, state the sponsor's or general partner's reasons for concluding that such an opinion is not necessary in order to permit the limited partners or shareholders to make an informed decision on the proposed transaction.

(c)   *Appraisals.* If the report, opinion or appraisal consists of an appraisal of the assets of the partnerships:

(1) Describe the purpose(s) for which the appraisals were obtained and their use in connection with the roll-up transaction;

(2) Describe which assets are covered by the appraisals and state the aggregate appraised value of the assets covered by the appraisals (including such value net of associated indebtedness). Provide a description of, and valuation of, any assets subject to any material qualifications by the appraiser and a summary of such qualifications;

(3) Identify the date as of which the appraisals were prepared. State whether and in what circumstances the appraisals will be updated. State whether any events have occurred or conditions have changed since the date of the appraisals that may have caused a material change in the value of the assets;

(4) Include as an appendix to the prospectus one or more tables setting forth the following information:

    (i) The appraised value of any separately appraised asset that is significant to the partnership holding such asset;

    (ii) If the appraiser considered different valuation approaches in preparing the appraisals of the assets identified in response to paragraph (c)(4)(i) of this Item, the value of each such asset under each valuation approach considered by the appraiser, identifying the valuation approach used by the appraiser in determining the appraised value and the reason such approach was chosen; and

    (iii) All material assumptions used by the appraiser in appraising the assets identified in response to paragraph (c)(4)(i) of this Item, and, if the appraiser used different assumptions for any of such assets, the reasons the different assumptions were chosen.

(5) For purposes of this Item and Item 902, an asset is "significant" to a partnership if it represents more than 10% of the value of the partnership's assets as of the end of the most recently-completed fiscal year or recently-completed interim period or if 10% or more of the partnership's cash flow or net income for the most recently-completed fiscal year or most recently-completed subsequent interim period was derived from such asset.

Instructions to Item 911. (1) The reports, opinions and appraisals required to be identified in response to paragraph (a) of this Item include any reports, opinions and appraisals which materially relate to the roll-up transaction whether or not relied upon, such as reports or opinions regarding alternatives to the roll-up transaction whether or not the alternatives were rejected.

(2) The information called for by paragraph (a)(2) of this Item should be given with respect to the firm which provides the report, opinion or appraisal rather than the employees of such firm who prepared it.

(3) With respect to appraisals, a summary prepared by the appraisers should not be included in lieu of the description of the appraisals required by paragraph (c) of this Item. A clear and concise summary description of the appraisals is required.

Item 912. Source and Amount of Funds and Transactional Expenses

(a) State the source and total amount of funds or other consideration to be used in the roll-up transaction.

(b)(1) Furnish a reasonably itemized statement of all expenses incurred or estimated to be incurred in connection with the roll-up transaction including, but not limited to, filing fees, legal, financial advisory, accounting and appraisal fees, solicitation expenses and printing costs. Identify the persons responsible for paying any or all of such expenses.

(2) State whether or not any partnership subject to the roll-up transaction will be, directly or indirectly, responsible for any or all of the expenses of the transaction. If any partnership will be so responsible, state the amount to be provided by each partnership and the sources of capital to finance such amount.

(c)   If all or any part of the consideration to be used by the sponsor or successor in the roll-up transaction is expected to be, directly or indirectly, provided by any partnership, state the amount to be provided by each partnership and the sources of capital to finance such amount.

(d)   If all or any part of the funds or other consideration is, or is expected to be, directly or indirectly borrowed by the sponsor or successor for the purpose of the roll-up transaction:

(1)   Provide a summary of each such loan agreement containing the identity of the parties, the term, the collateral, the stated and effective interest rates, and other material terms or conditions; and

(2)   Briefly describe any plans or arrangements to finance or repay such borrowing, or, if no plans or arrangements have been made, make a statement to that effect.

(e)   If the source of all or any part of the funds to be used in the roll-up transaction is a loan made in the ordinary course of business by a bank as defined by section 3(a)(6) of the Exchange Act and section 13(d) or 14(d) is applicable to such transaction, the name of such bank shall not be made available to the public if the person filing the statement so requests in writing and files such request, naming such bank, with the Secretary of the Commission.

Item 913.   Other Provisions of the Transaction

(a)   State whether or not appraisal rights are provided under applicable state law, under the partnership's governing instruments or will be voluntarily accorded by the successor, the general partner or the sponsor (or any of their affiliates) in connection with the roll-up transaction. If so, summarize such appraisal rights. If appraisal rights will not be available to investors who object to the transaction, briefly outline the rights which may be available to such investors under such law.

(b)   If any provision has been made to allow investors to obtain access to the books and records of the partnership or to obtain counsel or appraisal services at the expense of the successor, the general partner, the partnership, the sponsor (or any of their affiliates), describe such provision.

(c)   Discuss the investors' rights under federal and state law to obtain a partnership's list of investors.

Item 914.   Pro Forma Financial Statements: Selected Financial Data

(a)   In addition to the information required by Item 301 of Regulation S–K, Selected Financial Data, and Item 302 of Regulation S–K, Supplementary Financial Information, for each partnership proposed to be included in a roll-up transaction provide: Ratio of earnings to fixed charges, cash and cash equivalents, total assets at book value, total assets at the value assigned for purposes of the roll-up transaction (if applicable), total liabilities, general and limited partners' equity, net increase (decrease) in cash and cash equivalents, net cash provided by operating activities, distributions; and per unit data for net income (loss), book value, value assigned for purposes of the roll-up transaction (if applicable), and distributions (separately identifying distributions that represent a return of capital). This information should be provided for the same period(s) for which Selected Financial Data and Supplementary Financial Information are required to be provided. Additional or other information should be provided if material to an understanding of each partnership proposed to be included in a roll-up transaction.

(b)   Provide pro forma financial information (including oil and gas reserves and cash flow disclosure, if appropriate), assuming:

(1)   All partnerships participate in the roll-up transaction; and

(2)   Participation in a roll-up transaction of those partnerships that on a combined basis have the lowest combined net cash provided by operating activities for the last fiscal year of such partnerships, provided participation by such partnerships satisfies all conditions to consummation of the roll-up transaction. If the combination of all partnerships proposed to be included in a roll-up transaction results in such lowest combined net cash provided by operating activities, this shall be noted and no separate pro forma financial statements are required.

(c)   The pro forma financial statements required by paragraph (b) of this Item shall disclose the effect of the roll-up transaction on the successor's:

(1) Balance sheet as of the later of the end of the most recent fiscal year or the latest interim period;

(2) Statement of income (with separate line items to reflect income (loss) excluding and including the roll-up expenses and payments), earnings per share amounts, and ratio of earnings to fixed charges for the most recent fiscal year and the latest interim period;

(3) Statement of cash flows for the most recent fiscal year and the latest interim period; and

(4) Book value per share as of the later of the end of the most recent fiscal year or the latest interim period.

Instructions to Item 914. (1) Notwithstanding the provisions of this Item, any or all of the information required by paragraphs (b) and (c) of this Item that is not material for the exercise of prudent judgment in regard to the matter to be acted upon, may be omitted.

(2) If the roll-up transaction is structured to permit participation by portions of partnerships, consideration should be given to the effect of such participation in preparing the pro forma financial statements reflecting a partial roll-up.

Item 915.   Federal Income Tax Consequences

(a) Provide a brief, clear and understandable summary of the material Federal income tax consequences of the roll-up transaction and an investment in the successor. Where a tax opinion has been provided, briefly summarize the substance of such opinion, including identification of the material consequences upon which counsel has not been asked, or is unable, to opine. If any of the material Federal income tax consequences are not expected to be the same for investors in all partnerships, the differences shall be described.

(b) State whether or not the opinion of counsel is included as an appendix to the prospectus. If filed as an exhibit to the registration statement and not included as an appendix to the prospectus, include a statement to the effect that, upon receipt of a written request by an investor or his representative who has been so designated in writing, a copy of the opinion of counsel will be transmitted promptly, without charge, by the general partner or sponsor. The statement should include the name and address of the person to whom investors should make their request.

Subpart 1000—Mergers and Acquisitions
(Regulation M–A)

Item 1000.   Definitions

The following definitions shall apply to the terms used in Regulation M–A, unless specified otherwise:

(a) "Associate" has the same meaning as in Rule 12b–2 under the Securities Exchange Act of 1934;

(b) "Instruction C" means General Instruction C to Schedule 13E–3 and General Instruction C to Schedule TO;

(c) "Issuer tender offer" has the same meaning as in Rule 13e–3(a)(3) under the Securities Exchange Act;

(d) "Offeror" means any person who makes a tender offer or on whose behalf a tender offer is made;

(e) "Rule 13e–3 transaction" has the same meaning as in Rule 13e–3(a)(3) under the Securities Exchange Act;

(f) "Subject company" means the company or entity whose securities are sought to be acquired in the transaction (*e.g.,* the target), or that is otherwise the subject of the transaction;

(g) "Subject securities" means the securities or class of securities that are sought to be acquired in the transaction or that are otherwise the subject of the transaction; and

(h) "Third-party tender offer" means a tender offer that is not an issuer tender offer.

Item 1001.   Summary Term Sheet

Summary term sheet. Provide security holders with a summary term sheet that is written in plain English. The summary term sheet must briefly describe in bullet point format the most material terms of the proposed transaction. The summary term sheet must provide securities holders with sufficient information to understand the essential features and significance of the proposed transaction. The bullet points must cross-reference a more detailed discussion contained in the disclosure document that is disseminated to security holders.

Instruction to Item 1001:

1.   The summary term sheet must not recite all information contained in the disclosure document that will be provided to security holders. The summary term sheet is intended to serve as an overview of all material matters that are presented in the accompanying documents provided to security holders.

2.   The summary term sheet must begin on the first or second page of the disclosure document provided to security holders.

3.   Refer to Rule 421(b) and (d) of Regulation C of the Securities Act for a description of plain English disclosure.

Item 1002.   Subject Company Information

(a)   *Name and address.* State the name of the subject company (or the issuer in the case of an issuer tender offer), and the address and telephone number of its principal executive offices.

(b)   *Securities.* State the exact titles and number of shares outstanding of the subject class of equity securities as of the most recent practicable date. This may be based upon information in the most recently available filing with the Commission by the subject company unless the filing person has more current information.

(c)   *Trading market and price.* Identify the principal market in which the subject securities are traded and state the high and low sales prices for the subject securities in the principal market (or, if there is no principal market, the range of high and low bid quotations and the source of the quotations) for each quarter during the past two years. If there is no established trading market for the securities (except for limited or sporadic quotations), so state.

(d)   *Dividends.* State the frequency and amount of any dividends paid during the past two years with respect to the subject securities. Briefly describe any restriction on the subject company's current or future ability to pay dividends. If the filing person is not the subject company, furnish this information to the extent known after making reasonable inquiry.

(e)   *Prior public offerings.* If the filing person has made an underwritten public offering of the subject securities for cash during the past three years that was registered under the Securities Act of 1933 or exempt from registration under Regulation A, state the date of the offering, the amount of securities offered, the offering price per share (adjusted for stock splits, stock dividends, etc. as appropriate) and the aggregate proceeds received by the filing person.

(f)   *Prior stock purchases.* If the filing person purchased any subject securities during the past two years, state the amount of the securities purchased, the range of prices paid and the average purchase price for each quarter during that period. Affiliates need not give information for purchases made before becoming an affiliate.

Item 1003.   Identity and Background of Filing Person

(a)   *Name and address.* State the name, business address and business telephone number of each filing person. Also state the name and address of each person specified in Instruction C to the schedule (except for Schedule 14D–9). If the filing person is an affiliate of the subject company, state the nature of the affiliation. If the filing person is the subject company, so state.

(b)   *Business and background of entities.* If any filing person (other than the subject company) or any person specified in Instruction C to the schedule is not a natural person, state the person's principal business, state or other place of organization, and the information required by paragraphs (c)(3) and (c)(4) of this item for each person.

(c) *Business and background of natural persons.* If any filing person or any person specified in Instruction C to the schedule is a natural person, provide the following information for each person:

    (1)   Current principal occupation or employment and the name, principal business and address of any corporation or other organization in which the employment or occupation is conducted;

    (2)   Material occupations, positions, offices or employment during the past five years, giving the starting and ending dates of each and the name, principal business and address of any corporation or other organization in which the occupation, position, office or employment was carried on;

    (3)   A statement whether or not the person was convicted in a criminal proceeding during the past five years (excluding traffic violations or similar misdemeanors). If the person was convicted, described the criminal proceeding, including the dates, nature of conviction, name and location of court, and penalty imposed or other disposition of the case;

    (4)   A statement whether or not the person was a party to any judicial or administrative proceeding during the past five years (except for matters that were dismissed without sanction or settlement) that resulted in a judgment, decree or final order enjoining the person from future violations of, or prohibiting activities subject to, federal or state securities laws, or a finding of any violation of federal or state securities laws. Describe the proceeding, including a summary of the terms of the judgment, decree or final order; and

    (5)   Country of citizenship.

(d)   *Tender offer.* Identify the tender offer and the class of securities to which the offer relates, the name of the offeror and its address (which may be based on the offeror's Schedule TO filed with the Commission).

> *Instructions to Item 1003*
>
> If the filing person is making information relating to the transaction available on the Internet, state the address where the information can be found.

Item 1004.   Terms of the Transaction

  (a) *Material terms.* State the material terms of the transaction.

    (1) *Tender offers.* In the case of a tender offer, the information must include:

      (i)   The total number and class of securities sought in the offer;

      (ii)   The type and amount of consideration offered to security holders;

      (iii)   The scheduled expiration date;

      (iv)   Whether a subsequent offering period will be available, if the transaction is a third-party tender offer;

      (v)   Whether the offer may be extended, and if so, how it could be extended;

      (vi)   The dates before and after which security holders may withdraw securities tendered in the offer;

      (vii) The procedures for tendering and withdrawing securities;

      (viii) The manner in which securities will be accepted for payment;

      (ix)   If the offer is for less than all securities of a class, the periods for accepting securities on a pro rata basis and the offeror's present intentions in the event that the offer is oversubscribed;

      (x)   An explanation of any material differences in the rights of security holders as a result of the transaction, if material;

      (xi)   A brief statement as to the accounting treatment of the transaction, if material; and

      (xii) The federal income tax consequences of the transaction, if material.

(2) *Mergers or similar transactions.* In the case of a merger or similar transaction, the information must include:

    (i)   A brief description of the transaction;

    (ii)   The consideration offered to security holders;

    (iii)   The reasons for engaging in the transaction;

    (iv)   The vote required for approval of the transaction;

    (v)   An explanation of any material differences in the rights of security holders as a result of the transaction, if material;

    (vi)   A brief statement as to the accounting treatment of the transaction, if material; and

    (vii)   The federal income tax consequences of the transaction, if material.

Instructions of Item 1004(a):

If the consideration offered includes securities exempt from registration under the Securities Act of 1933, provide a description of the securities that complies with Item 202 of Regulation S–K. This description is not required if the issuer of the securities meets the requirements of General Instructions I.A, I.B.1 or I.B.2, as applicable, or I.C. of Form S–3 and elects to furnish information by incorporation by reference; only capital stock is to be issued, and securities of the same class are registered under section 12 of the Exchange Act and either are listed for trading or admitted to unlisted trading privileges on a national securities exchange; or are securities for which bid and offer quotations are reported in an automated quotations system operated by a national securities association.

    (b)   *Purchases.* State whether any securities are to be purchased from any officer, director or affiliate of the subject company and provide the details of each transaction.

    (c)   *Different terms.* Describe any term or arrangement in the Rule 13e–3 transaction that treats any subject security holders differently from other subject security holders.

    (d)   *Appraisal rights.* State whether or not dissenting security holders are entitled to any appraisal rights. If so, summarize the appraisal rights. If there are no appraisal rights available under state law for security holders who object to the transaction, briefly outline any other rights that may be available to security holders under the law.

    (e)   *Provisions for unaffiliated security holders.* Describe any provision made by the filing person in connection with the transaction to grant unaffiliated security holders access to the corporate files of the filing person or to obtain counsel or appraisal services at the expense of the filing person. If none, so state.

    (f)   *Eligibility for listing or trading.* If the transaction involves the offer of securities of the filing person in exchange for equity securities held by unaffiliated security holders of the subject company, describe whether or not the filing person will take steps to assure that the securities offered are or will be eligible for trading on an automated quotations system operated by a national securities association.

Item 1005.   Past Contacts, Transactions, Negotiations and Agreements

    (a)   *Transactions.* Briefly state the nature and approximate dollar amount of any transaction, other than those described in paragraphs (b) or (c) of this item, that occurred during the past two years, between the filing person (including any person specified in Instruction C of the schedule) and;

    (1)   The subject company or any of its affiliates that are not natural persons if the aggregate value of the transactions is more than one percent of the subject company's consolidated revenues for:

        (i)   The fiscal year when the transaction occurred; or

        (ii)   The past portion of the current fiscal year, if the transaction occurred in the current year; and

Instructions to Item 1005(a)(1):

The information required by this Item may be based on the information in the subject company's most recent filing with the Commission, unless the filing person has reason to believe the information is not accurate.

(2)   Any executive officer, director or affiliate of the subject company that is a natural person if the aggregate value of the transaction or series of similar transactions with that person exceeds $60,000.

(b)   *Significant corporate events.* Describe any negotiations, transactions or material contacts during the past two years between the filing person (including subsidiaries of the filing person and any person specified in Instruction C of the schedule) and the subject company or its affiliates concerning any:

     (1)   Merger;

     (2)   Consolidation;

     (3)   Acquisition;

     (4)   Tender offer for or other acquisition of any class of the subject company's securities;

     (5)   Election of the subject company's directors; or

     (6)   Sale or other transfer of a material amount of assets of the subject company.

(c)   *Negotiations or contacts.* Describe any negotiations or material contacts concerning the matters referred to in paragraph (b) of this item during the past two years between:

     (1)   Any affiliates of the subject company; or

     (2)   The subject company or any of its affiliates and any person not affiliated with the subject company who would have a direct interest in such matters.

Instruction to paragraphs (b) and (c) of Item 1005: Identify the person who initiated the contacts or negotiations.

(d)   *Conflicts of interest.* If material, describe any agreement, arrangement or understanding and any actual or potential conflict of interest between the filing person or its affiliates and:

     (1)   The subject company, its executive officers, directors or affiliates; or

     (2)   The offeror, its executive officers, directors or affiliates.

Instruction to Item 1005(d):

If the filing person is the subject company, no disclosure called for by this paragraph is required in the document disseminated to security holders, so long as substantially the same information was filed with the Commission previously and disclosed in a proxy statement, report or other communication sent to security holders by the subject company in the past year. The document disseminated to security holders, however, must refer specifically to the discussion in the proxy statement, report or other communication that was sent to security holders previously. The information also must be filed as an exhibit to the schedule.

(e)   *Agreements involving the subject company's securities.* Describe any agreement, arrangement, or understanding, whether or not legally enforceable, between the filing person (including any person specified in Instruction C of the schedule) and any other person with respect to any securities of the subject company. Name all persons that are a party to the agreements, arrangements, or understandings and describe all material provisions.

Instructions to Item 1005(e):

1.   The information required by this Item includes: the transfer or voting securities, joint ventures, loan or option arrangements, puts or calls, guarantees of loans, guarantees against loss, or the giving or withholding of proxies, consents or authorizations.

2.   Include information for any securities that are pledged or otherwise subject to a contingency, the occurrence of which would give another person the power to direct the voting or disposition of the subject securities. No disclosure, however, is required about standard default and similar provisions contained in loan agreements.

Item 1006.   Purposes of the Transaction and Plans or Proposals

(a)   *Purposes.* State the purposes of the transaction.

(b)   *Use of securities acquired.* Indicate whether the securities acquired in the transaction will be retained, retired, held in treasury, or otherwise disposed of.

(c)   *Plans.* Describe any plans, proposals or negotiations that relate to or would result in:

    (1)   Any extraordinary transaction, such as a merger, reorganization or liquidation, involving the subject company or any of its subsidiaries;

    (2)   Any purchase, sale or transfer of a material amount of assets of the subject company or any of its subsidiaries;

    (3)   Any material change in the present dividend rate or policy, or indebtedness or capitalization of the subject company;

    (4)   Any change in the present board of directors or management of the subject company, including, but not limited to, any plans or proposals to change the number or the term of directors or to fill any existing vacancies on the board or to change any material term of the employment contract of any executive officer;

    (5)   Any other material change in the subject company's corporate structure or business, including, if the subject company is a registered closed-end investment company, any plans or proposals to make any changes in its investment policy for which a vote would be required by section 13 of the Investment Company Act of 1940;

    (6)   Any class of equity securities of the subject company to be delisted from a national securities exchange or cease to be authorized to be quoted in an automated quotations system operated by a national securities association;

    (7)   Any class of equity securities of the subject company becoming eligible for termination of registration under section 12(g)(4) of the Act;

    (8)   The suspension of the subject company's obligation to file reports under section 15(d) of the Act;

    (9)   The acquisitions by any person of additional securities of the subject company, or the disposition of securities of the subject company; or

    (10) Any changes in the subject company's charter, bylaws or other governing instruments or other actions that could impede the acquisition of control of the subject company.

(d)   *Subject company negotiations.* If the filing person is the subject company:

    (1)   State whether or not that person is undertaking or engaged in any negotiations in response to the tender offer that relate to:

        (i)   A tender offer or other acquisition of the subject company's securities by the filing person, any of its subsidiaries, or any other person; or

        (ii)   Any of the matters referred to in paragraphs (c)(1) through (c)(3) of this item; and

    (2)   Describe any transaction, board resolution, agreement in principle, or signed contract that is entered into in response to the tender offer that relates to one or more of the matters referred to in paragraph (d)(1) of this item.

Instruction to Item 1006(d)(1):

    If an agreement in principle has not been reached at the time of filing, no disclosure under paragraph (d)(1) of this item is required of the possible terms of or the parties to the transaction if in the opinion of the board of directors of the subject company disclosure would jeopardize continuation of the negotiations. In that case, disclosure indicating that negotiations are being undertaken or are underway and are in the preliminary stages is sufficient.

Item 1007.   Source and Amount of Funds or Other Consideration

    (a)   *Source of funds.* State the specific sources and total amount of funds or other consideration to be used in the transaction. If the transaction involves a tender offer, disclose the amount of funds or other consideration required to purchase the maximum amount of securities sought in the offer.

(b) *Conditions.* State any material conditions to the financing discussed in response to paragraph (a) of this item. Disclose any alternative financing arrangements or alternative financing plans in the event the primary financing plans fall through. If none, so state.

(c) *Expenses.* Furnish a reasonably itemized statement of all expenses incurred or estimated to be incurred in connection with the transaction including, but not limited to, filing, legal, accounting and appraisal fees, solicitation expenses and printing costs and state whether or not the subject company has paid or will be responsible for paying any or all expenses.

(d) *Borrowed funds.* If all or any part of the funds or other consideration required is, or is expected, to be borrowed, directly or indirectly, for the purpose of the transaction:

(1) Provide a summary of each loan agreement or arrangement containing the identity of the parties, the term, the collateral, the stated and effective interest rates, and any other material terms or conditions of the loan; and

(2) Briefly describe any plans or arrangements to finance or repay the loan, or, if no plans or arrangements have been made, so state.

Instruction to Item 1007(d):

If the transaction is a third-party tender offer and the source of all or any part of the funds used in the transaction is to come from a loan made in the ordinary course of business by a bank as defined by section 3(a)(6) of the Act, the name of the bank will not be made available to the public if the filing person so requests in writing and files the request, naming the bank, with the Secretary of the Commission.

Item 1008.   Interest in Securities of the Subject Company

(a) *Securities ownership.* State the aggregate number and percentage of subject securities that are beneficially owned by each person named in response to Item 1003 of Regulation M–A and by each associate and majority-owned subsidiary of those persons. Give the name and address of any associate or subsidiary.

Instructions to Item 1008(a):

1. For purposes of this item, beneficial ownership is determined in accordance with Rule 13d–3 under the Exchange Act. Identify the shares that the person has a right to acquire.

2. The information required by this rule may be based on the number of outstanding securities disclosed in the subject company's most recently available filing with the Commission, unless the filing person has more current information.

3. The information required by this item with respect to officers, directors and associates of the subject company must be given to the extent known after making reasonable inquiry.

(b) *Securities transactions.* Describe any transaction in the subject securities during the past 60 days. The description of transactions required must include, but not necessarily be limited to:

(1) The identity of the persons specified in the Instruction to this rule who effected the transaction;

(2) The date of the transaction;

(3) The amount of securities involved;

(4) The price per share; and

(5) Where and how the transaction was effected.

Instructions to Item 1008(b):

1. Provide the required transaction information for the following persons:

(a) The filing person (for all schedules);

(b) Any person named in Instruction C of the schedule and any associate or majority-owned subsidiary of the issuer or filing person (for all schedules except Schedule 14D–9);

(c) Any executive officer, director, affiliate or subsidiary of the filing person (for Schedule 14D–9);

(d)   The issuer and any executive officer or director of any subsidiary of the issuer or filing person (for an issuer tender offer on Schedule TO); and

(e)   The issuer and any pension, profit-sharing or similar plan of the issuer or affiliate filing the schedule (for a going-private transaction on Schedule 13E–3).

2.   Provide the information required by this Item if it is available to the filing person at the time the statement is initially filed with the Commission. If the information is not initially available, it must be obtained and filed with the Commission promptly, but in no event later than three business days after the date of the initial filing, and if material, disclosed in a manner reasonably designed to inform security holders. The procedure specified by this instruction is provided to maintain the confidentiality of information in order to avoid possible misuse of inside information.

Item 1009.   Persons/Assets, Retained, Employed, Compensated or Used

(a)   *Solicitations or recommendations.* Identify all persons and classes of persons that are directly or indirectly employed, retained, or to be compensated to make solicitations or recommendations in connection with the transaction. Provide a summary of all material terms of employment, retainer or other arrangement for compensation.

(b)   *Employees and corporate assets.* Identify any officer, class of employees or corporate assets of the subject company that has been or will be employed or used by the filing person in connection with the transaction. Describe the purpose for their employment or use.

Instruction to Item 1009(b):

Provide all information required by this Item except for the information required by paragraph (a) of this item and Item 1007 of Regulation M–A.

Item 1010.   Financial Statements

(a)   *Financial information.* Furnish the following financial information:

(1)   Audited financial statements for the two fiscal years required to be filed with the company's most recent annual report under sections 13 and 15(d) of the Exchange Act;

(2)   Unaudited balance sheets, comparative year-to-date statements of comprehensive income (as defined in Item 1–02 of Regulation S–X) and related earnings per share data and statements of cash flows required to be included in the company's most recent quarterly report filed under the Exchange Act; and

(3)   [Removed and Reserved].

(4)   Book value per share as of the date of the most recent balance sheet presented.

(b)   *Pro forma information.* If material, furnish pro forma information disclosing the effect of the transaction on:

(1)   The company's balance sheet as of the date of the most recent balance sheet presented under paragraph (a) of this item;

(2)   The company's statement of comprehensive income and earnings per share for the most recent fiscal year and the latest interim period provided under paragraph (a)(2) of this Item; and

(3)   The company's book value per share as of the date of the most recent balance sheet presented under paragraph (a) of this item.

(c)   *Summary information.* Furnish a fair and adequate summary of the information specified in paragraphs (a) and (b) of this item for the same periods specified. A fair and adequate summary includes:

(1)   The summarized financial information specified in section Item 1–02(bb)(1) of Regulation S–X;

(2)   Income per common share from continuing operations (basic and diluted, if applicable);

(3)   Net income per common share (basic and diluted, if applicable);

(4)   [Removed and Reserved].

(5)   Book value per share as of the date of the most recent balance sheet; and

(6)   If material, pro forma data for the summarized financial information specified in paragraphs (c)(1) through (c)(5) of this item disclosing the effect of the transaction.

Item 1011.   Additional Information

(a)   *Agreements, regulatory requirements and legal proceedings.* If material to a security holder's decision whether to sell, tender or hold the securities sought in the tender offer, furnish the following information:

(1)   Any present or proposed material agreement, arrangement, understanding or relationship between the offeror or any of its executive officers, directors, controlling persons or subsidiaries (other than any agreement, arrangement or understanding disclosed under any other items of Regulation M–A);

Instruction to paragraph (a)(1):

In an issuer tender offer disclose any material agreement, arrangement, understanding or relationship between the offeror and any of its executive officers, directors, controlling persons or subsidiaries.

(2)   To the extent known by the offeror after reasonable investigation, the applicable regulatory requirements which must be complied with or approvals which must be obtained in connection with the tender offer;

(3)   The applicability of any anti-trust laws;

(4)   The applicability of margin requirements under section 7 of the Act and the applicable regulations; and

(5)   Any material pending legal proceedings relating to the tender offer, including the name and location of the court or agency in which the proceedings are pending, the date instituted, the principal parties, and a brief summary of the proceedings and the relief sought.

Instruction to Item 1011(a)(5):

A copy of any document relating to a major development (such as pleadings, an answer, complaint, temporary restraining order, injunction, opinion, judgement or order) in a material pending legal proceeding must be furnished promptly to the Commission staff on a supplemental basis.

(b)   Furnish the information required by Item 402(t)(2) and (3) of Regulation S–K and in the tabular format set forth in Item 402(t)(1) of Regulation S–K with respect to each named executive officer

(1)   Of the subject company in a Rule 13e–3 transaction; or

(2)   Of the issuer whose securities are the subject of a third-party tender offer, regarding any agreement or understanding, whether written or unwritten, between such named executive officer and the subject company, issuer, bidder, or the acquiring company, as applicable, concerning any type of compensation, whether present, deferred or contingent, that is based upon or otherwise relates to the Rule 13e–3 transaction or third-party tender offer.

Instructions to Item 1011(b):

1.   The obligation to provide the information in paragraph (b) of this rule shall not apply where the issuer whose securities are the subject of the Rule 13e–3 transaction or tender offer is a foreign private issuer, as defined in Rule 3b–4 under the Exchange Act of 1934, or an emerging growth company, as defined in Rule 405 of the Securities Act or Rule 12b–2 of the Exchange Act.

2.   For purposes of Instruction 1 to Item 402(t)(2) of this part: If the disclosure is included in a Schedule 13E–3 or Schedule 14D–9, the disclosure provided by this table shall be quantified assuming that the triggering event took place on the latest practicable date and that the price per share of the securities of the subject company in a Rule 13e–3 transaction, or of the issuer whose securities are the subject of the third-party tender offer, shall be determined as follows: If the shareholders are to receive a fixed dollar amount, the price per share shall be that fixed dollar amount, and if such value is not a fixed dollar amount, the price per share shall be the average closing market price of such securities over the first five business days following the first public announcement of the transaction. Compute the dollar value of in-the-money option awards for which vesting would be accelerated by determining the difference between this price and the exercise or base price of the options. Include only

compensation that is based on or otherwise relates to the subject transaction. Apply Instruction 1 to Item 402(t) with respect to those executive officers for whom disclosure was required in the most recent filing by the subject company in a Rule 13e–3 transaction or by the issuer whose securities are the subject of a third-party tender offer, with the Commission under the Securities Act of 1933 or Securities Exchange Act of 1934 that required disclosure pursuant to Item 402(c).

(c)   *Other material information.* Furnish such additional material information, if any, as may be necessary to make the required statements, in light of the circumstances under which they are made, not materially misleading.

Item 1012.   The Solicitation or Recommendation

(a)   *Solicitation or recommendation.* State the nature of the solicitation or the recommendation. If this statement relates to a recommendation, state whether the filing person is advising holders of the subject securities to accept or reject the tender offer or to take other action with respect to the tender offer and, if so, describe the other action recommended. If the filing person is the subject company and is not making a recommendation, state whether the subject company is expressing no opinion and is remaining neutral toward the tender offer or is unable to take a position with respect to the tender offer.

(b)   *Reasons.* State the reasons for the position (including the inability to take a position) stated in paragraph (a) of this item. Conclusory statements such as "The tender offer is in the best interests of shareholders" are not considered sufficient disclosure.

(c)   *Intent to tender.* To the extent known by the filing person after making reasonable inquiry, state whether the filing person or any executive officer, director, affiliate or subsidiary of the filing person currently intends to tender, sell or hold the subject securities that are held of record or beneficially owned by that person.

(d)   *Intent to tender or vote in a going-private transaction.* To the extent known by the filing person after making reasonable inquiry, state whether or not any executive officer, director or affiliate of the issuer (or any person specified in Instruction C to the schedule) currently intends to tender or sell subject securities owned or held by that person and/or how each person currently intends to vote subject securities, including any securities the person has proxy authority for. State the reasons for the intended action.

Instruction to Item 1012(d):

Provide the information required by this rule if it is available to the filing person at the time the statement is initially filed with the Commission. If the information is not available, it must be filed with the Commission promptly, but in no event later than three business days after the date of the initial filing, and if material, disclosed in a manner reasonably designed to inform security holders.

(e)   *Recommendations of others.* To the extent known by the filing person after making reasonable inquiry, state whether or not any person specified in paragraph (d) of this item has made a recommendation either in support of or opposed to the transaction and the reasons for the recommendation.

Item 1013.   Purposes, Alternatives, Reasons and Effects in a Going-Private Transaction

(a)   *Purposes.* State the purposes for the Rule 13e–3 transaction.

(b)   *Alternatives.* If the subject company or affiliate considered alternative means to accomplish the stated purposes, briefly describe the alternatives and state the reasons for their rejection.

(c)   *Reasons.* State the reasons for the structure of the Rule 13e–3 transaction and for undertaking the transaction at this time.

(d)   *Effects.* Describe the effects of the Rule 13e–3 transaction on the subject company, its affiliates and unaffiliated security holders, including the federal tax consequences of the transaction.

Instructions to Item 1013:

1.   Conclusory statements will not be considered sufficient disclosure in response to this item.

2.   The description required by paragraph (d) of this item must include a reasonably detailed discussion of both the benefits and detriments of the Rule 13e–3 transaction to the subject company, its affiliates and

unaffiliated security holders. The benefits and detriments of the Rule 13e–3 transaction must be quantified to the extent practicable.

3. If the statement is filed by an affiliate of the subject company, the description required by paragraph (d) of this item must include, but not limited to, the effect of the Rule 13e–3 transaction on the affiliate's interest in the net book value and net earnings of the subject company in terms of both dollar amounts and percentages.

Item 1014. Fairness of the Going-Private Transaction

(a) *Fairness.* State whether the subject company or affiliate filing the statement reasonably believes that the Rule 13e–3 transaction is fair or unfair to unaffiliated security holders. If any director dissented to or abstained from voting on the Rule 13e–3 transaction, identify the director, and indicate, if known, after making reasonable inquiry, the reasons for the dissent or abstention.

(b) *Factors considered in determining fairness.* Discuss in reasonable derail the material factors upon which the belief stated in paragraph (a) in this item is based and, to the extent practicable, the weight assigned to each factor. The discussion must include an analysis of the extent, if any, to which the filing person's beliefs are based on the factors described in Instruction 2 of this item, paragraphs (c), (d) and (e) of this item and Item 1015 of Regulation M–A.

(c) *Approval of security holders.* State whether or not the transaction is structured so that approval of at least a majority of unaffiliated security holders is required.

(d) *Unaffiliated representative.* State whether or not a majority of directors who are not employees of the subject company has retained an unaffiliated representative to act solely on behalf of unaffiliated security holders for purposes of negotiating the terms of the Rule 13e–3 transaction and/ or preparing a report concerning the fairness of the transaction.

(e) *Approval of directors.* State whether or not the Rule 13e–3 transaction was approved by a majority of the directors of the subject company who are not employees of the subject company.

(f) *Other offers.* If any offer of the type described in paragraph (viii) of Instruction 2 to this item has been received, describe the offer and state the reasons for its rejection.

Instructions to Item 1014:

1. A statement that the issuer or affiliate has no reasonable belief as to the fairness of the Rule 13e–3 transaction to unaffiliated security holders will not be considered sufficient disclosure in response to paragraph (a) of this item.

2. The factors that are important in determining the fairness of a transaction to unaffiliated security holders and the weight, if any, that should be given to them in a particular context will vary. Normally such factors will include, among others, those referred to in paragraphs (c), (d) and (e) of this item and whether the consideration offered to unaffiliated security holders constitutes fair value in relation to:

(i) Current market prices;

(ii) Historical market prices;

(iii) Net book value;

(iv) Going concern value;

(v) Liquidation value;

(vi) Purchase prices paid in previous purchases disclosed in response to Item 1002(f) of Regulation M–A;

(vii) Any report, opinion, or appraisal described in Item 1015 of Regulation M–A; and

(viii) Firm offers of which the subject company or affiliate is aware made by any unaffiliated person, other than the filing persons, during the past two years for:

(A) The merger or consolidation of the subject company with or into another company, or vice versa;

(B) The sale or other transfer of all or any substantial part of the assets of the subject company; or

(C) A purchase of the subject company's securities that would enable the holder to exercise control of the subject company.

3. Conclusory statements, such as "The Rule 13e–3 transaction is fair to unaffiliated security holders in relation to net book value, going concern value and future prospects of the issuer" will not be considered sufficient disclosure in response to paragraph (b) of this item.

Item 1015.   Reports, Opinions, Appraisals and Negotiations

(a) *Report, opinion or appraisal.* State whether or not the subject company or affiliate has received any report, opinion (other than an opinion of counsel) or appraisal from an outside party that is materially related to the Rule 13e–3 transaction, including, but not limited to: Any report, opinion or appraisal relating to the consideration or the fairness of the consideration to be offered to security holders or the fairness of the transaction to the issuer or affiliate or to security holders who are not affiliates.

(b) *Preparer and summary of the report, opinion or appraisal.* For each report, opinion or appraisal described in response to paragraph (a) of this item or any negotiation or report described in response to Item 1014(d) of Regulation M–A or Item 14(b)(6) of Schedule 14A concerning the terms of the transaction:

(1) Identify the outside party and/ or unaffiliated representative;

(2) Briefly describe the qualifications of the outside party and/ or unaffiliated representative;

(3) Describe the method of selection of the outside party and/ or unaffiliated representative;

(4) Describe any material relationship that existed during the past two years or is mutually understood to be contemplated and any compensation received or to be received as a result of the relationship between:

(i) The outside party, its affiliates, and/ or unaffiliated representative; and

(ii) The subject company or its affiliates;

(5) If the report, opinion or appraisal relates to the fairness of the consideration, state whether the subject company or affiliate determined the amount of consideration to be paid; and

(6) Furnish a summary concerning the negotiation, report, opinion or appraisal. The summary must include, but need not be limited to, the procedures followed; the findings and recommendations; the bases for and methods of arriving at such findings and recommendations; instructions received from the subject company or affiliate; and any limitation imposed by the subject company or affiliate on the scope of the investigation.

Instruction to Item 1015(b):

The information called for by paragraphs (b)(1), (2) and (3) of this item must be given with respect to the firm that provides the report, opinion appraisal rather than the employees of the firm that prepared the report.

(c) *Availability of documents.* Furnish a statement to the effect that the report, opinion and appraisal will be made available for inspection and copying at the principal executive offices of the subject company or affiliate during its regular business hours by any interested equity security holder of the subject company or representative who has been so designated in writing. This statement also may provide that a copy of the report, opinion or appraisal will be transmitted by the subject company or affiliate to any interested equity security holder of the subject company or representative who has been so designated in writing upon written request and at the expense of the requesting security holder.

Item 1016.   Exhibits

File as an exhibit to the schedule:

(a) Any disclosure materials furnished to security holders by or on behalf of the filing person, including:

(1) Tender offer materials (including transmittal letter);

(2) Solicitation or recommendation (including those referred to in Item 1012 of Regulation M–A);

(3)   Going-private disclosure document.

(4)   Prospectus used in connection with an exchange offer where securities are registered under the Securities Act of 1933; and

(5)   Any other disclosure materials;

(b)   Any loan agreement referred to in response to Item 1007(d) of Regulation M–A;

Instruction to Item 1016(b):

If the filing relates to a third-party tender offer and a request is made under Item 1007(d) of Regulation M–A, the identity of the bank providing financing may be omitted from the loan agreement filed as an exhibit.

(c)   Any report, opinion or appraisal referred to in response to Item 1014(d) or Item 1015 of Regulation M–A;

(d)   Any document setting forth the terms of any agreement, arrangement, understanding or relationship referred to in response to Item 1005(e) or Item 1011(a)(1) of Regulation M–A;

(e)   Any agreement, arrangement or understanding referred to in response to Item 1005(d), or the pertinent portions of any proxy statement, report or other communication containing the disclosure required by Item 1005(d) of Regulation M–A;

(f)   A detailed statement describing security holders' appraisal rights and the procedures for exercising those appraisal rights referred to in response to Item 1004(d) of Regulation M–A;

(g)   Any written instruction, form or other material that is furnished to persons making an oral solicitation or recommendation by or on behalf of the filing person for their use directly or indirectly in connection with the transaction; and

(h)   Any written opinion prepared by legal counsel at the filing person's request and communicated to the filing person pertaining to the tax consequences of the transaction.

Exhibit Table to Item 1016 of Regulation M–A [13E–3 to 14D–9]

Disclosure Material	X		X		X
Loan Agreement	X		X		
Report, Opinion or Appraisal	X				
Contracts, Arrangements or Understandings	X		X		X
Statement re: Appraisal Rights	X				
Oral Solicitation Materials	X		X		X
Tax Opinion		X			

Instructions to Item 1016:

1.   Schedules (or similar attachments) to the exhibits required by this Item are not required to be filed provided that they do not contain information material to an investment or voting decision and that information is not otherwise disclosed in the exhibit or the disclosure document. Each exhibit filed must contain a list briefly identifying the contents of all omitted schedules. Registrants need not prepare a separate list of omitted information if such information is already included within the exhibit in a manner that conveys the subject matter of the omitted schedules and attachments. In addition, the registrant must provide a copy of any omitted schedule to the Commission or its staff upon request.

2.   The registrant may redact information from exhibits required to be filed by this Item if disclosure of such information would constitute a clearly unwarranted invasion of personal privacy (e.g., disclosure of bank account numbers, social security numbers, home addresses and similar information).

[Regulation S–K, subpart 1100—Regulation AB—disclosure requirements for asset-backed securities—is omitted.]

REGULATION G

17 C.F.R. § 244.___

Rule 100.   General Rules Regarding Disclosure of Non-GAAP Financial Measures

(a)   Whenever a registrant, or person acting on its behalf, publicly discloses material information that includes a non-GAAP financial measure, the registrant must accompany that non-GAAP financial measure with:

    (1)   A presentation of the most directly comparable financial measure calculated and presented in accordance with Generally Accepted Accounting Principles (GAAP); and

    (2)   A reconciliation (by schedule or other clearly understandable method), which shall be quantitative for historical non-GAAP measures presented, and quantitative, to the extent available without unreasonable efforts, for forward-looking information, of the differences between the non-GAAP financial measure disclosed or released with the most comparable financial measure or measures calculated and presented in accordance with GAAP identified in paragraph (a)(1) of this rule.

(b)   A registrant, or a person acting on its behalf, shall not make public a non-GAAP financial measure that, taken together with the information accompanying that measure and any other accompanying discussion of that measure, contains an untrue statement of a material fact or omits to state a material fact necessary in order to make the presentation of the non-GAAP financial measure, in light of the circumstances under which it is presented, not misleading.

(c)   This rule shall not apply to a disclosure of a non-GAAP financial measure that is made by or on behalf of a registrant that is a foreign private issuer if the following conditions are satisfied:

    (1)   The securities of the registrant are listed or quoted on a securities exchange or inter-dealer quotation system outside the United States;

    (2)   The non-GAAP financial measure is not derived from or based on a measure calculated and presented in accordance with generally accepted accounting principles in the United States; and

    (3)   The disclosure is made by or on behalf of the registrant outside the United States, or is included in a written communication that is released by or on behalf of the registrant outside the United States.

(d)   This rule shall not apply to a non-GAAP financial measure included in disclosure relating to a proposed business combination, the entity resulting therefrom or an entity that is a party thereto, if the disclosure is contained in a communication that is subject to Rule 425 under the Securities Act, Rule 14a–12 or Rule 14d–2(b)(2) under the Exchange Act or Rule 1015 of Regulation S–K.

Notes to Rule 100:

1.   If a non-GAAP financial measure is made public orally, telephonically, by Web cast, by broadcast, or by similar means, the requirements of paragraphs (a)(1)(i) and (a)(1)(ii) of this rule will be satisfied if:

    (i)   The required information in those paragraphs is provided on the registrant's Web site at the time the non-GAAP financial measure is made public; and

    (ii)   The location of the web site is made public in the same presentation in which the non-GAAP financial measure is made public.

2.   The provisions of paragraph (c) of this rule shall apply notwithstanding the existence of one or more of the following circumstances:

    (i)   A written communication is released in the United States as well as outside the United States, so long as the communication is released in the United States contemporaneously with or after the release outside the United States and is not otherwise targeted at persons located in the United States;

    (ii)   Foreign journalists, U.S. journalists or other third parties have access to the information;

(iii)   The information appears on one or more web sites maintained by the registrant, so long as the web sites, taken together, are not available exclusively to, or targeted at, persons located in the United States; or

(iv)   Following the disclosure or release of the information outside the United States, the information is included in a submission by the registrant to the Commission made under cover of a Form 6–K.

Rule 101.   Definitions

This rule defines certain terms as used in Regulation G (Rules 100–102).

(a)(1)   Non-GAAP financial measure. A non-GAAP financial measure is a numerical measure of a registrant's historical or future financial performance, financial position or cash flows that:

(i)   Excludes amounts, or is subject to adjustments that have the effect of excluding amounts, that are included in the most directly comparable measure calculated and presented in accordance with GAAP in the statement of income, balance sheet or statement of cash flows (or equivalent statements) of the issuer; or

(ii)   Includes amounts, or is subject to adjustments that have the effect of including amounts, that are excluded from the most directly comparable measure so calculated and presented.

(2)   A non-GAAP financial measure does not include operating and other financial measures and ratios or statistical measures calculated using exclusively one or both of:

(i)   Financial measures calculated in accordance with GAAP; and

(ii)   Operating measures or other measures that are not non-GAAP financial measures.

(3)   A non-GAAP financial measure does not include financial measures required to be disclosed by GAAP, Commission rules, or a system of regulation of a government or governmental authority or self-regulatory organization that is applicable to the registrant.

(b)   GAAP. GAAP refers to generally accepted accounting principles in the United States, except that:

(1)   In the case of foreign private issuers whose primary financial statements are prepared in accordance with non-U.S. generally accepted accounting principles, GAAP refers to the principles under which those primary financial statements are prepared; and

(2)   In the case of foreign private issuers that include a non-GAAP financial measure derived from a measure calculated in accordance with U.S. generally accepted accounting principles, GAAP refers to U.S. generally accepted accounting principles for purposes of the application of the requirements of Regulation G to the disclosure of that measure.

(c)   Registrant. A registrant subject to this regulation is one that has a class of securities registered under Section 12 of the Securities Exchange Act of 1934, or is required to file reports under Section 15(d) of the Securities Exchange Act of 1934, excluding any investment company registered under Section 8 of the Investment Company Act of 1940.

(d)   United States. United States means the United States of America, its territories and possessions, any State of the United States, and the District of Columbia.

Rule 102.   No Effect on Antifraud Liability

Neither the requirements of this Regulation G nor a person's compliance or non-compliance with the requirements of this Regulation shall in itself affect any person's liability under Section 10(b) of the Securities Exchange Act of 1934 or Rule 10b–5 under the Exchange Act.

REGULATION S-X

QUALIFICATIONS AND REPORTS
OF ACCOUNTANTS

(Selected Provisions)

17 C.F.R. § 210.___

Item 2–01.   Qualifications of accountants
Preliminary Note to Item 2–01

1.   Item 2–01 is designed to ensure that auditors are qualified and independent of their audit clients both in fact and in appearance. Accordingly, the rule sets forth restrictions on financial, employment, and business relationships between an accountant and an audit client and restrictions on an accountant providing certain non-audit services to an audit client.

2.   Item 2–01(b) sets forth the general standard of auditor independence. Paragraphs (c)(1) to (c)(5) reflect the application of the general standard to particular circumstances. The rule does not purport to, and the Commission could not, consider all circumstances that raise independence concerns, and these are subject to the general standard in Item 2–01(b). In considering this standard, the Commission looks in the first instance to whether a relationship or the provision of a service: creates a mutual or conflicting interest between the accountant and the audit client; places the accountant in the position of auditing his or her own work; results in the accountant acting as management or an employee of the audit client; or places the accountant in a position of being an advocate for the audit client.

3.   These factors are general guidance only and their application may depend on particular facts and circumstances. For that reason, Item 2–01 provides that, in determining whether an accountant is independent, the Commission will consider all relevant facts and circumstances. For the same reason, registrants and accountants are encouraged to consult with the Commission's Office of the Chief Accountant before entering into relationships, including relationships involving the provision of services, that are not explicitly described in the rule.

(a)   The Commission will not recognize any person as a certified public accountant who is not duly registered and in good standing as such under the laws of the place of his residence or principal office. The Commission will not recognize any person as a public accountant who is not in good standing and entitled to practice as such under the laws of the place of his residence or principal office.

(b)   The Commission will not recognize an accountant as independent, with respect to an audit client, if the accountant is not, or a reasonable investor with knowledge of all relevant facts and circumstances would conclude that the accountant is not, capable of exercising objective and impartial judgment on all issues encompassed within the accountant's engagement. In determining whether an accountant is independent, the Commission will consider all relevant circumstances, including all relationships between the accountant and the audit client, and not just those relating to reports filed with the Commission.

(c)   This paragraph sets forth a non-exclusive specification of circumstances inconsistent with paragraph (b) of this Item.

(1)   *Financial Relationships.* An accountant is not independent if, at any point during the audit and professional engagement period, the accountant has a direct financial interest or a material indirect financial interest in the accountant's audit client, such as:

(i)   *Investments in Audit Clients.* An accountant is not independent when:

(A)   The accounting firm, any covered person in the firm, or any of his or her immediate family members, has any direct investment in an audit client, such as stocks, bonds, notes, options, or other securities. The term direct investment includes an investment in an audit client through an intermediary if:

(1)   The accounting firm, covered person, or immediate family member, alone or together with other persons, supervises or participates in the intermediary's investment decisions or has control over the intermediary; or

(2)   The intermediary is not a diversified management investment company, as defined by section 5(b)(1) of the Investment Company Act of 1940 and has an investment in the audit client that amounts to 20% or more of the value of the intermediary's total investments.

(B)   Any partner, principal, shareholder, or professional employee of the accounting firm, any of his or her immediate family members, any close family member of a covered person in the firm, or any group of the above persons has filed a Schedule 13D or 13G with the Commission indicating beneficial ownership of more than five percent of an audit client's equity securities or controls an audit client, or a close family member of a partner, principal, or shareholder of the accounting firm controls an audit client.

(C)   The accounting firm, any covered person in the firm, or any of his or her immediate family members, serves as voting trustee of a trust, or executor of an estate, containing the securities of an audit client, unless the accounting firm, covered person in the firm, or immediate family member has no authority to make investment decisions for the trust or estate.

(D)   The accounting firm, any covered person in the firm, any of his or her immediate family members, or any group of the above persons has any material indirect investment in an audit client. For purposes of this paragraph, the term material indirect investment does not include ownership by any covered person in the firm, any of his or her immediate family members, or any group of the above persons of 5% or less of the outstanding shares of a diversified management investment company, as defined by section 5(b)(1) of the Investment Company Act of 1940 that invests in an audit client.

(E)   The accounting firm, any covered person in the firm, or any of his or her immediate family members:

(1)   Has any direct or material indirect investment in an entity where:

(i)   An audit client has an investment in that entity that is material to the audit client and has the ability to exercise significant influence over that entity; or

(ii)   The entity has an investment in an audit client that is material to that entity and has the ability to exercise significant influence over that audit client;

(2)   Has any material investment in an entity over which an audit client has the ability to exercise significant influence; or

(3)   Has the ability to exercise significant influence over an entity that has the ability to exercise significant influence over an audit client.

(ii)   *Other Financial Interests in Audit Client.* An accountant is not independent when the accounting firm, any covered person in the firm, or any of his or her immediate family members has:

(A)   *Loans/Debtor-Creditor Relationship.* Any loan (including any margin loan) to or from an audit client, or an audit client's officers, directors, or record or beneficial owners of more than ten percent of the audit client's equity securities, except for the following loans obtained from a financial institution under its normal lending procedures, terms, and requirements:

(1)   Automobile loans and leases collateralized by the automobile;

(2)   Loans fully collateralized by the cash surrender value of an insurance policy;

(3)   Loans fully collateralized by cash deposits at the same financial institution; and

(4)   A mortgage loan collateralized by the borrower's primary residence provided the loan was not obtained while the covered person in the firm was a covered person.

(B) *Savings and Checking Accounts.* Any savings, checking, or similar account at a bank, savings and loan, or similar institution that is an audit client, if the account has a balance that exceeds the amount insured by the Federal Deposit Insurance Corporation or any similar insurer, except that an accounting firm account may have an uninsured balance provided that the likelihood of the bank, savings and loan, or similar institution experiencing financial difficulties is remote.

(C) *Broker-Dealer Accounts.* Brokerage or similar accounts maintained with a broker-dealer that is an audit client, if:

(1) Any such account includes any asset other than cash or securities (within the meaning of "security" provided in the Securities Investor Protection Act of 1970 ("SIPA"));

(2) The value of assets in the accounts exceeds the amount that is subject to a Securities Investor Protection Corporation advance, for those accounts, under Section 9 of SIPA; or

(3) With respect to non-U.S. accounts not subject to SIPA protection, the value of assets in the accounts exceeds the amount insured or protected by a program similar to SIPA.

(D) *Futures Commission Merchant Accounts.* Any futures, commodity, or similar account maintained with a futures commission merchant that is an audit client.

(E) *Credit Cards.* Any aggregate outstanding credit card balance owed to a lender that is an audit client that is not reduced to $10,000 or less on a current basis taking into consideration the payment due date and any available grace period.

(F) *Insurance Products.* Any individual policy issued by an insurer that is an audit client unless:

(1) The policy was obtained at a time when the covered person in the firm was not a covered person in the firm; and

(2) The likelihood of the insurer becoming insolvent is remote.

(G) *Investment Companies.* Any financial interest in an entity that is part of an investment company complex that includes an audit client.

(iii) *Exceptions.* Notwithstanding paragraphs (c)(1)(i) and (c)(1)(ii) of this Item, an accountant will not be deemed not independent if:

(A) *Inheritance and Gift.* Any person acquires an unsolicited financial interest, such as through an unsolicited gift or inheritance, that would cause an accountant to be not independent under paragraph (c)(1)(i) or (c)(1)(ii) of this Item, and the financial interest is disposed of as soon as practicable, but no later than 30 days after the person has knowledge of and the right to dispose of the financial interest.

(B) *New Audit Engagement.* Any person has a financial interest that would cause an accountant to be not independent under paragraph (c)(1)(i) or (c)(1)(ii) of this Item, and:

(1) The accountant did not audit the client's financial statements for the immediately preceding fiscal year; and

(2) The accountant is independent under paragraph (c)(1)(i) and (c)(1)(ii) of this Item before the earlier of:

(i) Signing an initial engagement letter or other agreement to provide audit, review, or attest services to the audit client; or

(ii) Commencing any audit, review, or attest procedures (including planning the audit of the client's financial statements).

(C) *Employee Compensation and Benefit Plans.* An immediate family member of a person who is a covered person in the firm only by virtue of paragraphs (f)(11)(iii) or (f)(11)(iv) of this Item has a financial interest that would cause an accountant to be not independent under paragraph (c)(1)(i) or (c)(1)(ii) of this Item, and the acquisition of the financial interest was an unavoidable consequence of participation in his or her employer's employee compensation or benefits program, provided that the financial interest, other than unexercised employee stock options, is disposed of as soon as practicable, but no later than 30 days after the person has the right to dispose of the financial interest.

(iv) *Audit Clients' Financial Relationships.* An accountant is not independent when:

(A) *Investments by the Audit Client in the Accounting Firm.* An audit client has, or has agreed to acquire, any direct investment in the accounting firm, such as stocks, bonds, notes, options, or other securities, or the audit client's officers or directors are record or beneficial owners of more than 5% of the equity securities of the accounting firm.

(B) *Underwriting.* An accounting firm engages an audit client to act as an underwriter, broker-dealer, market-maker, promoter, or analyst with respect to securities issued by the accounting firm.

(2) *Employment Relationships.* An accountant is not independent if, at any point during the audit and professional engagement period, the accountant has an employment relationship with an audit client, such as:

(i) *Employment at Audit Client of Accountant.* A current partner, principal, shareholder, or professional employee of the accounting firm is employed by the audit client or serves as a member of the board of directors or similar management or governing body of the audit client.

(ii) *Employment at Audit Client of Certain Relatives of Accountant.* A close family member of a covered person in the firm is in an accounting role or financial reporting oversight role at an audit client, or was in such a role during any period covered by an audit for which the covered person in the firm is a covered person.

(iii) *Employment at Audit Client of Former Employee of Accounting Firm.*

(A) A former partner, principal, shareholder, or professional employee of an accounting firm is in an accounting role or financial reporting oversight role at an audit client, unless the individual:

(1) Does not influence the accounting firm's operations or financial policies;

(2) Has no capital balances in the accounting firm; and

(3) Has no financial arrangement with the accounting firm other than one providing for regular payment of a fixed dollar amount (which is not dependent on the revenues, profits, or earnings of the accounting firm):

(i) Pursuant to a fully funded retirement plan, rabbi trust, or, in jurisdictions in which a rabbi trust does not exist, a similar vehicle; or

(ii) In the case of a former professional employee who was not a partner, principal, or shareholder of the accounting firm and who has been disassociated from the accounting firm for more than five years, that is immaterial to the former professional employee; and

(B) A former partner, principal, shareholder, or professional employee of an accounting firm is in a financial reporting oversight role at an issuer (as defined in section 10A(f) of the Securities Exchange Act of 1934), except an issuer that is an investment company registered under section 8 of the Investment Company Act of 1940, unless the individual:

(1) Employed by the issuer was not a member of the audit engagement team of the issuer during the one year period preceding the date that audit procedures commenced for the fiscal period that included the date of initial employment of the audit engagement team member by the issuer;

(2) For purposes of paragraph (c)(2)(iii)(B)(1) of this Item, the following individuals are not considered to be members of the audit engagement team:

(i) Persons, other than the lead partner and the concurring partner, who provided ten or fewer hours of audit, review, or attest services during the period covered by paragraph (c)(2)(iii)(B)(1) of this Item;

(ii) Individuals employed by the issuer as a result of a business combination between an issuer that is an audit client and the employing entity, provided employment was not in contemplation of the business combination and the audit committee of the successor issuer is aware of the prior employment relationship; and

(iii) Individuals that are employed by the issuer due to an emergency or other unusual situation provided that the audit committee determines that the relationship is in the interest of investors;

(3) For purposes of paragraph (c)(2)(iii)(B)(1) of this Item, audit procedures are deemed to have commenced for a fiscal period the day following the filing of the issuer's periodic annual report with the Commission covering the previous fiscal period; or

(C) A former partner, principal, shareholder, or professional employee of an accounting firm is in a financial reporting oversight role with respect to an investment company registered under section 8 of the Investment Company Act of 1940, if:

(1) The former partner, principal, shareholder, or professional employee of an accounting firm is employed in a financial reporting oversight role related to the operations and financial reporting of the registered investment company at an entity in the investment company complex, as defined in (f)(14) of this Item, that includes the registered investment company; and

(2) The former partner, principal, shareholder, or professional employee of an accounting firm employed by the registered investment company or any entity in the investment company complex was a member of the audit engagement team of the registered investment company or any other registered investment company in the investment company complex during the one year period preceding the date that audit procedures commenced that included the date of initial employment of the audit engagement team member by the registered investment company or any entity in the investment company complex.

(3) For purposes of paragraph (c)(2)(iii)(C)(2) of this Item, the following individuals are not considered to be members of the audit engagement team:

(i) Persons, other than the lead partner and concurring partner, who provided ten or fewer hours of audit, review or attest services during the period covered by paragraph (c)(2)(iii)(C)(2) of this Item;

(ii) Individuals employed by the registered investment company or any entity in the investment company complex as a result of a business combination between a registered investment company or any entity in the investment company complex that is an audit client and the employing entity, provided employment was not in contemplation of the business combination and the audit committee of the registered investment company is aware of the prior employment relationship; and

(iii) Individuals that are employed by the registered investment company or any entity in the investment company complex due to an emergency or other unusual situation provided that the audit committee determines that the relationship is in the interest of investors.

(iv) *Employment at accounting firm of former employee of audit client.* A former officer, director, or employee of an audit client becomes a partner, principal, shareholder, or professional employee of the accounting firm, unless the individual does not participate in, and is not in a position to influence, the audit of the financial statements of the audit client covering any period during which he or she was employed by or associated with that audit client.

(4) For purposes of paragraph (c)(2)(iii)(C)(2) of this Item, audit procedures are deemed to have commenced the day following the filing of the registered investment company's periodic annual report with the Commission.

(3) *Business Relationships.* An accountant is not independent if, at any point during the audit and professional engagement period, the accounting firm or any covered person in the firm has any direct or material indirect business relationship with an audit client, or with persons associated with the audit client in a decision-making capacity, such as an audit client's officers, directors, or substantial stockholders. The relationships described in this paragraph do not include a relationship in which the accounting firm or covered person in the firm provides professional services to an audit client or is a consumer in the ordinary course of business.

(4) *Non-audit Services.* An accountant is not independent if, at any point during the audit and professional engagement period, the accountant provides the following non-audit services to an audit client:

(i) *Bookkeeping or Other Services Related to the Accounting Records or Financial Statements of the Audit Client.* Any service, unless it is reasonable to conclude that the results of these services will not be subject to audit procedures during an audit of the audit client's financial statements, including:

(A) Maintaining or preparing the audit client's accounting records;

(B) Preparing the audit client's financial statements that are filed with the Commission or that form the basis of financial statements filed with the Commission; or

(C) Preparing or originating source data underlying the audit client's financial statements.

(ii) *Financial Information Systems Design and Implementation.* Any service, unless it is reasonable to conclude that the results of these services will not be subject to audit procedures during an audit of the audit client's financial statements, including:

(A) Directly or indirectly operating, or supervising the operation of, the audit client's information system or managing the audit client's local area network; or

(B) Designing or implementing a hardware or software system that aggregates source data underlying the financial statements or generates information that is significant to the audit client's financial statements or other financial information systems taken as a whole.

(iii) *Appraisal or Valuation Services, Fairness Opinions, or Contribution-in-Kind Reports.* Any appraisal service, valuation service, or any service involving a fairness opinion or contribution-in-kind report for an audit client, unless it is reasonable to conclude that the results of these services will not be subject to audit procedures during an audit of the audit client's financial statements.

(iv) *Actuarial Services.* Any actuarially-oriented advisory service involving the determination of amounts recorded in the financial statements and related accounts for the audit client other than assisting a client in understanding the methods, models, assumptions, and inputs used in computing an amount, unless it is reasonable to conclude that the results of these services will not be subject to audit procedures during an audit of the audit client's financial statements.

(v) *Internal Audit Outsourcing Services.* Any internal audit service that has been outsourced by the audit client that relates to the audit client's internal accounting controls, financial systems, or financial statements, for an audit client unless it is reasonable to conclude that the results of these services will not be subject to audit procedures during an audit of the audit client's financial statements.

(vi) *Management Functions.* Acting, temporarily or permanently, as a director, officer, or employee of an audit client, or performing any decision-making, supervisory, or ongoing monitoring function for the audit client.

(vii) *Human Resources.*

(A) Searching for or seeking out prospective candidates for managerial, executive, or director positions;

(B) Engaging in psychological testing, or other formal testing or evaluation programs;

(C) Undertaking reference checks of prospective candidates for an executive or director position;

(D) Acting as a negotiator on the audit client's behalf, such as determining position, status or title, compensation, fringe benefits, or other conditions of employment; or

(E) Recommending, or advising the audit client to hire, a specific candidate for a specific job (except that an accounting firm may, upon request by the audit client, interview candidates and advise the audit client on the candidate's competence for financial accounting, administrative, or control positions).

(viii) *Broker-Dealer, Investment Adviser, or Investment Banking Services.* Acting as a broker-dealer (registered or unregistered), promoter, or underwriter, on behalf of an audit client, making investment decisions on behalf of the audit client or otherwise having discretionary authority over an audit client's investments, executing a transaction to buy or sell an audit client's investment, or having custody of assets of the audit client, such as taking temporary possession of securities purchased by the audit client.

(ix) *Legal Services.* Providing any service to an audit client that, under circumstances in which the service is provided, could be provided only by someone licensed, admitted, or otherwise qualified to practice law in the jurisdiction in which the service is provided.

(x) *Expert Services Unrelated to the Audit.* Providing an expert opinion or other expert service for an audit client, or an audit client's legal representative, for the purpose of advocating an audit client's interests in litigation or in a regulatory or administrative proceeding or investigation. In any litigation or regulatory or administrative proceeding or investigation, an accountant's independence shall not be deemed to be impaired if the accountant provides factual accounts, including in testimony, of work performed or explains the positions taken or conclusions reached during the performance of any service provided by the accountant for the audit client.

(5) *Contingent fees.* An accountant is not independent if, at any point during the audit and professional engagement period, the accountant provides any service or product to an audit client for a contingent fee or a commission, or receives a contingent fee or commission from an audit client.

(6) *Partner rotation.*

(i) Except as provided in paragraph (c)(6)(ii) of this Item, an accountant is not independent of an audit client when:

(A) Any audit partner as defined in paragraph (f)(7)(ii) of this Item performs:

(1) The services of a lead partner, as defined in paragraph (f)(7)(ii)(A) of this Item, or concurring partner, as defined in paragraph (f)(7)(ii)(B) of this Item, for more than five consecutive years; or

(2) One or more of the services defined in paragraphs (f)(7)(ii)(C) and (D) of this Item for more than seven consecutive years;

(B) *Any Audit Partner*:

(1) Within the five consecutive year period following the performance of services for the maximum period permitted under paragraph (c)(6)(i)(A)(1) of this Item, performs for that audit client the services of a lead partner, as defined in paragraph (f)(7)(ii)(A) of this Item, or concurring partner, as defined in paragraph (f)(7)(ii)(B) of this Item, or a combination of those services, or

(2) Within the two consecutive year period following the performance of services for the maximum period permitted under paragraph (c)(6)(i)(A)(2) of this Item, performs one or more of the services defined in paragraph (f)(7)(ii) of this Item.

(ii)   Any accounting firm with less than five audit clients that are issuers (as defined in section 10A(f) of the Securities Exchange Act of 1934) and less than ten partners shall be exempt from paragraph (c)(6)(i) of this Item provided the Public Company Accounting Oversight Board conducts a review at least once every three years of each of the audit client engagements that would result in a lack of auditor independence under this paragraph.

(iii)   For purposes of paragraph (c)(6)(i) of this Item, an audit client that is an investment company registered under section 8 of the Investment Company Act of 1940, does not include an affiliate of the audit client that is an entity in the same investment company complex, as defined in paragraph (f)(14) of this Item, except for another registered investment company in the same investment company complex. For purposes of calculating consecutive years of service under paragraph (c)(6)(i) of this Item with respect to investment companies in an investment company complex, audits of registered investment companies with different fiscal year-ends that are performed in a continuous 12-month period count as a single consecutive year.

(7)   *Audit Committee Administration of the Engagement.* An accountant is not independent of an issuer (as defined in section 10A(f) of the Securities Exchange Act of 1934), other than an issuer that is an Asset-Backed Issuer as defined in Item 1101 of Regulation S–K, or an investment company registered under section 8 of the Investment Company Act of 1940, other than a unit investment trust as defined by section 4(2) of the Investment Company Act of 1940, unless:

(i)   In accordance with Section 10A(i) of the Securities Exchange Act of 1934 either:

(A)   Before the accountant is engaged by the issuer or its subsidiaries, or the registered investment company or its subsidiaries, to render audit or non-audit services, the engagement is approved by the issuer's or registered investment company's audit committee; or

(B)   The engagement to render the service is entered into pursuant to pre-approval policies and procedures established by the audit committee of the issuer or registered investment company, provided the policies and procedures are detailed as to the particular service and the audit committee is informed of each service and such policies and procedures do not include delegation of the audit committees responsibilities under the Securities Exchange Act of 1934 to management; or

(C)   With respect to the provision of services other than audit, review or attest services the pre-approval requirement is waived if:

(1)   The aggregate amount of all such services provided constitutes no more than five percent of the total amount of revenues paid by the audit client to its accountant during the fiscal year in which the services are provided;

(2)   Such services were not recognized by the issuer or registered investment company at the time of the engagement to be non-audit services; and

(3)   Such services are promptly brought to the attention of the audit committee of the issuer or registered investment company and approved prior to the completion of the audit by the audit committee or by one or more members of the audit committee who are members of the board of directors to whom authority to grant such approvals has been delegated by the audit committee.

(ii)   A registered investment company's audit committee also must pre-approve its accountant's engagements for non-audit services with the registered investment company's investment adviser (not including a sub-adviser whose role is primarily portfolio management and is sub-contracted or overseen by another investment adviser) and any entity controlling, controlled by, or under common control with the investment adviser that provides ongoing services to the registered investment company in accordance with paragraph (c)(7)(i) of this Item, if the engagement relates directly to the operations and financial reporting of the registered investment company, except that with respect to the waiver of the pre-approval requirement under paragraph (c)(7)(i)(C) of this Item, the aggregate amount of all services provided constitutes no more than five percent of the total amount of revenues paid to the registered investment company's accountant by the registered investment company, its investment adviser and any entity controlling, controlled by, or under common control with the investment adviser that provides ongoing services to the registered investment company during the fiscal year in which the services are provided that would have to be pre-approved by the registered investment company's audit committee pursuant to this rule.

(8)   *Compensation.* An accountant is not independent of an audit client if, at any point during the audit and professional engagement period, any audit partner earns or receives compensation based on the audit partner procuring engagements with that audit client to provide any products or services other than audit, review or attest services. Any accounting firm with fewer than ten partners and fewer than five audit clients that are issuers (as defined in section 10A(f) of the Securities Exchange Act of 1934) shall be exempt from the requirement stated in the previous sentence.

(d)   *Quality Controls.* An accounting firm's independence will not be impaired solely because a covered person in the firm is not independent of an audit client provided:

(1)   The covered person did not know of the circumstances giving rise to the lack of independence;

(2)   The covered person's lack of independence was corrected as promptly as possible under the relevant circumstances after the covered person or accounting firm became aware of it; and

(3)   The accounting firm has a quality control system in place that provides reasonable assurance, taking into account the size and nature of the accounting firm's practice, that the accounting firm and its employees do not lack independence, and that covers at least all employees and associated entities of the accounting firm participating in the engagement, including employees and associated entities located outside of the United States.

(4)   For an accounting firm that annually provides audit, review, or attest services to more than 500 companies with a class of securities registered with the Commission under section 12 of the Securities Exchange Act of 1934, a quality control system will not provide such reasonable assurance unless it has at least the following features:

(i)   Written independence policies and procedures;

(ii)   With respect to partners and managerial employees, an automated system to identify their investments in securities that might impair the accountant's independence;

(iii)   With respect to all professionals, a system that provides timely information about entities from which the accountant is required to maintain independence;

(iv)   An annual or on-going firm-wide training program about auditor independence;

(v)   An annual internal inspection and testing program to monitor adherence to independence requirements;

(vi)   Notification to all accounting firm members, officers, directors, and employees of the name and title of the member of senior management responsible for compliance with auditor independence requirements;

(vii)   Written policies and procedures requiring all partners and covered persons to report promptly to the accounting firm when they are engaged in employment negotiations with an audit client, and requiring the firm to remove immediately any such professional from that audit client's engagement and to review promptly all work the professional performed related to that audit client's engagement; and

(viii) A disciplinary mechanism to ensure compliance with this rule.

(e)(1)   *Transition and Grandfathering.* Provided the following relationships did not impair the accountant's independence under pre-existing requirements of the Commission, the Independence Standards, Board, or the accounting profession in the United States, the existence of the relationship on May 6, 2003 will not be deemed to impair an accountant's independence:

(i)   Employment relationships that commenced at the issuer prior to May 6, 2003 as described in paragraph (c)(2)(iii)(B) of this Item.

(ii)   Compensation earned or received, as described in paragraph (c)(8) of this Item during the fiscal year of the accounting firm that includes the effective date of this rule.

(iii) Until May 6, 2004, the provision of services described in paragraph (c)(4) of this Item provided those services are pursuant to contracts in existence on May 6, 2003.

(iv) The provision of services by the accountant under contracts in existence on May 6, 2003 that have not been pre-approved by the audit committee as described in paragraph (c)(7) of this Item.

(v) Until the first day of the issuer's fiscal year beginning after May 6, 2003 by a "lead" partner and other audit partner (other than the "concurring" partner) providing services in excess of those permitted under paragraph (c)(6) of this Item. An accountant's independence will not be deemed to be impaired until the first day of the issuer's fiscal year beginning after May 6, 2004 by a "concurring" partner providing services in excess of those permitted under paragraph (c)(6) of this Item. For the purposes of calculating periods of service under paragraph (c)(6) of this Item:

(A) For the "lead" and "concurring" partner, the period of service includes time served as the "lead" or "concurring" partner prior to May 6, 2003; and

(B) For audit partners other than the "lead" partner or "concurring" partner, and for audit partners in foreign firms, the period of service does not include time served on the audit engagement team prior to the first day of issuer's fiscal year beginning on or after May 6, 2003.

(2) *Settling Financial Arrangements With Former Professionals.* To the extent not required by pre-existing requirements of the Commission, the Independence Standards Board, or the accounting profession in the United States, the requirement in paragraph (c)(2)(iii) of this Item to settle financial arrangements with former professionals applies to situations that arise after the effective date of this rule.

(f) *Definitions of Terms.* For purposes of this rule:

(1) Accountant, as used in paragraphs (b) through (e) of this Item, means a registered public accounting firm, certified public accountant or public accountant performing services in connection with an engagement for which independence is required. References to the accountant include any accounting firm with which the certified public accountant or public accountant is affiliated.

(2) Accounting firm means an organization (whether it is a sole proprietorship, incorporated association, partnership, corporation, limited liability company, limited liability partnership, or other legal entity) that is engaged in the practice of public accounting and furnishes reports or other documents filed with the Commission or otherwise prepared under the securities laws, and all of the organization's departments, divisions, parents, subsidiaries, and associated entities, including those located outside of the United States. Accounting firm also includes the organization's pension, retirement, investment, or similar plans.

(3)(i) Accounting role means a role in which a person is in a position to or does exercise more than minimal influence over the contents of the accounting records or anyone who prepares them.

(ii) Financial reporting oversight role means a role in which a person is in a position to or does exercise influence over the contents of the financial statements or anyone who prepares them, such as when the person is a member of the board of directors or similar management or governing body, chief executive officer, president, chief financial officer, chief operating officer, general counsel, chief accounting officer, controller, director of internal audit, director of financial reporting, treasurer, or any equivalent position.

(4) Affiliate of the audit client means:

(i) An entity that has control over the audit client, or over which the audit client has control, or which is under common control with the audit client, including the audit client's parents and subsidiaries;

(ii) An entity over which the audit client has significant influence, unless the entity is not material to the audit client;

(iii) An entity that has significant influence over the audit client, unless the audit client is not material to the entity; and

(iv) Each entity in the investment company complex when the audit client is an entity that is part of an investment company complex.

(5)   Audit and professional engagement period includes both:

(i)   The period covered by any financial statements being audited or reviewed (the "audit period"); and

(ii)   The period of the engagement to audit or review the audit client's financial statements or to prepare a report filed with the Commission (the "professional engagement period"):

(A)   The professional engagement period begins when the accountant either signs an initial engagement letter (or other agreement to review or audit a client's financial statements) or begins audit, review, or attest procedures, whichever is earlier; and

(B)   The professional engagement period ends when the audit client or the accountant notifies the Commission that the client is no longer that accountant's audit client.

(iii)   For audits of the financial statements of foreign private issuers, the "audit and professional engagement period" does not include periods ended prior to the first day of the last fiscal year before the foreign private issuer first filed, or was required to file, a registration statement or report with the Commission, provided there has been full compliance with home country independence standards in all prior periods covered by any registration statement or report filed with the Commission.

(6)   Audit client means the entity whose financial statements or other information is being audited, reviewed, or attested and any affiliates of the audit client, other than, for purposes of paragraph (c)(1)(i) of this Item, entities that are affiliates of the audit client only by virtue of paragraph (f)(4)(ii) or (f)(4)(iii) of this Item.

(7)(i)   Audit engagement team means all partners, principals, shareholders and professional employees participating in an audit, review, or attestation engagement of an audit client, including audit partners and all persons who consult with others on the audit engagement team during the audit, review, or attestation engagement regarding technical or industry-specific issues, transactions, or events.

(ii)   Audit partner means a partner or persons in an equivalent position, other than a partner who consults with others on the audit engagement team during the audit, review, or attestation engagement regarding technical or industry-specific issues, transactions, or events, who is a member of the audit engagement team who has responsibility for decision-making on significant auditing, accounting, and reporting matters that affect the financial statements, or who maintains regular contact with management and the audit committee and includes the following:

(A)   The lead or coordinating audit partner having primary responsibility for the audit or review (the "lead partner");

(B)   The partner conducting a quality review under applicable professional standards and any applicable rules of the Commission to evaluate the significant judgments and the related conclusions reached in forming the overall conclusion on the audit or review engagement ("Engagement Quality Reviewer" or "Engagement Quality Control Reviewer");

(C)   Other audit engagement team partners who provide more than ten hours of audit, review, or attest services in connection with the annual or interim consolidated financial statements of the issuer or an investment company registered under section 8 of the Investment Company Act of 1940; and

(D)   Other audit engagement team partners who serve as the "lead partner" in connection with any audit or review related to the annual or interim financial statements of a subsidiary of the issuer whose assets or revenues constitute 20% or more of the assets or revenues of the issuer's respective consolidated assets or revenues.

(8)   Chain of command means all persons who:

(i)   Supervise or have direct management responsibility for the audit, including at all successively senior levels through the accounting firm's chief executive;

(ii)   Evaluate the performance or recommend the compensation of the audit engagement partner; or

(iii)   Provide quality control or other oversight of the audit.

(9)   Close family members means a person's spouse, spousal equivalent, parent, dependent, nondependent child, and sibling.

(10)   Contingent fee means, except as stated in the next sentence, any fee established for the sale of a product or the performance of any service pursuant to an arrangement in which no fee will be charged unless a specified finding or result is attained, or in which the amount of the fee is otherwise dependent upon the finding or result of such product or service. Solely for the purposes of this rule, a fee is not a "contingent fee" if it is fixed by courts or other public authorities, or, in tax matters, if determined based on the results of judicial proceedings or the findings of governmental agencies. Fees may vary depending, for example, on the complexity of services rendered.

(11)   Covered persons in the firm means the following partners, principals, shareholders, and employees of an accounting firm:

(i)   The "audit engagement team";

(ii)   The "chain of command";

(iii)   Any other partner, principal, shareholder, or managerial employee of the accounting firm who has provided ten or more hours of non-audit services to the audit client for the period beginning on the date such services are provided and ending on the date the accounting firm signs the report on the financial statements for the fiscal year during which those services are provided, or who expects to provide ten or more hours of non-audit services to the audit client on a recurring basis; and

(iv)   Any other partner, principal, or shareholder from an "office" of the accounting firm in which the lead audit engagement partner primarily practices in connection with the audit.

(12)   Group means two or more persons who act together for the purposes of acquiring, holding, voting, or disposing of securities of a registrant.

(13)   Immediate family members means a person's spouse, spousal equivalent, and dependents.

(14)   Investment company complex.

(i)   "Investment company complex" includes:

(A)   An investment company and its investment adviser or sponsor;

(B)   Any entity controlled by or controlling an investment adviser or sponsor in paragraph (f)(14)(i)(A) of this Item, or any entity under common control with an investment adviser or sponsor in paragraph (f)(14)(i)(A) of this Item if the entity:

(1)   Is an investment adviser or sponsor; or

(2)   Is engaged in the business of providing administrative, custodian, underwriting, or transfer agent services to any investment company, investment adviser, or sponsor; and

(C)   Any investment company or entity that would be an investment company but for the exclusions provided by section 3(c) of the Investment Company Act of 1940 that has an investment adviser or sponsor included in this definition by either paragraph (f)(14)(i)(A) or (f)(14)(i)(B) of this Item.

(ii)   An investment adviser, for purposes of this definition, does not include a sub-adviser whose role is primarily portfolio management and is subcontracted with or overseen by another investment adviser.

(iii)   Sponsor, for purposes of this definition, is an entity that establishes a unit investment trust.

(15)   Office means a distinct sub-group within an accounting firm, whether distinguished along geographic or practice lines.

(16) Rabbi trust means an irrevocable trust whose assets are not accessible to the accounting firm until all benefit obligations have been met, but are subject to the claims of creditors in bankruptcy or insolvency.

(17) Audit committee means a committee (or equivalent body) as defined in section 3(a)(58) of the Securities Exchange Act of 1934.

C. SEC PROCEDURAL RULES

RULES OF PRACTICE

17 C.F.R. § 201.___

Subpart A—Rules of Practice

[Removed and Reserved]

Subpart B—Regulations Pertaining to the Equal Access to Justice Act

[Omitted]

Subpart C—Procedures Pertaining to the Payment of Bounties Pursuant to Subsection 21A(e) of the Securities Exchange Act of 1934

[Reserved]

Subpart D—Rules of Practice General Rules

RULES OF PRACTICE

Subpart C—Procedures Pertaining to the Payment of Bounties Pursuant to Subsection 21A(e) of the Securities Exchange Act of 1934

[Reserved]

Subpart D—Rules of Practice

General Rules

Rule 100.   Scope of the Rules of Practice

(a)   Unless provided otherwise, these Rules of Practice govern proceedings before the Commission under the statutes that it administers.

(b)   These rules do not apply to:

(1)   Investigations, except where made specifically applicable by the Rules Relating to Investigations, part 203 of this chapter; or

(2)   Actions taken by the duty officer pursuant to delegated authority under 17 CFR section 200.43.

(3)   Initiation of proceedings for SRO proposed rule changes under Rule 700–701 of the Rules of Practice, except where made specifically applicable therein.

(c)   The Commission, upon its determination that to do so would serve the interests of justice and not result in prejudice to the parties to the proceeding, may by order direct, in a particular proceeding, that an alternative procedure shall apply or that compliance with an otherwise applicable rule is unnecessary.

Rule 101.   Definitions

(a)   For purposes of these Rules of Practice, unless explicitly stated to the contrary:

(1)   *Commission* means the United States Securities and Exchange Commission, or a panel of Commissioners constituting a quorum of the Commission, or a single Commissioner acting as duty officer pursuant to 17 CFR section 200.43;

(2)   *Counsel* means any attorney representing a party or any other person representing a party pursuant to Rule 102(b);

(3)   *Disciplinary proceeding* means an action pursuant to Rule 102(e);

(4)   *Enforcement proceeding* means an action, initiated by an order instituting proceedings, held for the purpose of determining whether or not a person is about to violate, has violated, has caused a violation of, or has aided or abetted a violation of any statute or rule administered by the Commission, or whether to impose a sanction as defined in Section 551(10) of the Administrative Procedure Act;

(5)   *Hearing officer* means an administrative law judge, a panel of Commissioners constituting less than a quorum of the Commission, an individual Commissioner, or any other person duly authorized to preside at a hearing;

(6)   *Interested division* means a division or an office assigned primary responsibility by the Commission to participate in a particular proceeding;

(7)   *Order instituting proceedings* means an order issued by the Commission commencing a proceeding or an order issued by the Commission to hold a hearing;

(8)   *Party* means the interested division, any person named as a respondent in an order instituting proceedings, any applicant named in the caption of any order, persons entitled to notice in a stop order proceeding as set forth in Rule 200(a)(2) or any person seeking Commission review of a decision;

(9)   *Proceeding* means any agency process initiated:

(i)   By an order instituting proceedings; or

(ii)   By the filing, pursuant to Rule 410, of a petition for review of an initial decision by a hearing officer; or

(iii) By the filing, pursuant to Rule 420, of an application for review of a self-regulatory organization determination; or

(iv)   By the filing, pursuant to Rule 430, of a notice of intention to file a petition for review of a determination made pursuant to delegated authority; or

(v)   By the filing, pursuant to Rule 440, of an application for review of a determination by the Public Company Accounting Oversight Board; or

(vi)   By the filing, pursuant to Rule 601 of Regulation NMS, of an application for review of an action or failure to act in connection with the implementation or operation of any effective transaction reporting plan; or

(vii) By the filing, pursuant to Rule 608 of Regulation NMS, of an application for review of an action taken or failure to act in connection with the implementation or operation of any effective national market system plan; or

(viii) By the filing, pursuant to Section 11A(b)(5) under the Securities Exchange Act of 1934, of an application for review of a determination of a registered securities information processor;

(10) *Secretary* means the Secretary of the Commission;

(11) *Temporary sanction* means a temporary cease-and-desist order or a temporary suspension of the registration of a broker, dealer, municipal securities dealer, government securities broker, government securities dealer, or transfer agent pending final determination whether the registration shall be revoked; and

(12) *Board* means the Public Company Accounting Oversight Board.

Rule 102.   Appearance and Practice Before the Commission

A person shall not be represented before the Commission or a hearing officer except as stated in paragraphs (a) and (b) of this rule or as otherwise permitted by the Commission or a hearing officer.

(a)   *Representing oneself.* In any proceeding, an individual may appear on his or her own behalf.

(b)   *Representing others.* In any proceeding, a person may be represented by an attorney at law admitted to practice before the Supreme Court of the United States or the highest court of any State (as defined in section 3(a)(16) of the Exchange Act); a member of a partnership may represent the partnership; a bona fide officer of a corporation, trust or association may represent the corporation, trust or association; and an officer or employee of a state commission or of a department or political subdivision of a state may represent the state commission or the department or political subdivision of the state.

(c)   *Former Commission employees.* Former employees of the Commission must comply with the restrictions on practice contained in the Commission's Conduct Regulation, Subpart M.

(d)   *Designation of address for service; notice of appearance; power of attorney; withdrawal.*

(1)   *Representing oneself.* When an individual first makes any filing or otherwise appears on his or her own behalf before the Commission or a hearing officer in a proceeding as defined in § 201.101(a), he or she shall file with the Commission, or otherwise state on the record, and keep current, a mailing address and email address at which any notice or other written communication required to be served upon him or her or furnished to him or her may be sent and a telephone number where he or she may be reached during business hours. Within ten days of April 12, 2021, any individual appearing on his or her own behalf before the Commission or hearing officer in a proceeding as defined in Rule 101(a) that is ongoing on that date shall electronically file a notice that complies with section (d)(1). Notices required by this Rule shall be served in accordance with § 201.150(a). Individuals shall electronically file a § 201.102(d) compliant notice in their ongoing proceedings even if a prior Rule 102(d) paper filing included the participant's email address.

(2) *Representing others.* When a person first makes any filing or otherwise appears in a representative capacity before the Commission or a hearing officer in a proceeding as defined in Rule 101(a), that person shall file with the Commission, and keep current, a written notice stating the name of the proceeding; the representative's name, business address, email address, and telephone number; and the name, email address, and address of the person or persons represented. Within ten days of April 12, 2021, any person appearing in a representative capacity before the Commission or hearing officer in a proceeding as defined in Rule 101(a) that is ongoing on that date shall electronically file a notice that complies with this section (d)(2).

Notices required by this section shall be served in accordance with § 201.150(a). Participants are directed to electronically file a Rule 102(d) compliant notice in their ongoing proceedings even if a prior § 201.102(d) paper filing included the participant's email address

(3) *Power of attorney.* Any individual appearing or practicing before the Commission in a representative capacity may be required to file a power of attorney with the Commission showing his or her authority to act in such capacity.

(4) *Withdrawal.* Any person seeking to withdraw his or her appearance in a representative capacity shall file a notice of withdrawal with the Commission or the hearing officer. The notice shall state the name, mailing address, email address, and telephone number of the withdrawing representative; the name, email address, address, and telephone number of the person for whom the appearance was made; and the effective date of the withdrawal. If the person seeking to withdraw knows the name, mailing address, email address, and telephone number of the new representative, or knows that the person for whom the appearance was made intends to represent him- or herself, that information shall be included in the notice. The notice must be served on the parties in accordance with Rule 150. The notice shall be filed at least five days before the proposed effective date of the withdrawal.

(e) *Suspension and disbarment.*

(1) *Generally.* The Commission may censure a person or deny, temporarily or permanently, the privilege of appearing or practicing before it in any way to any person who is found by the Commission after notice and opportunity for hearing in the matter:

(i)   Not to possess the requisite qualifications to represent others; or

(ii)   To be lacking in character or integrity or to have engaged in unethical or improper professional conduct; or

(iii)   To have willfully violated, or willfully aided and abetted the violation of any provision of the Federal securities laws or the rules and regulations thereunder.

(iv)   With respect to persons licensed to practice as accountants, "improper professional conduct" under Rule 102(e)(1)(ii) means:

(A)   Intentional or knowing conduct, including reckless conduct, that results in a violation of applicable professional standards; or

(B)   Either of the following two types of negligent conduct:

(1)   A single instance of highly unreasonable conduct that results in a violation of applicable professional standards in circumstances in which an accountant knows, or should know, that heightened scrutiny is warranted.

(2)   Repeated instances of unreasonable conduct, each resulting in a violation of applicable professional standards, that indicate a lack of competence to practice before the Commission.

(2) *Certain professionals and convicted persons.* Any attorney who has been suspended or disbarred by a court of the United States or of any State; or any person whose license to practice as an accountant, engineer, or other professional or expert has been revoked or suspended in any State; or any person who has been convicted of a felony or a misdemeanor involving moral turpitude shall be forthwith suspended from appearing or practicing before the Commission. A disbarment, suspension,

revocation or conviction within the meaning of this rule shall be deemed to have occurred when the disbarring, suspending, revoking or convicting agency or tribunal enters its judgment or order, including a judgment or order on a plea of nolo contendere, regardless of whether an appeal of such judgment or order is pending or could be taken.

(3) *Temporary suspensions.* An order of temporary suspension shall become effective upon service on the respondent. No order of temporary suspension shall be entered by the Commission pursuant to paragraph (e)(3)(i) of this rule more than 90 days after the date on which the final judgment or order entered in a judicial or administrative proceeding described in paragraph (e)(3)(i)(A) or (e)(3)(i)(B) of this rule has become effective, whether upon completion of review or appeal procedures or because further review or appeal procedures are no longer available.

(i) The Commission, with due regard to the public interest and without preliminary hearing, may, by order, temporarily suspend from appearing or practicing before it any attorney, accountant, engineer, or other professional or expert who has been by name:

(A) Permanently enjoined by any court of competent jurisdiction, by reason of his or her misconduct in an action brought by the Commission, from violating or aiding and abetting the violation of any provision of the Federal securities laws or of the rules and regulation thereunder; or

(B) Found by any court of competent jurisdiction in an action brought by the Commission to which he or she is a party or found by the Commission in any administrative proceeding to which he or she is a party to have violated (unless the violation was found not to have been willful) or aided and abetted the violation of any provision of the Federal securities laws or of the rules and regulations thereunder.

(ii) Any person temporarily suspended from appearing and practicing before the Commission in accordance with paragraph (e)(3)(i) of this rule may, within 30 days after service upon him or her of the order of temporary suspension, petition the Commission to lift the temporary suspension. If no petition has been received by the Commission within 30 days after service of the order, the suspension shall become permanent.

(iii) Within 30 days after the filing of a petition in accordance with paragraph (e)(3)(ii) of this rule, the Commission shall either lift the temporary suspension, or set the matter down for hearing at a time and place designated by the Commission, or both, and, after opportunity for hearing, may censure the petitioner or disqualify petitioner from appearing or practicing before the Commission for a period of time or permanently. In every case in which the temporary suspension has not been lifted, every hearing held and other action taken pursuant to this paragraph (e)(3) shall be expedited in accordance with Rule 500. If the hearing is held before a hearing officer, the time limits set forth in Rule 540 will govern review of the hearing officer's initial decision.

(iv) In any hearing held on a petition filed in accordance with paragraph (e)(3)(ii) of this rule, the staff of the Commission shall show either that the petitioner has been enjoined as described in paragraph (e)(3)(i)(A) of this rule or that the petitioner has been found to have committed or aided and abetted violations as described in paragraph (e)(3)(i)(B) of this rule and that showing, without more, may be the basis for censure or disqualification. Once that showing has been made, the burden shall be upon the petitioner to show cause why he or she should not be censured or temporarily or permanently disqualified from appearing and practicing before the Commission. In any such hearing, the petitioner may not contest any finding made against him or her or fact admitted by him or her in the judicial or administrative proceeding upon which the proceeding under this paragraph (e)(3) is predicated. A person who has consented to the entry of a permanent injunction as described in paragraph (e)(3)(i)(A) of this rule without admitting the facts set forth in the complaint shall be presumed for all purposes under this paragraph (e)(3) to have been enjoined by reason of the misconduct alleged in the complaint.

(4) *Filing of prior orders.* Any person appearing or practicing before the Commission who has been the subject of an order, judgment, decree, or finding as set forth in paragraph (e)(3) of this rule shall promptly file with the Secretary a copy thereof (together with any related opinion or statement

of the agency or tribunal involved). Failure to file any such paper, order, judgment, decree or finding shall not impair the operation of any other provision of this rule.

(5)   *Reinstatement.*

(i)   An application for reinstatement of a person permanently suspended or disqualified under paragraph (e)(1) or (e)(3) of this rule may be made at any time, and the applicant may, in the Commission's discretion, be afforded a hearing; however, the suspension or disqualification shall continue unless and until the applicant has been reinstated by the Commission for good cause shown.

(ii)   Any person suspended under paragraph (e)(2) of this rule shall be reinstated by the Commission, upon appropriate application, if all the grounds for application of the provisions of that paragraph are subsequently removed by a reversal of the conviction or termination of the suspension, disbarment, or revocation. An application for reinstatement on any other grounds by any person suspended under paragraph (e)(2) of this rule may be filed at any time and the applicant shall be accorded an opportunity for a hearing in the matter; however, such suspension shall continue unless and until the applicant has been reinstated by order of the Commission for good cause shown.

(6)   *Other proceedings not precluded.* A proceeding brought under paragraph (e)(1), (e)(2) or (e)(3) of this rule shall not preclude another proceeding brought under these same paragraphs.

(7)   *Public hearings.* All hearings held under this paragraph (e) shall be public unless otherwise ordered by the Commission on its own motion or after considering the motion of a party.

(f)   *Practice defined.* For the purposes of these Rules of Practice, practicing before the Commission shall include, but shall not be limited to:

(1)   Transacting any business with the Commission; and

(2)   The preparation of any statement, opinion or other paper by any attorney, accountant, engineer or other professional or expert, filed with the Commission in any registration statement, notification, application, report or other document with the consent of such attorney, accountant, engineer or other professional or expert.

Rule 103.   Construction of Rules

(a)   The Rules of Practice shall be construed and administered to secure the just, speedy, and inexpensive determination of every proceeding.

(b)   In any particular proceeding, to the extent that there is a conflict between these rules and a procedural requirement contained in any statute, or any rule or form adopted thereunder, the latter shall control.

(c)   For purposes of these rules:

(1)   Any term in the singular includes the plural, and any term in the plural includes the singular, if such use would be appropriate;

(2)   Any use of a masculine, feminine, or neuter gender encompasses such other genders as would be appropriate; and

(3)   Unless the context requires otherwise, counsel for a party may take any action required or permitted to be taken by such party.

Rule 104.   Business Hours

The Headquarters office of the Commission, at 100 F Street, N.E., Washington, D.C. 20549, is open each day, except Saturdays, Sundays, and Federal legal holidays, from 9 a.m. to 5:30 p.m., Eastern Standard Time or Eastern Daylight Saving Time, whichever is currently in effect in Washington, D.C. Federal legal holidays consist of New Year's Day; Birthday of Martin Luther King, Jr.; Presidents Day; Memorial Day;

Independence Day; Labor Day; Columbus Day; Veterans Day; Thanksgiving Day; Christmas Day; and any other day appointed as a holiday in Washington, D.C. by the President or the Congress of the United States.

Rule 110.   Presiding Officer

All proceedings shall be presided over by the Commission or, if the Commission so orders, by a hearing officer. When the Commission designates that the hearing officer shall be an administrative law judge, the Chief Administrative Law Judge shall select, pursuant to 17 CFR section 200.30–10, the administrative law judge to preside.

Rule 111.   Hearing Officer: Authority

The hearing officer shall have the authority to do all things necessary and appropriate to discharge his or her duties. No provision of these Rules of Practice shall be construed to limit the powers of the hearing officer provided by the Administrative Procedure Act. The powers of the hearing officer include, but are not limited to, the following:

(a)   Administering oaths and affirmations;

(b)   Issuing subpoenas authorized by law and revoking, quashing, or modifying any such subpoena;

(c)   Receiving relevant evidence and ruling upon the admission of evidence and offers of proof;

(d)   Regulating the course of a proceeding and the conduct of the parties and their counsel;

(e)   Holding prehearing and other conferences as set forth in Rule 221 and requiring the attendance at any such conference of at least one representative of each party who has authority to negotiate concerning the resolution of issues in controversy;

(f)   Recusing himself or herself upon motion made by a party or upon his or her own motion;

(g)   Ordering, in his or her discretion, in a proceeding involving more than one respondent, that the interested division indicate, on the record, at least one day prior to the presentation of any evidence, each respondent against whom that evidence will be offered;

(h)   Subject to any limitations set forth elsewhere in these Rules of Practice, considering and ruling upon all procedural and other motions, including a motion to correct a manifest error of fact in the initial decision. A motion to correct is properly filed under this Rule only if the basis for the motion is a patent misstatement of fact in the initial decision. Any motion to correct must be filed within ten days of the initial decision. A brief in opposition may be filed within five days of a motion to correct. The hearing officer shall have 20 days from the date of filing of any brief in opposition filed to rule on a motion to correct;

(i)   Preparing an initial decision as provided in Rule 360;

(j)   Upon notice to all parties, reopening any hearing prior to the filing of an initial decision therein, or, if no initial decision is to be filed, prior to the time fixed for the filing of final briefs with the Commission; and

(k)   Informing the parties as to the availability of one or more alternative means of dispute resolution, and encouraging the use of such methods.

Rule 112.   Hearing Officer: Disqualification and Withdrawal

(a)   *Notice of disqualification.* At any time a hearing officer believes himself or herself to be disqualified from considering a matter, the hearing officer shall issue a notice stating that he or she is withdrawing from the matter and setting forth the reasons therefor.

(b)   *Motion for withdrawal.* Any party who has a reasonable, good faith basis to believe that a hearing officer has a personal bias, or is otherwise disqualified from hearing a case, may make a motion to the hearing officer that the hearing officer withdraw. The motion shall be accompanied by an affidavit setting forth in detail the facts alleged to constitute grounds for disqualification. If the hearing officer finds himself or herself not disqualified, he or she shall so rule and shall continue to preside over the proceeding.

Rule 120.   *Ex parte* Communications

(a)   Except to the extent required for the disposition of *ex parte* matters as authorized by law, the person presiding over an evidentiary hearing may not:

(1)   Consult a person or party on a fact in issue, unless on notice and opportunity for all parties to participate; or

(2)   Be responsible to or subject to the supervision or direction of an employee or agent engaged in the performance of investigative or prosecuting functions for the Commission.

(b)   The Commission's code of behavior regarding *ex parte* communications between persons outside the Commission and decisional employees governs other prohibited communications during a proceeding conducted under the Rules of Practice.

Rule 121.   Separation of Functions

Any Commission officer, employee or agent engaged in the performance of investigative or prosecutorial functions for the Commission in a proceeding as defined in Rule 101(a) may not, in that proceeding or one that is factually related, participate or advise in the decision, or in Commission review of the decision pursuant to Section 557 of the Administrative Procedure Act except as a witness or counsel in the proceeding.

Rule 140.   Commission Orders and Decisions: Signature and Availability

(a)   *Signature required.* All orders and decisions of the Commission shall be signed by the Secretary or any other person duly authorized by the Commission.

(b)   *Availability for inspection.* Each order and decision shall be available for inspection by the public from the date of entry, unless the order or decision is nonpublic. A nonpublic order or decision shall be available for inspection by any person entitled to inspect it from the date of entry.

(c)   *Date of entry of orders.* The date of entry of a Commission order shall be the date the order is signed. Such date shall be reflected in the caption of the order, or if there is no caption, in the order itself.

Rule 141.   Orders and Decisions: Service of Orders Instituting Proceedings and Other Orders and Decisions

(a)   *Service of an order instituting proceedings.*

(1)   *By whom made.* The Secretary, or another duly authorized officer of the Commission, shall serve a copy of an order instituting proceedings on each person named in the order as a party. The Secretary may direct an interested division to assist in making service.

(2)   *How made.*

(i)   *To individuals.* Notice of a proceeding shall be made to an individual by delivering a copy of the order instituting proceedings to the individual or to an agent authorized by appointment or by law to receive such notice. *Delivery* means—handing a copy of the order to the individual; or leaving a copy at the individual's office with a clerk or other person in charge thereof; or leaving a copy at the individual's dwelling house or usual place of abode with some person of suitable age and discretion then residing therein; or sending a copy of the order addressed to the individual by U.S. Postal Service certified, registered or Express Mail and obtaining a confirmation of receipt; or giving confirmed telegraphic notice.

(ii)   *To corporations or entities.* Notice of a proceeding shall be made to a person other than a natural person by delivering a copy of the order instituting proceedings to an officer, managing or general agent, or any other agent authorized by appointment or law to receive such notice, by any method specified in paragraph (a)(2)(i) of this rule, or, in the case of an issuer of a class of securities registered with the Commission, by sending a copy of the order addressed to the most recent address shown on the entity's most recent filing with the Commission by U.S. Postal Service certified, registered, or Express Mail and obtaining a confirmation of attempted delivery.

(iii) *Upon persons registered with the Commission.* In addition to any other method of service specified in paragraph (a)(2) of this rule, notice may be made to a person currently registered with the Commission as a broker, dealer, municipal securities dealer, government securities broker, government securities dealer, investment adviser, investment company or transfer agent by sending a copy of the order addressed to the most recent business address shown on the person's registration form by U.S. Postal Service certified, registered or Express Mail and obtaining a confirmation of attempted delivery.

(iv) *Upon persons in a foreign country.* Notice of a proceeding to a person in a foreign country may be made by any of the following methods:

(A) Any method specified in paragraph (a)(2) of this rule that is not prohibited by the law of the foreign country; or

(B) By any internationally agreed means of service that is reasonably calculated to give notice, such as those authorized by the Hague Convention on the Service Abroad of Judicial and Extrajudicial Documents; or

(C) Any method that is reasonably calculated to give notice:

(1) As prescribed by the foreign country's law for service in that country in an action in its courts of general jurisdiction; or

(2) As the foreign authority directs in response to a letter rogatory or letter of request; or

(3) Unless prohibited by the foreign country's law, by delivering a copy of the order instituting proceedings to the individual personally, or using any form of mail that the Secretary or the interested division addresses and sends to the individual and that requires a signed receipt; or

(D) By any other means not prohibited by international agreement, as the Commission or hearing officer orders.

(v) *In stop order proceedings.* Notwithstanding any other provision of paragraph (a)(2) of this rule, in proceedings pursuant to sections 8 or 10 of the Securities Act of 1933, or sections 305 or 307 of the Trust Indenture Act of 1939, notice of the institution of proceedings shall be made by personal service or confirmed telegraphic notice, or a waiver obtain pursuant to paragraph (a)(4) of this rule.

(vi) *To persons registered with self-regulatory organizations.* Notice of a proceeding shall be made to a person registered with a self-regulatory organization by any method specified in paragraph (a)(2)(i) of this rule, or by sending a copy of the order addressed to the most recent address for the person shown in the Central Registration Depository by U.S. Postal Service certified, registered, or Express Mail and obtaining a confirmation of attempted delivery.

(3) *Record of service.* The Secretary shall maintain a record of service on parties (in hard copy or computerized format), identifying the party given notice, the method of service, the date of service, the address to which service was made, and the person who made service. If a division serves a copy of an order instituting proceedings, the division shall file with the Secretary either an acknowledgement of service by the person served or proof of service consisting of a statement by the person who made service certifying the date and manner of service; the names of the persons served; and their mail or electronic addresses, facsimile numbers, or the addresses of the places of delivery, as appropriate for the manner of service. If service is made in person, the certificate of service shall state, if available, the name of the individual to whom the order was given. If service is made by U.S. Postal Service certified or Express Mail, the Secretary shall maintain the confirmation of receipt or of attempted delivery, and tracking number. If service is made to an agent authorized by appointment to receive service, the certificate of service shall be accompanied by evidence of the appointment.

(4) *Waiver of service.* In lieu of service as set forth in paragraph (a)(2) of this rule, the party may be provided a copy of the order instituting proceedings by first class mail or other reliable means if a waiver of service is obtained from the party and placed in the record.

(b) *Service of orders or decisions other than an order instituting proceedings.* Written orders or decisions issued by the Commission or by a hearing officer shall be served promptly on each party pursuant to any method of service authorized under paragraph of this Rule or Rule 150(c) and (d). Such orders or decisions may also be served by facsimile transmission if the party to be served has agreed to accept such service in a writing, signed by the party, and has provided the Commission with information concerning the facsimile machine telephone number and hours of facsimile machine operation. Service of orders or decisions by the Commission, including those entered pursuant to delegated authority, shall be made by the Secretary or, as authorized by the Secretary, by a member of an interested division. Service of orders or decisions issued by a hearing officer shall be made by the Secretary or the hearing officer.

Rule 150.   Service of Papers by Parties

(a) *When required.* In every proceeding as defined in Rule 101(a), each paper, including each notice of appearance, written motion, brief, or other written communication, shall be served upon each party in the proceeding in accordance with the provisions of this rule; provided, however, that absent an order to the contrary, no service shall be required for motions which may be heard *ex parte*.

(b) *Upon a person represented by counsel.* Whenever service is required to be made upon a person represented by counsel who has filed a notice of appearance pursuant to Rule 102, service shall be made pursuant to paragraph (c) of this rule upon counsel, unless service upon the person represented is ordered by the Commission or the hearing officer.

(c) *How made.* Service shall be made electronically in the form and manner to be specified by the Office of the Secretary in the materials posted on the Commission's website. Persons serving each other shall have provided the Commission and the parties with notice of an email address.

(1) *Certification of inability to serve electronically.* If a person reasonably cannot serve electronically (due, for example, to a failure to have a functional email address or a lack of access to electronic transmission devices due to incarceration or otherwise), the person promptly shall file a certification under this paragraph that explains why the person reasonably cannot comply using any additional method of service listed in Rule 150(d). The filing also must indicate the expected duration of the person's reasonable inability to comply, such as whether the certification is intended to apply to a solitary instance of service or all instances of service made during the proceeding. The certification is immediately effective. Upon filing the certification, it will be part of the record of the proceeding, and the person may serve paper documents by any additional method listed in Rule 150(d).

(d) *Additional methods of service.* If a person reasonably cannot serve electronically, or if service is of an investigative subpoena pursuant to 17 CFR 203.8, service may be made by delivering a copy of the filing. *Delivery* means:

(1) Personal service—handing a copy to the person required to be served; or leaving a copy at the person's office with a clerk or other person in charge thereof, or, if there is no one in charge, leaving it in a conspicuous place therein; or, if the office is closed or the person to be served has no office, leaving it at the person's dwelling house or usual place of abode with some person of suitable age and discretion then residing therein;

(2) Mailing the papers through the U.S. Postal Service by first class, registered, or certified mail or Express Mail delivery addressed to the person;

(3) Sending the papers through a commercial courier service or express delivery service; or

(4) Transmitting the papers by facsimile transmission to the person required to be served.

The persons so serving each other shall have provided the Commission and the parties with notice of a facsimile machine telephone number.

(e) *When service is complete.* Electronic service is complete upon transmission, but is not effective if the sender learns that the transmission failed. Personal service, service by U.S. Postal Service express mail or service by a commercial courier or express delivery service is complete upon delivery. Service by mail is complete upon mailing. Service by facsimile is complete upon confirmation of transmission.

Rule 151.   Filing of Papers With the Commission: Procedure

(a) *When to file.* All papers required to be served upon any person shall also be filed contemporaneously with the Commission electronically pursuant to the requirements of Rule 152(a). The person making such filing is responsible for ensuring that the Commission receives a complete and legible filing within the time limit set for such filing. Documents that are attached to filings shall be filed in accordance with this section.

(b) *Where to file.* Filing of papers with the Commission shall be made by filing them with the Secretary. When a proceeding is assigned to a hearing officer, a person making a filing with the Secretary shall promptly provide to the hearing officer a copy of any such filing, provided, however, that the hearing officer may direct or permit filings to be made with him or her, in which event the hearing officer shall note thereon the filing date and promptly provide the Secretary with either the original or a copy of any such filings.

(c) *To whom to direct the filing.* Unless otherwise provided, where the Commission has assigned a case to a hearing officer, all motions, objections, applications or other filings made during a proceeding prior to the filing of an initial decision therein, or, if no initial decision is to be filed, prior to the time fixed for the filing of briefs with the Commission, shall be directed to and decided by the hearing officer.

(d) *Certificate of service.* Papers filed with the Commission or a hearing officer shall be accompanied by a certificate stating the name of the person or persons served, the date of service, the method of service, and the mailing address or email address to which service was made, if not made in person.

(e) *Sensitive personal information.* Sensitive personal information is defined as a Social Security number, taxpayer identification number, financial account number, credit card or debit card number, passport number, driver's license number, state-issued identification number, home address (other than city and state), telephone number, date of birth (other than year), names and initials of minor children, as well as any unnecessary health information identifiable by individual, such as an individual's medical records. Sensitive personal information shall not be included in, and must be redacted or omitted from, all filings subject to:

(1) *Exceptions.* The following information may be included and is not required to be redacted from filings:

(i) The last four digits of a financial account number, credit card or debit card number, passport number, driver's license number, and state-issued identification number;

(ii) Home addresses and telephone numbers of parties and persons filing documents with the Commission;

(iii) Business telephone numbers; and

(iv) Copies of unredacted filings by regulated entities or registrants that are available on the Commission's public website.

(2) *Confidential treatment of information.* If the person making any filing believes that sensitive personal information (as defined above) contained therein is necessary to the proceeding, the person shall file unredacted documents, along with a motion for a protective order with redacted documents, in accordance with § 201.322 to limit disclosure of unredacted sensitive personal information.

(3) *Certification.* Any filing must include a certification that any information described in paragraph (e) of this section has been omitted or redacted from the filing or, if necessary to the filing, has been filed under seal pursuant to Rule 322.

Rule 152.   Filing of Papers: Form

(a) *Electronic filing.* Papers filed in connection with any proceeding as defined in Rule 101(a) shall be filed electronically in the form and manner to be specified by the Office of the Secretary in the materials posted on the Commission's website. Papers filed electronically must be received by the Commission by midnight Eastern Time on the date the filing is due.

(1) *Certification of Inability to File Electronically.* If a person reasonably cannot comply with the requirements of this section, due to a lack of access to electronic transmission devices (due to incarceration or otherwise), the person promptly shall file a certification under this paragraph that explains why the person reasonably cannot comply using any additional method of filing listed in Rule 152(a)(2). The filing also must indicate the expected duration of the person's reasonable inability to comply, such as whether the certification is intended to apply to a solitary filing or all filings made during the proceeding. The certification is immediately effective. Upon filing the certification, it will be part of the record of the proceeding, and the person may file paper documents by any additional method listed in § 201.152(a)(2).

(2) *Additional methods of filing.* If a person reasonably cannot file electronically, filing may be made by hand delivering the filing by 5:30 p.m. Eastern Time through a commercial courier service or express delivery service; mailing the filing through the U.S. Postal Service by first class, certified, registered, or express mail delivery so that it is received by the Commission by 5:30 p.m. Eastern Time; or transmitting the filing by facsimile transmission so that it is received by the Commission by midnight Eastern Time.

(b) *Form.* Papers filed in connection with any proceeding as defined in Rule 101(a) shall:

(1) Reflect a page, electronically or otherwise, that measures 8 1/2 × 11 inches when printed, except that, to the extent that the reduction of larger documents would render them illegible when printed, such documents may be filed on larger paper;

(2) Use 12-point or larger typeface;

(3) Include at the head of the paper, or on a title page, the name of the Commission, the title of the proceeding, the names of the parties, the subject of the particular paper or pleading, and the file number assigned to the proceeding;

(4) Be paginated with left hand margins at least 1 inch wide, and other margins of at least 1 inch; and

(5) Be double-spaced, with single-spaced footnotes and single-spaced indented quotations.

(c) *Signature required.* All papers must be dated and signed as provided in Rule 153. Electronic filings that require a signature pursuant to Rule 153 may be signed with an "/s/" notation, but in that event, the use of the filer's log in and password to file a document shall be deemed the signature of the person making the filing for purposes of Rule 153.

(d) *Suitability for recordkeeping.* Documents which, in the opinion of the Office of the Secretary, are not suitable for computer scanning may be rejected.

(e) *Form of briefs.* All briefs containing more than 10 pages shall include a table of contents, an alphabetized table of cases, a table of statutes, and a table of other authorities cited, with references to the pages of the brief wherein they are cited.

(f) *Scandalous or impertinent matter.* Any scandalous or impertinent matter contained in any brief or pleading or in connection with any oral presentation in a proceeding may be stricken on order of the Commission or the hearing officer.

(g) [Reserved.]

Rule 153.   Filing of Papers: Signature Requirement and Effect

(a) *General requirements.* Following the issuance of an order instituting proceedings, every filing of a party represented by counsel shall be signed by at least one counsel of record in his or her name and shall state that counsel's business address and telephone number. A party who acts as his or her own counsel shall sign his or her individual name and state his or her address and telephone number on every filing.

(b) *Effect of signature.*

(1)   The signature of a counsel or party shall constitute a certification that:

(i)   The person signing the filing has read the filing;

(ii)   To the best of his or her knowledge, information, and belief, formed after reasonable inquiry, the filing is well grounded in fact and is warranted by existing law or a good faith argument for the extension, modification, or reversal of existing law; and

(iii)   The filing is not made for any improper purpose, such as to harass or to cause unnecessary delay or needless increase in the cost of adjudication.

(2)   If a filing is not signed, the hearing officer or the Commission shall strike the filing, unless it is signed promptly after the omission is called to the attention of the person making the filing.

Rule 154.   Motions

The requirements in this rule apply to motions and related filings except where another rule expressly governs.

(a)   *Generally.* Unless made during a hearing or conference, a motion shall be in writing, shall state with particularity the grounds therefor, shall set forth the relief or order sought, and shall be accompanied by a written brief of the points and authorities relied upon. All written motions shall be served in accordance with Rule 150, be filed in accordance with Rule 151, meet the requirements of Rule 152, and be signed in accordance with Rule 153. The Commission or the hearing officer may order that an oral motion be submitted in writing. Unless otherwise ordered by the Commission or the hearing officer, if a motion is properly made to the Commission concerning a proceeding to which a hearing officer is assigned, the proceeding before the hearing officer shall continue pending the determination of the motion by the Commission. No oral argument shall be heard on any motion unless the Commission or the hearing officer otherwise directs.

(b)   *Opposing and reply briefs.* Briefs in opposition to a motion shall be filed within five days after service of the motion. Reply briefs shall be filed within three days after service of the opposition.

(c)   *Length limitation.* No motion (together with the brief in support of the motion), brief in opposition to the motion, or reply brief shall exceed 7,000 words, exclusive of any table of contents or table of authorities. The word limit shall not apply to any addendum that consists solely of copies of applicable cases, pertinent legislative provisions or rules, or relevant exhibits. Requests for leave to file motions and briefs in excess of 7,000 words are disfavored. A motion or brief, together with any accompanying brief, that does not exceed 15 pages in length, exclusive of pages containing the table of contents, table of authorities, and any addendum that consists solely of copies of applicable cases, pertinent legislative provisions, or rules and exhibits, but inclusive of pleadings incorporated by reference, is presumptively considered to contain no more than 7,000 words. Any motion or brief that exceeds these page limits must include a certificate by the attorney, or an unrepresented party, stating that the document complies with the length limitation set forth in this paragraph and stating the number of words in the document. The person preparing the certificate may rely on the word count of a word-processing program to prepare the document.

Rule 155.   Default; Motion to Set Aside Default

(a)   A party to a proceeding may be deemed to be in default and the Commission or the hearing officer may determine the proceeding against that party upon consideration of the record, including the order instituting proceedings, the allegations of which may be deemed to be true, if that party fails:

(1)   To appear, in person or through a representative, at a hearing or conference of which that party has been notified;

(2)   To answer, to respond to a dispositive motion within the time provided, or otherwise to defend the proceeding; or

(3)   To cure a deficient filing within the time specified by the commission or the hearing officer pursuant to Rule 180(b).

(b)   A motion to set aside a default shall be made within a reasonable time, state the reasons for the failure to appear or defend, and specify the nature of the proposed defense in the proceeding. In order to prevent injustice and on such conditions as may be appropriate, the hearing officer, at any time prior to the filing of the initial decision, or the Commission, at any time, may for good cause shown set aside a default.

Rule 160.   Time Computation

(a)   *Computation.* In computing any period of time prescribed in or allowed by these Rules of Practice or by order of the Commission, the day of the act, event, or default from which the designated period of time begins to run shall not be included. The last day of the period so computed shall be included unless it is a Saturday, Sunday, or Federal legal holiday (as defined in Rule 104), in which event the period runs until the end of the next day that is not a Saturday, Sunday, or Federal legal holiday. Intermediate Saturdays, Sundays, and Federal legal holidays shall be excluded from the computation when the period of time prescribed or allowed is seven days or less, not including any additional time allowed for service by mail in paragraph (b) of this rule. If on the day a filing is to be made, weather or other conditions have caused the Secretary's office or other designated filing location to close, the filing deadline shall be extended to the end of the next day that is neither a Saturday, a Sunday, nor a Federal legal holiday.

(b)   *Additional time for service by mail.* If service is made by mail, three days shall be added to the prescribed period for response unless an order of the Commission or the hearing officer specifies a date certain for filing. In the event that an order of the Commission or the hearing officer specifies a date certain for filing, no time shall be added for service by mail.

Rule 161.   Extensions of Time, Postponements and Adjournments

(a)   *Availability.* Except as otherwise provided by law, the Commission, at any time, or the hearing officer, at any time prior to the filing of his or her initial decision or, if no initial decision is to be filed, at any time prior to the closing of the record, may, for good cause shown, extend or shorten any time limits prescribed by these Rules of Practice for the filing of any papers and may, consistent with paragraphs (b) and (c) of this rule, postpone or adjourn any hearing.

(b)   *Considerations in Determining Whether to Extend Time Limits or Grant Postponements, Adjournments and Extensions.*

(1)   In considering all motions or requests pursuant to paragraph (a) or (b) of this rule, the Commission or the hearing officer should adhere to a policy of strongly disfavoring such requests, except in circumstances where the requesting party makes a strong showing that the denial of the request or motion would substantially prejudice their case. In determining whether to grant any requests, the Commission or hearing officer shall consider, in addition to any other relevant factors:

(i)   The length of the proceeding to date;

(ii)   The number of postponements, adjournments or extensions already granted;

(iii)   The stage of the proceedings at the time of the request;

(iv)   The impact of the request on the hearing officer's ability to complete the proceeding in the time specified by the Commission; and

(v)   Any other such matters as justice may require.

(2)   To the extent that the Commission has chosen a timeline under which the hearing would occur beyond the statutory 60-day deadline, this policy of strongly disfavoring requests for postponement will not apply to a request by a respondent to postpone commencement of a cease and desist proceeding hearing beyond the statutory 60-day period.

(c)(1)   *Time Limit.* Postponements, adjournments or extensions of time for filing papers shall not exceed 21 days unless the Commission or the hearing officer states on the record or sets forth in a written order the reasons why a longer period of time is necessary.

(2)   *Stay Pending Commission Consideration of Offers of Settlement.* (i) If the Commission staff and one or more respondents in the proceeding file a joint motion notifying the hearing officer that

they have agreed in principle to a settlement on all major terms, then the hearing officer shall stay the proceeding as to the settling respondent(s), or in the discretion of the hearing officer as to all respondents, pending completion of Commission consideration of the settlement offer. Any such stay will be contingent upon:

    (A)   The settling respondent(s) submitting to the Commission staff, within fifteen business days of the stay, a signed offer of settlement in conformance with Rule 240 of the Rules of Practice; and

    (B)   Within twenty business days of receipt of the signed offer, the staff submitting the settlement offer and accompanying recommendation to the Commission for consideration.

    (ii)   If the parties fail to meet either of these deadlines or if the Commission rejects the offer of settlement, the hearing officer must be promptly notified and, upon notification of the hearing officer, the stay shall lapse and the proceeding will continue. In the circumstance where:

    (A)   A hearing officer has granted a stay because the parties have "agreed in principle to a settlement;"

    (B)   The agreement in principle does not materialize into a signed settlement offer within 15 business days of the stay; and

    (C)   The stay lapses, the hearing officer will not be required to grant another stay related to the settlement process until both parties have notified the hearing officer in writing that a signed settlement offer has been prepared, received by the Commission's staff, and will be submitted to the Commission.

    (iii)   The granting of any stay pursuant to this paragraph (c) shall stay the timeline pursuant to Rule 360(a) of the Rules of Practice.

Rule 180.   Sanctions

(a)   *Contemptuous Conduct.*

    (1)   *Subject to exclusion or suspension.* Contemptuous conduct by any person before the Commission or a hearing officer during any proceeding, including at or in connection with any conference, deposition or hearing, shall be grounds for the Commission or the hearing officer to:

    (i)   Exclude that person from such deposition, hearing or conference, or any portion thereof; and/or

    (ii)   Summarily suspend that person from representing others in the proceeding in which such conduct occurred for the duration, or any portion, of the proceeding.

    (2)   *Review procedure.* A person excluded from a deposition, hearing or conference, or a counsel summarily suspended from practice for the duration or any portion of a proceeding, may seek review of the exclusion or suspension by filing with the Commission, within three days of the exclusion or suspension order, a motion to vacate the order. The Commission shall consider such motion on an expedited basis as provided in Rule 500.

    (3)   *Adjournment.* Upon motion by a party represented by counsel subject to an order of exclusion or suspension, an adjournment shall be granted to allow the retention of new counsel. In determining the length of an adjournment, the Commission or hearing officer shall consider, in addition to the factors set forth in Rule 161, the availability of co-counsel for the party or of other members of a suspended counsel's firm.

(b)   *Deficient Filings; Leave to Cure Deficiencies.* The Commission or the hearing officer may reject, in whole or in part, any filing that fails to comply with any requirements of these Rules of Practice or of any order issued in the proceeding in which the filing was made. Any such filings shall not be part of the record. The Commission or the hearing officer may direct a party to cure any deficiencies and to resubmit the filing within a fixed time period.

(c)   *Failure to make required filing or to cure deficient filing.* The Commission or the hearing officer may enter a default pursuant to Rule 155, dismiss one or more claims, decide the particular claim(s) at issue against that person, or prohibit the introduction of evidence or exclude testimony concerning that claim if a person fails:

    (1)   To make a filing required under these Rules of Practice; or

    (2)   To cure a deficient filing within the time specified by the Commission or the hearing officer pursuant to paragraph (b) of this rule.

Rule 190.   Confidential Treatment of Information in Certain Filings

    (a)   *Application.* An application for confidential treatment pursuant to the provisions of Clause 30 of Schedule A of the Securities Act of 1933, and Rule 406 thereunder, section 24(b)(2) of the Securities Exchange Act of 1934, and Rule 24b–2 thereunder, and Rule 104 thereunder, section 45(a) of the Investment Company Act of 1940, and Rule 45a–1 thereunder, or section 210(a) of the Investment Advisers Act of 1940, shall be filed with the Secretary. The application shall be accompanied by a sealed copy of the materials as to which confidential treatment is sought.

    (b)   *Procedure for Supplying Additional Information.* The applicant may be required to furnish in writing additional information with respect to the grounds for objection to public disclosure. Failure to supply the information so requested within 14 days from the date of receipt by the applicant of a notice of the information required shall be deemed a waiver of the objection to public disclosure of that portion of the information to which the additional information relates, unless the Commission or the hearing officer shall otherwise order for good cause shown at or before the expiration of such 14-day period.

    (c)   *Confidentiality of Materials Pending Final Decision.* Pending the determination of the application for confidential treatment, transcripts, non-final orders including an initial decision, if any, and other materials in connection with the application shall be placed under seal; shall be for the confidential use only of the hearing officer, the Commission, the applicant, and any other parties and counsel; and shall be made available to the public only in accordance with orders of the Commission.

    (d)   *Public Availability of Orders.* Any final order of the Commission denying or sustaining an application for confidential treatment shall be made public. Any prior findings or opinions relating to an application for confidential treatment under this rule shall be made public at such time as the material as to which confidentiality was requested is made public.

Rule 191.   Adjudications Not Required to Be Determined on the Record After Notice and Opportunity for Hearing

    (a)   *Scope of the Rule.* This rule applies to every case of adjudication, as defined in 5 U.S.C.A. section 551, pursuant to any statute which the Commission administers, where adjudication is not required to be determined on the record after notice and opportunity for hearing and which the Commission has not chosen to determine on the record after notice and opportunity for hearing.

    (b)   *Procedure.* In every case of adjudication under paragraph (a) of this rule, the Commission shall give prompt notice of any adverse action or final disposition to any person who has requested the Commission to make (or not to make) any such adjudication, and furnish to any such person a written statement of reasons therefor. Additional procedures may be specified in rules relating to specific types of such adjudications. Where any such rule provides for the publication of a Commission order, notice of the action or disposition shall be deemed to be given by such publication.

    (c)   *Contents of the Record.* If the Commission provides notice and opportunity for the submission of written comments by parties to the adjudication or, as the case may be, by other interested persons, written comments received on or before the closing date for comments, unless accorded confidential treatment pursuant to statute or rule of the Commission, become a part of the record of the adjudication. The Commission, in its discretion, may accept and include in the record written comments filed with the Commission after the closing date.

Rule 192.   Rulemaking: Issuance, Amendment and Repeal of Rules of General Application

(a)   *By Petition.* Any person desiring the issuance, amendment or repeal of a rule of general application may file a petition therefor with the Secretary. Such petition shall include a statement setting forth the text or the substance of any proposed rule or amendment desired or specifying the rule the repeal of which is desired, and stating the nature of his or her interest and his or her reasons for seeking the issuance, amendment or repeal of the rule. The Secretary shall acknowledge, in writing, receipt of the petition and refer it to the appropriate division or office for consideration and recommendation. Such recommendations shall be transmitted with the petition to the Commission for such action as the Commission deems appropriate. The Secretary shall notify the petitioner of the action taken by the Commission.

(b)   *Notice of Proposed Issuance, Amendment or Repeal of Rules.* Except where the Commission finds that notice and public procedure are impracticable, unnecessary, or contrary to the public interest, whenever the Commission proposes to issue, amend, or repeal any rule or regulation of general application other than an interpretive rule; general statement of policy; or rule of agency organization, procedure, or practice; or any matter relating to agency management or personnel or to public property, loans, grants, benefits, or contracts, there shall first be published in the *Federal Register* a notice of the proposed action. Such notice shall include:

(1)   A statement of the time, place, and nature of the rulemaking proceeding, with particular reference to the manner in which interested persons shall be afforded the opportunity to participate in such proceeding;

(2)   Reference to the authority under which the rule is proposed; and

(3)   The terms or substance of the proposed rule or a description of the subjects and issues involved.

Rule 193.   Applications by Barred Individuals for Consent to Associate

(a)   *Preliminary note.* This section governs applications to the Commission bycertain persons, barred by Commission order from association with brokers, dealers, municipal securities dealers, government securities brokers, government securities dealers, investment advisers, investment companies or transfer agents, for consent to become so associated. Applications made pursuant to this section must show that the proposed association would be consistent with the public interest. In addition to the information specifically required by the section, applications should be supplemented, where appropriate, by written statements of individuals (other than the applicant) who are competent to attest to the applicant's character, employment performance, and other relevant information. Intentional misstatements or omissions of fact may constitute criminal violations of 18 U.S.C. 1001 *et seq.* and other provisions of law.

(1)   The nature of the supervision that an applicant will receive or exercise as an associated person with a registered entity is an important matter bearing upon the public interest. In meeting the burden of showing that the proposed association is consistent with the public interest, the application and supporting documentation must demonstrate that the proposed supervision, procedures, or terms and conditions of employment are reasonably designed to prevent a recurrence of the conduct that led to imposition of the bar. As an associated person, the applicant will be limited to association in a specified capacity with a particular registered entity and may also be subject to specific terms and conditions.

(2)   Normally, the applicant's burden of demonstrating that the proposed association is consistent with the public interest will be difficult to meet where the applicant is to be supervised by, or is to supervise, another barred individual. In addition, where an applicant wishes to become the sole proprietor of a registered entity and thus is seeking Commission consent notwithstanding an absence of supervision, the applicant's burden will be difficult to meet.

(3)   In addition to the factors set forth in paragraph (d) of this section, the Commission will consider the nature of the findings that resulted in the bar when making its determination as to whether the proposed association is consistent with the public interest. In this regard, attention is

directed to Rule 201.5(e) of the Commission's Rules on Informal and Other Procedures, Rule 201.5(e). Among other things, Rule 201.5(e) sets forth the Commission's policy "not to permit a * * * respondent [in an administrative proceeding] to consent to * * * [an] order that imposes a sanction while denying the allegations in the * * * order for proceedings." Consistent with the rationale underlying that policy, and in order to avoid the appearance that an application made pursuant to this section was granted on the basis of such denial, the Commission will not consider any application that attempts to reargue or collaterally attack the findings that resulted in the Commission's bar order.

(b)   *Scope of Rule.* Applications for Commission consent to associate, or to change the terms and conditions of association, with a registered broker, dealer, municipal securities dealer, government securities broker, government securities dealer, investment adviser, investment company or transfer agent may be made pursuant to this rule where a Commission order bars the individual from association with a registered entity and:

(1)   Such barred individual seeks to become associated with an entity that is not a member of a self-regulatory organization; or

(2)   The order contains a proviso that application may be made to the Commission after a specified period of time.

(c)   *Form of Application.* Each application shall be supported by an affidavit, signed by the applicant, that addresses the factors set forth in paragraph (d) of this section. The application shall be filed pursuant to §§ 201.151, 152 and 153. Each application shall include as exhibits:

(1)   A copy of the Commission order imposing the bar;

(2)   An undertaking by the applicant to notify immediately the Commission in writing if any information submitted in support of the application becomes materially false or misleading while the application is pending;

(3)   The following forms, as appropriate:

(i)   A copy of a completed Form U–4, where the applicant's proposed association is with a broker-dealer or municipal securities dealer;

(ii)   A copy of a completed Form MSD–4, where the applicant's proposed association is with a bank municipal securities dealer;

(iii)   The information required by Form ADV with respect to the applicant, where the applicant's proposed association is with an investment adviser;

(iv)   The information required by Form TA–1 with respect to the applicant, where the applicant's proposed association is with a transfer agent; and

(4)   A written statement by the proposed employer that describes:

(i)   The terms and conditions of employment and supervision to be exercised over such applicant and, where applicable, by such applicant;

(ii)   The qualifications, experience, and disciplinary records of the proposed supervisor(s) of the applicant;

(iii)   The compliance and disciplinary history, during the two years preceding the filing of the application, of the office in which the applicant will be employed; and

(iv)   The names of any other associated persons in the same office who have previously been barred by the Commission, and whether they are to be supervised by the applicant.

(d)   *Required Showing.* The applicant shall make a showing satisfactory to the Commission that the proposed association would be consistent with the public interest.

(e)   *Factors to Be Addressed.* The affidavit required by paragraph (b) of this rule shall address each of the following:

(1)   The time period since the imposition of the bar;

(2) Any restitution or similar action taken by the applicant to recompense any person injured by the misconduct that resulted in the bar;

(3) The applicant's compliance with the order imposing the bar;

(4) The applicant's employment during the period subsequent to imposition of the bar;

(5) The capacity or position in which the applicant proposes to be associated;

(6) The manner and extent of supervision to be exercised over such applicant and, where applicable, by such applicant;

(7) Any relevant courses, seminars, examinations or other actions completed by the applicant subsequent to imposition of the bar to prepare for his or her return to the securities business; and

(8) Any other information material to the application.

(f) *Notification to Applicant and Written Statement.* In the event an adverse recommendation is proposed by the staff with respect to an application made pursuant to this rule, the applicant shall be so advised and provided with a written statement of the reasons for such recommendation. The applicant shall then have 30 days to submit a written statement in response.

(g) *Concurrent Applications.* The Commission will not consider any application submitted pursuant to this rule if any other application for consent to associate concerning the same applicant is pending before any self-regulatory organization.

INITIATION OF PROCEEDINGS AND PREHEARING RULES

Rule 200.   Initiation of Proceedings

(a) *Order Instituting Proceedings; Notice and Opportunity for Hearing.*

(1) *Generally.* Whenever an order instituting proceedings is issued by the Commission, appropriate notice thereof shall be given to each party to the proceeding by the Secretary or another duly designated officer of the Commission. Each party shall be given notice of any hearing within a time reasonable in light of the circumstances, in advance of the hearing; provided, however, no prior notice need be given to a respondent if the Commission has authorized the Division of Enforcement to seek a temporary sanction *ex parte.*

(2) *Stop Order Proceedings: Additional Persons Entitled to Notice.* Any notice of a proceeding relating to the issuance of a stop order suspending the effectiveness of a registration statement pursuant to section 8(d) of the Securities Act of 1933, shall be sent to or served on the issuer; or, in the case of a foreign government or political subdivision thereof, sent to or served on the underwriter; or, in the case of a foreign or territorial person, sent to or served on its duly authorized representative in the United States named in the registration statement, properly directed in the case of telegraphic notice to the address given in such statement. In addition, if such proceeding is commenced within 90 days after the registration statement has become effective, notice of the proceeding shall be given to the agent for service named on the facing sheet of the registration statement and to each other person designated on the facing sheet of the registration statement as a person to whom copies of communications to such agent are to be sent.

(b) *Content of Order.* The order instituting proceedings shall:

(1) State the nature of any hearing;

(2) State the legal authority and jurisdiction under which the hearing is to be held;

(3) Contain a short and plain statement of the matters of fact and law to be considered and determined, unless the order directs an answer pursuant to Rule 220 in which case the order shall set forth the factual and legal basis alleged therefor in such detail as will permit a specific response thereto; and

(4) State the nature of any relief or action sought or taken.

(c)   *Time and Place of Hearing.* The time and place for any hearing shall be fixed with due regard for the public interest and the convenience and necessity of the parties, other participants, or their representatives.

(d)   *Amendment to Order Instituting Proceedings.*

(1)   *By the Commission.* Upon motion by a party, the Commission may, at any time, amend an order instituting proceedings to include new matters of fact or law.

(2)   *By the Hearing Officer.* Upon motion by a party, the hearing officer may, at any time prior to the filing of an initial decision or, if no initial decision is to be filed, prior to the time fixed for the filing of final briefs with the Commission, amend and order instituting proceedings to include new matters of fact or law that are within the scope of the original order instituting proceedings.

(e)   *Publication of Notice of Public Hearings.* Unless otherwise ordered by the Commission, notice of any public hearing shall be given general circulation by release to the public, by publication in the *SEC News Digest* and, where directed, by publication in the *Federal Register*.

Rule 201.   Consolidation and Severance of Proceedings

(a)   *Consolidation.* By order of the Commission or a hearing officer, proceedings involving a common question of law or fact may be consolidated for hearing of any or all the matters at issue in such proceedings. The Commission or the hearing officer may make such orders concerning the conduct of such proceedings as it deems appropriate to avoid unnecessary cost or delay. Consolidation shall not prejudice any rights under these Rules of Practice and shall not affect the right of any party to raise issues that could have been raised if consolidation had not occurred. For purposes of this rule, no distinction is made between joinder and consolidation of proceedings.

(b)   *Severance.* By order of the Commission, any proceeding may be severed with respect to one or more parties. Any motion to sever must be made solely to the Commission and must include a representation that a settlement offer is pending before the Commission or otherwise show good cause.

Rule 202.   Specification of Procedures by Parties in Certain Proceedings

(a)   *Motion to Specify Procedures.* In any proceeding other than an enforcement or disciplinary proceeding, a proceeding to review a determination by a self-regulatory organization pursuant to Rule 420 and Rule 421, or a proceeding to review a determination of the Board pursuant to Rule 440 and Rule 441, a party may, at any time up to 20 days prior to the start of a hearing, make a motion to specify the procedures necessary or appropriate for the proceeding with particular reference to:

(1)   Whether there should be an initial decision by a hearing officer;

(2)   Whether any interested division of the Commission may assist in the preparation of the Commission's decision; and

(3)   Whether there should be a 30-day waiting period between the issuance of the Commission's order and the date it is to become effective.

(b)   *Objections: Effect of Failure to Object.* Any other party may object to the procedures so specified, and such party may specify such additional procedures as it considers necessary or appropriate. In the absence of such objection or such specification of additional procedures, such other party may be deemed to have waived objection to the specified procedures.

(c)   *Approval Required.* Any proposal pursuant to paragraph (a) of this rule, even if not objected to by any party, shall be subject to the written approval of the hearing officer.

(d)   *Procedure Upon Agreement to Waive an Initial Decision.* If an initial decision is waived pursuant to paragraph (a) of this rule, the hearing officer shall notify the Secretary and, unless the Commission directs otherwise within 14 days, no initial decision shall be issued.

Rule 210.   Parties, Limited Participants and Amici Curiae

(a) *Parties in an Enforcement or Disciplinary Proceeding, a Proceeding to Review a Self-Regulatory Organization Determination, or a Proceeding to Review a Board Determination.*

(1) *Generally.* No person shall be granted leave to become a party or a non-party participant on a limited basis in an enforcement or disciplinary proceeding, a proceeding to review a determination by a self-regulatory organization pursuant to Rule 420 and Rule 421, or a proceeding to review a determination by the Board pursuant to Rule 440 and Rule 441, except as authorized by paragraph (c) of this rule.

(2) *Disgorgement Proceedings.* In an enforcement proceeding, a person may state his or her views with respect to a proposed plan of disgorgement or file a proof of claim pursuant to Rule 1103.

(b) *Intervention as a Party.*

(1) *Generally.* In any proceeding, other than an enforcement proceeding, a disciplinary proceeding, a proceeding to review a self-regulatory determination, or a proceeding to review a Board determination, any person may seek leave to intervene as a party by filing a motion setting forth the person's interest in the proceeding. No person, however, shall be admitted as a party to a proceeding by intervention unless it is determined that leave to participate pursuant to paragraph (c) of this rule would be inadequate for the protection of the person's interests. In a proceeding under the Investment Company Act of 1940, any representative of interested security holders, or any other person whose participation in the proceeding may be in the public interest or for the protection of investors, may be admitted as a party upon the filing of a written motion setting forth the person's interest in the proceeding.

(2) *Intervention as of Right.* In proceedings under the Investment Company Act of 1940, any interested State or State agency shall be admitted as a party to any proceeding upon the filing of a written motion requesting leave to be admitted.

(c) *Leave to Participate on a Limited Basis.* In any proceeding, other than an enforcement proceeding, a disciplinary proceeding, a proceeding to review a self-regulatory determination, or a proceeding to review a Board determination, any person may seek leave to participate on a limited basis as a non-party participant as to any matter affecting the person's interests:

(1) *Procedure.* Motions for leave to participate shall be in writing, shall set forth the nature and extent of the movant's interest in the proceeding, and, except where good cause for late filing is shown, shall be filed not later than 20 days prior to the date fixed for the commencement of the hearing. Leave to participate pursuant to this paragraph (c) may include such rights of a party as the hearing officer may deem appropriate. Persons granted leave to participate shall be served in accordance with Rule 150; provided, however, that a party to the proceeding may move that the extent of notice of filings or other papers to be provided to persons granted leave to participate be limited, or may move that the persons granted leave to participate bear the cost of being provided copies of any or all filings or other papers. Persons granted leave to participate shall be bound, except as may be otherwise determined by the hearing officer, by any stipulation between the parties to the proceeding with respect to procedure, including submission of evidence, substitution of exhibits, corrections of the record, the time within which briefs or exceptions may be filed or proposed findings and conclusions may be submitted, the filing of initial decisions, the procedure to be followed in the preparation of decisions and the effective date of the Commission's order in the case. Where the filing of briefs or exceptions or the submission of proposed findings and conclusions are waived by the parties to the proceedings, a person granted leave to participate pursuant to this paragraph (c) shall not be permitted to file a brief or exceptions or submit proposed findings and conclusions except by leave of the Commission or of the hearing officer.

(2) *Certain Persons Entitled to Leave to Participate.* The hearing officer is directed to grant leave to participate under this paragraph (c) to any person to whom it is proposed to issue any security in exchange for one or more bona fide outstanding securities, claims or property interests, or partly in such exchange and partly for cash, where the Commission is authorized to approve the terms and

conditions of such issuance and exchange after a hearing upon the fairness of such terms and conditions.

(3)   Leave to participate in certain Commission proceedings by a representative of the United States Department of Justice, a United States Attorney's Office, or a criminal prosecutorial authority of any State or any other political subdivision of a State. The Commission or the hearing officer may grant leave to participate on a limited basis to an authorized representative of the United States Department of Justice, an authorized representative of a United States Attorney, or an authorized representative of any criminal prosecutorial authority of any State or any other political subdivision of a State for the purpose of requesting a stay during the pendency of a criminal investigation or prosecution arising out of the same or similar facts that are at issue in the pending Commission enforcement or disciplinary proceeding. Upon a showing that such a stay is in the public interest or for the protection of investors, the motion for stay shall be favored. A stay granted under this paragraph (c)(3) may be granted for such a period and upon such conditions as the Commission or the hearing officer deems appropriate.

(d)   *Amicus Participation.*

(1)   *Availability.* An amicus brief may be filed only if:

(i)   A motion for leave to file the brief has been granted;

(ii)   The brief is accompanied by written consent of all parties;

(iii)   The brief is filed at the request of the Commission or the hearing officer; or

(iv)   The brief is presented by the United States or an officer or agency thereof, or by a State, Territory or Commonwealth.

(2)   *Procedure.* An amicus brief may be filed conditionally with the motion for leave. The motion for leave shall identify the interest of the movant and shall state the reasons why a brief of an amicus curiae is desirable. Except as all parties otherwise consent, any amicus curiae shall file its brief within the time allowed the party whose position the amicus will support, unless the Commission or hearing officer, for cause shown, grants leave for a later filing. In the event that a later filing is allowed, the order granting leave to file shall specify when an opposing party may reply to the brief. A motion of an amicus curiae to participate in oral argument will be granted only for extraordinary reasons.

(e)   *Permission to State Views.* Any person may make a motion seeking leave to file a memorandum or make an oral statement of his or her views. Any such communication may be included in the record; provided, however, that unless offered and admitted as evidence of the truth of the statements therein made, any assertions of fact submitted pursuant to the provisions of this paragraph (e) will be considered only to the extent that the statements therein made are otherwise supported by the record.

(f)   *Modification of Participation Provisions.* The Commission or the hearing officer may, by order, modify the provisions of this rule which would otherwise be applicable, and may impose such terms and conditions on the participation of any person in any proceeding as it may deem necessary or appropriate in the public interest.

Rule 220.   **Answer to Allegations**

(a)   *When required.* In its order instituting proceedings, the Commission may require any respondent to file an answer to each of the allegations contained therein. Even if not so ordered, any respondent in any proceeding may elect to file an answer. Any other person granted leave by the Commission or the hearing officer to participate on a limited basis in such proceedings pursuant to Rule 210(c) may be required to file an answer.

(b)   *When to file.* Except where a different period is provided by rule or by order, a respondent required to file an answer as provided in paragraph (a) of this Rule shall do so within 20 days after service upon the respondent of the order instituting proceedings. Persons granted leave to participate on a limited basis in the proceeding pursuant to Rule 210(c) may file an answer within a reasonable time, as determined by the Commission or the hearing officer. If the order instituting proceedings is amended, the Commission or the hearing officer may require that an amended answer be filed and, if such an answer is required, shall specify a date for the filing thereof.

(c)   *Contents; effect of failure to deny.* Unless otherwise directed by the hearing officer or the Commission, an answer shall specifically admit, deny, or state that the party does not have, and is unable to obtain, sufficient information to admit or deny each allegation in the order instituting proceedings. When a party intends in good faith to deny only a part of an allegation, the party shall specify so much of it as is true and shall deny only the remainder. A statement of a lack of information shall have the effect of a denial. Any allegation not denied shall be deemed admitted. A respondent must affirmatively state in the answer any avoidance or affirmative defense, including but not limited to res judicata and statute of limitations. In this regard, a respondent must state in the answer whether the respondent relied on the advice of counsel, accountants, auditors, or other professionals in connection with any claim, violation alleged or remedy sought. Failure to do so may be deemed a waiver.

(d)   *Motion for more definite statement.* A respondent may file with an answer a motion for a more definite statement of specified matters of fact or law to be considered or determined. Such motion shall state the respects in which, and the reasons why, each such matter of fact or law should be required to be made more definite. If the motion is granted, the order granting such motion shall set the periods for filing such a statement and any answer thereto.

(e)   *Amendments.* A respondent may amend its answer at any time by written consent of each adverse party or with leave of the Commission or the hearing officer. Leave shall be freely granted when justice so requires.

(f)   *Failure to file answer: default.* If a respondent fails to file an answer required by this Rule within the time provided, such respondent may be deemed in default pursuant to Rule 155(a). A party may make a motion to set aside a default pursuant to Rule 155(b).

Rule 221.   Prehearing Conferences

(a)   *Purposes of Conference.* The purposes of a prehearing conference include, but are not limited to:

(1)   Expediting the disposition of the proceeding;

(2)   Establishing early and continuing control of the proceeding by the hearing officer; and

(3)   Improving the quality of the hearing through more thorough preparation.

(b)   *Procedure.* On his or her own motion or at the request of a party, the hearing officer may, in his or her discretion, direct counsel or any party to meet for an initial, final or other prehearing conference. Such conferences may be held with or without the hearing officer present as the hearing officer deems appropriate. Where such a conference is held outside the presence of the hearing officer, the hearing officer shall be advised promptly by the parties of any agreements reached. Such conferences also may be held with one or more persons participating by telephone or other remote means.

(c)   *Subjects to be discussed.* At a prehearing conference consideration may be given and action taken with respect to any and all of the following:

(1)   Simplification and clarification of the issues;

(2)   Exchange of witness and exhibit lists and copies of exhibits;

(3)   Timing of expert witness disclosures and reports, if any;

(4)   Stipulations, admissions of fact, and stipulations concerning the contents, authenticity, or admissibility into evidence of documents;

(5)   Matters of which official notice may be taken;

(6)   The schedule for exchanging prehearing motions or briefs, if any;

(7)   The method of service for papers other than Commission orders;

(8)   The filing of any motion pursuant to Rule 250;

(9)   Settlement of any or all issues;

(10) Determination of hearing dates;

(11) Amendments to the order instituting proceedings or answers thereto;

(12) Production, and timing for completion of the production, of documents as set forth in Rule 230, and prehearing production of documents in response to subpoenas duces tecum as set forth in Rule 232;

(13) Specification of procedures as set forth in Rule 202;

(14) Depositions to be conducted, if any, and date by which depositions shall be completed; and

(15) Such other matters as may aid in the orderly and expeditious disposition of the proceeding.

(d) *Required Prehearing Conference.* Except where the emergency nature of a proceeding would make a prehearing conference clearly inappropriate, at least one prehearing conference should be held.

(e) *Prehearing Orders.* At or following the conclusion of any conference held pursuant to this rule, the hearing officer shall enter a ruling or order which recites the agreements reached and any procedural determinations made by the hearing officer.

(f) *Failure to Appear: Default.* Any person who is named in an order instituting proceedings as a person against whom findings may be made or sanctions imposed and who fails to appear, in person or through a representative, at a prehearing conference of which he or she has been duly notified may be deemed in default pursuant to Rule 155(a). A party may make a motion to set aside a default pursuant to Rule 155(b).

Rule 222.   Prehearing Submissions and Disclosures

(a) *Submissions Generally.* The hearing officer, on his or her own motion, or at the request of a party or other participant, may order any party, including the interested division, to furnish such information as deemed appropriate, including any or all of the following:

(1) An outline or narrative summary of its case or defense;

(2) The legal theories upon which it will rely;

(3) Copies and a list of documents that it intends to introduce at the hearing; and

(4) A list of witnesses who will testify on its behalf, including the witnesses' names, occupations, addresses and a brief summary of their expected testimony.

(b) *Expert witnesses—(1) Information to be supplied; reports.* Each party who intends to call an expert witness shall submit, in addition to the information required by paragraph (a)(4) of this Rule, a statement of the expert's qualifications, a listing of other proceedings in which the expert has given expert testimony during the previous four years, and a list of publications authored or co-authored by the expert in the previous ten years. Additionally, if the witness is one retained or specially employed to provide expert testimony in the case or one whose duties as the party's employee regularly involve giving expert testimony, then the party must include in the disclosure a written report—prepared and signed by the witness. The report must contain:

(i) A complete statement of all opinions the witness will express and the basis and reasons for them;

(ii) The facts or data considered by the witness in forming them;

(iii) Any exhibits that will be used to summarize or support them; and

(iv) A statement of the compensation to be paid for the study and testimony in the case.

(2) *Drafts and communications protected.* (i) Drafts of any report or other disclosure required under this Rule need not be furnished regardless of the form in which the draft is recorded.

(ii) Communications between a party's attorney and the party's expert witness who is required to provide a report under this Rule need not be furnished regardless of the form of the communications, except if the communications relate to compensation for the expert's study or testimony, identify facts or data that the party's attorney provided and that the expert considered in forming the opinions to be expressed, or identify assumptions that the party's attorney provided and that the expert relied on in forming the opinions to be expressed.

Rule 230.   Enforcement and Disciplinary Proceedings: Availability of Documents for Inspection and Copying

For purposes of this rule, the term *documents* shall include writings, drawings, graphs, charts, photographs, recordings and other data compilations, including data stored by computer, from which information can be obtained.

(a)   *Documents to be Available for Inspection and Copying.*

(1)   Unless otherwise provided by this rule, or by order of the Commission or the hearing officer, the Division of Enforcement shall make available for inspection and copying by any party documents obtained by the Division prior to the institution of proceedings, in connection with the investigation leading to the Division's recommendation to institute proceedings. Such documents shall include:

(i)   Each subpoena issued;

(ii)   Every other written request to persons not employed by the Commission to provide documents or to be interviewed;

(iii)   The documents turned over in response to any such subpoenas or other written requests;

(iv)   All transcripts and transcript exhibits;

(v)   Any other documents obtained from persons not employed by the Commission; and

(vi)   Any final examination or inspection reports prepared by the Office of Compliance Inspections and Examinations, the Division of Trading and Markets, or the Division of Investment Management, if the Division of Enforcement intends either to introduce any such report into evidence or to use any such report to refresh the recollection of any witness.

(2)   Nothing in this paragraph (a) shall limit the right of the Division to make available any other document, or shall limit the right of a respondent to seek access to or production pursuant to subpoena of any other document, or shall limit the authority of the hearing officer to order the production of any document pursuant to subpoena.

(b)   *Documents that may be withheld or redacted.*

(1)   The Division of Enforcement may withhold a document if:

(i)   The document is privileged;

(ii)   The document is an internal memorandum, note or writing prepared by a Commission employee, other than an examination or inspection report as specified in paragraph (a)(1)(vi) of this rule, or is otherwise attorney work product and will not be offered in evidence;

(iii)   The document would disclose the identity of a confidential source;

(iv)   The document reflects only settlement negotiations between the Division of Enforcement and a person or entity who is not a respondent in the proceeding; or

(v)   The hearing officer grants leave to withhold a document or category of documents as not relevant to the subject matter of the proceeding or otherwise, for good cause shown.

(2)   Unless the hearing officer orders otherwise upon motion, the Division of Enforcement may redact information from a document if:

(i)   The information is among the categories set forth in paragraphs (b)(1)(i) through (v) of this rule; or

(ii)   The information consists of the following with regard to a person other than the respondent to whom the information is being produced:

      (A) An individual's social-security number;

      (B) An individual's birth date;

      (C) The name of an individual known to be a minor; or

      (D) A financial account number, taxpayer-identification number, credit card or debit card number, passport number, driver's license number, or state-issued identification number other than the last four digits of the number.

    (3) Nothing in this paragraph (b) authorizes the Division of Enforcement in connection with an enforcement or disciplinary proceeding to withhold, contrary to the doctrine of *Brady v. Maryland,* 373 U.S. 83, 87, 83 S.Ct. 1194, 10 L.Ed.2d 215 (1963), documents that contain material exculpatory evidence.

    (c) *Withheld Document List.* The hearing officer may require the Division of Enforcement to submit for review a list of documents or categories of documents withheld pursuant to paragraphs (b)(1)(i) through (b)(1)(v) of this rule or to submit any document withheld, and may determine whether any such document should be made available for inspection and copying. When similar documents are withheld pursuant to paragraphs (b)(1)(i) through (b)(1)(v) of this rule, those documents may be identified by category instead of by individual document. The hearing officer retains discretion to determine when an identification by category is insufficient.

    (d) *Timing of Inspection and Copying.* Unless otherwise ordered by the Commission or the hearing officer, the Division of Enforcement shall commence making documents available to a respondent for inspection and copying pursuant to this rule no later than 7 days after service of the order instituting proceedings. In a proceeding in which a temporary cease-and-desist order is sought pursuant to Rule 510 or a temporary suspension of registration is sought pursuant to Rule 520, documents shall be made available no later than the day after service of the decision as to whether to issue a temporary cease-and-desist order or temporary suspension order.

    (e) *Place of Inspection and Copying.* Documents subject to inspection and copying pursuant to this rule shall be made available to the respondent for inspection and copying at the Commission office where they are ordinarily maintained, or at such other place as the parties, in writing, may agree. A respondent shall not be given custody of the documents or leave to remove the documents from the Commission's offices pursuant to the requirements of this rule other than by written agreement of the Division of Enforcement. Such agreement shall specify the documents subject to the agreement, the date they shall be returned and such other terms or conditions as are appropriate to provide for the safekeeping of the documents.

    (f) *Copying Costs and Procedures.* The respondent may obtain a photocopy of any documents made available for inspection. The respondent shall be responsible for the cost of photocopying. Unless otherwise ordered, charges for copies made by the Division of Enforcement at the request of the respondent will be at the rate charged pursuant to the fee schedule at 17 CFR section 200.80e for copies. The respondent shall be given access to the documents at the Commission's offices or such other place as the parties may agree during normal business hours for copying of documents at the respondent's expense.

    (g) *Issuance of Investigatory Subpoenas After Institution of Proceedings.* The Division of Enforcement shall promptly inform the hearing officer and each party if investigatory subpoenas are issued under the same investigation file number or pursuant to the same order directing private investigation ("formal order") under which the investigation leading to the institution of proceedings was conducted. The hearing officer shall order such steps as necessary and appropriate to assure that the issuance of investigatory subpoenas after the institution of proceedings is not for the purpose of obtaining evidence relevant to the proceedings and that any relevant documents that may be obtained through the use of investigatory subpoenas in a continuing investigation are made available to each respondent for inspection and copying on a timely basis.

    (h) *Failure to Make Documents Available—Harmless Error.* In the event that a document required to be made available to a respondent pursuant to this rule is not made available by the Division of Enforcement, no rehearing or redecision of a proceeding already heard or decided shall be required, unless the respondent shall establish that the failure to make the document available was not harmless error.

Rule 231. **Enforcement and Disciplinary Proceedings: Production of Witness Statements**

(a) *Availability.* Any respondent in an enforcement or disciplinary proceeding may move that the Division of Enforcement produce for inspection and copying any statement of any person called or to be called as a witness by the Division of Enforcement that pertains, or is expected to pertain, to his or her direct testimony and that would be required to be produced pursuant to the Jencks Act, 18 U.S.C. § 3500(e). For purposes of this rule, *statement* shall have the meaning set forth in 18 U.S.C. § 3500(e). Such production shall be made at a time and place fixed by the hearing officer and shall be made available to any party, provided, however, that the production shall be made under conditions intended to preserve the items to be inspected or copied.

(b) *Failure to Produce—Harmless Error.* In the event that a statement required to be made available for inspection and copying by a respondent is not turned over by the Division of Enforcement, no rehearing or redecision of a proceeding already heard or decided shall be required unless the respondent establishes that the failure to turn over the statement was not harmless error.

Rule 232. **Subpoenas**

(a) *Availability; procedure.* In connection with any hearing ordered by the Commission or any deposition permitted under Rule 233, a party may request the issuance of subpoenas requiring the attendance and testimony of witnesses at such depositions or at the designated time and place of hearing, and subpoenas requiring the production of documentary or other tangible evidence returnable at any designated time or place. Unless made on the record at a hearing, requests for issuance of a subpoena shall be made in writing and served on each party pursuant to Rule 150. A person whose request for a subpoena has been denied or modified may not request that any other person issue the subpoena.

(1) *Unavailability of Hearing Officer.* In the event that the hearing officer assigned to a proceeding is unavailable, the party seeking issuance of the subpoena may seek its issuance from the first available of the following persons: the Chief Administrative Law Judge, the law judge most senior in service as a law judge, the duty officer, any other member of the Commission, or any other person designated by the Commission to issue subpoenas. Requests for issuance of a subpoena made to the Commission, or any member thereof, must be submitted to the Secretary, not to an individual Commissioner.

(2) *Signing may be Delegated.* A hearing officer may authorize issuance of a subpoena, and may delegate the manual signing of the subpoena to any other person authorized to issue subpoenas.

(b) *Standards for Issuance.* Where it appears to the person asked to issue the subpoena that the subpoena sought may be unreasonable, oppressive, excessive in scope, or unduly burdensome, he or she may, in his or her discretion, as a condition precedent to the issuance of the subpoena, require the person seeking the subpoena to show the general relevance and reasonable scope of the testimony or other evidence sought. If after consideration of all the circumstances, the person requested to issue the subpoena determines that the subpoena or any of its terms is unreasonable, oppressive, excessive in scope, or unduly burdensome, he or she may refuse to issue the subpoena, or issue it only upon such conditions as fairness requires. In making the foregoing determination, the person issuing the subpoena may inquire of the other participants whether they will stipulate to the facts sought to be proved.

(c) *Service.* Service shall be made pursuant to the provisions of Rule 150(b)–(d). The provisions of this paragraph (c) shall apply to the issuance of subpoenas for purposes of investigations, as required by 17 CFR 203.8, as well as depositions and hearings.

(d) *Tender of fees required.* When a subpoena ordering the attendance of a person at a hearing or deposition is issued at the instance of anyone other than an officer or agency of the United States, service is valid only if the subpoena is accompanied by a tender to the subpoenaed person of the fees for one day's attendance and mileage specified by paragraph (f) of this rule.

(e) *Application to quash or modify.—(1) Procedure.* Any person to whom a subpoena or notice of deposition is directed, or who is an owner, creator or the subject of the documents that are to be produced pursuant to a subpoena, or any party may, prior to the time specified therein for compliance, but in no event more than 15 days after the date of service of such subpoena or notice, request that the subpoena or notice be quashed or modified. Such request shall be made by application filed with the Secretary and served on all parties pursuant to Rule 150. The party on whose behalf the subpoena or notice was issued may, within five days of service of the application, file an opposition to the application. If a hearing officer has been assigned to the proceeding, the application to quash shall be directed to that hearing officer for consideration, even if the subpoena or notice was issued by another person.

(2) *Standards governing application to quash or modify.* If compliance with the subpoena or notice of deposition would be unreasonable, oppressive, unduly burdensome or would unduly delay the hearing, the hearing officer or the Commission shall quash or modify the subpoena or notice, or may order a response to the subpoena, or appearance at a deposition, only upon specified conditions. These conditions may include but are not limited to a requirement that the party on whose behalf the subpoena was issued shall make reasonable compensation to the person to whom the subpoena was addressed for the cost of copying or transporting evidence to the place for return of the subpoena.

(3) *Additional standards governing application to quash deposition notices or subpoenas filed pursuant to Rule 233(a).* The hearing officer or the Commission shall quash or modify a deposition notice or subpoena filed or issued pursuant to Rule 233(a) unless the requesting party demonstrates that the deposition notice or subpoena satisfies the requirements of Rule 233(a), and:

(i) The proposed deponent was a witness of or participant in any event, transaction, occurrence, act, or omission that forms the basis for any claim asserted by the Division of Enforcement, any defense, or anything else required to be included in an answer pursuant to Rule 220(c) by any respondent in the proceeding (this excludes a proposed deponent whose only knowledge of these matters arises from the Division of Enforcement's investigation or the proceeding);

(ii) The proposed deponent is a designated as an "expert witness" under Rule 222(b); provided, however, that the deposition of an expert who is required to submit a written report under Rule 222(b) may only occur after such report is served; or

(iii) The proposed deponent has custody of documents or electronic data relevant to the claims or defenses of any party (this excludes Division of Enforcement or other Commission officers or personnel who have custody of documents or data that was produced by the Division to the respondent).

(f) *Witness fees and mileage.* Witnesses summoned before the Commission shall be paid the same fees and mileage that are paid to witnesses in the courts of the United States, and witnesses whose depositions are taken and the persons taking the same shall severally be entitled to the same fees as are paid for like services in the courts of the United States. Witness fees and mileage shall be paid by the party at whose instance the witnesses appear. Except for such witness fees and mileage, each party is responsible for paying any fees and expenses of the expert witnesses whom that party designates under Rule 222(b), for appearance at any deposition or hearing.

Rule 233.   Depositions Upon Oral Examination

(a) *Depositions upon written notice.* In any proceeding under the 120-day timeframe designated pursuant to Rule 360(a)(2), depositions upon written notice may be taken as set forth in this paragraph. No other depositions shall be permitted except as provided in paragraph (b) of this rule.

(1) If the proceeding involves a single respondent, the respondent may file written notices to depose no more than three persons, and the Division of Enforcement may file written notices to depose no more than three persons.

(2) If the proceeding involves multiple respondents, the respondents collectively may file joint written notices to depose no more than five persons, and the Division of Enforcement may file written notices to depose no more than five persons. The depositions taken under this paragraph (a)(2) shall not exceed a total of five depositions for the Division of Enforcement, and five depositions for all respondents collectively.

(3) *Additional depositions upon motion.* Any side may file a motion with the hearing officer seeking leave to notice up to two additional depositions beyond those permitted pursuant to paragraphs (a)(1) and (a)(2) of this rule.

(i) *Procedure.* (A) A motion for additional depositions must be filed no later than 90 days prior to the hearing date. Any party opposing the motion may submit an opposition within five days after service of the motion. No reply shall be permitted. The motion and any oppositions each shall not exceed seven pages in length. These limitations exclusively govern motions under this rule; notwithstanding Rule 154(a), any points and authorities shall be included in the motion or opposition, with no separate statement of points and authorities permitted, and none of the requirements in Rule 154(b) or (c) shall apply.

(B) Upon consideration of the motion and any opposing papers, the hearing officer will issue an order either granting or denying the motion. The hearing officer shall consider the motion on an expedited basis.

(C) The proceeding shall not automatically be stayed pending the determination of the motion.

(ii) *Grounds and standards for motion.* A motion under this paragraph (a)(3) shall not be granted unless the additional depositions satisfy Rule 232(e) and the moving side demonstrates a compelling need for the additional depositions by:

(A) Identifying each of the witnesses whom the moving side plans to depose pursuant to paragraphs (a)(1) or (a)(2) of this rule as well as the additional witnesses whom the side seeks to depose;

(B) Describing the role of each witness and proposed additional witness;

(C) Describing the matters concerning which each witness and proposed additional witness is expected to be questioned, and why the deposition of each witness and proposed additional witness is necessary for the moving side's arguments, claims, or defenses; and

(D) Showing that the additional deposition(s) requested will not be unreasonably cumulative or duplicative.

(iii) If the moving side proposes to take and submit the additional deposition(s) on written questions, as provided in Rule 234, the motion shall so state. The motion for additional depositions shall constitute a motion under Rule 234(a), and the moving party is required to submit its questions with its motion under this rule. The procedures for such a deposition shall be governed by Rule 234.

(4) A deponent's attendance may be ordered by subpoena issued pursuant to the procedures in Rule 232; and

(5) The Commission or hearing officer may rule on a motion that a deposition noticed under paragraphs (a)(1) or (a)(2) of this rule shall not be taken upon a determination under Rule 232(e). The fact that a witness testified during an investigation does not preclude the deposition of that witness.

(b) *Depositions when witness is unavailable.* In addition to depositions permitted under paragraph (a) of this rule, the Commission or the hearing officer may grant a party's request to file a written notice of deposition if the requesting party shows that the prospective witness will likely give testimony material to the proceeding; that it is likely the prospective witness, who is then within the United States, will be unable to attend or testify at the hearing because of age, sickness, infirmity, imprisonment, other disability, or absence from the United States, unless it appears that the absence of the witness was procured by the party requesting the deposition; and that the taking of a deposition will serve the interests of justice.

(c) *Service and contents of notice.* Notice of any deposition pursuant to this rule shall be made in writing and served on each party pursuant to Rule 150. A notice of deposition shall designate by name a deposition officer. The deposition officer may be any person authorized to administer oaths by the laws of the United States or of the place where the deposition is to be held. A notice of deposition also shall state:

(1) The name and address of the witness whose deposition is to be taken;

(2)　The time and place of the deposition; provided that a subpoena for a deposition may command a person to attend a deposition only as follows:

(i)　Within 100 miles of where the person resides, is employed, or regularly transacts business in person;

(ii)　Within the state where the person resides, is employed, or regularly transacts business in person, if the person is a party or a party's officer;

(iii)　At such other location that the parties and proposed deponent stipulate; or

(iv)　At such other location that the hearing officer or the Commission determines is appropriate; and

(3)　The manner of recording and preserving the deposition.

(d)　*Producing documents.* In connection with any deposition pursuant to Rule 233, a party may request the issuance of a subpoena duces tecum under Rule 232. The party conducting the deposition shall serve upon the deponent any subpoena duces tecum so issued. The materials designated for production, as set out in the subpoena, must be listed in the notice of deposition.

(e)　*Method of recording—(1) Method stated in the notice.* The party who notices the deposition must state in the notice the method for recording the testimony. Unless the hearing officer or Commission orders otherwise, testimony may be recorded by audio, audiovisual, or stenographic means. The noticing party bears the recording costs. Any party may arrange to transcribe a deposition, at that party's expense. Each party shall bear its own costs for obtaining copies of any transcripts or audio or audiovisual recordings.

(2)　*Additional method.* With prior notice to the deponent and other parties, any party may designate another method for recording the testimony in addition to that specified in the original notice. That party bears the expense of the additional record or transcript unless the hearing officer or the Commission orders otherwise.

(f)　*By remote means.* The parties may stipulate—or the hearing officer or Commission may on motion order—that a deposition be taken by telephone or other remote means. For the purpose of this rule, the deposition takes place where the deponent answers the questions.

(g)　*Deposition officer's duties—(1) Before the deposition.* The deposition officer designated pursuant to paragraph (c) of this rule must begin the deposition with an on-the-record statement that includes:

(i)　The deposition officer's name and business address;

(ii)　The date, time, and place of the deposition;

(iii)　The deponent's name;

(iv)　The deposition officer's administration of the oath or affirmation to the deponent; and

(v)　The identity of all persons present.

(2)　*Conducting the deposition; Avoiding distortion.* If the deposition is recorded non-stenographically, the deposition officer must repeat the items in paragraphs (g)(1)(i) through (iii) of this rule at the beginning of each unit of the recording medium. The deponent's and attorneys' appearance or demeanor must not be distorted through recording techniques.

(3)　*After the deposition.* At the end of a deposition, the deposition officer must state on the record that the deposition is complete and must set out any stipulations made by the attorneys about custody of the transcript or recording and of the exhibits, or about any other pertinent matters.

(h)　*Order and record of the examination—(1) Order of examination.* The examination and cross-examination of a deponent shall proceed as they would at the hearing. After putting the deponent under oath or affirmation, the deposition officer must record the testimony by the method designated under paragraph (e) of this rule. The testimony must be recorded by the deposition officer personally or by a person acting in the presence and under the direction of the deposition officer. The witness being deposed may have counsel present during the deposition.

(2)   *Form of objections stated during the deposition.* An objection at the time of the examination—whether to evidence, to a party's conduct, to the deposition officer's qualifications, to the manner of taking the deposition, or to any other aspect of the deposition—must be noted on the record, but the examination shall still proceed and the testimony shall be taken subject to any objection. An objection must be stated concisely in a nonargumentative and nonsuggestive manner. A person may instruct a deponent not to answer only when necessary to preserve a privilege, to enforce a limitation ordered by the hearing officer or the Commission, or to present a motion to the hearing officer or the Commission for a limitation on the questioning in the deposition.

(i)   *Waiver of objections—(1) To the notice.* An objection to an error or irregularity in a deposition notice is waived unless promptly served in writing on the party giving the notice.

(2)   *To the deposition officer's qualification.* An objection based on disqualification of the deposition officer before whom a deposition is to be taken is waived if not made:

(i)   Before the deposition begins; or

(ii)   Promptly after the basis for disqualification becomes known or, with reasonable diligence, could have been known.

(3)   *To the taking of the deposition.*

(i)   *Objection to competence, relevance, or materiality.* An objection to a deponent's competence—or to the competence, relevance, or materiality of testimony—is not waived by a failure to make the objection before or during the deposition, unless the ground for it might have been corrected at that time.

(ii)   *Objection to an error or irregularity.* An objection to an error or irregularity at an oral examination is waived if:

(A)   It relates to the manner of taking the deposition, the form of a question or answer, the oath or affirmation, a party's conduct, or other matters that might have been corrected at that time; and

(B)   It is not timely made during the deposition.

(4)   *To completing and returning the deposition.* An objection to how the deposition officer transcribed the testimony—or prepared, signed, certified, sealed, endorsed, sent, or otherwise dealt with the deposition—is waived unless a motion to suppress is made promptly after the error or irregularity becomes known or, with reasonable diligence, could have been known.

(j)   *Duration; cross-examination; motion to terminate or limit.* (1) *Duration.* Unless otherwise stipulated or ordered by the hearing officer or the Commission, a deposition is limited to one day of seven hours, including cross-examination as provided in this sub-rule. In a deposition conducted by or for a respondent, the Division of Enforcement shall be allowed a reasonable amount of time for cross-examination of the deponent. In a deposition conducted by the Division, the respondents collectively shall be allowed a reasonable amount of time for cross-examination of the deponent. The hearing officer or the Commission may allow additional time if needed to fairly examine the deponent or if the deponent, another person, or any other circumstance impedes or delays the examination.

(2)   *Motion to terminate or limit—(i) Grounds.* At any time during a deposition, the deponent or a party may move to terminate or limit it on the ground that it is being conducted in bad faith or in a manner that unreasonably annoys, embarrasses, or oppresses the deponent or party. If the objecting deponent or party so demands, the deposition must be suspended for the time necessary to present the motion to the hearing officer or the Commission.

(ii)   *Order.* Upon a motion under paragraph (j)(2)(i) of this rule, the hearing officer or the Commission may order that the deposition be terminated or may limit its scope. If terminated, the deposition may be resumed only by order of the hearing officer or the Commission.

(k)   *Review by the witness; changes. (1) Review; statement of changes.* On request by the deponent or a party before the deposition is completed, and unless otherwise ordered by the hearing officer or the

Commission, the deponent must be allowed 14 days after being notified by the deposition officer that the transcript or recording is available, unless a longer time is agreed to by the parties or permitted by the hearing officer, in which:

    (i)   To review the transcript or recording; and

    (ii)   If there are changes in form or substance, to sign a statement listing the changes and the reasons for making them.

    (2) *Changes indicated in the deposition officer's certificate.* The deposition officer must note in the certificate prescribed by paragraph (*l*)(1) of this rule whether a review was requested and, if so, must attach any changes the deponent makes during the 14-day period.

    (*l*) *Certification and delivery; exhibits; copies of the transcript or recording.* (1) *Certification and delivery.* The deposition officer must certify in writing that the witness was duly sworn and that the deposition accurately records the witness's testimony. The certificate must accompany the record of the deposition. Unless the hearing officer orders otherwise, the deposition officer must seal the deposition in an envelope or package bearing the title of the action and marked "Deposition of [witness's name]" and must promptly send it to the attorney or party who arranged for the transcript or recording. The attorney or party must store it under conditions that will protect it against loss, destruction, tampering, or deterioration.

    (2) *Documents and tangible things. (i) Originals and copies.* Documents and tangible things produced for inspection during a deposition must, on a party's request, be marked for identification and attached to the deposition. Any party may inspect and copy them. But if the person who produced them wants to keep the originals, the person may:

    (A) Offer copies to be marked, attached to the deposition, and then used as originals— after giving all parties a fair opportunity to verify the copies by comparing them with the originals; or

    (B) Give all parties a fair opportunity to inspect and copy the originals after they are marked—in which event the originals may be used as if attached to the deposition.

    (ii) *Order regarding the originals.* Any party may move for an order that the originals be attached to the deposition pending final disposition of the case.

    (3) *Copies of the transcript or recording.* Unless otherwise stipulated or ordered by the hearing officer or Commission, the deposition officer must retain the stenographic notes of a deposition taken stenographically or a copy of the recording of a deposition taken by another method. When paid reasonable charges, the deposition officer must furnish a copy of the transcript or recording to any party or the deponent, as directed by the party or person paying such charges.

    (m) *Presentation of Objections and Disputes.* Any party seeking relief with respect to disputes over conduct of the deposition may file a motion with the hearing officer to obtain relief as permitted by this part.

Rule 234.   Depositions Upon Written Questions

    (a) *Availability.* Any deposition permitted under Rule 233 may be taken and submitted on written questions upon motion of any party, for good cause shown, or as stipulated by the parties.

    (b) *Procedure.* Written questions shall be filed with the motion. Within 10 days after service of the motion and written questions, any party may file objections to such written questions and any party may file cross-questions. When a deposition is taken pursuant to this rule no persons other than the witness, counsel to the witness, the deposition officer, and, if the deposition officer does not act as reporter, a reporter, shall be present at the examination of the witness. No party shall be present or represented unless otherwise permitted by order. The deposition officer shall propound the questions and cross-questions to the witness in the order submitted.

    (c) *Additional requirements.* The order for deposition, filing of the deposition, form of the deposition and use of the deposition in the record shall be governed by paragraphs (c) through (*l*) of Rule 233, except that no cross-examination shall be made.

Rule 235.   Introducing Prior Sworn Statements of Witnesses Into the Record

(a)   At a hearing, any person wishing to introduce a prior, sworn deposition taken pursuant to Rule 233 or Rule 234, investigative testimony, or other sworn statement or a declaration pursuant to 28 U.S.C. 1746, of a witness, not a party, otherwise admissible in the proceeding, may make a motion setting forth the reasons therefor. If only part of a statement or declaration is offered in evidence, the hearing officer may require that all relevant portions of the statement or declaration be introduced. If all of a statement or declaration is offered in evidence, the hearing officer may require that portions not relevant to the proceeding be excluded. A motion to introduce a prior sworn statement or declaration may be granted if:

(1)   The witness is dead;

(2)   The witness is out of the United States, unless it appears that the absence of the witness was procured by the party offering the prior sworn statement or declaration;

(3)   The witness is unable to attend or testify because of age, sickness, infirmity, imprisonment or other disability;

(4)   The party offering the prior sworn statement or declaration has been unable to procure the attendance of the witness by subpoena; or

(5)   In the discretion of the Commission or the hearing officer, it would be desirable, in the interests of justice, to allow the prior sworn statement or declaration to be used. In making this determination, due regard shall be given to the presumption that witnesses will testify orally in an open hearing. If the parties have stipulated to accept a prior sworn statement or declaration in lieu of live testimony, consideration shall also be given to the convenience of the parties in avoiding unnecessary expense.

(b)   Sworn statement or declaration of party or agent. An adverse party may use for any purpose a deposition taken pursuant to Rule 233 or Rule 234, investigative testimony, or others worn statement or a declaration pursuant to 28 U.S.C. 1746, of a party or anyone who, when giving the sworn statement or declaration, was the party's officer, director, or managing agent.

Rule 240.   Settlement

(a)   *Availability.* Any person who is notified that a proceeding may or will be instituted against him or her, or any party to a proceeding already instituted, may, at any time, propose in writing an offer of settlement.

(b)   *Procedure.* An offer of settlement shall state that it is made pursuant to this rule; shall recite or incorporate as a part of the offer the provisions of paragraphs (c)(4) and (5) of this rule; shall be signed by the person making the offer, not by counsel; and shall be submitted to the interested division.

(c)   *Consideration of Offers of Settlement.*

(1)   Offers of settlement shall be considered by the interested division when time, the nature of the proceedings, and the public interest permit.

(2)   Where a hearing officer is assigned to a proceeding, the interested division and the party submitting the offer may request that the hearing officer express his or her views regarding the appropriateness of the offer of settlement. A request for the hearing officer to express his or her views on an offer of settlement or otherwise to participate in a settlement conference constitutes a waiver by the persons making the request of any right to claim bias or prejudgment by the hearing officer based on the views expressed.

(3)   The interested division shall present the offer of settlement to the Commission with its recommendation, except that, if the division's recommendation is unfavorable, the offer shall not be presented to the Commission unless the person making the offer so requests.

(4)   By submitting an offer of settlement, the person making the offer waives, subject to acceptance of the offer:

(i)   All hearings pursuant to the statutory provisions under which the proceeding is to be or has been instituted;

(ii)   The filing of proposed findings of fact and conclusions of law;

(iii)   Proceedings before, and an initial decision by, a hearing officer;

(iv)   All post-hearing procedures; and

(v)   Judicial review by any court.

(5)   By submitting an offer of settlement the person further waives:

(i)   Such provisions of the Rules of Practice or other requirements of law as may be construed to prevent any member of the Commission's staff from participating in the preparation of, or advising the Commission as to, any order, opinion, finding of fact, or conclusion of law to be entered pursuant to the offer; and

(ii)   Any right to claim bias or prejudgment by the Commission based on the consideration of or discussions concerning settlement of all or any part of the proceeding.

(6)   If the Commission rejects the offer of settlement, the person making the offer shall be notified of the Commission's action and the offer of settlement shall be deemed withdrawn. The rejected offer shall not constitute a part of the record in any proceeding against the person making the offer, provided, however, that rejection of an offer of settlement does not affect the continued validity of waivers pursuant to paragraph (c)(5) of this rule with respect to any discussions concerning the rejected offer of settlement.

(7)   Final acceptance of any offer of settlement will occur only upon the issuance of findings and an order by the Commission.

Rule 250.   Dispositive Motions

(a)   *Motion for a ruling on the pleadings.* No later than 14 days after a respondent's answer has been filed, any party may move for a ruling on the pleadings on one or more claims or defenses, asserting that, even accepting all of the non-movant's factual allegations as true and drawing all reasonable inferences in the non-movant's favor, the movant is entitled to a ruling as a matter of law. The hearing officer shall promptly grant or deny the motion.

(b)   *Motion for summary disposition in 30- and 75-day proceedings.* In any proceeding under the 30- or 75-day timeframe designated pursuant to Rule 360(a)(2), after a respondent's answer has been filed and documents have been made available to that respondent for inspection and copying pursuant to Rule 230, any party may make a motion for summary disposition on one or more claims or defenses, asserting that the undisputed pleaded facts, declarations, affidavits, documentary evidence or facts officially noted pursuant to Rule 323 show that there is no genuine issue with regard to any material fact and that the movant is entitled to summary disposition as a matter of law. The hearing officer shall promptly grant or deny the motion for summary disposition or shall defer decision on the motion. If it appears that a party, for good cause shown, cannot present prior to the hearing facts essential to justify opposition to the motion, the hearing officer shall deny or defer the motion.

(c)   *Motion for summary disposition in 120-day proceedings.* In any proceeding under the 120-day timeframe designated pursuant to Rule 360(a)(2), after a respondent's answer has been filed and documents have been made available to that respondent for inspection and copying pursuant to Rule 230, a party may make a motion for summary disposition on one or more claims or defenses, asserting that the undisputed pleaded facts, declarations, affidavits, deposition transcripts, documentary evidence or facts officially noted pursuant to Rule 323 show that there is no genuine issue with regard to any material fact and that the movant is entitled to summary disposition as a matter of law. A motion for summary disposition shall be made only with leave of the hearing officer. Leave shall be granted only for good cause shown and if consideration of the motion will not delay the scheduled start of the hearing. The hearing officer shall promptly grant or deny the motion for summary disposition or shall defer decision on the motion. If it appears that a party, for good cause shown, cannot present prior to the hearing facts essential to justify opposition to the motion, the hearing officer shall deny or defer the motion.

(d) *Motion for a ruling as a matter of law following completion of case in chief.* Following the interested division's presentation of its case in chief, any party may make a motion, asserting that the movant is entitled to a ruling as a matter of law on one or more claims or defenses.

(e) *Length limitation for dispositive motions.* Dispositive motions, together with any supporting memorandum of points and authorities (exclusive of any declarations, affidavits, deposition transcripts or other attachments), shall not exceed 9,800 words. Requests for leave to file motions and accompanying documents in excess of 9,800 words are disfavored. A double-spaced motion that does not, together with any accompanying memorandum of points and authorities, exceed 35 pages in length, inclusive of pleadings incorporated by reference (but excluding any declarations, affidavits, deposition transcripts or attachments) is presumptively considered to contain no more than 9,800 words. Any motion that exceeds this page limit must include a certificate by the attorney, or an unrepresented party, stating that the brief complies with the word limit set forth in this paragraph and stating the number of words in the motion. The person preparing the certificate may rely on the word count of a word-processing program to prepare the document.

(f) *Opposition and reply length limitations and response time.* A non-moving party may file an opposition to a dispositive motion and the moving party may thereafter file a reply.

(1) *Length limitations.* Any opposition must comply with the length limitations applicable to the movant's motion as set forth in paragraph (e) of this rule. Any reply must comply with the length limitations set forth in Rule 154(c).

(2) *Response Time.* (i) For motions under paragraphs (a), (b), and (d) of this rule, the response times set forth in Rule 154(b) apply to any opposition and reply briefs.

(ii) For motions under paragraph (c) of this rule, any opposition must be filed within 21 days after service of such a motion, and any reply must be filed within seven days after service of any opposition.

RULES REGARDING HEARINGS

Rule 300.   Hearings

Hearings for the purpose of taking evidence shall be held only upon order of the Commission. All hearings shall be conducted in a fair, impartial, expeditious and orderly manner.

Rule 301.   Hearings to Be Public

All hearings, except hearings on applications for confidential treatment filed pursuant to Rule 190, hearings held to consider a motion for a protective order pursuant to Rule 322, and hearings on *ex parte* application for a temporary cease-and-desist order, shall be public unless otherwise ordered by the Commission on its own motion or the motion of a party. No hearing shall be nonpublic where all respondents request that the hearing be made public.

Rule 302.   Record of Hearings

(a) *Recordation.* Unless ordered otherwise by the hearing officer or the Commission, all hearings shall be recorded and a written transcript thereof shall be prepared.

(b) *Availability of a Transcript.* Transcripts of public hearings shall be available for purchase at prescribed rates. Transcripts of nonpublic proceedings, and transcripts subject to a protective order pursuant to Rule 322, shall be available for purchase only by parties, provided, however, that any person compelled to submit data or evidence in a hearing may purchase a copy of his or her own testimony.

(c) *Transcript Correction.* Prior to the filing of post-hearing briefs or proposed findings and conclusions, or within such earlier time as directed by the Commission or the hearing officer, a party or witness may make a motion to correct the transcript. Proposed corrections of the transcript may be submitted to the hearing officer by stipulation pursuant to Rule 324, or by motion. Upon notice to all parties to the proceeding, the hearing officer may, by order, specify corrections to the transcript.

Rule 310.   Failure to Appear at Hearings: Default

Any person named in an order instituting proceedings as a person against whom findings may be made or sanctions imposed who fails to appear at a hearing of which he or she has been duly notified may be deemed to be in default pursuant to Rule 155(a). A party may make a motion to set aside a default pursuant to Rule 155(b).

Rule 320.   Evidence: Admissibility

(a)   Except as otherwise provided in this rule, the Commission or the hearing officer may receive relevant evidence and shall exclude all evidence that is irrelevant, immaterial, unduly repetitious, or unreliable.

(b)   Subject to Rule 235, evidence that constitutes hearsay may be admitted if it is relevant, material, and bears satisfactory indicia of reliability so that its use is fair.

Rule 321.   Evidence: Objections and Offers of Proof

(a)   *Objections.* Objections to the admission or exclusion of evidence must be made on the record and shall be in short form, stating the grounds relied upon. Exceptions to any ruling thereon by the hearing officer need not be noted at the time of the ruling. Such exceptions will be deemed waived on appeal to the Commission, however, unless raised:

(1)   Pursuant to interlocutory review in accordance with Rule 400;

(2)   In a proposed finding or conclusion filed pursuant to Rule 340; or

(3)   In a petition for Commission review of an initial decision filed in accordance with Rule 410.

(b)   *Offers of Proof.* Whenever evidence is excluded from the record, the party offering such evidence may make an offer of proof, which shall be included in the record. Excluded material shall be retained pursuant to Rule 350(b).

Rule 322.   Evidence: Confidential Information, Protective Orders

(a)   *Procedure.* In any proceeding as defined in Rule 101(a), a party, any person who is the owner, subject or creator of a document subject to subpoena or which may be introduced as evidence, or any witness who testifies at a hearing may file a motion requesting a protective order to limit from disclosure to other parties or to the public documents or testimony that contain confidential information. The motion should include a general summary or extract of the documents without revealing confidential details.

(b)   If review of the documents that are the subject of a request for a protective order is necessary to a ruling on the motion and the information as to which a protective order is sought is available to the movant, the motion shall be accompanied by:

(1)   A complete, sealed copy of the materials containing the information as to which a protective order is sought, with the allegedly confidential information marked as such, and with the first page of the document labeled "Under Seal." If the movant seeks a protective order against disclosure to other parties as well as the public, copies of the documents shall not be served on other parties; and

(2)   A redacted copy of the materials containing the information as to which a protective order is sought, with the allegedly confidential information redacted. The redacted version shall indicate any omissions with brackets or ellipses, and its pagination and depiction of text on each page shall be identical to that of the sealed version. A redacted copy need not accompany a motion requesting a protective order if the materials would be redacted in their entirety.

(c)   *Basis for Issuance.* Documents and testimony introduced in a public hearing are presumed to be public. A motion for a protective order shall be granted only upon a finding that the harm resulting from disclosure would outweigh the benefits of disclosure.

(d)   *Requests for Additional Information Supporting Confidentiality.* A movant under paragraph (a) of this rule may be required to furnish in writing additional information with respect to the grounds for confidentiality. Failure to supply the information so requested within five days from the date of receipt by the movant of a notice of the information required shall be deemed a waiver of the objection to public disclosure of that portion of the documents to which the additional information relates, unless the Commission or the hearing officer shall otherwise order for good cause shown at or before the expiration of such five-day period.

(e) *Confidentiality of Documents Pending Decision.* Pending a determination of a motion under this rule, the documents as to which confidential treatment is sought and any other documents that would reveal the confidential information in those documents shall be maintained under seal and shall be disclosed only in accordance with orders of the Commission or the hearing officer. Any order issued in connection with a motion under this rule shall be public unless the order would disclose information as to which a protective order has been granted, in which case that portion of the order that would reveal the protected information shall be nonpublic.

Rule 323.   Evidence: Official Notice

Official notice may be taken of any material fact which might be judicially noticed by a district court of the United States, any matter in the public official records of the Commission, or any matter which is peculiarly within the knowledge of the Commission as an expert body. If official notice is requested or taken of a material fact not appearing in the evidence in the record, the parties, upon timely request, shall be afforded an opportunity to establish the contrary.

Rule 324.   Evidence: Stipulations

The parties may, by stipulation, at any stage of the proceeding agree upon any pertinent facts in the proceeding. A stipulation may be received in evidence and, when received, shall be binding on the parties to the stipulation.

Rule 325.   Evidence: Presentation Under Oath or Affirmation

A witness at a hearing for the purpose of taking evidence shall testify under oath or affirmation.

Rule 326.   Evidence: Presentation, Rebuttal and Cross-Examination

In any proceeding in which a hearing is required to be conducted on the record after opportunity for hearing in accord with 5 U.S.C.A. section 556(a), a party is entitled to present its case or defense by oral or documentary evidence, to submit rebuttal evidence, and to conduct such cross-examination as, in the discretion of the Commission or the hearing officer, may be required for a full and true disclosure of the facts. The scope and form of evidence, rebuttal evidence, if any, and cross-examination, if any, in any other proceeding shall be determined by the Commission or the hearing officer in each proceeding.

Rule 340.   Proposed Findings, Conclusions and Supporting Briefs

(a) *Opportunity to File.* Before an initial decision is issued, each party shall have an opportunity, reasonable in light of all the circumstances, to file in writing proposed findings and conclusions together with, or as a part of, its brief.

(b) *Procedure.* Proposed findings of fact must be supported by citations to specific portions of the record. If successive filings are directed, the proposed findings and conclusions of the party assigned to file first shall be set forth in serially numbered paragraphs, and any counter statement of proposed findings and conclusions must, in addition to any other matter, indicate those paragraphs of the proposals already filed as to which there is no dispute. A reply brief may be filed by the party assigned to file first, or, where simultaneous filings are directed, reply briefs may be filed by each party, within the period prescribed therefor by the hearing officer. No further briefs may be filed except with leave of the hearing officer.

(c) *Time for Filing.* In any proceeding in which an initial decision is to be issued:

(1) At the end of each hearing, the hearing officer shall, by order, after consultation with the parties, prescribe the period within which proposed findings and conclusions and supporting briefs are to be filed. The party or parties directed to file first shall make its or their initial filing within 30 days

of the end of the hearing unless the hearing officer, for good cause shown, permits a different period and sets forth in the order the reasons why the different period is necessary.

(2)   The total period within which all such proposed findings and conclusions and supporting briefs and any counter statements of proposed findings and conclusions and reply briefs are to be filed shall be no longer than 90 days after the close of the hearing unless the hearing officer, for good cause shown, permits a different period and sets forth in an order the reasons why the different period is necessary.

Rule 350.   Record in Proceedings Before Hearing Officer; Retention of Documents; Copies

(a)   *Contents of the Record.* The record shall consist of:

(1)   The order instituting proceedings, each notice of hearing and any amendments;

(2)   Each application, motion, submission or other paper, and any amendments, motions, objections, and exceptions to or regarding them;

(3)   Each stipulation, transcript of testimony and document or other item admitted into evidence;

(4)   Each written communication accepted by the hearing officer pursuant to Rule 210;

(5)   With respect to a request to disqualify a hearing officer or to allow the hearing officer's withdrawal under Rule 112, each affidavit or transcript of testimony taken and the decision made in connection with the request;

(6)   All motions, briefs and other papers filed on interlocutory appeal;

(7)   All proposed findings and conclusions;

(8)   Each written order issued by the hearing officer or Commission; and

(9)   Any other document or item accepted into the record by the hearing officer.

(b)   *Retention of Documents not admitted.* Any document offered into evidence but excluded shall not be considered a part of the record. The Secretary shall retain any such document until the later of the date upon which a Commission order ending the proceeding becomes final, or the conclusion of any judicial review of the Commission's order.

(c)   *Substitution of Copies.* A true copy of a document may be substituted for any document in the record or any document retained pursuant to paragraph (b) of this rule.

Rule 351.   Transmittal of Documents to Secretary; Record Index; Certification

(a)   *Preparation, certification of record index.* Promptly after the close of the hearing, the hearing officer shall transmit to the Secretary an index of the originals of any motions, exhibits or any other documents filed with or accepted into evidence by the hearing officer that have not been previously transmitted to the Secretary, and the Secretary shall prepare a record index. Prior to issuance of an initial decision, or if no initial decision is to be prepared, within 30 days of the close of the hearing, the Secretary shall transmit the record index to the hearing officer and serve a copy of the record index on each party. Any person may file proposed corrections to the record index with the hearing officer within three days of service of the record index. Any opposition to the proposed corrections shall be filed within three days of service of the proposed corrections. The hearing officer shall, by order, direct whether any corrections to the record index shall be made. The Secretary shall make such corrections, if any, and issue a revised record index. If an initial decision is to be issued, the initial decision shall include a certification that the record consists of the items set forth in the record index or revised record index issued.

(b)   *Preparation, Certification of Record Index.* Promptly after the close of the hearing, the hearing officer shall transmit to the Secretary an index of the originals of any motions, exhibits or any other documents filed with or accepted into evidence by the hearing officer that have not been previously transmitted to the Secretary, and the Secretary shall prepare a record index. Prior to issuance of an initial decision, or if no initial decision is to be prepared, within 30 days of the close of the hearing, the Secretary shall transmit the record index to the hearing officer and serve a copy of the record index on each party. Any person may file proposed corrections to the record index with the hearing officer within 15 days of service of the record index. The hearing officer shall, by order, direct whether any corrections to the record index shall be made. The Secretary shall make such corrections, if any, and issue a revised record index. If an initial decision is to be issued, the initial decision shall include a certification that the record consists of the items set forth in the record index or revised record index issued by the Secretary.

(c)   *Electronic exhibits.* No later than five days after the Secretary serves a final record index, the parties shall submit electronically to the Secretary a copy of all exhibits that were admitted, or offered and not admitted, during the hearing, and any other exhibits that were admitted after the hearing. The parties shall submit such evidence in the form and manner to be specified by the Office of the Secretary in the materials posted on the Commission's website.

(1)   *Certification of Inability to Submit Exhibits Electronically.* A person who reasonably cannot submit exhibits electronically must file a certification under § 201.351(c)(1) that explains why the person reasonably cannot comply. The filing also must indicate the expected duration of the person's reasonable inability to comply, such as whether the certification is intended to apply to a solitary submission or all submissions made during the proceeding. The certification is immediately effective. Upon filing the certification, it will be part of the record of the proceeding, and the person shall submit originals of any exhibits that have not already been submitted to the Secretary by other means.

(2)   *Signature requirement.* Electronic submissions that require a signature pursuant to Rule 153 may be signed with an "/s/" notation, but in that event, the use of the filer's login and password to file a document shall be deemed the signature of the person making the submission for purposes of § 201.153.

(3)   *Certification.* The parties shall certify that exhibits and other documents or items submitted to the Secretary under this section are true and accurate copies of exhibits that were admitted, or offered and not admitted, during the hearing, or any other exhibits that were admitted after the hearing.

(d)   *Final Transmittal of Record Items to the Secretary.* After the close of the hearing, the hearing officer shall transmit to the Secretary originals of any motions, exhibits or any other documents filed with, or accepted into evidence by, the hearing officer, or any other portions of the record that have not already been transmitted to the Secretary. Prior to service of the initial decision by the Secretary, or if no initial decision is to be issued, within 60 days of the close of the hearing, the Secretary shall inform the hearing officer if any portions of the record are not in the Secretary's custody.

Rule 360.   Initial Decision of Hearing Officer and Timing of Hearing

(a)(1)   *When Required.* Unless the Commission directs otherwise, the hearing officer shall prepare an initial decision in any proceeding in which the Commission directs a hearing officer to preside at a hearing, provided, however, that an initial decision may be waived by the parties with the consent of the hearing officer pursuant to Rule 202.

(2)   *Time period for filing initial decision and for hearing—(i) Initial Decision.* In the order instituting proceedings, the Commission will specify a time period in which the hearing officer's initial decision must be filed with the Secretary. In the Commission's discretion, after consideration of the nature, complexity, and urgency of the subject matter, and with due regard for the public interest and the protection of investors, this time period will be either 30, 75, or 120 days. The time period will run from the occurrence of the following events: (A) The completion of post-hearing briefing in a proceeding where the hearing has been completed; or (B) The completion of briefing on a Rule 250 motion in the event the hearing officer has determined that no hearing is necessary; or (C) The determination by the hearing officer that, pursuant to Rule 155, a party is deemed to be in default and no hearing is necessary.

(ii)   *Hearing.* Under the 120-day timeline, the hearing officer shall issue an order scheduling the hearing to begin approximately four months (but no more than ten months) from the date of service of the order instituting the proceeding. Under the 75-day timeline, the hearing officer shall issue an order scheduling the hearing to begin approximately 2-1/2 months (but no more than six months) from the date of the service of the order instituting the proceeding. Under the 30-day timeline, the hearing officer shall issue an order scheduling the hearing to begin approximately one month (but no more than four months) from the date of the service of the order instituting the proceeding. These deadlines confer no substantive rights on respondents. If a stay is granted pursuant to Rule 161(c)(2)(i) or Rule 210(c)(3), the time period specified in the order instituting proceedings in which the hearing officer's initial decision must be filed with the Secretary, as well as any other time limits established in orders issued by the hearing officer in the proceeding, shall be automatically tolled during the period while the stay is in effect.

(3) *Certification of extension; motion for extension.* (i) In the event that the hearing officer presiding over the proceeding determines that it will not be possible to file the initial decision within the specified period of time, the hearing officer may certify to the Commission in writing the need to extend the initial decision deadline by up to 30 days for case management purposes. The certification must be issued no later than 30 days prior to the expiration of the time specified for the issuance of an initial decision and be served on the Commission and all parties in the proceeding. If the Commission has not issued an order to the contrary within 14 days after receiving the certification, the extension set forth in the hearing officer's certification shall take effect.

(ii) Either in addition to a certification of extension, or instead of a certification of extension, the Chief Administrative Law Judge may submit a motion to the Commission requesting an extension of the time period for filing the initial decision. First, the hearing officer presiding over the proceeding must consult with the Chief Administrative Law Judge. Following such consultation, the Chief Administrative Law Judge may determine, in his or her discretion, to submit a motion to the Commission requesting an extension of the time period for filing the initial decision. This motion may request an extension of any length but must be filed no later than 15 days prior to the expiration of the time specified in the certification of extension, or if there is no certification of extension, 30 days prior to the expiration of the time specified in the order instituting proceedings. The motion will be served upon all parties in the proceeding, who may file with the Commission statements in support of or in opposition to the motion. If the Commission determines that additional time is necessary or appropriate in the public interest, the Commission shall issue an order extending the time period for filing the initial decision.

(iii) The provisions of this paragraph (a)(3) confer no rights on respondents.

(b) *Content.* An initial decision shall include findings and conclusions, and the reasons or basis therefor, as to all the material issues of fact, law or discretion presented on the record and the appropriate order, sanction, relief, or denial thereof. The initial decision shall also state the time period, not to exceed 21 days after service of the decision, except for good cause shown, within which a petition for review of the initial decision may be filed. The reasons for any extension of time shall be stated in the initial decision. The initial decision shall also include a statement that, as provided in paragraph (d) of this rule:

(1) The Commission will enter an order of finality as to each party unless a party or an aggrieved person entitled to review timely files a petition for review of the initial decision or a motion to correct a manifest error of fact in the initial decision with the hearing officer, or the Commission determines on its own initiative to review the initial decision; and

(2) If a party or an aggrieved person entitled to review timely files a petition for review or a motion to correct a manifest error of fact in the initial decision with the hearing officer, or if the Commission takes action to review as to a party or an aggrieved person entitled to review, the initial decision shall not become final as to that party or person.

(c) *Filing, service and publication.* The Secretary shall promptly serve the initial decision upon the parties and shall promptly publish notice of the filing thereof on the SEC website; provided, however, that in nonpublic proceedings no notice shall be published unless the Commission otherwise directs.

(d) *Finality.*

(1) If a party or an aggrieved person entitled to review timely files a petition for review or a motion to correct a manifest error of fact in the initial decision, or if the Commission on its own initiative orders review of a decision with respect to a party or a person aggrieved who would be entitled to review, the initial decision shall not become final as to that party or person.

(2) If a party or aggrieved person entitled to review fails to file timely a petition for review or a motion to correct a manifest error of fact in the initial decision, and if the Commission does not order review of a decision on its own initiative, the Commission will issue an order that the decision has become final as to that party. The decision becomes final upon issuance of the order. The order of finality shall state the date on which sanctions, if any, take effect. Notice of the order shall be published on the SEC website.

APPEAL TO THE COMMISSION AND COMMISSION REVIEW

Rule 400. Interlocutory Review

(a) *Availability.* The Commission may, at any time, on its own motion, direct that any matter be submitted to it for review. Petitions by parties for interlocutory review are disfavored, and the Commission ordinarily will grant a petition to review a hearing officer ruling prior to its consideration of an initial decision only in extraordinary circumstances. The Commission may decline to consider a ruling certified by a hearing officer pursuant to paragraph (c) of this rule or the petition of a party who has been denied certification if it determines that interlocutory review is not warranted or appropriate under the circumstances. This rule is the exclusive remedy for review of a hearing officer's ruling prior to Commission consideration of the entire proceeding and is the sole mechanism for appeal of actions delegated pursuant to 17 C.F.R. sections 200.30–9 and 200.30–10.

(b) *Expedited Consideration.* Interlocutory review of a hearing officer's ruling shall be expedited in every way, consistent with the Commission's other responsibilities.

(c) *Certification Process.* A ruling submitted to the Commission for interlocutory review must be certified in writing by the hearing officer and shall specify the material relevant to the ruling involved. The hearing officer shall not certify a ruling unless:

(1) His or her ruling would compel testimony of Commission members, officers or employees or the production of documentary evidence in their custody; or

(2) Upon application by a party, within five days of the hearing officer's ruling, the hearing officer is of the opinion that:

(i) The ruling involves a controlling question of law as to which there is substantial ground for difference of opinion; and

(ii) An immediate review of the order may materially advance the completion of the proceeding.

(d) *Proceedings not Stayed.* The filing of an application for review or the grant of review shall not stay proceedings before the hearing officer unless he or she, or the Commission, shall so order. The Commission will not consider the motion for a stay unless the motion shall have first been made to the hearing officer.

Rule 401. Consideration of Stays

(a) *Procedure.* A request for a stay shall be made by written motion, filed pursuant to Rule 154, and served on all parties pursuant to Rule 150. The motion shall state the reasons for the relief requested and the facts relied upon, and, if the facts are subject to dispute, the motion shall be supported by affidavits or other sworn statements or copies thereof. Portions of the record relevant to the relief sought, if available to the movant, shall be filed with the motion. The Commission may issue a stay based on such motion or on its own motion.

(b) *Scope of Relief.* The Commission may grant a stay in whole or in part, and may condition relief under this rule upon such terms, or upon the implementation of such procedures, as it deems appropriate.

(c) *Stay of a Commission Order.* A motion for a stay of a Commission order may be made by any person aggrieved thereby who would be entitled to review in a federal court of appeals. A motion seeking to stay the effectiveness of a Commission order pending judicial review may be made to the Commission at any time during which the Commission retains jurisdiction over the proceeding.

(d)   *Stay of an Action by a Self-Regulatory Organization.*

(1)   *Availability.* A motion for a stay of an action by a self-regulatory organization for which the Commission is the appropriate regulatory agency, for which action review may be sought pursuant to Rule 420, may be made by any person aggrieved thereby at the time an application for review is filed in accordance with Rule 420 or thereafter.

(2)   *Summary Entry.* A stay may be entered summarily, without notice and opportunity for hearing.

(3)   *Expedited Consideration.* Where the action complained of has already taken effect and the motion for stay is filed within 10 days of the effectiveness of the action, or where the action complained of, will, by its terms, take effect within five days of the filing of the motion for stay, the consideration of and decision on the motion for a stay shall be expedited in every way, consistent with the Commission's other responsibilities. Where consideration will be expedited, persons opposing the motion for a stay may file a statement in opposition within two days of service of the motion unless the Commission, by written order, shall specify a different period.

(e)   *Lifting of stay of action by the Public Company Accounting Oversight Board.*

(1)   *Availability.* Any person aggrieved by a stay of action by the Board entered in accordance with 15 U.S.C. § 7215(e) for which review has been sought pursuant to Rule 440 or which the Commission has taken up on its motion pursuant to Rule 441 may make a motion to lift the stay. The Commission may, at any time, on its own motion determine whether to lift the automatic stay.

(2)   *Summary action.* The Commission may lift a stay summarily, without notice and opportunity for hearing.

(3)   *Expedited consideration.* The Commission may expedite consideration of a motion to lift a stay of Board action, consistent with the Commission's other responsibilities. Where consideration is expedited, persons opposing the lifting of the stay may file a statement in opposition within two days of service of the motion requesting lifting of the stay unless the Commission, by written order, shall specify a different period.

Rule 410.   Appeal of Initial Decisions by Hearing Officers

(a)   *Petition for Review: when Available.* In any proceeding in which an initial decision is made by a hearing officer, any party, and any other person who would have been entitled to judicial review of the decision entered therein if the Commission itself had made the decision, may file a petition for review of the decision with the Commission.

(b)   *Procedure.* The petition for review of an initial decision shall be filed with the Commission within such time after service of the initial decision as prescribed by the hearing officer pursuant to Rule 360(b) unless a party has filed a motion to correct an initial decision with the hearing officer. If such correction has been sought, a party shall have 21 days from the date of the hearing officer's order resolving the motion to correct to file a petition for review. The petition shall set forth a statement of the issues presented for review under Rule 411(b). In the event a petition for review is filed, any other party to the proceeding may file a cross-petition for review within the original time allowed for seeking review or within ten days from the date that the petition for review was filed, whichever is later.

(c)   *Length limitation.* Except with leave of the Commission, the petition for review shall not exceed three pages in length. Incorporation of pleadings or filings by reference is not permitted. Motions to file petitions in excess of those limitations are disfavored.

(d)   *Financial Disclosure Statement Requirement.* Any person who files a petition for review of an initial decision that asserts that person's inability to pay either disgorgement, interest or a penalty shall file with the opening brief a sworn financial disclosure statement containing the information specified in Rule 630(b).

(e)   *Prerequisite to Judicial Review.* Pursuant to section 704 of the Administrative Procedure Act, a petition to the Commission for review of an initial decision is a prerequisite to the seeking of judicial review of a final order entered pursuant to such decision.

Rule 411.   Commission Consideration of Initial Decisions by Hearing Officers

(a) *Scope of Review.* The Commission may affirm, reverse, modify, set aside or remand for further proceedings, in whole or in part, an initial decision by a hearing officer and may make any findings or conclusions that in its judgment are proper and on the basis of the record.

(b) *Standards for Granting Review Pursuant to a Petition for Review.*

(1) *Mandatory Review.* After a petition for review has been filed, the Commission shall review any initial decision that:

(i)   Denies any request for action pursuant to section 8(a) or section 8(c) of the Securities Act of 1933, or the first sentence of section 12(d) of the Exchange Act;

(ii) Suspends trading in a security pursuant to section 12(k) of the Exchange Act; or

(iii) Is in a case of adjudication (as defined in 5 U.S.C.A. section 551) not required to be determined on the record after notice and opportunity for hearing (except to the extent there is involved a matter described in 5 U.S.C.A. section 554(a)(1) through (6)).

(2) *Discretionary Review.* The Commission may decline to review any other decision. In determining whether to grant review, the Commission shall consider whether the petition for review makes a reasonable showing that:

(i)   A prejudicial error was committed in the conduct of the proceeding; or

(ii) The decision embodies:

(A) A finding or conclusion of material fact that is clearly erroneous; or

(B) A conclusion of law that is erroneous; or

(C) An exercise of discretion or decision of law or policy that is important and that the Commission should review.

(c) *Commission Review Other Than Pursuant to a Petition for Review.* The Commission may, on its own initiative, order review of any initial decision, or a portion of any initial decision, within 21 days after the end of the period established for filing a petition for review pursuant to Rule 410(b). A party who does not intend to file a petition for review, and who desires the Commission's determination whether to order review on its own initiative to be made in a shorter time, may make a motion for an expedited decision, accompanied by a written statement that the party waives its right to file a petition for review. The vote of one member of the Commission, conveyed to the Secretary, shall be sufficient to bring a matter before the Commission for review.

(d) *Limitations on matters reviewed.* Review by the Commission of an initial decision shall be limited to the issues specified in an opening brief that complies with Rule 450(b), or the issues, if any, specified in the briefing schedule order issued pursuant to Rule 450(a). Any exception to an initial decision not supported in an opening brief that complies with Rule 450(b) may, at the discretion of the Commission, be deemed to have been waived by the petitioner. On notice to all parties, however, the Commission may, at any time prior to issuance of its decision, raise and determine any other matters that it deems material, with opportunity for oral or written argument thereon by the parties.

(e) *Summary Affirmance.*

(1) At any time within 21 days after the filing of a petition for review pursuant to Rule 410(b), any party may file a motion in accordance with Rule 154 asking that the Commission summarily affirm an initial decision. Any party may file an opposition and reply to such motion in accordance with Rule 154. Pending determination of the motion for summary affirmance, the Commission, in its discretion, may delay issuance of a briefing schedule order pursuant to Rule 450.

(2) Upon consideration of the motion and any opposition or upon its own initiative, the Commission may summarily affirm an initial decision. The Commission may grant summary affirmance if it finds that no issue raised in the initial decision warrants consideration by the Commission of further oral or written argument. The Commission will decline to grant summary affirmance upon a reasonable showing that a prejudicial error was committed in the conduct of the

proceeding or that the decision embodies an exercise of discretion or decision of law or policy that is important and that the Commission should review.

(f)   *Failure to Obtain a Majority.* In the event a majority of participating Commissioners do not agree to a disposition on the merits, the initial decision shall be of no effect, and an order will be issued in accordance with this result.

Rule 420.   Appeal of Determinations by Self-Regulatory Organizations

(a)   *Application for review; when available.* An application for review by the Commission may be filed by any person who is aggrieved by a determination of a self-regulatory organization with respect to any

(1)   Final disciplinary sanction;

(2)   Denial or conditioning of membership or participation;

(3)   Prohibition or limitation in respect to access to services offered by that self-regulatory organization or a member thereof; or

(4)   Bar from association as to which a notice is required to be filed with the Commission pursuant to Section 19(d)(1) of the Exchange Act.

(b)   *Procedure.* As required by section 19(d)(1) of the Securities Exchange Act of 1934, an applicant must file an application for review with the Commission within 30 days after the notice of the determination is filed with the Commission and received by the aggrieved person applying for review. The Commission will not extend this 30-day period, absent a showing of extraordinary circumstances. This rule is the exclusive remedy for seeking an extension of the 30-day period.

(c)   *Application.* The application shall be filed with the Commission pursuant to Rule 151. The applicant shall serve the application on the self-regulatory organization. The application shall identify the determination complained of and set forth in summary form a brief statement of the alleged errors in the determination and supporting reasons therefor. The application shall state an address where the applicant can be served. The application should not exceed two pages in length. If the applicant will be represented by a representative, the application shall be accompanied by the notice of appearance required by Rule 102(d). Any exception to a determination not supported in an opening brief that complies with Rule 450(b) may, at the discretion of the Commission, be deemed to have been waived by the applicant.

(d)   *Determination not Stayed.* Filing an application for review with the Commission pursuant to paragraph (b) of this rule shall not operate as a stay of the complained of determination made by the self-regulatory organization unless the Commission otherwise orders either pursuant to a motion filed in accordance with Rule 401 or on its own motion.

(e)   *Certification of the record; service of the index.* Fourteen days after receipt of an application for review or a Commission order for review, the self-regulatory organization shall certify and file electronically in the form and manner to be specified by the Office of the Secretary in the materials posted on the Commission's website one unredacted copy of the record upon which the action complained of was taken.

(1)   The self-regulatory organization also shall file electronically with the Commission one copy of an index to such record, and shall serve upon each party one copy of the index. If such index contains any sensitive personal information, as defined in paragraph (e)(2) of this section, the self-regulatory organization also shall file electronically with the Commission one redacted copy of such index, subject to the requirements of paragraph (e)(2) of this rule.

(2)   *Sensitive personal information.* Sensitive personal information is defined as a Social Security number, taxpayer identification number, financial account number, credit card or debit card number, passport number, driver's license number, state-issued identification number, home address (other than city and state), telephone number, date of birth (other than year), names and initials of minor children, as well as any unnecessary health information identifiable by individual, such as an individual's medical records. Sensitive personal information shall not be included in, and must be redacted or omitted from, all filings subject to:

(i)   *Exceptions.* The following information may be included and is not required to be redacted from filings:

    (A) The last four digits of a financial account number, credit card or debit card number, passport number, driver's license number, and state-issued identification number;

    (B) Home addresses and telephone numbers of parties and persons filing documents with the Commission;

    (C) Business telephone numbers; and

    (D) Copies of unredacted filings by regulated entities or registrants that are available on the Commission's public website.

    (d) *Certification.* Any filing made pursuant to this section, other than the record upon which the action complained of was taken, must include a certification that any information described in paragraph (e)(2) of this rule has been omitted or redacted from the filing.

Rule 421.   Commission Consideration of Determinations by Self-Regulatory Organizations

    (a) *Commission Review other than Pursuant to a Petition for Review.* The Commission may, on its own initiative, order review of any determination by a self-regulatory organization that could be subject to an application for review pursuant to 420(a) within 40 days after notice thereof was filed with the Commission pursuant to section 19(d)(1) of the Exchange Act.

    (b) *Supplemental Briefing.* The Commission may at any time prior to issuance of its decision raise or consider any matter that it deems material, whether or not raised by the parties. Notice to the parties and an opportunity for supplemental briefing with respect to issues not briefed by the parties shall be given where the Commission believes that such briefing would significantly aid the decisional process.

Rule 430.   Appeal of Actions Made Pursuant to Delegated Authority

    (a) *Scope of Rule.* Any person aggrieved by an action made by authority delegated in 17 C.F.R. sections 200.30–1 through 200.30–8 or 17 C.F.R. sections 200.30–11 through 200.30–18 may seek review of the action pursuant to paragraph (b) of this rule.

    (b) *Procedure.*

    (1) *Notice of Intention to Petition for Review.* A party to an action made pursuant to delegated authority, or a person aggrieved by such action, may seek Commission review of the action by filing a written notice of intention to petition for review within five days after actual notice of the action to that party or aggrieved person, or 15 days after publication of the notice of action in the Federal Register, or five days after service of notice of the action on that party or aggrieved person pursuant to Rule 141(b), whichever is the earliest.

    (2) *Petition for Review.* Within five days after the filing of a notice of intention to petition for review pursuant to paragraph (b)(1) of this rule the person seeking review shall file a petition for review containing a clear and concise statement of the issues to be reviewed and the reasons why review is appropriate. The petition shall include exceptions to any findings of fact or conclusions of law made, together with supporting reasons for such exceptions based on appropriate citations to such record as may exist. These reasons may be stated in summary form.

    (c) *Prerequisite to Judicial Review.* Pursuant to Section 704 of the Administrative Procedure Act a petition to the Commission for review of an action made by authority delegated in 17 C.F.R. sections 200.30–1 through 200.30–18 is a prerequisite to the seeking of judicial review of a final order entered pursuant to such an action. Pursuant to 15 U.S.C. 7214(h)(2), any decision by the Commission pursuant to 200.30–11 shall not be reviewable under section 25 of the Securities Exchange Act of 1934 and shall not be deemed 'final agency action' for purposes of 5 U.S.C. 704.

Rule 431.   Commission Consideration of Actions Made Pursuant to Delegated Authority

    (a) *Scope of Review.* The Commission may affirm, reverse, modify, set aside or remand for further proceedings, in whole or in part, any action made pursuant to authority delegated in 17 C.F.R. sections 200.30–1 through 200.30–18.

(b) *Standards for Granting Review Pursuant to a Petition for Review.*

(1) *Mandatory review.* After a petition for review has been filed, the Commission shall review any action that it would be required to review pursuant to Rule 411(b)(1) if the action was made as the initial decision of a hearing officer.

(2) *Discretionary review.* The Commission may decline to review any other action. In determining whether to grant review, the Commission shall consider the factors set forth in Rule 411(b)(2).

(c) *Commission Review Other Than Pursuant to a Petition for Review.* The Commission may, on its own initiative, order review of any action made pursuant to delegated authority at any time, provided, however, that where there are one or more parties to the matter, such review shall not be ordered more than ten days after the action. The vote of one member of the Commission, conveyed to the Secretary, shall be sufficient to bring a matter before the Commission for review.

(d) *Required Items in an Order for Review.* In an order granting a petition for review or directing review on the Commissioner's own initiative, the Commission shall set forth the time within which any party or other person may file a statement in support of or in opposition to the action made by delegated authority and shall state whether a stay shall be granted, if none is in effect, or shall be continued, if in effect pursuant to paragraph (e) of this rule.

(e) *Automatic Stay of Delegated Action.* An action made pursuant to delegated authority shall have immediate effect and be deemed the action of the Commission. Upon filing with the Commission of a notice of intention to petition for review, or upon notice to the Secretary of the vote of a Commissioner that a matter be reviewed, an action made pursuant to delegated authority shall be stayed until the Commission orders otherwise, provided, however, there shall be no automatic stay of an action:

(1) To grant a stay of action by the Commission or a self-regulatory organization as authorized by 17 CFR sections 200.30–14(g)(5)–(6); or

(2) To commence a subpoena enforcement proceeding as authorized by 17 CFR section 200.30–4(a)(10).

(f) *Effectiveness of Stay or of Commission Decision to Modify or Reverse a Delegated Action.* As against any person who shall have acted in reliance upon any action at a delegated level, any stay or any modification or reversal by the Commission of such action shall be effective only from the time such person receives actual notice of such stay, modification or reversal.

Rule 440.   Appeal of Determinations by the Public Company Accounting Oversight Board

(a) *Application for Review; When Available.* Any person who is aggrieved by a determination of the Board with respect to any final disciplinary sanction, including disapproval of a completed application for registration of a public accounting firm, may file an application for review.

(b) *Procedure.* An aggrieved person may file an application for review with the Commission pursuant to Rule 151 within 30 days after the notice filed by the Board of its determination with the Commission pursuant to 17 CFR 240.19d–4 is received by the aggrieved person applying for review. The applicant shall serve the application on the Board at the same time. The application shall identify the determination complained of, set forth in summary form a brief statement of alleged errors in the determination and supporting reasons therefor, and state an address where the applicant can be served. The application should not exceed two pages in length. The notice of appearance required by Rule 102(d) shall accompany the application. Any exception to a determination not supported in an opening brief that complies with Rule 450(b) may, at the discretion of the Commission, be deemed to have been waived by the applicant.

(c) *Stay of Determination.* Filing an application for review with the Commission pursuant to paragraph (b) of this rule operates as a stay of the Board's determination unless the Commission otherwise orders either pursuant to a motion filed in accordance with Rule 401(e) or upon its own motion.

(d) *Certification of the record; service of the index.* Within fourteen days after receipt of an application for review, the Board shall certify and file electronically in the form and manner to be specified by the Office of the Secretary in the materials posted on the Commission's website one unredacted copy of the record upon which it took the complained-of action.

(1) The Board shall file electronically with the Commission one copy of an index of such record, and shall serve one copy of the index on each party. If such index contains any sensitive personal information, as defined in paragraph (d)(2) of this section, the Board also shall file electronically with the Commission one redacted copy of such index, subject to the requirements of paragraphs (d)(2) of this section.

(2) *Sensitive personal information.* Sensitive personal information is defined as a Social Security number, taxpayer identification number, financial account number, credit card or debit card number, passport number, driver's license number, state-issued identification number, home address (other than city and state), telephone number, date of birth (other than year), names and initials of minor children, as well as any unnecessary health information identifiable by individual, such as an individual's medical records. Sensitive personal information shall not be included in, and must be redacted or omitted from, all filings subject to:

(i) *Exceptions.* The following information may be included and is not required to be redacted from filings:

(A) The last four digits of a financial account number, credit card or debit card number, passport number, driver's license number, and state-issued identification number;

(B) Home addresses and telephone numbers of parties and persons filing documents with the Commission;

(C) Business telephone numbers; and

(D) Copies of unredacted filings by regulated entities or registrants that are available on the Commission's public website.

(e) *Certification.* Any filing made pursuant to this section, other than the record upon which the action complained of was taken, must include a certification that any information described in paragraph (d)(2) of this section has been omitted or redacted from the filing.

Rule 441. Commission Consideration of Board Determinations

(a) *Commission Review Other Than Pursuant to an Application for Review.* The Commission may, on its own initiative, order review of any final disciplinary sanction, including disapproval of a completed application for registration of a public accounting firm, imposed by the Board that could be subject to an application for review pursuant to Rule 440(a) within 40 days after the Board filed notice thereof pursuant to Rule 19d–4 under the Securities Exchange Act of 1934.

(b) *Supplemental Briefing.* The Commission may at any time prior to the issuance of its decision raise or consider any matter that it deems material, whether or not raised by the parties. The Commission will give notice to the parties and an opportunity for supplemental briefing with respect to issues not briefed by the parties where the Commission believes that such briefing could significantly aid the decisional process.

Rule 450. Briefs Filed With the Commission

(a) *Briefing Schedule Order.* Other than review ordered pursuant to Rule 431, if review of a determination is mandated by statute, rule, or judicial order or the Commission determines to grant review as a matter of discretion, the Commission shall issue a briefing schedule order directing the party or parties to file opening briefs and specifying particular issues, if any, as to which briefing should be limited or directed. Unless otherwise provided, opening briefs shall be filed within 30 days of the date of the briefing schedule order. Opposition briefs shall be filed within 30 days after the date opening briefs are due. Reply briefs shall be filed within 14 days after the date opposition briefs are due. No briefs in addition to those specified in the briefing schedule order may be filed except with leave of the Commission. The briefing schedule order shall be issued:

(1) At the time the Commission orders review on its own initiative pursuant to Rule 411 or Rule 421, or orders interlocutory review on its own motion pursuant to Rule 400(a); or

(2) Within 21 days, or such longer time as provided by the Commission, after:

(i) The last day permitted for filing a petition for review pursuant to Rule 410(b) or a brief in opposition to a petition for review pursuant to Rule 410(d);

(ii) Receipt by the Commission of an index to the record of a determination of a self-regulatory organization filed pursuant to Rule 420(d).

(iii) Receipt by the Commission of an index to the record of a determination by the Board filed pursuant to Rule 440(d);

(iv) Receipt by the Commission of the mandate of a court of appeals with respect to a judicial remand; or

(v) Certification of a ruling for interlocutory review pursuant to Rule 400(c).

(b) *Contents of briefs.* Briefs shall be confined to the particular matters at issue. Each exception to the findings or conclusions being reviewed shall be stated succinctly. Exceptions shall be supported by citation to the relevant portions of the record, including references to the specific pages relied upon, and by concise argument including citation of such statutes, decisions and other authorities as may be relevant. If the exception relates to the admission or exclusion of evidence, the substance of the evidence admitted or excluded shall be set forth in the brief, or by citation to the record. Reply briefs shall be confined to matters in opposition briefs of other parties; except as otherwise determined by the Commission in its discretion, any argument raised for the first time in a reply brief shall be deemed to have been waived.

(c) *Length limitation.* Except with leave of the Commission, opening and opposition briefs shall not exceed 14,000 words and reply briefs shall not exceed 7,000 words, exclusive of pages containing the table of contents, table of authorities, and any addendum that consists solely of copies of applicable cases, pertinent legislative provisions or rules, and exhibits. Incorporation of pleadings or filings by reference is not permitted. Motions to file briefs in excess of these limitations are disfavored.

(d) *Certificate of compliance.* An opening or opposition brief that does not exceed 30 pages in length, exclusive of pages containing the table of contents, table of authorities, and any addendum that consists solely of copies of applicable cases, pertinent legislative provisions, or rules and exhibits, is presumptively considered to contain no more than 14,000 words. A reply brief that does not exceed 15 pages in length, exclusive of pages containing the table of contents, table of authorities, and any addendum that consists solely of copies of applicable cases, pertinent legislative provisions, or rules and exhibits is presumptively considered to contain no more than 7,000 words. Any brief that exceeds these page limits must include a certificate by the party's representative, or an unrepresented party, stating that the brief complies with the requirements set forth in Rule 450(c) and stating the number of words in the brief. The person preparing the certificate may rely on the word count of the word-processing system used to prepare the brief.

Rule 451.   Oral Argument Before the Commission

(a) *Availability.* The Commission, on its own motion or the motion of a party or any other aggrieved person entitled to Commission review, may order oral argument with respect to any matter. Motions for oral argument with respect to whether to affirm all or part of an initial decision by a hearing officer shall be granted unless exceptional circumstances make oral argument impractical or inadvisable. The Commission will consider appeals, motions and other matters properly before it on the basis of the papers filed by the parties without oral argument unless the Commission determines that the presentation of facts and legal arguments in the briefs and record and the decisional process would be significantly aided by oral argument.

(b) *Procedure.* Requests for oral argument shall be made by separate motion accompanying the initial brief on the merits. The Commission shall issue an order as to whether oral argument is to be heard, and if so, the time and place therefor. If oral argument is granted, the time fixed for oral argument shall be changed only by written order of the Commission, for good cause shown. The order shall state at whose request the change is made and the reasons for any such changes. No visual aids may be used at oral argument unless copies have been provided to the Commission and all parties at least five business days before the argument is to be held.

(c) *Time Allowed.* Unless the Commission orders otherwise, not more than one half-hour per side will be allowed for oral argument. The Commission may, in its discretion, determine that several persons have a common interest, and that the interests represented will be considered a single side for purposes of allotting time for oral argument. Time will be divided equally among persons on a single side, provided, however, that by mutual agreement they may reallocate their time among themselves. A request for additional time must be made by motion filed reasonably in advance of the date fixed for argument.

(d) *Participation of Commissioners.* A member of the Commission who was not present at the oral argument may participate in the decision of the proceeding, provided that the member has reviewed the transcript of such argument prior to such participation. The decision shall state whether the required review was made.

Rule 452.   Additional Evidence

Upon its own motion or the motion of a party, the Commission may allow the submission of additional evidence. A party may file a motion for leave to adduce additional evidence at any time prior to issuance of a decision by the Commission. Such motion shall show with particularity that such additional evidence is material and that there were reasonable grounds for failure to adduce such evidence previously. The Commission may accept or hear additional evidence, may remand the proceeding to a self-regulatory organization, or may remand or refer the proceeding to a hearing officer for the taking of additional evidence, as appropriate.

Rule 460.   Record Before the Commission

The Commission shall determine each matter on the basis of the record.

(a) *Contents of the Record.*

(1) In proceedings for final decision before the Commission other than those reviewing a determination by a self-regulatory organization, the record shall consist of:

(i) All items part of the record below in accordance with Rule 350;

(ii) Any petitions for review, cross-petitions or oppositions; and

(iii) All briefs, motions, submissions and other papers filed on appeal or review.

(2) In a proceeding for final decision before the Commission reviewing a determination by a self-regulatory organization, the record shall consist of:

(i) The record certified pursuant to Rule 420(d) by the self-regulatory organization;

(ii) Any application for review; and

(iii) Any submissions, moving papers, and briefs filed on appeal or review.

(3) In a proceeding for final decision before the Commission reviewing a determination of the Board, the record shall consist of:

(i) The record certified pursuant to Rule 440(d) by the Board;

(ii) Any application for review; and

(iii) Any submissions, moving papers, and briefs filed on appeal or review.

(b) *Transmittal of Record to Commission.* Within 14 days after the last date set for filing briefs or such later date as the Commission directs, the Secretary shall transmit the record to the Commission.

(c) *Review of Documents not Admitted.* Any document offered in evidence but excluded by the hearing officer or the Commission and any document marked for identification but not offered as an exhibit shall not be considered a part of the record before the Commission on appeal but shall be transmitted to the Commission by the Secretary if so requested by the Commission. In the event that the Commission does not request the document, the Secretary shall retain the document not admitted into the record until the later of:

(1) The date upon which the Commission's order becomes final, or

(2)   The conclusion of any judicial review of that order.

Rule 470.   Reconsideration

(a)   *Scope of Rule.* A party or any person aggrieved by a determination in a proceeding may file a motion for reconsideration of a final order issued by the Commission.

(b)   *Procedure.* A motion for reconsideration shall be filed within 10 days after service of the order complained of, or within such time as the Commission may prescribe upon motion for extension of time filed by the person seeking reconsideration, if the motion is made within the foregoing 10-day period. The motion for reconsideration shall briefly and specifically state the matters of record alleged to have been erroneously decided, the grounds relied upon, and the relief sought. A motion for reconsideration shall conform to the requirements, including the limitation on the number of words, provided in Rule 154. No response to a motion for reconsideration shall be filed unless requested by the Commission. Any response so requested shall comply with Rule 154.

Rule 490.   Receipt of Petitions for Judicial Review Pursuant to 28 U.S.C.A. § 2112(a)(1)

The Commission officer and office designated pursuant to 28 U.S.C.A. section 2112(a)(1) to receive copies of petitions for review of Commission orders from the persons instituting review in a court of appeals, are the Secretary and the Office of the Secretary at the Commission's Headquarters. Ten copies of each petition shall be submitted. Each copy shall state on its face that it is being submitted to the Commission pursuant to 28 U.S.C.A. section 2112 by the person or persons who filed the petition in the court of appeals.

RULES RELATING TO TEMPORARY ORDERS AND SUSPENSIONS

Rule 500.   Expedited Consideration of Proceedings

Consistent with the Commission's or the hearing officer's other responsibilities, every hearing shall be held and every decision shall be rendered at the earliest possible time in connection with:

(a)   An application for a temporary sanction, as defined in Rule 101(a), or a proceeding to determine whether a temporary sanction should be made permanent;

(b)   A motion or application to review an order suspending temporarily the effectiveness of an exemption from registration pursuant to Regulations A, B, E or F under the Securities Act; or,

(c)   A motion to or petition to review an order suspending temporarily the privilege of appearing before the Commission under Rule 102(e)(3), or a sanction under Rule 180(a)(1).

Rule 510.   Temporary Cease-and-Desist Orders: Application Process

(a)   *Procedure.* A request for entry of a temporary cease-and-desist order shall be made by application filed by the Division of Enforcement. The application shall set forth the statutory provision or rule that each respondent is alleged to have violated; the temporary relief sought against each respondent, including whether the respondent would be required to take action to prevent the dissipation or conversion of assets; and whether the relief is sought *ex parte.*

(b)   *Accompanying Documents.* The application shall be accompanied by a declaration of facts signed by a person with knowledge of the facts contained therein, a memorandum of points and authorities, a proposed order imposing the temporary relief sought, and, unless relief is sought *ex parte,* a proposed notice of hearing and order to show cause whether the temporary relief should be imposed. If a proceeding for a permanent cease-and-desist order has not already been commenced, a proposed order instituting proceedings to determine whether a permanent cease-and-desist order should be imposed shall also be filed with the application.

(c)   *With Whom Filed.* The application shall be filed with the Secretary or, if the Secretary is unavailable, with the duty officer. In no event shall an application be filed with an administrative law judge.

(d)   *Record of Proceedings.* Hearings, including *ex parte* presentations made by the Division of Enforcement pursuant to Rule 513, shall be recorded or transcribed pursuant to Rule 302.

Rule 511.   Temporary Cease-and-Desist Orders: Notice; Procedures for Hearing

(a)   *Notice: How Given.* Notice of an application for a temporary cease-and-desist order shall be made by serving a notice of hearing and order to show cause pursuant to Rule 141(b) or, where timely service of a notice of hearing pursuant to Rule 141(b) is not practicable, by any other means reasonably calculated to give actual notice that a hearing will be held, including telephonic notification of the general subject matter, time, and place of the hearing. If an application is made *ex parte,* pursuant to Rule 513, no notice to a respondent need be given prior to the Commission's consideration of the application.

(b)   *Hearing Before the Commission.* Except as provided in paragraph (d) of this rule, hearings on an application for a temporary cease-and-desist order shall be held before the Commission.

(c)   *Presiding Officer: Designation.* The Chairman shall preside or designate a Commissioner to preside at the hearing. If the Chairman is absent or unavailable at the time of hearing and no other Commissioner has been designated to preside, the duty officer on the day the hearing begins shall preside or designate another Commissioner to preside.

(d)   *Procedure at Hearing.*

(1)   The presiding officer shall have all those powers of a hearing officer set forth in Rule 111 and shall rule on the admissibility of evidence and other procedural matters, including, but not limited to whether oral testimony will be heard; the time allowed each party for the submission of evidence or argument; and whether post-hearing submission of briefs, proposed findings of fact and conclusions of law will be permitted and if so, the procedures for submission; provided, however, that the person presiding may consult with other Commissioners participating in the hearing on these or any other question of procedure.

(2)   Each Commissioner present at the hearing shall be afforded a reasonable opportunity to ask questions of witnesses, if any, or of counsel.

(3)   A party or witness may participate by telephone. Alternative means of remote access, including a video link, shall be permitted in the Commission's discretion. Factors the Commission may consider in determining whether to permit alternative means of remote access include, but are not limited to, whether allowing an alternative means of access will delay the hearing, whether the alternative means is reliable, and whether the party proposing its use has made arrangements to pay for its cost.

(4)   After a hearing has begun, the Commission may, on its own motion, or the motion of a party, assign a hearing officer to preside at the taking of oral testimony or other evidence and to certify the record of such testimony or other evidence to the Commission within a fixed period of time. No recommended or initial decision shall be made by such a hearing officer.

Rule 512.   Temporary Cease-and-Desist Orders: Issuance After Notice and Opportunity for Hearing

(a)   *Basis for Issuance.* A temporary cease-and-desist order shall be issued only if the Commission determines that the alleged violation or threatened violation specified in an order instituting proceedings whether to enter a permanent cease-and-desist order pursuant to Securities Act Section 8A(a), Exchange Act section 21C(a), Investment Company Act section 9(f)(1), or Investment Advisers Act section 203(k)(1), or the continuation thereof, is likely to result in significant dissipation or conversion of assets, significant harm to investors, or substantial harm to the public interest, including, but not limited to, losses to the Securities Investor Protection Corporation, prior to the completion of proceedings on the permanent cease-and-desist order.

(b)   *Content, Scope and Form of Order.* Every temporary cease-and-desist order granted shall:

(1)   Describe the basis for its issuance, including the alleged or threatened violations and the harm that is likely to result without the issuance of an order;

(2)   Describe in reasonable detail, and not by reference to the order instituting proceedings or any other document, the act or acts the respondent is to take or refrain from taking; and

(3) Be indorsed with the date and hour of issuance.

(c) *Effective Upon Service.* A temporary cease-and-desist order is effective upon service upon the respondent.

(d) *Service: How Made.* Service of a temporary cease-and-desist order shall be made pursuant to Rule 141(a). The person who serves the order shall promptly file a declaration of service identifying the person served, the method of service, the date of service, the address to which service was made and the person who made service; provided, however, failure to file such a declaration shall have no effect on the validity of the service.

(e) *Commission Review.* At any time after the respondent has been served with a temporary cease-and-desist order, the respondent may apply to the Commission to have the order set aside, limited or suspended. The application shall set forth with specificity the facts that support the request.

Rule 513.   Temporary Cease-and-Desist Orders: Issuance Without Prior Notice and Opportunity for Hearing

In addition to the requirements for issuance of a temporary cease-and-desist order set forth in Rule 512, the following requirements shall apply if a temporary cease-and-desist order is to be entered without prior notice and opportunity for hearing:

(a) *Basis for Issuance Without Prior Notice and Opportunity for Hearing.* A temporary cease-and-desist order may be issued without notice and opportunity for hearing only if the Commission determines, from specific facts in the record of the proceeding, that notice and hearing prior to entry of an order would be impracticable or contrary to the public interest.

(b) *Content of the Order.* An *ex parte* temporary cease-and-desist order shall state specifically why notice and hearing would have been impracticable or contrary to the public interest.

(c) *Hearing Before the Commission.* If a respondent has been served with a temporary cease-and-desist order entered without a prior Commission hearing, the respondent may apply to the Commission to have the order set aside, limited, or suspended, and if the application is made within 10 days after the date on which the order was served, may request a hearing on such application. The Commission shall hold a hearing and render a decision on the respondent's application at the earliest possible time. The hearing shall begin within two days of the filing of the application unless the applicant consents to a longer period or the Commission, by order, for good cause shown, sets a later date. The Commission shall render a decision on the application within five calendar days of its filing, provided, however, that the Commission, by order, for good cause shown, may extend the time within which a decision may be rendered for a single period of five calendar days, or such longer time as consented to by the applicant. If the Commission does not render its decision within 10 days of the respondent's application or such longer time as consented to by the applicant, the temporary order shall be suspended until a decision is rendered.

(d) *Presiding Officer, Procedure at Hearing.* Procedures with respect to the selection of a presiding officer and the conduct of the hearing shall be in accordance with Rule 511.

Rule 514.   Temporary Cease-and-Desist Orders: Judicial Review; Duration

(a) *Availability of Judicial Review.* Judicial review of a temporary cease-and-desist order shall be available as provided in section 8A(d)(2) of the Securities Act, section 21C(d)(2) of the Exchange Act, section 9(f)(4)(B) of the Investment Company Act, or section 203(k)(4)(B) of the Investment Advisers Act.

(b) *Duration.* Unless set aside, limited, or suspended, either by order of the Commission, a court of competent jurisdiction, or a hearing officer acting pursuant to Rule 531, or by operation of Rule 513, a temporary cease-and-desist order shall remain effective and enforceable until the earlier of:

(1) The completion of the proceedings whether a permanent order shall be entered; or

(2) 180 days, or such longer time as consented to by the respondent, after issuance of a briefing schedule order pursuant to Rule 540(b), if an initial decision whether a permanent order should be entered is appealed.

Rule 520. Suspension of Registration of Brokers, Dealers, or Other Exchange Act—Registered Entities: Application

(a) *Procedure.* A request for suspension of a registered broker, dealer, municipal securities dealer, government securities broker, government securities dealer, or transfer agent pending a final determination whether the registration shall be revoked shall be made by application filed by the Division of Enforcement. The application shall set forth the statutory provision or rule that each respondent is alleged to have violated and the temporary suspension sought as to each respondent.

(b) *Accompanying Documents.* The application shall be accompanied by a declaration of facts signed by a person with knowledge of the facts contained therein, a memorandum of points and authorities, a proposed order imposing the temporary suspension of registration sought, and a proposed notice of hearing and order to show cause whether the temporary suspension of registration should be imposed. If a proceeding to determine whether to revoke the registration permanently has not already been commenced, a proposed order instituting proceedings to determine whether a permanent sanction should be imposed shall also be filed with the application.

(c) *With Whom Filed.* The application shall be filed with the Secretary or, if the Secretary is unavailable, with the duty officer. In no event shall an application be filed with an administrative law judge.

(d) *Record of Hearings.* All hearings shall be recorded or transcribed pursuant to Rule 302.

Rule 521. Suspension of Registration of Brokers, Dealers, or Other Exchange Act—Registered Entities: Notice and Opportunity for Hearing on Application

(a) *How Given.* Notice of an application to suspend a registration pursuant to Rule 520 shall be made by serving a notice of hearing and order to show cause pursuant to Rule 141(b) or, where timely service of a notice of hearing pursuant to Rule 141(b) is not practicable, by any other means reasonably calculated to give actual notice that a hearing will be held, including telephonic notification of the general subject matter, time, and place of the hearing.

(b) *Hearing: Before Whom Held.* Except as provided in paragraph (d) of this rule, hearings on an application to suspend a registration pursuant to Rule 520 shall be held before the Commission.

(c) *Presiding Officer: Designation.* The Chairman shall preside or designate a Commissioner to preside at the hearing. If the Chairman is absent or unavailable at the time of hearing and no other Commissioner has been designated to preside, the duty officer on the day the hearing begins shall preside or designate another Commissioner to preside.

(d) *Procedure at Hearing.*

(1) The presiding officer shall have all those powers of a hearing officer set forth in Rule 111 and shall rule on the admissibility of evidence and other procedural matters, including, but not limited to whether oral testimony will be heard; the time allowed each party for the submission of evidence or argument; and whether post-hearing submission of briefs, proposed findings of fact and conclusions of law will be permitted and if so, the procedures for submission; provided, however, that the person presiding may consult with other Commissioners participating in the hearing on these or any other question of procedure.

(2) Each Commissioner present at the hearing shall be afforded a reasonable opportunity to ask questions of witnesses, if any, or counsel.

(3) A party or witness may participate by telephone. Alternative means of remote access, including a video link, shall be permitted in the Commission's discretion. Factors the Commission may consider in determining whether to permit alternative means of remote access include, but are not limited to, whether allowing an alternative means of access will delay the hearing, whether the alternative means is reliable, and whether the party proposing its use has made arrangements to pay for its cost.

(4) After a hearing has begun, the Commission may, on its own motion or the motion of a party, assign a hearing officer to preside at the taking of oral testimony or other evidence and to certify the

record of such testimony or other evidence to the Commission within a fixed period of time. No recommended or initial decision shall be made.

Rule 522.   Suspension of Registration of Brokers, Dealers, or Other Exchange Act— Registered Entities: Issuance and Review of Order

(a)   *Basis for Issuance.* An order suspending a registration, pending final determination as to whether the registration shall be revoked shall be issued only if the Commission finds that the suspension is necessary or appropriate in the public interest or for the protection of investors.

(b)   *Content, Scope and Form of Order.* Each order suspending a registration shall:

(1)   Describe the basis for its issuance, including the alleged or threatened violations and the harm that is likely to result without the issuance of an order;

(2)   Describe in reasonable detail, and not by reference to the order instituting proceedings or any other document, the act or acts the respondent is to take or refrain from taking; and

(3)   Be indorsed with the date and hour of issuance.

(c)   *Effective Upon Service.* An order suspending a registration is effective upon service upon the respondent.

(d)   *Service: How Made.* Service of an order suspending a registration shall be made pursuant to Rule 141(a). The person who serves the order shall promptly file a declaration of service identifying the person served, the method of service, the date of service, the address to which service was made and the person who made service; provided, however, failure to file such a declaration shall have no effect on the validity of the service.

(e)   *Commission Review.* At any time after the respondent has been served with an order suspending a registration, the respondent may apply to the Commission or the hearing officer to have the order set aside, limited, or suspended. The application shall set forth with specificity the facts that support the request.

Rule 523.   [Reserved]

Rule 524.   Suspension of Registrations: Duration

Unless set aside, limited or suspended by order of the Commission, a court of competent jurisdiction, or a hearing officer acting pursuant to Rule 531, an order suspending a registration shall remain effective and enforceable until the earlier of:

(a)   The completion of the proceedings whether the registration shall be permanently revoked; or

(b)   180 days, or such longer time as consented to by the respondent, after issuance of a briefing schedule order pursuant to Rule 540(b), if an initial decision whether the registration shall be permanently revoked is appealed.

Rule 530.   Initial Decision on Permanent Order: Timing for Submitting Proposed Findings and Preparation of Decision

Unless otherwise ordered by the Commission or hearing officer, if a temporary cease-and-desist order or suspension of registration order is in effect, the following time limits shall apply to preparation of an initial decision as to whether such order should be made permanent:

(a)   Proposed findings and conclusions and briefs in support thereof shall be filed 30 days after the close of the hearing;

(b)   The record in the proceedings shall be served by the Secretary upon the hearing officer three days after the date for the filing of the last brief called for by the hearing officer; and

(c)   The initial decision shall be filed with the Secretary at the earliest possible time, but in no event more than 30 days after service of the record, unless the hearing officer, by order, shall extend the time for good cause shown for a period not to exceed 30 days.

Rule 531.   Initial Decision on Permanent Order: Effect on Temporary Order

(a)   *Specification of Permanent Sanction.* If, at the time an initial decision is issued, a temporary sanction is in effect as to any respondent, the initial decision shall specify:

(1)   Which terms or conditions of a temporary cease-and-desist order, if any, shall become permanent; and

(2)   Whether a temporary suspension of a respondent's registration, if any, shall be made a permanent revocation of registration.

(b)   *Modification of Temporary Order.* If any temporary sanction shall not become permanent under the terms of the initial decision, the hearing officer shall issue a separate order setting aside, limiting or suspending the temporary sanction then in effect in accordance with the terms of the initial decision. The hearing officer shall decline to suspend a term or condition of a temporary cease-and-desist order if it is found that the continued effectiveness of such term or condition is necessary to effectuate any term of the relief ordered in the initial decision, including the payment of disgorgement, interest or penalties. An order modifying temporary sanctions shall be effective 14 days after service. Within one week of service of the order modifying temporary sanctions any party may seek a stay or modification of the order from the Commission pursuant to Rule 401.

Rule 540.   Appeal and Commission Review of Initial Decision Making a Temporary Order Permanent

(a)   *Petition for Review.* Any person who seeks Commission review of an initial decision as to whether a temporary sanction shall be made permanent shall file a petition for review pursuant to Rule 410, provided, however, that the petition must be filed within 10 days after service of the initial decision.

(b)   *Review Procedure.* If the Commission determines to grant or order review, it shall issue a briefing schedule order pursuant to Rule 450. Unless otherwise ordered by the Commission, opening briefs shall be filed within 21 days of the order granting or ordering review, and opposition briefs shall be filed within 14 days after opening briefs are filed. Reply briefs shall be filed within seven days after opposition briefs are filed. Oral argument, if granted by the Commission, shall be held within 90 days of the issuance of the briefing schedule order.

Rule 550.   Summary Suspensions Pursuant to Exchange Act Section 12(k)(1)(A)

(a)   *Petition for Termination of Suspension.* Any person adversely affected by a suspension pursuant to section 12(k)(1)(A) of the Exchange Act, who desires to show that such suspension is not necessary in the public interest or for the protection of investors may file a sworn petition with the Secretary, requesting that the suspension be terminated. The petition shall set forth the reasons why the petitioner believes that the suspension of trading should not continue and state with particularity the facts upon which the petitioner relies.

(b)   *Commission Consideration of a Petition.* The Commission, in its discretion, may schedule a hearing on the matter, request additional written submissions, or decide the matter on the facts presented in the petition and any other relevant facts known to the Commission. If the petitioner fails to cooperate with, obstructs, or refuses to permit the making of an examination by the Commission, such conduct shall be grounds to deny the petition.

RULES REGARDING DISGORGEMENT AND PENALTY PAYMENTS

Rule 600.   Interest on Sums Disgorged

(a)   *Interest Required.* Prejudgment interest shall be due on any sum required to be paid pursuant to an order of disgorgement. The disgorgement order shall specify each violation that forms the basis for the disgorgement ordered; the date which, for purposes of calculating disgorgement, each such violation was deemed to have occurred; the amount to be disgorged for each such violation; and the total sum to be disgorged. Prejudgment interest shall be due from the first day of the month following each such violation through the last day of the month preceding the month in which payment of disgorgement is made. The order shall state the amount of prejudgment interest owed as of the date of the disgorgement order and that interest shall continue to accrue on all funds owed until they are paid.

(b)   *Rate of Interest.* Interest on the sum to be disgorged shall be computed at the underpayment rate of interest established under section 6621(a)(2) of the Internal Revenue Code, and shall be compounded quarterly. The Commission or the hearing officer may, by order, specify a lower rate of prejudgment interest as to any funds which the respondent has placed in an escrow or otherwise guaranteed for payment of disgorgement upon a final determination of the respondent's liability. Escrow and other guarantee arrangements must be approved by the Commission or the hearing officer prior to entry of the disgorgement order.

Rule 601.   Prompt Payment of Disgorgement, Interest and Penalties

(a)   *Timing of Payments.* Unless otherwise provided, funds due pursuant to an order by the Commission requiring the payment of disgorgement, interest or penalties shall be paid no later than 21 days after service of the order, and funds due pursuant to an order by a hearing officer shall be paid in accordance with the order of finality issued pursuant to Rule 360(d)(2).

(b)   *Stays.* A stay of any order requiring the payment of disgorgement, interest or penalties may be sought at any time pursuant to Rule 401.

(c)   *Method of Making Payment.* Payment shall be made by United States postal money order, wire transfer, certified check, bank cashier's check, or bank money order made payable to the Securities and Exchange Commission. The payment shall be mailed or delivered to the office designated by this Commission. Payment shall be accompanied by a letter that identifies the name and number of the case and the name of the respondent making payment. A copy of the letter and the instrument of payment shall be sent to counsel for the Division of Enforcement.

Rules 610 Through 614 and Rule 620. [Removed and Reserved]

Rule 630.   Inability to Pay Disgorgement, Interest or Penalties

(a)   *Generally.* In any proceeding in which an order requiring payment of disgorgement, interest or penalties may be entered, a respondent may present evidence of an inability to pay disgorgement, interest or a penalty. The Commission may, in its discretion, or the hearing officer may, in his or her discretion, consider evidence concerning ability to pay in determining whether disgorgement, interest or a penalty is in the public interest.

(b)   *Financial Disclosure Statement.* Any respondent who asserts an inability to pay disgorgement, interest or penalties may be required to file a sworn financial disclosure statement and to keep the statement current. The financial statement shall show the respondent's assets, liabilities, income or other funds received and expenses or other payments, from the date of the first violation alleged against that respondent in the order instituting proceedings, or such later date as specified by the Commission or a hearing officer, to the date of the order requiring the disclosure statement to be filed. By order, the Commission or the hearing officer may prescribe the use of the Disclosure of Assets and Financial Information Form or any other form, may specify other time periods for which disclosure is required, and may require such other information as deemed necessary to evaluate a claim of inability to pay.

(c)   *Confidentiality.* Any respondent submitting financial information pursuant to this rule or Rule 410(c) may make a motion, pursuant to Rule 322, for the issuance of a protective order against disclosure of the information submitted to the public or to any parties other than the Division of Enforcement. Prior to a ruling on the motion, no party receiving information as to which a motion for a protective order has been made may transfer or convey the information to any other person without the prior permission of the Commission or the hearing officer.

(d) *Service Required.* Notwithstanding any provision of Rule 322, a copy of the financial disclosure statement shall be served on the Division of Enforcement.

(e) *Failure to File Required Financial Information: Sanction.* Any respondent who, after making a claim of inability to pay either disgorgement, interest or a penalty, fails to file a financial disclosure statement when such a filing has been ordered or is required by rule may, in the discretion of the Commission or the hearing officer, be deemed to have waived the claim of inability to pay. No sanction pursuant to Rule 155 or Rule 180 shall be imposed for a failure to file such a statement.

Rule 700.   Initiation of Proceedings for SRO Proposed Rule Changes

(a) *Rules of Practice.* For purposes of these Rules of Practice contained at Rule 700 through 701, the following Rules of Practice apply:

(1)   Rule 103, (Construction of Rules);

(2)   Rule 104, (Business Hours); and

(3)   Rule 160, (Time Computation).

(b) *Institution of proceedings; notice and opportunity to submit written views.*

(1)   Generally. If the Commission determines to initiate proceedings to determine whether a self-regulatory organization's proposed rule change should be disapproved, it shall provide notice thereof to the self-regulatory organization that filed the proposed rule change, as well as all interested parties and the public, by publication in the Federal Register of the grounds for disapproval under consideration.

(i)   Prior to notice. If the Commission determines to institute proceedings prior to initial publication by the Commission of the notice of the self-regulatory organization's proposed rule change in the Federal Register, then the Commission shall publish notice of the proposed rule change simultaneously with a brief summary of the grounds for disapproval under consideration.

(ii)   Subsequent to notice. If the Commission determines to institute proceedings subsequent to initial publication by the Commission of the notice of the self-regulatory organization's proposed rule change in the Federal Register, then the Commission shall publish separately in the Federal Register a brief summary of the grounds for disapproval under consideration.

(iii)   Service of an order instituting proceedings. In addition to publication in the Federal Register of the grounds for disapproval under consideration, the Secretary, or another duly authorized officer of the Commission, shall serve a copy of the grounds for disapproval under consideration to the self-regulatory organization that filed the proposed rule change by serving notice to the person listed as the contact person on the cover page of the Form 19b–4 filing. Notice shall be made by delivering a copy of the order to such contact person either by any method specified in Rule 141(a) or by electronic means including e-mail.

(2)   Notice of the grounds for disapproval under consideration. The grounds for disapproval under consideration shall include a brief statement of the matters of fact and law on which the Commission instituted the proceedings, including the areas in which the Commission may have questions or may need to solicit additional information on the proposed rule change. The Commission may consider during the course of the proceedings additional matters of fact and law beyond what was set forth in its notice of the grounds for disapproval under consideration.

(3)   Demonstration of consistency with the Exchange Act. The burden to demonstrate that a proposed rule change is consistent with the Exchange Act and the rules and regulations issued thereunder that are applicable to the self-regulatory organization is on the self-regulatory organization that proposed the rule change. As reflected in the General Instructions to Form 19b–4, the Form is designed to elicit information necessary for the public to provide meaningful comment on the proposed rule change and for the Commission to determine whether the proposed rule change is consistent with the requirements of the Exchange Act and the rules and regulations thereunder applicable to the self-regulatory organization. The self-regulatory organization must provide all information elicited by the

Form, including the exhibits, and must present the information in a clear and comprehensible manner. In particular, the self-regulatory organization must explain why the proposed rule change is consistent with the requirements of the Exchange Act and the rules and regulations thereunder applicable to the self-regulatory organization. A mere assertion that the proposed rule change is consistent with those requirements, or that another self-regulatory organization has a similar rule in place, is not sufficient. Instead, the description of the proposed rule change, its purpose and operation, its effect, and a legal analysis of its consistency with applicable requirements must all be sufficiently detailed and specific to support an affirmative Commission finding. Any failure of the self-regulatory organization to provide the information elicited by Form 19b–4 may result in the Commission not having a sufficient basis to make an affirmative finding that a proposed rule change is consistent with the Exchange Act and the rules and regulations issued thereunder that are applicable to the self-regulatory organization.

(c)   *Conduct of hearings.*

(1)   Initial comment period in writing. Unless otherwise specified by the Commission in its notice of grounds for disapproval under consideration, all interested persons will be given an opportunity to submit written data, views, and arguments concerning the proposed rule change under consideration and whether the Commission should approve or disapprove the proposed rule change. The self-regulatory organization that submitted the proposed rule change may file a written statement in support of its proposed rule change demonstrating, in specific detail, how such proposed rule change is consistent with the requirements of the Exchange Act and the rules and regulations thereunder applicable to the self-regulatory organization, including a response to each of the grounds for disapproval under consideration. Such statement may include specific representations or undertakings by the self-regulatory organization. The Commission will specify in the summary of the grounds for disapproval under consideration the length of the initial comment period.

(2)   Oral. The Commission, in its sole discretion, may determine whether any issues relevant to approval or disapproval would be facilitated by the opportunity for an oral presentation of views.

(3)   Rebuttal. At the end of the initial comment period, the self-regulatory organization that filed the proposed rule change will be given an opportunity to respond to any comments received. The self-regulatory organization may voluntarily file, or the Commission may request a self-regulatory organization to file, a response to a comment received regarding any aspect of the proposed rule change under consideration to assist the Commission in determining whether the proposed rule change should be disapproved. The Commission will specify in the summary of the grounds for disapproval under consideration the length of the rebuttal period.

(4)   Non-response. Any failure by the self-regulatory organization to provide a complete response, within the applicable time period specified, to a comment letter received or to the Commission's grounds for disapproval under consideration may result in the Commission not having a sufficient basis to make an affirmative finding that a proposed rule change is consistent with the Exchange Act and the rules and regulations issued thereunder that are applicable to the self-regulatory organization.

(d)   *Record before the Commission.*

(1)   Filing of papers with the Commission. Filing of papers with the Commission shall be made by filing them with the Secretary, including through electronic means. In its notice setting forth the grounds for disapproval under consideration for a proposed rule change, the Commission shall inform interested parties of the methods by which they may submit written comments and arguments for or against Commission approval.

(2)   Public availability of materials received. During the conduct of the proceedings, the Commission generally will make available publicly all written comments it receives without change. In its notice setting forth the grounds for disapproval under consideration for a proposed rule change, the Commission shall inform interested parties of the methods by which they may view all written communications relating to the proposed rule change between the Commission and any person, other than those that may be withheld from the public in accordance with the provisions of 5 U.S.C. 552.

(3)   Record before the Commission. The Commission shall determine each matter on the basis of the record. The record shall consist of the proposed rule change filed on Form 19b–4 by the self-

regulatory organization, including all attachments and exhibits thereto, and all written materials received from any interested parties on the proposed rule change, including the self-regulatory organization that filed the proposed rule change, through the means identified by the Commission as provided in paragraph (1), as well as any written materials that reflect communications between the Commission and any interested parties.

(e) *Amended notice not required.* The Commission is not required to amend its notice of grounds for disapproval under consideration in order to consider, during the course of the proceedings, additional matters of fact and law beyond what was set forth in the notice of the grounds for disapproval under consideration.

Rule 701.   Issuance of Order

At any time following conclusion of the rebuttal period specified in Rule 700(b)(4), the Commission may issue an order approving or disapproving the self-regulatory organization's proposed rule change together with a written statement of the reasons therefor.

INFORMAL PROCEDURES AND SUPPLEMENTARY INFORMATION CONCERNING ADJUDICATORY PROCEEDINGS

Rule 900.   Informal Procedures and Supplementary Information Concerning Adjudicatory Proceedings

(a) *Guidelines for the timely completion of proceedings.* (1) Timely resolution of adjudicatory proceedings is one factor in assessing the effectiveness of the adjudicatory program in protecting investors, promoting public confidence in the securities markets and assuring respondents a fair hearing. Establishment of guidelines for the timely completion of key phases of contested administrative proceedings provides a standard for both the Commission and the public to gauge the Commission's adjudicatory program on this criterion. The Commission has directed that:

(i)   To the extent possible, a decision by the Commission on review of an interlocutory matter should be completed within 45 days of the date set for filing the final brief on the matter submitted for review.

(ii)   To the extent possible, a decision by the Commission on a motion to stay a decision that has already taken effect or that will take effect within five days of the filing of the motion, should be issued within five days of the date set for filing of the opposition to the motion for a stay. If the decision complained of has not taken effect, the Commission's decision should be issued within 45 days of the date set for filing of the opposition to the motion for a stay.

(iii)   Ordinarily, a decision by the Commission with respect to an appeal from the initial decision of a hearing officer, a review of a determination by a self-regulatory organization or the Public Company Accounting Oversight Board, or a remand of a prior Commission decision by a court of appeals will be issued within eight months from the completion of briefing on the petition for review, application for review, or remand order. If the Commission determines that the complexity of the issues presented in a petition for review, application for review, or remand order warrants additional time, the decision of the Commission in that matter may be issued within ten months of the completion of briefing.

(iv)   If the Commission determines that a decision by the Commission cannot be issued within the period specified in paragraph (a)(1)(iii) of this rule, the Commission may extend that period by orders as it deems appropriate in its discretion. The guidelines in this paragraph (a) confer no rights or entitlements on parties or other persons.

(2)   The guidelines in this paragraph (a) do not create a requirement that each portion of a proceeding or the entire proceeding be completed within the periods described. Among other reasons, Commission review may require additional time because a matter is unusually complex or because the record is exceptionally long. In addition, fairness is enhanced if the Commission's deliberative process is not constrained by an inflexible schedule. In some proceedings, deliberation may be delayed by the need to consider more urgent matters, to permit the preparation of dissenting opinions, or for other

good cause. The guidelines will be used by the Commission as one of several criteria in monitoring and evaluating its adjudicatory program. The guidelines will be examined periodically, and, if necessary, readjusted in light of changes in the pending caseload and the available level of staff resources.

(b)   *Reports to the Commission on pending cases.* The administrative law judges, the Secretary and the General Counsel have each been delegated authority to issue certain orders or adjudicate certain proceedings. See17 CFR 200.30–1et seq. Proceedings are also assigned to the General Counsel for the preparation of a proposed order or opinion which will then be recommended to the Commission for consideration. In order to improve accountability by and to the Commission for management of the docket, the Commission has directed that confidential status reports with respect to all filed adjudicatory proceedings shall be made periodically to the Commission. These reports will be made through the Secretary, with a minimum frequency established by the Commission. In connection with these periodic reports, if a proceeding pending before the Commission has not been concluded within 30 days of the guidelines established in paragraph (a) of this rule, the General Counsel shall specifically apprise the Commission of that fact, and shall describe the procedural posture of the case, project an estimated date for conclusion of the proceeding, and provide such other information as is necessary to enable the Commission to make a determination under paragraph (a)(1)(iv) of this rule or to determine whether additional steps are necessary to reach a fair and timely resolution of the matter.

(c)   *Publication of information concerning the pending case docket.* Ongoing disclosure of information about the adjudication program caseload increases awareness of the importance of the program, facilitates oversight of the program and promotes confidence in the efficiency and fairness of the program by investors, securities industry participants, self-regulatory organizations and other members of the public. The Commission has directed the Secretary to publish in the first and seventh months of each fiscal year summary statistical information about the status of pending adjudicatory proceedings and changes in the Commission's caseload over the prior six months. The report will include the number of cases pending before the administrative law judges and the Commission at the beginning and end of the six-month period. The report will also show increases in the caseload arising from new cases being instituted, appealed or remanded to the Commission and decreases in the caseload arising from the disposition of proceedings by issuance of initial decisions, issuance of final decisions issued on appeal of initial decisions, other dispositions of appeals of initial decisions, final decisions on review of self-regulatory organization determinations, other dispositions on review of self-regulatory organization determinations, and decisions with respect to stays or interlocutory motions. For each category of decision, the report shall also show the median age of the cases at the time of the decision, the number of cases decided within the guidelines for the timely completion of adjudicatory proceedings, and, with respect to appeals from initial decisions, reviews of determinations by self-regulatory organizations or the Public Company Accounting Oversight Board, and remands of prior Commission decisions, the median days from the completion of briefing to the time of the Commission's decision.

Rule 1100.   Creation of Fair Fund

In any agency process initiated by an order instituting proceedings in which the Commission or the hearing officer issues an order requiring the payment of disgorgement by a respondent and also assessing a civil money penalty against that respondent, the Commission or the hearing officer may order that the amount of disgorgement and of the civil penalty, together with any funds received pursuant to 15 U.S.C. 7246(b), be used to create a fund for the benefit of investors who were harmed by the violation.

Rule 1101.   Submission of Plan of Distribution; Contents of Plan

(a)   *Submission.* The Commission or the hearing officer may, at any time, order any party to submit a plan for the administration and distribution of funds in a Fair Fund or disgorgement fund. Unless ordered otherwise, the Division of Enforcement shall submit a proposed plan no later than 60 days after the respondent has turned over the funds or other assets pursuant to the Commission's order imposing disgorgement and, if applicable, a civil money penalty and any appeals of the Commission's order have been waived or completed, or appeal is no longer available.

(b) *Contents of Plan.* Unless otherwise ordered, a plan for the administration of a Fair Fund or a disgorgement fund shall include the following elements:

(1) Procedures for the receipt of additional funds, including the specification of any account where funds will be held, the instruments in which the funds may be invested; and, in the case of a Fair Fund, the receipt of any funds pursuant to 15 U.S.C. § 7246(b), if applicable;

(2) Specification of categories of persons potentially eligible to receive proceeds from the fund;

(3) Procedures for providing notice to such persons of the existence of the fund and their potential eligibility to receive proceeds of the fund;

(4) Procedures for making and approving claims, procedures for handling disputed claims, and a cut-off date for the making of claims;

(5) A proposed date for the termination of the fund, including provision for the disposition of any funds not otherwise distributed;

(6) Procedures for the administration of the fund, including selection, compensation, and, as necessary, indemnification of a fund administrator to oversee the fund, process claims, prepare accountings, file tax returns, and, subject to the approval of the Commission, make distributions from the fund to investors who were harmed by the violation; and

(7) Such other provisions as the Commission or the hearing officer may require.

Rule 1102.   Provisions for Payment

(a) *Payment to Registry of the Court or Court-Appointed Receiver.* Subject to such conditions as the Commission or the hearing officer shall deem appropriate, a plan for the administration of a Fair Fund or a disgorgement fund may provide for payment of funds into a court registry or to a court-appointed receiver in any case pending in federal or state court against a respondent or any other person based upon a complaint alleging violations arising from the same or substantially similar facts as those alleged in the Commission's order instituting proceedings.

(b) *Payment to the United States Treasury Under Certain Circumstances.* When, in the opinion of the Commission or the hearing officer, the cost of administering a plan of disgorgement relative to the value of the available disgorgement funds and the number of potential claimants would not justify distribution of the disgorgement funds to injured investors, the plan may provide that the disgorgement funds and any civil penalty shall be paid directly to the general fund of the United States Treasury.

Rule 1103.   Notice of Proposed Plan and Opportunity for Comment by Non-parties

Notice of a proposed plan of disgorgement or a proposed Fair Fund plan shall be published on the SEC website and in such other publications as the Commission or the hearing officer may require. The notice shall specify how copies of the proposed plan may be obtained and shall state that persons desiring to comment on the proposed plan may submit their views, in writing, to the Commission.

Rule 1104.   Order Approving, Modifying, or Disapproving Proposed Plan

At any time after 30 days following publication of notice of a proposed plan of disgorgement or of a proposed Fair Fund plan, the Commission shall, by order, approve, approve with modifications, or disapprove the proposed plan. In the discretion of the Commission, a proposed plan that is substantially modified prior to adoption may be republished for an additional comment period pursuant to Rule 1103. The order approving or disapproving the plan should be entered within 30 days after the end of the final period allowed for comments on the proposed plan unless the Commission or the hearing officer, by written order, allows a longer period for good cause shown.

Rule 1105.   Administration of Plan

(a) *Appointment and Removal of Administrator.* The Commission or the hearing officer shall have discretion to appoint any person, including a Commission employee, as administrator of a plan of disgorgement or a Fair Fund plan and to delegate to that person responsibility for administering the plan. An administrator may be removed at any time by order of the Commission or hearing officer.

(b) *Assistance by Respondent.* A respondent may be required or permitted to administer or assist in administering a plan of disgorgement subject to such terms and conditions as the Commission or the hearing officer deems appropriate to ensure the proper distribution of the funds.

(c) *Administrator to Post Bond.* If the administrator is not a Commission employee, the administrator shall be required to obtain a bond in the manner prescribed in 11 U.S.C. § 322, in an amount to be approved by the Commission. The cost of the bond may be paid for as a cost of administration. The Commission may waive posting of a bond for good cause shown.

(d) *Administrator's Fees.* If the administrator is a Commission employee, no fee shall be paid to the administrator for his or her services. If the administrator is not a Commission employee, the administrator may file an application for fees for completed services, and upon approval by the Commission or a hearing officer, may be paid a reasonable fee for those services. Any objections thereto shall be filed within 21 days of service of the application on the parties.

(e) *Source of Funds.* Unless otherwise ordered, fees and other expenses of administering the plan shall be paid first from the interest earned on the funds, and if the interest is not sufficient, then from the corpus.

(f) *Accountings.* During the first 10 days of each calendar quarter, or as otherwise directed by the Commission or the hearing officer, the administrator shall file an accounting of all monies earned or received and all monies spent in connection with the administration of the plan of disgorgement. A final accounting shall be submitted for approval of the Commission or hearing officer prior to discharge of the administrator and cancellation of the administrator's bond, if any.

(g) *Amendment.* A plan may be amended upon motion by any party or by the plan administrator or upon the Commission's or the hearing officer's own motion.

Rule 1106.   Right to Challenge

Other than in connection with the opportunity to submit comments as provided in Rule 1103, no person shall be granted leave to intervene or to participate or otherwise to appear in any agency proceeding or otherwise to challenge an order of disgorgement or creation of a Fair Fund; or an order approving, approving with modifications, or disapproving a plan of disgorgement or a Fair Fund plan; or any determination relating to a plan based solely upon that person's eligibility or potential eligibility to participate in a fund or based upon any private right of action such person may have against any person who is also a respondent in the proceeding.

INFORMAL AND OTHER PROCEDURES

17 C.F.R. § 202.___

Rule 1. General

(a) The statutes administered by the Commission provide generally

(1) For the filing with it of certain statements, such as registration statements, periodic and ownership reports, and proxy solicitation material, and for the filing of certain plans of reorganization, applications and declarations seeking Commission approvals;

(2) For Commission determination through formal procedures of matters initiated by private parties or by the Commission;

(3) For the investigation and examination of persons and records where necessary to carry out the purposes of the statutes and for enforcement of statutory provisions; and

(4) For the adoption of rules and regulations where necessary to effectuate the purposes of the statutes.

(b) In addition to the Commission's rules of practice, set forth in Part 201 of this chapter, the Commission has promulgated rules and regulations pursuant to the several statutes it administers (parts 230, 240, 260, 270 and 275 of this Act). These parts contain substantive provisions and include as well numerous provisions detailing the procedure for meeting specific standards embodied in the statutes. The Commission's rules and regulations under each of the statutes are available in pamphlet form upon request to the Superintendent of Documents, U.S. Government Printing Office, Washington, D.C., 20402.

(c) The statutes and the published rules, regulations and forms thereunder prescribe the course and method of formal procedures to be followed in Commission proceedings. These are supplemented where feasible by certain informal procedures designed to aid the public and facilitate the execution of the Commission's functions. There follows a brief description of procedures generally followed by the Commission which have not been formalized in rules.

(d) The informal procedures of the Commission are largely concerned with the rendering of advice and assistance by the Commission's staff to members of the public dealing with the Commission. While opinions expressed by members of the staff do not constitute an official expression of the Commission's views, they represent the views of persons who are continuously working with the provisions of the statute involved. And any statement by the director, associate director, assistant director, chief accountant, chief counsel, or chief financial analyst of a division can be relied upon as representing the views of that division. In certain instances an informal statement of the views of the Commission may be obtained. The staff, upon request or on its own motion, will generally present questions to the Commission which involve matters of substantial importance and where the issues are novel or highly complex, although the granting of a request for an informal statement by the Commission is entirely within its discretion.

Rule 2. Pre-filing Assistance and Interpretative Advice

The staff of the Commission renders interpretative and advisory assistance to members of the general public, prospective registrants, applicants and declarants. For example, persons having a question regarding the availability of an exemption may secure informal administrative interpretations of the applicable statute or rule as they relate to the particular facts and circumstances presented. Similarly, persons contemplating filings with the Commission may receive advice of a general nature as to the preparation thereof, including information as to the forms to be used and the scope of the items contained in the forms. Inquiries may be directed to an appropriate officer of the Commission's staff. In addition, informal discussions with members of the staff may be arranged whenever feasible, at the Commission's central office or, except in connection certain matters under the Investment Company Act of 1940, at one of its regional offices.

Rule 3. Processing of Filings

(a) Registration statements, proxy statements, letters of notification, periodic reports, applications for qualification of indentures, and similar documents filed with the Commission under the Securities Act of 1933 and the Trust Indenture Act of 1939, and certain filings under the Securities Exchange Act of 1934 are routed to the Division of Corporation Finance, which passes initially on the adequacy of disclosure and recommends the initial action to be taken. If the filing appears to afford inadequate disclosure, as for example through omission of material information or through violation of accepted accounting principles and practices, the usual practice is to bring the deficiency to the attention of the person who filed the document by letter from the Assistant Director assigned supervision over the particular filing, and to afford a reasonable opportunity to discuss the matter and make the necessary corrections. This informal procedure is not generally employed when the deficiencies appear to stem from careless disregard of the statutes and rules or a deliberate attempt to conceal or mislead or where the Commission deems formal proceedings necessary in the public interest. If an electronic filing is not prepared in accordance with the requirements of the current EDGAR Filer Manual, the filing may be suspended and the filer so notified. Reasonable opportunity will be afforded the filer to make the necessary corrections or resubmit the filing as needed. Where it appears that the filing affords adequate disclosure, acceleration of its effectiveness when appropriate normally will be granted. A similar procedure is followed with respect to filings under the Investment Company Act of 1940 and certain filings relating to investment companies under the Securities Act of 1933, the Securities Exchange Act of 1934, and the Trust Indenture Act of 1939, which are routed to the Division of Investment Management. A similar procedure is also followed in the Commission's Regional Offices with respect to registration statements on Forms SB–1, SB–2 and related filings under the Trust Indenture Act of 1939.

(b)(1) Applications for registration as brokers, dealers, investment advisers, municipal securities dealers and transfer agents are submitted to the Office of Filings and Information Services where they are examined to determine whether all necessary information has been supplied and whether all required financial statements and other documents have been furnished in proper form. Defective applications may be returned with a request for correction or held until corrected before being accepted as a filing. The files of the Commission and other sources of information are considered to determine whether any person connected with the applicant appears to have engaged in activities which would warrant commencement of proceedings on the question of denial of registration. The staff confers with applicants and makes suggestions in appropriate cases for amendments and supplemental information. Where it appears appropriate in the public interest and where a basis therefore exists, denial proceedings may be instituted. Within forty-five days of the date of the filing of a broker dealer, investment adviser or municipal securities dealer application (or within such longer period as to which the applicant consents), the Commission shall by order grant registration or institute proceedings to determine whether registration should be denied. An application for registration as a transfer agent shall become effective within 30 days after receipt of the application (or within such shorter period as the Commission may determine). The Office of Filings and Information Services is also responsible for the processing and substantive examination of statements of beneficial ownership of securities and changes in such ownership filed under the Securities Exchange Act of 1934, and the Investment Company Act of 1940, and for the examination of reports filed pursuant to Rule 144 under the Securities Act of 1933.

(2) Applications for registration as national securities exchanges, or exemption from registration as exchanges by reason of such exchanges' limited volume of transactions filed with the

Commission are routed to the Division of Market Regulation, which examines these applications to determine whether all necessary information has been supplied and whether all required financial statements and other documents have been furnished in proper form. Defective applications may be returned with a request for correction or held until corrected before being accepted as a filing. The files of the Commission and other sources of information are considered to determine whether any person connected with the applicant appears to have engaged in activities which would warrant commencement of proceedings on the question of denial of registration. The staff confers with applicants and makes suggestions in appropriate cases for amendments and supplemental information. Where it appears appropriate in the public interest and where a basis therefore exists, denial proceedings may be instituted. Within 90 days of the date of publication of a notice of the filing of an application for registration as a national securities exchange, or exemption from registration by reason of such exchanges' limited volume of transactions (or within such longer period as to which the applicant consents), the Commission shall by order grant registration, or institute proceedings to determine whether registration should be denied as provided in Rule 19(a)(1) under the Securities Exchange Act of 1934.

(3) Notice forms for registration as national securities exchanges pursuant to Section 6(g)(1) of the Securities Exchange Act of 1934 filed with the Commission are routed to the Division of Market Regulation, which examines these notices to determine whether all necessary information has been supplied and whether all other required documents have been furnished in proper form. Defective notices may be returned with a request for correction or held until corrected before being accepted as a filing.

Rule 3a. Instructions for Filing Fees

(a) *General instructions for remittance of filing fees.* Payment of filing fees specified by the following rules shall be made according to the directions listed in this rule: rule of this chapter, Rule 0–9 under the Exchange Act, and Rule 0–8 under the Investment Company Act of 1940. All such fees are to be paid through the U.S. Treasury designated lockbox depository and may be paid by wire transfer, certified check, bank cashier's check, United States postal money order, or bank money order pursuant to the specific instructions set forth in paragraph (b) of this rule. Personal checks will not be accepted for payment of fees. To ensure proper posting, all filers must include their Commission-assigned Central Index Key (CIK) number (also known as the Commission-assigned registrant or payor account number) on fee payments. If a third party submits a fee payment, the fee payment must specify the account number to which the fee is to be applied.

(b) *Instructions for payment of filing fees.* Except as provided in paragraph (c) of this rule, these instructions provide direction for remitting fees specified in paragraph (a) of this rule. You may contact the Fee Account Services Branch in the Office of Financial Management at (202) 551–8989 for additional information if you have questions.

(1) *Instructions for payment of fees by wire transfer (FEDWIRE).* U.S. Bank, N.A. in St. Louis, Missouri is the U.S. Treasury designated lockbox depository and financial agent for Commission filing fee payments. The hours of operation at U.S. Bank are 8:30 a.m. to 6 p.m. Eastern time for wire transfers. Any bank or wire transfer service may initiate wire transfers of filing fee payments through the FEDWIRE system to U.S. Bank. A filing entity does not need to establish an account at U.S. Bank in order to remit filing fee payments.

(i) To ensure proper credit and prompt filing acceptance, in all wire transfers of filing fees to the Commission, you must include:

(A) The Commission's account number at U.S. Bank (152307768324); and

(B) The payor's CIK number.

(ii) You may refer to the examples found on the Commission's Web site at www.sec.gov for the proper format.

(2) *Instructions for payment of fees by check or money order.* To remit a filing fee payment by check (certified or bank cashier's check) or money order (United States postal or bank money order), you must make it payable to the Securities and Exchange Commission, omitting the name or title of any official of the Commission. On the front of the check or money order, you must include the

Commission's account number (152307768324) and CIK number of the account to which the fee is to be applied. U.S. Bank does not accept walk-in deliveries by individuals. You must mail checks or money orders to the following U.S. Bank addresses:

(i)   Remittances through the U.S. Postal Service must be sent to the following address: Securities and Exchange Commission, P.O. Box 979081, St. Louis, MO 63197–9000.

(ii)   The following address can be used for remittances through other common carriers: U.S. Bank, Government Lockbox 979081, 1005 Convention Plaza, SL–MO–C2–GL, St. Louis, MO 63101.

Note to paragraph (b). Wire transfers are not instantaneous. The time required to process a wire transfer through the FEDWIRE system, from origination to receipt by U.S. Bank, varies substantially. Specified filings, such as registration statements pursuant to section 6(b) of the Securities Act of 1933 that provide for the registration of securities and mandate the receipt of the appropriate fee payment upon filing, and transactional filings pursuant to the Securities Exchange Act of 1934, such as many proxy statements involving extraordinary business transactions, will not be accepted if sufficient funds have not been received by the Commission at the time of filing. You should obtain from your bank or wire transfer service the reference number of the wire transfer. Having this number can greatly facilitate tracing the funds if any problems occur. If a wire transfer of filing fees does not contain the required information in the proper format, the Commission may not be able to identify the payor and the acceptance of filings may be delayed. To ensure proper credit, you must provide all required information to the sending bank or wire transfer service. Commission data must be inserted in the proper fields. The most critical data are the Commission's account number at U.S. Bank and the Commission-assigned account number identified as the CIK number.

(c)   *Special instructions for Rule 462(b) and Rule 110(d) of this chapter.* Notwithstanding paragraphs (a) and (b) of this rule, for registration statements filed pursuant to Rule 462(b) and Rule 110(d) of this chapter, payment of filing fees for the purposes of this rule may be made by:

(1)   The registrant or its agent instructing its bank or a wire transfer service to transmit to the Commission the applicable filing fee by a wire transfer of such amount from the issuer's account or its agent's account to the U.S. Treasury designated lockbox depository as soon as practicable, but no later than the close of the next business day following the filing of the registration statement; and

(2)   The registrant submitting with the registration statement at the time of filing a certification that:

(i)   The registrant or its agent has so instructed its bank or a wire transfer service;

(ii)   The registrant or its agent will not revoke such instructions; and

(iii)   The registrant or its agent has sufficient funds in such account to cover the amount of such filing fee.

Note to paragraph (c). Such instructions may be sent on the date of filing the registration statement after the close of business of such bank or wire transfer service, provided that the registrant undertakes in the certification sent to the Commission with the registration statement that it will confirm receipt of such instructions by the bank or wire transfer service during regular business hours on the following business day.

(d)   *Filing fee accounts.* A filing fee account is maintained for each filer who submits a filing requiring a fee on the Commission's EDGAR system or who submits funds to the U.S. Treasury designated depository in anticipation of paying a filing fee. Account statements are regularly prepared and provided to account holders. Account holders must maintain a current account address with the Commission to ensure timely access to these statements.

Note to paragraph (d). The deposit of money into a filing fee account does not constitute payment of a filing fee. Payment of the filing fee occurs at the time the filing is made, commensurate with the drawing down of the balance of the fee account.

(e)   *Return of funds from inactive accounts.* Funds held in any filing fee account in which there has not been a deposit, withdrawal or other adjustment for more than three years will be returned to the account holder, and account statements will not be sent again until a deposit, withdrawal or other adjustment is made with respect to the account. Filers must maintain a current account address to assure the timely return of funds. It may not be possible to return funds from inactive accounts if the Commission is unable to identify a current account address of an account holder after making reasonable efforts to do so.

Note to paragraph (e). A company must update its account and other addresses using the EDGAR Web site. This method ensures data integrity and the timeliest update. Simply changing an address in the text of the cover page of a filing made on the EDGAR system will not be sufficient to update the Commission's account address records.

Rule 4. Facilitating Administrative Hearings

(a) Applications, declarations, and other requests involving formal Commission action after opportunity for hearing are scrutinized by the appropriate division for conformance with applicable statutory standards and Commission rules and generally the filing party is advised of deficiencies. Prior to passing upon applications and declarations the Commission receives the views of all interested persons at public hearings whenever appropriate; hence, any applicant or declarant seeking Commission approval of proposed transactions by a particular time should file his application or declaration in time to allow for the presentation and consideration of such views.

(b) After the staff has had an opportunity to study an application or declaration, interested persons may informally discuss the problems therein raised to the extent that time and the nature of the case permit (e.g., consideration is usually given to whether the proceeding is contested and if so to the nature of the contest). In such event, the staff will, to the extent feasible, advise as to the nature of the issues raised by the filing, the necessity for any amendments to the documents filed, the type of evidence it believes should be presented at the hearing and, in some instances, the nature, form, and contents of documents to be submitted as formal exhibits. The staff will, in addition, generally advise as to Commission policy in past cases which dealt with the same subject matter as the filing under consideration.

(c) During the course of the hearings, the staff is generally available for informal discussions to reconcile bona fide divergent views not only between itself and other persons interested in the proceedings, but among all interested persons; and, when circumstances permit, an attempt is made to narrow, if possible, the issues to be considered at the formal hearing.

(d) In some instances the Commission in the order accompanying its findings and opinion reserves jurisdiction over certain matters relating to the proceeding, such as payment of fees and expenses, accounting entries, terms and conditions relating to securities to be issued, and other matters. In such cases, upon receipt of satisfactory information and data the Commission considers whether further hearing is required before releasing jurisdiction.

Rule 5. Enforcement Activities

(a) Where, from complaints received from members of the public, communications from Federal or State agencies, examination of filings made with the Commission, or otherwise, it appears that there may be violation of the acts administered by the Commission or the rules or regulations thereunder, a preliminary investigation is generally made. In such preliminary investigation no process is issued or testimony compelled. The Commission may, in its discretion, make such formal investigations and authorize the use of process as it deems necessary to determine whether any person has violated, is violating, or is about to violate any provision of the federal securities laws or the rules of a self-regulatory organization of which the person is a member or participant. Unless otherwise ordered by the Commission, the investigation or examination is non-public and the reports thereon are for staff and Commission use only.

(b) After investigation or otherwise the Commission may in its discretion take one or more of the following actions: institution of administrative proceedings looking to the imposition of remedial sanctions, initiation of injunctive proceedings in the courts, and, in the case of a willful violation, reference of the matter to the Department of Justice for criminal prosecution. The Commission may also, on some occasions, refer the matter to, or grant requests for access to its files made by, domestic and foreign governmental authorities, self-regulatory organizations such as stock exchanges or the National Association of Securities Dealers, Inc., and other persons or entities.

(c) Persons who become involved in preliminary or formal investigations may, on their own initiative, submit a written statement to the Commission setting forth their interests and position in regard to the subject matter of the investigation. Upon request, the staff, in its discretion, may advise such persons of the general nature of the investigation, including the indicated violations as they pertain to them, and the amount of time that may be available for preparing and submitting a statement prior to the presentation of a staff recommendation to the Commission for the commencement of an administrative or injunction proceeding. Submissions by interested persons should be forwarded to the appropriate Division Director or Regional Director with a copy to the staff members conducting the investigation and should be clearly referenced to the specific investigation to which they relate. In the event a recommendation for the commencement of an enforcement proceeding is presented by the staff, any submissions by interested persons will be forwarded to the Commission in conjunction with the staff memorandum.

(d) In instances where the staff has concluded its investigation of a particular matter and has determined that it will not recommend the commencement of an enforcement proceeding against a person, the staff, in its discretion, may advise the party that its formal investigation has been terminated. Such advice if given must in no way be construed as indicating that the party has been exonerated or that no action may ultimately result from the staff's investigation of the particular matter.

(e) The Commission has adopted the policy that in any civil lawsuit brought by it or in any administrative proceeding of an accusatory nature pending before it, it is important to avoid creating, or permitting to be created, an impression that a decree is being entered or a sanction imposed, when the conduct alleged did not, in fact, occur. Accordingly, it hereby announces its policy not to permit a defendant or respondent to consent to a judgment or order that imposes a sanction while denying the allegations in the complaint or order for proceedings. In this regard, the Commission believes that a refusal to admit the allegations is equivalent to a denial, unless the defendant or respondent states that he neither admits nor denies the allegations.

(f) In the course of the Commission's investigations, civil lawsuits, and administrative proceedings, the staff, with appropriate authorization, may discuss with persons involved the disposition of such matters by consent, by settlement, or in some other manner. It is the policy of the Commission, however, that the disposition of any such matter may not, expressly or impliedly, extend to any criminal charges that have been, or may be, brought against any such person or any recommendation with respect thereto. Accordingly, any person involved in an enforcement matter before the Commission who consents, or agrees to consent, to any judgment or order does so solely for the purpose of resolving the claims against him in that investigative, civil, or administrative matter and not for the purpose of resolving any criminal charges that have been, or might be, brought against him. This policy reflects the fact that neither the Commission nor its staff has the authority or responsibility for instituting, conducting, settling, or otherwise disposing of criminal proceedings. That authority and responsibility are vested in the Attorney General and representatives of the Department of Justice.

Rule 6. Adoption, Revision, and Rescission of Rules and Regulations of General Application

(a) The procedure followed by the Commission in connection with the adoption, revision, and rescission of rules of general application necessarily varies in accordance with the nature of the rule, the extent of public interest therein, and the necessity for speed in its adoption. Rules relating to Commission organization, procedure and management, for example, are generally adopted by the Commission without affording public discussion thereof. On the other hand, in the adoption of substantive rules materially affecting an industry or a segment of the public, such as accounting rules, every feasible effort is made in advance of adoption to receive the views of persons to be affected. In such cases, proposals for the adoption, revision, or rescission of rules are initiated either by the Commission or by members of the public, and to the extent practicable, the practices set forth in paragraph (b) of this rule are observed.

(b) After preliminary consideration by the Commission a draft of the proposed rule is published in the FEDERAL REGISTER and mailed to interested persons (e.g., other interested regulatory bodies, principal registrants or persons to be affected, stock exchanges, professional societies and leading authorities on the subject concerned and other persons requesting such draft) for comments. Unless accorded confidential treatment pursuant to statute or rule of the Commission, written comments filed with the Commission on or before the closing date for comments become a part of the public record upon the proposed rule. The Commission, in its discretion, may accept and include in the public record written comments received by the Commission after the closing date.

(c) Following analysis of comments received, the rule may be adopted in the form published or in a revised form in the light of such comments. In some cases, a revised draft is prepared and published and, where appropriate, an oral hearing may be held before final action upon the proposal. Any interested person may appear at the hearing and/or may submit written comment for consideration in accordance with the Commission's notice of the rulemaking procedure to be followed. The rule in the form in which it is adopted by the Commission is publicly released and is published in the FEDERAL REGISTER.

Rule 7. Submittals

(a) All required statements, reports, applications, etc. must be filed with the principal office of the Commission unless otherwise specified in the Commission's rules, schedules and forms. Reports by exchange members, brokers and dealers required by Rule 17a–5 under the Securities Exchange Act of 1934 must be filed with the appropriate regional office as provided in Rule 255(a) under the Securities Act of 1933, and with the principal office of the Commission and the appropriate regional office as provided under Rule 17a–5(a) et seq. under the Securities Exchange Act of 1934.

(b) *Electronic filings.* All documents required to be filed in electronic format with the Commission pursuant to the federal securities laws or the rules and regulations thereunder shall be filed at the principal office in Washington, D.C. via EDGAR by delivery to the Commission of a magnetic tape or diskette, or by direct transmission.

Rule 140.   Interim Commission Review of PCAOB Inspection Reports

(a) Definitions.

(1) Board or PCAOB means the Public Company Accounting Oversight Board.

(2) Registered public accounting firm or Firm shall have the meaning set forth in section 2(a)(12) of the Sarbanes-Oxley Act of 2002.

(3) Associated person means a person associated with the registered public accounting firm as defined in section 2(a)(9) of the Sarbanes-Oxley Act of 2002.

(b) Reviewable matters. A registered public accounting firm may request interim Commission review of an assessment or determination by the PCAOB contained in an inspection report prepared under section 104 of the Sarbanes-Oxley Act of 2002 and relating to that firm, if the firm:

(1) Has provided the PCAOB with a response, pursuant to the rules of the PCAOB, to the substance of particular items in a draft inspection report and disagrees with the assessments relating to those items contained in any final inspection report prepared by the PCAOB following such response;

(2) Disagrees with an assessment contained in any final inspection report that was not contained in the draft inspection report provided to the firm under section 104 of the Sarbanes-Oxley Act of 2002 or the rules of the PCAOB; or

(3) Disagrees with the determination of the PCAOB that criticisms or defects in the quality control systems of the firm that were identified in an inspection report, but not disclosed to the public, have not been addressed to the satisfaction of the PCAOB within 12 months after the date of that inspection report.

(c) Procedures for requesting interim Commission review.

(1) A request for interim Commission review with respect to matters described in paragraph (b) of this rule must be submitted to the Commission's Office of the Secretary within 30 calendar days of the following:

(i) The date the firm is provided a copy of the final inspection report described in paragraph (b)(1) or (b)(2) of this rule; or

(ii) The date the firm receives notice of the PCAOB's determination described in paragraph (b)(3) of this rule.

(2) The PCAOB shall not make publicly available the final inspection report or criticisms or defects in the quality control systems of the firm subject to a determination described in paragraph (b) of this rule, as applicable, during the 30-day period during which the firm may request interim Commission review, unless the firm consents in writing to earlier publication of the report.

(3)   A request for interim Commission review ("request" or "submission") must be marked "Request for Interim Commission Review With Respect to PCAOB Inspection Report." The request must focus on the specific matters for which relief is requested and succinctly address the issues raised by the PCAOB. The request, to the extent possible, should include, for example:

(i)   A copy of the particular inspection report that is the subject of the request;

(ii)   The specific assessments or determinations that are the subject of the request;

(iii)   The alleged errors or deficiencies in the PCAOB's assessments or determination and the reasons for the firm's position;

(iv)   If the matter is being reviewed under paragraph (b)(3) of this rule, any actions taken by the registered public accounting firm to address criticisms or defects identified in the inspection report; and

(v)   Any supporting documentation relevant to the review.

(4)   The firm must provide a copy of its review request to the PCAOB simultaneously with its submission to the Commission.

(5)   A timely review request by a firm will operate as a stay of publication of those portions of the final inspection report or criticisms or defects in the quality control systems of the firm subject to a determination described in paragraph (b) of this rule, as applicable, that are the subject of the firm's review request, unless the Commission otherwise determines in its own discretion. Upon expiration of the 30-day period during which the firm may request interim Commission review, the PCAOB shall make publicly available the remainder of the final inspection report or criticisms or defects in the quality control systems of the firm that were identified in an inspection report, as applicable, that are not the subject of the firm's review request, unless the Commission otherwise determines that such a result would not be necessary or appropriate.

(6)   If the firm fails to make a timely review request, pursuant to Section 104(g)(2) of the Sarbanes-Oxley Act of 2002, the PCAOB shall make publicly available the final inspection report or criticisms or defects in the quality control systems of the firm that were identified in an inspection report, as applicable.

(d)   Procedures for granting or denying the review request. Within 30 calendar days of a timely review request, the Commission will notify the firm and the PCAOB as to whether the Commission will exercise its discretion to grant the request for an interim review. If the Commission does not grant the review request, the stay of publication is terminated upon notification to the firm and the PCAOB. If the Commission does grant the review request, the stay of publication shall continue unless the Commission determines otherwise in its own discretion, or unless the firm consents in writing to the PCAOB, with a copy to the Commission, to earlier publication.

(e)   Procedures where a review request has been granted.

(1)   Where the Commission has notified the firm and the PCAOB that it is granting the request for an interim review, the PCAOB may submit responsive information and documents with the Commission within 15 calendar days of receipt of such notice. The PCAOB must provide a copy of such information and documents simultaneously to the firm.

(2)   During the course of the interim review, the Commission may request additional information relating to the PCAOB's assessments or determination under review, and provide a period of up to seven calendar days to respond to such request, from the PCAOB, the firm, and any associated person of the firm. The Commission may grant the firm or the PCAOB a period of up to seven calendar days to respond to any information obtained pursuant to this paragraph. The firm or the PCAOB, as applicable, shall provide simultaneously to the other party all information provided as a result of a request for additional information or responses thereto. The firm with which any associated person from whom information is requested shall provide simultaneously to the PCAOB all information provided as a result of a request for additional information or responses thereto. If the firm (including any associated person) or the PCAOB fails to respond timely to a request from the Commission, such failure may serve as the basis for the Commission to conclude its review and make a determination adverse to the non-responsive party.

(3)   The Commission, based on the information submitted by the firm, the PCAOB and any associated persons, shall consider whether the PCAOB's assessments or determination are arbitrary and capricious, or otherwise not consistent with the purposes of the Act.

(4)   At the conclusion of its review, the Commission shall inform the firm and the PCAOB in writing that the Commission:

(i)   Does not object to all or part of the assessments or determination of the PCAOB and the stay of publication is terminated; or

(ii)   Remands to the PCAOB with instructions that the stay of publication is permanent or that the PCAOB take such other actions as the Commission deems necessary or appropriate with respect to publication, including, but not limited to, revising the final inspection report or determinations before publication.

(5)   The review pursuant to this rule shall be completed and a written notice pursuant to this rule shall be sent no more than 75 calendar days after notification to the firm and the PCAOB that the Commission is granting the request for an interim review, unless the Commission extends the period for good cause.

(f)   Treatment of review.

(1)   Time periods in this rule shall be computed as provided in the Commission's Rules of Practice, Rule 160.

(2)   Unless otherwise determined by the Commission, the decision to grant or deny a review request and the conclusions of the Commission's review shall be non-public, and the information or documents submitted, created, or obtained by the Commission or its staff in the course of the review shall be deemed non-public. Nothing in this rule shall be construed to impair or limit the ability of any party to request confidential treatment under the Freedom of Information Act, section 105(b)(5) of the Sarbanes-Oxley Act of 2002, or any other applicable law.

(3)   Pursuant to section 104(h)(2) of the Sarbanes-Oxley Act of 2002, any decision of the Commission as a result of an interim review with respect to a PCAOB inspection report, including whether a request for review is granted or denied, shall not be reviewable under section 25 of the Securities Exchange Act of 1934 and shall not be deemed to be "final agency action" for purposes of 5 U.S.C. 704.

(4)   Any action taken by the Commission relates solely to the publication of the relevant inspection report and does not affect the ability of the Commission or PCAOB to take appropriate action.

(g)   Designation of address; Representation.

(1)   When a registered public accounting firm first submits a request for interim Commission review, or an associated person first submits information related to a request, the firm or associated person shall submit to the Commission, and keep current, an address at which any notice or other written communication furnished to the firm or associated person may be sent, a contact name and telephone number where the firm or associated person may be reached during business hours and, if represented, the representative's name, business address, and telephone number.

(2)   If the firm, PCAOB, or associated person will be represented by a representative, the initial submission of that person shall be accompanied by the notice of appearance required by Rule 102(d) of the Rules of Practice. The other provisions of Rule 102 of the Rules of Practice with respect to representation before the Commission shall apply.

Rule 170.   Initiation of Disapproval Proceedings for PCAOB Proposed Rules

Initiation of disapproval proceedings for proposed rules of the Public Company Accounting Oversight Board as defined by section 107 of the Sarbanes-Oxley Act of 2002 are subject to the provisions of Rules 700 and 701 of the Rules of Practice as fully as if it were a registered securities association, except that:

(a)   Demonstration of Consistency with the Sarbanes-Oxley Act of 2002. For purposes of proposed rules of the Public Company Accounting Oversight Board, apply this paragraph in lieu of paragraph (b)(3) of Rule 700 of the Rules of Practice. The burden to demonstrate that a proposed rule is consistent with the requirements of title I of the Sarbanes-Oxley Act of 2002, and the rules and regulations issued thereunder, or as necessary or appropriate in the public interest or for the protection of investors, is on the Public Company Accounting Oversight Board. In its filing the Public Company Accounting Oversight Board must explain in a clear and comprehensible manner why the proposed rule change is consistent with the requirements of title I of the Sarbanes-Oxley Act of 2002 and the rules and regulations thereunder, or as necessary or appropriate in the public interest or for the protection of investors. A mere assertion that the proposed rule change is consistent with those requirements is not sufficient. Instead, the description of the proposed rule, its purpose and operation, its effect, and a legal analysis of its consistency with applicable requirements must all be sufficiently detailed and specific to support an affirmative Commission finding. Any failure by the Public Company Accounting Oversight Board in its proposed rule filing with the Commission may result in the Commission not having a sufficient basis to make an affirmative finding that a proposed rule change is consistent with the title I of the Sarbanes-Oxley Act of 2002, and the rules and regulations issued thereunder, or as necessary or appropriate in the public interest or for the protection of investors.

(b) For each reference to "the Exchange Act and the rules and regulations thereunder applicable to the self-regulatory organization" apply "title I of the Sarbanes-Oxley Act of 2002, and the rules and regulations issued thereunder applicable to such organization, or as necessary or appropriate in the public interest or for the protection of investors."

RULES RELATING TO INVESTIGATIONS

17 C.F.R. § 203.___

A.   In General

A.   IN GENERAL

Rule 1.   Application of the Rules of This Part

The rules of this part apply only to investigations conducted by the Commission. They do not apply to adjudicative or rulemaking proceedings.

Rule 2.   Information Obtained in Investigations and Examinations

Information or documents obtained by the Commission in the course of any investigation or examination, unless made a matter of public record, shall be deemed non-public, but the Commission approves the practice whereby officials of the Divisions of Enforcement, Corporation Finance, Market Regulation and Investment Management and the Office of International Affairs, at the level of Assistant Director or higher, and officials in Regional Offices at the level of Assistant Regional Director or higher, may engage in and may authorize members of the Commission's staff to engage in discussions with persons identified in Rule 24c-1(b) under the Securities Exchange Act of 1934 concerning information obtained in individual investigations conducted pursuant to Commission order.

Rule 3.   Suspension and Disbarment

The provisions of Rule 102(e) of the Commission's rules of practice are hereby made specifically applicable to all investigations.

B.   FORMAL INVESTIGATIVE PROCEEDINGS

Rule 4.   Applicability of Rules 4 Through 8

(a)   Rules 4 through 8 shall be applicable to a witness who is sworn in a proceeding pursuant to a Commission order for investigation or examination, such proceeding being hereinafter referred to as a "formal investigative proceeding."

(b)   Formal investigative proceedings may be held before the Commission, before one or more of its members, or before any officer designated by it for the purpose of taking testimony of witnesses and received other evidence. The term "officer conducting the investigation" shall mean any of the foregoing.

Rule 5.   Non-public Formal Investigative Proceedings

Unless otherwise ordered by the Commission, all formal investigative proceedings shall be non-public.

Rule 6. Transcripts

Transcripts, if any, of formal investigative proceedings shall be recorded solely by the official reporter, or by any other person or means designated by the officer conducting the investigation. A person who has submitted documentary evidence or testimony in a formal investigative proceeding shall be entitled, upon written request, to procure a copy of his documentary evidence or a transcript of his testimony on payment of the appropriate fees: *Provided, however,* That in a nonpublic formal investigative proceeding the Commission may for good cause deny such request. In any event, any witness, upon proper identification, shall have the right to inspect the official transcript of the witness' own testimony.

Rule 7. Rights of Witnesses

(a)   Any person who is compelled or requested to furnish documentary evidence or testimony at a formal investigative proceeding shall, upon request, be shown the Commission's order of investigation. Copies of formal orders of investigation shall not be furnished, for their retention, to such persons requesting the same except with the express approval of officials in the Regional Offices at the level of Assistant Regional Director or higher, or officials in the Division or Divisions conducting or supervising the investigation at the level of Assistant Director or higher. Such approval shall not be given unless the person granting such approval, in his or her discretion, is satisfied that there exist reasons consistent both with the protection of privacy of persons involved in the investigation and with the unimpeded conduct of the investigation.

(b)   Any person compelled to appear, or who appears by request or permission of the Commission, in person at a formal investigative proceeding may be accompanied, represented and advised by counsel, as defined in Rule 101(a) of the Commission's rules of practice: *Provided, however,* That all witnesses shall be sequestered, and unless permitted in the discretion of the officer conducting the investigation no witness or the counsel accompanying any such witness shall be permitted to be present during the examination of any other witness called in such proceeding.

(c)   The right to be accompanied, represented and advised by counsel shall mean the right of a person testifying to have an attorney present with him during any formal investigative proceeding and to have this attorney

(1)   Advise such person before, during and after the conclusion of such examination,

(2)   Question such person briefly at the conclusion of the examination to clarify any of the answers such person has given, and

(3)   Make summary notes during such examination solely for the use of such person.

(d)   Unless otherwise ordered by the Commission, in any public formal investigative proceeding, if the record shall contain implications of wrongdoing by any person, such person shall have the right to appear on the record; and in addition to the rights afforded other witnesses hereby, he shall have a reasonable opportunity of cross-examination and production of rebuttal testimony or documentary evidence. "Reasonable" shall mean permitting persons as full an opportunity to assert their position as may be granted consistent with administrative efficiency and with avoidance of undue delay. The determination of reasonableness in each instance shall be made in the discretion of the officer conducting the investigation.

(e)   The officer conducting the investigation may report to the Commission any instances where any witness or counsel has been guilty of dilatory, obstructionist or contumacious conduct during the course of an investigation or any other instance of violation of these rules. The Commission will thereupon take such further action as the circumstances may warrant, including suspension or disbarment of counsel from further appearance or practice before it, in accordance with Rule 102(e) of the Commission's rules of practice, or exclusion from further participation in the particular investigation.

Rule 8. Service of Subpoenas

Service of subpoenas issued in formal investigative proceedings shall be effected in the manner prescribed by Rule 232(c) of the Commission's Rules of Practice.

D. STANDARDS OF PROFESSIONAL CONDUCT FOR ATTORNEYS APPEARING AND PRACTICING BEFORE THE COMMISSION IN THE REPRESENTATION OF AN ISSUER

17 C.F.R. § 205.____

Rule 1. Purpose and Scope

This part sets forth minimum standards of professional conduct for attorneys appearing and practicing before the Commission in the representation of an issuer. These standards supplement applicable standards of any jurisdiction where an attorney is admitted or practices and are not intended to limit the ability of any jurisdiction to impose additional obligations on an attorney not inconsistent with the application of this part. Where the standards of a state or other United States jurisdiction where an attorney is admitted or practices conflict with this part, this part shall govern.

Rule 2. Definitions

For purposes of this part, the following definitions apply:

(a) Appearing and practicing before the Commission:

(1) Means:

(i) Transacting any business with the Commission, including communications in any form;

(ii) Representing an issuer in a Commission administrative proceeding or in connection with any Commission investigation, inquiry, information request, or subpoena;

(iii) Providing advice in respect of the United States securities laws or the Commission's rules or regulations thereunder regarding any document that the attorney has notice will be filed with or submitted to, or incorporated into any document that will be filed with or submitted to, the Commission, including the provision of such advice in the context of preparing, or participating in the preparation of, any such document; or

(iv) Advising an issuer as to whether information or a statement, opinion, or other writing is required under the United States securities laws or the Commission's rules or regulations thereunder to be filed with or submitted to, or incorporated into any document that will be filed with or submitted to, the Commission; but

(2) Does not include an attorney who:

(i) Conducts the activities in paragraphs (a)(1)(i) through (a)(1)(iv) of this rule other than in the context of providing legal services to an issuer with whom the attorney has an attorney-client relationship; or

(ii) Is a non-appearing foreign attorney.

647

(b)   Appropriate response means a response to an attorney regarding reported evidence of a material violation as a result of which the attorney reasonably believes:

(1)   That no material violation, as defined in paragraph (i) of this rule, has occurred, is ongoing, or is about to occur;

(2)   That the issuer has, as necessary, adopted appropriate remedial measures, including appropriate steps or sanctions to stop any material violations that are ongoing, to prevent any material violation that has yet to occur, and to remedy or otherwise appropriately address any material violation that has already occurred and to minimize the likelihood of its recurrence; or

(3)   That the issuer, with the consent of the issuer's board of directors, a committee thereof to whom a report could be made pursuant to Rule 3(b)(3), or a qualified legal compliance committee, has retained or directed an attorney to review the reported evidence of a material violation and either:

(i)   Has substantially implemented any remedial recommendations made by such attorney after a reasonable investigation and evaluation of the reported evidence; or

(ii)   Has been advised that such attorney may, consistent with his or her professional obligations, assert a colorable defense on behalf of the issuer (or the issuer's officer, director, employee, or agent, as the case may be) in any investigation or judicial or administrative proceeding relating to the reported evidence of a material violation.

(c)   Attorney means any person who is admitted, licensed, or otherwise qualified to practice law in any jurisdiction, domestic or foreign, or who holds himself or herself out as admitted, licensed, or otherwise qualified to practice law.

(d)   Breach of fiduciary duty refers to any breach of fiduciary or similar duty to the issuer recognized under an applicable Federal or State statute or at common law, including but not limited to misfeasance, nonfeasance, abdication of duty, abuse of trust, and approval of unlawful transactions.

(e)   Evidence of a material violation means credible evidence, based upon which it would be unreasonable, under the circumstances, for a prudent and competent attorney not to conclude that it is reasonably likely that a material violation has occurred, is ongoing, or is about to occur.

(f)   Foreign government issuer means a foreign issuer as defined in Rule 405 eligible to register securities on Schedule B of the Securities Act of 1933.

(g)   In the representation of an issuer means providing legal services as an attorney for an issuer, regardless of whether the attorney is employed or retained by the issuer.

(h)   Issuer means an issuer (as defined in section 3 of the Securities Exchange Act of 1934), the securities of which are registered under section 12 of that Act, or that is required to file reports under section 15(d) of that Act, or that files or has filed a registration statement that has not yet become effective under the Securities Act of 1933, and that it has not withdrawn, but does not include a foreign government issuer. For purposes of paragraphs (a) and (g) of this rule, the term "issuer" includes any person controlled by an issuer, where an attorney provides legal services to such person on behalf of, or at the behest, or for the benefit of the issuer, regardless of whether the attorney is employed or retained by the issuer.

(i)   Material violation means a material violation of an applicable United States federal or state securities law, a material breach of fiduciary duty arising under United States federal or state law, or a similar material violation of any United States federal or state law.

(j)   Non-appearing foreign attorney means an attorney:

(1)   Who is admitted to practice law in a jurisdiction outside the United States;

(2)   Who does not hold himself or herself out as practicing, and does not give legal advice regarding, United States federal or state securities or other laws (except as provided in paragraph (j)(3)(ii) of this rule); and

(3)   Who:

(i)   Conducts activities that would constitute appearing and practicing before the Commission only incidentally to, and in the ordinary course of, the practice of law in a jurisdiction outside the United States; or

(ii)   Is appearing and practicing before the Commission only in consultation with counsel, other than a non-appearing foreign attorney, admitted or licensed to practice in a state or other United States jurisdiction.

(k)   Qualified legal compliance committee means a committee of an issuer (which also may be an audit or other committee of the issuer) that:

(1)   Consists of at least one member of the issuer's audit committee (or, if the issuer has no audit committee, one member from an equivalent committee of independent directors) and two or more members of the issuer's board of directors who are not employed, directly or indirectly, by the issuer and who are not, in the case of a registered investment company, "interested persons" as defined in section 2(a)(19) of the Investment Company Act of 1940;

(2)   Has adopted written procedures for the confidential receipt, retention, and consideration of any report of evidence of a material violation under Rule 3;

(3)   Has been duly established by the issuer's board of directors, with the authority and responsibility:

(i)   To inform the issuer's chief legal officer and chief executive officer (or the equivalents thereof) of any report of evidence of a material violation (except in the circumstances described in Rule 3(b)(4));

(ii)   To determine whether an investigation is necessary regarding any report of evidence of a material violation by the issuer, its officers, directors, employees or agents and, if it determines an investigation is necessary or appropriate, to:

(A)   Notify the audit committee or the full board of directors;

(B)   Initiate an investigation, which may be conducted either by the chief legal officer (or the equivalent thereof) or by outside attorneys; and

(C)   Retain such additional expert personnel as the committee deems necessary; and

(iii)   At the conclusion of any such investigation, to:

(A)   Recommend, by majority vote, that the issuer implement an appropriate response to evidence of a material violation; and

(B)   Inform the chief legal officer and the chief executive officer (or the equivalents thereof) and the board of directors of the results of any such investigation under this rule and the appropriate remedial measures to be adopted; and

(4)   Has the authority and responsibility, acting by majority vote, to take all other appropriate action, including the authority to notify the Commission in the event that the issuer fails in any material respect to implement an appropriate response that the qualified legal compliance committee has recommended the issuer to take.

(*l*)   Reasonable or reasonably denotes, with respect to the actions of an attorney, conduct that would not be unreasonable for a prudent and competent attorney.

(m)   Reasonably believes means that an attorney believes the matter in question and that the circumstances are such that the belief is not unreasonable.

(n)   Report means to make known to directly, either in person, by telephone, by e-mail, electronically, or in writing.

Rule 3.   Issuer as Client

(a)   *Representing an Issuer.* An attorney appearing and practicing before the Commission in the representation of an issuer owes his or her professional and ethical duties to the issuer as an organization. That the attorney may work with and advise the issuer's officers, directors, or employees in the course of representing the issuer does not make such individuals the attorney's clients.

(b)   *Duty to Report Evidence of a Material Violation.*

(1)   If an attorney, appearing and practicing before the Commission in the representation of an issuer, becomes aware of evidence of a material violation by the issuer or by any officer, director, employee, or agent of the issuer, the attorney shall report such evidence to the issuer's chief legal officer (or the equivalent thereof) or to both the issuer's chief legal officer and its chief executive officer (or the equivalents thereof) forthwith. By communicating such information to the issuer's officers or directors, an attorney does not reveal client confidences or secrets or privileged or otherwise protected information related to the attorney's representation of an issuer.

(2)   The chief legal officer (or the equivalent thereof) shall cause such inquiry into the evidence of a material violation as he or she reasonably believes is appropriate to determine whether the material violation described in the report has occurred, is ongoing, or is about to occur. If the chief legal officer (or the equivalent thereof) determines no material violation has occurred, is ongoing, or is about to occur, he or she shall notify the reporting attorney and advise the reporting attorney of the basis for such determination. Unless the chief legal officer (or the equivalent thereof) reasonably believes that no material violation has occurred, is ongoing, or is about to occur, he or she shall take all reasonable steps to cause the issuer to adopt an appropriate response, and shall advise the reporting attorney thereof. In lieu of causing an inquiry under this paragraph (b), a chief legal officer (or the equivalent thereof) may refer a report of evidence of a material violation to a qualified legal compliance committee under paragraph (c)(2) of this rule if the issuer has duly established a qualified legal compliance committee prior to the report of evidence of a material violation.

(3)   Unless an attorney who has made a report under paragraph (b)(1) of this rule reasonably believes that the chief legal officer or the chief executive officer of the issuer (or the equivalent thereof) has provided an appropriate response within a reasonable time, the attorney shall report the evidence of a material violation to:

(i)   The audit committee of the issuer's board of directors;

(ii)   Another committee of the issuer's board of directors consisting solely of directors who are not employed, directly or indirectly, by the issuer and are not, in the case of a registered investment company, "interested persons" as defined in section 2(a)(19) of the Investment Company Act of 1940 (if the issuer's board of directors has no audit committee); or

(iii)   The issuer's board of directors (if the issuer's board of directors has no committee consisting solely of directors who are not employed, directly or indirectly, by the issuer and are not, in the case of a registered investment company, "interested persons" as defined in section 2(a)(19) of the Investment Company Act of 1940).

(4)   If an attorney reasonably believes that it would be futile to report evidence of a material violation to the issuer's chief legal officer and chief executive officer (or the equivalents thereof) under paragraph (b)(1) of this rule, the attorney may report such evidence as provided under paragraph (b)(3) of this rule.

(5)   An attorney retained or directed by an issuer to investigate evidence of a material violation reported under paragraph (b)(1), (b)(3), or (b)(4) of this rule shall be deemed to be appearing and practicing before the Commission. Directing or retaining an attorney to investigate reported evidence of a material violation does not relieve an officer or director of the issuer to whom such evidence has been reported under paragraph (b)(1), (b)(3), or (b)(4) of this rule from a duty to respond to the reporting attorney.

(6)   An attorney shall not have any obligation to report evidence of a material violation under this paragraph (b) if:

(i)   The attorney was retained or directed by the issuer's chief legal officer (or the equivalent thereof) to investigate such evidence of a material violation and:

(A)   The attorney reports the results of such investigation to the chief legal officer (or the equivalent thereof); and

(B)   Except where the attorney and the chief legal officer (or the equivalent thereof) each reasonably believes that no material violation has occurred, is ongoing, or is about to occur, the chief legal officer (or the equivalent thereof) reports the results of the investigation to the issuer's board of directors, a committee thereof to whom a report could be made pursuant to paragraph (b)(3) of this rule, or a qualified legal compliance committee; or

(ii)   The attorney was retained or directed by the chief legal officer (or the equivalent thereof) to assert, consistent with his or her professional obligations, a colorable defense on behalf of the issuer (or the issuer's officer, director, employee, or agent, as the case may be) in any investigation or judicial or administrative proceeding relating to such evidence of a material violation, and the chief legal officer (or the equivalent thereof) provides reasonable and timely reports on the progress and outcome of such proceeding to the issuer's board of directors, a committee thereof to whom a report could be made pursuant to paragraph (b)(3) of this rule, or a qualified legal compliance committee.

(7)   An attorney shall not have any obligation to report evidence of a material violation under this paragraph (b) if such attorney was retained or directed by a qualified legal compliance committee:

(i)   To investigate such evidence of a material violation; or

(ii)   To assert, consistent with his or her professional obligations, a colorable defense on behalf of the issuer (or the issuer's officer, director, employee, or agent, as the case may be) in any investigation or judicial or administrative proceeding relating to such evidence of a material violation.

(8)   An attorney who receives what he or she reasonably believes is an appropriate and timely response to a report he or she has made pursuant to paragraph (b)(1), (b)(3), or (b)(4) of this rule need do nothing more under this rule with respect to his or her report.

(9)   An attorney who does not reasonably believe that the issuer has made an appropriate response within a reasonable time to the report or reports made pursuant to paragraph (b)(1), (b)(3), or (b)(4) of this rule shall explain his or her reasons therefor to the chief legal officer (or the equivalent thereof), the chief executive officer (or the equivalent thereof), and directors to whom the attorney reported the evidence of a material violation pursuant to paragraph (b)(1), (b)(3), or (b)(4) of this rule.

(10) An attorney formerly employed or retained by an issuer who has reported evidence of a material violation under this part and reasonably believes that he or she has been discharged for so doing may notify the issuer's board of directors or any committee thereof that he or she believes that he or she has been discharged for reporting evidence of a material violation under this rule.

(c)   *Alternative Reporting Procedures for Attorneys Retained or Employed by an Issuer that has Established a Qualified Legal Compliance Committee.*

(1)   If an attorney, appearing and practicing before the Commission in the representation of an issuer, becomes aware of evidence of a material violation by the issuer or by any officer, director, employee, or agent of the issuer, the attorney may, as an alternative to the reporting requirements of paragraph (b) of this rule, report such evidence to a qualified legal compliance committee, if the issuer has previously formed such a committee. An attorney who reports evidence of a material violation to such a qualified legal compliance committee has satisfied his or her obligation to report such evidence and is not required to assess the issuer's response to the reported evidence of a material violation.

(2)   A chief legal officer (or the equivalent thereof) may refer a report of evidence of a material violation to a previously established qualified legal compliance committee in lieu of causing an inquiry to be conducted under paragraph (b)(2) of this rule. The chief legal officer (or the equivalent thereof) shall inform the reporting attorney that the report has been referred to a qualified legal compliance committee. Thereafter, pursuant to the requirements under Rule 2(k), the qualified legal compliance committee shall be responsible for responding to the evidence of a material violation reported to it under this paragraph (c).

(d)   *Issuer Confidences.*

(1)   Any report under this rule (or the contemporaneous record thereof) or any response thereto (or the contemporaneous record thereof) may be used by an attorney in connection with any investigation, proceeding, or litigation in which the attorney's compliance with this part is in issue.

(2) An attorney appearing and practicing before the Commission in the representation of an issuer may reveal to the Commission, without the issuer's consent, confidential information related to the representation to the extent the attorney reasonably believes necessary:

(i)   To prevent the issuer from committing a material violation that is likely to cause substantial injury to the financial interest or property of the issuer or investors;

(ii) To prevent the issuer, in a Commission investigation or administrative proceeding from committing perjury, proscribed in 18 U.S.C. 1621; suborning perjury, proscribed in 18 U.S.C. 1622; or committing any act proscribed in 18 U.S.C. 1001 that is likely to perpetrate a fraud upon the Commission; or

(iii) To rectify the consequences of a material violation by the issuer that caused, or may cause, substantial injury to the financial interest or property of the issuer or investors in the furtherance of which the attorney's services were used.

Rule 4. Responsibilities of Supervisory Attorneys

(a) An attorney supervising or directing another attorney who is appearing and practicing before the Commission in the representation of an issuer is a supervisory attorney. An issuer's chief legal officer (or the equivalent thereof) is a supervisory attorney under this rule.

(b) A supervisory attorney shall make reasonable efforts to ensure that a subordinate attorney, as defined in Rule 5(a), that he or she supervises or directs conforms to this part. To the extent a subordinate attorney appears and practices before the Commission in the representation of an issuer, that subordinate attorney's supervisory attorneys also appear and practice before the Commission.

(c) A supervisory attorney is responsible for complying with the reporting requirements in Rule 3 when a subordinate attorney has reported to the supervisory attorney evidence of a material violation.

(d) A supervisory attorney who has received a report of evidence of a material violation from a subordinate attorney under Rule 3 may report such evidence to the issuer's qualified legal compliance committee if the issuer has duly formed such a committee.

Rule 5. Responsibilities of a Subordinate Attorney

(a) An attorney who appears and practices before the Commission in the representation of an issuer on a matter under the supervision or direction of another attorney (other than under the direct supervision or direction of the issuer's chief legal officer (or the equivalent thereof)) is a subordinate attorney.

(b) A subordinate attorney shall comply with this part notwithstanding that the subordinate attorney acted at the direction of or under the supervision of another person.

(c) A subordinate attorney complies with Rule 3 if the subordinate attorney reports to his or her supervising attorney under Rule 3(b) evidence of a material violation of which the subordinate attorney has become aware in appearing and practicing before the Commission.

(d) A subordinate attorney may take the steps permitted or required by Rule 3(b) or (c) if the subordinate attorney reasonably believes that a supervisory attorney to whom he or she has reported evidence of a material violation under Rule 3(b) has failed to comply with Rule 3.

Rule 6. Sanctions and Discipline

(a) A violation of this part by any attorney appearing and practicing before the Commission in the representation of an issuer shall subject such attorney to the civil penalties and remedies for a violation of the federal securities laws available to the Commission in an action brought by the Commission thereunder.

(b) An attorney appearing and practicing before the Commission who violates any provision of this part is subject to the disciplinary authority of the Commission, regardless of whether the attorney may also be subject to discipline for the same conduct in a jurisdiction where the attorney is admitted or practices. An administrative disciplinary proceeding initiated by the Commission for violation of this part may result in an attorney being censured, or being temporarily or permanently denied the privilege of appearing or practicing before the Commission.

(c)   An attorney who complies in good faith with the provisions of this part shall not be subject to discipline or otherwise liable under inconsistent standards imposed by any state or other United States jurisdiction where the attorney is admitted or practices.

(d)   An attorney practicing outside the United States shall not be required to comply with the requirements of this part to the extent that such compliance is prohibited by applicable foreign law.

Rule 7.   No Private Right of Action

(a)   Nothing in this part is intended to, or does, create a private right of action against any attorney, law firm, or issuer based upon compliance or noncompliance with its provisions.

(b)   Authority to enforce compliance with this part is vested exclusively in the Commission.

E. SECURITIES EXCHANGE ACT OF 1934*, SELECTED RULES, AND FORMS

---

* Including the Sarbanes-Oxley Act of 2002.

Short Title

Sec. 1. This act may be cited as the ["Securities Exchange Act of 1934"].

Necessity for Regulation

Sec. 2. For the reasons hereinafter enumerated, transactions in securities as commonly conducted upon securities exchanges and over-the-counter markets are effected with a national public interest which makes it necessary to provide for regulation and control of such transactions and of practices and matters related thereto, including transactions by officers, directors, and principal security holders, to require appropriate reports, to remove impediments to and perfect the mechanisms of a national market system for securities and a national system for the clearance and settlement of securities transactions and the safeguarding of securities and funds related thereto, and to impose requirements necessary to make such regulation and control reasonably complete and effective, in order to protect interstate commerce, the national credit, the Federal taxing power, to protect and make more effective the national banking system and Federal Reserve System, and to insure the maintenance of fair and honest markets in such transactions:

(1)   Such transactions

(a)   are carried on in large volume by the public generally and in large part originate outside the States in which the exchanges and over-the-counter markets are located and/or are effected by means of the mails and instrumentalities of interstate commerce;

(b)   constitute an important part of the current of interstate commerce;

(c)   involve in large part the securities of issuers engaged in interstate commerce;

(d)   involve the use of credit, directly affect the financing of trade, industry, and transportation in interstate commerce, and directly affect and influence the volume of interstate commerce; and affect the national credit.

(2)   The prices established and offered in such transactions are generally disseminated and quoted throughout the United States and foreign countries and constitute a basis for determining and establishing the prices at which securities are bought and sold, the amount of certain taxes owing to the United States and to the several States by owners, buyers, and sellers of securities, and the value of collateral for bank loans.

(3)   Frequently the prices of securities on such exchanges and markets are susceptible to manipulation and control, and the dissemination of such prices gives rise to excessive speculation, resulting in sudden and unreasonable fluctuations in the prices of securities which

(a)   cause alternately unreasonable expansion and unreasonable contraction of the volume of credit available for trade, transportation, and industry in interstate commerce,

(b)   hinder the proper appraisal of the value of securities and thus prevent a fair calculation of taxes owing to the United States and to the several States by owners, buyers, and sellers of securities, and

(c)   prevent the fair valuation of collateral for bank loans and/or obstruct the effective operation of the national banking system and Federal Reserve System.

(4)   National emergencies, which produce widespread unemployment and the dislocation of trade, transportation, and industry, and which burden interstate commerce and adversely affect the general welfare, are precipitated, intensified, and prolonged by manipulation and sudden and unreasonable fluctuations of security prices and by excessive speculation on such exchanges and markets, and to meet such emergencies the Federal Government is put to such great expense as to burden the national credit.

Definitions and Application

Sec. 3.   (a)   When used in this Act, unless the context otherwise requires—

(1)   The term "exchange" means any organization, association, or group of persons, whether incorporated or unincorporated, which constitutes, maintains, or provides a market place or facilities for bringing together purchasers and sellers of securities or for otherwise performing with respect to securities the functions commonly performed by a stock exchange as that term is generally understood, and includes the market place and the market facilities maintained by such exchange.

(2)   The term "facility" when used with respect to an exchange includes its premises, tangible or intangible property whether on the premises or not, any right to the use of such premises or property or any service thereof for the purpose of effecting or reporting a transaction on an exchange (including, among other things, any system of communication to or from the exchange, by ticker or otherwise, maintained by or with the consent of the exchange), and any right of the exchange to the use of any property or service.

(3)(A)   The term "member" when used with respect to a national securities exchange means

(i)   any natural person permitted to effect transactions on the floor of the exchange without the services of another person acting as broker,

(ii) any registered broker or dealer with which such a natural person is associated,

(iii) any registered broker or dealer permitted to designate as a representative such a natural person, and

(iv) any other registered broker or dealer which agrees to be regulated by such exchange and with respect to which the exchange undertakes to enforce compliance with the provisions of this Act, the rules and regulations thereunder, and its own rules. For purposes of sections 6(b)(1), 6(b)(4), 6(b)(6), 6(b)(7), 6(d), 17(d), 19(d), 19(e), 19(g), 19(h), and 21 of this Act, the term "member" when used with respect to a national securities exchange also means, to the extent of the rules of the exchange specified by the Commission, any person required by the Commission to comply with such rules pursuant to section 6(f) of this Act.

(B) The term "member" when used with respect to a registered securities association means any broker or dealer who agrees to be regulated by such association and with respect to whom the association undertakes to enforce compliance with the provisions of this Act, the rules and regulations thereunder, and its own rules.

(4) Broker.—

(A) In general.—

The term "broker" means any person engaged in the business of effecting transactions in securities for the account of others.

(B) Exception for certain bank activities.—

A bank shall not be considered to be a broker because the bank engages in any one or more of the following activities under the conditions described:

(i) Third party brokerage agreements.—

The bank enters into a contractual or other written arrangement with a broker or dealer registered under this title under which the broker or dealer offers brokerage services on or off the premises of the bank if—

(I) such broker or dealer is clearly identified as the person performing the brokerage services;

(II) the broker or dealer performs brokerage services in an area that is clearly marked and, to the extent practicable, physically separate from the routine deposit-taking activities of the bank;

(III) any materials used by the bank to advertise or promote generally the availability of brokerage services under the arrangement clearly indicate that the brokerage services are being provided by the broker or dealer and not by the bank;

(IV) any materials used by the bank to advertise or promote generally the availability of brokerage services under the arrangement are in compliance with the Federal securities laws before distribution;

(V) bank employees (other than associated persons of a broker or dealer who are qualified pursuant to the rules of a self-regulatory organization) perform only clerical or ministerial functions in connection with brokerage transactions including scheduling appointments with the associated persons of a broker or dealer, except that bank employees may forward customer funds or securities and may describe in general terms the types of investment vehicles available from the bank and the broker or dealer under the arrangement;

(VI) bank employees do not receive incentive compensation for any brokerage transaction unless such employees are associated persons of a broker or dealer and are qualified pursuant to the rules of a self-regulatory organization, except that the bank employees may receive compensation for the referral of any customer if the compensation is a nominal one-time cash fee of a fixed dollar amount and the payment of the fee is not contingent on whether the referral results in a transaction;

(VII) such services are provided by the broker or dealer on a basis in which all customers that receive any services are fully disclosed to the broker or dealer;

(VIII) the bank does not carry a securities account of the customer except as permitted under clause (ii) or (viii) of this subparagraph;

(IX) the bank, broker, or dealer informs each customer that the brokerage services are provided by the broker or dealer and not by the bank and that the securities are not deposits or other obligations of the bank, are not guaranteed by the bank, and are not insured by the Federal Deposit Insurance Corporation.

(ii)   Trust activities.—

The bank effects transactions in a trustee capacity, or effects in a fiduciary capacity in its trust department or other department that is regularly examined by bank examiners for compliance with fiduciary principles and standards, and—

(I)   is chiefly compensated for such transactions, consistent with fiduciary principles and standards, on the basis of an administration or annual fee (payable monthly, quarterly, or other basis), a percentage of assets management, or a flat or capped per order processing fee equal to not more that the cost incurred by the bank in connection with executing securities transactions for trustee and fiduciary customers, or any combination of such fees; and

(II)   does not publicly solicit brokerage business, other than by advertising its other trust activities.

(iii)   Permissible securities transactions.—

The bank effects transactions in—

(I)   commercial paper, bankers acceptances, or commercial bills;

(II)   exempted securities;

(III)   qualified Canadian government obligations as defined in section 5136 of the Revised Statutes, in conformity with section 15C of this Act and the rules and regulations thereunder, or obligations of the North American Development Bank; or

(IV)   any standardized, credit enhanced debt security issued by a foreign government pursuant to the March 1989 plan of then Secretary of the Treasury Brady, used by such foreign government to retire outstanding commercial bank loans.

(iv)   Certain stock purchase plans.—

(I)   Employee benefit plans.—

The bank effects transactions, as part of its transfer agency activities, in the securities of an issuer as part of any pension, retirement, profit-sharing, bonus, thrift, savings, incentive, or other similar benefit plan for the employees of that issuer or its affiliates (as defined in section 2 of the Bank Holding Company Act of 1956), if the bank does not solicit transactions or provide investment advice with respect to the purchase or sale of securities in connection with the plan.

(II)   Dividend reinvestment plans.—

The bank effects transactions, as part of its transfer agency activities, in the securities of an issuer as part of that issuer's dividend reinvestment plan, if—

(aa)   the bank does not solicit transactions or provide investment advice with respect to the purchase or sale of securities in connection with the plan; and

(bb)   the bank does not net shareholders' buy and sell orders, other than for programs for odd-lot holders or plans registered with the Commission.

(III)   Issuer plans.—

The bank effects transactions, as part of its transfer agency activities, in the securities of an issuer as part of a plan or program for the purchase or sale of that issuer's shares, if—

(aa) the bank does not solicit transactions or provide investment advice with respect to the purchase or sale of securities in connection with the plan or program; and

(bb) the bank does not net shareholders' buy and sell orders, other than for programs for odd-lot holders or plans registered with the Commission.

(IV) Permissible delivery of materials.—

The exception to being considered a broker for a bank engaged in activities described in subclauses (I), (II), and (III) will not be affected by delivery of written or electronic plan materials by a bank to employees of the issuer, shareholders of the issuer, or members of affinity groups of the issuer, so long as such materials are—

(aa) comparable in scope and nature to that permitted by the Commission as of the date of enactment of the Gramm-Leach-Bliley Act; or

(bb) otherwise permitted by the Commission.

(v) Sweep accounts.—

The bank effects transactions as part of a program for the investment or reinvestment of deposit funds into any no-load, open-end management investment company registered under the Investment Company Act of 1940 that holds itself out as a money market fund.

(vi) Affiliate transactions.—

The bank effects transactions for the account of any affiliate of the bank (as defined in section 2 of the Bank Holding Company Act of 1956) other than—

(I) a registered broker or dealer; or

(II) an affiliate that is engaged in merchant banking, as described in section 4(k)(4)(H) of the Bank Holding Company Act of 1956.

(vii) Private securities offerings.—

The bank

(I) effects sales as part of the primary offering of securities not involving a public offering, pursuant to section 3(b), 4(2), or 4(5) of the Securities Act of 1933 or the rules and regulations thereunder;

(II) at any time after the date that is 1 year after the date of the enactment of the Gramm-Leach-Bliley Act, is not affiliated with a broker or dealer that has been registered for more than 1 year in accordance with this Act, and engages in dealing, market making, or underwriting activities, other than with respect to exempted securities; and

(III) if the bank is not affiliated with a broker or dealer, does not effect any primary offering described in subclause (I) the aggregate amount of which exceeds 25 percent of the capital of the bank, except that the limitation of this subclause shall not apply with respect to any sale of government securities or municipal securities.

(viii) Safekeeping and custody activities.—

(I) In general.—

The bank, as part of customary banking activities—

(aa) provides safekeeping or custody services with respect to securities, including the exercise of warrants and other rights on behalf of customers;

(bb) facilitates the transfer of funds or securities, as a custodian or a clearing agency, in connection with the clearance and settlement of its customers' transactions in securities;

(cc) effects securities lending or borrowing transactions with or on behalf of customers as part of services provided to customers pursuant to division (aa) or (bb) or invests cask collateral pledged in connection with such transactions;

(dd) holds securities pledged by a customer to another person or securities subject to purchase or resale agreements involving a customer, or facilitates the pledging or transfer of such securities by book entry or as otherwise provided under applicable law, if the bank maintains records separately identifying the securities and the customer; or

(ee) serves as a custodian or provider of other related administrative services to any individual retirement account, pension, retirement, profit sharing, bonus, thrift savings, incentive, or other similar benefit plan.

(II) Exception for carrying broker activities.—

The exception to being considered a broker for a bank engaged in activities described in subclause (I) shall not apply if the bank, in connection with such activities, acts in the United States as a carrying broker (as such term, and different formulations thereof, are used in section 15(c)(3) of this Act and the rules and regulations thereunder) for any broker or dealer, unless such carrying broker activities are engaged in with respect to government securities (as defined in paragraph (42) of this subsection).

(ix) Identified banking products.—

The bank effects transactions in identified banking products as defined in section 206 of the Gramm-Leach-Bliley Act.

(x) Municipal securities.—

The bank effects transactions in municipal securities.

(xi) De minimis exception.—

The bank effects, other than in transactions referred to in clauses (i) through (x), not more than 500 transactions in securities in any calendar year, and such transactions are not effected by an employee of the bank who is also an employee of a broker or dealer.

(C) Execution by broker or dealer.—

The exception to being considered a broker for a bank engaged in activities described in clauses (ii), (iv), and (viii) of subparagraph (B) shall not apply if the activities described in such provisions result in the trade in the United States of any security that is publicly traded security in the United States, unless—

(i) the bank directs such trade to a registered broker or dealer for execution;

(ii) the trade is a cross trade or other substantially similar trade of a security that—

(I) is made by the bank or between the bank and an affiliated fiduciary; and

(II) is not in contravention of fiduciary principles established under applicable Federal or State law; or

(iii) the trade is conducted in some other manner permitted under rules, regulations, or orders as the Commission may prescribe or issue.

(D) Fiduciary capacity.—

For purposes of subparagraph (B)(ii), the term "fiduciary capacity" means—

(i) in the capacity as trustee, executor, administrator, registrar of stocks and bonds, transfer agent, guardian, assignee, receiver, or custodian under a uniform gift to minor act, or as an investment adviser if the bank receives a fee for its investment advice;

(ii) in any capacity in which the bank possesses investment discretion on behalf of another; or

(iii) in any other similar capacity.

(E) Exception for entities subject to section 15(f).—

The term "broker" does not include a bank that—

(i) was, on the day before the date of enactment of the Gramm-Leach-Bliley Act, subject to section 15(f); and

(ii) is subject to such restrictions and requirements as the Commission considers appropriate. [effective May 12, 2001]

(F) Joint rulemaking required.—

Joint Rulemaking Required.—The Commission and the Board of Governors of the Federal Reserve System shall jointly adopt a single set of rules or regulations to implement the exceptions in subparagraph (B).

(5) Dealer.—

(A) In general.—

The term "dealer" means any person engaged in the business of buying and selling securities not including security-based swaps, other than security-based swaps with or for persons that are not eligible contract participants for such person's own account through a broker or otherwise.

(B) Exception for person not engaged in the business of dealing.—

The term "dealer" does not include a person that buys or sells securities not including security-based swaps, other than security-based swaps with or for persons that are not eligible contract participants for such person's own account, either individually or in a fiduciary capacity, but not as a part of a regular business.

(C) Exception for certain bank activities.—

A bank shall not be considered to be a dealer because the bank engages in any of the following activities under the conditions described:

(i) Permissible securities transactions.—

The bank buys or sells—

(I) commercial paper, bankers acceptances, or commercial bills;

(II) exempted securities;

(III) qualified Canadian government obligations as defined in section 5136 of the Revised Statutes of the United States, in conformity with section 15C of this Act and the rules and regulations thereunder, or obligations of the North American Development Bank; or

(IV) any standardized, credit enhanced debt security issued by a foreign government pursuant to the March 1989 plan of then Secretary of the Treasury Brady, used by such foreign government to retire outstanding commercial bank loans.

(ii) Investment, trustee, and fiduciary transactions.—

The bank buys or sells securities for investment purposes—

(I) for the bank; or

(II) for accounts for which the bank acts as a trustee or fiduciary.

(iii) Asset-backed transactions.—

The bank engages in the issuance or sale to qualified investors, through a grantor trust or other separate entity, of securities backed by or representing an interest in notes, drafts, acceptances, loans, leases, receivables, other obligations (other than securities of which the bank is not the issuer), or pools of any such obligations predominantly originated by—

(I)   the bank;

(II)   an affiliate of any such bank other than a broker or dealer; or

(III)   a syndicate of banks of which the bank is a member, if the obligations or pool of obligations consists of mortgage obligations or consumer-related receivables.

(iv)   Identified banking products.—

The bank buys or sells identified banking products as defined in section 206 of the Gramm-Leach-Bliley Act.

(6)   The term "bank" means

(A)   a banking institution organized under the laws of the United States or a Federal savings association, as defined in section 2(5) of the Home Owners' Loan Act,

(B)   a member bank of the Federal Reserve System,

(C)   any other banking institution or savings association, as defined in section 2(4) of the Home Owners' Loan Act, whether incorporated or not, doing business under the laws of any State or of the United States, a substantial portion of the business of which consists of receiving deposits or exercising fiduciary powers similar to those permitted to national banks under the authority of the Comptroller of the Currency pursuant to the first section of Public Law 87–722, and which is supervised and examined by State or Federal authority having supervision over banks or savings associations, and which is not operated for the purpose of evading the provisions of this Act, and

(D)   a receiver, conservator, or other liquidating agent of any institution or firm included in clauses (A), (B), or (C) of this paragraph.

(7)   The term "director" means any director of a corporation or any person performing similar functions with respect to any organization, whether incorporated or unincorporated.

(8)   The term "issuer" means any person who issues or proposes to issue any security; except that with respect to certificates of deposit for securities, voting-trust certificates, or collateral-trust certificates, or with respect to certificates of interest or shares in an unincorporated investment trust not having a board of directors or of the fixed, restricted management, or unit type, the term "issuer" means the person or persons performing the acts and assuming the duties of depositor or manager pursuant to the provisions of the trust or other agreement or instrument under which such securities are issued; and except that with respect to equipment-trust certificates or like securities, the term "issuer" means the person by whom the equipment or property is, or is to be, used.

(9)   The term "person" means a natural person, company, government, or political subdivision, agency, or instrumentality of a government.

(10)   The term "security" means any note, stock, treasury stock, security future, security-based swap, bond, debenture, certificate of interest or participation in any profit-sharing agreement or in any oil, gas, or other mineral royalty or lease, any collateral-trust certificate, preorganization certificate or subscription, transferable share, investment contract, voting-trust certificate, certificate of deposit for a security, any put, call, straddle, option, or privilege on any security, certificate of deposit, or group or index of securities (including any interest therein or based on the value thereof), or any put, call, straddle, option, or privilege entered into on a national securities exchange relating to foreign currency, or in general, any instrument commonly known as a "security"; or any certificate of interest or participation in, temporary or interim certificate for, receipt for, or warrant or right to subscribe to or purchase, any of the foregoing; but shall not include currency or any note, draft, bill of exchange, or banker's acceptance which has a maturity at the time of issuance of not exceeding nine months, exclusive of days of grace, or any renewal thereof the maturity of which is likewise limited.

(11)   The term "equity security" means any stock or similar security; or any security future on any such security; or any security convertible, with or without consideration, into such a security, or carrying any warrant or right to subscribe to or purchase such a security; or any such warrant or right; or any other security which the Commission shall deem to be of similar nature and consider necessary or appropriate, by such rules and regulations as it may prescribe in the public interest or for the protection of investors, to treat as an equity security.

(12)(A)   The term "exempted security" or "exempted securities" includes—

(i)   government securities, as defined in paragraph (42) of this subsection;

(ii)   municipal securities, as defined in paragraph (29) of this subsection;

(iii)   any interest or participation in any common trust fund or similar fund that is executed from the definition of the term "investment company" under section 3(c)(3) of the Investment Company Act of 1940;

(iv)   any interest or participation in a single trust fund, or a collective trust fund maintained by a bank, or any security arising out of a contract issued by an insurance company, which interest, participation, or security is issued in connection with a qualified plan as defined in subparagraph (C) of this paragraph;

(v)   any security issued by or any interest or participation in any pooled income fund, collective trust fund, collective investment fund, or similar fund that is excluded from the definition of an investment company under section 3(c)(10)(B) of the Investment Company Act of 1940;

(vi)   solely for purposes of sections 12, 13, 14, and 16 of this Act, any security issued by or any interest or participation in any church plan, company, or account that is excluded from the definition of an investment company under section 3(c)(14) of the Investment Company Act of 1940; and

(vii)   such other securities (which may include, among others, unregistered securities, the market in which is predominantly intrastate) as the Commission may, by such rules and regulations as it deems consistent with the public interest and the protection of investors, either unconditionally or upon specified terms and conditions or for stated periods, exempt from the operation of any one or more provisions of this Act which by their terms do not apply to an "exempted security" or to "exempted securities".

(B)(i)   Notwithstanding subparagraph (A)(i) of this paragraph, government securities shall not be deemed to be "exempted securities" for the purposes of section 17A of this Act.

(ii)   Notwithstanding subparagraph (A)(ii) of this paragraph, municipal securities shall not be deemed to be "exempted securities" for the purposes of sections 15 and 17A of this Act.

(C)   For purposes of subparagraph (A)(iv) of this paragraph, the term "qualified plan" means

(i)   a stock bonus, pension, or profit-sharing plan which meets the requirements for qualification under section 401 of the Internal Revenue Code of 1954,

(ii)   an annuity plan which meets the requirements for the deduction of the employer's contribution under section 404(a)(2) of such Code,

(iii)   a governmental plan as defined in section 414(d) of such Code which has been established by an employer for the exclusive benefit of its employees or their beneficiaries for the purpose of distributing to such employees or their beneficiaries the corpus and income of the funds accumulated under such plan, if under such plan it is impossible, prior to the satisfaction of all liabilities with respect to such employees and their beneficiaries, for any part of the corpus or income to be used for, or diverted to, purposes other than the exclusive benefit of such employees or their beneficiaries, or

(iv)   a church plan, company, or account that is excluded from the definition of an investment company under section 3(c)(14) of the Investment Company Act of 1940, other than any plan described in clause (i), (ii), or (iii) of this subparagraph which (I) covers employees some or all of whom are employees within the meaning of section 401(c) of such Code, or (II) is a plan funded by an annuity contract described in section 403(b) of such Code.

(13)   The terms "buy" and "purchase" each include any contract to buy, purchase or otherwise acquire. For security futures products, such term includes any contract agreement or transaction for future delivery. For security-based swaps, such terms include the execution, termination (prior to its scheduled maturity date), assignment, exchange, or similar transfer or conveyance of, or extinguishing of rights or obligations under, a security-based swap, as the context may require.

(14) The terms "sale" and "sell" each include any contract to sell or otherwise dispose of. For security futures products, such term includes any contract, agreement or transaction for future delivery. For security-based swaps, such terms include the execution, termination (prior to its scheduled maturity date), assignment, exchange, or similar transfer or conveyance of, or extinguishing of rights or obligations under, a security-based swap, as the context may require.

(15) The term "Commission" means the Securities and Exchange Commission established by section 4 of this Act.

(16) The term "State" means any State of the United States, the District of Columbia, Puerto Rico, the Virgin Islands, or any other possession of the United States.

(17) The term "interstate commerce" means trade, commerce, transportation, or communication among the several States, or between any foreign country and any State, or between any State and any place or ship outside thereof. The term includes intrastate use of

    (A) any facility of a national securities exchange or of a telephone or other interstate means of communication, or

    (B) any other interstate instrumentality.

(18) The term "person associated with a broker or dealer" or "associated person of a broker or dealer" means any partner, officer, director, or branch manager of such broker or dealer (or any person occupying a similar status or performing similar functions), any person directly or indirectly controlling, controlled by, or under common control with such broker or dealer, or any employee of such broker or dealer, except that any person associated with a broker or dealer whose functions are solely clerical or ministerial shall not be included in the meaning of such term for purposes of section 15(b) of this Act (other than paragraph (6) thereof).

(19) The terms "investment company", "affiliated person", "insurance company", "separate account", and "company" have the same meanings as in the Investment Company Act of 1940.

(20) The terms "investment adviser" and "underwriter" have the same meanings as in the Investment Advisers Act of 1940.

(21) The term "person associated with a member" or "associated person of a member" when used with respect to a member of a national securities exchange or registered securities association means any partner, officer, director, or branch manager of such member (or any person occupying a similar status or performing similar functions), any person directly or indirectly controlling, controlled by, or under common control with such member, or any employee of such member.

(22)(A) The term "securities information processor" means any person engaged in the business of

    (i) collecting, processing, or preparing for distribution or publication, or assisting, participating in, or coordinating the distribution or publication of, information with respect to transactions in or quotations for any security (other than an exempted security) or

    (ii) distributing or publishing (whether by means of a ticker tape, a communications network, a terminal display device, or otherwise) on a current and continuing basis, information with respect to such transactions or quotations. The term "securities information processor" does not include any bona fide newspaper, news magazine, or business or financial publication of general and regular circulation, any self-regulatory organization, any bank, broker, dealer, building and loan, savings and loan, or homestead association, or cooperative bank, if such bank, broker, dealer, association, or cooperative bank would be deemed to be a securities information processor solely by reason of functions performed by such institutions as part of customary banking, brokerage, dealing, association, or cooperative bank activities, or any common carrier, as defined in section 3 of the Communications Act of 1934, subject to the jurisdiction of the Federal Communications Commission or a State commission, as defined in section 3 of that Act, unless the Commission determines that such carrier is engaged in the business of collecting, processing, or preparing for distribution or publication, information with respect to transactions in or quotations for any security.

(B) The term "exclusive processor" means any securities information processor or self-regulatory organization which, directly or indirectly, engages on an exclusive basis on behalf of any national securities exchange or registered securities association, or any national securities exchange or registered securities association which engages on an exclusive basis on its own behalf, in collecting, processing, or preparing for distribution or publication any information with respect to

(i) transactions or quotations on or effected or made by means of any facility of such exchange or

(ii) quotations distributed or published by means of any electronic system operated or controlled by such association.

(23)(A) The term "clearing agency" means any person who acts as an intermediary in making payments or deliveries or both in connection with transactions in securities or who provides facilities for comparison of data respecting the terms of settlement of securities transactions, to reduce the number of settlements of securities transactions, or for the allocation of securities settlement responsibilities. Such term also means any person, such as a securities depository, who

(i) acts as a custodian of securities in connection with a system for the central handling of securities whereby all securities of a particular class or series of any issuer deposited within the system are treated as fungible and may be transferred, loaned, or pledged by bookkeeping entry without physical delivery of securities certificates, or

(ii) otherwise permits or facilitates the settlement of securities transactions or the hypothecation or lending of securities without physical delivery of securities certificates.

(B) The term "clearing agency" does not include

(i) any Federal Reserve bank, Federal home loan bank, or Federal land bank;

(ii) any national securities exchange or registered securities association solely by reason of its providing facilities for comparison of data respecting the terms of settlement of securities transactions effected on such exchange or by means of any electronic system operated or controlled by such association;

(iii) any bank, broker, dealer, building and loan, savings and loan, or homestead association, or cooperative bank if such bank, broker, dealer, association, or cooperative bank would be deemed to be a clearing agency solely by reason of functions performed by such institution as part of customary banking, brokerage, dealing, association, or cooperative banking activities, or solely by reason of acting on behalf of a clearing agency or a participant therein in connection with the furnishing by the clearing agency of services to its participants or the use of services of the clearing agency by its participants, unless the Commission, by rule otherwise provides as necessary or appropriate to assure the prompt and accurate clearance and settlement of securities transactions or to prevent evasion of this title;

(iv) any life insurance company, its registered separate accounts, or a subsidiary of such insurance company solely by reason of functions commonly performed by such entities in connection with variable annuity contracts or variable life policies issued by such insurance company or its separate accounts;

(v) any registered open-end investment company or unit investment trust solely by reason of functions commonly performed by it in connection with shares in such registered open-end investment company or unit investment trust, or

(vi) any person solely by reason of its performing functions described in paragraph (25)(E) of this subsection.

(24) The term "participant" when used with respect to a clearing agency means any person who uses a clearing agency to clear or settle securities transactions or to transfer, pledge, lend, or hypothecate securities. Such term does not include a person whose only use of a clearing agency is

(A) through another person who is a participant or

(B) as a pledgee of securities.

(25) The term "transfer agent" means any person who engages on behalf of an issuer of securities or on behalf of itself as an issuer of securities in

(A) countersigning such securities upon issuance;

(B) monitoring the issuance of such securities with a view to preventing unauthorized issuance, a function commonly performed by a person called a registrar;

(C) registering the transfer of such securities;

(D) exchanging or converting such securities; or

(E) transferring record ownership of securities by bookkeeping entry without physical issuance of securities certificates. The term "transfer agent" does not include any insurance company or separate account which performs such functions solely with respect to variable annuity contracts or variable life policies which it issues or any registered clearing agency which performs such functions solely with respect to options contracts which it issues.

(26) The term "self-regulatory organization" means any national securities exchange, registered securities association, or registered clearing agency, or (solely for purposes of sections 19(b), 19(c), and 23(b) of this Act) the Municipal Securities Rulemaking Board established by section 15B of this Act.

(27) The term "rules of an exchange", "rules of an association", or "rules of a clearing agency" means the constitution, articles of incorporation, bylaws, and rules, or instruments corresponding to the foregoing, of an exchange, association of brokers and dealers, or clearing agency, respectively, and such of the stated policies, practices, and interpretations of such exchange, association, or clearing agency as the Commission, by rule, may determine to be necessary or appropriate in the public interest or for the protection of investors to be deemed to be rules of such exchange, association, or clearing agency.

(28) The term "rules of a self-regulatory organization" means the rules of an exchange which is a national securities exchange, the rules of an association of brokers and dealers which is a registered securities association, the rules of a clearing agency which is a registered clearing agency, or the rules of the Municipal Securities Rulemaking Board.

(29) The term "municipal securities" means securities which are direct obligations of, or obligations guaranteed as to principal or interest by, a State or any political subdivision thereof, or any agency or instrumentality of a State or any political subdivision thereof, or any municipal corporate instrumentality of one or more States, or any security which is an industrial development bond (as defined in section 103(c)(2) of the Internal Revenue Code of 1954) the interest on which is excludable from gross income under section 103(a)(1) of such code if, by reason of the application of paragraph (4) or (6) of section 103(c) of such code (determined as if paragraphs (4)(A), (5), and (7) were not included in such section 103(c)), paragraph (1) of such section 103(c) does not apply to such security.

(30) The term "municipal securities dealer" means any person (including a separately identifiable department or division of a bank) engaged in the business of buying and selling municipal securities for his own account, through a broker or otherwise, but does not include—

(A) any person insofar as he buys or sells such securities for his own account, either individually or in some fiduciary capacity, but not as a part of a regular business; or

(B) a bank, unless the bank is engaged in the business of buying and selling municipal securities for its own account other than in a fiduciary capacity, through a broker or otherwise: *Provided, however,* That if the bank is engaged in such business through a separately identifiable department or division (as defined by the Municipal Securities Rulemaking Board in accordance with section 15B(b)(2)(H) of this Act) the department or division and not the bank itself shall be deemed to be the municipal securities dealer.

(31) The term "municipal securities broker" means a broker engaged in the business of effecting transactions in municipal securities for the account of others.

(32) The term "person associated with a municipal securities dealer" when used with respect to a municipal securities dealer which is a bank or a division or department of a bank means any person directly engaged in the management, direction, supervision, or performance of any of the municipal

securities dealer's activities with respect to municipal securities, and any person directly or indirectly controlling such activities or controlled by the municipal securities dealer in connection with such activities.

(33) The term "municipal securities investment portfolio" means all municipal securities held for investment and not for sale as part of a regular business by a municipal securities dealer or by a person, directly or indirectly, controlling, controlled by, or under common control with a municipal securities dealer.

(34) The term "appropriate regulatory agency" means—

(A) When used with respect to a municipal securities dealer:

(i) the Comptroller of the Currency, in the case of a national bank, a subsidiary or a department or division of any such bank, a Federal savings association (as defined in section 3(b)(2) of the Federal Deposit Insurance Act (12 U.S.C. 1813(b)(2))), the deposits of which are insured by the Federal Deposit Insurance Corporation, or a subsidiary or department or division of any such Federal savings association;

(ii) the Board of Governors of the Federal Reserve System, in the case of a State member bank of the Federal Reserve System, a subsidiary thereof, a bank holding company, or a subsidiary of a bank holding company which is a bank other than a bank specified in clause (i), (iii), or (iv) of this subparagraph, a subsidiary or a department or division of such subsidiary, or a savings and loan holding company;

(iii) the Federal Deposit Insurance Corporation, in the case of a bank insured by the Federal Deposit Insurance Corporation (other than a member of the Federal Reserve System), a subsidiary or department or division of any such bank, a State savings association (as defined in section 3(b)(3) of the Federal Deposit Insurance Act (12 U.S.C. 1813(b)(3))), the deposits of which are insured by the Federal Deposit Insurance Corporation, or a subsidiary or a department or division of any such State savings association; and

(iv) the Commission in the case of all other municipal securities dealers.

(B) When used with respect to a clearing agency or transfer agent:

(i) the Comptroller of the Currency, in the case of a national bank, a subsidiary of any such bank, a Federal savings association (as defined in section 3(b)(2) of the Federal Deposit Insurance Act (12 U.S.C. 1813(b)(2))), the deposits of which are insured by the Federal Deposit Insurance Corporation, or a subsidiary of any such Federal savings association;

(ii) the Board of Governors of the Federal Reserve System, in the case of a State member bank of the Federal Reserve System, a subsidiary thereof, a bank holding company, a subsidiary of a bank holding company that is a bank other than a bank specified in clause (i) or (iii) of this subparagraph, or a savings and loan holding company;

(iii) the Federal Deposit Insurance Corporation, in the case of a bank insured by the Federal Deposit Insurance Corporation (other than a member of the Federal Reserve System, a subsidiary of any such bank, a State savings association (as defined in section 3(b)(3) of the Federal Deposit Insurance Act (12 U.S.C. 1813(b)(3))), the deposits of which are insured by the Federal Deposit Insurance Corporation, or a subsidiary of any such State savings association; and

(iv) the Commission in the case of all other clearing agencies and transfer agents.

(C) When used with respect to a participant or applicant to become a participant in a clearing agency or a person requesting or having access to services offered by a clearing agency:

(i) the Comptroller of the Currency, in the case of a national bank or a Federal savings association (as defined in section 3(b)(2) of the Federal Deposit Insurance Act (12 U.S.C. 1813(b)(2))), the deposits of which are insured by the Federal Deposit Insurance Corporation when the appropriate regulatory agency for such clearing agency is not the Commission;

(ii) the Board of Governors of the Federal Reserve System in the case of a State member bank of the Federal Reserve System, a bank holding company, a subsidiary of a bank holding company that is a bank other than a bank specified in clause (i) or (iii) of this subparagraph, or a savings and loan holding company when the appropriate regulatory agency for such clearing agency is not the Commission;

(iii) the Federal Deposit Insurance Corporation, in the case of a bank insured by the Federal Deposit Insurance Corporation (other than a member of the Federal Reserve System) or a State savings association (as defined in section 3(b)(3) of the Federal Deposit Insurance Act (12 U.S.C. 1813(b)(3))), the deposits of which are insured by the Federal Deposit Insurance Corporation; and when the appropriate regulatory agency for such clearing agency is not the Commission;

(iv) the Commission in all other cases.

(D) When used with respect to an institutional investment manager which is a bank the deposits of which are insured in accordance with the Federal Deposit Insurance Act:

(i) the Comptroller of the Currency, in case of a national bank or a Federal savings association (as defined in section 3(b)(2) of the Federal Deposit Insurance Act (12 U.S.C. 1813(b)(2))), the deposits of which are insured by the Federal Deposit Insurance Corporation;

(ii) the Board of Governors of the Federal Reserve System, in the case of any other member bank of the Federal Reserve System; and

(iii) the Federal Deposit Insurance Corporation, in the case of any other insured bank or a State savings association (as defined in section 3(b)(3) of the Federal Deposit Insurance Act (12 U.S.C. 1813(b)(3))), the deposits of which are insured by the Federal Deposit Insurance Corporation.

(E) When used with respect to a national securities exchange or registered securities association, member thereof, person associated with a member thereof, applicant to become a member thereof or to become associated with a member thereof, or person requesting or having access to services offered by such exchange or association or member thereof, or the Municipal Securities Rulemaking Board, the Commission.

(F) When used with respect to a person exercising investment discretion with respect to an account;

(i) the Comptroller of the Currency, in the case of a national bank or a Federal savings association (as defined in section 3(b)(2) of the Federal Deposit Insurance Act (12 U.S.C. 1813(b)(2))), the deposits of which are insured by the Federal Deposit Insurance Corporation;

(ii) the Board of Governors of the Federal Reserve System in the case of any other member bank of the Federal Reserve System;

(iii) the Federal Deposit Insurance Corporation, in the case of any other bank the deposits of which are insured in accordance with the Federal Deposit Insurance Act or a State savings association (as defined in section 3(b)(3) of the Federal Deposit Insurance Act (12 U.S.C. 1813(b)(3))), the deposits of which are insured by the Federal Deposit Insurance Corporation; and

(iv) the Commission in the case of all other such persons.

(G) When used with respect to a government securities broker or government securities dealer, or person associated with a government securities broker or government securities dealer:

(i) the Comptroller of the Currency, in the case of a national bank, a Federal savings association (as defined in section 3(b)(2) of the Federal Deposit Insurance Act), the deposits of which are insured by the Federal Deposit Insurance Corporation, or a Federal branch or Federal agency of a foreign bank (as such terms are used in the International Banking Act of 1978);

(ii) the Board of Governors of the Federal Reserve System, in the case of a State member bank of the Federal Reserve System, a foreign bank, an uninsured State branch or State agency of a foreign bank, a commercial lending company owned or controlled by a foreign bank (as such terms are used in the International Banking Act of 1978), or a corporation organized or having an agreement with the Board of Governors of the Federal Reserve System pursuant to section 25 or section 25A of the Federal Reserve Act;

(iii)   the Federal Deposit Insurance Corporation, in the case of a bank insured by the Federal Deposit Insurance Corporation (other than a member of the Federal Reserve System or a Federal savings bank), a State savings association (as defined in section 3(b)(3) of the Federal Deposit Insurance Act), the deposits of which are insured by the Federal Deposit Insurance Corporation, or an insured State branch of a foreign bank (as such terms are used in the International Banking Act of 1978); and

(iv)   the Commission, in the case of all other government securities brokers and government securities dealers.

(H)   When used with respect to an institution described in subparagraph (D), (F), or (G) of section 2(c)(2), or held under section 4(f), of the Bank Holding Company Act of 1956—

(i)   the Comptroller of Currency, in the case of a national bank;

(ii)   the Board of Governors of Federal Reserve System, in the case of a state member bank of the Federal Reserve System or any corporation chartered under section 25A of the Federal Reserve Act;

(iii)   the Federal Deposit Insurance Corporation, in the case of any other bank the deposits of which are insured in accordance with the Federal Deposit Insurance Act; or

(iv)   the Commission in the case of all other such institutions

As used in this paragraph, the terms "bank holding company" and "subsidiary of a bank holding company" have the meanings given them in section 2 of the Bank Holding Company Act of 1956.

As used in this paragraph, the term "savings and loan holding company" has the same meaning as in section 10(a) of the Home Owners' Loan Act (12 U.S.C. § 1467a(a)).

(35) A person exercises "investment discretion" with respect to an account if, directly or indirectly, such person

(A)   is authorized to determine what securities or other property shall be purchased or sold by or for the account,

(B)   makes decisions as to what securities or other property shall be purchased or sold by or for the account even though some other person may have responsibility for such investment decisions, or

(C)   otherwise exercises such influence with respect to the purchase and sale of securities or other property by or for the account as the Commission, by rule, determines, in the public interest or for the protection of investors, should be subject to the operation of the provisions of this title and the rules and regulations thereunder.

(36) A class of persons or markets is subject to "equal regulation" if no member of the class has a competitive advantage over any other member thereof resulting from a disparity in their regulation under this Act which the Commission determines is unfair and not necessary or appropriate in furtherance of the purposes of this Act.

(37) The term "records" means accounts, correspondence, memorandums, tapes, discs, papers, books, and other documents or transcribed information of any type, whether expressed in ordinary or machine language.

(38) The term "market maker" means any specialist permitted to act as a dealer, any dealer acting in the capacity of block positioner, and any dealer who, with respect to a security, holds himself out (by entering quotations in an inter-dealer communications system or otherwise) as being willing to buy and sell such security for his own account on a regular or continuous basis.

(39) A person is subject to a "statutory disqualification" with respect to membership or participation in, or association with a member of, a self-regulatory organization, if such person—

(A)   has been and is expelled or suspended from membership or participation in, or barred or suspended from being associated with a member of, any self-regulatory organization, foreign equivalent of a self-regulatory organization, foreign or international securities exchange, contract market designated pursuant to section 5 of the Commodity Exchange Act, or any substantially equivalent foreign statute or regulation or futures association registered under section 17 of such Act, or any substantially foreign statute or regulation or has been and is denied trading privileges on any such contract market or foreign equivalent;

(B) is subject to—

(i) an order of the Commission, other appropriate regulatory agency, or foreign financial regulatory authority—

(I) denying, suspending for a period not exceeding 12 months, or revoking his registration as a broker, dealer, municipal securities dealer, government securities broker, government securities dealer, security-based swap dealer, or major security-based swap participant or limiting his activities as a foreign person performing a function substantially equivalent to any of the above; or

(II) barring or suspending for a period not exceeding 12 months his being associated with a broker, dealer, municipal securities dealer, government securities broker, government securities dealer, security-based swap dealer, major security-based swap participant, or foreign person performing a function substantially equivalent to any of the above;

(ii) an order of the Commodity Futures Trading Commission denying, suspending, or revoking his registration under the Commodity Exchange Act; or

(iii) an order by a foreign financial regulatory authority denying, suspending, or revoking the person's authority to engage in transactions in contracts of sale of a commodity for future delivery or other instruments traded on or subject to the rules of a contract market, board of trade, or foreign equivalent thereof;

(C) by his conduct while associated with a broker, dealer, municipal securities dealer, government securities broker, government securities dealer, security-based swap dealer, or major security-based swap participant, or while associated with an entity or person required to be registered under the Commodity Exchange Act, has been found to be a cause of any effective suspension, expulsion, or order of the character described in subparagraph (A) or (B) of this paragraph, and in entering such a suspension, expulsion, or order, the Commission, an appropriate regulatory agency, or any such self-regulatory organization shall have jurisdiction to find whether or not any person was a cause thereof;

(D) by his conduct while associated with any broker, dealer, municipal securities dealer, government securities broker, government securities dealer, security-based swap dealer, major security-based swap participant, or any other entity engaged in transactions in securities, or while associated with an entity engaged in transactions in contracts of sale of a commodity for future delivery or other instruments traded on or subject to the rules of a contract market, board of trade, or foreign equivalent thereof, has been found to be a cause of any effective suspension, expulsion, or order by a foreign or international securities exchange or foreign financial regulatory authority empowered by a foreign government to administer or enforce its laws relating to financial transactions as described in subparagraph (A) or (B) of this paragraph;

(E) has associated with him any person who is known, or in the exercise of reasonable care should be known, to him to be a person described by subparagraph (A), (B), (C), or (D) of this paragraph; or

(F) has committed or omitted any act, or is subject to an order or finding enumerated in subparagraph[3] (D), (E), (G), or (H) of paragraph (4) of section 15(b) of this Act, has been convicted of any offense specified in subparagraph (B) of such paragraph (4) or any other felony within ten years of the date of the filing of an application for membership or participation in, or to become associated with a member of, such self-regulatory organization, is enjoined from any action, conduct, or practice specified in subparagraph (C) of such paragraph (4), has willfully made or caused to be made in any application for membership or participation in, or to become associated with a member of, a self-regulatory organization, report required to be filed with a self-regulatory

---

[3] Original included sections (D) and (E).

organization, or proceeding before a self-regulatory organization, any statement which was at the time, and in the light of the circumstances under which it was made, false or misleading with respect to any material fact, or has omitted to state in any such application, report, or proceeding any material fact which is required to be stated therein.

(40) The term "financial responsibility rules" means the rules and regulations of the Commission or the rules and regulations prescribed by any self-regulatory organization relating to financial responsibility and related practices which are designated by the Commission, by rule or regulation, to be financial responsibility rules.

(41) The term "mortgage related security" means a security that meets standards of creditworthiness as established by the Commission and either:

(A) represents ownership of one or more promissory notes or certificates of interest or participation in such notes (including any rights designed to assure servicing of, or the receipt or timeliness of receipt by the holders of such notes, certificates, or participations of amounts payable under, such notes, certificates, or participations), which notes:

(i) are directly secured by a first lien on a single parcel of real estate, including stock allocated to a dwelling unit in a residential cooperative housing corporation, upon which is located a dwelling or mixed residential and commercial structure, on a residential manufactured home as defined in section 603(6) of the National Manufactured Housing Construction and Safety Standards Act of 1974, whether such manufactured home is considered real or personal property under the laws of the State in which it is to be located, or on one or more parcels of real estate upon which is located one or more commercial structures; and

(ii) were originated by a savings and loan association, savings bank, commercial bank, credit union, insurance company, or similar institution which is supervised and examined by a Federal or State authority, or by a mortgagee approved by the Secretary of Housing and Urban Development pursuant to sections 203 and 211 of the National Housing Act, or, where such notes involve a lien on the manufactured home, by any such institution or by any financial institution approved for insurance by the Secretary of Housing and Urban Development pursuant to section 2 of the National Housing Act; or

(B) is secured by one or more promissory notes or certificates of interest or participations in such notes (with or without recourse to the issuer thereof) and, by its terms, provides for payments of principal in relation to payments, or reasonable projections of payments, on notes meeting the requirements of subparagraphs (A)(i) and (ii) or certificates of interest or participations in promissory notes meeting such requirements.[4]

For the purpose of this paragraph, the term "promissory note", when used in connection with a manufactured home, shall also include a loan, advance, or credit sale as evidenced by a retail installment sales contract or other instrument.

(42) The term "government securities" means—

(A) securities which are direct obligations of, or obligations guaranteed as to principal or interest by, the United States;

(B) securities which are issued or guaranteed by the Tennessee Valley Authority or by corporations in which the United States has a direct or indirect interest and which are designated by the Secretary of the Treasury for exemption as necessary or appropriate in the public interest or for the protection of investors;

(C) securities issued or guaranteed as to principal or interest by any corporation the securities of which are designated, by statute specifically naming such corporation, to constitute exempt securities within the meaning of the laws administered by the Commission;

(D) for purposes of sections 15C and 17A, any put, call, straddle, option, or privilege on a security described in subparagraph (A), (B), or (C) other than a put, call, straddle, option, or privilege—

---

[4] Original said 'evidence'.

(i) that is traded on one or more national securities exchanges; or

(ii) for which quotations are disseminated through an automated quotation system operated by a registered securities association; or

(E) for purposes of section 15, 15C, and 17A as applied to a bank, a qualified Canadian government obligation as defined in section 5136 of the Revised Statutes of the United States.

(43) The term "government securities broker" means any person regularly engaged in the business of effecting transactions in government securities for the account of others, but does not include—

(A) any corporation the securities of which are government securities under subparagraph (B) or (C) of paragraph (42) of this subsection; or

(B) any person registered with the Commodity Futures Trading Commission, any contract market designated by the Commodity Futures Trading Commission, such contract market's affiliated clearing organization, or any floor trader on such contract market, solely because such person effects transactions in government securities that the Commission, after consultation with the Commodity Futures Trading Commission, has determined by rule or order to be incidental to such person's futures-related business.

(44) The term "government securities dealer" means any person engaged in the business of buying and selling government securities for his own account, through a broker or otherwise, but does not include—

(A) any person insofar as he buys or sells such securities for his own account, either individually or in some fiduciary capacity, but not as a part of a regular business;

(B) any corporation the securities of which are government securities under subparagraph (B) or (C) of paragraph (42) of this subsection;

(C) any bank, unless the bank is engaged in the business of buying and selling government securities for its own account other than in a fiduciary capacity, through a broker or otherwise; or

(D) any person registered with the Commodity Futures Trading Commission, any contract market designated by the Commodity Futures Trading Commission, such contract market's affiliated clearing organization, or any floor trader on such contract market, solely because such person effects transactions in government securities that the Commission, after consultation with the Commodity Futures Trading Commission, has determined by rule or order to be incidental to such person's futures-related business.

(45) The term "person associated with a government securities broker or government securities dealer" means any partner, officer, director, or branch manager of such government securities broker or government securities dealer (or any person occupying a similar status or performing similar functions), and any other employee of such government securities broker or government securities dealer who is engaged in the management, direction, supervision, or performance of any activities relating to government securities, and any person directly or indirectly controlling, controlled by, or under common control with such government securities broker or government securities dealer.

(46) The term "financial institution" means—

(A) a bank (as defined in paragraph (6) of this subsection);

(B) a foreign bank (as such term is used in the International Banking Act of 1978); and

(C) a savings association (as defined in section 3(b) of the Federal Deposit Insurance Act) the deposits of which are insured by the Federal Deposit Insurance Corporation.

(47) The term "securities laws" means the Securities Act of 1933, the Securities Exchange Act of 1934, the Sarbanes-Oxley Act of 2002, the Trust Indenture Act of 1939, the Investment Company Act of 1940, the Investment Advisers Act of 1940, and the Securities Investor Protection Act of 1970.

(48) The term "registered broker or dealer" means a broker or dealer registered or required to register pursuant to section 15 or 15B of this Act, except that in paragraph (3) of this subsection and

sections 6 and 15A of this Act the term means such a broker or dealer and a government securities broker or government securities dealer registered or required to register pursuant to section 15C(a)(1)(A) of this Act.

(49) The term "person associated with a transfer agent" and "associated person of a transfer agent" mean any person (except an employee whose functions are solely clerical or ministerial) directly engaged in the management, direction, supervision, or performance of any of the transfer agent's activities with respect to transfer agent functions, and any person directly or indirectly controlling such activities or controlled by the transfer agent in connection with such activities.

(50) The term "foreign securities authority" means any foreign government, or any governmental body or regulatory organization empowered by a foreign government to administer or enforce its laws as they relate to securities matters.

(51)(A) The term "penny stock" means any equity security other than a security that is—

(i)   registered or approved for registration and traded on a national securities exchange that meets such criteria as the Commission shall prescribe by rule or regulation for purposes of this paragraph;

(ii) authorized for quotation on an automated quotation system sponsored by a registered securities association, if such system

(I)   was established and in operation before January 1, 1990, and

(II) meets such criteria as the Commission shall prescribe by rule or regulation for purposes of this paragraph;

(iii) issued by an investment company registered under the Investment Company Act of 1940;

(iv) excluded, on the basis of exceeding a minimum price, net tangible assets of the issuer, or other relevant criteria, from the definition of such term by rule or regulation which the Commission shall prescribe for purposes of this paragraph; or

(v)   exempted, in whole or in part, conditionally or unconditionally, from the definition of such term by rule, regulation, or order prescribed by the Commission.

(B) The Commission may, by rule, regulation, or order, designate any equity security or class of equity securities described in clause (i) or (ii) of subparagraph (A) as within the meaning of the term "penny stock" if such security or class of securities is traded other than on a national securities exchange or through an automated quotation system described in clause (ii) of subparagraph (A).

(C) In exercising its authority under this paragraph to prescribe rules, regulations, and orders, the Commission shall determine that such rule, regulation, or order is consistent with the public interest and the protection of investors.

(52) The term "foreign financial regulatory authority" means any

(A) foreign securities authority,

(B) other governmental body or foreign equivalent of a self-regulatory organization empowered by a foreign government to administer or enforce its laws relating to the regulation of fiduciaries, trusts, commercial lending, insurance, trading in contracts of sale of a commodity for future delivery, or other instruments traded on or subject to the rules of a contract market, board of trade, or foreign equivalent, or other financial activities, or

(C) membership organization a function of which is to regulate participation of its members in activities listed above.

(53)(A) The term "small business related security" means a security that meets standards of credit-worthiness as established by the Commission, and either—

(i)   represents an interest in 1 or more promissory notes or leases of personal property evidencing the obligation of a small business concern and originated by an insured depository institution, insured credit union, insurance company, or similar institution which is supervised and examined by a Federal or State authority, or a finance company or leasing company; or

(ii)   is secured by an interest in 1 or more promissory notes or leases of personal property (with or without recourse to the issuer or lessee) and provides for payments of principal in relation to payments, or reasonable projections of payments, on notes or leases described in clause (i).

(B)   For purposes of this paragraph—

(i)   an "interest in a promissory note or a lease of personal property" includes ownership rights, certificates of interest or participation in such notes or leases, and rights designed to assure servicing of such notes or leases, or the receipt or timely receipt of amounts payable under such notes or leases;

(ii)   the term "small business concern" means a business that meets the criteria for a small business concern established by the Small Business Administration under section 3(a) of the Small Business Act;

(iii) the term "insured depository institution" has the same meaning as in section 3 of the Federal Deposit Insurance Act; and

(iv)   the term "insured credit union" has the same meaning as in section 101 of the Federal Credit Union Act.

(54)   Qualified investor.—

(A)   Definition.—

Except as provided in subparagraph (B), for the purposes of this Act, the term "qualified investor" means

(i)   any investment company registered with the Commission under section 8 of the Investment Company Act of 1940;

(ii)   any issuer eligible for an exclusion from the definition of investment company pursuant to section 3(c)(7) of the Investment Company Act of 1940;

(iii) any bank (as defined in paragraph (6) of this subsection), savings association (as defined in section (3)(b) of the federal Deposit Insurance Act), broker, dealer, insurance company (as defined in section 2(a)(13) of the Securities Act of 1933), or business development company (as defined in section 2(a)(48) of the Investment Company Act of 1940);

(iv)   any small business investment company licensed by the United States Small Business Administration under section 301(c) or (d) of the Small Business Investment Act of 1958;

(v)   any State sponsored employee benefit plan, or any other employee benefit plan, within the meaning of the Employee Retirement Income Security Act of 1974, other than an individual retirement account, if the investment decisions are made by a plan fiduciary, as defined in section 3(21) of that Act, which is either a bank, savings and loan association, insurance company, or registered investment adviser;

(vi)   any trust whose purchases of securities are directed by a person described in clauses (i) through (v) of this subparagraph;

(vii) any market intermediary exempt under section 3(c)(2) of the Investment Company Act of 1940;

(viii) any associated person of a broker or dealer other than a natural person;

(ix)   any foreign bank (as defined in section 1(b)(7) of the International Banking Act of 1978);

(x)   the government of any foreign country;

(xi)   any corporation, company, or partnership that owns and invests on a discretionary basis, not less than $25,000,000 in investments;

(xii) any natural person who owns and invests on a discretionary basis, not less than $25,000,000 in investments;

(xiii) any government or political subdivision, agency, or instrumentality of a government who owns and invests on a discretionary basis not less than $50,000,000 in investments; or

(xiv) any multinational or supranational entity or any agency or instrumentality thereof.

(B)   Altered thresholds for asset-backed securities and loan participations.—

For purposes of section 3(a)(5)(C)(iii) of this Act and section 206(a)(5) of the Gramm-Leach-Bliley Act, the term "qualified investor" has the meaning given such term by subparagraph (A) of this paragraph except that clauses (xi) and (xii) shall be applied by substituting "$10,000,000" for "$25,000,000."

(C)   Additional authority.—

The Commission may, by rule or order, define a "qualified investor" as any other person, taking into consideration such factors as the financial sophistication of the person, net worth, and knowledge and experience in financial matters.

(55)(A)   The term "security future" means a contract of sale for future delivery of a single security or of a narrow-based security index, including any interest therein or based on the value thereof, except an exempted security under section 3(a)(12) of this title as in effect on the date of the enactment of the Futures Trading Act of 1982 (other than any municipal security as defined in section 3(a)(29) as in effect on the date of the enactment of the Futures Trading Act of 1982). The term "security future" does not include any agreement, contract, or transaction excluded from the Commodity Exchange Act under section 2(c), 2(d), 2(f), or 2(g) of the Commodity Exchange Act (as in effect on the date of the enactment of the Commodity Futures Modernization Act of 2000) or Title IV of the Commodity Futures Modernization Act of 2000.

(B)   The term "narrow-based security index" means an index—

(i)   that has 9 or fewer component securities;

(ii)   in which a component security comprises more than 30 percent of the index's weighting;

(iii)   in which the five highest weighted component securities in the aggregate comprise more than 60 percent of the index's weighting; or

(iv)   in which the lowest weighted component securities comprising, in the aggregate, 25 percent of the index's weighting have an aggregate dollar value of average daily trading volume of less than $50,000,000 (or in the case of an index with 15 or more component securities, $30,000,000), except that if there are two or more securities with equal weighting that could be included in the calculation of the lowest weighted component securities comprising, in the aggregate, 25 percent of the index's weighting, such securities shall be ranked from lowest to highest dollar value of average daily trading volume and shall be included in the calculation based on their ranking starting with the lowest ranked security.

(C)   Notwithstanding subparagraph (B), an index is not a narrow-based security index if—

(i)(I) it has at least nine component securities;

(II)   no component security comprises more than 30 percent of the index's weighting; and

(III)   each component security is—

(aa)   registered pursuant to section 12 of the Securities Exchange Act of 1934;

(bb)   one of 750 securities with the largest market capitalization; and

(cc)   one of 675 securities with the largest dollar value of average daily trading volume;

(ii)   a board of trade was designated as a contract market by the Commodity Futures Trading Commission with respect to a contract of sale for future delivery on the index, before the date of the enactment of the Commodity Futures Modernization Act of 2000;

(iii)(I)   a contract of sale for future delivery on the index traded on a designated contract market or registered derivatives transaction execution facility for at least 30 days as a contract of sale for future delivery on an index that was not a narrow-based security index; and

(II)   it has been a narrow-based security index for no more than 45 business days over 3 consecutive calendar months;

(iv)   a contract of sale for future delivery on the index is traded on or subject to the rules of a foreign board of trade and meets such requirements as are jointly established by rule or regulation by the Commission and the Commodity Futures Trading Commission;

(v)   no more than 18 months have passed since the date of the enactment of the Commodity Futures Modernization Act of 2000 and—

(I)   it is traded on or subject to the rules of a foreign board of trade;

(II)   the offer and sale in the United States of a contract of sale for future delivery on the index was authorized before the date of the enactment of the Commodity Futures Modernization Act of 2000; and

(III)   the conditions of such authorization continue to be met; or

(vi)   a contract of sale for future delivery on the index is traded on or subject to the rules of a board of trade and meets such requirements as are jointly established by rule, regulation, or order by the Commission and the Commodity Futures Trading Commission.

(D)   Within 1 year after the enactment of the Commodity Futures Modernization Act of 2000, the Commission and the Commodity Futures Trading Commission jointly shall adopt rules or regulations that set forth the requirements under clause (iv) of subparagraph (C).

(E)   An index that is a narrow-based security index solely because it was a narrow-based security index for more than 45 business days over 3 consecutive calendar months pursuant to clause (iii) of subparagraph (C) shall not be a narrow-based security index for the 3 following calendar months.

(F)   For purposes of subparagraphs (B) and (C) of this paragraph—

(i)   the dollar value of average daily trading volume and the market capitalization shall be calculated as of the preceding 6 full calendar months; and

(ii)   the Commission and the Commodity Futures Trading Commission shall, by rule or regulation, jointly specify the method to be used to determine market capitalization and dollar value of average daily trading volume.

(56)   The term "security futures product" means a security future or any put, call, straddle, option, or privilege on any security future.

(57)(A)   The term "margin", when used with respect to a security futures product, means the amount, type, and form of collateral required to secure any extension or maintenance of credit, or the amount, type, and form of collateral required as a performance bond related to the purchase, sale, or carrying of a security futures product.

(B)   The terms "margin level" and "level of margin", when used with respect to a security futures product, mean the amount of margin required to secure any extension or maintenance of credit, or the amount of margin required as a performance bond related to the purchase, sale, or carrying of a security futures product.

(C)   The terms "higher margin level" and "higher level of margin", when used with respect to a security futures product, mean a margin level established by a national securities exchange registered pursuant to section 6(g) that is higher than the minimum amount established and in effect pursuant to section 7(c)(2)(B).

(58) Audit committee.—

The term "audit committee" means—

(A)   a committee (or equivalent body) established by and amongst the board of directors of an issuer for the purpose of overseeing the accounting and financial reporting processes of the issuer and audits of the financial statements of the issuer; and

(B)   if no such committee exists with respect to an issuer, the entire board of directors of the issuer.

(59) Registered public accounting firm.—

The term "registered public accounting firm" has the same meaning as in section 2 of the Sarbanes-Oxley Act of 2002.

(60) Credit rating.—

The term "credit rating" means an assessment of the creditworthiness of an obligor as an entity or with respect to specific securities or money market instruments.

(61) Credit rating agency.—

The term "credit rating agency" means any person—

(A)   engaged in the business of issuing credit ratings on the Internet or through another readily accessible means, for free or for a reasonable fee, but does not include a commercial credit reporting company;

(B)   employing either a quantitative or qualitative model, or both, to determine credit ratings; and

(C)   receiving fees from either issuers, investors, or other market participants, or a combination thereof.

(62) Nationally recognized statistical rating organization.—

The term "nationally recognized statistical rating organization" means a credit rating agency that—

(A)   issues credit ratings certified by qualified institutional buyers, in accordance with section 15e(a)(1)(B)(ix), with respect to—

(i)   financial institutions, brokers, or dealers;

(ii)   insurance companies;

(iii)   corporate issuers;

(iv)   issuers of asset-backed securities (as that term is defined in section 1101(c) of part 229 of title 17, Code of Federal Regulations, as in effect on the date of enactment of this paragraph);

(v)   issuers of government securities, municipal securities, or securities issued by a foreign government; or

(vi)   a combination of one or more categories of obligors described in any of clauses (i) through (v); and

(B)   is registered under section 15E.

(63) Person associated with a nationally recognized statistical rating organization.—

The term "person associated with" a nationally recognized statistical rating organization means any partner, officer, director, or branch manager of a nationally recognized statistical rating organization (or any person occupying a similar status or performing similar functions), any person directly or indirectly controlling, controlled by, or under common control with a nationally recognized statistical rating organization, or any employee of a nationally recognized statistical rating organization.

(64) Qualified institutional buyer.—

The term "qualified institutional buyer" has the meaning given such term in section 230.144A(a) of title 17, Code of Federal Regulations, or any successor thereto.

(65) Eligible contract participant.—

The term "eligible contract participant" has the same meaning as in section 1a of the Commodity Exchange Act (7 U.S.C. 1a).

(66) Major swap participant.—

The term "major swap participant" has the same meaning as in section 1a of the Commodity Exchange Act (7 U.S.C. 1a).

(67) Major security-based swap participant.—

(A) In general.—

The term "major security-based swap participant" means any person—

(i) who is not a security-based swap dealer; and

(ii)(I)who maintains a substantial position in security-based swaps for any of the major security-based swap categories, as such categories are determined by the Commission, excluding both positions held for hedging or mitigating commercial risk and positions maintained by any employee benefit plan (or any contract held by such a plan) as defined in paragraphs (3) and (32) of section 3 of the Employee Retirement Income Security Act of 1974 (29 U.S.C. 1002) for the primary purpose of hedging or mitigating any risk directly associated with the operation of the plan;

(II) whose outstanding security-based swaps create substantial counterparty exposure that could have serious adverse effects on the financial stability of the United States banking system or financial markets; or

(III) that is a financial entity that—

(aa) is highly leveraged relative to the amount of capital such entity holds and that is not subject to capital requirements established by an appropriate Federal banking agency; and

(bb) maintains a substantial position in outstanding security-based swaps in any major security-based swap category, as such categories are determined by the Commission.

(B) Definition of substantial position.—

For purposes of subparagraph (A), the Commission shall define, by rule or regulation, the term 'substantial position' at the threshold that the Commission determines to be prudent for the effective monitoring, management, and oversight of entities that are systemically important or can significantly impact the financial system of the United States. In setting the definition under this subparagraph, the Commission shall consider the person's relative position in uncleared as opposed to cleared security-based swaps and may take into consideration the value and quality of collateral held against counterparty exposures.

(C) Scope of designation.—

For purposes of subparagraph (A), a person may be designated as a major security-based swap participant for 1 or more categories of security-based swaps without being classified as a major security-based swap participant for all classes of security-based swaps.

(68) Security-based swap.—

(A) In general.—

Except as provided in subparagraph (B), the term "security-based swap" means any agreement, contract, or transaction that—

(i)   is a swap, as that term is defined under section 1a of the Commodity Exchange Act (without regard to paragraph (47)(B)(x) of such section); and

(ii)   is based on—

(I)   an index that is a narrow-based security index, including any interest therein or on the value thereof;

(II)   a single security or loan, including any interest therein or on the value thereof; or

(III) the occurrence, nonoccurrence, or extent of the occurrence of an event relating to a single issuer of a security or the issuers of securities in a narrow-based security index, provided that such event directly affects the financial statements, financial condition, or financial obligations of the issuer.

(B) Rule of construction regarding master agreements.—

The term "security-based swap" shall be construed to include a master agreement that provides for an agreement, contract, or transaction that is a security-based swap pursuant to subparagraph (A), together with all supplements to any such master agreement, without regard to whether the master agreement contains an agreement, contract, or transaction that is not a security-based swap pursuant to subparagraph (A), except that the master agreement shall be considered to be a security-based swap only with respect to each agreement, contract, or transaction under the master agreement that is a security-based swap pursuant to subparagraph (A).

(C) Exclusions.—

The term "security-based swap" does not include any agreement, contract, or transaction that meets the definition of a security-based swap only because such agreement, contract, or transaction references, is based upon, or settles through the transfer, delivery, or receipt of an exempted security under paragraph (12), as in effect on the date of enactment of the Futures Trading Act of 1982 (other than any municipal security as defined in paragraph (29) as in effect on the date of enactment of the Futures Trading Act of 1982), unless such agreement, contract, or transaction is of the character of, or is commonly known in the trade as, a put, call, or other option.

(D) Mixed swap.—

The term "security-based swap" includes any agreement, contract, or transaction that is as described in subparagraph (A) and also is based on the value of 1 or more interest or other rates, currencies, commodities, instruments of indebtedness, indices, quantitative measures, other financial or economic interest or property of any kind (other than a single security or a narrow-based security index), or the occurrence, non-occurrence, or the extent of the occurrence of an event or contingency associated with a potential financial, economic, or commercial consequence (other than an event described in subparagraph (A)(ii)(III)).

(E) Rule of construction regarding use of the term index.—

The term "index" means an index or group of securities, including any interest therein or based on the value thereof.

(69) Swap.—

The term "swap" has the same meaning as in section 1a of the Commodity Exchange Act (7 U.S.C. 1a).

(70) Person associated with a security-based swap dealer or major security-based swap participant.—

(A) In general.—

The term "person associated with a security-based swap dealer or major security-based swap participant" or "associated person of a security-based swap dealer or major security-based swap participant" means—

(i) any partner, officer, director, or branch manager of such security-based swap dealer or major security-based swap participant (or any person occupying a similar status or performing similar functions);

(ii) any person directly or indirectly controlling, controlled by, or under common control with such security-based swap dealer or major security-based swap participant; or

(iii) any employee of such security-based swap dealer or major security-based swap participant.

(B) Exclusion.—

Other than for purposes of section 15F(*l*)(2), the term "person associated with a security-based swap dealer or major security-based swap participant" or "associated person of a security-based swap dealer or major security-based swap participant" does not include any person associated with a security-based swap dealer or major security-based swap participant whose functions are solely clerical or ministerial.

(71) Security-based swap dealer.—

(A) In general.—

The term "security-based swap dealer" means any person who—

(i) holds themself out as a dealer in security-based swaps;

(ii) makes a market in security-based swaps;

(iii) regularly enters into security-based swaps with counterparties as an ordinary course of business for its own account; or

(iv) engages in any activity causing it to be commonly known in the trade as a dealer or market maker in security-based swaps.

(B) Designation by type or class.—

A person may be designated as a security-based swap dealer for a single type or single class or category of security-based swap or activities and considered not to be a security-based swap dealer for other types, classes, or categories of security-based swaps or activities.

(C) Exception.—

The term "security-based swap dealer" does not include a person that enters into security-based swaps for such person's own account, either individually or in a fiduciary capacity, but not as a part of regular business.

(D) De minimis exception.—

The Commission shall exempt from designation as a security-based swap dealer an entity that engages in a de minimis quantity of security-based swap dealing in connection with transactions with or on behalf of its customers. The Commission shall promulgate regulations to establish factors with respect to the making of any determination to exempt.

(72) Appropriate federal banking agency.—

The term "appropriate Federal banking agency" has the same meaning as in section 3(q) of the Federal Deposit Insurance Act (12 U.S.C. 1813(q)).

(73) Board.—

The term "Board" means the Board of Governors of the Federal Reserve System.

(74) Prudential regulator.—

The term "prudential regulator" has the same meaning as in section 1a of the Commodity Exchange Act (7 U.S.C. 1a).

(75) Security-based swap data repository.—

The term "security-based swap data repository" means any person that collects and maintains information or records with respect to transactions or positions in, or the terms and conditions of, security-based swaps entered into by third parties for the purpose of providing a centralized recordkeeping facility for security-based swaps.

(76) Swap dealer.—

The term "swap dealer" has the same meaning as in section 1a of the Commodity Exchange Act (7 U.S.C. 1a).

(77) Security-based swap execution facility.—

The term "security-based swap execution facility" means a trading system or platform in which multiple participants have the ability to execute or trade security-based swaps by accepting bids and offers made by multiple participants in the facility or system, through any means of interstate commerce, including any trading facility, that—

    (A)   facilitates the execution of security-based swaps between persons; and

    (B)   is not a national securities exchange.

(78) Security-based swap agreement.—

    (A)   In general.—

For purposes of sections 9, 10, 16, 20, and 21A of this Act, and section 17 of the Securities Act of 1933 (15 U.S.C. 77q), the term "security-based swap agreement" means a swap agreement as defined in section 206A of the Gramm-Leach-Bliley Act (15 U.S.C. 78c note) of which a material term is based on the price, yield, value, or volatility of any security or any group or index of securities, or any interest therein.

    (B)   Exclusions.—

The term "security-based swap agreement" does not include any security-based swap.

(79) Asset-backed security.—

The term "asset-backed security"—[5]

    (A)   means a fixed-income or other security collateralized by any type of self-liquidating financial asset (including a loan, a lease, a mortgage, or a secured or unsecured receivable) that allows the holder of the security to receive payments that depend primarily on cash flow from the asset, including—

        (i)   a collateralized mortgage obligation;

        (ii)   a collateralized debt obligation;

        (iii)   a collateralized bond obligation;

        (iv)   a collateralized debt obligation of asset-backed securities;

        (v)   a collateralized debt obligation of collateralized debt obligations; and

        (vi)   a security that the Commission, by rule, determines to be an asset-backed security for purposes of this section; and

    (B)   does not include a security issued by a finance subsidiary held by the parent company or a company controlled by the parent company, if none of the securities issued by the finance subsidiary are held by an entity that is not controlled by the parent company.

(80) Emerging growth company.—The term 'emerging growth company' means an issuer that had total annual gross revenues of less than $1,000,000,000 (as such amount is indexed for inflation every 5 years by the Commission to reflect the change in the Consumer Price Index for All Urban Consumers published by the Bureau of Labor Statistics, setting the threshold to the nearest 1,000,000) during its most recently completed fiscal year. An issuer that is an emerging growth company as of the

---

[5]   Original designated this section as a duplicate (77).

first day of that fiscal year shall continue to be deemed an emerging growth company until the earliest of—

(A) the last day of the fiscal year of the issuer during which it had total annual gross revenues of $1,000,000,000 (as such amount is indexed for inflation every 5 years by the Commission to reflect the change in the Consumer Price Index for All Urban Consumers published by the Bureau of Labor Statistics, setting the threshold to the nearest 1,000,000) or more;

(B) the last day of the fiscal year of the issuer following the fifth anniversary of the date of the first sale of common equity securities of the issuer pursuant to an effective registration statement under the Securities Act of 1933;

(C) the date on which such issuer has, during the previous 3-year period, issued more than $1,000,000,000 in non-convertible debt; or

(D) the date on which such issuer is deemed to be a 'large accelerated filer', as defined in Rule 12b–2, or any successor thereto.

(80)[6] Funding portal.—The term "funding portal" means any person acting as an intermediary in a transaction involving the offer or sale of securities for the account of others, solely pursuant to section 4(a)(6) of the Securities Act of 1933, that does not—

(A) offer investment advice or recommendations;

(B) solicit purchases, sales, or offers to buy the securities offered or displayed on its website or portal;

(C) compensate employees, agents, or other persons for such solicitation or based on the sale of securities displayed or referenced on its website or portal;

(D) hold, manage, possess, or otherwise handle investor funds or securities; or

(E) engage in such other activities as the Commission, by rule, determines appropriate.

(b) Power to define technical, trade, accounting, and other terms

The Commission and the Board of Governors of the Federal Reserve System, as to matters within their respective jurisdictions, shall have power by rules and regulations to define technical, trade, accounting, and other terms used in this act, consistently with the provisions and purposes of this act.

(c) Application to governmental departments or agencies.—

No provision of this act shall apply to, or be deemed to include, any executive department or independent establishment of the United States, or any lending agency which is wholly owned, directly or indirectly, by the United States, or any officer, agent, or employee of any such department, establishment, or agency, acting in the course of his official duty as such, unless such provision makes specific reference to such department, establishment, or agency.

(d) Issuers of municipal securities.—

No issuer of municipal securities or officer or employee thereof acting in the course of his official duties as such shall be deemed to be a "broker", "dealer", or "municipal securities dealer" solely by reason of buying, selling, or effecting transactions in the issuer's securities.

(e) Charitable organizations.—

(1) Exemption.—

Notwithstanding any other provision of this act, but subject to paragraph (2) of this subsection, a charitable organization, as defined in section 3(c)(10)(D) of the Investment Company Act of 1940, or any trustee, director, officer, employee, or volunteer of such a charitable organization acting within the scope of such person's employment or duties with such organization, shall not be deemed to be a "broker", "dealer", "municipal securities broker", "municipal securities dealer", "government securities broker", or "government securities dealer" for purposes of this act solely because such organization or

---

[6] So in original. Two pars. (80) have been enacted.

person buys, holds, sells, or trades in securities for its own account in its capacity as trustee or administrator of, or otherwise on behalf of or for the account of—

    (A)   such a charitable organization;

    (B)   a fund that is excluded from the definition of an investment company under section 3(c)(10)(B) of the Investment Company Act of 1940; or

    (C)   a trust or other donative instrument described in section 3(c)(10)(B) of the Investment Company Act of 1940, or the settlors (or potential settlors) or beneficiaries of any such trust or other instrument.

    (2)   Limitation on compensation.—

The exemption provided under paragraph (1) shall not be available to any charitable organization, or any trustee, director, officer, employee, or volunteer of such a charitable organization, unless each person who, on or after 90 days after December 8, 1995, solicits donations on behalf of such charitable organization from any donor to a fund that is excluded from the definition of an investment company under section 3(c)(10)(B) of the Investment Company Act of 1940, is either a volunteer or is engaged in the overall fund raising activities of a charitable organization and receives no commission or other special compensation based on the number or the value of donations collected for the fund.

    (f)   Consideration of promotion of efficiency, competition, and capital formation

Whenever pursuant to this act the Commission is engaged in rulemaking, or in the review of a rule of a self-regulatory organization, and is required to consider or determine whether an action is necessary or appropriate in the public interest, the Commission shall also consider, in addition to the protection of investors, whether the action will promote efficiency, competition, and capital formation.

    (g)   Church plans

No church plan described in section 414(e) of Title 26, no person or entity eligible to establish and maintain such a plan under Title 26, no company or account that is excluded from the definition of an investment company under section 3(c)(14) of the Investment Company Act of 1940, and no trustee, director, officer or employee of or volunteer for such plan, company, account, person, or entity, acting within the scope of that person's employment or activities with respect to such plan, shall be deemed to be a "broker", "dealer", "municipal securities broker", "municipal securities dealer", "government securities broker", "government securities dealer", "clearing agency", or "transfer agent" for purposes of this act—

    (1)   solely because such plan, company, person, or entity buys, holds, sells, trades in, or transfers securities or acts as an intermediary in making payments in connection with transactions in securities for its own account in its capacity as trustee or administrator of, or otherwise on behalf of, or for the account of, any church plan, company, or account that is excluded from the definition of an investment company under section 3(c)(14) of the Investment Company Act of 1940; and

    (2)   if no such person or entity receives a commission or other transaction-related sales compensation in connection with any activities conducted in reliance on the exemption provided by this subsection.

    (h)   Limited exemption for funding portals.—

    (1)   In general.—The Commission shall, by rule, exempt, conditionally or unconditionally, a registered funding portal from the requirement to register as a broker or dealer under section 15(a)(1), provided that such funding portal—

    (A)   remains subject to the examination, enforcement, and other rulemaking authority of the Commission;

    (B)   is a member of a national securities association registered under section 15A; and

    (C)   is subject to such other requirements under this title as the Commission determines appropriate under such rule.

    (2)   National securities association membership.—For purposes of sections 15(b)(8) and 15A, the term "broker or dealer" includes a funding portal and the term "registered broker or dealer" includes a registered funding portal, except to the extent that the Commission, by rule, determines otherwise,

provided that a national securities association shall only examine for and enforce against a registered funding portal rules of such national securities association written specifically for registered funding portals.

Swap Agreements

Sec. 3A. (a) [reserved]

(b) Security-Based Swap Agreements.—

(1) The definition of "security" in section 3(a)(10) of this Act does not include any security-based swap agreement.

(2) The Commission is prohibited from registering, or requiring, recommending, or suggesting, the registration under this Act of any security-based swap agreement. If the Commission becomes aware that a registrant has filed a registration application with respect to such a swap agreement, the Commission shall promptly so notify the registrant. Any such registration with respect to such a swap agreement shall be void and of no force or effect.

(3) Except as provided in section 16(a) with respect to reporting requirements, the Commission is prohibited from—

(A) promulgating, interpreting, or enforcing rules; or

(B) issuing orders of general applicability;

under this Act in a manner that imposes or specifies reporting or recordkeeping requirements, procedures, or standards as prophylactic measures against fraud, manipulation, or insider trading with respect to any security-based swap agreement.

(4) References in this Act to the "purchase" or "sale" of a security-based swap agreement shall be deemed to mean the execution, termination (prior to its scheduled maturity date), assignment, exchange, or similar transfer or conveyance of, or extinguishing of rights or obligations under, a security-based swap agreement, as the context may require.

Securities-Related Derivatives

Sec. 3B. (a) Any agreement, contract, or transaction (or class thereof) that is exempted by the Commodity Futures Trading Commission pursuant to section 4(c)(1) of the Commodity Exchange Act (7 U.S.C. 6(c)(1)) with the condition that the Commission exercise concurrent jurisdiction over such agreement, contract, or transaction (or class thereof) shall be deemed a security for purposes of the securities laws.

(b) With respect to any agreement, contract, or transaction (or class thereof) that is exempted by the Commodity Futures Trading Commission pursuant to section 4(c)(1) of the Commodity Exchange Act (7 U.S.C. 6(c)(1)) with the condition that the Commission exercise concurrent jurisdiction over such agreement, contract, or transaction (or class thereof), references in the securities laws to the "purchase" or "sale" of a security shall be deemed to include the execution, termination (prior to its scheduled maturity date), assignment, exchange, or similar transfer or conveyance of, or extinguishing of rights or obligations under such agreement, contract, or transaction, as the context may require.

Clearing for Security-Based Swaps

Sec. 3C. (a) In General.—

(1) Standard for clearing.—

It shall be unlawful for any person to engage in a security-based swap unless that person submits such security-based swap for clearing to a clearing agency that is registered under this Act or a clearing agency that is exempt from registration under this Act if the security-based swap is required to be cleared.

(2) Open access.—

The rules of a clearing agency described in paragraph (1) shall.—

(A) prescribe that all security-based swaps submitted to the clearing agency with the same terms and conditions are economically equivalent within the clearing agency and may be offset with each other within the clearing agency; and

(B) provide for non-discriminatory clearing of a security-based swap executed bilaterally or on or through the rules of an unaffiliated national securities exchange or security-based swap execution facility.

(b) Commission Review.—

(1) Commission-initiated review.—

(A) The Commission on an ongoing basis shall review each security-based swap, or any group, category, type, or class of security-based swaps to make a determination that such security-based swap, or group, category, type, or class of security-based swaps should be required to be cleared.

(B) The Commission shall provide at least a 30-day public comment period regarding any determination under subparagraph (A).

(2) Swap submissions.—

(A) A clearing agency shall submit to the Commission each security-based swap, or any group, category, type, or class of security-based swaps that it plans to accept for clearing and provide notice to its members (in a manner to be determined by the Commission) of such submission.

(B) Any security-based swap or group, category, type, or class of security-based swaps listed for clearing by a clearing agency as of the date of enactment of this subsection shall be considered submitted to the Commission.

(C) The Commission shall.—

(i) make available to the public any submission received under subparagraphs (A) and (B);

(ii) review each submission made under subparagraphs (A) and (B), and determine whether the security-based swap, or group, category, type, or class of security-based swaps, described in the submission is required to be cleared; and

(iii) provide at least a 30-day public comment period regarding its determination whether the clearing requirement under subsection (a)(1) shall apply to the submission.

(3) Deadline.—

The Commission shall make its determination under paragraph (2)(C) not later than 90 days after receiving a submission made under paragraphs (2)(A) and (2)(B), unless the submitting clearing agency agrees to an extension for the time limitation established under this paragraph.

(4) Determination.—

(A) In reviewing a submission made under paragraph (2), the Commission shall review whether the submission is consistent with section 17A.

(B) In reviewing a security-based swap, group of security-based swaps or class of security-based swaps pursuant to paragraph (1) or a submission made under paragraph (2), the Commission shall take into account the following factors:

(i) The existence of significant outstanding notional exposures, trading liquidity and adequate pricing data.

(ii) The availability of rule framework, capacity, operational expertise and resources, and credit support infrastructure to clear the contract on terms that are consistent with the material terms and trading conventions on which the contract is then traded.

(iii) The effect on the mitigation of systemic risk, taking into account the size of the market for such contract and the resources of the clearing agency available to clear the contract.

(iv) The effect on competition, including appropriate fees and charges applied to clearing.

(v) The existence of reasonable legal certainty in the event of the insolvency of the relevant clearing agency or 1 or more of its clearing members with regard to the treatment of customer and security-based swap counterparty positions, funds, and property.

(C) In making a determination under subsection (b)(1) or paragraph (2)(C) that the clearing requirement shall apply, the Commission may require such terms and conditions to the requirement as the Commission determines to be appropriate.

(5) Rules.—Not later than 1 year after the date of the enactment of this section, the Commission shall adopt rules for a clearing agency's submission for review, pursuant to this subsection, of a security-based swap, or a group, category, type, or class of security-based swaps, that it seeks to accept for clearing. Nothing in this paragraph limits the Commission from making a determination under paragraph (2)(C) for security-based swaps described in paragraph (2)(B).

(c) Stay of Clearing Requirement.—

(1) In general.—

After making a determination pursuant to subsection (b)(2), the Commission, on application of a counterparty to a security-based swap or on its own initiative, may stay the clearing requirement of subsection (a)(1) until the Commission completes a review of the terms of the security-based swap (or the group, category, type, or class of security-based swaps) and the clearing arrangement.

(2) Deadline.—

The Commission shall complete a review undertaken pursuant to paragraph (1) not later than 90 days after issuance of the stay, unless the clearing agency that clears the security-based swap, or group, category, type, or class of security-based swaps, agrees to an extension of the time limitation established under this paragraph.

(3) Determination.—

Upon completion of the review undertaken pursuant to paragraph (1), the Commission may—

(A) determine, unconditionally or subject to such terms and conditions as the Commission determines to be appropriate, that the security-based swap, or group, category, type, or class of security-based swaps, must be cleared pursuant to this subsection if it finds that such clearing is consistent with subsection (b)(4); or

(B) determine that the clearing requirement of subsection (a)(1) shall not apply to the security-based swap, or group, category, type, or class of security-based swaps.

(4) Rules.—

Not later than 1 year after the date of the enactment of this section, the Commission shall adopt rules for reviewing, pursuant to this subsection, a clearing agency's clearing of a security-based swap, or a group, category, type, or class of security-based swaps, that it has accepted for clearing.

(d) Prevention of Evasion.—

(1) In general.—

The Commission shall prescribe rules under this section (and issue interpretations of rules prescribed under this section), as determined by the Commission to be necessary to prevent evasions of the mandatory clearing requirements under this Act.

(2) Duty of commission to investigate and take certain actions.—

To the extent the Commission finds that a particular security-based swap or any group, category, type, or class of security-based swaps that would otherwise be subject to mandatory clearing but no clearing agency has listed the security-based swap or the group, category, type, or class of security-based swaps for clearing, the Commission shall—

    (A)   investigate the relevant facts and circumstances;

    (B)   within 30 days issue a public report containing the results of the investigation; and

    (C)   take such actions as the Commission determines to be necessary and in the public interest, which may include requiring the retaining of adequate margin or capital by parties to the security-based swap or the group, category, type, or class of security-based swaps.

    (3)   Effect on authority.—

Nothing in this subsection—

    (A)   authorizes the Commission to adopt rules requiring a clearing agency to list for clearing a security-based swap or any group, category, type, or class of security-based swaps if the clearing of the security-based swap or the group, category, type, or class of security-based swaps would threaten the financial integrity of the clearing agency; and

    (B)   affects the authority of the Commission to enforce the open access provisions of subsection (a)(2) with respect to a security-based swap or the group, category, type, or class of security-based swaps that is listed for clearing by a clearing agency.

    (e)   Reporting Transition Rules.—Rules adopted by the Commission under this section shall provide for the reporting of data, as follows:

    (1)   Security-based swaps entered into before the date of the enactment of this section shall be reported to a registered security-based swap data repository or the Commission no later than 180 days after the effective date of this section.

    (2)   Security-based swaps entered into on or after such date of enactment shall be reported to a registered security-based swap data repository or the Commission no later than the later of—

    (A)   90 days after such effective date; or

    (B)   such other time after entering into the security-based swap as the Commission may prescribe by rule or regulation.

    (f)   Clearing Transition Rules—

    (1)   Security-based swaps entered into before the date of the enactment of this section are exempt from the clearing requirements of this subsection if reported pursuant to subsection (e)(1).

    (2)   Security-based swaps entered into before application of the clearing requirement pursuant to this section are exempt from the clearing requirements of this section if reported pursuant to subsection (e)(2).

    (g)   Exceptions—

    (1)   In general.—

The requirements of subsection (a)(1) shall not apply to a security-based swap if 1 of the counterparties to the security-based swap—

    (A)   is not a financial entity;

    (B)   is using security-based swaps to hedge or mitigate commercial risk; and

    (C)   notifies the Commission, in a manner set forth by the Commission, how it generally meets its financial obligations associated with entering into non-cleared security-based swaps.

    (2)   Option to clear.—

The application of the clearing exception in paragraph (1) is solely at the discretion of the counterparty to the security-based swap that meets the conditions of subparagraphs (A) through (C) of paragraph (1).

(3)   Financial entity definition.—

(A)   In general.—

For the purposes of this subsection, the term "financial entity" means—

(i)   a swap dealer;

(ii)   a security-based swap dealer;

(iii) a major swap participant;

(iv)   a major security-based swap participant;

(v)   a commodity pool as defined in section 1a(10) of the Commodity Exchange Act;

(vi)   a private fund as defined in section 202(a) of the Investment Advisers Act of 1940 (15 U.S.C. 80–b–2(a));

(vii) an employee benefit plan as defined in paragraphs (3) and (32) of section 3 of the Employee Retirement Income Security Act of 1974 (29 U.S.C. 1002);

(viii) a person predominantly engaged in activities that are in the business of banking or financial in nature, as defined in section 4(k) of the Bank Holding Company Act of 1956.

(B)   Exclusion.—

The Commission shall consider whether to exempt small banks, savings associations, farm credit system institutions, and credit unions, including—

(i)   depository institutions with total assets of $10,000,000,000 or less;

(ii)   farm credit system institutions with total assets of $10,000,000,000 or less; or

(iii) credit unions with total assets of $10,000,000,000 or less.

(4)   Treatment of affiliates.—

(A)   In general.—An affiliate of a person that qualifies for an exception under this subsection (including affiliate entities predominantly engaged in providing financing for the purchase of the merchandise or manufactured goods of the person) may qualify for the exception only if the affiliate—

(i)   enters into the security-based swap to hedge or mitigate the commercial risk of the person or other affiliate of the person that is not a financial entity, and the commercial risk that the affiliate is hedging or mitigating has been transferred to the affiliate;

(ii)   is directly and wholly-owned by another affiliate qualified for the exception under this paragraph or an entity that is not a financial entity;

(iii) is not indirectly majority-owned by a financial entity;

(iv)   is not ultimately owned by a parent company that is a financial entity; and

(v)   does not provide any services, financial or otherwise, to any affiliate that is a nonbank financial company supervised by the Board of Governors (as defined under section 102 of the Financial Stability Act of 2010).

(B)   Limitation on qualifying affiliates.—The exception in subparagraph (A) shall not apply if the affiliate is—

(i)   a swap dealer;

(ii)   a security-based swap dealer;

(iii) a major swap participant;

(iv)   a major security-based swap participant;

(v)   a commodity pool;

(vi)   a bank holding company;

(vii) a private fund, as defined in section 202(a) of the Investment Advisers Act of 1940 (15 U.S.C. 80–b–2(a));

(viii) an employee benefit plan or government plan, as defined in paragraphs (3) and (32) of section 3 of the Employee Retirement Income Security Act of 1974 (29 U.S.C. 1002);

(ix) an insured depository institution;

(x) a farm credit system institution;

(xi) a credit union;

(xii) a nonbank financial company supervised by the Board of Governors (as defined under section 102 of the Financial Stability Act of 2010); or

(xiii) an entity engaged in the business of insurance and subject to capital requirements established by an insurance governmental authority of a State, a territory of the United States, the District of Columbia, a country other than the United States, or a political subdivision of a country other than the United States that is engaged in the supervision of insurance companies under insurance law.

(C) Limitation on affiliates' affiliates.—Unless the Commission determines, by order, rule, or regulation, that it is in the public interest, the exception in subparagraph (A) shall not apply with respect to an affiliate if such affiliate is itself affiliated with—

(i) a major security-based swap participant;

(ii) a security-based swap dealer;

(iii) a major swap participant; or

(iv) a swap dealer.

(D) Conditions on transactions.—With respect to an affiliate that qualifies for the exception in subparagraph (A)—

(i) such affiliate may not enter into any security-based swap other than for the purpose of hedging or mitigating commercial risk; and

(ii) neither such affiliate nor any person affiliated with such affiliate that is not a financial entity may enter into a security-based swap with or on behalf of any affiliate that is a financial entity or otherwise assume, net, combine, or consolidate the risk of security-based swaps entered into by any such financial entity, except one that is an affiliate that qualifies for the exception under subparagraph (A).

(E) Transition rule for affiliates.—

An affiliate, subsidiary, or a wholly owned entity of a person that qualifies for an exception under subparagraph (A) and is predominantly engaged in providing financing for the purchase or lease of merchandise or manufactured goods of the person shall be exempt from the margin requirement described in section 15F(e) and the clearing requirement described in subsection (a) with regard to security-based swaps entered into to mitigate the risk of the financing activities for not less than a 2-year period beginning on the date of enactment of this subparagraph.

(F) Risk management program.—Any security-based swap entered into by an affiliate that qualifies for the exception in subparagraph (A) shall be subject to a centralized risk management program of the affiliate, which is reasonably designed both to monitor and manage the risks associated with the security-based swap and to identify each of the affiliates on whose behalf a security-based swap was entered into.

(5) Election of counterparty.—

(A) Security-based swaps required to be cleared.—

With respect to any security-based swap that is subject to the mandatory clearing requirement under subsection (a) and entered into by a security-based swap dealer or a major security-based swap participant with a counterparty that is not a swap dealer, major swap participant, security-based swap dealer, or major security-based swap participant, the counterparty shall have the sole right to select the clearing agency at which the security-based swap will be cleared.

(B) Security-based swaps not required to be cleared.—

With respect to any security-based swap that is not subject to the mandatory clearing requirement under subsection (a) and entered into by a security-based swap dealer or a major security-based swap participant with a counterparty that is not a swap dealer, major swap participant, security-based swap dealer, or major security-based swap participant, the counterparty—

(i) may elect to require clearing of the security-based swap; and

(ii) shall have the sole right to select the clearing agency at which the security-based swap will be cleared.

(6) Abuse of exception.—

The Commission may prescribe such rules or issue interpretations of the rules as the Commission determines to be necessary to prevent abuse of the exceptions described in this subsection. The Commission may also request information from those persons claiming the clearing exception as necessary to prevent abuse of the exceptions described in this subsection.

(h) Trade Execution.—

(1) In general.—

With respect to transactions involving security-based swaps subject to the clearing requirement of subsection (a)(1), counterparties shall—

(A) execute the transaction on an exchange; or

(B) execute the transaction on a security-based swap execution facility registered under section 3D or a security-based swap execution facility that is exempt from registration under section 3D(e).

(2) Exception.—

The requirements of subparagraphs (A) and (B) of paragraph (1) shall not apply if no exchange or security-based swap execution facility makes the security-based swap available to trade or for security-based swap transactions subject to the clearing exception under subsection (g).

(i) Board Approval.—Exemptions from the requirements of this section to clear a security-based swap or execute a security-based swap through a national securities exchange or security-based swap execution facility shall be available to a counterparty that is an issuer of securities that are registered under section 12 or that is required to file reports pursuant to section 15(d), only if an appropriate committee of the issuer's board or governing body has reviewed and approved the issuer's decision to enter into security-based swaps that are subject to such exemptions.

(j) Designation of Chief Compliance Officer.—

(1) In general.—

Each registered clearing agency shall designate an individual to serve as a chief compliance officer.

(2) Duties.—

The chief compliance officer shall—

(A) report directly to the board or to the senior officer of the clearing agency;

(B) in consultation with its board, a body performing a function similar thereto, or the senior officer of the registered clearing agency, resolve any conflicts of interest that may arise;

(C) be responsible for administering each policy and procedure that is required to be established pursuant to this section;

(D) ensure compliance with this title (including regulations issued under this title) relating to agreements, contracts, or transactions, including each rule prescribed by the Commission under this section;

(E) establish procedures for the remediation of noncompliance issues identified by the compliance officer through any—

    (i)   compliance office review;

    (ii)   look-back;

    (iii)   internal or external audit finding;

    (iv)   self-reported error; or

    (v)   validated complaint; and

(F) establish and follow appropriate procedures for the handling, management response, remediation, retesting, and closing of noncompliance issues.

(3) Annual reports.—

(A) In general.—

In accordance with rules prescribed by the Commission, the chief compliance officer shall annually prepare and sign a report that contains a description of—

    (i)   the compliance of the registered clearing agency or security-based swap execution facility of the compliance officer with respect to this title (including regulations under this title); and

    (ii)   each policy and procedure of the registered clearing agency of the compliance officer (including the code of ethics and conflict of interest policies of the registered clearing agency).

(B) Requirements—A compliance report under subparagraph (A) shall—

    (i)   accompany each appropriate financial report of the registered clearing agency that is required to be furnished to the Commission pursuant to this section; and

    (ii)   include a certification that, under penalty of law, the compliance report is accurate and complete.

Security-Based Swap Execution Facilities

Sec. 3D. (a)   Registration.—

(1) In General.—No person may operate a facility for the trading or processing of security-based swaps, unless the facility is registered as a security-based swap execution facility or as a national securities exchange under this section.

(2) Dual Registration—Any person that is registered as a security-based swap execution facility under this section shall register with the Commission regardless of whether the person also is registered with the Commodity Futures Trading Commission as a swap execution facility.

(b) Trading and Trade Processing.—A security-based swap execution facility that is registered under subsection (a) may—

(1) make available for trading any security-based swap; and

(2) facilitate trade processing of any security-based swap.

(c) Identification of Facility Used To Trade Security-based Swaps by National Securities Exchanges.—A national securities exchange shall, to the extent that the exchange also operates a security-based swap execution facility and uses the same electronic trade execution system for listing and executing trades of security-based swaps on or through the exchange and the facility, identify whether electronic trading of such security-based swaps is taking place on or through the national securities exchange or the security-based swap execution facility.

(d)   Core Principles for Security-based Swap Execution Facilities.—

(1)(A)   To be registered, and maintain registration, as a security-based swap execution facility, the security-based swap execution facility shall comply with—

(i)   the core principles described in this subsection; and

(ii)   any requirement that the Commission may impose by rule or regulation.

(B)   Unless otherwise determined by the Commission, by rule or regulation, a security-based swap execution facility described in subparagraph (A) shall have reasonable discretion in establishing the manner in which it complies with the core principles described in this subsection.

(2)   Compliance with Rules.—A security-based swap execution facility shall—

(A)   establish and enforce compliance with any rule established by such security-based swap execution facility, including—

(i)   the terms and conditions of the security-based swaps traded or processed on or through the facility; and

(ii)   any limitation on access to the facility;

(B)   establish and enforce trading, trade processing, and participation rules that will deter abuses and have the capacity to detect, investigate, and enforce those rules, including means—

(i)   to provide market participants with impartial access to the market; and

(ii)   to capture information that may be used in establishing whether rule violations have occurred; and

(C)   establish rules governing the operation of the facility, including rules specifying trading procedures to be used in entering and executing orders traded or posted on the facility, including block trades.

(3)   Security-Based Swaps Not Readily Susceptible to Manipulation.—The security-based swap execution facility shall permit trading only in security-based swaps that are not readily susceptible to manipulation.

(4)   Monitoring of Trading and Trade Processing—The security-based swap execution facility shall.—

(A)   establish and enforce rules or terms and conditions defining, or specifications detailing—

(i)   trading procedures to be used in entering and executing orders traded on or through the facilities of the security-based swap execution facility; and

(ii)   procedures for trade processing of security-based swaps on or through the facilities of the security-based swap execution facility; and

(B)   monitor trading in security-based swaps to prevent manipulation, price distortion, and disruptions of the delivery or cash settlement process through surveillance, compliance, and disciplinary practices and procedures, including methods for conducting real-time monitoring of trading and comprehensive and accurate trade reconstructions.

(5)   Ability to Obtain Information.—The security-based swap execution facility shall—

(A)   establish and enforce rules that will allow the facility to obtain any necessary information to perform any of the functions described in this subsection;

(B)   provide the information to the Commission on request; and

(C)   have the capacity to carry out such international information-sharing agreements as the Commission may require.

(6) Financial Integrity of Transactions.—The security-based swap execution facility shall establish and enforce rules and procedures for ensuring the financial integrity of security-based swaps entered on or through the facilities of the security-based swap execution facility, including the clearance and settlement of security-based swaps pursuant to section 3C(a)(1).

(7) Emergency Authority.—The security-based swap execution facility shall adopt rules to provide for the exercise of emergency authority, in consultation or cooperation with the Commission, as is necessary and appropriate, including the authority to liquidate or transfer open positions in any security-based swap or to suspend or curtail trading in a security-based swap.

(8) Timely Publication of Trading Information.—

(A) In General.—The security-based swap execution facility shall make public timely information on price, trading volume, and other trading data on security-based swaps to the extent prescribed by the Commission.

(B) Capacity of Security-Based Swap Execution Facility.—The security-based swap execution facility shall be required to have the capacity to electronically capture and transmit and disseminate trade information with respect to transactions executed on or through the facility.

(9) Recordkeeping and Reporting.—

(A) In General.—A security-based swap execution facility shall—

(i) maintain records of all activities relating to the business of the facility, including a complete audit trail, in a form and manner acceptable to the Commission for a period of 5 years; and

(ii) report to the Commission, in a form and manner acceptable to the Commission, such information as the Commission determines to be necessary or appropriate for the Commission to perform the duties of the Commission under this title.

(B) Requirements.—The Commission shall adopt data collection and reporting requirements for security-based swap execution facilities that are comparable to corresponding requirements for clearing agencies and security-based swap data repositories.

(10) Antitrust Considerations.—Unless necessary or appropriate to achieve the purposes of this title, the security-based swap execution facility shall not—

(A) adopt any rules or taking any actions that result in any unreasonable restraint of trade; or

(B) impose any material anticompetitive burden on trading or clearing.

(11) Conflicts of Interest.—The security-based swap execution facility shall—

(A) establish and enforce rules to minimize conflicts of interest in its decision-making process; and

(B) establish a process for resolving the conflicts of interest.

(12) Financial Resources.—

(A) In General.—The security-based swap execution facility shall have adequate financial, operational, and managerial resources to discharge each responsibility of the security-based swap execution facility, as determined by the Commission.

(B) Determination of Resource Adequacy—The financial resources of a security-based swap execution facility shall be considered to be adequate if the value of the financial resources—

(i) enables the organization to meet its financial obligations to its members and participants notwithstanding a default by the member or participant creating the largest financial exposure for that organization in extreme but plausible market conditions; and

(ii) exceeds the total amount that would enable the security-based swap execution facility to cover the operating costs of the security-based swap execution facility for a 1-year period, as calculated on a rolling basis.

(13) System Safeguards.—The security-based swap execution facility shall—

(A) establish and maintain a program of risk analysis and oversight to identify and minimize sources of operational risk, through the development of appropriate controls and procedures, and automated systems, that—

(i) are reliable and secure; and

(ii) have adequate scalable capacity;

(B) establish and maintain emergency procedures, backup facilities, and a plan for disaster recovery that allow for—

(i) the timely recovery and resumption of operations; and

(ii) the fulfillment of the responsibilities and obligations of the security-based swap execution facility; and

(C) periodically conduct tests to verify that the backup resources of the security-based swap execution facility are sufficient to ensure continued—

(i) order processing and trade matching;

(ii) price reporting;

(iii) market surveillance; and

(iv) maintenance of a comprehensive and accurate audit trail.

(14) Designation of Chief Compliance Officer.—

(A) In General—Each security-based swap execution facility shall designate an individual to serve as a chief compliance officer.

(B) Duties.—The chief compliance officer shall—

(i) report directly to the board or to the senior officer of the facility;

(ii) review compliance with the core principles in this subsection;

(iii) in consultation with the board of the facility, a body performing a function similar to that of a board, or the senior officer of the facility, resolve any conflicts of interest that may arise;

(iv) be responsible for establishing and administering the policies and procedures required to be established pursuant to this section;

(v) ensure compliance with this title and the rules and regulations issued under this title, including rules prescribed by the Commission pursuant to this section;

(vi) establish procedures for the remediation of noncompliance issues found during—

(I) compliance office reviews;

(II) look backs;

(III) internal or external audit findings;

(IV) self-reported errors; or

(V) through validated complaints; and

(vii) establish and follow appropriate procedures for the handling, management response, remediation, retesting, and closing of noncompliance issues.

(C) Annual Reports.—

(i)   In General.—In accordance with rules prescribed by the Commission, the chief compliance officer shall annually prepare and sign a report that contains a description of—

(I)   the compliance of the security-based swap execution facility with this title; and

(II)   the policies and procedures, including the code of ethics and conflict of interest policies, of the security-based swap execution facility.

(ii)   Requirements.—The chief compliance officer shall—

(I)   submit each report described in clause (i) with the appropriate financial report of the security-based swap execution facility that is required to be submitted to the Commission pursuant to this section; and

(II)   include in the report a certification that, under penalty of law, the report is accurate and complete.

(e)   Exemptions.—The Commission may exempt, conditionally or unconditionally, a security-based swap execution facility from registration under this section if the Commission finds that the facility is subject to comparable, comprehensive supervision and regulation on a consolidated basis by the Commodity Futures Trading Commission.

(f)   Rules.—The Commission shall prescribe rules governing the regulation of security-based swap execution facilities under this section."

Segregation of Assets Held as Collateral in Security-Based Swap Transactions

Sec. 3E.   (a)   Registration Requirement.—It shall be unlawful for any person to accept any money, securities, or property (or to extend any credit in lieu of money, securities, or property) from, for, or on behalf of a security-based swaps customer to margin, guarantee, or secure a security-based swap cleared by or through a clearing agency (including money, securities, or property accruing to the customer as the result of such a security-based swap), unless the person shall have registered under this title with the Commission as a broker, dealer, or security-based swap dealer, and the registration shall not have expired nor been suspended nor revoked.

(b)   Cleared Security-based Swaps.—

(1)   Segregation Required.—A broker, dealer, or security-based swap dealer shall treat and deal with all money, securities, and property of any security-based swaps customer received to margin, guarantee, or secure a security-based swap cleared by or through a clearing agency (including money, securities, or property accruing to the security-based swaps customer as the result of such a security-based swap) as belonging to the security-based swaps customer.

(2)   Commingling Prohibited.—Money, securities, and property of a security-based swaps customer described in paragraph (1) shall be separately accounted for and shall not be commingled with the funds of the broker, dealer, or security-based swap dealer or be used to margin, secure, or guarantee any trades or contracts of any security-based swaps customer or person other than the person for whom the same are held.

(c)   Exceptions.—

(1)   Use of Funds.—

(A)   In General.—Notwithstanding subsection (b), money, securities, and property of a security-based swaps customer of a broker, dealer, or security-based swap dealer described in subsection (b) may, for convenience, be commingled and deposited in the same 1 or more accounts with any bank or trust company or with a clearing agency.

(B)   Withdrawal.—Notwithstanding subsection (b), such share of the money, securities, and property described in subparagraph (A) as in the normal course of business shall be necessary to margin, guarantee, secure, transfer, adjust, or settle a cleared security-based swap with a clearing agency, or with any member of the clearing agency, may be withdrawn and applied to such purposes, including the payment of commissions, brokerage, interest, taxes, storage, and other charges, lawfully accruing in connection with the cleared security-based swap.

(2) Commission Action.—Notwithstanding subsection (b), in accordance with such terms and conditions as the Commission may prescribe by rule, regulation, or order, any money, securities, or property of the security-based swaps customer of a broker, dealer, or security-based swap dealer described in subsection (b) may be commingled and deposited as provided in this section with any other money, securities, or property received by the broker, dealer, or security-based swap dealer and required by the Commission to be separately accounted for and treated and dealt with as belonging to the security-based swaps customer of the broker, dealer, or security-based swap dealer.

(d) Permitted Investments.—Money described in subsection (b) may be invested in obligations of the United States, in general obligations of any State or of any political subdivision of a State, and in obligations fully guaranteed as to principal and interest by the United States, or in any other investment that the Commission may by rule or regulation prescribe, and such investments shall be made in accordance with such rules and regulations and subject to such conditions as the Commission may prescribe.

(e) Prohibition.—It shall be unlawful for any person, including any clearing agency and any depository institution, that has received any money, securities, or property for deposit in a separate account or accounts as provided in subsection (b) to hold, dispose of, or use any such money, securities, or property as belonging to the depositing broker, dealer, or security-based swap dealer or any person other than the swaps customer of the broker, dealer, or security-based swap dealer.

(f) Segregation Requirements for Uncleared Security-based Swaps.—

(1) Segregation of Assets Held as Collateral in Uncleared Security-based Swap Transactions—

(A) Notification.—A security-based swap dealer or major security-based swap participant shall be required to notify the counterparty of the security-based swap dealer or major security-based swap participant at the beginning of a security-based swap transaction that the counterparty has the right to require segregation of the funds of other property supplied to margin, guarantee, or secure the obligations of the counterparty.

(B) Segregation and Maintenance of Funds—At the request of a counterparty to a security-based swap that provides funds or other property to a security-based swap dealer or major security-based swap participant to margin, guarantee, or secure the obligations of the counterparty, the security-based swap dealer or major security-based swap participant shall—

(i) segregate the funds or other property for the benefit of the counterparty; and

(ii) in accordance with such rules and regulations as the Commission may promulgate, maintain the funds or other property in a segregated account separate from the assets and other interests of the security-based swap dealer or major security-based swap participant.

(2) Applicability.—The requirements described in paragraph (1) shall—

(A) apply only to a security-based swap between a counterparty and a security-based swap dealer or major security-based swap participant that is not submitted for clearing to a clearing agency; and

(B)(i) not apply to variation margin payments; or

(ii) not preclude any commercial arrangement regarding—

(I) the investment of segregated funds or other property that may only be invested in such investments as the Commission may permit by rule or regulation; and

(II) the related allocation of gains and losses resulting from any investment of the segregated funds or other property.

(3) Use of Independent Third-Party Custodians.—The segregated account described in paragraph (1) shall be—

(A) carried by an independent third-party custodian; and

(B)   designated as a segregated account for and on behalf of the counterparty.

(4)   Reporting Requirement—If the counterparty does not choose to require segregation of the funds or other property supplied to margin, guarantee, or secure the obligations of the counterparty, the security-based swap dealer or major security-based swap participant shall report to the counterparty of the security-based swap dealer or major security-based swap participant on a quarterly basis that the back office procedures of the security-based swap dealer or major security-based swap participant relating to margin and collateral requirements are in compliance with the agreement of the counterparties.

(g)   Bankruptcy.—A security-based swap, as defined in section 3(a)(68) shall be considered to be a security as such term is used in section 101(53A)(B) and subchapter III of title 11, United States Code. An account that holds a security-based swap, other than a portfolio margining account referred to in section 15(c)(3)(C) shall be considered to be a securities account, as that term is defined in section 741 of title 11, United States Code. The definitions of the terms "purchase" and "sale" in section 3(a)(13) and (14) shall be applied to the terms "purchase" and "sale", as used in section 741 of title 11, United States Code. The term "customer", as defined in section 741 of title 11, United States Code, excludes any person, to the extent that such person has a claim based on any open repurchase agreement, open reverse repurchase agreement, stock borrowed agreement, non-cleared option, or non-cleared security-based swap except to the extent of any margin delivered to or by the customer with respect to which there is a customer protection requirement under section 15(c)(3) or a segregation requirement.

Securities and Exchange Commission

Sec. 4.   (a)   There is hereby established a Securities and Exchange Commission (hereinafter referred to as the "Commission") to be composed of five commissioners to be appointed by the President by and with the advice and consent of the Senate. Not more than three of such commissioners shall be members of the same political party, and in making appointments members of different political parties shall be appointed alternately as nearly as may be practicable. No commissioner shall engage in any other business, vocation, or employment than that of serving as commissioner, nor shall any commissioner participate, directly or indirectly, in any stock-market operations or transactions of a character subject to regulation by the Commission pursuant to this Act. Each commissioner shall hold office for a term of five years and until his successor is appointed and has qualified, except that he shall not so continue to serve beyond the expiration of the next session of Congress subsequent to the expiration of said fixed term of office, and except

(1)   any commissioner appointed to fill a vacancy occurring prior to the expiration of the term for which his predecessor was appointed shall be appointed for the remainder of such term, and

(2)   the terms of office of the commissioners first taking office after the enactment of this Act, shall expire as designated by the President at the time of nomination, one at the end of one year, one at the end of two years, one at the end of three years, one at the end of four years, and one at the end of five years, after the date of the enactment of this Act.

(b)   Appointment and Compensation of Staff and Leasing Authority.—

(1)   Appointment and compensation.—

The Commission shall appoint and compensate officers, attorneys, economists, examiners, and other employees in accordance with section 4802 of Title 5.

(2)   Reporting of information.—

In establishing and adjusting schedules of compensation and benefits for officers, attorneys, economists, examiners, and other employees of the Commission under applicable provisions of law, the Commission shall inform the heads of the agencies referred to under section 1833b of Title 12 and Congress of such compensation and benefits and shall seek to maintain comparability with such agencies regarding compensation and benefits.

(3)   Leasing authority.—

Notwithstanding any other provision of law, the Commission is authorized to enter directly into leases for real property for office, meeting, storage, and such other space as is necessary to carry out its functions, and shall be exempt from any General Services Administration space management regulations or directives.

(c) Notwithstanding any other provision of law, in accordance with regulations which the Commission shall prescribe to prevent conflicts of interest, the Commission may accept payment and reimbursement, in cash or in kind, from non-Federal agencies, organizations, and individuals for travel, subsistence, and other necessary expenses incurred by Commission members and employees in attending meetings and conferences concerning the functions or activities of the Commission. Any payment or reimbursement accepted shall be credited to the appropriated funds of the Commission. The amount of travel, subsistence, and other necessary expenses for members and employees paid or reimbursed under this subsection may exceed per diem amounts established in official travel regulations, but the Commission may include in its regulations under this subsection a limitation on such amounts.

(d) Notwithstanding any other provision of law, former employers of participants in the Commission's professional fellows programs may pay such participants their actual expenses for relocation to Washington, District of Columbia, to facilitate their participation in such programs, and program participants may accept such payments.

(e) Notwithstanding any other provision of law, whenever any fee is required to be paid to the Commission pursuant to any provision of the securities laws or any other law, the Commission may provide by rule that such fee shall be paid in a manner other than in cash and the Commission may also specify the time that such fee shall be determined and paid relative to the filing of any statement or document with the Commission.

(f) **Reimbursement of Expenses for Assisting Foreign Securities Authorities.—**

Notwithstanding any other provision of law, the Commission may accept payment and reimbursement, in cash or in kind, from a foreign securities authority, or made on behalf of such authority, for necessary expenses incurred by the Commission, its members, and employees in carrying out any investigation pursuant to section 21(a)(2) of this Act or in providing any other assistance to a foreign securities authority. Any payment or reimbursement accepted shall be considered a reimbursement to the appropriated funds of the Commission.

(g) Office of the Investor Advocate.—

(1) Office established.—

There is established within the Commission the Office of the Investor Advocate (in this subsection referred to as the "Office").

(2) Investor advocate.—

(A) In general.—

The head of the Office shall be the Investor Advocate, who shall—

(i) report directly to the Chairman; and

(ii) be appointed by the Chairman, in consultation with the Commission, from among individuals having experience in advocating for the interests of investors in securities and investor protection issues, from the perspective of investors.

(B) Compensation.—

The annual rate of pay for the Investor Advocate shall be equal to the highest rate of annual pay for other senior executives who report to the Chairman of the Commission.

(C) Limitation on service.—

An individual who serves as the Investor Advocate may not be employed by the Commission—

(i) during the 2-year period ending on the date of appointment as Investor Advocate; or

(ii) during the 5-year period beginning on the date on which the person ceases to serve as the Investor Advocate.

(3)   Staff of office.—

The Investor Advocate, after consultation with the Chairman of the Commission, may retain or employ independent counsel, research staff, and service staff, as the Investor Advocate deems necessary to carry out the functions, powers, and duties of the Office.

(4)   Functions of the investor advocate.—

The Investor Advocate shall—

   (A)   assist retail investors in resolving significant problems such investors may have with the Commission or with self-regulatory organizations;

   (B)   identify areas in which investors would benefit from changes in the regulations of the Commission or the rules of self-regulatory organizations;

   (C)   identify problems that investors have with financial service providers and investment products;

   (D)   analyze the potential impact on investors of—

      (i)   proposed regulations of the Commission; and

      (ii)   proposed rules of self-regulatory organizations registered under this title; and

   (E)   to the extent practicable, propose to the Commission changes in the regulations or orders of the Commission and to Congress any legislative, administrative, or personnel changes that may be appropriate to mitigate problems identified under this paragraph and to promote the interests of investors.

(5)   Access to documents.—

The Commission shall ensure that the Investor Advocate has full access to the documents of the Commission and any self-regulatory organization, as necessary to carry out the functions of the Office.

(6)   Annual reports.—

   (A)   Report on objectives.—

      (i)   In general.—
Not later than June 30 of each year after 2010, the Investor Advocate shall submit to the Committee on Banking, Housing, and Urban Affairs of the Senate and the Committee on Financial Services of the House of Representatives a report on the objectives of the Investor Advocate for the following fiscal year.

      (ii)   Contents.—
Each report required under clause (i) shall contain full and substantive analysis and explanation.

   (B)   Report on activities.—

      (i)   In General.—
Not later than December 31 of each year after 2010, the Investor Advocate shall submit to the Committee on Banking, Housing, and Urban Affairs of the Senate and the Committee on Financial Services of the House of Representatives a report on the activities of the Investor Advocate during the immediately preceding fiscal year.

      (ii)   Contents.—
Each report required under clause (i) shall include—

         (I)   appropriate statistical information and full and substantive analysis;

         (II)   information on steps that the Investor Advocate has taken during the reporting period to improve investor services and the responsiveness of the Commission and self-regulatory organizations to investor concerns;

(III) a summary of the most serious problems encountered by investors during the reporting period;

(IV) an inventory of the items described in subclause (III) that includes—

(aa) identification of any action taken by the Commission or the self-regulatory organization and the result of such action;

(bb) the length of time that each item has remained on such inventory; and

(cc) for items on which no action has been taken, the reasons for inaction, and an identification of any official who is responsible for such action;

(V) recommendations for such administrative and legislative actions as may be appropriate to resolve problems encountered by investors; and

(VI) any other information, as determined appropriate by the Investor Advocate.

(iii) Independence.—

Each report required under this paragraph shall be provided directly to the Committees listed in clause (i) without any prior review or comment from the Commission, any commissioner, any other officer or employee of the Commission, or the Office of Management and Budget.

(iv) Confidentiality.—

No report required under clause (i) may contain confidential information.

(7) Regulations.—

The Commission shall, by regulation, establish procedures requiring a formal response to all recommendations submitted to the Commission by the Investor Advocate, not later than 3 months after the date of such submission.

(8) Ombudsman

(A) Appointment

Not later than 180 days after the date on which the first Investor Advocate is appointed under paragraph (2)(A)(i), the Investor Advocate shall appoint an Ombudsman, who shall report directly to the Investor Advocate.

(B) Duties

The Ombudsman appointed under subparagraph (A) shall—

(i) act as a liaison between the Commission and any retail investor in resolving problems that retail investors may have with the Commission or with self-regulatory organizations;

(ii) review and make recommendations regarding policies and procedures to encourage persons to present questions to the Investor Advocate regarding compliance with the securities laws; and

(iii) establish safeguards to maintain the confidentiality of communications between the persons described in clause (ii) and the Ombudsman.

(C) Limitation

In carrying out the duties of the Ombudsman under subparagraph (B), the Ombudsman shall utilize personnel of the Commission to the extent practicable. Nothing in this paragraph shall be construed as replacing, altering, or diminishing the activities of any ombudsman or similar office of any other agency.

(D) Report

The Ombudsman shall submit a semiannual report to the Investor Advocate that describes the activities and evaluates the effectiveness of the Ombudsman during the preceding year. The

Investor Advocate shall include the reports required under this section in the reports required to be submitted by the Inspector Advocate under paragraph (6).

(h) Examiners.—

(1) Division of Trading and Markets—The Division of Trading and Markets of the Commission, or any successor organizational unit, shall have a staff of examiners who shall—

(A) perform compliance inspections and examinations of entities under the jurisdiction of that Division; and

(B) report to the Director of that Division.

(2) Division of Investment Management—The Division of Investment Management of the Commission, or any successor organizational unit, shall have a staff of examiners who shall—

(A) perform compliance inspections and examinations of entities under the jurisdiction of that Division; and

(B) report to the Director of that Division.

(i) Securities and Exchange Commission Reserve Fund.—

(1) Reserve fund established.—

There is established in the Treasury of the United States a separate fund, to be known as the "Securities and Exchange Commission Reserve Fund" (referred to in this subsection as the "Reserve Fund").

(2) Reserve fund amounts.—

(A) In general.—

Except as provided in subparagraph (B), any registration fees collected by the Commission under section 6(b) of the Securities Act of 1933 (15 U.S.C. 77f(b)) or section 24(f) of the Investment Company Act of 1940 (15 U.S.C. 80a–24(f)) shall be deposited into the Reserve Fund.

(B) Limitations.—

For any 1 fiscal year—

(i) the amount deposited in the Fund may not exceed $50,000,000; and

(ii) the balance in the Fund may not exceed $100,000,000.

(C) Excess fees.—

Any amounts in excess of the limitations described in subparagraph (B) that the Commission collects from registration fees under section 6(b) of the Securities Act of 1933 (15 U.S.C. 77f(b)) or section 24(f) of the Investment Company Act of 1940 (15 U.S.C. 80a–24(f)) shall be deposited in the General Fund of the Treasury of the United States and shall not be available for obligation by the Commission.

(3) Use of amounts in reserve fund.—

The Commission may obligate amounts in the Reserve Fund, not to exceed a total of $100,000,000 in any 1 fiscal year, as the Commission determines is necessary to carry out the functions of the Commission. Any amounts in the reserve fund shall remain available until expended. Not later than 10 days after the date on which the Commission obligates amounts under this paragraph, the Commission shall notify Congress of the date, amount, and purpose of the obligation.

(4) Rule of construction.—

Amounts collected and deposited in the Reserve Fund shall not be construed to be Government funds or appropriated monies and shall not be subject to apportionment for the purpose of chapter 15 of title 31, United States Code, or under any other authority.

(j) Office of the Advocate for Small Business Capital Formation.—

(1)   Office established.—There is established within the Commission the Office of the Advocate for Small Business Capital Formation (hereafter in this subsection referred to as the "Office").

(2)   Advocate for Small Business Capital Formation.—

(A)   In general.—The head of the Office shall be the Advocate for Small Business Capital Formation, who shall—

(i)   report directly to the Commission; and

(ii)   be appointed by the Commission, from among individuals having experience in advocating for the interests of small businesses and encouraging small business capital formation.

(B)   Compensation.—The annual rate of pay for the Advocate for Small Business Capital Formation shall be equal to the highest rate of annual pay for other senior executives who report directly to the commission.

(C)   No current employee of the commission.—An individual may not be appointed as the Advocate for Small Business Capital Formation if the individual is currently employed by the Commission.

(3)   Staff of Office.—The Advocate for Small Business Capital Formation, after consultation with the Commission, may retain or employ independent counsel, research staff, and service staff, as the Advocate for Small Business Capital Formation determines to be necessary to carry out the functions of the Office.

(4)   Functions of the Advocate for Small Business Capital Formation.—The Advocate for Small Business Capital Formation shall—

(A)   assist small businesses and small business investors in resolving significant problems such businesses and investors may have with the Commission or with self-regulatory organizations;

(B)   identify areas in which small businesses and small business investors would benefit from changes in the regulations of the Commission or the rules of self-regulatory organizations;

(C)   identify problems that small businesses have securing access to capital, including any unique challenges to minority-owned small businesses, women-owned small businesses, and small businesses affected by hurricanes or other natural disasters;

(D)   analyze the potential impact on small businesses and small business investors of—

(i)   proposed regulations of the Commission that are likely to have a significant economic impact on small businesses and small business capital formation; and

(ii)   proposed rules that are likely to have a significant economic impact on small businesses and small business capital formation of self-regulatory organizations registered under this title;

(E)   conduct outreach to small businesses and small business investors, including through regional roundtables, in order to solicit views on relevant capital formation issues;

(F)   to the extent practicable, propose to the Commission changes in the regulations or orders of the Commission and to Congress any legislative, administrative, or personnel changes that may be appropriate to mitigate problems identified under this paragraph and to promote the interests of small businesses and small business investors;

(G)   consult with the Investor Advocate on proposed recommendations made under subparagraph (F); and

(H)   advise the Investor Advocate on issues related to small businesses and small business Investors.

(5)   Access to documents.—The commission shall ensure that the Advocate for Small Business Capital Formation has full access to the documents and information of the Commission and any self-regulatory organization, as necessary to carry out the functions of the Office.

(6)   Annual report on activities.—

(A)   In general.—Not later than December 31 of each year after 2015, the Advocate for Small Business Capital Formation shall submit to the Committee on Banking, Housing, and Urban Affairs of the Senate and the Committee on Financial Services of the House of Representatives a report on the activities of the Advocate for Small Business Capital Formation during the immediately preceding fiscal year.

(B)   Contents.—Each report under subparagraph (A) shall include—

(i)   appropriate statistical information and full and substantive analysis;

(ii)   information on steps that the Advocate for Small Business Capital Formation has taken during the reporting period to improve small business services and the responsiveness of the Commission and self-regulatory organizations to small business and small business investor concerns;

(iii)   a summary of the most serious issues encountered by small businesses and small business investors, including any unique issues encountered by minority-owned small businesses, women-owned small businesses, and small businesses affected by hurricanes or other natural disasters and their investors, during the reporting period;

(iv)   an inventory of the items summarized under clause (iii) (including items summarized under such clause for any prior reporting period on which no action has been taken or that have not been resolved to the satisfaction of the Advocate for Small Business Capital Formation as of the beginning of the reporting period covered by the report) that includes—

(I)   identification of any action taken by the Commission or the self-regulatory organization and the result of such action;

(II)   the length of time that each item has maintained on such inventory; and

(III)   for items on which no action has been taken, the reasons for inaction, and an identification of any official who is responsible for such action;

(v)   recommendations for such changes to the regulations, guidance and order of the Commission and such legislative actions as may be appropriate to resolve problems with the Commission and self-regulatory organizations encountered by small businesses and small business investors and to encourage small business capital formation; and

(vi)   any other information, as determined appropriate by the Advocate for Small Business Capital Formation.

(C)   Confidentiality.—No report required by subparagraph (A) may contain confidential information.

(D)   Independence.—Each report required under subparagraph (A) shall be provided directly to the committees of Congress listed in such subparagraph without any prior review or comment from the Commission, any commissioner, any other officer or employee of the Commission, or the Office of Management and Budget.

(7)   Regulations.—The Commission shall establish procedures requiring a formal response to all recommendations submitted to the Commission by the Advocate for Small Business Capital Formation, not later than 3 months after the date of such submission.

(8)   Government-Business Forum on Small Business Capital Formation.—The Advocate for Small Business Capital Formation shall be responsible for planning, organizing, and executing the annual Government-Business Forum on Small Business Capital Formation described in section 503 of the Small Business Incentive Act of 1980 (15 U.S.C. 80c–1).

(9)   Rule of construction.—Nothing in this subsection may be construed as replacing or reducing the responsibilities of the Investor Advocate with respect to small business investors.

Delegation of Functions by Commission

Sec. 4A. (a)   In addition to its existing authority, the Securities and Exchange Commission shall have the authority to delegate, by published order or rule, any of its functions to a division of the Commission, an individual Commissioner, an administrative law judge, or an employee or employee board, including functions with respect to hearing, determining, ordering, certifying, reporting, or otherwise acting as to any work, business, or matter. Nothing in this section shall be deemed to supersede the provisions of section 556(b) of Title 5, or to authorize the delegation of the function of rule-making as defined in subchapter II of chapter 5 of Title 5, United States Code with reference to general rules as distinguished from rules of particular applicability, or of the making of any rule pursuant to section 19(c) of this Act.

(b)   With respect to the delegation of any of its functions, as provided in subsection (a) of this section, the Commission shall retain a discretionary right to review the action of any such division of the Commission, individual Commissioner, administrative law judge, employee, or employee board, upon its own initiative or upon petition of a party to or intervenor in such action, within such time and in such manner as the Commission by rule shall prescribe. The vote of one member of the Commission shall be sufficient to bring any such action before the Commission for review. A person or party shall be entitled to review by the Commission if he or it is adversely affected by action at a delegated level which

(1)   denies any request for action pursuant to section 8(a) or section 8(c) of the Securities Act of 1933 or the first sentence of section 12(d) of this Act;

(2)   suspends trading in a security pursuant to section 12(k) of this Act; or

(3)   is pursuant to any provision of this Act in a case of adjudication, as defined in section 551 of Title 5, United States Code, not required by this Act to be determined on the record after notice and opportunity for hearing (except to the extent there is involved a matter described in section 554(a)(1) through (6) of such Title 5).

(c)   If the right to exercise such review is declined, or if no such review is sought within the time stated in the rules promulgated by the Commission, then the action of any such division of the Commission, individual Commissioner, administrative law judge, employee, or employee board, shall, for all purposes, including appeal or review thereof, be deemed the action of the Commission.

Transfer of Functions With Respect to Assignment of Personnel to Chairman

Sec. 4B.   In addition to the functions transferred by the provisions of Reorganization Plan Numbered 10 of 1950 (64 Stat. 1265), there are hereby transferred from the Commission to the Chairman of the Commission the functions of the Commission with respect to the assignment of Commission personnel, including Commissioners, to perform such functions as may have been delegated by the Commission to the Commission personnel, including Commissioners, pursuant to section 4A of this Act.

Appearance and Practice Before the Commission

Sec. 4C. (a)   Authority to Censure.—

The Commission may censure any person, or deny, temporarily or permanently, to any person the privilege of appearing or practicing before the Commission in any way, if that person is found by the Commission, after notice and opportunity for hearing in the matter—

(1)   not to possess the requisite qualifications to represent others;

(2)   to be lacking in character or integrity, or to have engaged in unethical or improper professional conduct; or

(3)   to have willfully violated, or willfully aided and abetted the violation of, any provision of the securities laws or the rules and regulations issued thereunder.

(b)   Definition.—

With respect to any registered public accounting firm or associated person, for purposes of this section, the term "improper professional conduct" means—

(1)   intentional or knowing conduct, including reckless conduct, that results in a violation of applicable professional standards; and

(2)   negligent conduct in the form of—

(A)   a single instance of highly unreasonable conduct that results in a violation of applicable professional standards in circumstances in which the registered public accounting firm or associated person knows, or should know, that heightened scrutiny is warranted; or

(B)   repeated instances of unreasonable conduct, each resulting in a violation of applicable professional standards, that indicate a lack of competence to practice before the Commission.

Additional Duties of Inspector General

Sec. 4D.   (a)   Suggestion Submissions by Commission Employees—

(1)   Hotline established.—

The Inspector General of the Commission shall establish and maintain a telephone hotline or other electronic means for the receipt of—

(A)   suggestions by employees of the Commission for improvements in the work efficiency, effectiveness, and productivity, and the use of the resources, of the Commission; and

(B)   allegations by employees of the Commission of waste, abuse, misconduct, or mismanagement within the Commission.

(2)   Confidentiality.—

The Inspector General shall maintain as confidential—

(A)   the identity of any individual who provides information by the means established under paragraph (1), unless the individual requests otherwise, in writing; and

(B)   at the request of any such individual, any specific information provided by the individual.

(b)   Consideration of Reports.—The Inspector General shall consider any suggestions or allegations received by the means established under subsection (a)(1), and shall recommend appropriate action in relation to such suggestions or allegations.

(c)   Recognition.—The Inspector General may recognize any employee who makes a suggestion under subsection (a)(1) (or by other means) that would or does—

(1)   increase the work efficiency, effectiveness, or productivity of the Commission; or

(2)   reduce waste, abuse, misconduct, or mismanagement within the Commission.

(d)   Report.—The Inspector General of the Commission shall submit to Congress an annual report containing a description of—

(1)   the nature, number, and potential benefits of any suggestions received under subsection (a);

(2)   the nature, number, and seriousness of any allegations received under subsection (a);

(3)   any recommendations made or actions taken by the Inspector General in response to substantiated allegations received under subsection (a); and

(4)   any action the Commission has taken in response to suggestions or allegations received under subsection (a).

(e)   Funding.—The activities of the Inspector General under this subsection shall be funded by the Securities and Exchange Commission Investor Protection Fund established under section 21F.

Deadline for Completing Enforcement Investigations
and Compliance Examinations and Inspections

Sec. 4E. (a)   Enforcement Investigations.—

(1)   In general.—

Not later than 180 days after the date on which Commission staff provide a written Wells notification to any person, the Commission staff shall either file an action against such person or provide notice to the Director of the Division of Enforcement of its intent to not file an action.

(2)   Exceptions for certain complex actions.—

Notwithstanding paragraph (1), if the Director of the Division of Enforcement of the Commission or the Director's designee determines that a particular enforcement investigation is sufficiently complex such that a determination regarding the filing of an action against a person cannot be completed within the deadline specified in paragraph (1), the Director of the Division of Enforcement of the Commission or the Director's designee may, after providing notice to the Chairman of the Commission, extend such deadline as needed for one additional 180-day period. If after the additional 180-day period the Director of the Division of Enforcement of the Commission or the Director's designee determines that a particular enforcement investigation is sufficiently complex such that a determination regarding the filing of an action against a person cannot be completed within the additional 180-day period, the Director of the Division of Enforcement of the Commission or the Director's designee may, after providing notice to and receiving approval of the Commission, extend such deadline as needed for one or more additional successive 180-day periods.

(b)   Compliance Examinations and Inspections.—

(1)   In general.—

Not later than 180 days after the date on which Commission staff completes the on-site portion of its compliance examination or inspection or receives all records requested from the entity being examined or inspected, whichever is later, Commission staff shall provide the entity being examined or inspected with written notification indicating either that the examination or inspection has concluded, has concluded without findings, or that the staff requests the entity undertake corrective action.

(2)   Exceptions for certain complex actions.—

Notwithstanding paragraph (1), if the head of any division or office within the Commission responsible for compliance examinations and inspections or his designee determines that a particular compliance examination or inspection is sufficiently complex such that a determination regarding concluding the examination or inspection, or regarding the staff requests the entity undertake corrective action, cannot be completed within the deadline specified in paragraph (1), the head of any division or office within the Commission responsible for compliance examinations and inspections or his designee may, after providing notice to the Chairman of the Commission, extend such deadline as needed for one additional 180-day period.

Transactions on Unregistered Exchanges

Sec. 5.   It shall be unlawful for any broker, dealer, or exchange, directly or indirectly, to make use of the mails or any means or instrumentality of interstate commerce for the purpose of using any facility of an exchange within or subject to the jurisdiction of the United States to effect any transaction in a security, or to report any such transaction, unless such exchange

(1)   is registered as a national securities exchange under section 6 of this Act, or

(2)   is exempted from such registration upon application by the exchange because, in the opinion of the Commission, by reason of the limited volume of transactions effected on such exchange, it is not practicable and not necessary or appropriate in the public interest or for the protection of investors to require such registration.

National Securities Exchanges

Sec. 6.   (a)   An exchange may be registered as a national securities exchange under the terms and conditions hereinafter provided in this section and in accordance with the provisions of section 19(a) of this Act, by filing with the Commission an application for registration in such form as the Commission, by rule, may prescribe containing the rules of the exchange and such other information and documents as the Commission, by rule, may prescribe as necessary or appropriate in the public interest or for the protection of investors.

(b)   An exchange shall not be registered as a national securities exchange unless the Commission determines that—

(1)   Such exchange is so organized and has the capacity to be able to carry out the purposes of this Act and to comply, and (subject to any rule or order of the Commission pursuant to section 17(d) or 19(g)(2) of this Act) to enforce compliance by its members and persons associated with its members, with the provisions of this Act, the rules and regulations thereunder, and the rules of the exchange.

(2)   Subject to the provisions of subsection (c) of this section, the rules of the exchange provide that any registered broker or dealer or natural person associated with a registered broker or dealer may become a member of such exchange and any person may become associated with a member thereof.

(3)   The rules of the exchange assure a fair representation of its members in the selection of its directors and administration of its affairs and provide that one or more directors shall be representative of issuers and investors and not be associated with a member of the exchange, broker, or dealer.

(4)   The rules of the exchange provide for the equitable allocation of reasonable dues, fees, and other charges among its members and issuers and other persons using its facilities.

(5)   The rules of the exchange are designed to prevent fraudulent and manipulative acts and practices, to promote just and equitable principles of trade, to foster cooperation and coordination with persons engaged in regulating, clearing, settling, processing information with respect to, and facilitating transactions in securities, to remove impediments to and perfect the mechanism of a free and open market and a national market system, and, in general, to protect investors and the public interest; and are not designed to permit unfair discrimination between customers, issuers, brokers, or dealers, or to regulate by virtue of any authority conferred by this Act matters not related to the purposes of this Act or the administration of the exchange.

(6)   The rules of the exchange provide that (subject to any rule or order of the Commission pursuant to section 17(d) or 19(g)(2) of this Act) its members and persons associated with its members shall be appropriately disciplined for violation of the provisions of this Act, the rules or regulations thereunder, or the rules of the exchange, by expulsion, suspension, limitation of activities, functions, and operations, fine, censure, being suspended or barred from being associated with a member, or any other fitting sanction.

(7)   The rules of the exchange are in accordance with the provisions of subsection (d) of this section, and in general, provide a fair procedure for the disciplining of members and persons associated with members, the denial of membership to any person seeking membership therein, the barring of any person from becoming associated with a member thereof, and the prohibition or limitation by the exchange of any person with respect to access to services offered by the exchange or a member thereof.

(8)   The rules of the exchange do not impose any burden on competition not necessary or appropriate in furtherance of the purposes of this Act.

(9)(A)   The rules of the exchange prohibit the listing of any security issued in a limited partnership rollup transaction (as such term is defined in paragraphs (4) and (5) of section 14(h)), unless such transaction was conducted in accordance with procedures designed to protect the rights of limited partners, including—

(i)   the right of dissenting limited partners to one of the following:

(I)   an appraisal and compensation;

(II) retention of a security under substantially the same terms and conditions as the original issue;

(III) approval of the limited partnership rollup transaction by not less than 75 percent of the outstanding securities of each of the participating limited partnerships;

(IV) the use of a committee of limited partners that is independent, as determined in accordance with rules prescribed by the exchange, of the general partner or sponsor, that has been approved by a majority of the outstanding units of each of the participating limited partnerships, and that has such authority as is necessary to protect the interest of limited partners, including the authority to hire independent advisors, to negotiate with the general partner or sponsor on behalf of the limited partners, and to make a recommendation to the limited partners with respect to the proposed transaction; or

(V) other comparable rights that are prescribed by rule by the exchange and that are designed to protect dissenting limited partners;

(ii) the right not to have their voting power unfairly reduced or abridged;

(iii) the right not to bear an unfair portion of the costs of a proposed limited partnership rollup transaction that is rejected; and

(iv) restrictions on the conversion of contingent interests or fees into non-contingent interests or fees and restrictions on the receipt of a non-contingent equity interest in exchange for fees for services which have not yet been provided.

(B) As used in this paragraph, the term "dissenting limited partner" means a person who, on the date on which soliciting material is mailed to investors, is a holder of a beneficial interest in a limited partnership that is the subject of a limited partnership rollup transaction, and who casts a vote against the transaction and complies with procedures established by the exchange, except that for purposes of an exchange or tender offer, such person shall file an objection in writing under the rules of the exchange during the period during which the offer is outstanding.

(10)(A) The rules of the exchange prohibit any member that is not the beneficial owner of a security registered under section 12 from granting a proxy to vote the security in connection with a shareholder vote described in subparagraph (B), unless the beneficial owner of the security has instructed the member to vote the proxy in accordance with the voting instructions of the beneficial owner.

(B) A shareholder vote described in this subparagraph is a shareholder vote with respect to the election of a member of the board of directors of an issuer, executive compensation, or any other significant matter, as determined by the Commission, by rule, and does not include a vote with respect to the uncontested election of a member of the board of directors of any investment company registered under the Investment Company Act of 1940 (15 U.S.C. 80b–1 et seq.).

(C) Nothing in this paragraph shall be construed to prohibit a national securities exchange from prohibiting a member that is not the beneficial owner of a security registered under section 12 from granting a proxy to vote the security in connection with a shareholder vote not described in subparagraph (A).

(c)(1) A national securities exchange shall deny membership to

(A) any person, other than a natural person, which is not a registered broker or dealer or

(B) any natural person who is not, or is not associated with, a registered broker or dealer.

(2) A national securities exchange may, and in cases in which the Commission, by order, directs as necessary or appropriate in the public interest or for the protection of investors shall, deny membership to any registered broker or dealer or natural person associated with a registered broker or dealer, and bar from becoming associated with a member any person, who is subject to a statutory disqualification. A national securities exchange shall file notice with the Commission not less than thirty days prior to admitting any person to membership or permitting any person to become associated with a member, if the exchange knew, or in the exercise of reasonable care should have known, that

such person was subject to a statutory disqualification. The notice shall be in such form and contain such information as the Commission, by rule, may prescribe as necessary or appropriate in the public interest or for the protection of investors.

(3)(A)   A national securities exchange may deny membership to, or condition the membership of, a registered broker or dealer if

      (i)   such broker or dealer does not meet such standards of financial responsibility or operational capability or such broker or dealer or any natural person associated with such broker or dealer does not meet such standards of training, experience, and competence as are prescribed by the rules of the exchange or

      (ii)   such broker or dealer or person associated with such broker or dealer has engaged and there is a reasonable likelihood he may again engage in acts or practices inconsistent with just and equitable principles of trade. A national securities exchange may examine and verify the qualifications of an applicant to become a member and the natural persons associated with such an applicant in accordance with procedures established by the rules of the exchange.

(B)   A national securities exchange may bar a natural person from becoming a member or associated with a member, or condition the membership of a natural person or association of a natural person with a member, if such natural person

      (i)   does not meet such standards of training, experience, and competence as are prescribed by the rules of the exchange or

      (ii)   has engaged and there is a reasonable likelihood he may again engage in acts or practices inconsistent with just and equitable principles of trade. A national securities exchange may examine and verify the qualifications of an applicant to become a person associated with a member in accordance with procedures established by the rules of the exchange and require any person associated with a member, or any class of such persons, to be registered with the exchange in accordance with procedures so established.

(C)   A national securities exchange may bar any person from becoming associated with a member if such person does not agree

      (i)   to supply the exchange with such information with respect to its relationship and dealings with the member as may be specified in the rules of the exchange and

      (ii)   to permit the examination of its books and records to verify the accuracy of any information so supplied.

(4)   A national securities exchange may limit

(A)   the number of members of the exchange and

(B)   the number of members and designated representatives of members permitted to effect transactions on the floor of the exchange without the services of another person acting as broker: *Provided, however,* That no national securities exchange shall have the authority to decrease the number of memberships in such exchange, or the number of members and designated representatives of members permitted to effect transactions on the floor of such exchange without the services of another person acting as broker, below such number in effect on May 1, 1975, or the date such exchange was registered with the Commission, whichever is later: *And provided further,* That the Commission, in accordance with the provisions of section 19(c) of this Act, may amend the rules of any national securities exchange to increase (but not to decrease) or to remove any limitation on the number of memberships in such exchange or the number of members or designated representatives of members permitted to effect transactions on the floor of the exchange without the services of another person acting as broker, if the Commission finds that such limitation imposes a burden on competition not necessary or appropriate in furtherance of the purposes of this Act.

(d)(1)   In any proceeding by a national securities exchange to determine whether a member or person associated with a member should be disciplined (other than a summary proceeding pursuant to paragraph (3) of this subsection), the exchange shall bring specific charges, notify such member or person of, and give him an opportunity to defend against, such charges, and keep a record. A determination by the exchange to impose a disciplinary sanction shall be supported by a statement setting forth—

> (A)   any act or practice in which such member or person associated with a member has been found to have engaged, or which such member or person has been found to have omitted;

> (B)   the specific provision of this Act, the rules or regulations thereunder, or the rules of the exchange which any such act or practice, or omission to act, is deemed to violate; and

> (C)   the sanction imposed and the reasons therefor.

(2)   In any proceeding by a national securities exchange to determine whether a person shall be denied membership, barred from becoming associated with a member, or prohibited or limited with respect to access to services offered by the exchange or a member thereof (other than a summary proceeding pursuant to paragraph (3) of this subsection), the exchange shall notify such person of, and give him an opportunity to be heard upon, the specific grounds for denial, bar, or prohibition or limitation under consideration and keep a record. A determination by the exchange to deny membership, bar a person from becoming associated with a member, or prohibit or limit a person with respect to access to services offered by the exchange or a member thereof shall be supported by a statement setting forth the specific grounds on which the denial, bar, or prohibition or limitation is based.

(3)   A national securities exchange may summarily

> (A)   suspend a member or person associated with a member who has been and is expelled or suspended from any self-regulatory organization or barred or suspended from being associated with a member of any self-regulatory organization,

> (B)   suspend a member who is in such financial or operating difficulty that the exchange determines and so notifies the Commission that the member cannot be permitted to continue to do business as a member with safety to investors, creditors, other members, or the exchange, or

> (C)   limit or prohibit any person with respect to access to services offered by the exchange if subparagraph (A) or (B) of this paragraph is applicable to such person or, in the case of a person who is not a member, if the exchange determines that such person does not meet the qualification requirements or other prerequisites for such access and such person cannot be permitted to continue to have such access with safety to investors, creditors, members, or the exchange. Any person aggrieved by any such summary action shall be promptly afforded an opportunity for a hearing by the exchange in accordance with the provisions of paragraph (1) or (2) of this subsection. The Commission, by order, may stay any such summary action on its own motion or upon application by any person aggrieved thereby, if the Commission determines summarily or after notice and opportunity for hearing (which hearing may consist solely of the submission of affidavits or presentation of oral arguments) that such stay is consistent with the public interest and the protection of investors.

(e)(1)   On and after the date of enactment of the Securities Acts Amendments of 1975, no national securities exchange may impose any schedule or fix rates of commissions, allowances, discounts, or other fees to be charged by its members: *Provided, however,* That until May 1, 1976, the preceding provisions of this paragraph shall not prohibit any such exchange from imposing or fixing any schedule of commissions, allowances, discounts, or other fees to be charged by its members for acting as broker on the floor of the exchange or as odd-lot dealer: *And provided further,* That the Commission, in accordance with the provisions of section 19(b) of this Act as modified by the provisions of paragraph (3) of this subsection, may—

> (A)   permit a national securities exchange, by rule, to impose a reasonable schedule or fix reasonable rates of commissions, allowances, discounts, or other fees to be charged by its members for effecting transactions on such exchange prior to November 1, 1976, if the Commission finds that such schedule or fixed rates of commissions, allowances, discounts, or other fees are in the public interest; and

> (B)   permit a national securities exchange, by rule, to impose a schedule or fix rates of commissions, allowances, discounts, or other fees to be charged by its members for effecting transactions on such exchange after November 1, 1976, if the Commission finds that such schedule or fixed rates of commissions, allowances, discounts, or other fees

(i)   are reasonable in relation to the costs of providing the service for which such fees are charged (and the Commission publishes the standards employed in adjudging reasonableness) and

(ii)   do not impose any burden on competition not necessary or appropriate in furtherance of the purposes of this Act, taking into consideration the competitive effects of permitting such schedule or fixed rates weighed against the competitive effects of other lawful actions which the Commission is authorized to take under this Act.

(2)   Notwithstanding the provisions of section 19(c) of this Act, the Commission, by rule, may abrogate any exchange rule which imposes a schedule or fixes rates of commissions, allowances, discounts, or other fees, if the Commission determines that such schedule or fixed rates are no longer reasonable, in the public interest, or necessary to accomplish the purposes of this Act.

(3)(A)   Before approving or disapproving any proposed rule change submitted by a national securities exchange which would impose a schedule or fix rates of commissions, allowances, discounts, or other fees to be charged by its members for effecting transactions on such exchange, the Commission shall afford interested persons

(i)   an opportunity for oral presentation of data, views, and arguments and

(ii)   with respect to any such rule concerning transactions effected after November 1, 1976, if the Commission determines there are disputed issues of material fact, to present such rebuttal submissions and to conduct (or have conducted under subparagraph (B) of this paragraph) such cross-examination as the Commission determines to be appropriate and required for full disclosure and proper resolution of such disputed issues of material fact.

(B)   The Commission shall prescribe rules and make rulings concerning any proceeding in accordance with subparagraph (A) of this paragraph designed to avoid unnecessary costs or delay. Such rules or rulings may

(i)   impose reasonable time limits on each interested person's oral presentations, and

(ii)   require any cross-examination to which a person may be entitled under subparagraph (A) of this paragraph to be conducted by the Commission on behalf of that person in such manner as the Commission determines to be appropriate and required for full disclosure and proper resolution of disputed issues of material fact.

(C)(i)   If any class of persons, the members of which are entitled to conduct (or have conducted) cross-examination under subparagraphs (A) and (B) of this paragraph and which have, in the view of the Commission, the same or similar interests in the proceeding, cannot agree upon a single representative of such interests for purposes of cross-examination, the Commission may make rules and rulings specifying the manner in which such interests shall be represented and such cross-examination conducted.

(ii)   No member of any class of persons with respect to which the Commission has specified the manner in which its interests shall be represented pursuant to clause (i) of this subparagraph shall be denied, pursuant to such clause (i), the opportunity to conduct (or have conducted) cross-examination as to issues affecting his particular interests if he satisfies the Commission that he has made a reasonable and good faith effort to reach agreement upon group representation and there are substantial and relevant issues which would not be presented adequately by group representation.

(D)   A transcript shall be kept of any oral presentation and cross-examination.

(E)   In addition to the bases specified in section 25(a) of this Act, a reviewing Court may set aside an order of the Commission under section 19(b) of this Act approving an exchange rule imposing a schedule or fixing rates of commissions, allowances, discounts, or other fees, if the Court finds—

(1)   a Commission determination under subparagraph (A) of this paragraph that an interested person is not entitled to conduct cross-examination or make rebuttal submissions, or

(2)   a Commission rule or ruling under subparagraph (B) of this paragraph limiting the petitioner's cross-examination or rebuttal submissions,

has precluded full disclosure and proper resolution of disputed issues of material fact which were necessary for fair determination by the Commission.

(f)   The Commission, by rule or order, as it deems necessary or appropriate in the public interest and for the protection of investors, to maintain fair and orderly markets, or to assure equal regulation, may require—

(1)   any person not a member or a designated representative of a member of a national securities exchange effecting transactions on such exchange without the services of another person acting as a broker, or

(2)   any broker or dealer not a member of a national securities exchange effecting transactions on such exchange on a regular basis,

to comply with such rules of such exchange as the Commission may specify.

(g)   Notice Registration of Security Futures Product Exchanges.—

(1)   Registration Required.—An exchange that lists or trades security futures products may register as a national securities exchange solely for the purposes of trading security futures products if—

(A)   the exchange is a board of trade, as that term is defined by the Commodity Exchange Act, that had been designated a contract market by the Commodity Futures Trading Commission and such designation is not suspended by order of the Commodity Futures Trading Commission; and

(B)   such exchange does not serve as a market place for transactions in securities other than—

(i)   security futures products; or

(ii)   futures on exempted securities or groups or indexes of securities or options thereon that have been authorized under section 2(a)(1)(C) of the Commodity Exchange Act.

(2)   Registration by Notice Filing.—

(A)   Form and Content.—An exchange required to register only because such exchange lists or trades security futures products may register for purposes of this section by filing with the Commission a written notice in such form as the Commission, by rule, may prescribe containing the rules of the exchange and such other information and documents concerning such exchange, comparable to the information and documents required for national securities exchanges under section 6(a), as the Commission, by rule, may prescribe as necessary or appropriate in the public interest or for the protection of investors. If such exchange has filed documents with the Commodity Futures Trading Commission, to the extent that such documents contain information satisfying the Commission's informational requirements, copies of such documents may be filed with the Commission in lieu of the required written notice.

(B)   Immediate Effectiveness.—Such registration shall be effective contemporaneously with the submission of notice, in written or electronic form, to the Commission, except that such registration shall not be effective if such registration would be subject to suspension or revocation.

(C)   Termination.—Such registration shall be terminated immediately if any of the conditions for registration set forth in this subsection are no longer satisfied.

(3)   Public Availability.—The Commission shall promptly publish in the Federal Register an acknowledgment of receipt of all notices the Commission receives under this subsection and shall make all such notices available to the public.

(4)   Exemption of Exchanges From Specified Provisions.—

(A)   Transaction Exemptions.—An exchange that is registered under paragraph (1) of this subsection shall be exempt from, and shall not be required to enforce compliance by its members with, and its members shall not, solely with respect to those transactions effected on such exchange in security futures products, be required to comply with, the following provisions of this Act and the rules thereunder:

    (i)   Subsections (b)(2), (b)(3), (b)(4), (b)(7), (b)(9), (c), (d), and (e) of this section.

    (ii)   Section 8.

    (iii) Section 11.

    (iv) Subsections (d), (f), and (k) of section 17.

    (v)   Subsections (a), (f), and (h) of section 19.

    (B)   Rule Change Exemptions.—An exchange that registered under paragraph (1) of this subsection shall also be exempt from submitting proposed rule changes pursuant to section 19(b) of this Act, except that—

    (i)   such exchange shall file proposed rule changes related to higher margin levels, fraud or manipulation, recordkeeping, reporting, listing standards, or decimal pricing for security futures products, sales practices for security futures products for persons who effect transactions in security futures products, or rules effectuating such exchange's obligation to enforce the securities laws pursuant to section 19(b)(7);

    (ii)   such exchange shall file pursuant to sections 19(b)(1) and 19(b)(2) proposed rule changes related to margin, except for changes resulting in higher margin levels; and

    (iii) such exchange shall file pursuant to section 19(b)(1) proposed rule changes that have been abrogated by the Commission pursuant to section 19(b)(7)(C).

    (5)   Trading in Security Futures Products.—

    (A)   In General.—Subject to subparagraph (B), it shall be unlawful for any person to execute or trade a security futures product until the later of—

    (i)   1 year after the date of the enactment of the Commodity Futures Modernization Act of 2000; or

    (ii)   such date that a futures association registered under section 17 of the Commodity Exchange Act has met the requirements set forth in section 15A(k)(2) of this Act.

    (B)   Principal-to-Principal Transactions.—Notwithstanding subparagraph (A), a person may execute or trade a security futures product transaction if—

    (i)   the transaction is entered into—

    (I)   on a principal-to-principal basis between parties trading for their own accounts or as described in section 1a(18)(B)(ii) of the Commodity Exchange Act; and

    (II) only between eligible contract participants (as defined in subparagraphs (A), (B)(ii), and (C) of such section 1a(18)) at the time at which the persons enter into the agreement, contract, or transaction; and

    (ii)   the transaction is entered into on or after the later of—

    (I)   8 months after the date of the enactment of the Commodity Futures Modernization Act of 2000; or

    (II) such date that a futures association registered under section 17 of the Commodity Exchange Act has met the requirements set forth in section 15A(k)(2) of this Act.

  (h)   Trading in Security Futures Products.—

    (1)   Trading on Exchange or Association Required.—It shall be unlawful for any person to effect transactions in security futures products that are not listed on a national securities exchange or a national securities association registered pursuant to section 15A(a).

(2) Listing Standards Required.—Except as otherwise provided in paragraph (7), a national securities exchange or a national securities association registered pursuant to section 15A(a) may trade only security futures products that (A) conform with listing standards that such exchange or association files with the Commission under section 19(b) and (B) meet the criteria specified in section 2(a)(1)(D)(i) of the Commodity Exchange Act.

(3) Requirements for Listing Standards and Conditions for Trading.—Such listing standards shall—

(A) except as otherwise provided in a rule, regulation, or order issued pursuant to paragraph (4), require that any security underlying the security future, including each component security of a narrow-based security index, be registered pursuant to section 12 of this Act;

(B) require that if the security futures product is not cash settled, the market on which the security futures product is traded have arrangements in place with a registered clearing agency for the payment and delivery of the securities underlying the security futures product;

(C) be no less restrictive than comparable listing standards for options traded on a national securities exchange or national securities association registered pursuant to section 15A(a) of this Act;

(D) except as otherwise provided in a rule, regulation, or order issued pursuant to paragraph (4), require that the security future be based upon common stock and such other equity securities as the Commission and the Commodity Futures Trading Commission jointly determine appropriate;

(E) require that the security futures product is cleared by a clearing agency that has in place provisions for linked and coordinated clearing with other clearing agencies that clear security futures products, which permits the security futures product to be purchased on one market and offset on another market that trades such product;

(F) require that only a broker or dealer subject to suitability rules comparable to those of a national securities association registered pursuant to section 15A(a) effect transactions in the security futures product;

(G) require that the security futures product be subject to the prohibition against dual trading in section 4j of the Commodity Exchange Act and the rules and regulations thereunder or the provisions of section 11(a) of this Act and the rules and regulations thereunder, except to the extent otherwise permitted under this Act and the rules and regulations thereunder;

(H) require that trading in the security futures product not be readily susceptible to manipulation of the price of such security futures product, nor to causing or being used in the manipulation of the price of any underlying security, option on such security, or option on a group or index including such securities;

(I) require that procedures be in place for coordinated surveillance among the market on which the security futures product is traded, any market on which any security underlying the security futures product is traded, and other markets on which any related security is traded to detect manipulation and insider trading;

(J) require that the market on which the security futures product is traded has in place audit trails necessary or appropriate to facilitate the coordinated surveillance required in subparagraph (I);

(K) require that the market on which the security futures product is traded has in place procedures to coordinate trading halts between such market and any market on which any security underlying the security futures product is traded and other markets on which any related security is traded; and

(L) require that the margin requirements for a security futures product comply with the regulations prescribed pursuant to section 7(c)(2)(B), except that nothing in this subparagraph shall be construed to prevent a national securities exchange or national securities association from requiring higher margin levels for a security futures product when it deems such action to be necessary or appropriate.

(4)   Authority to Modify certain Listing Standard Requirements.—

(A)   Authority to Modify.—The Commission and the Commodity Futures Trading Commission, by rule, regulation, or order, may jointly modify the listing standard requirements specified in subparagraph (A) or (D) of paragraph (3) to the extent such modification fosters the development of fair and orderly markets in security futures products, is necessary or appropriate in the public interest, and is consistent with the protection of investors.

(B)   Authority to Grant Exemptions.—The Commission and the Commodity Futures Trading Commission, by order, may jointly exempt any person from compliance with the listing standard requirement specified in subparagraph (E) of paragraph (3) to the extent such exemption fosters the development of fair and orderly markets in security futures products, is necessary or appropriate in the public interest, and is consistent with the protection of investors.

(5)   Requirements for Other Persons Trading Security Future Products.—It shall be unlawful for any person (other than a national securities exchange or a national securities association registered pursuant to section 15A(a)) to constitute, maintain, or provide a marketplace or facilities for bringing together purchasers and sellers of security future products or to otherwise perform with respect to security future products the functions commonly performed by a stock exchange as that term is generally understood, unless a national securities association registered pursuant to section 15A(a) or a national securities exchange of which such person is a member—

(A)   has in place procedures for coordinated surveillance among such person, the market trading the securities underlying the security future products, and other markets trading related securities to detect manipulation and insider trading;

(B)   has rules to require audit trails necessary or appropriate to facilitate the coordinated surveillance required in subparagraph (A); and

(C)   has rules to require such person to coordinate trading halts with markets trading the securities underlying the security future products and other markets trading related securities.

(6)   Deferral of Options on Security Futures Trading.—No person shall offer to enter into, enter into, or confirm the execution of any put, call, straddle, option, or privilege on a security future, except that, after 3 years after the date of the enactment of this subsection, the Commission and the Commodity Futures Trading Commission may by order jointly determine to permit trading of puts, calls, straddles, options, or privileges on any security future authorized to be traded under the provisions of this Act and the Commodity Exchange Act.

(7)   Deferral of Linked and Coordinated Clearing.—

(A)   Notwithstanding paragraph (2), until the compliance date, a national securities exchange or national securities association registered pursuant to section 15A(a) may trade a security futures product that does not—

(i)   conform with any listing standard promulgated to meet the requirement specified in subparagraph (E) of paragraph (3); or

(ii)   meet the criterion specified in section 2(a)(1)(D)(i)(IV) of the Commodity Exchange Act.

(B)   The Commission and the Commodity Futures Trading Commission shall jointly publish in the Federal Register a notice of the compliance date no later than 165 days before the compliance date.

(C)   For purposes of this paragraph, the term "compliance date" means the later of—

(i)   180 days after the end of the first full calendar month period in which the average aggregate comparable share volume for all security futures products based on single equity securities traded on all national securities exchanges, any national securities associations registered pursuant to section 15A(a), and all other persons equals or exceeds 10 percent of the average aggregate comparable share volume of options on single equity securities traded on all national securities exchanges and any national securities associations registered pursuant to section 15A(a); or

(ii) 2 years after the date on which trading in any security futures product commences under this Act.

(i) Consistent with this Act, each national securities exchange registered pursuant to subsection (a) of this section shall issue such rules as are necessary to avoid duplicative or conflicting rules applicable to any broker or dealer registered with the Commission pursuant to section 15(b) (except paragraph (11) thereof), that is also registered with the Commodity Futures Trading Commission pursuant to section 4f(a) of the Commodity Exchange Act (except paragraph (2) thereof), with respect to the application of—

(1) rules of such national securities exchange of the type specified in section 15(c)(3)(B) involving security futures products; and

(2) similar rules of national securities exchanges registered pursuant to section 6(g) and national securities associations registered pursuant to section 15A(k) involving security futures products.

(j) Procedures and Rules for Security Future Products.—A national securities exchange registered pursuant to subsection (a) shall implement the procedures specified in section 6(h)(5)(A) of this Act and adopt the rules specified in subparagraphs (B) and (C) of section 6(h)(5) of this Act not later than 8 months after the date of receipt of a request from an alternative trading system for such implementation and rules.

(k)(1) To the extent necessary or appropriate in the public interest, to promote fair competition, and consistent with the promotion of market efficiency, innovation, and expansion of investment opportunities, the protection of investors, and the maintenance of fair and orderly markets, the Commission and the Commodity Futures Trading Commission shall jointly issue such rules, regulations, or orders as are necessary and appropriate to permit the offer and sale of a security futures product traded on or subject to the rules of a foreign board of trade to United States persons.

(2) The rules, regulations, or orders adopted under paragraph (1) shall take into account, as appropriate, the nature and size of the markets that the securities underlying the security futures product reflect.

(l) Security-Based Swaps

It shall be unlawful for any person to effect a transaction in a security-based swap with or for a person that is not an eligible contract participant, unless such transaction is effected on a national securities exchange registered pursuant to subsection (b).

Margin Requirements

Sec. 7. (a) For the purpose of preventing the excessive use of credit for the purchase or carrying of securities, the Board of Governors of the Federal Reserve System shall, prior to October 1, 1934, and from time to time thereafter, prescribe rules and regulations with respect to the amount of credit that may be initially extended and subsequently maintained on any security (other than an exempted security or a security futures product). For the initial extension of credit, such rules and regulations shall be based upon the following standard: An amount not greater than whichever is the higher of—

(1) 55 per centum of the current market price of the security, or

(2) 100 per centum of the lowest market price of the security during the preceding thirty-six calendar months, but not more than 75 per centum of the current market price.

Such rules and regulations may make appropriate provision with respect to the carrying of undermargined accounts for limited periods and under specified conditions; the withdrawal of funds or securities; the substitution or additional purchases of securities; the transfer of accounts from one lender to another; special or different margin requirements for delayed deliveries, short sales, arbitrage transactions, and securities to which paragraph (2) of this subsection does not apply; the bases and the methods to be used in calculating loans, and margins and market prices; and similar administrative adjustments and details. For the purposes of paragraph (2) of this subsection, until July 1, 1936, the lowest price at which a security has sold on or after July 1, 1933, shall be considered as the lowest price at which such security has sold during the preceding thirty-six calendar months.

(b)   Notwithstanding the provisions of subsection (a) of this section, the Board of Governors of the Federal Reserve System, may, from time to time, with respect to all or specified securities or transactions, or classes of securities, or classes of transactions, by such rules and regulations

(1)   prescribe such lower margin requirements for the initial extension or maintenance of credit as it deems necessary or appropriate for the accommodation of commerce and industry, having due regard to the general credit situation of the country, and

(2)   prescribe such higher margin requirements for the initial extension or maintenance of credit as it may deem necessary or appropriate to prevent the excessive use of credit to finance transactions in securities.

(c)   Unlawful Credit Extension to Customers.—

(1)   Prohibition.—

It shall be unlawful for any member of a national securities exchange or any broker or dealer, directly or indirectly, to extend or maintain credit or arrange for the extension or maintenance of credit to or for any customer—

(A)   on any security (other than an exempted security), except as provided in paragraph (2) in contravention of the rules and regulations which the Board of Governors of the Federal Reserve System (hereafter in this section referred to as the "Board") shall prescribe under subsections (a) and (b); or

(B)   without collateral or on any collateral other than securities, except in accordance with such rules and regulations as the Board may prescribe—

(i)   to permit under specified conditions and for a limited period any such member, broker, or dealer to maintain a credit initially extended in conformity with the rules and regulations of the Board; and

(ii)   to permit the extension or maintenance of credit in cases where the extension or maintenance of credit is not for the purpose of purchasing or carrying securities or of evading or circumventing the provisions of subparagraph (A).

(2)   Margin Regulations.—

(A)   Compliance With Margin Rules Required.—It shall be unlawful for any broker, dealer, or member of a national securities exchange to, directly or indirectly, extend or maintain credit to or for, or collect margin from any customer on, any security futures product unless such activities comply with the regulations—

(i)   which the Board shall prescribe pursuant to subparagraph (B); or

(ii)   if the Board determines to delegate the authority to prescribe such regulations, which the Commission and the Commodity Futures Trading Commission shall jointly prescribe pursuant to subparagraph (B).

If the Board delegates the authority to prescribe such regulations under clause (ii) and the Commission and the Commodity Futures Trading Commission have not jointly prescribed such regulations within a reasonable period of time after the date of such delegation, the Board shall prescribe such regulations pursuant to subparagraph (B).

(B)   Criteria for Issuance of Rules.—The Board shall prescribe, or, if the authority is delegated pursuant to subparagraph (A)(ii), the Commission and the Commodity Futures Trading Commission shall jointly prescribe, such regulations to establish margin requirements, including the establishment of levels of margin (initial and maintenance) for security futures products under such terms, and at such levels, as the Board deems appropriate, or as the Commission and the Commodity Futures Trading Commission jointly deem appropriate—

(i)   to preserve the financial integrity of markets trading security futures products;

(ii)   to prevent systemic risk;

(iii)   to require that—

(I)   the margin requirements for a security future product be consistent with the margin requirements for comparable option contracts traded on any exchange registered pursuant to section 6(a) of this Act; and

(II)   initial and maintenance margin levels for a security future product not be lower than the lowest level of margin, exclusive of premium, required for any comparable option contract traded on any exchange registered pursuant to section 6(a) of this Act, other than an option on a security future;

except that nothing in this subparagraph shall be construed to prevent a national securities exchange or national securities association from requiring higher margin levels for a security future product when it deems such action to be necessary or appropriate; and

(iv) to ensure that the margin requirements (other than levels of margin), including the type, form, and use of collateral for security futures products, are and remain consistent with the requirements established by the Board, pursuant to subparagraphs (A) and (B) of paragraph (1).

(3)   Exception.—

This subsection and the rules and regulations issued under this subsection shall not apply to any credit extended, maintained, or arranged by a member of a national securities exchange or a broker or dealer to or for a member of a national securities exchange or a registered broker or dealer—

(A)   a substantial portion of whose business consists of transactions with persons other than brokers or dealers; or

(B)   to finance its activities as a market maker or an underwriter;

except that the Board may impose such rules and regulations, in whole or in part, on any credit otherwise exempted by this paragraph if the Board determines that such action is necessary or appropriate in the public interest or for the protection of investors.

(d)   Unlawful credit extension in violation of rules and regulations; exceptions to application of rules, etc.—

(1)   Prohibition.—

It shall be unlawful for any person not subject to subsection (c) to extend or maintain credit or to arrange for the extension or maintenance of credit for the purpose of purchasing or carrying any security, in contravention of such rules and regulations as the Board shall prescribe to prevent the excessive use of credit for the purchasing or carrying of or trading in securities in circumvention of the other provisions of this section. Such rules and regulations may impose upon all loans made for the purpose of purchasing or carrying securities limitations similar to those imposed upon members, brokers, or dealers by subsection (c) and the rules and regulations thereunder.

(2)   Exceptions.—

This subsection and the rules and regulations issued under this subsection shall not apply to any credit extended, maintained, or arranged—

(A)   by a person not in the ordinary course of business;

(B)   on an exempted security;

(C)   to or for a member of a national securities exchange or a registered broker or dealer—

(i)   a substantial portion of whose business consists of transactions with persons other than brokers or dealers; or

(ii)   to finance its activities as a market maker or an underwriter;

(D)   by a bank on a security other than an equity security; or

(E)   as the Board shall, by such rules, regulations, or orders as it may deem necessary or appropriate in the public interest or for the protection of investors, exempt, either unconditionally or upon specified terms and conditions or for stated periods, from the operation of this subsection and the rules and regulations thereunder.

(3)　　Board authority.—

The Board may impose such rules and regulations, in whole or in part, on any credit otherwise exempted by subparagraph (C) if it determines that such action is necessary or appropriate in the public interest or for the protection of investors.

(e)　　The provisions of this section or the rules and regulations thereunder shall not apply on or before July 1, 1937, to any loan or extension of credit made prior to the enactment of this Act or to the maintenance, renewal, or extension of any such loan or credit, except to the extent that the Board of Governors of the Federal Reserve System may by rules and regulations prescribe as necessary to prevent the circumvention of the provisions of this section or the rules and regulations thereunder by means of withdrawals of funds or securities, substitutions of securities, or additional purchases or by any other device.

(f)(1)　　It is unlawful for any United States person, or any foreign person controlled by a United States person or acting on behalf of or in conjunction with such person, to obtain, receive, or enjoy the beneficial use of a loan or other extension of credit from any lender (without regard to whether the lender's office or place of business is in a State or the transaction occurred in whole or in part within a State) for the purpose of (A) purchasing or carrying United States securities, or (B) purchasing or carrying within the United States of any other securities, if, under this section or rules and regulations prescribed thereunder, the loan or other credit transaction is prohibited or would be prohibited if it had been made or the transaction had otherwise occurred in a lender's office or other place of business in a State.

(2)　　For the purpose of this subsection—

(A)　　The term "United States person" includes a person which is organized or exists under the laws of any State or, in the case of a natural person, a citizen or resident of the United States; a domestic estate; or a trust in which one or more of the foregoing persons has a cumulative direct or indirect beneficial interest in excess of 50 per centum of the value of the trust.

(B)　　The term "United States security" means a security (other than an exempted security) issued by a person incorporated under the laws of any State, or whose principal place of business is within a State.

(C)　　The term "foreign person controlled by a United States person" includes any noncorporate entity in which United States persons directly or indirectly have more than a 50 per centum beneficial interest, and any corporation in which one or more United States persons, directly or indirectly, own stock possessing more than 50 per centum of the total combined voting power of all classes of stock entitled to vote, or more than 50 per centum of the total value of shares of all classes of stock.

(3)　　The Board of Governors of the Federal Reserve System may, in its discretion and with due regard for the purposes of this section, by rule or regulation exempt any class of United States persons or foreign persons controlled by a United States person from the application of this subsection.

(g)　　Subject to such rules and regulations as the Board of Governors of the Federal Reserve System may adopt in the public interest and for the protection of investors, no member of a national securities exchange or broker or dealer shall be deemed to have extended or maintained credit or arranged for the extension or maintenance of credit for the purpose of purchasing a security, within the meaning of this section, by reason of a bona fide agreement for delayed delivery of a mortgage related security or a small business related security against full payment of the purchase price thereof upon such delivery within one hundred and eighty days after the purchase, or within such shorter period as the Board of Governors of the Federal Reserve System may prescribe by rule or regulation.

Restrictions on Borrowing and Lending by Members, Brokers and Dealers

Sec. 8.　　It shall be unlawful for any registered broker or dealer, member of a national securities exchange, or broker or dealer who transacts a business in securities through the medium of any member of a national securities exchange, directly or indirectly—

(a) In contravention of such rules and regulations as the Commission shall prescribe for the protection of investors to hypothecate or arrange for the hypothecation of any securities carried for the account of any customer under circumstances

(1) that will permit the commingling of his securities without his written consent with the securities of any other customer,

(2) that will permit such securities to be commingled with the securities of any person other than a bona fide customer, or

(3) that will permit such securities to be hypothecated, or subjected to any lien or claim of the pledgee, for a sum in excess of the aggregate indebtedness of such customers in respect of such securities.

(b) To lend or arrange for the lending of any securities carried for the account of any customer without the written consent of such customer or in contravention of such rules and regulations as the Commission shall prescribe for the protection of investors.

Prohibition Against Manipulation of Security Prices

Sec. 9.   (a) It shall be unlawful for any person, directly or indirectly, by the use of the mails or any means or instrumentality of interstate commerce, or of any facility of any national securities exchange, or for any member of a national securities exchange—

(1) For the purpose of creating a false or misleading appearance of active trading in any security other than a government security, or a false or misleading appearance with respect to the market for any such security,

(A) to effect any transaction in such security which involves no change in the beneficial ownership thereof, or

(B) to enter an order or orders for the purchase of such security with the knowledge that an order or orders of substantially the same size, at substantially the same time, and at substantially the same price, for the sale of any such security, has been or will be entered by or for the same or different parties, or

(C) to enter any order or orders for the sale of any such security with the knowledge that an order or orders of substantially the same size, at substantially the same time, and at substantially the same price, for the purchase of such security, has been or will be entered by or for the same or different parties.

(2) To effect, alone or with 1 or more other persons, a series of transactions in any security other than a government security, any security not so registered, or in connection with any security-based swap or security-based swap agreement with respect to such security creating actual or apparent active trading in such security, or raising or depressing the price of such security, for the purpose of inducing the purchase or sale of such security by others.

(3) If a dealer, broker, security-based swap dealer, major security-based swap participant, or other person selling or offering for sale or purchasing or offering to purchase the security, a security-based swap, or a security-based swap agreement with respect to such security, to induce the purchase or sale of any security other than a government security, any security not so registered, any security-based swap, or any security-based swap agreement with respect to such security by the circulation or dissemination in the ordinary course of business of information to the effect that the price of any such security will or is likely to rise or fall because of market operations of any 1 or more persons conducted for the purpose of raising or depressing the price of such security.

(4) If a dealer, broker, security-based swap dealer, major security-based swap participant, or other person selling or offering for sale or purchasing or offering to purchase the security, a security-based swap, or security-based swap agreement with respect to such security, to make, regarding any security other than a government security, any security not so registered, any security-based swap, or any security-based swap agreement with respect to such security, for the purpose of inducing the purchase or sale of such security, such security-based swap, or such security-based swap agreement any statement which was at the time and in the light of the circumstances under which it was made,

false or misleading with respect to any material fact, and which that person knew or had reasonable ground to believe was so false or misleading.

(5)   For a consideration, received directly or indirectly from a broker, dealer, security-based swap dealer, major security-based swap participant, or other person selling or offering for sale or purchasing or offering to purchase the security, a security-based swap, or security-based swap agreement with respect to such security, to induce the purchase of any security other than a government security, any security not so registered, any security-based swap, or any security-based swap agreement with respect to such security by the circulation or dissemination of information to the effect that the price of any such security will or is likely to rise or fall because of the market operations of any 1 or more persons conducted for the purpose of raising or depressing the price of such security

(6)   To effect either alone or with one or more other persons any series of transactions for the purchase and/or sale of any security other than a government security for the purpose of pegging, fixing, or stabilizing the price of such security in contravention of such rules and regulations as the Commission may prescribe as necessary or appropriate in the public interest or for the protection of investors.

(b)   It shall be unlawful for any person to effect, in contravention of such rules and regulations as the Commission may prescribe as necessary or appropriate in the public interest or for the protection of investors—

(1)   any transaction in connection with any security whereby any party to such transaction acquires—

(A)   any put, call, straddle, or other option or privilege of buying the security from or selling the security to another without being bound to do so;

(B)   any security futures product on the security; or

(C)   any security-based swap involving the security or the issuer of the security;

(2)   any transaction in connection with any security with relation to which such person has, directly or indirectly, any interest in any—

(A)   such put, call, straddle, option, or privilege;

(B)   such security futures product; or

(C)   such security-based swap; or

(3)   any transaction in any security for the account of any person who such person has reason to believe has, and who actually has, directly or indirectly, any interest in any—

(A)   such put, call, straddle, option, or privilege;

(B)   such security futures product with relation to such security; or

(C)   any security-based swap involving such security or the issuer of such security.

(c)   It shall be unlawful for any broker, dealer, or member of a national securities exchange directly or indirectly to endorse or guarantee the performance of any put, call, straddle, option, or privilege in relation to any security, other than a government security, in contravention of such rules and regulations as the Commission may prescribe as necessary or appropriate in the public interest or for the protection of investors.

(d)   Transactions Relating to Short Sales of Securities—It shall be unlawful for any person, directly or indirectly, by the use of the mails or any means or instrumentality of interstate commerce, or of any facility of any national securities exchange, or for any member of a national securities exchange to effect, alone or with one or more other persons, a manipulative short sale of any security. The Commission shall issue such other rules as are necessary or appropriate to ensure that the appropriate enforcement options and remedies are available for violations of this subsection in the public interest or for the protection of investors.

(e)   The terms "put", "call", "straddle", "option", or "privilege" as used in this section shall not include any registered warrant, right, or convertible security.

(f)   Any person who willfully participates in any act or transaction in violation of subsections (a), (b), or (c) of this section, shall be liable to any person who shall purchase or sell any security at a price which was affected by such act or transaction, and the person so injured may sue in law or in equity in any court of competent jurisdiction to recover the damages sustained as a result of any such act or transaction. In any such suit the court may, in its discretion, require an undertaking for the payment of the costs of such suit, and assess reasonable costs, including reasonable attorneys' fees, against either party litigant. Every person who becomes liable to make any payment under this subsection may recover contribution as in cases of contract from any person who, if joined in the original suit, would have been liable to make the same payment. No action shall be maintained to enforce any liability created under this section, unless brought within one year after the discovery of the facts constituting the violation and within three years after such violation.

(g)   The provisions of subsection (a) of this section shall not apply to an exempted security.

(h)(1)   Notwithstanding any other provision of law, the Commission shall have the authority to regulate the trading of any put, call, straddle, option, or privilege on any security, certificate of deposit, or group or index of securities (including any interest therein or based on the value thereof), or any put, call, straddle, option, or privilege entered into on a national securities exchange relating to foreign currency (but not, with respect to any of the foregoing, an option on a contract for future delivery other than a security futures product).

     (2)   Notwithstanding the Commodity Exchange Act, the Commission shall have the authority to regulate the trading of any security futures product to the extent provided in the securities laws.

(i)   Limitations on Practices That Affect Market Volatility.—

It shall be unlawful for any person, by the use of the mails or any means or instrumentality of interstate commerce or of any facility of any national securities exchange, to use or employ any act or practice in connection with the purchase or sale of any equity security in contravention of such rules or regulations as the Commission may adopt, consistent with the public interest, the protection of investors, and the maintenance of fair and orderly markets—

     (1)   to prescribe means reasonably designed to prevent manipulation of price levels of the equity securities market or a substantial segment thereof; and

     (2)   to prohibit or constrain, during periods of extraordinary market volatility, any trading practice in connection with the purchase or sale of equity securities that the Commission determines

         (A)   has previously contributed significantly to extraordinary levels of volatility that have threatened the maintenance of fair and orderly markets; and

         (B)   is reasonably certain to engender such levels of volatility if not prohibited or constrained.

In adopting rules under paragraph (2), the Commission shall, consistent with the purposes of this subsection, minimize the impact on the normal operations of the market and a natural person's freedom to buy or sell any equity security.

(j)   The authority of the Commission under this section with respect to security-based swap agreements shall be subject to the restrictions and limitations of section 3A(b) of this Act.

(k)   It shall be unlawful for any person, directly or indirectly, by the use of any means or instrumentality of interstate commerce or of the mails, or of any facility of any national securities exchange, to effect any transaction in, or to induce or attempt to induce the purchase or sale of, any security-based swap, in connection with which such person engages in any fraudulent, deceptive, or manipulative act or practice, makes any fictitious quotation, or engages in any transaction, practice, or course of business which operates as a fraud or deceit upon any person. The Commission shall, for the purposes of this subsection, by rules and regulations define, and prescribe means reasonably designed to prevent, such transactions, acts, practices, and courses of business as are fraudulent, deceptive, or manipulative, and such quotations as are fictitious.[7]

---

[7]   Marked as 9(j) in Dodd-Frank Act.

Manipulative and Deceptive Devices

Sec. 10. It shall be unlawful for any person, directly or indirectly, by the use of any means or instrumentality of interstate commerce or of the mails, or of any facility of any national securities exchange—

(a)(1)   To effect a short sale, or to use or employ any stop-loss order in connection with the purchase or sale, of any security, other than a government security, in contravention of such rules and regulations as the Commission may prescribe as necessary or appropriate in the public interest or for the protection of investors.

(2)   Paragraph (1) of this subsection shall not apply to security futures products.

(b)   To use or employ, in connection with the purchase or sale of any security registered on a national securities exchange or any security not so registered, or any securities based swap agreement any manipulative or deceptive device or contrivance in contravention of such rules and regulations as the Commission may prescribe as necessary or appropriate in the public interest or for the protection of investors.

(c)(1)   To effect, accept, or facilitate a transaction involving the loan or borrowing of securities in contravention of such rules and regulations as the Commission may prescribe as necessary or appropriate in the public interest or for the protection of investors.

(2)   Nothing in paragraph (1) may be construed to limit the authority of the appropriate Federal banking agency (as defined in section 3(q) of the Federal Deposit Insurance Act (12 U.S.C. 1813(q))), the National Credit Union Administration, or any other Federal department or agency having a responsibility under Federal law to prescribe rules or regulations restricting transactions involving the loan or borrowing of securities in order to protect the safety and soundness of a financial institution or to protect the financial system from systemic risk.

Rules promulgated under subsection (b) that prohibit fraud, manipulation, or insider trading (but not rules imposing or specifying reporting or recordkeeping requirements, procedures, or standards as prophylactic measures against fraud, manipulation, or insider trading), and judicial precedents decided under subsection (b) and rules promulgated thereunder that prohibit fraud, manipulation, or insider trading, shall apply to security-based swap agreements to the same extent as they apply to securities. Judicial precedents decided under section 17(a) of the Securities Act of 1933 and sections 9, 15, 16, 20, and 21A of this Act, and judicial precedents decided under applicable rules promulgated under such sections, shall apply to security-based swap agreements to the same extent as they apply to securities.

Audit Requirements

Sec. 10A.   (a)   In General.—

Each audit required pursuant to this Act of the financial statements of an issuer by a registered public accounting firm shall include, in accordance with generally accepted auditing standards, as may be modified or supplemented from time to time by the Commission—

(1)   procedures designed to provide reasonable assurance of detecting illegal acts that would have a direct and material effect on the determination of financial statement amounts;

(2)   procedures designed to identify related party transactions that are material to the financial statements or otherwise require disclosure therein; and

(3)   an evaluation of whether there is substantial doubt about the ability of the issuer to continue as a going concern during the ensuing fiscal year.

(b)   Required Response to Audit Discoveries.—

(1)   Investigation and report to management.—

If, in the course of conducting an audit pursuant to this Act to which subsection (a) applies, the registered public accounting firm detects or otherwise becomes aware of information indicating that an illegal act (whether or not perceived to have a material effect on the financial statements of the issuer) has or may have occurred, the accountant shall, in accordance with generally accepted auditing standards, as may be modified or supplemented from time to time by the Commission—

(A)(i)   determine whether it is likely that an illegal act has occurred; and

(ii)   if so, determine and consider the possible effect of the illegal act on the financial statements of the issuer, including any contingent monetary effects, such as fines, penalties, and damages; and

(B)   as soon as practicable, inform the appropriate level of the management of the issuer and assure that the audit committee of the issuer, or the board of the directors of the issuer in the absence of such a committee, is adequately informed with respect to illegal acts that have been detected or have otherwise come to the attention of such accountant in the course of the audit, unless the illegal act is clearly inconsequential.

(2)   Response to failure to take remedial action.—

If, after determining that the audit committee of the board of directors of the issuer, or the board of directors of the issuer in the absence of an audit committee, is adequately informed with respect to illegal acts that have been detected or have otherwise come to the attention of the firm in the course of the audit of such firm, the registered public accounting firm concludes that—

(A)   the illegal act has a material effect on the financial statements of the issuer;

(B)   the senior management has not taken, and the board of directors has not caused senior management to take, timely and appropriate remedial actions with respect to the illegal act; and

(C)   the failure to take remedial action is reasonably expected to warrant departure from a standard report of the auditor, when made, or warrant resignation from the audit engagement;

the registered public accounting firm shall, as soon as practicable, directly report its conclusions to the board of directors.

(3)   Notice to commission; response to failure to notify.—

An issuer whose board of directors receives a report under paragraph (2) shall inform the Commission by notice not later than 1 business day after the receipt of such report and shall furnish the registered public accounting firm making such report with a copy of the notice furnished to the Commission. If the registered public accounting firm fails to receive a copy of the notice before the expiration of the required 1-business-day period, the registered public accounting firm shall—

(A)   resign from the engagement; or

(B)   furnish to the Commission a copy of its report (or the documentation of any oral report given) not later than 1 business day following such failure to receive notice.

(4)   Report after resignation.—

If a registered public accounting firm resigns from an engagement under paragraph (3)(A), the firm shall, not later than 1 business day following the failure by the issuer to notify the Commission under paragraph (3), furnish to the Commission a copy of the firm's report (or the documentation of any oral report given).

(c)   Auditor liability limitation.—

No registered public accounting firm shall be liable in a private action for any finding, conclusion, or statement expressed in a report made pursuant to paragraph (3) or (4) of subsection (b), including any rule promulgated pursuant thereto.

(d)   Civil Penalties in Cease-And-Desist Proceedings.—

If the Commission finds, after notice and opportunity for hearing in a proceeding instituted pursuant to section 21C, that a registered public accounting firm has willfully violated paragraph (3) or (4) of subsection (b), the Commission may, in addition to entering an order under section 21C, impose a civil penalty against the registered public accounting firm and any other person that the Commission finds was a cause of such violation. The determination to impose a civil penalty and the amount of the penalty shall be governed by the standards set forth in section 21B.

(e)   Preservation of Existing Authority.—

Except as provided in subsection (d), nothing in this section shall be held to limit or otherwise affect the authority of the Commission under this Act.

(f)   Definitions.—

As used in this section, the term "illegal act" means an act or omission that violates any law, or any rule or regulation having the force of law.

As used in this section, the term "issuer" means an issuer (as defined in section 3), the securities of which are registered under section 12, or that is required to file reports pursuant to section 15(d), or that files or has filed a registration statement that has not yet become effective under the Securities Act of 1933 and that it has not withdrawn.

(g)   Prohibited Activities.—

Except as provided in subsection (h), it shall be unlawful for a registered public accounting firm (and any associated person of that firm, to the extent determined appropriate by the Commission) that performs for any issuer any audit required by this title or the rules of the Commission under this title or, beginning 180 days after the date of commencement of the operations of the Public Company Accounting Oversight Board established under section 101 of the Sarbanes-Oxley Act of 2002 (in this section referred to as the "Board"), the rules of the Board, to provide to that issuer, contemporaneously with the audit, any non-audit service, including—

(1)   bookkeeping or other services related to the accounting records or financial statements of the audit client;

(2)   financial information systems design and implementation;

(3)   appraisal or valuation services, fairness opinions, or contribution-in-kind reports;

(4)   actuarial services;

(5)   internal audit outsourcing services;

(6)   management functions or human resources;

(7)   broker or dealer, investment adviser, or investment banking services;

(8)   legal services and expert services unrelated to the audit; and

(9)   any other service that the Board determines, by regulation, is impermissible.

(h)   Preapproval Required for Non-Audit Services.—

A registered public accounting firm may engage in any non-audit service, including tax services, that is not described in any of paragraphs (1) through (9) of subsection (g) for an audit client, only if the activity is approved in advance by the audit committee of the issuer, in accordance with subsection (i).

(i)   Preapproval Requirements.—

(1)   In general.—

(A)   Audit committee action.—

All auditing services (which may entail providing comfort letters in connection with securities underwritings or statutory audits required for insurance companies for purposes of State law) and non-audit services, other than as provided in subparagraph (B), provided to an issuer by the auditor of the issuer shall be preapproved by the audit committee of the issuer.

(B)   De minimis exception.—

The preapproval requirement under subparagraph (A) is waived with respect to the provision of non-audit services for an issuer, if—

    (i)   the aggregate amount of all such non-audit services provided to the issuer constitutes not more than 5 percent of the total amount of revenues paid by the issuer to its auditor during the fiscal year in which the nonaudit services are provided;

    (ii)   such services were not recognized by the issuer at the time of the engagement to be non-audit services; and

    (iii)   such services are promptly brought to the attention of the audit committee of the issuer and approved prior to the completion of the audit by the audit committee or by 1 or more members of the audit committee who are members of the board of directors to whom authority to grant such approvals has been delegated by the audit committee.

    (2)   Disclosure to investors.—

Approval by an audit committee of an issuer under this subsection of a non-audit service to be performed by the auditor of the issuer shall be disclosed to investors in periodic reports required by section 13(a).

    (3)   Delegation authority.—

The audit committee of an issuer may delegate to 1 or more designated members of the audit committee who are independent directors of the board of directors, the authority to grant preapprovals required by this subsection. The decisions of any member to whom authority is delegated under this paragraph to preapprove an activity under this subsection shall be presented to the full audit committee at each of its scheduled meetings.

    (4)   Approval of audit services for other purposes.—

In carrying out its duties under subsection (m)(2), if the audit committee of an issuer approves an audit service within the scope of the engagement of the auditor, such audit service shall be deemed to have been preapproved for purposes of this subsection.

(j)   Audit Partner Rotation.—

It shall be unlawful for a registered public accounting firm to provide audit services to an issuer if the lead (or coordinating) audit partner (having primary responsibility for the audit), or the audit partner responsible for reviewing the audit, has performed audit services for that issuer in each of the 5 previous fiscal years of that issuer.

(k)   Reports to Audit Committees.—

Each registered public accounting firm that performs for any issuer any audit required by this title shall timely report to the audit committee of the issuer—

    (1)   all critical accounting policies and practices to be used;

    (2)   all alternative treatments of financial information within generally accepted accounting principles that have been discussed with management officials of the issuer, ramifications of the use of such alternative disclosures and treatments, and the treatment preferred by the registered public accounting firm; and

    (3)   other material written communications between the registered public accounting firm and the management of the issuer, such as any management letter or schedule of unadjusted differences.

(l)   Conflicts of Interest.—

It shall be unlawful for a registered public accounting firm to perform for an issuer any audit service required by this title, if a chief executive officer, controller, chief financial officer, chief accounting officer, or any person serving in an equivalent position for the issuer, was employed by that registered independent public accounting firm and participated in any capacity in the audit of that issuer during the 1-year period preceding the date of the initiation of the audit.

(m)   Standards Relating to Audit Committees.—

    (1)   Commission rules.—

    (A)   In general.—

Effective not later than 270 days after the date of enactment of this subsection, the Commission shall, by rule, direct the national securities exchanges and national securities associations to prohibit the listing of any security of an issuer that is not in compliance with the requirements of any portion of paragraphs (2) through (6).

(B)   Opportunity to cure defects.—

The rules of the Commission under subparagraph (A) shall provide for appropriate procedures for an issuer to have an opportunity to cure any defects that would be the basis for a prohibition under subparagraph (A), before the imposition of such prohibition.

(2)   Responsibilities relating to registered public accounting firms.—

The audit committee of each issuer, in its capacity as a committee of the board of directors, shall be directly responsible for the appointment, compensation, and oversight of the work of any registered public accounting firm employed by that issuer (including resolution of disagreements between management and the auditor regarding financial reporting) for the purpose of preparing or issuing an audit report or related work, and each such registered public accounting firm shall report directly to the audit committee.

(3)   Independence.—

(A)   In general.—

Each member of the audit committee of the issuer shall be a member of the board of directors of the issuer, and shall otherwise be independent.

(B)   Criteria.—

In order to be considered to be independent for purposes of this paragraph, a member of an audit committee of an issuer may not, other than in his or her capacity as a member of the audit committee, the board of directors, or any other board committee—

(i)   accept any consulting, advisory, or other compensatory fee from the issuer; or

(ii)   be an affiliated person of the issuer or any subsidiary thereof.

(C)   Exemption authority.—

The Commission may exempt from the requirements of subparagraph (B) a particular relationship with respect to audit committee members, as the Commission determines appropriate in light of the circumstances.

(4)   Complaints.—

Each audit committee shall establish procedures for—

(A)   the receipt, retention, and treatment of complaints received by the issuer regarding accounting, internal accounting controls, or auditing matters; and

(B)   the confidential, anonymous submission by employees of the issuer of concerns regarding questionable accounting or auditing matters.

(5)   Authority to engage advisors.—

Each audit committee shall have the authority to engage independent counsel and other advisers, as it determines necessary to carry out its duties.

(6)   Funding.—

Each issuer shall provide for appropriate funding, as determined by the audit committee, in its capacity as a committee of the board of directors, for payment of compensation—

(A)   to the registered public accounting firm employed by the issuer for the purpose of rendering or issuing an audit report; and

(B)   to any advisers employed by the audit committee under paragraph (5).

Position Limits and Position Accountability for Security-Based Swaps and Large Trader Reporting

Sec. 10B. (a) Position Limits—As a means reasonably designed to prevent fraud and manipulation, the Commission shall, by rule or regulation, as necessary or appropriate in the public interest or for the protection of investors, establish limits (including related hedge exemption provisions) on the size of positions in any security-based swap that may be held by any person. In establishing such limits, the Commission may require any person to aggregate positions in—

(1) any security-based swap and any security or loan or group of securities or loans on which such security-based swap is based, which such security-based swap references, or to which such security-based swap is related as described in paragraph (68) of section 3(a), and any other instrument relating to such security or loan or group or index of securities or loans; or

(2) any security-based swap and—

(A) any security or group or index of securities, the price, yield, value, or volatility of which, or of which any interest therein, is the basis for a material term of such security-based swap as described in paragraph (68) of section 3(a); and

(B) any other instrument relating to the same security or group or index of securities described under subparagraph (A).

(b) Exemptions—The Commission, by rule, regulation, or order, may conditionally or unconditionally exempt any person or class of persons, any security-based swap or class of security-based swaps, or any transaction or class of transactions from any requirement the Commission may establish under this section with respect to position limits.

(c) SRO Rules—

(1) In general.—

As a means reasonably designed to prevent fraud or manipulation, the Commission, by rule, regulation, or order, as necessary or appropriate in the public interest, for the protection of investors, or otherwise in furtherance of the purposes of this title, may direct a self-regulatory organization—

(A) to adopt rules regarding the size of positions in any security-based swap that may be held by—

(i) any member of such self-regulatory organization;

(ii) any person for whom a member of such self-regulatory organization effects transactions in such security-based swap; and

(B) to adopt rules reasonably designed to ensure compliance with requirements prescribed by the Commission under this subsection.

(2) Requirement to aggregate positions.—

In establishing the limits under paragraph (1), the self-regulatory organization may require such member or person to aggregate positions in—

(A) any security-based swap and any security or loan or group or narrow-based security index of securities or loans on which such security-based swap is based, which such security-based swap references, or to which such security-based swap is related as described in section 3(a)(68), and any other instrument relating to such security or loan or group or narrow-based security index of securities or loans; or

(B)(i) any security-based swap; and

(ii) any security-based swap and any other instrument relating to the same security or group or narrow-based security index of securities.

(d) Large Trader Reporting—The Commission, by rule or regulation, may require any person that effects transactions for such person's own account or the account of others in any securities-based swap or uncleared security-based swap and any security or loan or group or narrow-based security index of securities or loans as set forth in paragraphs (1) and (2) of subsection (a) under this section to report such information as the Commission may prescribe regarding any position or positions in any security-based swap or uncleared security-based swap and any security or loan or group or narrow-based security index of securities or loans and any other instrument relating to such security or loan or group or narrow-based security index of securities or loans as set forth in paragraphs (1) and (2) of subsection (a) under this section.

Compensation Committees

Sec. 10C.   (a) Independence of Compensation Committees—

    (1)   Listing standards.—

The Commission shall, by rule, direct the national securities exchanges and national securities associations to prohibit the listing of any equity security of an issuer, other than an issuer that is a controlled company, limited partnership, company in bankruptcy proceedings, open-ended management investment company that is registered under the Investment Company Act of 1940, or a foreign private issuer that provides annual disclosures to shareholders of the reasons that the foreign private issuer does not have an independent compensation committee, that does not comply with the requirements of this subsection.

    (2)   Independence of compensation committees.—

The rules of the Commission under paragraph (1) shall require that each member of the compensation committee of the board of directors of an issuer be—

      (A)   a member of the board of directors of the issuer; and

      (B)   independent.

    (3)   Independence.—

The rules of the Commission under paragraph (1) shall require that, in determining the definition of the term "independence" for purposes of paragraph (2), the national securities exchanges and the national securities associations shall consider relevant factors, including—

      (A)   the source of compensation of a member of the board of directors of an issuer, including any consulting, advisory, or other compensatory fee paid by the issuer to such member of the board of directors; and

      (B)   whether a member of the board of directors of an issuer is affiliated with the issuer, a subsidiary of the issuer, or an affiliate of a subsidiary of the issuer.

    (4)   Exemption authority.—

The rules of the Commission under paragraph (1) shall permit a national securities exchange or a national securities association to exempt a particular relationship from the requirements of paragraph (2), with respect to the members of a compensation committee, as the national securities exchange or national securities association determines is appropriate, taking into consideration the size of an issuer and any other relevant factors.

  (b)   Independence of Compensation Consultants and Other Compensation Committee Advisers—

    (1)   In general.—

The compensation committee of an issuer may only select a compensation consultant, legal counsel, or other adviser to the compensation committee after taking into consideration the factors identified by the Commission under paragraph (2).

    (2)   Rules.—

The Commission shall identify factors that affect the independence of a compensation consultant, legal counsel, or other adviser to a compensation committee of an issuer. Such factors shall be competitively neutral among categories of consultants, legal counsel, or other advisers and preserve the ability of compensation committees to retain the services of members of any such category, and shall include—

(A) the provision of other services to the issuer by the person that employs the compensation consultant, legal counsel, or other adviser;

(B) the amount of fees received from the issuer by the person that employs the compensation consultant, legal counsel, or other adviser, as a percentage of the total revenue of the person that employs the compensation consultant, legal counsel, or other adviser;

(C) the policies and procedures of the person that employs the compensation consultant, legal counsel, or other adviser that are designed to prevent conflicts of interest;

(D) any business or personal relationship of the compensation consultant, legal counsel, or other adviser with a member of the compensation committee; and

(E) any stock of the issuer owned by the compensation consultant, legal counsel, or other adviser.

(c) Compensation Committee Authority Relating to Compensation Consultants—

(1) Authority to retain compensation consultant.—

(A) In general.—

The compensation committee of an issuer, in its capacity as a committee of the board of directors, may, in its sole discretion, retain or obtain the advice of a compensation consultant.

(B) Direct responsibility of compensation committee.—

The compensation committee of an issuer shall be directly responsible for the appointment, compensation, and oversight of the work of a compensation consultant.

(C) Rule of construction.—

This paragraph may not be construed—

(i) to require the compensation committee to implement or act consistently with the advice or recommendations of the compensation consultant; or

(ii) to affect the ability or obligation of a compensation committee to exercise its own judgment in fulfillment of the duties of the compensation committee.

(2) Disclosure.—

In any proxy or consent solicitation material for an annual meeting of the shareholders (or a special meeting in lieu of the annual meeting) occurring on or after the date that is 1 year after the date of enactment of this section, each issuer shall disclose in the proxy or consent material, in accordance with regulations of the Commission, whether—

(A) the compensation committee of the issuer retained or obtained the advice of a compensation consultant; and

(B) the work of the compensation consultant has raised any conflict of interest and, if so, the nature of the conflict and how the conflict is being addressed.

(d) Authority To Engage Independent Legal Counsel and Other Advisers—

(1) In general.—

The compensation committee of an issuer, in its capacity as a committee of the board of directors, may, in its sole discretion, retain and obtain the advice of independent legal counsel and other advisers.

(2) Direct responsibility of compensation committee.—

The compensation committee of an issuer shall be directly responsible for the appointment, compensation, and oversight of the work of independent legal counsel and other advisers.

(3) Rule of construction.—

This subsection may not be construed—

    (A)   to require a compensation committee to implement or act consistently with the advice or recommendations of independent legal counsel or other advisers under this subsection; or

    (B)   to affect the ability or obligation of a compensation committee to exercise its own judgment in fulfillment of the duties of the compensation committee.

  (e)   Compensation of Compensation Consultants, Independent Legal Counsel, and Other Advisers— Each issuer shall provide for appropriate funding, as determined by the compensation committee in its capacity as a committee of the board of directors, for payment of reasonable compensation—

    (1)   to a compensation consultant; and

    (2)   to independent legal counsel or any other adviser to the compensation committee.

  (f)   Commission Rules—

    (1)   In general.—

Not later than 360 days after the date of enactment of this section, the Commission shall, by rule, direct the national securities exchanges and national securities associations to prohibit the listing of any security of an issuer that is not in compliance with the requirements of this section.

    (2)   Opportunity to cure defects.—

The rules of the Commission under paragraph (1) shall provide for appropriate procedures for an issuer to have a reasonable opportunity to cure any defects that would be the basis for the prohibition under paragraph (1), before the imposition of such prohibition.

    (3)   Exemption authority.—

      (A)   In general.—

The rules of the Commission under paragraph (1) shall permit a national securities exchange or a national securities association to exempt a category of issuers from the requirements under this section, as the national securities exchange or the national securities association determines is appropriate.

      (B)   Considerations.—

In determining appropriate exemptions under subparagraph (A), the national securities exchange or the national securities association shall take into account the potential impact of the requirements of this section on smaller reporting issuers.

  (g)   Controlled Company Exemption—

    (1)   In general.—

This section shall not apply to any controlled company.

    (2)   Definition.—

For purposes of this section, the term "controlled company" means an issuer—

      (A)   that is listed on a national securities exchange or by a national securities association; and

      (B)   that holds an election for the board of directors of the issuer in which more than 50 percent of the voting power is held by an individual, a group, or another issuer.

Recovery of Erroneously Awarded Compensation Policy

  Sec. 10D.   (a) Listing Standards—The Commission shall, by rule, direct the national securities exchanges and national securities associations to prohibit the listing of any security of an issuer that does not comply with the requirements of this section.

  (b)   Recovery of Funds—The rules of the Commission under subsection (a) shall require each issuer to develop and implement a policy providing—

(1) for disclosure of the policy of the issuer on incentive-based compensation that is based on financial information required to be reported under the securities laws; and

(2) that, in the event that the issuer is required to prepare an accounting restatement due to the material noncompliance of the issuer with any financial reporting requirement under the securities laws, the issuer will recover from any current or former executive officer of the issuer who received incentive-based compensation (including stock options awarded as compensation) during the 3-year period preceding the date on which the issuer is required to prepare an accounting restatement, based on the erroneous data, in excess of what would have been paid to the executive officer under the accounting restatement.

Trading by Members of Exchanges, Brokers, and Dealers

Sec. 11. (a)(1) It shall be unlawful for any member of a national securities exchange to effect any transaction on such exchange for its own account, the account of an associated person, or an account with respect to which it or an associated person thereof exercises investment discretion: Provided, however, That this paragraph shall not make unlawful—

(A) any transaction by a dealer acting in the capacity of market maker;

(B) any transaction for the account of an odd-lot dealer in a security in which he is so registered;

(C) any stabilizing transaction effected in compliance with rules under section 10(b) of this Act to facilitate a distribution of a security in which the member effecting such transaction is participating;

(D) any bona fide arbitrage transaction, any bona fide hedge transaction involving a long or short position in an equity security and a long or short position in a security entitling the holder to acquire or sell such equity security, or any risk arbitrage transaction in connection with a merger, acquisition, tender offer, or similar transaction involving a recapitalization;

(E) any transaction for the account of a natural person, the estate of a natural person, or a trust created by a natural person for himself or another natural person;

(F) any transaction to offset a transaction made in error;

(G) any other transaction for a member's own account provided that

(i) such member is primarily engaged in the business of underwriting and distributing securities issued by other persons, selling securities to customers, and acting as broker, or any one or more of such activities, and whose gross income normally is derived principally from such business and related activities and

(ii) such transaction is effected in compliance with rules of the Commission which, as a minimum, assure that the transaction is not inconsistent with the maintenance of fair and orderly markets and yields priority, parity, and precedence in execution to orders for the account of persons who are not members or associated with members of the exchange;

(H) any transaction for an account with respect to which such member or an associated person thereof exercises investment discretion if such member—

(i) has obtained, from the person or persons authorized to transact business for the account, express authorization for such member or associated person to effect such transactions prior to engaging in the practice of effecting such transactions;

(ii) furnishes the person or persons authorized to transact business for the account with a statement at least annually disclosing the aggregate compensation received by the exchange member in effecting such transactions; and

(iii) complies with any rules the Commission has prescribed with respect to the requirements of clauses (i) and (ii); and

(I)   any other transaction of a kind which the Commission, by rule, determines is consistent with the purposes of this paragraph, the protection of investors, and the maintenance of fair and orderly markets.

(2)   The Commission, by rule, as it deems necessary or appropriate in the public interest and for the protection of investors, to maintain fair and orderly markets, or to assure equal regulation of exchange markets and markets occurring otherwise than on an exchange, may regulate or prohibit:

(A)   transactions on a national securities exchange not unlawful under paragraph (1) of this subsection effected by any member thereof for its own account (unless such member is acting in the capacity of market maker or odd-lot dealer), the account of an associated person, or an account with respect to which such member or an associated person thereof exercises investment discretion;

(B)   transactions otherwise than on a national securities exchange effected by use of the mails or any means or instrumentality of interstate commerce by any member of a national securities exchange, broker, or dealer for the account of such member, broker, or dealer (unless such member, broker, or dealer is acting in the capacity of a market maker) the account of an associated person, or an account with respect to which such member, broker, or dealer or associated person thereof exercises investment discretion; and

(C)   transactions on a national securities exchange effected by any broker or dealer not a member thereof for the account of such broker or dealer (unless such broker or dealer is acting in the capacity of market maker), the account of an associated person, or an account with respect to which such broker or dealer or associated person thereof exercises investment discretion.

(3)   The provisions of paragraph (1) of this subsection insofar as they apply to transactions on a national securities exchange effected by a member thereof who was a member on February 1, 1978 shall not become effective until February 1, 1979. Nothing in this paragraph shall be construed to impair or limit the authority of the Commission to regulate or prohibit such transactions prior to February 1, 1979, pursuant to paragraph (2) of this subsection.

(b)   When not in contravention of such rules and regulations as the Commission may prescribe as necessary or appropriate in the public interest and for the protection of investors, to maintain fair and orderly markets, or to remove impediments to and perfect the mechanism of a national market system, the rules of a national securities exchange may permit

(1)   a member to be registered as an odd-lot dealer and as such to buy and sell for his own account so far as may be reasonably necessary to carry on such odd-lot transactions, and

(2)   a member to be registered as a specialist. Under the rules and regulations of the Commission a specialist may be permitted to act as a broker and dealer or limited to acting as a broker or dealer. It shall be unlawful for a specialist or an official of the exchange to disclose information in regard to orders placed with such specialist which is not available to all members of the exchange, to any person other than an official of the exchange, a representative of the Commission, or a specialist who may be acting for such specialist: *Provided, however,* That the Commission, by rule, may require disclosure to all members of the exchange of all orders placed with specialists, under such rules and regulations as the Commission may prescribe as necessary or appropriate in the public interest or for the protection of investors. It shall also be unlawful for a specialist permitted to act as a broker and dealer to effect on the exchange as broker any transaction except upon a market or limited price order.

(c)   If because of the limited volume of transactions effected on an exchange, it is in the opinion of the Commission impracticable and not necessary or appropriate in the public interest or for the protection of investors to apply any of the foregoing provisions of this section or the rules and regulations thereunder, the Commission shall have power, upon application of the exchange and on a showing that the rules of such exchange are otherwise adequate for the protection of investors, to exempt such exchange and its members from any such provision or rules and regulations.

(d)   It shall be unlawful for a member of a national securities exchange who is both a dealer and a broker, or for any person who both as a broker and a dealer transacts a business in securities through the medium of a member or otherwise, to effect through the use of any facility of a national securities exchange or of the mails or of any means or instrumentality of interstate commerce, or otherwise in the case of a member,

(1)   any transaction in connection with which, directly or indirectly, he extends or maintains or arranges for the extension or maintenance of credit to or for a customer on any security (other than an exempted security) which was a part of a new issue in the distribution of which he participated as a member of a selling syndicate or group within thirty days prior to such transaction: *Provided,* That credit shall not be deemed extended by reason of a bona fide delayed delivery of

(i)   any such security against full payment of the entire purchase price thereof upon such delivery within thirty-five days after such purchase or

(ii)   any mortgage related security or any small business related security against full payment of the entire purchase price thereof upon such delivery within one hundred and eighty days after such purchase, or within such shorter period as the Commission may prescribe by rule or regulation, or

(2)   any transaction with respect to any security (other than an exempted security) unless, if the transaction is with a customer, he discloses to such customer in writing at or before the completion of the transaction whether he is acting as a dealer for his own account, as a broker for such customer, or as a broker for some other person.

National Market System for Securities; Securities Information Processors

Sec. 11A.   (a)(1) The Congress finds that—

(A)   The securities markets are an important national asset which must be preserved and strengthened.

(B)   New data processing and communications techniques create the opportunity for more efficient and effective market operations.

(C)   It is in the public interest and appropriate for the protection of investors and the maintenance of fair and orderly markets to assure—

(i)   economically efficient execution of securities transactions;

(ii)   fair competition among brokers and dealers, among exchange markets, and between exchange markets and markets other than exchange markets;

(iii)   the availability to brokers, dealers, and investors of information with respect to quotations for and transactions in securities;

(iv)   the practicability of brokers executing investors' orders in the best market; and

(v)   an opportunity, consistent with the provisions of clauses (i) and (iv) of this subparagraph, for investors' orders to be executed without the participation of a dealer.

(D)   The linking of all markets for qualified securities through communication and data processing facilities will foster efficiency, enhance competition, increase the information available to brokers, dealers, and investors, facilitate the offsetting of investors' orders, and contribute to best execution of such orders.

(2)   The Commission is directed, therefore, having due regard for the public interest, the protection of investors, and the maintenance of fair and orderly markets, to use its authority under this Act to facilitate the establishment of a national market system for securities (which may include subsystems for particular types of securities with unique trading characteristics) in accordance with the findings and to carry out the objectives set forth in paragraph (1) of this subsection. The Commission, by rule, shall designate the securities or classes of securities qualified for trading in the national market system from among securities other than exempted securities. (Securities or classes of securities so designated hereinafter in this section referred to as "qualified securities".)

(3)   The Commission is authorized in furtherance of the directive in paragraph (2) of this subsection—

(A) to create one or more advisory committees pursuant to the Federal Advisory Committee Act (which shall be in addition to the National Market Advisory Board established pursuant to subsection (d) of this section) and to employ one or more outside experts;

(B) by rule or order, to authorize or require self-regulatory organizations to act jointly with respect to matters as to which they share authority under this Act in planning, developing, operating, or regulating a national market system (or a subsystem thereof) or one or more facilities thereof; and

(C) to conduct studies and make recommendations to the Congress from time to time as to the possible need for modifications of the scheme of self-regulation provided for in this Act so as to adapt it to a national market system.

(b)(1) Except as otherwise provided in this section, it shall be unlawful for any securities information processor unless registered in accordance with this subsection, directly or indirectly, to make use of the mails or any means or instrumentality of interstate commerce to perform the functions of a securities information processor. The Commission, by rule or order, upon its own motion or upon application, may conditionally or unconditionally exempt any securities information processor or class of securities information processors or security or class of securities from any provision of this section or the rules or regulations thereunder, if the Commission finds that such exemption is consistent with the public interest, the protection of investors, and the purposes of this section, including the maintenance of fair and orderly markets in securities and the removal of impediments to and perfection of the mechanism of a national market system: *Provided, however,* That a securities information processor not acting as the exclusive processor of any information with respect to quotations for or transactions in securities is exempt from the requirement to register in accordance with this subsection unless the Commission, by rule or order, finds that the registration of such securities information processor is necessary or appropriate in the public interest, for the protection of investors, or for the achievement of the purposes of this section.

(2) A securities information processor may be registered by filing with the Commission an application for registration in such form as the Commission, by rule, may prescribe containing the address of its principal office, or offices, the names of the securities and markets for which it is then acting and for which it proposes to act as a securities information processor, and such other information and documents as the Commission, by rule, may prescribe with regard to performance capability, standards and procedures for the collection, processing, distribution, and publication of information with respect to quotations for and transactions in securities, personnel qualifications, financial condition, and such other matters as the Commission determines to be germane to the provisions of this Act and the rules and regulations thereunder, or necessary or appropriate in furtherance of the purposes of this section.

(3) The Commission shall, upon the filing of an application for registration pursuant to paragraph (2) of this subsection, publish notice of the filing and afford interested persons an opportunity to submit written data, views, and arguments concerning such application. Within ninety days of the date of the publication of such notice (or within such longer period as to which the applicant consents) the Commission shall—

(A) by order grant such registration, or

(B) institute proceedings to determine whether registration should be denied. Such proceedings shall include notice of the grounds for denial under consideration and opportunity for hearing and shall be concluded within one hundred eighty days of the date of publication of notice of the filing of the application for registration. At the conclusion of such proceedings the Commission, by order, shall grant or deny such registration. The Commission may extend the time for the conclusion of such proceedings for up to sixty days if it finds good cause for such extension and publishes its reasons for so finding or for such longer periods as to which the applicant consents.

The Commission shall grant the registration of a securities information processor if the Commission finds that such securities information processor is so organized, and has the capacity, to be able to assure the prompt, accurate, and reliable performance of its functions as a securities information processor, comply with the provisions of this Act and the rules and regulations thereunder, carry out its functions in a manner consistent with the purposes of this section, and, insofar as it is acting as an exclusive processor, operate fairly and efficiently. The Commission shall deny the registration of a securities information processor if the Commission does not make any such finding.

(4) A registered securities information processor may, upon such terms and conditions as the Commission deems necessary or appropriate in the public interest or for the protection of investors, withdraw from registration by filing a written notice of withdrawal with the Commission. If the Commission finds that any registered securities information processor is no longer in existence or has ceased to do business in the capacity specified in its application for registration, the Commission, by order, shall cancel the registration.

(5)(A) If any registered securities information processor prohibits or limits any person in respect of access to services offered, directly or indirectly, by such securities information processor, the registered securities information processor shall promptly file notice thereof with the Commission. The notice shall be in such form and contain such information as the Commission, by rule, may prescribe as necessary or appropriate in the public interest or for the protection of investors. Any prohibition or limitation on access to services with respect to which a registered securities information processor is required by this paragraph to file notice shall be subject to review by the Commission on its own motion, or upon application by any person aggrieved thereby filed within thirty days after such notice has been filed with the Commission and received by such aggrieved person, or within such longer period as the Commission may determine. Application to the Commission for review, or the institution of review by the Commission on its own motion, shall not operate as a stay of such prohibition or limitation, unless the Commission otherwise orders, summarily or after notice and opportunity for hearing on the question of a stay (which hearing may consist solely of the submission of affidavits or presentation of oral arguments). The Commission shall establish for appropriate cases an expedited procedure for consideration and determination of the question of a stay.

(B) In any proceeding to review the prohibition or limitation of any person in respect of access to services offered by a registered securities information processor, if the Commission finds, after notice and opportunity for hearing, that such prohibition or limitation is consistent with the provisions of this Act and the rules and regulations thereunder and that such person has not been discriminated against unfairly, the Commission, by order, shall dismiss the proceeding. If the Commission does not make any such finding or if it finds that such prohibition or limitation imposes any burden on competition not necessary or appropriate in furtherance of the purposes of this Act, the Commission, by order, shall set aside the prohibition or limitation and require the registered securities information processor to permit such person access to services offered by the registered securities information processor.

(6) The Commission, by order, may censure or place limitations upon the activities, functions, or operations of any registered securities information processor or suspend for a period not exceeding twelve months or revoke the registration of any such processor, if the Commission finds, on the record after notice and opportunity for hearing, that such censure, placing of limitations, suspension, or revocation is in the public interest, necessary or appropriate for the protection of investors or to assure the prompt, accurate, or reliable performance of the functions of such securities information processor, and that such securities information processor has violated or is unable to comply with any provision of this Act or the rules or regulations thereunder.

(c)(1) No self-regulatory organization, member thereof, securities information processor, broker, or dealer shall make use of the mails or any means or instrumentality of interstate commerce to collect, process, distribute, publish, or prepare for distribution or publication any information with respect to quotations for or transactions in any security other than an exempted security, to assist, participate in, or coordinate the distribution or publication of such information, or to effect any transaction in, or to induce or attempt to induce the purchase or sale of, any such security in contravention of such rules and regulations as the Commission shall prescribe as necessary or appropriate in the public interest, for the protection of investors, or otherwise in furtherance of the purposes of this Act to—

(A) prevent the use, distribution, or publication of fraudulent, deceptive, or manipulative information with respect to quotations for and transactions in such securities;

(B)   assure the prompt, accurate, reliable, and fair collection, processing, distribution, and publication of information with respect to quotations for and transactions in such securities and the fairness and usefulness of the form and content of such information;

(C)   assure that all securities information processors may, for purposes of distribution and publication, obtain on fair and reasonable terms such information with respect to quotations for and transactions in such securities as is collected, processed, or prepared for distribution or publication by any exclusive processor of such information acting in such capacity;

(D)   assure that all exchange members, brokers, dealers, securities information processors, and, subject to such limitations as the Commission, by rule, may impose as necessary or appropriate for the protection of investors or maintenance of fair and orderly markets, all other persons may obtain on terms which are not unreasonably discriminatory such information with respect to quotations for and transactions in such securities as is published or distributed by any self-regulatory organization or securities information processor;

(E)   assure that all exchange members, brokers, and dealers transmit and direct orders for the purchase or sale of qualified securities in a manner consistent with the establishment and operation of a national market system; and

(F)   assure equal regulation of all markets for qualified securities and all exchange members, brokers, and dealers effecting transactions in such securities.

(2)   The Commission, by rule, as it deems necessary or appropriate in the public interest or for the protection of investors, may require any person who has effected the purchase or sale of any qualified security by use of the mails or any means or instrumentality of interstate commerce to report such purchase or sale to a registered securities information processor, national securities exchange, or registered securities association and require such processor, exchange, or association to make appropriate distribution and publication of information with respect to such purchase or sale.

(3)(A)   The Commission, by rule, is authorized to prohibit brokers and dealers from effecting transactions in securities registered pursuant to section 12(b) of this Act otherwise than on a national securities exchange, if the Commission finds, on the record after notice and opportunity for hearing, that—

(i)   as a result of transactions in such securities effected otherwise than on a national securities exchange the fairness or orderliness of the markets for such securities has been affected in a manner contrary to the public interest or the protection of investors;

(ii)   no rule of any national securities exchange unreasonably impairs the ability of any dealer to solicit or effect transactions in such securities for his own account or unreasonably restricts competition among dealers in such securities or between dealers acting in the capacity of market makers who are specialists in such securities and such dealers who are not specialists in such securities, and

(iii)   the maintenance or restoration of fair and orderly markets in such securities may not be assured through other lawful means under this Act.

The Commission may conditionally or unconditionally exempt any security or transaction or any class of securities or transactions from any such prohibition if the Commission deems such exemption consistent with the public interest, the protection of investors, and the maintenance of fair and orderly markets.

(B)   For the purposes of subparagraph (A) of this paragraph, the ability of a dealer to solicit or effect transactions in securities for his own account shall not be deemed to be unreasonably impaired by any rule of an exchange fairly and reasonably prescribing the sequence in which orders brought to the exchange must be executed or which has been adopted to effect compliance with a rule of the Commission promulgated under this Act.

(4)   The Commission is directed to review any and all rules of national securities exchanges which limit or condition the ability of members to effect transactions in securities otherwise than on such exchanges.

(5)   No national securities exchange or registered securities association may limit or condition the participation of any member in any registered clearing agency.

(6)   Tick size.—

(A)   Study and report.—The Commission shall conduct a study examining the transition to trading and quoting securities in one penny increments, also known as decimalization. The study shall examine the impact that decimalization has had on the number of initial public offerings since its implementation relative to the period before its implementation. The study shall also examine the impact that this change has had on liquidity for small and middle capitalization company securities and whether there is sufficient economic incentive to support trading operations in these securities in penny increments. Not later than 90 days after the date of enactment of this paragraph [enacted April 5, 2012], the Commission shall submit to Congress a report on the findings of the study.

(B)   Designation.—If the Commission determines that the securities of emerging growth companies should be quoted and traded using a minimum increment of greater than $0.01, the Commission may, by rule not later than 180 days after the date of enactment of this paragraph [enacted April 5, 2012], designate a minimum increment for the securities of emerging growth companies that is greater than $0.01 but less than $0.10 for use in all quoting and trading of securities in any exchange or other execution venue.

(d)(1)   Not later than one hundred eighty days after the date of enactment of Securities Act Amendment of 1975, June 4, 1975, the Commission shall establish a National Market Advisory Board (hereinafter in this section referred to as the "Advisory Board") to be composed of fifteen members, not all of whom shall be from the same geographical area of the United States, appointed by the Commission for a term specified by the Commission of not less than two years or more than five years. The Advisory Board shall consist of persons associated with brokers and dealers (who shall be a majority) and persons not so associated who are representative of the public and, to the extent feasible, have knowledge of the securities markets of the United States.

(2)   It shall be the responsibility of the Advisory Board to formulate and furnish to the Commission its views on significant regulatory proposals made by the Commission or any self-regulatory organization concerning the establishment, operation, and regulation of the markets for securities in the United States.

(3)(A)   The Advisory Board shall study and make recommendations to the Commission as to the steps it finds appropriate to facilitate the establishment of a national market system. In so doing, the Advisory Board shall assume the responsibilities of any advisory committee appointed to advise the Commission with respect to the national market system which is in existence at the time of the establishment of the Advisory Board.

(B)   The Advisory Board shall study the possible need for modifications of the scheme of self-regulation provided for in this Act so as to adapt it to a national market system, including the need for the establishment of a new self-regulatory organization (hereinafter in this section referred to as a "National Market Regulatory Board" or "Regulatory Board") to administer the national market system. In the event the Advisory Board determines a National Market Regulatory Board should be established, it shall make recommendations as to:

(i)   the point in time at which a Regulatory Board should be established;

(ii)   the composition of a Regulatory Board;

(iii)   the scope of the authority of a Regulatory Board;

(iv)   the relationship of a Regulatory Board to the Commission and to existing self-regulatory organizations; and

(v)   the manner in which a Regulatory Board should be funded.

The Advisory Board shall report to the Congress, on or before December 31, 1976, the results of such study and its recommendations, including such recommendations for legislation as it deems appropriate.

(C) In carrying out its responsibilities under this paragraph, the Advisory Board shall consult with self-regulatory organizations, brokers, dealers, securities information processors, issuers, investors, representatives of Government agencies, and other persons interested or likely to participate in the establishment, operation, or regulation of the national market system.

(e) National Markets System for Security Futures Products.—

(1) Consultation and cooperation required.—

With respect to security futures products, the Commission and the Commodity Futures Trading Commission shall consult and cooperate so that, to the maximum extent practicable, their respective regulatory responsibilities may be fulfilled and the rules and regulations applicable to security futures products may foster a national market system for security futures products if the Commission and the Commodity Futures Trading Commission jointly determine that such a system would be consistent with the congressional findings in subsection (a)(1). In accordance with this objective, the Commission shall, at least 15 days prior to the issuance for public comment of any proposed rule or regulation under this section concerning security futures products, consult and request the views of the Commodity Futures Trading Commission.

(2) No rule adopted pursuant to this section shall be applied to any person with respect to the trading of security futures products on an exchange that is registered under section 6(g) unless the Commodity Futures Trading Commission has issued an order directing that such rule is applicable to such persons.

Registration Requirements for Securities

Sec. 12. (a) It shall be unlawful for any member, broker, or dealer to effect any transaction in any security (other than an exempted security) on a national securities exchange unless a registration is effective as to such security for such exchange in accordance with the provisions of this Act and the rules and regulations thereunder. The provisions of this subsection shall not apply in respect of a security futures product traded on a national securities exchange.

(b) A security may be registered on a national securities exchange by the issuer filing an application with the exchange (and filing with the Commission such duplicate originals thereof as the Commission may require), which application shall contain—

(1) Such information, in such detail, as to the issuer and any person directly or indirectly controlling or controlled by, or under direct or indirect common control with, the issuer, and any guarantor of the security as to principal or interest or both, as the Commission may by rules and regulations require, as necessary or appropriate in the public interest or for the protection of investors, in respect of the following:

(A) the organization, financial structure, and nature of the business;

(B) the terms, position, rights, and privileges of the different classes of securities outstanding;

(C) the terms on which their securities are to be, and during the preceding three years have been, offered to the public or otherwise;

(D) the directors, officers, and underwriters, and each security holder of record holding more than 10 per centum of any class of any equity security of the issuer (other than an exempted security), their remuneration and their interests in the securities of, and their material contracts with, the issuer and any person directly or indirectly controlling or controlled by, or under direct or indirect common control with, the issuer;

(E) remuneration to others than directors and officers exceeding $20,000 per annum;

(F) bonus and profit-sharing arrangements;

(G) management and service contracts;

(H) options existing or to be created in respect of their securities;

(I) material contracts, not made in the ordinary course of business, which are to be executed in whole or in part at or after the filing of the application or which were made not more than two years before such filing, and every material patent or contract for a material patent right shall be deemed a material contract;

(J) balance sheets for not more than the three preceding fiscal years, certified if required by the rules and regulations of the Commission by a registered public accounting firm;

(K) profit and loss statements for not more than the three preceding fiscal years, certified if required by the rules and regulations of the Commission by a registered public accounting firm; and

(L) any further financial statements which the Commission may deem necessary or appropriate for the protection of investors.

(2) Such copies of articles of incorporation, bylaws, trust indentures, or corresponding documents by whatever name known, underwriting arrangements, and other similar documents of, and voting trust agreements with respect to, the issuer and any person directly or indirectly controlling or controlled by, or under direct or indirect common control with, the issuer as the Commission may require as necessary or appropriate for the proper protection of investors and to insure fair dealing in the security.

(3) Such copies of material contracts, referred to in paragraph (1)(I) above, as the Commission may require as necessary or appropriate for the proper protection of investors and to insure fair dealing in the security.

(c) If in the judgment of the Commission any information required under subsection (b) of this section is inapplicable to any specified class or classes of issuers, the Commission shall require in lieu thereof the submission of such other information of comparable character as it may deem applicable to such class of issuers.

(d) If the exchange authorities certify to the Commission that the security has been approved by the exchange for listing and registration, the registration shall become effective thirty days after the receipt of such certification by the Commission or within such shorter period of time as the Commission may determine. A security registered with a national securities exchange may be withdrawn or stricken from listing and registration in accordance with the rules of the exchange and, upon such terms as the Commission may deem necessary to impose for the protection of investors, upon application by the issuer or the exchange to the Commission; whereupon the issuer shall be relieved from further compliance with the provisions of this section and section 13 of this Act and any rules or regulations under such sections as to the securities so withdrawn or stricken. An unissued security may be registered only in accordance with such rules and regulations as the Commission may prescribe as necessary or appropriate in the public interest or for the protection of investors.

(e) Notwithstanding the foregoing provisions of this section, the Commission may by such rules and regulations as it deems necessary or appropriate in the public interest or for the protection of investors, permit securities listed on any exchange at the time the registration of such exchange as a national securities exchange becomes effective, to be registered for a period ending not later than July 1, 1935, without complying with the provisions of this section.

(f)(1)(A) Notwithstanding the preceding subsections of this section, any national securities exchange, in accordance with the requirements of this subsection and the rules hereunder, may extend unlisted trading privileges to—

(i) any security that is listed and registered on a national securities exchange, subject to subparagraph (B); and

(ii) any security that is otherwise registered pursuant to this section, or that would be required to be so registered except for the exemption from registration provided in subparagraph (B) or (G) of subsection (g)(2), subject to subparagraph (E) of this paragraph.

(B) A national securities exchange may not extend unlisted trading privileges to a security described in subparagraph (A)(i) during such interval, if any, after the commencement of an initial public offering of such security, as is or may be required pursuant to subparagraph (C).

(C)   Not later than 180 days after the date of enactment of the Unlisted Trading Privileges Act of 1994, the Commission shall prescribe, by rule or regulation, the duration of the interval referred to in subparagraph (B), if any, as the Commission determines to be necessary or appropriate for the maintenance of fair and orderly markets, the protection of investors and the public interest, or otherwise in furtherance of the purposes of this title. Until the earlier of the effective date of such rule or regulation or 240 days after such date of enactment, such interval shall begin at the opening of trading on the day on which such security commences trading on the national securities exchange with which such security is registered and end at the conclusion of the next day of trading.

(D)   The Commission may prescribe, by rule or regulation such additional procedures or requirements for extending unlisted trading privileges to any security as the Commission deems necessary or appropriate for the maintenance of fair and orderly markets, the protection of investors and the public interest, or otherwise in furtherance of the purposes of this title.

(E)   No extension of unlisted trading privileges to securities described in subparagraph (A)(ii) may occur except pursuant to a rule, regulation, or order of the Commission approving such extension or extensions. In promulgating such rule or regulation or in issuing such order, the Commission—

    (i)   shall find that such extension or extensions of unlisted trading privileges is consistent with the maintenance of fair and orderly markets, the protection of investors and the public interest, and otherwise in furtherance of the purposes of this title;

    (ii)   shall take account of the public trading activity in such securities, the character of such trading, the impact of such extension on the existing markets for such securities, and the desirability of removing impediments to and the progress that has been made toward the development of a national market system; and

    (iii)   shall not permit a national securities exchange to extend unlisted trading privileges to such securities if any rule of such national securities exchange would unreasonably impair the ability of a dealer to solicit or effect transactions in such securities for its own account, or would unreasonably restrict competition among dealers in such securities or between such dealers acting in the capacity of market makers who are specialists and such dealers who are not specialists.

(F)   An exchange may continue to extend unlisted trading privileges in accordance with this paragraph only if the exchange and the subject security continue to satisfy the requirements for eligibility under this paragraph, including any rules and regulations issued by the Commission pursuant to this paragraph, except that unlisted trading privileges may continue with regard to securities which had been admitted on such exchange prior to July 1, 1964, notwithstanding the failure to satisfy such requirements. If unlisted trading privileges in a security are discontinued pursuant to this subparagraph, the exchange shall cease trading in that security, unless the exchange and the subject security thereafter satisfy the requirements of this paragraph and the rules issued hereunder.

(G)   For purposes of this paragraph—

    (i)   a security is the subject of an initial public offering if—

        (I)   the offering of the subject security is registered under the Securities Act of 1933; and

        (II)   the issuer of the security, immediately prior to filing the registration statement with respect to the offering, was not subject to the reporting requirements of section 13 or 15(d) of this title; and

    (ii)   an initial public offering of such security commences at the opening of trading on the day on which such security commences trading on the national securities exchange with which such security is registered.

(2)(A)   At any time within 60 days of commencement of trading on an exchange of a security pursuant to unlisted trading privileges, the Commission may summarily suspend such unlisted trading privileges on the exchange. Such suspension shall not be reviewable under section 25 of this title and shall not be deemed to be a final agency action for purposes of section 704 of title 5, United States Code. Upon such suspension—

(i)   the exchange shall cease trading in the security by the close of business on the date of such suspension, or at such time as the Commission may prescribe by rule or order for the maintenance of fair and orderly markets, the protection of investors and the public interest, or otherwise in furtherance of the purposes of this title; and

(ii)   if the exchange seeks to extend unlisted trading privileges to the security, the exchange shall file an application to reinstate its ability to do so with the Commission pursuant to such procedures as the Commission may prescribe by rule or order for the maintenance of fair and orderly markets, the protection of investors and the public interest, or otherwise in furtherance of the purposes of this title.

(B)   A suspension under subparagraph (A) shall remain in effect until the Commission, by order, grants approval of an application to reinstate, as described in subparagraph (A)(ii).

(C)   A suspension under subparagraph (A) shall not affect the validity or force of an extension of unlisted trading privileges in effect prior to such suspension.

(D)   The Commission shall not approve an application by a national securities exchange to reinstate its ability to extend unlisted trading privileges to a security unless the Commission finds, after notice and opportunity for hearing, that the extension of unlisted trading privileges pursuant to such application is consistent with the maintenance of fair and orderly markets, the protection of investors and the public interest, and otherwise in furtherance of the purposes of this Act. If the application is made to reinstate unlisted trading privileges to a security described in paragraph (1)(A)(ii), the Commission—

(i)   shall take account of the public trading activity in such security, the character of such trading, the impact of such extension on the existing markets for such a security, and the desirability of removing impediments to and the progress that has been made toward the development of a national market system; and

(ii)   shall not grant any such application if any rule of the national securities exchange making application under this subsection would unreasonably impair the ability of a dealer to solicit or effect transactions in such security for its own account, or would unreasonably restrict competition among dealers in such security or between such dealers acting in the capacity of marketmakers who are specialists and such dealers who are not specialists.

(3)   Notwithstanding paragraph (2), the Commission shall by rules and regulations suspend unlisted trading privileges in whole or in part for any or all classes of securities for a period not exceeding twelve months, if it deems such suspension necessary or appropriate in the public interest or for the protection of investors or to prevent evasion of the purposes of this Act.

(4)   On the application of the issuer of any security for which unlisted trading privileges on any exchange have been continued or extended pursuant to this subsection, or of any broker or dealer who makes or creates a market for such security, or of any other person having a bona fide interest in the question of termination or suspension of such unlisted trading privileges, or on its own motion, the Commission shall by order terminate, or suspend for a period not exceeding twelve months, such unlisted trading privileges for such security if the Commission finds, after appropriate notice and opportunity for hearing, that such termination or suspension is necessary or appropriate in the public interest or for the protection of investors.

(5)   In any proceeding under this subsection in which appropriate notice and opportunity for hearing are required, notice of not less than ten days to the applicant in such proceeding, to the issuer of the security involved, to the exchange which is seeking to continue or extend or has continued or extended unlisted trading privileges for such security, and to the exchange, if any, on which such security is listed and registered, shall be deemed adequate notice, and any broker or dealer who makes or creates a market for such security, and any other person having a bona fide interest in such proceeding, shall upon application be entitled to be heard.

(6)   Any security for which unlisted trading privileges are continued or extended pursuant to this subsection shall be deemed to be registered on a national securities exchange within the meaning of this Act. The powers and duties of the Commission under this Act shall be applicable to the rules of an exchange in respect of any such security. The Commission may, by such rules and regulations as it

deems necessary or appropriate in the public interest or for the protection of investors, either unconditionally or upon specified terms and conditions, or for stated periods, exempt such securities from the operation of any provision of section 13, 14, or 16 of this Act.

(g)(1)   Every issuer which is engaged in interstate commerce, or in a business affecting interstate commerce, or whose securities are traded by use of the mails or any means or instrumentality of interstate commerce shall—

    (A)   within 120 days after the last day of its first fiscal year ended on which the issuer has total assets exceeding $10,000,000 and a class of equity security (other than an exempted security) held of record by either—

        (i)   2,000 persons, or

        (ii)   500 persons who are not accredited investors (as such term is defined by the Commission), and

    (B)   in the case of an issuer that is a bank, a savings and loan holding company (as defined in section 10 of the Home Owners' Loan Act), or a bank holding company, as such term is defined in section 2 of the Bank Holding Company Act of 1956, not later than 120 days after the last day of its first fiscal year ended after the effective date of this subsection, on which the issuer has total assets exceeding $10,000,000 and a class of equity security (other than an exempted security) held of record by 2,000 or more persons,

register such security by filing with the Commission a registration statement (and such copies thereof as the Commission may require) with respect to such security containing such information and documents as the Commission may specify comparable to that which is required in an application to register a security pursuant to subsection (b) of this section. Each such registration statement shall become effective sixty days after filing with the Commission or within such shorter period as the Commission may direct. Until such registration statement becomes effective it shall not be deemed filed for the purposes of section 18 of this Act. Any issuer may register any class of equity security not required to be registered by filing a registration statement pursuant to the provisions of this paragraph. The Commission is authorized to extend the date upon which any issuer or class of issuers is required to register a security pursuant to the provisions of this paragraph.

(2)   The provisions of this subsection shall not apply in respect of—

    (A)   any security listed and registered on a national securities exchange.

    (B)   any security issued by an investment company registered pursuant to section 8 of the Investment Company Act of 1940.

    (C)   any security, other than permanent stock, guaranty stock, permanent reserve stock, or any similar certificate evidencing nonwithdrawable capital, issued by a savings and loan association, building and loan association, cooperative bank, homestead association, or similar institution, which is supervised and examined by State or Federal authority having supervision over any such institution.

    (D)   any security of an issuer organized and operated exclusively for religious, educational, benevolent, fraternal, charitable, or reformatory purposes and not for pecuniary profit, and no part of the net earnings of which inures to the benefit of any private shareholder or individual; or any security of a fund that is excluded from the definition of an investment company under section 3(c)(10)(B) of the Investment Company Act of 1940.

    (E)   any security of an issuer which is a "cooperative association" as defined in the Agricultural Marketing Act, approved June 15, 1929, as amended, or a federation of such cooperative associations, if such federation possesses no greater powers or purposes than cooperative associations so defined.

    (F)   any security issued by a mutual or cooperative organization which supplies a commodity or service primarily for the benefit of its members and operates not for pecuniary profit, but only if the security is part of a class issuable only to persons who purchase commodities or services from the issuer, the security is transferable only to a successor in interest or occupancy of premises serviced or to be served by the issuer, and no dividends are payable to the holder of the security.

(G)   any security issued by an insurance company if all of the following conditions are met:

(i)   Such insurance company is required to and does file an annual statement with the Commissioner of Insurance (or other officer or agency performing a similar function) of its domiciliary State, and such annual statement conforms to that prescribed by the National Association of Insurance Commissioners or in the determination of such State commissioner, officer or agency substantially conforms to that so prescribed.

(ii)   Such insurance company is subject to regulation by its domiciliary State of proxies, consents, or authorizations in respect of securities issued by such company and such regulation conforms to that prescribed by the National Association of Insurance Commissioners.

(iii)   After July 1, 1966, the purchase and sales of securities issued by such insurance company by beneficial owners, directors, or officers of such company are subject to regulation (including reporting) by its domiciliary State substantially in the manner provided in section 16 of this Act.

(H)   any interest or participation in any collective trust funds maintained by a bank or in a separate account maintained by an insurance company which interest or participation is issued in connection with

(i)   a stock-bonus, pension, or profit-sharing plan which meets the requirements for qualification under section 401 of the Internal Revenue Code of 1954,

(ii)   an annuity plan which meets the requirements for deduction of the employer's contribution under section 404(a)(2) of such Code, or

(iii)   a church plan, company, or account that is excluded from the definition of an investment company under section 3(c)(14) of the Investment Company Act of 1940.

(3)   The Commission may by rules or regulations or, on its own motion, after notice and opportunity for hearing, by order, exempt from this subsection any security of a foreign issuer, including any certificate of deposit for such a security, if the Commission finds that such exemption is in the public interest and is consistent with the protection of investors.

(4)   Registration of any class of security pursuant to this subsection shall be terminated ninety days, or such shorter period as the Commission may determine, after the issuer files a certification with the Commission that the number of holders of record of such class of security is reduced to less than three hundred persons, or, in the case of a bank, a savings and loan holding company (as defined in section 10 of the Home Owners' Loan Act), or a bank holding company, as such term is defined in section 2 of the Bank Holding Company Act of 1956, 1,200 persons. The Commission shall after notice and opportunity for hearing deny termination of registration if it finds that the certification is untrue. Termination of registration shall be deferred pending final determination on the question of denial.

(5)   For the purposes of this subsection the term "class" shall include all securities of an issuer which are of substantially similar character and the holders of which enjoy substantially similar rights and privileges. The Commission may for the purpose of this subsection define by rules and regulations the terms "total assets" and "held of record" as it deems necessary or appropriate in the public interest or for the protection of investors in order to prevent circumvention of the provisions of this subsection. For purposes of this subsection, a security futures product shall not be considered a class of equity security of the issuer of the securities underlying the security futures product. For purposes of determining whether an issuer is required to register a security with the Commission pursuant to paragraph (1), the definition of 'held of record' shall not include securities held by persons who received the securities pursuant to an employee compensation plan in transactions exempted from the registration requirements of section 5 of the Securities Act of 1933.

(6)   Exclusion for persons holding certain securities.—The Commission shall, by rule, exempt, conditionally or unconditionally, securities acquired pursuant to an offering made under section 4(a)(6) of the Securities Act of 1933 from the provisions of this subsection.

(h)   The Commission may by rules and regulations, or upon application of an interested person, by order, after notice and opportunity for hearing, exempt in whole or in part any issuer or class of issuers from the provisions of subsection (g) of this section or from section 13, 14, or 15(d) or may exempt from section 16 any officer, director, or beneficial owner of securities of any issuer, any security of which is required to be registered pursuant to subsection (g) hereof, upon such terms and conditions and for such period as it deems necessary or appropriate, if the Commission finds, by reason of the number of public investors, amount of trading interest in the securities, the nature and extent of the activities of the issuer, income or assets of the issuer, or otherwise, that such action is not inconsistent with the public interest or the protection of investors. The Commission may, for the purposes of any of the above-mentioned sections or subsections of this Act, classify issuers and prescribe requirements appropriate for each such class.

(i)   In respect of any securities issued by banks and savings associations the deposits of which are insured in accordance with the Federal Deposit Insurance Act, the powers, functions, and duties vested in the Commission to administer and enforce this section and sections 10A(m), 12, 13, 14(a), 14(c), 14(d), 14(f), and 16 of this Act, and sections 302, 303, 304, 306, 401(b), 404, 406, and 407 of the Sarbanes-Oxley Act of 2002,

(1)   with respect to national banks and Federal savings associations, the accounts of which are insured by the Federal Deposit Insurance Corporation are vested in the Comptroller of the Currency,

(2)   with respect to all other member banks of the Federal Reserve System are vested in the Board of Governors of the Federal Reserve System,

(3)   with respect to all other insured banks and State savings associations, the accounts of which are insured by the Federal Deposit Insurance Corporation, are vested in the Federal Deposit Insurance Corporation,

(4)   The Comptroller of the Currency, the Board of Governors of the Federal Reserve System, and the Federal Deposit Insurance Corporation shall have the power to make such rules and regulations as may be necessary for the execution of the functions vested in them as provided in this subsection. In carrying out their responsibilities under this subsection, the agencies named in the first sentence of this subsection shall issue substantially similar regulations to regulations and rules issued by the Commission under this section and sections 10A(m), 12, 13, 14(a), 14(c), 14(d), 14(f), and 16 of this Act, and sections 302, 303, 304, 306, 401(b), 404, 406, and 407 of the Sarbanes-Oxley Act of 2002, unless they find that implementation of substantially similar regulations with respect to insured banks and insured institutions are not necessary or appropriate in the public interest or for protection of investors, and publish such findings, and the detailed reasons therefor, in the Federal Register. Such regulations of the above-named agencies, or the reasons for failure to publish such substantially similar regulations to those of the Commission, shall be published in the Federal Register within 120 days of October 28, 1974, and, thereafter, within 60 days of any changes made by the Commission in its relevant regulations and rules.

(j)   The Commission is authorized, by order, as it deems necessary or appropriate for the protection of investors to deny, to suspend the effective date of, to suspend for a period not exceeding twelve months, or to revoke the registration of a security, if the Commission finds, on the record after notice and opportunity for hearing, that the issuer, of such security has failed to comply with any provision of this Act or the rules and regulations thereunder. No member of a national securities exchange, broker, or dealer shall make use of the mails or any means or instrumentality of interstate commerce to effect any transaction in, or to induce the purchase or sale of, any security the registration of which has been and is suspended or revoked pursuant to the preceding sentence.

(k)   Trading Suspensions; Emergency Authority.—

(1)   Trading suspensions.—

If in its opinion the public interest and the protection of investors so require, the Commission is authorized by order—

(A)   summarily to suspend trading in any security (other than an exempted security) for a period not exceeding 10 business days, and

(B)   summarily to suspend all trading on any national securities exchange or otherwise, in securities other than exempted securities, for a period not exceeding 90 calendar days.

The action described in subparagraph (B) shall not take effect unless the Commission notifies the President of its decision and the President notifies the Commission that the President does not disapprove of such decision.

If the actions described in subparagraph (A) or (B) involve a security futures product, the Commission shall consult with and consider the views of the Commodity Futures Trading Commission.

(2)   Emergency orders.—

(A)   In general.—

The Commission, in an emergency, may by order summarily take such action to alter, supplement, suspend, or impose requirements or restrictions with respect to any matter or action subject to regulation by the Commission or a self-regulatory organization under the securities laws, as the Commission determines is necessary in the public interest and for the protection of investors—

(i)   to maintain or restore fair and orderly securities markets (other than markets in exempted securities); or

(ii)   to ensure prompt, accurate, and safe clearance and settlement of transactions in securities (other than exempted securities);

(iii)   to reduce, eliminate, or prevent the substantial disruption by the emergency of—

(I)   securities markets (other than markets in exempted securities), investment companies, or any other significant portion or segment of such markets; or

(II)   the transmission or processing of securities transactions (other than transactions in exempted securities).

(B)   Effective period.—

An order of the Commission under this paragraph shall continue in effect for the period specified by the Commission, and may be extended. Except as provided in subparagraph (C), an order of the Commission under this paragraph may not continue in effect for more than 10 business days, including extensions.

(C)   Extension.—

An order of the Commission under this paragraph may be extended to continue in effect for more than 10 business days if, at the time of the extension, the Commission finds that the emergency still exists and determines that the continuation of the order beyond 10 business days is necessary in the public interest and for the protection of investors to attain an objective described in clause (i), (ii), or (iii) of subparagraph (A). In no event shall an order of the Commission under this paragraph continue in effect for more than 30 calendar days.

(D)   Security futures.—

If the actions described in subparagraph (A) involve a security futures product, the Commission shall consult with and consider the views of the Commodity Futures Trading Commission.

(E)   Exemption.—

In exercising its authority under this paragraph, the Commission shall not be required to comply with the provisions of—

(i)   section 19(c) of this Act; or

(ii)   section 553 of Title 5.

(3)   Termination of emergency actions by president.—

The President may direct that action taken by the Commission under paragraph (1)(B) or paragraph (2) of this subsection shall not continue in effect.

(4)   Compliance with orders.—

No member of a national securities exchange, broker, or dealer shall make use of the mails or any means or instrumentality of interstate commerce to effect any transaction in, or to induce the purchase or sale of, any security in contravention of an order of the Commission under this subsection unless such order has been stayed, modified, or set aside as provided in paragraph (5) of this subsection or has ceased to be effective upon direction of the President as provided in paragraph (3).

(5)   Limitations on review of orders.—

An order of the Commission pursuant to this subsection shall be subject to review only as provided in section 25(a) of this Act. Review shall be based on an examination of all the information before the Commission at the time such order was issued. The reviewing court shall not enter a stay, writ of mandamus, or similar relief unless the court finds, after notice and hearing before a panel of the court, that the Commission's action is arbitrary, capricious, an abuse of discretion, or otherwise not in accordance with law.

(6)   Consultation.—

Prior to taking any action described in paragraph (1)(B), the Commission shall consult with and consider the views of the Secretary of the Treasury, the Board of Governors of the Federal Reserve System, and the Commodity Futures Trading Commission, unless such consultation is impracticable in light of the emergency.

(7)   Definition.—

For purposes of this subsection, the term "emergency" means—

     (A)   a major market disturbance characterized by or constituting—

         (i)   sudden and excessive fluctuations of securities prices generally, or a substantial threat thereof, that threaten fair and orderly markets; or

         (ii)   a substantial disruption of the safe or efficient operation of the national system for clearance and settlement of transactions in securities, or a substantial threat thereof; or

     (B)   a major disturbance that substantially disrupts, or threatens to substantially disrupt—

         (i)   the functioning of securities markets, investment companies, or any other significant portion or segment of the securities markets; or

         (ii)   the transmission or processing of securities transactions.

     (*l*)   It shall be unlawful for an issuer, any class of whose securities is registered pursuant to this section or would be required to be so registered except for the exemption from registration provided by subsection (g)(2)(B) or (g)(2)(G) of this section, by the use of any means or instrumentality of interstate commerce, or of the mails, to issue, either originally or upon transfer, any of such securities in a form or with a format which contravenes such rules and regulations as the Commission may prescribe as necessary or appropriate for the prompt and accurate clearance and settlement of transactions in securities. The provisions of this subsection shall not apply to variable annuity contracts or variable life policies issued by an insurance company or its separate accounts.

Periodical and Other Reports

     Sec. 13.   (a)   Every issuer of a security registered pursuant to section 12 of this Act shall file with the Commission, in accordance with such rules and regulations as the Commission may prescribe as necessary or appropriate for the proper protection of investors and to insure fair dealing in the security—

     (1)   such information and documents (and such copies thereof) as the Commission shall require to keep reasonably current the information and documents required to be included in or filed with an application or registration statement filed pursuant to section 12 of this Act, except that the Commission may not require the filing of any material contract wholly executed before July 1, 1962.

(2) such annual reports (and such copies thereof), certified if required by the rules and regulations of the Commission by independent public accountants, and such quarterly reports (and such copies thereof), as the Commission may prescribe.

Every issuer of a security registered on a national securities exchange shall also file a duplicate original of such information, documents, and reports with the exchange. In any registration statement, periodic report, or other reports to be filed with the Commission, an emerging growth company need not present selected financial data in accordance with section 301 of title 17, Code of Federal Regulations, for any period prior to the earliest audited period presented in connection with its first registration statement that became effective under this Act or the Securities Act of 1933 and, with respect to any such statement or reports, an emerging growth company may not be required to comply with any new or revised financial accounting standard until such date that a company that is not an issuer (as defined under section 2(a) of the Sarbanes-Oxley Act of 2002 is required to comply with such new or revised accounting standard, if such standard applies to companies that are not issuers.

(b)(1) The Commission may prescribe, in regard to reports made pursuant to this Act the form or forms in which the required information shall be set forth, the items or details to be shown in the balance sheet and the earnings statement, and the methods to be followed in the preparation of reports, in the appraisal or valuation of assets and liabilities, in the determination of depreciation and depletion, in the differentiation of recurring and nonrecurring income, in the differentiation of investment and operating income, and in the preparation, where the Commission deems it necessary or desirable, of separate and/or consolidated balance sheets or income accounts of any person directly or indirectly controlling or controlled by the issuer, or any person under direct or indirect common control with the issuer; but in the case of the reports of any person whose methods of accounting are prescribed under the provisions of any law of the United States, or any rule or regulation thereunder, the rules and regulations of the Commission with respect to reports shall not be inconsistent with the requirements imposed by such law or rule or regulation in respect of the same subject matter (except that such rules and regulations of the Commission may be inconsistent with such requirements to the extent that the Commission determines that the public interest or the protection of investors so requires).

(2) Every issuer which has a class of securities registered pursuant to section 12 of this Act and every issuer which is required to file reports pursuant to section 15(d) of this Act shall—

(A) make and keep books, records, and accounts, which, in reasonable detail, accurately and fairly reflect the transactions and dispositions of the assets of the issuer;

(B) devise and maintain a system of internal accounting controls sufficient to provide reasonable assurances that—

(i) transactions are executed in accordance with management's general or specific authorization;

(ii) transactions are recorded as necessary

(I) to permit preparation of financial statements in conformity with generally accepted accounting principles or any other criteria applicable to such statements, and

(II) to maintain accountability for assets;

(iii) access to assets is permitted only in accordance with management's general or specific authorization; and

(iv) the recorded accountability for assets is compared with the existing assets at reasonable intervals and appropriate action is taken with respect to any differences; and

(C) notwithstanding any other provision of law, pay the allocable share of such issuer of a reasonable annual accounting support fee or fees, determined in accordance with section 109 of the Sarbanes-Oxley Act of 2002.

(3)(A) With respect to matters concerning the national security of the United States, no duty or liability under paragraph (2) of this subsection shall be imposed upon any person acting in cooperation with the head of any Federal department or agency responsible for such matters if such act in cooperation with such head of a department or agency was done upon the specific, written directive of the head of such department or agency pursuant to Presidential authority to issue such directives.

Each directive issued under this paragraph shall set forth the specific facts and circumstances with respect to which the provisions of this paragraph are to be invoked. Each such directive shall, unless renewed in writing, expire one year after the date of issuance.

(B)   Each head of a Federal department or agency of the United States who issues a directive pursuant to this paragraph shall maintain a complete file of all such directives and shall, on October 1 of each year, transmit a summary of matters covered by such directives in force at any time during the previous year to the Permanent Select Committee on Intelligence of the House of Representatives and the Select Committee on Intelligence of the Senate.

(4)   No criminal liability shall be imposed for failing to comply with the requirements of paragraph (2) of this subsection except as provided in paragraph (5) of this subsection.

(5)   No person shall knowingly circumvent or knowingly fail to implement a system of internal accounting controls or knowingly falsify any book, record, or account described in paragraph (2).

(6)   Where an issuer which has a class of securities registered pursuant to section 12 of this Act or an issuer which is required to file reports pursuant to section 15(d) of this Act holds 50 per centum or less of the voting power with respect to a domestic or foreign firm, the provisions of paragraph (2) require only that the issuer proceed in good faith to use its influence, to the extent reasonable under the issuer's circumstances, to cause such domestic or foreign firm to devise and maintain a system of internal accounting controls consistent with paragraph (2). Such circumstances include the relative degree of the issuer's ownership of the domestic or foreign firm and the laws and practices governing the business operations of the country in which such firm is located. An issuer which demonstrates good faith efforts to use such influence shall be conclusively presumed to have complied with the requirements of paragraph (2).

(7)   For the purpose of paragraph (2) of this subsection, the terms "reasonable assurances" and "reasonable detail" mean such level of detail and degree of assurance as would satisfy prudent officials in the conduct of their own affairs.

(c)   If in the judgment of the Commission any report required under subsection (a) is inapplicable to any specified class or classes of issuers, the Commission shall require in lieu thereof the submission of such reports of comparable character as it may deem applicable to such class or classes of issuers.

(d)(1)   Any person who, after acquiring directly or indirectly the beneficial ownership of any equity security of a class which is registered pursuant to section 12 of this Act, or any equity security of an insurance company which would have been required to be so registered except for the exemption contained in section 12(g)(2)(G) of this Act, or any equity security issued by a closed-end investment company registered under the Investment Company Act of 1940 or any equity security issued by a Native Corporation pursuant to Section 37(d)(6) of the Alaska Native Claims Settlement Act, or otherwise becomes or is deemed to become a beneficial owner of any of the foregoing upon the purchase or sale of a security-based swap that the commission may define by rule, and is directly or indirectly the beneficial owner of more than 5 per centum of such class shall, within ten days after such acquisition, or within such shorter time as the Commission may establish by rule and file with the Commission, a statement containing such of the following information, and such additional information, as the Commission may by rules and regulations prescribe as necessary or appropriate in the public interest or for the protection of investors—

(A)   the background, and identity, residence, and citizenship of, and the nature of such beneficial ownership by, such person and all other persons by whom or on whose behalf the purchases have been or are to be effected;

(B)   the source and amount of the funds or other consideration used or to be used in making the purchases, and if any part of the purchase price is represented or is to be represented by funds or other consideration borrowed or otherwise obtained for the purpose of acquiring, holding, or trading such security, a description of the transaction and the names of the parties thereto, except that where a source of funds is a loan made in the ordinary course of business by a bank, as defined in section 3(a)(6) of this Act, if the person filing such statement so requests, the name of the bank shall not be made available to the public;

(C)   if the purpose of the purchases or prospective purchases is to acquire control of the business of the issuer of the securities, any plans or proposals which such persons may have to liquidate such issuer, to sell its assets to or merge it with any other persons, or to make any other major change in its business or corporate structure;

(D)   the number of shares of such security which are beneficially owned, and the number of shares concerning which there is a right to acquire, directly or indirectly, by

(i)   such person, and

(ii)   by each associate of such person, giving the background, identity, residence and citizenship of each such associate; and

(E)   information as to any contracts, arrangements, or understandings with any person with respect to any securities of the issuer, including but not limited to transfer of any of the securities, joint ventures, loan or option arrangements, puts or calls, guaranties of loans, guaranties against loss or guaranties of profits, division of losses or profits, or the giving or withholding of proxies, naming the persons with whom such contracts, arrangements, or understandings have been entered into, and giving the details thereof.

(2)   If any material change occurs in the facts set forth and in the statement filed with the Commission, an amendment shall be filed with the Commission, in accordance with such rules and regulations as the Commission may prescribe as necessary or appropriate in the public interest or for the protection of investors.

(3)   When two or more persons act as a partnership, limited partnership, syndicate, or other group for the purpose of acquiring, holding, or disposing of securities of an issuer, such syndicate or group shall be deemed a "person" for the purposes of this subsection.

(4)   In determining, for purposes of this subsection, any percentage of a class of any security, such class shall be deemed to consist of the amount of the outstanding securities of such class, exclusive of any securities of such class held by or for the account of the issuer or a subsidiary of the issuer.

(5)   The Commission, by rule or regulation or by order, may permit any person to file in lieu of the statement required by paragraph (1) of this subsection or the rules and regulations thereunder, a notice stating the name of such person, the number of shares of any equity securities subject to paragraph (1) which are owned by him, the date of their acquisition and such other information as the Commission may specify, if it appears to the Commission that such securities were acquired by such person in the ordinary course of his business and were not acquired for the purpose of and do not have the effect of changing or influencing the control of the issuer nor in connection with or as a participant in any transaction having such purpose or effect.

(6)   The provisions of this subsection shall not apply to—

(A)   any acquisition or offer to acquire securities made or proposed to be made by means of a registration statement under the Securities Act of 1933;

(B)   any acquisition of the beneficial ownership of a security which, together with all other acquisitions by the same person of securities of the same class during the preceding twelve months, does not exceed 2 per centum of that class;

(C)   any acquisition of an equity security by the issuer of such security;

(D)   any acquisition or proposed acquisition of a security which the Commission, by rules or regulations or by order, shall exempt from the provisions of this subsection as not entered into for the purpose of, and not having the effect of, changing or influencing the control of the issuer or otherwise as not comprehended within the purposes of this subsection.

(e)(1)   It shall be unlawful for an issuer which has a class of equity securities registered pursuant to section 12 of this Act, or which is a closed-end investment company registered under the Investment Company Act of 1940, to purchase any equity security issued by it if such purchase is in contravention of such rules and regulations as the Commission, in the public interest or for the protection of investors, may adopt

(A)   to define acts and practices which are fraudulent, deceptive, or manipulative, and

(B)   to prescribe means reasonably designed to prevent such acts and practices. Such rules and regulations may require such issuer to provide holders of equity securities of such class with such information relating to the reasons for such purchase, the source of funds, the number of shares to be purchased, the price to be paid for such securities, the method of purchase, and such additional information, as the Commission deems necessary or appropriate in the public interest or for the protection of investors, or which the Commission deems to be material to a determination whether such security should be sold.

(2)   For the purpose of this subsection, a purchase by or for the issuer or any person controlling, controlled by, or under common control with the issuer, or a purchase subject to control of the issuer or any such person, shall be deemed to be a purchase by the issuer. The Commission shall have power to make rules and regulations implementing this paragraph in the public interest and for the protection of investors, including exemptive rules and regulations covering situations in which the Commission deems it unnecessary or inappropriate that a purchase of the type described in this paragraph shall be deemed to be a purchase by the issuer for purposes of some or all of the provisions of paragraph (1) of this subsection.

(3)   At the time of filing such statement as the Commission may require by rule pursuant to paragraph (1) of this subsection, the person making the filing shall pay to the Commission a fee at a rate that, subject to paragraph (4), is equal to $92 per $1,000,000 of the value of securities proposed to be purchased. The fee shall be reduced with respect to securities in an amount equal to any fee paid with respect to any securities issued in connection with the proposed transaction under section 6(b) of the Securities Act of 1933, or the fee paid under that section shall be reduced in an amount equal to the fee paid to the Commission in connection with such transaction under this paragraph.

(4)   Annual adjustment.—

For each fiscal year, the Commission shall by order adjust the rate required by paragraph (3) for such fiscal year to a rate that is equal to the rate (expressed in dollars per million) that is applicable under section 6(b) of the Securities Act of 1933 for such fiscal year.

(5)   Fee collections.—

Fees collected pursuant to this subsection for fiscal year 2012 and each fiscal year thereafter shall be deposited and credited as general revenue of the Treasury and shall not be available for obligation.

(6)   Effective date; publication.—

In exercising its authority under this subsection, the Commission shall not be required to comply with the provisions of section 553 of title 5, United States Code. An adjusted rate prescribed under paragraph (4) shall be published and take effect in accordance with section 6(b) of the Securities Act of 1933 (15 U.S.C. 77f(b)).

(7)   pro rata application.—

The rates per $1,000,000 required by this subsection shall be applied pro rata to amounts and balances of less than $1,000,000.

(f)(1)   Every institutional investment manager which uses the mails, or any means or instrumentality of interstate commerce in the course of its business as an institutional investment manager and which exercises investment discretion with respect to accounts holding equity securities of a class described in subsection (d)(1) of this section or otherwise becomes or is deemed to become a beneficial owner of any security of a class described in subsection (d)(1) upon the purchase or sale of a security-based swap that the Commission may define by rule having an aggregate fair market value on the last trading day in any of the preceding twelve months of at least $100,000,000 or such lesser amount (but in no case less than $10,000,000) as the Commission, by rule, may determine, shall file reports with the Commission in such form, for such periods, and at such times after the end of such periods as the Commission, by rule, may prescribe, but in no event shall such reports be filed for periods longer than one year or shorter than one quarter. Such reports shall include for each such equity security held on the last day of the reporting period by accounts (in aggregate or by type as the Commission, by rule, may prescribe) with respect to which the institutional investment manager exercises investment discretion (other than securities held in amounts which the Commission, by rule, determines to be insignificant for purposes of this subsection), the name of the issuer and the title, class, CUSIP number, number of shares or principal amount, and aggregate fair market value of each such security. Such reports may also include for accounts (in aggregate or by type) with respect to which the institutional investment manager exercises investment discretion such of the following information as the Commission, by rule, prescribes—

    (A) the name of the issuer and the title, class, CUSIP number, number of shares or principal amount, and aggregate fair market value or cost or amortized cost of each other security (other than an exempted security) held on the last day of the reporting period by such accounts;

    (B) the aggregate fair market value or cost or amortized cost of exempted securities (in aggregate or by class) held on the last day of the reporting period by such accounts;

    (C) the number of shares of each equity security of a class described in subsection (d)(1) held on the last day of the reporting period by such accounts with respect to which the institutional investment manager possesses sole or shared authority to exercise the voting rights evidenced by such securities;

    (D) the aggregate purchases and aggregate sales during the reporting period of each security (other than an exempted security) effected by or for such accounts; and

    (E) with respect to any transaction or series of transactions having a market value of at least $500,000 or such other amount as the Commission, by rule, may determine, effected during the reporting period by or for such accounts in any equity security of a class described in subsection (d)(1)—

        (i) the name of the issuer and the title, class, and CUSIP number of the security;

        (ii) the number of shares or principal amount of the security involved in the transaction;

        (iii) whether the transaction was a purchase or sale;

        (iv) the per share price or prices at which the transaction was effected;

        (v) the date or dates of the transaction;

        (vi) the date or dates of the settlement of the transaction;

        (vii) the broker or dealer through whom the transaction was effected;

        (viii) the market or markets in which the transaction was effected; and

        (ix) such other related information as the Commission, by rule, may prescribe.

    (2) The Commission shall prescribe rules providing for the public disclosure of the name of the issuer and the title, class, CUSIP number, aggregate amount of the number of short sales of each security, and any additional information determined by the Commission following the end of the reporting period. At a minimum, such public disclosure shall occur every month.

    (3) The Commission, by rule or order, may exempt, conditionally or unconditionally, any institutional investment manager or security or any class of institutional investment managers or securities from any or all of the provisions of this subsection or the rules thereunder.

    (4) The Commission shall make available to the public for a reasonable fee a list of all equity securities of a class described in subsection (d)(1), updated no less frequently than reports are required to be filed pursuant to paragraph (1) of this subsection. The Commission shall tabulate the information contained in any report filed pursuant to this subsection in a manner which will, in the view of the Commission, maximize the usefulness of the information to other Federal and State authorities and the public. Promptly after the filing of any such report, the Commission shall make the information contained therein conveniently available to the public for a reasonable fee in such form as the Commission, by rule, may prescribe, except that the Commission, as it determines to be necessary or appropriate in the public interest or for the protection of investors, may delay or prevent public disclosure of any such information in accordance with section 552 of Title 5, United States Code. Notwithstanding the preceding sentence, any such information identifying the securities held by the account of a natural person or an estate or trust (other than a business trust or investment company) shall not be disclosed to the public.

(5)   In exercising its authority under this subsection, the Commission shall determine (and so state) that its action is necessary or appropriate in the public interest and for the protection of investors or to maintain fair and orderly markets or, in granting an exemption, that its action is consistent with the protection of investors and the purposes of this subsection. In exercising such authority the Commission shall take such steps as are within its power, including consulting with the Comptroller General of the United States, the Director of the Office of Management and Budget, the appropriate regulatory agencies, Federal and State authorities which, directly or indirectly, require reports from institutional investment managers of information substantially similar to that called for by this subsection, national securities exchanges, and registered securities associations,

(A)   to achieve uniform, centralized reporting of information concerning the securities holdings of and transactions by or for accounts with respect to which institutional investment managers exercise investment discretion, and

(B)   consistently with the objective set forth in the preceding subparagraph, to avoid unnecessarily duplicative reporting by, and minimize the compliance burden on, institutional investment managers. Federal authorities which, directly or indirectly, require reports from institutional investment managers of information substantially similar to that called for by this subsection shall cooperate with the Commission in the performance of its responsibilities under the preceding sentence. An institutional investment manager which is a bank, the deposits of which are insured in accordance with the Federal Deposit Insurance Act, shall file with the appropriate regulatory agency a copy of every report filed with the Commission pursuant to this subsection.

(6)(A)   For purposes of this subsection the term "institutional investment manager" includes any person, other than a natural person, investing in or buying and selling securities for its own account, and any person exercising investment discretion with respect to the account of any other person.

(B)   The Commission shall adopt such rules as it deems necessary or appropriate to prevent duplicative reporting pursuant to this subsection by two or more institutional investment managers exercising investment discretion with respect to the same account.[8]

(g)(1)   Any person who is directly or indirectly the beneficial owner of more than 5 per centum of any security of a class described in subsection (d)(1) of this section or otherwise becomes or is deemed to become a beneficial owner of any security of a class described in subsection (d)(1) upon the purchase or sale of a security-based swap that the Commission may define by rule and shall file with the Commission a statement setting forth, in such form and at such time as the Commission may, by rule, prescribe—

(A)   such person's identity, residence, and citizenship; and

(B)   the number and description of the shares in which such person has an interest and the nature of such interest.

(2)   If any material change occurs in the facts set forth in the statement filed with the Commission, an amendment shall be filed with the Commission, in accordance with such rules and regulations as the Commission may prescribe as necessary or appropriate in the public interest or for the protection of investors.

(3)   When two or more persons act as a partnership, limited partnership, syndicate, or other group for the purpose of acquiring, holding, or disposing of securities of an issuer, such syndicate or group shall be deemed a "person" for the purposes of this subsection.

(4)   In determining, for purposes of this subsection, any percentage of a class of any security, such class shall be deemed to consist of the amount of the outstanding securities of such class, exclusive of any securities of such class held by or for the account of the issuer or a subsidiary of the issuer.

(5)   In exercising its authority under this subsection, the Commission shall take such steps as it deems necessary or appropriate in the public interest or for the protection of investors

(A)   to achieve centralized reporting of information regarding ownership,

---

[8]   Original said 'amount' instead of 'account'.

(B) to avoid unnecessarily duplicative reporting by and minimize the compliance burden on persons required to report, and

(C) to tabulate and promptly make available the information contained in any report filed pursuant to this subsection in a manner which will, in the view of the Commission, maximize the usefulness of the information to other Federal and State agencies and the public.

(6) The Commission may, by rule or order, exempt, in whole or in part, any person or class of persons from any or all of the reporting requirements of this subsection as it deems necessary or appropriate in the public interest or for the protection of investors.

(h) Large Trader Reporting.—

(1) Identification requirements for large traders.—

For the purpose of monitoring the impact on the securities markets of securities transactions involving a substantial volume or a large fair market value or exercise value and for the purpose of otherwise assisting the Commission in the enforcement of this Act, each large trader shall—

(A) provide such information to the Commission as the Commission may by rule or regulation prescribe as necessary or appropriate, identifying such large trader and all accounts in or through which such large trader effects such transactions; and

(B) identify, in accordance with such rules or regulations as the Commission may prescribe as necessary or appropriate, to any registered broker or dealer by or through whom such large trader directly or indirectly effects securities transactions, such large trader and all accounts directly or indirectly maintained with such broker or dealer by such large trader in or through which such transactions are effected.

(2) Recordkeeping and reporting requirements for brokers and dealers.—

Every registered broker or dealer shall make and keep for prescribed periods such records as the Commission by rule or regulation prescribes as necessary or appropriate in the public interest, for the protection of investors, or otherwise in furtherance of the purposes of this Act, with respect to securities transactions that equal or exceed the reporting activity level effected directly or indirectly by or through such registered broker or dealer of or for any person that such broker or dealer knows is a large trader, or any person that such broker or dealer has reason to know is a large trader on the basis of transactions in securities effected by or through such broker or dealer. Such records shall be available for reporting to the Commission, or any self-regulatory organization that the Commission shall designate to receive such reports, on the morning of the day following the day the transactions were effected, and shall be reported to the Commission or a self-regulatory organization designated by the Commission immediately upon request by the Commission or such a self-regulatory organization. Such records and reports shall be in a format and transmitted in a manner prescribed by the Commission (including, but not limited to, machine readable form).

(3) Aggregation rules.—

The Commission may prescribe rules or regulations governing the manner in which transactions and accounts shall be aggregated for the purpose of this subsection, including aggregation on the basis of common ownership or control.

(4) Examination of broker and dealer records.—

All records required to be made and kept by registered brokers and dealers pursuant to this subsection with respect to transactions effected by large traders are subject at any time, or from time to time, to such reasonable periodic, special, or other examinations by representatives of the Commission as the Commission deems necessary or appropriate in the public interest, for the protection of investors, or otherwise in furtherance of the purposes of this Act.

(5) Factors to be considered in commission actions.—

In exercising its authority under this subsection, the Commission shall take into account—

(A) existing reporting systems;

(B) the costs associated with maintaining information with respect to transactions effected by large traders and reporting such information to the Commission or self-regulatory organizations; and

(C) the relationship between the United States and international securities markets.

(6) Exemptions.—

The Commission, by rule, regulation, or order, consistent with the purposes of this Act, may exempt any person or class of persons or any transaction or class of transactions, either conditionally or upon specified terms and conditions or for stated periods, from the operation of this subsection, and the rules and regulations thereunder.

(7) Authority of commission to limit disclosure of information.—

Notwithstanding any other provision of law, the Commission shall not be compelled to disclose any information required to be kept or reported under this subsection. Nothing in this subsection shall authorize the Commission to withhold information from Congress, or prevent the Commission from complying with a request for information from any other Federal department or agency requesting information for purposes within the scope of its jurisdiction, or complying with an order of a court of the United States in an action brought by the United States or the Commission. For purposes of section 552 of Title 5, United States Code, this subsection shall be considered a statute described in subsection (b)(3)(B) of such section 552.

(8) Definitions.—

For purposes of this subsection—

(A) the term "large trader" means every person who, for his own account or an account for which he exercises investment discretion, effects transactions for the purchase or sale of any publicly traded security or securities by use of any means or instrumentality of interstate commerce or of the mails, or of any facility of a national securities exchange, directly or indirectly by or through a registered broker or dealer in an aggregate amount equal to or in excess of the identifying activity level;

(B) the term "publicly traded security" means any equity security (including an option on individual equity securities, and an option on a group or index of such securities) listed, or admitted to unlisted trading privileges, on a national securities exchange, or quoted in an automated interdealer quotation system;

(C) the term "identifying activity level" means transactions in publicly traded securities at or above a level of volume, fair market value, or exercise value as shall be fixed from time to time by the Commission by rule or regulation, specifying the time interval during which such transactions shall be aggregated;

(D) the term "reporting activity level" means transactions in publicly traded securities at or above a level of volume, fair market value, or exercise value as shall be fixed from time to time by the Commission by rule, regulation, or order, specifying the time interval during which such transactions shall be aggregated; and

(E) the term "person" has the meaning given in section 3(a)(9) of this Act and also includes two or more persons acting as a partnership, limited partnership, syndicate, or other group, but does not include a foreign central bank.

(i) Accuracy of Financial Reports.—

Each financial report that contains financial statements, and that is required to be prepared in accordance with (or reconciled to) generally accepted accounting principles under this title and filed with the Commission shall reflect all material correcting adjustments that have been identified by a registered public accounting firm in accordance with generally accepted accounting principles and the rules and regulations of the Commission.

(j) Off-Balance Sheet Transactions.—

Not later than 180 days after the date of enactment of the Sarbanes-Oxley Act of 2002, the Commission shall issue final rules providing that each annual and quarterly financial report required to be filed with the Commission shall disclose all material off-balance sheet transactions, arrangements, obligations (including contingent obligations), and other relationships of the issuer with unconsolidated entities or other persons, that may have a material current or future effect on financial condition, changes in financial condition, results of operations, liquidity, capital expenditures, capital resources, or significant components of revenues or expenses.

(k)   Prohibition on Personal Loans to Executives.—

     (1)   In general.—

It shall be unlawful for any issuer (as defined in section 2 of the Sarbanes-Oxley Act of 2002), directly or indirectly, including through any subsidiary, to extend or maintain credit, to arrange for the extension of credit, or to renew an extension of credit, in the form of a personal loan to or for any director or executive officer (or equivalent thereof) of that issuer. An extension of credit maintained by the issuer on the date of enactment of this subsection shall not be subject to the provisions of this subsection, provided that there is no material modification to any term of any such extension of credit or any renewal of any such extension of credit on or after that date of enactment.

     (2)   Limitation.—

Paragraph (1) does not preclude any home improvement and manufactured home loans (as that term is defined in section 5 of the Home Owners' Loan Act, consumer credit (as defined in section 103 of the Truth in Lending Act, or any extension of credit under an open end credit plan (as defined in section 103 of the Truth in Lending Act, or a charge card (as defined in section 127(c)(4)(e) of the Truth in Lending Act, or any extension of credit by a broker or dealer registered under section 15 of this title to an employee of that broker or dealer to buy, trade, or carry securities, that is permitted under rules or regulations of the Board of Governors of the Federal Reserve System pursuant to section 7 of this title (other than an extension of credit that would be used to purchase the stock of that issuer), that is—

       (A)   made or provided in the ordinary course of the consumer credit business of such issuer;

       (B)   of a type that is generally made available by such issuer to the public; and

       (C)   made by such issuer on market terms, or terms that are no more favorable than those offered by the issuer to the general public for such extensions of credit.

     (3)   Rule of construction for certain loans.—

Paragraph (1) does not apply to any loan made or maintained by an insured depository institution (as defined in section 3 of the Federal Deposit Insurance Act, if the loan is subject to the insider lending restrictions of section 22(h) of the Federal Reserve Act (12 U.S.C. § 375b).

(*l*)   Real Time Issuer Disclosures.—

Each issuer reporting under section 13(a) or 15(d) shall disclose to the public on a rapid and current basis such additional information concerning material changes in the financial condition or operations of the issuer, in plain English, which may include trend and qualitative information and graphic presentations, as the Commission determines, by rule, is necessary or useful for the protection of investors and in the public interest.

(m)   Public Availability of Security-Based Swap Transaction Data.—

     (1)   In general.—

       (A)   Definition of real-time public reporting.—

In this paragraph, the term "real-time public reporting" means to report data relating to a security-based swap transaction, including price and volume, as soon as technologically practicable after the time at which the security-based swap transaction has been executed.

       (B)   Purpose.—

The purpose of this subsection is to authorize the Commission to make security-based swap transaction and pricing data available to the public in such form and at such times as the Commission determines appropriate to enhance price discovery.

(C) General rule.—

The Commission is authorized to provide by rule for the public availability of security-based swap transaction, volume, and pricing data as follows:

(i) With respect to those security-based swaps that are subject to the mandatory clearing requirement described in section 3C(a)(1) (including those security-based swaps that are excepted from the requirement pursuant to section 3C(g)), the Commission shall require real-time public reporting for such transactions.

(ii) With respect to those security-based swaps that are not subject to the mandatory clearing requirement described in section 3C(a)(1), but are cleared at a registered clearing agency, the Commission shall require real-time public reporting for such transactions.

(iii) With respect to security-based swaps that are not cleared at a registered clearing agency and which are reported to a security-based swap data repository or the Commission under section 3C(a)(6), the Commission shall require real-time public reporting for such transactions, in a manner that does not disclose the business transactions and market positions of any person.

(iv) With respect to security-based swaps that are determined to be required to be cleared under section 3C(b) but are not cleared, the Commission shall require real-time public reporting for such transactions.

(D) Registered entities and public reporting.—

The Commission may require registered entities to publicly disseminate the security-based swap transaction and pricing data required to be reported under this paragraph.

(E) Rulemaking required.—

With respect to the rule providing for the public availability of transaction and pricing data for security-based swaps described in clauses (i) and (ii) of subparagraph (C), the rule promulgated by the Commission shall contain provisions—

(i) to ensure such information does not identify the participants;

(ii) to specify the criteria for determining what constitutes a large notional security-based swap transaction (block trade) for particular markets and contracts;

(iii) to specify the appropriate time delay for reporting large notional security-based swap transactions (block trades) to the public; and

(iv) that take into account whether the public disclosure will materially reduce market liquidity.

(F) Timeliness of reporting.—

Parties to a security-based swap (including agents of the parties to a security-based swap) shall be responsible for reporting security-based swap transaction information to the appropriate registered entity in a timely manner as may be prescribed by the Commission.

(G) Reporting of swaps to registered security-based swap data repositories.—

Each security-based swap (whether cleared or uncleared) shall be reported to a registered security-based swap data repository.

(H) Registration of clearing agencies.—

A clearing agency may register as a security-based swap data repository.

(2) Semiannual and annual public reporting of aggregate security-based swap data.—

(A) In general.—

In accordance with subparagraph (B), the Commission shall issue a written report on a semiannual and annual basis to make available to the public information relating to—

(i)   the trading and clearing in the major security-based swap categories; and

(ii)   the market participants and developments in new products.

(B)   Use; consultation.—

In preparing a report under subparagraph (A), the Commission shall—

(i)   use information from security-based swap data repositories and clearing agencies; and

(ii)   consult with the Office of the Comptroller of the Currency, the Bank for International Settlements, and such other regulatory bodies as may be necessary.

(C)   Authority of commission.—

The Commission may, by rule, regulation, or order, delegate the public reporting responsibilities of the Commission under this paragraph in accordance with such terms and conditions as the Commission determines to be appropriate and in the public interest.

(n)   Security-Based Swap Data Repositories.—

Security-based Swap Data Repositories—

(1)   Registration requirement.—

It shall be unlawful for any person, unless registered with the Commission, directly or indirectly, to make use of the mails or any means or instrumentality of interstate commerce to perform the functions of a security-based swap data repository.

(2)   Inspection and examination.—

Each registered security-based swap data repository shall be subject to inspection and examination by any representative of the Commission.

(3)   Compliance with core principles.—

(A)   In general.—

To be registered, and maintain registration, as a security-based swap data repository, the security-based swap data repository shall comply with—

(i)   the requirements and core principles described in this subsection; and

(ii)   any requirement that the Commission may impose by rule or regulation.

(B)   Reasonable discretion of security-based swap data depository.—

Unless otherwise determined by the Commission, by rule or regulation, a security-based swap data repository described in subparagraph (A) shall have reasonable discretion in establishing the manner in which the security-based swap data repository complies with the core principles described in this subsection.

(4)   Standard Setting.—

(A)   Data identification.—

(i)   In general.—

In accordance with clause (ii), the Commission shall prescribe standards that specify the data elements for each security-based swap that shall be collected and maintained by each registered security-based swap data repository.

(ii)   Requirement.—

In carrying out clause (i), the Commission shall prescribe consistent data element standards applicable to registered entities and reporting counterparties.

(B)   Data collection and maintenance.—

The Commission shall prescribe data collection and data maintenance standards for security-based swap data repositories.

(C)   Comparability.—

The standards prescribed by the Commission under this subsection shall be comparable to the data standards imposed by the Commission on clearing agencies in connection with their clearing of security-based swaps.

(5)   Duties.—

A security-based swap data repository shall—

(A)   accept data prescribed by the Commission for each security-based swap under subsection (b);

(B)   confirm with both counterparties to the security-based swap the accuracy of the data that was submitted;

(C)   maintain the data described in subparagraph (A) in such form, in such manner, and for such period as may be required by the Commission;

(D)(i)   provide direct electronic access to the Commission (or any designee of the Commission, including another registered entity); and

(ii)   provide the information described in subparagraph (A) in such form and at such frequency as the Commission may require to comply with the public reporting requirements set forth in subsection (m);

(E)   at the direction of the Commission, establish automated systems for monitoring, screening, and analyzing security-based swap data;

(F)   maintain the privacy of any and all security-based swap transaction information that the security-based swap data repository receives from a security-based swap dealer, counterparty, or any other registered entity; and

(G)   on a confidential basis pursuant to section 24, upon request, and after notifying the Commission of the request, make available security-based swap data obtained by the security-based swap data repository, including individual counterparty trade and position data, to—

(i)   each appropriate prudential regulator;

(ii)   the Financial Stability Oversight Council;

(iii)   the Commodity Futures Trading Commission;

(iv)   the Department of Justice; and

(v)   any other person that the Commission determines to be appropriate, including—

(I)   foreign financial supervisors (including foreign futures authorities);

(II)   foreign central banks;

(III)   foreign ministries; and

(IV)   other foreign authorities.

(H)   Confidentiality agreement.—Before the security-based swap data repository may share information with any entity described in subparagraph (G), the security-based swap data repository shall receive a written agreement from each entity stating that the entity shall abide by the confidentiality requirements described in section 24 relating to the information on security-based swap transactions that is provided.

(6)   Designation of chief compliance officer.—

(A)   In general.—

Each security-based swap data repository shall designate an individual to serve as a chief compliance officer.

(B) Duties.—

The chief compliance officer shall—

(i) report directly to the board or to the senior officer of the security-based swap data repository;

(ii) review the compliance of the security-based swap data repository with respect to the requirements and core principles described in this subsection;

(iii) in consultation with the board of the security-based swap data repository, a body performing a function similar to the board of the security-based swap data repository, or the senior officer of the security-based swap data repository, resolve any conflicts of interest that may arise;

(iv) be responsible for administering each policy and procedure that is required to be established pursuant to this section;

(v) ensure compliance with this title (including regulations) relating to agreements, contracts, or transactions, including each rule prescribed by the Commission under this section;

(vi) establish procedures for the remediation of noncompliance issues identified by the chief compliance officer through any—

(I) compliance office review;

(II) look-back;

(III) internal or external audit finding;

(IV) self-reported error; or

(V) validated complaint; and

(vii) establish and follow appropriate procedures for the handling, management response, remediation, retesting, and closing of noncompliance issues.

(C) Annual reports.—

(i) In general.—

In accordance with rules prescribed by the Commission, the chief compliance officer shall annually prepare and sign a report that contains a description of—

(I) the compliance of the security-based swap data repository of the chief compliance officer with respect to this title (including regulations); and

(II) each policy and procedure of the security-based swap data repository of the chief compliance officer (including the code of ethics and conflict of interest policies of the security-based swap data repository).

(ii) Requirements.—

A compliance report under clause (i) shall—

(I) accompany each appropriate financial report of the security-based swap data repository that is required to be furnished to the Commission pursuant to this section; and

(II) include a certification that, under penalty of law, the compliance report is accurate and complete.

(7) Core principles applicable to security-based swap data repositories.—

(A) Antitrust considerations.—

Unless necessary or appropriate to achieve the purposes of this title, the swap data repository shall not—

    (i)   adopt any rule or take any action that results in any unreasonable restraint of trade; or

    (ii)   impose any material anticompetitive burden on the trading, clearing, or reporting of transactions.

(B)   Governance arrangements.—

Each security-based swap data repository shall establish governance arrangements that are transparent—

    (i)   to fulfill public interest requirements; and

    (ii)   to support the objectives of the Federal Government, owners, and participants.

(C)   Conflicts of interest.—

Each security-based swap data repository shall—

    (i)   establish and enforce rules to minimize conflicts of interest in the decision-making process of the security-based swap data repository; and

    (ii)   establish a process for resolving any conflicts of interest described in clause (i).

(D)   Additional duties developed by commission.—

    (i)   In general.—

The Commission may develop 1 or more additional duties applicable to security-based swap data repositories.

    (ii)   Consideration of evolving standards.—

In developing additional duties under subparagraph (A), the Commission may take into consideration any evolving standard of the United States or the international community.

    (iii)   Additional duties for commission designees.—

The Commission shall establish additional duties for any registrant described in section 13(m)(2)(C) in order to minimize conflicts of interest, protect data, ensure compliance, and guarantee the safety and security of the security-based swap data repository.

(8)   Required registration for security-based swap data repositories.—

Any person that is required to be registered as a security-based swap data repository under this subsection shall register with the Commission, regardless of whether that person is also licensed under the Commodity Exchange Act as a swap data repository.

(9)   Rules.—

The Commission shall adopt rules governing persons that are registered under this subsection.

(o)   Beneficial Ownership—For purposes of this section and section 16, a person shall be deemed to acquire beneficial ownership of an equity security based on the purchase or sale of a security-based swap, only to the extent that the Commission, by rule, determines after consultation with the prudential regulators and the Secretary of the Treasury, that the purchase or sale of the security-based swap, or class of security-based swap, provides incidents of ownership comparable to direct ownership of the equity security, and that it is necessary to achieve the purposes of this section that the purchase or sale of the security-based swaps, or class of security-based swap, be deemed the acquisition of beneficial ownership of the equity security.

(p)   Disclosures relating to conflict minerals originating in the Democratic Republic of the Congo

    (1)   Regulations.—

(A)   In general.—

Not later than 270 days after July 21, 2010, the Commission shall promulgate regulations requiring any person described in paragraph (2) to disclose annually, beginning with the person's first full fiscal year that begins after the date of promulgation of such regulations, whether conflict minerals that are necessary as described in paragraph (2)(B), in the year for which such reporting is required, did originate in the Democratic Republic of the Congo or an adjoining country and, in cases in which such conflict minerals did originate in any such country, submit to the Commission a report that includes, with respect to the period covered by the report—

(i)   a description of the measures taken by the person to exercise due diligence on the source and chain of custody of such minerals, which measures shall include an independent private sector audit of such report submitted through the Commission that is conducted in accordance with standards established by the Comptroller General of the United States, in accordance with rules promulgated by the Commission, in consultation with the Secretary of State; and

(ii)   a description of the products manufactured or contracted to be manufactured that are not DRC conflict free ("DRC conflict free" is defined to mean the products that do not contain minerals that directly or indirectly finance or benefit armed groups in the Democratic Republic of the Congo or an adjoining country), the entity that conducted the independent private sector audit in accordance with clause (i), the facilities used to process the conflict minerals, the country of origin of the conflict minerals, and the efforts to determine the mine or location of origin with the greatest possible specificity.

(B)   Certification.—

The person submitting a report under subparagraph (A) shall certify the audit described in clause (i) of such subparagraph that is included in such report. Such a certified audit shall constitute a critical component of due diligence in establishing the source and chain of custody of such minerals.

(C)   Unreliable determination.—

If a report required to be submitted by a person under subparagraph (A) relies on a determination of an independent private sector audit, as described under subparagraph (A)(i), or other due diligence processes previously determined by the Commission to be unreliable, the report shall not satisfy the requirements of the regulations promulgated under subparagraph (A)(i).

(D)   DRC conflict free.—

For purposes of this paragraph, a product may be labeled as "DRC conflict free" if the product does not contain conflict minerals that directly or indirectly finance or benefit armed groups in the Democratic Republic of the Congo or an adjoining country.

(E)   Information available to the public.—

Each person described under paragraph (2) shall make available to the public on the Internet website of such person the information disclosed by such person under subparagraph (A).

(2)   Person described.—

A person is described in this paragraph if—

(A)   the person is required to file reports with the Commission pursuant to paragraph (1)(A); and

(B)   conflict minerals are necessary to the functionality or production of a product manufactured by such person.

(3)   Revisions and waivers.—

The Commission shall revise or temporarily waive the requirements described in paragraph (1) if the President transmits to the Commission a determination that—

(A)   such revision or waiver is in the national security interest of the United States and the President includes the reasons therefor; and

(B)   establishes a date, not later than 2 years after the initial publication of such exemption, on which such exemption shall expire.

(4)   Termination of disclosure requirements.—

The requirements of paragraph (1) shall terminate on the date on which the President determines and certifies to the appropriate congressional committees, but in no case earlier than the date that is one day after the end of the 5-year period beginning on July 21, 2010, that no armed groups continue to be directly involved and benefitting from commercial activity involving conflict minerals.

(5)   Definitions.—

For purposes of this subsection, the terms "adjoining country", "appropriate congressional committees", "armed group", and "conflict mineral" have the meaning given those terms under section 1502 of the Dodd-Frank Wall Street Reform and Consumer Protection Act.

(q)   Disclosure of Payments by Resource Extraction Issuers.—

(1)   Definitions.—In this subsection—

(A)   the term "commercial development of oil, natural gas, or minerals" includes exploration, extraction, processing, export, and other significant actions relating to oil, natural gas, or minerals, or the acquisition of a license for any such activity, as determined by the Commission;

(B)   the term "foreign government" means a foreign government, a department, agency, or instrumentality of a foreign government, or a company owned by a foreign government, as determined by the Commission;

(C)   the term "payment"—

(i)   means a payment that is—

(I)   made to further the commercial development of oil, natural gas, or minerals; and

(II)   not de minimis; and

(ii)   includes taxes, royalties, fees (including license fees), production entitlements, bonuses, and other material benefits, that the Commission, consistent with the guidelines of the Extractive Industries Transparency Initiative (to the extent practicable), determines are part of the commonly recognized revenue stream for the commercial development of oil, natural gas, or minerals;

(D)   the term "resource extraction issuer" means an issuer that—

(i)   is required to file an annual report with the Commission; and

(ii)   engages in the commercial development of oil, natural gas, or minerals;

(E)   the term "interactive data format" means an electronic data format in which pieces of information are identified using an interactive data standard; and

(F)   the term "interactive data standard" means a standardized list of electronic tags that mark information included in the annual report of a resource extraction issuer.

(2)   Disclosure.—

(A)   Information required.—

Not later than 270 days after the date of enactment of the Dodd-Frank Wall Street Reform and Consumer Protection Act, the Commission shall issue final rules that require each resource extraction issuer to include in an annual report of the resource extraction issuer information relating to any payment made by the resource extraction issuer, a subsidiary of the resource extraction issuer, or an entity under the control of the resource extraction issuer to a foreign government or the Federal Government for the purpose of the commercial development of oil, natural gas, or minerals, including—

(i)   the type and total amount of such payments made for each project of the resource extraction issuer relating to the commercial development of oil, natural gas, or minerals; and

(ii)   the type and total amount of such payments made to each government.

(B)   Consultation in rulemaking.—

In issuing rules under subparagraph (A), the Commission may consult with any agency or entity that the Commission determines is relevant.

(C)   Interactive data format.—

The rules issued under subparagraph (A) shall require that the information included in the annual report of a resource extraction issuer be submitted in an interactive data format.

(D)   Interactive data standard.—

(i)   In general.—

The rules issued under subparagraph (A) shall establish an interactive data standard for the information included in the annual report of a resource extraction issuer.

(ii)   Electronic tags.—

The interactive data standard shall include electronic tags that identify, for any payments made by a resource extraction issuer to a foreign government or the Federal Government—

(I)   the total amounts of the payments, by category;

(II)   the currency used to make the payments;

(III)   the financial period in which the payments were made;

(IV)   the business segment of the resource extraction issuer that made the payments;

(V)   the government that received the payments, and the country in which the government is located;

(VI)   the project of the resource extraction issuer to which the payments relate; and

(VII) such other information as the Commission may determine is necessary or appropriate in the public interest or for the protection of investors.

(E)   International transparency efforts.—

To the extent practicable, the rules issued under subparagraph (A) shall support the commitment of the Federal Government to international transparency promotion efforts relating to the commercial development of oil, natural gas, or minerals.

(F)   Effective date.—

With respect to each resource extraction issuer, the final rules issued under subparagraph (A) shall take effect on the date on which the resource extraction issuer is required to submit an annual report relating to the fiscal year of the resource extraction issuer that ends not earlier than 1 year after the date on which the Commission issues final rules under subparagraph (A).

(3)   Public availability of information.—

(A)   In general.—

To the extent practicable, the Commission shall make available online, to the public, a compilation of the information required to be submitted under the rules issued under paragraph (2)(A).

(B) Other information.—

Nothing in this paragraph shall require the Commission to make available online information other than the information required to be submitted under the rules issued under paragraph (2)(A).

(4) Authorization of appropriations.—

There are authorized to be appropriated to the Commission such sums as may be necessary to carry out this subsection.

(r) Disclosure of Certain Activities Relating to Iran.—

(1) In general.—Each issuer required to file an annual or quarterly report under subsection (a) shall disclose in that report the information required by paragraph (2) if, during the period covered by the report, the issuer or any affiliate of the issuer—

(A) knowingly engaged in an activity described in subsection (a) or (b) of section 5 of the Iran Sanctions Act of 1996 (Public Law 104–172; 50 U.S.C. 1701 note);

(B) knowingly engaged in an activity described in subsection (c)(2) of section 104 of the Comprehensive Iran Sanctions, Accountability, and Divestment Act of 2010 (22 U.S.C. 8513) or a transaction described in subsection (d)(1) of that section;

(C) knowingly engaged in an activity described in section 105A(b)(2) of that Act; or

(D) knowingly conducted any transaction or dealing with—

(i) any person the property and interests in property of which are blocked pursuant to Executive Order No. 13224 (66 Fed. Reg. 49079; relating to blocking property and prohibiting transactions with persons who commit, threaten to commit, or support terrorism);

(ii) any person the property and interests in property of which are blocked pursuant to Order No. 13382 (70 Fed. Reg. 38567; relating to blocking of property of weapons of mass destruction proliferators and their supporters); or

(iii) any person or entity identified under section 560.304 of title 31, Code of Federal Regulations (relating to the definition of the Government of Iran) without the specific authorization of a Federal department or agency.

(2) Information required.—If an issuer or an affiliate of the issuer has engaged in any activity described in paragraph (1), the issuer shall disclose a detailed description of each such activity, including—

(A) the nature and extent of the activity;

(B) the gross revenues and net profits, if any, attributable to the activity; and

(C) whether the issuer or the affiliate of the issuer (as the case may be) intends to continue the activity.

(3) Notice of disclosures.—If an issuer reports under paragraph (1) that the issuer or an affiliate of the issuer has knowingly engaged in any activity described in that paragraph, the issuer shall separately file with the Commission, concurrently with the annual or quarterly report under subsection (a), a notice that the disclosure of that activity has been included in that annual or quarterly report that identifies the issuer and contains the information required by paragraph (2).

(4) Public disclosure of information.—Upon receiving a notice under paragraph (3) that an annual or quarterly report includes a disclosure of an activity described in paragraph (1), the Commission shall promptly—

(A) transmit the report to—

(i)   the President;

(ii)   the Committee on Foreign Affairs and the Committee on Financial Services of the House of Representatives; and

(iii) the Committee on Foreign Relations and the Committee on Banking, Housing, and Urban Affairs of the Senate; and

(B)   make the information provided in the disclosure and the notice available to the public by posting the information on the Internet website of the Commission.

(5)   Investigations.—Upon receiving a report under paragraph (4) that includes a disclosure of an activity described in paragraph (1) (other than an activity described in subparagraph (D)(iii) of that paragraph), the President shall—

(A)   initiate an investigation into the possible imposition of sanctions under the Iran Sanctions Act of 1996 (Public Law 104–172; 50 U.S.C. 1701 note), section 104 or 105A of the Comprehensive Iran Sanctions, Accountability, and Divestment Act of 2010, an Executive order specified in clause (i) or (ii) of paragraph (1)(D), or any other provision of law relating to the imposition of sanctions with respect to Iran, as applicable; and

(B)   not later than 180 days after initiating such an investigation, make a determination with respect to whether sanctions should be imposed with respect to the issuer or the affiliate of the issuer (as the case may be).

(6)   Sunset.—The provisions of this subsection shall terminate on the date that is 30 days after the date on which the President makes the certification described in section 401(a) of the Comprehensive Iran Sanctions, Accountability, and Divestment Act of 2010 (22 U.S.C. 8551(a)).

(b)   Effective Date.—The amendment made by subsection (a) shall take effect with respect to reports required to be filed with the Securities and Exchange Commission after the date that is 180 days after the date of the enactment of this Act.

Reporting and Recordkeeping for Certain Security-Based Swaps

Sec. 13A.   (a)   Required Reporting of Security-based Swaps Not Accepted by Any Clearing Agency or Derivatives Clearing Organization.—

(1)   In general.—

Each security-based swap that is not accepted for clearing by any clearing agency or derivatives clearing organization shall be reported to—

(A)   a security-based swap data repository described in section 13(n); or

(B)   in the case in which there is no security-based swap data repository that would accept the security-based swap, to the Commission pursuant to this section within such time period as the Commission may by rule or regulation prescribe.

(2)   Transition rule for preenactment security-based swaps.—

(A)   Security-based swaps entered into before the date of enactment of the wall street transparency and accountability act of 2010.—

Each security-based swap entered into before the date of enactment of the Wall Street Transparency and Accountability Act of 2010, the terms of which have not expired as of the date of enactment of that Act, shall be reported to a registered security-based swap data repository or the Commission by a date that is not later than—

(i)   30 days after issuance of the interim final rule; or

(ii)   such other period as the Commission determines to be appropriate.

(B)   Commission rulemaking.—

The Commission shall promulgate an interim final rule within 90 days of the date of enactment of this section providing for the reporting of each security-based swap entered into before the date of enactment as referenced in subparagraph (A).

(C)   Effective date.—

The reporting provisions described in this section shall be effective upon the date of the enactment of this section.

(3)   Reporting obligations.—

(A)   Security-based swaps in which only 1 counterparty is a security-based swap dealer or major security-based swap participant.—

With respect to a security-based swap in which only 1 counterparty is a security-based swap dealer or major security-based swap participant, the security-based swap dealer or major security-based swap participant shall report the security-based swap as required under paragraphs (1) and (2).

(B)   Security-based swaps in which 1 counterparty is a security-based swap dealer and the other a major security-based swap participant.—

With respect to a security-based swap in which counterparty is a security-based swap dealer and the other a major security-based swap participant, the security-based swap dealer shall report the security-based swap as required under paragraphs (1) and (2).

(C)   Other security-based swaps.—

With respect to any other security-based swap not described in subparagraph (A) or (B), the counterparties to the security-based swap shall select a counterparty to report the security-based swap as required under paragraphs (1) and (2).

(b)   Duties of Certain Individuals.—Any individual or entity that enters into a security-based swap shall meet each requirement described in subsection (c) if the individual or entity did not—

(1)   clear the security-based swap in accordance with section 3C(a)(1); or

(2)   have the data regarding the security-based swap accepted by a security-based swap data repository in accordance with rules (including timeframes) adopted by the Commission under this title.

(c)   Requirements.—An individual or entity described in subsection (b) shall—

(1)   upon written request from the Commission, provide reports regarding the security-based swaps held by the individual or entity to the Commission in such form and in such manner as the Commission may request; and

(2)   maintain books and records pertaining to the security-based swaps held by the individual or entity in such form, in such manner, and for such period as the Commission may require, which shall be open to inspection by—

(A)   any representative of the Commission;

(B)   an appropriate prudential regulator;

(C)   the Commodity Futures Trading Commission;

(D)   the Financial Stability Oversight Council; and

(E)   the Department of Justice.

(d)   Identical Data.—In prescribing rules under this section, the Commission shall require individuals and entities described in subsection (b) to submit to the Commission a report that contains data that is not less comprehensive than the data required to be collected by security-based swap data repositories under this title.

Proxies

Sec. 14. (a)(1) It shall be unlawful for any person, by the use of the mails or by any means or instrumentality of interstate commerce or of any facility of a national securities exchange or otherwise, in contravention of such rules and regulations as the Commission may prescribe as necessary or appropriate in the public interest or for the protection of investors, to solicit or to permit the use of his name to solicit any proxy or consent or authorization in respect of any security (other than an exempted security) registered pursuant to section 12 of this Act.

(2)   The rules and regulations prescribed by the Commission under paragraph (1) may include—

(A)   a requirement that a solicitation of proxy, consent, or authorization by (or on behalf of) an issuer include a nominee submitted by a shareholder to serve on the board of directors of the issuer; and

(B)   a requirement that an issuer follow a certain procedure in relation to a solicitation described in subparagraph (A).

(b)(1)   It shall be unlawful for any member of a national securities exchange, or any broker or dealer registered under this Act, or any bank, association, or other entity that exercises fiduciary powers, in contravention of such rules and regulations as the Commission may prescribe as necessary or appropriate in the public interest or for the protection of investors, to give, or to refrain from giving a proxy, consent, authorization, or information statement in respect of any security registered pursuant to section 12 of this Act, or any security issued by an investment company registered under the Investment Company Act of 1940, and carried for the account of a customer.

(2)   With respect to banks, the rules and regulations prescribed by the Commission under paragraph (1) shall not require the disclosure of the names of beneficial owners of securities in an account held by the bank on December 28, 1985, unless the beneficial owner consents to the disclosure. The provisions of this paragraph shall not apply in the case of a bank which the Commission finds has not made a good faith effort to obtain such consent from such beneficial owners.

(c)   Unless proxies, consents, or authorizations in respect of a security registered pursuant to section 12 of this Act, or a security issued by an investment company registered under the Investment Company Act of 1940, are solicited by or on behalf of the management of the issuer from the holders of record of such security in accordance with the rules and regulations prescribed under subsection (a) of this section, prior to any annual or other meeting of the holders of such security, such issuer shall, in accordance with rules and regulations prescribed by the Commission, file with the Commission and transmit to all holders of record of such security information substantially equivalent to the information which would be required to be transmitted if a solicitation were made, but no information shall be required to be filed or transmitted pursuant to this subsection before July 1, 1964.

(d)(1)   It shall be unlawful for any person, directly or indirectly, by use of the mails or by any means or instrumentality of interstate commerce or of any facility of a national securities exchange or otherwise, to make a tender offer for, or a request or invitation for tenders of, any class of any equity security which is registered pursuant to section 12 of this Act, or any equity security of an insurance company which would have been required to be so registered except for the exemption contained in section 12(g)(2)(G) of this Act, or any equity security issued by a closed-end investment company registered under the Investment Company Act of 1940, if, after consummation thereof, such person would, directly or indirectly, be the beneficial owner of more than 5 per centum of such class, unless at the time copies of the offer or request or invitation are first published or sent or given to security holders such person has filed with the Commission a statement containing such of the information specified in section 13(d) of this Act, and such additional information as the Commission may by rules and regulations prescribe as necessary or appropriate in the public interest or for the protection of investors. All requests or invitations for tenders or advertisements making a tender offer or requesting or inviting tenders of such a security shall be filed as a part of such statement and shall contain such of the information contained in such statement as the Commission may by rules and regulations prescribe. Copies of any additional material soliciting or requesting such tender offers subsequent to the initial solicitation or request shall contain such information as the Commission may by rules and regulations prescribe as necessary or appropriate in the public interest or for the protection of investors, and shall be filed with the Commission not later than the time copies of such material are first published or sent or given to security holders. Copies of all statements, in the form in which such material is furnished to security holders and the Commission, shall be sent to the issuer not later than the date such material is first published or sent or given to any security holders.

(2) When two or more persons act as a partnership, limited partnership, syndicate, or other group for the purpose of acquiring, holding, or disposing of securities of an issuer, such syndicate or group shall be deemed a "person" for purposes of this subsection.

(3) In determining, for purposes of this subsection, any percentage of a class of any security, such class shall be deemed to consist of the amount of the outstanding securities of such class, exclusive of any securities of such class held by or for the account of the issuer or a subsidiary of the issuer.

(4) Any solicitation or recommendation to the holders of such a security to accept or reject a tender offer or request or invitation for tenders shall be made in accordance with such rules and regulations as the Commission may prescribe as necessary or appropriate in the public interest or for the protection of investors.

(5) Securities deposited pursuant to a tender offer or request or invitation for tenders may be withdrawn by or on behalf of the depositor at any time until the expiration of seven days after the time definitive copies of the offer or request or invitation are first published or sent or given to security holders, and at any time after sixty days from the date of the original tender offer or request or invitation, except as the Commission may otherwise prescribe by rules, regulations, or order as necessary or appropriate in the public interest or for the protection of investors.

(6) Where any person makes a tender offer, or request or invitation for tenders, for less than all the outstanding equity securities of a class, and where a greater number of securities is deposited pursuant thereto within ten days after copies of the offer or request or invitation are first published or sent or given to security holders than such person is bound or willing to take up and pay for, the securities taken up shall be taken up as nearly as may be pro rata, disregarding fractions, according to the number of securities deposited by each depositor. The provisions of this subsection shall also apply to securities deposited within ten days after notice of an increase in the consideration offered to security holders, as described in paragraph (7), is first published or sent or given to security holders.

(7) Where any person varies the terms of a tender offer or request or invitation for tenders before the expiration thereof by increasing the consideration offered to holders of such securities, such person shall pay the increased consideration to each security holder whose securities are taken up and paid for pursuant to the tender offer or request or invitation for tenders whether or not such securities have been taken up by such person before the variation of the tender offer or request or invitation.

(8) The provisions of this subsection shall not apply to any offer for, or request or invitation for tenders of, any security—

(A) if the acquisition of such security, together with all other acquisitions by the same person of securities of the same class during the preceding twelve months, would not exceed 2 per centum of that class;

(B) by the issuer of such security; or

(C) which the Commission, by rules or regulations or by order, shall exempt from the provisions of this subsection as not entered into for the purpose of, and not having the effect of, changing or influencing the control of the issuer or otherwise as not comprehended within the purposes of this subsection.

(e) It shall be unlawful for any person to make any untrue statement of a material fact or omit to state any material fact necessary in order to make the statements made, in the light of the circumstances under which they are made, not misleading, or to engage in any fraudulent, deceptive, or manipulative acts or practices, in connection with any tender offer or request or invitation for tenders, or any solicitation of security holders in opposition to or in favor of any such offer, request, or invitation. The Commission shall, for the purposes of this subsection, by rules and regulations define, and prescribe means reasonably designed to prevent, such acts and practices as are fraudulent, deceptive, or manipulative.

(f) If, pursuant to any arrangement or understanding with the person or persons acquiring securities in a transaction subject to subsection (d) of this section or subsection (d) of section 13 of this Act, any persons are to be elected or designated as directors of the issuer, otherwise than at a meeting of security holders, and the persons so elected or designated will constitute a majority of the directors of the issuer, then, prior to the time any such person takes office as a director, and in accordance with rules and regulations prescribed by the Commission, the issuer shall file with the Commission, and transmit to all holders of record of securities of the issuer who would be entitled to vote at a meeting for election of directors, information substantially equivalent to the information which would be required by subsection (a) or (c) of this section to be transmitted if such person or persons were nominees for election as directors at a meeting of such security holders.

(g)(1)(A) At the time of filing such preliminary proxy solicitation material as the Commission may require by rule pursuant to subsection (a) of this section that concerns an acquisition, merger, consolidation, or proposed sale or other disposition of substantially all the assets of a company, the person making such filing, other than a company registered under the Investment Company Act of 1940, shall pay to the Commission the following fees:

(i) for preliminary proxy solicitation material involving an acquisition, merger, or consolidation, if there is a proposed payment of cash or transfer of securities or property to shareholders, a fee at a rate that, subject to paragraphs (4) is equal to $92 per $1,000,000 of such proposed payment, or of the value of such securities or other property proposed to be transferred; and

(ii) for preliminary proxy solicitation material involving a proposed sale or other disposition of substantially all of the assets of a company, a fee at a rate that, subject to paragraphs (4) is equal to $92 per $1,000,000 of the cash or of the value of any securities or other property proposed to be received upon such sale or disposition.

(B) The fee imposed under subparagraph (A) shall be reduced with respect to securities in an amount equal to any fee paid to the Commission with respect to such securities in connection with the proposed transaction under section 6(b) of the Securities Act of 1933, or the fee paid under that section shall be reduced in an amount equal to the fee paid to the Commission in connection with such transaction under this subsection. Where two or more companies involved in an acquisition, merger, consolidation, sale, or other disposition of substantially all the assets of a company must file such proxy material with the Commission, each shall pay a proportionate share of such fee.

(2) At the time of filing such preliminary information statement as the Commission may require by rule pursuant to subsection (c) of this section, the issuer shall pay to the Commission the same fee as required for preliminary proxy solicitation material under paragraph (1) of this subsection.

(3) At the time of filing such statement as the Commission may require by rule pursuant to subsection (d)(1) of this section, the person making the filing shall pay to the Commission a fee at a rate that, subject to paragraph (4), is equal to $92 per $1,000,000 of the aggregate amount of cash or of the value of securities or other property proposed to be offered. The fee shall be reduced with respect to securities in an amount equal to any fee paid with respect to such securities in connection with the proposed transaction under section 6(b) of the Securities Act of 1933, or the fee paid under that section shall be reduced in an amount equal to the fee paid to the Commission in connection with such transaction under this subsection.

(4) Annual adjustment.—

For each fiscal year, the Commission shall by order adjust the rate required by paragraphs (1) and (3) for such fiscal year to a rate that is equal to the rate (expressed in dollars per million) that is applicable under section 6(b) of the Securities Act of 1933 for such fiscal year.

(5) Fee collection.—

Fees collected pursuant to this subsection for fiscal year 2012 and each fiscal year thereafter shall be deposited and credited as general revenue of the Treasury and shall not be available for obligation.

(6) Review; effective date; publication.—

In exercising its authority under this subsection, the Commission shall not be required to comply with the provisions of section 553 of title 5, United States Code. An adjusted rate prescribed under paragraph (4) shall be published and take effect in accordance with section 6(b) of the Securities Act of 1933.

(7)   pro rata application.—

The rates per $1,000,000 required by this subsection shall be applied pro rata to amounts and balances of less than $1,000,000.

(8)   Notwithstanding any other provision of law, the Commission may impose fees, charges, or prices for matters not involving any acquisition, merger, consolidation, sale, or other disposition of assets described in this subsection, as authorized by section 9701 of Title 31, United States Code, or otherwise.

(h)   Proxy Solicitations and Tender Offers in Connection With Limited Partnership Rollup Transactions.—

(1)   Proxy rules to contain special provisions.—

It shall be unlawful for any person to solicit any proxy, consent, or authorization concerning a limited partnership rollup transaction, or to make any tender offer in furtherance of a limited partnership rollup transaction, unless such transaction is conducted in accordance with rules prescribed by the Commission under subsections (a) and (d) of this section as required by this subsection. Such rules shall—

(A)   permit any holder of a security that is the subject of the proposed limited partnership rollup transaction to engage in preliminary communications for the purpose of determining whether to solicit proxies, consents, or authorizations in opposition to the proposed limited partnership rollup transaction, without regard to whether any such communication would otherwise be considered a solicitation of proxies, and without being required to file soliciting material with the Commission prior to making that determination, except that—

(i)   nothing in this subparagraph shall be construed to limit the application of any provision of this Act prohibiting, or reasonably designed to prevent, fraudulent, deceptive, or manipulative acts or practices under this Act; and

(ii)   any holder of not less than 5 percent of the outstanding securities that are the subject of the proposed limited partnership rollup transaction who engages in the business of buying and selling limited partnership interests in the secondary market shall be required to disclose such ownership interests and any potential conflicts of interests in such preliminary communications;

(B)   require the issuer to provide to holders of the securities that are the subject of the limited partnership rollup transaction such list of the holders of the issuer's securities as the Commission may determine in such form and subject to such terms and conditions as the Commission may specify;

(C)   prohibit compensating any person soliciting proxies, consents, or authorizations directly from security holders concerning such a limited partnership rollup transaction—

(i)   on the basis of whether the solicited proxy, consent, or authorization either approves or disapproves the proposed limited partnership rollup transaction; or

(ii)   contingent on the approval, disapproval, or completion of the limited partnership rollup transaction;

(D)   set forth disclosure requirements for soliciting material distributed in connection with a limited partnership rollup transaction, including requirements for clear, concise, and comprehensible disclosure with respect to—

(i)   any changes in the business plan, voting rights, form of ownership interest, or the compensation of the general partner in the proposed limited partnership rollup transaction from each of the original limited partnerships;

(ii) the conflicts of interest, if any, of the general partner;

(iii) whether it is expected that there will be a significant difference between the exchange values of the limited partnerships and the trading price of the securities to be issued in the limited partnership rollup transaction;

(iv) the valuation of the limited partnerships and the method used to determine the value of the interests of the limited partners to be exchanged for the securities in the limited partnership rollup transaction;

(v) the differing risks and effects of the limited partnership rollup transaction for investors in different limited partnerships proposed to be included, and the risks and effects of completing the limited partnership rollup transaction with less than all limited partnerships;

(vi) the statement by the general partner required under subparagraph (E);

(vii) such other matters deemed necessary or appropriate by the Commission;

(E) require a statement by the general partner as to whether the proposed limited partnership rollup transaction is fair or unfair to investors in each limited partnership, a discussion of the basis for that conclusion, and an evaluation and a description by the general partner of alternatives to the limited partnership rollup transaction, such as liquidation;

(F) provide that, if the general partner or sponsor has obtained any opinion (other than an opinion of counsel), appraisal, or report that is prepared by an outside party and that is materially related to the limited partnership rollup transaction, such soliciting materials shall contain or be accompanied by clear, concise, and comprehensible disclosure with respect to—

(i) the analysis of the transaction, scope of review, preparation of the opinion, and basis for and methods of arriving at conclusions, and any representations and undertakings with respect thereto;

(ii) the identity and qualifications of the person who prepared the opinion, the method of selection of such person, and any material past, existing, or contemplated relationships between the person or any of its affiliates and the general partner, sponsor, successor, or any other affiliate;

(iii) any compensation of the preparer of such opinion, appraisal, or report that is contingent on the transaction's approval or completion; and

(iv) any limitations imposed by the issuer on the access afforded to such preparer to the issuer's personnel, premises, and relevant books and records;

(G) provide that, if the general partner or sponsor has obtained any opinion, appraisal, or report as described in subparagraph (F) from any person whose compensation is contingent on the transaction's approval or completion or who has not been given access by the issuer to its personnel and premises and relevant books and records, the general partner or sponsor shall state the reasons therefor;

(H) provide that, if the general partner or sponsor has not obtained any opinion on the fairness of the proposed limited partnership rollup transaction to investors in each of the affected partnerships, such soliciting materials shall contain or be accompanied by a statement of such partner's or sponsor's reasons for concluding that such an opinion is not necessary in order to permit the limited partners to make an informed decision on the proposed transaction;

(I) require that the soliciting material include a clear, concise, and comprehensible summary of the limited partnership rollup transaction (including a summary of the matters referred to in clauses (i) through (vii) of subparagraph (D) and a summary of the matter referred to in subparagraphs (F), (G), and (H)), with the risks of the limited partnership rollup transaction set forth prominently in the fore part thereof;

(J) provide that any solicitation or offering period with respect to any proxy solicitation, tender offer, or information statement in a limited partnership rollup transaction shall be for not less than the lesser of 60 calendar days or the maximum number of days permitted under applicable State law; and

(K) contain such other provisions as the Commission determines to be necessary or appropriate for the protection of investors in limited partnership rollup transactions.

(2) Exemptions.—

The Commission may, consistent with the public interest, the protection of investors, and the purposes of this Act, exempt by rule or order any security or class of securities, any transaction or class of transactions, or any person or class of persons, in whole or in part, conditionally or unconditionally, from the requirements imposed pursuant to paragraph (1) or from the definition contained in paragraph (4).

(3) Effect on commission authority.—

Nothing in this subsection limits the authority of the Commission under subsection (a) or (d) of this section or any other provision of this Act or precludes the Commission from imposing, under subsection (a) or (d) of this section or any other provision of this Act, a remedy or procedure required to be imposed under this subsection.

(4) Definition of limited partnership rollup transaction.—

Except as provided in paragraph (5), as used in this subsection, the term "limited partnership rollup transaction" means a transaction involving the combination or reorganization of one or more limited partnerships, directly or indirectly, in which—

(A) some or all of the investors in any of such limited partnerships will receive new securities, or securities in another entity, that will be reported under a transaction reporting plan declared effective before December 17, 1993, by the Commission under section 11A of this Act;

(B) any of the investors' limited partnership securities are not, as of the date of filing, reported under a transaction reporting plan declared effective before December 17, 1993, by the Commission under section 11A of this Act;

(C) investors in any of the limited partnerships involved in the transaction are subject to a significant adverse change with respect to voting rights, the term of existence of the entity, management compensation, or investment objectives; and

(D) any of such investors are not provided an option to receive or retain a security under substantially the same terms and conditions as the original issue.

(5) Exclusions from definition.—

Notwithstanding paragraph (4), the term "limited partnership rollup transaction" does not include—

(A) a transaction that involves only a limited partnership or partnerships having an operating policy or practice of retaining cash available for distribution and reinvesting proceeds from the sale, financing, or refinancing of assets in accordance with such criteria as the Commission determines appropriate;

(B) a transaction involving only limited partnerships wherein the interests of the limited partners are repurchased, recalled, or exchanged in accordance with the terms of the preexisting limited partnership agreements for securities in an operating company specifically identified at the time of the formation of the original limited partnership;

(C) a transaction in which the securities to be issued or exchanged are not required to be and are not registered under the Securities Act of 1933;

(D) a transaction that involves only issuers that are not required to register or report under section 12 of this Act, both before and after the transaction;

(E) a transaction, except as the Commission may otherwise provide by rule for the protection of investors, involving the combination or reorganization of one or more limited partnerships in which a non-affiliated party succeeds to the interests of a general partner or sponsor, if—

> (i)   such action is approved by not less than 66⅔ percent of the outstanding units of each of the participating limited partnerships; and

> (ii)   as a result of the transaction, the existing general partners will receive only compensation to which they are entitled as expressly provided for in the preexisting limited partnership agreements; or

(F)   a transaction, except as the Commission may otherwise provide by rule for the protection of investors, in which the securities offered to investors are securities of another entity that are reported under a transaction reporting plan declared effective before December 17, 1993, by the Commission under section 11A of this Act, if—

> (i)   such other entity was formed, and such class of securities was reported and regularly traded, not less than 12 months before the date on which soliciting material is mailed to investors; and

> (ii)   the securities of that entity issued to investors in the transaction do not exceed 20 percent of the total outstanding securities of the entity, exclusive of any securities of such class held by or for the account of the entity or a subsidiary of the entity.

(i)   Disclosure of pay versus performance.—

Disclosure of Pay Versus Performance—The Commission shall, by rule, require each issuer to disclose in any proxy or consent solicitation material for an annual meeting of the shareholders of the issuer a clear description of any compensation required to be disclosed by the issuer, for any issuer other than an emerging growth company under Item 402 of Regulation S–K (or any successor thereto), including information that shows the relationship between executive compensation actually paid and the financial performance of the issuer, taking into account any change in the value of the shares of stock and dividends of the issuer and any distributions. The disclosure under this subsection may include a graphic representation of the information required to be disclosed.

(j)   Disclosure of Hedging by Employees and Directors.—

Disclosure of Hedging by Employees and Directors.—The Commission shall, by rule, require each issuer to disclose in any proxy or consent solicitation material for an annual meeting of the shareholders of the issuer whether any employee or member of the board of directors of the issuer, or any designee of such employee or member, is permitted to purchase financial instruments (including prepaid variable forward contracts, equity swaps, collars, and exchange funds) that are designed to hedge or offset any decrease in the market value of equity securities—

(1)   granted to the employee or member of the board of directors by the issuer as part of the compensation of the employee or member of the board of directors; or

(2)   held, directly or indirectly, by the employee or member of the board of directors.

Shareholder Approval of Executive Compensation

Sec. 14A.   (a)   Separate Resolution Required.—

(1)   In general.—

Not less frequently than once every 3 years, a proxy or consent or authorization for an annual or other meeting of the shareholders for which the proxy solicitation rules of the Commission require compensation disclosure shall include a separate resolution subject to shareholder vote to approve the compensation of executives, as disclosed pursuant to section 229.402 of title 17, Code of Federal Regulations, or any successor thereto.

(2)   Frequency of vote.—

Not less frequently than once every 6 years, a proxy or consent or authorization for an annual or other meeting of the shareholders for which the proxy solicitation rules of the Commission require compensation disclosure shall include a separate resolution subject to shareholder vote to determine whether votes on the resolutions required under paragraph (1) will occur every 1, 2, or 3 years.

(3)   Effective date.—

The proxy or consent or authorization for the first annual or other meeting of the shareholders occurring after the end of the 6-month period beginning on the date of enactment of this section shall include—

(A)   the resolution described in paragraph (1); and

(B)   a separate resolution subject to shareholder vote to determine whether votes on the resolutions required under paragraph (1) will occur every 1, 2, or 3 years.

(b)   Shareholder Approval of Golden Parachute Compensation.—

(1)   Disclosure.—

In any proxy or consent solicitation material (the solicitation of which is subject to the rules of the Commission pursuant to subsection (a)) for a meeting of the shareholders occurring after the end of the 6-month period beginning on the date of enactment of this section, at which shareholders are asked to approve an acquisition, merger, consolidation, or proposed sale or other disposition of all or substantially all the assets of an issuer, the person making such solicitation shall disclose in the proxy or consent solicitation material, in a clear and simple form in accordance with regulations to be promulgated by the Commission, any agreements or understandings that such person has with any named executive officers of such issuer (or of the acquiring issuer, if such issuer is not the acquiring issuer) concerning any type of compensation (whether present, deferred, or contingent) that is based on or otherwise relates to the acquisition, merger, consolidation, sale, or other disposition of all or substantially all of the assets of the issuer and the aggregate total of all such compensation that may (and the conditions upon which it may) be paid or become payable to or on behalf of such executive officer.

(2)   Shareholder.—

Any proxy or consent or authorization relating to the proxy or consent solicitation material containing the disclosure required by paragraph (1) shall include a separate resolution subject to shareholder vote to approve such agreements or understandings and compensation as disclosed, unless such agreements or understandings have been subject to a shareholder vote under subsection (a).

(c)   Rule of Construction.—The shareholder vote referred to in subsections (a) and (b) shall not be binding on the issuer or the board of directors of an issuer, and may not be construed—

(1)   as overruling a decision by such issuer or board of directors;

(2)   to create or imply any change to the fiduciary duties of such issuer or board of directors;

(3)   to create or imply any additional fiduciary duties for such issuer or board of directors; or

(4)   to restrict or limit the ability of shareholders to make proposals for inclusion in proxy materials related to executive compensation.

(d)   Disclosure of Votes.—Every institutional investment manager subject to section 13(f) shall report at least annually how it voted on any shareholder vote pursuant to subsections (a) and (b), unless such vote is otherwise required to be reported publicly by rule or regulation of the Commission.

(1)   In general.—

Exemption—The Commission may, by rule or order, exempt any other issuer or class of issuers from the requirement under subsection (a) or (b). In determining whether to make an exemption under this subsection, the Commission shall take into account, among other considerations, whether the requirements under subsections (a) and (b) disproportionately burdens small issuers.

(2)   Treatment of emerging growth companies.—

(A)   In general.—An emerging growth company shall be exempt from the requirements of subsections (a) and (b).

(B)   Compliance after termination of emerging growth company treatment. An issuer that was an emerging growth company but is no longer an emerging growth company shall include the first separate resolution described under subsection (a)(1) not later than the end of—

(i)   in the case of an issuer that was an emerging growth company for less than 2 years after the date of first sale of common equity securities of the issuer pursuant to an effective registration statement under the Securities Act of 1933, the 3-year period beginning on such date; and

(ii)   in the case of any other issuer, the 1-year period beginning on the date the issuer is no longer an emerging growth company.

Corporate Governance

Sec. 14B.   Not later than 180 days after the date of enactment of this subsection, the Commission shall issue rules that require an issuer to disclose in the annual proxy sent to investors the reasons why the issuer has chosen—

(1)   the same person to serve as chairman of the board of directors and chief executive officer (or in equivalent positions); or

(2)   different individuals to serve as chairman of the board of directors and chief executive officer (or in equivalent positions of the issuer).

Registration and Regulation of Brokers and Dealers

Sec. 15.   (a)(1)   It shall be unlawful for any broker or dealer which is either a person other than a natural person or a natural person not associated with a broker or dealer which is a person other than a natural person (other than such a broker or dealer whose business is exclusively intrastate and who does not make use of any facility of a national securities exchange) to make use of the mails or any means or instrumentality of interstate commerce to effect any transactions in, or to induce or attempt to induce the purchase or sale of, any security (other than an exempted security or commercial paper, bankers' acceptances, or commercial bills) unless such broker or dealer is registered in accordance with subsection (b) of this section.

(2)   The Commission, by rule or order, as it deems consistent with the public interest and the protection of investors, may conditionally or unconditionally exempt from paragraph (1) of this subsection any broker or dealer or class of brokers or dealers specified in such rule or order.

(b)(1)   A broker or dealer may be registered by filing with the Commission an application for registration in such form and containing such information and documents concerning such broker or dealer and any persons associated with such broker or dealer as the Commission, by rule, may prescribe as necessary or appropriate in the public interest or for the protection of investors. Within forty-five days of the date of the filing of such application (or within such longer period as to which the applicant consents), the Commission shall—

(A)   by order grant registration, or

(B)   institute proceedings to determine whether registration should be denied. Such proceedings shall include notice of the grounds for denial under consideration and opportunity for hearing and shall be concluded within one hundred twenty days of the date of the filing of the application for registration. At the conclusion of such proceedings, the Commission, by order, shall grant or deny such registration. The Commission may extend the time for conclusion of such proceedings for up to ninety days if it finds good cause for such extension and publishes its reasons for so finding or for such longer period as to which the applicant consents.

The Commission shall grant such registration if the Commission finds that the requirements of this section are satisfied. The order granting registration shall not be effective until such broker or dealer has become a member of a registered securities association, or until such broker or dealer has become a member of a national securities exchange, if such broker or dealer effects transactions solely on that exchange, unless the Commission has exempted such broker or dealer, by rule or order, from such membership. The Commission shall deny such registration if it does not make such a finding or if it finds that if the applicant were so registered, its registration would be subject to suspension or revocation under paragraph (4) of this subsection.

(2)(A)   An application for registration of a broker or dealer to be formed or organized may be made by a broker or dealer to which the broker or dealer to be formed or organized is to be the successor. Such application, in such form as the Commission, by rule, may prescribe, shall contain such information and documents concerning the applicant, the successor, and any persons associated with the applicant or the successor, as the Commission, by rule, may prescribe as necessary or appropriate in the public interest or for the protection of investors. The grant or denial of registration to such an applicant shall be in accordance with the procedures set forth in paragraph (1) of this subsection. If the Commission grants such registration, the registration shall terminate on the forty-fifth day after the effective date thereof, unless prior thereto the successor shall, in accordance with such rules and regulations as the Commission may prescribe, adopt the application for registration as its own.

(B)   Any person who is a broker or dealer solely by reason of acting as a municipal securities dealer or municipal securities broker, who so acts through a separately identifiable department or division, and who so acted in such a manner on June 4, 1975, may, in accordance with such terms and conditions as the Commission, by rule, prescribes as necessary and appropriate in the public interest and for the protection of investors, register such separately identifiable department or division in accordance with this subsection. If any such department or division is so registered, the department or division and not such person himself shall be the broker or dealer for purposes of this Act.

(C)   Within six months of the date of the granting of registration to a broker or dealer, the Commission, or upon the authorization and direction of the Commission, a registered securities association or national securities exchange of which such broker or dealer is a member, shall conduct an inspection of the broker or dealer to determine whether it is operating in conformity with the provisions of this Act and the rules and regulations thereunder: *Provided, however,* That the Commission may delay such inspection of any class of brokers or dealers for a period not to exceed six months.

(3)   Any provision of this Act (other than section 5 of this Act and subsection (a) of this section) which prohibits any act, practice, or course of business if the mails or any means or instrumentality of interstate commerce is used in connection therewith shall also prohibit any such act, practice, or course of business by any registered broker or dealer or any person acting on behalf of such a broker or dealer, irrespective of any use of the mails or any means or instrumentality of interstate commerce in connection therewith.

(4)   The Commission, by order, shall censure, place limitations on the activities, functions, or operations of, suspend for a period not exceeding twelve months, or revoke the registration of any broker or dealer if it finds, on the record after notice and opportunity for hearing, that such censure, placing of limitations, suspension, or revocation is in the public interest and that such broker or dealer, whether prior or subsequent to becoming such, or any person associated with such broker or dealer, whether prior or subsequent to becoming so associated—

(A)   has willfully made or caused to be made in any application for registration or report required to be filed with the Commission or with any other appropriate regulatory agency under this Act, or in any proceeding before the Commission with respect to registration, any statement which was at the time and in the light of the circumstances under which it was made false or misleading with respect to any material fact, or has omitted to state in any such application or report any material fact which is required to be stated therein.

(B)   has been convicted within ten years preceding the filing of any application for registration or at any time thereafter of any felony or misdemeanor or of a substantially equivalent crime by a foreign court of competent jurisdiction which the Commission finds—

(i)   involves the purchase or sale of any security, the taking of a false oath, the making of a false report, bribery, perjury, burglary, any substantially equivalent activity however denominated by the laws of the relevant foreign government, or conspiracy to commit any such offense;

778

(ii)   arises out of the conduct of the business of a broker, dealer, municipal securities dealer, municipal advisor, government securities broker, government securities dealer, investment adviser, bank, insurance company, fiduciary, transfer agent, nationally recognized statistical rating organization, foreign person performing a function substantially equivalent to any of the above, or entity or person required to be registered under the Commodity Exchange Act or any substantially equivalent foreign statute or regulation;

(iii)   involves the larceny, theft, robbery, extortion, forgery, counterfeiting, fraudulent concealment, embezzlement, fraudulent conversion, or misappropriation of funds, or securities, or substantially equivalent activity however denominated by the laws of the relevant foreign government; or

(iv)   involves the violation of section 152, 1341, 1342, or 1343 or chapter 25 or 47 of Title 18, United States Code, or a violation of a substantially equivalent foreign statute.

(C)   is permanently or temporarily enjoined by order, judgment, or decree of any court of competent jurisdiction from acting as an investment adviser, underwriter, broker, dealer, municipal securities dealer, municipal advisor, government securities broker, government securities dealer, securities-based swap dealer, major security-based swap participant, transfer agent, nationally recognized statistical rating organization, foreign person performing a function substantially equivalent to any of the above, or entity or person required to be registered under the Commodity Exchange Act or any substantially equivalent foreign statute or regulation, or as an affiliated person or employee of any investment company, bank, insurance company, foreign entity substantially equivalent to any of the above, or entity or person required to be registered under the Commodity Exchange Act or any substantially equivalent foreign statute or regulation, or from engaging in or continuing any conduct or practice in connection with any such activity, or in connection with the purchase or sale of any security.

(D)   has willfully violated any provision of the Securities Act of 1933, the Investment Advisers Act of 1940, the Investment Company Act of 1940, the Commodity Exchange Act, this Act, the rules or regulations under any of such statutes, or the rules of the Municipal Securities Rulemaking Board, or is unable to comply with any such provision.

(E)   has willfully aided, abetted, counseled, commanded, induced, or procured the violation by any other person of any provision of the Securities Act of 1933, the Investment Advisers Act of 1940, the Investment Company Act of 1940, the Commodity Exchange Act, this Act, the rules or regulations under any of such statutes, or the rules of the Municipal Securities Rulemaking Board, or has failed reasonably to supervise, with a view to preventing violations of the provisions of such statutes, rules, and regulations, another person who commits such a violation, if such other person is subject to his supervision. For the purposes of this subparagraph (E) no person shall be deemed to have failed reasonably to supervise any other person, if—

(i)   there have been established procedures, and a system for applying such procedures, which would reasonably be expected to prevent and detect, insofar as practicable, any such violation by such other person, and

(ii)   such person has reasonably discharged the duties and obligations incumbent upon him by reason of such procedures and system without reasonable cause to believe that such procedures and system were not being complied with.

(F)   is subject to any order of the Commission barring or suspending the right of the person to be associated with a broker, dealer, security-based swap dealer, or a major security-based swap participant.

(G)   has been found a foreign financial regulatory authority to have—

(i)   made or caused to be made in any application for registration or report required to be filed with a foreign financial regulatory authority, or in any proceeding before a foreign financial regulatory authority with respect to registration, any statement that was at the time and in the light of the circumstances under which it was made false or misleading with respect to any material fact, or has omitted to state in any application or report to the foreign financial regulatory authority any material fact that is required to be stated therein;

(ii)   violated any foreign statute or regulation regarding transactions in securities, or contracts of sale of a commodity for future delivery, traded on or subject to the rules of a contract market or any board of trade;

(iii)   aided, abetted, counseled, commanded, induced, or procured the violation by any person of any provision of any statutory provisions enacted by a foreign government, or rules or regulations thereunder, empowering a foreign financial regulatory authority regarding transactions in securities, or contracts of sale of a commodity for future delivery, traded on or subject to the rules of a contract market or any board of trade, or has been found, by a foreign financial regulatory authority, to have failed reasonably to supervise, with a view to preventing violations of such statutory provisions, rules, and regulations, another person who commits such a violation, if such other person is subject to his supervision; or

(H)   is subject to any final order of a State securities commission (or any agency or officer performing like functions), State authority that supervises or examines banks, savings associations, or credit unions, State insurance commission (or any agency or office performing like functions), an appropriate Federal banking agency (as defined in section 3 of the Federal Deposit Insurance Act (12 U.S.C. § 1813(q))), or the National Credit Union Administration, that—

(i)   bars such person from association with an entity regulated by such commission, authority, agency, or officer, or from engaging in the business of securities, insurance, banking, savings association activities, or credit union activities; or

(ii)   constitutes a final order based on violations of any laws or regulations that prohibit fraudulent, manipulative, or deceptive conduct.

(5)   Pending final determination whether any registration under this subsection shall be revoked, the Commission, by order, may suspend such registration, if such suspension appears to the Commission, after notice and opportunity for hearing, to be necessary or appropriate in the public interest or for the protection of investors. Any registered broker or dealer may, upon such terms and conditions as the Commission deems necessary or appropriate in the public interest or for the protection of investors, withdraw from registration by filing a written notice of withdrawal with the Commission. If the Commission finds that any registered broker or dealer is no longer in existence or has ceased to do business as a broker or dealer, the Commission, by order, shall cancel the registration of such broker or dealer.

(6)(A)   With respect to any person who is associated, who is seeking to become associated, or, at the time of the alleged misconduct, who was associated or was seeking to become associated with a broker or dealer, or any person participating, or, at the time of the alleged misconduct, who was participating, in an offering of any penny stock, the Commission, by order, shall censure, place limitations on the activities or functions of such person, or suspend for a period not exceeding 12 months or bar any such person from being associated with a broker, dealer, investment adviser, municipal securities dealer, municipal advisor, transfer agent, or nationally recognized statistical rating organization, or from participating in an offering of penny stock, if the Commission finds, on the record after notice and opportunity for a hearing, that such censure, placing of limitations, suspension, or bar is in the public interest and that such person—

(i)   has committed or omitted any act, or is subject to an order or finding, enumerated in subparagraph (A), (D), (E), (H), or (G) of paragraph (4) of this subsection;

(ii)   has been convicted of any offense specified in subparagraph (B) of such paragraph (4) within 10 years of the commencement of the proceedings under this paragraph; or

(iii)   is enjoined from any action, conduct, or practice specified in subparagraph (C) of such paragraph (4).

(B)   It shall be unlawful—

(i)   for any person as to whom an order under subparagraph (A) is in effect, without the consent of the Commission, willfully to become, or to be, associated with a broker or dealer in contravention of such order, or to participate in an offering of penny stock in contravention of such order;

(ii) for any broker or dealer to permit such a person, without the consent of the Commission, to become or remain, a person associated with the broker or dealer in contravention of such order, if such broker or dealer knew, or in the exercise of reasonable care should have known, of such order; or

(iii) for any broker or dealer to permit such a person, without the consent of the Commission, to participate in an offering of penny stock in contravention of such order, if such broker or dealer knew, or in the exercise of reasonable care should have known, of such order and of such participation.

(C) For purposes of this paragraph, the term "person participating in an offering of penny stock" includes any person acting as any promoter, finder, consultant, agent, or other person who engages in activities with a broker, dealer, or issuer for purposes of the issuance or trading in any penny stock, or inducing or attempting to induce the purchase or sale of any penny stock. The Commission may, by rule or regulation, define such term to include other activities, and may, by rule, regulation, or order, exempt any person or class of persons, in whole or in part, conditionally or unconditionally, from such term.

(7) No registered broker or dealer or government securities broker or government securities dealer registered (or required to register) under section 15C(a)(1)(A) of this Act shall effect any transaction in, or induce the purchase or sale of, any security unless such broker or dealer meets such standards of operational capability and such broker or dealer and all natural persons associated with such broker or dealer meet such standards of training, experience, competence, and such other qualifications as the Commission finds necessary or appropriate in the public interest or for the protection of investors. The Commission shall establish such standards by rules and regulations, which may—

(A) specify that all or any portion of such standards shall be applicable to any class of brokers and dealers and persons associated with brokers and dealers;

(B) require persons in any such class to pass tests prescribed in accordance with such rules and regulations, which tests shall, with respect to any class of partners, officers, or supervisory employees (which latter term may be defined by the Commission's rules and regulations and as so defined shall include branch managers of brokers or dealers) engaged in the management of the broker or dealer, include questions relating to bookkeeping, accounting, internal control over cash and securities, supervision of employees, maintenance of records, and other appropriate matters; and

(C) provide that persons in any such class other than brokers and dealers and partners, officers, and supervisory employees of brokers or dealers, may be qualified solely on the basis of compliance with such standards of training and such other qualifications as the Commission finds appropriate.

The Commission, by rule, may prescribe reasonable fees and charges to defray its costs in carrying out this paragraph, including, but not limited to, fees for any test administered by it or under its direction. The Commission may cooperate with registered securities associations and national securities exchanges in devising and administering tests and may require registered brokers and dealers and persons associated with such brokers and dealers to pass tests administered by or on behalf of any such association or exchange and to pay such association or exchange reasonable fees or charges to defray the costs incurred by such association or exchange in administering such tests.

(8) It shall be unlawful for any registered broker or dealer to effect any transaction in, or induce or attempt to induce the purchase or sale of, any security (other than commercial paper, bankers' acceptances, or commercial bills), unless such broker or dealer is a member of a securities association registered pursuant to section 15A of this Act or effects transactions in securities solely on a national securities exchange of which it is a member.

(9) The Commission by rule or order, as it deems consistent with the public interest and the protection of investors, may conditionally or unconditionally exempt from paragraph (8) of this subsection any broker or dealer or class of brokers or dealers specified in such rule or order.

(10) For the purposes of determining whether a person is subject to a statutory disqualification under section 6(c)(2), 15A(g)(2), or 17A(b)(4)(A) of this Act, the term "Commission" in paragraph (4)(B) of this subsection shall mean "exchange", "association", or "clearing agency", respectively.

(11) broker/dealer registration with respect to transactions in security futures products.—

(A) Notice Registration.—

(i) Contents of notice.—

Notwithstanding paragraphs (1) and (2), a broker or dealer required to register only because it effects transactions in security futures products on an exchange registered pursuant to section 6(g) may register for purposes of this section by filing with the Commission a written notice in such form and containing such information concerning such broker or dealer and any persons associated with such broker or dealer as the Commission, by rule, may prescribe as necessary or appropriate in the public interest or for the protection of investors. A broker or dealer may not register under this paragraph unless that broker or dealer is a member of a national securities association registered under section 15A(k).

(ii) Immediate effectiveness.—

Such registration shall be effective contemporaneously with the submission of notice, in written or electronic form, to the Commission, except that such registration shall not be effective if the registration would be subject to suspension or revocation under paragraph (4).

(iii) Suspension.—

Such registration shall be suspended immediately if a national securities association registered pursuant to section 15A(k) of this Act suspends the membership of that broker or dealer.

(iv) Termination.—

Such registration shall be terminated immediately if any of the above stated conditions for registration set forth in this paragraph are no longer satisfied.

(B) Exemptions for registered brokers and dealers.—

A broker or dealer registered pursuant to the requirements of subparagraph (A) shall be exempt from the following provisions of this Act and the rules thereunder with respect to transactions in security futures products:

(i) Section 8.

(ii) Section 11.

(iii) Subsections (c)(3) and (c)(5) of this section.

(iv) Section 15B.

(v) Section 15C.

(vi) Subsections (d), (e), (f), (g), (h), and (i) of section 17.

(12) Exemption for security futures product exchange members.—

(A) Registration exemption.—

A natural person shall be exempt from the registration requirements of this section if such person—

(i) is a member of a designated contract market registered with the Commission as an exchange pursuant to section 6(g);

(ii) effects transactions only in securities on the exchange of which such person is a member; and

(iii) does not directly accept or solicit orders from public customers or provide advice to public customers in connection with the trading of security futures products.

(B) Other exemptions.—

A natural person exempt from registration pursuant to subparagraph (A) shall also be exempt from the following provisions of this Act and the rules thereunder:

(i) Section 8.

(ii) Section 11.

(iii) Subsections (c)(3), (c)(5), and (e) of this section.

(iv) Section 15B.

(v) Section 15C.

(vi) Subsections (d), (e), (f), (g), (h), and (i) of section 17.

(c)(1)(A) No broker or dealer shall make use of the mails or any means or instrumentality of interstate commerce to effect any transaction in, or to induce or attempt to induce the purchase or sale of, any security (other than commercial paper, bankers' acceptances, or commercial bills), or any security-based swap agreement, by means of any manipulative, deceptive, or other fraudulent device or contrivance.

(B) No broker, dealer, or municipal securities dealer shall make use of the mails or any means or instrumentality of interstate commerce to effect any transaction in, or to induce or attempt to induce the purchase or sale of, any municipal security or any security-based swap agreement involving a municipal security by means of any manipulative, deceptive, or other fraudulent device or contrivance.

(C) No government securities broker or government securities dealer shall make use of the mails or any means or instrumentality of interstate commerce to effect any transaction in, or to induce or to attempt to induce the purchase or sale of, any government security or any security-based swap agreement involving a government security by means of any manipulative, deceptive, or other fraudulent device or contrivance.

(2)(A) No broker or dealer shall make use of the mails or any means or instrumentality of interstate commerce to effect any transaction in, or to induce or attempt to induce the purchase or sale of, any security (other than an exempted security or commercial paper, bankers' acceptances, or commercial bills) otherwise than on a national securities exchange of which it is a member, in connection with which such broker or dealer engages in any fraudulent, deceptive, or manipulative act or practice, or makes any fictitious quotation.

(B) No broker, dealer, or municipal securities dealer shall make use of the mails or any means or instrumentality of interstate commerce to effect any transaction in, or to induce or attempt to induce the purchase or sale of, any municipality security in connection with which such broker, dealer, or municipal securities dealer engages in any fraudulent, deceptive, or manipulative act or practice, or makes any fictitious quotation.

(C) No government securities broker or government securities dealer shall make use of the mails or any means or instrumentality of interstate commerce to effect any transaction in, or induce or attempt to induce the purchase or sale of, any government security in connection with which such government securities broker or government securities dealer engages in any fraudulent, deceptive, or manipulative act or practice, or makes any fictitious quotation.

(D) The Commission shall, for the purposes of this paragraph, by rules and regulations define, and prescribe means reasonably designed to prevent, such acts and practices as are fraudulent, deceptive, or manipulative and such quotations as are fictitious.

(E) The Commission shall, prior to adopting any rule or regulation under subparagraph (C), consult with and consider the views of the Secretary of the Treasury and each appropriate regulatory agency. If the Secretary of the Treasury or any appropriate regulatory agency comments in writing on a proposed rule or regulation of the Commission under such subparagraph (C) that has been published for comment, the Commission shall respond in writing to such written comment before adopting the proposed rule. If the Secretary of the Treasury determines, and notifies the Commission, that such rule or regulation, if implemented, would, or as applied does

    (i)   adversely affect the liquidity or efficiency of the market for government securities; or

    (ii)   impose any burden on competition not necessary or appropriate in furtherance of the purposes of this section, the Commission shall, prior to adopting the proposed rule or regulation, find that such rule or regulation is necessary and appropriate in furtherance of the purposes of this section notwithstanding the Secretary's determination.

(3)(A)   No broker or dealer (other than a government securities broker or government securities dealer, except a registered broker or dealer) shall make use of the mails or any means or instrumentality of interstate commerce to effect any transaction in, or to induce or attempt to induce the purchase or sale of, any security (other than an exempted security (except a government security) or commercial paper, bankers' acceptances, or commercial bills) in contravention of such rules and regulations as the Commission shall prescribe as necessary or appropriate in the public interest or for the protection of investors to provide safeguards with respect to the financial responsibility and related practices of brokers and dealers including, but not limited to, the acceptance of custody and use of customers' securities and the carrying and use of customers' deposits or credit balances. Such rules and regulations shall (A) require the maintenance of reserves with respect to customers' deposits or credit balances, and (B) no later than September 1, 1975, establish minimum financial responsibility requirements for all brokers and dealers.

(B)   Consistent with this Act, the Commission, in consultation with the Commodity Futures Trading Commission, shall issue such rules, regulations, or orders as are necessary to avoid duplicative or conflicting regulations applicable to any broker or dealer registered with the Commission pursuant to section 15(b) (except paragraph (11) thereof), that is also registered with the Commodity Futures Trading Commission pursuant to section 4f(a) of the Commodity Exchange Act (except paragraph (2) thereof), with respect to the application of: (i) the provisions of section 8, section 15(c)(3), and section 17 of this Act and the rules and regulations thereunder related to the treatment of customer funds, securities, or property, maintenance of books and records, financial reporting, or other financial responsibility rules, involving security futures products; and (ii) similar provisions of the Commodity Exchange Act and rules and regulations thereunder involving security futures products.

(C)   Notwithstanding any provision of sections 2(a)(1)(C)(i) or 4d(a)(2) of the Commodity Exchange Act and the rules and regulations thereunder, and pursuant to an exemption granted by the Commission under section 36 of this title or pursuant to a rule or regulation, cash and securities may be held by a broker or dealer registered pursuant to subsection (b)(1) and also registered as a futures commission merchant pursuant to section 4f(a)(1) of the Commodity Exchange Act, in a portfolio margining account carried as a futures account subject to section 4d of the Commodity Exchange Act and the rules and regulations thereunder, pursuant to a portfolio margining program approved by the Commodity Futures Trading Commission, and subject to subchapter IV of chapter 7 of title 11 of the United States Code and the rules and regulations thereunder. The Commission shall consult with the Commodity Futures Trading Commission to adopt rules to ensure that such transactions and accounts are subject to comparable requirements to the extent practicable for similar products.

(4)   If the Commission finds, after notice and opportunity for a hearing, that any person subject to the provisions of sections 12, 13, 14 or subsection (d) of section 15 of this Act or any rule or regulation thereunder has failed to comply with any such provision, rule, or regulation in any material respect, the Commission may publish its findings and issue an order requiring such person, and any person who was a cause of the failure to comply due to an act or omission the person knew or should have known would contribute to the failure to comply, to comply, or to take steps to effect compliance, with such provision or such rule or regulation thereunder upon such terms and conditions and within such time as the Commission may specify in such order.

(5)   No dealer (other than a specialist registered on a national securities exchange) acting in the capacity of market maker or otherwise shall make use of the mails or any means or instrumentality of interstate commerce to effect any transaction in, or to induce or attempt to induce the purchase or sale of, any security (other than an exempted security or a municipal security) in contravention of such specified and appropriate standards with respect to dealing as the Commission, by rule, shall prescribe as necessary or appropriate in the public interest and for the protection of investors, to maintain fair and orderly markets, or to remove impediments to and perfect the mechanism of a national market system. Under the rules of the Commission a dealer in a security may be prohibited from acting as a broker in that security.

(6)   No broker or dealer shall make use of the mails or any means or instrumentality of interstate commerce to effect any transaction in, or to induce or attempt to induce the purchase or sale of, any security (other than an exempted security, municipal security, commercial paper, bankers' acceptances, or commercial bills) in contravention of such rules and regulations as the Commission shall prescribe as necessary or appropriate in the public interest and for the protection of investors or to perfect or remove impediments to a national system for the prompt and accurate clearance and settlement of securities transactions, with respect to the time and method of, and the form and format of documents used in connection with, making settlements of and payments for transactions in securities, making transfers and deliveries of securities, and closing accounts. Nothing in this paragraph shall be construed (A) to affect the authority of the Board of Governors of the Federal Reserve System, pursuant to section 7 of this Act, to prescribe rules and regulations for the purpose of preventing the excessive use of credit for the purchase or carrying of securities, or (B) to authorize the Commission to prescribe rules or regulations for such purpose.

(7)   In connection with any bid for or purchase of a government security related to an offering of government securities by or on behalf of an issuer, no government securities broker, government securities dealer, or bidder for or purchaser of securities in such offering shall knowingly or willfully make any false or misleading written statement or omit any fact necessary to make any written statement made not misleading.

(8)   Prohibition of Referral Fees.—

No broker or dealer, or person associated with a broker or dealer, may solicit or accept, directly or indirectly, remuneration for assisting an attorney in obtaining the representation of any person in any private action arising under this Act or under the Securities Act of 1933.

(d)   Supplementary and Periodic Information—

(1)   In general.—

Each issuer which has filed a registration statement containing an undertaking which is or becomes operative under this subsection as in effect prior to August 20, 1964, and each issuer which shall after such date file a registration statement which has become effective pursuant to the Securities Act of 1933, as amended, shall file with the Commission, in accordance with such rules and regulations as the Commission may prescribe as necessary or appropriate in the public interest or for the protection of investors, such supplementary and periodic information, documents, and reports as may be required pursuant to section 13 of this Act in respect of a security registered pursuant to section 12 of this Act. The duty to file under this subsection shall be automatically suspended if and so long as any issue of securities of such issuer is registered pursuant to section 12 of this Act. The duty to file under this subsection shall also be automatically suspended as to any fiscal year, other than the fiscal year within which such registration statement became effective, if, at the beginning of such fiscal year, the securities of each class other than any class asset-based securities, to which the registration statement relates are held of record by less than 300 persons, or, in the case of a bank, a savings and loan holding company (as defined in section 10 of the Home Owners' Loan Act), or a bank holding company, as such term is defined in section 2 of the Bank Holding Company Act of 1956, 1,200 persons. For the purposes of this subsection, the term "class" shall be construed to include all securities of an issuer which are of substantially similar character and the holders of which enjoy substantially similar rights and privileges. The Commission may, for the purpose of this subsection, define by rules and regulations the term "held of record" as it deems necessary or appropriate in the public interest or for the protection of investors in order to prevent circumvention of the provisions of this subsection. Nothing in this subsection shall apply to securities issued by a foreign government or political subdivision thereof.

(2)   Asset-backed securities.—

(A)   Suspension of duty to file.—

The Commission may, by rule or regulation, provide for the suspension or termination of the duty to file under this subsection for any class of asset-backed security, on such terms and conditions and for such period or periods as the Commission deems necessary or appropriate in the public interest or for the protection of investors.

(B)   Classification of issuers.—

The Commission may, for purposes of this subsection, classify issuers and prescribe requirements appropriate for each class of issuers of asset-backed securities.

(e)   Notices to Customers Regarding Securities Lending.—Every registered broker or dealer shall provide notice to its customers that they may elect not to allow their fully paid securities to be used in connection with short sales. If a broker or dealer uses a customer's securities in connection with short sales, the broker or dealer shall provide notice to its customer that the broker or dealer may receive compensation in connection with lending the customer's securities. The Commission, by rule, as it deems necessary or appropriate in the public interest and for the protection of investors, may prescribe the form, content, time, and manner of delivery of any notice required under this paragraph.

(f)   The Commission, by rule, as it deems necessary or appropriate in the public interest and for the protection of investors or to assure equal regulation, may require any member of a national securities exchange not required to register under this section and any person associated with any such member to comply with any provision of this Act (other than subsection (a)) or the rules or regulations thereunder which by its terms regulates or prohibits any act, practice, or course of business by a "broker or dealer" or "registered broker or dealer" or a "person associated with a broker or dealer," respectively.

(g)   Every registered broker or dealer shall establish, maintain, and enforce written policies and procedures reasonably designed, taking into consideration the nature of such broker's or dealer's business, to prevent the misuse in violation of this Act, or the rules or regulations thereunder, of material, nonpublic information by such broker or dealer or any person associated with such broker or dealer. The Commission, as it deems necessary or appropriate in the public interest or for the protection of investors, shall adopt rules or regulations to require specific policies or procedures reasonably designed to prevent misuse in violation of this Act (or the rules or regulations thereunder) of material, nonpublic information.

(h)   Requirements for transactions in penny stocks.—

(1)   In general.—

No broker or dealer shall make use of the mails or any means or instrumentality of interstate commerce to effect any transaction in, or to induce or attempt to induce the purchase or sale of, any penny stock by any customer except in accordance with the requirements of this subsection and the rules and regulations prescribed under this subsection.

(2)   Risk disclosure with respect to penny stocks—

Prior to effecting any transaction in any penny stock, a broker or dealer shall give the customer a risk disclosure document that—

(A)   contains a description of the nature and level of risk in the market for penny stocks in both public offerings and secondary trading;

(B)   contains a description of the broker's or dealer's duties to the customer and of the rights and remedies available to the customer with respect to violations of such duties or other requirements of Federal securities laws;

(C)   contains a brief, clear, narrative description of a dealer market, including "bid" and "ask" prices for penny stocks and the significance of the spread between the bid and ask prices;

(D)   contains the toll free telephone number for inquiries on disciplinary actions established pursuant to section 15A(i) of this Act;

(E)   defines significant terms used in the disclosure document or in the conduct of trading in penny stocks; and

(F)   contains such other information, and is in such form (including language, type size, and format), as the Commission shall require by rule or regulation.

(3)   Commission rules relating to disclosure.—

The Commission shall adopt rules setting forth additional standards for the disclosure by brokers and dealers to customers of information concerning transactions in penny stocks. Such rules—

(A)   shall require brokers and dealers to disclose to each customer, prior to effecting any transaction in, and at the time of confirming any transaction with respect to any penny stock, in accordance with such procedures and methods as the Commission may require consistent with the public interest and the protection of investors—

(i)   the bid and ask prices for penny stock, or such other information as the Commission may, by rule, require to provide customers with more useful and reliable information relating to the price of such stock;

(ii)   the number of shares to which such bid and ask prices apply, or other comparable information relating to the depth and liquidity of the market for such stock; and

(iii)   the amount and a description of any compensation that the broker or dealer and the associated person thereof will receive or has received in connection with such transaction;

(B)   shall require brokers and dealers to provide, to each customer whose account with the broker or dealer contains penny stocks, a monthly statement indicating the market value of the penny stocks in that account or indicating that the market value of such stock cannot be determined because of the unavailability of firm quotes; and

(C)   may, as the Commission finds necessary or appropriate in the public interest or for the protection of investors, require brokers and dealers to disclose to customers additional information concerning transactions in penny stocks.

(4)   Exemptions.—

The Commission, as it determines consistent with the public interest and the protection of investors, may by rule, regulation, or order exempt in whole or in part, conditionally or unconditionally, any person or class of persons, or any transaction or class of transactions, from the requirements of this subsection. Such exemptions shall include an exemption for brokers and dealers based on the minimal percentage of the broker's or dealer's commissions, commission-equivalents, and markups received from transactions in penny stocks.

(5)   Regulations.—

It shall be unlawful for any person to violate such rules and regulations as the Commission shall prescribe in the public interest or for the protection of investors or to maintain fair and orderly markets—

(A)   as necessary or appropriate to carry out this subsection; or

(B)   as reasonably designed to prevent fraudulent, deceptive, or manipulative acts and practices with respect to penny stocks.

(i)   Limitations on State Law.—

(1)   Capital, margin, books and records, bonding, and reports.—

No law, rule, regulation, or order, or other administrative action of any State or political subdivision thereof shall establish capital, custody, margin, financial responsibility, making and keeping records, bonding, or financial or operational reporting requirements for brokers, dealers, municipal securities dealers, government securities brokers, or government securities dealers that differ from, or are in addition to, the requirements in those areas established under this title. The Commission shall consult periodically the securities commissions (or any agency or office performing like functions) of the States concerning the adequacy of such requirements as established under this Act.

(2) Funding portals.—

(A) Limitation on State laws.—Except as provided in subparagraph (B), no State or political subdivision thereof may enforce any law, rule, regulation, or other administrative action against a registered funding portal with respect to its business as such.

(B) Examination and enforcement authority.—Subparagraph (A) does not apply with respect to the examination and enforcement of any law, rule, regulation, or administrative action of a State or political subdivision thereof in which the principal place of business of a registered funding portal is located, provided that such law, rule, regulation, or administrative action is not in addition to or different from the requirements for registered funding portals established by the Commission.

(C) Definition.—For purposes of this paragraph, the term "State" includes the District of Columbia and the territories of the United States.

(3) De minimis transactions by associated persons.—

No law, rule, regulation, or order, or other administrative action of any State or political subdivision thereof may prohibit an associated person of a broker or dealer from effecting a transaction described in paragraph (3) for a customer in such State if—

(A) such associated person is not ineligible to register with such State for any reason other than such a transaction;

(B) such associated person is registered with a registered securities association and at least one State; and

(C) the broker or dealer with which such person is associated is registered with such State.

(4) Described transactions.—

(A) In general.—

A transaction is described in this paragraph if—

(i) such transaction is effected—

(I) on behalf of a customer that, for 30 days prior to the day of the transaction, maintained an account with the broker or dealer; and

(II) by an associated person of the broker or dealer—

(aa) to which the customer was assigned for 14 days prior to the day of the transaction; and

(bb) who is registered with a State in which the customer was a resident or was present for at least 30 consecutive days during the 1-year period prior to the day of the transaction; or

(ii) the transaction is effected—

(I) on behalf of a customer that, for 30 days prior to the day of the transaction, maintained an account with the broker or dealer; and

(II) during the period beginning on the date on which such associated person files an application for registration with the State in which the transaction is effected and ending on the earlier of—

(aa) 60 days after the date on which the application is filed; or

(bb) the date on which such State notifies the associated person that it has denied the application for registration or has stayed the pendency of the application for cause.

(B)   Rules of construction.—

For purposes of subparagraph (A)(i)(II)—

(i)   each of up to 3 associated persons of a broker or dealer who are designated to effect transactions during the absence or unavailability of the principal associated person for a customer may be treated as an associated person to which such customer is assigned; and

(ii)   if the customer is present in another State for 30 or more consecutive days or has permanently changed his or her residence to another State, a transaction is not described in this paragraph, unless the associated person of the broker or dealer files an application for registration with such State not later than 10 business days after the later of the date of the transaction, or the date of the discovery of the presence of the customer in the other State for 30 or more consecutive days or the change in the customer's residence.

(j)   Rulemaking to Extend Requirements to New Hybrid Products.—

(1)   Consultation.—

Prior to commencing a rulemaking under this subsection, the Commission shall consult with and seek the concurrence of the Board concerning the imposition of broker or dealer registration requirements with respect to any new hybrid product. In developing and promulgating rules under this subsection, the Commission shall consider the views of the Board, including views with respect to the nature of the new hybrid product; the history, purpose, extent, and appropriateness of the regulation of the new product under the Federal banking laws; and the impact of the proposed rule on the banking industry.

(2)   Limitation.—

The Commission shall not—

(A)   require a bank to register as a broker or dealer under this section because the bank engages in any transaction in, or buys or sells, a new hybrid product; or

(B)   brings an action against a bank for a failure to comply with a requirement described in subparagraph (A), unless the Commission has imposed such requirement by rule or regulation issued in accordance with this section.

(3)   Criteria for rulemaking.—

The Commission shall not impose a requirement under paragraph (2) of this subsection with respect to any new hybrid product unless the Commission determines that—

(A)   the new hybrid product is a security; and

(B)   imposing such requirement is necessary and appropriate in the public interest and for protection of investors.

(4)   Considerations.—

In making a determination under paragraph (3), the Commission shall consider—

(A)   the nature of the new hybrid product; and

(B)   the history, purpose, extent, and appropriateness of the regulation of the new hybrid product under the Federal Securities laws and under the Federal Banking laws.

(5)   Objection to commission regulation.—

(A)   Filing of petition for review.—

The Board may obtain review of any final regulation described in paragraph (2) in the United States Court of Appeals for the District of Columbia Circuit by filing in such court, not later than 60 days after the date of publication of the final regulation, a written petition requesting that the regulation be set aside. Any proceeding to challenge any such rule shall be expedited by the Court of Appeals.

(B)   Transmittal of petition and record.—

A copy of a petition described in such paragraph (A) shall be transmitted as soon as possible by the Clerk of the Court to an officer or employee of the Commission designated for that purpose. Upon receipt of the petition, the Commission shall file with the Court the regulation under review and any documents referred to therein, and any other relevant materials prescribed by the Court.

(C)   Exclusive jurisdiction.—

On the date of the filing of the petition under subparagraph (A), the Court has jurisdiction, which becomes exclusive on the filing of the materials set forth in subparagraph (B), to affirm and enforce or to set aside the regulation at issue.

(D)   Standard of review.—

The Court shall determine to affirm and enforce or set aside a regulation of the Commission under this subsection, based on the determination of the Court as to whether—

     (i)   the subject product is a new hybrid product, as defined in this subsection;

     (ii)   the subject product is a security;

     (iii)   imposing a requirement to register as a broker or dealer for banks engaging in transactions in such product is appropriate in light of the history, purpose, and extent of regulation under the Federal securities laws and under the Federal banking laws, giving deference neither to the views of the Commission nor the Board.

(E)   Judicial stay.—

The filing of a petition by the Board pursuant to subparagraph (A) shall operate as a judicial stay, until the date on which the determination of the Court is final (including any appeal of such determination).

(F)   Other authority to challenge.—

Any aggrieved party may seek judicial review of the Commission's rulemaking under the subsection pursuant to section 25 of this Act.

    (6)   Definitions.—

For purposes of this subsection:

(A)   New hybrid product.—

The term "new hybrid product" means a product that

     (i)   was not subjected to regulation by the Commission as a security prior to the date of the enactment of the Gramm-Leach-Bliley Act;

     (ii)   is not an identified banking product as such term is defined in section 206 of such Act; and

     (iii)   is not an equity swap within the meaning of section 206(a)(6) of such Act.

(B)   Board.—

The term "Board" means the Board of Governors of the Federal Reserve System. [effective May 12, 2001]

   (j)[9]   The authority of the Commission under this section with respect to security-based swap agreements shall be subject to the restrictions and limitations of section 3A(b) of this Act.

   (k)   Registration or succession to a United States broker or dealer.—

In determining whether to permit a foreign person or an affiliate of a foreign person to register as a United States broker or dealer, or succeed to the registration of a United States broker or dealer, the

---

    [9]   Two (j)s have been enacted.

Commission may consider whether, for a foreign person, or an affiliate of a foreign person that presents a risk to the stability of the United States financial system, the home country of the foreign person has adopted, or made demonstrable progress toward adopting, an appropriate system of financial regulation to mitigate such risk.

(*l*)   Termination of a United States broker or dealer.—For a foreign person or an affiliate of a foreign person that presents such a risk to the stability of the United States financial system, the Commission may determine to terminate the registration of such foreign person or an affiliate of such foreign person as a broker or dealer in the United States, if the Commission determines that the home country of the foreign person has not adopted, or made demonstrable progress toward adopting, an appropriate system of financial regulation to mitigate such risk.

(k)[10] Standard of conduct.—

(1)   In general

Notwithstanding any other provision of this act or the Investment Advisers Act of 1940, the Commission may promulgate rules to provide that, with respect to a broker or dealer, when providing personalized investment advice about securities to a retail customer (and such other customers as the Commission may by rule provide), the standard of conduct for such broker or dealer with respect to such customer shall be the same as the standard of conduct applicable to an investment adviser under section 211 of the Investment Advisers Act of 1940. The receipt of compensation based on commission or other standard compensation for the sale of securities shall not, in and of itself, be considered a violation of such standard applied to a broker or dealer. Nothing in this section shall require a broker or dealer or registered representative to have a continuing duty of care or loyalty to the customer after providing personalized investment advice about securities.

(2)   Disclosure of range of products offered.—

Where a broker or dealer sells only proprietary or other limited range of products, as determined by the Commission, the Commission may by rule require that such broker or dealer provide notice to each retail customer and obtain the consent or acknowledgment of the customer. The sale of only proprietary or other limited range of products by a broker or dealer shall not, in and of itself, be considered a violation of the standard set forth in paragraph (1).

(*l*)   Termination of a United States broker or dealer.—

For a foreign person or an affiliate of a foreign person that presents such a risk to the stability of the United States financial system, the Commission may determine to terminate the registration of such foreign person or an affiliate of such foreign person as a broker or dealer in the United States, if the Commission determines that the home country of the foreign person has not adopted, or made demonstrable progress toward adopting, an appropriate system of financial regulation to mitigate such risk.

(*l*)[11] Other matters.—

The Commission shall—

(1)   facilitate the provision of simple and clear disclosures to investors regarding the terms of their relationships with brokers, dealers, and investment advisers, including any material conflicts of interest; and

(2)   examine and, where appropriate, promulgate rules prohibiting or restricting certain sales practices, conflicts of interest, and compensation schemes for brokers, dealers, and investment advisers that the Commission deems contrary to the public interest and the protection of investors.

(m)   Harmonization of enforcement.—

The enforcement authority of the Commission with respect to violations of the standard of conduct applicable to a broker or dealer providing personalized investment advice about securities to a retail customer shall include—

---

[10]   Two (k)s have been enacted.
[11]   Two (*l*)s have been enacted.

    (1) the enforcement authority of the Commission with respect to such violations provided under this act; and

    (2) the enforcement authority of the Commission with respect to violations of the standard of conduct applicable to an investment adviser under the Investment Advisers Act of 1940, including the authority to impose sanctions for such violations, and

the Commission shall seek to prosecute and sanction violators of the standard of conduct applicable to a broker or dealer providing personalized investment advice about securities to a retail customer under this act to same extent as the Commission prosecutes and sanctions violators of the standard of conduct applicable to an investment advisor under the Investment Advisers Act of 1940.

  (n) Disclosures to Retail Investors.—

    (1) In general.—

Notwithstanding any other provision of the securities laws, the Commission may issue rules designating documents or information that shall be provided by a broker or dealer to a retail investor before the purchase of an investment product or service by the retail investor.

    (2) Considerations.—

In developing any rules under paragraph (1), the Commission shall consider whether the rules will promote investor protection, efficiency, competition, and capital formation.

    (3) Form and contents of documents and information.—

Any documents or information designated under a rule promulgated under paragraph (1) shall—

      (A) be in a summary format; and

      (B) contain clear and concise information about—

        (i) investment objectives, strategies, costs, and risks; and

        (ii) any compensation or other financial incentive received by a broker, dealer, or other intermediary in connection with the purchase of retail investment products.

  (o) Authority to Restrict Mandatory Pre-dispute Arbitration—The Commission, by rule, may prohibit, or impose conditions or limitations on the use of, agreements that require customers or clients of any broker, dealer, or municipal securities dealer to arbitrate any future dispute between them arising under the Federal securities laws, the rules and regulations thereunder, or the rules of a self-regulatory organization if it finds that such prohibition, imposition of conditions, or limitations are in the public interest and for the protection of investors.

Registered Securities Associations

  Sec. 15A.   (a) An association of brokers and dealers may be registered as a national securities association pursuant to subsection (b) of this section, or as an affiliated securities association pursuant to subsection (d) of this section, under the terms and conditions hereinafter provided in this section and in accordance with the provisions of section 19(a) of this Act, by filing with the Commission an application for registration in such form as the Commission, by rule, may prescribe containing the rules of the association and such other information and documents as the Commission, by rule, may prescribe as necessary or appropriate in the public interest or for the protection of investors.

  (b) An association of brokers and dealers shall not be registered as a national securities association unless the Commission determines that—

    (1) By reason of the number and geographical distribution of its members and the scope of their transactions, such association will be able to carry out the purposes of this section.

    (2) Such association is so organized and has the capacity to be able to carry out the purposes of this Act and to comply, and (subject to any rule or order of the Commission pursuant to section 17(d) or 19(g)(2) of this Act) to enforce compliance by its members and persons associated with its members, with the provisions of this Act, the rules and regulations thereunder, the rules of the Municipal Securities Rulemaking Board, and the rules of the association.

(3)   Subject to the provisions of subsection (g) of this section, the rules of the association provide that any registered broker or dealer may become a member of such association and any person may become associated with a member thereof.

(4)   The rules of the association assure a fair representation of its members in the selection of its directors and administration of its affairs and provide that one or more directors shall be representative of issuers and investors and not be associated with a member of the association, broker, or dealer.

(5)   The rules of the association provide for the equitable allocation of reasonable dues, fees, and other charges among members and issuers and other persons using any facility or system which the association operates or controls.

(6)   The rules of the association are designed to prevent fraudulent and manipulative acts and practices, to promote just and equitable principles of trade, to foster cooperation and coordination with persons engaged in regulating, clearing, settling, processing information with respect to, and facilitating transactions in securities, to remove impediments to and perfect the mechanism of a free and open market and a national market system, and, in general, to protect investors and the public interest; and are not designed to permit unfair discrimination between customers, issuers, brokers, or dealers, to fix minimum profits, to impose any schedule or fix rates of commissions, allowances, discounts, or other fees to be charged by its members, or to regulate by virtue of any authority conferred by this Act matters not related to the purposes of this Act or the administration of the association.

(7)   The rules of the association provide that (subject to any rule or order of the Commission pursuant to section 17(d) or 19(g)(2) of this Act) its members and persons associated with its members shall be appropriately disciplined for violation of any provision of this Act, the rules or regulations thereunder, the rules of the Municipal Securities Rulemaking Board, or the rules of the association, by expulsion, suspension, limitation of activities, functions, and operations, fine, censure, being suspended or barred from being associated with a member, or any other fitting sanction.

(8)   The rules of the association are in accordance with the provisions of subsection (h) of this section, and, in general, provide a fair procedure for the disciplining of members and persons associated with members, the denial of membership to any person seeking membership therein, the barring of any person from becoming associated with a member thereof, and the prohibition or limitation by the association of any person with respect to access to services offered by the association or a member thereof.

(9)   The rules of the association do not impose any burden on competition not necessary or appropriate in furtherance of the purposes of this Act.

(10)   The requirements of subsection (c) of this section, insofar as these may be applicable, are satisfied.

(11)   The rules of the association include provisions governing the form and content of quotations relating to securities sold otherwise than on a national securities exchange which may be distributed or published by any member or person associated with a member, and the persons to whom such quotations may be supplied. Such rules relating to quotations shall be designed to produce fair and informative quotations, to prevent fictitious or misleading quotations, and to promote orderly procedures for collecting, distributing, and publishing quotations.

(12)   The rules of the association to promote just and equitable principles of trade, as required by paragraph (6), include rules to prevent members of the association from participating in any limited partnership rollup transaction (as such term is defined in paragraphs (4) and (5) of section 14(h) of this Act) unless such transaction was conducted in accordance with procedures designed to protect the rights of limited partners, including—

(A)   the right of dissenting limited partners to one of the following:

(i)   an appraisal and compensation;

(ii)   retention of a security under substantially the same terms and conditions as the original issue;

(iii) approval of the limited partnership rollup transaction by not less than 75 percent of the outstanding securities of each of the participating limited partnerships;

(iv) the use of a committee that is independent, as determined in accordance with rules prescribed by the association, of the general partner or sponsor, that has been approved by a majority of the outstanding securities of each of the participating partnerships, and that has such authority as is necessary to protect the interest of limited partners, including the authority to hire independent advisors, to negotiate with the general partner or sponsor on behalf of the limited partners, and to make a recommendation to the limited partners with respect to the proposed transaction; or

(v) other comparable rights that are prescribed by rule by the association and that are designed to protect dissenting limited partners;

(B) the right not to have their voting power unfairly reduced or abridged;

(C) the right not to bear an unfair portion of the costs of a proposed limited partnership rollup transaction that is rejected; and

(D) restrictions on the conversion of contingent interests or fees into non-contingent interests or fees and restrictions on the receipt of a non-contingent equity interest in exchange for fees for services which have not yet been provided.

As used in this paragraph, the term "dissenting limited partner" means a person who, on the date on which soliciting material is mailed to investors, is a holder of a beneficial interest in a limited partnership that is the subject of a limited partnership rollup transaction, and who casts a vote against the transaction and complies with procedures established by the association, except that for purposes of an exchange or tender offer, such person shall file an objection in writing under the rules of the association during the period in which the offer is outstanding.

(13) The rules of the association prohibit the authorization for quotation on an automated interdealer quotation system sponsored by the association of any security designated by the Commission as a national market system security resulting from a limited partnership rollup transaction (as such term is defined in paragraphs (4) and (5) of section 14(h) of this Act), unless such transaction was conducted in accordance with procedures designed to protect the rights of limited partners, including—

(A) the right of dissenting limited partners to one of the following:

(i) an appraisal and compensation;

(ii) retention of a security under substantially the same terms and conditions as the original issue;

(iii) approval of the limited partnership rollup transaction by not less than 75 percent of the outstanding securities of each of the participating limited partnerships;

(iv) the use of a committee that is independent, as determined in accordance with rules prescribed by the association, of the general partner or sponsor, that has been approved by a majority of the outstanding securities of each of the participating partnerships, and that has such authority as is necessary to protect the interest of limited partners, including the authority to hire independent advisors, to negotiate with the general partner or sponsor on behalf of the limited partners, and to make a recommendation to the limited partners with respect to the proposed transaction; or

(v) other comparable rights that are prescribed by rule by the association and that are designed to protect dissenting limited partners;

(B) the right not to have their voting power unfairly reduced or abridged;

(C) the right not to bear an unfair portion of the costs of a proposed limited partnership rollup transaction that is rejected; and

(D) restrictions on the conversion of contingent interests or fees into non-contingent interests or fees and restrictions on the receipt of a non-contingent equity interest in exchange for fees for services which have not yet been provided.

As used in this paragraph, the term "dissenting limited partner" means a person who, on the date on which soliciting material is mailed to investors, is a holder of a beneficial interest in a limited partnership that is the subject of a limited partnership rollup transaction, and who casts a vote against the transaction and complies with procedures established by the association, except that for purposes of an exchange or tender offer, such person shall file an objection in writing under the rules of the association during the period during which the offer is outstanding.

(14) The rules of the association include provisions governing the sales, or offers of sales, of securities on the premises of any military installation to any member of the Armed Forces or a dependent thereof, which rules require—

(A) the broker or dealer performing brokerage services to clearly and conspicuously disclose to potential investors—

(i) that the securities offered are not being offered or provided by the broker or dealer on behalf of the Federal Government, and that its offer is not sanctioned, recommended, or encouraged by the Federal Government; and

(ii) the identity of the registered broker-dealer offering the securities;

(B) such broker or dealer to perform an appropriate suitability determination, including consideration of costs and knowledge about securities, prior to making a recommendation of a security to a member of the Armed Forces or a dependent thereof; and

(C) that no person receive any referral fee or incentive compensation in connection with a sale or offer of sale of securities, unless such person is an associated person of a registered broker or dealer and is qualified pursuant to the rules of a self-regulatory organization.

(15) The rules of the association provide that the association shall—

(A) request guidance from the Municipal Securities Rulemaking Board in interpretation of the rules of the Municipal Securities Rulemaking Board; and

(B) provide information to the Municipal Securities Rulemaking Board about the enforcement actions and examinations of the association under section 15B(b)(2)(E), so that the Municipal Securities Rulemaking Board may—

(i) assist in such enforcement actions and examinations; and

(ii) evaluate the ongoing effectiveness of the rules of the Board.

(c) The Commission may permit or require the rules of an association applying for registration pursuant to subsection (b) of this section, to provide for the admission of an association registered as an affiliated securities association pursuant to subsection (d) of this section, to participation in said applicant association as an affiliate thereof, under terms permitting such powers and responsibilities to such affiliate, and under such other appropriate terms and conditions, as may be provided by the rules of said applicant association, if such rules appear to the Commission to be necessary or appropriate in the public interest or for the protection of investors and to carry out the purposes of this section. The duties and powers of the Commission with respect to any national securities association or any affiliated securities association shall in no way be limited by reason of any such affiliation.

(d) An applicant association shall not be registered as an affiliated securities association unless it appears to the Commission that—

(1) such association, notwithstanding that it does not satisfy the requirements set forth in paragraph (1) of subsection (b) of this section, will, forthwith upon the registration thereof, be admitted to affiliation with an association registered as a national securities association pursuant to subsection (b) of this section, in the manner and under the terms and conditions provided by the rules of said national securities association in accordance with subsection (c) of this section; and

(2) such association and its rules satisfy the requirements set forth in paragraphs (2) to (10), inclusive, and paragraph (12), of subsection (b) of this section; except that in the case of any such association any restrictions upon membership therein of the type authorized by paragraph (3) of subsection (b) of this section shall not be less stringent than in the case of the national securities association with which such association is to be affiliated.

(e)(1) The rules of a registered securities association may provide that no member thereof shall deal with any nonmember professional (as defined in paragraph (2) of this subsection) except at the same prices, for the same commissions or fees, and on the same terms and conditions as are by such member accorded to the general public.

(2) For the purposes of this subsection, the term "nonmember professional" shall include

(A) with respect to transactions in securities other than municipal securities, any registered broker or dealer who is not a member of any registered securities association, except such a broker or dealer who deals exclusively in commercial paper, bankers' acceptances, and commercial bills, and

(B) with respect to transactions in municipal securities, any municipal securities dealer (other than a bank or division or department of a bank) who is not a member of any registered securities association and any municipal securities broker who is not a member of any such association.

(3) Nothing in this subsection shall be so construed or applied as to prevent

(A) any member of a registered securities association from granting to any other member of any registered securities association any dealer's discount, allowance, commission, or special terms, in connection with the purchase or sale of securities, or

(B) any member of a registered securities association or any municipal securities dealer which is a bank or a division or department of a bank from granting to any member of any registered securities association or any such municipal securities dealer any dealer's discount, allowance, commission, or special terms in connection with the purchase or sale of municipal securities: *Provided, however,* That the granting of any such discount, allowance, commission, or special terms in connection with the purchase or sale of municipal securities shall be subject to rules of the Municipal Securities Rulemaking Board adopted pursuant to section 15B(b)(2)(K) of this Act.

(f) Nothing in subsection (b)(6) or (b)(11) of this section shall be construed to permit a registered securities association to make rules concerning any transaction by a registered broker or dealer in a municipal security.

(g)(1) A registered securities association shall deny membership to any person who is not a registered broker or dealer.

(2) A registered securities association may, and in cases in which the Commission, by order, directs as necessary or appropriate in the public interest or for the protection of investors shall, deny membership to any registered broker or dealer, and bar from becoming associated with a member any person, who is subject to a statutory disqualification. A registered securities association shall file notice with the Commission not less than thirty days prior to admitting any registered broker or dealer to membership or permitting any person to become associated with a member, if the association knew, or in the exercise of reasonable care should have known, that such broker or dealer or person was subject to a statutory disqualification. The notice shall be in such form and contain such information as the Commission, by rule, may prescribe as necessary or appropriate in the public interest or for the protection of investors.

(3)(A) A registered securities association may deny membership to, or condition the membership of, a registered broker or dealer if (i) such broker or dealer does not meet such standards of financial responsibility or operational capability or such broker or dealer or any natural person associated with such broker or dealer does not meet such standards of training, experience, and competence as are prescribed by the rules of the association or (ii) such broker or dealer or person associated with such broker or dealer has engaged and there is a reasonable likelihood he will again engage in acts or practices inconsistent with just and equitable principles of trade. A registered securities association may examine and verify the qualifications of an applicant to become a member and the natural persons associated with such an applicant in accordance with procedures established by the rules of the association.

(B) A registered securities association may bar a natural person from becoming associated with a member or condition the association of a natural person with a member if such natural person

(i) does not meet such standards of training, experience, and competence as are prescribed by the rules of the association or

(ii) has engaged and there is a reasonable likelihood he will again engage in acts or practices inconsistent with just and equitable principles of trade. A registered securities association may examine and verify the qualifications of an applicant to become a person associated with a member in accordance with procedures established by the rules of the association and require a natural person associated with a member, or any class of such natural persons, to be registered with the association in accordance with procedures so established.

(C) A registered securities association may bar any person from becoming associated with a member if such person does not agree

(i) to supply the association with such information with respect to its relationship and dealings with the member as may be specified in the rules of the association and

(ii) to permit examination of its books and records to verify the accuracy of any information so supplied.

(D) Nothing in subparagraph (A), (B), or (C) of this paragraph shall be construed to permit a registered securities association to deny membership to or condition the membership of, or bar any person from becoming associated with or condition the association of any person with, a broker or dealer that engages exclusively in transactions in municipal securities.

(4) A registered securities association may deny membership to a registered broker or dealer not engaged in a type of business in which the rules of the association require members to be engaged: *Provided, however,* That no registered securities association may deny membership to a registered broker or dealer by reason of the amount of such type of business done by such broker or dealer or the other types of business in which he is engaged.

(h)(1) In any proceeding by a registered securities association to determine whether a member or person associated with a member should be disciplined (other than a summary proceeding pursuant to paragraph (3) of this subsection) the association shall bring specific charges, notify such member or person of, and give him an opportunity to defend against, such charges, and keep a record. A determination by the association to impose a disciplinary sanction shall be supported by a statement setting forth—

(A) any act or practice in which such member or person associated with a member has been found to have engaged, or which such member or person has been found to have omitted;

(B) the specific provision of this Act, the rules or regulations thereunder, the rules of the Municipal Securities Rulemaking Board, or the rules of the association which any such act or practice, or omission to act, is deemed to violate; and

(C) the sanction imposed and the reason therefor.

(2) In any proceeding by a registered securities association to determine whether a person shall be denied membership, barred from becoming associated with a member, or prohibited or limited with respect to access to services offered by the association or a member thereof (other than a summary proceeding pursuant to paragraph (3) of this subsection), the association shall notify such person of and give him an opportunity to be heard upon, the specific grounds for denial, bar, or prohibition or limitation under consideration and keep a record. A determination by the association to deny membership, bar a person from becoming associated with a member, or prohibit or limit a person with respect to access to services offered by the association or a member thereof shall be supported by a statement setting forth the specific grounds on which the denial, bar, or prohibition or limitation is based.

(3)   A registered securities association may summarily

(A)   suspend a member or person associated with a member who has been and is expelled or suspended from any self-regulatory organization or barred or suspended from being associated with a member of any self-regulatory organization,

(B)   suspend a member who is in such financial or operating difficulty that the association determines and so notifies the Commission that the member cannot be permitted to continue to do business as a member with safety to investors, creditors, other members, or the association, or

(C)   limit or prohibit any person with respect to access to services offered by the association if subparagraph (A) or (B) of this paragraph is applicable to such person or, in the case of a person who is not a member, if the association determines that such person does not meet the qualification requirements or other prerequisites for such access and such person cannot be permitted to continue to have such access with safety to investors, creditors, members, or the association. Any person aggrieved by any such summary action shall be promptly afforded an opportunity for a hearing by the association in accordance with the provisions of paragraph (1) or (2) of this subsection. The Commission, by order, may stay any such summary action on its own motion or upon application by any person aggrieved thereby, if the Commission determines summarily or after notice and opportunity for hearing (which hearing may consist solely of the submission of affidavits or presentation of oral arguments) that such stay is consistent with the public interest and the protection of investors.

(i)   Obligation to maintain registration, disciplinary, and other data.—

(1)   Maintenance of system to respond to inquiries.—

A registered securities association shall—

(A)   establish and maintain a system for collecting and retaining registration information;

(B)   establish and maintain a toll-free telephone listing, and a readily accessible electronic or other process, to receive and promptly respond to inquiries regarding—

(i)   registration information on its members and their associated persons; and

(ii)   registration information on the members and their associated persons of any registered national securities exchange that uses the system described in subparagraph (A) for the registration of its members and their associated persons; and

(C)   adopt rules governing the process for making inquiries and the type, scope, and presentation of information to be provided in response to such inquiries in consultation with any registered national securities exchange providing information pursuant to subparagraph (B)(ii).

(2)   Recovery of costs.—

A registered securities association may charge persons making inquiries described in paragraph (1)(B), other than individual investors, reasonable fees for responses to such inquiries.

(3)   Process for disputed information.—

Each registered securities association shall adopt rules establishing an administrative process for disputing the accuracy of information provided in response to inquiries under this subsection in consultation with any registered national securities exchange providing information pursuant to paragraph (1)(B)(ii).

(4)   Limitation on liability.—

A registered securities association, or an exchange reporting information to such an association, shall not have any liability to any person for any actions taken or omitted in good faith under this subsection.

(5)   Definition.—

For purposes of this subsection, the term "registration information" means the information reported in connection with the registration or licensing of brokers and dealers and their associated persons, including disciplinary actions, regulatory, judicial, and arbitration proceedings, and other information required by law, or exchange or association rule, and the source and status of such information.

(j)   Registration for Sales of Private Securities Offerings.—

A registered securities association shall create a limited qualification category for any associated person of a member who effects sales as part of a primary offering of securities not involving a public offering, pursuant to section 3(b), 4(2), or 4(6) of the Securities Act of 1933 and the rules and regulations thereunder, and shall deem qualified in such limited qualification category, without testing, any bank employee who, in the six month period preceding the date of enactment of the Gramm-Leach-Bliley Act, engaged in effecting such sales. [effective May 12, 2001]

(k)   Limited Purpose National Securities Association.—

(1)   Regulation of Members With Respect to Security Futures Products.—A futures association registered under section 17 of the Commodity Exchange Act shall be a registered national securities association for the limited purpose of regulating the activities of members who are registered as brokers or dealers in security futures products pursuant to section 15(b)(11).

(2)   Requirements for Registration.—Such a securities association shall—

(A)   be so organized and have the capacity to carry out the purposes of the securities laws applicable to security futures products and to comply, and (subject to any rule or order of the Commission pursuant to section 19(g)(2)) to enforce compliance by its members and persons associated with its members, with the provisions of the securities laws applicable to security futures products, the rules and regulations thereunder, and its rules;

(B)   have rules that—

(i)   are designed to prevent fraudulent and manipulative acts and practices, to promote just and equitable principles of trade, and, in general, to protect investors and the public interest, including rules governing sales practices and the advertising of security futures products reasonably comparable to those of other national securities associations registered pursuant to subsection (a) that are applicable to security futures products; and

(ii)   are not designed to regulate by virtue of any authority conferred by this Act matters not related to the purposes of this Act or the administration of the association;

(C)   have rules that provide that (subject to any rule or order of the Commission pursuant to section 19(g)(2)) its members and persons associated with its members shall be appropriately disciplined for violation of any provision of the securities laws applicable to security futures products, the rules or regulations thereunder, or the rules of the association, by expulsion, suspension, limitation of activities, functions, and operations, fine, censure, being suspended or barred from being associated with a member, or any other fitting sanction; and

(D)   have rules that ensure that members and natural persons associated with members meet such standards of training, experience, and competence necessary to effect transactions in security futures products and are tested for their knowledge of securities and security futures products.

(3)   Exemption From Rule Change Submission.—Such a securities association shall be exempt from submitting proposed rule changes pursuant to section 19(b) of this Act, except that—

(A)   the association shall file proposed rule changes related to higher margin levels, fraud or manipulation, recordkeeping, reporting, listing standards, or decimal pricing for security futures products, sales practices for, advertising of, or standards of training, experience, competence, or other qualifications for security futures products for persons who effect transactions in security futures products, or rules effectuating the association's obligation to enforce the securities laws pursuant to section 19(b)(7);

(B)   the association shall file pursuant to sections 19(b)(1) and 19(b)(2) proposed rule changes related to margin, except for changes resulting in higher margin levels; and

(C)   the association shall file pursuant to section 19(b)(1) proposed rule changes that have been abrogated by the Commission pursuant to section 19(b)(7)(C).

(4) Other Exemptions.—Such a securities association shall be exempt from and shall not be required to enforce compliance by its members, and its members shall not, solely with respect to their transactions effected in security futures products, be required to comply, with the following provisions of this Act and the rules thereunder:

(A) Section 8.

(B) Subsections (b)(1), (b)(3), (b)(4), (b)(5), (b)(8), (b)(10), (b)(11), (b)(12), (b)(13), (c), (d), (e), (f), (g), (h), and (i) of this section.

(C) Subsections (d), (f), and (k) of section 17.

(D) Subsections (a), (f), and (h) of section 19.

(*l*) Consistent with this Act, each national securities association registered pursuant to subsection (a) of this section shall issue such rules as are necessary to avoid duplicative or conflicting rules applicable to any broker or dealer registered with the Commission pursuant to section 15(b) (except paragraph (11) thereof), that is also registered with the Commodity Futures Trading Commission pursuant to section 4f(a) of the Commodity Exchange Act (except paragraph (2) thereof), with respect to the application of—

(1) rules of such national securities association of the type specified in section 15(c)(3)(B) involving security futures products; and

(2) similar rules of national securities associations registered pursuant to subsection (k) of this section and national securities exchanges registered pursuant to section 6(g) involving security futures products.

(m) Procedures and Rules for Security Future Products.—A national securities association registered pursuant to subsection (a) shall, not later than 8 months after the date of the enactment of the Commodity Futures Modernization Act of 2000, implement the procedures specified in section 6(h)(5)(A) of this Act and adopt the rules specified in subparagraphs (B) and (C) of section 6(h)(5) of this Act.

Municipal Securities

Sec. 15B.   (a)(1)(A) It shall be unlawful for any municipal securities dealer (other than one registered as a broker or dealer under section 15 of this Act) to make use of the mails or any means or instrumentality of interstate commerce to effect any transaction in, or to induce or attempt to induce the purchase or sale of, any municipal security unless such municipal securities dealer is registered in accordance with this subsection.

(B) It shall be unlawful for a municipal advisor to provide advice to or on behalf of a municipal entity or obligated person with respect to municipal financial products or the issuance of municipal securities, or to undertake a solicitation of a municipal entity or obligated person, unless the municipal advisor is registered in accordance with this subsection.

(2) A municipal securities dealer or municipal advisor may be registered by filing with the Commission an application for registration in such form and containing such information and documents concerning such municipal securities dealer or municipal advisor and any persons associated with such municipal securities dealer or municipal advisor as the Commission, by rule, may prescribe as necessary or appropriate in the public interest or for the protection of investors. Within forty-five days of the date of the filing of such application (or within such longer period as to which the applicant consents), the Commission shall—

(A) by order grant registration, or

(B) institute proceedings to determine whether registration should be denied. Such proceedings shall include notice of the grounds for denial under consideration and opportunity for hearing and shall be concluded within one hundred twenty days of the date of the filing of the application for registration. At the conclusion of such proceedings the Commission, by order, shall grant or deny such registration. The Commission may extend the time for the conclusion of such proceedings for up to ninety days if it finds good cause for such extension and publishes its reasons for so finding or for such longer period as to which the applicant consents.

The Commission shall grant the registration of a municipal securities dealer or municipal advisor if the Commission finds that the requirements of this section are satisfied. The Commission shall deny such registration if it does not make such a finding or if it finds that if the applicant were so registered, its registration would be subject to suspension or revocation under subsection (c) of this section.

(3)   Any provision of this Act (other than section 5 of this Act or paragraph (1) of this subsection) which prohibits any act, practice, or course of business if the mails or any means or instrumentality of interstate commerce is used in connection therewith shall also prohibit any such act, practice, or course of business by any registered municipal securities dealer or municipal advisor or any person acting on behalf of such municipal securities dealer or municipal advisor, irrespective of any use of the mails or any means or instrumentality of interstate commerce in connection therewith.

(4)   The Commission, by rule or order, upon its own motion or upon application, may conditionally or unconditionally exempt any broker, dealer, municipal securities dealer, or municipal advisor, or class of brokers, dealers, municipal securities dealers, or municipal advisors from any provision of this section or the rules or regulations thereunder, if the Commission finds that such exemption is consistent with the public interest, the protection of investors, and the purposes of this section.

(5)   No municipal advisor shall make use of the mails or any means or instrumentality of interstate commerce to provide advice to or on behalf of a municipal entity or obligated person with respect to municipal financial products, the issuance of municipal securities, or to undertake a solicitation of a municipal entity or obligated person, in connection with which such municipal advisor engages in any fraudulent, deceptive, or manipulative act or practice.

(b)(1)   The Municipal Securities Rulemaking Board shall be composed of 15 members, or such other number of members as specified by rules of the Board pursuant to paragraph (2)(B), which shall perform the duties set forth in this section. The members of the Board shall serve as members for a term of 3 years or for such other terms as specified by rules of the Board pursuant to paragraph (2)(B), and shall consist of (A) 8 individuals who are independent of any municipal securities broker, municipal securities dealer, or municipal advisor, at least 1 of whom shall be representative of institutional or retail investors in municipal securities, at least 1 of whom shall be representative of municipal entities, and at least 1 of whom shall be a member of the public with knowledge of or experience in the municipal industry (which members are hereinafter referred to as "public representatives"); and (B) 7 individuals who are associated with a broker, dealer, municipal securities dealer, or municipal advisor, including at least 1 individual who is associated with and representative of brokers, dealers, or municipal securities dealers that are not banks or subsidiaries or departments or divisions of banks (which members are hereinafter referred to as "broker-dealer representatives"), at least 1 individual who is associated with and representative of municipal securities dealers which are banks or subsidiaries or departments or divisions of banks (which members are hereinafter referred to as "bank representatives"), and at least 1 individual who is associated with a municipal advisor (which members are hereinafter referred to as "advisor representatives" and, together with the broker-dealer representatives and the bank representatives, are referred to as "regulated representatives"). Each member of the board shall be knowledgeable of matters related to the municipal securities markets. The members of the Board shall serve as members for a term of two years, and shall consist of

     (A)   five individuals who are not associated with any broker, dealer, or municipal securities dealer (other than by reason of being under common control with, or indirectly controlling, any broker or dealer which is not a municipal securities broker or municipal securities dealer), at least one of whom shall be representative of investors in municipal securities, and at least one of whom shall be representative of issuers of municipal securities (which members are hereinafter referred to as "public representatives");

     (B)   five individuals who are associated with and representative of municipal securities brokers and municipal securities dealers which are not banks or subsidiaries or departments or divisions of banks (which members are hereinafter referred to as "broker-dealer representatives"); and

(C) five individuals who are associated with and representative of municipal securities dealers which are banks or subsidiaries or departments or divisions of banks (which members are hereinafter referred to as "bank representatives"). Prior to the expiration of the terms of office of the initial members of the Board, an election shall be held under rules adopted by the Board (pursuant to subsection (b)(2)(B) of this section) of the members to succeed such initial members.

(2) The Board shall propose and adopt rules to effect the purposes of this Act with respect to transactions in municipal securities effected by brokers, dealers, and municipal securities dealers and advice provided to or on behalf of municipal entities or obligated persons by brokers, dealers, municipal securities dealers, and municipal advisors with respect to municipal financial products, the issuance of municipal securities, and solicitations of municipal entities or obligated persons undertaken by brokers, dealers, municipal securities dealers, and municipal advisors. The rules of the Board, as a minimum, shall:

(A) provide that no municipal securities broker or municipal securities dealer shall effect any transaction in, or induce or attempt to induce the purchase or sale of, any municipal security, and no broker, dealer, municipal securities dealer, or municipal advisor shall provide advice to or on behalf of a municipal entity or obligated person with respect to municipal financial products or the issuance of municipal securities, unless such municipal securities broker or municipal securities dealer meets such standards of operational capability and such municipal securities broker or municipal securities dealer and every natural person associated with such municipal securities broker or municipal securities dealer meet such standards of training, experience, competence, and such other qualifications as the Board finds necessary or appropriate in the public interest or for the protection of investors and municipal entities or obligated persons. In connection with the definition and application of such standards the Board may—

(i) appropriately classify municipal securities brokers, municipal securities dealers and municipal advisors (taking into account relevant matters, including types of business done, nature of securities other than municipal securities sold, and character of business organization), and persons associated with municipal securities brokers, municipal securities dealers, and municipal advisors.

(ii) specify that all or any portion of such standards shall be applicable to any such class; and

(iii) require persons in any such class to pass tests administered in accordance with subsection (c)(7) of this section.

(B) establish fair procedures for the nomination and election of members of the Board and assure fair representation in such nominations and elections of public representatives, broker dealer representatives, bank representatives, and advisor representatives. Such rules—

(i) shall provide that the number of public representatives of the Board shall at all times exceed the total number of regulated representatives and that the membership shall at all times be as evenly divided in number as possible between public representatives and regulated representatives;

(ii) shall specify the length or lengths of terms members shall serve;

(iii) may increase the number of members which shall constitute the whole Board, provided that such number is an odd number; and

(iv) shall establish requirements regarding the independence of public representatives.

(C) be designed to prevent fraudulent and manipulative acts and practices, to promote just and equitable principles of trade, to foster cooperation and coordination with persons engaged in regulating, clearing, settling, processing information with respect to, and facilitating transactions in municipal securities and municipal financial products, to remove impediments to and perfect the mechanism of a free and open market in municipal securities and municipal financial products, and, in general, to protect investors, and municipal entities, obligated persons, and the public interest; and not be designed to permit unfair discrimination among customers, municipal entities, obligated persons, municipal securities brokers, municipal securities dealers, or municipal advisors, to fix minimum profits, to impose any schedule or fix rates of commissions, allowances, discounts, or other fees to be charged by municipal securities brokers, municipal securities dealers, or municipal advisors, to regulate by virtue of any authority conferred by this Act matters not related to the purposes of this Act or the administration of the Board, or to impose any burden on competition not necessary or appropriate in furtherance of the purposes of this Act.

(D) if the Board deems appropriate, provide for the arbitration of claims, disputes, and controversies relating to transactions in municipal securities and advice concerning municipal financial products: *Provided, however,* that no person other than a municipal securities broker, municipal securities dealer, municipal advisor, or person associated with such a municipal securities broker, municipal securities dealer, or municipal advisor may be compelled to submit to such arbitration except at his instance and in accordance with section 29 of this Act.

(E) provide for the periodic examination in accordance with subsection (c)(7) of this section of municipal securities brokers, municipal securities dealers and municipal advisors to determine compliance with applicable provisions of this Act, the rules and regulations thereunder, and the rules of the Board. Such rules shall specify the minimum scope and frequency of such examinations and shall be designed to avoid unnecessary regulatory duplication or undue regulatory burdens for any such municipal securities broker, municipal securities dealer or municipal advisors.

(F) include provisions governing the form and content of quotations relating to municipal securities which may be distributed or published by any municipal securities broker, municipal securities dealer, or person associated with such a municipal securities broker or municipal securities dealer, and the persons to whom such quotations may be supplied. Such rules relating to quotations shall be designed to produce fair and informative quotations, to prevent fictitious or misleading quotations, and to promote orderly procedures for collecting, distributing, and publishing quotations.

(G) prescribe records to be made and kept by municipal securities brokers, municipal securities dealers and municipal advisors and the periods for which such records shall be preserved.

(H) define the term "separately identifiable department or division", as that term is used in section 3(a)(30) of this Act, in accordance with specified and appropriate standards to assure that a bank is not deemed to be engaged in the business of buying and selling municipal securities through a separately identifiable department or division unless such department or division is organized and administered so as to permit independent examination and enforcement of applicable provisions of this Act, the rules and regulations thereunder, and the rules of the Board. A separately identifiable department or division of a bank may be engaged in activities other than those relating to municipal securities.

(I) provide for the operation and administration of the Board, including the selection of a Chairman from among the members of the Board, the compensation of the members of the Board, and the appointment and compensation of such employees, attorneys, and consultants as may be necessary or appropriate to carry out the Board's functions under this section.

(J) provide that each municipal securities broker, municipal securities dealer and municipal advisor shall pay to the Board such reasonable fees and charges as may be necessary or appropriate to defray the costs and expenses of operating and administering the Board. Such rules shall specify the amount of such fees and charges, which may include charges for failure to submit to the Board, or to any information system operated by the Board, within the prescribed timeframes, any items of information or documents required to be submitted under any rule issued by the Board.

(K) establish the terms and conditions under which any broker, dealer, or municipal securities dealer may sell, or prohibit any broker, dealer, or municipal securities dealer from selling, any part of a new issue of municipal securities to a related account of a broker, dealer, or municipal securities dealer during the underwriting period.

(L)   with respect to municipal advisors—

     (i)   prescribe means reasonably designed to prevent acts, practices, and courses of business as are not consistent with a municipal advisor's fiduciary duty to its clients;

     (ii)   provide continuing education requirements for municipal advisors;

     (iii)   provide professional standards; and

     (iv)   not impose a regulatory burden on small municipal advisors that is not necessary or appropriate in the public interest and for the protection of investors, municipal entities, and obligated persons, provided that there is robust protection of investors against fraud.'

(3)   The Board, in conjunction with or on behalf of any Federal financial regulator or self-regulatory organization, may—

(A)   establish information systems; and

(B)   assess such reasonable fees and charges for the submission of information to, or the receipt of information from, such systems from any persons which systems may be developed for the purposes of serving as a repository of information from municipal market participants or otherwise in furtherance of the purposes of the Board, a Federal financial regulator, or a self-regulatory organization, except that the Board—

     (i)   may not charge a fee to municipal entities or obligated persons to submit documents or other information to the Board or charge a fee to any person to obtain, directly from the Internet site of the Board, documents or information submitted by municipal entities, obligated persons, brokers, dealers, municipal securities dealers, or municipal advisors, including documents submitted under the rules of the Board or the Commission; and

     (ii)   shall not be prohibited from charging commercially reasonable fees for automated subscription-based feeds or similar services, or for charging for other data or document-based services customized upon request of any person, made available to commercial enterprises, municipal securities market professionals, or the general public, whether delivered through the Internet or any other means, that contain all or part of the documents or information, subject to approval of the fees by the Commission under section 19(b).

(4)   The Board may provide guidance and assistance in the enforcement of, and examination for, compliance with the rules of the Board to the Commission, a registered securities association under section 15A, or any other appropriate regulatory agency, as applicable.

(5)   The Board, the Commission, and a registered securities association under section 15A, or the designees of the Board, the Commission, or such association, shall meet not less frequently than 2 times a year—

(A)   to describe the work of the Board, the Commission, and the registered securities association involving the regulation of municipal securities; and

(B)   to share information about—

     (i)   the interpretation of the Board, the Commission, and the registered securities association of Board rules; and

     (ii)   examination and enforcement of compliance with Board rules

(7)[12] Nothing in this section shall be construed to impair or limit the power of the Commission under this Act.

(c)(1)   No broker, dealer, or municipal securities dealer shall make use of the mails or any means or instrumentality of interstate commerce to effect any transaction in, or to induce or attempt to induce the purchase or sale of, any municipal security, and no broker, dealer, municipal securities dealer, or municipal advisor shall make use of the mails or any means or instrumentality of interstate commerce to provide advice to or on behalf of a municipal entity or obligated person with respect to municipal financial products,

---

[12] So in original. No par. (6) enacted.

the issuance of municipal securities, or to undertake a solicitation of a municipal entity or obligated person, in contravention of any rule of the Board. A municipal advisor and any person associated with such municipal advisor shall be deemed to have a fiduciary duty to any municipal entity for whom such municipal advisor acts as a municipal advisor, and no municipal advisor may engage in any act, practice, or course of business which is not consistent with a municipal advisor's fiduciary duty or that is in contravention of any rule of the Board.

(2)   The Commission, by order, shall censure, place limitations on the activities, functions, or operations, suspend for a period not exceeding twelve months, or revoke the registration of any municipal securities dealer or municipal advisor, if it finds, on the record after notice and opportunity for hearing, that such censure, placing of limitations, denial, suspension, or revocation, is in the public interest and that such municipal securities dealer or municipal advisor has committed or omitted any act, or is subject to an order or finding, enumerated in subparagraph (A), (D), (E), (G), or (H) of paragraph (4) of section 15(b) of this Act, has been convicted of any offense specified in subparagraph (B) of such paragraph (4) within ten years of the commencement of the proceedings under this paragraph, or is enjoined from any action, conduct, or practice specified in subparagraph (C) of such paragraph (4).

(3)   Pending final determination whether any registration under this section shall be revoked, the Commission, by order, may suspend such registration, if such suspension appears to the Commission, after notice and opportunity for hearing, to be necessary or appropriate in the public interest or for the protection of investors or municipal entities or obligated person. Any registered municipal securities dealer or municipal advisor may, upon such terms and conditions as the Commission may deem necessary in the public interest or for the protection of investors or municipal entities or obligated person, withdraw from registration by filing a written notice of withdrawal with the Commission. If the Commission finds that any registered municipal securities dealer or municipal advisor is no longer in existence or has ceased to do business as a municipal securities dealer or municipal advisor, the Commission, by order, shall cancel the registration of such municipal securities dealer or municipal advisor.

(4)   The Commission, by order, shall censure or place limitations on the activities or functions of any person associated, seeking to become associated, or, at the time of the alleged misconduct, associated or seeking to become associated with a municipal securities dealer, or suspend for a period not exceeding 12 months or bar any such person from being associated with a broker, dealer, investment adviser, municipal securities dealer, municipal adviser, transfer agent, or nationally recognized statistical rating organization, if the Commission finds, on the record after notice and opportunity for hearing, that such censure, placing of limitations, suspension, or bar is in the public interest and that such person has committed any act, or is subject to an order or finding, enumerated in subparagraph (A), (D), (E), (G), or (H) of paragraph (4) of section 15(b) of this Act, has been convicted of any offense specified in subparagraph (B) of such paragraph (4) within 10 years of the commencement of the proceedings under this paragraph, or is enjoined from any action, conduct, or practice specified in subparagraph (C) of such paragraph (4). It shall be unlawful for any person as to whom an order entered pursuant to this paragraph or paragraph (5) of this subsection suspending or barring him from being associated with a municipal securities dealer is in effect willfully to become, or to be, associated with a municipal securities dealer without the consent of the Commission, and it shall be unlawful for any municipal securities dealer to permit such a person to become, or remain, a person associated with him without the consent of the Commission, if such municipal securities dealer knew, or, in the exercise of reasonable care should have known, of such order.

(5)   With respect to any municipal securities dealer for which the Commission is not the appropriate regulatory agency, the appropriate regulatory agency for such municipal securities dealer may sanction any such municipal securities dealer in the manner and for the reasons specified in paragraph (2) of this subsection and any person associated with such municipal securities dealer in the manner and for the reasons specified in paragraph (4) of this subsection. In addition, such appropriate regulatory agency may, in accordance with section 8 of the Federal Deposit Insurance Act, enforce compliance by such municipal securities dealer or any person associated with such municipal securities dealer with the provisions of this section, section 17 of this Act, the rules of the Board, and the rules of the Commission pertaining to municipal securities dealers, persons associated with municipal securities dealers, and transactions in municipal securities. For purposes of the preceding

sentence, any violation of any such provision shall constitute adequate basis for the issuance of any order under section 8(b) or 8(c) of the Federal Deposit Insurance Act, and the customers of any such municipal securities dealer shall be deemed to be "depositors" as that term is used in section 8(c) of that Act. Nothing in this paragraph shall be construed to affect in any way the powers of such appropriate regulatory agency to proceed against such municipal securities dealer under any other provision of law.

(6)(A) The Commission, prior to the entry of an order of investigation, or commencement of any proceedings, against any municipal securities dealer, or person associated with any municipal securities dealer, for which the Commission is not the appropriate regulatory agency, for violation of any provision of this section, section 15(c)(1) or 15(c)(2) of this Act, any rule or regulation under any such section, or any rule of the Board, shall

(i) give notice to the appropriate regulatory agency for such municipal securities dealer, of the identity of such municipal securities dealer or person associated with such municipal securities dealer, the nature of and basis for such proposed action, and whether the Commission is seeking a monetary penalty against such municipal securities dealer or such associated person pursuant to section 21B of this Act; and

(ii) consult with such appropriate regulatory agency concerning the effect of such proposed action on sound banking practices and the feasibility and desirability of coordinating such action with any proceeding or proposed proceeding by such appropriate regulatory agency against such municipal securities dealer or associated person.

(B) The appropriate regulatory agency for a municipal securities dealer (if other than the Commission), prior to the entry of an order of investigation, or commencement of any proceedings, against such municipal securities dealer or person associated with such municipal securities dealer, for violation of any provision of this section, the rules of the Board, or the rules or regulations of the Commission pertaining to municipal securities dealers, persons associated with municipal securities dealers, or transactions in municipal securities shall

(i) give notice to the Commission of the identity of such municipal securities dealer or person associated with such municipal securities dealer and the nature of and basis for such proposed action and

(ii) consult with the Commission concerning the effect of such proposed action on the protection of investors or municipal entities or obligated person and the feasibility and desirability of coordinating such action with any proceeding or proposed proceeding by the Commission against such municipal securities dealer or associated person.

(C) Nothing in this paragraph shall be construed to impair or limit (other than by the requirement of prior consultation) the power of the Commission or the appropriate regulatory agency for a municipal securities dealer to initiate any action of a class described in this paragraph or to affect in any way the power of the Commission or such appropriate regulatory agency to initiate any other action pursuant to this Act or any other provision of law.

(7)(A) Tests required pursuant to subsection (b)(2)(A)(iii) of this section shall be administered by or on behalf of and periodic examinations pursuant to subsection (b)(2)(E) of this section shall be conducted by—

(i) a registered securities association, in the case of municipal securities brokers and municipal securities dealers who are members of such association; and

(ii) the appropriate regulatory agency for any municipal securities broker or municipal securities dealer, in the case of all other municipal securities brokers and municipal securities dealers;

(iii) the Commission, or its designee, in the case of municipal advisors.

(B) A registered securities association shall make a report of any examination conducted pursuant to subsection (b)(2)(E) of this section and promptly furnish the Commission a copy thereof and any data supplied to it in connection with such examination. Subject to such limitations as the Commission, by rule, determines to be necessary or appropriate in the public interest or for the protection of investors or municipal entities or obligated person, the Commission shall, on request, make available to the Board a copy of any report of an examination of a municipal securities broker or municipal securities dealer made by or furnished to pursuant to this paragraph or section 17(c)(3) of this Act.

(8) The Commission is authorized, by order, if in its opinion such action is necessary or appropriate in the public interest, for the protection of investors, or otherwise, in furtherance of the purposes of this Act, to remove from office or censure any person who is, or at the time of the alleged violation or abuse was, a member or employee of the Board, who, the Commission finds, on the record after notice and opportunity for hearing, has willfully

    (A) violated any provision of this Act, the rules and regulations thereunder, or the rules of the Board or

    (B) abused his authority.

(9)(A) Fines collected by the Commission for violations of the rules of the Board shall be equally divided between the Commission and the Board.

    (B) Fines collected by a registered securities association under section 15A(7) with respect to violations of the rules of the Board shall be accounted for by such registered securities association separately from other fines collected under section 15A(7) and shall be allocated between such registered securities association and the Board, and such allocation shall require the registered securities association to pay to the Board 1/3 of all fines collected by the registered securities association reasonably allocable to violations of the rules of the Board, or such other portion of such fines as may be directed by the Commission upon agreement between the registered securities association and the Board.

(d)(1) Neither the Commission nor the Board is authorized under this Act, by rule or regulation, to require any issuer of municipal securities, directly or indirectly through a purchaser or prospective purchaser of securities from the issuer, to file with the Commission or the Board prior to the sale of such securities by the issuer any application, report, or document in connection with the issuance, sale, or distribution of such securities.

(2) The Board is not authorized under this Act to require any issuer of municipal securities, directly or indirectly through a municipal securities broker, municipal securities dealer, municipal advisor or otherwise, to furnish to the Board or to a purchaser or a prospective purchaser of such securities any application, report, document, or information with respect to such issuer: *Provided, however,* That the Board may require municipal securities brokers and municipal securities dealers or municipal advisor to furnish to the Board or to a purchaser or prospective purchaser of municipal securities applications, reports, documents, and information with respect to the issuer thereof which are generally available from a source other than such issuer. Nothing in this paragraph shall be construed to impair or limit the power of the Commission under any provision of this Act.

(e) Definitions—For purposes of this section—

(1) the term "Board" means the Municipal Securities Rulemaking Board established under subsection (b)(1);

(2) the term "guaranteed investment contract" includes any investment that has specified withdrawal or reinvestment provisions and a specifically negotiated or bid interest rate, and also includes any agreement to supply investments on 2 or more future dates, such as a forward supply contract;

(3) the term "investment strategies" includes plans or programs for the investment of the proceeds of municipal securities that are not municipal derivatives, guaranteed investment contracts, and the recommendation of and brokerage of municipal escrow investments;

(4) the term "municipal advisor"—

    (A) means a person (who is not a municipal entity or an employee of a municipal entity) that—

(i) provides advice to or on behalf of a municipal entity or obligated person with respect to municipal financial products or the issuance of municipal securities, including advice with respect to the structure, timing, terms, and other similar matters concerning such financial products or issues; or

(ii) undertakes a solicitation of a municipal entity;

(B) includes financial advisors, guaranteed investment contract brokers, third-party marketers, placement agents, solicitors, finders, and swap advisors, if such persons are described in any of clauses (i) through (iii) of subparagraph (A); and

(C) does not include a broker, dealer, or municipal securities dealer serving as an underwriter (as defined in section 2(a)(11) of the Securities Act of 1933) (15 U.S.C. 77b(a)(11)), any investment adviser registered under the Investment Advisers Act of 1940, or persons associated with such investment advisers who are providing investment advice, any commodity trading advisor registered under the Commodity Exchange Act or persons associated with a commodity trading advisor who are providing advice related to swaps, attorneys offering legal advice or providing services that are of a traditional legal nature, or engineers providing engineering advice;

(5) the term "municipal financial product" means municipal derivatives, guaranteed investment contracts, and investment strategies;

(6) the term "rules of the Board" means the rules proposed and adopted by the Board under subsection (b)(2);

(7) the term "person associated with a municipal advisor" or "associated person of an advisor" means—

(A) any partner, officer, director, or branch manager of such municipal advisor (or any person occupying a similar status or performing similar functions);

(B) any other employee of such municipal advisor who is engaged in the management, direction, supervision, or performance of any activities relating to the provision of advice to or on behalf of a municipal entity or obligated person with respect to municipal financial products or the issuance of municipal securities; and

(C) any person directly or indirectly controlling, controlled by, or under common control with such municipal advisor;

(8) the term "municipal entity" means any State, political subdivision of a State, or municipal corporate instrumentality of a State, including—

(A) any agency, authority, or instrumentality of the State, political subdivision, or municipal corporate instrumentality;

(B) any plan, program, or pool of assets sponsored or established by the State, political subdivision, or municipal corporate instrumentality or any agency, authority, or instrumentality thereof; and

(C) any other issuer of municipal securities;

(9) the term "solicitation of a municipal entity or obligated person" means a direct or indirect communication with a municipal entity or obligated person made by a person, for direct or indirect compensation, on behalf of a broker, dealer, municipal securities dealer, municipal advisor, or investment adviser (as defined in section 202 of the Investment Advisers Act of 1940) that does not control, is not controlled by, or is not under common control with the person undertaking such solicitation for the purpose of obtaining or retaining an engagement by a municipal entity or obligated person of a broker, dealer, municipal securities dealer, or municipal advisor for or in connection with municipal financial products, the issuance of municipal securities, or of an investment adviser to provide investment advisory services to or on behalf of a municipal entity; and

(10) the term "obligated person" means any person, including an issuer of municipal securities, who is either generally or through an enterprise, fund, or account of such person, committed by contract

or other arrangement to support the payment of all or part of the obligations on the municipal securities to be sold in an offering of municipal securities.

Government Securities Brokers and Dealers

Sec. 15C. (a)(1)(A) It shall be unlawful for any government securities broker or government securities dealer (other than a registered broker or dealer or a financial institution) to make use of the mails or any means or instrumentality of interstate commerce to effect any transaction in, or to induce or attempt to induce the purchase or sale of, any government security unless such government securities broker or government securities dealer is registered in accordance with paragraph (2) of this subsection.

(B)(i) It shall be unlawful for any government securities broker or government securities dealer that is a registered broker or dealer or a financial institution to make use of the mails or any means or instrumentality of interstate commerce to effect any transaction in, or to induce or attempt to induce the purchase or sale of, any government security unless such government securities broker or government securities dealer has filed with the appropriate regulatory agency written notice that it is a government securities broker or government securities dealer. When such a government securities broker or government securities dealer ceases to act as such it shall file with the appropriate regulatory agency a written notice that it is no longer acting as a government securities broker or government securities dealer.

(ii) Such notices shall be in such form and contain such information concerning a government securities broker or government securities dealer that is a financial institution and any persons associated with such government securities broker or government securities dealer as the Board of Governors of the Federal Reserve System shall, by rule, after consultation with each appropriate regulatory agency (including the Commission), prescribe as necessary or appropriate in the public interest or for the protection of investors. Such notices shall be in such form and contain such information concerning a government securities broker or government securities dealer that is a registered broker or dealer and any persons associated with such government securities broker or government securities dealer as the Commission shall, by rule, prescribe as necessary or appropriate in the public interest or for the protection of investors.

(iii) Each appropriate regulatory agency (other than the Commission) shall make available to the Commission the notices which have been filed with it under this subparagraph, and the Commission shall maintain and make available to the public such notices and the notices it receives under this subparagraph.

(2) A government securities broker or a government securities dealer subject to the registration requirement of paragraph (1)(A) of this subsection may be registered by filing with the Commission an application for registration in such form and containing such information and documents concerning such government securities broker or government securities dealer and any persons associated with such government securities broker or government securities dealer as the Commission, by rule, may prescribe as necessary or appropriate in the public interest or for the protection of investors. Within 45 days of the date of filing of such application (or within such longer period as to which the applicant consents), the Commission shall—

(A) by order grant registration, or

(B) institute proceedings to determine whether registration should be denied. Such proceedings shall include notice of the grounds for denial under consideration and opportunity for hearing and shall be concluded within 120 days of the date of the filing of the application for registration. At the conclusion of such proceedings, the Commission, by order, shall grant or deny such registration. The Commission may extend the time for the conclusion of such proceedings for up to 90 days if it finds good cause for such extension and publishes its reasons for so finding or for such longer period as to which the applicant consents.

The Commission shall grant the registration of a government securities broker or a government securities dealer if the Commission finds that the requirements of this section are satisfied. The order granting registration shall not be effective until such government securities broker or government securities dealer has become a member of a national securities exchange registered under section 6 of this title, or a securities association registered under section 15A of this title, unless the Commission has exempted such government securities broker or government securities dealer, by rule or order, from such membership. The Commission shall deny such registration if it does not make such a finding or if it finds that if the applicant were so registered, its registration would be subject to suspension or revocation under subsection (c) of this section.

(3) Any provision of this Act (other than section 5 of this Act or paragraph (1) of this subsection) which prohibits any act, practice, or course of business if the mails or any means or instrumentality of interstate commerce is used in connection therewith shall also prohibit any such act, practice, or course of business by any government securities broker or government securities dealer registered or having filed notice under paragraph (1) of this subsection or any person acting on behalf of such government securities broker or government securities dealer, irrespective of any use of the mails or any means or instrumentality of interstate commerce in connection therewith.

(4) No government securities broker or government securities dealer that is required to register under paragraph (1)(A) of this subsection and that is not a member of the Securities Investor Protection Corporation shall effect any transaction in any security in contravention of such rules as the Commission shall prescribe pursuant to this subsection to assure that its customers receive complete, accurate, and timely disclosure of the inapplicability of Securities Investor Protection Corporation coverage to their accounts.

(5) The Secretary of the Treasury (hereinafter in this section referred to as the "Secretary"), by rule or order, upon the Secretary's own motion or upon application, may conditionally or unconditionally exempt any government securities broker or government securities dealer, or class of government securities brokers or government securities dealers, from any provision of subsection (a), (b), or (d) of this section, other than subsection (d)(3) of this section, or the rules thereunder, if the Secretary finds that such exemption is consistent with the public interest, the protection of investors, and the purposes of this Act.

(b)(1) The Secretary shall propose and adopt rules to effect the purposes of this Act with respect to transactions in government securities effected by government securities brokers and government securities dealers as follows:

(A) Such rules shall provide safeguards with respect to the financial responsibility and related practices of government securities brokers and government securities dealers including, but not limited to, capital adequacy standards, the acceptance of custody and use of customers' securities, the carrying and use of customers' deposits or credit balances, and the transfer and control of government securities subject to repurchase agreements and in similar transactions.

(B) Such rules shall require every government securities broker and government securities dealer to make reports to and furnish copies of records to the appropriate regulatory agency, and to file with the appropriate regulatory agency, annually or more frequently, a balance sheet and income statement certified by an independent public accountant, prepared on a calendar or fiscal year basis, and such other financial statements (which shall, as the Secretary specifies, be certified) and information concerning its financial condition as required by such rules.

(C) Such rules shall require records to be made and kept by government securities brokers and government securities dealers and shall specify the periods for which such records shall be preserved.

(2) Risk assessment for Holding Company Systems.—

(A) Obligations to obtain, maintain, and report information.—

Every person who is registered as a government securities broker or government securities dealer under this section shall obtain such information and make and keep such records as the Secretary by rule prescribes concerning the registered person's policies, procedures, or systems for monitoring and controlling financial and operational risks to it resulting from the activities of any of its associated persons, other than a natural person. Such records shall describe, in the aggregate, each of the financial and securities activities conducted by, and customary sources of capital and funding of, those of its associated persons whose business activities are reasonably likely to have a material impact on the financial or operational condition of such registered person, including its capital, its liquidity, or its ability to conduct or finance its operations. The Secretary, by rule, may require summary reports of such information to be filed with the registered person's appropriate regulatory agency no more frequently than quarterly.

(B)   Authority to require additional information.—

If, as a result of adverse market conditions or based on reports provided pursuant to subparagraph (A) of this paragraph or other available information, the appropriate regulatory agency reasonably concludes that it has concerns regarding the financial or operational condition of any government securities broker or government securities dealer registered under this section, such agency may require the registered person to make reports concerning the financial and securities activities of any of such person's associated persons, other than a natural person, whose business activities are reasonably likely to have a material impact on the financial or operational condition of such registered person. The appropriate regulatory agency, in requiring reports pursuant to this subparagraph, shall specify the information required, the period for which it is required, the time and date on which the information must be furnished, and whether the information is to be furnished directly to the appropriate regulatory agency or to a self-regulatory organization with primary responsibility for examining the registered person's financial and operational condition.

(C)   Special provisions with respect to associated persons subject to federal banking agency regulation.—

(i)   Cooperation in implementation.—

In developing and implementing reporting requirements pursuant to subparagraph (A) of this paragraph with respect to associated persons subject to examination by or reporting requirements of a Federal banking agency, the Secretary shall consult with and consider the views of each such Federal banking agency. If a Federal banking agency comments in writing on a proposed rule of the Secretary under this paragraph that has been published for comment, the Secretary shall respond in writing to such written comment before adopting the proposed rule. The Secretary shall, at the request of a Federal banking agency, publish such comment and response in the Federal Register at the time of publishing the adopted rule.

(ii)   Use of banking agency reports.—

A registered government securities broker or government securities dealer shall be in compliance with any recordkeeping or reporting requirement adopted pursuant to subparagraph (A) of this paragraph concerning an associated person that is subject to examination by or reporting requirements of a Federal banking agency if such government securities broker or government securities dealer utilizes for such recordkeeping or reporting requirement copies of reports filed by the associated person with the Federal banking agency pursuant to section 5211 of the Revised Statutes, section 9 of the Federal Reserve Act, section 7(a) of the Federal Deposit Insurance Act, section 10(b) of the Home Owners' Loan Act, or section 8 of the Bank Holding Company Act of 1956. The Secretary may, however, by rule adopted pursuant to subparagraph (A), require any registered government securities broker or government securities dealer filing such reports with the appropriate regulatory agency to obtain, maintain, or report supplemental information if the Secretary makes an explicit finding, based on information provided by the appropriate regulatory agency, that such supplemental information is necessary to inform the appropriate regulatory agency regarding potential risks to such government securities broker or government securities dealer. Prior to requiring any such supplemental information, the Secretary shall first request the Federal banking agency to expand its reporting requirements to include such information.

(iii)   Procedure for requiring additional information.—

Prior to making a request pursuant to subparagraph (B) of this paragraph for information with respect to an associated person that is subject to examination by or reporting requirements of a Federal banking agency, the appropriate regulatory agency shall—

(I) notify such banking agency of the information required with respect to such associated person; and

(II) consult with such agency to determine whether the information required is available from such agency and for other purposes, unless the appropriate regulatory agency determines that any delay resulting from such consultation would be inconsistent with ensuring the financial and operational condition of the government securities broker or government securities dealer or the stability or integrity of the securities markets.

(iv) **Exclusion for examination reports.—**

Nothing in this subparagraph shall be construed to permit the Secretary or an appropriate regulatory agency to require any registered government securities broker or government securities dealer to obtain, maintain, or furnish any examination report of any Federal banking agency or any supervisory recommendations or analysis contained therein.

(v) **Confidentiality of information provided.—**

No information provided to or obtained by an appropriate regulatory agency from any Federal banking agency pursuant to a request under clause (iii) of this subparagraph regarding any associated person which is subject to examination by or reporting requirements of a Federal banking agency may be disclosed to any other person (other than a self-regulatory organization), without the prior written approval of the Federal banking agency. Nothing in this clause shall authorize the Secretary or any appropriate regulatory agency to withhold information from Congress, or prevent the Secretary or any appropriate regulatory agency from complying with a request for information from any other Federal department or agency requesting the information for purposes within the scope of its jurisdiction, or complying with an order of a court of the United States in an action brought by the United States or the Commission.

(vi) **Notice to banking agencies concerning financial and operational condition concerns.—**

The Secretary or appropriate regulatory agency shall notify the Federal banking agency of any concerns of the Secretary or the appropriate regulatory agency regarding significant financial or operational risks resulting from the activities of any government securities broker or government securities dealer to any associated person thereof which is subject to examination by or reporting requirements of the Federal banking agency.

(vii) **Definition.—**

For purposes of this subparagraph, the term "Federal banking agency" shall have the same meaning as the term "appropriate Federal banking agency" in section 3(q) of the Federal Deposit Insurance Act.

(D) **Exemptions.—**

The Secretary by rule or order may exempt any person or class of persons, under such terms and conditions and for such periods as the Secretary shall provide in such rule or order, from the provisions of this paragraph, and the rules thereunder. In granting such exemptions, the Secretary shall consider, among other factors—

(i) whether information of the type required under this paragraph is available from a supervisory agency (as defined in section 1101(6) of the Right to Financial Privacy Act of 1978) a State insurance commission or similar State agency, the Commodity Futures Trading Commission, or a similar foreign regulator;

(ii)   the primary business of any associated person;

(iii)   the nature and extent of domestic or foreign regulation of the associated person's activities;

(iv)   the nature and extent of the registered person's securities transactions; and

(v)   with respect to the registered person and its associated persons, on a consolidated basis, the amount and proportion of assets devoted to, and revenues derived from, activities in the United States securities markets.

(E)   Conformity with requirements under section 17(h).—

In exercising authority pursuant to subparagraph (A) of this paragraph concerning information with respect to associated persons of government securities brokers and government securities dealers who are also associated persons of registered brokers or dealers reporting to the Commission pursuant to section 17(h) of this Act, the requirements relating to such associated persons shall conform, to the greatest extent practicable, to the requirements under section 17(h).

(F)   Authority to limit disclosure of information.—

Notwithstanding any other provision of law, the Secretary and any appropriate regulatory agency shall not be compelled to disclose any information required to be reported under this paragraph, or any information supplied to the Secretary or any appropriate regulatory agency by any domestic or foreign regulatory agency that relates to the financial or operational condition of any associated person of a registered government securities broker or a government securities dealer. Nothing in this paragraph shall authorize the Secretary or any appropriate regulatory agency to withhold information from Congress, or prevent the Secretary or any appropriate regulatory agency from complying with a request for information from any other Federal department or agency requesting the information for purposes within the scope of its jurisdiction, or complying with an order of a court of the United States in an action brought by the United States or the Commission. For purposes of section 552 of Title 5, United States Code, this paragraph shall be considered a statute described in subsection (b)(3)(B) of such section 552.

(3)(A)   With respect to any financial institution that has filed notice as a government securities broker or government securities dealer or that is required to file notice under subsection (a)(1)(B) of this section, the appropriate regulatory agency for such government securities broker or government securities dealer may issue such rules and regulations with respect to transactions in government securities as may be necessary to prevent fraudulent and manipulative acts and practices and to promote just and equitable principles of trade. If the Secretary of the Treasury determines, and notifies the appropriate regulatory agency, that such rule or regulation, if implemented, would, or as applied does

(i)   adversely affect the liquidity or efficiency of the market for government securities; or

(ii)   impose any burden on competition not necessary or appropriate in furtherance of the purposes of this section, the appropriate regulatory agency shall, prior to adopting the proposed rule or regulation, find that such rule or regulation is necessary and appropriate in furtherance of the purposes of this section notwithstanding the Secretary's determination.

(B)   The appropriate regulatory agency shall consult with and consider the views of the Secretary prior to approving or amending a rule or regulation under this paragraph, except where the appropriate regulatory agency determines that an emergency exists requiring expeditious and summary action and publishes its reasons therefor. If the Secretary comments in writing to the appropriate regulatory agency on a proposed rule or regulation that has been published for comment, the appropriate regulatory agency shall respond in writing to such written comment before approving the proposed rule or regulation.

(C)   In promulgating rules under this section, the appropriate regulatory agency shall consider the sufficiency and appropriateness of then existing laws and rules applicable to government securities brokers, government securities dealers, and persons associated with government securities brokers and government securities dealers.

(4) Rules promulgated and orders issued under this section shall—

(A) be designed to prevent fraudulent and manipulative acts and practices and to protect the integrity, liquidity, and efficiency of the market for government securities, investors, and the public interest; and

(B) not be designed to permit unfair discrimination between customers, issuers, government securities brokers, or government securities dealers, or to impose any burden on competition not necessary or appropriate in furtherance of the purposes of this Act.

(5) In promulgating rules and issuing orders under this section, the Secretary—

(A) may appropriately classify government securities brokers and government securities dealers (taking into account relevant matters, including types of business done, nature of securities other than government securities purchased or sold, and character of business organization) and persons associated with government securities brokers and government securities dealers;

(B) may determine, to the extent consistent with paragraph (2) of this subsection and with the public interest, the protection of investors, and the purposes of this Act, not to apply, in whole or in part, certain rules under this section, or to apply greater, lesser, or different standards, to certain classes of government securities brokers, government securities dealers, or persons associated with government securities brokers or government securities dealers;

(C) shall consider the sufficiency and appropriateness of then existing laws and rules applicable to government securities brokers, government securities dealers, and persons associated with government securities brokers and government securities dealers; and

(D) shall consult with and consider the views of the Commission and the Board of Governors of the Federal Reserve System, except where the Secretary determines that an emergency exists requiring expeditious or summary action and publishes its reasons for such determination.

(6) If the Commission or the Board of Governors of the Federal Reserve System comments in writing on a proposed rule of the Secretary that has been published for comment, the Secretary shall respond in writing to such written comment before approving the proposed rule.

(7) No government securities broker or government securities dealer shall make use of the mails or any means or instrumentality of interstate commerce to effect any transaction in, or to induce or attempt to induce the purchase or sale of, any government security in contravention of any rule under this section.

(c)(1) With respect to any government securities broker or government securities dealer registered or required to register under subsection (a)(1)(A) of this section—

(A) The Commission, by order, shall censure, place limitations on the activities, functions, or operations of, suspend for a period not exceeding 12 months, or revoke the registration of such government securities broker or government securities dealer, if it finds, on the record after notice and opportunity for hearing, that such censure, placing of limitations, suspension, or revocation is in the public interest and that such government securities broker or government securities dealer, or any person associated with such government securities broker or government securities dealer (whether prior or subsequent to becoming so associated), has committed or omitted any act, or is subject to an order or finding, enumerated in subparagraph (A), (D), (E), (G), or (H) of paragraph (4) of section 15(b) of this Act, has been convicted of any offense specified in subparagraph (B) of such paragraph (4) within 10 years of the commencement of the proceedings under this paragraph, or is enjoined from any action, conduct, or practice specified in subparagraph (C) of such paragraph (4).

(B) Pending final determination whether registration of any government securities broker or government securities dealer shall be revoked, the Commission, by order, may suspend such registration, if such suspension appears to the Commission, after notice and opportunity for hearing, to be necessary or appropriate in the public interest or for the protection of investors. Any registered government securities broker or registered government securities dealer may, upon such terms and conditions as the Commission may deem necessary in the public interest or for the protection of investors, withdraw from registration by filing a written notice of withdrawal with the Commission. If the Commission finds that any registered government securities broker or registered government securities dealer is no longer in existence or has ceased to do business as a government securities broker or government securities dealer, the Commission, by order, shall cancel the registration of such government securities broker or government securities dealer.

(C)   The Commission, by order, shall censure or place limitations on the activities or functions of any person who is, or at the time of the alleged misconduct was, associated or seeking to become associated, with a government securities broker or government securities dealer registered or required to register under subsection (a)(1)(A) of this section or suspend for a period not exceeding 12 months or bar any such person from being associated with such a government securities broker or government securities dealer, if the Commission finds, on the record after notice and opportunity for hearing, that such censure, placing of limitations, suspension, or bar is in the public interest and that such person has committed or omitted any act, or is subject to an order or finding, enumerated in subparagraph (A), (D), (E), (G) or (H) of paragraph (4) of section 15(b) of this Act, has been convicted of any offense specified in subparagraph (B) of such paragraph (4) within 10 years of the commencement of the proceedings under this paragraph, or is enjoined from any action, conduct, or practice specified in subparagraph (C) of such paragraph (4).

(2)(A)   With respect to any government securities broker or government securities dealer which is not registered or required to register under subsection (a)(1)(A) of this section, the appropriate regulatory agency for such government securities broker or government securities dealer may, in the manner and for the reasons specified in paragraph (1)(A) of this subsection, censure, place limitations on the activities, functions, or operations of, suspend for a period not exceeding 12 months, or bar from acting as a government securities broker or government securities dealer any such government securities broker or government securities dealer, and may sanction any person associated, seeking to become associated, or, at the time of the alleged misconduct, associated or seeking to become associated with such government securities broker or government securities dealer in the manner and for the reasons specified in paragraph (1)(C) of this subsection.

(B)   In addition, where applicable, such appropriate regulatory agency may, in accordance with section 8 of the Federal Deposit Insurance Act, section 5 of the Home Owners' Loan Act of 1933, or section 407 of the National Housing Act, enforce compliance by such government securities broker or government securities dealer or any person associated, seeking to become associated, or, at the time of the alleged misconduct, associated or seeking to become associated with such government securities broker or government securities dealer with the provisions of this section and the rules thereunder.

(C)   For purposes of subparagraph (B) of this paragraph, any violation of any such provision shall constitute adequate basis for the issuance of any order under section 8(b) or 8(c) of the Federal Deposit Insurance Act, section 5(d)(2) or 5(d)(3) of the Home Owners' Loan Act of 1933, or section 407(e) or 407(f) of the National Housing Act, and the customers of any such government securities broker or government securities dealer shall be deemed, respectively, "depositors" as that term is used in section 8(c) of the Federal Deposit Insurance Act, "savings account holders" as that term is used in section 5(d)(3) of the Home Owners' Loan Act of 1933, or "insured members" as that term is used in section 407(f) of the National Housing Act.

(D)   Nothing in this paragraph shall be construed to affect in any way the powers of such appropriate regulatory agency to proceed against such government securities broker or government securities dealer under any other provision of law.

(E)   Each appropriate regulatory agency (other than the Commission) shall promptly notify the Commission after it has imposed any sanction under this paragraph on a government securities broker or government securities dealer, or a person associated with a government securities broker or government securities dealer, and the Commission shall maintain, and make available to the public, a record of such sanctions and any sanctions imposed by it under this subsection.

(3)   It shall be unlawful for any person as to whom an order entered pursuant to paragraph (1) or (2) of this subsection suspending or barring him from being associated with a government securities broker or government securities dealer is in effect willfully to become, or to be, associated with a government securities broker or government securities dealer without the consent of the appropriate regulatory agency, and it shall be unlawful for any government securities broker or government securities dealer to permit such a person to become, or remain, a person associated with it without the consent of the appropriate regulatory agency, if such government securities broker or government securities dealer knew, or, in the exercise of reasonable care should have known, of such order.

(d)(1)   All records of a government securities broker or government securities dealer are subject at any time, or from time to time, to such reasonable periodic, special, or other examinations by representatives of the appropriate regulatory agency for such government securities broker or government securities dealer as such appropriate regulatory agency deems necessary or appropriate in the public interest, for the protection of investors, or otherwise in furtherance of the purposes of this Act.

(2)   Information received by an appropriate regulatory agency, the Secretary, or the Commission from or with respect to any government securities broker, government securities dealer, any person associated with a government securities broker or government securities dealer, or any other person subject to this section or rules promulgated thereunder, may be made available by the Secretary or the recipient agency to the Commission, the Secretary, the Department of Justice, the Commodity Futures Trading Commission, any appropriate regulatory agency, any self-regulatory organization, or any Federal Reserve Bank.

(3)   Government Securities Trade Reconstruction.—

(A)   Furnishing records.—

Every government securities broker and government securities dealer shall furnish to the Commission on request such records of government securities transactions, including records of the date and time of execution of trades, as the Commission may require to reconstruct trading in the course of a particular inquiry or investigation being conducted by the Commission for enforcement or surveillance purposes. In requiring information pursuant to this paragraph, the Commission shall specify the information required, the period for which it is required, the time and date on which the information must be furnished, and whether the information is to be furnished directly to the Commission, to the Federal Reserve Bank of New York, or to an appropriate regulatory agency or self-regulatory organization with responsibility for examining the government securities broker or government securities dealer. The Commission may require that such information be furnished in machine readable form notwithstanding any limitation in subparagraph (B). In utilizing its authority to require information in machine readable form, the Commission shall minimize the burden such requirement may place on small government securities brokers and dealers.

(B)   Limitation; construction.—

The Commission shall not utilize its authority under this paragraph to develop regular reporting requirements, except that the Commission may require information to be furnished under this paragraph as frequently as necessary for particular inquiries or investigations for enforcement or surveillance purposes. This paragraph shall not be construed as requiring, or as authorizing the Commission to require, any government securities broker or government securities dealer to obtain or maintain any information for purposes of this paragraph which is not otherwise maintained by such broker or dealer in accordance with any other provision of law or usual and customary business practice. The Commission shall, where feasible, avoid requiring any information to be furnished under this paragraph that the Commission may obtain from the Federal Reserve Bank of New York.

(C)   Procedures for requiring information.—

At the time the Commission requests any information pursuant to subparagraph (A) with respect to any government securities broker or government securities dealer for which the Commission is not the appropriate regulatory agency, the Commission shall notify the appropriate regulatory agency for such government securities broker or government securities dealer and, upon request, furnish to the appropriate regulatory agency any information supplied to the Commission.

(D)   Consultation.—

Within 90 days after December 17, 1993, and annually thereafter, or upon the request of any other appropriate regulatory agency, the Commission shall consult with the other appropriate regulatory agencies to determine the availability of records that may be required to be furnished under this paragraph and, for those records available directly from the other appropriate regulatory agencies, to develop a procedure for furnishing such records expeditiously upon the Commission's request.

(E)   Exclusion for examination reports.—

Nothing in this paragraph shall be construed so as to permit the Commission to require any government securities broker or government securities dealer to obtain, maintain, or furnish any examination report of any appropriate regulatory agency other than the Commission or any supervisory recommendations or analysis contained in any such examination report.

(F)   Authority to limit disclosure of information.—

Notwithstanding any other provision of law, the Commission and the appropriate regulatory agencies shall not be compelled to disclose any information required or obtained under this paragraph. Nothing in this paragraph shall authorize the Commission or any appropriate regulatory agency to withhold information from Congress, or prevent the Commission or any appropriate regulatory agency from complying with a request for information from any other Federal department or agency requesting information for purposes within the scope of its jurisdiction, or from complying with an order of a court of the United States in an action brought by the United States, the Commission, or the appropriate regulatory agency. For purposes of section 552 of Title 5, United States Code, this subparagraph shall be considered a statute described in subsection (b)(3)(B) of such section 552.

(e)(1)   It shall be unlawful for any government securities broker or government securities dealer registered or required to register with the Commission under subsection (a)(1)(A) of this section to effect any transaction in, or induce or attempt to induce the purchase or sale of, any government security, unless such government securities broker or government securities dealer is a member of a national securities exchange registered under section 6 of this Act or a securities association registered under section 15A of this Act.

(2)   The Commission, after consultation with the Secretary, by rule or order, as it deems consistent with the public interest and the protection of investors, may conditionally or unconditionally exempt from paragraph (1) of this subsection any government securities broker or government securities dealer or class of government securities brokers or government securities dealers specified in such rule or order.

(f)   Large Position Reporting.—

(1)   Reporting requirements.—

The Secretary may adopt rules to require specified persons holding, maintaining, or controlling large positions in to-be-issued or recently issued Treasury securities to file such reports regarding such positions as the Secretary determines to be necessary and appropriate for the purpose of monitoring the impact in the Treasury securities market of concentrations of positions in Treasury securities and for the purpose of otherwise assisting the Commission in the enforcement of this Act, taking into account any impact of such rules on the efficiency and liquidity of the Treasury securities market and the cost to taxpayers of funding the Federal debt. Unless otherwise specified by the Secretary, reports required under this subsection shall be filed with the Federal Reserve Bank of New York, acting as agent for the Secretary. Such reports shall, on a timely basis, be provided directly to the Commission by the person with whom they are filed.

(2)   Recordkeeping requirements.—

Rules under this subsection may require persons holding, maintaining, or controlling large positions in Treasury securities to make and keep for prescribed periods such records as the Secretary determines are necessary or appropriate to ensure that such persons can comply with reporting requirements under this subsection.

(3)   Aggregation rules.—

Rules under this subsection—

(A)   may prescribe the manner in which positions and accounts shall be aggregated for the purpose of this subsection, including aggregation on the basis of common ownership or control; and

(B)   may define which persons (individually or as a group) hold, maintain, or control large positions.

(4)   Definitional authority; determination of reporting threshold.—

(A)   In prescribing rules under this subsection, the Secretary may, consistent with the purpose of this subsection, define terms used in this subsection that are not otherwise defined in section 3 of this Act.

(B)   Rules under this subsection shall specify—

(i)   the minimum size of positions subject to reporting under this subsection, which shall be no less than the size that provides the potential for manipulation or control of the supply or price, or the cost of financing arrangements, of an issue or the portion thereof that is available for trading;

(ii)   the types of positions (which may include financing arrangements) to be reported;

(iii)   the securities to be covered; and

(iv)   the form and manner in which reports shall be transmitted, which may include transmission in machine readable form.

(5)   Exemptions.—

Consistent with the public interest and the protection of investors, the Secretary by rule or order may exempt in whole or in part, conditionally or unconditionally, any person or class of persons, or any transaction or class of transactions, from the requirements of this subsection.

(6)   Limitation on disclosure of information.—

Notwithstanding any other provision of law, the Secretary and the Commission shall not be compelled to disclose any information required to be kept or reported under this subsection. Nothing in this subsection shall authorize the Secretary or the Commission to withhold information from Congress, or prevent the Secretary or the Commission from complying with a request for information from any other Federal department or agency requesting information for purposes within the scope of its jurisdiction, or from complying with an order of a court of the United States in an action brought by the United States, the Secretary, or the Commission. For purposes of section 552 of Title 5, United States Code, this paragraph shall be considered a statute described in subsection (b)(3)(B) of such section 552.

(g)(1)   Nothing in this section except paragraph (2) of this subsection shall be construed to impair or limit the authority under any other provision of law of the Commission, the Secretary of the Treasury, the Board of Governors of the Federal Reserve System, the Comptroller of the Currency, the Federal Deposit Insurance Corporation, the Secretary of Housing and Urban Development, and the Government National Mortgage Association.

(2)   Notwithstanding any other provision of this Act, the Commission shall not have any authority to make investigations of, require the filing of a statement by, or take any other action under this Act against a government securities broker or government securities dealer, or any person associated with a government securities broker or government securities dealer, for any violation or

threatened violation of the provisions of this section, other than subsection (d)(3) of this section or the rules or regulations thereunder, unless the Commission is the appropriate regulatory agency for such government securities broker or government securities dealer. Nothing in the preceding sentence shall be construed to limit the authority of the Commission with respect to violations or threatened violations of any provision of this Act other than this (except subsection (d)(3)), or the rules or regulations under any such other provision, or investigations pursuant to section 21(a)(2) of this Act to assist a foreign securities authority.

(h)   Emergency Authority.—

The Secretary may, by order, take any action with respect to a matter or action subject to regulation by the Secretary under this section, or the rules of the Secretary under this section, involving a government security or a market therein (or significant portion or segment of that market), that the Commission may take under section 78l(k)(2) of this title with respect to transactions in securities (other than exempted securities) or a market therein (or significant portion or segment of that market).

Securities Analysts and Research Reports

Sec. 15D.   (a)   Analyst Protections.—

The Commission, or upon the authorization and direction of the Commission, a registered securities association or national securities exchange, shall have adopted, not later than 1 year after the date of enactment of this section, rules reasonably designed to address conflicts of interest that can arise when securities analysts recommend equity securities in research reports and public appearances, in order to improve the objectivity of research and provide investors with more useful and reliable information, including rules designed—

(1)   to foster greater public confidence in securities research, and to protect the objectivity and independence of securities analysts, by—

(A)   restricting the prepublication clearance or approval of research reports by persons employed by the broker or dealer who are engaged in investment banking activities, or persons not directly responsible for investment research, other than legal or compliance staff;

(B)   limiting the supervision and compensatory evaluation of securities analysts to officials employed by the broker or dealer who are not engaged in investment banking activities; and

(C)   requiring that a broker or dealer and persons employed by a broker or dealer who are involved with investment banking activities may not, directly or indirectly, retaliate against or threaten to retaliate against any securities analyst employed by that broker or dealer or its affiliates as a result of an adverse, negative, or otherwise unfavorable research report that may adversely affect the present or prospective investment banking relationship of the broker or dealer with the issuer that is the subject of the research report, except that such rules may not limit the authority of a broker or dealer to discipline a securities analyst for causes other than such research report in accordance with the policies and procedures of the firm;

(2)   to define periods during which brokers or dealers who have participated, or are to participate, in a public offering of securities as underwriters or dealers should not publish or otherwise distribute research reports relating to such securities or to the issuer of such securities;

(3)   to establish structural and institutional safeguards within registered brokers or dealers to assure that securities analysts are separated by appropriate informational partitions within the firm from the review, pressure, or oversight of those whose involvement in investment banking activities might potentially bias their judgment or supervision; and

(4)   to address such other issues as the Commission, or such association or exchange, determines appropriate.

(b)   Disclosure.—

The Commission, or upon the authorization and direction of the Commission, a registered securities association or national securities exchange, shall have adopted, not later than 1 year after the date of enactment of this section, rules reasonably designed to require each securities analyst to disclose in public appearances, and each registered broker or dealer to disclose in each research report, as applicable, conflicts of interest that are known or should have been known by the securities analyst or the broker or dealer, to exist at the time of the appearance or the date of distribution of the report, including—

(1) the extent to which the securities analyst has debt or equity investments in the issuer that is the subject of the appearance or research report;

(2) whether any compensation has been received by the registered broker or dealer, or any affiliate thereof, including the securities analyst, from the issuer that is the subject of the appearance or research report, subject to such exemptions as the Commission may determine appropriate and necessary to prevent disclosure by virtue of this paragraph of material non-public information regarding specific potential future investment banking transactions of such issuer, as is appropriate in the public interest and consistent with the protection of investors;

(3) whether an issuer, the securities of which are recommended in the appearance or research report, currently is, or during the 1-year period preceding the date of the appearance or date of distribution of the report has been, a client of the registered broker or dealer, and if so, stating the types of services provided to the issuer;

(4) whether the securities analyst received compensation with respect to a research report, based upon (among any other factors) the investment banking revenues (either generally or specifically earned from the issuer being analyzed) of the registered broker or dealer; and

(5) such other disclosures of conflicts of interest that are material to investors, research analysts, or the broker or dealer as the Commission, or such association or exchange, determines appropriate.

(c) Limitation.—Notwithstanding subsection (a) or any other provision of law, neither the Commission nor any national securities association registered under section 15A may adopt or maintain any rule or regulation in connection with an initial public offering of the common equity of an emerging growth company—

(1) restricting, based on functional role, which associated persons of a broker, dealer, or member of a national securities association, may arrange for communications between a securities analyst and a potential investor; or

(2) restricting a securities analyst from participating in any communications with the management of an emerging growth company that is also attended by any other associated person of a broker, dealer, or member of a national securities association whose functional role is other than as a securities analyst.

(d) Definitions.—

(1) the term "securities analyst" means any associated person of a registered broker or dealer that is principally responsible for, and any associated person who reports directly or indirectly to a securities analyst in connection with, the preparation of the substance of a research report, whether or not any such person has the job title of "securities analyst"; and

(2) the term "research report" means a written or electronic communication that includes an analysis of equity securities of individual companies or industries, and that provides information reasonably sufficient upon which to base an investment decision.

Registration of Nationally Recognized Statistical Rating Organizations

Sec. 15E. (a) Registration Procedures.—

(1) Application for registration.—

(A) In general.—

A credit rating agency that elects to be treated as a nationally recognized statistical rating organization for purposes of this title (in this section referred to as the "applicant"), shall furnish to the Commission an application for registration, in such form as the Commission shall require, by rule or regulation issued in accordance with subsection (n), and containing the information described in subparagraph (B).

(B) Required information.—

An application for registration under this section shall contain information regarding—

    (i) credit ratings performance measurement statistics over short-term, mid-term, and long-term periods (as applicable) of the applicant;

    (ii) the procedures and methodologies that the applicant uses in determining credit ratings;

    (iii) policies or procedures adopted and implemented by the applicant to prevent the misuse, in violation of this title (or the rules and regulations hereunder), of material, nonpublic information;

    (iv) the organizational structure of the applicant;

    (v) whether or not the applicant has in effect a code of ethics, and if not, the reasons therefor;

    (vi) any conflict of interest relating to the issuance of credit ratings by the applicant;

    (vii) the categories described in any of clauses (i) through (v) of section 3(a)(62)(B) with respect to which the applicant intends to apply for registration under this section;

    (viii) on a confidential basis, a list of the 20 largest issuers and subscribers that use the credit rating services of the applicant, by amount of net revenues received therefrom in the fiscal year immediately preceding the date of submission of the application;

    (ix) on a confidential basis, as to each applicable category of obligor described in any of clauses (i) through (v) of section 3(a)(62)(B), written certifications described in subparagraph (C), except as provided in subparagraph (D); and

    (x) any other information and documents concerning the applicant and any person associated with such applicant as the Commission, by rule, may prescribe as necessary or appropriate in the public interest or for the protection of investors.

(C) Written certifications.—

Written certifications required by subparagraph (B)(ix)—

    (i) shall be provided from not fewer than 10 qualified institutional buyers, none of which is affiliated with the applicant;

    (ii) may address more than one category of obligors described in any of clauses (i) through (v) of section 3(a)(62)(B);

    (iii) shall include not fewer than 2 certifications for each such category of obligor; and

    (iv) shall state that the qualified institutional buyer—

        (I) meets the definition of a qualified institutional buyer under section 3(a)(64); and

        (II) has used the credit ratings of the applicant for at least the 3 years immediately preceding the date of the certification in the subject category or categories of obligors.

(D) Exemption from certification requirement.—

A written certification under subparagraph (B)(ix) is not required with respect to any credit rating agency which has received, or been the subject of, a no-action letter from the staff of the Commission prior to August 2, 2006, stating that such staff would not recommend enforcement action against any broker or dealer that considers credit ratings issued by such credit rating agency to be ratings from a nationally recognized statistical rating organization.

(E)   Limitation on liability of qualified institutional buyers.—

No qualified institutional buyer shall be liable in any private right of action for any opinion or statement expressed in a certification made pursuant to subparagraph (B)(ix).

(2)   Review of application.—

(A)   Initial determination.—

Not later than 90 days after the date on which the application for registration is furnished to the Commission under paragraph (1) (or within such longer period as to which the applicant consents) the Commission shall—

(i)   by order, grant such registration for ratings in the subject category or categories of obligors, as described in clauses (i) through (v) of section 3(a)(62)(B); or

(ii)   institute proceedings to determine whether registration should be denied.

(B)   Conduct of proceedings.—

(i)   Content.—

Proceedings referred to in subparagraph (A)(ii) shall—

(I)   include notice of the grounds for denial under consideration and an opportunity for hearing; and

(II)   be concluded not later than 120 days after the date on which the application for registration is furnished to the Commission under paragraph (1).

(ii)   Determination.—

At the conclusion of such proceedings, the Commission, by order, shall grant or deny such application for registration.

(iii)   Extension authorized.—

The Commission may extend the time for conclusion of such proceedings for not longer than 90 days, if it finds good cause for such extension and publishes its reasons for so finding, or for such longer period as to which the applicant consents.

(C)   Grounds for decision.—

The Commission shall grant registration under this subsection—

(i)   if the Commission finds that the requirements of this section are satisfied; and

(ii)   unless the Commission finds (in which case the Commission shall deny such registration) that—

(I)   the applicant does not have adequate financial and managerial resources to consistently produce credit ratings with integrity and to materially comply with the procedures and methodologies disclosed under paragraph (1)(B) and with subsections (g), (h), (i), and (j); or

(II)   if the applicant were so registered, its registration would be subject to suspension or revocation under subsection (d).

(3)   Public availability of information.—

Subject to section 24, the Commission shall, by rule, require a nationally recognized statistical rating organization, upon the granting of registration under this section, to make the information and documents submitted to the Commission in its completed application for registration, or in any amendment submitted under paragraph (1) or (2) of subsection (b), publicly available on its website, or through another comparable, readily accessible means, except as provided in clauses (viii) and (ix) of paragraph (1)(B).

(b)   Update of registration.—

(1)   Update.—

Each nationally recognized statistical rating organization shall promptly amend its application for registration under this section if any information or document provided therein becomes materially inaccurate, except that a nationally recognized statistical rating organization is not required to amend—

(A)   the information required to be filed under subsection (a)(1)(B)(i) by filing information under this paragraph, but shall amend such information in the annual submission of the organization under paragraph (2) of this subsection; or

(B)   the certifications required to be provided under subsection (a)(1)(B)(ix) by filing information under this paragraph.

(2)   Certification.—

Not later than 90 days after the end of each calendar year, each nationally recognized statistical rating organization shall file with the Commission an amendment to its registration, in such form as the Commission, by rule, may prescribe as necessary or appropriate in the public interest or for the protection of investors—

(A)   certifying that the information and documents in the application for registration of such nationally recognized statistical rating organization (other than the certifications required under subsection (a)(1)(B)(ix)) continue to be accurate; and

(B)   listing any material change that occurred to such information or documents during the previous calendar year.

(c)   Accountability for Ratings Procedures.—

(1)   Authority.—

The Commission shall have exclusive authority to enforce the provisions of this section in accordance with this title with respect to any nationally recognized statistical rating organization, if such nationally recognized statistical rating organization issues credit ratings in material contravention of those procedures relating to such nationally recognized statistical rating organization, including procedures relating to the prevention of misuse of nonpublic information and conflicts of interest, that such nationally recognized statistical rating organization—

(A)   includes in its application for registration under subsection (a)(1)(B)(ii); or

(B)   makes and disseminates in reports pursuant to section 17(a) or the rules and regulations thereunder.

(2)   Limitation.—

The rules and regulations that the Commission may prescribe pursuant to this title, as they apply to nationally recognized statistical rating organizations, shall be narrowly tailored to meet the requirements of this title applicable to nationally recognized statistical rating organizations. Notwithstanding any other provision of this section, or any other provision of law, neither the Commission nor any State (or political subdivision thereof) may regulate the substance of credit ratings or the procedures and methodologies by which any nationally recognized statistical rating organization determines credit ratings. Nothing in this paragraph may be construed to afford a defense against any action or proceeding brought by the Commission to enforce the antifraud provisions of the securities laws.

(3)   Internal controls over processes for determining credit ratings.—

(A)   In general.—

Each nationally recognized statistical rating organization shall establish, maintain, enforce, and document an effective internal control structure governing the implementation of and adherence to policies, procedures, and methodologies for determining credit ratings, taking into consideration such factors as the Commission may prescribe, by rule.

(B)   Attestation requirement.—

The Commission shall prescribe rules requiring each nationally recognized statistical rating organization to submit to the Commission an annual internal controls report, which shall contain—

(i)   a description of the responsibility of the management of the nationally recognized statistical rating organization in establishing and maintaining an effective internal control structure under subparagraph (A);

(ii)   an assessment of the effectiveness of the internal control structure of the nationally recognized statistical rating organization; and

(iii) In General.—the attestation of the chief executive officer, or equivalent individual, of the nationally recognized statistical rating organization

(d)   Censure, Denial, or Suspension of Registration; Notice and Hearing.—

(1)   In general.—

The Commission, by order, shall censure, place limitations on the activities, functions, or operations of, suspend for a period not exceeding 12 months, or revoke the registration of any nationally recognized statistical rating organization, or with respect to any person who is associated with, who is seeking to become associated with, or, at the time of the alleged misconduct, who was associated or was seeking to become associated with a nationally recognized statistical rating organization, the Commission, by order, shall censure, place limitations on the activities or functions of such person, suspend for a period not exceeding 1 year, or bar such person from being associated with a nationally recognized statistical rating organization, if the Commission finds, on the record after notice and opportunity for hearing, that such censure, placing of limitations, suspension, bar or revocation is necessary for the protection of investors and in the public interest and that such nationally recognized statistical rating organization, or any person associated with such an organization, whether prior to or subsequent to becoming so associated—

(A)   has committed or omitted any act, or is subject to an order or finding, enumerated in subparagraph (A), (D), (E), (H), or (G) of section 15(b)(4), has been convicted of any offense specified in section 15(b)(4)(B), or is enjoined from any action, conduct, or practice specified in subparagraph (C) of section 15(b)(4), during the 10-year period preceding the date of commencement of the proceedings under this subsection, or at any time thereafter;

(B)   has been convicted during the 10-year period preceding the date on which an application for registration is filed with to the Commission under this section, or at any time thereafter, of—

(i)   any crime that is punishable by imprisonment for 1 or more years, and that is not described in section 15(b)(4)(B); or

(ii)   a substantially equivalent crime by a foreign court of competent jurisdiction;

(C)   is subject to any order of the Commission barring or suspending the right of the person to be associated with a nationally recognized statistical rating organization;

(D)   fails to file the certifications required under subsection (b)(2);

(E)   fails to maintain adequate financial and managerial resources to consistently produce credit ratings with integrity;

(F)   has failed reasonably to supervise, with a view to preventing a violation of the securities laws, an individual who commits such a violation, if the individual is subject to the supervision of that person.

(2)   Suspension or revocation for particular class of securities.—

(A)   In general.—

The Commission may temporarily suspend or permanently revoke the registration of a nationally recognized statistical rating organization with respect to a particular class or subclass of securities, if the Commission finds, on the record after notice and opportunity for hearing, that the nationally recognized statistical rating organization does not have adequate financial and managerial resources to consistently produce credit ratings with integrity.

(B) Considerations.—

In making any determination under subparagraph (A), the Commission shall consider—

(i) whether the nationally recognized statistical rating organization has failed over a sustained period of time, as determined by the Commission, to produce ratings that are accurate for that class or subclass of securities; and

(ii) such other factors as the Commission may determine.

(e) Termination of Registration.—

(1) Voluntary withdrawal.—

A nationally recognized statistical rating organization may, upon such terms and conditions as the Commission may establish as necessary in the public interest or for the protection of investors, withdraw from registration by furnishing a written notice of withdrawal to the Commission.

(2) Commission authority.—

In addition to any other authority of the Commission under this title, if the Commission finds that a nationally recognized statistical rating organization is no longer in existence or has ceased to do business as a credit rating agency, the Commission, by order, shall cancel the registration under this section of such nationally recognized statistical rating organization.

(f) Representations.—

(1) Ban on representations of sponsorship by united states or agency thereof.—

It shall be unlawful for any nationally recognized statistical rating organization to represent or imply in any manner whatsoever that such nationally recognized statistical rating organization has been designated, sponsored, recommended, or approved, or that the abilities or qualifications thereof have in any respect been passed upon, by the United States or any agency, officer, or employee thereof.

(2) Ban on representation as NRSRO of unregistered credit rating agencies.—

It shall be unlawful for any credit rating agency that is not registered under this section as a nationally recognized statistical rating organization to state that such credit rating agency is a nationally recognized statistical rating organization registered under this title.

(3) Statement of registration under securities exchange act of 1934 provisions.—

No provision of paragraph (1) shall be construed to prohibit a statement that a nationally recognized statistical rating organization is a nationally recognized statistical rating organization under this title, if such statement is true in fact and if the effect of such registration is not misrepresented.

(g) Prevention of Misuse of Nonpublic Information.—

(1) Organization policies and procedures.—

Each nationally recognized statistical rating organization shall establish, maintain, and enforce written policies and procedures reasonably designed, taking into consideration the nature of the business of such nationally recognized statistical rating organization, to prevent the misuse in violation of this title, or the rules or regulations hereunder, of material, nonpublic information by such nationally recognized statistical rating organization or any person associated with such nationally recognized statistical rating organization.

(2) Commission authority.—

The Commission shall issue final rules in accordance with subsection (n) to require specific policies or procedures that are reasonably designed to prevent misuse in violation of this title (or the rules or regulations hereunder) of material, nonpublic information.

(h)   Management of Conflicts of Interest.—

(1)   Organization policies and procedures.—

Each nationally recognized statistical rating organization shall establish, maintain, and enforce written policies and procedures reasonably designed, taking into consideration the nature of the business of such nationally recognized statistical rating organization and affiliated persons and affiliated companies thereof, to address and manage any conflicts of interest that can arise from such business.

(2)   Commission authority.—

The Commission shall issue final rules in accordance with subsection (n) to prohibit, or require the management and disclosure of, any conflicts of interest relating to the issuance of credit ratings by a nationally recognized statistical rating organization, including, without limitation, conflicts of interest relating to—

(A)   the manner in which a nationally recognized statistical rating organization is compensated by the obligor, or any affiliate of the obligor, for issuing credit ratings or providing related services;

(B)   the provision of consulting, advisory, or other services by a nationally recognized statistical rating organization, or any person associated with such nationally recognized statistical rating organization, to the obligor, or any affiliate of the obligor;

(C)   business relationships, ownership interests, or any other financial or personal interests between a nationally recognized statistical rating organization, or any person associated with such nationally recognized statistical rating organization, and the obligor, or any affiliate of the obligor;

(D)   any affiliation of a nationally recognized statistical rating organization, or any person associated with such nationally recognized statistical rating organization, with any person that underwrites the securities or money market instruments that are the subject of a credit rating; and

(E)   any other potential conflict of interest, as the Commission deems necessary or appropriate in the public interest or for the protection of investors.

(3)   Separation of ratings from sales and marketing.—

(A)   Rules required.—

The Commission shall issue rules to prevent the sales and marketing considerations of a nationally recognized statistical rating organization from influencing the production of ratings by the nationally recognized statistical rating organization.

(B)   Contents of rules—The rules issued under subparagraph (A) shall provide for—

(i)   exceptions for small nationally recognized statistical rating organizations with respect to which the Commission determines that the separation of the production of ratings and sales and marketing activities is not appropriate; and

(ii)   suspension or revocation of the registration of a nationally recognized statistical rating organization, if the Commission finds, on the record, after notice and opportunity for a hearing, that—

(I)   the nationally recognized statistical rating organization has committed a violation of a rule issued under this subsection; and

(II)   the violation of a rule issued under this subsection affected a rating.

(4)   Look-back requirement.—

(A)   Review by the nationally recognized statistical rating organization.—

Each nationally recognized statistical rating organization shall establish, maintain, and enforce policies and procedures reasonably designed to ensure that, in any case in which an employee of a person subject to a credit rating of the nationally recognized statistical rating organization or the issuer, underwriter, or sponsor of a security or money market instrument subject to a credit rating of the nationally recognized statistical rating organization was employed by the nationally recognized statistical rating organization and participated in any capacity in determining credit ratings for the person or the securities or money market instruments during the 1-year period preceding the date an action was taken with respect to the credit rating, the nationally recognized statistical rating organization shall—

    (i)   conduct a review to determine whether any conflicts of interest of the employee influenced the credit rating; and

    (ii)   take action to revise the rating if appropriate, in accordance with such rules as the Commission shall prescribe.

    (B) Review by commission.—

        (i) In general.—

The Commission shall conduct periodic reviews of the policies described in subparagraph (A) and the implementation of the policies at each nationally recognized statistical rating organization to ensure they are reasonably designed and implemented to most effectively eliminate conflicts of interest.

        (ii) Timing of reviews.—

The Commission shall review the code of ethics and conflict of interest policy of each nationally recognized statistical rating organization—

            (I)   not less frequently than annually; and

            (II)   whenever such policies are materially modified or amended.

  (5)   Report to commission on certain employment transitions.—

    (A) Report required.—

Each nationally recognized statistical rating organization shall report to the Commission any case such organization knows or can reasonably be expected to know where a person associated with such organization within the previous 5 years obtains employment with any obligor, issuer, underwriter, or sponsor of a security or money market instrument for which the organization issued a credit rating during the 12-month period prior to such employment, if such employee—

        (i)   was a senior officer of such organization;

        (ii)   participated in any capacity in determining credit ratings for such obligor, issuer, underwriter, or sponsor; or

        (iii)   supervised an employee described in clause (ii).

    (B) Public disclosure.—

Upon receiving such a report, the Commission shall make such information publicly available.

(i)   Prohibited conduct.—

  (1)   Prohibited acts and practices.—

The Commission shall issue final rules in accordance with subsection (n) to prohibit any act or practice relating to the issuance of credit ratings by a nationally recognized statistical rating organization that the Commission determines to be unfair, coercive, or abusive, including any act or practice relating to—

    (A)   conditioning or threatening to condition the issuance of a credit rating on the purchase by the obligor or an affiliate thereof of other services or products, including pre-credit rating assessment products, of the nationally recognized statistical rating organization or any person associated with such nationally recognized statistical rating organization;

(B) lowering or threatening to lower a credit rating on, or refusing to rate, securities or money market instruments issued by an asset pool or as part of any asset-backed or mortgage-backed securities transaction, unless a portion of the assets within such pool or part of such transaction, as applicable, also is rated by the nationally recognized statistical rating organization; or

(C) modifying or threatening to modify a credit rating or otherwise departing from its adopted systematic procedures and methodologies in determining credit ratings, based on whether the obligor, or an affiliate of the obligor, purchases or will purchase the credit rating or any other service or product of the nationally recognized statistical rating organization or any person associated with such organization.

(2) Rule of construction.—

Nothing in paragraph (1), or in any rules or regulations adopted thereunder, may be construed to modify, impair, or supersede the operation of any of the antitrust laws (as defined in the first section of the Clayton Act, except that such term includes section 5 of the Federal Trade Commission Act, to the extent that such section 5 applies to unfair methods of competition).

(j) Designation of Compliance Officer.—

(1) In general.—

In General.—Each nationally recognized statistical rating organization shall designate an individual responsible for administering the policies and procedures that are required to be established pursuant to subsections (g) and (h), and for ensuring compliance with the securities laws and the rules and regulations thereunder, including those promulgated by the Commission pursuant to this section.

(2) Limitations.—

(A) In general.—

Except as provided in subparagraph (B), an individual designated under paragraph (1) may not, while serving in the designated capacity—

(i) perform credit ratings;

(ii) participate in the development of ratings methodologies or models;

(iii) perform marketing or sales functions; or

(iv) participate in establishing compensation levels, other than for employees working for that individual.

(B) Exception.—

The Commission may exempt a small nationally recognized statistical rating organization from the limitations under this paragraph, if the Commission finds that compliance with such limitations would impose an unreasonable burden on the nationally recognized statistical rating organization.

(3) Other duties.—

Each individual designated under paragraph (1) shall establish procedures for the receipt, retention, and treatment of—

(A) complaints regarding credit ratings, models, methodologies, and compliance with the securities laws and the policies and procedures developed under this section; and

(B) confidential, anonymous complaints by employees or users of credit ratings.

(4) Compensation.—

The compensation of each compliance officer appointed under paragraph (1) shall not be linked to the financial performance of the nationally recognized statistical rating organization and shall be arranged so as to ensure the independence of the officer's judgment.

(5)   Annual reports required.—

     (A)   Annual reports required.—

Each individual designated under paragraph (1) shall submit to the nationally recognized statistical rating organization an annual report on the compliance of the nationally recognized statistical rating organization with the securities laws and the policies and procedures of the nationally recognized statistical rating organization that includes—

         (i)   a description of any material changes to the code of ethics and conflict of interest policies of the nationally recognized statistical rating organization; and

         (ii)   a certification that the report is accurate and complete.

     (B)   Submission of reports to the commission.—

Each nationally recognized statistical rating organization shall file the reports required under subparagraph (A) together with the financial report that is required to be submitted to the Commission under this section.

(k)   Statements of Financial Condition.—

Each nationally recognized statistical rating organization shall, on a confidential basis, file with the Commission, at intervals determined by the Commission, such financial statements, certified (if required by the rules or regulations of the Commission) by an independent public accountant, and information concerning its financial condition, as the Commission, by rule, may prescribe as necessary or appropriate in the public interest or for the protection of investors.

(*l*)   Sole Method of Registration.—

(1)   In general.—

On and after the effective date of this section, a credit rating agency may only be registered as a nationally recognized statistical rating organization for any purpose in accordance with this section.

(2)   Prohibition on reliance on no-action relief.—

On and after the effective date of this section—

     (A)   an entity that, before that date, received advice, approval, or a no-action letter from the Commission or staff thereof to be treated as a nationally recognized statistical rating organization pursuant to the commission rule at section 240.15c3–1 of title 17, Code of Federal Regulations, may represent itself or act as a nationally recognized statistical rating organization only—

         (i)   during Commission consideration of the application, if such entity has filed an application for registration under this section; and

         (ii)   on and after the date of approval of its application for registration under this section; and

     (B)   the advice, approval, or no-action letter described in subparagraph (A) shall be void.

(3)   Notice to other agencies.—

Not later than 30 days after the date of enactment of this section, the Commission shall give notice of the actions undertaken pursuant to this section to each Federal agency which employs in its rules and regulations the term "nationally recognized statistical rating organization" (as that term is used under Commission rule 15c3–1 (17 C.F.R. 240.15c3–1), as in effect on the date of enactment of this section).

(m)   Accountability.—

(1)   In general.—

The enforcement and penalty provisions of this title shall apply to statements made by a credit rating agency in the same manner and to the same extent as such provisions apply to statements made by a registered public accounting firm or a securities analyst under the securities laws, and such statements shall not be deemed forward-looking statements for the purposes of section 21E.

(2)   Rulemaking.—

The Commission shall issue such rules as may be necessary to carry out this subsection.

(n)   Regulations.—

(1)   New provisions.—

Such rules and regulations as are required by this section or are otherwise necessary to carry out this section, including the application form required under subsection (a)—

(A)   shall be issued by the Commission in final form, not later than 270 days after the date of enactment of this section; and

(B)   shall become effective not later than 270 days after the date of enactment of this section.

(2)   Review of existing regulations.—

Not later than 270 days after the date of enactment of this section, the Commission shall—

(A)   review its existing rules and regulations which employ the term "nationally recognized statistical rating organization" or "NRSRO"; and

(B)   amend or revise such rules and regulations in accordance with the purposes of this section, as the Commission may prescribe as necessary or appropriate in the public interest or for the protection of investors.

(o)   NRSROs Subject to Commission Authority.—

(1)   In general.—

No provision of the laws of any State or political subdivision thereof requiring the registration, licensing, or qualification as a credit rating agency or a nationally recognized statistical rating organization shall apply to any nationally recognized statistical rating organization or person employed by or working under the control of a nationally recognized statistical rating organization.

(2)   Limitation.—

Nothing in this subsection prohibits the securities commission (or any agency or office performing like functions) of any State from investigating and bringing an enforcement action with respect to fraud or deceit against any nationally recognized statistical rating organization or person associated with a nationally recognized statistical rating organization.

(p)   Regulation of Nationally Recognized Statistical Rating Organizations—

(1)   Establishment of office of credit ratings.—

(A)   Office established.—

The Commission shall establish within the Commission an Office of Credit Ratings (referred to in this subsection as the "Office") to administer the rules of the Commission—

(i)   with respect to the practices of nationally recognized statistical rating organizations in determining ratings, for the protection of users of credit ratings and in the public interest;

(ii)   to promote accuracy in credit ratings issued by nationally recognized statistical rating organizations; and

(iii)   to ensure that such ratings are not unduly influenced by conflicts of interest.

(B)   Director of the office.—

The head of the Office shall be the Director, who shall report to the Chairman.

(2) Staffing.—

The Office established under this subsection shall be staffed sufficiently to carry out fully the requirements of this section. The staff shall include persons with knowledge of and expertise in corporate, municipal, and structured debt finance.

(3) Commission examinations.—

(A) Annual examinations required.—

The Office shall conduct an examination of each nationally recognized statistical rating organization at least annually.

(B) Conduct of examinations.—

Each examination under subparagraph (A) shall include a review of—

(i) whether the nationally recognized statistical rating organization conducts business in accordance with the policies, procedures, and rating methodologies of the nationally recognized statistical rating organization;

(ii) the management of conflicts of interest by the nationally recognized statistical rating organization;

(iii) implementation of ethics policies by the nationally recognized statistical rating organization;

(iv) the internal supervisory controls of the nationally recognized statistical rating organization;

(v) the governance of the nationally recognized statistical rating organization;

(vi) the activities of the individual designated by the nationally recognized statistical rating organization under subsection (j)(1);

(vii) the processing of complaints by the nationally recognized statistical rating organization; and

(viii) the policies of the nationally recognized statistical rating organization governing the post-employment activities of former staff of the nationally recognized statistical rating organization.

(C) Inspection reports.—

The Commission shall make available to the public, in an easily understandable format, an annual report summarizing—

(i) the essential findings of all examinations conducted under subparagraph (A), as deemed appropriate by the Commission;

(ii) the responses by the nationally recognized statistical rating organizations to any material regulatory deficiencies identified by the Commission under clause (i); and

(iii) whether the nationally recognized statistical rating organizations have appropriately addressed the recommendations of the Commission contained in previous reports under this subparagraph.

(4) Rulemaking authority.—

The Commission shall—

(A) establish, by rule, fines, and other penalties applicable to any nationally recognized statistical rating organization that violates the requirements of this section and the rules thereunder; and

(B) issue such rules as may be necessary to carry out this section.

(q) Transparency of Ratings Performance.—

(1) Rulemaking required.—

The Commission shall, by rule, require that each nationally recognized statistical rating organization publicly disclose information on the initial credit ratings determined by the nationally recognized statistical rating organization for each type of obligor, security, and money market instrument, and any subsequent changes to such credit ratings, for the purpose of allowing users of credit ratings to evaluate the accuracy of ratings and compare the performance of ratings by different nationally recognized statistical rating organizations.

(2)   Content.—

The rules of the Commission under this subsection shall require, at a minimum, disclosures that—

(A)   are comparable among nationally recognized statistical rating organizations, to allow users of credit ratings to compare the performance of credit ratings across nationally recognized statistical rating organizations;

(B)   are clear and informative for investors having a wide range of sophistication who use or might use credit ratings;

(C)   include performance information over a range of years and for a variety of types of credit ratings, including for credit ratings withdrawn by the nationally recognized statistical rating organization;

(D)   are published and made freely available by the nationally recognized statistical rating organization, on an easily accessible portion of its website, and in writing, when requested;

(E)   are appropriate to the business model of a nationally recognized statistical rating organization; and

(F)   each nationally recognized statistical rating organization include an attestation with any credit rating it issues affirming that no part of the rating was influenced by any other business activities, that the rating was based solely on the merits of the instruments being rated, and that such rating was an independent evaluation of the risks and merits of the instrument.

(r)   Credit Ratings Methodologies.—The Commission shall prescribe rules, for the protection of investors and in the public interest, with respect to the procedures and methodologies, including qualitative and quantitative data and models, used by nationally recognized statistical rating organizations that require each nationally recognized statistical rating organization—

(1)   to ensure that credit ratings are determined using procedures and methodologies, including qualitative and quantitative data and models, that are—

(A)   approved by the board of the nationally recognized statistical rating organization, a body performing a function similar to that of a board; and

(B)   in accordance with the policies and procedures of the nationally recognized statistical rating organization for the development and modification of credit rating procedures and methodologies;

(2)   to ensure that when material changes to credit rating procedures and methodologies (including changes to qualitative and quantitative data and models) are made, that—

(A)   the changes are applied consistently to all credit ratings to which the changed procedures and methodologies apply;

(B)   to the extent that changes are made to credit rating surveillance procedures and methodologies, the changes are applied to then-current credit ratings by the nationally recognized statistical rating organization within a reasonable time period determined by the Commission, by rule; and

(C)   the nationally recognized statistical rating organization publicly discloses the reason for the change; and

(3)   to notify users of credit ratings—

(A) of the version of a procedure or methodology, including the qualitative methodology or quantitative inputs, used with respect to a particular credit rating;

(B) when a material change is made to a procedure or methodology, including to a qualitative model or quantitative inputs;

(C) when a significant error is identified in a procedure or methodology, including a qualitative or quantitative model, that may result in credit rating actions; and

(D) of the likelihood of a material change described in subparagraph (B) resulting in a change in current credit ratings.

(s) Transparency of Credit Rating Methodologies and Information Reviewed.—

(1) Form for disclosures.—

The Commission shall require, by rule, each nationally recognized statistical rating organization to prescribe a form to accompany the publication of each credit rating that discloses—

(A) information relating to—

(i) the assumptions underlying the credit rating procedures and methodologies;

(ii) the data that was relied on to determine the credit rating; and

(iii) if applicable, how the nationally recognized statistical rating organization used servicer or remittance reports, and with what frequency, to conduct surveillance of the credit rating; and

(B) information that can be used by investors and other users of credit ratings to better understand credit ratings in each class of credit rating issued by the nationally recognized statistical rating organization.

(2) Format.—

The form developed under paragraph (1) shall—

(A) be easy to use and helpful for users of credit ratings to understand the information contained in the report;

(B) require the nationally recognized statistical rating organization to provide the content described in paragraph (3)(B) in a manner that is directly comparable across types of securities; and

(C) be made readily available to users of credit ratings, in electronic or paper form, as the Commission may, by rule, determine.

(3) Content of form.—

(A) Qualitative content.—

Each nationally recognized statistical rating organization shall disclose on the form developed under paragraph (1)—

(i) the credit ratings produced by the nationally recognized statistical rating organization;

(ii) the main assumptions and principles used in constructing procedures and methodologies, including qualitative methodologies and quantitative inputs and assumptions about the correlation of defaults across underlying assets used in rating structured products;

(iii) the potential limitations of the credit ratings, and the types of risks excluded from the credit ratings that the nationally recognized statistical rating organization does not comment on, including liquidity, market, and other risks;

(iv) information on the uncertainty of the credit rating, including—

(I) information on the reliability, accuracy, and quality of the data relied on in determining the credit rating; and

(II) a statement relating to the extent to which data essential to the determination of the credit rating were reliable or limited, including—

(aa) any limits on the scope of historical data; and

(bb) any limits in accessibility to certain documents or other types of information that would have better informed the credit rating;

(v) whether and to what extent third party due diligence services have been used by the nationally recognized statistical rating organization, a description of the information that such third party reviewed in conducting due diligence services, and a description of the findings or conclusions of such third party;

(vi) a description of the data about any obligor, issuer, security, or money market instrument that were relied upon for the purpose of determining the credit rating;

(vii) a statement containing an overall assessment of the quality of information available and considered in producing a rating for an obligor, security, or money market instrument, in relation to the quality of information available to the nationally recognized statistical rating organization in rating similar issuances;

(viii) information relating to conflicts of interest of the nationally recognized statistical rating organization; and

(ix) such additional information as the Commission may require.

(B) Quantitative content.—

Each nationally recognized statistical rating organization shall disclose on the form developed under this subsection—

(i) an explanation or measure of the potential volatility of the credit rating, including—

(I) any factors that might lead to a change in the credit ratings; and

(II) the magnitude of the change that a user can expect under different market conditions;

(ii) information on the content of the rating, including—

(I) the historical performance of the rating; and

(II) the expected probability of default and the expected loss in the event of default;

(iii) information on the sensitivity of the rating to assumptions made by the nationally recognized statistical rating organization, including—

(I) 5 assumptions made in the ratings process that, without accounting for any other factor, would have the greatest impact on a rating if the assumptions were proven false or inaccurate; and

(II) an analysis, using specific examples, of how each of the 5 assumptions identified under subclause (I) impacts a rating;

(iv) such additional information as may be required by the Commission.

(4) Due diligence services for asset-backed securities.—

(A) Findings.—

The issuer or underwriter of any asset-backed security shall make publicly available the findings and conclusions of any third-party due diligence report obtained by the issuer or underwriter.

(B)   Certification required.—

In any case in which third-party due diligence services are employed by a nationally recognized statistical rating organization, an issuer, or an underwriter, the person providing the due diligence services shall provide to any nationally recognized statistical rating organization that produces a rating to which such services relate, written certification, as provided in subparagraph (C).

(C)   Format and content.—

The Commission shall establish the appropriate format and content for the written certifications required under subparagraph (B), to ensure that providers of due diligence services have conducted a thorough review of data, documentation, and other relevant information necessary for a nationally recognized statistical rating organization to provide an accurate rating.

(D)   Disclosure of certification.—

The Commission shall adopt rules requiring a nationally recognized statistical rating organization, at the time at which the nationally recognized statistical rating organization produces a rating, to disclose the certification described in subparagraph (B) to the public in a manner that allows the public to determine the adequacy and level of due diligence services provided by a third party.

(t)   Corporate Governance, Organization, and Management of Conflicts of Interest.—

(1)   Board of directors.—

Each nationally recognized statistical rating organization shall have a board of directors.

(2)   Independent directors.—

(A)   In general.—

At least 1/2 of the board of directors, but not fewer than 2 of the members thereof, shall be independent of the nationally recognized statistical rating agency. A portion of the independent directors shall include users of ratings from a nationally recognized statistical rating organization.

(B)   Independence determination.—

In order to be considered independent for purposes of this subsection, a member of the board of directors of a nationally recognized statistical rating organization—

(i)   may not, other than in his or her capacity as a member of the board of directors or any committee thereof—

(I)   accept any consulting, advisory, or other compensatory fee from the nationally recognized statistical rating organization; or

(II)   be a person associated with the nationally recognized statistical rating organization or with any affiliated company thereof; and

(ii)   shall be disqualified from any deliberation involving a specific rating in which the independent board member has a financial interest in the outcome of the rating.

(C)   Compensation and term.—

The compensation of the independent members of the board of directors of a nationally recognized statistical rating organization shall not be linked to the business performance of the nationally recognized statistical rating organization, and shall be arranged so as to ensure the independence of their judgment. The term of office of the independent directors shall be for a pre-agreed fixed period, not to exceed 5 years, and shall not be renewable.

(3)   Duties of board of directors.—

In addition to the overall responsibilities of the board of directors, the board shall oversee—

(A) the establishment, maintenance, and enforcement of policies and procedures for determining credit ratings;

(B) the establishment, maintenance, and enforcement of policies and procedures to address, manage, and disclose any conflicts of interest;

(C) the effectiveness of the internal control system with respect to policies and procedures for determining credit ratings; and

(D) the compensation and promotion policies and practices of the nationally recognized statistical rating organization.

(4)   Treatment of NRSRO subsidiaries.—

If a nationally recognized statistical rating organization is a subsidiary of a parent entity, the board of the directors of the parent entity may satisfy the requirements of this subsection by assigning to a committee of such board of directors the duties under paragraph (3), if—

(A) at least 1/2 of the members of the committee (including the chairperson of the committee) are independent, as defined in this section; and

(B) at least 1 member of the committee is a user of ratings from a nationally recognized statistical rating organization.

(5)   Exception authority.—

If the Commission finds that compliance with the provisions of this subsection present an unreasonable burden on a small nationally recognized statistical rating organization, the Commission may permit the nationally recognized statistical rating organization to delegate such responsibilities to a committee that includes at least one individual who is a user of ratings of a nationally recognized statistical rating organization.

(u)   Duty To Report Tips Alleging Material Violations of Law.—

(1) Duty to report.—

Each nationally recognized statistical rating organization shall refer to the appropriate law enforcement or regulatory authorities any information that the nationally recognized statistical rating organization receives from a third party and finds credible that alleges that an issuer of securities rated by the nationally recognized statistical rating organization has committed or is committing a material violation of law that has not been adjudicated by a Federal or State court.

(2)   Rule of construction.—

Nothing in paragraph (1) may be construed to require a nationally recognized statistical rating organization to verify the accuracy of the information described in paragraph (1).

(v)   Information From Sources Other Than the Issuer.—In producing a credit rating, a nationally recognized statistical rating organization shall consider information about an issuer that the nationally recognized statistical rating organization has, or receives from a source other than the issuer or underwriter, that the nationally recognized statistical rating organization finds credible and potentially significant to a rating decision.

Registration and Regulation of Security-Based Swap Dealers and Major Security-Based Swap Participants

Sec. 15F.   (a)   Registration.—

(1) Security-based swap dealers.—

It shall be unlawful for any person to act as a security-based swap dealer unless the person is registered as a security-based swap dealer with the Commission.

(2) Major security-based swap participants.—

It shall be unlawful for any person to act as a major security-based swap participant unless the person is registered as a major security-based swap participant with the Commission.

(b) Requirements.—

(1) In general.—

A person shall register as a security-based swap dealer or major security-based swap participant by filing a registration application with the Commission.

(2) Contents.—

(A) In general.—

The application shall be made in such form and manner as prescribed by the Commission, and shall contain such information, as the Commission considers necessary concerning the business in which the applicant is or will be engaged.

(B) Continual reporting.—

A person that is registered as a security-based swap dealer or major security-based swap participant shall continue to submit to the Commission reports that contain such information pertaining to the business of the person as the Commission may require.

(3) Expiration.—

Each registration under this section shall expire at such time as the Commission may prescribe by rule or regulation.

(4) Rules.—

Except as provided in subsections (d) and (e), the Commission may prescribe rules applicable to security-based swap dealers and major security-based swap participants, including rules that limit the activities of non-bank security-based swap dealers and major security-based swap participants.

(5) Transition.—

Not later than 1 year after the date of enactment of the Wall Street Transparency and Accountability Act of 2010, the Commission shall issue rules under this section to provide for the registration of security-based swap dealers and major security-based swap participants.

(6) Statutory disqualification.—

Except to the extent otherwise specifically provided by rule, regulation, or order of the Commission, it shall be unlawful for a security-based swap dealer or a major security-based swap participant to permit any person associated with a security-based swap dealer or a major security-based swap participant who is subject to a statutory disqualification to effect or be involved in effecting security-based swaps on behalf of the security-based swap dealer or major security-based swap participant, if the security-based swap dealer or major security-based swap participant knew, or in the exercise of reasonable care should have known, of the statutory disqualification.

(c) Dual Registration.—

(1) Security-based swap dealer.—

Any person that is required to be registered as a security-based swap dealer under this section shall register with the Commission, regardless of whether the person also is registered with the Commodity Futures Trading Commission as a swap dealer.

(2) Major security-based swap participant.—

Any person that is required to be registered as a major security-based swap participant under this section shall register with the Commission, regardless of whether the person also is registered with the Commodity Futures Trading Commission as a major swap participant.

(d) Rulemaking.—

(1) In general.—

The Commission shall adopt rules for persons that are registered as security-based swap dealers or major security-based swap participants under this section.

(2) Exception for prudential requirements.—

(A) In general.—

The Commission may not prescribe rules imposing prudential requirements on security-based swap dealers or major security-based swap participants for which there is a prudential regulator.

(B) Applicability.—

Subparagraph (A) does not limit the authority of the Commission to prescribe rules as directed under this section.

(e) Capital and Margin Requirements.—

(1) In general.—

(A) Security-based swap dealers and major security-based swap participants that are banks.—

Each registered security-based swap dealer and major security-based swap participant for which there is not a prudential regulator shall meet such minimum capital requirements and minimum initial and variation margin requirements as the prudential regulator shall by rule or regulation prescribe under paragraph (2)(A).

(B) Security-based swap dealers and major security-based swap participants that are not banks.—

Each registered security-based swap dealer and major security-based swap participant for which there is not a prudential regulator shall meet such minimum capital requirements and minimum initial and variation margin requirements as the Commission shall by rule or regulation prescribe under paragraph (2)(B).

(2) Rules.—

(A) Security-based swap dealers and major security-based swap participants that are banks.—

The prudential regulators, in consultation with the Commission and the Commodity Futures Trading Commission, shall adopt rules for security-based swap dealers and major security-based swap participants, with respect to their activities as a swap dealer or major swap participant, for which there is a prudential regulator imposing—

(i) capital requirements; and

(ii) both initial and variation margin requirements on all security-based swaps that are not cleared by a registered clearing agency.

(B) Security-based swap dealers and major security-based swap participants that are not banks.—

The Commission shall adopt rules for security-based swap dealers and major security-based swap participants, with respect to their activities as a swap dealer or major swap participant, for which there is not a prudential regulator imposing—

(i) capital requirements; and

(ii) both initial and variation margin requirements on all swaps that are not cleared by a registered clearing agency.

(C) Capital.—

In setting capital requirements for a person that is designated as a security-based swap dealer or a major security-based swap participant for a single type or single class or category of security-based swap or activities, the prudential regulator and the Commission shall take into account the risks associated with other types of security-based swaps or classes of security-based swaps or categories of security-based swaps engaged in and the other activities conducted by that person that are not otherwise subject to regulation applicable to that person by virtue of the status of the person.

(3) Standards for capital and margin.—

(A) In general.—

To offset the greater risk to the security-based swap dealer or major security-based swap participant and the financial system arising from the use of security-based swaps that are not cleared, the requirements imposed under paragraph (2) shall—

    (i) help ensure the safety and soundness of the security-based swap dealer or major security-based swap participant; and

    (ii) be appropriate for the risk associated with the non-cleared security-based swaps held as a security-based swap dealer or major security-based swap participant.

(B) Rule of construction.—

    (i) In general.—

Nothing in this section shall limit, or be construed to limit, the authority—

        (I) of the Commission to set financial responsibility rules for a broker or dealer registered pursuant to section 15(b) (except for section 15(b)(11) thereof) in accordance with section 15(c)(3); or

        (II) of the Commodity Futures Trading Commission to set financial responsibility rules for a futures commission merchant or introducing broker registered pursuant to section 4f(a) of the Commodity Exchange Act (except for section 4f(a)(3) thereof) in accordance with section 4f(b) of the Commodity Exchange Act.

    (ii) Futures commission merchants and other dealers.—

A futures commission merchant, introducing broker, broker, or dealer shall maintain sufficient capital to comply with the stricter of any applicable capital requirements to which such futures commission merchant, introducing broker, broker, or dealer is subject to under this title or the Commodity Exchange Act.

(C) Margin requirements.—

In prescribing margin requirements under this subsection, the prudential regulator with respect to security-based swap dealers and major security-based swap participants that are depository institutions, and the Commission with respect to security-based swap dealers and major security-based swap participants that are not depository institutions shall permit the use of noncash collateral, as the regulator or the Commission determines to be consistent with—

    (i) preserving the financial integrity of markets trading security-based swaps; and

    (ii) preserving the stability of the United States financial system.

(D) Comparability of capital and margin requirements.—

    (i) In general.—

The prudential regulators, the Commission, and the Securities and Exchange Commission shall periodically (but not less frequently than annually) consult on minimum capital requirements and minimum initial and variation margin requirements.

    (ii) Comparability.—

The entities described in clause (i) shall, to the maximum extent practicable, establish and maintain comparable minimum capital requirements and minimum initial and variation margin requirements, including the use of noncash collateral, for—

        (I) security-based swap dealers; and

           (II)   major security-based swap participants.

    (4)   Applicability with Respect to Counterparties.—

The requirements of paragraphs (2)(A)(ii) and (2)(B)(ii) shall not apply to a security-based swap in which a counterparty qualifies for an exception under section 3C(g)(1) or satisfies the criteria in section 3C(g)(4)

  (f)   Reporting and Recordkeeping.—

    (1)   In general.—

Each registered security-based swap dealer and major security-based swap participant—

        (A)   shall make such reports as are required by the Commission, by rule or regulation, regarding the transactions and positions and financial condition of the registered security-based swap dealer or major security-based swap participant;

        (B)(i)   for which there is a prudential regulator, shall keep books and records of all activities related to the business as a security-based swap dealer or major security-based swap participant in such form and manner and for such period as may be prescribed by the Commission by rule or regulation; and

           (ii)   for which there is no prudential regulator, shall keep books and records in such form and manner and for such period as may be prescribed by the Commission by rule or regulation; and

        (C)   shall keep books and records described in subparagraph (B) open to inspection and examination by any representative of the Commission.

    (2)   Rules.—

The Commission shall adopt rules governing reporting and recordkeeping for security-based swap dealers and major security-based swap participants.

  (g)   Daily Trading Records.—

    (1)   In general.—

Each registered security-based swap dealer and major security-based swap participant shall maintain daily trading records of the security-based swaps of the registered security-based swap dealer and major security-based swap participant and all related records (including related cash or forward transactions) and recorded communications, including electronic mail, instant messages, and recordings of telephone calls, for such period as may be required by the Commission by rule or regulation.

    (2)   Information requirements.—

The daily trading records shall include such information as the Commission shall require by rule or regulation.

    (3)   Counterparty records.—

Each registered security-based swap dealer and major security-based swap participant shall maintain daily trading records for each counterparty in a manner and form that is identifiable with each security-based swap transaction.

    (4)   Audit trail.—

Each registered security-based swap dealer and major security-based swap participant shall maintain a complete audit trail for conducting comprehensive and accurate trade reconstructions.

    (5)   Rules.—

The Commission shall adopt rules governing daily trading records for security-based swap dealers and major security-based swap participants.

  (h)   Business Conduct Standards.—

(1)   In general.—

Each registered security-based swap dealer and major security-based swap participant shall conform with such business conduct standards as prescribed in paragraph (3) and as may be prescribed by the Commission by rule or regulation that relate to—

(A)   fraud, manipulation, and other abusive practices involving security-based swaps (including security-based swaps that are offered but not entered into);

(B)   diligent supervision of the business of the registered security-based swap dealer and major security-based swap participant;

(C)   adherence to all applicable position limits; and

(D)   such other matters as the Commission determines to be appropriate.

(2)   Responsibilities with respect to special entities.—

(A)   Advising special entities.—

A security-based swap dealer or major security-based swap participant that acts as an advisor to special entity regarding a security-based swap shall comply with the requirements of paragraph (4) with respect to such special entity.

(B)   Entering of security-based swaps with respect to special entities.—

A security-based swap dealer that enters into or offers to enter into security-based swap with a special entity shall comply with the requirements of paragraph (5) with respect to such special entity.

(C)   Special entity defined.—

For purposes of this subsection, the term 'special entity' means—

(i)   a Federal agency;

(ii)   a State, State agency, city, county, municipality, or other political subdivision of a State or;

(iii)   any employee benefit plan, as defined in section 3 of the Employee Retirement Income Security Act of 1974 (29 U.S.C. 1002);

(iv)   any governmental plan, as defined in section 3 of the Employee Retirement Income Security Act of 1974 (29 U.S.C. 1002); or

(v)   any endowment, including an endowment that is an organization described in section 501(c)(3) of the Internal Revenue Code of 1986.

(3)   Business conduct requirements.—

Business conduct requirements adopted by the Commission shall—

(A)   establish a duty for a security-based swap dealer or major security-based swap participant to verify that any counterparty meets the eligibility standards for an eligible contract participant;

(B)   require disclosure by the security-based swap dealer or major security-based swap participant to any counterparty to the transaction (other than a security-based swap dealer, major security-based swap participant, security-based swap dealer, or major security-based swap participant) of—

(i)   information about the material risks and characteristics of the security-based swap;

(ii)   any material incentives or conflicts of interest that the security-based swap dealer or major security-based swap participant may have in connection with the security-based swap; and (iii)(I)   for cleared security-based swaps, upon the request of the counterparty, receipt of the daily mark of the transaction from the appropriate derivatives clearing organization; and

(II)   for uncleared security-based swaps, receipt of the daily mark of the transaction from the security-based swap dealer or the major security-based swap participant;

(C)   establish a duty for a security-based swap dealer or major security-based swap participant to communicate in a fair and balanced manner based on principles of fair dealing and good faith; and

(D)   establish such other standards and requirements as the Commission may determine are appropriate in the public interest, for the protection of investors, or otherwise in furtherance of the purposes of this Act.

(4)   Special requirements for security-based swap dealers acting as advisors.—

(A)   In general.—

It shall be unlawful for a security-based swap dealer or major security-based swap participant—

(i)   to employ any device, scheme, or artifice to defraud any special entity or prospective customer who is a special entity;

(ii)   to engage in any transaction, practice, or course of business that operates as a fraud or deceit on any special entity or prospective customer who is a special entity; or

(iii)   to engage in any act, practice, or course of business that is fraudulent, deceptive, or manipulative.

(B)   Duty.—

Any security-based swap dealer that acts as an advisor to a special entity shall have a duty to act in the best interests of the special entity.

(C)   Reasonable efforts.—

Any security-based swap dealer that acts as an advisor to a special entity shall make reasonable efforts to obtain such information as is necessary to make a reasonable determination that any security-based swap recommended by the security-based swap dealer is in the best interests of the special entity, including information relating to—

(i)   the financial status of the special entity;

(ii)   the tax status of the special entity;

(iii)   the investment or financing objectives of the special entity; and

(iv)   any other information that the Commission may prescribe by rule or regulation.

(5)   Special requirements for security-based swap dealers as counterparties to special entities.—

(A)   In general.—

Any security-based swap dealer or major security-based swap participant that offers to or enters into a security-based swap with a special entity shall—

(i)   comply with any duty established by the Commission for a security-based swap dealer or major security-based swap participant, with respect to a counterparty that is an eligible contract participant within the meaning of subclause (I) or (II) of clause (vii) of section 1a(18) of the Commodity Exchange Act, that requires the security-based swap dealer or major security-based swap participant to have a reasonable basis to believe that the counterparty that is a special entity has an independent representative that—

(I)   has sufficient knowledge to evaluate the transaction and risks;

(II)   is not subject to a statutory disqualification;

(III) is independent of the security-based swap dealer or major security-based swap participant;

(IV) undertakes a duty to act in the best interests of the counterparty it represents;

(V) makes appropriate disclosures;

(VI) will provide written representations to the special entity regarding fair pricing and the appropriateness of the transaction; and

(VII) in the case of employee benefit plans subject to the Employee Retirement Income Security Act of 1974, is a fiduciary as defined in section 3 of that Act (29 U.S.C. 1002); and

(ii) before the initiation of the transaction, disclose to the special entity in writing the capacity in which the security-based swap dealer is acting.

(B) Commission authority.—

The Commission may establish such other standards and requirements under this paragraph as the Commission may determine are appropriate in the public interest, for the protection of investors, or otherwise in furtherance of the purposes of this Act.

(6) Rules.—

The Commission shall prescribe rules under this subsection governing business conduct standards for security-based swap dealers and major security-based swap participants.

(7) Applicability.—

This subsection shall not apply with respect to a transaction that is—

(A) initiated by a special entity on an exchange or security-based swaps execution facility; and

(B) the security-based swap dealer or major security-based swap participant does not know the identity of the counterparty to the transaction.'

(i) Documentation Standards.—

(1) In general.—

Each registered security-based swap dealer and major security-based swap participant shall conform with such standards as may be prescribed by the Commission, by rule or regulation, that relate to timely and accurate confirmation, processing, netting, documentation, and valuation of all security-based swaps.

(2) Rules.—

The Commission shall adopt rules governing documentation standards for security-based swap dealers and major security-based swap participants.

(j) Duties.—Each registered security-based swap dealer and major security-based swap participant shall, at all times, comply with the following requirements:

(1) Monitoring of trading.—

The security-based swap dealer or major security-based swap participant shall monitor its trading in security-based swaps to prevent violations of applicable position limits.

(2) Risk management procedures.—

The security-based swap dealer or major security-based swap participant shall establish robust and professional risk management systems adequate for managing the day-to-day business of the security-based swap dealer or major security-based swap participant.

(3) Disclosure of general information.—

The security-based swap dealer or major security-based swap participant shall disclose to the Commission and to the prudential regulator for the security-based swap dealer or major security-based swap participant, as applicable, information concerning—

    (A) terms and conditions of its security-based swaps;

    (B) security-based swap trading operations, mechanisms, and practices;

    (C) financial integrity protections relating to security-based swaps; and

    (D) other information relevant to its trading in security-based swaps.

(4) **Ability to obtain information.—**

The security-based swap dealer or major security-based swap participant shall—

    (A) establish and enforce internal systems and procedures to obtain any necessary information to perform any of the functions described in this section; and

    (B) provide the information to the Commission and to the prudential regulator for the security-based swap dealer or major security-based swap participant, as applicable, on request.

(5) **Conflicts of interest.—**

The security-based swap dealer and major security-based swap participant shall implement conflict-of-interest systems and procedures that—

    (A) establish structural and institutional safeguards to ensure that the activities of any person within the firm relating to research or analysis of the price or market for any security-based swap or acting in a role of providing clearing activities or making determinations as to accepting clearing customers are separated by appropriate informational partitions within the firm from the review, pressure, or oversight of persons whose involvement in pricing, trading, or clearing activities might potentially bias their judgment or supervision and contravene the core principles of open access and the business conduct standards described in this title; and

    (B) address such other issues as the Commission determines to be appropriate.

(6) **Antitrust considerations.—**

Unless necessary or appropriate to achieve the purposes of this title, the security-based swap dealer or major security-based swap participant shall not—

    (A) adopt any process or take any action that results in any unreasonable restraint of trade; or

    (B) impose any material anticompetitive burden on trading or clearing.

(7) **Rules.—**

The Commission shall prescribe rules under this subsection governing duties of security-based swap dealers and major security-based swap participants.

(k) **Designation of Chief Compliance Officer.—**

(1) **In general.—**Each security-based swap dealer and major security-based swap participant shall designate an individual to serve as a chief compliance officer.

(2) **Duties.—**The chief compliance officer shall—

    (A) report directly to the board or to the senior officer of the security-based swap dealer or major security-based swap participant;

    (B) review the compliance of the security-based swap dealer or major security-based swap participant with respect to the security-based swap dealer and major security-based swap participant requirements described in this section;

    (C) in consultation with the board of directors, a body performing a function similar to the board, or the senior officer of the organization, resolve any conflicts of interest that may arise;

(D) be responsible for administering each policy and procedure that is required to be established pursuant to this section;

(E) ensure compliance with this title (including regulations) relating to security-based swaps, including each rule prescribed by the Commission under this section;

(F) establish procedures for the remediation of noncompliance issues identified by the chief compliance officer through any—

    (i) compliance office review;

    (ii) look-back;

    (iii) internal or external audit finding;

    (iv) self-reported error; or

    (v) validated complaint; and

(G) establish and follow appropriate procedures for the handling, management response, remediation, retesting, and closing of noncompliance issues.

(3) Annual reports.—

(A) In general.—

In accordance with rules prescribed by the Commission, the chief compliance officer shall annually prepare and sign a report that contains a description of—

    (i) the compliance of the security-based swap dealer or major swap participant with respect to this title (including regulations); and

    (ii) each policy and procedure of the security-based swap dealer or major security-based swap participant of the chief compliance officer (including the code of ethics and conflict of interest policies).

(B) Requirements.—

A compliance report under subparagraph (A) shall—

    (i) accompany each appropriate financial report of the security-based swap dealer or major security-based swap participant that is required to be furnished to the Commission pursuant to this section; and

    (ii) include a certification that, under penalty of law, the compliance report is accurate and complete.

(*l*) Enforcement and Administrative Proceeding Authority.—

(1) Primary enforcement authority.—

(A) Securities and exchange commission.—

Except as provided in subparagraph (B), (C), or (D), the Commission shall have primary authority to enforce subtitle B, and the amendments made by subtitle B of the Wall Street Transparency and Accountability Act of 2010, with respect to any person.

(B) Prudential regulators.—

The prudential regulators shall have exclusive authority to enforce the provisions of subsection (e) and other prudential requirements of this title (including risk management standards), with respect to security-based swap dealers or major security-based swap participants for which they are the prudential regulator.

(C) Referral.—

    (i) Violations of nonprudential requirements.—

If the appropriate Federal banking agency for security-based swap dealers or major security-based swap participants that are depository institutions has cause to believe that such security-based swap dealer or major security-based swap participant may have engaged in conduct that constitutes a violation of the nonprudential requirements of this section or rules adopted by the Commission thereunder, the agency may recommend in writing to the Commission that the Commission initiate an enforcement proceeding as authorized under this title. The recommendation shall be accompanied by a written explanation of the concerns giving rise to the recommendation.

(ii)   Violations of prudential requirements.—

If the Commission has cause to believe that a securities-based swap dealer or major securities-based swap participant that has a prudential regulator may have engaged in conduct that constitute a violation of the prudential requirements of subsection (e) or rules adopted thereunder, the Commission may recommend in writing to the prudential regulator that the prudential regulator initiate an enforcement proceeding as authorized under this title. The recommendation shall be accompanied by a written explanation of the concerns giving rise to the recommendation.

(D)   Backstop enforcement authority.—

(i)   Initiation of enforcement proceeding by prudential regulator.—

If the Commission does not initiate an enforcement proceeding before the end of the 90-day period beginning on the date on which the Commission receives a written report under subsection (C)(i), the prudential regulator may initiate an enforcement proceeding.

(ii)   Initiation of enforcement proceeding by commission.—

If the prudential regulator does not initiate an enforcement proceeding before the end of the 90-day period beginning on the date on which the prudential regulator receives a written report under subsection (C)(ii), the Commission may initiate an enforcement proceeding.

(2)   Censure, denial, suspension; notice and hearing.—

The Commission, by order, shall censure, place limitations on the activities, functions, or operations of, or revoke the registration of any security-based swap dealer or major security-based swap participant that has registered with the Commission pursuant to subsection (b) if the Commission finds, on the record after notice and opportunity for hearing, that such censure, placing of limitations, or revocation is in the public interest and that such security-based swap dealer or major security-based swap participant, or any person associated with such security-based swap dealer or major security-based swap participant effecting or involved in effecting transactions in security-based swaps on behalf of such security-based swap dealer or major security-based swap participant, whether prior or subsequent to becoming so associated—

(A)   has committed or omitted any act, or is subject to an order or finding, enumerated in subparagraph (A), (D), or (E) of paragraph (4) of section 15(b);

(B)   has been convicted of any offense specified in subparagraph (B) of such paragraph (4) within 10 years of the commencement of the proceedings under this subsection;

(C)   is enjoined from any action, conduct, or practice specified in subparagraph (C) of such paragraph (4);

(D)   is subject to an order or a final order specified in subparagraph (F) or (H), respectively, of such paragraph (4); or

(E)   has been found by a foreign financial regulatory authority to have committed or omitted any act, or violated any foreign statute or regulation, enumerated in subparagraph (G) of such paragraph (4).

(3)   Associated persons.—

With respect to any person who is associated, who is seeking to become associated, or, at the time of the alleged misconduct, who was associated or was seeking to become associated with a security-based swap dealer or major security-based swap participant for the purpose of effecting or being involved in effecting security-based swaps on behalf of such security-based swap dealer or major security-based swap participant, the Commission, by order, shall censure, place limitations on the activities or functions of such person, or suspend for a period not exceeding 12 months, or bar such person from being associated with a security-based swap dealer or major security-based swap participant, if the Commission finds, on the record after notice and opportunity for a hearing, that such censure, placing of limitations, suspension, or bar is in the public interest and that such person—

(A) has committed or omitted any act, or is subject to an order or finding, enumerated in subparagraph (A), (D), or (E) of paragraph (4) of section 15(b);

(B) has been convicted of any offense specified in subparagraph (B) of such paragraph (4) within 10 years of the commencement of the proceedings under this subsection;

(C) is enjoined from any action, conduct, or practice specified in subparagraph (C) of such paragraph (4);

(D) is subject to an order or a final order specified in subparagraph (F) or (H), respectively, of such paragraph (4); or

(E) has been found by a foreign financial regulatory authority to have committed or omitted any act, or violated any foreign statute or regulation, enumerated in subparagraph (G) of such paragraph (4).

(4) Unlawful conduct.—

(A) for any person as to whom an order under paragraph (3) is in effect, without the consent of the Commission, willfully to become, or to be, associated with a security-based swap dealer or major security-based swap participant in contravention of such order; or

(B) for any security-based swap dealer or major security-based swap participant to permit such a person, without the consent of the Commission, to become or remain a person associated with the security-based swap dealer or major security-based swap participant in contravention of such order, if such security-based swap dealer or major security-based swap participant knew, or in the exercise of reasonable care should have known, of such order.

Credit Risk Retention

Sec. 15G.   (a)   Definitions.—In this section—

(1) the term "Federal banking agencies" means the Office of the Comptroller of the Currency, the Board of Governors of the Federal Reserve System, and the Federal Deposit Insurance Corporation;

(2) the term "insured depository institution" has the same meaning as in section 3(c) of the Federal Deposit Insurance Act (12 U.S.C. 1813(c));

(3) the term "securitizer" means—

(A) an issuer of an asset-backed security; or

(B) a person who organizes and initiates an asset-backed securities transaction by selling or transferring assets, either directly or indirectly, including through an affiliate, to the issuer; and

(4) the term "originator" means a person who—

(A) through the extension of credit or otherwise, creates a financial asset that collateralizes an asset-backed security; and

(B) sells an asset directly or indirectly to a securitizer.

(b) Regulations Required.—

(1) In general.—

Not later than 270 days after the date of enactment of this section, the Federal banking agencies and the Commission shall jointly prescribe regulations to require any securitizer to retain an economic interest in a portion of the credit risk for any asset that the securitizer, through the issuance of an asset-backed security, transfers, sells, or conveys to a third party.

(2)   Residential mortgages.—

Not later than 270 days after the date of the enactment of this section, the Federal banking agencies, the Commission, the Secretary of Housing and Urban Development, and the Federal Housing Finance Agency, shall jointly prescribe regulations to require any securitizer to retain an economic interest in a portion of the credit risk for any residential mortgage asset that the securitizer, through the issuance of an asset-backed security, transfers, sells, or conveys to a third party.

(c)   Standards for Regulations.—

     (1)   Standards.—

         (A)   prohibit a securitizer from directly or indirectly hedging or otherwise transferring the credit risk that the securitizer is required to retain with respect to an asset;

         (B)   require a securitizer to retain—

             (i)   not less than 5 percent of the credit risk for any asset—

                 (I)   that is not a qualified residential mortgage that is transferred, sold, or conveyed through the issuance of an asset-backed security by the securitizer; or

                 (II)   that is a qualified residential mortgage that is transferred, sold, or conveyed through the issuance of an asset-backed security by the securitizer, if 1 or more of the assets that collateralize the asset-backed security are not qualified residential mortgages; or

             (ii)   less than 5 percent of the credit risk for an asset that is not a qualified residential mortgage that is transferred, sold, or conveyed through the issuance of an asset-backed security by the securitizer, if the originator of the asset meets the underwriting standards prescribed under paragraph (2)(B);

         (C)   specify—

             (i)   the permissible forms of risk retention for purposes of this section;

             (ii)   the minimum duration of the risk retention required under this section; and

             (iii)   that a securitizer is not required to retain any part of the credit risk for an asset that is transferred, sold or conveyed through the issuance of an asset-backed security by the securitizer, if all of the assets that collateralize the asset-backed security are qualified residential mortgages;

         (D)   apply, regardless of whether the securitizer is an insured depository institution;

         (E)   with respect to a commercial mortgage, specify the permissible types, forms, and amounts of risk retention that would meet the requirements of subparagraph (B), which in the determination of the Federal banking agencies and the Commission may include—

             (i)   retention of a specified amount or percentage of the total credit risk of the asset;

             (ii)   retention of the first-loss position by a third-party purchaser that specifically negotiates for the purchase of such first loss position, holds adequate financial resources to back losses, provides due diligence on all individual assets in the pool before the issuance of the asset-backed securities, and meets the same standards for risk retention as the Federal banking agencies and the Commission require of the securitizer;

             (iii)   a determination by the Federal banking agencies and the Commission that the underwriting standards and controls for the asset are adequate; and

(iv) provision of adequate representations and warranties and related enforcement mechanisms; and

(F) establish appropriate standards for retention of an economic interest with respect to collateralized debt obligations, securities collateralized by collateralized debt obligations, and similar instruments collateralized by other asset-backed securities; and

(G) provide for—

(i) a total or partial exemption of any securitization, as may be appropriate in the public interest and for the protection of investors;

(ii) a total or partial exemption for the securitization of an asset issued or guaranteed by the United States, or an agency of the United States, as the Federal banking agencies and the Commission jointly determine appropriate in the public interest and for the protection of investors, except that, for purposes of this clause, the Federal National Mortgage Association and the Federal Home Loan Mortgage Corporation are not agencies of the United States;

(iii) a total or partial exemption for any asset-backed security that is a security issued or guaranteed by any State of the United States, or by any political subdivision of a State or territory, or by any public instrumentality of a State or territory that is exempt from the registration requirements of the Securities Act of 1933 by reason of section 3(a)(2) of that Act (15 U.S.C. 77c(a)(2)), or a security defined as a qualified scholarship funding bond in section 150(d)(2) of the Internal Revenue Code of 1986, as may be appropriate in the public interest and for the protection of investors; and

(iv) the allocation of risk retention obligations between a securitizer and an originator in the case of a securitizer that purchases assets from an originator, as the Federal banking agencies and the Commission jointly determine appropriate.

(2) Asset classes.—

(A) Asset classes.—

The regulations prescribed under subsection (b) shall establish asset classes with separate rules for securitizers of different classes of assets, including residential mortgages, commercial mortgages, commercial loans, auto loans, and any other class of assets that the Federal banking agencies and the Commission deem appropriate.

(B) Contents.—

For each asset class established under subparagraph (A), the regulations prescribed under subsection (b) shall include underwriting standards established by the Federal banking agencies that specify the terms, conditions, and characteristics of a loan within the asset class that indicate a low credit risk with respect to the loan.

(d) Originators.—In determining how to allocate risk retention obligations between a securitizer and an originator under subsection (c)(1)(E)(iv), the Federal banking agencies and the Commission shall—

(1) reduce the percentage of risk retention obligations required of the securitizer by the percentage of risk retention obligations required of the originator; and

(2) consider—

(A) whether the assets sold to the securitizer have terms, conditions, and characteristics that reflect low credit risk;

(B) whether the form or volume of transactions in securitization markets creates incentives for imprudent origination of the type of loan or asset to be sold to the securitizer; and

(C) the potential impact of the risk retention obligations on the access of consumers and businesses to credit on reasonable terms, which may not include the transfer of credit risk to a third party.

(e) Exemptions, Exceptions, and Adjustments.—

(1)   In general.—

The Federal banking agencies and the Commission may jointly adopt or issue exemptions, exceptions, or adjustments to the rules issued under this section, including exemptions, exceptions, or adjustments for classes of institutions or assets relating to the risk retention requirement and the prohibition on hedging under subsection (c)(1).

(2)   Applicable standards.—

Any exemption, exception, or adjustment adopted or issued by the Federal banking agencies and the Commission under this paragraph shall—

(A)   help ensure high quality underwriting standards for the securitizers and originators of assets that are securitized or available for securitization; and

(B)   encourage appropriate risk management practices by the securitizers and originators of assets, improve the access of consumers and businesses to credit on reasonable terms, or otherwise be in the public interest and for the protection of investors.

(3)   Certain institutions and programs exempt.—

(A)   Farm credit system institutions.—

Notwithstanding any other provision of this section, the requirements of this section shall not apply to any loan or other financial asset made, insured, guaranteed, or purchased by any institution that is subject to the supervision of the Farm Credit Administration, including the Federal Agricultural Mortgage Corporation.

(B)   Other federal programs.—

This section shall not apply to any residential, multifamily, or health care facility mortgage loan asset, or securitization based directly or indirectly on such an asset, which is insured or guaranteed by the United States or an agency of the United States. For purposes of this subsection, the Federal National Mortgage Association, the Federal Home Loan Mortgage Corporation, and the Federal home loan banks shall not be considered an agency of the United States.

(4)   Exemption for qualified residential mortgages.—

(A)   In general.—

The Federal banking agencies, the Commission, the Secretary of Housing and Urban Development, and the Director of the Federal Housing Finance Agency shall jointly issue regulations to exempt qualified residential mortgages from the risk retention requirements of this subsection.

(B)   Qualified residential mortgage.—

The Federal banking agencies, the Commission, the Secretary of Housing and Urban Development, and the Director of the Federal Housing Finance Agency shall jointly define the term "qualified residential mortgage" for purposes of this subsection, taking into consideration underwriting and product features that historical loan performance data indicate result in a lower risk of default, such as—

(i)   documentation and verification of the financial resources relied upon to qualify the mortgagor;

(ii)   standards with respect to—

(I)   the residual income of the mortgagor after all monthly obligations;

(II)   the ratio of the housing payments of the mortgagor to the monthly income of the mortgagor;

(III) the ratio of total monthly installment payments of the mortgagor to the income of the mortgagor;

(iii) mitigating the potential for payment shock on adjustable rate mortgages through product features and underwriting standards;

(iv) mortgage guarantee insurance or other types of insurance or credit enhancement obtained at the time of origination, to the extent such insurance or credit enhancement reduces the risk of default; and

(v) prohibiting or restricting the use of balloon payments, negative amortization, prepayment penalties, interest-only payments, and other features that have been demonstrated to exhibit a higher risk of borrower default.

(C) Limitation on definition.—

The Federal banking agencies, the Commission, the Secretary of Housing and Urban Development, and the Director of the Federal Housing Finance Agency in defining the term "qualified residential mortgage", as required by subparagraph (B), shall define that term to be no broader than the definition "qualified mortgage" as the term is defined under section 129C(c)(2) of the Truth in Lending Act, as amended by the Consumer Financial Protection Act of 2010, and regulations adopted thereunder.

(5) Condition for qualified residential mortgage exemption.—

The regulations issued under paragraph (4) shall provide that an asset-backed security that is collateralized by tranches of other asset-backed securities shall not be exempt from the risk retention requirements of this subsection.

(6) Certification.—

The Commission shall require an issuer to certify, for each issuance of an asset-backed security collateralized exclusively by qualified residential mortgages, that the issuer has evaluated the effectiveness of the internal supervisory controls of the issuer with respect to the process for ensuring that all assets that collateralize the asset-backed security are qualified residential mortgages.

(f) Enforcement—The regulations issued under this section shall be enforced by.—

(1) the appropriate Federal banking agency, with respect to any securitizer that is an insured depository institution; and

(2) the Commission, with respect to any securitizer that is not an insured depository institution.

(g) Authority of Commission.—The authority of the Commission under this section shall be in addition to the authority of the Commission to otherwise enforce the securities laws.

(h) Authority to Coordinate on Rulemaking.—The Chairperson of the Financial Stability Oversight Council shall coordinate all joint rulemaking required under this section.

(i) Effective Date of Regulations.—The regulations issued under this section shall become effective—

(1) with respect to securitizers and originators of asset-backed securities backed by residential mortgages, 1 year after the date on which final rules under this section are published in the Federal Register; and

(2) with respect to securitizers and originators of all other classes of asset-backed securities, 2 years after the date on which final rules under this section are published in the Federal Register.

Directors, Officers, and Principal Stockholders

Sec. 16. (a) Disclosures Required.—

(1) Directors, officers, and principal stockholders required to file.—

Every person who is directly or indirectly the beneficial owner of more than 10 percent of any class of any equity security (other than an exempted security) which is registered pursuant to section 12, or who is a director or an officer of the issuer of such security, shall file the statements required by this subsection with the Commission.

(2)   Time of filing.—

The statements required by this subsection shall be filed—

(A)   at the time of the registration of such security on a national securities exchange or by the effective date of a registration statement filed pursuant to section 12(g);

(B)   within 10 days after he or she becomes such beneficial owner, director, or officer, or within such shorter time as the commission may establish by rule;

(C)   if there has been a change in such ownership, or if such person shall have purchased or sold a security-based swap agreement involving such equity security, before the end of the second business day following the day on which the subject transaction has been executed, or at such other time as the Commission shall establish, by rule, in any case in which the Commission determines that such 2-day period is not feasible.

(3)   Contents of statements.—

A statement filed—

(A)   under subparagraph (A) or (B) of paragraph (2) shall contain a statement of the amount of all equity securities of such issuer of which the filing person is the beneficial owner; and

(B)   under subparagraph (C) of such paragraph shall indicate ownership by the filing person at the date of filing, any such changes in such ownership, and such purchases and sales of the security-based swap agreements or security-based swaps as have occurred since the most recent such filing under such subparagraph.

(4)   Electronic filing and availability.—

Beginning not later than 1 year after the date of enactment of the Sarbanes-Oxley Act of 2002—

(A)   a statement filed under subparagraph (C) of paragraph (2) shall be filed electronically;

(B)   the Commission shall provide each such statement on a publicly accessible Internet site not later than the end of the business day following that filing; and

(C)   the issuer (if the issuer maintains a corporate website) shall provide that statement on that corporate website, not later than the end of the business day following that filing.

(b)   For the purpose of preventing the unfair use of information which may have been obtained by such beneficial owner, director, or officer by reason of his relationship to the issuer, any profit realized by him from any purchase and sale, or any sale and purchase, of any equity security of such issuer (other than an exempted security) or a security-based swap agreement involving any such equity security within any period of less than six months, unless such security or security-based swap agreement was acquired in good faith in connection with a debt previously contracted, shall inure to and be recoverable by the issuer, irrespective of any intention on the part of such beneficial owner, director, or officer in entering into such transaction of holding the security or security-based swap agreement purchased or of not repurchasing the security or security-based swap agreement sold for a period exceeding six months. Suit to recover such profit may be instituted at law or in equity in any court of competent jurisdiction by the issuer, or by the owner of any security of the issuer in the name and in behalf of the issuer if the issuer shall fail or refuse to bring such suit within sixty days after request or shall fail diligently to prosecute the same thereafter; but no such suit shall be brought more than two years after the date such profit was realized. This subsection shall not be construed to cover any transaction where such beneficial owner was not such both at the time of the purchase and sale, or the sale and purchase, of the security or security-based swap agreement or a security-based swap involved, or any transaction or transactions which the Commission by rules and regulations may exempt as not comprehended within the purpose of this subsection.

(c)   It shall be unlawful for any such beneficial owner, director, or officer, directly or indirectly, to sell any equity security of such issuer (other than an exempted security), if the person selling the security or his principal

(1)   does not own the security sold, or

(2)   if owning the security, does not deliver it against such sale within twenty days thereafter, or does not within five days after such sale deposit it in the mails or other usual channels of

transportation; but no person shall be deemed to have violated this subsection if he proves that notwithstanding the exercise of good faith he was unable to make such delivery or deposit within such time, or that to do so would cause undue inconvenience or expense.

(d)   The provisions of subsection (b) of this section shall not apply to any purchase and sale, or sale and purchase, and the provisions of subsection (c) of this section shall not apply to any sale, of an equity security not then or theretofore held by him in an investment account, by a dealer in the ordinary course of his business and incident to the establishment or maintenance by him of a primary or secondary market (otherwise than on a national securities exchange or an exchange exempted from registration under section 5 of this Act) for such security. The Commission may, by such rules and regulations as it deems necessary or appropriate in the public interest, define and prescribe terms and conditions with respect to securities held in an investment account and transactions made in the ordinary course of business and incident to the establishment or maintenance of a primary or secondary market.

(e)   The provisions of this section shall not apply to foreign or domestic arbitrage transactions unless made in contravention of such rules and regulations as the Commission may adopt in order to carry out the purposes of this section.

(f)   Treatment of Transactions in Security Futures Products.—The provisions of this section shall apply to ownership of and transactions in security futures products.

(g)   The authority of the Commission under this section with respect to security-based swap agreements shall be subject to the restrictions and limitations of section 3A(b) of this Act.

Records and Reports

Sec. 17. (a)(1)   Every national securities exchange, member thereof, broker or dealer who transacts a business in securities through the medium of any such member, registered securities association, registered broker or dealer, registered municipal securities dealer, municipal advisor, registered securities information processor, registered transfer agent, nationally recognized statistical rating organization, and registered clearing agency and the Municipal Securities Rulemaking Board shall make and keep for prescribed periods such records, furnish such copies thereof, and make and disseminate such reports as the Commission, by rule, prescribes as necessary or appropriate in the public interest, for the protection of investors, or otherwise in furtherance of the purposes of this Act. Any report that a nationally recognized statistical rating organization is required by Commission rules under this paragraph to make and disseminate to the Commission shall be deemed furnished to the Commission.

(2)   Every registered clearing agency shall also make and keep for prescribed periods such records, furnish such copies thereof, and make and disseminate such reports, as the appropriate regulatory agency for such clearing agency, by rule, prescribes as necessary or appropriate for the safeguarding of securities and funds in the custody or control of such clearing agency or for which it is responsible.

(3)   Every registered transfer agent shall also make and keep for prescribed periods such records, furnish such copies thereof, and make such reports as the appropriate regulatory agency for such transfer agent, by rule, prescribes as necessary or appropriate in furtherance of the purposes of section 17A of this Act.

(b)   Records Subject to Examination.—

(1)   Procedures for cooperation with other agencies.—

All records of persons described in subsection (a) of this section are subject at any time, or from time to time, to such reasonable periodic, special, or other examinations by representatives of the Commission and the appropriate regulatory agency for such persons as the Commission or the appropriate regulatory agency for such persons deems necessary or appropriate in the public interest, for the protection of investors, or otherwise in furtherance of the purposes of this Act: *Provided*, however, That the Commission shall, prior to conducting any such examination of a—

(A)   registered clearing agency, registered transfer agent, or registered municipal securities dealer for which it is not the appropriate regulatory agency, give notice to the appropriate regulatory agency for such clearing agency, transfer agent, or municipal securities dealer of such proposed examination and consult with such appropriate regulatory agency concerning the feasibility and desirability of coordinating such examination with examinations conducted by such appropriate regulatory agency with a view to avoiding unnecessary regulatory duplication or undue regulatory burdens for such clearing agency, transfer agent, or municipal securities dealer; or

(B) broker or dealer registered pursuant to section 15(b)(11) of this Act, exchange registered pursuant to section 6(g) of this Act, or national securities association registered pursuant to section 15A(k) of this Act, give notice to the Commodity Futures Trading Commission of such proposed examination and consults with the Commodity Futures Trading Commission concerning the feasibility and desirability of coordinating such examination with examinations conducted by the Commodity Futures Trading Commission in order to avoid unnecessary regulatory duplication or undue regulatory burdens for such broker or dealer or exchange.

(2) Furnishing data and reports to CFTC.—

The Commission shall notify the Commodity Futures Trading Commission of any examination conducted of any broker or dealer registered pursuant to section 15(b)(11) of this Act, exchange registered pursuant to section 6(g) of this Act, or national securities association registered pursuant to section 15A(k) of this Act and, upon request, furnish to the Commodity Futures Trading Commission any examination report and data supplied to, or prepared by, the Commission in connection with such examination.

(3) Use of CFTC reports.—

Prior to conducting an examination under paragraph (1), the Commission shall use the reports of examinations, if the information available therein is sufficient for the purposes of the examination, of—

(A) any broker or dealer registered pursuant to section 15(b)(11) of this Act;

(B) an exchange registered pursuant to section 6(g) of this Act; or[13]

(C) a national securities association registered pursuant to section 15A(k) of this Act;

that is made by the Commodity Futures Trading Commission, a national securities association registered pursuant to section 15A(k) of this Act, or an exchange registered pursuant to section 6(g) of this Act.

(4) Rules of construction.—

(A) Notwithstanding any other provision of this subsection, the records of a broker or dealer registered pursuant to section 15(b)(11) of this Act, an exchange registered pursuant to section 6(g) of this Act, or a national securities association registered pursuant to section 15A(k) of this Act described in this subparagraph shall not be subject to routine periodic examinations by the Commission.

(B) Any recordkeeping rules adopted under this subsection for a broker or dealer registered pursuant to section 15(b)(11) of this Act, an exchange registered pursuant to section 6(g) of this Act, or a national securities association registered pursuant to section 15A(k) of this Act shall be limited to records with respect to persons, accounts, agreements, contracts, and transactions involving security futures products.

(C) Nothing in the proviso in paragraph (1) shall be construed to impair or limit (other than by the requirement of prior consultation) the power of the Commission under this subsection to examine any clearing agency, transfer agent, or municipal securities dealer or to affect in any way the power of the Commission under any other provision of this Act or otherwise to inspect, examine, or investigate any such clearing agency, transfer agent, or municipal securities dealer.

(c)(1) Every clearing agency, transfer agent, and municipal securities dealer for which the Commission is not the appropriate regulatory agency shall

---

[13] Included "an" in 17(b)(3)(B) and "a" in 17(b)(3)(C) to correct the Statute's grammatical error.

(A)   file with the appropriate regulatory agency for such clearing agency, transfer agent, or municipal securities dealer a copy of any application, notice, proposal, report, or document filed with the Commission by reason of its being a clearing agency, transfer agent, or municipal securities dealer and

(B)   file with the Commission a copy of any application, notice, proposal, report, or document filed with such appropriate regulatory agency by reason of its being a clearing agency, transfer agent, or municipal securities dealer. The Municipal Securities Rulemaking Board shall file with each agency enumerated in section 3(a)(34)(A) of this Act copies of every proposed rule change filed with the Commission pursuant to section 19(b) of this Act.

(2)   The appropriate regulatory agency for a clearing agency, transfer agent, or municipal securities dealer for which the Commission is not the appropriate regulatory agency shall file with the Commission notice of the commencement of any proceeding and a copy of any order entered by such appropriate regulatory agency against any clearing agency, transfer agent, municipal securities dealer, or person associated with a transfer agent or municipal securities dealer, and the Commission shall file with such appropriate regulatory agency, if any, notice of the commencement of any proceeding and a copy of any order entered by the Commission against the clearing agency, transfer agent, or municipal securities dealer, or against any person associated with a transfer agent or municipal securities dealer for which the agency is the appropriate regulatory agency.

(3)   The Commission and the appropriate regulatory agency for a clearing agency, transfer agent, or municipal securities dealer for which the Commission is not the appropriate regulatory agency shall each notify the other and make a report of any examination conducted by it of such clearing agency, transfer agent, or municipal securities dealer, and, upon request, furnish to the other a copy of such report and any data supplied to it in connection with such examination.

(4)   The Commission or the appropriate regulatory agency may specify that documents required to be filed pursuant to this subsection with the Commission or such agency, respectively, may be retained by the originating clearing agency, transfer agent, or municipal securities dealer, or filed with another appropriate regulatory agency. The Commission or the appropriate regulatory agency (as the case may be) making such a specification shall continue to have access to the document on request.

(d)(1)   The Commission, by rule or order, as it deems necessary or appropriate in the public interest and for the protection of investors, to foster cooperation and coordination among self-regulatory organizations, or to remove impediments to and foster the development of a national market system and national system for the clearance and settlement of securities transactions, may—

(A)   with respect to any person who is a member of or participant in more than one self-regulatory organization, relieve any such self-regulatory organization of any responsibility under this Act

(i)   to receive regulatory reports from such person,

(ii)   to examine such person for compliance, or to enforce compliance by such person, with specified provisions of this Act, the rules and regulations thereunder, and its own rules, or

(iii)   to carry out other specified regulatory functions with respect to such person, and

(B)   allocate among self-regulatory organizations the authority to adopt rules with respect to matters as to which, in the absence of such allocation, such self-regulatory organizations share authority under this Act.

In making any such rule or entering any such order, the Commission shall take into consideration the regulatory capabilities and procedures of the self-regulatory organizations, availability of staff, convenience of location, unnecessary regulatory duplication, and such other factors as the Commission may consider germane to the protection of investors, cooperation and coordination among self-regulatory organizations, and the development of a national market system and a national system for the clearance and settlement of securities transactions. The Commission, by rule or order, as it deems necessary or appropriate in the public interest and for the protection of investors, may require any self-regulatory organization relieved of any responsibility pursuant to this paragraph, and any person with respect to whom such responsibility relates, to take such steps as are specified in any such rule or order to notify customers of, and persons doing business with, such person of the limited nature of such self-regulatory organization's responsibility for such person's acts, practices, and course of business.

(2)   A self-regulatory organization shall furnish copies of any report of examination of any person who is a member of or a participant in such self-regulatory organization to any other self-regulatory organization of which such person is a member or in which such person is a participant upon the request of such person, such other self-regulatory organization, or the Commission.

(e)(1)(A)   Every registered broker or dealer shall annually file with the Commission a balance sheet and income statement certified by an independent public accounting firm, or by a registered public accounting firm if the firm is required to be registered under the Sarbanes-Oxley Act of 2002, prepared on a calendar or fiscal year basis, and such other financial statements (which shall, as the Commission specifies, be certified) and information concerning its financial condition as the Commission, by rule may prescribe as necessary or appropriate in the public interest or for the protection of investors.

(B)   Every registered broker and dealer shall annually send to its customers its certified balance sheet and such other financial statements and information concerning its financial condition as the Commission, by rule, may prescribe pursuant to subsection (a) of this section.

(C)   The Commission, by rule or order, may conditionally or unconditionally exempt any registered broker or dealer, or class of such brokers or dealers, from any provision of this paragraph if the Commission determines that such exemption is consistent with the public interest and the protection of investors.

(2)   The Commission, by rule, as it deems necessary or appropriate in the public interest or for the protection of investors, may prescribe the form and content of financial statements filed pursuant to this Act and the accounting principles and accounting standards used in their preparation.

(f)(1)   Every national securities exchange, member thereof, registered securities association, broker, dealer, municipal securities dealer, government securities broker, government securities dealer, registered transfer agent, registered clearing agency, participant therein, member of the Federal Reserve System, and bank whose deposits are insured by the Federal Deposit Insurance Corporation shall—

(A)   report to the Commission or other person designated by the Commission and to the Secretary of the Treasury such information about securities that are missing, lost, counterfeit, stolen, or cancelled, in such form and within such time as the Commission, by rule, determines is necessary or appropriate in the public interest or for the protection of investors; such information shall be available on request for a reasonable fee, to any such exchange, member, association, broker, dealer, municipal securities dealer, transfer agent, clearing agency, participant, member of the Federal Reserve System, or insured bank, and such other persons as the Commission, by rule, designates; and

(B)   make such inquiry with respect to information reported pursuant to this subsection as the Commission, by rule, prescribes as necessary or appropriate in the public interest or for the protection of investors, to determine whether securities in their custody or control, for which they are responsible, or in which they are effecting, clearing, or settling a transaction have been reported as missing, lost, counterfeit, stolen, cancelled, or reported in such other manner as the Commission, by rule, may prescribe.

(2)   Every member of a national securities exchange, broker, dealer, registered transfer agent, registered clearing agency, registered securities information processor, national securities exchange, and national securities association require that each of its partners, directors, officers, and employees be fingerprinted and shall submit such fingerprints, or cause the same to be submitted, to the Attorney General of the United States for identification and appropriate processing. The Commission, by rule, may exempt from the provisions of this paragraph upon specified terms, conditions, and periods, any class of partners, directors, officers, or employees of any such member, broker, dealer, transfer agent, clearing agency, securities information processor, national securities exchange, or national securities association, if the Commission finds that such action is not inconsistent with the public interest or the protection of investors. Notwithstanding any other provision of law, in providing identification and

processing functions, the Attorney General shall provide the Commission and self-regulatory organizations designated by the Commission with access to all criminal history record information.

(3)(A)   In order to carry out the authority under paragraph (1) above, the Commission or its designee may enter into agreement with the Attorney General to use the facilities of the National Crime Information Center ("NCIC") to receive, store, and disseminate information in regard to missing, lost, counterfeit, or stolen securities and to permit direct inquiry access to NCIC's file on such securities for the financial community.

(B)   In order to carry out the authority under paragraph (1) of this subsection, the Commission or its designee and the Secretary of the Treasury shall enter into an agreement whereby the Commission or its designee will receive, store, and disseminate information in the possession, and which comes into the possession, of the Department of the Treasury in regard to missing, lost, counterfeit, or stolen securities.

(4)   In regard to paragraphs (1), (2), and (3), above insofar as such paragraphs apply to any bank or member of the Federal Reserve System, the Commission may delegate its authority to:

(A)   the Comptroller of the Currency as to national banks;

(B)   the Federal Reserve Board in regard to any member of the Federal Reserve System which is not a national bank; and

(C)   the Federal Deposit Insurance Corporation for any State bank which is insured by the Federal Deposit Insurance Corporation but which is not a member of the Federal Reserve System.

(5)   The Commission shall encourage the insurance industry to require their insured to report expeditiously instances of missing, lost, counterfeit, or stolen securities to the Commission or to such other person as the Commission may, by rule, designate to receive such information.

(g)   Any broker, dealer, or other person extending credit who is subject to the rules and regulations prescribed by the Board of Governors of the Federal Reserve System pursuant to this Act shall make such reports to the Board as it may require as necessary or appropriate to enable it to perform the functions conferred upon it by this Act. If any such broker, dealer, or other person shall fail to make any such report or fail to furnish full information therein, or, if in the judgment of the Board it is otherwise necessary, such broker, dealer, or other person shall permit such inspections to be made by the Board with respect to the business operations of such broker, dealer, or other person as the Board may deem necessary to enable it to obtain the required information.

(h)   Risk Assessment for Holding Company Systems.—

(1)   Obligations to obtain, maintain, and report information.—

Every person who is

(A)   a registered broker or dealer, or

(B)   a registered municipal securities dealer for which the Commission is the appropriate regulatory agency, shall obtain such information and make and keep such records as the Commission by rule prescribes concerning the registered person's policies, procedures, or systems for monitoring and controlling financial and operational risks to it resulting from the activities of any of its associated persons, other than a natural person. Such records shall describe, in the aggregate, each of the financial and securities activities conducted by and the customary sources of capital and funding of, those of its associated persons whose business activities are reasonably likely to have a material impact on the financial or operational condition of such registered person, including its net capital, its liquidity, or its ability to conduct or finance its operations. The Commission, by rule, may require summary reports of such information to be filed with the Commission no more frequently than quarterly.

(2)   Authority to require additional information.—

If, as a result of adverse market conditions or based on reports provided to the Commission pursuant to paragraph (1) of this subsection or other available information, the Commission reasonably concludes that it has concerns regarding the financial or operational condition of (A) any registered broker or dealer, or (B) any registered municipal securities dealer, government securities broker, or government securities dealer for which the Commission is the appropriate regulatory agency, the Commission may require the registered person to make reports concerning the financial and securities activities of any of such person's associated persons, other than a natural person, whose business activities are reasonably likely to have a material impact on the financial or operational condition of such registered person. The Commission, in requiring reports pursuant to this paragraph, shall specify the information required, the period for which it is required, the time and date on which the information must be furnished, and whether the information is to be furnished directly to the Commission or to a self-regulatory organization with primary responsibility for examining the registered person's financial and operational condition.

(3) Special provisions with respect to associated persons subject to federal banking agency regulation.—

(A) Cooperation in implementation.—

In developing and implementing reporting requirements pursuant to paragraph (1) of this subsection with respect to associated persons subject to examination by or reporting requirements of a Federal banking agency, the Commission shall consult with and consider the views of each such Federal banking agency. If a Federal banking agency comments in writing on a proposed rule of the Commission under this subsection that has been published for comment, the Commission shall respond in writing to such written comment before adopting the proposed rule. The Commission shall, at the request of the Federal banking agency, publish such comment and response in the Federal Register at the time of publishing the adopted rule.

(B) Use of banking agency reports.—

A registered broker, dealer, or municipal securities dealer shall be in compliance with any recordkeeping or reporting requirement adopted pursuant to paragraph (1) of this subsection concerning an associated person that is subject to examination by or reporting requirements of a Federal banking agency if such broker, dealer, or municipal securities dealer utilizes for such recordkeeping or reporting requirement copies of reports filed by the associated person with the Federal banking agency pursuant to section 5211 of the Revised Statutes, section 9 of the Federal Reserve Act, section 7(a) of the Federal Deposit Insurance Act, section 10(b) of the Home Owners' Loan Act, or section 8 of the Bank Holding Company Act of 1956. The Commission may, however, by rule adopted pursuant to paragraph (1), require any broker, dealer, or municipal securities dealer filing such reports with the Commission to obtain, maintain, or report supplemental information if the Commission makes an explicit finding that such supplemental information is necessary to inform the Commission regarding potential risks to such broker, dealer, or municipal securities dealer. Prior to requiring any such supplemental information, the Commission shall first request the Federal banking agency to expand its reporting requirements to include such information.

(C) Procedure for requiring additional information.—

Prior to making a request pursuant to paragraph (2) of this subsection for information with respect to an associated person that is subject to examination by or reporting requirements of a Federal banking agency, the Commission shall—

(i) notify such agency of the information required with respect to such associated person; and

(ii) consult with such agency to determine whether the information required is available from such agency and for other purposes, unless the Commission determines that any delay resulting from such consultation would be inconsistent with ensuring the financial and operational condition of the broker, dealer, municipal securities dealer, government securities broker, or government securities dealer or the stability or integrity of the securities markets.

(D) Exclusion for examination reports.—

Nothing in this subsection shall be construed to permit the Commission to require any registered broker or dealer, or any registered municipal securities dealer, government securities broker, or government securities dealer for which the Commission is the appropriate regulatory agency, to obtain, maintain, or furnish any examination report of any Federal banking agency or any supervisory recommendations or analysis contained therein.

(E) Confidentiality of information provided.—

No information provided to or obtained by the Commission from any Federal banking agency pursuant to a request by the Commission under subparagraph (C) of this paragraph regarding any associated person which is subject to examination by or reporting requirements of a Federal banking agency may be disclosed to any other person (other than a self-regulatory organization), without the prior written approval of the Federal banking agency. Nothing in this subsection shall authorize the Commission to withhold information from Congress, or prevent the Commission from complying with a request for information from any other Federal department or agency requesting the information for purposes within the scope of its jurisdiction, or complying with an order of a court of the United States in an action brought by the United States or the Commission.

(F) Notice to banking agencies concerning financial and operational condition concerns.—

The Commission shall notify the Federal banking agency of any concerns of the Commission regarding significant financial or operational risks resulting from the activities of any registered broker or dealer, or any registered municipal securities dealer, government securities broker, or government securities dealer for which the Commission is the appropriate regulatory agency, to any associated person thereof which is subject to examination by or reporting requirements of the Federal banking agency.

(G) Definition.—

For purposes of this paragraph, the term "Federal banking agency" shall have the same meaning as the term "appropriate Federal bank agency" in section 3(q) of the Federal Deposit Insurance Act.

(4) Exemptions.—

The Commission by rule or order may exempt any person or class of persons, under such terms and conditions and for such periods as the Commission shall provide in such rule or order, from the provisions of this subsection, and the rules thereunder. In granting such exemptions, the Commission shall consider, among other factors—

(A) whether information of the type required under this subsection is available from a supervisory agency (as defined in section 1101(6) of the Right to Financial Privacy Act of 1978), a State insurance commission or similar State agency, the Commodity Futures Trading Commission, or a similar foreign regulator;

(B) the primary business of any associated person;

(C) the nature and extent of domestic or foreign regulation of the associated person's activities;

(D) the nature and extent of the registered person's securities activities; and

(E) with respect to the registered person and its associated persons, on a consolidated basis, the amount and proportion of assets devoted to, and revenues derived from, activities in the United States securities markets.

(5) Authority to limit disclosure of information.—

Notwithstanding any other provision of law, the Commission shall not be compelled to disclose any information required to be reported under this subsection, or any information supplied to the Commission by any domestic or foreign regulatory agency that relates to the financial or operational condition of any associated person of a registered broker, dealer, government securities broker, government securities dealer, or municipal securities dealer. Nothing in this subsection shall authorize the Commission to withhold information from Congress, or prevent the Commission from complying with a request for information from any other Federal department or agency requesting the information for purposes within the scope of its jurisdiction, or complying with an order of a court of the United States in an action brought by the United States or the Commission. For purposes of section 552 of Title 5, United States Code, this subsection shall be considered a statute described in subsection (b)(3)(B) of such section 552. In prescribing regulations to carry out the requirements of this subsection, the Commission shall designate information described in or obtained pursuant to subparagraph (B) or (C) of paragraph (3) of this subsection as confidential information for purposes of section 24(b)(2) of this Act.

(i)   Authority to limit Disclosure of Information.—

Notwithstanding any other provision of law, the Commission shall not be compelled to disclose any information required to be reported under subsection (h) or (i) or any information supplied to the Commission by any domestic or foreign regulatory agency that relates to the financial or operational condition of any associated person of a broker or dealer, investment bank holding company, or any affiliate of an investment bank holding company. Nothing in this subsection shall authorize the Commission to withhold information from Congress, or prevent the Commission from complying with a request for information from any other Federal department or agency or any self-regulatory organization requesting the information for purposes within the scope of its jurisdiction, or complying with an order of the Court of the United States in an action brought by the United States or the Commission. For purposes of section 552 of Title 5, United States Code, this subsection shall be considered a statute described in subsection (b)(3)(B) of such section 552. In prescribing regulations to carry out the requirements of the subsection the Commission shall designate information described in or obtained pursuant to subparagraph (A), (B), and (C) if subsection (i)(3) as confidential information for purposes of section 24(b)(2) of this Act.

(j)   Coordination of Examining Authorities.—

    (1)   Elimination of duplication.—

The Commission and the examining authorities, through cooperation and coordination of examination and oversight activities, shall eliminate any unnecessary and burdensome duplication in the examination process.

    (2)   Coordination of examinations.—

The Commission and the examining authorities shall share such information, including reports of examinations, customer complaint information, and other nonpublic regulatory information, as appropriate to foster a coordinated approach to regulatory oversight of brokers and dealers that are subject to examination by more than one examining authority.

    (3)   Examinations for cause.—

At any time, any examining authority may conduct an examination for cause of any broker or dealer subject to its jurisdiction.

    (4)   Confidentiality.—

        (A)   In general.—

Section 24 shall apply to the sharing of information in accordance with this subsection. The Commission shall take appropriate action under section 24(c) to ensure that such information is not inappropriately disclosed.

        (B)   Appropriate Disclosure not prohibited.—

Nothing in this paragraph authorizes the Commission or any examining authority to withhold information from the Congress, or prevent the Commission or any examining authority from complying with a request for information from any other Federal department or agency requesting the information for purposes within the scope of its jurisdiction, or complying with an order of a court of the United States in an action brought by the United States or the Commission.

    (5)   Definition.—

For purposes of this subsection, the term "examining authority" means a self-regulatory organization registered with the Commission under this Act (other than a registered clearing agency) with the authority to examine, inspect, and otherwise oversee the activities of a registered broker or dealer.

National System for Clearance and Settlement of Securities Transactions

Sec. 17A.   (a)(1) The Congress finds that—

(A) The prompt and accurate clearance and settlement of securities transactions, including the transfer of record ownership and the safeguarding of securities and funds related thereto, are necessary for the protection of investors and persons facilitating transactions by and acting on behalf of investors.

(B) Inefficient procedures for clearance and settlement impose unnecessary costs on investors and persons facilitating transactions by and acting on behalf of investors.

(C) New data processing and communications techniques create the opportunity for more efficient, effective, and safe procedures for clearance and settlement.

(D) The linking of all clearance and settlement facilities and the development of uniform standards and procedures for clearance and settlement will reduce unnecessary costs and increase the protection of investors and persons facilitating transactions by and acting on behalf of investors.

(2)(A) The Commission is directed, therefore, having due regard for the public interest, the protection of investors, the safeguarding of securities and funds, and maintenance of fair competition among brokers and dealers, clearing agencies, and transfer agents, to use its authority under this Act—

(i) to facilitate the establishment of a national system for the prompt and accurate clearance and settlement of transactions in securities (other than exempt securities); and

(ii) to facilitate the establishment of linked or coordinated facilities for clearance and settlement of transactions in securities, securities options, contracts of sale for future delivery and options thereon, and commodity options;

in accordance with the findings and to carry out the objectives set forth in paragraph (1) of this subsection.

(B) The Commission shall use its authority under this Act to assure equal regulation under this Act of registered clearing agencies and registered transfer agents. In carrying out its responsibilities set forth in subparagraph (A)(ii) of this paragraph, the Commission shall coordinate with the Commodity Futures Trading Commission and consult with the Board of Governors of the Federal Reserve System.

(b)(1) Except as otherwise provided in this section, it shall be unlawful for any clearing agency, unless registered in accordance with this subsection, directly or indirectly, to make use of the mails or any means or instrumentality of interstate commerce to perform the functions of a clearing agency with respect to any security (other than an exempted security). The Commission, by rule or order, upon its own motion or upon application, may conditionally or unconditionally exempt any clearing agency or security or any class of clearing agencies or securities from any provisions of this section or the rules or regulations thereunder, if the Commission finds that such exemption is consistent with the public interest, the protection of investors, and the purposes of this section, including the prompt and accurate clearance and settlement of securities transactions and the safeguarding of securities and funds. A clearing agency or transfer agent shall not perform the functions of both a clearing agency and a transfer agent unless such clearing agency or transfer agent is registered in accordance with this subsection and subsection (c) of this section.

(2) A clearing agency may be registered under the terms and conditions hereinafter provided in this subsection and in accordance with the provisions of section 19(a) of this Act, by filing with the Commission an application for registration in such form as the Commission, by rule, may prescribe containing the rules of the clearing agency and such other information and documents as the Commission, by rule, may prescribe as necessary or appropriate in the public interest or for the prompt and accurate clearance and settlement of securities transactions.

(3) A clearing agency shall not be registered unless the Commission determines that—

(A) Such clearing agency is so organized and has the capacity to be able to facilitate the prompt and accurate clearance and settlement of securities transactions and derivative agreements, contracts, and transactions for which it is responsible, to safeguard securities and funds in its custody or control or for which it is responsible, to comply with the provisions of this Act and the rules and regulations thereunder, to enforce (subject to any rule or order of the Commission pursuant to section 17(d) or 19(g)(2) of this Act) compliance by its participants with the rules of the clearing agency, and to carry out the purposes of this section.

(B) Subject to the provisions of paragraph (4) of this subsection, the rules of the clearing agency provide that any

    (i) registered broker or dealer,

    (ii) other registered clearing agency,

    (iii) registered investment company,

    (iv) bank,

    (v) insurance company, or

    (vi) other person or class of persons as the Commission, by rule, may from time to time designate as appropriate to the development of a national system for the prompt and accurate clearance and settlement of securities transactions may become a participant in such clearing agency.

(C) The rules of the clearing agency assure a fair representation of its shareholders (or members) and participants in the selection of its directors and administration of its affairs. (The Commission may determine that the representation of participants is fair if they are afforded a reasonable opportunity to acquire voting stock of the clearing agency, directly or indirectly, in reasonable proportion to their use of such clearing agency.)

(D) The rules of the clearing agency provide for the equitable allocation of reasonable dues, fees, and other charges among its participants.

(E) The rules of the clearing agency do not impose any schedule of prices, or fix rates or other fees, for services rendered by its participants.

(F) The rules of the clearing agency are designed to promote the prompt and accurate clearance and settlement of securities transactions and, to the extent applicable, derivative agreements, contracts, and transactions, to assure the safeguarding of securities and funds which are in the custody or control of the clearing agency or for which it is responsible, to foster cooperation and coordination with persons engaged in the clearance and settlement of securities transactions and, to the extent applicable, derivative agreements, contracts and transactions to remove impediments to and perfect the mechanism of a national system for the prompt and accurate clearance and settlement of securities transactions, and, in general, to protect investors and the public interest; and are not designed to permit unfair discrimination in the admission of participants or among participants in the use of the clearing agency, or to regulate by virtue of any authority conferred by this Act matters not related to the purposes of this section or the administration of the clearing agency.

(G) The rules of the clearing agency provide that (subject to any rule or order of the Commission pursuant to section 17(d) or 19(g)(2) of this Act) its participants shall be appropriately disciplined for violation of any provision of the rules of the clearing agency by expulsion, suspension, limitation of activities, functions, and operations, fine, censure, or any other fitting sanction.

(H) The rules of the clearing agency are in accordance with the provisions of paragraph (5) of this subsection, and, in general, provide a fair procedure with respect to the disciplining of participants, the denial of participation to any person seeking participation therein, and the prohibition or limitation by the clearing agency of any person with respect to access to services offered by the clearing agency.

(I)   The rules of the clearing agency do not impose any burden on competition not necessary or appropriate in furtherance of the purposes of this Act.

(4)(A)   A registered clearing agency may, and in cases in which the Commission, by order, directs as appropriate in the public interest shall, deny participation to any person subject to a statutory disqualification. A registered clearing agency shall file notice with the Commission not less than thirty days prior to admitting any person to participation, if the clearing agency knew, or in the exercise of reasonable care should have known, that such person was subject to a statutory disqualification. The notice shall be in such form and contain such information as the Commission, by rule, may prescribe as necessary or appropriate in the public interest or for the protection of investors.

(B)   A registered clearing agency may deny participation to, or condition the participation of, any person if such person does not meet such standards of financial responsibility, operational capability, experience, and competence as are prescribed by the rules of the clearing agency. A registered clearing agency may examine and verify the qualifications of an applicant to be a participant in accordance with procedures established by the rules of the clearing agency.

(5)(A)   In any proceeding by a registered clearing agency to determine whether a participant should be disciplined (other than a summary proceeding pursuant to subparagraph (C) of this paragraph), the clearing agency shall bring specific charges, notify such participant of, and give him an opportunity to defend against such charges, and keep a record. A determination by the clearing agency to impose a disciplinary sanction shall be supported by a statement setting forth—

(i)   any act or practice in which such participant has been found to have engaged, or which such participant has been found to have omitted;

(ii)   the specific provisions of the rules of the clearing agency which any such act or practice, or omission to act, is deemed to violate; and

(iii)   the sanction imposed and the reasons therefor.

(B)   In any proceeding by a registered clearing agency to determine whether a person shall be denied participation or prohibited or limited with respect to access to services offered by the clearing agency, the clearing agency shall notify such person of, and give him an opportunity to be heard upon, the specific grounds for denial or prohibition or limitation under consideration and keep a record. A determination by the clearing agency to deny participation or prohibit or limit a person with respect to access to services offered by the clearing agency shall be supported by a statement setting forth the specific grounds on which the denial or prohibition or limitation is based.

(C)   A registered clearing agency may summarily suspend and close the accounts of a participant who

(i)   has been and is expelled or suspended from any self-regulatory organization,

(ii)   is in default of any delivery of funds or securities to the clearing agency, or

(iii)   is in such financial or operating difficulty that the clearing agency determines and so notifies the appropriate regulatory agency for such participant that such suspension and closing of accounts are necessary for the protection of the clearing agency, its participants, creditors, or investors. A participant so summarily suspended shall be promptly afforded an opportunity for a hearing by the clearing agency in accordance with the provisions of subparagraph (A) of this paragraph. The appropriate regulatory agency for such participant, by order, may stay any such summary suspension on its own motion or upon application by any person aggrieved thereby, if such appropriate regulatory agency determines summarily or after notice and opportunity for hearing (which hearing may consist solely of the submission of affidavits or presentation of oral arguments) that such stay is consistent with the public interest and protection of investors.

(6)   No registered clearing agency shall prohibit or limit access by any person to services offered by any participant therein.

(7)(A)   A clearing agency that is regulated directly or indirectly by the Commodity Futures Trading Commission through its association with a designated contract market for security futures products that is a national securities exchange registered pursuant to section 6(g), and that would be required to register pursuant to paragraph (1) of this subsection only because it performs the functions of a clearing agency with respect to security futures products effected pursuant to the rules of the designated contract market with which such agency is associated, is exempted from the provisions of this section and the rules and regulations thereunder, except that if such a clearing agency performs the functions of a clearing agency with respect to a security futures product that is not cash settled, it must have arrangements in place with a registered clearing agency to effect the payment and delivery of the securities underlying the security futures product.

    (B) Any clearing agency that performs the functions of a clearing agency with respect to security futures products must coordinate with and develop fair and reasonable links with any and all other clearing agencies that perform the functions of a clearing agency with respect to security futures products, in order to permit, as of the compliance date (as defined in section 6(h)(6)(C)), security futures products to be purchased on one market and offset on another market that trades such products.

    (8) A registered clearing agency shall be permitted to provide facilities for the clearance and settlement of any derivative agreements, contracts, or transactions that are excluded from the Commodity Exchange Act, subject to the requirements of this section and to such rules and regulations as the Commission may prescribe as necessary or appropriate in the public interest, for the protection of investors, or otherwise in furtherance of the purposes of this Act.

    (c)(1) Except as otherwise provided in this section, it shall be unlawful for any transfer agent, unless registered in accordance with this section, directly or indirectly, to make use of the mails or any means or instrumentality of interstate commerce to perform the function of a transfer agent with respect to any security registered under section 12 of this Act or which would be required to be registered except for the exemption from registration provided by subsection (g)(2)(B) or (g)(2)(G) of that section. The appropriate regulatory agency, by rule or order, upon its own motion or upon application, may conditionally or unconditionally exempt any person or security or class of persons or securities from any provision of this section or any rule or regulation prescribed under this section, if the appropriate regulatory agency finds

    (A) that such exemption is in the public interest and consistent with the protection of investors and the purposes of this section, including the prompt and accurate clearance and settlement of securities transactions and the safeguarding of securities and funds, and

    (B) the Commission does not object to such exemption.

    (2) A transfer agent may be registered by filing with the appropriate regulatory agency for such transfer agent an application for registration in such form and containing such information and documents concerning such transfer agent and any persons associated with the transfer agent as such appropriate regulatory agency may prescribe as necessary or appropriate in furtherance of the purposes of this section. Except as hereinafter provided, such registration shall become effective 45 days after receipt of such application by such appropriate regulatory agency or within such shorter period of time as such appropriate regulatory agency may determine.

    (3) The appropriate regulatory agency for a transfer agent, by order, shall deny registration to, censure, place limitations on the activities, functions, or operations of, suspend for a period not exceeding 12 months, or revoke the registration of such transfer agent, if such appropriate regulatory agency finds, on the record after notice and opportunity for hearing, that such denial, censure, placing of limitations, suspension, or revocation is in the public interest and that such transfer agent, whether prior or subsequent to becoming such, or any person associated with such transfer agent, whether prior or subsequent to becoming so associated—

    (A) has committed or omitted any act, or is subject to an order or finding, enumerated in subparagraph (A), (D), (E), (G), or (H) of paragraph (4) of section 15(b) of this Act, has been convicted of any offense specified in subparagraph (B) of such paragraph (4) within ten years of the commencement of the proceedings under this paragraph, or is enjoined from any action, conduct, or practice specified in subparagraph (C) of such paragraph (4); or

    (B) is subject to an order entered pursuant to subparagraph (C) of paragraph (4) of this subsection barring or suspending the right of such person to be associated with a transfer agent.

(4)(A)   Pending final determination whether any registration by a transfer agent under this subsection shall be denied, the appropriate regulatory agency for such transfer agent, by order, may postpone the effective date of such registration for a period not to exceed fifteen days, but if, after notice and opportunity for hearing (which may consist solely of affidavits and oral arguments), it shall appear to such appropriate regulatory agency to be necessary or appropriate in the public interest or for the protection of investors to postpone the effective date of such registration until final determination, such appropriate regulatory agency shall so order. Pending final determination whether any registration under this subsection shall be revoked, such appropriate regulatory agency, by order, may suspend such registration, if such suspension appears to such appropriate regulatory agency, after notice and opportunity for hearing, to be necessary or appropriate in the public interest or for the protection of investors.

(B)   A registered transfer agent may, upon such terms and conditions as the appropriate regulatory agency for such transfer agent deems necessary or appropriate in the public interest, for the protection of investors, or in furtherance of the purposes of this section, withdraw from registration by filing a written notice of withdrawal with such appropriate regulatory agency. If such appropriate regulatory agency finds that any transfer agent for which it is the appropriate regulatory agency, is no longer in existence or has ceased to do business as a transfer agent, such appropriate regulatory agency, by order, shall cancel or deny the registration.

(C)   The appropriate regulatory agency for a transfer agent, by order, shall censure or place limitations on the activities or functions of any person associated, seeking to become associated, or, at the time of the alleged misconduct, associated or seeking to become associated with the transfer agent, or suspend for a period not exceeding 12 months or bar any such person from being associated with the transfer agent, broker, dealer, investment adviser, municipal securities dealer, municipal advisor, or nationally recognized statistical rating organization, if the appropriate regulatory agency finds, on the record after notice and opportunity for hearing, that such censure, placing of limitations, suspension, or bar is in the public interest and that such person has committed or omitted any act, or is subject to an order or finding, enumerated in subparagraph (A), (D), (E), (G), or (H) or paragraph (4) of section 15(b) of this Act, has been convicted of any offense specified in subparagraph (B) of such paragraph (4) within ten years of the commencement of the proceedings under this paragraph, or is enjoined from any action, conduct, or practice specified in subparagraph (C) of such paragraph (4). It shall be unlawful for any person as to whom such an order suspending or barring him from being associated with a transfer agent is in effect willfully to become, or to be, associated with a transfer agent without the consent of the appropriate regulatory agency that entered the order and the appropriate regulatory agency for that transfer agent. It shall be unlawful for any transfer agent to permit such a person to become, or remain, a person associated with it without the consent of such appropriate regulatory agencies, if the transfer agent knew, or in the exercise of reasonable care should have known, of such order. The Commission may establish, by rule, procedures by which a transfer agent reasonably can determine whether a person associated or seeking to become associated with it is subject to any such order, and may require, by rule, that any transfer agent comply with such procedures.

(d)(1)   No registered clearing agency or registered transfer agent shall, directly or indirectly, engage in any activity as clearing agency or transfer agent in contravention of such rules and regulations

(A)   as the Commission may prescribe as necessary or appropriate in the public interest, for the protection of investors, or otherwise in furtherance of the purposes of this Act, or

(B)   as the appropriate regulatory agency for such clearing agency or transfer agent may prescribe as necessary or appropriate for the safeguarding of securities and funds.

(2)   With respect to any clearing agency or transfer agent for which the Commission is not the appropriate regulatory agency, the appropriate regulatory agency for such clearing agency or transfer agent may, in accordance with section 8 of the Federal Deposit Insurance Act, enforce compliance by such clearing agency or transfer agent with the provisions of this section, sections 17 and 19 of this Act, and the rules and regulations thereunder. For purposes of the preceding sentence, any violation of any such provision shall constitute adequate basis for the issuance of an order under section 8(b) or 8(c) of the Federal Deposit Insurance Act, and the participants in any such clearing agency and the

persons doing business with any such transfer agent shall be deemed to be "depositors" as that term is used in section 8(c) of that Act.

(3)(A)   With respect to any clearing agency or transfer agent for which the Commission is not the appropriate regulatory agency, the Commission and the appropriate regulatory agency for such clearing agency or transfer agent shall consult and cooperate with each other, and, as may be appropriate, with State banking authorities having supervision over such clearing agency or transfer agent toward the end that, to the maximum extent practicable, their respective regulatory responsibilities may be fulfilled and the rules and regulations applicable to such clearing agency or transfer agent may be in accord with both sound banking practices and a national system for the prompt and accurate clearance and settlement of securities transactions. In accordance with this objective—

(i)   the Commission and such appropriate regulatory agency shall, at least fifteen days prior to the issuance for public comment of any proposed rule or regulation or adoption of any rule or regulation concerning such clearing agency or transfer agent, consult and request the views of the other; and

(ii)   such appropriate regulatory agency shall assume primary responsibility to examine and enforce compliance by such clearing agency or transfer agent with the provisions of this section and sections 17 and 19 of this Act.

(B)   Nothing in the preceding subparagraph or elsewhere in this Act shall be construed to impair or limit (other than by the requirement of notification) the Commission's authority to make rules under any provision of this Act or to enforce compliance pursuant to any provision of this Act by any clearing agency, transfer agent, or person associated with a transfer agent with the provisions of this Act and the rules and regulations thereunder.

(4)   Nothing in this section shall be construed to impair the authority of any State banking authority or other State or Federal regulatory authority having jurisdiction over a person registered as a clearing agency, transfer agent, or person associated with a transfer agent, to make and enforce rules governing such person which are not inconsistent with this Act and the rules and regulations thereunder.

(5)   A registered transfer agent may not, directly or indirectly, engage in any activity in connection with the guarantee of a signature of an endorser of a security, including the acceptance or rejection of such guarantee, in contravention of such rules and regulations as the Commission may prescribe as necessary or appropriate in the public interest, for the protection of investors, to facilitate the equitable treatment of financial institutions which issue such guarantees, or otherwise in furtherance of the purposes of this Act.

(e)   The Commission shall use its authority under this Act to end the physical movement of securities certificates in connection with the settlement among brokers and dealers of transactions in securities consummated by means of the mails or any means or instrumentalities of interstate commerce.

(f)(1)   Notwithstanding any provision of State law, except as provided in paragraph (3), if the Commission makes each of the findings described in paragraph (2)(A), the Commission may adopt rules concerning—

(A)   the transfer of certificated or uncertificated securities (other than government securities issued pursuant to chapter 31 of Title 31, United States Code, or securities otherwise processed within a book-entry system operated by the Federal Reserve banks pursuant to a Federal book-entry regulation) or limited interests (including security interest) therein; and

(B)   rights and obligations of purchasers, sellers, owners, lenders, borrowers, and financial intermediaries (including brokers, dealers, banks, and clearing agencies) involved in or affected by such transfers, and the rights of third parties whose interests in such securities devolve from such transfers.

(2)(A)   The findings described in this paragraph are findings by the Commission that—

(i)   such rule is necessary or appropriate for the protection of investors or in the public interest and is reasonably designed to promote the prompt, accurate, and safe clearance and settlement of securities transactions;

(ii)   in the absence of a uniform rule, the safe and efficient operation of the national system for clearance and settlement of securities transactions will be, or is, substantially impeded; and

(iii) to the extent such rule will impair or diminish, directly or indirectly, rights of persons specified in paragraph (1)(B) under State law concerning transfers of securities (or limited interests therein), the benefits of such rule outweigh such impairment or diminution of rights.

(B) In making the findings described in subparagraph (A), the Commission shall give consideration to the recommendations of the Advisory Committee established under paragraph (4), and it shall consult with and consider the views of the Secretary of the Treasury and the Board of Governors of the Federal Reserve System. If the Secretary of the Treasury objects, in writing, to any proposed rule of the Commission on the basis of the Secretary's view on the issues described in clauses (i), (ii), and (iii) of subparagraph (A), the Commission shall consider all feasible alternatives to the proposed rule, and it shall not adopt any such rule unless the Commission makes an explicit finding that the rule is the most practicable method for achieving safe and efficient operation of the national clearance and settlement system.

(3)   Any State may, prior to the expiration of 2 years after the Commission adopts a rule under this subsection, enact a statute that specifically refers to this subsection and the specific rule thereunder and establishes, prospectively from the date of enactment of the State statute, a provision that differs from that applicable under the Commission's rule.

(4)(A)   Within 90 days after the date of enactment of this subsection, the Commission shall (and at such times thereafter as the Commission may determine, the Commission may), after consultation with the Secretary of the Treasury and the Board of Governors of the Federal Reserve System, establish an advisory committee under the Federal Advisory Committee Act. The Advisory Committee shall be directed to consider and report to the Commission on such matters as the Commission, after consultation with the Secretary of the Treasury and the Board of Governors of the Federal Reserve System, determines, including the areas, if any, in which State commercial laws and related Federal laws concerning the transfer of certificated or uncertificated securities, limited interests (including security interests) in such securities, or the creation or perfection of security interests in such securities do not provide the necessary certainty, uniformity, and clarity for purchasers, sellers, owners, lenders, borrowers, and financial intermediaries concerning their respective rights and obligations.

(B)   The Advisory Committee shall consist of 15 members, of which—

(i)   11 shall be designated by the Commission in accordance with the Federal Advisory Committee Act; and

(ii)   2 each shall be designated by the Board of Governors of the Federal Reserve System and the Secretary of the Treasury.

(C)   The Advisory Committee shall conduct its activities in accordance with the Federal Advisory Committee Act. Within 6 months of its designation, or such longer time as the Commission may designate, the Advisory Committee shall issue a report to the Commission, and shall cause copies of that report to be delivered to the Secretary of the Treasury and the Chairman of the Board of Governors of the Federal Reserve System.

(g)   Registration Requirement.—It shall be unlawful for a clearing agency, unless registered with the Commission, directly or indirectly to make use of the mails or any means or instrumentality of interstate commerce to perform the functions of a clearing agency with respect to a security-based swap.

(g)[14] Due Diligence for the Delivery of Dividends, Interest, and Other Valuable Property Rights—

---

[14] Two (g)s have been enacted.

(1) The Commission shall revise its regulations in section 240.17Ad–17 of title 17, Code of Federal Regulations, as in effect on December 8, 1997, to extend the application of such section to brokers and dealers and to provide for the following:

(A) A requirement that the paying agent provide a single written notification to each missing security holder that the missing security holder has been sent a check that has not yet been negotiated. The written notification may be sent along with a check or other mailing subsequently sent to the missing security holder but must be provided no later than 7 months after the sending of the not yet negotiated check.

(B) An exclusion for paying agents from the notification requirements when the value of the not yet negotiated check is less than $25.

(C) A provision clarifying that the requirements described in subparagraph (A) shall have no effect on State escheatment laws.

(D) For purposes of such revised regulations—

(i) a security holder shall be considered a 'missing security holder' if a check is sent to the security holder and the check is not negotiated before the earlier of the paying agent sending the next regularly scheduled check or the elapsing of 6 months after the sending of the not yet negotiated check; and

(ii) the term 'paying agent' includes any issuer, transfer agent, broker, dealer, investment adviser, indenture trustee, custodian, or any other person that accepts payments from the issuer of a security and distributes the payments to the holders of the security.

(2) The Commission shall adopt such rules, regulations, and orders necessary to implement this subsection no later than 1 year after the date of enactment of this subsection. In proposing such rules, the Commission shall seek to minimize disruptions to current systems used by or on behalf of paying agents to process payment to account holders and avoid requiring multiple paying agents to send written notification to a missing security holder regarding the same not yet negotiated check.

(h) Voluntary Registration.—A person that clears agreements, contracts, or transactions that are not required to be cleared under this title may register with the Commission as a clearing agency.

(i) Standards for Clearing Agencies Clearing Security-based Swap Transactions.—To be registered and to maintain registration as a clearing agency that clears security-based swap transactions, a clearing agency shall comply with such standards as the Commission may establish by rule. In establishing any such standards, and in the exercise of its oversight of such a clearing agency pursuant to this title, the Commission may conform such standards or oversight to reflect evolving United States and international standards. Except where the Commission determines otherwise by rule or regulation, a clearing agency shall have reasonable discretion in establishing the manner in which it complies with any such standards.

(j) Rules.—The Commission shall adopt rules governing persons that are registered as clearing agencies for security-based swaps under this title.

(k) Exemptions.—The Commission may exempt, conditionally or unconditionally, a clearing agency from registration under this section for the clearing of security-based swaps if the Commission determines that the clearing agency is subject to comparable, comprehensive supervision and regulation by the Commodity Futures Trading Commission or the appropriate government authorities in the home country of the agency. Such conditions may include, but are not limited to, requiring that the clearing agency be available for inspection by the Commission and make available all information requested by the Commission.

(l) Existing Depository Institutions and Derivative Clearing Organizations.—

(1) In general.—

A depository institution or derivative clearing organization registered with the Commodity Futures Trading Commission under the Commodity Exchange Act that is required to be registered as a clearing agency under this section is deemed to be registered under this section solely for the purpose of clearing security-based swaps to the extent that, before the date of enactment of this subsection—

(A)   the depository institution cleared swaps as a multilateral clearing organization; or

(B)   the derivative clearing organization cleared swaps pursuant to an exemption from registration as a clearing agency.

(2)   Conversion of depository institutions.—

A depository institution to which this subsection applies may, by the vote of the shareholders owning not less than 51 percent of the voting interests of the depository institution, be converted into a State corporation, partnership, limited liability company, or similar legal form pursuant to a plan of conversion, if the conversion is not in contravention of applicable State law.

(3)   Sharing of information.—

The Commodity Futures Trading Commission shall make available to the Commission, upon request, all information determined to be relevant by the Commodity Futures Trading Commission regarding a derivatives clearing organization deemed to be registered with the Commission under paragraph (1).

(m)   Modification of Core Principles—The Commission may conform the core principles established in this section to reflect evolving United States and international standards.

(n)(1)   Revision of rules required.—The Commission shall revise its regulations in section 240.17Ad–17 of title 17, Code of Federal Regulations, as in effect on December 8, 1997, to extend the application of such section to brokers and dealers and to provide for the following: (A) A requirement that the paying agent provide a single written notification to each missing security holder that the missing security holder has been sent a check that has not yet been negotiated. The written notification may be sent along with a check or other mailing subsequently sent to the missing security holder but must be provided no later than 7 months after the sending of the not yet negotiated check. (B) An exclusion for paying agents from the notification requirements when the value of the not yet negotiated check is less than $25. (C) A provision clarifying that the requirements described in subparagraph (A) shall have no effect on State escheatment laws. (D) For purposes of such revised regulations—(i) a security holder shall be considered a "missing security holder" if a check is sent to the security holder and the check is not negotiated before the earlier of the paying agent sending the next regularly scheduled check or the elapsing of 6 months after the sending of the not yet negotiated check; and (ii) the term "paying agent" includes any issuer, transfer agent, broker, dealer, investment adviser, indenture trustee, custodian, or any other person that accepts payments from the issuer of a security and distributes the payments to the holders of the security.

(2)   Rulemaking—The Commission shall adopt such rules, regulations, and orders necessary to implement this subsection no later than 1 year after the date of enactment of this subsection. In proposing such rules, the Commission shall seek to minimize disruptions to current systems used by or on behalf of paying agents to process payment to account holders and avoid requiring multiple paying agents to send written notification to a missing security holder regarding the same not yet negotiated check.

Automated Quotation Systems for Penny Stocks

Sec. 17B.   (a)   Findings.—

The Congress finds that—

(1)   the market for penny stocks suffers from a lack of reliable and accurate quotation and last sale information available to investors and regulators;

(2)   it is in the public interest and appropriate for the protection of investors and the maintenance of fair and orderly markets to improve significantly the information available to brokers, dealers, investors, and regulators with respect to quotations for and transactions in penny stocks; and

(3)   a fully implemented automated quotation system for penny stocks would meet the information needs of investors and market participants and would add visibility and regulatory and surveillance data to that market.

(b)   Mandate to Facilitate the Establishment of Automated Quotation Systems.—

(1)   In general.—

The Commission shall facilitate the widespread dissemination of reliable and accurate last sale and quotation information with respect to penny stocks in accordance with the findings set forth in subsection (a), with a view toward establishing, at the earliest feasible time, one or more automated quotation systems that will collect and disseminate information regarding all penny stocks.

(2)   Characteristics of systems.—

Each such automated quotation system shall—

(A)   be operated by a registered securities association or a national securities exchange in accordance with such rules as the Commission and these entities shall prescribe;

(B)   collect and disseminate quotation and transaction information;

(C)   except as provided in subsection (c), provide bid and ask quotations of participating brokers or dealers, or comparably accurate and reliable pricing information, which shall constitute firm bids or offers for at least such minimum numbers of shares or minimum dollar amounts as the Commission and the registered securities association or national securities exchange shall require; and

(D)   provide for the reporting of the volume of penny stock transactions, including last sale reporting, when the volume reaches appropriate levels that the Commission shall specify by rule or order.

(c)   Exemptive Authority.—

The Commission may, by rule or order, grant such exemptions, in whole or in part, conditionally or unconditionally, to any penny stock or class of penny stocks from the requirements of subsection (b) as the Commission determines to be consistent with the public interest, the protection of investors, and the maintenance of fair and orderly markets.

(d)   Commission Reporting Requirements.—

The Commission shall, in each of the first 5 annual reports (under section 23(b)(1) of this Act) submitted more than 12 months after the date of enactment of this section, include a description of the status of the penny stock automated quotation system or systems required by subsection (b). Such description shall include—

(1)   a review of the development, implementation, and progress of the project, including achievement of significant milestones and current project schedule; and

(2)   a review of the activities of registered securities associations and national securities exchanges in the development of the system.

Liability for Misleading Statements

Sec. 18.   (a)   Any person who shall make or cause to be made any statement in any application, report, or document filed pursuant to this Act or any rule or regulation thereunder or any undertaking contained in a registration statement as provided in subsection (d) of section 15 of this Act, which statement was at the time and in the light of the circumstances under which it was made false or misleading with respect to any material fact, shall be liable to any person (not knowing that such statement was false or misleading) who, in reliance upon such statement, shall have purchased or sold a security at a price which was affected by such statement, for damages caused by such reliance, unless the person sued shall prove that he acted in good faith and had no knowledge that such statement was false or misleading. A person seeking to enforce such liability may sue at law or in equity in any court of competent jurisdiction. In any such suit the court may, in its discretion, require an undertaking for the payment of the costs of such suit, and assess reasonable costs, including reasonable attorneys' fees, against either party litigant.

(b)   Every person who becomes liable to make payment under this section may recover contribution as in cases of contract from any person who, if joined in the original suit, would have been liable to make the same payment.

(c)   No action shall be maintained to enforce any liability created under this section unless brought within one year after the discovery of the facts constituting the cause of action and within three years after such cause of action accrued.

Registration, Responsibilities, and Oversight of Self-Regulatory Organizations

Sec. 19. (a)(1)   The Commission shall, upon the filing of an application for registration as a national securities exchange, registered securities association, or registered clearing agency, pursuant to section 6, 15A, or 17A of this Act, respectively, publish notice of such filing and afford interested persons an opportunity to submit written data, views, and arguments concerning such application. Within ninety days of the date of publication of such notice (or within such longer period as to which the applicant consents), the Commission shall—

(A)   by order grant such registration, or

(B)   institute proceedings to determine whether registration should be denied. Such proceedings shall include notice of the grounds for denial under consideration and opportunity for hearing and shall be concluded within one hundred eighty days of the date of a publication of notice of the filing of the application for registration. At the conclusion of such proceedings the Commission, by order, shall grant or deny such registration. The Commission may extend the time for conclusion of such proceedings for up to ninety days if it finds good cause for such extension and publishes its reasons for so finding or for such longer period as to which the applicant consents.

The Commission shall grant such registration if it finds that the requirements of this Act and the rules and regulations thereunder with respect to the applicant are satisfied. The Commission shall deny such registration if it does not make such finding.

(2)   With respect to an application for registration filed by a clearing agency for which the Commission is not the appropriate regulatory agency—

(A)   The Commission shall not grant registration prior to the sixtieth day after the date of publication of notice of the filing of such application unless the appropriate regulatory agency for such clearing agency has notified the Commission of such appropriate regulatory agency's determination that such clearing agency is so organized and has the capacity to be able to safeguard securities and funds in its custody or control or for which it is responsible and that the rules of such clearing agency are designed to assure the safeguarding of such securities and funds.

(B)   The Commission shall institute proceedings in accordance with paragraph (1)(B) of this subsection to determine whether registration should be denied if the appropriate regulatory agency for such clearing agency notifies the Commission within sixty days of the date of publication of notice of the filing of such application of such appropriate regulatory agency's

(i)   determination that such clearing agency may not be so organized or have the capacity to be able to safeguard securities or funds in its custody or control or for which it is responsible or that the rules of such clearing agency may not be designed to assure the safeguarding of such securities and funds and

(ii)   reasons for such determination.

(C)   The Commission shall deny registration if the appropriate regulatory agency for such clearing agency notifies the Commission prior to the conclusion of proceedings instituted in accordance with paragraph (1)(B) of this subsection of such appropriate regulatory agency's

(i)   determination that such clearing agency is not so organized or does not have the capacity to be able to safeguard securities or funds in its custody or control or for which it is responsible or that the rules of such clearing agency are not designed to assure the safeguarding of such securities or funds and

(ii)   reasons for such determination.

(3)   A self-regulatory organization may, upon such terms and conditions as the Commission, by rule, deems necessary or appropriate in the public interest or for the protection of investors, withdraw

from registration by filing a written notice of withdrawal with the Commission. If the Commission finds that any self-regulatory organization is no longer in existence or has ceased to do business in the capacity specified in its application for registration, the Commission, by order, shall cancel its registration. Upon the withdrawal of a national securities association from registration or the cancellation, suspension, or revocation of the registration of a national securities association, the registration of any association affiliated therewith shall automatically terminate.

(b)(1)   Each self-regulatory organization shall file with the Commission, in accordance with such rules as the Commission may prescribe, copies of any proposed rule or any proposed change in, addition to, or deletion from the rules of such self-regulatory organization (hereinafter in this subsection collectively referred to as a "proposed rule change") accompanied by a concise general statement of the basis and purpose of such proposed rule change. The Commission shall, as soon as practicable after the date of the filing of any proposed rule change, publish notice thereof together with the terms of substance of the proposed rule change or a description of the subjects and issues involved. The Commission shall give interested persons an opportunity to submit written data, views, and arguments concerning such proposed rule change. No proposed rule change shall take effect unless approved by the Commission or otherwise permitted in accordance with the provisions of this subsection.

(2)   Approval process.—

(A)   Approval process established.—

(i)   In general.—

Except as provided in clause (ii), not later than 45 days after the date of publication of a proposed rule change under paragraph (1), the Commission shall—

(I)   by order, approve or disapprove the proposed rule change; or

(II)   institute proceedings under subparagraph (B) to determine whether the proposed rule change should be disapproved.

(ii)   Extension of time period.—

The Commission may extend the period established under clause (i) by not more than an additional 45 days, if—

(I)   the Commission determines that a longer period is appropriate and publishes the reasons for such determination; or

(II)   the self-regulatory organization that filed the proposed rule change consents to the longer period.

(B)   Proceedings.—

(i)   Notice and hearing.—

If the Commission does not approve or disapprove a proposed rule change under subparagraph (A), the Commission shall provide to the self-regulatory organization that filed the proposed rule change—

(I)   notice of the grounds for disapproval under consideration; and

(II)   opportunity for hearing, to be concluded not later than 180 days after the date of publication of notice of the filing of the proposed rule change.

(ii)   Order of approval or disapproval.—

(I)   In general.—

Except as provided in subclause (II), not later than 180 days after the date of publication under paragraph (1), the Commission shall issue an order approving or disapproving the proposed rule change.

(II)   Extension of time period.—

The Commission may extend the period for issuance under clause (I) by not more than 60 days, if—

    (aa) the Commission determines that a longer period is appropriate and publishes the reasons for such determination; or

    (bb) the self-regulatory organization that filed the proposed rule change consents to the longer period.

(C)   Standards for approval and disapproval.—

(i)   Approval.—

The Commission shall approve a proposed rule change of a self-regulatory organization if it finds that such proposed rule change is consistent with the requirements of this title and the rules and regulations issued under this title that are applicable to such organization.

(ii)   Disapproval.—

The Commission shall disapprove a proposed rule change of a self-regulatory organization if it does not make a finding described in clause (i).

(iii)   Time for approval.—

The Commission may not approve a proposed rule change earlier than 30 days after the date of publication under paragraph (1), unless the Commission finds good cause for so doing and publishes the reason for the finding.

(D)   Result of failure to institute or conclude proceedings.—

A proposed rule change shall be deemed to have been approved by the Commission, if—

(i)   the Commission does not approve or disapprove the proposed rule change or begin proceedings under subparagraph (B) within the period described in subparagraph (A); or

(ii)   the Commission does not issue an order approving or disapproving the proposed rule change under subparagraph (B) within the period described in subparagraph (B)(ii).

(E)   Publication date based on federal register publishing.—

For purposes of this paragraph, if, after filing a proposed rule change with the Commission pursuant to paragraph (1), a self-regulatory organization publishes a notice of the filing of such proposed rule change, together with the substantive terms of such proposed rule change, on a publicly accessible website, the Commission shall thereafter send the notice to the Federal Register for publication thereof under paragraph (1) within 15 days of the date on which such website publication is made. If the Commission fails to send the notice for publication thereof within such 15 day period, then the date of publication shall be deemed to be the date on which such website publication was made.

(F)   Rulemaking.—

(i)   In general.—

Not later than 180 days after the date of enactment of the Investor Protection and Securities Reform Act of 2010, after consultation with other regulatory agencies, the Commission shall promulgate rules setting forth the procedural requirements of the proceedings required under this paragraph.

(ii)   Notice and comment not required.—

The rules promulgated by the Commission under clause (i) are not required to include republication of proposed rule changes or solicitation of public comment.

(3)(A)   Notwithstanding the provisions of paragraph (2) of this subsection, a proposed rule change shall take effect upon filing with the Commission if designated by the self-regulatory organization on any person, whether or not the person is a member of the self-regulatory organization as

(i)   constituting a stated policy, practice, or interpretation with respect to the meaning, administration, or enforcement of an existing rule of the self-regulatory organization,

(ii)   establishing or changing a due, fee, or other charge imposed by the self-regulatory organization on any person, whether or not the person is a member of the self-regulatory organization, or

(iii)   concerned solely with the administration of the self-regulatory organization or other matters which the Commission, by rule, consistent with the public interest and the purposes of this subsection, may specify as without the provisions of such paragraph (2).

(B)   Notwithstanding any other provision of this subsection, a proposed rule change may be put into effect summarily if it appears to the Commission that such action is necessary for the protection of investors, the maintenance of fair and orderly markets, or the safeguarding of securities or funds. Any proposed rule change so put into effect shall be filed promptly thereafter in accordance with the provisions of paragraph (1) of this subsection.

(C)   Any proposed rule change of a self-regulatory organization which has taken effect pursuant to the subparagraph (A) or (B) of this paragraph may be enforced by such organization to the extent it is not inconsistent with the provisions of this Act, the rules and regulations thereunder, and applicable Federal and State law. At any time within the 60-day period beginning on the date of filing of such a proposed rule change in accordance with the provisions of paragraph (1), the Commission summarily may temporarily suspend the change in the rules of the self-regulatory organization made thereby, if it appears to the Commission that such action is necessary or appropriate in the public interest, for the protection of investors, or otherwise in furtherance of the purposes of this title. If the Commission takes such action, the Commission shall institute proceedings under paragraph (2)(B) to determine whether the proposed rule should be approved or disapproved. Commission action pursuant to this subparagraph shall not affect the validity or force of the rule change during the period it was in effect and shall not be reviewable under the section 25 of this Act nor deemed to be "final agency action" for purposes of section 704 of Title 5, United States Code.

(4)   With respect to a proposed rule change filed by a registered clearing agency for which the Commission is not the appropriate regulatory agency—

(A)   The Commission shall not approve any such proposed rule change prior to the thirtieth day after the date of publication of notice of the filing thereof unless the appropriate regulatory agency for such clearing agency has notified the Commission of such appropriate regulatory agency's determination that the proposed rule change is consistent with the safeguarding of securities and funds in the custody or control of such clearing agency or for which it is responsible.

(B)   The Commission shall institute proceedings in accordance with paragraph (2)(B) of this subsection to determine whether any such proposed rule change should be disapproved, if the appropriate regulatory agency for such clearing agency notifies the Commission within thirty days of the date of publication of notice of the filing of the proposed rule change of such appropriate regulatory agency's

(i)   determination that the proposed rule change may be inconsistent with the safeguarding of securities or funds in the custody or control of such clearing agency or for which it is responsible and

(ii)   reasons for such determination.

(C)   The Commission shall disapprove any such proposed rule change if the appropriate regulatory agency for such clearing agency notifies the Commission prior to the conclusion of proceedings instituted in accordance with paragraph (2)(B) of this subsection of such appropriate regulatory agency's

(i)   determination that the proposed rule change is inconsistent with the safeguarding of securities or funds in the custody or control of such clearing agency or for which it is responsible and

(ii)   reasons for such determination.

(D)(i)   The Commission shall order the temporary suspension of any change in the rules of a clearing agency made by a proposed rule change that has taken effect under paragraph (3), if the appropriate regulatory agency for the clearing agency notifies the Commission not later than 30 days after the date on which the proposed rule change was filed of—

(I)   the determination by the appropriate regulatory agency that the rules of such clearing agency, as so changed, may be inconsistent with the safeguarding of securities or funds in the custody or control of such clearing agency or for which it is responsible; and

(II)   the reasons for the determination described in subclause (I).

(ii)   If the Commission takes action under clause (i), the Commission shall institute proceedings under paragraph (2)(B) to determine if the proposed rule change should be approved or disapproved

(5)   The Commission shall consult with and consider the views of the Secretary of the Treasury prior to approving a proposed rule filed by a registered securities association that primarily concerns conduct related to transactions in government securities except where the Commission determines that an emergency exists requiring expeditious or summary action and publishes its reasons therefor. If the Secretary of the Treasury comments in writing to the Commission on a proposed rule that has been published for comment, the Commission shall respond in writing to such written comment before approving the proposed rule. If the Secretary of the Treasury determines, and notifies the Commission that such rule, if implemented, would, or as applied does

(i)   adversely affect the liquidity or efficiency of the market for government securities; or

(ii)   impose any burden on competition not necessary or appropriate in furtherance of the purposes of this section, the Commission shall, prior to adopting the proposed rule, find that such rule is necessary and appropriate in furtherance of the purposes of this section notwithstanding the Secretary's determination.

(6)   In approving rules described in paragraph (5), the Commission shall consider the sufficiency and appropriateness of then existing laws and rules applicable to government securities brokers, government securities dealers, and persons associated with government securities brokers and government securities dealers.

(7)   Security Futures Product Rule Changes.—

(A)   Filing Required.—A self-regulatory organization that is an exchange registered with the Commission pursuant to section 6(g) of this Act or that is a national securities association registered pursuant to section 15A(k) of this Act shall file with the Commission, in accordance with such rules as the Commission may prescribe, copies of any proposed rule change or any proposed change in, addition to, or deletion from the rules of such self-regulatory organization (hereinafter in this paragraph collectively referred to as a "proposed rule change") that relates to higher margin levels, fraud or manipulation, recordkeeping, reporting, listing standards, or decimal pricing for security futures products, sales practices for security futures products for persons who effect transactions in security futures products, or rules effectuating such self-regulatory organization's obligation to enforce the securities laws. Such proposed rule change shall be accompanied by a concise general statement of the basis and purpose of such proposed rule change. The Commission shall, upon the filing of any proposed rule change, promptly publish notice thereof together with the terms of substance of the proposed rule change or a description of the subjects and issues involved. The Commission shall give interested persons an opportunity to submit data, views, and arguments concerning such proposed rule change.

(B)   Filing With CFTC.—A proposed rule change filed with the Commission pursuant to subparagraph (A) shall be filed concurrently with the Commodity Futures Trading Commission. Such proposed rule change may take effect upon filing of a written certification with the Commodity Futures Trading Commission under section 5c(c) of the Commodity Exchange Act, upon a determination by the Commodity Futures Trading Commission that review of the proposed rule change is not necessary, or upon approval of the proposed rule change by the Commodity Futures Trading Commission.

(C) Abrogation of rule Changes.—Any proposed rule change of a self-regulatory organization that has taken effect pursuant to subparagraph (B) may be enforced by such self-regulatory organization to the extent such rule is not inconsistent with the provisions of this Act, the rules and regulations thereunder, and applicable Federal law. At any time within 60 days of the date of the filing of a written certification with the Commodity Futures Trading Commission under section 5c(c) of the Commodity Exchange Act, the date the Commodity Futures Trading Commission determines that review of such proposed rule change is not necessary, or the date the Commodity Futures Trading Commission approves such proposed rule change, the Commission, after consultation with the Commodity Futures Trading Commission, may summarily abrogate the proposed rule change and require that the proposed rule change be refiled in accordance with the provisions of paragraph (1), if it appears to the Commission that such proposed rule change unduly burdens competition or efficiency, conflicts with the securities laws, or is inconsistent with the public interest and the protection of investors. Commission action pursuant to the preceding sentence shall not affect the validity or force of the rule change during the period it was in effect and shall not be reviewable under section 25 of this Act nor deemed to be a final agency action for purposes of section 704 of title 5, United States Code.

(D) Review of Resubmitted Abrogated Rules.—

(i) Proceedings.—Within 35 days of the date of publication of notice of the filing of a proposed rule change that is abrogated in accordance with subparagraph (C) and refiled in accordance with paragraph (1), or within such longer period as the Commission may designate up to 90 days after such date if the Commission finds such longer period to be appropriate and publishes its reasons for so finding or as to which the self-regulatory organization consents, the Commission shall—

(I) by order approve such proposed rule change; or

(II) after consultation with the Commodity Futures Trading Commission, institute proceedings to determine whether the proposed rule change should be disapproved. Proceedings under subclause (II) shall include notice of the grounds for disapproval under consideration and opportunity for hearing and be concluded within 180 days after the date of publication of notice of the filing of the proposed rule change. At the conclusion of such proceedings, the Commission, by order, shall approve or disapprove such proposed rule change. The Commission may extend the time for conclusion of such proceedings for up to 60 days if the Commission finds good cause for such extension and publishes its reasons for so finding or for such longer period as to which the self-regulatory organization consents.

(ii) Grounds for Approval.—The Commission shall approve a proposed rule change of a self-regulatory organization under this subparagraph if the Commission finds that such proposed rule change does not unduly burden competition or efficiency, does not conflict with the securities laws, and is not inconsistent with the public interest or the protection of investors. The Commission shall disapprove such a proposed rule change of a self-regulatory organization if it does not make such finding. The Commission shall not approve any proposed rule change prior to the 30th day after the date of publication of notice of the filing thereof, unless the Commission finds good cause for so doing and publishes its reasons for so finding.

(8) Decimal Pricing.—Not later than 9 months after the date on which trading in any security futures product commences under this Act, all self-regulatory organizations listing or trading security futures products shall file proposed rule changes necessary to implement decimal pricing of security futures products. The Commission may not require such rules to contain equal minimum increments in such decimal pricing.

(9) Consultation With CFTC.—

(A) Consultation Required.—The Commission shall consult with and consider the views of the Commodity Futures Trading Commission prior to approving or disapproving a proposed rule change filed by a national securities association registered pursuant to section 15A(a) or a national securities exchange subject to the provisions of subsection (a) that primarily concerns conduct related to transactions in security futures products, except where the Commission determines that an emergency exists requiring expeditious or summary action and publishes its reasons therefor.

(B) Responses to CFTC Comments and Findings.—If the Commodity Futures Trading Commission comments in writing to the Commission on a proposed rule that has been published for comment, the Commission shall respond in writing to such written comment before approving or disapproving the proposed rule. If the Commodity Futures Trading Commission determines, and notifies the Commission, that such rule, if implemented or as applied, would—

    (i) adversely affect the liquidity or efficiency of the market for security futures products; or

    (ii) impose any burden on competition not necessary or appropriate in furtherance of the purposes of this section,

the Commission shall, prior to approving or disapproving the proposed rule, find that such rule is necessary and appropriate in furtherance of the purposes of this section notwithstanding the Commodity Futures Trading Commission's determination.

(10) Rule of construction relating to filing date of proposed rule changes.—

(A) In general.—

For purposes of this subsection, the date of filing of a proposed rule change shall be deemed to be the date on which the Commission receives the proposed rule change.

(B) Exception.—

A proposed rule change has not been received by the Commission for purposes of subparagraph (A) if, not later than 7 business days after the date of receipt by the Commission, the Commission notifies the self-regulatory organization that such proposed rule change does not comply with the rules of the Commission relating to the required form of a proposed rule change, except that if the Commission determines that the proposed rule change is unusually lengthy and is complex or raises novel regulatory issues, the Commission shall inform the self-regulatory organization of such determination not later than 7 business days after the date of receipt by the Commission and, for the purposes of subparagraph (A), a proposed rule change has not been received by the Commission, if, not later than 21 days after the date of receipt by the Commission, the Commission notifies the self-regulatory organization that such proposed rule change does not comply with the rules of the Commission relating to the required form of a proposed rule change.

(11) Notwithstanding paragraph (2), the time period within which the Commission is required by order to approve a proposed rule change or institute proceedings to determine whether the proposed rule change should be disapproved is stayed pending a determination by the Commission upon the request of the Commodity Futures Trading Commission or its Chairman that the Commission issue a determination as to whether a product that is the subject of such proposed rule change is a security pursuant to section 8306 of the Wall Street Transparency and Accountability Act.

(c) The Commission, by rule, may abrogate, add to, and delete from (hereinafter in this subsection collectively referred to as "amend") the rules of a self-regulatory organization (other than a registered clearing agency) as the Commission deems necessary or appropriate to insure the fair administration of the self-regulatory organization, to conform its rules to requirements of this Act and the rules and regulations thereunder applicable to such organization, or otherwise in furtherance of the purposes of this Act, in the following manner:

(1) The Commission shall notify the self-regulatory organization and publish notice of the proposed rulemaking in the Federal Register. The notice shall include the text of the proposed

amendment to the rules of the self-regulatory organization and a statement of the Commission's reasons, including any pertinent facts, for commencing such proposed rulemaking.

(2)   The Commission shall give interested persons an opportunity for the oral presentation of data, views, and arguments, in addition to an opportunity to make written submissions. A transcript shall be kept of any oral presentation.

(3)   A rule adopted pursuant to this subsection shall incorporate the text of the amendment to the rules of the self-regulatory organization and a statement of the Commission's basis for and purpose in so amending such rules. This statement shall include an identification of any facts on which the Commission considers its determination so to amend the rules of the self-regulatory agency to be based, including the reasons for the Commission's conclusions as to any of such facts which were disputed in the rulemaking.

(4)(A)   Except as provided in paragraphs (1) through (3) of this subsection, rulemaking under this subsection shall be in accordance with the procedures specified in section 553 of Title 5, United States Code, for rulemaking not on the record.

(B)   Nothing in this subsection shall be construed to impair or limit the Commission's power to make, or to modify or alter the procedures the Commission may follow in making, rules and regulations pursuant to any other authority under this Act.

(C)   Any amendment to the rules of a self-regulatory organization made by the Commission pursuant to this subsection shall be considered for all purposes of this Act to be part of the rules of such self-regulatory organization and shall not be considered to be a rule of the Commission.

(5)   With respect to rules described in subsection (b)(5), the Commission shall consult with and consider the views of the Secretary of the Treasury before abrogating, adding to, and deleting from such rules, except where the Commission determines that an emergency exists requiring expeditious or summary action and publishes its reasons therefor.

(d)(1)   If any self-regulatory organization imposes any final disciplinary sanction on any member thereof or participant therein, denies membership or participation to any applicant, or prohibits or limits any person in respect to access to services offered by such organization or member thereof or if any self-regulatory organization (other than a registered clearing agency) imposes any final disciplinary sanction on any person associated with a member or bars any person from becoming associated with a member, the self-regulatory organization shall promptly file notice thereof with the appropriate regulatory agency for the self-regulatory organization and (if other than the appropriate regulatory agency for the self-regulatory organization) the appropriate regulatory agency for such member, participant, applicant, or other person. The notice shall be in such form and contain such information as the appropriate regulatory agency for the self-regulatory organization, by rule, may prescribe as necessary or appropriate in furtherance of the purposes of this Act.

(2)   Any action with respect to which a self-regulatory organization is required by paragraph (1) of this subsection to file notice shall be subject to review by the appropriate regulatory agency for such member, participant, applicant, or other person, on its own motion, or upon application by any person aggrieved thereby filed within thirty days after the date such notice was filed with such appropriate regulatory agency and received by such aggrieved person, or within such longer period as such appropriate regulatory agency may determine. Application to such appropriate regulatory agency for review, or the institution of review by such appropriate regulatory agency on its own motion, shall not operate as a stay of such action unless such appropriate regulatory agency otherwise orders, summarily or after notice and opportunity for hearing on the question of a stay (which hearing may consist solely of the submission of affidavits or presentation of oral arguments). Each appropriate regulatory agency shall establish for appropriate cases an expedited procedure for consideration and determination of the question of a stay.

(3)   The provisions of this subsection shall apply to an exchange registered pursuant to section 6(g) of this Act or a national securities association registered pursuant to section 15A(k) of this Act only to the extent that such exchange or association imposes any final disciplinary sanction for—

(A)   a violation of the Federal securities laws or the rules and regulations thereunder; or

(B)   a violation of a rule of such exchange or association, as to which a proposed change would be required to be filed under section 19 of this Act, except that, to the extent that the exchange or association rule violation relates to any account, agreement, contract, or transaction, this subsection shall apply only to the extent such violation involves a security futures product.

(e)(1)   In any proceeding to review a final disciplinary sanction imposed by a self-regulatory organization on a member thereof or participant therein or a person associated with such a member, after notice and opportunity for hearing (which hearing may consist solely of consideration of the record before the self-regulatory organization and opportunity for the presentation of supporting reasons to affirm, modify, or set aside the sanction)—

(A)   if the appropriate regulatory agency for such member, participant, or person associated with a member finds that such member, participant, or person associated with a member has engaged in such acts or practices, or has omitted such acts, as the self-regulatory organization has found him to have engaged in or omitted, that such acts or practices or omissions to act, are in violation of such provisions of this Act, the rules or regulations thereunder, the rules of the self-regulatory organization, or, in the case of a registered securities association, the rules of the Municipal Securities Rulemaking Board as have been specified in the determination of the self-regulatory organization, and that such provisions are, and were applied in a manner, consistent with the purposes of this Act, such appropriate regulatory agency, by order, shall so declare and, as appropriate, affirm the sanction imposed by the self-regulatory organization, modify the sanction in accordance with paragraph (2) of this subsection, or remand to the self-regulatory organization for further proceedings; or

(B)   if such appropriate regulatory agency does not make any such finding it shall, by order, set aside the sanction imposed by the self-regulatory organization and, if appropriate, remand to the self-regulatory organization for further proceedings.

(2)   If the appropriate regulatory agency for a member, participant, or person associated with a member, having due regard for the public interest and the protection of investors, finds after a proceeding in accordance with paragraph (1) of this subsection that a sanction imposed by a self-regulatory organization upon such member, participant, or person associated with a member imposes any burden on competition not necessary or appropriate in furtherance of the purposes of this Act or is excessive or oppressive, the appropriate regulatory agency may cancel, reduce, or require the remission of such sanction.

(f)   In any proceeding to review the denial of membership or participation in a self-regulatory organization to any applicant, the barring of any person from becoming associated with a member of a self-regulatory organization, or the prohibition or limitation by a self-regulatory organization of any person with respect to access to services offered by the self-regulatory organization or any member thereof, if the appropriate regulatory agency for such applicant or person, after notice and opportunity for hearing (which hearing may consist solely of consideration of the record before the self-regulatory organization and opportunity for the presentation of supporting reasons to dismiss the proceeding or set aside the action of the self-regulatory organization) finds that the specific grounds on which such denial, bar, or prohibition or limitation is based exist in fact, that such denial, bar, or prohibition or limitation is in accordance with the rules of the self-regulatory organization, and that such rules are, and were applied in a manner, consistent with the purposes of this Act, such appropriate regulatory agency, by order, shall dismiss the proceeding. If such appropriate regulatory agency does not make any such finding or if it finds that such denial, bar, or prohibition or limitation imposes any burden on competition not necessary or appropriate in furtherance of the purposes of this Act, such appropriate regulatory agency, by order, shall set aside the action of the self-regulatory organization and require it to admit such applicant to membership or participation, permit such person to become associated with a member, or grant such person access to services offered by the self-regulatory organization or member thereof.

(g)(1)   Every self-regulatory organization shall comply with the provisions of this Act, the rules and regulations thereunder, and its own rules, and (subject to the provisions of section 17(d) of this Act, paragraph (2) of this subsection, and the rules thereunder) absent reasonable justification or excuse enforce compliance—

(A) in the case of a national securities exchange, with such provisions by its members and persons associated with its members;

(B) in the case of a registered securities association, with such provisions and the provisions of the rules of the Municipal Securities Rulemaking Board by its members and persons associated with its members; and

(C) in the case of a registered clearing agency, with its own rules by its participants.

(2) The Commission, by rule, consistent with the public interest, the protection of investors, and the other purposes of this Act, may relieve any self-regulatory organization of any responsibility under this Act to enforce compliance with any specified provision of this Act or the rules or regulations thereunder by any member of such organization or person associated with such a member, or any class of such members or persons associated with a member.

(h)(1) The appropriate regulatory agency for a self-regulatory organization is authorized, by order, if in its opinion such action is necessary or appropriate in the public interest, for the protection of investors, or otherwise in furtherance of the purposes of this Act, to suspend for a period not exceeding twelve months or revoke the registration of such self-regulatory organization, or to censure or impose limitations upon the activities, functions, and operations of such self-regulatory organization, if such appropriate regulatory agency finds, on the record after notice and opportunity for hearing, that such self-regulatory organization has violated or is unable to comply with any provision of this Act, the rules or regulations thereunder, or its own rules or without reasonable justification or excuse has failed to enforce compliance—

(A) in the case of a national securities exchange, with any such provision by a member thereof or a person associated with a member thereof;

(B) in the case of a registered securities association, with any such provision or any provision of the rules of the Municipal Securities Rulemaking Board by a member thereof or a person associated with a member thereof; or

(C) in the case of a registered clearing agency, with any provision of its own rules by a participant therein.

(2) The appropriate regulatory agency for a self-regulatory organization is authorized, by order, if in its opinion such action is necessary or appropriate in the public interest, for the protection of investors, or otherwise in furtherance of the purposes of this Act, to suspend for a period not exceeding twelve months or expel from such self-regulatory organization any member thereof or participant therein, if such member or participant is subject to an order of the Commission pursuant to section 15(b)(4) of this Act or if such appropriate regulatory agency finds, on the record after notice and opportunity for hearing, that such member or participant has willfully violated or has effected any transaction for any other person who, such member or participant had reason to believe, was violating with respect to such transaction—

(A) in the case of a national securities exchange, any provision of the Securities Act of 1933, the Investment Advisers Act of 1940, the Investment Company Act of 1940, this Act, or the rules or regulations under any of such statutes;

(B) in the case of a registered securities association, any provision of the Securities Act of 1933, the Investment Advisers Act of 1940, the Investment Company Act of 1940, this Act, the rules or regulations under any of such statutes, or the rules of the Municipal Securities Rulemaking Board; or

(C) in the case of a registered clearing agency, any provision of the rules of the clearing agency.

(3) The appropriate regulatory agency for a national securities exchange or registered securities association is authorized, by order, if in its opinion such action is necessary or appropriate in the public interest, for the protection of investors, or otherwise in furtherance of the purposes of this Act, to suspend for a period not exceeding twelve months or to bar any person from being associated with a member of such national securities exchange or registered securities association, if such person is subject to an order of the Commission pursuant to section 15(b)(6) of this Act or if such appropriate regulatory agency finds, on the record after notice and opportunity for hearing, that such person has

willfully violated or has effected any transaction for any other person who, such person associated with a member had reason to believe, was violating with respect to such transaction—

    (A)   in the case of a national securities exchange, any provision of the Securities Act of 1933, the Investment Advisers Act of 1940, the Investment Company Act of 1940, this Act, or the rules or regulations under any of such statutes; or

    (B)   in the case of a registered securities association, any provision of the Securities Act of 1933, the Investment Advisers Act of 1940, the Investment Company Act of 1940, this Act, the rules or regulations under any of the statutes, or the rules of the Municipal Securities Rulemaking Board.

    (4)   The appropriate regulatory agency for a self-regulatory organization is authorized, by order, if in its opinion such action is necessary or appropriate in the public interest, for the protection of investors, or otherwise in furtherance of the purposes of this Act, to remove from office or censure any person who is, or at the time of the alleged misconduct was, an officer or director of such self-regulatory organization, if such appropriate regulatory agency finds, on the record after notice and opportunity for hearing, that such person has willfully violated any provision of this Act, the rules or regulations thereunder, or the rules of such self-regulatory organization, willfully abused his authority, or without reasonable justification or excuse has failed to enforce compliance—

    (A)   in the case of a national securities exchange, with any such provision by any member or person associated with a member;

    (B)   in the case of a registered securities association, with any such provision or any provision of the rules of the Municipal Securities Rulemaking Board by any member or person associated with a member; or

    (C)   in the case of a registered clearing agency, with any provision of the rules of the clearing agency by any participant.

    (i)   If a proceeding under subsection (h)(1) of this section results in the suspension or revocation of the registration of a clearing agency, the appropriate regulatory agency for such clearing agency may, upon notice to such clearing agency, apply to any court of competent jurisdiction specified in section 21(d) or 27 of this Act for the appointment of a trustee. In the event of such an application, the court may, to the extent it deems necessary or appropriate, take exclusive jurisdiction of such clearing agency and the records and assets thereof, wherever located; and the court shall appoint the appropriate regulatory agency for such clearing agency or a person designated by such appropriate regulatory agency as trustee with power to take possession and continue to operate or terminate the operations of such clearing agency in an orderly manner for the protection of participants and investors, subject to such terms and conditions as the court may prescribe.

Liability of Controlling Persons and Persons Who Aid and Abet Violations

    Sec. 20.   (a)   Every person who, directly or indirectly, controls any person liable under any provision of this Act or of any rule or regulation thereunder shall also be liable jointly and severally with and to the same extent as such controlled person to any person to whom such controlled person is liable (including to the Commission in any action brought under paragraph (1) or (3) of section 21(d)), unless the controlling person acted in good faith and did not directly or indirectly induce the act or acts constituting the violation or cause of action.

    (b)   It shall be unlawful for any person, directly or indirectly, to do any act or thing which it would be unlawful for such person to do under the provisions of this Act or any rule or regulation thereunder through or by means of any other person.

    (c)   It shall be unlawful for any director or officer of, or any owner of any securities issued by, any issuer required to file any document, report, or information under this Act or any rule or regulation thereunder without just cause to hinder, delay, or obstruct the making or filing of any such document, report, or information.

    (d)   Wherever communicating, or purchasing or selling a security while in possession of, material nonpublic information would violate, or result in liability to any purchaser or seller of the security under any provisions of this Act, or any rule or regulation thereunder, such conduct in connection with a purchase or sale of a put, call, straddle, option, privilege or security-based swap agreement with respect to such security or with respect to a group or index of securities including such security, shall also violate and result in comparable liability to any purchaser or seller of that security under such provision, rule, or regulation.

(e)   Prosecution of Persons Who Aid and Abet Violations.—

For purposes of any action brought by the Commission under paragraph (1) or (3) of section 21(d), any person that knowingly or recklessly provides substantial assistance to another person in violation of a provision of this Act, or of any rule or regulation issued under this Act, shall be deemed to be in violation of such provision to the same extent as the person to whom such assistance is provided.

(f)   The authority of the Commission under this section with respect to security-based swap agreements shall be subject to the restrictions and limitations of section 3A(b) of this Act.

Liability to Contemporaneous Traders for Insider Trading

Sec. 20A.   (a)   Private Rights of Action Based on Contemporaneous Trading.—

Any person who violates any provision of this Act or the rules or regulations thereunder by purchasing or selling a security while in possession of material, nonpublic information shall be liable in an action in any court of competent jurisdiction to any person who, contemporaneously with the purchase or sale of securities that is the subject of such violation, has purchased (where such violation is based on a sale of securities) or sold (where such violation is based on a purchase of securities) securities of the same class.

(b)   Limitations on Liability.—

(1)   Contemporaneous trading actions limited to profit gained or loss avoided.—

The total amount of damages imposed under subsection (a) shall not exceed the profit gained or loss avoided in the transaction or transactions that are the subject of the violation.

(2)   Offsetting disgorgements against liability.—

The total amount of damages imposed against any person under subsection (a) shall be diminished by the amounts, if any, that such person may be required to disgorge, pursuant to a court order obtained at the instance of the Commission, in a proceeding brought under section 21(d) of this Act relating to the same transaction or transactions.

(3)   Controlling person liability.—

No person shall be liable under this section solely by reason of employing another person who is liable under this section, but the liability of a controlling person under this section shall be subject to section 20(a) of this Act.

(4)   Statute of limitations.—

No action may be brought under this section more than 5 years after the date of the last transaction that is the subject of the violation.

(c)   Joint and Several Liability for Communicating.—

Any person who violates any provision of this Act or the rules or regulations thereunder by communicating material, nonpublic information shall be jointly and severally liable under subsection (a) with, and to the same extent as, any person or persons liable under subsection (a) to whom the communication was directed.

(d)   Authority Not to Restrict Other Express or Implied Rights of action.—

Nothing in this section shall be construed to limit or condition the right of any person to bring an action to enforce a requirement of this Act or the availability of any cause of action implied from a provision of this Act.

(e)   Provisions Not to Affect Public Prosecutions.—

This section shall not be construed to bar or limit in any manner any action by the Commission or the Attorney General under any other provision of this Act, nor shall it bar or limit in any manner any action to recover penalties, or to seek any other order regarding penalties.

Investigations and Actions

Sec. 21. (a)(1)   The Commission may, in its discretion, make such investigations as it deems necessary to determine whether any person has violated, is violating, or is about to violate any provision of this Act, the rules or regulations thereunder, the rules of a national securities exchange or registered securities association of which such person is a member or a person associated, or, as to any act or practice, or omission to act, while associated with a member, formerly associated with a member, the rules of a registered clearing agency in which such person is a participant, or, as to any act or practice, or omission to act, while a participant, was a participant, the rules of the Public Company Accounting Oversight Board, of which such person is a registered public accounting firm, a person associated with such a firm, or, as to any act, practice, or omission to act, while associated with such firm, a person formerly associated with such a firm or the rules of the Municipal Securities Rulemaking Board, and may require or permit any person to file with it a statement in writing, under oath or otherwise as the Commission shall determine, as to all the facts and circumstances concerning the matter to be investigated. The Commission is authorized in its discretion, to publish information concerning any such violations, and to investigate any facts, conditions, practices, or matters which it may deem necessary or proper to aid in the enforcement of such provisions, in the prescribing of rules and regulations under this Act, or in securing information to serve as a basis for recommending further legislation concerning the matters to which this Act relates.

(2)   On request from a foreign securities authority, the Commission may provide assistance in accordance with this paragraph if the requesting authority states that the requesting authority is conducting an investigation which it deems necessary to determine whether any person has violated, is violating, or is about to violate any laws or rules relating to securities matters that the requesting authority administers or enforces. The Commission may, in its discretion, conduct such investigation as the Commission deems necessary to collect information and evidence pertinent to the request for assistance. Such assistance may be provided without regard to whether the facts stated in the request would also constitute a violation of the laws of the United States. In deciding whether to provide such assistance, the Commission shall consider whether

(A)   the requesting authority has agreed to provide reciprocal assistance in securities matters to the Commission; and

(B)   compliance with the request would prejudice the public interest of the United States.

(b)   For the purpose of any such investigation, or any other proceeding under this Act, any member of the Commission or any officer designated by it is empowered to administer oaths and affirmations, subpoena witnesses, compel their attendance, take evidence, and require the production of any books, papers, correspondence, memoranda, or other records which the Commission deems relevant or material to the inquiry. Such attendance of witnesses and the production of any such records may be required from any place in the United States or any State at any designated place of hearing.

(c)   In case of contumacy by, or refusal to obey a subpena issued to, any person, the Commission may invoke the aid of any court of the United States within the jurisdiction of which such investigation or proceeding is carried on, or where such person resides or carries on business, in requiring the attendance and testimony of witnesses and the production of books, papers, correspondence, memoranda, and other records. And such court may issue an order requiring such person to appear before the Commission or member or officer designated by the Commission, there to produce records, if so ordered, or to give testimony touching the matter under investigation or in question; and any failure to obey such order of the court may be punished by such court as a contempt thereof. All process in any such case may be served in the judicial district whereof such person is an inhabitant or wherever he may be found. Any person who shall, without just cause, fail or refuse to attend and testify or to answer any lawful inquiry or to produce books, papers, correspondence, memoranda, and other records, if in his power so to do, in obedience to the subpena of the Commission, shall be guilty of a misdemeanor and, upon conviction, shall be subject to a fine of not more than $1,000 or to imprisonment for a term of not more than one year, or both.

(d)(1)   Whenever it shall appear to the Commission that any person is engaged or is about to engage in acts or practices constituting a violation of any provision of this Act, the rules or regulations thereunder, the rules of a national securities exchange or registered securities association of which such person is a member or a person associated with a member, the rules of a registered clearing agency in which such person is a participant, the rules of the Public Company Accounting Oversight Board, of which such person is a registered public accounting firm or a person associated with such a firm, or the rules of the Municipal Securities Rulemaking Board, it may in its discretion bring an action in the proper district court of the United States, the United States District Court for the District of Columbia, or the United States courts of any territory or other place subject to the jurisdiction of the United States, to enjoin such acts or practices, and upon a proper showing a permanent or temporary injunction or restraining order shall be granted without bond. The Commission may transmit such evidence as may be available concerning such acts or practices as may constitute a violation of any provision of this Act or the rules or regulations thereunder to the Attorney General, who may, in his discretion, institute the necessary criminal proceedings under this Act.

(2)   Authority of A Court to Prohibit Persons From Serving As Officers and Directors.—

In any proceeding under paragraph (1) of this subsection, the court may prohibit, conditionally or unconditionally, and permanently or for such period of time as it shall determine, any person who violated section 10(b) of this Act or the rules or regulations thereunder from acting as an officer or director of any issuer that has a class of securities registered pursuant to section 12 of this Act or that is required to file reports pursuant to section 15(d) of this Act if the person's conduct demonstrates unfitness to serve as an officer or director of any such issuer.

(3)   Civil Money Penalties and Authority to Seek Disgorgement.—

(A)   Authority of commission.—

Whenever it shall appear to the Commission that any person has violated any provision of this Act, the rules or regulations thereunder, or a cease-and-desist order entered by the Commission pursuant to section 21C of this Act, other than by committing a violation subject to a penalty pursuant to section 21A, the Commission may bring an action in a United States district court to seek, and the court shall have jurisdiction to—

(i)   impose, upon a proper showing, a civil penalty to be paid by the person who committed such violation; and

(ii)   require disgorgement under paragraph (7) of any unjust enrichment by the person who received such unjust enrichment as a result of such violation.

(B)   Amount of penalty.—

(i)   First tier.—

The amount of a civil penalty imposed under subparagraph (A)(i) shall be determined by the court in light of the facts and circumstances. For each violation, the amount of the penalty shall not exceed the greater of

(I) $5,000 for a natural person or $50,000 for any other person, or

(II)   the gross amount of pecuniary gain to such defendant as a result of the violation.

(ii)   Second tier.—

Notwithstanding clause (i), the amount of a civil penalty imposed under subparagraph (a)(i) for each such violation shall not exceed the greater of

(I)   of $50,000 for a natural person or $250,000 for any other person, or

(II)   the gross amount of pecuniary gain to such defendant as a result of the violation, if the violation described in subparagraph (A) involved fraud, deceit, manipulation, or deliberate or reckless disregard of a regulatory requirement.

(iii)   Third tier.—

Notwithstanding clauses (i) and (ii), the amount of a civil penalty imposed under subparagraph (a)(i) for each violation described in that subparagraph shall not exceed the greater of

    (I) $100,000 for a natural person or $500,000 for any other person, or

    (II) the gross amount of pecuniary gain to such defendant as a result of the violation, if—

        (aa) the violation described in subparagraph (A) involved fraud, deceit, manipulation, or deliberate or reckless disregard of a regulatory requirement; and

        (bb) such violation directly or indirectly resulted in substantial losses or created a significant risk of substantial losses to other persons.

  (C) Procedures for collection.—

    (i) Payment of penalty to treasury.—

A penalty imposed under this section shall be payable into the Treasury of the United States, except as otherwise provided in section 308 of the Sarbanes-Oxley Act of 2002 and section 21F of this title.

    (ii) Collection of penalties.—

If a person upon whom such a penalty is imposed shall fail to pay such penalty within the time prescribed in the court's order, the Commission may refer the matter to the Attorney General who shall recover such penalty by action in the appropriate United States district court.

    (iii) Remedy not exclusive.—

The actions authorized by this paragraph may be brought in addition to any other action that the Commission or the Attorney General is entitled to bring.

    (iv) Jurisdiction and venue.—

For purposes of section 27 of this Act, actions under this paragraph shall be actions to enforce a liability or a duty created by this Act.

  (D) Special provisions relating to a violation of a cease-and-desist order.—

In an action to enforce a cease-and-desist order entered by the Commission pursuant to section 21C, each separate violation of such order shall be a separate offense, except that in the case of a violation through a continuing failure to comply with the order, each day of the failure to comply shall be deemed a separate offense.

  (4) prohibition of attorneys' fees paid from commission disgorgement funds.—

Except as otherwise ordered by the court upon motion by the Commission, or, in the case of an administrative action, as otherwise ordered by the Commission, funds disgorged under paragraph (7) as the result of an action brought by the Commission in Federal court, or as a result of any Commission administrative action, shall not be distributed as payment for attorneys' fees or expenses incurred by private parties seeking distribution of the disgorged funds.

  (5) Equitable Relief.—

In any action or proceeding brought or instituted by the Commission under any provision of the securities laws, the Commission may seek, and any Federal court may grant, any equitable relief that may be appropriate or necessary for the benefit of investors.

  (6) Authority of A Court to Prohibit Persons From Participating in An Offering of Penny Stock.—

  (A) In general.—

In any proceeding under paragraph (1) against any person participating in, or, at the time of the alleged misconduct who was participating in, an offering of penny stock, the court may prohibit that person from participating in an offering of penny stock, conditionally or unconditionally, and permanently or for such period of time as the court shall determine.

(B) Definition.—

For purposes of this paragraph, the term "person participating in an offering of penny stock" includes any person engaging in activities with a broker, dealer, or issuer for purposes of issuing, trading, or inducing or attempting to induce the purchase or sale of, any penny stock. The Commission may, by rule or regulation, define such term to include other activities, and may, by rule, regulation, or order, exempt any person or class of persons, in whole or in part, conditionally or unconditionally, from inclusion in such term.

(7) Disgorgement.—In any action or proceeding brought by the Commission under any provision of the securities laws, the Commission may seek, and any Federal court may order disgorgement.

(8) Limitations periods.—

(A) Disgorgement.—The Commission may bring a claim for disgorgement under paragraph (7)—

    (i) not later than 5 years after the latest date of the violation that gives rise to the action or proceeding in which the Commission seeks occurs; or

    (ii) not later than 10 years after the latest date of the violation that gives rise to the action or proceeding in which the Commission seeks the claim if the violation involves conduct that violates—

        (I) section 10(b);

        (II) section 17(a)(1) of the Securities Act of 1933

        (III) section 206(1) of the Investment Company Act of 1940; or

        (IV) any other provision of the securities laws for which scienter must be established.

(B) Equitable remedies.—The Commission may seek a claim for any equitable remedy including for an injunction or for a bar. Suspension, or cease and desist order, not later than 10 years after the latest date on which a violation that gives rise to the claim occurs.

(C) Calculation.—For the purposes of calculating any limitations period under this paragraph with respect to an action or claim, any time in which the person against which the action or claim, as applicable, is brought is outside of the United States shall not count towards the accrual of that period.

(9) Rule of construction.—Nothing in paragraph (7) may be construed as altering any right that any private party may have to maintain a suit for violation of this Act.

(e) Upon application of the Commission the district courts of the United States, and the United States courts of any territory or other place subject to the jurisdiction of the United States shall have jurisdiction to issue writs of mandamus, injunctions, and orders commanding

    (1) any person to comply with the provisions of this Act, the rules, regulations, and orders thereunder, the rules of a national securities exchange or registered securities association of which such person is a member or person associated with a member, the rules of a registered clearing agency in which such person is a participant, the rules of the Public Company Accounting Oversight Board, of which such person is a registered public accounting firm or a person associated with such a firm, the rules of the Municipal Securities Rulemaking Board, or any undertaking contained in a registration statement as provided in subsection (d) of section 15 of this Act,

    (2) any national securities exchange or registered securities association to enforce compliance by its members and persons associated with its members with the provisions of this Act, the rules, regulations, and orders thereunder, and the rules of such exchange or association, or

    (3) any registered clearing agency to enforce compliance by its participants with the provisions of the rules of such clearing agency.

(f)   Notwithstanding any other provision of this Act, the Commission shall not bring any action pursuant to subsection (d) or (e) of this section against any person for violation of, or to command compliance with, the rules of a self-regulatory organization or the Public Company Accounting Oversight Board unless it appears to the Commission that

(1)   such self-regulatory organization or the Public Company Accounting Oversight Board is unable or unwilling to take appropriate action against such person in the public interest and for the protection of investors, or

(2)   such action is otherwise necessary or appropriate in the public interest or for the protection of investors.

(g)   Notwithstanding the provisions of section 1407(a) of Title 28, United States Code, or any other provision of law, no action for equitable relief instituted by the Commission pursuant to the securities laws shall be consolidated or coordinated with other actions not brought by the Commission, even though such other actions may involve common questions of fact, unless such consolidation is consented to by the Commission.

(h)(1)   The Right to Financial Privacy Act of 1978 shall apply with respect to the Commission, except as otherwise provided in this subsection.

(2)   Notwithstanding section 1105 or 1107 of the Rights to Financial Privacy Act of 1978, the Commission may have access to and obtain copies of, or the information contained in financial records of a customer from a financial institution without prior notice to the customer upon an ex parte showing to an appropriate United States district court that the Commission seeks such financial records pursuant to a subpena issued in conformity with the requirements of section 19(b) of the Securities Act of 1933, section 21(b) of the Securities Exchange Act of 1934, section 42(b) of the Investment Company Act of 1940, or section 209(b) of the Investment Advisers Act of 1940, and that the Commission has reason to believe that—

(A)   delay in obtaining access to such financial records, or the required notice, will result in—

(i)   flight from prosecution;

(ii)   destruction of or tampering with evidence;

(iii)   transfer of assets or records outside the territorial limits of the United States;

(iv)   improper conversion of investor assets; or

(v)   impeding the ability of the Commission to identify or trace the source or disposition of funds involved in any securities transaction;

(B)   such financial records are necessary to identify or trace the record or beneficial ownership interest in any security;

(C)   the acts, practices or course of conduct under investigation involve—

(i)   the dissemination of materially false or misleading information concerning any security, issuer, or market, or the failure to make disclosures required under the securities laws, which remain uncorrected; or

(ii)   a financial loss to investors or other persons protected under the securities laws which remains substantially uncompensated; or

(D)   the acts, practices or course of conduct under investigation—

(i)   involve significant financial speculation in securities; or

(ii)   endanger the stability of any financial or investment intermediary.

(3)   Any application under paragraph (2) for a delay in notice shall be made with reasonable specificity.

(4)(A)   Upon a showing described in paragraph (2), the presiding judge or magistrate shall enter an ex parte order granting the requested delay for a period not to exceed ninety days and an order prohibiting the financial institution involved from disclosing that records have been obtained or that a request for records has been made.

(B)   Extensions of the period of delay of notice provided in subparagraph (A) of up to ninety days each may be granted by the court upon application, but only in accordance with this subsection or section 1109(a), (b)(1), or (b)(2) of the Right to Financial Privacy Act of 1978.

(C)   Upon expiration of the period of delay of notification ordered under subparagraph (A) or (B), the customer shall be served with or mailed a copy of the subpena insofar as it applies to the customer together with the following notice which shall describe with reasonable specificity the nature of the investigation for which the Commission sought the financial records:

"Records or information concerning your transactions which are held by the financial institution named in the attached subpena were supplied to the Securities and Exchange Commission on (date). Notification was withheld pursuant to a determination by the (title of court so ordering) under section 21(h) of the Securities Exchange Act of 1934 that (state reason). The purpose of the investigation or official proceeding was (state purpose)."

(5)   Upon application by the Commission, all proceedings pursuant to paragraphs (2) and (4) shall be held in camera and the records thereof sealed until expiration of the period of delay or such other date as the presiding judge or magistrate may permit.

(6)   Repealed.

(7)(A)   Following the expiration of the period of delay of notification ordered by the court pursuant to paragraph (4) of this subsection, the customer may, upon motion, reopen the proceeding in the district court which issued the order. If the presiding judge or magistrate finds that the movant is the customer to whom the records obtained by the Commission pertain, and that the Commission has obtained financial records or information contained therein in violation of this subsection, other than paragraph (1), it may order that the customer be granted civil penalties against the Commission in an amount equal to the sum of—

(i) $100 without regard to the volume of records involved;

(ii)   any out-of-pocket damages sustained by the customer as a direct result of the disclosure; and

(iii) if the violation is found to have been willful, intentional, and without good faith, such punitive damages as the court may allow, together with the costs of the action and reasonable attorney's fees as determined by the court.

(B)   Upon a finding that the Commission has obtained financial records or information contained therein in violation of this subsection, other than paragraph (1), the court, in its discretion, may also or in the alternative issue injunctive relief to require the Commission to comply with this subsection with respect to any subpena which the Commission issues in the future for financial records of such customer for purposes of the same investigation.

(C)   Whenever the court determines that the Commission has failed to comply with this subsection, other than paragraph (1), and the court finds that the circumstances raise questions of whether an officer or employee of the Commission acted in a willful and intentional manner and without good faith with respect to the violation, the Office of Personnel Management shall promptly initiate a proceeding to determine whether disciplinary action is warranted against the agent or employee who was primarily responsible for the violation. After investigating and considering the evidence submitted, the Office of Personnel Management shall submit its findings and recommendations to the Commission and shall send copies of the findings and recommendations to the officer or employee or his representative. The Commission shall take the corrective action that the Office of Personnel Management recommends.

(8)   The relief described in paragraphs (7) and (10) shall be the only remedies or sanctions available to a customer for a violation of this subsection, other than paragraph (1), and nothing herein or in the Right to Financial Privacy Act of 1978 shall be deemed to prohibit the use in any investigation or proceeding of financial records, or the information contained therein, obtained by a subpena issued by the Commission. In the case of an unsuccessful action under paragraph (7), the court shall award

the costs of the action and attorney's fees to the Commission if the presiding judge or magistrate finds that the customer's claims were made in bad faith.

(9)(A)   The Commission may transfer financial records or the information contained therein to any government authority if the Commission proceeds as a transferring agency in accordance with section 1112 of the Right to Financial Privacy Act of 1978, except that the customer notice required under section 1112(b) or (c) of such Act may be delayed upon a showing by the Commission, in accordance with the procedure set forth in paragraphs (4) and (5), that one or more of subparagraphs (A) through (D) of paragraph (2) apply.

(B)   The Commission may, without notice to the customer pursuant to section 1112 of the Right to Financial Privacy Act of 1978, transfer financial records or the information contained therein to a State securities agency or to the Department of Justice. Financial records or information transferred by the Commission to the Department of Justice or to a State securities agency pursuant to the provisions of this subparagraph may be disclosed or used only in an administrative, civil, or criminal action or investigation by the Department of Justice or the State securities agency which arises out of or relates to the acts, practices, or courses of conduct investigated by the Commission, except that if the Department of Justice or the State securities agency determines that the information should be disclosed or used for any other purpose, it may do so if it notifies the customer, except as otherwise provided in the Right to Financial Privacy Act of 1978, within 30 days of its determination, or complies with the requirements of section 1109 of such Act regarding delay of notice.

(10) Any government authority violating paragraph (9) shall be subject to the procedures and penalties applicable to the Commission under paragraph (7)(A) with respect to a violation by the Commission in obtaining financial records.

(11) Notwithstanding the provisions of this subsection, the Commission may obtain financial records from a financial institution or transfer such records in accordance with provisions of the Right to Financial Privacy Act of 1978.

(12) Nothing in this subsection shall enlarge or restrict any rights of a financial institution to challenge requests for records made by the Commission under existing law. Nothing in this subsection shall entitle a customer to assert any rights of a financial institution.

(13) Unless the context otherwise requires, all terms defined in the Right to Financial Privacy Act of 1978 which are common to this subsection shall have the same meaning as in such Act.

(i)   Information to CFTC.—The Commission shall provide the Commodity Futures Trading Commission with notice of the commencement of any proceeding and a copy of any order entered by the Commission against any broker or dealer registered pursuant to section 15(b)(11), any exchange registered pursuant to section 6(g), or any national securities association registered pursuant to section 15A(k).

Civil Penalties for Insider Trading

Sec. 21A.   (a)   Authority to Impose Civil Penalties.—

(1)   Judicial actions by commission authorized.—

Whenever it shall appear to the Commission that any person has violated any provision of this Act or the rules or regulations thereunder by purchasing or selling a security or security-based swap agreement while in possession of material, nonpublic information in, or has violated any such provision by communicating such information in connection with, a transaction on or through the facilities of a national securities exchange or from or through a broker or dealer, and which is not part of a public offering by an issuer of securities other than standardized options or security futures products, the Commission—

(A)   may bring an action in a United States district court to seek, and the court shall have jurisdiction to impose, a civil penalty to be paid by the person who committed such violation; and

(B)   may, subject to subsection (b)(1) bring an action in a United States district court to seek, and the court shall have jurisdiction to impose, a civil penalty to be paid by a person who, at the time of the violation directly or indirectly controlled the person who committed such violation.

(2)   Amount of penalty for person who committed violation.—

The amount of the penalty which may be imposed on the person who committed such violation shall be determined by the court in light of the fact and circumstances, but shall not exceed three times the profit gained or loss avoided as a result of such unlawful purchase, sale, or communication.

(3)   Amount of penalty for controlling person.—

The amount of the penalty which may be imposed on any person who, at the time of the violation, directly or indirectly controlled the person who committed such violation, shall be determined by the court in light of the facts and circumstances, but shall not exceed the greater of $1,000,000, or three times the amount of the profit gained or loss avoided as a result of such controlled person's violation. If such controlled person's violation was a violation by communication, the profit gained or loss avoided as a result of the violation shall, for purposes of this paragraph only, be deemed to be limited to the profit gained or loss avoided by the person or persons to whom the controlled person directed such communication.

(b)   Limitations on Liability.—

(1)   Liability of controlling persons.—

No controlling person shall be subject to a penalty under subsection (a)(1)(B) unless the Commission establishes that—

(A)   such controlling person knew or recklessly disregarded the fact that such controlled person was likely to engage in the act or acts constituting the violation and failed to take appropriate steps to prevent such act or acts before they occurred; or

(B)   such controlling person knowingly or recklessly failed to establish, maintain, or enforce any policy or procedure required under section 15(f) of this Act or section 204A of the Investment Advisers Act of 1940 and such failure substantially contributed to or permitted the occurrence of the act or acts constituting the violation.

(2)   Additional restrictions on liability.—

No person shall be subject to a penalty under subsection (a) solely by reason of employing another person who is subject to a penalty under such subsection, unless such employing person is liable as a controlling person under paragraph (1) of this subsection. Section 20(a) of this Act shall not apply to actions under subsection (a) of this section.

(c)   Authority of Commission.—

The Commission, by such rules, regulations, and orders as it considers necessary or appropriate in the public interest or for the protection of investors, may exempt, in whole or in part, either unconditionally or upon specific terms and conditions, any person or transaction or class of persons or transactions from this section.

(d)   Procedures for Collection.—

(1)   Payment of penalty to treasury.—

A penalty imposed under this section shall be payable into the Treasury of the United States, except as otherwise provided in section 308 of the Sarbanes-Oxley Act of 2002 and section 21F of this title.

(2)   Collection of penalties.—

If a person upon whom such a penalty is imposed shall fail to pay such penalty within the time prescribed in the court's order, the Commission may refer the matter to the Attorney General who shall recover such penalty by action in the appropriate United States district court.

(3)   Remedy not exclusive.—

The actions authorized by this section may be brought in addition to any other actions that the Commission or the Attorney General are entitled to bring.

(4)   Jurisdiction and venue.—

For purposes of section 27 of this Act, actions under this section shall be actions to enforce a liability or a duty created by this Act.

(5)   Statute of limitations.—

No action may be brought under this section more than 5 years after the date of the purchase or sale. This section shall not be construed to bar or limit in any manner any action by the Commission or the Attorney General under any other provision of this Act, nor shall it bar or limit in any manner any action to recover penalties, or to seek any other order regarding penalties, imposed in an action commenced within 5 years of such transaction.

(e)   Definition.—

For purposes of this section, "profit gained" or "loss avoided" is the difference between the purchase or sale price of the security and the value of that security as measured by the trading price of the security a reasonable period after public dissemination of the nonpublic information.

(f)   The authority of the Commission under this section with respect to security-based swap agreements shall be subject to the restrictions and limitations of section 3A(b) of this Act.

(g)   Duty of Members and Employees of Congress.—

(1)   In general.—Subject to the rule of construction under section 10 of the STOCK Act and solely for purposes of the insider trading prohibitions arising under this Act, including section 10(b) and Rule 10b–5 thereunder, each Member of Congress or employee of Congress owes a duty arising from a relationship of trust and confidence to the Congress, the United States Government, and the citizens of the United States with respect to material, nonpublic information derived from such person's position as a Member of Congress or employee of Congress or gained from the performance of such person's official responsibilities.

(2)   Definitions.—In this subsection—

(A)   the term "Member of Congress" means a member of the Senate or House of Representatives, a Delegate to the House of Representatives, and the Resident Commissioner from Puerto Rico; and

(B)   the term "employee of Congress" means—

(i)   any individual (other than a Member of Congress), whose compensation is disbursed by the Secretary of the Senate or the Chief Administrative Officer of the House of Representatives; and

(ii)   any other officer or employee of the legislative branch (as defined in section 109(11) of the Ethics in Government Act of 1978).

(3)   Rule of construction.—Nothing in this subsection shall be construed to impair or limit the construction of the existing antifraud provisions of the securities laws or the authority of the Commission under those provisions.

(h)   Duty of Other Federal Officials.—

(1)   In general.—Subject to the rule of construction under section 10 of the STOCK Act and solely for purposes of the in-sider trading prohibitions arising under this Act, including section 10(b), and Rule 10b–5 thereunder, each executive branch employee, each judicial officer, and each judicial employee owes a duty arising from a relationship of trust and confidence to the United States Government and the citizens of the United States with respect to material, nonpublic information derived from such person's position as an executive branch employee, judicial officer, or judicial employee or gained from the performance of such person's official responsibilities.

(2)   Definitions.—In this Rule—

(A)   the term "executive branch employee"—

(i)   has the meaning given the term "employee" under section 2105 of title 5, United States Code;

(ii)   includes—

(I)   the President;

(II)   the Vice President; and

(III) an employee of the United States Postal Service or the Postal Regulatory Commission;

(B)   the term "judicial employee" has the meaning given that term in section 109(8) of the Ethics in Government Act of 1978; and

(C)   the term "judicial officer" has the meaning given that term under section 109(10) of the Ethics in Government Act of 1978.

(3)   Rule of construction.—Nothing in this subsection shall be construed to impair or limit the construction of the existing antifraud provisions of the securities laws or the authority of the Commission under those provisions.

(i)   Participation in Initial Public Offerings.—An individual described in section 101(f) of the Ethics in Government Act of 1978 may not purchase securities that are the subject of an initial public offering (within the meaning given such term in section 12(f)(1)(G)(i)) in any manner other than is available to members of the public generally.

Civil Remedies in Administrative Proceedings

Sec. 21B.   (a)   Commission Authority to Assess Money Penalties.—

(1)   In general.—

In any proceeding instituted pursuant to sections 15(b)(4), 15(b)(6), 15B, 15C, 15D, 15E, or 17A of this Act against any person, the Commission or the appropriate regulatory agency may impose a civil penalty if it finds, on the record after notice and opportunity for hearing, that such penalty is in the public interest and that such person—

(A)   has willfully violated any provision of the Securities Act of 1933, the Investment Company Act of 1940, the Investment Advisers Act of 1940, or this Act, or the rules or regulations thereunder, or the rules of the Municipal Securities Rulemaking Board;

(B)   has willfully aided, abetted, counseled, commanded, induced, or procured such a violation by any other person;

(C)   has willfully made or caused to be made in any application for registration or report required to be filed with the Commission or with any other appropriate regulatory agency under this Act, or in any proceeding before the Commission with respect to registration, any statement which was, at the time and in the light of the circumstances under which it was made, false or misleading with respect to any material fact, or has omitted to state in any such application or report any material fact which is required to be stated therein; or

(D)   has failed reasonably to supervise, within the meaning of section 15(b)(4)(E) of this Act, with a view to preventing violations of the provisions of such statutes, rules and regulations, another person who commits such a violation, if such other person is subject to his supervision;

(2)   Cease-and-desist proceedings—In any proceeding instituted under section 21C against any person, the Commission may impose a civil penalty, if the Commission finds, on the record after notice and opportunity for hearing, that such person—

(A)   is violating or has violated any provision of this title, or any rule or regulation issued under this title; or

(B)   is or was a cause of the violation of any provision of this title, or any rule or regulation issued under this title.

(b)   Maximum amount of Penalty.—

(1) First tier.—

The maximum amount of penalty for each act or omission described in subsection (a) shall be $5,000 for a natural person or $50,000 for any other person.

(2) Second tier.—

Notwithstanding paragraph (1), the maximum amount of penalty for each such act or omission shall be $50,000 for a natural person or $250,000 for any other person if the act or omission described in subsection (a) involved fraud, deceit, manipulation, or deliberate or reckless disregard of a regulatory requirement.

(3) Third tier.—

Notwithstanding paragraphs (1) and (2), the maximum amount of penalty for each such act or omission shall be $100,000 for a natural person or $500,000 for any other person if—

    (A) the act or omission described in subsection (a) involved fraud, deceit, manipulation, or deliberate or reckless disregard of a regulatory requirement; and

    (B) such act or omission directly or indirectly resulted in substantial losses or created a significant risk of substantial losses to other persons or resulted in substantial pecuniary gain to the person who committed the act or omission.

(c) Determination of Public Interest.—

In considering under this section whether a penalty is in the public interest, the Commission or the appropriate regulatory agency may consider—

    (1) whether the act or omission for which such penalty is assessed involved fraud, deceit, manipulation, or deliberate or reckless disregard of a regulatory requirement;

    (2) the harm to other persons resulting either directly or indirectly from such act or omission;

    (3) the extent to which any person was unjustly enriched, taking into account any restitution made to persons injured by such behavior;

    (4) whether such person previously has been found by the Commission, another appropriate regulatory agency, or a self-regulatory organization to have violated the Federal securities laws, State securities laws, or the rules of a self-regulatory organization, has been enjoined by a court of competent jurisdiction from violations of such laws or rules, or has been convicted by a court of competent jurisdiction of violations of such laws or of any felony or misdemeanor described in section 15(b)(4)(B) of this Act;

    (5) the need to deter such person and other persons from committing such acts or omissions; and

    (6) such other matters as justice may require.

(d) Evidence Concerning Ability to Pay.—

In any proceeding in which the Commission or the appropriate regulatory agency may impose a penalty under this section, a respondent may present evidence of the respondent's ability to pay such penalty. The Commission or the appropriate regulatory agency may, in its discretion, consider such evidence in determining whether such penalty is in the public interest. Such evidence may relate to the extent of such person's ability to continue in business and the collectability of a penalty, taking into account any other claims of the United States or third parties upon such person's assets and the amount of such person's assets.

(e) Authority to Enter An Order Requiring An Accounting and Disgorgement.—

In any proceeding in which the Commission or the appropriate regulatory agency may impose a penalty under this section, the Commission or the appropriate regulatory agency may enter an order requiring accounting and disgorgement, including reasonable interest. The Commission is authorized to adopt rules, regulations, and orders concerning payments to investors, rates of interest, periods of accrual, and such other matters as it deems appropriate to implement this subsection.

(f)   Security-based Swaps.—

(1)   Clearing agency.—

Any clearing agency that knowingly or recklessly evades or participates in or facilitates an evasion of the requirements of section 3C shall be liable for a civil money penalty in twice the amount otherwise available for a violation of section 3C.

(2)   Security-based swap dealer or major security-based swap participant.—

Any security-based swap dealer or major security-based swap participant that knowingly or recklessly evades or participates in or facilitates an evasion of the requirements of section 3C shall be liable for a civil money penalty in twice the amount otherwise available for a violation of section 3C.

Cease-and-Desist Proceedings

Sec. 21C.   (a)   Authority of the Commission.—

If the Commission finds, after notice and opportunity for hearing, that any person is violating, has violated or is about to violate any provision of this Act, or any rule or regulation thereunder, the Commission may publish its findings and enter an order requiring such person, and any other person that is, was, or would be a cause of the violation, due to an act or omission the person knew or should have known would contribute to such violation, to cease and desist from committing or causing such violation and any future violation of the same provision, rule, or regulation. Such order may, in addition to requiring a person to cease and desist from committing or causing a violation, require such person to comply, or to take steps to effect compliance, with such provision, rule or regulation, upon such terms and conditions and within such time as the Commission may specify in such order. Any such order may, as the Commission deems appropriate, require future compliance or steps to effect future compliance, either permanently or for such period of time as the Commission may specify, with such provision, rule, or regulation with respect to any security, any issuer, or any other person.

(b)   Hearing.—

The notice instituting proceedings pursuant to subsection (a) shall fix a hearing date not earlier than 30 days nor later than 60 days after service of the notice unless an earlier or a later date is set by the Commission with the consent of any respondent so served.

(c)   Temporary Order.—

(1)   In general.—

Whenever the Commission determines that the alleged violation or threatened violation specified in the notice instituting proceedings pursuant to subsection (a), or the continuation thereof, is likely to result in significant dissipation or conversion of assets, significant harm to investors, or substantial harm to the public interest, including, but not limited to, losses to the Securities Investor Protection Corporation, prior to the completion of the proceedings, the Commission may enter a temporary order requiring the respondent to cease and desist from the violation or threatened violation and to take such action to prevent the violation or threatened violation and to prevent dissipation or conversion of assets, significant harm to investors, or substantial harm to the public interest as the Commission deems appropriate pending completion of such proceedings. Such an order shall be entered only after notice and opportunity for a hearing, unless the Commission determines that notice and hearing prior to entry would be impracticable or contrary to the public interest. A temporary order shall become effective upon service upon the respondent and, unless set aside, limited, or suspended by the Commission or a court of competent jurisdiction, shall remain effective and enforceable pending the completion of the proceedings.

(2)   Applicability.—

Paragraph 1 shall apply only to a respondent that acts, or, at the time of the alleged misconduct acted, as a broker, dealer, investment adviser, investment company, municipal securities dealer, government securities broker, government securities dealer, registered public accounting firm (as defined in section 2 of the Sarbanes-Oxley Act of 2002), or transfer agent, or is, or was at the time of the alleged misconduct, an associated person of, or a person seeking to become associated with, any of the foregoing.

(3)   Temporary freeze.—

     (A)   In general.—

         (i)   Issuance of temporary order.—

Whenever, during the course of a lawful investigation involving possible violations of the Federal securities laws by an issuer of publicly traded securities or any of its directors, officers, partners, controlling persons, agents, or employees, it shall appear to the Commission that it is likely that the issuer will make extraordinary payments (whether compensation or otherwise) to any of the foregoing persons, the Commission may petition a Federal district court for a temporary order requiring the issuer to escrow, subject to court supervision, those payments in an interest-bearing account for 45 days.

         (ii)   Standard.—

A temporary order shall be entered under clause (i), only after notice and opportunity for a hearing, unless the court determines that notice and hearing prior to entry of the order would be impracticable or contrary to the public interest.

         (iii)   Effective period.—

A temporary order issued under clause (i) shall—

         (I)   become effective immediately;

         (II)   be served upon the parties subject to it; and

         (III)   unless set aside, limited or suspended by a court of competent jurisdiction, shall remain effective and enforceable for 45 days.

         (iv)   Extensions authorized.—

The effective period of an order under this subparagraph may be extended by the court upon good cause shown for not longer than 45 additional days, provided that the combined period of the order shall not exceed 90 days.

     (B)   Process on determination of violations.—

         (i)   Violations charged.—

If the issuer or other person described in subparagraph (A) is charged with any violation of the Federal securities laws before the expiration of the effective period of a temporary order under subparagraph (A) (including any applicable extension period), the order shall remain in effect, subject to court approval, until the conclusion of any legal proceedings related thereto, and the affected issuer or other person, shall have the right to petition the court for review of the order.

         (ii)   Violations not charged.—

If the issuer or other person described in subparagraph (A) is not charged with any violation of the Federal securities laws before the expiration of the effective period of a temporary order under subparagraph (A) (including any applicable extension period), the escrow shall terminate at the expiration of the 45-day effective period (or the expiration of any extension period, as applicable), and the disputed payments (with accrued interest) shall be returned to the issuer or other affected person.

(d)   Review of Temporary Orders.—

     (1)   Commission review.—

At any time after the respondent has been served with a temporary cease-and-desist order pursuant to subsection (c), the respondent may apply to the Commission to have the order set aside, limited, or suspended. If the respondent has been served with a temporary cease-and-desist order entered without a prior Commission hearing, the respondent may, within 10 days after the date on which the order was served, request a hearing on such application and the Commission shall hold a hearing and render a decision on such application at the earliest possible time.

(2) Judicial review.—

(A) 10 days after the date the respondent was served with a temporary cease-and-desist order entered with a prior Commission hearing, or

(B) 10 days after the Commission renders a decision on an application and hearing under paragraph (1), with respect to any temporary cease-and-desist order entered without a prior Commission hearing;

the respondent may apply to the United States district court for the district in which the respondent resides or has its principal place of business, or for the District of Columbia, for an order setting aside, limiting, or suspending the effectiveness or enforcement of the order, and the court shall have jurisdiction to enter such an order. A respondent served with a temporary cease-and-desist order entered without a prior Commission hearing may not apply to the court except after hearing and decision by the Commission on the respondent's application under paragraph (1) of this subsection.

(3) No automatic stay of temporary order.—

The commencement of proceedings under paragraph (2) of this subsection shall not, unless specifically ordered by the court, operate as a stay of the Commission's order.

(4) Exclusive review.—

Section 25 of this Act shall not apply to a temporary order entered pursuant to this section.

(e) Authority to Enter An Order Requiring An Accounting and Disgorgement.—

In any cease-and-desist proceeding under subsection (a), the Commission may enter an order requiring accounting and disgorgement, including reasonable interest. The Commission is authorized to adopt rules, regulations, and orders concerning payments to investors, rates of interest, periods of accrual, and such other matters as it deems appropriate to implement this subsection.

(f) Authority of the Commission to Prohibit Persons From Serving As Officers or Directors.—

In any cease-and-desist proceeding under subsection (a), the Commission may issue an order to prohibit, conditionally or unconditionally, and permanently or for such period of time as it shall determine, any person who has violated section 10(b) or the rules or regulations thereunder, from acting as an officer or director of any issuer that has a class of securities registered pursuant to section 12, or that is required to file reports pursuant to section 15(d), if the conduct of that person demonstrates unfitness to serve as an officer or director of any such issuer.

Private Securities Litigation

Sec. 21D.   (a)   Private Class Actions.—

(1) In general.—

The provisions of this subsection shall apply in each private action arising under this Act that is brought as a plaintiff class action pursuant to the Federal Rules of Civil Procedure.

(2) Certification filed with complaint.—

(A) In general.—

Each plaintiff seeking to serve as a representative party on behalf of a class shall provide a sworn certification, which shall be personally signed by such plaintiff and filed with the complaint, that—

(i)   states that the plaintiff has reviewed the complaint and authorized its filing;

(ii) states that the plaintiff did not purchase the security that is the subject of the complaint at the direction of plaintiff's counsel or in order to participate in any private action arising under this Act;

(iii) states that the plaintiff is willing to serve as a representative party on behalf of a class, including providing testimony at deposition and trial, if necessary;

(iv) sets forth all of the transactions of the plaintiff in the security that is the subject of the complaint during the class period specified in the complaint;

(v) identifies any other action under this Act, filed during the 3-year period preceding the date on which the certification is signed by the plaintiff, in which the plaintiff has sought to serve as a representative party on behalf of a class; and

(vi) states that the plaintiff will not accept any payment for serving as a representative party on behalf of a class beyond the plaintiff's pro rata share of any recovery, except as ordered or approved by the court in accordance with paragraph (4).

(B) Nonwaiver of attorney-client privilege.—

The certification filed pursuant to subparagraph (A) shall not be construed to be a waiver of the attorney-client privilege.

(3) Appointment of lead plaintiff.—

(A) Early notice to class members.—

(i) In general.—

Not later than 20 days after the date on which the complaint is filed, the plaintiff or plaintiffs shall cause to be published, in a widely circulated national business-oriented publication or wire service, a notice advising members of the purported plaintiff class—

(I) of the pendency of the action, the claims asserted therein, and the purported class period; and

(II) that, not later than 60 days after the date on which the notice is published, any member of the purported class may move the court to serve as lead plaintiff of the purported class.

(ii) Multiple actions.—

If more than one action on behalf of a class asserting substantially the same claim or claims arising under this Act is filed, only the plaintiff or plaintiffs in the first filed action shall be required to cause notice to be published in accordance with clause (i).

(iii) Additional notices may be required under federal rules.—

Notice required under clause (i) shall be in addition to any notice required pursuant to the Federal Rules of Civil Procedure.

(B) Appointment of lead plaintiff.—

(i) In general.—

Not later than 90 days after the date on which a notice is published under subparagraph (A)(i), the court shall consider any motion made by a purported class member in response to the notice, including any motion by a class member who is not individually named as a plaintiff in the complaint or complaints, and shall appoint as lead plaintiff the member or members of the purported plaintiff class that the court determines to be most capable of adequately representing the interests of class members (hereafter in this paragraph referred to as the "most adequate plaintiff") in accordance with this subparagraph.

(ii) Consolidated actions.—

If more than one action on behalf of a class asserting substantially the same claim or claims arising under this Act has been filed, and any party has sought to consolidate those actions for pretrial purposes or for trial, the court shall not make the determination required by clause (i) until after the decision on the motion to consolidate is rendered. As soon as practicable after such decision is rendered, the court shall appoint the most adequate plaintiff as lead plaintiff for the consolidated actions in accordance with this paragraph.

(iii)   Rebuttable presumption.—

    (I)   In general.—

Subject to subclause (II), for purposes of clause (i), the court shall adopt a presumption that the most adequate plaintiff in any private action arising under this Act is the person or group of persons that—

    (aa)   has either filed the complaint or made a motion in response to a notice under subparagraph (A)(i);

    (bb)   in the determination of the court, has the largest financial interest in the relief sought by the class; and

    (cc)   otherwise satisfies the requirements of Rule 23 of the Federal Rules of Civil Procedure.

    (II)   Rebuttable evidence.—

The presumption described in subclause (I) may be rebutted only upon proof by a member of the purported plaintiff class that the presumptively most adequate plaintiff—

    (aa)   will not fairly and adequately protect the interests of the class; or

    (bb)   is subject to unique defenses that render such plaintiff incapable of adequately representing the class.

(iv)   Discovery.—

For purposes of this subparagraph, discovery relating to whether a member or members of the purported plaintiff class is the most adequate plaintiff may be conducted by a plaintiff only if the plaintiff first demonstrates a reasonable basis for a finding that the presumptively most adequate plaintiff is incapable of adequately representing the class.

(v)   Selection of lead counsel.—

The most adequate plaintiff shall, subject to the approval of the court, select and retain counsel to represent the class.

(vi)   Restrictions on professional plaintiffs.—

Except as the court may otherwise permit, consistent with the purposes of this section, a person may be a lead plaintiff, or an officer, director, or fiduciary of a lead plaintiff, in no more than 5 securities class actions brought as plaintiff class actions pursuant to the Federal Rules of Civil Procedure during any 3-year period.

(4)   Recovery by plaintiffs.—

The share of any final judgment or of any settlement that is awarded to a representative party serving on behalf of a class shall be equal, on a per share basis, to the portion of the final judgment or settlement awarded to all other members of the class. Nothing in this paragraph shall be construed to limit the award of reasonable costs and expenses (including lost wages) directly relating to the representation of the class, to any representative party serving on behalf of a class.

(5)   Restrictions on settlements under seal.—

The terms and provisions of any settlement agreement of a class action shall not be filed under seal, except that on motion of any party to the settlement, the court may order filing under seal for those portions of a settlement agreement as to which good cause is shown for such filing under seal. For purposes of this paragraph, good cause shall exist only if publication of a term or provision of a settlement agreement would cause direct and substantial harm to any party.

(6) Restrictions on payment of attorneys' fees and expenses.—

Total attorneys' fees and expenses awarded by the court to counsel for the plaintiff class shall not exceed a reasonable percentage of the amount of any damages and prejudgment interest actually paid to the class.

(7) Disclosure of settlement terms to class members.—

Any proposed or final settlement agreement that is published or otherwise disseminated to the class shall include each of the following statements, along with a cover page summarizing the information contained in such statements:

(A) Statement of plaintiff recovery.—

The amount of the settlement proposed to be distributed to the parties to the action, determined in the aggregate and on an average per share basis.

(B) Statement of potential outcome of case.—

(i) Agreement on amount of damages.—

If the settling parties agree on the average amount of damages per share that would be recoverable if the plaintiff prevailed on each claim alleged under this Act, a statement concerning the average amount of such potential damages per share.

(ii) Disagreement on amount of damages.—

If the parties do not agree on the average amount of damages per share that would be recoverable if the plaintiff prevailed on each claim alleged under this Act, a statement from each settling party concerning the issue or issues on which the parties disagree.

(iii) Inadmissibility for certain purposes.—

A statement made in accordance with clause (i) or (ii) concerning the amount of damages shall not be admissible in any Federal or State judicial action or administrative proceeding, other than an action or proceeding arising out of such statement.

(C) Statement of attorneys' fees or costs sought.—

If any of the settling parties or their counsel intend to apply to the court for an award of attorneys' fees or costs from any fund established as part of the settlement, a statement indicating which parties or counsel intend to make such an application, the amount of fees and costs that will be sought (including the amount of such fees and costs determined on an average per share basis), and a brief explanation supporting the fees and costs sought. Such information shall be clearly summarized on the cover page of any notice to a party of any proposed or final settlement agreement.

(D) Identification of lawyers' representatives.—

The name, telephone number, and address of one or more representatives of counsel for the plaintiff class who will be reasonably available to answer questions from class members concerning any matter contained in any notice of settlement published or otherwise disseminated to the class.

(E) Reasons for settlement.—

A brief statement explaining the reasons why the parties are proposing the settlement.

(F) Other information.—

Such other information as may be required by the court.

(8) Security for payment of costs in class actions.—

In any private action arising under this Act that is certified as a class action pursuant to the Federal Rules of Civil Procedure, the court may require an undertaking from the attorneys for the plaintiff class, the plaintiff class, or both, or from the attorneys for the defendant, the defendant, or both, in such proportions and at such times as the court determines are just and equitable, for the payment of fees and expenses that may be awarded under this subsection.

(9)   Attorney conflict of interest.—

If a plaintiff class is represented by an attorney who directly owns or otherwise has a beneficial interest in the securities that are the subject of the litigation, the court shall make a determination of whether such ownership or other interest constitutes a conflict of interest sufficient to disqualify the attorney from representing the plaintiff class.

(b)   Requirements for Securities Fraud Actions.—

(1)   Misleading statements and omissions.—

In any private action arising under this Act in which the plaintiff alleges that the defendant—

    (A)   made an untrue statement of a material fact; or

    (B)   omitted to state a material fact necessary in order to make the statements made, in light of the circumstances in which they were made, not misleading;

the complaint shall specify each statement alleged to have been misleading, the reason or reasons why the statement is misleading, and, if an allegation regarding the statement or omission is made on information and belief, the complaint shall state with particularity all facts on which that belief is formed.

(2)   Required state of mind.—

    (A)   In general—Except as provided in subparagraph (B), in any private action arising under this Act in which the plaintiff may recover money damages only on proof that the defendant acted with a particular state of mind, the complaint shall, with respect to each act or omission alleged to violate this Act, state with particularity facts giving rise to a strong inference that the defendant acted with the required state of mind.

    (B)   Exception—In the case of an action for money damages brought against a credit rating agency or a controlling person under this title, it shall be sufficient, for purposes of pleading any required state of mind in relation to such action, that the complaint state with particularity facts giving rise to a strong inference that the credit rating agency knowingly or recklessly failed—

        (i)   to conduct a reasonable investigation of the rated security with respect to the factual elements relied upon by its own methodology for evaluating credit risk; or

        (ii)   to obtain reasonable verification of such factual elements (which verification may be based on a sampling technique that does not amount to an audit) from other sources that the credit rating agency considered to be competent and that were independent of the issuer and underwriter.

(3)   Motion to dismiss; stay of discovery.—

    (A)   Dismissal for failure to meet pleading requirements.—

In any private action arising under this Act, the court shall, on the motion of any defendant, dismiss the complaint if the requirements of paragraphs (1) and (2) are not met.

    (B)   Stay of discovery.—

In any private action arising under this Act, all discovery and other proceedings shall be stayed during the pendency of any motion to dismiss, unless the court finds upon the motion of any party that particularized discovery is necessary to preserve evidence or to prevent undue prejudice to that party.

    (C)   Preservation of evidence.—

        (i)   In general.—

During the pendency of any stay of discovery pursuant to this paragraph, unless otherwise ordered by the court, any party to the action with actual notice of the allegations contained in the complaint shall treat all documents, data compilations (including electronically recorded or stored data), and tangible objects that are in the custody or control of such person and that are relevant to the allegations, as if they were the subject of a continuing request for production of documents from an opposing party under the Federal Rules of Civil Procedure.

(ii)   Sanction for willful violation.—

A party aggrieved by the willful failure of an opposing party to comply with clause (i) may apply to the court for an order awarding appropriate sanctions.

(D)   Circumvention of stay of discovery.—

Upon a proper showing, a court may stay discovery proceedings in any private action in a state court, as necessary in aid of its jurisdiction, or to protect or effectuate its judgements, in an action subject to a stay of discovery pursuant to this paragraph.

(4)   Loss causation.—

In any private action arising under this Act, the plaintiff shall have the burden of proving that the act or omission of the defendant alleged to violate this Act caused the loss for which the plaintiff seeks to recover damages.

(c)   Sanctions for Abusive Litigation.—

(1)   Mandatory review by court.—

In any private action arising under this Act, upon final adjudication of the action, the court shall include in the record specific findings regarding compliance, by each party and each attorney representing any party, with each requirement of Rule 11(b) of the Federal Rules of Civil Procedure as to any complaint, responsive pleading, or dispositive motion.

(2)   Mandatory sanctions.—

If the court makes a finding under paragraph (1) that a party or attorney violated any requirement of Rule 11(b) of the Federal Rules of Civil Procedure as to any complaint, responsive pleading, or dispositive motion, the court shall impose sanctions on such party or attorney in accordance with Rule 11 of the Federal Rules of Civil Procedure. Prior to making a finding that any party or attorney has violated Rule 11 of the Federal Rules of Civil Procedure, the court shall give such party or attorney notice and an opportunity to respond.

(3)   Presumption in favor of attorneys' fees and costs.—

(A)   In general.—

Subject to subparagraphs (B) and (C), for purposes of paragraph (2), the court shall adopt a presumption that the appropriate sanction—

(i)   for failure of any responsive pleading or dispositive motion to comply with any requirement of Rule 11(b) of the Federal Rules of Civil Procedure is an award to the opposing party of the reasonable attorneys' fees and other expenses incurred as a direct result of the violation; and

(ii)   for substantial failure of any complaint to comply with any requirement of Rule 11(b) of the Federal Rules of Civil Procedure is an award to the opposing party of the reasonable attorneys' fees and other expenses incurred in the action.

(B)   Rebuttal evidence.—

The presumption described in subparagraph (A) may be rebutted only upon proof by the party or attorney against whom sanctions are to be imposed that—

(i)   the award of attorneys' fees and other expenses will impose an unreasonable burden on that party or attorney and would be unjust, and the failure to make such an award would not impose a greater burden on the party in whose favor sanctions are to be imposed; or

      (ii)   the violation of Rule 11(b) of the Federal Rules of Civil Procedure was de minimis.

   (C)   Sanctions.—

If the party or attorney against whom sanctions are to be imposed meets its burden under subparagraph (B), the court shall award the sanctions that the court deems appropriate pursuant to Rule 11 of the Federal Rules of Civil Procedure.

  (d)   Defendant's Right to Written Interrogatories.—

In any private action arising under this Act in which the plaintiff may recover money damages, the court shall, when requested by a defendant, submit to the jury a written interrogatory on the issue of each such defendant's state of mind at the time the alleged violation occurred.

  (e)   Limitation on Damages.—

   (1)   In general.—

Except as provided in paragraph (2), in any private action arising under this Act in which the plaintiff seeks to establish damages by reference to the market price of a security, the award of damages to the plaintiff shall not exceed the difference between the purchase or sale price paid or received, as appropriate, by the plaintiff for the subject security and the mean trading price of that security during the 90-day period beginning on the date on which the information correcting the misstatement or omission that is the basis for the action is disseminated to the market.

   (2)   Exception.—

In any private action arising under this Act in which the plaintiff seeks to establish damages by reference to the market price of a security, if the plaintiff sells or repurchases the subject security prior to the expiration of the 90-day period described in paragraph (1), the plaintiff's damages shall not exceed the difference between the purchase or sale price paid or received, as appropriate, by the plaintiff for the security and the mean trading price of the security during the period beginning immediately after dissemination of information correcting the misstatement or omission and ending on the date on which the plaintiff sells or repurchases the security.

   (3)   Definition.—

For purposes of this subsection, the "mean trading price" of a security shall be an average of the daily trading price of that security, determined as of the close of the market each day during the 90-day period referred to in paragraph (1).

  (f)   Proportionate Liability.—

   (1)   Applicability.—

Nothing in this subsection shall be construed to create, affect, or in any manner modify, the standard for liability associated with any action arising under the securities laws.

   (2)   Liability for damages.—

   (A)   Joint and several liability.—

Any covered person against whom a final judgment is entered in a private action shall be liable for damages jointly and severally only if the trier of fact specifically determines that such covered person knowingly committed a violation of the securities laws.

   (B)   Proportionate liability.—

      (i)   In general.—

Except as provided in subparagraph (A), a covered person against whom a final judgment is entered in a private action shall be liable solely for the portion of the judgment that corresponds to the percentage of responsibility of that covered person, as determined under paragraph (3).

(ii) Recovery by and costs of covered person.—

In any case in which a contractual relationship permits, a covered person that prevails in any private action may recover the attorney's fees and costs of that covered person in connection with the action.

(3) Determination of responsibility.—

(A) In general.—

In any private action, the court shall instruct the jury to answer special interrogatories, or if there is no jury, shall make findings, with respect to each covered person and each of the other persons claimed by any of the parties to have caused or contributed to the loss incurred by the plaintiff, including persons who have entered into settlements with the plaintiff or plaintiffs, concerning—

(i) whether such person violated the securities laws;

(ii) the percentage of responsibility of such person, measured as a percentage of the total fault of all persons who caused or contributed to the loss incurred by the plaintiff; and

(iii) whether such person knowingly committed a violation of the securities laws.

(B) Contents of special interrogatories or findings.—

The responses to interrogatories, or findings, as appropriate, under subparagraph (A) shall specify the total amount of damages that the plaintiff is entitled to recover and the percentage of responsibility of each covered person found to have caused or contributed to the loss incurred by the plaintiff or plaintiffs.

(C) Factors for consideration.—

In determining the percentage of responsibility under this paragraph, the trier of fact shall consider—

(i) the nature of the conduct of each covered person found to have caused or contributed to the loss incurred by the plaintiff or plaintiffs; and

(ii) the nature and extent of the causal relationship between the conduct of each such person and the damages incurred by the plaintiff or plaintiffs.

(4) Uncollectible share.—

(A) In general.—

Notwithstanding paragraph (2)(B), (if) upon motion made not later than 6 months after a final judgment is entered in any private action, the court determines that all or part of the share of the judgment of the covered person is not collectible against that covered person, and is also not collectible against a covered person described in paragraph (2)(A), each covered person described in paragraph (2)(B) shall be liable for the uncollectible share as follows:

(i) Percentage of net worth.—

Each covered person shall be jointly and severally liable for the uncollectible share if the plaintiff establishes that—

(I) the plaintiff is an individual whose recoverable damages under final judgment are equal to more than 10 percent of the net worth of the plaintiff; and

(II) the net worth of the plaintiff is equal to less than $200,000.

(ii) Other plaintiffs.—

With respect to any plaintiff not described in subclauses (I) and (II) of clause (i), each covered person shall be liable for the uncollectible share in proportion to the percentage of responsibility of that covered person, except that the total liability of a covered person under this clause may not exceed 50 percent of the proportionate share of that covered person, as determined under paragraph (3)(B).

(iii)   Net worth.—

For purposes of this subparagraph, net worth shall be determined as of the date immediately preceding the date of the purchase or sale (as applicable) by the plaintiff of the security that is the subject of the action, and shall be equal to the fair market value of assets, minus liabilities, including the net value of the investments of the plaintiff in real and personal property (including personal residences).

(B)   Overall limit.—

In no case shall the total payments required pursuant to subparagraph (A) exceed the amount of the uncollectible share.

(C)   Covered persons subject to contribution.—

A covered person against whom judgment is not collectible shall be subject to contribution and to any continuing liability to the plaintiff on the judgment.

(5)   Right of contribution.—

To the extent that a covered person is required to make an additional payment pursuant to paragraph (4), that covered person may recover contribution—

(A)   from the covered person originally liable to make the payment;

(B)   from any covered person liable jointly and severally pursuant to paragraph (2)(A);

(C)   from any covered person held proportionately liable pursuant to this paragraph who is liable to make the same payment and has paid less than his or her proportionate share of that payment; or

(D)   from any other person responsible for the conduct giving rise to the payment that would have been liable to make the same payment.

(6)   Nondisclosure to jury.—

The standard for allocation of damages under paragraphs (2) and (3) and the procedure for reallocation of uncollectible shares under paragraph (4) shall not be disclosed to members of the jury.

(7)   Settlement discharge.—

(A)   In general.—

A covered person who settles any private action at any time before final verdict or judgment shall be discharged from all claims for contribution brought by other persons. Upon entry of the settlement by the court, the court shall enter a bar order constituting the final discharge of all obligations to the plaintiff of the settling covered person arising out of the action. The order shall bar all future claims for contribution arising out of the action—

(i)   by any person against the settling covered person; and

(ii)   by the settling covered person against any person, other than a person whose liability has been extinguished by the settlement of the settling covered person.

(B)   Reduction.—

If a covered person enters into a settlement with the plaintiff prior to final verdict or judgment, the verdict or judgment shall be reduced by the greater of—

(i)   an amount that corresponds to the percentage of responsibility of that covered person; or

(ii)   the amount paid to the plaintiff by that covered person.

(8)   Contribution.—

904

A covered person who becomes jointly and severally liable for damages in any private action may recover contribution from any other person who, if joined in the original action, would have been liable for the same damages. A claim for contribution shall be determined based on the percentage of responsibility of the claimant and of each person against whom a claim for contribution is made.

(9) Statute of limitations for contribution.—

In any private action determining liability, an action for contribution shall be brought not later than 6 months after the entry of a final, nonappealable judgment in the action, except that an action for contribution brought by a covered person who was required to make an additional payment pursuant to paragraph (4) may be brought not later than 6 months after the date on which such payment was made.

(10) Definitions.—

For purposes of this subsection

    (A) a covered person "knowingly commits a violation of the securities laws"—

        (i) with respect to an action that is based on an untrue statement of material fact or omission of a material fact necessary to make the statement not misleading, if—

            (I) that covered person makes an untrue statement of a material fact, with actual knowledge that the representation is false, or omits to state a fact necessary in order to make the statement made not misleading, with actual knowledge that, as a result of the omission, one of the material representations of the covered person is false; and

            (II) persons are likely to reasonably rely on that misrepresentation or omission; and

        (ii) with respect to an action that is based on any conduct that is not described in clause (i), if that covered person engages in that conduct with actual knowledge of the facts and circumstances that make the conduct of that covered person a violation of the securities laws;

    (B) reckless conduct by a covered person shall not be construed to constitute a knowing commission of a violation of the securities laws by that covered person;

    (C) the term "covered person" means—

        (i) a defendant in any private action arising under this Act; or

        (ii) a defendant in any private action arising under section 11 of the Securities Act of 1933, who is an outside director of the issuer of the securities that are the subject of the action; and

    (D) the term "outside director" shall have the meaning given such term by rule or regulation of the Commission.

Application of Safe Harbor for Forward-Looking Statements

Sec. 21E.   (a) Applicability.—

This section shall apply only to a forward-looking statement made by—

    (1) an issuer that, at the time that the statement is made, is subject to the reporting requirements of section 13(a) or section 15(d);

    (2) a person acting on behalf of such issuer;

    (3) an outside reviewer retained by such issuer making a statement on behalf of such issuer; or

    (4) an underwriter, with respect to information provided by such issuer or information derived from information provided by such issuer.

(b) Exclusions.—

Except to the extent otherwise specifically provided by rule, regulation, or order of the Commission, this section shall not apply to a forward-looking statement—

    (1)   that is made with respect to the business or operations of the issuer, if the issuer—

        (A)   during the 3-year period preceding the date on which the statement was first made—

            (i)   was convicted of any felony or misdemeanor described in clauses (i) through (iv) of section 15(b)(4)(B); or

            (ii)   has been made the subject of a judicial or administrative decree or order arising out of a governmental action that—

                (I)   prohibits future violations of the antifraud provisions of the securities laws;

                (II)   requires that the issuer cease and desist from violating the antifraud provisions of the securities laws; or

                (III)   determines that the issuer violated the antifraud provisions of the securities laws;

        (B)   makes the forward-looking statement in connection with an offering of securities by a blank check company;

        (C)   issues penny stock;

        (D)   makes the forward-looking statement in connection with a rollup transaction; or

        (E)   makes the forward-looking statement in connection with a going private transaction; or

    (2)   that is—

        (A)   included in a financial statement prepared in accordance with generally accepted accounting principles;

        (B)   contained in a registration statement of, or otherwise issued by, an investment company;

        (C)   made in connection with a tender offer;

        (D)   made in connection with an initial public offering;

        (E)   made in connection with an offering by, or relating to the operations of, a partnership, limited liability company, or a direct participation investment program; or

        (F)   made in a disclosure of beneficial ownership in a report required to be filed with the Commission pursuant to section 13(d).

  (c)   Safe Harbor.—

    (1)   In general.—

Except as provided in subsection (b), in any private action arising under this Act that is based on an untrue statement of a material fact or omission of a material fact necessary to make the statement not misleading, a person referred to in subsection (a) shall not be liable with respect to any forward-looking statement, whether written or oral, if and to the extent that—

        (A)   the forward-looking statement is—

            (i)   identified as a forward-looking statement, and is accompanied by meaningful cautionary statements identifying important factors that could cause actual results to differ materially from those in the forward-looking statement; or

            (ii)   immaterial; or

        (B)   the plaintiff fails to prove that the forward-looking statement—

            (i)   if made by a natural person, was made with actual knowledge by that person that the statement was false or misleading; or

    (ii)   if made by a business entity; was

        (I)   made by or with the approval of an executive officer of that entity; and

        (II)   made or approved by such officer with actual knowledge by that officer that the statement was false or misleading.

    (2)   Oral forward-looking statements.—

In the case of an oral forward-looking statement made by an issuer that is subject to the reporting requirements of section 13(a) or section 15(d), or by a person acting on behalf of such issuer, the requirement set forth in paragraph (1)(A) shall be deemed to be satisfied—

    (A)   if the oral forward-looking statement is accompanied by a cautionary statement—

        (i)   that the particular oral statement is a forward-looking statement; and

        (ii)   that the actual results might differ materially from those projected in the forward-looking statement; and

    (B)   if—

        (i)   the oral forward-looking statement is accompanied by an oral statement that additional information concerning factors that could cause actual results to materially differ from those in the forward-looking statement is contained in a readily available written document, or portion thereof;

        (ii)   the accompanying oral statement referred to in clause (i) identifies the document, or portion thereof, that contains the additional information about those factors relating to the forward-looking statement; and

        (iii)   the information contained in that written document is a cautionary statement that satisfies the standard established in paragraph (1)(A).

    (3)   Availability.—

Any document filed with the Commission or generally disseminated shall be deemed to be readily available for purposes of paragraph (2).

    (4)   Effect on other safe harbors.—

The exemption provided for in paragraph (1) shall be in addition to any exemption that the Commission may establish by rule or regulation under subsection (g).

(d)   Duty to Update.—

Nothing in this section shall impose upon any person a duty to update a forward-looking statement.

(e)   Dispositive Motion.—

On any motion to dismiss based upon subsection (c)(1), the court shall consider any statement cited in the complaint and any cautionary statement accompanying the forward-looking statement, which are not subject to material dispute, cited by the defendant.

(f)   Stay Pending Decision on Motion.—

In any private action arising under this Act, the court shall stay discovery (other than discovery that is specifically directed to the applicability of the exemption provided for in this section) during the pendency of any motion by a defendant for summary judgment that is based on the grounds that—

    (1)   the statement or omission upon which the complaint is based is a forward-looking statement within the meaning of this section; and

    (2)   the exemption provided for in this section precludes a claim for relief.

(g)   Exemption Authority.—

In addition to the exemptions provided for in this section, the Commission may, by rule or regulation, provide exemptions from or under any provision of this Act, including with respect to liability that is based on a statement or that is based on projections or other forward-looking information, if and to the extent that any such exemption is consistent with the public interest and the protection of investors, as determined by the Commission.

(h)   Effect on Other Authority of Commission.—

Nothing in this section limits, either expressly or by implication, the authority of the Commission to exercise similar authority or to adopt similar rules and regulations with respect to forward-looking statements under any other statute under which the Commission exercises rulemaking authority.

(i)   Definitions.—

For purposes of this section, the following definitions shall apply:

(1)   Forward-looking statement.—

The term "forward-looking statement" means—

(A)   a statement containing a projection of revenues, income (including income loss), earnings (including earnings loss) per share, capital expenditures, dividends, capital structure, or other financial items;

(B)   a statement of the plans and objectives of management for future operations, including plans or objectives relating to the products or services of the issuer;

(C)   a statement of future economic performance, including any such statement contained in a discussion and analysis of financial condition by the management or in the results of operations included pursuant to the rules and regulations of the Commission;

(D)   any statement of the assumptions underlying or relating to any statement described in subparagraph (A), (B) or (C);

(E)   any report issued by an outside reviewer retained by an issuer, to the extent that the report assesses a forward-looking statement made by the issuer; or

(F)   a statement containing a projection or estimate of such other items as may be specified by rule or regulation of the Commission.

(2)   Investment company.—

The term "investment company" has the same meaning as in section 3(a) of the Investment Company Act of 1940.

(3)   Going private transaction.—

The term "going private transaction" has the meaning given that term under the rules or regulations of the Commission issued pursuant to section 13(e).

(4)   Person acting on behalf of an issuer.—

The term "person acting on behalf of an issuer" means any officer, director, or employee of such issuer.

(5)   Other terms.—

The terms "blank check company", "rollup transaction", "partnership", "limited liability company", "executive officer of an entity" and "direct participation investment program", have the meanings given those terms by rule or regulation of the Commission.

Securities Whistleblower Incentives and Protection

Sec. 21F.   (a)   Definitions.—In this section the following definitions shall apply:

(1)   Covered judicial or administrative action.—

The term 'covered judicial or administrative action' means any judicial or administrative action brought by the Commission under the securities laws that results in monetary sanctions exceeding $1,000,000.

(2)   Fund.—

The term 'Fund' means the Securities and Exchange Commission Investor Protection Fund.

(3)   Original information.—

The term 'original information' means information that—

(A)   is derived from the independent knowledge or analysis of a whistleblower;

(B)   is not known to the Commission from any other source, unless the whistleblower is the original source of the information; and

(C)   is not exclusively derived from an allegation made in a judicial or administrative hearing, in a governmental report, hearing, audit, or investigation, or from the news media, unless the whistleblower is a source of the information.

(4)   Monetary sanctions.—

The term 'monetary sanctions', when used with respect to any judicial or administrative action, means—

(A)   any monies, including penalties, disgorgement, and interest, ordered to be paid; and

(B)   any monies deposited into a disgorgement fund or other fund pursuant to section 308(b) of the Sarbanes-Oxley Act of 2002, as a result of such action or any settlement of such action.

(5)   Related action.—

The term 'related action', when used with respect to any judicial or administrative action brought by the Commission under the securities laws, means any judicial or administrative action brought by an entity described in subclauses (I) through (IV) of subsection (h)(2)(D)(i) that is based upon the original information provided by a whistleblower pursuant to subsection (a) that led to the successful enforcement of the Commission action.

(6)   Whistleblower.—

The term 'whistleblower' means any individual who provides, or 2 or more individuals acting jointly who provide, information relating to a violation of the securities laws to the Commission, in a manner established, by rule or regulation, by the Commission.

(b)   Awards.—

(1)   In general.—

In any covered judicial or administrative action, or related action, the Commission, under regulations prescribed by the Commission and subject to subsection (c), shall pay an award or awards to 1 or more whistleblowers who voluntarily provided original information to the Commission that led to the successful enforcement of the covered judicial or administrative action, or related action, in an aggregate amount equal to—

(A)   not less than 10 percent, in total, of what has been collected of the monetary sanctions imposed in the action or related actions; and

(B)   not more than 30 percent, in total, of what has been collected of the monetary sanctions imposed in the action or related actions.

(2)   Payment of awards.—

Any amount paid under paragraph (1) shall be paid from the Fund.

(c)   Determination of Amount of Award; Denial of Award.—

(1)   Determination of amount of award.—

(A)   Discretion.—

The determination of the amount of an award made under subsection (b) shall be in the discretion of the Commission.

(B)   Criteria.—

In determining the amount of an award made under subsection (b), the Commission—

(i)   shall take into consideration—

(I)   the significance of the information provided by the whistleblower to the success of the covered judicial or administrative action;

(II)   the degree of assistance provided by the whistleblower and any legal representative of the whistleblower in a covered judicial or administrative action;

(III)   the programmatic interest of the Commission in deterring violations of the securities laws by making awards to whistleblowers who provide information that lead to the successful enforcement of such laws; and

(IV)   such additional relevant factors as the Commission may establish by rule or regulation; and

(ii)   shall not take into consideration the balance of the Fund.

(2)   Denial of award.—

No award under subsection (b) shall be made—

(A)   to any whistleblower who is, or was at the time the whistleblower acquired the original information submitted to the Commission, a member, officer, or employee of—

(i)   an appropriate regulatory agency;

(ii)   the Department of Justice;

(iii)   a self-regulatory organization;

(iv)   the Public Company Accounting Oversight Board; or

(v)   a law enforcement organization;

(B)   to any whistleblower who is convicted of a criminal violation related to the judicial or administrative action for which the whistleblower otherwise could receive an award under this section;

(C)   to any whistleblower who gains the information through the performance of an audit of financial statements required under the securities laws and for whom such submission would be contrary to the requirements of section 10A of the Securities Exchange Act of 1934; or

(D)   to any whistleblower who fails to submit information to the Commission in such form as the Commission may, by rule, require.

(d)   Representation.—

(1)   Permitted representation.—

Any whistleblower who makes a claim for an award under subsection (b) may be represented by counsel.

(2)   Required representation.—

(A)   In general.—

Any whistleblower who anonymously makes a claim for an award under subsection (b) shall be represented by counsel if the whistleblower anonymously submits the information upon which the claim is based.

(B)   Disclosure of identity.—

Prior to the payment of an award, a whistleblower shall disclose the identity of the whistleblower and provide such other information as the Commission may require, directly or through counsel for the whistleblower.

(e)   No contract with the Commission is necessary for any whistleblower to receive an award under subsection (b), unless otherwise required by the Commission by rule or regulation.

(f) Any determination made under this section, including whether, to whom, or in what amount to make awards, shall be in the discretion of the Commission. Any such determination, except the determination of the amount of an award if the award was made in accordance with subsection (b), may be appealed to the appropriate court of appeals of the United States not more than 30 days after the determination is issued by the Commission. The court shall review the determination made by the Commission in accordance with section 706 of title 5, United States Code.

(g) Investor Protection Fund.—

    (1) Fund established.—

There is established in the Treasury of the United States a fund to be known as the 'Securities and Exchange Commission Investor Protection Fund'.

    (2) Use of fund.—

The Fund shall be available to the Commission, without further appropriation or fiscal year limitation, for—

        (A) paying awards to whistleblowers as provided in subsection (b); and

        (B) funding the activities of the Inspector General of the Commission under section 4(i).

    (3) Deposits and credits.—

        (A) In general.—

There shall be deposited into or credited to the Fund an amount equal to—

        (i) any monetary sanction collected by the Commission in any judicial or administrative action brought by the Commission under the securities laws that is not added to a disgorgement fund or other fund under section 308 of the Sarbanes-Oxley Act of 2002 or otherwise distributed to victims of a violation of the securities laws, or the rules and regulations thereunder, underlying such action, unless the balance of the Fund at the time the monetary sanction is collected exceeds $300,000,000;

        (ii) any monetary sanction added to a disgorgement fund or other fund under section 308 of the Sarbanes-Oxley Act of 2002 that is not distributed to the victims for whom the Fund was established, unless the balance of the disgorgement fund at the time the determination is made not to distribute the monetary sanction to such victims exceeds $200,000,000; and

        (iii) all income from investments made under paragraph (4).

        (B) Additional amounts.—

If the amounts deposited into or credited to the Fund under subparagraph (A) are not sufficient to satisfy an award made under subsection (b), there shall be deposited into or credited to the Fund an amount equal to the unsatisfied portion of the award from any monetary sanction collected by the Commission in the covered judicial or administrative action on which the award is based.

    (4) Investments.—

        (A) Amounts in fund may be invested.—

The Commission may request the Secretary of the Treasury to invest the portion of the Fund that is not, in the discretion of the Commission, required to meet the current needs of the Fund.

        (B) Eligible investments.—

Investments shall be made by the Secretary of the Treasury in obligations of the United States or obligations that are guaranteed as to principal and interest by the United States, with maturities suitable to the needs of the Fund as determined by the Commission on the record.

        (C) Interest and proceeds credited.—

The interest on, and the proceeds from the sale or redemption of, any obligations held in the Fund shall be credited to the Fund.

(5)   Reports to congress.—

Not later than October 30 of each fiscal year beginning after the date of enactment of this subsection, the Commission shall submit to the Committee on Banking, Housing, and Urban Affairs of the Senate, and the Committee on Financial Services of the House of Representatives a report on—

(A)   the whistleblower award program, established under this section, including—

(i)   a description of the number of awards granted; and

(ii)   the types of cases in which awards were granted during the preceding fiscal year;

(B)   the balance of the Fund at the beginning of the preceding fiscal year;

(C)   the amounts deposited into or credited to the Fund during the preceding fiscal year;

(D)   the amount of earnings on investments made under paragraph (4) during the preceding fiscal year;

(E)   the amount paid from the Fund during the preceding fiscal year to whistleblowers pursuant to subsection (b);

(F)   the balance of the Fund at the end of the preceding fiscal year; and

(G)   a complete set of audited financial statements, including—

(i)   a balance sheet;

(ii)   income statement; and

(iii)   cash flow analysis.

(h)   Protection of Whistleblowers.—

(1)   Prohibition against retaliation.—

(A)   In general.—

No employer may discharge, demote, suspend, threaten, harass, directly or indirectly, or in any other manner discriminate against, a whistleblower in the terms and conditions of employment because of any lawful act done by the whistleblower—

(i)   in providing information to the Commission in accordance with this section;

(ii)   in initiating, testifying in, or assisting in any investigation or judicial or administrative action of the Commission based upon or related to such information; or

(iii)   in making disclosures that are required or protected under the Sarbanes-Oxley Act of 2002, the Securities Exchange Act of 1934, including section 10A(m) of such Act, section 1513(e) of title 18, United States Code, and any other law, rule, or regulation subject to the jurisdiction of the Commission.

(B)   Enforcement.—

(i)   Cause of action.—

An individual who alleges discharge or other discrimination in violation of subparagraph (A) may bring an action under this subsection in the appropriate district court of the United States for the relief provided in subparagraph (C).

(ii)   Subpoenas.—

A subpoena requiring the attendance of a witness at a trial or hearing conducted under this section may be served at any place in the United States.

(iii)   Statute of limitations.—

(I)   In general.—

An action under this subsection may not be brought—

    (aa) more than 6 years after the date on which the violation of subparagraph (A) occurred; or

    (bb) more than 3 years after the date when facts material to the right of action are known or reasonably should have been known by the employee alleging a violation of subparagraph (A).

(II)   Required action within 10 years.—

Notwithstanding subclause (I), an action under this subsection may not in any circumstance be brought more than 10 years after the date on which the violation occurs.

(C)   Relief.—

Relief for an individual prevailing in an action brought under subparagraph (B) shall include—

    (i)   reinstatement with the same seniority status that the individual would have had, but for the discrimination;

    (ii)   2 times the amount of back pay otherwise owed to the individual, with interest; and

    (iii)   compensation for litigation costs, expert witness fees, and reasonable attorneys' fees.

(2)   Confidentiality.—

(A)   In general.—

Except as provided in subparagraphs (B) and (C), the Commission and any officer or employee of the Commission shall not disclose any information, including information provided by a whistleblower to the Commission, which could reasonably be expected to reveal the identity of a whistleblower, except in accordance with the provisions of section 552a of title 5, United States Code, unless and until required to be disclosed to a defendant or respondent in connection with a public proceeding instituted by the Commission or any entity described in subparagraph (C). For purposes of section 552 of title 5, United States Code, this paragraph shall be considered a statute described in subsection (b)(3)(B) of such section.

(B)   Exempted statute.—

For purposes of section 552 of title 5, United States Code, this paragraph shall be considered a statute described in subsection (b)(3)(B) of such section 552.

(C)   Rule of construction.—

Nothing in this section is intended to limit, or shall be construed to limit, the ability of the Attorney General to present such evidence to a grand jury or to share such evidence with potential witnesses or defendants in the course of an ongoing criminal investigation.

(D)   Availability to government agencies.—

(i)   In general.—

Without the loss of its status as confidential in the hands of the Commission, all information referred to in subparagraph (A) may, in the discretion of the Commission, when determined by the Commission to be necessary to accomplish the purposes of this Act and to protect investors, be made available to—

    (I)   the Attorney General of the United States;

    (II)   an appropriate regulatory authority;

(III)   a self-regulatory organization;

(IV)   a State attorney general in connection with any criminal investigation;

(V)   any appropriate State regulatory authority;

(VI)   the Public Company Accounting Oversight Board;

(VII)   a foreign securities authority; and

(VIII) a foreign law enforcement authority.

(ii)(I)   Each of the entities described in subclauses (I) through (VI) of clause (i) shall maintain such information as confidential in accordance with the requirements established under subparagraph (A).

(II)   Each of the entities described in subclauses (VII) and (VIII) of clause (i) shall maintain such information in accordance with such assurances of confidentiality as the Commission determines appropriate.

(3)   Rights retained.—

Nothing in this section shall be deemed to diminish the rights, privileges, or remedies of any whistleblower under any Federal or State law, or under any collective bargaining agreement.

(i)   Provision of False Information.—

A whistleblower shall not be entitled to an award under this section if the whistleblower (1) knowingly and willfully makes any false, fictitious, or fraudulent statement or representation; or (2) uses any false writing or document knowing the writing or document contains any false, fictitious, or fraudulent statement or entry.

(j)   Rulemaking authority.—

The Commission shall have the authority to issue such rules and regulations as may be necessary or appropriate to implement the provisions of this section consistent with the purposes of this section.

Hearings by Commission

Sec. 22.   Hearings may be public and may be held before the Commission, any member or members thereof, or any officer or officers of the Commission designated by it, and appropriate records thereof shall be kept.

Rules, Regulations, and Orders; Annual Reports

Sec. 23.   (a)(1)   The Commission, the Board of Governors of the Federal Reserve System, and the other agencies enumerated in section 3(a)(34) of this Act shall each have power to make such rules and regulations as may be necessary or appropriate to implement the provisions of this act for which they are responsible or for the execution of the functions vested in them by this Act, and may for such purposes classify persons, securities, transactions, statements, applications, reports, and other matters within their respective jurisdictions, and prescribe greater, lesser, or different requirements for different classes thereof. No provision of this Act imposing any liability shall apply to any act done or omitted in good faith in conformity with a rule, regulation, or order of the Commission, the Board of Governors of the Federal Reserve System, other agency enumerated in section 3(a)(34) of this Act, or any self-regulatory organization, notwithstanding that such rule, regulation, or order may thereafter be amended or rescinded or determined by judicial or other authority to be invalid for any reason.

(2)   The Commission and the Secretary of the Treasury, in making rules and regulations pursuant to any provisions of this Act, shall consider among other matters the impact any such rule or regulation would have on competition. The Commission and the Secretary of the Treasury shall not adopt any such rule or regulation which would impose a burden on competition not necessary or appropriate in furtherance of the purposes of this Act. The Commission and the Secretary of the Treasury shall include in the statement of basis and purpose incorporated in any rule or regulation adopted under this Act, the reasons for the Commission's or the Secretary's determination that any

burden on competition imposed by such rule or regulation is necessary or appropriate in furtherance of the purposes of this Act.

(3)   The Commission and the Secretary, in making rules and regulations pursuant to any provision of this Act, considering any application for registration in accordance with section 19(a) of this Act, or reviewing any proposed rule change of a self-regulatory organization in accordance with section 19(b) of this Act, shall keep in a public file and make available for copying all written statements filed with the Commission and the Secretary and all written communications between the Commission or the Secretary and any person relating to the proposed rule, regulation, application, or proposed rule change; *Provided, however,* That the Commission and the Secretary shall not be required to keep in a public file or make available for copying any such statement or communication which it may withhold from the public in accordance with the provisions of section 552 of Title 5, United States Code.

(b)(1)   The Commission, the Board of Governors of the Federal Reserve System, and the other agencies enumerated in section 3(a)(34) of this Act, shall each make an annual report to the Congress on its work for the preceding year, and shall include in each such report whatever information, data, and recommendations for further legislation it considers advisable with regard to matters within its respective jurisdiction under this Act.

(2)   The appropriate regulatory agency for a self-regulatory organization shall include in its annual report to the Congress for each fiscal year, a summary of its oversight activities under this Act with respect to such self-regulatory organization, including a description of any examination conducted as part of such activities of any such organization, any material recommendation presented as part of such activities to such organization for changes in its organization or rules, and any action by such organization in response to any such recommendation.

(3)   The appropriate regulatory agency for any class of municipal securities dealers shall include in its annual report to the Congress for each fiscal year a summary of its regulatory activities pursuant to this Act with respect to such municipal securities dealers, including the nature of and reason for any sanction imposed pursuant to this Act against any such municipal securities dealer.

(4)   The Commission shall also include in its annual report to the Congress for each fiscal year—

(A)   a summary of the Commission's oversight activities with respect to self-regulatory organizations for which it is not the appropriate regulatory agency, including a description of any examination of any such organization, any material recommendation presented to any such organization for changes in its organization or rules, and any action by any such organization in response to any such recommendations;

(B)   a statement and analysis of the expenses and operations of each self-regulatory organization in connection with the performance of its responsibilities under this Act, for which purpose data pertaining to such expenses and operations shall be made available by such organization to the Commission at its request;

(C)   the steps the Commission has taken and the progress it has made toward ending the physical movement of the securities certificate in connection with the settlement of securities transactions, and its recommendations, if any, for legislation to eliminate the securities certificate;

(D)   the number of requests for exemptions from provisions of this Act received, the number granted, and the basis upon which any such exemption was granted;

(E)   a summary of the Commission's regulatory activities with respect to municipal securities dealers for which it is not the appropriate regulatory agency, including the number and nature of, and reason for, any sanction imposed in proceedings against such municipal securities dealers;

(F)   a statement of the time elapsed between the filing of reports pursuant to section 13(f) of this Act and the public availability of the information contained therein, the costs involved in the Commission's processing of such reports and tabulating such information, the manner in which the Commission uses such information, and the steps the Commission has taken and the progress it has made toward requiring such reports to be filed and such information to be made available to the public in machine language;

    (G) information concerning

        (i) the effects its rules and regulations are having on the viability of small brokers and dealers;

        (ii) its attempts to reduce any unnecessary reporting burden on such brokers and dealers; and

        (iii) its efforts to help to assure the continued participation of small brokers and dealers in the United States securities markets;

    (H) a statement detailing its administration of the Freedom of Information Act, section 552 of Title 5, United States Code, including a copy of the report filed pursuant to subsection (d) of such section; and

    (I) the steps that have been taken and the progress that has been made in promoting the timely public dissemination and availability for analytical purposes (on a fair, reasonable, and nondiscriminatory basis) of information concerning government securities transactions and quotations, and its recommendations, if any, for legislation to assure timely dissemination of

        (i) information on transactions in regularly traded government securities sufficient to permit the determination of the prevailing market price for such securities, and

        (ii) reports of the highest published bids and lowest published offers for government securities (including the size at which persons are willing to trade with respect to such bids and offers).

    (c) The Commission, by rule, shall prescribe the procedure applicable to every case pursuant to this Act of adjudication (as defined in section 551 of Title 5, United States Code) not required to be determined on the record after notice and opportunity for hearing. Such rules shall, as a minimum, provide that prompt notice shall be given of any adverse action or final disposition and that such notice and the entry of any order shall be accompanied by a statement of written reasons.

    (d) Cease-And-Desist Procedures

Within 1 year after the date of enactment of this subsection, the Commission shall establish regulations providing for the expeditious conduct of hearings and rendering of decisions under section the 21C of this Act, section 8A of the Securities Act of 1933, section 9(f) of the Investment Company Act of 1940, and section 203(k) of the Investment Advisers Act of 1940.

Public Availability of Information

    Sec. 24. (a) For purposes of section 552 of Title 5, United States Code, the term "records" includes all applications, statements, reports, contracts, correspondence, notices, and other documents filed with or otherwise obtained by the Commission pursuant to this Act or otherwise.

    (b) It shall be unlawful for any member, officer, or employee of the Commission to disclose to any person other than a member, officer, or employee of the Commission, or to use for personal benefit, any information contained in any application, statement, report, contract, correspondence, notice, or other document filed with or otherwise obtained by the Commission

    (1) in contravention of the rules and regulations of the Commission under section 552 of Title 5, United States Code, or

    (2) in circumstances where the Commission has determined pursuant to such rules to accord confidential treatment to such information.

    (c) Confidential Disclosures.—

The Commission may, in its discretion and upon a showing that such information is needed, provide all "records" (as defined in subsection (a)) and other information in its possession to such persons, both domestic and foreign, as the Commission by rule deems appropriate if the person receiving such records or information provides such assurances of confidentiality as the Commission deems appropriate.

(d)   Records Obtained From Foreign Securities Authorities.—

Except as provided in subsection (g), the Commission shall not be compelled to disclose records obtained from a foreign securities authority if

(1)   the foreign securities authority has in good faith determined and represented to the Commission that public disclosure of such records would violate the laws applicable to that foreign securities authority, and

(2)   the Commission obtains such records pursuant to

(A)   such procedure as the Commission may authorize for use in connection with the administration or enforcement of the securities laws, or

(B)   a memorandum of understanding. For purposes of section 552 of Title 5, United States Code, this subsection shall be considered a statute described in subsection (b)(3)(B) of such section 552.

(e)   Freedom of Information Act.—

For purposes of section 552(b)(8) of Title 5, (commonly referred to as the Freedom of Information Act)—

(1)   the Commission is an agency responsible for the regulation or supervision of financial institutions; and

(2)   any entity for which the Commission is responsible for regulating, supervising, or examining under this title is a financial institution.

(f)   Sharing privileged information with other authorities.—

(1)   Privileged information provided by the commission.—The Commission shall not be deemed to have waived any privilege applicable to any information by transferring that information to or permitting that information to be used by—

(A)   any agency (as defined in section 6 of title 18, United States Code);

(B)   the Public Company Accounting Oversight Board;

(C)   any self-regulatory organization;

(D)   any foreign securities authority;

(E)   any foreign law enforcement authority; or

(F)   any State securities or law enforcement authority.

(2)   Nondisclosure of privileged information provided to the commission.—The Commission shall not be compelled to disclose privileged information obtained from any foreign securities authority, or foreign law enforcement authority, if the authority has in good faith determined and represented to the Commission that the information is privileged.

(3)   Nonwaiver of privileged information provided to the commission.—

(A)   In general.—Federal agencies, State securities and law enforcement authorities, self-regulatory organizations, and the Public Company Accounting Oversight Board shall not be deemed to have waived any privilege applicable to any information by transferring that information to or permitting that information to be used by the Commission.

(B)   Exception.—The provisions of subparagraph (A) shall not apply to a self-regulatory organization or the Public Company Accounting Oversight Board with respect to information used by the Commission in an action against such organization.

(4)   Definitions.—For purposes of this subsection—

(A)   the term "privilege" includes any work-product privilege, attorney-client privilege, governmental privilege, or other privilege recognized under Federal, State, or foreign law;

(B)   the term "foreign law enforcement authority" means any foreign authority that is empowered under foreign law to detect, investigate or prosecute potential violations of law; and

(C) the term "State securities or law enforcement authority" means the authority of any State or territory that is empowered under State or territory law to detect, investigate, or prosecute potential violations of law.

(g) Savings Provisions.—

(1) alter the Commission's responsibilities under the Right to Financial Privacy Act, as limited by section 21(h) of this Act, with respect to transfers of records covered by such statutes, or

(2) authorize the Commission to withhold information from the Congress or prevent the Commission from complying with an order of a court of the United States in an action commenced by the United States or the Commission.

Court Review of Orders and Rules

Sec. 25. (a)(1) A person aggrieved by a final order of the Commission entered pursuant to this Act may obtain review of the order in the United States Court of Appeals for the circuit in which he resides or has his principal place of business, or for the District of Columbia Circuit, by filing in such court, within sixty days after the entry of the order, a written petition requesting that the order be modified or set aside in whole or in part.

(2) A copy of the petition shall be transmitted forthwith by the clerk of the court to a member of the Commission or an officer designated by the Commission for that purpose. Thereupon the Commission shall file in the court the record on which the order complained of is entered, as provided in section 2112 of Title 28, United States Code, and the Federal Rules of Appellate Procedure.

(3) On the filing of the petition, the court has jurisdiction, which becomes exclusive on the filing of the record, to affirm or modify and enforce or to set aside the order in whole or in part.

(4) The findings of the Commission as to the facts, if supported by substantial evidence, are conclusive.

(5) If either party applies to the court for leave to adduce additional evidence and shows to the satisfaction of the court that the additional evidence is material and that there was reasonable ground for failure to adduce it before the Commission, the court may remand the case to the Commission for further proceedings, in whatever manner and on whatever conditions the court considers appropriate. If the case is remanded to the Commission, it shall file in the court a supplemental record containing any new evidence, any further or modified findings, and any new order.

(b)(1) A person adversely affected by a rule of the Commission promulgated pursuant to section 6, 9(h)(2), 11, 11A, 15(c)(5) or (6), 15A, 17, 17A, or 19 of this Act may obtain review of this rule in the United States Court of Appeals for the circuit in which he resides or has his principal place of business or for the District of Columbia Circuit, by filing in such court, within sixty days after the promulgation of the rule, a written petition requesting that the rule be set aside.

(2) A copy of the petition shall be transmitted forthwith by the clerk of the court to a member of the Commission or an officer designated for that purpose. Thereupon, the Commission shall file in the court the rule under review and any documents referred to therein, the Commission's notice of proposed rulemaking and any documents referred to therein, all written submissions and the transcript of any oral presentations in the rulemaking, factual information not included in the foregoing that was considered by the Commission in the promulgation of the rule or proffered by the Commission as pertinent to the rule, the report of any advisory committee received or considered by the Commission in the rulemaking, and any other materials prescribed by the court.

(3) On the filing of the petition, the court has jurisdiction, which becomes exclusive on the filing of the materials set forth in paragraph (2) of this subsection, to affirm and enforce or to set aside the rule.

(4) The findings of the Commission as to the facts identified by the Commission as the basis, in whole or in part, of the rule, if supported by substantial evidence, are conclusive. The court shall affirm and enforce the rule unless the Commission's action in promulgating the rule is found to be arbitrary, capricious, an abuse of discretion, or otherwise not in accordance with law; contrary to constitutional

right, power, privilege, or immunity; in excess of statutory jurisdiction, authority, or limitations, or short of statutory right; or without observance of procedure required by law.

(5)   If proceedings have been instituted under this subsection in two or more courts of appeals with respect to the same rule, the Commission shall file the materials set forth in paragraph (2) of this subsection in that court in which a proceeding was first instituted. The other courts shall thereupon transfer all such proceedings to the court in which the materials have been filed. For the convenience of the parties in the interest of justice that court may thereafter transfer all the proceedings to any other court of appeals.

(c)(1)   No objection to an order or rule of the Commission, for which review is sought under this section, may be considered by the court unless it was urged before the Commission or there was reasonable ground for failure to do so.

(2)   The filing of a petition under this section does not operate as a stay of the Commission's order or rule. Until the court's jurisdiction becomes exclusive, the Commission may stay its order or rule pending judicial review if it finds that justice so requires. After the filing of a petition under this section, the court, on whatever conditions may be required and to the extent necessary to prevent irreparable injury, may issue all necessary and appropriate process to stay the order or rule or to preserve status or rights pending its review; but (notwithstanding section 705 of Title 5, United States Code) no such process may be issued by the court before the filing of the record or the materials set forth in subsection (b)(2) of this section unless: (A) the Commission has denied a stay or failed to grant requested relief, (B) a reasonable period has expired since the filing of an application for a stay without a decision by the Commission, or (C) there was reasonable ground for failure to apply to the Commission.

(3)   When the same order or rule is the subject of one or more petitions for review filed under this section and an action for enforcement filed in a district court of the United States under section 21(d) or (e) of this Act, that court in which the petition or the action is first filed has jurisdiction with respect to the order or rule to the exclusion of any other court, and thereupon all such proceedings shall be transferred to that court; but, for the convenience of the parties in the interest of justice, that court may thereafter transfer all the proceedings to any other court of appeals or district court of the United States, whether or not a petition for review or an action for enforcement was originally filed in the transferee court. The scope of review by a district court under section 21(d) or (e) of this Act is in all cases the same as by a court of appeals under this section.

(d)(1)   For purposes of the preceding subsections of this section, the term "Commission" includes the agencies enumerated in section 3(a)(34) of this Act insofar as such agencies are acting pursuant to this Act and the Secretary of the Treasury insofar as he is acting pursuant to section 15C of this Act.

(2)   For purposes of subsection (a)(4) of this section and section 706 of Title 5, United States Code, an order of the Commission pursuant to section 19(a) of this Act denying registration to a clearing agency for which the Commission is not the appropriate regulatory agency or pursuant to section 19(b) of this Act disapproving a proposed rule change by such a clearing agency shall be deemed to be an order of the appropriate regulatory agency for such clearing agency insofar as such order was entered by reason of a determination by such appropriate regulatory agency pursuant to section 19(a)(2)(C) or 19(b)(4)(C) of this Act that such registration or proposed rule change would be inconsistent with the safeguarding of securities or funds.

Unlawful Representations

Sec. 26. No action or failure to act by the Commission or the Board of Governors of the Federal Reserve System, in the administration of this Act shall be construed to mean that the particular authority has in any way passed upon the merits of, or given approval to, any security or any transaction or transactions therein, nor shall such action or failure to act with regard to any statement or report filed with or examined by such authority pursuant to this Act or rules and regulations thereunder, be deemed a finding by such authority that such statement or report is true and accurate on its face or that it is not false or misleading. It shall be unlawful to make, or cause to be made, to any prospective purchaser or seller of a security any representation that any such action or failure to act by any such authority is to be so construed or has such effect.

Jurisdiction of Offenses and Suits

Sec. 27. (a) In General—The district courts of the United States and the United States courts of any Territory or other place subject to the jurisdiction of the United States shall have exclusive jurisdiction of violations of this Act or the rules and regulations thereunder, and of all suits in equity and actions at law brought to enforce any liability or duty created by this Act or the rules and regulations thereunder. Any criminal proceeding may be brought in the district wherein any act or transaction constituting the violation occurred. Any suit or action to enforce any liability or duty created by this Act or rules and regulations thereunder, or to enjoin any violation of such Act or rules and regulations, may be brought in any such district or in the district wherein the defendant is found or is an inhabitant or transacts business, and process in such cases may be served in any other district of which the defendant is an inhabitant or wherever the defendant may be found. In any action or proceeding instituted by the Commission under this title in a United States district court for any judicial district, a subpoena issued to compel the attendance of a witness or the production of documents or tangible things (or both) at a hearing or trial may be served at any place within the United States. Rule 45(c)(3)(A)(ii) of the Federal Rules of Civil Procedure shall not apply to a subpoena issued under the preceding sentence. Judgments and decrees so rendered shall be subject to review as provided in sections 1254, 1291, 1292, and 1294 of Title 28, United States Code. No costs shall be assessed for or against the Commission in any proceeding under this Act brought by or against it in the Supreme Court or such other courts.

(b) Extraterritorial Jurisdiction—The district courts of the United States and the United States courts of any Territory shall have jurisdiction of an action or proceeding brought or instituted by the Commission or the United States alleging a violation of the antifraud provisions of this title involving—

(1) conduct within the United States that constitutes significant steps in furtherance of the violation, even if the securities transaction occurs outside the United States and involves only foreign investors; or

(2) conduct occurring outside the United States that has a foreseeable substantial effect within the United States.

Effect on Existing Law

Sec. 28. (a) Limitation on Judgments.—

(1) In general.—No person permitted to maintain a suit for damages under the provisions of this title shall recover, through satisfaction of judgment in 1 or more actions, a total amount in excess of the actual damages to that person on account of the act complained of. Except as otherwise specifically provided in this title, nothing in this title shall affect the jurisdiction of the securities commission (or any agency or officer performing like functions) of any State over any security or any person insofar as it does not conflict with the provisions of this title or the rules and regulations under this title.

(2) Rule of construction.—Except as provided in subsection (f), the rights and remedies provided by this title shall be in addition to any and all other rights and remedies that may exist at law or in equity.

(3) State bucket shop laws.—No State law which prohibits or regulates the making or promoting of wagering or gaming contracts, or the operation of "bucket shops" or other similar or related activities, shall invalidate—

(A) any put, call, straddle, option, privilege, or other security subject to this title (except any security that has a pari-mutuel payout or otherwise is determined by the Commission, acting by rule, regulation, or order, to be appropriately subject to such laws), or apply to any activity which is incidental or related to the offer, purchase, sale, exercise, settlement, or closeout of any such security;

(B) any security-based swap between eligible contract participants; or

(C) any security-based swap effected on a national securities exchange registered pursuant to section 6(b).

(4)   Other state provisions.—No provision of State law regarding the offer, sale, or distribution of securities shall apply to any transaction in a security-based swap or a security futures product, except that this paragraph may not be construed as limiting any State antifraud law of general applicability. A security-based swap may not be regulated as an insurance contract under any provision of State law.

(b)   Nothing in this Act shall be construed to modify existing law with regard to the binding effect

(1)   on any member of or participant in any self-regulatory organization of any action taken by the authorities of such organization to settle disputes between its members or participants,

(2)   on any municipal securities dealer or municipal securities broker of any action taken pursuant to a procedure established by the Municipal Securities Rulemaking Board to settle disputes between municipal securities dealers and municipal securities brokers, or

(3)   of any action described in paragraph (1) or (2) on any person who has agreed to be bound thereby.

(c)   The stay, setting aside, or modification pursuant to section 19(e) of this Act of any disciplinary sanction imposed by a self-regulatory organization on a member thereof, person associated with a member, or participant therein, shall not affect the validity or force of any action taken as a result of such sanction by the self-regulatory organization prior to such stay, setting aside, or modification: *Provided,* That such action is not inconsistent with the provisions of this Act or the rules or regulations thereunder. The rights of any person acting in good faith which arise out of any such action shall not be affected in any way by such stay, setting aside, or modification.

(d)   No State or political subdivision thereof shall impose any tax on any change in beneficial or record ownership of securities effected through the facilities of a registered clearing agency or registered transfer agent or any nominee thereof or custodian therefor or upon the delivery or transfer of securities to or through or receipt from such agency or agent or any nominee thereof or custodian therefor, unless such change in beneficial or record ownership or such transfer or delivery or receipt would otherwise be taxable by such State or political subdivision if the facilities of such registered clearing agency, registered transfer agent, or any nominee thereof or custodian therefor were not physically located in the taxing State or political subdivision. No State or political subdivision thereof shall impose any tax on securities which are deposited in or retained by a registered clearing agency, registered transfer agent, or any nominee thereof or custodian therefor, unless such securities would otherwise be taxable by such State or political subdivision if the facilities of such registered clearing agency, registered transfer agent, or any nominee thereof or custodian therefor were not physically located in the taxing State or political subdivision.

(e)(1)   No person using the mails, or any means or instrumentality of interstate commerce, in the exercise of investment discretion with respect to an account shall be deemed to have acted unlawfully or to have breached a fiduciary duty under State or Federal law unless expressly provided to the contrary by a law enacted by the Congress or any State subsequent to June 4, 1975, solely by reason of his having caused the account to pay a member of an exchange, broker, or dealer an amount of commission for effecting a securities transaction in excess of the amount of commission another member of an exchange, broker, or dealer would have charged for effecting that transaction, if such person determined in good faith that such amount of commission was reasonable in relation to the value of the brokerage and research services provided by such member, broker, or dealer, viewed in terms of either that particular transaction or his overall responsibilities with respect to the accounts as to which he exercises investment discretion. This subsection is exclusive and plenary insofar as conduct is covered by the foregoing, unless otherwise expressly provided by contract: *Provided, however,* That nothing in this subsection shall be construed to impair or limit the power of the Commission under any other provision of this Act or otherwise.

(2)   A person exercising investment discretion with respect to an account shall make such disclosure of his policies and practices with respect to commissions that will be paid for effecting securities transactions, at such times and in such manner, as the appropriate regulatory agency, by rule, may prescribe as necessary or appropriate in the public interest or for the protection of investors.

(3)   For purposes of this subsection a person provides brokerage and research services insofar as he—

(A) furnishes advice, either directly or through publications or writings, as to the value of securities, the advisability of investing in, purchasing, or selling securities, and the availability of securities or purchasers or sellers of securities;

(B) furnishes analyses and reports concerning issuers, industries, securities, economic factors and trends, portfolio strategy, and the performance of accounts; or

(C) effects securities transactions and performs functions incidental thereto (such as clearance, settlement, and custody) or required in connection therewith by rules of the Commission or a self-regulatory organization of which such person is a member or person associated with a member or in which such person is a participant.

(4) The provisions of this Rule shall not apply with regard to securities that are security futures products.

(f) Limitations on remedies.—

(1) Class action limitations.—

No covered class action based upon the statutory or common law of any State or subdivision thereof may be maintained in any State or Federal court by any private party alleging—

(A) a misrepresentation or omission of a material fact in connection with the purchase or sale of a covered security; or

(B) that the defendant used or employed any manipulative or deceptive device or contrivance in connection with the purchase or sale of a covered security.

(2) Removal of covered class actions.—

Any covered class action brought in any State court involving a covered security, as set forth in paragraph (1), shall be removable to the Federal district court for the district in which the action is pending, and shall be subject to paragraph (1).

(3) Preservations of certain actions.—

(A) Actions under state law of state of incorporation.—

(i) Actions preserved.—

Notwithstanding paragraph (1) or (2), a covered class action described in clause (ii) of this subparagraph that is based upon the statutory or common law of the State in which the issuer is incorporated (in the case of a corporation) or organized (in the case of any other entity) may be maintained in a State or Federal court by a private party.

(ii) Permissible actions.—

A covered class action is described in this clause if it involves—

(I) the purchase or sale of securities by the issuer or an affiliate of the issuer exclusively from or to holders of equity securities of the issuer; or

(II) any recommendation, position, or other communication with respect to the sale of securities of an issuer that—

(aa) is made by or on behalf of the issuer or an affiliate of the issuer to holders of equity securities of the issuer; and

(bb) concerns decisions of such equity holders with respect to voting their securities, acting in response to a tender or exchange offer, or exercising dissenters' or appraisal rights.

(B) State actions.—

(i) In general.—

Notwithstanding any other provision of this subsection, nothing in this subsection may be construed to preclude a State or political subdivision thereof or a State pension plan from bringing an action involving a covered security on its own behalf, or as a member of a class comprised solely of other States, political subdivisions, or State pension plans that are named plaintiffs, and that have authorized participation, in such action.

(ii)   State pension plan defined.—

For purposes of this subparagraph, the term "State pension plan" means a pension plan established and maintained for its employees by the government of a State or political subdivision thereof, or by any agency or instrumentality thereof.

(C)   Actions under contractual agreements between issuers and indenture trustees.—

Notwithstanding paragraph (1) or (2), a covered class action that seeks to enforce a contractual agreement between an issuer and an indenture trustee may be maintained in a State or Federal court by a party to the agreement or a successor to such party.

(D)   Remand of removed actions.—

In an action that has been removed from a State court pursuant to paragraph (2), if the Federal court determines that the action may be maintained in State court pursuant to this subsection, the Federal court shall remand such action to such State court.

(4)   Preservation of state jurisdiction.—

The securities commission (or any agency or office performing like functions) of any State shall retain jurisdiction under the laws of such State to investigate and bring enforcement actions.

(5)   Definitions.—

For purposes of this subsection, the following definitions shall apply:

(A)   Affiliate of the issuer.—

The term "affiliate of the issuer" means a person that directly or indirectly, through one or more intermediaries, controls or is controlled by or is under common control with, the issuer.

(B)   Covered class action.—

The term "covered class action" means—

(i)   any single lawsuit in which—

(I)   damages are sought on behalf of more than 50 persons or prospective class members, and questions of law or fact common to those persons or members of the prospective class, without reference to issues of individualized reliance on an alleged misstatement or omission, predominate over any questions affecting only individual persons or members; or

(II)   one or more named parties seek to recover damages on a representative basis on behalf of themselves and other unnamed parties similarly situated, and questions of law or fact common to those persons or members of the prospective class predominate over any questions affecting only individual persons or members; or

(ii)   any group of lawsuits filed in or pending in the same court and involving common questions of law or fact, in which—

(I)   damages are sought on behalf of more than 50 persons; and

(II)   the lawsuits are joined, consolidated, or otherwise proceed as a single action for any purpose.

(C)   Exception for derivative actions.—

Notwithstanding subparagraph (B), the term "covered class action" does not include an exclusively derivative action brought by one or more shareholders on behalf of a corporation.

(D)   Counting of certain class members.—

For purposes of this paragraph, a corporation, investment company, pension plan, partnership, or other entity, shall be treated as one person or prospective class member, but only if the entity is not established for the purpose of participating in the action.

(E) Covered security.—

The term "covered security" means a security that satisfies the standards for a covered security specified in paragraph (1) or (2) of section 18(b) of the Securities Act of 1933, at the time during which it is alleged that the misrepresentation, omission, or manipulative or deceptive conduct occurred, except that such term shall not include any debt security that is exempt from registration under the Securities Act of 1933 pursuant to rules issued by the Commission under section 4(2) of this Act.

(F) Rule of construction.—

Nothing in this paragraph shall be construed to affect the discretion of a State court in determining whether actions filed in such court should be joined, consolidated, or otherwise allowed to proceed as a single action.

Validity of Contracts

Sec. 29. (a) Any condition, stipulation, or provision binding any person to waive compliance with any provision of this Act or of any rule or regulation thereunder, or of any rule of a self-regulatory organization, shall be void.

(b) Every contract made in violation of any provision of this Act or of any rule or regulation thereunder, and every contract (including any contract for listing a security on an exchange) heretofore or hereafter made, the performance of which involves the violation of, or the continuance of any relationship or practice in violation of, any provision of this Act or any rule or regulation thereunder, shall be void

(1) as regards the rights of any person who, in violation of any such provision, rule, or regulation, shall have made or engaged in the performance of any such contract, and

(2) as regards the rights of any person who, not being a party to such contract, shall have acquired any right thereunder with actual knowledge of the facts by reason of which the making or performance of such contract was in violation of any such provision, rule, or regulation:

Provided,

(A) That no contract shall be void by reason of this subsection because of any violation of any rule or regulation prescribed pursuant to paragraph (3) of subsection (c) of section 15 of this Act, and

(B) that no contract shall be deemed to be void by reason of this subsection in any action maintained in reliance upon this subsection, by any person to or for whom any broker or dealer sells, or from or for whom any broker or dealer purchases, a security in violation of any rule or regulation prescribed pursuant to paragraph (1) or (2) of subsection (c) of section 15 of this Act, unless such action is brought within one year after the discovery that such sale or purchase involves such violation and within three years after such violation. The Commission may, in a rule or regulation prescribed pursuant to such paragraph (2) of such section 15(c), designate such rule or regulation, or portion thereof, as a rule or regulation, or portion thereof, a contract in violation of which shall not be void by reason of this subsection.

(c) Nothing in this Act shall be construed

(1) to affect the validity of any loan or extension of credit (or any extension or renewal thereof) made or of any lien created prior or subsequent to the enactment of this Act, unless at the time of the making of such loan or extension of credit (or extension or renewal thereof) or the creating of such lien, the person making such loan or extension of credit (or extension or renewal thereof) or acquiring such lien shall have actual knowledge of facts by reason of which the making of such loan or extension of credit (or extension or renewal thereof) or the acquisition of such lien is a violation of the provisions of this Act or any rule or regulation thereunder, or

(2) to afford a defense to the collection of any debt or obligation or the enforcement of any lien by any person who shall have acquired such debt, obligation, or lien in good faith for value and without

actual knowledge of the violation of any provision of this Act or any rule or regulation thereunder affecting the legality of such debt, obligation, or lien.

Foreign Securities Exchanges

Sec. 30. (a) It shall be unlawful for any broker or dealer, directly or indirectly, to make use of the mails or of any means or instrumentality of interstate commerce for the purpose of effecting on an exchange not within or subject to the jurisdiction of the United States, any transaction in any security the issuer of which is a resident of, or is organized under the laws of, or has its principal place of business in, a place within or subject to the jurisdiction of the United States, in contravention of such rules and regulations as the Commission may prescribe as necessary or appropriate in the public interest or for the protection of investors or to prevent the evasion of this Act.

(b) The provisions of this Act or of any rule or regulation thereunder shall not apply to any person insofar as he transacts a business in securities without the jurisdiction of the United States, unless he transacts such business in contravention of such rules and regulations as the Commission may prescribe as necessary or appropriate to prevent the evasion of this Act.

(c) Rule of Construction—No provision of this title that was added by the Wall Street Transparency and Accountability Act of 2010, or any rule or regulation thereunder, shall apply to any person insofar as such person transacts a business in security-based swaps without the jurisdiction of the United States, unless such person transacts such business in contravention of such rules and regulations as the Commission may prescribe as necessary or appropriate to prevent the evasion of any provision of this title that was added by the Wall Street Transparency and Accountability Act of 2010. This subsection shall not be construed to limit the jurisdiction of the Commission under any provision of this title, as in effect prior to the date of enactment of the Wall Street Transparency and Accountability Act of 2010.

Prohibited Foreign Trade Practices by Issuers—FRCP § 104

Sec. 30A. (a) Prohibition.—

It shall be unlawful for any issuer which has a class of securities registered pursuant to section 12 of this Act or which is required to file reports under section 15(d) of this Act, or for any officer, director, employee, or agent of such issuer or any stockholder thereof acting on behalf of such issuer, to make use of the mails or any means or instrumentality of interstate commerce corruptly in furtherance of an offer, payment, promise to pay, or authorization of the payment of any money, or offer, gift, promise to give, or authorization of the giving of anything of value to—

  (1) any foreign official for purposes of—

    (A)(i) influencing any act or decision of such foreign official in his official capacity, or

    (ii) inducing such foreign official to do or omit to do any act in violation of the lawful duty of such official, or

    (iii) securing any improper advantage; or

    (B) inducing such foreign official to use his influence with a foreign government or instrumentality thereof to affect or influence any act or decision of such government or instrumentality,

in order to assist such issuer in obtaining or retaining business for or with, or directing business to, any person;

  (2) any foreign political party or official thereof or any candidate for foreign political office for purposes of—

    (A)(i) influencing any act or decision of such party, official, or candidate in its or his official capacity, or

    (ii) inducing such party, official, or candidate to do or omit to do an act in violation of the lawful duty of such party, official, or candidate, or

    (iii) securing any improper advantage; or

(B) inducing such party, official, or candidate to use its or his influence with a foreign government or instrumentality thereof to affect or influence any act or decision of such government or instrumentality,

in order to assist such issuer in obtaining or retaining business for or with, or directing business to, any person; or

(3) any person, while knowing that all or a portion of such money or thing of value will be offered, given, or promised, directly or indirectly, to any foreign official, to any foreign political party or official thereof, or to any candidate for foreign political office, for purposes of—

(A)(i) influencing any act or decision of such foreign official, political party, party official, or candidate in his or its official capacity, or

(ii) inducing such foreign official, political party, party official, or candidate to do or omit to do any act in violation of the lawful duty of such foreign official, political party, party official, or candidate, or

(iii) securing any improper advantage; or

(B) inducing such foreign official, political party, party official, or candidate to use his or its influence with a foreign government or instrumentality thereof to affect or influence any act or decision of such government or instrumentality,

in order to assist such issuer in obtaining or retaining business for or with, or directing business to, any person.

(b) Exception for Routine Governmental Action.—

Subsection (a) and (g) shall not apply to any facilitating or expediting payment to a foreign official, political party, or party official the purpose of which is to expedite or to secure the performance of a routine governmental action by a foreign official, political party, or party official.

(c) Affirmative Defenses.—

It shall be an affirmative defense to actions under subsection (a) or (g) that—

(1) the payment, gift, offer, or promise of anything of value that was made, was lawful under the written laws and regulations of the foreign official's, political party's, party official's, or candidate's country; or

(2) the payment, gift, offer, or promise of anything of value that was made, was a reasonable and bona fide expenditure, such as travel and lodging expenses, incurred by or on behalf of a foreign official, party, party official, or candidate and was directly related to—

(A) the promotion, demonstration, or explanation of products or services; or

(B) the execution or performance of a contract with a foreign government or agency thereof.

(d) Guidelines by the Attorney General.—

Not later than one year after the date of the enactment of the Foreign Corrupt Practices Act Amendments of 1988, the Attorney General, after consultation with the Commission, the Secretary of Commerce, the United States Trade Representative, the Secretary of State, and the Secretary of the Treasury, and after obtaining the views of all interested persons through public notice and comment procedures, shall determine to what extent compliance with this section would be enhanced and the business community would be assisted by further clarification of the preceding provisions of this section and may, based on such determination and to the extent necessary and appropriate, issue—

(1) guidelines describing specific types of conduct, associated with common types of export sales arrangements and business contracts, which for purposes of the Department of Justice's present enforcement policy, the Attorney General determines would be in conformance with the preceding provisions of this section; and

(2) general precautionary procedures which issuers may use on a voluntary basis to conform their conduct to the Department of Justice's present enforcement policy regarding the preceding provisions of this section.

The Attorney General shall issue the guidelines and procedures referred to in the preceding sentence in accordance with the provisions of subchapter II of chapter 5 of Title 5, United States Code, and those guidelines and procedures shall be subject to the provisions of chapter 7 of that Title.

(e)   Opinions of the Attorney General.—

(1)   The Attorney General, after consultation with appropriate departments and agencies of the United States and after obtaining the views of all interested persons through public notice and comment procedures, shall establish a procedure to provide responses to specific inquiries by issuers concerning conformance of their conduct with the Department of Justice's present enforcement policy regarding the preceding provisions of this section. The Attorney General shall, within 30 days after receiving such a request, issue an opinion in response to that request. The opinion shall state whether or not certain specified prospective conduct would, for purposes of the Department of Justice's present enforcement policy, violate the preceding provisions of this section. Additional requests for opinions may be filed with the Attorney General regarding other specified prospective conduct that is beyond the scope of conduct specified in previous requests. In any action brought under the applicable provisions of this section, there shall be a rebuttable presumption that conduct, which is specified in a request by an issuer and for which the Attorney General has issued an opinion that such conduct is in conformity with the Department of Justice's present enforcement policy, is in compliance with the preceding provisions of this section. Such a presumption may be rebutted by a preponderance of the evidence. In considering the presumption for purposes of this paragraph, a court shall weigh all relevant factors, including but not limited to whether the information submitted to the Attorney General was accurate and complete and whether it was within the scope of the conduct specified in any request received by the Attorney General. The Attorney General shall establish the procedures required by this paragraph in accordance with the provisions of subchapter II of chapter 5 of Title 5, United States Code, and that procedure shall be subject to the provisions of chapter 7 of that Title.

(2)   Any document or other material which is provided to, received by, or prepared in the Department of Justice or any other department or agency of the United States in connection with a request by an issuer under the procedure established under paragraph (1), shall be exempt from disclosure under section 552 of Title 5, United States Code, and shall not, except with the consent of the issuer, be made publicly available, regardless of whether the Attorney General responds to such a request or the issuer withdraws such request before receiving a response.

(3)   Any issuer who has made a request to the Attorney General under paragraph (1) may withdraw such request prior to the time the Attorney General issues an opinion in response to such request. Any request so withdrawn shall have no force or effect.

(4)   The Attorney General shall, to the maximum extent practicable, provide timely guidance concerning the Department of Justice's present enforcement policy with respect to the preceding provisions of this section to potential exporters and small businesses that are unable to obtain specialized counsel on issues pertaining to such provisions. Such guidance shall be limited to responses to requests under paragraph (1) concerning conformity of specified prospective conduct with the Department of Justice's present enforcement policy regarding the preceding provisions of this section and general explanations of compliance responsibilities and of potential liabilities under the preceding provisions of this section.

(f)   Definitions.—

For purposes of this section:

(1)(A)   The term "foreign official" means any officer or employee of a foreign government or any department, agency, or instrumentality thereof, or of a public international organization, or any person acting in an official capacity for or on behalf of any such government or department, agency, or instrumentality, or for or on behalf of any such public international organization.

(B)   For purposes of subparagraph (A), the term "public international organization" means—

(i)   an organization that is designated by Executive order pursuant to section 1 of the International Organizations Immunities Act; or

    (ii)   any other international organization that is designated by the President by Executive order for the purposes of this section, effective as of the date of publication of such order in the Federal Register.

    (2)(A)   A person's state of mind is "knowing" with respect to conduct, a circumstance, or a result if—

    (i)   such person is aware that such person is engaging in such conduct, that such circumstance exists, or that such result is substantially certain to occur; or

    (ii)   such person has a firm belief that such circumstance exists or that such result is substantially certain to occur.

    (B)   When knowledge of the existence of a particular circumstance is required for an offense, such knowledge is established if a person is aware of a high probability of the existence of such circumstance, unless the person actually believes that such circumstance does not exist.

    (3)(A)   The term "routine governmental action" means only an action which is ordinarily and commonly performed by a foreign official in—

    (i)   obtaining permits, licenses, or other official documents to qualify a person to do business in a foreign country;

    (ii)   processing governmental papers, such as visas and work orders;

    (iii)   providing police protection, mail pick-up and delivery, or scheduling inspections associated with contract performance or inspections related to transit of goods across country;

    (iv)   providing phone service, power and water supply, loading and unloading cargo, or protecting perishable products or commodities from deterioration; or

    (v)   actions of a similar nature.

    (B)   The term "routine governmental action" does not include any decision by a foreign official whether, or on what terms, to award new business to or to continue business with a particular party, or any action taken by a foreign official involved in the decisionmaking process to encourage a decision to award new business to or continue business with a particular party.

(g)   Alternative Jurisdiction.—

    (1)   It shall also be unlawful for any issuer organized under the laws of the United States, or a State, territory, possession, or commonwealth of the United States or a political subdivision thereof and which has a class of securities registered pursuant to section 12 of this Act or which is required to file reports under section 15(d) of this Act, or for any United States person that is an officer, director, employee, or agent of such issuer or a stockholder thereof acting on behalf of such issuer, to corruptly do any act outside the United States in furtherance of an offer, payment, promise to pay, or authorization of the payment of any money, or offer, gift, promise to give, or authorization of the giving of anything of value to any of the persons or entities set forth in paragraphs (1), (2), and (3) of subsection (a) of this section for the purposes set forth therein, irrespective of whether such issuer or such officer, director, employee, agent, or stockholder makes use of the mails or any means or instrumentality of interstate commerce in furtherance of such offer, gift, payment, promise, or authorization.

    (2)   As used in this subsection, the term "United States person" means a national of the United States (as defined in section 101 of the Immigration and Nationality Act) or any corporation, partnership, association, joint-stock company, business trust, unincorporated organization, or sole proprietorship organized under the laws of the United States or any State, territory, possession, or commonwealth of the United States, or any political subdivision thereof.

Prohibited Foreign Trade Practices by Domestic Concerns—FRCP § 103(a)

    Sec. 30B.   (a)   Prohibition.—It shall be unlawful for any domestic concern, other than an issuer which is subject to section 30A of this Act, or for any officer, director, employee, or agent of such domestic concern or any stockholder thereof acting on behalf of such domestic concern, to make use of the mails or any means or instrumentality of interstate commerce corruptly in furtherance of an offer, payment, promise to pay, or authorization of the payment of any money, or offer, gift, promise to give, or authorization of the giving of anything of value to—

(1)   any foreign official for purposes of—

(A)(i)   influencing any act or decision of such foreign official in his official capacity, (ii) inducing such foreign official to do or omit to do any act in violation of the lawful duty of such official, or (iii) securing any improper advantage; or

(B)   inducing such foreign official to use his influence with a foreign government or instrumentality thereof to affect or influence any act or decision of such government or instrumentality,

in order to assist such domestic concern in obtaining or retaining business for or with, or directing business to, any person;

(2)   any foreign political party or official thereof or any candidate for foreign political office for purposes of—

(A)(i)   influencing any act or decision of such party, official, or candidate in its or his official capacity, (ii) inducing such party, official, or candidate to do or omit to do an act in violation of the lawful duty of such party, official, or candidate, or (iii) securing any improper advantage; or

(B)   inducing such party, official, or candidate to use its or his influence with a foreign government or instrumentality thereof to affect or influence any act or decision of such government or instrumentality,

in order to assist such domestic concern in obtaining or retaining business for or with, or directing business to, any person; or

(3)   any person, while knowing that all or a portion of such money or thing of value will be offered, given, or promised, directly or indirectly, to any foreign official, to any foreign political party or official thereof, or to any candidate for foreign political office, for purposes of—

(A)(i)   influencing any act or decision of such foreign official, political party, party official, or candidate in his or its official capacity, (ii) inducing such foreign official, political party, party official, or candidate to do or omit to do any act in violation of the lawful duty of such foreign official, political party, party official, or candidate, or (iii) securing any improper advantage; or

(B)   inducing such foreign official, political party, party official, or candidate to use his or its influence with a foreign government or instrumentality thereof to affect or influence any act or decision of such government or instrumentality,

in order to assist such domestic concern in obtaining or retaining business for or with, or directing business to, any person.

(b)   Exception for routine governmental action.—Subsections (a) and (i) of this section shall not apply to any facilitating or expediting payment to a foreign official, political party, or party official the purpose of which is to expedite or to secure the performance of a routine governmental action by a foreign official, political party, or party official.

(c)   Affirmative defenses.—It shall be an affirmative defense to actions under subsection (a) or (i) of this section that—

(1)   the payment, gift, offer, or promise of anything of value that was made, was lawful under the written laws and regulations of the foreign official's, political party's, party official's, or candidate's country; or

(2)   the payment, gift, offer, or promise of anything of value that was made, was a reasonable and bona fide expenditure, such as travel and lodging expenses, incurred by or on behalf of a foreign official, party, party official, or candidate and was directly related to—

(A)   the promotion, demonstration, or explanation of products or services; or

(B)   the execution or performance of a contract with a foreign government or agency thereof.

(d)   Injunctive relief.—

(1)   When it appears to the Attorney General that any domestic concern to which this section applies, or officer, director, employee, agent, or stockholder thereof, is engaged, or about to engage, in any act or practice constituting a violation of subsection (a) or (i) of this section, the Attorney General may, in his discretion, bring a civil action in an appropriate district court of the United States to enjoin such act or practice, and upon a proper showing, a permanent injunction or a temporary restraining order shall be granted without bond.

(2)   For the purpose of any civil investigation which, in the opinion of the Attorney General, is necessary and proper to enforce this section, the Attorney General or his designee are empowered to administer oaths and affirmations, subpoena witnesses, take evidence, and require the production of any books, papers, or other documents which the Attorney General deems relevant or material to such investigation. The attendance of witnesses and the production of documentary evidence may be required from any place in the United States, or any territory, possession, or commonwealth of the United States, at any designated place of hearing.

(3)   In case of contumacy by, or refusal to obey a subpoena issued to, any person, the Attorney General may invoke the aid of any court of the United States within the jurisdiction of which such investigation or proceeding is carried on, or where such person resides or carries on business, in requiring the attendance and testimony of witnesses and the production of books, papers, or other documents. Any such court may issue an order requiring such person to appear before the Attorney General or his designee, there to produce records, if so ordered, or to give testimony touching the matter under investigation. Any failure to obey such order of the court may be punished by such court as a contempt thereof.

All process in any such case may be served in the judicial district in which such person resides or may be found. The Attorney General may make such rules relating to civil investigations as may be necessary or appropriate to implement the provisions of this subsection.

(e)   Guidelines by Attorney General.—Not later than 6 months after August 23, 1988, the Attorney General, after consultation with the Securities and Exchange Commission, the Secretary of Commerce, the United States Trade Representative, the Secretary of State, and the Secretary of the Treasury, and after obtaining the views of all interested persons through public notice and comment procedures, shall determine to what extent compliance with this section would be enhanced and the business community would be assisted by further clarification of the preceding provisions of this section and may, based on such determination and to the extent necessary and appropriate, issue—

(1)   guidelines describing specific types of conduct, associated with common types of export sales arrangements and business contracts, which for purposes of the Department of Justice's present enforcement policy, the Attorney General determines would be in conformance with the preceding provisions of this section; and

(2)   general precautionary procedures which domestic concerns may use on a voluntary basis to conform their conduct to the Department of Justice's present enforcement policy regarding the preceding provisions of this section.

The Attorney General shall issue the guidelines and procedures referred to in the preceding sentence in accordance with the provisions of subchapter II of chapter 5 of Title 5 and those guidelines and procedures shall be subject to the provisions of chapter 7 of that title.

(f)   Opinions of Attorney General.—

(1)   The Attorney General, after consultation with appropriate departments and agencies of the United States and after obtaining the views of all interested persons through public notice and comment procedures, shall establish a procedure to provide responses to specific inquiries by domestic concerns concerning conformance of their conduct with the Department of Justice's present enforcement policy regarding the preceding provisions of this section. The Attorney General shall, within 30 days after receiving such a request, issue an opinion in response to that request. The opinion shall state whether or not certain specified prospective conduct would, for purposes of the Department of Justice's present enforcement policy, violate the preceding provisions of this section. Additional requests for opinions may be filed with the Attorney General regarding other specified prospective conduct that is beyond the scope of conduct specified in previous requests. In any action brought under

the applicable provisions of this section, there shall be a rebuttable presumption that conduct, which is specified in a request by a domestic concern and for which the Attorney General has issued an opinion that such conduct is in conformity with the Department of Justice's present enforcement policy, is in compliance with the preceding provisions of this section. Such a presumption may be rebutted by a preponderance of the evidence. In considering the presumption for purposes of this paragraph, a court shall weigh all relevant factors, including but not limited to whether the information submitted to the Attorney General was accurate and complete and whether it was within the scope of the conduct specified in any request received by the Attorney General. The Attorney General shall establish the procedure required by this paragraph in accordance with the provisions of subchapter II of chapter 5 of Title 5 and that procedure shall be subject to the provisions of chapter 7 of that title.

(2)   Any document or other material which is provided to, received by, or prepared in the Department of Justice or any other department or agency of the United States in connection with a request by a domestic concern under the procedure established under paragraph (1), shall be exempt from disclosure under section 552 of Title 5 and shall not, except with the consent of the domestic concern, by made publicly available, regardless of whether the Attorney General response to such a request or the domestic concern withdraws such request before receiving a response.

(3)   Any domestic concern who has made a request to the Attorney General under paragraph (1) may withdraw such request prior to the time the Attorney General issues an opinion in response to such request. Any request so withdrawn shall have no force or effect.

(4)   The Attorney General shall, to the maximum extent practicable, provide timely guidance concerning the Department of Justice's present enforcement policy with respect to the preceding provisions of this section to potential exporters and small businesses that are unable to obtain specialized counsel on issues pertaining to such provisions. Such guidance shall be limited to responses to requests under paragraph (1) concerning conformity of specified prospective conduct with the Department of Justice's present enforcement policy regarding the preceding provisions of this section and general explanations of compliance responsibilities and of potential liabilities under the preceding provisions of this section.

(g)   Penalties.—

(1)(A)   Any domestic concern that is not a natural person and that violates subsection (a) or (i) of this section shall be fined not more than $2,000,000.

(B)   Any domestic concern that is not a natural person and that violates subsection (a) or (i) of this section shall be subject to a civil penalty of not more than $10,000 imposed in an action brought by the Attorney General.

(2)(A)   Any natural person that is an officer, director, employee, or agent of a domestic concern, or stockholder acting on behalf of such domestic concern, who willfully violates subsection (a) or (i) of this section shall be fined not more than $100,000 or imprisoned not more than 5 years, or both.

(B)   Any natural person that is an officer, director, employee, or agent of a domestic concern, or stockholder acting on behalf of such domestic concern, who violates subsection (a) or (i) of this section shall be subject to a civil penalty of not more than $10,000 imposed in an action brought by the Attorney General.

(3)   Whenever a fine is imposed under paragraph (2) upon any officer, director, employee, agent, or stockholder of a domestic concern, such fine may not be paid, directly or indirectly, by such domestic concern.

(h)   Definitions.—For purposes of this section:

(1)   The term "domestic concern" means—

(A)   any individual who is a citizen, national, or resident of the United States; and

(B)   any corporation, partnership, association, joint-stock company, business trust, unincorporated organization, or sole proprietorship which has its principal place of business in the United States, or which is organized under the laws of a State of the United States or a territory, possession, or commonwealth of the United States.

(2)(A)   The term "foreign official" means any officer or employee of a foreign government or any department, agency, or instrumentality thereof, or of a public international organization, or any person acting in an official capacity for or on behalf of any such government or department, agency, or instrumentality, or for or on behalf of any such public international organization.

(B)   For purposes of subparagraph (A), the term "public international organization" means—

(i)   an organization that is designated by Executive order pursuant to section 1 of the International Organizations Immunities Act (22 U.S.C. § 288); or

(ii)   any other international organization that is designated by the President by Executive order for the purposes of this section, effective as of the date of publication of such order in the Federal Register.

(3)(A)   A person's state of mind is "knowing" with respect to conduct, a circumstance, or a result if—

(i)   such person is aware that such person is engaging in such conduct, that such circumstance exists, or that such result is substantially certain to occur; or

(ii)   such person has a firm belief that such circumstance exists or that such result is substantially certain to occur.

(B)   When knowledge of the existence of a particular circumstance is required for an offense, such knowledge is established if a person is aware of a high probability of the existence of such circumstance, unless the person actually believes that such circumstance does not exist.

(4)(A)   The term "routine governmental action" means only an action which is ordinarily and commonly performed by a foreign official in—

(i)   obtaining permits, licenses, or other official documents to qualify a person to do business in a foreign country;

(ii)   processing governmental papers, such as visas and work orders;

(iii)   providing police protection, mail pick-up and delivery, or scheduling inspections associated with contract performance or inspections related to transit of goods across country;

(iv)   providing phone service, power and water supply, loading and unloading cargo, or protecting perishable products or commodities from deterioration; or

(v)   actions of a similar nature.

(B)   The term "routine governmental action" does not include any decision by a foreign official whether, or on what terms, to award new business to or to continue business with a particular party, or any action taken by a foreign official involved in the decision-making process to encourage a decision to award new business to or continue business with a particular party.

(5)   The term "interstate commerce" means trade, commerce, transportation, or communication among the several States, or between any foreign country and any State or between any State and any place or ship outside thereof, and such term includes the intrastate use of—

(A)   a telephone or other interstate means of communication, or

(B)   any other interstate instrumentality.

(i)   Alternative jurisdiction.—

(1)   It shall also be unlawful for any United States person to corruptly do any act outside the United States in furtherance of an offer, payment, promise to pay, or authorization of the payment of any money, or offer, gift, promise to give, or authorization of the giving of anything of value to any of the persons or entities set forth in paragraphs (1), (2), and (3) of subsection (a), for the purposes set forth therein, irrespective of whether such United States person makes use of the mails or any means or instrumentality of interstate commerce in furtherance of such offer, gift, payment, promise, or authorization.

(2)   As used in this subsection, the term "United States person" means a national of the United States (as defined in section 101 of the Immigration and Nationality Act or any corporation, partnership, association, joint-stock company, business trust, unincorporated organization, or sole proprietorship organized under the laws of the United States or any State, territory, possession, or commonwealth of the United States, or any political subdivision thereof;

Prohibited Foreign Trade Practices by Persons Other than Issuers or Domestic Concerns—FRCP § 104A

Sec. 30C.   (a)   Prohibition.—It shall be unlawful for any person other than an issuer that is subject to section 30A of this Act or a domestic concern (as defined in section 30B of this Act), or for any officer, director, employee, or agent of such person or any stockholder thereof acting on behalf of such person, while in the territory of the United States, corruptly to make use of the mails or any means or instrumentality of interstate commerce or to do any other act in furtherance of an offer, payment, promise to pay, or authorization of the payment of any money, or offer, gift, promise to give, or authorization of the giving of anything of value to—

(1)   any foreign official for purposes of—

(A)(i)   influencing any act or decision of such foreign official in his official capacity, (ii) inducing such foreign official to do or omit to do any act in violation of the lawful duty of such official, or (iii) securing any improper advantage; or

(B)   inducing such foreign official to use his influence with a foreign government or instrumentality thereof to affect or influence any act or decision of such government or instrumentality,

in order to assist such person in obtaining or retaining business for or with, or directing business to, any person;

(2)   any foreign political party or official thereof or any candidate for foreign political office for purposes of—

(A)(i)   influencing any act or decision of such party, official, or candidate in its or his official capacity, (ii) inducing such party, official, or candidate to do or omit to do an act in violation of the lawful duty of such party, official, or candidate, or (iii) securing any improper advantage; or

(B)   inducing such party, official, or candidate to use its or his influence with a foreign government or instrumentality thereof to affect or influence any act or decision of such government or instrumentality,

in order to assist such person in obtaining or retaining business for or with, or directing business to, any person; or

(3)   any person, while knowing that all or a portion of such money or thing of value will be offered, given, or promised, directly or indirectly, to any foreign official, to any foreign political party or official thereof, or to any candidate for foreign political office, for purposes of—

(A)(i)   influencing any act or decision of such foreign official, political party, party official, or candidate in his or its official capacity, (ii) inducing such foreign official, political party, party official, or candidate to do or omit to do any act in violation of the lawful duty of such foreign official, political party, party official, or candidate, or (iii) securing any improper advantage; or

(B)   inducing such foreign official, political party, party official, or candidate to use his or its influence with a foreign government or instrumentality thereof to affect or influence any act or decision of such government or instrumentality, in order to assist such person in obtaining or retaining business for or with, or directing business to, any person.

(b)   Exception for routine governmental action.—Subsection (a) of this section shall not apply to any facilitating or expediting payment to a foreign official, political party, or party official the purpose of which is to expedite or to secure the performance of a routine governmental action by a foreign official, political party, or party official.

(c)   Affirmative defenses.—It shall be an affirmative defense to actions under subsection (a) of this section that—

    (1)   the payment, gift, offer, or promise of anything of value that was made, was lawful under the written laws and regulations of the foreign official's, political party's, party official's, or candidate's country; or

    (2)   the payment, gift, offer, or promise of anything of value that was made, was a reasonable and bona fide expenditure, such as travel and lodging expenses, incurred by or on behalf of a foreign official, party, party official, or candidate and was directly related to—

      (A)   the promotion, demonstration, or explanation of products or services; or

      (B)   the execution or performance of a contract with a foreign government or agency thereof.

(d)   Injunctive relief.—

    (1)   When it appears to the Attorney General that any person to which this section applies, or officer, director, employee, agent, or stockholder thereof, is engaged, or about to engage, in any act or practice constituting a violation of subsection (a) of this section, the Attorney General may, in his discretion, bring a civil action in an appropriate district court of the United States to enjoin such act or practice, and upon a proper showing, a permanent injunction or a temporary restraining order shall be granted without bond.

    (2)   For the purpose of any civil investigation which, in the opinion of the Attorney General, is necessary and proper to enforce this section, the Attorney General or his designee are empowered to administer oaths and affirmations, subpoena witnesses, take evidence, and require the production of any books, papers, or other documents which the Attorney General deems relevant or material to such investigation. The attendance of witnesses and the production of documentary evidence may be required from any place in the United States, or any territory, possession, or commonwealth of the United States, at any designated place of hearing.

    (3)   In case of contumacy by, or refusal to obey a subpoena issued to, any person, the Attorney General may invoke the aid of any court of the United States within the jurisdiction of which such investigation or proceeding is carried on, or where such person resides or carries on business, in requiring the attendance and testimony of witnesses and the production of books, papers, or other documents. Any such court may issue an order requiring such person to appear before the Attorney General or his designee, there to produce records, if so ordered, or to give testimony touching the matter under investigation. Any failure to obey such order of the court may be punished by such court as a contempt thereof.

    (4)   All process in any such case may be served in the judicial district in which such person resides or may be found. The Attorney General may make such rules relating to civil investigations as may be necessary or appropriate to implement the provisions of this subsection.

(e)   Penalties.—

    (1)(A)   Any juridical person that violates subsection (a) of this section shall be fined not more than $2,000,000.

      (B)   Any juridical person that violates subsection (a) of this section shall be subject to a civil penalty of not more than $10,000 imposed in an action brought by the Attorney General.

    (2)(A)   Any natural person who willfully violates subsection (a) of this section shall be fined not more than $100,000 or imprisoned not more than 5 years, or both.

      (B)   Any natural person who violates subsection (a) of this section shall be subject to a civil penalty of not more than $10,000 imposed in an action brought by the Attorney General.

    (3)   Whenever a fine is imposed under paragraph (2) upon any officer, director, employee, agent, or stockholder of a person, such fine may not be paid, directly or indirectly, by such person.

(f)   Definitions.—For purposes of this section:

    (1)   The term "person", when referring to an offender, means any natural person other than a national of the United States (as defined in section 101 of the Immigration and Nationality Act (8

U.S.C. § 1101) or any corporation, partnership, association, joint-stock company, business trust, unincorporated organization, or sole proprietorship organized under the law of a foreign nation or a political subdivision thereof.

(2)(A)   The term "foreign official" means any officer or employee of a foreign government or any department, agency, or instrumentality thereof, or of a public international organization, or any person acting in an official capacity for or on behalf of any such government or department, agency, or instrumentality, or for or on behalf of any such public international organization.

(B)   For purposes of subparagraph (A), the term "public international organization" means—

(i)   an organization that is designated by Executive order pursuant to section 1 of the International Organizations Immunities Act (22 U.S.C. § 288); or

(ii)   any other international organization that is designated by the President by Executive order for the purposes of this section, effective as of the date of publication of such order in the Federal Register.

(3)(A)   A person's state of mind is knowing, with respect to conduct, a circumstance or a result if—

(i)   such person is aware that such person is engaging in such conduct, that such circumstance exists, or that such result is substantially certain to occur; or

(ii)   such person has a firm belief that such circumstance exists or that such result is substantially certain to occur.

(B)   When knowledge of the existence of a particular circumstance is required for an offense, such knowledge is established if a person is aware of a high probability of the existence of such circumstance, unless the person actually believes that such circumstance does not exist.

(4)(A)   The term "routine governmental action" means only an action which is ordinarily and commonly performed by a foreign official in—

(i)   obtaining permits, licenses, or other official documents to qualify a person to do business in a foreign country;

(ii)   processing governmental papers, such as visas and work orders;

(iii)   providing police protection, mail pick-up and delivery, or scheduling inspections associated with contract performance or inspections related to transit of goods across country;

(iv)   providing phone service, power and water supply, loading and unloading cargo, or protecting perishable products or commodities from deterioration; or

(v)   actions of a similar nature.

(B)   The term "routine governmental action" does not include any decision by a foreign official whether, or on what terms, to award new business to or to continue business with a particular party, or any action taken by a foreign official involved in the decision-making process to encourage a decision to award new business to or continue business with a particular party.

(5)   The term "interstate commerce" means trade, commerce, transportation, or communication among the several States, or between any foreign country and any State or between any State and any place or ship outside thereof, and such term includes the intrastate use of—

(A)   a telephone or other interstate means of communication, or

(B)   any other interstate instrumentality.

Transaction Fees

Sec. 31. (a)   Recovery of Costs of Annual Appropriation.—The Commission shall, in accordance with this section, collect transaction fees and assessments that are designed to recover the costs to the Government of the annual appropriation to the Commission by Congress.

(b)   Exchange-Traded Securities.—

Subject to subsection (j), each national securities exchange shall pay to the Commission a fee at a rate equal to $15 per $1,000,000 of the aggregate dollar amount of sales of securities (other than bonds, debentures, other evidences of indebtedness, security futures products, and options on securities indexes (excluding a narrow-based security index)) transacted on such national securities exchange.

(c)   Off-Exchange Trades of Exchange Registered and Last-Sale Reported Securities.—

Subject to subsection (j), each national securities association shall pay to the Commission a fee at a rate equal to $15 per $1,000,000 of the aggregate dollar amount of sales transacted by or through any member of such association otherwise than on a national securities exchange of securities (other than bonds, debentures, other evidences of indebtedness, security futures products, and options on securities indexes (excluding a narrow-based security index)) registered on a national securities exchange or subject to prompt last sale reporting pursuant to the rules of the Commission or a registered national securities association.

(d)   Assessments on Security Futures Transactions.—

Each national securities exchange and national securities association shall pay to the Commission an assessment equal to $0.009 for each round turn transaction (treated as including one purchase and one sale of a contract of sale for future delivery) on a security future traded on such national securities exchange or by or through any member of such association otherwise than on a national securities exchange, except that for fiscal year 2007 and each succeeding fiscal year such assessment shall be equal to $0.0042 for each such transaction.

(e)   Dates for payments.—

The fees and assessments required by subsections (b), (c), and (d) of this section shall be paid—

(1)   on or before March 15, with respect to transactions and sales occurring during the period beginning on the preceding September 1 and ending at the close of the preceding December 31; and

(2)   on or before September 25, with respect to transactions and sales occurring during the period beginning on the preceding January 1 and ending at the close of the preceding August 31.

(f)   Exemptions.—

The Commission, by rule, may exempt any sale of securities or any class of sales of securities from any fee or assessments imposed by this section, if the Commission finds that such exemption is consistent with the public interest, the equal regulation of markets and brokers and dealers, and the development of a national market system.

(g)   Publication.—

The Commission shall publish in the Federal Register notices of the fee and assessments rates applicable under this section for each fiscal year not later than 30 days after the date on which an Act making a regular appropriation to the Commission for such fiscal year is enacted together with any estimates or projections on which such fees are based.

(h)   Pro Rata Application.—

The rates per $1,000,000 required by this section shall be applied pro rata to amounts and balances of less than $1,000,000.

(i)   Deposit of Fees.—

(1)   Offsetting collections.—

Fees collected pursuant to subsections (b), (c), and (d) of this section for any fiscal year—

(A)   shall be deposited and credited as offsetting collections to the account providing appropriations to the Commission; and

(B)   except as provided in subsection (k) of this section, shall not be collected for any fiscal year except to the extent provided in advance in appropriation Acts.

(2)   General revenues prohibited.—

No fees collected pursuant to subsections (b), (c), and (d) of this section for fiscal year 2002 or any succeeding fiscal year shall be deposited and credited as general revenue of the Treasury.

(j)   Adjustments to Fee Rates.—

(1)   Annual adjustment.—

Subject to subsections (i)(1)(B) and (k), for each fiscal year, the Commission shall by order adjust each of the rates applicable under subsections (b) and (c) for such fiscal year to a uniform adjusted rate that, when applied to the baseline estimate of the aggregate dollar amount of sales for such fiscal year, is reasonably likely to produce aggregate fee collections under this section (including assessments collected under subsection (d) of this section) that are equal to the regular appropriation to the Commission by Congress for such fiscal year.

(2)   Mid-year adjustment.—

Subject to subsections (i)(1)(B) and (k), for each fiscal year, the Commission shall determine, by March 1 of such fiscal year, whether, based on the actual aggregate dollar volume of sales during the first 5 months of such fiscal year, the baseline estimate of the aggregate dollar volume of sales used under paragraph (1) for such fiscal year is reasonably likely to be 10 percent (or more) greater or less than the actual aggregate dollar volume of sales for such fiscal year. If the Commission so determines, the Commission shall by order, no later than March 1, adjust each of the rates applicable under subsections (b) and (c) for such fiscal year to a uniform adjusted rate that, when applied to the revised estimate of the aggregate dollar amount of sales for the remainder of such fiscal year, is reasonably likely to produce aggregate fee collections under this section (including fees collected during such five-month period and assessments collected under subsection (d) of this section) that are equal to the revised estimate of the regular appropriation to the Commission by Congress for such fiscal year. In making such revised estimate, the Commission shall, after consultation with the Congressional Budget Office and the Office of Management and Budget, use the same methodology required by subsection (l).

(3)   Review.—

In exercising its authority under this subsection, the Commission shall not be required to comply with the provisions of section 553 of title 5, United States Code. An adjusted rate prescribed under paragraph (1) or (2) and published under subsection (g) shall not be subject to judicial review.

(4)   Effective date.—

(A)   Annual adjustment.—

Subject to subsections (i)(1)(B) and (k), an adjusted rate prescribed under paragraph (1) shall take effect on the later of—

(i)   the first day of the fiscal year to which such rate applies; or

(ii)   60 days after the date on which an Act making a regular appropriation to the Commission for such fiscal year is enacted.

(B)   Mid-year adjustment.—

An adjusted rate prescribed under paragraph (2) shall take effect on April 1 of the fiscal year to which such rate applies.

(k)   Lapse of Appropriation.—

If on the first day of a fiscal year a regular appropriation to the Commission has not been enacted, the Commission shall continue to collect (as offsetting collections) the fees and assessments under subsections (b), (c), and (d) of this section at the rate in effect during the preceding fiscal year, until 60 days after the date such a regular appropriation is enacted.

(l)   Baseline Estimate of the Aggregate Dollar Amount of Sales.—

Baseline estimate of the aggregate dollar amount of sales.—The baseline estimate of the aggregate dollar amount of sales for any fiscal year is the baseline estimate of the aggregate dollar amount of sales of securities (other than bonds, debentures, other evidences of indebtedness, security futures products, and options on securities indexes (excluding a narrow-based security index)) to be transacted on each national securities exchange and by or through any member of each national securities association (otherwise than on a national securities exchange) during such fiscal year as determined by the Commission, after consultation with the Congressional Budget Office and the Office of Management and Budget, using the methodology required for making projections pursuant to section 257 of the Balanced Budget and Emergency Deficit Control Act of 1985.

(m)   Transmittal of Commission Budget Requests—

    (1)   Budget required.—

For fiscal year 2012, and each fiscal year thereafter, the Commission shall prepare and submit a budget to the President. Whenever the Commission submits a budget estimate or request to the President or the Office of Management and Budget, the Commission shall concurrently transmit copies of the estimate or request to the Committee on Appropriations of the Senate, the Committee on Appropriations of the House of Representatives, the Committee on Banking, Housing, and Urban Affairs of the Senate, and the Committee on Financial Services of the House of Representatives.

    (2)   Submission to congress.—

The President shall submit each budget submitted under paragraph (1) to Congress, in unaltered form, together with the annual budget for the Administration submitted by the President.

    (3)   Contents.—

The Commission shall include in each budget submitted under paragraph (1)—

        (A)   an itemization of the amount of funds necessary to carry out the functions of the Commission.

        (B)   an amount to be designated as contingency funding to be used by the Commission to address unanticipated needs; and

        (C)   a designation of any activities of the Commission for which multi-year budget authority would be suitable.

Penalties

Sec. 32.   (a)   Any person who willfully violates any provision of this Act (other than section 30A), or any rule or regulation thereunder the violation of which is made unlawful or the observance of which is required under the terms of this Act, or any person who willfully and knowingly makes, or causes to be made, any statement in any application, report, or document required to be filed under this Act or any rule or regulation thereunder or any undertaking contained in a registration statement as provided in subsection (d) of section 15 of this Act or by any self-regulatory organization in connection with an application for membership or participation therein or to become associated with a member thereof, which statement was false or misleading with respect to any material fact, shall upon conviction be fined not more than $5,000,000 or imprisoned not more than 20 years, or both, except that when such person is a person other than a natural person, a fine not exceeding $25,000,000 may be imposed; but no person shall be subject to imprisonment under this section for the violation of any rule or regulation if he proves that he had no knowledge of such rule or regulation.

(b)   Any issuer which fails to file information, documents, or reports required to be filed under subsection (d) of section 15 of this Act or any rule or regulation thereunder shall forfeit to the United States the sum of $100 for each and every day such failure to file shall continue. Such forfeiture, which shall be in lieu of any criminal penalty for such failure to file which might be deemed to arise under subsection (a) of this section, shall be payable into the Treasury of the United States and shall be recoverable in a civil suit in the name of the United States.

(c)(1)(A)   Any issuer that violates section 30A(a) or (g) shall be fined not more than $2,000,000.

    (B)   Any issuer that violates section 30A(a) or (g) shall be subject to a civil penalty of not more than $10,000 imposed in an action brought by the Commission.

(2)(A)   Any officer, director, employee, or agent of an issuer, or stockholder acting on behalf of such issuer, who willfully violates section 30A(a) or (g) of this Act shall be fined not more than $100,000, or imprisoned not more than 5 years, or both.

(B)   Any officer, director, employee, or agent of an issuer, or stockholder acting on behalf of such issuer, who violates section 30A(a) or (g) of this Act shall be subject to a civil penalty of not more than $10,000 imposed in an action brought by the Commission.

(3)   Whenever a fine is imposed under paragraph (2) upon any officer, director, employee, agent, or stockholder of an issuer, such fine may not be paid, directly or indirectly, by such issuer.

Separability of Provision

Sec. 33.   If any provision of this Act, or the application of such provision to any person or circumstances, shall be held invalid, the remainder of the Act and the application of such provision to persons or circumstances other than those as to which it is held invalid, shall not be affected thereby.

Effective Date

Sec. 34.   This Act shall become effective on July 1, 1934, except that sections 6 and 12 (b to e) of this Act shall become effective on September 1, 1934; and sections 5, 7, 8, 9(a)(6), 10, 11, 12(a), 13, 14, 15, 16, 17, 18, 19, and 30 of this Act shall become effective on October 1, 1934.

Authorization of Appropriations

Sec. 35.   In addition to any other funds authorized to be appropriated to the Commission, there are authorized to be appropriated to carry out the functions, powers, and duties of the Commission—

(1)   for fiscal year 2011, $1,300,000,000;

(2)   for fiscal year 2012, $1,500,000,000;

(3)   for fiscal year 2013, $1,750,000,000;

(4)   for fiscal year 2014, $2,000,000,000; and

(5)   for fiscal year 2015, $2,250,000,000.

Requirements for the EDGAR System

Sec. 35A.   The Commission, by rule or regulation—

(1)   shall provide that any information in the EDGAR system that is required to be disseminated by the contractor—

(A)   may be sold or disseminated by the contractor only pursuant to a uniform schedule of fees prescribed by the Commission;

(B)   may be obtained by a purchaser by direct interconnection with the EDGAR system;

(C)   shall be equally available on equal terms to all persons; and

(D)   may be used, resold, or redisseminated by any person who has lawfully obtained such information without restriction and without payment of additional fees or royalties; and

(2)   shall require that persons, or classes of persons, required to make filings with the Commission submit such filings in a form and manner suitable for entry into the EDGAR system and shall specify the date that such requirement is effective with respect to that person or class; except that the Commission may exempt persons or classes of persons, or filings or classes of filings, from such rules or regulations in order to prevent hardships or to avoid imposing unreasonable burdens or as otherwise may be necessary or appropriate.

General Exemptive Authority

Sec. 36.   (a)   Authority.—

(1)   In general.—

Except as provided in subsection (b), but notwithstanding any other provision of this title, the Commission, by rule, regulation, or order, may conditionally or unconditionally exempt any person, security, or transaction, or any class or classes of persons, securities, or transactions, from any provision or provisions of this title or of any rule or regulation thereunder, to the extent that such exemption is necessary or appropriate in the public interest, and is consistent with the protection of investors.

(2)   Procedures.—

The Commission shall, by rule or regulation, determine the procedures under which an exemptive order under this section shall be granted and may, in its sole discretion, decline to entertain any application for an order of exemption under this section.

(b)   Limitation.—

The Commission may not, under this section, exempt any person, security, or transaction, or any class or classes of persons, securities, or transactions from section 15C or the rules or regulations issued thereunder or (for purposes of section 15C and the rules and regulations issued thereunder) from any definition in paragraph (42), (43), (44), or (45) of section 3(a).

(c)   Derivatives.—Unless the Commission is expressly authorized by any provision described in this subsection to grant exemptions, the Commission shall not grant exemptions, with respect to amendments made by subtitle B of the Wall Street Transparency and Accountability Act of 2010, with respect to paragraphs (65), (66), (68), (69), (70), (71), (72), (73), (74), (75), (76), and (79) of section 3(a), and sections 10B(a), 10B(b), 10B(c), 13A, 15F, 17A(g), 17A(h), 17A(i), 17A(j), 17A(k), and 17A(*l*); provided that the Commission shall have exemptive authority under this title with respect to security-based swaps as to the same matters that the Commodity Futures Trading Commission has under the Wall Street Transparency and Accountability Act of 2010 with respect to swaps, including under section 4(c) of the Commodity Exchange Act.

Tennessee Valley Authority

Sec. 37.   (a)   In general. Commencing with the issuance by the Tennessee Valley Authority of an annual report on Commission Form 10–K (or any successor thereto) for fiscal year 2006 and thereafter, the Tennessee Valley Authority shall file with the Commission, in accordance with such rules and regulations as the Commission has prescribed or may prescribe, such periodic, current, and supplementary information, documents, and reports as would be required pursuant to section 13 of this Act title if the Tennessee Valley Authority were an issuer of a security registered pursuant to section 12 of this Act. Notwithstanding the preceding sentence, the Tennessee Valley Authority shall not be required to register any securities under this Act, and shall not be deemed to have registered any securities under this Act.

(b)   Limited treatment as issuer. Commencing with the issuance by the Tennessee Valley Authority of an annual report on Commission Form 10–K (or any successor thereto) for fiscal year 2006 and thereafter, the Tennessee Valley Authority shall be deemed to be an issuer for purposes of section 10A of this Act, other than for subsection (m)(1) or (m)(3) of section 10A of this Act. The Tennessee Valley Authority shall not be required by this subsection to comply with the rules issued by any national securities exchange or national securities association in response to rules issued by the Commission pursuant to section 10A(m)(1) of this Act.

(c)   No effect on TVA authority. Nothing in this section shall be construed to diminish, impair, or otherwise affect the authority of the Board of Directors of the Tennessee Valley Authority to carry out its statutory functions under the Tennessee Valley Authority Act of 1933.

Federal National Mortgage Association, Federal Home Loan Mortgage Corporation, Federal Home Loan Banks

Sec. 38.   (a)   Federal National Mortgage Association and Federal Home Loan Mortgage Corporation.—No class of equity securities of the Federal National Mortgage Association or the Federal Home Loan Mortgage Corporation shall be treated as an exempted security for purposes of section 12, 13, 14, or 16.

(b)   Federal Home Loan Banks.—

(1) Registration.—Each Federal Home Loan Bank shall register a class of its common stock under section 12(g), not later than 120 days after the date of enactment of the Federal Housing Finance Regulatory Reform Act of 2008, and shall thereafter maintain such registration and be treated for purposes of this title as an "issuer", the securities of which are required to be registered under section 12, regardless of the number of members holding such stock at any given time.

(2) Standards Relating to Audit Committees.—Each Federal Home Loan Bank shall comply with the rules issued by the Commission under section 10A(m).

(c) Definitions.—For purposes of this section, the following definitions shall apply:

(1) Federal Home Loan Bank; Member.—The terms "Federal Home Loan Bank" and "member", have the same meanings as in section 2 of the Federal Home Loan Bank Act.

(2) Federal National Mortgage Association.—The term "Federal National Mortgage Association" means the corporation created by the Federal National Mortgage Association Charter Act.

(3) Federal Home Loan Mortgage Corporation.—The term "Federal Home Loan Mortgage Corporation" means the corporation created by the Federal Home Loan Mortgage Corporation Act.

Investor Advisory Committee

Sec. 39. (a) Establishment and Purpose.—

(1) Establishment.—

There is established within the Commission the Investor Advisory Committee (referred to in this section as the "Committee").

(2) Purpose.—

The Committee shall—

    (A) advise and consult with the Commission on—

        (i) regulatory priorities of the Commission;

        (ii) issues relating to the regulation of securities products, trading strategies, and fee structures, and the effectiveness of disclosure;

        (iii) initiatives to protect investor interest; and

        (iv) initiatives to promote investor confidence and the integrity of the securities marketplace; and

    (B) submit to the Commission such findings and recommendations as the Committee determines are appropriate, including recommendations for proposed legislative changes.

(b) Membership.—

(1) In general.—

The members of the Committee shall be—

    (A) the Investor Advocate;

    (B) a representative of State securities commissions;

    (C) a representative of the interests of senior citizens; and

    (D) not fewer than 10, and not more than 20, members appointed by the Commission, from among individuals who—

        (i) represent the interests of individual equity and debt investors, including investors in mutual funds;

        (ii) represent the interests of institutional investors, including the interests of pension funds and registered investment companies;

        (iii) are knowledgeable about investment issues and decisions; and

(iv) have reputations of integrity.

(2) Term.—

Each member of the Committee appointed under paragraph (1)(B) shall serve for a term of 4 years.

(3) Members not commission employees.—

Members appointed under paragraph (1)(B) shall not be deemed to be employees or agents of the Commission solely because of membership on the Committee.

(c) Chairman; Vice Chairman; Secretary; Assistant Secretary.—

(1) In general.—

The members of the Committee shall elect, from among the members of the Committee—

(A) a chairman, who may not be employed by an issuer;

(B) a vice chairman, who may not be employed by an issuer;

(C) a secretary; and

(D) an assistant secretary.

(2) Term.—

Each member elected under paragraph (1) shall serve for a term of 3 years in the capacity for which the member was elected under paragraph (1).

(d) Meetings.—

(1) Frequency of meetings.—

The Committee shall meet—

(A) not less frequently than twice annually, at the call of the chairman of the Committee; and

(B) from time to time, at the call of the Commission.

(2) Notice.—

The chairman of the Committee shall give the members of the Committee written notice of each meeting, not later than 2 weeks before the date of the meeting.

(e) Compensation and Travel Expenses.—Each member of the Committee who is not a full-time employee of the United States shall—

(1) be entitled to receive compensation at a rate not to exceed the daily equivalent of the annual rate of basic pay in effect for a position at level V of the Executive Schedule under section 5316 of title 5, United States Code, for each day during which the member is engaged in the actual performance of the duties of the Committee; and

(2) while away from the home or regular place of business of the member in the performance of services for the Committee, be allowed travel expenses, including per diem in lieu of subsistence, in the same manner as persons employed intermittently in the Government service are allowed expenses under section 5703(b) of title 5, United States Code.

(f) Staff.—The Commission shall make available to the Committee such staff as the chairman of the Committee determines are necessary to carry out this section.

(g) Review by Commission.—The Commission shall—

(1) review the findings and recommendations of the Committee; and

(2) each time the Committee submits a finding or recommendation to the Commission, promptly issue a public statement—

(A) assessing the finding or recommendation of the Committee; and

(B)   disclosing the action, if any, the Commission intends to take with respect to the finding or recommendation.

(h)   Committee Findings.—Nothing in this section shall require the Commission to agree to or act upon any finding or recommendation of the Committee.

(i)   Federal Advisory Committee Act.—The Federal Advisory Committee Act (5 U.S.C. App.) shall not apply with respect to the Committee and its activities.

(j)   Authorization of Appropriations.—There is authorized to be appropriated to the Commission such sums as are necessary to carry out this section.

SARBANES-OXLEY ACT OF 2002

PL 107–204 (HR 3763), 107th Cong., 2d sess. (July 30, 2002)

Selected Provisions

An Act To protect investors by improving the accuracy and reliability of corporate disclosures made pursuant to the securities laws, and for other purposes.

Sec. 1. Short title; table of contents (15 U.S.C.A. § 7201)

(a) Short title.—This Act may be cited as the "Sarbanes-Oxley Act of 2002".

(b) Table of contents.—The table of contents for this Act is as follows:

Sec. 2. Definitions (15 U.S.C.A. § 7201)

(a) In general.—Except as otherwise specifically provided in this Act, the following definitions shall apply:

(1) Appropriate state regulatory authority.—The term "appropriate State regulatory authority" means the State agency or other authority responsible for the licensure or other regulation of the practice of accounting in the State or States having jurisdiction over a registered public accounting firm or associated person thereof, with respect to the matter in question.

(2) Audit.—The term "audit" means an examination of the financial statements of any issuer by an independent public accounting firm in accordance with the rules of the Board or the Commission (or, for the period preceding the adoption of applicable rules of the Board under section 103, in

accordance with then-applicable generally accepted auditing and related standards for such purposes), for the purpose of expressing an opinion on such statements.

(3) Audit committee.—The term "audit committee" means—

(A) a committee (or equivalent body) established by and amongst the board of directors of an issuer for the purpose of overseeing the accounting and financial reporting processes of the issuer and audits of the financial statements of the issuer; and

(B) if no such committee exists with respect to an issuer, the entire board of directors of the issuer.

(4) Audit report.—The term "audit report" means a document or other record—

(A) prepared following an audit performed for purposes of compliance by an issuer with the requirements of the securities laws; and

(B) in which a public accounting firm either—

(i) sets forth the opinion of that firm regarding a financial statement, report, or other document; or

(ii) asserts that no such opinion can be expressed.

(5) Board.—The term "Board" means the Public Company Accounting Oversight Board established under section 101.

(6) Commission.—The term "Commission" means the Securities and Exchange Commission.

(7) Issuer.—The term "issuer" means an issuer (as defined in section 3 of the Securities Exchange Act of 1934 (15 U.S.C. 78c)), the securities of which are registered under section 12 of that Act (15 U.S.C. 78*l*), or that is required to file reports under section 15(d) (15 U.S.C. 78o(d)), or that files or has filed a registration statement that has not yet become effective under the Securities Act of 1933 (15 U.S.C. 77a et seq.), and that it has not withdrawn.

(8) Non-audit services.—The term "non-audit services" means any professional services provided to an issuer by a registered public accounting firm, other than those provided to an issuer in connection with an audit or a review of the financial statements of an issuer.

(9) Person associated with a public accounting firm.—

(A) In general.—The terms "person associated with a public accounting firm" (or with a "registered public accounting firm") and "associated person of a public accounting firm" (or of a "registered public accounting firm") mean any individual proprietor, partner, shareholder, principal, accountant, or other professional employee of a public accounting firm, or any other independent contractor or entity that, in connection with the preparation or issuance of any audit report—

(i) shares in the profits of, or receives compensation in any other form from, that firm; or

(ii) participates as agent or otherwise on behalf of such accounting firm in any activity of that firm.

(B) Exemption authority.—The Board may, by rule, exempt persons engaged only in ministerial tasks from the definition in subparagraph (A), to the extent that the Board determines that any such exemption is consistent with the purposes of this Act, the public interest, or the protection of investors.

(C) Investigative and enforcement authority—For purposes of sections 3(c), 101(c), 105, and 107(c) and the rules of the Board and Commission issued thereunder, except to the extent specifically excepted by such rules, the terms defined in subparagraph (A) shall include any person associated, seeking to become associated, or formerly associated with a public accounting firm, except that—

(i) the authority to conduct an investigation of such person under section 105(b) shall apply only with respect to any act or practice, or omission to act, by the person while such person was associated or seeking to become associated with a registered public accounting firm; and

    (ii)   the authority to commence a disciplinary proceeding under section 105(c)(1), or impose sanctions under section 105(c)(4), against such person shall apply only with respect to—

        (I)   conduct occurring while such person was associated or seeking to become associated with a registered public accounting firm; or

        (II)   non-cooperation, as described in section 105(b)(3), with respect to a demand in a Board investigation for testimony, documents, or other information relating to a period when such person was associated or seeking to become associated with a registered public accounting firm.

    (10) Professional standards.—The term "professional standards" means—

    (A)   accounting principles that are—

        (i)   established by the standard setting body described in section 19(b) of the Securities Act of 1933, as amended by this Act, or prescribed by the Commission under section 19(a) of that Act (15 U.S.C. 17a(s)) or section 13(b) of the Securities Exchange Act of 1934 (15 U.S.C. 78a(m)); and

        (ii)   relevant to audit reports for particular issuers, or dealt with in the quality control system of a particular registered public accounting firm; and

    (B)   auditing standards, standards for attestation engagements, quality control policies and procedures, ethical and competency standards, and independence standards (including rules implementing title II) that the Board or the Commission determines—

        (i)   relate to the preparation or issuance of audit reports for issuers; and

        (ii)   are established or adopted by the Board under section 103(a), or are promulgated as rules of the Commission.

    (11) Public accounting firm.—The term "public accounting firm" means—

    (A)   a proprietorship, partnership, incorporated association, corporation, limited liability company, limited liability partnership, or other legal entity that is engaged in the practice of public accounting or preparing or issuing audit reports; and

    (B)   to the extent so designated by the rules of the Board, any associated person of any entity described in subparagraph (A).

    (12) Registered public accounting firm.—The term "registered public accounting firm" means a public accounting firm registered with the Board in accordance with this Act.

    (13) Rules of the board.—The term "rules of the Board" means the bylaws and rules of the Board (as submitted to, and approved, modified, or amended by the Commission, in accordance with section 107), and those stated policies, practices, and interpretations of the Board that the Commission, by rule, may deem to be rules of the Board, as necessary or appropriate in the public interest or for the protection of investors.

    (14) Security.—The term "security" has the same meaning as in section 3(a) of the Securities Exchange Act of 1934 (15 U.S.C.A. § 78c(a)).

    (15) Securities laws.—The term "securities laws" means the provisions of law referred to in section 3(a)(47) of the Securities Exchange Act of 1934 (15 U.S.C.A. § 78c(a)(47)), as amended by this Act, and includes the rules, regulations, and orders issued by the Commission thereunder.

    (16) State.—The term "State" means any State of the United States, the District of Columbia, Puerto Rico, the Virgin Islands, or any other territory or possession of the United States.

    (17) Foreign auditor oversight authority.—The term "foreign auditor oversight authority" means any governmental body or other entity empowered by a foreign government to conduct inspections of

public accounting firms or otherwise to administer or enforce laws related to the regulation of public accounting firms.

(b)   Conforming amendment.—[see Section 3(a)(47) of the Securities Exchange Act of 1934 (15 U.S.C.A. § 78c(a)(47))]

Sec. 3.   Commission rules and enforcement (15 U.S.C.A. § 7202)

(a)   Regulatory action.—The Commission shall promulgate such rules and regulations, as may be necessary or appropriate in the public interest or for the protection of investors, and in furtherance of this Act.

(b)   Enforcement.—

(1)   In general.—A violation by any person of this Act, any rule or regulation of the Commission issued under this Act, or any rule of the Board shall be treated for all purposes in the same manner as a violation of the Securities Exchange Act of 1934 (15 U.S.C.A. §§ 78a et seq.) or the rules and regulations issued thereunder, consistent with the provisions of this Act, and any such person shall be subject to the same penalties, and to the same extent, as for a violation of that Act or such rules or regulations.

(2)   Investigations, injunctions, and prosecution of offenses.—[amending Section 21 of the Securities Exchange Act of 1934 (15 U.S.C.A. § 78u)]

(3)   Cease-and-desist proceedings.—[amending Section 21C(c)(2) of the Securities Exchange Act of 1934 (15 U.S.C.A. § 78u–3(c)(2))] is amended by inserting "after "government securities dealer,".

(4)   Enforcement by federal banking agencies.—[amending Section 12(i) of the Securities Exchange Act of 1934 (15 U.S.C.A. § 78l(i))]

(c)   Effect on commission authority.—Nothing in this Act or the rules of the Board shall be construed to impair or limit—

(1)   the authority of the Commission to regulate the accounting profession, accounting firms, or persons associated with such firms for purposes of enforcement of the securities laws;

(2)   the authority of the Commission to set standards for accounting or auditing practices or auditor independence, derived from other provisions of the securities laws or the rules or regulations thereunder, for purposes of the preparation and issuance of any audit report, or otherwise under applicable law; or

(3)   the ability of the Commission to take, on the initiative of the Commission, legal, administrative, or disciplinary action against any registered public accounting firm or any associated person thereof.

TITLE I—PUBLIC COMPANY ACCOUNTING OVERSIGHT BOARD

Sec. 101. Establishment; administrative provisions (15 U.S.C.A. § 7211)

(a)   Establishment of board.—There is established the Public Company Accounting Oversight Board, to oversee the audit of companies that are subject to the securities laws, and related matters, in order to protect the interests of investors and further the public interest in the preparation of informative, accurate, and independent audit reports. The Board shall be a body corporate, operate as a nonprofit corporation, and have succession until dissolved by an Act of Congress.

(b)   Status.—The Board shall not be an agency or establishment of the United States Government, and, except as otherwise provided in this Act, shall be subject to, and have all the powers conferred upon a nonprofit corporation by, the District of Columbia Nonprofit Corporation Act. No member or person employed by, or agent for, the Board shall be deemed to be an officer or employee of or agent for the Federal Government by reason of such service.

(c)   Duties of the board.—The Board shall, subject to action by the Commission under section 107, and once a determination is made by the Commission under subsection (d) of this section—

(1) register public accounting firms that prepare audit reports for issuers, brokers, and dealers in accordance with section 102;

(2) establish or adopt, or both, by rule, auditing, quality control, ethics, independence, and other standards relating to the preparation of audit reports for issuers, brokers, and dealers in accordance with section 103;

(3) conduct inspections of registered public accounting firms, in accordance with section 104 and the rules of the Board;

(4) conduct investigations and disciplinary proceedings concerning, and impose appropriate sanctions where justified upon, registered public accounting firms and associated persons of such firms, in accordance with section 105;

(5) perform such other duties or functions as the Board (or the Commission, by rule or order) determines are necessary or appropriate to promote high professional standards among, and improve the quality of audit services offered by, registered public accounting firms and associated persons thereof, or otherwise to carry out this Act, in order to protect investors, or to further the public interest;

(6) enforce compliance with this Act, the rules of the Board, professional standards, and the securities laws relating to the preparation and issuance of audit reports and the obligations and liabilities of accountants with respect thereto, by registered public accounting firms and associated persons thereof; and

(7) set the budget and manage the operations of the Board and the staff of the Board.

(d) Commission determination.—The members of the Board shall take such action (including hiring of staff, proposal of rules, and adoption of initial and transitional auditing and other professional standards) as may be necessary or appropriate to enable the Commission to determine, not later than 270 days after the date of enactment of this Act, that the Board is so organized and has the capacity to carry out the requirements of this title, and to enforce compliance with this title by registered public accounting firms and associated persons thereof. The Commission shall be responsible, prior to the appointment of the Board, for the planning for the establishment and administrative transition to the Board's operation.

(e) Board membership.—

(1) Composition.—The Board shall have 5 members, appointed from among prominent individuals of integrity and reputation who have a demonstrated commitment to the interests of investors and the public, and an understanding of the responsibilities for and nature of the financial disclosures required of issuers, brokers, and dealers under the securities laws and the obligations of accountants with respect to the preparation and issuance of audit reports with respect to such disclosures.

(2) Limitation.—Two members, and only 2 members, of the Board shall be or have been certified public accountants pursuant to the laws of 1 or more States, provided that, if 1 of those 2 members is the chairperson, he or she may not have been a practicing certified public accountant for at least 5 years prior to his or her appointment to the Board.

(3) Full-time independent service.—Each member of the Board shall serve on a full-time basis, and may not, concurrent with service on the Board, be employed by any other person or engage in any other professional or business activity. No member of the Board may share in any of the profits of, or receive payments from, a public accounting firm (or any other person, as determined by rule of the Commission), other than fixed continuing payments, subject to such conditions as the Commission may impose, under standard arrangements for the retirement of members of public accounting firms.

(4) Appointment of board members.—

(A) Initial board.—Not later than 90 days after the date of enactment of this Act, the Commission, after consultation with the Chairman of the Board of Governors of the Federal Reserve System and the Secretary of the Treasury, shall appoint the chairperson and other initial members of the Board, and shall designate a term of service for each.

(B) Vacancies.—A vacancy on the Board shall not affect the powers of the Board, but shall be filled in the same manner as provided for appointments under this section.

(5) Term of service.—

(A) In general.—The term of service of each Board member shall be 5 years, and until a successor is appointed, except that—

(i) the terms of office of the initial Board members (other than the chairperson) shall expire in annual increments, 1 on each of the first 4 anniversaries of the initial date of appointment; and

(ii) any Board member appointed to fill a vacancy occurring before the expiration of the term for which the predecessor was appointed shall be appointed only for the remainder of that term.

(B) Term limitation.—No person may serve as a member of the Board, or as chairperson of the Board, for more than 2 terms, whether or not such terms of service are consecutive.

(6) Removal from office.—A member of the Board may be removed by the Commission from office, in accordance with section 107(d)(3), for good cause shown before the expiration of the term of that member.

(f) Powers of the board.—In addition to any authority granted to the Board otherwise in this Act, the Board shall have the power, subject to section 107—

(1) to sue and be sued, complain and defend, in its corporate name and through its own counsel, with the approval of the Commission, in any Federal, State, or other court;

(2) to conduct its operations and maintain offices, and to exercise all other rights and powers authorized by this Act, in any State, without regard to any qualification, licensing, or other provision of law in effect in such State (or a political subdivision thereof);

(3) to lease, purchase, accept gifts or donations of or otherwise acquire, improve, use, sell, exchange, or convey, all of or an interest in any property, wherever situated;

(4) to appoint such employees, accountants, attorneys, and other agents as may be necessary or appropriate, and to determine their qualifications, define their duties, and fix their salaries or other compensation (at a level that is comparable to private sector self-regulatory, accounting, technical, supervisory, or other staff or management positions);

(5) to allocate, assess, and collect accounting support fees established pursuant to section 109, for the Board, and other fees and charges imposed under this title; and

(6) to enter into contracts, execute instruments, incur liabilities, and do any and all other acts and things necessary, appropriate, or incidental to the conduct of its operations and the exercise of its obligations, rights, and powers imposed or granted by this title.

(g) Rules of the board.—The rules of the Board shall, subject to the approval of the Commission—

(1) provide for the operation and administration of the Board, the exercise of its authority, and the performance of its responsibilities under this Act;

(2) permit, as the Board determines necessary or appropriate, delegation by the Board of any of its functions to an individual member or employee of the Board, or to a division of the Board, including functions with respect to hearing, determining, ordering, certifying, reporting, or otherwise acting as to any matter, except that—

(A) the Board shall retain a discretionary right to review any action pursuant to any such delegated function, upon its own motion;

(B) a person shall be entitled to a review by the Board with respect to any matter so delegated, and the decision of the Board upon such review shall be deemed to be the action of the Board for all purposes (including appeal or review thereof); and

(C) if the right to exercise a review described in subparagraph (A) is declined, or if no such review is sought within the time stated in the rules of the Board, then the action taken by the holder of such delegation shall for all purposes, including appeal or review thereof, be deemed to be the action of the Board;

(3)   establish ethics rules and standards of conduct for Board members and staff, including a bar on practice before the Board (and the Commission, with respect to Board-related matters) of 1 year for former members of the Board, and appropriate periods (not to exceed 1 year) for former staff of the Board; and

(4)   provide as otherwise required by this Act.

(h)   Annual report to the commission.—The Board shall submit an annual report (including its audited financial statements) to the Commission, and the Commission shall transmit a copy of that report to the Committee on Banking, Housing, and Urban Affairs of the Senate, and the Committee on Financial Services of the House of Representatives, not later than 30 days after the date of receipt of that report by the Commission.

Sec. 102.   Registration with the board (15 U.S.C.A. § 7212)

(a)   Mandatory registration.—It shall be unlawful for any person that is not a registered public accounting firm to prepare or issue, or to participate in the preparation or issuance of, any audit report with respect to any issuer, broker or dealer.

(b)   Applications for registration.—

(1)   Form of application.—A public accounting firm shall use such form as the Board may prescribe, by rule, to apply for registration under this section.

(2)   Contents of applications.—Each public accounting firm shall submit, as part of its application for registration, in such detail as the Board shall specify—

(A)   the names of all issuers, brokers, and dealers for which the firm prepared or issued audit reports during the immediately preceding calendar year, and for which the firm expects to prepare or issue audit reports during the current calendar year;

(B)   the annual fees received by the firm from each such issuer, broker, or dealer for audit services, other accounting services, and non-audit services, respectively;

(C)   such other current financial information for the most recently completed fiscal year of the firm as the Board may reasonably request;

(D)   a statement of the quality control policies of the firm for its accounting and auditing practices;

(E)   a list of all accountants associated with the firm who participate in or contribute to the preparation of audit reports, stating the license or certification number of each such person, as well as the State license numbers of the firm itself;

(F)   information relating to criminal, civil, or administrative actions or disciplinary proceedings pending against the firm or any associated person of the firm in connection with any audit report;

(G)   copies of any periodic or annual disclosure filed by an issuer, broker, or dealer with the Commission during the immediately preceding calendar year which discloses accounting disagreements between such issuer, broker, or dealer and the firm in connection with an audit report furnished or prepared by the firm for such issuer, broker, or dealer; and

(H)   such other information as the rules of the Board or the Commission shall specify as necessary or appropriate in the public interest or for the protection of investors.

(3)   Consents.—Each application for registration under this subsection shall include—

(A)   a consent executed by the public accounting firm to cooperation in and compliance with any request for testimony or the production of documents made by the Board in the furtherance of its authority and responsibilities under this title (and an agreement to secure and enforce similar consents from each of the associated persons of the public accounting firm as a condition of their continued employment by or other association with such firm); and

(B)   a statement that such firm understands and agrees that cooperation and compliance, as described in the consent required by subparagraph (A), and the securing and enforcement of such consents from its associated persons, in accordance with the rules of the Board, shall be a condition to the continuing effectiveness of the registration of the firm with the Board.

(c)   Action on applications.—

(1)   Timing.—The Board shall approve a completed application for registration not later than 45 days after the date of receipt of the application, in accordance with the rules of the Board, unless the Board, prior to such date, issues a written notice of disapproval to, or requests more information from, the prospective registrant.

(2)   Treatment.—A written notice of disapproval of a completed application under paragraph (1) for registration shall be treated as a disciplinary sanction for purposes of sections 105(d) and 107(c).

(d)   Periodic reports.—Each registered public accounting firm shall submit an annual report to the Board, and may be required to report more frequently, as necessary to update the information contained in its application for registration under this section, and to provide to the Board such additional information as the Board or the Commission may specify, in accordance with subsection (b)(2).

(e)   Public availability.—Registration applications and annual reports required by this subsection, or such portions of such applications or reports as may be designated under rules of the Board, shall be made available for public inspection, subject to rules of the Board or the Commission, and to applicable laws relating to the confidentiality of proprietary, personal, or other information contained in such applications or reports, provided that, in all events, the Board shall protect from public disclosure information reasonably identified by the subject accounting firm as proprietary information.

(f)   Registration and annual fees.—The Board shall assess and collect a registration fee and an annual fee from each registered public accounting firm, in amounts that are sufficient to recover the costs of processing and reviewing applications and annual reports.

Sec. 103. Auditing, quality control, and independence standards and rules (15 U.S.C.A. § 7213)

(a)   Auditing, quality control, and ethics standards.—

(1)   In general.—The Board shall, by rule, establish, including, to the extent it determines appropriate, through adoption of standards proposed by 1 or more professional groups of accountants designated pursuant to paragraph (3)(A) or advisory groups convened pursuant to paragraph (4), and amend or otherwise modify or alter, such auditing and related attestation standards, such quality control standards, such ethics standards, and such independence standards to be used by registered public accounting firms in the preparation and issuance of audit reports, as required by this Act or the rules of the Commission, or as may be necessary or appropriate in the public interest or for the protection of investors.

(2)   Rule requirements.—In carrying out paragraph (1), the Board—

(A)   shall include in the auditing standards that it adopts, requirements that each registered public accounting firm shall—

(i)   prepare, and maintain for a period of not less than 7 years, audit work papers, and other information related to any audit report, in sufficient detail to support the conclusions reached in such report;

(ii)   provide a concurring or second partner review and approval of such audit report (and other related information), and concurring approval in its issuance, by a qualified person (as prescribed by the Board) associated with the public accounting firm, other than the person in charge of the audit, or by an independent reviewer (as prescribed by the Board); and

(iii)   in each audit report for an issuer, describe the scope of the auditor's testing of the internal control structure and procedures of the issuer, required by section 404(b), and present (in such report or in a separate report)—

(I)   the findings of the auditor from such testing;

(II)   an evaluation of whether such internal control structure and procedures—

(aa) include maintenance of records that in reasonable detail accurately and fairly reflect the transactions and dispositions of the assets of the issuer;

(bb) provide reasonable assurance that transactions are recorded as necessary to permit preparation of financial statements in accordance with generally accepted accounting principles, and that receipts and expenditures of the issuer are being made only in accordance with authorizations of management and directors of the issuer; and

(III) a description, at a minimum, of material weaknesses in such internal controls, and of any material noncompliance found on the basis of such testing.

(B) shall include, in the quality control standards that it adopts with respect to the issuance of audit reports, requirements for every registered public accounting firm relating to—

(i) monitoring of professional ethics and independence from issuers, brokers, or dealers on behalf of which the firm issues audit reports;

(ii) consultation within such firm on accounting and auditing questions;

(iii) supervision of audit work;

(iv) hiring, professional development, and advancement of personnel;

(v) the acceptance and continuation of engagements;

(vi) internal inspection; and

(vii) such other requirements as the Board may prescribe, subject to subsection (a)(1).

(3) Authority to adopt other standards.—

(A) In general.—In carrying out this subsection, the Board—

(i) may adopt as its rules, subject to the terms of section 107, any portion of any statement of auditing standards or other professional standards that the Board determines satisfy the requirements of paragraph (1), and that were proposed by 1 or more professional groups of accountants that shall be designated or recognized by the Board, by rule, for such purpose, pursuant to this paragraph or 1 or more advisory groups convened pursuant to paragraph (4); and

(ii) notwithstanding clause (i), shall retain full authority to modify, supplement, revise, or subsequently amend, modify, or repeal, in whole or in part, any portion of any statement described in clause (i).

(B) Initial and transitional standards.—The Board shall adopt standards described in subparagraph (A)(i) as initial or transitional standards, to the extent the Board determines necessary, prior to a determination of the Commission under section 101(d), and such standards shall be separately approved by the Commission at the time of that determination, without regard to the procedures required by section 107 that otherwise would apply to the approval of rules of the Board.

(C) Transition period for emerging growth companies.—Any rules of the Board requiring mandatory audit firm rotation or a supplement to the auditor's report in which the auditor would be required to provide additional information about the audit and the financial statements of the issuer (auditor discussion and analysis) shall not apply to an audit of an emerging growth company, as defined in section 3 of the Securities Exchange Act of 1934. Any additional rules adopted by the Board after the date of enactment of this subparagraph shall not apply to an audit of any emerging growth company, unless the Commission determines that the application of such additional requirements is necessary or appropriate in the public interest, after considering the protection of investors and whether the action will promote efficiency, competition, and capital formation.

(4) Advisory groups.—The Board shall convene, or authorize its staff to convene, such expert advisory groups as may be appropriate, which may include practicing accountants and other experts, as well as representatives of other interested groups, subject to such rules as the Board may prescribe

to prevent conflicts of interest, to make recommendations concerning the content (including proposed drafts) of auditing, quality control, ethics, independence, or other standards required to be established under this section.

(b)   Independence standards and rules.—The Board shall establish such rules as may be necessary or appropriate in the public interest or for the protection of investors, to implement, or as authorized under, title II of this Act.

(c)   Cooperation with designated professional groups of accountants and advisory groups.—

(1)   In general.—The Board shall cooperate on an ongoing basis with professional groups of accountants designated under subsection (a)(3)(A) and advisory groups convened under subsection (a)(4) in the examination of the need for changes in any standards subject to its authority under subsection (a), recommend issues for inclusion on the agendas of such designated professional groups of accountants or advisory groups, and take such other steps as it deems appropriate to increase the effectiveness of the standard setting process.

(2)   Board responses.—The Board shall respond in a timely fashion to requests from designated professional groups of accountants and advisory groups referred to in paragraph (1) for any changes in standards over which the Board has authority.

(d)   Evaluation of standard setting process.—The Board shall include in the annual report required by section 101(h) the results of its standard setting responsibilities during the period to which the report relates, including a discussion of the work of the Board with any designated professional groups of accountants and advisory groups described in paragraphs (3)(A) and (4) of subsection (a), and its pending issues agenda for future standard setting projects.

Sec. 104. Inspections of registered public accounting firms (15 U.S.C.A. § 7214)

(a)   In general.—(1) Inspections generally—The Board shall conduct a continuing program of inspections to assess the degree of compliance of each registered public accounting firm and associated persons of that firm with this Act, the rules of the Board, the rules of the Commission, or professional standards, in connection with its performance of audits, issuance of audit reports, and related matters involving issuers.

(2)   Inspections of audit reports for brokers and dealers—

(A)   The Board may, by rule, conduct and require a program of inspection in accordance with paragraph (1), on a basis to be determined by the Board, of registered public accounting firms that provide one or more audit reports for a broker or dealer. The Board, in establishing such a program, may allow for differentiation among classes of brokers and dealers, as appropriate.

(B)   If the Board determines to establish a program of inspection pursuant to subparagraph (A), the Board shall consider in establishing any inspection schedules whether differing schedules would be appropriate with respect to registered public accounting firms that issue audit reports only for one or more brokers or dealers that do not receive, handle, or hold customer securities or cash or are not a member of the Securities Investor Protection Corporation.

(C)   Any rules of the Board pursuant to this paragraph shall be subject to prior approval by the Commission pursuant to section 107(b) before the rules become effective, including an opportunity for public notice and comment.

(D)   Notwithstanding anything to the contrary in section 102 of this Act, a public accounting firm shall not be required to register with the Board if the public accounting firm is exempt from the inspection program which may be established by the Board under subparagraph (A).

(b)   Inspection frequency.—

(1)   In general.—Subject to paragraph (2), inspections required by this section shall be conducted—

(A)   annually with respect to each registered public accounting firm that regularly provides audit reports for more than 100 issuers; and

(B) not less frequently than once every 3 years with respect to each registered public accounting firm that regularly provides audit reports for 100 or fewer issuers.

(2) Adjustments to schedules.—The Board may, by rule, adjust the inspection schedules set under paragraph (1) if the Board finds that different inspection schedules are consistent with the purposes of this Act, the public interest, and the protection of investors. The Board may conduct special inspections at the request of the Commission or upon its own motion.

(c) Procedures.—The Board shall, in each inspection under this section, and in accordance with its rules for such inspections—

(1) identify any act or practice or omission to act by the registered public accounting firm, or by any associated person thereof, revealed by such inspection that may be in violation of this Act, the rules of the Board, the rules of the Commission, the firm's own quality control policies, or professional standards;

(2) report any such act, practice, or omission, if appropriate, to the Commission and each appropriate State regulatory authority; and

(3) begin a formal investigation or take disciplinary action, if appropriate, with respect to any such violation, in accordance with this Act and the rules of the Board.

(d) Conduct of inspections.—In conducting an inspection of a registered public accounting firm under this section, the Board shall—

(1) inspect and review selected audit and review engagements of the firm (which may include audit engagements that are the subject of ongoing litigation or other controversy between the firm and 1 or more third parties), performed at various offices and by various associated persons of the firm, as selected by the Board;

(2) evaluate the sufficiency of the quality control system of the firm, and the manner of the documentation and communication of that system by the firm; and

(3) perform such other testing of the audit, supervisory, and quality control procedures of the firm as are necessary or appropriate in light of the purpose of the inspection and the responsibilities of the Board.

(e) Record retention.—The rules of the Board may require the retention by registered public accounting firms for inspection purposes of records whose retention is not otherwise required by section 103 or the rules issued thereunder.

(f) Procedures for review.—The rules of the Board shall provide a procedure for the review of and response to a draft inspection report by the registered public accounting firm under inspection. The Board shall take such action with respect to such response as it considers appropriate (including revising the draft report or continuing or supplementing its inspection activities before issuing a final report), but the text of any such response, appropriately redacted to protect information reasonably identified by the accounting firm as confidential, shall be attached to and made part of the inspection report.

(g) Report.—A written report of the findings of the Board for each inspection under this section, subject to subsection (h), shall be—

(1) transmitted, in appropriate detail, to the Commission and each appropriate State regulatory authority, accompanied by any letter or comments by the Board or the inspector, and any letter of response from the registered public accounting firm; and

(2) made available in appropriate detail to the public (subject to section 105(b)(5)(A), and to the protection of such confidential and proprietary information as the Board may determine to be appropriate, or as may be required by law), except that no portions of the inspection report that deal with criticisms of or potential defects in the quality control systems of the firm under inspection shall be made public if those criticisms or defects are addressed by the firm, to the satisfaction of the Board, not later than 12 months after the date of the inspection report.

(h) Interim commission review.—

(1) Reviewable matters.—A registered public accounting firm may seek review by the Commission, pursuant to such rules as the Commission shall promulgate, if the firm—

(A) has provided the Board with a response, pursuant to rules issued by the Board under subsection (f), to the substance of particular items in a draft inspection report, and disagrees with the assessments contained in any final report prepared by the Board following such response; or

(B) disagrees with the determination of the Board that criticisms or defects identified in an inspection report have not been addressed to the satisfaction of the Board within 12 months of the date of the inspection report, for purposes of subsection (g)(2).

(2) Treatment of review.—Any decision of the Commission with respect to a review under paragraph (1) shall not be reviewable under section 25 of the Securities Exchange Act of 1934 (15 U.S.C. 78y), or deemed to be "final agency action" for purposes of section 704 of title 5, United States Code.

(3) Timing.—Review under paragraph (1) may be sought during the 30-day period following the date of the event giving rise to the review under subparagraph (A) or (B) of paragraph (1).

Sec. 105. Investigations and disciplinary proceedings (15 U.S.C.A. § 7215)

(a) In general.—The Board shall establish, by rule, subject to the requirements of this section, fair procedures for the investigation and disciplining of registered public accounting firms and associated persons of such firms.

(b) Investigations.—

(1) Authority.—In accordance with the rules of the Board, the Board may conduct an investigation of any act or practice, or omission to act, by a registered public accounting firm, any associated person of such firm, or both, that may violate any provision of this Act, the rules of the Board, the provisions of the securities laws relating to the preparation and issuance of audit reports and the obligations and liabilities of accountants with respect thereto, including the rules of the Commission issued under this Act, or professional standards, regardless of how the act, practice, or omission is brought to the attention of the Board.

(2) Testimony and document production.—In addition to such other actions as the Board determines to be necessary or appropriate, the rules of the Board may—

(A) require the testimony of the firm or of any person associated with a registered public accounting firm, with respect to any matter that the Board considers relevant or material to an investigation;

(B) require the production of audit work papers and any other document or information in the possession of a registered public accounting firm or any associated person thereof, wherever domiciled, that the Board considers relevant or material to the investigation, and may inspect the books and records of such firm or associated person to verify the accuracy of any documents or information supplied;

(C) request the testimony of, and production of any document in the possession of, any other person, including any client of a registered public accounting firm that the Board considers relevant or material to an investigation under this section, with appropriate notice, subject to the needs of the investigation, as permitted under the rules of the Board; and

(D) provide for procedures to seek issuance by the Commission, in a manner established by the Commission, of a subpoena to require the testimony of, and production of any document in the possession of, any person, including any client of a registered public accounting firm, that the Board considers relevant or material to an investigation under this section.

(3) Noncooperation with investigations.—

(A) In general.—If a registered public accounting firm or any associated person thereof refuses to testify, produce documents, or otherwise cooperate with the Board in connection with an investigation under this section, the Board may—

(i) suspend or bar such person from being associated with a registered public accounting firm, or require the registered public accounting firm to end such association;

(ii) suspend or revoke the registration of the public accounting firm; and

(iii) invoke such other lesser sanctions as the Board considers appropriate, and as specified by rule of the Board.

(B) Procedure.—Any action taken by the Board under this paragraph shall be subject to the terms of section 107(c).

(4) Coordination and referral of investigations.—

(A) Coordination.—The Board shall notify the Commission of any pending Board investigation involving a potential violation of the securities laws, and thereafter coordinate its work with the work of the Commission's Division of Enforcement, as necessary to protect an ongoing Commission investigation.

(B) Referral.—The Board may refer an investigation under this section—

(i) to the Commission;

(ii) to a self-regulatory organization, in the case of an investigation that concerns an audit report for a broker or dealer that is under the jurisdiction of such self-regulatory organization;

(iii) to any other Federal functional regulator (as defined in section 509 of the Gramm-Leach-Bliley Act (15 U.S.C. 6809)), in the case of an investigation that concerns an audit report for an institution that is subject to the jurisdiction of such regulator; and

(iv) at the direction of the Commission, to—

(I) the Attorney General of the United States;

(II) the attorney general of 1 or more States; and

(III) the appropriate State regulatory authority.

(5) Use of documents.—

(A) Confidentiality.—Except as provided in subparagraph (B) and (C), all documents and information prepared or received by or specifically for the Board, and deliberations of the Board and its employees and agents, in connection with an inspection under section 104 or with an investigation under this section, shall be confidential and privileged as an evidentiary matter (and shall not be subject to civil discovery or other legal process) in any proceeding in any Federal or State court or administrative agency, and shall be exempt from disclosure, in the hands of an agency or establishment of the Federal Government, under the Freedom of Information Act (5 U.S.C. 552a), or otherwise, unless and until presented in connection with a public proceeding or released in accordance with subsection (c).

(B) Availability to government agencies.—Without the loss of its status as confidential and privileged in the hands of the Board, all information referred to in subparagraph (A) may—

(i) be made available to the Commission; and

(ii) in the discretion of the Board, when determined by the Board to be necessary to accomplish the purposes of this Act or to protect investors, be made available to—

(I) the Attorney General of the United States;

(II) the appropriate Federal functional regulator (as defined in section 509 of the Gramm-Leach-Bliley Act (15 U.S.C. 6809)), other than the Commission, with respect to an audit report for an institution subject to the jurisdiction of such regulator;

(III) State attorneys general in connection with any criminal investigation;

(IV) any appropriate State regulatory authority, each of which shall maintain such information as confidential and privileged; and

(V) a self-regulatory organization, with respect to an audit report for a broker or dealer that is under the jurisdiction of such self-regulatory organization,

(C) Availability to foreign oversight authorities.—Without the loss of its status as confidential and privileged in the hands of the Board, all information referred to in subparagraph (A) that relates to a public accounting firm that a foreign government has empowered a foreign auditor oversight authority to inspect or otherwise enforce laws with respect to, may, at the discretion of the Board, be made available to the foreign auditor oversight authority, if—

    (i) the Board finds that it is necessary to accomplish the purposes of this Act or to protect investors;

    (ii) the foreign auditor oversight authority provides—

      (I) such assurances of confidentiality as the Board may request;

      (II) a description of the applicable information systems and controls of the foreign auditor oversight authority; and

      (III) a description of the laws and regulations of the foreign government of the foreign auditor oversight authority that are relevant to information access; and

    (iii) the Board determines that it is appropriate to share such information.

(6) Immunity.—Any employee of the Board engaged in carrying out an investigation under this Act shall be immune from any civil liability arising out of such investigation in the same manner and to the same extent as an employee of the Federal Government in similar circumstances.

(c) Disciplinary procedures.—

(1) Notification; recordkeeping.—The rules of the Board shall provide that in any proceeding by the Board to determine whether a registered public accounting firm, or an associated person thereof, should be disciplined, the Board shall—

(A) bring specific charges with respect to the firm or associated person;

(B) notify such firm or associated person of, and provide to the firm or associated person an opportunity to defend against, such charges; and

(C) keep a record of the proceedings.

(2) Public hearings.—Hearings under this section shall not be public, unless otherwise ordered by the Board for good cause shown, with the consent of the parties to such hearing.

(3) Supporting statement.—A determination by the Board to impose a sanction under this subsection shall be supported by a statement setting forth—

(A) each act or practice in which the registered public accounting firm, or associated person, has engaged (or omitted to engage), or that forms a basis for all or a part of such sanction;

(B) the specific provision of this Act, the securities laws, the rules of the Board, or professional standards which the Board determines has been violated; and

(C) the sanction imposed, including a justification for that sanction.

(4) Sanctions.—If the Board finds, based on all of the facts and circumstances, that a registered public accounting firm or associated person thereof has engaged in any act or practice, or omitted to act, in violation of this Act, the rules of the Board, the provisions of the securities laws relating to the preparation and issuance of audit reports and the obligations and liabilities of accountants with respect thereto, including the rules of the Commission issued under this Act, or professional standards, the Board may impose such disciplinary or remedial sanctions as it determines appropriate, subject to applicable limitations under paragraph (5), including—

(A) temporary suspension or permanent revocation of registration under this title;

(B) temporary or permanent suspension or bar of a person from further association with any registered public accounting firm;

(C) temporary or permanent limitation on the activities, functions, or operations of such firm or person (other than in connection with required additional professional education or training);

(D) a civil money penalty for each such violation, in an amount equal to—

(i) not more than $100,000 for a natural person or $2,000,000 for any other person; and

(ii) in any case to which paragraph (5) applies, not more than $750,000 for a natural person or $15,000,000 for any other person;

(E) censure;

(F) required additional professional education or training; or

(G) any other appropriate sanction provided for in the rules of the Board.

(5) Intentional or other knowing conduct.—The sanctions and penalties described in subparagraphs (A) through (C) and (D)(ii) of paragraph (4) shall only apply to—

(A) intentional or knowing conduct, including reckless conduct, that results in violation of the applicable statutory, regulatory, or professional standard; or

(B) repeated instances of negligent conduct, each resulting in a violation of the applicable statutory, regulatory, or professional standard.

(6) Failure to supervise.—

(A) In general.—The Board may impose sanctions under this section on a registered accounting firm or upon any person who is, or at the time of the alleged failure reasonably to supervise was, a supervisory person of such firm, if the Board finds that—

(i) the firm has failed reasonably to supervise an associated person, either as required by the rules of the Board relating to auditing or quality control standards, or otherwise, with a view to preventing violations of this Act, the rules of the Board, the provisions of the securities laws relating to the preparation and issuance of audit reports and the obligations and liabilities of accountants with respect thereto, including the rules of the Commission under this Act, or professional standards; and

(ii) such associated person commits a violation of this Act, or any of such rules, laws, or standards.

(B) Rule of construction.—No current or former supervisory person of a registered public accounting firm shall be deemed to have failed reasonably to supervise any associated person for purposes of subparagraph (A), if—

(i) there have been established in and for that firm procedures, and a system for applying such procedures, that comply with applicable rules of the Board and that would reasonably be expected to prevent and detect any such violation by such associated person; and

(ii) such person has reasonably discharged the duties and obligations incumbent upon that person by reason of such procedures and system, and had no reasonable cause to believe that such procedures and system were not being complied with.

(7) Effect of suspension.—

(A) Association with a public accounting firm.—It shall be unlawful for any person that is suspended or barred from being associated with a registered public accounting firm under this subsection willfully to become or remain associated with any registered public accounting firm, or for any registered public accounting firm that knew, or, in the exercise of reasonable care should have known, of the suspension or bar, to permit such an association, without the consent of the Board or the Commission.

(B) Association with an issuer, broker, or dealer.—It shall be unlawful for any person that is suspended or barred from being associated with a registered public accounting firm under this subsection willfully to become or remain associated with any issuer, broker, or dealer in an accountancy or a financial management capacity, and for any issuer, broker, or dealer that knew, or in the exercise of reasonable care should have known, of such suspension or bar, to permit such an association, without the consent of the Board or the Commission.

(d)   Reporting of sanctions.—

(1)   Recipients.—If the Board imposes a disciplinary sanction, in accordance with this section, the Board shall report the sanction to—

(A)   the Commission;

(B)   any appropriate State regulatory authority or any foreign accountancy licensing board with which such firm or person is licensed or certified; and

(C)   the public (once any stay on the imposition of such sanction has been lifted).

(2)   Contents.—The information reported under paragraph (1) shall include—

(A)   the name of the sanctioned person;

(B)   a description of the sanction and the basis for its imposition; and

(C)   such other information as the Board deems appropriate.

(e)   Stay of sanctions.—

(1)   In general.—Application to the Commission for review, or the institution by the Commission of review, of any disciplinary action of the Board shall operate as a stay of any such disciplinary action, unless and until the Commission orders (summarily or after notice and opportunity for hearing on the question of a stay, which hearing may consist solely of the submission of affidavits or presentation of oral arguments) that no such stay shall continue to operate.

(2)   Expedited procedures.—The Commission shall establish for appropriate cases an expedited procedure for consideration and determination of the question of the duration of a stay pending review of any disciplinary action of the Board under this subsection.

Sec. 106.   Foreign public accounting firms (15 U.S.C.A. § 7216)

(a)   Applicability to certain foreign firms.—

(1)   In general.—Any foreign public accounting firm that prepares or furnishes an audit report with respect to any issuer, broker, or dealer shall be subject to this Act and the rules of the Board and the Commission issued under this Act, in the same manner and to the same extent as a public accounting firm that is organized and operates under the laws of the United States or any State, except that registration pursuant to section 102 shall not by itself provide a basis for subjecting such a foreign public accounting firm to the jurisdiction of the Federal or State courts, other than with respect to controversies between such firms and the Board.

(2)   Board authority.—The Board may, by rule, determine that a foreign public accounting firm (or a class of such firms) that does not issue audit reports nonetheless plays such a substantial role in the preparation and furnishing of such reports for particular issuers, brokers, or dealers that it is necessary or appropriate, in light of the purposes of this Act and in the public interest or for the protection of investors, that such firm (or class of firms) should be treated as a public accounting firm (or firms) for purposes of registration under, and oversight by the Board in accordance with, this title.

(b)   Production of documents—

(1)   Production by foreign firms

If a foreign public accounting firm performs material services upon which a registered public accounting firm relies in the conduct of an audit or interim review, issues an audit report, performs audit work, or conducts interim reviews, the foreign public accounting firm shall—

(A)   produce the audit work papers of the foreign public accounting firm and all other documents of the firm related to any such audit work or interim review to the Commission or the Board, upon request of the Commission or the Board; and

(B) be subject to the jurisdiction of the courts of the United States for purposes of enforcement of any request for such documents.

(2) Other production

Any registered public accounting firm that relies, in whole or in part, on the work of a foreign public accounting firm in issuing an audit report, performing audit work, or conducting an interim review, shall—

(A) produce the audit work papers of the foreign public accounting firm and all other documents related to any such work in response to a request for production by the Commission or the Board; and

(B) secure the agreement of any foreign public accounting firm to such production, as a condition of the reliance by the registered public accounting firm on the work of that foreign public accounting firm.

(c) Exemption authority.—The Commission, and the Board, subject to the approval of the Commission, may, by rule, regulation, or order, and as the Commission (or Board) determines necessary or appropriate in the public interest or for the protection of investors, either unconditionally or upon specified terms and conditions exempt any foreign public accounting firm, or any class of such firms, from any provision of this Act or the rules of the Board or the Commission issued under this Act.

(d) Service of requests or process.

(1) In general. Any foreign public accounting firm that performs work for a domestic registered public accounting firm shall furnish to the domestic registered public accounting firm a written irrevocable consent and power of attorney that designates the domestic registered public accounting firm as an agent upon whom may be served any request by the Commission or the Board under this section or upon whom may be served any process, pleadings, or other papers in any action brought to enforce this section.

(2) Specific audit work. Any foreign public accounting firm that performs material services upon which a registered public accounting firm relies in the conduct of an audit or interim review, issues an audit report, performs audit work, or, performs interim reviews, shall designate to the Commission or the Board an agent in the United States upon whom may be served any request by the Commission or the Board under this section or upon whom may be served any process, pleading, or other papers in any action brought to enforce this section.

(e) Sanctions. A willful refusal to comply, in whole in or in part, with any request by the Commission or the Board under this section, shall be deemed a violation of this Act.

(f) Other means of satisfying production obligations. Notwithstanding any other provisions of this section, the staff of the Commission or the Board may allow a foreign public accounting firm that is subject to this section to meet production obligations under this section through alternate means, such as through foreign counterparts of the Commission or the Board.

(g) Definition.—In this section, the term "foreign public accounting firm" means a public accounting firm that is organized and operates under the laws of a foreign government or political subdivision thereof.

Sec. 107. Commission oversight of the board (15 U.S.C.A. § 7217)

(a) General oversight responsibility.—The Commission shall have oversight and enforcement authority over the Board, as provided in this Act. The provisions of section 17(a)(1) of the Securities Exchange Act of 1934 (15 U.S.C. 78q(a)(1)), and of section 17(b)(1) of the Securities Exchange Act of 1934 (15 U.S.C. 78q(b)(1)) shall apply to the Board as fully as if the Board were a "registered securities association" for purposes of those sections 17(a)(1) and 17(b)(1).

(b) Rules of the board.—

(1) Definition.—In this section, the term "proposed rule" means any proposed rule of the Board, and any modification of any such rule.

(2) Prior approval required.—No rule of the Board shall become effective without prior approval of the Commission in accordance with this section, other than as provided in section 103(a)(3)(B) with respect to initial or transitional standards.

(3) Approval criteria.—The Commission shall approve a proposed rule, if it finds that the rule is consistent with the requirements of this Act and the securities laws, or is necessary or appropriate in the public interest or for the protection of investors.

(4) Proposed rule procedures.—The provisions of paragraphs (1) through (3) of section 19(b) of the Securities Exchange Act of 1934 (15 U.S.C.A. § 78s(b)) shall govern the proposed rules of the Board, as fully as if the Board were a "registered securities association" for purposes of that section 19(b), except that, for purposes of this paragraph—

    (A) the phrase "consistent with the requirements of this title and the rules and regulations thereunder applicable to such organization" in section 19(b)(2) of that Act shall be deemed to read "consistent with the requirements of title I of the Sarbanes-Oxley Act of 2002, and the rules and regulations issued thereunder applicable to such organization, or as necessary or appropriate in the public interest or for the protection of investors"; and

    (B) the phrase "otherwise in furtherance of the purposes of this title" in section 19(b)(3)(C) of that Act shall be deemed to read "otherwise in furtherance of the purposes of title I of the Sarbanes-Oxley Act of 2002".

(5) Commission authority to amend rules of the board.—The provisions of section 19(c) of the Securities Exchange Act of 1934 (15 U.S.C. 78s(c)) shall govern the abrogation, deletion, or addition to portions of the rules of the Board by the Commission as fully as if the Board were a "registered securities association" for purposes of that section 19(c), except that the phrase "to conform its rules to the requirements of this title and the rules and regulations thereunder applicable to such organization, or otherwise in furtherance of the purposes of this title" in section 19(c) of that Act shall, for purposes of this paragraph, be deemed to read "to assure the fair administration of the Public Company Accounting Oversight Board, conform the rules promulgated by that Board to the requirements of title I of the Sarbanes-Oxley Act of 2002, or otherwise further the purposes of that Act, the securities laws, and the rules and regulations thereunder applicable to that Board".

(c) Commission review of disciplinary action taken by the board.—

(1) Notice of sanction.—The Board shall promptly file notice with the Commission of any final sanction on any registered public accounting firm or on any associated person thereof, in such form and containing such information as the Commission, by rule, may prescribe.

(2) Review of sanctions.—The provisions of sections 19(d)(2) and 19(e)(1) of the Securities Exchange Act of 1934 (15 U.S.C. 78s (d)(2) and (e)(1)) shall govern the review by the Commission of final disciplinary sanctions imposed by the Board (including sanctions imposed under section 105(b)(3) of this Act for noncooperation in an investigation of the Board), as fully as if the Board were a self-regulatory organization and the Commission were the appropriate regulatory agency for such organization for purposes of those sections 19(d)(2) and 19(e)(1), except that, for purposes of this paragraph—

    (A) section 105(e) of this Act (rather than that section 19(d)(2)) shall govern the extent to which application for, or institution by the Commission on its own motion of, review of any disciplinary action of the Board operates as a stay of such action;

    (B) references in that section 19(e)(1) to "members" of such an organization shall be deemed to be references to registered public accounting firms;

    (C) the phrase "consistent with the purposes of this title" in that section 19(e)(1) shall be deemed to read "consistent with the purposes of this title and title I of the Sarbanes-Oxley Act of 2002";

    (D) references to rules of the Municipal Securities Rulemaking Board in that section 19(e)(1) shall not apply; and

    (E) the reference to section 19(e)(2) of the Securities Exchange Act of 1934 shall refer instead to section 107(c)(3) of this Act.

(3) Commission modification authority.—The Commission may enhance, modify, cancel, reduce, or require the remission of a sanction imposed by the Board upon a registered public accounting firm or associated person thereof, if the Commission, having due regard for the public interest and the protection of investors, finds, after a proceeding in accordance with this subsection, that the sanction—

(A) is not necessary or appropriate in furtherance of this Act or the securities laws; or

(B) is excessive, oppressive, inadequate, or otherwise not appropriate to the finding or the basis on which the sanction was imposed.

(d) Censure of the board; other sanctions.—

(1) Rescission of board authority.—The Commission, by rule, consistent with the public interest, the protection of investors, and the other purposes of this Act and the securities laws, may relieve the Board of any responsibility to enforce compliance with any provision of this Act, the securities laws, the rules of the Board, or professional standards.

(2) Censure of the board; limitations.—The Commission may, by order, as it determines necessary or appropriate in the public interest, for the protection of investors, or otherwise in furtherance of the purposes of this Act or the securities laws, censure or impose limitations upon the activities, functions, and operations of the Board, if the Commission finds, on the record, after notice and opportunity for a hearing, that the Board—

(A) has violated or is unable to comply with any provision of this Act, the rules of the Board, or the securities laws; or

(B) without reasonable justification or excuse, has failed to enforce compliance with any such provision or rule, or any professional standard by a registered public accounting firm or an associated person thereof.

(3) Censure of board members; removal from office.—The Commission may, as necessary or appropriate in the public interest, for the protection of investors, or otherwise in furtherance of the purposes of this Act or the securities laws, remove from office or censure any person who is, or at the time of the alleged conduct was, a member of the Board, if the Commission finds, on the record, after notice and opportunity for a hearing, that such member—

(A) has willfully violated any provision of this Act, the rules of the Board, or the securities laws;

(B) has willfully abused the authority of that member; or

(C) without reasonable justification or excuse, has failed to enforce compliance with any such provision or rule, or any professional standard by any registered public accounting firm or any associated person thereof.

Sec. 108. Accounting standards (15 U.S.C.A. § 7218)

(a) Amendment to Securities Act of 1933 [amending Section 19 of the Securities Act of 1933 (15 U.S.C.A. § 77s)]

(b) Commission authority.—The Commission shall promulgate such rules and regulations to carry out section 19(b) of the Securities Act of 1933, as added by this section, as it deems necessary or appropriate in the public interest or for the protection of investors.

(c) No effect on commission powers.—Nothing in this Act, including this section and the amendment made by this section, shall be construed to impair or limit the authority of the Commission to establish accounting principles or standards for purposes of enforcement of the securities laws.

(d) Study and report on adopting principles-based accounting.—

(1) Study.—

(A) In general.—The Commission shall conduct a study on the adoption by the United States financial reporting system of a principles-based accounting system.

(B) Study topics.—The study required by subparagraph (A) shall include an examination of—

(i) the extent to which principles-based accounting and financial reporting exists in the United States;

(ii) the length of time required for change from a rules-based to a principles-based financial reporting system;

(iii) the feasibility of and proposed methods by which a principles-based system may be implemented; and

(iv) a thorough economic analysis of the implementation of a principles-based system.

(2) Report.—Not later than 1 year after the date of enactment of this Act, the Commission shall submit a report on the results of the study required by paragraph (1) to the Committee on Banking, Housing, and Urban Affairs of the Senate and the Committee on Financial Services of the House of Representatives.

Sec. 109. Funding (15 U.S.C.A. § 7219)

(a) In general.—The Board, and the standard setting body designated pursuant to section 19(b) of the Securities Act of 1933, as amended by section 108, shall be funded as provided in this section.

(b) Annual budgets.—The Board and the standard setting body referred to in subsection (a) shall each establish a budget for each fiscal year, which shall be reviewed and approved according to their respective internal procedures not less than 1 month prior to the commencement of the fiscal year to which the budget pertains (or at the beginning of the Board's first fiscal year, which may be a short fiscal year). The budget of the Board shall be subject to approval by the Commission. The budget for the first fiscal year of the Board shall be prepared and approved promptly following the appointment of the initial five Board members, to permit action by the Board of the organizational tasks contemplated by section 101(d).

(c) Sources and uses of funds.—

(1) Recoverable budget expenses.—The budget of the Board (reduced by any registration or annual fees received under section 102(e) for the year preceding the year for which the budget is being computed), and all of the budget of the standard setting body referred to in subsection (a), for each fiscal year of each of those 2 entities, shall be payable from annual accounting support fees, in accordance with subsections (d) and (e). Accounting support fees and other receipts of the Board and of such standard-setting body shall not be considered public monies of the United States.

(2) Funds generated from the collection of monetary penalties.—Subject to the availability in advance in an appropriations Act, and notwithstanding subsection (j), all funds collected by the Board as a result of the assessment of monetary penalties shall be used to fund a merit scholarship program for undergraduate and graduate students enrolled in accredited accounting degree programs, which program is to be administered by the Board or by an entity or agent identified by the Board.

(d) Annual accounting support fee for the board.—

(1) Establishment of fee.—The Board shall establish, with the approval of the Commission, a reasonable annual accounting support fee (or a formula for the computation thereof), as may be necessary or appropriate to establish and maintain the Board. Such fee may also cover costs incurred in the Board's first fiscal year (which may be a short fiscal year), or may be levied separately with respect to such short fiscal year.

(2) Assessments.—The rules of the Board under paragraph (1) shall provide for the equitable allocation, assessment, and collection by the Board (or an agent appointed by the Board) of the fee established under paragraph (1), among issuers, in accordance with subsection (g), and among brokers and dealers, in accordance with subsection (h), and allowing for differentiation among classes of issuers, brokers and dealers, as appropriate.

(3) Brokers and dealers—The Board shall begin the allocation, assessment, and collection of fees under paragraph (2) with respect to brokers and dealers with the payment of support fees to fund

the first full fiscal year beginning after the date of enactment of the Investor Protection and Securities Reform Act of 2010.

(e) Annual accounting support fee for standard setting body.—The annual accounting support fee for the standard setting body referred to in subsection (a)—

(1) shall be allocated in accordance with subsection (g), and assessed and collected against each issuer, on behalf of the standard setting body, by 1 or more appropriate designated collection agents, as may be necessary or appropriate to pay for the budget and provide for the expenses of that standard setting body, and to provide for an independent, stable source of funding for such body, subject to review by the Commission; and

(2) may differentiate among different classes of issuers.

(f) Limitation on fee.—The amount of fees collected under this section for a fiscal year on behalf of the Board or the standards setting body, as the case may be, shall not exceed the recoverable budget expenses of the Board or body, respectively (which may include operating, capital, and accrued items), referred to in subsection (c)(1).

(g) Allocation of accounting support fees among issuers.—Any amount due from issuers (or a particular class of issuers) under this section to fund the budget of the Board or the standard setting body referred to in subsection (a) shall be allocated among and payable by each issuer (or each issuer in a particular class, as applicable) in an amount equal to the total of such amount, multiplied by a fraction—

(1) the numerator of which is the average monthly equity market capitalization of the issuer for the 12-month period immediately preceding the beginning of the fiscal year to which such budget relates; and

(2) the denominator of which is the average monthly equity market capitalization of all such issuers for such 12-month period.

(h) Allocation of Accounting Support Fees Among Brokers and Dealers—

(1) Obligation to pay—Each broker or dealer shall pay to the Board the annual accounting support fee allocated to such broker or dealer under this section.

(2) Allocation—Any amount due from a broker or dealer (or from a particular class of brokers and dealers) under this section shall be allocated among brokers and dealers and payable by the broker or dealer (or the brokers and dealers in the particular class, as applicable).

(3) Proportionality—The amount due from a broker or dealer shall be in proportion to the net capital of the broker or dealer (before or after any adjustments), compared to the total net capital of all brokers and dealers (before or after any adjustments), in accordance with rules issued by the Board.

(i) Conforming amendments.—[amending Section 13(b)(2) of the Securities Exchange Act of 1934 (15 U.S.C.A. § 78m(b)(2))] is amended—

(j) Rule of construction.—Nothing in this section shall be construed to render either the Board, the standard setting body referred to in subsection (a), or both, subject to procedures in Congress to authorize or appropriate public funds, or to prevent such organization from utilizing additional sources of revenue for its activities, such as earnings from publication sales, provided that each additional source of revenue shall not jeopardize, in the judgment of the Commission, the actual and perceived independence of such organization.

(k) Start-up expenses of the board.—From the unexpended balances of the appropriations to the Commission for fiscal year 2003, the Secretary of the Treasury is authorized to advance to the Board not to exceed the amount necessary to cover the expenses of the Board during its first fiscal year (which may be a short fiscal year).

Sec. 110. Definitions (15 U.S.C.A. § 7220)

For the purposes of this title, the following definitions shall apply:

(1) Audit—The term "audit" means an examination of the financial statements, reports, documents, procedures, controls, or notices of any issuer, broker, or dealer by an independent public

accounting firm in accordance with the rules of the Board or the Commission, for the purpose of expressing an opinion on the financial statements or providing an audit report.

(2)   Audit report—The term "audit report" means a document, report, notice, or other record—

(A)   prepared following an audit performed for purposes of compliance by an issuer, broker, or dealer with the requirements of the securities laws; and

(B)   in which a public accounting firm either—

(i)   sets forth the opinion of that firm regarding a financial statement, report, notice, or other document, procedures, or controls; or

(ii)   asserts that no such opinion can be expressed.

(3)   Broker—The term "broker" means a broker (as such term is defined in section 3(a)(4) of the Securities Exchange Act of 1934 (15 U.S.C. 78c(a)(4))) that is required to file a balance sheet, income statement, or other financial statement under section 17(e)(1)(A) of such Act (15 U.S.C. 78q(e)(1)(A)), where such balance sheet, income statement, or financial statement is required to be certified by a registered public accounting firm.

(4)   Dealer—The term "dealer" means a dealer (as such term is defined in section 3(a)(5) of the Securities Exchange Act of 1934 (15 U.S.C. 78c(a)(5))) that is required to file a balance sheet, income statement, or other financial statement under section 17(e)(1)(A) of such Act (15 U.S.C. 78q(e)(1)(A)), where such balance sheet, income statement, or financial statement is required to be certified by a registered public accounting firm.

(5)   Professional standards—The term "professional standards" means—

(A)   accounting principles that are—

(i)   established by the standard setting body described in section 19(b) of the Securities Act of 1933, as amended by this Act, or prescribed by the Commission under section 19(a) of that Act (15 U.S.C. 17a(s)) or section 13(b) of the Securities Exchange Act of 1934 (15 U.S.C. 78a(m)); and

(ii)   relevant to audit reports for particular issuers, brokers, or dealers, or dealt with in the quality control system of a particular registered public accounting firm; and

(B)   auditing standards, standards for attestation engagements, quality control policies and procedures, ethical and competency standards, and independence standards (including rules implementing title II) that the Board or the Commission determines—

(i)   relate to the preparation or issuance of audit reports for issuers, brokers, or dealers; and

(ii)   are established or adopted by the Board under section 103(a), or are promulgated as rules of the Commission.

(6)   Self-regulatory organization—The term "self-regulatory organization" has the same meaning as in section 3(a) of the Securities Exchange Act of 1934 (15 U.S.C. 78c(a)).

TITLE III—CORPORATE RESPONSIBILITY

Sec. 301. Public company audit committees

[amending Section 10A of the Securities Exchange Act of 1934 (15 U.S.C.A. § 78j–1)]

Sec. 302. Corporate responsibility for financial reports (15 U.S.C.A. § 7241)

(a)   Regulations required.—The Commission shall, by rule, require, for each company filing periodic reports under section 13(a) or 15(d) of the Securities Exchange Act of 1934 (15 U.S.C. 78m, 78o(d)), that the principal executive officer or officers and the principal financial officer or officers, or persons performing similar functions, certify in each annual or quarterly report filed or submitted under either such section of such Act that—

(1)   the signing officer has reviewed the report;

(2)   based on the officer's knowledge, the report does not contain any untrue statement of a material fact or omit to state a material fact necessary in order to make the statements made, in light of the circumstances under which such statements were made, not misleading;

(3)   based on such officer's knowledge, the financial statements, and other financial information included in the report, fairly present in all material respects the financial condition and results of operations of the issuer as of, and for, the periods presented in the report;

(4)   the signing officers—

(A)   are responsible for establishing and maintaining internal controls;

(B)   have designed such internal controls to ensure that material information relating to the issuer and its consolidated subsidiaries is made known to such officers by others within those entities, particularly during the period in which the periodic reports are being prepared;

(C)   have evaluated the effectiveness of the issuer's internal controls as of a date within 90 days prior to the report; and

(D)   have presented in the report their conclusions about the effectiveness of their internal controls based on their evaluation as of that date;

(5)   the signing officers have disclosed to the issuer's auditors and the audit committee of the board of directors (or persons fulfilling the equivalent function)—

(A)   all significant deficiencies in the design or operation of internal controls which could adversely affect the issuer's ability to record, process, summarize, and report financial data and have identified for the issuer's auditors any material weaknesses in internal controls; and

(B)   any fraud, whether or not material, that involves management or other employees who have a significant role in the issuer's internal controls; and

(6)   the signing officers have indicated in the report whether or not there were significant changes in internal controls or in other factors that could significantly affect internal controls subsequent to the date of their evaluation, including any corrective actions with regard to significant deficiencies and material weaknesses.

(b)   Foreign reincorporations have no effect.—Nothing in this section 302 shall be interpreted or applied in any way to allow any issuer to lessen the legal force of the statement required under this section 302, by an issuer having reincorporated or having engaged in any other transaction that resulted in the transfer of the corporate domicile or offices of the issuer from inside the United States to outside of the United States.

(c)   Deadline.—The rules required by subsection (a) shall be effective not later than 30 days after the date of enactment of this Act.

Sec. 303. Improper influence on conduct of audits (15 U.S.C.A. § 7242)

(a)   Rules to prohibit.—It shall be unlawful, in contravention of such rules or regulations as the Commission shall prescribe as necessary and appropriate in the public interest or for the protection of investors, for any officer or director of an issuer, or any other person acting under the direction thereof, to take any action to fraudulently influence, coerce, manipulate, or mislead any independent public or certified accountant engaged in the performance of an audit of the financial statements of that issuer for the purpose of rendering such financial statements materially misleading.

(b)   Enforcement.—In any civil proceeding, the Commission shall have exclusive authority to enforce this section and any rule or regulation issued under this section.

(c)   No preemption of other law.—The provisions of subsection (a) shall be in addition to, and shall not supersede or preempt, any other provision of law or any rule or regulation issued thereunder.

(d)   Deadline for rulemaking.—The Commission shall—

(1)   propose the rules or regulations required by this section, not later than 90 days after the date of enactment of this Act; and

(2)   issue final rules or regulations required by this section, not later than 270 days after that date of enactment.

Sec. 304. Forfeiture of certain bonuses and profits (15 U.S.C.A. § 7243)

(a)   Additional compensation prior to noncompliance with commission financial reporting requirements.—If an issuer is required to prepare an accounting restatement due to the material noncompliance of the issuer, as a result of misconduct, with any financial reporting requirement under the securities laws, the chief executive officer and chief financial officer of the issuer shall reimburse the issuer for—

(1)   any bonus or other incentive-based or equity-based compensation received by that person from the issuer during the 12-month period following the first public issuance or filing with the Commission (whichever first occurs) of the financial document embodying such financial reporting requirement; and

(2)   any profits realized from the sale of securities of the issuer during that 12-month period.

(b)   Commission exemption authority.—The Commission may exempt any person from the application of subsection (a), as it deems necessary and appropriate.

Sec. 305. Officer and director bars and penalties

(a)   Unfitness standard. [amending Section 21(d)(2) of the Securities Exchange Act of 1934 (15 U.S.C.A. § 78u(d)(2)) and Section 20(e) of the Securities Act of 1933 (15 U.S.C.A. § 77t(e))].

(b)   Equitable relief. [amending Section 21(d) of the Securities Exchange Act of 1934 (15 U.S.C.A. § 78u(d))].

Sec. 306. Insider trades during pension fund blackout periods (15 U.S.C.A. § 7244)

(a)   Prohibition of insider trading during pension fund blackout periods.—

(1)   In general.—Except to the extent otherwise provided by rule of the Commission pursuant to paragraph (3), it shall be unlawful for any director or executive officer of an issuer of any equity security (other than an exempted security), directly or indirectly, to purchase, sell, or otherwise acquire or transfer any equity security of the issuer (other than an exempted security) during any blackout period with respect to such equity security if such director or officer acquires such equity security in connection with his or her service or employment as a director or executive officer.

(2)   Remedy.—

(A)   In general.—Any profit realized by a director or executive officer referred to in paragraph (1) from any purchase, sale, or other acquisition or transfer in violation of this subsection shall inure to and be recoverable by the issuer, irrespective of any intention on the part of such director or executive officer in entering into the transaction.

(B)   Actions to recover profits.—An action to recover profits in accordance with this subsection may be instituted at law or in equity in any court of competent jurisdiction by the issuer, or by the owner of any security of the issuer in the name and in behalf of the issuer if the issuer fails or refuses to bring such action within 60 days after the date of request, or fails diligently to prosecute the action thereafter, except that no such suit shall be brought more than 2 years after the date on which such profit was realized.

(3)   Rulemaking authorized.—The Commission shall, in consultation with the Secretary of Labor, issue rules to clarify the application of this subsection and to prevent evasion thereof. Such rules shall provide for the application of the requirements of paragraph (1) with respect to entities treated as a single employer with respect to an issuer under section 414(b), (c), (m), or (o) of the Internal Revenue Code of 1986 to the extent necessary to clarify the application of such requirements and to prevent evasion thereof. Such rules may also provide for appropriate exceptions from the requirements

of this subsection, including exceptions for purchases pursuant to an automatic dividend reinvestment program or purchases or sales made pursuant to an advance election.

(4) Blackout period.—For purposes of this subsection, the term "blackout period", with respect to the equity securities of any issuer—

(A) means any period of more than 3 consecutive business days during which the ability of not fewer than 50 percent of the participants or beneficiaries under all individual account plans maintained by the issuer to purchase, sell, or otherwise acquire or transfer an interest in any equity of such issuer held in such an individual account plan is temporarily suspended by the issuer or by a fiduciary of the plan; and

(B) does not include, under regulations which shall be prescribed by the Commission—

(i) a regularly scheduled period in which the participants and beneficiaries may not purchase, sell, or otherwise acquire or transfer an interest in any equity of such issuer, if such period is—

(I) incorporated into the individual account plan; and

(II) timely disclosed to employees before becoming participants under the individual account plan or as a subsequent amendment to the plan; or

(ii) any suspension described in subparagraph (A) that is imposed solely in connection with persons becoming participants or beneficiaries, or ceasing to be participants or beneficiaries, in an individual account plan by reason of a corporate merger, acquisition, divestiture, or similar transaction involving the plan or plan sponsor.

(5) Individual account plan.—For purposes of this subsection, the term "individual account plan" has the meaning provided in section 3(34) of the Employee Retirement Income Security Act of 1974 (29 U.S.C. 1002(34)), except that such term shall not include a one-participant retirement plan (within the meaning of section 101(i)(8)(B) of such Act (29 U.S.C. 1021(i)(8)(B))).

(6) Notice to directors, executive officers, and the commission.—In any case in which a director or executive officer is subject to the requirements of this subsection in connection with a blackout period (as defined in paragraph (4)) with respect to any equity securities, the issuer of such equity securities shall timely notify such director or officer and the Securities and Exchange Commission of such blackout period.

(b) Notice requirements to participants and beneficiaries under ERISA.—* * *

Sec. 307. Rules of professional responsibility for attorneys (15 U.S.C.A. § 7245)

Not later than 180 days after the date of enactment of this Act, the Commission shall issue rules, in the public interest and for the protection of investors, setting forth minimum standards of professional conduct for attorneys appearing and practicing before the Commission in any way in the representation of issuers, including a rule—

(1) requiring an attorney to report evidence of a material violation of securities law or breach of fiduciary duty or similar violation by the company or any agent thereof, to the chief legal counsel or the chief executive officer of the company (or the equivalent thereof); and

(2) if the counsel or officer does not appropriately respond to the evidence (adopting, as necessary, appropriate remedial measures or sanctions with respect to the violation), requiring the attorney to report the evidence to the audit committee of the board of directors of the issuer or to another committee of the board of directors comprised solely of directors not employed directly or indirectly by the issuer, or to the board of directors.

Sec. 308. Fair funds for investors (15 U.S.C.A. § 7246)

(a) Civil penalties to be used for the relief of victims—If, in any judicial or administrative action brought by the Commission under the securities laws, the Commission obtains a civil penalty against any person for a violation of such laws, or such person agrees, in settlement of any such action, to such civil penalty, the amount of such civil penalty shall, on the motion or at the direction of the Commission, be added to and become part of a disgorgement fund or other fund established for the benefit of the victims of such violation.

(b)   Acceptance of additional donations.—The Commission is authorized to accept, hold, administer, and utilize gifts, bequests and devises of property, both real and personal, to the United States for a disgorgement fund or other fund described in subsection (a). Such gifts, bequests, and devises of money and proceeds from sales of other property received as gifts, bequests, or devises shall be deposited in such fund and shall be available for allocation in accordance with subsection (a).

(c)   Study required.—

(1)   Subject of study.—The Commission shall review and analyze—

(A)   enforcement actions by the Commission over the five years preceding the date of the enactment of this Act that have included proceedings to obtain civil penalties or disgorgements to identify areas where such proceedings may be utilized to efficiently, effectively, and fairly provide restitution for injured investors; and

(B)   other methods to more efficiently, effectively, and fairly provide restitution to injured investors, including methods to improve the collection rates for civil penalties and disgorgements.

(2)   Report required.—The Commission shall report its findings to the Committee on Financial Services of the House of Representatives and the Committee on Banking, Housing, and Urban Affairs of the Senate within 180 days after of the date of the enactment of this Act, and shall use such findings to revise its rules and regulations as necessary. The report shall include a discussion of regulatory or legislative actions that are recommended or that may be necessary to address concerns identified in the study.

(d)   Conforming amendments.—[amending various sections of the 1933 and 1934 Acts]

Each of the following provisions is amended by inserting ", except as otherwise provided in section 308 of the Sarbanes-Oxley Act of 2002" after "Treasury of the United States".

SELECTED RULES AND REGULATIONS UNDER SECURITIES EXCHANGE ACT OF 1934

17 C.F.R. § 240.___

1934 ACT RULES

HYPOTHECATION OF CUSTOMERS' SECURITIES

STANDARDIZED OPTIONS

MANIPULATIVE AND DECEPTIVE DEVICES AND CONTRIVANCES

REPORTS UNDER SECTION 10A

REQUIREMENTS UNDER SECTION 10C

REQUIREMENTS UNDER SECTION 10D

MARKETS

EXEMPTIONS FROM EXCHANGE ACT REGISTRATION

1934 ACT RULES

1934 ACT RULES

1934 ACT RULES

EXEMPTION OF CERTAIN ISSUERS FROM
SECTION 15(d) OF THE ACT

PENNY STOCK RULES

NATIONAL AND AFFILIATED SECURITIES ASSOCIATION

REPORTS OF DIRECTORS

1934 ACT RULES

PRESERVATION OF RECORDS AND REPORTS OF CERTAIN STABILIZING ACTIVITIES

SUPERVISED INVESTMENT BANK HOLDING COMPANY RULES

POWERS WITH RESPECT TO EXCHANGES AND SECURITIES

SECURITIES WHISTLEBLOWER INCENTIVES AND PROTECTION

INSPECTION AND PUBLICATION OF INFORMATION FILED UNDER THE ACT

ATTENTION ELECTRONIC FILERS

THIS REGULATION SHOULD BE READ IN CONJUNCTION WITH REGULATION S–T (PART 232 OF THIS CHAPTER), WHICH GOVERNS THE PREPARATION AND SUBMISSION OF DOCUMENTS IN ELECTRONIC FORMAT. MANY PROVISIONS RELATING TO THE PREPARATION AND SUBMISSION OF DOCUMENTS IN PAPER FORMAT CONTAINED IN THIS REGULATION ARE SUPERSEDED BY THE PROVISIONS OF REGULATION S–T FOR DOCUMENTS REQUIRED TO BE FILED IN ELECTRONIC FORMAT.

RULES OF GENERAL APPLICATION

Rule 0–1. Definitions

(a) As used in the Rules and Regulations, prescribed by the Commission pursuant to Title I of the Securities Exchange Act of 1934, unless the context otherwise specifically requires:

(1) The term "Commission" means the Securities and Exchange Commission.

(2) The term "Act" means Title I of the Securities Exchange Act of 1934.

(3) The term "section" refers to a section of the Securities Exchange Act of 1934.

(4) The term "rules and regulations" refers to all rules and regulations adopted by the Commission pursuant to the act, including the forms for registration and reports and the accompanying instructions thereto.

(5) The term "electronic filer" means a person or an entity that submits filings electronically pursuant to Rules 100 and 101 of Regulation S–T of this chapter, respectively.

(6) The term "electronic filing" means a document under the federal securities laws that is transmitted or delivered to the Commission in electronic format.

(b) Unless otherwise specifically stated, the terms used in the Rules and Regulations shall have the meaning defined in the Act.

(c) A Rule or Regulation which defines a term without express reference to the Act or to the Rules and Regulations, or to a portion thereof, defines such term for all purposes as used both in the Act and in the Rules and Regulations, unless the context otherwise specifically requires.

(d)   Unless otherwise specified or the context otherwise requires, the term "prospectus" means a prospectus meeting the requirements of section 10(a) of the Securities Act of 1933 as amended.

Rule 0–2.   Business Hours of the Commission

(a)   The principal office of the Commission, at 100 F Street, NE, Washington, D.C. 20549, is open each day, except Saturdays, Sundays and federal holidays, from 9:00 a.m. to 5:30 p.m., Eastern Standard Time or Eastern Daylight Saving Time, whichever is currently in effect, *provided that* hours for the filing of documents pursuant to the Act or the rules and regulations thereunder are as set forth in paragraphs (b) and (c) of this rule.

(b)   *Submissions Made in Paper.* Paper documents filed with or otherwise furnished to the Commission may be submitted to the commission each day, except Saturdays, Sundays and federal holidays, from 8 a.m. to 5:30 p.m., Eastern Standard Time or Eastern Daylight Saving Time, whichever is currently in effect.

(c)   *Filings by Direct Transmission.* Filings made by direct transmission may be submitted to the Commission each day, except Saturdays, Sundays and federal holidays, from 8:00 a.m. to 10:00 p.m., Eastern Standard Time or Eastern Daylight Saving Time, whichever is currently in effect.

Rule 0–3.   Filing of Material With the Commission

(a)   All papers required to be filed with the Commission pursuant to the Act or the rules and regulations thereunder shall be filed at the principal office in Washington, D.C. Material may be filed by delivery to the Commission, through the mails or otherwise. The date on which papers are actually received by the Commission shall be the date of filing thereof if all of the requirements with respect to the filing have been complied with, except that if the last day on which papers can be accepted as timely filed falls on a Saturday, Sunday or holiday, such papers may be filed on the first business day following.

(b)   The manually signed original (or in the case of duplicate originals, one duplicate original) of all registrations, applications, statements, reports, or other documents filed under the Securities Exchange Act of 1934, as amended, shall be numbered sequentially (in addition to any internal numbering which otherwise may be present) by handwritten, typed, printed, or other legible form of notation from the facing page of the document through the last page of that document and any exhibits or attachments thereto. Further, the total number of pages contained in a numbered original shall be set forth on the first page of the document.

(c)   Each document filed shall contain an exhibit index, which should immediately precede the exhibits filed with such document. The index shall list each exhibit filed and identify by handwritten, typed, printed, or other legible form of notation in the manually signed original, the page number in the sequential numbering system described in paragraph (b) of this rule where such exhibit can be found or where it is stated that the exhibit is incorporated by reference. Further, the first page of the manually signed document shall list the page in the filing where the exhibit index is located.

Rule 0–4.   Non-disclosure of Information Obtained in the Course of Examinations and Investigations

Information or documents obtained by officers or employees of the Commission in the course of any examination or investigation pursuant to Section 17(a) or 21(a) shall, unless made a matter of public record, be deemed confidential. Except as provided by 17 CFR 203.2, officers and employees are hereby prohibited from making such confidential information or documents or any other non-public records of the Commission available to anyone other than a member, officer or employee of the Commission, unless the Commission or the General Counsel, pursuant to delegated authority, authorizes the disclosure of such information or the production of such documents as not being contrary to the public interest. Any officer or employee who is served with a subpoena requiring the disclosure of such information or the production of such documents shall appear in court and, unless the authorization described in the preceding sentence shall have been given, shall respectfully decline to disclose the information or produce the documents called for, basing his refusal upon this rule. Any officer or employee who is served with such a subpoena shall promptly advise the General Counsel of the service of such subpoena, the nature of the information or documents sought, and any circumstances which may bear upon the desirability of making available such information or documents.

Rule 0–5. Reference to Rule by Obsolete Designation

Wherever in any rule, form, or instruction book specific reference is made to a rule by number or other designation which is now obsolete, such reference shall be deemed to be made to the corresponding rule or rules in the existing general rules and regulations.

Rule 0–6. Disclosure Detrimental to the National Defense or Foreign Policy

(a) Any requirement to the contrary notwithstanding, no registration statement, report, proxy statement or other document filed with the Commission or any securities exchange shall contain any document or information which, pursuant to Executive order, has been classified by an appropriate department or agency of the United States for protection in the interests of national defense or foreign policy.

(b) Where a document or information is omitted pursuant to paragraph (a) of this rule, there shall be filed, in lieu of such document or information, a statement from an appropriate department or agency of the United States to the effect that such document or information has been classified or that the status thereof is awaiting determination. Where a document is omitted pursuant to paragraph (a) of this rule, but information relating to the subject matter of such document is nevertheless included in material filed with the Commission pursuant to a determination of an appropriate department or agency of the United States that disclosure of such information would not be contrary to the interests of national defense or foreign policy, a statement from such department or agency to that effect shall be submitted for the information of the Commission. A registrant may rely upon any such statement in filing or omitting any document or information to which the statement relates.

(c) The Commission may protect any information in its possession which may require classification in the interests of national defense or foreign policy pending determination by an appropriate department or agency as to whether such information should be classified.

(d) It shall be the duty of the registrant to submit the documents or information referred to in paragraph (a) of this rule to the appropriate department or agency of the United States prior to filing them with the Commission and to obtain and submit to the Commission, at the time of filing such documents or information, or in lieu thereof, as the case may be, the statements from such department or agency required by paragraph (b) of this rule. All such statements shall be in writing.

Rule 0–8. Application of Rules to Registered Broker-Dealers

Any provision of any rule or regulation under the Act which prohibits any act, practice, or course of business by any person if the mails or any means or instrumentality of interstate commerce are used in connection therewith, shall also prohibit any such act, practice, or course of business by any broker or dealer registered pursuant to section 15(b) of the Act, or any person acting on behalf of such a broker or dealer, irrespective of any use of the mails or any means or instrumentality of interstate commerce.

Rule 0–9. Payment of Fees

All payments of fees for registration statements under the Act shall be made by wire transfer, or by certified check, bank cashier's check, United States postal money order, or bank money order payable to the Securities and Exchange Commission, omitting the name or title of any official of the Commission. There will be no refunds. Payment of fees required by this Rule shall be made in accordance with the directions set forth in § 202.3a of this chapter.

Rule 0–10. Small Entities for Purposes of the Regulatory Flexibility Act

For purposes of Commission rulemaking in accordance with the provisions of Chapter Six of the Administrative Procedure Act, and unless otherwise defined for purposes of a particular rulemaking proceeding, the term "small business" or "small organization" shall:

(a) When used with reference to an "issuer" or a "person," other than an investment company, mean an "issuer" or "person" that, on the last day of its most recent fiscal year, had total assets of $5 million or less;

(b) When used with reference to an "issuer" or a "person" that is an investment company, have the meaning ascribed to those terms by Rule 0–10 of the Investment Company Act of 1940;

(c) When used with reference to a broker or dealer, mean a broker or dealer that:

(1) Had total capital (net worth plus subordinated liabilities) of less than $500,000 on the date in the prior fiscal year as of which its audited financial statements were prepared pursuant to Rule 17a–5(d) or, if not required to file such statements, a broker or dealer that had total capital (net worth plus subordinated liabilities) of less than $500,000 on the last business day of the preceding fiscal year (or in the time that it has been in business, if shorter); and

(2) Is not affiliated with any person (other than a natural person) that is not a small business or small organization as defined in this rule;

(d) When used with reference to a clearing agency, mean a clearing agency that:

(1) Compared, cleared and settled less than $500 million in securities transactions during the preceding fiscal year (or in the time that it has been in business, if shorter);

(2) Had less than $200 million of funds and securities in its custody or control at all times during the preceding fiscal year (or in the time that it has been in business, if shorter); and

(3) Is not affiliated with any person (other than a natural person) that is not a small business or small organization as defined in this rule;

(e) When used with reference to an exchange, mean any exchange that;

(1) has been exempted from the reporting requirements of Rule 601 of Regulation NMS; and

(2) Is not affiliated with any person (other than a natural person) that is not a small business or small organization as defined in this rule;

(f) When used with reference to a municipal securities dealer that is a bank (including any separately identifiable department or division of a bank), mean any such municipal securities dealer that:

(1) Had, or is a department of a bank that had, total assets of less than $10 million dollars at all times during the preceding fiscal year (or in the time that it has been in business, if shorter);

(2) Had an average monthly volume of municipal securities transactions in the preceding fiscal year (or in the time it has been registered, if shorter) of less than $100,000; and

(3) Is not affiliated with any person (other than a natural person) that is not a small business or small organization as defined in this rule;

(g) When used with reference to a securities information processor, mean a securities information processor that:

(1) Had gross revenues of less than $10 million during the preceding fiscal year (or in the time it has been in business, if shorter);

(2) Provided service to less than 100 interrogation devices or moving tickers at all times during the preceding fiscal year (or in the time that it has been in business, if shorter); and

(3) Is not affiliated with any person (other than a natural person) that is not a small business or small organization as defined in this rule; and

(h) When used with reference to a transfer agent, mean a transfer agent that:

(1) Received less than 500 items for transfer and less than 500 items for processing during the preceding six months (or in the time that it has been in business, if shorter);

(2)   Transferred items only of issuers that would be deemed "small businesses" or "small organizations" as defined in this rule; and

(3)   Maintained master shareholder files that in the aggregate contained less than 1,000 shareholder accounts or was the named transfer agent for less than 1,000 shareholder accounts at all times during the preceding fiscal year (or in the time that it has been in business, if shorter); and

(4)   Is not affiliated with any person (other than a natural person) that is not a small business or small organization under this rule.

(i)   For purposes of paragraph (c) of this rule, a broker or dealer is affiliated with another person if:

(1)   Such broker or dealer controls, is controlled by, or is under common control with such other person; a person shall be deemed to control another person if that person has the right to vote 25 percent or more of the voting securities of such other person or is entitled to receive 25 percent or more of the net profits of such other person or is otherwise able to direct or cause the direction of the management or policies of such other person; or

(2)   Such broker or dealer introduces transactions in securities, other than registered investment company securities or interests or participations in insurance company separate accounts, to such other person, or introduces accounts of customers or other brokers or dealers, other than accounts that hold only registered investment company securities or interests or participations in insurance company separate accounts, to such other person that carries such accounts on a fully disclosed basis.

(j)   For purposes of paragraphs (d) through (h) of this rule, a person is affiliated with another person if that person controls, is controlled by, or is under common control with such other person; a person shall be deemed to control another person if that person has the right to vote 25 percent or more of the voting securities of such other person or is entitled to receive 25 percent or more of the net profits of such other person or is otherwise able to direct or cause the direction of the management or policies of such other person.

(k)   For purposes of paragraph (g) of this rule, "interrogation device" shall refer to any device that may be used to read or receive securities information, including quotations, indications of interest, last sale data and transaction reports, and shall include proprietary terminals or personal computers that receive securities information via computer-to-computer interfaces or gateway access.

Rule 0–11.   Filing Fees for Certain Acquisitions, Dispositions and Similar Transactions

(a)   *General.*

(1)   At the time of filing a disclosure document described in paragraphs (b) through (d) of this rule relating to certain acquisitions, dispositions, business combinations, consolidations or similar transactions, the person filing the specified document shall pay a fee payable to the Commission to be calculated as set forth in paragraphs (b) through (d) of this rule.

(2)   Only one fee per transaction is required to be paid. A required fee shall be reduced in an amount equal to any fee paid with respect to such transaction pursuant to either section 6(b) of the Securities Act of 1933 or any applicable provision of this rule; the fee requirements under section 6(b) shall be reduced in an amount equal to the fee paid the Commission with respect to a transaction under this regulation. No part of a filing fee is refundable.

(3)   If at any time after the initial payment the aggregate consideration offered is increased, an additional filing fee based upon such increase shall be paid with the required amended filing.

(4)   When the fee is based upon the market value of securities, such market value shall be established by either the average of the high and low prices reported in the consolidated reporting system (for exchange traded securities and last sale reported over-the-counter securities) or the average of the bid and asked price (for other over-the-counter securities) as of a specified date within 5 business days prior to the date of the filing. If there is no market for the securities, the value shall be based upon the book value of the securities computed as of the latest practicable date prior to the

date of the filing, unless the issuer of the securities is in bankruptcy or receivership or has an accumulated capital deficit, in which case one-third of the principal amount, par value or stated value of the securities shall be used.

(5)   The cover page of the filing shall set forth the calculation of the fee in tabular format, as well as the amount offset by a previous filing and the identification of such filing, if applicable.

(b)   *Section 13(e)(1) filings.* At the time of filing such statement as the Commission may require pursuant to section 13(e)(1) of the Act, a fee of one-fiftieth of one percent of the value of the securities proposed to be acquired by the acquiring person. The value of the securities proposed to be acquired shall be determined as follows:

(1)   The value of the securities to be acquired solely for cash shall be the amount of cash to be paid for them:

(2)   The value of the securities to be acquired with securities or other non-cash consideration, whether or not in combination with a cash payment for the same securities, shall be based upon the market value of the securities to be received by the acquiring person as established in accordance with paragraph (a)(4) of this rule.

(c)   *Proxy and information statement filings.* At the time of filing a preliminary proxy statement pursuant to Rule 14a–6(a) or preliminary information statement pursuant to Rule 14c–5(a) that concerns a merger, consolidation, acquisition of a company, or proposed sale or other disposition of substantially all the assets of the registrant (including a liquidation), the following fee:

(1)   For preliminary material involving a vote upon a merger, consolidation or acquisition of a company, a fee of one-fiftieth of one percent of the proposed cash payment or of the value of the securities and other property to be transferred to security holders in the transaction. The fee is payable whether the registrant is acquiring another company or being acquired.

(i)   The value of securities or other property to be transferred to security holders, whether or not in combination with a cash payment for the same securities, shall be based upon the market value of the securities to be received by the acquiring person as established in accordance with paragraph (a)(4) of this rule.

(ii)   Notwithstanding the above, where the acquisition, merger or consolidation is for the sole purpose of changing the registrant's domicile no filing fee is required to be paid.

(2)   For preliminary material involving a vote upon a proposed sale or other disposition of substantially all the assets of the registrant, a fee of one-fiftieth of one percent of the aggregate of the cash and the value of the securities (other than its own) and other property to be received by the registrant. In the case of a disposition in which the registrant will not receive any property, such as at liquidation or spin-off, the fee shall be one-fiftieth of one percent of the aggregate of the cash and the value of the securities and other property to be distributed to security holders.

(i)   The value of the securities to be received (or distributed in the case of a spin-off or liquidation) shall be based upon the market value of such securities as established in accordance with paragraph (a)(4) of this rule.

(ii)   The value of other property shall be a bona fide estimate of the fair market value of such property.

(3)   Where two or more companies are involved in the transaction, each shall pay a proportionate share of such fee, determined by the persons involved.

(4)   Notwithstanding the above, the fee required by this paragraph (c) shall not be payable for a proxy statement filed by a company registered under the Investment Company Act of 1940.

(d)   *Section 14(d)(1) filings.* At the time of filing such statement as the Commission may require pursuant to section 14(d)(1) of the Act, a fee of one-fiftieth of one percent of the aggregate of the cash or of the value of the securities or other property offered by the bidder. Where the bidder is offering securities or other non-cash consideration for some or all of the securities to be acquired, whether or not in combination with a cash payment for the same securities, the value of the consideration to be offered for such securities shall be based upon the market value of the securities to be received by the bidder as established in accordance with paragraph (a)(4) of this rule.

Rule 0–12. Commission Procedures for Filing Applications for Orders for Exemptive Relief Under Section 36 of the Exchange Act

(a) The application shall be in writing in the form of a letter, must include any supporting documents necessary to make the application complete, and otherwise must comply with Rule 0–3. All applications must be submitted to the Office of the Secretary of the Commission. Requestors may seek confidential treatment of their applications to the extent provided under § 200.81 of this chapter. If an application is incomplete, the Commission, through the Division handling the application, may request that the application be withdrawn unless the applicant can justify, based on all the facts and circumstances, why supporting materials have not been submitted and undertakes to submit the omitted materials promptly.

(b) An applicant may submit a request electronically. The electronic mailbox to use for these applications is described on the Commission's Web site at http://www.sec.gov in the "Exchange Act Exemptive Applications" section. In the event the electronic mailbox is revised in the future, applicants can find the appropriate mailbox by accessing the "Electronic Mailboxes at the Commission" section.

(c) An applicant also may submit a request in paper format. Five copies of every paper application and every amendment to such an application must be submitted to the Office of the Secretary at 100 F Street, NE., Washington, DC 20549–1090. Applications must be on white paper no larger than 8 1/2 by 11 inches in size. The left margin of applications must be at least 1 1/2 inches wide, and if the application is bound, it must be bound on the left side. All typewritten or printed material must be on one side of the paper only and must be set forth in black ink so as to permit photocopying.

(d) Every application (electronic or paper) must contain the name, address and telephone number of each applicant and the name, address, and telephone number of a person to whom any questions regarding the application should be directed. The Commission will not consider hypothetical or anonymous requests for exemptive relief. Each applicant shall state the basis for the relief sought, and identify the anticipated benefits for investors and any conditions or limitations the applicant believes would be appropriate for the protection of investors. Applicants should also cite to and discuss applicable precedent.

(e) Amendments to the application should be prepared and submitted as set forth in these procedures and should be marked to show what changes have been made.

(f) After the filing is complete, the applicable Division will review the application. Once all questions and issues have been answered to the satisfaction of the Division, the staff will make an appropriate recommendation to the Commission. After consideration of the recommendation by the Commission, the Commission's Office of the Secretary will issue an appropriate response and will notify the applicant. If the application pertains to a section of the Exchange Act pursuant to which the Commission has delegated its authority to the appropriate Division, the Division Director or his or her designee will issue an appropriate response and notify the applicant.

(g) The Commission, in its sole discretion, may choose to publish in the Federal Register a notice that the application has been submitted. The notice would provide that any person may, within the period specified therein, submit to the Commission any information that relates to the Commission action requested in the application. The notice also would indicate the earliest date on which the Commission would take final action on the application, but in no event would such action be taken earlier than 25 days following publication of the notice in the Federal Register.

(h) The Commission may, in its sole discretion, schedule a hearing on the matter addressed by the application.

Rule 0–13. Commission Procedures for Filing Applications to Request a Substituted Compliance Order Under the Exchange Act

(a) The application shall be in writing in the form of a letter, must include any supporting documents necessary to make the application complete, and otherwise must comply with Rule 0–3. All applications must be submitted to the Office of the Secretary of the Commission, by a party that potentially would comply with requirements under the Exchange Act pursuant to a substituted compliance order, or by the relevant foreign financial regulatory authority or authorities. If an application is incomplete, the Commission may request that the application be withdrawn unless the applicant can justify, based on all the facts and circumstances, why supporting materials have not been submitted and undertakes to submit the omitted materials promptly.

(b)   An applicant may submit a request electronically. The electronic mailbox to use for these applications is described on the Commission's Web site at *www.sec.gov* in the "Exchange Act Substituted Compliance Applications" section. In the event electronic mailboxes are revised in the future, applicants can find the appropriate mailbox by accessing the "Electronic Mailboxes at the Commission" section.

(c)   All filings and submissions filed pursuant to this rule must be in the English language. If a filing or submission filed pursuant to this rule requires the inclusion of a document that is in a foreign language, a party must submit instead a fair and accurate English translation of the entire foreign language document. A party may submit a copy of the unabridged foreign language document when including an English translation of a foreign language document in a filing or submission filed pursuant to this rule. A party must provide a copy of any foreign language document upon the request of Commission staff.

(d)   An applicant also may submit a request in paper format. Five copies of every paper application and every amendment to such an application must be submitted to the Office of the Secretary at 100 F Street NE., Washington, DC 20549–1090. Applications must be on white paper no larger than 8 1/2 by 11 inches in size. The left margin of applications must be at least 1 1/2 inches wide, and if the application is bound, it must be bound on the left side. All typewritten or printed material must be set forth in black ink so as to permit photocopying.

(e)   Every application (electronic or paper) must contain the name, address, telephone number, and email address of each applicant and the name, address, telephone number, and email address of a person to whom any questions regarding the application should be directed. The Commission will not consider hypothetical or anonymous requests for a substituted compliance order. Each applicant shall provide the Commission with any supporting documentation it believes necessary for the Commission to make such determination, including information regarding applicable requirements established by the foreign financial regulatory authority or authorities, as well as the methods used by the foreign financial regulatory authority or authorities to monitor and enforce compliance with such rules. Applicants should also cite to and discuss applicable precedent.

(f)   Amendments to the application should be prepared and submitted as set forth in these procedures and should be marked to show what changes have been made.

(g)   After the filing is complete, the staff will review the application. Once all questions and issues have been answered to the satisfaction of the staff, the staff will make an appropriate recommendation to the Commission. After consideration of the recommendation and a vote by the Commission, the Commission's Office of the Secretary will issue an appropriate response and will notify the applicant.

(h)   The Commission shall publish in the Federal Register a notice that a complete application has been submitted. The notice will provide that any person may, within the period specified therein, submit to the Commission any information that relates to the Commission action requested in the application. The notice also will indicate the earliest date on which the Commission would take final action on the application, but in no event would such action be taken earlier than 25 days following publication of the notice in the Federal Register.

(i)   The Commission may, in its sole discretion, schedule a hearing on the matter addressed by the application

Rule 3a1–1.   Exemption From the Definition of "Exchange" Under Section 3(a)(1) of the Act

(a)   An organization, association, or group of persons shall be exempt from the definition of the term "exchange" under section 3(a)(1) of the Securities Exchange Act of 1934 (the Exchange Act) if such organization, association, or group of persons:

    (1)   Is operated by a national securities association;

    (2)   Is in compliance with Regulation ATS; or

(3)   Pursuant to paragraph (a) of Rule 301 of Regulation ATS, is not required to comply with Regulation ATS.

(b)   Notwithstanding paragraph (a) of this rule, an organization, association, or group of persons shall not be exempt under this rule from the definition of "exchange," if:

(1)   During three of the preceding four calendar quarters such organization, association, or group of persons had:

(i)   Fifty percent or more of the average daily dollar trading volume in any security and five percent or more of the average daily dollar trading volume in any class of securities; or

(ii)   Forty percent or more of the average daily dollar trading volume in any class of securities; and

(2)   The Commission determines, after notice to the organization, association, or group of persons, and an opportunity for such organization, association, or group of persons to respond, that such an exemption would not be necessary or appropriate in the public interest or consistent with the protection of investors taking into account the requirements for exchange registration under section 6 of the Exchange Act and the objectives of the national market system under section 11A of the Exchange Act.

(3)   For purposes of paragraph (b) of this rule, each of the following shall be considered a "class of securities":

(i)   Equity securities, which shall have the same meaning as in Rule 3a11–1 under the Exchange Act;

(ii)   Listed options, which shall mean any options traded on a national securities exchange or automated facility of a national securities exchange;

(iii)   Unlisted options, which shall mean any options other than those traded on a national securities exchange or automated facility of a national securities association;

(iv)   Municipal securities, which shall have the same meaning as in section 3(a)(29) of the Act;

(v)   Corporate debt securities, which shall mean any securities that:

(A)   Evidence a liability of the issuer of such securities;

(B)   Have a fixed maturity date that is at least one year following the date of issuance; and

(C)   Are not exempted securities, as defined in section 3(a)(12) of the Act, (15 U.S.C. 78c(a)(12));

(vi)   Foreign corporate debt securities, which shall mean any securities that:

(A)   Evidence a liability of the issuer of such debt securities;

(B)   Are issued by a corporation or other organization incorporated or organized under the laws of any foreign country; and

(C)   Have a fixed maturity date that is at least one year following the date of issuance; and

(vii)   Foreign sovereign debt securities, which shall mean any securities that:

(A)   Evidence a liability of the issuer of such debt securities;

(B)   Are issued or guaranteed by the government of a foreign country, any political subdivision of a foreign country or any supranational entity; and

(C)   Do not have a maturity date of a year or less following the date of issuance.

Rule 3a4–1. Associated Persons of an Issuer Deemed Not to Be Brokers

(a)   An associated person of an issuer of securities shall not be deemed to be a broker solely by reason of his participation in the sale of the securities of such issuer if the associated person:

(1)   Is not subject to a statutory disqualification, as that term is defined in section 3(a)(39) of the Act, at the time of his participation; and

(2)   Is not compensated in connection with his participation by the payment of commissions or other remuneration based either directly or indirectly on transactions in securities; and

(3)   Is not at the time of his participation an associated person of a broker or dealer; and

(4)   Meets the conditions of any one of paragraph (a)(4)(i), (ii), or (iii) of this rule.

(i)   The associated person restricts his participation to transactions involving offers and sales of securities:

(A)   To a registered broker or dealer; a registered investment company (or registered separate account); an insurance company; a bank; a savings and loan association; a trust company or similar institution supervised by a state or federal banking authority; or a trust for which a bank, a savings and loan association, a trust company, or a registered investment adviser either is the trustee or is authorized in writing to make investment decisions; or

(B)   That are exempted by reason of section 3(a)(7), 3(a)(9) or 3(a)(10) of the Securities Act of 1933 from the registration provisions of that Act; or

(C)   That are made pursuant to a plan or agreement submitted for the vote or consent of the security holders who will receive securities of the issuer in connection with a reclassification of securities of the issuer, a merger or consolidation or a similar plan of acquisition involving an exchange of securities, or a transfer of assets of any other person to the issuer in exchange for securities of the issuer; or

(D)   That are made pursuant to a bonus, profit-sharing, pension, retirement, thrift, savings, incentive, stock purchase, stock ownership, stock appreciation, stock option, dividend reinvestment or similar plan for employees of an issuer or a subsidiary of the issuer;

(ii)   The associated person meets all of the following conditions:

(A)   The associated person primarily performs, or is intended primarily to perform at the end of the offering, substantial duties for or on behalf of the issuer otherwise than in connection with transactions in securities; and

(B)   The associated person was not a broker or dealer, or an associated person of a broker or dealer, within the preceding 12 months; and

(C)   The associated person does not participate in selling an offering of securities for any issuer more than once every 12 months other than in reliance on paragraph (a)(4)(i) or (iii) of this rule, except that for securities issued pursuant to Rule 415 under the Securities Act of 1933, the 12 months shall begin with the last sale of any security included within one Rule 415 registration.

(iii)   The associated person restricts his participation to any one or more of the following activities:

(A)   Preparing any written communication or delivering such communication through the mails or other means that does not involve oral solicitation by the associated person of a potential purchaser; *Provided, however,* that the content of such communication is approved by a partner, officer or director of the issuer;

(B)   Responding to inquiries of a potential purchaser in a communication initiated by the potential purchaser; *Provided, however,* That the content of such responses are limited to information contained in a registration statement filed under the Securities Act of 1933 or other offering document; or

(C)   Performing ministerial and clerical work involved in effecting any transaction.

(b) No presumption shall arise that an associated person of an issuer has violated section 15(a) of the Act solely by reason of his participation in the sale of securities of the issuer if he does not meet the conditions specified in paragraph (a) of this rule.

(c) *Definitions.* When used in this rule:

(1) The term "associated person of an issuer" means any natural person who is a partner, officer, director, or employee of:

(i) The issuer;

(ii) A corporate general partner of a limited partnership that is the issuer;

(iii) A company or partnership that controls, is controlled by, or is under common control with, the issuer; or

(iv) An investment adviser registered under the Investment Advisers Act of 1940 to an investment company registered under the Investment Company Act of 1940 which is the issuer.

(2) The term "associated person of a broker or dealer" means any partner, officer, director, or branch manager of such broker or dealer (or any person occupying a similar status or performing similar functions), any person directly or indirectly controlling, controlled by, or under common control with such broker or dealer, or any employee of such broker or dealer, except that any person associated with a broker or dealer whose functions are solely clerical or ministerial and any person who is required under the laws of any State to register as a broker or dealer in that State solely because such person is an issuer of securities or associated person of an issuer of securities shall not be included in the meaning of such term for purposes of this rule.

Rule 3a4–2.   **[Removed and Reserved]**

Rule 3a4–3.   **[Removed and Reserved]**

Rule 3a4–4.   **[Removed and Reserved]**

Rule 3a4–5.   **[Removed and Reserved]**

Rule 3a4–6.   **[Removed and Reserved]**

Rule 3a5–1.   Exemption From the Definition of "Dealer" for a Bank Engaged in Riskless Principal Transactions

(a) A bank is exempt from the definition of the term "dealer" to the extent that it engages in or effects riskless principal transactions if the number of such riskless principal transactions during a calendar year combined with transactions in which the bank is acting as an agent for a customer pursuant to section 3(a)(4)(B)(xi) of the Act during that same year does not exceed 500.

(b) For purposes of this rule, the term riskless principal transaction means a transaction in which, after having received an order to buy from a customer, the bank purchased the security from another person to offset a contemporaneous sale to such customer or, after having received an order to sell from a customer, the bank sold the security to another person to offset a contemporaneous purchase from such customer.

Rule 3a5–2.   Exemption From the Definition of "Dealer" for Banks Effecting Transactions in Securities Issued Pursuant to Regulation S

(a) A bank is exempt from the definition of the term "dealer" under section 3(a)(5) of the Act, to the extent that, in a riskless principal transaction, the bank:

(1) Purchases an eligible security from an issuer or a broker-dealer and sells that security in compliance with the requirements of Rule 903 under the Securities Act of 1933 to a purchaser who is not in the United States;

(2) Purchases from a person who is not a U.S. person under Rule 902(k) under the Securities Act of 1933 an eligible security after its initial sale with a reasonable belief that the eligible security

was initially sold outside of the United States within the meaning of and in compliance with the requirements of Rule 903 under the Securities Act of 1933, and resells that security to a purchaser who is not in the United States or to a registered broker or dealer, provided that if the resale is made prior to the expiration of any applicable distribution compliance period specified in Rule 903(b)(2) or (b)(3) under the Securities Act of 1933, the resale is made in compliance with the requirements of Rule 904 under the Securities Act of 1933; or

(3)   Purchases from a registered broker or dealer an eligible security after its initial sale with a reasonable belief that the eligible security was initially sold outside of the United States within the meaning of and in compliance with the requirements of Rule 903 under the Securities Act of 1933, and resells that security to a purchaser who is not in the United States, *provided that* if the resale is made prior to the expiration of any applicable distribution compliance period specified in Rule 903(b)(2) or (b)(3) under the Securities Act of 1933, the resale is made in compliance with the requirements of Rule 904 under the Securities Act of 1933.

(b)   *Definitions.* For purposes of this Rule:

(1)   *Distributor* has the same meaning as in Rule 902(d) under the Securities Act of 1933.

(2)   *Eligible security* means a security that:

(i)   Is not being sold from the inventory of the bank or an affiliate of the bank; and

(ii)   Is not being underwritten by the bank or an affiliate of the bank on a firm-commitment basis, unless the bank acquired the security from an unaffiliated distributor that did not purchase the security from the bank or an affiliate of the bank.

(3)   *Purchaser* means a person who purchases an eligible security and who is not a U.S. person under Rule 902(k) under the Securities Act of 1933.

(4)   *Riskless principal transaction* means a transaction in which, after having received an order to buy from a customer, the bank purchased the security from another person to offset a contemporaneous sale to such customer or, after having received an order to sell from a customer, the bank sold the security to another person to offset a contemporaneous purchase from such customer.

Rule 3a5–3.   Exemption From the Definition of "Dealer" for Banks Engaging in Securities Lending Transactions

(a)   A bank is exempt from the definition of the term "dealer" under section 3(a)(5) of the Act, to the extent that, as a conduit lender, it engages in or effects securities lending transactions, and any securities lending services in connection with such transactions, with or on behalf of a person the bank reasonably believes to be:

(1)   A qualified investor as defined in section 3(a)(54)(A) of the Act; or

(2)   Any employee benefit plan that owns and invests, on a discretionary basis, not less than $25,000,000 in investments.

(b)   *Securities lending transaction* means a transaction in which the owner of a security lends the security temporarily to another party pursuant to a written securities lending agreement under which the lender retains the economic interests of an owner of such securities, and has the right to terminate the transaction and to recall the loaned securities on terms agreed by the parties.

(c)   *Securities lending services* means:

(1)   Selecting and negotiating with a borrower and executing, or directing the execution of the loan with the borrower;

(2)   Receiving, delivering, or directing the receipt or delivery of loaned securities;

(3)   Receiving, delivering, or directing the receipt or delivery of collateral;

(4)   Providing mark-to-market, corporate action, recordkeeping or other services incidental to the administration of the securities lending transaction;

(5)   Investing, or directing the investment of, cash collateral; or

(6) Indemnifying the lender of securities with respect to various matters.

(d) For the purposes of this Rule, the term *conduit lender* means a bank that borrows or loans securities, as principal, for its own account, and contemporaneously loans or borrows the same securities, as principal, for its own account. A bank that qualifies under this definition as a conduit lender at the commencement of a transaction will continue to qualify, notwithstanding whether:

(1) The lending or borrowing transaction terminates and so long as the transaction is replaced within one business day by another lending or borrowing transaction involving the same securities; and

(2) Any substitutions of collateral occur.

DEFINITION OF "EQUITY SECURITY" AS USED IN SECTIONS 12(g) AND 16

Rule 3a11–1. Definition of the Term "Equity Security"

The term "equity security" is hereby defined to include any stock or similar security, certificate of interest or participation in any profit sharing agreement, preorganization certificate or subscription, transferable share, voting trust certificate or certificate of deposit for an equity security, limited partnership interest, interest in a joint venture, or certificate of interest in a business trust; any security future on any such security; or any security convertible, with or without consideration into such a security, or carrying any warrant or right to subscribe to or purchase such a security; or any such warrant or right; or any put, call, straddle, or other option or privilege of buying such a security from or selling such a security to another without being bound to do so.

MISCELLANEOUS EXEMPTIONS

Rule 3a12–1. Exemption of Certain Mortgages and Interests in Mortgages

Mortgages, as defined in section 302(d) of the Emergency Home Finance Act of 1970, which are or have been sold by the Federal Home Loan Mortgage Corporation are hereby exempted from the operation of such provisions of the Act as by their terms do not apply to an "exempted security" or to "exempted securities".

Rule 3a12–3. Exemption From Sections 14(a), 14(b), 14(c), 14(f) and 16 for Securities of Certain Foreign Issuers

(a) Securities for which the filing of registration statements on Form 18 are authorized shall be exempt from the operation of sections 14 and 16 of the Act.

(b) Securities registered by a foreign private issuer, as defined in Rule 3b–4 shall be exempt from sections 14(a), 14(b), 14(c), 14(f) and 16 of the Act.

Rule 3a12–4. Exemptions From Sections 15(a) and 15(c)(3) for Certain Mortgage Securities

(a) When used in this Rule the following terms shall have the meanings indicated:

(1) The term "whole loan mortgage" means an evidence of indebtedness secured by mortgage, deed of trust, or other lien upon real estate or upon leasehold interests therein where the entire mortgage, deed or other lien is transferred with the entire evidence of indebtedness.

(2) The term "aggregated whole loan mortgage" means two or more whole loan mortgages that are grouped together and sold to one person in one transaction.

(3) The term "participation interest" means an undivided interest representing one of only two such interests in a whole loan mortgage or in an aggregated whole loan mortgage, provided that the other interest is retained by the originator of such participation interest.

(4) The term "commitment" means a contract to purchase a whole loan mortgage, an aggregated whole loan mortgage or a participation interest which by its terms requires that the contract be fully executed within 2 years.

(5)   The term "mortgage security" means a whole loan mortgage, an aggregated whole loan mortgage, a participation interest, or a commitment.

(b)   A mortgage security shall be deemed an "exempted security" for purposes of subsections (a) and (c)(3) of section 15 of the Act provided that, in the case of and at the time of any sale of the mortgage security by a broker or dealer, such mortgage security is not in default and has an unpaid principal amount of at least $50,000.

Rule 3a12–5. Exemption of Certain Investment Contract Securities From Sections 7(c) and 11(d)(1)

(a)   An investment contract security involving the direct ownership of specified residential real property shall be exempted from the provisions of sections 7(c) and 11(d)(1) of the Act with respect to any transaction by a broker or dealer who, directly or indirectly, arranges for the extension or maintenance of credit on the security to or from a customer, if the credit:

(1)   Is secured by a lien, mortgage, deed of trust, or any other similar security interest related only to real property: *Provided, however,* That this provision shall not prevent a lender from requiring

(i)   A security interest in the common areas and recreational facilities or furniture and fixtures incidental to the investment contract if the purchase of such furniture and fixtures is required by, or subject to the approval of, the issuer, as a condition of purchase; or

(ii)   An assignment of future rentals in the event of default by the purchaser or a co-signer or guarantor on the debt obligation other than the issuer, its affiliates, or any broker or dealer offering such securities;

(2)   Is to be repaid by periodic payments of principal and interest pursuant to an amortization schedule established by the governing instruments: *Provided, however,* That this provision shall not prevent the extension of credit on terms which require the payment of interest only, if extended in compliance with the other provisions of this rule; and

(3)   Is extended by a lender which is not, directly or indirectly controlling, controlled by, or under common control with the broker or dealer or the issuer of the securities or affiliates thereof.

(b)   For purposes of this rule:

(1)   "Residential real property" shall mean real property containing living accommodations, whether used on a permanent or transient basis, and may include furniture or fixtures if required as a condition of purchase of the investment contract or if subject to the approval of the issuer.

(2)   "Direct ownership" shall mean ownership of a fee or leasehold estate or a beneficial interest in a trust the purchase of which, under applicable local law, is financed and secured by a security interest therein similar to a mortgage or deed of trust, but it shall not include an interest in a real estate investment trust, an interest in a general or limited partnership, or similar indirect interest in the ownership of real property.

Rule 3a12–6. Definition of "Common Trust Fund" as Used in Section 3(a)(12) of the Act

The term "common trust fund" as used in section 3(a)(12) of the Act shall include a common trust fund which is maintained by a bank which is a member of an affiliated group, as defined in section 1504(a) of the Internal Revenue Code of 1954, and which is maintained exclusively for the collective investment and reinvestment of monies contributed thereto by one or more bank members of such affiliated group in the capacity of trustee, executor, administrator, or guardian; *Provided,* That:

(a)   The common trust fund is operated in compliance with the same state and federal regulatory requirements as would apply if the bank maintaining such fund and any other contributing banks were the same entity; and

(b)   The rights of persons for whose benefit a contributing bank acts as trustee, executor, administrator, or guardian would not be diminished by reason of the maintenance of such common trust fund by another bank member of the affiliated group.

Rule 3a12–7. Exemption for Certain Derivative Securities Traded Otherwise Than on a National Securities Exchange

Any put, call, straddle, option, or privilege traded exclusively otherwise than on a national securities exchange and for which quotations are not disseminated through an automated quotation system of a registered securities association, which relates to any securities which are direct obligations of, or obligations guaranteed as to principal or interest by, the United States, or securities issued or guaranteed by a corporation in which the United States has a direct or indirect interest as shall be designated for exemption by the Secretary of the Treasury pursuant to section 3(a)(12) of the Act, shall be exempt from all provisions of the Act which by their terms do not apply to any "exempted security" or "exempted securities," provided that the securities underlying such put, call, straddle, option or privilege represent an obligation equal to or exceeding $250,000 principal amount.

Rule 3a12–8. Exemption for Designated Foreign Government Securities for Purposes of Futures Trading

(a) When used in this rule, the following terms shall have the meaning indicated:

(1) the term "designated foreign government security" shall mean a security not registered under the Securities Act of 1933 nor the subject of any American depositary receipt so registered, and representing a debt obligation of the government of

    (i) the United Kingdom of Great Britain and Northern Ireland; or

    (ii) Canada;

    (iii) Japan;

    (iv) the Commonwealth of Australia;

    (v) the Republic of France;

    (vi) New Zealand;

    (vii) the Republic of Austria;

    (viii) the Kingdom of Denmark;

    (ix) the Republic of Finland;

    (x) the Kingdom of the Netherlands;

    (xi) Switzerland;

    (xii) Federal Republic of Germany;

    (xiii) the Republic of Ireland;

    (xiv) the Republic of Italy;

    (xv) the Kingdom of Spain;

    (xvi) the United Mexican States;

    (xvii) the Federative Republic of Brazil;

    (xviii) the Republic of Argentina;

    (xix) the Republic of Venezuela;

    (xx) the Kingdom of Belgium; or

    (xxi) the Kingdom of Sweden.

(2) The term "qualifying foreign futures contracts" shall mean any contracts for the purchase or sale of a designated foreign government security for future delivery, as "future delivery" is defined in 7 U.S.C. section 2, provided such contracts require delivery outside the United States, any of its possessions or territories, and are traded on or through a board of trade, as defined at 7 U.S.C. section 2.

(b)   Any designated foreign government security shall, for purposes only of the offer, sale or confirmation of sale of qualifying foreign futures contracts, be exempted from all provisions of the Act which by their terms do not apply to an "exempted security" or "exempted securities."

Rule 3a12–9. Exemption of Certain Direct Participation Program Securities From the Arranging Provisions of Sections 7(c) and 11(d)(1)

(a)   Direct participation program securities sold on a basis whereby the purchase price is paid to the issuer in one or more mandatory deferred payments shall be deemed to be exempted securities for purposes of the arranging provisions of sections 7(c) and 11(d)(1) of the Act, provided that:

(1)   The securities are registered under the Securities Act of 1933 or are sold or offered exclusively on an intrastate basis in reliance upon section 3(a)(11) of that Act;

(2)   The mandatory deferred payments bear a reasonable relationship to the capital needs and program objectives described in a business development plan disclosed to investors in a registration statement filed with the Commission under the Securities Act of 1933 or, where no registration statement is required to be filed with the Commission, as part of a statement filed with the relevant state securities administrator;

(3)   Not less than 50 percent of the purchase price of the direct participation program security is paid by the investor at the time of sale;

(4)   The total purchase price of the direct participation program security is due within three years in specified property programs or two years in non-specified property programs. Such pay-in periods are to be measured from the earlier of the completion of the offering or one year following the effective date of the offering.

(b)   For purposes of this rule:

(1)   "Direct participation program" shall mean a program financed through the sale of securities, other than securities that are listed on an exchange, quoted on NASDAQ, or will otherwise be actively traded during the pay-in period as a result of efforts by the issuer, underwriter, or other participants in the initial distribution of such securities, that provides for flow-through tax consequences to its investors; *Provided, however,* That the term "direct participation program" does not include real estate investment trusts, Subchapter S corporate offerings, tax qualified pension and profit sharing plans under sections 401 and 403(a) of the Internal Revenue Code ("Code"), tax shelter annuities under section 403(b) of the Code, individual retirement plans under section 408 of the Code, and any issuer, including a separate account, that is registered under the Investment Company Act of 1940.

(2)   "Business development plan" shall mean a specific plan describing the program's anticipated economic development and the amounts of future capital contributions, in the form of mandatory deferred payments, to be required at specified times or upon the occurrence of certain events.

(3)   "Specified property program" shall mean a direct participation program in which, at the date of effectiveness, more than 75 percent of the net proceeds from the sale of program securities are committed to specific purchases or expenditures. "Non-specified property program" shall mean any other direct participation program.

Rule 3a12–10.   Exemption of Certain Securities Issued by the Resolution Funding Corporation

Securities that are issued by the Resolution Funding Corporation pursuant to section 21B(f) of the Federal Home Loan Bank Act are exempt from the operation of all provisions of the Act that by their terms do not apply to any "exempted security" or to "exempted securities."

Rule 3a12–12.   Exemption From Certain Provisions of Section 16 of the Act for Asset-Backed Securities

Asset-backed securities, as defined in Item 1101 of Regulation AB, are exempt from section 16 of the Act.

(a) Debt securities that are listed for trading on a national securities exchange shall be exempt from the restrictions on borrowing of section 8(a) of the Act.

(b) Debt securities registered pursuant to the provisions of section 12(b) of the Act shall be exempt from sections 14(a), 14(b), and 14(c) of the Act, except that Rules 14a–1, 14a–2, 14a–9, 14a–13, 14b–1, 14b–2, 14c–1, 14c–6 and 14c–7 shall continue to apply.

(c) For purposes of this rule, "debt securities" is defined to mean any securities that are not "equity securities" as defined in section 3(a)(11) of the Act and Rule 3a11–1 thereunder.

Rule 3a40–1. Designation of Financial Responsibility Rules

The term "financial responsibility rules" for purposes of the Securities Investor Protection Act of 1970 shall include:

(a) Any rule adopted by the Commission pursuant to sections 8, 15(c)(3), 17(a) or 17(e)(1)(A) of the Act;

(b) Any rule adopted by the Commission relating to hypothecation or lending of customer securities;

(c) Any rule adopted by any self-regulatory organization relating to capital, margin, recordkeeping, hypothecation or lending requirements; and

(d) Any other rule adopted by the Commission or any self-regulatory organization relating to the protection of funds or securities.

Rule 3a43–1. Customer-Related Government Securities Activities Incidental to the Futures-Related Business of a Futures Commission Merchant Registered With the Commodity Futures Trading Commission

(a) A futures commission merchant registered with the Commodity Futures Trading Commission ("CFTC") is not a government securities broker or government securities dealer solely because such futures commission merchant effects transactions in government securities that are defined in paragraph (b) of this rule as incidental to such person's futures-related business.

(b) Provided that the futures commission merchant

(i) Maintains in a regulated account all funds and securities associated with such government securities transactions (except funds and securities associated with transactions under paragraph (b)(1)(i) below) and

(ii) Does not advertise that it is in the business of effecting transactions in government securities otherwise than in connection with futures or options on futures trading or the investment of margin or excess funds related to such trading or the trading of any other instrument subject to CFTC jurisdiction, the following transactions in government securities are incidental to the futures-related business of such a futures commission merchant:

(1) Transactions as agent for a customer—

(i) To effect delivery pursuant to a futures contract; or

(ii) For risk reduction or arbitrage of existing or contemporaneously created positions in futures or options on futures;

(2) Transactions as agent for a customer for investment of margin and excess funds related to futures or options on futures trading or the trading of other instruments subject to CFTC jurisdiction, provided further that,

(i) Such transactions involve Treasury securities with a maturity of less than 93 days at the time of the transaction,

(ii) Such transactions generate no monetary profit for the futures commission merchant in excess of the costs of executing such transactions, or

(iii) Such transactions are unsolicited, and commissions and other income generated on transactions pursuant to this subparagraph (iii) (including transactional fees paid by the futures commission merchant and charged to its customer) do not exceed 2% of such futures commission merchant's total commission revenues;

(3) Exchange of futures for physicals transactions as agent for or as principal with a customer; and

(4) Any transaction or transactions that the Commission exempts, either unconditionally or on specified terms and conditions, as incidental to the futures-related business of a specified futures commission merchant, a specified category of futures commission merchants, or futures commission merchants generally.

(c) *Definitions.*

(1) "Customer" means any person for whom the futures commission merchant effects or intends to effect transactions in futures, options on futures, or any other instruments subject to CFTC jurisdiction.

(2) "Regulated account" means a customer segregation account subject to the regulations of the CFTC; provided, however, that, where such regulations do not permit to be maintained in such an account or require to be maintained in a separate regulated account funds or securities in proprietary accounts or funds or securities used as margin for or excess funds related to futures contracts, options on futures or any other instruments subject to CFTC jurisdiction that trade outside the United States, its territories, or possessions, the term "regulated account" means such separate regulated account or any other account subject to record-keeping regulations of the CFTC.

(3) "Unsolicited transaction" means a transaction that is not effected in a discretionary account or recommended to a customer by the futures commission merchant, an associated person of a futures commission merchant, a business affiliate that is controlled by, controlling, or under common control with the futures commission merchant, or an introducing broker that is guaranteed by the futures commission merchant.

(4) "Futures" and "futures contracts" mean contracts of sale of a commodity for future delivery traded on or subject to the rules of a contract market designated by the CFTC or traded on or subject to the rules of any board of trade located outside the United States, its territories, or possessions.

(5) "Options on futures" means puts or calls on a futures contract traded on or subject to the rules of a contract market designated by the CFTC or traded or subject to the rules of any board of trade located outside the United States, its territories, or possessions.

Rule 3a44–1. Proprietary Government Securities Transactions Incidental to the Futures-Related Business of a CFTC-Regulated Person

(a) A person registered with the Commodity Futures Trading Commission ("CFTC"), a contract market designated by the CFTC, such a contract market's affiliated clearing organization, or any floor trader or such a contract market (hereinafter referred to collectively as a "CFTC-regulated person") is not a government securities dealer solely because such person effects transactions for its own account in government securities that are defined in paragraph (b) of this rule as incidental to such person's futures-related business.

(b) Provided that a CFTC-regulated person does not advertise or otherwise hold itself out as a government securities dealer except as permitted under Rule 3a43–1 the following transactions in government securities for its own account are incidental to the futures-related business of such a CFTC-regulated person:

(1) Transactions to effect delivery of a government security pursuant to a futures contract;

(2) Exchange of futures for physicals transactions with

(i) A government securities broker or government securities dealer that has registered with the Commission or filed notice pursuant to section 15C(a) of the Act or

(ii) A CFTC-regulated person;

(3) Transactions (including repurchase agreements and reverse repurchase agreements) involving segregated customer funds and securities or funds and securities held by a clearing organization with

    (i) A government securities broker or government securities dealer that has registered with the Commission of filed notice pursuant to section 15C(a) of the Act or

    (ii) A bank;

(4) Transactions for risk reduction or arbitrage of existing or contemporaneously created positions in futures or options on futures with

    (i) A government securities broker or government securities dealer that has registered with the Commission or filed notice pursuant to section 15C(a) of the Act or

    (ii) A CFTC-regulated person;

(5) Repurchase and reverse repurchase agreement transactions between a futures commission merchant acting in a proprietary capacity and another CFTC-regulated person acting in a proprietary capacity and contemporaneous offsetting transactions between such a futures commission merchant and

    (i) A government securities broker or government securities dealer that has registered with the Commission or filed notice pursuant to section 15C(a) of the Act,

    (ii) A bank, or

    (iii) A CFTC-regulated person acting in a proprietary capacity; and

(6) Any transaction or transactions that the Commission exempts, either unconditionally or on specified terms and conditions, as incidental to the futures related business of a specified CFTC-regulated person, a specified category of CFTC-regulated persons, or CFTC-regulated persons generally.

(c) Definitions:

    (1) "Segregated customer funds" means funds subject to CFTC segregation requirements.

    (2) "Futures" and "futures contracts" means contracts of sale of a commodity for future delivery traded on or subject to the rules of a contract market designated by the CFTC or traded on or subject to the rules of any board of trade located outside the United States, its territories, or possessions.

    (3) "Options on futures" means puts or calls on a futures contract traded on or subject to the rules of a contract market designated by the CFTC or traded on or subject to the rules of any board of trade located outside the United States, its territories, or possessions.

Rule 3a51–1. Definition of "Penny Stock"

For purposes of section 3(a)(51) of the Act, the term "penny stock" shall mean any equity security other than a security:

    (a) That is an NMS stock, as defined in Rule 600(b)(47) of Regulation NMS, provided that:

    (1) The security is registered, or approved for registration upon notice of issuance, on a national securities exchange that has been continuously registered as a national securities exchange since April 20, 1992 (the date of the adoption of Rule 3a51–1 by the Commission); and the national securities exchange has maintained quantitative listing standards that are substantially similar to or stricter than those listing standards that were in place on that exchange on January 8, 2004; or

    (2) The security is registered, or approved for registration upon notice of issuance, on a national securities exchange, or is listed, or approved for listing upon notice of issuance on, an automated quotation system sponsored by a registered national securities association, that:

    (i) Has established initial listing standards that meet or exceed the following criteria:

    (A) The issuer shall have:

    (1) Stockholders' equity of $5,000,000;

(2)   Market value of listed securities of $50 million for 90 consecutive days prior to applying for the listing (market value means the closing bid price multiplied by the number of securities listed); or

(3)   Net income of $750,000 (excluding non-recurring items) in the most recently completed fiscal year or in two of the last three most recently completed fiscal years;

(B)   The issuer shall have an operating history of at least one year or a market value of listed securities of $50 million (market value means the closing bid price multiplied by the number of securities listed);

(C)   The issuer's stock, common or preferred, shall have a minimum bid price of $4 per share;

(D)   In the case of common stock, there shall be at least 300 round lot holders of the security (a round lot holder means a holder of a normal unit of trading);

(E)   In the case of common stock, there shall be at least 1,000,000 publicly held shares and such shares shall have a market value of at least $5 million (market value means the closing bid price multiplied by number of publicly held shares, and shares held directly or indirectly by an officer or director of the issuer and by any person who is the beneficial owner of more than 10 percent of the total shares outstanding are not considered to be publicly held);

(F)   In the case of a convertible debt security, there shall be a principal amount outstanding of at least $10 million;

(G)   In the case of rights and warrants, there shall be at least 100,000 issued and the underlying security shall be registered on a national securities exchange or listed on an automated quotation system sponsored by a registered national securities association and shall satisfy the requirements of paragraph (a) or (e) of this rule;

(H)   In the case of put warrants (that is, instruments that grant the holder the right to sell to the issuing company a specified number of shares of the company's common stock, at a specified price until a specified period of time), there shall be at least 100,000 issued and the underlying security shall be registered on a national securities exchange or listed on an automated quotation system sponsored by a registered national securities association and shall satisfy the requirements of paragraph (a) or (e) of this rule;

(I)   In the case of units (that is, two or more securities traded together), all component parts shall be registered on a national securities exchange or listed on an automated quotation system sponsored by a registered national securities association and shall satisfy the requirements of paragraph (a) or (e) of this rule; and

(J)   In the case of equity securities (other than common and preferred stock, convertible debt securities, rights and warrants, put warrants, or units), including hybrid products and derivative securities products, the national securities exchange or registered national securities association shall establish quantitative listing standards that are substantially similar to those found in paragraphs (a)(2)(i)(A) through (a)(2)(i)(I) of this rule; and

(ii)   Has established quantitative continued listing standards that are reasonably related to the initial listing standards set forth in paragraph (a)(2)(i) of this rule, and that are consistent with the maintenance of fair and orderly markets;

(b)   That is issued by an investment company registered under the Investment Company Act of 1940;

(c)   That is a put or call option issued by the Options Clearing Corporation;

(d)   Except for purposes of section 7(b) of the Securities Act and Rule 419, that has a price of five dollars or more;

(1)   For purposes of paragraph (d) of this rule:

(i)   A security has a price of five dollars or more for a particular transaction if the security is purchased or sold in that transaction at a price of five dollars or more, excluding any broker or dealer commission, commission equivalent, markup, or mark-down; and

(ii)   Other than in connection with a particular transaction, a security has a price of five dollars or more at a given time if the inside bid quotation is five dollars or more; *provided, however,* that if there is no such inside bid quotation, a security has a price of five dollars or more at a given time if the average of three or more interdealer bid quotations at specified prices displayed at that time in an interdealer quotation system, as defined in Rule 15c2–7(c)(1), by three or more market makers in the security, is five dollars or more.

(iii)   The term "inside bid quotation" shall mean the highest bid quotation for the security displayed by a market maker in the security on an automated interdealer quotation system that has the characteristics set forth in section 178(b)(2) of the Act, or such other automated interdealer quotation system designated by the Commission for purposes of this rule, at any time in which at least two market makers are contemporaneously displaying on such system bid and offer quotations for the security at specified prices.

(2)   If a security is a unit composed of one or more securities, the unit price divided by the number of shares of the unit that are not warrants, options, rights, or similar securities must be five dollars or more, as determined in accordance with paragraph (d)(1) of this rule, and any share of the unit that is a warrant, option, right, or similar security, or a convertible security, must have an exercise price or conversion price of five dollars or more;

(e)(1)   That is registered, or approved for registration upon notice of issuance, on a national securities exchange that makes transaction reports available pursuant to Rule 601 of Regulation NMS, provided that:

(i)   Price and volume information with respect to transactions in that security is required to be reported on a current and continuing basis and is made available to vendors of market information pursuant to the rules of the national securities exchange;

(ii)   The security is purchased or sold in a transaction that is effected on or through the facilities of the national securities exchange, or that is part of the distribution of the security; and

(iii)   The security satisfies the requirements of paragraph (a)(1) or (a)(2) of this rule;

(2)   A security that satisfies the requirements of this paragraph, but does not otherwise satisfy the requirements of paragraphs (a), (b), (c), (d), (f), or (g) of this rule, shall be a penny stock for purposes of section 15(b)(6) of the Act;

(f)   That is a security futures product listed on a national securities exchange or an automated quotation system sponsored by a registered national securities association; or

(g)   Whose issuer has:

(1)   Net tangible assets (*i.e.,* total assets less intangible assets and liabilities) in excess of $2,000,000, if the issuer has been in continuous operation for at least three years, or $5,000,000, if the issuer has been in continuous operation for less than three years; or

(2)   Average revenue of at least $6,000,000 for the last three years.

(3)   For purposes of paragraph (g) of this rule, net tangible assets or average revenues must be demonstrated by financial statements dated less than fifteen months prior to the date of the transaction that the broker or dealer has reviewed and has a reasonable basis for believing are accurate in relation to the date of the transaction, and:

(i)   If the issuer is other than a foreign private issuer, are the most recent financial statements for the issuer that have been audited and reported on by an independent public accountant in accordance with the provisions of 17 CFR 210.2–02; or

(ii)   If the issuer is a foreign private issuer, are the most recent financial statements for the issuer that have been filed with the Commission or furnished to the Commission pursuant to Rule 12g3–2(b) of this Act; *provided, however,* that if financial statements for the issuer dated less than fifteen months prior to the date of the transaction have not been filed with or furnished to the Commission, financial statements dated within fifteen months prior to the transaction shall be prepared in accordance with generally accepted accounting principles in the country of incorporation, audited in compliance with the requirements of that jurisdiction, and reported on by an accountant duly registered and in good standing in accordance with the regulations of that jurisdiction;

(4)   The broker or dealer shall preserve, as part of its records, copies of the financial statements required by paragraph (g)(3) of this rule for the period specified in Rule 17a–4(b) of this Act.

Rule 3a55–1. Method for Determining Market Capitalization and Dollar Value of Average Daily Trading Volume; Application of the Definition of Narrow-Based Security Index

(a)   For purposes of Section 3(a)(55)(C)(i)(III)(bb) of the Act:

(1)   On a particular day, a security shall be 1 of 750 securities with the largest market capitalization as of the preceding 6 full calendar months when it is included on a list of such securities designated by the Commission and the CFTC as applicable for that day.

(2)   In the event that the Commission and the CFTC have not designated a list under paragraph (a)(1) of this Rule:

(i)   The method to be used to determine market capitalization of a security as of the preceding 6 full calendar months is to sum the values of the market capitalization of such security for each U.S. trading day of the preceding 6 full calendar months, and to divide this sum by the total number of such trading days.

(ii)   The 750 securities with the largest market capitalization shall be identified from the universe of all NMS securities as defined in Rule 600 that are common stock or depositary shares.

(b)(1)   For purposes of Section 3(a)(55)(B) of the Act:

(i)(A)   The method to be used to determine the dollar value of ADTV of a security is to sum the dollar value of ADTV of all reported transactions in such security in each jurisdiction as calculated pursuant to paragraphs (b)(1)(ii) and (iii).

(B)   The dollar value of ADTV of a security shall include the value of all reported transactions for such security and for any depositary share that represents such security.

(C)   The dollar value of ADTV of a depositary share shall include the value of all reported transactions for such depositary share and for the security that is represented by such depositary share.

(ii)   For trading in a security in the United States, the method to be used to determine the dollar value of ADTV as of the preceding 6 full calendar months is to sum the value of all reported transactions in such security for each U.S. trading day during the preceding 6 full calendar months, and to divide this sum by the total number of such trading days.

(iii)(A)   For trading in a security in a jurisdiction other than the United States, the method to be used to determine the dollar value of ADTV as of the preceding 6 full calendar months is to sum the value in U.S. dollars of all reported transactions in such security in such jurisdiction for each trading day during the preceding 6 full calendar months, and to divide this sum by the total number of trading days in such jurisdiction during the preceding 6 full calendar months.

(B)   If the value of reported transactions used in calculating the ADTV of securities under paragraph (b)(1)(iii)(A) is reported in a currency other than U.S. dollars, the total value of each day's transactions in such currency shall be converted into U.S. dollars on the basis of a spot rate of exchange for that day obtained from at least one independent entity that provides or disseminates foreign exchange quotations in the ordinary course of its business.

(iv)   The dollar value of ADTV of the lowest weighted 25% of an index is the sum of the dollar value of ADTV of each of the component securities comprising the lowest weighted 25% of such index.

(2)   For purposes of Section 3(a)(55)(C)(i)(III)(cc) of the Act:

(i) On a particular day, a security shall be 1 of 675 securities with the largest dollar value of ADTV as of the preceding 6 full calendar months when it is included on a list of such securities designated by the Commission and the CFTC as applicable for that day.

(ii) In the event that the Commission and the CFTC have not designated a list under paragraph (b)(2) of this Rule:

(A) The method to be used to determine the dollar value of ADTV of a security as of the preceding 6 full calendar months is to sum the value of all reported transactions in such security in the United States for each U.S. trading day during the preceding 6 full calendar months, and to divide this sum by the total number of such trading days.

(B) The 675 securities with the largest dollar value of ADTV shall be identified from the universe of all NMS securities as defined in Rule 600 that are common stock or depositary shares.

(c) For purposes of Section 3(a)(55)(C) of the Act, the requirement that each component security of an index be registered pursuant to Section 12 of the Act shall be satisfied with respect to any security that is a depositary share if the deposited securities underlying the depositary share are registered pursuant to Section 12 of the Act and the depositary share is registered under the Securities Act of 1933 on Form F–6.

(d) For purposes of this Rule:

(1) CFTC means Commodity Futures Trading Commission.

(2) Closing price of a security means:

(i) If reported transactions in the security have taken place in the United States, the price at which the last transaction in such security took place in the regular trading session of the principal market for the security in the United States.

(ii) If no reported transactions in a security have taken place in the United States, the closing price of such security shall be the closing price of any depositary share representing such security divided by the number of shares represented by such depositary share.

(iii) If no reported transactions in a security or in a depositary share representing such security have taken place in the United States, the closing price of such security shall be the price at which the last transaction in such security took place in the regular trading session of the principal market for the security. If such price is reported in a currency other than U.S. dollars, such price shall be converted into U.S. dollars on the basis of a spot rate of exchange relevant for the time of the transaction obtained from at least one independent entity that provides or disseminates foreign exchange quotations in the ordinary course of its business.

(3) Depositary share has the same meaning as in Rule 12b–2.

(4) Foreign financial regulatory authority has the same meaning as in Section 3(a)(52) of the Act.

(5) With respect to any particular day, the lowest weighted component securities comprising, in the aggregate, 25% of an index's weighting for purposes of Section 3(a)(55)(B)(iv) of the Act ("lowest weighted 25% of an index") means those securities:

(i) That are the lowest weighted securities when all the securities in such index are ranked from lowest to highest based on the index's weighting methodology; and

(ii) For which the sum of the weight of such securities is equal to, or less than, 25% of the index's total weighting.

(6) Market capitalization of a security on a particular day:

(i) If the security is not a depositary share, is the product of:

(A) The closing price of such security on that same day; and

(B) The number of outstanding shares of such security on that same day.

(ii) If the security is a depositary share, is the product of:

(A) The closing price of the depositary share on that same day divided by the number of deposited securities represented by such depositary share; and

(B) The number of outstanding shares of the security represented by the depositary share on that same day.

(7) Outstanding shares of a security means the number of outstanding shares of such security as reported on the most recent Form 10–K, Form 10–Q, Form 10–KSB, Form 10–QSB, or Form 20–F filed with the Commission by the issuer of such security, including any change to such number of outstanding shares subsequently reported by the issuer on a Form 8–K.

(8) Preceding 6 full calendar months means, with respect to a particular day, the period of time beginning on the same day of the month 6 months before and ending on the day prior to such day.

(9) Principal market for a security means the single securities market with the largest reported trading volume for the security during the preceding 6 full calendar months.

(10) Reported transaction means:

(i) With respect to securities transactions in the United States, any transaction for which a transaction report is collected, processed, and made available pursuant to an effective transaction reporting plan, or for which a transaction report, last sale data, or quotation information is disseminated through an automated quotation system as described in Section 3(a)(51)(A)(ii) of the Act; and

(ii) With respect to securities transactions outside the United States, any transaction that has been reported to a foreign financial regulatory authority in the jurisdiction where such transaction has taken place.

(11) U.S. trading day means any day on which a national securities exchange is open for trading.

(12) Weighting of a component security of an index means the percentage of such index's value represented, or accounted for, by such component security.

Rule 3a55–2. Indexes Underlying Futures Contracts Trading for Fewer Than 30 Days

(a) An index on which a contract of sale for future delivery is trading on a designated contract market, registered derivatives transaction execution facility, or foreign board of trade is not a narrow-based security index under Section 3(a)(55) of the Act for the first 30 days of trading, if:

(1) Such index would not have been a narrow-based security index on each trading day of the preceding 6 full calendar months with respect to a date no earlier than 30 days prior to the commencement of trading of such contract;

(2) On each trading day of the preceding 6 full calendar months with respect to a date no earlier than 30 days prior to the commencement of trading such contract:

(i) Such index had more than 9 component securities;

(ii) No component security in such index comprised more than 30 percent of the index's weighting;

(iii) The 5 highest weighted component securities in such index did not comprise, in the aggregate, more than 60 percent of the index's weighting; and

(iv) The dollar value of the trading volume of the lowest weighted 25% of such index was not less than $50 million (or in the case of an index with 15 or more component securities, $30 million); or

(3) On each trading day of the preceding 6 full calendar months, with respect to a date no earlier than 30 days prior to the commencement of trading such contract:

(i) Such index had at least 9 component securities;

(ii) No component security in such index comprised more than 30 percent of the index's weighting; and

      (iii) Each component security in such index was:

          (A) Registered pursuant to Section 12 of the Act or was a depositary share representing a security registered pursuant to Section 12 of the Act;

          (B) 1 of 750 securities with the largest market capitalization that day; and

          (C) 1 of 675 securities with the largest dollar value of trading volume that day.

  (b) An index that is not a narrow-based security index for the first 30 days of trading pursuant to paragraph (a) of this Rule, shall become a narrow-based security index if such index has been a narrow-based security index for more than 45 business days over 3 consecutive calendar months.

  (c) An index that becomes a narrow-based security index solely because it was a narrow-based security index for more than 45 business days over 3 consecutive calendar months pursuant to paragraph (b) of this Rule shall not be a narrow-based security index for the following 3 calendar months.

  (d) For purposes of this Rule:

      (1) Market capitalization has the same meaning as in Rule 3a55–1(d)(6).

      (2) Dollar value of trading volume of a security on a particular day is the value in U.S. dollars of all reported transactions in such security on that day. If the value of reported transactions used in calculating dollar value of trading volume is reported in a currency other than U.S. dollars, the total value of each day's transactions shall be converted into U.S. dollars on the basis of a spot rate of exchange for that day obtained from at least one independent entity that provides or disseminates foreign exchange quotations in the ordinary course of its business.

      (3) Lowest weighted 25% of an index has the same meaning as in Rule 3a55–1(d)(5).

      (4) Preceding 6 full calendar months has the same meaning as in Rule 3a55–1(d)(8).

      (5) Reported transaction has the same meaning as in Rule 3a55–1(d)(10).

Rule 3a55–3. Futures Contracts on Security Indexes Trading on or Subject to the Rules of a Foreign Board of Trade

  When a contract of sale for future delivery on a security index is traded on or subject to the rules of a foreign board of trade, such index shall not be a narrow-based security index if it would not be a narrow-based security index if a futures contract on such index were traded on a designated contract market or registered derivatives transaction execution facility.

Rule 3a55–4. Exclusion From Definition of Narrow-Based Security Index for Indexes Composed of Debt Securities

  (a) An index is not a narrow-based security index if:

      (1)(i) Each of the securities of an issuer included in the index is a security, as defined in section 2(a)(1) of the Securities Act of 1933 and section 3(a)(10) of the Act and the respective rules promulgated thereunder, that is a note, bond, debenture, or evidence of indebtedness;

      (ii) None of the securities of an issuer included in the index is an equity security, as defined in section 3(a)(11) of the Act and the rules promulgated thereunder;

      (iii) The index is comprised of more than nine securities that are issued by more than nine non-affiliated issuers;

      (iv) The securities of any issuer included in the index do not comprise more than 30 percent of the index's weighting;

      (v) The securities of any five non-affiliated issuers included in the index do not comprise more than 60 percent of the index's weighting;

      (vi) Except as provided in paragraph (a)(1)(viii) of this rule, for each security of an issuer included in the index one of the following criteria is satisfied:

(A)   The issuer of the security is required to file reports pursuant to section 13 or section 15(d) of the Act;

(B)   The issuer of the security has a worldwide market value of its outstanding common equity held by non-affiliates of $71 million or more;

(C)   The issuer of the security has outstanding securities that are notes, bonds, debentures, or evidences of indebtedness having a total remaining principal amount of at least $1 billion;

(D)   The security is an exempted security as defined in section 3(a)(12) of the Act and the rules promulgated thereunder; or

(E)   The issuer of the security is a government of a foreign country or a political subdivision of a foreign country;

(vii) Except as provided in paragraph (a)(1)(viii) of this rule, for each security of an issuer included in the index one of the following criteria is satisfied:

(A)   The security has a total remaining principal amount of at least $250,000,000; or

(B)   The security is a municipal security, as defined in section 3(a)(29) of the Act and the rules promulgated thereunder that has a total remaining principal amount of at least $200,000,000 and the issuer of such municipal security has outstanding securities that are notes, bonds, debentures, or evidences of indebtedness having a total remaining principal amount of at least $1 billion; and

(viii) Paragraphs (a)(1)(vi) and (a)(1)(vii) of this rule will not apply to securities of an issuer included in the index if:

(A)   All securities of such issuer included in the index represent less than five percent of the index's weighting; and

(B)   Securities comprising at least 80 percent of the index's weighting satisfy the provisions of paragraphs (a)(1)(vi) and (a)(1)(vii) of this rule; or

(2)(i) The index includes exempted securities, other than municipal securities, as defined in section 3(a)(29) of the Act and the rules promulgated thereunder, that are:

(A)   Notes, bonds, debentures, or evidences of indebtedness; and

(B)   Not equity securities, as defined in section 3(a)(11) of the Act and the rules promulgated thereunder; and

(ii)   Without taking into account any portion of the index composed of such exempted securities, other than municipal securities, the remaining portion of the index would not be a narrow-based security index meeting all the conditions under paragraph (a)(1) of this rule.

(b)   For purposes of this rule:

(1)   An issuer is affiliated with another issuer if it controls, is controlled by, or is under common control with, that issuer.

(2)   For purposes of this rule, control means ownership of 20 percent or more of an issuer's equity, or the ability to direct the voting of 20 percent or more of the issuer's voting equity.

(3)   The term issuer includes a single issuer or group of affiliated issuers.

DEFINITIONS

Rule 3b–1.   Definition of "Listed"

The term "listed" means admitted to full trading privileges upon application by the issuer or its fiscal agent or, in the case of the securities of a foreign corporation, upon application by a banker engaged in distributing them; and includes securities for which authority to add to the list on official notice of issuance has been granted.

Rule 3b–2. Definition of "Officer"

The term "officer" means a president, vice president, secretary, treasury or principal financial officer, comptroller or principal accounting officer, and any person routinely performing corresponding functions with respect to any organization whether incorporated or unincorporated.

Rule 3b–3. [Removed and Reserved]

Rule 3b–4. Definition of "Foreign Government," "Foreign Issuer" and "Foreign Private Issuer"

(a) *Foreign government:* The term "foreign government" means the government of any foreign country or of any political subdivision of a foreign country.

(b) *Foreign issuer:* The term "foreign issuer" means any issuer which is a foreign government, a national of any foreign country or a corporation or other organization incorporated or organized under the laws of any foreign country.

(c) *Foreign private issuer:* The term "foreign private issuer" means any foreign issuer other than a foreign government except for an issuer meeting the following conditions as of the last business day of its most recently completed second fiscal quarter:

    (1) More than 50 percent of the issuer's outstanding voting securities are directly or indirectly held of record by residents of the United States; and

    (2) Any of the following:

        (i) The majority of the executive officers or directors are United States citizens or residents;

        (ii) more than 50 percent of the assets of the issuer are located in the United States; or

        (iii) The business of the issuer is administered principally in the United States.

Instructions to paragraph (c)(1): To determine the percentage of outstanding voting securities held by U.S. residents:

    A. Use the method of calculating record ownership in Rule 12g3–2(a) under the Act, except that:

        (1) your inquiry as to the amount of shares represented by accounts of customers resident in the United States may be limited to brokers, dealer, banks and other nominees located in:

            (i) The United States,

            (ii) Your jurisdiction of incorporation, and,

            (iii) The jurisdiction that is the primary trading market for your voting securities, if different than your jurisdiction of incorporation; and

        (2) Notwithstanding § 240.12g5–1(a)(8) of this chapter, you shall not exclude securities held by persons who received the securities pursuant to an employee compensation plan

    B. If, after reasonable inquiry, you are unable to obtain information about the amount of shares represented by accounts of customers resident in the United states, you may assume, for purposes of this definition, that the customers are residents of the jurisdiction in which the nominee has its principal place of business.

    C. Count shares of voting securities beneficially owned by residents of the United States as reported on reports of beneficial ownership provided to you or filed publicly and based on information otherwise provided to you.

(d) Notwithstanding paragraph (c) of this rule, in the case of a new registrant with the Commission, the determination of whether an issuer is a foreign private issuer will be made as of a date within 30 days prior to the issuer's filing of an initial registration statement under either the Act or the Securities Act of 1933.

(e)   Once an issuer qualifies as a foreign private issuer, it will immediately be able to use the forms and rules designated for foreign private issuers until it fails to qualify for this status at the end of its most recently completed second fiscal quarter. An issuer's determination that it fails to qualify as a foreign private issuer governs its eligibility to use the forms and rules designated for foreign private issuers beginning on the first day of the fiscal year following the determination date. Once an issuer fails to qualify for foreign private issuer status, it will remain unqualified unless it meets the requirements for foreign private issuer status as of the last business day of its second fiscal quarter.

Rule 3b–5.   Non-exempt Securities Issued Under Governmental Obligations

(a)   Any part of an obligation evidenced by any bond, note, debenture, or other evidence of indebtedness issued by any governmental unit specified in section 3(a)(12) of the Act which is payable from payments to be made in respect of property or money which is or will be used, under a lease, sale, or loan arrangement, by or for industrial or commercial enterprise, shall be deemed to be a separate "security" within the meaning of section 3(a)(10) of the Act, issued by the lessee or obligor under the lease, sale or loan arrangement.

(b)   An obligation shall not be deemed a separate "security" as defined in paragraph (a) of this rule if,

(1)   The obligation is payable from the general revenues of a governmental unit, specified in section 3(a)(12) of the Act, having other resources which may be used for the payment of the obligation, or

(2)   the obligation relates to a public project or facility owned and operated by or on behalf of and under the control of a governmental unit specified in such section, or

(3)   the obligation relates to a facility which is leased to and under the control of an industrial or commercial enterprise but is a part of a public project which, as a whole, is owned by and under the general control of a governmental unit specified in such section, or an instrumentality thereof.

(c)   This rule shall apply to transactions of the character described in paragraph (a) of this rule only with respect to bonds, notes, debentures or other evidences of indebtedness sold after December 31, 1968.

Rule 3b–6.   Liability for Certain Statements by Issuers

(a)   A statement within the coverage of paragraph (b) of this rule which is made by or on behalf of an issuer or by an outside reviewer retained by the issuer shall be deemed not to be a fraudulent statement (as defined in paragraph (d) of this rule), unless it is shown that such statement was made or reaffirmed without a reasonable basis or was disclosed other than in good faith.

(b)   This rule applies to the following statements:

(1)   A forward-looking statement (as defined in paragraph (c) of this rule) made in a document filed with the Commission, in Part I of a quarterly report on Form 10–Q or in an annual report to shareholders meeting the requirements of Rules 14a–3(b) and (c) or 14c–3(a) and (b), a statement reaffirming such forward-looking statement after the date the document was filed or the annual report was made publicly available, or a forward-looking statement made before the date the document was filed or the date the annual report was publicly available if such statement is reaffirmed in a filed document, in Part I of a quarterly report on Form 10–Q, or in an annual report made publicly available within a reasonable time after the making of such forward-looking statement; *Provided,* That:

(i)   At the time such statements are made or reaffirmed, either the issuer is subject to the reporting requirements of Rule 13(a) or 15(d) of the Act and has complied with the requirements of Rule 13a–1 or 15d–1 thereunder, if applicable, to file its most recent annual report on Form 10–K, Form 20–F or Form 40–F; or if the issuer is not subject to the reporting requirements of section 13(a) or 15(d) of the Act, the statements are made in a registration statement filed under the Securities Act of 1933 offering statement or solicitation of interest, written document or broadcast script under Regulation A or pursuant to section 12(b) or (g) of the Securities Act of 1934; and

(ii)   The statements are not made by or on behalf of an issuer that is an investment company registered under the Investment Company Act of 1940; and

(2)   Information that is disclosed in a document filed with the Commission in Part I of a quarterly report on Form 10–Q or in an annual report to security holders meeting the requirements of Rules 14a–3(b) and (c) or 14c–3(a) and (b) under the Act and that relates to

(i)   The effects of changing prices on the business enterprise, presented voluntarily or pursuant to Item 303 of Regulation S–K, "Management's Discussion and Analysis of Financial Conditions and Results of Operations" Item 5 of Form 20–F, "Operating and Financial Review and Prospectus," or Item 302 of Regulation S–K "Supplementary Financial Information," or Rule 3–20(c) of Regulation S–X; or

(ii)   The value of proved oil and gas reserves (such as a standardized measure of discounted future net cash flows relating to proved oil and gas reserves as set forth in paragraphs 932–235–50–29 through 932–235–50–36 (Extractive Activities—Oil and Gas Topic), presented voluntarily or pursuant to Item 302 of Regulation S–K.

(c)   For the purpose of this rule, the term "forward-looking statement" shall mean and shall be limited to:

(1)   A statement containing a projection of revenues, income (loss), earnings (loss) per share, capital expenditures, dividends, capital structure or other financial items;

(2)   A statement of management's plans and objectives for future operations;

(3)   A statement of future economic performance contained in management's discussion and analysis of financial condition and results of operations included pursuant to Item 303 of Regulation S–K or Item 5 of Form 20–F; or

(4)   Disclosed statements of the assumptions underlying or relating to any of the statements described in paragraphs (c)(1), (2), or (3) of this rule.

(d)   For the purpose of this rule the term "fraudulent statement" shall mean a statement which is an untrue statement of a material fact, a statement false or misleading with respect to any material fact, an omission to state a material fact necessary to make a statement not misleading, or which constitutes the employment of a manipulative, deceptive, or fraudulent device, contrivance, scheme, transaction, act, practice, course of business, or an artifice to defraud, as those terms are used in the Act or the rules or regulations promulgated thereunder.

Rule 3b–7.   Definition of "Executive Officer"

The term "executive officer," when used with reference to a registrant, means its president, any vice president of the registrant in charge of a principal business unit, division of function (such as sales, administration or finance), any other officer who performs a policy making function or any other person who performs similar policy making functions for the registrant. Executive officers of subsidiaries may be deemed executive officers of the registrant if they perform such policy making functions for the registrant.

Rule 3b–8.   Definitions of "Qualified OTC Market Maker," "Qualified Third Market Maker" and "Qualified Block Positioner"

For the purposes of Regulation U under the Act:

(a)   The term "Qualified OTC Market Maker" in an over-the-counter ("OTC") margin security means a dealer in any "OTC Margin Security" [as that term is defined in section 2(j) of Regulation U] who

(1)   Is a broker or dealer registered pursuant to section 15 of the Act,

(2)   Is subject to and is in compliance with Rule 15c3–1,

(3)   Has and maintains minimum net capital, as defined in Rule 15c3–1, of the lesser of

(i) $250,000 or

(ii) $25,000 plus $5,000 for each security in excess of five with regard to which the broker or dealer is, or is seeking to become a Qualified OTC Market Maker, and

(4)   Except when such activity is unlawful, meets all of the following conditions with respect to such security:

    (i)   He regularly publishes bona fide, competitive bid and offer quotations in a recognized inter-dealer quotation system,

    (ii)   He furnishes bona fide, competitive bid and offer quotations to other brokers and dealers on request,

    (iii)   He is ready, willing and able to effect transactions in reasonable amounts, and at his quoted prices, with other brokers and dealers, and

    (iv)   He has a reasonable average rate of inventory turnover in such security.

(b)   The term "Qualified Third Market Maker" means a dealer in any stock registered on a national securities exchange ("exchange") who

(1)   Is a broker or dealer registered pursuant to section 15 of the Act,

(2)   Is subject to and is in compliance with Rule 15c3–1,

(3)   Has and maintains minimum net capital, as defined in Rule 15c3–1, of the lesser of

    (i) $500,000 or

    (ii) $100,000 plus $20,000 for each security in excess of five with regard to which the broker or dealer is, or is seeking to become, a Qualified Third Market Maker, and

(4)   Except when such activity is unlawful, meets all of the following conditions with respect to such security:

    (i)   He furnishes bona fide, competitive bid and offer quotations at all times to other brokers and dealers on request,

    (ii)   He is ready, willing and able to effect transactions for his own account in reasonable amounts, and at his quoted prices with other brokers and dealers, and

    (iii)   He has a reasonable average rate of inventory turnover in such security.

(c)   The term "Qualified Block Positioner" means a dealer who

(1)   Is a broker or dealer registered pursuant to section 15 of the Act,

(2)   Is subject to and in compliance with Rule 15c3–1,

(3)   Has and maintains minimum net capital, as defined in Rule 15c3–1 of $1,000,000 and

(4)   Except when such activity is unlawful, meets all of the following conditions:

    (i)   He engages in the activity of purchasing long or selling short, from time to time, from or to a customer (other than a partner or a joint venture or other entity in which a partner, the dealer, or a person associated with such dealer, as defined in section 3(a)(18) of the Act, participates) a block of stock with a current market value of $200,000 or more in a single transaction, or in several transactions at approximately the same time, from a single source to facilitate a sale or purchase by such customer,

    (ii)   He has determined in the exercise of reasonable diligence that the block could not be sold to or purchased from others on equivalent or better terms, and

    (iii)   He sells the shares comprising the block as rapidly as possible commensurate with the circumstances.

Rule 3b–11. Definitions Relating to Limited Partnership Roll-up Transactions for Purposes of Sections 6(b)(9), 14(h), and 15A(b)(12)–(13)

(a)   The term "limited partnership roll-up transaction" does not include a transaction involving only entities that are not "finite-life" as defined in Item 901(b)(2) of Regulation S–K.

(b)   The term "limited partnership roll-up transaction" does not include a transaction involving only entities registered under the Investment Company Act of 1940 or any Business Development Company as defined in section 2(a)(48) of that Act.

(c)   The term "regularly traded" shall be defined as in Item 901(c)(2)(v)(C) of Regulation S–K.

Rule 3b–12.   Definition of OTC Derivatives Dealer

The term OTC derivatives dealer means any dealer that is affiliated with a registered broker or dealer (other than an OTC derivatives dealer), and whose securities activities:

(a)   Are limited to:

(1)   Engaging in dealer activities in eligible OTC derivative instruments that are securities;

(2)   Issuing and reacquiring securities that are issued by the dealer, including warrants on securities, hybrid securities, and structured notes;

(3)   Engaging in cash management securities activities;

(4)   Engaging in ancillary portfolio management securities activities; and

(5)   Engaging in such other securities activities that the Commission designates by order pursuant to Rule 15a–1(b)(1) under the Act; and

(b)   Consist primarily of the activities described in paragraphs (a)(1), (a)(2), and (a)(3) of this rule; and

(c)   Do not consist of any other securities activities, including engaging in any transaction in any security that is not an eligible OTC derivative instrument, except as permitted under paragraphs (a)(3), (a)(4), and (a)(5) of this rule.

(d)   For purposes of this rule, the term hybrid security means a security that incorporates payment features economically similar to options, forwards, futures, swap agreements, or collars involving currencies, interest or other rates, commodities, securities, indices, quantitative measures, or other financial or economic interests or property of any kind, or any payment or delivery that is dependent on the occurrence or nonoccurrence of any event associated with a potential financial, economic, or commercial consequence (or any combination, permutation, or derivative of such contract or underlying interest).

Rule 3b–13.   Definition of Eligible OTC Derivative Instrument

(a)   Except as otherwise provided in paragraph (b) of this rule, the term eligible OTC derivative instrument means any contract, agreement, or transaction that:

(1)   Provides, in whole or in part, on a firm or contingent basis, for the purchase or sale of, or is based on the value of, or any interest in, one or more commodities, securities, currencies, interest or other rates, indices, quantitative measures, or other financial or economic interests or property of any kind; or

(2)   Involves any payment or delivery that is dependent on the occurrence or nonoccurrence of any event associated with a potential financial, economic, or commercial consequence; or

(3)   Involves any combination or permutation of any contract, agreement, or transaction or underlying interest, property, or event described in paragraphs (a)(1) or (a)(2) of this rule.

(b)   The term eligible OTC derivative instrument does not include any contract, agreement, or transaction that:

(1)   Provides for the purchase or sale of a security, on a firm basis, unless:

(i)   The settlement date for such purchase or sale occurs at least one year following the trade date or, in the case of an eligible forward contract, at least four months following the trade date; or

(ii)   The material economic features of the contract, agreement, or transaction consist primarily of features of a type described in paragraph (a) of this rule other than the provision for the purchase or sale of a security on a firm basis; or

(2)   Provides, in whole or in part, on a firm or contingent basis, for the purchase or sale of, or is based on the value of, or any interest in, any security (or group or index of securities), and is:

(i)   Listed on, or traded on or through, a national securities exchange or registered national securities association, or facility or market thereof; or

(ii)   Except as otherwise determined by the Commission by order pursuant to Rule 15a–1(b)(2) under the Act, one of a class of fungible instruments that are standardized as to their material economic terms.

(c)   The Commission may issue an order pursuant to Rule 15a–1(b)(3) under the Act clarifying whether certain contracts, agreements, or transactions are within the scope of eligible OTC derivative instrument.

(d)   For purposes of this rule, the term eligible forward contract means a forward contract that provides for the purchase or sale of a security other than a government security, provided that, if such contract provides for the purchase or sale of margin stock (as defined in Regulation U of the Regulations of the Board of Governors of the Federal Reserve System), such contract either:

(1)   Provides for the purchase or sale of such stock by the issuer thereof (or an affiliate that is not a bank or a broker or dealer); or

(2)   Provides for the transfer of transaction collateral in an amount that would satisfy the requirements, if any, that would be applicable assuming the OTC derivatives dealer party to such transaction were not eligible for the exemption from Regulation T of the Regulations of the Board of Governors of the Federal Reserve System, set forth in Rule 36a1–1 under the Act.

Rule 3b–14.   Definition of Cash Management Securities Activities

The term cash management securities activities means securities activities that are limited to transactions involving:

(a)   Any taking possession of, and any subsequent sale or disposition of, collateral provided by a counterparty, or any acquisition of, and any subsequent sale or disposition of, collateral to be provided to a counterparty, in connection with any securities activities of the dealer permitted under Rule 15a–1 of the Act or any non-securities activities of the dealer that involve eligible OTC derivative instruments or other financial instruments;

(b)   Cash management, in connection with any securities activities of the dealer permitted under Rule 15a–1 of the Act or any non-securities activities of the dealer that involve eligible OTC derivative instruments or other financial instruments; or

(c)   Financing of positions of the dealer acquired in connection with any securities activities of the dealer permitted under Rule 15a–1 of the Act or any non-securities activities that involve eligible OTC derivative instruments or other financial instruments.

Rule 3b–15.   Definition of Ancillary Portfolio Management Securities Activities

(a)   The term ancillary portfolio management securities activities means securities activities that:

(1)   Are limited to transactions in connection with:

(i)   Dealer activities in eligible OTC derivative instruments;

(ii)   The issuance of securities by the dealer; or

(iii)   Such other securities activities that the Commission designates by order pursuant to Rule 15a–1(b)(1) of the Act; and

(2)   Are conducted for the purpose of reducing the market or credit risk of the dealer or consist of incidental trading activities for portfolio management purposes; and

(3)   Are limited to risk exposures within the market, credit, leverage, and liquidity risk parameters set forth in:

    (i) The trading authorizations granted to the associated person (or to the supervisor of such associated person) who executes a particular transaction for, or on behalf of, the dealer; and

    (ii) The written guidelines approved by the governing body of the dealer and included in the internal risk management control system for the dealer pursuant to Rule 15c3–4 of the Act; and

    (4) Are conducted solely by one or more associated persons of the dealer who perform substantial duties for, or on behalf of, the dealer in connection with its dealer activities in eligible OTC derivative instruments.

    (b) The Commission may issue an order pursuant to Rule 15a–1(b)(4) of the Act clarifying whether certain securities activities are within the scope of ancillary portfolio management securities activities.

Rule 3b–16. Definitions of Terms Used in Section 3(a)(1) of the Act

    (a) An organization, association, or group of persons shall be considered to constitute, maintain, or provide "a market place or facilities for bringing together purchasers and sellers of securities or for otherwise performing with respect to securities the functions commonly performed by a stock exchange," as those terms are used in section 3(a)(1) of the Act, if such organization, association, or group of persons:

    (1) Brings together the orders for securities of multiple buyers and sellers; and

    (2) Uses established, non-discretionary methods (whether by providing a trading facility or by setting rules) under which such orders interact with each other, and the buyers and sellers entering such orders agree to the terms of a trade.

    (b) An organization, association, or group of persons shall not be considered to constitute, maintain, or provide "a market place or facilities for bringing together purchasers and sellers of securities or for otherwise performing with respect to securities the functions commonly performed by a stock exchange," solely because such organization, association, or group of persons engages in one or more of the following activities:

    (1) Routes orders to a national securities exchange, a market operated by a national securities association, or a broker-dealer for execution; or

    (2) Allows persons to enter orders for execution against the bids and offers of a single dealer; and

    (i) As an incidental part of these activities, matches orders that are not displayed to any person other than the dealer and its employees; or

    (ii) In the course of acting as a market maker registered with a self-regulatory organization, displays the limit orders of such market maker's, or other broker-dealer's, customers; and

    (A) Matches customer orders with such displayed limit orders; and

    (B) As an incidental part of its market making activities, crosses or matches orders that are not displayed to any person other than the market maker and its employees.

    (c) For purposes of this rule the term order means any firm indication of a willingness to buy or sell a security, as either principal or agent, including any bid or offer quotation, market order, limit order, or other priced order.

    (d) For the purposes of this rule, the terms bid and offer shall have the same meaning as under Rule 600 of Regulation NMS.

    (e) The Commission may conditionally or unconditionally exempt any organization, association, or group of persons from the definition in paragraph (a) of this rule.

Rule 3b–17. [Removed and Reserved]

Rule 3b–18. Definitions of Terms Used in Section 3(a)(5) of the Act

For purposes of Section 3(a)(5)(C) of the Act:

(a)   The term affiliate means any company that controls, is controlled by, or is under common control with another company.

(b)   The term consumer-related receivable means any obligation incurred by any natural person to pay money arising out of a transaction in which the money, property, insurance, or services (being purchased) are primarily for personal, family, or household purposes.

(c)   The term member as it relates to the term "syndicate of banks" means a bank that is a participant in a syndicate of banks and together with its affiliates, other than its broker or dealer affiliates, originates no less than 10% of the value of the obligations in a pool of obligations used to back the securities issued through a grantor trust or other separate entity.

(d)   The term obligation means any note, draft, acceptance, loan, lease, receivable, or other evidence of indebtedness that is not a security issued by a person other than the bank.

(e)   The term originated means:

(1)   Funding an obligation at the time that the obligation is created; or

(2)   Initially approving and underwriting the obligation, or initially agreeing to purchase the obligation, provided that:

(i)   The obligation conforms to the underwriting standards or is evidenced by the loan documents of the bank or its affiliates, other than its broker or dealer affiliates; and

(ii)   The bank or its affiliates, other than its broker or dealer affiliates, fund the obligation in a timely manner, not to exceed six months after the obligation is created.

(f)   The term pool means more than one obligation or type of obligation grouped together to provide collateral for a securities offering.

(g)   The term predominantly originated means that no less than 85% of the value of the obligations in any pool were originated by:

(1)   The bank or its affiliates, other than its broker or dealer affiliates; or

(2)   Banks that are members of a syndicate of banks and affiliates of such banks, other than their broker or dealer affiliates, if the obligations or pool of obligations consist of mortgage obligations or consumer-related receivables.

(3)   For this purpose, the bank and its affiliates include any financial institution with which the bank or its affiliates have merged but does not include the purchase of a pool of obligations or the purchase of a line of business.

(h)   The term syndicate of banks means a group of banks that acts jointly, on a temporary basis, to issue through a grantor trust or other separate entity, securities backed by obligations originated by each of the individual banks or their affiliates, other than their broker or dealer affiliates.

Rule 3b–19.   Definition of "Issuer" in Section 3(a)(8) of the Act in Relation to Asset-Backed Securities

The following applies with respect to asset-backed securities under the Act. Terms used in this rule have the same meaning as in Item 1101 of Regulation AB.

(a)   The depositor for the asset-backed securities acting solely in its capacity as depositor to the issuing entity is the "issuer" for purposes of the asset-backed securities of that issuing entity.

(b)   The person acting in the capacity as the depositor specified in paragraph (a) of this rule is a different "issuer" from that same person acting as a depositor for another issuing entity or for purposes of that person's own securities.

REGISTRATION AND EXEMPTION OF EXCHANGES

Rule 6a–1.   Application for Registration as a National Securities Exchange or Exemption From Registration Based on Limited Volume

(a)   An application for registration as a national securities exchange, or for exemption from such registration based on limited volume, shall be filed on Form 1, in accordance with the instructions contained therein.

(b)   Promptly after the discovery that any information filed on Form 1 was inaccurate when filed, the exchange shall file with the Commission an amendment correcting such inaccuracy.

(c)   Promptly after the discovery that any information in the statement, any exhibit, or any amendment was inaccurate when filed, the exchange shall file with the Commission an amendment correcting such inaccuracy.

(d)   Whenever the number of changes to be reported in an amendment, or the number of amendments filed, are so great that the purpose of clarity will be promoted by the filing of a new complete statement and exhibits, an exchange may, at its election, or shall, upon request of the Commission, file as an amendment a complete new statement together with all exhibits which are prescribed to be filed in connection with Form 1.

Rule 6a–2.   Amendments to Application

(a)   A national securities exchange, or an exchange exempted from such registration based on limited volume, shall file an amendment to Form 1, which shall set forth the nature and effective date of the action taken and shall provide any new information and correct any information rendered inaccurate, on Form 1 within 10 days after any action is taken that renders inaccurate, or that causes to be incomplete, any of the following:

(1)   Information filed on the Execution Page of Form 1, or amendment thereto; or

(2)   Information filed as part of Exhibits C, F, G, H, J, K or M, or any amendments thereto.

(b)   On or before June 30 of each year, a national securities exchange, or an exchange exempted from such registration based on limited volume, shall file, as an amendment to Form 1, the following:

(1)   Exhibits D and I as of the end of the latest fiscal year of the exchange; and

(2)   Exhibits K, M, and N, which shall be up to date as of the latest date practicable within 3 months of the date the amendment is filed.

(c)   On or before June 30, 2001 and every 3 years thereafter, a national securities exchange, or an exchange exempted from such registration based on limited volume, shall file, as an amendment to Form 1, complete Exhibits A, B, C and J. The information filed under this paragraph (c) shall be current as of the latest practicable date, but shall, at a minimum, be up to date within 3 months as of the date the amendment is filed.

(d)(1)   If an exchange, on an annual or more frequent basis, publishes, or cooperates in the publication of, any of the information required to be filed by paragraphs (b)(2) and (c) of this rule, in lieu of filing such information, an exchange may:

(i)   Identify the publication in which such information is available, the name, address, and telephone number of the person from whom such publication may be obtained, and the price of such publication; and

(ii)   Certify to the accuracy of such information as of its publication date.

(2)   If an exchange keeps the information required under paragraphs (b)(2) and (c) of this rule up to date and makes it available to the Commission and the public upon request, in lieu of filing such information, an exchange may certify that the information is kept up to date and is available to the Commission and the public upon request.

(3)   If the information required to be filed under paragraphs (b)(2) and (c) of this rule is available continuously on an Internet web site controlled by an exchange, in lieu of filing such information with the Commission, such exchange may:

    (i)   Indicate the location of the Internet web site where such information may be found; and

    (ii)   Certify that the information available at such location is accurate as of its date.

(e)   The Commission may exempt a national securities exchange, or an exchange exempted from such registration based on limited volume, from filing the amendment required by this rule for any affiliate or subsidiary listed in Exhibit C of the exchange's application for registration, as amended, that either:

    (1)   Is listed in Exhibit C of the application for registration, as amended, of one or more other national securities exchanges; or

    (2)   Was an inactive subsidiary throughout the subsidiary's latest fiscal year.

Any such exemption may be granted upon terms and conditions the Commission deems necessary or appropriate in the public interest or for the protection of investors, provided however, that at least one national securities exchange shall be required to file the amendments required by this rule for an affiliate or subsidiary described in paragraph (e)(1) of this rule.

(f)   A national securities exchange registered pursuant to Section 6(g)(1) of the Act shall be exempt from the requirements of this rule.

Rule 6a–3.   Supplemental Material to Be Filed by Exchanges

(a)(1)   A national securities exchange, or an exchange exempted from such registration based on limited volume, shall file with the Commission any material (including notices, circulars, bulletins, lists, and periodicals) issued or made generally available to members of, or participants or subscribers to, the exchange. Such material shall be filed with the Commission within 10 days after issuing or making such material available to members, participants or subscribers.

    (2)   If the information required to be filed under paragraph (a)(1) of this rule is available continuously on an Internet web site controlled by an exchange, in lieu of filing such information with the Commission, such exchange may:

        (i)   Indicate the location of the Internet web site where such information may be found; and

        (ii)   Certify that the information available at such location is accurate as of its date.

(b)   Within 15 days after the end of each calendar month, a national securities exchange or an exchange exempted from such registration based on limited volume, shall file a report concerning the securities sold on such exchange during the calendar month. Such report shall set forth:

    (1)   The number of shares of stock sold and the aggregate dollar amount of such stock sold;

    (2)   The principal amount of bonds sold and the aggregate dollar amount of such bonds sold; and

    (3)   The number of rights and warrants sold and the aggregate dollar amount of such rights and warrants sold.

(c)   A national securities exchange registered pursuant to Section 6(g)(1) of the Act shall be exempt from the requirements of this rule.

Rule 6a–4.   Notice of Registration Under Section 6(g) of the Act, Amendment to Such Notice, and Supplemental Materials to Be Filed by Exchanges Registered Under Section 6(g) of the Act

(a)   Notice of registration. (1) An exchange may register as a national securities exchange solely for the purposes of trading security futures products by filing Form 1–N ("notice of registration"), in accordance with the instructions contained therein, if:

(i)   The exchange is a board of trade, as that term is defined in the Commodity Exchange Act, that:

(A)   Has been designated a contract market by the Commodity Futures Trading Commission and such designation is not suspended by order of the Commodity Futures Trading Commission; or

(B)   Is registered as a derivative transaction execution facility under Section 5a of the Commodity Exchange Act and such registration is not suspended by the Commodity Futures Trading Commission; and

(ii)   Such exchange does not serve as a market place for transactions in securities other than:

(A)   Security futures products; or

(B)   Futures on exempted securities or on groups or indexes of securities or options thereon that have been authorized under Section 2(a)(1)(C) of the Commodity Exchange Act.

(2)   Promptly after the discovery that any information filed on Form 1–N was inaccurate when filed, the exchange shall file with the Commission an amendment correcting such inaccuracy.

(b)   Amendment to notice of registration. (1) A national securities exchange registered pursuant to Section 6(g)(1) of the Act ("Security Futures Product Exchange") shall file an amendment to Form 1–N, which shall set forth the nature and effective date of the action taken and shall provide any new information and correct any information rendered inaccurate, on Form 1–N, within:

(i)   Ten days after any action is taken that renders inaccurate, or that causes to be incomplete, any information filed on the Execution Page of Form 1–N, or amendment thereto; or

(ii)   30 days after any action is taken that renders inaccurate, or that causes to be incomplete, any information filed as part of Exhibit F to Form 1–N, or any amendments thereto.

(2)   A Security Futures Product Exchange shall maintain records relating to changes in information required in Exhibits C and E to Form 1–N which shall be current of as of the latest practicable date, but shall, at a minimum, be up-to-date within 30 days. A Security Futures Product Exchange shall make such records available to the Commission and the public upon request.

(3)   On or before June 30, 2002, and by June 30 every year thereafter, a Security Futures Product Exchange shall file, as an amendment to Form 1–N, Exhibits F, H, and I, which shall be current of as of the latest practicable date, but shall, at a minimum, be up-to-date within three months as of the date the amendment is filed.

(4)   On or before June 30, 2004, and by June 30 every three years thereafter, a Security Futures Product Exchange shall file, as an amendment to Form 1–N, complete Exhibits A, B, C, and E, which shall be current of as of the latest practicable date, but shall, at a minimum, be up-to-date within three months as of the date the amendment is filed.

(5)(i)   If a Security Futures Product Exchange, on an annual or more frequent basis, publishes, or cooperates in the publication of, any of the information required to be filed by paragraphs (b)(3) and (b)(4) of this rule, in lieu of filing such information, a Security Futures Product Exchange may satisfy this filing requirement by:

(A)   Identifying the publication in which such information is available, the name, address, and telephone number of the person from whom such publication may be obtained, and the price of such publication; and

(B)   Certifying to the accuracy of such information as of its publication date.

(ii)   If a Security Futures Product Exchange keeps the information required under paragraphs (b)(3) and (b)(4) of this rule up-to-date and makes it available to the Commission and the public upon request, in lieu of filing such information, a Security Futures Product Exchange may satisfy this filing requirement by certifying that the information is kept up-to-date and is available to the Commission and the public upon request.

(iii)   If the information required to be filed under paragraphs (b)(3) and (b)(4) of this rule is available continuously on an Internet web site controlled by a Security Futures Product

Exchange, in lieu of filing such information with the Commission, such Security Futures Product Exchange may satisfy this filing requirement by:

(A)   Indicating the location of the Internet web site where such information may be found; and

(B)   Certifying that the information available at such location is accurate as of its date.

(6)(i)   The Commission may exempt a Security Futures Product Exchange from filing the amendment required by this rule for any affiliate or subsidiary listed in Exhibit C to Form 1–N (§ 249.10 of this chapter), as amended, that either:

(A)   Is listed in Exhibit C to Form 1 or to Form 1–N, as amended, of one or more other national securities exchanges; or

(B)   Was an inactive affiliate or subsidiary throughout the affiliate's or subsidiary's latest fiscal year.

(ii)   Any such exemption may be granted upon terms and conditions the Commission deems necessary or appropriate in the public interest or for the protection of investors, provided however, that at least one national securities exchange shall be required to file the amendments required by this rule for an affiliate or subsidiary described in paragraph (b)(6)(i) of this rule.

(7)   If a Security Futures Product Exchange has filed documents with the Commodity Futures Trading Commission, to the extent that such documents contain information satisfying the Commission's informational requirements, copies of such documents may be filed with the Commission in lieu of the required written notice.

(c)   Supplemental material to be filed by Security Futures Product Exchanges.

(1)(i)   A Security Futures Product Exchange shall file with the Commission any material related to the trading of security futures products (including notices, circulars, bulletins, lists, and periodicals) issued or made generally available to members of, participants in, or subscribers to, the exchange. Such material shall be filed with the Commission within ten days after issuing or making such material available to members, participants, or subscribers.

(ii)   If the information required to be filed under paragraph (c)(1)(i) of this rule is available continuously on an Internet web site controlled by an exchange, in lieu of filing such information with the Commission, such exchange may:

(A)   Indicate the location of the Internet web site where such information may be found; and

(B)   Certify that the information available at such location is accurate as of its date.

(2)   Within 15 days after the end of each calendar month, a Security Futures Product Exchange shall file a report concerning the security futures products traded on such exchange during the previous calendar month. Such a report shall:

(i)   For each contract of sale for future delivery of a single security, the number of contracts traded on such exchange during the relevant calendar month and the total number of shares underlying such contracts traded; and

(ii)   For each contract of sale for future delivery of a narrow-based security index, the number of contracts traded on such exchange during the relevant calendar month and the total number of shares represented by the index underlying such contracts traded.

Rule 6h–1.   Settlement and Regulatory Halt Requirements for Security Futures Products

(a)   For the purposes of this Rule:

(1)   *Opening price* means the price at which a security opened for trading, or a price that fairly reflects the price at which a security opened for trading, during the regular trading session of the national securities exchange or national securities association that lists the security. If the security is not listed on a national securities exchange or a national securities association, then *opening price*

shall mean the price at which a security opened for trading, or a price that fairly reflects the price at which a security opened for trading, on the primary market for the security.

(2) *Regular trading session* of a security means the normal hours for business of a national securities exchange or national securities association that lists the security.

(3) *Regulatory halt* means a delay, halt, or suspension in the trading of a security, that is instituted by the national securities exchange or national securities association that lists the security, as a result of:

(i) A determination that there are matters relating to the security or issuer that have not been adequately disclosed to the public, or that there are regulatory problems relating to the security which should be clarified before trading is permitted to continue; or

(ii) The operation of circuit breaker procedures to halt or suspend trading in all equity securities trading on that national securities exchange or national securities association.

(b)(1) The final settlement price of a cash-settled security futures product must fairly reflect the opening price of the underlying security or securities.

(2) Notwithstanding paragraph (b)(1) of this Rule, if an opening price for one or more securities underlying a security futures product is not readily available, the final settlement price of the security futures product shall fairly reflect:

(i) The price of the underlying security or securities during the most recent regular trading session for such security or securities; or

(ii) The next available opening price of the underlying security or securities.

(3) Notwithstanding paragraph (b)(1) or (b)(2) of this Rule, if a clearing agency registered under Section 17A of the Act, or exempt from registration pursuant to Section 17A(b)(7) of the Act, to which the final settlement price of a security futures product is or would be reported determines, pursuant to its rules, that such final settlement price is not consistent with the protection of investors and the public interest, taking into account such factors as fairness to buyers and sellers of the affected security futures product, the maintenance of a fair and orderly market in such security futures product, and consistency of interpretation and practice, the clearing agency shall have the authority to determine, under its rules, a final settlement price for such security futures product.

(c) *Regulatory trading halts.* The rules of a national securities exchange or national securities association registered pursuant to Section 15A(a) of the Act that lists or trades one or more security futures products must include the following provisions:

(1) Trading of a security futures product based on a single security shall be halted at all times that a regulatory halt has been instituted for the underlying security; and

(2) Trading of a security futures product based on a narrow-based security index shall be halted at all times that a regulatory halt has been instituted for one or more underlying securities that constitute 50 percent or more of the market capitalization of the narrow-based security index.

(d) The Commission may exempt from the requirements of this Rule, either unconditionally or on specified terms and conditions, any national securities exchange or national securities association, if the Commission determines that such exemption is necessary or appropriate in the public interest and consistent with the protection of investors. An exemption granted pursuant to this paragraph shall not operate as an exemption from any Commodity Futures Trading Commission rules. Any exemption that may be required from such rules must be obtained separately from the Commodity Futures Trading Commission.

Rule 6h–2. Security Future Based on Note, Bond, Debenture, or Evidence of Indebtedness

A security future may be based upon a security that is a note, bond, debenture, or evidence of indebtedness or a narrow-based security index composed of such securities.

HYPOTHECATION OF CUSTOMERS' SECURITIES

Rule 8c-1.　Hypothecation of Customers' Securities

(a)　*General provisions.* No member of a national securities exchange, and no broker or dealer who transacts a business in securities through the medium of any such member shall, directly or indirectly, hypothecate or arrange for or permit the continued hypothecation of any securities carried for the account of any customer under circumstances:

(1)　That will permit the commingling of securities carried for the account of any such customer with securities carried for the account of any other customer, without first obtaining the written consent of each such customer to such hypothecation;

(2)　That will permit such securities to be commingled with securities carried for the account of any person other than a bona fide customer of such member, broker or dealer under a lien for a loan made to such member, broker or dealer; or

(3)　That will permit securities carried for the account of customers to be hypothecated or subjected to any lien or liens or claim or claims of the pledges or pledgees, for a sum which exceeds the aggregate indebtedness of all customers in respect of securities carried for their accounts; except that this clause shall not be deemed to be violated by reason of an excess arising on any day through the reduction of the aggregate indebtedness of customers on such day, provided that funds or securities in an amount sufficient to eliminate such excess are paid or placed in transfer to pledgees for the purpose of reducing the sum of the liens or claims to which securities carried for the account of customers are subjected as promptly as practicable after such reduction occurs, but before the lapse of one-half hour after the commencement of banking hours on the next banking day at the place where the largest principal amount of loans of such member, broker or dealer are payable and, in any event, before such member, broker or dealer on such day has obtained or increased any bank loan collateralized by securities carried for the account of customers.

(b)　*Definitions.* For the purposes of this rule:

(1)　The term customer shall not include any general or special partner or any director or officer of such member, broker or dealer, or any participant, as such, in any joint, group or syndicate account with such member, broker or dealer or with any partner, officer or director thereof. The term also shall not include any counterparty who has delivered collateral to an OTC derivatives dealer pursuant to a transaction in an eligible OTC derivative instrument, or pursuant to the OTC derivatives dealer's cash management securities activities or ancillary portfolio management securities activities, and who has received a prominent written notice from the OTC derivatives dealer that:

(i)　Except as otherwise agreed in writing by the OTC derivatives dealer and the counterparty, the dealer may repledge or otherwise use the collateral in its business;

(ii)　In the event of the OTC derivatives dealer's failure, the counterparty will likely be considered an unsecured creditor of the dealer as to that collateral;

(iii)　The Securities Investor Protection Act of 1970 does not protect the counterparty; and

(iv)　The collateral will not be subject to the requirements of Rule 8c-1, Rule 15c2-1, Rule 15c3-2, or Rule 15c3-3 of the Act;

(2)　The term "securities carried for the account of any customer" shall be deemed to mean:

(i)　Securities received by or on behalf of such member, broker or dealer for the account of any customer;

(ii)　Securities sold and appropriated by such member, broker or dealer to a customer, except that if such securities were subject to a lien when appropriated to a customer they shall not be deemed to be "securities carried for the account of any customer" pending their release from such lien as promptly as practicable;

(iii)　Securities sold, but not appropriated, by such member, broker or dealer to a customer who has made any payment therefor, to the extent that such member, broker or dealer owns and has received delivery of securities of like kind, except that if such securities were subject to a lien when such payment was made they shall not be deemed to be "securities carried for the account of any customer" pending their release from such lien as promptly as practicable;

(3) "Aggregate indebtedness" shall not be deemed to be reduced by reason of uncollected items. In computing aggregate indebtedness, related guaranteed and guarantor accounts shall be treated as a single account and considered on a consolidated basis, and balances in accounts carrying both long and short positions shall be adjusted by treating the market value of the securities required to cover such short positions as though such market value were a debit; and

(4) In computing the sum of the liens or claims to which securities carried for the account of customers of a member, broker or dealer are subject, any rehypothecation of such securities by another member, broker or dealer who is subject to this rule or to Rule 15c2–1 shall be disregarded.

(c) *Exemption for cash accounts.* The provisions of paragraph (a)(1) of this rule shall not apply to any hypothecation of securities carried for the account of a customer in a special cash account within the meaning of 12 CFR § 220.4(c): *Provided,* That at or before the completion of the transaction of purchase of such securities for, or of sale of such securities to, such customer, written notice is given or sent to such customer disclosing that such securities are or may be hypothecated under circumstances which will permit the commingling thereof with securities carried for the account of other customers. The term "the completion of the transaction" shall have the meaning given to such term by Rule 15c1–1(b).

(d) *Exemption for clearinghouse liens.* The provisions of paragraphs (a)(2), (a)(3), and (f) of this rule shall not apply to any lien or claim of the clearing corporation, or similar department or association, of a national securities exchange or a registered national securities association for a loan made and to be repaid on the same calendar day, which is incidental to the clearing of transactions in securities or loans through such corporation, department, or association: *Provided, however,* That for the purpose of paragraph (a)(3) of this rule, "aggregate indebtedness of all customers in respect of securities carried for their accounts" shall not include indebtedness in respect of any securities subject to any lien or claim exempted by this paragraph.

(e) *Exemption for certain liens on securities of noncustomers.* The provisions of paragraph (a)(2) of this rule shall not be deemed to prevent such member, broker or dealer from permitting securities not carried for the account of a customer to be subjected

(1) To a lien for a loan made against securities carried for the account of customers, or

(2) To a lien for a loan made and to be repaid on the same calendar day. For the purpose of this exemption, a loan shall be deemed to be "made against securities carried for the account of customers" if only securities carried for the account of customers are used to obtain or to increase such loan or as substitutes for other securities carried for the account of customers.

(f) *Notice and certification requirements.* No person subject to this rule shall hypothecate any security carried for the account of a customer unless at or prior to the time of each such hypothecation, he gives written notice to the pledgee that the security pledged is carried for the account of a customer and that such hypothecation does not contravene any provision of this rule, except that in the case of an omnibus account the members, broker or dealer for whom such account is carried may furnish a signed statement to the person carrying such account that all securities carried therein by such member, broker or dealer will be securities carried for the account of his customers and that the hypothecation thereof by such member, broker or dealer will not contravene any provision of this rule. The provisions of this paragraph shall not apply to any hypothecation of securities under any lien or claim of a pledgee securing a loan made and to be repaid on the same calendar day.

(g) The fact that securities carried for the accounts of customers and securities carried for the accounts of others are represented by one or more certificates in the custody of a clearing corporation or other subsidiary organization of either a national securities exchange or of a registered national securities association, or of a custodian bank, in accordance with a system for the central handling of securities established by a national securities exchange or a registered national securities association, pursuant to which system the hypothecation of such securities is effected by bookkeeping entries without physical delivery of such securities, shall not, in and of itself, result in a commingling of securities prohibited by paragraph (a)(1) or (a)(2) of this rule, whenever a participating member, broker or dealer hypothecates securities in accordance with such system: *Provided, however,* That

(1) Any such custodian of any securities held by or for such system shall agree that it will not for any reason, including the assertion of any claim, right or lien of any kind, refuse to refrain from promptly delivering any such securities (other than securities then hypothecated in accordance with such system) to such clearing corporation or other subsidiary organization or as directed by it, except that nothing in such agreement shall be deemed to require the custodian to deliver any securities in contravention of any notice of levy, seizure or similar notice, or order or judgment, issued or directed by a governmental agency or court, or officer thereof, having jurisdiction over such custodian, which on its face affects such securities;

(2) Such systems shall have safeguards in the handling, transfer and delivery of securities and provisions for fidelity bond coverage of the employees and agents of the clearing corporation or other subsidiary organization and for periodic examinations by independent public accountants; and

(3) The provisions of this paragraph shall not be effective with respect to any particular system unless the agreement required by paragraph (g)(1) of this rule and the safeguards and provisions required by paragraph (g)(2) of this rule shall have been deemed adequate by the Commission for the protection of investors, and unless any subsequent amendments to such agreement, safeguards or provisions shall have been deemed adequate by the Commission for the protection of investors.

STANDARDIZED OPTIONS

Rule 9b–1.   Options Disclosure Document

(a) *Definitions.* The following definitions shall apply for the purpose of this rule.

(1) "Options market" means a national securities exchange, an automated quotation system of a registered securities association or a foreign securities exchange on which standardized options are traded.

(2) "Options class" means all options contracts covering the same underlying instrument.

(3) "Options disclosure document" means a document, including all amendments and supplements thereto, prepared by one or more options markets which has been filed with the Commission or distributed in accordance with paragraph (b) of this Rule. "Definitive options disclosure document" or "document" means an options disclosure document furnished to customers in accordance with paragraph (b) of this Rule.

(4) "Standardized options" are options contracts trading on a national securities exchange, an automated quotation system of a registered securities association, or a foreign securities exchange which relate to options classes the terms of which are limited to specific expiration dates and exercise prices, or such other securities as the Commission may, by order, designate.

(b)(1) Five preliminary copies of an options disclosure document containing the information specified in paragraph (c) of this rule shall be filed with the Commission by an options market at least 60 days prior to the date definitive copies are furnished to customers, unless the commission determines otherwise having due regard to the adequacy of the information disclosed and the public interest and protection of investors. Five copies of the definitive options disclosure document shall be filed with the Commission not later than the date the options disclosure document is furnished to customers. Notwithstanding the above, the use of an options disclosure document shall not be permitted unless the options class to which such document relates is the subject of an effective registration statement on Form S–20 under the Securities Act of 1933, or is exempt from registration under the Securities Act of 1933.

(2)(i) If the information contained in the options disclosure document becomes or will become materially inaccurate or incomplete or there is or will be an omission of material information necessary to make the options disclosure document not misleading, the options market shall amend or supplement its options disclosure document by filing five copies of an amendment or supplement to such options disclosure document with the Commission at least 30 days prior to the date definitive copies are furnished to customers, unless the Commission determines otherwise having due regard to the adequacy of the information disclosed and the public interest and protection of investors. Five copies of the definitive options disclosure document, as amended or supplemented, shall be filed with the Commission not later than the date the amendment or supplement, or the amended options disclosure document, is furnished to customers.

(ii) Notwithstanding paragraph (b)(2)(i) of this Rule, an options market may distribute an amendment or supplement to an options disclosure document prior to such 30 day period if it determines, in good faith, that such delivery is necessary to ensure timely and accurate disclosure with respect to one or more of the options classes covered by the document. Five copies of any amendment or supplement distributed pursuant to this paragraph shall be filed with the Commission at the time of distribution. In that instance, if the Commission determines, having given due regard to the adequacy of the information disclosed and the public interest and the protection of investors, it may require refiling of the amendment pursuant to paragraph (b)(2)(i) of this Rule.

(c) Information required in an options disclosure document. An options disclosure document shall contain the following information, unless otherwise provided by the Commission, with respect to the options classes covered by the document:

(1)   A glossary of terms;

(2)   A discussion of the mechanics of exercising the options;

(3)   A discussion of the risks of being a holder or writer of the options;

(4)   The identification of the market or markets in which the options are traded;

(5)   A brief reference to the transaction costs, margin requirements and tax consequences of options trading;

(6)   The identification of the issuer of the options;

(7)   A general identification of the type of instrument or instruments underlying the options class or classes covered by the document;

(8)   If the options are not exempt from registration under the Securities Act of 1933, the registration of the options on Form S-20 and the availability of the prospectus and the information in Part II of the registration statement; and

(9)   Such other information as the Commission may specify.

(d)   Broker-dealer obligations. (1) No broker or dealer shall accept an order from a customer to purchase or sell an option contract relating to an options class that is the subject of a definitive options disclosure document, or approve the customer's account for the trading of such option, unless the broker or dealer furnishes or has furnished to the customer a copy of the definitive options disclosure document.

(2)   If a definitive options disclosure document relating to an options class is amended or supplemented, each broker and dealer shall promptly send a copy of the definitive amendment or supplement or a copy of the definitive options disclosure document as amended to each customer whose account is approved for trading the options class or classes to which the amendment or supplement relates.

MANIPULATIVE AND DECEPTIVE DEVICES AND CONTRIVANCES

Rule 10a-1.   Short Sales [Reserved]

Rule 10b-1.   Prohibition of Use of Manipulative or Deceptive Devices or Contrivances With Respect to Certain Securities Exempted From Registration

The term "manipulative or deceptive device or contrivance," as used in section 10(b) of this Act, is hereby defined to include any act or omission to act with respect to any security exempted from the operation of section 12(a) of this Act pursuant to any section in this part which specifically provides that this rule shall be applicable to such security if such act or omission to act would have been unlawful under section 9(a) of this Act, or any rule or regulation heretofore or hereafter prescribed thereunder, if done or omitted to be done with respect to a security registered on a national securities exchange, and the use of any means or instrumentality of interstate commerce or of the mails or of any facility of any national securities exchange to use or employ any such device or contrivance in connection with the purchase or sale of any such security is hereby prohibited.

Rule 10b–3. Employment of Manipulative and Deceptive Devices by Brokers or Dealers

(a)   It shall be unlawful for any broker or dealer, directly or indirectly, by the use of any means or instrumentality of interstate commerce, or of the mails, or of any facility of any national securities exchange, to use or employ, in connection with the purchase or sale of any security otherwise than on a national securities exchange, any act, practice, or course of business defined by the Commission to be included within the term "manipulative, deceptive, or other fraudulent device or contrivance", as such term is used in section 15(c)(1) of the Act.

(b)   It shall be unlawful for any municipal securities dealer directly or indirectly, by the use of any means or instrumentality of interstate commerce, or of the mails, or of any facility of any national securities exchange, to use or employ, in connection with the purchase or sale of any municipal security, any act, practice, or course of business defined by the Commission to be included within the term "manipulative, deceptive, or other fraudulent device or contrivance," as such term is used in section 15(c)(1) of the Act.

Rule 10b–5. Employment of Manipulative and Deceptive Devices

It shall be unlawful for any person, directly or indirectly, by the use of any means or instrumentality of interstate commerce, or of the mails or of any facility of any national securities exchange,

(a)   To employ any device, scheme, or artifice to defraud,

(b)   To make any untrue statement of a material fact or to omit to state a material fact necessary in order to make the statements made, in the light of the circumstances under which they were made, not misleading, or

(c)   To engage in any act, practice, or course of business which operates or would operate as a fraud or deceit upon any person,

in connection with the purchase or sale of any security.

Rule 10b5–1. Trading "on the Basis of" Material Nonpublic Information in Insider Trading Cases

Preliminary Note to Rule 10b5–1: This provision defines when a purchase or sale constitutes trading "on the basis of" material nonpublic information in insider trading cases brought under Section 10(b) of the Act and Rule 10b–5 thereunder. The law of insider trading is otherwise defined by judicial opinions construing Rule 10b–5, and Rule 10b5–1 does not modify the scope of insider trading law in any other respect.

(a)   General. The "manipulative and deceptive devices" prohibited by Section 10(b) of the Act and Rule10b–5 thereunder include, among other things, the purchase or sale of a security of any issuer, on the basis of material nonpublic information about that security or issuer, in breach of a duty of trust or confidence that is owed directly, indirectly, or derivatively, to the issuer of that security or the shareholders of that issuer, or to any other person who is the source of the material nonpublic information.

(b)   Definition of "on the basis of." Subject to the affirmative defenses in paragraph (c) of this rule, a purchase or sale of a security of an issuer is "on the basis of" material nonpublic information about that security or issuer if the person making the purchase or sale was aware of the material nonpublic information when the person made the purchase or sale.

(c)   Affirmative defenses.

(1)(i)   Subject to paragraph (c)(1)(ii) of this rule, a person's purchase or sale is not "on the basis of" material nonpublic information if the person making the purchase or sale demonstrates that:

(A)   before becoming aware of the information, the person had:

(1)   entered into a binding contract to purchase or sell the security,

(2)   instructed another person to purchase or sell the security for the instructing person's account, or

(3)   adopted a written plan for trading securities;

(B)   the contract, instruction, or plan described in paragraph (c)(1)(i)(A) of this rule:

(1)   specified the amount of securities to be purchased or sold and the price at which and the date on which the securities were to be purchased or sold;

(2)   included a written formula or algorithm, or computer program, for determining the amount of securities to be purchased or sold and the price at which and the date on which the securities were to be purchased or sold; or

(3)   did not permit the person to exercise any subsequent influence over how, when, or whether to effect purchases or sales; provided, in addition, that any other person who, pursuant to the contract, instruction, or plan, did exercise such influence must not have been aware of the material nonpublic information when doing so; and

(C)   the purchase or sale that occurred was pursuant to the contract, instruction, or plan. A purchase or sale is not "pursuant to a contract, instruction, or plan" if, among other things, the person who entered into the contract, instruction, or plan altered or deviated from the contract, instruction, or plan to purchase or sell securities (whether by changing the amount, price, or timing of the purchase or sale), or entered into or altered a corresponding or hedging transaction or position with respect to those securities.

(ii)   Paragraph (c)(1)(i) of this rule is applicable only when the contract, instruction, or plan to purchase or sell securities was given or entered into in good faith and not as part of a plan or scheme to evade the prohibitions of this rule.

(iii)   This paragraph (c)(1)(iii) defines certain terms as used in paragraph (c) of this rule.

(A)   Amount. "Amount" means either a specified number of shares or other securities or a specified dollar value of securities.

(B)   Price. "Price" means the market price on a particular date or a limit price, or a particular dollar price.

(C)   Date. "Date" means, in the case of a market order, the specific day of the year on which the order is to be executed (or as soon thereafter as is practicable under ordinary principles of best execution). "Date" means, in the case of a limit order, a day of the year on which the limit order is in force.

(2)   A person other than a natural person also may demonstrate that a purchase or sale of securities is not "on the basis of" material nonpublic information if the person demonstrates that:

(i)   The individual making the investment decision on behalf of the person to purchase or sell the securities was not aware of the information; and

(ii)   The person had implemented reasonable policies and procedures, taking into consideration the nature of the person's business, to ensure that individuals making investment decisions would not violate the laws prohibiting trading on the basis of material nonpublic information. These policies and procedures may include those that restrict any purchase, sale, and causing any purchase or sale of any security as to which the person has material nonpublic information, or those that prevent such individuals from becoming aware of such information.

Rule 10b5–2. Duties of Trust or Confidence in Misappropriation Insider Trading Cases

Preliminary Note to Rule 10b5–2: This rule provides a non-exclusive definition of circumstances in which a person has a duty of trust or confidence for purposes of the "misappropriation" theory of insider trading under Section 10(b) of the Act and Rule 10b–5. The law of insider trading is otherwise defined by judicial opinions construing Rule 10b–5, and Rule 10b5–2 does not modify the scope of insider trading law in any other respect.

(a)   Scope of Rule. This rule shall apply to any violation of Section 10(b) of the Act and Rule 10b–5 thereunder that is based on the purchase or sale of securities on the basis of, or the communication of, material nonpublic information misappropriated in breach of a duty of trust or confidence.

(b)   Enumerated "duties of trust or confidence." For purposes of this rule, a "duty of trust or confidence" exists in the following circumstances, among others:

(1)   Whenever a person agrees to maintain information in confidence;

(2)   Whenever the person communicating the material nonpublic information and the person to whom it is communicated have a history, pattern, or practice of sharing confidences, such that the recipient of the information knows or reasonably should know that the person communicating the material nonpublic information expects that the recipient will maintain its confidentiality; or

(3)   Whenever a person receives or obtains material nonpublic information from his or her spouse, parent, child, or sibling; provided, however, that the person receiving or obtaining the information may demonstrate that no duty of trust or confidence existed with respect to the information, by establishing that he or she neither knew nor reasonably should have known that the person who was the source of the information expected that the person would keep the information confidential, because of the parties' history, pattern, or practice of sharing and maintaining confidences, and because there was no agreement or understanding to maintain the confidentiality of the information.

Rule 10b–9.   Prohibited Representations in Connection With Certain Offerings

(a)   It shall constitute a "manipulative or deception device or contrivance", as used in section 10(b) of the Act, for any person, directly or indirectly, in connection with the offer or sale of any security, to make any representation:

(1)   To the effect that the security is being offered or sold on an "all-or-none" basis, unless the security is part of an offering or distribution being made on the condition that all or a specified amount of the consideration paid for such security will be promptly refunded to the purchaser unless

(i)   All of the securities being offered are sold at a specified price within a specified time, and

(ii)   The total amount due to the seller is received by him by a specified date; or

(2)   To the effect that the security is being offered or sold on any other basis whereby all or part of the consideration paid for any such security will be refunded to the purchaser if all or some of the securities are not sold, unless the security is part of an offering or distribution being made on the condition that all or a specified part of the consideration paid for such security will be promptly refunded to the purchaser unless

(i)   A specified number of units of the security are sold at a specified price within a specified time, and

(ii)   The total amount due to the seller is received by him by a specified date.

(b)   This rule shall not apply to any offer or sale of securities as to which the seller has a firm commitment from underwriters or others (subject only to customary conditions precedent, including "market outs") for the purchase of all the securities being offered.

Rule 10b–10.   Confirmation of Transactions

Preliminary Note. This rule requires broker-dealers to disclose specified information in writing to customers at or before completion of a transaction. The requirements under this rule that particular information be disclosed is not determinative of a broker-dealer's obligation under the general antifraud provisions of the federal securities laws to disclose additional information to a customer at the time of the customer's investment decision.

(a)   It shall be unlawful for any broker or dealer to effect for or with the account of a customer any transaction in, or to induce the purchase or sale by such customer of, any security (other than U.S. Savings Bonds or municipal securities) unless such broker or dealer, at or before completion of such transaction, gives or sends to such customer written notification disclosing:

(1)   The date and time of the transaction (or the fact that the time of the transaction will be furnished upon written request to such customer) and the identity, price, and number of shares or units (or principal amount) of such security purchased or sold by such customer; and

(2)   Whether the broker or dealer is acting as agent for such customer, as agent for some other person, as agent for both such customer and some other person, or as principal for its own account; and if the broker or dealer is acting as principal, whether it is a market maker in the security (other than by reason of acting as a block positioner); and

    (i)   If the broker or dealer is acting as agent for such customer, for some other person, or for both such customer and some other person:

        (A)   The name of the person from whom the security was purchased, or to whom it was sold, for such customer or the fact that the information will be furnished upon written request of such customer; and

        (B)   The amount of any remuneration received or to be received by the broker from such customer in connection with the transaction unless remuneration paid by such customer is determined pursuant to written agreement with such customer, otherwise than on a transaction basis; and

        (C)   For a transaction in any NMS stock as defined in Rule 600 of Regulation NMS or a security authorized for quotation on an automated interdealer quotation system that has the characteristics set forth in section 17B of the Act, a statement whether payment for order flow is received by the broker or dealer for transactions in such securities and the fact that the source and nature of the compensation received in connection with the particular transaction will be furnished upon written request of the customer; provided, however, that brokers or dealers that do not receive payment for order flow in connection with any transaction have no disclosure obligations under this paragraph; and

        (D)   The source and amount of any other remuneration received or to be received by the broker in connection with the transaction: *Provided, however,* that if, in the case of a purchase, the broker was not participating in a distribution, or in the case of a sale, was not participating in a tender offer, the written notification may state whether any other remuneration has been or will be received and the fact that the source and amount of such other remuneration will be furnished upon written request of such customer; or

    (ii)   If the broker or dealer is acting as principal for its own account:

        (A)   In the case where such broker or dealer is not a market maker in that security and, if, after having received an order to buy from a customer, the broker or dealer purchased the equity security from another person to offset a contemporaneous sale to such customer or, after having received an order to sell from a customer, the broker or dealer sold the security to another person to offset a contemporaneous purchase from such customer, the difference between the price to the customer and the dealer's contemporaneous purchase (for customer purchases) or sale price (for customer sales); or

        (B)   In the case of any other transaction in an NMS stock as defined by Rule 600 of Regulation NMS, or an equity security that is traded on a national securities exchange and that is subject to last sale reporting, the reported trade price, the price to the customer in the transaction, and the difference, if any, between the reported trade price and the price to the customer.

(3)   Whether any odd-lot differential or equivalent fee has been paid by such customer in connection with the execution of an order for an odd-lot number of shares or units (or principal amount) of a security and the fact that the amount of any such differential or fee will be furnished upon oral or written request: *Provided, however,* that such disclosure need not be made if the differential or fee is included in the remuneration disclosure, or exempted from disclosure, pursuant to paragraph (a)(2)(i)(B) of this rule; and

(4)   In the case of any transaction in a debt security subject to redemption before maturity, a statement to the effect that such debt security may be redeemed in whole or in part before maturity, that such a redemption could affect the yield represented and the fact that additional information is available upon request; and

(5)   In the case of a transaction in a debt security effected exclusively on the basis of a dollar price:

(i)   The dollar price at which the transaction was effected, and

(ii)   The yield to maturity calculated from the dollar price: *Provided, however,* that this paragraph (a)(5)(ii) shall not apply to a transaction in a debt security that either:

(A)   Has a maturity date that may be extended by the issuer thereof, with a variable interest payable thereon; or

(B)   Is an asset-backed security, that represents an interest in or is secured by a pool of receivables or other financial assets that are subject continuously to prepayment; and

(6)   In the case of a transaction in a debt security effected on the basis of yield:

(i)   The yield at which the transaction was effected, including the percentage amount and its characterization (e.g., current yield, yield to maturity, or yield to call) and if effected at yield to call, the type of call, the call date and call price; and

(ii)   The dollar price calculated from the yield at which the transaction was effected; and

(iii)   If effected on a basis other than yield to maturity and the yield to maturity is lower than the represented yield, the yield to maturity as well as the represented yield; *Provided, however,* that this paragraph (a)(6)(iii) shall not apply to a transaction in a debt security that either:

(A)   Has a maturity date that may be extended by the issuer thereof, with a variable interest rate payable thereon; or

(B)   Is an asset-backed security, that represents an interest in or is secured by a pool of receivables or other financial assets that are subject continuously to prepayment; and

(7)   In the case of a transaction in a debt security that is an asset-backed security, which represents an interest in or is secured by a pool of receivables or other financial assets that are subject continuously to prepayment, a statement indicating that the actual yield of such asset-backed security may vary according to the rate at which the underlying receivables or other financial assets are prepaid and a statement of the fact that information concerning the factors that affect yield (including at a minimum estimated yield, weighted average life, and the prepayment assumptions underlying yield) will be furnished upon written request of such customer; and

(8)   That the broker or dealer is not a member of the Securities Investor Protection Corporation (SIPC), or that the broker or dealer clearing or carrying the customer account is not a member of SIPC, if such is the case: *Provided, however,* that this paragraph (a)(9) shall not apply in the case of a transaction in shares of a registered open-end investment company or unit investment trust if:

(i)   The customer sends funds or securities directly to, or receives funds or securities directly from, the registered open-end investment company or unit investment trust, its transfer agent, its custodian, or other designated agent, and such person is not an associated person of the broker or dealer required by paragraph (a) of this rule to send written notification to the customer; and

(ii)   The written notification required by paragraph (a) of this rule is sent on behalf of the broker or dealer to the customer by a person described in paragraph (a)(9)(i) of this rule.

(b)   *Alternative Periodic Reporting.* A broker or dealer may effect transactions for or with the account of a customer without giving or sending to such customer the written notification described in paragraph (a) of this rule if:

(1)   Such transactions are effected pursuant to a periodic plan or an investment company plan, or effected in shares of any open-end management investment company registered under the Investment Company Act of 1940 that holds itself out as a money market fund and attempts to maintain a stable net asset value per share: *Provided, however,* that no sales load is deducted upon the purchase or redemption of shares in the money market fund; and

(2)   Such broker or dealer gives or sends to such customer within five business days after the end of each quarterly period, for transactions involving investment company and periodic plans, and after the end of each monthly period, for other transactions described in paragraph (b)(1) of this rule,

a written statement disclosing each purchase or redemption, effected for or with, and each dividend or distribution credited to or reinvested for, the account of such customer during the month; the date of such transaction; the identity, number, and price of any securities purchased or redeemed by such customer in each such transaction; the total number of shares of such securities in such customer's account; any remuneration received or to be received by the broker or dealer in connection therewith; and that any other information required by paragraph (a) of this rule will be furnished upon written request: *Provided, however,* that the written statement may be delivered to some other person designated by the customer for distribution to the customer; and

(3) Such customer is provided with prior notification in writing disclosing the intention to send the written information referred to in paragraph (b)(1) of this rule in lieu of an immediate confirmation.

(c) A broker or dealer shall give or send to a customer information requested pursuant to this rule within 5 business days of receipt of the request: *Provided, however,* That in the case of information pertaining to a transaction effected more than 30 days prior to receipt of the request, the information shall be given or sent to the customer within 15 business days.

(d) *Definitions.* For the purposes of this rule—

(1) "Customer" shall not include a broker or dealer;

(2) "Completion of the transaction" shall have the meaning provided in Rule 15c1–1 under the Act;

(3) "Time of the transaction" means the time of execution, to the extent feasible, of the customer's order;

(4) "Debt security" as used in paragraphs (a)(3), (4), and (5) only, means any security, such as a bond, debenture, note, or any other similar instrument which evidences a liability of the issuer (including any such security that is convertible into stock or a similar security) and fractional or participation interests in one or more of any of the foregoing: *Provided, however,* That securities issued by an investment company registered under the Investment Company Act of 1940 shall not be included in this definition;

(5) "Periodic plan" means any written authorization for a broker acting as agent to purchase or sell for a customer a specific security or securities (other than securities issued by an open end investment company or unit investment trust registered under the Investment Company Act of 1940), in specific amounts (calculated in security units or dollars), at specific time intervals and setting forth the commissions or charges to be paid by the customer in connection therewith (or the manner of calculating them); and

(6) "Investment company plan" means any plan under which securities issued by an open-end investment company or unit investment trust registered under the Investment Company Act of 1940 are purchased by a customer (the payments being made directly to, or made payable to, the registered investment company, or the principal underwriter, custodian, trustee, or other designated agent of the registered investment company), or sold by a customer pursuant to—

(i) An individual retirement or individual pension plan qualified under the Internal Revenue Code;

(ii) A contractual or systematic agreement under which the customer purchases at the applicable public offering price, or redeems at the applicable redemption price, such securities in specified amounts (calculated in security units or dollars) at specified time intervals and setting forth the commissions or charges to be paid by such customer in connection therewith (or the manner of calculating them); or

(iii) Any other arrangement involving a group of two or more customers and contemplating periodic purchases of such securities by each customer through a person designated by the group: *Provided,* That such arrangement requires the registered investment company or its agent—

(A) To give or send to the designated person, at or before the completion of the transaction for the purchase of such securities, a written notification of the receipt of the total amount paid by the group;

(B)   To send to anyone in the group who was a customer in the prior quarter and on whose behalf payment has not been received in the current quarter a quarterly written statement reflecting that a payment was not received on his behalf; and

(C)   To advise each customer in the group if a payment is not received from the designated person on behalf of the group within 10 days of a date certain specified in the arrangement for delivery of that payment by the designated person and thereafter to send to each such customer the written notification described in paragraph (a) of this rule for the next three succeeding payments.

(7)   "NMS stock" shall have the meaning provided in Rule 600 of Regulation NMS.

(8)   Payment for order flow shall mean any monetary payment, service, property, or other benefit that results in remuneration, compensation, or consideration to a broker or dealer from any broker or dealer, national securities exchange, registered securities association, or exchange member in return for the routing of customer orders by such broker or dealer to any broker or dealer, national securities exchange, registered securities association, or exchange member for execution, including but not limited to: research, clearance, custody, products or services; reciprocal agreements for the provision of order flow; adjustment of a broker or dealer's unfavorable trading errors; offers to participate as underwriter in public offerings; stock loans or shared interest accrued thereon; discounts, rebates, or any other reductions of or credits against any fee to, or expense or other financial obligation of, the broker or dealer routing a customer order that exceeds that fee, expense or financial obligation.

(9)   Asset-backed security means a security that is primarily serviced by the cashflows of a discrete pool of receivables or other financial assets, either fixed or revolving, that by their terms convert into cash within a finite time period plus any rights or other assets designed to assure the servicing or timely distribution of proceeds to the security holders.

(e)   The provisions of paragraphs (a) and (b) of this Rule shall not apply to a broker or dealer registered pursuant to section 15(b)(11)(A) of the Act to the extent that it effects transactions for customers in security futures products in a futures account (as that term is defined in Rule 15c3–3(a)(15)) and a broker or dealer registered pursuant to section 15(b)(1) of the Act that is also a futures commission merchant registered pursuant to section 4f(a)(1) of the Commodity Exchange Act, to the extent that it effects transactions for customers in security futures products in a futures account (as that term is defined in Rule 15c3–3(a)(15)), Provided that:

(1)   The broker or dealer that effects any transaction for a customer in security futures products in a futures account gives or sends to the customer no later than the next business day after execution of any futures securities product transaction, written notification disclosing:

(i)   The date the transaction was executed, the identity of the single security or narrow-based security index underlying the contract for the security futures product, the number of contracts of such security futures product purchased or sold, the price, and the delivery month;

(ii)   The source and amount of any remuneration received or to be received by the broker or dealer in connection with the transaction, including, but not limited to, markups, commissions, costs, fees, and other charges incurred in connection with the transaction, provided, however, that if no remuneration is to be paid for an initiating transaction until the occurrence of the corresponding liquidating transaction, that the broker or dealer may disclose the amount of remuneration only on the confirmation for the liquidating transaction;

(iii)   The fact that information about the time of the execution of the transaction, the identity of the other party to the contract, and whether the broker or dealer is acting as agent for such customer, as agent for some other person, as agent for both such customer and some other person, or as principal for its own account, and if the broker or dealer is acting as principal, whether it is engaging in a block transaction or an exchange of security futures products for physical securities, will be available upon written request of the customer; and

(iv)   Whether payment for order flow is received by the broker or dealer for such transactions, the amount of this payment and the fact that the source and nature of the compensation received in connection with the particular transaction will be furnished upon written request of the customer; provided, however, that brokers or dealers that do not receive payment for order flow have no disclosure obligation under this paragraph.

(2)   Transitional provision.

(i)   Broker-dealers are not required to comply with paragraph (e)(1)(iii) of this Rule until June 1, 2003, Provided that, if, not withstanding the absence of the disclosure required in that paragraph, the broker-dealer receives a written request from a customer for the information described in paragraph (e)(1)(iii) of this rule, the broker-dealer must make the information available to the customer; and

(ii)   Broker-dealers are not required to comply with paragraph (e)(1)(iv) of this Rule until June 1, 2003.

(f)   The Commission may exempt any broker or dealer from the requirements of paragraphs (a) and (b) of this rule with regard to specific transactions of specific classes of transactions for which the broker or dealer will provide alternative procedures to effect the purposes of this rule; any such exemption may be granted subject to compliance with such alternative procedures and upon such other stated terms and conditions as the Commission may impose.

Rule 10b–16. Disclosure of Credit Terms in Margin Transactions

(a)   It shall be unlawful for any broker or dealer to extend credit, directly or indirectly, to any customer in connection with any securities transaction unless such broker or dealer has established procedures to assure that each customer:

(1)   Is given or sent at the time of opening the account, a written statement or statements disclosing

(i)   The conditions under which an interest charge will be imposed;

(ii)   The annual rate or rates of interest that can be imposed;

(iii)   The method of computing interest;

(iv)   If rates of interest are subject to change without prior notice, the specific conditions under which they can be changed;

(v)   The method of determining the debit balance or balances on which interest is to be charged and whether credit is to be given for credit balances in cash accounts;

(vi)   What other charges resulting from the extension of credit, if any, will be made and under what conditions; and

(vii)   The nature of any interest or lien retained by the broker or dealer in the security or other property held as collateral and the conditions under which additional collateral can be required: *Provided, however,* That the requirements of this subparagraph will be met in any case where the account is opened by telephone if the information required to be disclosed is orally communicated to the customer at that time and the required written statement or statements are sent to the customer immediately thereafter: *And provided, further,* That in the case of customers to whom credit is already being extended on the effective date of this rule, the written statement or statements required hereunder must be given or sent to said customers within 90 days after the effective date of this rule; and

(2)   Is given or sent a written statement or statements, at least quarterly, for each account in which credit was extended, disclosing

(i)   The balance at the beginning of the period; the date, amount and a brief description of each debit and credit entered during such period; the closing balance; and, if interest is charged for a period different from the period covered by the statement, the balance as of the last day of the interest period;

(ii)   The total interest charge for the period during which interest is charged (or, if interest is charged separately for separate accounts, the total interest charge for each such account), itemized to show the dates on which the interest period began and ended; the annual rate or rates of interest charged and the interest charge for each such different annual rate of interest; and either each different debit balance on which an interest calculation was based or the average debit balance for the interest period, except that if an average debit balance is used, a separate average debit balance must be disclosed for each interest rate applied; and

(iii) All other charges resulting from the extension of credit in that account: *Provided, however,* That if the interest charge disclosed on a statement is for a period different from the period covered by the statement, there must be printed on the statement appropriate language to the effect that it should be retained for use in conjunction with the next statement containing the remainder of the required information: *And provided further,* That in the case of "equity funding programs" registered under the Securities Act of 1933, the requirements of this paragraph will be met if the broker or dealer furnishes to the customer, within 1 month after each extension of credit, a written statement or statements containing the information required to be disclosed under this paragraph.

(b) It shall be unlawful for any broker or dealer to make any changes in the terms and conditions under which credit charges will be made (as described in the initial statement made under paragraph (a) of this rule), unless the customer shall have been given not less than thirty (30) days written notice of such changes, except that no such prior notice shall be necessary where such changes are required by law: *Provided, however,* That if any change for which prior notice would otherwise be required under this paragraph results in a lower interest charge to the customer than would have been imposed before the change, notice of such change may be given within a reasonable time after the effective date of the change.

Rule 10b–17. Untimely Announcements of Record Dates

(a) It shall constitute a "manipulative or deceptive device or contrivance" as used in section 10(b) of the Act for any issuer of a class of securities publicly traded by the use of any means or instrumentality of interstate commerce or of the mails or of any facility of any national securities exchange to fail to give notice in accordance with paragraph (b) of this rule of the following actions relating to such class of securities:

(1) A dividend or other distribution in cash or in kind, except an ordinary interest payment on a debt security, but including a dividend or distribution of any security of the same or another issuer;

(2) A stock split or reverse split; or

(3) A rights or other subscription offering.

(b) Notice shall be deemed to have been given in accordance with this rule only if:

(1) Given to the National Association of Securities Dealers, Inc., no later than 10 days prior to the record date involved or, in case of a rights subscription or other offering if such 10 days advance notice is not practical, on or before the record date and in no event later than the effective date of the registration statement to which the offering relates, and such notice includes:

(i) Title of the security to which the declaration relates;

(ii) Date of declaration;

(iii) Date of record for determining holders entitled to receive the dividend or other distribution or to participate in the stock or reverse split;

(iv) Date of payment or distribution or, in the case of a stock or reverse split or rights or other subscription offering, the date of delivery;

(v) For a dividend or other distribution including a stock or reverse split or rights or other subscription offering:

(a) In cash, the amount of cash to be paid or distributed per share, except if exact per share cash distributions cannot be given because of existing conversion rights which may be exercised during the notice period and which may affect the per share cash distribution, then a reasonable approximation of the per share distribution may be provided so long as the actual per share distribution is subsequently provided on the record date,

(b) In the same security, the amount of the security outstanding immediately prior to and immediately following the dividend or distribution and the rate of the dividend or distribution,

(c) In any other security of the same issuer, the amount to be paid or distributed and the rate of the dividend or distribution,

(d) In any security of another issuer, the name of the issuer and title of that security, the amount to be paid or distributed, and the rate of the dividend or distribution and if that security is a right or a warrant, the subscription price,

(e) In any other property (including securities not covered under paragraphs (b)(1)(v) (b) through (d) of this rule) the identity of the property and its value and basis for assigning that value;

(vi) Method of settlement of fractional interests;

(vii) Details of any condition which must be satisfied or Government approval which must be secured to enable payment of distribution; and in

(viii) The case of stock or reverse split in addition to the aforementioned information;

(a) The name and address of the transfer or exchange agent; or

(2) The Commission, upon written request or upon its own motion, exempts the issuer from compliance with paragraph (b)(1) of this rule either unconditionally or on specified terms or conditions, as not constituting a manipulative or deceptive device or contrivance comprehended within the purpose of this rule; or

(3) Given in accordance with procedures of the national securities exchange or exchanges upon which a security of such issuer is registered pursuant to section 12 of the Act which contain requirements substantially comparable to those set forth in paragraph (b)(1) of this rule.

(c) The provisions of this rule shall not apply, however, to redeemable securities issued by open-end investment companies and unit investment trusts registered with the Commission under the Investment Company Act of 1940.

Rule 10b–18. Purchases of Certain Equity Securities by the Issuer and Others

Preliminary Notes to Rule 10b–18:

1. Rule 10b–18 provides an issuer (and its affiliated purchasers) with a "safe harbor" from liability for manipulation under sections 9(a)(2) of the Act and Rule 10b–5 under the Act *solely* by reason of the manner, timing, price, and volume of their repurchases when they repurchase the issuer's common stock in the market in accordance with the rule's manner, timing, price, and volume conditions. As a safe harbor, compliance with Rule 10b–18 is voluntary. To come within the safe harbor, however, an issuer's repurchases must satisfy (on a daily basis) each of the rule's four conditions. Failure to meet any one of the four conditions will remove all of the issuer's repurchases from the safe harbor for that day. The safe harbor, moreover, is not available for repurchases that, although made in technical compliance with the rule, are part of a plan or scheme to evade the federal securities laws.

2. Regardless of whether the repurchases are effected in accordance with Rule 10b–18, reporting issuers must report their repurchasing activity as required by Item 703 of Regulations S–K and S–B and Item 15(e) of Form 20–F (regarding foreign private issuers), and closed-end management investment companies that are registered under the Investment Company Act of 1940 must report their repurchasing activity as required by Item 8 of Form N–CSR.

(a) *Definitions.* Unless otherwise provided, all terms used in this rule shall have the same meaning as in the Act. In addition, the following definitions shall apply:

(1) *ADTV* means the average daily trading volume reported for the security during the four calendar weeks preceding the week in which the Rule 10b–18 purchase is to be effected.

(2) *Affiliate* means any person that directly or indirectly controls, is controlled by, or is under common control with, the issuer.

(3) *Affiliated purchaser* means:

(i) A person acting, directly or indirectly, in concert with the issuer for the purpose of acquiring the issuer's securities; or

(ii) An affiliate who, directly or indirectly, controls the issuer's purchases of such securities, whose purchases are controlled by the issuer, or whose purchases are under common control with those of the issuer; *Provided, however,* that "affiliated purchaser" shall not include a broker, dealer, or other person solely by reason of such broker, dealer, or other person effecting Rule 10b–18 purchases on behalf of the issuer or for its account, and shall not include an officer or director of the issuer solely by reason of that officer or director's participation in the decision to authorize Rule 10b–18 purchases by or on behalf of the issuer.

(4) *Agent independent of the issuer* has the meaning contained in Rule 100 under Regulation M.

(5) *Block* means a quantity of stock that either:

(i) Has a purchase price of $200,000 or more; or

(ii) Is at least 5,000 shares and has a purchase price of at least $50,000; or

(iii) Is at least 20 round lots of the security and totals 150 percent or more of the trading volume for that security or, in the event that trading volume data are unavailable, is at least 20 round lots of the security and totals at least one-tenth of one percent (.001) of the outstanding shares of the security, exclusive of any shares owned by any affiliate; *Provided, however,* That a block under paragraph (a)(5)(i), (ii), and (iii) shall not include any amount a broker or dealer, acting as principal, has accumulated for the purpose of sale or resale to the issuer or to any affiliated purchaser of the issuer if the issuer or such affiliated purchaser knows or has reason to know that such amount was accumulated for such purpose, nor shall it include any amount that a broker or dealer has sold short to the issuer or to any affiliated purchaser of the issuer if the issuer or such affiliated purchaser knows or has reason to know that the sale was a short sale.

(6) *Consolidated system* means a consolidated transaction or quotation reporting system that collects and publicly disseminates on a current and continuous basis transaction or quotation information in common equity securities pursuant to an effective transaction reporting plan or a national market system plan (as defined in Rule 600 of Regulation NMS).

(7) *Market-wide trading suspension* means a market-wide trading halt of 30 minutes or more that is:

(i) Imposed pursuant to the rules of a national securities exchange or a national securities association in response to a market-wide decline during a single trading session; or

(ii) Declared by the Commission pursuant to its authority under section 12(k) of the Act.

(8) *Plan* has the meaning contained in Rule 100 under Regulation M.

(9) *Principal market* for a security means the single securities market with the largest reported trading volume for the security during the six full calendar months preceding the week in which the Rule 10b–18 purchase is to be effected.

(10) *Public float value* has the meaning contained in Rule 100 under Regulation M.

(11) *Purchase price* means the price paid per share as reported, exclusive of any commission paid to a broker acting as agent, or commission equivalent, mark-up, or differential paid to a dealer.

(12) *Riskless principal transaction* means a transaction in which a broker or dealer after having received an order from an issuer to buy its security, buys the security as principal in the market at the same price to satisfy the issuer's buy order. The issuer's buy order must be effected at the same price per-share at which the broker or dealer bought the shares to satisfy the issuer's buy order, exclusive of any explicitly disclosed markup or markdown, commission equivalent, or other fee. In addition, only the first leg of the transaction, when the broker or dealer buys the security in the market as principal, is reported under the rules of a self-regulatory organization or under the Act. For purposes of this rule, the broker or dealer must have written policies and procedures in place to assure that, at a minimum, the issuer's buy order was received prior to the offsetting transaction; the offsetting transaction is

allocated to a riskless principal account or the issuer's account within 60 seconds of the execution; and the broker or dealer has supervisory systems in place to produce records that enable the broker or dealer to accurately and readily reconstruct, in a time-sequenced manner, all orders effected on a riskless principal basis.

(13) *Rule 10b–18 purchase* means a purchase (or any bid or limit order that would effect such purchase) of an issuer's common stock (or an equivalent interest, including a unit of beneficial interest in a trust or limited partnership or a depository share) by or for the issuer or any affiliated purchaser (including riskless principal transactions). However, it does *not* include any purchase of such security:

(i) Effected during the applicable restricted period of a distribution that is subject to Rule 102 under Regulation M;

(ii) Effected by or for an issuer plan by an agent independent of the issuer;

(iii) Effected as a fractional share purchase (a fractional interest in a security) evidenced by a script certificate, order form, or similar document;

(iv) Effected during the period from the time of public announcement (as defined in Rule 165(f) under the Securities Act of 1933) of a merger, acquisition, or similar transaction involving a recapitalization, until the earlier of the completion of such transaction or the completion of the vote by target shareholders. This exclusion does not apply to Rule 10b–18 purchases:

(A) Effected during such transaction in which the consideration is solely cash and there is no valuation period; or

(B) Where:

(1) The total volume of Rule 10b–18 purchases effected on any single day does not exceed the lesser of 25% of the security's four-week ADTV or the issuer's average daily Rule 10b–18 purchases during the three full calendar months preceding the date of the announcement of such transaction;

(2) The issuer's block purchases effected pursuant to paragraph (b)(4) of this rule do not exceed the average size and frequency of the issuer's block purchases effected pursuant to paragraph (b)(4) of this rule during the three full calendar months preceding the date of the announcement of such transaction; and

(3) Such purchases are not otherwise restricted or prohibited;

(v) Effected pursuant to Rule 13e–1;

(vi) Effected pursuant to a tender offer that is subject to Rule 13e–4 or specifically excepted from Rule 13e–4; or

(vii) Effected pursuant to a tender offer that is subject to section 14(d) of the Act and the rules and regulations thereunder.

(b) *Conditions to be met.* Rule 10b–18 purchases shall not be deemed to have violated the anti-manipulation provisions of sections 9(a)(2) or 10(b) of the Act, or Rule 10b–5 under the Act, solely by reason of the time, price, or amount of the Rule 10b–18 purchases, or the number of brokers or dealers used in connection with such purchases, if the issuer or affiliated purchaser of the issuer effects the Rule 10b–18 purchases according to each of the following conditions:

(1) *One broker or dealer.* Rule 10b–18 purchases must be effected from or through only one broker or dealer on any single day; *Provided, however,* that:

(i) The "one broker or dealer" condition shall not apply to Rule 10b–18 purchases that are not solicited by or on behalf of the issuer or its affiliated purchaser(s);

(ii) Where Rule 10b–18 purchases are effected by or on behalf of more than one affiliated purchaser of the issuer (or the issuer and one or more of its affiliated purchasers) on a single day, the issuer and all affiliated purchasers must use the same broker or dealer; and

(iii) Where Rule 10b–18 purchases are effected on behalf of the issuer by a broker-dealer that is not an electronic communication network (ECN) or other alternative trading system (ATS), that broker-dealer can access ECN or other ATS liquidity in order to execute repurchases on behalf of the issuer (or any affiliated purchaser of the issuer) on that day.

(2)   *Time of purchases.* Rule 10b–18 purchases must not be:

(i)   The opening (regular way) purchase reported in the consolidated system;

(ii)   Effected during the 10 minutes before the scheduled close of the primary trading session in the principal market for the security, and the 10 minutes before the scheduled close of the primary trading session in the market where the purchase is effected, for a security that has an ADTV value of $1 million or more and a public float value of $150 million or more; and

(iii)   Effected during the 30 minutes before the scheduled close of the primary trading session in the principal market for the security, and the 30 minutes before the scheduled close of the primary trading session in the market where the purchase is effected, for all other securities;

(iv)   However, for purposes of this rule, Rule 10b–18 purchases may be effected following the close of the primary trading session until the termination of the period in which last sale prices are reported in the consolidated system so long as such purchases are effected at prices that do not exceed the lower of the closing price of the primary trading session in the principal market for the security and any lower bids or sale prices subsequently reported in the consolidated system, and all of this rule's conditions are met. However, for purposes of this rule, the issuer may use one broker or dealer to effect Rule 10b–18 purchases during this period that may be different from the broker or dealer that it used during the primary trading session. However, the issuer's Rule 10b–18 purchase may not be the opening transaction of the session following the close of the primary trading session.

(3)   *Price of purchases.* Rule 10b–18 purchases must be effected at a purchase price that:

(i)   Does not exceed the highest independent bid or the last independent transaction price, whichever is higher, quoted or reported in the consolidated system at the time the Rule 10b–18 purchase is effected;

(ii)   For securities for which bids and transaction prices are not quoted or reported in the consolidated system, Rule 10b–18 purchases must be effected at a purchase price that does not exceed the highest independent bid or the last independent transaction price, whichever is higher, displayed and disseminated on any national securities exchange or on any inter-dealer quotation system (as defined in Rule 15c2–11) that displays at least two priced quotations for the security, at the time the Rule 10b–18 purchase is effected; and

(iii)   For all other securities, Rule 10b–18 purchases must be effected at a price no higher than the highest independent bid obtained from three independent dealers.

(4)   *Volume of purchases.* The total volume of Rule 10b–18 purchases effected by or for the issuer and any affiliated purchasers effected on any single day must not exceed 25 percent of the ADTV for that security; *However*, once each week, in lieu of purchasing under the 25 percent of ADTV limit for that day, the issuer or an affiliated purchaser of the issuer may effect one block purchase if:

(i)   No other Rule 10b–18 purchases are effected that day, and

(ii)   The block purchase is not included when calculating a security's four week ADTV under this rule.

(c)   *Alternative conditions.* The conditions of paragraph (b) of this rule shall apply in connection with Rule 10b–18 purchases effected during a trading session following the imposition of a market-wide trading suspension, except:

(1)   That the time of purchases condition in paragraph (b)(2) of this rule shall not apply, either:

(i)   From the reopening of trading until the scheduled close of trading on the day that the market-wide trading suspension is imposed; or

(ii)   At the opening of trading on the next trading day until the scheduled close of trading that day, if a market-wide trading suspension was in effect at the close of trading on the preceding day; and

(2)   The volume of purchases condition in paragraph (b)(4) of this rule is modified so that the amount of Rule 10b–18 purchases must not exceed 100 percent of the ADTV for that security.

(d)   *Other purchases.* No presumption shall arise that an issuer or an affiliated purchaser has violated the anti-manipulation provisions of sections 9(a)(2) or 10(b) of the Act, or Rule 10b–5 under the Act, if the Rule 10b–18 purchases of such issuer or affiliated purchaser do not meet the conditions specified in paragraph (b) or (c) of this rule.

Rule 10b–21.   Deception in Connection with a Seller's Ability or Intent to Deliver Securities on the Date Delivery is Due

PRELIMINARY NOTE to Rule 10b–21: This rule is not intended to limit, or restrict, the applicability of the general antifraud provisions of the federal securities laws, such as section 10(b) of the Act and rule 10b–5 thereunder.

(a)   It shall also constitute a "manipulative or deceptive device or contrivance" as used in section 10(b) of this Act for any person to submit an order to sell an equity security if such person deceives a broker or dealer, a participant of a registered clearing agency, or a purchaser about its intention or ability to deliver the security on or before the settlement date, and such person fails to deliver the security on or before the settlement date.

(b)   For purposes of this rule, the term *settlement date* shall mean the business day on which delivery of a security and payment of money is to be made through the facilities of a registered clearing agency in connection with the sale of a security.

REPORTS UNDER SECTION 10A

Rule 10A–1.   Notice to the Commission Pursuant to Section 10A of the Act

(a)(1)   If any issuer with a reporting obligation under the Act receives a report requiring a notice to the Commission in accordance with section 10A(b)(3) of the Act, the issuer shall submit such notice to the Commission's Office of the Chief Accountant within the time period prescribed in that section. The notice may be provided by facsimile, telegraph, personal delivery, or any other means, provided it is received by the Office of the Chief Accountant within the required time period.

(2)   The notice specified in paragraph (a)(1) of this rule shall be in writing and:

(i)   Shall identify the issuer (including the issuer's name, address, phone number, and file number assigned to the issuer's filings by the Commission) and the independent accountant (including the independent accountant's name and phone number, and the address of the independent accountant's principal office);

(ii)   Shall state the date that the issuer received from the independent accountant the report specified in section 10A(b)(2) of the Act;

(iii)   Shall provide, at the election of the issuer, either:

(A)   A summary of the independent accountant's report, including a description of the act that the independent accountant has identified as a likely illegal act and the possible effect of that act on all affected financial statements of the issuer or those related to the most current three-year period, whichever is shorter; or

(B)   A copy of the independent accountant's report; and

(iv)   May provide additional information regarding the issuer's views of and response to the independent accountant's report.

(3)   Reports of the independent accountant submitted by the issuer to the Commission's Office of the Chief Accountant in accordance with paragraph (a)(2)(iii)(B) of this rule shall be deemed to have been made pursuant to section 10A(b)(3) or section 10A(b)(4) of the Act, for purposes of the safe harbor provided by section 10A(c) of the Act.

(4)   Submission of the notice in paragraphs (a)(1) and (a)(2) of this rule shall not relieve the issuer from its obligations to comply fully with all other reporting requirements, including, without limitation:

(i)   The filing requirements of Form 8–K and Form N–CSR regarding a change in the issuer's certifying accountant and

(ii)   The disclosure requirements of Item 304 of Regulation S–K.

(b)(1)   Any independent accountant furnishing to the Commission a copy of a report (or the documentation of any oral report) in accordance with section 10A(b)(3) or section 10A(b)(4) of the Act, shall submit that report (or documentation) to the Commission's Office of the Chief Accountant within the time period prescribed by the appropriate section of the Act. The report (or documentation) may be submitted to the Commission's Office of the Chief Accountant by facsimile, telegraph, personal delivery, or any other means, provided it is received by the Office of the Chief Accountant within the time period set forth in section 10A(b)(3) or 10A(b)(4) of the Act, whichever is applicable in the circumstances.

(2)   If the report (or documentation) submitted to the Office of the Chief Accountant in accordance with paragraph (b)(1) of this rule does not clearly identify both the issuer (including the issuer's name, address, phone number, and file number assigned to the issuer's filings with the Commission) and the independent accountant (including the independent accountant's name and phone number, and the address of the independent accountant's principal office), then the independent accountant shall place that information in a prominent attachment to the report (or documentation) and shall submit that attachment to the Office of the Chief Accountant at the same time and in the same manner as the report (or documentation) is submitted to that Office.

(3)   Submission of the report (or documentation) by the independent accountant as described in paragraphs (b)(1) and (b)(2) of this rule shall not replace, or otherwise satisfy the need for, the newly engaged and former accountants' letters under Items 304(a)(2)(D) and 304(a)(3) of Regulation S–K, respectively, and shall not limit, reduce, or affect in any way the independent accountant's obligations to comply fully with all other legal and professional responsibilities, including, without limitation, those under generally accepted auditing standards and the rules or interpretations of the Commission that modify or supplement those auditing standards.

(c)   A notice or report submitted to the Office of the Chief Accountant in accordance with paragraphs (a) and (b) of this rule shall be deemed to be an investigative record and shall be non-public and exempt from disclosure pursuant to the Freedom of Information Act to the same extent and for the same periods of time that the Commission's investigative records are non-public and exempt from disclosure under, among other applicable provisions, 5 U.S.C. 552(b)(7) and § 200.80(b)(7) of this chapter. Nothing in this paragraph, however, shall relieve, limit, delay, or affect in any way, the obligation of any issuer or any independent accountant to make all public disclosures required by law, by any Commission disclosure item, rule, report, or form, or by any applicable accounting, auditing, or professional standard.

Instruction to Paragraph (c): Issuers and independent accountants may apply for additional bases for confidential treatment for a notice, report, or part thereof, in accordance with § 200.83 of this chapter. That section indicates, in part, that any person who, pursuant to any requirement of law, submits any information or causes or permits any information to be submitted to the Commission, may request that the Commission afford it confidential treatment by reason of personal privacy or business confidentiality, or for any other reason permitted by Federal law.

Rule 10A–3.   Listing Standards Related to Audit Committees

(a)   Pursuant to section 10A(m) of the Act and section 3 of the Sarbanes-Oxley Act of 2002:

(1)   *National securities exchanges.* The rules of each national securities exchange registered pursuant to section 6 of the Act must, in accordance with the provisions of this rule, prohibit the initial or continued listing of any security of an issuer that is not in compliance with the requirements of any portion of paragraph (b) or (c) of this rule.

(2)   *National securities associations.* The rules of each national securities association registered pursuant to section 15A of the Act must, in accordance with the provisions of this rule, prohibit the

initial or continued listing in an automated inter-dealer quotation system of any security of an issuer that is not in compliance with the requirements of any portion of paragraph (b) or (c) of this rule.

(3) *Opportunity to cure defects.* The rules required by paragraphs (a)(1) and (a)(2) of this rule must provide for appropriate procedures for a listed issuer to have an opportunity to cure any defects that would be the basis for a prohibition under paragraph (a) of this rule, before the imposition of such prohibition. Such rules also may provide that if a member of an audit committee ceases to be independent in accordance with the requirements of this rule for reasons outside the member's reasonable control, that person, with notice by the issuer to the applicable national securities exchange or national securities association, may remain an audit committee member of the listed issuer until the earlier of the next annual shareholders meeting of the listed issuer or one year from the occurrence of the event that caused the member to be no longer independent.

(4) *Notification of noncompliance.* The rules required by paragraphs (a)(1) and (a)(2) of this rule must include a requirement that a listed issuer must notify the applicable national securities exchange or national securities association promptly after an executive officer of the listed issuer becomes aware of any material noncompliance by the listed issuer with the requirements of this rule.

(5) *Implementation.*

(i) The rules of each national securities exchange or national securities association meeting the requirements of this rule must be operative, and listed issuers must be in compliance with those rules, by the following dates:

(A) July 31, 2005 for foreign private issuers and smaller reporting companies (as defined in Rule 12b–2); and

(B) For all other listed issuers, the earlier of the listed issuer's first annual shareholders meeting after January 15, 2004, or October 31, 2004.

(ii) Each national securities exchange and national securities association must provide to the Commission, no later than July 15, 2003, proposed rules or rule amendments that comply with this rule.

(iii) Each national securities exchange and national securities association must have final rules or rule amendments that comply with this rule approved by the Commission no later than December 1, 2003.

(b) *Required standards.*—

(1) *Independence.*

(i) Each member of the audit committee must be a member of the board of directors of the listed issuer, and must otherwise be independent; provided that, where a listed issuer is one of two dual holding companies, those companies may designate one audit committee for both companies so long as each member of the audit committee is a member of the board of directors of at least one of such dual holding companies.

(ii) Independence requirements for non-investment company issuers. In order to be considered to be independent for purposes of this paragraph (b)(1), a member of an audit committee of a listed issuer that is not an investment company may not, other than in his or her capacity as a member of the audit committee, the board of directors, or any other board committee:

(A) Accept directly or indirectly any consulting, advisory, or other compensatory fee from the issuer or any subsidiary thereof, provided that, unless the rules of the national securities exchange or national securities association provide otherwise, compensatory fees do not include the receipt of fixed amounts of compensation under a retirement plan (including deferred compensation) for prior service with the listed issuer (provided that such compensation is not contingent in any way on continued service); or

(B) Be an affiliated person of the issuer or any subsidiary thereof.

(iii) Independence requirements for investment company issuers. In order to be considered to be independent for purposes of this paragraph (b)(1), a member of an audit committee of a listed issuer that is an investment company may not, other than in his or her capacity as a member of the audit committee, the board of directors, or any other board committee:

(A) Accept directly or indirectly any consulting, advisory, or other compensatory fee from the issuer or any subsidiary thereof, provided that, unless the rules of the national securities exchange or national securities association provide otherwise, compensatory fees do not include the receipt of fixed amounts of compensation under a retirement plan (including deferred compensation) for prior service with the listed issuer (provided that such compensation is not contingent in any way on continued service); or

(B) Be an "interested person" of the issuer as defined in section 2(a)(19) of the Investment Company Act of 1940.

(iv) *Exemptions from the independence requirements.*

(A) For an issuer listing securities pursuant to a registration statement under section 12 of the Act or for an issuer that has a registration statement under the Securities Act of 1933 covering an initial public offering of securities to be listed by the issuer, where in each case the listed issuer was not, immediately prior to the effective date of such registration statement, required to file reports with the Commission pursuant to section 13(a) or 15(d) of the Act:

(1) All but one of the members of the listed issuer's audit committee may be exempt from the independence requirements of paragraph (b)(1)(ii) of this rule for 90 days from the date of effectiveness of such registration statement; and

(2) A minority of the members of the listed issuer's audit committee may be exempt from the independence requirements of paragraph (b)(1)(ii) of this rule for one year from the date of effectiveness of such registration statement.

(B) An audit committee member that sits on the board of directors of a listed issuer and an affiliate of the listed issuer is exempt from the requirements of paragraph (b)(1)(ii)(B) of this rule if the member, except for being a director on each such board of directors, otherwise meets the independence requirements of paragraph (b)(1)(ii) of this rule for each such entity, including the receipt of only ordinary-course compensation for serving as a member of the board of directors, audit committee or any other board committee of each such entity.

(C) An employee of a foreign private issuer who is not an executive officer of the foreign private issuer is exempt from the requirements of paragraph (b)(1)(ii) of this rule if the employee is elected or named to the board of directors or audit committee of the foreign private issuer pursuant to the issuer's governing law or documents, an employee collective bargaining or similar agreement or other home country legal or listing requirements.

(D) An audit committee member of a foreign private issuer may be exempt from the requirements of paragraph (b)(1)(ii)(B) of this rule if that member meets the following requirements:

(1) The member is an affiliate of the foreign private issuer or a representative of such an affiliate;

(2) The member has only observer status on, and is not a voting member or the chair of, the audit committee; and

(3) Neither the member nor the affiliate is an executive officer of the foreign private issuer.

(E) An audit committee member of a foreign private issuer may be exempt from the requirements of paragraph (b)(1)(ii)(B) of this rule if that member meets the following requirements:

(1) The member is a representative or designee of a foreign government or foreign governmental entity that is an affiliate of the foreign private issuer; and

(2) The member is not an executive officer of the foreign private issuer.

(F) In addition to paragraphs (b)(1)(iv)(A) through (E) of this rule, the Commission may exempt from the requirements of paragraphs (b)(1)(ii) or (b)(1)(iii) of this rule a particular relationship with respect to audit committee members, as the Commission determines appropriate in light of the circumstances.

(2) *Responsibilities relating to registered public accounting firms.* The audit committee of each listed issuer, in its capacity as a committee of the board of directors, must be directly responsible for the appointment, compensation, retention and oversight of the work of any registered public accounting firm engaged (including resolution of disagreements between management and the auditor regarding financial reporting) for the purpose of preparing or issuing an audit report or performing other audit, review or attest services for the listed issuer, and each such registered public accounting firm must report directly to the audit committee.

(3) *Complaints.* Each audit committee must establish procedures for:

(i) The receipt, retention, and treatment of complaints received by the listed issuer regarding accounting, internal accounting controls, or auditing matters; and

(ii) The confidential, anonymous submission by employees of the listed issuer of concerns regarding questionable accounting or auditing matters.

(4) *Authority to engage advisers.* Each audit committee must have the authority to engage independent counsel and other advisers, as it determines necessary to carry out its duties.

(5) *Funding.* Each listed issuer must provide for appropriate funding, as determined by the audit committee, in its capacity as a committee of the board of directors, for payment of:

(i) Compensation to any registered public accounting firm engaged for the purpose of preparing or issuing an audit report or performing other audit, review or attest services for the listed issuer;

(ii) Compensation to any advisers employed by the audit committee under paragraph (b)(4) of this rule; and

(iii) Ordinary administrative expenses of the audit committee that are necessary or appropriate in carrying out its duties.

(c) *General exemptions.*

(1) At any time when an issuer has a class of securities that is listed on a national securities exchange or national securities association subject to the requirements of this rule, the listing of other classes of securities of the listed issuer on a national securities exchange or national securities association is not subject to the requirements of this rule.

(2) At any time when an issuer has a class of common equity securities (or similar securities) that is listed on a national securities exchange or national securities association subject to the requirements of this rule, the listing of classes of securities of a direct or indirect consolidated subsidiary or an at least 50% beneficially owned subsidiary of the issuer (except classes of equity securities, other than non-convertible, non-participating preferred securities, of such subsidiary) is not subject to the requirements of this rule.

(3) The listing of securities of a foreign private issuer is not subject to the requirements of paragraphs (b)(1) through (b)(5) of this rule if the foreign private issuer meets the following requirements:

(i) The foreign private issuer has a board of auditors (or similar body), or has statutory auditors, established and selected pursuant to home country legal or listing provisions expressly requiring or permitting such a board or similar body;

(ii) The board or body, or statutory auditors is required under home country legal or listing requirements to be either:

(A) Separate from the board of directors; or

(B) Composed of one or more members of the board of directors and one or more members that are not also members of the board of directors;

(iii) The board or body, or statutory auditors, are not elected by management of such issuer and no executive officer of the foreign private issuer is a member of such board or body, or statutory auditors;

(iv) Home country legal or listing provisions set forth or provide for standards for the independence of such board or body, or statutory auditors, from the foreign private issuer or the management of such issuer;

(v) Such board or body, or statutory auditors, in accordance with any applicable home country legal or listing requirements or the issuer's governing documents, are responsible, to the extent permitted by law, for the appointment, retention and oversight of the work of any registered public accounting firm engaged (including, to the extent permitted by law, the resolution of disagreements between management and the auditor regarding financial reporting) for the purpose of preparing or issuing an audit report or performing other audit, review or attest services for the issuer; and

(vi) The audit committee requirements of paragraphs (b)(3), (b)(4) and (b)(5) of this rule apply to such board or body, or statutory auditors, to the extent permitted by law.

(4) The listing of a security futures product cleared by a clearing agency that is registered pursuant to section 17A of the Act or that is exempt from the registration requirements of section 17A pursuant to paragraph (b)(7)(A) of such section is not subject to the requirements of this rule.

(5) The listing of a standardized option, as defined in Rule 9b–1(a)(4), issued by a clearing agency that is registered pursuant to section 17A of the Act is not subject to the requirements of this rule.

(6) The listing of securities of the following listed issuers are not subject to the requirements of this rule:

(i) Asset-Backed Issuers (as defined in Item 1101 of Regulation S–K);

(ii) Unit investment trusts (as defined in 15 U.S.C. 80a–4(2)); and

(iii) Foreign governments (as defined in Rule 3b–4(a)).

(7) The listing of securities of a listed issuer is not subject to the requirements of this rule if:

(i) The listed issuer, as reflected in the applicable listing application, is organized as a trust or other unincorporated association that does not have a board of directors or persons acting in a similar capacity; and

(ii) The activities of the listed issuer that is described in paragraph (c)(7)(i) of this rule are limited to passively owning or holding (as well as administering and distributing amounts in respect of) securities, rights, collateral or other assets on behalf of or for the benefit of the holders of the listed securities.

(d) *Disclosure.* Any listed issuer availing itself of an exemption from the independence standards contained in paragraph (b)(1)(iv) of this rule (except paragraph (b)(1)(iv)(B)), the general exemption contained in paragraph (c)(3) or the last sentence of paragraph (a)(3) of this rule, must:

(1) Disclose its reliance on the exemption and its assessment of whether, and if so, how, such reliance would materially adversely affect the ability of the audit committee to act independently and to satisfy the other requirements of this rule in any proxy or information statement for a meeting of shareholders at which directors are elected that is filed with the Commission pursuant to the requirements of section 14 of the Act; and

(2) Disclose the information specified in paragraph (d)(1) of this rule in, or incorporate such information by reference from such proxy or information statement filed with the Commission into, its annual report filed with the Commission pursuant to the requirements of section 13(a) or 15(d) of the Act.

(e) *Definitions.* Unless the context otherwise requires, all terms used in this rule have the same meaning as in the Act. In addition, unless the context otherwise requires, the following definitions apply for purposes of this rule:

(1)(i)   The term *affiliate* of, or a person *affiliated* with, a specified person, means a person that directly, or indirectly through one or more intermediaries, controls, or is controlled by, or is under common control with, the person specified.

    (ii)(A)   A person will be deemed not to be in control of a specified person for purposes of this rule if the person:

        (1)   Is not the beneficial owner, directly or indirectly, of more than 10% of any class of voting equity securities of the specified person; and

        (2)   Is not an executive officer of the specified person.

    (B)   Paragraph (e)(1)(ii)(A) of this rule only creates a safe harbor position that a person does not control a specified person. The existence of the safe harbor does not create a presumption in any way that a person exceeding the ownership requirement in paragraph (e)(1)(ii)(A)(1) of this rule controls or is otherwise an affiliate of a specified person.

    (iii)   The following will be deemed to be affiliates:

        (A)   An executive officer of an affiliate;

        (B)   A director who also is an employee of an affiliate;

        (C)   A general partner of an affiliate; and

        (D)   A managing member of an affiliate.

    (iv)   For purposes of paragraph (e)(1)(i) of this rule, dual holding companies will not be deemed to be affiliates of or persons affiliated with each other by virtue of their dual holding company arrangements with each other, including where directors of one dual holding company are also directors of the other dual holding company, or where directors of one or both dual holding companies are also directors of the businesses jointly controlled, directly or indirectly, by the dual holding companies (and, in each case, receive only ordinary-course compensation for serving as a member of the board of directors, audit committee or any other board committee of the dual holding companies or any entity that is jointly controlled, directly or indirectly, by the dual holding companies).

(2)   In the case of foreign private issuers with a two-tier board system, the term *board of directors* means the supervisory or non-management board.

(3)   In the case of a listed issuer that is a limited partnership or limited liability company where such entity does not have a board of directors or equivalent body, the term *board of directors* means the board of directors of the managing general partner, managing member or equivalent body.

(4)   The term *control* (including the terms *controlling, controlled by* and under *common control with*) means the possession, direct or indirect, of the power to direct or cause the direction of the management and policies of a person, whether through the ownership of voting securities, by contract, or otherwise.

(5)   The term *dual holding companies* means two foreign private issuers that:

    (i)   Are organized in different national jurisdictions;

    (ii)   Collectively own and supervise the management of one or more businesses which are conducted as a single economic enterprise; and

    (iii)   Do not conduct any business other than collectively owning and supervising such businesses and activities reasonably incidental thereto.

(6)   The term *executive officer* has the meaning set forth in Rule 3b–7.

(7)   The term *foreign private issuer* has the meaning set forth in Rule 3b–4(c).

(8)   The term *indirect acceptance* by a member of an audit committee of any consulting, advisory or other compensatory fee includes acceptance of such a fee by a spouse, a minor child or stepchild or a child or stepchild sharing a home with the member or by an entity in which such member is a partner, member, an officer such as a managing director occupying a comparable position or executive officer,

or occupies a similar position (except limited partners, non-managing members and those occupying similar positions who, in each case, have no active role in providing services to the entity) and which provides accounting, consulting, legal, investment banking or financial advisory services to the issuer or any subsidiary of the issuer.

(9)   The terms *listed* and *listing* refer to securities listed on a national securities exchange or listed in an automated inter-dealer quotation system of a national securities association or to issuers of such securities.

Instructions to Rule 10A–3

1.   The requirements in paragraphs (b)(2) through (b)(5), (c)(3)(v) and (c)(3)(vi) of this rule do not conflict with, and do not affect the application of, any requirement or ability under a listed issuer's governing law or documents or other home country legal or listing **provisions that** requires or permits shareholders to ultimately vote on, approve or ratify such requirements. The requirements instead relate to the assignment of responsibility as between the audit committee and management. In such an instance, however, if the listed issuer provides a recommendation or nomination regarding such responsibilities to shareholders, the audit committee of the listed issuer, or body performing similar functions, must be responsible for making the recommendation or nomination.

2.   The requirements in paragraphs (b)(2) through (b)(5), (c)(3)(v), (c)(3)(vi) and Instruction 1 of this rule do not conflict with any legal or listing requirement in a listed issuer's home jurisdiction that prohibits the full board of directors from delegating such responsibilities to the listed issuer's audit committee or limits the degree of such delegation. In that case, the audit committee, or body performing similar functions, must be granted such responsibilities, which can include advisory powers, with respect to such matters to the extent permitted by law, including submitting nominations or recommendations to the full board.

3.   The requirements in paragraphs (b)(2) through (b)(5), (c)(3)(v) and (c)(3)(vi) of this rule do not conflict with any legal or listing requirement in a listed issuer's home jurisdiction that vests such responsibilities with a government entity or tribunal. In that case, the audit committee, or body performing similar functions, must be granted such responsibilities, which can include advisory powers, with respect to such matters to the extent permitted by law.

4.   For purposes of this rule, the determination of a person's beneficial ownership must be made in accordance with Rule 13d–3.

REQUIREMENTS UNDER SECTION 10C

Rule 10C–1. Listing Standards Relating to Compensation Committees

(a)   Pursuant to section 10C(a) of the Act and section 952 of the Dodd-Frank Wall Street Reform and Consumer Protection Act of 2010:

(1)   *National securities exchanges.* The rules of each national securities exchange registered pursuant to section 6 of the Act, to the extent such national securities exchange lists equity securities, must, in accordance with the provisions of this rule, prohibit the initial or continued listing of any equity security of an issuer that is not in compliance with the requirements of any portion of paragraph (b) or (c) of this rule.

(2)   *National securities associations.* The rules of each national securities association registered pursuant to section 15A of the Act, to the extent such national securities association lists equity securities in an automated inter-dealer quotation system, must, in accordance with the provisions of this rule, prohibit the initial or continued listing in an automated inter-dealer quotation system of any equity security of an issuer that is not in compliance with the requirements of any portion of paragraph (b) or (c) of this rule.

(3)   *Opportunity to cure defects.* The rules required by paragraphs (a)(1) and (a)(2) of this rule must provide for appropriate procedures for a listed issuer to have a reasonable opportunity to cure any defects that would be the basis for a prohibition under paragraph (a) of this rule, before the imposition of such prohibition. Such rules may provide that if a member of a compensation committee ceases to be independent in accordance with the requirements of this rule for reasons outside the member's reasonable control, that person, with notice by the issuer to the applicable national securities exchange or national securities association, may remain a compensation committee member of the

listed issuer until the earlier of the next annual shareholders meeting of the listed issuer or one year from the occurrence of the event that caused the member to be no longer independent.

    (4)   *Implementation.*

        (i)   Each national securities exchange and national securities association that lists equity securities must provide to the Commission, no later than 90 days after publication of this rule in the Federal Register, proposed rules or rule amendments that comply with this rule. Each submission must include, in addition to any other information required under section 19(b) of the Act and the rules thereunder, a review of whether and how existing or proposed listing standards satisfy the requirements of this rule, a discussion of the consideration of factors relevant to compensation committee independence conducted by the national securities exchange or national securities association, and the definition of independence applicable to compensation committee members that the national securities exchange or national securities association proposes to adopt or retain in light of such review.

        (ii)   Each national securities exchange and national securities association that lists equity securities must have rules or rule amendments that comply with this rule approved by the Commission no later than one year after publication of this rule in the Federal Register.

  (b) · *Required standards.* The requirements of this rule apply to the compensation committees of listed issuers.

    (1)   *Independence.*

        (i)   Each member of the compensation committee must be a member of the board of directors of the listed issuer, and must otherwise be independent.

        (ii)   *Independence requirements.* In determining independence requirements for members of compensation committees, the national securities exchanges and national securities associations shall consider relevant factors, including, but not limited to:

           (A)   The source of compensation of a member of the board of directors of an issuer, including any consulting, advisory or other compensatory fee paid by the issuer to such member of the board of directors; and

           (B)   Whether a member of the board of directors of an issuer is affiliated with the issuer, a subsidiary of the issuer or an affiliate of a subsidiary of the issuer.

        (iii)   *Exemptions from the independence requirements.*

           (A)   The listing of equity securities of the following categories of listed issuers is not subject to the requirements of paragraph (b)(1) of this rule:

               (1)   Limited partnerships;

               (2)   Companies in bankruptcy proceedings;

               (3)   Open-end management investment companies registered under the Investment Company Act of 1940; and

               (4)   Any foreign private issuer that discloses in its annual report the reasons that the foreign private issuer does not have an independent compensation committee. (B) In addition to the issuer exemptions set forth in paragraph (b)(1)(iii)(A) of this rule, a national securities exchange or a national securities association, pursuant to section 19(b) of the Act and the rules thereunder, may exempt from the requirements of paragraph (b)(1) of this rule a particular relationship with respect to members of the compensation committee, as each national securities exchange or national securities association determines is appropriate, taking into consideration the size of an issuer and any other relevant factors.

    (2)   Authority to retain compensation consultants, independent legal counsel and other compensation advisers.

(i)   The compensation committee of a listed issuer, in its capacity as a committee of the board of directors, may, in its sole discretion, retain or obtain the advice of a compensation consultant, independent legal counsel or other adviser.

(ii)   The compensation committee shall be directly responsible for the appointment, compensation and oversight of the work of any compensation consultant, independent legal counsel and other adviser retained by the compensation committee.

(iii)   Nothing in this paragraph shall be construed:

(A)   To require the compensation committee to implement or act consistently with the advice or recommendations of the compensation consultant, independent legal counsel or other adviser to the compensation committee; or

(B)   To affect the ability or obligation of a compensation committee to exercise its own judgment in fulfillment of the duties of the compensation committee.

(3)   *Funding.* Each listed issuer must provide for appropriate funding, as determined by the compensation committee, in its capacity as a committee of the board of directors, for payment of reasonable compensation to a compensation consultant, independent legal counsel or any other adviser retained by the compensation committee.

(4)   *Independence of compensation consultants and other advisers.* The compensation committee of a listed issuer may select a compensation consultant, legal counsel or other adviser to the compensation committee only after taking into consideration the following factors, as well as any other factors identified by the relevant national securities exchange or national securities association in its listing standards:

(i)   The provision of other services to the issuer by the person that employs the compensation consultant, legal counsel or other adviser;

(ii)   The amount of fees received from the issuer by the person that employs the compensation consultant, legal counsel or other adviser, as a percentage of the total revenue of the person that employs the compensation consultant, legal counsel or other adviser;

(iii)   The policies and procedures of the person that employs the compensation consultant, legal counsel or other adviser that are designed to prevent conflicts of interest;

(iv)   Any business or personal relationship of the compensation consultant, legal counsel or other adviser with a member of the compensation committee;

(v)   Any stock of the issuer owned by the compensation consultant, legal counsel or other adviser; and

(vi)   Any business or personal relationship of the compensation consultant, legal counsel, other adviser or the person employing the adviser with an executive officer of the issuer.

Instruction to Paragraph (b)(4) of this rule: A listed issuer's compensation committee is required to conduct the independence assessment outlined in paragraph (b)(4) with respect to any compensation consultant, legal counsel or other adviser that provides advice to the compensation committee, other than in-house legal counsel.

(5)   *General exemptions.*

(i)   The national securities exchanges and national securities associations, pursuant to section 19(b) of the Act and the rules thereunder, may exempt from the requirements of this rule certain categories of issuers, as the national securities exchange or national securities association determines is appropriate, taking into consideration, among other relevant factors, the potential impact of such requirements on smaller reporting issuers.

(ii)   The requirements of this rule shall not apply to any controlled company or to any smaller reporting company.

(iii)   The listing of a security futures product cleared by a clearing agency that is registered pursuant to section 17A of the Act or that is exempt from the registration requirements of section 17A(b)(7)(A) is not subject to the requirements of this rule.

(iv) The listing of a standardized option, as defined in Rule 9b–1(a)(4), issued by a clearing agency that is registered pursuant to section 17A of the Act is not subject to the requirements of this rule.

(c) *Definitions.* Unless the context otherwise requires, all terms used in this rule have the same meaning as in the Act and the rules and regulations thereunder. In addition, unless the context otherwise requires, the following definitions apply for purposes of this rule:

(1) In the case of foreign private issuers with a two-tier board system, the term board of directors means the supervisory or non-management board.

(2) The term compensation committee means:

(i) a committee of the board of directors that is designated as the compensation committee; or

(ii) in the absence of a committee of the board of directors that is designated as the compensation committee, a committee of the board of directors performing functions typically performed by a compensation committee, including oversight of executive compensation, even if it is not designated as the compensation committee or also performs other functions; or

(iii) for purposes of this rule other than paragraphs (b)(2)(i) and (b)(3), in the absence of a committee as described in (i) or (ii) above, the members of the board of directors who oversee executive compensation matters on behalf of the board of directors.

(3) The term controlled company means an issuer:

(i) That is listed on a national securities exchange or by a national securities association; and

(ii) Of which more than 50 percent of the voting power for the election of directors is held by an individual, a group or another company.

(4) The terms listed and listing refer to equity securities listed on a national securities exchange or listed in an automated inter-dealer quotation system of a national securities association or to issuers of such securities.

(5) The term open-end management investment company means an open-end company, as defined by Section 5(a)(1) of the Investment Company Act of 1940, that is registered under that Act.

REQUIREMENTS UNDER SECTION 10D

Rule 10D–1. Listing Standards Relating to Recovery of Erroneously Awarded Compensation

(a) Each national securities exchange registered pursuant to section 6 of the Act (15 U.S.C. 78f) and each national securities association registered pursuant to section 15A of the Act (15 U.S.C. 78o–3), to the extent such national securities exchange or association lists securities, must:

(1) In accordance with the provisions of this section, prohibit the initial or continued listing of any security of an issuer that is not in compliance with the requirements of any portion of this section;

(2) No later than [INSERT DATE 90 DAYS AFTER DATE OF PUBLICATION IN THE FEDERAL REGISTER], propose rules or rule amendments that comply with this section. Such rules or rule amendments that comply with this section must be effective no later than one year after [INSERT DATE OF PUBLICATION IN THE FEDERAL REGISTER];

(3) Require that each listed issuer:

(i) Adopt the recovery policy required by this section no later than 60 days following the effective date of the listing standard referenced in paragraph (a)(2) of this section to which the issuer is subject;

(ii) Comply with that recovery policy for all incentive-based compensation received (as defined in paragraph (d) of this section) by executive officers on or after the effective date of the applicable listing standard;

(iii) Provide the disclosures required by this section and in the applicable Commission filings required on or after the effective date of the listing standard referenced in paragraph (a)(2) of this section to which the issuer is subject.

(b)   *Recovery of Erroneously Awarded Compensation.* The issuer must:

(1)   Adopt and comply with a written policy providing that the issuer will recover reasonably promptly the amount of erroneously awarded incentive-based compensation in the event that the issuer is required to prepare an accounting restatement due to the material noncompliance of the issuer with any financial reporting requirement under the securities laws, including any required accounting restatement to correct an error in previously issued financial statements that is material to the previously issued financial statements, or that would result in a material misstatement if the error were corrected in the current period or left uncorrected in the current period.

(i)   The issuer's recovery policy must apply to all incentive-based compensation received by a person:

(A)   After beginning service as an executive officer;

(B)   Who served as an executive officer at any time during the performance period for that incentive-based compensation;

(C)   While the issuer has a class of securities listed on a national securities exchange or a national securities association; and

(D)   During the three completed fiscal years immediately preceding the date that the issuer is required to prepare an accounting restatement as described in paragraph (b)(1) of this section. In addition to these last three completed fiscal years, the recovery policy must apply to any transition period (that results from a change in the issuer's fiscal year) within or immediately following those three completed fiscal years. However, a transition period between the last day of the issuer's previous fiscal year end and the first day of its new fiscal year that comprises a period of nine to 12 months would be deemed a completed fiscal year. An issuer's obligation to recover erroneously awarded compensation is not dependent on if or when the restated financial statements are filed.

(ii)   For purposes of determining the relevant recovery period, the date that an issuer is required to prepare an accounting restatement as described in paragraph (b)(1) of this section is the earlier to occur of:

(A)   The date the issuer's board of directors, a committee of the board of directors, or the officer or officers of the issuer authorized to take such action if board action is not required, concludes, or reasonably should have concluded, that the issuer is required to prepare an accounting restatement as described in paragraph (b)(1) of this section; or

(B)   The date a court, regulator, or other legally authorized body directs the issuer to prepare an accounting restatement as described in paragraph (b)(1) of this section.

(iii) The amount of incentive-based compensation that must be subject to the issuer's recovery policy ("erroneously awarded compensation") is the amount of incentive-based compensation received that exceeds the amount of incentive-based compensation that otherwise would have been received had it been determined based on the restated amounts, and must be computed without regard to any taxes paid. For incentive-based compensation based on stock price or total shareholder return, where the amount of erroneously awarded compensation is not subject to mathematical recalculation directly from the information in an accounting restatement:

(A)   The amount must be based on a reasonable estimate of the effect of the accounting restatement on the stock price or total shareholder return upon which the incentive-based compensation was received; and

(B)   The issuer must maintain documentation of the determination of that reasonable estimate and provide such documentation to the exchange or association.

(iv)   The issuer must recover erroneously awarded compensation in compliance with its recovery policy except to the extent that the conditions of paragraphs (b)(1)(iv)(A), (B), or (C) of this section are met, and the issuer's committee of independent directors responsible for executive compensation decisions, or in the absence of such a committee, a majority of the independent directors serving on the board, has made a determination that recovery would be impracticable.

(A) The direct expense paid to a third party to assist in enforcing the policy would exceed the amount to be recovered. Before concluding that it would be impracticable to recover any amount of erroneously awarded compensation based on expense of enforcement, the issuer must make a reasonable attempt to recover such erroneously awarded compensation, document such reasonable attempt(s) to recover, and provide that documentation to the exchange or association.

(B) Recovery would violate home country law where that law was adopted prior to [INSERT DATE OF PUBLICATION IN THE FEDERAL REGISTER]. Before concluding that it would be impracticable to recover any amount of erroneously awarded compensation based on violation of home country law, the issuer must obtain an opinion of home country counsel, acceptable to the applicable national securities exchange or association, that recovery would result in such a violation, and must provide such opinion to the exchange or association.

(C) Recovery would likely cause an otherwise tax-qualified retirement plan, under which benefits are broadly available to employees of the registrant, to fail to meet the requirements of 26 U.S.C. 401(a)(13) or 26 U.S.C. 411(a) and regulations thereunder.

(v) The issuer is prohibited from indemnifying any executive officer or former executive officer against the loss of erroneously awarded compensation.

(2) File all disclosures with respect to such recovery policy in accordance with the requirements of the Federal securities laws, including the disclosure required by the applicable Commission filings.

(c) *General Exemptions.* The requirements of this section do not apply to the listing of:

(1) A security futures product cleared by a clearing agency that is registered pursuant to section 17A of the Act (15 U.S.C. 78q–1) or that is exempt from the registration requirements of section 17A(b)(7)(A) (15 U.S.C. 78q–1(b)(7)(A));

(2) A standardized option, as defined in 17 CFR 240.9b–1(a)(4), issued by a clearing agency that is registered pursuant to section 17A of the Act (15 U.S.C. 78q–1);

(3) Any security issued by a unit investment trust, as defined in 15 U.S.C. 80a–4(2);

(4) Any security issued by a management company, as defined in 15 U.S.C. 80a–4(3), that is registered under section 8 of the Investment Company Act of 1940 (15 U.S.C. 80a–8), if such management company has not awarded incentive-based compensation to any executive officer of the company in any of the last three fiscal years, or in the case of a company that has been listed for less than three fiscal years, since the listing of the company.

(d) *Definitions.* Unless the context otherwise requires, the following definitions apply for purposes of this section:

Executive Officer. An *executive officer* is the issuer's president, principal financial officer, principal accounting officer (or if there is no such accounting officer, the controller), any vice-president of the issuer in charge of a principal business unit, division, or function (such as sales, administration, or finance), any other officer who performs a policy-making function, or any other person who performs similar policy-making functions for the issuer. Executive officers of the issuer's parent(s) or subsidiaries are deemed executive officers of the issuer if they perform such policy making functions for the issuer. In addition, when the issuer is a limited partnership, officers or employees of the general partner(s) who perform policy-making functions for the limited partnership are deemed officers of the limited partnership. When the issuer is a trust, officers, or employees of the trustee(s) who perform policy-making functions for the trust are deemed officers of the trust. Policy-making function is not intended to include policy-making functions that are not significant. Identification of an executive officer for purposes of this section would include at a minimum executive officers identified pursuant to 17 CFR 229.401(b).

Financial Reporting Measures. *Financial reporting measures* are measures that are determined and presented in accordance with the accounting principles used in preparing the issuer's financial statements, and any measures that are derived wholly or in part from such measures. Stock price and total shareholder return are also financial reporting measures. A financial reporting measure need not be presented within the financial statements or included in a filing with the Commission.

Incentive-Based Compensation. Incentive-based compensation is any compensation that is granted, earned, or vested based wholly or in part upon the attainment of a financial reporting measure.

Received. Incentive-based compensation is deemed received in the issuer's fiscal period during which the financial reporting measure specified in the incentive-based compensation award is attained, even if the payment or grant of the incentive-based compensation occurs after the end of that period.

MARKETS

Rule 11a–1. Regulation of Floor Trading

(a)   No member of a national securities exchange, while on the floor of such exchange, shall initiate, directly or indirectly, any transaction in any security admitted to trading on such exchange, for any account in which such member has an interest, or for any such account with respect to which such member has discretion as to the time of execution, the choice of security to be bought or sold, the total amount of any security to be bought or sold, or whether any such transaction shall be one of purchase or sale.

(b)   The provisions of paragraph (a) of this rule shall not apply to:

(1)   Any transaction by a registered specialist in a security in which he is so registered on such exchange;

(2)   Any transaction for the account of an odd-lot dealer in a security in which he is so registered on such exchange;

(3)   Any stabilizing transaction effected in compliance with Rule 104 of Regulation M to facilitate a distribution of such security in which such member is participating;

(4)   Any bona fide arbitrage transaction;

(5)   Any transaction made with the prior approval of a floor official of such exchange to permit such member to contribute to the maintenance of a fair and orderly market in such security, or any purchase or sale to reverse any such transaction;

(6)   Any transaction to offset a transaction made in error; or

(7)   Any transaction effected in conformity with a plan designed to eliminate floor trading activities which are not beneficial to the market and which plan has been adopted by an exchange and declared effective by the Commission. For the purpose of this rule, a plan filed with the Commission by a national securities exchange shall not become effective unless the Commission, having due regard for the maintenance of fair and orderly markets, for the public interest, and for the protection of investors, declares the plan to be effective.

(c)   For the purpose of this rule the term "on the floor of such exchange" shall include the trading floor; the rooms, lobbies, and other premises immediately adjacent thereto for use of members generally; other rooms, lobbies and premises made available primarily for use by members generally; and the telephone and other facilities in any such place.

(d)   Any national securities exchange may apply for an exemption from the provisions of this rule in compliance with the provisions of section 11(c) of the Act.

Rule 11a1–1(T).   Transactions Yielding Priority, Parity, and Precedence

(a)   A transaction effected on a national securities exchange for the account of a member which meets the requirements of section 11(a)(1)(G)(i) of the Act shall be deemed, in accordance with the requirements of section 11(a)(1)(G)(ii), to be not inconsistent with the maintenance of fair and orderly markets and to yield priority, parity, and precedence in execution to orders for the account of persons who are not members or associated with members of the exchange if such transaction is effected in compliance with each of the following requirements:

(1)   A member shall disclose that a bid or offer for its account is for its account to any member with whom such bid or offer is placed or to whom it is communicated, and any member through whom that bid or offer is communicated shall disclose to others participating in effecting the order that it is for the account of a member.

(2)   Immediately before executing the order, a member (other than the specialist in such security) presenting any order for the account of a member on the exchange shall clearly announce or otherwise indicate to the specialist and to other members then present for the trading in such security on the exchange that he is presenting an order for the account of a member.

(3)   Notwithstanding rules of priority, parity, and precedence otherwise applicable, any member presenting for execution a bid or offer for its own account or for the account of another member shall grant priority to any bid or offer at the same price for the account of a person who is not, or is not associated with, a member, irrespective of the size of any such bid or offer or the time when entered.

(b)   A member shall be deemed to meet the requirements of section 11(a)(1)(G)(i) of the Act if during its preceding fiscal year more than 50 percent of its gross revenues was derived from one or more of the sources specified in that section. In addition to any revenue which independently meets the requirements of section 11(a)(1)(G)(i), revenue derived from any transaction specified in paragraph (A), (B), or (D) of section 11(a)(1) of the Act or specified in Rule 11a1–4(T) shall be deemed to be revenue derived from one or more of the sources specified in section 11(a)(1)(G)(i). A member may rely on a list of members which are stated to meet the requirements of section 11(a)(1)(G)(i) if such list is prepared, and updated at least annually, by the exchange. In preparing any such list, an exchange may rely on a report which sets forth a statement of gross revenues of a member if covered by a report of independent accountants for such member to the effect that such report has been prepared in accordance with generally accepted accounting principles.

Rule 11a1–2. Transactions for Certain Accounts of Associated Persons of Members

A transaction effected by a member of a national securities exchange for the account of an associated person thereof shall be deemed to be of a kind which is consistent with the purposes of section 11(a)(1) of the Act, the protection of investors, and the maintenance of fair and orderly markets if the transaction is effected:

(a)   For the account of and for the benefit of an associated person, if, assuming such transaction were for the account of a member, or

(b)   For the account of an associated person but for the benefit of an account carried by such associated person, if, assuming such account were carried on the same basis by a member, the member would have been permitted, under section 11(a) of the Act and the other rules thereunder, to effect the transaction: *Provided, however,* That a transaction may not be effected by a member for the account of and for the benefit of an associated person under section 11(a)(1)(G) of the Act and Rule 11a1–1(T) thereunder unless the associated person derived, during its preceding fiscal year, more than 50 percent of its gross revenues from one or more of the sources specified in section 11(a)(1)(G)(i) of the Act.

Rule 11a1–3(T).   Bona Fide Hedge Transactions in Certain Securities

A bona fide hedge transaction effected on a national securities exchange by a member for its own account or an account of an associated person thereof and involving a long or short position in a security entitling the holder to acquire or sell an equity security, and a long or short position in one or more other securities entitling the holder to acquire or sell such equity security, shall be deemed to be of a kind which is consistent with the purposes of section 11(a)(1) of the Act, the protection of investors, and the maintenance of fair and orderly markets.

Rule 11a1–4(T).   Bond Transactions on National Securities Exchanges

A transaction in a bond, note, debenture, or other form of indebtedness effected on a national securities exchange by a member for its own account or the account of an associated person thereof shall be deemed to be of a kind which is consistent with the purposes of section 11(a)(1) of the Act, the protection of investors, and the maintenance of fair and orderly markets.

Rule 11a1–5. Transactions by Registered Competitive Market Makers and Registered Equity Market Makers

Any transaction by a New York Stock Exchange registered competitive market maker or an American Stock Exchange registered equity market maker effected in compliance with their respective governing rules shall be deemed to be of a kind which is consistent with the purposes of section 11(a)(1) of the Act, the protection of investors, and the maintenance of fair and orderly markets.

Rule 11a1–6. Transactions for Certain Accounts of OTC Derivatives Dealers

A transaction effected by a member of a national securities exchange for the account of an OTC derivatives dealer that is an associated person of that member shall be deemed to be of a kind that is consistent with the purposes of section 11(a)(1) of the Act, the protection of investors, and the maintenance of fair and orderly markets if, assuming such transaction were for the account of a member, the member would have been permitted, under section 11(a) of the Act and the other rules thereunder (with the exception of Rule 11a1–2), to effect the transaction.

Rule 11a2–2(T). Transactions Effected by Exchange Members Through Other Members

(a) A member of a national securities exchange (the "initiating member") may not effect a transaction on that exchange for its own account, the account of an associated person, or an account with respect to which it or an associated person thereof exercises investment discretion unless:

(1) The transaction is of a kind described in paragraphs A through H of section 11(a)(1) of the Act and is effected in accordance with applicable rules and regulations thereunder; or

(2) The transaction is effected in compliance with each of the following conditions:

(i) The transaction is executed on the floor, or through use of the facilities, of the exchange by a member (the "executing member") which is not an associated person of the initiating member;

(ii) The order for the transaction is transmitted from off the exchange floor;

(iii) Neither the initiating member nor an associated person of the initiating member participates in the execution of the transaction at any time after the order for the transaction has been so transmitted; and

(iv) In the case of a transaction effected for an account with respect to which the initiating member or an associated person thereof exercises investment discretion, neither the initiating member nor any associated person thereof retains any compensation in connection with effecting the transaction: *Provided, however,* That this condition shall not apply to the extent that the person or persons authorized to transact business for the account have expressly provided otherwise by written contract referring to section 11(a) of the Act and this rule executed on or after March 15, 1978, by each of them and by such exchange member or associated person exercising investment discretion.

(b) For purposes of this rule, a member "effects" a securities transaction when it performs any function in connection with the processing of that transaction, including, but not limited to,

(1) Transmission of an order for execution,

(2) Execution of the order,

(3) Clearance and settlement of the transaction, and

(4) Arranging for the performance of any such function.

(c) For purposes of this rule, the term "compensation in connection with effecting the transaction" refers to compensation directly or indirectly received or calculated on a transaction-related basis for the performance of any function involved in effecting a securities transaction.

(d) A member, or an associated person of a member, authorized by written contract to retain compensation in connection with effecting transactions pursuant to paragraph (a)(2)(iv) of this rule shall furnish at least annually to the person or persons authorized to transact business for the account a statement setting forth the total amount of all compensation retained by the member or any associated person thereof in connection with effecting transactions for that account during the period covered by the statement, which amount shall be exclusive of all amounts paid to others during that period for services rendered in effecting such transactions.

(e) A transaction effected in compliance with the requirements of this rule shall be deemed to be one of a kind which is consistent with the purposes of section 11(a)(1) of the Act, the protection of investors, and the maintenance of fair and orderly markets.

(f) The provisions of this rule shall not apply to transactions by exchange members to which, by operation of section 11(a)(3) of the Act, section 11(a)(1) of the Act is not effective.

Rule 11b–1. Regulation of Specialists

(a)(1) The rules of a national securities exchange may permit a member of such exchange to register as a specialist and to act as a dealer.

(2) The rules of a national securities exchange permitting a member of such exchange to register as a specialist and to act as a dealer shall include:

(i) Adequate minimum capital requirements in view of the markets for securities on such exchange;

(ii) Requirements, as a condition of a specialist's registration, that a specialist engage in a course of dealings for his own account to assist in the maintenance, so far as practicable, of a fair and orderly market, and that a finding by the exchange of any substantial or continued failure by a specialist to engage in such a course of dealings will result in the suspension or cancellation of such specialist's registration in one or more of the securities in which such specialist is registered;

(iii) Provisions restricting his dealings so far as practicable to those reasonably necessary to permit him to maintain a fair and orderly market or necessary to permit him to act as an odd-lot dealer;

(iv) Provisions stating the responsibilities of a specialist acting as a broker in securities in which he is registered; and

(v) Procedures to provide for the effective and systematic surveillance of the activities of specialists.

(b) If after appropriate notice and opportunity for hearing the Commission finds that a member of a national securities exchange registered with such exchange as a specialist in specified securities has, for any account in which he, his member organization, or any participant therein has any beneficial interest, direct or indirect, effected transactions in such securities which were not part of a course of dealings reasonably necessary to permit such specialist to maintain a fair and orderly market, or to act as an odd-lot dealer, in the securities in which he is registered and were not effected in a manner consistent with the rules adopted by such exchange pursuant to paragraph (a)(2)(iii) of this rule, the Commission may by order direct such exchange to cancel, or to suspend for such period as the Commission may determine, such specialist's registration in one or more of the securities in which such specialist is registered: *Provided, however,* If such exchange has itself suspended or cancelled such specialist's registration in one or more of the securities in which such specialist is registered, no further sanction shall be imposed pursuant to this paragraph (b) except in a case where the Commission finds substantial or continued misconduct by a specialist: *And provided, further,* That the provisions of this paragraph (b) shall not apply to a member of a national securities exchange exempted pursuant to the provisions of paragraph (d) of this rule.

(c) For the purposes of this rule, the term "rules" of an exchange shall mean its constitution, articles of incorporation, by-laws, or rules or instruments corresponding thereto, whatever the name, and its stated policies.

(d) Any national securities exchange may apply for an exemption from the provisions of this rule in compliance with the provisions of section 11(c) of the Act.

Rule 11d1–1. Exemption of Certain Securities From Section 11(d)(1)

A security shall be exempt from the provisions of section 11(d)(1) with respect to any transaction by a broker and dealer who, directly or indirectly extends or maintains or arranges for the extension or maintenance of credit on the security to or for a customer if:

(a)   The broker and dealer has not sold the security to the customer or bought the security for the customer's account; or

(b)   The security is acquired by the customer in exchange with the issuer thereof for an outstanding security of the same issuer on which credit was lawfully maintained for the customer at the time of the exchange; or

(c)   The customer is a broker or dealer or bank; or

(d)   The security is acquired by the customer through the exercise of a right evidenced by a warrant or certificate expiring within 90 days after issuance, provided such right was originally issued to the customer as a stockholder of the corporation issuing the security upon which credit is to be extended. The right shall be deemed to be issued to the customer as a stockholder if he actually owned the stock giving rise to the right when such right accrued, even though such stock was not registered in his name; and in determining such fact the broker and dealer may rely upon a signed statement of the customer which the broker and dealer accepts in good faith; or

(e)   Such broker and dealer would otherwise be subject to the prohibition of section 11(d)(1) with respect to 50 percent or less of all the securities of the same class which are outstanding or currently being distributed, and such broker and dealer sold the security to the customer or bought the security for the customer's account on a day when he was not participating in the distribution of any new issue of such security. A broker-dealer shall be deemed to be participating in a distribution of a new issue if

(1)   He owns, directly or indirectly, any undistributed security of such issue, or

(2)   He is engaged in any stabilizing activities to facilitate a distribution of such issue, or

(3)   He is a party to any syndicate agreement under which such stabilizing activities are being or may be undertaken, or

(4)   He is a party to an executory agreement to purchase or distribute such issue.

Rule 11d1–2. Exemption From Section 11(d)(1) for Certain Investment Company Securities Held by Broker-Dealers as Collateral in Margin Accounts

Any securities issued by a registered open-end investment company or unit investment trust as defined in the Investment Company Act of 1940 shall be exempted from the provisions of section 11(d)(1) with respect to any transaction by a person who is a broker and a dealer who, directly or indirectly, extends or maintains or arranges for the extension or maintenance of credit on such security, provided such security has been owned by the person to whom credit would be provided for more than 30 days, or purchased by such person pursuant to a plan for the automatic reinvestment of the dividends of such company or trust.

Rule 11d2–1. Exemption From Section 11(d)(2) for Certain Broker-Dealers Effecting Transactions for Customers Security Futures Products in Futures Accounts

A broker or dealer registered pursuant to section 15(b)(1) of the Act that is also a futures commission merchant registered pursuant to section 4f(a)(1) of the Commodity Exchange Act, to the extent that it effects transactions for customers in security futures products in a futures account (as that term is defined in Rule 15c3–3(a)(15)), is exempt from section 11(d)(2) of the Act.

EXEMPTIONS FROM EXCHANGE ACT REGISTRATION

Rule 12a–4.   Exemption of Certain Warrants From Section 12(a)

(a)   When used in this rule, the following terms shall have the meaning indicated unless the context otherwise requires:

(1)   The term "warrant" means any warrant or certificate evidencing a right to subscribe to or otherwise acquire another security, issued or unissued.

(2)   The term "beneficiary security" means a security to the holders of which a warrant or right to subscribe to or otherwise acquire another security is granted.

(3)   The term "subject security" means a security which is the subject of a warrant or right to subscribe to or otherwise acquire such security.

(4)   The term "in the process of admission to dealing", in respect of a specified security means that

(i)   An application has been filed pursuant to section 12(b) and (c) of the Act for the registration of such security on a national securities exchange; or

(ii)   The Commission has granted an application made pursuant to section 12(f) of the Act to continue or extend unlisted trading privileges to such security on a national securities exchange; or

(iii)   Written notice has been filed with the Commission by a national securities exchange to the effect that such security has been approved for admission to dealing as a security exempted from the operation of section 12(a) of the Act.

(b)   Any issued or unissued warrant granted to the holders of a security admitted to dealing on a national securities exchange, shall be exempt from the operation of section 12(a) of the Act to the extent necessary to render lawful the effecting of transactions therein on any national securities exchange

(i)   On which the beneficiary security is admitted to dealing or

(ii)   On which the subject security is admitted to dealing or is in the process of admission to dealing, subject to the following terms and conditions:

(1)   Such warrant by its terms expires within 90 days after the issuance thereof;

(2)   A registration statement under the Securities Act of 1933 is in effect as to such warrant and as to each subject security, or the applicable terms of any exemption from such registration have been met in respect to such warrant and each subject security; and

(3)   Within five days after the exchange has taken official action to admit such warrant to dealing, it shall notify the Commission of such action.

(c)   Notwithstanding paragraph (b) of this rule no exemption pursuant to this rule shall be available for transactions in any such warrant on any exchange on which the beneficiary security is admitted to dealing unless:

(1)   Each subject security is admitted to dealing or is in process of admission to dealing on a national securities exchange; or

(2)   There is available from a registration statement and periodic reports or other data filed by the issuer of the subject security, pursuant to any act administered by the Commission, information substantially equivalent to that available with respect to a security listed and registered on a national securities exchange.

(d)   Notwithstanding the foregoing, an unissued warrant shall not be exempt pursuant to this rule unless:

(1)   Formal or official announcement has been made by the issuer specifying

(i)   The terms upon which such warrant and each subject security is to be issued,

(ii)   The date, if any, as of which the security holders entitled to receive such warrant will be determined,

(iii)   The approximate date of the issuance of such warrant, and

(iv)   The approximate date of the issuance of each subject security; and,

(2)   The members of the exchange are subject to rules which provide that the performance of the contract to purchase and sell an unissued warrant shall be conditioned upon the issuance of such warrant.

(e)   The Commission may by order deny or revoke the exemption of a warrant under this rule, if, after appropriate notice and opportunity for hearing to the issuer of such warrant and to the exchange or exchanges on which such warrant is admitted to dealing as an exempted security, it finds that:

(1)   Any of the terms or conditions of this rule have not been met with respect to such exemption, or

(2)   At any time during the period of such exemption transactions have been effected on any such exchanges in such warrant which

(i)   Create or induce a false, misleading or artificial appearance of activity,

(ii)   Unduly or improperly influence the market price, or

(iii)   Make a price which does not reflect the true state of the market; or

(3)   Any other facts exist which make such denial or revocation necessary or appropriate in the public interest or for the protection of investors.

(f)   If it appears necessary or appropriate in the public interest or for the protection of investors, the Commission may summarily suspend the exemption of such warrant pending the determination by the Commission whether such exemption shall be denied or revoked.

(g)   Rule 10b–1 shall be applicable to any warrant exempted by this rule.

Rule 12a–5. Temporary Exemption of Substituted or Additional Securities

(a)(1)   Subject to the conditions of paragraph (a)(2) of this rule, whenever the holders of a security admitted to trading on a national securities exchange (hereinafter called the original security) obtain the right, by operation of law or otherwise, to acquire all or any part of a class of another or substitute security of the same or another issuer, or an additional amount of the original security, then:

(i)   All or any part of the class of such other or substituted security shall be temporarily exempted from the operation of section 12(a) to the extent necessary to render lawful transactions therein on an issued or "when-issued" basis on any national securities exchange on which the original, the other or the substituted security is lawfully admitted to trading; and

(ii)   The additional amount of the original security shall be temporarily exempted from the operation of section 12(a) to the extent necessary to render lawful transactions therein on a "when-issued" basis on any national securities exchange on which the original security is lawfully admitted to trading.

(2)   The exemptions provided by paragraph (a)(1) of this rule shall be available only if the following conditions are met:

(i)   A registration statement is in effect under the Securities Act of 1933 to the extent required as to the security which is the subject of such exemption, or the terms of any applicable exemption from registration under such act have been complied with, if required;

(ii)   Any stockholder approval necessary to the issuance of the security which is the subject of the exemption, has been obtained; and

(iii)   All other necessary official action, other than the filing or recording of charter amendments or other documents with the appropriate state authorities, has been taken to authorize and assure the issuance of the security which is the subject of such exemption.

(b)   The exemption provided by this rule shall terminate on the earliest of the following dates:

(1)   When registration of the exempt security on the exchange become effective;

(2)   When the exempt security is granted unlisted trading privileges on the exchange;

(3)   The close of business on the tenth day after

(i)   Withdrawal of an application for registration of the exempt security on the exchange;

(ii)   Withdrawal by the exchange of its certification of approval of the exempt security for listing and registration;

(iii)   Withdrawal of an application for admission of the exempt security to unlisted trading privileges on the exchange; or

(iv)   The sending to the exchange of notice of the entry of an order by the Commission denying any application for admission of the exempt security to unlisted trading privileges on the exchange;

(4)   The close of business on the one hundred and twentieth day after the date on which the exempt security was admitted by action of the exchange to trading thereon as a security exempted from the operation of section 12(a) by this rule, unless prior thereto an application for registration of the exempt security or for admission of the exempt security to unlisted trading privileges on the exchange has been filed.

(c)   Notwithstanding paragraph (b) of this rule, the Commission, having due regard for the public interest and the protection of investors, may at any time extend the period of exemption of any security by this rule or may sooner terminate the exemption upon notice to the exchange and to the issuer of the extension or termination thereof.

(d)   The Exchange shall file with the Commission a notification on Form 26 promptly after taking action to admit any security to trading under this rule: *Provided, however,* That no notification need be filed under this rule concerning the admission or proposed admission to trading of additional amounts of a class of security admitted to trading on such exchange.

(e)   Rule 10b–1 shall be applicable to all securities exempted from the operation of section 12(a) of the Act by this rule.

Rule 12a–6.   Exemption of Securities Underlying Certain Options From Section 12(a)

(a)   When used in this rule, the following terms shall have the meanings indicated unless the context otherwise requires:

(1)   The term "option" shall include any put, call, spread, straddle, or other option or privilege of buying a security from or selling a security to another without being bound to do so, but such term shall not include any such option where the writer is: The issuer of the security which may be purchased or sold upon exercise of the option, or is a person that directly, or indirectly, through one or more intermediaries, controls, or is controlled by, or is under common control with such issuer;

(2)   The term "underlying security" means a security which relates to or is the subject of an option.

(b)   Any underlying security shall be exempt from the operation of section 12(a) of the Act if all of the following terms and conditions are met:

(1)   The related option is duly listed and registered on a national securities exchange;

(2)   The only transactions on such exchange with respect to such underlying securities consist of the delivery of and payment for such underlying securities pursuant to the terms of such options relating to the exercise thereof; and

(3)   Such underlying security is

(i)   Duly listed and registered on another national securities exchange at the time the option is issued; or

(ii)   Duly quoted on the National Association of Securities Dealers Automated Quotation System ("NASDAQ") at the time the option is issued.

Rule 12a–7. Exemption of Stock Contained in Standardized Market Baskets From Section 12(a) of the Act

(a)   Any component stock of a standardized market basket shall be exempt from the registration requirement of section 12(a) of the Act, solely for the purpose of inclusion in a standardized market basket, provided that all of the following terms and conditions are met:

    (1)   The standardized market basket has been duly approved by the Commission for listing on a national securities exchange pursuant to the requirements of section 19(b) of the Act; and

    (2)   The stock is an NMS Stock as defined in Rule 600 of Regulation NMS and is either

        (i)   Listed and registered for trading on a national securities exchange by the issuer or

        (ii)   Quoted on the National Association of Securities Dealers Automated Quotation System;

(b)   When used in this rule, the term "standardized market basket" means a group of at least 100 stocks purchased or sold in a single execution and at a single trading location with physical delivery and transfer of ownership of each component stock resulting from such execution.

Rule 12a–8. Exemption of Depositary Shares

Depositary shares (as that term is defined in Rule 12b–2) registered on Form F–6, but not the underlying deposited securities, shall be exempt from the operation of section 12(a) of the Act.

Rule 12a–9. Exemption of Standardized Options From Section 12(a) of the Act

The provisions of section 12(a) of the Act do not apply in respect of any standardized option, as defined by Rule 9b–1(a)(4), issued by a clearing agency registered under section 17A of the Act and traded on a national securities exchange registered pursuant to section 6(a) of the Act.

Rule 12a–10. Exemption of Security-based Swaps from Section 12(a) of the Act

The provisions of Section 12(a) of the Act do not apply to any security-based swap that:

(a)   Is issued or will be issued by a clearing agency registered as a clearing agency under Section 17A of the Act or exempt from registration under Section 17A of the Act pursuant to a rule, regulation, or order of the Commission, in its function as a central counterparty with respect to the security-based swap;

(b)   The Commission has determined is required to be cleared or that is permitted to be cleared pursuant to the clearing agency's rules;

(c)   Is sold to an eligible contract participant (as defined in Section 1a(18) of the Commodity Exchange Act in reliance on Rule 239 under the Securities Act of 1933; and

(d)   Is traded on a national securities exchange registered pursuant to Section 6(a) of the Act.

Rule 12a–11. Exemption of Security-based Swaps Sold in Reliance on Securities Act of 1933 Rule 240 from Section 12(a) of the Act

(a)   The provisions of Section 12(a) of the Act do not apply to any security-based swap offered and sold in reliance on Rule 240 under the Securities Act of 1933.

(b)   This rule will expire on February 11, 2014. In such event, the Commission will publish a rule removing this rule from 17 CFR part 240 or modifying it as appropriate.

REGULATION 12B—REGISTRATION AND REPORTING

Rule 12b–1. Scope of Regulation

The rules contained in this regulation shall govern all registration statements pursuant to sections 12(b) and 12(g) of the Act and all reports filed pursuant to sections 13 and 15(d) of the Act, including all amendments to such statements and reports, except that any provision in a form covering the same subject matter as any such rule shall be controlling.

Rule 12b–2. Definitions

Unless the context otherwise requires, the following terms, when used in the rules contained in this regulation or in Regulation 13A or 15D or in the forms for statements and reports filed pursuant to sections 12, 13 or 15(d) of the Act, shall have the respective meanings indicated in this rule:

Accelerated filer and large accelerated filer. (1) *Accelerated filer.* The term "accelerated filer" means an issuer after it first meets the following conditions as of the end of its fiscal year:

(i) The issuer had an aggregate worldwide market value of the voting and non-voting common equity held by its non-affiliates of $75 million or more, but less than $700 million, as of the last business day of the issuer's most recently completed second fiscal quarter;

(ii) The issuer has been subject to the requirements of section 13(a) or 15(d) of the Act for a period of at least twelve calendar months; and

(iii) The issuer has filed at least one annual report pursuant to section 13(a) or 15(d) of the Act and

(iv) The issuer is not eligible to use the requirements for smaller reporting companies under the revenue test in paragraph (2) or (3)(iii)(B) of the "smaller reporting company" definition in this rule, as applicable.

(2) *Large accelerated filer.* The term "large accelerated filer" means an issuer after it first meets the following conditions as of the end of its fiscal year:

(i) The issuer had an aggregate worldwide market value of the voting and non-voting common equity held by its non-affiliates of $700 million or more, as of the last business day of the issuer's most recently completed second fiscal quarter;

(ii) The issuer has been subject to the requirements of section 13(a) or 15(d) of the Act for a period of at least twelve calendar months; and

(iii) The issuer has filed at least one annual report pursuant to section 13(a) or 15(d) of the Act and

(iv) The issuer is not eligible to use the requirements for smaller reporting companies under the revenue test in paragraph (2) or (3)(iii)(B) of the "smaller reporting company" definition in this rule, as applicable.

(3) *Entering and exiting accelerated filer and large accelerated filer status.*

(i) The determination at the end of the issuer's fiscal year for whether a non-accelerated filer becomes an accelerated filer, or whether a non-accelerated filer or accelerated filer becomes a large accelerated filer, governs the deadlines for the annual report to be filed for that fiscal year, the quarterly and annual reports to be filed for the subsequent fiscal year and all annual and quarterly reports to be filed thereafter while the issuer remains an accelerated filer or large accelerated filer.

(ii) Once an issuer becomes an accelerated filer, it will remain an accelerated filer unless: the issuer determines, at the end of a fiscal year, that the aggregate worldwide market value of the voting and non-voting common equity held by its non-affiliates was less than $60 million, as of the last business day of the issuer's most recently completed second fiscal quarter; or it determines that it is eligible to use the requirements for smaller reporting companies under the revenue test in paragraph (2) or (3)(iii)(B) of the "smaller reporting company" definition in this rule, as applicable. An issuer that makes either of these determinations becomes a nonaccelerated filer. The issuer will not become an accelerated filer again unless it subsequently meets the conditions in paragraph (1) of this definition.

(iii) Once an issuer becomes a large accelerated filer, it will remain a large accelerated filer unless: it determines, at the end of a fiscal year, that the aggregate worldwide market value of the voting and non-voting common equity held by its non-affiliates ("aggregate worldwide market value") was less than $560 million, as of the last business day of the issuer's most recently completed second fiscal quarter or it determines that it is eligible to use the requirements for smaller reporting companies under the revenue test in paragraph (2) or (3)(iii)(B) of the "smaller reporting company" definition in this rule, as applicable. If the issuer's aggregate worldwide market value was $60 million or more, but less than $560 million, as of the last business day of the issuer's most recently completed second fiscal quarter, and it is not eligible to use the requirements for smaller reporting companies under the revenue test in paragraph (2) or (3)(iii)(B) of the "smaller reporting company" definition in this rule, as applicable, it becomes an accelerated filer. If the issuer's aggregate worldwide market value was less than $60 million, as of the last business day of the issuer's most recently completed second fiscal quarter, or it is eligible to use the requirements for smaller reporting companies under the revenue test in paragraph (2) or (3)(iii)(B) of the "smaller reporting company" definition in this rule, it becomes a non-accelerated filer. An issuer will not become a large accelerated filer again unless it subsequently meets the conditions in paragraph (2) of this definition.

(iv)   The determination at the end of the issuer's fiscal year for whether an accelerated filer becomes a non-accelerated filer, or a large accelerated filer becomes an accelerated filer or a non-accelerated filer, governs the deadlines for the annual report to be filed for that fiscal year, the quarterly and annual reports to be filed for the subsequent fiscal year and all annual and quarterly reports to be filed thereafter while the issuer remains an accelerated filer or non-accelerated filer.

NOTE to paragraphs (1), (2) and (3): The aggregate worldwide market value of the issuer's outstanding voting and non-voting common equity shall be computed by use of the price at which the common equity was last sold, or the average of the bid and asked prices of such common equity, in the principal market for such common equity.

(4)   For purposes of paragraphs (1), (2), and (3) of this definition only, a business development company is considered to be eligible to use the requirements for smaller reporting companies under the revenue test in paragraph (2) or (3)(iii)(B) of the "smaller reporting company" definition in this rule, provided that the business development company meets the requirements of the test using annual investment income under Rule 6–07.1 of Regulation S–X as the measure of its "annual revenues" for purposes of the test.

Affiliate. An "affiliate" of, or a person "affiliated" with, a specified person, is a person that directly, or indirectly through one or more intermediaries, controls, or is controlled by, or is under common control with, the person specified.

Amount. The term "amount," when used in regard to securities, means the principal amount if relating to evidences of indebtedness, the number of shares if relating to shares, and the number of units if relating to any other kind of security.

Associate. The term "associate" used to indicate a relationship with any person, means

(1)   Any corporation or organization (other than the registrant or a majority-owned subsidiary of the registrant) of which such person is an officer or partner or is, directly or indirectly, the beneficial owner of 10 percent or more of any class of equity securities,

(2)   Any trust or other estate in which such person has a substantial beneficial interest or as to which such person serves as trustee or in a similar fiduciary capacity, and

(3)   Any relative or spouse of such person, or any relative of such spouse, who has the same home as such person or who is a director or officer of the registrant or any of its parents or subsidiaries.

Business combination related shell company: The term business combination related shell company means a shell company (as defined in Item 12b–2) that is:

(1)   Formed by an entity that is not a shell company solely for the purpose of changing the corporate domicile of that entity solely within the United States; or

(2)   Formed by an entity that is not a shell company solely for the purpose of completing a business combination transaction (as defined in Item 165(f)) among one or more entities other than the shell company, none of which is a shell company.

Certified. The term "certified," when used in regard to financial statements, means examined and reported upon with an opinion expressed by an independent public or certified public accountant.

Charter. The term "charter" includes articles of incorporation, declarations of trust, articles of association or partnership, or any similar instrument, as amended, effecting (either with or without filing with any governmental agency) the organization or creation of an incorporated or unincorporated person.

Common equity. The term "common equity" means any class of common stock or an equivalent interest, including but not limited to a unit of beneficial interest in a trust or a limited partnership interest.

Control. The term "control" (including the terms "controlling," "controlled by" and "under common control with") means the possession, direct or indirect, of the power to direct or cause the direction of the management and policies of a person, whether through the ownership of voting securities, by contract, or otherwise.

Depositary share. The term "depositary share" means a security, evidenced by an American Depositary Receipt, that represents a foreign security or a multiple of or fraction thereof deposited with a depositary.

Emerging growth company. (1) The term *emerging growth company* means an issuer that had total annual gross revenues of less than $1,070,000,000 during its most recently completed fiscal year.

(2) An issuer that is an emerging growth company as of the first day of that fiscal year shall continue to be deemed an emerging growth company until the earliest of:

(i) the last day of the fiscal year of the issuer during which it had total annual gross revenues of $1,070,000,000 or more;

(ii) the last day of the fiscal year of the issuer following the fifth anniversary of the date of the first sale of common equity securities of the issuer pursuant to an effective registration statement under the Securities Act of 1933;

(iii) the date on which the issuer has, during the previous three year period, issued more than $1,000,000,000 in non-convertible debt; or

(iv) the date on which such issuer is deemed to be a large accelerated filer, as defined in Rule 12b–2, or any successor thereto.

Employee. The term "employee" does not include a director, trustee, or officer.

Fiscal year. The term "fiscal year" means the annual accounting period or, if no closing date has been adopted, the calendar year ending on December 31.

Majority-owned subsidiary. The term "majority-owned subsidiary" means a subsidiary more than 50 percent of whose outstanding securities representing the right, other than as affected by events of default, to vote for the election of directors, is owned by the subsidiary's parent and/or one or more of the parent's other majority-owned subsidiaries.

Managing underwriter. The term "managing underwriter" includes an underwriter (or underwriters) who, by contract or otherwise, deals with the registrant; organizes the selling effort; receives some benefit directly or indirectly in which all other underwriters similarly situated do not share in proportion to their respective interests in the underwriting; or represents any other underwriters in such matters as maintaining the records of the distribution, arranging the allotments of securities offered or arranging for appropriate stabilization activities, if any.

Material. The term "material," when used to qualify a requirement for the furnishing of information as to any subject, limits the information required to those matters to which there is a substantial likelihood that a reasonable investor would attach importance in determining whether to buy or sell the securities registered.

Material weakness. The term "material weakness" is a deficiency, or a combination of deficiencies, in internal control over financial reporting such that there is a reasonable possibility that a material misstatement of the registrant's annual or interim financial statements will not be prevented or detected on a timely basis.

Parent. A "parent" of a specified person is an affiliate controlling such person directly, or indirectly through one or more intermediaries.

Predecessor. The term "predecessor" means a person the major portion of the business and assets of which another person acquired in a single succession or in a series of related successions in each of which the acquiring person acquired the major portion of the business and assets of the acquired person.

Previously filed or reported. The terms "previously filed" and "previously reported" mean previously filed with, or reported in, a statement under section 12, a report under section 13 or 15(d), a definitive proxy statement or information statement under section 14 of the Act, or a registration statement under the Securities Act of 1933: *Provided,* That information contained in any such document shall be deemed to have been previously filed with, or reported to, an exchange only if such document is filed with such exchange.

Principal underwriter. The term "principal underwriter" means an underwriter in privity of contract with the issuer of the securities as to which he is underwriter.

Promoter.

(1) The term "promoter" includes:

    (i) Any person who, acting alone or in conjunction with one or more other persons, directly or indirectly takes initiative in founding and organizing the business or enterprise of an issuer; or

    (ii) Any person who, in connection with the founding and organizing of the business or enterprise of an issuer, directly or indirectly receives in consideration of services or property, or both services and property, 10 percent or more of any class of securities of the issuer or 10 percent or more of the proceeds from the sale of any class of such securities. However, a person who receives such securities or proceeds either solely as underwriting commissions or solely in consideration of property shall not be deemed a promoter within the meaning of this paragraph if such person does not otherwise take part in founding and organizing the enterprise.

(2) All persons coming within the definition of "promoter" in paragraph (1) of this definition may be referred to as "founders" or "organizers" or by another term provided that such term is reasonably descriptive of those persons' activities with respect to the issuer.

Prospectus. Unless otherwise specified or the context otherwise requires, the term "prospectus" means a prospectus meeting the requirements of section 10(a) of the Securities Act of 1933 as amended.

Registrant. The term "registrant" means an issuer of securities with respect to which a registration statement or report is to be filed.

Registration statement. The term "registration statement" or "statement", when used with reference to registration pursuant to section 12 of the Act, includes both an application for registration of securities on a national securities exchange pursuant to section 12(b) of the Act and a registration statement filed pursuant to section 12(g) of the Act.

Share. The term "share" means a share of stock in a corporation or unit of interest in an unincorporated person.

Shell company. The term shell company means a registrant, other than an asset-backed issuer as defined in Item 1101(b) of Regulation AB, that has:

    (1) No or nominal operations; and

    (2) Either:

        (i) No or nominal assets;

        (ii) Assets consisting solely of cash and cash equivalents; or

        (iii) Assets consisting of any amount of cash and cash equivalents and nominal other assets.

Note: For purposes of this definition, the determination of a registrant's assets (including cash and cash equivalents) is based solely on the amount of assets that would be reflected on the registrant's balance sheet prepared in accordance with generally accepted accounting principles on the date of that determination.

Significant deficiency. The term "significant deficiency" is a deficiency, or a combination of deficiencies, in internal control over financial reporting that is less severe than a material weakness, yet important enough to merit attention by those responsible for oversight of the registrant's financial reporting.

Significant subsidiary. The term "significant subsidiary" means a subsidiary, including its subsidiaries, which meets any of the following conditions:

(1)   The registrant's and its other subsidiaries' investments in and advances to the subsidiary exceed 10 percent of the total assets of the registrant and its subsidiaries consolidated as of the end of the most recently completed fiscal year (for a proposed business combination to be accounted for as a pooling of interests, this condition is also met when the number of common shares exchanged or to be exchanged by the registrant exceeds 10 percent of its total common shares outstanding at the date the combination is initiated); or

(2)   The registrant's and its other subsidiaries' proportionate share of the total assets (after intercompany eliminations) of the subsidiary exceeds 10 percent of the total assets of the registrants and its subsidiaries consolidated as of the end of the most recently completed fiscal year; or

(3)   The registrant's and its other subsidiaries' equity in the income from continuing operations before income taxes of the subsidiary exclusive of amounts attributable to any noncontrolling interests exceeds 10 percent of such income of the registrant and its subsidiaries consolidated for the most recently completed fiscal year.

NOTE 1: A registrant that files its financial statements in accordance with or provides a reconciliation to U.S. Generally Accepted Accounting Principles shall make the prescribed tests using amounts determined under U.S. Generally Accepted Accounting Principles. A foreign private issuer that files its financial statements in accordance with IFRS as issued by the IASB shall make the prescribed tests using amounts determined under IFRS as issued by the IASB.

COMPUTATIONAL NOTE 1 to paragraph (3): For purposes of making the prescribed income test the following guidance should be applied:

1.   When a loss exclusive of amounts attributable to any noncontrolling interests has been incurred by either the parent and its subsidiaries consolidated or the tested subsidiary, but not both, the equity in the income or loss of the tested subsidiary should be excluded from the income of the registrant and its subsidiaries consolidated for purposes of the computation.

2.   If income of the registrant and its subsidiaries consolidated exclusive of amounts attributable to any noncontrolling interests for the most recent fiscal year is at least 10 percent lower than the average of the income for the last five fiscal years, such average income should be substituted for purposes of the computation. Any loss years should be omitted for purposes of computing average income.

Smaller reporting company. As used in this part, the term *smaller reporting company* means an issuer that is not an investment company, an asset-backed issuer (as defined in § 229.1101 of this chapter), or a majority-owned subsidiary of a parent that is not a smaller reporting company and that:

(1)   Had a public float of less than $250 million; or

(2)   Had annual revenues of less than $100 million and either:

(i)   No public float; or

(ii)   A public float of less than $700 million.

(3)   *Determination.* Whether an issuer is a smaller reporting company is determined on an annual basis.

(i)   For issuers that are required to file reports under section 13(a) or 15(d) of the Exchange Act:

(A)   Public float is measured as of the last business day of the issuer's most recently completed second fiscal quarter and computed by multiplying the aggregate worldwide number of shares of its voting and non-voting common equity held by non-affiliates by the price at which the common equity was last sold, or the average of the bid and asked prices of common equity, in the principal market for the common equity;

(B)   Annual revenues are as of the most recently completed fiscal year for which audited financial statements are available; and

(C)   An issuer must reflect the determination of whether it came within the definition of smaller reporting company in its quarterly report on Form 10–Q for the first fiscal quarter of the next year, indicating on the cover page of that filing, and in subsequent filings for that fiscal year, whether it is a smaller reporting company, except that, if a determination based on public float indicates that the issuer is newly eligible to be a smaller reporting company, the issuer may choose to reflect this determination beginning with its first quarterly report on Form 10–Q following the determination, rather than waiting until the first fiscal quarter of the next year.

(ii)   For determinations based on an initial registration statement under the Securities Act or Exchange Act for shares of its common equity:

   (A)   Public float is measured as of a date within 30 days of the date of the filing of the registration statement and computed by multiplying the aggregate worldwide number of shares of its voting and non-voting common equity held by non-affiliates before the registration plus, in the case of a Securities Act registration statement, the number of shares of its voting and non-voting common equity included in the registration statement by the estimated public offering price of the shares;

   (B)   Annual revenues are as of the most recently completed fiscal year for which audited financial statements are available; and

   (C)   The issuer must reflect the determination of whether it came within the definition of smaller reporting company in the registration statement and must appropriately indicate on the cover page of the filing, and subsequent filings for the fiscal year in which the filing is made, whether it is a smaller reporting company. The issuer must re-determine its status at the end of its second fiscal quarter and then reflect any change in status as provided in paragraph (3)(i)(C) of this rule. In the case of a determination based on an initial Securities Act registration statement, an issuer that was not determined to be a smaller reporting company has the option to re-determine its status at the conclusion of the offering covered by the registration statement based on the actual offering price and number of shares sold.

(iii)   Once an issuer determines that it does not qualify for smaller reporting company status because it exceeded one or more of the current thresholds, it will remain unqualified unless when making its annual determination either:

   (A)   It determines that its public float was less than $200 million; or

   (B)   It determines that its public float and its annual revenues meet the requirements for subsequent qualification included in the chart below:

Prior Annual Revenues	Prior Public Float	
	None or less than $700 million	$700 million or more
Less than $100 million	Neither threshold exceeded	Public float Less than $560 million; and
		Revenues Less than $100 million.
$100 million or more	Public float None or less than $700 million; and	Public float Less than $560 million; and
	Revenues Less than $80 million.	Revenues Less than $80 million.

Instruction to definition of "smaller reporting company": A registrant that qualifies as a smaller reporting company under the public float thresholds identified in paragraphs (1) and (3)(iii)(A) of this rule will qualify as a smaller reporting company regardless of its revenues.

Instruction 2 to definition of "smaller reporting company": A foreign private issuer is not eligible to use the requirements for smaller reporting companies unless it uses the forms and rules designated for domestic issuers and provides financial statements prepared in accordance with U.S. Generally Accepted Accounting Principles.

Subsidiary. A "subsidiary" of a specified person is an affiliate controlled by such person directly, or indirectly through one or more intermediaries. (See also "majority-owned subsidiary," "significant subsidiary," and "totally-held subsidiary.")

Succession. The term succession means the direct acquisition of the assets comprising a going business, whether by merger, consolidation, purchase, or other direct transfer; or the acquisition of control of a shell company in a transaction required to be reported on Form 8–K in compliance with Item 5.01 of that Form or on Form 20–F in compliance with Rule 13a–19 or Rule 15d–19. Except for an acquisition of control of a shell company, the term does not include the acquisition of control of a business unless followed by the direct acquisition of its assets. The terms succeed and successor have meanings correlative to the foregoing.

Totally held subsidiary. The term "totally held subsidiary" means a subsidiary

(1) Substantially all of whose outstanding securities are owned by its parent and/or the parent's other totally held subsidiaries, and

(2) Which is not indebted to any person other than its parent and/or the parent's other totally held subsidiaries in an amount which is material in relation to the particular subsidiary, excepting indebtedness incurred in the ordinary course of business which is not overdue and which matures within one year from the date of its creation, whether evidenced by securities or not.

Voting securities. The term "voting securities" means securities the holders of which are presently entitled to vote for the election of directors.

Wholly-owned subsidiary. The term "wholly-owned subsidiary" means a subsidiary substantially all of whose outstanding voting securities are owned by its parent and/or the parent's other wholly-owned subsidiaries.

Rule 12b-3. Title of Securities

Wherever the title of securities is required to be stated there shall be given such information as will indicate the type and general character of the securities, including the following:

(a) In the case of shares, the par or stated value, if any; the rate of dividends, if fixed, and whether cumulative or noncumulative; a brief indication of the preference, if any; and if convertible, a statement to that effect.

(b) In the case of funded debt, the rate of interest; the date of maturity, or if the issue matures serially, a brief indication of the serial maturities, such as "maturing serially from 1950 to 1960"; if the payment of principal or interest is contingent, an appropriate indication of such contingency; a brief indication of the priority of the issue; and if convertible, a statement to that effect.

(c) In the case of any other kind of security, appropriate information of comparable character.

Rule 12b-4. Supplemental Information

The Commission or its staff may, where it is deemed appropriate, request supplemental information concerning the registrant, a registration statement or a periodic or other report under the Act. This information shall not be required to be filed with or deemed part of the registration statement or report. The information shall be returned to the registrant upon request, provided that:

(a) Such request is made at the time such information is furnished to the staff;

(b) The return of such information is consistent with the protection of investors; and

(c) The return of such information is consistent with the provisions of the Freedom of Information Act.

Rule 12b-5. Determination of Affiliates of Banks

In determining whether a person is an "affiliate" or "parent" of a bank or whether a bank is a "subsidiary" or "majority-owner subsidiary" of a person within the meaning of those terms as defined in Rule 12b-2, voting securities of the bank held by a corporation all of the stock of which is directly owned by the United States Government shall not be taken into consideration.

Rule 12b–6. When Securities Are Deemed to Be Registered

A class of securities with respect to which a registration statement has been filed pursuant to section 12 of the Act shall be deemed to be registered for the purposes of sections 13, 14, 15(d) and 16 of the Act and the rules and regulations thereunder only when such statement has become effective as provided in section 12, and securities of said class shall not be subject to sections 13, 14 and 16 of the Act until such statement has become effective as provided in section 12.

Rule 12b–10. Requirements as to Proper Form

Every statement or report shall be on the form prescribed therefor by the Commission, as in effect on the date of filing. Any statement or report shall be deemed to be filed on the proper form unless objection to the form is made by the Commission within thirty days after the date of filing.

Rule 12b–11. Number of Copies—Signatures—Binding

(a) Except as provided in a particular form, three complete copies of each statement or report, including exhibits and all other papers and documents filed as a part thereof, shall be filed with the Commission. At least one complete copy of each statement shall be filed with each exchange on which the securities covered thereby are to be registered. At least one complete copy of each report under Section 13 of the Act shall be filed with each exchange on which the registrant has securities registered.

(b) At least one copy of each statement or report filed with the Commission and one copy thereof filed with each exchange shall be signed in the manner prescribed by the appropriate form.

(c) Each copy of a statement or report filed with the Commission or with an exchange shall be bound in one or more parts. Copies filed with the Commission shall be bound without stiff covers. The statement or report shall be bound on the left side in such a manner as to leave the reading matter legible.

(d) Where the Act or the rules, forms, reports, or schedules thereunder, including paragraph (b) of this rule, require a document filed with or furnished to the Commission to be signed, such document shall be manually signed, or signed using either typed signatures or duplicated or facsimile versions of manual signatures. Where typed, duplicated or facsimile signatures are used, each signatory to the filing shall manually sign a signature page or other document authenticating, acknowledging or otherwise adopting his or her signature that appears in the filing. Such document shall be executed before or at the time the filing is made and shall be retained by the filer for a period of five years. Upon request, the filer shall furnish to the Commission or its staff a copy of any or all documents retained pursuant to this rule.

Rule 12b–12. Requirements as to Paper, Printing and Language

(a) Statements and reports shall be filed on good quality, unglazed white paper, no larger than $8\frac{1}{2}$ × 11 inches in size, insofar as practicable. To the extent that the reduction of larger documents would render them illegible, such documents may be filed on paper larger than $8\frac{1}{2}$ × 11 inches in size.

(b) The statement or report and, insofar as practicable, all papers and documents filed as a part thereof, shall be printed, lithographed, mimeographed, or typewritten. However, the statement or report or any portion thereof may be prepared by any similar process which, in the opinion of the Commission, produces copies suitable for a permanent record and microfilming. Irrespective of the process used, all copies of any such material shall be clear, easily readable and suitable for repeated photocopying. Debits in credit categories and credits in debit categories shall be designated so as to be clearly distinguishable as such on photocopies.

(c) The body of all printed statements and reports and all notes to financial statements and other tabular data included therein shall be in roman type at least as large and as legible as 10-point modern type. However, to the extent necessary for convenient presentation, financial statements and other tabular data, including tabular data in notes, may be in roman type at least as large and as legible as 8-point modern type. All such type shall be leaded at least 2 points.

(d)(1) All Exchange Act filings and submissions must be in the English language, except as otherwise provided by this Rule. If a filing or submission requires the inclusion of a document that is in a foreign language, a party must submit instead a fair and accurate English translation of the entire foreign language document, except as provided by paragraph (d)(3) of this Rule.

(2) If a filing or submission subject to review by the Division of Corporation Finance requires the inclusion of a foreign language document as an exhibit or attachment, a party must submit a fair and accurate English translation of the foreign language document if consisting of any of the following, or an amendment of any of the following:

(i) Articles of incorporation, memoranda of association, bylaws, and other comparable documents, whether original or restated;

(ii) Instruments defining the rights of security holders, including indentures qualified or to be qualified under the Trust Indenture Act of 1939;

(iii) Voting agreements, including voting trust agreements;

(iv) Contracts to which directors, officers, promoters, voting trustees or security holders named in a registration statement, report or other document are parties;

(v) Contracts upon which a filer's business is substantially dependent;

(vi) Audited annual and interim consolidated financial information; and

(vii) Any document that is or will be the subject of a confidential treatment request under Rule 24b–2 of this Act or Rule 406 of the Securities Act of 1933.

(3)(i) A party may submit an English summary instead of an English translation of a foreign language document as an exhibit or attachment to a filing or submission subject to review by the Division of Corporation Finance, as long as:

(A) The foreign language document does not consist of any of the subject matter enumerated in paragraph (d)(2) of this Rule; or

(B) The applicable form permits the use of an English summary.

(ii) Any English summary submitted under paragraph (d)(3) of this Rule must:

(A) Fairly and accurately summarize the terms of each material provision of the foreign language document; and

(B) Fairly and accurately describe the terms that have been omitted or abridged.

(4) When submitting an English summary or English translation of a foreign language document under this Rule, a party must identify the submission as either an English summary or English translation. A party may submit a copy of the unabridged foreign language document when including an English summary or English translation of a foreign language document in a filing or submission. A party must provide a copy of any foreign language document upon the request of Commission staff.

(5) A foreign government or its political subdivision must provide a fair and accurate English translation of its latest annual budget submitted as Exhibit B to Form 18 or Exhibit (c) to Form 18–K only if one is available. If no English translation is available, a filer must provide a copy of the foreign language version of its latest annual budget as an exhibit.

(6) A Canadian issuer may file an exhibit, attachment or other part of a Form 40–F registration statement or annual report, Schedule 13E–4F, Schedule 14D–1F, or Schedule 14D–9F, that contains text in both French and English if the issuer included the French text to comply with the requirements of the Canadian securities administrator or other Canadian authority and, for an electronic filing, if the filing is an HTML document, as defined in Regulation S–T Rule 11.

(e) Where a statement or report is distributed to investors through an electronic medium, issuers may satisfy legibility requirements applicable to printed documents, such as paper size and type size and font, by presenting all required information in a format readily communicated to investors.

Rule 12b–13. Preparation of Statement or Report

The statement or report shall contain the numbers and captions of all items of the appropriate form, but the text of the items may be omitted provided the answers thereto are so prepared as to indicate to the reader the coverage of the items without the necessity of his referring to the text of the items or instructions thereto. However, where any item requires information to be given in tabular form, it shall be given in substantially the tabular form specified in the item. All instructions, whether appearing under the items of the form or elsewhere therein, are to be omitted. Unless expressly provided otherwise, if any item is inapplicable or the answer thereto is in the negative, an appropriate statement to that effect shall be made.

Rule 12b–14. Riders—Inserts

Riders shall not be used. If the statement or report is typed on a printed form, and the space provided for the answer to any given item is insufficient, reference shall be made in such space to a full insert page or pages on which the item number and caption and the complete answer are given.

Rule 12b–15. Amendments

All amendments must be filed under cover of the form amended, marked with the letter "A" to designate the document as an amendment, e.g., "10–K/A," and in compliance with pertinent requirements applicable to statements and reports. Amendments filed pursuant to this rule must set forth the complete text of each item as amended. Amendments must be numbered sequentially and be filed separately for each statement or report amended. Amendments to a statement may be filed either before or after registration becomes effective. Amendments must be signed on behalf of the registrant by a duly authorized representative of the registrant. An amendment to any report required to include the certifications as specified in Rule 13a–14(a) or Rule 15d–14(a) must include new certifications by each principal executive and principal financial officer of the registrant, and an amendment to any report required to be accompanied by the certifications as specified in Rule 13a–14(b) or Rule 15d–14(b) must be accompanied by new certifications by each principal executive and principal financial officer of the registrant. An amendment to any report required to include the certifications as specified in Rules 13a–14(d) or Rules 15d–14(d) of the Securities Exchange Act of 1934 must include a new certification by an individual specified in Rules 13a–14(e), or Rules 15d–14(e) of the Securities Exchange Act of 1934, as applicable. The requirements of the form being amended will govern the number of copies to be filed in connection with a paper format amendment. Electronic filers satisfy the provisions dictating the number of copies by filing one copy of the amendment in electronic format. See Rule 309 of Regulation S–T.

Rule 12b–20. Additional Information

In addition to the information expressly required to be included in a statement or report, there shall be added such further material information, if any, as may be necessary to make the required statements, in the light of the circumstances under which they are made not misleading.

Rule 12b–21. Information Unknown or Not Available

Information required need be given only insofar as it is known or reasonably available to the registrant. If any required information is unknown and not reasonably available to the registrant, either because the obtaining thereof would involve unreasonable effort or expense, or because it rests peculiarly within the knowledge of another person not affiliated with the registrant, the information may be omitted, subject to the following conditions.

(a)   The registrant shall give such information on the subject as it possesses or can acquire without unreasonable effort or expense, together with the sources thereof.

(b)   The registrant shall include a statement either showing that unreasonable effort or expense would be involved or indicating the absence of any affiliation with the person within whose knowledge the information rests and stating the result of a request made to such person for the information.

Rule 12b–22. Disclaimer of Control

If the existence of control is open to reasonable doubt in any instance, the registrant may disclaim the existence of control and any admission thereof; in such case, however, the registrant shall state the material facts pertinent to the possible existence of control.

Rule 12b–23. Incorporation by Reference

(a) *Registration statement or report.* Except as provided by this rule or in the appropriate form, information may be incorporated by reference in answer, or partial answer, to any item of a registration statement or report.

(b) *Financial information.* Except as provided in the Commission's rules, financial information required to be given in comparative form for two or more fiscal years or periods must not be incorporated by reference unless the information incorporated by reference includes the entire period for which the comparative data is given. In the financial statements, incorporating by reference, or cross-referencing to, information outside of the financial statements is not permitted unless otherwise specifically permitted or required by the Commission's rules or by U.S. Generally Accepted Accounting Principles or International Financial Reporting Standards as issued by the International Accounting Standards Board, whichever is applicable.

(c) *Exhibits.* Any document or part thereof filed with the Commission pursuant to any Act administered by the Commission may be incorporated by reference as an exhibit to any statement or report filed with the Commission by the same or any other person. Any document or part thereof filed with an exchange pursuant to the Act may be incorporated by reference as an exhibit to any statement or report filed with the exchange by the same or any other person. If any modification has occurred in the text of any document incorporated by reference since the filing thereof, the registrant must file with the reference a statement containing the text of any such modification and the date thereof.

(d) *Hyperlinks.* You must include an active hyperlink to information incorporated into a registration statement or report by reference if such information is publicly available on the Commission's Electronic Data Gathering, Analysis and Retrieval System ("EDGAR") at the time the registration statement or form is filed. For hyperlinking to exhibits, please refer to Item 601 of Regulation S–K or the appropriate form.

(e) *General.* Include an express statement clearly describing the specific location of the information you are incorporating by reference. The statement must identify the document where the information was originally filed or submitted and the location of the information within that document. The statement must be made at the particular place where the information is required, if applicable. Information must not be incorporated by reference in any case where such incorporation would render the disclosure incomplete, unclear, or confusing. For example, unless expressly permitted or required, disclosure must not be incorporated by reference from a second document if that second document incorporates information pertinent to such disclosure by reference to a third document.

Rule 12b–25. Notification of Inability to Timely File All or Any Required Portion of a Form 10–K, 20–F, 11–K, N–SAR, N–CSR, 10–Q, or 10–D

(a) If all or any required portion of an annual or transition report on Form 10–K, 20–F or 11–K, a quarterly or transition report on Form 10–Q or a distribution report on Form 10–D required to be filed pursuant to section 13 or 15(d) of the Act and rules thereunder, or if all or any required portion of a semi-annual, annual or transition report on Form N–CSR or Form N–CEN required to be filed pursuant to section 13 or 15(d) of the Act or section 30 of the Investment Company Act of 1940 and the rules thereunder, is not filed within the time period prescribed for such report, the registrant, no later than one business day after the due date for such report, shall file a Form 12b–25 with the Commission which shall contain disclosure of its inability to file the report timely and the reasons therefor in reasonable detail.

(b) With respect to any report or portion of any report described in paragraph (a) of this rule which is not timely filed because the registrant is unable to do so without unreasonable effort or expense, such report shall be deemed to be filed on the prescribed due date for such report if:

(1) The registrant files the Form 12b–25 in compliance with paragraph (a) of this rule and, when applicable, furnishes the exhibit required by paragraph (c) of this rule;

(2) The registrant represents in the Form 12b–25 that:

(i) The reason(s) causing the inability to file timely could not be eliminated by the registrant without unreasonable effort or expense; and

(ii)   The subject annual report, semi-annual report or transition report on Form 10–K, 20–F, 11–K, N–CEN, or N–CSR, or portion thereof, will be filed no later than the fifteenth calendar day following the prescribed due date; or the subject quarterly report or transition report on Form 10–Q or distribution report on Form 10–D, or portion thereof, will be filed no later than the fifth calendar day following the prescribed due date; and

(3)   The report/portion thereof is actually filed within the period specified by paragraph (b)(2)(ii) of this rule.

(c)   If paragraph (b) of this rule is applicable and the reason the subject report/portion thereof cannot be filed timely without unreasonable effort or expense relates to the inability of any person, other than the registrant, to furnish any required opinion, report or certification, the Form 12b–25 shall have attached as an exhibit a statement signed by such person stating the specific reasons why such person is unable to furnish the required opinion, report or certification on or before the date such report must be filed.

(d)   Notwithstanding paragraph (b) of this rule, a registrant will not be eligible to use any registration statement form under the Securities Act of 1933 the use of which is predicated on timely filed reports until the subject report is actually filed pursuant to paragraph (b)(3) of this rule.

(e)   If a Form 12b–25 filed pursuant to paragraph (a) of this rule relates only to a portion of a subject report, the registrant shall:

(1)   File the balance of such report and indicate on the cover page thereof which disclosure items are omitted; and

(2)   Include, on the upper right corner of the amendment to the report which includes the previously omitted information, the following statement:

The following items were the subject of a Form 12b–25 and are included herein: (*List Item Numbers*)

(f)   The provisions of this rule shall not apply to financial statements to be filed by amendment to a Form 10–K as provided for by paragraph (a) of Item 3–09 of Regulation S–K or schedules to be filed by amendment in accordance with General Instruction A to Form 10–K.

(g)   *Electronic filings.* The provisions of this rule shall not apply to reports required to be filed in electronic format if the sole reason the report is not filed within the time period prescribed is that the filer is unable to file the report in electronic format. Filers unable to submit a report in electronic format within the time period prescribed solely due to difficulties with electronic filing should comply with either Rule 201 or 202 of Regulation S–T, or apply for an adjustment of filing date pursuant to Rule 13(b) of Regulation S–T.

(h)   Interactive data submissions. The provisions of this rule shall not apply to the submission or posting of an Interactive Data File. Filers unable to submit or post an Interactive Data File within the time period prescribed should comply with either Rule 201 or 202 of Regulation S–T.

Rule 12b–30. Additional Exhibits

The registrant may file such exhibits as it may desire, in addition to those required by the appropriate form. Such exhibits shall be so marked as to indicate clearly the subject matters to which they refer.

Rule 12b–31. Omission of Substantially Identical Documents

In any case where two or more indentures, contracts, franchises, or other documents required to be filed as exhibits are substantially identical in all material respects except as to the parties thereto, the dates of execution, or other details, the registrant need file a copy of only one of such documents, with a schedule identifying the other documents omitted and setting forth the material details in which such documents differ from the document of which a copy is filed. The Commission may at any time in its discretion require the filing of copies of any documents so omitted.

Rule 12b–32. [Removed and Reserved]

Rule 12b–33. Annual Reports to Other Federal Agencies

Notwithstanding any rule or other requirement to the contrary, whenever copies of an annual report by a registrant to any other Federal agency are required or permitted to be filed as an exhibit to an application or report filed by such registrant with the Commission or with a securities exchange, only one copy of such annual report need be filed with the Commission and one copy thereof with each such exchange, provided appropriate reference to such copy is made in each copy of the application or report filed with the Commission or with such exchange.

Rule 12b–36. Use of Financial Statements Filed Under Other Acts

Where copies of certified financial statements filed under other acts administered by the Commission are filed with a statement or report, the accountant's certificate shall be manually signed or manually signed copies of the certificate shall be filed with the financial statements. Where such financial statements are incorporated by reference in a statement or report, the written consent of the accountant to such incorporation by reference shall be filed with the statement or report. Such consent shall be dated and signed manually.

CERTIFICATION BY EXCHANGES AND EFFECTIVENESS OF REGISTRATION

Rule 12d1–1. Registration Effective as to Class or Series

(a) An application filed pursuant to section 12(b) and (c) of the Act for registration of a security on a national securities exchange shall be deemed to apply for registration of the entire class of such security. Registration shall become effective, as provided in section 12(d) of the Act,

(1) As to the shares or amounts of such class then issued, and

(2) Without further application for registration, upon issuance as to additional shares or amounts of such class then or thereafter authorized.

(b) This rule shall apply to classes of securities of which a specified number of shares or amounts was registered or registered upon notice of issuance, and to applications for registration filed, prior to the close of business on January 28, 1954, as well as to classes registered, or applications filed, thereafter.

(c) This rule shall not affect the right of a national securities exchange to require the issuer of a registered security to file documents with or pay fees to the exchange in connection with the modification of such security or the issuance of additional shares or amounts.

(d) If a class of security is issuable in two or more series with different terms, each such series shall be deemed a separate class for the purposes of this rule.

Rule 12d1–2. Effectiveness of Registration

(a) A request for acceleration of the effective date of registration pursuant to section 12(d) of the Act and Rule 12d1–1 shall be made in writing by either the registrant, the exchange, or both and shall briefly describe the reasons therefor.

(b) A registration statement on Form 8–A for the registration of a class of securities under section 12(b) of the Act shall become effective:

(1) If a class of securities is not concurrently being registered under the Securities Act of 1933 ("Securities Act"), upon the later of receipt by the Commission of certification from the national securities exchange or the filing of the Form 8–A with the Commission; or

(2) If a class of securities is concurrently being registered under the Securities Act, upon the later of the filing of the Form 8–A with the Commission, receipt by the Commission of certification from the national securities exchange listed on the Form 8–A or effectiveness of the Securities Act registration statement relating to the class of securities.

(c) A registration statement on Form 8–A for the registration of a class of securities under section 12(g) of the Act shall become effective:

(1)   If a class of securities is not concurrently being registered under the Securities Act, upon the filing of the Form 8–A with the Commission; or

(2)   If class of securities is concurrently being registered under the Securities Act, upon the later of the filing of the Form 8–A with the Commission or the effectiveness of the Securities Act registration statement relating to the class of securities.

Rule 12d1–3. Requirements as to Certification

(a)   Certification that a security has been approved by an exchange for listing and registration pursuant to section 12(d) of the Act and Rule 12d1–1 shall be made by the governing committee or other corresponding authority of the exchange.

(b)   The certification shall specify

(1)   The approval of the exchange for listing and registration;

(2)   The title of the security so approved;

(3)   The date of filing with the exchange of the application for registration and of any amendments thereto; and

(4)   Any conditions imposed on such certification. The exchange shall promptly notify the Commission of the partial or complete satisfaction of any such conditions.

(c)   The certification must be filed in electronic format via the Commission's Electronic Data Gathering, Analysis, and Retrieval (EDGAR) system in accordance with the EDGAR rules set forth in § 232 of this chapter (Regulation S–T).

Rule 12d1–4. Date of Receipt of Certification by Commission

The date of receipt by the Commission of the certification approving a security for listing and registration shall be the date on which the certification is actually received by the Commission or the date on which the application for registration to which the certification relates is actually received by the Commission, whichever date is later.

Rule 12d1–5. Operation of Certification on Subsequent Amendments

If an amendment to the application for registration of a security is filed with the exchange and with the Commission after the receipt by the Commission of the certification of the exchange approving the security for listing and registration, the certification, unless withdrawn, shall be deemed made with reference to the application as amended.

Rule 12d1–6. Withdrawal of Certification

An exchange may, by notice to the Commission, withdraw its certification prior to the time that the registration to which it relates first becomes effective pursuant to Rule 12d1–1.

SUSPENSION OF TRADING, WITHDRAWAL, AND STRIKING FROM LISTING AND REGISTRATION

Rule 12d2–1. Suspension of Trading

(a)   A national securities exchange may suspend from trading a security listed and registered thereon in accordance with its rules. Such exchange shall promptly notify the Commission of any such suspension, the effective date thereof, and the reasons therefor.

(b)   Any such suspension may be continued until such time as it shall appear to the Commission that such suspension is designed to evade the provisions of section 12(d) of the Act and the rules and regulations thereunder relating to the withdrawal and striking of a security from listing and registration. During the continuance of such suspension the exchange shall notify the Commission promptly of any change in the reasons for the suspension. Upon the restoration to trading of any security suspended under this rule, the exchange shall notify the Commission promptly of the effective date thereof.

(c) Suspension of trading shall not terminate the registration of any security.

Rule 12d2-2. Removal From Listing and Registration

Preliminary Notes: 1. The filing of the Form 25 by an issuer relates solely to the withdrawal of a class of securities from listing on a national securities exchange and/or from registration under section 12(b) of the Act, and shall not affect its obligation to be registered under section 12(g) of the Act and/or reporting obligations under section 15(d) of the Act.

2. Implementation. The rules of each national securities exchange must be designed to meet the requirements of this rule and must be operative no later than April 24, 2006. Each national securities exchange must submit to the Commission a proposed rule change that complies with section 19(b) of the Act and Rule 19b-4 thereunder, and this rule no later than October 24, 2005.

(a) A national securities exchange must file with the Commission an application on Form 25 to strike a class of securities from listing on a national securities exchange and/or registration under section 12(b) of the Act within a reasonable time after the national securities exchange is reliably informed that any of the following conditions exist with respect to such a security:

(1) The entire class of the security has been called for redemption, maturity or retirement; appropriate notice thereof has been given; funds sufficient for the payment of all such securities have been deposited with an agency authorized to make such payments; and such funds have been made available to security holders.

(2) The entire class of the security has been redeemed or paid at maturity or retirement.

(3) The instruments representing the securities comprising the entire class have come to evidence, by operation of law or otherwise, other securities in substitution therefor and represent no other right, except, if such be the fact, the right to receive an immediate cash payment (the right of dissenters to receive the appraised or fair value of their holdings shall not prevent the application of this provision).

(4) All rights pertaining to the entire class of the security have been extinguished; *Provided, however,* that where such an event occurs as the result of an order of a court or other governmental authority, the order shall be final, all applicable appeal periods shall have expired, and no appeals shall be pending.

Effective Date: Such an application shall be deemed to be granted and shall become effective at the opening of business on such date as the exchange shall specify in said application, but not less than 10 days following the date on which said application is filed with the Commission; *Provided, however,* That in the event removal is being effected under paragraph (a)(3) of this rule and the exchange has admitted or intends to admit a successor security to trading under the temporary exemption provided for by Rule 12a-5, such date shall not be earlier than the date on which the successor security is removed from its exempt status.

(b)(1) In cases not provided for in paragraph (a) of this rule, a national securities exchange may file an application on Form 25 to strike a class of securities from listing and/or withdraw the registration of such securities, in accordance with its rules, if the rules of such exchange, at a minimum, provide for:

(i) Notice to the issuer of the exchange's decision to delist its securities;

(ii) An opportunity for appeal to the national securities exchange's board of directors, or to a committee designated by the board; and

(iii) Public notice of the national securities exchange's final determination to remove the security from listing and/or registration, by issuing a press release and posting notice on its Web site. Public notice under this paragraph shall be disseminated no fewer than 10 days before the delisting becomes effective pursuant to paragraph (d)(1) of this rule, and must remain posted on its Web site until the delisting is effective.

(2) A national securities exchange must promptly deliver a copy of the application on Form 25 to the issuer.

(c)(1) The issuer of a class of securities listed on a national securities exchange and/or registered under section 12(b) of the Act may file an application on Form 25 to notify the Commission of its withdrawal of such securities from listing on such national securities exchange and its intention to withdraw the securities from registration under section 12(b) of the Act.

(2)   An issuer filing Form 25 under this paragraph must satisfy the requirements in paragraph (c)(2) of this rule and represent on the Form 25 that such requirements have been met:

(i)   The issuer must comply with all applicable laws in effect in the state in which it is incorporated and with the national securities exchange's rules governing an issuer's voluntary withdrawal of a class of securities from listing and/or registration.

(ii)   No fewer than 10 days before the issuer files an application on Form 25 with the Commission, the issuer must provide written notice to the national securities exchange of its determination to withdraw the class of securities from listing and/or registration on such exchange. Such written notice must set forth a description of the security involved, together with a statement of all material facts relating to the reasons for withdrawal from listing and/or registration.

(iii)   Contemporaneous with providing written notice to the exchange of its intent to withdraw a class of securities from listing and/or registration, the issuer must publish notice of such intention, along with its reasons for such withdrawal, via a press release and, if it has a publicly accessible Web site, posting such notice on that Web site. Any notice provided on an issuer's Web site under this paragraph shall remain available until the delisting on Form 25 has become effective pursuant to paragraph (d)(1) of this rule. If the issuer has not arranged for listing and/or registration on another national securities exchange or for quotation of its security in a quotation medium (as defined in Rule 15c2–11), then the press release and posting on the Web site must contain this information.

(3)   A national securities exchange, that receives, pursuant to paragraph (c)(2)(ii) of this rule, written notice from an issuer that such issuer has determined to withdraw a class of securities from listing and/or registration on such exchange, must provide notice on its Web site of the issuer's intent to delist and/or withdraw from registration its securities by the next business day. Such notice must remain posted on the exchange's Web site until the delisting on Form 25 is effective pursuant to paragraph (d)(1) of this rule.

(d)(1)   An application on Form 25 to strike a class of securities from listing on a national securities exchange will be effective 10 days after Form 25 is filed with the Commission.

(2)   An application on Form 25 to withdraw the registration of a class of securities under section 12(b) of the Act will be effective 90 days, or such shorter period as the Commission may determine, after filing with the Commission.

(3)   Notwithstanding paragraphs (d)(1) and (d)(2) of this rule, the Commission may, by written notice to the exchange and issuer, postpone the effectiveness of an application to delist and/or to deregister to determine whether the application on Form 25 to strike the security from registration under section 12(b) of the Act has been made in accordance with the rules of the exchange, or what terms should be imposed by the Commission for the protection of investors.

(4)   Notwithstanding paragraph (d)(2) of this rule, whenever the Commission commences a proceeding against an issuer under section 12 of the Act prior to the withdrawal of the registration of a class of securities, such security will remain registered under section 12(b) of the Act until the final decision of such proceeding or until the Commission otherwise determines to suspend the effective date of, or revoke, the registration of a class of securities.

(5)   An issuer's duty to file any reports under section 13(a) of the Act and the rules and regulations thereunder solely because of such security's registration under section 12(b) of the Act will be suspended upon the effective date for the delisting pursuant to paragraph (d)(1) of this rule. If, following the effective date of delisting on Form 25, the Commission, an exchange, or an issuer delays the withdrawal of a security's registration under section 12(b) of the Act, an issuer shall, within 60 days of such delay, file any reports that would have been required under section 13(a) of the Act and the rules and regulations thereunder, had the Form 25 not been filed. The issuer also shall timely file any subsequent reports required under section 13(a) of the Act for the duration of the delay.

(6)   An issuer whose reporting responsibilities under section 13(a) of the Act are suspended for a class of securities under paragraph (d)(5) of this rule is, nevertheless, required to file any reports that an issuer with such a class of securities registered under section 12 of the Act would be required to file under section 13(a) of the Act if such class of securities:

(i)   Is registered under section 12(g) of the Act; or

(ii)   Would be registered, or would be required to be registered, under section 12(g) of the Act but for the exemption from registration under section 12(g) of the Act provided by section 12(g)(2)(A) of the Act.

(7)(i)   An issuer whose reporting responsibilities under section 13(a) of the Act are suspended under paragraph (d)(5) of this rule is, nevertheless, required to file any reports that would be required under section 15(d) of the Act but for the fact that the reporting obligations are:

(A)   Suspended for a class of securities under paragraph (d)(5) of this rule; and

(B)   Suspended, terminated, or otherwise absent under section 12(g) of the Act.

(ii)   The reporting responsibilities of an issuer under section 15(d) of the Act shall continue until the issuer is required to file reports under section 13(a) of the Act or the issuer's reporting responsibilities under section 15(d) of the Act are otherwise suspended.

(8)   In the event removal is being effected under paragraph (a)(3) of this rule and the national securities exchange has admitted or intends to admit a successor security to trading under the temporary exemption provided for by Rule 12a–5, the effective date of the Form 25, as set forth in paragraph (d)(1) of this rule, shall not be earlier than the date the successor security is removed from its exempt status.

(e)   The following are exempt from section 12(d) of the Act and the provisions of this rule:

(1)   Any standardized option, as defined in Rule 9b–1, that is:

(i)   Issued by a clearing agency registered under section 17A of the Act; and

(ii)   Traded on a national securities exchange registered pursuant to section 6(a) of the Act; and

(2)   Any security futures product that is:

(i)   Traded on a national securities exchange registered under section 6(a) of the Act or on a national securities association registered pursuant to section 15A(a) of the Act; and

(ii)   Cleared by a clearing agency registered as a clearing agency pursuant to section 17A of the Act or is exempt from registration under section 17A(b)(7) of the Act.

UNLISTED TRADING

Rule 12f–1.   Applications for Permission to Reinstate Unlisted Trading Privileges

(a)   An application to reinstate unlisted trading privileges may be made to the Commission by any national securities exchange for the extension of unlisted trading privileges to any security for which such unlisted trading privileges have been suspended by the Commission, pursuant to section 12(f)(2)(A) of the Act. One copy of such application, executed by a duly authorized officer of the exchange, shall be filed and shall set forth:

(1)   Name of issuer;

(2)   Title of security;

(3)   The name of each national securities exchange, if any, on which such security is listed or admitted to unlisted trading privileges;

(4)   Whether transaction information concerning such security is reported pursuant to an effective transaction reporting plan contemplated by Rule 601 of Regulation NMS.

(5)   The date of the Commission's suspension of unlisted trading privileges in the security on the exchange;

(6)   Any other information which is deemed pertinent to the question of whether the reinstatement of unlisted trading privileges in such security is consistent with the maintenance of fair and orderly markets and the protection of investors; and

(7)   That a copy of the instant application has been mailed, or otherwise personally provided, to the issuer of the securities for which unlisted trading privileges are sought and to each exchange listed in Item (3) of this rule.

Rule 12f–2.   Extending Unlisted Trading Privileges to a Security That Is the Subject of an Initial Public Offering

(a)   *General Provision*—A national securities exchange may extend unlisted trading privileges to a subject security when at least one transaction in the subject security has been effected on the national securities exchange upon which the security is listed and the transaction has been reported pursuant to an effective transaction reporting plan, as defined in Rule 600 of Regulation NMS.

(b)   The extension of unlisted trading privileges pursuant to this rule shall be subject to all the provisions set forth in section 12(f) of the Act, as amended, and any rule or regulation promulgated thereunder, or which may be promulgated thereunder while the extension is in effect.

(c)   *Definitions.* For the purposes of this rule:

(1)   The term "subject security" shall mean a security that is the subject of an initial public offering, as that term is defined in section 12(f)(1)(G)(i) of the Act, and

(2)   An initial public offering commences at such time as is described in section 12(f)(1)(G)(ii) of the Act.

Rule 12f–3.   Termination or Suspension of Unlisted Trading Privileges

(a)   The issuer of any security for which unlisted trading privileges on any exchange have been continued or extended, or any broker or dealer who makes or creates a market for such security, or any other person having a bona fide interest in the question of termination or suspension of such unlisted trading privileges, may make application to the Commission for the termination or suspension of such unlisted trading privileges. One duly executed copy of such application shall be filed, and it shall contain the following information:

(1)   Name and address of applicant;

(2)   A brief statement of the applicant's interest in the question of termination or suspension of such unlisted trading privileges;

(3)   Title of security;

(4)   Names of issuer;

(5)   Amount of such security issued and outstanding (number of shares of stock or principal amount of bonds), stating source of information;

(6)   Annual volume of public trading in such security (number of shares of stock or principal amount of bonds) on such exchange for each of the three calendar years immediately preceding the date of such application, and monthly volume of trading in such security for each of the twelve calendar months immediately preceding the date of such application;

(7)   Price range on such exchange for each of the twelve calendar months immediately preceding the date of such application;

(8)   A brief statement of the information in the applicant's possession, and the source thereof, with respect to

(i)   the extent of public trading in such security on such exchange, and

(ii)   the character of trading in such security on such exchange; and

(9)   A brief statement that a copy of the instant application has been mailed, or otherwise personally provided, to the exchange from which the suspension or termination of unlisted trading privileges is sought, and to any other exchange on which such security is listed or traded pursuant to unlisted trading privileges.

(b)   Unlisted trading privileges in any security on any national securities exchange may be suspended or terminated by such exchange in accordance with its rules.

Rule 12f–4.   Exemption of Securities Admitted to Unlisted Trading Privileges From Sections 13, 14 and 16

(a)   Any security for which unlisted trading privileges on any national securities exchange have been continued or extended pursuant to section 12(f) of the Act shall be exempt from section 13 of the act unless

(1)   such security or another security of the same issuer is listed and registered on a national securities exchange or registered pursuant to section 12(g) of the Act, or

(2)   such issuer would be required to file information, documents and reports pursuant to section 15(d) of the Act but for the fact that securities of the issuer are deemed to be "registered on a national securities exchange" within the meaning of section 12(f)(6) of the Act.

(b)   Any security for which unlisted trading privileges on any national securities exchange have been continued or extended pursuant to section 12(f) of the Act shall be exempt from section 14 of the Act unless such security is also listed and registered on a national securities exchange or registered pursuant to section 12(g) of the Act.

(c)(1)   Any equity security for which unlisted trading privileges on any national securities exchange have been continued or extended pursuant to section 12(f) of the Act shall be exempt from section 16 of the Act unless such security or another equity security of the same issuer is listed and registered on a national securities exchange or registered pursuant to section 12(g) of the Act.

(2)   Any equity security for which unlisted trading privileges on any national securities exchange have been continued or extended pursuant to section 12(f) of the Act and which is not listed and registered on any other such exchange or registered pursuant to section 12(g) of the Act shall be exempt from section 16 of the Act insofar as that section would otherwise apply to any person who is directly or indirectly the beneficial owner of more than 10 percent of such security, unless another equity security of the issuer of such unlisted security is so listed or registered and such beneficial owner is a director or officer of such issuer or directly or indirectly the beneficial owner of more than 10 percent of any such listed security.

(d)   Any reference in this rule to a security registered pursuant to section 12(g) of the Act shall include, and any reference to a security not so registered shall exclude, any security as to which a registration statement pursuant to such section is at the time required to be effective.

Rule 12f–5.   Exchange Rules for Securities to Which Unlisted Trading Privileges Are Extended

A national securities exchange shall not extend unlisted trading privileges to any security unless the national securities exchange has in effect a rule or rules providing for transactions in the class or type of security to which the exchange extends unlisted trading privileges.

EXTENSIONS AND TEMPORARY EXEMPTIONS; DEFINITIONS

Rule 12g–2.   Securities Deemed to Be Registered Pursuant to Section 12(g)(1) Upon Termination of Exemption Pursuant to Section 12(g)(2)(A) or (B)

Any class of securities which would have been required to be registered pursuant to section 12(g)(1) of the Act except for the fact that it was exempt from such registration by section 12(g)(2)(A) because it was listed and registered on a national securities exchange, or by section 12(g)(2)(B) because it was issued by an investment company registered pursuant to section 8 of the Investment Company Act of 1940, shall upon the termination of the listing and registration of such class or the termination of the registration of such company and without the filing of an additional registration statement be deemed to be registered pursuant to said section 12(g)(1) if at the time of such termination

(i)   The issuer of such class of securities has elected to be regulated as a business development company pursuant to sections 55 through 65 of the Investment Company Act of 1940 and such election has not been withdrawn, or

(ii)   Securities of the class are not exempt from such registration pursuant to section 12 of the Act or rules thereunder and all securities of such class are held of record by 300 or more persons, or 1,200 or more persons in the case of a bank; a savings and loan holding company, as such term is defined in section 10 of the Home Owners' Loan Act; or a bank holding company, as such term is defined in section 2 of the Bank Holding Company Act of 1956.

Rule 12g–3.   Registration of Securities of Successor Issuers

(a)   Where in connection with a succession by merger, consolidation, exchange of securities, acquisition of assets or otherwise, securities of an issuer that are not already registered pursuant to section 12 of the Act are issued to the holders of any class of securities of another issuer that is registered pursuant to either section 12(b) or (g) of the Act, the class of securities so issued shall be deemed to be registered under the same paragraph of section 12 of the Act unless upon consummation of the succession:

(1)   Such class is exempt from such registration other than by Rule 12g3–2;

(2)   All securities of such class are held of record by fewer than 300 persons, or 1,200 persons in the case of a bank; a savings and loan holding company, as such term is defined in section 10 of the Home Owners' Loan Act (12 U.S.C. 1461); or a bank holding company, as such term is defined in section 2 of the Bank Holding Company Act of 1956 (12 U.S.C. 1841); or

(3)   The securities issued in connection with the succession were registered on Form F–8 or Form F–80 and following succession the successor would not be required to register such class of securities under section 12 of the Act but for this rule.

(b)   Where in connection with a succession by merger, consolidation, exchange of securities, acquisition of assets or otherwise, securities of an issuer that are not already registered pursuant to section 12 of the Act are issued to the holders of any class of securities of another issuer that is required to file a registration statement pursuant to either section 12(b) or (g) of the Act but has not yet done so, the duty to file such statement shall be deemed to have been assumed by the issuer of the class of securities so issued. The successor issuer shall file a registration statement pursuant to the same paragraph of section 12 of the Act with respect to such class within the period of time the predecessor issuer would have been required to file such a statement unless upon consummation of the succession:

(1)   Such class is exempt from such registration other than by Rule 12g3–2;

(2)   All securities of such class are held of record by fewer than 300 persons, or 1,200 persons in the case of a bank; a savings and loan holding company, as such term is defined in section 10 of the Home Owners' Loan Act (12 U.S.C. 1461); or a bank holding company, as such term is defined in section 2 of the Bank Holding Company Act of 1956 (12 U.S.C. 1841); or

(3)   The securities issued in connection with the succession were registered on Form F–8 or Form F–80 and following the succession the successor would not be required to register such class of securities under section 12 of the Act but for this rule.

(c)   Where in connection with a succession by merger, consolidation, exchange of securities, acquisition of assets or otherwise, securities of an issuer that are not already registered pursuant to section 12 of the Act are issued to the holders of classes of securities of two or more other issuers that are each registered pursuant to section 12 of the Act, the class of securities so issued shall be deemed to be registered under section 12 of the Act unless upon consummation of the succession:

(1)   Such class is exempt from such registration other than by Rule 12g3–2;

(2)   All securities of such class are held of record by fewer than 300 persons, or 1,200 persons in the case of a bank; a savings and loan holding company, as such term is defined in section 10 of the Home Owners' Loan Act (12 U.S.C. 1461); or a bank holding company, as such term is defined in section 2 of the Bank Holding Company Act of 1956 (12 U.S.C. 1841); or

(3)   The securities issued in connection with the succession were registered on Form F–8 or Form F–80 and following succession the successor would not be required to register such class of securities under section 12 of the Act but for this rule.

(d)   If the classes of securities issued by two or more predecessor issuers (as described in paragraph (c) of this rule) are registered under the same paragraph of section 12 of the Act, the class of securities issued by the successor issuer shall be deemed registered under the same paragraph of section 12 of the Act. If the classes of securities issued by the predecessor issuers are not registered under the same paragraph of section 12 of the Act, the class of securities issued by the successor issuer shall be deemed registered under section 12(g) of the Act.

(e)   An issuer that is deemed to have a class of securities registered pursuant to section 12 of the Act according to paragraph (a), (b), (c) or (d) of this rule shall file reports on the same forms and such class of securities shall be subject to the provisions of sections 14 and 16 of the Act to the same extent as the predecessor issuers, except as follows:

(1)   An issuer that is not a foreign issuer shall not be eligible to file on Form 20–F or to use the exemption in Rule 3a12–3.

(2)   A foreign private issuer shall be eligible to file on Form 20–F and to use the exemption in Rule 3a12–3.

(f)   An issuer that is deemed to have a class of securities registered pursuant to section 12 of the Act according to paragraphs (a), (b), (c) or (d) of this rule shall indicate in the Form 8–K report filed with the Commission in connection with the succession, pursuant to the requirements of Form 8–K, the paragraph of section 12 of the Act under which the class of securities issued by the successor issuer is deemed registered by operation of paragraphs (a), (b), (c) or (d) of this rule. If a successor issuer that is deemed registered under section 12(g) of the Act by paragraph (d) of this rule intends to list a class of securities on a national securities exchange, it must file a registration statement pursuant to section 12(b) of the Act with respect to that class of securities.

(g)   An issuer that is deemed to have a class of securities registered pursuant to section 12 of the Act according to paragraph (a), (b), (c) or (d) of this rule shall file an annual report for each fiscal year beginning on or after the date as of which the succession occurred. Annual reports shall be filed within the period specified in the appropriate form. Each such issuer shall file an annual report for each of its predecessors that had securities registered pursuant to section 12 of the Act covering the last full fiscal year of the predecessor before the registrant's succession, unless such report has been filed by the predecessor. Such annual report shall contain information that would be required if filed by the predecessor.

Rule 12g3–2. Exemptions for American Depositary Receipts and Certain Foreign Securities

(a)   Securities of any class issued by any foreign private issuer shall be exempt from section 12(g) of the Act if the class has fewer than 300 holders resident in the United States. This exemption shall continue until the next fiscal year end at which the issuer has a class of equity securities held by 300 or more persons resident in the United States. For the purpose of determining whether a security is exempt pursuant to this paragraph:

(1)   Securities held of record by persons resident in the United States shall be determined as provided in Rule 12g5–1 except that securities held of record by a broker, dealer, bank or nominee for any of them for the accounts of customers resident in the United States shall be counted as held in the United States by the number of separate accounts for which the securities are held. The issuer may rely in good faith on information as to the number of such separate accounts supplied by all owners of the class of its securities which are brokers, dealers, or banks or a nominee for any of them.

(2)   Persons in the United States who hold securities only through a Canadian Retirement Account (as that term is defined in Rule 237(a)(2) under the Securities Act of 1933), shall not be counted as holders resident in the United States.

(b)(1)   A foreign private issuer shall be exempt from the requirement to register a class of equity securities under section 12(g) of the Act if:

(i)   The issuer is not required to file or furnish reports under section 13(a) of the Act or section 15(d) of the Act;

(ii)   The issuer currently maintains a listing of the subject class of securities on one or more exchanges in a foreign jurisdiction that, either singly or together with the trading of the same class of the issuer's securities in another foreign jurisdiction, constitutes the primary trading market for those securities; and

(iii)   The issuer has published in English, on its Internet Web site or through an electronic information delivery system generally available to the public in its primary trading market, information that, since the first day of its most recently completed fiscal year, it:

(A)   Has made public or been required to make public pursuant to the laws of the country of its incorporation, organization or domicile;

(B)   Has filed or been required to file with the principal stock exchange in its primary trading market on which its securities are traded and which has been made public by that exchange; and

(C)   Has distributed or been required to distribute to its security holders.

Note 1 to Paragraph (b)(1): For the purpose of paragraph (b) of this rule, primary trading market means that at least 55 percent of the trading in the subject class of securities on a worldwide basis took place in, on or through the facilities of a securities market or markets in a single foreign jurisdiction or in no more than two foreign jurisdictions during the issuer's most recently completed fiscal year. If a foreign private issuer aggregates the trading of its subject class of securities in two foreign jurisdictions for the purpose of this paragraph, the trading for the issuer's securities in at least one of the two foreign jurisdictions must be larger than the trading in the United States for the same class of the issuer's securities. When determining an issuer's primary trading market under this paragraph, calculate average daily trading volume in the United States and on a worldwide basis as under Rule 12h–6 under the Act.

Note 2 to Paragraph (b)(1): Paragraph (b)(1)(iii) of this rule does not apply to an issuer when claiming the exemption under paragraph (b) upon the effectiveness of the termination of its registration of a class of securities under section 12(g) of the Act, or the termination of its obligation to file or furnish reports under section 15(d) of the Act.

Note 3 to Paragraph (b)(1): Compensatory stock options for which the underlying securities are in a class exempt under paragraph (b) of this rule are also exempt under that paragraph.

(2)(i)   In order to maintain the exemption under paragraph (b) of this rule, a foreign private issuer shall publish, on an ongoing basis and for each subsequent fiscal year, in English, on its Internet Web site or through an electronic information delivery system generally available to the public in its primary trading market, the information specified in paragraph (b)(1)(iii) of this rule.

(ii)   An issuer must electronically publish the information required by paragraph (b)(2) of this rule promptly after the information has been made public.

(3)(i)   The information required to be published electronically under paragraph (b) of this rule is information that is material to an investment decision regarding the subject securities, such as information concerning:

(A)   Results of operations or financial condition;

(B)   Changes in business;

(C)   Acquisitions or dispositions of assets;

(D)   The issuance, redemption or acquisition of securities;

(E)   Changes in management or control;

(F)   The granting of options or the payment of other remuneration to directors or officers; and

(G)   Transactions with directors, officers or principal security holders.

(ii)   At a minimum, a foreign private issuer shall electronically publish English translations of the following documents required to be published under paragraph (b) of this rule if in a foreign language:

(A)   Its annual report, including or accompanied by annual financial statements;

(B)   Interim reports that include financial statements;

(C)   Press releases; and

(D)   All other communications and documents distributed directly to security holders of each class of securities to which the exemption relates.

(c)   The exemption under paragraph (b) of this rule shall remain in effect until:

(1)   The issuer no longer satisfies the electronic publication condition of paragraph (b)(2) of this rule;

(2)   The issuer no longer maintains a listing of the subject class of securities on one or more exchanges in a primary trading market, as defined under paragraph (b)(1) of this rule; or

(3)   The issuer registers a class of securities under section 12 of the Act or incurs reporting obligations under section 15(d) of the Act.

(d)   Depositary shares registered on Form F–6 (§ 239.36 of this chapter), but not the underlying deposited securities, are exempt from section 12(g) of the Act under this paragraph.

Rule 12g–4. Certifications of Termination of Registration Under Section 12(g)

(a)   Termination of registration of a class of securities under section 12(g) of the Act shall take effect 90 days, or such shorter period as the Commission may determine, after the issuer certifies to the Commission on Form 15 that the class of securities is held of record by:

(1)   Fewer than 300 persons, or in the case of a bank; a savings and loan holding company, as such term is defined in section 10 of the Home Owners' Loan Act; or a bank holding company, as such term is defined in section 2 of the Bank Holding Company Act of 1956, 1,200 persons; or

(2)   Fewer than 500 persons, where the total assets of the issuer have not exceeded $10 million on the last day of each of the issuer's most recent three fiscal years.

(b)   The issuer's duty to file any reports required under section 13(a) shall be suspended immediately upon filing a certification on Form 15; *Provided, however,* That if the certification on Form 15 is subsequently withdrawn or denied, the issuer shall, within 60 days after the date of such withdrawal or denial, file with the Commission all reports which would have been required had the certification on Form 15 not been filed. If the suspension resulted from the issuer's merger into, or consolidation with, another issuer or issuers, the certification shall be filed by the successor issuer.

Rule 12g5–1. Definition of Securities "Held of Record"

(a)   For the purpose of determining whether an issuer is subject to the provisions of sections 12(g) and 15(d) of the Act, securities shall be deemed to be "held of record" by each person who is identified as the owner of such securities on records of security holders maintained by or on behalf of the issuer subject to the following:

(1)   In any case where the records of security holders have not been maintained in accordance with accepted practice, any additional person who would be identified as such an owner on such records if they had been maintained in accordance with accepted practice shall be included as a holder of record.

(2)   Except as specified in paragraph (a)(9) of this section, securities identified as held of record by a corporation, a partnership, a trust whether or not the trustees are named, or other organization shall be included as so held by one person.

(3)   Securities identified as held of record by one or more persons as trustees, executors, guardians, custodians or in other fiduciary capacities with respect to a single trust, estate or account shall be included as held of record by one person.

(4)   Securities held by two or more persons as coowners shall be included as held by one person.

(5)   Each outstanding unregistered or bearer certificate shall be included as held of record by a separate person, except to the extent that the issuer can establish that, if such securities were registered, they would be held of record, under the provisions of this rule, by a lesser number of persons.

(6)   Securities registered in substantially similar names where the issuer has reason to believe because of the address or other indications that such names represent the same person, may be included as held of record by one person.

(7)   Other than when determining compliance with Rule 257(d)(2) of the Securities Act of 1933, the definition of "held of record" shall not include securities issued in a Tier 2 offering pursuant to Regulation A by an issuer that:

(i)   Is required to file reports pursuant to Rule 257(b) of Regulation A;

(ii)   Is current in filing annual, semiannual and special financial reports pursuant to such rule as of its most recently completed fiscal year end;

(iii) Has engaged a transfer agent registered pursuant to Section 17A(c) of the Act to perform the function of a transfer agent with respect to such securities; and

(iv)   Had a public float of less than $75 million as of the last business day of its most recently completed semiannual period, computed by multiplying the aggregate worldwide number of shares of its common equity securities held by non-affiliates by the price at which such securities were last sold (or the average bid and asked prices of such securities) in the principal market for such securities or, in the event the result of such public float calculation was zero, had annual revenues of less than $50 million as of its most recently completed fiscal year. An issuer that would be required to register a class of securities under Section 12(g) of the Act as a result of exceeding the applicable threshold in this paragraph (a)(7)(iv), may continue to exclude the relevant securities from the definition of "held of record" for a transition period ending on the penultimate day of the fiscal year two years after the date it became ineligible. The transition period terminates immediately upon the failure of an issuer to timely file any periodic report due pursuant to Rule 257 of the Securities Act of 1933 at which time the issuer must file a registration statement that registers that class of securities under the Act within 120 days.

(8)(i)   For purposes of determining whether an issuer is required to register a class of equity securities with the Commission pursuant to section 12(g)(1) of the Act (15 U.S.C. 78l(g)(1)), an issuer may exclude securities:

(A)   Held by persons who received the securities pursuant to an employee compensation plan in transactions exempt from, or not subject to, the registration requirements of section 5 of the Securities Act of 1933 (15 U.S.C. 77e); and

(B)   Held by persons who received the securities in a transaction exempt from, or not subject to, the registration requirements of section 5 of the Securities Act (15 U.S.C. 77e) from the issuer, a predecessor of the issuer or an acquired company in substitution or exchange for excludable securities under paragraph (a)(8)(i)(A) of this rule, as long as the persons were eligible to receive securities pursuant to § 230.701(c) of this chapter at the time the excludable securities were originally issued to them.

(ii)   As a non-exclusive safe harbor under this paragraph (a)(8):

(A)   An issuer may deem a person to have received the securities pursuant to an employee compensation plan if such plan and the person who received the securities pursuant to the plan met the plan and participant conditions of § 230.701(c) of this chapter; and

(B)   An issuer may, solely for the purposes of Section 12(g) of the Act (15 U.S.C. 78l(g)(1)), deem the securities to have been issued in a transaction exempt from, or not subject to, the registration requirements of Section 5 of the Securities Act (15 U.S.C. 77e) if the issuer had a reasonable belief at the time of the issuance that the securities were issued in such a transaction.

(9)   For purposes of determining whether a crowdfunding issuer, as defined in § 270.3a–9(b)(1) of this chapter, or a crowdfunding vehicle, as defined in § 270.3a–9(b)(2) of this chapter, is required to register a class of equity securities with the Commission pursuant to section 12(g)(1) of the Act, both the crowdfunding issuer and the crowdfunding vehicle:

(i)   May exclude securities issued by a crowdfunding vehicle, as defined in § 270.3a–9(b)(2) of this chapter, in an offering under §§ 227.100 through 227.504 (Regulation Crowdfunding) in which the crowdfunding vehicle and the crowdfunding issuer are deemed to be co-issuers under the Securities Act (15 U.S.C. 77a *et seq.*) and that are held by natural persons; and

(ii)   Shall include securities issued by a crowdfunding vehicle, as defined in Rules 3a–9(b)(2), in an offering under Regulation Crowdfunding in which the crowdfunding vehicle and the crowdfunding issuer are deemed to be co-issuers under the Securities Act and that are held by investors that are not natural persons.

(b)   Notwithstanding paragraph (a) of this rule:

(1)   Securities held, to the knowledge of the issuer, subject to a voting trust, deposit agreement or similar arrangement shall be included as held of record by the record holders of the voting trust certificates, certificates of deposit, receipts or similar evidences of interest in such securities: *Provided, however,* That the issuer may rely in good faith on such information as is received in response to its request from a non-affiliated issuer of the certificates or evidences of interest.

(2)   Whole or fractional securities issued by a savings and loan association, building and loan association, cooperative bank, homestead association, or similar institution for the sole purpose of qualifying a borrower for membership in the issuer, and which are to be redeemed or repurchased by the issuer when the borrower's loan is terminated, shall not be included as held of record by any person.

(3)   If the issuer knows or has reason to know that the form of holding securities of record is used primarily to circumvent the provisions of section 12(g) or 15(d) of the Act, the beneficial owners of such securities shall be deemed to be the record owners thereof.

Rule 12g5–2.   Definition of "Total Assets"

For the purpose of section 12(g)(1) of the Act, the term "total assets" shall mean the total assets as shown on the issuer's balance sheet or the balance sheet of the issuer and its subsidiaries consolidated, whichever is larger, as required to be filed on the form prescribed for registration under this rule and prepared in accordance with the pertinent provisions of Regulation S–X. Where the security is a certificate of deposit, voting trust certificate, or certificate or other evidence of interest in a similar trust or agreement, the "total assets" of the issuer of the security held under the trust or agreement shall be deemed to be the "total assets" of the issuer of such certificate or evidence of interest.

Rule 12h–1.   Exemptions From Registration Under Section 12(g) of the Act

Issuers shall be exempt from the provisions of section 12(g) of the Act with respect to the following securities:

(a)   Any interest or participation in an employee stock bonus, stock purchase, profit sharing, pension, retirement, incentive, thrift, savings or similar plan which is not transferable by the holder except in the event of death or mental incompetency, or any security issued solely to fund such plans;

(b)   Any interest or participation in any common trust fund or similar fund maintained by a bank exclusively for the collective investment and reinvestment of monies contributed thereto by the bank in its capacity as a trustee, executor, administrator, or guardian. For purposes of this paragraph (b), the term "common trust fund" shall include a common trust fund which is maintained by a bank which is a member of an affiliated group, as defined in section 1504(a) of the Internal Revenue Code of 1954, and which is maintained exclusively for the investment and reinvestment of monies contributed thereto by one or more bank members of such affiliated group in the capacity of trustee, executor, administrator, or guardian; *Provided,* That:

(1)   The common trust fund is operated in compliance with the same state and Federal regulatory requirements as would apply if the bank maintaining such fund and any other contributing banks were the same entity; and

(2)   The rights of persons for whose benefit a contributing bank acts as trustee, executor, administrator or guardian would not be diminished by reason of the maintenance of such common trust fund by another bank member of the affiliated group;

(c)   Any class of equity security which would not be outstanding 60 days after a registration statement would be required to be filed with respect thereto;

(d)   Any standardized option, as that term is defined in Rule 9b–1(a)(4) of the Exchange Act, that is issued by a clearing agency registered under section 17A of the Act and traded on a national securities exchange registered pursuant to section 6(a) of the Act or on a national securities association registered pursuant to section 15A(a) of the Act;

(e)   Any security futures product that is traded on a national securities exchange registered pursuant to section 6 of the Act or on a national securities association registered pursuant to section 15A(a) of the Act and cleared by a clearing agency that is registered pursuant to section 17A of the Act or is exempt from registration under section 17A(b)(7) of the Act;

(f)(1)   Stock options issued under written compensatory stock option plans under the following conditions:

(i)   The issuer of the equity security underlying the stock options does not have a class of security registered under section 12 of the Act and is not required to file reports pursuant to section 15(d) of the Act;

(ii)   The stock options have been issued pursuant to one or more written compensatory stock option plans established by the issuer, its parents, its majority-owned subsidiaries or majority-owned subsidiaries of the issuer's parents;

NOTE to paragraph (f)(1)(ii): All stock options issued under all written compensatory stock option plans on the same class of equity security of the issuer will be considered part of the same class of equity security for purposes of the provisions of paragraph (f) of this Rule.

(iii)   The stock options are held only by those persons described in Rule 701(c) under the Securities Act or their permitted transferees as provided in paragraph (f)(1)(iv) of this Rule;

(iv)   The stock options and, prior to exercise, the shares to be issued on exercise of the stock options are restricted as to transfer by the optionholder other than to persons who are family members (as defined in Rule 701(c)(3) under the Securities Act) through gifts or domestic relations orders, or to an executor or guardian of the optionholder upon the death or disability of the optionholder until the issuer becomes subject to the reporting requirements of section 13 or 15(d) of the Act or is no longer relying on the exemption pursuant to this Rule; provided that the optionholder may transfer the stock options to the issuer, or in connection with a change of control or other acquisition transaction involving the issuer, if after such transaction the stock options no longer will be outstanding and the issuer no longer will be relying on the exemption pursuant to this Rule;

NOTE to paragraph (f)(1)(iv): For purposes of this Rule, optionholders may include any permitted transferee under paragraph (f)(1)(iv) of this Rule; provided that such permitted transferees may not further transfer the stock options.

(v)   The stock options and the shares issuable upon exercise of such stock options are restricted as to any pledge, hypothecation, or other transfer, including any short position, any "put equivalent position" (as defined in Rule 16a–1(h) of this chapter), or any "call equivalent position" (as defined in Rule 16a–1(b) of this chapter) by the optionholder prior to exercise of an option, except in the circumstances permitted in paragraph (f)(1)(iv) of this Rule, until the issuer becomes subject to the reporting requirements of section 13 or 15(d) of the Act or is no longer relying on the exemption pursuant paragraph (f)(1) of this Rule; and

NOTE to paragraphs (f)(1)(iv) and (f)(1)(v): The transferability restrictions in paragraphs (f)(1)(iv) and (f)(1)(v) of this Rule must be contained in a written compensatory stock option plan, individual written compensatory stock option agreement, other stock purchase or stockholder agreement to which the issuer and the optionholder are a signatory or party, other enforceable agreement by or against the issuer and the optionholder, or in the issuer's by-laws or certificate or articles of incorporation.

    (vi)   The issuer has agreed in the written compensatory stock option plan, the individual written compensatory stock option agreement, or another agreement enforceable against the issuer to provide the following information to optionholders once the issuer is relying on the exemption pursuant to paragraph (f)(1) of this Rule until the issuer becomes subject to the reporting requirements of section 13 or 15(d) of the Act or is no longer relying on the exemption pursuant paragraph (f)(1) of this Rule:

        The information described in Rules 701(e)(3), (4), and (5) under the Securities Act, every six months with the financial statements being not more than 180 days old and with such information provided either by physical or electronic delivery to the optionholders or by written notice to the optionholders of the availability of the information on an Internet site that may be password-protected and of any password needed to access the information.

NOTE to paragraph (f)(1)(vi): The issuer may request that the optionholder agree to keep the information to be provided pursuant to this Rule confidential. If an optionholder does not agree to keep the information to be provided pursuant to this Rule confidential, then the issuer is not required to provide the information.

    (2)   If the exemption provided by paragraph (f)(1) of this Rule ceases to be available, the issuer of the stock options that is relying on the exemption provided by this Rule must file a registration statement to register the class of stock options under section 12 of the Act within 120 calendar days after the exemption provided by paragraph (f)(1) of this Rule ceases to be available; and

    (g)(1)   Stock options issued under written compensatory stock option plans under the following conditions:

        (i)   The issuer of the equity security underlying the stock options has registered a class of security under section 12 of the Act or is required to file periodic reports pursuant to section 15(d) of the Act;

        (ii)   The stock options have been issued pursuant to one or more written compensatory stock option plans established by the issuer, its parents, its majority-owned subsidiaries or majority-owned subsidiaries of the issuer's parents;

NOTE to paragraph (g)(1)(ii): All stock options issued under all of the written compensatory stock option plans on the same class of equity security of the issuer will be considered part of the same class of equity security of the issuer for purposes of the provisions of paragraph (g) of this Rule.

        (iii)   The stock options are held only by those persons described in Rule 701(c) under the Securities Act or those persons specified in General Instruction A.1(a) of Form S–8; provided that an issuer can still rely on this exemption if there is an insignificant deviation from satisfaction of the condition in this paragraph (g)(1)(iii) and after December 7, 2007 the issuer has made a good faith and reasonable attempt to comply with the conditions of this paragraph (g)(1)(iii). For purposes of this paragraph (g)(1)(iii), an insignificant deviation exists if the number of optionholders that do not meet the condition in this paragraph (g)(1)(iii) are insignificant both as to the aggregate number of optionholders and number of outstanding stock options.

    (2)   If the exemption provided by paragraph (g)(1) of this Rule ceases to be available, the issuer of the stock options that is relying on the exemption provided by this Rule must file a registration statement to register the class of stock options or a class of security under section 12 of the Act within 60 calendar days after the exemption provided in paragraph (g)(1) of this Rule ceases to be available.

    (h)   Any security-based swap that is issued by a clearing agency registered as a clearing agency under Section 17A of the Act or exempt from registration under Section 17A of the Act pursuant to a rule, regulation, or order of the Commission in its function as a central counterparty that the Commission has determined must be cleared or that is permitted to be cleared pursuant to the clearing agency's rules, and that was sold to an eligible contract participant (as defined in Section 1a(18) of the Commodity Exchange Act) in reliance on Rule 239 under the Securities Act of 1933.

(i)   Any security-based swap offered and sold in reliance on Rule 240 under the Securities Act of 1933. This rule will expire on February 11, 2014. In such event, the Commission will publish a rule removing this paragraph (i) from 17 CFR part 240 or modifying it as appropriate.

Rule 12h–3.   Suspension of Duty to File Reports Under Section 15(d)

(a)   Subject to paragraphs (c) and (d) of this rule, the duty under section 15(d) to file reports required by section 13(a) of the Act with respect to a class of securities specified in paragraph (b) of this rule shall be suspended for such class of securities immediately upon filing with the Commission a certification on Form 15 if the issuer of such class has filed all reports required by section 13(a), without regard to Rule 12b–25, for the shorter of its most recent three fiscal years and the portion of the current year preceding the date of filing Form 15, or the period since the issuer became subject to such reporting obligation. If the certification on Form 15 is subsequently withdrawn or denied, the issuer shall, within 60 days, file with the Commission all reports which would have been required if such certification had not been filed.

(b)   The classes of securities eligible for the suspension provided in paragraph (a) of this rule are:

Note to Paragraph (b): The suspension of classes of asset-backed securities addressed in Rule 15d–22.

(1)   Any class of securities, other than any class of asset-backed securities, held of record by:

(i)   Fewer than 300 persons, or in the case of a bank; a savings and loan holding company, as such term is defined in section 10 of the Home Owners' Loan Act; or a bank holding company, as such term is defined in section 2 of the Bank Holding Company Act of 1956, 1,200 persons; or

(ii)   Fewer than 500 persons, where the total assets of the issuer have not exceeded $10 million on the last day of each of the issuer's three most recent fiscal years; and

(2)   Any class or securities deregistered pursuant to section 12(d) of the Act if such class would not thereupon be deemed registered under section 12(g) of the Act or the rules thereunder.

(c)   This rule shall not be available for any class of securities for a fiscal year in which a registration statement relating to that class becomes effective under the Securities Act of 1933, or is required to be updated pursuant to section 10(a)(3) of the Act, and, in the case of paragraph (b)(1)(ii), the two succeeding fiscal years; *Provided, however,* That this paragraph shall not apply to the duty to file reports which arises solely from a registration statement filed by an issuer with no significant assets, for the reorganization of a non-reporting issuer into a one subsidiary holding company in which equity security holders receive the same proportional interest in the holding company as they held in the non-reporting issuer, except for changes resulting from the exercise of dissenting shareholder rights under state law.

(d)   The suspension provided by this rule relates only to the reporting obligation under section 15(d) with respect to a class of securities, does not affect any other duties imposed on that class of securities, and shall continue as long as either criteria (i) or (ii) of paragraph (b)(1) is met on the first day of any subsequent fiscal year; *Provided, however,* That such criteria need not be met if the duty to file reports arises solely from a registration statement filed by an issuer with no significant assets in a reorganization of a non-reporting company into a one subsidiary holding company in which equity security holders receive the same proportional interest in the holding company as they held in the non-reporting issuer except for changes resulting from the exercise of dissenting shareholder rights under state law.

(e)   If the suspension provided by this rule is discontinued because a class of securities does not meet the eligibility criteria of paragraph (b) on the first day of an issuer's fiscal year, then the issuer shall resume periodic reporting pursuant to section 15(d) by filing an annual report on Form 10–K for its preceding fiscal year, not later than 120 days after the end of such fiscal year.

Rule 12h–4.   Exemption From Duty to File Reports Under Section 15(d)

An issuer shall be exempt from the duty under section 15(d) of the Act to file reports required by section 13(a) of the Act with respect to securities registered under the Securities Act of 1933 on Form F–7, Form F–8 or Form F–80, provided that the issuer is exempt from the obligations of section 12(g) of the Act pursuant to Rule 12g3–2(b).

Rule 12h–5. Exemption for Subsidiary Issuers of Guaranteed Securities and Subsidiary Guarantors

(a)   Any issuer of a guaranteed security, or guarantor of a security, that is permitted to omit financial statements by 210.3–10 of Regulation S–X of this chapter is exempt from the requirements of Section 13(a) or 15(d) of the Act.

(b)   Any issuer of a guaranteed security, or guarantor of a security, that would be permitted to omit financial statements by 210.3–10 of Regulation S–X of this chapter, but is required to file financial statements in accordance with the operation of 210.3–10(g) of Regulation S–X of this chapter, is exempt from the requirements of Section 13(a) or 15(d) of the Act.

Rule 12h–6. Certification by a Foreign Private Issuer Regarding the Termination of Registration of a Class of Securities Under Section 12(g) or the Duty to File Reports Under Section 13(a) or Section 15(d)

(a)   A foreign private issuer may terminate the registration of a class of securities under section 12(g) of the Act, or terminate the obligation under section 15(d) of the Act to file or furnish reports required by section 13(a) of the Act with respect to a class of equity securities, or both, after certifying to the Commission on Form 15F that:

(1)   The foreign private issuer has had reporting obligations under section 13(a) or section 15(d) of the Act for at least the 12 months preceding the filing of the Form 15F, has filed or furnished all reports required for this period, and has filed at least one annual report pursuant to section 13(a) of the Act;

(2)   The foreign private issuer's securities have not been sold in the United States in a registered offering under the Securities Act of 1933 during the 12 months preceding the filing of the Form 15F, other than securities issued:

(i)   To the issuer's employees;

(ii)   By selling security holders in non-underwritten offerings;

(iii)   Upon the exercise of outstanding rights granted by the issuer if the rights are granted pro rata to all existing security holders of the class of the issuer's securities to which the rights attach;

(iv)   Pursuant to a dividend or interest reinvestment plan; or

(v)   Upon the conversion of outstanding convertible securities or upon the exercise of outstanding transferable warrants issued by the issuer;

NOTE to Paragraph (a)(2): The exceptions in paragraphs (a)(2)(iii) through (v) do not apply to securities issued pursuant to a standby underwritten offering or other similar arrangement in the United States.

(3)   The foreign private issuer has maintained a listing of the subject class of securities for at least the 12 months preceding the filing of the Form 15F on one or more exchanges in a foreign jurisdiction that, either singly or together with the trading of the same class of the issuer's securities in another foreign jurisdiction, constitutes the primary trading market for those securities; and

(4)(i)   The average daily trading volume of the subject class of securities in the United States for a recent 12-month period has been no greater than 5 percent of the average daily trading volume of that class of securities on a worldwide basis for the same period; or

(ii)   On a date within 120 days before the filing date of the Form 15F, a foreign private issuer's subject class of equity securities is either held of record by:

(A)   Less than 300 persons on a worldwide basis; or

(B)   Less than 300 persons resident in the United States.

NOTE to Paragraph (a)(4): If an issuer's equity securities trade in the form of American Depositary Receipts in the United States, for purposes of paragraph (a)(4)(i), it must calculate the trading volume of its American Depositary Receipts in terms of the number of securities represented by those American Depositary Receipts.

(b)   A foreign private issuer must wait at least 12 months before it may file a Form 15F to terminate its section 13(a) or 15(d) reporting obligations in reliance on paragraph (a)(4)(i) of this rule if:

(1)   The issuer has delisted a class of equity securities from a national securities exchange or inter-dealer quotation system in the United States, and at the time of delisting, the average daily trading volume of that class of securities in the United States exceeded 5 percent of the average daily trading volume of that class of securities on a worldwide basis for the preceding 12 months; or

(2)   The issuer has terminated a sponsored American Depositary Receipts facility, and at the time of termination the average daily trading volume in the United States of the American Depositary Receipts exceeded 5 percent of the average daily trading volume of the underlying class of securities on a worldwide basis for the preceding 12 months.

(c)   A foreign private issuer may terminate its duty to file or furnish reports pursuant to section 13(a) or section 15(d) of the Act with respect to a class of debt securities after certifying to the Commission on Form 15F that:

(1)   The foreign private issuer has filed or furnished all reports required by section 13(a) or section 15(d) of the Act, including at least one annual report pursuant to section 13(a) of the Act; and

(2)   On a date within 120 days before the filing date of the Form 15F, the class of debt securities is either held of record by:

(i)   Less than 300 persons on a worldwide basis; or

(ii)   Less than 300 persons resident in the United States.

(d)(1)   Following a merger, consolidation, exchange of securities, acquisition of assets or otherwise, a foreign private issuer that has succeeded to the registration of a class of securities under section 12(g) of the Act of another issuer pursuant to Rule 12g–3, or to the reporting obligations of another issuer under section 15(d) of the Act pursuant to Rule 15d–5, may file a Form 15F to terminate that registration or those reporting obligations if:

(i)   Regarding a class of equity securities, the successor issuer meets the conditions under paragraph (a) of this rule; or

(ii)   Regarding a class of debt securities, the successor issuer meets the conditions under paragraph (c) of this rule.

(2)   When determining whether it meets the prior reporting requirement under paragraph (a)(1) or paragraph (c)(1) of this rule, a successor issuer may take into account the reporting history of the issuer whose reporting obligations it has assumed pursuant to Rule 12g–3 or Rule 15d–5.

(e)   *Counting method.* When determining under this rule the number of United States residents holding a foreign private issuer's equity or debt securities:

(1)(i)   Use the method for calculating record ownership Rule 12g3–2(a), except that you may limit your inquiry regarding the amount of securities represented by accounts of customers resident in the United States to brokers, dealers, banks and other nominees located in:

(A)   The United States;

(B)   The foreign private issuer's jurisdiction of incorporation, legal organization or establishment; and

(C)   The foreign private issuer's primary trading market, if different from the issuer's jurisdiction of incorporation, legal organization or establishment.

(ii)   If you aggregate the trading volume of the issuer's securities in two foreign jurisdictions for the purpose of complying with paragraph (a)(3) of this rule, you must include both of those foreign jurisdictions when conducting your inquiry under paragraph (e)(1)(i) of this rule.

(2)   If, after reasonable inquiry, you are unable without unreasonable effort to obtain information about the amount of securities represented by accounts of customers resident in the United States, for purposes of this rule, you may assume that the customers are the residents of the jurisdiction in which the nominee has its principal place of business.

(3) You must count securities as owned by United States holders when publicly filed reports of beneficial ownership or other reliable information that is provided to you indicates that the securities are held by United States residents.

(4) When calculating under this rule the number of your United States resident security holders, you may rely in good faith on the assistance of an independent information services provider that in the regular course of its business assists issuers in determining the number of, and collecting other information concerning, their security holders.

(f) *Definitions.* For the purpose of this rule:

(1) *Debt security* means any security other than an equity security as defined under Rule 3a11–1, including:

(i) Non-participatory preferred stock, which is defined as non-convertible capital stock, the holders of which are entitled to a preference in payment of dividends and in distribution of assets on liquidation, dissolution, or winding up of the issuer, but are not entitled to participate in residual earnings or assets of the issuer; and

(ii) Notwithstanding Rule 3a11–1, any debt security described in paragraph (f)(3)(i) and (ii) of this rule;

(2) *Employee* has the same meaning as the definition of employee provided in Form S–8.

(3) *Equity security* means the same as under Rule 3a11–1, but, for purposes of paragraphs (a)(3) and (a)(4)(i) of this rule, does not include:

(i) Any debt security that is convertible into an equity security, with or without consideration;

(ii) Any debt security that includes a warrant or right to subscribe to or purchase an equity security;

(iii) Any such warrant or right; or

(iv) Any put, call, straddle, or other option or privilege that gives the holder the option of buying or selling a security but does not require the holder to do so.

(4) *Foreign private issuer* has the same meaning as under Rule 3b–4.

(5) *Primary trading market* means that:

(i) At least 55 percent of the trading in a foreign private issuer's class of securities that is the subject of Form 15F took place in, on or through the facilities of a securities market or markets in a single foreign jurisdiction or in no more than two foreign jurisdictions during a recent 12-month period; and

(ii) If a foreign private issuer aggregates the trading of its subject class of securities in two foreign jurisdictions for the purpose of paragraph (a)(3) of this rule, the trading for the issuer's securities in at least one of the two foreign jurisdictions must be larger than the trading in the United States for the same class of the issuer's securities.

(6) *Recent 12-month period* means a 12-calendar-month period that ended no more than 60 days before the filing date of the Form 15F.

(g)(1) Suspension of a foreign private issuer's duty to file reports under section 13(a) or section 15(d) of the Act shall occur immediately upon filing the Form 15F with the Commission if filing pursuant to paragraph (a), (c) or (d) of this rule. If there are no objections from the Commission, 90 days, or such shorter period as the Commission may determine, after the issuer has filed its Form 15F, the effectiveness of any of the following shall occur:

(i) The termination of registration of a class of securities under section 12(g); and

(ii) The termination of a foreign private issuer's duty to file reports under section 13(a) or section 15(d) of the Act.

(2)   If the Form 15F is subsequently withdrawn or denied, the issuer shall, within 60 days after the date of the withdrawal or denial, file with or submit to the Commission all reports that would have been required had the issuer not filed the Form 15F.

(h)   As a condition to termination of registration or reporting under paragraph (a), (c) or (d) of this rule, a foreign private issuer must, either before or on the date that it files its Form 15F, publish a notice in the United States that discloses its intent to terminate its registration of a class of securities under section 12(g) of the Act, or its reporting obligations under section 13(a) or section 15(d) of the Act, or both. The issuer must publish the notice through a means reasonably designed to provide broad dissemination of the information to the public in the United States. The issuer must also submit a copy of the notice to the Commission, either under cover of a Form 6–K (17 C.F.R. § 249.306) before or at the time of filing of the Form 15F, or as an exhibit to the Form 15F.

(i)(1)   A foreign private issuer that, before the effective date of this rule, terminated the registration of a class of securities under section 12(g) of the Act or suspended its reporting obligations regarding a class of equity or debt securities under section 15(d) of the Act may file a Form 15F in order to:

(i)   Terminate under this rule the registration of a class of equity securities that was the subject of a Form 15 filed by the issuer pursuant to Rule 12g–4; or

(ii)   Terminate its reporting obligations under section 15(d) of the Act, which had been suspended by the terms of that section or by the issuer's filing of a Form 15 pursuant to Rule 12h–3, regarding a class of equity or debt securities.

(2)   In order to be eligible to file a Form 15F under this paragraph:

(i)   If a foreign private issuer terminated the registration of a class of securities pursuant to Rule 12g–4 or suspended its reporting obligations pursuant to Rule 12h–3 or section 15(d) of the Act regarding a class of equity securities, the issuer must meet the requirements under paragraph (a)(3) and paragraph (a)(4)(i) or (a)(4)(ii) of this rule; or

(ii)   If a foreign private issuer suspended its reporting obligations pursuant to Rule 12h–3 or section 15(d) of the Act regarding a class of debt securities, the issuer must meet the requirements under paragraph (c)(2) of this rule.

(3)(i)   If the Commission does not object, 90 days after the filing of a Form 15F under this paragraph, or such shorter period as the Commission may determine, the effectiveness of any of the following shall occur:

(A)   The termination under this rule of the registration of a class of equity securities, which was the subject of a Form 15 filed pursuant to Rule 12g–4, and the duty to file reports required by section 13(a) of the Act regarding that class of securities; or

(B)   The termination of a foreign private issuer's reporting obligations under section 15(d) of the Act, which had previously been suspended by the terms of that section or by the issuer's filing of a Form 15 pursuant to Rule 12h–3, regarding a class of equity or debt securities.

(ii)   If the Form 15F is subsequently withdrawn or denied, the foreign private issuer shall, within 60 days after the date of the withdrawal or denial, file with or submit to the Commission all reports that would have been required had the issuer not filed the Form 15F.

Note to rule 12h–6: The suspension of classes of asset-backed securities is addressed in Rule 15d–22.

Rule 12h–7.   Exemption for Issuers of Securities That are Subject to Insurance Regulation

An issuer shall be exempt from the duty under section 15(d) of the Act to file reports required by section 13(a) of the Act with respect to securities registered under the Securities Act of 1933, provided that:

(a)   The issuer is a corporation subject to the supervision of the insurance commissioner, bank commissioner, or any agency or officer performing like functions, of any State;

(b)   The securities do not constitute an equity interest in the issuer and are either subject to regulation under the insurance laws of the domiciliary State of the issuer or are guarantees of securities that are subject to regulation under the insurance laws of that jurisdiction;

(c)　The issuer files an annual statement of its financial condition with, and is supervised and its financial condition examined periodically by, the insurance commissioner, bank commissioner, or any agency or officer performing like functions, of the issuer's domiciliary State;

(d)　The securities are not listed, traded, or quoted on an exchange, alternative trading system, interdealer quotation system, electronic communications network, or any other similar system, network, or publication for trading or quoting;

(e)　The issuer takes steps reasonably designed to ensure that a trading market for the securities does not develop, including, except to the extent prohibited by the law of any State or by action of the insurance commissioner, bank commissioner, or any agency or officer performing like functions of any State, requiring written notice to, and acceptance by, the issuer prior to any assignment or other transfer of the securities and reserving the right to refuse assignments or other transfers at any time on a non-discriminatory basis; and

(f)　The prospectus for the securities contains a statement indicating that the issuer is relying on the exemption provided by this rule.

REGULATION 13A—REPORTS OF ISSUERS OF SECURITIES REGISTERED PURSUANT TO SECTION 12

Rule 13a–1.　Requirements of Annual Reports

Every issuer having securities registered pursuant to section 12 of the Act shall file an annual report on the appropriate form authorized or prescribed therefor for each fiscal year after the last full fiscal year for which financial statements were filed in its registration statement. Annual reports shall be filed within the period specified in the appropriate form.

Rule 13a–2.　[Reserved]

Rule 13a–3.　Reporting by Form 40–F Registrant

A registrant that is eligible to use Forms 40–F and 6–K and files reports in accordance therewith shall be deemed to satisfy the requirements of Regulation 13A.

Rule 13a–10.　Transition Reports

(a)　Every issuer that changes its fiscal closing date shall file a report covering the resulting transition period between the closing date of its most recent fiscal year and the opening date of its new fiscal year; *Provided, however,* that an issuer shall file an annual report for any fiscal year that ended before the date on which the issuer determined to change its fiscal year end. In no event shall the transition report cover a period of 12 or more months.

(b)　The report pursuant to this rule shall be filed for the transition period not more than the number of days specified in paragraph (j) of this rule after either the close of the transition period or the date of the determination to change the fiscal closing date, whichever is later. The report shall be filed on the form appropriate for annual reports of the issuer, shall cover the period from the close of the last fiscal year end and shall indicate clearly the period covered. The financial statements for the transition period filed therewith shall be audited. Financial statements, which may be unaudited, shall be filed for the comparable period of the prior year, or a footnote, which may be unaudited, shall state for the comparable period of the prior year, revenues, gross profits, income taxes, income or loss from continuing operations and net income or loss. The effects of any discontinued operations as classified under the provisions of generally accepted accounting principles also shall be shown, if applicable. Per share data based upon such income or loss and net income or loss shall be presented in conformity with applicable accounting standards. Where called for by the time span to be covered, the comparable period financial statements or footnote shall be included in subsequent filings.

(c)　If the transition period covers a period of less than six months, in lieu of the report required by paragraph (b) of this rule, a report may be filed for the transition period on Form 10–Q not more than the number of days specified in paragraph (j) of this rule after either the close of the transition period or the date of the determination to change the fiscal closing date, whichever is later. The report on Form 10–Q shall cover the period from the close of the last fiscal year end and shall indicate clearly the period covered. The financial statements filed therewith need not be audited but, if they are not audited, the issuer shall file with the first annual report for the newly adopted fiscal year separate audited statements of income and cash flows covering the transition period. The notes to financial statements for the transition period included in such first annual report may be integrated with the notes to financial statements for the full fiscal period. A separate audited balance sheet as of the end of the transition period shall be filed in the annual report only if the audited balance sheet as of the end of the fiscal year prior to the transition period is not filed. Schedules need not be filed in transition reports on Form 10–Q.

(d)   Notwithstanding the foregoing in paragraphs (a), (b), and (c) of this rule, if the transition period covers a period of one month or less, the issuer need not file a separate transition report if either:

     (1)   The first report required to be filed by the issuer for the newly adopted fiscal year after the date of the determination to change the fiscal year end is an annual report, and that report covers the transition period as well as the fiscal year; or

     (2)(i)   The issuer files with the first annual report for the newly adopted fiscal year separate audited statements of income and cash flows covering the transition period; and

     (ii)   The first report required to be filed by the issuer for the newly adopted fiscal year after the date of the determination to change the fiscal year end is a quarterly report on Form 10–Q; and

     (iii)   Information on the transition period is included in the issuer's quarterly report on Form 10–Q for the first quarterly period (except the fourth quarter) of the newly adopted fiscal year that ends after the date of the determination to change the fiscal year. The information covering the transition period required by Part II and Item 2 of Part I may be combined with the information regarding the quarter. However, the financial statements required by Part I, which may be unaudited, shall be furnished separately for the transition period.

(e)   Every issuer required to file quarterly reports on Form 10–Q pursuant to Rule 13a–13 of this chapter that changes its fiscal year end shall:

     (1)   File a quarterly report on Form 10–Q within the time period specified in General Instruction A.1. to that form for any quarterly period (except the fourth quarter) of the old fiscal year that ends before the date on which the issuer determined to change its fiscal year end, except that the issuer need not file such quarterly report if the date on which the quarterly period ends also is the date on which the transition period ends;

     (2)   File a quarterly report on Form 10–Q within the time specified in General Instruction A.1. to that form for each quarterly period of the old fiscal year within the transition period. In lieu of a quarterly report for any quarter of the old fiscal year within the transition period, the issuer may file a quarterly report on Form 10–Q for any period of three months within the transition period that coincides with a quarter of the newly adopted fiscal year if the quarterly report is filed within the number of days specified in paragraph (j) of this rule after the end of such three month period, provided the issuer thereafter continues filing quarterly reports on the basis of the quarters of the newly adopted fiscal year;

     (3)   Commence filing quarterly reports for the quarters of the new fiscal year no later than the quarterly report for the first quarter of the new fiscal year that ends after the date on which the issuer determined to change the fiscal year end; and

     (4)   Unless such information is or will be included in the transition report, or the first annual report on Form 10–K for the newly adopted fiscal year, include in the initial quarterly report on Form 10–Q for the newly adopted fiscal year information on any period beginning on the first day subsequent to the period covered by the issuer's final quarterly report on Form 10–Q or annual report on Form 10–K for the old fiscal year. The information covering such period required by Part II and Item 2 of Part I may be combined with the information regarding the quarter. However, the financial statements required by Part I, which may be unaudited, shall be furnished separately for such period.

NOTE to paragraphs (c) and (e): If it is not practicable or cannot be cost-justified to furnish in a transition report on Form 10–Q or a quarterly report for the newly adopted fiscal year financial statements for corresponding periods of the prior year where required, financial statements may be furnished for the quarters of the preceding fiscal year that most nearly are comparable if the issuer furnishes an adequate discussion of seasonal and other factors that could affect the comparability of information or trends reflected, an assessment of the comparability of the data, and a representation as to the reason recasting has not been undertaken.

(f)   Every successor issuer with securities registered under section 12 of the Act that has a different fiscal year from that of its predecessor(s) shall file a transition report pursuant to this rule, containing the required information about each predecessor, for the transition period, if any, between the close of the fiscal year covered by the last annual report of each predecessor and the date of succession. The report shall be filed for the transition period on the form appropriate for annual reports of the issuer not more than the number of days specified in paragraph (j) of this rule after the date of the succession, with financial statements in conformity with the requirements set forth in paragraph (b) of this rule. If the transition period covers a period of less than six months, in lieu of a transition report on the form appropriate for the issuer's annual reports, the report may be filed for the transition period on Form 10–Q and Form 10–QSB not more than the number of days specified in paragraph (j) of this rule after the date of the succession, with financial statements in conformity with the requirements set forth in paragraph (c) of this rule. Notwithstanding the foregoing, if the transition period covers a period of one month or less, the successor issuer need not file a separate transition report if the information is reported by the successor issuer in conformity with the requirements set forth in paragraph (d) of this rule.

(g)(1)   Paragraphs (a) through (f) of this rule shall not apply to foreign private issuers.

(2)   Every foreign private issuer that changes its fiscal closing date shall file a report covering the resulting transition period between the closing date of its most recent fiscal year and the opening date of its new fiscal year. In no event shall a transition report cover a period longer than 12 months.

(3)   The report for the transition period shall be filed on Form 20–F responding to all items to which such issuer is required to respond when Form 20–F is used as an annual report. The financial statements for the transition period filed therewith shall be audited. The report shall be filed within four months after either the close of the transition period or the date on which the issuer made the determination to change the fiscal closing date, whichever is later.

(i)   Within six months after either the close of the transition period or the date on which the issuer made the determination to change the fiscal closing date, whichever is later, for new fiscal years ending before December 15, 2011; and

(ii)   Within four months after either the close of the transition period or the date on which the issuer made the determination to change the fiscal closing date, whichever is later, for new fiscal years ending on or after December 15, 2011.

(4)   If the transition period covers a period of six or fewer months, in lieu of the report required by paragraph (g)(3) of this rule, a report for the transition period may be filed on Form 20–F responding to Items 5, 8.A.7, 13, 14, and 17 or 18 within three months after either the close of the transition period or the date on which the issuer made the determination to change the fiscal closing date, whichever is later. The financial statements required by either Item 17 or Item 18 shall be furnished for the transition period. Such financial statements may be unaudited and condensed as permitted in Article 10 of Regulation S–X, but if the financial statements are unaudited and condensed, the issuer shall file with the first annual report for the newly adopted fiscal year separate audited statements of income and cash flows covering the transition period.

(5)   Notwithstanding the foregoing in paragraphs (g)(2), (g)(3), and (g)(4) of this rule, if the transition period covers a period of one month or less, a foreign private issuer need not file a separate transition report if the first annual report for the newly adopted fiscal year covers the transition period as well as the fiscal year.

(h)   The provisions of this rule shall not apply to investment companies required to file reports pursuant to Rule 30a–1 under the Investment Company Act of 1940.

(i)   No filing fee shall be required for a transition report filed pursuant to this rule.

(j)(1)   For transition reports to be filed on the form appropriate for annual reports of the issuer, the number of days shall be:

(i)   60 days (75 days for fiscal years ending before December 15, 2006) for large accelerated filers (as defined in Rule12b–2);

(ii)   75 days for accelerated filers (as defined in Rule 12b–2); and

(iii) 90 days for all other issuers; and

(2)   For transition reports to be filed on Form 10–Q the number of days shall be:

(i)   40 days for large accelerated filers and accelerated filers (as defined in Rule 12b–2); and

(ii)   45 days for all other issuers.

(k)(1)   Paragraphs (a) through (g) of this rule shall not apply to asset-backed issuers.

(2)   Every asset-backed issuer that changes its fiscal closing date shall file a report covering the resulting transition period between the closing date of its most recent fiscal year and the opening date of its new fiscal year. In no event shall a transition report cover a period longer than 12 months.

(3)   The report for the transition period shall be filed on Form 10–K responding to all items to which such asset-backed issuer is required to respond pursuant to General Instruction J. of Form 10–K. Such report shall be filed within 90 days after the later of either the close of the transition period or the date on which the issuer made the determination to change the fiscal closing date.

(4)   Notwithstanding the foregoing in paragraphs (k)(2) and (k)(3) of this rule, if the transition period covers a period of one month or less, an asset-backed issuer need not file a separate transition report if the first annual report for the newly adopted fiscal year covers the transition period as well as the fiscal year.

(5)   Any obligation of the asset-backed issuer to file distribution reports pursuant to Rule 13a–17 will continue to apply regardless of a change in the asset-backed issuer's fiscal closing date.

NOTE 1: In addition to the report or reports required to be filed pursuant to this rule, every issuer, except a foreign private issuer or an investment company required to file reports pursuant to Rule 30a–1 under the Investment Company Act of 1940, that changes its fiscal closing date is required to file a Form 8–K report that includes the information required by Item 5.03 of Form 8–K within the period specified in General Instruction B.1. to that form.

NOTE 2: The report or reports to be filed pursuant to this rule must include the certification required by Rule 13a–14.

Rule 13a–11. Current Reports on Form 8–K

(a)   Except as provided in paragraph (b) of this rule, every registrant subject to Rule 13a–1 shall file a current report on Form 8–K within the period specified in that form unless substantially the same information as that required by Form 8–K has been previously reported by the registrant.

(b)   This rule shall not apply to foreign governments, foreign private issuers required to make reports on Form 6–K pursuant to Rule 13a–16, issuers of American Depositary Receipts for securities of any foreign issuer, or investment companies required to file reports pursuant to Rule 30a–1 of this chapter under the Investment Company Act of 1940, except where such an investment company is required to file:

(1)   Notice of a blackout period pursuant to § 245.104 of this chapter;

(2)   Disclosure pursuant to Instruction 2 to Rule 14a–11(b)(1) of information concerning outstanding shares and voting; or

(3)   Disclosure pursuant to Instruction 2 to Rule 14a–11(b)(10) of the date by which a nominating shareholder or nominating shareholder group must submit the notice required pursuant to Rule 14a–11(b)(10).

(c)   No failure to file a report on Form 8–K that is required solely pursuant to Item 1.01, 1.02, 2.03, 2.04, 2.05, 2.06, 4.02(a), 502(e) or 6.03 of Form 8–K shall be deemed to be a violation of section 10(b) and Rule 10b–5.

Rule 13a–13. Quarterly Reports on Form 10–Q

(a)   Except as provided in paragraphs (b) and (c) of this rule, every issuer that has securities registered pursuant to section 12 of the Act and is required to file annual reports pursuant to section 13 of the Act, and has filed or intends to file such reports on Form 10–K shall file a quarterly report on Form 10–Q within the period specified in General Instruction A.1. to that form for each of the first three quarters of each fiscal year of the issuer, commencing with the first fiscal quarter following the most recent fiscal year for which full financial statements were included in the registration statement, or, if the registration statement included financial statements for an interim period subsequent to the most recent fiscal year end meeting the requirements of Article 10 of Regulation S–X and Rule 8–03 of Regulation S–X for smaller reporting companies, for the first fiscal quarter subsequent to the quarter reported upon in the registration statement. The first quarterly report of the issuer shall be filed either within 45 days after the effective date of the registration statement or on or before the date on which such report would have been required to be filed if the issuer has been required to file reports on Form 10–Q as of its last fiscal quarter, whichever is later.

(b)   The provisions of this rule shall not apply to the following issuers:

(1)   Investment companies required to file reports pursuant to Rule 30a–1;

(2)   Foreign private issuers required to file reports pursuant to Rule 13a–16; and

(3)   Asset-backed issuers required to file reports pursuant to Rule 13a–17 of the Securities Exchange Act of 1934.

(c)   Part I of the quarterly report on Form 10–Q need not be filed by:

(1)   Mutual life insurance companies; or

(2)   Mining companies not in the production stage but engaged primarily in the exploration for the development of mineral deposits other than oil, gas or coal, if all the following conditions are met:

(i)   The registrant has not been in production during the current fiscal year or the two years immediately prior thereto: except that being in production for an aggregate period of not more than eight months over the three-year period shall not be a violation of this condition.

(ii)   Receipts from the sale of mineral products or from the operations of mineral producing properties by the registrant and its subsidiaries combined have not exceeded $500,000 in any of the most recent six years and have not aggregated more than $1,500,000 in the most recent six fiscal years.

(d)   Notwithstanding the foregoing provisions of this rule, the financial information required by Part I of Form 10–Q shall not be deemed to be "filed" for the purpose of section 18 of the Act or otherwise subject to the liabilities of that section of the Act, but shall be subject to all other provisions of the Act.

Rule 13a–14. Certification of Disclosure in Annual and Quarterly Reports

(a)   Each report, including transition reports, filed on Form 10–Q, Form 10–K, Form 20–F or Form 40–F under section 13(a) of the Act, other than a report filed by an Asset-Backed Issuer (as defined in Item 1101 of Regulation AB), or a report on Form 20–F filed under Rule 13a–19, must include certifications in the form specified in the applicable exhibit filing requirements of such report and such certifications must be filed as an exhibit to such report. Each principal executive and principal financial officer of the issuer, or persons performing similar functions, at the time of filing of the report must sign a certification. The principal executive and principal financial officers of an issuer may omit the portion of the introductory language in paragraph 4 as well as language in paragraph 4(b) of the certification that refers to the certifying officers' responsibility for designing, establishing and maintaining internal control over financial reporting for the issuer until the issuer becomes subject to the internal control over financial reporting requirements in Rule 13a–15 or Rule 15d–15.

(b)   Each periodic report containing financial statements filed by an issuer pursuant to section 13(a) of the Act must be accompanied by the certifications required by Section 1350 of Chapter 63 of Title 18 of the United States Code and such certifications must be furnished as an exhibit to such report as specified in the applicable exhibit requirements for such report. Each principal executive and principal financial officer of the issuer (or equivalent thereof) must sign a certification. This requirement may be satisfied by a single certification signed by an issuer's principal executive and principal financial officers.

(c)   A person required to provide the certification specified in paragraph (a), (b) or (d) of this Rule may not have the certification signed on his or her behalf pursuant to a power of attorney or other form of confirming authority.

(d)   Each annual report and transition report filed on Form 10–K by an asset-backed issuer under section 13(a) of the Act must include a certification in the form specified in the applicable exhibit filing requirements of such report and such certification must be filed as an exhibit to such report. Terms used in paragraphs (d) and (e) of this rule have the same meaning as in Item 1101 of Regulation AB.

(e)   With respect to asset-backed issuers, the certification required by paragraph (d) of this rule must be signed by either:

(1)   The senior officer in charge of securitization of the depositor if the depositor is signing the report; or

(2)   The senior officer in charge of the servicing function of the servicer if the servicer is signing the report on behalf of the issuing entity. If multiple servicers are involved in servicing the pool assets, the senior officer in charge of the servicing function of the master servicer (or entity performing the equivalent function) must sign if a representative of the servicer is to sign the report on behalf of the issuing entity.

(f)   The certification requirements of this rule do not apply to an Interactive Data File, as defined in Rule 11 of Regulation S–T.

Rule 13a–15. Controls and Procedures

(a)   Every issuer that has a class of securities registered pursuant to section 12 of the Act, other than an Asset-Backed Issuer (as defined in Item 1101 of Regulation S–K), a small business investment company registered on Form N–5, or a unit investment trust as defined in section 4(2) of the Investment Company Act of 1940, must maintain disclosure controls and procedures (as defined in paragraph (e) of this rule) and, if the issuer either had been required to file an annual report pursuant to section 13(a) or 15(d) of the Act for the prior fiscal year or had filed an annual report with the Commission for the prior fiscal year, internal control over financial reporting (as defined in paragraph (f) of this rule).

(b)   Each such issuer's management must evaluate, with the participation of the issuer's principal executive and principal financial officers, or persons performing similar functions, the effectiveness of the issuer's disclosure controls and procedures, as of the end of each fiscal quarter, except that management must perform this evaluation:

(1)   In the case of a foreign private issuer (as defined in Rule 3b–4) as of the end of each fiscal year; and

(2)   In the case of an investment company registered under section 8 of the Investment Company Act of 1940, within the 90-day period prior to the filing date of each report requiring certification under Rule 30a–2 of the Investment Company Act of 1940.

(c)   The management of each such issuer that either had been required to file an annual report pursuant to section 13(a) or 15(d) of the Act for the prior fiscal year or previously had filed an annual report with the Commission for the prior fiscal year, other than an investment company registered under section 8 of the Investment Company Act of 1940, must evaluate, with the participation of the issuer's principal executive and principal financial officers, or persons performing similar functions, the effectiveness, as of the end of each fiscal year, of the issuer's internal control over financial reporting. The framework on which management's evaluation of the issuer's internal control over financial reporting is based must be a suitable, recognized control framework that is established by a body or group that has followed due-process procedures, including the broad distribution of the framework for public comment. Although there are many different ways to conduct an evaluation of the effectiveness of internal control over financial reporting to meet the requirements of this paragraph, an evaluation that is conducted in accordance with the interpretive guidance issued by the Commission in Release No. 34–55929 will satisfy the evaluation required by this paragraph.

(d)   The management of each such issuer that either had been required to file an annual report pursuant to section 13(a) or 15(d) of the Act for the prior fiscal year or had filed an annual report with the Commission for the prior fiscal year, other than an investment company registered under section 8 of the Investment Company Act of 1940, must evaluate, with the participation of the issuer's principal executive and principal financial officers, or persons performing similar functions, any change in the issuer's internal control over financial reporting, that occurred during each of the issuer's fiscal quarters, or fiscal year in the case of a foreign private issuer, that has materially affected, or is reasonably likely to materially affect, the issuer's internal control over financial reporting.

(e)   For purposes of this rule, the term disclosure controls and procedures means controls and other procedures of an issuer that are designed to ensure that information required to be disclosed by the issuer in the reports that it files or submits under the Act is recorded, processed, summarized and reported, within the time periods specified in the Commission's rules and forms. Disclosure controls and procedures include, without limitation, controls and procedures designed to ensure that information required to be disclosed by an issuer in the reports that it files or submits under the Act is accumulated and communicated to the issuer's management, including its principal executive and principal financial officers, or persons performing similar functions, as appropriate to allow timely decisions regarding required disclosure.

(f)   The term internal control over financial reporting is defined as a process designed by, or under the supervision of, the issuer's principal executive and principal financial officers, or persons performing similar functions, and effected by the issuer's board of directors, management and other personnel, to provide reasonable assurance regarding the reliability of financial reporting and the preparation of financial statements for external purposes in accordance with generally accepted accounting principles and includes those policies and procedures that:

(1)   Pertain to the maintenance of records that in reasonable detail accurately and fairly reflect the transactions and dispositions of the assets of the issuer;

(2)   Provide reasonable assurance that transactions are recorded as necessary to permit preparation of financial statements in accordance with generally accepted accounting principles, and that receipts and expenditures of the issuer are being made only in accordance with authorizations of management and directors of the issuer; and

(3)   Provide reasonable assurance regarding prevention or timely detection of unauthorized acquisition, use or disposition of the issuer's assets that could have a material effect on the financial statements.

Rule 13a-16. Reports of Foreign Private Issuers on Form 6-K

(a)   Every foreign private issuer which is subject to Rule 13a-1 shall make reports on Form 6-K, except that this rule shall not apply to:

(1)   Investment companies required to file reports pursuant to Rule 30a-1; or

(2)   Issuers of American Depositary Receipts for securities of any foreign issuer;

(3)   Issuers filing periodic reports on Forms 10-K, 10-Q, and 8-K; or

(4)   Asset-backed issuers, as defined in Item 1101 of Regulation S-K.

(b)   Such reports shall be transmitted promptly after the information required by Form 6-K is made public by the issuer, by the country of its domicile or under the laws of which it was incorporated or organized, or by a foreign securities exchange with which the issuer has filed the information.

(c)   Reports furnished pursuant to this rule shall not be deemed to be "filed" for the purpose of section 18 of the Act or otherwise subject to the liabilities of that section.

Rule 13a-17. Reports of Asset-Backed Issuers on Form 10-D

Every asset-backed issuer subject to Rule 13a-1 of the Securities Exchange Act of 1934 shall make reports on Form 10-D. Such reports shall be filed within the period specified in Form 10-D.

Rule 13a–18. Compliance With Servicing Criteria for Asset-Backed Securities

(a)   This rule applies to every class of asset-backed securities subject to the reporting requirements of section 13(a) of the Act. Terms used in this rule have the same meaning as in Item 1101 of Regulation AB.

(b)   Reports on assessments of compliance with servicing criteria for asset-backed securities required. With regard to a class of asset-backed securities subject to the reporting requirements of section 13(a) of the Act, the annual report on Form 10–K for such class must include from each party participating in the servicing function a report regarding its assessment of compliance with the servicing criteria specified in paragraph (d) of Item 1122 of Regulation AB, as of and for the period ending the end of each fiscal year, with respect to asset-backed securities transactions taken as a whole involving the party participating in the servicing function and that are backed by the same asset type backing the class of asset-backed securities (including the asset-backed securities transaction that is to be the subject of the report on Form 10–K for that fiscal year).

(c)   Attestation reports on assessments of compliance with servicing criteria for asset-backed securities required. With respect to each report included pursuant to paragraph (b) of this rule, the annual report on Form 10–K must also include a report by a registered public accounting firm that attests to, and reports on, the assessment made by the asserting party. The attestation report on assessment of compliance with servicing criteria for asset-backed securities must be made in accordance with standards for attestation engagements issued or adopted by the Public Company Accounting Oversight Board.

Note to Rule 13a–18. If multiple parties are participating in the servicing function, a separate assessment report and attestation report must be included for each party participating in the servicing function. A party participating in the servicing function means any entity (e.g., master servicer, primary servicers, trustees) that is performing activities that address the criteria in paragraph (d) of Item 1122 of Regulation AB, unless such entity's activities relate only to 5% or less of the pool assets.

Rule 13a–19. Reports by Shell Companies on Form 20–F

Every foreign private issuer that was a shell company, other than a business combination related shell company, immediately before a transaction that causes it to cease to be a shell company shall, within four business days of completion of that transaction, file a report on Form 20–F containing the information that would be required if the issuer were filing a form for registration of securities on Form 20–F to register under the Act all classes of the issuer's securities subject to the reporting requirements of section 13 or section 15(d) of the Act upon consummation of the transaction, with such information reflecting the registrant and its securities upon consummation of the transaction.

Rule 13a–20. Plain English Presentation of Specified Information

(a)   Any information included or incorporated by reference in a report filed under section 13(a) of the Act that is required to be disclosed pursuant to Item 402, 403, 404 or 407 of Regulation S–K must be presented in a clear, concise and understandable manner. You must prepare the disclosure using the following standards:

(1)   Present information in clear, concise sections, paragraphs and sentences;

(2)   Use short sentences;

(3)   Use definite, concrete, everyday words;

(4)   Use the active voice;

(5)   Avoid multiple negatives;

(6)   Use descriptive headings and subheadings;

(7)   Use a tabular presentation or bullet lists for complex material, wherever possible;

(8)   Avoid legal jargon and highly technical business and other terminology;

(9)   Avoid frequent reliance on glossaries or defined terms as the primary means of explaining information. Define terms in a glossary or other section of the document only if the meaning is unclear from the context. Use a glossary only if it facilitates understanding of the disclosure; and

(10) In designing the presentation of the information you may include pictures, logos, charts, graphs and other design elements so long as the design is not misleading and the required information is clear. You are encouraged to use tables, schedules, charts and graphic illustrations that present relevant data in an understandable manner, so long as such presentations are consistent with applicable disclosure requirements and consistent with other information in the document. You must draw graphs and charts to scale. Any information you provide must not be misleading.

(b)   Reserved.

Note to Rule 13a–20. In drafting the disclosure to comply with this rule, you should avoid the following:

1.   Legalistic or overly complex presentations that make the substance of the disclosure difficult to understand;

2.   Vague "boilerplate" explanations that are imprecise and readily subject to different interpretations;

3.   Complex information copied directly from legal documents without any clear and concise explanation of the provision(s); and

4.   Disclosure repeated in different sections of the document that increases the size of the document but does not enhance the quality of the information.

REGULATION 13B–2—MAINTENANCE OF RECORDS AND PREPARATION OF REQUIRED REPORTS

Rule 13b2–1. Falsification of Accounting Records

No person shall directly or indirectly, falsify or cause to by falsified, any book, record or account subject to section 13(b)(2)(A) of the Act.

Rule 13b2–2. Representations and Conduct in Connection With the Preparation of Required Reports and Documents

(a)   No director or officer of an issuer shall, directly or indirectly:

(1)   Make or cause to be made a materially false or misleading statement to an accountant in connection with; or

(2)   Omit to state, or cause another person to omit to state, any material fact necessary in order to make statements made, in light of the circumstances under which such statements were made, not misleading, to an accountant in connection with:

(i)   Any audit, review or examination of the financial statements of the issuer required to be made pursuant to this subpart; or

(ii)   The preparation or filing of any document or report required to be filed with the Commission pursuant to this subpart or otherwise.

(b)(1)   No officer or director of an issuer, or any other person acting under the direction thereof, shall directly or indirectly take any action to coerce, manipulate, mislead, or fraudulently influence any independent public or certified public accountant engaged in the performance of an audit or review of the financial statements of that issuer that are required to be filed with the Commission pursuant to this subpart or otherwise if that person knew or should have known that such action, if successful, could result in rendering the issuer's financial statements materially misleading.

(2)   For purposes of paragraphs (b)(1) and (c)(2) of this rule, actions that, "if successful, could result in rendering the issuer's financial statements materially misleading" include, but are not limited to, actions taken at any time with respect to the professional engagement period to coerce, manipulate, mislead, or fraudulently influence an auditor:

(i)   To issue or reissue a report on an issuer's financial statements that is not warranted in the circumstances (due to material violations of generally accepted accounting principles, the standards of the PCAOB, or other professional or regulatory standards);

(ii)   Not to perform audit, review or other procedures required by the standards of the PCAOB or other professional standards;

(iii)   Not to withdraw an issued report; or

(iv)   Not to communicate matters to an issuer's audit committee.

(c)   In addition, in the case of an investment company registered under section 8 of the Investment Company Act of 1940, or a business development company as defined in section 2(a)(48) of the Investment Company Act of 1940, no officer or director of the company's investment adviser, sponsor, depositor, trustee, or administrator (or, in the case of paragraph (c)(2) of this rule, any other person acting under the direction thereof) shall, directly or indirectly:

(1)(i)   Make or cause to be made a materially false or misleading statement to an accountant in connection with; or

(ii)   Omit to state, or cause another person to omit to state, any material fact necessary in order to make statements made, in light of the circumstances under which such statements were made, not misleading to an accountant in connection with:

(A)   Any audit, review, or examination of the financial statements of the investment company required to be made pursuant to this subpart; or

(B)   The preparation or filing of any document or report required to be filed with the Commission pursuant to this subpart or otherwise; or

(2)   Take any action to coerce, manipulate, mislead, or fraudulently influence any independent public or certified public accountant engaged in the performance of an audit or review of the financial statements of that investment company that are required to be filed with the Commission pursuant to this subpart or otherwise if that person knew or should have known that such action, if successful, could result in rendering the investment company's financial statements materially misleading.

REGULATIONS 13D-G

Rule 13d-1.   Filing of Schedules 13D and 13G

(a)   Any person who, after acquiring directly or indirectly the beneficial ownership of any equity security of a class which is specified in paragraph (i) of this rule, is directly or indirectly the beneficial owner of more than 5 percent of such class shall, within 10 days after such acquisition, file with the Commission, a statement containing the information required by Schedule 13D.

(b)(1)   A person who would otherwise be obligated under paragraph (a) of this rule to file a statement on Schedule 13D may, in lieu thereof, file with the Commission, a short form statement on Schedule 13G *Provided* That:

(i)   Such person has acquired such securities in the ordinary course of his business and not with the purpose nor with the effect of changing or influencing the control of the issuer, nor in connection with or as a participant in any transaction having such purpose or effect, including any transaction subject to Rule 13d-3(b), other than activities solely in connection with a nomination under Rule 14a-11; and

(ii)   Such person is:

(A)   A broker or dealer registered under section 15 of the Act;

(B)   A bank as defined in section 3(a)(6) of the Act;

(C)   An insurance company as defined in section 3(a)(19) of the Act;

(D)   An investment company registered under section 8 of the Investment Company Act of 1940;

(E)   An investment adviser registered under section 203 of the Investment Advisers Act of 1940 or under the laws of any state;

    (F) An employee benefit plan as defined in section 3(3) of the Employee Retirement Income Security Act of 1974, as amended, ("ERISA") that is subject to the provisions of ERISA or any such plan that is not subject to ERISA that is maintained primarily for the benefit of the employees of a state or local government or instrumentality, or an endowment fund;

    (G) A parent holding company or control person, provided the aggregate amount held directly by the parent or control person, and directly and indirectly by their subsidiaries or affiliates that are not persons specified in Rule 13d–1(b)(1)(ii)(A) through (J), does not exceed one percent of the securities of the subject class;

    (H) A savings association as defined in section 3(b) of the Federal Deposit Insurance Act;

    (I) A church plan that is excluded from the definition of an investment company under section 3(c)(14) of the Investment Company Act of 1940; and

    (J) A non-U.S. institution that is the functional equivalent of any of the institutions listed in paragraphs (b)(1)(ii)(A) through (I) of this rule, so long as the non-U.S. institution is subject to a regulatory scheme that is substantially comparable to the regulatory scheme applicable to the equivalent U.S. institution; and

    (K) A group, provided that all the members are persons specified in Rule 13d 1(b)(1)(ii)(A) through (J).

    (iii) Such person has promptly notified any other person (or group within the meaning of section 13(d)(3) of the Act) on whose behalf it holds, on a discretionary basis, securities exceeding five percent of the class, of any acquisition or transaction on behalf of such other person which might be reportable by that person under section 13(d) of the Act. This paragraph only requires notice to the account owner of information which the filing person reasonably should be expected to know and which would advise the account owner of an obligation he may have to file a statement pursuant to section 13(d) of the Act or an amendment thereto.

Instruction 1 to paragraph (b)(1): For purposes of paragraph (b)(1)(i) of this rule, the exception for activities solely in connection with a nomination under Rule 14a–11 will not be available after the election of directors.

    (2) The Schedule 13G filed pursuant to paragraph (b)(1) of this rule shall be filed within 45 days after the end of the calendar year in which the person became obligated under paragraph (b)(1) of this rule to report the person's beneficial ownership as of the last day of the calendar year, Provided, That it shall not be necessary to file a Schedule 13G unless the percentage of the class of equity security specified in paragraph (i) of this rule beneficially owned as of the end of the calendar year is more than five percent; However, if the person's direct or indirect beneficial ownership exceeds 10 percent of the class of equity securities prior to the end of the calendar year, the initial Schedule 13G shall be filed within 10 days after the end of the first month in which the person's direct or indirect beneficial ownership exceeds 10 percent of the class of equity securities, computed as of the last day of the month.

    (c) A person who would otherwise be obligated under paragraph (a) of this rule to file a statement on Schedule 13D may, in lieu thereof, file with the Commission, within 10 days after an acquisition described in paragraph (a) of this rule, a short-form statement on Schedule 13G. Provided, That the person:

    (1) Has not acquired the securities with any purpose, or with the effect, of changing or influencing the control of the issuer, or in connection with or as a participant in any transaction having that purpose or effect, including any transaction subject to Rule 13d–3(b), other than activities solely in connection with a nomination under Rule 14a–11;

Instruction 1 to paragraph (c)(1): For purposes of paragraph (c)(1) of this rule, the exception for activities solely in connection with a nomination under Rule 14a–11 will not be available after the election of directors.

    (2) Is not a person reporting pursuant to paragraph (b)(1) of this rule; and

    (3) Is not directly or indirectly the beneficial owner of 20 percent or more of the class.

    (d) Any person who, as of December 31, 1978, or as of the end of any calendar year thereafter, is directly or indirectly the beneficial owner of more than 5 percent of any equity security of a class specified in paragraph (d) of this rule and who is not required to file a statement under paragraph (a) of this rule by virtue of the exemption provided by section 13(d)(6)(A) or (B) of the Act, or because such beneficial ownership was acquired prior to December 22, 1970, or because such person otherwise (except for the exemption provided by section 13(d)(6)(c) of the Act) is not required to file such statement, shall, within 45 days after the end of the calendar year in which such person became obligated to report under this paragraph, send to the issuer of the security at its principal executive office, by registered or certified mail, and file with the Commission a statement containing the information required by Schedule 13G.

(e)(1) Notwithstanding paragraphs (b) and (c) of this rule and Rule 13d-2(b), a person that has reported that it is the beneficial owner of more than five percent of a class of equity securities in a statement on Schedule 13G pursuant to paragraph (b) or (c) of this rule, or is required to report the acquisition but has not yet filed the schedule, shall immediately become subject to Rules 13d-1(a) and 13d-2(a) and shall file a statement on Schedule 13D within 10 days if, and shall remain subject to those requirements for so long as, the person:

 (i) Has acquired or holds the securities with a purpose or effect of changing or influencing control of the issuer, or in connection with or as a participant in any transaction having that purpose or effect, including any transaction subject to Rule 13d-3(b); and

 (ii) Is at that time the beneficial owner of more than five percent of a class of equity securities described in Rule 13d-1(i).

 (2) From the time the person has acquired or holds the securities with a purpose or effect of changing or influencing control of the issuer, or in connection with or as a participant in any transaction having that purpose or effect until the expiration of the tenth day from the date of the filing of the Schedule 13D pursuant to this rule, that person shall not:

 (i) Vote or direct the voting of the securities described therein; or

 (ii) Acquire an additional beneficial ownership interest in any equity securities of the issuer of the securities, nor of any person controlling the issuer.

(f)(1) Notwithstanding paragraph (c) of this rule and Rule 13d-2(b), persons reporting on Schedule 13G pursuant to paragraph (c) of this rule shall immediately become subject to Rules 13d-1(a) and 13d-2(a) and shall remain subject to those requirements for so long as, and shall file a statement on Schedule 13D within 10 days of the date on which, the person's beneficial ownership equals or exceeds 20 percent of the class of equity securities.

 (2) From the time of the acquisition of 20 percent or more of the class of equity securities until the expiration of the tenth day from the date of the filing of the Schedule 13D pursuant to this rule, the person shall not:

 (i) Vote or direct the voting of the securities described therein, or

 (ii) Acquire an additional beneficial ownership interest in any equity securities of the issuer of the securities, nor of any person controlling the issuer.

(g) Any person who has reported an acquisition of securities in a statement on Schedule 13G pursuant to paragraph (b) of this rule, or has become obligated to report on the Schedule 13G but has not yet filed the Schedule, and thereafter ceases to be a person specified in paragraph (b)(1)(ii) of this rule or determines that it no longer has acquired or holds the securities in the ordinary course of business shall immediately become subject to Rule 13d-1(a) or 13d-1(c) (if the person satisfies the requirements specified in 13d-1(c)), and 13d-2(a), (b) or (d), and shall file, within 10 days thereafter, a statement on Schedule 13D or amendment to Schedule 13G, as applicable, if the person is a beneficial owner at that time of more than five percent of the class of equity securities.

(h) Any person who has filed a Schedule 13D pursuant to paragraph (e), (f) or (g) of this rule may again report its beneficial ownership on Schedule 13G pursuant to paragraphs (b) or (c) of this rule provided the person qualifies thereunder, as applicable, by filing a Schedule 13G once the person determines that the provisions of paragraph (e), (f) or (g) of this rule no longer apply.

(i) For the purpose of this regulation, the term "equity security" means any equity security of a class which is registered pursuant to section 12 of that Act, or any equity security of any insurance company which would have been required to be so registered except for the exemption contained in section 12(g)(2)(G) of the Act, or any equity security issued by a closed-end investment company registered under the Investment Company Act of 1940; *Provided,* Such term shall not include securities of a class of non-voting securities.

(j) For the purpose of sections 13(d) and 13(g), any person, in determining the amount of outstanding securities of a class of equity securities, may rely upon information set forth in the issuer's most recent quarterly or annual report, and any current report subsequent thereto, filed with the Commission pursuant to this Act, unless he knows or has reason to believe that the information contained therein is inaccurate.

(k)(1) Whenever two or more persons are required to file a statement containing the information required by Schedule 13D or Schedule 13G with respect to the same securities, only one statement need be filed: *Provided,* That:

(i) Each person on whose behalf the statement is filed is individually eligible to use the Schedule on which the information is filed;

(ii) Each person on whose behalf the statement is filed is responsible for the timely filing of such statement and any amendments thereto, and for the completeness and accuracy of the information concerning such person contained therein; such person is not responsible for the completeness or accuracy of the information concerning the other persons making the filing, unless such person knows or has reason to believe that such information is inaccurate; and

(iii) Such statement identifies all such persons, contains the required information with regard to each such person, indicates that such statement is filed on behalf of all such persons, and includes, as an exhibit, their agreement in writing that such a statement is filed on behalf of each of them.

(2) A group's filing obligation may be satisfied either by a single joint filing or by each of the group's members making an individual filing. If the group's members elect to make their own filings, each such filing should identify all members of the group but the information provided concerning the other persons making the filing need only reflect information which the filing person knows or has reason to know.

Rule 13d–2. Filing of Amendments to Schedules 13D or 13G

(a) Schedule 13D—If any material change occurs in the facts set forth in the statement required by Rule 13d–1(a), including, but not limited to, any material increase or decrease in the percentage of the class beneficially owned, the person or persons who were required to file such statement shall promptly file or cause to be filed with the Commission an amendment disclosing such change. An acquisition or disposition of beneficial ownership of securities in an amount equal to one percent or more of the class of securities shall be deemed "material" for purposes of this rule; acquisitions or dispositions of less than such amounts may be material, depending upon the facts and circumstances.

(b) Schedule 13G—Notwithstanding paragraph (a) of this rule, and provided that the person or persons filing a statement pursuant to Rule 13d–1(b) or 13d–1(c) continues to meet the requirements set forth therein, any person who has filed a short form statement on Schedule 13G pursuant to Rules 13d–1(b), 13d–1(c) or 13d–1(d) shall amend such statement within forty-five days after the end of each calendar year if, as of the end of such calendar year, there are any changes in the information reported in the previous filing on that Schedule; *Provided, however,* That such amendment need not be filed with respect to a change in the percent of class outstanding previously reported if such change results solely from a change in the aggregate number of securities outstanding. Once an amendment has been filed reflecting beneficial ownership of five percent or less of the class of securities, no additional filings are required unless the person thereafter becomes the beneficial owner of more than five percent of the class and is required to file pursuant to Rule 13d–1.

(c) Any person relying on Rule 13d–1(b) that has filed its initial Schedule 13G pursuant to that paragraph shall, in addition to filing any amendments pursuant to Rule 13d–2(b), file an amendment on Schedule 13G within 10 days after the end of the first month in which the person's direct or indirect beneficial ownership, computed as of the last day of the month, exceeds 10 percent of the class of equity securities. Thereafter, that person shall, in addition to filing any amendments pursuant to Rule 13d–2(b), file an amendment on Schedule 13G within 10 days after the end of the first month in which the person's direct or indirect beneficial ownership, computed as of the last day of the month, increases or decreases by more than five percent of the class of equity securities. Once an amendment has been filed reflecting beneficial ownership of five percent or less of the class of securities, no additional filings are required by this paragraph (c).

(d) Any person relying on Rule 13d–1(c) and has filed its initial Schedule 13G pursuant to that paragraph shall, in addition to filing any amendments pursuant to Rule 13d–2(b), file an amendment on Schedule 13G promptly upon acquiring, directly or indirectly, greater than 10 percent of a class of equity securities specified in Rule 13d–1(d), and thereafter promptly upon increasing or decreasing its beneficial ownership by more than five percent of the class of equity securities. Once an amendment has been filed reflecting beneficial ownership of five percent or less of the class of securities, no additional filings are required by this paragraph (d).

(e) The first electronic amendment to a paper format Schedule 13D or Schedule 13G shall restate the entire text of the Schedule 13D or Schedule 13G, but previously filed paper exhibits to such Schedules are not required to be restated electronically. See Rule 102 of Regulation S–T regarding amendments to exhibits previously filed in paper format. Notwithstanding the foregoing, if the sole purpose of filing the first electronic Schedule 13D or 13G amendment is to report a change in beneficial ownership that would terminate the filer's obligation to report, the amendment need not include a restatement of the entire text of the Schedule being amended.

NOTE to Rule 13d–2: For persons filing a short form statement pursuant to Rule 13d–1(b) or (c), see also Rule 13d–1(e), (f), and (g).

Rule 13d–3. Determination of Beneficial Owner

(a) For the purposes of sections 13(d) and 13(g) of the Act a beneficial owner of a security includes any person who, directly or indirectly, through any contract, arrangement, understanding, relationship, or otherwise has or shares:

(1) Voting power which includes the power to vote, or to direct the voting of, such security; and/or,

(2) Investment power which includes the power to dispose, or to direct the disposition of, such security.

(b) Any person who, directly or indirectly, creates or uses a trust, proxy, power of attorney, pooling arrangement or any other contract, arrangement, or device with the purpose or effect of divesting such person of beneficial ownership of a security or preventing the vesting of such beneficial ownership as part of a plan or scheme to evade the reporting requirements of section 13(d) or (g) of the Act shall be deemed for purposes of such Sections to be the beneficial owner of such security.

(c) All securities of the same class beneficially owned by a person, regardless of the form which such beneficial ownership takes, shall be aggregated in calculating the number of shares beneficially owned by such person.

(d) Notwithstanding the provisions of paragraphs (a) and (c) of this rule:

(1)(i) A person shall be deemed to be the beneficial owner of a security, subject to the provisions of paragraph (b) of this rule, if that person has the right to acquire beneficial ownership of such security, as defined in Rule 13d–3(a) within sixty days, including but not limited to any right to acquire:

(A) Through the exercise of any option, warrant or right;

(B) Through the conversion of a security;

(C) Pursuant to the power to revoke a trust, discretionary account, or similar arrangement; or

(D) Pursuant to the automatic termination of a trust, discretionary account or similar arrangement; provided, however, any person who acquires a security or power specified in paragraphs (d)(1)(i)(A), (B) or (C) of this rule, with the purpose or effect of changing or influencing the control of the issuer, or in connection with or as a participant in any transaction having such purpose or effect, immediately upon such acquisition shall be deemed to be the beneficial owner of the securities which may be acquired through the exercise or conversion of such security or power. Any securities not outstanding which are subject to such options, warrants, rights or conversion privileges shall be deemed to be outstanding for the purpose of computing the percentage of outstanding securities of the class owned by such person but shall not be deemed to be outstanding for the purpose of computing the percentage of the class by any other person.

(ii)   Paragraph (i) remains applicable for the purpose of determining the obligation to file with respect to the underlying security even though the option, warrant, right or convertible security is of a class of equity security, as defined in Rule 13d–1(i), and may therefore give rise to a separate obligation to file.

(2)   A member of a national securities exchange shall not be deemed to be a beneficial owner of securities held directly or indirectly by it on behalf of another person solely because such member is the record holder of such securities and, pursuant to the rules of such exchange, may direct the vote of such securities, without instruction, on other than contested matters or matters that may affect substantially the rights or privileges of the holders of the securities to be voted, but is otherwise precluded by the rules of such exchange from voting without instruction.

(3)   A person who in the ordinary course of his business is a pledgee of securities under a written pledge agreement shall not be deemed to be the beneficial owner of such pledged securities until the pledgee has taken all formal steps necessary which are required to declare a default and determines that the power to vote or to direct the vote or to dispose or to direct the disposition of such pledged securities will be exercised, provided, that:

(i)   The pledgee agreement is bona fide and was not entered into with the purpose nor with the effect of changing or influencing the control of the issuer, nor in connection with any transaction having such purpose or effect, including any transaction subject to Rule 13d–3(b);

(ii)   The pledgee is a person specified in Rule 13d–1(b)(ii), including persons meeting the conditions set forth in paragraph (G) thereof; and

(iii)   The pledgee agreement, prior to default, does not grant to the pledgee:

(A)   The power to vote or to direct the vote of the pledged securities; or

(B)   The power to dispose or direct the disposition of the pledged securities, other than the grant of such power(s) pursuant to a pledge agreement under which credit is extended subject to regulation T and in which the pledgee is a broker or dealer registered under section 15 of the Act.

(4)   A person engaged in business as an underwriter of securities who acquires securities through his participation in good faith in a firm commitment underwriting registered under the Securities Act of 1933 shall not be deemed to be the beneficial owner of such securities until the expiration of forty days after the date of such acquisition.

Rule 13d–4.   Disclaimer of Beneficial Ownership

Any person may expressly declare in any statement filed that the filing of such statement shall not be construed as an admission that such person is, for the purposes of sections 13(d) or 13(g) of the Act, the beneficial owner of any securities covered by the statement.

Rule 13d–5.   Acquisition of Securities

(a)   A person who becomes a beneficial owner of securities shall be deemed to have acquired such securities for purposes of section 13(d)(1) of the Act, whether such acquisition was through purchase or otherwise. However, executors or administrators of a decedent's estate generally will be presumed not to have acquired beneficial ownership of the securities in the decedent's estate until such time as such executors or administrators are qualified under local law to perform their duties.

(b)(1)   When two or more persons agree to act together for the purpose of acquiring, holding, voting or disposing of equity securities of an issuer, the group formed thereby shall be deemed to have acquired beneficial ownership, for purposes of sections 13(d) and (g) of the Act, as of the date of such agreement, of all equity securities of that issuer beneficially owned by any such persons.

(2) Notwithstanding the previous paragraph, a group shall be deemed not to have acquired any equity securities beneficially owned by the other members of the group solely by virtue of their concerted actions relating to the purchase of equity securities directly from an issuer in a transaction not involving a public offering: *Provided,* That:

(i) All the members of the group are persons specified in Rule 13d–1(b)(1)(ii);

(ii) The purchase is in the ordinary course of each member's business and not with the purpose nor with the effect of changing or influencing control of the issuer, nor in connection with or as a participant in any transaction having such purpose or effect, including any transaction subject to Rule 13d–3(b);

(iii) There is no agreement among, or between any members of the group to act together with respect to the issuer or its securities except for the purpose of facilitating the specific purchase involved; and

(iv) The only actions among or between any members of the group with respect to the issuer or its securities subsequent to the closing date of the non-public offering are those which are necessary to conclude ministerial matters directly related to the completion of the offer or sale of the securities.

Rule 13d–6. Exemption of Certain Acquisitions

The acquisition of securities of an issuer by a person who, prior to such acquisition, was a beneficial owner of more than five percent of the outstanding securities of the same class as those acquired shall be exempt from section 13(d) of the Act, *Provided,* that:

(a) The acquisition is made pursuant to preemptive subscription rights in an offering made to all holders of securities of the class to which the preemptive subscription rights pertain;

(b) Such person does not acquire additional securities except through the exercise of his pro rata share of the preemptive subscription rights; and

(c) The acquisition is duly reported, if required, pursuant to Section 16(a) of the Act and the rules and regulations thereunder.

Rule 13d–7. Dissemination

One copy of the Schedule filed pursuant to Rules 13d–1 and 13d–2 shall be sent to the issuer of the security at its principal executive office, by registered or certifies mail. A copy of Schedules filed pursuant to Rules 13d–1(a) 13d–2(a) shall also be sent to each national securities exchange where the security is traded.

Rule 13e–1. Purchases of Securities by the Issuer During a Third-Party Tender Offer

An issuer that has received notice that it is the subject of a tender offer made under section 14(d)(1) of the Act, that has commenced under Rule 14d–2 must not purchase any of its equity securities during the tender offer unless the issuer first:

(a) Files a statement with the Commission containing the following information:

(1) The title and number of securities to be purchases;

(2) The names of the persons or classes of persons from whom the issuer will purchase the securities;

(3) The name of any exchange, interdealer quotation system or any other market on or through which the securities will be purchased;

(4) The purpose of the purchase;

(5) Whether the issuer will retire the securities, hold the securities in its treasury, or dispose of the securities. If the issuer intends to dispose of the securities, describe how it intends to do so; and

(6)   The source and amount of funds or other consideration to make the purchase. If the issuer borrows any funds or other consideration to make the purchase or enters any agreement for the purpose of acquiring, holding, or trading the securities, describe the transaction and agreement and identify the parties; and

(b)   Pays the fee required by Rule 0–11 when it files the initial statement.

(c)   This rule does not apply to periodic repurchases in connection with an employee benefit plan or other similar plan of the issuer so long as the purchases are made in the ordinary course and not in response to the tender offer.

Instructions to Rule 13e–1: File eight copies if paper filing is permitted.

Rule 13e–3.   Going Private Transactions by Certain Issuers or Their Affiliates

(a)   *Definitions.* Unless indicated otherwise or the context otherwise requires, all terms used in this rule and in Schedule 13E–3 shall have the same meaning as in the Act or elsewhere in the General Rules and Regulations thereunder. In addition, the following definitions apply:

(1)   An "affiliate" of an issuer is a person that directly or indirectly through one or more intermediaries controls, is controlled by, or is under common control with such issuer. For the purposes of this rule only, a person who is not an affiliate of an issuer at the commencement of such person's tender offer for a class of equity securities of such issuer will not be deemed an affiliate of such issuer prior to the stated termination of such tender offer and any extensions thereof;

(2)   The term "purchase" means any acquisition for value including, but not limited to,

(i)   Any acquisition pursuant to the dissolution of an issuer subsequent to the sale or other disposition of substantially all the assets of such issuer to its affiliate,

(ii)   Any acquisition pursuant to a merger,

(iii)   Any acquisition of fractional interests in connection with a reverse stock split, and

(iv)   any acquisition subject to the control of an issuer or an affiliate of such issuer;

(3)   A "Rule 13e–3 transaction" is any transaction or series of transactions involving one or more of the transactions described in paragraph (a)(3)(i) of this rule which has either a reasonable likelihood or a purpose of producing, either directly or indirectly, any of the effects described in paragraph (a)(3)(ii) of this rule;

(i)   The transactions referred to in paragraph (a)(3) of this rule are:

(A)   A purchase of any equity security by the issuer of such security or by an affiliate of such issuer;

(B)   A tender offer for or request or invitation for tenders of any equity security made by the issuer of such class of securities or by an affiliate of such issuer; or

(C)   A solicitation subject to Regulation 14A of any proxy, consent or authorization of, or a distribution subject to Regulation 14C of information statements to, any equity security holder by the issuer of the class of securities or by an affiliate of such issuer, in connection with: a merger, consolidation, reclassification, recapitalization, reorganization or similar corporate transaction of an issuer or between an issuer (or its subsidiaries) and its affiliate; a sale of substantially all the assets of an issuer to its affiliate or group of affiliates; or a reverse stock split of any class of equity securities of the issuer involving the purchase of fractional interests.

(ii)   The effects referred to in paragraph (a)(3) of this rule are:

(A)   Causing any class of equity securities of the issuer which is subject to section 12(g) or section 15(d) of the Act to become eligible for termination of registration under Rule 12g–4 or Rule 12h–6, or causing the reporting obligations with respect to such class to become eligible for termination under Rule 12h–6; or suspension under Rule 12h–3 (§ 240.12h–3) or section 15(d); or

(B)   Causing any class of equity securities of the issuer which is either listed on a national securities exchange or authorized to be quoted in an inter-dealer quotation system of a registered national securities association to be neither listed on any national securities exchange nor authorized to be quoted on an inter-dealer quotation system of any registered national securities association.

(4)   An "unaffiliated security holder" is any security holder of an equity security subject to a Rule 13e–3 transaction who is not an affiliate of the issuer of such security.

(b)   *Application of section to an issuer (or an affiliate of such issuer) subject to section 12 of the Act.*

(1)   It shall be a fraudulent, deceptive or manipulative act or practice, in connection with a Rule 13e–3 transaction, for an issuer which has a class of equity securities registered pursuant to section 12 of the Act or which is a closed-end investment company registered under the Investment Company Act of 1940, or an affiliate of such issuer, directly or indirectly

(i)   To employ any device, scheme or artifice to defraud any person;

(ii)   To make any untrue statement of a material fact or to omit to state a material fact necessary in order to make the statements made, in light of the circumstances under which they were made, not misleading; or

(iii)   To engage in any act, practice or course of business which operates or would operate as a fraud or deceit upon any person.

(2)   As a means reasonably designed to prevent fraudulent, deceptive or manipulative acts or practices in connection with any Rule 13e–3 transaction, it shall be unlawful for an issuer which has a class of equity securities registered pursuant to section 12 of the Act, or an affiliate of such issuer, to engage, directly or indirectly, in a Rule 13e–3 transaction unless:

(i)   Such issuer or affiliate complies with the requirements of paragraphs (d), (e) and (f) of this rule; and

(ii)   The Rule 13e–3 transaction is not in violation of paragraph (b)(1) of this rule.

(c)   *Application of section to an issuer (or an affiliate of such issuer) subject to section 15(d) of the Act.*

(1)   It shall be unlawful as a fraudulent, deceptive or manipulative act or practice for an issuer which is required to file periodic reports pursuant to section 15(d) of the Act, or an affiliate of such issuer, to engage, directly or indirectly, in a Rule 13e–3 transaction unless such issuer or affiliate complies with the requirements of paragraphs (d), (e) and (f) of this rule.

(2)   An issuer or affiliate which is subject to paragraph (c)(1) of this rule and which is soliciting proxies or distributing information statements in connection with a transaction described in paragraph (a)(3)(i)(A) of this rule may elect to use the timing procedures for conducting a solicitation subject to Regulation 14A or a distribution subject to Regulation 14C in complying with paragraphs (d), (e) and (f) of this rule, provided that if an election is made, such solicitation or distribution is conducted in accordance with the requirements of the respective regulations, including the filing of preliminary copies of soliciting materials or an information statement at the time specified in Regulation 14A or 14C, respectively.

(d)   *Material required to be filed.* The issuer or affiliate engaging in a Rule 13e–3 transaction must file with the Commission:

(1)   A Schedule 13E–3 including all exhibits;

(2)   An amendment to Schedule 13E–3 reporting promptly any material changes in the information set forth in the schedule previously filed; and

(3)   A final amendment to Schedule 13E–3 reporting promptly the results of the Rule 13e–3 transaction.

(e)   *Disclosure of information to security holders.* (1) In addition to disclosing the information required by any other applicable rule or regulation under the federal securities laws, the issuer or affiliate engaging in a Rule 13e–3 transaction must disclose to security holders of the class that is the subject of the transaction, as specified in paragraph (f) of this rule, the following:

(i)   The information required by Item 1 of Schedule 13E–3 (Summary Term Sheet);

(ii)   The information required by Items 7, 8, and 9 of Schedule 13E–3, which must be prominently disclosed in a "Special Factors" section in the front of the disclosure document;

(iii)   A prominent legend on the outside front cover page that indicates that neither the Securities and Exchange Commission nor any state securities commission has: approved or disapproved of the transaction; passed upon the merits or fairness of the transaction; or passed upon the adequacy or accuracy of the disclosure in the document. The legend also must make it clear that any representation to the contrary is a criminal offense;

(iv)   The information concerning appraisal rights required by Item 1016(f) of Regulation S–K;

(v)   The information required by the remaining items of Schedule 13E–3, except for Item 1016 of Regulation S–K (exhibits), or a fair and adequate summary of the information.

Instructions to paragraph (e)(1): 1. If the Rule 13e–3 transaction also is subject to Regulation 14A or 14C, the registration provisions and rules of the Securities Act of 1933, Regulation 14D or Rule 13e–4, the information required by paragraph (e)(1) of this rule must be combined with the proxy statement, information statement, prospectus or tender offer material sent or given to security holders.

2.   If the Rule 13e–3 involves a registered securities offering, the legend required by Item 501(b)(7) of Regulation S–K must be combined with the legend required by paragraph (e)(1)(iii) of this rule.

3.   The required legend must be written in clear, plain language.

(2)   If there is any material change in the information previously disclosed to security holders, the issuer of affiliate must disclose the change promptly to security holders as specified in paragraph (f)(1)(iii) of this rule.

* * *

(f)   *Dissemination of information to security holders.*

(1)   If the Rule 13e–3 transaction involves a purchase as described in paragraph (a)(3)(i)(A) of this rule or a vote, consent, authorization, or distribution of information statements as described in paragraph (a)(3)(i)(C) of this rule, the issuer or affiliate engaging in the Rule 13e–3 transaction shall:

(i)   Provide the information required by paragraph (e) of this rule:

(A)   In accordance with the provisions of any applicable Federal or State law, but in no event later than 20 days prior to: any such purchase; any such vote, consent or authorization; or with respect to the distribution of information statements, the meeting date, or if corporate action is to be taken by means of the written authorization or consent of security holders, the earliest date on which corporate action may be taken: *Provided, however,* That if the purchase subject to this rule is pursuant to a tender offer excepted from Rule 13e–4 by paragraph (g)(5) of Rule 13e–4, the information required by paragraph (e) of this rule shall be disseminated in accordance with paragraph (e) of Rule 13e–4 no later than 10 business days prior to any purchase pursuant to such tender offer,

(B)   to each person who is a record holder of a class of equity securities subject to the Rule 13e–3 transaction as of a date not more than 20 days prior to the date of dissemination of such information.

(ii)   If the issuer or affiliate knows that securities of the class of securities subject to the Rule 13e–3 transaction are held of record by a broker, dealer, bank or voting trustee or their nominees, such issuer or affiliate shall (unless Rule 14a–13(a) or 14c–7 is applicable) furnish the number of copies of the information required by paragraph (e) of this rule that are requested by such persons (pursuant to inquiries by or on behalf of the issuer or affiliate), instruct such persons to forward such information to the beneficial owners of such securities in a timely manner and undertake to pay the reasonable expenses incurred by such persons in forwarding such information; and

(iii)   Promptly disseminate disclosure of material changes to the information required by paragraph (d) of this rule in a manner reasonably calculated to inform security holders.

(2)   If the Rule 13e–3 transaction is a tender offer or a request or invitation for tenders of equity securities which is subject to Regulation 14D or Rule 13e–4, the tender offer containing the information required by paragraph (e) of this rule, and any material change with respect thereto, shall be published, sent or given in accordance with Regulation 14D or Rule 13e–4, respectively, to security holders of the class of securities being sought by the issuer or affiliate.

(g)   *Exceptions.* This rule shall not apply to:

(1)   Any Rule 13e–3 transaction by or on behalf of a person which occurs within one year of the date of termination of a tender offer in which such person was the bidder and became an affiliate of the issuer as a result of such tender offer: *Provided,* That the consideration offered to unaffiliated security holders in such Rule 13e–3 transaction is at least equal to the highest consideration offered during such tender offer and *Provided further,* That:

(i)   If such tender offer was made for any or all securities of a class of the issuer;

(A)   Such tender offer fully disclosed such person's intention to engage in a Rule 13e–3 transaction, the form and effect of such transaction and, to the extent known, the proposed terms thereof; and

(B)   Such Rule 13e–3 transaction is substantially similar to that described in such tender offer; or

(ii)   If such tender offer was made for less than all the securities of a class of the issuer:

(A)   Such tender offer fully disclosed a plan of merger, a plan of liquidation or a similar binding agreement between such person and the issuer with respect to a Rule 13e–3 transaction; and

(B)   Such Rule 13e–3 transaction occurs pursuant to the plan of merger, plan of liquidation or similar binding agreement disclosed in the bidder's tender offer.

(2)   Any Rule 13e–3 transaction in which the security holders are offered or receive only an equity security *Provided,* That:

(i)   Such equity security has substantially the same rights as the equity security which is the subject of the Rule 13e–3 transaction including, but not limited to, voting, dividends, redemption and liquidation rights except that this requirement shall be deemed to be satisfied if unaffiliated security holders are offered common stock;

(ii)   Such equity security is registered pursuant to section 12 of the Act or reports are required to be filed by the issuer thereof pursuant to section 15(d) of the Act; and

(iii)   If the security which is the subject of the Rule 13e–3 transaction was either listed on a national securities exchange or authorized to be quoted in an interdealer quotation system of a registered national securities association, such equity security is either listed on a national securities exchange or authorized to be quoted in an inter-dealer quotation system of a registered national securities association.

(3)   [Removed and Reserved]

(4)   Redemptions, calls or similar purchases of an equity security by an issuer pursuant to specific provisions set forth in the instrument(s) creating or governing that class of equity securities; or

(5)   Any solicitation by an issuer with respect to a plan of reorganization under Chapter XI of the Bankruptcy Act, as amended, if made after the entry of an order approving such plan pursuant to section 1125(b) of that Act and after, or concurrently with, the transmittal of information concerning such plan as required by section 1125(b) of that Act.

(6)   Any tender offer or business combination made in compliance with 1933 Act Rule 802, Rule 13e–4(h)(8) or Rule 14d–1(c) or any other kind of transaction that otherwise meets the conditions for

reliance on the cross-border exemptions set forth in Rule 13e–4(h)(8), Rule 14d–1(c) or Rule 802 except for the fact that it is not technically subject to those rules.

Instruction to Rule 13e–3(g)(6): To the extent applicable, the acquiror must comply with the conditions set forth in Rule 802, and Rules 13e–4(h)(8) and 14d–1(c). If the acquiror publishes or otherwise disseminates an informational document to the holders of the subject securities in connection with the transaction, the acquiror must furnish an English translation of that informational document, including any amendments thereto, to the Commission under cover of Form CB (§ 239.800 of this chapter) by the first business day after publication or dissemination. If the acquiror is a foreign entity, it must also file a Form F–X (§ 239.42 of this chapter) with the Commission at the same time as the submission of the Form CB to appoint an agent for service in the United States.

Rule 13e–4.   Tender Offers by Issuers

(a) *Definitions.* Unless the context otherwise requires, all terms used in this rule and in Schedule TO shall have the same meaning as in the Act or elsewhere in the General Rules and Regulations thereunder. In addition, the following definitions shall apply:

(1) The term "issuer" means any issuer which has a class of equity security registered pursuant to section 12 of the Act, or which is required to file periodic reports pursuant to section 15(d) of the Act, or which is a closed-end investment company registered under the Investment Company Act of 1940.

(2) The term "issuer tender offer" refers to a tender offer for, or a request or invitation for tenders of, any class of equity security, made by the issuer of such class of equity security or by an affiliate of such issuer.

(3) As used in this rule and in Schedule TO the term "business day" means any day, other than Saturday, Sunday, or a Federal holiday, and shall consist of the time period from 12:01 a.m. through 12:00 midnight Eastern Time. In computing any time period under this Rule or Schedule TO the date of the event that begins the running of such time period shall be included *except that* if such event occurs on other than a business day such period shall begin to run on and shall include the first business day thereafter.

(4) The term "commencement" means 12:01 a.m. on the date that the issuer or affiliate has first published, sent or given the means to tender to security holders. For purposes of this rule, the means to tender includes the transmittal form or a statement regarding how the transmittal form may be obtained.

(5) The term "termination" means the date after which securities may not be tendered pursuant to an issuer tender offer.

(6) The term "security holders" means holders of record and beneficial owners of securities of the class of equity security which is the subject of an issuer tender offer.

(7) The term "security position listing" means, with respect to the securities of any issuer held by a registered clearing agency in the name of the clearing agency or its nominee, a list of those participants in the clearing agency on whose behalf the clearing agency holds the issuer's securities and of the participants' respective positions in such securities as of a specified date.

* * *

(b) *Filing, disclosure and dissemination.* As soon as practicable on the date of commencement of the issuer tender offer, the issuer or affiliate making the issuer tender offer must comply with:

(1) The filing requirements of paragraph (c)(2) of this rule;

(2) The disclosure requirements of paragraph (d)(1) of this rule; and

(3) The dissemination requirements of paragraph (e) of this rule.

(c) *Material required to be filed.* The issuer or affiliate making the issuer tender offer must file with the Commission:

(1)   All written communications made by the issuer or affiliate relating to the issuer tender offer, from and including the first public announcement, as soon as practicable on the date of the communication;

(2)   A Schedule TO including all exhibits;

(3)   An amendment to Schedule TO reporting promptly any material changes in the information set forth in the schedule previously filed; and

(4)   A final amendment to Schedule TO reporting promptly the results of the issuer tender offer.

Instructions to Rule 13e–4(c):

1.   Pre-commencement communications must be filed under cover of Schedule TO and the box on the cover page of the schedule must be marked.

2.   Any communications made in connection with an exchange offer registered under the Securities Act of 1933 need only be filed under Rule 425 of that Act and will be deemed filed under this rule.

3.   Each pre-commencement written communication must include a prominent legend in clear, plain language advising security holders to read the tender offer statement when it is available because it contains important information. The legend also must advise investors that they can get the tender offer statement and other filed documents for free at the Commission's web site and explain which documents are free from the issuer.

4.   See Rules 135, 165 and 166 under the Securities Act for pre-commencement communications made in connection with registered exchange offers.

5.   "Public announcement" is any oral or written communication by the issuer, affiliate or any person authorized to act on their behalf that is reasonably designed to, or has the effect of, informing the public or security holders in general about the issuer tender offer.

(d)   *Disclosure of tender offer information to security holders.*

(1)   The issuer or affiliate making the issuer tender offer must disclose, in a manner prescribed by paragraph (e)(1) of this rule, the following:

(i)   The information required by Item 1 of Schedule TO (summary term sheet); and

(ii)   The information required by the remaining items of Schedule TO for issuer tender offers, except for Item 12 (exhibits), or a fair and adequate summary of the information.

(2)   If there are any material changes in the information previously disclosed to security holders, the issuer or affiliate must disclose the changes promptly to security holders in a manner specified in paragraph (e)(3) of this rule.

(3)   If the issuer or affiliate disseminates the issuer tender offer by means of summary publication as described in paragraph (e)(1)(iii) of this rule, the summary advertisement must not include a transmittal letter that would permit security holders to tender securities sought in the offer and must disclose at least the following information:

(i)   The identity of the issuer or affiliate making the issuer tender offer;

(ii)   The information required by Item 1004(a)(1) and Item 1006(a) of Regulation S–K;

(iii)   Instructions on how security holders can obtain promptly a copy of the statement required by paragraph (d)(1) of this rule, at the issuer or affiliate's expense; and

(iv)   A statement that the information contained in the statement required by paragraph (d)(1) of this rule is incorporated by reference.

(e)   *Dissemination of tender offers to security holders.* An issuer tender offer will be deemed to be published, sent or given to security holders if the issuer or affiliate making the issuer tender offer complies fully with one or more of the methods described in this rule.

(1)   For issuer tender offers in which the consideration offered consists solely of cash and/or securities exempt from registration under section 3 of the Securities Act of 1933:

(i)   Dissemination of cash issuer tender offers by long-form publication: By making adequate publication of the information required by paragraph (d)(1) of this rule in a newspaper or newspapers, on the date of commencement of the issuer tender offer.

(ii)   Dissemination of any issuer tender offer by use of stockholder and other lists:

(A)   By mailing or otherwise furnishing promptly a statement containing the information required by paragraph (d)(1) of this rule to each security holder who name appears on the most recent stockholder list of the issuer;

(B)   By contacting each participant on the most recent security position listing of any clearing agency within the possession or access of the issuer or affiliate making the issuer tender offer, and making inquiry of each participant as to the approximate number of beneficial owners of the securities sought in the offer that are held by the participant;

(C)   By furnishing to each participant a sufficient number of copies of the statement required by paragraph (d)(1) of this rule for transmittal to the beneficial owners; and

(D)   By agreeing to reimburse each participant promptly for its reasonable expenses incurred in forwarding the statement to beneficial owners.

(iii)   Dissemination of certain cash issuer tender offers by summary publication:

(A)   If the issuer tender offer is not subject to Rule 13e–3, by making adequate publication of a summary advertisement containing the information required by paragraph (d)(3) of this rule in a newspaper or newspapers, on the date of commencement of the issuer tender offer; and

(B)   By mailing or otherwise furnishing promptly the statement required by paragraph (d)(1) of this rule and a transmittal letter to any security holder who requests a copy of the statement or transmittal letter.

Instruction to paragraph (e)(1): For purposes of paragraphs (e)(1)(i) and (e)(1)(iii) of this rule, adequate publication of the issuer tender offer may require publication in a newspaper with a national circulation, a newspaper with metropolitan or regional circulation, or a combination of the two, depending upon the facts and circumstances involved.

(2)   For tender offers in which the consideration consists solely or partially of securities registered under the Securities Act of 1933, a registration statement containing all of the required information, including pricing information, has been filed and a preliminary prospectus that meets the requirements of section 10(a) of the Securities Act, including a letter of transmittal, is delivered to security holders. However, for going-private transactions (as defined in Rule 13e–3) and roll-up transactions (as described by Item 901 of Regulation S–K), a registration statement registering the securities to be offered must have become effective and only a prospectus that meets the requirements of section 10(a) of the Securities Act may be delivered to security holders on the date of commencement.

Instructions to paragraph (e)(2)

1.   If the prospectus is being delivered by mail, mailing on the date of commencement is sufficient.

2.   A preliminary prospectus used under this rule may not omit information under Rule 430 or Rule 430A under the Securities Act.

3.   If a preliminary prospectus is used under this rule and the issuer must disseminate material changes, the tender offer must remain open for the period specified in paragraph (e)(3) of this rule.

4.   If a preliminary prospectus is used under this rule, tenders may be requested in accordance with Rule 162(a) under the Securities Act of 1933.

(3)   If a material change occurs in the information published, sent or given to security holders, the issuer or affiliate must disseminate promptly disclosure of the change in a manner reasonably calculated to inform security holders of the change. In a registered securities offer where the issuer or affiliate disseminates the preliminary prospectus as permitted by paragraph (e)(2) of this rule, the offer must remain open from the date that material changes to the tender offer materials are disseminated to security holders, as follows:

(i) Five business days for a prospectus supplement containing a material change other than price or share levels;

(ii) Ten business days for a prospectus supplement containing a change in price, the amount of securities sought, the dealer's soliciting fee, or other similarly significant change;

(iii) Ten business days for a prospectus supplement included as part of a post-effective amendment; and

(iv) Twenty business days for a revised prospectus when the initial prospectus was materially deficient.

(f) *Manner of making tender offer.*

(1) The issuer tender offer, unless withdrawn, shall remain open until the expiration of:

(i) At least twenty business days from its commencement; and

(ii) At least ten business days from the date that notice of an increase or decrease in the percentage of the class of securities being sought or the consideration offered or the dealer's soliciting fee to be given is first published, sent or given to security holders.

Provided, however, That, for purposes of this paragraph, the acceptance for payment by the issuer or affiliate of an additional amount of securities not to exceed two percent of the class of securities that is the subject of the tender offer shall not be deemed to be an increase. For purposes of this paragraph, the percentage of a class of securities shall be calculated in accordance with section 14(d)(3) of the Act.

(2) The issuer or affiliate making the issuer tender offer shall permit securities tendered pursuant to the issuer tender offer to be withdrawn:

(i) At any time during the period such issuer tender offer remains open; and

(ii) If not yet accepted for payment, after the expiration of forty business days from the commencement of the issuer tender offer.

(3) If the issuer or affiliate makes a tender offer for less than all of the outstanding equity securities of a class, and if a greater number of securities is tendered pursuant thereto than the issuer or affiliate is bound or willing to take up and pay for, the securities taken up and paid for shall be taken up and paid for as nearly as may be pro rata, disregarding fractions, according to the number of securities tendered by each security holder during the period such offer remains open; *Provided, however,* That this provision shall not prohibit the issuer or affiliate making the issuer tender offer from:

(i) Accepting all securities tendered by persons who own, beneficially or of record, an aggregate of not more than a specified number which is less than one hundred shares of such security and who tender all their securities, before prorating securities tendered by others; or

(ii) Accepting by lot securities tendered by security holders who tender all securities held by them and who, when tendering their securities, elect to have either all or none or at least a minimum amount or none accepted, if the issuer or affiliate first accepts all securities tendered by security holders who do not so elect;

(4) In the event the issuer or affiliate making the issuer tender increases the consideration offered after the issuer tender offer has commenced, such issuer or affiliate shall pay such increased consideration to all security holders whose tendered securities are accepted for payment by such issuer or affiliate.

(5) The issuer or affiliate making the tender offer shall either pay the consideration offered, or return the tendered securities, promptly after the termination or withdrawal of the tender offer.

(6) Until the expiration of at least ten business days after the date of termination of the issuer tender offer, neither the issuer nor any affiliate shall make any purchases, otherwise than pursuant to the tender offer, of:

(i) Any security which is the subject of the issuer tender offer, or any security of the same class and series, or any right to purchase any such securities; and

(ii)   In the case of an issuer tender offer which is an exchange offer, any security being offered pursuant to such exchange offer, or any security of the same class and series, or any right to purchase any such security.

(7)   The time periods for the minimum offering periods pursuant to this rule shall be computed on a concurrent as opposed to a consecutive basis.

(8)   No issuer or affiliate shall make a tender offer unless:

(i)   The tender offer is open to all security holders of the class of securities subject to the tender offer; and

(ii)   The consideration paid to any security holder for securities tendered in the tender offer is the highest consideration paid to any other security holder for securities tendered in the tender offer.

(9)   Paragraph (f)(8)(i) of this rule shall not:

(i)   Affect dissemination under paragraph (e) of this rule; or

(ii)   Prohibit an issuer or affiliate from making a tender offer excluding all security holders in a state where the issuer or affiliate is prohibited from making the tender offer by administrative or judicial action pursuant to a state statute after a good faith effort by the issuer or affiliate to comply with such statute.

(10)   Paragraph (f)(8)(ii) of this rule shall not prohibit the offer of more than one type of consideration in a tender offer, provided that:

(i)   Security holders are afforded equal right to elect among each of the types of consideration offered; and

(ii)   The highest consideration of each type paid to any security holder is paid to any other security holder receiving that type of consideration.

(11)   If the offer and sale of securities constituting consideration offered in an issuer tender offer is prohibited by the appropriate authority of a state after a good faith effort by the issuer or affiliate to register or qualify the offer and sale of such securities in such state:

(i)   The issuer or affiliate may offer security holders in such state an alternative form of consideration; and

(ii)   Paragraph (f)(10) of this rule shall not operate to require the issuer or affiliate to offer or pay the alternative form of consideration to security holders in any other state.

(12)(i)   Paragraph (f)(8)(ii) of this rule shall not prohibit the negotiation, execution or amendment of an employment compensation, severance or other employee benefit arrangement, or payments made or to be made or benefits granted or to be granted according to such an arrangement, with respect to any security holder of the issuer, where the amount payable under the arrangement:

(A)   Is being paid or granted as compensation for past services performed, future services to be performed, or future services to be refrained from performing, by the security holder (and matters incidental thereto); and

(B)   Is not calculated based on the number of securities tendered or to be tendered in the tender offer by the security holder.

(ii)   The provisions of paragraph (f)(12)(i) of this rule shall be satisfied and, therefore, pursuant to this non-exclusive safe harbor, the negotiation, execution or amendment of an arrangement and any payments made or to be made or benefits granted or to be granted according to that arrangement shall not be prohibited by paragraph (f)(8)(ii) of this rule, if the arrangement is approved as an employment compensation, severance or other employee benefit arrangement solely by independent directors as follows:

(A)   The compensation committee or a committee of the board of directors that performs functions similar to a compensation committee of the issuer approves the arrangement, regardless of whether the issuer is a party to the arrangement, or, if an affiliate is a party to the arrangement, the compensation committee or a committee of the board of directors that performs functions similar to a compensation committee of the affiliate approves the arrangement; or

(B)   If the issuer's or affiliate's board of directors, as applicable, does not have a compensation committee or a committee of the board of directors that performs functions similar to a compensation committee or if none of the members of the issuer's or affiliate's compensation committee or committee that performs functions similar to a compensation committee is independent, a special committee of the board of directors formed to consider and approve the arrangement approves the arrangement; or

(C)   If the issuer or affiliate, as applicable, is a foreign private issuer, any or all members of the board of directors or any committee of the board of directors authorized to approve employment compensation, severance or other employee benefit arrangements under the laws or regulations of the home country approves the arrangement.

Instructions to paragraph (f)(12)(ii): For purposes of determining whether the members of the committee approving an arrangement in accordance with the provisions of paragraph (f)(12)(ii) of this rule are independent, the following provisions shall apply:

1.   If the issuer or affiliate, as applicable, is a listed issuer (as defined in Rule 10A–3) whose securities are listed either on a national securities exchange registered pursuant to section 6(a) of the Exchange Act or in an inter-dealer quotation system of a national securities association registered pursuant to section 15A(a) of the Exchange Act that has independence requirements for compensation committee members that have been approved by the Commission (as those requirements may be modified or supplemented), apply the issuer's or affiliate's definition of independence that it uses for determining that the members of the compensation committee are independent in compliance with the listing standards applicable to compensation committee members of the listed issuer.

2.   If the issuer or affiliate, as applicable, is not a listed issuer (as defined in Rule 10A–3), apply the independence requirements for compensation committee members of a national securities exchange registered pursuant to section 6(a) of the Exchange Act or an inter-dealer quotation system of a national securities association registered pursuant to section 15A(a) of the Exchange Act that have been approved by the Commission (as those requirements may be modified or supplemented). Whatever definition the issuer or affiliate, as applicable, chooses, it must apply that definition consistently to all members of the committee approving the arrangement.

3.   Notwithstanding Instructions 1 and 2 to paragraph (f)(12)(ii), if the issuer or affiliate, as applicable, is a closed-end investment company registered under the Investment Company Act of 1940, a director is considered to be independent if the director is not, other than in his or her capacity as a member of the board of directors or any board committee, an "interested person" of the investment company, as defined in section 2(a)(19) of the Investment Company Act of 1940.

4.   If the issuer or affiliate, as applicable, is a foreign private issuer, apply either the independence standards set forth in Instructions 1 and 2 to paragraph (f)(12)(ii) or the independence requirements of the laws, regulations, codes or standards of the home country of the issuer or affiliate, as applicable, for members of the board of directors or the committee of the board of directors approving the arrangement.

5.   A determination by the issuer's or affiliate's board of directors, as applicable, that the members of the board of directors or the committee of the board of directors, as applicable, approving an arrangement in accordance with the provisions of paragraph (f)(12)(ii) are independent in accordance with the provisions of this instruction to paragraph (f)(12)(ii) shall satisfy the independence requirements of paragraph (f)(12)(ii).

Instruction to paragraph (f)(12): The fact that the provisions of paragraph (f)(12) of this rule extend only to employment compensation, severance and other employee benefit arrangements and not to other arrangements, such as commercial arrangements, does not raise any inference that a payment under any such other arrangement constitutes consideration paid for securities in a tender offer.

(13)   *Electronic filings*. If the issuer or affiliate is an electronic filer, the minimum offering periods set forth in paragraph (f)(1) of this rule shall be tolled for any period during which it fails to file in electronic format, absent a hardship exemption, the Schedule TO Issuer Tender Offer Statement, the tender offer material specified in Item 1016(a)(1) of Regulation M–A, and any amendments thereto. If such documents were filed in paper pursuant to a temporary hardship exemption, the minimum

offering periods shall be tolled for any period during which a required confirming electronic copy of such Schedule and tender offer material is delinquent.

(g)   The requirements of section 13(e)(1) of the Act and Rule 13e–4 and Schedule 13e–4 thereunder shall be deemed satisfied with respect to any issuer tender offer, including any exchange offer, where the issuer is incorporated or organized under the laws of Canada or any Canadian province or territory, is a foreign private issuer, and is not an investment company registered or required to be registered under the Investment Company Act of 1940, if less than 40 percent of the class of securities that is the subject of the tender offer is held by U.S. holders, and the tender offer is subject to, and the issuer complies with, the laws, regulations and policies of Canada and/or any of its provinces or territories governing the conduct of the offer (unless the issuer has received an exemption(s) from, and the issuer tender offer does not comply with, requirements that otherwise would be prescribed by this rule), *provided that:*

(1)   Where the consideration for an issuer tender offer subject to this paragraph consists solely of cash, the entire disclosure document or documents required to be furnished to holders of the class of securities to be acquired shall be filed with the Commission on Schedule 13E–4F and disseminated to shareholders residing in the United States in accordance with such Canadian laws, regulations and policies; or

(2)   Where the consideration for an issuer tender offer subject to this paragraph includes securities to be issued pursuant to the offer, any registration statement and/or prospectus relating thereto shall be filed with the Commission along with the Schedule 13E–4F referred to in paragraph (g)(1) of this rule, and shall be disseminated, together with the home jurisdiction document(s) accompanying such Schedule, to shareholders of the issuer residing in the United States in accordance with such Canadian laws, regulations and policies.

NOTE: Notwithstanding the grant of an exemption from one or more of the applicable Canadian regulatory provisions imposing requirements that otherwise would be prescribed by this rule, the issuer tender offer will be eligible to proceed in accordance with the requirements of this rule if the Commission by order determines that the applicable Canadian regulatory provisions are adequate to protect the interest of investors.

(h)   This rule shall not apply to:

(1)   Calls or redemptions of any security in accordance with the terms and conditions of its governing instruments;

(2)   Offers to purchase securities evidenced by a scrip certificate, order form or similar document which represents a fractional interest in a share of stock or similar security;

(3)   Offers to purchase securities pursuant to a statutory procedure for the purchase of dissenting security holders' securities;

(4)   Any tender offer which is subject to section 14(d) of the Act;

(5)   Offers to purchase from security holders who own an aggregate of not more than a specified number of shares that is less than one hundred: *Provided, however,* that:

(i)   The offer complies with paragraph (f)(8)(i) of this rule with respect to security holders who own a number of shares equal to or less than the specified number of shares, except that an issuer can elect to exclude participants in a plan as that term is defined in Regulation M, or to exclude security holders who do not own their shares as of a specified date determined by the issuer; and

(ii)   The offer complies with paragraph (f)(8)(ii) of this rule or the consideration paid pursuant to the offer is determined on the basis of a uniformly applied formula based on the market price of the subject security;

(6)   An issuer tender offer made solely to effect a rescission offer: *Provided, however,* That the offer is registered under the Securities Act of 1933, and the consideration is equal to the price paid by each security holder, plus legal interest if the issuer elects to or is required to pay legal interest;

(7)   Offers by closed-end management investment companies to repurchase equity securities pursuant to Rule 23c–3 of the Investment Company Act of 1940;

(8) *Cross-border tender offers (Tier 1)*. Any issuer tender offer (including any exchange offer) where the issuer is a foreign private issuer as defined in Rule 3b–4 if the following conditions are satisfied.

(i) Except in the case of an issuer tender offer that is commenced during the pendency of a tender offer made by a third party in reliance on Rule 14d–1(c), U.S. holders do not hold more than 10 percent of the subject class sought in the offer (as determined under Instructions 2 or 3 to paragraph (h)(8) and paragraph (i) of this rule);

(ii) The issuer or affiliate must permit U.S. holders to participate in the offer on terms at least as favorable as those offered any other holder of the same class of securities that is subject to the offer, however:

(A) *Registered exchange offers*. If the issuer or affiliate offers securities registered under the Securities Act of 1933, the issuer or affiliate need not extend the offer to security holders in those states or jurisdictions that prohibit the offer or sale of securities after the issuer or affiliate has made a good faith effort to register or qualify the offer and sale of securities in that state or jurisdiction, except that the issuer or affiliate must offer the same cash alternative to security holders in any such state or jurisdiction that it has offered to security holders in any other state or jurisdiction.

(B) *Exempt exchange offers*. If the issuer or affiliate offers securities exempt from registration under Rule 802 under the Securities Act of 1933, the issuer or affiliate need not extend the offer to security holders in those states or jurisdictions that require registration or qualification, except that the issuer or affiliate must offer the same cash alternative to security holders in any such state or jurisdiction that it has offered to security holders in any other state or jurisdiction.

(C) *Cash only consideration*. The issuer or affiliate may offer U.S. holders cash only consideration for the tender of the subject securities, notwithstanding the fact that the issuer or affiliate is offering security holders outside the United States a consideration that consists in whole or in part of securities of the issuer or affiliate, if the issuer or affiliate has a reasonable basis for believing that the amount of cash is substantially equivalent to the value of the consideration offered to non-U.S. holders, and either of the following conditions are satisfied:

(1) The offered security is a "margin security" within the meaning of Regulation T and the issuer or affiliate undertakes to provide, upon the request of any U.S. holder or the Commission staff, the closing price and daily trading volume of the security on the principal trading market for the security as of the last trading day of each six months preceding the announcement of the offer and each of the trading days thereafter; or

(2) If the offered security is not a "margin security" within the meaning of Regulation T, the issuer or affiliate undertakes to provide, upon the request of any U.S. holder or the Commission staff, an opinion of an independent expert stating that the cash consideration offered security holders outside the United States.

(D) *Disparate tax treatments*. If the issuer or affiliate offers "loan notes" solely to offer sellers tax advantages not available in the United States and these notes are neither listed on any organized securities market nor registered under the Securities Act of 1933, the loan notes need not be offered to U.S. holders.

(iii) *Informational documents*. (A) If the issuer or affiliate publishes or otherwise disseminates an informational document to the holders of the securities in connection with the issuer tender offer (including any exchange offer), the issuer or affiliate must furnish the informational document, including any amendments thereto, in English, to the Commission on Form CB by the first business day after publication or dissemination. If the issuer of affiliate is a foreign company, it must also file a Form F–X with the Commission at the same time as the submission of Form CB to appoint an agent for service in the United States.

(B) The issuer or affiliate must disseminate any informational document to U.S. holders, including any amendments thereto, in English, on a comparable basis to that provided to security holders in the home jurisdiction.

(C) If the issuer or affiliate disseminates by publication in its home jurisdiction, the issuer or affiliate must publish the information in the United States in a manner reasonably calculated to inform U.S. holders of the offer.

(iv) An investment company registered or required to be registered under the Investment Company Act of 1940, other than a registered closed-end investment company, may not use this paragraph (h)(8); or

* * *

(9) Any other transaction or transactions, if the Commission, upon written request or upon its own motion, exempts such transaction or transactions, either unconditionally, or on specified terms and conditions, as not constituting a fraudulent, deceptive or manipulative act or practice comprehended within the purpose of this rule.

(i) *Cross-border tender offers* (Tier II). Any issuer tender offer (including any exchange offer) that meets the conditions in paragraph (i)(1) of this rule shall be entitled to the exemptive relief specified in paragraph (i)(2) of this rule, provided that such issuer tender offer complies with all the requirements of this rule other than those for which an exemption has been specifically provided in paragraph (i)(2) of this rule. In addition, any issuer tender offer (including any exchange offer) subject only to the requirements of section 14(e) of the Act and Regulation 14E thereunder that meets the conditions in paragraph (i)(1) of this rule also shall be entitled to the exemptive relief specified in paragraph (i)(2) of this rule, to the extent needed under the requirements of Regulation 14E, so long as the tender offer complies with all requirements of Regulation 14E other than those for which an exemption has been specifically provided in paragraph (i)(2) of this Rule:

(1) *Conditions.* (i) The issuer is a foreign private issuer as defined in Rule 3b–4 and is not an investment company registered or required to be registered under the Investment Company Act of 1940, other than a registered closed-end investment company, and

(ii) Except in the case of an issuer tender offer commenced during the pendency of a tender offer made by a third party in reliance on Rule 14d–1(d), U.S. holders do not hold more than 40 percent of the class of securities sought in the offer (as determined in accordance with Instructions 2 or 3 to paragraphs (h)(8) and (i) of this rule).

(2) *Exemptions.* The issuer tender offer shall comply with all requirements of this rule other than the following:

(i) *Equal treatment-loan notes.* If the issuer or affiliate offers loan notes solely to offer sellers tax advantages not available in the United States and these notes are neither listed on any organized securities market nor registered under the Securities Act, the loan notes need not be offered to U.S. holders, notwithstanding paragraphs (f)(8) and (h)(9) of this rule.

(ii) *Equal treatment—separate U.S. and foreign offers.* Notwithstanding the provisions of paragraph (f)(8) of this rule, an issuer or affiliate conducting an issuer tender offer meeting the conditions of paragraph (i)(1) of this rule may separate the offer into multiple offers: one offer made to U.S. holders, which also may include all holders of American Depositary Shares representing interests in the subject securities, and one or more offers made to non-U.S. holders. The U.S. offer must be made on terms at least as favorable as those offered any other holder of the same class of securities that is the subject of the tender offers. U.S. holders may be included in the foreign offer(s) only where the laws of the jurisdiction governing such foreign offer(s) expressly preclude the exclusion of U.S. holders from the foreign offer(s) and where the offer materials distributed to U.S. holders fully and adequately disclose the risks of participating in the foreign offer(s).

(iii) *Notice of extensions.* Notice of extensions made in accordance with the requirements of the home jurisdiction law or practice will satisfy the requirements of Rule 14e–1(d).

(iv) *Prompt of Payment.* Payment made in accordance with the requirements of the home jurisdiction law or practice will satisfy the requirements of Rule 14c–1(c).

(v) *Suspension of withdrawal rights during counting of tendered securities.* The issuer or affiliate may suspend withdrawal rights required under paragraph (f)(2) of this rule at the end of the offer and during the period that securities tendered into the offer are being counted, provided that:

(A) The issuer or affiliate has provided an offer period, including withdrawal rights, for a period of at least 20 U.S. business days;

(B) At the time withdrawal rights are suspended, all offer conditions have been satisfied or waived, except to the extent that the issuer or affiliate is in the process of determining whether a minimum acceptance condition included in the terms of the offer has been satisfied by counting tendered securities; and

(C) Withdrawal rights are suspended only during the counting process and are reinstated immediately thereafter, except to the extent that they are terminated through the acceptance of tendered securities.

(vi) *Early termination of an initial offering period.* An issuer or affiliate conducting an issuer tender offer may terminate an initial offering period, including a voluntary extension of that period, if at the time the initial offering period and withdrawal rights terminate, the following conditions are met:

(A) The initial offering period has been open for at least 20 U.S. business days;

(B) The issuer or affiliate has adequately discussed the possibility of and the impact of the early termination in the original offer materials;

(C) The issuer or affiliate provides a subsequent offering period after the termination of the initial offering period;

(D) All offer conditions are satisfied as of the time when the initial offering period ends; and

(E) The issuer or affiliate does not terminate the initial offering period or any extension of that period during any mandatory extension required under U.S. tender offer rules.

Instructions to paragraph (h)(8) and (i) of this rule:

1. "Home jurisdiction" means both the jurisdiction of the issuer's incorporation, organization or chartering and the principal foreign market where the issuer's securities are listed or quoted.

2. "U.S. holder" means any security holder resident to the United States. To determine the percentage of outstanding securities held by U.S. holders:

i. Calculate the U.S. ownership as of a date no more than 60 days before and no more than 30 days after the public announcement of the tender offer. If you are unable to calculate as of a date within these time frames, the calculation may be made as of the most recent practicable date before public announcement, but in no event earlier than 120 days before announcement;

ii. Include securities underlying American Depositary Shares convertible or exchangeable into the securities that are the subject of the tender offer when calculating the number of subject securities outstanding, as well as the number held by U.S. holders. Exclude from the calculations other types of securities that are convertible or exchangeable into the securities that are the subject of the tender offer, such as warrants, options and convertible securities;

iii. Use the method of calculating record ownership in Rule 12g3–2(a), except that your inquiry as to the amount of securities represented by accounts of customers resident in the United States may be limited to brokers, dealers, banks and other nominees located in the United States, your jurisdiction of incorporation, and the jurisdiction that is the primary trading market for the subject securities, if different than your jurisdiction of incorporation;

iv. If, after reasonable inquiry, you are unable to obtain information about the amount of securities represented by accounts of customers resident in the United States, you may assume, for purposes of this definition, that the customers are residents of the jurisdiction in which the nominee has its principal place of business; and

v.   Count securities as beneficially owned by residents of the United States as reported on reports of beneficial ownership that are provided to you or publicly fixed and based on information otherwise provided to you.

3.   If you are unable to conduct the analysis of U.S. ownership set forth in Instruction 2 above, U.S. holders will be presumed to hold 10 percent or less of the outstanding subject securities (40 percent for Tier II) so long as there is a primary trading market outside the United States, as defined in Rule 12h–6(f)(5), unless:

i.   Average daily trading volume of the subject securities in the United States for a recent twelve-month period ending on a date no more than 60 days before the public announcement of the tender offer exceeds 10 percent (or 40 percent) of the average daily trading volume of that class of securities on a worldwide basis for the same period; or

ii.   The most recent annual report or annual information filed or submitted by the issuer with securities regulators of the home jurisdiction or with the Commission or any jurisdiction in which the subject securities trade before the public announcement of the offer indicates that U.S. holders hold more than 10 percent (or 40 percent) of the outstanding subject class of securities; or

iii.   You know or have reason to know, before the public announcement of the offer, that the level of U.S. ownership of the subject securities exceeds 10 percent (or 40 percent) of such securities. As an example, you are deemed to know information about U.S. ownership of the subject class of securities that is publicly available and that appears in any filing with the Commission or any regulatory body in the home jurisdiction and, if different, the non-U.S. jurisdiction in which the primary trading market for the subject class of securities is located. You are also deemed to know information obtained or readily available from any other source that is reasonably reliable, including from persons you have retained to advise you about the transaction, as well as from third-party information providers. These examples are not intended to be exclusive.

4.   United States means the United States of America, its territories and possessions, any State of the United States, and the District of Columbia.

5.   The exemptions provided by paragraphs (h)(8) and (i) of this rule are not available for any securities transaction or series of transactions that technically complies with paragraph (h)(8) and (i) of this rule but are part of a plan or scheme to evade the provisions of this rule.

(j)(1)   It shall be a fraudulent, deceptive or manipulative act or practice, in connection with an issuer tender offer, for an issuer or an affiliate of such issuer, in connection with an issuer tender offer:

(i)   To employ any device, scheme or artifice to defraud any person;

(ii)   To make any untrue statement of a material fact or to omit to state a material fact necessary in order to make the statements made, in the light of the circumstances under which they were made, not misleading; or

(iii)   To engage in any act, practice or course of business which operates or would operate as a fraud or deceit upon any person.

(2)   As a means reasonably designed to prevent fraudulent, deceptive or manipulative acts or practices in connection with any issuer tender offer, it shall be unlawful for an issuer or an affiliate of such issuer to make an issuer tender offer unless:

(i)   Such issuer or affiliate complies with the requirements of paragraphs (b), (c), (d), (e) and (f) of this rule; and

(ii)   The issuer tender offer is not in violation of paragraph (j)(1) of this rule.

Rule 13f–1.   Reporting by Institutional Investment Managers of Information With Respect to Accounts Over Which They Exercise Investment Discretion

(a)(1)   Every institutional investment manager which exercises investment discretion with respect to accounts holding section 13(f) securities, as defined in paragraph (c) of this rule, having an aggregate fair market value on the last trading day of any month of any calendar year of at least $100,000,000 shall file a report on Form 13F with the Commission within 45 days after the last day of such calendar year and within 45 days after the last day of each of the first three calendar quarters of the subsequent calendar year.

(2)   An amendment to a Form 13F report, other than one reporting only holdings that were not previously reported in a public filing for the same period, must set forth the complete text of the Form 13F. Amendments must be numbered sequentially.

(b)   For the purposes of this rule, "investment discretion" has the meaning set forth in section 3(a)(35) of the Act. An institutional investment manager shall also be deemed to exercise "investment discretion" with respect to all accounts over which any person under its control exercises investment discretion.

(c)   For purposes of this rule "section 13(f) securities" shall mean equity securities of a class described in section 13(d)(1) of the Act that are admitted to trading on a national securities exchange or quoted on the automated quotation system of a registered securities association. In determining what classes of securities are section 13(f) securities, an institutional investment manager may rely on the most recent list of such securities published by the Commission pursuant to section 13(f)(4) of the Act. Only securities of a class on such list shall be counted in determining whether an institutional investment manager must file a report under this rule and only those securities shall be reported in such report. Where a person controls the issuer of a class of equity securities which are "section 13(f) securities" as defined in this rule, those securities shall not be deemed to be "section 13(f) securities" with respect to the controlling person, provided that such person does not otherwise exercise investment discretion with respect to accounts with fair market value of at least $100,000,000 within the meaning of paragraph (a) of this rule.

Rule 13h–1.   Large Trader Reporting

(a)   *Definitions.* For purposes of this rule:

(1)   The term large trader means any person that:

(i)   Directly or indirectly, including through other persons controlled by such person, exercises investment discretion over one or more accounts and effects transactions for the purchase or sale of any NMS security for or on behalf of such accounts, by or through one or more registered broker-dealers, in an aggregate amount equal to or greater than the identifying activity level; or

(ii)   Voluntarily registers as a large trader by filing electronically with the Commission Form 13H.

(2)   The term person has the same meaning as in Section 13(h)(8)(E) of the Securities Exchange Act of 1934.

(3)   The term control (including the terms controlling, controlled by and under common control with) means the possession, direct or indirect, of the power to direct or cause the direction of the management and policies of a person, whether through the ownership of securities, by contract, or otherwise. For purposes of this rule only, any person that directly or indirectly has the right to vote or direct the vote of 25% or more of a class of voting securities of an entity or has the power to sell or direct the sale of 25% or more of a class of voting securities of such entity, or in the case of a partnership, has the right to receive, upon dissolution, or has contributed, 25% or more of the capital, is presumed to control that entity.

(4)   The term investment discretion has the same meaning as in Section 3(a)(35) of the Securities Exchange Act of 1934. A person's employees who exercise investment discretion within the scope of their employment are deemed to do so on behalf of such person.

(5)   The term NMS security has the meaning provided for in Regulation NMS Rule 600(b)(47).

(6)   The term transaction or transactions means all transactions in NMS securities, excluding the purchase or sale of such securities pursuant to exercises or assignments of option contracts. For the sole purpose of determining whether a person is a large trader, the following transactions are excluded from this definition:

(i)   Any journal or bookkeeping entry made to an account in order to record or memorialize the receipt or delivery of funds or securities pursuant to the settlement of a transaction;

(ii)   Any transaction that is part of an offering of securities by or on behalf of an issuer, or by an underwriter on behalf of an issuer, or an agent for an issuer, whether or not such offering is subject to registration under the Securities Act of 1933, provided, however, that this exemption shall not include an offering of securities effected through the facilities of a national securities exchange;

(iii)   Any transaction that constitutes a gift;

(iv)   Any transaction effected by a court appointed executor, administrator, or fiduciary pursuant to the distribution of a decedent's estate;

(v)   Any transaction effected pursuant to a court order or judgment;

(vi)   Any transaction effected pursuant to a rollover of qualified plan or trust assets subject to Section 402(a)(5) of the Internal Revenue Code (26 U.S.C. 1 et seq.);

(vii)   Any transaction between an employer and its employees effected pursuant to the award, allocation, sale, grant, or exercise of a NMS security, option or other right to acquire securities at a pre-established price pursuant to a plan which is primarily for the purpose of an issuer benefit plan or compensatory arrangement; or

(viii) Any transaction to effect a business combination, including a reclassification, merger, consolidation, or tender offer subject to Section 14(d) of the Securities Exchange Act of 1934; an issuer tender offer or other stock buyback by an issuer; or a stock loan or equity repurchase agreement.

(7)   The term identifying activity level means: aggregate transactions in NMS securities that are equal to or greater than:

(i)   During a calendar day, either two million shares or shares with a fair market value of $20 million; or

(ii)   During a calendar month, either twenty million shares or shares with a fair market value of $200 million.

(8)   The term reporting activity level means:

(i)   Each transaction in NMS securities, effected in a single account during a calendar day, that is equal to or greater than 100 shares;

(ii)   Any transaction in NMS securities for fewer than 100 shares, effected in a single account during a calendar day, that a registered broker-dealer may deem appropriate; or

(iii)   Such other amount that may be established by order of the Commission from time to time.

(9)   The term Unidentified Large Trader means each person who has not complied with the identification requirements of paragraphs (b)(1) and (b)(2) of this rule that a registered broker-dealer knows or has reason to know is a large trader. For purposes of determining under this rule whether a registered broker-dealer has reason to know that a person is large trader, a registered broker-dealer need take into account only transactions in NMS securities effected by or through such broker-dealer.

(b)   *Identification requirements for large traders.*

(1)   *Form 13H.* Except as provided in paragraph (b)(3) of this rule, each large trader shall file electronically Form 13H with the Commission, in accordance with the instructions contained therein:

(i)   Promptly after first effecting aggregate transactions, or after effecting aggregate transactions subsequent to becoming inactive pursuant to paragraph (b)(3) of this rule, equal to or greater than the identifying activity level;

(ii)   Within 45 days after the end of each full calendar year; and

(iii)   Promptly following the end of a calendar quarter in the event that any of the information contained in a Form 13H filing becomes inaccurate for any reason.

(2) *Disclosure of large trader status.* Each large trader shall disclose to the registered broker-dealers effecting transactions on its behalf its large trader identification number and each account to which it applies. A large trader on Inactive Status pursuant to paragraph (b)(3) of this rule must notify broker-dealers promptly after filing for reactivated status with the Commission.

(3) *Filing requirement.*

(i) Compliance by controlling person. A large trader shall not be required to separately comply with the requirements of this paragraph (b) if a person who controls the large trader complies with all of the requirements under paragraphs (b)(1), (b)(2), and (b)(4) of this rule applicable to such large trader with respect to all of its accounts.

(ii) Compliance by controlled person. A large trader shall not be required to separately comply with the requirements of this paragraph (b) if one or more persons controlled by such large trader collectively comply with all of the requirements under paragraphs (b)(1), (b)(2), and (b)(4) of this rule applicable to such large trader with respect to all of its accounts.

(iii) Inactive status. A large trader that has not effected aggregate transactions at any time during the previous full calendar year in an amount equal to or greater than the identifying activity level shall become inactive upon filing a Form 13H and thereafter shall not be required to file Form 13H or disclose its large trader status unless and until its transactions again are equal to or greater than the identifying activity level. A large trader that has ceased operations may elect to become inactive by filing an amended Form 13H to indicate its terminated status.

(4) Other information. Upon request, a large trader must promptly provide additional descriptive or clarifying information that would allow the Commission to further identify the large trader and all accounts through which the large trader effects transactions.

(c) *Aggregation.*

(1) *Transactions.* For the purpose of determining whether a person is a large trader, the following shall apply:

(i) The volume or fair market value of transactions in equity securities and the volume or fair market value of the equity securities underlying transactions in options on equity securities, purchased and sold, shall be aggregated;

(ii) The fair market value of transactions in options on a group or index of equity securities (or based on the value thereof), purchased and sold, shall be aggregated; and

(iii) Under no circumstances shall a person subtract, offset, or net purchase and sale transactions, in equity securities or option contracts, and among or within accounts, when aggregating the volume or fair market value of transactions for purposes of this rule.

(2) *Accounts.* Under no circumstances shall a person disaggregate accounts to avoid the identification requirements of this rule.

(d) *Recordkeeping requirements for broker and dealers.*

(1) *Generally.* Every registered broker-dealer shall maintain records of all information required under paragraphs (d)(2) and (d)(3) of this rule for all transactions effected directly or indirectly by or through:

(i) An account such broker-dealer carries for a large trader or an Unidentified Large Trader, or

(ii) If the broker-dealer is a large trader, any proprietary or other account over which such broker-dealer exercises investment discretion.

(iii) Additionally, where a non-broker-dealer carries an account for a large trader or an Unidentified Large Trader, the broker-dealer effecting transactions directly or indirectly for such large trader or Unidentified Large Trader shall maintain records of all of the information required under paragraphs (d)(2) and (d)(3) of this rule for those transactions.

(2) *Information.* The information required to be maintained for all transactions shall include:

(i) The clearing house number or alpha symbol of the broker or dealer submitting the information and the clearing house numbers or alpha symbols of the entities on the opposite side of the transaction;

(ii) Identifying symbol assigned to the security;

(iii) Date transaction was executed;

(iv) The number of shares or option contracts traded in each specific transaction; whether each transaction was a purchase, sale, or short sale; and, if an option contract, whether the transaction was a call or put option, an opening purchase or sale, a closing purchase or sale, or an exercise or assignment;

(v) Transaction price;

(vi) Account number;

(vii) Identity of the exchange or other market center where the transaction was executed.

(viii) A designation of whether the transaction was effected or caused to be effected for the account of a customer of such registered broker-dealer, or was a proprietary transaction effected or caused to be effected for the account of such broker-dealer;

(ix) If part or all of an account's transactions at the registered broker-dealer have been transferred or otherwise forwarded to one or more accounts at another registered broker-dealer, an identifier for this type of transaction; and if part or all of an account's transactions at the reporting broker-dealer have been transferred or otherwise received from one or more other registered broker-dealers, an identifier for this type of transaction;

(x) If part or all of an account's transactions at the reporting broker-dealer have been transferred or otherwise received from another account at the reporting broker-dealer, an identifier for this type of transaction; and if part or all of an account's transactions at the reporting broker-dealer have been transferred or otherwise forwarded to one or more other accounts at the reporting broker-dealer, an identifier for this type of transaction;

(xi) If a transaction was processed by a depository institution, the identifier assigned to the account by the depository institution;

(xii) The time that the transaction was executed; and

(xiii) The large trader identification number(s) associated with the account, unless the account is for an Unidentified Large Trader.

(3) *Information relating to Unidentified Large Traders.* With respect to transactions effected directly or indirectly by or through the account of an Unidentified Large Trader, the information required to be maintained for all transactions also shall include such Unidentified Large Trader's name, address, date the account was opened, and tax identification number(s).

(4) *Retention.* The records and information required to be made and kept pursuant to the provisions of this rule shall be kept for such periods of time as provided in Rule 17a–4(b) under the Securities Exchange Act of 1934.

(5) *Availability of information.* The records and information required to be made and kept pursuant to the provisions of this rule shall be available on the morning after the day the transactions were effected (including Saturdays and holidays).

(e) *Reporting requirements for brokers and dealers.* Upon the request of the Commission, every registered broker-dealer who is itself a large trader or carries an account for a large trader or an Unidentified Large Trader shall electronically report to the Commission, using the infrastructure supporting Rule 17a–25 under the Securities Exchange Act of 1934, in machine-readable form and in accordance with instructions issued by the Commission, all information required under paragraphs (d)(2) and (d)(3) of this rule for all transactions effected directly or indirectly by or through accounts carried by such broker-dealer for large traders and Unidentified Large Traders, equal to or greater than the reporting activity level. Additionally, where a non-broker-dealer carries an account for a large trader or an Unidentified Large Trader, the broker-dealer effecting such transactions directly or indirectly for a large trader shall electronically report using the infrastructure supporting Rule 17a–25 under the Securities Exchange Act of 1934, in machine-readable form and in accordance with instructions issued by the Commission, all information required under paragraphs (d)(2) and (d)(3) of this rule for such transactions equal to or greater than the reporting activity level. Such reports shall be submitted to the Commission no later than the day and time specified in the request for transaction information, which shall be no earlier than the opening of business of the day following such request, unless in unusual circumstances the same-day submission of information is requested.

(f)   *Monitoring safe harbor.* For the purposes of this rule, a registered broker-dealer shall be deemed not to know or have reason to know that a person is a large trader if it does not have actual knowledge that a person is a large trader and it establishes policies and procedures reasonably designed to:

(1)   Identify persons who have not complied with the identification requirements of paragraphs (b)(1) and (b)(2) of this rule but whose transactions effected through an account or a group of accounts carried by such broker-dealer or through which such broker-dealer executes transactions, as applicable (and considering account name, tax identification number, or other identifying information available on the books and records of such broker-dealer) equal or exceed the identifying activity level;

(2)   Treat any persons identified in paragraph (f)(1) of this rule as an Unidentified Large Trader for purposes of this rule; and

(3)   Inform any person identified in paragraph (f)(1) of this rule of its potential obligations under this rule.

(g)   *Exemptions.* Upon written application or upon its own motion, the Commission may by order exempt, upon specified terms and conditions or for stated periods, any person or class of persons or any transaction or class of transactions from the provisions of this rule to the extent that such exemption is consistent with the purposes of the Securities Exchange Act of 1934.

Rule 13k–1.   Foreign Bank Exemption From the Insider Lending Prohibition Under Section 13(k)

(a)   For the purpose of this rule:

(1)   *Foreign bank* means an institution:

(i)   The home jurisdiction of which is other than the United States;

(ii)   That is regulated as a bank in its home jurisdiction; and

(iii)   That engages directly in the business of banking.

(2)   *Home jurisdiction* means the country, political subdivision or other place in which a foreign bank is incorporated or organized.

(3)   *Engages directly in the business of banking* means that an institution engages directly in banking activities that are usual for the business of banking in its home jurisdiction.

(4)   *Affiliate, parent* and *subsidiary* have the same meaning as under Rule 12b–2.

(b)   An issuer that is a foreign bank or the parent or other affiliate of a foreign bank is exempt from the prohibition of extending, maintaining, arranging for, or renewing credit in the form of a personal loan to or for any of its directors or executive officers under section 13(k) of the Act with respect to any such loan made by the foreign bank as long as:

(1)   Either:

(i)   The laws or regulations of the foreign bank's home jurisdiction require the bank to insure its deposits or be subject to a deposit guarantee or protection scheme; or

(ii)   The Board of Governors of the Federal Reserve System has determined that the foreign bank or another bank organized in the foreign bank's home jurisdiction is subject to comprehensive supervision or regulation on a consolidated basis by the bank supervisor in its home jurisdiction under 12 CFR § 211.24(c); and

(2)   The loan by the foreign bank to any of its directors or executive officers or those of its parent or other affiliate:

(i)   Is on substantially the same terms as those prevailing at the time for comparable transactions by the foreign bank with other persons who are not executive officers, directors or employees of the foreign bank, its parent or other affiliate; or

(ii)   Is pursuant to a benefit or compensation program that is widely available to the employees of the foreign bank, its parent or other affiliate and does not give preference to any of the executive officers or directors of the foreign bank, its parent or other affiliate over any other employees of the foreign bank, its parent or other affiliate; or

(iii)   Has received express approval by the bank supervisor in the foreign bank's home jurisdiction.

NOTES to paragraph (b):

1.   The exemption provided in paragraph (b) of this rule applies to a loan by the subsidiary of a foreign bank to a director or executive officer of the foreign bank, its parent or other affiliate as long as the subsidiary is under the supervision or regulation of the bank supervisor in the foreign bank's home jurisdiction, the subsidiary's loan meets the requirements of paragraph (b)(2) of this rule, and the foreign bank meets the requirements of paragraph (b)(1) of this rule.

2.   For the purpose of paragraph (b)(1)(ii) of this rule, a foreign bank may rely on a determination by the Board of Governors of the Federal Reserve System that another bank in the foreign bank's home jurisdiction is subject to comprehensive supervision or regulation on a consolidated basis by the bank supervisor under 12 CFR § 211.24(c) as long as the foreign bank is under substantially the same banking supervision or regulation as the other bank in their home jurisdiction.

(c)   As used in paragraph (1) of section 13(k) of the Act, *issuer* does not include a foreign government, as defined under Rule 405 of the Securities Act of 1933, that files a registration statement under the Securities Act of 1933 on Schedule B.

Rule 13p–1.   Requirement of Report Regarding Disclosure of Registrant's Supply Chain Information Regarding Conflict Minerals

Every registrant that files reports with the Commission under Sections 13(a) (15 U.S.C. § 78m(a)) or 15(d) (15 U.S.C. § 78o(d)) of the Exchange Act, having conflict minerals that are necessary to the functionality or production of a product manufactured or contracted by that registrant to be manufactured, shall file a report on Form SD within the period specified in that Form disclosing the information required by the applicable items of Form SD as specified in that Form (17 C.F.R. § 249b.400).

Rule 13q–1.   Disclosure of Payments Made by Resource Extraction Issuers

(a)   *Resource extraction issuers.* Every issuer that is required to file an annual report with the Commission on Form 10–K (17 CFR 249.310), Form 20–F (17 CFR 249.220f), or Form 40–F (17 CFR 249.240f) pursuant to Section 13 or 15(d) of the Exchange Act and engages in the commercial development of oil, natural gas, or minerals must furnish a report on Form SD (17 CFR 249b.400) within the period specified in that Form disclosing the information required by the applicable items of Form SD as specified in that Form.

(b)   *Anti-evasion.* Disclosure is required under this section in circumstances in which an activity related to the commercial development of oil, natural gas, or minerals, or a payment or series of payments made by a resource extraction issuer to a foreign government or the Federal Government for the purpose of commercial development of oil, natural gas, or minerals, is not, in form or characterization, within one of the categories of activities or payments specified in Form SD, but is part of a plan or scheme to evade the disclosure required under this section.

(c)   *Alternative reporting.* An application for recognition by the Commission that an alternative reporting regime requires disclosure that satisfies the transparency objectives of Section 13(q) (15 U.S.C. 78m(q)), for purposes of alternative reporting pursuant to Item 2.01(c) of Form SD, must be filed in accordance with the procedures set forth in Rule 0–13, except that, for purposes of this paragraph (c), applications may be submitted by resource extraction issuers, governments, industry groups, or trade associations.

(d)   *Exemptions.* (1) *Conflicts of law.* A resource extraction issuer that is prohibited by the law of the jurisdiction where the project is located from providing the payment information required by Form SD may exclude such disclosure, subject to the following conditions:

(i)   The issuer has taken all reasonable steps to seek and use any exemptions or other relief under the applicable law of the foreign jurisdiction, and has been unable to obtain or use such an exemption or other relief;

(ii)   The issuer must disclose on Form SD:

(A)   The foreign jurisdiction for which it is omitting the disclosure pursuant to this paragraph (d)(1);

(B)   The particular law of that jurisdiction that prevents the issuer from providing such disclosure; and

(C)   The efforts the issuer has undertaken to seek and use exemptions or other relief under the applicable law of that jurisdiction, and the results of those efforts; and

(iii)   The issuer must furnish as an exhibit to Form SD a legal opinion from counsel that opines on the issuer's inability to provide such disclosure without violating the foreign jurisdiction's law.

(2)   *Conflicts with pre-existing contracts.* A resource extraction issuer that is unable to provide the payment information required by Form SD without violating one or more contract terms that were in effect prior to the effective date of this section may exclude such disclosure, subject to the following conditions:

(i)   The issuer has taken all reasonable steps to obtain the consent of the relevant contractual parties, or to seek and use another contractual exception or other relief, to disclose the payment information, and has been unable to obtain such consent or other contractual exception or relief;

(ii)   The issuer must disclose on Form SD:

(A)   The jurisdiction for which it is omitting the disclosure pursuant to this paragraph (d)(2);

(B)   The particular contract terms that prohibit the issuer from providing such disclosure; and

(C)   The efforts the issuer has undertaken to obtain the consent of the contracting parties, or to seek and use another contractual exception or relief, to disclose the payment information, and the results of those efforts; and

(iii)   The issuer must furnish as an exhibit to Form SD a legal opinion from counsel that opines on the issuer's inability to provide such disclosure without violating the contractual terms.

(3)   *Exemption for emerging growth companies and smaller reporting companies.* An issuer that is an emerging growth company or a smaller reporting company, each as defined under Rule 12b–2, is exempt from, and need not comply with, the requirements of this section, unless it is subject to the resource extraction payment disclosure requirements of an alternative reporting regime, which has been deemed by the Commission to require disclosure that satisfies the transparency objectives of Section 13(q), pursuant to Rule 13q–1(c).

(4)   *Case-by-case exemption.* A resource extraction issuer may file an application for exemptive relief under this section in accordance with the procedures set forth in Rule 0–12.

(e)   *Compilation.* To the extent practicable, the staff will periodically make a compilation of the information required to be submitted under this section publicly available online. The staff may determine the form, manner and timing of the compilation, except that no information included therein may be anonymized (whether by redacting the names of the resource extraction issuers or otherwise).

REGULATION 14A—SOLICITATION OF PROXIES

Rule 14a-1. Definitions

Unless the context otherwise requires, all terms used in this regulation have the same meanings as in the Act or elsewhere in the general rules and regulations thereunder. In addition, the following definitions apply unless the context otherwise requires:

(a) *Associate.* The term "associate," used to indicate a relationship with any person, means

(1) Any corporation or organization (other than the registrant or a majority owned subsidiary of the registrant) of which such person is an officer or partner or is, directly or indirectly, the beneficial owner of 10 percent or more of any class of equity securities;

(2) Any trust or other estate in which such person has a substantial beneficial interest or as to which such person serves as trustee or in a similar fiduciary capacity; and

(3) Any relative or spouse of such person, or any relative of such spouse, who has the same home as such person or who is a director or officer of the registrant or any of its parents or subsidiaries.

(b) *Employee benefit plan.* For purposes of Rules 14a-13, 14b-1 and 14b-2, the term "employee benefit plan" means any purchase, savings, option, bonus, appreciation, profit sharing, thrift, incentive, pension or similar plan primarily for employees, directors, trustees or officers.

(c) *Entity that exercises fiduciary powers.* The term "entity that exercises fiduciary powers" means any entity that holds securities in nominee name or otherwise on behalf of a beneficial owner but does not include a clearing agency registered pursuant to section 17A of the Act or a broker or a dealer.

(d) *Exempt employee benefit plan securities.* For purposes of Rules 14a-13, 14b-1 and 14b-2, the term "exempt employee benefit plan securities" means:

(1) Securities of the registrant held by an employee benefit plan, as defined in paragraph (b) of this rule, where such plan is established by the registrant; or

(2) If notice regarding the current solicitation has been given pursuant to Rule 14a-13(a)(1)(ii)(C) or if notice regarding the current request for a list of names, addresses and securities positions of beneficial owners has been given pursuant to Rule 14a-13(b)(3), securities of the registrant held by an employee benefit plan, as defined in paragraph (b) of this rule, where such plan is established by an affiliate of the registrant.

(e) *Last fiscal year.* The term "last fiscal year" of the registrant means the last fiscal year of the registrant ending prior to the date of the meeting for which proxies are to be solicited or if the solicitation involves written authorizations or consents in lieu of a meeting, the earliest date they may be used to effect corporate action.

(f) *Proxy.* The term "proxy" includes every proxy, consent or authorization within the meaning of section 14(a) of the Act. The consent or authorization may take the form of failure to object or to dissent.

(g) *Proxy statement.* The term "proxy statement" means the statement required by Rule 14a-3(a) whether or not contained in a single document.

(h) *Record date.* The term "record date" means the date as of which the record holders of securities entitled to vote at a meeting or by written consent or authorization shall be determined.

(i) *Record holder.* For purposes of Rules 14a-13, 14b-1 and 14b-2, the term "record holder" means any broker, dealer, voting trustee, bank, association or other entity that exercises fiduciary powers which holds securities of record in nominee name or otherwise or as a participant in a clearing agency registered pursuant to section 17A of the Act.

(j) *Registrant.* The term "registrant" means the issuer of the securities in respect of which proxies are to be solicited.

(k)   *Respondent bank.* For purposes of Rules 14-13, 14b-1 and 14b-2, the term "respondent bank" means any bank, association or other entity that exercises fiduciary powers which holds securities on behalf of beneficial owners and deposits such securities for safekeeping with another bank, association or other entity that exercises fiduciary powers.

(l)   *Solicitation.*

(1)   The terms "solicit" and "solicitation" include:

(i)   Any request for a proxy whether or not accompanied by or included in a form of proxy;

(ii)   Any request to execute or not to execute, or to revoke, a proxy; or

(iii)   The furnishing of a form of proxy or other communication to security holders under circumstances reasonably calculated to result in the procurement, withholding or revocation of a proxy, including:

(A)   Any proxy voting advice that makes a recommendation to a security holder as to its vote, consent, or authorization on a specific matter for which security holder approval is solicited, and that is furnished by a person that markets its expertise as a provider of such proxy voting advice, separately from other forms of investment advice, and sells such proxy voting advice for a fee.

(B)   [Reserved]

(2)   The terms do not apply, however, to:

(i)   The furnishing of a form of proxy to a security holder upon the unsolicited request of such security holder;

(ii)   The performance by the registrant of acts required by Rule 14a-7;

(iii)   The performance by any person of ministerial acts on behalf of a person soliciting a proxy; or

(iv)   A communication by a security holder who does not otherwise engage in a proxy solicitation (other than a solicitation exempt under Rule 14a-2) stating how the security holder intends to vote and the reasons therefor, provided that the communication:

(A)   Is made by means of speeches in public forums, press releases, published or broadcast opinions, statements, or advertisements appearing in a broadcast media, or newspaper, magazine or other bona fide publication disseminated on a regular basis,

(B)   Is directed to persons to whom the security holder owes a fiduciary duty in connection with the voting of securities of a registrant held by the security holder, or

(C)   Is made in response to unsolicited requests for additional information with respect to a prior communication by the security holder made pursuant to this paragraph (l)(2)(iv).

(v)   The furnishing of any proxy voting advice by a person who furnishes such advice only in response to an unprompted request.

Rule 14a-2.   Solicitations to Which Rules 14a-3 to 14a-15 Apply

Rules 14a-3 to 14a-14 except as specified, apply to every solicitation of a proxy with respect to securities registered pursuant to section 12 of the Act, whether or not trading in such securities has been suspended. To the extent specified below, certain of these sections also apply to roll-up transactions that do not involve an entity with securities registered pursuant to section 12 of the Act.

(a)   Rules 14a-3 to 14a-15 do not apply to the following:

(1)   Any solicitation by a person in respect to securities carried in his name or in the name of his nominee (otherwise than as voting trustee) or held in his custody, if such person—

(i)   Receives no commission or remuneration for such solicitation, directly or indirectly, other than reimbursement of reasonable expenses,

(ii) Furnishes promptly to the person solicited (or such person's household in accordance with Rule 14a–3(e)(1)) a copy of all soliciting material with respect to the same subject matter or meeting received from all persons who shall furnish copies thereof for such purpose and who shall, if requested, defray the reasonable expenses to be incurred in forwarding such material, and

(iii) In addition, does no more than impartially instruct the person solicited to forward a proxy to the person, if any, to whom the person solicited desires to give a proxy, or impartially request from the person solicited instructions as to the authority to be conferred by the proxy and state that a proxy will be given if no instructions are received by a certain date.

(2) Any solicitation by a person in respect of securities of which he is the beneficial owner;

(3) Any solicitation involved in the offer and sale of securities registered under the Securities Act of 1933: *Provided,* That this paragraph shall not apply to securities to be issued in any transaction of the character specified in paragraph (a) of Rule 145 under that Act;

(4) Any solicitation with respect to a plan of reorganization under Chapter 11 of the Bankruptcy Reform Act of 1978, as amended, if made after the entry of an order approving the written disclosure statement concerning a plan of reorganization pursuant to section 1125 of said Act and after, or concurrently with, the transmittal of such disclosure statement as required by section 1125 of said Act;

(5) [Removed and Reserved]

(6) Any solicitation through the medium of a newspaper advertisement which informs security holders of a source from which they may obtain copies of a proxy statement, form of proxy and any other soliciting material and does no more than:

(i) Name the registrant,

(ii) State the reason for the advertisement, and

(iii) Identify the proposal or proposals to be acted upon by security holders.

(b) Rules 14a–3 to 14a–6 (other than 14a–6(g) and 14a–6(p)), 14a–8 and 14a–10 to 14a–15 do not apply to the following:

(1) Any solicitation by or on behalf of any person who does not, at any time during such solicitation, seek directly or indirectly, either on its own or another's behalf, the power to act as proxy for a security holder and does not furnish or otherwise request, or act on behalf of a person who furnishes or requests, a form of revocation, abstention, consent or authorization. Provided, however, That the exemption set forth in this paragraph shall not apply to:

(i) The registrant or an affiliate or associate of the registrant (other than an officer or director or any person serving in a similar capacity);

(ii) An officer or director of the registrant or any person serving in a similar capacity engaging in a solicitation financed directly or indirectly by the registrant;

(iii) An officer, director, affiliate or associate of a person that is ineligible to rely on the exemption set forth in this paragraph (other than persons specified in paragraph (b)(1)(i) of this rule), or any person serving in a similar capacity;

(iv) Any nominee for whose election as a director proxies are solicited;

(v) Any person soliciting in opposition to a merger, recapitalization, reorganization, sale of assets or other extraordinary transaction recommended or approved by the board of directors of the registrant who is proposing or intends to propose an alternative transaction to which such person or one of its affiliates is a party;

(vi) Any person who is required to report beneficial ownership of the registrant's equity securities on a Schedule 13D, unless such person has filed a Schedule 13D and has not disclosed pursuant to Item 4 thereto an intent, or reserved the right, to engage in a control transaction, or any contested solicitation for the election of directors;

(vii) Any person who receives compensation from an ineligible person directly related to the solicitation of proxies, other than pursuant to Rule 14a–13;

(viii) Where the registrant is an investment company registered under the Investment Company Act of 1940, an "interested person" of that investment company, as that term is defined in section 2(a)(19) of the Investment Company Act;

(ix) Any person who, because of a substantial interest in the subject matter of the solicitation, is likely to receive a benefit from a successful solicitation that would not be shared pro rata by all other holders of the same class of securities, other than a benefit arising from the person's employment with the registrant; and

(x) Any person acting on behalf of any of the foregoing.

(2) Any solicitation made otherwise than on behalf of the registrant where the total number of persons solicited is not more than ten;

(3) The furnishing of proxy voting advice by any person (the "advisor") to any other person with whom the advisor has a business relationship, if:

(i) The advisor renders financial advice in the ordinary course of his business;

(ii) The advisor discloses to the recipient of the advice any significant relationship with the registrant or any of its affiliates, or a security holder proponent of the matter on which advice is given, as well as any material interests of the advisor in such matter;

(iii) The advisor receives no special commission or remuneration for furnishing the proxy voting advice from any person other than a recipient of the advice and other persons who receive similar advice under this subsection; and

(iv) The proxy voting advice is not furnished on behalf of any person soliciting proxies or on behalf of a participant in an election subject to the provisions of Rule 14a–12(c);

(4) Any solicitation in connection with a roll-up transaction as defined in Item 901(c) of Regulation S–K in which the holder of a security that is the subject of a proposed roll-up transaction engages in preliminary communications with other holders of securities that are the subject of the same limited partnership roll-up transaction for the purpose of determining whether to solicit proxies, consents, or authorizations in opposition to the proposed limited partnership roll-up transaction; *provided, however,* that:

(i) This exemption shall not apply to a security holder who is an affiliate of the registrant or general partner or sponsor; and

(ii) This exemption shall not apply to a holder of five percent (5%) or more of the outstanding securities of a class that is the subject of the proposed roll-up transaction who engages in the business of buying and selling limited partnership interests in the secondary market unless that holder discloses to the persons to whom the communications are made such ownership interest and any relations of the holder to the parties of the transaction or to the transaction itself, as required by Rule 14a–6(n)(1) and specified in the Notice of Exempt Preliminary Roll-up Communication. If the communication is oral, this disclosure may be provided to the security holder orally. Whether the communication is written or oral, the notice required by Rule 14a–6(n) and the Notice of Exempt Preliminary Roll-up Communication shall be furnished to the Commission.

(5) Publication or distribution by a broker or a dealer of a research report in accordance with Rule 138 or Rule 139 during a transaction in which the broker or dealer or its affiliate participates or acts in an advisory role.

(6) Any solicitation by or on behalf of any person who does not seek directly or indirectly, either on its own or another's behalf, the power to act as proxy for a shareholder and does not furnish or otherwise request, or act on behalf of a person who furnishes or requests, a form of revocation, abstention, consent, or authorization in an electronic shareholder forum that is established, maintained or operated pursuant to the provisions of Rule 14a–17, provided that the solicitation is made more than 60 days prior to the date announced by a registrant for its next

annual or special meeting of shareholders. If the registrant announces the date of its next annual or special meeting of shareholders less than 60 days before the meeting date, then the solicitation may not be made more than two days following the date of the registrant's announcement of the meeting date. Participation in an electronic shareholder forum does not eliminate a person's eligibility to solicit proxies after the date that this exemption is no longer available, or is no longer being relied upon, provided that any such solicitation is conducted in accordance with this regulation.

(7)   Any solicitation by or on behalf of any shareholder in connection with the formation of a nominating shareholder group pursuant to Rule 14a–11, provided that:

(i)   The soliciting shareholder is not holding the registrant's securities with the purpose, or with the effect, of changing control of the registrant or to gain a number of seats on the board of directors that exceeds the maximum number of nominees that the registrant could be required to include under Rule 14a–11(d);

(ii)   Each written communication includes no more than:

(A)   A statement of each soliciting shareholder's intent to form a nominating shareholder group in order to nominate one or more directors under Rule 14a–11;

(B)   Identification of, and a brief statement regarding, the potential nominee or nominees or, where no nominee or nominees have been identified, the characteristics of the nominee or nominees that the shareholder intends to nominate, if any;

(C)   The percentage of voting power of the registrant's securities that are entitled to be voted on the election of directors that each soliciting shareholder holds or the aggregate percentage held by any group to which the shareholder belongs; and

(D)   The means by which shareholders may contact the soliciting party.

(iii)   Any written soliciting material published, sent or given to shareholders in accordance with this paragraph must be filed by the shareholder with the Commission, under the registrant's Exchange Act file number, or, in the case of a registrant that is an investment company registered under the Investment Company Act of 1940 (15 U.S.C. 80a–1 et seq.), under the registrant's Investment Company Act file number, no later than the date the material is first published, sent or given to shareholders. Three copies of the material must at the same time be filed with, or mailed for filing to, each national securities exchange upon which any class of securities of the registrant is listed and registered. The soliciting material must include a cover page in the form set forth in Schedule 14N (§ 240.14n–101) and the appropriate box on the cover page must be marked.

(iv)   In the case of an oral solicitation made in accordance with the terms of this rule, the nominating shareholder must file a cover page in the form set forth in Schedule 14N (§ 240.14n–101), with the appropriate box on the cover page marked, under the registrant's Exchange Act file number (or in the case of an investment company registered under the Investment Company Act of 1940 (15 U.S.C. 80a–1 et seq.), under the registrant's Investment Company Act file number), no later than the date of the first such communication.

Instruction to paragraph (b)(7): The exemption provided in paragraph (b)(7) of this rule shall not apply to a shareholder that subsequently engages in soliciting or other nominating activities outside the scope of Rules 14a–2(b)(8) and 14a–11 in connection with the subject election of directors or is or becomes a member of any other group, as determined under section 13(d)(3) of the Securities Exchange Act of 1934 and Rule 13d–5(b), or otherwise, with persons engaged in soliciting or other nominating activities in connection with the subject election of directors.

(8)   Any solicitation by or on behalf of a nominating shareholder or nominating shareholder group in support of its nominee that is included or that will be included on the registrant's form of proxy in accordance with Rule 14a–11 or for or against the registrant's nominee or nominees, provided that:

(i)   The soliciting party does not, at any time during such solicitation, seek directly or indirectly, either on its own or another's behalf, the power to act as proxy for a shareholder and does not furnish or otherwise request, or act on behalf of a person who furnishes or requests, a form of revocation, abstention, consent or authorization;

(ii)   Any written communication includes:

(A)   The identity of each nominating shareholder and a description of his or her direct or indirect interests, by security holdings or otherwise;

(B)   A prominent legend in clear, plain language advising shareholders that a shareholder nominee is or will be included in the registrant's proxy statement and that they should read the registrant's proxy statement when available because it includes important information (or, if the registrant's proxy statement is publicly available, advising shareholders of that fact and encouraging shareholders to read the registrant's proxy statement because it includes important information). The legend also must explain to shareholders that they can find the registrant's proxy statement, other soliciting material, and any other relevant documents at no charge on the Commission's Web site; and

(iii)   Any written soliciting material published, sent or given to shareholders in accordance with this paragraph must be filed by the nominating shareholder or nominating shareholder group with the Commission, under the registrant's Exchange Act file number, or, in the case of a registrant that is an investment company registered under the Investment Company Act of 1940 (15 U.S.C. 80a–1 et seq.), under the registrant's Investment Company Act file number, no later than the date the material is first published, sent or given to shareholders. Three copies of the material must at the same time be filed with, or mailed for filing to, each national securities exchange upon which any class of securities of the registrant is listed and registered. The soliciting material must include a cover page in the form set forth in Schedule 14N (§ 240.14n–101) and the appropriate box on the cover page must be marked.

Instruction 1 to paragraph (b)(8): A nominating shareholder or nominating shareholder group may rely on the exemption provided in paragraph (b)(8) of this rule only after receiving notice from the registrant in accordance with Rule 14a–11(g)(1) or 14a–11(g)(3)(iv) that the registrant will include the nominating shareholder's or nominating shareholder group's nominee or nominees in its form of proxy.

Instruction 2 to paragraph (b)(8): Any solicitation by or on behalf of a nominating shareholder or nominating shareholder group in support of its nominee included or to be included on the registrant's form of proxy in accordance with Rule 14a–11 or for or against the registrant's nominee or nominees must be made in reliance on the exemption provided in paragraph (b)(8) of this rule and not on any other exemption.

Instruction 3 to paragraph (b)(8): The exemption provided in paragraph (b)(8) of this rule shall not apply to a person that subsequently engages in soliciting or other nominating activities outside the scope of Rule 14a–11 in connection with the subject election of directors or is or becomes a member of any other group, as determined under section 13(d)(3) of the Securities Exchange Act of 1934 and Rule 13d–5(b), or otherwise, with persons engaged in soliciting or other nominating activities in connection with the subject election of directors.

(9)   Paragraphs (b)(1) and (b)(3) of this section shall not be available to a person furnishing proxy voting advice covered by Rule 240.14a–1(*l*)(1)(iii)(A) ("proxy voting advice business") unless the proxy voting advice business includes in its proxy voting advice or in an electronic medium used to deliver the proxy voting advice prominent disclosure of:

(i)   Any information regarding an interest, transaction, or relationship of the proxy voting advice business (or its affiliates) that is material to assessing the objectivity of the proxy voting advice in light of the circumstances of the particular interest, transaction, or relationship; and

(ii)   Any policies and procedures used to identify, as well as the steps taken to address, any such material conflicts of interest arising from such interest, transaction, or relationship.

Rule 14a–3.   Information to Be Furnished to Security Holders

(a)   No solicitation subject to this regulation shall be made unless each person solicited is concurrently furnished or has previously been furnished with:

(1)   A publicly-filed preliminary or definitive written proxy statement, in the form and manner described in Rule 14a–16, containing the information specified in Schedule 14A;

(2)   A preliminary or definitive proxy statement included in a registration statement file under the Securities Act of 1933 on Form S–4 or F–4 (17 C.F.R. § 239.34) or Form N–14 (17 C.F.R. § 239.23) containing the information specified in such Form; or

(3)   A publicly-filed preliminary or definitive proxy statement, not in the form and manner described in Rule 14a–16, containing the information specified in Schedule 14A, if:

   (i)   The solicitation relates to a business combination transaction as defined in Rule 165 under the Securities Act of 1933, as well as transactions for cash consideration requiring disclosure under Item 14 of Schedule 14A; or

   (ii)   The solicitation may not follow the form and manner described in Rule 14a–16 pursuant to the laws of the state of incorporation of the registrant;

(b)   If the solicitation is made on behalf of the registrant, other than an investment company registered under the Investment Company Act of 1940, and relates to an annual (or special meeting in lieu of the annual) meeting of security holders, or written consent in lieu of such meeting, at which directors are to be elected, each proxy statement furnished pursuant to paragraph (a) of this rule shall be accompanied or preceded by an annual report to security holders as follows:

(1)   The report shall include, for the registrant and its subsidiaries, consolidated and audited balance sheets as of the end of the two most recent fiscal years and audited statements of income and cash flows for each of the three most recent fiscal years prepared in accordance with Regulation S–X, except that the provisions of Article 3 (other than Rules 3–03(e), 3–04 and 3–20 of Regulation S–X) and Article 11 shall not apply. Any financial statement schedules or exhibits or separate financial statements which may otherwise be required in filings with the Commission may be omitted. If the financial statements of the registrant and its subsidiaries consolidated in the annual report filed or to be filed with the Commission are not required to be audited, the financial statements required by this paragraph may be unaudited. A smaller reporting company may provide the information in Article 8 of Regulation S–X in lieu of the financial information required by this paragraph 9(b)(1).

NOTE 1 to Paragraph (b)(1): If the financial statements for a period prior to the most recently completed fiscal year have been examined by a predecessor accountant, the separate report of the predecessor accountant may be omitted in the report to security holders, provided the registrant has obtained from the predecessor accountant a reissued report covering the prior period presented and the successor accountant clearly indicates in the scope paragraph of his or her report (a) that the financial statements of the prior period were examined by other accountants, (b) the date of their report, (c) the type of opinion expressed by the predecessor accountant and (d) the substantive reasons therefore, if it was other than unqualified. It should be noted, however, that the separate report of any predecessor accountant is required in filings with the Commission. If, for instance, the financial statements in the annual report to security holders are incorporated by reference in a Form 10–K, the separate report of a predecessor accountant shall be filed in Part II or in Part IV as a financial statement schedule.

NOTE 2 to Paragraph (b)(1): For purposes of complying with Rule 14a–3, if the registrant has changed its fiscal closing date, financial statements covering two years and one period of 9 to 12 months shall be deemed to satisfy the requirements for statements of income and cash flows for the three most recent fiscal years.

(2)(i)   Financial statements and notes thereto shall be presented in roman type at least as large and as legible as 10-point modern type. If necessary for convenient presentation, the financial statements may be in roman type as large and as legible as 8-point modern type. All type shall be leaded at least 2 points.

   (ii)   Where the annual report to security holders is delivered through an electronic medium, issuers may satisfy legibility requirements applicable to printed documents, such as type size and font, by presenting all required information in a format readily communicated to investors.

(3)   The report shall contain the supplementary financial information required by item 302 of Regulation S–K.

(4)   The report shall contain information concerning changes in and disagreements with accountants on accounting and financial disclosure required by Item 304 of Regulation S–K.

(5)(i)   The report shall contain the selected financial data required by Item 301 of Regulation S–K.

(ii)   The report shall contain management's discussion and analysis of financial condition and results of operations required by Item 303 of Regulation S–K.

(iii)   The report shall contain the quantitative and qualitative disclosures about market risk required by Item 305 of Regulation S–K.

(6)   The report shall contain a brief description of the business done by the registrant and its subsidiaries during the most recent fiscal year which will, in the opinion of management, indicate the general nature and scope of the business of the registrant and its subsidiaries.

(7)   The report shall contain information relating to the registrant's industry segments, classes of similar products or services, foreign and domestic operations and exports sales required by paragraphs (b), (c)(1)(i) and (d) of Item 101 of Regulation S–K.

(8)   The report shall identify each of the registrant's directors and executive officers, and shall indicate the principal occupation or employment of each such person and the name and principal business of any organization by which such person is employed.

(9)   The report shall contain the market price of and dividends on the registrant's common equity and related security holder matters required by Items 201(a), (b) and (c) of Regulation S–K. If the report precedes or accompanies a proxy statement or information statement relating to an annual meeting of security holders at which directors are to be elected (or special meeting or written consents in lieu of such meeting), furnish the performance graph required by Item 201(e).

(10)   The registrant's proxy statement, or the report, shall contain an undertaking in bold face or otherwise reasonably prominent type to provide without charge to each person solicited upon the written request of any such person, a copy of the registrant's annual report on Form 10–K, including the financial statements and the financial statement schedules, required to be filed with the Commission pursuant to Rule 13a–1 under the Act for the registrant's most recent fiscal year, and shall indicate the name and address (including title or department) of the person to whom such a written request is to be directed. In the discretion of management, a registrant need not undertake to furnish without charge copies of all exhibits to its Form 10–K, provided that the copy of the annual report on Form 10–K furnished without charge to requesting security holders is accompanied by a list briefly describing all the exhibits not contained therein and indicating that the registrant will furnish any exhibit upon the payment of a specified reasonable fee, which fee shall be limited to the registrant's reasonable expenses in furnishing such exhibit. If the registrant's annual report to security holders complies with all of the disclosure requirements of Form 10–K and is filed with the Commission in satisfaction of its Form 10–K filing requirements, such registrant need not furnish a separate Form 10–K to security holders who receive a copy of such annual report.

NOTE to paragraph(b)(10): Pursuant to the undertaking required by paragraph (b)(10) of this rule, a registrant shall furnish a copy of its annual report on Form 10–K to a beneficial owner of its securities upon receipt of a written request from such person. Each request must set forth a good faith representation that, as of the record date for the solicitation requiring the furnishing of the annual report to security holders pursuant to paragraph (b) of this rule, the person making the request was a beneficial owner of securities entitled to vote.

(11)   Subject to the foregoing requirements, the report may be in any form deemed suitable by management and the information required by paragraphs (b)(5) to (10) of this rule may be presented in an appendix or other separate section of the report, provided that the attention of security holders is called to such presentation.

NOTE: Registrants are encouraged to utilize tables, schedules, charts and graphic illustrations of present financial information in an understandable manner. Any presentation of financial information must be consistent with the data in the financial statements contained in the report and, if appropriate, should refer to relevant portions of the financial statements and notes thereto.

(12)   [Reserved.]

(13)   Paragraph (b) of this rule shall not apply, however, to solicitations made on behalf of the registrant before the financial statements are available if a solicitation is being made at the same time

in opposition to the registrant and if the registrant's proxy statement includes an undertaking in bold face type to furnish such annual report to all persons being solicited at least 20 calendar days before the date of the meeting or, if the solicitation refers to a written consent or authorization in lieu of a meeting, at least 20 calendar days prior to the earliest date on which it may be used to effect corporate action.

(c)   The report sent to security holders pursuant to this rule shall be submitted in electronic format, in accordance with the EDGAR Filer Manual, to the Commission, solely for its information, not later than the date on which such report is first sent or given to security holders or the date on which preliminary copies, or definitive copies, if preliminary filing was not required, of solicitation material are filed with the Commission pursuant to Rule 4a–6, whichever date is later. The report is not deemed to be "soliciting material" or to be "filed" with the Commission or subject to this regulation otherwise than as provided in this Rule, or to the liabilities of section 18 of the Act, except to the extent that the registrant specifically requests that it be treated as a part of the proxy soliciting material or incorporates it in the proxy statement or other filed report by reference

(d)   An annual report to security holders prepared on an integrated basis pursuant to General Instruction H to Form 10–K may also be submitted in satisfaction of this rule. When filed as the annual report on Form 10–K, responses to the Items of that form are subject to Section 18 of the Act notwithstanding paragraph (c) of this rule.

(e)   Notwithstanding paragraphs (a) and (b) of this rule:

(e)(1)(i)   A registrant will be considered to have delivered an annual report to security holders, proxy statement or Notice of Internet Availability of Proxy Materials, as described in Rule 14a–16, to all security holders of record who share an address if:

(A)   The registrant delivers one annual report to security holders, proxy statement or Notice of Internet Availability of Proxy Materials, as applicable, to the shared address;

(B)   The registrant addresses the annual report to security holders, proxy statement or Notice of Internet Availability of Proxy Materials, as applicable, to the security holders as a group (for example, "ABC Fund [or Corporation] Security Holders," "Jane Doe and Household," "The Smith Family"), to each of the security holders individually (for example, "John Doe and Richard Jones") or to the security holders in a form to which each of the security holders has consented in writing;

NOTE to paragraph (e)(1)(i)(B): Unless the registrant addresses the annual report to security holders, proxy statement or Notice of Internet Availability of Proxy Materials to the security holders as a group or to each of the security holders individually, it must obtain, from each security holder to be included in the household group, a separate affirmative written consent to the specific form of address the registrant will use.

(C)   The security holders consent, in accordance with paragraph (e)(1)(ii) of this rule, to delivery of one annual report to security holders or proxy statement, as applicable;

(D)   With respect to delivery of the proxy statement or Notice of Internet Availability of Proxy Materials, the registrant delivers, together with or subsequent to delivery of the proxy statement, a separate proxy card for each security holder at the shared address; and

(E)   The registrant includes an undertaking in the proxy statement to deliver promptly upon written or oral request a separate copy of the annual report to security holders, proxy statement or Notice of Internet Availability of Proxy Materials, as applicable, to a security holder at a shared address to which a single copy of the document was delivered.

(ii)   *Consent.*

(A)   *Affirmative written consent.* Each security holder must affirmatively consent, in writing, to delivery of one annual report to security holders or proxy statement, as applicable. A security holder's affirmative written consent will be considered valid only if the security holder has been informed of:

(1)   The duration of the consent;

(2)   The specific types of documents to which the consent will apply;

(3)   The procedures the security holder must follow to revoke consent; and

(4)   The registrant's obligation to begin sending individual copies to a security holder within thirty days after the security holder revokes consent.

(B)   *Implied consent.* The registrant need not obtain affirmative written consent from a security holder for purposes of paragraph (e)(1)(ii)(A) of this Rule if all of the following conditions are met:

(1)   The security holder has the same last name as the other security holders at the shared address or the registrant reasonably believes that the security holders are members of the same family;

(2)   The registrant has sent the security holder a notice at least 60 days before the registrant begins to rely on this rule concerning delivery of annual reports to security holders, proxy statements or Notices of Internet Availability of Proxy Materials to that security holder. The notice must:

(i)   Be a separate written document;

(ii)   State that only one annual report to security holders, proxy statement or Notice of Internet Availability of Proxy Materials, as applicable, will be delivered to the shared address unless the registrant receives contrary instructions;

(iii)   Include a toll-free telephone number, or be accompanied by a reply form that is pre-addressed with postage provided, that the security holder can use to notify the registrant that the security holder wishes to receive a separate annual report to security holders, proxy statement or Notice of Internet Availability of Proxy Materials;

(iv)   State the duration of the consent;

(v)   Explain how a security holder can revoke consent;

(vi)   State that the registrant will begin sending individual copies to a security holder within thirty days after the security holder revokes consent; and

(vii)   Contain the following prominent statement, or similar clear and understandable statement, in bold-face type: "Important Notice Regarding Delivery of Security Holder Documents." This statement also must appear on the envelope in which the notice is delivered. Alternatively, if the notice is delivered separately from other communications to security holders, this statement may appear either on the notice or on the envelope in which the notice is delivered.

NOTE to paragraph (e)(1)(ii)(B)(2): The notice should be written in plain English. See Rule 421(d)(2) of this chapter for a discussion of plain English principles.

(3)   The registrant has not received the reply form or other notification indicating that the security holder wishes to continue to receive an individual copy of the annual report to security holders, proxy statement or Notice of Internet Availability of Proxy Materials, as applicable, within 60 days after the registrant sent the notice required by paragraph (e)(1)(ii)(B)(2) of this rule; and

(4)   The registrant delivers the document to a post office box or residential street address.

NOTE to paragraph (e)(1)(ii)(B)(4): The registrant can assume that a street address is residential unless the registrant has information that indicates the street address is a business.

(iii)   *Revocation of consent.* If a security holder, orally or in writing, revokes consent to delivery of one annual report to security holders, proxy statement or Notice of Internet Availability of Proxy Materials to a shared address, the registrant must begin sending individual copies to that security holder within 30 days after the registrant receives revocation of the security holder's consent.

(iv)   *Definition of address.* Unless otherwise indicated, for purposes of this Rule, address means a street address, a post office box number, an electronic mail address, a facsimile telephone number or other similar destination to which paper or electronic documents are delivered, unless otherwise provided in this Rule. If the registrant has reason to believe that the address is a street address of a multi-unit building, the address must include the unit number.

NOTE to paragraph (e)(1): A person other than the registrant making a proxy solicitation may deliver a single proxy statement to security holders of record or beneficial owners who have separate accounts and share an address if: (a) the registrant or intermediary has followed the procedures in this Rule; and (b) the registrant or intermediary makes available the shared address information to the person in accordance with Rule 14a–7(a)(2)(i) and (ii).

(2)   Notwithstanding paragraphs (a) and (b) of this rule, unless state law requires otherwise, a registrant is not required to send an annual report to security holders, proxy statement or Notice of Internet Availability of Proxy Materials to a security holder if:

(i)   An annual report to security holders and a proxy statement, or a Notice of Internet Availability of Proxy Materials, for two consecutive annual meetings; or

(ii)   All, and at least two, payments (if sent by first class mail) of dividends or interest on securities, or dividend reinvestment confirmations, during a twelve month period, have been mailed to such security holder's address and have been returned as undeliverable. If any such security holder delivers or causes to be delivered to the registrant written notice setting forth his then current address for security holder communications purposes, the registrant's obligation to deliver an annual report to security holders, a proxy statement or a Notice of Internet Availability of Proxy Materials under this rule is reinstated.

(f)   The provisions of paragraph (a) of this rule shall not apply to a communication made by means of speeches in public forums, press releases, published or broadcast opinions, statements, or advertisements appearing in a broadcast media, newspaper, magazine or other bona fide publication disseminated on a regular basis, provided that:

(1)   No form of proxy, consent or authorization or means to execute the same is provided to a security holder in connection with the communication; and

(2)   At the time the communication is made, a definitive proxy statement is on file with the Commission pursuant to Rule 14a–6(b).

Rule 14a–4.   Requirements as to Proxy

(a)   The form of proxy

(1)   shall indicate in bold-face type whether or not the proxy is solicited on behalf of the registrant's board of directors or, if provided other than by a majority of the board of directors, shall indicate in bold-face type on whose behalf the solicitation is made;

(2)   Shall provide a specifically designated blank space for dating the proxy card; and

(3)   Shall identify clearly and impartially each matter intended to be acted upon, whether or not related to or conditioned on the approval of other matters, and whether proposed by the registrant or by security holders. No reference need be made, however, to proposals as to which discretionary authority is conferred pursuant to paragraph (c) of this rule.

NOTE to paragraph (a)(3) (electronic filers): Electronic filers shall satisfy the filing requirements of Rule 14a–6(a) or (b) with respect to the form of proxy by filing the form of proxy as an appendix at the end of the proxy statement. Forms of proxy shall not be filed as exhibits or separate documents within an electronic submission.

(b)(1)   Means shall be provided in the form of proxy whereby the person solicited is afforded an opportunity to specify by boxes a choice between approval or disapproval of, or abstention with respect to each separate matter referred to therein as intended to be acted upon, other than elections to office and votes to determine the frequency of shareholder votes on executive compensation pursuant to Rule 14a–21(b) of this chapter. A proxy may confer discretionary authority with respect to matters as to which a choice is not specified by the security holder provided that the form of proxy states in bold-face type how it is intended to vote the shares represented by the proxy in each such case.

(2)   A form of proxy that provides for the election of directors shall set forth the names of persons nominated for election as directors, including any person whose nomination by a shareholder or

shareholder group satisfies the requirements of an applicable state or foreign law provision, or a registrant's governing documents asthey relate to the inclusion of shareholder director nominees in the registrant's proxymaterials.

(3) Except as otherwise provided in § 240.14a–19, a form of proxy that provides for the election of directors may provide a means for the security holder to grant authorityto vote for the nominees set forth, as a group, provided that there is a similar means for the security holder to withhold authority to vote for such group of nominees (or, when applicable state law gives legal effect to votes cast against a nominee, a similar means forthe security holder to vote against such group of nominees and a means for security holders to abstain from voting for such group of nominees). Any such form of proxy which is executed by the security holder in such manner as not to withhold authority to vote for the election of any nominee, or not to grant authority to vote against the election of any nominee, shall be deemed to grant authority to vote for the election of any nominee, provided that the form of proxy so states in bold-face type. Means to grant authority to vote for any nominees as a group or to withhold authority for any nominees as a group or to vote against any nominees as a group may not be provided if the form of proxy includes one or more shareholder nominees in accordance with an applicable state or foreign law provision, or a registrant's governing documents as they relate to the inclusion of shareholder director nominees in the registrant's proxy materials.

(4) When applicable state law gives legal effect to votes cast against a nominee,then in lieu of providing a means for security holders to withhold authority to vote, the form of proxy shall provide a means for security holders to vote against each nominee and a means for security holders to abstain from voting. When applicable state law does not give legal effect to votes cast against a nominee, such form of proxy shall not providea means for security holders to vote against any nominee and such form of proxy shall clearly provide any of the following means for security holders to withhold authority to vote for each nominee:

(i) A box opposite the name of each nominee which may be marked to indicate that authority to vote for such nominee is withheld; or

(ii) An instruction in bold-face type which indicates that the security holder may withhold authority to vote for any nominee by lining through or otherwise striking out the name of any nominee; or

(iii) Designated blank spaces in which the security holder may enter the names of nominees with respect to whom the security holder chooses to withhold authority to vote; or

(iv) Any other similar means, provided that clear instructions are furnished indicating how the security holder may withhold authority to vote for any nominee.

Instruction to paragraphs (b)(2), (3), and (4): These paragraphs do not apply in the case of a merger, consolidation or other plan if the election of directors isan integral part of the plan.

(b)(5) A form of proxy which provides for a shareholder vote on the frequency of shareholder votes to approve the compensation of executives required by section 14A(a)(2) of the Securities Exchange Act of 1934 shall provide means whereby the person solicited is afforded an opportunity to specify by boxes a choice among 1, 2 or 3 years, or abstain.

Instructions. 1. Paragraph (2) does not apply in the case of a merger, consolidation or other plan if the election of directors is an integral part of the plan.

2. If applicable state law gives legal effect to votes cast against a nominee, then in lieu of, or in addition to, providing a means for security holders to withhold authority to vote, the issuer should provide a similar means for security holders to vote against each nominee.

(c) A proxy may confer discretionary authority to vote with respect to any of the following matters:

(1) For an annual meeting of shareholders, if the registrant did not have notice of the matter at least 45 days before the date on which the registrant first sent its proxy materials for the prior year's annual meeting of shareholders (or date specified by an advance notice provision), and a specific statement to that effect is made in the proxy statement or form of proxy. If during the prior year the registrant did not hold an annual meeting, or if the date of the meeting has changed more than 30 days

from the prior year, then notice must not have been received a reasonable time before the registrant sends its proxy materials for the current year.

(2) In the case in which the registrant has received timely notice in connection with an annual meeting of shareholders (as determined under paragraph (c)(1) of this rule), if the registrant includes, in the proxy statement, advice on the nature of the matter and how the registrant intends to exercise its discretion to vote on each matter. However, even if the registrant includes this information in its proxy statement, it may not exercise discretionary voting authority on a particular proposal if the proponent:

(i) Provides the registrant with a written statement, within the time-frame determined under paragraph (c)(1) of this rule, that the proponent intends to deliver a proxy statement and form of proxy to holders of at least the percentage of the company's voting shares required under applicable law to carry the proposal;

(ii) Includes the same statement in its proxy materials filed under Rule 14a–6; and

(iii) Immediately after soliciting the percentage of shareholders required to carry the proposal, provides the registrant with a statement from any solicitor or other person with knowledge that the necessary steps have been taken to deliver a proxy statement and form of proxy to holders of at least the percentage of the company's voting shares required under applicable law to carry out the proposal.

(3) For solicitations other than for annual meetings or for solicitations by persons other than the registrant, matters which the persons making the solicitation do not know, a reasonable time before the solicitation, are to be presented at the meeting, if a specific statement to that effect is made in the proxy statement or form of proxy.

(4) Approval of the minutes of the prior meeting if such approval does not amount to ratification of the action taken at that meeting;

(5) The election of any person to any office for which a bona fide nominee is named in a proxy statement and such nominee is unable to serve or for good cause will not serve.

(6) Any proposal omitted from the proxy statement and form of proxy pursuant to Rules 14a–8 or 14a–9 of this chapter.

(7) Matters incident to the conduct of the meeting.

(d) No proxy shall confer authority:

(1) To vote for the election of any person to any office for which a bona fide nominee is not named in the proxy statement,

(i) A person shall not be deemed to be a bona fide nominee and shall not be named as such unless the person has consented to being named in a proxy statement relating to the registrant's next annual meeting of shareholders at which directors are to be elected (or a special meeting in lieu of such meeting) and to serve if elected.

(ii) Notwithstanding paragraph (d)(1)(i) of this section, if the registrant is an investment company registered under the Investment Company Act of 1940 (15 U.S.C. 80a–1 *et seq.*) or a business development company as defined by section 2(a)(48) of the Investment Company Act of 1940 (15 U.S.C. 80a–2(a)(48)), a person shall not be deemed to be a bona fide nominee and shall not be named as such unless the person has consented to being named in the proxy statement and to serve if elected. Provided, however, that nothing in this § 240.14a–4 shall prevent any person soliciting in support of nominees who, if elected, would constitute a minority of the board of directors of an investment company registered under the Investment Company Act of 1940 or a business development company as defined by section 2(a)(48) of the Investment Company Act of 1940, from seeking authority to vote for nominees named in the registrant's proxy statement, so long as the soliciting party:

(A) Seeks authority to vote in the aggregate for the number of director positions then subject to election;

(B)   Represents that it will vote for all the registrant nominees, other than those registrant nominees specified by the soliciting party;

(C)   Provides the security holder an opportunity to withhold authority with respect to any other registrant nominee by writing the name of that nominee on the form of proxy; and

(D)   States on the form of proxy and in the proxy statement that there is no assurance that the registrant's nominees will serve if elected with any of the soliciting party's nominees.

(2)   To vote at any annual meeting other than the next annual meeting (or any adjournment thereof) to be held after the date on which the proxy statement and form of proxy are first sent or given to security holders,

(3)   To vote with respect to more than one meeting (and any adjournment thereof) or more than one consent solicitation or

(4)   To consent to or authorize any action other than the action proposed to be taken in the proxy statement, or matters referred to in paragraph (c) of this rule. A person shall not be deemed to be a bona fide nominee and he shall not be named as such unless he has consented to being named in the proxy statement and to serve if elected. Provided, however, That nothing in this Rule 14a–4 shall prevent any person soliciting in support of nominees who, if elected, would constitute a minority of the board of directors, from seeking authority to vote for nominees named in the registrant's proxy statement, so long as the soliciting party:

(i)   Seeks authority to vote in the aggregate for the number of director positions then subject to election;

(ii)   Represents that it will vote for all the registrant nominees, other than those registrant nominees specified by the soliciting party;

(iii)   Provides the security holder an opportunity to withhold authority with respect to any other registrant nominee by writing the name of that nominee on the form of proxy; and

(iv)   States on the form of proxy and in the proxy statement that there is no assurance that the registrant's nominees will serve if elected with any of the soliciting party's nominees.

(e)   The proxy statement or form of proxy shall provide, subject to reasonable specified conditions, that the shares represented by the proxy will be voted and that where the person solicited specifies by means of a ballot provided pursuant to paragraph (b) of this rule a choice with respect to any matter to be acted upon, the shares will be voted in accordance with the specifications so made.

(f)   No person conducting a solicitation subject to this regulation shall deliver a form of proxy, consent or authorization to any security holder unless the security holder concurrently receives, or has previously received, a definitive proxy statement that has been filed with the Commission pursuant to Rule 14a–6(b).

Rule 14a–5.   Presentation of Information in Proxy Statement

(a)   The information included in the proxy statement shall be clearly presented and the statements made shall be divided into groups according to subject matter and the various groups of statements shall be preceded by appropriate headings. The order of items and sub-items in the schedule need not be followed. Where practicable and appropriate, the information shall be presented in tabular form. All amounts shall be stated in figures. Information required by more than one applicable item need not be repeated. No statement need be made in response to any item or sub-item which is inapplicable.

(b)   Any information required to be included in the proxy statement as to terms of securities or other subject matter which from a standpoint of practical necessity must be determined in the future may be stated in terms of present knowledge and intention. To the extent practicable, the authority to be conferred concerning each such matter shall be confined within limits reasonably related to the need for discretionary authority. Subject to the foregoing, information which is not known to the persons on whose behalf the solicitation is to be made and which it is not reasonably within the power of such persons to ascertain or procure may be omitted, if a brief statement of the circumstances rendering such information unavailable is made.

(c)   Any information contained in any other proxy soliciting material which has been or will be furnished to each person solicited in connection with the same meeting or subject matter may be omitted from the proxy statement, if a clear reference is made to the particular document containing such information.

(d)(1)   All printed proxy statements shall be in roman type at least as large and as legible as 10-point modern type, except that to the extent necessary for convenient presentation financial statements and other tabular data, but not the notes thereto, may be in roman type at least as large and as legible as 8-point modern type. All such type shall be leaded at least 2 points.

(2)   Where a proxy statement is delivered through an electronic medium, issuers may satisfy legibility requirements applicable to printed documents, such as type size and font, by presenting all required information in a format readily communicated to investors.

(e)   All proxy statements shall disclose, under an appropriate caption, the following dates:

(1)   The deadline for submitting shareholder proposals for inclusion in the registrant's proxy statement and form of proxy for the registrant's next annual meeting, calculated in the manner provided in 14a–8(d) (Question 5);

(2)   The date after which notice of a shareholder proposal submitted outside the processes of 14a–8 is considered untimely, either calculated in the manner provided by 14a–4(c)(1) or as established by the registrant's advance notice provision, if any, authorized by applicable state law; and

(3)   The deadline for submitting nominees for inclusion in the registrant's proxy statement and form of proxy pursuant to Rule 14a–11, an applicable state or foreign law provision, or a registrant's governing documents as they relate to the inclusion of shareholder director nominees in the registrant's proxy materials for the registrant's next annual meeting of shareholders.

(4)   The deadline for providing notice of a solicitation of proxies in support of director nominees other than the registrant's nominees pursuant to Rule 14a–19 for the registrant's next annual meeting unless the registrant is an investment company registered under the Investment Company Act of 1940 or a business development company as defined by section 2(a)(48) of the Investment Company Act of 1940.

(f)   If the date of the next annual meeting is subsequently advanced or delayed by more than 30 calendar days from the date of the annual meeting to which the proxy statement relates, the registrant shall, in a timely manner, inform shareholders of such change, and the new dates referred to in paragraphs (e)(1) and (e)(2) of this rule, by including a notice, under Item 5, in its earliest possible quarterly report on Form 10–Q, or, in the case of investment companies, in a shareholder report under Rule 30d–1 under the Investment Company Act of 1940, or, if impracticable, any means reasonably calculated to inform shareholders.

Rule 14a–6. Filing Requirements

(a)   *Preliminary proxy statement.* Five preliminary copies of the proxy statement and form of proxy shall be filed with the Commission at least 10 calendar days prior to the date definitive copies of such material are first sent or given to security holders, or such shorter period prior to that date as the Commission may authorize upon a showing of good cause thereunder. A registrant, however, shall not file with the Commission a preliminary proxy statement, form of proxy or other soliciting material to be furnished to security holders concurrently therewith if the solicitation relates to an annual (or special meeting in lieu of the annual) meeting, or for an investment company registered under the Investment Company Act of 1940 or a business development company, if the solicitation relates to any meeting of security holders at which the only matters to be acted upon are:

(1)   The election of directors;

(2)   The election, approval or ratification of accountant(s);

(3)   A security holder proposal included pursuant to Rule 14a–8;

(4)   A shareholder nominee for director included pursuant to Rule 14a–11, an applicable state or foreign law provision, or a registrant's governing documents as they relate to the inclusion of shareholder director nominees in the registrant's proxy materials.

(5)   the approval or ratification of a plan as defined in paragraph (a)(6)(ii) of Item 402 of Regulation S–K or amendments to such a plan;

(6)   With respect to an investment company registered under the Investment Company Act of 1940 or a business development company, a proposal to continue, without change, any advisory or other contract or agreement that previously has been the subject of a proxy solicitation for which proxy material was filed with the Commission pursuant to this rule;

(7)   A vote to approve the compensation of executives as required pursuant to section 14A(a)(1) of the Securities Exchange Act of 1934 and Rule 14a–21(a) of this chapter, or pursuant to section 111(e)(1) of the Emergency Economic Stabilization Act of 2008 and Rule 14a–20 of this chapter, a vote to determine the frequency of shareholder votes to approve the compensation of executives as required pursuant to Rule 14A(a)(2) of the Securities Exchange Act of 1934 and Rule 14a–21(b) of this Act, or any other shareholder advisory vote on executive compensation.

(8)   A vote to approve the compensation of executives as required pursuant to Section 111(e)(1) of the Emergency Economic Stabilization Act of 2008 and Rule 14a–20.

This exclusion from filing preliminary proxy material does not apply if the registrant comments upon or refers to a solicitation in opposition in connection with the meeting in its proxy material.

NOTE 1: The filing of revised material does not recommence the ten day time period unless the revised material contains material revisions or material new proposal(s) that constitute a fundamental change in the proxy material.

NOTE 2: The official responsible for the preparation of the proxy material should make every effort to verify the accuracy and completeness of the information required by the applicable rules. The preliminary material should be filed with the Commission at the earliest practicable date.

NOTE 3: Solicitation in Opposition. For purposes of the exclusion from filing preliminary proxy material, a "solicitation in opposition" includes: (a) Any solicitation opposing a proposal supported by the registrant; (b) any solicitation supporting a proposal that the registrant does not expressly support, other than a securityholder proposal included in the registrant's proxy material pursuant to Rule 14a–8; and (c) any solicitation subject to Rule 14a–19. The inclusion of a security holder proposal in the registrant's proxy material pursuant to Rule 14a–8 does not constitute a "solicitation in opposition," even if the registrant opposes the proposal and/or includes a statement in opposition to the proposal. The inclusion of a shareholder nominee in the registrant's proxy materials pursuant to an applicable state or foreign law provision, or a registrant's governing documents as they relate to the inclusion of shareholder director nominees in the registrant's proxy materials does not constitute a "solicitation in opposition" for purposes of Rule 14a–6(a), even if the registrant opposes the shareholder nominee and solicits against the shareholder nominee and in favor of a registrant nominee.

NOTE 4: A registrant that is filing proxy material in preliminary form only because the registrant has commented on or referred to a solicitation in opposition should indicate that fact in a transmittal letter when filing the preliminary material with the Commission.

(b)   *Definitive proxy statement and other soliciting material.* Eight definitive copies of the proxy statement, form of proxy and all other soliciting materials, in the same form as the materials sent to security holders, must be filed with the Commission no later than the date they are first sent or given to security holders. Three copies of these materials also must be filed with, or mailed for filing to, each national securities exchange on which the registrant has a class of securities listed and registered.

(c)   *Personal solicitation materials.* If part or all of the solicitation involves personal solicitation, then eight copies of all written instructions or other materials that discuss, review or comment on the merits of any matter to be acted on, that are furnished to persons making the actual solicitation for their use directly or indirectly in connection with the solicitation, must be filed with the Commission no later than the date the materials are first sent or given to these persons.

(d)   *Release dates.* All preliminary proxy statements and forms filed pursuant to paragraph (a) of this rule shall be accompanied by a statement of the date on which definitive copies therefor filed pursuant to paragraph (b) of this rule are intended to be released to security holders. All definitive material filed pursuant to paragraph (b) of this rule shall be accompanied by a statement of the date on which copies of such material have been released to security holders, or, if not released, the date on which copies thereof are intended to be released. All material filed pursuant to paragraph (c) of this rule shall be accompanied by a statement of the date on which copies thereof were released to the individual who will make the actual solicitation, or if not released, the date on which copies thereof are intended to be released.

(e)(1) *Public Availability of Information.* All copies of preliminary proxy statements and forms of proxy filed pursuant to paragraph (a) of this rule shall be clearly marked "Preliminary Copies," and shall be deemed immediately available for public inspection unless confidential treatment is obtained pursuant to paragraph (e)(2) of this rule.

(2) *Confidential treatment.* If action will be taken on any matter specified in Item 14 of Schedule 14A, all copies of the preliminary proxy statement and form of proxy filed under paragraph (a) of this rule will be for the information of the Commission only and will not be deemed available for public inspection until filed with the Commission in definitive form so long as:

(i) The proxy statement does not relate to a matter of proposal subject to Rule 13e–3 or a roll-up transaction as defined in Item 901(c) of Regulation S–K;

(ii) Neither the parties to the transaction nor any persons authorized to act on their behalf have made any public communications relating to the transaction except for statements where the content is limited to the information specified in Rule 135 under the Securities Act; and

(iii) The materials are filed in paper and marked "Confidential, For Use of the Commission Only." In all cases, the materials may be disclosed to any department or agency of the United States Government and to the Congress, and the Commission may make any inquiries or investigation into the materials as may be necessary to conduct an adequate review by the Commission.

Instruction to paragraph (e)(2): If communications are made publicly that go beyond the information specified in Rule 135, the preliminary proxy materials must be re-filed promptly with the Commission as public materials.

* * *

(f) *Communications not required to be filed.* Copies of replies to inquiries from security holders requesting further information and copies of communications which do no more than request that forms of proxy theretofore solicited be signed and returned need not be filed pursuant to this rule.

(g) *Solicitations Subject to Rule 14a–2(b)(1).*

(1) Any person who:

(i) Engages in a solicitation pursuant to Rule 14a–2(b)(1), and

(ii) At the commencement of that solicitation owns beneficially securities of the class which is the subject of the solicitation with a market value of over $5 million,

Shall furnish or mail to the Commission, not later than three days after the date the written solicitation is first sent or given to any security holder, five copies of a statement containing the information specified in the Notice of Exempt Solicitation which statement shall attach as an exhibit all written soliciting materials. Five copies of an amendment to such statement shall be furnished or mailed to the Commission, in connection with dissemination of any additional communications, not later than three days after the date the additional material is first sent or given to any security holder. Three copies of the Notice of Exempt Solicitation and amendments thereto shall, at the same time the materials are furnished or mailed to the Commission, be furnished or mailed to each national securities exchange upon which any class of securities of the registrant is listed and registered.

(2) Notwithstanding paragraph (g)(1) of this Rule, no such submission need be made with respect to oral solicitations (other than with respect to scripts used in connection with such oral solicitations), speeches delivered in a public forum, press releases, published or broadcast opinions, statements, and advertisements appearing in a broadcast media, or a newspaper, magazine or other bona fide publication disseminated on a regular basis.

(h) *Revised material.* Where any proxy statement, form of proxy or other material filed pursuant to this rule is amended or revised, two of the copies of such amended or revised material filed pursuant to this rule (or in the case of investment companies registered under the Investment Company Act of 1940, three of such copies) shall be marked to indicate clearly and precisely the changes effected therein. If the amendment or revision alters the text of the material the changes in such text shall be indicated by means of underscoring or in some other appropriate manner.

(i)   *Fees.* At the time of filing the proxy solicitation material, the persons upon whose behalf the solicitation is made, other than investment companies registered under the Investment Company Act of 1940, shall pay to the Commission the following applicable fee:

(1)   For preliminary proxy material involving acquisitions, mergers, spin-offs, consolidations or proposed sales or other dispositions of substantially all the assets of the company, a fee established in accordance with Rule 0–11 shall be paid. No refund shall be given.

(2)   For all other proxy submissions and submissions made pursuant to Rule 14a–6(g), no fee shall be required.

(j)   *Merger proxy materials.* (1) Any proxy statement, form of proxy or other soliciting material required to be filed by this rule that also is either

(i)   Included in a registration statement filed under the Securities Act of 1933 on Forms S–4, F–4 or N–14; or

(ii)   Filed under Rule 424, Rule 425 or Rule 497 under the Securities Act of 1933 is required to be filed only under the Securities Act, and is deemed filed under this rule.

(2)   Under paragraph (j)(1) of this rule, the fee required by paragraph (i) of this rule need not be paid.

(k)   *Computing time periods.* In computing time periods beginning with the filing date specified in Regulation 14A, the filing date shall be counted as the first day of the time period and midnight of the last day shall constitute the end of the specified time period.

(l)   *Roll-up transactions.* If a transaction is a roll-up transaction as defined in Item 901(c) of Regulation S–K and is registered (or authorized to be registered) on Form S–4 or Form F–4, the proxy statement of the sponsor or the general partner as defined in Item 901(d) and Item 901(a), respectively, of Regulation S–K must be distributed to security holders no later than the lesser of 60 calendar days prior to the date on which the meeting of security holders is held or action is taken, or the maximum number of days permitted for giving notice under applicable state law.

(m)   *Cover Page.* Proxy materials filed with the Commission shall include a cover page in the form set forth in Schedule 14A. The cover page required by this paragraph need not be distributed to security holders.

(n)   *Solicitations subject to Rule 14a–2(b)(4).* Any person who:

(1)   Engages in a solicitation pursuant to Rule 14a–2(b)(4); and

(2)   At the commencement of that solicitation both owns five percent (5%) or more of the outstanding securities of a class that is the subject of the proposed roll-up transaction, and engages in the business of buying and selling limited partnership interests in the secondary market, shall furnish or mail to the Commission, not later than three days after the date an oral or written solicitation by that person is first made, sent or provided to any security holder, five copies of a statement containing the information specified in the Notice of Exempt Preliminary Roll-up Communication. Five copies of any amendment to such statement shall be furnished or mailed to the Commission not later than three days after a communication containing revised material is first made, sent or provided to any security holder.

(o)   *Solicitations before furnishing a definitive proxy statement.* Solicitations that are published, sent or given to security holders before they have been furnished a definitive proxy statement must be made in accordance with Rule 14a–12 unless there is an exemption available under Rule 14a–2.

(p)   *Solicitations subject to Rule 14a–11.* Any soliciting material that is published, sent or given to shareholders in connection with Rule 14a–2(b)(7) or (b)(8) must be filed with the Commission as specified in that section.

Rule 14a–7. Obligations of Registrants to Provide a List of, or Mail Soliciting Material to, Security Holders

(a)   If the registrant has made or intends to make a proxy solicitation in connection with a security holder meeting or action by consent or authorization, upon the written request by any record or beneficial holder of securities of the class entitled to vote at the meeting or to execute a consent or authorization to provide a list of security holders or to mail the requesting security holder's materials, regardless of whether the request references this rule, the registrant shall:

    (1)   Deliver to the requesting security holder within five business days after receipt of the request:

        (i)   Notification as to whether the registrant has elected to mail the security holder's soliciting materials or provide a security holder list if the election under paragraph (b) of this rule is to be made by the registrant;

        (ii)   A statement of the approximate number of record holders and beneficial holders, separated by type of holder and class, owning securities in the same class or classes as holders which have been or are to be solicited on management's behalf, or any more limited group of such holders designated by the security holder if available or retrievable under the registrant's or its transfer agent's security holder data systems; and

        (iii)   The estimated cost of mailing a proxy statement, form of proxy or other communication to such holders, including to the extent known or reasonably available, the estimated costs of any bank, broker, and similar person through whom the registrant has solicited or intends to solicit beneficial owners in connection with the security holder meeting or action;

    (2)   Perform the acts set forth in either paragraphs (a)(2)(i) or (a)(2)(ii) of this rule, at the registrant's or requesting security holder's option, as specified in paragraph (b) of this rule:

        (i)   Send copies of any proxy statement, form of proxy, or other soliciting material, including a Notice of Internet Availability of Proxy Materials (as described in Rule 14a–16), furnished by the security holder to the record holders, including banks, brokers, and similar entities, designated by the security holder. A sufficient number of copies must be sent to the banks, brokers, and similar entities for distribution to all beneficial owners designated by the security holder. The security holder may designate only record holders and/or beneficial owners who have not requested paper and/ or e-mail copies of the proxy statement. If the registrant has received affirmative written or implied consent to deliver a single proxy statement to security holders at a shared address in accordance with the procedures in Rule 14a–3(e)(1), a single copy of the proxy statement or Notice of Internet Availability of Proxy Materials furnished by the security holder shall be sent to that address, provided that if multiple copies of the Notice of Internet Availability of Proxy Materials are furnished by the security holder for that address, the registrant shall deliver those copies in a single envelope to that address. The registrant shall send the security holder material with reasonable promptness after tender of the material to be sent, envelopes or other containers therefore, postage or payment for postage and other reasonable expenses of effecting such distribution. The registrant shall not be responsible for the content of the material; or

        (ii)   Deliver the following information to the requesting security holder within five business days of receipt of the request:

           (A)   A reasonably current list of the names, addresses and security positions of the record holders, including banks, brokers and similar entities holding securities in the same class or classes as holders which have been or are to be solicited on management's behalf, or any more limited group of such holders designated by the security holder if available or retrievable under the registrant's or its transfer agent's security holder data systems;

           (B)   The most recent list of names, addresses and security positions of beneficial owners as specified in Rule 14a–13(b), in the possession, or which subsequently comes into the possession, of the registrant;

(C)   The names of security holders at a shared address that have consented to delivery of a single copy of proxy materials to a shared address, if the registrant has received written or implied consent in accordance with Rule 14a–3(e)(1); and

(D)   If the registrant has relied on Rule 14a–16, the names of security holders who have requested paper copies of the proxy materials for all meetings and the names of security holders who, as of the date that the registrant receives the request, have requested paper copies of the proxy materials only for the meeting to which the solicitation relates.

(iii)   All security holder list information shall be in the form requested by the security holder to the extent that such form is available to the registrant without undue burden or expense. The registrant shall furnish the security holder with updated record holder information on a daily basis or, if not available on a daily basis, at the shortest reasonable intervals; provided, however, the registrant need not provide beneficial or record holder information more current than the record date for the meeting or action.

(b)(1)   The requesting security holder shall have the options set forth in paragraph (a)(2) of this rule, and the registrant shall have corresponding obligations, if the registrant or general partner or sponsor is soliciting or intends to solicit with respect to:

(i)   A proposal that is subject to Rule 13e–3;

(ii)   A roll-up transaction as defined in Item 901(c) of Regulation S–K that involves an entity with securities registered pursuant to section 12 of the Act; or

(iii)   A roll-up transaction as defined in Item 901(c) of Regulation S–K that involves a limited partnership, unless the transaction involves only:

(A)   Partnerships whose investors will receive new securities or securities in another entity that are not reported under a transaction reporting plan declared effective before December 17, 1993 by the Commission under Section 11A of the Act; or

(B)   Partnerships whose investors' securities are reported under a transaction reporting plan declared effective before December 17, 1993 by the Commission under Section 11A of the Act.

(2)   With respect to all other requests pursuant to this rule, the registrant shall have the option to either mail the security holder's material or furnish the security holder list as set forth in this rule.

(c)   At the time of a list request, the security holder making the request shall:

(1)   If holding the registrant's securities through a nominee, provide the registrant with a statement by the nominee or other independent third party, or a copy of a current filing made with the Commission and furnished to the registrant, confirming such holder's beneficial ownership; and

(2)   Provide the registrant with an affidavit, declaration, affirmation or other similar document provided for under applicable state law identifying the proposal or other corporate action that will be the subject of the security holder's solicitation or communication and attesting that:

(i)   The security holder will not use the list information for any purpose other than to solicit security holders with respect to the same meeting or action by consent or authorization for which the registrant is soliciting or intends to solicit or to communicate with security holders with respect to a solicitation commenced by the registrant; and

(ii)   The security holder will not disclose such information to any person other than a beneficial owner for whom the request was made and an employee or agent to the extent necessary to effectuate the communication or solicitation.

(d)   The security holder shall not use the information furnished by the registrant pursuant to paragraph (a)(2)(ii) of this rule for any purpose other than to solicit security holders with respect to the same meeting or action by consent or authorization for which the registrant is soliciting or intends to solicit or to communicate with security holders with respect to a solicitation commenced by the registrant; or disclose such information to any person other than an employee, agent, or beneficial owner for whom a request was made to the extent necessary to effectuate the communication or solicitation. The security holder shall return the information provided pursuant to paragraph (a)(2)(ii) of this rule and shall not retain any copies thereof or of any information derived from such information after the termination of the solicitation.

(e)   The security holder shall reimburse the reasonable expenses incurred by the registrant in performing the acts requested pursuant to paragraph (a) of this rule.

NOTES to Rule 14a–7.

NOTE 1 to Rule14a–7.   Reasonably prompt methods of distribution to security holders may be used instead of mailing. If an alternative distribution method is chosen, the costs of that method should be considered where necessary rather than the costs of mailing.

NOTE 2 to Rule 14a–7.   When providing the information required by Rule 14a–7(a)(1)(ii), if the registrant has received affirmative written or implied consent to delivery of a single copy of proxy materials to a shared address in accordance with Rule 14a–3(e)(1), it shall exclude from the number of record holders those to whom it does not have to deliver a separate proxy statement.

Rule 14a–8.   Shareholder Proposals

This rule addresses when a company must include a shareholder's proposal in its proxy statement and identify the proposal in its form of proxy when the company holds an annual or special meeting of shareholders. In summary, in order to have your shareholder proposal included on a company's proxy card, and included along with any supporting statement in its proxy statement, you must be eligible and follow certain procedures. Under a few specific circumstances, the company is permitted to exclude your proposal, but only after submitting its reasons to the Commission. We structured this rule in a question-and-answer format so that it is easier to understand. The references to "you" are to a shareholder seeking to submit the proposal.

(a)   Question 1: What is a proposal? A shareholder proposal is your recommendation or requirement that the company and/or its board of directors take action, which you intend to present at a meeting of the company's shareholders. Your proposal should state as clearly as possible the course of action that you believe the company should follow. If your proposal is placed on the company's proxy card, the company must also provide in the form of proxy means for shareholders to specify by boxes a choice between approval or disapproval, or abstention. Unless otherwise indicated, the word "proposal" as used in this rule refers both to your proposal, and to your corresponding statement in support of your proposal (if any).

(b)   Question 2: Who is eligible to submit a proposal, and how do I demonstrate to the company that I am eligible?

(1)   To be eligible to submit a proposal, you must satisfy the following requirements:

(i)   You must have continuously held:

(A)   At least $2,000 in market value of the company's securities entitled to vote on the proposal for at least three years; or

(B)   At least $15,000 in market value of the company's securities entitled to vote on theproposal for at least two years; or

(C)   At least $25,000 in market value of the company's securities entitled to vote on theproposal for at least one year; or

(D)   The amounts specified in paragraph (b)(3) of this section. This paragraph (b)(1)(i)(D) will expire on the same date that § 240.14a–8(b)(3) expires; and

(ii)   You must provide the company with a written statement that you intend to continue tohold the requisite amount of securities, determined in accordance with paragraph (b)(1)(i)(A) through (C) of this rule, through the date of the shareholders' meeting for which the proposal is submitted; and

(iii)   You must provide the company with a written statement that you are able to meet with the company in person or via teleconference no less than 10 calendar days, nor more than 30 calendar days, after submission of the shareholder proposal. You must include your contact information as well as business days and specific times that you are available to discuss the proposal with the company. You must identify times that are within the regular business hours of the company's principal executive offices. If these hours are not disclosed in the company's proxy statement for the prior year's annual meeting, you must identify times that are between 9 a.m. and 5:30 p.m. in the time zone of the company's principal executive offices. If you elect to co-file a proposal, all co-filers must either:

    (A)   Agree to the same dates and times of availability, or

    (B)   Identify a single lead filer who will provide dates and times of the lead filer's availability to engage on behalf of all co-filers; and

    (iv)   If you use a representative to submit a shareholder proposal on your behalf, you must provide the company with written documentation that:

    (A)   Identifies the company to which the proposal is directed;

    (B)   Identifies the annual or special meeting for which the proposal is submitted;

    (C)   Identifies you as the proponent and identifies the person acting on your behalf as your representative;

    (D)   Includes your statement authorizing the designated representative to submit the proposal and otherwise act on your behalf;

    (E)   Identifies the specific topic of the proposal to be submitted;

    (F)   Includes your statement supporting the proposal; and

    (G)   Is signed and dated by you.

    (v)   The requirements of paragraph (b)(1)(iv) of this rule shall not apply to shareholders that are entities so long as the representative's authority to act on the shareholder's behalf is apparent and self-evident such that a reasonable person would understand that the agent has authority to submit the proposal and otherwise act on the shareholder's behalf.

    (vi)   For purposes of paragraph (b)(1)(i) of this rule, you may not aggregate your holdings with those of another shareholder or group of shareholders to meet the requisite amount of securities necessary to be eligible to submit a proposal.

    (2)   One of the following methods must be used to demonstrate your eligibility to submit a proposal:

    (i)   If you are the registered holder of your securities, which means that your name appears in the company's records as a shareholder, the company can verify your eligibility on its own, although you will still have to provide the company with a written statement that you intend to continue to hold the requisite amount of securities, determined in accordance with paragraph (b)(1)(i)(A) through (C) of this rule, through the date of the meeting of shareholders.

    (ii)   If, like many shareholders, you are not a registered holder, the company likely does not know that you are a shareholder, or how many shares you own. In this case, at the time you submit your proposal, you must prove your eligibility to the company in one of two ways:

    (A)   The first way is to submit to the company a written statement from the "record" holder of your securities (usually a broker or bank) verifying that, at the time you submitted your proposal, you continuously held at least $2,000, $15,000, or $25,000 in market value of the company's securities entitled to vote on the proposal for at least three years, two years, or one year, respectively. You must also include your own written statement that you intend to continue to hold the requisite amount of securities, determined in accordance with paragraph (b)(1)(i)(A) through (C) of this rule, through the date of the shareholders' meeting for which the proposal is submitted; or

    (B)   The second way to prove ownership applies only if you were required to file, and filed, a Schedule 13D (§ 240.13d–101), Schedule 13G (§ 240.13d–102), Form 3 (§ 249.103 of this chapter), Form 4 (§ 249.104 of this chapter), and/or Form 5 (§ 249.105 of this chapter), or amendments to those documents or updated forms, demonstrating that you meet at least one of the share ownership requirements under paragraph (b)(1)(i)(A) through (C) of this rule. If you have filed one or more of these documents with the SEC, you may demonstrate youreligibility to submit a proposal by submitting to the company:

(1) A copy of the schedule(s) and/or form(s), and any subsequent amendments reporting a change in your ownership level;

(2) Your written statement that you continuously held at least $2,000, $15,000, or $25,000 in market value of the company's securities entitled to vote on the proposal for at leastthree years, two years, or one year, respectively; and

(3) Your written statement that you intend to continue to hold the requisite amount of securities, determined in accordance with paragraph (b)(1)(i)(A) through (C) of this section, through the date of the company's annual or special meeting.

(4) If you continuously held at least $2,000 of a company's securities entitled to vote on the proposal for at least one year as of January 4, 2021, and you have continuously maintained a minimum investment ofat least $2,000 of such securities from January 4, 2021 through the date the proposal is submitted to the company, you will be eligible to submit a proposal to such company for an annual or special meeting to be heldprior to January 1, 2023. If you rely on this provision, you must provide the company with yourwritten statement that you intend to continue to hold at least $2,000 of such securities through the date of the shareholders' meeting for which the proposal is submitted. You must also followthe procedures set forth in paragraph (b)(2) of this section to demonstrate that:

(i) You continuously held at least $2,000 of the company's securities entitled to vote onthe proposal for at least one year as of January 4, 2021; and

(ii) You have continuously maintained a minimum investment of at least $2,000 of suchsecurities from January 4, 2021through the date the proposal is submitted to the company.

(iii) This paragraph (b)(3) will expire on January 1, 2023.

(3) If you continuously held at least $2,000 of a company's securities entitled to vote on the proposal for at least one year as of January 4, 2021 and you have continuously maintained a minimum investment of at least $2,000 of such securities from January 4, 2021 through the date the proposal is submitted to the company, you will be eligible to submit a proposal to such company for an annual or special meeting to be held prior to January 1, 2023. If you rely on this provision, you must provide the company with your written statement that you intend to continue to hold at least $2,000 of such securities through the date of the shareholders' meeting for which the proposal is submitted. You must also follow the procedures set forth in paragraph (b)(2) of this rule to demonstrate that:

(i) You continuously held at least $2,000 of the company's securities entitled to vote on the proposal for at least one year as of 60 days after publication in the federal register]; and

(ii) You have continuously maintained a minimum investment of at least $2,000 of such securities from [60 days after publication in the federal register] through the date the proposal is submitted to the company.

(iii) This paragraph (b)(3) will expire on January 1, 2023.

(c) Question 3: How many proposals may I submit? Each person may submit no more than one proposal, directly or indirectly, to a company for a particular shareholders' meeting. A person may not rely on the securities holdings of another person for the purpose of meeting the eligibility requirements and submitting multiple proposals for a particular shareholders' meeting.

(d) Question 4: How long can my proposal be? The proposal, including any accompanying supporting statement, may not exceed 500 words.

(e) Question 5: What is the deadline for submitting a proposal?

(1) If you are submitting your proposal for the company's annual meeting, you can in most cases find the deadline in last year's proxy statement. However, if the company did not hold an

annual meeting last year, or has changed the date of its meeting for this year more than 30 days from last year's meeting, you can usually find the deadline in one of the company's quarterly reports on Form 10–Q, or in shareholder reports of investment companies under Rule 30d–1 of the Investment Company Act of 1940. In order to avoid controversy, shareholders should submit their proposals by means, including electronic means, that permit them to prove the date of delivery.

(2)   The deadline is calculated in the following manner if the proposal is submitted for a regularly scheduled annual meeting. The proposal must be received at the company's principal executive offices not less than 120 calendar days before the date of the company's proxy statement released to shareholders in connection with the previous year's annual meeting. However, if the company did not hold an annual meeting the previous year, or if the date of this year's annual meeting has been changed by more than 30 days from the date of the previous year's meeting, then the deadline is a reasonable time before the company begins to print and send its proxy materials.

(3)   If you are submitting your proposal for a meeting of shareholders other than a regularly scheduled annual meeting, the deadline is a reasonable time before the company begins to print and send its proxy materials.

(f)   Question 6: What if I fail to follow one of the eligibility or procedural requirements explained in answers to Questions 1 through 4 of this rule?

(1)   The company may exclude your proposal, but only after it has notified you of the problem, and you have failed adequately to correct it. Within 14 calendar days of receiving your proposal, the company must notify you in writing of any procedural or eligibility deficiencies, as well as of the time frame for your response. Your response must be postmarked, or transmitted electronically, no later than 14 days from the date you received the company's notification. A company need not provide you such notice of a deficiency if the deficiency cannot be remedied, such as if you fail to submit a proposal by the company's properly determined deadline. If the company intends to exclude the proposal, it will later have to make a submission under Rule 14a–8 and provide you with a copy under Question 10 below, Rule14a–8(j).

(2)   If you fail in your promise to hold the required number of securities through the date of the meeting of shareholders, then the company will be permitted to exclude all of your proposals from its proxy materials for any meeting held in the following two calendar years.

(g)   Question 7: Who has the burden of persuading the Commission or its staff that my proposal can be excluded? Except as otherwise noted, the burden is on the company to demonstrate that it is entitled to exclude a proposal.

(h)   Question 8: Must I appear personally at the shareholders' meeting to present the proposal?

(1)   Either you, or your representative who is qualified under state law to present the proposal on your behalf, must attend the meeting to present the proposal. Whether you attend the meeting yourself or send a qualified representative to the meeting in your place, you should make sure that you, or your representative, follow the proper state law procedures for attending the meeting and/or presenting your proposal.

(2)   If the company holds it shareholder meeting in whole or in part via electronic media, and the company permits you or your representative to present your proposal via such media, then you may appear through electronic media rather than traveling to the meeting to appear in person.

(3)   If you or your qualified representative fail to appear and present the proposal, without good cause, the company will be permitted to exclude all of your proposals from its proxy materials for any meetings held in the following two calendar years.

(i)   Question 9: If I have complied with the procedural requirements, on what other bases may a company rely to exclude my proposal?

(1)   Improper under state law: If the proposal is not a proper subject for action by shareholders under the laws of the jurisdiction of the company's organization;

NOTE to paragraph (i)(1): Depending on the subject matter, some proposals are not considered proper under state law if they would be binding on the company if approved by shareholders. In our experience, most proposals that are cast as recommendations or requests that the board of directors take specified action are proper under state law. Accordingly, we will assume that a proposal drafted as a recommendation or suggestion is proper unless the company demonstrates otherwise.

(2)   Violation of law: If the proposal would, if implemented, cause the company to violate any state, federal, or foreign law to which it is subject;

NOTE to paragraph (i)(2): We will not apply this basis for exclusion to permit exclusion of a proposal on grounds that it would violate foreign law if compliance with the foreign law could result in a violation of any state or federal law.

(3)   Violation of proxy rules: If the proposal or supporting statement is contrary to any of the Commission's proxy rules, including Rule 14a–9, which prohibits materially false or misleading statements in proxy soliciting materials;

(4)   Personal grievance: special interest: If the proposal relates to the redress of a personal claim or grievance against the company or any other person, or if it is designed to result in a benefit to you, or to further a personal interest, which is not shared by the other shareholders at large;

(5)   Relevance: If the proposal relates to operations which account for less than 5 percent of the company's total assets at the end of its most recent fiscal year, and for less than 5 percent of its net earnings and gross sales for its most recent fiscal year, and is not otherwise significantly related to the company's business;

(6)   Absence of power/authority: If the company would lack the power or authority to implement the proposal;

(7)   Management functions: If the proposal deals with a matter relating to the company's ordinary business operations;

(8)   Director elections: If the proposal:

(i)   Would disqualify a nominee who is standing for election;

(ii)   Would remove a director from office before his or her term expired;

(iii)   Questions the competence, business judgment, or character of one or more nominees or directors;

(iv)   Seeks to include a specific individual in the company's proxy materials for election to the board of directors; or

(v)   Otherwise could affect the outcome of the upcoming election of directors.

(9)   Conflicts with company's proposal: If the proposal directly conflicts with one of the company's own proposals to be submitted to shareholders at the same meeting.

NOTE to paragraph (i)(9): A company's submission to the Commission under this rule should specify the points of conflict with the company's proposal.

(10)   Substantially implemented: If the company has already substantially implemented the proposal;

NOTE to paragraph (i)(10): A company may exclude a shareholder proposal that would provide an advisory vote or seek future advisory votes to approve the compensation of executives as disclosed pursuant to Item 402 of Regulation S–K or any successor to Item 402 (a "say-on-pay vote") or that relates to the frequency of say-on-pay votes, provided that in the most recent shareholder vote required by Rule 14a–21(b) of this chapter a single year (i.e., one, two, or three years) received approval of a majority of votes cast on the matter and the company has adopted a policy on the frequency of say-on-pay votes that is consistent with the choice of the majority of votes cast in the most recent shareholder vote required by Rule 14a–21(b) of this chapter.

(11)   Duplication: If the proposal substantially duplicates another proposal previously submitted to the company by another proponent that will be included in the company's proxy materials for the same meeting;

(12) *Resubmissions.* If the proposal addresses substantially the same subject matter as a proposal, or proposals, previously included in the company's proxy materials within the preceding five calendar years if the most recent vote occurred within the preceding three calendar years and the most recent vote was:

    (i)   Less than 5 percent of the votes cast if previously voted on once;

    (ii) Less than 15 percent of the votes cast if previously voted on twice; or

    (iii) Less than 25 percent of the votes cast if previously voted on three or more times.

(13) Specific amount of dividends: If the proposal relates to specific amounts of cash or stock dividends.

(j)   Question 10: What procedures must the company follow if it intends to exclude my proposal?

(1)   If the company intends to exclude a proposal from its proxy materials, it must file its reasons with the Commission no later than 80 calendar days before it files its definitive proxy statement and form of proxy with the Commission. The company must simultaneously provide you with a copy of its submission. The Commission staff may permit the company to make its submission later than 80 days before the company files its definitive proxy statement and form of proxy, if the company demonstrates good cause for missing the deadline.

(2)   The company must file six paper copies of the following:

    (i)   The proposal;

    (ii) An explanation of why the company believes that it may exclude the proposal, which should, if possible, refer to the most recent applicable authority, such as prior Division letters issued under the rule; and

    (iii) A supporting opinion of counsel when such reasons are based on matters of state or foreign law.

(k) Question 11: May I submit my own statement to the Commission responding to the company's arguments? Yes, you may submit a response, but it is not required. You should try to submit any response to us, with a copy to the company, as soon as possible after the company makes its submission. This way, the Commission staff will have time to consider fully your submission before it issues its response. You should submit six paper copies of your response.

(*l*)   Question 12: If the company includes my shareholder proposal in its proxy materials, what information about me must it include along with the proposal itself?

(1)   The company's proxy statement must include your name and address, as well as the number of the company's voting securities that you hold. However, instead of providing that information, the company may instead include a statement that it will provide the information to shareholders promptly upon receiving an oral or written request.

(2)   The company is not responsible for the contents of your proposal or supporting statement.

(m) Question 13: What can I do if the company includes in its proxy statement reasons why it believes shareholders should not vote in favor of my proposal, and I disagree with some of its statements?

(1)   The company may elect to include in its proxy statement reasons why it believes shareholders should vote against your proposal. The company is allowed to make arguments reflecting its own point of view, just as you may express your own point of view in your proposal's supporting statement.

(2)   However, if you believe that the company's opposition to your proposal contains materially false or misleading statements that may violate our anti-fraud rule, 14a–9, you should promptly send to the Commission staff and the company a letter explaining the reasons for your view, along with a copy of the company's statements opposing your proposal. To the extent possible, your letter should include specific factual information demonstrating the inaccuracy of

the company's claims. Time permitting, you may wish to try to work out your differences with the company by yourself before contacting the Commission staff.

(3) We require the company to send you a copy of its statements opposing your proposal before it sends its proxy materials, so that you may bring to our attention any materially false or misleading statements, under the following timeframes:

(i) If our no-action response requires that you make revisions to your proposal or supporting statement as a condition to requiring the company to include it in its proxy materials, then the company must provide you with a copy of its opposition statements no later than 5 calendar days after the company receives a copy of your revised proposal; or

(ii) In all other cases, the company must provide you with a copy of its opposition statements no later than 30 calendar days before its files definitive copies of its proxy statement and form of proxy under Rule 14a–6.

Rule 14a–9. False or Misleading Statements

(a) No solicitation subject to this regulation shall be made by means of any proxy statement, form of proxy, notice of meeting or other communication, written or oral, containing any statement which, at the time and in the light of the circumstances under which it is made, is false or misleading with respect to any material fact, or which omits to state any material fact necessary in order to make the statements therein not false or misleading or necessary to correct any statement in any earlier communication with respect to the solicitation of a proxy for the same meeting or subject matter which has become false or misleading.

(b) The fact that a proxy statement, form of proxy or other soliciting material has been filed with or examined by the Commission shall not be deemed a finding by the Commission that such material is accurate or complete or not false or misleading, or that the Commission has passed upon the merits of or approved any statement contained therein or any matter to be acted upon by security holders. No representation contrary to the foregoing shall be made.

(c) No nominee, nominating shareholder or nominating shareholder group, or any member thereof, shall cause to be included in a registrant's proxy materials, either pursuant to the federal proxy rules, an applicable state or foreign law provision, or a registrant's governing documents as they relate to including shareholder nominees for director in a registrant's proxy materials, include in a notice on Schedule 14N (§ 240.14n–101), or include in any other related communication, any statement which, at the time and in the light of the circumstances under which it is made, is false or misleading with respect to any material fact, or which omits to state any material fact necessary in order to make the statements therein not false or misleading or necessary to correct any statement in any earlier communication with respect to a solicitation for the same meeting or subject matter which has become false or misleading.

NOTE: The following are some examples of what, depending upon particular facts and circumstances, may be misleading within the meaning of this rule.

a. Predictions as to specific future market values.

b. Material which directly or indirectly impugns character, integrity or personal reputation, or directly or indirectly makes charges concerning improper, illegal or immoral conduct or associations, without factual foundation.

c. Failure to so identify a proxy statement, form of proxy and other soliciting material as to clearly distinguish it from the soliciting material of any other person or persons soliciting for the same meeting or subject matter.

d. Claims made prior to a meeting regarding the results of a solicitation.

Rule 14a–10. Prohibition of Certain Solicitations

No person making a solicitation which is subject to Rules 14a–1 to 14a–10 shall solicit:

(a) Any undated or postdated proxy; or

(b) Any proxy which provides that it shall be deemed to be dated as of any date subsequent to the date on which it is signed by the security holder.

Rule 14a–12. Solicitation Prior to Furnishing Required Proxy Statement

(a)   Notwithstanding the provisions of Rule 14a–3(a), a solicitation may be made before furnishing security holders with a proxy statement meeting the requirements of Rule 14a–3(a) if:

(1)   Each written communication includes:

(i)   The identity of the participants in the solicitation (as defined in Instruction 3 to Item 4 of Schedule 14A) and a description of their direct or indirect interests, by security holdings or otherwise, or a prominent legend in clear, plain language advising security holders where they can obtain that information; and

(ii)   A prominent legend in clear, plain language advising security holders to read the proxy statement when it is available because it contains important information. The legend also must explain to investors that they can get the proxy statement, and any other relevant documents, for free at the Commission's web site and describe which documents are available free from the participants; and

(2)   A definitive proxy statement meeting the requirements of Rule 14a–3(a) is sent or given to security holders solicited in reliance on this rule before or at the same time as the forms of proxy, consent or authorization are furnished to or requested from security holders.

(b)   Any soliciting material published, sent or given to security holders in accordance with paragraph (a) of this rule must be filed with the Commission no later than the date the material is first published, sent or given to security holders. Three copies of the material must at the same time be filed with, or mailed for filing to, each national securities exchange upon which any class of securities of the registrant is listed and registered. The soliciting material must include a cover page in the form set forth in Schedule 14A and the appropriate box on the cover page must be marked. Soliciting material in connection with a registered offering is required to be filed only under Rule 424 or Rule 425 of the Securities Act of 1933, and will be deemed filed under this rule.

(c)   Solicitations by any person or group of persons for the purpose of opposing a solicitation subject to this regulation by any person or group of persons with respect to the election or removal of directors at any annual or special meeting of security holders also are subject to the following provisions:

(1)   *Application of this rule to annual report to security holders.* Notwithstanding the provisions of Rule 14a–3(b) and (c), any portion of the annual report to security holders referred to in Rule 14a–3(b) that comments upon or refers to any solicitation subject to this rule, or to any participant in the solicitation, other than the solicitation by the management, must be filed with the Commission as proxy material subject to this regulation. This must be filed in electronic format unless an exemption is available under Rules 201 or 202 of Regulation S–T.

(2)   *Use of reprints or reproductions.* In any solicitation subject to this Rule 14a–12(c), soliciting material that includes, in whole or part, any reprints or reproductions of any previously published material must:

(i)   State the name of the author and publication, the date of prior publication, and identify any person who is quoted without being named in the previously published material.

(ii)   Except in the case of a public or official document or statement, state whether or not the consent of the author and publication has been obtained to the use of the previously published material as proxy soliciting material.

(iii)   If any participant using the previously published material, or anyone on his or her behalf, paid, directly or indirectly, for the preparation or prior publication of the previously published material, or has made or proposes to made any payments or give any other consideration in connection with the publication or republication of the material, state the circumstances.

Instructions to Rule 14a–12

1.   If paper filing is permitted, file eight copies of the soliciting material with the Commission, except that only three copies of the material specified by Rule 14a–12(c)(1) need be filed.

2.   Any communications made under this rule after the definitive proxy statement is on file but before it is disseminated also must specify that the proxy statement is publicly available and the anticipated date of dissemination.

3.   Inclusion of a nominee pursuant to Rule 14a–11, an applicable state or foreign law provision, or a registrant's governing documents as they relate to the inclusion of shareholder director nominees in the registrant's proxy materials, or solicitations by a nominating shareholder or nominating shareholder group that are made in connection with that nomination constitute solicitations in opposition subject to Rule 14a–12(c), except for purposes of Rule 14a–6(a).

Rule 14a–13. Obligation of Registrants in Communicating With Beneficial Owners

(a)   If the registrant knows that securities of any class entitled to vote at a meeting (or by written consents or authorizations if no meeting is held) with respect to which the registrant intends to solicit proxies, consents or authorizations are held of record by a broker, dealer, voting trustee, bank, association, or other entity that exercises fiduciary powers in nominee name or otherwise, the registrant shall:

(1)   By first class mail or other equally prompt means:

(i)   Inquire of each such record holder:

(A)   Whether other persons are the beneficial owners of such securities and if so, the number of copies of the proxy and other soliciting material necessary to supply such material to such beneficial owners;

(B)   In the case of an annual (or special meeting in lieu of the annual) meeting, or written consents in lieu of such meeting, at which directors are to be elected, the number of copies of the annual report to security holders necessary to supply such report to beneficial owners to whom such reports are to be distributed by such record holder or its nominee and not by the registrant; and

(C)   If the record holder has an obligation under Rule 14b–1(b)(3) or Rule 14b–2(b)(4)(ii) and (iii); and (3), whether an agent has been designated to act on its behalf in fulfilling such obligation and, if so, the name and address of such agent; and

(D)   Whether it holds the registrant's securities on behalf of any respondent bank and, if so, the name and address of each such respondent bank; and

(ii)   Indicate to each such record holder:

(A)   Whether the registrant, pursuant to paragraph (c) of this rule, intends to distribute the annual report to security holders to beneficial owners of its securities whose names, addresses and securities positions are disclosed pursuant to Rules 14b–1(b)(3) and 14b–2(b)(4)(ii) and (iii);

(B)   The record date; and

(C)   At the option of the registrant, any employee benefit plan established by an affiliate of the registrant that holds securities of the registrant that the registrant elects to treat as exempt employee benefit plan securities;

(2)   Upon receipt of a record holder's or respondent bank's response indicating, pursuant to Rule 14b–2(b)(1)(i), the names and addresses of its respondent banks, within one business day after the date such response is received, make an inquiry of and give notification to each such respondent bank in the same manner required by paragraph (a)(1) of this rule; *Provided, however,* the inquiry required by paragraphs (a)(1) and (a)(2) of this rule shall not cover beneficial owners of exempt employee benefit plan securities;

(3)   Make the inquiry required by paragraph (a)(1) of this rule at least 20 business days prior to the record date of the meeting of security holders, or

(i)   If such inquiry is impracticable 20 business days prior to the record date of a special meeting, as many days before the record date of such meeting as is practicable or,

(ii)   If consents or authorizations are solicited, and such inquiry is impracticable 20 business days before the earliest date on which they may be used to effect corporate action, as many days before that date as is practicable, or

(iii)   At such later time as the rules of a national securities exchange on which the class of securities in question is listed may permit for good cause shown; *Provided, however,* That if a record holder or respondent bank has informed the registrant that a designated office(s) or department(s) is to receive such inquiries, the inquiry shall be made to such designated office(s) or department(s); and

(4)   Supply, in a timely manner, each record holder and respondent bank of whom the inquiries required by paragraphs (a)(1) and (a)(2) of this rule are made with copies of the proxy, other proxy soliciting material, and/or the annual report to security holders, in such quantities, assembled in such form and at such place(s), as the record holder or respondent bank may reasonably request in order to send such material to each beneficial owner of securities who is to be furnished with such material by the record holder or respondent bank; and

(5)   Upon the request of any record holder or respondent bank that is supplied with proxy soliciting material and/or annual reports to security holders pursuant to paragraph (a)(4) of this rule, pay its reasonable expenses for completing the sending of such material to beneficial owners.

NOTE 1: If the registrant's list of security holders indicates that some of its securities are registered in the name of a clearing agency registered pursuant to Section 17A of the Act (*e.g.,* "Cede & Co.," nominee for the Depository Trust Company), the registrant shall make appropriate inquiry of the clearing agency and thereafter of the participants in such clearing agency who may hold on behalf of a beneficial owner or respondent bank, and shall comply with the above paragraph with respect to any such participant (see Rule 14a–1(i)).

NOTE 2: The attention of registrants is called to the fact that each broker, dealer, bank, association and other entity that exercises fiduciary powers has an obligation pursuant to Rule 14b–1(b), Rule 14b–2(b) (except as provided therein with respect to employee benefit plan securities held in nominee name) and, with respect to brokers and dealers, applicable self-regulatory organization requirements to obtain and forward, within the time periods prescribed therein, (a) proxies (or in lieu thereof requests for voting instructions) and proxy soliciting materials to all beneficial owners on whose behalf it holds securities, and (b) annual reports to security holders to beneficial owners on whose behalf it holds securities, unless the registrant has notified the record holder or respondent bank that it has assumed responsibility to send such material to beneficial owners whose names, addresses and securities positions are disclosed pursuant to Rule 14b–1(b)(3) and Rule 14b–2(b)(4)(ii) and (iii).

NOTE 3: The attention of registrants is called to the fact that registrants have an obligation, pursuant to paragraph (d) of this rule, to cause proxies (or in lieu thereof requests for voting instructions), proxy soliciting material and annual reports to security holders to be furnished, in a timely manner, to beneficial owners of exempt employee benefit plan securities.

(b)   Any registrant requesting pursuant to Rule 14b–1(b)(3) and Rule 14b–2(b)(4)(ii) and (iii) a list of names, addresses and securities positions of beneficial owners of its securities who either have consented or have not objected to disclosure of such information shall:

(1)   By first class mail or other equally prompt means, inquire of each record holder and each respondent bank identified to the registrant pursuant to Rule 14b–2(b)(4)(i) whether such record holder or respondent bank holds the registrant's securities on behalf of any respondent banks and, if so, the name and address of each such respondent bank;

(2)   Request such list to be compiled as of a date no earlier than five business days after the date the registrant's request is received by the record holder or respondent bank; *Provided, however,* That if the record holder or respondent bank has informed the registrant that a designated office(s) or department(s) is to receive such requests, the request shall be made to such designated office(s) or department(s);

(3)   Make such request to the following persons that hold the registrant's securities on behalf of beneficial owners; all brokers, dealers, banks, associations and other entities that exercise fiduciary powers; *Provided, however,* such request shall not cover beneficial owners of exempt employee benefit plan securities as defined in Rule 14a–1(d)(1); and, at the option of the registrant, such request may give notice of any employee benefit plan established by an affiliate of the registrant that holds securities of the registrant that the registrant elects to treat as exempt employee benefit plan securities;

(4)   Use the information furnished in response to such request exclusively for purposes of corporate communications; and

(5)   Upon the request of any record holder or respondent bank to whom such request is made, pay the reasonable expenses, both direct and indirect, of providing beneficial owner information.

NOTE: A registrant will be deemed to have satisfied its obligations under paragraph (b) of this rule by requesting consenting and non-objecting beneficial owner lists from a designated agent acting on behalf of the record holder or respondent bank and paying to that designated agent the reasonable expenses of providing the beneficial owner information.

(c)   A registrant, at its option, may send its annual report to security holders to the beneficial owners whose identifying information is provided by record holders and respondent banks, pursuant to Rule 14b–1(b)(3) and 14b–2(b)(4)(ii) and (iii), provided that such registrant notifies the record holders and respondent banks, at the time it makes the inquiry required by paragraph (a) of this rule, that the registrant will send the annual report to security holders to the beneficial owners so identified.

(d)   If a registrant solicits proxies, consents or authorizations from record holders and respondent banks who hold securities on behalf of beneficial owners, the registrant shall cause proxies (or in lieu thereof requests for voting instructions), proxy soliciting material and annual reports to security holders to be furnished, in a timely manner, to beneficial owners of exempt employee benefit plan securities.

Rule 14a–14. Modified or Superseded Documents

(a)   Any statement contained in a document incorporated or deemed to be incorporated by reference shall be deemed to be modified or superseded, for purposes of the proxy statement, to the extent that a statement contained in the proxy statement or in any other subsequently filed document that also is or is deemed to be incorporated by reference modifies or replaces such statement.

(b)   The modifying or superseding statement may, but need not, state it has modified or superseded a prior statement or include any other information set forth in the document that is not so modified or superseded. The making of a modifying or superseding statement shall not be deemed an admission that the modified or superseded statement, when made, constituted an untrue statement of a material fact, an omission to state a material fact necessary to make a statement not misleading, or the employment of a manipulative, deceptive, or fraudulent device, contrivance, scheme, transaction, act, practice, course of business or artifice to defraud, as those terms are used in the Securities Act of 1933, the Securities Exchange Act of 1934 ("the Act"), the Investment Company Act of 1940, or the rules and regulations thereunder.

(c)   Any statement so modified shall not be deemed in its unmodified form to constitute part of the proxy statement for purposes of the Act. Any statement so superseded shall not be deemed to constitute a part of the proxy statement for purposes of the Act.

Rule 14a–15. Differential and Contingent Compensation in Connection With Roll-up Transactions

(a)   It shall be unlawful for any person to receive compensation for soliciting proxies, consents, or authorizations directly from security holders in connection with a roll-up transaction as provided in paragraph (b) of this rule, if the compensation is:

(1)   Based on whether the solicited proxy, consent, or authorization either approves or disapproves the proposed roll-up transaction; or

(2)   Contingent on the approval, disapproval, or completion of the roll-up transaction.

(b)   This rule is applicable to a roll-up transaction as defined in Item 901(c) of Regulation S–K, except for a transaction involving only:

(1)   Finite-life entities that are not limited partnerships;

(2)   Partnerships whose investors will receive new securities or securities in another entity that are not reported under a transaction reporting plan declared effective before December 17, 1993 by the Commission under section 11A of the Act; or

(3)   Partnerships whose investors' securities are reported under a transaction reporting plan declared effective before December 17, 1993 by the Commission under section 11A of the Act.

Rule 14a–16. Internet Availability of Proxy Materials

(a)(1)   A registrant may furnish a proxy statement pursuant to Rule 14a–3(a), or an annual report to security holders pursuant to Rule 14a–3(b), to a security holder by sending the security holder a Notice of Internet Availability of Proxy Materials, as described in this rule, 40 calendar days or more prior to the security holder meeting date, or if no meeting is to be held, 40 calendar days or more prior to the date the votes, consents or authorizations may be used to effect the corporate action, and complying with all other requirements of this rule.

(2)   Unless the registrant chooses to follow the full set delivery option set forth in paragraph (n) of this rule, it must provide the record holder or respondent bank with all information listed in paragraph (d) of this rule in sufficient time for the record holder or respondent bank to prepare, print and send a Notice of Internet Availability of Proxy Materials to beneficial owners at least 40 calendar days before the meeting date.

(b)(1)   All materials identified in the Notice of Internet Availability of Proxy Materials must be publicly accessible, free of charge, at the Web site address specified in the notice on or before the time that the notice is sent to the security holder and such materials must remain available on that Web site through the conclusion of the meeting of security holders.

(2)   All additional soliciting materials sent to security holders or made public after the Notice of Internet Availability of Proxy Materials has been sent must be made publicly accessible at the specified Web site address no later than the day on which such materials are first sent to security holders or made public.

(3)   The Web site address relied upon for compliance under this rule may not be the address of the Commission's electronic filing system.

(4)   The registrant must provide security holders with a means to execute a proxy as of the time the Notice of Internet Availability of Proxy Materials is first sent to security holders.

(c)   The materials must be presented on the Web site in a format, or formats, convenient for both reading online and printing on paper.

(d)   The Notice of Internet Availability of Proxy Materials must contain the following:

(1)   A prominent legend in bold-face type that states "Important Notice Regarding the Availability of Proxy Materials for the Shareholder Meeting To Be Held on [insert meeting date]";

"Important Notice Regarding the Availability of Proxy Materials for the Shareholder Meeting To Be Held on [insert meeting date].

1.   This communication presents only an overview of the more complete proxy materials that are available to you on the Internet. We encourage you to access and review all of the important information contained in the proxy materials before voting.

2.   The [proxy statement] [information statement] [annual report to security holders] [is/are] available at [Insert Web site address].

3.   If you want to receive a paper or e-mail copy of these documents, you must request one. There is no charge to you for requesting a copy. Please make your request for a copy as instructed below on or before [Insert a date] to facilitate timely delivery.";

(2)   An indication that the communication is not a form for voting and presents only an overview of the more complete proxy materials, which contain important information and are available on the Internet or by mail, and encouraging a security holder to access and review the proxy materials before voting;

(3)   The Internet Web site address where the proxy materials are available;

(4) Instructions regarding how a security holder may request a paper or email copy of the proxy materials at no charge, including the date by which they should make the request to facilitate timely delivery, and an indication that they will not otherwise receive a paper or email copy;

(5) The date, time, and location of the meeting, or if corporate action is to be taken by written consent, the earliest date on which the corporate action may be effected;

(6) A clear and impartial identification of each separate matter intended to be acted on and the soliciting person's recommendations, if any, regarding those matters, but no supporting statements;

(7) A list of the materials being made available at the specified Web site;

(8) A toll-free telephone number, an e-mail address, and an Internet Web site where the security holder can request a copy of the proxy statement, annual report to security holders, and form of proxy, relating to all of the registrant's future security holder meetings and for the particular meeting to which the proxy materials being furnished relate;

(9) Any control/identification numbers that the security holder needs to access his or her form of proxy;

(10) Instructions on how to access the form of proxy, provided that such instructions do not enable a security holder to execute a proxy without having access to the proxy statement and, if required by Rule 14a–3(b), the annual report to security holders; and

(11) Information on how to obtain directions to be able to attend the meeting and vote in person.

(e)(1) The Notice of Internet Availability of Proxy Materials may not be incorporated into, or combined with, another document, except that it may be incorporated into, or combined with, a notice of security holder meeting required under state law, unless state law prohibits such incorporation or combination.

(2) The Notice of Internet Availability of Proxy Materials may contain only the information required by paragraph (d) of this rule and any additional information required to be included in a notice of security holders meeting under state law; provided that:

(i) The registrant must revise the information on the Notice of Internet Availability of Proxy Materials, including any title to the document, to reflect the fact that:

(A) The registrant is conducting a consent solicitation rather than a proxy solicitation; or

(B) The registrant is not soliciting proxy or consent authority, but is furnishing an information statement pursuant to Rule 14c–2; and

(ii) The registrant may include a statement on the Notice to educate security holders that no personal information other than the identification or control number is necessary to execute a proxy.

(f)(1) Except as provided in paragraph (h) of this rule, the Notice of Internet Availability of Proxy Materials must be sent separately from other types of security holder communications and may not accompany any other document or materials, including the form of proxy.

(2) Notwithstanding paragraph (f)(1) of this rule, the registrant may accompany the Notice of Internet Availability of Proxy Materials with:

(i) A pre-addressed, postage-paid reply card for requesting a copy of the proxy materials;

(ii) A copy of any notice of security holder meeting required under state law if that notice is not combined with the Notice of Internet Availability of Proxy Materials; and

(iii) In the case of an investment company registered under the Investment Company Act of 1940, the company's prospectus, a summary prospectus that satisfies the requirements of Rule 498(b) or § 230.498A(c) of the 1933 Act, a Notice under § 270.30e–3 of this chapter, or a report that is required to be transmitted to stockholders by section 30(e) of the Investment Company and the rules thereunder; and

(iv) An explanation of the reasons for a registrant's use of the rules detailed in this rule and the process of receiving and reviewing the proxy materials and voting as detailed in this rule.

(g) *Plain English.*

(1) To enhance the readability of the Notice of Internet Availability of Proxy Materials, the registrant must use plain English principles in the organization, language, and design of the notice.

(2) The registrant must draft the language in the Notice of Internet Availability of Proxy Materials so that, at a minimum, it substantially complies with each of the following plain English writing principles:

(i) Short sentences;

(ii) Definite, concrete, everyday words;

(iii) Active voice;

(iv) Tabular presentation or bullet lists for complex material, whenever possible;

(v) No legal jargon or highly technical business terms; and

(vi) No multiple negatives.

(3) In designing the Notice of Internet Availability of Proxy Materials, the registrant may include pictures, logos, or similar design elements so long as the design is not misleading and the required information is clear.

(h) The registrant may send a form of proxy to security holders if:

(1) At least 10 calendar days or more have passed since the date it first sent the Notice of Internet Availability of Proxy Materials to security holders and the form of proxy is accompanied by a copy of the Notice of Internet Availability of Proxy Materials; or

(2) The form of proxy is accompanied or preceded by a copy, via the same medium, of the proxy statement and any annual report to security holders that is required by Rule 14a-3(b).

(i) The registrant must file a form of the Notice of Internet Availability of Proxy Materials with the Commission pursuant to Rule 14a-6(b) no later than the date that the registrant first sends the notice to security holders.

(j) *Obligation to provide copies.*

(1) The registrant must send, at no cost to the record holder or respondent bank and by U.S. first class mail or other reasonably prompt means, a paper copy of the proxy statement, information statement, annual report to security holders, and form of proxy (to the extent each of those documents is applicable) to any record holder or respondent bank requesting such a copy within three business days after receiving a request for a paper copy.

(2) The registrant must send, at no cost to the record holder or respondent bank and via e-mail, an electronic copy of the proxy statement, information statement, annual report to security holders, and form of proxy (to the extent each of those documents is applicable) to any record holder or respondent bank requesting such a copy within three business days after receiving a request for an electronic copy via e-mail.

(3) The registrant must provide copies of the proxy materials for one year after the conclusion of the meeting or corporate action to which the proxy materials relate, provided that, if the registrant receives the request after the conclusion of the meeting or corporate action to which the proxy materials relate, the registrant need not send copies via First Class mail and need not respond to such request in three business days.

(4) The registrant must maintain records of security holder requests to receive materials in paper or via e-mail for future solicitations and must continue to provide copies of the materials to a security holder who has made such a request until the security holder revokes such request.

(k) *Security holder information.*

(1) A registrant or its agent shall maintain the Internet Web site on which it posts its proxy materials in a manner that does not infringe on the anonymity of a person accessing such Web site.

(2) The registrant and its agents shall not use any e-mail address obtained from a security holder solely for the purpose of requesting a copy of proxy materials pursuant to paragraph (j) of this rule for any purpose other than to send a copy of those materials to that security holder. The registrant shall not disclose such information to any person other than an employee or agent to the extent necessary to send a copy of the proxy materials pursuant to paragraph (j) of this rule.

(*l*) A person other than the registrant may solicit proxies pursuant to the conditions imposed on registrants by this rule, provided that:

(1) A soliciting person other than the registrant is required to provide copies of its proxy materials only to security holders to whom it has sent a Notice of Internet Availability of Proxy Materials; and

(2) A soliciting person other than the registrant must send its Notice of Internet Availability of Proxy Materials by the later of:

(i) 40 Calendar days prior to the security holder meeting date or, if no meeting is to be held, 40 calendar days prior to the date the votes, consents, or authorizations may be used to effect the corporate action; or

(ii) The date on which it files its definitive proxy statement with the Commission, provided its preliminary proxy statement is filed no later than 10 calendar days after the date that the registrant files its definitive proxy statement.

(3) *Content of the soliciting person's Notice of Internet Availability of Proxy Materials.*

(i) If, at the time a soliciting person other than the registrant sends its Notice of Internet Availability of Proxy Materials, the soliciting person is not aware of all matters on the registrant's agenda for the meeting of security holders, the soliciting person's Notice on Internet Availability of Proxy Materials must provide a clear and impartial identification of each separate matter on the agenda to the extent known by the soliciting person at that time. The soliciting person's notice also must include a clear statement indicating that there may be additional agenda items of which the soliciting person is not aware and that the security holder cannot direct a vote for those items on the soliciting person's proxy card provided at that time.

(ii) If a soliciting person other than the registrant sends a form of proxy not containing all matters intended to be acted upon, the Notice of Internet Availability of Proxy Materials must clearly state whether execution of the form of proxy will invalidate a security holder's prior vote on matters not presented on the form of proxy.

(m) This rule shall not apply to a proxy solicitation in connection with a business combination transaction, as defined in Rule 165 of the Securities Act of 1933, as well as transactions for cash consideration requiring disclosure under Item 14 of Schedule 14A.

(n) *Full Set Delivery Option.*

(1) For the purposes of this paragraph (n), the term full set of proxy materials shall include all of the following documents:

(i) A copy of the proxy statement;

(ii) A copy of the annual report to security holders is required by Rule 14a–3(b); and

(iii) A form of proxy.

(2) Notwithstanding paragraphs (e) and (f)(2) of this rule, a registrant or other soliciting person may:

(i) Accompany the Notice of Internet Availability of Proxy Materials with a full set of proxy materials; or

(ii) Send a full set of proxy materials without a Notice of Internet Availability of Proxy Materials if all of the information required in a Notice of Internet Availability of Proxy Materials pursuant to paragraphs (d) and (n)(4) is incorporated in the proxy statement and the form of proxy.

(3)   A registrant or other soliciting person that sends a full set of proxy materials to a security holder pursuant to this paragraph (n) need not comply with

    (i)   The timing provisions of paragraphs (a) and (*l*)(2); and

    (ii)   The obligation to provide copies pursuant to paragraph (j).

(4)   A registrant or other soliciting person that sends a full set of proxy materials to a security holder pursuant to this paragraph (n) need not include in its Notice of Internet Availability of Proxy Materials, proxy statement, or form of proxy the following disclosures:

    (i)   Instructions regarding the nature of the communication pursuant to paragraph (d)(2) of this rule;

    (ii)   Instructions on how to request a copy of the proxy materials; and

    (iii)   Instructions on how to access the form of proxy pursuant to paragraph (d)(10).

Rule 14a–17. Electronic Shareholder Forums

(a)   A shareholder, registrant, or third party acting on behalf of a shareholder or registrant may establish, maintain, or operate an electronic shareholder forum to facilitate interaction among the registrant's shareholders and between the registrant and its shareholders as the shareholder or registrant deems appropriate. Subject to paragraphs (b) and (c) of this Rule, the forum must comply with the federal securities laws, including Section 14(a) of the Act and its associated regulations, other applicable federal laws, applicable state laws, and the registrant's governing documents.

(b)   No shareholder, registrant, or third party acting on behalf of a shareholder or registrant, by reason of establishing, maintaining, or operating an electronic shareholder forum, will be liable under the federal securities laws for any statement or information provided by another person to the electronic shareholder forum. Nothing in this Rule prevents or alters the application of the federal securities laws, including the provisions for liability for fraud, deception, or manipulation, or other applicable federal and state laws to the person or persons that provide a statement or information to an electronic shareholder forum.

(c)   Reliance on the exemption in Rule 14a–2(b)(6) to participate in an electronic shareholder forum does not eliminate a person's eligibility to solicit proxies after the date that the exemption in Rule 14a–2(b)(6) is no longer available, or is no longer being relied upon, provided that any such solicitation is conducted in accordance with this regulation.

Rule 14a–18. Disclosure Regarding Nominating Shareholders and Nominees Submitted for Inclusion in a Registrant's Proxy Materials Pursuant to Applicable State or Foreign Law, or a Registrant's Governing Documents

To have a nominee included in a registrant's proxy materials pursuant to a procedure set forth under applicable state or foreign law, or the registrant's governing documents addressing the inclusion of shareholder director nominees in the registrant's proxy materials, the nominating shareholder or nominating shareholder group must provide notice to the registrant of its intent to do so on a Schedule 14N (§ 240.14n–101) and file that notice, including the required disclosure, with the Commission on the date first transmitted to the registrant. This notice shall be postmarked or transmitted electronically to the registrant by the date specified by the registrant's advance notice provision or, where no such provision is in place, no later than 120 calendar days before the anniversary of the date that the registrant mailed its proxy materials for the prior year's annual meeting, except that, if the registrant did not hold an annual meeting during the prior year, or if the date of the meeting has changed by more than 30 calendar days from the prior year, then the nominating shareholder or nominating shareholder group must provide notice a reasonable time before the registrant mails its proxy materials, as specified by the registrant in a Form 8–K (§ 249.308 of this chapter) filed pursuant to Item 5.08 of Form 8–K.

Rule 14a–19. Solicitation of proxies in support of director nominees other than the registrant's nominees.

(a)   No person may solicit proxies in support of director nominees other than the registrant's nominees unless such person:

(1)   Provides notice to the registrant in accordance with paragraph (b) of this section unless the information required by paragraph (b) of this section has been provided in a preliminary or definitive proxy statement previously filed by such person;

(2)   Files a definitive proxy statement with the Commission in accordance with § 240.14a–6(b) by the later of:

(i)   25 calendar days prior to the security holder meeting date; or

(ii)   Five (5) calendar days after the date that the registrant files its definitive proxy statement; and

(3)   Solicits the holders of shares representing at least 67% of the voting power of shares entitled to vote on the election of directors and includes a statement to that effect in the proxy statement or form of proxy.

(b)   The notice shall:

(1)   Be postmarked or transmitted electronically to the registrant at its principal executive office no later than 60 calendar days prior to the anniversary of the previous year's annual meeting date, except that, if the registrant did not hold an annual meeting during the previous year, or if the date of the meeting has changed by more than 30 calendar days from the previous year, then notice must be provided by the later of 60 calendar days prior to the date of the annual meeting or the 10th calendar day following the day on which public announcement of the date of the annual meeting is first made by the registrant;

(2)   Include the names of all nominees for whom such person intends to solicit proxies; and

(3)   Include a statement that such person intends to solicit the holders of shares representing at least 67% of the voting power of shares entitled to vote on the election of directors in support of director nominees other than the registrant's nominees.

(c)   If any change occurs with respect to such person's intent to solicit the holders of shares representing at least 67% of the voting power of shares entitled to vote on the election of directors in support of director nominees other than the registrant's nominees or with respect to the names of such person's nominees, such person shall notify the registrant promptly.

(d)   A registrant shall notify the person conducting a proxy solicitation subject to this section of the names of all nominees for whom the registrant intends to solicit proxies unless the names have been provided in a preliminary or definitive proxy statement previously filed by the registrant. The notice shall be postmarked or transmitted electronically no later than 50 calendar days prior to the anniversary of the previous year's annual meeting date, except that, if the registrant did not hold an annual meeting during the previous year, or if the date of the meeting has changed by more than 30 calendar days from the previous year, then notice must be provided no later than 50 calendar days prior to the date of the annual meeting. If any change occurs with respect to the names of the registrant's nominees, the registrant shall notify the person conducting a proxy solicitation subject to this section promptly.

(e)   Notwithstanding the provisions of § 240.14a–4(b)(2), if any person is conducting a proxy solicitation subject to this section, the form of proxy of the registrant and the form of proxy of any person soliciting proxies pursuant to this section shall:

(1)   Set forth the names of all persons nominated for election by the registrant and by any person or group of persons that has complied with this section and the name of any person whose nomination by a shareholder or shareholder group satisfies the requirements of an applicable state or foreign law provision or a registrant's governing documents as they relate to the inclusion of shareholder director nominees in the registrant's proxy materials;

(2)   Provide a means for the security holder to grant authority to vote for thenominees set forth;

(3)   Clearly distinguish between the nominees of the registrant, the nominees ofthe person or group of persons that has complied with this section and the nominees ofany shareholder or shareholder group whose nominees are included in a registrant's proxy materials pursuant to the requirements of an applicable state or foreign law provision or a registrant's governing documents;

(4)   Within each group of nominees referred to in paragraph (e)(3) of this section,list nominees in alphabetical order by last name;

(5)   Use the same font type, style and size for all nominees;

(6)   Prominently disclose the maximum number of nominees for which authorityto vote can be granted; and

(7)   Prominently disclose the treatment and effect of a proxy executed in a manner that grants authority to vote for the election of fewer or more nominees than the number of directors being elected and the treatment and effect of a proxy executed in a manner that does not grant authority to vote with respect to any nominees.

(f)   If any person is conducting a proxy solicitation subject to this section, the formof proxy of the registrant and the form of proxy of any person soliciting proxies pursuant to this section may provide a means for the security holder to grant authority to vote for the nominees of the registrant set forth, as a group, and a means for the security holder to grant authority to vote for the nominees of any other soliciting person set forth, as a group, provided that there is a similar means for the security holder to withhold authority to vote for such groups of nominees unless the number of nominees of the registrant or ofany other soliciting person is less than the number of directors being elected. Means to grant authority to vote for any nominees as a group or to withhold authority for any nominees as a group may not be provided if the form of proxy includes one or more shareholder nominees in accordance with an applicable state or foreign law provision or aregistrant's governing documents as they relate to the inclusion of shareholder director nominees in the registrant's proxy materials.

(g)   This section shall not apply to:

(1)   A consent solicitation; or

(2)   A solicitation in connection with an election of directors at an investment company registered under the Investment Company Act of 1940 or a business development company as defined by section 2(a)(48) of the Investment Company Act of 1940.

Instruction to paragraphs (b)(1) and (d): Where the deadline falls ona Saturday, Sunday or holiday, the deadline will be treated as the first business day following the Saturday, Sunday or holiday.

Instruction to paragraph (f): Where applicable state law gives legal effect to votes cast against a nominee, the form of proxy may provide a means for the security holder to grant authority to vote for the nominees of the registrant set forth, as agroup, and a means for the security holder to grant authority to vote for the nominees of any other soliciting person set forth, as a group, provided that, in lieu of the ability to withhold authority to vote as a group, there is a similar means for the security holder to vote against such group of nominees as well as a means for security holders to abstain from voting for such group of nominees).

Rule 14a–20. Shareholder Approval of Executive Compensation of TARP Recipients

If a solicitation is made by a registrant that is a TARP recipient, as defined in section 111(a)(3) of the Emergency Economic Stabilization Act of 2008 (12 U.S.C. 5221(a)(3)), during the period in which any obligation arising from financial assistance provided under the TARP, as defined in section 3(8) of the Emergency Economic Stabilization Act of 2008 (12 U.S.C. 5202(8)), remains outstanding and the solicitation relates to an annual (or special meeting in lieu of the annual) meeting of security holders for which proxies will be solicited for the election of directors, as required pursuant to section 111(e)(1) of the Emergency Economic Stabilization Act of 2008 (12 U.S.C. 5221(e)(1)), the registrant shall provide a separate shareholder vote to approve the compensation of executives, as disclosed pursuant to Item 402 of Regulation

S–K, including the compensation discussion and analysis, the compensation tables, and any related material.

Note to Rule 14a–20: TARP recipients that are smaller reporting companies entitled to provide scaled disclosure pursuant to Item 402(*l*) of Regulation S–K are not required to include a compensation discussion and analysis in their proxy statements in order to comply with this rule. In the case of these smaller reporting companies, the required vote must be to approve the compensation of executives as disclosed pursuant to Item 402(m) through (q) of Regulation S–K.

Rule 14a–21. Shareholder Approval of Executive Compensation, Frequency of Votes for Approval of Executive Compensation and Shareholder Approval of Golden Parachute Compensation

(a) If a solicitation is made by a registrant, other than an emerging growth company as defined in Rule 12b–2, and the solicitation relates to an annual or other meeting of shareholders at which directors will be elected and for which the rules of the Commission require executive compensation disclosure pursuant to Item 402 of Regulation S–K, the registrant shall, for the first annual or other meeting of shareholders on or after January 21, 2011, or for the first annual or other meeting of shareholders on or after January 21, 2013 if the registrant is a smaller reporting company, and thereafter no later than the annual or other meeting of shareholders held in the third calendar year after the immediately preceding vote under this subsection, include a separate resolution subject to shareholder advisory vote to approve the compensation of its named executive officers, as disclosed pursuant to Item 402 of Regulation S–K.

Instruction to paragraph (a):

The registrant's resolution shall indicate that the shareholder advisory vote under this subsection is to approve the compensation of the registrant's named executive officers as disclosed pursuant to Item 402 of Regulation S–K. The following is a non-exclusive example of a resolution that would satisfy the requirements of this subsection: "RESOLVED, that the compensation paid to the company's named executive officers, as disclosed pursuant to Item 402 of Regulation S–K, including the Compensation Discussion and Analysis, compensation tables and narrative discussion is hereby APPROVED."

(b) If a solicitation is made by a registrant, other than an emerging growth company as defined in Rule 12b–2, and the solicitation relates to an annual or other meeting of shareholders at which directors will be elected and for which the rules of the Commission require executive compensation disclosure pursuant to Item 402 of Regulation S–K, the registrant shall, for the first annual or other meeting of shareholders on or after January 21, 2011, or for the first annual or other meeting of shareholders on or after January 21, 2013 if the registrant is a smaller reporting company, and thereafter no later than the annual or other meeting of shareholders held in the sixth calendar year after the immediately preceding vote under this subsection, include a separate resolution subject to shareholder advisory vote as to whether the shareholder vote required by paragraph (a) of this rule should occur every 1, 2 or 3 years. Registrants required to provide a separate shareholder vote pursuant to Rule 14a–20 of this chapter shall include the separate resolution required by this rule for the first annual or other meeting of shareholders after the registrant has repaid all obligations arising from financial assistance provided under the TARP, as defined in section 3(8) of the Emergency Economic Stabilization Act of 2008 (12 U.S.C. 5202(8)), and thereafter no later than the annual or other meeting of shareholders held in the sixth calendar year after the immediately preceding vote under this subsection.

(c) If a solicitation is made by a registrant, other than an emerging growth company as defined in Rule 12b–2, for a meeting of shareholders at which shareholders are asked to approve an acquisition, merger, consolidation or proposed sale or other disposition of all or substantially all the assets of the registrant, the registrant shall include a separate resolution subject to shareholder advisory vote to approve any agreements or understandings and compensation disclosed pursuant to Item 402(t) of Regulation S–K, unless such agreements or understandings have been subject to a shareholder advisory vote under paragraph (a) of this rule. Consistent with section 14A(b) of the Securities Exchange Act of 1934, any agreements or understandings between an acquiring company and the named executive officers of the registrant, where the registrant is not the acquiring company, are not required to be subject to the separate shareholder advisory vote under this paragraph.

Instructions to Rule 14a–21:

1.   Disclosure relating to the compensation of directors required by Item 402(k) and Item 402(r) of Regulation S–K is not subject to the shareholder vote required by paragraph (a) of this rule. If a registrant includes disclosure pursuant to Item 402(s) of Regulation S–K about the registrant's compensation policies and practices as they relate to risk management and risk-taking incentives, these policies and practices would not be subject to the shareholder vote required by paragraph (a) of this rule. To the extent that risk considerations are a material aspect of the registrant's compensation policies or decisions for named executive officers, the registrant is required to discuss them as part of its Compensation Discussion and Analysis under Item 402(b) of Regulation S–K, and therefore such disclosure would be considered by shareholders when voting on executive compensation.

2.   If a registrant includes disclosure of golden parachute compensation arrangements pursuant to Item 402(t) in an annual meeting proxy statement, such disclosure would be subject to the shareholder advisory vote required by paragraph (a) of this rule.

3.   Registrants that are smaller reporting companies entitled to provide scaled disclosure in accordance with Item 402(*l*) of Regulation S–K are not required to include a Compensation Discussion and Analysis in their proxy statements in order to comply with this rule. For smaller reporting companies, the vote required by paragraph (a) of this rule must be to approve the compensation of the named executive officers as disclosed pursuant to Item 402(m) through (q) of Regulation S–K.

4.   A registrant that has ceased being an emerging growth company shall include the first separate resolution described under Rule 14a–21(a) not later than the end of (i) in the case of a registrant that was an emerging growth company for less than two years after the date of first sale of common equity securities of the registrant pursuant to an effective registration statement under the Securities Act of 1933, the three-year period beginning on such date; and (ii) in the case of any other registrant, the one-year period beginning on the date the registrant is no longer an emerging growth company.

Rule 14b–1.   Obligation of Registered Brokers and Dealers in Connection With the Prompt Forwarding of Certain Communications to Beneficial Owners

(a)   *Definitions.* Unless the context otherwise requires, all terms used in this rule shall have the same meanings as in the Act and, with respect to proxy soliciting material, as in Rule 14a–1 thereunder and, with respect to information statements, as in Rule 14c–1 thereunder. In addition, as used in this rule, the term "registrant" means:

(1)   The issuer of a class of securities registered pursuant to section 12 of the Act; or

(2)   An investment company registered under the Investment Company Act of 1940.

(b)   *Dissemination and beneficial owner information requirements.* A broker or dealer registered under section 15 of the Act shall comply with the following requirements for disseminating certain communications to beneficial owners and providing beneficial owner information to registrants.

(1)   The broker or dealer shall respond, by first class mail or other equally prompt means, directly to the registrant no later than seven business days after the date it receives an inquiry made in accordance with Rule 14a–13(a) or Rule 14c–7(a) by indicating, by means of a search card or otherwise:

(i)   The approximate number of customers of the broker or dealer who are beneficial owners of the registrant's securities that are held of record by the broker, dealer, or its nominee;

(ii)   The number of customers of the broker or dealer who are beneficial owners of the registrant's securities who have objected to disclosure of their names, addresses, and securities positions if the registrant has indicated, pursuant to Rule 14a–13(a)(1)(ii)(A) or Rule 14c–7(a)(1)(ii)(A), that it will distribute the annual report to security holders to beneficial owners of its securities whose names, addresses and securities positions are disclosed pursuant to paragraph (b)(3) of this rule; and

(iii)   The identity of the designated agent of the broker or dealer, if any, acting on its behalf in fulfilling its obligations under paragraph (b)(3) of this rule; *Provided, however,* that if the broker or dealer has informed the registrant that a designated office(s) or department(s) is to receive such inquiries, receipt for purposes of paragraph (b)(1) of this rule shall mean receipt by such designated office(s) or department(s).

(2)   The broker or dealer shall, upon receipt of the proxy, other proxy soliciting material, information statement, and/or annual report to security holders from the registrant or other soliciting person, forward such materials to its customers who are beneficial owners of the registrant's securities no later than five business days after receipt of the proxy material, information statement or annual report to security holders.

NOTE to Paragraph (b)(2): At the request of a registrant, or on its own initiative so long as the registrant does not object, a broker or dealer may, but is not required to, deliver one annual report to security holders, proxy statement, information statement, or Notice of Internet Availability of Proxy Materials to more than one beneficial owner sharing an address if the requirements set forth in Rule 14a–3(e)(1) (with respect to annual reports to security holders, proxy statements, and Notices of Internet Availability of Proxy Materials) and Rule 14c–3(c) (with respect to annual reports to security holders, information statements, and Notices of Internet Availability of Proxy Materials) applicable to registrants, with the exception of Rule 14a–3(e)(1)(i)(E), are satisfied instead by the broker or dealer.

(3)   The broker or dealer shall, through its agent or directly:

(i)   Provide the registrant, upon the registrant's request, with the names, addresses, and securities positions, compiled as of a date specified in the registrant's request which is no earlier than five business days after the date the registrant's request is received, of its customers who are beneficial owners of the registrant's securities and who have not objected to disclosure of such information; *Provided, however,* that if the broker or dealer has informed the registrant that a designated office(s) or department(s) is to receive such requests, receipt shall mean receipt by such designated office(s) or department(s); and

(ii)   Transmit the data specified in paragraph (b)(3)(i) of this rule to the registrant no later than five business days after the record date or other date specified by the registrant.

NOTE 1: Where a broker or dealer employs a designated agent to act on its behalf in performing the obligations imposed on the broker or dealer by paragraph (b)(3) of this rule, the five business day time period for determining the date as of which the beneficial owner information is to be compiled is calculated from the date the designated agent receives the registrant's request. In complying with the registrant's request for beneficial owner information under paragraph (b)(3) of this rule, a broker or dealer need only supply the registrant with the names, addresses, and securities positions of non-objecting beneficial owners.

NOTE 2: If a broker or dealer receives a registrant's request less than five business days before the requested compilation date, it must provide a list compiled as of a date that is no more than five business days after receipt and transmit the list within five business days after the compilation date.

(c)   *Exceptions to dissemination and beneficial owner information requirements.* A broker or dealer registered under section 15 of the Act shall be subject to the following with respect to its dissemination and beneficial owner information requirements.

(1)   With regard to beneficial owners of exempt employee benefit plan securities, the broker or dealer shall:

(i)   Not include information in its response pursuant to paragraph (b)(1) of this rule or forward proxies (or in lieu thereof requests for voting instructions), proxy soliciting material, information statements, or annual reports to security holders pursuant to paragraph (b)(2) of this rule to such beneficial owners; and

(ii)   Not include in its response, pursuant to paragraph (b)(3) of this rule, data concerning such beneficial owners.

(2)   A broker or dealer need not satisfy:

(i)   Its obligations under paragraphs (b)(2), (b)(3) and (d) of this rule if the registrant or other soliciting person, as applicable, does not provide assurance of reimbursement of the broker's or dealer's reasonable expenses, both direct and indirect, incurred in connection with performing the obligations imposed by paragraphs (b)(2), (b)(3) and (d) of this rule; or

(ii)   Its obligation under paragraph (b)(2) of this rule to forward annual reports to security holders to non-objecting beneficial owners identified by the broker or dealer, through its agent or directly, pursuant to paragraph (b)(3) of this rule if the registrant notifies the broker or dealer pursuant to Rule 14a–13(c) or Rule 14c–7(c) that the registrant will send the annual report to security holders to such non-objecting beneficial owners identified by the broker or dealer and delivered in a list to the registrant pursuant to paragraph (b)(3) of this rule.

(3)   In its response pursuant to paragraph (b)(1) of this Rule, a broker or dealer shall not include information about annual reports to security holders, proxy statements or information statements that will not be delivered to security holders sharing an address because of the broker or dealer's reliance on the procedures referred to in the Note to paragraph (b)(2) of this Rule.

(d)   Upon receipt from the soliciting person of all the information listed in Rule 14a–16(d), the broker or dealer shall:

(1)   Prepare and send a Notice of Internet Availability of Proxy Materials containing the information required in paragraph (e) of this rule to beneficial owners no later than:

(i)   With respect to a registrant, 40 calendar days prior to the security holder meeting date or, if no meeting is to be held, 40 calendar days prior to the date the votes, consents, or authorizations may be used to effect the corporate action; and

(ii)   With respect to a soliciting person other than the registrant, the later of:

(A)   40 calendar days prior to the security holder meeting date or, if no meeting is to be held, 40 calendar days prior to the date the votes, consents, or authorizations may be used to effect the corporate action; or

(B)   10 calendar days after the date that the registrant first sends its proxy statement or Notice of Internet Availability of Proxy Materials to security holders.

(2)   Establish a Web site at which beneficial owners are able to access the broker or dealer's request for voting instructions and, at the broker or dealer's option, establish a Web site at which beneficial owners are able to access the proxy statement and other soliciting materials, provided that such Web sites are maintained in a manner consistent with paragraphs (b), (c), and (k) of Rule 14a–16;

(3)   Upon receipt of a request from the registrant or other soliciting person, send to security holders specified by the registrant or other soliciting person a copy of the request for voting instructions accompanied by a copy of the intermediary's Notice of Internet Availability of Proxy Materials 10 calendar days or more after the broker or dealer sends its Notice of Internet Availability of Proxy Materials pursuant to paragraph (d)(1); and

(4)   Upon receipt of a request for a copy of the materials from a beneficial owner:

(i)   Request a copy of the soliciting materials from the registrant or other soliciting person, in the form requested by the beneficial owner, within three business days after receiving the beneficial owner's request;

(ii)   Forward a copy of the soliciting materials to the beneficial owner, in the form requested by the beneficial owner, within three business days after receiving the materials from the registrant or other soliciting person; and

(iii)   Maintain records of security holder requests to receive a paper or e-mail copy of the proxy materials in connection with future proxy solicitations and provide copies of the proxy materials to a security holder who has made such a request for all securities held in the account of that security holder until the security holder revokes such request.

(5)   Notwithstanding any other provisions in this paragraph (d), if the broker or dealer receives copies of the proxy statement and annual report to security holders (if applicable) from the soliciting person with instructions to forward such materials to beneficial owners, the broker or dealer:

(i)   Shall either:

(A)   Prepare a Notice of Internet Availability of Proxy Materials and forward it with the proxy statement and annual report to security holders (if applicable); or

(B)   Incorporate any information required in the Notice of Internet Availability of Proxy Materials that does not appear in the proxy statement into the broker or dealer's request for voting instructions to be sent with the proxy statement and annual report (if applicable);

(ii)   Need not comply with the following provisions:

     (A)   The timing provisions of paragraph (d)(1)(ii); and

     (B)   Paragraph (d)(4); and

(iii)   Need not include in its Notice of Internet Availability of Proxy Materials or request for voting instructions the following disclosures:

     (A)   Legends 1 and 3 of Rule 14a–16(d)(1); and

     (B)   Instructions on how to request a copy of the proxy materials.

(e)   *Content of Notice of Internet Availability of Proxy Materials.* The broker or dealer's Notice of Internet Availability of Proxy Materials shall:

(1)   Include all information, as it relates to beneficial owners, required in a registrant's Notice of Internet Availability of Proxy Materials under Rule 14a–16(d), provided that the broker or dealer shall provide its own, or its agent's, toll-free telephone number, an e-mail address, and an Internet Web site to service requests for copies from beneficial owners;

(2)   Include a brief description, if applicable, of the rules that permit the broker or dealer to vote the securities if the beneficial owner does not return his or her voting instructions; and

(3)   Otherwise be prepared and sent in a manner consistent with paragraphs (e), (f), and (g) of Rule 14a–16.

Rule 14b–2. Obligations of Banks, Associations and Other Entities That Exercise Fiduciary Powers in Connection With the Prompt Forwarding of Certain Communications to Beneficial Owners

(a)   *Definitions.* Unless the context otherwise requires, all terms used in this rule shall have the same meanings as in the Act and, with respect to proxy soliciting material, as in Rule 14a–1 thereunder and, with respect to information statements, as in Rule 14c–1 thereunder. In addition, as used in this rule, the following terms shall apply:

(1)   The term "banks" means a bank, association, or other entity that exercises fiduciary powers.

(2)   The term "beneficial owner" includes any person who has or shares, pursuant to an instrument, agreement, or otherwise, the power to vote, or to direct the voting of a security.

NOTE 1: If more than one person shares voting power, the provisions of the instrument creating that voting power shall govern with respect to whether consent to disclosure of beneficial owner information has been given.

NOTE 2: If more than one person shares voting power or if the instrument creating that voting power provides that such power shall be exercised by different persons depending on the nature of the corporate action involved, all persons entitled to exercise such power shall be deemed beneficial owners; *Provided, however,* that only one such beneficial owner need be designated among the beneficial owners to receive proxies or requests for voting instructions, other proxy soliciting material, information statements, and/or annual reports to security holders, if the person so designated assumes the obligation to disseminate, in a timely manner, such materials to the other beneficial owners.

(3)   The term "registrant" means:

     (i)   The issuer of a class of securities registered pursuant to Section 12 of the Act; or

     (ii)   An investment company registered under the Investment Company Act of 1940.

(b)   *Dissemination and beneficial owner information requirements.* A bank shall comply with the following requirements for disseminating certain communications to beneficial owners and providing beneficial owner information to registrants.

(1)   The bank shall:

(i)   Respond, by first class mail or other equally prompt means, directly to the registrant, no later than one business day after the date it receives an inquiry made in accordance with Rule 14a–13(a) or Rule 14c–7(a) by indicating the name and address of each of its respondent banks that holds the registrant's securities on behalf of beneficial owners, if any; and

(ii)   Respond, by first class mail or other equally prompt means, directly to the registrant no later than seven business days after the date it receives an inquiry made in accordance with Rule 14a–13(a) or Rule 14c–7(a) by indicating, by means of a search card or otherwise:

(A)   The approximate number of customers of the bank who are beneficial owners of the registrant's securities that are held of record by the bank or its nominee;

(B)   If the registrant has indicated, pursuant to Rule 14a–13(a)(1)(ii)(A) or Rule 14c–7(a)(1)(ii)(A), that it will distribute the annual report to security holders to beneficial owners of its securities whose names, addresses, and securities positions are disclosed pursuant to paragraphs (b)(4)(ii) and (iii) of this rule:

(1)   With respect to customer accounts opened on or before December 28, 1986, the number of beneficial owners of the registrant's securities who have affirmatively consented to disclosure of their names, addresses, and securities positions; and

(2)   With respect to customer accounts opened after December 28, 1986, the number of beneficial owners of the registrant's securities who have not objected to disclosure of their names, addresses, and securities positions; and

(C)   The identity of its designated agent, if any, acting on its behalf in fulfilling its obligations under paragraphs (b)(4)(ii) and (iii) of this rule;

Provided, however, that, if the bank or respondent bank has informed the registrant that a designated office(s) or department(s) is to receive such inquiries, receipt for purposes of paragraphs (b)(1)(i) and (ii) of this rule shall mean receipt by such designated office(s) or department(s).

(2)   Where proxies are solicited, the bank shall, within five business days after the record date:

(i)   Execute an omnibus proxy, including a power of substitution, in favor of its respondent banks and forward such proxy to the registrant; and

(ii)   Furnish a notice to each respondent bank in whose favor an omnibus proxy has been executed that it has executed such a proxy, including a power of substitution, in its favor pursuant to paragraph (b)(2)(i) of this rule.

(3)   Upon receipt of the proxy, other proxy soliciting material, information statement, and/or annual report to security holders from the registrant or other soliciting person, the bank shall forward such materials to each beneficial owner on whose behalf it holds securities, no later than five business days after the date it receives such material and, where a proxy is solicited, the bank shall forward, with the other proxy soliciting material and/or the annual report to security holders, either:

(i)   A properly executed proxy:

(A)   Indicating the number of securities held for such beneficial owner;

(B)   Bearing the beneficial owner's account number or other form of identification, together with instructions as to the procedures to vote the securities;

(C)   Briefly stating which other proxies, if any, are required to permit securities to be voted under the terms of the instrument creating that voting power or applicable state law; and

(D)   Being accompanied by an envelope addressed to the registrant or its agent, if not provided by the registrant; or

(ii)   A request for voting instructions (for which registrant's form of proxy may be used and which shall be voted by the record holder bank or respondent bank in accordance with the instructions received), together with an envelope addressed to the record holder bank or respondent bank.

NOTE to Paragraph (b)(3): At the request of a registrant, or on its own initiative so long as the registrant does not object, a bank may, but is not required to, deliver one annual report to security holders, proxy statement, information statement, or Notice of Internet Availability of Proxy Materials to more than one beneficial owner sharing an address if the requirements set forth in Rule 14a–3(e)(1) (with respect to annual reports to security holders, proxy statements, and Notices of Internet Availability of Proxy Materials) and Rule 14c–3(c) (with respect to annual reports to security holders, information statements, and Notices of Internet Availability of Proxy Materials) applicable to registrants, with the exception of Rule 14a–3(e)(1)(i)(E), are satisfied instead by the bank.

(4)   The bank shall:

(i)   Respond, by first class mail or other equally prompt means, directly to the registrant no later than one business day after the date it receives an inquiry made in accordance with Rule 14a–13(b)(1) or Rule 14c–7(b)(1) by indicating the name and address of each of its respondent banks that holds the registrant's securities on behalf of beneficial owners, if any;

(ii)   Through its agent or directly, provide the registrant, upon the registrant's request, and within the time specified in paragraph (b)(4)(iii) of this rule, with the names, addresses, and securities position, compiled as of a date specified in the registrant's request which is no earlier than five business days after the date the registrant's request is received, of:

(A)   With respect to customer accounts opened on or before December 28, 1986, beneficial owners of the registrant's securities on whose behalf it holds securities who have consented affirmatively to disclosure of such information, subject to paragraph (b)(5) of this rule; and

(B)   With respect to customer accounts opened after December 28, 1986, beneficial owners of the registrant's securities on whose behalf it holds securities who have not objected to disclosure of such information;

Provided, however, that if the record holder bank or respondent bank has informed the registrant that a designated office(s) or department(s) is to receive such requests, receipt for purposes of paragraphs (b)(4)(i) and (ii) of this rule shall mean receipt by such designated office(s) or department(s); and

(iii)   Through its agent or directly, transmit the data specified in paragraph (b)(4)(ii) of this rule to the registrant no later than five business days after the date specified by the registrant.

NOTE 1: Where a record holder bank or respondent bank employs a designated agent to act on its behalf in performing the obligations imposed on it by paragraphs (b)(4)(ii) and (iii) of this rule, the five business day time period for determining the date as of which the beneficial owner information is to be compiled is calculated from the date the designated agent receives the registrant's request. In complying with the registrant's request for beneficial owner information under paragraphs (b)(4)(ii) and (iii) of this rule, a record holder bank or respondent bank need only supply the registrant with the names, addresses and securities positions of affirmatively consenting and non-objecting beneficial owners.

NOTE 2: If a record holder bank or respondent bank receives a registrant's request less than five business days before the requested compilation date, it must provide a list compiled as of a date that is no more than five business days after receipt and transmit the list within five business days after the compilation date.

(5)   For customer accounts opened on or before December 28, 1986, unless the bank has made a good faith effort to obtain affirmative consent to disclosure of beneficial owner information pursuant to paragraph (b)(4)(ii) of this rule, the bank shall provide such information as to beneficial owners who do not object to disclosure of such information. A good faith effort to obtain affirmative consent to disclosure of beneficial owner information shall include, but shall not be limited to, making an inquiry:

(i)   Phrased in neutral language, explaining the purpose of the disclosure and the limitations on the registrant's use thereof;

(ii)   Either in at least one mailing separate from other account mailings or in repeated mailings; and

(iii)   In a mailing that includes a return card, postage paid enclosure.

(c)   *Exceptions to dissemination and beneficial owner information requirements.* The bank shall be subject to the following with respect to its dissemination and beneficial owner requirements.

(1)   With regard to beneficial owners of exempt employee benefit plan securities, the bank shall not:

(i)   Include information in its response pursuant to paragraph (b)(1) of this rule; or forward proxies (or in lieu thereof requests for voting instructions), proxy soliciting material, information statements, or annual reports to security holders pursuant to paragraph (b)(3) of this rule to such beneficial owners; or

(ii)   Include in its response pursuant to paragraphs (b)(4) and (b)(5) of this rule data concerning such beneficial owners.

(2)   The bank need not satisfy:

(i)   Its obligations under paragraphs (b)(2), (b)(3), (b)(4) and (d) of this rule if the registrant or other soliciting person, as applicable, does not provide assurance of reimbursement of its reasonable expenses, both direct and indirect, incurred in connection with performing the obligations imposed by paragraphs (b)(2), (b)(3), (b)(4) and (d) of this rule; or

(ii)   Its obligation under paragraph (b)(3) of this rule to forward annual reports to security holders to consenting and non-objecting beneficial owners identified pursuant to paragraphs (b)(4)(ii) and (iii) of this rule if the registrant notifies the record holder bank or respondent bank, pursuant to Rule 14a–13(c) or Rule 14c–7(c), that the registrant will send the annual report to security holders to beneficial owners whose names addresses and securities positions are disclosed pursuant to paragraphs (b)(4)(ii) and (iii) of this rule.

(3)   For the purposes of determining the fees which may be charged to registrants pursuant to Rule 14a–13(b)(5), Rule 14c–7(a)(5), and paragraph (c)(2) of this rule for performing obligations under paragraphs (b)(2), (b)(3), and (b)(4) of this rule: an amount no greater than that permitted to be charged by brokers or dealers for reimbursement of their reasonable expenses, both direct and indirect, incurred in connection with performing the obligations imposed by paragraphs (b)(2) and (b)(3) of Rule 14b–1, shall be deemed to be reasonable.

(4)   In its response pursuant to paragraph (b)(1)(ii)(A) of this rule, a bank shall not include information about annual reports to security holders, proxy statements or information statements that will not be delivered to security holders sharing an address because of the bank's reliance on the procedures referred to in the Note to paragraph (b)(3) of this rule.

(d)   Upon receipt from the soliciting person of all the information listed in Rule 14a–16(d), the bank shall:

(1)   Prepare and send a Notice of Internet Availability of Proxy Materials containing the information required in paragraph (e) of this rule to beneficial owners no later than:

(i)   With respect to a registrant, 40 calendar days prior to the security holder meeting date or, if no meeting is to be held, 40 calendar days prior to the date the votes, consents, or authorizations may be used to effect the corporate action; and

(ii)   With respect to a soliciting person other than the registrant, the later of:

(A)   40 calendar days prior to the security holder meeting date or, if no meeting is to be held, 40 calendar days prior to the date the votes, consents, or authorizations may be used to effect the corporate action; or

(B)   10 calendar days after the date that the registrant first sends its proxy statement or Notice of Internet Availability of Proxy Materials to security holders.

(2)   Establish a Web site at which beneficial owners are able to access the bank's request for voting instructions and, at the bank's option, establish a Web site at which beneficial owners are able to access the proxy statement and other soliciting materials, provided that such Web sites are maintained in a manner consistent with paragraphs (b), (c), and (k) of Rule 14a–16;

(3)   Upon receipt of a request from the registrant or other soliciting person, send to security holders specified by the registrant or other soliciting person a copy of the request for voting instructions accompanied by a copy of the intermediary's Notice of Internet Availability of Proxy Materials 10 days

or more after the bank sends its Notice of Internet Availability of Proxy Materials pursuant to paragraph (d)(1); and

(4) Upon receipt of a request for a copy of the materials from a beneficial owner:

(i) Request a copy of the soliciting materials from the registrant or other soliciting person, in the form requested by the beneficial owner, within three business days after receiving the beneficial owner's request;

(ii) Forward a copy of the soliciting materials to the beneficial owner, in the form requested by the beneficial owner, within three business days after receiving the materials from the registrant or other soliciting person; and

(iii) Maintain records of security holder requests to receive a paper or e-mail copy of the proxy materials in connection with future proxy solicitations and provide copies of the proxy materials to a security holder who has made such a request for all securities held in the account of that security holder until the security holder revokes such request.

(5) Notwithstanding any other provisions in this paragraph (d), if the bank receives copies of the proxy statement and annual report to security holders (if applicable) from the soliciting person with instructions to forward such materials to beneficial owners, the bank:

(i) Shall either:

(A) Prepare a Notice of Internet Availability of Proxy Materials and forward it with the proxy statement and annual report to security holders (if applicable); or

(B) Incorporate any information required in the Notice of Internet Availability of Proxy Materials that does not appear in the proxy statement into the bank's request for voting instructions to be sent with the proxy statement and annual report (if applicable);

(ii) Need not comply with the following provisions:

(A) The timing provisions of paragraph (d)(1)(ii); and

(B) Paragraph (d)(4); and

(iii) Need not include in its Notice of Internet Availability of Proxy Materials or request for voting instructions the following disclosures:

(A) Legends 1 and 3 of Rule 14a–16(d)(1); and

(B) Instructions on how to request a copy of the proxy materials.

(e) *Content of Notice of Internet Availability of Proxy Materials.* The bank's Notice of Internet Availability of Proxy Materials shall:

(1) Include all information, as it relates to beneficial owners, required in a registrant's Notice of Internet Availability of Proxy Materials under Rule 14a–16(d), provided that the bank shall provide its own, or its agent's, toll-free telephone number, e-mail address, and Internet Web site to service requests for copies from beneficial owners; and

(2) Otherwise be prepared and sent in a manner consistent with paragraphs (e), (f), and (g) of Rule 14a.

REGULATION 14C—DISTRIBUTION OF INFORMATION PURSUANT TO SECTION 14(c)

Rule 14c–1. Definitions

Unless the context otherwise requires, all terms used in this regulation have the same meanings as in the Act or elsewhere in the general rules and regulations thereunder. In addition, the following definitions apply unless the context otherwise requires:

(a) *Associate.* The term "associate," used to indicate a relationship with any person, means:

(1) Any corporation or organization (other than the registrant or a majority owned subsidiary of the registrant) of which such person is an officer or partner or is, directly or indirectly, the beneficial owner of 10 percent or more of any class of equity securities;

(2) Any trust or other estate in which such person has a substantial beneficial interest or as to which such person serves as trustee or in a similar fiduciary capacity; and

(3) Any relative or spouse of such person, or any relative of such spouse, who has the same home as such person or who is a director or officer of the registrant or any of its parents or subsidiaries.

(b) *Employee benefit plan.* For purposes of Rule 14c–7, the term "employee benefit plan" means any purchase, savings, option, bonus, appreciation, profit sharing, thrift, incentive, pension or similar plan primarily for employees, directors, trustees or officers.

(c) *Entity that exercises fiduciary powers.* The term "entity that exercises fiduciary powers" means any entity that holds securities in nominee name or otherwise on behalf of a beneficial owner but does not include a clearing agency registered pursuant to section 17A of the Act, or a broker or a dealer.

(d) *Exempt employee benefit plan securities.* For purposes of Rule 14c–7, the term "exempt employee benefit plan securities" means:

(1) Securities of the registrant held by an employee benefit plan, as defined in paragraph (b) of this rule, where such plan is established by the registrant; or

(2) If notice regarding the current distribution of information statements has been given pursuant to Rule 14c–7(a)(1)(ii)(C) or if notice regarding the current request for a list of names, addresses and securities positions of beneficial owners has been given pursuant to Rule 14c–7(b)(3), securities of the registrant held by an employee benefit plan, as defined in paragraph (b) of this rule, where such plan is established by an affiliate of the registrant.

(e) *Information statement.* The term "information statement" means the statement required by Rule 14c–2, whether or not contained in a single document.

(f) *Last fiscal year.* The term "last fiscal year" of the registrant means the last fiscal year of the registrant ending prior to the date of the meeting with respect to which an information statement is required to be distributed, or if the information statement involves consents or authorizations in lieu of a meeting, the earliest date on which they may be used to effect corporate action.

(g) *Proxy.* The term "proxy" includes every proxy, consent or authorization within the meaning of section 14(a) of the Act. The consent or authorization may take the form of failure to object or to dissent.

(h) *Record date.* The term "record date" means the date as of which the record holders of securities entitled to vote at a meeting or by written consent or authorization shall be determined.

(i) *Record holder.* For purposes of Rule 14c–7, the term "record holder" means any broker, dealer, voting trustee, bank, association or other entity that exercises fiduciary powers which holds securities of record in nominee name or otherwise or as a participant in a clearing agency registered pursuant to section 17A of the Act.

(j) *Registrant.* The term "registrant" means

(1) The issuer of a class of securities registered pursuant to Section 12 of the Act; or

(2) An investment company registered under the Investment Company Act of 1940 that has made a public offering of its securities.

(k) *Respondent bank.* For purposes of Rule 14c–7, the term "respondent bank" means any bank, association or other entity that exercises fiduciary powers which holds securities on behalf of beneficial owners and deposits such securities for safekeeping with another bank, association or other entity that exercises fiduciary powers.

Rule 14c–2. Distribution of Information Statement

(a)(1)   In connection with every annual or other meeting of the holders of the class of securities registered pursuant to section 12 of the Act or of a class of securities issued by an investment company registered under the Investment Company Act of 1940 that has made a public offering of securities, including the taking of corporate action by the written authorization or consent of security holders, the registrant shall transmit to every security holder of the class that is entitled to vote or give an authorization or consent in regard to any matter to be acted upon and from whom proxy authorization or consent is not solicited on behalf of the registrant pursuant to section 14(a) of the Act:

(i)   A written information statement containing the information specified in Schedule 14C;

(ii)   A publicly-filed information statement, in the form and manner described in Rule 14c–3(d), containing the information specified in Schedule 14C; or

(iii)   A written information statement included in a registration statement filed under the Securities Act of 1933 on Form S–4 or F–4 (17 C.F.R. § 239.34) or Form N–14 (17 C.F.R. § 239.23) and containing the information specified in such Form.

(2)   Notwithstanding paragraph (a)(1) of this rule:

(i)   In the case of a class of securities in unregistered or bearer form, such statements need to be transmitted only to those security holders whose names are known to the registrant; and

(ii)   No such statements need to be transmitted to a security holder if a registrant would be excused from delivery of an annual report to security holders or a proxy statement under Rule 14a–3(e)(2) if such rule were applicable.

(b)   The information statement shall be sent or given at least 20 calendar days prior to the meeting date or, in the case of corporate action taken pursuant to the consents or authorizations of security holders, at least 20 calendar days prior to the earliest date on which the corporate action may be taken.

(c)   If a transaction is a roll-up transaction as defined in Item 901(c) of Regulation S–K and is registered (or authorized to be registered) on Form S–4 or Form F–4, the information statement must be distributed to security holders no later than the lesser of 60 calendar days prior to the date on which the meeting of security holders is held or action is taken, or the maximum number of days permitted for giving notice under applicable state law.

(d)   A registrant shall transmit an information statement to security holders pursuant to paragraph (a) of this rule by satisfying the requirements set forth in Rule 14a–16; provided, however, that the registrant shall revise the information required in the Notice of Internet Availability of Proxy Materials to reflect the fact that the registrant is not soliciting proxies for the meeting.

Rule 14c–3. Annual Report to Be Furnished Security Holders

(a)   If the information statement relates to an annual (or special meeting in lieu of the annual) meeting, or written consent in lieu of such meeting, of security holders at which directors of the registrant, other than an investment company registered under the Investment Company Act of 1940, are to be elected, it shall be accompanied or preceded by an annual report to security holders.

(1)   The annual report to security holders shall contain the information specified in paragraphs (b)(1) through (b)(11) of Rule 14a–3.

(2)   [Reserved]

(b)   The report sent to security holders pursuant to this rule shall be submitted in electronic format, in accordance with the EDGAR Filer Manual, to the Commission, solely for its information, not later than the date on which such report is first sent or given to security holders or the date on which preliminary copies, or definitive copies, if preliminary filing was not required, of the information statement are filed with the Commission pursuant Rule 14c–5, whichever date is later. The report is not deemed to be "filed" with the Commission or subject to this regulation otherwise than as provided in this rule, or to the liabilities of section 18 of the Act, except to the extent that the registrant specifically requests that it be treated as a part of the information statement or incorporates it in the information statement or other filed report by reference.

(c) A registrant will be considered to have delivered a Notice of Internet Availability of Proxy Materials, annual report to security holders or information statement to security holders of record who share an address if the requirements set forth in Rule 14a–3(e)(1) are satisfied with respect to the Notice of Internet Availability of Proxy Materials, annual report to security holders or information statement, as applicable.

(d) A registrant shall furnish an annual report to security holders pursuant to paragraph (a) of this rule by satisfying the requirements set forth in Rule 14a–16.

Rule 14c-4. Presentation of Information in Information Statement

(a) The information included in the information statement shall be clearly presented and the statements made shall be divided into groups according to subject matter and the various groups of statements shall be preceded by appropriate headings. The order of items and sub-items in the schedule need not be followed. Where practicable and appropriate, the information shall be presented in tabular form. All amounts shall be stated in figures. Information required by more than one applicable item need not be repeated. No statement need be made in response to any item or sub-item which is inapplicable.

(b) Any information required to be included in the information statement as to terms of securities or other subject matters which from a standpoint of practical necessity must be determined in the future may be stated in terms of present knowledge and intention. Subject to the foregoing, information which is not known to the registrant and which it is not reasonably within the power of the registrant to ascertain or procure may be omitted, if a brief statement of the circumstances rendering such information unavailable is made.

(c) All printed information statements shall be in roman type at least as large and as legible as 10-point modern type except that to the extent necessary for convenient presentation, financial statements and other tabular data, but not the notes thereto, may be in roman type at least as large and as legible as 8-point modern type. All such type shall be leaded at least 2 points.

(d) Where an information statement is delivered through an electronic medium, issuers may satisfy legibility requirements applicable to printed documents, such as type size and font, by presenting all required information in a format readily communicated to investors.

Rule 14c-5. Filing Requirements

(a) *Preliminary information statement.* Five preliminary copies of the information statement shall be filed with the Commission at least 10 calendar days prior to the date definitive copies of such statement are first sent or given to security holders, or such shorter period prior to that date as the Commission may authorize upon a showing of good cause therefor. In computing the 10-day period, the filing date of the preliminary copies is to be counted as the first day and the 11th day is the date on which definitive copies of the information statement may be sent to security holders. A registrant, however, shall not file with the Commission a preliminary information statement if it relates to an annual (or special meeting in lieu of the annual) meeting, of security holders at which the only matters to be acted upon are:

(1) The election of directors;

(2) The election, approval or ratification of accountant(s);

(3) A security holder proposal identified in the registrant's information statement pursuant to Item 4 of Schedule 14C; and/or

(4) The approval or ratification of a plan as defined in paragraph (a)(6)(ii) of Item 402 of Regulation S–K or amendments to such a plan.

This exclusion from filing a preliminary information statement does not apply if the registrant comments upon or refers to a solicitation in opposition in connection with the meeting in its information statement.

NOTE 1: The filing of revised material does not recommence the ten day time period unless the revised material contains material revisions or material new proposal(s) that constitute a fundamental change in the information statement.

NOTE 2: The officials responsible for the preparation of the information statement should make every effort to verify the accuracy and completeness of the information required by the applicable rules. The preliminary statement should be filed with the Commission at the earliest practicable date.

NOTE 3: Solicitation in Opposition—For purposes of the exclusion from filing a preliminary information statement, a "solicitation in opposition" includes: (a) Any solicitation opposing a proposal supported by the registrant; and (b) any solicitation supporting a proposal that the registrant does not expressly support, other than a security holder proposal identified in the registrant's information statement pursuant to Item 4 of Schedule 14C. The identification of a security holder proposal in the registrant's information statement does not constitute a "solicitation in opposition," even if the registrant opposes the proposal and/or includes a statement in opposition to the proposal.

NOTE 4: A registrant that is filing an information statement in preliminary form only because the registrant has commented on or referred to an opposing solicitation should indicate that fact in a transmittal letter when filing the preliminary material with the Commission.

(b) *Definitive information statement.* Eight definitive copies of the information statement, in the form in which it is furnished to security holders, must be filed with the Commission no later than the date the information statement is first sent or given to security holders. Three copies of these materials also must be filed with, or mailed for filing to, each national securities exchange on which the registrant has a class of securities listed and registered.

(c) *Release dates.* All preliminary material filed pursuant to paragraph (a) of this rule shall be accompanied by a statement of the date on which copies thereof filed pursuant to paragraph (b) of this rule are intended to be released to security holders. All definitive material filed pursuant to paragraph (b) of this rule shall be accompanied by a statement of the date on which copies of such material have been released to security holders or, if not released, the date on which copies thereof are intended to be released.

(d)(1) *Public availability of information.* All copies of material filed pursuant to paragraph (a) of this rule shall be clearly marked "Preliminary Copies," and shall be deemed immediately available for public inspection unless confidential treatment is obtained pursuant to paragraph (d)(2) of this rule.

(2) *Confidential Treatment.* If action will be taken on any matter specified in Item 14 of Schedule 14A, all copies of the preliminary information statement filed under paragraph (a) of this rule will be for the information of the Commission only and will not be deemed available for public inspection until filed with the Commission in definitive form so long as:

(i) The information statement does not relate to a matter or proposal subject to Rule 13e–3 or a roll-up transaction as defined in Item 901(c) of Regulation S–K;

(ii) Neither the parties to the transaction nor any persons authorized to act on their behalf have made any public communications relating to the transaction except for statements where the content is limited to the information specified in Rule 135 under the Securities Act; and

(iii) The materials are filed in paper and marked "Confidential, For Use of the Commission Only." In all cases, the materials may be disclosed to any department or agency of the United States Government and to the Congress, and the Commission may make any inquiries or investigation into the materials as may be necessary to conduct an adequate review by the Commission.

Instruction to paragraph (d)(2): If communications are made publicly that go beyond the information specified in Rule 135, the materials must be re-filed publicly with the Commission.

(e) *Revised information statements.* Where any information statement filed pursuant to this rule is amended or revised, two of the copies of such amended or revised material filed pursuant to this rule shall be marked to indicate clearly and precisely the changes effected therein. If the amendment or revision alters the text of the material, the changes in such text shall be indicated by means of underscoring or in some other appropriate manner.

(f) *Merger material.* Notwithstanding the foregoing provisions of this rule, any information statement or other material included in a registration statement filed under the Securities Act of 1933 on Form N–14, S–4, or F–4 shall be deemed filed both for the purposes of that Act and for the purposes of this rule, but separate copies of such material need not be furnished pursuant to this rule, nor shall any fee be required under paragraph (a) of this rule. However, any additional material used after the effective date of the registration statement on Form N–14, S–4, or F–4 shall be filed in accordance with this rule, unless separate copies of such material are required to be filed as an amendment of such registration statement.

(g)   *Fees.* At the time of filing a preliminary information statement regarding an acquisition, merger, spin-off, consolidation or proposed sale or other disposition of substantially all the assets of the company, the registrant shall pay the Commission a fee, no part of which shall be refunded, established in accordance with Rule 0–11.

(h)   *Cover page.* Each information statement filed with the Commission shall include a cover page in the form set forth in Schedule 14C. The cover page required by this paragraph need not be distributed to security holders.

Rule 14c–6. False or Misleading Statements

(a)   No information statement shall contain any statement which, at the time and in the light of the circumstances under which it is made, is false or misleading with respect to any material fact, or which omits to state any material fact necessary in order to make the statements therein not false or misleading or necessary to correct any statement in any earlier communication with respect to the same meeting or subject matter which has become false or misleading.

(b)   The fact that an information statement has been filed with or examined by the Commission shall not be deemed a finding by the Commission that such material is accurate or complete or not false or misleading, or that the Commission has passed upon the merits of or approved any statement contained therein or any matter to be acted upon by security holders. No representation contrary to the foregoing shall be made.

Rule 14c–7. Providing Copies of Material for Certain Beneficial Owners

(a)   If the registrant knows that securities of any class entitled to vote at a meeting, or by written authorizations or consents if no meeting is held, are held of record by a broker, dealer, voting trustee, or bank, association, or other entity that exercises fiduciary powers in nominee name or otherwise, the registrant shall:

(1)   By first class mail or other equally prompt means:

(i)   Inquire of each such record holder:

(A)   Whether other persons are the beneficial owners of such securities and, if so, the number of copies of the information statement necessary to supply such material to such beneficial owners; and

(B)   In the case of an annual (or special meeting in lieu of the annual) meeting, or written consents in lieu of such meeting, at which directors are to be elected, the number of copies of the annual report to security holders, necessary to supply such report to such beneficial owners for whom proxy material has not been and is not to be made available and to whom such reports are to be distributed by such record holder or its nominee and not by the registrant; and

(C)   If the record holder or respondent bank has an obligation under Rule 14b–1(b)(3) or Rule 14b–2(b)(4)(ii) and (iii), whether an agent has been designated to act on its behalf in fulfilling such obligation, and, if so, the name and address of such agent; and

(D)   Whether it holds the registrant's securities on behalf of any respondent bank and, if so, the name and address of each such respondent bank; and

(ii)   Indicate to each such record holder:

(A)   Whether the registrant, pursuant to paragraph (c) of this rule, intends to distribute the annual report to security holders to beneficial owners of its securities whose names, addresses and securities positions are disclosed pursuant to Rule 14b–1(b)(3) and Rule 14b–2(b)(4)(ii) and (iii);

(B)   The record date; and

(C) At the option of the registrant, any employee benefit plan established by an affiliate of the registrant that holds securities of the registrant that the registrant elects to treat as exempt employee benefit plan securities;

(2) Upon receipt of a record holder's or respondent bank's response indicating, pursuant to Rule 14b–2(b)(1)(i), the names and addresses of its respondent banks, within one business day after the date such response is received, make an inquiry of and give notification to each such respondent bank in the same manner required by paragraph (a)(1) of this rule; *Provided, however,* the inquiry required by paragraphs (a)(1) and (a)(2) of this rule shall not cover beneficial owners of exempt employee benefit plan securities;

(3) Make the inquiry required by paragraph (a)(1) of this rule on the earlier of:

(i) At least 20 business days prior to the record date of the meeting of security holders or the record date of written consents in lieu of a meeting; or

(ii) At least 20 business days prior to the date the information statement is required to be sent or given pursuant to Rule 14c–2(b);

Provided, however, That, if a record holder or respondent bank has informed the registrant that a designated office(s) or department(s) is to receive such inquires, the inquiry shall be made to such designated office(s) or department(s);

(4) Supply, in a timely manner, each record holder and respondent bank of whom the inquiries required by paragraphs (a)(1) and (a)(2) of this rule are made with copies of the information statement and/or the annual report to security holders, in such quantities, assembled in such form and at such place(s), as the record holder or respondent bank may reasonably request in order to send such material to each beneficial owner of securities who is to be furnished with such material by the record holder or respondent bank; and

(5) Upon the request of any record holder or respondent bank that is supplied with Notices of Internet Availability of Proxy Materials, information statements and/or annual reports to security holders pursuant to paragraph (a)(3) of this rule, pay its reasonable expenses for completing the sending of such material to beneficial owners.

NOTE 1: If the registrant's list of security holders indicates that some of its securities are registered in the name of a clearing agency registered pursuant to Section 17A of the Act (*e.g.,* "Cede & Co.," nominee for the Depository Trust Company), the registrants shall make appropriate inquiry of the clearing agency and thereafter of the participants in such clearing agency who may hold on behalf of a beneficial owner or respondent bank, and shall comply with the above paragraph with respect to any such participant (*see* Rule 14c–1(h)).

NOTE 2: The attention of registrants is called to the fact that each broker, dealer, bank, association, and other entity that exercises fiduciary powers has an obligation pursuant to Rule 14b–1 and Rule 14b–2 (except as provided therein with respect to exempt employee benefit plan securities held in nominee name) and, with respect to brokers and dealers, applicable self-regulatory organization requirements, to obtain and forward, within the time periods prescribed therein, (a) information statements to beneficial owners on whose behalf it holds securities, and (b) annual reports to security holders to beneficial owners on whose behalf it holds securities, unless the registrant has notified the record holder or respondent bank that it has assumed responsibility to send such material to beneficial owners whose names, addresses and securities positions are disclosed pursuant to Rule 14b–1(b)(3) and Rule 14b–2(b)(4)(ii) and (iii).

NOTE 3: The attention of registrants is called to the fact that registrants have an obligation, pursuant to paragraph (d) of this rule, to cause information statements and annual reports to security holders to be furnished, in accordance with Rule 14c–2 to beneficial owners of exempt employee benefit plan securities.

(b) Any registrant requesting pursuant to Rule 14b–1(b)(3) and Rule 14b–2(b)(4)(ii) and (iii) a list of names, addresses and securities positions of beneficial owners of its securities who either have consented or have not objected to disclosure of such information shall:

(1) By first class mail or other equally prompt means, inquire of each record holder and each respondent bank identified to the registrant pursuant to Rule 14b–2(e)(1) whether such record holder or respondent bank holds the registrant's securities on behalf of any respondent banks and, if so, the name and address of each such respondent bank;

(2)   Request such list be compiled as of a date no earlier than five business days after the date the registrant's request is received by the record holder or respondent bank; *Provided, however,* That if the record holder or respondent bank has informed the registrant that a designated office(s) or department(s) is to receive such requests, the request shall be made to such designated office(s) or department(s);

(3)   Make such request to the following persons that hold the registrant's securities on behalf of beneficial owners: all brokers, dealers, banks, associations and other entities that exercise fiduciary powers; *Provided, however,* such request shall not cover beneficial owners of exempt employee benefit plan securities as defined in Rule 14a–1(d)(1); and at the option of the registrant, such request may give notice of any employee benefit plan established by an affiliate of the registrant that holds securities of the registrant that the registrant elects to treat as exempt employee benefit plan securities;

(4)   Use the information furnished in response to such request exclusively for purposes of corporate communications; and

(5)   Upon the request of any record holder or respondent bank to whom such request is made, pay the reasonable expenses, both direct and indirect, of providing beneficial owner information.

NOTE: A registrant will be deemed to have satisfied its obligations under paragraph (b) of this rule by requesting consenting and non-objecting beneficial owner lists from a designated agent acting on behalf of the record holder or respondent bank and paying to that designated agent the reasonable expenses of providing the beneficial owner information.

(c)   A registrant, at its option, may send by mail or other equally prompt means its annual report to security holders to the beneficial owners whose identifying information is provided by record holders and respondent banks, pursuant to Rule 14b–1(b)(3) and Rule 14b–2(b)(4)(ii) and (iii), provided that such registrant notifies the record holders and respondent banks at the time it makes the inquiry required by paragraph (a) of this rule that the registrant will send the annual report to security holders to the beneficial owners so identified.

(d)   If a registrant furnishes information statements to record holders and respondent banks who hold securities on behalf of beneficial owners, the registrant shall cause information statements and annual reports to security holders to be furnished, in accordance with Rule 14c–2, to beneficial owners of exempt employee benefit plan securities.

REGULATION 14D

Rule 14d–1. Scope of and Definitions Applicable to Regulations 14D and 14E

(a)   *Scope.* Regulation 14D shall apply to any tender offer that is subject to section 14(d)(1) of the Act, including, but not limited to, any tender offer for securities of a class described in that section that is made by an affiliate of the issuer of such class. Regulation 14E shall apply to any tender offer for securities (other than exempted securities) unless otherwise noted therein.

(b)   The requirements imposed by sections 14(d)(1) through 14(d)(7) of the Act, Regulation 14D and Schedules TO and 14D–9 thereunder, and Rule 14e–1 of Regulation 14E under the Act, shall be deemed satisfied with respect to any tender offer, including any exchange offer, for the securities of an issuer incorporated or organized under the laws of Canada or any Canadian province or territory, if such issuer is a foreign private issuer and is not an investment company registered or required to be registered under the Investment Company Act of 1940, if less than 40 percent of the class of securities outstanding that is the subject of the tender offer is held by U.S. holders, and the tender offer is subject to, and the bidder complies with, the laws, regulations and policies of Canada and/or any of its provinces or territories governing the conduct of the offer (unless the bidder has received an exemption(s) from, and the tender offer does not comply with, requirements that otherwise would be prescribed by Regulation 14D or 14E), *provided that:*

(1)   In the case of tender offers subject to section 14(d)(1) of the Act, where the consideration for a tender offer subject to this rule consists solely of cash, the entire disclosure document or documents required to be furnished to holders of the class of securities to be acquired shall be filed with the Commission on Schedule 14D–1F and disseminated to shareholders of the subject company residing in the United States in accordance with such Canadian laws, regulations and policies; or

(2) Where the consideration for a tender offer subject to this rule includes securities of the bidder to be issued pursuant to the offer, any registration statement and/or prospectus relating thereto shall be filed with the Commission along with the Schedule 14D–1F referred to in paragraph (b)(1) of this rule, and shall be disseminated, together with the home jurisdiction document(s) accompanying such Schedule, to shareholders of the subject company residing in the United States in accordance with such Canadian laws, regulations and policies.

NOTES: 1. For purposes of any tender offer, including any exchange offer, otherwise eligible to proceed in accordance with Rule 14d–1(b) under the Act, the issuer of the subject securities will be presumed to be a foreign private issuer and U.S. holders will be presumed to hold less than 40 percent of such outstanding securities, *unless* (a) the aggregate trading volume of that class on national securities exchanges in the United States and on NASDAQ exceeded its aggregate trading volume on securities exchanges in Canada and on the Canadian Dealing Network, Inc. ("CDN") over the 12 calendar month period prior to commencement of this offer, or if commenced in response to a prior offer, over the 12 calendar month period prior to the commencement of the initial offer (based on volume figures published by such exchanges and NASDAQ and CDN); (b) the most recent annual report or annual information form filed or submitted by the issuer with securities regulators of Ontario, Quebec, British Columbia or Alberta (or, if the issuer of the subject securities is not a reporting issuer in any of such provinces, with any other Canadian securities regulator) or with the Commission indicates that U.S. holders hold 40 percent or more of the outstanding subject class of securities; or (c) the offeror has actual knowledge that the level of U.S. ownership equals or exceeds 40 percent of such securities.

2. Notwithstanding the grant of an exemption from one or more of the applicable Canadian regulatory provisions imposing requirements that otherwise would be prescribed by Regulation 14D or 14E, the tender offer will be eligible to proceed in accordance with the requirements of this rule if the Commission by order determines that the applicable Canadian regulatory provisions are adequate to protect the interest of investors.

(c) *Tier 1.* Any tender offer for the securities of a foreign private issuer as defined in § 240.3b–4 is exempt from the requirements of Rules 14(d)(1) through 14(d)(7) of the Act, Regulation 14D and Schedules TO and 14D–9 thereunder, and Rule 14e–1 and 14e–2 of Regulation 14E under the Act if the following conditions are satisfied:

(1) *U.S. ownership limitation.* Except the in case of a tender offer that is commenced during the pendency of a tender offer made by a prior bidder in reliance on this paragraph or Rule 13e–4(h)(8), U.S. holders do not hold more than 10 percent of the class of securities sought in the offer (as determined under Instructions 2 or 3 to paragraphs (c) and (d) of this rule).

(2) *Equal treatment.* The bidder must permit U.S. holders to participate in the offer on terms at least as favorable as those offered any other holder of the same class of securities that is subject to the offer, however:

(i) *Registered exchange offers.* If the bidder offers securities registered under the Securities Act of 1933, the bidder need not extend the offer to security holders in those states or jurisdictions that prohibit the offer or sale of securities after the bidder has made a good faith effort to register or qualify the offer and sale of securities in that state or jurisdiction, except that the bidder must offer the same cash alternative to security holders in any such state or jurisdiction that it has offered to security holders in any other state or jurisdiction.

(ii) *Exempt exchange offers.* If the bidder offers securities exempt from registration under Rule 802 under the Securities Act of 1933, the bidder need not extend the offer to security holders in those states or jurisdictions that require registration or qualification, except that the bidder must offer the same cash alternative to security holders in any such state or jurisdiction that it has offered to security holders in any other state or jurisdiction.

(iii) *Cash only consideration.* The bidder may offer U.S. holders cash only consideration for the tender of the subject securities, notwithstanding the fact that the bidder is offering security holders outside the United States a consideration that consists in whole or in part of securities of the bidder, so long as the bidder has a reasonable basis for believing that the amount of cash is substantially equivalent to the value of the consideration offered to non-U.S. holders, and either of the following conditions are satisfied:

(A) The offered security is a "margin security" within the meaning of Regulation T and the issuer or affiliate undertakes to provide, upon the request of any U.S. holder or the

Commission staff, the closing price and daily trading volume of the security on the principal trading market for the security as of the last trading day of each six months preceding the announcement of the offer and each of the trading days thereafter; or

(B) If the offered security is not a "margin security" within the meaning of Regulation T, the issuer or affiliate undertakes to provide, upon the request of any U.S. holder or the Commission staff, an opinion of an independent expert stating that the cash consideration offered security holders outside the United States.

(iv) *Disparate tax treatments.* If the bidder offers "loan notes" solely to offer sellers tax advantages not available in the United States and these notes are neither listed on any organized securities market nor registered under the Securities Act of 1933, the loan notes need not be offered to U.S. holders.

(3) *Informational documents.* (i) The bidder must disseminate any informational documents to U.S. holders, including any amendments thereto, in English, or an comparable basis to that provided to security holders in the home jurisdiction.

(ii) If the bidder disseminates by publication in its home jurisdiction, the bidder must publish the information in the United States in a manner reasonably calculated to inform U.S. holders of the offer.

(iii) In the case of tender offers for securities described in section 14(d)(1) of the Act, if the bidder publishes or otherwise disseminates an informational document to the holders of the securities in connection with the issuer tender offer (including any exchange offer), the bidder must furnish the informational document, including any amendments thereto, in English, to the Commission on Form CB by the first business day after publication or dissemination. If the bidder is a foreign company, it must also file a Form F–X with the Commission at the same time as the submission of Form CB to appoint an agent for service in the United States.

(4) *Investment companies.* The issuer of the securities that are the subject of the tender offer is not an investment company registered or required to be registered under the Investment Company Act of 1940, other than a registered closed-end investment company.

(d) *Tier II.* A person conducting a tender offer (including any exchange offer) that meets the conditions in paragraph (d)(1) of this rule shall be entitled to the exemptive relief specified in paragraph (d)(2) of this rule, provided that such tender offer complies with all the requirements of this rule other than those for which an exemption has been specifically provided in paragraph (d)(2) of this rule. In addition, a person conducting a tender offer subject only to the requirements of section 14(e) of the Act and Regulation 14E thereunder that meets the conditions in paragraph (d)(1) of the rule also shall be entitled to the exemptive relief specified in paragraph (d)(2) of this rule, to the extent needed under the requirements of Regulation 14E, so long as the tender offer complies with all requirements of Regulation 14E other than those for which an exemption has been specifically provided in paragraph (d)(2) of this rule:

(1) *Conditions.* (i) The subject company is a foreign private issuer as defined in Rule 3b–4 and is not an investment company registered or required to be registered under the Investment Company Act of 1940, other than a registered closed-end investment company, and

(ii) Except in the case of a tender offer that is commenced during the pendency of a tender offer made by a prior bidder in reliance on this paragraph or Rule 13e–4(i), U.S. holders do not hold more than 40 percent of the class of securities sought in the offer (as determined under Instructions 2 or 3 to paragraphs (c) and (d) of this rule); and

(iii) The bidder complies with all applicable U.S. tender offer laws and regulations, other than those for which an exemption has been provided for in paragraph (d)(2) of this rule.

(2) *Exemptions.*—(i) *Equal treatment—loan notes.* If the bidder offers loan notes solely to offer sellers tax advantages not available in the United States and these notes are neither listed on any organized securities market nor registered under the Securities Act, the loan notes need not be offered to U.S. holders (like 13e–4(i)(2)(i)), notwithstanding Rule 14d–10.

(ii) *Equal treatment—separate U.S. and foreign offers.* Notwithstanding the provisions of Rule 14d–10, a bidder conducting a tender offer meeting the conditions of paragraph (d)(1) of this rule may separate the offer into multiple offers: one offer made to U.S. holders, which also may include all holders of American Depositary Shares representing interests in the subject securities, and one or more offers made to non-U.S. holders. The U.S. offer must be made on terms at least as favorable as those offered any other holder of the same class of securities that is the subject of the tender offers. U.S. holders may be included in the foreign offer(s) only where the laws of the jurisdiction governing such foreign offer(s) expressly preclude the exclusion of U.S. holders from the foreign offer(s) and where the offer materials distributed to U.S. holders fully and adequately disclose the risks of participating in the foreign offer(s).

(iii) *Notice of extensions.* Notice of extensions made in accordance with the requirements of the home jurisdiction law or practice will satisfy the requirements of Rule 14e–1(d).

(iv) *Prompt payment.* Payment made in accordance with the requirements of the home jurisdiction law or practice will satisfy the requirements of Rule 14e–1(c). Where payment may not be made on a more expedited basis under home jurisdiction law or practice, payment for securities tendered during any subsequent offering period within 20 business days of the date of tender will satisfy the prompt payment requirements of Rule 14d–11(e). For purposes of this paragraph, a business day is determined with reference to the target's home jurisdiction.

(v) *Subsequent offering period/ Withdrawal rights.* A bidder will satisfy the announcement and prompt payment requirements of Rule 14d–11(d), if the bidder announces the results of the tender offer, including the approximate number of securities deposited to date, and pays for tendered securities in accordance with the requirements of the home jurisdiction law or practice and the subsequent offering period commences immediately following such announcements. Notwithstanding section 14(d)(5) of the Act, the bidder need not extend withdrawal rights following the close of the offer and prior to the commencement of the subsequent offering period.

(vi) *Payment of interest on securities tendered during subsequent offering period.* Notwithstanding the requirements of Rule 14d–11(f), the bidder may pay interest on securities tendered during a subsequent offering period, if required under applicable foreign law. Paying interest on securities tendered during a subsequent offering period in accordance with this rule will not be deemed to violate Rule 14d–10(a)(2).

(vii) *Suspension of withdrawal rights during counting of tendered securities.* The bidder may suspend withdrawal rights required under Rule 14(d)(5) of the Act at the end of the offer and during the period that securities tendered into the offer are being counted, provided that:

(A) The bidder has provided an offer period including withdrawal rights for a period of at least 20 U.S. business days;

(B) At the time withdrawal rights are suspended, all offer conditions have been satisfied or waived, except to the extent that the bidder is in the process of determining whether a minimum acceptance condition included in the terms of the offer has been satisfied by counting tendered securities; and

(C) Withdrawal rights are suspended only during the counting process and are reinstated immediately thereafter, except to the extent that they are terminated through the acceptance of tendered securities.

(viii) *Mix and match elections and the subsequent offering period.* Notwithstanding the requirements of Rule 14d–11(b), where the bidder offers target security holders a choice between different forms of consideration, it may establish a ceiling on one or more forms of consideration offered. Notwithstanding the requirements of Rule 14d–11(f), a bidder that establishes a ceiling on one or more forms of consideration offered pursuant to this subsection may offset elections of tendering security holders against one another, subject to proration, so that elections are satisfied to the greatest extent possible and pro rated to the extent that they cannot be satisfied in full. Such a bidder also may separately offset and pro rate securities tendered during the initial offering period and those tendered during any subsequent offering period, notwithstanding the requirements of Rule 14d–10(c).

(ix) *Early termination of an initial offering period*. A bidder may terminate an initial offering period, including a voluntary extension of that period, if at the time the initial offering period and withdrawal rights terminate, the following conditions are met:

(A) The initial offering period has been open for at least 20 U.S. business days;

(B) The bidder has adequately discussed the possibility of and the impact of the early termination in the original offer materials;

(C) The bidder provides a subsequent offering period after the termination of the initial offering period;

(D) All offer conditions are satisfied as of the time when the initial offering period ends; and

(E) The bidder does not terminate the initial offering period or any extension of that period during any mandatory extension required under U.S. tender offer rules.

Instructions to paragraph (c) and (d) of this rule:

1. "Home jurisdiction" means both the jurisdiction of the subject company's incorporation, organization or chartering and the principal foreign market where the issuer's securities are listed or quoted.

2. "U.S. holder" means any security holder resident to the United States. Except as otherwise provided in Instruction 3 below, to determine the percentage of outstanding securities held by U.S. holders:

i. Calculate the U.S. ownership as of a date no more than 60 before and no more than 30 days after public announcement of the tender offer. If you are unable to calculate as of a date within these time frames, the calculation may be made as of the most recent practicable date before public announcement, but in no event earlier than 120 days before announcement;

ii. Include securities underlying American Depositary Shares convertible or exchangeable into the securities that are the subject of the tender offer when calculating the number of subject securities outstanding, as well as the number held by U.S. holders. Exclude from the calculations other types of securities that are convertible or exchangeable into the securities that are the subject of the tender offer, such as warrants, options and convertible securities. Exclude from those calculations securities held by the bidder;

iii. Use the method of calculating record ownership in Rule 12g3–2(a), except that your inquiry as to the amount of securities represented by accounts of customers resident in the United States may be limited to brokers, dealers, banks and other nominees located in the United States, the subject company's jurisdiction of incorporation or that of each participant in a business combination, and the jurisdiction that is the primary trading market for the subject securities, if different from the subject company's jurisdiction of incorporation;

iv. If, after reasonable inquiry, you are unable to obtain information about the amount of securities represented by accounts of customers resident in the United States, you may assume, for purposes of this definition, that the customers are residents of the jurisdiction in which the nominee has its principal place of business; and

v. Count securities as beneficially owned by residents of the United States as reported on reports of beneficial ownership that are provided to you or publicly fixed and based on information otherwise provided to you.

3. In a tender offer by a bidder other than an affiliate of the issuer of the subject securities that is not made pursuant to an agreement with the issuer of the subject securities, the issuer of the subject securities will be presumed to be a foreign private issuer and U.S. holders will be presumed to hold less than 10 percent (40 percent in the case of paragraph (d) of this rule) of such outstanding securities, unless paragraphs i., ii., or iii. of this rule indicate otherwise. In addition, where the bidder is unable to conduct the analysis of U.S. ownership set forth in Instruction 2 above, the bidder may presume that the percentage of securities held by U.S. holders is less than 10 percent (40 percent in the case of paragraph (d) of this rule) of the outstanding securities so long as there is a primary trading market for the subject securities outside the U.S., as defined in Rule 12h–6(f)(5), unless:

i. Average daily trading volume of the subject securities in the United States for a recent twelve-month period ending on a date no more than 60 days before the public announcement of the offer exceeds 10 percent (40 percent in the case of paragraph (d) of this rule) of the average daily trading volume of that class of securities on a worldwide basis for the same period; or

ii. The most recent annual report or annual information filed or submitted by the issuer with securities regulators of the home jurisdiction or with the Commission or any jurisdiction in which the subject securities trade before the public announcement of the offer indicates that U.S. holders hold more than 10 percent (40 percent in the case of paragraph (d) of this rule) of the outstanding subject class of securities; or

iii. The bidder knows or has reason to know, before the public announcement of the offer, that the level of U.S. ownership exceeds 10 percent (40 percent in the case of paragraph (d) of this rule) of such securities. As an example, a bidder is deemed to know information about U.S. ownership of the subject class of securities that is publicly available and that appears in any filing with the Commission or any regulatory body in the issuer's jurisdiction of incorporation or (if different) the non-U.S. jurisdiction in which the primary trading market for the subject securities is located. The bidder is deemed to know information about U.S. ownership available from the issuer or obtained or readily available from any other source that is reasonably reliable, including from persons it has retained to advise it about the transaction, as well as from third-party information providers. These examples are not intended to be exclusive.

4. "United States" means the United States of America, its territories and possessions, any state of the United States, and the District of Columbia.

5. The exemptions provided in paragraphs (c) and (d) of this rule are not available for any securities transaction or series of transactions that technically complies with paragraph (c) or (d) of this rule but are part of a plan or scheme to evade the provisions of Regulations 14D or 14E.

(e) Notwithstanding paragraph (a) of this rule, the requirements imposed by sections 14(d)(1) through 14(d)(7) of the Act, Regulation 14D promulgated thereunder shall not apply by virtue of the fact that a bidder for the securities of a foreign private issuer, as defined in Rule 3b–4, the subject company of such a tender offer, their representatives, or any other person specified in Rule 240.14d–9(d), provides any journalist with access to its press conferences held outside of the United States, to meetings with its representatives conducted outside of the United States, or to written press-related materials released outside the United States, at or in which a present or proposed tender offer is discussed, if:

(1) Access is provided to both U.S. and foreign journalists; and

(2) With respect to any written press-related materials released by the bidder or its representatives that discuss a present or proposed tender offer for equity securities registered under section 12 of the Act, the written press-related materials must state that these written press-related materials are not an extension of a tender offer in the United States for a class of equity securities of the subject company. If the bidder intends to extend the tender offer in the United States at some future time, a statement regarding this intention, and that the procedural and filing requirements of the Williams Act will be satisfied at that time, also must be included in these written press-related materials. No means to tender securities, or coupons that could be returned to indicate interest in the tender offer, may be provided as part of, or attached to, these written press-related materials.

(f) For the purpose of Rule 14d–1(e), a bidder may presume that a target company qualifies as a foreign private issuer if the target company is a foreign issuer and files registration statements or reports on the disclosure forms specifically designated for foreign private issuers, claims the exemption from registration under the Act pursuant to Rule 12g3–2(b), or is not reporting in the United States.

(g) *Definitions.* Unless the context otherwise requires, all terms used in Regulation 14D and Regulation 14E have the same meaning as in the Act and in Rule 12b–2 promulgated thereunder. In addition, for purposes of sections 14(d) and 14(e) of the Act and Regulations 14D and 14E, the following definitions apply:

(1) The term "beneficial owner" shall have the same meaning as that set forth in Rule 13d–3: *Provided, however,* That, except with respect to Rule 14d–3 and Rule 14d–9(d), the term shall not include a person who does not have or share investment power or who is deemed to be a beneficial owner by virtue of Rule 13d–3(d)(1);

(2) The term "bidder" means any person who makes a tender offer or on whose behalf a tender offer is made: *Provided, however,* That the term does not include an issuer which makes a tender offer for securities of any class of which it is the issuer;

(3) The term "business day" means any day, other than Saturday, Sunday or a federal holiday, and shall consist of the time period from 12:01 a.m. through 12:00 midnight Eastern time. In computing

any time period under section 14(d)(5) or section 14(d)(6) of the Act or under Regulation 14D or Regulation 14E, the date of the event which begins the running of such time period shall be included *except that* if such event occurs on other than a business day such period shall begin to run on and shall include the first business day thereafter; and

(4) The term "initial offering period" means the period from the time the offer commences until all minimum time periods, including extensions, required by Regulation 14D and 14E have been satisfied and all conditions to the offer have been satisfied or waived within these time periods.

(5) The term "security holders" means holders of record and beneficial owners of securities which are the subject of a tender offer;

(6) The term "security position listing" means, with respect to securities of any issuer held by a registered clearing agency in the name of the clearing agency or its nominee, a list of those participants in the clearing agency on whose behalf the clearing agency holds the issuer's securities and of the participants' respective positions in such securities as of a specified date.

(7) The term "subject company" means any issuer of securities which are sought by a bidder pursuant to a tender offer;

(8) The term "subsequent offering period" means the period immediately following the initial offering period meeting the conditions specified in Rule 14d–11.

(9) The term "tender offer material" means:

(i) The bidder's formal offer, including all the material terms and conditions of the tender offer and all amendments thereto;

(ii) The related transmittal letter (whereby securities of the subject company which are sought in the tender offer may be transmitted to the bidder or its depositary) and all amendments thereto; and

(iii) Press releases, advertisements, letters and other documents published by the bidder or sent or given by the bidder to security holders which, directly or indirectly, solicit, invite or request tenders of the securities being sought in the tender offer.

(h) *Signatures.* Where the Act or the rules, forms, reports or schedules thereunder require a document filed with or furnished to the Commission to be signed, such document shall be manually signed, or signed using either typed signatures or duplicated or facsimile versions of manual signatures. Where typed, duplicated or facsimile signatures are used, each signatory to the filing shall manually sign a signature page or other document authenticating, acknowledging or otherwise adopting his or her signature that appears in the filing. Such document shall be executed before or at the time the filing is made and shall be retained by the filer for a period of five years. Upon request, the filer shall furnish to the Commission or its staff a copy of any or all documents retained pursuant to this rule.

Rule 14d–2. Commencement of a Tender Offer

(a) *Date of commencement.* A bidder will have commenced its tender offer for purposes of section 14(d) of the Act and the rules under that section at 12:01 a.m. on the date when the bidder has first published, sent or given the means to tender to security holders. For purposes of this rule, the means to tender includes the transmittal form or a statement regarding how the transmittal form may be obtained.

(b) *Pre-commencement communications.* A communication by the bidder will not be deemed to constitute commencement of a tender offer if:

(1) It does not include the means for security holders to tender their shares into the offer; and

(2) All written communications relating to the tender offer, from and including the first public announcement, are filed under cover of Schedule TO with the Commission no later than the date of the communication. The bidder also must deliver to the subject company and any other bidder for the same class of securities the first communication relating to the transaction that is filed, or required to be filed with the Commission.

Instructions to paragraph (b)(2)

1. The box on the front of Schedule TO indicating that the filing contains pre-commencement communications must be checked.

2. Any communications made in connection with an exchange offer registered under the Securities Act of 1933 need only be filed under Rule 425 of that Act and will be deemed filed under this rule.

3. Each pre-commencement written communication must include a prominent legend in clear, plain language advising security holders to read the tender offer statement when it is available because it contains important information. The legend also must advise investors that they can get the tender offer statement and other filed documents for free at the Commission's web site and explain which documents are free from the offeror.

4. See Rules 135, 165 and 166 under the Securities Act for pre-commencement communications made in connection with registered exchange offers.

5. "Public announcement" is any oral or written communication by the bidder, or any person authorized to act on the bidder's behalf, that is reasonably designed to, or has the effect of, informing the public or security holders in general about the tender offer.

(c) *Filing and other obligations triggered by commencement.* As soon as practicable on the date of commencement, a bidder must comply with the filing requirements of Rule 14d–3(a), the dissemination requirements of Rule 14d–4(a) or (b), and the disclosure requirements of Rule 14d–6(a).

Rule 14d–3. Filing and Transmission of Tender Offer Statement

(a) *Filing and transmittal.* No bidder shall make a tender offer if, after consummation thereof, such bidder would be the beneficial owner of more than 5 percent of the class of the subject company's securities for which the tender offer is made, unless as soon as practicable on the date of the commencement of the tender offer such bidder:

(1) Files with the Commission a Tender Offer Statement on Schedule TO, including all exhibits thereto;

(2) Delivers a copy of such Schedule TO, including all exhibits thereto:

(i) To the subject company at its principal executive office; and

(ii) To any other bidder, which has filed a Schedule TO with the Commission relating to a tender offer which has not yet terminated for the same class of securities of the subject company, at such bidder's principal executive office or at the address of the person authorized to receive notices and communications (which is disclosed on the cover sheet of such other bidder's Schedule TO);

(3) Gives telephonic notice of the information required by Rule 14d–6(e)(2)(i) and (ii) and mails by means of first class mail a copy of such Schedule TO, including all exhibits thereto:

(i) To each national securities exchange where such class of the subject company's securities is registered and listed for trading (which may be based upon information contained in the subject company's most recent Annual Report on Form 10–K filed with the Commission unless the bidder has reason to believe that such information is not current), which telephonic notice shall be made when practicable prior to the opening of each such exchange; and

(ii) To the National Association of Securities Dealers, Inc. ("NASD") if such class of the subject company's securities is authorized for quotation in the NASDAQ interdealer quotation system.

(b) *Post-commencement amendments and additional materials.* The bidder making the tender offer must file with the Commission:

(1) An amendment to Schedule TO reporting promptly any material changes in the information set forth in the schedule previously filed and including copies of any additional tender offer materials as exhibits; and

(2) A final amendment to Schedule TO reporting promptly to results of the tender offer.

Instruction to paragraph (b): A copy of any additional tender offer materials or amendment filed under this rule must be sent promptly to the subject company and to any exchange and/or NASD, as required by paragraph (a) of this rule, but in no event later than the date the materials are first published, sent or given to security holders.

(c)   *Certain announcements.* Notwithstanding the provisions of paragraph (b) of this rule, if the additional tender offer material or an amendment to Schedule 14d–1 discloses only the number of shares deposited to date, and/or announces an extension of the time during which shares may be tendered, then the bidder may file such tender offer material or amendment and send a copy of such tender offer material or amendment to the subject company, any exchange and/or the NASD, as required by paragraph (a) of this rule, promptly after the date such tender offer material is first published or sent or given to security holders.

Rule 14d–4.   Dissemination of Tender Offers to Security Holders

As soon as practicable on the date of commencement of a tender offer, the bidder must publish, send or give the disclosure required by Rule 14d–6 to security holders of the class of securities that is the subject of the offer, by complying with all of the requirements of any of the following:

(a)   *Cash tender offers and exempt securities offers.* For tender offers in which the consideration consists solely of cash and/or securities exempt from registration under section 3 of the Securities Act of 1933.

(1)   *Long-form publication.* The bidder makes adequate publication in a newspaper or newspapers of long-form publication of the tender offer.

(2)   *Summary publication.*

(i)   If the tender offer is not subject to Rule 13e–3, the bidder makes adequate publication in a newspaper or newspapers of a summary advertisement of the tender offer; and

(ii)   Mails by first class mail or otherwise furnishes with reasonable promptness the bidder's tender offer materials to any security holder who requests such tender offer materials pursuant to the summary advertisement or otherwise.

(3)   *Use of stockholder lists and security position listings.* Any bidder using stockholder lists and security position listings under Rule 14d–5 must comply with paragraph (a)(1) or (2) of this rule on or before the date of the bidder's request under Rule 14d–5(a).

Instruction to paragraph (a): Tender offers may be published or sent or given to security holders by other methods, but with respect to summary publication and the use of stockholder lists and security position listings under Rule 14d–5, paragraphs (a)(2) and (a)(3) of this rule are exclusive.

(b)   *Registered securities offers.* For tender offers in which the consideration consists solely or partially of securities registered under the Securities Act of 1933, a registration statement containing all of the required information, including pricing information, has been filed and a preliminary prospectus or a prospectus that meets the requirements of section 10(a) of the Securities Act, including a letter of transmittal, is delivered to security holders. However, for going-private transactions (as defined by Item 901 of Regulation S–K), a registration statement registering the securities to be offered must have become effective and only a prospectus that meets the requirements of section 10(a) of the Securities Act may be delivered to security holders on the date of commencement.

Instructions to paragraph (b):

1.   If the prospectus is being delivered by mail, mailing on the date of commencement is sufficient.

2.   A preliminary prospectus used under this rule may not omit information under Rule 430 or Rule 430A under the Securities Act of 1933.

3.   If a preliminary prospectus is used under this rule and the bidder must disseminate material changes, the tender offer must remain open for the period specified in paragraph (d)(2) of this rule.

4.   If a preliminary prospectus is used under this rule, tenders may be requested in accordance with Rule 162(a) under the Securities Act.

(c)   *Adequate publication.* Depending on the facts and circumstances involved, adequate publication of a tender offer pursuant to this rule may require publication in a newspaper with a national circulation or may only require publication in a newspaper with metropolitan or regional circulation or may require publication in a combination thereof: *Provided, however,* That publication in all editions of a daily newspaper with a national circulation shall be deemed to constitute adequate publication.

(d)(1)   *Publications of changes and extension of the offers.* If a tender offer has been published or sent or given to security holders by one or more of the methods enumerated in this rule, a material change in the information published, sent or given to security holders shall be promptly disseminated to security holders in a manner reasonably designed to inform security holders of such change; *Provided, however,* That if the bidder has elected pursuant to Rule 14d-5(f)(1) of this rule to require the subject company to disseminate amendments disclosing material changes to the tender offer materials pursuant to Rule 14d-5, the bidder shall disseminate material changes in the information published or sent or given to security holders at least pursuant to Rule 14d-5.

(2)   In a registered securities offer where the bidder disseminates the preliminary prospectus as permitted by paragraph (b) of this rule, the offer must remain open from the date that material changes to the tender offer materials are disseminated to security holders, as follows:

(i)   Five business days for a prospectus supplement containing a material change other than price or share levels;

(ii)   Ten business days for a prospectus supplement containing a change in price, the amount of securities sought, the dealer's soliciting fee, or other similarly significant change;

(iii)   Ten business days for a prospectus supplement included as part of a post-effective amendment; and

(iv)   Twenty business days for a revised prospectus when the initial prospectus was materially deficient.

Rule 14d-5.   Dissemination of Certain Tender Offers by the Use of Stockholder Lists and Security Position Listings

(a)   *Obligations of the subject company.* Upon receipt by a subject company at its principal executive offices of a bidder's written request, meeting the requirements of paragraph (e) of this rule, the subject company shall comply with the following sub-paragraphs.

(1)   The subject company shall notify promptly transfer agents and any other person who will assist the subject company in complying with the requirements of this rule of the receipt by the subject company of a request by a bidder pursuant to this rule.

(2)   The subject company shall promptly ascertain whether the most recently prepared stockholder list, written or otherwise, within the access of the subject company was prepared as of a date earlier than ten business days before the date of the bidder's request and, if so, the subject company shall promptly prepare or cause to be prepared a stockholder list as of the most recent practicable date which shall not be more than ten business days before the date of the bidder's request.

(3)   The subject company shall make an election to comply and shall comply with all of the provisions of either paragraph (b) or paragraph (c) of this rule. The subject company's election once made shall not be modified or revoked during the bidder's tender offer and extensions thereof.

(4)   No later than the second business day after the date of the bidder's request, the subject company shall orally notify the bidder, which notification shall be confirmed in writing, of the subject company's election made pursuant to paragraph (a)(3) of this rule. Such notification shall indicate

(i)   The approximate number of security holders of the class of securities being sought by the bidder and,

(ii)   If the subject company elects to comply with paragraph (b) of this rule, appropriate information concerning the location for delivery of the bidder's tender offer materials and the approximate direct costs incidental to the mailing to security holders of the bidder's tender offer materials computed in accordance with paragraph (g)(2) of this rule.

(b)   *Mailing of tender offer materials by the subject company.* A subject company which elects pursuant to paragraph (a)(3) of this rule to comply with the provisions of this paragraph shall perform the acts prescribed by the following paragraphs.

(1)   The subject company shall promptly contact each participant named on the most recent security position listing of any clearing agency within the access of the subject company and make inquiry of each such participant as to the approximate number of beneficial owners of the subject company securities being sought in the tender offer held by each such participant.

(2)   No later than the third business day after delivery of the bidder's tender offer materials pursuant to paragraph (g)(1) of this rule, the subject company shall begin to mail or cause to be mailed by means of first class mail a copy of the bidder's tender offer materials to each person whose name appears as a record holder of the class of securities for which the offer is made on the most recent stockholder list referred to in paragraph (a)(2) of this rule. The subject company shall use its best efforts to complete the mailing in a timely manner but in no event shall such mailing be completed in a substantially greater period of time than the subject company would complete a mailing to security holders of its own materials relating to the tender offer.

(3)   No later than the third business day after the delivery of the bidder's tender offer materials pursuant to paragraph (g)(1) of this rule, the subject company shall begin to transmit or cause to be transmitted a sufficient number of sets of the bidder's tender offer materials to the participants named on the security position listings described in paragraph (b)(1) of this rule. The subject company shall use its best efforts to complete the transmittal in a timely manner but in no event shall such transmittal be completed in a substantially greater period of time than the subject company would complete a transmittal to such participants pursuant to security position listings of clearing agencies of its own material relating to the tender offer.

(4)   The subject company shall promptly give oral notification to the bidder, which notification shall be confirmed in writing, of the commencement of the mailing pursuant to paragraph (b)(2) of this rule and of the transmittal pursuant to paragraph (b)(3) of this rule.

(5)   During the tender offer and any extension thereof the subject company shall use reasonable efforts to update the stockholder list and shall mail or cause to be mailed promptly following each update a copy of the bidder's tender offer materials (to the extent sufficient sets of such materials have been furnished by the bidder) to each person who has become a record holder since the later of

    (i)   The date of preparation of the most recent stockholder list referred to in paragraph (a)(2) of this rule or

    (ii)   The last preceding update.

(6)   If the bidder has elected pursuant to paragraph (f)(1) of this rule to require the subject company to disseminate amendments disclosing material changes to the tender offer materials pursuant to this rule, the subject company, promptly following delivery of each such amendment, shall mail or cause to be mailed a copy of each such amendment to each record holder whose name appears on the shareholder list described in paragraphs (a)(2) and (b)(5) of this rule and shall transmit or cause to be transmitted sufficient copies of such amendment to each participant named on security position listings who received sets of the bidder's tender offer materials pursuant to paragraph (b)(3) of this rule.

(7)   The subject company shall not include any communication other than the bidder's tender offer materials or amendments thereto in the envelopes or other containers furnished by the bidder.

(8)   Promptly following the termination of the tender offer, the subject company shall reimburse the bidder the excess, if any, of the amounts advanced pursuant to paragraph (f)(3)(iii) over the direct costs incidental to compliance by the subject company and its agents in performing the acts required by this rule computed in accordance with paragraph (g)(2) of this rule.

(c)   *Delivery of stockholder lists and security position listings.* A subject company which elects pursuant to paragraph (a)(3) of this rule to comply with the provisions of this paragraph shall perform the acts prescribed by the following paragraphs.

(1) No later than the third business day after the date of the bidder's request, the subject company must furnish to the bidder at the subject company's principal executive office a copy of the names and addresses of the record holders on the most recent stockholder list referred to in paragraph (a)(2) of this rule; the names and addresses of participants identified on the most recent security position listing of any clearing agency that is within the access of the subject company; and the most recent list of names, addresses and security positions of beneficial owners as specified in Rule 14a–13(b), in the possession of the subject company, or that subsequently comes into its possession. All security holder list information must be in the format requested by the bidder to the extent the format is available to the subject company without under burden or expense.

(2) If the bidder has elected pursuant to paragraph (f)(1) of this rule to require the subject company to disseminate amendments disclosing material changes to the tender offer materials, the subject company shall update the stockholder list by furnishing the bidder with the name and address of each record holder named on the stockholder list, and not previously furnished to the bidder, promptly after such information becomes available to the subject company during the tender offer and any extensions thereof.

(d) *Liability of subject company and others.* Neither the subject company nor any affiliate or agent of the subject company nor any clearing agency shall be:

(1) Deemed to have made a solicitation or recommendation respecting the tender offer within the meaning of section 14(d)(4) based solely upon the compliance or noncompliance by the subject company or any affiliate or agent of the subject company with one or more requirements of this rule;

(2) Liable under any provision of the Federal securities laws to the bidder or to any security holder based solely upon the inaccuracy of the current names or addresses on the stockholder list or security position listing, unless such inaccuracy results from a lack of reasonable care on the part of the subject company or any affiliate or agent of the subject company;

(3) Deemed to be an "underwriter" within the meaning of section 2(a)(11) of the Securities Act of 1933 for any purpose of that Act or any rule or regulation promulgated thereunder based solely upon the compliance or noncompliance by the subject company or any affiliate or agent of the subject company with one or more of the requirements of this rule;

(4) Liable under any provision of the Federal securities laws for the disclosure in the bidder's tender offer materials, including any amendment thereto, based solely upon the compliance or noncompliance by the subject company or any affiliate or agent of the subject company with one or more of the requirements of this rule.

(e) *Content of the bidder's request.* The bidder's written request referred to in paragraph (a) of this rule shall include the following:

(1) The identity of the bidder;

(2) The title of the class of securities which is the subject of the bidder's tender offer;

(3) A statement that the bidder is making a request to the subject company pursuant to paragraph (a) of this rule for the use of the stockholder list and security position listings for the purpose of disseminating a tender offer to security holders;

(4) A statement that the bidder is aware of and will comply with the provisions of paragraph (f) of this rule;

(5) A statement as to whether or not it has elected pursuant to paragraph (f)(1) of this rule to disseminate amendments disclosing material changes to the tender offer materials pursuant to this rule; and

(6) The name, address and telephone number of the person whom the subject company shall contact pursuant to paragraph (a)(4) of this rule.

(f) *Obligations of the bidder.* Any bidder who requests that a subject company comply with the provisions of paragraph (a) of this rule shall comply with the following paragraphs.

(1) The bidder shall make an election whether or not to require the subject company to disseminate amendments disclosing material changes to the tender offer materials pursuant to this

rule, which election shall be included in the request referred to in paragraph (a) of this rule and shall not be revocable by the bidder during the tender offer and extensions thereof.

(2)   With respect to a tender offer subject to section 14(d)(1) of the Act in which the consideration consists solely of cash and/or securities exempt from registration under section 3 of the Securities Act of 1933, the bidder shall comply with the requirements of Rule 14d–4(a)(3).

(3)   If the subject company elects to comply with paragraph (b) of this rule,

(i)   The bidder shall promptly deliver the tender offer materials after receipt of the notification from the subject company as provided in paragraph (a)(4) of this rule;

(ii)   The bidder shall promptly notify the subject company of any amendment to the bidder's tender offer materials requiring compliance by the subject company with paragraph (b)(6) of this rule and shall promptly deliver such amendment to the subject company pursuant to paragraph (g)(1) of this rule;

(iii)   The bidder shall advance to the subject company an amount equal to the approximate cost of conducting mailings to security holders computed in accordance with paragraph (g)(2) of this rule;

(iv)   The bidder shall promptly reimburse the subject company for the direct costs incidental to compliance by the subject company and its agents in performing the acts required by this rule computed in accordance with paragraph (g)(2) of this rule which are in excess of the amount advanced pursuant to paragraph (f)(2)(iii) of this rule; and

(v)   The bidder shall mail by means of first class mail or otherwise furnish with reasonable promptness the tender offer materials to any security holder who requests such materials.

(4)   If the subject company elects to comply with paragraph (c) of this rule,

(i)   The subject company shall use the stockholder list and security position listings furnished to the bidder pursuant to paragraph (c) of this rule exclusively in the dissemination of tender offer materials to security holders in connection with the bidder's tender offer and extensions thereof;

(ii)   The bidder shall return the stockholder lists and security position listings furnished to the bidder pursuant to paragraph (c) of this rule promptly after the termination of the bidder's tender offer;

(iii)   The bidder shall accept, handle and return the stockholder lists and security position listings furnished to the bidder pursuant to paragraph (c) of this rule to the subject company on a confidential basis;

(iv)   The bidder shall not retain any stockholder list or security position listing furnished by the subject company pursuant to paragraph (c) of this rule, or any copy thereof, nor retain any information derived from any such list or listing or copy thereof after the termination of the bidder's tender offer;

(v)   The bidder shall mail by means of first class mail, at its own expense, a copy of its tender offer materials to each person whose identity appears on the stockholder list as furnished and updated by the subject company pursuant to paragraphs (c)(1) and (2) of this rule;

(vi)   The bidder shall contact the participants named on the security position listing of any clearing agency, make inquiry of each participant as to the approximate number of sets of tender offer materials required by each such participant, and furnish, at its own expense, sufficient sets of tender offer materials and any amendment thereto to each such participant for subsequent transmission to the beneficial owners of the securities being sought by the bidder;

(vii)   The bidder shall mail by means of first class mail or otherwise furnish with reasonable promptness the tender offer materials to any security holder who requests such materials; and

(viii)   The bidder shall promptly reimburse the subject company for direct costs incidental to compliance by the subject company and its agents in performing the acts required by this rule computed in accordance with paragraph (g)(2) of this rule.

(g) *Delivery of materials, computation of direct costs.*

(1) Whenever the bidder is required to deliver tender offer materials or amendments to tender offer materials, the bidder shall deliver to the subject company at the location specified by the subject company in its notice given pursuant to paragraph (a)(4) of this rule a number of sets of the materials or of the amendment, as the case may be, at least equal to the approximate number of security holders specified by the subject company in such notice, together with appropriate envelopes or other containers therefor: *Provided, however,* That such delivery shall be deemed not to have been made unless the bidder has complied with paragraph (f)(3)(iii) of this rule at the time the materials or amendments, as the case may be, are delivered.

(2) The approximate direct cost of mailing the bidder's tender offer materials shall be computed by adding

(i) the direct cost incidental to the mailing of the subject company's last annual report to shareholders (excluding employee time), less the costs of preparation and printing of the report, and postage, plus

(ii) the amount of first class postage required to mail the bidder's tender offer materials. The approximate direct costs incidental to the mailing of the amendments to the bidder's tender offer materials shall be computed by adding

(iii) the estimated direct costs of preparing mailing labels, of updating shareholder lists and of third party handling charges plus

(iv) the amount of first class postage required to mail the bidder's amendment. Direct costs incidental to the mailing of the bidder's tender offer materials and amendments thereto when finally computed may include all reasonable charges paid by the subject company to third parties for supplies or services, including costs attendant to preparing shareholder lists, mailing labels, handling the bidder's materials, contacting participants named on security position listings and for postage, but shall exclude indirect costs, such as employee time which is devoted to either contesting or supporting the tender offer on behalf of the subject company. The final billing for direct costs shall be accompanied by an appropriate accounting in reasonable detail.

NOTE. Reasonably prompt methods of distribution to security holders may be used instead of mailing. If alternative methods are chosen, the approximate direct costs of distribution shall be computed by adding the estimated direct costs of preparing the document for distribution through the chosen medium (including updating of shareholder lists) plus the estimated reasonable cost of distribution through that medium. Direct costs incidental to the distribution of tender offer materials and amendments thereto may include all reasonable charges paid by the subject company to third parties for supplies or services, including costs attendant to preparing shareholder lists, handling the bidder's materials, and contacting participants named on security position listings, but shall not include indirect costs, such as employee time which is devoted to either contesting or supporting the tender offer on behalf of the subject company.

Rule 14d–6. Disclosure of Tender Offer Information to Security Holders

(a) *Information required on date of commencement—*

(1) *Long-form publication.* If a tender offer is published, sent or given to security holders on the date of commencement by means of long-form publication under Rule 14d–4(a)(1), the long-form publication must include the information required by paragraph (d)(1) of this rule.

(2) *Summary publication.* If a tender offer is published, sent or given to security holders on the date of commencement by means of summary publication under Rule 14d–4(a)(2):

(i) The summary advertisement must contain at least the information required by paragraph (d)(2) of this rule; and

(ii) The tender offer materials furnished by the bidder upon the request of any security holder must include the information required by paragraph (d)(1) of this rule.

(3) *Use of stockholder lists and security position listings.* If a tender offer is published, sent or given to security holders on the date of commencement by the use of stockholders lists and security position listings under Rule 14d–4(a)(3):

(i)   The summary advertisement must contain the information required by paragraph (d)(2) of this rule; and

(ii)   The tender offer materials transmitted to security holders pursuant to such lists and security position listings and furnished by the bidder upon the request of any security holder must include the information required by paragraph (d)(1) of this rule.

(4)   *Other tender offers.* If a tender offer is published or sent or given to security holders other than pursuant to Rule 14d–4(a), the tender offer materials that are published or sent or given to security holders on the date of commencement of such offer must include the information required by paragraph (d)(1) of this rule.

(b)   *Information required in other tender offer materials published after commencement.* Except for tender offer materials described in paragraphs (a)(2)(ii) and (a)(3)(ii) of this rule, additional tender offer materials published, sent or given to security holders after commencement must include:

(1)   The identities of the bidder and subject company;

(2)   The amount and class of securities being sought;

(3)   The type and amount of consideration being offered; and

(4)   The scheduled expiration date of the tender offer may be extended and, if so, the procedures for extension of the tender offer.

Instruction to paragraph (b): If the additional tender offer materials are summary advertisements, they also must include the information required by paragraphs (d)(2)(v) of this rule.

(c)   *Material changes.* A material change in the information published or sent or given to security holders must be promptly disclosed to security holders in additional tender offer materials.

(d)   *Information to be included.*—(1) *Tender offer materials other than summary publication.* The following information is required by paragraphs (a)(1), (a)(2)(ii), (a)(3)(ii) and (a)(4) of this rule:

(i)   The information required by Item 1 to Schedule TO (Summary Term Sheet); and

(ii)   The information required by the remaining items of Schedule TO for third-party tender offers, except for Item 12 (exhibits) of Schedule TO, or a fair and adequate summary of the information.

(2)   *Summary Publication.* The following information is required in a summary advertisement under paragraphs (a)(2)(i) and (a)(3)(i) of this rule:

(i)   The identity of the bidder and the subject company;

(ii)   The information required by Item 1004(a)(1) of Regulation M–A;

(iii)   If the tender offer is for less than all of the outstanding securities of a class of equity securities, a statement as to whether the purpose or one of the purposes of the tender offer is to acquire or influence control of the business of the subject company;

(iv)   A statement that the information required by paragraph (d)(1) of this rule is incorporated by reference into the summary advertisement;

(v)   Appropriate instructions as to how security holders may obtain promptly, at the bidder's expense, the bidder's tender offer materials; and

(vi)   In a tender offer published or sent or given to security holder by the use of stockholder lists and security position listings under Rule 14d–4(a)(3), a statement that a request is being made for such lists and listings. The summary publication also must state that tender offer materials will be mailed to record holders and will be furnished to brokers, banks and similar persons whose name appears or who nominee appears on the list of security holders or, if applicable, who are listed as participants in a clearing agency's security position listing for subsequent transmittal to beneficial owners of such securities. If the list furnished to the bidder also included beneficial owners pursuant to Rule 14d–5(c)(1) and tender offer materials will be mailed directly to beneficial holders, include a statement to that effect.

(3) *No transmittal letter.* Neither the initial summary advertisement nor any subsequent summary advertisement may include a transmittal letter (the letter furnished to security holders for transmission of securities sought in the tender offer) or any amendment to the transmittal letter.

Rule 14d–7. Additional Withdrawal Rights

(a)(1) *Rights.* In addition to the provisions of section 14(d)(5) of the Act, any person who has deposited securities pursuant to a tender offer has the right to withdraw any such securities during the period such offer request or invitation remains open.

(2) *Exemption during subsequent offering period.* Notwithstanding the provisions of section 14(d)(5) of the Act and paragraph (a) of this rule, the bidder need not offer withdrawal rights during a subsequent offering period.

(b) *Notice of withdrawal.* Notice of withdrawal pursuant to this rule shall be deemed to be timely upon the receipt by the bidder's depositary of a written notice of withdrawal specifying the name(s) of the tendering stockholder(s), the number or amount of the securities to be withdrawn and the name(s) in which the certificate(s) is (are) registered, if different from that of the tendering security holder(s). A bidder may impose other reasonable requirements, including certificate numbers and a signed request for withdrawal accompanied by a signature guarantee, as conditions precedent to the physical release of withdrawn securities.

Rule 14d–8. Exemption From Statutory Pro Rata Requirements

Notwithstanding the pro rata provisions of section 14(d)(6) of the Act, if any person makes a tender offer or request or invitation for tenders, for less than all of the outstanding equity securities of a class, and if a greater number of securities are deposited pursuant thereto than such person is bound or willing to take up and pay for, the securities taken up and paid for shall be taken up and paid for as nearly as may be pro rata, disregarding fractions, according to the number of securities deposited by each depositor during the period such offer, request or invitation remains open.

Rule 14d–9. Recommendation or Solicitation by the Subject Company and Others

(a) *Pre-commencement communications.* A communication by a person described in paragraph (e) of this rule with respect to a tender offer will not be deemed to constitute a recommendation or solicitation under this rule if:

(1) The tender offer has not commenced under Rule 14d–2; and

(2) The communication is filed under cover of Schedule 14D–9 with the Commission no later than the date of the communication.

Instructions to paragraph (a)(2):

1. The box on the front of Schedule 14D–9 indicating that the filing contains pre-commencement communications must be checked.

2. Any communications made in connection with an exchange off registered under the Securities Act of 1933 need only be filed under Rule 425 of that Act and will be deemed filed under this rule.

3. Each pre-commencement written communication must include a prominent legend in clear, plain language advising security holders to read the company's solicitation/ recommendation statement when it is available because it contains important information. The legend also must advise investors that they can get the recommendation and other filed documents for free at the Commission's web site and explain which documents are free from the filer.

4. See Rule 135, 165 and 166 under the Securities Act for pre-commencement communications made in connection with registered exchange offers.

(b) *Post-commencement communications.* After commencement by a bidder under Rule 14d–2, no solicitation or recommendation to security holders may be made by any person described in paragraph (e) of this rule with respect to a tender offer for such securities unless as soon as practicable on the date such solicitation or recommendation is first published or sent or given to security holders such person complies with the following:

(1) Such person shall file with the Commission a Tender Offer Solicitation/Recommendation Statement on Schedule 14D–9, including all exhibits thereto; and

(2) If such person is either the subject company or an affiliate of the subject company,

(i) Such person shall hand deliver a copy of the Schedule 14D–9 to the bidder at its principal office or at the address of the person authorized to receive notices and communications (which is set forth on the cover sheet of the bidder's Schedule TO filed with the Commission); and

(ii) Such person shall give telephonic notice (which notice to the extent possible shall be given prior to the opening of the market) of the information required by Items 1003(d) and 1012(a) of Regulation M–A and shall mail a copy of the Schedule to each national securities exchange where the class of securities is registered and listed for trading and, if the class is authorized for quotation in the NASDAQ interdealer quotation system, to the National Association of Securities Dealers, Inc. ("NASD").

(3) If such person is neither the subject company nor an affiliate of the subject company,

(i) Such person shall mail a copy of the schedule to the bidder at its principal office or at the address of the person authorized to receive notices and communications (which is set forth on the cover sheet of the bidder's Schedule TO filed with the Commission); and

(ii) Such person shall mail a copy of the Schedule to the subject company at its principal office.

(c) *Amendments.* If any material change occurs in the information set forth in the Schedule 14D–9 required by this rule, the person who filed such Schedule 14D–9 shall:

(1) File with the Commission an amendment on Schedule 14D–9 disclosing such change promptly, but not later than the date such material is first published, sent or given to security holders; and

(2) Promptly deliver copies and give notice of the amendment in the same manner as that specified in paragraph (b)(2) or (3) of this rule, whichever is applicable; and

(3) Promptly disclose and disseminate such change in a manner reasonably designed to inform security holders of such change.

(d) *Information required in solicitation or recommendation.* Any solicitation or recommendation to holders of a class of securities referred to in section 14(d)(1) of the Act with respect to a tender offer for such securities shall include the name of the person making such solicitation or recommendation and the information required by Items 1 through 8 of Schedule 14D–9 or a fair and adequate summary thereof: *Provided, however,* That such solicitation or recommendation may omit any of such information previously furnished to security holders of such class of securities by such person with respect to such tender offer.

(e) *Applicability.*

(1) Except as is provided in paragraphs (e)(2) and (f) of this rule, this rule shall only apply to the following persons:

(i) The subject company, any director, officer, employee, affiliate or subsidiary of the subject company;

(ii) Any record holder or beneficial owner of any security issued by the subject company, by the bidder, or by any affiliate of either the subject company or the bidder; and

(iii) Any person who makes a solicitation or recommendation to security holders on behalf of any of the foregoing or on behalf of the bidder other than by means of a solicitation or recommendation to security holders which has been filed with the Commission pursuant to this rule or Rule 14d–3.

(2) Notwithstanding paragraph (e)(1) of this rule, this rule shall not apply to the following persons:

(i) A bidder who has filed a Schedule TO pursuant to Rule 14d–3;

(ii)   Attorneys, banks, brokers, fiduciaries or investment advisers who are not participating in a tender offer in more than a ministerial capacity and who furnish information and/or advice regarding such tender offer to their customers or clients on the unsolicited request of such customers or clients or solely pursuant to a contract or a relationship providing for advice to the customer or client to whom the information and/or advice is given.

(iii)   Any person specified in paragraph (e)(1) of this rule if:

(A)   The subject company is the subject of a tender offer conducted under Rule 14d–1(c);

(B)   Any person specified in paragraph (e)(1) of this rule furnishes to the Commission of Form CB the entire informational document it publishes or otherwise disseminates to holders of the class of securities in connection with the tender offer no later than the next business day after publication or dissemination;

(C)   Any person specified in paragraph (e)(1) of this rule disseminates information documents to U.S. holders, including any amendments thereto, in English, on a comparable basis to that provided to security holders in the issuer's home jurisdiction; and

(D)   Any person specified in paragraph (e)(1) of this rule disseminates by publication in its home jurisdiction, such person must publish the information in the United States in a manner reasonably calculated to inform U.S. security holders of the offer.

(f)   *Stop-look-and-listen communication.* This rule shall not apply to the subject company with respect to a communication by the subject company to its security holders which only:

(1)   Identifies the tender offer by the bidder;

(2)   States that such tender offer is under consideration by the subject company's board of directors and/or management;

(3)   States that on or before a specified date (which shall be no later than 10 business days from the date of commencement of such tender offer) the subject company will advise such security holders of

(i)   whether the subject company recommends acceptance or rejection of such tender offer; expresses no opinion and remains neutral toward such tender offer; or is unable to take a position with respect to such tender offer and

(ii)   the reason(s) for the position taken by the subject company with respect to the tender offer (including the inability to take a position); and

(4)   Requests such security holders to defer making a determination whether to accept or reject such tender offer until they have been advised of the subject company's position with respect thereto pursuant to paragraph (f)(3) of this rule.

(g)   *Statement of management's position.* A statement by the subject company's of its position with respect to a tender offer which is required to be published or sent or given to security holders pursuant to Rule 14e–2 shall be deemed to constitute a solicitation or recommendation within the meaning of this rule and section 14(d)(4) of the Act.

Rule 14d–10. Equal Treatment of Security Holders

(a)   No bidder shall make a tender offer unless:

(1)   The tender offer is open to all security holders of the class of securities subject to the tender offer; and

(2)   The consideration paid to any security holder for securities tendered in the tender offer is the highest consideration paid to any other security holder for securities tendered in the tender offer.

(b)   Paragraph (a)(1) of this rule shall not:

(1)   Affect dissemination under Rule 14d–4; or

(2)   Prohibit a bidder from making a tender offer excluding all security holders in a state where the bidder is prohibited from making the tender offer by administrative or judicial action pursuant to a state statute after a good faith effort by the bidder to comply with such statute.

(c)   Paragraph (a)(2) of this rule shall not prohibit the offer of more than one type of consideration in a tender offer, *Provided,* That:

(1)   Security holders are afforded equal right to elect among each of the types of consideration offered; and

(2)   The highest consideration of each type paid to any security holder is paid to any other security holder receiving that type of consideration.

(d)(1)   Paragraph (a)(2) of this rule shall not prohibit the negotiation, execution or amendment of an employment compensation, severance or other employee benefit arrangement, or payments made or to be made or benefits granted or to be granted according to such an arrangement, with respect to any security holder of the subject company, where the amount payable under the arrangement:

(i)   Is being paid or granted as compensation for past services performed, future services to be performed, or future services to be refrained from performing, by the security holder (and matters incidental thereto); and

(ii)   Is not calculated based on the number of securities tendered or to be tendered in the tender offer by the security holder.

(2)   The provisions of paragraph (d)(1) of this rule shall be satisfied and, therefore, pursuant to this non-exclusive safe harbor, the negotiation, execution or amendment of an arrangement and any payments made or to be made or benefits granted or to be granted according to that arrangement shall not be prohibited by paragraph (a)(2) of this rule, if the arrangement is approved as an employment compensation, severance or other employee benefit arrangement solely by independent directors as follows:

(i)   The compensation committee or a committee of the board of directors that performs functions similar to a compensation committee of the subject company approves the arrangement, regardless of whether the subject company is a party to the arrangement, or, if the bidder is a party to the arrangement, the compensation committee or a committee of the board of directors that performs functions similar to a compensation committee of the bidder approves the arrangement; or

(ii)   If the subject company's or bidder's board of directors, as applicable, does not have a compensation committee or a committee of the board of directors that performs functions similar to a compensation committee or if none of the members of the subject company's or bidder's compensation committee or committee that performs functions similar to a compensation committee is independent, a special committee of the board of directors formed to consider and approve the arrangement approves the arrangement; or

(iii)   If the subject company or bidder, as applicable, is a foreign private issuer, any or all members of the board of directors or any committee of the board of directors authorized to approve employment compensation, severance or other employee benefit arrangements under the laws or regulations of the home country approves the arrangement.

Instructions to paragraph (d)(2): For purposes of determining whether the members of the committee approving an arrangement in accordance with the provisions of paragraph (d)(2) of this rule are independent, the following provisions shall apply:

1.   If the bidder or subject company, as applicable, is a listed issuer (as defined in 17 C.F.R. § 240.10A–3) whose securities are listed either on a national securities exchange registered pursuant to section 6(a) of the Exchange Act or in an inter-dealer quotation system of a national securities association registered pursuant to section 15A(a) of the Exchange Act that has independence requirements for compensation committee members that have been approved by the Commission (as those requirements may be modified or supplemented), apply the bidder's or subject company's definition of independence that it uses for determining that the members of the compensation committee are independent in compliance with the listing standards applicable to compensation committee members of the listed issuer.

2. If the bidder or subject company, as applicable, is not a listed issuer (as defined in 17 C.F.R. § 240.10A–3), apply the independence requirements for compensation committee members of a national securities exchange registered pursuant to section 6(a) of the Exchange Act or an inter-dealer quotation system of a national securities association registered pursuant to section 15A(a) of the Exchange Act that have been approved by the Commission (as those requirements may be modified or supplemented). Whatever definition the bidder or subject company, as applicable, chooses, it must apply that definition consistently to all members of the committee approving the arrangement.

3. Notwithstanding Instructions 1 and 2 to paragraph (d)(2), if the bidder or subject company, as applicable, is a closed-end investment company registered under the Investment Company Act of 1940, a director is considered to be independent if the director is not, other than in his or her capacity as a member of the board of directors or any board committee, an "interested person" of the investment company, as defined in section 2(a)(19) of the Investment Company Act of 1940.

4. If the bidder or the subject company, as applicable, is a foreign private issuer, apply either the independence standards set forth in Instructions 1 and 2 to paragraph (d)(2) or the independence requirements of the laws, regulations, codes or standards of the home country of the bidder or subject company, as applicable, for members of the board of directors or the committee of the board of directors approving the arrangement.

5. A determination by the bidder's or the subject company's board of directors, as applicable, that the members of the board of directors or the committee of the board of directors, as applicable, approving an arrangement in accordance with the provisions of paragraph (d)(2) are independent in accordance with the provisions of this instruction to paragraph (d)(2) shall satisfy the independence requirements of paragraph (d)(2).

Instruction to paragraph (d): The fact that the provisions of paragraph (d) of this rule extend only to employment compensation, severance and other employee benefit arrangements and not to other arrangements, such as commercial arrangements, does not raise any inference that a payment under any such other arrangement constitutes consideration paid for securities in a tender offer.

(e) If the offer and sale of securities constituting consideration offered in a tender offer is prohibited by the appropriate authority of a state after a good faith effort by the bidder to register or qualify the offer and sale of such securities in such state:

(1) The bidder may offer security holders in such state an alternative form of consideration; and

(2) Paragraph (c) of this rule shall not operate to require the bidder to offer or pay the alternative form of consideration to security holders in any other state.

(f) This rule shall not apply to any tender offer with respect to which the Commission, upon written request or upon its own motion, either unconditionally or on specified terms and conditions, determines that compliance with this rule is not necessary or appropriate in the public interest or for the protection of investors.

Rule 14d–11. Subsequent Offering Period

A bidder may elect to provide a subsequent offering period of at least three business days during which tenders will be accepted if:

(a) The initial offering period of at least 20 business days has expired;

(b) The offer is for all outstanding securities of the class that is subject of the tender offer, and if the bidder is offering security holders a choice of different forms of consideration, there is no ceiling on any form of consideration offered;

(c) The bidder immediately accepts and promptly pays for all securities tendered during the initial offering period;

(d) The bidder announces the results of the tender offer, including the approximate number and percentage of securities deposited to date, no later than 9:00 a.m. Eastern time on the next business day after the expiration date of the initial offering period and immediately begins the subsequent offering period;

(e) The bidder immediately accepts and promptly pays for all securities as they are tendered during the subsequent offering period; and

(f)   The bidder offers the same form and amount of consideration to security holders in both the initial and the subsequent offering period.

NOTE: No withdrawal rights apply during the subsequent offering period in accordance with Rule 14d–7(a)(2).

REGULATION 14E

Rule 14e–1. Unlawful Tender Offer Practices

As a means reasonably designed to prevent fraudulent, deceptive or manipulative acts or practices within the meaning of section 14(e) of the Act, no person who makes a tender offer shall:

(a)   Hold such tender offer open for less than twenty business days from the date such tender offer is first published or sent to security holders; provided, however, that if the tender offer involves a roll-up transaction as defined in Item 901(c) of Regulation S–K and the securities being offered are registered (or authorized to be registered) on Form S–4 or Form F–4, the offer shall not be open for less than sixty calendar days from the date the tender offer is first published or sent to security holders;

(b)   Increase or decrease the percentage of the class of securities being sought or the consideration offered or the dealer's soliciting fee to be given in a tender offer unless such tender offer remains open for at least ten business days from the date that notice of such increase or decrease is first published or sent or given to security holders.

Provided, however, That, for purposes of this paragraph, the acceptance for payment of an additional amount of securities not to exceed two percent of the class of securities that is the subject of the tender offer shall not be deemed to be an increase. For purposes of this paragraph, the percentage of a class of securities shall be calculated in accordance with section 14(d)(3) of the Act.

(c)   Fail to pay the consideration offered or return the securities deposited by or on behalf of security holders promptly after the termination or withdrawal of a tender offer.

This paragraph does not prohibit a bidder electing to offer a subsequent offering period under Rule 14d–11 from paying for securities during the subsequent offering period in accordance with that rule.

(d)   Extend the length of a tender offer without issuing a notice of such extension by press release or other public announcement, which notice shall include disclosure of the approximate number of securities deposited to date and shall be issued no later than the earlier of:

(i)   9:00 a.m. Eastern time, on the next business day after the scheduled expiration date of the offer or

(ii)   If the class of securities which is the subject of the tender offer is registered on one or more national securities exchanges, the first opening of any one of such exchanges on the next business day after the scheduled expiration date of the offer.

(e)   The periods of time required by paragraphs (a) and (b) of this rule shall be tolled for any period during which the bidder has failed to file in electronic format, absent a hardship exemption (§§ 232.201 and 232.202 of this chapter), the Schedule TO Tender Offer Statement, any tender offer material required to be filed by Item 12 of that Schedule pursuant to paragraph (a) of Item 1016 of Regulation M–A (17 C.F.R. § 229.1016(a)), and any amendments thereto. If such documents were filed in paper pursuant to a hardship exemption (see § 232.201 and § 232.202(d)), the minimum offering periods shall be tolled for any period during which a required confirming electronic copy of such Schedule and tender offer material is delinquent.

Rule 14e–2. Position of Subject Company With Respect to a Tender Offer

(a)   *Position of subject company.* As a means reasonably designed to prevent fraudulent, deceptive or manipulative acts or practices within the meaning of section 14(e) of the Act, the subject company, no later than 10 business days from the date the tender offer is first published or sent or given, shall publish, send or give to security holders a statement disclosing that the subject company:

(1)   Recommends acceptance or rejection of the bidder's tender offer;

(2)   Expresses no opinion and is remaining neutral toward the bidder's tender offer; or

(3)   Is unable to take a position with respect to the bidder's tender offer. Such statement shall also include the reason(s) for the position (including the inability to take a position) disclosed therein.

(b)   *Material change.* If any material change occurs in the disclosure required by paragraph (a) of this rule, the subject company shall promptly publish or send or give a statement disclosing such material change to security holders.

(c)   Any issuer, a class of the securities of which is the subject of a tender offer filed with the Commission on Schedule 14D–1F and conducted in reliance upon and in conformity with Rule 14d–1(b) under the Act, and any director or officer of such issuer where so required by the laws, regulations and policies of Canada and/or any of its provinces or territories, in lieu of the statements called for by paragraph (a) of this rule and Rule 14d–9 under the Act, shall file with the Commission on Schedule 14D–9F the entire disclosure document(s) required to be furnished to holders of securities of the subject issuer by the laws, regulations and policies of Canada and/or any of its provinces or territories governing the conduct of the tender offer, and shall disseminate such document(s) in the United States in accordance with such laws, regulations and policies.

(d)   *Exemption for cross-border tender offers.* The subject company shall be exempt from this rule with respect to a tender offer conducted under Rule 14d–1(c).

Rule 14e–3.   Transactions in Securities on the Basis of Material, Nonpublic Information in the Context of Tender Offers

(a)   If any person has taken a substantial step or steps to commence, or has commenced, a tender offer (the "offering person"), it shall constitute a fraudulent, deceptive or manipulative act or practice within the meaning of section 14(e) of the Act for any other person who is in possession of material information relating to such tender offer which information he knows or has reason to know is nonpublic and which he knows or has reason to know has been acquired directly or indirectly from:

(1)   The offering person,

(2)   The issuer of the securities sought or to be sought by such tender offer, or

(3)   Any officer, director, partner or employee or any other person acting on behalf of the offering person or such issuer,

to purchase or sell or cause to be purchased or sold any of such securities or any securities convertible into or exchangeable for any such securities or any option or right to obtain or to dispose of any of the foregoing securities, unless within a reasonable time prior to any purchase or sale such information and its source are publicly disclosed by press release or otherwise.

(b)   A person other than a natural person shall not violate paragraph (a) of this rule if such person shows that:

(1)   The individual(s) making the investment decision on behalf of such person to purchase or sell any security described in paragraph (a) of this rule or to cause any such security to be purchased or sold by or on behalf of others did not know the material, nonpublic information; and

(2)   Such person had implemented one or a combination of policies and procedures, reasonable under the circumstances, taking into consideration the nature of the person's business, to ensure that individual(s) making investment decision(s) would not violate paragraph (a) of this rule, which policies and procedures may include, but are not limited to,

(i)   those which restrict any purchase, sale and causing any purchase and sale of any such security or

(ii)   those which prevent such individual(s) from knowing such information.

(c)   Notwithstanding anything in paragraph (a) of this rule to the contrary, the following transactions shall not be violations of paragraph (a) of this rule:

(1)   Purchase(s) of any security described in paragraph (a) of this rule by a broker or by another agent on behalf of an offering person; or

(2)   Sale(s) by any person of any security described in paragraph (a) of this rule to the offering person.

(d)(1)   As a means reasonably designed to prevent fraudulent, deceptive or manipulative acts or practices within the meaning of section 14(e) of the Act, it shall be unlawful for any person described in paragraph (d)(2) of this rule to communicate material, nonpublic information relating to a tender offer to any other person under circumstances in which it is reasonably foreseeable that such communication is likely to result in a violation of this rule *except* that this paragraph shall not apply to a communication made in good faith,

    (i)   To the officers, directors, partners or employees of the offering person, to its advisors or to other persons, involved in the planning, financing, preparation or execution of such tender offer;

    (ii)   To the issuer whose securities are sought or to be sought by such tender offer, to its officers, directors, partners, employees or advisors or to other persons, involved in the planning, financing, preparation or execution of the activities of the issuer with respect to such tender offer; or

    (iii)   To any person pursuant to a requirement of any statute or rule or regulation promulgated thereunder.

(2)   The persons referred to in paragraph (d)(1) of this rule are:

    (i)   The offering person or its officers, directors, partners, employees or advisors;

    (ii)   The issuer of the securities sought or to be sought by such tender offer or its officers, directors, partners, employees or advisors;

    (iii)   Anyone acting on behalf of the persons in paragraph (d)(2)(i) of this rule or the issuer or persons in paragraph (d)(2)(ii) of this rule; and

    (iv)   Any person in possession of material information relating to a tender offer which information he knows or has reason to know is nonpublic and which he knows or has reason to know has been acquired directly or indirectly from any of the above.

Rule 14e–4.   Prohibited Transactions in Connection With Partial Tender Offers

(a)   *Definitions.* For purposes of this rule:

(1)   The amount of a person's "net long position" in a subject security shall equal the excess, if any, of such person's "long position" over such person's "short position." For the purposes of determining the net long position as of the end of the proration period and for tendering concurrently to two or more partial tender offers, securities that have been tendered in accordance with the rule and not withdrawn are deemed to be part of the person's long position.

    (i)   Such person's "long position," is the amount of subject securities that such person:

        (A)   Or his agent has title to or would have title to but for having lent such securities; or

        (B)   Has purchased, or has entered into an unconditional contract, binding on both parties thereto, to purchase but has not yet received; or

        (C)   Has exercised a standardized call option for; or

        (D)   Has converted, exchanged, or exercised an equivalent security for; or

        (E)   Is entitled to receive upon conversion, exchange, or exercise of an equivalent security.

    (ii)   Such person's "short position," is the amount of subject securities or subject securities underlying equivalent securities that such person:

        (A)   Has sold, or has entered into an unconditional contract, binding on both parties thereto, to sell; or

        (B)   Has borrowed; or

(C) Has written a non-standardized call option, or granted any other right pursuant to which his shares may be tendered by another person; or

(D) Is obligated to deliver upon exercise of a standardized call option sold on or after the date that a tender offer is first publicly announced or otherwise made known by the bidder to holders of the security to be acquired, if the exercise price of such option is lower than the highest tender offer price or stated amount of the consideration offered for the subject security. For the purpose of this paragraph, if one or more tender offers for the same security are ongoing on such date, the announcement date shall be that of the first announced offer.

(2) The term "equivalent security" means

(i) Any security (including any option, warrant, or other right to purchase the subject security), issued by the person whose securities are the subject of the offer, that is immediately convertible into, or exchangeable or exercisable for, a subject security, or

(ii) Any other right or option (other than a standardized call option) that entitles the holder thereof to acquire a subject security, but only if the holder thereof reasonably believes that the maker or writer of the right or option has title to and possession of the subject security and upon exercise will promptly deliver the subject security.

(3) The term "subject security" means a security that is the subject of any tender offer or request or invitation for tenders.

(4) For purposes of this rule, a person shall be deemed to "tender" a security if he

(i) Delivers a subject security pursuant to an offer,

(ii) Causes such delivery to be made,

(iii) Guarantees delivery of a subject security pursuant to a tender offer,

(iv) Causes a guarantee of such delivery to be given by another person, or

(v) Uses any other method by which acceptance of a tender offer may be made.

(5) The term *partial tender offer* means a tender offer or request or invitation for tenders for less than all of the outstanding securities subject to the offer in which tenders are accepted either by lot or on a *pro rata* basis for a specified period, or a tender offer for all of the outstanding shares that offers a choice of consideration in which tenders for different forms of consideration may be accepted either by lot or on a *pro rata* basis for a specified period.

(6) The term "standardized call option" means any call option that is traded on an exchange, or for which quotation information is disseminated in an electronic interdealer quotation system of a registered national securities association.

(b) It shall be unlawful for any person acting alone or in concert with others, directly or indirectly, to tender any subject security in a partial tender offer:

(1) For his own account unless at the time of tender, and at the end of the proration period or period during which securities are accepted by lot (including any extensions thereof), he has a net long position equal to or greater than the amount tendered in:

(i) The subject security and will deliver or cause to be delivered such security for the purpose of tender to the person making the offer within the period specified in the offer; or

(ii) An equivalent security and, upon the acceptance of his tender will acquire the subject security by conversion, exchange, or exercise of such equivalent security to the extent required by the terms of the offer, and will deliver or cause to be delivered the subject security so acquired for the purpose of tender to the person making the offer within the period specified in the offer; or

(2) For the account of another person unless the person making the tender possesses the subject security or an equivalent security, or has a reasonable belief that, upon information furnished by the person on whose behalf the tender is made, such person owns the subject security or an equivalent security and will promptly deliver the subject security or such equivalent security for the purpose of tender to the person making the tender.

(c)   This rule shall not prohibit any transaction or transactions which the Commission, upon written request or upon its own motion, exempts, either unconditionally or on specified terms and conditions.

Rule 14e–5.   Prohibiting Purchases Outside of a Tender Offer

(a)   *Unlawful activity.* As a means reasonably designed to prevent fraudulent, deceptive or manipulative acts or practices in connection with a tender offer for equity securities, no covered person may directly or indirectly purchase or arrange to purchase any subject securities or any related securities except as part of the tender offer. This prohibition applies from the time of public announcement of the tender offer until the tender offer expires. This prohibition does not apply to any purchases or arrangements to purchase made during the time of any subsequent offering period as provided for in Rule 14d–11 if the consideration paid or to be paid for the purchases or arrangements to purchase is the same in form and amount as the consideration offered in the tender offer.

(b)   *Excepted activity.* The following transactions in subject securities or related securities are not prohibited by paragraph (a) of this rule:

(1)   *Exercises of securities.* Transactions by covered persons to convert, exchange, or exercise related securities before public announcement;

(2)   *Purchases for plans.* Purchases or arrangements to purchase by or for a plan that are made by an agent independent of the issuer;

(3)   *Purchases during odd-lot offers.* Purchases or arrangements to purchase if the tender offer is excepted under Rule 13e–4(h)(5);

(4)   *Purchases as intermediary.* Purchases by or through a dealer-manager or its affiliates that are made in the ordinary course of business and made either:

(i)   On an agency basis not for a covered person; or

(ii)   As principal for its own account if the dealer-manager or its affiliate is not a market-maker, and the purchase is made to offset a contemporaneous sale after having received an unsolicited order to buy from a customer who is not a covered person;

(5)   *Basket transactions.* Purchases or arrangements to purchase a basket of securities containing a subject security or a related security if the following conditions are satisfied:

(i)   The purchase or arrangement to purchase is made in the ordinary course of business and not to facilitate the tender offer;

(ii)   The basket contains 20 or more securities; and

(iii)   Covered securities and related securities do not comprise more that 5% of the value of the basket;

(6)   *Covering transactions.* Purchases or arrangements to purchase that are made to satisfy an obligation to deliver a subject security or a related security arising from a short sale or from the exercise of an option by a non-covered person if:

(i)   The short sale or option transaction was made in the ordinary course of business and not to facilitate the offer;

(ii)   In the case of a short sale, the short sale was entered into before public announcement of the tender offer; and

(iii)   In the case of an exercise of an option, the covered person wrote the option before public announcement of the tender offer;

(7)   *Purchases pursuant to contractual obligations.* Purchases or arrangements to purchase pursuant to a contract if the following conditions are satisfied:

(i)   The contract was entered into before public announcement of the tender offer;

(ii)   The contract is unconditional and binding on both parties; and

(iii) The existence of the contract and all material terms including quantity, price and parties are disclosed in the offering materials;

(8) *Purchases or arrangements to purchase by an affiliate of the dealer-manager.* Purchases or arrangements to purchase by an affiliate of a dealer-manager if the following conditions are satisfied:

(i) The dealer-manager maintains and enforces written policies and procedures reasonably designed to prevent the flow of information to or from the affiliate that might result in a violation of the federal securities laws and regulations;

(ii) The dealer-manager is registered as a broker or dealer under section 15(a) of the Act;

(iii) The affiliate has no officers (or persons performing similar functions) or employees (other than clerical, ministerial, or supported personnel) in common with the dealer-manager that direct, effect, or recommend transactions in securities; and

(iv) The purchases or arrangements to purchase are not made to facilitate the tender offer;

(9) *Purchases by connected exempt market makers or connected exempt principal traders.* Purchases or arrangements to purchase if the following conditions are satisfied:

(i) The issuer of the subject security is a foreign private issuer, as defined in Rule 3b–4(c);

(ii) The tender offer is subject to the United Kingdom's City Code on Takeovers and Mergers;

(iii) The purchase or arrangement to purchase is effected by a connected exempt market maker or a connected exempt principal trader, as those terms are used in the United Kingdom's City Code on Takeovers and Mergers;

(iv) The connected exempt market maker or the connected exempt principal trader complies with the applicable provisions of the United Kingdom's City Code on Takeovers and Mergers; and

(v) The tender offer documents disclose the identity of the connected exempt market making or principal purchases by such market maker or principal trader to the extent that this information is required to be made public in the United Kingdom;

(10) *Purchases during cross-border tender offers.* Purchases or arrangements to purchase if the following conditions are satisfied:

(i) The tender offer is excepted under Rule 13e–4(h)(8) or 14d–1(c);

(ii) The offering documents furnished to U.S. holders prominently disclose the possibility of any purchases, or arrangements to purchase, or the intent to make such purchases;

(iii) The offering documents disclose the manner in which any information about any such purchases or arrangements to purchase will be disclosed;

(iv) The offeror discloses information in the United States about any such purchases or arrangements to purchase in a manner comparable to the disclosure made in the home jurisdiction, as defined in Rule 13e–4(i)(3); and

(v) The purchases comply with the applicable tender offer laws and regulations of the home jurisdiction;

(11) Purchases or arrangements to purchase pursuant to a foreign tender offer(s). Purchases or arrangements to purchase pursuant to a foreign offer(s) where the offeror seeks to acquire subject securities through a U.S. tender offer and a concurrent or substantially concurrent foreign offer(s), if the following conditions are satisfied:

(i) The U.S. and foreign tender offer(s) meet the conditions for reliance on the Tier II cross-border exemptions set forth in Rule 14d–1(d);

(ii) The economic terms and consideration in the U.S. tender offer and foreign tender offer(s) are the same, provided that any cash consideration to be paid to U.S. security holders may be converted from the currency to be paid in the foreign tender offer(s) to U.S. dollars at an exchange rate disclosed in the U.S. offering documents;

(iii) The procedural terms of the U.S. tender offer are at least as favorable as the terms of the foreign tender offer(s);

(iv) The intention of the offeror to make purchases pursuant to the foreign tender offer(s) is disclosed in the U.S. offering documents; and

(v) Purchases by the offeror in the foreign tender offer(s) are made solely pursuant to the foreign tender offer(s) and not pursuant to an open market transaction(s), a private transaction(s), or other transaction(s); and

(12) Purchases or arrangements to purchase by an affiliate of the financial advisor and an offeror and its affiliates.

(i) Purchases or arrangements to purchase by an affiliate of a financial advisor and an offeror and its affiliates that are permissible under and will be conducted in accordance with the applicable laws of the subject company's home jurisdiction, if the following conditions are satisfied:

(A) The subject company is a foreign private issuer as defined in Rule 3b–4(c);

(B) The covered person reasonably expects that the tender offer meets the conditions for reliance on the Tier II cross-border exemptions set forth in Rule 14d–1(d);

(C) No purchases or arrangements to purchase otherwise than pursuant to the tender offer are made in the United States;

(D) The United States offering materials disclose prominently the possibility of, or the intention to make, purchases or arrangements to purchase subject securities or related securities outside of the tender offer, and if there will be public disclosure of purchases of subject or related securities, the manner in which information regarding such purchases will be disseminated;

(E) There is public disclosure in the United States, to the extent that such information is made public in the subject company's home jurisdiction, of information regarding all purchases of subject securities and related securities otherwise than pursuant to the tender offer from the time of public announcement of the tender offer until the tender offer expires;

(F) Purchases or arrangements to purchase by an offeror and its affiliates must satisfy the following additional condition: the tender offer price will be increased to match any consideration paid outside of the tender offer that is greater than the tender offer price; and

(G) Purchases or arrangements to purchase by an affiliate of a financial advisor must satisfy the following additional conditions:

(1) The financial advisor and the affiliate maintain and enforce written policies and procedures reasonably designed to prevent the transfer of information among the financial advisor and affiliate that might result in a violation of U.S. federal securities laws and regulations through the establishment of information barriers;

(2) The financial advisor has an affiliate that is registered as a broker or dealer under section 15(a) of the Act;

(3) The affiliate has no officers (or persons performing similar functions) or employees (other than clerical, ministerial, or support personnel) in common with the financial advisor that direct, effect, or recommend transactions in the subject securities or related securities who also will be involved in providing the offeror or subject company with financial advisory services or dealer-manager services; and

(4) The purchases or arrangements to purchase are not made to facilitate the tender offer.

(ii) Reserved.

(c)   *Definitions.* For purposes of this rule, the term:

(1)   "Affiliate" has the same meaning as in Rule 12b–2;

(2)   "Agent independent of the issuer" has the same meaning as in Rule 100(b) of Regulation M;

(3)   "Covered person" means:

(i)   The offeror and its affiliates;

(ii)   The offeror's dealer-manager and its affiliates;

(iii) Any advisor to any of the persons specified in paragraph (c)(3)(i) and (ii) of this rule, whose compensation is dependent of the completion of the offer; and

(iv)   Any person acting, directly or indirectly, in concert with any of the persons specified in this paragraph (c)(3) in connection with any purchase or arrangement to purchase any subject securities or any related securities;

(4)   "Plan" has the same meaning as in Rule 100(b) of Regulation M;

(5)   "Public announcement" is any oral or written communication by the offeror or any person authorized to act on the offeror's behalf that is reasonably designed to, or has the effect of, informing the public or security holders in general about the tender offer;

(6)   "Related securities" means securities that are immediately convertible into, exchangeable for, or exercisable for subject securities;

(7)   "Subject securities" has the same meaning as in Item 1000 of Regulation S–K;

(8)   Subject company has the same meaning as in Regulation M–A of this chapter; and

(9)   Home jurisdiction has the same meaning as in the Instructions to paragraphs (c) and (d) of Rule 14d–1.

(d)   *Exemptive authority.* Upon written application or upon its own motion, the commission may grant an exemption from the provisions of this rule, either unconditionally or on specified terms or conditions, to any transaction or class of transactions or any security or class of security, or any person or class of persons.

Rule 14e–6.   Repurchase Offers by Certain Closed-End Registered Investment Companies

Rules 14e–1 and 14e–2 shall not apply to any offer by a closed-end management investment company to repurchase equity securities of which it is the issuer pursuant to Rule 23c–3 of the Investment Company Act.

Rule 14e–7.   Unlawful Tender Offer Practices in Connection With Roll-ups

In order to implement section 14(h) of the Act:

(a)(1)   It shall be unlawful for any person to receive compensation for soliciting tenders directly from security holders in connection with a roll-up transaction as provided in paragraph (a)(2) of this rule, if the compensation is:

(i)   Based on whether the solicited person participates in the tender offer; or

(ii)   Contingent on the success of the tender offer.

(2)   Paragraph (a)(1) of this rule is applicable to a roll-up transaction as defined in Item 901(c) of Regulation S–K, structured as a tender offer, except for a transaction involving only:

(i)   Finite-life entities that are not limited partnerships;

(ii)   Partnerships whose investors will receive new securities or securities in another entity that are not reported under a transaction reporting plan declared effective before December 17, 1993 by the Commission under section 11A of the Act; or

(iii) Partnerships whose investors' securities are reported under a transaction reporting plan declared effective before December 17, 1993 by the Commission under section 11A of the Act.

(b)(1)   It shall be unlawful for any finite-life entity that is the subject of a roll-up transaction as provided in paragraph (b)(2) of this rule to fail to provide a security holder list or mail communications related to a tender offer that is in furtherance of the roll-up transaction, at the option of a requesting security holder, pursuant to the procedures set forth in Rule 14a–7.

(2)   Paragraph (b)(1) of this rule is applicable to a roll-up transaction as defined in Item 901(c) of Regulation S–K, structured as a tender offer, that involves:

(i)   An entity with securities registered pursuant to section 12 of the Act; or

(ii)   A limited partnership, unless the transaction involves only:

(A)   Partnerships whose investors will receive new securities or securities in another entity that are not reported under a transaction reporting plan declared effective before December 17, 1993 by the Commission under Section 11A of the Act; or

(B)   Partnerships whose investors' securities are reported under a transaction reporting plan declared effective before December 17, 1993 by the Commission under Section 11A of the Act.

Rule 14e–8.   Prohibited Conduct in Connection With Precommencement Communications

It is a fraudulent, deceptive or manipulative act or practice within the meaning of section 14(e) of the Act for any person to publicly announce that the person (or a party on whose behalf the person is acting) plans to make a tender offer that has not yet been commenced, if the person:

(a)   Is making the announcement of a potential tender offer without the intention to commence the offer within a reasonable time and complete the offer;

(b)   Intends, directly or indirectly, for the announcement to manipulate the market price of the stock of the bidder or subject company; or

(c)   Does not have the reasonable belief that the person will have the means to purchase securities to complete the offer.

Rule 14f–1.   Change in Majority of Directors

If, pursuant to any arrangement or understanding with the person or persons acquiring securities in a transaction subject to section 13(d) or 14(d) of the Act, any persons are to be elected or designated as directors of the issuer, otherwise than at a meeting of security holders, and the persons so elected or designated will constitute a majority of the directors of the issuer, then, not less than 10 days prior to the date any such person take office as a director, or such shorter period prior to that date as the Commission may authorize upon a showing of good cause therefor, the issuer shall file with the Commission and transmit to all holders of record of securities of the issuer who would be entitled to vote at a meeting for election of directors, information substantially equivalent to the information which would be required by Items 6(a), (d) and (e), 7 and 8 of Schedule 14A of Regulation 14A to be transmitted if such person or persons were nominees for election as directors at a meeting of such security holders. Eight copies of such information shall be filed with the Commission.

Rule 14n–1.   Filing of Schedule 14N

(a)   A shareholder or group of shareholders that submits a nominee or nominees in accordance with Rule 14a–11 or a procedure set forth under applicable state or foreign law, or a registrant's governing documents providing for the inclusion of shareholder director nominees in the registrant's proxy materials shall file with the Commission a statement containing the information required by Schedule 14N and simultaneously provide the notice on Schedule 14N to the registrant.

(b)(1)   Whenever two or more persons are required to file a statement containing the information required by Schedule 14N, only one statement need be filed. The statement must identify all such persons, contain the required information with regard to each such person, indicate that the statement is filed on behalf of all such persons, and include, as an appendix, their agreement in writing that the statement is filed on behalf of each of them. Each person on whose behalf the statement is filed is responsible for the timely filing of that statement and any amendments thereto, and for the completeness and accuracy of the information concerning such person contained therein; such person is not responsible for the completeness or accuracy of the information concerning the other persons making the filing.

(2) If the group's members elect to make their own filings, each filing should identify all members of the group but the information provided concerning the other persons making the filing need only reflect information which the filing person knows or has reason to know.

Rule 14n–2. Filing of Amendments to Schedule 14N

(a) If any material change occurs with respect to the nomination, or in the disclosure or certifications set forth in the Schedule 14N required by Rule 14n–1(a), the person or persons who were required to file the statement shall promptly file or cause to be filed with the Commission an amendment disclosing that change.

(b) An amendment shall be filed within 10 calendar days of the final results of the election being announced by the registrant stating the nominating shareholder's or the nominating shareholder group's intention with regard to continued ownership of their shares.

Rule 14n–3. Dissemination

One copy of Schedule 14N filed pursuant to Rules 14n–1 and 14n–2 shall be mailed by registered or certified mail or electronically transmitted to the registrant at its principal executive office. Three copies of the material must at the same time be filed with, or mailed for filing to, each national securities exchange upon which any class of securities of the registrant is listed and registered.

EXEMPTION OF CERTAIN SECURITIES FROM SECTION 15(a)

Rule 15a–1. Securities Activities of OTC Derivatives Dealers

Preliminary Note: OTC derivatives dealers are a special class of broker-dealers that are exempt from certain broker-dealer requirements, including membership in a self-regulatory organization (Rule 15b9–2 of the Act), regular broker-dealer margin rules (Rule 36a1–1 of the Act), and application of the Securities Investor Protection Act of 1970 (Rule 36a1–2 of the Act). OTC derivative dealers are subject to special requirements, including limitations on the scope of their securities activities (Rule 15a–1 of the Act), specified internal risk management control systems (Rule 15c3–4 of the Act), recordkeeping obligations (Rule 17a–3(a)(10) of the Act), and reporting responsibilities (Rule 17a–12 of the Act). They are also subject to alternative net capital treatment (Rule 15c3–1(a)(5) of the Act). This rule 15a–1 uses a number of defined terms in setting forth the securities activities in which an OTC derivatives dealer may engage: "OTC derivatives dealer," "eligible OTC derivative instrument," "cash management securities activities," and "ancillary portfolio management securities activities." These terms are defined under Rules 3b–12 through 3b–15 of the Act.

(a) The securities activities of an OTC derivatives dealer shall:

(1) Be limited to:

(i) Engaging in dealer activities in eligible OTC derivative instruments that are securities;

(ii) Issuing and reacquiring securities that are issued by the dealer, including warrants on securities, hybrid securities, and structured notes;

(iii) Engaging in cash management securities activities;

(iv) Engaging in ancillary portfolio management securities activities; and

(v) Engaging in such other securities activities that the Commission designates by order pursuant to paragraph (b)(1) of this rule; and

(2) Consist primarily of the activities described in paragraphs (a)(1)(i), (a)(1)(ii), and (a)(1)(iii) of this rule; and

(3) Not consist of any other securities activities, including engaging in any transaction in any security that is not an eligible OTC derivative instrument, except as permitted under paragraphs (a)(1)(iii), (a)(1)(iv), and (a)(1)(v) of this rule.

(b)   The Commission, by order, entered upon its own initiative or after considering an application for exemptive relief, may clarify or expand the scope of eligible OTC derivative instruments and the scope of permissible securities activities of an OTC derivatives dealer. Such orders may:

(1)   Identify other permissible securities activities;

(2)   Determine that a class of fungible instruments that are standardized as to their material economic terms is within the scope of eligible OTC derivative instrument;

(3)   Clarify whether certain contracts, agreements, or transactions are within the scope of eligible OTC derivative instrument; or

(4)   Clarify whether certain securities activities are within the scope of ancillary portfolio management securities activities.

(c)   To the extent an OTC derivatives dealer engages in any securities transaction pursuant to paragraphs (a)(1)(i) through (a)(1)(v) of this rule, such transaction shall be effected through a registered broker or dealer (other than an OTC derivatives dealer) that, in the case of any securities transaction pursuant to paragraphs (a)(1)(i), or (a)(1)(iii) through (a)(1)(v) of this rule, is an affiliate of the OTC derivatives dealer, except that this paragraph (c) shall not apply if:

(1)   The counterparty to the transaction with the OTC derivatives dealer is acting as principal and is:

(i)   A registered broker or dealer;

(ii)   A bank acting in a dealer capacity, as permitted by U.S. law;

(iii)   A foreign broker or dealer; or

(iv)   An affiliate of the OTC derivatives dealer; or

(2)   The OTC derivatives dealer is engaging in an ancillary portfolio management securities activity, and the transaction is in a foreign security, and a registered broker or dealer, a bank, or a foreign broker or dealer is acting as agent for the OTC derivatives dealer.

(d)   To the extent an OTC derivatives dealer induces or attempts to induce any counterparty to enter into any securities transaction pursuant to paragraphs (a)(1)(i) through (a)(1)(v) of this rule, any communication or contact with the counterparty concerning the transaction (other than clerical and ministerial activities conducted by an associated person of the OTC derivatives dealer) shall be conducted by one or more registered persons that, in the case of any securities transaction pursuant to paragraphs (a)(1)(i), or (a)(1)(iii) through (a)(1)(v) of this rule, is associated with an affiliate of the OTC derivatives dealer, except that this paragraph (d) shall not apply if the counterparty to the transaction with the OTC derivatives dealer is:

(1)   A registered broker or dealer;

(2)   A bank acting in a dealer capacity, as permitted by U.S. law;

(3)   A foreign broker or dealer; or

(4)   An affiliate of the OTC derivatives dealer.

(e)   For purposes of this rule, the term hybrid security means a security that incorporates payment features economically similar to options, forwards, futures, swap agreements, or collars involving currencies, interest or other rates, commodities, securities, indices, quantitative measures, or other financial or economic interests or property of any kind, or any payment or delivery that is dependent on the occurrence or nonoccurrence of any event associated with a potential financial, economic, or commercial consequence (or any combination, permutation, or derivative of such contract or underlying interest).

(f)   For purposes of this rule, the term affiliate means any organization (whether incorporated or unincorporated) that directly or indirectly controls, is controlled by, or is under common control with, the OTC derivatives dealer.

(g)   For purposes of this rule, the term foreign broker or dealer means any person not resident in the United States (including any U.S. person engaged in business as a broker or dealer entirely outside the United States, except as otherwise permitted by Rule 15a–6 of the Act) that is not an office or branch of, or a natural person associated with, a registered broker or dealer, whose securities activities, if conducted in the United States, would be described by the definition of "broker" in section 3(a)(4) of the Act or "dealer" in section 3(a)(5) of the Act.

(h) For purposes of this rule, the term foreign security means any security including a depositary share issued by a United States bank, provided that the depositary share is initially offered and sold outside the United States in accordance with Regulation S issued by a person not organized or incorporated under the laws of the United States, provided the transaction that involves such security is not effected on a national securities exchange or on a market operated by a registered national securities association; or a debt security (including a convertible debt security) issued by an issuer organized or incorporated under the laws of the United States that is initially offered and sold outside the United States in accordance with Regulation S.

(i) For purposes of this rule, the term registered person is:

(A) A natural person who is associated with a registered broker or dealer and is registered or approved under the rules of a self-regulatory organization of which such broker or dealer is a member; or

(B) If the counterparty to the transaction with the OTC derivatives dealer is a resident of a jurisdiction other than the United States, a natural person who is not resident in the United States and is associated with a broker or dealer that is registered or licensed by a foreign financial regulatory authority in the jurisdiction in which such counterparty is resident or in which such natural person is located, in accordance with applicable legal requirements, if any.

Rule 15a–2. Exemption of Certain Securities of Cooperative Apartment Houses From Section 15(a)

Shares of a corporation which represent ownership, or entitle the holders thereof to possession and occupancy, of specific apartment units in property owned by such corporations and organized and operated on a cooperative basis are hereby exempted from the operation of section 15(a) of the Securities Exchange Act of 1934, when such shares are sold by or through a real estate broker licensed under the laws of the political subdivision in which the property is located.

Rule 15a–4. Forty-Five Day Exemption From Registration for Certain Members of National Securities Exchanges

(a) A natural person who is a member of a national securities exchange shall, upon termination of his association with a registered broker-dealer, be exempt, for a period of forty-five days after such termination, from the registration requirement of section 15(a) of the Act solely for the purpose of continuing to effect transactions on the floor of such exchange if (1) such person has filed with the Commission an application for registration as a broker-dealer and such person complies in all material respects with rules of the Commission applicable to registered brokers and dealers and (2) such exchange has filed with the Commission a statement that it has reviewed such application and that there do not appear to be grounds for its denial.

(b) The exemption from registration provided by this rule shall not be available to any person while there is pending before the Commission any proceeding involving any such person pursuant to section 15(b)(1)(B) of the Act.

Rule 15a–5. Exemption of Certain Non-Bank Lenders

A lender approved under the rules and regulations of the Small Business Administration shall be exempt from the registration requirement of section 15(a)(1) of the Act if it does not engage in the business of effecting transactions in securities or of buying and selling securities for its own account except in respect of receiving notes evidencing loans to small business concerns and selling the portion of such notes guaranteed by the Small Business Administration through or to a registered broker or dealer or to a bank, a savings institution, an insurance company, or an account over which an investment adviser registered pursuant to the Investment Advisers Act of 1940 exercises investment discretion.

Rule 15a–6.   Exemption of Certain Foreign Brokers or Dealers

(a)   A foreign broker or dealer shall be exempt from the registration requirements of sections 15(a)(1) or 15B(a)(1) of the Act to the extent that the foreign broker or dealer:

(1)   Effects transactions in securities with or for persons that have not been solicited by the foreign broker or dealer; or

(2)   Furnishes research reports to major U.S. institutional investors, and effects transactions in the securities discussed in the research reports with or for those major U.S. institutional investors, provided that:

(i)   The research reports do not recommend the use of the foreign broker or dealer to effect trades in any security;

(ii)   The foreign broker or dealer does not initiate contact with those major U.S. institutional investors to follow up on the research reports, and does not otherwise induce or attempt to induce the purchase or sale of any security by those major U.S. institutional investors;

(iii)   If the foreign broker or dealer has a relationship with a registered broker or dealer that satisfies the requirements of paragraph (a)(3) of this rule, any transactions with the foreign broker or dealer in securities discussed in the research reports are effected only through that registered broker or dealer, pursuant to the provisions of paragraph (a)(3); and

(iv)   The foreign broker or dealer does not provide research to U.S. persons pursuant to any express or implied understanding that those U.S. persons will direct commission income to the foreign broker or dealer; or

(3)   Induces or attempts to induce the purchase or sale of any security by a U.S. institutional investor or a major U.S. institutional investor, provided that:

(i)   The foreign broker or dealer:

(A)   Effects any resulting transactions with or for the U.S. institutional investor or the major U.S. institutional investor through a registered broker or dealer in the manner described by paragraph (a)(3)(iii) of this rule; and

(B)   Provides the Commission (upon request or pursuant to agreements reached between any foreign securities authority, including any foreign government, as specified in section 3(a)(50) of the Act, and the Commission or the U.S. Government) with any information or documents within the possession, custody, or control of the foreign broker or dealer, any testimony of foreign associated persons, and any assistance in taking the evidence of other persons, wherever located, that the Commission requests and that relates to transactions under paragraph (a)(3) of this rule, except that if, after the foreign broker or dealer has exercised its best efforts to provide the information, documents, testimony, or assistance, including requesting the appropriate governmental body and, if legally necessary, its customers (with respect to customer information) to permit the foreign broker or dealer to provide the information, documents, testimony, or assistance to the Commission, the foreign broker or dealer is prohibited from providing this information, documents, testimony, or assistance by applicable foreign law or regulations, then this paragraph (a)(3)(i)(B) shall not apply and the foreign broker or dealer will be subject to paragraph (c) of this rule;

(ii)   The foreign associated person of the foreign broker or dealer effecting transactions with the U.S. institutional investor or the major U.S. institutional investor:

(A)   Conducts all securities activities from outside the U.S., except that the foreign associated persons may conduct visits to U.S. institutional investors and major U.S. institutional investors within the United States, provided that:

(1)   The foreign associated person is accompanied on these visits by an associated person of a registered broker or dealer that accepts responsibility for the foreign associated person's communications with the U.S. institutional investor or the major U.S. institutional investor; and

(2) Transactions in any securities discussed during the visit by the foreign associated person are effected only through the registered broker or dealer, pursuant to paragraph (a)(3) of this rule; and

(B) Is determined by the registered broker or dealer to:

(1) Not be subject to a statutory disqualification specified in section 3(a)(39) of the Act, or any substantially equivalent foreign

(i) Expulsion or suspension from membership,

(ii) Bar or suspension from association,

(iii) Denial of trading privileges,

(iv) Order denying, suspending, or revoking registration or barring or suspending association, or

(v) Finding with respect to causing any such effective foreign suspension, expulsion, or order;

(2) Not to have been convicted of any foreign offense, enjoined from any foreign act, conduct, or practice, or found to have committed any foreign act substantially equivalent to any of those listed in sections 15(b)(4)(B), (C), (D), or (E) of the Act; and

(3) *Not* to have been found to have made or caused to be made any false foreign statement or omission substantially equivalent to any of those listed in section 3(a)(39)(E) of the Act; and

(iii) The registered broker or dealer through which the transaction with the U.S. institutional investor or the major U.S. institutional investor is effected:

(A) Is responsible for:

(1) Effecting the transactions conducted under paragraph (a)(3) of this rule, other than negotiating their terms;

(2) Issuing all required confirmations and statements to the U.S. institutional investor or the major U.S. institutional investor;

(3) As between the foreign broker or dealer and the registered broker or dealer, extending or arranging for the extension of any credit to the U.S. institutional investor or the major U.S. institutional investor in connection with the transactions;

(4) Maintaining required books and records relating to the transactions, including those required by Rules 17a–3 and 17a–4 under the Act;

(5) Complying with Rule 15c3–1 under the Act with respect to the transactions; and

(6) Receiving, delivering, and safeguarding funds and securities in connection with the transactions on behalf of the U.S. institutional investor or the major U.S. institutional investor in compliance with Rule 15c3–3 under the Act;

(B) Participates through an associated person in all oral communications between the foreign associated person and the U.S. institutional investor, other than a major U.S. institutional investor;

(C) Has obtained from the foreign broker or dealer, with respect to each foreign associated person, the types of information specified in Rule 17a–3(a)(12) under the Act, provided that the information required by paragraph (a)(12)(d) of that rule shall include sanctions imposed by foreign securities authorities, exchanges, or associations, including without limitation those described in paragraph (a)(3)(ii)(B) of this rule;

(D) Has obtained from the foreign broker or dealer and each foreign associated person written consent to service of process for any civil action brought by or proceeding before the Commission or a self-regulatory organization (as defined in section 3(a)(26) of the Act), providing that process may be served on them by service on the registered broker or dealer in the manner set forth on the registered broker's or dealer's current Form BD; and

(E) Maintains a written record of the information and consents required by paragraphs (a)(3)(iii)(C) and (D) of this rule, and all records in connection with trading activities of the U.S. institutional investor or the major U.S. institutional investor involving the foreign broker or dealer conducted under paragraph (a)(3) of this rule, in an office of the registered broker or dealer located in the United States (with respect to nonresident registered brokers or dealers, pursuant to Rule 17a–7(a) under the Act) and makes these records available to the Commission upon request; or

(4) Effects transactions in securities with or for, or induces or attempts to induce the purchase or sale of any security by:

(i) A registered broker or dealer, whether the registered broker or dealer is acting as principal for its own account or as agent for others, or a bank acting pursuant to an exception or exemption from the definition of "broker" or "dealer" in sections 3(a)(4)(B), 3(a)(4)(E), or 3(a)(5)(C) of the Act or the rules thereunder;

(ii) The African Development Bank, the Asian Development Bank, the Inter-American Development Bank, the International Bank for Reconstruction and Development, the International Monetary Fund, the United Nations, and their agencies, affiliates, and pension funds;

(iii) A foreign person temporarily present in the United States, with whom the foreign broker or dealer had a bona fide, preexisting relationship before the foreign person entered the United States;

(iv) Any agency or branch of a U.S. person permanently located outside the United States, provided that the transactions occur outside the United States; or

(v) U.S. citizens resident outside the United States, provided that the transactions occur outside the United States, and that the foreign broker or dealer does not direct its selling efforts toward identifiable groups of U.S. citizens resident abroad.

(b) When used in this rule,

(1) The term "family of investment companies" shall mean:

(i) Except for insurance company separate accounts, any two or more separately registered investment companies under the Investment Company Act of 1940 that share the same investment adviser or principal underwriter and hold themselves out to investors as related companies for purposes of investment and investor services; and

(ii) With respect to insurance company separate accounts, any two or more separately registered separate accounts under the Investment Company Act of 1940 that share the same investment adviser or principal underwriter and function under operational or accounting or control systems that are substantially similar.

(2) The term "foreign associated person" shall mean any natural person domiciled outside the United States who is an associated person, as defined in section 3(a)(18) of the Act, of the foreign broker or dealer, and who participates in the solicitation of a U.S. institutional investor or a major U.S. institutional investor under paragraph (a)(3) of this rule.

(3) The term "foreign broker or dealer" shall mean any non-U.S. resident person (including any U.S. person engaged in business as a broker or dealer entirely outside the United States, except as otherwise permitted by this rule) that is not an office or branch of, or a natural person associated with, a registered broker or dealer, whose securities activities, if conducted in the United States, would be described by the definition of "broker" or "dealer" in sections 3(a)(4) or 3(a)(5) of the Act.

(4) The term "major U.S. institutional investor" shall mean a person that is:

(i) A U.S. institutional investor that has, or has under management, total assets in excess of $100 million; provided, however, that for purposes of determining the total assets of an investment company under this rule, the investment company may include the assets of any family of investment companies of which it is a part; or

(ii)   An investment adviser registered with the Commission under section 203 of the Investment Advisers Act of 1940 that has total assets under management in excess of $100 million.

(5)   The term "registered broker or dealer" shall mean a person that is registered with the Commission under sections 15(b), 15B(a)(2), or 15C(a)(2) of the Act.

(6)   The term "United States" shall means the United States of America, including the States and any territories and other areas subject to its jurisdiction.

(7)   The term "U.S. institutional investor" shall mean a person that is:

(i)   An investment company registered with the Commission under section 8 of the Investment Company Act of 1940; or

(ii)   A bank, savings and loan association, insurance company, business development company, small business investment company, or employee benefit plan defined in Rule 501(a)(1) of Regulation D under the Securities Act of 1933; a private business development company defined in Rule 501(a)(2); an organization described in section 501(c)(3) of the Internal Revenue Code, as defined in Rule 501(a)(3); or a trust defined in Rule 501(a)(7).

(c)   The Commission, by order after notice and opportunity for hearing, may withdraw the exemption provided in paragraph (a)(3) of this rule with respect to the subsequent activities of a foreign broker or dealer or class of foreign brokers or dealers conducted from a foreign country, if the Commission finds that the laws or regulations of that foreign country have prohibited the foreign broker or dealer, or one of a class of foreign brokers or dealers, from providing, in response to a request from the Commission, information or documents within its possession, custody, or control, testimony of foreign associated persons, or assistance in taking the evidence of other persons, wherever located, related to activities exempted by paragraph (a)(3) of this rule.

Rule 15a–7.   [Removed and Reserved]

Rule 15a–8.   [Removed and Reserved]

Rule 15a–9.   [Removed and Reserved]

Rule 15a–10. Exemption of Certain Brokers or Dealers With Respect to Security Futures Products

(a)   A broker or dealer that is registered by notice with the Commission pursuant to Section 15(b)(11)(A) of the Act and that is not a member of either a national securities exchange registered pursuant to Section 6(a) of the Act or a national securities association registered pursuant to Section 15A(a) of the Act will be exempt from the registration requirement of Section 15(a)(1) of the Act solely to act as a broker or a dealer in security futures products.

(b)   A broker or dealer that is registered by notice with the Commission pursuant to Section 15(b)(11)(A) of the Act and that is a member of either a national securities exchange registered pursuant to Section 6(a) of the Act or a national securities association registered pursuant to Section 15A(a) of the Act will be exempt from the registration requirement of Section 15(a)(1) of the Act solely to act as a broker or a dealer in security futures products, if:

(1)   The rules of any such exchange or association of which the broker or dealer is a member provides specifically for a broker or dealer that is registered by notice with the Commission pursuant to Section 15(b)(11)(A) of the Act to become a member of such exchange or association; and

(2)   The broker or dealer complies with Section 11(a)–(c) of the Act with respect to any transactions in security futures products on a national securities exchange registered pursuant to Section 6(a) of the Act of which it is a member, notwithstanding Section 15(b)(11)(B)(ii) of the Act.

Rule 15a–11. [Removed and Reserved]

REGISTRATION OF BROKERS AND DEALERS

Rule 15b1–1. Application for Registration of Broker or Dealer

(a)   An application for registration of a broker or dealer that is filed pursuant to section 15(b) of the Act shall be filed on Form BD in accordance with the instructions to the form. A broker or dealer that is an OTC derivatives dealer shall indicate where appropriate on Form BD that the type of business in which it is engaged is that of acting as an OTC derivatives dealer.

(b)   Every application for registration of a broker or dealer that is filed on or after January 25, 1993, shall be filed with the Central Registration Depository operated by the Financial Industry Regulatory Authority, Inc.

(c)   An application for registration that is filed with the Central Registration Depository pursuant to this rule shall be considered a "report" filed with the Commission for purposes of sections 15(b), 17(a), 18(a), 32(a) of the Act and other applicable provisions of the Act.

Rule 15b1–3. Registration of Successor to Registered Broker or Dealer

(a)   In the event that a broker or dealer succeeds to and continues the business of a broker or dealer registered pursuant to section 15(b) of the Act, the registration of the predecessor shall be deemed to remain effective as the registration of the successor if the successor, within 30 days after such succession, files an application for registration on Form BD, and the predecessor files a notice of withdrawal from registration on Form BDW; *Provided, however,* That the registration of the predecessor broker or dealer will cease to be effective as the registration of the successor broker or dealer 45 days after the application for registration on Form BD is filed by such successor.

(b)   Notwithstanding paragraph (a) of this rule, if a broker or dealer succeeds to and continues the business of a registered predecessor broker or dealer, and the succession is based solely on a change in the predecessor's date or state of incorporation, form of organization, or composition of a partnership, the successor may, within 30 days after the succession, amend the registration of the predecessor broker or dealer on Form BD to reflect these changes. This amendment shall be deemed an application for registration filed by the predecessor and adopted by the successor.

Rule 15b1–4. Registration of Fiduciaries

The registration of a broker or dealer shall be deemed to be the registration of any executor, administrator, guardian, conservator, assignee for the benefit of creditors, receiver, trustee in insolvency or bankruptcy, or other fiduciary, appointed or qualified by order, judgment, or decree of a court of competent jurisdiction to continue the business of such registered broker or dealer; *Provided,* That such fiduciary files with the Commission, within 30 days after entering upon the performance of his duties, a statement setting forth as to such fiduciary substantially the information required by Form BD.

Rule 15b1–5. Consent to Service of Process to Be Furnished by Non-resident Brokers or Dealers and by Non-resident General Partners or Managing Agents of Brokers or Dealers

(a)   Each nonresident broker or dealer registered or applying for registration pursuant to section 15(b) of the Act, each nonresident general partner of a broker or dealer partnership which is registered or applying for registration, and each nonresident managing agent of any other unincorporated broker or dealer which is registered or applying for registration, shall furnish to the Commission, in a form prescribed by or acceptable to it, a written irrevocable consent and power of attorney which

(1)   Designates the Securities and Exchange Commission as an agent upon whom may be served any process, pleadings, or other papers in any civil suit or action brought in any appropriate court in any place subject to the jurisdiction of the United States, with respect to any cause of action

(i)   Which accrues during the period beginning when such broker or dealer becomes registered pursuant to section 15 of the Act 1934 and the rules and regulations thereunder and ending either when such registration is cancelled or revoked, or when the Commission receives from such broker or dealer a notice to withdraw from such registration, whichever is earlier,

(ii) Which arises out of any activity, in any place subject to the jurisdiction of the United States, occurring in connection with the conduct of business of a broker or dealer, and

(iii) Which is founded directly or indirectly, upon the provisions of the Securities Act of 1933, the Securities Exchange Act of 1934, the Trust Indenture Act of 1939, the Investment Company Act of 1940, the Investment Advisers Act of 1940, or any rule or regulation under any of said Acts; and

(2) Stipulates and agrees that any such civil suit or action may be commenced by the service of process upon the Commission and the forwarding of a copy thereof as provided in paragraph (c) of this rule, and that the service as aforesaid of any such process, pleadings, or other papers upon the Commission shall be taken and held in all courts to be as valid and binding as if due personal service thereof had been made.

(b) The required consent and power of attorney shall be furnished to the Commission within the following period of time:

(1) Each nonresident broker or dealer registered at the time this rule becomes effective, and each nonresident general partner or managing agent of an unincorporated broker or dealer registered at the time this rule becomes effective, shall furnish such consent and power of attorney within 60 days after such date;

(2) Each broker or dealer applying for registration after the effective date of this rule shall furnish, at the time of filing such application, all the consents and powers of attorney required to be furnished by such broker or dealer and by each general partner or managing agent thereof; *Provided, however,* That where an application for registration of a broker or dealer is pending at the time this rule becomes effective such consents and powers of attorney shall be furnished within 30 days after this rule becomes effective.

(3) Each broker or dealer registered or applying for registration who or which becomes a nonresident broker or dealer after the effective date of this rule, and each general partner or managing agent, of an unincorporated broker or dealer registered or applying for registration, who becomes a nonresident after the effective date of this rule, shall furnish such consent and power of attorney within 30 days thereafter.

(c) Service of any process, pleadings or other papers on the Commission under this part shall be made by delivering the requisite number of copies thereof to the Secretary of the Commission or to such other person as the Commission may authorize to act in its behalf. Whenever any process, pleadings or other papers as aforesaid are served upon the Commission, it shall promptly forward a copy thereof by registered or certified mail to the appropriate defendants at their last address of record filed with the Commission. The Commission shall be furnished a sufficient number of copies for such purpose, and one copy for its file.

(d) For purposes of this rule the following definitions shall apply:

(1) The term "broker" shall have the meaning set out in section 3(a)(4) of the Act.

(2) The term "dealer" shall have the meaning set out in section 3(a)(5) of the Act.

(3) The term "managing agent" shall mean any person, including a trustee, who directs or manages or who participated in the directing or managing of the affairs of any unincorporated organization or association which is not a partnership.

(4) The term "nonresident broker or dealer" shall mean

(A) In the case of an individual, one who resides in or has his principal place of business in any place not subject to the jurisdiction of the United States;

(B) In the case of a corporation, one incorporated in or having its principal place of business in any place not subject to the jurisdiction of the United States;

(C) In the case of a partnership or other unincorporated organization or association, one having its principal place of business in any place not subject to the jurisdiction of the United States.

(5) A general partner or managing agent of a broker or dealer shall be deemed to be a nonresident if he resides in any place not subject to the jurisdiction of the United States.

Rule 15b1–6. Notice to Brokers and Dealers of Requirements Regarding Lost Securityholders and Unresponsive Payees

Brokers and dealers are hereby notified of Rule 17Ad–17 (§ 240.17Ad–17), which addresses certain requirements with respect to lost securityholders and unresponsive payees that may be applicable to them.

Rule 15b2–2. Inspection of Newly Registered Brokers and Dealers

(a) *Definition.* For the purpose of this rule the term "applicable financial responsibility rules" shall include: (1) Any rule adopted by the Commission pursuant to sections 8, 15(c)(3), 17(a), or 17(e)(1)(A) of the Act; (2) any rule adopted by the Commission relating to hypothecation or lending of customer securities; (3) any other rule adopted by the Commission relating to the protection of funds or securities; and (4) any rule adopted by the Secretary of the Treasury pursuant to section 15C(b)(1) of the Act.

(b) Each self-regulatory organization that has responsibility for examining a broker or dealer member (including members that are government securities brokers or government securities dealers registered pursuant to section 15C(a)(1)(A) of the Act) for compliance with applicable financial responsibility rules is authorized and directed to conduct an inspection of the member, within six months of the member's registration with the Commission, to determine whether the member is operating in conformity with applicable financial responsibility rules.

(c) The examining self-regulatory organization is further authorized and directed to conduct an inspection of the member no later than twelve months from the member's registration with the Commission, to determine whether the member is operating in conformity with all other applicable provisions of the Act and rules thereunder.

(d) In each case where the examining self-regulatory organization determines that a broker or dealer member has not commenced actual operations within six months of the member's registration with the Commission, it shall delay the inspection pursuant to this rule until the second six month period from the member's registration with the Commission.

(e) No inspection need be conducted as provided for in paragraphs (b) and (c) of this rule if:

(1) The member was registered with the Commission prior to April 26, 1982;

(2) An inspection of the member has already been conducted by another self-regulatory organization pursuant to this rule;

(3) An inspection of the member has already been conducted by the Commission pursuant to section 15(b)(2)(C) of the Act, or

(4) The member is registered with the Commission pursuant to section 15(b)(11)(A) of the Act.

Rule 15b3–1. Amendments to Applications

(a) If the information contained in any application for registration as a broker or dealer, or in any amendment thereto, is or becomes inaccurate for any reason, the broker or dealer shall promptly file with the Central Registration Depository (operated by the Financial Industry Regulatory Authority, Inc.) an amendment on Form BD correcting such information.

(b) Every amendment filed with the Central Registration Depository pursuant to this rule shall constitute a "report" filed with the Commission within the meaning of sections 15(b), 17(a), 18(a), 32(a) of the Act and other applicable provisions of the Act.

Rule 15b5–1. Extension of Registration for Purposes of the Securities Investor Protection Act of 1970 After Cancellation or Revocation

Commission revocation or cancellation of the registration of a broker or dealer pursuant to section 15(b) of the Act: (i) shall be effective for all purposes, except as hereinafter provided, on the date of the order of revocation or cancellation or, if such order is stayed, on the date the stay is terminated; and (ii) shall be effective six months after the date of the order of revocation or cancellation (or, if such order is stayed, the date the stay is terminated) with respect to a broker's or dealer's registration status as a member within the meaning of Section 3(a)(2) of the Securities Investor Protection Act of 1970 for purposes of the application of sections 5, 6, and 7 thereof to customer claims arising prior to the date of the order of revocation or cancellation (or, if such order is stayed, the date the stay is terminated).

Rule 15b6–1. Withdrawal From Registration

(a) Notice of withdrawal from registration as a broker or dealer pursuant to section 15(b) of the Act shall be filed on Form BDW in accordance with the instructions contained therein. Every notice of withdrawal from registration as a broker or dealer shall be filed with the Central Registration Depository (operated by the Financial Industry Regulatory Authority, Inc.) in accordance with applicable filing requirements. Prior to filing a notice of withdrawal from registration on Form BDW, a broker or dealer shall amend Form BD in accordance with Rule 15b3–1(a) under the Act to update any inaccurate information.

(b) A notice of withdrawal from registration filed by a broker or dealer pursuant to section 15(b) of the Act shall become effective for all matters (except as provided in this paragraph (b) and in paragraph (c) of this rule) on the 60th day after the filing thereof with the Commission, within such longer period of time as to which such broker or dealer consents or which the Commission by order may determine as necessary or appropriate in the public interest or for the protection of investors, or within such shorter period of time as the Commission may determine. If a notice of withdrawal from registration is filed with the Commission at any time subsequent to the date of the issuance of a Commission order instituting proceedings pursuant to section 15(b) of the Act to censure, place limitations on the activities, functions or operations of, or suspend or revoke the registration of, such broker or dealer, or if prior to the effective date of the notice of withdrawal pursuant to this paragraph (b), the Commission institutes such a proceeding or a proceeding to impose terms or conditions upon such withdrawal, the notice of withdrawal shall not become effective pursuant to this paragraph (b) except at such time and upon such terms and conditions as the Commission deems necessary or appropriate in the public interest or for the protection of investors.

(c) With respect to a broker's or dealer's registration status as a member within the meaning of section 3(a)(2) of the Securities Investor Protection Act of 1970 for purposes of the application of Sections 5, 6, and 7 thereof to customer claims arising prior to the effective date of withdrawal pursuant to paragraph (b) of this rule, the effective date of a broker's or dealer's withdrawal from registration pursuant to this paragraph (c) shall be six months after the effective date of withdrawal pursuant to paragraph (b) of this rule or such shorter period of time as the Commission may determine.

(d) Every notice of withdrawal filed with the Central Registration Depository pursuant to this rule shall constitute a "report" filed with the Commission within the meaning of sections 15(b), 17(a), 18(a), 32(a) of the Act and other applicable provisions of the Act.

(e) The Commission, by order, may exempt any broker or dealer from the filing requirements provided in Form BDW under conditions that differ from the filing instructions contained in Form BDW.

Rule 15b7–1. Compliance With Qualification Requirements of Self-Regulatory Organizations

No registered broker or dealer shall effect any transaction in, or induce the purchase or sale of, any security unless any natural person associated with such broker or dealer who effects or is involved in effecting such transaction is registered or approved in accordance with the standards of training, experience, competence, and other qualification standards (including but not limited to submitting and maintaining all required forms, paying all required fees, and passing any required examinations) established by the rules of any national securities exchange or national securities association of which such broker or dealer is a member or under the rules of the Municipal Securities Rulemaking Board (if it is subject to the rules of that organization).

Rule 15b9–1. Exemption for Certain Exchange Members

(a) Any broker or dealer required by section 15(b)(8) of the Act to become a member of a registered national securities association shall be exempt from such requirement if it:

(1) Is a member of a national securities exchange,

    (2)   Carries no customer accounts, and

    (3)   Has annual gross income derived from purchases and sales of securities otherwise than on a national securities exchange of which it is a member in an amount no greater than $1,000.

    (b)   The gross income limitation contained in paragraph (a) of this rule, shall not apply to income derived from transactions

    (1)   For the dealer's own account with or through another registered broker or dealer or

    (2)   Through the Intermarket Trading System.

    (c)   For purposes of this rule, the term "Intermarket Trading System" shall mean the intermarket communications linkage operated jointly by certain self-regulatory organizations pursuant to a plan filed with, and approved by, the Commission pursuant to Rule 608 of Regulation NMS.

Rule 15b9–2. Exemption From SRO Membership for OTC Derivatives Dealers

An OTC derivatives dealer, as defined in Rule 3b–12 under the Exchange, shall be exempt from any requirement under section 15(b)(8) of the Act to become a member of a registered national securities association.

Rule 15b11–1. Registration by Notice of Security Futures Product Broker-Dealers

    (a)   A broker or dealer may register by notice pursuant to section 15(b)(11)(A) of the Act if it:

    (1)   Is registered with the Commodity Futures Trading Commission as a futures commission merchant or an introducing broker, as those terms are defined in the Commodity Exchange Act respectively;

    (2)   Is a member of the National Futures Association or another national securities association registered under section 15A(k) of the Act; and

    (3)   Is not required to register as a broker or dealer in connection with transactions in securities other than security futures products.

    (b)   A broker or dealer registering by notice pursuant to section 15(b)(11)(A) of the Act must file Form BD–N (17 CFR 249.501b) in accordance with the instructions to the form. A broker or dealer registering by notice pursuant to this rule must indicate where appropriate on Form BD–N that it satisfies all of the conditions in paragraph (a) of this rule.

    (c)   If the information contained in any notice of registration filed on Form BD–N (17 CFR 249.501b) pursuant to this rule is or becomes inaccurate for any reason, the broker or dealer shall promptly file an amendment on Form BD–N correcting such information.

    (d)   An application for registration by notice, and any amendments thereto, that are filed on Form BD–N (17 CFR 249.501b) pursuant to this rule will be considered a "report" filed with the Commission for purposes of sections 15(b), 17(a), 18(a), 32(a) and other applicable provisions of the Act.

RULES RELATING TO OVER-THE-COUNTER MARKETS

Rule 15c1–1. Definitions

As used in any rule adopted pursuant to section 15(c)(1) of the Act:

    (a)   The term "customer" shall not include a broker or dealer or a municipal securities dealer; provided, however, that the term "customer" shall include a municipal securities dealer (other than a broker or dealer) with respect to transactions in securities other than municipal securities.

    (b)   The term "the completion of the transaction" means:

    (1)   In the case of a customer who purchases a security through or from a broker, dealer or municipal securities dealer, except as provided in paragraph (b)(2) of this rule, the time when such customer pays the broker, dealer or municipal securities dealer any part of the purchase

price, or, if payment is effected by a bookkeeping entry, the time when such bookkeeping entry is made by the broker, dealer or municipal securities dealer for any part of the purchase price;

(2)   In the case of a customer who purchases a security through or from a broker, dealer or municipal securities dealer and who makes payment therefor prior to the time when payment is requested or notification is given that payment is due, the time when such broker, dealer or municipal securities dealer delivers the security to or into the account of such customer;

(3)   In the case of a customer who sells a security through or to a broker, dealer or municipal securities dealer except as provided in paragraph (b)(4) of this rule, if the security is not in the custody of the broker, dealer or municipal securities dealer at the time of sale, the time when the security is delivered to the broker, dealer or municipal securities dealer at the time of sale, the time when the broker, dealer or municipal securities dealer transfers the security from the account of such customer;

(4)   In the case of a customer who sells a security through or to a broker, dealer or municipal securities dealer and who delivers such security to such broker, dealer or municipal securities dealer prior to the time when delivery is requested or notification is given that delivery is due, the time when such broker, dealer or municipal securities dealer makes payment to or into the account of such customer.

Rule 15c1-2. Fraud and Misrepresentation

(a)   The term "manipulative, deceptive, or other fraudulent device or contrivance", as used in section 15(c)(1) of the Act, is hereby defined to include any act, practice, or course of business which operates or would operate as a fraud or deceit upon any person.

(b)   The term "manipulative, deceptive, or other fraudulent device or contrivance", as used in section 15(c)(1) of the Act, is hereby defined to include any untrue statement of a material fact and any omission to state a material fact necessary in order to make the statements made, in the light of the circumstances under which they are made, not misleading, which statement or omission is made with knowledge or reasonable grounds to believe that it is untrue or misleading.

(c)   The scope of this Rule shall not be limited by any specific definitions of the term "manipulative, deceptive, or other fraudulent device or contrivance" contained in other rules adopted pursuant to section 15(c)(1) of the Act.

Rule 15c1-3. Misrepresentation by Brokers, Dealers and Municipal Securities Dealers as to Registration

The term "manipulative, deceptive, or other fraudulent device or contrivance," as used in section 15(c)(1) of the Act, is hereby defined to include any representation by a broker, dealer or municipal securities dealer that the registration of a broker or dealer, pursuant to section 15(b) of the Act, or the registration of a municipal securities dealer pursuant to section 15B(a) of the Act, or the failure of the Commission to deny or revoke such registration, indicates in any way that the Commission has passed upon or approved the financial standing, business, or conduct of such registered broker, dealer or municipal securities dealer or the merits of any security or any transaction or transactions therein.

Rule 15c1-5. Disclosure of Control

The term "manipulative, deceptive, or other fraudulent device or contrivance," as used in section 15(c)(1) of the Act, is hereby defined to include any act of any broker, dealer or municipal securities dealer controlled by, controlling, or under common control with, the issuer of any security, designed to effect with or for the account of a customer any transaction in, or to induce the purchase or sale by such customer of, such security unless such broker, dealer or municipal securities dealer, before entering into any contract with or for such customer for the purchase or sale of such security, discloses to such customer the existence of such control, and unless such disclosure, if not made in writing, is supplemented by the giving or sending of written disclosure at or before the completion of the transaction.

Rule 15c1–6. Disclosure of Interest in Distribution

The term "manipulative, deceptive, or other fraudulent device or contrivance," as used in section 15(c)(1) of the Act, is hereby defined to include any act of any broker who is acting for a customer or for both such customer and some other person, or of any dealer or municipal securities dealer who receives or has promise of receiving a fee from a customer for advising such customer with respect to securities, designed to effect with or for the account of such customer any transaction in, or to induce the purchase or sale by such customer of, any security in the primary or secondary distribution of which such broker, dealer or municipal securities dealer is participating or is otherwise financially interested unless such broker, dealer or municipal securities dealer, at or before the completion of each such transaction gives or sends to such customer written notification of the existence of such participation or interest.

Rule 15c1–7. Discretionary Accounts

(a)   The term "manipulative, deceptive, or other fraudulent device or contrivance," as used in section 15(c) of the Act, is hereby defined to include any act of any broker, dealer or municipal securities dealer designed to effect with or for any customer's account in respect to which such broker, dealer or municipal securities dealer or his agent or employee is vested with any discretionary power any transactions or purchase or sale which are excessive in size or frequency in view of the financial resources and character of such account.

(b)   The term "manipulative, deceptive, or other fraudulent device or contrivance," as used in section 15(c)(1) of the Act, is hereby defined to include any act of any broker, dealer or municipal securities dealer designed to effect with or for any customer's account in respect to which such broker, dealer or municipal securities dealer or his agent or employee is vested with any discretionary power any transaction of purchase or sale unless immediately after effecting such transaction such broker, dealer or municipal securities dealer makes a record of such transaction which record includes the name of such customer, the name, amount and price of the security, and the date and time when such transaction took place.

Rule 15c1–8. Sales at the Market

The term "manipulative, deceptive, or other fraudulent device or contrivance," as used in section 15(c)(1) of the Act, is hereby defined to include any representation made to a customer by a broker, dealer or municipal securities dealer who is participating or otherwise financially interested in the primary or secondary distribution of any security which is not admitted to trading on a national securities exchange that such security is being offered to such customer "at the market" or at a price related to the market price unless such broker, dealer or municipal securities dealer knows or has reasonable grounds to believe that a market for such security exists other than that made, created, or controlled by him, or by any person for whom he is acting or with whom he is associated in such distribution, or by any person controlled by, controlling or under common control with him.

Rule 15c1–9. Use of Pro Forma Balance Sheets

The term "manipulative, deceptive, or other fraudulent device or contrivance", as used in section 15(c)(1) of the Act, is hereby defined to include the use of financial statements purporting to give effect to the receipt and application of any part of the proceeds from the sale or exchange of securities, unless the assumptions upon which each such financial statement is based are clearly set forth as part of the caption to each such statement in type at least as large as that used generally in the body of the statement.

Rule 15c2–1. Hypothecation of Customers' Securities

(a)   *General provisions.* The term "fraudulent, deceptive, or manipulative act or practice", as used in section 15(c)(2) of the Act, is hereby defined to include the direct or indirect hypothecation by a broker or dealer, or his arranging for or permitting, directly or indirectly, the continued hypothecation of any securities carried for the account of any customer under circumstances:

(1)   That will permit the commingling of securities carried for the account of any such customer with securities carried for the account of any other customer, without first obtaining the written consent of each such customer to such hypothecation;

(2)   That will permit such securities to be commingled with securities carried for the account of any person other than a bona fide customer of such broker or dealer under a lien for a loan made to such broker or dealer; or

(3)   That will permit securities carried for the account of customers to be hypothecated, or subjected to any lien or liens or claims or claims of the pledgee or pledgees, for a sum which exceeds the aggregate indebtedness of all customers in respect of securities carried for their accounts; except that this clause shall not be deemed to be violated by reason of an excess arising on any day through the reduction of the aggregate indebtedness of customers on such day, provided that funds or securities in an amount sufficient to eliminate such excess are paid or placed in transfer to pledgees for the purpose of reducing the sum of the liens or claims to which securities carried for the account of customers are subject as promptly as practicable after such reduction occurs, but before the lapse of one half hour after the commencement of banking hours on the next banking day at the place where the largest principal amount of loans of such broker or dealer are payable and, in any event, before such broker or dealer on such day has obtained or increased any bank loan collateralized by securities carried for the account of customers.

(b)   *Definitions.* For the purposes of this rule:

(1)   The term customer shall not include any general or special partner or any director or officer of such broker or dealer, or any participant, as such, in any joint, group or syndicate account with such broker or dealer or with any partner, officer or director thereof. The term also shall not include a counterparty who has delivered collateral to an OTC derivatives dealer pursuant to a transaction in an eligible OTC derivative instrument, or pursuant to the OTC derivatives dealer's cash management securities activities or ancillary portfolio management securities activities, and who has received a prominent written notice from the OTC derivatives dealer that:

(i)   Except as otherwise agreed in writing by the OTC derivatives dealer and the counterparty, the dealer may repledge or otherwise use the collateral in its business;

(ii)   In the event of the OTC derivatives dealer's failure, the counterparty will likely be considered an unsecured creditor of the dealer as to that collateral;

(iii)   The Securities Investor Protection Act of 1970 does not protect the counterparty; and

(iv)   The collateral will not be subject to the requirements of Rules 8c–1, 15c2–1, 15c3–2, or 15c3–3 under the Exchange Act;

(2)   The term "securities carried for the account of any customer" shall be deemed to mean:

(i)   Securities received by or on behalf of such broker or dealer for the account of any customer;

(ii)   Securities sold and appropriated by such broker or dealer to a customer, except that if such securities were subject to a lien when appropriated to a customer they shall not be deemed to be "securities carried for the account of any customer" pending their release from such lien as promptly as practicable;

(iii)   Securities sold, but not appropriated, by such broker or dealer to a customer who has made any payment therefor, to the extent that such broker or dealer owns and has received delivery of securities of like kind, except that if such securities were subject to a lien when such payment was made they shall not be deemed to be "securities carried for the account of any customer" pending their release from such lien as promptly as practicable;

(3)   "Aggregate indebtedness" shall not be deemed to be reduced by reason of uncollected items. In computing aggregate indebtedness, related guaranteed and guarantor accounts shall be treated as a single account and considered on a consolidated basis, and balances in accounts carrying both long and short positions shall be adjusted by treating the market value of the securities required to cover such short positions as though such market value were a debit; and

(4)   In computing the sum of the liens or claims to which securities carried for the account of customers of a broker or dealer are subject, any rehypothecation of such securities by another broker or dealer who is subject to this rule or to Rule 8c–1 shall be disregarded.

(c)   *Exemption for cash accounts.* The provisions of paragraph (a)(1) of this rule shall not apply to any hypothecation of securities carried for the account of a customer in a special cash account within the meaning of Item 4(c) of Regulation T: *Provided,* That at or before the completion of the transaction of purchase of such securities for, or of sale of such securities to, such customer, written notice is given or sent to such customer disclosing that such securities are or may be hypothecated under circumstances which will permit the commingling thereof with securities carried for the account of other customers. The term "the completion of the transaction" shall have the meaning given to such term by Rule 15c1-1(b).

(d)   *Exemption for clearing house liens.* The provisions of paragraphs (a)(2), (a)(3), and (f) of this rule shall not apply to any lien or claim of the clearing corporation, or similar department or association, of a national securities exchange or a registered national securities association, for a loan made and to be repaid on the same calendar day, which is incidental to the clearing of transactions in securities or loans through such corporation, department, or association: *Provided, however,* That for the purpose of paragraph (a)(3) of this rule, "aggregate indebtedness of all customers in respect of securities carried for their accounts" shall not include indebtedness in respect of any securities subject to any lien or claim exempted by this paragraph.

(e)   *Exemption for certain liens on securities of noncustomers.* The provisions of paragraph (a)(2) of this rule shall not be deemed to prevent such broker or dealer from permitting securities not carried for the account of a customer to be subjected (1) to a lien for a loan made against securities carried for the account of customers, or (2) to a lien for a loan made and to be repaid on the same calendar day. For the purpose of this exemption, a loan shall be deemed to be "made against securities carried for the account of customers" if only securities carried for the account of customers are used to obtain or to increase such loan or as substitutes for other securities carried for the account of customers.

(f)   *Notice and certification requirements.* No person subject to this rule shall hypothecate any security carried for the account of a customer unless, at or prior to the time of each such hypothecation, he gives written notice to the pledgee that the security pledged is carried for the account of a customer and that such hypothecation does not contravene any provision of this rule, except that in the case of an omnibus account the broker or dealer for whom such account is carried may furnish a signed statement to the person carrying such account that all securities carried therein by such broker or dealer will be securities carried for the account of his customers and that the hypothecation thereof by such broker or dealer will not contravene any provision of this rule. The provisions of this paragraph shall not apply to any hypothecation of securities under any lien or claim of a pledgee securing a loan made and to be repaid on the same calendar day.

(g)   The fact that securities carried for the accounts of customers and securities carried for the accounts of others are represented by one or more certificates in the custody of a clearing corporation or other subsidiary organization of either a national securities exchange or of a registered national securities association, or of a custodian bank, in accordance with a system for the central handling of securities established by a national securities exchange or a registered national securities association, pursuant to which system the hypothecation of such securities is effected by bookkeeping entries without physical delivery of such securities, shall not, in and of itself, result in a commingling of securities prohibited by paragraph (a)(1) or (a)(2) of this rule, whenever a participating member, broker or dealer hypothecates securities in accordance with such system: *Provided, however,* That

(1)   Any such custodian of any securities held by or for such system shall agree that it will not for any reason, including the assertion of any claim, right or lien of any kind, refuse or refrain from promptly delivering any such securities (other than securities then hypothecated in accordance with such system) to such clearing corporation or other subsidiary organization or as directed by it, except that nothing in such agreement shall be deemed to require the custodian to deliver any securities in contravention of any notice of levy, seizure or similar notice, or order or judgment, issued or directed by a governmental agency or court, or officer thereof, having jurisdiction over such custodian, which on its face affects such securities;

(2)   Such systems shall have safeguards in the handling, transfer and delivery of securities and provisions for fidelity bond coverage of the employees and agents of the clearing corporation or other subsidiary organization and for periodic examinations by independent public accountants; and

(3)   The provisions of this paragraph (g) shall not be effective with respect to any particular system unless the agreement required by paragraph (g)(1) of this rule and the safeguards and

provisions required by paragraph (g)(2) of this rule shall have been deemed adequate by the Commission for the protection of investors, and unless any subsequent amendments to such agreement, safeguards or provisions shall have been deemed adequate by the Commission for the protection of investors.

Rule 15c2–4. Transmission or Maintenance of Payments Received in Connection With Underwritings

It shall constitute a "fraudulent, deceptive, or manipulative act or practice" as used in section 15(c)(2) of the Act, for any broker, dealer or municipal securities dealer participating in any distribution of securities, other than a firm-commitment underwriting, to accept any part of the sale price of any security being distributed unless:

(a) The money or other consideration received is promptly transmitted to the persons entitled thereto; or

(b) If the distribution is being made on an "all-or-none" basis, or on any other basis which contemplates that payment is not to be made to the person on whose behalf the distribution is being made until some further event or contingency occurs,

(1) The money or other consideration received is promptly deposited in a separate bank account, as agent or trustee for the persons who have the beneficial interests therein, until the appropriate event or contingency has occurred, and then the funds are promptly transmitted or returned to the persons entitled thereto, or

(2) All such funds are promptly transmitted to a bank which has agreed in writing to hold all such funds in escrow for the persons who have the beneficial interests therein and to transmit or return such funds directly to the persons entitled thereto when the appropriate event or contingency has occurred.

Rule 15c2–5. Disclosure and Other Requirements When Extending or Arranging Credit in Certain Transactions

(a) It shall constitute a "fraudulent, deceptive, or manipulative act or practice" as used in section 15(c)(2) of the Act for any broker or dealer to offer or sell any security to, or to attempt to induce the purchase of any security by, any person, in connection with which such broker or dealer directly or indirectly offers to extend any credit to or to arrange any loan for such person, or extends to or participates in arranging any loan for such person, unless such broker or dealer, before any purchase, loan or other related element of the transaction is entered into:

(1) Delivers to such person a written statement setting forth the exact nature and extent of

(i) Such person's obligations under the particular loan arrangement, including among other things, the specific charges which such person will incur under such loan in each period during which the loan may continue or be extended,

(ii) The risks and disadvantages which such person will incur in the entire transaction, including the loan arrangement,

(iii) All commissions, discounts, and other remuneration received and to be received in connection with the entire transaction including the loan arrangement, by the broker or dealer, by any person controlling, controlled by, or under common control with the broker or dealer, and by any other person participating in the transaction; *Provided, however,* That the broker or dealer shall be deemed to be in compliance with this paragraph if the customer, before any purchase, loan, or other related element of the transaction is entered into in a manner legally binding upon the customer, receives a statement from the lender, or receives a prospectus or offering circular from the broker or dealer, which statement, prospectus or offering circular contains the information required by this subparagraph; and

(2) Obtains from such person information concerning his financial situation and needs, reasonably determines that the entire transaction, including the loan arrangement, is suitable for such person, and retains in his files a written statement setting forth the basis upon which the broker or

dealer made such determination; *Provided, however,* That the written statement referred to in this paragraph must be made available to the customer on request.

(b)   This rule shall not apply to any credit extended or any loan arranged by any broker or dealer subject to the provisions of Regulation T if such credit is extended or such loan is arranged, in compliance with the requirements of such regulation, only for the purpose of purchasing or carrying the security offered or sold: *Provided, however,* That notwithstanding this paragraph, the provisions of paragraph (a) shall apply in full force with respect to any transaction involving the extension of or arrangement for credit by a broker or dealer (i) in a special insurance premium funding account within the meaning of section 4(k) of Regulation T or (ii) in compliance with the terms of Rule 13a12–5.

(c)   This rule shall not apply to any offer to extend credit or arrange any loan, or to any credit extended or loan arranged, in connection with any offer or sale, or attempt to induce the purchase, of any municipal security.

(d)   This rule shall not apply to a transaction involving the extension of credit by an OTC derivatives dealer, as defined in Rule 3b–12 under the Act, if the transaction is exempt from the provisions of section 7(c) of the Act pursuant to Rule 36a1–1 under the Act.

Rule 15c2–6. [Reserved]

Rule 15c2–7. Identification of Quotations

(a)   It shall constitute an attempt to induce the purchase or sale of a security by making a "fictitious quotation" within the meaning of section 15(c)(2) of the Act, for any broker or dealer to furnish or submit, directly or indirectly, any quotation for a security (other than a municipal security) to an inter-dealer quotation system unless:

(1)   The inter-dealer-quotation-system is informed, if such is the case, that the quotation is furnished or submitted;

(i)   By a correspondent broker or dealer for the account or in behalf of another broker or dealer, and if so, the identity of such other broker or dealer; and/or

(ii)   In furtherance of one or more other arrangements (including a joint account, guarantee of profit, guarantee against loss, commission, markup, markdown, indication of interest and accommodation arrangement) between or among brokers or dealers, and if so, the identity of each broker or dealer participating in any such arrangement or arrangements: *Provided, however,* That the provisions of this subparagraph shall not apply if only one of the brokers or dealers participating in any such arrangement or arrangements furnishes or submits a quotation with respect to the security to an inter-dealer-quotation-system.

(2)   The inter-dealer-quotation-system to which the quotation is furnished or submitted makes it a general practice to disclose with each published quotation, by appropriate symbol or otherwise, the category or categories (paragraph (a)(1)(i) and/or (ii) of this rule) in furtherance of which the quotation is submitted, and the identities of all other brokers and dealers referred to in paragraph (a)(1) of this rule where such information is supplied to the inter-dealer-quotation-system under the provisions of paragraph (a)(1) of this rule.

(b)   It shall constitute an attempt to induce the purchase or sale of a security by making a "fictitious quotation," within the meaning of section 15(c)(2) of the Act, for a broker or dealer to enter into any correspondent or other arrangement (including a joint account, guarantee of profit, guarantee against loss, commission, markup, markdown, indication of interest and accommodation arrangement) in furtherance of which two or more brokers or dealers furnish or submit quotations with respect to a particular security unless such broker or dealer informs all brokers or dealers furnishing or submitting such quotations of the existence of such correspondent and other arrangements, and the identity of the parties thereto.

(c)   For purposes of this rule:

(1)   The term "inter-dealer-quotation-system" shall mean any system of general circulation to brokers and dealers which regularly disseminates quotations of identified brokers or dealers but shall not include a quotation sheet prepared and distributed by a broker or dealer in the regular course of his business and containing only quotations of such broker or dealer.

(2)   The term "quotation" shall mean any bid or offer, or any indication of interest (such as OW or BW) in any bid or offer.

(3)   The term "correspondent" shall mean a broker or dealer who has a direct line of communication to another broker or dealer located in a different city or geographic area.

Rule 15c2–8. Delivery of Prospectus

(a)   It shall constitute a deceptive act or practice, as those terms are used in section 15(c)(2) of the Act, for a broker or dealer to participate in a distribution of securities with respect to which a registration statement has been filed under the Securities Act of 1933 unless he complies with the requirements set forth in paragraphs (b) through (h) of this rule. For the purposes of this rule, a broker or dealer participating in the distribution shall mean any underwriter and any member or proposed member of the selling group.

(b)   In connection with an issue of securities, the issuer of which has not previously been required to file reports pursuant to sections 13(a) or 15(d) of the Act, unless such issuer has been exempted from the requirement to file reports thereunder pursuant to section 12(h) of the Act, such broker or dealer shall deliver a copy of the preliminary prospectus to any person who is expected to receive a confirmation of sale at least 48 hours prior to the sending of such confirmation. This paragraph (b) does not apply with respect to asset-backed securities that meet the requirements of General Instruction I.B.5 of Form S–3. Provided, however, this paragraph (b) shall apply to all issuances of asset-backed securities (as defined in Rule 1101(c) of this chapter) regardless of whether the issuer has previously been required to file reports pursuant to sections 13(a) or 15(d) of the Securities Exchange Act of 1934, or exempted from the requirement to file reports thereunder pursuant to section 12(h) of the Act.

(c)   Such broker or dealer shall take reasonable steps to furnish to any person who makes written request for a preliminary prospectus between the filing date and a reasonable time prior to the effective date of the registration statement to which such prospectus relates, a copy of the latest preliminary prospectus on file with the Commission. Reasonable steps shall include receiving an undertaking by the managing underwriter or underwriters to send such copy to the address given in the requests.

(d)   Such broker or dealer shall take reasonable steps to comply promptly with the written request of any person for a copy of the final prospectus relating to such securities during the period between the effective date of the registration statement and the later of either the termination of such distribution, or the expiration of the applicable 40- or 90-day period under section 4(3) of the Securities Act of 1933. Reasonable steps shall include receiving an undertaking by the managing underwriter or underwriters to send such copy to the address given in the requests. (The 40-day period referred to above shall be deemed to apply for purposes of this rule irrespective of the provisions of paragraph (b) of Rule 174 of the Securities Act of 1933.)

(e)   Such broker or dealer shall take reasonable steps

(1)   To make available a copy of the preliminary prospectus relating to such securities to each of his associated persons who is expected, prior to the effective date, to solicit customers' orders for such securities before the making of any such solicitation by such associated persons and

(2)   To make available to each such associated person a copy of any amended preliminary prospectus promptly after the filing thereof.

(f)   Such broker or dealer shall take reasonable steps to make available a copy of the final prospectus relating to such securities to each of his associated persons who is expected, after the effective date, to solicit customers orders for such securities prior to the making of any such solicitation by such associated persons, unless a preliminary prospectus which is substantially the same as the final prospectus except for matters relating to the price of the stocks, has been so made available.

(g)   If the broker or dealer is a managing underwriter of such distribution, he shall take reasonable steps to see to it that all other brokers or dealers participating in such distribution are promptly furnished with sufficient copies, as requested by them, of each preliminary prospectus, each amended preliminary prospectus and the final prospectus to enable them to comply with paragraphs (b), (c), (d), and (e) of this rule.

(h)   If the broker or dealer is a managing underwriter of such distribution, he shall take reasonable steps to see that any broker or dealer participating in the distribution or trading in the registered security is furnished reasonable quantities of the final prospectus relating to such securities, as requested by him, in order to enable him to comply with the prospectus delivery requirements of section 5(b)(1) and (2) of the Securities Act of 1933.

(i)   This rule shall not require the furnishing of prospectuses in any state where such furnishing would be unlawful under the laws of such state: *Provided, however,* That this provision is not to be construed to relieve a broker or dealer from complying with the requirements of section 5(b)(1) and (2) of the Securities Act of 1933.

Rule 15c2–11.   Publication or Submission of Quotations Without Specified Information

(a)   *Unlawful activity.* As a means reasonably designed to prevent fraudulent, deceptive, or manipulative acts or practices, it shall be unlawful for:

(1)   *Brokers or dealers.* A broker or dealer to publish any quotation for a security or, directly or indirectly, to submit any such quotation for publication, in any quotation medium, unless:

(i)(A)Such broker or dealer has in its records the documents and information specified in paragraph (b) of this rule;

(B)   Such documents and information specified in paragraph (b) of this rule (excluding paragraphs (b)(5)(i)(N) through (P) of this rule) are current and publicly available; and

(C)   Based upon a review of the documents and information specified in paragraph (b) of this rule, together with any other documents and information required by paragraph (c) of this rule, such broker or dealer has a reasonable basis under the circumstances for believing that:

(1)   The documents and information specified in paragraph (b) of this rule are accurate in all material respects; and

(2)   The sources of the documents and information specified in paragraph (b) of this rule are reliable; or

(ii)(A)   The quotation medium is a qualified interdealer quotation system that made a publicly available determination that it has performed the activities described in paragraph (a)(2)(i) through (iii) of this rule; and

(B)   Such quotation is published or submitted for publication within three business days after such qualified interdealer quotation system makes such publicly available determination.

(2)   *Qualified interdealer quotation systems.* A qualified interdealer quotation system to make known to others the quotation of a broker or dealer that is published or submitted for publication pursuant to paragraph (a)(1)(ii) of this rule, unless:

(i)   Such qualified interdealer quotation system has in its records the documents and information specified in paragraph (b) of this rule (excluding paragraphs (b)(5)(i)(N) through (P) of this rule except where the qualified interdealer quotation system has knowledge or possession of this information);

(ii)   Such documents and information specified in paragraph (b) of this rule (excluding paragraphs (b)(5)(i)(N) through (P) of this rule) are current and publicly available;

(iii)   Based upon a review of the documents and information specified in paragraph (b) of this rule (excluding paragraphs (b)(5)(i)(N) through (P) of this rule, except where the qualified interdealer quotation system has knowledge or possession of this information), together with any other documents and information required by paragraph (c) of this rule, such qualified interdealer quotation system has a reasonable basis under the circumstances for believing that:

(A)   The documents and information specified in paragraph (b) of this rule are accurate in all material respects; and

(B) The sources of the documents and information specified in paragraph (b) of this rule are reliable; and

(iv) The qualified interdealer quotation system makes a publicly available determination that it has performed the activities described in paragraphs (i) through (iii) of this paragraph (a)(2); or

(3) *Qualified interdealer quotation systems or registered national securities Associations.* A qualified interdealer quotation system or registered national securities association to make a publicly available determination described in paragraph (f)(2)(iii)(B), (f)(3)(ii)(A), or (f)(7) of this rule, unless such qualified interdealer quotation system or registered national securities association establishes, maintains, and enforces reasonably designed written policies and procedures to determine whether:

(i) The documents and information specified in paragraph (b) of this rule are current and publicly available; and

(ii) The requirements of an exception under paragraph (f) of this rule are met, if it makes a publicly available determination described in paragraph (f)(7) of this rule.

(b) *Specified information.* (1) A copy of the prospectus specified by section 10(a) of the Securities Act of 1933 for an issuer that has filed a registration statement under the Securities Act of 1933, other than a registration statement on Form F–6, that became effective less than 90 calendar days prior to the day on which such broker or dealer publishes or submits the quotation to the quotation medium; *Provided,* That such registration statement has not thereafter been the subject of a stop order that is still in effect when the quotation is published or submitted; or

(2) A copy of the offering circular provided for under Regulation A (§§ 230.251 through 230.263 of this chapter) for an issuer that has filed an offering statement under Regulation A that was qualified less than 40 calendar days prior to the day on which such broker or dealer publishes or submits the quotation to the quotation medium; *Provided,* That the Regulation A exemption, with respect to such issuer, has not thereafter become subject to a suspension order that is still in effect when the quotation is published or submitted; or

(3) A current copy of:

(i) An annual report filed pursuant to section 13 or 15(d) of the Act, together with any periodic and current reports that have been filed thereafter under the Act by the issuer, except for current reports filed during the three business days prior to the publication or submission of the quotation; *Provided, however,* That, until such issuer has filed its first such annual report, the broker, dealer, or qualified interdealer quotation system has in its records a copy of the registration statement filed by the issuer under the Securities Act of 1933, other than a registration statement on Form F–6, that became effective within the prior 16 months, or a copy of any registration statement filed by the issuer under section 12 of the Act that became effective within the prior 16 months, together with any periodic and current reports filed thereafter under section 13 or 15(d) of the Act;

(ii) An annual report filed pursuant to Regulation A, together with any periodic and current reports filed thereafter under Regulation A by the issuer, except for current reports filed during the three business days prior to the publication or submission of the quotation; *Provided, however,* That, until such issuer has filed its first such annual report, the broker, dealer, or qualified interdealer quotation system has in its records a copy of the offering statement filed by the issuer under Regulation A, that was qualified within the prior 16 months, together with any periodic and current reports filed thereafter under Regulation A;

(iii) An annual report filed pursuant to Regulation Crowdfunding (§§ 227.100 through 227.503 of this chapter); *Provided, however,* That, until such issuer has filed its first such annual report, the broker, dealer, or qualified interdealer quotation system has in its records a copy of the Form C filed by the issuer under Regulation Crowdfunding within the prior 16 months, together with any Form C/A and Form C/U filed thereafter under Regulation Crowdfunding;

(iv) An annual statement referred to in section 12(g)(2)(G)(i) of the Act (in the case of an issuer required to file reports pursuant to section 13 or 15(d) of the Act), together with any periodic and current reports filed thereafter under the Act by the issuer, except for current reports filed during the three business days prior to the publication or submission of the quotation; *Provided, however,* That, until such issuer has filed its first such annual statement, the broker, dealer, or qualified interdealer quotation system has in its records a copy of the registration statement filed by the issuer under the Securities Act of 1933, other than a registration statement on Form F–6, that became effective within the prior 16 months, or a copy of any registration statement filed by the issuer under section 12 of the Act, that became effective within the prior 16 months, together with any periodic and current reports filed thereafter under section 13 or 15(d) of the Act; or

(v)   An annual statement referred to in section 12(g)(2)(G)(i) of the Act (in the case of an issuer of a security that falls within the provisions of section 12(g)(2)(G) of the Act); or

(4)   A copy of the information that, since the first day of its most recently completed fiscal year, the issuer has published as required to establish the exemption from registration under section 12(g) of the Act pursuant to § 240.12g3–2(b) of this chapter, which the broker or dealer must make available upon the request of a person expressing an interest in a proposed transaction in the issuer's security with the broker or dealer, such as by providing the requesting person with appropriate instructions regarding how to obtain the information electronically; or

(5)(i) The following information, which must be (excluding paragraphs (b)(5)(i)(N) through (P) of this rule) as of a date within 12 months prior to the publication or submission of the quotation, unless otherwise specified:

(A)   The name of the issuer and any predecessors during the past five years;

(B)   The address(es) of the issuer's principal executive office and of its principal place of business;

(C)   The state of incorporation or registration of the issuer and of each of its predecessors (if any) during the past five years;

(D)   The title, class, and ticker symbol (if assigned) of the security;

(E)   The par or stated value of the security;

(F)   The number of shares or total amount of the securities outstanding as of the end of the issuer's most recent fiscal year;

(G)   The name and address of the transfer agent;

(H)   A description of the issuer's business;

(I)   A description of products or services offered by the issuer;

(J)   A description and extent of the issuer's facilities;

(K)   The name and title of all company insiders;

(L)   The issuer's most recent balance sheet (as of a date less than 16 months before the publication or submission of the quotation) and profit and loss and retained earnings statements (for the 12 months preceding the date of the most recent balance sheet);

(M)   Similar financial information for such part of the two preceding fiscal years as the issuer or its predecessors has been in existence;

(N)   Whether the broker or dealer or any associated person of the broker or dealer is affiliated, directly or indirectly, with the issuer;

(O)   Whether the quotation is being published or submitted on behalf of any other broker or dealer and, if so, the name of such broker or dealer; and

(P)   Whether the quotation is being submitted or published, directly or indirectly, by or on behalf of the issuer or a company insider and, if so, the name of such person and the basis for any exemption under the federal securities laws for any sales of such securities on behalf of such person.

(ii)   The broker or dealer must make the documents and information specified in paragraph (b)(5)(i) of this rule available upon the request of a person expressing an interest in a proposed transaction in the issuer's security with the broker or dealer, such as by providing the requesting person with appropriate instructions regarding how to obtain such publicly available documents and information electronically. If such information is made available to others upon request pursuant to this paragraph, such delivery, unless otherwise represented, shall not constitute a representation by such broker or dealer that such information is accurate but shall constitute a representation by such broker or dealer that the information is current in relation to the day the quotation is submitted, the broker or dealer has a reasonable basis under the circumstances for believing the information is accurate in all material respects, and the information was obtained from sources that the broker or dealer has a reasonable basis under the circumstances for believing are reliable. The documents and information specified in paragraph (b)(5) of this rule must be reviewed where paragraphs (b)(1) through (b)(4) of this rule do not apply to such issuer. For purposes of compliance with paragraph (a)(1)(i)(B) or (a)(2)(ii) of this rule, the documents and information specified in paragraph (b)(5) of this rule must be reviewed for an issuer for which the documents and information specified in paragraph (b)(1), (b)(2), (b)(3), or (b)(4) of this rule regarding such issuer are not current.

(c)   *Supplemental information.* With respect to any security the quotation of which is within the provisions of this rule, the broker or dealer submitting or publishing such quotation, or any qualified interdealer quotation system that makes known to others the quotation of a broker or dealer pursuant to paragraph (a)(2) of this rule, shall have in its records the following documents and information:

    (1)   Records related to the submission or publication of such quotation, including the identity of the person or persons for whom the quotation is being published or submitted, whether such person or persons is the issuer or a company insider, and any information regarding the transactions provided to the broker, dealer, or qualified interdealer quotation system by such person or persons;

    (2)   A copy of any trading suspension order issued by the Commission pursuant to section 12(k) of the Act regarding any securities of the issuer or its predecessor (if any) during the 12 months preceding the date of the publication or submission of the quotation or a copy of the public release issued by the Commission announcing such trading suspension order; and

    (3)   A copy or a written record of any other material information (including adverse information) regarding the issuer that comes to the knowledge or possession of the broker, dealer, or qualified interdealer quotation system before the publication or submission of the quotation.

(d)   *Recordkeeping.* (1)(i) The following persons shall preserve for a period of not less than three years, the first two years in an easily accessible place, the documents and information required under paragraphs (a), (b), and (c) of this rule, except for the documents and information that are available on the Commission's *Electronic Data Gathering, Analysis and Retrieval System* (EDGAR):

      (A)   Any broker or dealer that publishes or submits a quotation pursuant to paragraph (a)(1) of this rule for a security; or

      (B)   Any qualified interdealer quotation system that makes known to others the quotation of a broker or dealer pursuant to paragraph (a)(2) of this rule for a security;

      (ii)   Any broker or dealer that publishes or submits a quotation pursuant to paragraph (a)(1)(ii) of this rule shall preserve for a period of not less than three years, the first two years in an easily accessible place, the name of the qualified interdealer quotation system that made a publicly available determination that it has performed the activities described in paragraph (a)(2)(i) through (iii) of this rule.

    (2)   The following persons shall preserve for a period of not less than three years, the first two years in an easily accessible place, the documents and information that demonstrate that the requirements for an exception under paragraph (f)(2), (f)(3), (f)(5), (f)(6), or (f)(7) of this rule are met, except for the documents and information that are available on EDGAR:

      (i)   Any qualified interdealer quotation system or registered national securities association that makes a publicly available determination described in paragraph (f)(2)(iii)(B), (f)(3)(ii)(A), or (f)(7) of this rule; and

      (ii)   Any broker or dealer that publishes or submits a quotation pursuant to paragraph (f) of this rule; *Provided, however,* That any broker or dealer that relies on a publicly available determination described in paragraph (f)(2)(iii)(B) or (f)(3)(ii)(A) of this rule shall preserve only a record of the name of the qualified interdealer quotation system or registered national securities association that determined whether the documents and information specified in paragraph (b) of this rule are current and publicly available in addition to the documents and information that demonstrate that the other requirements of the exception provided in paragraph (f)(2) or (f)(3), respectively, are met; and that any broker or dealer that relies on a publicly available determination described in paragraph (f)(7) of this rule shall preserve only a record of the exception provided in paragraph (f)(1), (f)(3)(i), (f)(4), or (f)(5) for which the publicly available determination is made and the name of the qualified interdealer quotation system or registered national securities association that determined that the requirements of that exception are met.

(e) *Definitions.* For purposes of this rule:

(1) *Company insider* shall mean any officer or director of the issuer, or person that performs a similar function, or any person who is, directly or indirectly, the beneficial owner of more than 10 percent of the outstanding units or shares of any class of any equity security of the issuer.

(2) *Current* shall mean, for the documents and information specified in:

(i) Paragraph (b)(1), (b)(2), (b)(4), or (b)(5) of this rule, filed, published, or are as of a date in accordance with the time frames specified in the applicable paragraph for such documents and information; or

(ii) Paragraph (b)(3) of this rule, the most recently required annual report or statement filed pursuant to section 13 or 15(d) of the Act and any rule(s) thereunder, Regulation A, Regulation Crowdfunding, or section 12(G)(2)(g) of the Act, together with any subsequently required periodic reports or statements, filed pursuant to section 13 or 15(d) of the Act and any rule(s) thereunder, Regulation A, Regulation Crowdfunding, or section 12(G)(2)(g) of the Act.

(3) *Interdealer quotation system* shall mean any system of general circulation to brokers or dealers that regularly disseminates quotations of identified brokers or dealers.

(4) *Issuer*, in the case of quotations for American Depositary Receipts, shall mean the issuer of the deposited shares represented by such American Depositary Receipts.

(5) *Publicly available* shall mean available on EDGAR; on the website of a state or federal agency, a qualified interdealer quotation system, a registered national securities association, an issuer, or a registered broker or dealer; or through an electronic information delivery system that is generally available to the public in the primary trading market of a foreign private issuer as defined in § 240.3b–4 of this chapter; *Provided, however,* That *publicly available* shall mean where access is not restricted by user name, password, fees, or other restraints.

(6) *Qualified interdealer quotation system* shall mean any interdealer quotation system that meets the definition of an "alternative trading system" under § 242.300(a) of this chapter and operates pursuant to the exemption from the definition of an "exchange" under § 240.3a1–1(a)(2) of this chapter.

(7) Except as otherwise specified in this rule, *quotation* shall mean any bid or offer at a specified price with respect to a security, or any indication of interest by a broker or dealer in receiving bids or offers from others for a security, or any indication by a broker or dealer that wishes to advertise its general interest in buying or selling a particular security.

(8) *Quotation medium* shall mean any "interdealer quotation system" or any publication or electronic communications network or other device that is used by brokers or dealers to make known to others their interest in transactions in any security, including offers to buy or sell at a stated price or otherwise, or invitations of offers to buy or sell.

(9) *Shell company* shall mean any issuer, other than a business combination related shell company, as defined in § 230.405 of this chapter, or an asset-backed issuer as defined in Item 1101(b) of Regulation AB (§ 229.1101(b) of this chapter), that has:

(i) No or nominal operations; and

(ii) Either:

(A) No or nominal assets;

(B) Assets consisting solely of cash and cash equivalents; or

(C) Assets consisting of any amount of cash and cash equivalents and nominal other assets.

(f) *Exceptions.* Except as provided in paragraph (d)(2) of this rule, the provisions of this rule shall not apply to:

(1) The publication or submission of a quotation for a security that is admitted to trading on a national securities exchange and that is traded on such an exchange on the same day as, or on the business day next preceding, the day the quotation is published or submitted.

(2)(i) The publication or submission by a broker or dealer, solely on behalf of a customer (other than a person acting as or for a dealer), of a quotation that represents the customer's unsolicited indication of interest;

(ii) *Provided, however,* That this paragraph (f)(2) shall not apply to a quotation:

(A) Consisting of both a bid and an offer, each of which is at a specified price, unless the quotation medium specifically identifies the quotation as representing such an unsolicited customer interest; or

(B) Published or submitted, directly or indirectly on behalf of a company insider or affiliate as defined in § 230.144(a)(1) of this chapter, unless the documents and information specified in paragraph (b) of this rule are current and publicly available.

(iii) For purposes of this paragraph (f)(2)(ii)(B), a broker or dealer that publishes or submits quotations may rely on either a:

(A) Written representation from the customer's broker that such customer is not a company insider or an affiliate if:

(1) Such representation is received prior to, and on the same day that, the quotation representing the customer's unsolicited indication of interest is published or submitted; and

(2) The broker or dealer has a reasonable basis under the circumstances for believing that the customer's broker is a reliable source; or

(B) Publicly available determination by a qualified interdealer quotation system or registered national securities association that the documents and information specified in paragraph (b) of this rule are current and publicly available.

(3)(i)(A) The publication or submission, in an interdealer quotation system that specifically identifies as such unsolicited customer indications of interest of the kind described in paragraph (f)(2) of this rule, of a quotation for a security that has been the subject of a bid or offer quotation (exclusive of any identified customer interests) in such a system at a specified price, with no more than four business days in succession without such a quotation;

(B) *Provided, however,* That this paragraph (f)(3) shall not apply to a quotation that is published or submitted by a broker or dealer for the security of an issuer that:

(1) Was the subject of a trading suspension order issued by the Commission pursuant to section 12(k) of the Act until 60 calendar days after the expiration of such order;

(2) Such broker or dealer, or any qualified interdealer quotation system or registered national securities association, has a reasonable basis under the circumstances for believing is a shell company, unless such quotation is published or submitted within the 18 months following the initial quotation for such issuer's security that is the subject of a bid or offer quotation in an interdealer quotation system at a specified price;

(C) *Provided further,* That this paragraph (f)(3) shall apply to the publication or submission of a quotation for a security of an issuer only if the documents and information regarding such issuer that are specified in:

(1)   Paragraph (b)(3)(i), (b)(3)(iv), or (b)(3)(v) of this rule are filed within 180 calendar days from the end of the issuer's most recent fiscal year or any quarterly reporting period that is covered by a report required by section 13 or 15(d) of the Act, as applicable;

(2)   Paragraph (b)(3)(ii) or (b)(3)(iii) of this rule are timely filed;

(3)   Paragraph (b)(4) or (b)(5)(i) (excluding paragraphs (b)(5)(i)(N) through (P)) are current and publicly available; or

(4)   Paragraph (b)(3)(i), (b)(3)(ii), (b)(3)(iii), (b)(3)(iv), or (b)(3)(v) are filed within 15 calendar days starting on the date on which a publicly available determination is made pursuant to paragraph (f)(3)(ii)(A) of this rule; or

(ii) If the documents and information specified in paragraph (b) of this rule (excluding paragraphs (b)(5)(i)(N) through (P)) regarding an issuer are no longer current and publicly available, timely filed, or filed within 180 calendar days, as specified in paragraph (f)(3)(i)(C) of this rule, a broker or dealer may continue to publish or submit a quotation for such issuer's security in an interdealer quotation system during the time frame specified in in paragraph (f)(3)(ii)(C) if:

(A)   Within the first four business days that such documents and information are no longer current and publicly available, timely filed, or filed within 180 calendar days, as applicable, a qualified interdealer quotation system or registered national securities association makes a publicly available determination that:

(1)   Such documents and information are no longer current and publicly available, timely filed, or filed within 180 calendar days, as specified in paragraph (f)(3)(i)(C) of this rule; and

(2)   The exception provided in paragraph (f)(3)(ii) of this rule is available only during the 15 calendar days starting on the date on which the publicly available determination described in paragraph (f)(3)(ii)(A)(*1*) of this rule is made; and

(B)   The broker or dealer complies with the requirements of paragraphs (d)(2) and (f)(3)(i) of this rule, except for the requirement that the documents and information specified in paragraph (b) (excluding paragraphs (b)(5)(i)(N) through (P)) regarding such issuer be current and publicly available, timely filed, or filed within 180 calendar days, as applicable;

(C)   *Provided, however,* That the provisions of this paragraph (f)(3)(ii) shall apply only during the shorter of the period beginning with the date on which a qualified interdealer quotation system or registered national securities association makes a publicly available determination identified in paragraph (f)(3)(ii)(A) and ending on:

(1)   The date on which the documents and information specified in paragraph (b) (excluding paragraphs (b)(5)(i)(N) through (P)) regarding such issuer become current and publicly available or filed; or

(2)   The fourteenth calendar day following the date on which such publicly available determination was made.

(3)   The publication or submission of a quotation for a municipal security.

(4)   The publication or submission of a quotation for:

(i)   A security with a worldwide average daily trading volume value of at least $100,000 reported during the 60 calendar days immediately before the publication of the quotation of such security; and

(ii) The issuer of such security has at least $50 million in total assets and $10 million in shareholders' equity as reflected in the issuer's publicly available audited balance sheet issued within six months after the end of its most recent fiscal year.

(6)   The publication or submission of a quotation for a security by a broker or dealer that is named as an underwriter in a registration statement for an offering of that class of security referenced in paragraph (b)(1) of this rule or in an offering statement for an offering of that class of security referenced in paragraph (b)(2) of this rule; *Provided, however,* That this paragraph (f)(6) shall apply only to the publication or submission of a quotation for such security within the time frames specified in paragraph (b)(1) or (b)(2) of this rule.

(7)   The publication or submission of a quotation by a broker or dealer that relies on a publicly available determination by a qualified interdealer quotation system or registered national securities association that the requirements of an exception provided in paragraph (f)(1), (f)(3)(i), (f)(4), or (f)(5) of this rule are met; *Provided, however,* That any qualified interdealer quotation system or registered national securities association that makes a publicly available determination that the requirements of the exception provided in paragraph (f)(3)(i) of this rule are met must subsequently make a publicly available determination under paragraph (f)(3)(ii)(A) of this rule, as applicable.

(g)   *Exemptive authority.* Upon written application or upon its own motion, the Commission may, conditionally or unconditionally, exempt by order any person, security, or transaction, or any class or classes of persons, securities, or transactions, from any provision or provisions of this rule, to the extent that such exemption is necessary or appropriate in the public interest, and is consistent with the protection of investors.

Rule 15c2–12.   Municipal Securities Disclosure

Preliminary Note: For a discussion of disclosure obligations relating to municipal securities, issuers, brokers, dealers, and municipal securities dealers should refer to Securities Act Release No. 7049, Securities Exchange Act Release No. 33741, FR–42 (March 9, 1994). For a discussion of the obligations of underwriters to have a reasonable basis for recommending municipal securities, brokers, dealers, and municipal securities dealers should refer to Securities Exchange Act Release No. 26100 (Sept. 22, 1988) and Securities Exchange Act Release No. 26985 (June 28, 1989).

(a)   *General.* As a means reasonably designed to prevent fraudulent, deceptive, or manipulative acts or practices, it shall be unlawful for any broker, dealer, or municipal securities dealer (a "Participating Underwriter" when used in connection with an Offering) to act as an underwriter in a primary offering of municipal securities with an aggregate principal amount of $1,000,000 or more (an "Offering") unless the Participating Underwriter complies with the requirements of this rule or is exempted from the provisions of this rule.

(b)   *Requirements.*

(1)   Prior to the time the Participating Underwriter bids for, purchases, offers, or sells municipal securities in an Offering, the Participating Underwriter shall obtain and review an official statement that an issuer of such securities deems final as of its date, except for the omission of no more than the following information: the offering price(s), interest rate(s), selling compensation, aggregate principal amount, principal amount per maturity, delivery dates, any other terms or provisions required by an issuer of such securities to be specified in a competitive bid, ratings, other terms of the securities depending on such matters, and the identity of the underwriter(s).

(2)   Except in competitively bid offerings, from the time the Participating Underwriter has reached an understanding with an issuer of municipal securities that it will become a Participating Underwriter in an Offering until a final official statement is available, the Participating Underwriter shall send no later than the next business day, by first class mail or other equally prompt means, to any potential customer, on request, a single copy of the most recent preliminary official statement, if any.

(3)   The Participating Underwriter shall contract with an issuer of municipal securities or its designated agent to receive, within seven business days after any final agreement to purchase, offer, or sell the municipal securities in an Offering and in sufficient time to accompany any confirmation

that requests payment from any customer, copies of a final official statement in sufficient quantity to comply with paragraph (b)(4) of this rule and the rules of the Municipal Securities Rulemaking Board.

(4)   From the time the final official statement becomes available until the earlier of (i) ninety days from the end of the underwriting period or (ii) the time when the official statement is available to any person from a nationally recognized municipal securities information repository, but in no case less than twenty five days following the end of the underwriting period, the Participating Underwriter in an Offering shall send no later than the next business day, by first class mail or other equally prompt means, to any potential customer, on request, a single copy of the final official statement.

(5)(i)   A Participating Underwriter shall not purchase or sell municipal securities in connection with an Offering unless the Participating Underwriter has reasonably determined that an issuer of municipal securities, or an obligated person for whom financial or operating data is presented in the final official statement has undertaken, either individually or in combination with other issuers of such municipal securities or obligated persons, in a written agreement or contract for the benefit of holders of such securities, to provide, either directly or indirectly through an indenture trustee or a designated agent:

(A)   To each nationally recognized municipal securities information repository and to the appropriate state information depository, if any, annual financial information for each obligated person for whom financial information or operating data is presented in the final official statement, or, for each obligated person meeting the objective criteria specified in the undertaking and used to select the obligated persons for whom financial information or operating data is presented in the final official statement, except that, in the case of pooled obligations, the undertaking shall specify such objective criteria;

(B)   If not submitted as part of the annual financial information, then when and if available, to each nationally recognized municipal securities information repository and to the appropriate state information depository, audited financial statements for each obligated person covered by paragraph (b)(5)(i)(A) of this rule;

(C)   In a timely manner not in excess of ten business days after the occurrence of the event, notice of any of the following events with respect to the securities being offered in the Offering:

(1)   Principal and interest payment delinquencies;

(2)   Non-payment related defaults, if material;

(3)   Unscheduled draws on debt service reserves reflecting financial difficulties;

(4)   Unscheduled draws on credit enhancements reflecting financial difficulties;

(5)   Substitution of credit or liquidity providers, or their failure to perform;

(6)   Adverse tax opinions, the issuance by the Internal Revenue Service of proposed or final determinations of taxability, Notices of Proposed Issue (IRS Form 5701–TEB) or other material notices or determinations with respect to the tax status of the security, or other material events affecting the tax status of the security;

(7)   Modifications to rights of security holders, if material;

(8)   Bond calls, if material, and tender offers;

(9)   Defeasances;

(10)   Release, substitution, or sale of property securing repayment of the securities, if material;

(11)   Rating changes;

(12)   Bankruptcy, insolvency, receivership or similar event of the obligated person;

NOTE to paragraph (b)(5)(i)(C)(12): For the purposes of the event identified in subparagraph (b)(5)(i)(C)(12), the event is considered to occur when any of the following occur: the appointment of a receiver, fiscal agent or similar officer for an obligated person in a proceeding under the U.S. Bankruptcy Code or in any other proceeding under state or federal law in which a court or governmental authority has assumed jurisdiction over substantially all of the assets or business of the obligated person, or if such jurisdiction has been assumed by leaving the existing governing body and officials or officers in possession but subject to the supervision and orders of a court or governmental authority, or the entry of an order confirming a plan of reorganization, arrangement or liquidation by a court or governmental authority having supervision or jurisdiction over substantially all of the assets or business of the obligated person;

(13) The consummation of a merger, consolidation, or acquisition involving an obligated person or the sale of all or substantially all of the assets of the obligated person, other than in the ordinary course of business, the entry into a definitive agreement to undertake such an action or the termination of a definitive agreement relating to any such actions, other than pursuant to its terms, if material;

(14) Appointment of a successor or additional trustee or the change of name of a trustee, if material;

(15) Incurrence of a financial obligation of the obligated person, if material, or agreement to covenants, events of default, remedies, priority rights, or other similar terms of a financial obligation of the obligated person, any of which affect security holders, if material; and

(16) Default, event of acceleration, termination event, modification of terms, or other similar events under the terms of a financial obligation of the obligated person, any of which reflect financial difficulties; and

(D) In a timely manner, to each nationally recognized municipal securities information repository or to the Municipal Securities Rulemaking Board, and to the appropriate state information depository, if any, notice of a failure of any person specified in paragraph (b)(5)(i)(A) of this rule to provide required annual financial information, on or before the date specified in the written agreement or contract.

(ii) The written agreement or contract for the benefit of holders of such securities also shall identify each person for whom annual financial information and notices of material events will be provided, either by name or by the objective criteria used to select such persons, and, for each such person shall:

(A) Specify, in reasonable detail, the type of financial information and operating data to be provided as part of annual financial information;

(B) Specify, in reasonable detail, the accounting principles pursuant to which financial statements will be prepared, and whether the financial statements will be audited; and

(C) Specify the date on which the annual financial information for the preceding fiscal year will be provided, and to whom it will be provided.

(iii) Such written agreement or contract for the benefit of holders of such securities also may provide that the continuing obligation to provide annual financial information and notices of events may be terminated with respect to any obligated person, if and when such obligated person no longer remains an obligated person with respect to such municipal securities.

(c) *Recommendations.* As a means reasonably designed to prevent fraudulent, deceptive, or manipulative acts or practices, it shall be unlawful for any broker, dealer, or municipal securities dealer to recommend the purchase or sale of a municipal security unless such broker, dealer, or municipal securities dealer has procedures in place that provide reasonable assurance that it will receive prompt notice of any event disclosed pursuant to paragraph (b)(5)(i)(C), paragraph (b)(5)(i)(D), and paragraph (d)(2)(ii)(B) of this rule with respect to that security.

(d) *Exemptions.*

(1) This rule shall not apply to a primary offering of municipal securities in authorized denominations of $100,000 or more, if such securities:

(i) Are sold to no more than thirty five persons each of whom the Participating Underwriter reasonably believes

(A) Has such knowledge and experience in financial and business matters that it is capable of evaluating the merits and risks of the prospective investment and

(B) Is not purchasing for more than one account or with a view to distributing the securities; or

(ii) Have a maturity of nine months or less.

(2) Paragraph (b)(5) of this rule shall not apply to an Offering of municipal securities if, at such time as an issuer of such municipal securities delivers the securities to the Participating Underwriters:

(i) No obligated person will be an obligated person with respect to more than $10,000,000 in aggregate amount of outstanding municipal securities, including the offered securities and excluding municipal securities that were offered in a transaction exempt from this rule pursuant to paragraph (d)(1) of this rule;

(ii) An issuer of municipal securities or obligated person has undertaken, either individually or in combination with other issuers of municipal securities or obligated persons, in a written agreement or contract for the benefit of holders of such municipal securities, to provide:

(A) Upon request to any person or at least annually to the appropriate state information depository, if any, financial information or operating data regarding each obligated person for which financial information or operating data is presented in the final official statement, as specified in the undertaking, which financial information and operating data shall include, at a minimum, that financial information and operating data which is customarily prepared by such obligated person and is publicly available; and

(B) In a timely manner not in excess of ten business days after the occurrence of the event, notice of events specified in paragraph (b)(5)(i)(C) of this rule with respect to the securities that are the subject of the Offering; and

(iii) the final official statement identifies by name, address, and telephone number the persons from which the foregoing information, data, and notices can be obtained.

(3) The provisions of paragraph (b)(5) of this rule, other than paragraph (b)(5)(i)(C) of this rule, shall not apply to an Offering of municipal securities, if such municipal securities have a stated maturity of 18 months or less.

(4) The provisions of paragraph (c) of this rule shall not apply to municipal securities:

(i) Sold in an Offering to which paragraph (b)(5) of this rule did not apply, other than Offerings exempt under paragraph (d)(2)(ii) of this rule; or

(ii) Sold in an Offering exempt from this rule under paragraph (d)(1) of this rule.

(5) With the exception of paragraphs (b)(1)–(4), this rule shall apply to a primary offering of municipal securities in authorized denominations of $100,000 or more if such securities may, at the option of the holder thereof, be tendered to an issuer of such securities or its designated agent for redemption or purchase at par value or more at least as frequently as every nine months until maturity, earlier redemption, or purchase by an issuer or its designated agent; provided, however, that paragraphs (b)(5) and (c) shall not apply to such securities outstanding on November 30, 2010 for so long as they continuously remain in authorized denominations of $100,000 or more and may, at the option of the holder thereof, be tendered to an issuer of such securities or its designated agent for redemption or purchase at par value or more at least as frequently as every nine months until maturity, earlier redemption, or purchase by an issuer or its designated agent.

(e) *Exemptive Authority.* The Commission, upon written request, or upon its own motion, may exempt any broker, dealer, or municipal securities dealer, whether acting in the capacity of a Participating Underwriter or otherwise, that is a participant in a transaction or class of transactions from any requirement of this rule, either unconditionally or on specified terms and conditions, if the Commission determines that such an exemption is consistent with the public interest and the protection of investors.

(f) *Definitions.* For the purposes of this rule—

(1)   The term "authorized denominations of $100,000 or more" means municipal securities with a principal amount of $100,000 or more and with restrictions that prevent the sale or transfer of such securities in principal amounts of less than $100,000 other than through a primary offering; except that, for municipal securities with an original issue discount of 10 percent or more, the term means municipal securities with a minimum purchase price of $100,000 or more and with restrictions that prevent the sale or transfer of such securities, in principal amounts that are less than the original principal amount at the time of the primary offering, other than through a primary offering.

(2)   The term "end of the underwriting period" means the later of such time as (i) the issuer of municipal securities delivers the securities to the Participating Underwriters or (ii) the Participating Underwriter does not retain, directly or as a member of an underwriting syndicate, an unsold balance of the securities for sale to the public.

(3)   The term "final official statement" means a document or set of documents prepared by an issuer of municipal securities or its representatives that is complete as of the date delivered to the Participating Underwriter(s) and that sets forth information concerning the terms of the proposed issue of securities; information, including financial information or operating data, concerning such issuers of municipal securities and those other entities, enterprises, funds, accounts, and other persons material to an evaluation of the Offering; and a description of the undertakings to be provided pursuant to paragraph (b)(5)(i), paragraph (d)(2)(ii), and paragraph (d)(2)(iii) of this rule, if applicable, and of any instances in the previous five years in which each person specified pursuant to paragraph (b)(5)(ii) of this rule failed to comply, in all material respects, with any previous undertakings in a written contract or agreement specified in paragraph (b)(5)(i) of this rule. Financial information or operating data may be set forth in the document or set of documents, or may be included by specific reference to documents previously provided to each nationally recognized municipal securities information repository, and to a state information depository, if any, or filed with the Commission. If the document is a final official statement, it must be available from the Municipal Securities Rulemaking Board.

(4)   The term "issuer of municipal securities" means the governmental issuer specified in section 3(a)(29) of the Act and the issuer of any separate security, including a separate security as defined in Rule 3b–5(a) under the Act.

(5)   The term "potential customer" means (i) any person contacted by the Participating Underwriter concerning the purchase of municipal securities that are intended to be offered or have been sold in an Offering, (ii) any person who has expressed an interest to the Participating Underwriter in possibly purchasing such municipal securities, and (iii) any person who has a customer account with the Participating Underwriter.

(6)   The term "preliminary official statement" means an official statement prepared by or for an issuer of municipal securities for dissemination to potential customers prior to the availability of the final official statement.

(7)   The term "primary offering" means an offering of municipal securities directly or indirectly by or on behalf of an issuer of such securities, including any remarketing of municipal securities (i) that is accompanied by a change in the authorized denomination of such securities from $100,000 or more to less than $100,000, or (ii) that is accompanied by a change in the period during which such securities may be tendered to an issuer of such securities or its designated agent for redemption or purchase from a period of nine months or less to a period of more than nine months.

(8)   The term "underwriter" means any person who has purchased from an issuer of municipal securities with a view to, or offers or sells for an issuer of municipal securities in connection with, the offering of any municipal security, or participates or has a direct or indirect participation in any such undertaking, or participates or has a participation in the direct or indirect underwriting of any such undertaking; except, that such term shall not include a person whose interest is limited to a commission, concession, or allowance from an underwriter, broker, dealer, or municipal securities dealer not in excess of the usual and customary distributors' or sellers' commission, concession, or allowance.

(9)   The term annual financial information means financial information or operating data, provided at least annually, of the type included in the final official statement with respect to an obligated person, or in the case where no financial information or operating data was provided in the

final official statement with respect to such obligated person, of the type included in the final official statement with respect to those obligated persons that meet the objective criteria applied to select the persons for which financial information or operating data will be provided on an annual basis. Financial information or operating data may be set forth in the document or set of documents, or may be included by specific reference to documents previously provided to each nationally recognized municipal securities information repository, and to a state information depository, if any, or filed with the Commission. If the document is a final official statement, it must be available from the Municipal Securities Rulemaking Board.

(10) The term obligated person means any person, including an issuer of municipal securities, who is either generally or through an enterprise, fund, or account of such person committed by contract or other arrangement to support payment of all, or part of the obligations on the municipal securities to be sold in the Offering (other than providers of municipal bond insurance, letters of credit, or other liquidity facilities).

(11)(i) The term financial obligation means a:

    (A) Debt obligation;

    (B) Derivative instrument entered into in connection with, or pledged as security or a source of payment for, an existing or planned debt obligation; or

    (C) Guarantee of paragraph (f)(11)(i)(A) or (B).

    (ii) The term financial obligation shall not include municipal securities as to which a final official statement has been provided to the Municipal Securities Rulemaking Board consistent with this rule.

(g) *Transitional Provision.* If on July 28, 1989 a Participating Underwriter was contractually committed to act as underwriter in an Offering of municipal securities originally issued before July 29, 1989, the requirements of paragraphs (b)(3) and (b)(4) shall not apply to the Participating Underwriter in connection with such an Offering. Paragraph (b)(5) of this rule shall not apply to a Participating Underwriter that has contractually committed to act as an underwriter in an Offering of municipal securities before July 3, 1995; except that paragraph (b)(5)(i)(A) and paragraph (b)(5)(i)(B) shall not apply with respect to fiscal years ending prior to January 1, 1996. Paragraph (c) shall become effective on January 1, 1996. Paragraph (d)(2)(ii) and paragraph (d)(2)(iii) of this rule shall not apply to an Offering of municipal securities commencing prior to January 1, 1996.

Rule 15c3-1. Net Capital Requirements for Brokers or Dealers

(a) Every broker or dealer must at all times have and maintain net capital no less than the greater of the highest minimum requirement applicable to its ratio requirement under paragraph (a)(1) of this rule, or to any of its activities under paragraph (a)(2) of this rule, and must otherwise not be "insolvent" as that term is defined in paragraph (c)(16) of this rule. In lieu of applying paragraphs (a)(1) and (a)(2) of this rule, an OTC derivatives dealer shall maintain net capital pursuant to paragraph (a)(5) of this rule. Each broker or dealer also shall comply with the supplemental requirements of paragraphs (a)(4) and (a)(9) of this rule, to the extent either paragraph is applicable to its activities. In addition, a broker or dealer shall maintain net capital of not less than its own net capital requirement plus the sum of each broker's or dealer's subsidiary or affiliate minimum net capital requirements, which is consolidated pursuant to Appendix C, Rule 15c3-1c.

Ratio Requirements

Aggregate Indebtedness Standard

(1)(i) No broker or dealer, other than one that elects the provisions of paragraph (a)(1)(ii) of this rule, shall permit its aggregate indebtedness to all other persons to exceed 1500 percent of its net capital (or 800 percent of its net capital for 12 months after commencing business as a broker or dealer).

Alternative Standard

(ii) A broker or dealer may elect not to be subject to the Aggregate Indebtedness Standard of paragraph (a)(1)(i) of this rule. That broker or dealer shall not permit its net capital to be less than the greater of $250,000 or 2 percent of aggregate debit items computed in accordance with the Formula for Determination of Reserve Requirements for Brokers and Dealers (Exhibit A to Rule 15c3–3). Such broker or dealer shall notify its Examining Authority, in writing, of its election to operate under this paragraph (a)(1)(ii). Once a broker or dealer has notified its Examining Authority, it shall continue to operate under this paragraph unless a change is approved upon application to the Commission. A broker or dealer that elects this standard and is not exempt from Rule 15c3–3 shall:

(A)   Make the computation required by Rule 15c3–3(e) and set forth in Exhibit A, Rule 15c3–3a, on a weekly basis and, in lieu of the 1 percent reduction of certain debit items required by Note E(3) in the computation of its Exhibit A requirement, reduce aggregate debit items in such computation by 3 percent;

(B)   Include in Items 7 and 8 of Exhibit A, the market value of items specified therein more than 7 business days old;

(C)   Exclude credit balances in accounts representing amounts payable for securities not yet received from the issuer or its agent which securities are specified in paragraphs (c)(2)(vi)(A) and (E) of this rule and any related debit items from the Exhibit A requirement for 3 business days; and

(D)   Deduct from net worth in computing net capital 1 percent of the contract value of all failed to deliver contracts or securities borrowed that were allocated to failed to receive contracts of the same issue and which thereby were excluded from Items 11 or 12 of Exhibit A.

Futures Commission Merchants

(iii)   No broker or dealer registered as a futures commission merchant shall permit its net capital to be less than the greater of its requirement under paragraph (a)(1)(i) or (ii) of this rule, or 4 percent of the funds required to be segregated pursuant to the Commodity Exchange Act and the regulations thereunder (less the market value of commodity options purchased by option customers on or subject to the rules of a contract market, each such deduction not to exceed the amount of funds in the customer's account).

* * *

[The net capital rule which is extremely complex is only excerpted here. The rule contains different or additional computation formulas for: brokers who do not generally carry customer accounts (Rule 15c3–1(a)(2)), brokers or dealers engaged solely in the sale of redeemable shares of registered investment company and certain other share accounts (Rule 15c3–1(a)(3)), market makers (Rule 15c3–1(a)(4), (6)), brokers or dealers engaged in the sale of options (Rule 15c3–1(a)(5)), specialists (Rule 15c3–1(a)(7)), municipal securities brokers' brokers (Rule 15c–3(a)(8)), and brokers or dealers engaged in reverse repurchase agreements (Rule 15c3–1(a)(9)). The rule also contains five appendices that are not included herein.]

Rule 15c3–3. Customer Protection—Reserves and Custody of Securities

[The reserve requirements of this customer protection rule are omitted.]

Rule 15c3–4. Internal Risk Management Control Systems for OTC Derivatives Dealers

[Omitted]

Rule 15c3–5. Risk Management Controls for Brokers or Dealers With Market Access

(a)   For the purpose of this rule:

(1)   The term market access shall mean:

(i)   Access to trading in securities on an exchange or alternative trading system as a result of being a member or subscriber of the exchange or alternative trading system, respectively; or

(ii)   Access to trading in securities on an alternative trading system provided by a broker-dealer operator of an alternative trading system to a non-broker-dealer.

(2)   The term regulatory requirements shall mean all federal securities laws, rules and regulations, and rules of self-regulatory organizations, that are applicable in connection with market access.

(b)   A broker or dealer with market access, or that provides a customer or any other person with access to an exchange or alternative trading system through use of its market participant identifier or otherwise, shall establish, document, and maintain a system of risk management controls and supervisory procedures reasonably designed to manage the financial, regulatory, and other risks of this business activity. Such broker or dealer shall preserve a copy of its supervisory procedures and a written description of its risk management controls as part of its books and records in a manner consistent with Rule 17a–4(e)(7). A broker-dealer that routes orders on behalf of an exchange or alternative trading system for the purpose of accessing other trading centers with protected quotations in compliance with Rule 611 of Regulation NMS for NMS stocks, or in compliance with a national market system plan for listed options, shall not be required to comply with this rule with regard to such routing services, except with regard to paragraph (c)(1)(ii) of this rule.

(c)   The risk management controls and supervisory procedures required by paragraph (b) of this rule shall include the following elements:

(1)   Financial risk management controls and supervisory procedures. The risk management controls and supervisory procedures shall be reasonably designed to systematically limit the financial exposure of the broker or dealer that could arise as a result of market access, including being reasonably designed to:

(i)   Prevent the entry of orders that exceed appropriate pre-set credit or capital thresholds in the aggregate for each customer and the broker or dealer and, where appropriate, more finely-tuned by sector, security, or otherwise by rejecting orders if such orders would exceed the applicable credit or capital thresholds; and

(ii)   Prevent the entry of erroneous orders, by rejecting orders that exceed appropriate price or size parameters, on an order-by-order basis or over a short period of time, or that indicate duplicative orders.

(2)   Regulatory risk management controls and supervisory procedures. The risk management controls and supervisory procedures shall be reasonably designed to ensure compliance with all regulatory requirements, including being reasonably designed to:

(i)   Prevent the entry of orders unless there has been compliance with all regulatory requirements that must be satisfied on a pre-order entry basis;

(ii)   Prevent the entry of orders for securities for a broker or dealer, customer, or other person if such person is restricted from trading those securities;

(iii)   Restrict access to trading systems and technology that provide market access to persons and accounts pre-approved and authorized by the broker or dealer; and

(iv)   Assure that appropriate surveillance personnel receive immediate post-trade execution reports that result from market access.

(d)   The financial and regulatory risk management controls and supervisory procedures described in paragraph (c) of this rule shall be under the direct and exclusive control of the broker or dealer that is subject to paragraph (b) of this rule.

(1)   Notwithstanding the foregoing, a broker or dealer that is subject to paragraph (b) of this rule may reasonably allocate, by written contract, after a thorough due diligence review, control over specific regulatory risk management controls and supervisory procedures described in paragraph (c)(2) of this rule to a customer that is a registered broker or dealer, provided that such broker or dealer subject to paragraph (b) of this rule has a reasonable basis for determining that such customer, based on its position in the transaction and relationship with an ultimate customer, has better access than the broker or dealer to that ultimate customer and its trading information such that it can more effectively implement the specified controls or procedures.

(2)   Any allocation of control pursuant to paragraph (d)(1) of this rule shall not relieve a broker or dealer that is subject to paragraph (b) of this rule from any obligation under this rule, including the overall responsibility to establish, document, and maintain a system of risk management controls and supervisory procedures reasonably designed to manage the financial, regulatory, and other risks of market access.

(e)   A broker or dealer that is subject to paragraph (b) of this rule shall establish, document, and maintain a system for regularly reviewing the effectiveness of the risk management controls and supervisory procedures required by paragraphs (b) and (c) of this rule and for promptly addressing any issues.

(1)   Among other things, the broker or dealer shall review, no less frequently than annually, the business activity of the broker or dealer in connection with market access to assure the overall effectiveness of such risk management controls and supervisory procedures. Such review shall be conducted in accordance with written procedures and shall be documented. The broker or dealer shall preserve a copy of such written procedures, and documentation of each such review, as part of its books and records in a manner consistent with Rules 17a–4(e)(7) and 17a–4(b), respectively.

(2)   The Chief Executive Officer (or equivalent officer) of the broker or dealer shall, on an annual basis, certify that such risk management controls and supervisory procedures comply with paragraphs (b) and (c) of this rule, and that the broker or dealer conducted such review, and such certifications shall be preserved by the broker or dealer as part of its books and records in a manner consistent with Rule 17a–4(b).

(f)   The Commission, by order, may exempt from the provisions of this rule, either unconditionally or on specified terms and conditions, any broker or dealer, if the Commission determines that such exemption is necessary or appropriate in the public interest consistent with the protection of investors.

Rule 15c6–1. Settlement Cycle

(a)   Except as provided in paragraphs (b), (c), and (d) of this rule, a broker or dealer shall not effect or enter into a contract for the purchase or sale of a security (other than an exempted security, government security, municipal security, commercial paper, bankers' acceptances, or commercial bills) that provides for payment of funds and delivery of securities later than the second business day after the date of the contract unless otherwise expressly agreed to by the parties at the time of the transaction.

(b)   Paragraphs (a) and (c) of this rule shall not apply to contracts:

(1)   For the purchase or sale of limited partnership interests that are not listed on an exchange or for which quotations are not disseminated through an automated quotation system of a registered securities association;

(2)   For the purchase or sale of securities that the Commission may from time to time, taking into account then existing market practices, exempt by order from the requirements of paragraph (a) of this rule, either unconditionally or on specified terms and conditions, if the Commission determines that such exemption is consistent with the public interest and the protection of investors.

(c)   Paragraph (a) of this rule shall not apply to contracts for the sale for cash of securities that are priced after 4:30 p.m. Eastern time on the date such securities are priced and that are sold by an issuer to an underwriter pursuant to a firm commitment underwritten offering registered under the Securities Act of 1933 or sold to an initial purchaser by a broker-dealer participating in such offering provided that a broker or dealer shall not effect or enter into a contract for the purchase or sale of such securities that provides for payment of funds and delivery of securities later than the fourth business day after the date of the contract unless otherwise expressly agreed to by the parties at the time of the transaction.

(d)   For the purposes of paragraphs (a) and (c) of this rule, the parties to a contract shall be deemed to have expressly agreed to an alternate date for payment of funds and delivery of securities at the time of the transaction for a contract for the sale for cash of securities pursuant to a firm commitment offering if the managing underwriter and the issuer have agreed to such date for all securities sold pursuant to such offering and the parties to the contract have not expressly agreed to another date for payment of funds and delivery of securities at the time of the transaction.

REGULATION 15D—REPORTS OF REGISTRANTS
UNDER THE SECURITIES ACT OF 1933

Rule 15d–1.   Requirement of Annual Reports

Every registrant under the Securities Act of 1933 shall file an annual report, on the appropriate form authorized or prescribed therefor, for the fiscal year in which the registration statement under the Securities Act of 1933 became effective and for each fiscal year thereafter, unless the registrant is exempt from such filing by section 15(d) of the Act or rules thereunder. Annual reports shall be filed within the period specified in the appropriate report form.

Rule 15d–2.   Special Financial Report

(a)   If the registration statement under the Securities Act of 1933 did not contain certified financial statements for the registrant's last full fiscal year (or for the life of the registrant if less than a full fiscal year) preceding the fiscal year in which the registration statement became effective, the registrant shall, within 90 days after the effective date of the registration statement, file a special report furnishing certified financial statements for such last full fiscal year or other period, as the case may be, meeting the requirements of the form appropriate for annual reports of the registrant. If the registrant is a foreign private issuer as defined in Rule 405 of the Securities Act, then the special financial report shall be filed on the appropriate form for annual reports of the registrant and shall be filed by the later of 90 days after the date on which the registration statement became effective, or four months following the end of the registrant's latest full fiscal year.

(b)   The report shall be filed under cover of the facing sheet of the form appropriate for annual reports of the registrant, shall indicate on the facing sheet that it contains only financial statements for the fiscal year in question, and shall be signed in accordance with the requirements of the annual report form.

Rule 15d–3.   Reports for Depositary Shares Registered on Form F–6

Annual and other reports are not required with respect to Depositary Shares registered on Form F–6. The exemption in this rule does not apply to any deposited securities registered on any other form under the Securities Act of 1933.

Rule 15d–4.   Reporting by Form 40–F Registrants

A registrant that is eligible to use Forms 40–F and 6–K and files reports in accordance therewith shall be deemed to satisfy the requirements of Regulation 15D.

Rule 15d–5.   Reporting by Successor Issuers

(a)   Where in connection with a succession by merger, consolidation, exchange of securities or acquisition of assets, securities of any issuer that is not required to file reports pursuant to Section 15(d) of the Act, are issued to the holders of any class of securities of another issuer that is required to file such reports, the duty to file reports pursuant to such section shall be deemed to have been assumed by the issuer of the class of securities so issued. The successor issuer shall, after the consummation of the succession, file reports in accordance with section 15(d) of the Act and the rules and regulations thereunder, unless that issuer is exempt from filing such reports or the duty to file such reports is suspended under section 15(d) of the Act.

(b)   An issuer that is deemed to be a successor issuer according to paragraph (a) of this rule shall file reports on the same forms as the predecessor issuer except as follows:

(1)   An issuer that is not a foreign issuer shall not be eligible to file on Form 20–F.

(2)   A foreign private issuer shall be eligible to file on Form 20–F.

(c)   The provisions of paragraph (a) of this rule shall not apply to an issuer of securities in connection with a succession that was registered on Form F–8 or Form F–10 or Form F–80.

Rule 15d–6. Suspension of Duty to File Reports

If the duty of an issuer to file reports pursuant to section 15(d) of the Act as to any fiscal year is suspended as provided in Section 15(d) of the Act, such issuer shall, within 30 days after the beginning of the first fiscal year, file a notice on Form 15 informing the Commission of such suspension unless Form 15 has already been filed pursuant to Rule 12h–3. If the suspension resulted from the issuer's merger into, or consolidation with, another issuer or issuers, the notice shall be filed by the successor issuer.

OTHER REPORTS

Rule 15d–10. Transition Reports

(a)   Every issuer that changes its fiscal closing date transition shall file a report covering the resulting transition period between the closing date of its most recent fiscal year and the opening date of its new fiscal year; *Provided, however,* that an issuer shall file an annual report for any fiscal year that ended before the date on which the issuer determined to change its fiscal year end. In no event shall the transition report cover a period of 12 or more months.

(b)   The report pursuant to this rule shall be filed for the transition period not more than the number of days specified in paragraph (j) of this rule after either the close of the transition period or the date of the determination to change the fiscal closing date, whichever is later. The report shall be filed on the form appropriate for annual reports of the issuer, shall cover the period from the close of the last fiscal year end and shall indicate clearly the period covered. The financial statements for the transition period filed therewith shall be audited. Financial statements, which may be unaudited, shall be filed for the comparable period of the prior year, or a footnote, which may be unaudited, shall state for the comparable period of the prior year, revenues, gross profits, income taxes, income or loss from continuing operations and net income or loss. The effects of any discontinued operations as classified under the provisions of generally accepted accounting principles also shall be shown, if applicable. Per share data based upon such income or loss and net income or loss shall be presented in conformity with applicable accounting standards. Where called for by the time span to be covered, the comparable period financial statements or footnote shall be included in subsequent filings.

(c)   If the transition period covers a period of less than six months, in lieu of the report required by paragraph (b) of this rule, a report may be filed for the transition period on Form 10–Q not more than the number of days specified in paragraph (j) of this Rule after either the close of the transition period or the date of the determination to change the fiscal closing date, whichever is later. The report on Form 10–Q shall cover the period from the close of the last fiscal year end and shall indicate clearly the period covered. The financial statements filed therewith need not be audited but, if they are not audited, the issuer shall file with the first annual report for the newly adopted fiscal year separate audited statements of income and cash flows covering the transition period. The notes to financial statements for the transition period included in such first annual report may be integrated with the notes to financial statements for the full fiscal period. A separate audited balance sheet as of the end of the transition period shall be filed in the annual report only if the audited balance sheet as of the end of the fiscal year prior to the transition period is not filed. Schedules need not be filed in transition reports on Form 10–Q.

(d)   Notwithstanding the foregoing in paragraphs (a), (b), and (c) of this rule, if the transition period covers a period of one month or less, the issuer need not file a separate transition report if either:

(1)   The first report required to be filed by the issuer for the newly adopted fiscal year after the date of the determination to change the fiscal year end is an annual report, and that report covers the transition period as well as the fiscal year; or

(2)(i)   The issuer files with the first annual report for the newly adopted fiscal year separate audited statements of income and cash flows covering the transition period; and

(ii)   The first report required to be filed by the issuer for the newly adopted fiscal year after the date of the determination to change the fiscal year end is a quarterly report on Form 10–Q; and

(iii)   Information on the transition period is included in the issuer's quarterly report on Form 10–Q for the first quarterly period (except the fourth quarter) of the newly adopted fiscal year that ends after the date of the determination to change the fiscal year. The information covering the transition period required by Part II and Item 2 of Part I may be combined with the information regarding the quarter. However, the financial statements required by Part I, which may be unaudited, shall be furnished separately for the transition period.

(e)   Every issuer required to file quarterly reports on Form 10–Q pursuant to Rule 15d–13 that changes its fiscal year end shall:

(1)   File a quarterly report on Form 10–Q within the time period specified in General Instruction A.1. to that form for any quarterly period (except the fourth quarter) of the old fiscal year that ends before the date on which the issuer determined to change its fiscal year end, except that the issuer need not file such quarterly report if the date on which the quarterly period ends also is the date on which the transition period ends;

(2)   File a quarterly report on Form 10–Q within the time specified in General Instruction A.1. to that form for each quarterly period of the old fiscal year within the transition period. In lieu of a quarterly report for any quarter of the old fiscal year within the transition period, the issuer may file a quarterly report on Form 10–Q for any period of three months within the transition period that coincides with a quarter of the newly adopted fiscal year if the quarterly report is filed within the number of days specified in paragraph (j) of this Rule after the end of such three month period, provided the issuer thereafter continues filing quarterly reports on the basis of the quarters of the newly adopted fiscal year;

(3)   Commence filing quarterly reports for the quarters of the new fiscal year no later than the quarterly report for the first quarter of the new fiscal year that ends after the date on which the issuer determined to change the fiscal year end; and

(4)   unless such information is or will be included in the transition report, or the first annual report on Form 10–K for the newly adopted fiscal year, include in the initial quarterly report on Form 10–Q for the newly adopted fiscal year information on any period beginning on the first day subsequent to the period covered by the issuer's final quarterly report on Form 10–Q or annual report on Form 10–K for the old fiscal year. The information covering such period required by Part II and Item 2 of Part I may be combined with the information regarding the quarter. However, the financial statements required by Part I, which may be unaudited, shall be furnished separately for such period.

NOTE to paragraphs (c) and (e): If it is not practicable or cannot be cost-justified to furnish in a transition report on Form 10–Q or a quarterly report for the newly adopted fiscal year financial statements for corresponding periods of the prior year where required, financial statements may be furnished for the quarters of the preceding fiscal year that most nearly are comparable if the issuer furnishes an adequate discussion of seasonal and other factors that could affect the comparability of information or trends reflected, an assessment of the comparability of the data, and a representation as to the reason recasting has not been undertaken.

(f)   Every successor issuer that has a different fiscal year from that of its predecessor(s) shall file a transition report pursuant to this rule, containing the required information about each predecessor, for the transition period, if any, between the close of the fiscal year covered by the last annual report of each predecessor and the date of succession. The report shall be filed for the transition period on the form appropriate for annual reports of the issuer not more than the number of days specified in paragraph (j) of this Rule after the date of the succession, with financial statements in conformity with the requirements set forth in paragraph (b) of this rule. If the transition period covers a period of less than six months, in lieu of a transition report on the form appropriate for the issuer's annual reports, the report may be filed for the transition period on Form 10–Q not more than the number of days specified in paragraph (j) of this rule after the date of the succession, with financial statements in conformity with the requirements set forth in paragraph (c) of this rule. Notwithstanding the foregoing, if the transition period covers a period of one month or less, the successor issuer need not file a separate transition report if the information is reported by the successor issuer in conformity with the requirements set forth in paragraph (d) of this rule.

(g)(1)   Paragraphs (a) through (f) of this rule shall not apply to foreign private issuers.

(2)   Every foreign private issuer that changes its fiscal closing date shall file a report covering the resulting transition period between the closing date of its most recent year and the opening date of its new fiscal year. In no event shall a transition report cover a period longer than 12 months.

(3) The report for the transition period shall be filed on Form 20–F responding to all items to which such issuer is required to respond when Form 20–F is used as an annual report. The financial statements for the transition period filed therewith shall be audited. The report shall be filed within four months after either the close of the transition period or the date on which the issuer made the determination to change the fiscal closing date, whichever is later.

(4) If the transition period covers a period of six or fewer months, in lieu of the report required by paragraph (g)(3) of this rule, a report for the transition period may be filed on Form 20–F responding to Items 5, 8.A.7., 13, 14, and 17 or 18 within three months after either the close of the transition period or the date on which the issuer made the determination to change the fiscal closing date, whichever is later. The financial statements required by either Item 17 or Item 18 shall be furnished for the transition period. Such financial statements may be unaudited and condensed as permitted in Article 10 of Regulation S–X, but if the financial statements are unaudited and condensed, the issuer shall file with the first annual report for the newly adopted fiscal year separate audited statements of income and cash flows covering the transition period.

(5) Notwithstanding the foregoing in paragraphs (g)(2), (g)(3), and (g)(4) of this rule, if the transition period covers a period of one month or less, a foreign private issuer need not file a separate transition report if the first annual report for the newly adopted fiscal year covers the transition period as well as the fiscal year.

(h) The provisions of this rule shall not apply to investment companies required to file reports pursuant to Rule 30a–1 under the Investment Company Act of 1940.

(i) No filing fee shall be required for a transition report filed pursuant to this rule.

(j)(1) For transition reports to be filed on the form appropriate for annual reports of the issuer, the number of days shall be:

    (i) 60 days (75 days for fiscal years ending before December 15, 2006) for large accelerated filers (as defined in Rule 12b–2);

    (ii) 75 days for accelerated filers (as defined in Rule 12b–2); and

    (iii) 90 days for all other issuers; and

(2) For transition reports to be filed on Form 10–Q, the number of days shall be:

    (i) 40 days for large accelerated filers and accelerated filers (as defined in Rule 12b–2); and

    (ii) 45 days for all other issuers.

(k)(1) Paragraphs (a) through (g) of this rule shall not apply to asset-backed issuers.

(2) Every asset-backed issuer that changes its fiscal closing date shall file a report covering the resulting transition period between the closing date of its most recent fiscal year and the opening date of its new fiscal year. In no event shall a transition report cover a period longer than 12 months.

(3) The report for the transition period shall be filed on Form 10–K responding to all items which such asset-backed issuer is required to respond pursuant to General Instruction J of Form 10–K. Such report shall be filed within 90 days after the later of either the close of the transition period or the date on which the issuer made the determination to change the fiscal closing date.

(4) Notwithstanding the foregoing in paragraphs (k)(2) and (k)(3) of this rule, if the transition period covers a period of one month or less, an asset-backed issuer need not file a separate transition report if the first annual report for the newly adopted fiscal year covers the transition period as well as the fiscal year.

(5) Any obligation of the asset-backed issuer to file distribution reports pursuant to Rule 15d–17 will continue to apply regardless of a change in the asset-backed issuer's fiscal closing date.

NOTE 1: In addition to the report or reports required to be filed pursuant to this rule, every issuer, except a foreign private issuer or an investment company required to file reports pursuant to Rule 30b1–1 under the Investment Company Act of 1940, that changes its fiscal closing date is required to file a Form 8–

K report that includes the information required by Item 5.03 of Form 8–K within the period specified in General Instruction B.1. to that form.

NOTE 2: The report or reports to be filed pursuant to this rule must include the certification required by Rule 15d–14.

Rule 15d–11. Current Reports on Form 8–K

(a)   Except as provided in paragraph (b) of this rule, every registrant subject to Rule 15d–1 shall file a current report on Form 8–K within the period specified in that form unless substantially the same information as that required by Form 8–K has been previously reported by the registrant.

(b)   This rule shall not apply to foreign governments, foreign private issuers required to make reports on Form 6–K pursuant to Rule 15d–16, issuers of American Depositary Receipts for securities of any foreign issuer, or investment companies required to file reports pursuant to Rule 30a–1 of this chapter under the Investment Company Act of 1940, except where such an investment company is required to file:

(1)   Notice of a blackout period pursuant to § 245.104 of this chapter;

(2)   Disclosure pursuant to Instruction 2 to Rule 14a–11(b)(1) of information concerning outstanding shares and voting; or

(3)   Disclosure pursuant to Instruction 2 to Rule 14a–11(b)(10) of the date by which a nominating shareholder or nominating shareholder group must submit the notice required pursuant to Rule 14a–11(b)(10).

(c)   No failure to file a report on Form 8–K that is required solely pursuant to Item 1.01, 1.02, 2.03, 2.04, 2.05, 2.06, 4.02(a), 502(e) or 6.03 of Form 8–K shall be deemed to be a violation of section 10(b) and Rule 10b–5.

Rule 15d–13. Quarterly Reports on Form 10–Q

(a)   Except as provided in paragraphs (b) and (c) of this rule, every issuer that has securities registered pursuant to the Securities Act of 1933 and is required to file annual reports pursuant to section 15(d) of the Securities Exchange Act of 1934 on Form 10–K shall file a quarterly report on Form 10–Q within the period specified in General Instruction A.1. to that form for each of the first three quarters of each fiscal year of the issuer, commencing with the first fiscal quarter following the most recent fiscal year for which full financial statements were included in the registration statement, or, if the registration statement included financial statements for an interim period after the most recent fiscal year end meeting the requirements of Article 10 of Regulation S–X, or Rule 8–03 of Regulation S–X for smaller reporting companies, for the first fiscal quarter after the quarter reported upon in the registration statement. The first quarterly report of the issuer shall be filed either within 45 days after the effective date of the registration statement or on or before the date on which such report would have been required to be filed if the issuer had been required to file reports on Form 10–Q as of its last fiscal quarter, whichever is later.

(b)   The provisions of this rule shall not apply to the following issuers:

(1)   Investment companies required to file reports pursuant to Rule 30a–1;

(2)   Foreign private issuers required to file reports pursuant to Rule 15d–16; and.

(3)   Asset-backed issuers required to file reports pursuant to Rule 15d–17 of the Securities Exchange Act of 1934.

(c)   Part I of the quarterly report on Form 10–Q need not be filed by:

(1)   Mutual life insurance companies; or

(2)   Mining companies not in the production stage but engaged primarily in the exploration for the development of mineral deposits other than oil, gas or coal, if all of the following conditions are met:

(i)   The registrant has not been in production during the current fiscal year or the two years immediately prior thereto; except that being in production for an aggregate period of no more than eight months over the three-year period shall not be a violation of this condition.

(ii)   Receipts from the sale of mineral products or from the operations of mineral producing properties by the registrant and its subsidiaries combined have not exceeded $500,000 in any of the most recent six years and have not aggregated more than $1,500,000 in the most recent six fiscal years.

(d)   Notwithstanding the foregoing provisions of this rule, the financial information required by Part I of Form 10–Q shall not be deemed to be "filed" for the purpose of section 18 of the Act or otherwise subject to the liabilities of that section of the Act, but shall be subject to all other provisions of the Act.

(e)   Notwithstanding the foregoing provisions of this rule, the financial information required by Part I of Form 10–Q, or financial information submitted in lieu thereof pursuant to paragraph (d) of this rule, shall not be deemed to be "filed" for the purpose of section 18 of the Act or otherwise subject to the liabilities of that section of the Act, but shall be subject to all other provisions of the Act.

Rule 15d–14. Certification of Disclosure in Annual and Quarterly Reports

(a)   Each report, including transition reports, filed on Form 10–Q, Form 10–K, Form 20–F or Form 40–F under section 15(d) of the Act, other than a report filed by an Asset-Backed Issuer (as defined in Item 1101 of Regulation AB), or a report on Form 20–F filed under Rule 15d–19, must include certifications in the form specified in the applicable exhibit filing requirements of such report, and such certifications must be filed as an exhibit to such report. Each principal executive and principal financial officer of the issuer, or persons performing similar functions, at the time of filing of the report must sign a certification. The principal executive and principal financial officers of an issuer may omit the portion of the introductory language in paragraph 4 as well as language in paragraph 4(b) of the certification that refers to the certifying officers' responsibility for designing, establishing and maintaining internal control over financial reporting for the issuer until the issuer becomes subject to the internal control over financial reporting requirements in Rule 13a–15 or Rule 15d–15.

(b)   Each periodic report containing financial statements filed by an issuer pursuant to section 15(d) of the Act must be accompanied by the certifications required by Section 1350 of Chapter 63 of Title 18 of the United States Code and such certifications must be furnished as an exhibit to such report as specified in the applicable exhibit requirements for such report. Each principal executive and principal financial officer of the issuer (or equivalent thereof) must sign a certification. This requirement may be satisfied by a single certification signed by an issuer's principal executive and principal financial officers.

(c)   A person required to provide the certification specified in paragraph (a), (b) or (d) of this Rule may not have the certification signed on his or her behalf pursuant to a power of attorney or other form of confirming authority.

(d)   Each annual report and transition report filed on Form 10–K by an asset-backed issuer under section 15(d) of the Act must include a certification in the form specified in the applicable exhibit filing requirements of such report and such certification must be filed as an exhibit to such report. Terms used in paragraphs (d) and (e) of this rule have the same meaning as in Item 1101 of Regulation AB.

(e)   With respect to asset-backed issuers, the certification required by paragraph (d) of this rule must be signed by either:

(1)   The senior officer in charge of securitization of the depositor if the depositor is signing the report; or

(2)   The senior officer in charge of the servicing function of the servicer if the servicer is signing the report on behalf of the issuing entity. If multiple servicers are involved in servicing the pool assets, the senior officer in charge of the servicing function of the master servicer (or entity performing the equivalent function) must sign if a representative of the servicer is to sign the report on behalf of the issuing entity.

(f)   The certification requirements of this rule do not apply to:

(1)   An Interactive Data File, as defined in Rule 11 of Regulation S–T; or

(2)   XBRL-Related Documents, as defined in Rule 11 of Regulation S–T.

Rule 15d–15. Controls and Procedures

(a)   Every issuer that files reports under section 15(d) of the Act, other than an Asset-Backed Issuer (as defined in Item 1101 of Regulation S–K), a small business investment company registered on Form N–5, or a unit investment trust as defined in section 4(2) of the Investment Company Act of 1940, must maintain disclosure controls and procedures (as defined in paragraph (e) of this rule) and, if the issuer either had been required to file an annual report pursuant to section 13(a) or 15(d) of the Act for the prior fiscal year or had filed an annual report with the Commission for the prior fiscal year, internal control over financial reporting (as defined in paragraph (f) of this rule).

(b)   Each such issuer's management must evaluate, with the participation of the issuer's principal executive and principal financial officers, or persons performing similar functions, the effectiveness of the issuer's disclosure controls and procedures, as of the end of each fiscal quarter, except that management must perform this evaluation:

(1)   In the case of a foreign private issuer (as defined in Rule 3b–4) as of the end of each fiscal year; and

(2)   In the case of an investment company registered under section 8 of the Investment Company Act of 1940, within the 90-day period prior to the filing date of each report requiring certification under Rule 30a–2 of the Investment Company Act of 1940.

(c)   The management of each such issuer that either had been required to file an annual report pursuant to section 13(a) or 15(d) of the Act for the prior fiscal year or had filed an annual report with the Commission for the prior fiscal year, other than an investment company registered under section 8 of the Investment Company Act of 1940, must evaluate, with the participation of the issuer's principal executive and principal financial officers, or persons performing similar functions, the effectiveness, as of the end of each fiscal year, of the issuer's internal control over financial reporting. The framework on which management's evaluation of the issuer's internal control over financial reporting is based must be a suitable, recognized control framework that is established by a body or group that has followed due-process procedures, including the broad distribution of the framework for public comment. Although there are many different ways to conduct an evaluation of the effectiveness of internal control over financial reporting to meet the requirements of this paragraph, an evaluation that is conducted in accordance with the interpretive guidance issued by the Commission in Release No. 34–55929 will satisfy the evaluation required by this paragraph.

(d)   The management of each such issuer that previously either had been required to file an annual report pursuant to section 13(a) or 15(d) of the Act for the prior fiscal year or previously had filed an annual report with the Commission for the prior fiscal year, other than an investment company registered under section 8 of the Investment Company Act of 1940, must evaluate, with the participation of the issuer's principal executive and principal financial officers, or persons performing similar functions, any change in the issuer's internal control over financial reporting, that occurred during each of the issuer's fiscal quarters, or fiscal year in the case of a foreign private issuer, that has materially affected, or is reasonably likely to materially affect, the issuer's internal control over financial reporting.

(e)   For purposes of this rule, the term disclosure controls and procedures means controls and other procedures of an issuer that are designed to ensure that information required to be disclosed by the issuer in the reports that it files or submits under the Act is recorded, processed, summarized and reported, within the time periods specified in the Commission's rules and forms. Disclosure controls and procedures include, without limitation, controls and procedures designed to ensure that information required to be disclosed by an issuer in the reports that it files or submits under the Act is accumulated and communicated to the issuer's management, including its principal executive and principal financial officers, or persons performing similar functions, as appropriate to allow timely decisions regarding required disclosure.

(f)   The term internal control over financial reporting is defined as a process designed by, or under the supervision of, the issuer's principal executive and principal financial officers, or persons performing similar functions, and effected by the issuer's board of directors, management and other personnel, to provide reasonable assurance regarding the reliability of financial reporting and the preparation of financial statements for external purposes in accordance with generally accepted accounting principles and includes those policies and procedures that:

(1) Pertain to the maintenance of records that in reasonable detail accurately and fairly reflect the transactions and dispositions of the assets of the issuer;

(2) Provide reasonable assurance that transactions are recorded as necessary to permit preparation of financial statements in accordance with generally accepted accounting principles, and that receipts and expenditures of the issuer are being made only in accordance with authorizations of management and directors of the issuer; and

(3) Provide reasonable assurance regarding prevention or timely detection of unauthorized acquisition, use or disposition of the issuer's assets that could have a material effect on the financial statements.

Rule 15d–16. Reports of Foreign Private Issuers on Form 6–K

(a) Every foreign private issuer which is subject to Rule 15d–1 shall make reports on Form 6–K, except that this rule shall not apply to:

(1) Investment companies required to file reports pursuant to Rule 30a–1;

(2) Issuers of American depositary receipts for securities of any foreign issuer; or.

(3) Asset-backed issuers, as defined in Item 1101 of Regulation S–K.

(b) Such reports shall be transmitted promptly after the information required by Form 6–K is made public by the issuer, by the country of its domicile or under the laws of which it was incorporated or organized or by a foreign securities exchange with which the issuer has filed the information.

(c) Reports furnished pursuant to this rule shall not be deemed to be "filed" for the purpose of Section 18 of the Act or otherwise subject to the liabilities of that section.

Rule 15d–19. Reports by Shell Companies on Form 20–F

Every foreign private issuer that was a shell company, other than a business combination related shell company, immediately before a transaction that causes it to cease to be a shell company shall, within four business days of completion of that transaction, file a report on Form 20–F containing the information that would be required if the issuer were filing a form for registration of securities on Form 20–F to register under the Act all classes of the issuer's securities subject to the reporting requirements of section 13 or section 15(d) of the Act upon consummation of the transaction, with such information reflecting the registrant and its securities upon consummation of the transaction.

Rule 15d–20. Plain English Presentation of Specified Information

(a) Any information included or incorporated by reference in a report filed under section 15(d) of the Act that is required to be disclosed pursuant to Item 402, 403, 404 or 407 of Regulation S–K must be presented in a clear, concise and understandable manner. You must prepare the disclosure using the following standards:

(1) Present information in clear, concise sections, paragraphs and sentences;

(2) Use short sentences;

(3) Use definite, concrete, everyday words;

(4) Use the active voice;

(5) Avoid multiple negatives;

(6) Use descriptive headings and subheadings;

(7) Use a tabular presentation or bullet lists for complex material, wherever possible;

(8) Avoid legal jargon and highly technical business and other terminology;

(9) Avoid frequent reliance on glossaries or defined terms as the primary means of explaining information. Define terms in a glossary or other section of the document only if the meaning is unclear from the context. Use a glossary only if it facilitates understanding of the disclosure; and

(10) In designing the presentation of the information you may include pictures, logos, charts, graphs and other design elements so long as the design is not misleading and the required information is clear. You are encouraged to use tables, schedules, charts and graphic illustrations that present relevant data in an understandable manner, so long as such presentations are consistent with applicable disclosure requirements and consistent with other information in the document. You must draw graphs and charts to scale. Any information you provide must not be misleading.

(b)   Reserved.

Note to Rule 15d–20. In drafting the disclosure to comply with this rule, you should avoid the following:

1.   Legalistic or overly complex presentations that make the substance of the disclosure difficult to understand;

2.   Vague "boilerplate" explanations that are imprecise and readily subject to different interpretations;

3.   Complex information copied directly from legal documents without any clear and concise explanation of the provision(s); and

4.   Disclosure repeated in different sections of the document that increases the size of the document but does not enhance the quality of the information.

EXEMPTION OF CERTAIN ISSUERS FROM SECTION 15(d) OF THE ACT

Rule 15d–21. Reports for Employee Stock Purchase, Savings and Similar Plans

(a)   Separate annual and other reports need not be filed pursuant to section 15(d) of the Act with respect to any employee stock purchase, savings or similar plan, *provided:*

(1)   The issuer of the stock or other securities offered to employees through their participation in the plan files annual reports on Form 10–K; and

(2)   Such issuer furnishes, as a part of its annual report on such form or as an amendment thereto, the information, financial statements and exhibits required by Form 11–K with respect to the plan.

(b)   If the procedure permitted by this Rule is followed, the financial statements required by Form 11–K with respect to the plan shall be filed within 120 days after the end of the fiscal year of the plan, either as a part of or as an amendment to the annual report of the issuer for its last fiscal year, *provided that* if the fiscal year of the plan ends within 62 days prior to the end of the fiscal year of the issuer, such information, financial statements and exhibits may be furnished as a part of the issuer's next annual report. If a plan subject to the Employee Retirement Income Security Act of 1974 uses the procedure permitted by this Rule, the financial statements required by Form 11–K shall be filed within 180 days after the plan's fiscal year end.

PENNY STOCK RULES

Rule 15g–1. Exemptions for Certain Transactions

The following transactions shall be exempt from Rule 15g–2, Rule 15g–3, Rule 15g–4, Rule 15g–5, and Rule 15g–6:

(a)   Transactions by a broker or dealer:

(1)   Whose commissions, commission equivalents, mark-ups, and mark-downs from transactions in penny stocks during each of the immediately preceding three months and during eleven or more of the preceding twelve months, or during the immediately preceding six months, did not exceed five percent of its total commissions, commission equivalents, mark-ups, and mark-downs from transactions in securities during those months; and

(2)   Who has not been a market maker in the penny stock that is the subject of the transaction in the immediately preceding twelve months.

NOTE: Prior to April 28, 1993, commissions, commission equivalents, mark-ups, and mark-downs from transactions in designated securities, as defined in Rule 15c2–6(d)(2) as of April 15, 1992, may be considered to be commissions, commission equivalents, mark-ups, mark-downs from transactions in penny stocks for purposes of paragraph (a)(1) of this rule.

(b)   Transactions in which the customer is an institutional accredited investor, as defined in Rule 501(a)(1), (2), (3), (7), (8), (9), (12), or (13).

Note 1 to paragraph (b): Though the definition of "family client" from rule 501(a)(13) includes both natural persons and institutions, only family clients that are institutions may be considered institutional accredited investors.

(c)   Transactions that meet the requirements of Regulation D, or transactions with an issuer not involving any public offering pursuant to section 4(a)(2) of the Securities Act of 1933.

(d)   Transactions in which the customer is the issuer, or a director, officer, general partner, or direct or indirect beneficial owner of more than five percent of any class of equity security of the issuer, of the penny stock that is the subject of the transaction.

(e)   Transactions that are not recommended by the broker or dealer.

(f)   Any other transaction or class of transactions or persons or class of persons that, upon prior written request or upon its own motion, the Commission conditionally or unconditionally exempts by order as consistent with the public interest and the protection of investors.

Rule 15g–2.   Penny Stock Disclosure Document Relating to the Penny Stock Market

(a)   It shall be unlawful for a broker or dealer to effect a transaction in any penny stock for or with the account of a customer unless, prior to effecting such transaction, the broker or dealer has furnished to the customer a document containing the information set forth in Schedule 15G and has obtained from the customer a signed and dated written acknowledgement of receipt of the document.

(b)   Regardless of the form of acknowledgment used to satisfy the requirements of paragraph (a) of this rule, it shall be unlawful for a broker or dealer to effect a transaction in any penny stock for or with the account of a customer less than two business days after the broker or dealer sends such document.

(c)   The broker or dealer shall preserve, as part of its records, a copy of the written acknowledgment required by paragraph (a) of this rule for the period specified in Rule 17a–4(b) of this Act.

(d)   Upon request of the customer, the broker or dealer shall furnish the customer with a copy of the information set forth on the Commission's Web site at http://www.sec.gov/investor/pubs/microcapstock.htm.

Rule 15g–3.   Broker or Dealer Disclosure of Quotations and Other Information Relating to the Penny Stock Market

(a)   *Requirement.* It shall be unlawful for a broker or dealer to effect a transaction in any penny stock with or for the account of a customer unless such broker or dealer discloses to such customer, within the time periods and in the manner required by paragraph (b) of this rule, the following information:

(1)   The inside bid quotation and the inside offer quotation for the penny stock.

(2)   If paragraph (a)(1) of this rule does not apply because of the absence of an inside bid quotation and an inside offer quotation:

(i)   With respect to a transaction effected with or for a customer on a principal basis (other than as provided in paragraph (a)(2)(ii) of this rule):

(A)   The dealer shall disclose its offer price for the security:

(*1*)   If during the previous five days the dealer has effected no fewer than three bona fide sales to other dealers consistently at its offer price for the security current at the time of those sales, and

(*2*)   If the dealer reasonably believes in good faith at the time of the transaction with the customer that its offer price accurately reflects the price at which it is willing to sell one or more round lots to another dealer.

For purposes of this paragraph (a)(2)(i)(A), "consistently" shall constitute, at a minimum, seventy-five percent of the dealer's bona fide interdealer sales during the previous five-day period, and, if the dealer has effected only three bona fide interdealer sales during such period, all three of such sales.

(B) The dealer shall disclose its bid price for the security:

(1) If during the previous five days the dealer has effected no fewer than three bona fide purchases from other dealers consistently at its bid price for the security current at the time of those purchases, and

(2) If the dealer reasonably believes in good faith at the time of the transaction with the customer that its bid price accurately reflects the price at which it is willing to buy one or more round lots from another dealer.

For purposes of this paragraph (a)(2)(i)(B), "consistently" shall constitute, at a minimum, seventy-five percent of the dealer's bona fide interdealer purchases during the previous five-day period, and, if the dealer has effected only three bona fide interdealer purchases during such period, all three of such purchases.

(C) If the dealer's bid or offer prices to the customer do not satisfy the criteria of paragraphs (a)(2)(i)(A) or (a)(2)(i)(B) of this rule, the dealer shall disclose to the customer:

(1) That it has not effected inter-dealer purchases or sales of the penny stock consistently at its bid or offer price, and

(2) The price at which it last purchased the penny stock from, or sold the penny stock to, respectively, another dealer in a bona fide transaction.

(ii) With respect to transactions effected by a broker or dealer with or for the account of the customer:

(A) On an agency basis or

(B) On a basis other than as a market maker in the security, where, after having received an order from the customer to purchase a penny stock, the dealer effects the purchase from another person to offset a contemporaneous sale of the penny stock to such customer, or, after having received an order from the customer to sell the penny stock, the dealer effects the sale to another person to offset a contemporaneous purchase from such customer, the broker or dealer shall disclose the best independent interdealer bid and offer prices for the penny stock that the broker or dealer obtains through reasonable diligence. A broker-dealer shall be deemed to have exercised reasonable diligence if it obtains quotations from three market makers in the security (or all known market makers if there are fewer than three).

(3) With respect to bid or offer prices and transaction prices disclosed pursuant to paragraph (a) of this rule, the broker or dealer shall disclose the number of shares to which the bid and offer prices apply.

(b) *Timing.*

(1) The information described in paragraph (a) of this rule:

(i) Shall be provided to the customer orally or in writing prior to effecting any transaction with or for the customer for the purchase or sale of such penny stock; and

(ii) Shall be given or sent to the customer in writing, at or prior to the time that any written confirmation of the transaction is given or sent to the customer pursuant to Rule 10b–10 of this chapter.

(2) A broker or dealer, at the time of making the disclosure pursuant to paragraph (b)(1)(i) of this rule, shall make and preserve as part of its records, a record of such disclosure for the period specified in Rule 17a–4(b) of this Act.

(c) *Definitions.* For purposes of this rule:

(1)   The term "bid price" shall mean the price most recently communicated by the dealer to another broker or dealer at which the dealer is willing to purchase one or more round lots of the penny stock, and shall not include indications of interest.

(2)   The term "offer price" shall mean the price most recently communicated by the dealer to another broker or dealer at which the dealer is willing to sell one or more round lots of the penny stock, and shall not include indications of interest.

(3)   The term "inside bid quotation" for a security shall mean the highest bid quotation for the security displayed by a market maker in the security on a Qualifying Electronic Quotation System, at any time in which at least two market makers are contemporaneously displaying on such system bid and offer quotations for the security at specified prices.

(4)   The term "inside offer quotation" for a security shall mean the lowest offer quotation for the security displayed by a market maker in the security on a Qualifying Electronic Quotation System, at any time in which at least two market makers are contemporaneously displaying on such system bid and offer quotations for the security at specified prices.

(5)   The term "Qualifying Electronic Quotation System" shall mean an automated interdealer quotation system that has the characteristics set forth in section 17B(b)(2) of the Act, or such other automated interdealer quotation system designated by the Commission for purposes of this rule.

Rule 15g–4.   Disclosure of Compensation to Brokers or Dealers

Preliminary Note: Brokers and dealers may wish to refer to Securities Exchange Act Release No. 30608 (April 20, 1992) for a discussion of the procedures for computing compensation in active and competitive markets, inactive and competitive markets, and dominated and controlled markets.

(a)   *Disclosure Requirement.* It shall be unlawful for any broker or dealer to effect a transaction in any penny stock for or with the account of a customer unless such broker or dealer discloses to such customer, within the time periods and in the manner required by paragraph (b) of this rule, the aggregate amount of any compensation received by such broker or dealer in connection with such transaction.

(b)   *Timing.*

(1)   The information described in paragraph (a) of this rule:

(i)   Shall be provided to the customer orally or in writing prior to effecting any transaction with or for the customer for the purchase or sale of such penny stock; and

(ii)   Shall be given or sent to the customer in writing, at or prior to the time that any written confirmation of the transaction is given or sent to the customer pursuant to Rule 10b–10 of this Act.

(2)   A broker or dealer, at the time of making the disclosure pursuant to paragraph (b)(1)(i) of this rule, shall make and preserve as part of its records, a record of such disclosure for the period specified in Rule 17a–4(b) of this Act.

(c)   *Definition of Compensation.* For purposes of this rule, "compensation" means, with respect to a transaction in a penny stock:

(1)   If a broker is acting as agent for a customer, the amount of any remuneration received or to be received by it from such customer in connection with such transaction;

(2)   If, after having received a buy order from a customer, a dealer other than a market maker purchased the penny stock as principal from another person to offset a contemporaneous sale to such customer or, after having received a sell order from a customer, sold the penny stock as principal to another person to offset a contemporaneous purchase from such customer, the difference between the price to the customer and such contemporaneous purchase or sale price; or

(3)   If the dealer otherwise is acting as principal for its own account, the difference between the price to the customer and the prevailing market price.

(d)   *"Active and Competitive" Market.* For purposes of this rule only, a market may be deemed to be "active and competitive" in determining the prevailing market price with respect to a transaction by a market maker in a penny stock if the aggregate number of transactions effected by such market maker in the penny stock in the five business days preceding such transaction is less than twenty percent of the aggregate number of all transactions in the penny stock reported on a Qualifying Electronic Quotation System (as defined in Rule 15g–3(c)(5)) during such five-day period. No presumption shall arise that a market is not "active and competitive" solely by reason of a market maker not meeting the conditions specified in this paragraph.

Rule 15g–5. Disclosure of Compensation of Associated Persons in Connection With Penny Stock Transactions

(a)   *General.*

(1)   It shall be unlawful for a broker or dealer to effect a transaction in any penny stock for or with the account of a customer unless the broker or dealer discloses to such customer, within the time periods and in the manner required by paragraph (b) of this rule, the aggregate amount of cash compensation that any associated person of the broker or dealer who is a natural person and has communicated with the customer concerning the transaction at or prior to receipt of the customer's transaction order, other than any person whose function is solely clerical or ministerial, has received or will receive from any source in connection with the transaction and that is determined at or prior to the time of the transaction, including separate disclosure, if applicable, of the source and amount of such compensation that is not paid by the broker or dealer.

(b)   *Timing.*

(1)   The information described in paragraph (a) of this rule:

(i)   Shall be provided to the customer orally or in writing prior to effecting any transaction with or for the customer for the purchase or sale of such penny stock; and

(ii)   Shall be given or sent to the customer in writing, at or prior to the time that any written confirmation of the transaction is given or sent to the customer pursuant to Rule 10b–10 of this chapter.

(2)   A broker or dealer, at the time of making the disclosure pursuant to paragraph (b)(1)(i) of this rule, shall make and preserve as part of its records, a record of such disclosure for the period specified in Rule 17a–4(b) of this Act.

(c)   *Contingent Compensation Arrangements.* Where a portion or all of the cash or other compensation that the associated person may receive in connection with the transaction may be determined and paid following the transaction based on aggregate sales volume levels or other contingencies, the written disclosure required by paragraph (b)(1)(ii) of this rule shall state that fact and describe the basis upon which such compensation is determined.

Rule 15g–6. Account Statements for Penny Stock Customers

(a)   *Requirement.* It shall be unlawful for any broker or dealer that has effected the sale to any customer, other than in a transaction that is exempt pursuant to Rule 15g–1 of this Act, of any security that is a penny stock on the last trading day of any calendar month, or any successor of such broker or dealer, to fail to give or send to such customer a written statement containing the information described in paragraphs (c) and (d) of this rule with respect to each such month in which such security is held for the customer's account with the broker or dealer, within ten days following the end of such month.

(b)   *Exemptions.* A broker or dealer shall be exempted from the requirement of paragraph (a) of this rule under either of the following circumstances:

(1)   If the broker or dealer does not effect any transactions in penny stocks for or with the account of the customer during a period of six consecutive calendar months, then the broker or dealer shall not be required to provide monthly statements for each quarterly period that is immediately subsequent to such six-month period and in which the broker or dealer does not effect any transaction in penny stocks for or with the account of the customer, *provided* that the broker or dealer gives or sends to the customer written statements containing the information described in paragraphs (d) and (e) of this rule on a quarterly basis, within ten days following the end of each such quarterly period.

(2) If, on all but five or fewer trading days of any quarterly period, a security has a price of five dollars or more, the broker or dealer shall not be required to provide a monthly statement covering the security for subsequent quarterly periods, until the end of any such subsequent quarterly period on the last trading day of which the price of the security is less than five dollars.

(c) *Price Determinations.* For purposes of paragraphs (a) and (b) of this rule, the price of a security on any trading day shall be determined at the close of business in accordance with the provisions of Rule 3a51–1(d)(1) of this Act.

(d) *Market and Price Information.* The statement required by paragraph (a) of this rule shall contain at least the following information with respect to each penny stock covered by paragraph (a) of this rule, as of the last trading day of the period to which the statement relates:

(1) The identity and number of shares or units of each such security held for the customer's account; and

(2) The estimated market value of the security, to the extent that such estimated market value can be determined in accordance with the following provisions:

(i) The highest inside bid quotation for the security on the last trading day of the period to which the statement relates, multiplied by the number of shares or units of the security held for the customer's account; or

(ii) If paragraph (d)(2)(i) of this rule is not applicable because of the absence of an inside bid quotation, and if the broker or dealer furnishing the statement has effected at least ten separate Qualifying Purchases in the security during the last five trading days of the period to which the statement relates, the weighted average price per share paid by the broker or dealer in all Qualifying Purchases effected during such five-day period, multiplied by the number of shares or units of the security held for the customer's account; or

(iii) If neither of paragraphs (d)(2)(i) nor (d)(2)(ii) of this rule is applicable, a statement that there is "no estimated market value" with respect to the security.

(e) *Legend.* In addition to the information required by paragraph (d) of this rule, the written statement required by paragraph (a) of this rule shall include a conspicuous legend that is identified with the penny stocks described in the statement and that contains the following language:

IF THIS STATEMENT CONTAINS AN ESTIMATED VALUE, YOU SHOULD BE AWARE THAT THIS VALUE MAY BE BASED ON A LIMITED NUMBER OF TRADES OR QUOTES. THEREFORE, YOU MAY NOT BE ABLE TO SELL THESE SECURITIES AT A PRICE EQUAL OR NEAR TO THE VALUE SHOWN. HOWEVER, THE BROKER-DEALER FURNISHING THIS STATEMENT MAY NOT REFUSE TO ACCEPT YOUR ORDER TO SELL THESE SECURITIES. ALSO, THE AMOUNT YOU RECEIVE FROM A SALE GENERALLY WILL BE REDUCED BY THE AMOUNT OF ANY COMMISSIONS OR SIMILAR CHARGES. IF AN ESTIMATED VALUE IS NOT SHOWN FOR A SECURITY, A VALUE COULD NOT BE DETERMINED BECAUSE OF A LACK OF INFORMATION.

(f) *Preservation of Records.* Any broker or dealer subject to this rule shall preserve, as part of its records, copies of the written statements required by paragraph (a) of this rule and keep such records for the periods specified in Rule 17a–4(b) of this Act.

(g) *Definitions.* For purposes of this rule:

(1) The term "Quarterly period" shall mean any period of three consecutive full calendar months.

(2) The "inside bid quotation" for a security shall mean the highest bid quotation for the security displayed by a market maker in the security on a Qualifying Electronic Quotation System, at any time in which at least two market makers are contemporaneously displaying on such system bid and offer quotations for the security at specified prices.

(3) The term "Qualifying Electronic Quotation System" shall mean an automated interdealer quotation system that has the characteristics set forth in section 17B(b)(2) of the Act, or such other automated interdealer quotation system designated by the Commission for purposes of this rule.

(4)   The term "Qualifying Purchases" shall mean bona fide purchases by a broker or dealer of a penny stock for its own account, each of which involves at least 100 shares, but excluding any block purchase involving more than one percent of the outstanding shares or units of the security.

Rule 15g–8. Sales of Escrowed Securities of Blank Check Companies

As a means reasonably designed to prevent fraudulent, deceptive, or manipulative acts or practices, it shall be unlawful for any person to sell or offer to sell any security that is deposited and held in an escrow or trust account pursuant to Rule 419 under the Securities Act of 1933, or any interest in or related to such security, other than pursuant to a qualified domestic relations order as defined by the Internal Revenue Code of 1986, as amended, or Title I of the Employee Retirement Income Security Act, or the rules thereunder.

Rule 15g–9. Sales Practice Requirements for Certain Low Priced Securities

(a)   As a means reasonably designed to prevent fraudulent, deceptive, or manipulative acts or practices, it shall be unlawful for a broker or dealer to sell a designated security to, or to effect the purchase of a designated security by, any person unless:

(1)   The transaction is exempt under paragraph (c) of this rule; or

(2)   prior to the transaction:

(i)   The broker or dealer has approved the person's account for transactions in penny stocks in accordance with the procedures set forth in paragraph (b) of this rule; and

(ii)(A)   The broker or dealer has received from the person an agreement to the transaction setting forth the identity and quantity of the penny stock to be purchased; and

(B)   Regardless of the form of agreement used to satisfy the requirements of paragraph (a)(2)(ii)(A) of this rule, it shall be unlawful for such broker or dealer to sell a penny stock to, or to effect the purchase of a penny stock by, for or with the account of a customer less than two business days after the broker or dealer sends such agreement.

(b)   In order to approve a person's account for transactions in penny stocks the broker or dealer must:

(1)   Obtain from the person information concerning the person's financial situation, investment experience, and investment objectives;

(2)   Reasonably determine, based on the information required by paragraph (b)(1) of this rule and any other information known by the broker-dealer, that transactions in penny stock are suitable for the person, and that the person (or the person's independent adviser in these transactions) has sufficient knowledge and experience in financial matters that the person (or the person's independent adviser in these transactions) reasonably may be expected to be capable of evaluating the risks of transactions in designated penny stocks;

(3)   Deliver to the person a written statement:

(i)   Setting forth the basis on which the broker or dealer made the determination required by paragraph (b)(2) of this rule;

(ii)   Stating in a highlighted format that it is unlawful for the broker or dealer to effect a transaction in a penny stock subject to the provisions of paragraph (a)(2) of this rule unless the broker or dealer has received, prior to the transaction, a written agreement to the transaction from the person; and

(iii)   Stating in a highlighted format immediately preceding the customer signature line that:

(A)   The broker or dealer is required by this rule to provide the person with the written statement; and

(B)   The person should not sign and return the written statement to the broker or dealer if it does not accurately reflect the person's financial situation, investment experience, and investment objectives; and

(4)(i)   Obtain from the person a signed and dated copy of the statement required by paragraph (b)(3) of this rule; and

(ii)   Regardless of the form of statement used to satisfy the requirements of paragraph (b)(4)(i) of this rule, it shall be unlawful for such broker or dealer to sell a penny stock to, or to effect the purchase of a penny stock by, for or with the account of a customer less than two business days after the broker or dealer sends such statement.

(c)   For purposes of this rule, the following transactions shall be exempt:

(1)   Transactions that are exempt under Rules 15g–1(a), (b), (d), (e), and (f).

(2)   Transactions that meet the requirements of Rule 506 of the Securities Act of 1933 (including, where applicable, the requirements of Rules 501 through 503, and 507 through 508), or transactions with an issuer not involving any public offering pursuant to section 4(a)(2) of the Securities Act of 1933.

(3)   Transactions in which the purchaser is an established customer of the broker or dealer.

(d)   For purposes of this rule:

(1)   The term penny stock shall have the same meaning as in Rule 3a51–1.

(2)   The term established customer shall mean any person for whom the broker or dealer, or a clearing broker on behalf of such broker or dealer, carries an account, and who in such account:

(i)   Has effected a securities transaction, or made a deposit of funds or securities, more than one year previously; or

(ii)   Has made three purchases of penny stocks that occurred on separate days and involved different issuers.

Rule 15l–1.   Regulation Best Interest

(a)   Best interest obligation. (1) A broker, dealer, or a natural person who is an associated person of a broker or dealer, when making a recommendation of any securities transaction or investment strategy involving securities (including account recommendations) to a retail customer, shall act in the best interest of the retail customer at the time the recommendation is made, without placing the financial or other interest of the broker, dealer, or natural person who is an associated person of a broker or dealer making the recommendation ahead of the interest of the retail customer.

(2)   The best interest obligation in paragraph (a)(1) of this rule shall be satisfied if:

(i)   Disclosure obligation. The broker, dealer, or natural person who is an associated person of a broker or dealer, prior to or at the time of the recommendation, provides the retail customer, in writing, full and fair disclosure of:

(A)   All material facts relating to the scope and terms of the relationship with the retail customer, including:

(1)   That the broker, dealer, or such natural person is acting as a broker, dealer, or an associated person of a broker or dealer with respect to the recommendation;

(2)   The material fees and costs that apply to the retail customer's transactions, holdings, and accounts; and

(3)   The type and scope of services provided to the retail customer, including any material limitations on the securities or investment strategies involving securities that may be recommended to the retail customer; and

(B)   All material facts relating to conflicts of interest that are associated with the recommendation.

(ii)   Care obligation. The broker, dealer, or natural person who is an associated person of a broker or dealer, in making the recommendation, exercises reasonable diligence, care, and skill to:

(A) Understand the potential risks, rewards, and costs associated with the recommendation, and have a reasonable basis to believe that the recommendation could be in the best interest of at least some retail customers;

(B) Have a reasonable basis to believe that the recommendation is in the best interest of a particular retail customer based on that retail customer's investment profile and the potential risks, rewards, and costs associated with the recommendation and does not place the financial or other interest of the broker, dealer, or such natural person ahead of the interest of the retail customer;

(C) Have a reasonable basis to believe that a series of recommended transactions, even if in the retail customer's best interest when viewed in isolation, is not excessive and is in the retail customer's best interest when taken together in light of the retail customer's investment profile and does not place the financial or other interest of the broker, dealer, or such natural person making the series of recommendations ahead of the interest of the retail customer.

(iii) Conflict of interest obligation. The broker or dealer establishes, maintains, and enforces written policies and procedures reasonably designed to:

(A) Identify and at a minimum disclose, in accordance with paragraph (a)(2)(i) of this rule, or eliminate, all conflicts of interest associated with such recommendations;

(B) Identify and mitigate any conflicts of interest associated with such recommendations that create an incentive for a natural person who is an associated person of a broker or dealer to place the interest of the broker, dealer, or such natural person ahead of the interest of the retail customer;

(C)(1)   Identify and disclose any material limitations placed on the securities or investment strategies involving securities that may be recommended to a retail customer and any conflicts of interest associated with such limitations, in accordance with subparagraph (a)(2)(i), and

(2) Prevent such limitations and associated conflicts of interest from causing the broker, dealer, or a natural person who is an associated person of the broker or dealer to make recommendations that place the interest of the broker, dealer, or such natural person ahead of the interest of the retail customer; and

(D) Identify and eliminate any sales contests, sales quotas, bonuses, and non-cash compensation that are based on the sales of specific securities or specific types of securities within a limited period of time. (iv) Compliance obligation. In addition to the policies and procedures required by paragraph (a)(2)(iii) of this rule, the broker or dealer establishes, maintains, and enforces written policies and procedures reasonably designed to achieve compliance with Regulation Best Interest.

(b) Definitions. Unless otherwise provided, all terms used in this rule shall have the same meaning as in the Securities Exchange Act of 1934. In addition, the following definitions shall apply for purposes of this rule:

(1) Retail customer means a natural person, or the legal representative of such natural person, who:

(i) Receives a recommendation of any securities transaction or investment strategy involving

securities from a broker, dealer, or a natural person who is an associated person of a broker or dealer; and

(ii) Uses the recommendation primarily for personal, family, or household purposes.

(2) Retail customer investment profile includes, but is not limited to, the retail customer's age, other investments, financial situation and needs, tax status, investment objectives, investment experience, investment time horizon, liquidity needs, risk tolerance, and any other information the

retail customer may disclose to the broker, dealer, or a natural person who is an associated person of a broker or dealer in connection with a recommendation.

(3)   Conflict of interest means an interest that might incline a broker, dealer, or a natural person who is an associated person of a broker or dealer—consciously or unconsciously—to make a recommendation that is not disinterested.

NATIONAL AND AFFILIATED SECURITIES ASSOCIATION

Rule 15Aa-1. Registration of a National or an Affiliated Securities Association

Any application for registration of an association as a national, or as an affiliated, securities association shall be made in triplicate on Form X–15AA–1 accompanied by three copies of the exhibits prescribed by the Commission to be filed in connection therewith.

Rule 15Aj-1. Amendments and Supplements to Registration Statements of Securities Associations

Every association applying for registration or registered as a national securities association or as an affiliated securities association shall keep its registration statement up-to-date in the manner prescribed below:

(a)   *Amendments.* Promptly after the discovery of any inaccuracy in the registration statement or in any amendment or supplement thereto the association shall file with the Commission an amendment correcting such inaccuracy.

(b)   *Current supplements.* Promptly after any change which renders no longer accurate any information contained or incorporated in the registration statement or in any amendment or supplement thereto the association shall file with the Commission a current supplement setting forth such change, except that:

(1)   Supplements setting forth changes in the information called for in Exhibit C need not be filed until 10 days after the calendar month in which the changes occur.

(2)   No current supplements need be filed with respect to changes in the information called for in Exhibit B.

(3)   If changes in the information called for in items (1) and (2) of Exhibit C are reported in any record which is published at least once a month by the association and promptly filed in triplicate with the Commission, no current supplement need be filed with respect thereto.

(c)   *Annual supplements.*

(1)   Promptly after March 1 of each year, the association shall file with the Commission an annual consolidated supplement as of such date on Form X–15Aj–2 except that:

(i)   If the securities association publishes or cooperates in the publication of the information required in Items 6(a) and 6(b) of Form X–15Aj–2 on an annual or more frequent basis, in lieu of filing such an item the securities association may:

(A)   Identify the publication in which such information is available, the name, address, and telephone number of the person from whom such publication may be obtained, and the price thereof; and

(B)   Certify to the accuracy of such information as of its date.

(ii)   Promptly after March 1, 1995, and every three years thereafter each association shall file complete Exhibit A to Form X–15Aj–2. The information contained in this exhibit shall be up to date as of the latest practicable date within 3 months of the date on which these exhibits are filed. If the association publishes or cooperates in the publication of the information required in this exhibit on an annual or more frequent basis, in lieu of filing such exhibit the association may:

(A)   Identify the publication in which such information is available, the name, address, and telephone number of the person from whom such publication may be obtained, and the price thereof; and

(B)   Certify to the accuracy of such information as of its date. If a securities association keeps the information required in this exhibit up to date and makes it available to the Commission and the public upon request, in lieu of filing such an exhibit a securities association may certify that the information is kept up to date and is available to the Commission and the public upon request.

(2)   Promptly after the close of each fiscal year of the association, it shall file with the Commission a supplement setting forth its balance sheet as of the close of such year and its income and expense statement for such year.

(d)   *Filing, dating, etc.* Each amendment or supplement shall be filed in triplicate, at least one of which must be signed and attested, in the same manner as required in the case of the original registration statement, and must conform to the requirements of Form X–15Aj–1, except that the annual consolidated supplement shall be filed on Form X–15Aj–2. All amendments and supplements shall be dated and numbered in order of filing. One amendment or supplement may include any number of changes. In addition to the formal filing of amendments and supplements above described, each association shall send to the Commission three copies of any notices, reports, circulars, loose-leaf insertions, riders, new additions, lists or other records of changes covered by amendments or supplements when, as and if such records are made available to members of the association.

REPORTS OF DIRECTORS

Rule 16a–1.   Definition of Terms

Terms defined in this rule shall apply solely to section 16 of the Act and the rules thereunder. These terms shall not be limited to section 16(a) of the Act but also shall apply to all other subsections under section 16 of the Act.

(a)   The term "beneficial owner" shall have the following applications:

(1)   Solely for purposes of determining whether a person is a beneficial owner of more than ten percent of any class of equity securities registered pursuant to section 12 of the Act, the term "beneficial owner" shall mean any person who is deemed a beneficial owner pursuant to section 13(d) of the Act and the rules thereunder; *provided, however,* that the following institutions or persons shall not be deemed the beneficial owner of securities of such class held for the benefit of third parties or in customer or fiduciary accounts in the ordinary course of business (or in the case of an employee benefit plan specified in subparagraph (vi) below, of securities of such class allocated to plan participants where participants have voting power) as long as such shares are acquired by such institutions or persons without the purpose or effect of changing or influencing control of the issuer or engaging in any arrangement subject to Rule 13d–3(b):

(i)   A broker or dealer registered under section 15 of the Act;

(ii)   A bank as defined in section 3(a)(6) of the Act;

(iii)   An insurance company as defined in section 3(a)(19) of the Act;

(iv)   An investment company registered under section 8 of the Investment Company Act of 1940;

(v)   An investment adviser registered under section 203 of the Investment Advisers Act of 1940;

(vi)   An employee benefit plan as defined in section 3(3) of the Employee Retirement Income Security Act of 1974, as amended, ("ERISA") that is subject to the provisions of ERISA, or any such plan that is not subject to ERISA that is maintained primarily for the benefit of the employees of a state or local government or instrumentality, or an endowment fund;

(vii)   A parent holding company, provided the aggregate amount held directly by the parent, and directly and indirectly by its subsidiaries that are not persons specified in Rule 16a–1(a)(1)(i) through (x), does not exceed one percent of the securities of the subject class;

(viii)   A savings association as defined in section 3(b) of the Federal Deposit Insurance Act;

(ix) A church plan that is excluded from the definition of an investment company under section 3(c)(14) of the Investment Company Act of 1940; and

(x) A non-U.S. institution that is the functional equivalent of any of the institutions listed in paragraphs (a)(1)(i) through (ix) of this rule, so long as the non-U.S. institution is subject to a regulatory scheme that is substantially comparable to the regulatory scheme applicable to the equivalent U.S. institution and the non-U.S. institution is eligible to file a Schedule 13G pursuant to Rule 13d–1(b)(1)(ii)(J); and

(xi) A group, provided that all the members are persons specified in Rule 16a–1(a)(1)(i) through (x).

NOTE to paragraph (a). Pursuant to this rule, a person deemed a beneficial owner of more than ten percent of any class of equity securities registered under section 12 of the Act would file a Form 3, but the securities holdings disclosed on Form 3, and changes in beneficial ownership reported on subsequent Forms 4 or 5, would be determined by the definition of "beneficial owner" in paragraph (a)(2) of this rule.

(2) Other than for purposes of determining whether a person is a beneficial owner of more than ten percent of any class of equity securities registered under section 12 of the Act, the term "beneficial owner" shall mean any person who, directly or indirectly, through any contract, arrangement, understanding, relationship or otherwise, has or shares a direct or indirect pecuniary interest in the equity securities, subject to the following:

(i) The term "pecuniary interest" in any *class of equity* securities shall mean the opportunity, directly or indirectly, to profit or share in any profit derived from a transaction in the subject securities.

(ii) The term "indirect pecuniary interest" in any class of equity securities shall include, but not be limited to:

(A) Securities held by members of a person's immediate family sharing the same household; *provided, however,* that the presumption of such beneficial ownership may be rebutted; *see* Rule 16a–1(a)(4);

(B) A general partner's proportionate interest in the portfolio securities held by a general or limited partnership. The general partner's proportionate interest, as evidenced by the partnership agreement in effect at the time of the transaction and the partnership's most recent financial statements, shall be the greater of:

(*1*) The general partner's share of the partnership's profits, including profits attributed to any limited partnership interests held by the general partner and any other interests in profits that arise from the purchase and sale of the partnership's portfolio securities; or

(*2*) The general partner's share of the partnership capital account, including the share attributable to any limited partnership interest held by the general partner.

(C) A performance-related fee, other than an asset-based fee, received by any broker, dealer, bank, insurance company, investment company, investment adviser, investment manager, trustee or person or entity performing a similar function; *provided, however,* that no pecuniary interest shall be present where:

(*1*) The performance-related fee, regardless of when payable, is calculated based upon net capital gains and/or net capital appreciation generated from the portfolio or from the fiduciary's overall performance over a period of one year or more; and

(*2*) Equity securities of the issuer do not account for more than ten percent of the market value of the portfolio. A right to a nonperformance-related fee alone shall not represent a pecuniary interest in the securities;

(D) A person's right to dividends that is separated or separable from the underlying securities. Otherwise, a right to dividends alone shall not represent a pecuniary interest in the securities;

(E) A person's interest in securities held by a trust, as specified in Rule 16a–8(b); and

(F) A person's right to acquire equity securities through the exercise or conversion of any derivative security, whether or not presently exercisable.

(iii) A shareholder shall not be deemed to have a pecuniary interest in the portfolio securities held by a corporation or similar entity in which the person owns securities if the shareholder is not a controlling shareholder of the entity and does not have or share investment control over the entity's portfolio.

(3) Where more than one person subject to section 16 of the Act is deemed to be a beneficial owner of the same equity securities, all such persons must report as beneficial owners of the securities, either separately or jointly, as provided in Rule 16a–3(j). In such cases, the amount of short-swing profit recoverable shall not be increased above the amount recoverable if there were only one beneficial owner.

(4) Any person filing a statement pursuant to section 16(a) of the Act may state that the filing shall not be deemed an admission that such person is, for purposes of section 16 of the Act or otherwise, the beneficial owner of any equity securities covered by the statement.

(5) The following interests are deemed not to confer beneficial ownership for purposes of section 16 of the Act:

(i) Interests in portfolio securities held by any investment company registered under the Investment Company Act of 1940, and

(ii) Interests in securities comprising part of a broad-based, publicly traded market basket or index of stocks, approved for trading by the appropriate federal governmental authority.

(b) The term "call equivalent position" shall mean a derivative security position that increases in value as the value of the underlying equity increases, including, but not limited to, a long convertible security, a long call option, and a short put option position.

(c) The term "derivative securities" shall mean any option, warrant, convertible security, stock appreciation right, or similar right with an exercise or conversion privilege at a price related to an equity security, or similar securities with a value derived from the value of an equity security, but shall not include:

(1) Rights of a pledgee of securities to sell the pledged securities;

(2) Rights of all holders of a class of securities of an issuer to receive securities pro rata, or obligations to dispose of securities, as a result of a merger, exchange offer, or consolidation involving the issuer of the securities;

(3) Rights or obligations to surrender a security, or have a security withheld, upon the receipt or exercise of a derivative security or the receipt or vesting of equity securities, in order to satisfy the exercise price or the tax withholding consequences of receipt, exercise or vesting;

(4) Interests in broad-based index options, broad-based index futures, and broad-based publicly traded market baskets of stocks approved for trading by the appropriate federal governmental authority;

(5) Interests or rights to participate in employee benefit plans of the issuer;

(6) Rights with an exercise or conversion privilege at a price that is not fixed; or

(7) Options granted to an underwriter in a registered public offering for the purpose of satisfying over-allotments in such offering.

(d) The term "equity security of such issuer" shall mean any equity security or derivative security relating to an issuer, whether or not issued by that issuer.

(e) The term "immediate family" shall mean any child, stepchild, grandchild, parent, stepparent, grandparent, spouse, sibling, mother-in-law, father-in-law, son-in-law, daughter-in-law, brother-in-law, or sister-in-law, and shall include adoptive relationships.

(f) The term "officer" shall mean an issuer's president, principal financial officer, principal accounting officer (or, if there is no such accounting officer, the controller), any vice-president of the issuer in charge of a principal business unit, division or function (such as sales, administration or finance), any other officer who performs a policy-making function, or any other person who performs similar policy-making functions for the issuer. Officers of the issuer's parent(s) or subsidiaries shall be deemed officers of the issuer if they perform such policy-making functions for the issuer. In addition, when the issuer is a limited partnership, officers or employees of the general partner(s) who perform policy-making functions for the limited partnership are deemed officers of the limited partnership. When the issuer is a trust, officers or employees of the trustee(s) who perform policy-making functions for the trust are deemed officers of the trust.

NOTE: "Policy-making function" is not intended to include policy-making functions that are not significant. If pursuant to Item 401(b) of Regulation S–K the issuer identifies a person as an "executive officer," it is presumed that the Board of Directors has made that judgment and that the persons so identified are the officers for purposes of Section 16 of the Act, as are such other persons enumerated in this paragraph (f) but not in Item 401(b).

(g)   The term "portfolio securities" shall mean all securities owned by an entity, other than securities issued by the entity.

(h)   The term "put equivalent position" shall mean a derivative security position that increases in value as the value of the underlying equity decreases, including, but not limited to, a long put option and a short call option position.

Rule 16a–2.   Persons and Transactions Subject to Section 16

Any person who is the beneficial owner, directly or indirectly, of more than ten percent of any class of equity securities ("ten percent beneficial owner") registered pursuant to section 12 of the Act, any director or officer of the issuer of such securities, and any person specified in section 30(h) of the Investment Company Act of 1940, including any person specified in Rule 16a–8, shall be subject to the provisions of section 16 of the Act. The rules under section 16 of the Act apply to any class of equity securities of an issuer whether or not registered under section 12 of the Act. The rules under section 16 of the Act also apply to non-equity securities as provided by the Investment Company Act of 1940. With respect to transactions by persons subject to section 16 of the Act:

(a)   A transaction(s) carried out by a director or officer in the six months prior to the director or officer becoming subject to section 16 of the Act shall be subject to section 16 of the Act and reported on the first required Form 4 only if the transaction(s) occurred within six months of the transaction giving rise to the Form 4 filing obligation and the director or officer became subject to section 16 of the Act solely as a result of the issuer registering a class of equity securities pursuant to section 12 of the Act.

(b)   A transaction(s) following the cessation of director or officer status shall be subject to section 16 of the Act only if:

(1)   Executed within a period of less than six months of an opposite transaction subject to section 16(b) of the Act that occurred while that person was a director or officer; and

(2)   Not otherwise exempted from section 16(b) of the Act pursuant to the provision of this chapter.

NOTE to paragraph (b): For purposes of this paragraph, an acquisition and a disposition each shall be an opposite transaction with respect to the other.

(c)   The transaction that results in a person becoming a ten percent beneficial owner is not subject to section 16 of the Act unless the person otherwise is subject to section 16 of the Act. A ten percent beneficial owner not otherwise subject to section 16 of the Act must report only those transactions conducted while the beneficial owner of more than ten percent of a class of equity securities of the issuer registered pursuant to section 12 of the Act.

(d)(1)   Transactions by a person or entity shall be exempt from the provisions of section 16 of the Act for the 12 months following appointment and qualification, to the extent such person or entity is acting as:

(i)   Executor or administrator of the estate of a decedent;

(ii)   Guardian or member of a committee for an incompetent;

(iii) Receiver, trustee in bankruptcy, assignee for the benefit of creditors, conservator, liquidating agent, or other similar person duly authorized by law to administer the estate or assets of another person; or

(iv) Fiduciary in a similar capacity.

(2) Transactions by such person or entity acting in a capacity specified in paragraph (d)(1) of this rule after the period specified in that paragraph shall be subject to section 16 of the Act only where the estate, trust or other entity is a beneficial owner of more than ten percent of any class of equity security registered pursuant to section 12 of the Act.

Rule 16a-3. Reporting Transactions and Holdings

(a) Initial statements of beneficial ownership of equity securities required by section 16(a) of the Act shall be filed on Form 3. Statements of changes in beneficial ownership required by that section shall be filed on Form 4. Annual statements shall be filed on Form 5. At the election of the reporting person, any transaction required to be reported on Form 5 may be reported on an earlier filed Form 4. All such statements shall be prepared and filed in accordance with the requirements of the applicable form.

(b) A person filing statements pursuant to section 16(a) of the Act with respect to any class of equity securities registered pursuant to section 12 of the Act need not file an additional statement on Form 3:

(1) When an additional class of equity securities of the same issuer becomes registered pursuant to section 12 of the Act; or

(2) When such person assumes a different or an additional relationship to the same issuer (for example, when an officer becomes a director).

(c) Any issuer that has equity securities listed on more than one national securities exchange may designate one exchange as the only exchange with which reports pursuant to section 16(a) of the Act need be filed. Such designation shall be made in writing and shall be filed with the Commission and with each national securities exchange on which any equity security of the issuer is listed at the time of such election. The reporting person's obligation to file reports with each national securities exchange on which any equity security of the issuer is listed shall be satisfied by filing with the exchange so designated.

(d) Any person required to file a statement with respect to securities of a single issuer under both section 16(a) of the Act and section 30(h) of the Investment Company Act of 1940 may file a single statement containing the required information, which will be deemed to be filed under both Acts.

(e) [Removed and Reserved].

(f)(1) A Form 5 shall be filed by every person who at any time during the issuer's fiscal year was subject to section 16 of the Act with respect to such issuer, except as provided in paragraph (2) below. The Form shall be filed within 45 days after the issuer's fiscal year end, and shall disclose the following holdings and transactions not reported previously on Forms 3, 4 or 5:

(i) All transactions during the most recent fiscal year that were exempt from section 16(b) of the Act, except:

(A) Exercises and conversions of derivative securities exempt under either Rule 16b-3 or Rule 16b-6(b), and any transaction exempt under Rule 16b-3(d), Rule 16b-3(e), or Rule 16b-3(f) (these are required to be reported on Form 4);

(B) Transactions exempt from section 16(b) of the Act pursuant to Rule 16b-3(c), which shall be exempt from section 16(a) of the Act; and

(C) Transactions exempt from section 16(a) of the Act pursuant to another rule;

(ii) Transactions that constituted small acquisitions pursuant to Rule 16a-6(a);

(iii) All holdings and transactions that should have been reported during the most recent fiscal year, but were not; and

(iv) With respect to the first Form 5 requirement for a reporting person, all holdings and transactions that should have been reported in each of the issuer's last two fiscal years but were not, based on the reporting person's reasonable belief in good faith in the completeness and accuracy of the information.

(2)   Notwithstanding the above, no Form 5 shall be required where all transactions otherwise required to be reported on the Form 5 have been reported before the due date of the Form 5.

NOTE: Persons no longer subject to section 16 of the Act, but who were subject to the section at any time during the issuer's fiscal year, must file a Form 5 unless paragraph (f)(2) is satisfied. *See also* Rule 16a–2(b) regarding the reporting obligations of persons ceasing to be officers or directors.

(g)(1)   A Form 4 must be filed to report: All transactions not exempt from section 16(b) of the Act; All transactions exempt from section 16(b) of the Act pursuant to Rule 16b–3(d), Rule 16b–3(e), or Rule 16b–3(f); and all exercises and conversions of derivative securities, regardless of whether exempt from section 16(b) of the Act. Form 4 must be filed before the end of the second business day following the day on which the subject transaction has been executed.

(2)   Solely for purposes of section 16(a)(2)(C) of the Act and paragraph (g)(1) of this Rule, the date on which the executing broker, dealer or plan administrator notifies the reporting person of the execution of the transaction is deemed the date of execution for a transaction where the following conditions are satisfied:

(i)   the transaction is pursuant to a contract, instruction or written plan for the purchase or sale of equity securities of the issuer (as defined in Rule 16a–1(d)) that satisfies the affirmative defense conditions of Rule 10b5–1(c) of this chapter; and

(ii)   the reporting person does not select the date of execution.

(3)   Solely for purposes of section 16(a)(2)(C) of the Act and paragraph (g)(1) of this Rule, the date on which the plan administrator notifies the reporting person that the transaction has been executed is deemed the date of execution for a discretionary transaction (as defined in Rule 16b–3(b)(1)) for which the reporting person does not select the date of execution.

(4)   In the case of the transactions described in paragraphs (g)(2) and (g)(3) of this Rule, if the notification date is later than the third business day following the trade date of the transaction, the date of execution is deemed to be the third business day following the trade date of the transaction.

(5)   At the option of the reporting person, transactions that are reportable on Form 5 may be reported on Form 4, so long as the Form 4 is filed no later than the due date of the Form 5 on which the transaction is otherwise required to be reported.

(h)   The date of filing with the Commission shall be the date of receipt by the Commission.

(i)   *Signatures.* Where section 16 of the Act, or the rules or forms thereunder, require a document filed with or furnished to the Commission to be signed, such document shall be manually signed, or signed using either typed signatures or duplicated or facsimile versions of manual signatures. Where typed, duplicated or facsimile signatures are used, each signatory to the filing shall manually sign a signature page or other document authenticating, acknowledging or otherwise adopting his or her signature that appears in the filing. Such document shall be executed before or at the time the filing is made and shall be retained by the filer for a period of five years. Upon request, the filer shall furnish to the Commission or its staff a copy of any or all documents retained pursuant to this rule.

(j)   Where more than one person subject to section 16 of the Act is deemed to be a beneficial owner of the same equity securities, all such persons must report as beneficial owners of the securities, either separately or jointly. Where persons in a group are deemed to be beneficial owners of equity securities pursuant to Rule 16a–1(a)(1) due to the aggregation of holdings, a single Form 3, 4 or 5 may be filed on behalf of all persons in the group. Joint and group filings must include all required information for each beneficial owner, and such filings must be signed by each beneficial owner, or on behalf of such owner by an authorized person.

(k)   Any issuer that maintains a corporate Web site shall post on that Web site by the end of the business day after filing any Form 3, 4 or 5 filed under section 16(a) of the Act as to the equity securities of that issuer. Each such form shall remain accessible on such issuer's Web site for at least a 12-month period. In the case of an issuer that is an investment company and that does not maintain its own Web site, if any of the issuer's investment adviser, sponsor, depositor, trustee, administrator, principal underwriter, or any affiliated person of the investment company maintains a Web site that includes the name of the issuer, the issuer shall comply with the posting requirements by posting the forms on one such Web site.

Rule 16a–4.   Derivative Securities

(a)   For purposes of section 16 of the Act, both derivative securities and the underlying securities to which they relate shall be deemed to be the same class of equity securities, *except that* the acquisition or disposition of any derivative security shall be separately reported.

(b)   The exercise or conversion of a call equivalent position shall be reported on Form 4 and treated for reporting purposes as:

(1)   A purchase of the underlying security; and

(2)   A closing of the derivative security position.

(c)   The exercise or conversion of a put equivalent position shall be reported on Form 4 and treated for reporting purposes as:

(1)   A sale of the underlying security; and

(2)   A closing of the derivative security position.

(d)   The disposition or closing of a long derivative security position, as a result of cancellation or expiration, shall be exempt from section 16(a) of the Act if exempt from section 16(b) of the Act pursuant to Rule 16b–6(d).

NOTE to Rule 16a–4: A purchase or sale resulting from an exercise or conversion of a derivative security may be exempt from section 16(b) of the Act pursuant to Rule 16b–3 or Rule 16b–6(b).

Rule 16a–5.   Odd-Lot Dealers

Transactions by an odd-lot dealer (a) in odd-lots as reasonably necessary to carry on odd-lot transactions, or (b) in round lots to offset odd-lot transactions previously or simultaneously executed or reasonably anticipated in the usual course of business, shall be exempt from the provisions of section 16(a) of the Act with respect to participation by such odd-lot dealer in such transaction.

Rule 16a–6.   Small Acquisitions

(a)   Any acquisition of an equity security or the right to acquire such securities, other than an acquisition from the issuer (including an employee benefit plan sponsored by the issuer), not exceeding $10,000 in market value shall be reported on Form 5 subject to the following conditions:

(1)   Such acquisition, when aggregated with other acquisitions of securities of the same class (including securities underlying derivative securities, but excluding acquisitions exempted by rule from section 16(b) or previously reported on Form 4 or Form 5) within the prior six months, does not exceed a total of $10,000 in market value; and

(2)   The person making the acquisition does not within six months thereafter make any disposition, other than by a transaction exempt from section 16(b) of the Act.

(b)   If an acquisition no longer qualifies for the reporting deferral in paragraph (a) of this rule, all such acquisitions that have not yet been reported must be reported on a Form 4 before the end of the second business day following the day on which the conditions of paragraph (a) are no longer met.

Rule 16a–7.   Transactions Effected in Connection With a Distribution

(a)   Any purchase and sale, or sale and purchase, of a security that is made in connection with the distribution of a substantial block of securities shall be exempt from the provisions of section 16(a) of the Act, to the extent specified in this Rule, subject to the following conditions:

(1)   The person effecting the transaction is engaged in the business of distributing securities and is participating in good faith, in the ordinary course of such business, in the distribution of such block of securities; and

(2)   The security involved in the transaction is:

   (i)   Part of such block of securities and is acquired by the person effecting the transaction, with a view to distribution thereof, from the issuer or other person on whose behalf such securities are being distributed or from a person who is participating in good faith in the distribution of such block of securities; or

   (ii)   A security purchased in good faith by or for the account of the person effecting the transaction for the purpose of stabilizing the market price of securities of the class being distributed or to cover an over-allotment or other short position created in connection with such distribution.

(b)   Each person participating in the transaction must qualify on an individual basis for an exemption pursuant to this rule.

Rule 16a–8.   Trusts

(a)   *Persons subject to section 16.*

   (1)   *Trusts.* A trust shall be subject to section 16 of the Act with respect to securities of the issuer if the trust is a beneficial owner, pursuant to Rule 16a–1(a)(1), of more than ten percent of any class of equity securities of the issuer registered pursuant to section 12 of the Act ("ten percent beneficial owner").

   (2)   *Trustees, Beneficiaries, and Settlors.* In determining whether a trustee, beneficiary, or settlor is a ten percent beneficial owner with respect to the issuer:

   (i)   Such persons shall be deemed the beneficial owner of the issuer's securities held by the trust, to the extent specified by Rule 16a–1(a)(1); and

   (ii)   Settlors shall be deemed the beneficial owner of the issuer's securities held by the trust where they have the power to revoke the trust without the consent of another person.

(b)   *Trust Holdings and Transactions.* Holdings and transactions in the issuer's securities held by a trust shall be reported by the trustee on behalf of the trust, if the trust is subject to section 16 of the Act, except as provided below. Holdings and transactions in the issuer's securities held by a trust (whether or not subject to section 16 of the Act) may be reportable by other parties as follows:

   (1)   *Trusts.* The trust need not report holdings and transactions in the issuer's securities held by the trust in an employee benefit plan subject to the Employee Retirement Income Security Act over which no trustee exercises investment control.

   (2)   *Trustees.* If, as provided by Rule 16a–1(a)(2), a trustee subject to section 16 of the Act has a pecuniary interest in any holding or transaction in the issuer's securities held by the trust, such holding or transaction shall be attributed to the trustee and shall be reported by the trustee in the trustee's individual capacity, as well as on behalf of the trust. With respect to performance fees and holdings of the trustee's immediate family, trustees shall be deemed to have a pecuniary interest in the trust holdings and transactions in the following circumstances:

   (i)   A performance fee is received that does not meet the proviso of Rule 16a–1(a)(2)(ii)(C); or

   (ii)   At least one beneficiary of the trust is a member of the trustee's immediate family. The pecuniary interest of the immediate family member(s) shall be attributed to and reported by the trustee.

   (3)   *Beneficiaries.* A beneficiary subject to section 16 of the Act shall have or share reporting obligations with respect to transactions in the issuer's securities held by the trust, if the beneficiary is a beneficial owner of the securities pursuant to Rule 16a–1(a)(2), as follows:

   (i)   If a beneficiary shares investment control with the trustee with respect to a trust transaction, the transaction shall be attributed to and reported by both the beneficiary and the trust;

(ii)   If a beneficiary has investment control with respect to a trust transaction without consultation with the trustee, the transaction shall be attributed to and reported by the beneficiary only; and

(iii)   In making a determination as to whether a beneficiary is the beneficial owner of the securities pursuant to Rule 16a-1(a)(2), beneficiaries shall be deemed to have a pecuniary interest in the issuer's securities held by the trust to the extent of their pro rata interest in the trust where the trustee does not exercise exclusive investment control.

NOTE to paragraph (b)(3): Transactions and holdings attributed to a trust beneficiary may be reported by the trustee on behalf of the beneficiary, provided that the report is signed by the beneficiary or other authorized person. Where the transactions and holdings are attributed both to the trustee and trust beneficiary, a joint report may be filed in accordance with Rule 16a-3(j).

(4)   *Settlors.* If a settlor subject to section 16 of the Act reserves the right to revoke the trust without the consent of another person, the trust holdings and transactions shall be attributed to and reported by the settlor instead of the trust; *provided, however,* that if the settlor does not exercise or share investment control over the issuer's securities held by the trust, the trust holdings and transactions shall be attributed to and reported by the trust instead of the settlor.

(c)   *Remainder interests.* Remainder interests in a trust are deemed not to confer beneficial ownership for purposes of section 16 of the Act, provided that the persons with the remainder interests have no power, directly or indirectly, to exercise or share investment control over the trust.

(d)   A trust, trustee, beneficiary or settlor becoming subject to section 16(a) of the Act pursuant to this Rule also shall be subject to sections 16(b) and 16(c) of the Act.

Rule 16a-9.   Stock Splits, Stock Dividends, and Pro Rata Rights

The following shall be exempt from section 16 of the Act:

(a)   The increase or decrease in the number of securities held as a result of a stock split or stock dividend applying equally to all securities of a class, including a stock dividend in which equity securities of a different issuer are distributed; and

(b)   The acquisition of rights, such as shareholder or pre-emptive rights, pursuant to a pro rata grant to all holders of the same class of equity securities registered under section 12 of the Act.

NOTE: The exercise or sale of a pro rata right shall be reported pursuant to Rule 16a-4 and the exercise shall be eligible for exemption from section 16(b) of the Act pursuant to Rule 16b-6(b).

Rule 16a-10.   Exemptions Under Section 16(a)

Except as provided in Rule 16a-6, any transaction exempted from the requirements of section 16(a) of the Act, insofar as it is otherwise subject to the provisions of section 16(b), shall be likewise exempt from section 16(b) of the Act.

Rule 16a-11.   Dividend or Interest Reinvestment Plans

Any acquisition of securities resulting from the reinvestment of dividends or interest on securities of the same issuer shall be exempt from section 16 of the Act if the acquisition is made pursuant to a plan providing for the regular reinvestment of dividends or interest and the plan provides of broad-based participation, does not discriminate in favor of employees of the issuer, and operates on substantially the same terms for all plan participants.

Rule 16a-12.   Domestic Relations Orders

The acquisition or disposition of equity securities pursuant to a domestic relations order, as defined in the Internal Revenue Code or Title 1 of the Employee Retirement Income Security Act, or the rules thereunder, shall be exempt from section 16 of the Act.

Rule 16a–13. Change in Form of Beneficial Ownership

A transaction, other than the exercise or conversion of a derivative security or deposit into or withdrawal from a voting trust, that effects only a change in the form of beneficial ownership without changing a person's pecuniary interest in the subject equity securities shall be exempt from section 16 of the Act.

Rule 16b–1. Transactions Approved by a Regulatory Authority

Any purchase and sale, or sale and purchase, of a security shall be exempt from section 16(b) of the Act, if the transaction is effected by an investment company registered under the Investment Company Act of 1940 and both the purchase and sale of such security have been exempted from the provisions of section 17(a) of the Investment Company Act of 1940, by rule or order of the Commission.

Rule 16b–3. Transactions Between an Issuer and Its Officers or Directors

(a) *General.* A transaction between the issuer (including an employee benefit plan sponsored by the issuer) and an officer or director of the issuer that involves issuer equity securities shall be exempt from section 16(b) of the Act if the transaction satisfies the applicable conditions set forth in this rule.

(b) *Definitions.*

(1) A "Discretionary Transaction" shall mean a transaction pursuant to an employee benefit plan that:

(i) Is at the volition of a plan participant;

(ii) Is not made in connection with the participant's death, disability, retirement or termination of employment;

(iii) Is not required to be made available to a plan participant pursuant to a provision of the Internal Revenue Code; and

(iv) Results in either an intra-plan transfer involving an issuer equity securities fund, or a cash distribution funded by a volitional disposition of an issuer equity security.

(2) An "Excess Benefit Plan" shall mean an employee benefit plan that is operated in conjunction with a Qualified Plan, and provides only the benefits or contributions that would be provided under a Qualified Plan but for any benefit or contribution limitations set forth in the Internal Revenue Code of 1986, or any successor provisions thereof.

(3)(i) A "Non-Employee Director" shall mean a director who:

(A) Is not currently an officer (as defined in Rule 16a–1(f)) of the issuer or a parent or subsidiary of the issuer, or otherwise currently employed by the issuer or a parent or subsidiary of the issuer;

(B) Does not receive compensation, either directly or indirectly, from the issuer or a parent or subsidiary, for services rendered as a consultant or in any capacity other than as a director, except for an amount that does not exceed the dollar amount for which disclosure would be required pursuant to Item 404(a) of Regulation S–K; and

(C) Does not possess an interest in any other transaction for which disclosure would be required pursuant to Item 404(a) of Regulation S–K.

(ii) Notwithstanding paragraph (b)(3)(i) of this rule, a Non-Employee Director of a closed end investment company shall mean a director who is not an "interested person" of the issuer, as that term is defined in section 2(a)(19) of the Investment Company Act of 1940.

(4) A "Qualified Plan" shall mean an employee benefit plan that satisfies the coverage and participation requirements of section 410 and 401(a)(26) of the Internal Revenue Code of 1986, or any successor provisions thereof.

(5)   A "Stock Purchase Plan" shall mean an employee benefit plan that satisfies the coverage and participation requirements of sections 423(b)(3) and 423(b)(5), or section 410 of the Internal Revenue Code of 1986, or any successor provisions thereof.

(c)   *Tax-conditioned plans.* Any transaction (other than a Discretionary Transaction) pursuant to a Qualified Plan, an Excess Benefit Plan, or a Stock Purchase Plan shall be exempt without condition.

(d)   *Acquisitions from the issuer.* Any transaction, other than a Discretionary Transaction, involving an acquisition from the issuer (including without limitation a grant or award), whether or not intended for a compensatory or other particular purpose, shall be exempt if:

(1)   The transaction is approved by the board of directors of the issuer, or a committee of the board of directors that is composed solely of two or more Non-Employee Directors;

(2)   The transaction is approved or ratified, in compliance with section 14 of the Act, by either; the affirmative votes of the holders of a majority of the securities of the issuer present, or represented, and entitled to vote at a meeting duly held in accordance with the applicable laws of the state or other jurisdiction in which the issuer is incorporated; or the written consent of the holders of a majority of the securities of the issuer entitled to vote; provided that such ratification occurs no later than the date of the next annual meeting of shareholders; or

(3)   The issuer equity securities so acquired are held by the officer or director for a period of six months following the date of such acquisition, provided that this condition shall be satisfied with respect to a derivative security if at least six months elapse from the date of acquisition of the derivative security to the date of disposition of the derivative security (other than upon exercise or conversion) or its underlying equity security.

(e)   *Dispositions to the issuer.* Any transaction, other than a Discretionary Transaction, involving the disposition to the issuer of issuer equity securities, whether or not intended for a compensatory or other particular purpose, shall be exempt, provided that the terms of such disposition are approved in advance in the manner prescribed by either paragraph (d)(1) or paragraph (d)(2) of this rule.

(f)   *Discretionary Transactions.* A Discretionary Transaction shall be exempt only if effected pursuant to an election made at least six months following the date of the most recent election, with respect to any plan of the issuer, that effected a Discretionary Transaction that was:

(i)   An acquisition, if the transaction to be exempted would be a disposition; or

(ii)   A disposition, if the transaction to be exempted would be an acquisition.

NOTES to Rule 16b–3

NOTE (1): The exercise or conversion of a derivative security that does not satisfy the conditions of this rule is eligible for exemption from section 16(b) of the Act to the extent that the conditions of Rule 16b–6(b) are satisfied.

NOTE (2): Section 16(a) reporting requirements applicable to transactions exempt pursuant to this rule are set forth in Rule 16a–3(f) and (g) and Rule 16a–4.

NOTE (3): The approval conditions of paragraphs (d)(1), (d)(2) and (e) of this rule require the approval of each specific transaction, and are not satisfied by approval of a plan in its entirety except for the approval of a plan pursuant to which the terms and conditions of each transaction are fixed in advance, such as a formula plan. Where the terms of a subsequent transaction (such as the exercise price of an option, or the provision of an exercise or tax withholding right) are provided for in a transaction as initially approved pursuant to paragraphs (d)(1), (d)(2) or (e), such subsequent transaction shall not require further specific approval.

NOTE (4): For purposes of determining a director's status under those portions of paragraph (b)(3)(i) that reference Item 404(a), an issuer may rely on the disclosure provided under Item 404(a) of Regulation S–K for the issuer's most recent fiscal year contained in the most recent filing in which disclosure required under Item 404(a) is presented. Where a transaction disclosed in that filing was terminated before the director's proposed service as a Non-Employee Director, that transaction will not bar such service. The issuer must believe in good faith that any current or contemplated transaction in which the director participates will not be required to be disclosed under Item 404(a), based on information readily available to the issuer and the director at the time such director proposes to act as a Non-Employee Director. At such time as the issuer believes in good faith, based on readily available information, that a current or contemplated transaction with a director will be required to be disclosed under Item 404(a) in a future filing, the director no longer is eligible to serve as a Non-Employee Director; provided, however, that this determination does not result in retroactive loss of a Rule 16b–3 exemption for a transaction previously approved by the director while serving as a Non-Employee Director consistent with this note. In making the determinations specified in this Note, the issuer may rely on information it obtains from the director, for example, pursuant to a response to an inquiry.

Rule 16b–5. Bona Fide Gifts and Inheritance

Both the acquisition and the disposition of equity securities shall be exempt from the operation of section 16(b) of the Act if they are: (a) bona fide gifts; or (b) transfers of securities by will or the laws of descent and distribution.

Rule 16b–6. Derivative Securities

(a) The establishment of or increase in a call equivalent position or liquidation of or decrease in a put equivalent position shall be deemed a purchase of the underlying security for purposes of section 16(b) of the Act, and the establishment of or increase in a put equivalent position or liquidation of or decrease in a call equivalent position shall be deemed a sale of the underlying securities for purposes of section 16(b) of the Act; *provided, however,* that if the increase or decrease occurs as a result of the fixing of the exercise price of a right initially issued without a fixed price, where the date the price is fixed is not known in advance and is outside the control of the recipient, the increase or decrease shall be exempt from section 16(b) of the Act with respect to any offsetting transaction within the six months prior to the date the price is fixed.

(b) The closing of a derivative security position as a result of its exercise or conversion shall be exempt from the operation of section 16(b) of the Act, and the acquisition of underlying securities at a fixed exercise price due to the exercise or conversion of a call equivalent position or the disposition of underlying securities at a fixed exercise price due to the exercise of a put equivalent position shall be exempt from the operation of section 16(b) of the Act; *provided, however,* that the acquisition of underlying securities from the exercise of an out-of-the-money option, warrant, or right shall not be exempt unless the exercise is necessary to comport with the sequential exercise provisions of the Internal Revenue Code.

NOTE to paragraph (b): The exercise or conversion of a derivative security that does not satisfy the conditions of this rule is eligible for exemption from section 16(b) of the Act to the extent that the conditions of Rule 16b–3 are satisfied.

(c) In determining the short-swing profit recoverable pursuant to section 16(b) of the Act from transactions involving the purchase and sale or sale and purchase of derivative and other securities, the following rules apply:

(1) Short-swing profits in transactions involving the purchase and sale or sale and purchase of derivative securities that have identical characteristics (*e.g.,* purchases and sales of call options of the same strike price and expiration date, or purchases and sales of the same series of convertible debentures) shall be measured by the actual prices paid or received in the short-swing transactions.

(2) Short-swing profits in transactions involving the purchase and sale or sale and purchase of derivative securities having different characteristics but related to the same underlying security (*e.g.,* the purchase of a call option and the sale of a convertible debenture) or derivative securities and underlying securities shall not exceed the difference in price of the underlying security on the date of purchase or sale and the date of sale or purchase. Such profits may be measured by calculating the short-swing profits that would have been realized had the subject transactions involved purchases and sales solely of the derivative security that was purchased or solely of the derivative security that was sold, valued as of the time of the matching purchase or sale, and calculated for the lesser of the number of underlying securities actually purchased or sold.

(d) Upon cancellation or expiration of an option within six months of the writing of the option, any profit derived from writing the option shall be recoverable under section 16(b) of the Act. The profit shall not exceed the premium received for writing the option. The disposition or closing of a long derivative security position, as a result of cancellation or expiration, shall be exempt from section 16(b) of the Act where no value is received from the cancellation or expiration.

Rule 16b–7. Mergers, Reclassifications, and Consolidations

(a) The following transactions shall be exempt from the provisions of section 16(b) of the Act:

(1)   The acquisition of a security of a company, pursuant to a merger, reclassification or consolidation, in exchange for a security of a company that before the merger, reclassification or consolidation, owned 85 percent or more of either:

(i)   The equity securities of all other companies involved in the merger, reclassification or consolidation, or in the case of a consolidation, the resulting company; or

(ii)   The combined assets of all the companies involved in the merger, reclassification or consolidation, computed according to their book values before the merger, reclassification or consolidation as determined by reference to their most recent available financial statements for a 12 month period before the merger, reclassification or consolidation, or such shorter time as the company has been in existence.

(2)   The disposition of a security, pursuant to a merger, reclassification or consolidation, of a company that before the merger, reclassification or consolidation, owned 85 percent or more of either:

(i)   The equity securities of all other companies involved in the merger, reclassification or consolidation or, in the case of a consolidation, the resulting company; or

(ii)   The combined assets of all the companies undergoing merger, reclassification or consolidation, computed according to their book values before the merger, reclassification or consolidation as determined by reference to their most recent available financial statements for a 12 month period before the merger, reclassification or consolidation.

(b)   A merger within the meaning of this rule shall include the sale or purchase of substantially all the assets of one company by another in exchange for equity securities which are then distributed to the security holders of the company that sold its assets.

(c)   The exemption provided by this rule applies to any securities transaction that satisfies the conditions specified in this rule and is not conditioned on the transaction satisfying any other conditions.

(d)   Notwithstanding the foregoing, if a person subject to section 16 of the Act makes any non-exempt purchase of a security in any company involved in the merger, reclassification or consolidation and any non-exempt sale of a security in any company involved in the merger, reclassification or consolidation within any period of less than six months during which the merger, reclassification or consolidation took place, the exemption provided by this rule shall be unavailable to the extent of such purchase and sale.

Rule 16b–8.   Voting Trusts

Any acquisition or disposition of an equity security or certificate representing equity securities involved in the deposit or withdrawal from a voting trust or deposit agreement shall be exempt from section 16(b) of the Act if substantially all of the assets held under the voting trust or deposit agreement immediately after the deposit or immediately prior to the withdrawal consisted of equity securities of the same class as the security deposited or withdrawn; *provided, however,* that this exemption shall not apply if there is a non-exempt purchase or sale of an equity security of the class deposited within six months (including the date of withdrawal or deposit) of a nonexempt sale or purchase, respectively, of any certificate representing such equity security (other than the actual deposit or withdrawal).

Rule 16c–1.   Brokers

Any transaction shall be exempt from section 16(c) of the Act to the extent necessary to render lawful the execution by a broker of an order for an account in which the broker has no direct or indirect interest.

Rule 16c–2.   Transactions Effected in Connection With a Distribution

Any transaction shall be exempt from section 16(c) of the Act to the extent necessary to render lawful any sale made by or on behalf of a dealer in connection with a distribution of a substantial block of securities, where the sale is represented by an over-allotment in which the dealer is participating as a member of an underwriting group, or the dealer or a person acting on the dealer's behalf intends in good faith to offset such sale with a security to be acquired by or on behalf of the dealer as a participant in an underwriting, selling, or soliciting-dealer group of which the dealer is a member at the time of the sale, whether or not the security to be acquired is subject to a prior offering to existing security holders or some other class of persons.

Rule 16c–3. Exemption of Sales of Securities to Be Acquired

(a)   Whenever any person is entitled, incident to ownership of an issued security and without the payment of consideration, to receive another security "when issued" or "when distributed," the sale of the security to be acquired shall be exempt from the operation of section 16(c) of the Act, *provided that:*

(1)   The sale is made subject to the same conditions as those attaching to the right of acquisition;

(2)   Such person exercises reasonable diligence to deliver such security to the purchaser promptly after the right of acquisition matures; and

(3)   Such person reports the sale on the appropriate form for reporting transactions by persons subject to section 16(a) of the Act.

(b)   This rule shall not exempt transactions involving both a sale of the issued security and a sale of a security "when issued" or "when distributed" if the combined transactions result in a sale of more securities than the aggregate of issued securities owned by the seller plus those to be received for the other security "when issued" or "when distributed."

Rule 16c–4. Derivative Securities

Establishing or increasing a put equivalent position shall be exempt from section 16(c) of the Act, so long as the amount of securities underlying the put equivalent position does not exceed the amount of underlying securities otherwise owned.

Rule 16e–1. Arbitrage Transactions Under Section 16

It shall be unlawful for any director or officer of an issuer of an equity security which is registered pursuant to section 12 of the Act to effect any foreign or domestic arbitrage transaction in any equity security of such issuer, whether registered or not, unless he shall include such transaction in the statements required by section 16(a) and shall account to such issuer for the profits arising from such transaction, as provided in section 16(b). The provision of section 16(c) shall not apply to such arbitrage transactions. The provisions of section 16 shall not apply to any bona fide foreign or domestic arbitrage transaction insofar as it is effected by any person other than such director or officer of the issuer of such security.

PRESERVATION OF RECORDS AND REPORTS
OF CERTAIN STABILIZING ACTIVITIES

(Selected Provisions)

Rule 17a–1. Recordkeeping Rule for National Securities Exchanges, National Securities Associations, Registered Clearing Agencies and the Municipal Securities Rulemaking Board

(a)   Every national securities exchange, national securities association, registered clearing agency and the Municipal Securities Rulemaking Board shall keep and preserve at least one copy of all documents, including all correspondence, memoranda, papers, books, notices, accounts, and other such records as shall be made or received by it in the course of its business as such and in the conduct of its self-regulatory activity.

(b)   Every national securities exchange, national securities association, registered clearing agency and the Municipal Securities Rulemaking Board shall keep all such documents for a period of not less than five years, the first two years in an easily accessible place, subject to the destruction and disposition provisions of Rule 17a–6.

(c)   Every national securities exchange, registered securities association, registered clearing agency and the Municipal Securities Rulemaking Board shall, upon request of any representative of the Commission, promptly furnish to the possession of such representative copies of any documents required to be kept and preserved by it pursuant to paragraphs (a) and (b) of this Rule.

Rule 17a–3. Records to Be Made by Certain Exchange Members, Brokers and Dealers

This rule applies to the following types of entities: a member of a national securities exchange who transacts a business in securities directly with others than members of a national securities exchange; a broker or dealer who transacts a business in securities through the medium of a member of a national securities exchange; a broker or dealer, including an OTC derivatives dealer as that term is defined in Rule 3b–12, registered pursuant to section 15 of the Act; a security-based swap dealer registered pursuant to section 15F of the Act that is also a broker or dealer, including an OTC derivatives dealer, registered pursuant to section 15 of the Act; and a major security-based swap participant registered pursuant to section 15F of the Act that is also a broker or dealer, including an OTC derivatives dealer, registered pursuant to section 15 of the Act. Rule 18a–5 (rather than this rule) applies to the following types of entities: a security-based swap dealer registered pursuant to section 15F of the Act that is not also a broker or dealer, including an OTC derivatives dealer, registered pursuant to section 15 of the Act; and a major security-based swap participant registered pursuant to section 15F of the Act that is not also a broker or dealer, including an OTC derivatives dealer, registered pursuant to section 15 of the Act.

(a) Every member of a national securities exchange who transacts a business in securities directly with others than members of a national securities exchange, every broker or dealer who transacts a business in securities through the medium of any such member, and every broker or dealer registered pursuant to section 15 of the Act must make and keep current the following books and records relating to its business:

* * *

Rule 17a–5. Reports to Be Made by Certain Brokers and Dealers

This rule applies to the following types of entities: except as provided in this introductory text, a broker or dealer, including an OTC derivatives dealer as that term is defined in Rule 3b–12 registered pursuant to section 15 of the Act; a broker or dealer, other than an OTC derivatives dealer, registered pursuant to section 15 of the Act that is also a security-based swap dealer registered pursuant to section 15F of the Act; and a broker or dealer, including an OTC derivatives dealer, registered pursuant to section 15 of the Act that is also a major-security-based swap participant registered pursuant to section 15F of the Act. Rule 18a–7 (rather than this rule) applies to the following types of entities: a security-based swap dealer registered pursuant to section 15F of the Act that is not also a broker or dealer, other than an OTC derivatives dealer, registered pursuant to section 15 of the Act; a security-based swap dealer registered pursuant to section 15F of the Act that is also an OTC derivatives dealer; and a major security-based swap participant registered pursuant to section 15F of the Act that is not also a broker or dealer, including an OTC derivatives dealer, registered pursuant to section 15 of the Act.

* * *

Rule 17a–14. Form CRS, for Preparation, Filing and Delivery of Form CRS

(a) Scope of Rule. This rule shall apply to every broker or dealer registered with the Commission pursuant to section 15 of the Act that offers services to a retail investor.

(b) Form CRS. You must:

(1) Prepare Form CRS 17 CFR 249.640, by following the instructions in the form.

(2) File your current Form CRS electronically with the Commission through the Central Registration Depository ("Web CRD®") operated by the Financial Industry Regulatory Authority, Inc., and thereafter, file an amended Form CRS in accordance with the instructions in Form CRS.

(3) Amend your Form CRS as required by the instructions in the form.

(c) *Delivery of Form CRS.* You must:

(1) Deliver to each retail investor your current Form CRS before or at the earliest of:

(i) A recommendation of an account type, a securities transaction; or an investment strategy involving securities;

(ii) Placing an order for the retail investor; or

    (iii) The opening of a brokerage account for the retail investor.

    (2) Deliver to each retail investor who is an existing customer your current Form CRS before or at the time you:

    (i) Open a new account that is different from the retail investor's existing account(s);

    (ii) Recommend that the retail investor roll over assets from a retirement account into a new or existing account or investment; or

    (iii) Recommend or provide a new brokerage service or investment that does not necessarily involve the opening of a new account and would not be held in an existing account.

    (3) Post the current Form CRS prominently on your public Website, if you have one, in a location and format that is easily accessible for retail investors.

    (4) Communicate any changes made to Form CRS to each retail investor who is an existing customer within 60 days after the amendments are required to be made and without charge. The communication can be made by delivering the amended Form CRS or by communicating the information through another disclosure that is delivered to the retail investor.

    (5) Deliver a current Form CRS to each retail investor within 30 days upon request.

    (d) *Other disclosure obligations.* Delivering a Form CRS in compliance with this rule does not relieve you of any other disclosure obligations arising under the federal securities laws and regulations or other laws or regulations (including the rules of a self-regulatory organization).

    (e) *Definitions.* For purposes of this rule:

    (1) *Current Form CRS* means the most recent version of the Form CRS.

    (2) *Retail investor* means a natural person, or the legal representative of such natural person, who seeks to receive or receives services primarily for personal, family or household purposes.

    (f) *Transition rule.* (1) If you are registered with the Commission prior to June 30, 2020, pursuant to Section 15 of the Act, you must file your initial Form CRS with the Commission in accordance with section (b)(2) of this rule, beginning on May 1, 2020 and by no later than June 30, 2020.

    (2) On or after June 30, 2020, if you file an application for registration with the Commission or have an application for registration pending with the Commission as a broker or dealer pursuant to Section 15 of the Act, you must begin to comply with this rule by the date on which your registration application becomes effective pursuant to Section 15 of the Act, including by filing your Form CRS in accordance with paragraph (b)(2) of this rule.

    (3) Within 30 days after the date by which you are first required by paragraph (f) of this rule to electronically file your initial Form CRS with the Commission, you must deliver to each of your existing customers who is a retail investor your current Form CRS.

    (4) As of the date by which you are first required to electronically file your Form CRS with the Commission pursuant to this rule, you must begin using your Form CRS as required to comply with paragraph (c) of this rule.

Rule 17d–2. Program for Allocation of Regulatory Responsibility

    (a) Any two or more self-regulatory organizations may file with the Commission within ninety (90) days of the effective date of this rule, and thereafter as changes in designation are necessary or appropriate, a plan for allocating among the self-regulatory organizations the responsibility to receive regulatory reports from persons who are members or participants of more than one of such self-regulatory organizations to examine such persons for compliance, or to enforce compliance by such persons, with specified provisions of the Act, the rules and regulations thereunder, and the rules of such self-regulatory organizations, or to carry out other specified regulatory functions with respect to such persons.

    (b) Any plan filed hereunder may contain provisions for the allocation among the parties of expenses reasonably incurred by the self-regulatory organization having regulatory responsibilities under the plan.

(c)   After appropriate notice and opportunity for comment, the Commission may, by written notice, declare such a plan, or any part of the plan, effective if it finds the plan, or any part thereof, necessary or appropriate in the public interest and for the protection of investors, to foster cooperation and coordination among self-regulatory organizations, or to remove impediments to and foster the development of the national market system and a national system for the clearance and settlement of securities transactions and in conformity with the factors set forth in section 17(d) of the Act.

(d)   Upon the effectiveness of such a plan or part thereof, any self-regulatory organization which is a party to the plan shall be relieved of responsibility as to any person for whom such responsibility is allocated under the plan to another self-regulatory organization to the extent of such allocation.

(e)   Nothing herein shall preclude any self-regulatory organization from entering into more than one plan filed hereunder.

(f)   After the Commission has declared a plan or part thereof effective pursuant to paragraph (c) of this rule or acted pursuant to paragraph (g) of this rule, a self-regulatory organization relieved of responsibility may notify customers of, and persons doing business with, such member or participant of the limited nature of its responsibility for such member's or participant's acts, practices, and course of business.

(g)   In the event that plans declared effective pursuant to paragraph (c) of this rule do not provide for all members or participants or do not allocate all regulatory responsibilities, the Commission may, after due consideration of the factors enumerated in section 17(d)(1) and notice and opportunity for comment, designate one or more of the self-regulatory organizations responsible for specified regulatory responsibilities with respect to such members or participants.

SUPERVISED INVESTMENT BANK HOLDING COMPANY RULES

Preliminary Note: Rules 17i–1 through 17i–8 set forth a program of supervision at the holding company level for supervised investment bank holding companies. This program is designed to reduce the likelihood that financial and operational weakness in a supervised investment bank holding company will destabilize broker or dealer or the broader financial system. The focus of this supervision of the supervised investment bank holding company is its financial and operational condition and its risk management controls and methodologies.

[Rules 17i–1 through 17i–8 are omitted]

Rule 17Ab2–1.   Registration of Clearing Agencies

(a)   An application for registration or for exemption from registration as a clearing agency, as defined in section 3(a)(23) of the Act, or an amendment to any such application shall be filed with the Commission on Form CA–1, in accordance with the instructions thereto.

* * *

Rule 17Ac2–1.   Application for Registration of Transfer Agents

(a)   An application for registration, pursuant to section 17A(c) of the Act, of a transfer agent for which the Commission is the appropriate regulatory agency, as defined in section 3(a)(34)(B) of the Act, shall be filed with the Commission on Form TA–1, in accordance with the instructions contained therein and shall become effective on the thirtieth day following the date on which the application is filed, unless the Commission takes affirmative action to accelerate, deny or postpone such registration in accordance with the provisions of section 17A(c) of the Act.

* * *

POWERS WITH RESPECT TO EXCHANGES AND SECURITIES

Rule 19b–4. Filings With Respect to Proposed Rule Changes by Self-Regulatory Organizations

(a)   *Definitions.* As used in this rule:

(1)   The term *advance notice* means a notice required to be made by a designated clearing agency pursuant to Section 806(e) of the Payment, Clearing and Settlement Supervision Act (12 U.S.C. 5465(e));

(2)   The term *designated clearing agency* means a clearing agency that is registered with the Commission, and for which t Commission is the Supervisory Agency (as determined in accordance with section 803(8) of the Payment, Clearing and Settlement Supervision Act (12 U.S.C. 5462(8)), that has been designated by the Financial Stability Oversight Council pursuant to section 804 of the Payment, Clearing and Settlement Supervision Act (12 U.S.C. 5463) as systemically important or likely to become systemically important;

(3)   The term *Payment, Clearing and Settlement Supervision Act* means Title VIII of the Dodd-Frank Wall Street Reform and Consumer Protection Act (124 Stat. 1802, 1803, 1807, 1809, 1811, 1814, 1816, 1818, 1820, 1821; 12 U.S.C. 5461 *et seq.*);

(4)   The term *proposed rule change* has the meaning set forth in Section 19(b)(1) of the Act (15 U.S.C. 78s(b)(1));

(5)   The term *security-based swap submission* means a submission of identifying information required to be made by a clearing agency pursuant to section 3C(b)(2) of the Act (15 U.S.C. 78c–3(b)(2)) for each security-based swap, or any group, category, type or class of security-based swaps, that such clearing agency plans to accept for clearing;

(6)   The term *stated policy, practice, or interpretation* means:

    (i)   Any material aspect of the operation of the facilities of the self-regulatory organization; or

    (ii)   Any statement made generally available to the membership of, to all participants in, or to persons having or seeking access (including, in the case of national securities exchanges or registered securities associations, through a member) to facilities of, the self-regulatory organization ("specified persons"), or to a group or category of specified persons, that establishes or changes any standard, limit, or guideline with respect to:

        (A)   The rights, obligations, or privileges of specified persons or, in the case of national securities exchanges or registered securities associations, persons associated with specified persons; or

        (B)   The meaning, administration, or enforcement of an existing rule.

(b)(1)   Filings with respect to proposed rule changes by a self-regulatory organization, except filings with respect to proposed rules changes by self-regulatory organizations submitted pursuant to section 19(b)(7) of the Act (15 U.S.C. 78s(b)(7)), shall be made electronically on Form 19b–4 (17 CFR 249.819).

(2)   For purposes of Section 19(b) of the Act and this rule, a "business day" is any day other than a Saturday, Sunday, Federal holiday, a day that the Office of Personnel Management has announced that Federal agencies in the Washington, DC area are closed to the public, a day on which the Commission is subject to a Federal government shutdown or a day on which the Commission's Washington, DC office is otherwise not open for regular business.

(c)   A stated policy, practice, or interpretation of the self-regulatory organization shall be deemed to be a proposed rule change unless (1) it is reasonably and fairly implied by an existing rule of the self-regulatory organization or (2) it is concerned solely with the administration of the self-regulatory organization and is not a stated policy, practice, or interpretation with respect to the meaning, administration, or enforcement of an existing rule of the self-regulatory organization.

(d)   Regardless of whether it is made generally available, an interpretation of an existing rule of the self-regulatory organization shall be deemed to be a proposed rule change if (1) it is approved or ratified by the governing body of the self-regulatory organization and (2) it is not reasonably and fairly implied by that rule.

(e)   For the purposes of this paragraph, *new derivative securities product* means any type of option, warrant, hybrid securities product or any other security, other than a single equity option or a security futures product, whose value is based, in whole or in part, upon the performance of, or interest in, an underlying instrument.

(1)   The listing and trading of a new derivative securities product by a self-regulatory organization shall not be deemed a proposed rule change, pursuant to paragraph (c)(1) of this rule, if the Commission has approved, pursuant to section 19(b) of the Act (15 U.S.C. 78s(b)), the self-regulatory organization's trading rules, procedures and listing standards for the product class that would include the new derivative securities product and the self-regulatory organization has a surveillance program for the product class.

(2)   Recordkeeping and reporting:

(i)   Self-regulatory organizations shall retain at their principal place of business a file, available to Commission staff for inspection, of all relevant records and information pertaining to each new derivative securities product traded pursuant to this paragraph (e) for a period of not less than five years, the first two years in an easily accessible place, as prescribed in § 240.17a–1.

(ii)   When relying on this paragraph (e), a self-regulatory organization shall submit Form 19b–4(e) (17 CFR 249.820) to the Commission within five business days after commencement of trading a new derivative securities product.

(f)   A proposed rule change may take effect upon filing with the Commission pursuant to Section 19(b)(3)(A) of the Act, 15 U.S.C. 78s(b)(3)(A), if properly designated by the self-regulatory organization as:

(1)   Constituting a stated policy, practice, or interpretation with respect to the meaning, administration, or enforcement of an existing rule;

(2)   Establishing or changing a due, fee, or other charge applicable only to a member;

(3)   Concerned solely with the administration of the self-regulatory organization;

(4)   Effecting a change in an existing service of a registered clearing agency that either:

(i)(A)   Does not adversely affect the safeguarding of securities or funds in the custody or control of the clearing agency or for which it is responsible; and

(B)   Does not significantly affect the respective rights or obligations of the clearing agency or persons using the service; or

(ii)(A)   Primarily affects the clearing operations of the clearing agency with respect to products that are not securities, including futures that are not security futures, swaps that are not security-based swaps or mixed swaps, and forwards that are not security forwards; and

(B)   Either

(1)   Does not significantly affect any securities clearing operations of the clearing agency or any rights or obligations of the clearing agency with respect to securities clearing or persons using such securities-clearing service, or

(2)   Does significantly affect any securities clearing operations of the clearing agency or the rights or obligations of the clearing agency with respect to securities clearing or persons using such securities-clearing service, but is necessary to maintain fair and orderly markets for products that are not securities, including futures that are not security futures, swaps that are not security-based swaps or mixed swaps, and forwards that are not security forwards. Proposed rule changes filed pursuant to this subparagraph II must also be filed in accordance with the procedures of Section 19(b)(1) for approval pursuant to Section 19(b)(2) and the regulations thereunder within fifteen days of being filed under Section 19(b)(3)(A).

(5)   Effecting a change in an existing order-entry or trading system of a self-regulatory organization that:

(i)   Does not significantly affect the protection of investors or the public interest;

(ii)   Does not impose any significant burden on competition; and

(iii)   Does not have the effect of limiting the access to or availability of the system; or

(6) Effecting a change that:

   (i) Does not significantly affect the protection of investors or the public interest;

   (ii) Does not impose any significant burden on competition; and

   (iii) By its terms, does not become operative for 30 days after the date of the filing, or such shorter time as the Commission may designate if consistent with the protection of investors and the public interest; provided that the self-regulatory organization has given the Commission written notice of its intent to file the proposed rule change, along with a brief description and text of the proposed rule change, at least five business days prior to the date of filing of the proposed rule change, or such shorter time as designated by the Commission.

(g) Proceedings to determine whether a proposed rule change should be disapproved will be conducted pursuant to 17 CFR 201.700–701 (Initiation of Proceedings for SRO Proposed Rule Changes).

(h) Notice of orders issued pursuant to section 19(b) of the Act will be given by prompt publication thereof, together with a statement of written reasons therefor.

(i) Self-regulatory organizations shall retain at their principal place of business a file, available to interested persons for public inspection and copying, of all filings, notices and submissions made pursuant to this rule and all correspondence and other communications reduced to writing (including comment letters) to and from such self-regulatory organization concerning any such filing, notice or submission, whether such correspondence and communications are received or prepared before or after the filing, notice or submission of the proposed rule change, advance notice or security-based swap submission, as applicable.

(j) Filings by a self-regulatory organization submitted on Form 19b–4 (17 CFR 249.819) electronically shall contain an electronic signature. For the purposes of this rule, the term *electronic signature* means an electronic entry in the form of a magnetic impulse or other form of computer data compilation of any letter or series of letters or characters comprising a name, executed, adopted or authorized as a signature. The signatory to an electronically submitted rule filing shall manually sign a signature page or other document, in the manner prescribed by Form 19b–4, authenticating, acknowledging or otherwise adopting his or her signature that appears in typed form within the electronic filing. Such document shall be executed before or at the time the rule filing is electronically submitted and shall be retained by the filer in accordance with § 240.17a–1.

(k) If the conditions of this rule and Form 19b–4 (17 CFR 249.819) are otherwise satisfied, all filings submitted electronically on or before 5:30 p.m. Eastern Standard Time or Eastern Daylight Saving Time, whichever is currently in effect, on a business day, shall be deemed filed on that business day, and all filings submitted after 5:30 p.m. Eastern Standard Time or Eastern Daylight Saving Time, whichever is currently in effect, shall be deemed filed on the next business day.

(*l*) The self-regulatory organization shall post each proposed rule change, and any amendments thereto, on its Web site within two business days after the filing of the proposed rule change, and any amendments thereto, with the Commission. If a self-regulatory organization does not post a proposed rule change on its Web site on the same day that it filed the proposal with the Commission, then the self-regulatory organization shall inform the Commission of the date on which it posted such proposal on its Web site. Such proposed rule change and amendments shall be maintained on the self-regulatory organization's Web site until:

   (1) In the case of a proposed rule change filed under section 19(b)(2) of the Act (15 U.S.C. 78s(b)(2)), the Commission approves or disapproves the proposed rule change or the self-regulatory organization withdraws the proposed rule change, or any amendments, or is notified that the proposed rule change is not properly filed; or

   (2) In the case of a proposed rule change filed under section 19(b)(3)(A) of the Act (15 U.S.C. 78s(b)(3)(A)), or any amendment thereto, 60 days after the date of filing, unless the self-regulatory organization withdraws the proposed rule change or is notified that the proposed rule change is not properly filed; and

   (3) In the case of proposed rule changes approved by the Commission pursuant to section 19(b)(2) of the Act (15 U.S.C. 78s(b)(2)) or noticed by the Commission pursuant to section 19(b)(3)(A)

of the Act (15 U.S.C. 78s(b)(3)(A)), the self-regulatory organization updates its rule text as required by paragraph (m) of this rule; and

(4)   In the case of a proposed rule change, or any amendment thereto, that has been disapproved, withdrawn or not properly filed, the self-regulatory organization shall remove the proposed rule change, or any amendment, from its Web site within two business days of notification of disapproval, improper filing, or withdrawal by the SRO of the proposed rule change.

(m)(1)   Each self-regulatory organization shall post and maintain a current and complete version of its rules on its Web site.

(2)   A self-regulatory organization, other than a self-regulatory organization that is registered with the Commission under section 6(g) of the Act (15 U.S.C. 78f(g)) or pursuant to section 15A(k) of the Act (15 U.S.C. 78 o–1(k)), shall update its Web site to reflect rule changes filed pursuant to section 19(b)(2) of the Act (15 U.S.C. 78s(b)(2)) within two business days after it has been notified of the Commission's approval of a proposed rule change, and to reflect rule changes filed pursuant to section 19(b)(3)(A) of the Act (15 U.S.C. 78s(b)(3)(A)) within two business days of the Commission's notice of such proposed rule change.

(3)   A self-regulatory organization that is registered with the Commission under section 6(g) of the Act (15 U.S.C. 78f(g)) or pursuant to section 15A(k) of the Act (15 U.S.C. 78 o–1(k)), shall update its Web site to reflect rule changes filed pursuant to section 19(b)(2) of the Act by two business days after the later of:

(A)   Notification that the Commission has approved a proposed rule change; and

(B)(i)   The filing of a written certification with the Commodity Futures Trading Commission under section 5c(c) of the Commodity Exchange Act (7 U.S.C. 7a–2(c));

(ii)   Receipt of notice from the Commodity Futures Trading Commission that it has determined that review of the proposed rule change is not necessary; or

(iii)   Receipt of notice from the Commodity Futures Trading Commission that it has approved the proposed rule change.

(4)   If a rule change is not effective for a certain period, the self-regulatory organization shall clearly indicate the effective date in the relevant rule text.

(n)(1)(i)   A designated clearing agency shall provide an advance notice to the Commission of any proposed change to its rules, procedures, or operations that could materially affect the nature or level of risks presented by such designated clearing agency. Except as provided in paragraph (n)(1)(ii) of this rule, such advance notice shall be submitted to the Commission electronically on Form 19b–4 (referenced in 17 CFR 249.819). The Commission shall, upon the filing of any advance notice, provide for prompt publication thereof.

(ii)   Any designated clearing agency that files an advance notice with the Commission prior to December 10, 2013, shall file such advance notice in electronic format to a dedicated email address to be established by the Commission. The contents of an advance notice filed pursuant to this paragraph (n)(1)(ii) shall contain the information required to be included for advance notices in the General Instructions for Form 19b–4 (referenced in 17 CFR 249.819).

(2)(i)   For purposes of this paragraph (n), the phrase *materially affect the nature or level of risks presented,* when used to qualify determinations on a change to rules, procedures, or operations at the designated clearing agency, means matters as to which there is a reasonable possibility that the change could affect the performance of essential clearing and settlement functions or the overall nature or level of risk presented by the designated clearing agency.

(ii)   Changes to rules, procedures, or operations that could materially affect the nature or level of risks presented by a designated clearing agency may include, but are not limited to, changes that materially affect participant and product eligibility, risk management, daily or intraday settlement procedures, default procedures, system safeguards, governance or financial resources of the designated clearing agency.

(iii)   Changes to rules, procedures, or operations that may not materially affect the nature or level of risks presented by a designated clearing agency include, but are not limited to:

(A)   Changes to an existing procedure, control, or service that do not modify the rights or obligations of the designated clearing agency or persons using its payment, clearing, or settlement services and that do not adversely affect the safeguarding of securities, collateral, or funds in the custody or control of the designated clearing agency or for which it is responsible; or

(B)   Changes concerned solely with the administration of the designated clearing agency or related to the routine, daily administration, direction, and control of employees;

(3)   The designated clearing agency shall post the advance notice, and any amendments thereto, on its Web site within two business days after the filing of the advance notice, and any amendments thereto, with the Commission. Such advance notice and amendments shall be maintained on the designated clearing agency's Web site until the earlier of:

(i)   The date the designated clearing agency withdraws the advance notice or is notified that the advance notice is not properly filed; or

(ii)   The date the designated clearing agency posts a notice of effectiveness as required by paragraph (n)(4)(ii) of this rule.

(4)(i)   The designated clearing agency shall post a notice on its Web site within two business days of the date that any change to its rules, procedures, or operations referred to in an advance notice has been permitted to take effect as such date is determined in accordance with Section 806(e) of the Payment, Clearing and Settlement Supervision Act (12 U.S.C. 5465).

(ii)   The designated clearing agency shall post a notice on its Web site within two business days of the effectiveness of any change to its rules, procedures, or operations referred to in an advance notice.

(5)   A designated clearing agency shall provide copies of all materials submitted to the Commission relating to an advance notice with the Board of Governors of the Federal Reserve System contemporaneously with such submission to the Commission.

(6)   The publication and Web site posting requirements contained in paragraphs (n)(1), (n)(3), and (n)(4) of this rule do not apply to any information contained in an advance notice for which a designated clearing agency has requested confidential treatment following the procedures set forth in § 240.24b–2.

(o)(1)   Every clearing agency that is registered with the Commission that plans to accept a security-based swap, or any group, category, type, or class of security-based swaps for clearing shall submit to the Commission a security-based swap submission and provide notice to its members of such security-based swap submission.

(2)(i)   Except as provided in paragraph (o)(2)(ii) of this rule, a clearing agency shall submit each security-based swap submission to the Commission electronically on Form 19b–4 (referenced in 17 CFR 249.819) with the information required to be submitted for a security-based swap submission, as provided in § 240.19b–4 and Form 19b–4. Any information submitted to the Commission electronically on Form 19b–4 that is not complete or otherwise in compliance with this rule and Form 19b–4 shall not be considered a security-based swap submission and the Commission shall so inform the clearing agency within twenty-one business days of the submission on Form 19b–4 (referenced in 17 CFR 249.819).

(ii)   Any clearing agency that files a security-based swap submission with the Commission prior to December 10, 2013, shall file such security-based swap submission in electronic format to a dedicated email address to be established by the Commission. The contents of a security-based swap submission filed pursuant to this paragraph (o)(2)(ii) shall contain the information required to be included for security-based swap submissions in the General Instructions for Form 19b–4.

(3)   A security-based swap submission submitted by a clearing agency to the Commission shall include a statement that includes, but is not limited to:

(i)   How the security-based swap submission is consistent with Section 17A of the Act (15 U.S.C. 78q–1);

(ii)   Information that will assist the Commission in the quantitative and qualitative assessment of the factors specified in Section 3C of the Act (15 U.S.C. 78c–3), including, but not limited to:

(A)   The existence of significant outstanding notional exposures, trading liquidity, and adequate pricing data;

(B)   The availability of a rule framework, capacity, operational expertise and resources, and credit support infrastructure to clear the contract on terms that are consistent with the material terms and trading conventions on which the contract is then traded;

(C)   The effect on the mitigation of systemic risk, taking into account the size of the market for such contract and the resources of the clearing agency available to clear the contract;

(D)   The effect on competition, including appropriate fees and charges applied to clearing; and

(E)   The existence of reasonable legal certainty in the event of the insolvency of the relevant clearing agency or one or more of its clearing members with regard to the treatment of customer and security-based swap counterparty positions, funds, and property;

(iii)   A description of how the rules of the clearing agency prescribe that all security-based swaps submitted to the clearing agency with the same terms and conditions are economically equivalent within the clearing agency and may be offset with each other within the clearing agency, as applicable to the security-based swaps described in the security-based swap submission; and

(iv)   A description of how the rules of the clearing agency provide for non-discriminatory clearing of a security-based swap executed bilaterally or on or through the rules of an unaffiliated national securities exchange or security-based swap execution facility, as applicable to the security-based swaps described in the security-based swap submission.

(4)   A clearing agency shall submit security-based swaps to the Commission for review by group, category, type or class of security-based swaps, to the extent reasonable and practicable to do so.

(5)   A clearing agency shall post each security-based swap submission, and any amendments thereto, on its Web site within two business days after the submission of the security-based swap submission, and any amendments thereto, with the Commission. Such security-based swap submission and amendments shall be maintained on the clearing agency's Web site until the Commission makes a determination regarding the security-based swap submission or the clearing agency withdraws the security-based swap submission, or is notified that the security-based swap submission is not properly filed.

(6)   In connection with any security-based swap submission that is submitted by a clearing agency to the Commission, the clearing agency shall provide any additional information requested by the Commission as necessary to assess any of the factors it determines to be appropriate in order to make the determination of whether the clearing requirement applies.

(7)   Notices of orders issued pursuant to Section 3C of the Act (15 U.S.C. 78c–3), regarding security-based swap submissions will be given by prompt publication thereof, together with a statement of written reasons therefor.

Rule 19b–5.   Temporary Exemption From the Filing Requirements of Section 19(b) of the Act

Preliminary Notes

1.   The following rule provides for a temporary exemption from the rule filing requirement for self-regulatory organizations that file proposed rule changes concerning the operation of a pilot trading system

pursuant to section 19(b) of the Act. All other requirements under the Act that are applicable to self-regulatory organizations continue to apply.

2. The disclosures made pursuant to the provisions of this rule are in addition to any other applicable disclosure requirements under the federal securities laws.

[The text of the rule is omitted]

Rule 19b–7. Filings With Respect to Proposed Rule Changes Submitted Pursuant to Section 19(b)(7) of the Act

Preliminary Note: A self-regulatory organization also must refer to Form 19b–7 for further requirements with respect to the filing of proposed rule changes.

(a) Filings with respect to proposed rule changes required to be submitted pursuant to Section 19(b)(7) of the Act, shall be made on Form 19b–7 (§ 249.822 of this chapter).

(b) A proposed rule change will not be deemed filed on the date it is received by the Commission unless:

(1) A completed Form 19b–7 (§ 249.822 of this chapter) is submitted electronically; and

(2) In order to elicit meaningful comment, it is accompanied by:

(i) A clear and accurate statement of the basis and purpose of such rule change, including the impact on competition or efficiency, if any; and

(ii) A summary of any written comments (including e-mail) received by the self-regulatory organization on the proposed rule change.

(c) Self-regulatory organizations shall retain at their principle place of business a file, available to interested persons for public inspection and copying, of all filings made pursuant to this rule and all correspondence and other communications reduced to writing (including comment letters) to and from such self-regulatory organization concerning such filing, whether such correspondence and communications are received or prepared before or after the filing of the proposed rule change.

Rule 19c–1. Governing Certain Off-Board Agency Transactions by Members of National Securities Exchanges

The rules of each national securities exchange shall provide as follows:

No rule, stated policy, or practice of this exchange shall prohibit or condition, or be construed to prohibit or condition or otherwise limit, directly or indirectly, the ability of any member acting as agent to effect any transaction otherwise than on this exchange with another person (except when such member also is acting as agent for such other person in such transaction), in any equity security listed on this exchange or to which unlisted trading privileges on this exchange have been extended.

Rule 19c–3. Governing Off-Board Trading by Members of National Securities Exchanges

The rules of each national securities exchange shall provide as follows:

(a) No rule, stated policy or practice of this exchange shall prohibit or condition, or be construed to prohibit, condition or otherwise limit, directly or indirectly, the ability of any member to effect any transaction otherwise than on this exchange in any reported security listed and registered on this exchange or as to which unlisted trading privileges on this exchange have been extended (other than a put option or call option issued by the Options Clearing Corporation) which is not a covered security.

(b) For purposes of this rule,

(1) The term "Act" shall mean the Securities Exchange Act of 1934, as amended.

(2) The term "exchange" shall mean a national securities exchange registered as such with the Securities and Exchange Commission pursuant to Section 6 of the Act.

(3) The term "covered security" shall mean (i) Any equity security or class of equity securities which

    (A)   Was listed and registered on an exchange on April 26, 1979, and

    (B)   Remains listed and registered on at least one exchange continuously thereafter;

   (ii)   Any equity security or class of equity securities which

    (A)   Was traded on one or more exchanges on April 26, 1979, pursuant to unlisted trading privileges permitted by section 12(f)(1)(A) of the Act, and

    (B)   Remains traded on any such exchange pursuant to such unlisted trading privileges continuously thereafter; and

   (iii)   Any equity security or class of equity securities which

    (A)   Is issued in connection with a statutory merger, consolidation or similar plan or reorganization (including a reincorporation or change of domicile) in exchange for an equity security or class of equity securities described in paragraph (b)(3)(i) or (ii) of this rule.

    (B)   Is listed and registered on an exchange after April 26, 1979, and

    (C)   Remains listed and registered on at least one exchange continuously thereafter.

   (4)   The term "reported security" shall mean any security or class of securities for which transaction reports are collected, processed and made available pursuant to an effective transaction reporting plan.

   (5)   The term "transaction report" shall mean a report containing the price and volume associated with a completed transaction involving the purchase or sale of a security.

   (6)   The term "effective transaction reporting plan" shall mean any plan approved by the Commission pursuant to Rule 601 of Regulation NMS for collecting, processing and making available transaction reports with respect to transactions in an equity security or class of equity securities.

Rule 19c–5.   Governing the Multiple Listing of Options on National Securities Exchanges

   (a)   The rules of each national securities exchange that provides a trading market in standardized put or call options shall provide as follows:

   (1)   On and after January 22, 1990, but not before, no rule, stated policy, practice, or interpretation of this exchange shall prohibit or condition, or be construed to prohibit or condition or otherwise limit, directly or indirectly, the ability of this exchange to list any stock options class first listed on an exchange on or after January 22, 1990, because that options class is listed on another options exchange.

   (2)   During the period from January 22, 1990, to January 21, 1991, but not before, no rule, stated policy, practice, or interpretation of this exchange shall prohibit or condition, or be construed to prohibit or condition or otherwise limit, directly or indirectly, the ability of this exchange to list up to ten classes of standardized stock options overlying exchange-listed stocks that were listed on another options exchange before January 22, 1990. These ten classes shall be in addition to any option on an exchange-listed stock trading on this exchange that was traded on more than one options exchange before January 22, 1990.

   (3)   On and after January 21, 1991, but not before, no rule, stated policy, practice, or interpretation of this exchange shall prohibit or condition, or be construed to prohibit or condition or otherwise limit, directly or indirectly, the ability of this exchange to list any stock options class because that options class is listed on another options exchange.

   (b)   For purposes of paragraph (a)(2) of this rule, if any options class is delisted from an options exchange as a result of a merger of the equity security underlying the option or a failure of the underlying security to satisfy that exchange's options listing standards, then the exchange is permitted to select a replacement option from among those standardized options overlying exchange-listed stocks that were listed on another options exchange before January 22, 1990.

   (c)   For purposes of this rule, the term "exchange" shall mean a national securities exchange, registered as such with the Commission pursuant to section 6 of the Act, as amended.

(d)   For purposes of this rule, the term "standardized option" shall have the same meaning as that term is defined in Rule 9b–1 under the Act, as amended.

(e)   For purposes of this rule, the term "options class" shall have the same meaning as that term is defined in Rule 9b–1 under the Act, as amended.

Rule 19d–1. Notices by Self-Regulatory Organizations of Final Disciplinary Actions, Denials, Bars, or Limitations Respecting Membership, Association, Participation, or Access to Services, and Summary Suspensions

(a)   *General.* If any self-regulatory organization for which the Commission is the appropriate regulatory agency takes any action described in this rule to which the person affected thereby has consented and such action:

(1)   Conditions or limits membership or participation in, association with a member of, or access to services offered by, such organization or a member thereof and

(2)   Is based upon a statutory disqualification defined in section 3(a)(39) of the Act, notice thereof shall be filed under Rule 19h–1 and not under this rule.

(b)   The notice requirement of section 19(d)(1) of the Act, concerning an action subject to such section taken by a self-regulatory organization for which the Commission is the appropriate regulatory agency, shall be satisfied by any notice with respect to such action (including a notice filed pursuant to this rule) which contains the information required in the statement supporting the organization's determination required by section 6(d)(1) or (2), section 15A(h)(1) or (2), or section 17A(b)(5)(A) or (B) of the Act, as appropriate.

(c)(1)   Any self-regulatory organization for which the Commission is the appropriate regulatory agency that takes any final disciplinary action with respect to any person shall promptly file a notice thereof with the Commission in accordance with paragraph (d) of this rule. For the purposes of this rule, a "final disciplinary action" shall mean the imposition of any final disciplinary sanction pursuant to section 6(b)(6), 15A(b)(7), or 17A(b)(3)(G) of the Act or other action of a self-regulatory organization which, after notice and opportunity for hearing, results in any final disposition of charges of:

(i)   One or more violations of—

(A)   The rules of such organization;

(B)   The provisions of the Act or rules thereunder; or

(C)   In the case of a municipal securities broker or dealer, the rules of the Municipal Securities Rulemaking Board;

(ii)   Acts or practices constituting a statutory disqualification of a type defined in subparagraph (D) or (E) (except prior convictions) of section 3(a)(39) of the Act; or

(iii)   In the case of a proceeding by a national securities exchange or registered securities association based on section 6(c)(3)(A)(ii), 6(c)(3)(B)(ii), 15A(g)(3)(A)(ii), or 15A(g)(3)(B)(ii) of the Act, acts or practices inconsistent with just and equitable principles of trade.

Provided, however, That in the case of a disciplinary action in which a national securities exchange imposes a fine not exceeding $1000 or suspends floor privileges of a clerical employee for not more than five days for violation of any of its regulations concerning personal decorum on a trading floor, the disposition shall not be considered "final" for purposes of this paragraph if the sanctioned person has not sought an adjudication, including a hearing, or otherwise exhausted his administrative remedies at the exchange with respect to the matter. *Provided further,* That this exemption from the notice requirement of this paragraph shall not be available where a decorum sanction is imposed at, or results from, a hearing on the matter.

(2)   Any disciplinary action, other than a decorum sanction not deemed "final" under paragraph (c)(1) of this rule, taken by a self-regulatory organization for which the Commission is the appropriate regulatory agency against any person for violation of a rule of the self-regulatory organization which has been designated as a minor rule violation pursuant to a plan or any amendment thereto filed with and declared effective by the Commission under this paragraph, shall not be considered "final" for purposes of paragraph (c)(1) of this rule if the sanction imposed consists of a fine not exceeding $2500 and the sanctioned person has not sought an adjudication, including a hearing, or otherwise exhausted

his administrative remedies at the self-regulatory organization with respect to the matter. After appropriate notice of the terms of substance of the filing or a description of the subjects and issues involved and opportunity for interested persons to submit written comment, the Commission may, by order, declare such plan or amendment effective if it finds that such plan or amendment is consistent with the public interest, the protection of investors, or otherwise in furtherance of the purposes of the Act. The Commission in its order may restrict the categories of violations to be designated as minor rule violations and may impose any other terms or conditions to the plan (including abbreviated reporting of selected minor rule violations) and to the period of its effectiveness which it deems necessary or appropriate in the public interest, for the protection of investors or otherwise in furtherance of the purposes of the Act.

(d) *Contents of notice required by paragraph (c)(1).* Any notice filed pursuant to paragraph (c)(1) of this rule, shall consist of the following, as appropriate:

(1) The name of the respondent concerned together with his last known place of residence or business as reflected on the records of the self-regulatory organization and the name of the person, committee, or other organizational unit which brought the charges involved; except that, as to any respondent who has been found not to have violated a provision covered by a charge, identifying information with respect to such person may be deleted insofar as the notice reports the disposition of that charge, unless, prior to the filing of the notice, the respondent requests otherwise;

(2) A statement describing the investigative or other origin of the action;

(3) As charged in the proceeding, the specific provisions of the Act, the rules or regulations thereunder, the rules of the organization, and, in the case of a registered securities association, the rules of the Municipal Securities Rulemaking Board, and, in the event a violation of other statutes or rules constitutes a violation of any rule of the organization, such other statutes or rules; and a statement describing the answer of the respondent to the charges;

(4) A statement setting forth findings of fact with respect to any act or practice which such respondent was charged with having engaged in or omitted; the conclusion of the organization as to whether such respondent is deemed to have violated any provision covered by the charges; and a statement of the organization in support of the resolution of the principal issues raised in the proceedings;

(5) A statement describing any sanction imposed, the reasons therefor, and the date upon which such sanction has or will become effective, together with a finding if appropriate, as to whether such respondent was a cause of any sanction imposed upon any other person; and

(6) Such other matters as the organization may deem relevant.

(e) *Notice of final denial, bar, prohibition, termination or limitation based on qualification or administrative rules.* Any final action of a self-regulatory organization for which the Commission is the appropriate regulatory agency that is taken with respect to any person constituting a denial, bar, prohibition, or limitation of membership, participation or association with a member, or of access to services offered by a self-regulatory organization or a member thereof, and which is based on an alleged failure of any person to:

(1) Pass any test or examination required by the rules of the Commission or such organization;

(2) Comply with other qualification standards established by rules of the Commission or such organization; or

(3) Comply with any administrative requirements of such organization (including failure to pay entry or other dues or fees or to file prescribed forms or reports) not involving charges of violations which may lead to a disciplinary sanction.

Shall not be considered a "disciplinary action" for purposes of paragraph (c) of this rule; but notice thereof shall be promptly filed with the Commission in accordance with paragraph (f) of this rule, *Provided, however,* That no disposition of a matter shall be considered "final" pursuant to this paragraph which results merely from a notice of such failure to the person affected, if such person has not sought an adjudication, including a hearing, or otherwise exhausted his administrative remedies within such organization with respect to such a matter.

(f)   *Contents of notice required by paragraph (e).* Any notice filed pursuant to paragraph (e) of this rule shall consist of the following, as appropriate:

(1)   The name of each person concerned together with his last known place of residence or business as reflected on the records of the organization;

(2)   The specific provisions of the Act, the rules or regulations thereunder, the rules of the organization, and, in the case of a registered securities association, the rules of the Municipal Securities Rulemaking Board, upon which the action of the organization was based, and a statement describing the answer of the person concerned;

(3)   A statement setting forth findings of fact and conclusions as to each alleged failure of the person to pass any required examination, comply with other qualification standards, or comply with administrative obligations, and a statement of the organization in support of the resolution of the principal issues raised in the proceeding;

(4)   The date upon which such action has or will become effective; and

(5)   Such other matters as the organization may deem relevant.

(g)   *Notice of final action based upon prior adjudicated statutory disqualifications.* Any self-regulatory organization for which the Commission is the appropriate regulatory agency that takes any final action with respect to any person which:

(1)   Denies or conditions membership or participation in, or association with a member of, such organization or prohibits or limits access to services offered by such organization or a member thereof; and

(2)   Is based upon a statutory disqualification of a type defined in subparagraph (A), (B), or (C) of section 3(a)(39) of the Act or consisting of a prior conviction, as described in subparagraph (E) of said section 3(a)(39), shall promptly file a notice of such action with the Commission in accordance with paragraph (h) of this rule, *provided, however,* That no disposition of a matter shall be considered "final" pursuant to this paragraph where such person has not sought an adjudication, including a hearing, or otherwise exhausted his administrative remedies within such organization with respect to such a matter.

(h)   *Contents of notice required by paragraph (g).* Any notice filed pursuant to paragraph (g) of this rule shall consist of the following, as appropriate:

(1)   The name of the person concerned together with his last known place of residence or business as reflected on the record of the organization;

(2)   A statement setting forth the principal issues raised, the answer of any person concerned, and a statement of the organization in support of the resolution of the principal issues raised in the proceeding;

(3)   Any description furnished by or on behalf of the person concerned of the activities engaged in by the person since the adjudication upon which the disqualification is based;

(4)   Any description furnished by or on behalf of the person concerned of the prospective business or employment in which the person plans to engage and the manner and extent of supervision to be exercised over and by such person;

(5)   A copy of the order or decision of the court, the Commission or the self-regulatory organization which adjudicated the matter giving rise to such statutory disqualification;

(6)   The nature of the action taken and the date upon which such action is to be made effective; and

(7)   Such other matters as the organization deems relevant.

(i)   *Notice of summary suspension of membership, participation, or association, or summary limitation or prohibition of access to services.* If any self-regulatory organization for which the Commission is the appropriate regulatory agency summarily suspends a member, participant, or person associated with a member, or summarily limits or prohibits any person with respect to access to or services offered by the organization or (in the case of a national securities exchange or a registered securities association) a member thereof pursuant to the provisions of section 6(d)(3), 15A(h)(3) or 17A(b)(5)(C) of the Act, such organization shall, within 24 hours of the effectiveness of such summary suspension, limitation or prohibition notify the Commission of such action, which notice shall contain at least the following information:

(1)   The name of the person concerned together with his last known place of residence or business as reflected on the records of the organization;

(2)   The date upon which such summary action has or will become effective;

(3)   If such summary action is based upon the provisions of section 6(d)(3)(A), 15A(h)(3)(A), or 17A(b)(5)(C)(i) of the Act, a copy of the relevant order or decision of the self-regulatory organization;

(4)   If such summary action is based upon the provisions of section 6(d)(3)(B) or (C), 15A(h)(3)(B) or (C), or 17A(b)(5)(C)(ii) or (iii) of the Act, a statement describing, as appropriate:

(i)   The financial or operating difficulty of the member or participant upon which such organization determined the member or participant could not be permitted to continue to do business with safety to investors, creditors, other members or participants, or the organization;

(ii)   The pertinent failure to meet qualification requirements or other prerequisites for access and the basis upon which such organization determined that the person concerned could not be permitted to have access with safety to investors, creditors, other members, or the organization; or

(iii)   The default of any delivery of funds or securities to a clearing agency by a participant.

(5)   The nature and effective date of the suspension, limitation or prohibition; and

(6)   Such other matters as the organization deems relevant.

(j)   *Notice of limitation or prohibition of access to services by delisting of security.* Any national securities exchange for which the Commission is the appropriate regulatory agency that delists a security pursuant to section 12(d) of the Act, and Rule 12d2–2 must file a notice with the Commission in accordance with paragraph (k) of this rule.

(k)   *Contents of notice required by paragraph (j) of this rule.* The national securities exchange shall file notice pursuant to paragraph (j) of this rule on Form 25. Form 25 shall serve as notification to the Commission of such limitation or prohibition of access to services. The national securities exchange must attach a copy of its delisting determination to Form 25 and file Form 25 with the attachment on EDGAR.

Rule 19d–2.   Applications for Stays of Disciplinary Sanctions or Summary Suspensions by a Self-Regulatory Organization

If any self-regulatory organization imposes any final disciplinary sanction as to which a notice is required to be filed with the Commission pursuant to section 19(d)(1) of the Act, pursuant to section 6(b)(6), 15A(b)(7) or 17A(b)(3)(G) of the Act, or summarily suspends or limits or prohibits access pursuant to section 6(d)(3), 15A(h)(3) or 17A(b)(5)(C) of the Act, any person aggrieved thereby for which the Commission is the appropriate regulatory agency may file with the Commission a written motion for a stay of imposition of such action pursuant to Rule 401 of the Commission's Rules of Practice.

Rule 19d–3.   Applications for Review of Final Disciplinary Sanctions, Denials of Memberships, Participation or Association, or Prohibitions or Limitations of Access to Services Imposed by Self-Regulatory Organizations

Applications to the Commission for review of any final disciplinary sanction, denial or conditioning of membership, participation, bar from association, or prohibition or limitation with respect to access to services offered by a self-regulatory organization or a member thereof by any such organization shall be made pursuant to Rule 420 of the Commission's Rules of Practice.

Rule 19d–4.   Notice by the Public Company Accounting Oversight Board of Disapproval of Registration or of Disciplinary Action

(a)   *Definitions.*

(1)   *Board* means the Public Company Accounting Oversight Board.

(2) *Public accounting firm* shall have the meaning set forth in 15 U.S.C. § 7201(a)(11).

(3) *Registered public accounting firm* shall have the meaning set forth in 15 U.S.C. § 7201(a)(12).

(4) *Associated person* shall mean a person associated with a registered public accounting firm as defined in 15 U.S.C. § 7201(a)(9).

(b)(1) *Notice of disapproval of registration.* If the Board disapproves a completed application for registration by a public accounting firm, the Board shall file a notice of its disapproval with the Commission within 30 days and serve a copy on the public accounting firm.

(2) *Contents of the notice.* The notice required by paragraph (b)(1) of this rule shall provide the following information:

(i) The name of the public accounting firm and the public accounting firm's last known address as reflected in the Board's records;

(ii) The basis for the Board's disapproval, and a copy of the Board's written notice of disapproval; and

(iii) Such other information as the Board may deem relevant.

(c)(1) *Notice of disciplinary action.* If the Board imposes any final disciplinary sanction on any registered public accounting firm or any associated person of a registered public accounting firm under 15 U.S.C. § 7215(b)(3) or § 7215(c), the Board shall file a notice of the disciplinary sanction with the Commission within 30 days and serve a copy on the person sanctioned.

(2) *Contents of the notice.* The notice required by paragraph (c)(1) of this rule shall provide the following information:

(i) The name of the registered public accounting firm or the associated person, together with the firm's or the person's last known address as reflected in the Board's records;

(ii) A description of the acts or practices, or omissions to act, upon which the sanction is based;

(iii) A statement of the sanction imposed, the reasons therefor, or a copy of the Board's statement justifying the sanction, and the effective date of such sanction; and

(iv) Such other information as the Board may deem relevant.

Rule 19g2–1. Enforcement of Compliance by National Securities Exchanges and Registered Securities Associations With the Act and Rules and Regulations Thereunder

(a) In enforcing compliance, within the meaning of section 19(g) of the Act, with the Act and the rules and regulations thereunder by its members and persons associated with its members, a national securities exchange or registered securities association is not required:

(1) To enforce compliance with sections 12 (other than sections 12(j) and 12(k)), 13, 14 (other than section 14(b)), 15(d) and 16 of the Act and the rules thereunder except to the extent of any action normally taken with respect to any person which is not a member or a person associated with a member;

(2) To enforce compliance with respect to persons associated with a member, other than securities persons or persons who control a member; and

(3) To conduct examinations as to qualifications of, require filing of periodic reports by, or conduct regular inspections (including examinations of books and records) of, persons associated with a member, other than securities persons whose functions are not solely clerical or ministerial.

(b) For the purpose of this rule:

(1) A "securities person" is a person who is a general partner or officer (or person occupying a similar status or performing similar functions) or employee of a member; *Provided, however,* That a registered broker or dealer which controls, is controlled by, or is under common control with, the member and the general partners and officers (and persons occupying similar status or performing

similar functions) and employees of such a registered broker or dealer shall be securities persons if they effect, directly or indirectly, transactions in securities through the member by use of facilities maintained or supervised by such exchange or association; and

(2) "Control" means the power to direct or cause the direction of the management or policies of a company whether through ownership of securities, by contract or otherwise; *Provided, however,* That:

(i) Any person who, directly or indirectly, (A) has the right to vote 25 percent or more of the voting securities, (B) is entitled to receive 25 percent or more of the net profits, or (C) is a director (or person occupying a similar status or performing similar functions) of a company shall be presumed to be a person who controls such company;

(ii) Any person not covered by paragraph (b)(2)(i) of this rule shall be presumed not to be a person who controls such company; and

(iii) Any presumption may be rebutted on an appropriate showing.

Rule 19h–1. Notice by a Self-Regulatory Organization of Proposed Admission to or Continuance in Membership or Participation or Association With a Member of Any Person Subject to a Statutory Disqualification, and Applications to the Commission for Relief Therefrom

(a) *Notice of admission or continuance notwithstanding a statutory disqualification.*

(1) Any self-regulatory organization proposing, conditionally or unconditionally, to admit to, or continue any person in, membership or participation or (in the case of a national securities exchange or registered securities association) association with a member, notwithstanding a statutory disqualification, as defined in section 3(a)(39) of the Act, with respect to such person, shall file a notice with the Commission of such proposed admission or continuance. If such disqualified person has not consented to the terms of such proposal, notice of the organization's action shall be filed pursuant to Rule 19d–1 under the Act and not this rule.

(2) With respect to a person associated with a member of a national securities exchange or registered securities association, notices need be filed with the Commission pursuant to this rule only if such person:

(i) Controls such member, is a general partner or officer (or person occupying a similar status or performing similar functions) of such member, is an employee who, on behalf of such member, is engaged in securities advertising, public relations, research, sales, trading, or training or supervision of other employees who engage or propose to engage in such activities, except clerical and ministerial persons engaged in such activities, or is an employee with access to funds, securities or books and records, or

(ii) Is a broker or dealer not registered with the Commission, or controls such (unregistered) broker or dealer or is a general partner or officer (or person occupying a similar status or performing similar functions) of such broker or dealer.

(3) A notice need not be filed with the Commission pursuant to this rule if:

(i) The person subject to the statutory disqualification is already a participant in, a member of, or a person associated with a member of, a self-regulatory organization, and the terms and conditions of the proposed admission by another self-regulatory organization are the same in all material respects as those imposed or not disapproved in connection with such person's prior admission or continuance pursuant to an order of the Commission under paragraph (d) of this rule or other substantially equivalent written communication.

(ii) The self-regulatory organization finds, after reasonable inquiry, that except for the identity of the employer concerned, the terms and conditions of the proposed admission or continuance are the same in all material respects as those imposed or not disapproved in connection with a prior admission or continuance of the person subject to the statutory disqualification pursuant to an order of the Commission under paragraph (d) of this rule or other substantially equivalent written communication and that there is no intervening conduct or other circumstance that would cause the employment to be inconsistent with the public interest or the protection of investors;

(iii)   The disqualification consists of

(A)   An injunction from engaging in any action, conduct, or practice specified in section 15(b)(4)(C) of the Act, which injunction was entered 10 or more years prior to the proposed admission or continuance—*Provided, however,* That in the case of a final or permanent injunction which was preceded by a preliminary injunction against the same person in the same court proceeding, such ten-year period shall begin to run from the date of such preliminary injunction—and/or

(B)   A finding by the Commission or a self-regulatory organization of a willful violation of the Act, the Securities Act of 1933, the Investment Advisers Act of 1940, the Investment Company Act of 1940, or a rule or regulation under one or more of such Acts and the sanction for such violation is no longer in effect;

(iv)   The disqualification previously

(A)   Was a basis for the institution of an administrative proceeding pursuant to a provision of the federal securities laws, and

(B)   Was considered by the Commission in determining a sanction against such person in the proceeding; and the Commission concluded in such proceeding that it would not restrict or limit the future securities activities of such person in the capacity now proposed or, if it imposed any such restrictions or limitations for a specified time period, such time period has elapsed;

(v)   The disqualification consists of a court order or judgment of injunction or conviction, and such order or judgment

(A)   Expressly includes a provision that, on the basis of such order or judgment, the Commission will not institute a proceeding against such person pursuant to section 15(b) or 15B of the Act or that the future securities activities of such persons in the capacity now proposed will not be restricted or limited or

(B)   Includes such restrictions or limitations for a specified time period and such time period has elapsed; or

(vi)   In the case of a person seeking to become associated with a broker or dealer or municipal securities dealer, the Commission has previously consented to such proposed association pursuant to section 15(b)(6) or 15B(c)(4) of the Act.

In the case of an admission to membership, participation, or association, if an exception provided for in this paragraph (a)(3) is applicable, the self-regulatory organization shall, pursuant to its rules, determine when the admission to membership, participation, or association shall become effective.

(4)   If a self-regulatory organization determines to admit to, or continue any person in, membership, participation, or association with a member pursuant to an exception from the notice requirements provided in paragraph (a)(3)(ii), (iv) or (v) of this rule, such organization shall, within 14 calendar days of its making of such determination, furnish to the Commission, by letter, a notification setting forth, as appropriate:

(i)   The name of the person subject to the statutory disqualification;

(ii)   The name of the person's prospective and immediately preceding employers who are (were) brokers or dealers or municipal securities dealers;

(iii)   The name of the person's prospective supervisor(s);

(iv)   The respective places of such employments as reflected on the records of the self-regulatory organization;

(v)   If applicable, the findings of the self-regulatory organization referred to in paragraph (a)(3)(ii) of this rule and the nature (including relevant dates) of the previous Commission or court determination referred to in paragraph (a)(3)(iv) or (v) of this rule; and

(vi)   An identification of any other self-regulatory organization which has indicated its agreement with the terms and conditions of the proposed admission or continuance;

(5)   If a notice or notification has been previously filed or furnished pursuant to this rule by a self-regulatory organization, any other such organization need not file or furnish a separate notice or notification pursuant to this rule with respect to the same matter if such other organization agrees with the terms and conditions of the membership, participation or association reflected in the notice or notification so filed or furnished, and such agreement is set forth in the notice or notification.

(6)   The notice requirements of sections 6(c)(2), 15A(g)(2), and 17A(b)(4)(A) of the Act concerning an action of a self-regulatory organization subject to one (or more) of such sections and this paragraph (a) shall be satisfied by a notice with respect to such action filed in accordance with paragraph (c) of this rule.

(7)   The Commission, by written notice to a self-regulatory organization on or before the thirtieth day after receipt of a notice under this rule, may direct that such organization not admit to membership, participation, or association with a member any person who is subject to a statutory disqualification for a period not to exceed an additional 60 days beyond the initial 30 day notice period in order that the Commission may extend its consideration of the proposal; *Provided, however,* That during such extended period of consideration, the Commission will not direct the self-regulatory organization to bar the proposed admission to membership, participation or association with a member pursuant to section 6(c)(2), 15A(g)(2), or 17A(b)(4)(A) of the Act, and the Commission will not institute proceedings pursuant to section 15(b) or 15B of the Act on the basis of such disqualification if the self-regulatory organization has permitted the admission to membership, participation or association with a member, on a temporary basis, pending a final Commission determination.

(b)   *Preliminary notifications.* Promptly after receiving an application for admission to, or continuance in, participation or membership in, or association with a member of, a self-regulatory organization which would be required to file with the Commission a notice thereof pursuant to paragraph (a) of this rule if such admission or continuance is ultimately proposed by such organization, the organization shall file with the Commission a notification of such receipt. Such notification shall include, as appropriate:

(1)   The date of such receipt;

(2)   The names of the person subject to the statutory disqualification and the prospective employer concerned together with their respective last known places of residence or business as reflected on the records of the organization;

(3)   The basis for any such disqualification including (if based on a prior adjudication) a copy of the order or decision of the court, the Commission, or the self-regulatory organization which adjudicated the matter giving rise to the disqualification; and

(4)   The capacity in which the person concerned is proposed to be employed.

(c)   *Contents of notice of admission or continuance.* A notice filed with the Commission pursuant to paragraph (a) of this rule shall contain the following, as appropriate:

(1)   The name of the person concerned together with his last known place of residence or business as reflected on the records of the self-regulatory organization;

(2)   The basis for any such disqualification from membership, participation or association including (if based on a prior adjudication) a copy of the order or decision of the court, the Commission or the self-regulatory organization which adjudicated the matter giving rise to such disqualification;

(3)   In the case of an admission, the date upon which it is proposed by the organization that such membership, participation or association shall become effective, which shall be not less than 30 days from the date upon which the Commission receives the notice;

(4)   A description by or on behalf of the person concerned of the activities engaged in by the person since the disqualification arose, the prospective business or employment in which the person plans to engage and the manner and extent of supervision to be exercised over and by such person. This description shall be accompanied by a written statement submitted to the self-regulatory organization by the proposed employer setting forth the terms and conditions of such employment and supervision. The description also shall include

(i)   The qualifications, experience and disciplinary records of the proposed supervisors of the person and their family relationship (if any) to that person;

(ii)   The findings and results of all examinations conducted, during the two years preceding the filing of the notice, by self-regulatory organizations of the main office of the proposed employer and of the branch office(s) in which the employment will occur or be subject to supervisory controls;

(iii)   A copy of a completed Form U–4 with respect to the proposed association of such person and a certification by the self-regulatory organization that such person is fully qualified under all applicable requirements to engage in the proposed activities; and

(iv)   The name and place of employment of any other associated person of the proposed employer who is subject to a statutory disqualification (other than a disqualification specified in paragraph (a)(3)(iii) of this rule);

(5)   If a hearing on the matter has been held by the organization, a certified record of the hearing together with copies of any exhibits introduced therein;

(6)   All written submissions not included in a certified oral hearing record which were considered by the organization in its disposition of the matter;

(7)   An identification of any other self-regulatory organization which has indicated its agreement with the terms and conditions of the proposed admission or continuance;

(8)   All information furnished in writing to the self-regulatory organization by the staff of the Commission for consideration by the organization in its disposition of the matter or the incorporation by reference of such information, and a statement of the organization's views thereon; and

(9)   Such other matters as the organization or person deems relevant.

If the notice contains assertions of material facts not a matter of record before the self-regulatory organization, such facts shall be sworn to by affidavit of the person or organization offering such facts for Commission consideration. The notice may be accompanied by a brief.

(d)   *Application to the Commission for relief from certain statutory disqualifications.* The filing of a notice pursuant to paragraph (a) of this rule shall neither affect nor foreclose any action which the Commission may take with respect to such person pursuant to the provisions of section 15(b), 15B or 19(h) of the Act or any rule thereunder. Accordingly, a notice filed pursuant to paragraph (a) of this rule with respect to the membership, participation, or association of any person subject to an "applicable disqualification," as defined in paragraph (f) of this rule, may be accompanied by an application by or on behalf of the person concerned to the Commission for an order declaring, as applicable, that notwithstanding such disqualification, the Commission:

(1)   Will not institute proceedings pursuant to section 15(b)(1)(B), 15(b)(4), 15(b)(6), 15B(a)(2), 15B(c)(2), 19(h)(2) or 19(h)(3) of the Act if such person seeks to obtain or continue registration as a broker or dealer or municipal securities dealer or association with a broker or dealer or municipal securities dealer so registered, or membership or participation in a self-regulatory organization;

(2)   Will not direct otherwise, as provided in section 6(c)(2), 15A(g)(2) or 17A(b)(4)(A) of the Act; and

(3)   Will deem such person qualified pursuant to Rule G–4 of the Municipal Securities Rulemaking Board under the Act.

If a Commission consent is required in order to render a proposed association lawful under section 15(b)(6) or 15B(c)(4) of the Act, an application by or on behalf of the person seeking such consent shall accompany the notice of the proposed association filed pursuant to paragraph (a) of this rule. The

Commission may, in its discretion and subject to such terms and conditions as it deems necessary, issue such an order and consent should the Commission determine not to object to the position of the self-regulatory organization set forth in the notice or application; *Provided, however,* That nothing herein shall foreclose the right of any person, at his election, to apply directly to the Commission for such consent, if he makes such application pursuant to the terms of an existing order of the Commission under section 15(b)(6) or 15B(c)(4) of the Act limiting his association with a broker or dealer or municipal securities dealer but explicitly granting him such a right to apply for entry or reentry at a later time.

(e) *Contents of application to the Commission.* An application to the Commission pursuant to paragraph (d) of this rule shall consist of the following, as appropriate:

(1) The name of the person subject to the disqualification together with his last known place of residence or business as reflected on the records of the self-regulatory organization;

(2) A copy of the order or decision of the court, the Commission or the self-regulatory organization which adjudicated the matter giving rise to such "applicable disqualification";

(3) The nature of the relief sought and the reasons therefor;

(4) A description of the activities engaged in by the person since the disqualification arose;

(5) A description of the prospective business or employment in which the person plans to engage and the manner and extent of supervision to be exercised over and by such person. This description shall be accompanied by a written statement submitted to the self-regulatory organization by the proposed employer setting forth the terms and conditions of such employment and supervision. The description also shall include

(i) The qualifications, experience, and disciplinary records of the proposed supervisors of the person and their family relationship (if any) to that person;

(ii) The findings and results of all examinations conducted, during the two years preceding the filing of the application, by self-regulatory organizations of the main office of the proposed employer and of the branch office(s) in which the employment will occur or be subject to supervisory controls;

(iii) A copy of a completed Form U–4 with respect to the proposed association of such person and a certification by the self-regulatory organization that such person is fully qualified under all applicable requirements to engage in the proposed activities; and

(iv) The name and place of employment of any other associated person of the proposed employer who is subject to a statutory disqualification (other than a disqualification specified in paragraph (a)(3)(iii) of this rule);

(6) If a hearing on the matter has been held by the organization, a certified copy of the hearing record, together with copies of any exhibits introduced therein;

(7) All written submissions not included in a certified oral hearing record which were considered by the organization in its disposition of the matter;

(8) All information furnished in writing to the self-regulatory organization by the staff of the Commission for consideration by the organization in its disposition of the matter or the incorporation by reference of such information, and a statement of the organization's views thereon; and

(9) Such other matters as the organization or person deems relevant.

If the application contains assertions of material facts not a matter of record before the organization, such facts shall be sworn to by affidavit of the person or organization offering such facts for Commission consideration.

(f) *Definitions.* For purposes of this rule:

(1) The term "applicable disqualification" shall mean:

(i) Any effective order of the Commission pursuant to section 15(b)(4) or (6), 15B(c)(2) or (4) or 19(h)(2) or (3) of the Act—

(A) Revoking, suspending or placing limitations on the registration, activities, functions, or operations of a broker or dealer;

(B) Suspending, barring, or placing limitations on the association, activities, or functions of an associated person of a broker or dealer;

(C) Suspending or expelling any person from membership or participation in a self-regulatory organization; or

(D) Suspending or barring any person from being associated with a member of a national securities exchange or registered securities association;

(ii) Any conviction of injunction of a type described in section 15(b)(4)(B) or (C) of the Act; or

(iii) A failure under the provisions of Rule G–4 of the Municipal Securities Rulemaking Board under the Act, to meet qualifications standards, and such failure may be remedied by a finding or determination by the Commission pursuant to such rule(s) that the person affected nevertheless meets such standards.

(2) The term "control" shall mean the power to direct or cause the direction of the management or policies of a company whether through ownership of securities, by contract or otherwise; *Provided, however,* That

(i) Any person who, directly or indirectly, (A) has the right to vote 10 percent or more of the voting securities, (B) is entitled to receive 10 percent or more of the net profits, or (C) is a director (or person occupying a similar status or performing similar functions) of a company shall be presumed to be a person who controls such company;

(ii) Any person not covered by paragraph (i) shall be presumed not to be a person who controls such company; and

(iii) Any presumption may be rebutted on an appropriate showing.

(g) Where it deems appropriate to do so, the Commission may determine whether to (1) direct, pursuant to section 6(c)(2), 15A(g)(2) or 17A(b)(4)(A) of the Act, that a proposed admission covered by a notice filed pursuant to paragraph (a) of this rule shall be denied or an order barring a proposed association issued or (2) grant or deny an application filed pursuant to paragraph (d) of this rule on the basis of the notice or application filed by the self-regulatory organization, the person subject to the disqualification, or other applicant (such as the proposed employer) on behalf of such person, without oral hearing. Any request for oral hearing or argument should be submitted with the notice or application.

(h) The Rules of Practice shall apply to proceedings under this rule to the extent that they are not inconsistent with this rule.

Rule 21F–1. General

Section 21F of the Securities Exchange Act of 1934, entitled "Securities Whistleblower Incentives and Protection," requires the Securities and Exchange Commission ("Commission") to pay awards, subject to certain limitations and conditions, to whistleblowers who provide the Commission with original information about violations of the federal securities laws. These rules describe the whistleblower program that the Commission has established to implement the provisions of Section 21F, and explain the procedures you will need to follow in order to be eligible for an award. You should read these procedures carefully because the failure to take certain required steps within the time frames described in these rules may disqualify you from receiving an award for which you otherwise may be eligible. Unless expressly provided for in these rules, no person is authorized to make any offer or promise, or otherwise to bind the Commission with respect to the payment of any award or the amount thereof. The Securities and Exchange Commission's Office of the Whistleblower administers our whistleblower program. Questions about the program or these rules should be directed to the SEC Office of the Whistleblower, 100 F Street, N.E., Washington, DC 20549–5631.

Rule 21F-2. Whistleblower Status, Award Eligibility, Confidentiality, and Retaliation Protections

(a) *Whistleblower status.* (1) You are a whistleblower for purposes of Section 21F of the Exchange Act as of the time that, alone or jointly with others, you provide the Commission with information in writing that relates to a possible violation of the federal securities laws (including any law, rule, or regulation subject to the jurisdiction of the Commission) that has occurred, is ongoing, or is about to occur.

(2) A whistleblower must be an individual. A company or other entity is not eligible to be a whistleblower.

(b) *Award eligibility.* To be eligible for an award under Section 21F(b) of the Exchange Act (15 U.S.C. 78u-6(b)) based on any information you provide that relates to a possible violation of the federal securities laws, you must comply with the procedures and the conditions described in §§ 240.21F-4, 240.21F-8, and 240.21F-9. You should carefully review those rules before you submit any information that you may later wish to rely upon to claim an award.

(c) *Confidentiality protections.* To qualify for the confidentiality protections afforded by Section 21F(h)(2) of the Exchange Act (15 U.S.C. 78u-6(h)(2)) based on any information you provide that relates to a possible violation of the federal securities laws, you must comply with the procedures and the conditions described in Rule 21F-9(a).

(d) *Retaliation protections.* (1) To qualify for the retaliation protections afforded by Section 21F(h)(1) of the Exchange Act (15 U.S.C. 78u-6(h)(1)), you must satisfy all of the following criteria:

(i) You must qualify as a whistleblower under paragraph (a) of this section before experiencing the retaliation for which you seek redress;

(ii) You must reasonably believe that the information you provide to the Commission under paragraph (a) of this section relates to a possible violation of the federal securities laws; and

(iii) You must perform a lawful act that meets the following two criteria:

(A) First, the lawful act must be performed in connection with any of the activities described in Section 21F(h)(1)(A)(i) through (iii) of the Exchange Act; and

(B) Second, the lawful act must relate to the subject matter of your submission to the Commission under paragraph (a) of this section.

(2) To receive retaliation protection for a lawful act described in paragraph (d)(1)(iii) of this section, you do not need to qualify as a whistleblower under paragraph (a) of this section before performing the lawful act, but you must qualify as a whistleblower under paragraph (a) of this section before experiencing retaliation for the lawful act.

(3) To qualify for retaliation protection, you do not need to satisfy the procedures and conditions for award eligibility in Rules 21F-4, 21F-8, and F-9.

(4) Section 21F(h)(1) of the Exchange Act, including any rules promulgated thereunder, shall be enforceable in an action or proceeding brought by the Commission.

Rule 21F-3. Payment of Awards

(a) *Commission actions.* Subject to the eligibility requirements described in Rules 21F-2, 21F-8, and 21F-16, the Commission will pay an award or awards to one or more whistleblowers who:

(1) Voluntarily provide the Commission

(2) With original information

(3) That leads to the successful enforcement by the Commission of a federal court or administrative action

(4) In which the Commission obtains monetary sanctions totaling more than $1,000,000.

Note to paragraph (a): The terms voluntarily, original information, leads to successful enforcement, action, and monetary sanctions are defined in Rule 21F-4.

(b) *Related actions.* The Commission will also pay an award based on amounts collected in certain related actions.

(1)   A *related action* is a judicial or administrative action that is brought by one of the governmental entities listed in paragraphs (i) through (iii) of this section or a self-regulatory organization as specified in paragraph (iv) of this section (collectively "governmental/SRO authority"), that yields monetary sanctions, and that is based upon information that either the whistleblower provided directly to a governmental/SRO entity or the Commission itself passed along to the governmental/SRO entity pursuant to the Commission's procedures for sharing information, and which is the same original information that the whistleblower voluntarily provided to the Commission and that led the Commission to obtain monetary sanctions totaling more than $1,000,000.

(i)   The Attorney General of the United States;

(ii)   An appropriate regulatory authority (as defined in Rule 21F-4); or

(iii) A state Attorney General in a criminal case; or

(iv)   A self-regulatory organization (as defined in Rule 21F-4).

Note to paragraph (b): The terms appropriate regulatory authority and self-regulatory organization are defined in Rule 21F-4.

(2)   In order for the Commission to make an award in connection with a related action, the Commission must determine that the same original information that the whistleblower gave to the Commission also led to the successful enforcement of the related action under the same criteria described in these rules for awards made in connection with Commission actions. The Commission may seek assistance and confirmation from the authority bringing the related action in making this determination. The Commission will deny an award in connection with the related action if:

(i)   The Commission determines that the criteria for an award are not satisfied; or

(ii)   The Commission is unable to make a determination because the Office of the Whistleblower could not obtain sufficient and reliable information that could be used as the basis for an award determination pursuant to Rule 21F-12(a). Additional procedures apply to the payment of awards in related actions. These procedures are described in Rules 21F-11 and 21F-14.

(3)   The following provision shall apply where a claimant's application for a potential related action may also involve a potential recovery from another whistleblower award program for that same action.

(i)   Notwithstanding paragraph (b)(1) of this rule, if a judicial or administrative action is subject to a separate monetary award program established by the Federal Government, a state government, or a self-regulatory organization, the Commission will deem the action a related action only if the Commission finds (based on the facts and circumstances of the action) that its whistleblower program has the more direct or relevant connection to the action.

(ii)   In determining whether a potential related action has a more direct or relevant connection to the Commission's whistleblower program than another award program, the Commission will consider the nature, scope, and impact of the misconduct charged in the potential related action, and its relationship to the Federal securities laws. This inquiry may include consideration of, among other things:

(A) The relative extent to which the misconduct charged in the potential related action implicates the public policy interests underlying the Federal securities laws (such as investor protection) rather than other law-enforcement or regulatory interests (such as tax collection or fraud against the Federal Government);

(B) The degree to which the monetary sanctions imposed in the potential related action are attributable to conduct that also underlies the Federal securities law violations that were the subject of the Commission's enforcement action; and

(C)   Whether the potential related action involves state-law claims and the extent to which the state may have a whistleblower award program that potentially applies to that type of law-enforcement action.

(iii)   If the Commission determines to deem the action a related action, the Commission will not make an award to you for the related action if you have already been granted an award by the governmental/SRO entity responsible for administering the other whistleblower award program. Further, if you were denied an award by the other award program, you will not be permitted to readjudicate any issues before the Commission that the governmental/SRO entity responsible for administering the other whistleblower award program resolved against you as part of the award denial. Additionally, if the Commission makes an award before an award determination is finalized by the governmental/SRO entity responsible for administering the other award program, the Commission shall condition its award on the meritorious whistleblower making a prompt, irrevocable waiver of any claim to an award from the other award program.

Rule 21F–4.   Other Definitions

(a)   *Voluntary submission of information.*

(1)   Your submission of information is made voluntarily within the meaning of Rules 21F–1 through 21F–17 if you provide your submission before a request, inquiry, or demand that relates to the subject matter of your submission is directed to you or anyone representing you (such as an attorney):

(i)   By the Commission;

(ii)   In connection with an investigation, inspection, or examination by the Public Company Accounting Oversight Board, or any self-regulatory organization; or

(iii) In connection with an investigation by Congress, any other authority of the federal government, or a state Attorney General or securities regulatory authority.

(2)   If the Commission or any of these other authorities direct a request, inquiry, or demand as described in paragraph (1) of this rule to you or your representative first, your submission will not be considered voluntary, and you will not be eligible for an award, even if your response is not compelled by subpoena or other applicable law. However, your submission of information to the Commission will be considered voluntary if you voluntarily provided the same information to one of the other authorities identified above prior to receiving a request, inquiry, or demand from the Commission.

(3)   In addition, your submission will not be considered voluntary if you are required to report your original information to the Commission as a result of a pre-existing legal duty, a contractual duty that is owed to the Commission or to one of the other authorities set forth in paragraph (1) of this rule, or a duty that arises out of a judicial or administrative order.

(b)   *Original information.*

(1)   In order for your whistleblower submission to be considered original information, it must be:

(i)   Derived from your independent knowledge or independent analysis;

(ii)   Not already known to the Commission from any other source, unless you are the original source of the information;

(iii) Not exclusively derived from an allegation made in a judicial or administrative hearing, in a governmental report, hearing, audit, or investigation, or from the news media, unless you are a source of the information; and

(iv)   Provided to the Commission for the first time after July 21, 2010 (the date of enactment of the *Dodd-Frank Wall Street Reform and Consumer Protection Act*).

(2)   Independent knowledge means factual information in your possession that is not derived from publicly available sources. You may gain independent knowledge from your experiences, communications and observations in your business or social interactions.

(3)   Independent analysis means your own analysis, whether done alone or in combination with others. Analysis means your examination and evaluation of information that may be publicly available, but which reveals information that is not generally known or available to the public.

(4)   The Commission will not consider information to be derived from your independent knowledge or independent analysis in any of the following circumstances:

(i)   If you obtained the information through a communication that was subject to the attorney-client privilege, unless disclosure of that information would otherwise be permitted by an attorney pursuant to Rule 3(d)(2) of the Standards of Professional Conduct, the applicable state attorney conduct rules, or otherwise;

(ii)   If you obtained the information in connection with the legal representation of a client on whose behalf you or your employer or firm are providing services, and you seek to use the information to make a whistleblower submission for your own benefit, unless disclosure would otherwise be permitted by an attorney pursuant to Rule 3(d)(2) of the Standards of Professional Conduct chapter, the applicable state attorney conduct rules, or otherwise; or

(iii)   In circumstances not covered by paragraphs (b)(4)(i) or (b)(4)(ii) of this rule, if you obtained the information because you were:

(A)   An officer, director, trustee, or partner of an entity and another person informed you of allegations of misconduct, or you learned the information in connection with the entity's processes for identifying, reporting, and addressing possible violations of law;

(B)   An employee whose principal duties involve compliance or internal audit responsibilities, or you were employed by or otherwise associated with a firm retained to perform compliance or internal audit functions for an entity;

(C)   Employed by or otherwise associated with a firm retained to conduct an inquiry or investigation into possible violations of law; or

(D)   An employee of, or other person associated with, a public accounting firm, if you obtained the information through the performance of an engagement required of an independent public accountant under the federal securities laws (other than an audit subject to Rule 21F–8(c)(4)), and that information related to a violation by the engagement client or the client's directors, officers or other employees.

(iv)   If you obtained the information by a means or in a manner that is determined by a United States court to violate applicable federal or state criminal law; or

(v)   *Exceptions.* Paragraph (b)(4)(iii) of this rule shall not apply if:

(A)   You have a reasonable basis to believe that disclosure of the information to the Commission is necessary to prevent the relevant entity from engaging in conduct that is likely to cause substantial injury to the financial interest or property of the entity or investors;

(B)   You have a reasonable basis to believe that the relevant entity is engaging in conduct that will impede an investigation of the misconduct; or

(C)   At least 120 days have elapsed since you provided the information to the relevant entity's audit committee, chief legal officer, chief compliance officer (or their equivalents), or your supervisor, or since you received the information, if you received it under circumstances indicating that the entity's audit committee, chief legal officer, chief compliance officer (or their equivalents), or your supervisor was already aware of the information.

(vi)   If you obtained the information from a person who is subject to this rule, unless the information is not excluded from that person's use pursuant to this rule, or you are providing the Commission with information about possible violations involving that person.

(5)   The Commission will consider you to be an original source of the same information that we obtain from another source if the information satisfies the definition of original information and the other source obtained the information from you or your representative. In order to be considered an original source of information that the Commission receives from Congress, any other authority of the

federal government, a state Attorney General or securities regulatory authority, any self-regulatory organization, or the Public Company Accounting Oversight Board, you must have voluntarily given such authorities the information within the meaning of these rules. You must establish your status as the original source of information to the Commission's satisfaction. In determining whether you are the original source of information, the Commission may seek assistance and confirmation from one of the other authorities described above, or from another entity (including your employer), in the event that you claim to be the original source of information that an authority or another entity provided to the Commission.

(6)   If the Commission already knows some information about a matter from other sources at the time you make your submission, and you are not an original source of that information under paragraph (b)(5) of this rule, the Commission will consider you an original source of any information you provide that is derived from your independent knowledge or analysis and that materially adds to the information that the Commission already possesses.

(7)   If you provide information to the Congress, any other authority of the federal government, a state Attorney General or securities regulatory authority, any self-regulatory organization, or the Public Company Accounting Oversight Board, or to an entity's internal whistleblower, legal, or compliance procedures for reporting allegations of possible violations of law, and you, within 120 days, submit the same information to the Commission pursuant to Rule 21F–9, as you must do in order for you to be eligible to be considered for an award, then, for purposes of evaluating your claim to an award under Rules 21F–10 and 21F–11, the Commission will consider that you provided information as of the date of your original disclosure, report or submission to one of these other authorities or persons. You must establish the effective date of any prior disclosure, report, or submission, to the Commission's satisfaction. The Commission may seek assistance and confirmation from the other authority or person in making this determination.

(c)   *Information that leads to successful enforcement.* The Commission will consider that you provided original information that led to the successful enforcement of a judicial or administrative action in any of the following circumstances:

(1)   You gave the Commission original information that was sufficiently specific, credible, and timely to cause the staff to commence an examination, open an investigation, reopen an investigation that the Commission had closed, or to inquire concerning different conduct as part of a current examination or investigation, and the Commission brought a successful judicial or administrative action based in whole or in part on conduct that was the subject of your original information; or

(2)   You gave the Commission original information about conduct that was already under examination or investigation by the Commission, the Congress, any other authority of the federal government, a state Attorney General or securities regulatory authority, any self-regulatory organization, or the PCAOB (except in cases where you were an original source of this information as defined in paragraph (b)(5) of this rule), and your submission significantly contributed to the success of the action.

(3)   You reported original information through an entity's internal whistleblower, legal, or compliance procedures for reporting allegations of possible violations of law before or at the same time you reported them to the Commission; the entity later provided your information to the Commission, or provided results of an audit or investigation initiated in whole or in part in response to information you reported to the entity; and the information the entity provided to the Commission satisfies either paragraph (c)(1) or (c)(2) of this rule. Under this paragraph (c)(3), you must also submit the same information to the Commission in accordance with the procedures set forth in Rule 21F–9 within 120 days of providing it to the entity.

(d)   An action generally means a single captioned judicial or administrative proceeding brought by the Commission. Notwithstanding the foregoing:

(1)   For purposes of making an award under Rule 21F–10, the Commission will treat as a Commission action two or more administrative or judicial proceedings brought by the Commission if these proceedings arise out of the same nucleus of operative facts; or

(2) For purposes of determining the payment on an award under Rule 21F–14, the Commission will deem as part of the Commission action upon which the award was based any subsequent Commission proceeding that, individually, results in a monetary sanction of $1,000,000 or less, and that arises out of the same nucleus of operative facts.

(3) For purposes of making an award under Rules 21F–10 and 21F–11, the following will be deemed to be an administrative action and any money required to be paid thereunder will be deemed a monetary sanction under Rule 21F–4(e):

(i) A non-prosecution agreement or deferred prosecution agreement entered into by the U.S. Department of Justice; or

(ii) A similar settlement agreement entered into by the Commission outside of the context of a judicial or administrative proceeding to address violations of the securities laws.

(e) *Monetary sanctions* means:

(1) An order to pay money that results from a Commission action or related action and which is either:

(i) Expressly designated as a penalty, disgorgement, or interest; or

(ii) Otherwise ordered as relief for the violations that are the subject of the covered action or related action; or

Any money deposited into a disgorgement fund or other fund pursuant to section 308(b) of the Sarbanes-Oxley Act of 2002 (15 U.S.C. 7246(b)), as a result of such action or any settlement of such action

(f) Appropriate regulatory agency means the Commission, the Comptroller of the Currency, the Board of Governors of the Federal Reserve System, the Federal Deposit Insurance Corporation, the Office of Thrift Supervision, and any other agencies that may be defined as appropriate regulatory agencies under Section 3(a)(34) of the Securities Exchange Act of 1934.

(g) Appropriate regulatory authority means an appropriate regulatory agency other than the Commission.

(h) Self-regulatory organization means any national securities exchange, registered securities association, registered clearing agency, the Municipal Securities Rulemaking Board, and any other organizations that may be defined as self-regulatory organizations under Section 3(a)(26) of the Securities Exchange Act of 1934.

Rule 21F–5. Amount of Award

(a) The determination of the amount of an award is in the discretion of the Commission.

(b) If all of the conditions are met for a whistleblower award in connection with a Commission action or a related action, the Commission will then decide the percentage amount of the award applying the criteria set forth in Rule 21F–6 and pursuant to the procedures set forth in Rules 21F–10 and 21F–11. The amount will be at least 10 percent and no more than 30 percent of the monetary sanctions that the Commission and the other authorities are able to collect. The percentage awarded in connection with a Commission action may differ from the percentage awarded in connection with a related action.

(c) If the Commission makes awards to more than one whistleblower in connection with the same action or related action, the Commission will determine an individual percentage award for each whistleblower, but in no event will the total amount awarded to all whistleblowers in the aggregate be less than 10 percent or greater than 30 percent of the amount the Commission or the other authorities collect.

Rule 21F–6. Criteria for Determining Amount of Award

In exercising its discretion to determine the appropriate award, the Commission may consider the following factors (and only the following factors) in relation to the facts and circumstances of each case in setting the dollar or percentage amount of the award.

(a) *Factors that may increase the amount of a whistleblower's award.* In determining whether to increase the amount of an award, the Commission will consider the following factors, which are not listed in order of importance.

(1) *Significance of the information provided by the whistleblower.* The Commission will assess the significance of the information provided by a whistleblower to the success of the Commission action or related action. In considering this factor, the Commission may take into account, among other things:

(i) The nature of the information provided by the whistleblower and how it related to the successful enforcement action, including whether the reliability and completeness of the information provided to the Commission by the whistleblower resulted in the conservation of Commission resources;

(ii) The degree to which the information provided by the whistleblower supported one or more successful claims brought in the Commission or related action.

(2) *Assistance provided by the whistleblower.* The Commission will assess the degree of assistance provided by the whistleblower and any legal representative of the whistleblower in the Commission action or related action. In considering this factor, the Commission may take into account, among other things:

(i) Whether the whistleblower provided ongoing, extensive, and timely cooperation and assistance by, for example, helping to explain complex transactions, interpreting key evidence, or identifying new and productive lines of inquiry;

(ii) The timeliness of the whistleblower's initial report to the Commission or to an internal compliance or reporting system of business organizations committing, or impacted by, the securities violations, where appropriate;

(iii) The resources conserved as a result of the whistleblower's assistance;

(iv) Whether the whistleblower appropriately encouraged or authorized others to assist the staff of the Commission who might otherwise not have participated in the investigation or related action;

(v) The efforts undertaken by the whistleblower to remediate the harm caused by the violations, including assisting the authorities in the recovery of the fruits and instrumentalities of the violations; and

(vi) Any unique hardships experienced by the whistleblower as a result of his or her reporting and assisting in the enforcement action.

(3) *Law enforcement interest.* The Commission will assess its programmatic interest in deterring violations of the securities laws by making awards to whistleblowers who provide information that leads to the successful enforcement of such laws. In considering this factor, the Commission may take into account, among other things:

(i) The degree to which an award enhances the Commission's ability to enforce the federal securities laws and protect investors; and

(ii) The degree to which an award encourages the submission of high quality information from whistleblowers by appropriately rewarding whistleblowers' submission of significant information and assistance, even in cases where the monetary sanctions available for collection are limited or potential monetary sanctions were reduced or eliminated by the Commission because an entity self-reported a securities violation following the whistleblower's related internal disclosure, report, or submission.

(iii) Whether the subject matter of the action is a Commission priority, whether the reported misconduct involves regulated entities or fiduciaries, whether the whistleblower exposed an industry-wide practice, the type and severity of the securities violations, the age and duration of misconduct, the number of violations, and the isolated, repetitive, or ongoing nature of the violations; and

(iv)   The dangers to investors or others presented by the underlying violations involved in the enforcement action, including the amount of harm or potential harm caused by the underlying violations, the type of harm resulting from or threatened by the underlying violations, and the number of individuals or entities harmed.

(4)   *Participation in internal compliance systems.* The Commission will assess whether, and the extent to which, the whistleblower and any legal representative of the whistleblower participated in internal compliance systems. In considering this factor, the Commission may take into account, among other things:

(i)   Whether, and the extent to which, a whistleblower reported the possible securities violations through internal whistleblower, legal or compliance procedures before, or at the same time as, reporting them to the Commission; and

(ii)   Whether, and the extent to which, a whistleblower assisted any internal investigation or inquiry concerning the reported securities violations.

(b)   *Factors that may decrease the amount of a whistleblower's award.* In determining whether to decrease the amount of an award, the Commission will consider the following factors, which are not listed in order of importance.

(1)   *Culpability.* The Commission will assess the culpability or involvement of the whistleblower in matters associated with the Commission's action or related actions. In considering this factor, the Commission may take into account, among other things:

(i)   The whistleblower's role in the securities violations;

(ii)   The whistleblower's education, training, experience, and position of responsibility at the time the violations occurred;

(iii)   Whether the whistleblower acted with scienter, both generally and in relation to others who participated in the violations;

(iv)   Whether the whistleblower financially benefitted from the violations;

(v)   Whether the whistleblower is a recidivist;

(vi)   The egregiousness of the underlying fraud committed by the whistleblower; and

(vii)   Whether the whistleblower knowingly interfered with the Commission's investigation of the violations or related enforcement actions.

(2)   *Unreasonable reporting delay.* The Commission will assess whether the whistleblower unreasonably delayed reporting the securities violations. In considering this factor, the Commission may take into account, among other things:

(i)   Whether the whistleblower was aware of the relevant facts but failed to take reasonable steps to report or prevent the violations from occurring or continuing;

(ii)   Whether the whistleblower was aware of the relevant facts but only reported them after learning about a related inquiry, investigation, or enforcement action; and

(iii)   Whether there was a legitimate reason for the whistleblower to delay reporting the violations.

(c)   *Additional considerations in connection with certain awards of $5 million or less.*

(1)   This subpart applies when the Commission is considering any meritorious award application where:

(i)   the statutory maximum award of 30 percent of the monetary sanctions collected in any covered and related action(s), in the aggregate, is $5 million or less, and the Commission determines that it does not reasonably anticipate that future collections would cause the statutory maximum award to be paid to any whistleblower to exceed $5 million in the aggregate;

(ii)   none of the negative award factors specified in paragraphs Rule 21F–6(b)(1) or Rule 21F–6(b)(3) were found present with respect to the claimant's award application, and the award claim does not trigger Rule 21F–16 (concerning awards to whistleblowers who engage in culpable conduct);

(iii)   the claimant did not engage in unreasonable reporting delay under § 240.21F–6(b)(2) (although the Commission, in its sole discretion, may in certain limited circumstances determine to waive this criterion if the claimant can demonstrate that doing so based on the facts and circumstances of the matter is consistent with the public interest, the promotion of investor protection, and the objectives of the whistleblower program); and

(iv)   the Commission does not otherwise determine in its sole discretion that application of the enhancement afforded by this subpart would be inappropriate because either:

(a)   the whistleblower's assistance in the covered action or related action (as assessed under § 240.21F–6(a) of this section) was, under the relevant facts and circumstances, limited; or

(b)   providing the enhancement would be inconsistent with the public interest, the promotion of investor protection, or the objectives of the whistleblower program.

(2)   If the Commission determines that the criteria Rule 21F–6(c)(1) are satisfied, the resulting payout to a claimant for the original information that the claimant provided that led to one or more successful covered or related action(s), collectively, will be the maximum allowed under the statute.

(3)   Notwithstanding Rule 21F–6(c)(2), if two or more claimants qualify for an award in connection with any covered action or related action and at least one of those claimant's award applications qualifies under § 240.21F–6(c)(1), the aggregate amount awarded to all meritorious claimants will be the statutory maximum. In allocating that amount among the meritorious claimants, the Commission will consider whether an individual claimant's award application satisfies Rules 21F–6(c)(1)(ii), 21F–6(c)(1)(iii).

(3)   *Interference with internal compliance and reporting systems.* The Commission will assess, in cases where the whistleblower interacted with his or her entity's internal compliance or reporting system, whether the whistleblower undermined the integrity of such system. In considering this factor, the Commission will take into account whether there is evidence provided to the Commission that the whistleblower knowingly:

(i)   Interfered with an entity's established legal, compliance, or audit procedures to prevent or delay detection of the reported securities violation;

(ii)   Made any material false, fictitious, or fraudulent statements or representations that hindered an entity's efforts to detect, investigate, or remediate the reported securities violations; and

(iii)   Provided any false writing or document knowing the writing or document contained any false, fictitious or fraudulent statements or entries that hindered an entity's efforts to detect, investigate, or remediate the reported securities violations.

Rule 21F–7.   Confidentiality of Submissions

(a)   Pursuant to Section 21F(h)(2) of the Exchange and Rule 21F–2(c), the Commission will not disclose information that could reasonably be expected to reveal the identity of a whistleblower provided that the whistleblower has submitted information utilizing the processes specified Rule 21F–9(a), except that the Commission may disclose such information in the following circumstances:

(1)   When disclosure is required to a defendant or respondent in connection with a federal court or administrative action that the Commission files or in another public action or proceeding that is filed by an authority to which we provide the information, as described below;

(2)   When the Commission determines that it is necessary to accomplish the purposes of the Securities Exchange Act of 1934 and to protect investors, it may provide your information to the Department of Justice, an appropriate regulatory authority, a self-regulatory organization, a state attorney general in connection with a criminal investigation, any appropriate state regulatory authority, the Public Company Accounting Oversight Board, or foreign securities and law enforcement

authorities. Each of these entities other than foreign securities and law enforcement authorities is subject to the confidentiality requirements set forth in Section 21F(h) of the Securities Exchange Act of 1934. The Commission will determine what assurances of confidentiality it deems appropriate in providing such information to foreign securities and law enforcement authorities.

    (3)   The Commission may make disclosures in accordance with the Privacy Act of 1974 (5 U.S.C. 552a).

    (b)   You may submit information to the Commission anonymously. If you do so, however, you must also do the following:

    (1)   You must have an attorney represent you in connection with both your submission of information and your claim for an award, and your attorney's name and contact information must be provided to the Commission at the time you submit your information;

    (2)   You and your attorney must follow the procedures set forth in Rule 21F-9 for submitting original information anonymously; and

    (3)   Before the Commission will pay any award to you, you must disclose your identity to the Commission and your identity must be verified by the Commission as set forth in Rule 21F-10.

Rule 21F-8. Eligibility

    (a)   To be eligible for a whistleblower award, you must give the Commission information in the form and manner that the Commission requires. The procedures for submitting information and making a claim for an award are described in Rule 21F-9 through 21F-11. You should read these procedures carefully because you need to follow them in order to be eligible for an award, except that the Commission may, in its sole discretion, waive any of these procedures based upon a showing of extraordinary circumstances.

    (b)   In addition to any forms required by these rules, the Commission may also require that you provide certain additional information. You may be required to:

    (1)   Provide explanations and other assistance in order that the staff may evaluate and use the information that you submitted;

    (2)   Provide all additional information in your possession that is related to the subject matter of your submission in a complete and truthful manner, through follow-up meetings, or in other forms that our staff may agree to;

    (3)   Provide testimony or other evidence acceptable to the staff relating to whether you are eligible, or otherwise satisfy any of the conditions, for an award; and

    (4)   Enter into a confidentiality agreement in a form acceptable to the Office of the Whistleblower, covering any non-public information that the Commission provides to you, and including a provision that a violation of the agreement may lead to your ineligibility to receive an award.

    (c)   You are not eligible to be considered for an award if you do not satisfy the requirements of paragraphs (a) and (b) of this rule. In addition, you are not eligible if:

    (1)   You are, or were at the time you acquired the original information provided to the Commission, a member, officer, or employee of the Commission, the Department of Justice, an appropriate regulatory agency, a self-regulatory organization, the Public Company Accounting Oversight Board, or any law enforcement organization;

    (2)   You are, or were at the time you acquired the original information provided to the Commission, a member, officer, or employee of a foreign government, any political subdivision, department, agency, or instrumentality of a foreign government, or any other foreign financial regulatory authority as that term is defined in Section 3(a)(52) of the Securities Exchange Act of 1934;

    (3)   You are convicted of a criminal violation that is related to the Commission action or to a related action (as defined in Rule 21F-4) for which you otherwise could receive an award;

(4)   You obtained the original information that you gave the Commission through an audit of a company's financial statements, and making a whistleblower submission would be contrary to requirements of Section 10A of the Securities Exchange Act of 1934.

(5)   You are the spouse, parent, child, or sibling of a member or employee of the Commission, or you reside in the same household as a member or employee of the Commission;

(6)   You acquired the original information you gave the Commission from a person:

(i)   Who is subject to paragraph (c)(4) of this rule, unless the information is not excluded from that person's use, or you are providing the Commission with information about possible violations involving that person; or

(ii)   With the intent to evade any provision of these rules; or

(7)   The Commission or a court of competent jurisdiction finds that, in your whistleblower submission, your other dealings with the Commission (including your dealings beyond the whistleblower program and covered action), or your dealings with another governmental/SRO entity (as specified in Rule 21F-3(b)(1)) in connection with a related action, you knowingly and willfully made any materially false, fictitious, or fraudulent statement or representation, or used any false writing or document knowing that it contains any materially false, fictitious, or fraudulent statement or entry with intent to mislead or otherwise hinder the Commission or another governmental/SRO entity, provided that this provision should not apply if the Commission, in its discretion, finds it consistent with the public interest, the promotion of investor protection, and the objectives of the whistleblower program.

Rule 21F-9.   Procedures for Submitting Original Information

(a)   To submit information in a manner that satisfies Rules 21F-2(b) and R21F-2(c) of this chapter you must submit your information to the Commission by any of these methods:

(1)   Online, through the Commission's website located at www.sec.gov, using the Commission's electronic TCR portal (Tip, Complaint, or Referral);

(2)   Mailing or faxing a Form TCR to the SEC Office of the Whistleblower at the mailing address or fax number designated on the SEC's webpage for making such submissions; or

(3)   By any other such method that the Commission may expressly designate on its website as a mechanism that satisfies Rules 21F-2(b) and 240.21F-2(c) of this chapter. For a 30-day period following the Commission's designation of any new forms by placing them on the Commission's website, the Commission shall also continue to accept submissions made using the prior version of the forms.

(b)   Further, to be eligible for an award, you must declare under penalty of perjury at the time you submit your information pursuant to paragraph (a)(1), (a)(2), or (a)(3) of this rule that your information is true and correct to the best of your knowledge and belief.

(c)   Notwithstanding paragraphs (a) and (b) of this rule, if you are providing your original information to the Commission anonymously, then your attorney must submit your information on your behalf pursuant to the procedures specified in paragraph (a) of this rule. Prior to your attorney's submission, you must provide your attorney with a completed Form TCR that you have signed under penalty of perjury. When your attorney makes her submission on your behalf, your attorney will be required to certify that he or she:

(1)   Has verified your identity;

(2)   Has reviewed your completed and signed Form TCR for completeness and accuracy and that the information contained therein is true, correct and complete to the best of the attorney's knowledge, information and belief;

(3)   Has obtained your non-waivable consent to provide the Commission with your original completed and signed Form TCR in the event that the Commission requests it due to concerns that you may have knowingly and willfully made false, fictitious, or fraudulent statements or representations, or used any false writing or document knowing that the writing or document contains any false fictitious or fraudulent statement or entry; and

(4)   Consents to be legally obligated to provide the signed Form TCR within seven (7) calendar days of receiving such request from the Commission.

(d)   If you submitted original information in writing to the Commission after July 21, 2010 (the date of enactment of the Dodd-Frank Wall Street Reform and Consumer Protection Act) but before the effective date of these rules, your submission will be deemed to satisfy the requirements set forth in paragraphs (a) and (b) of this rule. If you were an anonymous whistleblower, however, you must provide your attorney with a completed and signed copy of Form TCR within 60 days of the effective date of these rules, your attorney must retain the signed form in his or her records, and you must provide of copy of the signed form to the Commission staff upon request by Commission staff prior to any payment of an award to you in connection with your submission. Notwithstanding the foregoing, you must follow the procedures and conditions for making a claim for a whistleblower award described in Rules 21F–10 and 21F–11.

(e)   You must follow the procedures specified in paragraphs (a) and (b) of this rule within 30 days of when you first provide the Commission with original information that you rely upon as a basis for claiming an award. If you fail to do so, then you will be deemed ineligible for an award in connection with that information (even if you later resubmit that information in accordance with paragraphs (a) and (b) of this rule). Notwithstanding the foregoing, the Commission shall waive your noncompliance with paragraphs (a) and (b) of this section if:

(1)   You demonstrate to the satisfaction of the Commission that you complied with the requirements of paragraphs (a) and (b) of this rule within 30 days of first obtaining actual or constructive notice about those requirements (or 30 days from the date you retain counsel to represent you in connection with your submission of original information, whichever occurs first); and

(2)   The Commission can readily develop an administrative record that unambiguously demonstrates that you would otherwise qualify for an award.

Rule 21F–10. Procedures for Making a Claim for a Whistleblower Award in SEC Actions that Result in Monetary Sanctions in Excess of $1,000,000

(a)   Whenever a Commission action results in monetary sanctions totaling more than $1,000,000, the Office of the Whistleblower will cause to be published on the Commission's website a "Notice of Covered Action." Such Notice will be published subsequent to the entry of a final judgment or order that alone, or collectively with other judgments or orders previously entered in the Commission action, exceeds $1,000,000; or, in the absence of such judgment or order subsequent to the deposit of monetary sanctions exceeding $1,000,000 into a disgorgement or other fund pursuant to Section 308(b) of the Sarbanes-Oxley Act of 2002. A claimant will have ninety (90) days from the date of the Notice of Covered Action to file a claim for an award based on that action, or the claim will be barred.

(b)   To file a claim for a whistleblower award, you must file Form WB-APP (as specified in Rule 21F–8(d)(2). You must sign this form as the claimant and submit it to the Office of the Whistleblower by mail, email (as a PDF attachment), or fax (or any other manner that the Office permits).

(1)   All claim forms, including any attachments, must be received by the Office of the Whistleblower within ninety (90) calendar days of the date of the Notice of Covered Action in order to be considered for an award.

(2)   Notwithstanding paragraphs (a) and (b)(1) of this section, the time period to file an application for an award based on a Commission settlement agreement covered by Rule 21F–4(d) shall be governed exclusively by Rule 21F–11(b)(1 if the settlement agreement was entered into after July 21, 2010 but before the effective date of this section as amended in 2020.

(c)   If you provided your original information to the Commission anonymously, you must disclose your identity on the Form WB-APP, and your identity must be verified in a form and manner that is acceptable to the Office of the Whistleblower prior to the payment of any award.

(d)   Once the time for filing any appeals of the Commission's judicial or administrative action has expired, or where an appeal has been filed, after all appeals in the action have been concluded, one or more staff members designated by the Director of the Division of Enforcement ("Claims Review Staff") will evaluate all timely whistleblower award claims submitted on Form WB-APP in accordance with the criteria set forth in these rules. In connection with this process, the Office of the Whistleblower may require that you provide additional information relating to your eligibility for an award or satisfaction of any of the conditions for an award, as set forth in Rule 21F–8(b). Following a determination by the Claims Review Staff (and an opportunity for the Commission to review that determination), the Office of the Whistleblower will send you a Preliminary Determination setting forth a preliminary assessment as to whether the claim should be allowed or denied and, if allowed, setting forth the proposed award dollar and percentage amount, and the grounds therefore.

(e) You may contest the Preliminary Determination made by the Claims Review Staff by submitting a written response to the Office of the Whistleblower setting forth the grounds for your objection to either the denial of an award or the proposed amount of an award. The response must be in the form and manner that the Office of the Whistleblower shall require. You may also include documentation or other evidentiary support for the grounds advanced in your response. In applying the award factors specified in Rule 21F–6 and determining the award dollar and percentage amounts set forth in the Preliminary Determination, the award factors may be considered by the SEC staff and the Commission in dollar terms, percentage terms or some combination thereof. Should you choose to contest a Preliminary Determination, you may set forth the reasons for your objection to the proposed amount of an award, including the grounds therefore, in dollar terms, percentage terms or some combination thereof.

(1) Before determining whether to contest a Preliminary Determination, you may:

(i) Within thirty (30) days of the date of the Preliminary Determination, request that the Office of the Whistleblower make available for your review the materials from among those set forth in Rule 21F–12(a) that formed the basis of the Claims Review Staff's Preliminary Determination.

(ii) Within thirty (30) calendar days of the date of the Preliminary Determination, request a meeting with the Office of the Whistleblower; however, such meetings are not required and the office may in its sole discretion decline the request.

(2) If you decide to contest the Preliminary Determination, you must submit your written response and supporting materials within sixty (60) calendar days of the date of the Preliminary Determination, or if a request to review materials is made pursuant to paragraph (e)(1) of this rule, then within sixty (60) calendar days of the Office of the Whistleblower making those materials available for your review.

(f) If you fail to submit a timely response pursuant to paragraph (e) of this rule, then the Preliminary Determination will become the Final Order of the Commission (except where the Preliminary Determination recommended an award, in which case the Preliminary Determination will be deemed a Proposed Final Determination for purposes of paragraph (h) of this rule). Your failure to submit a timely response contesting a Preliminary Determination will constitute a failure to exhaust administrative remedies, and you will be prohibited from pursuing an appeal pursuant to Rule 21F–13.

(g) If you submit a timely response pursuant to paragraph (e) of this rule, then the Claims Review Staff will consider the issues and grounds advanced in your response, along with any supporting documentation you provided, and will make its Proposed Final Determination.

(h) The Office of the Whistleblower will then notify the Commission of each Proposed Final Determination. Within thirty 30 days thereafter, any Commissioner may request that the Proposed Final Determination be reviewed by the Commission. If no Commissioner requests such a review within the 30-day period, then the Proposed Final Determination will become the Final Order of the Commission. In the event a Commissioner requests a review, the Commission will review the record that the staff relied upon in making its determinations, including your previous submissions to the Office of the Whistleblower, and issue its Final Order.

(i) The Office of the Whistleblower will provide you with the Final Order of the Commission.

Rule 21F–11. Procedures for Determining Awards Based upon a Related Action

(a) If you are eligible to receive an award following a Commission action that results in monetary sanctions totaling more than $1,000,000, you also may be eligible to receive an award based on the monetary sanctions that are collected from a related action (as defined in Rule 21F–3).

(b)   You must also use Form WB-APP (as specified in Rule 21F-8(d)(2)) to submit a claim for an award in a potential related action. You must sign this form as the claimant and submit it to the Office of the Whistleblower by mail, email (as a PDF attachment), or fax (or any other manner that the Office permits) as follows:

(1)   If a final order imposing monetary sanctions has been entered in a potential related action at the time you submit your claim for an award in connection with a Commission action, you must submit your claim for an award in that related action on the same Form WB-APP that you use for the Commission action. For purposes of this paragraph and paragraph (b)(2) of this rule, a final order imposing monetary sanctions is entered on the date of a court or administrative order imposing the monetary sanctions; however, with respect to any agreement covered by Rule 21F-4(d) (such as a deferred prosecution agreement or a nonprosecution agreement entered by the Department of Justice), the Commission will deem the date of the entry of the final order to be the later of either:

(i)   the effective date of this section as amended in 2020; or

(ii)   the date of the earliest public availability of the instrument reflecting the arrangement if evidenced by a press release or similar dated publication notice (or otherwise, the date of the last signature necessary for the agreement).

(2)   If a final order imposing monetary sanctions in a potential related action has not been entered at the time you submit your claim for an award in connection with a Commission action, you must submit your claim on Form WB-APP within ninety (90) days of the issuance of a final order imposing sanctions in the potential related action.

(c)   The Office of the Whistleblower may request additional information from you in connection with your claim for an award in a related action to demonstrate that you directly (or through the Commission) voluntarily provided the governmental/SRO entity (as specified in Rule 21F-3(b)(1)) the same original information that led to the Commission's successful covered action, and that this information led to the successful enforcement of the related action. Further, the Office of the Whistleblower, in its discretion, may seek assistance and confirmation from the governmental/SRO entity in making an award determination.

(d)   Once the time for filing any appeals of the final judgment or order in a potential related action has expired, or if an appeal has been filed, after all appeals in the action have been concluded, the Claims Review Staff (as specified in Rule 21F-10(d) will evaluate all timely whistleblower award claims submitted on Form WB-APP in connection with the related action. The evaluation will be undertaken pursuant to the criteria set forth in these rules. In connection with this process, the Office of the Whistleblower may require that you provide additional information relating to your eligibility for an award or satisfaction of any of the conditions for an award, as set forth in Rule 21F-(8)(b). Following a determination by the Claims Review Staff (and an opportunity for the Commission to review that determination), the Office of the Whistleblower will send you a Preliminary Determination setting forth a preliminary assessment as to whether the claim should be allowed or denied and, if allowed, setting forth the proposed award percentage amount.

(e)   You may contest the Preliminary Determination made by the Claims Review Staff by submitting a written response to the Office of the Whistleblower setting forth the grounds for your objection to either the denial of an award or the proposed amount of an award. The response must be in the form and manner that the Office of the Whistleblower shall require. You may also include documentation or other evidentiary support for the grounds advanced in your response. In applying the award factors specified in Rule 21F-6 and determining the award dollar and percentage amounts set forth in the Preliminary Determination, the award factors may be considered by the SEC staff and the Commission in dollar terms, percentage terms or some combination thereof. Should you choose to contest a Preliminary Determination, you may set forth the reasons for your objection to the proposed amount of an award, including the grounds therefore, in dollar terms, percentage terms or some combination thereof.

(1)   Before determining whether to contest a Preliminary Determination, you may:

(i)   Within thirty (30) days of the date of the Preliminary Determination, request that the Office of the Whistleblower make available for your review the materials from among those set forth in Rule 21F-12(a) that formed the basis of the Claims Review Staff's Preliminary Determination.

(ii)   Within thirty (30) days of the date of the Preliminary Determination, request a meeting with the Office of the Whistleblower; however, such meetings are not required and the office may in its sole discretion decline the request.

(2)   If you decide to contest the Preliminary Determination, you must submit your written response and supporting materials within sixty (60) calendar days of the date of the Preliminary Determination, or if a request to review materials is made pursuant to paragraph (e)(1)(i) of this section, then within sixty (60) calendar days of the Office of the Whistleblower making those materials available for your review.

(f)   If you fail to submit a timely response pursuant to paragraph (e) of this rule, then the Preliminary Determination will become the Final Order of the Commission (except where the Preliminary Determination recommended an award, in which case the Preliminary Determination will be deemed a Proposed Final Determination for purposes of paragraph (h) of this rule). Your failure to submit a timely response contesting a Preliminary Determination will constitute a failure to exhaust administrative remedies, and you will be prohibited from pursuing an appeal pursuant to Rule 21F–13.

(g)   If you submit a timely response pursuant to paragraph (e) of this rule, then the Claims Review Staff will consider the issues and grounds that you advanced in your response, along with any supporting documentation you provided, and will make its Proposed Final Determination.

(h)   The Office of the Whistleblower will notify the Commission of each Proposed Final Determination. Within thirty 30 days thereafter, any Commissioner may request that the Proposed Final Determination be reviewed by the Commission. If no Commissioner requests such a review within the 30-day period, then the Proposed Final Determination will become the Final Order of the Commission. In the event a Commissioner requests a review, the Commission will review the record that the staff relied upon in making its determinations, including your previous submissions to the Office of the Whistleblower, and issue its Final Order. (i) The Office of the Whistleblower will provide you with the Final Order of the Commission.

Rule 21F–12. Materials that May Form the Basis of an Award Determination and that May Comprise the Record on Appeal

(a)   The following items constitute the materials that the Commission, the Claims Review Staff (as specified in Rule 21F–10(d)), and the Office of the Whistleblower may rely upon to make an award determination pursuant to Rules 21F–10, 21F–11, and F–18:

(1)   Any publicly available materials from the covered action or related action, including:

(i)   The complaint, notice of hearing, answers and any amendments thereto;

(ii)   The final judgment, consent order, or final administrative order;

(iii)   Any transcripts of the proceedings, including any exhibits;

(iv)   Any items that appear on the docket; and

(v)   Any appellate decisions or orders.

(2)   The whistleblower's Form TCR, including attachments, and other related materials provided by the whistleblower to assist the Commission with the investigation or examination;

(3)   The whistleblower's Form WB-APP, including attachments, any supplemental materials submitted by the whistleblower before the deadline to file a claim for a whistleblower award for the relevant Notice of Covered Action, and any other materials timely submitted by the whistleblower in response either

(i)   to a request from the Office of the Whistleblower or the Commission; or

(ii)   to the Preliminary Determination or Preliminary Summary Disposition that was provided to the claimant;

(4)   Sworn declarations (including attachments) from the Commission staff regarding any matters relevant to the award determination;

(5)   With respect to an award claim involving a related action, any statements or other information that the entity provides or identifies in connection with an award determination, provided

the entity has authorized the Commission to share the information with the claimant. (Neither the Commission nor the Claims Review Staff may rely upon information that the entity has not authorized the Commission to share with the claimant); and

(6)   Any other documents or materials from third parties (including sworn declarations) that are received or obtained by the Office of the Whistleblower to resolve the claimant's award application, including information related to the claimant's eligibility. (The Commission, the Claims Review Staff, and the Office of the Whistleblower may not rely upon information that the third party has not authorized the Commission to share with the claimant.)

(b)   These rules do not entitle claimants to obtain from the Commission any materials (including any pre-decisional or internal deliberative process materials that are prepared exclusively to assist the Commission in deciding the claim) other than those listed in paragraph (a) of this rule. Moreover, the Office of the Whistleblower may make redactions as necessary to comply with any statutory restrictions, to protect the Commission's law enforcement and regulatory functions, and to comply with requests for confidential treatment from other law enforcement and regulatory authorities. The Office of the Whistleblower may also require you to sign a confidentiality agreement, as set forth in Rule 21F–(8)(b)(4), before providing these materials.

Rule 21F–13. Appeals

(a)   Section 21F of the Securities Exchange Act of 1934 commits determinations of whether, to whom, and in what amount to make awards to the Commission's discretion. A determination of whether or to whom to make an award may be appealed within 30 days after the Commission issues its final decision to the United States Court of Appeals for the District of Columbia Circuit, or to the circuit where the aggrieved person resides or has his principal place of business. Where the Commission makes an award based on the factors set forth in Rule 21F–6 of not less than 10 percent and not more than 30 percent of the monetary sanctions collected in the Commission or related action, the Commission's determination regarding the amount of an award (including the allocation of an award as between multiple whistleblowers, and any factual findings, legal conclusions, policy judgments, or discretionary assessments involving the Commission's consideration of the factors in Rule 21F–6) is not appealable.

(b)   The record on appeal shall consist of the Final Order, any materials that were considered by the Commission in issuing the Final Order, and any materials that were part of the claims process leading from the Notice of Covered Action to the Final Order (including, but not limited to, the Notice of Covered Action, whistleblower award applications filed by the claimant, the Preliminary Determination or Preliminary Summary Disposition, materials that were considered by the Claims Review Staff in issuing the Preliminary Determination or that were provided to the claimant by the Office of the Whistleblower in connection with a Preliminary Summary Disposition, and materials that were timely submitted by the claimant in response to the Preliminary Determination or Preliminary Summary Disposition). The record on appeal shall not include any pre-decisional or internal deliberative process materials that are prepared exclusively to assist the Commission and the Claims Review Staff (as specified in Rule 21F–10(d)) in deciding the claim (including the staff's Proposed Final Determination or the Office of the Whistleblower's Proposed Final Summary Disposition, or any Draft Preliminary Determination or Draft Summary Disposition that were provided to the Commission for review). When more than one claimant has sought an award based on a single Notice of Covered Action, the Commission may exclude from the record on appeal any materials that do not relate directly to the claimant who is seeking judicial review.

Rule 21F–14. Procedures Applicable to the Payment of Awards

(a)   Any award made pursuant to these rules will be paid from the Securities and Exchange Commission Investor Protection Fund (the "Fund").

(b)   A recipient of a whistleblower award is entitled to payment on the award only to the extent that a monetary sanction is collected in the Commission action or in a related action upon which the award is based.

(c)   Payment of a whistleblower award for a monetary sanction collected in a Commission action or related action shall be made following the later of:

(1)   The date on which the monetary sanction is collected; or

(2)   The completion of the appeals process for all whistleblower award claims arising from:

(i)   The Notice of Covered Action, in the case of any payment of an award for a monetary sanction collected in a Commission action; or

(ii)   The related action, in the case of any payment of an award for a monetary sanction collected in a related action.

(d)   If there are insufficient amounts available in the Fund to pay the entire amount of an award payment within a reasonable period of time from the time for payment specified by paragraph (c) of this rule, then subject to the following terms, the balance of the payment shall be paid when amounts become available in the Fund, as follows:

(1)   Where multiple whistleblowers are owed payments from the Fund based on awards that do not arise from the same Notice of Covered Action (or related action), priority in making these payments will be determined based upon the date that the collections for which the whistleblowers are owed payments occurred. If two or more of these collections occur on the same date, those whistleblowers owed payments based on these collections will be paid on a pro rata basis until sufficient amounts become available in the Fund to pay their entire payments.

(2)   Where multiple whistleblowers are owed payments from the Fund based on awards that arise from the same Notice of Covered Action (or related action), they will share the same payment priority and will be paid on a pro rata basis until sufficient amounts become available in the Fund to pay their entire payments.

Rule 21F–15. No Amnesty

The Securities Whistleblower Incentives and Protection provisions do not provide amnesty to individuals who provide information to the Commission. The fact that you may become a whistleblower and assist in Commission investigations and enforcement actions does not preclude the Commission from bringing an action against you based upon your own conduct in connection with violations of the federal securities laws. If such an action is determined to be appropriate, however, the Commission will take your cooperation into consideration in accordance with its Policy Statement Concerning Cooperation by Individuals in Investigations and Related Enforcement Actions (17 CFR § 202.12).

Rule 21F–16. Awards to Whistleblowers who Engage in Culpable Conduct

In determining whether the required $1,000,000 threshold has been satisfied (this threshold is further explained in Rule 21F–10) for purposes of making any award, the Commission will not take into account any monetary sanctions that the whistleblower is ordered to pay, or that are ordered against any entity whose liability is based substantially on conduct that the whistleblower directed, planned, or initiated. Similarly, if the Commission determines that a whistleblower is eligible for an award, any amounts that the whistleblower or such an entity pays in sanctions as a result of the action or related actions will not be included within the calculation of the amounts collected for purposes of making payments.

Rule 21F–17. Staff Communications With Individuals Reporting Possible Securities Law Violations

(a)   No person may take any action to impede an individual from communicating directly with the Commission staff about a possible securities law violation, including enforcing, or threatening to enforce, a confidentiality agreement (other than agreements dealing with information covered by Rules 21F–4(b)(4)(i) and 21F–4(b)(4)(ii) related to the legal representation of a client) with respect to such communications.

(b)   If you are a director, officer, member, agent, or employee of an entity that has counsel, and you have initiated communication with the Commission relating to a possible securities law violation, the staff is authorized to communicate directly with you regarding the possible securities law violation without seeking the consent of the entity's counsel.

Rule 21F–18. Summary Disposition

(a)   Notwithstanding the procedures specified in Rule 21F–10(d) through (g) and in Rule 21F–11(d) through (g), the Office of the Whistleblower may determine that an award application that meets any of the following conditions for denial shall be resolved through the summary disposition process described further in paragraph (b) of this section:

    (1)   You submitted an untimely award application;

    (2)   You did not comply with the requirements of Rule 21F–9 when submitting the tip upon which your award claim is based, and you otherwise are not eligible for a waiver under either Rule 21F–9(e) or the Commission's other waiver authorities;

    (3)   The information that you submitted was never provided to or used by the staff handling the covered action or the underlying investigation (or examination), and those staff members otherwise had no contact with you;

    (4)   You did not comply with Rule 21F–8(b);

    (5)   You failed to specify in the award application the submission pursuant to Rule 21F–9(a) upon which your claim to an award is based;

    (6)   Your application does not raise any novel or important legal or policy questions.

    (b)   The following procedures shall apply to any award application designated for summary disposition:

    (1)   The Office of the Whistleblower shall issue a Preliminary Summary Disposition that notifies you that your award application has been designated for resolution through the summary disposition process. The Preliminary Summary Disposition shall also state that the Office has preliminarily determined to recommend that the Commission deny the award application and identify the basis for the denial.

    (2)   Prior to issuing the Preliminary Summary Disposition, the Office of the Whistleblower shall prepare a staff declaration that sets forth any pertinent facts regarding the Office's recommendation to deny your application. At the same time that it provides you with the Preliminary Summary Disposition, the Office of the Whistleblower shall, in its sole discretion, either

        (i)   Provide you with the staff declaration; or

        (ii)   Notify you that a staff declaration has been prepared and advise you that you may obtain the declaration only if within fifteen (15) calendar days you sign and complete a confidentiality agreement in a form and manner acceptable to the Office of the Whistleblower pursuant to Rule 21F–8(b)(4). If you fail to return the signed confidentiality agreement within fifteen (15) calendar days, you will be deemed to have waived your ability to receive the staff declaration.

    (3)   You may reply to the Preliminary Summary Disposition by submitting a response to the Office of the Whistleblower within thirty (30) calendar days of the later of:

        (i)   The date of the Preliminary Summary Disposition, or

        (ii)   The date that the Office of the Whistleblower sends the staff declaration to you following your timely return of a signed confidentiality agreement. The response must identify the grounds for your objection to the denial (or in the case of item (a)(5) of this rule, correct the defect). The response must be in the form and manner that the Office of the Whistleblower shall require. You may include documentation or other evidentiary support for the grounds advanced in your response.

        (iii)   If you fail to submit a timely response pursuant to paragraph (b)(3) of this rule, the Preliminary Summary Disposition will become the Final Order of the Commission. Your failure to submit a timely written response will constitute a failure to exhaust administrative remedies.

    (4)   If you submit a timely response pursuant to paragraph (b)(3) of this section, the Office of the Whistleblower will consider the issues and grounds advanced in your response, along with any supporting documentation that you provided, and will prepare a Proposed Final Summary Disposition. The Office of the Whistleblower may supplement the administrative record as appropriate. (This provision does not prevent the Office of the Whistleblower from determining that, based on your

written response, the award claim is no longer appropriate for summary disposition and that it should be resolved through the claims adjudication procedures specified in either Rule 21F-10 or 21F-11).

(5)   The Office of the Whistleblower will then notify the Commission of the Proposed Final Summary Disposition. Within thirty (30) calendar days thereafter, any Commissioner may request that the Proposed Final Summary Disposition be reviewed by the Commission. If no Commissioner requests such a review within the 30-day period, then the Proposed Final Summary Disposition will become the Final Order of the Commission. In the event a Commissioner requests a review, the Commission will consider the award application and issue a Final Order.

(6)   The Office of the Whistleblower will provide you with the Final Order of the Commission.

(7)   In considering an award determination pursuant to this rule, the Office of the Whistleblower and the Commission may rely upon the items specified in Rule 21F-12(a). Further, Rule 21F-12(b) shall apply to summary dispositions.

INSPECTION AND PUBLICATION OF INFORMATION FILED UNDER THE ACT

Rule 24b-1.   Documents to Be Kept Public by Exchanges

Upon action of the Commission granting an exchange's application for registration or exemption, the exchange shall make available to public inspection at its offices during reasonable office hours a copy of the statement and exhibits filed with the Commission (including any amendments thereto) except those portions thereof to the disclosure of which the exchange shall have filed objection pursuant to Rule 24b-2 which objection shall not have been overruled by the Commission pursuant to section 24(b) of the Act.

Rule 24b-2.   Non-disclosure of Information Filed With the Commission and With Any Exchange

Preliminary Note: Except as otherwise provided in this rule, confidential treatment requests shall be submitted in paper format only, whether or not the filer is required to submit a filing in electronic format.

(a)   Any person filing any registration statement, report, application, statement, correspondence, notice or other document (herein referred to as the material filed) pursuant to the Act may make written objection to the public disclosure of any information contained therein in accordance with the procedure set forth below. The procedure provided in this rule shall be the exclusive means of requesting confidential treatment of information required to be filed under the Act.

(b)   Except as otherwise provided in paragraphs (g) and (h) of this rule, the person shall omit from material filed the portion thereof which it desires to keep undisclosed (hereinafter called the confidential portion). In lieu thereof, it shall indicate at the appropriate place in the material filed that the confidential portion has been so omitted and filed separately with the Commission. The person shall file with the copies of the material filed with the Commission:

(1)   One copy of the confidential portion, marked "Confidential Treatment," of the material filed with the Commission. The copy shall contain an appropriate identification of the item or other requirement involved and, notwithstanding that the confidential portion does not constitute the whole of the answer, the entire answer thereto; except that in case where the confidential portion is part of a financial statement or schedule, only the particular financial statement or schedule need be included. The copy of the confidential portion shall be in the same form as the remainder of the material filed;

(2)   An application making objection to the disclosure of the confidential portion. Such application shall be on a sheet or sheets separate from the confidential portion, and shall contain

(i)   An identification of the portion;

(ii)   A statement of the grounds of objection referring to, and containing an analysis of, the applicable exemption(s) from disclosure under the Commission's rules and regulations adopted under the Freedom of Information Act, and a justification of the period of time for which confidential treatment is sought;

(iii) A written consent to the furnishing of the confidential portion to other government agencies, offices or bodies and to the Congress; and

(iv) The name of each exchange, if any, with which the material is filed.

(3) The copy of the confidential portion and the application filed in accordance with this paragraph (b) shall be enclosed in a separate envelope marked "Confidential Treatment" and addressed to The Secretary, Securities and Exchange Commission, Washington, D.C., 20549.

(c) Pending a determination as to the objection filed the material for which confidential treatment has been applied will not be made available to the public.

(d)(1) If it is determined that the objection should be sustained, a notation to that effect will be made at the appropriate place in the material filed. Such a determination will not preclude reconsideration whenever appropriate, such as upon receipt of any subsequent request under the Freedom of Information Act and, if appropriate, revocation of the confidential status of all or a portion of the information in question. Where an initial determination has been made under this rule to sustain objections to disclosure, the Commission will attempt to give the person requesting confidential treatment advance notice, wherever possible, if confidential treatment is revoked.

(2) In any case where an objection to disclosure has been disallowed or where a prior grant of confidential treatment has been revoked, the person who requested such treatment will be so informed by registered or certified mail to the person or his agent for service. Pursuant to Rule 431, persons making objections to disclosure may petition the Commission for review of a determination by the Division disallowing objections or revoking confidential treatment.

(e) The confidential portion shall be made available to the public at the time and according to the conditions specified in paragraphs (d)(1) and (2) of this rule:

(1) Upon the lapse of five days after the dispatch of notice by registered or certified mail of a determination disallowing an objection, if prior to the lapse of such five days the person shall not have communicated to the Secretary of the Commission his intention to seek review by the Commission under Rule 431 of the determination made by the Division; or

(2) If such a petition for review shall have been filed under Rule 431, upon final disposition thereof adverse to the petitioner.

(f) If the confidential portion is made available to the public, one copy thereof shall be attached to each copy of the material filed with the Commission and with each exchange.

(g) An SCI entity (as defined in § 242.1000 of this chapter) shall not omit the confidential portion from the material filed in electronic format on Form SCI pursuant to Regulation SCI, and, in lieu of the procedures described in paragraph (b) of this rule, may request confidential treatment of all information provided on Form SCI by completing Section IV of Form SCI.

(h) A security-based swap data repository shall not omit the confidential portion from the material filed in electronic format pursuant to section 13(n) of the Securities Exchange Act of 1934 and the rules and regulations thereunder. In lieu of the procedures described in paragraph (b) of this rule, a security-based swap data repository shall request confidential treatment electronically for any material filed in electronic format pursuant to section 13(n) of the Securities Exchange Act of 1934 and the rules and regulations thereunder.

Rule 24b–3. Information Filed by Issuers and Others Under Sections 12, 13, 14, and 16

(a) Except as otherwise provided in this rule and in Rule 17a–6, each exchange shall keep available to the public under reasonable regulations as to the manner of inspection, during reasonable office hours, all information regarding a security registered on such exchange which is filed with it pursuant to sections 12, 13, 14, or 16, or any rules or regulations thereunder. This requirement shall not apply to any information to the disclosure of which objection has been filed pursuant to Rule 24b–2, which objection shall not have been overruled by the Commission pursuant to section 24(b). The making of such information available pursuant to this rule shall not be deemed a representation by any exchange as to the accuracy, completeness, or genuineness thereof.

(b)   In the case of an application for registration of a security pursuant to section 12 an exchange may delay making available the information contained therein until it has certified to the Commission its approval of such security for listing and registration.

Rule 24c-1. Access to Nonpublic Information

(a)   For purposes of this rule, the term "nonpublic information" means records, as defined in section 24(a) of the Act, and other information in the Commission's possession, which are not available for public inspection and copying.

(b)   The Commission may, in its discretion and upon a showing that such information is needed, provide nonpublic information in its possession to any of the following persons if the person receiving such nonpublic information provides such assurances of confidentiality as the Commission deems appropriate:

(1)   A federal, state, local or foreign government or any political subdivision, authority, agency or instrumentality of such government;

(2)   A self-regulatory organization as defined in section 3(a)(26) of the Act, or any similar organization empowered with self-regulatory responsibilities under the federal securities laws (as defined in section 3(a)(47) of the Act), the Commodity Exchange Act, or any substantially equivalent foreign statute or regulation;

(3)   A foreign financial regulatory authority as defined in section 3(a)(51) of the Act;

(4)   The Securities Investor Protection Corporation or any trustee or counsel for a trustee appointed pursuant to section 5(b) of the Securities Investor Protection Act of 1970;

(5)   A trustee in bankruptcy;

(6)   A trustee, receiver, master, special counsel or other person that is appointed by a court of competent jurisdiction or as a result of an agreement between the parties in connection with litigation or an administrative proceeding involving allegations of violations of the securities laws (as defined in section 3(a)(47) of the Act) or the Commission's Rules of Practice, or otherwise, where such trustee, receiver, master, special counsel or other person is specifically designated to perform particular functions with respect to, or as a result of, the litigation or proceeding or in connection with the administration and enforcement by the Commission of the federal securities laws or the Commission's Rules of Practice;

(7)   A bar association, state accountancy board or other federal, state, local or foreign licensing or oversight authority, or a professional association or self-regulatory authority to the extent that it performs similar functions; or

(8)   A duly authorized agent, employee or representative of any of the above persons.

(c)   Nothing contained in this rule shall affect:

(1)   The Commission's authority or discretion to provide or refuse to provide access to, or copies of, nonpublic information in its possession in accordance with such other authority or discretion as the Commission possesses by statute, rule or regulation; or

(2)   The Commission's responsibilities under the Privacy Act of 1974, or the Right to Financial Privacy Act of 1978 as limited by section 21(h) of the Act.

Rule 31. Section 31 Transaction Fees

(a)   *Definitions.* For the purpose of this rule, the following definitions shall apply:

(1)   *Assessment charge* means the amount owed by a covered SRO for a covered round turn transaction pursuant to section 31(d) of the Act.

(2)   *Billing period* means, for a single calendar year:

(i)   January 1 through August 31 ("billing period 1"); or

(ii)   September 1 through December 31 ("billing period 2").

(3) *Charge date* means the date on which a covered sale or covered round turn transaction occurs for purposes of determining the liability of a covered SRO pursuant to section 31 of the Act. The charge date is:

    (i) The settlement date, with respect to any covered sale (other than a covered sale resulting from the exercise of an option settled by physical delivery or from the maturation of a security future settled by physical delivery) or covered round turn transaction that a covered SRO is required to report to the Commission based on data that the covered SRO receives from a designated clearing agency;

    (ii) The exercise date, with respect to a covered sale resulting from the exercise of an option settled by physical delivery;

    (iii) The maturity date, with respect to a covered sale resulting from the maturation of a security future settled by physical delivery; and

    (iv) The trade date, with respect to all other covered sales and covered round turn transactions.

(4) *Covered association* means any national securities association by or through any member of which covered sales or covered round turn transactions occur otherwise than on a national securities exchange.

(5) *Covered exchange* means any national securities exchange on which covered sales or covered round turn transactions occur.

(6) *Covered sale* means a sale of a security, other than an exempt sale or a sale of a security future, occurring on a national securities exchange or by or through any member of a national securities association otherwise than on a national securities exchange.

(7) *Covered round turn transaction* means a round turn transaction in a security future, other than a round turn transaction in a future on a narrow-based security index, occurring on a national securities exchange or by or through a member of a national securities association otherwise than on a national securities exchange.

(8) *Covered SRO* means a covered exchange or covered association.

(9) *Designated clearing agency* means a clearing agency registered under section 17A of the Act that clears and settles covered sales or covered round turn transactions.

(10) *Due date* means:

    (i) March 15, with respect to the amounts owed by covered SROs under section 31 of the Act for covered sales and covered round turn transactions having a charge date in billing period 2; and

    (ii) September 30, with respect to the amounts owed by covered SROs under section 31 of the Act for covered sales and covered round turn transactions having a charge date in billing period 1.

(11) *Exempt sale* means:

    (i) Any sale of a security offered pursuant to an effective registration statement under the Securities Act of 1933 (except a sale of a put or call option issued by the Options Clearing Corporation) or offered in accordance with an exemption from registration afforded by section 3(a) or 3(b) of the Securities Act of 1933, or a rule thereunder;

    (ii) Any sale of a security by an issuer not involving any public offering within the meaning of section 4(2) of the Securities Act of 1933;

    (iii) Any sale of a security pursuant to and in consummation of a tender or exchange offer;

    (iv) Any sale of a security upon the exercise of a warrant or right (except a put or call), or upon the conversion of a convertible security;

(v)   Any sale of a security that is executed outside the United States and is not reported, or required to be reported, to a transaction reporting association as defined in Rule 600 of Regulation NMS and any approved plan filed thereunder;

(vi)   Any sale of an option on a security index (including both a narrow-based security index and a non-narrow-based security index);

(vii)   Any sale of a bond, debenture, or other evidence of indebtedness; and

(viii) Any recognized riskless principal sale.

(12)   *Fee rate* means the fee rate applicable to covered sales under section 31(b) or (c) of the Act, as adjusted from time to time by the Commission pursuant to section 31(j) of the Act.

(13)   *Narrow-based security index* means the same as in section 3(a)(55)(B) and (C) of the Act.

(14)   *Recognized riskless principal sale* means a sale of a security where all of the following conditions are satisfied:

(i)   A broker-dealer receives from a customer an order to buy (sell) a security;

(ii)   The broker-dealer engages in two contemporaneous offsetting transactions as principal, one in which the broker-dealer buys (sells) the security from (to) a third party and the other in which the broker-dealer sells (buys) the security to (from) the customer; and

(iii)   The Commission, pursuant to section 19(b)(2) of the Act, has approved a proposed rule change submitted by the covered SRO on which the second of the two contemporaneous offsetting transactions occurs that permits that transaction to be reported as riskless.

(15)   *Round turn transaction in a security future* means one purchase and one sale of a contract of sale for future delivery.

(16)   *Physical delivery exchange-traded option* means a securities option that is listed and registered on a national securities exchange and settled by the physical delivery of the underlying securities.

(17)   *Section 31 bill* means the bill sent by the Commission to a covered SRO pursuant to section 31 of the Act showing the total amount due from the covered SRO for the billing period, as calculated by the Commission based on the data submitted by the covered SRO in its Form R31 submissions for the months of the billing period.

(18)   *Trade reporting system* means an automated facility operated by a covered SRO used to collect or compare trade data.

(b)   *Reporting of covered sales and covered round turn transactions.*

(1)   Each covered SRO shall submit a completed Form R31 to the Commission within ten business days after the end of each month.

(2)   A covered exchange shall provide on Form R31 the following data on covered sales and covered round turn transactions occurring on that exchange and having a charge date in that month:

(i)   The aggregate dollar amount of covered sales that it reported to a designated clearing agency, as reflected in the data provided by the designated clearing agency;

(ii)   The aggregate dollar amount of covered sales resulting from the exercise of physical delivery exchange-traded options or from matured security futures, as reflected in the data provided by a designated clearing agency that clears and settles options or security futures;

(iii)   The aggregate dollar amount of covered sales that it captured in a trade reporting system but did not report to a designated clearing agency;

(iv)   The aggregate dollar amount of covered sales that it neither captured in a trade reporting system nor reported to a designated clearing agency; and

(v)   The total number of covered round turn transactions that it reported to a designated clearing agency, as reflected in the data provided by the designated clearing agency.

(3) A covered association shall provide on Form R31 the following data on covered sales and covered round turn transactions occurring by or through any member of such association otherwise than on a national securities exchange and having a charge date in that month:

(i)   The aggregate dollar amount of covered sales that it captured in a trade reporting system;

(ii)   The aggregate dollar amount of covered sales that it did not capture in a trade reporting system; and

(iii)   The total number of covered round turn transactions that it reported to a designated clearing agency, as reflected in the data provided by the designated clearing agency.

(4) *Duties of designated clearing agency.*

(i)   A designated clearing agency shall provide a covered SRO, upon request, the data in its possession needed by the covered SRO to complete Part I of Form R31.

(ii)   If a covered exchange trades physical delivery exchange-traded options or security futures that settle by physical delivery of the underlying securities, the designated clearing agency that clears and settles such transactions shall provide that covered exchange with the data in its possession relating to the covered sales resulting from the exercise of such options or from the matured security futures. If, during a particular month, the designated clearing agency cannot determine the covered exchange on which the options or security futures originally were traded, the designated clearing agency shall assign covered sales resulting from exercises or maturations as follows. To provide Form R31 data to the covered exchange for a particular month, the designated clearing agency shall:

(A) Calculate the aggregate dollar amount of all covered sales in the previous calendar month resulting from exercises and maturations, respectively, occurring on all covered exchanges for which it clears and settles transactions;

(B) Calculate, for the previous calendar month, the aggregate dollar amount of covered sales of physical delivery exchange-traded options occurring on each covered exchange for which it clears and settles transactions, and the aggregate dollar amount of covered sales of physical delivery exchange-traded options occurring on all such exchanges collectively;

(C) Calculate, for the previous calendar month, the total number of covered round turn transactions in security futures that settle by physical delivery that occurred on each covered exchange for which it clears and settles transactions, and the total number of covered round turn transactions in security futures that settle by physical delivery that occurred on all such exchanges collectively;

(D) Determine for the previous calendar month each covered exchange's percentage of the total dollar volume of physical delivery exchange-traded options ("exercise percentage") and each covered exchange's percentage of the total number of covered round turn transactions in security futures that settle by physical delivery ("maturation percentage"); and

(E) In the current month, assign to each covered exchange for which it clears and settles covered sales the exercise percentage of the aggregate dollar amount of covered sales on all covered exchanges resulting from the exercise of physical delivery exchange-traded options and the maturation percentage of all covered sales on all covered exchanges resulting from the maturation of security futures that settle by physical delivery.

(5) A covered SRO shall provide in Part I of Form R31 only the data supplied to it by a designated clearing agency.

(c) *Calculation and billing of section 31 fees.*

(1)   The amount due from a covered SRO for a billing period, as reflected in its Section 31 bill, shall be the sum of the monthly amounts due for each month in the billing period.

(2)   The monthly amount due from a covered SRO shall equal:

(i)   The aggregate dollar amount of its covered sales that have a charge date in that month, times the fee rate; plus

(ii)   The total number of its covered round turn transactions that have a charge date in that month, times the assessment charge.

(3)   By the due date, each covered SRO shall pay the Commission, either directly or through a designated clearing agency acting as agent, the entire amount due for the billing period, as reflected in its Section 31 bill.

Rule 36a1–1. Exemption From Section 7 for OTC Derivatives Dealers

Preliminary Note: OTC derivatives dealers are a special class of broker-dealers that are exempt from certain broker-dealer requirements, including membership in a self-regulatory organization (Rule 15b9–2), regular broker-dealer margin rules (Rule 36a1–1), and application of the Securities Investor Protection Act of 1970 (Rule 36a1–2). OTC derivative dealers are subject to special requirements, including limitations on the scope of their securities activities (Rule 15a–1), specified internal risk management control systems (Rule 15c3–4), recordkeeping obligations (Rule 17a–3(a)(10)), and reporting responsibilities (Rule 17a–12). They are also subject to alternative net capital treatment (Rule 15c3–1(a)(5)).

(a)   Except as otherwise provided in paragraph (b) of this rule, transactions involving the extension of credit by an OTC derivatives dealer shall be exempt from the provisions of section 7(c) of the Act, provided that the OTC derivatives dealer complies with section 7(d) of the Act.

(b)   The exemption provided under paragraph (a) of this rule shall not apply to extensions of credit made directly by a registered broker or dealer (other than an OTC derivatives dealer) in connection with transactions in eligible OTC derivative instruments for which an OTC derivatives dealer acts as counterparty.

Rule 36a1–2. Exemption From SIPA for OTC Derivatives Dealers

Preliminary Note: OTC derivatives dealers are a special class of broker-dealers that are exempt from certain broker-dealer requirements, including membership in a self-regulatory organization (Rule 15b9–2), regular broker-dealer margin rules (Rule 36a1–1), and application of the Securities Investor Protection Act of 1970 (Rule 36a1–2). OTC derivative dealers are subject to special requirements, including limitations on the scope of their securities activities (Rule 15a–1), specified internal risk management control systems (Rule15c3–4), recordkeeping obligations (Rule 17a–3(a)(10)), and reporting responsibilities (Rule 17a–12). They are also subject to alternative net capital treatment (Rule 15c3–1(a)(5)).

OTC derivatives dealers, as defined in Rule 3b–12, shall be exempt from the provisions of the Securities Investor Protection Act of 1970.

SELECTED FORMS UNDER THE SECURITIES EXCHANGE ACT OF 1934

17 C.F.R. § 249.___

A. FORM 3

17 C.F.R. § 249.103

INITIAL STATEMENT OF BENEFICIAL OWNERSHIP BY OFFICERS, DIRECTORS AND TEN PERCENT BENEFICIAL OWNERS OF A CLASS OF EQUITY SECURITIES SUBJECT TO THE 1934 ACT REPORTING REQUIREMENTS (PURSUANT TO SECTION 16(a))

UNITED STATES
SECURITIES AND EXCHANGE COMMISSION
Washington, D.C. 20549

FORM 3
INITIAL STATEMENT OF BENEFICIAL OWNERSHIP OF SECURITIES

THE COMMISSION IS AUTHORIZED TO SOLICIT THE INFORMATION REQUIRED BY THIS FORM PURSUANT TO SECTIONS 16(a) AND 23(a) OF THE SECURITIES EXCHANGE ACT OF 1934; AND SECTIONS 30(h) AND 38 OF THE INVESTMENT COMPANY ACT OF 1940, AND THE RULES AND REGULATIONS THEREUNDER.

DISCLOSURE OF INFORMATION SPECIFIED ON THIS FORM IS MANDATORY. THE INFORMATION WILL BE USED FOR THE PRIMARY PURPOSE OF DISCLOSING THE HOLDINGS OF DIRECTORS, OFFICERS, AND BENEFICIAL OWNERS OF REGISTERED COMPANIES. INFORMATION DISCLOSED WILL BE A MATTER OF PUBLIC RECORD AND AVAILABLE FOR INSPECTION BY MEMBERS OF THE PUBLIC. THE COMMISSION CAN USE IT IN INVESTIGATIONS OR LITIGATION INVOLVING THE FEDERAL SECURITIES LAWS OR OTHER CIVIL, CRIMINAL, OR REGULATORY STATUTES OR PROVISIONS, AS WELL AS FOR REFERRAL TO OTHER GOVERNMENTAL AUTHORITIES AND SELF-REGULATORY ORGANIZATIONS. FAILURE TO DISCLOSE REQUIRED INFORMATION MAY RESULT IN CIVIL OR CRIMINAL ACTION AGAINST PERSONS INVOLVED FOR VIOLATIONS OF THE FEDERAL SECURITIES LAWS AND RULES.

1934 ACT FORMS

GENERAL INSTRUCTIONS

1. **Who Must File**

    (a)   This Form must be filed by the following persons ("reporting person"):

    (i)   any director or officer of an issuer with a class of equity securities registered pursuant to section 12 of the Securities Exchange Act of 1934 ("Exchange Act"); (*Note*: Title is not determinative for purposes of determining "officer" status. *See* Rule 16a–1(f) for the definition of "officer");

    (ii)   any beneficial owner of greater than 10% of a class of equity securities registered under section 12 of the Exchange Act, as determined by voting or investment control over the securities pursuant to Rule 16a–1(a)(1) ("ten percent holder");

    (iii)   any officer or director of a registered holding company pursuant to Section 17(a) of the Public Utility Holding Company Act of 1935;

    (iv)   any officer, director, member of an advisory board, investment adviser, affiliated person of an investment adviser, or beneficial owner of more than 10% of any class of outstanding securities (other than short-term paper) of a registered closed-end investment company, under section 30(f) of the Investment Company Act of 1940; and

    (v)   any trust, trustee, beneficiary or settlor required to report pursuant to Rule 16a–8.

    (b)   If a reporting person is not an officer, director, or 10% holder, the person should check "other" in Item 5 (Relationship of Reporting Person to Issuer) and describe the reason for reporting status in the space provided.

    (c)   If a person described above does not beneficially own any securities required to be reported (*see* Rule 16a–1 and Instruction 5), the person is required to file this Form and state that no securities are beneficially owned.

2. **When Form Must Be Filed**

    (a)   This Form must be filed within 10 days after the event by which the person becomes a reporting person (*i.e.*, officer, director, ten percent holder or other person). This Form and any amendment is deemed filed with the Commission or the Exchange on the date it is received by the Commission or the Exchange, respectively. *See*, however, Rule 16a–3(h) regarding delivery to a third party business that guarantees delivery of the filing no later than the specified due date.

    (b)   A reporting person of an issuer that is registering securities for the first time under section 12 of the Exchange Act must file this Form no later than the effective date of the registration statement.

    (c)   A separate Form shall be filed to reflect beneficial ownership of securities of each issuer, except that a single statement shall be filed with respect to the securities of a registered public utility holding company and all of its subsidiary companies.

3. **Where Form Must Be Filed**

    (a)   A reporting person must file this Form in electronic format via the Commission's Electronic Data Gathering Analysis and Retrieval System (EDGAR) in accordance with EDGAR rules set forth in Regulation S–T, except that a filing person that has obtained a hardship exception under Regulation S–T Rule 202 may file the Form in paper. For assistance with technical questions about EDGAR or to request an access code, call the EDGAR Filer Support Office at (202) 942–8900. For assistance with questions about the EDGAR rules, call the Office of EDGAR and Information Analysis at (202) 942–2940.

    (b)   At the time this Form or any amendment is filed with the Commission, file one copy with each Exchange on which any class of securities of the issuer is registered. If the issuer has designated a single Exchange to receive section 16 filings, the copy shall be filed with that Exchange only.

    (c)   [Removed and Reserved].

    NOTE: If filing pursuant to a hardship exception under Regulation S–T Rule 202, file three copies of this Form or any amendment, at least one of which is signed, with the Securities and Exchange Commission, 450 5th Street, NW., Washington, D.C., 20549. (Acknowledgement of receipt by the Commission may be obtained by enclosing a self-addressed stamped postcard identifying the Form or amendment filed.)

FORM 3

4. Class of Securities Reported

(a)(i)   Persons reporting pursuant to section 16(a) of the Exchange Act shall include information as to their beneficial ownership of any class of equity securities of the issuer, even though one or more of such classes may not be registered pursuant to section 12 of the Exchange Act.

(ii)   Removed and reserved.

(iii)   Persons reporting pursuant to section 30(f) of the Investment Company Act of 1940 shall include information as to their beneficial ownership of any class of securities (equity or debt) of the registered closed-end investment company (other than "short-term paper" as defined in section 2(a)(38) of the Investment Company Act).

(b)   The title of the security should clearly identify the class, even if the issuer has only one class of securities outstanding; for example, "Common Stock," "Class A Common Stock," "Class B Convertible Preferred Stock," etc.

(c)   The amount of securities beneficially owned should state the face amount of debt securities (U.S. Dollars) or the number of equity securities, whichever is appropriate.

5. Holdings Required to be Reported

(a)   General Requirements

Report holdings of each class of securities of the issuer beneficially owned as of the date of the event requiring the filing of this Form. See Instruction 4 as to securities required to be reported.

(b)   Beneficial Ownership Reported (Pecuniary Interest)

(i)   Although, for purposes of determining status as a ten percent holder, a person is deemed to beneficially own securities over which that person has voting or investment control (see Rule 16a–1(a)(1)), for reporting purposes, a person is deemed to be the beneficial owner of securities if that person has or shares the opportunity, directly or indirectly, to profit or share in any profit derived from a transaction in the securities ("pecuniary interest"). See Rule 16a–1(a)(2). See also Rule 16a–8 for application of the beneficial ownership definition to trust holdings and transactions.

(ii)   Both direct and indirect beneficial ownership of securities shall be reported. Securities beneficially owned directly are those held in the reporting person's name or in the name of a bank, broker or nominee for the account of the reporting person. In addition, securities held as joint tenants, tenants in common, tenants by the entirety, or as community property are to be reported as held directly. If a person has a pecuniary interest, by reason of any contract, understanding or relationship (including a family relationship or arrangement), in securities held in the name of another person, that person is an indirect beneficial owner of those securities. See Rule 16a–1(a)(2)(ii) for certain indirect beneficial ownerships.

(iii)   Report securities beneficially owned directly on a separate line from those beneficially owned indirectly. Report different forms of indirect ownership on separate lines. The nature of indirect ownership shall be stated as specifically as possible; for example, "By Self as Trustee for X," "By Spouse," "By X Trust," "By Y Corporation," etc.

(iv)   In stating the amount of securities owned indirectly through a partnership, corporation, trust, or other entity, report the number of securities representing the reporting person's proportionate interest in securities beneficially owned by that entity. Alternatively, at the option of the reporting person, the entire amount of the entity's interest may be reported. See Rule 16a–1(a)(2)(ii)(B) and Rule 16a–1(a)(2)(iii).

(v)   Where more than one person beneficially owns the same equity securities, such owners may file Form 3 individually or jointly. Joint and group filings may be made by any designated beneficial owner. Holdings of securities owned separately by any joint or group filer are permitted to be included in the joint filing. Indicate only the name and address of the designated filer in Item 1 of Form 3 and attach a list of the names and addresses of each other reporting person. Joint and group filings must include all required information for each beneficial owner, and such filings must be signed by each beneficial owner, or on behalf of such owner by an authorized person. If this Form is being filed in paper pursuant to a hardship exemption and the space provided for signatures is insufficient, attach a signature page. If this Form is being filed in paper, submit any attached listing of names or signatures on another Form 3, copy of Form 3 or separate page of 8 1/2 by 11 inch white paper, indicate the number of pages comprising the report (Form plus attachments) at the bottom of each report page (e.g., 1 of 3, 2 of 3, 3 of 3), and include the name of the designated filer and information required by Items 2 and 3 of the Form on the attachment. *See* Rule 16a–3(i) regarding signatures.

(c)   *Non-Derivative and Derivative Securities*

(i)   Report non-derivative securities beneficially owned in Table I and derivative securities (*e.g.*, puts, calls, options, warrants, convertible securities, or other rights or obligations to buy or sell securities) beneficially owned in Table II. Derivative securities beneficially owned that are both equity securities and convertible or exchangeable for other equity securities (*e.g.*, convertible preferred securities) should be reported only on Table II.

(ii)   The title of a derivative security and the title of the equity security underlying the derivative security should be shown separately in the appropriate columns in Table II. The "puts" and "calls" reported in Table II include, in addition to separate puts and calls, any combination of the two, such as spreads and straddles. In reporting an option in Table II, state whether it represents a right to buy, a right to sell, an obligation to buy, or an obligation to sell the equity securities subject to the option.

(iii)   Describe in the appropriate columns in Table II characteristics of derivative securities, including title, exercise or conversion price, date exercisable, expiration date, and the title and amount of securities underlying the derivative security.

(iv)   Securities constituting components of a unit shall be reported separately on the applicable table (*e.g.*, if a unit has a non-derivative security component and a derivative security component, the non-derivative security component shall be reported in Table I and the derivative security component shall be reported in Table II). The relationship between individual securities comprising the unit shall be indicated in the space provided for explanation of responses.

6.   Additional Information

(a)   If the space provided in the line items on the electronic Form is insufficient, use the space provided for footnotes. If the space provided for footnotes is insufficient, create a footnote that refers to an exhibit to the form that contains the additional information.

(b)   If the space provided in the line items on the paper Form or space provided for additional comments is insufficient, attach another Form 3, copy of Form 3 or separate 8 1/2 by 11 inch white paper to Form 3, completed as appropriate to include the additional comments. Each attached page must include information required in Items 1, 2 and 3 of the Form. The number of pages comprising the report (Form plus attachments) shall be indicated at the bottom of each report page (e.g., 1 of 3, 2 of 3, 3 of 3).

(c)   If one or more exhibits are included, whether due to a lack of space or because the exhibit is, by nature, a separate document (e.g., a power of attorney), provide a sequentially numbered list of the exhibits in the Form. Use the number "24" for any power of attorney and the number "99" for any other exhibit. If there is more than one of either such exhibit, then use numerical subparts. If the exhibit is being filed as a confirming electronic copy under Regulation S–T Rule 202(d), then place the designation "CE" (confirming exhibit) next to the name of the exhibit in the exhibit list. If the exhibit is being filed in paper pursuant to a hardship exception under Regulation S–T Rule 202, then place the designation "P" (paper) next to the name of the exhibit in the exhibit list.

(d)   If additional information is not reported as provided in paragraph (a), (b) or (c) of this instruction, whichever apply, it will be assumed that no additional information was provided.

7.   Signature

(a)   If the Form is filed for an individual, it shall be signed by that person or specifically on behalf of the individual by a person authorized to sign for the individual. If signed on behalf of the individual by another person, the authority of such person to sign the Form shall be confirmed to the Commission in writing in an attachment to the Form or as soon as practicable in an amendment by the individual for whom the Form is filed, unless such a confirmation still in effect is on file with the Commission. The confirming statement need only indicate that the reporting person authorizes and designates the named person or persons to file the Form on the reporting person's behalf, and state the duration of the authorization.

(b)   If the Form is filed for a corporation, partnership, trust, or other entity, the capacity in which the individual signed shall be set forth. (*e.g.*, John Smith, Secretary, on behalf of X Corporation).

8.   Amendments

(a)   If this Form is filed as an amendment in order to add one or more lines of ownership information to Table I or Table II of the Form being amended, provide each line being added, together with one or more footnotes, as necessary, to explain the addition of the line or lines. Do not repeat lines of ownership information that were disclosed in the original Form and are not being amended.

(b)   If this Form is filed as an amendment in order to amend one or more lines of ownership information that already were disclosed in Table I or Table II of the Form being amended, provide the complete line or lines being amended, as amended, together with one or more footnotes, as necessary, to explain the amendment of the line or lines. Do not repeat lines of ownership information that were disclosed in the original Form and are not being amended.

(c)   If this Form is filed as an amendment for any purpose other than or in addition to the purposes described in paragraphs (a) and (b) of this General Instruction 8, provide one or more footnotes, as necessary, to explain the amendment.

FORM 3

UNITED STATES SECURITIES AND EXCHANGE COMMISSION
Washington, D.C. 20549
Form 3

INITIAL STATEMENT OF BENEFICIAL OWNERSHIP OF SECURITIES

Filed pursuant to Section 16(a) of the Securities Exchange Act of 1934, Section 17(a) of the Public Utility Holding Company Act of 1935 or Section 30(h) of the Investment Company Act of 1940

OMB APPROVAL	
OMB Number:	3235-0104
Expires:	January 31, 2005
Estimated average burden hours per response......	0.5

(Print or Type Responses)

1. Name and Address of Reporting Person*

(Last) (First) (Middle)

(Street)

(City) (State) (Zip)

2. Date of Event Requiring Statement (Month/Day/Year)

3. Issuer Name and Ticker or Trading Symbol

4. Relationship of Reporting Person(s) to Issuer
(Check all applicable)

____ Director ____ 10% Owner
____ Officer (give title below) ____ Other (specify below)

5. If Amendment, Date Original Filed (Month/Day/Year)

6. Individual or Joint/Group Filing (Check Applicable Line)
____ Form filed by One Reporting Person
____ Form filed by More than One Reporting Person

Table I — Non-Derivative Securities Beneficially Owned

1. Title of Security (Instr. 4)	2. Amount of Securities Beneficially Owned (Instr. 4)	3. Ownership Form: Direct (D) or Indirect (I) (Instr. 5)	4. Nature of Indirect Beneficial Ownership (Instr. 5)

Reminder: Report on a separate line for each class of securities beneficially owned directly or indirectly.
* If the form is filed by more than one reporting person, *see* Instruction 5(b)(v).

Potential persons who are to respond to the collection of information contained in this form are not required to respond unless the form displays a currently valid OMB control number.

SEC 1473 (6-03) (Over)

FORM 3 (continued)

Table II — Derivative Securities Beneficially Owned (*e.g.*, puts, calls, warrants, options, convertible securities)

1. Title of Derivative Security (Instr. 4)	2. Date Exercisable and Expiration Date (Month/Day/Year)		3. Title and Amount of Securities Underlying Derivative Security (Instr. 4)		4. Conversion or Exercise Price of Derivative Security	5. Ownership Form of Derivative Security: Direct (D) or Indirect (I) (Instr. 5)	6. Nature of Indirect Beneficial Ownership (Instr. 5)
	Date Exercisable	Expiration Date	Title	Amount or Number of Shares			

_____ _____
**Signature of Reporting Person   Date

Explanation of Responses:

** Intentional misstatements or omissions of facts constitute Federal Criminal Violations.
See 18 U.S.C. 1001 and 15 U.S.C. 78ff(a).

Note: File three copies of this Form, one of which must be manually signed. If space is insufficient, *See* Instruction 6 for procedure.

Potential persons who are to respond to the collection of information contained in this form are not required to respond unless the form displays a currently valid OMB Number.

B. FORM 4

17 C.F.R. § 249.104

CHANGES IN BENEFICIAL OWNERSHIP OF SECURITIES
(PURSUANT TO SECTION 16(a))

UNITED STATES
SECURITIES AND EXCHANGE COMMISSION
Washington, D.C. 20549

FORM 4
STATEMENT OF CHANGES OF BENEFICIAL
OWNERSHIP OF SECURITIES

THE COMMISSION IS AUTHORIZED TO SOLICIT THE INFORMATION REQUIRED BY THIS FORM PURSUANT TO SECTIONS 16(a) AND 23(a) OF THE SECURITIES EXCHANGE ACT OF 1934; AND SECTIONS 30(h) AND 38 OF THE INVESTMENT COMPANY ACT OF 1940, AND THE RULES AND REGULATIONS THEREUNDER.

DISCLOSURE OF INFORMATION SPECIFIED ON THIS FORM IS MANDATORY. THE INFORMATION WILL BE USED FOR THE PRIMARY PURPOSE OF DISCLOSING THE TRANSACTIONS AND HOLDINGS OF DIRECTORS, OFFICERS, AND BENEFICIAL OWNERS OF REGISTERED COMPANIES. INFORMATION DISCLOSED WILL BE A MATTER OF PUBLIC RECORD AND AVAILABLE FOR INSPECTION BY MEMBERS OF THE PUBLIC. THE COMMISSION CAN USE IT IN INVESTIGATIONS OR LITIGATION INVOLVING THE FEDERAL SECURITIES LAWS OR OTHER CIVIL, CRIMINAL, OR REGULATORY STATUTES OR PROVISIONS, AS WELL AS FOR REFERRAL TO OTHER GOVERNMENTAL AUTHORITIES AND SELF-REGULATORY ORGANIZATIONS. FAILURE TO DISCLOSE REQUIRED INFORMATION MAY RESULT IN CIVIL OR CRIMINAL ACTION AGAINST PERSONS INVOLVED FOR VIOLATIONS OF THE FEDERAL SECURITIES LAWS AND RULES.

GENERAL INSTRUCTIONS

1. **When Form Must Be Filed**

   (a)   This Form must be filed before the end of the second business day following the day on which a transaction resulting in a change in beneficial ownership has been executed (see Rule 16a–1(a)(2) and Instruction 4 regarding the meaning of "beneficial owner," and Rule 16a–3(g) regarding determination of the date of execution for specified transactions). This Form and any amendment is deemed filed with the Commission or the Exchange on the date it is received by the Commission or the Exchange, respectively. *See*, however, Rule 16a–3(h) regarding delivery to a third party business that guarantees delivery of the filing no later than the specified due date.

   (b)   A reporting person no longer subject to section 16 of the Securities Exchange Act of 1934 ("Exchange Act") must check the exit box appearing on this Form. However, Form 4 and Form 5 obligations may continue to be applicable. *See* Rules 16a–3(f) and 16a–2(b). Form 5 transactions to date may be included on this Form and subsequent Form 5 transactions may be reported on a later Form 4 or Form 5, provided all transactions are reported by the required date.

   (c)   A separate Form shall be filed to reflect beneficial ownership of securities of each issuer, except that a single statement shall be filed with respect to the securities of a registered public utility holding company and all of its subsidiary companies.

   (d)   If a reporting person is not an officer, director, or 10% holder, the person should check "other" in Item 6 (Relationship of Reporting Person to Issuer) and describe the reason for reporting status in the space provided.

2. **Where Form Must Be Filed**

   (a)   A reporting person must file this Form in electronic format via the Commission's Electronic Data Gathering Analysis and Retrieval System (EDGAR) in accordance with EDGAR rules set forth in Regulation S–T, except that a filing person that has obtained a hardship exception under Regulation S–T Rule 202 may file the Form in paper. For assistance with technical questions about EDGAR or to request an access code,

FORM 4

call the EDGAR Filer Support Office at (202) 942–8900. For assistance with questions about the EDGAR rules, call the Office of EDGAR and Information Analysis at (202) 942–2940.

(b)   At the time this Form or any amendment is filed with the Commission, file one copy with each Exchange on which any class of securities of the issuer is registered. If the issuer has designated a single Exchange to receive section 16 filings, the copy shall be filed with that Exchange only.

(c)   [Removed and Reserved].

NOTE: If filing pursuant to a hardship exception under Regulation S–T Rule 202, file three copies of this Form or any amendment, at least one of which is signed, with the Securities and Exchange Commission, 450 5th Street, NW., Washington, D.C., 20549. (Acknowledgement of receipt by the Commission may be obtained by enclosing a self-addressed stamped postcard identifying the Form or amendment filed.)

3.   Class of Securities Reported

(a)(i)   Persons reporting pursuant to section 16(a) of the Exchange Act shall report each transaction resulting in a change in beneficial ownership of any class of equity securities of the issuer and the beneficial ownership of that class of securities following the reported transaction(s), even though one or more of such classes may not be registered pursuant to section 12 of the Exchange Act.

(ii)   Persons reporting pursuant to section 17(a) of the Public Utility Holding Company Act of 1935 shall report each transaction resulting in a change in beneficial ownership of any class of securities (equity or debt) of the registered holding company and of all of its subsidiary companies and the beneficial ownership of that class of securities following the reported transaction(s). Specify the name of the parent or subsidiary issuing the securities.

(iii)   Persons reporting pursuant to section 30(h) of the Investment Company Act of 1940 shall report each transaction resulting in a change in beneficial ownership of any class of securities (equity or debt) of the registered closed-end investment company (other than "short-term paper" as defined in section 2(a)(38) of the Investment Company Act) and the beneficial ownership of that class of securities following the reported transaction(s).

(b)   The title of the security should clearly identify the class, even if the issuer has only one class of securities outstanding; for example, "Common Stock," "Class A Common Stock," "Class B Convertible Preferred Stock," etc.

(c)   The amount of securities beneficially owned should state the face amount of debt securities (U.S. Dollars) or the number of equity securities, whichever is appropriate.

4.   Transactions and Holdings Required to Be Reported

(a)   *General Requirements*

(i)   Report, in accordance with Rule 16a–3(g): (1) all transactions not exempt from Section 16(b); (2) all transactions exempt from Section 16(b) pursuant to Rule 16b–3(d), Rule 16b–3(e), or Rule 16b–3(f); and (3) all exercises and conversions of derivative securities, regardless of whether exempt from Section 16(b) of the Act. Every transaction must be reported even though acquisitions and dispositions are equal. Report total beneficial ownership following the reported transaction(s) for each class of securities in which a transaction was reported.

NOTE: The amount of securities beneficially owned following the reported transaction(s) specified in Column 5 of Table I and Column 9 of Table II should reflect those holdings reported or required to be reported by the date of the Form. Transactions and holdings eligible for deferred reporting on Form 5 need not be reflected in the month end total unless the transactions were reported earlier or are included on this Form.

(ii)   Each transaction should be reported on a separate line. Transaction codes specified in Instruction 8 should be used to identify the nature of the transaction resulting in an acquisition or disposition of a security. A deemed execution date must be reported in Column 2A of Table I or Column 3A of Table II only if the execution date for the transaction is calculated pursuant to Rule 16a–3(g)(2) or Rule 16a–3(g)(3).

NOTE: Transactions reportable on Form 5 may, at the option of the reporting person, be reported on a Form 4 filed before the due date of the Form 5. (*See* Instruction 8 for the code for voluntarily reported transactions.)

(b) *Beneficial Ownership Reported (Pecuniary Interest)*

(i)   Although for purposes of determining status as a ten percent holder, a person is deemed to beneficially own securities over which that person has voting or investment control (*see* Rule 16a–1(a)(1)), for reporting transactions and holdings, a person is deemed to be the beneficial owner of securities if that person has or shares the opportunity, directly or indirectly, to profit or share in any profit derived from a transaction in the securities ("pecuniary interest"). *See* Rule 16a–1(a)(2). *See also* Rule 16a–8 for the application of the beneficial ownership definition to trust holdings and transactions.

(ii)   Both direct and indirect beneficial ownership of securities shall be reported. Securities beneficially owned directly are those held in the reporting person's name or in the name of a bank, broker or nominee for the account of the reporting person. In addition, securities held as joint tenants, tenants in common, tenants by the entirety, or as community property are to be reported as held directly. If a person has a pecuniary interest, by reason of any contract, understanding, or relationship (including a family relationship or arrangement), in securities held in the name of another person, that person is an indirect beneficial owner of the securities. *See* Rule 16a–1(a)(2)(ii) for certain indirect beneficial ownerships.

(iii)   Report transactions in securities beneficially owned directly on separate lines from those beneficially owned indirectly. Report different forms of indirect ownership on separate lines. The nature of indirect ownership shall be stated as specifically as possible; for example, "By Self as Trustee for X," "By Spouse," "By X Trust," "By Y Corporation," etc.

(iv)   In stating the amount of securities acquired, disposed of, or beneficially owned indirectly through a partnership, corporation, trust, or other entity, report the number of securities representing the reporting person's proportionate interest in transactions conducted by that entity or holdings of that entity. Alternatively, at the option of the reporting person, the entire amount of the entity's interest may be reported. *See* Rule 16a–1(a)(2)(ii)(B) and Rule 16a–1(a)(2)(iii).

(v)   Where more than one beneficial owner of the same equity securities must report the same transaction on Form 4, such owners may file Form 4 individually or jointly. Joint and group filings may be made by any designated beneficial owner. Transactions with respect to securities owned separately by any joint or group filer are permitted to be included in the joint filing. Indicate only the name and address of the designated filer in Item 1 of Form 4 and attach a list of the names and addresses of each other reporting person. Joint and group filings must include all required information for each beneficial owner, and such filings must be signed by each beneficial owner, or on behalf of such owner by an authorized person. If this Form is being filed in paper pursuant to a hardship exemption and the space provided for signatures is insufficient, attach a signature page. If this Form is being filed in paper, submit any attached listing of names or signatures on another Form 4, copy of Form 4 or separate page of 8 1/2 by 11 inch white paper, indicate the number of pages comprising the report (Form plus attachments) at the bottom of each report page (e.g., 1 of 3, 2 of 3, 3 of 3), and include the name of the designated filer and information required by Items 2 and 3 of the Form on the attachment. *See* Rule 16a–3(i) regarding signatures.

(c)   *Non-Derivative and Derivative Securities*

(i)   Report acquisitions or dispositions and holdings of non-derivative securities in Table I. Report acquisitions or dispositions and holdings of derivative securities (*e.g.*, puts, calls, options, warrants, convertible securities, or other rights or obligations to buy or sell securities) in Table II. Report the exercise or conversion of a derivative security in Table II (as a disposition of the derivative security) and report in Table I the holdings of the underlying security. Report acquisitions or dispositions and holdings of derivative securities that are both equity securities and convertible or exchangeable for other equity securities (*e.g.*, convertible preferred securities) only on Table II.

(ii)   The title of a derivative security and the title of the equity security underlying the derivative security should be shown separately in the appropriate columns in Table II. The "puts" and "calls" reported in Table II include, in addition to separate puts and calls, any combination of the two, such as spreads and straddles. In reporting an option in Table II, state whether it represents a right to buy, a right to sell, an obligation to buy, or an obligation to sell the equity securities subject to the option.

(iii) Describe in the appropriate columns in Table II characteristics of derivative securities, including title, exercise or conversion price, date exercisable, expiration date, and the title and amount of securities underlying the derivative security. If the transaction reported is a purchase or sale of a derivative security, the purchase or sale price of that derivative security shall be reported in column 8. If the transaction is the exercise or conversion of a derivative security, leave column 8 blank and report the exercise or conversion price of the derivative security in column 2.

(iv) Securities constituting components of a unit shall be reported separately on the applicable table (*e.g.*, if a unit has a non-derivative security component and a derivative security component, the non-derivative security component shall be reported in Table I and the derivative security component shall be reported in Table II). The relationship between individual securities comprising the unit shall be indicated in the space provided for explanation of responses. When securities are purchased or sold as a unit, state the purchase or sale price per unit and other required information regarding the unit securities.

5. Price of Securities

(a) Prices of securities shall be reported in U.S. dollars on a per share basis, not an aggregate basis, except that the aggregate price of debt shall be stated. Amounts reported shall exclude brokerage commissions and other costs of execution.

(b) If consideration other than cash was paid for the security, describe the consideration, including the value of the consideration, in the space provided for explanation of responses.

6. Additional Information

(a) If the space provided in the line items on the electronic Form is insufficient, use the space provided for footnotes. If the space provided for footnotes is insufficient, create a footnote that refers to an exhibit to the form that contains the additional information.

(b) If the space provided in the line items on the paper Form or space provided for additional comments is insufficient, attach another Form 4, copy of Form 4 or separate 8 1/2 by 11 inch white paper to Form 4, completed as appropriate to include the additional comments. Each attached page must include information required in Items 1, 2 and 3 of the Form. The number of pages comprising the report (Form plus attachments) shall be indicated at the bottom of each report page (e.g., 1 of 3, 2 of 3, 3 of 3).

(c) If one or more exhibits are included, whether due to a lack of space or because the exhibit is, by nature, a separate document (e.g., a power of attorney), provide a sequentially numbered list of the exhibits in the Form. Use the number "24" for any power of attorney and the number "99" for any other exhibit. If there is more than one of either such exhibit, then use numerical subparts. If the exhibit is being filed as a confirming electronic copy under Regulation S–T Rule 202(d), then place the designation "CE" (confirming exhibit) next to the name of the exhibit in the exhibit list. If the exhibit is being filed in paper pursuant to a hardship exception under Regulation S–T Rule 202, then place the designation "P" (paper) next to the name of the exhibit in the exhibit list.

(d) If additional information is not reported as provided in paragraph (a), (b) or (c) of this instruction, whichever apply, it will be assumed that no additional information was provided.

7. Signature

(a) If the Form is filed for an individual, it shall be signed by that person or specifically on behalf of the individual by a person authorized to sign for the individual. If signed on behalf of the individual by another person, the authority of such person to sign the Form shall be confirmed to the Commission in writing in an attachment to the Form or as soon as practicable in an amendment by the individual for whom the Form is filed, unless such a confirmation still in effect is on file with the Commission. The confirming statement need only indicate that the reporting person authorizes and designates the named person or persons to file the Form on the reporting person's behalf, and state the duration of the authorization.

(b) If the Form is filed for a corporation, partnership, trust, or other entity, the capacity in which the individual signed shall be set forth (*e.g.*, John Smith, Secretary, on behalf of X Corporation).

8. Transaction Codes

Use the codes listed below to indicate in Table I, Column 3 and Table II, Column 4 the character of the transaction reported. Use the code that most appropriately describes the transaction. If the transaction is not specifically listed, use transaction Code "J" and describe the nature of the transaction in the space for explanation of responses. If a transaction is voluntarily reported earlier than required, place "V" in the appropriate column to so indicate; otherwise, the column should be left blank. If a transaction involves an equity swap or instrument with similar characteristics, use transaction Code "K" in addition to the code(s) that most appropriately describes the transaction, e.g., "S/K" or "P/K."

General Transaction Codes

P—Open market or private purchase of non-derivative or derivative security

S—Open market or private sale of non-derivative or derivative security

V—Transaction voluntarily reported earlier than required

Rule 16b–3 Transaction Codes

A—Grant, award or other acquisition pursuant to Rule 16b–3(d)

D—Disposition to the issuer of issuer equity securities pursuant to Rule 16b–3(e)

F—Payment of exercise price or tax liability by delivering or withholding securities incident to the receipt, exercise, or vesting of a security issued in accordance with Rule 16b–3

I—Discretionary transaction in accordance with Rule 16b–3(f) resulting in acquisition or disposition of issuer securities

M—Exercise or conversion of derivative security exempted pursuant to Rule 16b–3

Derivative Securities Codes (Except for transactions exempted pursuant to Rule 16b–3)

C—Conversion of derivative security

E—Expiration of short derivative position

H—Expiration (or cancellation) of long derivative position with value received

O—Exercise of out-of-the-money derivative security

X—Exercise of in-the-money or at-the-money derivative security

Other Section 16(b) Exempt Transaction and Small Acquisition Codes (except for Rule 16b–3 codes above)

G—Bona fide gift

L—Small acquisition under Rule 16a–6

W—Acquisition or disposition by will or the laws of descent and distribution

Z—Deposit into or withdrawal from voting trust

Other Transaction Codes

J—Other acquisition or disposition (describe transaction)

K—Transaction in equity swap or instrument with similar characteristics

U—Dispositions pursuant to a tender of shares in a change of control transaction

9. Amendments

(a) If this Form is filed as an amendment in order to add one or more lines of transaction information to Table I or Table II of the Form being amended, provide each line being added, together with one or more footnotes, as necessary, to explain the addition of the line or lines. Do not repeat lines of transaction information that were disclosed in the original Form and are not being amended.

(b)   If this Form is filed as an amendment in order to amend one or more lines of transaction information that already were disclosed in Table I or Table II of the Form being amended, provide the complete line or lines being amended, as amended, together with one or more footnotes, as necessary, to explain the amendment of the line or lines. Do not repeat lines of transaction information that were disclosed in the original Form and are not being amended.

(c)   If this Form is filed as an amendment for any purpose other than or in addition to the purposes described in paragraphs (a) and (b) of this General Instruction 9, provide one or more footnotes, as necessary, to explain the amendment.

FORM 4

☐ Check this box if no longer subject to Section 16. Form 4 or Form 5 obligations may continue. *See Instruction 1(b).*

(Print or Type Responses)

UNITED STATES SECURITIES AND EXCHANGE COMMISSION
Washington, D.C. 20549

STATEMENT OF CHANGES IN BENEFICIAL OWNERSHIP

Filed pursuant to Section 16(a) of the Securities Exchange Act of 1934, Section 17(a) of the Public Utility Holding Company Act of 1935 or Section 30(h) of the Investment Company Act of 1940

OMB APPROVAL
OMB Number: 3235-0287
Expires: January 31, 2008
Estimated average burden hours per response 0.5

1. Name and Address of Reporting Person*

(Last)   (First)   (Middle)

(Street)

(City)   (State)   (Zip)

2. Issuer Name and Ticker or Trading Symbol

5. Relationship of Reporting Person(s) to Issuer
(Check all applicable)

_____ Director   _____ 10% Owner
_____ Officer (give   _____ Other (specify
       title below)   below)

6. Individual or Joint/Group Filing (Check Applicable Line)
_____ Form filed by One Reporting Person
_____ Form filed by More than One Reporting Person

Table I — Non-Derivative Securities Acquired, Disposed of, or Beneficially Owned

1. Title of Security (Instr. 3)	2. Trans-action Date (Month/Day/Year)	2A. Deemed Execution Date, if any (Month/Day/Year)	3. Trans-action Code (Instr. 8)		4. Securities Acquired (A) or Disposed of (D) (Instr. 3, 4 and 5)			5. Amount of Securities Beneficially Owned Following Reported Transaction(s) (Instr. 3 and 4)	6. Owner-ship Form: Direct (D) or Indirect (I) (Instr. 4)	7. Nature of Indirect Beneficial Owner-ship (Instr. 4)
			Code	V	Amount	(A) or (D)	Price			

3. Date of Earliest Transaction Required to be Reported (Month/Day/Year)

4. If Amendment, Date Original Filed (Month/Day/Year)

Reminder: Report on a separate line for each class of securities beneficially owned directly or indirectly.
* If the form is filed by more than one reporting person, *see* Instruction 4(b)(v).

(If this Form is filed as an amendment, describe in paragraphs (a) and (b) of the General Instruction to explain the amendment.)

(If this Form is used to report a transaction information that already were disclosed in Part I and/or of the amendment line or lines being amended, set out with those lines with explain the amendment of the line or Part I, not representatives, the in the original Form and prior to being disclosed.)

FORM 4

FORM 4 (continued)

Page 2

Table II — Derivative Securities Acquired, Disposed of, or Beneficially Owned
(e.g. puts, calls, warrants, options, convertible securities)

1. Title of Derivative Security (Instr. 3)	2. Conversion or Exercise Price of Derivative Security	3. Transaction Date (Month/Day/Year)	3A. Deemed Execution Date, if any (Month/Day/Year)	4. Transaction Code (Instr. 8)		5. Number of Derivative Securities Acquired (A) or Disposed of (D) (Instr. 3, 4, and 5)		6. Date Exercisable and Expiration Date (Month/Day/Year)		7. Title and Amount of Underlying Securities (Instr. 3 and 4)		8. Price of Derivative Security (Instr. 5)	9. Number of derivative Securities Beneficially Owned following Reported Transaction(s)(Instr. 4)	10. Ownership Form of Derivative Security: Direct (D) or Indirect (I) (Instr. 4)	11. Nature of Indirect Beneficial Ownership (Instr. 4)
				Code	V	(A)	(D)	Date Exercisable	Expiration Date	Title	Amount or Number of Shares				

Explanation of Responses:

_____

** Signature of Reporting Person   Date

** Intentional misstatements or omissions of facts constitute Federal Criminal Violations.
See 18 U.S.C. 1001 and 15 U.S.C. 78ff(a).

Note: File three copies of this Form, one of which must be manually signed. If space is insufficient,
see Instruction 6 for procedure.

Potential persons who are to respond to the collection of information contained in this form are not
required to respond unless the form displays a currently valid OMB Number.

C. FORM 5

17 C.F.R. § 249.105

ANNUAL STATEMENT OF CHANGES IN BENEFICIAL OWNERSHIP
(PURSUANT TO SECTION 16(a))

UNITED STATES
SECURITIES AND EXCHANGE COMMISSION
Washington, D.C. 20549

FORM 5
ANNUAL STATEMENT OF BENEFICIAL OWNERSHIP OF SECURITIES

THE COMMISSION IS AUTHORIZED TO SOLICIT THE INFORMATION REQUIRED BY THIS FORM PURSUANT TO SECTIONS 16(a) AND 23(a) OF THE SECURITIES EXCHANGE ACT OF 1934, AND SECTIONS 30(h) AND 38 OF THE INVESTMENT COMPANY ACT OF 1940, AND THE RULES AND REGULATIONS THEREUNDER.

DISCLOSURE OF INFORMATION SPECIFIED ON THIS FORM IS MANDATORY. THE INFORMATION WILL BE USED FOR THE PRIMARY PURPOSE OF DISCLOSING THE TRANSACTIONS AND HOLDINGS OF DIRECTORS, OFFICERS, AND BENEFICIAL OWNERS OF REGISTERED COMPANIES. INFORMATION DISCLOSED WILL BE A MATTER OF PUBLIC RECORD AND AVAILABLE FOR INSPECTION BY MEMBERS OF THE PUBLIC. THE COMMISSION CAN USE IT IN INVESTIGATIONS OR LITIGATION INVOLVING THE FEDERAL SECURITIES LAWS OR OTHER CIVIL, CRIMINAL, OR REGULATORY STATUTES OR PROVISIONS, AS WELL AS FOR REFERRAL TO OTHER GOVERNMENTAL AUTHORITIES AND SELF-REGULATORY ORGANIZATIONS. FAILURE TO DISCLOSE REQUIRED INFORMATION MAY RESULT IN CIVIL OR CRIMINAL ACTION AGAINST PERSONS INVOLVED FOR VIOLATIONS OF THE FEDERAL SECURITIES LAWS AND RULES.

GENERAL INSTRUCTIONS

1. When Form Must Be Filed

(a)   This Form must be filed on or before the 45th day after the end of the issuer's fiscal year in accordance with Rule 16a–3(f). This Form and any amendment is deemed filed with the Commission or the Exchange on the date it is received by the Commission or the Exchange, respectively. *See*, however, Rule 16a–3(h) regarding delivery to a third party business that guarantees delivery of the filing no later than the specified due date.

(b)   A reporting person no longer subject to section 16 of the Securities Exchange Act of 1934 ("Exchange Act") must check the exit box appearing on this Form. Transactions and holdings previously reported are not required to be included on this Form. Form 4 or Form 5 obligations may continue to be applicable. *See* Rules 16a–3(f) and 16a–2(b).

(c)   A separate Form shall be filed to reflect beneficial ownership of securities of each issuer.

(d)   If a reporting person is not an officer, director, or 10% holder, the person should check "other" in Item 6 (Relationship of Reporting Person to Issuer) and describe the reason for reporting status in the space provided.

2. Where Form Must Be Filed

(a)   A reporting person must file this Form in electronic format via the Commission's Electronic Data Gathering Analysis and Retrieval System (EDGAR) in accordance with EDGAR rules set forth in Regulation S–T, except that a filing person that has obtained a hardship exception under Regulation S–T Rule 202 may file the Form in paper. For assistance with technical questions about EDGAR or to request an access code, call the EDGAR Filer Support Office at (202) 942–8900. For assistance with questions about the EDGAR rules, call the Office of EDGAR and Information Analysis at (202) 942–2940.

(b)   At the time this Form or any amendment is filed with the Commission, file one copy with each Exchange on which any class of securities of the issuer is registered. If the issuer has designated a single Exchange to receive section 16 filings, the copy shall be filed with that Exchange only.

(c)   [Removed and Reserved].

FORM 5

NOTE: If filing pursuant to a hardship exception under Regulation S–T Rule 202, file three copies of this Form or any amendment, at least one of which is signed, with the Securities and Exchange Commission, 450 5th Street, NW., Washington, D.C., 20549. (Acknowledgement of receipt by the Commission may be obtained by enclosing a self-addressed stamped postcard identifying the Form or amendment filed.)

3. Class of Securities Reported

(a)(i)   Persons reporting pursuant to section 16(a) of the Exchange Act shall include information as to transactions and holdings required to be reported in any class of equity securities of the issuer and the beneficial ownership at the end of the year of that class of equity securities, even though one or more of such classes may not be registered pursuant to Section 12 of the Exchange Act.

(ii)   Removed and Reserved.

(iii)   Persons reporting pursuant to section 30(h) of the Investment Company Act of 1940 shall include transactions and holdings required to be reported in any class of securities (equity or debt) of the registered closed-end investment company (other than "short-term paper" as defined in section 2(a)(38) of the Act) and the beneficial ownership at the end of the year of that class of securities.

(b)   The title of the security should clearly identify the class, even if the issuer has only one class of securities outstanding; for example, "Common Stock," "Class A Common Stock," "Class B Convertible Preferred Stock," etc.

(c)   The amount of securities beneficially owned should state the face amount of debt securities (U.S. Dollars) or the number of equity securities, whichever is appropriate.

4. Transactions and Holdings Required to Be Reported

(a)   *General Requirements*

(i)   Pursuant to Rule 16a–3(f), if not previously reported, the following transactions, and total beneficial ownership as of the end of the issuer's fiscal year (or the earlier date applicable to a person ceasing to be an insider during the fiscal year) for any class of securities for which a transaction is reported, shall be reported:

(A)   any transaction during the issuer's most recent fiscal year that was exempt from section 16(b) of the Act, except: (1) any transaction exempt from Section 16(b) pursuant to Rules 16b–3(d), 16b–3(e), or 16b–3(f) (these are required to be reported on Form 4); (2) any exercise or conversion of derivative securities exempt under either Rule 16b–3 or 16b–6(b) (these are required to be reported on Form 4); (3) any transaction exempt from Section 16(b) of the Act pursuant to Rule 16b–3(c), which is exempt from Section 16(a) of the Act; and (4) any transaction exempt from Section 16 of the Act pursuant to another Section 16(a) rule;

(B)   any small acquisition or series of acquisitions in a six month period during the issuer's fiscal year not exceeding $10,000 in market value (*see* Rule 16a–6); and

(C)   any transactions or holdings that should have been reported during the issuer's fiscal year on a Form 3 or Form 4, but were not reported. The first Form 5 filing obligation shall include all holdings and transactions that should have been reported in each of the issuer's last two fiscal years but were not. *See* Instruction 8 for the code to identify delinquent Form 3 holdings or Form 4 transactions reported on this Form 5.

NOTE: A required Form 3 or Form 4 must be filed within the time specified by the Form. Form 3 holdings or Form 4 transactions reported on Form 5 represent delinquent Form 3 and Form 4 filings.

(ii)   Each transaction should be reported on a separate line. Transaction codes specified in Instruction 8 should be used to identify the nature of the transaction resulting in an acquisition or disposition of a security. A deemed execution date must be reported in Column 2A of Table I or Column 3A of Table II only if the execution date for the transaction is calculated pursuant to Rule 16a–3(g)(2) or Rule 16a–3(g)(3).

(iii)   Every transaction shall be reported even though acquisitions and dispositions with respect to a class of securities are equal. Report total beneficial ownership as of the end of the issuer's fiscal year for all classes of securities in which a transaction was reported.

(b)   *Beneficial Ownership Reported (Pecuniary Interest)*

(i)   Although, for purposes of determining status as a ten percent holder, a person is deemed to beneficially own securities over which that person has voting or investment control (*see* Rule 16a–1(a)(1)), for reporting transactions and holdings, a person is deemed to be the beneficial owner of securities if that person has or shares the opportunity, directly or indirectly, to profit or share in any profit derived from a transaction in the securities ("pecuniary interest"). *See* Rule 16a–1(a)(2). *See also* Rule 16a–8 for the application of the beneficial ownership definition to trust holdings and transactions.

(ii)   Both direct and indirect beneficial ownership of securities shall be reported. Securities beneficially owned directly are those held in the reporting person's name or in the name of a bank, broker or nominee for the account of the reporting person. In addition, securities held as joint tenants, tenants in common, tenants by the entirety, or as community property are to be reported as held directly. If a person has a pecuniary interest, by reason of any contract, understanding, or relationship (including a family relationship or arrangement), in securities held in the name of another person, that person is an indirect beneficial owner of the securities. *See* Rule 16a–1(a)(2)(ii) for certain indirect beneficial ownerships.

(iii)   Report transactions in securities beneficially owned directly on separate lines from those beneficially owned indirectly. Report different forms of indirect ownership on separate lines. The nature of indirect ownership shall be stated as specifically as possible; for example, "By Self as Trustee for X," "By Spouse," "By X Trust," "By Y Corporation," etc.

(iv)   In stating the amount of securities acquired, disposed of, or beneficially owned indirectly through a partnership, corporation, trust, or other entity, report the number of securities representing the reporting person's proportionate interest in transactions conducted by that entity or holdings of that entity. Alternatively, at the option of the reporting person, the entire amount of the entity's interest may be reported. *See* Rule 16a–1(a)(2)(ii)(B) and Rule 16a–1(a)(2)(iii).

(v)   Where more than one beneficial owner of the same equity securities must report the same transaction or holding on Form 5, such owners may file Form 5 individually or jointly. Joint and group filings may be made by any designated beneficial owner. Transactions and holdings with respect to securities owned separately by any joint or group filer are permitted to be included in the joint filing. Indicate only the name and address of the designated filer in Item 1 of Form 5 and attach a list of the names and addresses of each other reporting person. Joint and group filings must include all required information for each beneficial owner, and such filings must be signed by each beneficial owner, or on behalf of such owner by an authorized person. If this Form is being filed in paper pursuant to a hardship exemption and the space provided for signatures is insufficient, attach a signature page. If this Form is being filed in paper, submit any attached listing of names or signatures on another Form 5, copy of Form 5 or separate page of 8 1/2 by 11 inch white paper, indicate the number of pages comprising the report (Form plus attachments) at the bottom of each report page (e.g., 1 of 3, 2 of 3, 3 of 3), and include the name of the designated filer and information required by Items 2 and 3 of the Form on the attachment.

See Rule 16a–3(i) regarding signatures.

(c)   *Non-Derivative and Derivative Securities*

(i)   Report acquisitions or dispositions and holdings of non-derivative securities in Table I. Report acquisitions or dispositions and holdings of derivative securities (*e.g.*, puts, calls, options, warrants, convertible securities, or other rights or obligations to buy or sell securities) in Table II. Report the exercise or conversion of a derivative security in Table II (as a disposition of the derivative security) and report in Table I the holdings of the underlying security. Report acquisitions or dispositions and holdings of derivative securities that are both equity securities and convertible or exchangeable for other equity securities (*e.g.*, convertible preferred securities) only on Table II.

(ii)   The title of a derivative security and the title of the equity security underlying the derivative security should be shown separately in the appropriate columns in Table II. The "puts" and "calls" reported in Table II include, in addition to separate puts and calls, any combination of the two, such as spreads and straddles. In reporting an option in Table II, state whether it represents a right to buy, a right to sell, an obligation to buy, or an obligation to sell the equity securities subject to the option.

(iii) Describe in the appropriate columns in Table II characteristics of derivative securities, including title, exercise or conversion price, date exercisable, expiration date, and the title and amount of securities underlying the derivative security. If the transaction reported is a purchase or sale of a derivative security, the purchase or sale price of the derivative security shall be reported in column 8. If the transaction is the exercise or conversion of a derivative security, leave column 8 blank and report the exercise or conversion price of the derivative security in column 2.

(iv) Securities constituting components of a unit shall be reported separately on the applicable table (e.g., if a unit has a non-derivative security component and a derivative security component, the non-derivative security component shall be reported in Table I and the derivative security component shall be reported in Table II). The relationship between individual securities comprising the unit shall be indicated in the space provided for explanation of responses. When securities are purchased or sold as a unit, state the purchase or sale price per unit and other required information regarding the unit securities.

5. Price of Securities

(a) Prices of securities shall be reported in U.S. dollars and on a per share basis, not an aggregate basis, except that the aggregate price of debt shall be stated. Amounts reported shall exclude brokerage commissions and other costs of execution.

(b) If consideration other than cash was paid for the security, describe the consideration, including the value of the consideration in the space provided for explanation of responses.

6. Additional Information

(a) If the space provided in the line items on the electronic Form is insufficient, use the space provided for footnotes. If the space provided for footnotes is insufficient, create a footnote that refers to an exhibit to the form that contains the additional information.

(b) If the space provided in the line items on the paper Form or space provided for additional comments is insufficient, attach another Form 5, copy of Form 5 or separate 8 1/2 by 11 inch white paper to Form 5, completed as appropriate to include the additional comments. Each attached page must include information required in Items 1, 2 and 3 of the Form. The number of pages comprising the report (Form plus attachments) shall be indicated at the bottom of each report page (e.g., 1 of 3, 2 of 3, 3 of 3).

(c) If one or more exhibits are included, whether due to a lack of space or because the exhibit is, by nature, a separate document (e.g., a power of attorney), provide a sequentially numbered list of the exhibits in the Form. Use the number "24" for any power of attorney and the number "99" for any other exhibit. If there is more than one of either such exhibit, then use numerical subparts. If the exhibit is being filed as a confirming electronic copy under Regulation S–T Rule 202(d), then place the designation "CE" (confirming exhibit) next to the name of the exhibit in the exhibit list. If the exhibit is being filed in paper pursuant to a hardship exception under Regulation S–T Rule 202, then place the designation "P" (paper) next to the name of the exhibit in the exhibit list.

(d) If additional information is not reported as provided in paragraph (a), (b) or (c) of this instruction, whichever apply, it will be assumed that no additional information was provided.

7. Signature

(a) If the Form is filed for an individual, it shall be signed by that person or specifically on behalf of the individual by a person authorized to sign for the individual. If signed on behalf of the individual by another person, the authority of such person to sign the Form shall be confirmed to the Commission in writing in an attachment to the Form or as soon as practicable in an amendment by the individual for whom the Form is filed, unless such a confirmation still in effect is on file with the Commission. The confirming statement need only indicate that the reporting person authorizes and designates the named person or persons to file the Form on the reporting person's behalf, and state the duration of the authorization.

(b) If the Form is filed for a corporation, partnership, trust, or other entity, the capacity in which the individual signed shall be set forth (e.g., John Smith, Secretary, on behalf of X Corporation).

8. Transaction Codes

Use the codes listed below to indicate in Table I, Column 3 and Table II, Column 4 the character of the transaction reported. Use the code that most appropriately describes the transaction. If the transaction is not specifically listed, use transaction Code "J" and describe the nature of the transaction in the space for explanation of responses. If a transaction involves an equity swap or instrument with similar characteristics, use transaction Code "K" in addition to the code(s) that most appropriately describes the transaction, e.g., "S/K" or "P/K."

General Transaction Codes

P—Open market or private purchase of non-derivative or derivative security

S—Open market or private sale of non-derivative or derivative security

Rule 16b–3 Transaction Codes

A—Grant, award or other acquisition pursuant to Rule 16b–3(d)

D—Disposition to the issuer of issuer equity securities pursuant to Rule 16b–3(e)

F—Payment of exercise price or tax liability by delivering or withholding securities incident to the receipt, exercise, or vesting of a security issued in accordance with Rule 16b–3

I—Discretionary transaction in accordance with Rule 16b–3(f) resulting in acquisition or disposition of issuer securities

M—Exercise or conversion of derivative security exempted pursuant to Rule 16b–3

Derivative Securities Codes (Except for transactions exempted pursuant to Rule 16b–3)

C—Conversion of derivative security

E—Expiration of short derivative position

H—Expiration (or cancellation) of long derivative position with value received

O—Exercise of out-of-the-money derivative security

X—Exercise of in-the-money or at-the-money derivative security

Other Section 16(b) Exempt Transaction and Small Acquisition Codes (except for Rule 16b–3 codes above)

G—Bona fide gift

L—Small acquisition under Rule 16a–6

W—Acquisition or disposition by will or the laws of descent and distribution

Z—Deposit into or withdrawal from voting trust

Other Transaction Codes

J—Other acquisition or disposition (describe transaction)

K—Transaction in equity swap or instrument with similar characteristics

U—Dispositions pursuant to a tender of shares in a change of control transaction

9. Amendments

(a) If this Form is filed as an amendment in order to add one or more lines of transaction or ownership information to Table I or Table II of the Form being amended, provide each line being added, together with one or more footnotes, as necessary, to explain the addition of the line or lines. Do not repeat lines of transaction or ownership information that were disclosed in the original Form and are not being amended.

(b) If this Form is filed as an amendment in order to amend one or more lines of transaction or ownership information that already were disclosed in Table I or Table II of the Form being amended, provide

FORM 5

the complete line or lines being amended, as amended, together with one or more footnotes, as necessary, to explain the amendment of the line or lines. Do not repeat lines of transaction or ownership information that were disclosed in the original Form and are not being amended.

(c) If this Form is filed as an amendment for any purpose other than or in addition to the purposes described in paragraphs (a) and (b) of this General Instruction 9, provide one or more footnotes, as necessary, to explain the amendment.

Form 3, 4 or 5 Holdings or Transactions
Not Previously Reported

To indicate that a holding should have been reported previously on Form 3, place a "3" in Table I, column 3 or Table II, column 4, as appropriate. Indicate in the space provided for explanation of responses the event triggering the Form 3 filing obligation. To indicate that a transaction should have been reported previously on Form 4, place a "4" next to the transaction code reported in Table I, column 3 or Table II, column 4 (*e.g.*, an open market purchase of a non-derivative security that should have been reported previously on Form 4 should be designated as "P4"). To indicate that a transaction should have been reported on a previous Form 5, place a "5" in Table I, column 3 or Table II, column 4 as appropriate. In addition, the appropriate box on the front page of the Form should be checked.

FORM 5

☐ Check box if no longer subject to Section 16. Form 4 or Form 5 obligations may continue. See Instruction 1(b).
☐ Form 3 Holdings Reported
☐ Form 4 Transactions Reported

UNITED STATES SECURITIES AND EXCHANGE COMMISSION
Washington, D.C. 20549

ANNUAL STATEMENT OF CHANGES IN BENEFICIAL OWNERSHIP OF SECURITIES

Filed pursuant to Section 16(a) of the Securities Exchange Act of 1934, Section 17(a) of the Public Utility Holding Company Act of 1935 or Section 30(h) of the Investment Company Act of 1940

OMB APPROVAL	
OMB Number:	3235-0362
Expires: January 31, 2008	
Estimated average burden hours per response.......	1.0

1. Name and Address of Reporting Person*

(Last) (First) (Middle)

(Street)

(City) (State) (Zip)

2. Issuer Name and Ticker or Trading Symbol

3. Statement for Issuer's Fiscal Year Ended (Month/Day/Year)

4. If Amendment, Date Original Filed (Month/Day/Year)

5. Relationship of Reporting Person(s) to Issuer (Check all applicable)

___ Director ___ 10% Owner
___ Officer (give title below) ___ Other (specify below)

6. Individual or Joint/Group Reporting (check applicable line)
___ Form Filed by One Reporting Person
___ Form Filed by More than One Reporting Person

Table I — Non-Derivative Securities Acquired, Disposed of, or Beneficially Owned

1. Title of Security (Instr. 3)	2. Transaction Date (Month/Day/Year)	2A. Deemed Execution Date, if any (Month/Day/Year)	3. Transaction Code (Instr. 8)		4. Securities Acquired (A) or Disposed of (D) (Instr. 3, 4 and 5)			5. Amount of Securities Beneficially Owned at end of Issuer's Fiscal Year (Instr. 3 and 4)	6. Ownership Form: Direct (D) or Indirect (I) (Instr. 4)	7. Nature of Indirect Beneficial Ownership (Instr. 4)
					Amount	(A) or (D)	Price			

Reminder: Report on a separate line for each class of securities beneficially owned directly or indirectly.

* If the form is filed by more than one reporting person, see Instruction 4(b)(v).

SEC 2270 (7-03)

FORM 5 (continued)

Table II — Derivative Securities Acquired, Disposed of, or Beneficially Owned
(e.g., puts, calls, warrants, options, convertible securities)

1. Title of Derivative Security (Instr. 3)	2. Conversion or Exercise Price of Derivative Security	3. Transaction Date (Month/Day/Year)	3A. Deemed Execution Date, if any (Month/Day/Year)	4. Transaction Code (Instr. 8)	5. Number of Derivative Securities Acquired (A) or Disposed of (D) (Instr. 3, 4, and 5)		6. Date Exercisable and Expiration Date (Month/Day/Year)		7. Title and Amount of Underlying Securities (Instr. 3 and 4)		8. Price of Derivative Security (Instr. 5)	9. Number of Derivative Securities Beneficially Owned at End of Issuer's Fiscal Year (Instr. 4)	10. Ownership Form of Derivative Securities: Direct (D) or Indirect (I) (Instr. 4)	11. Nature of Indirect Beneficial Ownership (Instr. 4)
					(A)	(D)	Date Exercisable	Expiration Date	Title	Amount or Number of Shares				

Explanation of Responses:

_____

_____   _____
** Signature of Reporting Person   Date

** Intentional misstatements or omissions of facts constitute Federal Criminal Violations.
See 18 U.S.C. 1001 and 15 U.S.C. 78ff(a).

Note: File three copies of this Form, one of which must be manually signed.
         If space provided is insufficient, *see* Instruction 6 for procedure.

Potential persons who are to respond to the collection of information contained in this form are not required to respond unless the form displays a currently valid OMB number.

1934 ACT FORMS

D. FORM 8–K

17 C.F.R. § 249.308

CURRENT REPORT FOR ISSUERS SUBJECT TO THE 1934 ACT REPORTING REQUIREMENTS

FORM 8–K

SECURITIES AND EXCHANGE COMMISSION

Washington, D.C. 20549

CURRENT REPORT

Pursuant to Section 13 or 15(d) of the Securities Exchange Act of 1934

Date of Report (Date of earliest event reported) _____

_____

(Exact name of registrant as specified in its charter)

| (State or other jurisdiction of incorporation) | (Commission File Number) | (IRS Employer Identification No.) |

(Address of principal executive offices)   (Zip Code)

Registrant's telephone number, including area code _____

_____

(Former name or former address, if changed since last report.)

Check the appropriate box below if the Form 8–K filing is intended to simultaneously satisfy the filing obligation of the registrant under any of the following provisions (*see* General Instruction A.2. below):

Written communications pursuant to Rule 425 under the Securities Act

☐ Soliciting material pursuant to Rule 14a–12 under the Exchange Act

☐ Pre-commencement communications pursuant to Rule 14d–2(b) under the Exchange Act

☐ Pre-commencement communications pursuant to Rule 13e–4(c) under the Exchange Act

Securities registered pursuant to Section 12(b) of the Act:

Title of each class	Trading symbol(s)	Name of each exchange on which registered

Indicate by check mark whether the registrant is an emerging growth company as defined in Rule 405 of the Securities Act of 1933 or Rule 12b–2 of the Securities Exchange Act of 1934.

Emerging growth company ☐

If an emerging growth company, indicate by check mark if the registrant has elected not to use the extended transition period for complying with any new or revised financial accounting standards provided pursuant to Section 13(a) of the Exchange Act. ☐

FORM 8–K

GENERAL INSTRUCTIONS

A. Rules as to Use of Form 8–K

1. Form 8–K shall be used for current reports under section 13 or 15(d) of the Securities Exchange Act of 1934, filed pursuant to Rule 13a–11 or Rule 15d–11, and for reports of nonpublic information required to be disclosed by Regulation FD.

2. Form 8–K may be used by a registrant to satisfy its filing obligations pursuant to Rule 425 under the Securities Act, regarding written communications related to business combination transactions, or Rule 14a–12(b) or Rule 14d–2(b) under the Exchange Act, relating to soliciting materials and pre-commencement communications pursuant to tender offers, respectively, provided that the Form 8–K filing satisfies all the substantive requirements of those rules (other than the Rule 425(c) requirement to include certain specified information in any prospectus filed pursuant to such rule). Such filing is also deemed to be filed pursuant to any rule for which the box is checked. A registrant is not required to check the box in connection with Rule 14a–12(b) or Rule 14d–2(b) if the communication is filed pursuant to Rule 425. Communications filed pursuant to Rule 425 are deemed filed under the other applicable items. See Note 2 to Rule 425, Rule 14a–12(b) and Instruction 2 to Rule 14d–2(b)(2).

B. Events to Be Reported and Time for Filing of Reports

1. A report on this form is required to be filed or furnished, as applicable, upon the occurrence of any one or more of the events specified in the items in Items 1–6 and 9 of this form. Unless otherwise specified, a report is to be filed or furnished within four business days after occurrence of the event. If the event occurs on a Saturday, Sunday or holiday on which the Commission is not open for business, then the four business day period shall begin to run on, and include, the first business day thereafter. A registrant either furnishing a report on this form under Item 7.01 (Regulation FD Disclosure) or electing to file a report on this form under Item 8.01 (Other Events) solely to satisfy its obligations under Regulation FD must furnish such report or make such filing, as applicable, in accordance with the requirements of Rule 100(a) of Regulation FD, including the deadline for furnishing or filing such report. A report pursuant to Item 5.08 is to be filed within four business days after the registrant determines the anticipated meeting date.

2. The information in a report furnished pursuant to Item 2.02 (Results of Operations and Financial Condition) or Item 7.01 (Regulation FD Disclosure) shall not be deemed to be "filed" for purposes of Section 18 of the Exchange Act or otherwise subject to the liabilities of that section, unless the registrant specifically states that the information is to be considered "filed" under the Exchange Act or incorporates it by reference into a filing under the Securities Act or the Exchange Act. If a report on Form 8–K contains disclosures under Item 2.02 or Item 7.01, whether or not the report contains disclosures regarding other items, all exhibits to such report relating to Item 2.02 or Item 7.01 will be deemed furnished, and not filed, unless the registrant specifies, under Item 9.01 (Financial Statements and Exhibits), which exhibits, or portions of exhibits, are intended to be deemed filed rather than furnished pursuant to this instruction.

3. If the registrant previously has reported substantially the same information as required by this form, the registrant need not make an additional report of the information on this form. To the extent that an item calls for disclosure of developments concerning a previously reported event or transaction, any information required in the new report or amendment about the previously reported event or transaction may be provided by incorporation by reference to the previously filed report. The term *previously reported* is defined in Rule 12b–2.

4. Copies of agreements, amendments or other documents or instruments required to be filed pursuant to Form 8–K are not required to be filed or furnished as exhibits to the Form 8–K unless specifically required to be filed or furnished by the applicable Item. This instruction does not affect the requirement to otherwise file such agreements, amendments or other documents or instruments, including as exhibits to registration statements and periodic reports pursuant to the requirements of Item 601 of Regulation S–K.

5. When considering current reporting on this form, particularly of other events of material importance pursuant to Item 7.01 (Regulation FD Disclosure) and Item 8.01(Other Events), registrants should have due regard for the accuracy, completeness and currency of the information in registration statements filed under the Securities Act which incorporate by reference information in reports filed pursuant to the Exchange Act, including reports on this form.

6.   A registrant's report under Item 7.01 (Regulation FD Disclosure) or Item 8.01 (Other Events) will not be deemed an admission as to the materiality of any information in the report that is required to be disclosed solely by Regulation FD.

C.   Application of General Rules and Regulations

1.   The General Rules and Regulations under the Act contain certain general requirements which are applicable to reports on any form. These general requirements should be carefully read and observed in the preparation and filing of reports on this form.

2.   Particular attention is directed to Regulation 12B which contains general requirements regarding matters such as the kind and size of paper to be used, the legibility of the report, the information to be given whenever the title of securities is required to be stated, and the filing of the report. The definitions contained in Rule 12b–2 should be especially noted. See also Regulations 13A and 15D.

D.   Preparation of Report

This form is not to be used as a blank form to be filled in, but only as a guide in the preparation of the report on paper meeting the requirements of Rule 12b–12. The report shall contain the numbers and captions of all applicable items, but the text of such items may be omitted, provided the answers thereto are prepared in the manner specified in Rule 12b–13. To the extent that Item 1.01 and one or more other items of the form are applicable, registrants need not provide the number and caption of Item 1.01 so long as the substantive disclosure required by Item 1.01 is disclosed in the report and the number and caption of the other applicable item(s) are provided. All items that are not required to be answered in a particular report may be omitted and no reference thereto need be made in the report. All instructions should also be omitted.

E.   Signature and Filing of Report

Three complete copies of the report, including any financial statements, exhibits or other papers or documents filed as a part thereof, and five additional copies which need not include exhibits, shall be filed with the Commission. At least one complete copy of the report, including any financial statements, exhibits or other papers or documents filed as a part thereof, shall be filed, with each exchange on which any class of securities of the registrant is registered. At least one complete copy of the report filed with the Commission and one such copy filed with each exchange shall be manually signed. Copies not manually signed shall bear typed or printed signatures.

F.   Incorporation by Reference

If the registrant makes available to its stockholders or otherwise publishes, within the period prescribed for filing the report, a press release or other document or statement containing information meeting some or all of the requirements of this form, the information called for may be incorporated by reference to such published document or statement, in answer or partial answer to any item or items of this form, provided copies thereof are filed as an exhibit to the report on this form.

G.   Use of This Form by Asset-Backed Issuers.

The following applies to registrants that are asset-backed issuers. Terms used in this General Instruction G. have the same meaning as in Item 1101 of Regulation AB.

1.   *Reportable Events That May Be Omitted.* The registrant need not file a report on this Form upon the occurrence of any one or more of the events specified in the following:

(a)   Item 2.01, Completion of Acquisition or Disposition of Assets;

(b)   Item 2.02, Results of Operations and Financial Condition;

(c)   Item 2.03, Creation of a Direct Financial Obligation or an Obligation under an Off-Balance Sheet Arrangement of a Registrant;

(d)   Item 2.05, Costs Associated with Exit or Disposal Activities;

(e)   Item 2.06, Material Impairments;

(f)   Item 3.01, Notice of Delisting or Failure to Satisfy a Continued Listing Rule or Standard; Transfer of Listing;

(g)   Item 3.02, Unregistered Sales of Equity Securities;

(h)   Item 4.01, Changes in Registrant's Certifying Accountant;

(i)   Item 4.02, Non-Reliance on Previously Issued Financial Statements or a Related Audit Report or Completed Interim Review;

(j)   Item 5.01, Changes in Control of Registrant;

(k)   Item 5.02, Departure of Directors or Principal Officers; Election of Directors; Appointment of Principal Officers;

(*l*)   Item 5.04, Temporary Suspension of Trading Under Registrant's Employee Benefit Plans; and

(m)   Item 5.05, Amendments to the Registrant's Code of Ethics, or Waiver of a Provision of the Code of Ethics.

2.   *Additional Disclosure for the Form 8-K Cover Page.* Immediately after the name of the issuing entity on the cover page of the Form 8-K, as separate line items, identify the exact name of the depositor as specified in its charter and the exact name of the sponsor as specified in its charter. Include a Central Index Key number for the depositor and the issuing entity, and if available, the sponsor.

3.   *Signatures.* The Form 8-K must be signed by the depositor. In the alternative, the Form 8-K may be signed on behalf of the issuing entity by a duly authorized representative of the servicer. If multiple servicers are involved in servicing the pool assets, a duly authorized representative of the master servicer (or entity performing the equivalent function) must sign if a representative of the servicer is to sign the report on behalf of the issuing entity.

INFORMATION TO BE INCLUDED IN THE REPORT

Section 1—Registrant's Business and Operations

Item 1.01.   Entry into a Material Definitive Agreement

(a)   If the registrant has entered into a material definitive agreement not made in the ordinary course of business of the registrant, or into any amendment of such agreement that is material to the registrant, disclose the following information:

(1)   the date on which the agreement was entered into or amended, the identity of the parties to the agreement or amendment and a brief description of any material relationship between the registrant or its affiliates and any of the parties, other than in respect of the material definitive agreement or amendment; and

(2)   a brief description of the terms and conditions of the agreement or amendment that are material to the registrant.

(b)   For purposes of this Item 1.01, a *material definitive agreement* means an agreement that provides for obligations that are material to and enforceable against the registrant, or rights that are material to the registrant and enforceable by the registrant against one or more other parties to the agreement, in each case whether or not subject to conditions.

Instructions.

1.   Any material definitive agreement of the registrant not made in the ordinary course of the registrant's business must be disclosed under this Item 1.01. An agreement is deemed to be not made in the ordinary course of a registrant's business even if the agreement is such as ordinarily accompanies the kind of business conducted by the registrant if it involves the subject matter identified in Item 601(b)(10)(ii)(A)—(D) of Regulation S-K. An agreement involving the subject matter identified in Item 601(b)(10)(iii)(A) or (B) need not be disclosed under this Item.

2.   A registrant must provide disclosure under this Item 1.01 if the registrant succeeds as a party to the agreement or amendment to the agreement by assumption or assignment (other than in connection with a merger or acquisition or similar transaction).

3.   With respect to asset-backed securities, as defined in Item 1101 of Regulation AB, disclosure is required under this Item 1.01 regarding the entry into or an amendment to a definitive agreement that is material to the

asset-backed securities transaction, even if the registrant is not a party to such agreement (e.g., a servicing agreement with a servicer contemplated by Item 1108(a)(3) of Regulation AB).

4.   To the extent a material definitive agreement is filed as an exhibit under this Item 1.01, schedules (or similar attachments) to the exhibits are not required to be filed unless they contain information material to an investment or voting decision and that information is not otherwise disclosed in the exhibit or the disclosure document. Each exhibit filed must contain a list briefly identifying the contents of all omitted schedules. Registrants need not prepare a separate list of omitted information if such information is already included within the exhibit in a manner that conveys the subject matter of the omitted schedules and attachments. In addition, the registrant must provide a copy of any omitted schedule to the Commission or its staff upon request.

5.   To the extent a material definitive agreement is filed as an exhibit under this Item 1.01, the registrant may redact information from the exhibit if disclosure of such information would constitute a clearly unwarranted invasion of personal privacy (e.g., disclosure of bank account numbers, social security numbers, home addresses and similar information).

6.   To the extent a material definitive agreement is filed as an exhibit under this Item 1.01, the registrant may redact specific provisions or terms of the exhibit if the registrant customarily and actually treats that information as private or confidential and if the omitted information is not material, provided that the registrant intends to incorporate by reference this filing into its future periodic reports or registration statements, as applicable, in satisfaction of Item 601(b)(10) of Regulation S–K. If it does so, the registrant should mark the exhibit index to indicate that portions of the exhibit have been omitted and include a prominent statement on the first page of the redacted exhibit that certain identified information has been excluded from the exhibit because it is both not material and is the type that the registrant treats as private or confidential. The registrant also must include brackets indicating where the information is omitted from the filed version of the exhibit. If requested by the Commission or its staff, the registrant must promptly provide on a supplemental basis an unredacted copy of the exhibit and its materiality and privacy or confidentiality analyses. Upon evaluation of the registrant's supplemental materials, the Commission or its staff may require the registrant to amend its filing to include in the exhibit any previously redacted information that is not adequately supported by the registrant's analyses. The registrant may request confidential treatment of the supplemental material submitted under this instruction pursuant to Rule 83 (§ 200.83) while it is in the possession of the Commission or its staff. After completing its review of the supplemental information, the Commission or its staff will return or destroy it if the registrant complies with the procedures outlined in Rules 418 or 12b–4.

If requested by the Commission or its staff, the registrant must promptly provide an unredacted copy of the exhibit on a supplemental basis. The Commission or its staff also may request the registrant to provide its materiality and competitive harm analyses on a supplemental basis. Upon evaluation of the registrant's supplemental materials, the Commission or its staff may request the registrant to amend its filing to include in the exhibit any previously redacted information that is not adequately supported by the registrant's materiality and competitive harm analyses.

The registrant may request confidential treatment of the supplemental material submitted under Instruction 6 of this Item pursuant to Rule 83 while it is in the possession of the Commission or its staff. After completing its review of the supplemental information, the Commission or its staff will return or destroy it at the request of the registrant, if the registrant complies with the procedures outlined in Rules 418 of the Securities Act or 12b–4 of the Exchange Act.

Item 1.02.   Termination of a Material Definitive Agreement

(a)   If a material definitive agreement which was not made in the ordinary course of business of the registrant and to which the registrant is a party is terminated otherwise than by expiration of the agreement on its stated termination date, or as a result of all parties completing their obligations under such agreement, and such termination of the agreement is material to the registrant, disclose the following information:

(1)   the date of the termination of the material definitive agreement, the identity of the parties to the agreement and a brief description of any material relationship between the registrant or its affiliates and any of the parties other than in respect of the material definitive agreement;

(2)   a brief description of the terms and conditions of the agreement that are material to the registrant;

(3)   a brief description of the material circumstances surrounding the termination; and

(4) any material early termination penalties incurred by the registrant.

(b) For purposes of this Item 1.02, the term *material definitive agreement* shall have the same meaning as set forth in Item 1.01(b).

Instructions.

1. No disclosure is required solely by reason of this Item 1.02 during negotiations or discussions regarding termination of a material definitive agreement unless and until the agreement has been terminated.

2. No disclosure is required solely by reason of this Item 1.02 if the registrant believes in good faith that the material definitive agreement has not been terminated, unless the registrant has received a notice of termination pursuant to the terms of agreement.

3. With respect to asset-backed securities, as defined in Item 1101 of Regulation AB, disclosure is required under this Item 1.02 regarding the termination of a definitive agreement that is material to the asset-backed securities transaction (otherwise than by expiration of the agreement on its stated termination date or as a result of all parties completing their obligations under such agreement), even if the registrant is not a party to such agreement (e.g., a servicing agreement with a servicer contemplated by Item 1108(a)(3) of Regulation AB).

Item 1.03. Bankruptcy or Receivership

(a) If a receiver, fiscal agent or similar officer has been appointed for a registrant or its parent, in a proceeding under the U.S. Bankruptcy Code or in any other proceeding under state or federal law in which a court or governmental authority has assumed jurisdiction over substantially all of the assets or business of the registrant or its parent, or if such jurisdiction has been assumed by leaving the existing directors and officers in possession but subject to the supervision and orders of a court or governmental authority, disclose the following information:

(1) the name or other identification of the proceeding;

(2) the identity of the court or governmental authority;

(3) the date that jurisdiction was assumed; and

(4) the identity of the receiver, fiscal agent or similar officer and the date of his or her appointment.

(b) If an order confirming a plan of reorganization, arrangement or liquidation has been entered by a court or governmental authority having supervision or jurisdiction over substantially all of the assets or business of the registrant or its parent, disclose the following:

(1) the identity of the court or governmental authority;

(2) the date that the order confirming the plan was entered by the court or governmental authority;

(3) a summary of the material features of the plan and, pursuant to Item 9.01 (Financial Statements and Exhibits), a copy of the plan as confirmed;

(4) the number of shares or other units of the registrant or its parent issued and outstanding, the number reserved for future issuance in respect of claims and interests filed and allowed under the plan, and the aggregate total of such numbers; and

(5) information as to the assets and liabilities of the registrant or its parent as of the date that the order confirming the plan was entered, or a date as close thereto as practicable.

Instructions.

1. The information called for in paragraph (b)(5) of this Item 1.03 may be presented in the form in which it was furnished to the court or governmental authority.

2. With respect to asset-backed securities, disclosure also is required under this Item 1.03 if the depositor (or servicer if the servicer signs the report on Form 10–K of the issuing entity) becomes aware of any instances described in paragraph (a) or (b) of this Item with respect to the sponsor, depositor, servicer contemplated by Item 1108(a)(3) of Regulation AB, trustee, significant obligor, enhancement or support provider contemplated by Items 1114(b) or 1115 of Regulation AB or other material party contemplated by Item 1101(d)(1) of Regulation AB. Terms used in this Instruction 2 have the same meaning as in Item 1101 of Regulation AB.

Item 1.04.   Mine Safety—Reporting of Shutdowns and Patterns of Violations

(a)   If the registrant or a subsidiary of the registrant has received, with respect to a coal or other mine of which the registrant or a subsidiary of the registrant is an operator

• an imminent danger order issued under section 107(a) of the Federal Mine Safety and Health Act of 1977;

• a written notice from the Mine Safety and Health Administration that the coal or other mine has a pattern of violations of mandatory health or safety standards that are of such nature as could have significantly and substantially contributed to the cause and effect of coal or other mine health or safety hazards under section 104(e) of such Act; or

• a written notice from the Mine Safety and Health Administration that the coal or other mine has the potential to have such a pattern,

disclose the following information:

(1)   The date of receipt by the issuer or a subsidiary of such order or notice.

(2)   The category of the order or notice.

(3)   The name and location of the mine involved.

Instructions to Item 1.04.

1.   The term *"coal or other mine"* means a coal or other mine, as defined in section 3 of the Federal Mine Safety and Health Act of 1977, that is subject to the provisions of such Act.

2.   The term *"operator"* has the meaning given the term in section 3 of the Federal Mine Safety and Health Act of 1977.

Section 2—Financial Information

Item 2.01.   Completion of Acquisition or Disposition of Assets

If the registrant or any of its majority-owned subsidiaries has completed the acquisition or disposition of a significant amount of assets, otherwise than in the ordinary course of business, disclose the following information:

(a)   the date of completion of the transaction;

(b)   a brief description of the assets involved;

(c)   the identity of the person(s) from whom the assets were acquired or to whom they were sold and the nature of any material relationship, other than in respect of the transaction, between such person(s) and the registrant or any of its affiliates, or any director or officer of the registrant, or any associate of any such director or officer;

(d)   the nature and amount of consideration given or received for the assets and, if any material relationship is disclosed pursuant to paragraph (c) of this Item 2.01, the formula or principle followed in determining the amount of such consideration;

(e)   if the transaction being reported is an acquisition and if a material relationship exists between the registrant or any of its affiliates and the source(s) of the funds used in the acquisition, the identity of the source(s) of the funds unless all or any part of the consideration used is a loan made in the ordinary course of business by a bank as defined by Section 3(a)(6) of the Act, in which case the identity of such bank may be omitted provided the registrant; and

(1)   has made a request for confidentiality pursuant to Section 13(d)(1)(B) of the Act; and

(2)   states in the report that the identity of the bank has been so omitted and filed separately with the Commission; and

(f)   If the registrant was a shell company, other than a business combination related shell company, as those terms are defined in Rule 12b–2 under the Exchange Act, immediately before the transaction, the information that would be required if the registrant were filing a general form for registration of securities on Form 10 reflecting all classes of the registrant's securities subject to the reporting requirements of Section

13 or Section 15(d) of such Act upon consummation of the transaction, with such information reflecting the registrant and its securities upon consummation of the transaction. Notwithstanding General Instruction B.3. to Form 8–K, if any disclosure required by this Item 2.01(f) is previously reported, as that term is defined in Rule 12b–2 under the Exchange Act, the registrant may identify the filing in which that disclosure is included instead of including that disclosure in this report.

Instructions.

1.   No information need be given as to:

(i)   any transaction between any person and any wholly-owned subsidiary of such person;

(ii)   any transaction between two or more wholly-owned subsidiaries of any person; or

(iii)   the redemption or other acquisition of securities from the public, or the sale or other disposition of securities to the public, by the issuer of such securities or by a wholly-owned subsidiary of that issuer.

2.   The term *acquisition* includes every purchase, acquisition by lease, exchange, merger, consolidation, succession or other acquisition, except that the term does not include the construction or development of property by or for the registrant or its subsidiaries or the acquisition of materials for such purpose. The term *disposition* includes every sale, disposition by lease, exchange, merger, consolidation, mortgage, assignment or hypothecation of assets, whether for the benefit of creditors or otherwise, abandonment, destruction, or other disposition.

3.   The information called for by this Item 2.01 is to be given as to each transaction or series of related transactions of the size indicated. The acquisition or disposition of securities is deemed the indirect acquisition or disposition of the assets represented by such securities if it results in the acquisition or disposition of control of such assets.

4.   An acquisition or disposition shall be deemed to involve a significant amount of assets:

(i)   if the registrant's and its other subsidiaries' equity in the net book value of such assets or the amount paid or received for the assets upon such acquisition or disposition exceeded 10% of the total assets of the registrant and its consolidated subsidiaries; or

(ii)   if it involved a business (see 17 CFR § 210.11–01(d)) that is significant (see 17 CFR § 210.11–01(b)).

Acquisitions of individually insignificant businesses are not required to be reported pursuant to this Item 2.01 unless they are related businesses (see 17 CFR § 210.3–05(a)(3)) and are significant in the aggregate.

5.   Attention is directed to the requirements in Item 9.01 (Financial Statements and Exhibits) with respect to the filing of:

(i)   financial statements of businesses acquired;

(ii)   *pro forma* financial information; and

(iii)   copies of the plans of acquisition or disposition as exhibits to the report.

Item 2.02.   Results of Operations and Financial Condition

(a)   If a registrant, or any person acting on its behalf, makes any public announcement or release (including any update of an earlier announcement or release) disclosing material non-public information regarding the registrant's results of operations or financial condition for a completed quarterly or annual fiscal period, the registrant shall disclose the date of the announcement or release, briefly identify the announcement or release and include the text of that announcement or release as an exhibit.

(b)   A Form 8–K is not required to be furnished to the Commission under this Item 2.02 in the case of disclosure of material non-public information that is disclosed orally, telephonically, by webcast, by broadcast, or by similar means if:

(1)   the information is provided as part of a presentation that is complementary to, and initially occurs within 48 hours after, a related, written announcement or release that has been furnished on Form 8–K pursuant to this Item 2.02 prior to the presentation;

(2)   the presentation is broadly accessible to the public by dial-in conference call, by webcast, by broadcast or by similar means;

(3)   the financial and other statistical information contained in the presentation is provided on the registrant's website, together with any information that would be required under Rule 100 under Regulation G; and

(4)   the presentation was announced by a widely disseminated press release, that included instructions as to when and how to access the presentation and the location on the registrant's Web site where the information would be available.

Instructions.

1.   The requirements of this Item 2.02 are triggered by the disclosure of material non-public information regarding a completed fiscal year or quarter. Release of additional or updated material non-public information regarding a completed fiscal year or quarter would trigger an additional Item 2.02 requirement.

2.   The requirements of paragraph (e)(1)(i) of Item 10 of Regulation S–K shall apply to disclosures under this Item 2.02.

3.   Issuers that make earnings announcements or other disclosures of material non-public information regarding a completed fiscal year or quarter in an interim or annual report to shareholders are permitted to specify which portion of the report contains the information required to be furnished under this Item 2.02.

4.   This Item 2.02 does not apply in the case of a disclosure that is made in a quarterly report filed with the Commission on Form 10–Q or an annual report filed with the Commission on Form 10–K.

Item 2.03.   Creation of a Direct Financial Obligation or an Obligation Under an Off-Balance Sheet Arrangement of a Registrant

(a)   If the registrant becomes obligated on a direct financial obligation that is material to the registrant, disclose the following information:

(1)   the date on which the registrant becomes obligated on the direct financial obligation and a brief description of the transaction or agreement creating the obligation;

(2)   the amount of the obligation, including the terms of its payment and, if applicable, a brief description of the material terms under which it may be accelerated or increased and the nature of any recourse provisions that would enable the registrant to recover from third parties; and

(3)   a brief description of the other terms and conditions of the transaction or agreement that are material to the registrant.

(b)   If the registrant becomes directly or contingently liable for an obligation that is material to the registrant arising out of an off-balance sheet arrangement, disclose the following information:

(1)   the date on which the registrant becomes directly or contingently liable on the obligation and a brief description of the transaction or agreement creating the arrangement and obligation;

(2)   a brief description of the nature and amount of the obligation of the registrant under the arrangement, including the material terms whereby it may become a direct obligation, if applicable, or may be accelerated or increased and the nature of any recourse provisions that would enable the registrant to recover from third parties;

(3)   the maximum potential amount of future payments (undiscounted) that the registrant may be required to make, if different; and

(4)   a brief description of the other terms and conditions of the obligation or arrangement that are material to the registrant.

(c)   For purposes of this Item 2.03, *direct financial obligation* means any of the following:

(1)   a long-term debt obligation, as defined in Item 303(a)(5)(ii)(A) of Regulation S–K;

(2)   a capital lease obligation, as defined in Item 303(a)(5)(ii)(B) of Regulation S–K;

(3)   an operating lease obligation, as defined in Item 303(a)(5)(ii)(C) of Regulation S–K; or

(4)   a short-term debt obligation that arises other than in the ordinary course of business.

(d)   For purposes of this Item 2.03, *off-balance sheet arrangement* has the meaning set forth in Item 303(a)(4)(ii) of Regulation S–K.

(e)   For purposes of this Item 2.03, *short-term debt obligation* means a payment obligation under a borrowing arrangement that is scheduled to mature within one year, or, for those registrants that use the operating cycle concept of working capital, within a registrant's operating cycle that is longer than one year, as discussed in Accounting Research Bulletin No. 43, Chapter 3A, *Working Capital*.

Instructions.

1.   A registrant has no obligation to disclose information under this Item 2.03 until the registrant enters into an agreement enforceable against the registrant, whether or not subject to conditions, under which the direct financial obligation will arise or be created or issued. If there is no such agreement, the registrant must provide the disclosure within four business days after the occurrence of the closing or settlement of the transaction or arrangement under which the direct financial obligation arises or is created.

2.   A registrant must provide the disclosure required by paragraph (b) of this Item 2.03 whether or not the registrant is also a party to the transaction or agreement creating the contingent obligation arising under the off-balance sheet arrangement. In the event that neither the registrant nor any affiliate of the registrant is also a party to the transaction or agreement creating the contingent obligation arising under the off-balance sheet arrangement in question, the four business day period for reporting the event under this Item 2.03 shall begin on the earlier of (i) the fourth business day after the contingent obligation is created or arises, and (ii) the day on which an executive officer, as defined in Rule 3b–7 under the Securities Exchange Act of 1934, of the registrant becomes aware of the contingent obligation.

3.   In the event that an agreement, transaction or arrangement requiring disclosure under this Item 2.03 comprises a facility, program or similar arrangement that creates or may give rise to direct financial obligations of the registrant in connection with multiple transactions, the registrant shall:

    (i)   disclose the entering into of the facility, program or similar arrangement if the entering into of the facility is material to the registrant; and

    (ii)   as direct financial obligations arise or are created under the facility or program, disclose the required information under this Item 2.03 to the extent that the obligations are material to the registrant (including when a series of previously undisclosed individually immaterial obligations become material in the aggregate).

4.   For purposes of Item 2.03(b)(3), the maximum amount of future payments shall not be reduced by the effect of any amounts that may possibly be recovered by the registrant under recourse or collateralization provisions in any guarantee agreement, transaction or arrangement.

5.   If the obligation required to be disclosed under this Item 2.03 is a security, or a term of a security, that has been or will be sold pursuant to an effective registration statement of the registrant, the registrant is not required to file a Form 8–K pursuant to this Item 2.03, *provided* that the prospectus relating to that sale contains the information required by this Item 2.03 and is filed within the required time period under Securities Act Rule 424.

Item 2.04.   Triggering Events That Accelerate or Increase a Direct Financial Obligation or an Obligation Under an Off-Balance Sheet Arrangement

(a)   If a triggering event causing the increase or acceleration of a direct financial obligation of the registrant occurs and the consequences of the event, taking into account those described in paragraph (a)(4) of this Item 2.04, are material to the registrant, disclose the following information:

    (1)   the date of the triggering event and a brief description of the agreement or transaction under which the direct financial obligation was created and is increased or accelerated;

    (2)   a brief description of the triggering event;

    (3)   the amount of the direct financial obligation, as increased if applicable, and the terms of payment or acceleration that apply; and

    (4)   any other material obligations of the registrant that may arise, increase, be accelerated or become direct financial obligations as a result of the triggering event or the increase or acceleration of the direct financial obligation.

(b)   If a triggering event occurs causing an obligation of the registrant under an off-balance sheet arrangement to increase or be accelerated, or causing a contingent obligation of the registrant under an off-balance sheet arrangement to become a direct financial obligation of the registrant, and the consequences of the event, taking into account those described in paragraph (b)(4) of this Item 2.04, are material to the registrant, disclose the following information:

(1)   the date of the triggering event and a brief description of the off-balance sheet arrangement;

(2)   a brief description of the triggering event;

(3)   the nature and amount of the obligation, as increased if applicable, and the terms of payment or acceleration that apply; and

(4)   any other material obligations of the registrant that may arise, increase, be accelerated or become direct financial obligations of the registrant as a result of the triggering event or the increase or acceleration of the obligation under the off-balance sheet arrangement or its becoming a direct financial obligation of the registrant.

(c)   For purposes of this Item 2.04, the term *direct financial obligation* has the meaning provided in Item 2.03 of this form, but shall also include an obligation arising out of an off-balance sheet arrangement that is accrued under FASB Statement of Financial Accounting Standards No. 5 *Accounting for Contingencies* (SFAS No. 5) as a probable loss contingency.

(d)   For purposes of this Item 2.04, the term *off-balance sheet arrangement* has the meaning provided in Item 2.03 of this form.

(e)   For purposes of this Item 2.04, a *triggering event* is an event, including an event of default, event of acceleration or similar event, as a result of which a direct financial obligation of the registrant or an obligation of the registrant arising under an off-balance sheet arrangement is increased or becomes accelerated or as a result of which a contingent obligation of the registrant arising out of an off-balance sheet arrangement becomes a direct financial obligation of the registrant.

Instructions.

1.   Disclosure is required if a triggering event occurs in respect of an obligation of the registrant under an off-balance sheet arrangement and the consequences are material to the registrant, whether or not the registrant is also a party to the transaction or agreement under which the triggering event occurs.

2.   No disclosure is required under this Item 2.04 unless and until a triggering event has occurred in accordance with the terms of the relevant agreement, transaction or arrangement, including, if required, the sending to the registrant of notice of the occurrence of a triggering event pursuant to the terms of the agreement, transaction or arrangement and the satisfaction of all conditions to such occurrence, except the passage of time.

3.   No disclosure is required solely by reason of this Item 2.04 if the registrant believes in good faith that no triggering event has occurred, unless the registrant has received a notice described in Instruction 2 to this Item 2.04.

4.   Where a registrant is subject to an obligation arising out of an off-balance sheet arrangement, whether or not disclosed pursuant to Item 2.03 of this form, if a triggering event occurs as a result of which under that obligation an accrual for a probable loss is required under SFAS No. 5, the obligation arising out of the off-balance sheet arrangement becomes a direct financial obligation as defined in this Item 2.04. In that situation, if the consequences as determined under Item 2.04(b) are material to the registrant, disclosure is required under this Item 2.04.

5.   With respect to asset-backed securities, as defined in, disclosure also is required under this Item 2.04 if an early amortization, performance trigger or other event, including an event of default, has occurred under the transaction agreements for the asset-backed securities that would materially alter the payment priority or distribution of cash flows regarding the asset-backed securities or the amortization schedule for the asset-backed securities. In providing the disclosure required by this Item, identify the changes to the payment priorities, flow of funds or asset-backed securities as a result. Disclosure is required under this Item whether or not the registrant is a party to the transaction agreement that results in the occurrence identified.

Item 2.05.   Costs Associated With Exit or Disposal Activities

If the registrant's board of directors, a committee of the board of directors or the officer or officers of the registrant authorized to take such action if board action is not required, commits the registrant to an exit or disposal plan, or otherwise disposes of a long-lived asset or terminates employees under a plan of termination described in paragraph 8 of FASB Statement of Financial Accounting Standards No. 146 *Accounting for Costs Associated with Exit or Disposal Activities* (SFAS No. 146), under which material charges will be incurred under generally accepted accounting principles applicable to the registrant, disclose the following information:

(a)   the date of the commitment to the course of action and a description of the course of action, including the facts and circumstances leading to the expected action and the expected completion date;

(b)   for each major type of cost associated with the course of action (for example, one-time termination benefits, contract termination costs and other associated costs), an estimate of the total amount or range of amounts expected to be incurred in connection with the action;

(c)   an estimate of the total amount or range of amounts expected to be incurred in connection with the action; and

(d)   the registrant's estimate of the amount or range of amounts of the charge that will result in future cash expenditures, *provided, however,* that if the registrant determines that at the time of filing it is unable in good faith to make a determination of an estimate required by paragraphs (b), (c) or (d) of this Item 2.05, no disclosure of such estimate shall be required; *provided further, however,* that in any such event, the registrant shall file an amended report on Form 8–K under this Item 2.05 within four business days after it makes a determination of such an estimate or range of estimates.

Item 2.06.   Material Impairments

If the registrant's board of directors, a committee of the board of directors or the officer or officers of the registrant authorized to take such action if board action is not required, concludes that a material charge for impairment to one or more of its assets, including, without limitation, impairments of securities or goodwill, is required under generally accepted accounting principles applicable to the registrant, disclose the following information:

(a)   the date of the conclusion that a material charge is required and a description of the impaired asset or assets and the facts and circumstances leading to the conclusion that the charge for impairment is required;

(b)   the registrant's estimate of the amount or range of amounts of the impairment charge; and

(c)   the registrant's estimate of the amount or range of amounts of the impairment charge that will result in future cash expenditures, *provided, however,* that if the registrant determines that at the time of filing it is unable in good faith to make a determination of an estimate required by paragraphs (b) or (c) of this Item 2.06, no disclosure of such estimate shall be required; *provided further, however,* that in any such event, the registrant shall file an amended report on Form 8–K under this Item 2.06 within four business days after it makes a determination of such an estimate or range of estimates.

Instruction.

No filing is required under this Item 2.06 if the conclusion is made in connection with the preparation, review or audit of financial statements required to be included in the next periodic report due to be filed under the Exchange Act, the periodic report is filed on a timely basis and such conclusion is disclosed in the report.

Section 3—Securities and Trading Markets

Item 3.01.   Notice of Delisting or Failure to Satisfy a Continued Listing Rule or Standard; Transfer of Listing

(a)   If the registrant has received notice from the national securities exchange or national securities association (or a facility thereof) that maintains the principal listing for any class of the registrant's common equity (as defined in Exchange Act Rule 12b–2) that:

- the registrant or such class of the registrant's securities does not satisfy a rule or standard for continued listing on the exchange or association;

- the exchange has submitted an application under Exchange Act Rule 12d2–2 to the Commission to delist such class of the registrant's securities; or

- the association has taken all necessary steps under its rules to delist the security from its automated inter-dealer quotation system,

the registrant must disclose:

    (i)   the date that the registrant received the notice;

    (ii)   the rule or standard for continued listing on the national securities exchange or national securities association that the registrant fails, or has failed to, satisfy; and

    (iii)   any action or response that, at the time of filing, the registrant has determined to take in response to the notice.

    (b)   If the registrant has notified the national securities exchange or national securities association (or a facility thereof) that maintains the principal listing for any class of the registrant's common equity (as defined in Exchange Act Rule 12b–2 that the registrant is aware of any material noncompliance with a rule or standard for continued listing on the exchange or association, the registrant must disclose):

    (i)   the date that the registrant provided such notice to the exchange or association;

    (ii)   the rule or standard for continued listing on the exchange or association that the registrant fails, or has failed, to satisfy; and

    (iii)   any action or response that, at the time of filing, the registrant has determined to take regarding its noncompliance.

    (c)   If the national securities exchange or national securities association (or a facility thereof) that maintains the principal listing for any class of the registrant's common equity (as defined in Exchange Act Rule 12b–2), in lieu of suspending trading in or delisting such class of the registrant's securities, issues a public reprimand letter or similar communication indicating that the registrant has violated a rule or standard for continued listing on the exchange or association, the registrant must state the date, and summarize the contents of the letter or communication.

    (d)   If the registrant's board of directors, a committee of the board of directors or the officer or officers of the registrant authorized to take such action if board action is not required, has taken definitive action to cause the listing of a class of its common equity to be withdrawn from the national securities exchange, or terminated from the automated inter-dealer quotation system of a registered national securities association, where such exchange or association maintains the principal listing for such class of securities, including by reason of a transfer of the listing or quotation to another securities exchange or quotation system, describe the action taken and state the date of the action.

Instructions.

1.   The registrant is not required to disclose any information required by paragraph (a) of this Item 3.01 where the delisting is a result of one of the following:

- the entire class of the security has been called for redemption, maturity or retirement; appropriate notice thereof has been given; if required by the terms of the securities, funds sufficient for the payment of all such securities have been deposited with an agency authorized to make such payments; and such funds have been made available to security holders;

- the entire class of the security has been redeemed or paid at maturity or retirement;

- the instruments representing the entire class of securities have come to evidence, by operation of law or otherwise, other securities in substitution therefor and represent no other right, except, if true, the right to receive an immediate cash payment (the right of dissenters to receive the appraised or fair value of their holdings shall not prevent the application of this provision); or

- all rights pertaining to the entire class of the security have been extinguished; provided, however, that where such an event occurs as the result of an order of a court or other governmental authority, the order shall be final, all applicable appeal periods shall have expired and no appeals shall be pending.

2.   A registrant must provide the disclosure required by paragraph (a) or (b) of this Item 3.01, as applicable, regarding any failure to satisfy a rule or standard for continued listing on the national securities exchange or national securities association (or a facility thereof) that maintains the principal listing for any class of the registrant's common equity (as defined in Exchange Act Rule 12b–2) even if the registrant has the benefit of a grace period or similar extension period during which it may cure the deficiency that triggers the disclosure requirement.

3.   Notices or other communications subsequent to an initial notice sent to, or by, a registrant under Item 3.01(a), (b) or (c) that continue to indicate that the registrant does not comply with the same rule or standard for continued listing that was the subject of the initial notice are not required to be filed, but may be filed voluntarily.

4.   Registrants whose securities are quoted exclusively (i.e., the securities are not otherwise listed on an exchange or association) on automated inter-dealer quotation systems are not subject to this Item 3.01 and such registrants are thus not required to file a Form 8–K pursuant to this Item 3.01 if the securities are no longer quoted on such quotation system. If a security is listed on an exchange or association and is also quoted on an automated inter-dealer quotation system, the registrant is subject to the disclosure obligations of Item 3.01 if any of the events specified in Item 3.01 occur.

Item 3.02.   Unregistered Sales of Equity Securities

(a)   If the registrant sells equity securities in a transaction that is not registered under the Securities Act, furnish the information set forth in paragraphs (a) and (c) through (e) of Item 701 of Regulation S–K. For purposes of determining the required filing date for the Form 8–K under this Item 3.02(a), the registrant has no obligation to disclose information under this Item 3.02 until the registrant enters into an agreement enforceable against the registrant, whether or not subject to conditions, under which the equity securities are to be sold. If there is no such agreement, the registrant must provide the disclosure within four business days after the occurrence of the closing or settlement of the transaction or arrangement under which the equity securities are to be sold.

(b)   No report need be filed under this Item 3.02 if the equity securities sold, in the aggregate since its last report filed under this Item 3.02 or its last periodic report, whichever is more recent, constitute less than 1% of the number of shares outstanding of the class of equity securities sold. In the case of a smaller reporting company no report need be filed if the equity securities sold, in the aggregate since its last report filed under this Item 3.02 or its last periodic report, whichever is more recent, constitute less than 5% of the number of shares outstanding of the class of equity securities sold.

Instructions.

1.   For purposes of this Item 3.02, "the number of shares outstanding" refers to the actual number of shares of equity securities of the class outstanding and does not include outstanding securities convertible into or exchangeable for such equity securities.

2.   A smaller reporting company is defined in Item 10(f)(1) of Regulation S–K.

Item 3.03.   Material Modification to Rights of Security Holders

(a)   If the constituent instruments defining the rights of the holders of any class of registered securities of the registrant have been materially modified, disclose the date of the modification, the title of the class of securities involved and briefly describe the general effect of such modification upon the rights of holders of such securities.

(b)   If the rights evidenced by any class of registered securities have been materially limited or qualified by the issuance or modification of any other class of securities by the registrant, briefly disclose the date of the issuance or modification, the general effect of the issuance or modification of such other class of securities upon the rights of the holders of the registered securities.

Instruction.

Working capital restrictions and other limitations upon the payment of dividends must be reported pursuant to this Item 3.03.

Section 4—Matters Related to Accountants and Financial Statements

Item 4.01.   Changes in Registrant's Certifying Accountant

(a)   If an independent accountant who was previously engaged as the principal accountant to audit the registrant's financial statements, or an independent accountant upon whom the principal accountant expressed reliance in its report regarding a significant subsidiary, resigns (or indicates that it declines to stand for re-appointment after completion of the current audit) or is dismissed, disclose the information required by Item 304(a)(1) of Regulation S–K, including compliance with Item 304(a)(3) of Regulation S–K.

(b)   If a new independent accountant has been engaged as either the principal accountant to audit the registrant's financial statements or as an independent accountant on whom the principal accountant is expected to express reliance in its report regarding a significant subsidiary, the registrant must disclose the information required by Item 304(a)(2) of Regulation S–K.

Instruction.

The resignation or dismissal of an independent accountant, or its refusal to stand for re-appointment, is a reportable event separate from the engagement of a new independent accountant. On some occasions, two reports on Form 8–K are required for a single change in accountants, the first on the resignation (or refusal to stand for re-appointment) or dismissal of the former accountant and the second when the new accountant is engaged. Information required in the second Form 8–K in such situations need not be provided to the extent that it has been reported previously in the first Form 8–K.

Item 4.02.   Non-Reliance on Previously Issued Financial Statements or a Related Audit Report or Completed Interim Review

(a)   If the registrant's board of directors, a committee of the board of directors or the officer or officers of the registrant authorized to take such action if board action is not required, concludes that any previously issued financial statements, covering one or more years or interim periods for which the registrant is required to provide financial statements under Regulation S–X should no longer be relied upon because of an error in such financial statements as addressed in Accounting Principles Board Opinion No. 20, as may be modified, supplemented or succeeded, disclose the following information:

(1)   the date of the conclusion regarding the non-reliance and an identification of the financial statements and years or periods covered that should no longer be relied upon;

(2)   a brief description of the facts underlying the conclusion to the extent known to the registrant at the time of filing; and

(3)   a statement of whether the audit committee, or the board of directors in the absence of an audit committee, or authorized officer or officers, discussed with the registrant's independent accountant the matters disclosed in the filing pursuant to this Item 4.02(a).

(b)   If the registrant is advised by, or receives notice from, its independent accountant that disclosure should be made or action should be taken to prevent future reliance on a previously issued audit report or completed interim review related to previously issued financial statements, disclose the following information:

(1)   the date on which the registrant was so advised or notified;

(2)   identification of the financial statements that should no longer be relied upon;

(3)   a brief description of the information provided by the accountant; and

(4)   a statement of whether the audit committee, or the board of directors in the absence of an audit committee, or authorized officer or officers, discussed with the independent accountant the matters disclosed in the filing pursuant to this Item 4.02(b).

(c)   If the registrant receives advisement or notice from its independent accountant requiring disclosure under paragraph (b) of this Item 4.02, the registrant must:

(1)   provide the independent accountant with a copy of the disclosures it is making in response to this Item 4.02 that the independent accountant shall receive no later than the day that the disclosures are filed with the Commission;

(2)   request the independent accountant to furnish to the registrant as promptly as possible a letter addressed to the Commission stating whether the independent accountant agrees with the statements made by the registrant in response to this Item 4.02 and, if not, stating the respects in which it does not agree; and

(3)   amend the registrant's previously filed Form 8–K by filing the independent accountant's letter as an exhibit to the filed Form 8–K no later than two business days after the registrant's receipt of the letter.

Section 5—Corporate Governance and Management

Item 5.01.   Changes in Control of Registrant

(a)   If, to the knowledge of the registrant's board of directors, a committee of the board of directors or authorized officer or officers of the registrant, a change in control of the registrant has occurred, furnish the following information:

(1)   the identity of the person(s) who acquired such control;

(2)   the date and a description of the transaction(s) which resulted in the change in control;

(3)   the basis of the control, including the percentage of voting securities of the registrant now beneficially owned directly or indirectly by the person(s) who acquired control;

(4)   the amount of the consideration used by such person(s);

(5)   the source(s) of funds used by the person(s), *unless* all or any part of the consideration used is a loan made in the ordinary course of business by a bank as defined by Section 3(a)(6) of the Act, in which case the identity of such bank may be omitted provided the person who acquired control:

(i)   has made a request for confidentiality pursuant to Section 13(d)(1)(B) of the Act; and

(ii)   states in the report that the identity of the bank has been so omitted and filed separately with the Commission.

(6)   the identity of the person(s) from whom control was assumed;

(7)   any arrangements or understandings among members of both the former and new control groups and their associates with respect to election of directors or other matters; and

(8)   if the registrant was a shell company, other than a business combination related shell company, as those terms are defined in Rule 12b–2 under the Exchange Act, immediately before the change in control, the information that would be required if the registrant were filing a general form for registration of securities on Form 10 under the Exchange Act reflecting all classes of the registrant's securities subject to the reporting requirements of Section 13 or Section 15(d) of such Act upon consummation of the change in control, with such information reflecting the registrant and its securities upon consummation of the transaction. Notwithstanding General Instruction B.3. to Form 8–K, if any disclosure required by this Item 5.01(a)(8) is previously reported, as that term is defined in Rule 12b–2 under the Exchange Act, the registrant may identify the filing in which that disclosure is included instead of including that disclosure in this report.

(b)   Furnish the information required by Item 403(c) of Regulation S–K.

Item 5.02.   Departure of Directors or Principal Officers; Election of Directors; Appointment of Principal Officers

(a)(1)   If a director has resigned or refuses to stand for re-election to the board of directors since the date of the last annual meeting of shareholders because of a disagreement with the registrant, known to an executive officer of the registrant, as defined in Rule 3b–7 under the Securities Exchange Act of 1934, on any matter relating to the registrant's operations, policies or practices, or if a director has been removed for cause from the board of directors, disclose the following information:

(i)   the date of such resignation, refusal to stand for re-election or removal;

(ii)   any positions held by the director on any committee of the board of directors at the time of the director's resignation, refusal to stand for re-election or removal; and

(iii)   a brief description of the circumstances representing the disagreement that the registrant believes caused, in whole or in part, the director's resignation, refusal to stand for re-election or removal.

(2)   If the director has furnished the registrant with any written correspondence concerning the circumstances surrounding his or her resignation, refusal or removal, the registrant shall file a copy of the document as an exhibit to the report on Form 8–K.

(3)   The registrant also must:

(i)   provide the director with a copy of the disclosures it is making in response to this Item 5.02 no later than the day the registrant file the disclosures with the Commission;

(ii)   provide the director with the opportunity to furnish the registrant as promptly as possible with a letter addressed to the registrant stating whether he or she agrees with the statements made by the registrant in response to this Item 5.02 and, if not, stating the respects in which he or she does not agree; and

(iii)   file any letter received by the registrant from the director with the Commission as an exhibit by an amendment to the previously filed Form 8–K within two business days after receipt by the registrant.

(b)   If the registrant's principal executive officer, president, principal financial officer, principal accounting officer, principal operating officer or any person performing similar functions, or any named executive officer, retires, resigns or is terminated from that position, or if a director retires, resigns, is removed, or refuses to stand for re-election (except in circumstances described in paragraph (a) of this Item 5.02), disclose the fact that the event has occurred and the date of the event.

(c)   If the registrant appoints a new principal executive officer, president, principal financial officer, principal accounting officer, principal operating officer, or person performing similar functions, disclose the following information with respect to the newly appointed officer:

(1)   the name and position of the newly appointed officer and the date of the appointment;

(2)   the information required by Items 401(b), (d), (e) and Item 404(a) of Regulation S–K; and

(3)   a brief description of any material plan, contract or arrangement (whether or not written) to which a covered officer is a party or in which he or she participates that is entered into or material amendment in connection with the triggering event or any grant or award to any such covered person or modification thereto, under any such plan, contract or arrangement in connection with any such event.

Instruction to paragraph (c). If the registrant intends to make a public announcement of the appointment other than by means of a report on Form 8–K, the registrant may delay filing the Form 8–K containing the disclosures required by this Item 5.02(c) until the day on which the registrant otherwise makes public announcement of the appointment of such officer.

(d)   If the registrant elects a new director, except by a vote of security holders at an annual meeting or special meeting convened for such purpose, disclose the following information:

(1)   the name of the newly elected director and the date of election;

(2)   a brief description of any arrangement or understanding between the new director and any other persons, naming such persons, pursuant to which such director was selected as a director;

(3)   the committees of the board of directors to which the new director has been, or at the time of this disclosure is expected to be, named; and

(4)   the information required by Item 404(a) of Regulation S–K.

(5)   a brief description of any material plan, contract or arrangement (whether or not written) to which the director is a party or in which he or she participates that is entered into or material amendment in connection with the triggering event or any grant or award to any such covered person or modification thereto, under any such plan, contract or arrangement in connection with any such event.

(e)   If the registrant enters into, adopts, or otherwise commences a material compensatory plan, contract or arrangement (whether or not written), as to which the registrant's principal executive officer, principal financial officer, or a named executive officer participates or is a party, or such compensatory plan, contract or arrangement is materially amended or modified, or a material grant or award under any such plan, contract or arrangement to any such person is made or materially modified, then the registrant shall provide a brief description of the terms and conditions of the plan, contract or arrangement and the amounts payable to the officer thereunder.

Instructions to paragraph (e).

1.   Disclosure under this Item 5.02(e) shall be required whether or not the specified event is in connection with events otherwise triggering disclosure pursuant to this Item 5.02.

2.   Grants or awards (or modifications thereto) made pursuant to a plan, contract or arrangement (whether involving cash or equity), that are materially consistent with the previously disclosed terms of such plan, contract or arrangement, need not be disclosed under this Item 5.02(e), provided the registrant has previously disclosed such terms and the grant, award or modification is disclosed when Item 402 of Regulation S–K requires such disclosure.

(f)(1)   If the salary or bonus of a named executive officer cannot be calculated as of the most recent practicable date and is omitted from the Summary Compensation Table as specified in Instruction 1 to Item 402(c)(2)(iii) and (iv) of Regulation S–K, disclose the appropriate information under this Item 5.02(f) when there is a payment, grant, award, decision or other occurrence as a result of which such amounts become calculable in whole or part. Disclosure under this Item 5.02(f) shall include a new total compensation figure for the named executive officer, using the new salary or bonus information to recalculate the information that was previously provided with respect to the named executive officer in the registrant's Summary Compensation Table for which the salary and bonus information was omitted in reliance on Instruction 1 to Item 402(c)(2)(iii) and (iv) of Regulation S–K.

(f)(2)   As specified in Instruction 6 to Item 402(u) of Regulation S–K (17 CFR 229.402(u)), disclosure under this Item 5.02(f) with respect to the salary or bonus of a principal executive officer shall include pay ratio disclosure pursuant to Item 402(u) of Regulation S–K calculated 294 using the new total compensation figure for the principal executive officer. Pay ratio disclosure is not required under this Item 5.02(f) until the omitted salary or bonus amounts for such principal executive officer become calculable in whole

Instructions to Item 5.02.

1.   The disclosure requirements of this Item 5.02 do not apply to a registrant that is a wholly-owned subsidiary of an issuer with a class of securities registered under Section 12 of the Exchange Act, or that is required to file reports under Section 15(d) of the Exchange Act.

2.   To the extent that any information called for in Item 5.02(c)(3) or Item 5.02(d)(3) or Item 5.02(d)(4) is not determined or is unavailable at the time of the required filing, the registrant shall include a statement this effect in the filing and then must file an amendment to its Form 8–K filing under this Item 5.02 containing such information within four business days after the information is determined or becomes available.

3.   The registrant need not provide information with respect to plans, contracts, and arrangements to the extent they do not discriminate in scope, terms or operation, in favor of executive officers or directors of the registrant and that are available generally to all salaried employees.

4.   For purposes of this Item, the term "named executive officer" shall refer to those executive officers for whom disclosure was required in the registrant's most recent filing with the Commission under the Securities Act or Exchange Act that required disclosure pursuant to Item 402(c) of Regulation S–K.

Item 5.03.   Amendments to Articles of Incorporation or Bylaws; Change in Fiscal Year

(a)   If a registrant with a class of equity securities registered under Section 12 of the Exchange Act amends its articles of incorporation or bylaws and a proposal for the amendment was not disclosed in a proxy statement or information statement filed by the registrant, disclose the following information:

(1)   The effective date of the amendment; and

(2)   A description of the provision adopted or changed by amendment and, if applicable, the previous provision.

(b)   If the registrant determines to change the fiscal year from that used in its most recent filing with the Commission other than by means of:

        (1)   A submission to a vote of security holders through the solicitation of proxies or otherwise; or

        (2)   An amendment to its articles of incorporation or bylaws, disclose the date of such determination, the date of the new fiscal year end and the form (for example, Form 10–K or Form 10–Q) on which the report covering the transition period will be filed.

Instruction to Item 5.03.

1.   Refer to Item 601(b)(3) of Regulation S–K regarding the filing of exhibits to this Item 5.03.

2.   With respect to asset-backed securities, as defined in Item 1101 of Regulation AB, disclosure is required under this Item 5.03 regarding any amendment to the governing documents of the issuing entity, regardless of whether the class of asset-backed securities is reporting under Section 13 or 15(d) of the Exchange Act.

Item 5.04.   Temporary Suspension of Trading Under Registrant's Employee Benefit Plans

(a)   No later than the fourth business day after which the registrant receives the notice required by section 101(i)(2)(E) of the Employment Retirement Income Security Act of 1974, or, if such notice is not received by the registrant, on the same date by which the registrant transmits a timely notice to an affected officer or director within the time period prescribed by Rule 104(b)(2)(i)(B) or 104(b)(2)(ii) of Regulation BTR, provide the information specified in Rule 104(b) and the date the registrant received the notice required by section 101(i)(2)(E) of the Employment Retirement Income Security Act of 1974, if applicable.

(b)   On the same date by which the registrant transmits a timely updated notice to an affected officer or director, as required by the time period under Rule 104(b)(2)(iii) of Regulation BTR, provide the information specified in Rule 104(b)(3)(iii).

Item 5.05.   Amendments to the Registrant's Code of Ethics, or Waiver of a Provision of the Code of Ethics

(a)   Briefly describe the date and nature of any amendment to a provision of the registrant's code of ethics that applies to the registrant's principal executive officer, principal financial officer, principal accounting officer or controller or persons performing similar functions and that relates to any element of the code of ethics definition enumerated in Item 406(b) of Regulation S–K.

(b)   If the registrant has granted a waiver, including an implicit waiver, from a provision of the code of ethics to an officer or person described in paragraph (a) of this Item 5.05, and the waiver relates to one or more of the elements of the code of ethics definition referred to in paragraph (a) of this Item 5.05, briefly describe the nature of the waiver, the name of the person to whom the waiver was granted, and the date of the waiver.

(c)   The registrant does not need to provide any information pursuant to this Item 5.05 if it discloses the required information on its Internet website within four business days following the date of the amendment or waiver and the registrant has disclosed in its most recently filed annual report its Internet address and intention to provide disclosure in this manner. If the registrant elects to disclose the information required by this Item 5.05 through its website, such information must remain available on the website for at least a 12-month period. Following the 12-month period, the registrant must retain the information for a period of not less than five years. Upon request, the registrant must furnish to the Commission or its staff a copy of any or all information retained pursuant to this requirement.

Instructions.

1.   The registrant does not need to disclose technical, administrative or other non-substantive amendments to its code of ethics.

2.   For purposes of this Item 5.05:

        (i)   The term *waiver* means the approval by the registrant of a material departure from a provision of the code of ethics; and

(ii)   The term *implicit waiver* means the registrant's failure to take action within a reasonable period of time regarding a material departure from a provision of the code of ethics that has been made known to an executive officer, as defined in Rule 3b–7 of the registrant.

Item 5.06.   Change in Shell Company Status

If a registrant that was a shell company, other than a business combination related shell company, as those terms are defined in Rule 12b–2 under the Exchange Act, has completed a transaction that has the effect of causing it to cease being a shell company, as defined in Rule 12b–2, disclose the material terms of the transaction. Notwithstanding General Instruction B.3. to Form 8–K, if any disclosure required by this Item 5.06 is previously reported, as that term is defined in Rule 12b–2 under the Exchange Act, the registrant may identify the filing in which that disclosure is included instead of including that disclosure in this report.

Item 5.07.   Submission of Matters to a Vote of Security Holders

If any matter was submitted to a vote of security holders, through the solicitation of proxies or otherwise, provide the following information:

(a)   The date of the meeting and whether it was an annual or special meeting. This information must be provided only if a meeting of security holders was held.

(b)   If the meeting involved the election of directors, the name of each director elected at the meeting, as well as a brief description of each other matter voted upon at the meeting; and state the number of votes cast for, against or withheld, as well as the number of abstentions and broker non-votes as to each such matter, including a separate tabulation with respect to each nominee for office. For the vote on the frequency of shareholder advisory votes on executive compensation required by section 14A(a)(2) of the Securities Exchange Act of 1934 and Rule 14a–21(b) under the Exchange Act of 1934, state the number of votes cast for each of 1 year, 2 years, and 3 years, as well as the number of abstentions.

(c)   A description of the terms of any settlement between the registrant and any other participant (as defined in Instruction 3 to Item 4 of Schedule 14A (17 CFR 240.14a–101)) terminating any solicitation subject to Rule 14a–12(c), including the cost or anticipated cost to the registrant.

(d)   No later than one hundred fifty calendar days after the end of the annual or other meeting of shareholders at which shareholders voted on the frequency of shareholder votes on the compensation of executives as required by section 14A(a)(2) of the Securities Exchange Act of 1934, but in no event later than sixty calendar days prior to the deadline for submission of shareholder proposals under Rule 240.14a–8 of the Exchange Act of 1934, as disclosed in the registrant's most recent proxy statement for an annual or other meeting of shareholders relating to the election of directors at which shareholders voted on the frequency of shareholder votes on the compensation of executives as required by section 14A(a)(2) of the Securities Exchange Act of 1934, by amendment to the most recent Form 8–K filed pursuant to (b) of this Item, disclose the company's decision in light of such vote as to how frequently the company will include a shareholder vote on the compensation of executives in its proxy materials until the next required vote on the frequency of shareholder votes on the compensation of executives.

Instruction 1 to Item 5.07. The four business day period for reporting the event under this Item 5.07, other than with respect to Item 5.07(d), shall begin to run on the day on which the meeting ended. * * *

Instruction 2 to Item 5.07. If any matter has been submitted to a vote of security holders otherwise than at a meeting of such security holders, corresponding information with respect to such submission shall be provided. The solicitation of any authorization or consent (other than a proxy to vote at a stockholders' meeting) with respect to any matter shall be deemed a submission of such matter to a vote of security holders within the meaning of this item.

Instruction 3 to Item 5.07. If the registrant did not solicit proxies and the board of directors as previously reported to the Commission was re-elected in its entirety, a statement to that effect in answer to paragraph (b) will suffice as an answer thereto regarding the election of directors.

Instruction 4 to Item 5.07. If the registrant has furnished to its security holders proxy soliciting material containing the information called for by paragraph (c), the paragraph may be answered by reference to the information contained in such material.

Instruction 5 to Item 5.07. A registrant may omit the information called for by this Item 5.07 if, on the date of the filing of its report on Form 8–K, the registrant meets the following conditions:

1. All of the registrant's equity securities are owned, either directly or indirectly, by a single person which is a reporting company under the Exchange Act and which has filed all the material required to be filed pursuant to Section 13, 14 or 15(d) thereof, as applicable; and

2. During the preceding thirty-six calendar months and any subsequent period of days, there has not been any material default in the payment of principal, interest, a sinking or purchase fund installment, or any other material default not cured within thirty days, with respect to any indebtedness of the registrant or its subsidiaries, and there has not been any material default in the payment of rentals under material long-term leases.

Item 5.08. Shareholder Director Nominations

(a) If the registrant did not hold an annual meeting the previous year, or if the date of this year's annual meeting has been changed by more than 30 calendar days from the date of the previous year's meeting, then the registrant is required to disclose the date by which a nominating shareholder or nominating shareholder group must submit the notice on Schedule 14N (§ 240.14n–101) required pursuant to Rule 14a–11(b)(10), which date shall be a reasonable time before the registrant mails its proxy materials for the meeting. Where a registrant is required to include shareholder director nominees in the registrant's proxy materials pursuant to either an applicable state or foreign law provision, or a provision in the registrant's governing documents, then the registrant is required to disclose the date by which a nominating shareholder or nominating shareholder group must submit the notice on Schedule 14N required pursuant to Rule 14a–18.

(b) If the registrant is a series company as defined in Rule 18f–2(a) under the Investment Company Act of 1940 (§ 270.18f–2 of this chapter), then the registrant is required to disclose in connection with the election of directors at an annual meeting of shareholders (or, in lieu of such an annual meeting, a special meeting of shareholders) the total number of shares of the registrant outstanding and entitled to be voted (or if the votes are to be cast on a basis other than one vote per share, then the total number of votes entitled to be voted and the basis for allocating such votes) on the election of directors at such meeting of shareholders as of the end of the most recent calendar quarter.

Section 6—Asset-Backed Securities

The Items in this rule apply only to asset-backed securities. Terms used in this rule have the same meaning as in Item 1101 of Regulation AB.

Item 6.01. ABS Informational and Computational Material

Report under this Item any ABS informational and computational material filed in, or as an exhibit to, this report.

Item 6.02. Change of Servicer or Trustee

If a servicer contemplated by Item 1108(a)(2) of Regulation AB or a trustee has resigned or has been removed, replaced or substituted, or if a new servicer contemplated by Item 1108(a)(2) of Regulation AB or trustee has been appointed, state the date the event occurred and the circumstances surrounding the change. In addition, provide the disclosure required by Item 1108(d) of Regulation AB, as applicable, regarding the servicer or trustee change. If a new servicer contemplated by Item 1108(a)(3) of this Regulation AB or a new trustee has been appointed, provide the information required by Item 1108(b) through (d) of Regulation AB regarding such servicer or Item 1109 of Regulation AB regarding such trustee, as applicable.

Instruction. To the extent that any information called for by this Item regarding such servicer or trustee is not determined or is unavailable at the time of the required filing, the registrant shall include a statement to this effect in the filing and then must file an amendment to its Form 8–K filing under this Item 6.02 containing such information within four business days after the information is determined or becomes available.

Item 6.03. Change in Credit Enhancement or Other External Support

(a) *Loss of existing enhancement or support.* If the depositor (or servicer if the servicer signs the report on Form 10–K of the issuing entity) becomes aware that any material enhancement or support specified in Item 1114(a)(1) through (3) of Regulation AB or Item 1115 of Regulation AB that was previously applicable regarding one or more classes of the asset-backed securities has terminated other than by expiration of the contract on its stated termination date or as a result of all parties completing their obligations under such agreement, then disclose:

(1) The date of the termination of the enhancement;

(2) The identity of the parties to the agreement relating to the enhancement or support;

(3) A brief description of the terms and conditions of the enhancement or support that are material to security holders;

(4) A brief description of the material circumstances surrounding the termination; and

(5) Any material early termination penalties paid or to be paid out of the cash flows backing the asset-backed securities.

(b) *Addition of new enhancement or support.* If the depositor (or servicer if the servicer signs the report on Form 10–K of the issuing entity) becomes aware that any material enhancement specified in Item 1114(a)(1) through (3) of Regulation AB or Item 1115 of Regulation AB has been added with respect to one or more classes of the asset-backed securities, then provide the date of addition of the new enhancement or support and the disclosure required by Items 1114 or 1115 of Regulation AB, as applicable, with respect to such new enhancement or support.

(c) *Material change to enhancement or support.* If the depositor (or servicer if the servicer signs the report on Form 10–K of the issuing entity) becomes aware that any existing material enhancement or support specified in Item 1114(a)(1) through (3) of Regulation AB or Item 1115 of Regulation AB with respect to one or more classes of the asset-backed securities has been materially amended or modified, disclose:

(1) The date on which the agreement or agreements relating to the enhancement or support was amended or modified;

(2) The identity of the parties to the agreement or agreements relating to the amendment or modification; and

(3) A brief description of the material terms and conditions of the amendment or modification.

Instructions.

1. Disclosure is required under this Item whether or not the registrant is a party to any agreement regarding the enhancement or support if the loss, addition or modification of such enhancement or support materially affects, directly or indirectly, the asset-backed securities, the pool assets or the cash flow underlying the asset-backed securities.

2. To the extent that any information called for by this Item regarding the enhancement or support is not determined or is unavailable at the time of the required filing, the registrant shall include a statement to this effect in the filing and then must file an amendment to its Form 8–K filing under this Item 6.03 containing such information within four business days after the information is determined or becomes available.

3. The instructions to Items 1.01 and 1.02 of this Form apply to this Item.

4. Notwithstanding Items 1.01 and 1.02 of this Form, disclosure regarding changes to material enhancement or support is to be reported under this Item 6.03 in lieu of those Items.

Item 6.04. Failure To Make a Required Distribution

If a required distribution to holders of the asset-backed securities is not made as of the required distribution date under the transaction documents, and such failure is material, identify the failure and state the nature of the failure to make the timely distribution.

Item 6.05.   Securities Act Updating Disclosure

Regarding an offering of asset-backed securities registered on Form S–F3, if any material pool characteristic of the actual asset pool at the time of issuance of the asset-backed securities differs by 5% or more (other than as a result of the pool assets converting into cash in accordance with their terms) from the description of the asset pool in the prospectus filed for the offering pursuant to Securities Act Rule 424, disclose the information required by Items 1111 and 1112 of Regulation AB regarding the characteristics of the actual asset pool. If applicable, also provide information required by Items 1108 and 1110 of Regulation AB regarding any new servicers or originators that would be required to be disclosed under those items regarding the pool assets.

Instruction.

No report is required under this Item if substantially the same information is provided in a post-effective amendment to the Securities Act registration statement or in a subsequent prospectus filed pursuant to Securities Act Rule 424.

Item 6.06.   Static Pool

Regarding an offering of asset-backed securities registered on Form SF–1 or Form SF–3, in lieu of providing the static pool information as required by Item 1105 of Regulation AB in a form of prospectus or prospectus, an issuer may file the required information in this report or as an exhibit to this report. The static pool disclosure must be filed by the time of effectiveness of a registration statement on Form SF–1, by the same date of the filing of a form of prospectus, as required by Rule 424(h), and by the same date of the filing of a final prospectus meeting the requirements of section 10(a) of the Securities Act filed in accordance with Rule 424(b).

Instructions.

1.   Refer to Item 601(b)(106) of Regulation S–K regarding the filing of exhibits to this Item 6.06.

2.   Refer to Item 10 of Form SF–1 (17 CFR 239.44) or Item 10 of Form SF–3 regarding incorporation by reference.

Section 7—Regulation FD

Item 7.01.   Regulation FD Disclosure

Unless filed under Item 8.01, disclose under this item only information that the registrant elects to disclose through Form 8–K pursuant to Regulation FD.

Section 8—Other Events

Item 8.01.   Other Events

The registrant may, at its option, disclose under this Item 8.01 any events, with respect to which information is not otherwise called for by this form, that the registrant deems of importance to security holders. The registrant may, at its option, file a report under this Item 8.01 disclosing the nonpublic information required to be disclosed by Regulation FD.

Section 9—Financial Statements and Exhibits

Item 9.01.   Financial Statements and Exhibits

List below the financial statements, pro forma financial information and exhibits, if any, filed as a part of this report.

(a)   *Financial statements of businesses acquired.*

(1)   For any business acquisition required to be described in answer to Item 2.01 of this form, financial statements of the business acquired shall be filed for the periods specified in Rule 3–05(b) of Regulation S–X or Rule 8–04(b) of Regulation S–X for smaller reporting companies.

(2)   The financial statements shall be prepared pursuant to Regulation S–X except that supporting schedules need not be filed. A manually signed accountant's report should be provided pursuant to Rule 2–02 of Regulation S–X.

(3)   With regard to the acquisition of one or more real estate properties, the financial statements and any additional information specified by Rule 3–14 or Rule 8–06 of Regulation S–X for smaller reporting companies.

(4)   Financial statements required by this item may be filed with the initial report, or by amendment not later than 71 calendar days after the date that the initial report on Form 8–K must be filed. If the financial statements are not included in the initial report, the registrant should so indicate in the Form 8–K report and state when the required financial statements will be filed. The registrant may, at its option, include unaudited financial statements in the initial report on Form 8–K.

(b)   *Pro forma financial information.*

(1)   For any transaction required to be described in answer to Item 2.01 of this form, furnish any pro forma financial information that would be required pursuant to Article 11 of Regulation S–X or Rule 8–05 of Regulation S–X for smaller reporting companies.

(2)   The provisions of paragraph (a)(4) of this Item 9.01 shall also apply to pro forma financial information relative to the acquired business.

(c)   *Shell company transactions.* The provisions of paragraph (a)(4) and (b)(2) of this Item shall not apply to the financial statements or pro forma financial information required to be filed under this Item with regard to any transaction required to be described in answer to Item 2.01 of this Form by a registrant that was a shell company, other than a business combination related shell company, as those terms are defined in Rule 12b–2 under the Exchange Act, immediately before that transaction. Accordingly, with regard to any transaction required to be described in answer to Item 2.01 of this Form by a registrant that was a shell company, other than a business combination related shell company, immediately before that transaction, the financial statements and pro forma financial information required by this Item must be filed in the initial report. Notwithstanding General Instruction B.3. to Form 8–K, if any financial statement or any financial information required to be filed in the initial report by this Item 9.01(c) is previously reported, as that term is defined in Rule 12b–2 under the Exchange Act, the registrant may identify the filing in which that disclosure is included instead of including that disclosure in the initial report.

(d)   *Exhibits.* The exhibits will be deemed to be filed or furnished, depending on the relevant item requiring such exhibit, in accordance with the provisions of Item 601 of Regulation S–K and Instruction B.2 to this form.

Instruction.

During the period after a registrant has reported a business combination pursuant to Item 2.01 of this form, until the date on which the financial statements specified by this Item 9.01 must be filed, the registrant will be deemed current for purposes of its reporting obligations under Section 13(a) or 15(d) of the Exchange Act. With respect to filings under the Securities Act, however, registration statements will not be declared effective and post-effective amendments to registrations statements will not be declared effective unless financial statements meeting the requirements of Rule 3–05 of Regulation S–X are provided. In addition, offerings should not be made pursuant to effective registration statements, or pursuant to Rule 506 of Regulation D where any purchasers are not accredited investors under Rule 501(a) of that Regulation, until the audited financial statements required by Rule 3–05 of Regulation S–X are filed; *provided, however,* that the following offerings or sales of securities may proceed notwithstanding that financial statements of the acquired business have not been filed:

(a)   offerings or sales of securities upon the conversion of outstanding convertible securities or upon the exercise of outstanding warrants or rights;

(b)   dividend or interest reinvestment plans;

(c)   employee benefit plans;

(d)   transactions involving secondary offerings; or

(e)   sales of securities pursuant to Rule 144.

Item 9.01

1934 ACT FORMS

SIGNATURES

Pursuant to the requirements of the Securities Exchange Act of 1934, the registrant has duly caused this report to be signed on its behalf by the undersigned hereunto duly authorized.

Date _____

(Registrant) _____

(Signature) * _____

---

*   Print name and title of the signing officer under his signature.

FORM 10

E. FORM 10

17 C.F.R. § 249.210

GENERAL FORM FOR REGISTRATION OF SECURITIES UNDER THE 1934 ACT

SECURITIES AND EXCHANGE COMMISSION

Washington, D.C. 20549

FORM 10

GENERAL FORM FOR REGISTRATION OF SECURITIES PURSUANT TO SECTION 12(b) OR (g) OF THE SECURITIES EXCHANGE ACT OF 1934

GENERAL INSTRUCTIONS

A. Rule as to Use of Form 10

Form 10 shall be used for registration pursuant to section 12(b) or (g) of the Securities Exchange Act of 1934 of classes of securities of issuers for which no other form is prescribed.

B. Application of General Rules and Regulations

(a) The General Rules and Regulations under the Act contain certain general requirements which are applicable to registration on any form. These general requirements should be carefully read and observed in the preparation and filing of registration statements on this form.

(b) Particular attention is directed to Regulation 12B which contains general requirements regarding matters such as the kind and size of paper to be used, the legibility of the registration statement, the information to be given whenever the title of securities is required to be stated, and the filing of the registration statement. The definitions contained in Rule 12b–2 should be especially noted.

C. Preparation of Registration Statement

(a) This form is not to be used as a blank form to be filled in, but only as a guide in the preparation of the registration statement on paper meeting the requirements of Rule 12b–12. The registration statement shall contain the item numbers and captions, but the text of the items may be omitted. The answers to the items shall be prepared in the manner specified in Rule 12b–13.

(b) Unless otherwise stated, the information required shall be given as of a date reasonably close to the date of filing the registration statement.

(c) Attention is directed to Rule 12b–20 which states: "In addition to the information expressly required to be included in a statement or report, there shall be added such further material information, if any, as may be necessary to make the required statements, in light of the circumstances under which they are made, not misleading."

D. Signature and Filing of Registration Statement

Three complete copies of the registration statement, including financial statements, exhibits and all other papers and documents filed as a part thereof, and five additional copies which need not include exhibits, shall be filed with the Commission. At least one complete copy of the registration statement, including financial statements, exhibits and all other papers and documents filed as a part thereof, shall be filed with each exchange on which any class of securities is to be registered. At least one complete copy of the registration statement filed with the Commission and one such copy filed with each exchange shall be manually signed. Copies not manually signed shall bear typed or printed signatures.

E. Omission of Information Regarding Foreign Subsidiaries

Information required by any item or other requirement of this form with respect to any foreign subsidiary may be omitted to the extent that the required disclosure would be detrimental to the registrant. However, financial statements, otherwise required, shall not be omitted pursuant to this instruction. Where information is omitted pursuant to this instruction, a statement shall be made that such information has been omitted and the names of the subsidiaries involved shall be separately furnished to the Commission.

The Commission may, in its discretion, call for justification that the required disclosure would be detrimental.

F.   Incorporation by Reference

Attention is directed to Rule 12b–23 which provides for the incorporation by reference of information contained in certain documents in answer or partial answer to any item of a registration statement.

SECURITIES AND EXCHANGE COMMISSION

Washington, D.C. 20549

FORM 10

**GENERAL FORM FOR REGISTRATION OF SECURITIES
PURSUANT TO SECTION 12(b) OR (g) OF THE
SECURITIES EXCHANGE ACT OF 1934**

_____

(Exact name of registrant as specified in its charter)

_____

(State or other jurisdiction of incorporation or organization)	(I.R.S. Employer Identification No.)

_____

(Address of principal executive offices)	(Zip Code)

Registrant's telephone number, including area code _____

Securities to be registered pursuant to Section 12(b) of the Act:

Title of each class to be so registered	Name of each exchange on which each class is to be registered

_____

_____

Securities to be registered pursuant to Section 12(g) of the Act:

_____

(Title of class)

_____

(Title of class)

Indicate by check mark whether the registrant is a large accelerated filer, an accelerated filer, a non-accelerated filer, a smaller reporting company, or an emerging growth company. See the definitions of "large accelerated filer," "accelerated filer," "smaller reporting company," and "emerging growth company" in Rule 12b–2 of the Exchange Act.

Large accelerated filer ☐
Non-accelerated filer ☐
Accelerated filer ☐
Smaller reporting company ☐

Emerging growth company ☐

If an emerging growth company, indicate by check mark if the registrant has elected not to use the extended transition period for complying with any new or revised financial accounting standards provided pursuant to Section 13(a) of the Exchange Act. ☐

If securities are registered pursuant to Section 12(b) of the Act, indicate by check mark whether the financial statements of the registrant included in the filing reflect the correction of an error to previously issued financial statements. ☐

Indicate by check mark whether any of those error corrections are restatements that required a recovery analysis of incentive-based compensation received by any of the registrant's executive officers during the relevant recovery period pursuant to § 240.10D–1(b). ☐

INFORMATION REQUIRED IN REGISTRATION STATEMENT

Item 1.   Business

Furnish the information required by Item 101 of Regulation S–K.

Item 1A. Risk Factors

Set forth, under the caption "Risk Factors," where appropriate, the risk factors described in Item 105 of Regulation S–K applicable to the registrant.

Item 2.   Financial Information

Furnish the information required by Items 301, 303, and 305 of Regulation S–K.

Item 3.   Properties

Furnish the information required by Item 102 of Regulation S–K.

Item 4.   Security Ownership of Certain Beneficial Owners and Management

Furnish the information required by Item 403 of Regulation S–K.

Item 5.   Directors and Executive Officers

Furnish the information required by Item 401 of Regulation S–K.

Item 6.   Executive Compensation

Furnish the information required by Item 402 of Regulation S–K and paragraph (e)(4) of Item 407 of Regulation S–K.

Item 7.   Certain Relationships and Related Transactions, and Director Independence

Furnish the information required by Item 404 of Regulation S–K and Item 407(a) of Regulation S–K.

Item 8.   Legal Proceedings

Furnish the information required by Item 103 of Regulation S–K.

Item 9.   Market Price of and Dividends on the Registrant's Common Equity and Related Stockholder Matters

Furnish the information required by Item 201 of Regulation S–K.

Item 10. Recent Sales of Unregistered Securities

Furnish the information required by Item 701 of Regulation S–K.

Item 11. Description of Registrant's Securities to Be Registered

Furnish the information required by Item 202 of Regulation S–K. If the class of securities to be registered will trade in the form of American Depositary Receipts, furnish Item 202(f) disclosure for such American Depositary Receipts as well.

Item 12. Indemnification of Directors and Officers

Furnish the information required by Item 702 of Regulation S–K.

Item 13. Financial Statements and Supplementary Data

Furnish all financial statements required by Regulation S–X and the supplementary financial information required by Item 302 of Regulation S–K. Smaller reporting companies may provide the financial information required by Article 8 of Regulation S–X in lieu of the information required by in other parts of Regulation S–X.

Item 14. Changes in and Disagreements With Accountants on Accounting and Financial Disclosure

Furnish the information required by Item 304 of Regulation S–K.

Item 15. Financial Statements and Exhibits

(a)   List separately all financial statements filed as part of the registration statement.

(b)   Furnish the exhibits required by Item 601 of Regulation S–K.

SIGNATURES

Pursuant to the requirements of Section 12 of the Securities Exchange Act of 1934, the registrant has duly caused this registration statement to be signed on its behalf by the undersigned, thereunto duly authorized.

(Registrant) _____

Date _____

By (Signature) * _____

---

*   Print name and title of the signing officer under his signature.

F.   FORM 10-Q

17 C.F.R. § 249.308a

QUARTERLY REPORT FOR ISSUERS SUBJECT TO THE 1934 ACT REPORTING REQUIREMENTS

FORM 10-Q

SECURITIES AND EXCHANGE COMMISSION

Washington, D.C. 20549

GENERAL INSTRUCTIONS

A.   Rule as to Use of Form 10-Q

1.   Form 10-Q shall be used for quarterly reports under section 13 or 15(d) of the Securities Exchange Act of 1934, required to be filed pursuant to Rule 13a–13 or Rule 15d–13. A quarterly report on this form pursuant to Rule 13a–13 or Rule 15d–13 shall be filed within the following period after the end of the first three fiscal quarters of each fiscal year, but no quarterly report need be filed for the fourth quarter of any fiscal year:

(a)   40 days after the end of the fiscal quarter for large accelerated filers and accelerated filers (as defined in Rule 12b–2); and

(b)   45 days after the end of the fiscal quarter for all other registrants.

B.   Application of General Rules and Regulations

1.   The General Rules and Regulations under the Act contain certain general requirements which are applicable to reports on any form. These general requirements should be carefully read and observed in the preparation and filing of reports on this form.

2.   Particular attention is directed to Regulation 12B which contains general requirements regarding matters such as the kind and size of paper to be used, the legibility of the report, the information to be given whenever the title of securities is required to be stated, and the filing of the report. The definitions contained in Rule 12b–2 should be especially noted. See also Regulations 13A and 15D.

C.   Preparation of Report

1.   This is not a blank form to be filled in. It is a guide copy to be used in preparing the report in accordance with Rules 12b–11 and 12b–12. The Commission does not furnish blank copies of this form to be filled in for filing.

2.   These general instructions are not to be filed with the report. The instructions to the various captions on the form are also to be omitted from the report as filed.

D.   Incorporation by Reference

1.   If the registrant makes available to its stockholders or otherwise publishes, within the period prescribed for filing the report, a document or statement containing information meeting some or all of the requirements of Part I of this form, the information called for may be incorporated by reference from such published document or statement, in answer or partial answer to any item or items of Part I of this form, provided copies thereof are filed as an exhibit to Part I of the report on this form.

2.   Other information may be incorporated by reference in answer or partial answer to any item or items of Part II of this form in accordance with the provisions of Rule 12b–23.

3.   If any information required by Part I or Part II is incorporated by reference into an electronic format document from the quarterly report to security holders as provided in General Instruction D, any portion of the quarterly report to security holders incorporated by reference shall be filed as an exhibit in electronic format, as required by Item 601(b)(13) of Regulation S–K.

E. Integrated Reports to Security Holders

Quarterly reports to security holders may be combined with the required information of Form 10–Q and will be suitable for filing with the Commission if the following conditions are satisfied:

1. The combined report contains full and complete answers to all items required by Part I of this form. When responses to a certain item of required disclosure are separated within the combined report, an appropriate cross-reference should be made.

2. If not included in the combined report, the cover page, appropriate responses to Part II, and the required signatures shall be included in the Form 10–Q. Additionally, as appropriate, a cross-reference sheet should be filed indicating the location of information required by the items of the form.

3. If an electronic filer files any portion of a quarterly report to security holders in combination with the required information of Form 10–Q, as provided in this instruction, only such portions filed in satisfaction of the Form 10–Q requirements shall be filed in electronic format.

F. Filed Status of Information Presented

1. Pursuant to Rule 13a–13(d) and Rule 15d–13(d), the information presented in satisfaction of the requirements of Items 1, 2 and 3 of Part I of this form, whether included directly in a report on this form, incorporated therein by reference from a report, document or statement filed as an exhibit to Part I of this form pursuant to Instruction D(1) above, included in an integrated report pursuant to Instruction E above, or contained in a statement regarding computation of per share earnings or a letter regarding a change in accounting principles filed as an exhibit to Part I pursuant to Item 601 of Regulation S–K, except as provided by Instruction F(2) below, shall not be deemed filed for the purpose of section 18 of the Act or otherwise subject to the liabilities of that section of the Act but shall be subject to the other provisions of the Act.

2. Information presented in satisfaction of the requirements of this form other than those of Items 1, 2 and 3 of Part I of this form shall be deemed filed for the purpose of section 18 of the Act; except that, where information presented in response to Items 1, 2 and 3 of Part I of this form (or as an exhibit thereto) is also used to satisfy Part II requirements through incorporation by reference, only that portion of Part I (or exhibit thereto) consisting of the information required by Part II shall be deemed so filed.

G. Signature and Filing of Report

If the report is filed in paper pursuant to a hardship exemption from electronic filing (see Item 201 et seq. of Regulation S–T), three complete copies of the report, including any financial statements, exhibits or other papers or documents filed as a part thereof, and five additional copies which need not include exhibits, shall be filed with the Commission. At least one complete copy of the report, including any financial statements, exhibits or other papers or documents filed as a part thereof, shall be filed with each exchange on which any class of securities of the registrant is registered. At least one complete copy of the report filed with the Commission and one such copy filed with each exchange shall be manually signed on the registrant's behalf by a duly authorized officer of the registrant and by the principal financial or chief accounting officer of the registrant. Copies not manually signed shall bear typed or printed signatures. In the case where the principal executive officer, principal financial officer or chief accounting officer is also duly authorized to sign on behalf of the registrant, one signature is acceptable provided that the registrant clearly indicates the dual responsibilities of the signatory.

H. Omission of Information by Certain Wholly-Owned Subsidiaries

If, on the date of the filing of its report on Form 10–Q, the registrant meets the conditions specified in paragraph (1) below, then such registrant may omit the information called for in the items specified in paragraph (2) below.

1. Conditions for availability of the relief specified in paragraph (2) below:

a. All of the registrant's equity securities are owned, either directly or indirectly, by a single person which is a reporting company under the Act and which has filed all the material required to be filed pursuant to section 13, 14 or 15(d) thereof, as applicable;

b. During the preceding thirty-six calendar months and any subsequent period of days, there has not been any material default in the payment of principal, interest, a sinking or purchase fund installment, or any other material default not cured within thirty days, with

FORM 10-Q

respect to any indebtedness of the registrant or its subsidiaries, and there has not been any material default in the payment of rentals under material long-term leases; and

    c.   There is prominently set forth, on the cover page of the Form 10-Q, a statement that the registrant meets the conditions set forth in General Instruction H(1)(a) and (b) of Form 10-Q and is therefore filing this Form with the reduced disclosure format.

2.   Registrants meeting the conditions specified in paragraph (1) above are entitled to the following relief:

    a.   Such registrants may omit the information called for by Item 2 of Part I, Management's Discussion and Analysis of Financial Condition and Results of Operations, provided that the registrant includes in the Form 10-Q a management's narrative analysis of the results of operations explaining the reasons for material changes in the amount of revenue and expense items between the most recent fiscal year-to-date period presented and the corresponding year-to-date period in the preceding fiscal year. Explanations of material changes should include, but not be limited to, changes in the various elements which determine revenue and expense levels such as unit sales volume, prices charged and paid, production levels, production cost variances, labor costs and discretionary spending programs. In addition, the analysis should include an explanation of the effect of any changes in accounting principles and practices or method of application that have a material effect on net income as reported.

    b.   Such registrants may omit the information called for in the following Part II Items: Item 2, Changes in Securities; Item 3, Defaults Upon Senior Securities.

    c.   Such registrants may omit the information called for by Item 3 of Part I, Quantitative and Qualitative Disclosures About Market Risk.

FORM 10-Q

SECURITIES AND EXCHANGE COMMISSION

Washington, D.C. 20549

(Mark One)

[   ]

QUARTERLY REPORT PURSUANT TO SECTION 13 OR 15(d)
OF THE SECURITIES EXCHANGE ACT OF 1934

For the quarterly period ended _____

OR

[   ]

TRANSITION REPORT PURSUANT TO SECTION 13 OR 15(d)
OF THE SECURITIES EXCHANGE ACT OF 1934

For the transition period from_____ to _____

Commission file number _____

_____

(Exact name of registrant as specified in its charter)

1934 ACT FORMS

(State or other jurisdiction of incorporation or organization)

(I.R.S. Employer Identification No.)

(Address of principal executive offices)

(Zip Code)

(Registrant's telephone number, including area code)

(Former name, former address and former fiscal year, if changed since last report)

Securities registered pursuant to Section 12(b) of the Act:

Title of each class	Trading symbol(s)	Name of each exchange on which registered

Indicate by check mark whether the registrant (1) has filed all reports required to be filed by Section 13 or 15(d) of the Securities Exchange Act of 1934 during the preceding 12 months (or for such shorter period that the registrant was required to file such reports), and (2) has been subject to such filing requirements for the past 90 days.

Yes ___ No ___

Indicate by check mark whether the registrant is a large accelerated filer, an accelerated filer, a non-accelerated filer, a smaller reporting company, or an emerging growth company. See the definitions of "large accelerated filer," "accelerated filer," "smaller reporting company," and "emerging growth company" in Rule 12b–2 of the Exchange Act.

Large accelerated filer □
Non-accelerated filer □
Accelerated filer □
Smaller reporting company □
Emerging growth company □

If an emerging growth company, indicate by check mark if the registrant has elected not to use the extended transition period for complying with any new or revised financial accounting standards provided pursuant to Rule 13(a) of the Exchange Act. □

Indicate by check mark whether the registrant is a shell company (as defined in Rule 12b–2 of the Exchange Act).

Yes ___ No ___

APPLICABLE ONLY TO ISSUERS INVOLVED IN BANKRUPTCY

PROCEEDINGS DURING THE PRECEDING FIVE YEARS:

Indicate by check mark whether the registrant has filed all documents and reports required to be filed by Sections 12, 13 or 15(d) of the Securities Exchange Act of 1934 subsequent to the distribution of securities under a plan confirmed by a court.

Yes ___ No ___

Indicate by check mark whether the registrant has submitted electronically a Indicate by check mark whether the registrant has submitted electronically every Interactive Data File required to be submitted pursuant to Rule 405 of Regulation S–T (§ 232.405 of this chapter) during the preceding 12 months (or for such shorter period that the registrant was required to submit such files).

Yes ___ No ___

APPLICABLE ONLY TO CORPORATE ISSUERS:

Indicate the number of shares outstanding of each of the issuer's classes of common stock, as of the latest practicable date.

Item 1. Financial Statements

Provide the information required by Rule 10–01 of Regulation S–X. A smaller reporting company, defined in Rule 12b–2, may provide the information required by Article 8–03 of Regulation S–X.

Item 2. Management's Discussion and Analysis of Financial Condition and Results of Operations

Furnish the information required by Item 303 of Regulation S–K.

Item 3. Quantitative and Qualitative Disclosures About Market Risk

Furnish the information required by Item 305 of Regulation S–K.

Item 4. Controls and Procedures

Furnish the information required by Item 307 of Regulation S–K and 308(c) of Regulation S–K.

PART II—OTHER INFORMATION

Instruction. The report shall contain the item numbers and captions of all applicable items of Part II, but the text of such items may be omitted provided the responses clearly indicate the coverage of the item. Any item which is inapplicable or to which the answer is negative may be omitted and no reference thereto need be made in the report. If substantially the same information has been previously reported by the registrant, an additional report of the information on this form need not be made. The term "previously reported" is defined in Rule 12b–2. A separate response need not be presented in Part II where information called for is already disclosed in the financial information provided in Part I and is incorporated by reference into Part II of the report by means of a statement to that effect in Part II which specifically identifies the incorporated information.

Item 1. Legal Proceedings

Furnish the information required by Item 103 of Regulation S–K. As to such proceedings which have been terminated during the period covered by the report, provide similar information, including the date of termination and a description of the disposition thereof with respect to the registrant and its subsidiaries.

Instruction. A legal proceeding need only be reported in the 10–Q filed for the quarter in which it first became a reportable event and in subsequent quarters in which there have been material developments. Subsequent Form 10–Q filings in the same fiscal year in which a legal proceeding or a material development is reported should reference any previous reports in that year.

Item 1A. Risk Factors

Set forth any material changes from risk factors as previously disclosed in the registrant's Form 10–K in response to Item 1A. to Part I of Form 10–K. Smaller reporting companies are not required to provide the information required by this item.

Item 2. Unregistered Sales of Equity Securities and Use of Proceeds

(a) Furnish the information required by Item 701 of Regulation S–K as to all equity securities of the registrant sold by the registrant during the period covered by the report that were not registered under the

Securities Act. If the Item 701 information previously has been included in a Current Report on Form 8–K, however, it need not be furnished.

(b)   If required pursuant to Rule 463 of the Securities Act of 1933, furnish the information required by Item 701(f) of Regulation S–K.

(c)   Furnish the information required by Item 703 of Regulation S–K for any repurchase made in the quarter covered by the report. Provide disclosures covering repurchases made on a monthly basis. For example, if the quarter began on January 16 and ended on April 15, the chart would show repurchases for the months from January 16 through February 15, February 16 through March 15, and March 16 through April 15.

Instruction. Working capital restrictions and other limitations upon the payment of dividends are to be reported hereunder.

Item 3.   Defaults Upon Senior Securities

(a)   If there has been any material default in the payment of principal, interest, a sinking or purchase fund installment, or any other material default not cured within 30 days, with respect to any indebtedness of the registrant or any of its significant subsidiaries exceeding 5 percent of the total assets of the registrant and its consolidated subsidiaries, identify the indebtedness and state the nature of the default. In the case of such a default in the payment of principal, interest, or a sinking or purchase fund installment, state the amount of the default and the total arrearage on the date of filing this report.

Instruction. This paragraph refers only to events which have become defaults under the governing instruments, i.e., after the expiration of any period of grace and compliance with any notice requirements.

(b)   If any material arrearage in the payment of dividends has occurred or if there has been any other material delinquency not cured within 30 days, with respect to any class of preferred stock of the registrant which is registered or which ranks prior to any class of registered securities, or with respect to any class of preferred stock of any significant subsidiary of the registrant, give the title of the class and state the nature of the arrearage or delinquency. In the case of an arrearage in the payment of dividends, state the amount and the total arrearage on the date of filing this report.

Instructions to Item 3.

1.   Item 3 need not be answered as to any default or arrearage with respect to any class of securities all of which is held by or for the account of the registrant or its totally held subsidiaries.

2.   The information required by Item 3 need not be made if previously disclosed on a report on Form 8–K.

Item 4.   Mine Safety Disclosures

If applicable, provide a statement that the information concerning mine safety violations or other regulatory matters required by Section 1503(a) of the Dodd-Frank Wall Street Reform and Consumer Protection Act and Item 104 of Regulation S–K is included in exhibit 95 to the quarterly report.

Item 5.   Other Information

(a)   The registrant must disclose under this item any information required to be disclosed in a report on Form 8–K during the period covered by this Form 10–Q, but not reported, whether or not otherwise required by this Form 10–Q. If disclosure of such information is made under this item, it need not be repeated in a report on Form 8–K which would otherwise be required to be filed with respect to such information or in a subsequent report on Form 10–Q; and

(b)   Furnish the information required by Item 407(c)(3) of Regulation S–K (§ 229.407 of this chapter).

Item 6.   Exhibits

Furnish the exhibits required by Item 601 of Regulation S–K.

SIGNATURES *

Pursuant to the requirements of the Securities Exchange Act of 1934, the registrant has duly caused this report to be signed on its behalf by the undersigned thereunto duly authorized.

Date _____

Date _____

(Registrant) _____

(Signature) ** _____

(Signature) ** _____

---

*   See General Instruction E.

**   Print name and title of the signing officer under his signature.

G.   FORM 10–K

17 C.F.R. § 249.310

ANNUAL REPORT FOR ISSUERS SUBJECT TO THE 1934 ACT REPORTING REQUIREMENTS

FORM 10–K

SECURITIES AND EXCHANGE COMMISSION

Washington, D.C. 20549

ANNUAL REPORT PURSUANT TO SECTION 13 OR 15(d) OF THE SECURITIES EXCHANGE ACT OF 1934

GENERAL INSTRUCTIONS

A.   Rule as to Use of Form 10–K

(1)   This form shall be used for annual reports pursuant to sections 13 or 15(d) of the Securities Exchange Act of 1934 (the "Act") for which no other form is prescribed. This form also shall be used for transition reports filed pursuant to section 13 or 15(d) of the Act.

(2)   Annual reports on this form shall be filed within the following period:

(a)   60 days after the end of the fiscal year covered by the report (75 days for fiscal years ending before December 15, 2006) for large accelerated filers (as defined in Rule 12b–2);

(b)   75 days after the end of the fiscal year covered by the report for accelerated filers (as defined in Rule 12b–2); and

(c)   90 days after the end of the fiscal year covered by the report for all other registrants.

(3)   Transition reports on this form shall be filed in accordance with the requirements set forth in Rule 13a–10 or Rule 15d–10 of this chapter applicable when the registrant changes its fiscal year end.

(4)   Notwithstanding paragraphs (2) and (3) of this General Instruction A., all schedules required by Article 12 of Regulation S–X may, at the option of the registrant, be filed as an amendment to the report not later than 30 days after the applicable due date of the report.

B.   Application of General Rules and Regulations

(1)   The General Rules and Regulations under the Act contain certain general requirements which are applicable to reports on any form. These general requirements should be carefully read and observed in the preparation and filing of reports on this Form.

(2)   Particular attention is directed to Regulation 12B which contains general requirements regarding matters such as the kind and size of paper to be used, the legibility of the report, the information to be given whenever the title of securities is required to be stated, and the filing of the report. The definitions contained in Rule 12b–2 should be especially noted. See also Regulations 13A and 15D.

C.   Preparation of Report

(1)   This Form is not to be used as a blank form to be filled in, but only as a guide in the preparation of the report on paper meeting the requirements of Rule 12b–12. Except as provided in General Instruction G, the answers to the items shall be prepared in the manner specified in Rule 12b–13.

(2)   Except where information is required to be given for the fiscal year or as of a specified date, it shall be given as of the latest practicable date.

(3)   Attention is directed to Rule 12b–20, which states: "In addition to the information expressly required to be included in a statement or report, there shall be added such further material information, if any, as may be necessary to make the required statements, in the light of the circumstances under which they are made, not misleading."

FORM 10–K

D. Signature and Filing of Report

(1)   Three complete copies of the report, including financial statements, financial statement schedules, exhibits, and all other papers and documents filed as a part thereof, and five additional copies which need not include exhibits, shall be filed with the Commission. At least one complete copy of the report, including financial statements, financial statement schedules, exhibits, and all other papers and documents filed as a part thereof, shall be filed with each exchange on which any class of securities of the registrant is registered. At least one complete copy of the report filed with the Commission and one such copy filed with each exchange shall be manually signed. Copies not manually signed shall bear typed or printed signatures.

(2)(a)   The report must be signed by the registrant, and on behalf of the registrant by its principal executive officer or officers its principal financial officer or officers, its controller or principal accounting officer, and by at least the majority of the board of directors or persons performing similar functions. Where the registrant is a limited partnership, the report shall be signed by the majority of the board of directors of any corporate general partner who signs the report.

(b)   The name of each person who signs the report shall be typed or printed beneath his signature. Any person who occupies more than one of the specified positions shall indicate each capacity in which he signs the report. Attention is directed to Rule 12b–11 concerning manual signatures and signatures pursuant to powers of attorney.

(3)   Registrants are requested to indicate in a transmittal letter with the Form 10–K whether the financial statements in the report reflect a change from the preceding year in any accounting principles or practices, or in the method of applying any such principles or practices.

E. Disclosure With Respect to Foreign Subsidiaries

Information required by any item or other requirement of this form with respect to any foreign subsidiary may be omitted to the extent that the required disclosure would be detrimental to the registrant. However, financial statements and financial statement schedules, otherwise required, shall not be omitted pursuant to this Instruction. Where information is omitted pursuant to this Instruction, a statement shall be made that such information has been omitted and the names of the subsidiaries involved shall be separately furnished to the Commission. The Commission may, in its discretion, call for justification that the required disclosure would be detrimental.

F. Information as to Employee Stock Purchase, Savings and Similar Plans

Attention is directed to Rule 15d–21 which provides that separate annual and other reports need not be filed pursuant to section 15(d) of the Act with respect to any employee stock purchase, savings or similar plan if the issuer of the stock or other securities offered to employees pursuant to the plan furnishes to the Commission the information and documents specified in the Rule.

G. Information to Be Incorporated by Reference

(1)   Attention is directed to Rule 12b–23 which provides for the incorporation by reference of information contained in certain documents in answer or partial answer to any item of a report.

(2)   The information called for by Parts I and II of this Form (Items 1 through 9A or any portion thereof) may, at the registrant's option, be incorporated by reference from the registrant's annual report to security holders furnished to the Commission pursuant to Rule 14a–3(b) or Rule 14c–3(a) or from the registrant's annual report to security holders, even if not furnished to the Commission pursuant to Rule 14a–3(b) or Rule 14c–3(a), provided such annual report contains the information required by Rule 14a–3.

NOTE 1: In order to fulfill the requirements of Part I of Form 10–K, the incorporated portion of the annual report to security holders must contain the information required by Items 1–3 of Form 10–K, to the extent applicable.

NOTE 2: If any information required by Part I or Part II is incorporated by reference into an electronic format document from the annual report to security holders as provided in General Instruction G, any portion of the annual report to security holders incorporated by reference shall be filed as an exhibit in electronic format, as required by Item 601(b)(13) of Regulation S–K.

(3)   The information required by Part III (Items 10, 11, 12, 13 and 14) shall be incorporated by reference from the registrant's definitive proxy statement (filed or to be filed pursuant to Regulation 14A)

or definitive information statement (filed or to be filed pursuant to Regulation 14C) which involves the election of directors, if such definitive proxy statement or information statement is filed with the Commission not later than 120 days after the end of the fiscal year covered by the Form 10–K. However, if such definitive proxy or information statement is not filed with the Commission in the 120-day period, or is not required to be filed with the Commission by virtue of Rule 3a12–3(b) under the Exchange Act, the Items comprising the Part III information must be filed as part of the Form 10–K, or as an amendment to the Form 10–K, not later than the end of the 120-day period. It should be noted that the information regarding executive officers required by Item 401 of Regulation S–K may be included in Part I of Form 10–K under an appropriate caption. See the Instruction to Item 401 of Regulation S–K.

(4)   No item numbers of captions of items need be contained in the material incorporated by reference into the report. When the registrant combines all of the information in Parts I and II of this Form (Items 1 through 9A) by incorporation by reference from the registrant's annual report to security holders and all of the information in Part III of this Form (Items 10 through 14) by incorporating by reference from a definitive proxy statement or information statement involving the election of directors, then, notwithstanding General Instruction C(1), this Form shall consist of the facing or cover page, those sections incorporated from the annual report to security holders, the proxy or information statement, and the information, if any, required by Part IV of this Form, signatures, and a cross reference sheet setting forth the item numbers and captions in Parts I, II and III of this Form and the page and/or pages in the referenced materials where the corresponding information appears.

H.   Integrated Reports to Security Holders

Annual reports to security holders may be combined with the required information of Form 10–K and will be suitable for filing with the Commission if the following conditions are satisfied:

(1)   The combined report contains full and complete answers to all items required by Form 10–K. When responses to a certain item of required disclosure are separated within the combined report, an appropriate cross-reference should be made. If the information required by Part III of Form 10–K is omitted by virtue of General Instruction G, a definitive proxy or information statement shall be filed.

(2)   The cover page and the required signatures are included. As appropriate, a cross-reference sheet should be filed indicating the location of information required by the items of the Form.

(3)   If an electronic filer files any portion of an annual report to security holders in combination with the required information of Form 10–K, as provided in this instruction, only such portions filed in satisfaction of the Form 10–K requirements shall be filed in electronic format.

I.   Omission of Information by Certain Wholly-Owned Subsidiaries

If, on the date of the filing of its report on Form 10–K, the registrant meets the conditions specified in paragraph (1) below, then such registrant may furnish the abbreviated narrative disclosure specified in paragraph (2) below.

(1)   Conditions for availability of the relief specified in paragraph (2) below.

(a)   All of the registrant's equity securities are owned, either directly or indirectly, by a single person which is a reporting company under the Act and which has filed all the material required to be filed pursuant to section 13, 14, or 15(d) thereof, as applicable, and which is named in conjunction with the registrant's description of its business;

(b)   During the preceding thirty-six calendar months and any subsequent period of days, there has not been any material default in the payment of principal, interest, a sinking or purchase fund installment, or any other material default not cured within thirty days, with respect to any indebtedness of the registrant or its subsidiaries, and there has not been any material default in the payment of rentals under material long-term leases; and

(c)   There is prominently set forth, on the cover page of the Form 10–K, a statement that the registrant meets the conditions set forth in General Instruction (I)(1)(a) and (b) of Form 10–K and is therefore filing this Form with the reduced disclosure format.

(d)   The registrant is not an asset-backed issuer, as defined in Item 1101 of Regulation AB.

FORM 10-K

(2) Registrants meeting the conditions specified in paragraph (1) above are entitled to the following relief:

(a) Such registrants may omit the information called for by Item 6, Selected Financial Data, and Item 7, Management's Discussion and Analysis of Financial Condition and Results of Operations provided that the registrant includes in the Form 10–K a management's narrative analysis of the results of operations explaining the reasons for material changes in the amount of revenue and expense items between the most recent fiscal year presented and the fiscal year immediately preceding it. Explanations of material changes should include, but not be limited to, changes in the various elements which determine revenue and expense levels such as unit sales volume, prices charged and paid, production levels, production cost variances, labor costs and discretionary spending programs. In addition, the analysis should include an explanation of the effect of any changes in accounting principles and practices or method of application that have a material effect on net income as reported.

(b) Such registrants may omit the list of subsidiaries exhibit required by Item 601 of Regulation S–K.

(c) Such registrants may omit the information called for by the following otherwise required Items: Item 10, Directors and Executive Officers of the Registrant; Item 11, Executive Compensation; Item 12, Security Ownership of Certain Beneficial Owners and Management; and Item 13, Certain Relationships and Related Transactions.

(d) In response to Item 1, Business, such registrant only need furnish a brief description of the business done by the registrant and its subsidiaries during the most recent fiscal year which will, in the opinion of management, indicate the general nature and scope of the business of the registrant and its subsidiaries, and in response to Item 2, Properties, such registrant only need furnish a brief description of the material properties of the registrant and its subsidiaries to the extent, in the opinion of the management, necessary to an understanding of the business done by the registrant and its subsidiaries.

J. Use of This Form by Asset-Backed Issuers

The following applies to registrants that are asset-backed issuers. Terms used in this General Instruction J. have the same meaning as in Item 1101 of Regulation AB.

(1) *Items that May be Omitted.* Such registrants may omit the information called for by the following otherwise required Items:

(a) Item 1, Business;

(b) Item 1A, Risk Factors;

(c) Item 2, Properties;

(d) Item 3, Legal Proceedings;

(e) [Removed and Reserved].

(f) Item 5, Market for Registrant's Common Equity, Related Stockholder Matters and Issuer Purchases of Equity Securities;

(g) Item 6, Selected Financial Data;

(h) Item 7, Management's Discussion and Analysis of Financial Condition and Results of Operations;

(i) Item 7A, Quantitative and Qualitative Disclosures About Market Risk;

(j) Item 8, Financial Statements and Supplementary Data;

(k) Item 9, Changes in and Disagreements With Accountants on Accounting and Financial Disclosure;

(l) Item 9A, Controls and Procedures;

(m)   If the issuing entity does not have any executive officers or directors, Item 10, Directors and Executive Officers of the Registrant, Item 11, Executive Compensation, Item 12, Security Ownership of Certain Beneficial Owners and Management, and Item 13, Certain Relationships and Related Transactions; and

(n)   Item 14, Principal Accountant Fees and Services.

(2)   *Substitute Information to be Included*. In addition to the Items that are otherwise required by this Form, the registrant must furnish in the Form 10–K the following information:

(a)   Immediately after the name of the issuing entity on the cover page of the Form 10–K, as separate line items, the exact name of the depositor as specified in its charter and the exact name of the sponsor as specified in its charter. Include a Central Index Key number for the depositor and the issuing entity, and if available, the sponsor.

(b)   Item 1112(b) of Regulation AB;

(c)   Items 1114(b)(2) and 1115(b) of Regulation AB;

(d)   Item 1117 of Regulation AB;

(e)   Item 1119 of Regulation AB;

(f)   Item 1122 of Regulation AB; and

(g)   Item 1123 of Regulation AB.

(3)   *Signatures*. The Form 10–K must be signed either:

(a)   On behalf of the depositor by the senior officer in charge of securitization of the depositor; or

(b)   On behalf of the issuing entity by the senior officer in charge of the servicing function of the servicer. If multiple servicers are involved in servicing the pool assets, the senior officer in charge of the servicing function of the master servicer (or entity performing the equivalent function) must sign if a representative of the servicer is to sign the report on behalf of the issuing entity.

FORM 10–K

SECURITIES AND EXCHANGE COMMISSION

Washington, D.C. 20549

(Mark One)

[   ]   **ANNUAL REPORT PURSUANT TO SECTION 13 OR 15(d) OF THE SECURITIES EXCHANGE ACT OF 1934**

For the fiscal year ended _____

OR

[   ]   **TRANSITION REPORT PURSUANT TO SECTION 13 OR 15(d) OF THE SECURITIES EXCHANGE ACT OF 1934**

For the transition period from _____ to _____

Commission file number _____

_____

(Exact name of registrant as specified in its charter)

_____   _____

(State or other jurisdiction of   (I.R.S. Employer
incorporation or organization)   Identification No.)

(Address of principal executive offices)   (Zip Code)

Registrant's telephone number, including area code _____

Securities registered pursuant to Section 12(b) of the Act:

Title of each class	Trading symbol(s)	Name of each exchange on which registered

Securities registered pursuant to section 12(g) of the Act:

_____

(Title of class)

_____

(Title of class)

Indicate by check mark if the registrant is a well-known seasoned issuer, as defined in Rule 405 of the Securities Act.

Yes ___ No___

Indicate by check mark if the registrant is not required to file reports pursuant to Section 13 or Section 15(d) of the Act.

Yes___ No___

NOTE: Checking the box above will not relieve any registrant required to file reports pursuant to Section 13 or 15(d) of the Exchange Act from their obligations under those Sections.

Indicate by check mark whether the registrant (1) has filed all reports required to be filed by Section 13 or 15(d) of the Securities Exchange Act of 1934 during the preceding 12 months (or for such shorter period that the registrant was required to file such reports), and (2) has been subject to such filing requirements for the past 90 days.

Yes ___ No ___

Indicate by check mark whether the registrant has submitted electronically every Interactive Data File required to be submitted pursuant to Rule 405 of Regulation S–T (§ 232.405 of this chapter) during the preceding 12 months (or for such shorter period that the registrant was required to submit such files).

Yes ___ No ___

Indicate by check mark whether the registrant is a large accelerated filer, an accelerated filer, a non-accelerated filer, a smaller reporting company, or an emerging growth company. See the definitions of "large accelerated filer," "accelerated filer," "smaller reporting company," and "emerging growth company" in Rule 12b–2 of the Exchange Act.

Large accelerated filer ☐
Non-accelerated filer ☐
Accelerated filer ☐
Smaller reporting company ☐
Emerging growth company ☐

If an emerging growth company, indicate by check mark if the registrant has elected not to use the extended transition period for complying with any new or revised financial accounting standards provided pursuant to Section 13(a) of the Exchange Act. ☐

Indicate by check mark whether the registrant has filed a report on and attestation to its management's assessment of the effectiveness of its internal control over financial reporting under Section 404(b) of the Sarbanes-Oxley Act by the registered public accounting firm that prepared or issued its audit report.☐

Indicate by check mark whether the registrant is a shell company (as defined in Rule 12b–2 of the Exchange Act).

Yes___ No___

State the aggregate market value of the voting and non-voting common equity held by non-affiliates computed by reference to the price at which the common equity was last sold, or the average bid and asked price of such common equity, as of the last business day of the registrant's most recently completed second fiscal quarter.

NOTE: If a determination as to whether a particular person or entity is an affiliate cannot be made without involving unreasonable effort and expense, the aggregate market value of the common stock held by non-affiliates may be calculated on the basis of assumptions reasonable under the circumstances, provided that the assumptions are set forth in this Form.

Indicate by check mark whether the registrant is a large accelerated filer, an accelerated filer, or a non-accelerated filer (as defined in Rule 12b–2 of the Exchange Act). Check one:

Large accelerated filer ___ Accelerated filer ___ Non-accelerated filer ___

APPLICABLE ONLY TO REGISTRANTS INVOLVED IN BANKRUPTCY PROCEEDINGS

DURING THE PRECEDING FIVE YEARS:

Indicate by check mark whether the registrant has filed all documents and reports required to be filed by Section 12, 13 or 15(d) of the Securities Exchange Act of 1934 subsequent to the distribution of securities under a plan confirmed by a court.

Yes ___ No ___

(APPLICABLE ONLY TO CORPORATE REGISTRANTS)

Indicate the number of shares outstanding of each of the registrant's classes of common stock, as of the latest practicable date.

DOCUMENTS INCORPORATED BY REFERENCE

List hereunder the following documents if incorporated by reference and the Part of the Form 10–K (e.g., Part I, Part II, etc.) into which the document is incorporated: (1) Any annual report to security holders; (2) Any proxy or information statement; and (3) Any prospectus filed pursuant to Rule 424(b) or (c) under the Securities Act of 1933. The listed documents should be clearly described for identification purposes (e.g., annual report to security holders for fiscal year ended December 24, 1980).

PART I

[See General Instruction G(2)]

Item 1. Business

Furnish the information required by Item 101 of Regulation S–K except that the discussion of the development of the registrant's business need only include developments since the beginning of the fiscal year for which this report is filed.

Item 1A. Risk Factors

Set forth, under the caption "Risk Factors," where appropriate, the risk factors described in Item 105 of Regulation S–K applicable to the registrant.

Item 1B. Unresolved Staff Comments

If the registrant is an accelerated filer or a large accelerated filer, as defined in Rule 12b–2 of the Exchange Act or is a well-known seasoned issuer as defined in Rule 405 of the Securities Act and has received written comments from the Commission staff regarding its periodic or current reports under the Act not less than 180 days before the end of its fiscal year to which the annual report relates, and such comments remain unresolved, disclose the substance of any such unresolved comments that the registrant believes are material. Such disclosure may provide other information including the position of the registrant with respect to any such comment.

Item 2.   Properties

Furnish the information required by Item 102 of Regulation S–K.

Item 3.   Legal Proceedings

(a)   Furnish the information required by Item 103 of Regulation S–K.

(b)   As to any proceeding that was terminated during the fourth quarter of the fiscal year covered by this report, furnish information similar to that required by Item 103 of Regulation S–K, including the date of termination and a description of the disposition thereof with respect to the registrant and its subsidiaries.

Item 4.   Mine Safety Disclosures

If applicable, provide a statement that the information concerning mine safety violations or other regulatory matters required by Section 1503(a) of the Dodd-Frank Wall Street Reform and Consumer Protection Act and Item 104 of Regulation S–K is included in exhibit 95 to the annual report.

PART II

[See General Instruction G(2)]

Item 5.   Market for Registrant's Common Equity, Related Stockholder Matters and Issuer Purchases of Equity Securities

(a)   Furnish the information required by Item 201 of Regulation S–K and Item 701 of Regulation S–K as to all equity securities of the registrant sold by the registrant during the period covered by the report that were not registered under the Securities Act. If the Item 701 information previously has been included in a Quarterly Report on Form 10–Q or in a Current Report on Form 8–K, it need not be furnished.

(b)   If required pursuant to Rule 463 of the Securities Act of 1933, furnish the information required by Item 701(f) of Regulation S–K.

(c)   Furnish the information required by Item 703 of Regulation S–K for any repurchase made in a month within the fourth quarter of the fiscal year covered by the report. Provide disclosures covering repurchases made on a monthly basis. For example, if the fourth quarter began on January 16 and ended on April 15, the chart would show repurchases for the months from January 16 through February 15, February 16 through March 15, and March 16 through April 15.

Item 6.   Selected Financial Data

Furnish the information required by Item 301 of Regulation S–K.

Item 7.   Management's Discussion and Analysis of Financial Condition and Results of Operation

Furnish the information required by Item 303 of Regulation S–K.

Item 7A. Quantitative and Qualitative Disclosures About Market Risk

Furnish the information required by Item 305 of Regulation S–K.

Item 8. Financial Statements and Supplementary Data

(a) Furnish financial statements meeting the requirements of Regulation S–X, except § 210.3–05 and Article 11 thereof, and the supplementary financial information required by Item 302 of Regulation S–K. Financial statements of the registrant and its subsidiaries consolidated (as required by Rule 14a–3(b)) shall be filed under this item. Other financial statements and schedules required under Regulation S–X may be filed as "Financial Statement Schedules" pursuant to Item 15, Exhibits, Financial Statement Schedules, and Reports on Form 8–K, of this Form.

(b) A smaller reporting company may provide the information required by Article 8 of Regulation S–X in lieu of any financial statements required by Item 8 of this Form.

Item 9. Changes in and Disagreements With Accountants on Accounting and Financial Disclosure

Furnish the information required by Item 304(b) of Regulation S–K.

Item 9A. Controls and Procedures

Furnish the information required by Items 307 and 308 of Regulation S–K.

Item 9A(T). Controls and Procedures

(a) If the registrant is neither a large accelerated filer nor an accelerated filer as those terms are defined in Rule 12b–2, furnish the information required by Items 307 and 308T of Regulation S–K with respect to an annual report that the registrant is required to file for a fiscal year ending on or after June 15, 2010.

(b) This temporary Item 9A(T) will expire on December 15, 2010

Item 9B. Other Information

The registrant must disclose under this item any information required to be disclosed in a report on Form 8–K during the fourth quarter of the year covered by this Form 10–K, but not reported, whether or not otherwise required by this Form 10–K. If disclosure of such information is made under this item, it need not be repeated in a report on Form 8–K which would otherwise be required to be filed with respect to such information or in a subsequent report on Form 10–K.

PART III

[See General Instruction G(3)]

Item 10. Directors and Executive Officers of the Registrant

Furnish the information required by Items 401, 405, 406, and 407(c)(3), (d)(4) and (d)(5) of Regulation S–K.

Item 11. Executive Compensation

Furnish the information required by Item 402 Regulation S–K and paragraphs (e)(4) and (e)(5) of Item 407 of Regulation S–K.

Item 12. Security Ownership of Certain Beneficial Owners and Management and Related Stockholder Matters

Furnish the information required by Item 201(d) of Regulation S–K and by Item 403 of Regulation S–K.

Item 13. Certain Relationships and Related Transactions, and Director Independence

Furnish the information required by Item 404 of Regulation S–K and Item 407(a) of Regulation S–K.

Item 14. Principal Accountant Fees and Services

Furnish the information required by Item 9(e) of Schedule 14A.

(1)   Disclose, under the caption *Audit Fees*, the aggregate fees billed for each of the last two fiscal years for professional services rendered by the principal accountant for the audit of the registrant's annual financial statements and review of financial statements included in the registrant's Form 10–Q or services that are normally provided by the accountant in connection with statutory and regulatory filings or engagements for those fiscal years.

(2)   Disclose, under the caption *Audit-Related Fees*, the aggregate fees billed in each of the last two fiscal years for assurance and related services by the principal accountant that are reasonably related to the performance of the audit or review of the registrant's financial statements and are not reported under Item 9(e)(1) of Schedule 14A. Registrants shall describe the nature of the services comprising the fees disclosed under this category.

(3)   Disclose under the caption *Tax Fees*, the aggregate fees billed in each of the last two fiscal years for professional services rendered by the principal accountant for tax compliance, tax advice, and tax planning. Registrants shall describe the nature of the services comprising the fees disclosed under this category.

(4)   Disclose, under the caption *All Other Fees*, the aggregate fees billed in each of the last two fiscal years for products and services provided by the principal accountant, other than the services reported in Items 9(e)(1) through 9(e)(3) of Schedule 14A. Registrants shall describe the nature of the services comprising the fees disclosed under this category.

(5)(i)   Disclose the audit committee's pre-approval policies and procedures described in paragraph (c)(7)(i) of Rule 2–01 of Regulation S–X.

(ii)   Disclose the percentage of services described in each of Items 9(e)(2) through 9(e)(4) of Schedule 14A that were approved by the audit committee pursuant to paragraph (c)(7)(i)(C) of Item 2–01 of Regulation S–X.

(6)   If greater than 50 percent, disclose the percentage of hours expended on the principal accountant's engagement to audit the registrant's financial statements for the most recent fiscal year that were attributed to work performed by persons other than the principal accountant's full-time, permanent employees.

Instruction to Item 14.

A registrant that is an Asset-Backed Issuer (as defined in Rule 13a–14(g) and Rule 15d–14(g) under the Exchange Act) is not required to disclose the information required by this Item.

PART IV

Item 15. Exhibits and Financial Statement Schedules

(a)   List the following documents filed as a part of the report:

1.   All financial statements;

2.   Those financial statement schedules required to be filed by Item 8 of this Form, and by paragraph (b) below.

3.   Those exhibits required by Item 601 of Regulation S–K and by paragraph (c) below. Identify in the list each management contract or compensatory plan or arrangement required to be filed as an exhibit to this form pursuant to Item 14(c) of this report.

(b)   Registrants shall file, as exhibits to this Form, the exhibits required by Item 601 of Regulation S–K.

(c)   Registrants shall file, as financial statement schedules to this Form, the financial statements required by Regulation S–X which are excluded from the annual report to shareholders by Rule 14a–3(b), including

(1) Separate financial statements of subsidiaries not consolidated and fifty percent or less owned persons;

(2) Separate financial statements of affiliates whose securities are pledged as collateral and

(3) Schedules.

SIGNATURES
[See General Instruction D]

Pursuant to the requirements of section 13 or 15(d) of the Securities Exchange Act of 1934, the registrant has duly caused this report to be signed on its behalf by the undersigned, thereunto duly authorized.

(Registrant) _____

By (Signature and Title) * _____

Date _____

Pursuant to the requirements of the Securities Exchange Act of 1934, this report has been signed below by the following persons on behalf of the registrant and in the capacities and on the dates indicated.

By (Signature and Title) * _____

Date _____

. . .

By (Signature and Title) * _____

Date _____

Supplemental Information to Be Furnished With Reports Filed Pursuant to Section 15(d) of the Act by Registrants Which Have Not Registered Securities Pursuant to Section 12 of the Act

(a) Except to the extent that the materials enumerated in (1) and/or (2) below are specifically incorporated into this Form by reference, every registrant which files an annual report on this Form pursuant to Section 15(d) of the Act must furnish to the Commission for its information, at the time of filing its report on this Form, four copies of the following:

(1) Any annual report to security holders covering the registrant's last fiscal year; and

(2) Every proxy statement, form of proxy or other proxy soliciting material sent to more than ten of the registrant's security holders with respect to any annual or other meeting of security holders.

(b) The foregoing material shall not be deemed to be "filed" with the Commission or otherwise subject to the liabilities of section 18 of the Act, except to the extent that the registrant specifically incorporates it in its annual report on this Form by reference.

(c) If no such annual report or proxy material has been sent to security holders, a statement to that effect shall be included under this caption. If such report or proxy material is to be furnished to security holders subsequent to the filing of the annual report of this Form, the registrant shall so state under this caption and shall furnish copies of such material to the Commission when it is sent to security holders.

---

* Print the name and title of each signing officer under his signature.

FORM 11–K

H. FORM 11–K

17 C.F.R. § 249.311

FOR ANNUAL REPORTS OF EMPLOYEE STOCK PURCHASE, SAVINGS AND SIMILAR PLANS PURSUANT TO SECTION 15(d) OF THE SECURITIES EXCHANGE ACT OF 1934

GENERAL INSTRUCTIONS

A.   Rule as to Use of Form 11–K

This form shall be used for annual reports pursuant to section 15(d) of the Securities Exchange Act of 1934 ("Exchange Act") with respect to employee stock purchase, savings and similar plans, interests in which constitute securities registered under the Securities Act of 1933. This form also shall be used for transition reports filed pursuant to section 15(d) of the Exchange Act. Such a report is required to be filed even though the issuer of the securities offered to employees pursuant to the plan also files annual reports pursuant to section 13(a) or 15(d) of the Exchange Act. However, attention is directed to Rule 15d–21, which provides that in certain cases the information required by this form may be furnished with respect to the plan as a part of the annual report of such issuer. Reports on this form shall be filed within 90 days after the end of the fiscal year of the plan, *provided that* plans subject to the Employee Retirement Income Security Act of 1974 ("ERISA") shall file the plan financial statements within 180 days after the plan's fiscal year end.

B.   Application of General Rules and Regulations

(a)   The General Rules and Regulations under the Exchange Act contain requirements applicable to reports on any form. These general requirements should be carefully read and observed in the preparation and filing of reports on this form.

(b)   Particular attention is directed to Regulation 12B, which contains general requirements regarding matters such as the kind and size of paper to be used, the legibility of the report, and the filing of the report. The definitions contained in Rule 12b–2 should be especially noted. See also Regulation 15D.

(c)   Four complete copies of each report on this form, including exhibits and all papers and documents filed as a part thereof, shall be filed with the Commission. At least one of the copies filed shall be manually signed. Copies not manually signed shall bear typed or printed signatures.

C.   Preparation of Report

This form is not to be used as a blank form to be filled in, but only as a guide in the preparation of the report on paper meeting the requirements of Rule 12b–12. The report may omit the text of Form 11–K specifying the information required provided the answers thereto are prepared in the manner specified in Rule 12b–13.

D.   Incorporation of Information in Report to Employees

Any financial statements contained in any plan annual report to employees covering the latest fiscal year of the plan may be incorporated by reference from such document in response to part or all of the requirements of this form, provided such financial statements substantially meet the requirements of this form and provided that such document is filed as an exhibit to this report on Form 11–K.

E.   Electronic Filers

Reports on this Form may be filed either in paper or in electronic format, at the filer's option. See Rule 101(b)(3) of Regulation S–T.

FORM 11–K

(Mark One)

[   ]   ANNUAL REPORT PURSUANT TO SECTION 15(d) OF THE SECURITIES EXCHANGE ACT OF 1934

For the fiscal year ended _____

1934 ACT FORMS

OR

[   ]   TRANSITION REPORT PURSUANT TO SECTION 15(d) OF THE SECURITIES EXCHANGE
ACT OF 1934

For the transition period from _____

to _____

Commission file number _____

    A.   Full title of the plan and the address of the plan, if different from that of the issuer named below:

    B.   Name of issuer of the securities held pursuant to the plan and the address of its principal
executive office:

REQUIRED INFORMATION

The following financial statements shall be furnished for the plan:

    1.   An audited statement of financial condition as of the end of the latest two fiscal years of the plan
(or such lesser period as the plan has been in existence).

    2.   An audited statement of comprehensive income (either in a single continuous financial statement
or in two separate but consecutive financial statements; or a statement of net income if there was no other
comprehensive income) and changes in plan equity for each of the latest three fiscal years of the plan (or
such lesser period as the plan has been in existence).

    3.   The statements required by Items 1 and 2 shall be prepared in accordance with the applicable
provisions of Article 6A of Regulation S–X.

    4.   In lieu of the requirements of Items 1–3 above, plans subject to ERISA may file plan financial
statements and schedules prepared in accordance with the financial reporting requirements of ERISA. To
the extent required by ERISA, the plan financial statements shall be examined by an independent
accountant, except that the "limited scope exemption" contained in section 103(a)(3)(C) of ERISA shall not
be available.

NOTE: A written consent of the accountant is required with respect to the plan annual financial statements
which have been incorporated by reference in a registration statement on Form S–8 under the Securities Act of
1933. The consent should be filed as an exhibit to this annual report. Such consent shall be currently dated and
manually signed.

SIGNATURES

The Plan. Pursuant to the requirements of the Securities Exchange Act of 1934, the trustees (or other
persons who administer the employee benefit plan) have duly caused this annual report to be signed
on its behalf by the undersigned hereunto duly authorized.

_____ (Name of Plan)

Date _____   _____ (Signature) *

*Print name and title of the signing official under the signature.

I. FORM FUNDING PORTAL

17 C.F.R. § 249.2000

APPLICATION OR AMENDMENT TO APPLICATION FOR REGISTRATION OR WITHDRAWAL FROM REGISTRATION AS FUNDING PORTAL UNDER THE SECURITIES EXCHANGE ACT OF 1934

WARNING: Failure to complete this form truthfully, to keep this form current and to file accurate supplementary information on a timely basis, or the failure to keep accurate books and records or otherwise to comply with the provisions of law applying to the conduct of business as a *funding portal*, would violate the Federal securities laws and may result in disciplinary, administrative, injunctive or criminal action.

Check the appropriate box:

This is:

☐   an initial application to register as a *funding portal* with the *SEC*.

☐   an amendment to any part of the *funding portal*'s most recent Form Funding Portal, including a *successor* registration.

☐   a withdrawal of the *funding portal*'s registration with the *SEC*.

Schedule A must be completed as part of all initial applications. Amendments to Schedule A must be provided on Schedule B. Schedule C must be completed by *nonresident funding portals*. If this is a withdrawal of a *funding portal*'s registration, complete Schedule D.

If this is an amendment to any part of the *funding portal's* most recent Form Funding Portal, provide an explanation describing the amendment: _____

_____

Item 1.   Identifying Information

Exact name, principal business address, mailing address, if different, and contact information of the *funding portal*:

A.   Full name of the *funding portal*: _____

B.   Name(s)/Website URL(s) under which business is conducted, if different from Item 1A:

_____

C.   IRS Empl. Ident. No.: _____

D.   If a name and/or website URL in (1A) or (1B) has changed since the *funding portal*'s most recent Form Funding Portal, enter the previous name and/or website URL and specify whether the name change is of the *funding portal* name (1A), or name/website URL (1B).

Previous name(s) or website URL(s): _____

E.   *Funding portal*'s main street address (Do not use a P.O. Box):

F.   Mailing address(es) (if different) and office locations (if more than one):

_____

_____

G.   Contact Information:

Telephone Number: _____

Fax Number: _____

Email Address: _____

H.   Contact Employee Information:

Name: _____

Title: _____

Direct Telephone Number: _____

Fax Number: _____

Direct Email Address: _____

I.   Month *applicant's* fiscal year ends: _____

J.   Registrations

Was the *applicant* previously registered on Form Funding Portal as a *funding portal* or with the Commission in any other capacity?

☐ Yes   SEC File No.: _____

☐ No

K.   Foreign registrations

(1)   Is the *applicant* registered with a *foreign financial regulatory authority*? Answer "no" even if affiliated with a business that is registered with a *foreign financial regulatory authority*.

☐ Yes   ☐ No

If "yes," complete Section K.2. below.

(2)   List the name, in English, of each *foreign financial regulatory authority* and country with which the *applicant* is registered. A separate entry must be completed for each *foreign financial regulatory authority* with which the *applicant* is registered.

English Name of Foreign Financial Regulatory Authority: _____

Registration Number (if any): _____

Name of Country: _____

Item 2.   Form of Organization

A.   Indicate legal status of *applicant*.

☐ Corporation   ☐ Limited Liability Company

☐ Sole Proprietorship   ☐ Other (please specify) _____

☐ Partnership

B.   If other than a sole proprietor, indicate date and place *applicant* obtained its legal status (*i.e.*, state or country where incorporated, where partnership agreement was filed, or where *applicant* entity was formed):

State/Country of formation: _____

Date of formation: _____

Item 3.   Successions

A.   Is the *applicant* at the time of this filing succeeding to the business of a currently registered *funding portal*?

☐ Yes   ☐ No

Do not report previous successions already reported on Form Funding Portal. If "yes," complete Section 3.B. below.

B.   Complete the following information if succeeding to the business of a currently-registered *funding portal*. If the *applicant* acquired more than one *funding portal* in the succession being reported on this Form Funding Portal, a separate entry must be completed for each acquired firm.

Name of Acquired *Funding Portal*: _____

Acquired *Funding Portal*'s *SEC* File No.: _____

C.   Briefly describe details of the succession including any assets or liabilities not assumed by the *successor*.

Item 4.   Control Relationships

In this Item, identify every *person* that, directly or indirectly, *controls* the *applicant*, *controls* management or policies of the *applicant*, or that the *applicant* directly or indirectly *controls*.

_____

_____

If this is an initial application, the *applicant* also must complete Schedule A. Schedule A asks for information about direct owners and executive officers. If this is an amendment updating information reported on the Schedule A filed with the *applicant*'s initial application, the *applicant* must complete Schedule B.

Item 5.   Disclosure Information

In this Item, provide information about the *applicant*'s disciplinary history and the disciplinary history of all *associated persons* or *control affiliates* of the *applicant* (as applicable). This information is used to decide whether to revoke registration, to place limitations on the *applicant*'s activities as a *funding portal*, and to identify potential problem areas on which to focus during examinations. One event may result in the requirement to answer "yes" to more than one of the questions below. Check all answers that apply. Refer to the Explanation of Terms section of Form Funding Portal Instructions for explanation of italicized terms.

If the answer is "yes" to any question in this Item, the *applicant* must complete the appropriate Disclosure Reporting Page ("DRP") (FP)—Criminal, Regulatory Action, Civil Judicial Action, Bankruptcy/SIPC, Bond, or Judgment/Lien, as applicable.

Criminal Disclosure

If the answer is "yes" to any question below, complete a Criminal DRP.

A.   In the past ten years, has the *applicant* or any *associated person*:

(1)   been convicted of any *felony*, or pled guilty or nolo contendere ("no contest") to any charge of a *felony*, in a domestic, foreign, or military court?

     ☐ Yes   ☐ No

The response to the following question may be limited to charges that are currently pending:

(2)   been *charged* with any *felony*?

     ☐ Yes   ☐ No

B.   In the past ten years, has the *applicant* or any *associated person*:

(1)   been convicted of any *misdemeanor*, or pled guilty or nolo contendere ("no contest"), in a domestic, foreign, or military court to any charge of a *misdemeanor* in a case involving: *investment-related* business, or any fraud, false statements, or omissions, wrongful taking of property, bribery, perjury, forgery, counterfeiting, extortion, or a conspiracy to commit any of these offenses?

     ☐ Yes   ☐ No

The response to the following question may be limited to charges that are currently pending:

(2)   been *charged* with a *misdemeanor* listed in Item 5–B(1)?

     ☐ Yes   ☐ No

Regulatory Action Disclosure

If the answer is "yes" to any question below, complete a Regulatory Action DRP.

C.   Has the *SEC* or the Commodities Futures Trading Commission ("CFTC") ever:

     (1)   *found the applicant* or any *associated person* to have made a false statement or omission?

        ☐ Yes   ☐ No

     (2)   *found the applicant* or any *associated person* to have been *involved* in a violation of any *SEC* or CFTC regulations or statutes?

        ☐ Yes   ☐ No

     (3)   *found the applicant* or any *associated person* to have been a cause of the denial, suspension, revocation, or restriction of the authorization of an *investment-related* business to operate?

        ☐ Yes   ☐ No

     (4)   entered an *order* against the *applicant* or *any associated person* in connection with *investment-related* activity?

        ☐ Yes   ☐ No

     (5)   imposed a civil money penalty on the *applicant* or any *associated person*, or ordered the *applicant* or any *associated person* to cease and desist from any activity?

        ☐ Yes   ☐ No

D.   Has any other federal regulatory agency, any state regulatory agency, or any *foreign financial regulatory authority*:

     (1)   ever *found* the *applicant* or any *associated person* to have made a false statement or omission, or been dishonest, unfair, or unethical?

        ☐ Yes   ☐ No

     (2)   ever *found* the *applicant* or any *associated person* to have been *involved* in a violation of *investment-related* regulations or statutes?

        ☐ Yes   ☐ No

     (3)   ever *found* the *applicant* or any *associated person* to have been the cause of a denial, suspension, revocation, or restriction of the authorization of an *investment-related* business to operate?

        ☐ Yes   ☐ No

     (4)   in the past ten years entered an *order* against the *applicant* or any *associated person* in connection with an *investment-related* activity?

        ☐ Yes   ☐ No

     (5)   ever denied, suspended, or revoked the registration or license of the *applicant* or that of any *associated person*, or otherwise prevented the *applicant* or any *associated person* of the *applicant*, by *order*, from associating with an *investment-related* business or restricted the activities of the *applicant* or any *associated person*?

        ☐ Yes   ☐ No

E.   Has any *self-regulatory organization* or commodities exchange ever:

     (1)   found the applicant or any associated person to have made a false statement or omission?

        ☐ Yes   ☐ No

(2) *found* the *applicant* or any *associated person* to have been *involved* in a violation of its rules (other than a violation designated as a *minor rule violation* under a plan approved by the *SEC*)?

☐ Yes   ☐ No

(3) *found* the *applicant* or any *associated person* to have been the cause of a denial, suspension, revocation or restriction of the authorization of an *investment-related* business to operate?

☐ Yes   ☐ No

(4) disciplined the *applicant* or any *associated person* by expelling or suspending the applicant or the associated person from membership, barring or suspending the *applicant* or the *associated person* from association with other members, or by otherwise restricting the activities of the *applicant* or the *associated person*?

☐ Yes   ☐ No

F. Has the *applicant* or any *associated person* ever had an authorization to act as an attorney, accountant, or federal contractor revoked or suspended?

☐ Yes   ☐ No

G. Is the *applicant* or any *associated person* currently the subject of any regulatory *proceeding* that could result in a "yes" answer to any part of Item 5C, 5–D, or 5–E?

☐ Yes   ☐ No

Civil Judicial Disclosure

If the answer is "yes" to a question below, complete a Civil Judicial Action DRP.

H. Has any domestic or foreign court:

(1) in the past ten years, *enjoined* the *applicant* or any *associated person* in connection with any *investment-related* activity?

☐ Yes   ☐ No

(2) ever *found* that the *applicant* or any *associated person* was *involved* in a violation of *investment-related* statutes or regulations?

☐ Yes   ☐ No

(3) ever dismissed, pursuant to a settlement agreement, an *investment-related* civil action brought against the *applicant* or any *associated person* by a state or *foreign financial regulatory authority*?

☐ Yes   ☐ No

I. Is the *applicant* or any *associated person* now the subject of any civil *proceeding* that could result in a "yes" answer to any part of Item 5–H(1)–(3)?

☐ Yes   ☐ No

Financial Disclosure

If the answer is "yes" to a question below, complete a Bankruptcy/Disclosure, Bond Disclosure or Judgment/Lien DRP, as applicable.

J. In the past ten years, has the *applicant* or a *control affiliate* of the *applicant* ever been a securities firm or a *control affiliate* of a securities firm that:

(1) has been the subject of a bankruptcy petition?

☐ Yes   ☐ No

(2) has had a trustee appointed or a direct payment procedure initiated under the Securities Investor Protection Act?

☐ Yes   ☐ No

K. Has a bonding company ever denied, paid out on, or revoked a bond for the *applicant*?

☐ Yes   ☐ No

L. Does the *applicant* have any unsatisfied judgments or liens against it?

☐ Yes   ☐ No

Item 6. Non-Securities Related Business

Does *applicant* engage in any non-securities related business?

☐ Yes   ☐ No

If "yes," briefly describe the non-securities business.

_____

_____

Item 7. Qualified Third Party Arrangements; Compensation Arrangements

A. Qualified Third Party Arrangements. Complete the following information for each *person* that will hold investor funds in escrow or otherwise pursuant to the requirements of Rule 303(e) of Regulation Crowdfunding (17 CFR 227.303(e)).

Name of *person*: _____

Address: _____

Phone Number: _____

B. Compensation. Please describe any compensation arrangements *funding portal* has with issuers.

_____

EXECUTION

The *funding portal* consents that service of any civil action brought by or notice of any proceeding before the Securities and Exchange Commission or any *self-regulatory organization* in connection with the *funding portal*'s investment-related business may be given by registered or certified mail to the *funding portal*'s contact *person* at the main address, or mailing address, if different, given in Items 1.E., 1.F., and 1.H. If the applicant is a *nonresident funding portal*, it must complete Schedule C to designate a U.S. agent for service of process.

The undersigned represents and warrants that he/she has executed this form on behalf of, and is duly authorized to bind, the *funding portal*. The undersigned and the *funding portal* represent that the information and statements contained herein and other information filed herewith, all of which are made a part hereof, are current, true and complete. The undersigned and the *funding portal* further represent that, if this is an amendment, to the extent that any information previously submitted is not amended, such information is currently accurate and complete.

Date: _____

Full Legal Name of *Funding Portal*: _____

By: _____
        (signature)

Title: _____

FORM FUNDING PORTAL

SCHEDULE A

Direct Owners and Executive Officers

1. Complete Schedule A only if submitting an initial application. Schedule A asks for information about the *applicant*'s direct owners and executive officers. Use Schedule B to amend this information.

2. Direct Owners and Executive Officers. List below the names of:

    (a) each Chief Executive Officer, Chief Financial Officer, Chief Operations Officer, Chief Legal Officer, Chief Compliance Officer, director and any other individuals with similar status or functions;

    (b) if *applicant* is organized as a corporation, each shareholder that is a direct owner of 5% or more of a class of the *applicant*'s voting securities, unless *applicant* is a public reporting company (a company subject to Section 13 or 15(d) of the Exchange Act);

    Direct owners include any *person* that owns, beneficially owns, has the right to vote, or has the power to sell or direct the sale of 5% or more of a class of the *applicant*'s voting securities. For purposes of this Schedule, a *person* beneficially owns any securities: (i) owned by his/her child, stepchild, grandchild, parent, stepparent, grandparent, spouse, sibling, mother-in-law, father-in-law, son-in-law, daughter-in-law, brother-in-law, or sister-in-law, sharing the same residence; or (ii) that he/she has the right to acquire, within 60 days, through the exercise of any option, warrant, or right to purchase the security.

    (c) if the *applicant* is organized as a partnership, <u>all</u> general partners and those limited and special partners that have the right to receive upon dissolution, or have contributed, 5% or more of the *applicant*'s capital;

    (d) in the case of a trust, (i) a *person* that directly owns 5% or more of a class of the *applicant*'s voting securities, or that has the right to receive upon dissolution, or has contributed, 5% or more of the *applicant*'s capital, (ii) the trust and (iii) each trustee; and

    (e) if the *applicant* is organized as a limited liability company ("LLC"), (i) those members that have the right to receive upon dissolution, or have contributed, 5% or more of the *applicant*'s capital, and (ii) if managed by elected managers, all elected managers.

3. In the DE/FE/NP column below, enter "DE" if the owner is a domestic entity, "FE" if the owner is an entity incorporated or domiciled in a foreign country, or "NP" if the owner or executive officer is a natural person.

4. Complete the Title or Status column by entering board/management titles; status as partner, trustee, sole proprietor, elected manager, shareholder, or member; and for shareholders or members, the class of securities owned (if more than one is issued).

5. Ownership codes are:

    NA—less than 5%   B—10% but less than 25%   D—50% but less than 75%

    A—5% but less than 10%   C—25% but less than 50%   E—75% or more

    G—Other (general partner, trustee, or elected member)

6. Control Person:

    (a) In the Control Person column, enter "Yes" if the *person* has *control* as defined in the Glossary of Terms to Form Funding Portal, and enter "No" if the *person* does not have *control*. Note that under this definition, most executive officers and all 25% owners, general partners, elected managers, and trustees are "control persons".

    (b) In the PR column, enter "PR" if the owner is a public reporting company under Section 13 or 15(d) of the Exchange Act.

7.　Complete each column.

FULL LEGAL NAME (Natural Persons: Last Name, First Name, Middle Name)	DE/FE/NP	Title or Status	Date Title or Status Acquired		Ownership Code	Control Person	CRD No. (If None: IRS Tax No. or IRS Employer ID No., if applicable, or if none, enter 0000000)
			MM	YYYY		Yes/No	PR

FORM FUNDING PORTAL
SCHEDULE B

Amendments to Schedule A

1.　Use Schedule B only to amend information requested on Schedule A. Refer to Schedule A for specific instructions for completing this Schedule B. Complete each column. File with a completed Execution Page.

2.　In the Type of Amendment column, indicate "A" (addition), "D" (deletion), or "C" (change in information about the same *person*).

3.　Ownership codes are:

NA—less than 5%　　　　B—10% but less than 25%　　　D—50% but less than 75%

A—5% but less than 10%　C—25% but less than 50%　　　E—75% or more

　　　　　　G—Other (general partner, trustee, or elected member)

4. List below all changes to Schedule A (Direct Owners and Executive Officers):

FULL LEGAL NAME (Natural Persons: Last Name, First Name, Middle	DE/FE/NP	Type of Amendment	Title or Status	Date Title or Status Acquired		Ownership Code	Control Person		CRD No. (If None: IRS Tax No. or IRS Employer ID No., if applicable, or if none, enter 0000000)
				MM	YYYY		Yes/No	PR	

FORM FUNDING PORTAL

SCHEDULE C

Nonresident Funding Portals

Service of Process and Certification Regarding Prompt Access to Books and Records and Ability to Submit to Inspections and Examinations

Each *nonresident funding portal applicant* shall use Schedule C of Form Funding Portal to: identify its United States agent for service of process, and certify that it can, as a matter of law and will: (1) provide the Commission and any registered national securities association of which it becomes a member with prompt access to its books and records, and (2) submit to onsite inspection and examination by the Commission and any registered national securities association of which it becomes a member.

A.   Agent for Service of Process:

1.   Name of United States *person applicant* designates and appoints as agent for service of process:

_____

2.   Address of United States *person applicant* designates and appoints as agent for service of process:

_____

The above identified agent for service of process may be served any process, pleadings, subpoenas, or other papers in:

(a)   any investigation or administrative proceeding conducted by the Commission that relates to the *applicant* or about which the *applicant* may have information; and

(b)   any civil or criminal suit or action or proceeding under the federal securities laws brought against the *applicant* or to which the *applicant* has been joined as defendant or respondent, in any appropriate court in any place subject to the jurisdiction of any state or of the United States or of any of its territories or possessions or of the District of Columbia. The *applicant* has stipulated and agreed that any such suit, action or administrative proceeding may be commenced by the service of process upon, and that service of an administrative subpoena shall be effected by service upon, the above-named agent for service of process, and that service as aforesaid shall be taken and held in all courts and administrative tribunals to be valid and binding as if personal service thereof had been made.

B.   Certification regarding access to records and ability to submit to inspections and examinations:

Applicant can, as a matter of law, and will:

1.   provide the Commission and any registered national securities association of which it becomes a member with prompt access to its books and records, and

2.   submit to onsite inspection and examination by the Commission and any registered national securities association of which it becomes a member.

Applicant must attach as an exhibit to this Form Funding Portal, Exhibit C, a copy of the opinion of counsel it is required to obtain in accordance with Rule 400(f) of Regulation Crowdfunding, i.e., the opinion of counsel that the nonresident funding portal can, as a matter of law, provide the Commission and any registered national securities association of which the nonresident funding portal becomes a member with prompt access to the books and records of such nonresident funding portal, and that the nonresident funding portal can, as a matter of law, submit to onsite inspection and examination by the Commission and any registered national securities association of which the nonresident funding portal becomes a member.

EXECUTION FOR NON-RESIDENT FUNDING PORTALS

The undersigned represents and warrants that he/she has executed this form on behalf of, and is duly authorized to bind, the *nonresident funding portal*. The undersigned and the *nonresident funding portal* represent that the information and statements contained herein and other information filed herewith, all of which are made a part hereof, are current, true and complete. The undersigned and the *nonresident funding portal* further represent that, if this is an amendment, to the extent that any information previously submitted is not amended, such information is currently accurate and complete.

The undersigned certifies that the *nonresident funding portal* can, as a matter of law, and will provide the Commission and any registered national securities association of which it becomes a member with prompt access to the books and records of such *nonresident funding portal* and can, as a matter of law, and will submit to onsite inspection and examination by the Commission and any registered national securities association of which it becomes a member. Finally, the undersigned authorizes any person having custody or possession of these books and records to make them available to federal regulatory representatives.

Signature: _____

Name and Title: _____

Date: _____

FORM FUNDING PORTAL
SCHEDULE D

If this is a withdrawal of registration:

A.   The date the *funding portal* ceased business or withdrew its registration request:

Date (MM/DD/YYYY): _____

B.   Location of Books and Records after Registration Withdrawal

Complete the following information for each location at which the *applicant* will keeps books and records after withdrawing its registration.

FORM FUNDING PORTAL

Name and address of entity where books and records are kept:

_____

_____

(area code) (telephone number)   (area code)   (fax number)

This is (check one):   ☐ one of *applicant's* branch offices or affiliates.

☐ a third party unaffiliated recordkeeper.

☐ other.

If this address is a private residence, check this box: ☐

Briefly describe the books and records kept at this location.

C.   Is the *funding portal* now the subject of or named in any *investment-related*

1.   Investigation

☐ Yes   ☐ No

2.   Investor initiated complaint

☐ Yes   ☐ No

3.   Private civil litigation

☐ Yes   ☐ No

CRIMINAL ACTION DISCLOSURE REPORTING PAGE (FP)

General Instructions

This Disclosure Reporting Page (DRP FP) is an ☐ INITIAL *OR* ☐ AMENDED response used to report details for affirmative responses to Items 5–A or 5–B of Form Funding Portal.

Check item(s) being responded to:	☐ 5–A(1)	☐ 5–A(2)	☐ 5–B(1)	☐ 5–B(2)

Use a separate DRP for each event or *proceeding*. The same event or *proceeding* may be reported for more than one *person* or entity using one DRP. File with a completed Execution Page.

Multiple counts of the same charge arising out of the same event(s) should be reported on the same DRP. Unrelated criminal actions, including separate cases arising out of the same event, must be reported on separate DRPs. Use this DRP to report all charges arising out of the same event. One event may result in more than one affirmative answer to the items listed above.

Part 1

Check all that apply:

1.   The *person*(s) or entity(ies) for whom this DRP is being filed is (are) the:

Select only one.

☐ *Applicant*

☐ *Applicant* and one or more *associated persons*

☐ One or more of *applicant's associated persons*

If this DRP is being filed for the *applicant*, and it is an amendment that seeks to remove a DRP concerning the *applicant* from the record, the reason the DRP should be removed is:

☐ The *applicant* is registered or applying for registration, and the event or *proceeding* was resolved in the *applicant's* favor.

1934 ACT FORMS

☐ The DRP was filed in error.

If this DRP is being filed for an *associated person*:

This *associated person* is:	☐ a firm	☐ a natural person
The *associated person* is:	☐ registered with the *SEC*	☐ not registered with the *SEC*

Full name of the *associated person* (including, for natural persons, last, first and middle names):
_____

If the *associated person* has a *CRD* number, provide that number. _____

If this is an amendment that seeks to remove a DRP concerning the *associated person*, the reason the DRP should be removed is:

☐ The *associated person*(s) is (are) no longer associated with the *applicant*.

☐ The event or *proceeding* was resolved in the *associated person*'s favor.

☐ The event or *proceeding* occurred more than ten years ago.

☐ The DRP was filed in error. Explain the circumstances:
_____
_____

Part 2

1. If charge(s) were brought against a firm or organization over which the *applicant* or an *associated person* exercise(s)(d) *control*:

   A. Enter the firm or organization's name _____

   B. Was the firm or organization engaged in an *investment-related* business?
      ☐ Yes   ☐ No

   C. What was the relationship of the *applicant* with the firm or organization? (In the case of a *associated person*, include any position or title with the firm or organization.)
   _____

2. Court where formal charge(s) were brought in: (include the name of Federal, Military, State or Foreign Court, Location of Court—City or County and State or Country, and Docket/Case number).

   A. Name of Court: _____

   B. Location of Court:

      Street Address: _____

      City or County: _____   State/Country: _____

      Postal Code: _____

3. Event Disclosure Detail (Use this for both organizational and individual charges.)

   A. Date First *Charged* (MM/D/YYYY): _____ ☐ Exact ☐ Explanation

   If not exact, provide explanation:
   _____

   B. Event Disclosure Detail (include charge(s)/charge Description(s), and for each charge provide: (1) number of counts, (2) *felony* or *misdemeanor*, (3) plea for each charge, and (4) product type if charge is *investment-related*).
   _____

C.   Did any of the charge(s) within the event *involve* a *felony*? ☐ Yes   ☐ No

D.   Current status of the event? ☐ Pending ☐ On Appeal ☐ Final

E.   Event status date (Complete unless status is pending)

    (MM/DD/YYYY): _____ ☐ Exact ☐ Explanation

If not exact, provide explanation:

_____

4.   Disposition Disclosure Detail: Include for each charge (a) Disposition Type *(e.g.,* convicted, acquitted, dismissed, pretrial, etc.), (b) Date, (c) Sentence/Penalty, (d) Duration (if sentence-suspension, probation, etc.), (e) Start Date of Penalty, (f) Penalty/Fine Amount, and (g) Date Paid.

_____

5.   Provide a brief summary of circumstances leading to the charge(s) as well as the disposition. Include the relevant dates when the conduct that was the subject of the charge(s) occurred. (The response must fit within the space provided.)

_____

_____

REGULATORY ACTION DISCLOSURE REPORTING PAGE (FP)

GENERAL INSTRUCTIONS

This Disclosure Reporting Page (DRP FP) is an ☐ INITIAL *OR* ☐ AMENDED response used to report details for affirmative responses to Item 5–C, 5–D, 5–E–5–F or 5–G of Form Funding Portal.

Check item(s) being responded to: ☐ 5–C(1)   ☐ 5–C(2)   ☐ 5–C(3)   ☐ 5–C(4)

☐ 5–C(5)   ☐ 5–D(1)   ☐ 5–D(2)   ☐ 5–D(3)   ☐ 5–D(4)   ☐ 5–D(5)

☐ 5–E(1)   ☐ 5–E(2)   ☐ 5–E(3)   ☐ 5–E(4)   ☐ 5–F   ☐ 5–G

Use a separate DRP for each event or *proceeding*. An event or *proceeding* may be reported for more than one *person* or entity using one DRP. File with a completed Execution Page.

One event may result in more than one affirmative answer to Items 5–C, 5–D, 5–E, 5–F or 5–G. Use only one DRP to report details related to the same event. If an event gives rise to actions by more than one regulator, provide details for each action on a separate DRP.

Part 1

The *person*(s) or entity(ies) for whom this DRP is being filed is (are) the:

    Select only one.

    ☐ *Applicant* (the *funding portal*)

    ☐ *Applicant* and one or more of the *applicant's associated person*(s)

    ☐ One or more of *applicant's associated person*(s)

If this DRP is being filed for the *applicant* and it is an amendment that seeks to remove a DRP concerning the *applicant* from the record, the reason the DRP should be removed is:

    ☐ The *applicant* is registered or applying for registration, and the event or *proceeding* was resolved in the *applicant's* favor.

    ☐ The DRP was filed in error.

1934 ACT FORMS

If this DRP is being filed for an *associated person*:

    This *associated person* is: ☐ a firm
                              ☐ a natural person

    The *associated person* is: ☐ registered with the *SEC*
                              ☐ not registered with the *SEC*

Full name of the *associated person* (including, for natural persons, last, first and middle names):

_____

If the *associated person* has a *CRD* number, provide that number. _____

If this is an amendment that seeks to remove a DRP concerning the *associated person*, the reason the DRP should be removed is:

    ☐   The *associated person*(s) is (are) no longer associated with the *applicant*.

    ☐   The event or *proceeding* was resolved in the *associated person*'s favor. The DRP was filed in error. Explain the circumstances:

Part 2

1.   Regulatory Action was initiated by:

☐ *SEC*   ☐ Other Federal Authority   ☐ *SRO*

☐ Foreign Authority   ☐ State

(Full name of regulator, *foreign financial regulatory authority*, federal authority, state or *SRO*)

_____

_____

_____

2.   Principal Sanction (check appropriate item):

☐ Civil and Administrative Penalty(ies)/Fine(s)

☐ Restitution   ☐ Expulsion   ☐ Disgorgement

☐ Bar   ☐ Revocation   ☐ Suspension

☐ Cease and Desist ☐ Injunction   ☐ Undertaking Censure

☐ Prohibition   ☐ Other

☐ Denial   ☐ Reprimand

Other Sanctions:

_____

_____

_____

3.   Date Initiated (MM/DD/YYYY): _____ ☐ Exact
                                        ☐ Explanation

If not exact, provide explanation:

_____

_____

_____

FORM FUNDING PORTAL

4. Docket/Case Number: _____

5. *Associated person*'s Employing Firm when activity occurred that led to the regulatory action (if applicable):

_____

_____

6. Principal Product Type (check appropriate item):

☐ Annuity(ies)—Fixed   ☐ Derivative(s)   ☐ Mutual Fund(s)

☐ Annuity(ies)—Variable   ☐ Direct Investment(s)—DPP & LP Interest(s)

☐ Money Market Fund(s)   ☐ Equity—OTC   ☐ Options

☐ CD(s) Equity Listed   ☐ (Common & Preferred Stock)   ☐ Penny Stock(s)

☐ Commodity Option(s)   ☐ Futures—Commodity   ☐ Unit Investment Trust(s)

☐ Debt—Asset Backed   ☐ Futures—Financial   ☐ Other

☐ Debt—Corporate   ☐ Index Option(s)   ☐ No Product

☐ Debt—Government   ☐ Insurance

☐ Debt—Municipal   ☐ Investment Contract(s)

Other Product Types:

_____

_____

_____

7. Describe the allegations related to this regulatory action. (The response must fit within the space provided.)

8. Current status? ☐ Pending   ☐ On Appeal   ☐ Final

9. If on appeal, to whom the regulatory action was appealed (*SEC, SRO*, Federal or State Court) and date appeal filed:

_____

If Final or On Appeal, complete all items below. For Pending Actions, complete Item 13 only.

10. How was matter resolved (check appropriate item):

☐ Acceptance, Waiver & Consent (AWC)   ☐ Dismissed   ☐ Vacated

☐ Consent   ☐ Withdrawn   ☐ *Order*

☐ Decision   ☐ Settled

☐ Decision & *Order* of Offer of Settlement   ☐ Stipulation and Consent   ☐ Other

11. Resolution Date (MM/DD/YYYY): _____ ☐ Exact ☐ Explanation

If not exact, provide explanation:

_____

_____

12. Resolution Detail:

 A. Were any of the following Sanctions Ordered (check all appropriate items)?

 ☐ Monetary/Fine ☐ Revocation/Expulsion/Denial ☐ Censure Amount: $ _____

 ☐ Disgorgement ☐ Suspension ☐ Bar

 ☐ Cease & Desist/Injunction

 B. Other Sanctions Ordered:

 _____

 _____

 C. Sanction detail: If suspended, *enjoined* or barred, provide duration including start date and capacities affected (General Securities Principal, Financial Operations Principal, etc.). If requalification by exam/retraining was a condition of the sanction, provide length of time given to requalify/retrain, type of exam required and whether condition has been satisfied. If disposition resulted in a fine, penalty, restitution, disgorgement or monetary compensation, provide total amount, portion levied against the *applicant* or an *associated person*, date paid and if any portion of penalty was waived:

 _____

 _____

13. Provide a brief summary of details related to the action status and (or) disposition, and include relevant terms, conditions and dates.

 _____

CIVIL JUDICIAL ACTION DISCLOSURE REPORTING PAGE (FP)

GENERAL INSTRUCTIONS

This Disclosure Reporting Page (DRP FP) is an ☐ INITIAL *OR* ☐ AMENDED response used to report details for affirmative responses to Item 5–H or 5–I of Form Funding Portal.

Check item(s) being responded to: ☐ 5–H(1) ☐ 5–H(2) ☐ 5–H(3) ☐ 5–I

Use a separate DRP for each event or *proceeding*. An event or *proceeding* may be reported for more than one *person* or entity using one DRP. File with a completed Execution Page.

One event may result in more than one affirmative answer to Item 5–H or 5–I. Use only one DRP to report details related to the same event. Unrelated civil judicial actions must be reported on separate DRPs.

Part 1

The *person*(s) or entity(ies) for whom this DRP is being filed is (are) the:

 Select only one.

 ☐ *Applicant* (the *funding portal*)

 ☐ *Applicant* and one or more of the applicant's *associated person*(s)

 ☐ One or more of the *applicant*'s associated *person*(s)

If this DRP is being filed for the *applicant* and it is an amendment that seeks to remove a DRP concerning the *applicant* from the record, the reason the DRP should be removed is:

 ☐ The *applicant* is registered or applying for registration, and the event or *proceeding* was resolved in the *applicant*'s favor.

 ☐ The DRP was filed in error.

FORM FUNDING PORTAL

If this DRP is being filed for an *associated person*:

    This *associated person* is: ☐ a firm ☐ a natural person

    The *associated person*: ☐ registered with the *SEC* ☐ not registered with the *SEC*

Full name of the *associated person* (including, for natural persons, last, first and middle names):

_____

If the *associated person* has a *CRD* number, provide that number. _____

If this is an amendment that seeks to remove a DRP concerning the *associated person*, the reason the DRP should be removed is:

    ☐   The *associated person*(s) is (are) no longer associated with the *applicant*.

    ☐   The event or *proceeding* was resolved in the *associated person*'s favor. The DRP was filed in error. Explain the circumstances:

_____

_____

Part 2

1.   Court Action initiated by: (Name of regulator, *foreign financial regulatory authority*, *SRO*, commodities exchange, agency, firm, private plaintiff, etc.)

2.   Principal Relief Sought (check appropriate item):

☐ Cease and Desist (Private/Civil Complaint)	☐ Disgorgement	☐ Money Damages
☐ Restraining Order	☐ Civil Penalty(ies)/Fine(s)	☐ Injunction
☐ Restitution	☐ Other _____	

Other Relief Sought: _____

3.   Filing Date of Court Action (MM/DD/YYYY): _____ ☐ Exact ☐ Explanation

    If not exact, provide explanation:

_____

4.   Principal Product Type (check appropriate item):

☐ Annuity(ies)—Fixed	☐ Derivative(s)	☐ Investment Contract(s)
☐ Annuity(ies)—Variable Direct	☐ Investment(s)—DPP & LP Interest(s)	☐ Money Market Fund(s) CD(s)
☐ Equity—OTC	☐ Mutual Fund(s)—Commodity	☐ Option(s) No Product
☐ Equity Listed (Common & Preferred Stock)	☐ Options	☐ Debt—Asset Backed
☐ Futures—Commodity Penny Stock(s)	☐ Debt—Corporate	☐ Futures—Financial Unit Investment
☐ Trust(s) Debt	☐ Government Index Option(s)	☐ Other Debt—Municipal
☐ Insurance		

Other Product Types:

_____

5. Formal Action was brought in (include the name of the Federal, State, or Foreign Court; Location of Court—City or County and State or Country; and Docket/Case Number

6. *Associated person*'s Employing Firm when activity occurred that led to the civil judicial action (if applicable):

7. Describe the allegations related to this civil action (the response must fit within the space provided):

8. Current status? ☐ Pending   ☐ On Appeal   ☐ Final

9. If on appeal, court to which the action was appealed (provide name of the court) and Date Appeal Filed (MM/DD/YYYY):

    _____

    _____

10. If pending, date notice/process was served (MM/DD/YYYY): _____

    ☐ Exact   ☐ Explanation

    If not exact, provide explanation:

    _____

If Final or On Appeal, complete all items below. For Pending Actions, complete Item 14 only.

11. How was matter resolved (check appropriate item):

    ☐ Consent   ☐ Judgment Rendered   ☐ Settled   ☐ Dismissed   ☐ Opinion

    ☐ Withdrawn   ☐ Other _____

12. Resolution Date(MM/DD/YYYY): _____ ☐ Exact   ☐ Explanation

    If not exact, provide explanation:

    _____

    _____

13. Resolution Detail:

    A. Were any of the following Sanctions Ordered or Relief Granted (check appropriate items)?

    ☐ Monetary/Fine Amount: ☐ Revocation/Expulsion/Denial   ☐ Disgorgement/Restitution
    $ _____

    ☐ Censure   ☐ Cease and Desist/Injunction   ☐ Bar

    ☐ Suspension

    B. Other Sanctions Ordered:

    _____

    C. Sanction detail: If suspended, *enjoined* or barred, provide duration including start date and capacities affected (General Securities Principal, Financial Operations Principal, etc.). If requalification by exam/retraining was a condition of the sanction, provide length of time given to requalify/retrain, type of exam required and whether condition has been satisfied. If disposition resulted in a fine, penalty, restitution, disgorgement or monetary compensation, provide total amount, portion levied against the *applicant* or an *associated person*, date paid and if any portion of penalty was waived:

    _____

    _____

FORM FUNDING PORTAL

_____
_____
_____
_____

14. Provide a brief summary of circumstances related to the action(s), allegation(s), disposition(s) and/or finding(s) disclosed above.

_____
_____
_____
_____

BANKRUPTCY/SIPC DISCLOSURE REPORTING PAGE (FP)

GENERAL INSTRUCTIONS

This Disclosure Reporting Page (DRP FP) is an ☐ INITIAL _OR_ ☐ AMENDED response used to report details for affirmative responses to Item 5–J of Form Funding Portal.

Check item(s) being responded to: ☐ 5–J(1)   ☐ 5–J(2)

Use a separate DRP for each event or _proceeding_. An event or _proceeding_ may be reported for more than one _person_ or entity using one DRP. File with a completed Execution Page.

One event may result in more than one affirmative answer to Item 5–J. Use only one DRP to report details related to the same event. Unrelated civil judicial actions must be reported on separate DRPs.

Part 1

1. The _person_(s) or entity(ies) for whom this DRP is being filed is (are) the:

    Select only one.

    ☐ _Applicant_

    ☐ Applicant and one or more control affiliate(s)

    ☐ One or more of _control affiliate_(s)

If this DRP is being filed for a _control affiliate_, give the full name of the _control affiliate_ below (for individuals, Last name, First name, Middle name).

If the _control affiliate_ is registered with the CRD, provide the CRD number. If not, indicate "non-registered" by checking the appropriate checkbox.

FP DRP—CONTROL AFFILIATE

Control Affiliate CRD Number   This _control affiliate_ is: a firm ☐
                                                           a natural person ☐

Registered: ☐ Yes   ☐ No

Full name of the _control affiliate_ (including, for natural persons, last, first and middle names):

_____

☐ This is an amendment that seeks to remove a DRP record because the _control affiliate_(s) is (are) no longer associated with the _funding portal_.

2. If the _control affiliate_ is registered through the CRD, has the _control affiliate_ submitted a DRP (with Form U–4) or BD DRP to the CRD System for the event? If the answer is "Yes," no other information on this DRP must be provided.

☐ Yes   ☐ No

NOTE: The completion of this Form does not relieve the *control affiliate* of its obligation to update its CRD records.

Part 2

1. Action Type: (check appropriate item)

   ☐ Bankruptcy   ☐ Declaration   ☐ Receivership
   ☐ Compromise   ☐ Liquidated   ☐ Other _____

2. Action Date (MM/DD/YYYY): _____ ☐ Exact ☐ Explanation

   If not exact, provide explanation: _____

3. If the financial action relates to an organization over which the *applicant* or *control affiliate person* exercise(s)(d) *control*, enter organization name and the *applicant*'s or *control affiliate*'s position, title or relationship:

   Was the Organization *investment-related*?   ☐ Yes   ☐ No

4. Court action brought in (Name of Federal, State or Foreign Court), Location of Court (City or County and State or Country), Docket/Case Number and Bankruptcy Chapter Number (if Federal Bankruptcy Filing):

5. Is action currently pending?   ☐ Yes   ☐ No

6. If not pending, provide Disposition Type: (check appropriate item)

   ☐ Direct Payment Procedure   ☐ Dismissed   ☐ Satisfied/Released
   ☐ Discharged Dissolved SIPA   ☐ Trustee   ☐ Appointed
   ☐ Other _____

7. Disposition Date (MM/DD/YYYY): ☐ Exact   ☐ Explanation

   If not exact, provide explanation: _____

8. Provide a brief summary of events leading to the action, and if not discharged, explain. (The information must fit within the space provided): _____

9. If a SIPA trustee was appointed or a direct payment procedure was begun, enter the amount paid by you; or the name of trustee:

   Currently Open?   ☐ Yes   ☐ No

   Date Direct Payment Initiated/Filed or Trustee Appointed (MM/DD/YYYY): _____

   ☐ Exact ☐ Explanation

   If not exact, provide explanation: _____

10. Provide details to any status disposition. Include details as to creditors, terms, conditions, amounts due and settlement schedule (if applicable): _____

BOND DISCLOSURE REPORTING PAGE (FP)

GENERAL INSTRUCTIONS

This Disclosure Reporting Page (DRP FP) is an ☐ INITIAL *OR* ☐ AMENDED response used to report details for affirmative responses to Item 5–K of Form Funding Portal.

Check item(s) being responded to: ☐ 5–K

FORM FUNDING PORTAL

Use a separate DRP for each event or *proceeding*. An event or *proceeding* may be reported for more than one *person* or entity using one DRP. File with a completed Execution Page.

One event may result in more than one affirmative answer to Item 5–K. Use only one DRP to report details related to the same event. If an event gives rise to actions by more than one regulator, provide details for each action on a separate DRP.

1.　Firm Name: (Policy Holder) _____

_____

2.　Bonding Company Name: _____

_____

3.　Disposition Type: (check appropriate item)

　　☐ Denied ☐ Payout ☐ Revoked

4.　Disposition Date (MM/DD/YYYY):　☐ Exact　☐ Explanation

　　If not exact, provide explanation:

_____

_____

5.　If disposition resulted in Payout, list Payout Amount and Date Paid:

_____

_____

6.　Summarize the details of circumstances leading to the necessity of the bonding company action:

_____

_____

_____

_____

JUDGMENT / LIEN DISCLOSURE REPORTING PAGE (FP)

GENERAL INSTRUCTIONS

This Disclosure Reporting Page (DRP FP) is an ☐ INITIAL *OR* ☐ AMENDED response used to report details for affirmative responses to Item 5–L of Form Funding Portal.

Check item(s) being responded to: ☐ 5–L

Use a separate DRP for each event or *proceeding*. An event or *proceeding* may be reported for more than one *person* or entity using one DRP. File with a completed Execution Page. One event may result in more than one affirmative answer to Item 5–L. Use only one DRP to report details related to the same event. If an event gives rise to actions by more than one regulator, provide details for each action on a separate DRP.

1.　Judgment/Lien Amount: _____

2.　Judgment/Lien Holder: _____

3.　Judgment/Lien Type: (check appropriate item)

　　☐ Civil　☐ Default　☐ Tax

4.　Date Field(MM/DD/YYYY): _____ ☐ Exact ☐ Explanation

　　If not exact, provide explanation: _____

5.　Is Judgment/Lien outstanding: ☐ Yes　☐ No

　　If No, how was matter resolved? (check appropriate item)

☐ Discharged ☐ Released ☐ Removed ☐ Satisfied

6. Court where judgment was given:

    A.   Name of Court _____

    B.   Location of Court:

        Street Address: _____

        City or County: _____ State/Country: _____

        Postal Code: _____

    C.   Docket/Case Number

7. Provide a brief summary of events leading to the action and any payment schedule details, including current status (if applicable): _____

FORM FUNDING PORTAL INSTRUCTIONS

A. GENERAL INSTRUCTIONS

1. EXPLANATION OF FORM

- This is the form that a *funding portal* must use to register with the Securities and Exchange Commission ("SEC" or "Commission"), to amend its registration and to withdraw from registration.

- The Commission may make publicly accessible all current Forms Funding Portal, including amendments and registration withdrawal requests, which may be searchable by the public, with the exception of certain personally identifiable information or other information with significant potential for misuse (including the contact employee's direct phone number, fax number and e-mail address and any IRS Tax Number, IRS Employer Identification Number, or any other similar information). If the *applicant* submits any attachments to Form Funding Portal in PDF format it is the responsibility of the *applicant* to redact certain personally identifiable information or other information with significant potential for misuse (including the contact employee's direct phone number, fax number and e-mail address and any IRS Tax Number, IRS Employer Identification Number, or any other similar information) from the PDF.

2. WHEN TO FILE FORM FUNDING PORTAL

- A *funding portal*'s registration must become effective before offering or selling any securities in reliance on Section 4(a)(6) through a platform. Under Rule 400, a *funding portal*'s registration will be effective the later of: (1) 30 calendar days after the date a complete Form Funding Portal is received by the Commission or (2) the date the *funding portal* is approved for membership by a national securities association registered under Section 15A of the Securities Exchange Act of 1934 ("Exchange Act").

- A registered *funding portal* must promptly file an amendment to Form Funding Portal when any information previously submitted on Form Funding Portal becomes inaccurate or incomplete for any reason.

- A *successor funding portal* may succeed to the registration of a registered *funding portal* by filing a registration on Form Funding Portal within 30 days after the succession.

- If a *funding portal* succeeds to and continues the business of a registered *funding portal* and the succession is based solely on a change of the predecessor's date or state of incorporation, form of organization, or composition of a partnership or similar reason, the *successor* may, within 30 days of the succession, amend the registration on Form Funding Portal to reflect these changes.

- A *funding portal* must also file a withdrawal on Form Funding Portal (and complete Schedule D) promptly upon ceasing to operate as a *funding portal*. Withdrawal will be effective on the

FORM FUNDING PORTAL

later of 30 days after receipt by the Commission, after the *funding portal* is no longer operational, or within such longer period of time as to which the *funding portal* consents or which the Commission by order may determine as necessary or appropriate in the public interest or for the protection of investors.

- A Form Funding Portal filing will not be considered complete unless it complies with all applicable requirements.

3.   **ELECTRONIC FILING**—The *applicant* must file Form Funding Portal electronically, and must utilize this system to file and amend Form Funding Portal electronically to assure the timely acceptance and processing of those filings.

4.   **CONTACT EMPLOYEE**—The individual listed as the contact employee must be authorized to receive all compliance information, communications, and mailings, and be responsible for disseminating it within the *applicant*'s organization.

5.   **FEDERAL INFORMATION LAW AND REQUIREMENTS**

- The principal purpose of this form is to provide a mechanism by which a *funding portal* can register with the Commission, amend its registration and withdraw from registration. The Commission maintains a file of the information on this form and will make certain information collected through the form publicly available. The SEC will not accept forms that do not include the required information.

- Section 4A(a) of the Securities Act of 1933 [15 U.S.C. § 77d–1(a)] and Sections 3(h) and 23(a) the Exchange Act [15 U.S.C. §§ 78c(h) and 78w(a)] authorize the SEC to collect the information required by Form Funding Portal. The SEC collects the information for regulatory purposes. Filing Form Funding Portal is mandatory for *persons* that are registering as *funding portals* with the SEC.

- Any member of the public may direct to the Commission any comments concerning the accuracy of the burden estimate on this Form and any suggestions for reducing this burden. This collection of information has been reviewed by the Office of Management and Budget in accordance with the clearance requirements of 44 U.S.C. § 3507. The information contained in this form is part of a system of records subject to the Privacy Act of 1974, as amended. The Securities and Exchange Commission has published in the Federal Register the Privacy Act Systems of Records Notice for these records.

B.   FILING INSTRUCTIONS

1.   FORMAT

- All fields requiring a response in Items 1–7 must be completed before the filing will be accepted.

- *Applicant* must complete the execution page certifying that Form Funding Portal and amendments thereto have been executed properly and that the information contained therein is accurate and complete.

- To amend information, the *applicant* must update the appropriate Form Funding Portal pages or Schedules.

- A paper copy, with original manual signatures, of the initial Form Funding Portal filing and amendments to Form Funding Portal and Disclosure Reporting Pages must be retained by the *applicant* and be made available for inspection upon a regulatory request.

2.   **DISCLOSURE REPORTING PAGES (DRP)**—Information concerning the *applicant* or *associated person* that relates to the occurrence of an event reportable under Item 5 must be provided on the *applicant*'s appropriate DRP (FP). If an *associated person* is an individual or organization registered through the CRD, such *associated person* need only complete the *associated person* name and CRD number of the *applicant*'s appropriate DRP. Details for the event must be submitted on the *associated person*'s appropriate DRP or DRP (U–4). If an *associated person* is an individual or organization <u>not</u> registered through the CRD, provide

complete answers to all of the questions and complete all fields requiring a response on the *associated person*'s appropriate DRP (FP).

3.   **DIRECT OWNERS**—Amend the Direct Owners and Executive Officers page when changes in ownership occur.

4.   **NONRESIDENT APPLICANTS**—Any *applicant* that is a *nonresident funding portal* must complete Schedule C and attach the opinion of counsel referred to therein.

C.   EXPLANATION OF TERMS

1.   GENERAL

APPLICANT—The *funding portal* applying on or amending this form.

ASSOCIATED PERSON—Any partner, officer, director or manager of the funding portal (or any person occupying a similar status or performing similar functions), any person directly or indirectly controlling or controlled by the funding portal, or any employee of the funding portal, except that any person associated with a funding portal whose functions are solely clerical or ministerial shall not be included in the meaning of such term for purposes of section 15(b) of the Exchange Act (other than paragraphs (4) and (6) thereof).

CONTROL—The power, directly or indirectly, to direct the management or policies of the *funding portal*, whether through contract, or otherwise. A *person* is presumed to *control* a *funding portal* if that *person*: (1) is a director, general partner or officer exercising executive responsibility (or has a similar status or functions); (2) directly or indirectly has the right to vote 25 percent or more of a class of a voting security or has the power to sell or direct the sale of 25 percent or more of a class of voting securities of the *funding portal*; or (3) in the case of a partnership, has contributed, or has a right to receive, 25 percent or more of the capital of the *funding portal*. (This definition is used solely for the purposes of Form Funding Portal).

CONTROL AFFILIATE—A *person* named in Item 4 or any other individual or organization that directly or indirectly controls, is under common control with, or is controlled by, the *applicant*, including any current employee of the *applicant* except one performing only clerical, administrative, support or similar functions, or who, regardless of title, performs no executive duties or has no senior policy making authority.

FOREIGN FINANCIAL REGULATORY AUTHORITY—Includes (1) a foreign securities authority; (2) other governmental body or foreign equivalent of a *self-regulatory organization* empowered by a foreign government to administer or enforce its laws relating to the regulation of *investment* or *investment-related* activities; and (3) a foreign membership organization, a function of which is to regulate the participation of its members in the activities listed above.

FUNDING PORTAL—A broker acting as an intermediary in a transaction involving the offer or sale of securities offered and sold in reliance on Section 4(a)(6), that does not, directly or indirectly: (1) offer *investment* advice or recommendations; (2) solicit purchases, sales or offers to buy the securities displayed on its platform; (3) compensate employees, agents, or other *persons* for such solicitation or based on the sale of securities displayed or referenced on its platform; or (4) hold, manage, possess, or otherwise handle investor funds or securities.

JURISDICTION—Any state of the United States, the District of Columbia, the Commonwealth of Puerto Rico, the U.S. Virgin Islands, any other territory of the United States, or any subdivision or regulatory body thereof.

NONRESIDENT FUNDING PORTAL—A *funding portal* incorporated in or organized under the laws of a jurisdiction outside of the United States or its territories, or having its principal place of business in any place not in the United States or its territories.

PERSON—An individual, partnership, corporation, trust, or other organization.

SELF-REGULATORY ORGANIZATION ("SRO")—A national securities association registered under Section 15A of the Exchange Act or any national securities exchange or registered clearing agency.

SUCCESSOR—A *funding portal* that assumes or acquires substantially all of the assets and liabilities, and that continues the business of, a registered predecessor *funding portal* that ceases its *funding portal* activities. *See* Rule 400(c) of Regulation Crowdfunding (17 CFR 227.400(c)).

2. **FOR THE PURPOSE OF ITEM 5 AND THE CORRESPONDING DISCLOSURE REPORTING PAGES (DRPs) (FP)**

CHARGED—Being accused of a crime in a formal complaint, information, or indictment (or equivalent formal charge).

ENJOINED—Includes being subject to a mandatory injunction, prohibitory injunction, preliminary injunction, or temporary restraining order.

FELONY—For *jurisdictions* that do not differentiate between a *felony* and a *misdemeanor*, a *felony* is an offense punishable by a sentence of at least one year imprisonment and/or a fine of at least $1,000. The term also includes a general court martial.

FOUND—Includes adverse final actions, including consent decrees in which the respondent has neither admitted nor denied the findings, but does not include agreements, deficiency letters, examination reports, memoranda of understanding, letters of caution, admonishments, and similar informal resolutions of matters.

INVESTMENT OR INVESTMENT-RELATED—Pertaining to securities, commodities, banking, savings association activities, credit union activities, insurance, or real estate (including, but not limited to, acting as or being associated with a *funding portal* broker-dealer, municipal securities dealer, government securities broker or dealer, issuer, investment company, investment adviser, futures sponsor, bank, security-based swap dealer, major security-based swap participant, savings association, credit union, insurance company, or insurance agency).

INVOLVED—Doing an act or aiding, abetting, counseling, commanding, inducing, conspiring with or failing reasonably to supervise another in doing an act.

MINOR RULE VIOLATION—A violation of a *self-regulatory organization* rule that has been designated as "minor" pursuant to a plan approved by the SEC or Commodity Futures Trading Commission. A rule violation may be designated as "minor" under a plan if the sanction imposed consists of a fine of $2,500 or less and if the sanctioned *person* does not contest the fine. (Check with the appropriate *self-regulatory organization* to determine if a particular rule violation has been designated as "minor" for these purposes).

MISDEMEANOR—For *jurisdictions* that do not differentiate between a *felony* and a *misdemeanor*, a *misdemeanor* is an offense punishable by a sentence of less than one year imprisonment and/or a fine of less than $1,000. The term also includes a special court martial.

ORDER—A written directive issued pursuant to statutory authority and procedures, including orders of denial, suspension, or revocation; does not include special stipulations, undertakings or agreements relating to payments, limitations on activity or other restrictions unless they are included in an *order*.

PROCEEDING—Includes a formal administrative or civil action initiated by a governmental agency, *self-regulatory organization* or a *foreign financial regulatory authority*; a *felony* criminal indictment or information (or equivalent formal charge); or a *misdemeanor* criminal information (or equivalent formal charge). Does not include other civil litigation, investigations, or arrests or similar charges effected in the absence of a formal criminal indictment or information (or equivalent formal charge).

SELECTED SCHEDULES UNDER THE SECURITIES EXCHANGE ACT OF 1934

SELECTED SCHEDULES UNDER THE SECURITIES EXCHANGE ACT OF 1934

A. SCHEDULE TO
17 C.F.R. § 240.14d–100

TENDER OFFER STATEMENT UNDER SECTION 14(d)(1) OR 13(e)(1) OF THE SECURITIES EXCHANGE ACT OF 1934

SECURITIES AND EXCHANGE COMMISSION

Washington, D.C. 20549

TENDER OFFER STATEMENT UNDER SECTION 14(d)(1) OR 13(e)(1) OF THE SECURITIES EXCHANGE ACT
(Amendment No. _____)

_____

(Name of Subject Company (issuer))

_____

(Name of Filing Persons (identifying status as offeror, issuer or other person))

_____

(Title of Class of Securities)

_____

(CUSIP Number of Class of Securities)

_____

(Name, address, and telephone numbers of person authorized to receive
to notices and communications of behalf of filing persons)

Calculation of Filing Fee

Transaction Valuation*	Amount of Filing Fee

* Set forth the amount on which the filing fee is calculated and state how it was determined.

☐ Check the box if any part of the fee is offset as provided by Rule 0–11(a)(2) and identify the filing with which the offsetting fee was previously paid. Identify the previous filing by registration statement number, or the Form or Schedule and the date of its filing.

Amount Previously Paid: _____

Form or Registration No.: _____

Filing Party: _____

Date Filed: _____

☐ Check the box if the filing relates solely to preliminary communications made before the commencement of a tender offer.

Check the appropriate boxes below to designate any transactions to which the statement relates:

☐ third-party tender offer subject to Rule 14d–1.

☐ issuer tender offer subject to Rule 13e–4.

☐ going-private transaction subject to Rule 13e–3.

☐ amendment to Schedule 13D under Rule 13d–2.

SCHEDULE TO

Check the following box if the filing is a final amendment reporting the results of the tender offer: ☐

If applicable, check the appropriate box(es) below to designate the appropriate rule provision(s) relied upon:

☐ Rule 13e–4(i) (Cross-Border Issuer Tender Offer)

☐ Rule 14d–1(d) (Cross-Border Third-Party Tender Offer)

GENERAL INSTRUCTIONS

A. File eight copies of the statement, including all exhibits with the Commission if paper filing is permitted.

B. This filing must be accompanied by a fee payable to the Commission as required by Rule 0–11.

C. If the statement is filed by a general or limited partnership, syndicate or other group, the information called for by Items 3 and 5–8 for a third-party tender offer and Items 5–8 for an issuer tender offer must be given with respect to: (i) Each partner of the general partnership; (ii) each partner who is, or functions as, a general partner of the limited partnership; (iii) each member of the syndicate or group; and (iv) each person controlling the partner or member. If the statement is filed by a corporation or if a person referred to in (i), (ii), (iii) or (iv) of this Instruction is a corporation, the information called for by the items specified above must be given with respect to: (a) Each executive officer and director of the corporation; (b) each person controlling the corporation; and (c) each executive officer and director of any corporation or other person ultimately in control of the corporation.

D. If the filing contains only preliminary communications made before the commencement of a tender offer, no signature or filing fee is required. The filer need not respond to the items in the schedule. Any pre-commencement communications that are filed under cover of this schedule need not be incorporated by reference into that schedule.

E. If an item is inapplicable or the answer is in the negative, so state. The statement published, sent or given to security holders may omit negative and not applicable responses. If the schedule includes any information that is not published, sent or given to security holders, provide that information or specifically incorporate it by reference under the appropriate item number and heading in the schedule. Do not recite the text of disclosure requirements in the schedule or any document published, sent or given to security holders. Indicate clearly the coverage of the requirements without referring to the text of the items.

F. Information contained in exhibits to the statement may be incorporated by reference in answer or partial answer to any item unless it would render the answer misleading, incomplete, unclear or confusing. A copy of any information that is incorporated by reference or a copy of the pertinent pages of a document containing the information must be submitted with this statement as an exhibit, unless it was previously filed with the Commission electronically on EDGAR. If an exhibit contains information responding to more than one item in the schedule, all information in that exhibit may be incorporated by reference once in response to the several items in the schedule for which it provides an answer. Information incorporated by reference is deemed filed with the Commission for all purposes of the Act.

G. A filing person may amend its previously filed Schedule 13D on Schedule TO if the appropriate box on the cover page is checked to indicate a combined filing and the information called for by the fourteen disclosure items on the cover page of Schedule 13D is provided on the cover page of the combined filing with respect to each filing person.

H. The final amendment required by Rule 14d–3(b)(2) and Rule 13e–4(c)(4) will satisfy the reporting requirements of section 13(d) of the Act with respect to all securities acquired by the offeror in the tender offer.

I. Amendments disclosing a material change in the information set forth in this statement may omit any information previously disclosed in this statement.

J. If the tender offer disclosed in this statement involves a going-private transaction, a combined Schedule TO and Schedule 13E–3 may be filed with the Commission under cover of Schedule TO. The Rule 13e–3 box on the cover page of the Schedule TO must be checked to indicate a combined filing. All information called for by both schedules must be provided except that Items 1–3, 5, 8 and 9 of Schedule TO may be omitted to the extent those items call for information that duplicates the item requirements in Schedule 13E–3.

K.   For purposes of this statement, the following definitions apply:

(1)   The term "offeror" means any person who makes a tender offer or on whose behalf a tender offer is made;

(2)   The term "issuer tender offer" has the same meaning as in Rule 13e–4(a)(2); and

(3)   The term "third-party tender offer" means a tender offer that is not an issuer tender offer.

Special Instructions for Complying With Schedule TO

Under sections 13(e), 14(d) and 23 of the Act and the rules and regulations of the Act, the Commission is authorized to solicit the information required to be supplied by this schedule.

Disclosure of the information specified in this schedule is mandatory. The information will be used for the primary purpose of disclosing tender offer and going-private transactions. This statement will be made a matter of public record. Therefore, any information given will be available for inspection by any member of the public.

Because of the public nature of the information, the Commission can use it for a variety of purposes, including referral to other governmental authorities or securities self-regulatory organizations for investigatory purposes or in connection with litigation involving the Federal securities laws or other civil, criminal or regulatory statutes or provisions.

Failure to disclose the information required by this schedule may result in civil or criminal action against the persons involved for violation of the Federal securities laws and rule.

Item 1.   Summary Term Sheet

Furnish the information required by Item 1001 of Regulation M–A unless information is disclosed to security holders in a prospectus that meets the requirements of Rule 421(d) of the Securities Act.

Item 2.   Subject Company Information

Furnish the information required by Item 1002(a) through (c) of Regulation M–A.

Item 3.   Identity and Background of Filing Person

Furnish the information required by Item 1003(a) through (c) of Regulation M–A for a third-party tender offer and the information required by Item 1003(a) of Regulation M–A for an issuer tender offer.

Item 4.   Terms of the Transaction

Furnish the information required by Item 1004(a) of Regulation M–A for a third-party tender offer and the information required by Item 1004(a) through (b) of Regulation M–A for an issuer tender offer.

Item 5.   Past Contacts, Transactions, Negotiations and Agreements

Furnish the information required by Item 1005(a) and (b) of Regulation M–A for a third-party tender offer and the information required by Item 1005(e) of Regulation M–A for an issuer tender offer.

Item 6.   Purposes of the Transaction and Plans or Proposals

Furnish the information required by Item 1006(a) and (c)(1) through (7) of Regulation M–A for a third-party tender offer and the information required by Item 1006(a) through (c) of Regulation M–A for an issuer tender offer.

Item 7.   Source and Amount of Funds or Other Consideration

Furnish the information required by Item 1007(a), (b) and (d) of Regulation M–A.

Item 8. Interest in Securities of the Subject Company

Furnish the information required by Item 1008 of Regulation M–A.

Item 9. Persons/Assets, Retained, Employed, Compensated or Used

Furnish the information required by Item 1009(a) of Regulation M–A.

Item 10. Financial Statements

If material, furnish the information required by Item 1010(a) and (b) of Regulation M–A for the issuer in an issuer tender offer and for the offeror in a third-party tender offer.

Instructions to Item 10:

1.   Financial statements must be provided when the offeror's financial condition is material to security holder's decision whether to sell, tender or hold the securities sought. The facts and circumstances of a tender offer, particularly the terms of the tender offer, may influence a determination as to whether financial statements are material, and thus required to be disclosed.

2.   Financial statements are *not* considered material when: (a) The consideration offered consists solely of cash; (b) the offer is not subject to any financing condition; *and* either: (c) the offeror is a public reporting company under Section 13(a) or 15(d) of the Act that files reports electronically on EDGAR, or (d) the offer is for all outstanding securities of the subject class. Financial information may be required, however, in a two-tier transaction. *See* Instruction 5 below.

3.   The filing person may incorporate by reference financial statements contained in any document filed with the Commission, solely for the purposes of this schedule, if: (a) The financial statements substantially meet the requirements of this item; (b) an express statement is made that the financial statements are incorporated by reference; (c) the information incorporated by reference is clearly identified by page, paragraph, caption or otherwise; and (d) if the information incorporated by reference is not filed with this schedule, an indication is made where the information may be inspected and copies obtained. Financial statements that are required to be presented in comparative form for two or more fiscal years or periods may not be incorporated by reference unless material incorporated by reference includes the entire period for which the comparative data is required to be given. *See* General Instruction F to this schedule.

4.   If the offeror in a third-party tender offer is a natural person, and such person's financial information is material, disclose the net worth of the offeror. If the offeror's net worth is derived from material amounts of assets that are not readily marketable or there are material guarantees and contingencies, disclose the nature and approximate amount of the individual's net worth that consists of illiquid assets and the magnitude of any guarantees or contingencies that may negatively affect the natural person's net worth.

5.   Pro forma financial information is required in a negotiated third-party cash tender offer when securities are intended to be offered in a subsequent merger or other transaction in which remaining target securities are acquired and the acquisition of the subject company is significant to the offeror under section 210.11–01(b)(1) of this chapter. The offeror must disclose the financial information specified in Item 3(f) and Item 5 of Form S–4 in the schedule filed with the Commission, but may furnish only the summary financial information specified in Item 3(d), (e) and (f) on Form S–4 in the disclosure document sent to security holders. If pro forma financial information is required by this instruction, the historical financial statements specified in Item 1010 of Regulation M–A are required for the bidder.

6.   The disclosure materials disseminated to security holder may contain the summarized financial information specified by Item 1010(c) of Regulation M–A instead of the financial information required by Item 1010(a) and (b). In that case, the financial information required by Item 1010(a) and (b) of Regulation M–A must be disclosed in the statement. If summarized financial information is disseminated to security holders, include appropriate instructions on how more complete financial information can be obtained. If the summarized financial information is prepared on the basis of a comprehensive body of accounting principles other than U.S. GAAP, the summarized financial information must be accompanied by a reconciliation as described in Instructions 8 of this Item.

7.   If the offeror is not subject to the periodic reporting requirements of the Act, the financial statements are not available or obtainable without unreasonable cost or expense. Make a statement to that effect and the reasons for their unavailability.

8. If the financial statements required by this Item are prepared on the basis of a comprehensive body of accounting principles other than U.S. GAAP, provide a reconciliation to U.S. GAAP in accordance with Item 17 of Form 20–F, unless a reconciliation is unavailable or not obtainable without unreasonable cost or expense. At a minimum, however, when financial statements are prepared on a basis other the U.S. GAAP, a narrative description of all material variations in accounting principles, practices and methods used in preparing the non-U.S. GAAP financial statements from those accepted in the U.S. must be presented.

Item 11. Additional Information

Furnish the information required by Item 1011(a) and (c) of Regulation M–A.

Item 12. Exhibits

File as an exhibit to the schedule all documents specified by Item 1016(a), (b), (d), (g) and (h) of Regulation M–A.

Item 13. Information Required by Schedule 13e–3

If the Schedule TO is combined with Schedule 13E–3, set forth the information required by Schedule 13E–3 that is not included or covered by the items in Schedule TO.

Signature

After due inquiry and to the best of my knowledge and belief, I certify that the information set forth in this statement is true, complete and correct.

_____

(Signature

_____

(Name and Title)

_____

(Date)

Instructions to Signature: The statement must be signed by the filing person or that person's by an authorized representative (other than an executive officer of a corporation or general partner of a partnership), evidence of the representative's authority to sign on behalf of the person must filed with the statement. The name and any title of each person who signs the statement must be typed or printed beneath the signature. See Rule 12b–11 and Rule 14d–1(h) with respect to signature requirements.

SCHEDULE 13D

B. SCHEDULE 13D
17 C.F.R. § 240.13d–101

INFORMATION REQUIREMENTS FOR FILINGS UPON ACQUISITION OF FIVE PERCENT OF A CLASS OF EQUITY SECURITIES SUBJECT TO THE REPORTING REQUIREMENTS OF THE 1934 ACT

SCHEDULE 13D

Under the Securities Exchange Act of 1934
(Amendment No. _____) *

_____
(Name of Issuer)

_____
(Title of Class of Securities)

_____
(CUSIP Number)

_____
(Name, Address and Telephone Number of Person Authorized
to Receive Notices and Communications)

_____
(Date of Event which Requires Filing of this Statement)

If the filing person has previously filed a statement on Schedule 13G to report the acquisition which is the subject of this Schedule 13D, and is filing this schedule because of Rule 13d–1(e), Rule 13d–1(f) or Rule 13d–1(g), check the following box [ ].

NOTE: Schedules filed in paper format shall include a signed original and five copies of the schedule, including all exhibits. See Rule 13d–7 for other parties to whom copies are to be sent.

* The remainder of this cover page shall be filed out for a reporting person's initial filing on this form with respect to the subject class of securities, and for any subsequent amendment containing information which would alter disclosures provided in a prior cover page.

The information required on the remainder of this cover page shall not be deemed to be "filed" for the purpose of Section 18 of the Securities Exchange Act of 1934 ("Act") or otherwise subject to the liabilities of that section of the Act but shall be subject to all other provisions of the Act (however, see the Notes).

CUSIP No. _____

(1)	Names of Reporting Persons. (entities only)	
(2)	Check the Appropriate Box if a Member of a Group (See Instructions)	(a) ___ (b) ___
(3)	SEC Use Only	
(4)	Source of Funds (See Instructions)	
(5)	Check if Disclosure of Legal Proceedings is Required Pursuant to Items 2(d) or 2(e)	
(6)	Citizenship or Place of Organization	

1429

Number of Shares Beneficially Owned by Each Reporting Person With	(7)	Sole Voting Power	
	(8)	Shared Voting Power	
	(9)	Sole Dispositive Power	
	(10)	Shared Dispositive Power	

(11)	Aggregate Amount Beneficially Owned by Each Reporting Person	
(12)	Check if the Aggregate Amount in Row (11) Excludes Certain Shares (See Instructions)	
(13)	Percent of Class Represented by Amount in Row (11)	
(14)	Type of Reporting Person (See Instructions)	

Instructions for Cover Page

(1) *Names of Reporting Persons*—Furnish the full legal name of each person for whom the report is filed—i.e., each person required to sign the schedule itself—including each member of a group. Do not include the name of a person required to be identified in the report but who is not a reporting person.

(2) If any of the shares beneficially owned by a reporting person are held as a member of a group and such membership is expressly affirmed, please check row 2(a). If the membership in a group is disclaimed or the reporting person describes a relationship with other persons but does not affirm the existence of a group, please check row 2(b) [unless a joint filing pursuant to Rule 13d–1(k)(1) in which case it may not be necessary to check row 2(b)].

(3) The 3rd row is for SEC internal use; please leave blank.

(4) Classify the source of funds or other consideration used or to be used in making the purchases as required to be disclosed pursuant to item 3 of Schedule 13D and insert the appropriate symbol (or symbols if more than one is necessary) in row (4):

Category of Source	Symbol
Subject Company (Company whose securities are being acquired)	SC
Bank	BK
Affiliate (of reporting person)	AF
Working Capital (of reporting person)	WC
Personal Funds (of reporting person)	PF
Other	OO

(5) If disclosure of legal proceedings or actions is required pursuant to either items 2(d) or 2(e) of Schedule 13D, row 5 should be checked.

(6) *Citizenship or Place of Organization*. Furnish citizenship if the named reporting person is a natural person. Otherwise, furnish place of organization. (See Item 2 of Schedule 13D).

(7)–(11), (13) *Aggregate Amount Beneficially Owned by Each Reporting Person, etc.* Rows (7) through (11), inclusive, and (13) are to be completed in accordance with the provisions of Item 5 of Schedule 13D. All percentages are to be rounded off to nearest tenth (one place after decimal point).

SCHEDULE 13D

(12) Check if the aggregate amount reported as beneficially owned in row (11) does not include shares which the reporting person discloses in the report but as to which beneficial ownership is disclaimed pursuant to Rule 13d–4 under the Securities Exchange Act of 1934.

(14) *Type of Reporting Person.* Please classify each "reporting person" according to the following breakdown and place the appropriate symbol (or symbols, i.e., if more than one is applicable, insert all applicable symbols) on the form:

Category	Symbol
Broker Dealer	BD
Bank	BK
Insurance Company	IC
Investment Company	IV
Investment Adviser	IA
Employee Benefit Plan, or Endowment Fund	EP
Church Plan	CP
Parent Holding Company/Control Person	HC
Corporation	CO
Partnership	PN
Individual	IN
Other	OO

NOTES: Attach as many copies of the second part of the cover page as are needed, one reporting person per page.

Filing persons may, in order to avoid unnecessary duplication, answer items on the schedules (Schedule 13D, 13G or TO) by appropriate cross references to an item or items on the cover page(s). This approach may only be used where the cover page item or items provide all the disclosure required by the schedule item. Moreover, such a use of a cover page item will result in the item becoming a part of the schedule and accordingly being considered as "filed" for purposes of Section 18 of the Securities Exchange Act or otherwise subject to the liabilities of that section of the Act.

Reporting persons may comply with their cover page filing requirements by filing either completed copies of the blank forms available from the Commission, printed or typed facsimiles, or computer printed facsimiles, provided the documents filed have identical formats to the forms prescribed in the Commission's regulations and meet existing Securities Exchange Act rules as to such matters as clarity and size (Securities Exchange Act Rule 12b–12).

SPECIAL INSTRUCTIONS FOR COMPLYING WITH SCHEDULE 13D

Under sections 13(d) and 23 of the Securities Exchange Act of 1934 and the rules and regulations thereunder, the Commission is authorized to solicit the information required to be supplied by this schedule by certain security holders of certain issuers.

Disclosure of the information specified in this schedule is mandatory. The information will be used for the primary purpose of determining and disclosing the holdings of certain beneficial owners of certain equity securities. This statement will be made a matter of public record. Therefore, any information given will be available for inspection by any member of the public.

Because of the public nature of the information, the Commission can utilize it for a variety of purposes, including referral to other governmental authorities or securities self-regulatory organizations for investigatory purposes or in connection with litigation involving the Federal securities laws or other civil, criminal or regulatory statements or provisions.

Failure to disclose the information requested by this schedule may result in civil or criminal action against the persons involved for violation of the Federal securities laws and rules promulgated thereunder.

SELECTED SCHEDULES UNDER THE
SECURITIES EXCHANGE ACT OF 1934

GENERAL INSTRUCTIONS

A. The item number and captions of the items shall be included but the text of the items is to be omitted. The answers to the items shall be so prepared as to indicate clearly the coverage of the items without referring to the text of the items. Answer every item. If an item is inapplicable or the answer is in the negative, so state.

B. Information contained in exhibits to the statement may be incorporated by reference in answer or partial answer to any item or sub-item of the statement unless it would render such answer misleading, incomplete, unclear or confusing. Material incorporated by reference shall be clearly identified in the reference by page, paragraph, caption or otherwise. An express statement that the specified matter is incorporated by reference shall be made at the particular place in the statement where the information is required. A copy of any information or a copy of the pertinent pages of a document containing such information which is incorporated by reference shall be submitted with this statement as an exhibit and shall be deemed to be filed with the Commission for all purposes of the Act.

C. If the statement is filed by a general or limited partnership, syndicate, or other group, the information called for by Items 2–6, inclusive, shall be given with respect to (i) each partner of such general partnership; (ii) each partner who is denominated as a general partner or who functions as a general partner of such limited partnership; (iii) each member of such syndicate or group; and (iv) each person controlling such partner or member. If the statement is filed by a corporation or if a person referred to in (i), (ii), (iii) or (iv) of this Instruction is a corporation, the information called for by the above mentioned items shall be given with respect to (a) each executive officer and director of such corporation; (b) each person controlling such corporation; and (c) each executive officer and director of any corporation or other person ultimately in control of such corporation.

Item 1. Security and Issuer

State the title of the class of equity securities to which this statement relates and the name and address of the principal executive offices of the issuer of such securities.

Item 2. Identity and Background

If the person filing this statement or any person enumerated in Instruction C of this statement is a corporation, general partnership, limited partnership, syndicate or other group of persons, state its name, the state or other place of its organization, its principal business, the address of its principal business, the address of its principal office and the information required by (d) and (e) of this Item. If the person filing this statement or any person enumerated in Instruction C is a natural person, provide the information specified in (a) through (f) of this Item with respect to such person(s).

(a) Name;

(b) Residence or business address;

(c) Present principal occupation or employment and the name, principal business and address of any corporation or other organization in which such employment is conducted;

(d) Whether or not, during the last five years, such person has been convicted in a criminal proceeding (excluding traffic violations or similar misdemeanors) and, if so, give the dates, nature of conviction, name and location of court, any penalty imposed, or other disposition of the case;

(e) Whether or not, during the last five years, such person was a party to a civil proceeding of a judicial or administrative body of competent jurisdiction and as a result of such proceeding was or is subject to a judgment, decree or final order enjoining future violations of, or prohibiting or mandating activities subject to, federal or state securities laws or finding any violation with respect to such laws; and, if so, identify and describe such proceedings and summarize the terms of such judgment, decree or final order; and

(f) Citizenship.

Item 3. Source and Amount of Funds or Other Consideration

State the source and the amount of funds or other consideration used or to be used in making the purchases, and if any part of the purchase price is or will be represented by funds or other consideration borrowed or otherwise obtained for the purpose of acquiring, holding, trading or voting the securities, a description of the transaction and the names of the parties thereto. Where material, such information should also be provided with respect to prior acquisitions not previously reported pursuant to this regulation. If the source of all or any part of the funds is a loan made in the ordinary course of business by a bank, as defined in Section 3(a)(6) of the Act, the name of the bank shall not be made available to the public if the person at the time of filing the statement so requests in writing and files such request, naming such bank, with the Secretary of the Commission. If the securities were acquired other than by purchase, describe the method of acquisition.

Item 4. Purpose of Transaction

State the purpose or purposes of the acquisition of securities of the issuer. Describe any plans or proposals which the reporting persons may have which relate to or would result in:

(a) The acquisition by any person of additional securities of the issuer, or the disposition of securities of the issuer;

(b) An extraordinary corporate transaction, such as a merger, reorganization or liquidation, involving the issuer or any of its subsidiaries;

(c) A sale or transfer of a material amount of assets of the issuer or of any of its subsidiaries;

(d) Any change in the present board of directors or management of the issuer, including any plans or proposals to change the number or term of directors or to fill any existing vacancies on the board;

(e) Any material change in the present capitalization or dividend policy of the issuer;

(f) Any other material change in the issuer's business or corporate structure, including but not limited to, if the issuer is a registered closed-end investment company, any plans or proposals to make any changes in its investment policy for which a vote is required by section 13 of the Investment Company Act of 1940;

(g) Changes in the issuer's charter, by-laws or instruments corresponding thereto or other actions which may impede the acquisition of control of the issuer by any person;

(h) Causing a class of securities of the issuer to be delisted from a national securities exchange or to cease to be authorized to be quoted in an inter-dealer quotation system of a registered national securities association;

(i) A class of equity securities of the issuer becoming eligible for termination of registration pursuant to Section 12(g)(4) of the Act; or

(j) Any action similar to any of those enumerated above.

Item 5. Interest in Securities of the Issuer

(a) State the aggregate number and percentage of the class of securities identified pursuant to Item 1 (which may be based on the number of securities outstanding as contained in the most recently available filing with the Commission by the issuer unless the filing person has reason to believe such information is not current) beneficially owned (identifying those shares which there is a right to acquire) by each person named in Item 2. The above mentioned information should also be furnished with respect to persons who, together with any of the persons named in Item 2, comprise a group within the meaning of section 13(d)(3) of the Act;

(b) For each person named in response to paragraph (a), indicate the number of shares as to which there is sole power to vote or to direct the vote, shared power to vote or to direct the vote, sole power to dispose or to direct the disposition, or shared power to dispose or to direct the disposition. Provide the applicable information required by Item 2 with respect to each person with whom the power to vote or to direct the vote or to dispose or direct the disposition is shared;

(c)   Describe any transactions in the class of securities reported on that were effected during the past sixty days or since the most recent filing on Schedule 13D, whichever is less, by the persons named in response to paragraph (a).

Instruction. The description of a transaction required by Item 5(c) shall include, but not necessarily be limited to: (1) the identity of the person covered by Item 5(c) who effected the transaction; (2) the date of the transaction; (3) the amount of securities involved; (4) the price per share or unit; and (5) where and how the transaction was effected.

(d)   If any other person is known to have the right to receive or the power to direct the receipt of dividends from, or the proceeds from the sale of, such securities, a statement to that effect should be included in response to this item and, if such interest relates to more than five percent of the class, such person should be identified. A listing of the shareholders of an investment company registered under the Investment Company Act of 1940 or the beneficiaries of an employee benefit plan, pension fund or endowment fund is not required.

(e)   If applicable, state the date on which the reporting person ceased to be the beneficial owner of more than five percent of the class of securities.

Instruction. For computations regarding securities which represent a right to acquire an underlying security, see Rule 13d–3(d)(1) and the note thereto.

Item 6.   Contracts, Arrangements, Understandings or Relationships With Respect to Securities of the Issuer

Describe any contracts, arrangements, understandings or relationships (legal or otherwise) among the persons named in Item 2 and between such persons and any person with respect to any securities of the issuer, including but not limited to transfer or voting of any of the securities, finder's fees, joint ventures, loan or option arrangements, puts or calls, guarantees of profits, division of profits or loss, or the giving or withholding of proxies, naming the persons with whom such contracts, arrangements, understandings or relationships have been entered into. Include such information for any of the securities that are pledged or otherwise subject to a contingency the occurrence of which would give another person voting power or investment power over such securities except that disclosure of standard default and similar provisions contained in loan agreements need not be included.

Item 7.   Material to Be Filed as Exhibits

The following shall be filed as exhibits: Copies of written agreements relating to the filing of joint acquisition statements as required by Rule 13d–1(k) and copies of all written agreements, contracts, arrangements, understandings, plans, or proposals relating to:

(1)   The borrowing of funds to finance the acquisition as disclosed in Item 3;

(2)   The acquisition of issuer control, liquidation, sale of assets, merger, or change in business or corporate structure, or any other matter as disclosed in Item 4; and

(3)   The transfer or voting of the securities, finder's fees, joint ventures, options, puts, calls, guarantees of loans, guarantees against loss or of profit, or the giving or withholding of any proxy as disclosed in Item 6.

SIGNATURE

After reasonable inquiry and to the best of my knowledge and belief, I certify that the information set forth in this statement is true, complete and correct.

(Date) _____

(Signature) _____

(Name/Title) _____

The original statement shall be signed by each person on whose behalf the statement is filed or his authorized representative. If the statement is signed on behalf of a person by his authorized representative (other than an executive officer or general partner of the filing person), evidence of the representative's authority to sign on behalf of such person shall be filed with the statement, *provided, however,* that a power of attorney for this purpose which is already on file with the Commission may be incorporated by reference. The name of any title of each person who signs the statement shall be typed or printed beneath his signature.

ATTENTION: Intentional misstatements or omissions of fact constitute Federal criminal violations (See 18 U.S.C.A. § 1001).

SELECTED SCHEDULES UNDER THE
SECURITIES EXCHANGE ACT OF 1934

C. SCHEDULE 13E–3
17 C.F.R. § 240.13e–100

TRANSACTION STATEMENT UNDER SECTION 13(e) OF
THE 1934 ACT AND RULE 13e–3 THEREUNDER

SECURITIES AND EXCHANGE COMMISSION
Washington, D.C. 20549

RULE 13e–3 TRANSACTION STATEMENT

(Pursuant to Section 13(e) of the Securities Exchange Act of 1934)

[Amendment No. _____]

_____

(Name of the Issuer)

_____

(Name of Person(s) Filing Statement)

_____

(Title of Class of Securities)

_____

(CUSIP Number of Class of Securities)

_____

(Name, Address and Telephone Number of Person Authorized to Receive Notices and
Communications on Behalf of Person(s) Filing Statement)

This statement is filed in connection with (check the appropriate box):

a. ☐ The filing of solicitation materials or an information statement subject to Regulation 14A, Regulation 14C or Rule 13e–3(c) under the Securities Exchange Act of 1934 ("the Act").

b. ☐ The filing of a registration statement under the Securities Act of 1933.

c. ☐ A tender offer.

d. ☐ None of the above.

Check the following box if the soliciting materials or information statement referred to in checking box (a) are preliminary copies: [ ]

Check the following box if the filing is a final amendment reporting the results of the transaction:
☐

Calculation of Filing Fee

Transaction valuation*	Amount of filing fee

* Set forth the amount on which the filing fee is calculated and state how it was determined.

☐ Check box if any part of the fee is offset as provided by Rule 0–11(a)(2) and identify the filing with which the offsetting fee was previously paid. Identify the previous filing by registration statement number, or the Form or Schedule and the date of its filing.

Amount Previously Paid: _____

Form or Registration No.: _____

Filing Party: _____

Date Filed: _____

SCHEDULE 13E-3

GENERAL INSTRUCTIONS

A. File eight copies of the statement, including all exhibits, with the Commission if paper filing is permitted.

B. This filing must be accompanied by a fee payable to the Commission as required by Rule 0–11(b).

C. If the statement is filed by a general or limited partnership, syndicate or other group, the information called for by Items 3, 5, 6 10 and 11 must be given with respect to: (i) Each partner of the general partnership; (ii) each partner who is, or functions as, a general partner of the limited partnership; (iii) each member of the syndicate or group; and (iv) each person controlling the partner or member. If the statement is filed by a corporation or if a person referred to in (i), (ii), (iii) or (iv) of this Instruction is a corporation, the information called for by the items specified above must be given with respect to: (a) Each executive officer and director of the corporation; (b) each person controlling the corporation; and (c) each executive officer and director of any corporation or other person ultimately in control of the corporation.

D. Depending on the type of Rule 13e–3 transaction, this statement must be filed with the Commission:

1. At the same time as filing preliminary or definitive soliciting materials or an information statement under Regulation 14A or 14C of the Act;

2. At the same time as filing a registration statement under the Securities Act of 1933;

3. As soon as practicable on the date a tender offer is first published, sent or given to security holders; or

4. At least 30 days before any purchase of securities of the class of securities subject to the Rule 13e–3 transaction, if the transaction does not involve a solicitation, an information statement, the registration of securities or a tender offer, as described in paragraphs 1, 2 or 3 of this Instruction; and

5. If the Rule 13e–3 transaction involves a series of transactions, the issuer or affiliate must filed this statement at the time indicated in paragraphs 1 through 4 of this Instruction for the first transaction and must amend the schedule promptly with respect to each subsequent transaction.

E. If an item is inapplicable or the answer is in the negative, so state. The statement published, sent or given to security holders may omit negative and not applicable responses, except that responses to Items 7, 8 and 9 of this schedule must be provided in full. If the schedule includes any information that is not published, sent or given to security holders, provide that information or specifically incorporate it by reference under the appropriate item number and heading in the schedule. Do not recite the text of disclosure requirements in the schedule or any document published, sent or given to security holders. Indicate clearly the coverage of the requirements without referring to the text of the items.

F. Information contained in exhibits to the statement may be incorporated by reference in answer or partial answer to any item unless it would render the answer misleading, incomplete, unclear or confusing. A copy of any information that is incorporated by reference or a copy of the pertinent pages of a document containing the information must be submitted with this statement as an exhibit, unless it was previously filed with the Commission electronically on EDGAR. If an exhibit contains information responding to more than one item in the schedule, all information in that exhibit may be incorporated by reference once in response to the several items in the schedule for which it provides an answer. Information incorporated by reference is deemed filed with the Commission for all purposes of the Act.

G. If the Rule 13e–3 transaction also involves a transaction subject to Regulation 14A or 14C of the Act, the registration of securities under the Securities Act of 1933 and the General Rules and Regulations of that Act, or a tender offer subject to Regulation 14D or Rule 13e–4, this statement must incorporate by reference the information contained in the proxy, information, registration or tender offer statement in answer to the items of this statement.

H. The information required by the items of this statement is intended to be in addition to any disclosure requirements of any other form or schedule that may be filed with the Commission in connection with the Rule 13e–3 transaction. If those forms or schedules require less information on any topic than this statement, the requirements of this statement control.

SELECTED SCHEDULES UNDER THE
SECURITIES EXCHANGE ACT OF 1934

Item 1

I.   If the Rule 13e–3 transaction involves a tender offer, then a combined statement on Schedules 13E–3 and TO may be filed with the Commission under cover of Schedule TO. See Instruction J of Schedule TO.

J.   Amendments disclosing a material change in the information set forth in this statement may omit any information previously disclosed in this statement.

Item 1.   Summary Term Sheet

Furnish the information required by Item 1001 of Regulation M–A unless information is disclosed to security holders in a prospectus that meets the requirements of Rule 421(d) under the Securities Act of 1933.

Item 2.   Subject Company Information

Furnish the information required by Item 1002 of Regulation M–A.

Item 3.   Identity and Background of Filing Person

Furnish the information required by Item 1003(a) through (c) of Regulation M–A.

Item 4.   Terms of the Transaction

Furnish the information required by Item 1004(a) and (c) through (f) of Regulation M–A.

Item 5.   Past Contacts, Transaction, Negotiations and Agreements

Furnish the information required by Item 1005(a) through (c) and (e) of Regulation M–A.

Item 6.   Purposes of the Transaction and Plans or Proposals

Furnish the information required by Item 1006(b) and (c)(1) through (8) of Regulation M–A.

Instruction to Item 6: In providing the information specified in Item 1006(c) for this item, discuss any activities or transactions that would occur after the Rule 13e–3 transaction.

Item 7.   Purposes, Alternatives, Reasons and Effects

Furnish the information required by Item 1013 of Regulation M–A.

Item 8.   Fairness of the Transaction

Furnish the information required by Item 1014 of Regulation M–A.

Item 9.   Reports, Opinions, Appraisals and Negotiations

Furnish the information required by Item 1015 of Regulation M–A.

Item 10.   Source and Amount of Funds or Other Consideration

Furnish the information required by Item 1007 of Regulation M–A.

Item 11.   Interest in Securities of the Subject Company

Furnish the information required by Item 1008 of Regulation M–A.

Item 12.   The Solicitation or Recommendation

Furnish the information required by Item 1012(d) and (e) of Regulation M–A.

Item 13.   Financial Statements

Furnish the information required by Item 1010(a) through (b) of Regulation M–A for the issuer of the subject class of securities.

Instructions to Item 13:

1.   The disclosure materials disseminated to security holders may contain the summarized financial information required by Item 1010(c) of Regulation M–A instead of the financial information required by Item 1010(a) and (b). In that case, the financial information required by Item 1010(a) and (b) of Regulation M–A must be disclosed directly or incorporated by reference in the statement. If summarized financial information is disseminated to security holders, include appropriate instructions on how more complete financial information can be obtained. If the summarized financial information is prepared on the basis of a comprehensive body of accounting principles other than U.S. GAAP, the summarized financial information must be accompanied by a reconciliation as described in Instruction 2.

2.   If the financial statements required by this Item are prepared on the basis of a comprehensive body of accounting principles other than U.S. GAAP, provide a reconciliation to U.S. GAAP in accordance with Item 17 of Form 20–F.

3.   The filing person may incorporate by reference financial statements contained in any document filed with the Commission, solely for the purposes of this schedule, if: (a) The financial statements substantially meet the requirements of this Item; (b) an express statement is made that the financial statements are incorporated by reference; (c) the matter incorporated by reference is clearly identified by page, paragraph, caption or otherwise; and (d) if the matter incorporated by reference is not filed with this Schedule, an indication is made where the information may be inspected and copies obtained. Financial statements that are required to be presented in comparative form for two or more fiscal years or periods may not be incorporated by reference unless the material incorporated by reference includes the entire period for which the comparative data is required to be given. *See* General Instruction F to this Schedule.

Item 14. Persons/Assets, Retained, Employed, Compensated or Used

Furnish the information required by Item 1009 of Regulation M–A.

Item 15. Additional Information

Furnish the information required by Item 1011(b) and (c) of Regulation M–A.

Item 16. Exhibits

File as an exhibit to the Schedule all documents specified in Item 1016(a) through (d), (f) and (g) of Regulation M–A.

SIGNATURE

After due inquiry and to the best of my knowledge and belief, I certify that the information set forth in this statement is true, complete and correct.

_____

(Signature)

_____

(Name and Title)

_____

(Date)

Instructions to Signature: The statement must be signed by the filing person or that person's authorized representative. If the statement is signed on behalf of a person by an authorized representative (other than an executive office of a corporation or general partner of a partnership), evidence of the representative's authority to sign on behalf of the person must be with the statement. The name and any title of each person who signs the statement must be typed or printed beneath the signature. See Rule 12b–11 with respect to signature requirements.

SELECTED SCHEDULES UNDER THE
SECURITIES EXCHANGE ACT OF 1934

D. SCHEDULE 13G
17 C.F.R. § 240.13d–102

ACQUISITION STATEMENT FOR SECURITIES PURCHASED
PURSUANT TO SECTION 13 OF THE 1934 ACT

SCHEDULE 13G

Under the Securities Exchange Act of 1934

(Amendment No. _____) *

_____
(Name of Issuer)

_____
(Title of Class of Securities)

_____
(CUSIP Number)

Check the appropriate box to designate the rule pursuant to which this Schedule is filed:

[ ] Rule 13d–1(b)

[ ] Rule 13d–1(c)

[ ] Rule 13d–1(d)

The information required in the remainder of this cover page shall not be deemed to be "filed" for the purpose of Section 18 of the Securities Exchange Act of 1934 ("Act") or otherwise subject to the liabilities of that section of the Act but shall be subject to all other provisions of the Act (however, see the Notes).

_____
CUSIP No. _____

(1)	Names of Reporting Persons.		
(2)	Check the Appropriate Box if a Member of a Group	(a)	
	(See Instructions)	(b)	
(3)	SEC Use Only		
(4)	Citizenship or Place of Organization		
Number of Shares Beneficially Owned by Each Reporting Person With	(5)	Sole Voting Power	
	(6)	Shared Voting Power	
	(7)	Sole Dispositive Power	
(8)	Shared Dispositive Power		
(9)	Aggregate Amount Beneficially Owned by Each Reporting Person		
(10)	Check if the Aggregate Amount in Row (9) Excludes Certain Shares (See Instructions)		

_____

*   The remainder of this cover page shall be filled out for a reporting person's initial filing on this form with respect to the subject class of securities, and for any subsequent amendment containing information which would alter the disclosures provided in a prior cover page.

(11)	Percent of Class Represented by Amount in Row (9)
(12)	Type of Reporting Person (See Instructions)

INSTRUCTIONS FOR SCHEDULE 13G

(1) *Names of Reporting Persons*—Furnish the full legal name of each person for whom the report is filed—i.e., each person required to sign the schedule itself—including each member of a group. Do not include the name of a person required to be identified in the report but who is not a reporting person.

(2) If any of the shares beneficially owned by a reporting person are held as a member of a group and such membership is expressly affirmed, please check row 2(a). If the membership in a group is disclaimed or the reporting person describes a relationship with other persons but does not affirm the existence of a group, please check row 2(b) [unless a joint filing pursuant to Rule 13d–1(e)(1) in which case it may not be necessary to check row 2(b)].

(3) The third row is for SEC internal use; please leave blank.

(4) *Citizenship or Place of Organization*. Furnish citizenship if the named reporting person is a natural person. Otherwise, furnish place of organization.

(5)–(9), (11) *Aggregate Amount Beneficially Owned By Each Reporting Person, etc.* Rows (5) through (9) inclusive, and (11) are to be completed in accordance with the provisions of Item 4 of Schedule 13G. All percentages are to be rounded off to the nearest tenth (one place after decimal point).

(10) Check if the aggregate amount reported as beneficially owned in row (9) does not include shares as to which beneficial ownership is disclaimed pursuant to Rule 13d–4 under the Securities Exchange Act of 1934.

(12) *Type of Reporting Person*. Please classify each "reporting person" according to the following breakdown (see Item 3 of Schedule 13G) and place the appropriate symbol on the form:

Category	Symbol
Broker Dealer	BD
Bank	BK
Insurance Company	IC
Investment Company	IV
Investment Adviser	IA
Employee Benefit Plan, Pension Fund, or Endowment Fund	EP
Parent Holding Company/Control Person	HC
Savings Association	SA
Church Plan	CP
Corporation	CO
Partnership	PN
Individual	IN
Non-U.S. Institution	FI
Other	OO

NOTES: Attach as many copies of the second part of the cover page as are needed, one reporting person per page.

Filing persons may, in order to avoid unnecessary duplication, answer items on the schedules (Schedule 13D, 13G or TO) by appropriate cross references to an item or items on the cover page(s). This approach may only be used where the cover page item or items provide all the disclosure required by the schedule item. Moreover, such a use of a cover page item will result in the item becoming a part of the schedule and accordingly being considered as "filed" for purposes of Section 18 of the Securities Exchange Act or otherwise subject to the liabilities of that section of the Act.

Reporting persons may comply with their cover page filing requirements by filing either completed copies of the blank forms available from the Commission, printed or typed facsimiles, or computer printed facsimiles, provided the documents filed have identical formats to the forms prescribed in the Commission's regulations and meet existing Securities Exchange Act rules as to such matters as clarity and size (Securities Exchange Act Rule 12b–12).

SPECIAL INSTRUCTIONS FOR COMPLYING WITH SCHEDULE 13G

Under sections 13(d), 13(g) and 23 of the Securities Exchange Act of 1934 and the rules and regulations thereunder, the Commission is authorized to solicit the information required to be supplied by this schedule by certain security holders of certain issuers.

Disclosure of the information specified in this schedule is mandatory. The information will be used for the primary purpose of determining and disclosing the holdings of certain beneficial owners of certain equity securities. This statement will be made a matter of public record. Therefore, any information given will be available for inspection by any member of the public.

Because of the public nature of the information, the Commission can utilize it for a variety of purposes, including referral to other governmental authorities or securities, self-regulatory organizations for investigatory purposes or in connection with litigation involving the Federal securities laws or other civil, criminal or regulatory statutes or provisions.

Failure to disclose the information requested by this schedule may result in civil or criminal action against the persons involved for violation of the Federal securities laws and rules promulgated thereunder.

GENERAL INSTRUCTIONS

A.   Statements filed pursuant to Rule 13d–1(b) containing the information required by this schedule shall be filed not later than February 14 following the calendar year covered by the statement or within the time specified in Rules 13d–1(b)(2) and 13d2(c). Statements filed pursuant to Rule 13d–1(c) shall be filed within the time specified in Rules 13d–1(c), 13d–2(b) and 13d–2(d). Statements filed pursuant to Rule 13d–1(d) shall be filed not later than February 14 following the calendar year covered by the statement pursuant to Rules 13d–1(d) and 13d–2(b).

B.   Information contained in a form which is required to be filed by rules under section 13(f) for the same calendar year as that covered by a statement on this Schedule may be incorporated by reference in response to any of the items of this Schedule. If such information is incorporated by reference in this Schedule, copies of the relevant pages of such form shall be filed as an exhibit to this Schedule.

C.   The item numbers and captions of the items shall be included but the text of the items is to be omitted. The answers to the items shall be so prepared as to indicate clearly the coverage of the items without referring to the text of the items. Answer every item. If an item is inapplicable or the answer is in the negative, so state.

Item 1(a).   **Name of Issuer**

_____

Item 1(b).   **Address of Issuer's Principal Executive Offices**

_____

Item 2(a).   **Name of Person Filing**

_____

Item 2(b).   **Address of Principal Business Office or, if None, Residence**

_____

Item 2(c).   **Citizenship**

_____

Item 2(d).   **Title of Class of Securities**

_____

Item 2(e).   **CUSIP No.**

_____

Item 3.   If This Statement Is Filed Pursuant to Rules 13d–1(b), or 13d–2(b), Check Whether the Person Filing Is a

(a)   [   ] Broker or Dealer registered under Section 15 of the Act

(b)   [   ] Bank as defined in section 3(a)(6) of the Act

(c)   [   ] Insurance Company as defined in section 3(a)(19) of the Act

(d)   [   ] Investment Company registered under section 8 of the Investment Company Act

(e)   [   ] Investment Adviser in accordance with Rule 13d–1(b)(1)(ii)(E)

(f)   [   ] Employee Benefit Plan or Endowment Fund in accordance with Rule 13d–1(b)(1)(ii)(F)

(g)   [   ] Parent Holding Company or control person in accordance with Rule 13d–1(b)(ii)(G)

(h)   [   ] A savings associations as defined in Section 3(b) of the Federal Deposit Insurance Act (12 U.S.C. 1813)

(i)   [   ] A church plan that is excluded from the definition of an investment company under section 3(c)(14) of the Investment Company Act of 1940

(j)   [   ] A non-U.S. institution in accordance with Rule 13d–1(b)(1)(ii)(J)

(k)   [   ] Group, in accordance with Rule 13d–1(b)(1)(ii)(K).

If filing as a non-U.S. institution in accordance with Rule 13d–1(b)(1)(ii)(J), please specify the type of institution: _____

Item 4.   Ownership

Provide the following information regarding the aggregate number and percentage of the class of securities of the issuer identified in Item 1.

SELECTED SCHEDULES UNDER THE
SECURITIES EXCHANGE ACT OF 1934

(a)   Amount Beneficially Owned:

(b)   Percent of Class:

(c)   Number of shares as to which such person has:

    (i)   sole power to vote or to direct the vote _____

    (ii)   shared power to vote or to direct the vote _____

    (iii)   sole power to dispose or to direct the disposition of _____

    (iv)   shared power to dispose or to direct the disposition of _____

Instruction. For computations regarding securities which represent a right to acquire an underlying security see Rule 13d–3(d)(1).

Item 5.   Ownership of Five Percent or Less of a Class

If this statement is being filed to report the fact that as of the date hereof the reporting person has ceased to be the beneficial owner of more than five percent of the class of securities, check the following [   ].

Instruction. Dissolution of a group requires a response to this item.

Item 6.   Ownership of More Than Five Percent on Behalf of Another Person

If any other person is known to have the right to receive or the power to direct the receipt of dividends from, or the proceeds from the sale of, such securities, a statement to that effect should be included in response to this item and, if such interest relates to more than five percent of the class, such person should be identified. A listing of the shareholders of an investment company registered under the Investment Company Act of 1940 or the beneficiaries of employee benefit plan, pension fund or endowment fund is not required.

Item 7.   Identification and Classification of the Subsidiary Which Acquired the Security Being Reported on by the Parent Holding Company

If a parent holding company has filed this schedule, pursuant to Rule 13d–1(b)(1)(ii)(G), so indicate under Item 3(g) and attach an exhibit stating the identity and the Item 3 classification of the relevant subsidiary. If a parent holding company has filed this schedule pursuant to Rule 13d–1(c) or Rule 13d–1(d), attach an exhibit stating the identification of the relevant subsidiary.

Item 8.   Identification and Classification of Members of the Group

If a group has filed this schedule pursuant to Rule 13d–1(b)(1)(ii)(J), so indicate under Item 3(h) and attach an exhibit stating the identity and Item 3 classification of each member of the group. If a group has filed this schedule pursuant to Rule 13d–1(c) or Rule 13d–1(d), attach an exhibit stating the identity of each member of the group.

Item 9.   Notice of Dissolution of Group

Notice of dissolution of a group may be furnished as an exhibit stating the date of the dissolution and that all further filings with respect to transactions in the security reported on will be filed, if required, by members of the group, in their individual capacity. See Item 5.

Item 10.   Certification

(a)   The following certification shall be included if the statement is filed pursuant to Rule 13d–1(b):

By signing below I certify that, to the best of my knowledge and belief, the securities referred to above were acquired and are held in the ordinary course of business and were not acquired and are not held for the purpose of or with the effect of changing or influencing the control of the issuer of the securities and were not acquired and are not held in connection with or as a participant in any transaction having that purpose or effect, other than activities solely in connection with a nomination under Rule 14a–11.

(b) The following certification shall be included if the statement is filed pursuant to Rule 13d–1(b)(1)(ii)(J), or if the statement is filed pursuant to Rule 13d–1(b)(1)(ii)(K) and a member of the group is a non-U.S. institution eligible to file pursuant to Rule 13d–1(b)(1)(ii)(J):

By signing below I certify that, to the best of my knowledge and belief, the securities referred to above were acquired and are held in the ordinary course of business and were not acquired and are not held for the purpose of or with the effect of changing or influencing the control of the issuer of the securities and were not acquired and are not held in connection with or as a participant in any transaction having that purpose or effect, other than activities solely in connection with a nomination under Rule 14a–11.

By signing below I certify that, to the best of my knowledge and belief, the foreign regulatory scheme applicable to [insert particular category of institutional investor] is substantially comparable to the regulatory scheme applicable to the functionally equivalent U.S. institution(s). I also undertake to furnish to the Commission staff, upon request, information that would otherwise be disclosed in a Schedule 13D.

(c) The following certification shall be included if the statement is filed pursuant to Rule 13d–1(c):

By signing below I certify that, to the best of my knowledge and belief, the securities referred to above were not acquired and are not held for the purpose of or with the effect of changing or influencing the control of the issuer of the securities and were not acquired and are not held in connection with or as a participant in any transaction having that purpose or effect, other than activities solely in connection with a nomination under Rule 14a–11.

SIGNATURE

After reasonable inquiry and to the best of my knowledge and belief, I certify that the information set forth in this statement is true, complete and correct.

_____
(Date)

_____
(Signature)

_____
(Name/Title)

The original statement shall be signed by each person on whose behalf the statement is filed or his authorized representative. If the statement is signed on behalf of a person by his authorized representative (other than an executive officer or general partner of the filing person), evidence of the representative's authority to sign on behalf of such person shall be filed with the statement, provided, however, that a power of attorney for this purpose which is already on file with the Commission may be incorporated by reference. The name and any title of each person who signs the statement shall be typed or printed beneath his signature.

NOTE: Schedules filed in paper format shall include a signed original and five copies of the schedule, including all exhibits. See Rule 13d–7 for other parties for whom copies are to be sent.

ATTENTION: Intentional misstatements or omissions of fact constitute Federal criminal violations (See 18 U.S.C.A. § 1001).

SELECTED SCHEDULES UNDER THE
SECURITIES EXCHANGE ACT OF 1934

E. SCHEDULE 14A
17 C.F.R. § 240.14a–101

INFORMATION REQUIRED IN PROXY STATEMENT

SCHEDULE 14A INFORMATION

Proxy Statement Pursuant to Section 14(a) of the Securities Exchange Act of 1934
(Amendment No.   )

Filed by the Registrant [   ]

Filed by a Party other than the Registrant [   ]

Check the appropriate box:

[   ]   Preliminary Proxy Statement

[   ]   Confidential, for Use of the Commission Only (as permitted by Rule 14a–6(e)(2))

[   ]   Definitive Proxy Statement

[   ]   Definitive Additional Materials

[   ]   Soliciting Material Under Rule 14a–12

_____

(Name of Registrant as Specified
In Its Charter)

_____

(Name of Person(s) Filing Proxy Statement
if other than the Registrant)

Payment of Filing Fee (Check the appropriate box):

[   ]   No fee required.

[   ]   Fee computed on table below per Exchange Act Rules 14a–6(i)(4) and 0–11.

    1)   Title of each class of securities to which transaction applies:

    _____

    2)   Aggregate number of securities to which transaction applies:

    _____

    3)   Per unit price or other underlying value of transaction computed pursuant to Exchange Act Rule 0–11 (Set forth the amount on which the filing fee is calculated and state how it was determined):

    _____

    4)   Proposed maximum aggregate value of transaction:

    _____

    5)   Total fee paid:

    _____

[   ]   Fee paid previously with preliminary materials.

[   ]   Check box if any part of the fee is offset as provided by Exchange Act Rule 0–11(a)(2) and identify the filing for which the offsetting fee was paid previously. Identify the previous filing by registration statement number, or the Form or Schedule and the date of its filing.

    1)   Amount Previously Paid:

SCHEDULE 14A

2) Form, Schedule or Registration Statement No.:

_____

3) Filing Party:

_____

4) Date Filed:

_____

NOTES.—A.   Where any item calls for information with respect to any matter to be acted upon and such matter involves other matters with respect to which information is called for by other items of this schedule, the information called for by such other items also shall be given. For example, where a solicitation of security holders is for the purpose of approving the authorization of additional securities which are to be used to acquire another specified company, and the registrants' security holders will not have a separate opportunity to vote upon the transaction, the solicitation to authorize the securities is also a solicitation with respect to the acquisition. Under those facts, information required by Items 11, 13 and 14 shall be furnished.

B.   Where any item calls for information with respect to any matter to be acted upon at the meeting, such item need be answered in the registrant's soliciting material only with respect to proposals to be made by or on behalf of the registrant.

C.   Except as otherwise specifically provided, where any item calls for information for a specified period with regard to directors, executive officers, officers or other persons holding specified positions or relationships, the information shall be given with regard to any person who held any of the specified positions or relationships at any time during the period. Information, other than information required by Item 404 of Regulation S–K, need not be included for any portion of the period during which such person did not hold any such position or relationship, provided a statement to that effect is made.

D.   Information may be incorporated by reference only in the manner and to the extent specifically permitted in the items of this schedule. Where incorporation by reference is used, the following shall apply:

1.   Any incorporation by reference of information pursuant to the provisions of this schedule shall be subject to the provisions of Item 10(d) of Regulation S–K restricting incorporation by reference of documents which incorporate by reference other information. A registrant incorporating any documents, or portions of documents, shall include a statement on the last page(s) of the proxy statement as to which documents, or portions of documents, are incorporated by reference. Information shall not be incorporated by reference in any case where such incorporation would render the statement incomplete, unclear or confusing.

2.   If a document is incorporated by reference but not delivered to security holders, include an undertaking to provide, without charge, to each person to whom a proxy statement is delivered, upon written or oral request of such person and by first class mail or other equally prompt means within one business day of receipt of such request, a copy of any and all of the information that has been incorporated by reference in the proxy statement (not including exhibits to the information that is incorporated by reference unless such exhibits are specifically incorporated by reference into the information that the proxy statement incorporates), and the address (including title or department) and telephone numbers to which such a request is to be directed. This includes information contained in documents filed subsequent to the date on which definitive copies of the proxy statement are sent or given to security holders, up to the date of responding to the request.

3.   If a document or portion of a document other than an annual report sent to security holders pursuant to the requirements of Rule 14a–3 with respect to the same meeting or solicitation of consents or authorizations as that to which the proxy statement relates is incorporated by reference in the manner permitted by Item 13(b) or 14(e)(1) of this schedule, the proxy statement must be sent to security holders no later than 20 business days prior to the date on which the meeting of such security holders is held or, if no meeting is held, at least 20 business days prior to the date the votes, consents or authorizations may be used to effect the corporate action.

4.   *Electronic filings.* If any of the information required by Items 13 or 14 of this Schedule is incorporated by reference from an annual or quarterly report to security holders, such report, or any portion

thereof incorporated by reference, shall be filed in electronic format with the proxy statement. This provision shall not apply to registered investment companies.

E.   In Item 13 of this Schedule, the reference to "meets the requirement of Form S–3" shall refer to a registrant who meets the following requirements:

(1)   The registrant or other person meets the requirements of General Instruction I.A. of Form S–3; and

(2)   One of the following is met:

(i)   The registrant or other person meets the aggregate market value requirement of General Instruction I.B.1 of Form S–3; or

(ii)   Action is to be taken as described in Items 11, 12, and 14 of this schedule which concerns non-convertible debt or preferred securities issued by a registrant meeting the requirements of General Instruction I.B.2. of Form S–3; or

(iii)   The registrant or other person is a majority-owned subsidiary and one of the conditions of General Instruction I.C. of Form S–3 is met.

Item 1.   Date, Time and Place Information

(a)   State the date, time and place of the meeting of security holders, and the complete mailing address, including ZIP Code, of the principal executive offices of the registrant, unless such information is otherwise disclosed in material furnished to security holders with or preceding the proxy statement. If action is to be taken by written consent, state the date by which consents are to be submitted if state law requires that such a date be specified or if the person soliciting intends to set a date.

(b)   On the first page of the proxy statement, as delivered to security holders, state the approximate date on which the proxy statement and form of proxy are first sent or given to security holders.

(c)   Furnish the information required to be in the proxy statement by Rule 14a–5(e).

Item 2.   Revocability of Proxy

State whether or not the person giving the proxy has the power to revoke it. If the right of revocation before the proxy is exercised is limited or is subject to compliance with any formal procedure, briefly describe such limitation or procedure.

Item 3.   Dissenters' Right of Appraisal

Outline briefly the rights of appraisal or similar rights of dissenters with respect to any matter to be acted upon and indicate any statutory procedure required to be followed by dissenting security holders in order to perfect such rights. Where such rights may be exercised only within a limited time after the date of adoption of a proposal, the filing of a charter amendment or other similar act, state whether the persons solicited will be notified of such date.

Instructions. 1.   Indicate whether a security holder's failure to vote against a proposal will constitute a waiver of his appraisal or similar rights and whether a vote against a proposal will be deemed to satisfy any notice requirements under State law with respect to appraisal rights. If the State law is unclear, state what position will be taken in regard to these matters.

2.   Open-end investment companies registered under the Investment Company Act of 1940 are not required to respond to this item.

Item 4.   Persons Making the Solicitation

(a)   *Solicitations not subject to Rule 14a–12(c).* (1) If the solicitation is made by the registrant, so state. Give the name of any director of the registrant who has informed the registrant in writing that he intends to oppose any action intended to be taken by the registrant and indicate the action which he intends to oppose.

(2) If the solicitation is made otherwise than by the registrant, so state and give the names of the participants in the solicitation, as defined in paragraphs (a)(iii), (iv), (v), and (vi) of Instruction 3 to this Item.

(3) If the solicitation is to be made otherwise than by the use of the mails or pursuant to Rule 14a–16, describe the methods to be employed. If the solicitation is to be made by specially engaged employees or paid solicitors, state

    (i) The material features of any contract or arrangement for such solicitation and identify the parties, and

    (ii) The cost or anticipated cost thereof.

(4) State the names of the persons by whom the cost of solicitation has been or will be borne, directly or indirectly.

(b) *Solicitations subject to Rule 14a–12(c).* (1) State by whom the solicitation is made and describe the methods employed and to be employed to solicit security holders.

(2) If regular employees of the registrant or any other participant in a solicitation have been or are to be employed to solicit security holders, describe the class or classes of employees to be so employed, and the manner and nature of their employment for such purpose.

(3) If specially engaged employees, representatives or other persons have been or are to be employed to solicit security holders, state

    (i) The material features of any contract or arrangement for such solicitation and the identity of the parties,

    (ii) The cost or anticipated cost thereof, and

    (iii) The approximate number of such employees or employees of any other person (naming such other person) who will solicit security holders.

(4) State the total amount estimated to be spent and the total expenditures to date for, in furtherance of, or in connection with the solicitation of security holders.

(5) State by whom the cost of the solicitation will be borne. If such cost is to be borne initially by any person other than the registrant, state whether reimbursement will be sought from the registrant, and, if so, whether the question of such reimbursement will be submitted to a vote of security holders.

(6) If any such solicitation is terminated pursuant to a settlement between the registrant and any other participant in such solicitation, describe the terms of such settlement, including the cost or anticipated cost thereof to the registrant.

Instructions. 1. With respect to solicitations subject to Rule 14a–12(c), costs and expenditures within the meaning of this Item 4 shall include fees for attorneys, accountants, public relations or financial advisers, solicitors, advertising, printing, transportation, litigation and other costs incidental to the solicitation, except that the registrant may exclude the amount of such costs represented by the amount normally expended for a solicitation for an election of directors in the absence of a contest, and costs represented by salaries and wages of regular employees and officers, provided a statement to that effect is included in the proxy statement.

2. The information required pursuant to paragraph (b)(6) of this Item should be included in any amended or revised proxy statement or other soliciting materials relating to the same meeting or subject matter furnished to security holders by the registrant subsequent to the date of settlement.

3. For purposes of this Item 4 and Item 5 of this Schedule 14A:

(a) The terms "participant" and "participant in a solicitation" include the following:

    (i) In the case of a solicitation made on behalf of the registrant, the registrant, each director of the registrant and each of the registrant's nominees for election as a director;

    (ii) In the case of a solicitation made otherwise than on behalf of the registrant, each of the soliciting person's nominees for election as a director;

(iii)   Any committee or group which solicits proxies, any member of such committee or group, and any person whether or not named as a member who, acting alone or with one or more other persons, directly or indirectly takes the initiative, or engages, in organizing, directing, or arranging for the financing of any such committee or group;

(iv)   Any person who finances or joins with another to finance the solicitation of proxies, except persons who contribute not more than $500 and who are not otherwise participants;

(v)   Any person who lends money or furnishes credit or enters into any other arrangements, pursuant to any contract or understanding with a participant, for the purpose of financing or otherwise inducing the purchase, sale, holding or voting of securities of the registrant by any participant or other persons, in support of or in opposition to a participant; except that such terms do not include a bank, broker or dealer who, in the ordinary course of business, lends money or executes orders for the purchase or sale of securities and who is not otherwise a participant; and

(vi)   Any person who solicits proxies.

(b)   The terms "participant" and "participant in a solicitation" do not include:

(i)   Any person or organization retained or employed by a participant to solicit security holders and whose activities are limited to the duties required to be performed in the course of such employment;

(ii)   Any person who merely transmits proxy soliciting material or performs other ministerial or clerical duties;

(iii)   Any person employed by a participant in the capacity of attorney, accountant, or advertising, public relations or financial adviser, and whose activities are limited to the duties required to be performed in the course of such employment;

(iv)   Any person regularly employed as an officer or employee of the registrant or any of its subsidiaries who is not otherwise a participant; or

(v)   Any officer or director of, or any person regularly employed by, any other participant, if such officer, director or employee is not otherwise a participant.

Item 5.   Interest of Certain Persons in Matters to Be Acted Upon

(a)   *Solicitations not subject to Rule 14a-12(c).* Describe briefly any substantial interest, direct or indirect, by security holdings or otherwise, of each of the following persons in any matter to be acted upon, other than elections to office:

(1)   If the solicitation is made on behalf of the registrant, each person who has been a director or executive officer of the registrant at any time since the beginning of the last fiscal year.

(2)   If the solicitation is made otherwise than on behalf of the registrant, each participant in the solicitation as defined in paragraphs (a)(iii), (iv), (v), and (vi) of Instruction 3 to Item 4.

(3)   Each nominee for election as a director of the registrant.

(4)   Each associate of any of the foregoing persons.

(5)   If the solicitation is made on behalf of the registrant, furnish the information required by Item 402(t) of Regulation S-K.

Instruction to paragraph (a). Except in the case of a solicitation subject to this regulation made in opposition to another solicitation subject to this regulation, the sub-item (a) shall not apply to any interest arising from the ownership of securities of the registrant where the security holder receives no extra or special benefit not shared on a pro rata basis by all other holders of the same class.

(b)   *Solicitation subject to Rule 14a-12(c).* With respect to any solicitation subject to Rule 14a-11:

(1)   Describe briefly any substantial interest, direct or indirect, by security holdings or otherwise, of each participant as defined in paragraphs (a)(ii), (iii), (iv), (v) and (vi) of Instruction 3 to Item 4 of this Schedule 14A, in any matter to be acted upon at the meeting, and include with respect to each participant the following information, or a fair and accurate summary thereof:

(i)   Name and business address of the participant.

(ii)   The participant's present principal occupation or employment and the name, principal business and address of any corporation or other organization in which such employment is carried on.

(iii)   State whether or not, during the past ten years, the participant has been convicted in a criminal proceeding (excluding traffic violations or similar misdemeanors) and, if so, give dates, nature of conviction, name and location of court, and penalty imposed or other disposition of the case. A negative answer need not be included in the proxy statement or other soliciting material.

(iv)   State the amount of each class of securities of the registrant which the participant owns beneficially, directly or indirectly.

(v)   State the amount of each class of securities of the registrant which the participant owns of record but not beneficially.

(vi)   State with respect to all securities of the registrant purchased or sold within the past two years, the dates on which they were purchased or sold and the amount purchased or sold on each such date.

(vii)   If any part of the purchase price or market value of any of the shares specified in paragraph (b)(1)(vi) of this Item is represented by funds borrowed or otherwise obtained for the purpose of acquiring or holding such securities, so state and indicate the amount of the indebtedness as of the latest practicable date. If such funds were borrowed or obtained otherwise than pursuant to a margin account or bank loan in the regular course of business of a bank, broker or dealer, briefly describe the transaction, and state the names of the parties.

(viii)   State whether or not the participant is, or was within the past year, a party to any contract, arrangements or understandings with any person with respect to any securities of the registrant, including, but not limited to joint ventures, loan or option arrangements, puts or calls, guarantees against loss or guarantees of profit, division of losses or profits, or the giving or withholding of proxies. If so, name the parties to such contracts, arrangements or understandings and give the details thereof.

(ix)   State the amount of securities of the registrant owned beneficially, directly or indirectly, by each of the participant's associates and the name and address of each such associate.

(x)   State the amount of each class of securities of any parent or subsidiary of the registrant which the participant owns beneficially, directly or indirectly.

(xi)   Furnish for the participant and associates of the participant the information required by Item 404(a) of Regulation S–K.

(xii)   State whether or not the participant or any associates of the participant have any arrangement or understanding with any person—

(A)   With respect to any future employment by the registrant or its affiliates; or

(B)   With respect to any future transactions to which the registrant or any of its affiliates will or may be a party.

If so, describe such arrangement or understanding and state the names of the parties thereto.

(2)   With respect to any person, other than a director or executive officer of the registrant acting solely in that capacity, who is a party to an arrangement or understanding pursuant to which a nominee for election as director is proposed to be elected, describe any substantial interest, direct or indirect, by security holdings or otherwise, that such person has in any matter to be acted upon at the meeting, and furnish the information called for by paragraphs (b)(1)(xi) and (xii) of this Item.

(3)   If the solicitation is made on behalf of the registrant, furnish the information required by Item 402(t) of Regulation S–K.

Instruction to paragraph (b). For purposes of this Item 5, beneficial ownership shall be determined in accordance with Rule 13d–3 under the Act.

Item 6.   Voting Securities and Principal Holders Thereof

(a)   As to each class of voting securities of the registrant entitled to be voted at the meeting (or by written consents or authorizations if no meeting is held), state the number of shares outstanding and the number of votes to which each class is entitled.

(b)   State the record date, if any, with respect to this solicitation. If the right to vote or give consent is not to be determined, in whole or in part, by reference to a record date, indicate the criteria for the determination of security holders entitled to vote or give consent.

(c)   If action is to be taken with respect to the election of directors and if the persons solicited have cumulative voting rights:

  (1)   Make a statement that they have such rights,

  (2)   briefly describe such rights,

  (3)   state briefly the conditions precedent to the exercise thereof, and

  (4)   if discretionary authority to cumulate votes is solicited, so indicate.

(d)   Furnish the information required by Item 403 of Regulation S–K to the extent known by the persons on whose behalf the solicitation is made.

(e)   If, to the knowledge of the persons on whose behalf the solicitation is made, a change in control of the registrant has occurred since the beginning of its last fiscal year, state the name of the person(s) who acquired such control, the amount and the source of the consideration used by such person or persons; the basis of the control, the date and a description of the transaction(s) which resulted in the change of control and the percentage of voting securities of the registrant now beneficially owned directly or indirectly by the person(s) who acquired control; and the identity of the person(s) from whom control was assumed. If the source of all or any part of the consideration used is a loan made in the ordinary course of business by a bank as defined by section 3(a)(6) of the Act, the identity of such bank shall be omitted provided a request for confidentiality has been made pursuant to section 13(d)(1)(B) of the Act by the person(s) who acquired control. In lieu thereof, the material shall indicate that the identity of the bank has been so omitted and filed separately with the Commission.

Instructions. 1.   State the terms of any loans or pledges obtained by the new control group for the purpose of acquiring control, and the names of the lenders or pledgees.

2.   Any arrangements or understandings among members of both the former and new control groups and their associates with respect to election of directors or other matters should be described.

Item 7.   Directors and Executive Officers

If action is to be taken with respect to the election of directors, furnish the following information in tabular form to the extent practicable. If, however, the solicitation is made on behalf of persons other than the registrant, the information required need be furnished only as to nominees of the persons making the solicitation.

(a)   The information required by Item 103(c)(2) of Regulation S–K with respect to directors and executive officers.

(b)   The information required by Items 401, 404(a) and (b), 405 and 407 of Regulation S–K, other than the information required by:

  (i)   Paragraph (c)(3) of Item 407 of Regulation S–K; and

  (ii)   Paragraphs (e)(4) and (e)(5) of Item 407 of Regulation S–K which are required by Item 8 of this Schedule 14A).

(c)   If a shareholder nominee or nominees are submitted to the registrant for inclusion in the registrant's proxy materials pursuant to Rule 14a–11 and the registrant is not permitted to exclude the nominee or nominees pursuant to the provisions of Rule 14a–11, the registrant must include in its proxy statement the disclosure required from the nominating shareholder or nominating shareholder group under Item 5 of Schedule 14N (§ 240.14n–101) with regard to the nominee or nominees and the nominating shareholder or nominating shareholder group.

(d)   If a registrant is required to include a shareholder nominee or nominees submitted to the registrant for inclusion in the registrant's proxy materials pursuant to a procedure set forth under applicable state or foreign law, or the registrant's governing documents providing for the inclusion of shareholder director nominees in the registrant's proxy materials, the registrant must include in its proxy statement the disclosure required from the nominating shareholder or nominating shareholder group under Item 6 of Schedule 14N (§ 240.14n–101) with regard to the nominee or nominees and the nominating shareholder or nominating shareholder group.

(e)   In lieu of the information required by this Item 7, investment companies registered under the Investment Company Act of 1940 must furnish the information required by Item 22(b) of this Schedule 14A.

(f)   If a person is conducting a solicitation that is subject to Rule 14a–19, the registrant must include in its proxy statement a statement directing shareholders to refer to any other soliciting person's proxy statement for information required by Item 7 of this Schedule 14A with regard to such person's nominee or nominees and a soliciting person other than the registrant must include in its proxy statement a statement directing shareholders to refer to the registrant's or other soliciting person's proxy statement for information required by Item 7 of this Schedule 14A with regard to the registrant's or other soliciting person's nominee or nominees. The statement must explain to shareholders that they can access the other soliciting person's proxy statement, and any other relevant documents, without cost on the Commission's website.

Instruction to Item 7. The information disclosed pursuant to paragraphs (c) and (d) of this Item 7 will not be deemed incorporated by reference into any filing under the Securities Act of 1933 (15 U.S.C. 77a et seq.), the Securities Exchange Act of 1934 (15 U.S.C. 78a et 102 seq.), or the Investment Company Act of 1940 (15 U.S.C. 80a–1 et seq.), except to the extent that the registrant specifically incorporates that information by reference.

Item 8.   Compensation of Directors and Executive Officers

(See Note C at the beginning of Schedule 14A).

Furnish the information required by Item 402 of Regulation S–K and paragraphs (e)(4) and (e)(5) of Item 407 of Regulation S–K if action is to be taken with regard to:

(a)   The election of directors;

(b)   Any bonus, profit sharing or other compensation plan, contract or arrangement in which any director, nominee for election as a director, or executive officer of the registrant will participate;

(c)   Any pension or retirement plan in which any such person will participate; or

(d)   The granting or extension to any such person of any options, warrants or rights to purchase any securities, other than warrants or rights issued to security holders as such, on a pro rata basis.

However, if the solicitation is made on behalf of persons other than the registrant, the information required need be furnished only as to nominees of the persons making the solicitation and associates of such nominees. In the case of investment companies registered under the Investment Company Act of 1940 and registrants that have elected to be regulated as business development companies, furnish the information required by Item 22(b)(13) of this Schedule.

Instruction. If an otherwise reportable compensation plan became subject to such requirements because of an acquisition or merger and, within one year of the acquisition or merger, such plan was terminated for purposes of prospective eligibility, the registrant may furnish a description of its obligation to the designated individuals pursuant to the compensation plan. Such description may be furnished in lieu of a description of the compensation plan in the proxy statement.

Item 9.   Independent Public Accountants

If the solicitation is made on behalf of the registrant and relates to

(1)   the annual (or special meeting in lieu of annual) meeting of security holders at which directors are to be elected, or a solicitation of consents or authorizations in lieu of such meeting or

(2)   the election, approval or ratification of the registrant's accountant, furnish the following information describing the registrant's relationship with its independent public accountant:

(a)   The name of the principal accountant selected or being recommended to security holders for election, approval or ratification for the current year. If no accountant has been selected or recommended, so state and briefly describe the reasons therefor.

(b)   The name of the principal accountant for the fiscal year most recently completed if different from the accountant selected or recommended for the current year or if no accountant has yet been selected or recommended for the current year.

(c)   The proxy statement shall indicate

(1)   Whether or not representatives of the principal accountant for the current year and for the most recently completed fiscal year are expected to be present at the security holders' meeting,

(2)   Whether or not they will have the opportunity to make a statement if they desire to do so and

(3)   Whether or not such representatives are expected to be available to respond to appropriate questions.

(d)   If during the registrant's two most recent fiscal years or any subsequent interim period,

(1)   An independent accountant who was previously engaged as the principal accountant to audit the registrant's financial statements, or an independent accountant on whom the principal accountant expressed reliance in its report regarding a significant subsidiary, has resigned (or indicated it has declined to stand for reelection after the completion of the current audit) or was dismissed, or

(2)   A new independent accountant has been engaged as either the principal accountant to audit the registrant's financial statements or as an independent accountant on whom the principal accountant has expressed or is expected to express reliance in its report regarding a significant subsidiary, then, notwithstanding any previous disclosure, provide the information required by Item 304(a) of Regulation S–K.

(e)(1)   Disclose, under the caption *Audit Fees*, the aggregate fees billed for each of the last two fiscal years for professional services rendered by the principal accountant for the audit of the registrant's annual financial statements and review of financial statements included in the registrant's Form 10–Q or services that are normally provided by the accountant in connection with statutory and regulatory filings or engagements for those fiscal years.

(2)   Disclose, under the caption *Audit-Related Fees*, the aggregate fees billed in each of the last two fiscal years for assurance and related services by the principal accountant that are reasonably related to the performance of the audit or review of the registrant's financial statements and are not reported under paragraph (e)(1) of this Item. Registrants shall describe the nature of the services comprising the fees disclosed under this category.

(3)   Disclose, under the caption *Tax Fees*, the aggregate fees billed in each of the last two fiscal years for professional services rendered by the principal accountant for tax compliance, tax advice, and tax planning. Registrants shall describe the nature of the services comprising the fees disclosed under this category.

(4)   Disclose, under the caption *All Other Fees*, the aggregate fees billed in each of the last two fiscal years for products and services provided by the principal accountant, other than the services reported in paragraphs (e)(1) through (e)(3) of this Item. Registrants shall describe the nature of the services comprising the fees disclosed under this category.

(5)(i)   Disclose the audit committee's pre-approval policies and procedures described in Item 2–01(c)(7)(I) of Regulation S–X.

(ii)   Disclose the percentage of services described in each of paragraphs (e)(2) through (e)(4) of this rule that were approved by the audit committee pursuant to Item 2–01(c)(7)(i)(C) of Regulation S–X.

(6)   If greater than 50 percent, disclose the percentage of hours expended on the principal accountant's engagement to audit the registrant's financial statements for the most recent fiscal year that were attributed to work performed by persons other than the principal accountant's full-time, permanent employees.

(7)   If the registrant is an investment company, disclose the aggregate non-audit fees billed by the registrant's accountant for services rendered to the registrant, and to the registrant's investment adviser (not including any subadviser whose role is primarily portfolio management and is subcontracted with or overseen by another investment adviser), and any entity controlling, controlled by, or under common control with the adviser that provides ongoing services to the registrant for each of the last two fiscal years of the registrant.

(8)   If the registrant is an investment company, disclose whether the audit committee of the board of directors has considered whether the provision of non-audit services that were rendered to the registrant's investment adviser (not including any subadviser whose role is primarily portfolio management and is subcontracted with or overseen by another investment adviser), and any entity controlling, controlled by, or under common control with the investment adviser that provides ongoing services to the registrant that were not pre-approved pursuant to Item 2–01(c)(7)(ii) of Regulation S–X is compatible with maintaining the principal accountant's independence.

Instruction to Item 9(e).

For purposes of Item 9(e)(2), (3), and (4), registrants that are investment companies must disclose fees billed for services rendered to the registrant and separately, disclose fees required to be approved by the investment company registrant's audit committee pursuant to Item 2–01(c)(7)(ii) of Regulation S–X. Registered investment companies must also disclose the fee percentages as required by Item 9(e)(5)(ii) for the registrant and separately, disclose the fee percentages as required by Item 9(e)(5)(ii) for the fees required to be approved by the investment company registrant's audit committee pursuant to Item 2–01(c)(7)(ii) of Regulation S–X.

Item 10. Compensation Plans

If action is to be taken with respect to any plan pursuant to which cash or noncash compensation may be paid or distributed, furnish the following information:

(a)   *Plans subject to security holder action.*

(1)   Describe briefly the material features of the plan being acted upon, identify each class of persons who will be eligible to participate therein, indicate the approximate number of persons in each such class, and state the basis of such participation.

(2)(i)   In the tabular format specified below, disclose the benefits or amounts that will be received by or allocated to each of the following under the plan being acted upon, if such benefits or amounts are determinable:

New Plan Benefits

Plan name

Name and position	Dollar value ($)	Number of units
CEO		
A		
B		
C		
D		
Executive Group		
Non-Executive Director Group		
Non-Executive Officer Employee Group		

    (ii)   The table required by paragraph (a)(2)(i) of this Item shall provide information as to the following persons:

        (A)   Each person (stating name and position) specified in paragraph (a)(3) of Item 402 of Regulation S–K;

Instruction: In the case of investment companies registered under the Investment Company Act of 1940, furnish the information for Compensated Persons as defined in Item 22(b)(13) of this Schedule in lieu of the persons specified in paragraph (a)(3) of Item 402 of Regulation S–K.

        (B)   All current executive officers as a group;

        (C)   All current directors who are not executive officers as a group; and

        (D)   All employees, including all current officers who are not executive officers, as a group.

Instruction to New Plan Benefits Table

Additional columns should be added for each plan with respect to which security holder action is to be taken.

    (iii)   If the benefits or amounts specified in paragraph (a)(2)(i) of this item are not determinable, state the benefits or amounts which would have been received by or allocated to each of the following for the last completed fiscal year if the plan had been in effect, if such benefits or amounts may be determined, in the table specified in paragraph (a)(2)(i) of this Item:

        (A)   Each person (stating name and position) specified in paragraph (a)(3) of Item 402 of Regulation S–K;

        (B)   All current executive officers as a group;

        (C)   All current directors who are not executive officers as a group; and

        (D)   All employees, including all current officers who are not executive officers, as a group.

    (3)   If the plan to be acted upon can be amended, otherwise than by a vote of security holders, to increase the cost thereof to the registrant or to alter the allocation of the benefits as between the persons and groups specified in paragraph (a)(2) of this item, state the nature of the amendments which can be so made.

(b)(1)   *Additional information regarding specified plans subject to security holder action.* With respect to any pension or retirement plan submitted for security holder action, state:

    (i)   The approximate total amount necessary to fund the plan with respect to past services, the period over which such amount is to be paid and the estimated annual payments necessary to pay the total amount over such period; and

(ii)   The estimated annual payment to be made with respect to current services. In the case of a pension or retirement plan, information called for by paragraph (a)(2) of this Item may be furnished in the format specified by paragraph (h)(2) of Item 402 of Regulation S–K.

Instruction. In the case of investment companies registered under the Investment Company Act of 1940, refer to Instruction 4 in Item 22(b)(13)(i) of this Schedule in lieu of paragraph (h)(2) of Item 402 of Regulation S–K.

(2)(i)   With respect to any specific grant of or any plan containing options, warrants or rights submitted for security holder action, state:

(A)   The title and amount of securities underlying such options, warrants or rights;

(B)   The prices, expiration dates and other material conditions upon which the options, warrants or rights may be exercised;

(C)   The consideration received or to be received by the registrant or subsidiary for the granting or extension of the options, warrants or rights;

(D)   The market value of the securities underlying the options, warrants, or rights as of the latest practicable date; and

(E)   In the case of options, the federal income tax consequences of the issuance and exercise of such options to the recipient and the registrant; and

(ii)   State separately the amount of such options received or to be received by the following persons if such benefits or amounts are determinable: (A) Each person (stating name and position) specified in paragraph (a)(3) of Item 402 of Regulation S–K; (B) All current executive officers as a group; (C) All current directors who are not executive officers as a group; (D) Each nominee for election as a director; (E) Each associate of any of such directors, executive officers or nominees; (F) Each other person who received or is to receive 5 percent of such options, warrants or rights; and (G) All employees, including all current officers who are not executive officers, as a group.

(c)   *Information regarding plans and other arrangements not subject to security holder action.* Furnish the information required by Item 201(d) of Regulation S–K.

Instructions to paragraph (c).

1.   If action is to be taken as described in paragraph (a) of this Item with respect to the approval of a new compensation plan under which equity securities of the registrant are authorized for issuance, information about the plan shall be disclosed as required under paragraphs (a) and (b) of this Item and shall not be included in the disclosure required by Item 201(d) of Regulation S–K. If action is to be taken as described in paragraph (a) of this Item with respect to the amendment or modification of an existing plan under which equity securities of the registrant are authorized for issuance, the registrant shall include information about securities previously authorized for issuance under the plan (including any outstanding options, warrants and rights previously granted pursuant to the plan and any securities remaining available for future issuance under the plan) in the disclosure required by Item 201(d) of Regulation S–K. Any additional securities that are the subject of the amendments or modification of the existing plan shall be disclosed as required under paragraphs (a) and (b) of this Item and shall not be included in the Item 201(d) disclosure.

Instructions

1.   The term "plan" as used in this Item means any plan as defined in paragraph (a)(6)(ii) of Item 402 of Regulation S–K.

2.   If action is to be taken with respect to a material amendment or modification of an existing plan, the item shall be answered with respect to the plan as proposed to be amended or modified and shall indicate any material differences from the existing plan.

3.   If the plan to be acted upon is set forth in a written document, three copies thereof shall be filed with the Commission at the time copies of the proxy statement and form of proxy are filed pursuant to paragraph (a) or (b) of Rule 14a–6. Electronic filers shall file with the Commission a copy of such written plan document in electronic format as an appendix to the proxy statement. It need not be provided to security holders unless it is a part of the proxy statement.

4. Paragraph (b)(2)(ii) does not apply to warrants or rights to be issued to security holders as such on a pro rata basis.

5. The Commission shall be informed, as supplemental information, when the proxy statement is first filed, as to when the options, warrants or rights and the shares called for thereby will be registered under the Securities Act or, if such registration is not contemplated, the section of the Securities Act or rule of the Commission under which exemption from such registration is claimed and the facts relied upon to make the exemption available.

Item 11. Authorization or Issuance of Securities Otherwise Than for Exchange

If action is to be taken with respect to the authorization or issuance of any securities otherwise than for exchange for outstanding securities of the registrant, furnish the following information:

(a) State the title and amount of securities to be authorized or issued.

(b) Furnish the information required by Item 202 of Regulation S–K. If the terms of the securities cannot be stated or estimated with respect to any or all of the securities to be authorized, because no offering thereof is contemplated in the proximate future, and if no further authorization by security holders for the issuance thereof is to be obtained, it should be stated that the terms of the securities to be authorized, including dividend or interest rates, conversion prices, voting rights, redemption prices, maturity dates, and similar matters will be determined by the board of directors. If the securities are additional shares of common stock of a class outstanding, the description may be omitted except for a statement of the preemptive rights, if any. Where the statutory provisions with respect to preemptive rights are so indefinite or complex that they cannot be stated in summarized form, it will suffice to make a statement in the form of an opinion of counsel as to the existence and extent of such rights.

(c) Describe briefly the transaction in which the securities are to be issued including a statement as to (1) the nature and approximate amount of consideration received or to be received by the registrant and (2) the approximate amount devoted to each purpose so far as determinable for which the net proceeds have been or are to be used. If it is impracticable to describe the transaction in which the securities are to be issued, state the reason, indicate the purpose of the authorization of the securities, and state whether further authorization for the issuance of the securities by a vote of security holders will be solicited prior to such issuance.

(d) If the securities are to be issued otherwise than in a public offering for cash, state the reasons for the proposed authorization or issuance and the general effect thereof upon the rights of existing security holders.

(e) Furnish the information required by Item 13(a) of this schedule.

Item 12. Modification or Exchange of Securities

If action is to be taken with respect to the modification of any class of securities of the registrant, or the issuance or authorization for issuance of securities of the registrant in exchange for outstanding securities of the registrant furnish the following information:

(a) If outstanding securities are to be modified, state the title and amount thereof. If securities are to be issued in exchange for outstanding securities, state the title and amount of securities to be so issued, the title and amount of outstanding securities to be exchanged therefor and the basis of the exchange.

(b) Describe any material differences between the outstanding securities and the modified or new securities in respect of any of the matters concerning which information would be required in the description of the securities in Item 202 of Regulation S–K.

(c) State the reasons for the proposed modification or exchange and the general effect thereof upon the rights of existing security holders.

(d) Furnish a brief statement as to arrears in dividends or as to defaults in principal or interest in respect to the outstanding securities which are to be modified or exchanged and such other information as may be appropriate in the particular case to disclose adequately the nature and effect of the proposed action.

(e) Outline briefly any other material features of the proposed modification or exchange. If the plan of proposed action is set forth in a written document, file copies thereof with the Commission in accordance with Rule 14a–8.

(f) Furnish the information required by Item 13(a) of this schedule.

Instruction. If the existing security is presently listed and registered on a national securities exchange, state whether the registrant intends to apply for listing and registration of the new or reclassified security on such exchange or any other exchange. If the registrant does not intend to make such application, state the effect of the termination of such listing and registration.

Item 13. Financial and Other Information

(*See* Notes D and E at the beginning of this Schedule.)

(a) *Information required.* If action is to be taken with respect to any matter specified in Item 11 or 12, furnish the following information:

(1) Financial statements meeting the requirements of Regulation S–X, including financial information required by Rule 3–05 and Article 11 of Regulation S–X with respect to transactions other than pursuant to which action is to be taken as described in this proxy statement (a smaller reporting company may provide the information in Rules 8–04 and 8–05 of Regulation S–X in lieu of the financial information required by Rule 3–05 and Article 11 of Regulation S–X);

(2) Item 302 of Regulation S–K, supplementary financial information;

(3) Item 303 of Regulation S–K, management's discussion and analysis of financial condition and results of operations;

(4) Item 304 of Regulation S–K, changes in and disagreements with accountants on accounting and financial disclosure;

(5) Item 305 of Regulation S–K, quantitative and qualitative disclosures about market risk; and

(6) A statement as to whether or not representatives of the principal accountants for the current year and for the most recently completed fiscal year:

(i) are expected to be present at the security holders' meeting;

(ii) will have the opportunity to make a statement if they desire to do so; and

(iii) are expected to be available to respond to appropriate questions.

(b) *Incorporation by reference.* The information required pursuant to paragraph (a) of this Item may be incorporated by reference into the proxy statement as follows:

(1) *S–3 registrants.* If the registrant meets the requirements of Form S–3 (*see* Note E to this Schedule), it may incorporate by reference to previously-filed documents any of the information required by paragraph (a) of this Item, provided that the requirements of paragraph (c) are met. Where the registrant meets the requirements of Form S–3 and has elected to furnish the required information by incorporation by reference, the registrant may elect to update the information so incorporated by reference to information in subsequently-filed documents.

(2) *All registrants.* The registrant may incorporate by reference any of the information required by paragraph (a) of this Item, provided that the information is contained in an annual report to security holders or a previously-filed statement or report, such report or statement is delivered to security holders with the proxy statement and the requirements of paragraph (c) are met.

(c) *Certain conditions applicable to incorporation by reference.* Registrants eligible to incorporate by reference into the proxy statement the information required by paragraph (a) of this Item in the manner specified by paragraphs (b)(1) and (b)(2) may do so only if:

(1) The information is not required to be included in the proxy statement pursuant to the requirement of another Item;

(2) The proxy statement identifies on the last page(s) the information incorporated by reference; and

(3) The material incorporated by reference substantially meets the requirements of this Item or the appropriate portions of this Item.

Instructions to Item 13. 1. Notwithstanding the provisions of this Item, any or all of the information required by paragraph (a) of this Item, not material for the exercise of prudent judgment in regard to the matter to be acted upon may be omitted. In the usual case the information is deemed material to the exercise of prudent judgment where the matter to be acted upon is the authorization or issuance of a material amount of senior securities, but the information is not deemed material where the matter to be acted upon is the authorization or issuance of common stock, otherwise than in an exchange, merger, consolidation, acquisition or similar transaction, the authorization of preferred stock without present intent to issue or the authorization of preferred stock for issuance for cash in an amount constituting fair value.

2. In order to facilitate compliance with Rule 2–02(a) of Regulation S–X, one copy of the definitive proxy statement filed with the Commission shall include a manually signed copy of the accountant's report. If the financial statements are incorporated by reference, a manually signed copy of the accountant's report shall be filed with the definitive proxy statement.

3. Notwithstanding the provisions of Regulation S–X, no schedules other than those prepared in accordance with Rules 12–15, 12–28 and 12–29 (or, for management investment companies, Rules 12–12 through 12–14) of that regulation need be furnished in the proxy statement.

4. Unless registered on a national securities exchange or otherwise required to furnish such information, registered investment companies need not furnish the information required by paragraphs (a)(2) or (3) of this Item.

5. If the registrant submits preliminary proxy material incorporating by reference financial statements required by this Item, the registrant should furnish a draft of the financial statements if the document from which they are incorporated has not been filed with or furnished to the Commission.

6. A registered investment company need not comply with paragraphs (a)(2), (a)(3), and (a)(5) of this Item 13.

Item 14. Mergers, Consolidations, Acquisitions and Similar Matters

(See Notes A, D and E at the beginning of the this Schedule.)

Instructions to Item 14.

1. In transactions in which the consideration offered to security holders consists wholly or in part of securities registered under the Securities Act of 1933, furnish the information required by Form S–4, Form F–4, or Form N–14, as applicable, instead of this Item. Only a Form S–4, Form F–4, or Form N–14 must be filed in accordance with Rule 14a–6(j) of the Securities Exchange Act.

2. (a) In transactions in which the consideration offered to security holders consists wholly of cash, the information required by paragraph (c)(1) of this Item for the acquiring company need not be provided unless the information is material to an informed voting decision (*e.g.,* the security holders of the target company are voting and financing is not assured).

(b) Additionally, if only the security holders of the target company are voting:

i. The financial information in paragraphs (b)(8)–(11) of this Item for the acquiring company and the target need not be provided; and

ii. The information in paragraph (c)(2) of this Item for the target company need not be provided.

If, however, the transaction is a going-private transaction (as defined by Rule 13e–3), then the information required by paragraph (c)(2) of this Item must be provided and to the extent that the going-private rules require the information specified in paragraph (b)(8)–(b)(11) of this Item, that information must be provided as well.

3. In transactions in which the consideration offered to security holders consists wholly of securities exempt from registration under the Securities Act of 1933 or a combination of exempt securities and case,

information about the acquiring company required by paragraph (c)(1) of this Item need not be provided if only the security holders of the acquiring company are voting, unless the information is material to an informed voting decision. If only the security holders of the target company are voting, information about the target company in paragraph (c)(2) of this Item need not be provided. However, the information required by paragraph (c)(2) of this Item must be provided if the transaction is a going-private (as defined by Rule 13e–3) or roll-up (as described by Item 901 of Regulation S–K) transaction.

4.   The information required by paragraphs (b)(8)–(11) and (c) need not be provided if the plan being voted on involves only the acquiring company and one or more of its totally held subsidiaries and does not involve a liquidation or a spin-off.

5.   To facilitate compliance with Rule 2–02(a) of Regulation S–X (technical requirements relating to accountant's reports), one copy of the definitive proxy statement filed with the Commission must include a signed copy of the accountants' reports, one copy of the definitive proxy statement filed with the Commission must include a signed copy of the accountant's report. If the financial statements are incorporated by reference, a signed copy of the accountant's report must be filed with the definitive proxy statement. Signatures may be typed if the document is filed electronically on EDGAR. See Rule 302 of Regulation S–T.

6.   Notwithstanding the provisions of Regulation S–X, no schedules other than those prepared in accordance with Item 12–15, Item 12–28 and Item 12–29 of Regulation S–X (or, for management investment companies, Items 12–12 through 12–14 of Regulation S–X) of that regulation need be furnished in the proxy statement.

7.   If the preliminary proxy material incorporates by reference financial statements required by this Item, a draft of the financial statements must be furnished to the Commission staff upon request if the document from which they are incorporated has not been filed with or furnished to the Commission.

(a)   *Applicability.* If action is to be taken with respect to any of the following transactions, provide the information required by the Item:

     (1)   A merger or consolidation;

     (2)   An acquisition of securities of another person;

     (3)   An acquisition of any other going business or the assets of a going business;

     (4)   A sale or other transfer of all or any substantial part of assets; or

     (5)   A liquidation or dissolution.

(b)   *Transaction information.* Provide the following information for each of the parties to the transaction unless otherwise specified:

     (1)   *Summary term sheet.* The information required by Item 1001 of Regulation M–A.

     (2)   *Contact information.* The name, complete mailing address and telephone number of the principal executive offices.

     (3)   *Business conducted.* A brief description of the general nature of the business conducted.

     (4)   *Terms of the transaction.* The information required by Item 1004(a)(2) of Regulation M–A.

     (5)   *Regulatory approvals.* A statement as to whether any federal or state regulatory requirements must be complied with or approval must be obtained in connection with the transaction and, if so, the status of the compliance or approval.

     (6)   *Reports, opinions, appraisals.* If a report, opinion or appraisal materially relating to the transaction has been received from an outside party, and is referred to in the proxy statement, furnish the information required by Item 1015(b) of Regulation M–A.

     (7)   *Past contacts, transactions or negotiations.* The information required by Items 1005(b) and 1011(a)(1) of Regulation M–A, for the parties to the transaction and their affiliates during the periods for which financial statements are presented or incorporated by reference under this Item.

     (8)   *Selected financial data.* The selected financial data required by Item 301 of Regulation S–K.

(9) *Pro forma selected financial data.* If material, the information required by Item 301 of Regulation S–K for the acquiring company, showing the pro forma effect of the transaction.

(10) *Pro forma information.* In a table designed to facilitate comparison, historical and pro forma per share data of the acquiring company and historical and equivalent pro forma per share data of the target company for the following Items:

(i)   Book value per share as of the date financial data is presented pursuant to Item 301 of Regulation S–K;

(ii)   Cash dividends declares per share for the periods for which financial data is presented pursuant to Item 301 of Regulation S–K; and

(iii)   Income (loss) per share from continuing operations for the periods for which financial data is presented pursuant to Item 301 of Regulation S–K.

Instructions to paragraphs (b)(8), (b)(9) and (b)(10):

1.   For a business combination, present the financial information required by paragraphs (b)(9) and (b)(10) only for the most recent fiscal year and interim period. For a combination between entities under common control, present the financial information required by paragraphs (b)(9) and (b)(10) (except for information with regard to book value) for the most recent three fiscal years and interim period. For purposes of these paragraphs, book value information need only be provided for the most recent balance sheet date.

2.   Calculate the equivalent pro forma per share amounts for one share of the company being acquired by multiplying the exchange ratio times each of:

(i)   The pro forma income (loss) per share before non-recurring charges or credits directly attributable to the transaction;

(ii)   The pro forma book value per share; and

(iii)   The pro forma dividends per share of the acquiring company.

3.   Unless registered on a national securities exchange or otherwise required to furnish such information, registered investment companies need not furnish the information required by paragraphs (b)(8) and (b)(9) of this Item.

(11) *Financial information.* If material, financial information required by Article 11 of Regulation S–X with respect to this transaction.

Instructions to paragraph (b)(11):

1.   Present any Article 11 information required with respect to transactions other than those being voted upon (where not incorporated by reference) together with the pro forma information relating to the transaction being voted upon. In presenting this information, you must clearly distinguish between the transaction being voted upon and any other transaction.

2.   If current pro forma financial information with respect to all other transactions is incorporated by reference, you need only present the pro forma effect of this transaction.

(c)   *Information about the parties to the transaction.*

(1)   *Acquiring company.* Furnish the information required by Part B (Registrant Information) of Form S–4 or Form F–4, as applicable, for the acquiring company. However, financial statements need only be presented for the latest two fiscal years and interim periods.

(2)   *Acquired company.* Furnish the information required by Part C (Information with Respect to the Company Being Acquired) of Form S–4 or Form F–4, as applicable.

(d)   *Information about parties to the transaction: registered investment companies and business development companies.* If the acquiring company or the acquired company is an investment company registered under the Investment Company Act of 1940 or a business development company as defined by section 2(a)(48) of the Investment Company Act of 1940, provide the following information for that company instead of the information specified by paragraph (c) of this Item:

(1)   Information required by Item 101 of Regulation S–K, description of business;

(2)   Information required by Item 102 of Regulation S–K, description of property;

(3)   Information required by Item 103 of Regulation S–K, legal proceedings;

(4)   Information required by Item 201 of Regulation S–K, market price of and dividends on the registrant's common equity and related stockholder matters;

(5)   Financial statements meeting the requirements of Regulation S–X, including financial information required by Rule 3–05 and Article 11 of Regulation S–X with respect to transactions other than that as to which action is to be taken as described in this proxy statement;

(6)   Information required by Item 301 of Regulation S–K, selected financial data;

(7)   Information required by Item 302 of Regulation S–K, supplementary financial information;

(8)   Information required Item 303 of Regulation S–K, management's discussion and analysis of financial condition and results of operations; and

(9)   Information required by Item 304 of Regulation S–K, changes in and disagreements with accountants on accounting and financial disclosure.

Instruction to paragraph (d) of Item 14: Unless registered on a national securities exchange or otherwise required to furnish such information, registered investment companies need not furnish the information required by paragraphs (d)(6), (d)(7) and (d)(8) of this Item.

(e)   *Incorporation by reference.*

(1)   The information required by paragraph (c) of this Item may be incorporated by reference into the proxy statement to the same extent as would be permitted by Form S–4 or Form F–4, as applicable.

(2)   Alternatively, the registrant may incorporate by reference into the proxy statement the information required by paragraph (c) of this Item if it is contained in an annual report sent to security holders in accordance with Rule 14a–3 of this chapter with respect to the same meeting or solicitation of consents or authorizations that the proxy statement relates to and the information substantially meets the disclosure requirements of Item 14 or Item 17 of Form S–4 or Form F–4, as applicable.

Item 15. Acquisition or Disposition of Property

If action is to be taken with respect to the acquisition or disposition of any property, furnish the following information:

(a)   Describe briefly the general character and location of the property.

(b)   State the nature and amount of consideration to be paid or received by the registrant or any subsidiary. To the extent practicable, outline briefly the facts bearing upon the question of the fairness of the consideration.

(c)   State the name and address of the transferor or transferee, as the case may be and the nature of any material relationship of such person to the registrant or any affiliate of the registrant.

(d)   Outline briefly any other material features of the contract or transaction.

Item 16. Restatement of Accounts

If action is to be taken with respect to the restatement of any asset, capital, or surplus account of the registrant, furnish the following information:

(a)   State the nature of the restatement and the date as of which it is to be effective.

(b)   Outline briefly the reasons for the restatement and for the selection of the particular effective date.

(c)   State the name and amount of each account (including any reserve accounts) affected by the restatement and the effect of the restatement thereon. Tabular presentation of the amounts shall be made when appropriate, particularly in the case of recapitalizations.

(d)   To the extent practicable, state whether and the extent, if any, to which the restatement will, as of the date thereof, alter the amount available for distribution to the holders of equity securities.

Item 17. Action With Respect to Reports

If action is to be taken with respect to any report of the registrant or of its directors, officers or committees or any minutes of a meeting of its security holders furnish the following information:

(a)   State whether or not such action is to constitute approval or disapproval of any of the matters referred to in such reports or minutes.

(b)   Identify each of such matters which it is intended will be approved or disapproved, and furnish the information required by the appropriate item or items of this schedule with respect to each such matter.

Item 18. Matters Not Required to Be Submitted

If action is to be taken with respect to any matter which is not required to be submitted to a vote of security holders, state the nature of such matter, the reasons for submitting it to a vote of security holders and what action is intended to be taken by the registrant in the event of a negative vote on the matter by the security holders.

Item 19. Amendment of Charter, Bylaws or Other Documents

If action is to be taken with respect to any amendment of the registrant's charter, bylaws or other documents as to which information is not required above, state briefly the reasons for and the general effect of such amendment.

Instructions. 1. Where the matter to be acted upon is the classification of directors, state whether vacancies which occur during the year may be filled by the board of directors to serve only until the next annual meeting or may be so filled for the remainder of the full term.

2.   Attention is directed to the discussion of disclosure regarding anti-takeover and similar proposals in Release No. 34–15230 (October 13, 1978).

Item 20. Other Proposed Action

If action is to be taken on any matter not specifically referred to in this Schedule 14A, describe briefly the substance of each such matter in substantially the same degree of detail as is required by Items 5 to 19, inclusive, of this Schedule, and, with respect to investment companies registered under the Investment Company Act of 1940, Item 22 of this Schedule. Registrants required to provide a separate shareholder vote pursuant to section 111(e)(1) of the Emergency Economic Stabilization Act of 2008 and Rule 14a–20 shall disclose that they are providing such a vote as required pursuant to the Emergency Economic Stabilization Act of 2008, and briefly explain the general effect of the vote, such as whether the vote is non-binding.

Item 21. Voting Procedures

As to each matter which is to be submitted to a vote of security holders, furnish the following information:

(a)   State the vote required for approval or election, other than for the approval of auditors.

(b)   Disclose the method by which votes will be counted, including the treatment and effect under applicable state law and registrant charter and bylaw provisions of abstentions, broker non-votes, and, to the extent applicable, a security holder's withholding of authority to vote for a nominee in an election of directors.

(c)   When applicable, disclose how the soliciting person intends to treat proxy authority granted in favor of any other soliciting person's nominees if such other soliciting person abandons its solicitation or fails to comply with § 240.14a–19.

Item 22. Information Required in Investment Company Proxy Statement

(a)   *General.*

(1)   *Definitions.* Unless the context otherwise requires, terms used in this Item that are defined in Rule 14a–1 under the Act (with respect to proxy soliciting material), in Rule 14c–1 (with respect to information statements), and in the Investment Company Act of 1940 shall have the same meanings provided therein and the following terms shall also apply:

(i)   *Administrator.* The term "Administrator" shall mean any person who provides significant administrative or business affairs management services to a Fund.

(ii)   *Affiliated broker.* The term "Affiliated Broker" shall mean any broker:

(A)   That is an affiliated person of the Fund;

(B)   That is an affiliated person of such person; or

(C)   An affiliated person of which is an affiliated person of the Fund, its investment adviser, principal underwriter, or Administrator.

(iii)   *Distribution plan.* The term "Distribution Plan" shall mean a plan adopted pursuant to Rule 12b–1 under the Investment Company Act of 1940.

(iv)   *Family of Investment Companies.* The term "Family of Investment Companies" shall mean any two or more registered investment companies that:

(A)   Share the same investment adviser or principal underwriter; and

(B)   Hold themselves out to investors as related companies for purposes of investment and investor services.

(v)   *Fund.* The term "Fund" shall mean a Registrant or, where the Registrant is a series company, a separate portfolio of the Registrant.

(vi)   *Fund complex.* The term "Fund Complex" shall mean two or more Funds that:

(A)   Hold themselves out to investors as related companies for purposes of investment and investor services; or

(B)   Have a common investment adviser or have an investment adviser that is an affiliated person of the investment adviser of any of the other Funds.

(vii)   *Immediate Family Member.* The term "Immediate Family Member" shall mean a person's spouse; child residing in the person's household (including step and adoptive children); and any dependent of the person, as defined in section 152 of the Internal Revenue Code.

(viii)   *Officer.* The term "Officer" shall mean the president, vice-president, secretary, treasurer, controller, or any other officer who performs policy-making functions.

(ix)   *Parent.* The term "Parent" shall mean the affiliated person of a specified person who controls the specified person directly or indirectly through one or more intermediaries.

(x)   *Registrant.* The term "Registrant" shall mean an investment company registered under the Investment Company Act of 1940 or a business development company as defined by section 2(a)(48) of the Investment Company Act of 1940.

(xi)   *Sponsoring Insurance Company.* The term "Sponsoring Insurance Company" of a Fund that is a separate account shall mean the insurance company that establishes and maintains the separate account and that owns the assets of the separate account.

(xii)   *Subsidiary.* The term "Subsidiary" shall mean an affiliated person of a specified person who is controlled by the specified person directly, or indirectly through one or more intermediaries.

(2)   Removed.

(3)   *General disclosure.* Furnish the following information in the proxy statement of a Fund or Funds:

(i)   State the name and address of the Fund's investment adviser, principal underwriter, and Administrator.

(ii)   When a Fund proxy statement solicits a vote on proposals affecting more than one Fund or class of securities of a Fund (unless the proposal or proposals are the same and affect all Fund or class shareholders), present a summary of all of the proposals in tabular form on one of the first three pages of the proxy statement and indicate which Fund or class shareholders are solicited with respect to each proposal.

(iii)   Unless the proxy statement is accompanied by a copy of the Fund's most recent annual report, state prominently in the proxy statement that the Fund will furnish, without charge, a copy of the annual report and the most recent semi-annual report succeeding the annual report, if any, to a shareholder upon request, providing the name, address, and toll-free telephone number of the person to whom such request shall be directed (or, if no toll-free telephone number is provided, a self-addressed postage paid card for requesting the annual report). The Fund should provide a copy of the annual report and the most recent semi-annual report succeeding the annual report, if any, to the requesting shareholder by first class mail, or other means designed to assure prompt delivery, within three business days of the request.

(iv)   If the action to be taken would, directly or indirectly, establish a new fee or expense or increase any existing fee or expense to be paid by the Fund or its shareholders, provide a table showing the current and pro forma fees (with the required examples) using the format prescribed in the appropriate registration statement form under the Investment Company Act of 1940 (for open-end management investment companies, Item 2 of Form N–1A; for closed-end management investment companies, Item 4 of Form N–2; and for separate accounts that offer variable annuity contracts, Item 4 of Form N–3).

Instructions. 1. Where approval is sought only for a change in asset breakpoints for a pre-existing fee that would not have increased the fee for the previous year (or have the effect of increasing fees or expenses, but for any other reason would not be reflected in a pro forma fee table), describe the likely effect of the change in lieu of providing pro forma fee information.

2.   An action would indirectly establish or increase a fee or expense where, for example, the approval of a new investment advisory contract would result in higher custodial or transfer agency fees.

3.   The tables should be prepared in a manner designed to facilitate understanding of the impact of any change in fees or expenses.

4.   A Fund that offers its shares exclusively to one or more separate accounts and thus is not required to include a fee table in its prospectus (see Item 2(a)(ii) of Form N–1A) should nonetheless prepare a table showing current and pro forma expenses and disclose that the table does not reflect separate account expenses, including sales load.

(v)   If action is to be taken with respect to the election of directors or the approval of an advisory contract, describe any purchases or sales of securities of the investment adviser or its Parents, or Subsidiaries of either, since the beginning of the most recently completed fiscal year by any director or any nominee for election as a director of the Fund.

Instructions. 1. Identify the parties, state the consideration, the terms of payment and describe any arrangement or understanding with respect to the composition of the board of directors of the Fund or of the investment adviser, or with respect to the selection of appointment of any person to any office with either such company.

2.   Transactions involving securities in an amount not exceeding one percent of the outstanding securities of any class of the investment adviser or any of its Parents or Subsidiaries may be omitted.

(b)   *Election of Directors.* If action is to be taken with respect to the election of directors of a Fund, furnish the following information in the proxy statement in addition to the information (and in the format) required by Item 7 and Item 8 of this Schedule.

Instructions to introductory text of paragraph (b). 1. Furnish information with respect to a prospective investment adviser to the extent applicable.

2.   If the solicitation is made by or on behalf of a person other than the Fund or an investment adviser of the Fund, provide information only as to nominees of the person making the solicitation.

3.   When providing information about directors and nominees for election as directors in response to this Item 22(b), furnish information for directors or nominees who are or would be "interested persons" of the Fund within the meaning of section 2(a)(19) of the Investment Company Act of 1940 separately from the information for directors or nominees who are not or would not be interested persons of the Fund. For example, when furnishing information in a table, you should provide separate tables (or separate sections of a single table) for directors and nominees who are or would be interested persons and for directors or nominees who are not or would not be interested persons. When furnishing information in narrative form, indicate by heading or otherwise the directors or nominees who are or would be interested persons and the directors or nominees who are not or would not be interested persons.

4.   No information need be given about any director whose term of office as a director will not continue after the meeting to which the proxy statement relates.

(1)   Provide the information required by the following table for each director, nominee for election as director, Officer of the Fund, person chosen to become an Officer of the Fund, and, if the Fund has an advisory board, member of the board. Explain in a footnote to the table any family relationship between the persons listed.

(1) Name, Address, and age.	(2) Position(s) Held with Fund.	(3) Term of Office and Length of Time Served.	(4) Principal Occupation(s) During Past 5 Years.	(5) Number of Portfolios in Fund Complex Overseen by Director or Nominee for Director.	(6) Other Directorships Held by Director or Nominee for Director.

Instructions to paragraph (b)(1). 1. For purposes of this paragraph, the term "family relationship" means any relationship by blood, marriage, or adoption, not more remote than first cousin.

2.   No nominee or person chosen to become a director or Officer who has not consented to act as such may be named in response to this Item. In this regard, see Rule 14a–4(d) under the Exchange Act.

3.   If fewer nominees are named than the number fixed by or pursuant to the governing instruments, state the reasons for this procedure and that the proxies cannot be voted for a greater number of persons than the number of nominees named.

4.   For each director or nominee for election as director who is or would be an "interested person" of the Fund within the meaning of section 2(a)(19) of the Investment Company Act of 1940, describe, in a footnote or otherwise, the relationship, events, or transactions by reason of which the director or nominee is or would be an interested person.

5.   State the principal business of any company listed under column (4) unless the principal business is implicit in its name.

6.   Include in column (5) the total number of separate portfolios that a nominee for election as director would oversee if he were elected.

7.   Indicate in column (6) directorships not included in column (5) that are held by a director or nominee for election as director in any company with a class of securities registered pursuant to section 12 of the Exchange Act, or subject to the requirements of section 15(d) of the Exchange Act, or any company registered as an investment company under the Investment Company Act of 1940, as amended, and name the companies in which the directorships are held. Where the other directorships include directorships overseeing two or more portfolios in the same Fund Complex, identify the Fund Complex and provide the number of portfolios overseen as a director in the Fund Complex rather than listing each portfolio separately.

(2)   For each individual listed in column (1) of the table required by paragraph (b)(1) of this Item, except for any director or nominee for election as director who is not or would not be an "interested person" of the Fund within the meaning of section 2(a)(19) of the Investment Company Act of 1940,

describe any positions, including as an officer, employee, director, or general partner, held with affiliated persons or principal underwriters of the Fund.

Instruction to paragraph (b)(2). When an individual holds the same position(s) with two or more registered investment companies that are part of the same Fund Complex, identify the Fund Complex and provide the number of registered investment companies for which the position(s) are held rather than listing each registered investment company separately.

(3) Describe briefly any arrangement or understanding between any director, nominee for election as director, Officer, or person chosen to become an Officer, and any other person(s) (naming the person(s)) pursuant to which he was or is to be selected as a director, nominee, or Officer.

Instruction to paragraph (b)(3). Do not include arrangements or understandings with directors or Officers acting solely in their capacities as such.

(4) Unless disclosed in the table required by paragraph (b)(1) of this Item, describe any positions, including as an officer, employee, director, or general partner, held by any director or nominee for election as director, who is not or would not be an "interested person" of the Fund within the meaning of section 2(a)(19) of the Investment Company Act of 1940, or Immediate Family Member of the director or nominee, during the past five years, with:

(i) The Fund;

(ii) An investment company, or a person that would be an investment company but for the exclusions provided by sections 3(c)(1) and 3(c)(7) of the Investment Company Act of 1940, having the same investment adviser, principal underwriter, or Sponsoring Insurance Company as the Fund or having an investment adviser, principal underwriter, or Sponsoring Insurance Company that directly or indirectly controls, is controlled by, or is under common control with an investment adviser, principal underwriter, or Sponsoring Insurance Company of the Fund;

(iii) An investment adviser, principal underwriter, Sponsoring Insurance Company, or affiliated person of the Fund; or

(iv) Any person directly or indirectly controlling, controlled by, or under common control with an investment adviser, principal underwriter, or Sponsoring Insurance Company of the Fund.

Instruction to paragraph (b)(4). When an individual holds the same position(s) with two or more portfolios that are part of the same Fund Complex, identify the Fund Complex and provide the number of portfolios for which the position(s) are held rather than listing each portfolio separately.

(5) For each director or nominee for election as director, state the dollar range of equity securities beneficially owned by the director or nominee as required by the following table:

(i) In the Fund; and

(ii) On an aggregate basis, in any registered investment companies overseen or to be overseen by the director or nominee within the same Family of Investment Companies as the Fund.

(1)	(2)	(3)
Name of Director or Nominee	Dollar Range of Equity Securities in the Fund	Aggregate Dollar Range of Equity Securities in All Funds Overseen or to be Overseen by Director or Nominee in Family of Investment Companies

Instructions to paragraph (b)(5). 1. Information should be provided as of the most recent practicable date. Specify the valuation date by footnote or otherwise.

2. Determine "beneficial ownership" in accordance with Rule 16a–1(a)(2) under the Exchange Act.

3. If action is to be taken with respect to more than one Fund, disclose in column (2) the dollar range of equity securities beneficially owned by a director or nominee in each such Fund overseen or to be overseen by the director or nominee.

4. In disclosing the dollar range of equity securities beneficially owned by a director or nominee in columns (2) and (3), use the following ranges: none, $1–$10,000, $10,001–$50,000, $50,001–$100,000, or over $100,000.

(6) For each director or nominee for election as director who is not or would not be an "interested person" of the Fund within the meaning of section 2(a)(19) of the Investment Company Act of 1940, and his Immediate Family Members, furnish the information required by the following table as to each class of securities owned beneficially or of record in:

(i) An investment adviser, principal underwriter, or Sponsoring Insurance Company of the Fund; or

(ii) A person (other than a registered investment company) directly or indirectly controlling, controlled by, or under common control with an investment adviser, principal underwriter, or Sponsoring Insurance Company of the Fund:

(1) Name of Director or Nominee	(2) Name of Owners and Relationships to Director or Nominee	(3) Company	(4) Title of Class	(5) Value of Securities	(6) Percent of Class

Instructions to paragraph (b)(6). 1. Information should be provided as of the most recent practicable date. Specify the valuation date by footnote or otherwise.

2. An individual is a "beneficial owner" of a security if he is a "beneficial owner" under either Rule 13d–3 or Rule 16a–1(a)(2) under the Exchange Act.

3. Identify the company in which the director, nominee, or Immediate Family Member of the director or nominee owns securities in column (3). When the company is a person directly or indirectly controlling, controlled by, or under common control with an investment adviser, principal underwriter, or Sponsoring Insurance Company, describe the company's relationship with the investment adviser, principal underwriter, or Sponsoring Insurance Company.

4. Provide the information required by columns (5) and (6) on an aggregate basis for each director (or nominee) and his Immediate Family Members.

(7) Unless disclosed in response to paragraph (b)(6) of this Item, describe any direct or indirect interest, the value of which exceeds $120,000, of each director or nominee for election as director who is not or would not be an "interested person" of the Fund within the meaning of section 2(a)(19) of the Investment Company Act of 1940, or Immediate Family Member of the director or nominee, during the past five years, in:

(i) An investment adviser, principal underwriter, or Sponsoring Insurance Company of the Fund; or

(ii) A person (other than a registered investment company) directly or indirectly controlling, controlled by, or under common control with an investment adviser, principal underwriter, or Sponsoring Insurance Company of the Fund.

Instructions to paragraph (b)(7). 1. A director, nominee, or Immediate Family Member has an interest in a company if he is a party to a contract, arrangement, or understanding with respect to any securities of, or interest in, the company.

2. The interest of the director (or nominee) and the interests of his Immediate Family Members should be aggregated in determining whether the value exceeds $120,000.

(8) Describe briefly any material interest, direct or indirect, of any director or nominee for election as director who is not or would not be an "interested person" of the Fund within the meaning of section 2(a)(19) of the Investment Company Act of 1940, or Immediate Family Member of the director or nominee, in any transaction, or series of similar transactions, since the beginning of the last two

completed fiscal years of the Fund, or in any currently proposed transaction, or series of similar transactions, in which the amount involved exceeds $120,000 and to which any of the following persons was or is to be a party:

    (i)   The Fund;

    (ii)   An Officer of the Fund;

    (iii)   An investment company, or a person that would be an investment company but for the exclusions provided by sections 3(c)(1) and 3(c)(7) of the Investment Company Act of 1940, having the same investment adviser, principal underwriter, or Sponsoring Insurance Company as the Fund or having an investment adviser, principal underwriter, or Sponsoring Insurance Company that directly or indirectly controls, is controlled by, or is under common control with an investment adviser, principal underwriter, or Sponsoring Insurance Company of the Fund;

    (iv)   An Officer of an investment company, or a person that would be an investment company but for the exclusions provided by sections 3(c)(1) and 3(c)(7) of the Investment Company Act of 1940, having the same investment adviser, principal underwriter, or Sponsoring Insurance Company as the Fund or having an investment adviser, principal underwriter, or Sponsoring Insurance Company that directly or indirectly controls, is controlled by, or is under common control with an investment adviser, principal underwriter, or Sponsoring Insurance Company of the Fund;

    (v)   An investment adviser, principal underwriter, or Sponsoring Insurance Company of the Fund;

    (vi)   An Officer of an investment adviser, principal underwriter, or Sponsoring Insurance Company of the Fund;

    (vii)   A person directly or indirectly controlling, controlled by, or under common control with an investment adviser, principal underwriter, or Sponsoring Insurance Company of the Fund; or

    (viii)   An Officer of a person directly or indirectly controlling, controlled by, or under common control with an investment adviser, principal underwriter, or Sponsoring Insurance Company of the Fund.

Instructions to paragraph (b)(8). 1. Include the name of each director, nominee, or Immediate Family Member whose interest in any transaction or series of similar transactions is described and the nature of the circumstances by reason of which the interest is required to be described.

2.   State the nature of the interest, the approximate dollar amount involved in the transaction, and, where practicable, the approximate dollar amount of the interest.

3.   In computing the amount involved in the transaction or series of similar transactions, include all periodic payments in the case of any lease or other agreement providing for periodic payments.

4.   Compute the amount of the interest of any director, nominee, or Immediate Family Member of the director or nominee without regard to the amount of profit or loss involved in the transaction(s).

5.   As to any transaction involving the purchase or sale of assets, state the cost of the assets to the purchaser and, if acquired by the seller within two years prior to the transaction, the cost to the seller. Describe the method used in determining the purchase or sale price and the name of the person making the determination.

6.   If the proxy statement relates to multiple portfolios of a series Fund with different fiscal years, then, in determining the date that is the beginning of the last two completed fiscal years of the Fund, use the earliest date of any series covered by the proxy statement.

7.   Disclose indirect, as well as direct, material interests in transactions. A person who has a position or relationship with, or interest in, a company that engages in a transaction with one of the persons listed in paragraphs (b)(8)(i) through (b)(8)(viii) of this Item may have an indirect interest in the transaction by reason of the position, relationship, or interest. The interest in the transaction, however, will not be deemed "material" within the meaning of paragraph (b)(8) of this Item where the interest of the director, nominee, or Immediate Family Member arises solely from the holding of an equity interest (including a limited partnership interest, but excluding a general partnership interest) or a creditor interest in a company that is a party to the transaction with

one of the persons specified in paragraphs (b)(8)(i) through (b)(8)(viii) of this Item, and the transaction is not material to the company.

8. The materiality of any interest is to be determined on the basis of the significance of the information to investors in light of all the circumstances of the particular case. The importance of the interest to the person having the interest, the relationship of the parties to the transaction with each other, and the amount involved in the transaction are among the factors to be considered in determining the significance of the information to investors.

9. No information need be given as to any transaction where the interest of the director, nominee, or Immediate Family Member arises solely from the ownership of securities of a person specified in paragraphs (b)(8)(i) through (b)(8)(viii) of this Item and the director, nominee, or Immediate Family Member receives no extra or special benefit not shared on a pro rata basis by all holders of the class of securities.

10. Transactions include loans, lines of credit, and other indebtedness. For indebtedness, indicate the largest aggregate amount of indebtedness outstanding at any time during the period, the nature of the indebtedness and the transaction in which it was incurred, the amount outstanding as of the latest practicable date, and the rate of interest paid or charged.

11. No information need be given as to any routine, retail transaction. For example, the Fund need not disclose that a director has a credit card, bank or brokerage account, residential mortgage, or insurance policy with a person specified in paragraphs (b)(8)(i) through (b)(8)(viii) of this Item unless the director is accorded special treatment.

(9) Describe briefly any direct or indirect relationship, in which the amount involved exceeds $120,000, of any director or nominee for election as director who is not or would not be an "interested person" of the Fund within the meaning of section 2(a)(19) of the Investment Company Act of 1940, or Immediate Family Member of the director or nominee, that exists, or has existed at any time since the beginning of the last two completed fiscal years of the Fund, or is currently proposed, with any of the persons specified in paragraphs (b)(8)(i) through (b)(8)(viii) of this Item. Relationships include:

(i) Payments for property or services to or from any person specified in paragraphs (b)(8)(i) through (b)(8)(viii) of this Item;

(ii) Provision of legal services to any person specified in paragraphs (b)(8)(i) through (b)(8)(viii) of this Item;

(iii) Provision of investment banking services to any person specified in paragraphs (b)(8)(i) through (b)(8)(viii) of this Item, other than as a participating underwriter in a syndicate; and

(iv) Any consulting or other relationship that is substantially similar in nature and scope to the relationships listed in paragraphs (b)(9)(i) through (b)(9)(iii) of this Item.

Instructions to paragraph (b)(9). 1. Include the name of each director, nominee, or Immediate Family Member whose relationship is described and the nature of the circumstances by reason of which the relationship is required to be described.

2. State the nature of the relationship and the amount of business conducted between the director, nominee, or Immediate Family Member and the person specified in paragraphs (b)(8)(i) through (b)(8)(viii) of this Item as a result of the relationship since the beginning of the last two completed fiscal years of the Fund or proposed to be done during the Fund's current fiscal year.

3. In computing the amount involved in a relationship, include all periodic payments in the case of any agreement providing for periodic payments.

4. If the proxy statement relates to multiple portfolios of a series Fund with different fiscal years, then, in determining the date that is the beginning of the last two completed fiscal years of the Fund, use the earliest date of any series covered by the proxy statement.

5. Disclose indirect, as well as direct, relationships. A person who has a position or relationship with, or interest in, a company that has a relationship with one of the persons listed in paragraphs (b)(8)(i) through (b)(8)(viii) of this Item may have an indirect relationship by reason of the position, relationship, or interest.

6. In determining whether the amount involved in a relationship exceeds $60,000, amounts involved in a relationship of the director (or nominee) should be aggregated with those of his Immediate Family Members.

7.   In the case of an indirect interest, identify the company with which a person specified in paragraphs (b)(8)(i) through (b)(8)(viii) of this Item has a relationship; the name of the director, nominee, or Immediate Family Member affiliated with the company and the nature of the affiliation; and the amount of business conducted between the company and the person specified in paragraphs (b)(8)(i) through (b)(8)(viii) of this Item since the beginning of the last two completed fiscal years of the Fund or proposed to be done during the Fund's current fiscal year.

8.   In calculating payments for property and services for purposes of paragraph (b)(9)(i) of this Item, the following may be excluded:

A.   Payments where the transaction involves the rendering of services as a common contract carrier, or public utility, at rates or charges fixed in conformity with law or governmental authority; or

B.   Payments that arise solely from the ownership of securities of a person specified in paragraphs (b)(8)(i) through (b)(8)(viii) of this Item and no extra or special benefit not shared on a pro rata basis by all holders of the class of securities is received.

9.   No information need be given as to any routine, retail relationship. For example, the Fund need not disclose that a director has a credit card, bank or brokerage account, residential mortgage, or insurance policy with a person specified in paragraphs (b)(8)(i) through (b)(8)(viii) of this Item unless the director is accorded special treatment.

(10)   If an Officer of an investment adviser, principal underwriter, or Sponsoring Insurance Company of the Fund, or an Officer of a person directly or indirectly controlling, controlled by, or under common control with an investment adviser, principal underwriter, or Sponsoring Insurance Company of the Fund, serves, or has served since the beginning of the last two completed fiscal years of the Fund, on the board of directors of a company where a director of the Fund or nominee for election as director who is not or would not be an "interested person" of the Fund within the meaning of section 2(a)(19) of the Investment Company Act of 1940, or Immediate Family Member of the director or nominee, is, or was since the beginning of the last two completed fiscal years of the Fund, an Officer, identify:

(i)   The company;

(ii)   The individual who serves or has served as a director of the company and the period of service as director;

(iii)   The investment adviser, principal underwriter, or Sponsoring Insurance Company or person controlling, controlled by, or under common control with the investment adviser, principal underwriter, or Sponsoring Insurance Company where the individual named in paragraph (b)(10)(ii) of this Item holds or held office and the office held; and

(iv)   The director of the Fund, nominee for election as director, or Immediate Family Member who is or was an Officer of the company; the office held; and the period of holding the office.

Instruction to paragraph (b)(10). If the proxy statement relates to multiple portfolios of a series Fund with different fiscal years, then, in determining the date that is the beginning of the last two completed fiscal years of the Fund, use the earliest date of any series covered by the proxy statement.

(11)   Provide in tabular form, to the extent practicable, the information required by Items 401(f) and (g), 404(a), and 405 of Regulation S–K.

Instruction to paragraph (b)(11). Information provided under paragraph (b)(8) of this Item 22 is deemed to satisfy the requirements of Item 404(a) of Regulation S–K for information about directors, nominees for election as directors, and Immediate Family Members of directors and nominees, and need not be provided under this paragraph (b)(11).

(12)   Describe briefly any material pending legal proceedings, other than ordinary routine litigation incidental to the Fund's business, to which any director or nominee for director or affiliated person of such director or nominee is a party adverse to the Fund or any of its affiliated persons or has a material interest adverse to the Fund or any of its affiliated persons. Include the name of the court where the case is pending, the date instituted, the principal parties, a description of the factual basis alleged to underlie the proceeding, and the relief sought.

(13) In the case of a Fund that is an investment company registered under the Investment Company Act of 1940, for all directors, and for each of the three highest-paid Officers that have aggregate compensation from the Fund for the most recently completed fiscal year in excess of $60,000 ("Compensated Persons"):

    (i)   Furnish the information required by the following table for the last fiscal year:

Compensation Table

(1)	(2)	(3)	(4)	(5)
Name of Person, Position	Aggregate Compensation From Fund	Pension or Retirement Benefits Accrued as Part of Fund Expenses	Estimated Annual Benefits Upon Retirement	Total Compensation From Fund and Complex Paid to Directors

Instructions to paragraph (b)(13)(i). 1. For column (1), indicate, if necessary, the capacity in which the remuneration is received. For Compensated Persons that are directors of the Fund, compensation is amounts received for service as a director.

2. If the Fund has not completed its first full year since its organization, furnish the information for the current fiscal year, estimating future payments that would be made pursuant to an existing agreement or understanding. Disclose in a footnote to the Compensation Table the period for which the information is furnished.

3. Include in column (2) amounts deferred at the election of the Compensated Person, whether pursuant to a plan established under Section 401(k) of the Internal Revenue Code or otherwise, for the fiscal year in which earned. Disclose in a footnote to the Compensation Table the total amount of deferred compensation (including interest) payable to or accrued for any Compensated Person.

4. Include in columns (3) and (4) all pension or retirement benefits proposed to be paid under any existing plan in the event of retirement at normal retirement date, directly or indirectly, by the Fund or any of its Subsidiaries, or by other companies in the Fund Complex. Omit column (4) where retirement benefits are not determinable.

5. For any defined benefit or actuarial plan under which benefits are determined primarily by final compensation (or average final compensation) and years of service, provide the information required in column (4) in a separate table showing estimated annual benefits payable upon retirement (including amounts attributable to any defined benefit supplementary or excess pension award plans) in specified compensation and years of service classifications. Also provide the estimated credited years of service for each Compensated Person.

6. Include in column (5) only aggregate compensation paid to a director for service on the board and other boards of investment companies in a Fund Complex specifying the number of such other investment companies.

    (ii)   Describe briefly the material provisions of any pension, retirement, or other plan or any arrangement other than fee arrangements disclosed in paragraph (b)(13)(i) of this Item pursuant to which Compensated Persons are or may be compensated for any services provided, including amounts paid, if any, to the Compensated Person under any such arrangements during the most recently completed fiscal year. Specifically include the criteria used to determine amounts payable under any plan, the length of service or vesting period required by the plan, the retirement age or other event that gives rise to payments under the plan, and whether the payment of benefits is secured or funded by the Fund.

(14) State whether or not the Fund has a separately designated audit committee established in accordance with section 3(a)(58)(A) of the Act. If the entire board of directors is acting as the Fund's audit committee as specified in section 3(a)(58)(B) of the Act, so state. If applicable, provide the disclosure required by Rule 10A–3(d) regarding an exemption from the listing standards for audit committees. Identify the other standing committees of the Fund's board of directors, and provide the following information about each committee, including any separately designated audit committee and any nominating committee:

    (i)   A concise statement of the functions of the committee;

(ii)   The members of the committee and, in the case of a nominating committee, whether or not the members of the committee are "interested persons" of the Fund as defined in section 2(a)(19) of the Investment Company Act of 1940; and

(iii)   The number of committee meetings held during the last fiscal year.

Instruction to paragraph (b)(14). For purposes of Item 22(b)(14), the term "nominating committee" refers not only to nominating committees and committees performing similar functions, but also to groups of directors fulfilling the role of a nominating committees, including the entire board of directors.

(15)(i)   Provide the information (and in the format) required by Items 407(b)(1), (b)(2) and (f) of Regulation S–K; and

(ii)   Provide the following regarding the requirements for the director nomination process:

(A)   The information (and in the format) required by Items 407(c)(1) and (c)(2) of Regulation S–K; and

(B)   If the Fund is a listed issuer (as defined in Rule 10A–3) whose securities are listed on a national securities exchange registered pursuant to section 6(a) of the Act or in an automated inter-dealer quotation system of a national securities association registered pursuant to section 15A of the Act that has independence requirements for nominating committee members, identify each director that is a member of the nominating committee that is not independent under the independence standards described in this paragraph. In determining whether the nominating committee members are independent, use the Fund's definition of independence that it uses for determining if the members of the nominating committee are independent in compliance with the independence standards applicable for the members of the nominating committee in the listing standards applicable to the Fund. If the Fund does not have independence standards for the nominating committee, use the independence standards for the nominating committee in the listing standards applicable to the Fund.

Instruction to paragraph (b)(15)(ii)(B).

If the national securities exchange or inter-dealer quotation system on which the Fund's securities are listed has exemptions to the independence requirements for nominating committee members upon which the Fund relied, disclose the exemption relied upon and explain the basis for the Fund's conclusion that such exemption is applicable.

(16)   In the case of a Fund that is a closed-end investment company:

(i)   Provide the information (and in the format) required by Item 407(d)(1), (d)(2) and (d)(3) of Regulation S–K; and

(ii)   Identify each director that is a member of the Fund's audit committee that is not independent under the independence standards described in this paragraph. If the Fund does not have a separately designated audit committee, or committee performing similar functions, the Fund must provide the disclosure with respect to all members of its board of directors.

(A)   If the Fund is a listed issuer (as defined in Rule 10A–3) whose securities are listed on a national securities exchange registered pursuant to section 6(a) of the Act or in an automated inter-dealer quotation system of a national securities association registered pursuant to section 15A of the Act that has independence requirements for audit committee members, in determining whether the audit committee members are independent, use the Fund's definition of independence that it uses for determining if the members of the audit committee are independent in compliance with the independence standards applicable for the members of the audit committee in the listing standards applicable to the Fund. If the Fund does not have independence standards for the audit committee, use the independence standards for the audit committee in the listing standards applicable to the Fund.

(B)   If the Fund is not a listed issuer whose securities are listed on a national securities exchange registered pursuant to section 6(a) of the Act or in an automated inter-dealer quotation system of a national securities association registered pursuant to section 15A of the Act, in determining whether the audit committee members are independent, use a definition of independence of a national securities exchange registered pursuant to section 6(a) of the Act or an automated inter-dealer quotation system of a national securities association registered pursuant to section 15A of the Act which has requirements that a majority of the board of directors be independent and that has been approved by the Commission, and state which definition is used. Whatever such definition the Fund chooses, it must use the same definition with respect to all directors and nominees for director. If the national securities exchange or national securities association whose standards are used has independence standards for the members of the audit committee, use those specific standards.

Instruction to paragraph (b)(16)(ii).

If the national securities exchange or inter-dealer quotation system on which the Fund's securities are listed has exemptions to the independence requirements for nominating committee members upon which the Fund relied, disclose the exemption relied upon and explain the basis for the Fund's conclusion that such exemption is applicable. The same disclosure should be provided if the Fund is not a listed issuer and the national securities exchange or inter-dealer quotation system selected by the Fund has exemptions that are applicable to the Fund.

(17) In the case of a Fund that is an investment company registered under the Investment Company Act of 1940, if a director has resigned or declined to stand for re-election to the board of directors since the date of the last annual meeting of security holders because of a disagreement with the registrant on any matter relating to the registrant's operations, policies or practices, and if the director has furnished the registrant with a letter describing such disagreement and requesting that the matter be disclosed, the registrant shall state the date of resignation or declination to stand for re-election and summarize the director's description of the disagreement. If the registrant believes that the description provided by the director is incorrect or incomplete, it may include a brief statement presenting its view of the disagreement.

(18) If a shareholder nominee or nominees are submitted to the Fund for inclusion in the Fund's proxy materials pursuant to Rule 14a–11 and the Fund is not permitted to exclude the nominee or nominees pursuant to the provisions of Rule 14a–11, the Fund must include in its proxy statement the disclosure required from the nominating shareholder or nominating shareholder group under Item 5 of Schedule 14N (§ 240.14n–101) with regard to the nominee or nominees and the nominating shareholder or nominating shareholder group.

(19) If a Fund is required to include a shareholder nominee or nominees submitted to the Fund for inclusion in the Fund's proxy materials pursuant to a procedure set forth under applicable state or foreign law or the Fund's governing documents providing for the inclusion of shareholder director nominees in the Fund's proxy materials, the Fund must include in its proxy statement the disclosure required from the nominating shareholder or nominating shareholder group under Item 6 of Schedule 14N § 240.14n–101 with regard to the nominee or nominees and the nominating shareholder or nominating shareholder group.

(20) In the case of a Fund that is an investment company registered under the Investment Company Act of 1940 (15 U.S.C. 80a) that is required to develop and implement a policy regarding the recovery of erroneously awarded compensation pursuant to § 240.10D–1(b)(1), if at any time during the last completed fiscal year the Fund was required to prepare an accounting restatement that required recovery of erroneously awarded compensation pursuant to the Fund's compensation recovery policy required by the listing standards adopted pursuant to 240.10D–1, or there was an outstanding balance as of the end of the last completed fiscal year of erroneously awarded compensation to be recovered from the application of the policy to a prior restatement, the Fund must provide the information required by Item 18 of Form N–CSR, as applicable.

(c) *Approval of investment advisory contract.* If action is to be taken with respect to an investment advisory contract, include the following information in the proxy statement.

Instruction. Furnish information with respect to a prospective investment adviser to the extent applicable (including the name and address of the prospective investment adviser).

(1) With respect to the existing investment advisory contract:

(i)   State the date of the contract and the date on which it was last submitted to a vote of security holders of the Fund, including the purpose of such submission;

(ii)   Briefly describe the terms of the contract, including the rate of compensation of the investment adviser;

(iii)   State the aggregate amount of the investment adviser's fee and the amount and purpose of any other material payments by the Fund to the investment adviser, or any affiliated person of the investment adviser, during the last fiscal year of the Fund;

(iv)   If any person is acting as an investment adviser of the Fund other than pursuant to a written contract that has been approved by the security holders of the company, identify the person and describe the nature of the services and arrangements;

(v)   Describe any action taken with respect to the investment advisory contract since the beginning of the Fund's last fiscal year by the board of directors of the Fund (unless described in response to paragraph (c)(1)(vi)) of this Item 22; and

(vi)   If an investment advisory contract was terminated or not renewed for any reason, state the date of such termination or non-renewal, identify the parties involved, and describe the circumstances of such termination or non-renewal.

(2)   State the name, address and principal occupation of the principal executive officer and each director or general partner of the investment adviser.

Instruction. If the investment adviser is a partnership with more than ten general partners, name:

(i)   The general partners with the five largest economic interests in the partnership, and, if different, those general partners comprising the management or executive committee of the partnership or exercising similar authority;

(ii)   The general partners with significant management responsibilities relating to the fund.

(3)   State the names and addresses of all Parents of the investment adviser and show the basis of control of the investment adviser and each Parent by its immediate Parent.

Instructions. 1. If any person named is a corporation, include the percentage of its voting securities owned by its immediate Parent.

2.   If any person named is a partnership, name the general partners having the three largest partnership interests (computed by whatever method is appropriate in the particular case).

(4)   If the investment adviser is a corporation and if, to the knowledge of the persons making the solicitation or the persons on whose behalf the solicitation is made, any person not named in answer to paragraph (c)(3) of this Item 22 owns, of record or beneficially, ten percent or more of the outstanding voting securities of the investment adviser, indicate that fact and state the name and address of each such person.

(5)   Name each officer or director of the Fund who is an officer, employee, director, general partner or shareholder of the investment adviser. As to any officer or director who is not a director or general partner of the investment adviser and who owns securities or has any other material direct or indirect interest in the investment adviser or any other person controlling, controlled by or under common control with the investment adviser, describe the nature of such interest.

(6)   Describe briefly and state the approximate amount of, where practicable, any material interest, direct or indirect, of any director of the Fund in any material transactions since the beginning of the most recently completed fiscal year, or in any material proposed transactions, to which the investment adviser of the Fund, any Parent or Subsidiary of the investment adviser (other than another Fund), or any Subsidiary of the Parent of such entities was or is to be a party.

Instructions. 1. Include the name of each person whose interest in any transaction is described and the nature of the relationship by reason of which such interest is required to be described. Where it is not practicable to state the approximate amount of the interest, indicate the approximate amount involved in the transaction.

2.   As to any transaction involving the purchase or sale of assets by or to the investment adviser, state the cost of the assets to the purchaser and the cost thereof to the seller if acquired by the seller within two years prior to the transaction.

3.   If the interest of any person arises from the position of the person as a partner in a partnership, the proportionate interest of such person in transactions to which the partnership is a party need not be set forth, but state the amount involved in the transaction with the partnership.

4.   No information need be given in response to this paragraph (c)(6) of Item 22 with respect to any transaction that is not related to the business or operations of the Fund and to which neither the Fund nor any of its Parents or Subsidiaries is a party.

(7)   Disclose any financial condition of the investment adviser that is reasonably likely to impair the financial ability of the adviser to fulfil its commitment to the fund under the proposed investment advisory contract.

(8)   Describe the nature of the action to be taken on the investment advisory contract and the reasons therefor, the terms of the contract to be acted upon, and, if the action is an amendment to, or a replacement of, an investment advisory contract, the material differences between the current and proposed contract.

(9)   If a change in the investment advisory fee is sought, state:

(i)   The aggregate amount of the investment adviser's fee during the last year;

(ii)   The amount that the adviser would have received had the proposed fee been in effect; and

(iii)   The difference between the aggregate amounts stated in response to paragraphs (i) and (ii) of this paragraph (c)(9) as a percentage of the amount stated in response to paragraph (i) of this paragraph (c)(9).

(10) If the investment adviser acts as such with respect to any other Fund having a similar investment objective, identify and state the size of such other Fund and the rate of the investment adviser's compensation. Also indicate for any Fund identified whether the investment adviser has waived, reduced, or otherwise agreed to reduce its compensation under any applicable contract.

Instruction. Furnish the information in response to this paragraph (c)(10) of Item 22 in tabular form.

(11) Discuss in reasonable detail the material factors and the conclusions with respect thereto that form the basis for the recommendation of the board of directors that the shareholders approve an investment advisory contract. Include the following in the discussion:

(i)   Factors relating to both the board's selection of the investment adviser and approval of the advisory fee and any other amounts to be paid by the Fund under the contract. This would include, but not be limited to, a discussion of the nature, extent, and quality of the services to be provided by the investment adviser; the investment performance of the Fund and the investment adviser; the costs of the services to be provided and profits to be realized by the investment adviser and its affiliates from the relationship with the Fund; the extent to which economies of scale would be realized as the Fund grows; and whether fee levels reflect these economies of scale for the benefit of Fund investors. Also indicate in the discussion whether the board relied upon comparisons of the services to be rendered and the amounts to be paid under the contract with those under other investment advisory contracts, such as contracts of the same and other investment advisers with other registered investment companies or other types of clients (e.g., pension funds and other institutional investors). If the board relied upon such comparisons, describe the comparisons that were relied on and how they assisted the board in determining to recommend that the shareholders approve the advisory contract; and

(ii)   If applicable, any benefits derived or to be derived by the investment adviser from the relationship with the Fund such as soft dollar arrangements by which brokers provide research to the Fund or its investment adviser in return for allocating Fund brokerage.

Instructions. 1. Conclusory statements or a list of factors will not be considered sufficient disclosure. Relate the factors to the specific circumstances of the Fund and the investment advisory contract for which approval is sought and state how the board evaluated each factor. For example, it is not sufficient to state that the board considered the amount of the investment advisory fee without stating what the board concluded about the amount of the fee and how that affected its determination to recommend approval of the contract.

2. If any factor enumerated in paragraph (c)(11)(i) of this Item 22 is not relevant to the board's evaluation of the investment advisory contract for which approval is sought, note this and explain the reasons why that factor is not relevant.

(12) Describe any arrangement or understanding made in connection with the proposed investment advisory contract with respect to the composition of the board of directors of the Fund or the investment adviser or with respect to the selection or appointment of any person to any office with either such company.

(13) For the most recently completed fiscal year, state:

(i) The aggregate amount of commissions paid to any Affiliated Broker; and

(ii) The percentage of the Fund's aggregate brokerage commissions paid to any such Affiliated Broker.

Instruction. Identify each Affiliated Broker and the relationships that cause the broker to be an Affiliated Broker.

(14) Disclose the amount of any fees paid by the Fund to the investment adviser, its affiliated persons or any affiliated person of such person during the most recent fiscal year for services provided to the Fund (other than under the investment advisory contract or for brokerage commissions). State whether these services will continue to be provided after the investment advisory contract is approved.

(d) *Approval of distribution plan.* If action is to be taken with respect to a Distribution Plan, include the following information in the proxy statement.

Instruction. Furnish information on a prospective basis to the extent applicable.

(1) Describe the nature of the action to be taken on the Distribution Plan and the reason therefor, the terms of the Distribution Plan to be acted upon, and, if the action is an amendment to, or a replacement of, a Distribution Plan, the material differences between the current and proposed Distribution Plan.

(2) If the Fund has a Distribution Plan in effect:

(i) Provide the date that the Distribution Plan was adopted and the date of the last amendment, if any;

(ii) Disclose the persons to whom payments may be made under the Distribution Plan, the rate of the distribution fee and the purposes for which such fee may be used;

(iii) Disclose the amount of distribution fees paid by the Fund pursuant to the plan during its most recent fiscal year, both in the aggregate and as a percentage of the Fund's average net assets during the period;

(iv) Disclose the name of, and the amount of any payments made under the Distribution Plan by the Fund during its most recent fiscal year to, any person who is an affiliated person of the Fund, its investment adviser, principal underwriter, or Administrator, an affiliated person of such person, or a person that during the most recent fiscal year received 10% or more of the aggregate amount paid under the Distribution Plan by the Fund;

(v) Describe any action taken with respect to the Distribution Plan since the beginning of the Fund's most recent fiscal year by the board of directors of the Fund; and

(vi) If a Distribution Plan was or is to be terminated or not renewed for any reason, state the date or prospective date of such termination or non-renewal, identify the parties involved, and describe the circumstances of such termination or non-renewal.

(3) Describe briefly and state the approximate amount of, where practicable, any material interest, direct or indirect, of any director or nominee for election as a director of the Fund in any material transactions since the beginning of the most recently completed fiscal year, or in any material

proposed transactions, to which any person identified in response to Item 22(d)(2)(iv) was or is to be a party.

Instructions. 1. Include the name of each person whose interest in any transaction is described and the nature of the relationship by reason of which such interest is required to be described. Where it is not practicable to state the approximate amount of the interest, indicate the approximate amount involved in the transaction.

2.   As to any transaction involving the purchase or sale of assets, state the cost of the assets to the purchaser and the cost thereof to the seller if acquired by the seller within two years prior to the transaction.

3.   If the interest of any person arises from the position of the person as a partner in a partnership, the proportionate interest of such person in transactions to which the partnership is a party need not be set forth but state the amount involved in the transaction with the partnership.

4.   No information need be given in response to this paragraph (d)(3) of Item 22 with respect to any transaction that is not related to the business or operations of the Fund and to which neither the Fund nor any of its Parents or Subsidiaries is a party.

(4)   Discuss in reasonable detail the material factors and the conclusions with respect thereto which form the basis for the conclusion of the board of directors that there is a reasonable likelihood that the proposed Distribution Plan (or amendment thereto) will benefit the Fund and its shareholders.

Instruction. Conclusory statements or a list of factors will not be considered sufficient disclosure.

Item 23. Delivery of Documents to Security Holders Sharing an Address

If one annual report to security holders, proxy statement, or Notice of Internet Availability of Proxy Materials is being delivered to two or more security holders who share an address in accordance with Rule 14a–3(e)(1), furnish the following information:

(a)   State that only one annual report to security holders, proxy statement, or Notice of Internet Availability of Proxy Materials, as applicable, is being delivered to multiple security holders sharing an address unless the registrant has received contrary instructions from one or more of the security holders;

(b)   Undertake to deliver promptly upon written or oral request a separate copy of the annual report to security holders, proxy statement, or Notice of Internet Availability of Proxy Materials, as applicable, to a security holder at a shared address to which a single copy of the documents was delivered and provide instructions as to how a security holder can notify the registrant that the security holder wishes to receive a separate copy of an annual report to security holders, proxy statement, or Notice of Internet Availability of Proxy Materials, as applicable;

(c)   Provide the phone number and mailing address to which a security holder can direct a notification to the registrant that the security holder wishes to receive a separate annual report to security holders, proxy statement, or Notice of Internet Availability of Proxy Materials, as applicable, in the future; and

(d)   Provide instructions how security holders sharing an address can request delivery of a single copy of annual reports to security holders, proxy statements, or Notices of Internet Availability of Proxy Materials if they are receiving multiple copies of annual reports to security holders, proxy statements, or Notices of Internet Availability of Proxy Materials.

Item 24. Shareholder Approval of Executive Compensation

Registrants required to provide any of the separate shareholder votes pursuant to Rule 14a–21 of this chapter shall disclose that they are providing each such vote as required pursuant to section 14A of the Securities Exchange Act of 1934, briefly explain the general effect of each vote, such as whether each such vote is non-binding, and, when applicable, disclose the current frequency of shareholder advisory votes on executive compensation required by Rule 14a–21(a) and when the next such shareholder advisory vote will occur.

F. SCHEDULE 14C
17 C.F.R. § 240.14c–101

INFORMATION REQUIRED IN INFORMATION STATEMENT

SCHEDULE 14C INFORMATION

Information Statement Pursuant to Section 14(c) of the Securities
Exchange Act of 1934 (Amendment No.   )

Check the appropriate box:

[   ]   Preliminary Information Statement

[   ]   Confidential, for Use of the Commission Only (as permitted by Rule 14c–5(d)(2))

[   ]   Definitive Information Statement

_____

(Name of Registrant As Specified In Its Charter)

_____

Payment of Filing Fee (Check the appropriate box):

[   ]   No fee required.

[   ]   Fee computed on table below per Exchange Act Rules 14c–5(g) and 0–11.

    1)   Title of each class of securities to which transaction applies:

_____

    2)   Aggregate number of securities to which transaction applies:

_____

    3)   Per unit price or other underlying value of transaction computed pursuant to Exchange Act Rule 0–11 (Set forth the amount on which the filing fee is calculated and state how it was determined):

_____

    4)   Proposed maximum aggregate value of transaction:

_____

    5)   Total fee paid:

_____

[   ]   Fee paid previously with preliminary materials.

[   ]   Check box if any part of the fee is offset as provided by Exchange Act Rule 0–11(a)(2) and identify the filing for which the offsetting fee was paid previously. Identify the previous filing by registration statement number, or the Form or Schedule and the date of its filing.

    1)   Amount Previously Paid:

_____

    2)   Form, Schedule or Registration Statement No.:

_____

    3)   Filing Party:

_____

_____

Note. Where any item, other than Item 4, calls for information with respect to any matter to be acted upon at the meeting or, if no meeting is being held, by written authorization or consent, such item need be answered only with respect to proposals to be made by the registrant. Registrants and acquirees that meet the definition of "smaller reporting company" under Rule 12b–2 of the Exchange Act shall refer to the disclosure items in Regulation S–K with specific attention to the scaled disclosure requirements for smaller reporting companies, if any. A smaller reporting company may provide the information in Article 8 of Regulation S–X in lieu of any financial statements required by Item 1 of Schedule 14C.

Item 1.   Information Required by Items of Schedule 14A

Furnish the information called for by all of the items of Schedule 14A of Regulation 14A (other than Items 1(c). 2, 4 and 5 thereof) which would be applicable to any matter to be acted upon at the meeting if proxies were to be solicited in connection with the meeting. Notes A, C, D, and E to Schedule 14A are also applicable to Schedule 14C.

Item 2.   Statement That Proxies Are Not Solicited

The following statement shall be set forth on the first page of the information statement in bold-face type:

We Are Not Asking You for a Proxy and You Are Requested Not to Send Us a Proxy

Item 3.   Interest of Certain Persons in or Opposition to Matters to Be Acted Upon

(a)   Describe briefly any substantial interest, direct or indirect, by security holdings or otherwise, of each of the following persons in any matter to be acted upon, other than elections to office:

(1)   each person who has been a director or officer of the registrant at any time since the beginning of the last fiscal year;

(2)   each nominee for election as a director of the registrant;

(3)   each associate of any of the foregoing persons.

(b)   Give the name of any director of the registrant who has informed the registrant in writing that he intends to oppose any action to be taken by the registrant at the meeting and indicate the action which he intends to oppose.

(c)   Furnish the information required by Item 402(t) of Regulation S–K.

Item 4.   Proposals by Security Holders

If any security holder entitled to vote at the meeting or by written authorization or consent has submitted to the registrant a reasonable time before the information statement is to be transmitted to security holders a proposal, other than elections to office, which is accompanied by notice of his intention to present the proposal for action at the meeting the registrant shall, if a meeting is held, make a statement to that effect, identify the proposal and indicate the disposition proposed to be made of the proposal by the registrant at the meeting.

Instructions. 1. This item need not be answered as to any proposal submitted with respect to an annual meeting if such proposal is submitted less than 60 days in advance of a day corresponding to the date of sending a proxy statement or information statement in connection with the last annual meeting of security holders.

2.   If the registrant intends to rule a proposal out of order, the Commission shall be so advised 20 calendar days prior to the date the definitive copies of the information statement are filed with the Commission, together with a statement of the reasons why the proposal is not deemed to be a proper subject for action by security holders.

Item 5.   Delivery of Documents to Security Holders Sharing an Address

If one annual report to security holders, information statement, or Notice of Internet Availability of Proxy Materials is being delivered to two or more security holders who share an address, furnish the following information in accordance with Rule 14a–3(e)(1):

(a)   State that only one annual report to security holders, information statement, or Notice of Internet Availability of Proxy Materials, as applicable, is being delivered to multiple security holders sharing an address unless the registrant has received contrary instructions from one or more of the security holders;

(b)   Undertake to deliver promptly upon written or oral request a separate copy of the annual report to security holders, information statement, or Notice of Internet Availability of Proxy Materials, as applicable, to a security holder at a shared address to which a single copy of the documents was delivered and provide instructions as to how a security holder can notify the registrant that the security holder wishes to receive a separate copy of an annual report to security holders, information statement, or Notice of Internet Availability of Proxy Materials, as applicable;

(c)   Provide the phone number and mailing address to which a security holder can direct a notification to the registrant that the security holder wishes to receive a separate annual report to security holders, information statement, or Notice of Availability of Proxy Materials, as applicable, in the future; and

(d)   Provide instructions how security holders sharing an address can request delivery of a single copy of annual reports to security holders, information statements, or Notices of Internet Availability of Proxy Materials if they are receiving multiple copies of annual reports to security holders, information statements, or Notices of Internet Availability of Proxy Materials.

G. SCHEDULE 14D-9
17 C.F.R. § 240.14d-101

SECURITIES AND EXCHANGE COMMISSION

Washington, D.C. 20549

Solicitation/Recommendation Statement Under Section 14(d)(4)
of the Securities Exchange Act of 1934

(Amendment No. _____)

_____

(Name of Subject Company)

_____

(Name of Person(s) Filing Statement)

_____

(Title of Class of Securities)

_____

(CUSIP Number of Class of Securities)

_____

(Name, address and telephone numbers of person authorized to receive notices
and communications on behalf of the persons filing statement)

[   ] Check box if the filing relates solely to preliminary communications made before the commencement of a tender offer.

GENERAL INSTRUCTIONS

A.   File eight copies of the statement, including all exhibits, with the Commission if paper filing is permitted.

B.   If the filing contains only preliminary communications made before the commencement of a tender offer, no signature is required. The filer need not respond to the items in the schedule. Any pre-commencement communications that are filed under cover of this schedule need not be incorporated by reference into the schedule.

C.   If an item is inapplicable or the answer is in the negative, so state. The statement published, sent or given to security holders may omit negative and not applicable responses. If the schedule includes any information that is not published, sent or given to security holders, provide that information or specifically incorporate it by reference under the appropriate item number and heading in the schedule. Do not recite the text of disclosure requirements in the schedule or any document published, sent or given to security holders. Indicate clearly the coverage of the requirements without referring to the text of the items.

D.   Information contained in exhibits to the statement may be incorporated by reference in answer or partial answer to any unless it would render the answer misleading, incomplete, unclear or confusing. A copy of any information that is incorporated by reference or a copy of the pertinent pages of a document containing the information must be submitted with this statement as an exhibit, unless it was previously filed with the Commission electronically on EDGAR. If an exhibit contains information responding to more than one item in the schedule, all information in that exhibit may be incorporated by reference once in response to the several items in the schedule for which it provides and answer. Information incorporated by reference is deemed filed with the Commission for all purposes of the Act.

E.   Amendments disclosing a material change in the information set forth in this statement may omit any information previously disclosed in this statement.

SELECTED SCHEDULES UNDER THE
SECURITIES EXCHANGE ACT OF 1934

Item 1.   Subject Company Information

Furnish the information required by Item 1002(a) and (b) of Regulation M–A.

Item 2.   Identity and Background of Filing Person

Furnish the information required by Item 1003(a) and (d) of Regulation M–A.

Item 3.   Past Contacts, Transactions, Negotiations and Agreements

Furnish the information required by Item 1005(d) of Regulation M–A.

Item 4.   The Solicitation or Recommendation

Furnish the information required by Item 1012(a) through (c) of Regulation M–A.

Item 5.   Person/Assets, Retained, Employed, Compensated or Used

Furnish the information required by Item 1009(a) of Regulation M–A.

Item 6.   Interest in Securities of the Subject Company

Furnish the information required by Item 1008(b) of Regulation M–A.

Item 7.   Purposes of the Transaction and Plans or Proposals

Furnish the information required by Item 1006(d) of Regulation M–A.

Item 8.   Additional Information

Furnish the information required by Item 1011(b) and (c) of Regulation M–A.

Item 9.   Exhibits

File as an exhibit to the Schedule all documents specified by Item 1016(a), (e) and (g) of Regulation M–A.

SIGNATURE

After due inquiry and to the best of my knowledge and belief, I certify that the information set forth in this statement is true, complete and correct.

_____
(Signature)

_____
(Name and Title)

_____
(Date)

Instruction to Signature: The statement must be signed by the filing person or that person's authorized representative. If the statement is signed on behalf of a person by an authorized representative (other than an executive officer of a corporation or general partner of a partnership), evidence of the representative's authority to sign on behalf of the person must be filed with the statement. The name and title of each person who signs the statement must be typed or printed beneath the signature. See Rule 14d–1(h) of the Securities Exchange Act of 1934 with respect to signature requirements.

H. SCHEDULE 15G
17 C.F.R. § 240.15g–100

PENNY STOCK DISCLOSURE STATEMENT
SCHEDULE 15G

**Information to be included in the document distributed
pursuant to Rule 15g–2**

SECURITIES AND EXCHANGE COMMISSION
Washington, D.C. 20549
SCHEDULE 15G

Under the Securities Exchange Act of 1934

Instructions to Schedule 15G

A.   Schedule 15G (Schedule) may be provided to customers in its entirety either on paper or electronically. It may also be provided to customers electronically through a link to the SEC's Web site.

    1.   If the Schedule is sent in paper form, the format and typeface of the Schedule must be reproduced exactly as presented. For example, words that are capitalized must remain capitalized, and words that are underlined or bold must remain underlined or bold. The typeface must be clear and easy to read. The Schedule may be reproduced either by photocopy or by printing.

    2.   If the Schedule is sent electronically, the e-mail containing the Schedule must have as a subject line "Important Information on Penny Stocks." The Schedule reproduced in the text of the e-mail must be clear, easy-to-read type presented in a manner reasonably calculated to draw the customer's attention to the language in the document, especially words that are capitalized, underlined or in bold.

    3.   If the Schedule is sent electronically using a hyperlink to the SEC Web site, the e-mail containing the hyperlink must have as a subject line: "Important Information on Penny Stocks." Immediately before the hyperlink, the text of the e-mail must reproduce the following statement in clear, easy-to-read type presented in a manner reasonably calculated to draw the customer's attention to the words: "We are required by the U.S. Securities and Exchange Commission to give you the following disclosure statement: http://www.sec.gov/investor/schedule15g.htm. It explains some of the risks of investing in penny stocks. Please read it carefully before you agree to purchase or sell a penny stock."

B.   Regardless of how the Schedule is provided to the customer, the communication must also provide the name, address, telephone number and e-mail address of the broker. E-mail messages may also include any privacy or confidentiality information that the broker routinely includes in e-mail messages sent to customers. No other information may be included in these communications, other than instructions on how to provide a signed and dated acknowledgement of receipt of the Schedule.

C.   The document entitled "Important Information on Penny Stocks" must be distributed as Schedule 15G and must be no more than two pages in length if provided in paper form.

D.   The disclosures made through the Schedule are in addition to any other disclosures that are required under the Federal securities laws.

E.   Recipients of the document must not be charged any fee for the document.

F.   The content of the Schedule is as follows:

Important Information on Penny Stocks

    •   The U.S. Securities and Exchange Commission (SEC) requires your broker to give this statement to you, and to obtain your signature to show that you have received it, before your first trade in a penny stock. This statement contains important information—and you should read it carefully before you sign it, and before you decide to purchase or sell a penny stock.

- In addition to obtaining your signature, the SEC requires your broker to wait at least two business days after sending you this statement before executing your first trade to give you time to carefully consider your trade.

Penny Stocks Can Be Very Risky

- Penny stocks are low-priced shares of small companies. Penny stocks may trade infrequently—which means that it may be difficult to sell penny stock shares once you have them. Because it may also be difficult to find quotations for penny stocks, they may be impossible to accurately price. Investors in penny stock should be prepared for the possibility that they may lose their whole investment.

- While penny stocks generally trade over-the-counter, they may also trade on U.S. securities exchanges, facilities of U.S. exchanges, or foreign exchanges. You should learn about the market in which the penny stock trades to determine how much demand there is for this stock and how difficult it will be to sell. Be especially careful if your broker is offering to sell you newly issued penny stock that has no established trading market.

- The securities you are considering have not been approved or disapproved by the SEC. Moreover, the SEC has not passed upon the fairness or the merits of this transaction nor upon the accuracy or adequacy of the information contained in any prospectus or any other information provided by an issuer or a broker or dealer.

Information You Should Get

- In addition to this statement, your broker is required to give you a statement of your financial situation and investment goals explaining why his or her firm has determined that penny stocks are a suitable investment for you. In addition, your broker is required to obtain your agreement to the proposed penny stock transaction.

- Before you buy penny stock, Federal law requires your salesperson to tell you the "offer" and the "bid" on the stock, and the "compensation" the salesperson and the firm receive for the trade. The firm also must send a confirmation of these prices to you after the trade. You will need this price information to determine what profit or loss, if any, you will have when you sell your stock.

- The offer price is the wholesale price at which the dealer is willing to sell stock to other dealers. The bid price is the wholesale price at which the dealer is willing to buy the stock from other dealers. In its trade with you, the dealer may add a retail charge to these wholesale prices as compensation (called a "markup" or "markdown").

- The difference between the bid and the offer price is the dealer's "spread." A spread that is large compared with the purchase price can make a resale of a stock very costly. To be profitable when you sell, the bid price of your stock must rise above the amount of this spread and the compensation charged by both your selling and purchasing dealers. Remember that if the dealer has no bid price, you may not be able to sell the stock after you buy it, and may lose your whole investment.

- After you buy penny stock, your brokerage firm must send you a monthly account statement that gives an estimate of the value of each penny stock in your account, if there is enough information to make an estimate. If the firm has not bought or sold any penny stocks for your account for six months, it can provide these statements every three months.

- Additional information about low-priced securities—including penny stocks—is available on the SEC's Web site at http://www.sec.gov/investor/pubs/microcapstock.htm. In addition, your broker will send you a copy of this information upon request. The SEC encourages you to learn all you can before making this investment.

Brokers' Duties and Customers' Rights and Remedies

- Remember that your salesperson is not an impartial advisor—he or she is being paid to sell you stock. Do not rely only on the salesperson, but seek outside advice before you buy any stock. You can get the disciplinary history of a salesperson or firm from NASD at 1-800-289-9999 or contact NASD via the Internet at http://www.nasd.com. You can also get additional information from your state securities official. The North American Securities Administrators Association, Inc. can give you contact

SCHEDULE 15G

information for your state. You can reach NASAA at (202) 737-0900 or via the Internet at http://www.nasaa.org.

- If you have problems with a salesperson, contact the firm's compliance officer. You can also contact the securities regulators listed above. Finally, if you are a victim of fraud, you may have rights and remedies under state and Federal law. In addition to the regulators listed above, you also may contact the SEC with complaints at (800)-SEC-0330 or via the Internet at help@sec.gov.

F. OTHER SELECTED REGULATIONS

REGULATION M

17 C.F.R. § 242.___

Anti-Manipulation Rules Concerning
Securities Offerings

PRELIMINARY NOTE: Any transaction or series of transactions, whether or not effected pursuant to the provisions of Regulation M, remain subject to the antifraud and antimanipulation provisions of the securities laws, including, without limitation, section 17(a) of the Securities Act of 1933 and sections 9, 10(b), and 15(c) of the Securities Exchange Act of 1934.

Rule 100.   Definitions

For purposes of this rule, the following definitions shall apply:

ADTV means the worldwide average daily trading volume during the two full calendar months immediately preceding, or any 60 consecutive calendar days ending within the 10 calendar days preceding, the filing of the registration statement; or, if there is no registration statement or if the distribution involves the sale of securities on a delayed basis pursuant to Rule 415 of this chapter, two full calendar months immediately preceding, or any consecutive 60 calendar days ending within the 10 calendar days preceding, the determination of the offering price.

Affiliated purchaser means:

(1)   A person acting, directly or indirectly, in concert with a distribution participant, issuer, or selling security holder in connection with the acquisition or distribution of any covered security; or

(2)   An affiliate, which may be a separately identifiable department or division of a distribution participant, issuer, or selling security holder, that, directly or indirectly, controls the purchases of any covered security by a distribution participant, issuer, or selling security holder, whose purchases are controlled by any such person, or whose purchases are under common control with any such person; or

(3)   An affiliate, which may be a separately identifiable department or division of a distribution participant, issuer, or selling security holder, that regularly purchases securities for its own account or for the account of others, or that recommends or exercises investment discretion with respect to the purchase or sale of securities; *Provided, however,* That this paragraph (3) shall not apply to such affiliate if the following conditions are satisfied:

(i)   The distribution participant, issuer, or selling security holder:

(A)   Maintains and enforces written policies and procedures reasonably designed to prevent the flow of information to or from the affiliate that might result in a violation of Rules 101, 102, and 104; and

(B)   Obtains an annual, independent assessment of the operation of such policies and procedures; and

(ii)   The affiliate has no officers (or persons performing similar functions) or employees (other than clerical, ministerial, or support personnel) in common with the distribution participant, issuer, or selling security holder that direct, effect, or recommend transactions in securities; and

(iii)   The affiliate does not, during the applicable restricted period, act as a market maker (other than as a specialist in compliance with the rules of a national securities exchange), or engage, as a broker or a dealer, in solicited transactions or proprietary trading, in covered securities.

Agent independent of the issuer means a trustee or other person who is independent of the issuer. The agent shall be deemed to be independent of the issuer only if:

(1)   The agent is not an affiliate of the issuer; and

(2)   Neither the issuer nor any affiliate of the issuer exercises any direct or indirect control or influence over the prices or amounts of the securities to be purchased, the timing of, or the manner in which, the securities are to be purchased, or the selection of a broker or dealer (other than the independent agent itself) through which purchases may be executed; *Provided, however,* That the issuer or its affiliate will not be deemed to have such control or influence solely because it revises not more than once in any three-month period the basis for determining the amount of its contributions to a plan or the basis for determining the frequency of its allocations to a plan, or any formula specified in a plan that determines the amount or timing of securities to be purchased by the agent.

Asset-backed security has the meaning contained in Item 1101 of Regulation S–K.

At-the-market offering means an offering of securities at other than a fixed price.

Business day refers to a 24 hour period determined with reference to the principal market for the securities to be distributed, and that includes a complete trading session for that market.

Completion of participation in a distribution. Securities acquired in the distribution for investment by any person participating in a distribution, or any affiliated purchaser of such person, shall be deemed to be distributed. A person shall be deemed to have completed its participation in a distribution as follows:

(1)   An issuer or selling security holder, when the distribution is completed;

(2)   An underwriter, when such person's participation has been distributed, including all other securities of the same class that are acquired in connection with the distribution, and any stabilization arrangements and trading restrictions in connection with the distribution have been terminated; *Provided, however,* That an underwriter's participation will not be deemed to have been completed if a syndicate overallotment option is exercised in an amount that exceeds the net syndicate short position at the time of such exercise; and

(3)   Any other person participating in the distribution, when such person's participation has been distributed.

Covered security means any security that is the subject of a distribution, or any reference security.

Current exchange rate means the current rate of exchange between two currencies, which is obtained from at least one independent entity that provides or disseminates foreign exchange quotations in the ordinary course of its business.

Distribution means an offering of securities, whether or not subject to registration under the Securities Act, that is distinguished from ordinary trading transactions by the magnitude of the offering and the presence of special selling efforts and selling methods.

Distribution participant means an underwriter, prospective underwriter, broker, dealer, or other person who has agreed to participate or is participating in a distribution.

Electronic communications network has the meaning contained in 600 of Regulation NMS.

Employee has the meaning contained in Form S–8 relating to employee benefit plans.

Exchange Act means the Securities Exchange Act of 1934.

Independent bid means a bid by a person who is not a distribution participant, issuer, selling security holder, or affiliated purchaser.

NASD means the National Association of Securities Dealers, Inc. or any of its subsidiaries.

Nasdaq means the electronic dealer quotation system owned and operated by The Nasdaq Stock Market, Inc.

Nasdaq security means a security that is authorized for quotation on Nasdaq, and such authorization is not suspended, terminated, or prohibited.

Net purchases means the amount by which a passive market maker's purchases exceed its sales.

Offering price means the price at which the security is to be or is being distributed.

Passive market maker means a market maker that effects bids or purchases in accordance with the provisions of Rule 103.

Penalty bid means an arrangement that permits the managing underwriter to reclaim a selling concession from a syndicate member in connection with an offering when the securities originally sold by the syndicate member are purchased in syndicate covering transactions.

Plan means any bonus, profit-sharing, pension, retirement, thrift, savings, incentive, stock purchase, stock option, stock ownership, stock appreciation, dividend reinvestment, or similar plan; or any dividend or interest reinvestment plan or employee benefit plan as defined in Rule 405 of the Securities Act.

Principal market means the single securities market with the largest aggregate reported trading volume for the class of securities during the 12 full calendar months immediately preceding the filing of the registration statement; or, if there is no registration statement or if the distribution involves the sale of securities on a delayed basis pursuant to Rule 415 of the Securities Act, during the 12 full calendar months immediately preceding the determination of the offering price. For the purpose of determining the aggregate trading volume in a security, the trading volume of depositary shares representing such security shall be included, and shall be multiplied by the multiple or fraction of the security represented by the depositary share. For purposes of this paragraph, depositary share means a security, evidenced by a depositary receipt, that represents another security, or a multiple or fraction thereof, deposited with a depositary.

Prospective underwriter means a person:

(1)   Who has submitted a bid to the issuer or selling security holder, and who knows or is reasonably certain that such bid will be accepted, whether or not the terms and conditions of the underwriting have been agreed upon; or

(2)   Who has reached, or is reasonably certain to reach, an understanding with the issuer or selling security holder, or managing underwriter that such person will become an underwriter, whether or not the terms and conditions of the underwriting have been agreed upon.

Public float value shall be determined in the manner set forth on the front page of Form 10–K, even if the issuer of such securities is not required to file Form 10–K, relating to the aggregate market value of common equity securities held by non-affiliates of the issuer.

Reference period means the two full calendar months immediately preceding the filing of the registration statement or, if there is no registration statement or if the distribution involves the sale of securities on a delayed basis pursuant to Rule 415 of the Securities Act, the two full calendar months immediately preceding the determination of the offering price.

Reference security means a security into which a security that is the subject of a distribution ("subject security") may be converted, exchanged, or exercised or which, under the terms of the subject security, may in whole or in significant part determine the value of the subject security.

Restricted period means:

(1)   For any security with an ADTV value of $100,000 or more of an issuer whose common equity securities have a public float value of $25 million or more, the period beginning on the later of one business day prior to the determination of the offering price or such time that a person becomes a distribution participant, and ending upon such person's completion of participation in the distribution; and

(2)   For all other securities, the period beginning on the later of five business days prior to the determination of the offering price or such time that a person becomes a distribution participant, and ending upon such person's completion of participation in the distribution.

(3)   In the case of a distribution involving a merger, acquisition, or exchange offer, the period beginning on the day proxy solicitation or offering materials are first disseminated to security holders, and ending upon the completion of the distribution.

Securities Act means the Securities Act of 1933.

Selling security holder means any person on whose behalf a distribution is made, other than an issuer.

Stabilize or stabilizing means the placing of any bid, or the effecting of any purchase, for the purpose of pegging, fixing, or maintaining the price of a security.

Syndicate covering transaction means the placing of any bid or the effecting of any purchase on behalf of the sole distributor or the underwriting syndicate or group to reduce a short position created in connection with the offering.

30% ADTV limitation means 30 percent of the market maker's ADTV in a covered security during the reference period, as obtained from the NASD.

Underwriter means a person who has agreed with an issuer or selling security holder:

(1)   To purchase securities for distribution; or

(2)   To distribute securities for or on behalf of such issuer or selling security holder; or

(3)   To manage or supervise a distribution of securities for or on behalf of such issuer or selling security holder.

Rule 101.   Activities by Distribution Participants

(a)   *Unlawful Activity.* In connection with a distribution of securities, it shall be unlawful for a distribution participant or an affiliated purchaser of such person, directly or indirectly, to bid for, purchase, or attempt to induce any person to bid for or purchase, a covered security during the applicable restricted period; *Provided, however,* That if a distribution participant or affiliated purchaser is the issuer or selling security holder of the securities subject to the distribution, such person shall be subject to the provisions of Rule 102, rather than this rule.

(b)   *Excepted Activity.* The following activities shall not be prohibited by paragraph (a) of this rule:

(1)   *Research.* The publication or dissemination of any information, opinion, or recommendation, if the conditions of Rule 138, 139, or 139b of the Securities Act are met; or

(2)   *Transactions complying with certain other sections.* Transactions complying with Rule 103 or Rule 104; or

(3)   *Odd-lot transactions.* Transactions in odd-lots; or transactions to offset odd-lots in connection with an odd-lot tender offer conducted pursuant to Rule 13e–4(h)(5) of the Exchange Act; or

(4)   *Exercises of securities.* The exercise of any option, warrant, right, or any conversion privilege set forth in the instrument governing a security; or

(5)   *Unsolicited transactions.* Unsolicited brokerage transactions; or unsolicited purchases that are not effected from or through a broker or dealer, on a securities exchange, or through an inter-dealer quotation system or electronic communications network; or

(6)   *Basket transactions.*

(i)   Bids or purchases, in the ordinary course of business, in connection with a basket of 20 or more securities in which a covered security does not comprise more than 5% of the value of the basket purchased; or

(ii)   Adjustments to such a basket in the ordinary course of business as a result of a change in the composition of a standardized index; or

(7)   *De minimis transactions.* Purchases during the restricted period, other than by a passive market maker, that total less than 2% of the ADTV of the security being purchased, or unaccepted bids; *Provided, however,* That the person making such bid or purchase has maintained and enforces written policies and procedures reasonably designed to achieve compliance with the other provisions of this rule; or

(8) *Transactions in connection with a distribution.* Transactions among distribution participants in connection with a distribution, and purchases of securities from an issuer or selling security holder in connection with a distribution, that are not effected on a securities exchange, or through an interdealer quotation system or electronic communications network; or

(9) *Offers to sell or the solicitation of offers to buy.* Offers to sell or the solicitation of offers to buy the securities being distributed (including securities acquired in stabilizing), or securities offered as principal by the person making such offer or solicitation; or

(10) *Transactions in Rule 144A securities.* Transactions in securities eligible for resale under Rule 144A(d)(3) of the Securities Act, or any reference security, if the Rule 144A securities are sold in the United States solely to:

(i)   buyers, as defined in Rule 144A(a)(1) of the Securities Act, or to purchasers that the seller and any person acting on behalf of the seller reasonably believes are qualified institutional buyers, in transactions exempt from registration under section 4(2) of the Securities Act or Rule 144A or Rule 500 of the Securities Act; or

(ii)   Persons not deemed to be "U.S. persons" for purposes of Rule 902(o)(2) or Rule 902(o)(7) [sic] of the Securities Act, during distribution qualifying under paragraph (b)(10)(i) of this rule.

(c)   *Excepted Securities.* The provisions of this rule shall not apply to any of the following securities:

(1)   *Actively-traded securities.* Securities that have an ADTV value of at least $1 million and are issued by an issuer whose common equity securities have a public float value of at least $150 million; *Provided, however,* That such securities are not issued by the distribution participant or an affiliate of the distribution participant; or

(2)   *Investment grade nonconvertible and asset-backed securities.* Nonconvertible debt securities, nonconvertible preferred securities, and asset-backed securities, that are rated by at least one nationally recognized statistical rating organization, as that term is used in Rule 15c3–1 of the Securities Act, in one of its generic rating categories that signifies investment grade; or

(3)   *Exempted securities.* "Exempted securities" as defined in section 3(a)(12) of the Exchange Act; or

(4)   *Face-amount certificates or securities issued by an open-end management investment company or unit investment trust.* Face-amount certificates issued by a face-amount certificate company, or redeemable securities issued by an open-end management investment company or a unit investment trust. Any terms used in this paragraph (c)(4) that are defined in the Investment Company Act of 1940 shall have the meanings specified in such Act.

(d)   *Exemptive Authority.* Upon written application or upon its own motion, the Commission may grant an exemption from the provisions of this rule either unconditionally or on specified terms and conditions, to any transaction or class of transactions, or to any security or class of securities.

Rule 102.   Activities by Issuers and Selling Security Holders During a Distribution

(a)   *Unlawful Activity.* In connection with a distribution of securities effected by or on behalf of an issuer or selling security holder, it shall be unlawful for such person, or any affiliated purchaser of such person, directly or indirectly, to bid for, purchase, or attempt to induce any person to bid for or purchase, a covered security during the applicable restricted period; *Except That* if an affiliated purchaser is a distribution participant, such affiliated purchaser may comply with Rule 101, rather than this rule.

(b)   *Excepted Activity.* The following activities shall not be prohibited by paragraph (a) of this rule.

(1)   *Odd-lot transactions.* Transactions in odd-lots, or transactions to offset odd-lots in connection with an odd-lot tender offer conducted pursuant to Rule 13e–4(h)(5) of the Exchange Act; or

(2)   *Transactions by closed-end investment companies.* (i) Transactions complying with Rule 23c–3 of the Exchange Act; or

(ii)   Periodic tender offers of securities, at net asset value, conducted pursuant to Rule 13e–4 of the Exchange Act by a closed-end investment company that engages in a continuous offering of its securities pursuant to Rule 415 of the Securities Act; *provided, however,* That such securities are not traded on a securities exchange or through an inter-dealer quotation system or electronic communications network; or

(3) *Redemptions by commodity pools or limited partnerships.* Redemptions by commodity pools or limited partnerships, at a price based on net asset value, which are effected in accordance with the terms and conditions of the instruments governing the securities; *Provided, however,* That such securities are not traded on a securities exchange, or through an inter-dealer quotation system or electronic communications network; or

(4) *Exercises of securities.* The exercise of any option, warrant, right, or any conversion privilege set forth in the instrument governing a security; or

(5) *Offers to sell or the solicitation of offers to buy.* Offers to sell or the solicitation of offers to buy the securities being distributed; or

(6) *Unsolicited purchases.* Unsolicited purchases that are not effected from or through a broker or dealer, on a securities exchange, or through an inter-dealer quotation system or electronic communications network; or

(7) *Transactions in Rule 144A securities.* Transactions in securities eligible for resale under Rule 144A(d)(3) of the Securities Act, or any reference security, if the Rule 144A securities are sold in the United States solely to:

(i) Qualified institutional buyers, as defined in Rule 144A(a)(1) of the Securities Act, or to purchasers that the seller and any person acting on behalf of the seller reasonably believes are qualified institutional buyers, in transactions exempt from registration under section 4(2) of the Securities Act or Rule 144A or Rule 500 of the Securities Act; or

(ii) Persons not deemed to be "U.S. persons" for purposes of Rule 902(*o*)(2) or Rule 902(*o*)(7) of the Securities Act, during a distribution qualifying under paragraph (b)(7)(i) of this rule.

(c) *Plans.*

(1) Paragraph (a) of this rule shall not apply to distributions of securities pursuant to a plan, which are made:

(i) Solely to employees or security holders of an issuer or its subsidiaries, or to a trustee or other person acquiring such securities for the accounts of such persons; or

(ii) To persons other than employees or security holders, if bids for or purchases of securities pursuant to the plan are effected solely by an agent independent of the issuer and the securities are from a source other than the issuer or an affiliated purchaser of the issuer.

(2) Bids for or purchases of any security made or effected by or for a plan shall be deemed to be a purchase by the issuer unless the bid is made, or the purchase is effected, by an agent independent of the issuer.

(d) *Excepted Securities.* The provisions of this rule shall not apply to any of the following securities:

(1) *Actively-traded reference securities.* Reference securities with an ADTV value of at least $1 million that are issued by an issuer whose common equity securities have a public float value of at least $150 million; *Provided, however,* That such securities are not issued by the issuer, or any affiliate of the issuer, of the security in distribution.

(2) *Investment grade nonconvertible and asset-backed securities.* Nonconvertible debt securities, nonconvertible preferred securities, and asset-backed securities, that are rated by at least one nationally recognized statistical rating organization, as that term is used in Rule 15c3–1 of the Exchange Act, in one of its generic rating categories that signifies investment grade; or

(3) *Exempted securities.* "Exempted securities" as defined in section 3(a)(12) of the Exchange Act; or

(4) *Face-amount certificates or securities issued by an open-end management investment company or unit investment trust.* Face-amount certificates issued by a face-amount certificate company, or redeemable securities issued by an open-end management investment company or a unit

investment trust. Any terms used in this paragraph (d)(4) that are defined in the Investment Company Act of 1940 shall have the meanings specified in such Act.

(e)   *Exemptive Authority.* Upon written application or upon its own motion, the Commission may grant an exemption from the provisions of this rule, either unconditionally or on specified terms and conditions, to any transaction or class of transactions, or to any security or class of securities.

Rule 103.   NASDAQ Passive Market Making

(a)   *Scope of Section.* This rule permits broker-dealers to engage in market making transactions in covered securities that are Nasdaq securities without violating the provisions of Rule 101; *Except That* this rule shall not apply to any security for which a stabilizing bid subject to Rule 104 is in effect, or during any at-the-market offering or best efforts offering.

(b)   *Conditions to be Met.*

(1)   *General limitations.* A passive market maker must effect all transactions in the capacity of a registered market maker on Nasdaq. A passive market maker shall not bid for or purchase a covered security at a price that exceeds the highest independent bid for the covered security at the time of the transaction, except as permitted by paragraph (b)(3) of this rule or required by a rule promulgated by the Commission or the NASD governing the handling of customer orders.

(2)   *Purchase limitation.* On each day of the restricted period, a passive market maker's net purchases shall not exceed the greater of its 30% ADTV limitation or 200 shares (together, "purchase limitation"); *Provided, however,* That a passive market maker may purchase all of the securities that are part of a single order that, when executed, results in its purchase limitation being equalled or exceeded. If a passive market maker's net purchases equal or exceed its purchase limitation, it shall withdraw promptly its quotations from Nasdaq. If a passive market maker withdraws its quotations pursuant to this paragraph, it may not effect any bid or purchase in the covered security for the remainder of that day, irrespective of any later sales during that day, unless otherwise permitted by Rule 101.

(3)   *Requirement to lower the bid.* If all independent bids for a covered security are reduced to a price below the passive market maker's bid, the passive market maker must lower its bid promptly to a level not higher than the then highest independent bid; *Provided, however,* That a passive market maker may continue to bid and effect purchases at its bid at a price exceeding the then highest independent bid until the passive market maker purchases an aggregate amount of the covered security that equals or, through the purchase of all securities that are part of a single order, exceeds the lesser of two times the minimum quotation size for the security, as determined by NASD rules, or the passive market maker's remaining purchasing capacity under paragraph (b)(2) of this rule.

(4)   *Limitation on displayed size.* At all times, the passive market maker's displayed bid size may not exceed the lesser of the minimum quotation size for the covered security, or the passive market maker's remaining purchasing capacity under paragraph (b)(2) of this rule; *Provided, however,* That a passive market maker whose purchasing capacity at any time is between one and 99 shares may display a bid size of 100 shares.

(5)   *Identification of a passive market making bid.* The bid displayed by a passive market maker shall be designated as such.

(6)   *Notification and reporting to the NASD.* A passive market maker shall notify the NASD in advance of its intention to engage in passive market making, and shall submit to the NASD information regarding passive market making purchases, in such form as the NASD shall prescribe.

(7)   *Prospectus disclosure.* The prospectus for any registered offering in which any passive market maker intends to effect transactions in any covered security shall contain the information required in Items 502, 508, of Regulation S–K or S–B.

(c)   *Transactions at Prices Resulting From Unlawful Activity.* No transaction shall be made at a price that the passive market maker knows or has reason to know is the result of activity that is fraudulent, manipulative, or deceptive under the securities laws, or any rule or regulation thereunder.

Rule 104.   Stabilizing and Other Activities in Connection With an Offering

(a)   *Unlawful Activity*. It shall be unlawful for any person, directly or indirectly, to stabilize, to effect any syndicate covering transaction, or to impose a penalty bid, in connection with an offering of any security, in contravention of the provisions of this rule. No stabilizing shall be effected at a price that the person stabilizing knows or has reason to know is in contravention of this rule, or is the result of activity that is fraudulent, manipulative, or deceptive under the securities laws, or any rule or regulation thereunder.

(b)   *Purpose*. Stabilizing is prohibited except for the purpose of preventing or retarding a decline in the market price of a security.

(c)   *Priority*. To the extent permitted or required by the market where stabilizing occurs, any person stabilizing shall grant priority to any independent bid at the same price irrespective of the size of such independent bid at the time that it is entered.

(d)   *Control of Stabilizing*. No sole distributor or syndicate or group stabilizing the price of a security or any member or members of such syndicate or group shall maintain more than one stabilizing bid in any one market at the same price at the same time.

(e)   *At-the-Market Offerings*. Stabilizing is prohibited in an at-the-market offering.

(f)   *Stabilizing Levels*.

(1)   *Maximum stabilizing bid*. Notwithstanding the other provisions of this paragraph (f), no stabilizing shall be made at a price higher than the lower of the offering price or the stabilizing bid for the security in the principal market (or, if the principal market is closed, the stabilizing bid in the principal market at its previous close).

(2)   *Initiating stabilizing*.

(i)   *Initiating stabilizing when the principal market is open*. After the opening of quotations for the security in the principal market, stabilizing may be initiated in any market at a price no higher than the last independent transaction price for the security in the principal market if the security has traded in the principal market on the day stabilizing is initiated or on the preceding business day and the current asked price in the principal market is equal to or greater than the last independent transaction price. If both conditions of the preceding sentence are not satisfied, stabilizing may be initiated in any market after the opening of quotations in the principal market at a price no higher than the highest current independent bid for the security in the principal market.

(ii)   *Initiating stabilizing when the principal market is closed*.

(A)   When the principal market for the security is closed, but immediately before the opening of quotations for the security in the market where stabilizing will be initiated, stabilizing may be initiated at a price no higher than the lower of:

(1)   The price at which stabilizing could have been initiated in the principal market for the security at its previous close; or

(2)   The most recent price at which an independent transaction in the security has been effected in any market since the close of the principal market, if the person stabilizing knows or has reason to know of such transaction.

(B)   When the principal market for the security is closed, but after the opening of quotations in the market where stabilizing will be initiated, stabilizing may be initiated at a price no higher than the lower of:

(1)   The price at which stabilization could have been initiated in the principal market for the security at its previous close; or

(2)   The last independent transaction price for the security in that market if the security has traded in that market on the day stabilizing is initiated or on the last preceding business day and the current asked price in that market is equal to or greater than the last independent transaction price. If both conditions of the preceding sentence are not satisfied, under this paragraph (f)(2)(ii)(B)(2), stabilizing may be

initiated at a price no higher than the highest current independent bid for the security in that market.

(iii) *Initiating stabilizing when there is no market for the security or before the offering price is determined.* If no bona fide market for the security being distributed exists at the time stabilizing is initiated, no stabilizing shall be initiated at a price in excess of the offering price. If stabilizing is initiated before the offering price is determined, then stabilizing may be continued after determination of the offering price at the price at which stabilizing then could be initiated.

(3) *Maintaining or carrying over a stabilizing bid.* stabilizing bid initiated pursuant to paragraph (f)(2) of this rule, which has not been discontinued, may be maintained, or carried over into another market, irrespective of changes in the independent bids or transaction prices for the security.

(4) *Increasing or reducing a stabilizing bid.* A stabilizing bid may be increased to a price no higher than the highest current independent bid for the security in the principal market if the principal market is open, or, if the principal market is closed, to a price no higher than the highest independent bid in the principal market at the previous close thereof. A stabilizing bid may be reduced, or carried over into another market at a reduced price, irrespective of changes in the independent bids or transaction prices for the security. If stabilizing is discontinued, it shall not be resumed at a price higher than the price at which stabilizing then could be initiated.

(5) *Initiating, maintaining, or adjusting a stabilizing bid to reflect the current exchange rate.* If a stabilizing bid is expressed in a currency other than the currency of the principal market for the security, such bid may be initiated, maintained, or adjusted to reflect the current exchange rate, consistent with the provisions of this rule. If, in initiating, maintaining, or adjusting a stabilizing bid pursuant to this paragraph (f)(5), the bid would be at or below the midpoint between two trading differentials, such stabilizing bid shall be adjusted downward to the lower differential.

(6) *Adjustments to stabilizing bid.* If a security goes ex-dividend, ex-rights, or ex-distribution, the stabilizing bid shall be reduced by an amount equal to the value of the dividend, right, or distribution. If, in reducing a stabilizing bid pursuant to this paragraph (f)(6), the bid would be at or below the midpoint between two trading differentials, such stabilizing bid shall be adjusted downward to the lower differential.

(7) *Stabilizing of components.* When two or more securities are being offered as a unit, the component securities shall not be stabilized at prices the sum of which exceeds the then permissible stabilizing price for the unit.

(8) *Special prices.* Any stabilizing price that otherwise meets the requirements of this rule need not be adjusted to reflect special prices available to any group or class of persons (including employees or holders of warrants or rights).

(g) *Offerings With no U.S. Stabilizing Activities.*

(1) Stabilizing to facilitate an offering of a security in the United States shall not be deemed to be in violation of this rule if all of the following conditions are satisfied:

(i) No stabilizing is made in the United States;

(ii) Stabilizing outside the United States is made in a jurisdiction with statutory or regulatory provisions governing stabilizing that are comparable to the provisions of this rule; and

(iii) No stabilizing is made at a price above the offering price in the United States, except as permitted by paragraph (f)(5) of this rule.

(2) For purposes of this paragraph (g), the Commission by rule, regulation, or order may determine whether a foreign statute or regulation is comparable to this rule considering, among other things, whether such foreign statute or regulation: specifies appropriate purposes for which stabilizing is permitted; provides for disclosure and control of stabilizing activities; places limitations on stabilizing levels; requires appropriate recordkeeping; provides other protections comparable to the provisions of this rule; and whether procedures exist to enable the Commission to obtain information concerning any foreign stabilizing transactions.

(h) *Disclosure and Notification.*

(1)   Any person displaying or transmitting a bid that such person knows is for the purpose of stabilizing shall provide prior notice to the market on which such stabilizing will be effected, and shall disclose its purpose to the person with whom the bid is entered.

(2)   Any person effecting a syndicate covering transaction or imposing a penalty bid shall provide prior notice to the self-regulatory organization with direct authority over the principal market in the United States for the security for which the syndicate covering transaction is effected or the penalty bid is imposed.

(3)   Any person subject to this rule who sells to, or purchases for the account of, any person any security where the price of such security may be or has been stabilized, shall send to the purchaser at or before the completion of the transaction, a prospectus, offering circular, confirmation, or other document containing a statement similar to that comprising the statement provided for in Item 502(d) of Regulation S–B or Item 502(d) of Regulation S–K.

(i)   *Recordkeeping Requirements.* A person subject to this rule shall keep the information and make the notification required by Rule 17a–2 of the Exchange Act.

(j)   *Excepted Securities.* The provisions of this rule shall not apply to:

(1)   *Exempted Securities.* "Exempted securities," as defined in section 3(a)(12) of the Exchange Act; or

(2)   *Transactions of Rule 144A securities.* Transactions in securities eligible for resale under Rule 144A(d)(3) of the Securities Act, if such securities are sold in the United States solely to:

(i)   Qualified institutional buyers, as defined in Rule 144A(a)(1) of the Securities Act, or to purchasers that the seller and any person acting on behalf of the seller reasonably believes are qualified institutional buyers, in a transaction exempt from registration under section 4(2) of the Securities Act or Rule 144A or Rule 500 of the Securities Act; or

(ii)   Persons not deemed to be "U.S. persons" for purposes of Rule 902(*o*)(2) or Rule 902(*o*)(7) of the Exchange Act, during a distribution qualifying under paragraph (j)(2)(i) of this rule.

(k)   *Exemptive Authority.* Upon written application or upon its own motion, the Commission may grant an exemption from the provisions of this rule, either unconditionally or on specified terms and conditions, to any transaction or class of transactions, or to any security or class of securities.

Rule 105.   Short Selling in Connection With a Public Offering

(a)   *Unlawful Activity.* In connection with an offering of equity securities for cash pursuant to a registration statement or a notification on Form 1–A or Form 1–E filed under the Securities Act of 1933 ("offered securities"), it shall be unlawful for any person to sell short (as defined in Rule 200(a) of Regulation SHO) the security that is the subject of the offering and purchase the offered securities from an underwriter or broker or dealer participating in the offering if such short sale was effected during the period ("Rule 105 restricted period") that is the shorter of the period:

(1)   Beginning five business days before the pricing of the offered securities and ending with such pricing; or

(2)   Beginning with the initial filing of such registration statement or notification on Form 1–A or Form 1–E and ending with the pricing.

(b)   *Excepted Activity.*

(1)   *Bona Fide Purchase.* It shall not be prohibited for such person to purchase the offered securities as provided in paragraph (a) of this rule if:

(i)   Such person makes a bona fide purchase(s) of the security that is the subject of the offering that is:

(A)   At least equivalent in quantity to the entire amount of the Rule 105 restricted period short sale(s);

(B)   Effected during regular trading hours;

(C)   Reported to an "effective transaction reporting plan" (as defined in Rule 600(b)(23) of Regulation NMS); and

(D)   Effected after the last Rule 105 restricted period short sale, and no later than the business day prior to the day of pricing; and

(ii)   Such person did not effect a short sale, that is reported to an effective transaction reporting plan, within the 30 minutes prior to the close of regular trading hours (as defined in Rule 600(b)(68) of Regulation NMS) on the business day prior to the day of pricing.

(2)   *Separate Accounts.* Paragraph (a) of this rule shall not prohibit the purchase of the offered security in an account of a person where such person sold short during the Rule 105 restricted period in a separate account, if decisions regarding securities transactions for each account are made separately and without coordination of trading or cooperation among or between the accounts.

(3)   *Investment Companies.* Paragraph (a) of this rule shall not prohibit an investment company (as defined by Section 3 of the Investment Company Act) that is registered under Section 8 of the Investment Company Act, or a series of such company (investment company) from purchasing an offered security where any of the following sold the offered security short during the Rule 105 restricted period:

(i)   An affiliated investment company, or any series of such a company; or

(ii)   A separate series of the investment company.

(c)   *Excepted Offerings.* This rule shall not apply to offerings that are not conducted on a firm commitment basis.

(d)   *Exemptive Authority.* Upon written application or upon its own motion, the Commission may grant an exemption from the provisions of this rule, either unconditionally or on specified terms and conditions, to any transaction or class of transactions, or to any security or class of securities.

REGULATION SHO

17 C.F.R. § 242.___

Regulation of Short Sales

Rule 200.   Definition of "Short Sale" and Marking Requirements

(a)   The term short sale shall mean any sale of a security which the seller does not own or any sale which is consummated by the delivery of a security borrowed by, or for the account of, the seller.

(b)   A person shall be deemed to own a security if:

(1)   The person or his agent has title to it; or

(2)   The person has purchased, or has entered into an unconditional contract, binding on both parties thereto, to purchase it, but has not yet received it; or

(3)   The person owns a security convertible into or exchangeable for it and has tendered such security for conversion or exchange; or

(4)   The person has an option to purchase or acquire it and has exercised such option; or

(5)   The person has rights or warrants to subscribe to it and has exercised such rights or warrants; or

(6)   The person holds a security futures contract to purchase it and has received notice that the position will be physically settled and is irrevocably bound to receive the underlying security.

(c)   A person shall be deemed to own securities only to the extent that he has a net long position in such securities.

(d)   A broker or dealer shall be deemed to own a security, even if it is not net long, if:

(1)   The broker or dealer acquired that security while acting in the capacity of a block positioner; and

(2)   If and to the extent that the broker or dealer's short position in the security is the subject of offsetting positions created in the course of bona fide arbitrage, risk arbitrage, or bona fide hedge activities.

(e)   A broker-dealer shall be deemed to own a security even if it is not net long, if:

(1)   The broker-dealer is unwinding index arbitrage position involving a long basket of stock and one or more short index futures traded on a board of trade or one or more standardized options contracts as defined in Rule 9b–1(a)(4) under the Securities Exchange Act of 1934; and

(2)   If and to the extent that the broker-dealer's short position in the security is the subject of offsetting positions created and maintained in the course of bona-fide arbitrage, risk arbitrage, or bona fide hedge activities; and

(3)   The sale does not occur during a period commencing at the time that the NYSE Composite Index has declined by two percent or more from its closing value on the previous day and terminating upon the end of the trading day. The two percent shall be calculated at the beginning of each calendar quarter and shall be two percent, rounded down to the nearest 10 points, of the average closing value of the NYSE Composite Index for the last month of the previous quarter.

(f)   In order to determine its net position, a broker or dealer shall aggregate all of its positions in a security unless it qualifies for independent trading unit aggregation, in which case each independent trading unit shall aggregate all of its positions in a security to determine its net position. Independent trading unit aggregation is available only if:

(1)   The broker or dealer has a written plan of organization that identifies each aggregation unit, specifies its trading objective(s), and supports its independent identity;

(2)   Each aggregation unit within the firm determines, at the time of each sale, its net position for every security that it trades;

(3)   All traders in an aggregation unit pursue only the particular trading objective(s) or strategy(s) of that aggregation unit and do not coordinate that strategy with any other aggregation unit; and

(4)   Individual traders are assigned to only one aggregation unit at any time.

(g)   A broker or dealer must mark all sell orders of any equity security as "long," "short," or "short exempt."

(1)   An order to sell shall be marked "long" only if the seller is deemed to own the security being sold pursuant to paragraphs (a) through (f) of this rule and either:

(i)   The security to be delivered is in the physical possession or control of the broker or dealer; or

(ii)   It is reasonably expected that the security will be in the physical possession or control of the broker or dealer no later than the settlement of the transaction.

(2)   A sale order shall be marked "short exempt" only if the provisions of Item 201(c) or (d) are met.

(h)   Upon written application or upon its own motion, the Commission may grant an exemption from the provisions of this rule, either unconditionally or on specified terms and conditions, to any transaction or class of transactions, or to any security or class of securities, or to any person or class of persons.

Rule 201.   Circuit Breaker

(a)   Definitions. For the purposes of this rule:

(1)   The term covered security shall mean any NMS stock as defined in Item 600(b)(48).

(2)   The term effective transaction reporting plan for a covered security shall have the same meaning as in Item 600(b)(23).

(3)   The term listing market shall have the same meaning as the term "listing market" as defined in the effective transaction reporting plan for the covered security.

(4)   The term national best bid shall have the same meaning as in Item 600(b)(43).

(5)   The term odd lot shall have the same meaning as in Item 600(b)(51).

(6)   The term plan processor shall have the same meaning as in Item 600(b)(59).

(7)   The term regular trading hours shall have the same meaning as in Item 600(b)(68).

(8)   The term riskless principal shall mean a transaction in which a broker or dealer, after having received an order to buy a security, purchases the security as principal at the same price to satisfy the order to buy, exclusive of any explicitly disclosed markup or markdown, commission equivalent, or other fee, or, after having received an order to sell, sells the security as principal at the same price to satisfy the order to sell, exclusive of any explicitly disclosed markup or markdown, commission equivalent, or other fee.

(9)   The term trading center shall have the same meaning as in Item 600(b)(82).

(b)(1)   A trading center shall establish, maintain, and enforce written policies and procedures reasonably designed to:

(i)   Prevent the execution or display of a short sale order of a covered security at a price that is less than or equal to the current national best bid if the price of that covered security 329 decreases by 10% or more from the covered security's closing price as determined by the listing market for the covered security as of the end of regular trading hours on the prior day; and

(ii)   Impose the requirements of paragraph (b)(1)(i) of this rule for the remainder of the day and the following day when a national best bid for the covered security is calculated and disseminated on a current and continuing basis by a plan processor pursuant to an effective national market system plan.

(iii)   Provided, however, that the policies and procedures must be reasonably designed to permit:

(A)   The execution of a displayed short sale order of a covered security by a trading center if, at the time of initial display of the short sale order, the order was at a price above the current national best bid; and

(B)   The execution or display of a short sale order of a covered security marked "short exempt" without regard to whether the order is at a price that is less than or equal to the current national best bid.

(2)   A trading center shall regularly surveil to ascertain the effectiveness of the policies and procedures required by paragraph (b)(1) of this rule and shall take prompt action to remedy deficiencies in such policies and procedures.

(3)   The determination regarding whether the price of a covered security has decreased by 10% or more from the covered security's closing price as determined by the listing market for the covered security as of the end of regular trading hours on the prior day shall be made by the listing market for the covered security and, if such decrease has occurred, the listing market shall immediately notify the single plan processor responsible for consolidation of information for the covered security pursuant to Item 603(b). The single plan processor must then disseminate this information.

(c)   Following any determination and notification pursuant to paragraph (b)(3) of this rule with respect to a covered security, a broker or dealer submitting a short sale order of the covered security in question to a trading center may mark the order "short exempt" if the broker or dealer identifies the order as being at a price above the current national best bid at the time of submission; provided, however:

(1)   The broker or dealer that identifies a short sale order of a covered security as "short exempt" in accordance with this paragraph (c) must establish, maintain, and enforce written policies and procedures reasonably designed to prevent incorrect identification of orders for purposes of this paragraph; and

(2)   The broker or dealer shall regularly surveil to ascertain the effectiveness of the policies and procedures required by paragraph (c)(1) of this rule and shall take prompt action to remedy deficiencies in such policies and procedures.

(d)   Following any determination and notification pursuant to paragraph (b)(3) of this rule with respect to a covered security, a broker or dealer may mark a short sale order of a covered security "short exempt" if the broker or dealer has a reasonable basis to believe that:

(1)   The short sale order of a covered security is by a person that is deemed to own the covered security pursuant to Item 200, provided that the person intends to deliver the security as soon as all restrictions on delivery have been removed.

(2)   The short sale order of a covered security is by a market maker to offset customer odd-lot orders or to liquidate an odd-lot position that changes such broker's or dealer's position by no more than a unit of trading.

(3)   The short sale order of a covered security is for a good faith account of a person who then owns another security by virtue of which he is, or presently will be, entitled to acquire an equivalent number of securities of the same class as the securities sold; provided such sale, or the purchase which such sale offsets, is effected for the bona fide purpose of profiting from a current difference between the price of the security sold and the security owned and that such right of acquisition was originally

attached to or represented by another security or was issued to all the holders of any such securities of the issuer.

(4)   The short sale order of a covered security is for a good faith account and submitted to profit from a current price difference between a security on a foreign securities market and a security on a securities market subject to the jurisdiction of the United States, provided that the short seller has an offer to buy on a foreign market that allows the seller to immediately cover the short sale at the time it was made. For the purposes of this paragraph (d)(4), a depository receipt of a security shall be deemed to be the same security as the security represented by such receipt.

(5)(i)   The short sale order of a covered security is by an underwriter or member of a syndicate or group participating in the distribution of a security in connection with an over-allotment of securities; or

(ii)   The short sale order of a covered security is for purposes of a lay-off sale by an underwriter or member of a syndicate or group in connection with a distribution of securities through a rights or standby underwriting commitment.

(6)   The short sale order of a covered security is by a broker or dealer effecting the execution of a customer purchase or the execution of a customer "long" sale on a riskless principal basis. In addition, for purposes of this paragraph (d)(6), a broker or dealer must have written policies and procedures in place to assure that, at a minimum:

(i)   The customer order was received prior to the offsetting transaction;

(ii)   The offsetting transaction is allocated to a riskless principal or customer account within 60 seconds of execution; and

(iii)   The broker or dealer has supervisory systems in place to produce records that enable the broker or dealer to accurately and readily reconstruct, in a time-sequenced manner, all orders on which a broker or dealer relies pursuant to this exception.

(7)   The short sale order is for the sale of a covered security at the volume weighted average price (VWAP) that meets the following criteria:

(i)   The VWAP for the covered security is calculated by:

(A)   Calculating the values for every regular way trade reported in the consolidated system for the security during the regular trading session, by multiplying each such price by the total number of shares traded at that price;

(B)   Compiling an aggregate sum of all values; and

(C)   Dividing the aggregate sum by the total number of reported shares for that day in the security.

(ii)   The transactions are reported using a special VWAP trade modifier.

(iii)   The VWAP matched security:

(A)   Qualifies as an "actively-traded security" pursuant to Item 101 and Item 102; or

(B)   The proposed short sale transaction is being conducted as part of a basket transaction of twenty or more securities in which the subject security does not comprise more than 5% of the value of the basket traded.

(iv)   The transaction is not effected for the purpose of creating actual, or apparent, active trading in or otherwise affecting the price of any security.

(v)   A broker or dealer shall be permitted to act as principal on the contra-side to fill customer short sale orders only if the broker's or dealer's position in the covered security, as committed by the broker or dealer during the pre-opening period of a trading day and aggregated across all of its customers who propose to sell short the same security on a VWAP basis, does not exceed 10% of the covered security's relevant average daily trading volume.

(e)   No self-regulatory organization shall have any rule that is not in conformity with, or conflicts with, this rule.

(f)   Upon written application or upon its own motion, the Commission may grant an exemption from the provisions of this rule, either unconditionally or on specified terms and conditions, to any person or class of persons, to any transaction or class of transactions, or to any security or class of securities to the extent that such exemption is necessary or appropriate, in the public interest, and is consistent with the protection of investors.

Rule 203.   Borrowing and Delivery Requirements

(a)   *Long Sales.*

(1)   If a broker or dealer knows or has reasonable grounds to believe that the sale of an equity security was or will be effected pursuant to an order marked "long," such broker or dealer shall not lend or arrange for the loan of any security for delivery to the purchaser's broker after the sale, or fail to deliver a security on the date delivery is due.

(2)   The provisions of paragraph (a)(1) of this rule shall not apply:

(i)   To the loan of any security by a broker or dealer through the medium of a loan to another broker or dealer;

(ii)   If the broker or dealer knows, or has been reasonably informed by the seller, that the seller owns the security, and that the seller would deliver the security to the broker or dealer prior to the scheduled settlement of the transaction, but the seller failed to do so; or

(iii)   If, prior to any loan or arrangement to loan any security for delivery, or failure to deliver, a national securities exchange, in the case of a sale effected thereon, or a national securities association, in the case of a sale not effected on an exchange, finds:

(A)   That such sale resulted from a mistake made in good faith;

(B)   That due diligence was used to ascertain that the circumstances specified in Rule 200(g) existed; and

(C)   Either that the condition of the market at the time the mistake was discovered was such that undue hardship would result from covering the transaction by a "purchase for cash" or that the mistake was made by the seller's broker and the sale was at a permissible price under any applicable short sale price test.

(b)   *Short Sales.*

(1)   A broker or dealer may not accept a short sale order in an equity security from another person, or effect a short sale in an equity security for its own account, unless the broker or dealer has:

(i)   Borrowed the security, or entered into a bona-fide arrangement to borrow the security; or

(ii)   Reasonable grounds to believe that the security can be borrowed so that it can be delivered on the date delivery is due; and

(iii)   Documented compliance with this paragraph (b)(1).

(2)   The provisions of paragraph (b)(1) of this rule shall not apply to:

(i)   A broker or dealer that has accepted a short sale order from another registered broker or dealer that is required to comply with paragraph (b)(1) of this rule, unless the broker or dealer relying on this exception contractually undertook responsibility for compliance with paragraph (b)(1) of this rule;

(ii)   Any sale of a security that a person is deemed to own pursuant to Rule 200, provided that the broker or dealer has been reasonably informed that the person intends to deliver such security as soon as all restrictions on delivery have been removed. If the person has not delivered such security within 35 days after the trade date, the broker-dealer that effected the sale must borrow securities or close out the short position by purchasing securities of like kind and quantity;

(iii)   Short sales effected by a market maker in connection with bona-fide market making activities in the security for which this exception is claimed; and

(iv) Transactions in Security Futures.

(3) If a participant of a registered clearing agency has a fail to deliver position at a registered clearing agency in a threshold security for thirteen consecutive settlement days, the participant shall immediately thereafter close out the fail to deliver position by purchasing securities of like kind and quantity:

(i) *Provided, however*, that a participant of a registered clearing agency that has a fail to deliver position at a registered clearing agency in a threshold security on the effective date of this amendment and which, prior to the effective date of this amendment, had been previously grandfathered from the close-out requirement in this paragraph (b)(3) (i.e., because the participant of a registered clearing agency had a fail to deliver position at a registered clearing agency on the settlement day preceding the day that the security became a threshold security), shall close out that fail to deliver position within thirty-five consecutive settlement days of the effective date of this amendment by purchasing securities of like kind and quantity;

(ii) *Provided, however*, that if a participant of a registered clearing agency has a fail to deliver position at a registered clearing agency in a threshold security that was sold pursuant to Rule 144 under the Securities Act for thirty-five consecutive settlement days, the participant shall immediately thereafter close out the fail to deliver position in the security by purchasing securities of like kind and quantity;

(iii) *Provided, however*, that a participant of a registered clearing agency that has a fail to deliver position at a registered clearing agency in a threshold security on the effective date of this amendment and which, prior to the effective date of this amendment, had been previously excepted from the close-out requirement in paragraph (b)(3) of this rule (i.e., because the participant of a registered clearing agency had a fail to deliver position in the threshold security that is attributed to short sales effected by a registered options market maker to establish or maintain a hedge on options positions that were created before the security became a threshold security), shall immediately close out that fail to deliver position, including any adjustments to the fail to deliver position, within 35 consecutive settlement days of the effective date of this amendment by purchasing securities of like kind and quantity;

(iv) If a participant of a registered clearing agency has a fail to deliver position at a registered clearing agency in a threshold security for thirteen consecutive settlement days, the participant and any broker or dealer for which it clears transactions, including any market maker that would otherwise be entitled to rely on the exception provided in paragraph (b)(2)(iii) of this rule, may not accept a short sale order in the threshold security from another person, or effect a short sale in the threshold security for its own account, without borrowing the security or entering into a bona-fide arrangement to borrow the security, until the participant closes out the fail to deliver position by purchasing securities of like kind and quantity;

(v) If a participant of a registered clearing agency entitled to rely on the 35 consecutive settlement day close-out requirement contained in paragraph (b)(3)(i), (b)(3)(ii), or (b)(3)(iii) of this rule has a fail to deliver position at a registered clearing agency in the threshold security for 35 consecutive settlement days, the participant and any broker or dealer for which it clears transactions, including any market maker, that would otherwise be entitled to rely on the exception provided in paragraph (b)(2)(ii) of this rule, may not accept a short sale order in the threshold security from another person, or effect a short sale in the threshold security for its own account, without borrowing the security or entering into a bona-fide arrangement to borrow the security, until the participant closes out the fail to deliver position by purchasing securities of like kind and quantity;

(vi) If a participant of a registered clearing agency reasonably allocates a portion of a fail to deliver position to another registered broker or dealer for which it clears trades or for which it is responsible for settlement, based on such broker or dealer's short position, then the provisions of this paragraph (b)(3) relating to such fail to deliver position shall apply to the portion of such registered broker or dealer that was allocated the fail to deliver position, and not to the participant; and

(vii) A participant of a registered clearing agency shall not be deemed to have fulfilled the requirements of this paragraph (b)(3) where the participant enters into an arrangement with another person to purchase securities as required by this paragraph (b)(3), and the participant knows or has reason to know that the other person will not deliver securities in settlement of the purchase.

(c) *Definitions.*

(1) For purposes of this rule, the term market maker has the same meaning as in section 3(a)(38) of the Securities Exchange Act of 1934.

(2) For purposes of this rule, the term participant has the same meaning as in section 3(a)(24) of the Exchange Act.

(3) For purposes of this rule, the term registered clearing agency means a clearing agency, as defined in section 3(a)(23)(A) of the Exchange Act, that is registered with the Commission pursuant to section 17A of the Exchange Act.

(4) For purposes of this rule, the term security future has the same meaning as in section 3(a)(55) of the Exchange Act.

(5) For purposes of this rule, the term settlement day means any business day on which deliveries of securities and payments of money may be made through the facilities of a registered clearing agency.

(6) For purposes of this rule, the term threshold security means any equity security of an issuer that is registered pursuant to section 12 of the Exchange Act or for which the issuer is required to file reports pursuant to section 15(d) of the Exchange Act:

(i) For which there is an aggregate fail to deliver position for five consecutive settlement days at a registered clearing agency of 10,000 shares or more, and that is equal to at least 0.5% of the issue's total shares outstanding;

(ii) Is included on a list disseminated to its members by a self-regulatory organization; and

(iii) Provided, however, that a security shall cease to be a threshold security if the aggregate fail to deliver position at a registered clearing agency does not exceed the level specified in paragraph (c)(6)(i) of this rule for five consecutive settlement days.

(d) *Exemptive Authority.* Upon written application or upon its own motion, the Commission may grant an exemption from the provisions of this rule, either unconditionally or on specified terms and conditions, to any transaction or class of transactions, or to any security or class of securities, or to any person or class of persons.

Rule 204.   Close-out Requirement

(a) A participant of a registered clearing agency must deliver securities to a registered clearing agency for clearance and settlement on a long or short sale in any equity security by settlement date, or if a participant of a registered clearing agency has a fail to deliver position at a registered clearing agency in any equity security for a long or short sale transaction in that equity security, the participant shall, by no later than the beginning of regular trading hours on the settlement day following the settlement date, immediately close out its fail to deliver position by borrowing or purchasing securities of like kind and quantity; Provided, however:

(1) If a participant of a registered clearing agency has a fail to deliver position at a registered clearing agency in any equity security and the participant can demonstrate on its books and records that such fail to deliver position resulted from a long sale, the participant shall by no later than the beginning of regular trading hours on the third consecutive settlement day following the settlement date, immediately close out the fail to deliver position by purchasing or borrowing securities of like kind and quantity;

(2) If a participant of a registered clearing agency has a fail to deliver position at a registered clearing agency in any equity security resulting from a sale of a security that a person is deemed to own pursuant to Item 200 and that such person intends to deliver as soon as all restrictions on delivery

have been removed, the participant shall, by no later than the beginning of regular trading hours on the thirty-fifth consecutive calendar day following the trade date for the transaction, immediately close out the fail to deliver position by purchasing securities of like kind and quantity; or

(3)   If a participant of a registered clearing agency has a fail to deliver position at a registered clearing agency in any equity security that is attributable to bona fide market making activities by a registered market maker, options market maker, or other market maker obligated to quote in the over-the-counter market, the participant shall by no later than the beginning of regular trading hours on the third consecutive settlement day following the settlement date, immediately close out the fail to deliver position by purchasing or borrowing securities of like kind and quantity.

(b)   If a participant of a registered clearing agency has a fail to deliver position in any equity security at a registered clearing agency and does not close out such fail to deliver position in accordance with the requirements of paragraph (a) of this rule, the participant and any broker or dealer from which it receives trades for clearance and settlement, including any market maker that would otherwise be entitled to rely on the exception provided in Item 203(b)(2)(iii), may not accept a short sale order in the equity security from another person, or effect a short sale in the equity security for its own account, to the extent that the broker or dealer submits its short sales to that participant for clearance and settlement, without first borrowing the security, or entering into a bona fide arrangement to borrow the security, until the participant closes out the fail to deliver position by purchasing securities of like kind and quantity and that purchase has cleared and settled at a registered clearing agency; Provided, however: A broker or dealer shall not be subject to the requirements of this paragraph if the broker or dealer timely certifies to the participant of a registered clearing agency that it has not incurred a fail to deliver position on settlement date for a long or short sale in an equity security for which the participant has a fail to deliver position at a registered clearing agency or that the broker or dealer is in compliance with paragraph (e) of this rule.

(c)   The participant must notify any broker or dealer from which it receives trades for clearance and settlement, including any market maker that would otherwise be entitled to rely on the exception provided in Item 203(b)(2)(iii):

(1)   That the participant has a fail to deliver position in an equity security at a registered clearing agency that has not been closed out in accordance with the requirements of paragraph (a) of this rule; and

(2)   When the purchase that the participant has made to close out the fail to deliver position has cleared and settled at a registered clearing agency.

(d)   If a participant of a registered clearing agency reasonably allocates a portion of a fail to deliver position to another registered broker or dealer for which it clears trades or from which it receives trades for settlement, based on such broker's or dealer's short position, the provisions of paragraphs (a) and (b) of this rule relating to such fail to deliver position shall apply to such registered broker or dealer that was allocated the fail to deliver position, and not to the participant. A broker or dealer that has been allocated a portion of a fail to deliver position that does not comply with the provisions of paragraph (a) of this rule must immediately notify the participant that it has become subject to the requirements of paragraph (b) of this rule.

(e)   Even if a participant of a registered clearing agency has not closed out a fail to deliver position at a registered clearing agency in accordance with paragraph (a) of this rule, or has not allocated a fail to deliver position to a broker or dealer in accordance with paragraph (d) of this rule, a broker or dealer shall not be subject to the requirements of paragraph (a) or (b) of this rule if the broker or dealer purchases or borrows the securities, and if:

(1)   The purchase or borrow is bona fide;

(2)   The purchase or borrow is executed after trade date but by no later than the end of regular trading hours on settlement date for the transaction;

(3)   The purchase or borrow is of a quantity of securities sufficient to cover the entire amount of that broker's or dealer's fail to deliver position at a registered clearing agency in that security; and

(4)   The broker or dealer can demonstrate that it has a net flat or net long position on its books and records on the day of the purchase or borrow.

(f)   A participant of a registered clearing agency shall not be deemed to have fulfilled the requirements of this rule where the participant enters into an arrangement with another person to purchase or borrow securities as required by this rule, and the participant knows or has reason to know that the other person will not deliver securities in settlement of the purchase or borrow.

(g)   *Definitions.* (1) For purposes of this rule, the term settlement date shall mean the business day on which delivery of a security and payment of money is to be made through the facilities of a registered clearing agency in connection with the sale of a security.

(2)   For purposes of this rule, the term regular trading hours has the same meaning as in Rule 600(b)(68) of Regulation NMS.

REGULATION ATS—ALTERNATIVE TRADING SYSTEMS

17 C.F.R. § 242.___

Preliminary Notes

1.   An alternative trading system is required to comply with the requirements in this Regulation ATS, unless such alternative trading system:

(a)   Is registered as a national securities exchange;

(b)   Is exempt from registration as a national securities exchange based on the limited volume of transactions effected on the alternative trading system; or

(c)   Trades only government securities and certain other related instruments.

All alternative trading systems must comply with the antifraud, antimanipulation, and other applicable provisions of the federal securities laws.

2.   The requirements imposed upon an alternative trading system by Regulation ATS are in addition to any requirements applicable to broker-dealers registered under section 15 of the Act, (15 U.S.C. 78o).

3.   An alternative trading system must comply with any applicable state law relating to the offer or sale of securities or the registration or regulation of persons or entities effecting transactions in securities.

4.   The disclosures made pursuant to the provisions of this rule are in addition to any other disclosure requirements under the federal securities laws.

Rule 300.   Definitions

For purposes of this rule, the following definitions shall apply:

(a)   Alternative trading system means any organization, association, person, group of persons, or system:

(1)   That constitutes, maintains, or provides a market place or facilities for bringing together purchasers and sellers of securities or for otherwise performing with respect to securities the functions commonly performed by a stock exchange within the meaning of Rule 3b–16 of the Exchange Act; and

(2)   That does not:

(i)   Set rules governing the conduct of subscribers other than the conduct of such subscribers' trading on such organization, association, person, group of persons, or system; or

(ii)   Discipline subscribers other than by exclusion from trading.

(b)   Subscriber means any person that has entered into a contractual agreement with an alternative trading system to access such alternative trading system for the purpose of effecting transactions in securities or submitting, disseminating, or displaying orders on such alternative trading system, including a customer, member, user, or participant in an alternative trading system. A subscriber, however, shall not include a national securities exchange or national securities association.

(c)   Affiliate of a subscriber means any person that, directly or indirectly, controls, is under common control with, or is controlled by, the subscriber, including any employee.

(d)   Debt security shall mean any security other than an equity security, as defined in Rule 3a11–1 under the Exchange Act, as well as non-participatory preferred stock.

(e)   Order means any firm indication of a willingness to buy or sell a security, as either principal or agent, including any bid or offer quotation, market order, limit order, or other priced order.

(f)   Control means the power, directly or indirectly, to direct the management or policies of the broker-dealer of an alternative trading system, whether through ownership of securities, by contract, or otherwise. A person is presumed to control the broker-dealer of an alternative trading system, if that person:

(1)   Is a director, general partner, or officer exercising executive responsibility (or having similar status or performing similar functions);

(2)   Directly or indirectly has the right to vote 25 percent or more of a class of voting security or has the power to sell or direct the sale of 25 percent or more of a class of voting securities of the broker-dealer of the alternative trading system; or

(3)   In the case of a partnership, has contributed, or has the right to receive upon dissolution, 25 percent or more of the capital of the broker-dealer of the alternative trading system.

(g)   NMS stock shall have the meaning provided in Rule 600 of Regulation NMS, provided, however, that a debt or convertible debt security shall not be deemed a covered security for purposes of Regulation ATS.

(h)   Effective transaction reporting plan shall have the meaning provided in Rule 600 of Regulation NMS.

(i)   Corporate debt security shall mean any security that:

(1)   Evidences a liability of the issuer of such security;

(2)   Has a fixed maturity that is at least on year following the date of issuance; and

(3)   Is not an exempted security as defined in section 3(a)(12) of the Act (15 U.S.C. 78c(a)(12)).

(4)   Is not an exempted security, as defined in section 3(a)(12) of the Act.

(j)   Commercial paper shall mean any note, draft, or bill of exchange which arises out of a current transaction or the proceeds of which have been or are to be used for current transactions, and which has a maturity at the time of issuance of not exceeding nine months, exclusive of days of grace, or any renewal thereof the maturity of which is likewise limited.

(k)   NMS Stock ATS means an alternative trading system, as defined in paragraph (a) of this rule, that trades NMS stocks, as defined in paragraph (g) of this rule.

Rule 301.   Requirements for Alternative Trading Systems

(a)   *Scope of Section.* An alternative trading system shall comply with the requirements in paragraph (b) of this rule, unless such alternative trading system:

(1)   Is registered as an exchange under section 6 of the Act;

(2)   Is exempted by the Commission from registration as an exchange based on the limited volume of transactions effected;

(3)   Is operated by a national securities association;

(4)(i)   Is registered as a broker-dealer under sections 15(b) or 15C of the Act, or is a bank, and

(ii)   Limits its securities activities to the following instruments:

(A)   Government securities, as defined in section 3(a)(42) of the Act;

(B)   Repurchase and reverse repurchase agreements solely involving securities included within paragraph (a)(4)(ii)(A) of this rule;

(C)   Any put, call, straddle, option, or privilege on a government security, other than a put, call, straddle, option, or privilege that:

(1)   Is traded on one or more national securities exchanges; or

(2)   For which quotations are disseminated through an automated quotation system operated by a registered securities association; and

(D)   Commercial paper.

(5)   Is exempted, conditionally or unconditionally, by Commission order, after application by such alternative trading system, from one or more of the requirements of paragraph (b) of this rule or Rule 304. The Commission will grant such exemption only after determining that such an order is consistent with the public interest, the protection of investors, and the removal of impediments to, and perfection of the mechanisms of, a national market system.

(b)   *Requirements.* Every alternative trading system subject to this Regulation ATS, pursuant to paragraph (a) of this rule, shall comply with the requirements in this paragraph (b).

(1)   *Broker-Dealer Registration.* The alternative trading system shall register as a broker-dealer under section 15 of the Act.

(2)   *Notice.*

(i)   The alternative trading system shall file an initial operation report on Form ATS, Rule 637 of the Exchange Act, in accordance with the instructions therein, at least 20 days prior to commencing operation as an alternative trading system.

(ii)   The alternative trading system shall file an amendment on Form ATS at least 20 calendar days prior to implementing a material change to the operation of the alternative trading system.

(iii)   If any information contained in the initial operation report filed under paragraph (b)(2)(i) of this rule becomes inaccurate for any reason and has not been previously reported to the Commission as an amendment on Form ATS, the alternative trading system shall file an amendment on Form ATS correcting such information within 30 calendar days after the end of each calendar quarter in which the alternative trading system has operated.

(iv)   The alternative trading system shall promptly file an amendment on Form ATS correcting information previously reported on Form ATS after discovery that any information filed under paragraphs (b)(2)(i), (ii) or (iii) of this rule was inaccurate when filed.

(v)   The alternative trading system shall promptly file a cessation of operations report on Form ATS in accordance with the instructions therein upon ceasing to operate as an alternative trading system.

(vi)   Every notice or amendment filed pursuant to this paragraph (b)(2) shall constitute a "report" within the meaning of sections 11A, 17(a), 18(a), and 32(a), and any other applicable provisions of the Act.

(vii)   The reports provided for in paragraph (b)(2) of this rule shall be considered filed upon receipt by the Division of Trading and Markets, at the Commission's principal office in Washington, DC. Duplicate originals of the reports provided for in paragraphs (b)(2)(i) through (v) of this rule must be filed with surveillance personnel designated as such by any self-regulatory organization that is the designated examining authority for the alternative trading system pursuant to Rule 17d–1 of the Exchange Act simultaneously with filing with the Commission. Duplicates of the reports required by paragraph (b)(9) of this rule shall be provided to surveillance personnel of such self-regulatory authority upon request. All reports filed pursuant to this paragraph (b)(2) and paragraph (b)(9) of this rule shall be deemed confidential when filed.

(viii)   An NMS Stock ATS that is operating pursuant to an initial operation report on Form ATS on file with the Commission as of January 7, 2019 ("Legacy NMS Stock ATS") shall be subject to the requirements of paragraphs (b)(2)(i) through (vii) of this rule until that ATS files an initial Form ATS-N with the Commission pursuant to Rule 304(a)(1)(iv)(A). Thereafter, the Legacy NMS Stock ATS shall file reports pursuant to Rule 304. An alternative trading system that trades NMS stocks and securities other than NMS stocks shall be subject to the requirements of Rule 304 of this chapter with respect to NMS stocks and paragraph (b)(2) of this rule with respect to non-NMS stocks. As of January 7, 2019, an entity seeking to operate as an NMS Stock ATS shall not be subject to the requirements of paragraphs (b)(2)(i) through (vii) of this rule and shall file reports pursuant to Rule 304.

(3)   *Order Display and Execution Access.*

    (i)   An alternative trading system shall comply with the requirements set forth in paragraph (b)(3)(ii) of this rule, with respect to any NMS stock in which the alternative trading system:

        (A)   Displays subscriber orders to any person (other than alternative trading system employees); and

        (B)   During at least 4 of the preceding 6 calendar months, had an average daily trading volume of 5 percent or more of the aggregate average daily share volume for such NMS stock as reported by an effective transaction reporting plan.

    (ii)   Such alternative trading system shall provide to a national securities exchange or national securities association the prices and sizes of the orders at the highest buy price and the lowest sell price for such NMS stock, displayed to more than one person in the alternative trading system, for inclusion in the quotation data made available by the national securities exchange or national securities association to vendors pursuant to Rule 602 of Regulation NMS.

    (iii)   With respect to any order displayed pursuant to paragraph (b)(3)(ii) of this rule, an alternative trading system shall provide to any broker-dealer that has access to the national securities exchange or national securities association to which the alternative trading system provides the prices and sizes of displayed orders pursuant to paragraph (b)(3)(ii) of this rule, the ability to effect a transaction with such orders that is:

        (A)   Equivalent to the ability of such broker-dealer to effect a transaction with other orders displayed on the exchange or by the association; and

        (B)   At the price of the highest priced buy order or lowest priced sell order displayed for the lesser of the cumulative size of such priced orders entered therein at such price, or the size of the execution sought by such broker-dealer.

(4)   *Fees.* The alternative trading system shall not charge any fee to broker-dealers that access the alternative trading system through a national securities exchange or national securities association, that is inconsistent with equivalent access to the alternative trading system required by paragraph (b)(3)(iii) of this rule. In addition, if the national securities exchange or national securities association to which an alternative trading system provides the prices and sizes of orders under paragraphs (b)(3)(ii) and (b)(3)(iii) of this rule establishes rules designed to assure consistency with standards for access to quotations displayed on such national securities exchange, or the market operated by such national securities association, the alternative trading system shall not charge any fee to members that is contrary to, that is not disclosed in the manner required by, or that is inconsistent with any standard of equivalent access established by such rules.

(5)   *Fair Access.*

    (i)   An alternative trading system shall comply with the requirements in paragraph (b)(5)(ii) of this rule, if during at least 4 of the preceding 6 calendar months, such alternative trading system had:

        (A)   With respect to any NMS stock, 5 percent or more of the average daily volume in that security reported by an effective transaction reporting plan;

        (B)   With respect to an equity security that is not an NMS stock and for which transactions are reported to a self-regulatory organization, 5 percent or more of the average daily trading volume in that security as calculated by the self-regulatory organization to which such transactions are reported;

        (C)   With respect to municipal securities, 5 percent or more of the average daily volume traded in the United States; or

        (D)   With respect to corporate debt securities, 5 percent or more of the average daily volume traded in the United States.

(ii) An alternative trading system shall:

(A) Establish written standards for granting access to trading on its system;

(B) Not unreasonably prohibit or limit any person in respect to access to services offered by such alternative trading system by applying the standards established under paragraph (b)(5)(ii)(A) of this rule in an unfair or discriminatory manner;

(C) Make and keep records of:

(1) All grants of access including, for all subscribers, the reasons for granting such access; and

(2) All denials or limitations of access and reasons, for each applicant, for denying or limiting access;

(D) Report the information required on Form ATS–R, Rule 638 of the Exchange Act, regarding grants, denials, and limitations of access.

(iii) Notwithstanding paragraph (b)(5)(i) of this rule, an alternative trading system shall not be required to comply with the requirements in paragraph (b)(5)(ii) of this rule, if such alternative trading system:

(A) Matches customer orders for a security with other customer orders;

(B) Such customers' orders are not displayed to any person, other than employees of the alternative trading system; and

(C) Such orders are executed at a price for such security disseminated by an effective transaction reporting plan, or derived from such prices.

(6) *Capacity, Integrity, and Security of Automated Systems.*

(i) The alternative trading system shall comply with the requirements in paragraph (b)(6)(ii) of this rule, if during at least 4 of the preceding 6 calendar months, such alternative trading system had:

(A) With respect to municipal securities, 20 percent or more of the average daily volume traded in the United States; or

(B) With respect to corporate debt securities, 20 percent or more of the average daily volume traded in the United States.

(ii) With respect to those systems that support order entry, order routing, order execution, transaction reporting, and trade comparison, the alternative trading system shall:

(A) Establish reasonable current and future capacity estimates;

(B) Conduct periodic capacity stress tests of critical systems to determine such system's ability to process transactions in an accurate, timely, and efficient manner;

(C) Develop and implement reasonable procedures to review and keep current its system development and testing methodology;

(D) Review the vulnerability of its systems and data center computer operations to internal and external threats, physical hazards, and natural disasters;

(E) Establish adequate contingency and disaster recovery plans;

(F) On an annual basis, perform an independent review, in accordance with established audit procedures and standards, of such alternative trading system's controls for ensuring that paragraphs (b)(6)(ii)(A) through (E) of this rule are met, and conduct a review by senior management of a report containing the recommendations and conclusions of the independent review; and

(G) Promptly notify the Commission staff of material systems outages and significant systems changes.

(iii)   Notwithstanding paragraph (b)(6)(i) of this rule, an alternative trading system shall not be required to comply with the requirements in paragraph (b)(6)(ii) of this rule, if such alternative trading system:

    (A)   Matches customer orders for a security with other customer orders;

    (B)   Such customers' orders are not displayed to any person, other than employees of the alternative trading system; and

    (C)   Such orders are executed at a price for such security disseminated by an effective transaction reporting plan, or derived from such prices.

(7)   *Examinations, Inspections, and Investigations.* The alternative trading system shall permit the examination and inspection of its premises, systems, and records, and cooperate with the examination, inspection, or investigation of subscribers, whether such examination is being conducted by the Commission or by a self-regulatory organization of which such subscriber is a member.

(8)   *Recordkeeping.* The alternative trading system shall:

(i)   Make and keep current the records specified in Rule 302; and

(ii)   Preserve the records specified in Rule 303.

(9)   *Reporting.* The alternative trading system shall:

(i)   Separately file the information required by Form ATS–R for transactions in NMS stocks, as defined in paragraph (g) of this rule, and transactions in securities other than NMS stocks within 30 calendar days after the end of each calendar quarter in which the market has operated after the effective date of this rule; and

(ii)   Separately file the information required by Form ATS–R for transactions in NMS stocks and transactions in securities other than NMS stocks within 10 calendar days after an alternative trading system ceases to operate.

(10)   *Written Procedures to Ensure the Confidential Treatment of Trading Information.*

(i)   The alternative trading system shall establish adequate written safeguards and written procedures to protect subscribers' confidential trading information. Such written safeguards and written procedures shall include:

    (A)   Limiting access to the confidential trading information of subscribers to those employees of the alternative trading system who are operating the system or responsible for its compliance with these or any other applicable rules;

    (B)   Implementing standards controlling employees of the alternative trading system trading for their own accounts; and

(ii)   The alternative trading system shall adopt and implement adequate written oversight procedures to ensure that the written safeguards and procedures established pursuant to paragraph (b)(10)(i) of this rule are followed.

(11)   *Name.* The alternative trading system shall not use in its name the word "exchange," or derivations of the word "exchange," such as the term "stock market."

Rule 302.   Recordkeeping Requirements for Alternative Trading Systems

To comply with the condition set forth in paragraph (b)(8) of Rule 301, an alternative trading system shall make and keep current the following records:

(a)   A record of subscribers to such alternative trading system (identifying any affiliations between the alternative trading system and subscribers to the alternative trading system, including common directors, officers, or owners);

(b)   Daily summaries of trading in the alternative trading system including:

(1)   Securities for which transactions have been executed;

(2)   Transaction volume, expressed with respect to equity securities in:

    (i)   Number of trades;

    (ii)   Number of shares traded; and

    (iii) Total settlement value in terms of U.S. dollars; and

  (3) Transaction volume, expressed with respect to debt securities in:

    (i)   Number of trades; and

    (ii)   Total U.S. dollar value; and

(c) Time-sequenced records of order information in the alternative trading system, including:

  (1) Date and time (expressed in terms of hours, minutes, and seconds) that the order was received;

  (2) Identity of the security;

  (3) The number of shares, or principal amount of bonds, to which the order applies;

  (4) An identification of the order as related to a program trade or an index arbitrage trade as defined in New York Stock Exchange Rule 80A;

  (5) The designation of the order as a buy or sell order;

  (6) The designation of the order as a short sale order;

  (7) The designation of the order as a market order, limit order, stop order, stop limit order, or other type or order;

  (8) Any limit or stop price prescribed by the order;

  (9) The date on which the order expires and, if the time in force is less than one day, the time when the order expires;

  (10) The time limit during which the order is in force;

  (11) Any instructions to modify or cancel the order;

  (12) The type of account, i.e., retail, wholesale, employee, proprietary, or any other type of account designated by the alternative trading system, for which the order is submitted;

  (13) Date and time (expressed in terms of hours, minutes, and seconds) that the order was executed;

  (14) Price at which the order was executed;

  (15) Size of the order executed (expressed in number of shares or units or principal amount); and

  (16) Identity of the parties to the transaction.

Rule 303.   Record Preservation Requirements for Alternative Trading Systems

(a) To comply with the condition set forth in paragraph (b)(8) of Rule 301, an alternative trading system shall preserve the following records:

  (1) For a period of not less than three years, the first two years in an easily accessible place, an alternative trading system shall preserve:

    (i)   All records required to be made pursuant to Rule 302;

    (ii)   All notices provided by such alternative trading system to subscribers generally, whether written or communicated through automated means, including, but not limited to, notices addressing hours of system operations, system malfunctions, changes to system procedures, maintenance of hardware and software, instructions pertaining to access to the market and denials of, or limitations on, access to the alternative trading system;

    (iii) If subject to paragraph (b)(5)(ii) of Rule 301, at least one copy of such alternative trading system's standards for access to trading, all documents relevant to the alternative trading systems decision to grant, deny, or limit access to any person, and all other documents made or received by the alternative trading system in the course of complying with paragraph (b)(5) of Rule 301; and

(iv) At least one copy of all documents made or received by the alternative trading system in the course of complying with paragraph (b)(6) of Rule 301, including all correspondence, memoranda, papers, books, notices, accounts, reports, test scripts, test results, and other similar records.

(v) At least one copy of the written safeguards and written procedures to protect subscribers' confidential trading information and the written oversight procedures created in the course of complying with paragraph (b)(10) of Rule 301.

(2) During the life of the enterprise and of any successor enterprise, an alternative trading system shall preserve:

(i) All partnership articles or, in the case of a corporation, all articles of incorporation or charter, minute books and stock certificate books; and

(ii) Copies of reports filed pursuant to paragraph (b)(2) of Rule 301 or Rule 304 and records made pursuant to paragraph (b)(5) of Rule 301.

(b) The records required to be maintained and preserved pursuant to paragraph (a) of this rule must be produced, reproduced, and maintained in paper form or in any of the forms permitted under Rule 17a–4(f) under the Exchange Act.

(c) Alternative trading systems must comply with any other applicable recordkeeping or reporting requirement in the Act, and the rules and regulations thereunder. If the information in a record required to be made pursuant to this rule is preserved in a record made pursuant to Rule 17a–3 or Rule 17a–4 under the Exchange Act, or otherwise preserved by the alternative trading system (whether in summary or some other form), this rule shall not require the sponsor to maintain such information in a separate file, provided that the sponsor can promptly sort and retrieve the information as if it had been kept in a separate file as a record made pursuant to this rule, and preserves the information in accordance with the time periods specified in paragraph (a) of this rule.

(d) The records required to be maintained and preserved pursuant to this rule may be prepared or maintained by a service bureau, depository, or other recordkeeping service on behalf of the alternative trading system. An agreement with a service bureau, depository, or other recordkeeping service shall not relieve the alternative trading system from the responsibility to prepare and maintain records as specified in this rule. The service bureau, depository, or other recordkeeping service shall file with the Commission a written undertaking in a form acceptable to the Commission, signed by a duly authorized person, to the effect that such records are the property of the alternative trading system required to be maintained and preserved and will be surrendered promptly on request of the alternative trading system, and shall include the following provision: With respect to any books and records maintained or preserved on behalf of (name of alternative trading system), the undersigned hereby undertakes to permit examination of such books and records at any time, or from time to time, during business hours by the staff of the Securities and Exchange Commission, any self-regulatory organization of which the alternative trading system is a member, or any State securities regulator having jurisdiction over the alternative trading system, and to promptly furnish to the Commission, self-regulatory organization of which the alternative trading system is a member, or any State securities regulator having jurisdiction over the alternative trading system a true, correct, complete and current hard copy of any, all, or any part of, such books and records.

(e) Every alternative trading system shall furnish to any representative of the Commission promptly upon request, legible, true, and complete copies of those records that are required to be preserved under this rule.

CUSTOMER MARGIN REQUIREMENTS FOR SECURITY FUTURES

17 C.F.R. § 242.___

Rule 400.   Customer Margin Requirements for Security Futures—Authority, Purpose, Interpretation, and Scope

(a)   *Authority and Purpose.* Rules 400 through 406 and 17 CFR 41.42 through 41.49 ("this Regulation, Rules 400 through 406") are issued by the Securities and Exchange Commission ("Commission") jointly with the Commodity Futures Trading Commission ("CFTC"), pursuant to authority delegated by the Board of Governors of the Federal Reserve System under section 7(c)(2)(A) of the Securities Exchange Act of 1934 ("Act"). The principal purpose of this Regulation is to regulate customer margin collected by brokers, dealers, and members of national securities exchanges, including futures commission merchants required to register as brokers or dealers under section 15(b)(11) of the Act, relating to security futures.

(b)   *Interpretation.* This Regulation shall be jointly interpreted by the Commission and the CFTC, consistent with the criteria set forth in clauses (i) through (iv) of section 7(c)(2)(B) of the Act and the provisions of Regulation T.

(c)   *Scope.*

(1)   This Regulation does not preclude a self-regulatory authority, under rules that are effective in accordance with section 19(b)(2) of the Act or section 19(b)(7) of the Act and, as applicable, section 5c(c) of the Commodity Exchange Act ("CEA"), or a security futures intermediary from imposing additional margin requirements on security futures, including higher initial or maintenance margin levels, consistent with this Regulation, or from taking appropriate action to preserve its financial integrity.

(2)   This Regulation does not apply to:

(i)   Financial relations between a customer and a security futures intermediary to the extent that they comply with a portfolio margining system under rules that meet the criteria set forth in section 7(c)(2)(B) of the Act and that are effective in accordance with section 19(b)(2) of the Act and, as applicable, section 5c(c) of the CEA;

(ii)   Financial relations between a security futures intermediary and a foreign person involving security futures traded on or subject to the rules of a foreign board of trade;

(iii)   Margin requirements that clearing agencies registered under section 17A of the Exchange Act or derivatives clearing organizations registered under section 5b of the CEA impose on their members;

(iv)   Financial relations between a security futures intermediary and a person based on a good faith determination by the security futures intermediary that such person is an exempted person; and

(v) Financial relations between a security futures intermediary and, or arranged by a security futures intermediary for, a person relating to trading in security futures by such person for its own account, if such person:

(A) Is a member of a national securities exchange or national securities association registered pursuant to section 15A(a) of the Act; and

(B) Is registered with such exchange or such association as a security futures dealer pursuant to rules that are effective in accordance with section 19(b)(2) of the Act and, as applicable, section 5c(c) of the CEA, that:

(1) Require such member to be registered as a floor trader or a floor broker with the CFTC under Section 4f(a)(1) of the CEA, or as a dealer with the Commission under section 15(b) of the Act;

(2) Require such member to maintain records sufficient to prove compliance with this paragraph (c)(2)(v) and the rules of the exchange or association of which it is a member;

(3) Require such member to hold itself out as being willing to buy and sell security futures for its own account on a regular or continuous basis; and

(4) Provide for disciplinary action, including revocation of such member's registration as a security futures dealer, for such member's failure to comply with this Regulation or the rules of the exchange or association.

(d) *Exemption.* The Commission may exempt, either unconditionally or on specified terms and conditions, financial relations involving any security futures intermediary, customer, position, or transaction, or any class of security futures intermediaries, customers, positions, or transactions, from one or more requirements of this Regulation (Rules 400–406), if the Commission determines that such exemption is necessary or appropriate in the public interest and consistent with the protection of investors. An exemption granted pursuant to this paragraph shall not operate as an exemption from any CFTC rules. Any exemption that may be required from such rules must be obtained separately from the CFTC.

Rule 401.   Definitions

(a) For purposes of this Regulation only, the following terms shall have the meanings set forth in this rule.

(1) Applicable margin rules and margin rules applicable to an account mean the rules and regulations applicable to financial relations between a security futures intermediary and a customer with respect to security futures and related positions carried in a securities account or futures account as provided in Rule 402(a) of this Regulation.

(2) Broker shall have the meaning provided in section 3(a)(4) of the Act.

(3) Contract multiplier means the number of units of a narrow-based security index expressed as a dollar amount, in accordance with the terms of the security future contract.

(4) Current market value means, on any day:

(i) With respect to a security future:

(A) If the instrument underlying such security future is a stock, the product of the daily settlement price of such security future as shown by any regularly published reporting or quotation service, and the applicable number of shares per contract; or

(B) If the instrument underlying such security future is a narrow-based security index, as defined in section 3(a)(55)(B) of the Act, the product of the daily settlement price of such security future as shown by any regularly published reporting or quotation service, and the applicable contract multiplier.

(ii) With respect to a security other than a security future, the most recent closing sale price of the security, as shown by any regularly published reporting or quotation service. If there is no recent closing sale price, the security futures intermediary may use any reasonable estimate of the market value of the security as of the most recent close of business.

(5)   Customer excludes an exempted person and includes:

(i)   Any person or persons acting jointly:

(A)   On whose behalf a security futures intermediary effects a security futures transaction or carries a security futures position; or

(B)   Who would be considered a customer of the security futures intermediary according to the ordinary usage of the trade;

(ii)   Any partner in a security futures intermediary that is organized as a partnership who would be considered a customer of the security futures intermediary absent the partnership relationship; and

(iii)   Any joint venture in which a security futures intermediary participates and which would be considered a customer of the security futures intermediary if the security futures intermediary were not a participant.

(6)   Daily settlement price means, with respect to a security future, the settlement price of such security future determined at the close of trading each day, under the rules of the applicable exchange, clearing agency, or derivatives clearing organization.

(7)   Dealer shall have the meaning provided in section 3(a)(5) of the Act.

(8)   Equity means the equity or margin equity in a securities or futures account, as computed in accordance with the margin rules applicable to the account and subject to adjustment under Rule 404(c), (d) and (e) of this Regulation.

(9)   Exempted person means:

(i)   A member of a national securities exchange, a registered broker or dealer, or a registered futures commission merchant, a substantial portion of whose business consists of transactions in securities, commodity futures, or commodity options with persons other than brokers, dealers, futures commission merchants, floor brokers, or floor traders, and includes a person who:

(A)   Maintains at least 1000 active accounts on an annual basis for persons other than brokers, dealers, persons associated with a broker or dealer, futures commission merchants, floor brokers, floor traders, and persons affiliated with a futures commission merchant, floor broker, or floor trader that are effecting transactions in securities, commodity futures, or commodity options;

(B)   Earns at least $10 million in gross revenues on an annual basis from transactions in securities, commodity futures, or commodity options with persons other than brokers, dealers, persons associated with a broker or dealer, futures commission merchants, floor brokers, floor traders, and persons affiliated with a futures commission merchant, floor broker, or floor trader; or

(C)   Earns at least 10 percent of its gross revenues on an annual basis from transactions in securities, commodity futures, or commodity options with persons other than brokers, dealers, persons associated with a broker or dealer, futures commission merchants, floor brokers, floor traders, and persons affiliated with a futures commission merchant, floor broker, or floor trader.

(ii)   For purposes of paragraph (a)(9)(i) of this rule only, persons affiliated with a futures commission merchant, floor broker, or floor trader means any partner, officer, director, or branch manager of such futures commission merchant, floor broker, or floor trader (or any person occupying a similar status or performing similar functions), any person directly or indirectly controlling, controlled by, or under common control with such futures commission merchant, floor broker, or floor trader, or any employee of such a futures commission merchant, floor broker, or floor trader.

(iii) A member of a national securities exchange, a registered broker or dealer, or a registered futures commission merchant that has been in existence for less than one year may meet the definition of exempted person based on a six-month period.

(10) Exempted security shall have the meaning provided in section 3(a)(12) of the Act.

(11) Floor broker shall have the meaning provided in Section 1a(16) of the CEA.

(12) Floor trader shall have the meaning provided in Section 1a(17) of the CEA.

(13) Futures account shall have the meaning provided in Rule 15c3–3(a) under the Exchange Act.

(14) Futures commission merchant shall have the meaning provided in Section 1a of the CEA.

(15) Good faith, with respect to making a determination or accepting a statement concerning financial relations with a person, means that the security futures intermediary is alert to the circumstances surrounding such financial relations, and if in possession of information that would cause a prudent person not to make the determination or accept the notice or certification without inquiry, investigates and is satisfied that it is correct.

(16) Listed option means a put or call option that is:

(i)   Issued by a clearing agency that is registered under section 17A of the Act or cleared and guaranteed by a derivatives clearing organization that is registered under Section 5b of the CEA; and

(ii)   Traded on or subject to the rules of a self-regulatory authority.

(17) Margin call means a demand by a security futures intermediary to a customer for a deposit of cash, securities or other assets to satisfy the required margin for security futures or related positions or a special margin requirement.

(18) Margin deficiency means the amount by which the required margin in an account is not satisfied by the equity in the account, as computed in accordance with Rule 404 of this Regulation.

(19) Margin equity security shall have the meaning provided in Regulation T.

(20) Margin security shall have the meaning provided in Regulation T.

(21) Member shall have the meaning provided in section 3(a)(3) of the Act, and shall include persons registered under section 15(b)(11) of the Act that are permitted to effect transactions on a national securities exchange without the services of another person acting as executing broker.

(22) Money market mutual fund means any security issued by an investment company registered under section 8 of the Investment Company Act of 1940 that is considered a money market fund under Rule 2a–7 of this Act.

(23) Persons associated with a broker or dealer shall have the meaning provided in section 3(a)(18) of the Act.

(24) Regulation T means Regulation T promulgated by the Board of Governors of the Federal Reserve System, 12 CFR part 220, as amended from time to time.

(25) Regulation T collateral value, with respect to a security, means the current market value of the security reduced by the percentage of required margin for a position in the security held in a margin account under Regulation T.

(26) Related position, with respect to a security future, means any position in an account that is combined with the security future to create an offsetting position as provided in Rule 403(b)(2) of this Regulation.

(27) Related transaction, with respect to a position or transaction in a security future, means:

(i)   Any transaction that creates, eliminates, increases or reduces an offsetting position involving a security future and a related position, as provided in Rule 403(b)(2) of this Regulation; or

(ii)   Any deposit or withdrawal of margin for the security future or a related position, except as provided in Rule 405(b) of this Regulation.

(28) Securities account shall have the meaning provided in Rule 15c3–3(a) of the Exchange Act.

(29) Security futures intermediary means any creditor as defined in Regulation T with respect to its financial relations with any person involving security futures.

(30) Self-regulatory authority means a national securities exchange registered under section 6 of the Act, a national securities association registered under section 15A of the Act, a contract market registered under Section 5 of the CEA or Section 5f of the CEA, or a derivatives transaction execution facility registered under Section 5a of the CEA.

(31) Special margin requirement shall have the meaning provided in Rule 404(e)(1)(ii) of this Regulation.

(32) Variation settlement means any credit or debit to a customer account, made on a daily or intraday basis, for the purpose of marking to market a security future or any other contract that is:

(i)   Issued by a clearing agency that is registered under section 17A of the Act or cleared and guaranteed by a derivatives clearing organization that is registered under Section 5b of the CEA; and

(ii)   Traded on or subject to the rules of a self-regulatory authority.

(b)   Terms used in this Regulation and not otherwise defined in this rule shall have the meaning set forth in the margin rules applicable to the account.

(c)   Terms used in this Regulation and not otherwise defined in this rule or in the margin rules applicable to the account shall have the meaning set forth in the Act and the CEA; if the definitions of a term in the Act and the CEA are inconsistent as applied in particular circumstances, such term shall have the meaning set forth in rules, regulations, or interpretations jointly promulgated by the Commission and the CFTC.

Rule 402.   General Provisions

(a)   *Applicable Margin Rules.* Except to the extent inconsistent with this Regulation:

(1)   A security futures intermediary that carries a security future on behalf of a customer in a securities account shall record and conduct all financial relations with respect to such security future and related positions in accordance with Regulation T and the margin rules of the self-regulatory authorities of which the security futures intermediary is a member.

(2)   A security futures intermediary that carries a security future on behalf of a customer in a futures account shall record and conduct all financial relations with respect to such security future and related positions in accordance with the margin rules of the self-regulatory authorities of which the security futures intermediary is a member.

(b)   *Separation and Consolidation of Accounts.*

(1)   The requirements for security futures and related positions in one account may not be met by considering items in any other account, except as permitted or required under paragraph (b)(2) of this rule or applicable margin rules. If withdrawals of cash, securities or other assets deposited as margin are permitted under this Regulation, bookkeeping entries shall be made when such cash, securities, or assets are used for purposes of meeting requirements in another account.

(2)   Notwithstanding paragraph (b)(1) of this rule, the security futures intermediary shall consider all futures accounts in which security futures and related positions are held that are within the same regulatory classification or account type and are owned by the same customer to be a single account for purposes of this Regulation. The security futures intermediary may combine such accounts with other futures accounts that are within the same regulatory classification or account type and are owned by the same customer for purposes of computing a customer's overall margin requirement, as permitted or required by applicable margin rules.

(c) *Accounts of Partners.* If a partner of the security futures intermediary has an account with the security futures intermediary in which security futures or related positions are held, the security futures intermediary shall disregard the partner's financial relations with the firm (as shown in the partner's capital and ordinary drawing accounts) in calculating the margin or equity of any such account.

(d) *Contribution to Joint Venture.* If an account in which security futures or related positions are held is the account of a joint venture in which the security futures intermediary participates, any interest of the security futures intermediary in the joint account in excess of the interest which the security futures intermediary would have on the basis of its right to share in the profits shall be margined in accordance with this Regulation.

(e) *Extensions of Credit.*

(1) No security futures intermediary may extend or maintain credit to or for any customer for the purpose of evading or circumventing any requirement under this Regulation (Rules 400–406).

(2) A security futures intermediary may arrange for the extension or maintenance of credit to or for any customer by any person, provided that the security futures intermediary does not willfully arrange credit that would constitute a violation of Regulation T, U or X of the Board of Governors of the Federal Reserve System by such person.

(f) *Change in Exempted Person Status.* Once a person ceases to qualify as an exempted person, it shall notify the security futures intermediary of this fact before entering into any new security futures transaction or related transaction that would require additional margin to be deposited under this Regulation. Financial relations with respect to any such transactions shall be subject to the provisions of this Regulation.

Rule 403.   Required Margin

(a) *Applicability.* Each security futures intermediary shall determine the required margin for the security futures and related positions held on behalf of a customer in a securities account or futures account as set forth in this rule.

(b) *Required Margin.—*

(1) *General Rule.* The required margin for each long or short position in a security future shall be twenty (20) percent of the current market value of such security future.

(2) *Offsetting Positions.* Notwithstanding the margin levels specified in paragraph (b)(1) of this rule, a self-regulatory authority may set the required initial or maintenance margin level for an offsetting position involving security futures and related positions at a level lower than the level that would be required under paragraph (b)(1) of this rule if such positions were margined separately, pursuant to rules that meet the criteria set forth in section 7(c)(2)(B) of the Act and are effective in accordance with section 19(b)(2) of the Act and, as applicable, Section 5c(c) of the CEA.

(c) *Procedures for Certain Margin Level Adjustments.* An exchange registered under section 6(g) of the Act, or a national securities association registered under section 15A(k) of the Act, may raise or lower the required margin level for a security future to a level not lower than that specified in this rule, in accordance with section 19(b)(7) of the Act.

Rule 404.   Type, Form and Use of Margin

(a) *When Margin is Required.* Margin is required to be deposited whenever the required margin for security futures and related positions in an account is not satisfied by the equity in the account, subject to adjustment under paragraph (c) of this rule.

(b) *Acceptable Margin Deposits.*

(1) The required margin may be satisfied by a deposit of cash, margin securities (subject to paragraph (b)(2) of this rule), exempted securities, any other asset permitted under Regulation T to satisfy a margin deficiency in a securities margin account, or any combination thereof, each as valued in accordance with paragraph (c) of this rule.

(2)   Shares of a money market mutual fund may be accepted as a margin deposit for purposes of this Regulation, provided that:

(i)   The customer waives any right to redeem the shares without the consent of the security futures intermediary and instructs the fund or its transfer agent accordingly;

(ii)   The security futures intermediary (or clearing agency or derivatives clearing organization with which the shares are deposited as margin) obtains the right to redeem the shares in cash, promptly upon request; and

(iii)   The fund agrees to satisfy any conditions necessary or appropriate to ensure that the shares may be redeemed in cash, promptly upon request.

(c)   *Adjustments.*

(1)   Futures accounts. For purposes of this rule, the equity in a futures account shall be computed in accordance with the margin rules applicable to the account, subject to the following:

(i)   A security future shall have no value;

(ii)   Each net long or short position in a listed option on a contract for future delivery shall be valued in accordance with the margin rules applicable to the account;

(iii)   Except as permitted in paragraph (e) of this rule, each margin equity security shall be valued at an amount no greater than its Regulation T collateral value;

(iv)   Each other security shall be valued at an amount no greater than its current market value reduced by the percentage specified for such security in Rule 15c3–1(c)(2)(vi) under the Exchange Act;

(v)   Freely convertible foreign currency may be valued at an amount no greater than its daily marked-to-market U.S. dollar equivalent;

(vi)   Variation settlement receivable (or payable) by an account at the close of trading on any day shall be treated as a credit (or debit) to the account on that day; and

(vii)   Each other acceptable margin deposit or component of equity shall be valued at an amount no greater than its value under Regulation T.

(2)   *Securities Accounts.* For purposes of this rule, the equity in a securities account shall be computed in accordance with the margin rules applicable to the account, subject to the following:

(i)   A security future shall have no value;

(ii)   Freely convertible foreign currency may be valued at an amount no greater than its daily mark-to-market U.S. dollar equivalent; and

(iii)   Variation settlement receivable (or payable) to an account at the close of trading on any day shall be treated as a credit (or debit) by the account on that day.

(d)   *Satisfaction Restriction.* Any transaction, position or deposit that is used to satisfy the required margin for security futures or related positions under this Regulation, including a related position, shall be unavailable to satisfy the required margin for any other position or transaction or any other requirement.

(e)   *Alternative Collateral Valuation for Margin Equity Securities in a Futures Account.*

(1)   Notwithstanding paragraph (c)(1)(iii) of this rule, a security futures intermediary need not value a margin equity security at its Regulation T collateral value when determining whether the required margin for the security futures and related positions in a futures account is satisfied, provided that:

(i)   The margin equity security is valued at an amount no greater than the current market value of the security reduced by the lowest percentage level of margin required for a long position in the security held in a margin account under the rules of a national securities exchange registered pursuant to section 6(a) of the Act;

(ii)   Additional margin is required to be deposited on any day when the day's security futures transactions and related transactions would create or increase a margin deficiency in the account if the margin equity securities were valued at their Regulation T collateral value, and shall be for the amount of the margin deficiency so created or increased (a "special margin requirement"); and

(iii)　Cash, securities, or other assets deposited as margin for the positions in an account are not permitted to be withdrawn from the account at any time that:

(A)　Additional cash, securities, or other assets are required to be deposited as margin under this rule for a transaction in the account on the same or a previous day; or

(B)　The withdrawal, together with other transactions, deposits, and withdrawals on the same day, would create or increase a margin deficiency if the margin equity securities were valued at their Regulation T collateral value.

(2)　All security futures transactions and related transactions on any day shall be combined to determine the amount of a special margin requirement. Additional margin deposited to satisfy a special margin requirement shall be valued at an amount no greater than its Regulation T collateral value.

(3)　If the alternative collateral valuation method set forth in paragraph (e) of this rule is used with respect to an account in which security futures or related positions are carried:

(i)　An account that is transferred from one security futures intermediary to another may be treated as if it had been maintained by the transferee from the date of its origin, if the transferee accepts, in good faith, a signed statement of the transferor (or, if that is not practicable, of the customer), that any margin call issued under this Regulation (Rules 400–406) has been satisfied; and

(ii)　An account that is transferred from one customer to another as part of a transaction, not undertaken to avoid the requirements of this Regulation, may be treated as if it had been maintained for the transferee from the date of its origin, if the security futures intermediary accepts in good faith and keeps with the transferee account a signed statement of the transferor describing the circumstances for the transfer.

(f)　*Guarantee of Accounts.* No guarantee of a customer's account shall be given any effect for purposes of determining whether the required margin in an account is satisfied, except as permitted under applicable margin rules.

Rule 405.　　Withdrawal of Margin

(a)　*By the Customer.* Except as otherwise provided in Rule 404(e)(1)(ii) of this Regulation, cash, securities, or other assets deposited as margin for positions in an account may be withdrawn, provided that the equity in the account after such withdrawal is sufficient to satisfy the required margin for the security futures and related positions in the account under this Regulation.

(b)　*By the Security Futures Intermediary.* Notwithstanding paragraph (a) of this rule, the security futures intermediary, in its usual practice, may deduct the following items from an account in which security futures or related positions are held if they are considered in computing the balance of such account:

(1)　Variation settlement payable, directly or indirectly, to a clearing agency that is registered under section 17A of the Act or a derivatives clearing organization that is registered under section 5b of the CEA;

(2)　Interest charged on credit maintained in the account;

(3)　Communication or shipping charges with respect to transactions in the account;

(4)　Payment of commissions, brokerage, taxes, storage and other charges lawfully accruing in connection with the positions and transactions in the account;

(5)　Any service charges that the security futures intermediary may impose; or

(6)　Any other withdrawals that are permitted from a securities margin account under Regulation T, to the extent permitted under applicable margin rules.

Rule 406.   Undermargined Accounts

(a)   *Failure to Satisfy Margin Call.* If any margin call required by this Regulation is not met in full, the security futures intermediary shall take the deduction required with respect to an undermargined account in computing its net capital under Commission or CFTC rules.

(b)   *Accounts that Liquidate to a Deficit.* If at any time there is a liquidating deficit in an account in which security futures are held, the security futures intermediary shall take steps to liquidate positions in the account promptly and in an orderly manner.

(c)   *Liquidation of Undermargined Accounts Not Required.* Notwithstanding Section 402(a) of this Regulation, section 220.4(d) of Regulation T respecting liquidation of positions in lieu of deposit shall not apply with respect to security futures carried in a securities account.

REGULATION AC—ANALYST CERTIFICATION

17 C.F.R. § 242.___

Rule 500.   Definitions

For purposes of Regulation AC (Rules 500–505 of this Regulation) the term:

Covered person of a broker or dealer means an associated person of that broker or dealer but does not include:

(1)   An associated person:

(i)   If the associated person has no officers (or persons performing similar functions) or employees in common with the broker or dealer who can influence the activities of research analysts or the content of research reports; and

(ii)   If the broker or dealer maintains and enforces written policies and procedures reasonably designed to prevent the broker or dealer, any controlling persons, officers (or persons performing similar functions), and employees of the broker or dealer from influencing the activities of research analysts and the content of research reports prepared by the associated person.

(2)   An associated person who is an investment adviser:

(i)   Not registered with the Commission as an investment adviser because of the prohibition of section 203A of the Investment Advisers Act of 1940; and

(ii)   Not registered or required to be registered with the Commission as a broker or dealer.

Note to definition of covered person: An associated person of a broker or dealer who is not a covered person continues to be subject to the federal securities laws, including the anti-fraud provisions of the federal securities laws.

Foreign person means any person who is not a U.S. person.

Foreign security means a security issued by a foreign issuer for which a U.S. market is not the principal trading market.

Public appearance means any participation by a research analyst in a seminar, forum (including an interactive electronic forum), or radio or television or other interview, in which the research analyst makes a specific recommendation or provides information reasonably sufficient upon which to base an investment decision about a security or an issuer.

Registered broker or dealer means a broker or dealer registered or required to register pursuant to section 15 or section 15B of the Securities Exchange Act of 1934 or a government securities broker or government securities dealer registered or required to register pursuant to section 15C(a)(1)(A) under the Securities Exchange Act of 1934.

Research analyst means any natural person who is primarily responsible for the preparation of the content of a research report.

Research report means a written communication (including an electronic communication) that includes an analysis of a security or an issuer and provides information reasonably sufficient upon which to base an investment decision.

Third party research analyst means:

(1)   With respect to a broker or dealer, any research analyst not employed by that broker or dealer or any associated person of that broker or dealer; and

(2)   With respect to a covered person of a broker or dealer, any research analyst not employed by that covered person, by the broker or dealer with whom that covered person is associated, or by any other associated person of the broker or dealer with whom that covered person is associated.

United States has the meaning contained in Rule 902(*l*) under the Securities Act.

U.S. person has the meaning contained in Rule 902(k) under the Securities Act.

Rule 501.   Certifications in Connection With Research Reports

(a)   A broker or dealer or covered person that publishes, circulates, or provides a research report prepared by a research analyst to a U.S. person in the United States shall include in that research report a clear and prominent certification by the research analyst containing the following:

(1)   A statement attesting that all of the views expressed in the research report accurately reflect the research analyst's personal views about any and all of the subject securities or issuers; and

(2)(i)   A statement attesting that no part of the research analyst's compensation was, is, or will be, directly or indirectly, related to the specific recommendations or views expressed by the research analyst in the research report; or

(ii)   A statement:

(A)   Attesting that part or all of the research analyst's compensation was, is, or will be, directly or indirectly, related to the specific recommendations or views expressed by the research analyst in the research report;

(B)   Identifying the source, amount, and purpose of such compensation; and

(C)   Further disclosing that the compensation could influence the recommendations or views expressed in the research report.

(b)   A broker or dealer or covered person that publishes, circulates, or provides a research report prepared by a third party research analyst to a U.S. person in the United States shall be exempt from the requirements of this rule with respect to such research report if the following conditions are satisfied:

(1)   The employer of the third party research analyst has no officers (or persons performing similar functions) or employees in common with the broker or dealer or covered person; and

(2)   The broker or dealer (or, with respect to a covered person, the broker or dealer with whom the covered person is associated) maintains and enforces written policies and procedures reasonably designed to prevent the broker or dealer, any controlling persons, officers (or persons performing similar functions), and employees of the broker or dealer from influencing the activities of the third party research analyst and the content of research reports prepared by the third party research analyst.

Rule 502.   Certifications in Connection With Public Appearances

(a)   If a broker or dealer publishes, circulates, or provides a research report prepared by a research analyst employed by the broker or dealer or covered person to a U.S. person in the United States, the broker or dealer must make a record within 30 days after any calendar quarter in which the research analyst made a public appearance that contains the following:

(1)   A statement by the research analyst attesting that the views expressed by the research analyst in all public appearances during the calendar quarter accurately reflected the research analyst's personal views at that time about any and all of the subject securities or issuers; and

(2) A statement by the research analyst attesting that no part of the research analyst's compensation was, is, or will be, directly or indirectly, related to the specific recommendations or views expressed by the research analyst in such public appearances.

(b) If the broker or dealer does not obtain a statement by the research analyst in accordance with paragraph (a) of this rule:

(1) The broker or dealer shall promptly notify in writing its examining authority, designated pursuant to section 17(d) of the Securities Exchange Act of 1934 and Rule 17d–2 of the Exchange Act, that the research analyst did not provide the certifications specified in paragraph (a) of this rule; and

(2) For 120 days following notification pursuant to paragraph (b)(1) of this rule, the broker or dealer shall disclose in any research report prepared by the research analyst and published, circulated, or provided to a U.S. person in the United States that the research analyst did not provide the certifications specified in paragraph (a) of this rule.

(c) In the case of a research analyst who is employed outside the United States by a foreign person located outside the United States, this rule shall only apply to a public appearance while the research analyst is physically present in the United States.

(d) A broker or dealer shall preserve the records specified in paragraphs (a) and (b) of this rule in accordance with Rule 17a–4 under the Exchange Act and for a period of not less than 3 years, the first 2 years in an accessible place.

Rule 503.   Certain Foreign Research Reports

A foreign person, located outside the United States and not associated with a registered broker or dealer, who prepares a research report concerning a foreign security and provides it to a U.S. person in the United States in accordance with the provisions of Rule 15a–6(a)(2) under the Exchange Act shall be exempt from the requirements of this regulation.

Rule 504.   Notification to Associated Persons

A broker or dealer shall notify any person with whom that broker or dealer is associated who publishes, circulates, or provides research reports:

(a) Whether the broker or dealer maintains and enforces written policies and procedures reasonably designed to prevent the broker or dealer, any controlling persons, officers (or persons performing similar functions), or employees of the broker or dealer from influencing the activities of research analysts and the content of research reports prepared by the associated person; and

(b) Whether the associated person has any officers (or persons performing similar functions) or employees in common with the broker or dealer who can influence the activities of research analysts or the content of research reports and, if so, the identity of those persons.

Rule 505.   Exclusion for News Media

No provision of this Regulation AC shall apply to any person who:

(a) Is the publisher of any bona fide newspaper, news magazine or business or financial publication of general and regular circulation; and

(b) Is not registered or required to be registered with the Commission as a broker or dealer or investment adviser.

17 C.F.R. § 242.___

Rule 600. NMS Security Designation and Definitions

(a) The term national market system security as used in section 11A(a)(2) of the Act shall mean any NMS security as defined in paragraph (b) of this rule.

(b) For purposes of Regulation NMS, the following definitions shall apply:

(1) Actionable indication of interest means any indication of interest that explicitly or implicitly conveys all of the following information with respect to any order available at the venue sending the indication of interest:

(i) Symbol;

(ii) Side (buy or sell);

(iii) A price that is equal to or better than the national best bid for buy orders and the national best offer for sell orders; and

(iv) A size that is at least equal to one round lot.

(2) Aggregate quotation size means the sum of the quotation sizes of all responsible brokers or dealers who have communicated on any national securities exchange bids or offers for an NMS security at the same price.

(3) Alternative trading system has the meaning provided in Rule 300(a) of Regulation M.

(4) Automated quotation means a quotation displayed by a trading center that:

(i) Permits an incoming order to be marked as immediate-or-cancel;

(ii) Immediately and automatically executes an order marked as immediate-or-cancel against the displayed quotation up to its full size;

(iii) Immediately and automatically cancels any unexecuted portion of an order marked as immediate-or-cancel without routing the order elsewhere;

(iv) Immediately and automatically transmits a response to the sender of an order marked as immediate-or-cancel indicating the action taken with respect to such order; and

(v)   Immediately and automatically displays information that updates the displayed quotation to reflect any change to its material terms.

(5)   Automated trading center means a trading center that:

(i)   Has implemented such systems, procedures, and rules as are necessary to render it capable of displaying quotations that meet the requirements for an automated quotation set forth in paragraph (b)(4) of this rule;

(ii)   Identifies all quotations other than automated quotations as manual quotations;

(iii)   Immediately identifies its quotations as manual quotations whenever it has reason to believe that it is not capable of displaying automated quotations; and

(iv)   Has adopted reasonable standards limiting when its quotations change from automated quotations to manual quotations, and vice versa, to specifically defined circumstances that promote fair and efficient access to its automated quotations and are consistent with the maintenance of fair and orderly markets.

(6)   Average effective spread means the share-weighted average of effective spreads for order executions calculated, for buy orders, as double the amount of difference between the execution price and the midpoint of the national best bid and national best offer at the time of order receipt and, for sell orders, as double the amount of difference between the midpoint of the national best bid and national best offer at the time of order receipt and the execution price.

(7)   Average realized spread means the share-weighted average of realized spreads for order executions calculated, for buy orders, as double the amount of difference between the execution price and the midpoint of the national best bid and national best offer five minutes after the time of order execution and, for sell orders, as double the amount of difference between the midpoint of the national best bid and national best offer five minutes after the time of order execution and the execution price; provided, however, that the midpoint of the final national best bid and national best offer disseminated for regular trading hours shall be used to calculate a realized spread if it is disseminated less than five minutes after the time of order execution.

(8)   Best bid and best offer mean the highest priced bid and the lowest priced offer.

(9)   Bid or offer means the bid price or the offer price communicated by a member of a national securities exchange or member of a national securities association to any broker or dealer, or to any customer, at which it is willing to buy or sell one or more round lots of an NMS security, as either principal or agent, but shall not include indications of interest.

(10)   Block size with respect to an order means it is:

(i)   Of at least 10,000 shares; or

(ii)   For a quantity of stock having a market value of at least $200,000.

(11)   Categorized by order size means dividing orders into separate categories for sizes from 100 to 499 shares, from 500 to 1999 shares, from 2000 to 4999 shares, and 5000 or greater shares.

(12)   Categorized by order type means dividing orders into separate categories for market orders, marketable limit orders, inside-the-quote limit orders, at-the-quote limit orders, and near-the-quote limit orders.

(13)   Categorized by security means dividing orders into separate categories for each NMS stock that is included in a report.

(14)   Consolidated display means:

(i)   The prices, sizes, and market identifications of the national best bid and national best offer for a security; and

(ii)   Consolidated last sale information for a security.

(15)   Consolidated last sale information means the price, volume, and market identification of the most recent transaction report for a security that is disseminated pursuant to an effective national market system plan.

(16) Covered order means any market order or any limit order (including immediate-or-cancel orders) received by a market center during regular trading hours at a time when a national best bid and national best offer is being disseminated, and, if executed, is executed during regular trading hours, but shall exclude any order for which the customer requests special handling for execution, including, but not limited to, orders to be executed at a market opening price or a market closing price, orders submitted with stop prices, orders to be executed only at their full size, orders to be executed on a particular type of tick or bid, orders submitted on a "not held" basis, orders for other than regular settlement, and orders to be executed at prices unrelated to the market price of the security at the time of execution.

(17) Customer means any person that is not a broker or dealer.

(18) Customer limit order means an order to buy or sell an NMS stock at a specified price that is not for the account of either a broker or dealer; provided, however, that the term customer limit order shall include an order transmitted by a broker or dealer on behalf of a customer.

(19) Customer order means an order to buy or sell an NMS security that is not for the account of a broker or dealer, but shall not include any order for a quantity of a security having a market value of at least $50,000 for an NMS security that is an option contract and a market value of at least $200,000 for any other NMS security.

(20) Directed order means an order from a customer that the customer specifically instructed the broker or dealer to route to a particular venue for execution.

(21) Dynamic market monitoring device means any service provided by a vendor on an interrogation device or other display that:

(i) Permits real-time monitoring, on a dynamic basis, of transaction reports, last sale data, or quotations with respect to a particular security; and

(ii) Displays the most recent transaction report, last sale data, or quotation with respect to that security until such report, data, or quotation has been superseded or supplemented by the display of a new transaction report, last sale data, or quotation reflecting the next reported transaction or quotation in that security.

(22) Effective national market system plan means any national market system plan approved by the Commission (either temporarily or on a permanent basis) pursuant to Rule 608.

(23) Effective transaction reporting plan means any transaction reporting plan approved by the Commission pursuant to Rule 601.

(24) Electronic communications network means, for the purposes of Rule 602(b)(5), any electronic system that widely disseminates to third parties orders entered therein by an exchange market maker or OTC market maker, and permits such orders to be executed against in whole or in part; except that the term electronic communications network shall not include:

(i) Any system that crosses multiple orders at one or more specified times at a single price set by the system (by algorithm or by any derivative pricing mechanism) and does not allow orders to be crossed or executed against directly by participants outside of such times; or

(ii) Any system operated by, or on behalf of, an OTC market maker or exchange market maker that executes customer orders primarily against the account of such market maker as principal, other than riskless principal.

(25) Exchange market maker means any member of a national securities exchange that is registered as a specialist or market maker pursuant to the rules of such exchange.

(26) Exchange-traded security means any NMS security or class of NMS securities listed and registered, or admitted to unlisted trading privileges, on a national securities exchange; provided, however, that securities not listed on any national securities exchange that are traded pursuant to unlisted trading privileges are excluded.

(27) Executed at the quote means, for buy orders, execution at a price equal to the national best offer at the time of order receipt and, for sell orders, execution at a price equal to the national best bid at the time of order receipt.

(28) Executed outside the quote means, for buy orders, execution at a price higher than the national best offer at the time of order receipt and, for sell orders, execution at a price lower than the national best bid at the time of order receipt.

(29) Executed with price improvement means, for buy orders, execution at a price lower than the national best offer at the time of order receipt and, for sell orders, execution at a price higher than the national best bid at the time of order receipt.

(30) Inside-the-quote limit order, at-the-quote limit order, and near-the-quote limit order mean non-marketable buy orders with limit prices that are, respectively, higher than, equal to, and lower by $0.10 or less than the national best bid at the time of order receipt, and non-marketable sell orders with limit prices that are, respectively, lower than, equal to, and higher by $0.10 or less than the national best offer at the time of order receipt.

(31) Intermarket sweep order means a limit order for an NMS stock that meets the following requirements:

(i) When routed to a trading center, the limit order is identified as an intermarket sweep order; and

(ii) Simultaneously with the routing of the limit order identified as an intermarket sweep order, one or more additional limit orders, as necessary, are routed to execute against the full displayed size of any protected bid, in the case of a limit order to sell, or the full displayed size of any protected offer, in the case of a limit order to buy, for the NMS stock with a price that is superior to the limit price of the limit order identified as an intermarket sweep order. These additional routed orders also must be marked as intermarket sweep orders.

(32) Interrogation device means any securities information retrieval system capable of displaying transaction reports, last sale data, or quotations upon inquiry, on a current basis on a terminal or other device.

(33) Joint self-regulatory organization plan means a plan as to which two or more self-regulatory organizations, acting jointly, are sponsors.

(34) Last sale data means any price or volume data associated with a transaction.

(35) Listed equity security means any equity security listed and registered, or admitted to unlisted trading privileges, on a national securities exchange.

(36) Listed option means any option traded on a registered national securities exchange or automated facility of a national securities association.

(37) Make publicly available means posting on an Internet Web site that is free and readily accessible to the public, furnishing a written copy to customers on request without charge, and notifying customers at least annually in writing that a written copy will be furnished on request.

(38) Manual quotation means any quotation other than an automated quotation.

(39) Market center means any exchange market maker, OTC market maker, alternative trading system, national securities exchange, or national securities association.

(40) Marketable limit order means any buy order with a limit price equal to or greater than the national best offer at the time of order receipt, or any sell order with a limit price equal to or less than the national best bid at the time of order receipt.

(41) Moving ticker means any continuous real-time moving display of transaction reports or last sale data (other than a dynamic market monitoring device) provided on an interrogation or other display device.

(42) Nasdaq security means any registered security listed on The Nasdaq Stock Market, Inc.

(43) National best bid and national best offer means, with respect to quotations for an NMS security, the best bid and best offer for such security that are calculated and disseminated on a current and continuing basis by a plan processor pursuant to an effective national market system plan; provided, that in the event two or more market centers transmit to the plan processor pursuant to such plan identical bids or offers for an NMS security, the best bid or best offer (as the case may be) shall

be determined by ranking all such identical bids or offers (as the case may be) first by size (giving the highest ranking to the bid or offer associated with the largest size), and then by time (giving the highest ranking to the bid or offer received first in time).

(44) National market system plan means any joint self-regulatory organization plan in connection with:

(i) The planning, development, operation or regulation of a national market system (or a subsystem thereof) or one or more facilities thereof; or

(ii) The development and implementation of procedures and/or facilities designed to achieve compliance by self-regulatory organizations and their members with any section of this Regulation NMS and part 240, subpart A of this chapter promulgated pursuant to section 11A of the Act.

(45) National securities association means any association of brokers and dealers registered pursuant to section 15A of the Act.

(46) National securities exchange means any exchange registered pursuant to section 6 of the Act.

(47) NMS security means any security or class of securities for which transaction reports are collected, processed, and made available pursuant to an effective transaction reporting plan, or an effective national market system plan for reporting transactions in listed options.

(48) NMS stock means any NMS security other than an option.

(49) Non-directed order means any order from a customer other than a directed order.

(50) Non-marketable limit order means any limit order other than a marketable limit order.

(51) Odd-lot means an order for the purchase or sale of an NMS stock in an amount less than a round lot.

(52) Options class means all of the put option or call option series overlying a security, as defined in section 3(a)(10) of the Act.

(53) Options series means the contracts in an options class that have the same unit of trade, expiration date, and exercise price, and other terms or conditions.

(54) Orders providing liquidity means orders that were executed against after resting at a trading center.

(55) Orders removing liquidity means orders that executed against resting trading interest at a trading center.

(56) OTC market maker means any dealer that holds itself out as being willing to buy from and sell to its customers, or others, in the United States, an NMS stock for its own account on a regular or continuous basis otherwise than on a national securities exchange in amounts of less than block size.

(57) Participants, when used in connection with a national market system plan, means any self-regulatory organization which has agreed to act in accordance with the terms of the plan but which is not a signatory of such plan.

(58) Payment for order flow has the meaning provided in Rule 10b–10 of the Securities Exchange Act of 1934.

(59) Plan processor means any self-regulatory organization or securities information processor acting as an exclusive processor in connection with the development, implementation and/or operation of any facility contemplated by an effective national market system plan.

(60) Profit-sharing relationship means any ownership or other type of affiliation under which the broker or dealer, directly or indirectly, may share in any profits that may be derived from the execution of non-directed orders.

(61) Protected bid or protected offer means a quotation in an NMS stock that:

(i) Is displayed by an automated trading center;

(ii)   Is disseminated pursuant to an effective national market system plan; and

(iii)   Is an automated quotation that is the best bid or best offer of a national securities exchange, the best bid or best offer of The Nasdaq Stock Market, Inc., or the best bid or best offer of a national securities association other than the best bid or best offer of The Nasdaq Stock Market, Inc.

(62)   Protected quotation means a protected bid or a protected offer.

(63)   Published aggregate quotation size means the aggregate quotation size calculated by a national securities exchange and displayed by a vendor on a terminal or other display device at the time an order is presented for execution to a responsible broker or dealer.

(64)   Published bid and published offer means the bid or offer of a responsible broker or dealer for an NMS security communicated by it to its national securities exchange or association pursuant to Rule 602 and displayed by a vendor on a terminal or other display device at the time an order is presented for execution to such responsible broker or dealer.

(65)   Published quotation size means the quotation size of a responsible broker or dealer communicated by it to its national securities exchange or association pursuant to Rule 602 and displayed by a vendor on a terminal or other display device at the time an order is presented for execution to such responsible broker or dealer.

(66)   Quotation means a bid or an offer.

(67)   Quotation size, when used with respect to a responsible broker's or dealer's bid or offer for an NMS security, means:

(i)   The number of shares (or units of trading) of that security which such responsible broker or dealer has specified, for purposes of dissemination to vendors, that it is willing to buy at the bid price or sell at the offer price comprising its bid or offer, as either principal or agent; or

(ii)   In the event such responsible broker or dealer has not so specified, a normal unit of trading for that NMS security.

(68)   Regular trading hours means the time between 9:30 a.m. and 4:00 p.m. Eastern Time, or such other time as is set forth in the procedures established pursuant to Rule 605(a)(2).

(69)   Responsible broker or dealer means:

(i)   When used with respect to bids or offers communicated on a national securities exchange, any member of such national securities exchange who communicates to another member on such national securities exchange, at the location (or locations) or through the facility or facilities designated by such national securities exchange for trading in an NMS security a bid or offer for such NMS security, as either principal or agent; provided, however, that, in the event two or more members of a national securities exchange have communicated on or through such national securities exchange bids or offers for an NMS security at the same price, each such member shall be considered a responsible broker or dealer for that bid or offer, subject to the rules of priority and precedence then in effect on that national securities exchange; and further provided, that for a bid or offer which is transmitted from one member of a national securities exchange to another member who undertakes to represent such bid or offer on such national securities exchange as agent, only the last member who undertakes to represent such bid or offer as agent shall be considered the responsible broker or dealer for that bid or offer; and

(ii)   When used with respect to bids and offers communicated by a member of an association to a broker or dealer or a customer, the member communicating the bid or offer (regardless of whether such bid or offer is for its own account or on behalf of another person).

(70)   Revised bid or offer means a market maker's bid or offer which supersedes its published bid or published offer.

(71)   Revised quotation size means a market maker's quotation size which supersedes its published quotation size.

(72) Self-regulatory organization means any national securities exchange or national securities association.

(73) Specified persons, when used in connection with any notification required to be provided pursuant to Rule 602(a)(3) and any election (or withdrawal thereof) permitted under Rule 602(a)(5), means:

(i) Each vendor;

(ii) Each plan processor; and

(iii) The processor for the Options Price Reporting Authority (in the case of a notification for a subject security which is a class of securities underlying options admitted to trading on any national securities exchange).

(74) Sponsor, when used in connection with a national market system plan, means any self-regulatory organization which is a signatory to such plan and has agreed to act in accordance with the terms of the plan.

(75) SRO display-only facility means a facility operated by or on behalf of a national securities exchange or national securities association that displays quotations in a security, but does not execute orders against such quotations or present orders to members for execution.

(76) SRO trading facility means a facility operated by or on behalf of a national securities exchange or a national securities association that executes orders in a security or presents orders to members for execution.

(77) Subject security means:

(i) With respect to a national securities exchange:

(A) Any exchange-traded security other than a security for which the executed volume of such exchange, during the most recent calendar quarter, comprised one percent or less of the aggregate trading volume for such security as reported pursuant to an effective transaction reporting plan or effective national market system plan; and

(B) Any other NMS security for which such exchange has in effect an election, pursuant to Rule 602(a)(5)(i), to collect, process, and make available to a vendor bids, offers, quotation sizes, and aggregate quotation sizes communicated on such exchange; and

(ii) With respect to a member of a national securities association:

(A) Any exchange-traded security for which such member acts in the capacity of an OTC market maker unless the executed volume of such member, during the most recent calendar quarter, comprised one percent or less of the aggregate trading volume for such security as reported pursuant to an effective transaction reporting plan or effective national market system plan; and

(B) Any other NMS security for which such member acts in the capacity of an OTC market maker and has in effect an election, pursuant to Rule 602(a)(5)(ii), to communicate to its association bids, offers, and quotation sizes for the purpose of making such bids, offers, and quotation sizes available to a vendor.

(78) Time of order execution means the time (to the second) that an order was executed at any venue.

(79) Time of order receipt means the time (to the second) that an order was received by a market center for execution.

(80) Time of the transaction has the meaning provided in Rule 10b–10 of the Securities Exchange Act of 1934 chapter.

(81) Trade-through means the purchase or sale of an NMS stock during regular trading hours, either as principal or agent, at a price that is lower than a protected bid or higher than a protected offer.

(82) Trading center means a national securities exchange or national securities association that operates an SRO trading facility, an alternative trading system, an exchange market maker, an OTC market maker, or any other broker or dealer that executes orders internally by trading as principal or crossing orders as agent.

(83) Trading rotation means, with respect to an options class, the time period on a national securities exchange during which:

(i) Opening, re-opening, or closing transactions in options series in such options class are not yet completed; and

(ii) Continuous trading has not yet commenced or has not yet ended for the day in options series in such options class.

(84) Transaction report means a report containing the price and volume associated with a transaction involving the purchase or sale of one or more round lots of a security.

(85) Transaction reporting association means any person authorized to implement or administer any transaction reporting plan on behalf of persons acting jointly under Rule 601(a).

(86) Transaction reporting plan means any plan for collecting, processing, making available or disseminating transaction reports with respect to transactions in securities filed with the Commission pursuant to, and meeting the requirements of, Rule 601.

(87) Vendor means any securities information processor engaged in the business of disseminating transaction reports, last sale data, or quotations with respect to NMS securities to brokers, dealers, or investors on a real-time or other current and continuing basis, whether through an electronic communications network, moving ticker, or interrogation device.

Rule 601.   Dissemination of Transaction Reports and Last Sale Data With Respect to Transactions in NMS Stocks

(a) Filing and effectiveness of transaction reporting plans.

(1) Every national securities exchange shall file a transaction reporting plan regarding transactions in listed equity and Nasdaq securities executed through its facilities, and every national securities association shall file a transaction reporting plan regarding transactions in listed equity and Nasdaq securities executed by its members otherwise than on a national securities exchange.

(2) Any transaction reporting plan, or any amendment thereto, filed pursuant to this rule shall be filed with the Commission, and considered for approval, in accordance with the procedures set forth in Rule 608(a) and (b). Any such plan, or amendment thereto, shall specify, at a minimum:

(i) The listed equity and Nasdaq securities or classes of such securities for which transaction reports shall be required by the plan;

(ii) Reporting requirements with respect to transactions in listed equity securities and Nasdaq securities, for any broker or dealer subject to the plan;

(iii) The manner of collecting, processing, sequencing, making available and disseminating transaction reports and last sale data reported pursuant to such plan;

(iv) The manner in which such transaction reports reported pursuant to such plan are to be consolidated with transaction reports from national securities exchanges and national securities associations reported pursuant to any other effective transaction reporting plan;

(v) The applicable standards and methods which will be utilized to ensure promptness of reporting, and accuracy and completeness of transaction reports;

(vi) Any rules or procedures which may be adopted to ensure that transaction reports or last sale data will not be disseminated in a fraudulent or manipulative manner;

(vii) Specific terms of access to transaction reports made available or disseminated pursuant to the plan; and

(viii) That transaction reports or last sale data made available to any vendor for display on an interrogation device identify the marketplace where each transaction was executed.

(3) No transaction reporting plan filed pursuant to this rule, or any amendment to an effective transaction reporting plan, shall become effective unless approved by the Commission or otherwise permitted in accordance with the procedures set forth in Rule 608.

(b) Prohibitions and reporting requirements.

(1) No broker or dealer may execute any transaction in, or induce or attempt to induce the purchase or sale of, any NMS stock:

(i) On or through the facilities of a national securities exchange unless there is an effective transaction reporting plan with respect to transactions in such security executed on or through such exchange facilities; or

(ii) Otherwise than on a national securities exchange unless there is an effective transaction reporting plan with respect to transactions in such security executed otherwise than on a national securities exchange by such broker or dealer.

(2) Every broker or dealer who is a member of a national securities exchange or national securities association shall promptly transmit to the exchange or association of which it is a member all information required by any effective transaction reporting plan filed by such exchange or association (either individually or jointly with other exchanges and/or associations).

(c) Retransmission of transaction reports or last sale data. Notwithstanding any provision of any effective transaction reporting plan, no national securities exchange or national securities association may, either individually or jointly, by rule, stated policy or practice, transaction reporting plan or otherwise, prohibit, condition or otherwise limit, directly or indirectly, the ability of any vendor to retransmit, for display in moving tickers, transaction reports or last sale data made available pursuant to any effective transaction reporting plan; provided, however, that a national securities exchange or national securities association may, by means of an effective transaction reporting plan, condition such retransmission upon appropriate undertakings to ensure that any charges for the distribution of transaction reports or last sale data in moving tickers permitted by paragraph (d) of this rule are collected.

(d) Charges. Nothing in this rule shall preclude any national securities exchange or national securities association, separately or jointly, pursuant to the terms of an effective transaction reporting plan, from imposing reasonable, uniform charges (irrespective of geographic location) for distribution of transaction reports or last sale data.

(e) Appeals. The Commission may, in its discretion, entertain appeals in connection with the implementation or operation of any effective transaction reporting plan in accordance with the provisions of Rule 608(d).

(f) Exemptions. The Commission may exempt from the provisions of this rule, either unconditionally or on specified terms and conditions, any national securities exchange, national securities association, broker, dealer, or specified security if the Commission determines that such exemption is consistent with the public interest, the protection of investors and the removal of impediments to, and perfection of the mechanisms of, a national market system.

Rule 602.   Dissemination of Quotations in NMS Securities

(a) Dissemination requirements for national securities exchanges and national securities associations.

(1) Every national securities exchange and national securities association shall establish and maintain procedures and mechanisms for collecting bids, offers, quotation sizes, and aggregate quotation sizes from responsible brokers or dealers who are members of such exchange or association, processing such bids, offers, and sizes, and making such bids, offers, and sizes available to vendors, as follows:

(i) Each national securities exchange shall at all times such exchange is open for trading, collect, process, and make available to vendors the best bid, the best offer, and aggregate quotation sizes for each subject security listed or admitted to unlisted trading privileges which is communicated on any national securities exchange by any responsible broker or dealer, but shall not include:

    (A) Any bid or offer executed immediately after communication and any bid or offer communicated by a responsible broker or dealer other than an exchange market maker which is cancelled or withdrawn if not executed immediately after communication; and

    (B) Any bid or offer communicated during a period when trading in that security has been suspended or halted, or prior to the commencement of trading in that security on any trading day, on that exchange.

    (ii) Each national securities association shall, at all times that last sale information with respect to NMS securities is reported pursuant to an effective transaction reporting plan, collect, process, and make available to vendors the best bid, best offer, and quotation sizes communicated otherwise than on an exchange by each member of such association acting in the capacity of an OTC market maker for each subject security and the identity of that member (excluding any bid or offer executed immediately after communication), except during any period when over-the-counter trading in that security has been suspended.

    (2) Each national securities exchange shall, with respect to each published bid and published offer representing a bid or offer of a member for a subject security, establish and maintain procedures for ascertaining and disclosing to other members of that exchange, upon presentation of orders sought to be executed by them in reliance upon paragraph (b)(2) of this rule, offer and the quotation size associated with it.

    (3)(i) If, at any time a national securities exchange is open for trading, such exchange determines, pursuant to rules approved by the Commission pursuant to section 19(b)(2) of the Act, that the level of trading activities or the existence of unusual market conditions is such that the exchange is incapable of collecting, processing, and making available to vendors the data for a subject security required to be made available pursuant to paragraph (a)(1) of this rule in a manner that accurately reflects the current state of the market on such exchange, such exchange shall immediately notify all specified persons of that determination. Upon such notification, responsible brokers or dealers that are members of that exchange shall be relieved of their obligation under paragraphs (b)(2) and (c)(3) of this rule and such exchange shall be relieved of its obligations under paragraphs (a)(1) and (2) of this rule for that security; provided, however, that such exchange will continue, to the maximum extent practicable under the circumstances, to collect, process, and make available to vendors data for that security in accordance with paragraph (a)(1) of this rule.

    (ii) During any period a national securities exchange, or any responsible broker or dealer that is a member of that exchange, is relieved of any obligation imposed by this rule for any subject security by virtue of a notification made pursuant to paragraph (a)(3)(i) of this rule, such exchange shall monitor the activity or conditions which formed the basis for such notification and shall immediately renotify all specified persons when that exchange is once again capable of collecting, processing, and making available to vendors the data for that security required to be made available pursuant to paragraph (a)(1) of this rule in a manner that accurately reflects the current state of the market on such exchange. Upon such renotification, any exchange or responsible broker or dealer which had been relieved of any obligation imposed by this rule as a consequence of the prior notification shall again be subject to such obligation.

    (4) Nothing in this rule shall preclude any national securities exchange or national securities association from making available to vendors indications of interest or bids and offers for a subject security at any time such exchange or association is not required to do so pursuant to paragraph (a)(1) of this rule.

    (5)(i) Any national securities exchange may make an election for purposes of the definition of subject security in Rule 600(b)(77) for any NMS security, by collecting, processing, and making available bids, offers, quotation sizes, and aggregate quotation sizes in that security; except that for any NMS security previously listed or admitted to unlisted trading privileges on only one exchange and not traded by any OTC market maker, such election shall be made by notifying all specified persons, and shall be effective at the opening of trading on the business day following notification.

(ii) Any member of a national securities association acting in the capacity of an OTC market maker may make an election for purposes of the definition of subject security in Rule 600(b)(77) for any NMS security, by communicating to its association bids, offers, and quotation sizes in that security; except that for any other NMS security listed or admitted to unlisted trading privileges on only one exchange and not traded by any other OTC market maker, such election shall be made by notifying its association and all specified persons, and shall be effective at the opening of trading on the business day following notification.

(iii) The election of a national securities exchange or member of a national securities association for any NMS security pursuant to this paragraph (a)(5) shall cease to be in effect if such exchange or member ceases to make available or communicate bids, offers, and quotation sizes in such security.

(b)   Obligations of responsible brokers and dealers.

(1)   Each responsible broker or dealer shall promptly communicate to its national securities exchange or national securities association, pursuant to the procedures established by that exchange or association, its best bids, best offers, and quotation sizes for any subject security.

(2)   Subject to the provisions of paragraph (b)(3) of this rule, each responsible broker or dealer shall be obligated to execute any order to buy or sell a subject security, other than an odd-lot order, presented to it by another broker or dealer, or any other person belonging to a category of persons with whom such responsible broker or dealer customarily deals, at a price at least as favorable to such buyer or seller as the responsible broker's or dealer's published bid or published offer (exclusive of any commission, commission equivalent or differential customarily charged by such responsible broker or dealer in connection with execution of any such order) in any amount up to its published quotation size.

(3)(i)   No responsible broker or dealer shall be obligated to execute a transaction for any subject security as provided in paragraph (b)(2) of this rule to purchase or sell that subject security in an amount greater than such revised quotation size if:

  (A)   Prior to the presentation of an order for the purchase or sale of a subject security, a responsible broker or dealer has communicated to its exchange or association, pursuant to paragraph (b)(1) of this rule, a revised quotation size; or

  (B)   At the time an order for the purchase or sale of a subject security is presented, a responsible broker or dealer is in the process of effecting a transaction in such subject security, and immediately after the completion of such transaction, it communicates to its exchange or association a revised quotation size, such responsible broker or dealer shall not be obligated by paragraph (b)(2) of this rule to purchase or sell that subject security in an amount greater than such revised quotation size.

(ii)   No responsible broker or dealer shall be obligated to execute a transaction for any subject security as provided in paragraph (b)(2) of this rule if:

  (A)   Before the order sought to be executed is presented, such responsible broker or dealer has communicated to its exchange or association pursuant to paragraph (b)(1) of this rule, a revised bid or offer; or

  (B)   At the time the order sought to be executed is presented, such responsible broker or dealer is in the process of effecting a transaction in such subject security, and, immediately after the completion of such transaction, such responsible broker or dealer communicates to its exchange or association pursuant to paragraph (b)(1) of this rule, a revised bid or offer; provided, however, that such responsible broker or dealer shall nonetheless be obligated to execute any such order in such subject security as provided in paragraph (b)(2) of this rule at its revised bid or offer in any amount up to its published quotation size or revised quotation size.

(4)   Subject to the provisions of paragraph (a)(4) of this rule:

(i)   No national securities exchange or OTC market maker may make available, disseminate or otherwise communicate to any vendor, directly or indirectly, for display on a terminal or other display device any bid, offer, quotation size, or aggregate quotation size for any NMS security which is not a subject security with respect to such exchange or OTC market maker; and

(ii) No vendor may disseminate or display on a terminal or other display device any bid, offer, quotation size, or aggregate quotation size from any national securities exchange or OTC market maker for any NMS security which is not a subject security with respect to such exchange or OTC market maker.

(5)(i) Entry of any priced order for an NMS security by an exchange market maker or OTC market maker in that security into an electronic communications network that widely disseminates such order shall be deemed to be:

(A) A bid or offer under this rule, to be communicated to the market maker's exchange or association pursuant to this paragraph (b) for at least the minimum quotation size that is required by the rules of the market maker's exchange or association if the priced order is for the account of a market maker, or the actual size of the order up to the minimum quotation size required if the priced order is for the account of a customer; and

(B) A communication of a bid or offer to a vendor for display on a display device for purposes of paragraph (b)(4) of this rule.

(ii) An exchange market maker or OTC market maker that has entered a priced order for an NMS security into an electronic communications network that widely disseminates such order shall be deemed to be in compliance with paragraph (b)(5)(i)(A) of this rule if the electronic communications network:

(A)(1) Provides to a national securities exchange or national securities association (or an exclusive processor acting on behalf of one or more exchanges or associations) the prices and sizes of the orders at the highest buy price and the lowest sell price for such security entered in, and widely disseminated by, the electronic communications network by exchange market makers and OTC market makers for the NMS security, and such prices and sizes are included in the quotation data made available by such exchange, association, or exclusive processor to vendors pursuant to this rule; and

(2) Provides, to any broker or dealer, the ability to effect a transaction with a priced order widely disseminated by the electronic communications network entered therein by an exchange market maker or OTC market maker that is:

(i) Equivalent to the ability of any broker or dealer to effect a transaction with an exchange market maker or OTC market maker pursuant to the rules of the national securities exchange or national securities association to which the electronic communications network supplies such bids and offers; and

(ii) At the price of the highest priced buy order or lowest priced sell order, or better, for the lesser of the cumulative size of such priced orders entered therein by exchange market makers or OTC market makers at such price, or the size of the execution sought by the broker or dealer, for such security; or

(B) Is an alternative trading system that:

(1) Displays orders and provides the ability to effect transactions with such orders under Rule 301(b)(3) of Regulation ATS; and

(2) Otherwise is in compliance with Regulation ATS.

(c) Transactions in listed options.

(1) A national securities exchange or national securities association:

(i) Shall not be required, under paragraph (a) of this rule, to collect from responsible brokers or dealers who are members of such exchange or association, or to make available to vendors, the quotation sizes and aggregate quotation sizes for listed options, if such exchange or association establishes by rule and periodically publishes the quotation size for which such responsible brokers or dealers are obligated to execute an order to buy or sell an options series that is a subject security at its published bid or offer under paragraph (b)(2) of this rule;

(ii) May establish by rule and periodically publish a quotation size, which shall not be for less than one contract, for which responsible brokers or dealers who are members of such exchange or association are obligated under paragraph (b)(2) of this rule to execute an order to buy or sell a listed option for the account of a broker or dealer that is in an amount different from the quotation size for which it is obligated to execute an order for the account of a customer; and

(iii) May establish and maintain procedures and mechanisms for collecting from responsible brokers and dealers who are members of such exchange or association, and making available to vendors, the quotation sizes and aggregate quotation sizes in listed options for which such responsible broker or dealer will be obligated under paragraph (b)(2) of this rule to execute an order from a customer to buy or sell a listed option and establish by rule and periodically publish the size, which shall not be less than one contract, for which such responsible brokers or dealers are obligated to execute an order for the account of a broker or dealer.

(2) If, pursuant to paragraph (c)(1) of this rule, the rules of a national securities exchange or national securities association do not require its members to communicate to it their quotation sizes for listed options, a responsible broker or dealer that is a member of such exchange or association shall:

(i) Be relieved of its obligations under paragraph (b)(1) of this rule to communicate to such exchange or association its quotation sizes for any listed option; and

(ii) Comply with its obligations under paragraph (b)(2) of this rule by executing any order to buy or sell a listed option, in an amount up to the size established by such exchange's or association's rules under paragraph (c)(1) of this rule.

(3) Thirty second response. Each responsible broker or dealer, within thirty seconds of receiving an order to buy or sell a listed option in an amount greater than the quotation size established by a national securities exchange's or national securities association's rules pursuant to paragraph (c)(1) of this rule, or its published quotation size must:

(i) Execute the entire order; or

(ii)(A) Execute that portion of the order equal to at least:

(1) The quotation size established by a national securities exchange's or national securities association's rules, pursuant to paragraph (c)(1) of this rule, to the extent that such exchange or association does not collect and make available to vendors quotation size and aggregate quotation size under paragraph (a) of this rule; or

(2) Its published quotation size; and

(B) Revise its bid or offer.

(4) Notwithstanding paragraph (c)(3) of this rule, no responsible broker or dealer shall be obligated to execute a transaction for any listed option as provided in paragraph (b)(2) of this rule if:

(i) Any of the circumstances in paragraph (b)(3) of this rule exist; or

(ii) The order for the purchase or sale of a listed option is presented during a trading rotation in that listed option.

(d) Exemptions. The Commission may exempt from the provisions of this rule, either unconditionally or on specified terms and conditions, any responsible broker or dealer, electronic communications network, national securities exchange, or national securities association if the Commission determines that such exemption is consistent with the public interest, the protection of investors and the removal of impediments to and perfection of the mechanism of a national market system.

Rule 603.   **Distribution, Consolidation, and Display of Information With Respect to Quotations for and Transactions in NMS Stocks**

(a) Distribution of information.

(1) Any exclusive processor, or any broker or dealer with respect to information for which it is the exclusive source, that distributes information with respect to quotations for or transactions in an NMS stock to a securities information processor shall do so on terms that are fair and reasonable.

(2) Any national securities exchange, national securities association, broker, or dealer that distributes information with respect to quotations for or transactions in an NMS stock to a securities information processor, broker, dealer, or other persons shall do so on terms that are not unreasonably discriminatory.

(b) *Consolidation of information.* Every national securities exchange on which an NMS stock is traded and national securities association shall act jointly pursuant to one or more effective national market system plans to disseminate consolidated information, including a national best bid and national best offer, on quotations for and transactions in NMS stocks. Such plan or plans shall provide for the dissemination of all consolidated information for an individual NMS stock through a single plan processor.

(c) *Display of information.*

(1) No securities information processor, broker, or dealer shall provide, in a context in which a trading or order-routing decision can be implemented, a display of any information with respect to quotations for or transactions in an NMS stock without also providing, in an equivalent manner, a consolidated display for such stock.

(2) The provisions of paragraph (c)(1) of this rule shall not apply to a display of information on the trading floor or through the facilities of a national securities exchange or to a display in connection with the operation of a market linkage system implemented in accordance with an effective national market system plan.

(d) *Exemptions.* The Commission, by order, may exempt from the provisions of this rule, either unconditionally or on specified terms and conditions, any person, security, or item of information, or any class or classes of persons, securities, or items of information, if the Commission determines that such exemption is necessary or appropriate in the public interest, and is consistent with the protection of investors.

Rule 604.   Display of Customer Limit Orders

(a) *Specialists and OTC market makers.* For all NMS stocks:

(1) Each member of a national securities exchange that is registered by that exchange as a specialist, or is authorized by that exchange to perform functions substantially similar to that of a specialist, shall publish immediately a bid or offer that reflects:

(i) The price and the full size of each customer limit order held by the specialist that is at a price that would improve the bid or offer of such specialist in such security; and

(ii) The full size of each customer limit order held by the specialist that:

(A) Is priced equal to the bid or offer of such specialist for such security;

(B) Is priced equal to the national best bid or national best offer; and

(C) Represents more than a de minimis change in relation to the size associated with the specialist's bid or offer.

(2) Each registered broker or dealer that acts as an OTC market maker shall publish immediately a bid or offer that reflects:

(i) The price and the full size of each customer limit order held by the OTC market maker that is at a price that would improve the bid or offer of such OTC market maker in such security; and

(ii) The full size of each customer limit order held by the OTC market maker that:

(A) Is priced equal to the bid or offer of such OTC market maker for such security;

(B) Is priced equal to the national best bid or national best offer; and

(C)   Represents more than a de minimis change in relation to the size associated with the OTC market maker's bid or offer.

(b)   Exceptions. The requirements in paragraph (a) of this rule shall not apply to any customer limit order:

(1)   That is executed upon receipt of the order.

(2)   That is placed by a customer who expressly requests, either at the time that the order is placed or prior thereto pursuant to an individually negotiated agreement with respect to such customer's orders, that the order not be displayed.

(3)   That is an odd-lot order.

(4)   That is a block size order, unless a customer placing such order requests that the order be displayed.

(5)   That is delivered immediately upon receipt to a national securities exchange or national securities association-sponsored system, or an electronic communications network that complies with the requirements of Rule 602(b)(5)(ii) with respect to that order.

(6)   That is delivered immediately upon receipt to another exchange member or OTC market maker that complies with the requirements of this rule with respect to that order.

(7)   That is an "all or none" order.

(c)   Exemptions. The Commission may exempt from the provisions of this rule, either unconditionally or on specified terms and conditions, any responsible broker or dealer, electronic communications network, national securities exchange, or national securities association if the Commission determines that such exemption is consistent with the public interest, the protection of investors and the removal of impediments to and perfection of the mechanism of a national market system.

Rule 605.   Disclosure of Order Execution Information

Rule 605 requires market centers to make available standardized, monthly reports of statistical information concerning their order executions. This information is presented in accordance with uniform standards that are based on broad assumptions about order execution and routing practices. The information will provide a starting point to promote visibility and competition on the part of market centers and broker-dealers, particularly on the factors of execution price and speed. The disclosures required by this rule do not encompass all of the factors that may be important to investors in evaluating the order routing services of a brokerdealer. In addition, any particular market center's statistics will encompass varying types of orders routed by different broker-dealers on behalf of customers with a wide range of objectives. Accordingly, the statistical information required by this rule alone does not create a reliable basis to address whether any particular broker-dealer failed to obtain the most favorable terms reasonably available under the circumstances for customer orders

(a)   Monthly electronic reports by market centers.

(1)   Every market center shall make available for each calendar month, in accordance with the procedures established pursuant to paragraph (a)(2) of this rule, a report on the covered orders in NMS stocks that it received for execution from any person. Such report shall be in electronic form; shall be categorized by security, order type, and order size; and shall include the following columns of information:

(i)   For market orders, marketable limit orders, inside-the-quote limit orders, at-the-quote limit orders, and near-the-quote limit orders:

(A)   The number of covered orders;

(B)   The cumulative number of shares of covered orders;

(C)   The cumulative number of shares of covered orders cancelled prior to execution;

(D)   The cumulative number of shares of covered orders executed at the receiving market center;

(E)   The cumulative number of shares of covered orders executed at any other venue;

(F)   The cumulative number of shares of covered orders executed from 0 to 9 seconds after the time of order receipt;

(G)   The cumulative number of shares of covered orders executed from 10 to 29 seconds after the time of order receipt;

(H)   The cumulative number of shares of covered orders executed from 30 seconds to 59 seconds after the time of order receipt;

(I)   The cumulative number of shares of covered orders executed from 60 seconds to 299 seconds after the time of order receipt;

(J)   The cumulative number of shares of covered orders executed from 5 minutes to 30 minutes after the time of order receipt; and

(K)   The average realized spread for executions of covered orders; and

(ii)   For market orders and marketable limit orders:

(A)   The average effective spread for executions of covered orders;

(B)   The cumulative number of shares of covered orders executed with price improvement;

(C)   For shares executed with price improvement, the share-weighted average amount per share that prices were improved;

(D)   For shares executed with price improvement, the share-weighted average period from the time of order receipt to the time of order execution;

(E)   The cumulative number of shares of covered orders executed at the quote;

(F)   For shares executed at the quote, the share-weighted average period from the time of order receipt to the time of order execution;

(G)   The cumulative number of shares of covered orders executed outside the quote;

(H)   For shares executed outside the quote, the share-weighted average amount per share that prices were outside the quote; and

(I)   For shares executed outside the quote, the share-weighted average period from the time of order receipt to the time of order execution.

(2)   Every national securities exchange on which NMS stocks are traded and each national securities association shall act jointly in establishing procedures for market centers to follow in making available to the public the reports required by paragraph (a)(1) of this rule in a uniform, readily accessible, and usable electronic form. In the event there is no effective national market system plan establishing such procedures, market centers shall prepare their reports in a consistent, usable, and machine-readable electronic format, and make such reports available for downloading from an Internet Web site that is free and readily accessible to the public. Every market center shall keep such reports posted on an Internet Web site that is free and readily accessible to the public for a period of three years from the initial date of posting on the Internet Web site.

(3)   A market center shall make available the report required by paragraph (a)(1) of this rule within one month after the end of the month addressed in the report.

(b)   Exemptions. The Commission may, by order upon application, conditionally or unconditionally exempt any person, security, or transaction, or any class or classes of persons, securities, or transactions, from any provision or provisions of this rule, if the Commission determines that such exemption is necessary or appropriate in the public interest, and is consistent with the protection of investors.

Rule 606.   Disclosure of Order Routing Information

(a)   Quarterly report on order routing.

(1)   Every broker or dealer shall make publicly available for each calendar quarter a report on its routing of non-directed orders in NMS securities during that quarter. For NMS stocks, such report shall be divided into three separate sections for securities that are listed on the New York Stock Exchange, Inc., securities that are qualified for inclusion in The Nasdaq Stock Market, Inc., and securities that are listed on the American Stock Exchange LLC or any other national securities exchange. Such report also shall include a separate section for NMS securities that are option contracts. Each of the four sections in a report shall include the following information:

(i)   The percentage of total customer orders for the section that were non-directed orders, and the percentages of total non-directed orders for the section that were market orders, limit orders, and other orders;

(ii)   The identity of the ten venues to which the largest number of total non-directed orders for the section were routed for execution and of any venue to which five percent or more of non-directed orders were routed for execution, the percentage of total non-directed orders for the section routed to the venue, and the percentages of total non-directed market orders, total non-directed limit orders, and total non-directed other orders for the section that were routed to the venue; and

(iii)   A discussion of the material aspects of the broker's or dealer's relationship with each venue identified pursuant to paragraph (a)(1)(ii) of this rule, including a description of any arrangement for payment for order flow and any profit-sharing relationship.

(2)   A broker or dealer shall make the report required by paragraph (a)(1) of this rule publicly available within one month after the end of the quarter addressed in the report.

(b)   Customer requests for information on order routing.

(1)   Every broker or dealer shall, on request of a customer, disclose to its customer, for:

(i)   Orders in NMS stocks that are submitted on a held basis;

(ii)   Orders in NMS stocks that are submitted on a not held basis and the broker or dealer is not required to provide the customer a report under subsection (3) below; and

(iii)   Orders in NMS securities that are option contracts, the identity of the venue to which the customer's orders were routed for execution in the six months prior to the request, whether the orders were directed orders or non-directed orders, and the time of the transactions, if any, that resulted from such orders. Such disclosure shall be made available using the most recent versions of the XML schema and the associated PDF renderer as published on the Commission's Web site for all reports required by this rule.

(2)   A broker or dealer shall notify customers in writing at least annually of the availability on request of the information specified in paragraph (b)(1) of this rule.

(3)   Except as provided for in paragraphs (b)(4) and (b)(5) of this rule, every broker or dealer shall, on request of a customer that places, directly or indirectly, one or more orders in NMS stocks that are submitted on a not held basis with the broker or dealer, disclose to such customer within seven business days of receiving the request, a report on its handling of such orders for that customer for the prior six months by calendar month. Such report shall be made available using the most recent versions of the XML schema and the associated PDF renderer as published on the Commission's Web site for all reports required by this rule. For purposes of such report, the handling of a NMS stock order submitted by a customer to a broker-dealer on a not held basis includes the handling of all child orders derived from that order. Such report shall be divided into two sections: one for directed orders and one for non-directed orders. Each section of such report shall include, with respect to such order flow sent by the customer to the broker or dealer, the total number of shares sent to the broker or dealer by the customer during the relevant period; the total number of shares executed by the broker or dealer as principal for its own account; the total number of orders exposed by the broker or dealer through an actionable indication of interest; and the venue or venues to which orders were exposed by the broker or dealer through an actionable indication of interest, provided that, where applicable, a broker or dealer must disclose that it exposed a customer's order through an actionable indication of interest to other customers but need not disclose the identity of such customers. Each section of such report also

shall include the following columns of information for each venue to which the broker or dealer routed such orders for the customer, in the aggregate:

    (i)   Information on Order Routing.

        (A)   Total shares routed;

        (B)   Total shares routed marked immediate or cancel;

        (C)   Total shares routed that were further routable; and

        (D)   Average order size routed.

    (ii)   Information on Order Execution.

        (A)   Total shares executed;

        (B)   Fill rate (shares executed divided by the shares routed);

        (C)   Average fill size;

        (D)   Average net execution fee or rebate (cents per 100 shares, specified to four decimal places);

        (E)   Total number of shares executed at the midpoint;

        (F)   Percentage of shares executed at the midpoint;

        (G)   Total number of shares executed that were priced on the side of the spread more favorable to the order;

        (H)   Percentage of total shares executed that were priced at the side of the spread more favorable to the order;

        (I)   Total number of shares executed that were priced on the side of the spread less favorable to the order; and

        (J)   Percentage of total shares executed that were priced on the side of the spread less favorable to the order.

    (iii)   Information on Orders that Provided Liquidity.

        (A)   Total number of shares executed of orders providing liquidity;

        (B)   Percentage of shares executed of orders providing liquidity;

        (C)   Average time between order entry and execution or cancellation, for orders providing liquidity (in milliseconds); and

        (D)   Average net execution rebate or fee for shares of orders providing liquidity (cents per 100 shares, specified to four decimal places).

    (iv)   Information on Orders that Removed Liquidity.

        (A)   Total number of shares executed of orders removing liquidity;

        (B)   Percentage of shares executed of orders removing liquidity; and

        (C)   Average net execution fee or rebate for shares of orders removing liquidity (cents per 100 shares, specified to four decimal places).

    (4)   Except as provided below, no broker or dealer shall be required to provide reports pursuant to paragraph (b)(3) of this rule if the percentage of shares of not held orders in NMS stocks the broker or dealer received from its customers over the prior six calendar months was less than five percent of the total shares in NMS stocks the broker or dealer received from its customers during that time (the "five percent threshold" for purposes of this paragraph). A broker or dealer that equals or exceeds this five percent threshold shall be required (subject to paragraph (b)(5)) to provide reports pursuant to paragraph (b)(3) of this rule for at least six calendar months ("Compliance Period") regardless of the percentage of shares of not held orders in NMS stocks the broker or dealer receives from its customers during the Compliance Period. The Compliance Period shall begin the first calendar day of the next

calendar month after the broker or dealer equaled or exceeded the five percent threshold, unless it is the first time the broker or dealer has equaled or exceeded the five percent threshold, in which case the Compliance Period shall begin the first calendar day four calendar months later. A broker or dealer shall not be required to provide reports pursuant to paragraph (b)(3) of this rule for orders that the broker or dealer did not receive during a Compliance Period. If, at any time after the end of a Compliance Period, the percentage of shares of not held orders in NMS stocks the broker or dealer received from its customers was less than five percent of the total shares in NMS stocks the broker or dealer received from its customers over the prior six calendar months, the broker or dealer shall not be required to provide reports pursuant to paragraph (b)(3) of this rule, except for orders that the broker or dealer received during the portion of a Compliance Period that remains covered by paragraph (b)(3) of this rule.

(5)   No broker or dealer shall be subject to the requirements of paragraph (b)(3) of this rule with respect to a customer that traded on average each month for the prior six months less than $1,000,000 of notional value of not held orders in NMS stocks through the broker or dealer.

(c)   Exemptions. The Commission may, by order upon application, conditionally or unconditionally exempt any person, security, or transaction, or any class or classes of persons, securities, or transactions, from any provision or provisions of this rule, if the Commission determines that such exemption is necessary or appropriate in the public interest, and is consistent with the protection of investors.

Rule 607.   Customer Account Statements

(a)   No broker or dealer acting as agent for a customer may effect any transaction in, induce or attempt to induce the purchase or sale of, or direct orders for purchase or sale of, any NMS stock or a security authorized for quotation on an automated inter-dealer quotation system that has the characteristics set forth in section 17B of the Act, unless such broker or dealer informs such customer, in writing, upon opening a new account and on an annual basis thereafter, of the following:

(1)   The broker's or dealer's policies regarding receipt of payment for order flow from any broker or dealer, national securities exchange, national securities association, or exchange member to which it routes customers' orders for execution, including a statement as to whether any payment for order flow is received for routing customer orders and a detailed description of the nature of the compensation received; and

(2)   The broker's or dealer's policies for determining where to route customer orders that are the subject of payment for order flow absent specific instructions from customers, including a description of the extent to which orders can be executed at prices superior to the national best bid and national best offer.

(b)   Exemptions. The Commission, upon request or upon its own motion, may exempt by rule or by order, any broker or dealer or any class of brokers or dealers, security or class of securities from the requirements of paragraph (a) of this rule with respect to any transaction or class of transactions, either unconditionally or on specified terms and conditions, if the Commission determines that such exemption is consistent with the public interest and the protection of investors.

Rule 608.   Filing and Amendment of National Market System Plans

(a)   Filing of national market system plans and amendments thereto.

(1)   Any two or more self-regulatory organizations, acting jointly, may file a national market system plan or may propose an amendment to an effective national market system plan ("proposed amendment") by submitting the text of the plan or amendment to the Secretary of the Commission, together with a statement of the purpose of such plan or amendment and, to the extent applicable, the documents and information required by paragraphs (a)(4) and (5) of this rule.

(2)   The Commission may propose amendments to any effective national market system plan by publishing the text thereof, together with a statement of the purpose of such amendment, in accordance with the provisions of paragraph (b) of this rule.

(3)   Self-regulatory organizations are authorized to act jointly in:

(i)   Planning, developing, and operating any national market subsystem or facility contemplated by a national market system plan;

(ii)   Preparing and filing a national market system plan or any amendment thereto; or

(iii)   Implementing or administering an effective national market system plan.

(4)   Every national market system plan filed pursuant to this rule, or any amendment thereto, shall be accompanied by:

(i)   Copies of all governing or constituent documents relating to any person (other than a self-regulatory organization) authorized to implement or administer such plan on behalf of its sponsors; and

(ii)   To the extent applicable:

(A)   A detailed description of the manner in which the plan or amendment, and any facility or procedure contemplated by the plan or amendment, will be implemented;

(B)   A listing of all significant phases of development and implementation (including any pilot phase) contemplated by the plan or amendment, together with the projected date of completion of each phase;

(C)   An analysis of the impact on competition of implementation of the plan or amendment or of any facility contemplated by the plan or amendment;

(D)   A description of any written understandings or agreements between or among plan sponsors or participants relating to interpretations of the plan or conditions for becoming a sponsor or participant in the plan; and

(E)   In the case of a proposed amendment, a statement that such amendment has been approved by the sponsors in accordance with the terms of the plan.

(5)   Every national market system plan, or any amendment thereto, filed pursuant to this rule shall include a description of the manner in which any facility contemplated by the plan or amendment will be operated. Such description shall include, to the extent applicable:

(i)   The terms and conditions under which brokers, dealers, and/or self-regulatory organizations will be granted or denied access (including specific procedures and standards governing the granting or denial of access);

(ii)   The method by which any fees or charges collected on behalf of all of the sponsors and/or participants in connection with access to, or use of, any facility contemplated by the plan or amendment will be determined and imposed (including any provision for distribution of any net proceeds from such fees or charges to the sponsors and/or participants) and the amount of such fees or charges;

(iii)   The method by which, and the frequency with which, the performance of any person acting as plan processor with respect to the implementation and/or operation of the plan will be evaluated; and

(iv)   The method by which disputes arising in connection with the operation of the plan will be resolved.

(6)   In connection with the selection of any person to act as plan processor with respect to any facility contemplated by a national market system plan (including renewal of any contract for any person to so act), the sponsors shall file with the Commission a statement identifying the person selected, describing the material terms under which such person is to serve as plan processor, and indicating the solicitation efforts, if any, for alternative plan processors, the alternatives considered and the reasons for selection of such person.

(7)   Any national market system plan (or any amendment thereto) which is intended by the sponsors to satisfy a plan filing requirement contained in any other section of this Regulation NMS and part 240, subpart A of this chapter shall, in addition to compliance with this rule, also comply with the requirements of such other section.

(8)(i)   A participant in an effective national market system plan shall ensure that a current and complete version of the plan is posted on a plan Web site or on a Web site designated by plan participants within two business days after notification by the Commission of effectiveness of the plan. Each participant in an effective national market system plan shall ensure that such Web site is updated to reflect amendments to such plan within two business days after the plan participants have been notified by the Commission of its approval of a proposed amendment pursuant to paragraph (b) of this rule. If the amendment is not effective for a certain period, the plan participants shall clearly indicate the effective date in the relevant text of the plan. Each plan participant also shall provide a link on its own Web site to the Web site with the current version of the plan.

(ii)   The plan participants shall ensure that any proposed amendments filed pursuant to paragraph (a) of this rule are posted on a plan Web site or a designated Web site no later than two business days after the filing of the proposed amendments with the Commission. The shall maintain any proposed amendment to the plan on a plan Web site or a designated Web site until the Commission approves the plan amendment and the plan participants update the Web site to reflect such amendment or the plan participants withdraw the proposed amendment. If the plan participants withdraw proposed amendments, the plan participants shall remove such amendments from the plan Web site or designated Web site within two business days of withdrawal. Each plan participant shall provide a link to the Web site with the current version of the plan.

(b)   Effectiveness of national market system plans.

(1)   The Commission shall publish notice of the filing of any national market system plan, or any proposed amendment to any effective national market system plan (including any amendment initiated by the Commission), together with the terms of substance of the filing or a description of the subjects and issues involved, and shall provide interested persons an opportunity to submit written comments. No national market system plan, or any amendment thereto, shall become effective unless approved by the Commission or otherwise permitted in accordance with paragraph (b)(3) of this rule.

(2)   Within 120 days of the date of publication of notice of filing of a national market system plan or an amendment to an effective national market system plan, or within such longer period as the Commission may designate up to 180 days of such date if it finds such longer period to be appropriate and publishes its reasons for so finding or as to which the sponsors consent, the Commission shall approve such plan or amendment, with such changes or subject to such conditions as the Commission may deem necessary or appropriate, if it finds that such plan or amendment is necessary or appropriate in the public interest, for the protection of investors and the maintenance of fair and orderly markets, to remove impediments to, and perfect the mechanisms of, a national market system, or otherwise in furtherance of the purposes of the Act. Approval of a national market system plan, or an amendment to an effective national market system plan (other than an amendment initiated by the Commission), shall be by order. Promulgation of an amendment to an effective national market system plan initiated by the Commission shall be by rule.

(3)   A proposed amendment may be put into effect upon filing with the Commission if designated by the sponsors as:

(i)   Establishing or changing a fee or other charge collected on behalf of all of the sponsors and/or participants in connection with access to, or use of, any facility contemplated by the plan or amendment (including changes in any provision with respect to distribution of any net proceeds from such fees or other charges to the sponsors and/or participants);

(ii)   Concerned solely with the administration of the plan, or involving the governing or constituent documents relating to any person (other than a self-regulatory organization) authorized to implement or administer such plan on behalf of its sponsors; or

(iii)   Involving solely technical or ministerial matters. At any time within 60 days of the filing of any such amendment, the Commission may summarily abrogate the amendment and require that such amendment be refiled in accordance with paragraph (a)(1) of this rule and reviewed in accordance with paragraph (b)(2) of this rule, if it appears to the Commission that such action is necessary or appropriate in the public interest, for the protection of investors, or the maintenance of fair and orderly markets, to remove impediments to, and perfect the mechanisms of, a national market system or otherwise in furtherance of the purposes of the Act.

(4)   Notwithstanding the provisions of paragraph (b)(1) of this rule, a proposed amendment may be put into effect summarily upon publication of notice of such amendment, on a temporary basis not to exceed 120 days, if the Commission finds that such action is necessary or appropriate in the public interest, for the protection of investors or the maintenance of fair and orderly markets, to remove impediments to, and perfect the mechanisms of, a national market system or otherwise in furtherance of the purposes of the Act.

(5)   Any plan (or amendment thereto) in connection with:

(i)   The planning, development, operation, or regulation of a national market system (or a subsystem thereof) or one or more facilities thereof; or

(ii)   The development and implementation of procedures and/or facilities designed to achieve compliance by self-regulatory organizations and/or their members of any section of this Regulation NMS and part 240, subpart A of this chapter promulgated pursuant to section 11A of the Act, approved by the Commission pursuant to section 11A of the Act (or pursuant to any rule or regulation thereunder) prior to the effective date of this rule (either temporarily or permanently) shall be deemed to have been filed and approved pursuant to this rule and no additional filing need be made by the sponsors with respect to such plan or amendment; provided, however, that all terms and conditions associated with any such approval (including time limitations) shall continue to be applicable; provided, further, that any amendment to such plan filed with or approved by the Commission on or after the effective date of this rule shall be subject to the provisions of, and considered in accordance with the procedures specified in, this rule.

(c)   Compliance with terms of national market system plans. Each self-regulatory organization shall comply with the terms of any effective national market system plan of which it is a sponsor or a participant. Each self-regulatory organization also shall, absent reasonable justification or excuse, enforce compliance with any such plan by its members and persons associated with its members.

(d)   Appeals. The Commission may, in its discretion, entertain appeals in connection with the implementation or operation of any effective national market system plan as follows:

(1)   Any action taken or failure to act by any person in connection with an effective national market system plan (other than a prohibition or limitation of access reviewable by the Commission pursuant to section 11A(b)(5) or section 19(d) of the Act) shall be subject to review by the Commission, on its own motion or upon application by any person aggrieved thereby (including, but not limited to, self-regulatory organizations, brokers, dealers, issuers, and vendors), filed not later than 30 days after notice of such action or failure to act or within such longer period as the Commission may determine.

(2)   Application to the Commission for review, or the institution of review by the Commission on its own motion, shall not operate as a stay of any such action unless the Commission determines otherwise, after notice and opportunity for hearing on the question of a stay (which hearing may consist only of affidavits or oral arguments).

(3)   In any proceedings for review, if the Commission, after appropriate notice and opportunity for hearing (which hearing may consist solely of consideration of the record of any proceedings conducted in connection with such action or failure to act and an opportunity for the presentation of reasons supporting or opposing such action or failure to act) and upon consideration of such other data, views, and arguments as it deems relevant, finds that the action or failure to act is in accordance with the applicable provisions of such plan and that the applicable provisions are, and were, applied in a manner consistent with the public interest, the protection of investors, the maintenance of fair and orderly markets, and the removal of impediments to, and the perfection of the mechanisms of a national market system, the Commission, by order, shall dismiss the proceeding. If the Commission does not make any such finding, or if it finds that such action or failure to act imposes any burden on competition not necessary or appropriate in furtherance of the purposes of the Act, the Commission, by order, shall set aside such action and/or require such action with respect to the matter reviewed as the Commission deems necessary or appropriate in the public interest, for the protection of investors, and the

maintenance of fair and orderly markets, or to remove impediments to, and perfect the mechanisms of, a national market system.

(e) Exemptions. The Commission may exempt from the provisions of this rule, either unconditionally or on specified terms and conditions, any self-regulatory organization, member thereof, or specified security, if the Commission determines that such exemption is consistent with the public interest, the protection of investors, the maintenance of fair and orderly markets and the removal of impediments to, and perfection of the mechanisms of, a national market system.

Rule 609. Registration of Securities Information Processors: Form of Application and Amendments

(a) An application for the registration of a securities information processor shall be filed on Form SIP in accordance with the instructions contained therein.

(b) If any information reported in items 1–13 or item 21 of Form SIP or in any amendment thereto is or becomes inaccurate for any reason, whether before or after the registration has been granted, the securities information processor shall promptly file an amendment on Form SIP correcting such information.

(c) The Commission, upon its own motion or upon application by any securities information processor, may conditionally or unconditionally exempt any securities information processor from any provision of the rules or regulations adopted under section 11A(b) of the Act.

(d) Every amendment filed pursuant to this rule shall constitute a "report" within the meaning of sections 17(a), 18(a) and 32(a) of the Act.

Rule 610. Access to Quotations

(a) Quotations of SRO trading facility. A national securities exchange or national securities association shall not impose unfairly discriminatory terms that prevent or inhibit any person from obtaining efficient access through a member of the national securities exchange or national securities association to the quotations in an NMS stock displayed through its SRO trading facility.

(b) Quotations of SRO display-only facility.

(1) Any trading center that displays quotations in an NMS stock through an SRO display-only facility shall provide a level and cost of access to such quotations that is substantially equivalent to the level and cost of access to quotations displayed by SRO trading facilities in that stock.

(2) Any trading center that displays quotations in an NMS stock through an SRO display-only facility shall not impose unfairly discriminatory terms that prevent or inhibit any person from obtaining efficient access to such quotations through a member, subscriber, or customer of the trading center.

(c) Fees for access to quotations. A trading center shall not impose, nor permit to be imposed, any fee or fees for the execution of an order against a protected quotation of the trading center or against any other quotation of the trading center that is the best bid or best offer of a national securities exchange, the best bid or best offer of The Nasdaq Stock Market, Inc., or the best bid or best offer of a national securities association other than the best bid or best offer of The Nasdaq Stock Market, Inc. in an NMS stock that exceed or accumulate to more than the following limits:

(1) If the price of a protected quotation or other quotation is $1.00 or more, the fee or fees cannot exceed or accumulate to more than $0.003 per share; or

(2) If the price of a protected quotation or other quotation is less than $1.00, the fee or fees cannot exceed or accumulate to more than 0.3% of the quotation price per share.

(d) Locking or crossing quotations. Each national securities exchange and national securities association shall establish, maintain, and enforce written rules that:

(1) Require its members reasonably to avoid:

(i) Displaying quotations that lock or cross any protected quotation in an NMS stock; and

(ii) Displaying manual quotations that lock or cross any quotation in an NMS stock disseminated pursuant to an effective national market system plan;

(2) Are reasonably designed to assure the reconciliation of locked or crossed quotations in an NMS stock; and

(3) Prohibit its members from engaging in a pattern or practice of displaying quotations that lock or cross any protected quotation in an NMS stock, or of displaying manual quotations that lock or cross any quotation in an NMS stock disseminated pursuant to an effective national market system plan, other than displaying quotations that lock or cross any protected or other quotation as permitted by an exception contained in its rules established pursuant to paragraph (d)(1) of this rule.

(e) Exemptions. The Commission, by order, may exempt from the provisions of this rule, either unconditionally or on specified terms and conditions, any person, security, quotations, orders, or fees, or any class or classes of persons, securities, quotations, orders, or fees, if the Commission determines that such exemption is necessary or appropriate in the public interest, and is consistent with the protection of investors.

Rule 611.   Order Protection Rule

(a) Reasonable policies and procedures.

(1) A trading center shall establish, maintain, and enforce written policies and procedures that are reasonably designed to prevent trade-throughs on that trading center of protected quotations in NMS stocks that do not fall within an exception set forth in paragraph (b) of this rule and, if relying on such an exception, that are reasonably designed to assure compliance with the terms of the exception.

(2) A trading center shall regularly surveil to ascertain the effectiveness of the policies and procedures required by paragraph (a)(1) of this rule and shall take prompt action to remedy deficiencies in such policies and procedures.

(b) Exceptions.

(1) The transaction that constituted the trade-through was effected when the trading center displaying the protected quotation that was traded through was experiencing a failure, material delay, or malfunction of its systems or equipment.

(2) The transaction that constituted the trade-through was not a "regular way" contract.

(3) The transaction that constituted the trade-through was a single-priced opening, reopening, or closing transaction by the trading center.

(4) The transaction that constituted the trade-through was executed at a time when a protected bid was priced higher than a protected offer in the NMS stock.

(5) The transaction that constituted the trade-through was the execution of an order identified as an intermarket sweep order.

(6) The transaction that constituted the trade-through was effected by a trading center that simultaneously routed an intermarket sweep order to execute against the full displayed size of any protected quotation in the NMS stock that was traded through.

(7) The transaction that constituted the trade-through was the execution of an order at a price that was not based, directly or indirectly, on the quoted price of the NMS stock at the time of execution and for which the material terms were not reasonably determinable at the time the commitment to execute the order was made.

(8) The trading center displaying the protected quotation that was traded through had displayed, within one second prior to execution of the transaction that constituted the trade-through, a best bid or best offer, as applicable, for the NMS stock with a price that was equal or inferior to the price of the trade-through transaction.

(9)   The transaction that constituted the trade-through was the execution by a trading center of an order for which, at the time of receipt of the order, the trading center had guaranteed an execution at no worse than a specified price (a "stopped order"), where:

      (i)   The stopped order was for the account of a customer;

      (ii)   The customer agreed to the specified price on an order-by-order basis; and

      (iii)   The price of the trade-through transaction was, for a stopped buy order, lower than the national best bid in the NMS stock at the time of execution or, for a stopped sell order, higher than the national best offer in the NMS stock at the time of execution.

(c)   Intermarket sweep orders. The trading center, broker, or dealer responsible for the routing of an intermarket sweep order shall take reasonable steps to establish that such order meets the requirements set forth in Rule 600(b)(31).

(d)   Exemptions. The Commission, by order, may exempt from the provisions of this rule, either unconditionally or on specified terms and conditions, any person, security, transaction, quotation, or order, or any class or classes of persons, securities, quotations, or orders, if the Commission determines that such exemption is necessary or appropriate in the public interest, and is consistent with the protection of investors.

Rule 612.   Minimum Pricing Increment

(a)   No national securities exchange, national securities association, alternative trading system, vendor, or broker or dealer shall display, rank, or accept from any person a bid or offer, an order, or an indication of interest in any NMS stock priced in an increment smaller than $0.01 if that bid or offer, order, or indication of interest is priced equal to or greater than $1.00 per share.

(b)   No national securities exchange, national securities association, alternative trading system, vendor, or broker or dealer shall display, rank, or accept from any person a bid or offer, an order, or an indication of interest in any NMS stock priced in an increment smaller than $0.0001 if that bid or offer, order, or indication of interest is priced less than $1.00 per share.

(c)   The Commission, by order, may exempt from the provisions of this rule, either unconditionally or on specified terms and conditions, any person, security, quotation, or order, or any class or classes of persons, securities, quotations, or orders, if the Commission determines that such exemption is necessary or appropriate in the public interest, and is consistent with the protection of investors.

Rule 613.   Consolidated Audit Trail

(a)   *Creation of a national market system plan governing a consolidated audit trail.*

(1)   Each national securities exchange and national securities association shall jointly file on or before 270 days from the date of publication of the Adopting Release in the Federal Register a national market system plan to govern the creation, implementation, and maintenance of a consolidated audit trail and central repository as required by this rule. The national market system plan shall discuss the following considerations:

      (i)   The method(s) by which data will be reported to the central repository including, but not limited to, the sources of such data and the manner in which the central repository will receive, extract, transform, load, and retain such data; and the basis for selecting such method(s);

      (ii)   The time and method by which the data in the central repository will be made available to regulators, in accordance with paragraph (e)(1) of this rule, to perform surveillance or analyses, or for other purposes as part of their regulatory and oversight responsibilities;

      (iii)   The reliability and accuracy of the data reported to and maintained by the central repository throughout its lifecycle, including transmission and receipt from market participants; data extraction, transformation and loading at the central repository; data maintenance and management at the central repository; and data access by regulators;

      (iv)   The security and confidentiality of the information reported to the central repository;

(v) The flexibility and scalability of the systems used by the central repository to collect, consolidate and store consolidated audit trail data, including the capacity of the consolidated audit trail to efficiently incorporate, in a cost-effective manner, improvements in technology, additional capacity, additional order data, information about additional securities or transactions, changes in regulatory requirements, and other developments;

(vi) The feasibility, benefits, and costs of broker-dealers reporting to the consolidated audit trail in a timely manner:

(A) The identity of all market participants (including broker-dealers and customers) that are allocated NMS securities, directly or indirectly, in a primary market transaction;

(B) The number of such securities each such market participant is allocated; and

(C) The identity of the broker-dealer making each such allocation;

(vii) The detailed estimated costs for creating, implementing, and maintaining the consolidated audit trail as contemplated by the national market system plan, which estimated costs should specify:

(A) An estimate of the costs to the plan sponsors for establishing and maintaining the central repository;

(B) An estimate of the costs to members of the plan sponsors, initially and on an ongoing basis, for reporting the data required by the national market system plan;

(C) An estimate of the costs to the plan sponsors, initially and on an ongoing basis, for reporting the data required by the national market system plan; and

(D) How the plan sponsors propose to fund the creation, implementation, and maintenance of the consolidated audit trail, including the proposed allocation of such estimated costs among the plan sponsors, and between the plan sponsors and members of the plan sponsors;

(viii) An analysis of the impact on competition, efficiency and capital formation of creating, implementing, and maintaining of the national market system plan;

(ix) A plan to eliminate existing rules and systems (or components thereof) that will be rendered duplicative by the consolidated audit trail, including identification of such rules and systems (or components thereof); to the extent that any existing rules or systems related to monitoring quotes, orders, and executions provide information that is not rendered duplicative by the consolidated audit trail, an analysis of:

(A) Whether the collection of such information remains appropriate;

(B) If still appropriate, whether such information should continue to be separately collected or should instead be incorporated into the consolidated audit trail; and

(C) If no longer appropriate, how the collection of such information could be efficiently terminated; the steps the plan sponsors propose to take to seek Commission approval for the elimination of such rules and systems (or components thereof); and a timetable for such elimination, including a description of how the plan sponsors propose to phase in the consolidated audit trail and phase out such existing rules and systems (or components thereof);

(x) Objective milestones to assess progress toward the implementation of the national market system plan;

(xi) The process by which the plan sponsors solicited views of their members and other appropriate parties regarding the creation, implementation, and maintenance of the consolidated audit trail, a summary of the views of such members and other parties, and how the plan sponsors took such views into account in preparing the national market system plan; and

(xii) Any reasonable alternative approaches to creating, implementing, and maintaining a consolidated audit trail that the plan sponsors considered in developing the national market system plan including, but not limited to, a description of any such alternative approach; the relative advantages and disadvantages of each such alternative, including an assessment of the alternative's costs and benefits; and the basis upon which the plan sponsors selected the approach reflected in the national market system plan.

(2)   The national market system plan, or any amendment thereto, filed pursuant to this rule shall comply with the requirements in Item 608(a), if applicable, and be filed with the Commission pursuant to Item 608.

(3)   The national market system plan submitted pursuant to this rule shall require each national securities exchange and national securities association to:

(i)   Within two months after effectiveness of the national market system plan jointly (or under the governance structure described in the plan) select a person to be the plan processor;

(ii)   Within four months after effectiveness of the national market system plan synchronize their business clocks and require members of each such exchange and association to synchronize their business clocks in accordance with paragraph (d) of this rule;

(iii)   Within one year after effectiveness of the national market system plan provide to the central repository the data specified in paragraph (c) of this rule;

(iv)   Within fourteen months after effectiveness of the national market system plan implement a new or enhanced surveillance system(s) as required by paragraph (f) of this rule;

(v)   Within two years after effectiveness of the national market system plan require members of each such exchange and association, except those members that qualify as small broker-dealers as defined in Rule 0–10(c) of the Securities Exchange Act of 1934, to provide to the central repository the data specified in paragraph (c) of this rule; and

(vi)   Within three years after effectiveness of the national market system plan require members of each such exchange and association that qualify as small broker-dealers as defined in Rule 0–10(c) of the Securities Exchange Act of 1934 to provide to the central repository the data specified in paragraph (c) of this rule.

(4)   Each national securities exchange and national securities association shall be a sponsor of the national market system plan submitted pursuant to this rule and approved by the Commission.

(5)   No national market system plan filed pursuant to this rule, or any amendment thereto, shall become effective unless approved by the Commission or otherwise permitted in accordance with the procedures set forth in Item 608. In determining whether to approve the national market system plan, or any amendment thereto, and whether the national market system plan or any amendment thereto is in the public interest under Item 608(b)(2), the Commission shall consider the impact of the national market system plan or amendment, as applicable, on efficiency, competition, and capital formation.

(b)   *Operation and administration of the national market system plan.*

(1)   The national market system plan submitted pursuant to this rule shall include a governance structure to ensure fair representation of the plan sponsors, and administration of the central repository, including the selection of the plan processor.

(2)   The national market system plan submitted pursuant to this rule shall include a provision addressing the requirements for the admission of new sponsors of the plan and the withdrawal of existing sponsors from the plan.

(3)   The national market system plan submitted pursuant to this rule shall include a provision addressing the percentage of votes required by the plan sponsors to effectuate amendments to the plan.

(4)   The national market system plan submitted pursuant to this rule shall include a provision addressing the manner in which the costs of operating the central repository will be allocated among the national securities exchanges and national securities associations that are sponsors of the plan, including a provision addressing the manner in which costs will be allocated to new sponsors to the plan.

(5)   The national market system plan submitted pursuant to this rule shall require the appointment of a Chief Compliance Officer to regularly review the operation of the central repository

to assure its continued effectiveness in light of market and technological developments, and make any appropriate recommendations for enhancements to the nature of the information collected and the manner in which it is processed.

(6)   The national market system plan submitted pursuant to this rule shall include a provision requiring the plan sponsors to provide to the Commission, at least every two years after effectiveness of the national market system plan, a written assessment of the operation of the consolidated audit trail. Such document shall include, at a minimum:

(i)   An evaluation of the performance of the consolidated audit trail including, at a minimum, with respect to data accuracy (consistent with paragraph (e)(6) of this rule), timeliness of reporting, comprehensiveness of data elements, efficiency of regulatory access, system speed, system downtime, system security (consistent with paragraph (e)(4) of this rule), and other performance metrics to be determined by the Chief Compliance Officer, along with a description of such metrics;

(ii)   A detailed plan, based on such evaluation, for any potential improvements to the performance of the consolidated audit trail with respect to any of the following: improving data accuracy; shortening reporting timeframes; expanding data elements; adding granularity and details regarding the scope and nature of Customer-IDs; expanding the scope of the national market system plan to include new instruments and new types of trading and order activities; improving the efficiency of regulatory access; increasing system speed; reducing system downtime; and improving performance under other metrics to be determined by the Chief Compliance Officer;

(iii)   An estimate of the costs associated with any such potential improvements to the performance of the consolidated audit trail, including an assessment of the potential impact on competition, efficiency, and capital formation; and

(iv)   An estimated implementation timeline for any such potential improvements, if applicable.

(7)   The national market system plan submitted pursuant to this rule shall include an Advisory Committee which shall function in accordance with the provisions set forth in this paragraph (b)(7). The purpose of the Advisory Committee shall be to advise the plan sponsors on the implementation, operation, and administration of the central repository.

(i)   The national market system plan submitted pursuant to this rule shall set forth the term and composition of the Advisory Committee, which composition shall include representatives of the member firms of the plan sponsors.

(ii)   Members of the Advisory Committee shall have the right to attend any meetings of the plan sponsors, to receive information concerning the operation of the central repository, and to provide their views to the plan sponsors; provided, however, that the plan sponsors may meet without the Advisory Committee members in executive session if, by affirmative vote of a majority of the plan sponsors, the plan sponsors determine that such an executive session is required.

(c)   *Data recording and reporting.*

(1)   The national market system plan submitted pursuant to this rule shall provide for an accurate, time-sequenced record of orders beginning with the receipt or origination of an order by a member of a national securities exchange or national securities association, and further documenting the life of the order through the process of routing, modification, cancellation, and execution (in whole or in part) of the order.

(2)   The national market system plan submitted pursuant to this rule shall require each national securities exchange, national securities association, and member to report to the central repository the information required by paragraph (c)(7) of this rule in a uniform electronic format, or in a manner that would allow the central repository to convert the data to a uniform electronic format, for consolidation and storage.

(3)   The national market system plan submitted pursuant to this rule shall require each national securities exchange, national securities association, and member to record the information required by

paragraphs (c)(7)(i) through (v) of this rule contemporaneously with the reportable event. The national market system plan shall require that information recorded pursuant to paragraphs (c)(7)(i) through (v) of this rule must be reported to the central repository by 8:00 a.m. Eastern Time on the trading day following the day such information has been recorded by the national securities exchange, national securities association, or member. The national market system plan may accommodate voluntary reporting prior to 8:00 a.m. Eastern Time, but shall not impose an earlier reporting deadline on the reporting parties.

(4)   The national market system plan submitted pursuant to this rule shall require each member of a national securities exchange or national securities association to record and report to the central repository the information required by paragraphs (c)(7)(vi) through (viii) of this rule by 8:00 a.m. Eastern Time on the trading day following the day the member receives such information. The national market system plan may accommodate voluntary reporting prior to 8:00 a.m. Eastern Time, but shall not impose an earlier reporting deadline on the reporting parties.

(5)   The national market system plan submitted pursuant to this rule shall require each national securities exchange and its members to record and report to the central repository the information required by paragraph (c)(7) of this rule for each NMS security registered or listed for trading on such exchange or admitted to unlisted trading privileges on such exchange.

(6)   The national market system plan submitted pursuant to this rule shall require each national securities association and its members to record and report to the central repository the information required by paragraph (c)(7) of this rule for each NMS security for which transaction reports are required to be submitted to the association.

(7)   The national market system plan submitted pursuant to this rule shall require each national securities exchange, national securities association, and any member of such exchange or association to record and electronically report to the central repository details for each order and each reportable event, including, but not limited to, the following information:

    (i)   For original receipt or origination of an order:

        (A)   Customer-ID(s) for each customer;

        (B)   The CAT-Order-ID;

        (C)   The CAT-Reporter-ID of the broker-dealer receiving or originating the order;

        (D)   Date of order receipt or origination;

        (E)   Time of order receipt or origination (using time stamps pursuant to paragraph (d)(3) of this rule); and

        (F)   Material terms of the order.

    (ii)   For the routing of an order, the following information:

        (A)   The CAT-Order-ID;

        (B)   Date on which the order is routed;

        (C)   Time at which the order is routed (using time stamps pursuant to paragraph (d)(3) of this rule);

        (D)   The CAT-Reporter-ID of the broker-dealer or national securities exchange routing the order;

        (E)   The CAT-Reporter-ID of the broker-dealer, national securities exchange, or national securities association to which the order is being routed;

        (F)   If routed internally at the broker-dealer, the identity and nature of the department or desk to which an order is routed; and

        (G)   Material terms of the order.

    (iii) For the receipt of an order that has been routed, the following information:

        (A)   The CAT-Order-ID;

(B)   Date on which the order is received;

(C)   Time at which the order is received (using time stamps pursuant to paragraph (d)(3) of this rule);

(D)   The CAT-Reporter-ID of the broker-dealer, national securities exchange, or national securities association receiving the order;

(E)   The CAT-Reporter-ID of the broker-dealer or national securities exchange routing the order; and

(F)   Material terms of the order.

(iv)   If the order is modified or cancelled, the following information:

(A)   The CAT-Order-ID;

(B)   Date the modification or cancellation is received or originated;

(C)   Time the modification or cancellation is received or originated (using time stamps pursuant to paragraph (d)(3) of this rule);

(D)   Price and remaining size of the order, if modified;

(E)   Other changes in material terms of the order, if modified; and

(F)   The CAT-Reporter-ID of the broker-dealer or Customer-ID of the person giving the modification or cancellation instruction.

(v)   If the order is executed, in whole or part, the following information:

(A)   The CAT-Order-ID;

(B)   Date of execution;

(C)   Time of execution (using time stamps pursuant to paragraph (d)(3) of this rule);

(D)   Execution capacity (principal, agency, riskless principal);

(E)   Execution price and size;

(F)   The CAT-Reporter-ID of the national securities exchange or broker-dealer executing the order; and

(G)   Whether the execution was reported pursuant to an effective transaction reporting plan or the Plan for Reporting of Consolidated Options Last Sale Reports and Quotation Information.

(vi)   If the order is executed, in whole or part, the following information:

(A)   The account number for any subaccounts to which the execution is allocated (in whole or part);

(B)   The CAT-Reporter-ID of the clearing broker or prime broker, if applicable; and

(C)   The CAT-Order-ID of any contra-side order(s).

(vii) If the trade is cancelled, a cancelled trade indicator.

(viii) For original receipt or origination of an order, the following information:

(A)   Information of sufficient detail to identify the customer; and

(B)   Customer account information.

(8)   All plan sponsors and their members shall use the same Customer-ID and CAT-Reporter-ID for each customer and broker-dealer.

(d)   *Clock synchronization and time stamps.* The national market system plan submitted pursuant to this rule shall require:

(1)   Each national securities exchange, national securities association, and member of such exchange or association to synchronize its business clocks that are used for the purposes of recording the date and time of any reportable event that must be reported pursuant to this rule to the time maintained by the National Institute of Standards and Technology, consistent with industry standards;

(2)   Each national securities exchange and national securities association to evaluate annually the clock synchronization standard to determine whether it should be shortened, consistent with changes in industry standards; and

(3)   Each national securities exchange, national securities association, and member of such exchange or association to utilize the time stamps required by paragraph (c)(7) of this rule, with at minimum the granularity set forth in the national market system plan submitted pursuant to this rule, which shall reflect current industry standards and be at least to the millisecond. To the extent that the relevant order handling and execution systems of any national securities exchange, national securities association, or member of such exchange or association utilize time stamps in increments finer than the minimum required by the national market system plan, the plan shall require such national securities exchange, national securities association, or member to utilize time stamps in such finer increments when providing data to the central repository, so that all reportable events reported to the central repository by any national securities exchange, national securities association, or member can be accurately sequenced. The national market system plan shall require the sponsors of the national market system plan to annually evaluate whether industry standards have evolved such that the required time stamp standard should be in finer increments.

(e)   *Central repository.*

(1)   The national market system plan submitted pursuant to this rule shall provide for the creation and maintenance of a central repository. Such central repository shall be responsible for the receipt, consolidation, and retention of all information reported pursuant to paragraph (c)(7) of this rule. The central repository shall store and make available to regulators data in a uniform electronic format, and in a form in which all events pertaining to the same originating order are linked together in a manner that ensures timely and accurate retrieval of the information required by paragraph (c)(7) of this rule for all reportable events for that order.

(2)   Each national securities exchange, national securities association, and the Commission shall have access to the central repository, including all systems operated by the central repository, and access to and use of the data reported to and consolidated by the central repository under paragraph (c) of this rule, for the purpose of performing its respective regulatory and oversight responsibilities pursuant to the federal securities laws, rules, and regulations. The national market system plan submitted pursuant to this rule shall provide that such access to and use of such data by each national securities exchange, national securities association, and the Commission for the purpose of performing its regulatory and oversight responsibilities pursuant to the federal securities laws, rules, and regulations shall not be limited.

(3)   The national market system plan submitted pursuant to this rule shall include a provision requiring the creation and maintenance by the plan processor of a method of access to the consolidated data stored in the central repository that includes the ability to run searches and generate reports.

(4)   The national market system plan submitted pursuant to this rule shall include policies and procedures, including standards, to be used by the plan processor to:

(i)   Ensure the security and confidentiality of all information reported to the central repository by requiring that:

(A)   All plan sponsors and their employees, as well as all employees of the central repository, agree to use appropriate safeguards to ensure the confidentiality of such data and agree not to use such data for any purpose other than surveillance and regulatory purposes, provided that nothing in this paragraph (e)(4)(i)(A) shall be construed to prevent a plan sponsor from using the data that it reports to the central repository for regulatory, surveillance, commercial, or other purposes as otherwise permitted by applicable law, rule, or regulation;

(B)   Each plan sponsor adopt and enforce rules that:

(*1*)   Require information barriers between regulatory staff and non-regulatory staff with regard to access and use of data in the central repository; and

(*2*)   Permit only persons designated by plan sponsors to have access to the data in the central repository;

(C)   The plan processor:

(*1*)   Develop and maintain a comprehensive information security program for the central repository, with dedicated staff, that is subject to regular reviews by the Chief Compliance Officer;

(*2*)   Have a mechanism to confirm the identity of all persons permitted to access the data; and

(*3*)   Maintain a record of all instances where such persons access the data; and

(D)   The plan sponsors adopt penalties for non-compliance with any policies and procedures of the plan sponsors or central repository with respect to information security.

(ii)   Ensure the timeliness, accuracy, integrity, and completeness of the data provided to the central repository pursuant to paragraph (c) of this rule; and

(iii)   Ensure the accuracy of the consolidation by the plan processor of the data provided to the central repository pursuant to paragraph (c) of this rule.

(5)   The national market system plan submitted pursuant to this rule shall address whether there will be an annual independent evaluation of the security of the central repository and:

(i)   If so, provide a description of the scope of such planned evaluation; and

(ii)   If not, provide a detailed explanation of the alternative measures for evaluating the security of the central repository that are planned instead.

(6)   The national market system plan submitted pursuant to this rule shall:

(i)   Specify a maximum error rate to be tolerated by the central repository for any data reported pursuant to paragraphs (c)(3) and (c)(4) of this rule; describe the basis for selecting such maximum error rate; explain how the plan sponsors will seek to reduce such maximum error rate over time; describe how the plan will seek to ensure compliance with such maximum error rate and, in the event of noncompliance, will promptly remedy the causes thereof;

(ii)   Require the central repository to measure the error rate each business day and promptly take appropriate remedial action, at a minimum, if the error rate exceeds the maximum error rate specified in the plan;

(iii)   Specify a process for identifying and correcting errors in the data reported to the central repository pursuant to paragraphs (c)(3) and (c)(4) of this rule, including the process for notifying the national securities exchanges, national securities association, and members who reported erroneous data to the central repository of such errors, to help ensure that such errors are promptly corrected by the reporting entity, and for disciplining those who repeatedly report erroneous data; and

(iv)   Specify the time by which data that has been corrected will be made available to regulators.

(7)   The national market system plan submitted pursuant to this rule shall require the central repository to collect and retain on a current and continuing basis and in a format compatible with the information consolidated and stored pursuant to paragraph (c)(7) of this rule:

(i)   Information, including the size and quote condition, on the national best bid and national best offer for each NMS security;

(ii)   Transaction reports reported pursuant to an effective transaction reporting plan filed with the Commission pursuant to, and meeting the requirements of, Item 601; and

(iii) Last sale reports reported pursuant to the Plan for Reporting of Consolidated Options Last Sale Reports and Quotation Information filed with the Commission pursuant to, and meeting the requirements of, Item 608.

(8) The national market system plan submitted pursuant to this rule shall require the central repository to retain the information collected pursuant to paragraphs (c)(7) and (e)(7) of this rule in a convenient and usable standard electronic data format that is directly available and searchable electronically without any manual intervention for a period of not less than five years.

(f) *Surveillance.* Every national securities exchange and national securities association subject to this rule shall develop and implement a surveillance system, or enhance existing surveillance systems, reasonably designed to make use of the consolidated information contained in the consolidated audit trail.

(g) *Compliance by members.*

(1) Each national securities exchange and national securities association shall file with the Commission pursuant to section 19(b)(2) of the Act (15 U.S.C. 78s(b)(2)) and Rule 19b–4 of the Securities Exchange Act of 1934 on or before 60 days from approval of the national market system plan a proposed rule change to require its members to comply with the requirements of this rule and the national market system plan approved by the Commission.

(2) Each member of a national securities exchange or national securities association shall comply with all the provisions of any approved national market system plan applicable to members.

(3) The national market system plan submitted pursuant to this rule shall include a provision requiring each national securities exchange and national securities association to agree to enforce compliance by its members with the provisions of any approved plan.

(4) The national market system plan submitted pursuant to this rule shall include a mechanism to ensure compliance with the requirements of any approved plan by the members of a national securities exchange or national securities association.

(h) *Compliance by national securities exchanges and national securities associations.*

(1) Each national securities exchange and national securities association shall comply with the provisions of the national market system plan approved by the Commission.

(2) Any failure by a national securities exchange or national securities association to comply with the provisions of the national market system plan approved by the Commission shall be considered a violation of this rule.

(3) The national market system plan submitted pursuant to this rule shall include a mechanism to ensure compliance by the sponsors of the plan with the requirements of any approved plan. Such enforcement mechanism may include penalties where appropriate.

(i) *Other securities and other types of transactions.* The national market system plan submitted pursuant to this rule shall include a provision requiring each national securities exchange and national securities association to jointly provide to the Commission within six months after effectiveness of the national market system plan a document outlining how such exchanges and associations could incorporate into the consolidated audit trail information with respect to equity securities that are not NMS securities, debt securities, primary market transactions in equity securities that are not NMS securities, and primary market transactions in debt securities, including details for each order and reportable event that may be required to be provided, which market participants may be required to provide the data, an implementation timeline, and a cost estimate.

(j) *Definitions.* As used in this rule:

(1) The term *CAT-Order-ID* shall mean a unique order identifier or series of unique order identifiers that allows the central repository to efficiently and accurately link all reportable events for an order, and all orders that result from the aggregation or disaggregation of such order.

(2) The term *CAT-Reporter-ID* shall mean, with respect to each national securities exchange, national securities association, and member of a national securities exchange or national securities association, a code that uniquely and consistently identifies such person for purposes of providing data to the central repository.

(3)   The term *customer* shall mean:

(i)   The account holder(s) of the account at a registered broker-dealer originating the order; and

(ii)   Any person from whom the broker-dealer is authorized to accept trading instructions for such account, if different from the account holder(s).

(4)   The term *customer account information* shall include, but not be limited to, account number, account type, customer type, date account opened, and large trader identifier (if applicable).

(5)   The term *Customer-ID* shall mean, with respect to a customer, a code that uniquely and consistently identifies such customer for purposes of providing data to the central repository.

(6)   The term *error rate* shall mean the percentage of reportable events collected by the central repository in which the data reported does not fully and accurately reflect the order event that occurred in the market.

(7)   The term *material terms of the order* shall include, but not be limited to, the NMS security symbol; security type; price (if applicable); size (displayed and non-displayed); side (buy/sell); order type; if a sell order, whether the order is long, short, short exempt; open/close indicator; time in force (if applicable); if the order is for a listed option, option type (put/call), option symbol or root symbol, underlying symbol, strike price, expiration date, and open/close; and any special handling instructions.

(8)   The term *order* shall include:

(i)   Any order received by a member of a national securities exchange or national securities association from any person;

(ii)   Any order originated by a member of a national securities exchange or national securities association; or

(iii)   Any bid or offer.

(9)   The term *reportable event* shall include, but not be limited to, the original receipt or origination, modification, cancellation, routing, and execution (in whole or in part) of an order, and receipt of a routed order.

REGULATION FD—SELECTIVE DISCLOSURE

17 C.F.R. § 243.___

Rule 100. General Rule Regarding Selective Disclosure

(a) Whenever an issuer, or any person acting on its behalf, discloses any material nonpublic information regarding that issuer or its securities to any person described in paragraph (b)(1) of this rule, the issuer shall make public disclosure of that information as provided Rule 101(e):

    (1) Simultaneously, in the case of an intentional disclosure; and

    (2) Promptly, in the case of a non-intentional disclosure.

(b)(1) Except as provided in paragraph (b)(2) of this rule, paragraph (a) of this rule shall apply to a disclosure made to any person outside the issuer:

    (i) Who is a broker or dealer, or a person associated with a broker or dealer, as those terms are defined in Section 3(a) of the Securities Exchange Act of 1934;

    (ii) Who is an investment adviser, as that term is defined in Section 202(a)(11) of the Investment Advisers Act of 1940; an institutional investment manager, as that term is defined in Section 13(f)(6) of the Securities Exchange Act of 1934, that filed a report on Form 13F with the Commission for the most recent quarter ended prior to the date of the disclosure; or a person associated with either of the foregoing. For purposes of this paragraph, a "person associated with an investment adviser or institutional investment manager" has the meaning set forth in Section 202(a)(17) of the Investment Advisers Act of 1940, assuming for these purposes that an institutional investment manager is an investment adviser;

    (iii) Who is a holder of the issuer's securities, under circumstances in which it is reasonably foreseeable that the person will purchase or sell the issuer's securities on the basis of the information.

    (2) Paragraph (a) of this rule shall not apply to a disclosure made:

        (i) To a person who owes a duty of trust or confidence to the issuer (such as an attorney, investment banker, or accountant);

        (ii) To a person who expressly agrees to maintain the disclosed information in confidence;

        (iii) In connection with a securities offering registered under the Securities Act, other than an offering of the type described in any of Rule 415(a)(1)(i) through (vi) under the Securities Act (except an offering of the type described in Rule 415(a)(1)(i) under the Securities Act also involving a registered offering, whether or not underwritten, for capital formation purposes for the account of the issuer (unless the issuer's offering is being registered for the purpose of evading the requirements of this rule)), if the disclosure is by any of the following means:

            (A) A registration statement filed under the Securities Act, including a prospectus contained therein;

            (B) A free writing prospectus used after filing of the registration statement for the offering or a communication falling within the exception to the definition of prospectus contained in clause (a) of section 2(a)(10) of the Securities Act;

            (C) Any other Section 10(b) prospectus;

            (D) A notice permitted by Rule 135 under the Securities Act;

(E)   A communication permitted by Rule 134 under the Securities Act; or

(F)   An oral communication made in connection with the registered securities offering after filing of the registration statement for the offering under the Securities Act.

Rule 101.   Definitions

This rule defines certain terms as used in Regulation FD.

(a)   Intentional. A selective disclosure of material nonpublic information is "intentional" when the person making the disclosure either knows, or is reckless in not knowing, that the information he or she is communicating is both material and nonpublic.

(b)   Issuer. An "issuer" subject to this regulation is one that has a class of securities registered under Section 12 of the Securities Exchange Act of 1934, or is required to file reports under Section 15(d) of the Securities Exchange Act of 1934, including any closed-end investment company (as defined in Section 5(a)(2) of the Investment Company Act of 1940), but not including any other investment company or any foreign government or foreign private issuer, as those terms are defined in Rule 405 under the Securities Act.

(c)   Person acting on behalf of an issuer. "Person acting on behalf of an issuer" means any senior official of the issuer (or, in the case of a closed-end investment company, a senior official of the issuer's investment adviser), or any other officer, employee, or agent of an issuer who regularly communicates with any person described in Rule 100(b)(1)(i), (ii), or (iii), or with holders of the issuer's securities. An officer, director, employee, or agent of an issuer who discloses material nonpublic information in breach of a duty of trust or confidence to the issuer shall not be considered to be acting on behalf of the issuer.

(d)   Promptly. "Promptly" means as soon as reasonably practicable (but in no event after the later of 24 hours or the commencement of the next day's trading on the New York Stock Exchange) after a senior official of the issuer (or, in the case of a closed-end investment company, a senior official of the issuer's investment adviser) learns that there has been a non-intentional disclosure by the issuer or person acting on behalf of the issuer of information that the senior official knows, or is reckless in not knowing, is both material and nonpublic.

(e)   Public disclosure.

(1)   Except as provided in paragraph (e)(2) of this rule, an issuer shall make the "public disclosure" of information required by Rule 100(a) by furnishing to or filing with the Commission a Form 8–K disclosing that information.

(2)   An issuer shall be exempt from the requirement to furnish or file a Form 8–K if it instead disseminates the information through another method (or combination of methods) of disclosure that is reasonably designed to provide broad, non-exclusionary distribution of the information to the public.

(f)   Senior official. "Senior official" means any director, executive officer (as defined in Rule 3b–7 of the Securities Exchange Act), investor relations or public relations officer, or other person with similar functions.

(g)   Securities offering. For purposes of Rule 100(b)(2)(iv):

(1)   Underwritten offerings. A securities offering that is underwritten commences when the issuer reaches an understanding with the broker-dealer that is to act as managing underwriter and continues until the later of the end of the period during which a dealer must deliver a prospectus or the sale of the securities (unless the offering is sooner terminated);

(2)   Non-underwritten offerings. A securities offering that is not underwritten:

(i)   If covered by Rule 415(a)(1)(x) of the Securities Act, commences when the issuer makes its first bona fide offer in a takedown of securities and continues until the later of the end of the period during which each dealer must deliver a prospectus or the sale of the securities in that takedown (unless the takedown is sooner terminated);

(ii)   If a business combination as defined in Rule 165(f)(1) of the Securities Act commences when the first public announcement of the transaction is made and continues until the completion of the vote or the expiration of the tender offer, as applicable (unless the transaction is sooner terminated);

(iii) If an offering other than those specified in paragraphs (a) and (b) of this rule, commences when the issuer files a registration statement and continues until the later of the end of the period during which each dealer must deliver a prospectus or the sale of the securities (unless the offering is sooner terminated).

Rule 102.   No Effect on Antifraud Liability

No failure to make a public disclosure required solely by Rule 100 shall be deemed to be a violation of Rule 10b–5 under the Securities Exchange Act.

Rule 103.   No Effect on Exchange Act Reporting Status

A failure to make a public disclosure required solely by Rule 100 shall not affect whether:

(a)   For purposes of Forms S–3, S–8 and SF–3 under the Securities Act of 1933, or Form N–2 under the Securities Act of 1933 and the Investment Company Act of, an issuer is deemed to have filed all the material required to be filed pursuant to Section 13 or 15(d) of the Securities Exchange Act of 1934 or where applicable, has made those filings in a timely manner; or

(b)   There is adequate current public information about the issuer for purposes of Rule 144(c) of the Securities Act.

REGULATION BTR—BLACKOUT TRADING RESTRICTION

17 C.F.R. § 245.___

Rule 100.   Definitions

As used in Regulation BTR (Rules 100–104), unless the context otherwise requires:

(a)   The term **acquired in connection with service or employment** as a director or executive officer, when applied to a director or executive officer, means that he or she acquired, directly or indirectly, an equity security:

    (1)   At a time when he or she was a director or executive officer, under a compensatory plan, contract, authorization or arrangement, including, but not limited to, an option, warrants or rights plan, a pension, retirement or deferred compensation plan or a bonus, incentive or profit-sharing plan (whether or not set forth in any formal plan document), including a compensatory plan, contract, authorization or arrangement with a parent, subsidiary or affiliate;

    (2)   At a time when he or she was a director or executive officer, as a result of any transaction or business relationship described in paragraph (a) of Item 404 of Regulation S–K or, in the case of a foreign private issuer, Item 7.B of Form 20–F (but without application of the disclosure thresholds of such provisions), to the extent that he or she has a pecuniary interest (as defined in paragraph (l) of this rule) in the equity securities;

    (3)   At a time when he or she was a director or executive officer, as directors' qualifying shares or other securities that he or she must hold to satisfy minimum ownership requirements or guidelines for directors or executive officers;

    (4)   Prior to becoming, or while, a director or executive officer where the equity security was acquired as a direct or indirect inducement to service or employment as a director or executive officer; or

    (5)   Prior to becoming, or while, a director or executive officer where the equity security was received as a result of a business combination in respect of an equity security of an entity involved in the business combination that he or she had acquired in connection with service or employment as a director or executive officer of such entity.

(b)   Except as provided in Rule 102, the term **blackout period:**

    (1)   With respect to the equity securities of any issuer (other than a foreign private issuer), means any period of more than three consecutive business days during which the ability to purchase, sell or otherwise acquire or transfer an interest in any equity security of such issuer held in an individual account plan is temporarily suspended by the issuer or by a fiduciary of the plan with respect to not fewer than 50% of the participants or beneficiaries located in the United States and its territories and possessions under all individual account plans (as defined in paragraph (j) of this rule) maintained by the issuer that permit participants or beneficiaries to acquire or hold equity securities of the issuer;

    (2)   With respect to the equity securities of any foreign private issuer (as defined in Rule 3b–4(c) under the Exchange Act), means any period of more than three consecutive business days during which both:

        (i)   The conditions of paragraph (b)(1) of this rule are met; and

1573

(ii)(A)   The number of participants and beneficiaries located in the United States and its territories and possessions subject to the temporary suspension exceeds 15% of the total number of employees of the issuer and its consolidated subsidiaries; or

(B)   More than 50,000 participants and beneficiaries located in the United States and its territories and possessions are subject to the temporary suspension.

(3)   In determining the individual account plans (as defined in paragraph (j) of this rule) maintained by an issuer for purposes of this paragraph (b):

(i)   The rules under section 414(b), (c), (m) and (o) of the Internal Revenue Code are to be applied; and

(ii)   An individual account plan that is maintained outside of the United States primarily for the benefit of persons substantially all of whom are nonresident aliens (within the meaning of section 104(b)(4) of the Employee Retirement Income Security Act of 1974) is not to be considered.

(4)   In determining the number of participants and beneficiaries in an individual account plan (as defined in paragraph (j) of this rule) maintained by an issuer:

(i)   The determination may be made as of any date within the 12-month period preceding the beginning date of the temporary suspension in question; provided that if there has been a significant change in the number of participants or beneficiaries in an individual account plan since the date selected, the determination for such plan must be made as of the most recent practicable date that reflects such change; and

(ii)   The determination may be made without regard to overlapping plan participation.

(c)(1)   The term director has, except as provided in paragraph (c)(2) of this rule, the meaning set forth in Rule 3(a)(7) under the Exchange Act.

(2)   In the case of a foreign private issuer (as defined in Rule 3b–4(c) under the Exchange Act), the term director means an individual within the definition set forth in Rule 3(a)(7) under the Exchange Act who is a management employee of the issuer.

(d)   The term derivative security has the meaning set forth in Rule 16a–1(c) under the Exchange Act.

(e)   The term equity security has the meaning set forth in Rule 3(a)(11) under the Exchange Act and Rule 3a11–1 under the Exchange Act.

(f)   The term equity security of the issuer means any equity security or derivative security relating to an issuer, whether or not issued by that issuer.

(g)   The term Exchange Act means the Securities Exchange Act of 1934.

(h)(1)   The term executive officer has, except as provided in paragraph (h)(2) of this rule, the meaning set forth in Rule 16a–1(f) under the Exchange Act.

(2)   In the case of a foreign private issuer (as defined in Rule 3b–4(c) under the Exchange Act), the term executive officer means the principal executive officer or officers, the principal financial officer or officers and the principal accounting officer or officers of the issuer.

(i)   The term exempt security has the meaning set forth in section 3(a)(12) of the Exchange Act.

(j)   The term individual account plan means a pension plan which provides for an individual account for each participant and for benefits based solely upon the amount contributed to the participant's account, and any income, expenses, gains and losses, and any forfeitures of accounts of other participants which may be allocated to such participant's account, except that such term does not include a one-participant retirement plan (within the meaning of section 101(i)(8)(B) of the Employee Retirement Income Security Act of 1974), nor does it include a pension plan in which participation is limited to directors of the issuer.

(k)   The term issuer means an issuer (as defined in section 3(a)(8) of the Exchange Act), the securities of which are registered under section 12 of the Exchange Act or that is required to file reports under section 15(d) of the Exchange Act or that files or has filed a registration statement that has not yet become effective under the Securities Act of 1933 and that it has not withdrawn.

(*l*) The term pecuniary interest has the meaning set forth in Rule 16a–1(a)(2)(i) under the Exchange Act and the term indirect pecuniary interest has the meaning set forth in Rule 16a–1(a)(2)(ii) under the Exchange Act. Rule 16a–1(a)(2)(iii) under the Exchange Act also shall apply to determine pecuniary interest for purposes of this regulation.

Rule 101. Prohibition of Insider Trading During Pension Fund Blackout Periods

(a) Except to the extent otherwise provided in paragraph (c) of this rule, it is unlawful under section 306(a)(1) of the Sarbanes-Oxley Act of 2002 for any director or executive officer of an issuer of any equity security (other than an exempt security), directly or indirectly, to purchase, sell or otherwise acquire or transfer any equity security of the issuer (other than an exempt security) during any blackout period with respect to such equity security, if such director or executive officer acquires or previously acquired such equity security in connection with his or her service or employment as a director or executive officer.

(b) For purposes of section 306(a)(1) of the Sarbanes-Oxley Act of 2002, any sale or other transfer of an equity security of the issuer during a blackout period will be treated as a transaction involving an equity security "acquired in connection with service or employment as a director or executive officer" (as defined in Rule 100(a)) to the extent that the director or executive officer has a pecuniary interest (as defined in Rule 100(*l*)) in such equity security, unless the director or executive officer establishes by specific identification of securities that the transaction did not involve an equity security "acquired in connection with service or employment as a director or executive officer." To establish that the equity security was not so acquired, a director or executive officer must identify the source of the equity securities and demonstrate that he or she has utilized the same specific identification for any purpose related to the transaction (such as tax reporting and any applicable disclosure and reporting requirements).

(c) The following transactions are exempt from section 306(a)(1) of the Sarbanes-Oxley Act of 2002:

(1) Any acquisition of equity securities resulting from the reinvestment of dividends in, or interest on, equity securities of the same issuer if the acquisition is made pursuant to a plan providing for the regular reinvestment of dividends or interest and the plan provides for broad-based participation, does not discriminate in favor of employees of the issuer and operates on substantially the same terms for all plan participants;

(2) Any purchase or sale of equity securities of the issuer pursuant to a contract, instruction or written plan entered into by the director or executive officer that satisfies the affirmative defense conditions of Rule 10b5–1(c) under the Exchange Act; provided that the director or executive officer did not enter into or modify the contract, instruction or written plan during the blackout period (as defined in Rule 100(b)) in question, or while aware of the actual or approximate beginning or ending dates of that blackout period (whether or not the director or executive officer received notice of the blackout period as required by Section 306(a)(6) of the Sarbanes-Oxley Act of 2002);

(3) Any purchase or sale of equity securities, other than a Discretionary Transaction (as defined in Rule 16b–3(b)(1) under the Exchange Act), pursuant to a Qualified Plan (as defined in Rule 16b–3(b)(4) under the Exchange Act), an Excess Benefit Plan (as defined in Rule 16b–3(b)(2) under the Exchange Act) or a Stock Purchase Plan (as defined in Rule 16b–3(b)(5) under the Exchange Act) (or, in the case of a foreign private issuer, pursuant to an employee benefit plan that either (i) has been approved by the taxing authority of a foreign jurisdiction, or (ii) is eligible for preferential treatment under the tax laws of a foreign jurisdiction because the plan provides for broad-based employee participation); provided that a Discretionary Transaction that meets the conditions of paragraph (c)(2) of this rule also shall be exempt;

(4) Any grant or award of an option, stock appreciation right or other equity compensation pursuant to a plan that, by its terms:

(i) Permits directors or executive officers to receive grants or awards; and

(ii) Either:

(A) States the amount and price of securities to be awarded to designated directors and executive officers or categories of directors and executive officers (though not necessarily to others who may participate in the plan) and specifies the timing of awards to directors and executive officers; or

(B) Sets forth a formula that determines the amount, price and timing, using objective criteria (such as earnings of the issuer, value of the securities, years of service, job classification, and compensation levels);

(5) Any exercise, conversion or termination of a derivative security that the director or executive officer did not write or acquire during the blackout period (as defined in Rule 100(b)) in question, or while aware of the actual or approximate beginning or ending dates of that blackout period (whether or not the director or executive officer received notice of the blackout period as required by Section 306(a)(6) of the Sarbanes-Oxley Act of 2002); and either:

(i) The derivative security, by its terms, may be exercised, converted or terminated only on a fixed date, with no discretionary provision for earlier exercise, conversion or termination; or

(ii) The derivative security is exercised, converted or terminated by a counterparty and the director or executive officer does not exercise any influence on the counterparty with respect to whether or when to exercise, convert or terminate the derivative security;

(6) Any acquisition or disposition of equity securities involving a bona fide gift or a transfer by will or the laws of descent and distribution;

(7) Any acquisition or disposition of equity securities pursuant to a domestic relations order, as defined in the Internal Revenue Code or Title I of the Employment Retirement Income Security Act of 1974, or the rules thereunder;

(8) Any sale or other disposition of equity securities compelled by the laws or other requirements of an applicable jurisdiction;

(9) Any acquisition or disposition of equity securities in connection with a merger, acquisition, divestiture or similar transaction occurring by operation of law;

(10) The increase or decrease in the number of equity securities held as a result of a stock split or stock dividend applying equally to all securities of that class, including a stock dividend in which equity securities of a different issuer are distributed; and the acquisition of rights, such as shareholder or pre-emptive rights, pursuant to a pro rata grant to all holders of the same class of equity securities; and

(11) Any acquisition or disposition of an asset-backed security, as defined in Item 1101 of Regulation S–K.

Rule 102.   Exceptions to Definition of Blackout Period

The term "blackout period," as defined in Rule 100(b), does not include:

(a) A regularly scheduled period in which participants and beneficiaries may not purchase, sell or otherwise acquire or transfer an interest in any equity security of an issuer, if a description of such period, including its frequency and duration and the plan transactions to be suspended or otherwise affected, is:

(1) Incorporated into the individual account plan or included in the documents or instruments under which the plan operates; and

(2) is closed to an employee before he or she formally enrolls, or within 30 days following formal enrollment, as a participant under the individual account plan or within 30 days after the adoption of an amendment to the plan. For purposes of this paragraph (a)(2), the disclosure may be provided in any graphic form that is reasonably accessible to the employee; or

(b) Any trading suspension described in Rule 100(b) that is imposed in connection with a corporate merger, acquisition, divestiture or similar transaction involving the plan or plan sponsor, the principal purpose of which is to permit persons affiliated with the acquired or divested entity to become participants or beneficiaries, or to cease to be participants or beneficiaries, in an individual account plan; provided that the persons who become participants or beneficiaries in an individual account plan are not able to participate in the same class of equity securities after the merger, acquisition, divestiture or similar transaction as before the transaction.

Rule 103.   Issuer Right of Recovery; Right of Action by Equity Security Owner

(a)   Recovery of profits. Section 306(a)(2) of the Sarbanes-Oxley Act of 2002 provides that any profit realized by a director or executive officer from any purchase, sale or other acquisition or transfer of any equity security of an issuer in violation of section 306(a)(1) of that Act will inure to and be recoverable by the issuer, regardless of any intention on the part of the director or executive officer in entering into the transaction.

(b)   Actions to recover profit. Section 306(a)(2) of the Sarbanes-Oxley Act of 2002 provides that an action to recover profit may be instituted at law or in equity in any court of competent jurisdiction by the issuer, or by the owner of any equity security of the issuer in the name and on behalf of the issuer if the issuer fails or refuses to bring such action within 60 days after the date of request, or fails diligently to prosecute the action thereafter, except that no such suit may be brought more than two years after the date on which such profit was realized.

(c)   Measurement of profit.

(1)   In determining the profit recoverable in an action undertaken pursuant to section 306(a)(2) of the Sarbanes-Oxley Act of 2002 from a transaction that involves a purchase, sale or other acquisition or transfer (other than a grant, exercise, conversion or termination of a derivative security) in violation of section 306(a)(1) of that Act of an equity security of an issuer that is registered pursuant to section 12(b) or 12(g) of the Exchange Act or (g) and listed on a national securities exchange or listed in an automated inter-dealer quotation system of a national securities association, profit (including any loss avoided) may be measured by comparing the difference between the amount paid or received for the equity security on the date of the transaction during the blackout period and the average market price of the equity security calculated over the first three trading days after the ending date of the blackout period.

(2)   In determining the profit recoverable in an action undertaken pursuant to section 306(a)(2) of the Sarbanes-Oxley Act of 2002 from a transaction that is not described in paragraph (c)(1) of this rule, profit (including any loss avoided) may be measured in a manner that is consistent with the objective of identifying the amount of any gain realized or loss avoided by a director or executive officer as a result of a transaction taking place in violation of section 306(a)(1) of that Act during the blackout period as opposed to taking place outside of such blackout period.

(3)   The terms of this rule do not limit in any respect the authority of the Commission to seek or determine remedies as the result of a transaction taking place in violation of section 306(a)(1) of the Sarbanes-Oxley Act.

Rule 104.   Notice

(a)   In any case in which a director or executive officer is subject to section 306(a)(1) of the Sarbanes-Oxley Act of 2002 in connection with a blackout period (as defined in Rule 100(b)) with respect to any equity security, the issuer of the equity security must timely notify each director or officer and the Commission of the blackout period.

(b)   For purposes of this rule:

(1)   The notice must include:

(i)   The reason or reasons for the blackout period;

(ii)   A description of the plan transactions to be suspended during, or otherwise affected by, the blackout period;

(iii)   A description of the class of equity securities subject to the blackout period;

(iv)   The length of the blackout period by reference to:

(A)   The actual or expected beginning date and ending date of the blackout period; or

(B)   The calendar week during which the blackout period is expected to begin and the calendar week during which the blackout period is expected to end, provided that the notice to directors and executive officers describes how, during such week or weeks, a director or executive officer may obtain, without charge, information as to whether the blackout period has begun or ended; and provided further that the notice to the Commission describes how, during the blackout period and for a period of two years after the ending date of the blackout period, a security holder or other interested person may obtain, without charge, the actual beginning and ending dates of the blackout period.

(C)   For purposes of this paragraph (b)(1)(iv), a calendar week means a seven-day period beginning on Sunday and ending on Saturday; and

(v)   The name, address and telephone number of the person designated by the issuer to respond to inquiries about the blackout period, or, in the absence of such a designation, the issuer's human resources director or person performing equivalent functions.

(2)(i)   Notice to an affected director or executive officer will be considered timely if the notice described in paragraph (b)(1) of this rule is provided (in graphic form that is reasonably accessible to the recipient):

(A)   No later than five business days after the issuer receives the notice required by section 101(i)(2)(E) of the Employment Retirement Income Security Act of 1974 (29 U.S.C. 1021(i)(2)(E)); or

(B)   If no such notice is received by the issuer, a date that is at least 15 calendar days before the actual or expected beginning date of the blackout period.

(ii)   Notwithstanding paragraph (b)(2)(i) of this rule, the requirement to give advance notice will not apply in any case in which the inability to provide advance notice of the blackout period is due to events that were unforeseeable to, or circumstances that were beyond the reasonable control of, the issuer, and the issuer reasonably so determines in writing. Determinations described in the preceding sentence must be dated and signed by an authorized representative of the issuer. In any case in which this exception to the advance notice requirement applies, the issuer must provide the notice described in paragraph (b)(1) of this rule, as well as a copy of the written determination, to all affected directors and executive officers as soon as reasonably practicable.

(iii)   If there is a subsequent change in the beginning or ending dates of the blackout period as provided in the notice to directors and executive officers under paragraph (b)(2)(i) of this rule, an issuer must provide directors and executive officers with an updated notice explaining the reasons for the change in the date or dates and identifying all material changes in the information contained in the prior notice. The updated notice is required to be provided as soon as reasonably practicable, unless such notice in advance of the termination of a blackout period is impracticable.

(3)   Notice to the Commission will be considered timely if:

(i)   The issuer, except as provided in paragraph (b)(3)(ii) of this rule, files a current report on Form 8–K within the time prescribed for filing the report under the instructions for the form; or

(ii)   In the case of a foreign private issuer (as defined in Rule 3b–4(c) under the Exchange Act), the issuer includes the information set forth in paragraph (b)(1) of this rule in the first annual report on Form 20–F or 40–F required to be filed after the receipt of the notice of a blackout period required by 29 CFR 2520.101–3(c) within the time prescribed for filing the report under the instructions for the form or in an earlier filed report on Form 6–K.

(iii)   If there is a subsequent change in the beginning or ending dates of the blackout period as provided in the notice to the Commission under paragraph (b)(3)(i) of this rule, an issuer must file a current report on Form 8–K containing the updated beginning or ending dates of the blackout period, explaining the reasons for the change in the date or dates and identifying all material changes in the information contained in the prior report. The updated notice is required to be provided as soon as reasonably practicable.

REGULATION R—EXEMPTIONS AND DEFINITIONS RELATED TO THE EXCEPTIONS FOR BANKS FROM THE DEFINITION OF BROKER

17 C.F.R. § 247.___

Rule 100. Definition

For purposes of this part, the following definition shall apply: *Act* means the Securities Exchange Act of 1934.

Rule 700. Defined Terms Relating to the Networking Exception From the Definition of "Broker"

When used with respect to the Third Party Brokerage Arrangements ("Networking") Exception from the definition of the term "broker" in section 3(a)(4)(B)(i) of the Act in the context of transactions with a customer, the following terms shall have the meaning provided:

(a) *Contingent on whether the referral results in a transaction* means dependent on whether the referral results in a purchase or sale of securities; whether an account is opened with a broker or dealer; whether the referral results in a transaction resulting in a particular type of security; or whether it results in multiple security transactions; *provided, however,* that a referral fee may be contingent on whether a customer:

(1) Contacts or keeps an appointment with a broker or dealer as a result of the referral; or

(2) Meets any objective, baseline qualification criteria established by the bank or broker or dealer for customer referrals, including such criteria as minimum assets, net worth, income, or marginal federal or state income tax rate, or any requirement for citizenship or residency that the

broker or dealer, or the bank, may have established generally for referrals for securities brokerage accounts.

(b)(1) *Incentive Compensation* means compensation that is intended to encourage a bank employee to refer customers to a broker or dealer or give a bank employee an interest in the success of a securities transaction at a broker or dealer. The term does not include compensation paid by a bank under a bonus or similar plan that is:

    (i)   Paid on a discretionary basis; and

    (ii)   Based on multiple factors or variables and:

        (A)   Those factors or variables include multiple significant factors or variables that are not related to securities transactions at the broker or dealer;

        (B)   A referral made by the employee is not a factor or variable in determining the employee's compensation under the plan; and

        (C)   The employee's compensation under the plan is not determined by reference to referrals made by any other person.

    (2)   Nothing in this paragraph (b) shall be construed to prevent a bank from compensating an officer, director or employee under a bonus or similar plan on the basis of any measure of the overall profitability or revenue of:

        (i)   The bank, either on a stand-alone or consolidated basis;

        (ii)   Any affiliate of the bank (other than a broker or dealer), or any operating unit of the bank or an affiliate (other than a broker or dealer), if the affiliate or operating unit does not over time predominately engage in the business of making referrals to broker or dealer; or

        (iii) A broker or dealer if:

            (A)   Such measure or overall profitability or revenue is only one of multiple factors or variables used to determine the compensation of the officer, director or employee;

            (B)   The factors or variables used to determine the compensation of the officer, director or employee include multiple significant factors or variable that are not related to the profitability or revenue of the broker or dealer;

            (C)   A referral made by the employee is not a factor or variable in determining the employee's compensation under the benefit plan; and

            (D)   The employee's compensation under the plan is not determined by reference to referrals made by any other person.

(c) *Nominal one-time cash fee of a fixed dollar amount* means a cash payment for a referral, to bank employee who was personally involved in referring the customer to the broker or dealer, in an amount that meets any of the following standards:

    (1)   The payment does not exceed:

        (i)   Twice the average of the minimum and maximum hourly wage established by the bank for the current or prior year for the job family that includes the employee; or

        (ii)   1/1000th of the average of the minimum and maximum annual base salary established by the bank for the current or prior year for the job family that includes the employee; or

    (2)   The payment does not exceed twice the employee's actual base hourly wage or 1/1000th of the employee's actual annual base salary; or

    (3)   The payment does not exceed twenty five dollars ($25), as adjusted in accordance with paragraph (f) of this rule.

(d) *Job family* means a group of jobs or positions involving similar responsibilities, or requiring similar skills, education or training, that a bank, or a separate unit, branch or department of a bank, has established and uses in the ordinary course of its business to distinguish among its employees for purposes of hiring, promotion, and compensation.

(e) *Referral* means the action taken by one or more bank employees to direct a customer of the bank to a broker or dealer for the purchase or sale of securities for the customer's account.

(f) *Inflation adjustment*—(1) *In general.* On April 1, 2012, and on the 1st day of each subsequent 5-year period, the dollar amount referred to in paragraph (c)(3) of this rule shall be adjusted by:

(i) Dividing the annual value of the Employment Cost Index For Wages and Salaries, Private Industry Workers (or any successor index thereto), as published by the Bureau of Labor Statistics, for the calendar year preceding the calendar year in which the adjustment is being made by the annual value of such index (or successor) for the calendar year ending December 31, 2006; and

(ii) Multiplying the dollar amount by the quotient obtained in paragraph (f)(1)(i) of this rule.

(2) *Rounding.* If the adjusted dollar amount determined under paragraph (f)(1) of this rule for any period is not a multiple of $1, the amount so determined shall be rounded to the nearest multiple of $1.

Rule 701. Exemption From the Definition of "Broker" for Certain Institutional Referrals

(a) *General.* A bank that meets the requirements for the exception from the definition of "broker" under section 3(a)(4)(B)(i) of the Act, other than section 3(a)(4)(B)(i)(VI) of the Act, is exempt from the conditions of section 3(a)(4)(B)(i)(VI) of the Act solely to the extent that a bank employee receives a referral fee for referring a high net worth customer or institutional customer to a broker or dealer with which the bank has a contractual or other written arrangement of the type specified in section 3(a)(4)(B)(i) of the Act, if:

(1) *Bank employee.*

(i) The bank employee is:

(A) Not registered or approved, or otherwise required to be registered or approved, in accordance with the qualification standards established by the rules of any self-regulatory organization;

(B) Predominantly engaged in banking activities other than making referrals to a broker or dealer; and

(C) Not subject to statutory disqualification, as that term is defined in section 3(a)(39) of the Act, except subparagraph (E) of that section; and

(ii) The high net worth customer or institutional customer is encountered by the bank employee in the ordinary course of the employee's assigned duties for the bank.

(2) *Bank determinations and obligations.*

(i) *Disclosures.* The bank provides the high net worth customer or institutional customer the information set forth in paragraph (b) of this rule

(A) In writing prior to or at the time of the referral; or

(B) Orally prior to or at the time of the referral and

(1) The bank provides such information to the customer in writing within 3 business days of the date on which the bank employee refers the customer to the broker or dealer; or

(2) The written agreement between the bank and the broker or dealer provides for the broker or dealer to provide such information to the customer in writing in accordance with paragraph (a)(3)(i) of this rule.

(ii) *Customer qualification.* (A) In the case of a customer that is a not a natural person, the bank has a reasonable basis to believe that the customer is an institutional customer before the referral fee is paid to the bank employee.

(B)   In the case of a customer that is a natural person, the bank has a reasonable basis to believe that the customer is a high net worth customer prior to or at the time of the referral.

(iii) *Employee qualification information.* Before a referral fee is paid to a bank employee under this rule, the bank provides the broker or dealer the name of the employee and such other identifying information that may be necessary for the broker or dealer to determine whether the bank employee is registered or approved, or otherwise required to be registered or approved, in accordance with the qualification standards established by the rules of any self-regulatory organization or is subject to statutory disqualification, as that term is defined in section 3(a)(39) of the Act, except subparagraph (E) of that section.

(iv) *Good faith compliance and corrections.* A bank that acts in good faith and that has reasonable policies and procedures in place to comply with the requirements of this rule shall not be considered a "broker" under section 3(a)(4) of the Act solely because the bank fails to comply with the provisions of this paragraph (a)(2) with respect to a particular customer if the bank:

(A)   Takes reasonable and prompt steps to remedy the error (such as, for example, by promptly making the required determination or promptly providing the broker or dealer the required information); and

(B)   Makes reasonable efforts to reclaim the portion of the referral fee paid to the bank employee for the referral that does not, following any required remedial action, meet the requirements of this rule and that exceeds the amount otherwise permitted under section 3(a)(4)(B)(i)(VI) of the Act and Rule 700.

(3) *Provisions of written agreement.* The written agreement between the bank and the broker or dealer shall require that:

(i) *Broker-dealer written disclosures.* If, pursuant to paragraph (a)(2)(i)(B)(2) of this rule, the broker or dealer is to provide the customer in writing the disclosures set forth in paragraph (b) of this rule, the broker or dealer provides such information to the customer in writing:

(A)   Prior to or at the time the customer begins the process of opening an account at the broker or dealer, if the customer does not have an account with the broker or dealer; or

(B)   Prior to the time the customer places an order for a securities transaction with the broker or dealer as a result of the referral, if the customer already has an account at the broker or dealer.

(ii) *Customer and employee qualifications.* Before the referral fee is paid to the bank employee:

(A)   The broker or dealer determine that the bank employee is not subject to statutory disqualification, as that term is defined in section 3(a)(39) of the Act, except subparagraph (E) of that section; and

(B)   The broker or dealer has a reasonable basis to believe that the customer is a high net worth customer or an institutional customer.

(iii) *Suitability or sophistication determination by broker or dealer.*

(A) *Contingent referral fees.* In any case in which payment of the referral fee is contingent on completion of a securities transaction at the broker or dealer, the broker or dealer, before such securities transaction is conducted, perform a suitability analysis of the securities transaction in accordance with the rules of the broker or dealer's applicable self-regulatory organization as if the broker or dealer had recommended the securities transaction.

(B) *Non-contingent referral fees.* In any case in which payment of the referral fee is not contingent on the completion of a securities transaction at the broker or dealer, the broker or dealer, before the referral fee is paid, either:

(1)   Determine that the customer:

            (i)   Has the capability to evaluate investment risk and make independent decisions; and

            (ii)   Is exercising independent judgment based on the customer's own independent assessment of the opportunities and risks presented by a potential investment, market factors and other investment considerations; or

       (2)   Perform a suitability analysis of all securities transactions requested by the customer contemporaneously with the referral in accordance with the rules of the broker or dealer's applicable self-regulatory organization as if the broker or dealer had recommended the securities transaction.

    (iv)   *Notice to the customer.* The broker or dealer inform the customer if the broker or dealer determines that the customer or the securities transaction(s) to be conducted by the customer does not meet the applicable standard set forth in paragraph (a)(3)(iii) of this rule.

    (v)   *Notice to the bank.* The broker or dealer promptly inform the bank if the broker or dealer determines that:

       (A)   The customer is not a high net worth customer or institutional customer, as applicable; or

       (B)   The bank employee is subject to statutory disqualification, as that term is defined in section 3(a)(39) of the Act, except subparagraph (E) of that section.

(b)   *Required disclosures.* The disclosures provided to the high net worth customer or institutional customer pursuant to paragraphs (a)(2)(i) or (a)(3)(i) of this rule shall clearly and conspicuously disclose

    (1)   The name of the broker or dealer; and

    (2)   That the bank employee participates in an incentive compensation program under which the bank employee may receive a fee of more than a nominal amount for referring the customer to the broker or dealer and payment of this fee may be contingent on whether the referral results in a transaction with the broker or dealer.

(c)   *Receipt of other compensation.* Nothing in this rule prevents or prohibits a bank from paying or a bank employee from receiving any type of compensation that would not be considered incentive compensation under Rule 700(b)(1) or that is described in Rule 700(b)(2).

(d)   *Definitions.* When used in this rule:

    (1)   *High net worth customer.*

      (i)   *General. High net worth customer* means:

       (A)   Any natural person who, either individually or jointly with his or her spouse, has at least $5 million in net worth excluding the primary residence and associated liabilities of the person and, if applicable, his or her spouse; and

       (B)   Any revocable, inter vivos or living trust the settlor of which is a natural person who, either individually or jointly with his or her spouse, meets the net worth standard set forth in paragraph (d)(1)(i)(A) of this rule.

      (ii)   *Individual and spousal assets.* In determining whether any person is a high net worth customer, there may be included in the assets of such person

       (A)   Any assets held individually;

       (B)   If the person is acting jointly with his or her spouse, any assets of the person's spouse (whether or not such assets are held jointly); and

       (C)   If the person is not acting jointly with his or her spouse, fifty percent of any assets held jointly with such person's spouse and any assets in which such person shares with such person's spouse a community property or similar shared ownership interest.

    (2)   *Institutional customer* means any corporation, partnership, limited liability company, trust or other non-natural person that has, or is controlled by a non-natural person that has, at least:

(i) $10 million in investments; or

(ii) $20 million in revenues; or

(iii) $15 million in revenues if the bank employee refers the customer to the broker or dealer for investment banking services.

(3)   *Investment banking services* includes, without limitation, acting as an underwriter in an offering for an issuer; acting as a financial adviser in a merger, acquisition, tender-offer or similar transaction; providing venture capital, equity lines of credit, private investment-private equity transactions or similar investments; serving as placement agent for an issuer; and engaging in similar activities.

(4)   *Referral fee* means a fee (paid in one or more installments) for the referral of a customer to a broker or dealer that is:

(i)   A predetermined dollar amount, or a dollar amount determined in accordance with a predetermined formula (such as a fixed percentage of the dollar amount of total assets placed in an account with the broker or dealer), that does not vary based on:

(A)   The revenue generated by or the profitability of securities transactions conducted by the customer with the broker or dealer; or

(B)   The quantity, price, or identity of securities transactions conducted over time by the customer with the broker or dealer; or

(C)   The number of customer referrals made; or

(ii)   A dollar amount based on a fixed percentage of the revenues received by the broker or dealer for investment banking services provided to the customer.

(e)   *Inflation adjustments.*

(1)   *In general.* On April 1, 2012, and on the 1st day of each subsequent 5-year period, each dollar amount in paragraphs (d)(1) and (d)(2) of this rule shall be adjusted by:

(i)   Dividing the annual value of the Personal Consumption Expenditures Chain-Type Price Index (or any successor index thereto), as published by the Department of Commerce, for the calendar year preceding the calendar year in which the adjustment is being made by the annual value of such index (or successor) for the calendar year ending December 31, 2006; and

(ii)   Multiplying the dollar amount by the quotient obtained in paragraph (e)(1)(i) of this rule.

(2)   *Rounding.* If the adjusted dollar amount determined under paragraph (e)(1) of this rule for any period is not a multiple of $100,000, the amount so determined shall be rounded to the nearest multiple of $100,000.

Rule 721.   Defined Terms Relating to the Trust and Fiduciary Activities Exception From the Definition of "Broker"

(a)   *Defined terms for chiefly compensated test.* For purposes of this part and section 3(a)(4)(B)(ii) of the Act, the following terms shall have the meaning provided:

(1)   *Chiefly compensated—account-by-account test. Chiefly compensated* shall mean the *relationship-total compensation percentage* for each *trust or fiduciary account* of the bank greater than 50 percent.

(2)   The *relationship-total compensation percentage* for a *trust or fiduciary account* shall be the mean of the *yearly compensation percentage* for the account for the immediately preceding year and the *yearly compensation percentage* for the account for the year immediately preceding that year.

(3)   The *yearly compensation percentage* for a *trust or fiduciary account* shall be

(i)   Equal to the relationship compensation attributable to the *trust or fiduciary account* during the year divided by the total compensation attributable to the *trust or fiduciary account* during that year, with the quotient expressed as a percentage; and

(ii) Calculated within 60 days of the end of the year.

(4) *Relationship compensation* means any compensation a bank receives attributable to a trust or fiduciary account that consists of:

(i) An administration fee, including, without limitation, a fee paid—

(A) For personal services, tax preparation, or real estate settlement services;

(B) For disbursing funds from, or for recording receipt of payments to, a trust or fiduciary account;

(C) In connection with securities lending or borrowing transactions;

(D) For custody services; or

(E) In connection with an investment in shares of an investment company for personal service, the maintenance of shareholder accounts or any service described in paragraph (a)(4)(iii)(C) of this rule;

(ii) An annual fee (payable on a monthly, quarterly or other basis), including, without limitation, a fee paid for assessing investment performance or for reviewing compliance with applicable investment guidelines or restrictions;

(iii) A fee based on a percentage of assets under management, including, without limitation, a fee paid

(A) Pursuant to a plan under Rule 12b–1 of the Investment Company Act of 1940;

(B) In connection with an investment in shares of an investment company for personal service or the maintenance of shareholder accounts;

(C) Based on a percentage of assets under management for any of the following services—

(I) Providing transfer agent or sub-transfer agent services for beneficial owners of investment company shares;

(II) Aggregating and processing purchase and redemption orders for investment company shares;

(III) Providing beneficial owners with account statements showing their purchases, sales, and positions in the investment company;

(IV) Processing dividend payments for the investment company;

(V) Providing sub-accounting services to the investment company for shares held beneficially;

(VI) Forwarding communications from the investment company to the beneficial owners, including proxies, shareholder reports, dividend and tax notices, and updated prospectuses; or

(VII) Receiving, tabulating, and transmitting proxies executed by beneficial owners of investment company shares;

(D) Based on the financial performance of the assets in an account; or

(E) For the types of services described in paragraph (a)(4)(i)(C) or (D) of this rule if paid based on a percentage of assets under management;

(iv) A flat or capped per order processing fee, paid by or on behalf of a customer or beneficiary, that is equal to not more than the cost incurred by the bank in connection with executing securities transactions for trust or fiduciary accounts; or

(v) Any combination of such fees.

(5) *Trust or fiduciary account* means an account for which the bank acts in a trustee or fiduciary capacity as defined in section 3(a)(4)(D) of the Act.

(6) *Year* means a calendar year, or fiscal year consistently used by the bank for recordkeeping and reporting purposes.

(b) *Revenues derived from transactions conducted under other exceptions or exemptions.* For purposes of calculating the *yearly compensation percentage* for a *trust or fiduciary account*, a bank may at its election exclude the compensation associated with any securities transaction conducted in accordance with the exceptions in section 3(a)(4)(B)(i) or sections 3(a)(4)(B)(iii)–(xi) of the Act and the rules issued thereunder, including any exemption related to such exceptions jointly adopted by the Commission and the Board, provided that if the bank elects to exclude such compensation, the bank must exclude the compensation from both the relationship compensation (if applicable) and total compensation for the account.

(c) *Advertising restrictions.*

(1) *In general.* A bank complies with the advertising restriction in section 3(a)(4)(B)(ii)(II) of the Act if advertisements by or on behalf of the bank do not advertise—

(i) That the bank provides securities brokerage services for trust or fiduciary accounts except as part of advertising the bank's broader trust or fiduciary services; and

(ii) The securities brokerage services provided by the bank to trust or fiduciary accounts more prominently than the other aspects of the trust or fiduciary services provided to such accounts.

(2) *Advertisement.* For purposes of this rule, the term advertisement has the same meaning as in Rule 760(h)(2).

Rule 722. Exemption Allowing Banks to Calculate Trust and Fiduciary Compensation on a Bank-Wide Basis

(a) *General.* A bank is exempt from meeting the "chiefly compensated" condition in section 3(a)(4)(B)(ii)(I) of the Act to the extent that it effects transactions in securities for any account in a trustee or fiduciary capacity within the scope of section 3(a)(4)(D) of the Act if:

(1) The bank meets the other conditions for the exception from the definition of the term "broker" under sections 3(a)(4)(B)(ii) and 3(a)(4)(C) of the Act, including the advertising restrictions in section 3(a)(4)(B)(ii)(II) of the Act as implemented by Rule 721(c); and

(2) The aggregate relationship-total compensation percentage for the bank's trust and fiduciary business is at least 70 percent.

(b) *Aggregate relationship-total compensation percentage.* For purposes of this rule, the *aggregate relationship-total compensation percentage* for a bank's trust and fiduciary business shall be the mean of the bank's *yearly bank-wide compensation percentage* for the immediately preceding year and the bank's *yearly bank-wide compensation percentage* for the year immediately preceding that year.

(c) *Yearly bank-wide compensation percentage.* For purposes of this rule, a bank's yearly bank-wide compensation percentage for a year shall be

(1) Equal to the *relationship compensation* attributable to the bank's trust and fiduciary business as a whole during the year divided by the total compensation attributable to the bank's trust and fiduciary business as a whole during that year, with the quotient expressed as a percentage; and

(2) Calculated within 60 days of the end of the year.

(d) *Revenues derived from transactions conducted under other exceptions or exemptions.* For purposes of calculating the *yearly compensation percentage* for a *trust or fiduciary account*, a bank may at its election exclude the compensation associated with any securities transaction conducted in accordance with the exceptions in section 3(a)(4)(B)(i) or sections 3(a)(4)(B)(iii)—(xi) of the Act and the rules issued thereunder, including any exemption related to such sections jointly adopted by the Commission and the Board, *provided that* if the bank elects to exclude such compensation, the bank must exclude the compensation from both the relationship compensation (if applicable) and total compensation of the bank.

Rule 723.   Exemptions for Special Accounts, Transferred Accounts, Foreign Branches and a De Minimis Number of Accounts

(a)   *Short-term accounts.* A bank may, in determining its compliance with the chiefly compensated test in Rule 721(a)(1) or Rule 722(a)(2), exclude any trust or fiduciary account that had been open for a period of less than 3 months during the relevant year.

(b)   *Accounts acquired as part of a business combination or asset acquisition.* For purposes of determining compliance with the chiefly compensated test in Rule 721(a)(1) or Rule 722(a)(2), any *trust or fiduciary account* that a bank acquired from another person as part of a merger, consolidation, acquisition, purchase of assets or similar transaction may be excluded by the bank for 12 months after the date the bank acquired the account from the other person.

(c)   *Non-shell foreign branches.*

(1)   *Exemption.* For purposes of determining compliance with the chiefly compensated test in Rule 722(a)(2), a bank may exclude the *trust or fiduciary accounts* held at a non-shell foreign branch of the bank if the bank has reasonable cause to believe that trust or fiduciary accounts of the foreign branch held by or for the benefit of a U.S. person as defined in Rule 902(k) under the Securities Act of 1933 constitute less than 10 percent of the total number of trust or fiduciary accounts of the foreign branch.

(2)   *Rules of construction.* Solely for purposes of this paragraph (c), a bank will be deemed to have reasonable cause to believe that a trust or fiduciary account of a foreign branch of the bank is not held by or for the benefit of a U.S. person if

(i)   The principal mailing address maintained and used by the foreign branch for the accountholder(s) and beneficiary(ies) of the account is not in the United States; or

(ii)   The records of the foreign branch indicate that the accountholder(s) and beneficiary(ies) of the account is not a U.S. person as defined in Rule 902(k) under the Securities Act of 1933.

(3)   *Non-shell foreign branch.* Solely for purposes of this paragraph (c), a non-shell foreign branch of a bank means a branch of the bank

(i)   That is located outside the United States and provides banking services to residents of the foreign jurisdiction in which the branch is located; and

(ii)   For which the decisions relating to day-to-day operations and business of the branch are made at that branch and are not made by an office of the bank located in the United States.

(d)   *Accounts transferred to a broker or dealer or other unaffiliated entity.* Notwithstanding section 3(a)(4)(B)(ii)(I) of the Act and Rule 721(a)(1) of this part, a bank operating under Rule 721(a)(1) shall not be considered a broker for purposes of section 3(a)(4) of the Act solely because a *trust or fiduciary account* does not meet the chiefly compensated standard in Rule 721(a)(1) if, within 3 months of the end of the year in which the account fails to meet such standard, the bank transfers the account or the securities held by or on behalf of the account to a broker or dealer registered under section 15 of the Act or another entity that is not an affiliate of the bank and is not required to be registered as a broker or dealer.

(e)   *De minimis exclusion.* A bank may, in determining its compliance with the chiefly compensated test in Rule 721(a)(1), exclude a *trust or fiduciary account* if:

(1)   The bank maintains records demonstrating that the securities transactions conducted by or on behalf of the account were undertaken by the bank in the exercise of its trust or fiduciary responsibilities with respect to the account;

(2)   The total number of accounts excluded by the bank under this paragraph (d) does not exceed the lesser of—

(i)   1 percent of the total number of trust or fiduciary accounts held by the bank, *provided that* if the number so obtained is less than 1 the amount shall be rounded up to 1; or

(ii)   500; and

(3) The bank did not rely on this paragraph (e) with respect to such account during the immediately preceding year.

Rule 740.   Defined Terms Relating to the Sweep Accounts Exception From the Definition of "Broker"

For purposes of section 3(a)(4)(B)(v) of the Act, the following terms shall have the meaning provided:

(a) *Deferred sales load* has the same meaning as in Rule 6c–10 under the Investment Company Act of 1940.

(b) *Money market fund* means an open-end company registered under the Investment Company Act of 1940 that is regulated as a money market fund pursuant to Rule 2a–7 under the Investment Company Act of 1940.

(c)(1) *No-load*, in the context of an investment company or the securities issued by an investment company, means, for securities of the class or series in which a bank effects transactions, that:

(i)   That class or series is not subject to a sales load or a deferred sales load; and

(ii) Total charges against net assets of that class or series of the investment company's securities for sales or sales promotion expenses, for personal service, or for the maintenance of shareholder accounts do not exceed 0.25 of 1% of average net assets annually.

(2) For purposes of this definition, charges for the following will not be considered charges against net assets of a class or series of an investment company's securities for sales or sales promotion expenses, for personal service, or for the maintenance of shareholder accounts:

(i)   Providing transfer agent or sub-transfer agent services for beneficial owners of investment company shares;

(ii) Aggregating and processing purchase and redemption orders for investment company shares;

(iii) Providing beneficial owners with account statements showing their purchases, sales, and positions in the investment company;

(iv) Processing dividend payments for the investment company;

(v)   Providing sub-accounting services to the investment company for shares held beneficially;

(vi) Forwarding communications from the investment company to the beneficial owners, including proxies, shareholder reports, dividend and tax notices, and updated prospectuses; or

(vii) Receiving, tabulating, and transmitting proxies executed by beneficial owners of investment company shares.

(d) *Open-end company* has the same meaning as in section 5(a)(1) of the Investment Company Act of 1940.

(e) *Sales load* has the same meaning as in section 2(a)(35) of the Investment Company Act of 1940.

Rule 741.   Exemption for Banks Effecting Transactions in Money Market Funds

(a) A bank is exempt from the definition of the term "broker" under section 3(a)(4) of the Act to the extent that it effects transactions on behalf of a customer in securities issued by a money market fund, provided that:

(1) The bank either

(A) Provides the customer, directly or indirectly, any other product or service, the provision of which would not, in and of itself, require the bank to register as a broker or dealer under section 15(a) of the Act; or

(B) Effects the transactions on behalf of another bank as part of a program for the investment or reinvestment of deposit funds of, or collected by, the other bank; and

    (2)(i)   The class or series of securities is no-load; or

        (ii) If the class or series of securities is not no-load:

           (A) The bank or, if applicable, the other bank described in paragraph (a)(1)(B) of this rule provides the customer, not later than at the time the customer authorizes the securities transactions, a prospectus for the securities; and

           (B) The bank and, if applicable, the other bank described in paragraph (a)(1)(B) of this rule do not characterize or refer to the class or series of securities as no-load.

  (b) *Definitions.* For purposes of this rule:

    (1) *Money market fund* has the same meaning as in Rule 740(b).

    (2) *No-load* has the same meaning as in Rule 740(c).

Rule 760.   Exemption From Definition of "Broker" for Banks Accepting Orders to Effect Transactions in Securities From or on Behalf of Custody Accounts

  (a) *Employee benefit plan accounts and individual retirement accounts or similar accounts.* A bank is exempt from the definition of the term "broker" under section 3(a)(4) of the Act to the extent that, as part of its customary banking activities, the bank accepts orders to effect transactions in securities for an employee benefit plan account or an individual retirement account or similar account for which the bank acts as a custodian if:

    (1) *Employee compensation restriction and additional conditions.* The bank complies with the employee compensation restrictions in paragraph (c) of this rule and the other conditions in paragraph (d) of this rule;

    (2) *Advertisements.* Advertisements by or on behalf of the bank do not:

        (i) Advertise that the bank accepts orders for securities transactions for employee benefit plan accounts or individual retirement accounts or similar accounts, except as part of advertising the other custodial or safekeeping services the bank provides to these accounts; or

        (ii) Advertise that such accounts are securities brokerage accounts or that the bank's safekeeping and custody services substitute for a securities brokerage account; and

    (3) *Advertisements and sales literature for individual retirement or similar accounts.* Advertisements and sales literature issued by or on behalf of the bank do not describe the securities order-taking services provided by the bank to individual retirement accounts or similar accounts more prominently than the other aspects of the custody or safekeeping services provided by the bank to these accounts.

  (b) *Accommodation trades for other custodial accounts.* A bank is exempt from the definition of the term "broker" under section 3(a)(4) of the Act to the extent that, as part of its customary banking activities, the bank accepts orders to effect transactions in securities for an account for which the bank acts as custodian other than an employee benefit plan account or an individual retirement account or similar account if:

    (1) *Accommodation.* The bank accepts orders to effect transactions in securities for the account only as an accommodation to the customer;

    (2) *Employee compensation restriction and additional conditions.* The bank complies with the employee compensation restrictions in paragraph (c) of this rule and the other conditions in paragraph (d) of this rule;

    (3) *Bank fees.* Any fee charged or received by the bank for effecting a securities transaction for the account does not vary based on:

        (i) Whether the bank accepted the order for the transaction; or

        (ii) The quantity or price of the securities to be bought or sold;

    (4) *Advertisements.* Advertisements by or on behalf of the bank do not state that the bank accepts orders for securities transactions for the account;

(5) *Sales literature.* Sales literature issued by or on behalf of the bank:

(i) Does not state that the bank accepts orders for securities transactions for the account except as part of describing the other custodial or safekeeping services the bank provides to the account; and

(ii) Does not describe the securities order-taking services provided to the account more prominently than the other aspects of the custody or safekeeping services provided by the bank to the account; and

(6) *Investment advice and recommendations.* The bank does not provide investment advice or research concerning securities to the account, make recommendations to the account concerning securities or otherwise solicit securities transactions from the account; *provided, however,* that nothing in this paragraph (b)(6) shall prevent a bank from:

(i) Publishing, using or disseminating advertisements and sales literature in accordance with paragraphs (b)(4) and (b)(5) of this rule; and

(ii) Responding to customer inquiries regarding the bank's safekeeping and custody services by providing:

(A) Advertisements or sales literature consistent with the provisions of paragraphs (b)(4) and (b)(5) of this rule describing the safekeeping, custody and related services that the bank offers;

(B) A prospectus prepared by a registered investment company, or sales literature prepared by a registered investment company or by the broker or dealer that is the principal underwriter of the registered investment company pertaining to the registered investment company's products;

(C) Information based on the materials described in paragraphs (b)(6)(ii)(A) and (B) of this rule; or

(iii) Responding to inquiries regarding the bank's safekeeping, custody or other services, such as inquiries concerning the customer's account or the availability of sweep or other services, so long as the bank does not provide investment advice or research concerning securities to the account or make a recommendation to the account concerning securities.

(c) *Employee compensation restriction.* A bank may accept orders pursuant to this rule for a securities transaction for an account described in paragraph (a) or (b) of this rule only if no bank employee receives compensation, including a fee paid pursuant to a plan under Rule 12b–1 under the Investment Company Act of 1940, from the bank, the executing broker or dealer, or any other person that is based on whether a securities transaction is executed for the account or that is based on the quantity, price, or identity of securities purchased or sold by such account, *provided that* nothing in this paragraph shall prohibit a bank employee from receiving compensation that would not be considered incentive compensation under Rule 700(b)(1) as if a referral had been made by the bank employee, or any compensation described in Rule 700(b)(2).

(d) *Other conditions.* A bank may accept orders for a securities transaction for an account for which the bank acts as a custodian under this rule only if the bank:

(1) Does not act in a trustee or fiduciary capacity (as defined in section 3(a)(4)(D) of the Act) with respect to the account, other than as a directed trustee;

(2) Complies with section 3(a)(4)(C) of the Act in handling any order for a securities transaction for the account; and

(3) Complies with section 3(a)(4)(B)(viii)(II) of the Act regarding carrying broker activities.

(e) *Non-fiduciary administrators and recordkeepers.* A bank that acts as a non-fiduciary and non-custodial administrator or recordkeeper for an employee benefit plan account for which another bank acts as custodian may rely on the exemption provided in this rule if:

(1) Both the custodian bank and the administrator or recordkeeper bank comply with paragraphs (a), (c) and (d) of this rule; and

(2)   The administrator or recordkeeper bank does not execute a cross-trade with or for the employee benefit plan account or net orders for securities for the employee benefit plan account, other than:

(i)   Crossing or netting orders for shares of open-end investment companies not traded on an exchange, or

(ii)   Crossing orders between or netting orders for accounts of the custodian bank that contracted with the administrator or recordkeeper bank for services.

(f)   *Subcustodians.* A bank that acts as a subcustodian for an account for which another bank acts as custodian may rely on the exemptions provided in this rule if:

(1)   For employee benefit plan accounts and individual retirement accounts or similar accounts, both the custodian bank and the subcustodian bank meet the requirements of paragraphs (a), (c) and (d) of this rule;

(2)   For other custodial accounts, both the custodian bank and the subcustodian bank meet the requirements of paragraphs (b), (c) and (d) of this rule; and

(3)   The subcustodian bank does not execute a cross-trade with or for the account or net orders for securities for the account, other than:

(i)   Crossing or netting orders for shares of open-end investment companies not traded on an exchange, or

(ii)   Crossing orders between or netting orders for accounts of the custodian bank.

(g)   *Evasions.* In considering whether a bank meets the terms of this rule, both the form and substance of the relevant account(s), transaction(s) and activities (including advertising activities) of the bank will be considered in order to prevent evasions of the requirements of this rule.

(h)   *Definitions.* When used in this rule:

(1)   *Account for which the bank acts as a custodian* means an account that is:

(i)   An employee benefit plan account for which the bank acts as a custodian;

(ii)   An individual retirement account or similar account for which the bank acts as a custodian;

(iii)   An account established by a written agreement between the bank and the customer that sets forth the terms that will govern the fees payable to, and rights and obligations of, the bank regarding the safekeeping or custody of securities; or

(iv)   An account for which the bank acts as a directed trustee.

(2)   *Advertisement* means any material that is published or used in any electronic or other public media, including any Web site, newspaper, magazine or other periodical, radio, television, telephone or tape recording, videotape display, signs or billboards, motion pictures, or telephone directories (other than routine listings).

(3)   *Directed trustee* means a trustee that does not exercise investment discretion with respect to the account.

(4)   *Employee benefit plan account* means a pension plan, retirement plan, profit sharing plan, bonus plan, thrift savings plan, incentive plan, or other similar plan, including, without limitation, an employer-sponsored plan qualified under section 401(a) of the Internal Revenue Code (26 U.S.C. 401(a)), a governmental or other plan described in section 457 of the Internal Revenue Code (26 U.S.C. 457), a tax-deferred plan described in section 403(b) of the Internal Revenue Code (26 U.S.C. 403(b)), a church plan, governmental, multiemployer or other plan described in section 414(d), (e) or (f) of the Internal Revenue Code (26 U.S.C. 414(d), (e) or (f)), an incentive stock option plan described in section 422 of the Internal Revenue Code (26 U.S.C. 422); a Voluntary Employee Beneficiary Association Plan described in section 501(c)(9) of the Internal Revenue Code (26 U.S.C. 501(c)(9)), a non-qualified deferred compensation plan (including a rabbi or secular trust), a supplemental or mirror plan, and a supplemental unemployment benefit plan.

(5)   *Individual retirement account or similar account* means an individual retirement account as defined in section 408 of the Internal Revenue Code (26 U.S.C. 408), Roth IRA as defined in section 408A of the Internal Revenue Code (26 U.S.C. 408A), health savings account as defined in section 223(d) of the Internal Revenue Code (26 U.S.C. 223(d)), Archer medical savings account as defined in section 220(d) of the Internal Revenue Code (26 U.S.C. 220(d)), Coverdell education savings account as defined in section 530 of the Internal Revenue Code (26 U.S.C. 530), or other similar account.

(6)   *Sales literature* means any written or electronic communication, other than an advertisement, that is generally distributed or made generally available to customers of the bank or the public, including circulars, form letters, brochures, telemarketing scripts, seminar texts, published articles, and press releases concerning the bank's products or services.

(7)   *Principal underwriter* has the same meaning as in section 2(a)(29) of the Investment Company Act of 1940.

Rule 771.   Exemption From the Definition of "Broker" for Banks Effecting Transactions in Securities Issued Pursuant to Regulation S

(a)   A bank is exempt from the definition of the term "broker" under section 3(a)(4) of the Act, to the extent that, as agent, the bank:

(1)   Effects a sale in compliance with the requirements of Rule 903 under the Securities Act of 1933 of an eligible security to a purchaser who is not in the United States;

(2)   Effects, by or on behalf of a person who is not a U.S. person under Rule 902(k) under the Securities Act of 1933, a resale of an eligible security after its initial sale with a reasonable belief that the eligible security was initially sold outside of the United States within the meaning of and in compliance with the requirements of Rule 903 under the Securities Act of 1933 to a purchaser who is not in the United States or a registered broker or dealer, provided that if the resale is made prior to the expiration of any applicable distribution compliance period specified in Rule 903(b)(2) or (b)(3) under the Securities Act of 1933, the resale is made in compliance with the requirements of Rule 904 under the Securities Act of 1933; or

(3)   Effects, by or on behalf of a registered broker or dealer, a resale of an eligible security after its initial sale with a reasonable belief that the eligible security was initially sold outside of the United States within the meaning of and in compliance with the requirements of Rule 903 under the Securities Act of 1933 to a purchaser who is not in the United States, provided that if the resale is made prior to the expiration of any applicable distribution compliance period specified in Rule 903(b)(2) or (b)(3) under the Securities Act of 1933, the resale is made in compliance with the requirements of Rule 904 under the Securities Act of 1933.

(b)   *Definitions.* For purposes of this rule:

(1)   *Distributor* has the same meaning as in Rule 902(d) under the Securities Act of 1933.

(2)   *Eligible security* means a security that:

(i)   Is not being sold from the inventory of the bank or an affiliate of the bank; and

(ii)   Is not being underwritten by the bank or an affiliate of the bank on a firm-commitment basis, unless the bank acquired the security from an unaffiliated distributor that did not purchase the security from the bank or an affiliate of the bank.

(3)   *Purchaser* means a person who purchases an eligible security and who is not a U.S. person under Rule 902(k) under the Securities Act of 1933.

Rule 772.   Exemption From the Definition of "Broker" for Banks Engaging in Securities Lending Transactions

(a)   A bank is exempt from the definition of the term "broker" under section 3(a)(4) of the Act, to the extent that, as an agent, it engages in or effects securities lending transactions, and any securities lending services in connection with such transactions, with or on behalf of a person the bank reasonably believes to be:

(1)   A qualified investor as defined in section 3(a)(54)(A) of the Act; or

(2)   Any employee benefit plan that owns and invests on a discretionary basis, not less than $25,000,000 in investments.

(b)   *Securities lending transaction* means a transaction in which the owner of a security lends the security temporarily to another party pursuant to a written securities lending agreement under which the lender retains the economic interests of an owner of such securities, and has the right to terminate the transaction and to recall the loaned securities on terms agreed by the parties.

(c)   *Securities lending services* means:

(1)   Selecting and negotiating with a borrower and executing, or directing the execution of the loan with the borrower;

(2)   Receiving, delivering, or directing the receipt or delivery of loaned securities;

(3)   Receiving, delivering, or directing the receipt or delivery of collateral;

(4)   Providing mark-to-market, corporate action, recordkeeping or other services incidental to the administration of the securities lending transaction;

(5)   Investing, or directing the investment of, cash collateral; or

(6)   Indemnifying the lender of securities with respect to various matters.

Rule 775.   Exemption From the Definition of "Broker" for Banks Effecting Certain Excepted or Exempted Transactions in Investment Company Securities

(a)   A bank that meets the conditions for an exception or exemption from the definition of the term "broker" except for the condition in section 3(a)(4)(C)(i) of the Act, is exempt from such condition to the extent that it effects a transaction in a *covered security*, if:

(1)   Any such security is neither traded on a national securities exchange nor through the facilities of a national securities association or an interdealer quotation system;

(2)   The security is distributed by a registered broker or dealer, or the sales charge is no more than the amount permissible for a security sold by a registered broker or dealer pursuant to any applicable rules adopted pursuant to section 22(b)(1) of the Investment Company Act of 1940 by a securities association registered under section 15A of the Act; and

(3)   Any such transaction is effected:

(i)   Through the National Securities Clearing Corporation; or

(ii)   Directly with a transfer agent or with an insurance company or separate account that is excluded from the definition of transfer agent in Section 3(a)(25) of the Act.

(b)   *Definitions.* For purposes of this rule:

(1)   *Covered security* means:

(i)   Any security issued by an open-end company, as defined by section 5(a)(1) of the Investment Company Act, that is registered under that Act; and

(ii)   Any variable insurance contract funded by a separate account, as defined by section 2(a)(37) of the Investment Company Act, that is registered under that Act.

(2)   *Interdealer quotation system* has the same meaning as in Rule 15c2–11 under the Securities Exchange Act of 1934.

(3)   *Insurance company* has the same meaning as in 15 U.S.C. 77b(a)(13).

Rule 776.   **Exemption From the Definition of "Broker" for Banks Effecting Certain Excepted or Exempted Transactions in a Company's Securities for Its Employee Benefit Plans**

(a)   A bank that meets the conditions for an exception or exemption from the definition of the term "broker" except for the condition in section 3(a)(4)(C)(i) of the Act, is exempt from such condition to the extent that it effects a transaction in the securities of a company directly with a transfer agent acting for the company that issued the security, if:

     (1)   No commission is charged with respect to the transaction;

     (2)   The transaction is conducted by the bank solely for the benefit of an employee benefit plan account;

     (3)   Any such security is obtained directly from:

         (i)   The company; or

         (ii)   An employee benefit plan of the company; and

     (4)   Any such security is transferred only to:

         (i)   The company; or

         (ii)   An employee benefit plan of the company.

(b)   For purposes of this rule, the term *employee benefit plan* account has the same meaning as in Rule 760(h)(4).

Rule 780.   **Exemption for Banks From Liability Under Section 29 of the Securities Exchange Act of 1934**

(a)   No contract entered into before March 31, 2009, shall be void or considered voidable by reason of section 29(b) of the Act because any bank that is a party to the contract violated the registration requirements of section 15(a) of the Act, any other applicable provision of the Act, or the rules and regulations thereunder based solely on the bank's status as a broker when the contract was created.

(b)   No contract shall be void or considered voidable by reason of section 29(b) of the Act because any bank that is a party to the contract violated the registration requirements of section 15(a) of the Act or the rules and regulations thereunder based solely on the bank's status as a broker when the contract was created, if:

     (1)   At the time the contract was created, the bank acted in good faith and had reasonable policies and procedures in place to comply with section 3(a)(4)(B) of the Act and the rules and regulations thereunder; and

     (2)   At the time the contract was created, any violation of the registration requirements of section 15(a) of the Act by the bank did not result in any significant harm or financial loss or cost to the person seeking to void the contract.

Rule 781.   **Exemption From the Definition of "Broker" for Banks for a Limited Period of Time**

A bank is exempt from the definition of the term "broker" under section 3(a)(4) of the Act until the first day of its first fiscal year commencing after September 30, 2008.

REGULATIONS S–P AND S–AM—PRIVACY OF CONSUMER FINANCIAL INFORMATION

17 C.F.R. § 248.___

Subpart A—Regulation S–P: Privacy of Consumer Financial Information and Safeguarding Personal Information

REGULATION S–P

Subpart C—Regulation S–ID: Identity Theft Red Flags

REGULATIONS S–P AND S–AM

Subpart A—Regulation S–P: Privacy of Consumer Financial Information and Safeguarding Personal Information

Rule 1. Purpose and Scope

(a) *Authority.* This part (Regulation VV) is issued by the Board under section 13 of the Bank Holding Company Act of 1956, as amended, as well as under the Federal Reserve Act, as amended; section 8 of the Federal Deposit Insurance Act, as amended; the Bank Holding Company Act of 1956, as amended; and the International Banking Act of 1978, as amended.

(b) *Purpose.* Section 13 of the Bank Holding Company Act establishes prohibitions and restrictions on proprietary trading and on investments in or relationships with covered funds by certain banking entities, including state member banks, bank holding companies, savings and loan holding companies, other companies that control and insured depository institution, foreign banking organizations, and certain subsidiaries thereof. This part implements section 13 of the Bank Holding Company Act by defining terms used in the statute and related terms, establishing prohibitions and restrictions on proprietary trading and on investments in or relationships with covered funds, and explaining the statute's requirements.

(c) *Scope.* This part implements section 13 of the Bank Holding Company Act with respect to banking entities for which the Board is authorized to issue regulations under section 13(b)(2) of the Bank Holding Company Act and take actions under section 13(e) of that Act. These include any state bank that is a member of the Federal Reserve System, any company that controls an insured depository institution (including a bank holding company and savings and loan holding company), any company that is treated as a bank holding company for purposes of section 8 of the International Banking Act, and any subsidiary of the foregoing other than for which the OCC, FDIC, CFTC, or SEC is the primary financial regulatory agency (as defined in section 2(12) of the Dodd-Frank Wall Street Reform and Consumer Protection Act of 2010).

(d) *Relationship to other authorities.* Except as otherwise provided under section 13 of the BHC Act or this part, and notwithstanding any other provision of law, the prohibitions and restrictions under section 13 of BHC Act and this part shall apply to the activities of a banking entity, even if such activities are authorized for the banking entity under the applicable provisions of law.

(e) *Preservation of authority.* Nothing in this part limits in any way the authority of the Board to impose on a banking entity identified in paragraph (c) of this rule additional requirements or restrictions with respect to any activity, investment, or relationship covered under section 13 of the Bank Holding Company Act or this part, or additional penalties for violation of this part provided under any other applicable provisions of law.

Rule 2. Model Privacy Form: Rule of Construction

(a) Model privacy form. Use of the model privacy form in Appendix A to Subpart A of this part, consistent with the instructions in Appendix A to Subpart A, constitutes compliance with the notice content requirements of §§ 248.6 and 248.7 of this part, although use of the model privacy form is not required.

(b) Examples. The examples in this part provide guidance concerning the rule's application in ordinary circumstances. The facts and circumstances of each individual situation, however, will determine whether compliance with an example, to the extent practicable, constitutes compliance with this part.

(c) Substituted compliance with CFTC financial privacy rules by futures commission merchants and introducing brokers. Except with respect to Item 30(b), any futures commission merchant or introducing broker (as those terms are defined in the Commodity Exchange Act registered by notice with the Commission for the purpose of conducting business in security futures products pursuant to section 15(b)(11)(A) of the Securities Exchange Act of 1934 that is subject to and in compliance with the financial privacy rules of the Commodity Futures Trading Commission (17 CFR part 160) will be deemed to be in compliance with this part).

Rule 3. Definitions

As used in this regulation, unless the context requires otherwise:

(a) "Affiliate" of a broker, dealer, or investment company, or an investment adviser registered with the Commission means any company that controls, is controlled by, or is under common control with the broker, dealer, or investment company, or investment adviser registered with the Commission. In addition, a broker, dealer, or investment company, or an investment adviser registered with the Commission will be deemed an affiliate of a company for purposes of this subpart if:

(1) That company is regulated under Title V of the GLBA by the Federal Trade Commission of by a Federal functional regulator other than the Commission; and

(2) Rule adopted by the Federal Trade Commission or another federal functional regulator under Title V of the GLBA treat the broker, dealer, or investment company, or investment adviser registered with the Commission as an affiliate of that company.

(b) "Broker" has the same meaning as in section 3(a)(4) of the Securities Exchange Act of 1934.

(c)(1) "Clear and conspicuous" means that a notice is reasonably understandable and designed to call attention to the nature and significance of the information in the notice.

(2) *Examples.* (i) *Reasonably understandable.* You make your notice reasonably understandable if you:

(A) Present the information in the notice in clear, concise sentences, paragraphs, and sections;

(B) Use short explanatory sentences or bullet lists whenever possible;

(C) Use definite, concrete, everyday words and active voice whenever possible;

(D) Avoid multiple negatives;

(E) Avoid legal and highly technical business terminology whenever possible; and

(F) Avoid explanations that are imprecise and readily subject to different interpretations.

(ii) *Designed to call attention.* You design you notice to call attention to the nature and significance of the information in it if you:

(A) Use a plain-language heading to call attention to the notice;

(B) Use a typeface and type size that are easy to read;

(C) Provide wide margins and ample line spacing;

(D) Use boldface or italics for key words; and

(E) Use distinctive type size, style, and graphic devices, such as shading or sidebars when you combine your notice with other information.

(iii) *Notices on web sites.* If you provide a notice on a web page, you design your notice to call attention to the nature and significance of the information in it if you use text or visual cues to encourage scrolling down the page if necessary to view the entire notice and ensure that other elements on the web site (such as text, graphics, hyperlinks, or sound) do not distract attention from the notice, and you either:

(A)   Place the notice on a screen that consumers frequently access, such as a page on which transactions are conducted; or

(B)   Place a link on a screen that consumers frequently access, such as a page on which transactions are conducted, that connects directly to the notice and is labeled appropriately to convey the importance, nature, and relevance of the notice.

(d)   "Collect" means to obtain information that you organize or can retrieve by the name of an individual or by identifying number, symbol, or other identifying particular assigned to the individual, irrespective of the source of the underlying information.

(e)   "Commission" means the Securities and Exchange Commission.

(f)   "Company" means any corporation, limited liability company, business trust, general or limited partnership, association, or similar organization.

(g)(1)   "Consumer" means an individual who obtains or has obtained a financial product or service from you that is to be used primarily for personal, family, or household purposes, or that individual's legal representative.

(2)   *Examples.* (i) An individual is your consumer if her or she provides nonpublic personal information to you in connection with obtaining or seeking to obtain brokerage services or investment advisory services, whether or not you provide brokerage services to the individual or establish a continuing relationship with the individual.

(ii)   An individual is not your consumer if he or she provides you only with his or her name, address, and general areas of investment interest in connection with a request for a prospectus, and investment adviser brochure, or other information about financial products or services.

(iii)   An individual is not your consumer if he or she has an account with another broker or dealer (the introducing broker-dealer) that carries securities for the individual in a special omnibus account with you (the clearing broker-dealer) in the name of the introducing broker-dealer, and when you receive only the account numbers and transaction information of the introducing broker-dealer's consumers in order to clear transactions.

(iv)   If you are an investment company, an individual is not your consumer when the individual purchases an interest in shares you have issued only through a broker or dealer or investment adviser who is the record owner of those shares.

(v)   An individual who is a consumer of another financial institution is not your consumer solely because you act as agent for, or provide processing or other services to, that financial institution.

(vi)   An individual is not your consumer solely because he or she has designated you as trustee for a trust.

(vii)   An individual is not your consumer solely because he or she is a beneficiary of a trust for which you are a trustee.

(viii) An individual is not your consumer solely because he or she is a participant or a beneficiary of an employee benefit plan that you sponsor or for which you act as a trustee or fiduciary.

(h)   "Consumer reporting agency" has the same meaning as in section 603(f) of the Fair Credit Reporting Act.

(i)   "Control" of a company means the power to exercise a controlling influence over the management or policies of a company whether through ownership of securities, by contact, or otherwise. Any person who owns beneficially, either directly or through one or more controlled companies, more than 25 percent of the voting securities of any company will be presumed not to control the company. Any presumption regarding control may be rebutted by evidence, but, in the case of an investment company, will continue until the

Commission makes a decision to the contrary according to the procedures described in section 2(a)(9) of the Investment Company Act of 1940.

(j) "Customer" means a consumer who has a customer relationship with you.

(k)(1) "Customer relationship" means a continuing relationship between a consumer and your under which you provide one or more financial products or services to the consumer that are to be used primarily for personal, family, or household purposes.

(2) *Examples.* (i) *Continuing relationship.* A consumer has a continuing relationship with you if:

(A) The consumer has a brokerage account with you, or if a consumer's account is transferred to you from another broker-dealer;

(B) The consumer has an investment advisory contract with you (whether written or oral);

(C) The consumer is the record owner of securities you have issued if you are an investment company;

(D) The consumer holds an investment product through you, such as when you act as a custodian for securities or for assets in an Individual Retirement Agreement;

(E) The consumer purchases a variable annuity from you;

(F) The consumer has an account with an introducing broker or dealer that clears transactions with and for its customers through you on a fully disclosed basis;

(G) You hold securities or other assets as collateral for a loan made to the consumer, even if you did not make the loan or do not effect any transactions on behalf of the consumer; or

(H) You regularly effect or engage in securities transactions with or for a consumer even if you do not hold any assets of the consumer.

(ii) *No continuing relationship.* A consumer does not, however, have a continuing relationship with you if you open an account for the consumer solely for the purpose of liquidating or purchasing securities as an accommodation, *i.e.*, on a one time basis, without the expectation of engaging in other transactions.

(*l*) *Dealer* has the same meaning as in section 3(a)(5) of the Securities Exchange Act of 1934.

(m) *Federal functional regulator* means:

(1) The Board of Governors of the Federal Reserve System;

(2) The Office of the Comptroller of the Currency.

(3) The Board of Directors of the Federal Deposit Insurance Corporation;

(4) The Director of the Office of Thrift Supervision;

(5) The National Credit Union Administration Board;

(6) The Securities and Exchange Commission; and

(7) The Commodity Futures Trading Commission.

(n)(1) *Financial Institution* means any institution the business of which is engaging in activities that are financial in nature or incidental to such financial activities as described in section 4(k) of the Bank Holding Company Act of 1956.

(2) *Financial Institution* does not include:

(i) The Federal Agricultural Mortgage Corporation or any entity chartered and operating under the Farm Credit Act of 1971; or

(ii) Institutions chartered by Congress specifically to engage in securitizations, secondary market sales (including sales of servicing rights), or similar transactions related to a transaction of a consumer, as long as such institutions do not sell or transfer nonpublic personal information to a nonaffiliated third party.

(*o*)(1) *Financial product or service* means any product or service that a financial holding company could offer by engaging in an activity that is financial in nature or incidental to such a financial activity under section 4(k) of the Bank Holding Company Act of 1956.

(2) *Financial Service* includes your evaluation or brokerage of information that you collect in connection with a request or an application from a consumer for a financial product or service.

(p) *GLBA* means the Gramm-Leach Bliley Act (Pub. L. No. 106–112, 113 Stat. 1338 (1999)).

(q) *Investment adviser* has the same meaning as in section 202(a)(11) of the Investment Advisers Act of 1940.

(r) *Investment company* has the same meaning as in section 3 of the Investment Company Act of 1940, and includes a separate series of the investment company.

(s)(1) *Nonaffiliated third party* means any person except:

(i) Your affiliate; or

(ii) A person employed jointly by you and any company that is not your affiliate (but *nonaffiliated third party* includes the other company that jointly employs the person).

(2) *Nonaffiliated third party* includes any company that is an affiliate solely by virtue of your or your affiliate's direct or indirect ownership or control of the company in conducting merchant banking or investment activities of the type described in section 4(k)(4)(H) or insurance company investment activities of the type described in section 4(k)(4)(I) of the Bank Holding Company Act.

(t)(1) *Nonpublic personal information* means:

(i) Personally identifiable financial information; and

(ii) Any list, description, or other grouping of consumers (and publicly available information pertaining to them) that is derived using any personally identifiable financial information that is not publicly available information.

(2) *Nonpublic personal information* does not include:

(i) Publicly available information except as included on a list described in paragraph (t)(1)(ii) of this Item or when the publicly available information is disclosed in a manner that indicates the individual is or has been your consumer; or

(ii) Any list, description or other grouping of consumers (and publicly available information pertaining to them) that is derived without using any personally identifiable financial information that is not publicly available information

(3) *Examples of lists.* (i) Nonpublic personal information includes any list of individuals' names and street addresses that is derived in whole or in part using personally identifiable financial information that is not publicly available information, such as account numbers.

(ii) Nonpublic personal information does not include any list of individuals' names and addresses that contains only publicly available information, is not derived in whole or in part using personally identifiable financial information that is not publicly available information, and is not disclosed in a manner that indicates that any of the individuals on the list is a consumer of a financial institution.

(u)(1) *Personally identifiable financial information* means any information:

(i) A consumer provides to you to obtain a financial product or service from you;

(ii) About a consumer resulting from any transaction involving a financial product or service from you;

(iii) You otherwise obtain about a consumer in connection with providing a financial product or service to that consumer.

(2) *Examples* (i) *Information included.* Personally identifiable financial information includes:

(A) Information a consumer provides to you on an application to obtain a loan, credit card, or other financial product or service;

(B) Account balance information, payment history, overdraft history, and credit or debit card purchase information;

(C) The fact that an individual is or has been one of your customers or has obtained a financial product or service from you;

(D) Any information about your consumer if it is disclosed in a manner that indicates that the individual is or has been your consumers;

(E) Any information that a consumer provides to you or that you or your agent otherwise obtain in connection with collecting on a loan or servicing a loan;

(F) Any information you collect through an Internet "Cookie" (an information collecting device from a web server); and

(G) Information from a consumer report.

(ii) *Information not included.* Personally identifiable financial information does not include:

(A) A list of names and addresses of customers of an entity that is not a financial institution; or

(B) Information that does not identify a consumer, such as aggregate information or blind data that does not contain personal identifiers such as account numbers, names, or addresses.

(v)(1) *Publicly available information* means any information that you reasonably believe is lawfully made available to the general public from:

(i) Federal, State, or local government records:

(ii) Widely distributes media; or

(iii) Disclosures to the general public that are required to be made by federal, State, or local law.

(2) *Examples* (i) *Reasonable Belief.* (A) You have a reasonable belief that information about your consumer is made available to the general public if you have confirmed, or your consumer has represented to you, that the information is publicly available from a source described in paragraphs (v)(1)(i)–(iii) of this Item;

(B) You have a reasonable belief that information about your consumer is made available to the general public if you have taken steps to submit the information, in accordance with your internal procedures and policies and with applicable law, to a keeper of federal, State, or local government records that is required by law to make the information publicly available.

(C) You have a reasonable belief that an individual's telephone number is lawfully made available to the general public if you have located the telephone number in the telephone book or the consumer has informed you that the telephone number is not unlisted.

(D) You do not have a reasonable belief that information about a consumer is publicly available solely because that information would normally be recorded with a keeper of federal, State, or local government records that is required by law to make the information publicly available, if the consumer has the ability in accordance with applicable law to keep that information nonpublic, such as where a consumer may record a deed in the name of a blind trust.

(ii) *Government records.* Publicly available information in government records includes information in government real estate records and security interest filings.

(iii) *Widely distributed media.* Publicly available information from widely distribute media includes information from a telephone book, a television or radio program, a newspaper, or a web site that is available to the general public on an unrestricted basis. A web site is not restricted merely because an Internet service provider or a site operator requires a fee or a password, so long as access is available to the general public.

(w)   *You* means:

(1)   Any broker or dealer;

(2)   Any investment company; and

(3)   Any investment adviser registered with the Commission under the Investment Advisers Act of 1940.

PRIVACY AND OPT OUT NOTICES

Rule 4.   Initial Privacy Notice to Consumers Required

(a)   *Initial notice requirement.* You must provide a clear and conspicuous notice that accurately reflects your privacy policies and practices to:

(1)   *Customer* An individual who becomes your customer, not later than when you establish a customer relationship, except as provided in paragraph (e) of this Item; and

(2)   *Consumer.* A consumer, before you disclose any nonpublic personal information about the consumer to any nonaffiliated third party, if you make such a disclosure other that as authorized by Items 14 and 15.

(b)   *When initial notice to consumer is not required.* You are not required to provide an initial notice to a consumer under paragraph (a) of this Item if:

(1)   You do not disclose any nonpublic personal information about the consumer to any nonaffiliated third party, other than as authorized by Items 14 and 15.

(2)   You do not have a customer relationship with the consumer.

(c)   *When you establish a customer relationship.* (1) *General rule.* You establish a customer relationship when you and the consumer enter into a continuing relationship.

(2)   *Special rule of loans.* You do not have customer relationship with a consumer if you buy a loan made to the consumer but do not have the servicing rights for that loan.

(3)   *Examples of establishing customer relationship.* You establish a customer relationship when the consumer:

(i)   Effects a securities transaction with you or opens a brokerage account with you under your procedures;

(ii)   Opens a brokerage account with an introducing broker or dealer that clears transactions with and for its customers through you on a fully disclosed basis;

(iii)   Enters into an advisory contract with you (whether in writing or orally);

(iv)   Purchases shares you have issued (and the consumers is the record owner of the shares), if you are an investment company.

(d)   *Existing customers.* When an existing customer obtains a new financial product or service from you that is to be used primarily for personal, family, or household purposes, you satisfy the initial notice requirements of paragraph (a) of this Item as follows:

(1)   You may provide a revised privacy notice, under Item 8, that covers the customer's new financial product or service; or

(2)   If the initial, revised, or annual notice that you most recently provided to that customer was accurate with respect to the new financial product or service, you do not need to provide a new privacy notice under paragraph (a) of this Item.

(e)   *Exceptions to allow subsequent delivery of notice.* (1) You may provide the initial notice required by paragraph (a)(1) of this Item within a reasonable time after you establish a customer relationship if:

(i) Establishing the customer relationship is not at the customer's election;

(ii) Providing notice not later than when you establish a customer relationship would substantially delay the customer's transaction and the customer agrees to receive the notice at a later time; or

(iii) A nonaffiliated broker or dealer or investment adviser establishes a customer relationship between you and a consumer without your prior knowledge.

(2) *Examples of exceptions.* (i) Not at customer's election. Establishing a customer relationship is not at the customer's election if the customer's account is transferred to you by a trustee selected by the Securities Investor Protection Corporation ("SIPC") and appointed by a United States Court.

(ii) *Substantial delay of customer's transaction.* Providing notice not later than when you establish a customer relationship would substantially delay the customer's transaction when you and the individual agree over the telephone to enter into a customer relationship involving prompt delivery of the financial product or service.

(iii) *No substantial delay of customer's transaction.* Providing notice not later than when you establish a customer relationship would not substantially delay the customer's transaction when the relationship is initiated in person at your office or through other means by which the customer may view the notice, such as on a web site.

(f) *Delivery.* When you are required to deliver an initial privacy notice by this rule, you must deliver it according to Item 9. If you use a short-form initial notice for non-customers according to Item 6(d), you may deliver your privacy notice according to Item 6(d)(3).

Rule 5. Annual Privacy Notice to Customers Required

(a)(1) *General rule.* You must provide a clear and conspicuous notice to customers that accurately reflects your privacy policies and practices not less than annually during the continuation of the customer relationship. *Annually* means at least once in any period of 12 consecutive months during which that relationship exists. You may define the 12-consecutive-month period, but you must apply it to the customer on a consistent basis.

(2) *Example.* You provide a notice annually if you define the 12-consecutive-month period as a calendar year and provide the annual notice to the customer once in each calendar year following the calendar year in which you provided the initial notice. For example, if a customer opens an account on any day of year 1, you must provide an annual notice to that customer by December 31 of year 2.

(b)(1) *Termination of customer relationship.* You are not required to provide an annual notice to a former customer.

(2) *Examples.* Your customer becomes a former customer when:

(i) The individual's brokerage account is closed;

(ii) The individual's investment advisory contract is terminated;

(iii) You are an investment company and the individual is no longer the record owner of securities you have issued; or

(iv) You are an investment company and your customer has been determined to be a lost securityholder as defined in Rule 17a–24(b) under the Exchange Act.

(c) *Special rule for loans.* If you do not have a customer relationship with a consumer under the special provision for loans in Item 4(c)(2), then you need not provide an annual notice to that consumer under this rule.

(d) *Delivery.* When you are required to deliver an annual privacy notice by this rule, you must deliver it according to Item 9.

Rule 6. Information to Be Included in Privacy Notices

(a) *General rule.* The initial, annual, and revised privacy notices that you provide under Items 4, 5, and 8 must include each of the following items of information that applies to you or to the consumers to whom you send your privacy notice, in addition to any other information you wish to provide:

(1)   The categories of nonpublic personal information that you collect;

(2)   The categories of nonpublic personal information that you disclose;

(3)   The categories of affiliates and nonaffiliated third parties to whom you disclose nonpublic personal information, other than those parties to whom you disclose information under Items 14 and 15;

(4)   The categories of nonpublic personal information about your former customers that you disclose and the categories of affiliates and nonaffiliated third parties to whom you disclose nonpublic personal information about your former customers, other than those parties to whom you disclose information under Items 14 and 15;

(5)   If you disclose nonpublic personal information to a nonaffiliated third party under Item 13 (and no other exception applies to that disclosure), a separate statement of the categories of information you disclose and the categories of third parties with whom you have contracted;

(6)   An explanation of the consumer's right under Item 10(a) to opt out of the disclosure of nonpublic personal information to nonaffiliated third parties, including the method(s) by which the consumer may exercise that right at that time;

(7)   Any disclosures that you make under section 603(d)(2)(A)(iii) of the Fair Credit Reporting Act (that is, notices regarding the ability to opt out of disclosures of information among affiliates);

(8)   Your policies and practices with respect to protecting the confidentiality and security of nonpublic personal information; and

(9)   Any disclosure that you make under paragraph (b) of this Item.

(b) *Description of nonaffiliated third parties subject to exceptions.* If you disclose nonpublic personal information to third parties as authorized under §§ 248.14 and 248.15, you are not required to list those exceptions in the initial or annual privacy notices required by §§ 248.4 and 248.5. When describing the categories with respect to those parties, it is sufficient to state that you make disclosures to other nonaffiliated companies:

(1)   For your everyday business purposes such as [include all that apply] to process transactions, maintain account(s), respond to court orders and legal investigations, or report to credit bureaus; or

(2)   As permitted by law.

(c) *Examples.* (1) *Categories of nonpublic personal information that you collect.* You satisfy the requirement to categorize the nonpublic personal information that you collect if you list the following categories, as applicable:

(i)   Information from the consumer;

(ii)   Information about the consumer's transactions with you or your affiliates;

(iii)   Information about the consumer's transactions with nonaffiliated third parties; and

(iv)   Information from a consumer-reporting agency.

(2) *Categories of nonpublic personal information you disclose.* (i) You satisfy the requirement to categorize the nonpublic personal information that you disclose if you list the categories described in paragraph (e)(1) of this Item, as applicable, and a few examples to illustrate the types of information in each category.

(ii)   If you reserve the right to disclose all of the nonpublic personal information about consumers that you collect, you may simply state that fact without describing the categories or examples of the nonpublic personal information you disclose.

(3) *Categories of affiliates and nonaffiliated third parties to whom you disclose.* You satisfy the requirement to categorize the affiliates and nonaffiliated third parties to whom you disclose nonpublic personal information if you list the following categories, as applicable, and a few examples to illustrate the types of third parties in each category:

    (i)   Financial service providers;

    (ii)   Non-financial companies; and

    (iii) Others.

(4) *Disclosures under exception for service providers and joint marketers.* If you disclose nonpublic personal information under the exception in Item 13 to a nonaffiliated third party to market products or services that you offer alone or jointly with another financial institution, you satisfy the disclosure requirement of paragraph (a)(5) of this rule if you:

    (i)   List the categories of nonpublic personal information you disclose, using the same categories and examples you used to meet the requirements of paragraph (a)(2) of this Item, as applicable; and

    (ii)   State whether the third party is:

        (A)   A service provider that performs marketing services on your behalf or on behalf of you and another financial institution; or

        (B)   A financial institution with which you have a joint marketing agreement.

(5) *Simplified notices.* If you do not disclose, and do not wish to reserve the right to disclose, nonpublic personal information to affiliates or nonaffiliated third parties except as authorized under Items 14 and 15, you may simply state that fact, in addition to the information you must provide under paragraphs (a)(1), (a)(8), (a)(9), and (b) of this Item.

(6) *Confidentiality and security.* You describe your policies and practices with respect to protecting the confidentiality and security of nonpublic personal information if you do both of the following:

    (i)   Describe in general terms who is authorized to have access to the information; and

    (ii)   State whether you have security practices and procedures in place to ensure the confidentiality of the information in accordance with your policy. You are not required to describe technical information about the safeguards you use.

(d)   *Short-form initial notice with opt out notice for non-customers.* (1) You may satisfy the initial notice requirements in Items 4(a)(2), 7(b), and 7(c) for a consumer who is not a customer by providing a short-form initial notice at the same time as you deliver an opt out notice as required in Item 7.

    (2)   A short-form initial notice must:

        (i)   Be clear and conspicuous;

        (ii)   State that your privacy notice is available upon request; and

        (iii) Explain a reasonable means by which the consumer may obtain the privacy notice.

    (3)   You must deliver your short-form initial notice according to Item 9. You are not required to deliver your privacy notice with your short-form initial notice. You instead may simply provide the consumer a reasonable means to obtain your privacy notice. If a consumer who receives your short-form notice requests your privacy notice, you must deliver your privacy notice according to Item 9.

    (4)   *Examples of obtaining privacy notice.* You provide a reasonable means by which a consumer may obtain a copy of your privacy notice if you:

        (i)   Provide a toll-free telephone number that the consumer may call to request the notice; or

        (ii)   For a consumer who conducts business in person at your office, maintain copies of the notice on hand that you provide to the consumer immediately upon request.

(e)   *Future disclosures.* Your notice may include:

    (1)   Categories of nonpublic personal information that you reserve the right to disclose in the future, but do not currently disclose; and

    (2)   Categories of affiliates or nonaffiliated third parties to whom you reserve the right in the future to disclose, but to whom you do not currently disclose, nonpublic personal information.

(f)   *Model privacy form.* Pursuant to § 248.2(a) and Appendix A to Subpart A of this part, Form S–P meets the notice content requirements of this rule.

Rule 7.   Form of Opt Out Notice to Consumers; Opt Out Methods

    (a)(1)   *Form of opt out notice.* If you are required to provide an opt out notice under Item 10(a), you must provide a clear and conspicuous notice to each of your consumers that accurately explains the right to opt out under that section. The notice must state:

    (i)   That you disclose or reserve the right to disclose nonpublic personal information about your consumer to a nonaffiliated third party;

    (ii)   That the consumer has the right to opt out of that disclosure; and

    (iii)   A reasonable means by which the consumer may exercise the opt out right.

    (2)   *Examples.* (i) *Adequate opt out notice.* You provide adequate notice that the consumer can opt out of the disclosure of nonpublic personal information to a nonaffiliated third party if you:

    (A)   Identify all of the categories of nonpublic personal information that you disclose or reserve the right to disclose, and all of the categories of nonaffiliated third parties to which you disclose the information, as described in Item 6(a)(2) and (3) and state that the consumer can opt out of the disclosure of that information; and

    (B)   Identify the financial products or services that the consumer obtains from you, either singly or jointly, to which the opt out direction would apply.

    (ii)   *Reasonable opt out means.* You provide a reasonable means to exercise an opt out right if you:

    (A)   Designate check-off boxes in a prominent position on the relevant forms with the opt out notice;

    (B)   Include a reply form together with the opt out notice;

    (C)   Provide an electronic means to opt out, such as a form that can be sent via electronic mail or a process at your web site, if the consumer agrees to the electronic delivery of information; or

    (D)   Provide a toll-free telephone number that consumers may call to opt out.

    (iii)   *Unreasonable opt out means.* You do not provide a reasonable means of opting out if:

    (A)   The only means of opting out is for the consumer to write his or her own letter to exercise that opt out right; or

    (B)   The only means of opting out as described in any notice subsequent to the initial notice is to use a check-off box that you provided with the initial notice but did not include with the subsequent notice.

    (iv)   *Specific opt out means.* You may require each consumer to opt out through a specific means, as long as that means is reasonable for that consumer.

(b)   *Same form as initial notice permitted.* You may provide the opt out notice together with or on the same written or electronic form as the initial notice you provide in accordance with Item 4.

(c)   *Initial notice required when opt out notice delivered subsequent to initial notice.* If you provide the opt out notice after the initial notice in accordance with Item 4, you must also include a copy of the initial notice with the opt out notice in writing or, if the consumer agrees, electronically.

(d) *Joint relationships.* (1) If two or more consumers jointly obtain a financial product or service from you, you may provide a single opt out notice. Your opt out notice must explain how you will treat an opt out direction by a joint consumer.

(2) Any of the joint consumers may exercise the right to opt out. You may either:

(i) Treat an opt out direction by a joint consumer as applying to all of the associated joint consumers; or

(ii) Permit each joint consumer to opt out separately.

(3) If you permit each joint consumer to opt out separately, you must permit one of the joint consumers to opt out on behalf of all of the joint consumers.

(4) You may not require *all* joint consumers to opt out before you implement any opt out direction.

(5) *Example.* If John and Mary have a joint brokerage account with you and arrange for you to send statements to John's address, you may do any of the following, but you must explain in your opt out notice which opt out policy you will follow:

(i) Send a single opt out notice to John's address, but you must accept an opt out direction from either John or Mary;

(ii) Treat an opt out direction by either John or Mary as applying to the entire account. If you do so, and John opts out, you may not require Mary to opt out as well before implementing John's opt out direction; or

(iii) Permit John and Mary to make different opt out directions. If you do so:

(A) You must permit John and Mary to opt out for each other.

(B) If both opt out, you must permit both to notify you in a single response (such as on a form or through a telephone call).

(C) If John opts out and Mary does not, you may only disclose nonpublic personal information about Mary, but not about John and not about John and Mary jointly.

(e) *Time to comply with opt out.* You must comply with a consumer's opt out direction as soon as reasonably practicable after you receive it.

(f) *Continuing right to opt out.* A consumer may exercise the right to opt out at any time.

(g) *Duration of consumer's opt out direction.* (1) A consumer's direction to opt out under this rule is effective until the consumer revokes it in writing or, if the consumer agrees, electronically.

(2) When a customer relationship terminates, the customer's opt out direction continues to apply to the nonpublic personal information that you collected during or related to that relationship. If the individual subsequently establishes a new customer relationship with you, the opt out direction that applied to the former relationship does not apply to the new relationship.

(h) *Delivery.* When you are required to deliver an opt out notice by this rule, you must deliver it according to Item 9.

(i) *Model privacy form.* Pursuant to § 248.2(a) and Appendix A to Subpart A of this part, Form S–P meets the notice content requirements of this rule.

Rule 8. Revised Privacy Notices

(a) *General rule.* Except as otherwise authorized in this subpart, you must not, directly or through any affiliate, disclose any nonpublic personal information about a consumer to a nonaffiliated third party other than as described in the initial notice that you provided to that consumer under Item 4, unless:

(1) You have provided to the consumer a clear and conspicuous revised notice that accurately describes your policies and practices;

(2) You have provided to the consumer a new opt out notice;

(3) You have given the consumer a reasonable opportunity, before you disclose the information to the nonaffiliated third party, to opt out of the disclosure; and

(4) The consumer does not opt out.

(b) *Examples.* (1) Except as otherwise permitted by Items 13, 14 and 15, you must provide a revised notice before you:

(i) Disclose a new category of nonpublic personal information to any nonaffiliated third party;

(ii) Disclose nonpublic personal information to a new category of nonaffiliated third party; or

(iii) Disclose nonpublic personal information about a former customer to a nonaffiliated third party, if that former customer has not had the opportunity to exercise an opt out right regarding that disclosure.

(2) A revised notice is not required if you disclose nonpublic personal information to a new nonaffiliated third party that you adequately described in your prior notice.

(c) *Delivery.* When you are required to deliver a revised privacy notice by this rule, you must deliver it according to Item 9.

Rule 9. Delivering Privacy and Opt Out Notices

(a) *How to provide notices.* You must provide any privacy notices and opt out notices, including short-form initial notices that this subpart requires so that each consumer can reasonably be expected to receive actual notice in writing or, if the consumer agrees, electronically.

(b)(1) *Examples of reasonable expectation of actual notice.* You may reasonably expect that a consumer will receive actual notice if you:

(i) Hand-deliver a printed copy of the notice to the consumer;

(ii) Mail a printed copy of the notice to the last known address of the consumer;

(iii) For the consumer who conducts transactions electronically, post the notice on the electronic site and require the consumer to acknowledge receipt of the notice as a necessary step to obtaining a particular financial product or service; or

(iv) For an isolated transaction with the consumer, such as an ATM transaction, post the notice on the ATM screen and require the consumer to acknowledge receipt of the notice as a necessary step to obtaining the particular financial product or service.

(2) *Examples of unreasonable expectation of actual notice.* You may not, however, reasonably expect that a consumer will receive actual notice of your privacy policies and practices if you:

(i) Only post a sign in your branch or office or generally publish advertisements of your privacy policies and practices; or

(ii) Send the notice via electronic mail to a consumer who does not obtain a financial product or service from you electronically.

(c) *Annual notices only.* (1) You may reasonably expect that a customer will receive actual notice of your annual privacy notice if:

(i) The customer uses your web site to access financial products and services electronically and agrees to receive notices at the web site and you post your current privacy notice continuously in a clear and conspicuous manner on the web site; or

(ii) The customer has requested that you refrain from sending any information regarding the customer relationship, and your current privacy notice remains available to the customer upon request.

(2) *Example of reasonable expectation of receipt of annual privacy notice.* You may reasonably expect that consumers who share an address will receive actual notice of your annual privacy notice if

you deliver the notice with or in a stockholder or shareholder report under the conditions in Rule 30d–1(f) under the Investment Company Act or Rule 30d–2(b) under that Act, or with or in a prospectus under the conditions in Rule 159 under the Securities Act.

(d) *Oral description of notice insufficient.* You may not provide any notice required by this subpart solely by orally explaining the notice, either in person or over the telephone.

(e) *Retention or accessibility of notices for customers.* (1) For customers only, you must provide the initial notice required by Item 4(a)(1), the annual notice required by Item 5(a), and the revised notice required by Item 8, so that the customer can retain them or obtain them later in writing or, if the customer agrees, electronically.

(2) *Examples of retention or accessibility.* You provide a privacy notice to the customer so that the customer can retain it or obtain it later if you:

(i) Hand-deliver a printed copy of the notice to the customer;

(ii) Mail a printed copy of the notice to the last known address of the customer; or

(iii) Make your current privacy notice available on a web site (or a link to another web site) for the customer who obtains a financial product or service electronically and agrees to receive the notice at the web site.

(f) *Joint notice with other financial institutions.* You may provide a joint notice from you and one or more of your affiliates or other financial institutions, as identified in the notice, as long as the notice is accurate with respect to you and the other institutions.

(g) *Joint relationships.* If two or more consumers jointly obtain a financial product or service from you, you may satisfy the initial, annual, and revised notice requirements of paragraph (a) of this Item by providing one notice to those consumers jointly.

LIMITS ON DISCLOSURES

Rule 10. Limits on Disclosure of Nonpublic Personal Information to Nonaffiliated Third Parties

(a)(1) *Conditions for disclosure.* Except as otherwise authorized in this subpart, you may not, directly or through any affiliate, disclose any nonpublic personal information about a consumer to a nonaffiliated third party unless:

(i) You have provided to the consumer an initial notice as required under Item 4;

(ii) You have provided to the consumer an opt out notice as required in Item 7;

(iii) You have given the consumer a reasonable opportunity, before you disclose the information to the nonaffiliated third party, to opt out of the disclosure; and

(iv) The consumer does not opt out.

(2) *Opt out definition.* Opt out means a direction by the consumer that you not disclose nonpublic personal information about that consumer to a nonaffiliated third party, other than as permitted by Items 13, 14, and 15.

(3) *Examples of reasonable opportunity to opt out.* You provide a consumer with a reasonable opportunity to opt out if:

(i) *By mail.* You mail the notices required in paragraph (a)(1) of this Item to the consumer and allow the consumer to opt out by mailing a form, calling a toll-free telephone number, or any other reasonable means within 30 days after the date you mailed the notices.

(ii) *By electronic means.* A customer opens an on-line account with you and agrees to receive the notices required in paragraph (a)(1) of this Item electronically, and you allow the customer to opt out by any reasonable means within 30 days after the date that the customer acknowledges receipt of the notices in conjunction with opening the account.

(iii) *Isolated transaction with consumer.* For an isolated transaction, such as the provision of brokerage services to a consumer as an accommodation, you provide the consumer with a reasonable opportunity to opt out if you provide the notices required in paragraph (a)(1) of this Item at the time of the transaction and request that the consumer decide, as a necessary part of the transaction, whether to opt out before completing the transaction.

(b) *Application of opt out to all consumers and all nonpublic personal information.* (1) You must comply with this rule, regardless of whether you and the consumer have established a customer relationship.

(2) Unless you comply with this rule, you may not, directly or through any affiliate, disclose any nonpublic personal information about a consumer that you have collected, regardless of whether you collected it before or after receiving the direction to opt out from the consumer.

(c) *Partial opt out.* You may allow a consumer to select certain nonpublic personal information or certain nonaffiliated third parties with respect to which the consumer wishes to opt out.

Rule 11. Limits on Redisclosure and Reuse of Information

(a)(1) *Information you receive under an exception.* If you receive nonpublic personal information from a nonaffiliated financial institution under an exception in Items 14 or 15, your disclosure and use of that information is limited as follows:

(i) You may disclose the information to the affiliates of the financial institution from which you received the information;

(ii) You may disclose the information to your affiliates, but your affiliates may, in turn, disclose and use the information only to the extent that you may disclose and use the information; and

(iii) You may disclose and use the information pursuant to an exception in Items 14 or 15 in the ordinary course of business to carry out the activity covered by the exception under which you received the information.

(2) *Example.* If you receive a customer list from a nonaffiliated financial institution in order to provide account-processing services under the exception in Item 14(a), you may disclose that information under any exception in Items 14 or 15 in the ordinary course of business in order to provide those services. You could also disclose that information in response to a properly authorized subpoena or in the ordinary course of business to your attorneys, accountants, and auditors. You could not disclose that information to a third party for marketing purposes or use that information for your own marketing purposes.

(b)(1) *Information you receive outside of an exception.* If you receive nonpublic personal information from a nonaffiliated financial institution other than under an exception in Items 14 or 15, you may disclose the information only:

(i) To the affiliates of the financial institution from which you received the information;

(ii) To your affiliates, but your affiliates may, in turn, disclose the information only to the extent that you can disclose the information; and

(iii) To any other person, if the disclosure would be lawful if made directly to that person by the financial institution from which you received the information.

(2) *Example.* If you obtain a customer list from a nonaffiliated financial institution outside of the exceptions in Items 14 or 15:

(i) You may use that list for your own purposes;

(ii) You may disclose that list to another nonaffiliated third party only if the financial institution from which you purchased the list could have lawfully disclosed the list to that third party. That is, you may disclose the list in accordance with the privacy policy of the financial institution from which you received the list, as limited by the opt out direction of each consumer whose nonpublic personal information you intend to disclose, and you may disclose the list in accordance with an exception in Items 14 or 15, such as in the ordinary course of business to your attorneys, accountants, or auditors.

(c) *Information you disclose under an exception.* If you disclose nonpublic personal information to a nonaffiliated third party under an exception in Items 14 or 15, the third party may disclose and use that information only as follows:

(1) The third party may disclose the information to your affiliates;

(2) The third party may disclose the information to its affiliates, but its affiliates may, in turn, disclose and use the information only to the extent that the third party may disclose and use the information; and

(3) The third party may disclose and use the information pursuant to an exception in Items 14 or 15 in the ordinary course of business to carry out the activity covered by the exception under which it received the information.

(d) *Information you disclose outside of an exception.* If you disclose nonpublic personal information to a nonaffiliated third party other than under an exception in Items 14 or 15, the third party may disclose the information only:

(1) To your affiliates;

(2) To its affiliates, but its affiliates, in turn, may disclose the information only to the extent the third party can disclose the information; and

(3) To any other person, if the disclosure would be lawful if you made it directly to that person.

Rule 12. Limits on Sharing Account Number Information for Marketing Purposes

(a) *General prohibition on disclosure of account numbers.* You must not, directly or through an affiliate, disclose, other than to a consumer reporting agency, an account number or similar form of access number or access code for a consumer's credit card account, deposit account, or transaction account to any nonaffiliated third party for use in telemarketing, direct mail marketing, or other marketing through electronic mail to the consumer.

(b) *Exceptions.* Paragraph (a) of this Item does not apply if you disclose an account number or similar form of access number or access code:

(1) To your agent or service provider solely in order to perform marketing for your own products or services, as long as the agent or service provider is not authorized to directly initiate charges to the account; or

(2) To a participant in a private label credit card program or an affinity or similar program where the participants in the program are identified to the customer when the customer enters into the program.

(c) *Example—Account number.* An account number, or similar form of access number or access code, does not include a number or code in an encrypted form, as long as you do not provide the recipient with a means to decode the number or code.

EXCEPTIONS

Rule 13. Exception to Opt Out Requirements for Service Providers and Joint Marketing

(a) *General rule.* (1) The opt out requirements in Items 7 and 10 do not apply when you provide nonpublic personal information to a nonaffiliated third party to perform services for you or functions on your behalf, if you:

(i) Provide the initial notice in accordance with Item 4; and

(ii) Enter into a contractual agreement with the third party that prohibits the third party from disclosing or using the information other than to carry out the purposes for which you disclosed the information, including use under an exception in Items 14 or 15 in the ordinary course of business to carry out those purposes.

(2) *Example.* If you disclose nonpublic personal information under this rule to a financial institution with which you perform joint marketing, your contractual agreement with that institution meets the

requirements of paragraph (a)(1)(ii) of this Item if it prohibits the institution from disclosing or using the nonpublic personal information except as necessary to carry out the joint marketing or under an exception in Items 14 or 15 in the ordinary course of business to carry out that joint marketing.

(b) *Service may include joint marketing.* The services a nonaffiliated third party performs for you under paragraph (a) of this Item may include marketing of your own products or services or marketing of financial products or services offered pursuant to joint agreements between you and one or more financial institutions.

(c) *Definition of joint agreement.* For purposes of this rule, *joint agreement* means a written contract pursuant to which you and one or more financial institutions jointly offer, endorse, or sponsor a financial product or service.

Rule 14. Exceptions to Notice and Opt Out Requirements for Processing and Servicing Transactions

(a) *Exceptions for processing and servicing transactions at consumer's request.* The requirements for initial notice in Item 4(a)(2), for the opt out in Items 7 and 10, and for initial notice in Item 13 in connection with service providers and joint marketing, do not apply if you disclose nonpublic personal information as necessary to effect, administer, or enforce a transaction that a consumer requests or authorizes, or in connection with:

(1) Processing or servicing a financial product or service that a consumer requests or authorizes;

(2) Maintaining or servicing the consumer's account with you, or with another entity as part of a private label credit card program or other extension of credit on behalf of such entity; or

(3) A proposed or actual securitization, secondary market sale (including sales of servicing rights), or similar transaction related to a transaction of the consumer.

(b) *Necessary to effect, administer, or enforce a transaction* means that the disclosure is:

(1) Required, or is one of the lawful or appropriate methods, to enforce your rights or the rights of other persons engaged in carrying out the financial transaction or providing the product or service; or

(2) Required, or is a usual, appropriate, or acceptable method:

(i) To carry out the transaction or the product or service business of which the transaction is a part, and record, service, or maintain the consumer's account in the ordinary course of providing the financial service or financial product;

(ii) To administer or service benefits or claims relating to the transaction or the product or service business of which it is a part;

(iii) To provide a confirmation, statement, or other record of the transaction, or information on the status or value of the financial service or financial product to the consumer or the consumer's agent or broker;

(iv) To accrue or recognize incentives or bonuses associated with the transaction that are provided by you or any other party;

(v) To underwrite insurance at the consumer's request or for reinsurance purposes, or for any of the following purposes as they relate to a consumer's insurance: Account administration, reporting, investigating, or preventing fraud or material misrepresentation, processing premium payments, processing insurance claims, administering insurance benefits (including utilization review activities), participating in research projects, or as otherwise required or specifically permitted by federal or State law; or

(vi) In connection with:

(A) The authorization, settlement, billing, processing, clearing, transferring, reconciling or collection of amounts charged, debited, or otherwise paid using a debit, credit, or other payment card, check, or account number, or by other payment means;

(B) The transfer of receivables, accounts, or interests therein; or

(C)   The audit of debit, credit, or other payment information.

Rule 15. Other Exceptions to Notice and Opt Out Requirements

(a)   *Exceptions to notice and opt out requirements.* The requirements for initial notice in Item 4(a)(2), for the opt out in Items 7 and 10, and for initial notice in Item 13 in connection with service providers and joint marketing do not apply when you disclose nonpublic personal information:

(1)   With the consent or at the direction of the consumer, provided that the consumer has not revoked the consent or direction;

(2)(i)   To protect the confidentiality or security of your records pertaining to the consumer, service, product, or transaction;

(ii)   To protect against or prevent actual or potential fraud, unauthorized transactions, claims, or other liability;

(iii)   For required institutional risk control or for resolving consumer disputes or inquiries;

(iv)   To persons holding a legal or beneficial interest relating to the consumer; or

(v)   To persons acting in a fiduciary or representative capacity on behalf of the consumer;

(3)   To provide information to insurance rate advisory organizations, guaranty funds or agencies, agencies that are rating you, persons that are assessing your compliance with industry standards, and your attorneys, accountants, and auditors;

(4)   To the extent specifically permitted or required under other provisions of law and in accordance with the Right to Financial Privacy Act of 1978, to law enforcement agencies (including a federal functional regulator, the Secretary of the Treasury, with respect to 31 U.S.C.A. Chapter 53, Subchapter II (Records and Reports on Monetary Instruments and Transactions) and Financial Recordkeeping, a State insurance authority, with respect to any person domiciled in that insurance authority's State that is engaged in providing insurance, and the Federal Trade Commission), self-regulatory organizations, or for an investigation on a matter related to public safety;

(5)(i)   To a consumer reporting agency in accordance with the Fair Credit Reporting Act, or

(ii)   From a consumer report reported by a consumer reporting agency;

(6)   In connection with a proposed or actual sale, merger, transfer, or exchange of all or a portion of a business or operating unit if the disclosure of nonpublic personal information concerns solely consumers of such business or unit; or

(7)(i)   To comply with federal, State, or local laws, rules and other applicable legal requirements;

(ii)   To comply with a properly authorized civil, criminal, or regulatory investigation, or subpoena or summons by federal, State, or local authorities; or

(iii)   To respond to judicial process or government regulatory authorities having jurisdiction over you for examination, compliance, or other purposes as authorized by law.

(b)   *Examples of consent and revocation of consent.* (1) A consumer may specifically consent to your disclosure to a nonaffiliated mortgage lender of the value of the assets in the consumer's brokerage or investment advisory account so that the lender can evaluate the consumer's application for a mortgage loan.

(2)   A consumer may revoke consent by subsequently exercising the right to opt out of future disclosures of nonpublic personal information as permitted under Item 7(f).

RELATION TO OTHER LAWS; EFFECTIVE DATE

Rule 16. Protection of Fair Credit Reporting Act

Nothing in this subpart shall be construed to modify, limit, or supersede the operation of the Fair Credit Reporting Act, and no inference shall be drawn on the basis of the provisions of this part regarding whether information is transaction or experience information under section 603 of that Act.

Rule 17. Relation to State Laws

(a) *In general.* This subpart shall not be construed as superseding, altering, or affecting any statute, regulation, order, or interpretation in effect in any State, except to the extent that such State statute, regulation, order, or interpretation is inconsistent with the provisions of this subpart, and then only to the extent of the inconsistency.

(b) *Greater protection under State law.* For purposes of this rule, a State statute, regulation, order, or interpretation is not inconsistent with the provisions of this subpart if the protection such statute, regulation, order, or interpretation affords any consumer is greater than the protection provided under this subpart, as determined by the Federal Trade Commission, after consultation with the Commission, on the Federal Trade Commission's own motion, or upon the petition of any interested party.

Rule 18. Effective Date; Transition Rule

(a) *Effective date.* This subpart is effective November 13, 2000. In order to provide sufficient time for you to establish policies and systems to comply with the requirements of this part, the compliance date for this subpart is July 1, 2001.

(b)(1) *Notice requirement for consumers who are your customers on the compliance date.* By July 1, 2001, you must have provided an initial notice, as required by Item 4, to consumers who are your customers on July 1, 2001.

(2) *Example.* You provide an initial notice to consumers who are your customers on July 1, 2001, if, by that date, you have established a system for providing an initial notice to all new customers and have mailed the initial notice to all your existing customers.

(c) *Two-year grandfathering of service agreements.* Until July 1, 2002, a contract that you have entered into with a nonaffiliated third party to perform services for you or functions on your behalf satisfies the provisions of Item 13(a)(2), even if the contract does not include a requirement that the third party maintain the confidentiality of nonpublic personal information, as long as you entered into the agreement on or before July 1, 2000.

Rules 19–29. [Reserved]

Rule 30. Procedures to Safeguard Customer Records and Information; Disposal of Consumer Report Information

(a) Every broker, dealer, and investment company, and every investment adviser registered with the Commission must adopt written policies and procedures that address administrative, technical, and physical safeguards for the protection of customer records and information. These written policies and procedures must be reasonably designed to:

(1) Insure the security and confidentiality of customer records and information;

(2) Protect against any anticipated threats or hazards to the security or integrity of customer records and information; and

(3) Protect against unauthorized access to or use of customer records or information that could result in substantial harm or inconvenience to any customer.

(b) Disposal of consumer report information and records—

(1) Definitions

(i) Consumer report has the same meaning as in section 603(d) of the Fair Credit Reporting Act.

(ii) Consumer report information means any record about an individual, whether in paper, electronic or other form, that is a consumer report or is derived from a consumer report. Consumer report information also means a compilation of such records. Consumer report information does not include information that does not identify individuals, such as aggregate information or blind data.

    (iii) Disposal means:

        (A) The discarding or abandonment of consumer report information; or

        (B) The sale, donation, or transfer of any medium, including computer equipment, on which consumer report information is stored.

    (iv) Notice-registered broker-dealers means a broker or dealer registered by notice with the Commission under section 15(b)(11) of the Securities Exchange Act of 1934.

    (v) Transfer agent has the same meaning as in section 3(a)(25) of the Securities Exchange Act of 1934.

  (2) Proper disposal requirements—

    (i) Standard. Every broker and dealer other than notice-registered broker-dealers, every investment company, and every investment adviser and transfer agent registered with the Commission, that maintains or otherwise possesses consumer report information for a business purpose must properly dispose of the information by taking reasonable measures to protect against unauthorized access to or use of the information in connection with its disposal.

    (ii) Relation to other laws. Nothing in this rule shall be construed:

        (A) To require any broker, dealer, or investment company, or any investment adviser or transfer agent registered with the Commission to maintain or destroy any record pertaining to an individual that is not imposed under other law; or

        (B) To alter or affect any requirement imposed under any other provision of law to maintain or destroy any of those records.

Rules 31-100.   [Reserved]

Subpart B—Regulation S-AM: Limitations on Affiliate Marketing

Rule 101.   Purpose and scope

  (a) Purpose. The purpose of this subpart is to implement section 624 of the Fair Credit Reporting Act, 15 U.S.C. 1681, et seq. ("FCRA"). Section 624, which was added to the FCRA by section 214 of the Fair and Accurate Credit Transactions Act of 2003, Pub. L. No. 108-159, 117 Stat. 1952 (2003) ("FACT Act" or "Act"), regulates the use of consumer information received from an affiliate to make marketing solicitations.

  (b) Scope. This subpart applies to any broker or dealer other than a notice-registered broker or dealer, to any investment company, and to any investment adviser or transfer agent registered with the Commission. These entities are referred to in this subpart as "you."

Rule 102.   Examples

  The examples in this subpart are not exclusive. The examples in this subpart provide guidance concerning the rules' application in ordinary circumstances. The facts and circumstances of each individual situation, however, will determine whether compliance with an example, to the extent applicable, constitutes compliance with this subpart. Examples in a paragraph illustrate only the issue described in the paragraph and do not illustrate any other issue that may arise under this subpart. Similarly, the examples do not illustrate any issues that may arise under other laws or regulations.

Rules 103-119.   [Reserved]

Rule 120.   Definitions

  As used in this subpart, unless the context requires otherwise:

  (a) Affiliate of a broker, dealer, or investment company, or an investment adviser or transfer agent registered with the Commission means any person that is related by common ownership or common control with the broker, dealer, or investment company, or the investment adviser or transfer agent registered with the Commission. In addition, a broker, dealer, or investment company, or an investment adviser or transfer agent registered with the Commission will be deemed an affiliate of a company for purposes of this subpart if:

(1)   That company is regulated under section 214 of the FACT Act, Pub. L. No. 108–159, 117 Stat. 1952 (2003), by a government regulator other than the Commission; and

(2)   Rules adopted by the other government regulator under section 214 of the FACT Act treat the broker, dealer, or investment company, or investment adviser or transfer agent registered with the Commission as an affiliate of that company.

(b)   Broker has the same meaning as in section 3(a)(4) of the Securities Exchange Act of 1934 (15 U.S.C. 78c(a)(4)). A "broker" does not include a broker registered by notice with the Commission under section 15(b)(11) of the Securities Exchange Act of 1934 (15 U.S.C. 78o(b)(11)).

(c)   Clear and conspicuous means reasonably understandable and designed to call attention to the nature and significance of the information presented.

(d)   Commission means the Securities and Exchange Commission.

(e)   Company means any corporation, limited liability company, business trust, general or limited partnership, association, or similar organization.

(f)   Concise. (1) In general. The term "concise" means a reasonably brief expression or statement.

(2)   Combination with other required disclosures. A notice required by this subpart may be concise even if it is combined with other disclosures required or authorized by federal or state law.

(g)   Consumer means an individual.

(h)   Control of a company means the power to exercise a controlling influence over the management or policies of a company whether through ownership of securities, by contract, or otherwise. Any person who owns beneficially, either directly or through one or more controlled companies, more than 25 percent of the voting securities of any company is presumed to control the company. Any person who does not own more than 25 percent of the voting securities of any company will be presumed not to control the company. Any presumption regarding control may be rebutted by evidence, but, in the case of an investment company, will continue until the Commission makes a decision to the contrary according to the procedures described in section 2(a)(9) of the Investment Company Act of 1940 (15 U.S.C. 80a–2(a)(9)).

(i)   Dealer has the same meaning as in section 3(a)(5) of the Securities Exchange Act of 1934 (15 U.S.C. 78c(a)(5)). A "dealer" does not include a dealer registered by notice with the Commission under section 15(b)(11) of the Securities Exchange Act of 1934 (15 U.S.C. 78o(b)(11)).

(j)   Eligibility information means any information the communication of which would be a consumer report if the exclusions from the definition of "consumer report" in section 603(d)(2)(A) of the FCRA did not apply. Eligibility information does not include aggregate or blind data that does not contain personal identifiers such as account numbers, names, or addresses.

(k)   FCRA means the Fair Credit Reporting Act (15 U.S.C. 1681, et seq.).

(l)   GLBA means the Gramm-Leach-Bliley Act (15 U.S.C. 6801, et seq.).

(m)   Investment adviser has the same meaning as in section 202(a)(11) of the Investment Advisers Act of 1940 (15 U.S.C. 80b–2(a)(11)).

(n)   Investment company has the same meaning as in section 3 of the Investment Company Act of 1940 (15 U.S.C. 80a–3) and includes a separate series of the investment company.

(o)   Marketing solicitation. (1) In general. The term "marketing solicitation" means the marketing of a product or service initiated by a person to a particular consumer that is:

(i)   Based on eligibility information communicated to that person by its affiliate as described in this subpart; and

(ii)   Intended to encourage the consumer to purchase or obtain such product or service.

(2)   Exclusion of marketing directed at the general public. A marketing solicitation does not include marketing communications that are directed at the general public. For example, television,

general circulation magazine, billboard advertisements and publicly available Web sites that are not directed to particular consumers would not constitute marketing solicitations, even if those communications are intended to encourage consumers to purchase products and services from the person initiating the communications.

(3) *Examples of marketing solicitations.* A marketing solicitation would include, for example, a telemarketing call, direct mail, e-mail, or other form of marketing communication directed to a particular consumer that is based on eligibility information received from an affiliate.

(p) *Person* means any individual, partnership, corporation, trust, estate, cooperative, association, government or governmental subdivision or agency, or other entity.

(q) *Pre-existing business relationship.* (1) *In general.* The term "pre-existing business relationship" means a relationship between a person, or a person's licensed agent, and a consumer based on:

(i) A financial contract between the person and the consumer which is in force on the date on which the consumer is sent a solicitation covered by this subpart;

(ii) The purchase, rental, or lease by the consumer of the person's goods or services, or a financial transaction (including holding an active account or a policy in force or having another continuing relationship) between the consumer and the person, during the 18-month period immediately preceding the date on which the consumer is sent a solicitation covered by this subpart; or

(iii) An inquiry or application by the consumer regarding a product or service offered by that person during the three-month period immediately preceding the date on which the consumer is sent a solicitation covered by this subpart.

(2) *Examples of pre-existing business relationships.* (i) If a consumer has a brokerage account with a broker-dealer that is currently in force, the broker-dealer has a pre-existing business relationship with the consumer and can use eligibility information it receives from its affiliates to make solicitations to the consumer about its products or services.

(ii) If a consumer has an investment advisory contract with a registered investment adviser, the investment adviser has a pre-existing business relationship with the consumer and can use eligibility information it receives from its affiliates to make solicitations to the consumer about its products or services.

(iii) If a consumer was the record owner of securities issued by an investment company, but the consumer redeems these securities, the investment company has a pre-existing business relationship with the consumer and can use eligibility information it receives from its affiliates to make solicitations to the consumer about its products or services for 18 months after the date the consumer redeemed the investment company's securities.

(iv) If a consumer applies for a margin account offered by a broker-dealer, but does not obtain a product or service from or enter into a financial contract or transaction with the broker-dealer, the broker-dealer has a pre-existing business relationship with the consumer and can therefore use eligibility information it receives from its affiliates to make solicitations to the consumer about its products or services for three months after the date of the application.

(v) If a consumer makes a telephone inquiry to a broker-dealer about its products or services and provides contact information to the broker-dealer, but does not obtain a product or service from or enter into a financial contract or transaction with the institution, the broker-dealer has a pre-existing business relationship with the consumer and can therefore use eligibility information it receives from its affiliates to make solicitations to the consumer about its products or services for three months after the date of the inquiry.

(vi) If a consumer makes an inquiry by e-mail to a broker-dealer about one of its affiliated investment company's products or services but does not obtain a product or service from, or enter into a financial contract or transaction with the broker-dealer or the investment company, the broker-dealer and the investment company both have a pre-existing business relationship with the consumer and can therefore use eligibility information they receive from their affiliates to make solicitations to the consumer about their products or services for three months after the date of the inquiry.

(vii) If a consumer who has a pre-existing business relationship with an investment company that is part of a group of affiliated companies makes a telephone call to the centralized call center for the affiliated companies to inquire about products or services offered by a broker-dealer affiliated with the investment company, and provides contact information to the call center, the call constitutes an inquiry to the broker-dealer. In these circumstances, the broker-dealer has a pre-existing business relationship with the consumer and can therefore use eligibility information it receives from the investment company to make solicitations to the consumer about its products or services for three months after the date of the inquiry.

(3) *Examples where no pre-existing business relationship is created.* (i) If a consumer makes a telephone call to a centralized call center for a group of affiliated companies to inquire about the consumer's existing account at a broker-dealer, the call does not constitute an inquiry to any affiliate other than the broker-dealer that holds the consumer's account and does not establish a pre-existing business relationship between the consumer and any affiliate of the account-holding broker-dealer.

(ii) If a consumer who has an advisory contract with a registered investment adviser makes a telephone call to an affiliate of the investment adviser to ask about the affiliate's retail locations and hours, but does not make an inquiry about the affiliate's products or services, the call does not constitute an inquiry and does not establish a pre-existing business relationship between the consumer and the affiliate. Also, the affiliate's capture of the consumer's telephone number does not constitute an inquiry and does not establish a pre-existing business relationship between the consumer and the affiliate.

(iii) If a consumer makes a telephone call to a broker-dealer in response to an advertisement offering a free promotional item to consumers who call a toll-free number, but the advertisement does not indicate that the broker-dealer's products or services will be marketed to consumers who call in response, the call does not create a pre-existing business relationship between the consumer and the broker-dealer because the consumer has not made an inquiry about a product or service offered by the institution, but has merely responded to an offer for a free promotional item.

(r) *Transfer agent* has the same meaning as in section 3(a)(25) of the Securities Exchange Act of 1934 (15 U.S.C. 78c(a)(25)).

(s) *You* means:

(1) Any broker or dealer other than a broker or dealer registered by notice with the Commission under section 15(b)(11) of the Securities Exchange Act of 1934 (15 U.S.C. 78*o*(b)(11));

(2) Any investment company;

(3) Any investment adviser registered with the Commission under the Investment Advisers Act of 1940 (15 U.S.C. 80b–1, et seq.); and

(4) Any transfer agent registered with the Commission under section 17A of the Securities Exchange Act of 1934 (15 U.S.C. 78q–1).

Rule 121.   Affiliate Marketing Opt Out and Exceptions

(a) *Initial notice and opt out requirement.* (1) *In general.* You may not use eligibility information about a consumer that you receive from an affiliate to make a marketing solicitation to the consumer, unless:

(i) It is clearly and conspicuously disclosed to the consumer in writing or, if the consumer agrees, electronically, in a concise notice that you may use eligibility information about that consumer received from an affiliate to make marketing solicitations to the consumer;

(ii) The consumer is provided a reasonable opportunity and a reasonable and simple method to "opt out," or the consumer prohibits you from using eligibility information to make marketing solicitations to the consumer; and

(iii) The consumer has not opted out.

(2) Example. A consumer has a brokerage account with a broker-dealer. The broker-dealer furnishes eligibility information about the consumer to its affiliated investment adviser. Based on that eligibility information, the investment adviser wants to make a marketing solicitation to the consumer about its discretionary advisory accounts. The investment adviser does not have a pre-existing business relationship with the consumer and none of the other exceptions apply. The investment adviser is prohibited from using eligibility information received from its broker-dealer affiliate to make marketing solicitations to the consumer about its discretionary advisory accounts unless the consumer is given a notice and opportunity to opt out and the consumer does not opt out.

(3) Affiliates who may provide the notice. The notice required by this paragraph must be provided:

(i) By an affiliate that has or has previously had a pre-existing business relationship with the consumer; or

(ii) As part of a joint notice from two or more members of an affiliated group of companies, provided that at least one of the affiliates on the joint notice has or has previously had a pre-existing business relationship with the consumer.

(b) Making marketing solicitations. (1) In general. For purposes of this subpart, you make a marketing solicitation if:

(i) You receive eligibility information from an affiliate;

(ii) You use that eligibility information to do one or more of the following:

(A) Identify the consumer or type of consumer to receive a marketing solicitation;

(B) Establish criteria used to select the consumer to receive a marketing solicitation; or

(C) Decide which of your products or services to market to the consumer or tailor your marketing solicitation to that consumer; and

(iii) As a result of your use of the eligibility information, the consumer is provided a marketing solicitation.

(2) Receiving eligibility information from an affiliate, including through a common database. You may receive eligibility information from an affiliate in various ways, including when the affiliate places that information into a common database that you may access.

(3) Receipt or use of eligibility information by your service provider. Except as provided in paragraph (b)(5) of this rule, you receive or use an affiliate's eligibility information if a service provider acting on your behalf (whether an affiliate or a nonaffiliated third party) receives or uses that information in the manner described in paragraph (b)(1)(i) or (b)(1)(ii) of this rule. All relevant facts and circumstances will determine whether a person is acting as your service provider when it receives or uses an affiliate's eligibility information in connection with marketing your products and services.

(4) Use by an affiliate of its own eligibility information. Unless you have used eligibility information that you receive from an affiliate in the manner described in paragraph (b)(1)(ii) of this rule, you do not make a marketing solicitation subject to this subpart if your affiliate:

(i) Uses its own eligibility information that it obtained in connection with a pre-existing business relationship it has or had with the consumer to market your products or services to the affiliate's consumer; or

(ii) Directs its service provider to use the affiliate's own eligibility information that it obtained in connection with a pre-existing business relationship it has or had with the consumer to market your products or services to the consumer, and you do not communicate directly with the service provider regarding that use.

(5) Use of eligibility information by a service provider. (i) In general. You do not make a marketing solicitation subject to this subpart if a service provider (including an affiliated or third-party service provider that maintains or accesses a common database that you may access) receives eligibility information from your affiliate that your affiliate obtained in connection with a pre-existing business

relationship it has or had with the consumer and uses that eligibility information to market your products or services to that affiliate's consumer, so long as:

(A) Your affiliate controls access to and use of its eligibility information by the service provider (including the right to establish the specific terms and conditions under which the service provider may use such information to market your products or services);

(B) Your affiliate establishes specific terms and conditions under which the service provider may access and use your affiliate's eligibility information to market your products and services (or those of affiliates generally) to your affiliate's consumers, such as the identity of the affiliated companies whose products or services may be marketed to the affiliate's consumers by the service provider, the types of products or services of affiliated companies that may be marketed, and the number of times your affiliate's consumers may receive marketing materials, and periodically evaluates the service provider's compliance with those terms and conditions;

(C) Your affiliate requires the service provider to implement reasonable policies and procedures designed to ensure that the service provider uses your affiliate's eligibility information in accordance with the terms and conditions established by your affiliate relating to the marketing of your products or services;

(D) Your affiliate is identified on or with the marketing materials provided to the consumer; and

(E) You do not directly use your affiliate's eligibility information in the manner described in paragraph (b)(1)(ii) of this rule.

(ii) Writing requirements. (A) The requirements of paragraphs (b)(5)(i)(A) and (C) of this rule must be set forth in a written agreement between your affiliate and the service provider; and

(B) The specific terms and conditions established by your affiliate as provided in paragraph (b)(5)(i)(B) of this rule must be set forth in writing.

(6) Examples of making marketing solicitations. (i) A consumer has an investment advisory contract with a registered investment adviser that is affiliated with a broker-dealer. The broker-dealer receives eligibility information about the consumer from the investment adviser. The broker-dealer uses that eligibility information to identify the consumer to receive a marketing solicitation about brokerage products and services, and, as a result, the broker-dealer provides a marketing solicitation to the consumer about its brokerage services. Pursuant to paragraph (b)(1) of this rule, the broker-dealer has made a marketing solicitation to the consumer.

(ii) The same facts as in the example in paragraph (b)(6)(i) of this rule, except that after using the eligibility information to identify the consumer to receive a marketing solicitation about brokerage products and services, the broker-dealer asks the registered investment adviser to send the marketing solicitation to the consumer and the investment adviser does so. Pursuant to paragraph (b)(1) of this rule, the broker-dealer has made a marketing solicitation to the consumer because it used eligibility information about the consumer that it received from an affiliate to identify the consumer to receive a marketing solicitation about its products or services, and, as a result, a marketing solicitation was provided to the consumer about the broker-dealer's products and services.

(iii) The same facts as in the example in paragraph (b)(6)(i) of this rule, except that eligibility information about consumers who have an investment advisory contract with a registered investment adviser is placed into a common database that all members of the affiliated group of companies may independently access and use. Without using the investment adviser's eligibility information, the broker-dealer develops selection criteria and provides those criteria, marketing materials, and related instructions to the investment adviser. The investment adviser reviews eligibility information about its own consumers using the selection criteria provided by the broker-dealer to determine which consumers should receive the broker-dealer's marketing materials and sends the broker-dealer's marketing materials to those consumers. Even though the broker-dealer has received eligibility information through the common database as provided in paragraph (b)(2) of this rule, it did not use that information to identify consumers or establish selection criteria; instead, the investment adviser used its own eligibility information. Therefore, pursuant to paragraph (b)(4)(i) of this rule, the broker-dealer has not made a marketing solicitation to the consumer.

(iv) The same facts as in the example in paragraph (b)(6)(iii) of this rule, except that the registered investment adviser provides the broker-dealer's criteria to the investment adviser's service provider and directs the service provider to use the investment adviser's eligibility information to identify investment adviser consumers who meet the criteria and to send the broker-dealer's marketing materials to those consumers. The broker-dealer does not communicate directly with the service provider regarding the use of the investment adviser's information to market its products or services to the investment adviser's consumers. Pursuant to paragraph (b)(4)(ii) of this rule, the broker-dealer has not made a marketing solicitation to the consumer.

(v) An affiliated group of companies includes an investment company, a principal underwriter for the investment company, a retail broker-dealer, and a transfer agent that also acts as a service provider. Each affiliate in the group places information about its consumers into a common database. The service provider has access to all information in the common database. The investment company controls access to and use of its eligibility information by the service provider. This control is set forth in a written agreement between the investment company and the service provider. The written agreement also requires the service provider to establish reasonable policies and procedures designed to ensure that the service provider uses the investment company's eligibility information in accordance with specific terms and conditions established by the investment company relating to the marketing of the products and services of all affiliates, including the principal underwriter and the retail broker-dealer. In a separate written communication, the investment company specifies the terms and conditions under which the service provider may use the investment company's eligibility information to market the retail broker-dealer's products and services to the investment company's consumers. The specific terms and conditions are: a list of affiliated companies (including the retail broker-dealer) whose products or services may be marketed to the investment company's consumers by the service provider; the specific products or services or types of products or services that may be marketed to the investment company's consumers by the service provider; the categories of eligibility information that may be used by the service provider in marketing products or services to the investment company's consumers; the types or categories of the investment company's consumers to whom the service provider may market products or services of investment company affiliates; the number and types of marketing communications that the service provider may send to the investment company's consumers; and the length of time during which the service provider may market the products or services of the investment company's affiliates to its consumers. The investment company periodically evaluates the service provider's compliance with these terms and conditions. The retail broker-dealer asks the service provider to market brokerage services to certain of the investment company's consumers. Without using the investment company's eligibility information, the retail broker-dealer develops selection criteria and provides those criteria, its marketing materials, and related instructions to the service provider. The service provider uses the investment company's eligibility information from the common database to identify the investment company's consumers to whom brokerage services will be marketed. When the retail broker-dealer's marketing materials are provided to the identified consumers, the name of the investment company is displayed on the retail broker-dealer's marketing materials, an introductory letter that accompanies the marketing materials, an account statement that accompanies the marketing materials, or the envelope containing the marketing materials. The requirements of paragraph (b)(5) of this rule have been satisfied, and the retail broker-dealer has not made a marketing solicitation to the consumer.

(vi) The same facts as in the example in paragraph (b)(6)(v) of this rule, except that the terms and conditions permit the service provider to use the investment company's eligibility information to market the products and services of other affiliates to the investment company's consumers whenever the service provider deems it appropriate to do so. The service provider uses the investment company's eligibility information in accordance with the discretion afforded to it by the terms and conditions. Because the terms and conditions are not specific, the requirements of paragraph (b)(5) of this rule have not been satisfied.

(c) Exceptions. The provisions of this subpart do not apply to you if you use eligibility information that you receive from an affiliate:

(1) To make a marketing solicitation to a consumer with whom you have a pre-existing business relationship;

(2) To facilitate communications to an individual for whose benefit you provide employee benefit or other services pursuant to a contract with an employer related to and arising out of the current employment relationship or status of the individual as a participant or beneficiary of an employee benefit plan;

(3) To perform services on behalf of an affiliate, except that this paragraph shall not be construed as permitting you to send marketing solicitations on behalf of an affiliate if the affiliate would not be permitted to send the marketing solicitation as a result of the election of the consumer to opt out under this subpart;

(4) In response to a communication about your products or services initiated by the consumer;

(5) In response to an authorization or request by the consumer to receive solicitations; or 144

(6) If your compliance with this subpart would prevent you from complying with any provision of State insurance laws pertaining to unfair discrimination in any State in which you are lawfully doing business.

(d) Examples of exceptions. (1) Example of the pre-existing business relationship exception. A consumer has a brokerage account with a broker-dealer. The consumer also has a deposit account with the broker-dealer's affiliated depository institution. The broker-dealer receives eligibility information about the consumer from its depository institution affiliate and uses that information to make a marketing solicitation to the consumer about the broker-dealer's college savings accounts. The broker-dealer may make this marketing solicitation even if the consumer has not been given a notice and opportunity to opt out because the broker-dealer has a pre-existing business relationship with the consumer.

(2) Examples of service provider exception. (i) A consumer has a brokerage account with a broker-dealer. The broker-dealer furnishes eligibility information about the consumer to its affiliate, a registered investment adviser. Based on that eligibility information, the investment adviser wants to make a marketing solicitation to the consumer about its advisory services. The investment adviser does not have a pre-existing business relationship with the consumer and none of the other exceptions in paragraph (c) of this rule apply. The consumer has been given an opt out notice and has elected to opt out of receiving such marketing solicitations. The investment adviser asks a service provider to send the marketing solicitation to the consumer on its behalf. The service provider may not send the marketing solicitation on behalf of the investment adviser because, as a result of the consumer's opt out election, the investment adviser is not permitted to make the marketing solicitation.

(ii) The same facts as in paragraph (d)(2)(i) of this rule, except the consumer has been given an opt out notice, but has not elected to opt out. The investment adviser asks a service provider to send the solicitation to the consumer on its behalf. The service provider may send the marketing solicitation on behalf of the investment adviser because, as a result of the consumer's not opting out, the investment adviser is permitted to make the marketing solicitation.

(3) Examples of consumer-initiated communications. (i) A consumer who is the record owner of shares in an investment company initiates a communication with an affiliated registered investment adviser about advisory services. The affiliated investment adviser may use eligibility information about the consumer it obtains from the investment company or any other affiliate to make marketing solicitations regarding the affiliated investment adviser's services in response to the consumer-initiated communication.

(ii) A consumer who has a brokerage account with a broker-dealer contacts the broker-dealer to request information about how to save and invest for a child's college education without specifying the type of savings or investment vehicle in which the consumer may be interested. Information about a range of different products or services offered by the broker-dealer and one or more of its affiliates may be responsive to that communication. Such products, services, and investments may include the following: investments in affiliated investment companies; investments in section 529 plans offered by the broker-dealer; or trust services offered by a different financial institution in the affiliated group. Any affiliate offering products or services that would be responsive to the consumer's request for information about saving and investing for a child's college education may use eligibility information to make marketing solicitations to the consumer in response to this communication.

(iii) A registered investment adviser makes a marketing call to the consumer without using eligibility information received from an affiliate. The investment adviser leaves a voice-mail message that invites the consumer to call a toll-free number to receive information about services offered by the investment adviser. If the consumer calls the toll-free number to inquire about the investment advisory services, the call is a consumer-initiated communication about a product or service, and the investment adviser may now use eligibility information it receives from its affiliates to make marketing solicitations to the consumer.

(iv) A consumer calls a broker-dealer to ask about retail locations and hours, but does not request information about its products or services. The broker-dealer may not use eligibility information it receives from an affiliate to make marketing solicitations to the consumer because the consumer-initiated communication does not relate to the broker-dealer's products or services. Thus, the use of eligibility information received from an affiliate would not be responsive to the communication and the exception does not apply.

(v) A consumer calls a broker-dealer to ask about retail locations and hours. The customer service representative asks the consumer if there is a particular product or service about which the consumer is seeking information. The consumer responds that the consumer wants to stop in and find out about mutual funds (i.e., registered open-end investment companies). The customer service representative offers to provide that information by telephone and mail additional information to the consumer. The consumer agrees and provides or confirms contact information for receipt of the materials to be mailed. The broker-dealer may use eligibility information it receives from an affiliate to make marketing solicitations to the consumer about mutual funds because such marketing solicitations would respond to the consumer-initiated communication about mutual funds.

(4) Examples of consumer authorization or request for marketing solicitations. (i) A consumer who has a brokerage account with a broker-dealer authorizes or requests information about life insurance offered by the broker-dealer's insurance affiliate. The authorization or request, whether given to the broker-dealer or the insurance affiliate, would permit the insurance affiliate to use eligibility information about the consumer it obtains from the broker-dealer or any other affiliate to make marketing solicitations to the consumer about life insurance.

(ii) A consumer completes an online application to open an online brokerage account with a broker-dealer. The broker-dealer's online application contains a blank check box that the consumer may check to authorize or request information from the broker-dealer's affiliates. The consumer checks the box. The consumer has authorized or requested marketing solicitations from the broker-dealer's affiliates.

(iii) A consumer completes an online application to open an online brokerage account with a broker-dealer. The broker-dealer's online application contains a check box indicating that the consumer authorizes or requests information from the broker-dealer's affiliates. The consumer does not deselect the check box. The consumer has not authorized or requested marketing solicitations from the broker-dealer's affiliates.

(iv) The terms and conditions of a brokerage account agreement contain preprinted boilerplate language stating that by applying to open an account the consumer authorizes or requests to receive solicitations from the broker-dealer's affiliates. The consumer has not authorized or requested marketing solicitations from the broker-dealer's affiliates.

(e) Relation to affiliate-sharing notice and opt out. Nothing in this subpart limits the responsibility of a person to comply with the notice and opt out provisions of Section 603(d)(2)(A)(iii) of the FCRA (15 U.S.C. 1681a(d)(2)(A)(iii)) where applicable.

Rule 122.   **Scope and Duration of Opt Out**

(a)   Scope of opt out. (1) In general. Except as otherwise provided in this rule, the consumer's election to opt out prohibits any affiliate covered by the opt out notice from using eligibility information received from another affiliate as described in the notice to make marketing solicitations to the consumer.

(2)   Continuing relationship. (i) In general. If the consumer establishes a continuing relationship with you or your affiliate, an opt out notice may apply to eligibility information obtained in connection with:

(A)   A single continuing relationship or multiple continuing relationships that the consumer establishes with you or your affiliates, including continuing relationships established subsequent to delivery of the opt out notice, so long as the notice adequately describes the continuing relationships covered by the opt out; or

(B)   Any other transaction between the consumer and you or your affiliates as described in the notice.

(ii)   Examples of continuing relationships. A consumer has a continuing relationship with you or your affiliate if the consumer:

(A)   Opens a brokerage account or enters into an advisory contract with you or your affiliate;

(B)   Obtains a loan for which you or your affiliate owns the servicing rights;

(C)   Purchases investment company shares in his or her own name;

(D)   Holds an investment through you or your affiliate; such as when you act or your affiliate acts as a custodian for securities or for assets in an individual retirement arrangement;

(E)   Enters into an agreement or understanding with you or your affiliate whereby you or your affiliate undertakes to arrange or broker a home mortgage loan for the consumer;

(F)   Enters into a lease of personal property with you or your affiliate; or

(G)   Obtains financial, investment, or economic advisory services from you or your affiliate for a fee.

(3)   No continuing relationship. (i) In general. If there is no continuing relationship between a consumer and you or your affiliate, and you or your affiliate obtain eligibility information about a consumer in connection with a transaction with the consumer, such as an isolated transaction or an application that is denied, an opt out notice provided to the consumer only applies to eligibility information obtained in connection with that transaction.

(ii)   Examples of isolated transactions. An isolated transaction occurs if:

(A)   The consumer uses your or your affiliate's ATM to withdraw cash from an account at another financial institution; or

(B)   A broker-dealer opens a brokerage account for the consumer solely for the purpose of liquidating or purchasing securities as an accommodation, i.e., on a one-time basis, without the expectation of engaging in other transactions.

(4)   Menu of alternatives. A consumer may be given the opportunity to choose from a menu of alternatives when electing to prohibit solicitations, such as by electing to prohibit solicitations from certain types of affiliates covered by the opt out notice but not other types of affiliates covered by the notice, electing to prohibit marketing solicitations based on certain types of eligibility information but not other types of eligibility information, or electing to prohibit marketing solicitations by certain methods of delivery but not other methods of delivery. However, one of the alternatives must allow the consumer to prohibit all marketing solicitations from all of the affiliates that are covered by the notice.

(5)   Special rule for a notice following termination of all continuing relationships. (i) In general. A consumer must be given a new opt out notice if, after all continuing relationships with you or your affiliate(s) are terminated, the consumer subsequently establishes another continuing relationship

with you or your affiliate(s) and the consumer's eligibility information is to be used to make a marketing solicitation. The new opt out notice must apply, at a minimum, to eligibility information obtained in connection with the new continuing relationship. Consistent with paragraph (b) of this rule, the consumer's decision not to opt out after receiving the new opt out notice would not override a prior opt out election by the consumer that applies to eligibility information obtained in connection with a terminated relationship, regardless of whether the new opt out notice applies to eligibility information obtained in connection with the terminated relationship.

    (ii)   Example. A consumer has an advisory contract with a company that is registered with the Commission as both a broker-dealer and an investment adviser, and that is part of an affiliated group. The consumer terminates the advisory contract. One year after terminating the advisory contract, the consumer opens a brokerage account with the same company. The consumer must be given a new notice and opportunity to opt out before the company's affiliates may make marketing solicitations to the consumer using eligibility information obtained by the company in connection with the new brokerage account relationship, regardless of whether the consumer opted out in connection with the advisory contract.

  (b)   Duration of opt out. The election of a consumer to opt out must be effective for a period of at least five years (the "opt out period") beginning when the consumer's opt out election is received and implemented, unless the consumer subsequently revokes the opt out in writing or, if the consumer agrees, electronically. An opt out period of more than five years may be established, including an opt out period that does not expire unless revoked by the consumer.

  (c)   Time of opt out. A consumer may opt out at any time.

Rule 123.   Contents of Opt Out Notice; Consolidated and Equivalent Notices

  (a)   Contents of opt out notice. (1) In general. A notice must be clear, conspicuous, and concise, and must accurately disclose:

    (i)   The name of the affiliate(s) providing the notice. If the notice is provided jointly by multiple affiliates and each affiliate shares a common name, such as "ABC," then the notice may indicate that it is being provided by multiple companies with the ABC name or multiple companies in the ABC group or family of companies, for example, by stating that the notice is provided by "all of the ABC companies," "the ABC banking, credit card, insurance, and securities companies," or by listing the name of each affiliate providing the notice. But if the affiliates providing the joint notice do not all share a common name, then the notice must either separately identify each affiliate by name or identify each of the common names used by those affiliates, for example, by stating that the notice is provided by "all of the ABC and XYZ companies" or by "the ABC bank and securities companies and the XYZ insurance companies";

    (ii)   A list of the affiliates or types of affiliates whose use of eligibility information is covered by the notice, which may include companies that become affiliates after the notice is provided to the consumer. If each affiliate covered by the notice shares a common name, such as "ABC," then the notice may indicate that it applies to multiple companies with the ABC name or multiple companies in the ABC group or family of companies, for example, by stating that the notice is provided by "all of the ABC companies," "the ABC banking, credit card, insurance, and securities companies," or by listing the name of each affiliate providing the notice. But if the affiliates covered by the notice do not all share a common name, then the notice must either separately identify each covered affiliate by name or identify each of the common names used by those affiliates, for example, by stating that the notice applies to "all of the ABC and XYZ companies" or to "the ABC banking and securities companies and the XYZ insurance companies";

    (iii) A general description of the types of eligibility information that may be used to make marketing solicitations to the consumer;

    (iv) That the consumer may elect to limit the use of eligibility information to make marketing solicitations to the consumer;

(v)   That the consumer's election will apply for the specified period of time stated in the notice and, if applicable, that the consumer will be allowed to renew the election once that period expires;

(vi)   If the notice is provided to consumers who may have previously opted out, such as if a notice is provided to consumers annually, that the consumer who has chosen to limit marketing solicitations does not need to act again until the consumer receives a renewal notice; and

(vii) A reasonable and simple method for the consumer to opt out.

(2)   Joint relationships. (i) If two or more consumers jointly obtain a product or service, a single opt out notice may be provided to the joint consumers. Any of the joint consumers may exercise the right to opt out.

(ii)   The opt out notice must explain how an opt out direction by a joint consumer will be treated. An opt out direction by a joint consumer may be treated as applying to all of the associated joint consumers, or each joint consumer may be permitted to opt out separately. If each joint consumer is permitted to opt out separately, one of the joint consumers must be permitted to opt out on behalf of all of the joint consumers and the joint consumers must be permitted to exercise their separate rights to opt out in a single response.

(iii) It is impermissible to require all joint consumers to opt out before implementing any opt out direction.

(3)   Alternative contents. If the consumer is afforded a broader right to opt out of receiving marketing than is required by this subpart, the requirements of this rule may be satisfied by providing the consumer with a clear, conspicuous, and concise notice that accurately discloses the consumer's opt out rights.

(4)   Model notices. Model notices are provided in the Appendix to this subpart.

(b)   Coordinated and consolidated notices. A notice required by this subpart may be coordinated and consolidated with any other notice or disclosure required to be issued under any other provision of law by the entity providing the notice, including but not limited to the notice described in section 603(d)(2)(A)(iii) of the FCRA (15 U.S.C. 1681a(d)(2)(A)(iii)) and the GLBA privacy notice.

(c)   Equivalent notices. A notice or other disclosure that is equivalent to the notice required by this subpart, and that is provided to a consumer together with disclosures required by any other provision of law, satisfies the requirements of this rule.

Rule 124.   Reasonable Opportunity to Opt Out

(a)   In general. You must not use eligibility information that you receive from an affiliate to make marketing solicitations to a consumer about your products or services unless the consumer is provided a reasonable opportunity to opt out, as required by § 248.121(a)(1)(ii).

(b)   Examples of a reasonable opportunity to opt out. The consumer is given a reasonable opportunity to opt out if:

(1)   By mail. The opt out notice is mailed to the consumer. The consumer is given 30 days from the date the notice is mailed to elect to opt out by any reasonable means.

(2)   By electronic means.

(i)   The opt out notice is provided electronically to the consumer, such as by posting the notice at an Internet Web site at which the consumer has obtained a product or service. The consumer acknowledges receipt of the electronic notice. The consumer is given 30 days after the date the consumer acknowledges receipt to elect to opt out by any reasonable means.

(ii)   The opt out notice is provided to the consumer by e-mail where the consumer has agreed to receive disclosures by e-mail from the person sending the notice. The consumer is given 30 days after the e-mail is sent to elect to opt out by any reasonable means.

(3)   At the time of an electronic transaction. The opt out notice is provided to the consumer at the time of an electronic transaction, such as a transaction conducted on an Internet Web site. The

consumer is required to decide, as a necessary part of proceeding with the transaction, whether to opt out before completing the transaction. There is a simple process that the consumer may use to opt out at that time using the same mechanism through which the transaction is conducted.

(4)   At the time of an in-person transaction. The opt out notice is provided to the consumer in writing at the time of an in-person transaction. The consumer is required to decide, as a necessary part of proceeding with the transaction, whether to opt out before completing the transaction, and is not permitted to complete the transaction without making a choice. There is a simple process that the consumer may use during the course of the in-person transaction to opt out, such as completing a form that requires consumers to write a "yes" or "no" to indicate their opt out preference or that requires the consumer to check one of two blank check boxes—one that allows consumers to indicate that they want to opt out and one that allows consumers to indicate that they do not want to opt out.

(5)   By including in a privacy notice. The opt out notice is included in a GLBA privacy notice. The consumer is allowed to exercise the opt out within a reasonable period of time and in the same manner as the opt out under that privacy notice.

Rule 125.   Reasonable and Simple Methods of Opting Out

(a)   In general. You must not use eligibility information about a consumer that you receive from an affiliate to make a marketing solicitation to the consumer about your products or services, unless the consumer is provided a reasonable and simple method to opt out, as required by § 248.121(a)(1)(ii).

(b)   Examples. (1) Reasonable and simple opt out methods. Reasonable and simple methods for exercising the opt out right include:

(i)   Designating a check-off box in a prominent position on the opt out form;

(ii)   Including a reply form and a self-addressed envelope together with the opt out notice;

(iii)   Providing an electronic means to opt out, such as a form that can be electronically mailed or processed at an Internet Web site, if the consumer agrees to the electronic delivery of information;

(iv)   Providing a toll-free telephone number that consumers may call to opt out; or

(v)   Allowing consumers to exercise all of their opt out rights described in a consolidated opt out notice that includes the GLBA privacy, FCRA affiliate sharing, and FCRA affiliate marketing opt outs, by a single method, such as by calling a single toll-free telephone number.

(2)   Opt out methods that are not reasonable and simple. Reasonable and simple methods for exercising an opt out right do not include:

(i)   Requiring the consumer to write his or her own letter; 156

(ii)   Requiring the consumer to call or write to obtain a form for opting out, rather than including the form with the opt out notice; or

(iii)   Requiring the consumer who receives the opt out notice in electronic form only, such as through posting at an Internet Web site, to opt out solely by paper mail or by visiting a different Web site without providing a link to that site.

(c)   Specific opt out means. Each consumer may be required to opt out through a specific means, as long as that means is reasonable and simple for that consumer.

Rule 126.   Delivery of Opt Out Notices

(a)   In general. The opt out notice must be provided so that each consumer can reasonably be expected to receive actual notice. For opt out notices provided electronically, the notice may be provided in compliance with either the electronic disclosure provisions in this subpart or the provisions in section 101 of the Electronic Signatures in Global and National Commerce Act, 15 U.S.C. 7001, et seq.

(b)   Examples of reasonable expectation of actual notice. A consumer may reasonably be expected to receive actual notice if the affiliate providing the notice:

(1)   Hand-delivers a printed copy of the notice to the consumer;

(2)   Mails a printed copy of the notice to the last known mailing address of the consumer;

(3)   Provides a notice by e-mail to a consumer who has agreed to receive electronic disclosures by e-mail from the affiliate providing the notice; or

(4)   Posts the notice on the Internet Web site at which the consumer obtained a product or service electronically and requires the consumer to acknowledge receipt of the notice.

(c)   Examples of no reasonable expectation of actual notice. A consumer may not reasonably be expected to receive actual notice if the affiliate providing the notice:

(1)   Only posts the notice on a sign in a branch or office or generally publishes the notice in a newspaper;

(2)   Sends the notice by e-mail to a consumer who has not agreed to receive electronic disclosures by e-mail from the affiliate providing the notice; or

(3)   Posts the notice on an Internet Web site without requiring the consumer to acknowledge receipt of the notice.

Rule 127.   Renewal of Opt Out Elections

(a)   Renewal notice and opt out requirement. (1) In general. After the opt out period expires, you may not make marketing solicitations to a consumer who previously opted out, unless:

(i)   The consumer has been given a renewal notice that complies with the requirements of this rule and §§ 248.124 through 248.126, and a reasonable opportunity and a reasonable and simple method to renew the opt out, and the consumer does not renew the opt out; or

(ii)   An exception in § 248.121(c) applies.

(2)   Renewal period. Each opt out renewal must be effective for a period of at least five years as provided in § 248.122(b).

(3)   Affiliates who may provide the notice. The notice required by this paragraph must be provided:

(i)   By the affiliate that provided the previous opt out notice, or its successor; or

(ii)   As part of a joint renewal notice from two or more members of an affiliated group of companies, or their successors, that jointly provided the previous opt out notice.

(b)   Contents of renewal notice. The renewal notice must be clear, conspicuous, and concise, and must accurately disclose:

(1)   The name of the affiliate(s) providing the notice. If the notice is provided jointly by multiple affiliates and each affiliate shares a common name, such as "ABC," then the notice may indicate it is being provided by multiple companies with the ABC name or multiple companies in the ABC group or family of companies, for example, by stating that the notice is provided by "all of the ABC companies," "the ABC banking, credit card, insurance, and securities companies," or by listing the name of each affiliate providing the notice. But if the affiliates providing the joint notice do not all share a common name, then the notice must either separately identify each affiliate by name or identify each of the common names used by those affiliates, for example, by stating that the notice is provided by "all of the ABC and XYZ companies" or by "the ABC banking and securities companies and the XYZ insurance companies";

(2)   A list of the affiliates or types of affiliates whose use of eligibility information is covered by the notice, which may include companies that become affiliates after the notice is provided to the consumer. If each affiliate covered by the notice shares a common name, such as "ABC," then the notice may indicate that it applies to multiple companies with the ABC name or multiple companies in the ABC group or family of companies, for example, by stating that the notice is provided by "all of the ABC companies," "the ABC banking, credit card, insurance, and securities companies," or by listing the name of each affiliate providing the notice. But if the affiliates covered by the notice do not all share a common name, then the notice must either separately identify each covered affiliate by name

or identify each of the common names used by those affiliates, for example, by stating that the notice applies to "all of the ABC and XYZ companies" or to "the ABC banking and securities companies and the XYZ insurance companies";

(3)   A general description of the types of eligibility information that may be used to make marketing solicitations to the consumer;

(4)   That the consumer previously elected to limit the use of certain information to make marketing solicitations to the consumer;

(5)   That the consumer's election has expired or is about to expire;

(6)   That the consumer may elect to renew the consumer's previous election;

(7)   If applicable, that the consumer's election to renew will apply for the specified period of time stated in the notice and that the consumer will be allowed to renew the election once that period expires; and

(8)   A reasonable and simple method for the consumer to opt out.

(c)   Timing of the renewal notice. (1) In general. A renewal notice may be provided to the consumer either:

(i)   A reasonable period of time before the expiration of the opt out period; or

(ii)   Any time after the expiration of the opt out period but before marketing solicitations that would have been prohibited by the expired opt out are made to the consumer.

(2)   Combination with annual privacy notice. If you provide an annual privacy notice under the GLBA, providing a renewal notice with the last annual privacy notice provided to the consumer before expiration of the opt out period is a reasonable period of time before expiration of the opt out in all cases.

(d)   No effect on opt out period. An opt out period may not be shortened by sending a renewal notice to the consumer before expiration of the opt out period, even if the consumer does not renew the opt out.

Rule 128.   Effective Date, Compliance Date, and Prospective Application

(a)   Effective date. This subpart is effective September 10, 2009.

(b)   Mandatory compliance date. Compliance with this subpart is required not later than January 1, 2010.

(c)   Prospective application. The provisions of this subpart do not prohibit you from using eligibility information that you receive from an affiliate to make a marketing solicitation to a consumer if you receive such information prior to January 1, 2010. For purposes of this rule, you are deemed to receive eligibility information when such information is placed into a common database and is accessible by you.

Appendix to Subpart B—Model Forms

a.   Although you and your affiliates are not required to use the model forms in this Appendix, use of a model form (if applicable to each person that uses it) complies with the requirement in section 624 of the FCRA for clear, conspicuous, and concise notices.

b.   Although you may need to change the language or format of a model form to reflect your actual policies and procedures, any such changes may not be so extensive as to affect the substance, clarity, or meaningful sequence of the language in the model forms. Acceptable changes include, for example:

1.   Rearranging the order of the references to "your income," "your account history," and "your credit score."

2.   Substituting other types of information for "income," "account history," or "credit score" for accuracy, such as "payment history," "credit history," "payoff status," or "claims history."

3.   Substituting a clearer and more accurate description of the affiliates providing or covered by the notice for phrases such as "the [ABC] group of companies."

4. Substituting other types of affiliates covered by the notice for "credit card," "insurance," or "securities" affiliates.

5. Omitting items that are not accurate or applicable. For example, if a person does not limit the duration of the opt out period, the notice may omit information about the renewal notice.

6. Adding a statement informing the consumer how much time they have to opt out before shared eligibility information may be used to make solicitations to them.

7. Adding a statement that the consumer may exercise the right to opt out at any time.

8. Adding the following statement, if accurate: "If you previously opted out, you do not need to do so again."

9. Providing a place on the form for the consumer to fill in identifying information, such as his or her name and address.

10. Adding disclosures regarding the treatment of opt-outs by joint consumers to comply with § 248.123(a)(2), if applicable.

A–1 Model Form for Initial Opt Out Notice (Single-Affiliate Notice)

A–2 Model Form for Initial Opt Out Notice (Joint Notice)

A–3 Model Form for Renewal Notice (Single-Affiliate Notice)

A–4 Model Form for Renewal Notice (Joint Notice)

A–5 Model Form for Voluntary "No Marketing" Notice

A–1—Model Form for Initial Opt Out Notice (Single-Affiliate Notice)—[Your Choice to Limit Marketing]/[Marketing Opt Out]

- [Name of Affiliate] is providing this notice.

- [Optional: Federal law gives you the right to limit some but not all marketing from our affiliates. Federal law also requires us to give you this notice to tell you about your choice to limit marketing from our affiliates.]

- You may limit our affiliates in the [ABC] group of companies, such as our [investment adviser, broker, transfer agent, and investment company] affiliates, from marketing their products or services to you based on your personal information that we collect and share with them. This information includes your [income], your [account history with us], and your [credit score].

- Your choice to limit marketing offers from our affiliates will apply [until you tell us to change your choice]/[for x years from when you tell us your choice]/[for at least 5 years from when you tell us your choice]. [Include if the opt out period expires.] Once that period expires, you will receive a renewal notice that will allow you to continue to limit marketing offers from our affiliates for [another x years]/[at least another 5 years].

- [Include, if applicable, in a subsequent notice, including an annual notice, for consumers who may have previously opted out.] If you have already made a choice to limit marketing offers from our affiliates, you do not need to act again until you receive the renewal notice.

To limit marketing offers, contact us [include all that apply]:

- **By telephone:** 1-877-###-####

- **On the Web:** www.——.com

- **By mail:** check the box and complete the form below, and send the form to:

    [Company name]

    [Company address]

☐ Do not allow your affiliates to use my personal information to market to me.

A-2—Model Form for Initial Opt Out Notice (Joint Notice)—[Your Choice to Limit Marketing]/[Marketing Opt Out]

- The [ABC group of companies] is providing this notice.

- [Optional: Federal law gives you the right to limit some but not all marketing from the [ABC] companies. Federal law also requires us to give you this notice to tell you about your choice to limit marketing from the [ABC] companies.]

- You may limit the [ABC] companies, such as the [ABC investment companies, investment advisers, transfer agents, and broker-dealers] affiliates, from marketing their products or services to you based on your personal information that they receive from other [ABC] companies. This information includes your [income], your [account history], and your [credit score].

- Your choice to limit marketing offers from the [ABC] companies will apply [until you tell us to change your choice]/[for x years from when you tell us your choice]/[for at least 5 years from when you tell us your choice]. [Include if the opt out period expires.] Once that period expires, you will receive a renewal notice that will allow you to continue to limit marketing offers from the [ABC] companies for [another x years]/[at least another 5 years].

- [Include, if applicable, in a subsequent notice, including an annual notice, for consumers who may have previously opted out.] If you have already made a choice to limit marketing offers from the [ABC] companies, you do not need to act again until you receive the renewal notice.

To limit marketing offers, contact us [include all that apply]:

- **By telephone:** 1–877-###-####

- **On the Web:** www.——.com

- **By mail:** check the box and complete the form below, and send the form to:

    [Company name]

    [Company address]

☐ Do not allow any company [in the ABC group of companies] to use my personal information to market to me.

A-3—Model Form for Renewal Notice (Single-Affiliate Notice)—[Renewing Your Choice to Limit Marketing]/[Renewing Your Marketing Opt Out]

- [Name of Affiliate] is providing this notice.

- [Optional: Federal law gives you the right to limit some but not all marketing from our affiliates. Federal law also requires us to give you this notice to tell you about your choice to limit marketing from our affiliates.]

- You previously chose to limit our affiliates in the [ABC] group of companies, such as our

[investment adviser, investment company, transfer agent, and broker-dealer] affiliates, from marketing their products or services to you based on your personal information that we share with them. This information includes your [income], your [account history with us], and your [credit score].

- • Your choice has expired or is about to expire.

To renew your choice to limit marketing for [x] more years, contact us [include all that apply]:

- **By telephone:** 1–877-###-####

- **On the Web:** www.——.com

- **By mail: check the box and complete the form below, and send the form to:**

    [Company name]

    [Company address]

☐ Renew my choice to limit marketing for [x] more years.

A–4—Model Form for Renewal Notice (Joint Notice)—[Renewing Your Choice to Limit Marketing]/[Renewing Your Marketing Opt Out]

- The [ABC group of companies] is providing this notice.

- [Optional: Federal law gives you the right to limit some but not all marketing from the [ABC] companies. Federal law also requires us to give you this notice to tell you about your choice to limit marketing from the [ABC] companies.]

- You previously chose to limit the [ABC] companies, such as the [ABC investment adviser, investment company, transfer agent, and broker-dealer] affiliates, from marketing their products or services to you based on your personal information that they receive from other ABC companies. This information includes your [income], your [account history], and your [credit score].

- Your choice to limit marketing offers from the [ABC] companies has expired or is about to expire.

To renew your choice to limit marketing for [x] more years, contact us [include all that apply]:

- **By telephone:** 1–877-###-####

- **On the Web:** www.——.com

- **By mail:** check the box and complete the form below, and send the form to:

    [Company name]

    [Company address]

☐   Renew my choice to limit marketing for [x] more years.

A–5—Model Form for Voluntary "No Marketing" Notice—Your Choice to Stop Marketing

- [Name of Affiliate] is providing this notice.

- You may choose to stop all marketing from us and our affiliates.

- [Your choice to stop marketing from us and our affiliates will apply until you tell us to change your choice.]

To stop all marketing, contact us [include all that apply]:

- **By telephone:** 1–877-###-####

- **On the Web:** www.——.com

- **By mail:** check the box and complete the form below, and send the form to:

    [Company name]
    [Company address]

☐   Do not send me marketing material.

Appendix A to Subpart A—Forms

A.   Any person may view and print this form at: http://www.sec.gov/about/forms/secforms.htm.

B.   Use of Form S–P by brokers, dealers, and investment companies, and investment advisers registered with the Commission constitutes compliance with the notice content requirements of §§ 248.6 and 248.7 of this part.

FORM S–P—Model Privacy Form.

A.   **The model Privacy form**

[FORMS]

B.   **General Instructions**

1.   **How the model privacy form is used.**

(a)   The model form may be used, at the option of a financial institution, including a group of financial institutions that use a common privacy notice, to meet the content requirements of the privacy notice and opt-out notice set forth in §§ 248.6 and 248.7 of this part.

(b)   The model form is a standardized form, including page layout, content, format, style, pagination, and shading. Institutions seeking to obtain the safe harbor through use of the model form may modify it only as described in these instructions.

(c)   Note that disclosure of certain information, such as assets, income, and information from a consumer reporting agency, may give rise to obligations under the Fair Credit Reporting Act [15 U.S.C. 1681–1681x] (FCRA), such as a requirement to permit a consumer to opt out of disclosures to affiliates or designation as a consumer reporting agency if disclosures are made to nonaffiliated third parties.

(d)   The word "customer" may be replaced by the word "member" whenever it appears in the model form, as appropriate.

2.   **The contents of the model privacy form.**

The model form consists of two pages, which may be printed on both sides of a single sheet of paper, or may appear on two separate pages. Where an institution provides a long list of institutions at the end of the model form in accordance with Instruction C.3(a)(1), or provides additional information in accordance with Instruction C.3(c), and such list or additional information exceeds the space available on page two of the model form, such list or additional information may extend to a third page.

(a)   *Page One.* The first page consists of the following components:

     (1)   Date last revised (upper right-hand corner).

     (2)   Title.

     (3)   Key frame (Why?, What?, How?).

     (4)   Disclosure table ("Reasons we can share your personal information").

     (5)   "To limit our sharing" box, as needed, for the financial institution's opt-out information.

     (6)   "Questions" box, for customer service contact information.

     (7)   Mail-in opt-out form, as needed.

(b)   *Page Two.* The second page consists of the following components:

     (1)   Heading (Page 2).

     (2)   Frequently Asked Questions ("Who we are" and "What we do").

     (3)   Definitions.

     (4)   "Other important information" box, as needed.

3.   **The format of the model privacy form.**

The format of the model form may be modified only as described below.

(a)   *Easily readable type font.* Financial institutions that use the model form must use an easily readable type font. While a number of factors together produce easily readable type font, institutions are required to use a minimum of 10-point font (unless otherwise expressly permitted in these Instructions) and sufficient spacing between the lines of type.

(b)   *Logo.* A financial institution may include a corporate logo on any page of the notice, so long as it does not interfere with the readability of the model form or the space constraints of each page.

(c) *Page size and orientation.* Each page of the model form must be printed on paper in portrait orientation, the size of which must be sufficient to meet the layout and minimum font size requirements, with sufficient white space on the top, bottom, and sides of the content.

(d) *Color.* The model form must be printed on white or light color paper (such as cream) with black or other contrasting ink color. Spot color may be used to achieve visual interest, so long as the color contrast is distinctive and the color does not detract from the readability of the model form. Logos may also be printed in color.

(e) *Languages.* The model form may be translated into languages other than English.

C. Information Required in the Model Privacy Form

The information in the model form may be modified only as described below:

1. Name of the institution or group of affiliated institutions providing the notice.

Insert the name of the financial institution providing the notice or a common identity of affiliated institutions jointly providing the notice on the form wherever [**name of financial institution**] appears.

2. Page one.

(a) *Last revised date.* The financial institution must insert in the upper right-hand corner the date on which the notice was last revised. The information shall appear in minimum 8-point font as "rev. [month/year]" using either the name or number of the month, such as "rev. July 2009" or "rev. 7/09".

(b) *General instructions for the "What?" box.*

(1) The bulleted list identifies the types of personal information that the institution collects and shares. All institutions must use the term "Social Security number" in the first bullet.

(2) Institutions must use five (5) of the following terms to complete the bulleted list: Income; account balances; payment history; transaction history; transaction or loss history; credit history; credit scores; assets; investment experience; credit-based insurance scores; insurance claim history; medical information; overdraft history; purchase history; account transactions; risk tolerance; medical-related debts; credit card or other debt; mortgage rates and payments; retirement assets; checking account information; employment information; wire transfer instructions.

(c) *General instructions for the disclosure table.* The left column lists reasons for sharing or using personal information. Each reason correlates to a specific legal provision described in paragraph C.2(d) of this Instruction. In the middle column, each institution must provide a "Yes" or "No" response that accurately reflects its information sharing policies and practices with respect to the reason listed on the left. In the right column, each institution must provide in each box one of the following three (3) responses, as applicable, that reflects whether a consumer can limit such sharing: "Yes" if it is required to or voluntarily provides an opt-out; "No" if it does not provide an opt-out; or "We don't share" if it answers "No" in the middle column. Only the sixth row ("For our affiliates to market to you") may be omitted at the option of the institution. See paragraph C.2(d)(6) of this Instruction.

(d) *Specific disclosures and corresponding legal provisions.*

(1) *For our everyday business purposes.* This reason incorporates sharing information under §§ 248.14 and 248.15 and with service providers pursuant to § 248.13 of this part other than the purposes specified in paragraphs C.2(d)(2) or C.2(d)(3) of these Instructions.

(2) *For our marketing purposes.* This reason incorporates sharing information with service providers by an institution for its own marketing to § 248.13 of this part. An institution that shares for this reason may choose to provide an opt-out.

(3) *For joint marketing with other financial companies.* This reason incorporates sharing information under joint marketing agreements between two or more financial institutions and with any service provider used in connection with such agreements pursuant to § 248.13 of this part. An institution that shares for this reason may choose to provide an opt-out.

(4) *For our affiliates' everyday business purposes—information about transactions and experiences.* This reason incorporates sharing information specified in sections 603(d)(2)(A)(i) and (ii) of the FCRA. An institution that shares for this reason may choose to provide an opt-out.

(5) *For our affiliates' everyday business purposes—information about creditworthiness.* This reason incorporates sharing information pursuant to section 603(d)(2)(A)(iii) of the FCRA. An institution that shares for this reason must provide an opt-out.

(6) *For our affiliates to market to you.* This reason incorporates sharing information specified in section 624 of the FCRA. This reason may be omitted from the disclosure table when: the institution does not have affiliates (or does not disclose personal information to its affiliates); the institution's affiliates do not use personal information in a manner that requires an opt-out; or the institution provides the affiliate marketing notice separately. Institutions that include this reason must provide an opt-out of indefinite duration. An institution that is required to provide an affiliate marketing opt-out, but does not include that opt-out in the model form under this part, must comply with section 624 of the FCRA and 17 CFR Part 248, Subpart B, with respect to the initial notice and opt-out and any subsequent renewal notice and opt-out. An institution not required to provide an opt-out under this subparagraph may elect to include this reason in the model form.

(7) *For nonaffiliates to market to you.* This reason incorporates sharing described in §§ 248.7 and 248.10(a) of this part. An institution that shares personal information for this reason must provide an opt-out.

(e) *To limit our sharing*: A financial institution must include this rule of the model form only if it provides an opt-out. The word "choice" may be written in either the singular or plural, as appropriate. Institutions must select one or more of the applicable opt-out methods described: telephone, such as by a toll-free number; a Website; or use of a mail-in opt-out form. Institutions may include the words "toll-free" before telephone, as appropriate. An institution that allows consumers to opt out online must provide either a specific Web address that takes consumers directly to the opt-out page or a general Web address that provides a clear and conspicuous direct link to the opt-out page. The opt-out choices made available to the consumer who contacts the institution through these methods must correspond accurately to the "Yes" responses in the third column of the disclosure table. In the part titled "Please note" institutions may insert a number that is 30 or greater in the space marked "[30]." Instructions on voluntary or state privacy law opt-out information are in paragraph C.2(g)(5) of these Instructions.

(f) *Questions box.* Customer service contact information must be inserted as appropriate, where **[phone number]** or **[website]** appear. Institutions may elect to provide either a phone number, such as a toll-free number, or a Web address, or both. Institutions may include the words "toll-free" before the telephone number, as appropriate.

(g) *Mail-in opt-out form.* Financial institutions must include this mail-in form only if they state in the "To limit our sharing" box that consumers can opt out by mail. The mail-in form must provide opt-out options that correspond accurately to the "Yes" responses in the third column in the disclosure table. Institutions that require customers to provide only name and address may omit the section identified as "[account #]." Institutions that require additional or different information, such as a random opt-out number or a truncated account number, to implement an opt-out election should modify the "[account #]" reference accordingly. This includes institutions that require customers with multiple accounts to identify each account to which the opt-out should apply. An institution must enter its opt-out mailing address: in the far right of this form (see version 3); or below the form (see version 4). The reverse side of the mail-in opt-out form must not include any content of the model form.

(1) *Joint accountholder.* Only institutions that provide their joint accountholders the choice to opt out for only one accountholder, in accordance with paragraph C.3(a)(5) of these Instructions, must include in the far left column of the mail-in form the following statement: "If you have a joint account, your choice(s) will apply to everyone on your account unless you mark below. [ ] Apply my choice(s) only to me." The word "choice" may be written in either the singular or plural, as appropriate. Financial institutions that provide insurance products or services, provide this option, and elect to use the model form may substitute the word "policy" for "account" in this statement. Institutions that do not provide this option may eliminate this left column from the mail-in form.

(2) *FCRA Section 603(d)(2)(A)(iii) opt-out.* If the institution shares personal information pursuant to section 603(d)(2)(A)(iii) of the FCRA, it must include in the mail-in opt-out form the following statement: "[ ] Do not share information about my creditworthiness with your affiliates for their everyday business purposes."

(3)   *FCRA Section 624 opt-out.* If the institution incorporates section 624 of the FCRA in accord with paragraph C.2(d)(6) of these Instructions, it must include in the mail-in opt-out form the following statement: "[ ] Do not allow your affiliates to use my personal information to market to me."

(4)   *Nonaffiliate opt-out.* If the financial institution shares personal information pursuant to § 248.10(a) of this part, it must include in the mail-in opt-out form the following statement: "[ ] Do not share my personal information with nonaffiliates to market their products and services to me."

(5)   *Additional opt-outs.* Financial institutions that use the disclosure table to provide opt-out options beyond those required by Federal law must provide those opt-outs in this rule of the model form. A financial institution that chooses to offer an opt-out for its own marketing in the mail-in opt-out form must include one of the two following statements: "[ ] Do not share my personal information to market to me." or "[ ] Do not use my personal information to market to me." A financial institution that chooses to offer an opt-out for joint marketing must include the following statement: "[ ] Do not share my personal information with other financial institutions to jointly market to me."

(h)   *Barcodes.* A financial institution may elect to include a barcode and/or "tagline" (an internal identifier) in 6-point font at the bottom of page one, as needed for information internal to the institution, so long as these do not interfere with the clarity or text of the form.

3.   Page Two

(a)   *General Instructions for the Questions.* Certain of the Questions may be customized as follows:

(1)   *"Who is providing this notice?"* This question may be omitted where only one financial institution provides the model form and that institution is clearly identified in the title on page one. Two or more financial institutions that jointly provide the model form must use this question to identify themselves as required by § 248.9(f) of this part. Where the list of institutions exceeds four (4) lines, the institution must describe in the response to this question the general types of institutions jointly providing the notice and must separately identify those institutions, in minimum 8-point font, directly following the "Other important information" box, or, if that box is not included in the institution's form, directly following the "Definitions." The list may appear in a multi-column format.

(2)   *"How does [name of financial institution] protect my personal information?"* The financial institution may only provide additional information pertaining to its safeguards practices following the designated response to this question. Such information may include information about the institution's use of cookies or other measures it uses to safeguard personal information. Institutions are limited to a maximum of 30 additional words.

(3)   *"How does [name of financial institution] collect my personal information?"* Institutions must use five (5) of the following terms to complete the bulleted list for this question: open an account; deposit money; pay your bills; apply for a loan; use your credit or debit card; seek financial or tax advice; apply for insurance; pay insurance premiums; file an insurance claim; seek advice about your investments; buy securities from us; sell securities to us; direct us to buy securities; direct us to sell your securities; make deposits or withdrawals from your account; enter into an investment advisory contract; give us your income information; provide employment information; give us your employment history; tell us about your investment or retirement portfolio; tell us about your investment or retirement earnings; apply for financing; apply for a lease; provide account information; give us your contact information; pay us by check; give us your wage statements; provide your mortgage information; make a wire transfer; tell us who receives the money; tell us where to send the money; show your government-issued ID; show your driver's license; order a commodity futures or option trade. Institutions that collect personal information from their affiliates and/or credit bureaus must include after the bulleted list the following statement: "We also collect your personal information from others, such as credit bureaus, affiliates, or other companies." Institutions that do not collect personal information from their affiliates or credit bureaus but do collect information from other companies must include the following statement instead: "We also collect your personal information from other companies." Only institutions that do not collect any personal information from affiliates, credit bureaus, or other companies can omit both statements.

(4) *"Why can't I limit all sharing?"* Institutions that describe state privacy law provisions in the *"Other important information"* box must use the bracketed sentence: "See below for more on your rights under state law." Other institutions must omit this sentence.

(5) *"What happens when I limit sharing for an account I hold jointly with someone else?"* Only financial institutions that provide opt-out options must use this question. Other institutions must omit this question. Institutions must choose one of the following two statements to respond to this question: "Your choices will apply to everyone on your account." or "Your choices will apply to everyone on your account—unless you tell us otherwise." Financial institutions that provide insurance products or services and elect to use the model form may substitute the word "policy" for "account" in these statements.

(b) *General Instructions for the Definitions.* The financial institution must customize the space below the responses to the three definitions in this rule. This specific information must be in italicized lettering to set off the information from the standardized definitions.

(1) *Affiliates.* As required by § 248.6(a)(3) of this part, where [*affiliate information*] appears, the financial institution must:

(i) If it has no affiliates, state: "[*name of financial institution*] *has no affiliates*";

(ii) If it has affiliates but does not share personal information, state: "*[name of financial institution] does not share with our affiliates*"; or

(iii) If it shares with its affiliates, state, as applicable: "*Our affiliates include companies with a [common corporate identity of financial institution] name; financial companies such as [insert illustrative list of companies]; nonfinancial companies, such as [insert illustrative list of companies;] and others, such as [insert illustrative list]."*

(2) *Nonaffiliates.* As required by § 248.6(c)(3) of this part, where [*nonaffiliate information*] appears, the financial institution must:

(i) If it does not share with nonaffiliated third parties, state: "*[name of financial institution] does not share with nonaffiliates so they can market to you*"; or

(ii) If it shares with nonaffiliated third parties, state, as applicable: "*Nonaffiliates we share with can include [list categories of companies such as mortgage companies, insurance companies, direct marketing companies, and nonprofit organizations]."*

(3) *Joint Marketing.* As required by § 248.13 of this part, where [*joint marketing*] appears, the financial institution must:

(i) If it does not engage in joint marketing, state: "*[name of financial institution] doesn't jointly market*"; or

(ii) If it shares personal information for joint marketing, state, as applicable: "*Our joint marketing partners include [list categories of companies such as credit card companies]."*

(c) *General instructions for the "Other important information" box.* This box is optional. The space provided for information in this box is not limited. Only the following types of information can appear in this box.

(1) State and/or international privacy law information; and/or

(2) Acknowledgment of receipt form.

Appendix B to Subpart A—Sample Clauses

This Appendix only applies to privacy notices provided before January 11, 2011. Financial institutions, including a group of financial holding company affiliates that use a common privacy notice, may use the following sample clauses, if the clause is accurate for each institution that uses the notice. (Note that disclosure of certain information, such as assets, income, and information from a consumer reporting agency, may give rise to obligations under the Fair Credit Reporting Act, such as a requirement to permit a consumer to opt out of disclosures to affiliates or designation as a consumer reporting agency if disclosures are made to nonaffiliated third parties.)

A–1—Categories of Information You Collect (All Institutions)

You may use this clause, as applicable, to meet the requirement of Item 6(a)(1) to describe the categories of nonpublic personal information you collect.

Sample Clause A–1:

We collect nonpublic personal information about you from the following sources:

- Information we receive from you on applications or other forms;
- Information about your transactions with us, our affiliates, or others; and
- Information we receive from a consumer reporting agency.

A–2—Categories of Information You Disclose (Institutions That Disclose Outside of the Exceptions)

You may use one of these clauses, as applicable, to meet the requirement of Item 6(a)(2) to describe the categories of nonpublic personal information you disclose. You may use these clauses if you disclose nonpublic personal information other than as permitted by the exceptions in items 13, 14, and 15.

Sample Clause A–2, Alternative 1:

We may disclose the following kinds of nonpublic personal information about you:

- Information we receive from you on applications or other forms, such as [*provide illustrative examples, such as "your name, address, social security number, assets, and income"*];
- Information about your transactions with us, our affiliates, or others, such as [*provide illustrative examples, such as "your account balance, payment history, parties to transactions, and credit card usage"*]; and
- Information we receive from a consumer reporting agency, such as [*provide illustrative examples, such as "your creditworthiness and credit history"*].

Sample Clause A–2, Alternative 2:

We may disclose all of the information that we collect, as described [*describe location in the notice, such as "above" or "below"*].

A–3—Categories of Information You Disclose and Parties to Whom You Disclose (Institutions That Do Not Disclose Outside of the Exceptions)

You may use this clause, as applicable, to meet the requirements of Items 6(a)(2), (3), and (4) to describe the categories of nonpublic personal information about customers and former customers that you disclose and the categories of affiliates and nonaffiliated third parties to whom you disclose. You may use this clause if you do not disclose nonpublic personal information to any party, other than as permitted by the exceptions in Items 14 and 15.

Sample Clause A–3:

We do not disclose any nonpublic personal information about our customers or former customers to anyone, except as permitted by law.

A–4—Categories of Parties to Whom You Disclose (Institutions That Disclose Outside of the Exceptions)

You may use this clause, as applicable, to meet the requirement of Item 6(a)(3) to describe the categories of affiliates and nonaffiliated third parties to whom you disclose nonpublic personal information. You may use this clause if you disclose nonpublic personal information other than as permitted by the exceptions in Items, 13, 14, and 15, as well as when permitted by the exceptions in Items 13, 14, and 15.

Sample Clause A–4:

We may disclose nonpublic personal information about you to the following types of third parties:

- Financial service providers, such as [*provide illustrative examples such as "mortgage bankers, securities broker-dealers, and insurance agents"*];

- Non-financial companies, such as [*provide illustrative examples, such as "retailers, direct marketers, airlines, and publishers"*]; and

- Others, such as [*provide illustrative examples, such as "non-profit organizations"*].

We may also disclose nonpublic personal information about you to nonaffiliated third parties as permitted by law.

A–5—Service Provider/Joint Marketing Exception

You may use one of these clauses, as applicable, to meet the requirements of Item 6(a)(5) related to the exception for service providers and joint marketers in Item 13. If you disclose nonpublic personal information under this exception, you must describe the categories of nonpublic personal information you disclose and the categories of third parties with whom you have contracted.

Sample Clause A–5, Alternative 1:

We may disclose the following information to companies that perform marketing services on our behalf or to other financial institutions with which we have joint marketing agreements:

- Information we receive from you on applications or other forms, such as [*provide illustrative examples, such as "your name, address, social security number, assets, and income"*];

- Information about your transactions with us, our affiliates, or others, such as [*provide illustrative examples, such as "your account balance, payment history, parties to transactions, and credit card usage"*]; and

- Information we receive from a consumer reporting agency, such as [*provide illustrative examples, such as "your creditworthiness and credit history"*].

Sample Clause A–5, Alternative 2:

We may disclose all of the information we collect, as described [*describe location in the notice, such as "above" or "below"*] to companies that perform marketing services on our behalf or to other financial institutions with whom we have joint marketing agreements.

A–6—Explanation of Opt Out Right (Institutions That Disclose Outside of the Exceptions)

You may use this clause, as applicable, to meet the requirement of Item 6(a)(6) to provide an explanation of the consumer's right to opt out of the disclosure of nonpublic personal information to nonaffiliated third parties, including the method(s) by which the consumer may exercise that right. You may use this clause if you disclose nonpublic personal information other than as permitted by the exceptions in Items 13, 14, and 15.

Sample Clause A–6:

If you prefer that we not disclose nonpublic personal information about you to nonaffiliated third parties, you may opt out of those disclosures, that is, you may direct us not to make those disclosures (other than disclosures permitted by law). If you wish to opt out of disclosures to nonaffiliated third parties, you may [*describe a reasonable means of opting out, such as "call the following toll-free number: (insert number)"*].

A–7—Confidentiality and Security (All Institutions)

You may use this clause, as applicable, to meet the requirement of Item 6(a)(8) to describe your policies and practices with respect to protecting the confidentiality and security of nonpublic personal information.

Sample Clause A–7:

We restrict access to nonpublic personal information about you to [*provide an appropriate description, such as "those employees who need to know that information to provide products or services to you"*]. We maintain physical, electronic, and procedural safeguards that comply with federal standards to guard your nonpublic personal information.

Subpart C—Regulation S–ID: Identity Theft Red Flags

§ 248.201   Duties Regarding the Detection, Prevention, and Mitigation of Identity Theft.

(a)   *Scope.* This rule applies to a *financial institution* or *creditor,* as defined in the Fair Credit Reporting Act (15 U.S.C. 1681), that is:

(1)   A broker, dealer or any other person that is registered or required to be registered under the Securities Exchange Act of 1934;

(2)   An investment company that is registered or required to be registered under the Investment Company Act of 1940, that has elected to be regulated as a business development company under that Act, or that operates as an employees' securities company under that Act; or

(3)   An investment adviser that is registered or required to be registered under the Investment Advisers Act of 1940.

(b)   *Definitions.* For purposes of this subpart, and Appendix A of this subpart, the following definitions apply:

(1)   *Account* means a continuing relationship established by a person with a financial institution or creditor to obtain a product or service for personal, family, household or business purposes. Account includes a brokerage account, a *mutual fund* account (*i.e.,* an account with an open-end investment company), and an investment advisory account.

(2)   The term *board of directors* includes:

(i)   In the case of a branch or agency of a foreign financial institution or creditor, the managing official of that branch or agency; and

(ii)   In the case of a financial institution or creditor that does not have a board of directors, a designated employee at the level of senior management.

(3)   *Covered account* means:

(i)   An account that a financial institution or creditor offers or maintains, primarily for personal, family, or household purposes, that involves or is designed to permit multiple payments or transactions, such as a brokerage account with a broker-dealer or an account maintained by a mutual fund (or its agent) that permits wire transfers or other payments to third parties; and

(ii)   Any other account that the financial institution or creditor offers or maintains for which there is a reasonably foreseeable risk to customers or to the safety and soundness of the financial institution or creditor from identity theft, including financial, operational, compliance, reputation, or litigation risks.

(4)   *Credit* has the same meaning as in 15 U.S.C. 1681a(r)(5).

(5)   *Creditor* has the same meaning as in 15 U.S.C. 1681m(e)(4).

(6)   *Customer* means a person that has a covered account with a financial institution or creditor.

(7)   *Financial institution* has the same meaning as in 15 U.S.C. 1681a(t).

(8)   *Identifying information* means any name or number that may be used, alone or in conjunction with any other information, to identify a specific person, including any—

(i)   Name, Social Security number, date of birth, official State or government issued driver's license or identification number, alien registration number, government passport number, employer or taxpayer identification number;

(ii)   Unique biometric data, such as fingerprint, voice print, retina or iris image, or other unique physical representation;

(iii)   Unique electronic identification number, address, or routing code; or

(iv)   Telecommunication identifying information or access device (as defined in 18 U.S.C. 1029(e)).

(9) *Identity theft* means a fraud committed or attempted using the identifying information of another person without authority.

(10) *Red Flag* means a pattern, practice, or specific activity that indicates the possible existence of identity theft.

(11) *Service provider* means a person that provides a service directly to the financial institution or creditor.

(12) *Other definitions.*

(i) *Broker* has the same meaning as in section 3(a)(4) of the Securities Exchange Act of 1934 (15 U.S.C. 78c(a)(4)).

(ii) *Commission* means the Securities and Exchange Commission.

(iii) *Dealer* has the same meaning as in section 3(a)(5) of the Securities Exchange Act of 1934 (15 U.S.C. 78c(a)(5)).

(iv) *Investment adviser* has the same meaning as in section 202(a)(11) of the Investment Advisers Act of 1940 (15 U.S.C. 80b–2(a)(11)).

(v) *Investment company* has the same meaning as in section 3 of the Investment Company Act of 1940 (15 U.S.C. 80a–3), and includes a separate series of the investment company.

(vi) Other terms not defined in this subpart have the same meaning as in the Fair Credit Reporting Act (15 U.S.C. 1681 *et seq.*).

(c) *Periodic identification of covered accounts.* Each financial institution or creditor must periodically determine whether it offers or maintains covered accounts. As a part of this determination, a financial institution or creditor must conduct a risk assessment to determine whether it offers or maintains covered accounts described in paragraph (b)(3)(ii) of this rule, taking into consideration:

(1) The methods it provides to open its accounts;

(2) The methods it provides to access its accounts; and

(3) Its previous experiences with identity theft.

(d) *Establishment of an Identity Theft Prevention Program—*

(1) *Program requirement.* Each financial institution or creditor that offers or maintains one or more covered accounts must develop and implement a written Identity Theft Prevention Program (Program) that is designed to detect, prevent, and mitigate identity theft in connection with the opening of a covered account or any existing covered account. The Program must be appropriate to the size and complexity of the financial institution or creditor and the nature and scope of its activities.

(2) *Elements of the Program.* The Program must include reasonable policies and procedures to:

(i) Identify relevant Red Flags for the covered accounts that the financial institution or creditor offers or maintains, and incorporate those Red Flags into its Program;

(ii) Detect Red Flags that have been incorporated into the Program of the financial institution or creditor;

(iii) Respond appropriately to any Red Flags that are detected pursuant to paragraph (d)(2)(ii) of this rule to prevent and mitigate identity theft; and

(iv) Ensure the Program (including the Red Flags determined to be relevant) is updated periodically, to reflect changes in risks to customers and to the safety and soundness of the financial institution or creditor from identity theft.

(e) *Administration of the Program.* Each financial institution or creditor that is required to implement a Program must provide for the continued administration of the Program and must:

(1) Obtain approval of the initial written Program from either its board of directors or an appropriate committee of the board of directors;

(2)   Involve the board of directors, an appropriate committee thereof, or a designated employee at the level of senior management in the oversight, development, implementation and administration of the Program;

(3)   Train staff, as necessary, to effectively implement the Program; and

(4)   Exercise appropriate and effective oversight of service provider arrangements.

(f)   *Guidelines.* Each financial institution or creditor that is required to implement a Program must consider the guidelines in Appendix A to this subpart and include in its Program those guidelines that are appropriate.

§ 248.202   Duties of Card Issuers Regarding Changes of Address.

(a)   *Scope.* This rule applies to a person described in § 248.201(a) that issues a credit or debit card (card issuer).

(b)   *Definitions.* For purposes of this rule:

(1)   *Cardholder* means a consumer who has been issued a *credit card* or *debit card* as defined in 15 U.S.C. 1681a(r).

(2)   *Clear and conspicuous* means reasonably understandable and designed to call attention to the nature and significance of the information presented.

(3)   Other terms not defined in this subpart have the same meaning as in the Fair Credit Reporting Act (15 U.S.C. 1681 *et seq.*).

(c)   *Address validation requirements.* A card issuer must establish and implement reasonable written policies and procedures to assess the validity of a change of address if it receives notification of a change of address for a consumer's debit or credit card account and, within a short period of time afterwards (during at least the first 30 days after it receives such notification), the card issuer receives a request for an additional or replacement card for the same account. Under these circumstances, the card issuer may not issue an additional or replacement card, until, in accordance with its reasonable policies and procedures and for the purpose of assessing the validity of the change of address, the card issuer:

(1)(i)   Notifies the cardholder of the request:

(A)   At the cardholder's former address; or

(B)   By any other means of communication that the card issuer and the cardholder have previously agreed to use; and

(ii)   Provides to the cardholder a reasonable means of promptly reporting incorrect address changes; or

(2)   Otherwise assesses the validity of the change of address in accordance with the policies and procedures the card issuer has established pursuant to § 248.201.

(d)   *Alternative timing of address validation.* A card issuer may satisfy the requirements of paragraph (c) of this rule if it validates an address pursuant to the methods in paragraph (c)(1) or (c)(2) of this rule when it receives an address change notification, before it receives a request for an additional or replacement card.

(e)   *Form of notice.* Any written or electronic notice that the card issuer provides under this paragraph must be clear and conspicuous and be provided separately from its regular correspondence with the cardholder.

Appendix A to Subpart C of Part 248—Interagency Guidelines on Identity Theft Detection, Prevention, and Mitigation Section 248.201 requires each financial institution and creditor that offers or maintains one or more covered accounts, as defined in § 248.201(b)(3), to develop and provide for the continued administration of a written Program to detect, prevent, and mitigate identity theft in connection with the opening of a covered account or any existing covered account. These guidelines are intended to assist financial institutions and creditors in the formulation and maintenance of a Program that satisfies the requirements of § 248.201.

I.   The Program

In designing its Program, a financial institution or creditor may incorporate, as appropriate, its existing policies, procedures, and other arrangements that control reasonably foreseeable risks to customers or to the safety and soundness of the financial institution or creditor from identity theft.

II.   Identifying Relevant Red Flags

(a)   *Risk Factors.* A financial institution or creditor should consider the following factors in identifying relevant Red Flags for covered accounts, as appropriate:

(1)   The types of covered accounts it offers or maintains;

(2)   The methods it provides to open its covered accounts;

(3)   The methods it provides to access its covered accounts; and

(4)   Its previous experiences with identity theft.

(b)   *Sources of Red Flags.* Financial institutions and creditors should incorporate relevant Red Flags from sources such as:

(1)   Incidents of identity theft that the financial institution or creditor has experienced;

(2)   Methods of identity theft that the financial institution or creditor has identified that reflect changes in identity theft risks; and

(3)   Applicable regulatory guidance.

(c)   *Categories of Red Flags.* The Program should include relevant Red Flags from the following categories, as appropriate. Examples of Red Flags from each of these categories are appended as Supplement A to this Appendix A.

(1)   Alerts, notifications, or other warnings received from consumer reporting agencies or service providers, such as fraud detection services;

(2)   The presentation of suspicious documents;

(3)   The presentation of suspicious personal identifying information, such as a suspicious address change;

(4)   The unusual use of, or other suspicious activity related to, a covered account; and

(5)   Notice from customers, victims of identity theft, law enforcement authorities, or other persons regarding possible identity theft in connection with covered accounts held by the financial institution or creditor.

III.   Detecting Red Flags

The Program's policies and procedures should address the detection of Red Flags in connection with the opening of covered accounts and existing covered accounts, such as by:

(a)   Obtaining identifying information about, and verifying the identity of, a person opening a covered account, for example, using the policies and procedures regarding identification and verification set forth in the Customer Identification Program rules implementing 31 U.S.C. 5318(*l*) (31 CFR 1023.220 (broker-dealers) and 1024.220 (mutual funds)); and

(b)   Authenticating customers, monitoring transactions, and verifying the validity of change of address requests, in the case of existing covered accounts.

IV.   Preventing and Mitigating Identity Theft

The Program's policies and procedures should provide for appropriate responses to the Red Flags the financial institution or creditor has detected that are commensurate with the degree of risk posed. In determining an appropriate response, a financial institution or creditor should consider aggravating factors that may heighten the risk of identity theft, such as a data security incident that results in unauthorized access to a customer's account records held by the financial institution, creditor, or third party, or notice that a customer has provided information related to a covered account held by the financial institution or creditor to someone fraudulently claiming to represent the financial institution or creditor or to a fraudulent Web site. Appropriate responses may include the following:

(a)   Monitoring a covered account for evidence of identity theft;

(b)   Contacting the customer;

(c)   Changing any passwords, security codes, or other security devices that permit access to a covered account;

(d)   Reopening a covered account with a new account number;

(e)   Not opening a new covered account;

(f)   Closing an existing covered account;

(g)   Not attempting to collect on a covered account or not selling a covered account to a debt collector;

(h)   Notifying law enforcement; or

(i)   Determining that no response is warranted under the particular circumstances.

V.   Updating the Program

Financial institutions and creditors should update the Program (including the Red Flags determined to be relevant) periodically, to reflect changes in risks to customers or to the safety and soundness of the financial institution or creditor from identity theft, based on factors such as:

(a)   The experiences of the financial institution or creditor with identity theft;

(b)   Changes in methods of identity theft;

(c)   Changes in methods to detect, prevent, and mitigate identity theft;

(d)   Changes in the types of accounts that the financial institution or creditor offers or maintains; and

(e)   Changes in the business arrangements of the financial institution or creditor, including mergers, acquisitions, alliances, joint ventures, and service provider arrangements.

VI.   Methods for Administering the Program

(a)   *Oversight of Program.* Oversight by the board of directors, an appropriate committee of the board, or a designated employee at the level of senior management should include:

(1)   Assigning specific responsibility for the Program's implementation;

(2)   Reviewing reports prepared by staff regarding compliance by the financial institution or creditor with § 248.201; and

(3)   Approving material changes to the Program as necessary to address changing identity theft risks.

(b)   *Reports.*

(1)   *In general.* Staff of the financial institution or creditor responsible for development, implementation, and administration of its Program should report to the board of directors, an appropriate committee of the board, or a designated employee at the level of senior management, at least annually, on compliance by the financial institution or creditor with § 248.201.

(2)   *Contents of report.* The report should address material matters related to the Program and evaluate issues such as: The effectiveness of the policies and procedures of the financial institution or creditor in addressing the risk of identity theft in connection with the opening of covered accounts and with respect to existing covered accounts; service provider arrangements; significant incidents involving identity theft and management's response; and recommendations for material changes to the Program.

(c)   *Oversight of service provider arrangements.* Whenever a financial institution or creditor engages a service provider to perform an activity in connection with one or more covered accounts the financial institution or creditor should take steps to ensure that the activity of the service provider is conducted in accordance with reasonable policies and procedures designed to detect, prevent, and mitigate the risk of identity theft. For example, a financial institution or creditor could require the service provider by contract to have policies and procedures to detect relevant Red Flags that may arise in the performance of the service provider's activities, and either report the Red Flags to the financial institution or creditor, or to take appropriate steps to prevent or mitigate identity theft.

VII. Other Applicable Legal Requirements

Financial institutions and creditors should be mindful of other related legal requirements that may be applicable, such as:

(a)   For financial institutions and creditors that are subject to 31 U.S.C. 5318(g), filing a Suspicious Activity Report in accordance with applicable law and regulation;

(b)   Implementing any requirements under 15 U.S.C. 1681c–1(h) regarding the circumstances under which credit may be extended when the financial institution or creditor detects a fraud or active duty alert;

(c)   Implementing any requirements for furnishers of information to consumer reporting agencies under 15 U.S.C. 1681s–2, for example, to correct or update inaccurate or incomplete information, and to not report information that the furnisher has reasonable cause to believe is inaccurate; and

(d)   Complying with the prohibitions in 15 U.S.C. 1681m on the sale, transfer, and placement for collection of certain debts resulting from identity theft.

Supplement A to Appendix A

In addition to incorporating Red Flags from the sources recommended in section II.b. of the Guidelines in Appendix A to this subpart, each financial institution or creditor may consider incorporating into its Program, whether singly or in combination, Red Flags from the following illustrative examples in connection with covered accounts:

Alerts, Notifications or Warnings From a Consumer Reporting Agency

1.   A fraud or active duty alert is included with a consumer report.

2.   A consumer reporting agency provides a notice of credit freeze in response to a request for a consumer report.

3.   A consumer reporting agency provides a notice of address discrepancy, as referenced in Sec. 605(h) of the Fair Credit Reporting Act (15 U.S.C. 1681c(h)).

4.   A consumer report indicates a pattern of activity that is inconsistent with the history and usual pattern of activity of an applicant or customer, such as:

   a.   A recent and significant increase in the volume of inquiries;

   b.   An unusual number of recently established credit relationships;

   c.   A material change in the use of credit, especially with respect to recently established credit relationships; or

   d.   An account that was closed for cause or identified for abuse of account privileges by a financial institution or creditor.

Suspicious Documents

5.   Documents provided for identification appear to have been altered or forged.

6.   The photograph or physical description on the identification is not consistent with the appearance of the applicant or customer presenting the identification.

7.   Other information on the identification is not consistent with information provided by the person opening a new covered account or customer presenting the identification.

8.   Other information on the identification is not consistent with readily accessible information that is on file with the financial institution or creditor, such as a signature card or a recent check.

9.   An application appears to have been altered or forged, or gives the appearance of having been destroyed and reassembled.

Suspicious Personal Identifying Information

10. Personal identifying information provided is inconsistent when compared against external information sources used by the financial institution or creditor. For example:

    a.   The address does not match any address in the consumer report; or

    b.   The Social Security Number (SSN) has not been issued, or is listed on the Social Security Administration's Death Master File.

11. Personal identifying information provided by the customer is not consistent with other personal identifying information provided by the customer. For example, there is a lack of correlation between the SSN range and date of birth.

12. Personal identifying information provided is associated with known fraudulent activity as indicated by internal or third-party sources used by the financial institution or creditor. For example:

    a.   The address on an application is the same as the address provided on a fraudulent application; or

    b.   The phone number on an application is the same as the number provided on a fraudulent application.

13. Personal identifying information provided is of a type commonly associated with fraudulent activity as indicated by internal or third-party sources used by the financial institution or creditor. For example:

    a.   The address on an application is fictitious, a mail drop, or a prison; or

    b.   The phone number is invalid, or is associated with a pager or answering service.

14. The SSN provided is the same as that submitted by other persons opening an account or other customers.

15. The address or telephone number provided is the same as or similar to the address or telephone number submitted by an unusually large number of other persons opening accounts or by other customers.

16. The person opening the covered account or the customer fails to provide all required personal identifying information on an application or in response to notification that the application is incomplete.

17. Personal identifying information provided is not consistent with personal identifying information that is on file with the financial institution or creditor.

18. For financial institutions and creditors that use challenge questions, the person opening the covered account or the customer cannot provide authenticating information beyond that which generally would be available from a wallet or consumer report.

Unusual Use of, or Suspicious Activity Related to, the Covered Account

19. Shortly following the notice of a change of address for a covered account, the institution or creditor receives a request for a new, additional, or replacement means of accessing the account or for the addition of an authorized user on the account.

20. A covered account is used in a manner that is not consistent with established patterns of activity on the account. There is, for example:

    a.   Nonpayment when there is no history of late or missed payments;

    b.   A material increase in the use of available credit;

    c.   A material change in purchasing or spending patterns; or

    d.   A material change in electronic fund transfer patterns in connection with a deposit account.

21. A covered account that has been inactive for a reasonably lengthy period of time is used (taking into consideration the type of account, the expected pattern of usage and other relevant factors).

22. Mail sent to the customer is returned repeatedly as undeliverable although transactions continue to be conducted in connection with the customer's covered account.

23. The financial institution or creditor is notified that the customer is not receiving paper account statements.

24. The financial institution or creditor is notified of unauthorized charges or transactions in connection with a customer's covered account.

**Notice From Customers, Victims of Identity Theft, Law Enforcement Authorities,
or Other Persons Regarding Possible Identity Theft in Connection With
Covered Accounts Held by the Financial Institution or Creditor**

25. The financial institution or creditor is notified by a customer, a victim of identity theft, a law enforcement authority, or any other person that it has opened a fraudulent account for a person engaged in identity theft.

G. INVESTMENT COMPANY ACT OF 1940 AND SELECTED RULES

TITLE I—INVESTMENT COMPANIES

TITLE I—INVESTMENT COMPANIES
Findings and Declaration of Policy

Sec. 1. (a) Findings.—

Upon the basis of facts disclosed by the record and reports of the Securities and Exchange Commission made pursuant to section 30 of the Public Utility Holding Company Act of 1935, the facts otherwise disclosed and ascertained, it is hereby found that investment companies are affected with a national public interest in that, among other things—

(1) the securities issued by such companies, which constitute a substantial part of all securities publicly offered, are distributed, purchased, paid for, exchanged, transferred, redeemed, and repurchased by use of the mails and means and instrumentalities of interstate commerce, and in the case of the numerous companies which issue redeemable securities this process of distribution and redemption is continuous;

(2) the principal activities of such companies—investing, reinvesting, and trading in securities—are conducted by use of the mails and means and instrumentalities of interstate commerce, including the facilities of national securities exchanges, and constitute a substantial part of all transactions effected in the securities markets of the Nation;

(3) such companies customarily invest and trade in securities issued by, and may dominate and control or otherwise affect the policies and management of, companies engaged in business in interstate commerce;

(4) such companies are media for the investment in the national economy of a substantial part of the national savings and may have a vital effect upon the flow of such savings into the capital markets; and

(5) the activities of such companies, extending over many States, their use of the instrumentalities of interstate commerce and the wide geographic distribution of their security holders, make difficult, if not impossible, effective State regulation of such companies in the interest of investors.

(b) Policy.—

Upon the basis of facts disclosed by the record and reports of the Securities and Exchange Commission made pursuant to section 30 of the Public Utility Holding Company Act of 1935, and facts otherwise disclosed and ascertained, it is hereby declared that the national public interest and the interest of investors are adversely affected—

(1) when investors purchase, pay for, exchange, receive dividends upon, vote, refrain from voting, sell, or surrender securities issued by investment companies without adequate, accurate, and explicit information, fairly presented, concerning the character of such securities and the circumstances, policies, and financial responsibility of such companies and their management;

(2) when investment companies are organized, operated, managed, or their portfolio securities are selected, in the interest of directors, officers, investment advisers, depositors, or other affiliated persons thereof, in the interest of underwriters, brokers, or dealers, in the interest of special classes of their security holders, or in the interest of other investment companies or persons engaged in other lines of business, rather than in the interest of all classes of such companies' security holders;

(3) when investment companies issue securities containing inequitable or discriminatory provisions, or fail to protect the preferences and privileges of the holders of their outstanding securities;

(4) when the control of investment companies is unduly concentrated through pyramiding or inequitable methods of control, or is inequitably distributed, or when investment companies are managed by irresponsible persons;

(5) when investment companies, in keeping their accounts, in maintaining reserves, and in computing their earnings and the asset value of their outstanding securities, employ unsound or misleading methods, or are not subjected to adequate independent scrutiny;

(6) when investment companies are reorganized, become inactive, or change the character of their business, or when the control or management thereof is transferred, without the consent of their security holders;

(7) when investment companies by excessive borrowing and the issuance of excessive amounts of senior securities increase unduly the speculative character of their junior securities; or

(8) when investment companies operate without adequate assets or reserves.

It is hereby declared that the policy and purposes of this Act, in accordance with which the provisions of this Act shall be interpreted, are to mitigate and, so far as is feasible, to eliminate the conditions enumerated in this section which adversely affect the national public interest and the interest of investors.

General Definitions

Sec. 2.   (a)   Definitions.—

When used in this Act, unless the context otherwise requires—

(1) "Advisory board" means a board, whether elected or appointed, which is distinct from the board of directors or board of trustees, of an investment company, and which is composed solely of persons who do not serve such company in any other capacity, whether or not the functions of such board are such as to render its members "directors" within the definition of that term, which board has advisory functions as to investments but has no power to determine that any security or other investment shall be purchased or sold by such company.

(2) "Affiliated company" means a company which is an affiliated person.

(3) "Affiliated person" of another person means

(A) any person directly or indirectly owning, controlling, or holding with power to vote, 5 per centum or more of the outstanding voting securities of such other person;

(B) any person 5 per centum or more of whose outstanding voting securities are directly or indirectly owned, controlled, or held with power to vote, by such other person

(C) any person directly or indirectly controlling, controlled by, or under common control with, such other person;

(D) any officer, director, partner, copartner, or employee of such other person;

(E)   if such other person is an investment company, any investment adviser thereof or any member of an advisory board thereof; and

(F)   if such other person is an unincorporated investment company not having a board of directors, the depositor thereof.

(4)   "Assignment" includes any direct or indirect transfer of hypothecation of a contract or chose in action by the assignor, or of a controlling block of the assignor's outstanding voting securities by a security holder of the assignor; but does not include an assignment of partnership interests incidental to the death or withdrawal of a minority of the members of the partnership having only a minority interest in the partnership business or to the admission to the partnership of one or more members who, after such admission, shall be only a minority of the members and shall have only a minority interest in the business.

(5)   "Bank" means

(A)   a depository institution (as defined in section 1813 of Title 12, United States Code) or a branch or agency of a foreign bank (as such terms are defined in section 3101 of Title 12, United States Code).

(B)   a member bank of the Federal Reserve System,

(C)   any other banking institution or trust company, whether incorporated or not, doing business under the laws of any State or of the United States, a substantial portion of the business of which consists of receiving deposits or exercising fiduciary powers similar to those permitted to national banks under the authority of the Comptroller of the Currency, and which is supervised and examined by State or Federal authority having supervision over banks, and which is not operated for the purpose of evading the provisions of this Act, and

(D)   a receiver, conservator, or other liquidating agent of any institution or firm included in clauses (A), (B), or (C) of this paragraph.

(6)   The term "broker" has the same meaning as given in section 3 of the Securities Exchange Act of 1934, except that such term does not include any person solely by reason of the fact that such person is an underwriter for one or more investment companies.

(7)   "Commission" means the Securities and Exchange Commission.

(8)   "Company" means a corporation, a partnership, an association, a joint-stock company, a trust, a fund, or any organized group of persons whether incorporated or not; or any receiver, trustee in a case under Title 11 of the United States Code or similar official or any liquidating agent for any of the foregoing, in his capacity as such.

(9)   "Control" means the power to exercise a controlling influence over the management or policies of a company, unless such power is solely the result of an official position with such company.

Any person who owns beneficially, either directly or through one or more controlled companies, more than 25 per centum of the voting securities of a company shall be presumed to control such company. Any person who does not so own more than 25 per centum of the voting securities of any company shall be presumed not to control such company. A natural person shall be presumed not to be a controlled person within the meaning of this Act. Any such presumption may be rebutted by evidence, but except as hereinafter provided, shall continue until a determination to the contrary made by the Commission by order either on its own motion or on application by an interested person. If an application filed hereunder is not granted or denied by the Commission within sixty days after filing thereof, the determination sought by the application shall be deemed to have been temporarily granted pending final determination of the Commission thereon. The Commission, upon its own motion or upon application, may by order revoke or modify any order issued under this paragraph whenever it shall find that the determination embraced in such original order is no longer consistent with the facts.

(10)   "Convicted" includes a verdict, judgment, or plea of guilty, or a finding of guilt on a plea of nolo contendere, if such verdict, judgment, plea, or finding has not been reversed, set aside, or withdrawn, whether or not sentence has been imposed.

(11) The term "dealer" has the same meaning as given in the Securities Exchange Act of 1934, but does not include an insurance company or investment company.

(12) "Director" means any director of a corporation or any person performing similar functions with respect to any organization, whether incorporated or unincorporated, including any natural person who is a member of a board of trustees of a management company created as a common-law trust.

(13) "Employees' securities company" means any investment company or similar issuer all of the outstanding securities of which (other than short-term paper) are beneficially owned

    (A) by the employees or persons on retainer of a single employer or of two or more employers each of which is an affiliated company of the other,

    (B) by former employees of such employer or employers,

    (C) by members of the immediate family of such employees, persons on retainer, or former employees,

    (D) by any two or more of the foregoing classes of persons, or

    (E) by such employer or employers together with any one or more of the foregoing classes of persons.

(14) "Exchange" means any organization, association, or group of persons, whether incorporated or unincorporated, which constitutes, maintains, or provides a market place or facilities for bringing together purchasers and sellers of securities or for otherwise performing with respect to securities the functions commonly performed by a stock exchange as that term is generally understood, and includes the market place and the market facilities maintained by such exchange.

(15) "Face-amount certificate" means any certificate, investment contract, or other security which represents an obligation on the part of its issuer to pay a stated or determinable sum or sums at a fixed or determinable date or dates more than twenty-four months after the date of issuance, in consideration of the payment of periodic installments of a stated or determinable amount (which security shall be known as a face-amount certificate of the "installment type"); or any security which represents a similar obligation on the part of a face-amount certificate company, the consideration for which is the payment of a single lump sum (which security shall be known as a "fully paid" face-amount certificate).

(16) "Government security" means any security issued or guaranteed as to principal or interest by the United States, or by a person controlled or supervised by and acting as an instrumentality of the Government of the United States pursuant to authority granted by the Congress of the United States; or any certificate of deposit for any of the foregoing.

(17) "Insurance company" means a company which is organized as an insurance company, whose primary and predominant business activity is the writing of insurance or the reinsuring of risks underwritten by insurance companies, and which is subject to supervision by the insurance commissioner or a similar official or agency of a State; or any receiver or similar official of any liquidating agent for such a company, in his capacity as such.

(18) "Interstate commerce" means trade, commerce, transportation, or communication among the several States, or between any foreign country and any State, or between any State and any place or ship outside thereof.

(19) "Interested person" of another person means—

    (A) when used with respect to an investment company—

    (i) any affiliated person of such company,

    (ii) any member of the immediate family of any natural person who is an affiliated person of such company,

    (iii) any interested person of any investment adviser of or principal underwriter for such company,

(iv) any person or partner or employee of any person who at any time since the beginning of the last two completed fiscal years of such company has acted as legal counsel for such company,

(v) any person or any affiliated person of a person (other than a registered investment company) that, at any time during the 6-month period preceding the date of the determination of whether that person or affiliated person is an interested person, has executed any portfolio transactions for, engaged in any principal transactions with, or distributed shares for—

    (I) the investment company;

    (II) any other investment company having the same investment adviser as such investment company or holding itself out to investors as a related company for purposes of investment or investor services; or

    (III) any account over which the investment company's investment adviser brokerage placement discretion

(vi) any person or any affiliated person of a person (other than a registered investment company) that, at any time during the 6-month period preceding the date of the determination of whether that person or affiliated person is an interested person, has loaned money or other property to—

    (I) the investment company;

    (II) any other investment company having the same investment adviser as such investment company or holding itself out to investors as a related company or holding itself out to investors as a related company for purposes of investment or investor services; or

    (III) any account for which the investment company's investment adviser has borrowing authority, and

(vii) any natural person whom the Commission by order shall have determined to be an interested person by reason of having had, at any time since the beginning of the last two completed fiscal years of such company, a material business or professional relationship with such company or with the principal executive officer of such company or with any other investment company having the same investment adviser or principal underwriter or with the principal executive officer of such other investment company:

Provided, That no person shall be deemed to be an interested person of an investment company solely by reason of (aa) his being a member of its board of directors or advisory board or an owner of its securities, or (bb) his membership in the immediate family of any person specified in clause (aa) of this proviso; and

    (B) when used with respect to an investment adviser of or principal underwriter for any investment company—

    (i) any affiliated person of such investment adviser or principal underwriter,

    (ii) any member of the immediate family of any natural person who is an affiliated person of such investment adviser or principal underwriter,

    (iii) any person who knowingly has any direct or indirect beneficial interest in, or who is designated as trustee, executor, or guardian of any legal interest in, any security issued either by such investment adviser or principal underwriter or by a controlling person of such investment adviser or principal underwriter,

    (iv) any person or partner or employee of any person who at any time since the beginning of the last two completed fiscal years of such investment company has acted as legal counsel for such investment adviser or principal underwriter,

    (v) any person or any affiliated person of a person (other than a registered investment company) that, at any time during the 6-month period preceding the date of the determination of whether that person or affiliated person is an interested person, has executed any portfolio transactions for, engaged in any principal transactions with, or distributed shares for—

(I) any investment company for which the investment adviser or principal underwriter serves as such;

(II) any investment company holding itself out to investors, for purposes of investment or investor services, as a company related to any investment company for which the investment adviser or principal underwriters serve as such; or

(III) any account over which the investment adviser has brokerage placement discretion

(vi) any person or any affiliated person of a person (other than a registered investment company) that, at any time during the 6-month period preceding the date of the determination of whether that person or affiliated person is an interested person, has loaned money or other property to—

(I) any investment company for which the investment advisor or principal underwriter serves as such;

(II) any investment company holding itself out to investors, for purposes of investment or investor services, as a company related to any investment company for which the investment advisor or principal underwriter serves as such; or

(III) any account for which the investment company's investment adviser has borrowing authority, and

(vii) any natural person whom the Commission by order shall have determined to be an interested person by reason of having had at any time since the beginning of the last two completed fiscal years of such investment company a material business or professional relationship with such investment adviser or principal underwriter or with the principal executive officer or any controlling person of such investment adviser or principal underwriter.

For the purpose of this paragraph (19), "member of the immediate family" means any parent, spouse of a parent, child, spouse of a child, spouse, brother, or sister, and includes step and adoptive relationships. The Commission may modify or revoke any order issued under clause (vii) of subparagraph (A) or (B) of this paragraph whenever it finds that such order is no longer consistent with the facts. No order issued pursuant to clause (vii) of subparagraph (A) or (B) of this paragraph shall become effective until at least sixty days after the entry thereof, and no such order shall affect the status of any person for the purposes of this Act or for any other purpose for any period prior to the effective date of such order.

(20) "Investment adviser" of an investment company means (A) any person (other than a bona fide officer, director, trustee, member of an advisory board, or employee of such company, as such) who pursuant to contract with such company regularly furnishes advice to such company with respect to the desirability of investing in, purchasing or selling securities or other property, or is empowered to determine what securities or other property shall be purchased or sold by such company, and (B) any other person who pursuant to contract with a person described in clause (A) regularly performs substantially all of the duties undertaken by such person described in clause (A); but does not include

(i) a person whose advice is furnished solely through uniform publications distributed to subscribers thereto,

(ii) a person who furnishes only statistical and other factual information, advice regarding economic factors and trends, or advice as to occasional transactions in specific securities, but without generally furnishing advice or making recommendations regarding the purchase or sale of securities,

(iii) a company furnishing such services at cost to one or more investment companies, insurance companies, or other financial institutions,

(iv) any person the character and amount of whose compensation for such services must be approved by a court, or

(v) such other persons as the Commission may by rules and regulations or order determine not to be within the intent of this definition.

(21) "Investment banker" means any person engaged in the business of underwriting securities issued by other persons, but does not include an investment company, any person who acts as an underwriter in isolated transactions but not as a part of a regular business, or any person solely by reason of the fact that such person is an underwriter for one or more investment companies.

(22) "Issuer" means every person who issues or proposes to issue any security, or has outstanding any security which it has issued.

(23) "Lend" includes a purchase coupled with an agreement by the vendor to repurchase; "borrow" includes a sale coupled with a similar agreement.

(24) "Majority-owned subsidiary" of a person means a company 50 per centum or more of the outstanding voting securities of which are owned by such person, or by a company which, within the meaning of this paragraph, is a majority-owned subsidiary of such person.

(25) "Means of instrumentality of interstate commerce" includes any facility of a national securities exchange.

(26) "National securities exchange" means an exchange registered under section 6 of the Securities Exchange Act of 1934.

(27) "Periodic payment plan certificate" means (A) any certificate, investment contract, or other security providing for a series of periodic payments by the holder, and representing an undivided interest in certain specified securities or in a unit or fund of securities purchased wholly or partly with the proceeds of such payments, and (B) any security the issuer of which is also issuing securities of the character described in clause (A) and the holder of which has substantially the same rights and privileges as those which holders of securities of the character described in clause (A) have upon completing the periodic payments for which such securities provide.

(28) "Person" means a natural person or a company.

(29) "Principal underwriter" of or for any investment company other than a closed-end company, or of any security issued by such a company, means any underwriter who as principal purchases from such company, or pursuant to contract has the right (whether absolute or conditional) from time to time to purchase from such company, any such security for distribution, or who as agent for such company sells or has the right to sell any such security to a dealer or to the public or both, but does not include a dealer who purchases from such company through a principal underwriter acting as agent for such company. "Principal underwriter" of or for a closed-end company or any issuer which is not an investment company, or of any security issued by such a company or issuer, means any underwriter who, in connection with a primary distribution of securities, (A) is in privity of contract with the issuer or an affiliated person of the issuer; (B) acting alone or in concert with one or more other persons, initiates or directs the formation of an underwriting syndicate; or (C) is allowed a rate of gross commission, spread, or other profit greater than the rate allowed another underwriter participating in the distribution.

(30) "Promoter" of a company or a proposed company means a person who, acting alone or in concert with other persons, is initiating or directing, or has within one year initiated or directed, the organization of such company.

(31) "Prospectus", as used in section 22, means a written prospectus intended to meet the requirements of section 10(a) of the Securities Act of 1933 and currently in use. As used elsewhere, "prospectus" means a prospectus as defined in the Securities Act of 1933.

(32) "Redeemable security" means any security, other than short-term paper, under the terms of which the holder upon its presentation to the issuer or to a person designated by the issuer, is entitled (whether absolutely or only out of surplus) to receive approximately his proportionate share of the issuer's current net assets, or the cash equivalent thereof.

(33) "Reorganization" means

    (A)   a reorganization under the supervision of a court of competent jurisdiction;

    (B)   a merger or consolidation;

    (C)   a sale of 75 per centum or more in value of the assets of a company;

(D) a restatement of the capital of a company, or an exchange of securities issued by a company for any of its own outstanding securities;

(E) a voluntary dissolution or liquidation of a company;

(F) a recapitalization or other procedure or transaction which has for its purpose the alteration, modification, or elimination of any of the rights, preferences, or privileges of any class of securities issued by a company, as provided in its charter or other instrument creating or defining such rights, preferences, and privileges;

(G) an exchange of securities issued by a company for outstanding securities issued by another company or companies, preliminary to and for the purpose of effecting or consummating any of the foregoing; or

(H) any exchange of securities by a company which is not an investment company for securities issued by a registered investment company.

(34) "Sale", "sell," "offer to sell", or "offer for sale" includes every contract of sale or disposition of, attempt or offer to dispose of, or solicitation of an offer to buy, a security or interest in a security, for value. Any security given or delivered with, or as a bonus on account of, any purchase of securities or any other thing, shall be conclusively presumed to constitute a part of the subject of such purchase and to have been sold for value.

(35) "Sales load" means the difference between the price of a security to the public and that portion of the proceeds from its sale which is received and invested or held for investment by the issuer (or in the case of a unit investment trust, by the depositor or trustee), less any portion of such difference deducted for trustee's or custodian's fees, insurance premiums, issue taxes, or administrative expenses or fees which are not properly chargeable to sales or promotional activities. In the case of a periodic payment plan certificate, "sales load" includes the sales load on any investment company securities in which the payments made on such certificate are invested, as well as the sales load on the certificate itself.

(36) "Security" means any note, stock, treasury stock, security future, bond, debenture, evidence of indebtedness, certificate of interest or participation in any profit-sharing agreement, collateral-trust certificate, preorganization certificate or subscription, transferable share, investment contract, voting-trust certificate, certificate of deposit for a security, fractional undivided interest in oil, gas, or other mineral rights, any put, call, straddle, option, or privilege on any security (including a certificate of deposit) or on any group or index of securities (including any interest therein or based on the value thereof), or any put, call, straddle, option, or privilege entered into on a national securities exchange relating to foreign currency, or, in general, any interest or instrument commonly known as a "security," or any certificate of interest or participation in, temporary or interim certificate for, receipt for, guarantee of, or warrant or right to subscribe to or purchase, any of the foregoing.

(37) "Separate account" means an account established and maintained by an insurance company pursuant to the laws of any State or territory of the United States, or of Canada or any province thereof, under which income, gains and losses, whether or not realized, from assets allocated to such account, are, in accordance with the applicable contract, credited to or charged against such account without regard to other income, gains, or losses of the insurance company.

(38) "Short-term paper" means any note, draft, bill of exchange, or banker's acceptance payable on demand or having a maturity at the time of issuance of not exceeding nine months, exclusive of days of grace, or any renewal thereof payable on demand or having a maturity likewise limited; and such other classes of securities, of a commercial rather than an investment character, as the Commission may designate by rules and regulations.

(39) "State" means any State of the United States, the District of Columbia, Puerto Rico, the Virgin Islands, or any other possession of the United States.

(40) "Underwriter" means any person who has purchased from an issuer with a view to, or sells for an issuer in connection with, the distribution of any security, or participates or has a direct or indirect participation in any such undertaking, or participates or has a participation in the direct or indirect underwriting of any such undertaking; but such term shall not include a person whose interest is limited to a commission from an underwriter or dealer not in excess of the usual and customary

distributor's or seller's commission. As used in this paragraph the term "issuer" shall include, in addition to an issuer, any person directly or indirectly controlling or controlled by the issuer, or any person under direct or indirect common control with the issuer. When the distribution of the securities in respect of which any person is an underwriter is completed such person shall cease to be an underwriter in respect of such securities or the issuer thereof.

(41) "Value", with respect to assets of registered investment companies, except as provided in subsection (b) of section 28 of this Act, means—

(A)   as used in sections 3, 5, and 12 of this Act,

(i)   with respect to securities owned at the end of the last preceding fiscal quarter for which market quotations are readily available, the market value at the end of such quarter;

(ii) with respect to other securities and assets owned at the end of the last preceding fiscal quarter, fair value at the end, of such quarter, as determined in good faith by the board of directors; and

(iii) with respect to securities and other assets acquired after the end of the last preceding fiscal quarter, the cost thereof; and

(B)   as used elsewhere in this Act,

(i)   with respect to securities for which market quotations are readily available, the market value of such securities; and

(ii) with respect to other securities and assets, fair value as determined in good faith by the board of directors;

in each case as of such time or times as determined pursuant to this Act, and the rules and regulations issued by the Commission hereunder. Notwithstanding the fact that market quotations for securities issued by controlled companies are available, the board of directors may in good faith determine the value of such securities: *Provided,* That the value so determined is not in excess of the higher of market value or asset value of such securities in the case of majority-owned subsidiaries, and is not in excess of market value in the case of other controlled companies.

For purposes of the valuation of those assets of a registered diversified company which are not subject to the limitations provided for in section 5(b)(1), the Commission may, by rules and regulations or orders, permit any security to be carried at cost, if it shall determine that such procedure is consistent with the general intent and purposes of this Act. For purposes of sections 5 and 12, in lieu of values determined as provided in clause (A) above, the Commission shall by rules and regulations permit valuation of securities at cost or other basis in cases where it may be more convenient for such company to make its computations on such basis by reason of the necessity or desirability of complying with the provisions of any United States revenue laws or rules and regulations issued thereunder, or the laws or the rules and regulations issued thereunder of any State in which the securities of such company may be qualified for sale.

The foregoing definition shall not derogate from the authority of the Commission with respect to the reports, information, and documents to be filed with the Commission by any registered company, or with respect to the accounting policies and principles to be followed by any such company, as provided in sections 8, 30, and 31.

(42) "Voting security" means any security presently entitling the owner or holder thereof to vote for the election of directors of a company. A specified percentage of the outstanding voting securities of a company means such amount of its outstanding voting securities as entitles the holder or holders thereof to cast said specified percentage of the aggregate votes which the holders of all the outstanding voting securities of such company are entitled to cast. The vote of a majority of the outstanding voting securities of a company means the vote, at the annual or a special meeting of the security holders of such company duly called,

(A)   of 67 per centum or more of the voting securities present at such meeting, if the holders of more than 50 per centum of the outstanding voting securities of such company are present or represented by proxy; or

(B) of more than 50 per centum of the outstanding voting securities of such company, whichever is the less.

(43) "Wholly-owned subsidiary" of a person means a company 95 per centum or more of the outstanding voting securities of which are owned by such person, or by a company which, within the meaning of this paragraph, is a wholly-owned subsidiary of such person.

(44) "Securities Act of 1933", "Securities Exchange Act of 1934", and "Trust Indenture Act of 1939" means those Acts, respectively, as heretofore or hereafter amended.

(45) "Savings and loan association" means a savings and loan association, building and loan association, cooperative bank, homestead association, or similar institution, which is supervised and examined by State or Federal authority having supervision over any such institution, and a receiver, conservator, or other liquidating agent of any such institution.

(46) "Eligible portfolio company" means any issuer which—

(A) is organized under the laws of, and has its principal place of business in, any State or States;

(B) is neither an investment company as defined in section 3 (other than a small business investment company which is licensed by the Small Business Administration to operate under the Small Business Investment Act of 1958 and which is a wholly-owned subsidiary of the business development company) nor a company which would be an investment company except for the exclusion from the definition of investment company in section 3(c); and

(C) satisfies one of the following:

(i) it does not have any class of securities with respect to which a member of a national securities exchange, broker, or dealer may extend or maintain credit to or for a customer pursuant to rules or regulations adopted by the Board of Governors of the Federal Reserve System under section 7 of the Securities Exchange Act of 1934;

(ii) it is controlled by a business development company, either alone or as part of a group acting together, and such business development company in fact exercises a controlling influence over the management or policies of such eligible portfolio company and, as a result of such control, has an affiliated person who is a director of such eligible portfolio company;

(iii) it has total assets of not more than $4,000,000, and capital and surplus (shareholders' equity less retained earnings) of not less than $2,000,000, except that the Commission may adjust such amounts by rule, regulation, or order to reflect changes in 1 or more generally accepted indices or other indicators for small businesses; or

(iv) it meets such other criteria as the Commission may, by rule, establish as consistent with the public interest, the protection of investors, and the purposes fairly intended by the policy and provisions of this Act.

(47) "Making available significant managerial assistance" by a business development company means—

(A) any arrangement whereby a business development company, through its directors, officers, employees, or general partners, offers to provide, and, if accepted, does so provide, significant guidance and counsel concerning the management, operations, or business objectives and policies of a portfolio company;

(B) the exercise by a business development company of a controlling influence over the management or policies of a portfolio company by the business development company acting individually or as part of a group acting together which controls such portfolio company; or

(C) with respect to a small business investment company licensed by the Small Business Administration to operate under the Small Business Investment Act of 1958, the making of loans to a portfolio company.

For purposes of subparagraph (A), the requirement that a business development company make available significant managerial assistance shall be deemed to be satisfied with respect to any particular portfolio company where the business development company purchases securities of such portfolio company in conjunction with one or more other persons acting together, and at least one of the persons in the group makes available significant managerial assistance to such portfolio company, except that such requirement will not be deemed to be satisfied if the business development company, in all cases, makes available significant managerial assistance solely in the manner described in this sentence.

(48) "Business development company" means any closed-end company which—

(A) is organized under the laws of, and has its principal place of business in, any State or States;

(B) is operated for the purpose of making investments in securities described in paragraphs (1) through (3) of section 54(a), and makes available significant managerial assistance with respect to the issuers of such securities, provided that a business development company must make available significant managerial assistance only with respect to the companies which are treated by such business development company as satisfying the 70 per centum of the value of its total assets condition of section 54; and provided further that a business development company need not make available significant managerial assistance with respect to any company described in paragraph (46)(C)(iii), or with respect to any other company that meets such criteria as the Commission may by rule, regulation, or order permit, as consistent with the public interest, the protection of investors, and the purposes of this title; and

(C) has elected pursuant to section 53(a) to be subject to the provisions of sections 54 through 64.

(49) "Foreign securities authority" means any foreign government or any governmental body or regulatory organization empowered by a foreign government to administer or enforce its laws as they relate to securities matters.

(50) "Foreign financial regulatory authority" means any

(A) foreign securities authority,

(B) other governmental body or foreign equivalent of a self-regulatory organization empowered by a foreign government to administer or enforce its laws relating to the regulation of fiduciaries, trusts, commercial lending, insurance, trading in contracts of sale of a commodity for future delivery, or other instruments traded on or subject to the rules of a contract market, board of trade or foreign equivalent, or other financial activities, or

(C) membership organization a function of which is to regulate the participation of its members in activities listed above.

(51)(A) "Qualified purchaser" means—

(i) any natural person (including any person who holds a joint, community property, or other similar shared ownership interest in an issuer that is excepted under section 3(c)(7) with that person's qualified purchaser spouse) who owns not less than $5,000,000 in investments, as defined by the Commission;

(ii) any company that owns not less than $5,000,000 in investments and that is owned directly or indirectly by or for 2 or more natural persons who are related as siblings or spouse (including former spouses), or direct lineal descendants by birth or adoption, spouses of such persons, the estates of such persons, or foundations, charitable organizations, or trusts established by or for the benefit of such persons;

(iii) any trust that is not covered by clause (ii) and that was not formed for the specific purpose of acquiring the securities offered, as to which the trustee or other person authorized to make decisions with respect to the trust, and each settlor or other person who has contributed assets to the trust, is a person described in clause (i), (ii), or (iv); or

(iv) any person, acting for its own account or the accounts of other qualified purchasers, who in the aggregate owns and invests on a discretionary basis, not less than $25,000,000 in investments.

(B) The Commission may adopt such rules and regulations applicable to the persons and trusts specified in clauses (i) through (iv) of subparagraph (A) as it determines are necessary or appropriate in the public interest or for the protection of investors.

(C) The term "qualified purchaser" does not include a company that, but for the exceptions provided for in paragraph (1) or (7) of section 3(c), would be an investment company (hereafter in this paragraph referred to as an "excepted investment company"), unless all beneficial owners of its outstanding securities (other than short-term paper), determined in accordance with section 3(c)(1)(A), that acquired such securities on or before April 30, 1996 (hereafter in this paragraph referred to as "pre-amendment beneficial owners"), and all pre-amendment beneficial owners of the outstanding securities (other than short-term paper) of any excepted investment company that, directly or indirectly, owns any outstanding securities of such excepted investment company, have consented to its treatment as a qualified purchaser. Unanimous consent of all trustees, directors, or general partners of a company or trust referred to in clause (ii) or (iii) of subparagraph (A) shall constitute consent for purposes of this subparagraph.

(52) The terms "security future" and "narrow-based security index" have the same meanings as provided in section 3(a)(55) of the Securities Exchange Act of 1934.

(b) Applicability to government.—

No provision in this Act shall apply to, or be deemed to include, the United States, a State, or any political subdivision of a State, or any agency, authority, or instrumentality of any one or more of the foregoing, or any corporation which is wholly owned directly or indirectly by any one or more of the foregoing, or any officer, agent, or employee of any of the foregoing acting as such in the course of his official duty, unless such provision makes specific reference thereto.

(c) Consideration of Promotion of Efficiency, Competition, and Capital Formation.—

Whenever pursuant to this title the Commission is engaged in rulemaking and is required to consider or determine whether an action is consistent with the public interest, the Commission shall also consider, in addition to the protection of investors, whether the action will promote efficiency, competition, and capital formation.

(53) The term "credit rating agency" has the same meaning as in section 3 of the Securities Exchange Act of 1934.

(54) The terms 'commodity pool', 'commodity pool operator', 'commodity trading advisor', 'major swap participant', 'swap', 'swap dealer', and 'swap execution facility' have the same meanings as in section 1a of the Commodity Exchange Act (7 U.S.C. 1a).

Definition of Investment Company

Sec. 3. (a) Definitions.—

(1) When used in this Act, "investment company" means any issuer which—

(A) is or holds itself out as being engaged primarily, or proposes to engage primarily, in the business of investing, reinvesting, or trading in securities;

(B) is engaged or proposes to engage in the business of issuing face-amount certificates of the installment type, or has been engaged in such business and has any such certificates outstanding; or

(C) is engaged or proposes to engage in the business of investing, reinvesting, owning, holding, or trading in securities, and owns or proposes to acquire investment securities having a value exceeding 40 per centum of the value of such issuer's total assets (exclusive of Government securities and cash items) on an unconsolidated basis.

(2) As used in this section, "investment securities" includes all securities except (A) Government securities, (B) securities issued by employees' securities companies, and (C) securities issued by majority-owned subsidiaries of the owner which (i) are not investment companies, and (ii) are not relying on the exception from the definition of investment company in paragraph (1) or (7) of subsection (c).

(b)   Exemption from provisions.—

Notwithstanding paragraph (i)(C) of subsection (a), none of the following persons is an investment company within the meaning of this Act:

(1)   Any issuer primarily engaged, directly or through a wholly-owned subsidiary or subsidiaries, in a business or businesses other than that of investing, reinvesting, owning, holding, or trading in securities.

(2)   Any issuer which the Commission, upon application by such issuer, finds and by order declares to be primarily engaged in a business or businesses other than that of investing, reinvesting, owning, holding, or trading in securities either directly or

(A)   through majority-owned subsidiaries or

(B)   through controlled companies conducting similar types of businesses. The filing of an application under this paragraph in good faith by an issuer other than a registered investment company shall exempt the applicant for a period of sixty days from all provisions of this Act applicable to investment companies as such. For cause shown, the Commission by order may extend such period of exemption for an additional period or periods. Whenever the Commission, upon its own motion or upon application, finds that the circumstances which gave rise to the issuance of an order granting an application under this paragraph no longer exist, the Commission shall by order revoke such order.

(3)   Any issuer all the outstanding securities of which (other than short-term paper and directors' qualifying shares) are directly or indirectly owned by a company excepted from the definition of investment company by paragraph (1) or (2) of this subsection.

(c)   Further exemptions.—

Notwithstanding subsection (a), none of the following persons is an investment company within the meaning of this Act:

(1)   Any issuer whose outstanding securities (other than short-term paper) are beneficially owned by not more than one hundred persons or, in the case of a qualifying venture capital fund, 250 persons and which is not making and does not presently propose to make a public offering of its securities. Such issuer shall be deemed to be an investment company for purposes of the limitations set forth in subparagraphs (A)(i) and (B)(i) of section 12(d)(1) governing the purchase or other acquisition by such issuer of any security issued by any registered investment company and the sale of any security issued by any registered open-end investment company to any such issuer. For purposes of this paragraph:

(A)   Beneficial ownership by a company shall be deemed to be beneficial ownership by one person, except that, if such company owns 10 per centum or more of the outstanding voting securities of the issuer, and is or, but for the exception provided for in this paragraph or paragraph (7), would be an investment company, the beneficial ownership shall be deemed to be that of the holders of such company's outstanding securities (other than short-term paper).

(B)   Beneficial ownership by any person who acquires securities or interests in securities of an issuer described in the first sentence of this paragraph shall be deemed to be beneficial ownership by the person from whom such transfer was made, pursuant to such rules and regulations as the Commission shall prescribe as necessary or appropriate in the public interest and consistent with the protection of investors and the purposes fairly intended by the policy and provisions of this Act, where the transfer was caused by legal separation, divorce, death, or other involuntary event.

(C)(i) The term 'qualifying venture capital fund' means a venture capital fund that has not more than $10,000,000 in aggregate capital contributions and uncalled committed capital, with such dollar amount to be indexed for inflation once every 5 years by the Commission, beginning from a measurement made by the Commission on a date selected by the Commission, rounded to the nearest $1,000,000.

(ii)   The term 'venture capital fund' has the meaning given the term in section 275.203(l)–1 of title 17, Code of Federal Regulations, or any successor regulation.

(2)(A) Any person primarily engaged in the business of underwriting and distributing securities issued by other persons, selling securities to customers, acting as broker, and acting as market intermediary, or any one or more of such activities, whose gross income normally is derived principally from such business and related activities.

(B) For purposes of this paragraph—

(i) the term "market intermediary" means any person that regularly holds itself out as being willing contemporaneously to engage in, and that is regularly engaged in, the business of entering into transactions on both sides of the market for a financial contract or one or more such financial contracts; and

(ii) the term "financial contract" means any arrangement that—

(I) takes the form of an individually negotiated contract, agreement, or option to buy, sell, lend, swap, or repurchase, or other similar individually negotiated transaction commonly entered into by participants in the financial markets;

(II) is in respect of securities, commodities, currencies, interest or other rates, other measures of value, or any other financial or economic interest similar in purpose or function to any of the foregoing; and

(III) is entered into in response to a request from a counter party for a quotation, or is otherwise entered into and structured to accommodate the objectives of the counter party to such arrangement.

(3) Any bank or insurance company; any savings and loan association, building and loan association, cooperative bank, homestead association, or similar institution, or any receiver, conservator, liquidator, liquidating agent, or similar official or person thereof or therefor; or any common trust fund or similar fund maintained by a bank exclusively for the collective investment and reinvestment of moneys contributed thereto by the bank in its capacity as a trustee, executor, administrator, or guardian, if

(A) such fund is employed by the bank solely as an aid to the administration of trusts, estates, or other accounts created and maintained for a fiduciary purpose;

(B) except in connection with the ordinary advertising of the bank's fiduciary services, interests in such fund are not—

(i) advertised; or

(ii) offered for sale to the general public; and

(C) fees and expenses charged by such fund are not in contravention of fiduciary principles established under applicable Federal or state law.

(4) Any person substantially all of whose business is confined to making small loans, industrial banking, or similar businesses.

(5) Any person who is not engaged in the business of issuing redeemable securities, face-amount certificates of the installment type or periodic payment plan certificates, and who is primarily engaged in one or more of the following businesses:

(A) Purchasing or otherwise acquiring notes, drafts, acceptances, open accounts receivable, and other obligations representing part or all of the sales price of merchandise, insurance, and services;

(B) making loans to manufacturers, wholesalers, and retailers of, and to prospective purchasers of, specified merchandise, insurance, and services; and

(C) purchasing or otherwise acquiring mortgages and other liens on and interests in real estate.

(6) Any company primarily engaged, directly or through majority-owned subsidiaries, in one or more of the businesses described in paragraphs (3), (4), and (5), or in one or more of such businesses (from which not less than 25 per centum of such company's gross income during its last fiscal year was

derived) together with an additional business or businesses other than investing, reinvesting, owning, holding, or trading in securities.

(7)(A)   Any issuer, the outstanding securities of which are owned exclusively by persons who, at the time of acquisition of such securities, are qualified purchasers, and which is not making and does not at that time propose to make a public offering of such securities. Securities that are owned by persons who received the securities from a qualified purchaser as a gift or bequest, or in a case in which the transfer was caused by legal separation, divorce, death, or other involuntary event, shall be deemed to be owned by a qualified purchaser, subject to such rules, regulations, and orders as the Commission may prescribe as necessary or appropriate in the public interest or for the protection of investors.

(B)   Notwithstanding subparagraph (A), an issuer is within the exception provided by this paragraph if—

(i)   in addition to qualified purchasers, outstanding securities of that issuer are beneficially owned by not more than 100 persons who are not qualified purchasers, if—

(I)   such persons acquired any portion of the securities of such issuer on or before September 1, 1996; and

(II)   at the time at which such persons initially acquired the securities of such issuer, the issuer was excepted by paragraph (1); and

(ii)   prior to availing itself of the exception provided by this paragraph—

(I)   such issuer has disclosed to each beneficial owner, as determined under paragraph (1), that future investors will be limited to qualified purchasers, and that ownership in such issuer is no longer limited to not more than 100 persons; and

(II)   concurrently with or after such disclosure, such issuer has provided each beneficial owner, as determined under paragraph (1), with a reasonable opportunity to redeem any part or all of their interests in the issuer, notwithstanding any agreement to the contrary between the issuer and such persons, for that person's proportionate share of the issuer's net assets.

(C)   Each person that elects to redeem under subparagraph (B)(ii)(II) shall receive an amount in cash equal to that person's proportionate share of the issuer's net assets, unless the issuer elects to provide such person with the option of receiving, and such person agrees to receive, all or a portion of such person's share in assets of the issuer. If the issuer elects to provide such persons with such an opportunity, disclosure concerning such opportunity shall be made in the disclosure required by subparagraph (B)(ii)(I).

(D)   An issuer that is excepted under this paragraph shall nonetheless be deemed to be an investment company for purposes of the limitations set forth in subparagraphs (A)(i) and (B)(i) of section 12(d)(1) relating to the purchase or other acquisition by such issuer of any security issued by any registered investment company and the sale of any security issued by any registered open-end investment company to any such issuer.

(E)   For purposes of determining compliance with this paragraph and paragraph (1), an issuer that is otherwise excepted under this paragraph and an issuer that is otherwise excepted under paragraph (1) shall not be treated by the Commission as being a single issuer for purposes of determining whether the outstanding securities of the issuer excepted under paragraph (1) are beneficially owned by not more than 100 persons or whether the outstanding securities of the issuer excepted under this paragraph are owned by persons that are not qualified purchasers. Nothing in this subparagraph shall be construed to establish that a person is a bona fide qualified purchaser for purposes of this paragraph or a bona fide beneficial owner for purposes of paragraph (1).

(8)   [Repealed]

(9)   Any person substantially all of whose business consists of owning or holding oil, gas, or other mineral royalties or leases, or fractional interests therein, or certificates of interest or participation in or investment contracts relative to such royalties, leases, or fractional interests.

(10)(A) Any company organized and operated exclusively for religious, educational, benevolent, fraternal, charitable, or reformatory purposes—

    (i) no part of the net earnings of which inures to the benefit of any private shareholder or individual; or

    (ii) which is or maintains a fund described in subparagraph (B).

(B) For the purposes of subparagraph (A)(ii), a fund is described in this subparagraph if such fund is a pooled income fund, collective trust fund, collective investment fund, or similar fund maintained by a charitable organization exclusively for the collective investment and reinvestment of one or more of the following:

    (i) assets of the general endowment fund or other funds of one or more charitable organizations;

    (ii) assets of a pooled income fund;

    (iii) assets contributed to a charitable organization in exchange for the issuance of charitable gift annuities;

    (iv) assets of a charitable remainder trust or of any other trust, the remainder interests of which are irrevocably dedicated to any charitable organization;

    (v) assets of a charitable lead trust;

    (vi) assets of a trust, the remainder interests of which are revocably dedicated to or for the benefit of 1 or more charitable organizations, if the ability to revoke the dedication is limited to circumstances involving—

        (I) an adverse change in the financial circumstances of a settlor or an income beneficiary of the trust;

        (II) a change in the identity of the charitable organization or organizations having the remainder interest, provided that the new beneficiary is also a charitable organization; or

        (III) both the changes described in subclauses (I) and (II):

    (vii) assets of a trust not described in clauses (i) through (v), the remainder interests of which are revocably dedicated to a charitable organization, subject to subparagraph (C); or

    (viii) such assets as the Commission may prescribe by rule, regulation, or order in accordance with section 6(c).

(C) A fund that contains assets described in clause (vii) of subparagraph (B) shall be excluded from the definition of an investment company for a period of 3 years after the date of enactment of this subparagraph, but only if—

    (i) such assets were contributed before the date which is 60 days after the date of enactment of this subparagraph; and

    (ii) such assets are commingled in the fund with assets described in one or more of clauses (i) through (vi) and (viii) of subparagraph (B).

(D) For purposes of this paragraph—

    (i) a trust or fund is "maintained" by a charitable organization if the organization serves as a trustee or administrator of the trust or fund or has the power to remove the trustees or administrators of the trust or fund and to designate new trustees or administrators;

    (ii) the term "pooled income fund" has the same meaning as in section 642(c)(5) of the Internal Revenue Code of 1986;

    (iii) the term "charitable organization" means an organization described in paragraphs (1) through (5) of section 170(c) or section 501(c)(3) of the Internal Revenue Code of 1986;

    (iv) the term "charitable lead trust" means a trust described in section 170(f)(2)(B), 2055(e)(2)(B), or 2522(c)(2)(B) of the Internal Revenue Code of 1986;

(v)   the term "charitable remainder trust" means a charitable remainder annuity trust or a charitable remainder unitrust, as those terms are defined in section 664(d) of the Internal Revenue Code of 1986; and

(vi)   the term "charitable gift annuity" means an annuity issued by a charitable organization that is described in section 501(m)(5) of the Internal Revenue Code of 1986.

(11)   Any employee's stock bonus, pension, or profit-sharing trust which meets the requirements for qualification under section 401 of Title 26; or any governmental plan described in section 3(a)(2)(C) of the Securities Act of 1933; or any collective trust fund maintained by a bank consisting solely of assets of one or more of such trusts, government plans, or church plans, companies or accounts that are excluded from the definition of an investment company under paragraph (14) of this subsection; or any separate account the assets of which are derived solely from

(A)   contributions under pension or profit-sharing plans which meet the requirements of section 401 of the Internal Revenue Code of 1986 or the requirements for deduction of the employer's contribution under section 404(a)(2) of such Code,

(B)   contributions under governmental plans in connection with which interests, participations, or securities are exempted from the registration provisions of section 5 of the Securities Act of 1933 by section 3(a)(2)(C) of such Act, and

(C)   advances made by an insurance company in connection with the operation of such separate account.

(12)   Any voting trust the assets of which consist exclusively of securities of a single issuer which is not an investment company.

(13)   Any security holders' protective committee or similar issuer having outstanding and issuing no securities other than certificates of deposit and short-term paper.

(14)   Any church plan described in section 414(e) of the Internal Revenue Code of 1986, if, under any such plan, no part of the assets may be used for, or diverted to, purposes other than the exclusive benefit of plan participants or beneficiaries, or any company or account that is—

(A)   established by a person that is eligible to establish and maintain such a plan under section 414(e) of the Internal Revenue Code of 1986; and

(B)   substantially all of the activities of which consist of—

(i)   managing or holding assets contributed to such church plans or other assets which are permitted to be commingled with the assets of church plans under the Internal Revenue Code of 1986; or

(ii)   administering or providing benefits pursuant to church plans.

Protection of Philanthropy Under State Law

Sec. 3a.   (a)   Registration requirements.—

A security issued by or any interest or participation in any pooled income fund, collective trust fund, collective investment fund, or similar fund that is excluded from the definition. of an investment company under section 80a–(c)(10)(B) of this title, and the offer or sale thereof, shall be exempt from any statute or regulation of a state that requires registration or qualification of securities.

(b)   Treatment of charitable organizations.—

No charitable organization, or any trustee, director, officer, employee, or volunteer of a charitable organization action within the scope of such person's employment or duties, shall be required to register as, or be subject to regulation as, a dealer, broker, agent, or investment adviser under the securities laws of any state because such organization or person buys, holds, sells, or trades in securities for its own account in its capacity as trustee or administrator of, or otherwise on behalf of or for the account of one or more of the following:

(1)   a charitable organization;

(2) a fund that is excluded from the definition of an investment company under section 80a–3(c)(10)(B) of this title; or

(3) a trust or other donative instrument described in section 80(c)(10)(B) of this title, or the settlors (or potential settlors) or beneficiaries of any such trusts or other instruments.

(c) State action.—

Notwithstanding subsections (a) and (b) of this section, during the 3-year period beginning on December 8, 1995, a state may enact a statute that specifically refers to this section and provides prospectively that this section shall not preempt the laws of that state referred to in this section

(d) Definitions.—

For purposes of this section—

(1) the term "charitable organization" means an organization described in paragraphs (1) through (5) of section 170(c) or section 501(c)(3) of the title 26;

(2) the term "security" has the same meaning as in section 78c of this title; and

(3) the term "State" means each of the several states of the United States, the District of Columbia, the Commonwealth of Puerto Rico, the Virgin Islands, Guam, American Samoa, and the Commonwealth of the Northern Mariana Islands.

Classification of Investment Companies

Sec. 4.   For the purposes of this Act, investment companies are divided into three principal classes, defined as follows:

(1) "Face-amount certificate company" means an investment company which is engaged or proposes to engage in the business of issuing face-amount certificates of the installment type, or which has been engaged in such business and has any such certificate outstanding.

(2) "Unit investment trust" means an investment company which

(A) is organized under a trust indenture, contract of custodianship or agency, or similar instrument,

(B) does not have a board of directors, and

(C) issues only redeemable securities, each of which represents an undivided interest in a unit of specified securities; but does not include a voting trust.

(3) "Management company" means any investment company other than a face-amount certificate company or a unit investment trust.

Subclassification of Management Companies

Sec. 5.   (a) Open-end and closed-end companies.—

For the purpose of this Act, management companies are divided into open-end and closed-end companies, defined as follows:

(1) "Open-end company" means a management company which is offering for sale or has outstanding any redeemable security of which it is the issuer.

(2) "Closed-end company" means any management company other than an open-end company.

(b) Diversified and non-diversified companies.—

Management companies are further divided into diversified companies and non-diversified companies, defined as follows:

(1) "Diversified company" means a management company which meets the following requirements: At least 75 per centum of the value of its total assets is represented by cash and cash items (including receivables), Government securities, securities of other investment companies, and other securities for the purposes of this calculation limited in respect of any one issuer to an amount

not greater in value than 5 per centum of the value of the total assets of such management company and to not more than 10 per centum of the outstanding voting securities of such issuer.

(2) "Non-diversified company" means any management company other than a diversified company.

(c)   Loss of status as diversified company.—

A registered diversified company which at the time of its qualification as such meets the requirements of paragraph (1) and subsection (b) shall not lose its status as a diversified company because of any subsequent discrepancy between the value of its various investments and the requirements of said paragraph, so long as any such discrepancy existing immediately after its acquisition of any security or other property is neither wholly nor partly the result of such acquisition.

Exemptions

Sec. 6.   (a)   Exemption of specified investment companies.—

The following investment companies are exempt from the provisions of this Act:

(1)   Any company which since the effective date of this Act or within five years prior to such date has been reorganized under the supervision of a court of competent jurisdiction, if

(A)   such company was not an investment company at the commencement of such reorganization proceedings,

(B)   at the conclusion of such proceedings all outstanding securities of such company were owned by creditors of such company or by persons to whom such securities were issued on account of creditors' claims, and

(C)   more than 50 per centum of the voting securities of such company, and securities representing more than 50 per centum of the net asset value of such company, are currently owned beneficially by not more than twenty-five persons; but such exemption shall terminate if any security of which such company is the issuer is offered for sale or sold to the public after the conclusion of such proceedings by the issuer or by or through any underwriter. For the purposes of this paragraph, any new company organized as part of the reorganization shall be deemed the same company as its predecessor; and beneficial ownership shall be determined in the manner provided in section 3(c)(1).

(2)   Any issuer as to which there is outstanding a writing filed with the Commission by the Federal Savings and Loan Insurance Corporation stating that exemption of such issuer from the provisions of this Act is consistent with the public interest and the protection of investors and is necessary or appropriate by reason of the fact that such issuer holds or proposes to acquire any assets or any product of any assets which have been segregated

(A)   from assets of any company which at the filing of such writing is an insured institution within the meaning of section 401(a) of the National Housing Act, as heretofore or hereafter amended, or

(B)   as a part of or in connection with any plan for or condition to the insurance of accounts of any company by said corporation or the conversion of any company into a Federal savings and loan association. Any such writing shall expire when canceled by a writing similarly filed or at the expiration of two years after the date of its filing, whichever first occurs; but said corporation may, nevertheless, before, at, or after the expiration of any such writing file another writing or writings with respect to such issuer.

(3)   Any company which prior to March 15, 1940, was and now is a wholly-owned subsidiary of a registered face-amount certificate company and was prior to said date and now is organized and operating under the insurance laws of any State and subject to supervision and examination by the insurance commissioner thereof, and which prior to March 15, 1940, was and now is engaged, subject to such laws, in business substantially all of which consists of issuing and selling only to residents of such State and investing the proceeds from, securities providing for or representing participations or interests in intangible assets consisting of mortgages or other liens on real estate or notes or bonds

secured thereby or in a fund or deposit of mortgages or other liens on real estate or notes or bonds secured thereby or having outstanding such securities so issued and sold.

(4)(A) Any company that is not engaged in the business of issuing redeemable securities, the operations of which are subject to regulation by the State in which the company is organized under a statute governing entities that provide financial or managerial assistance to enterprises doing business, or proposing to do business, in that State if—

(i) the organizational documents of the company state that the activities of the company are limited to the promotion of economic, business, or industrial development in the State through the provision of financial or managerial assistance to enterprises doing business, or proposing to do business, in that State, and such other activities that are incidental or necessary to carry out that purpose;

(ii) immediately following each sale of the securities of the company by the company or any underwriter for the company, not less than 80 percent of the securities of the company being offered in such sale, on a class-by-class basis, are held by persons who reside or who have a substantial business presence in that State;

(iii) the securities of the company are sold, or proposed to be sold, by the company or by any underwriter for the company, solely to accredited investors, as that term is defined in section 2(a)(15) of the Securities Act of 1933, or to such other persons that the Commission, as necessary or appropriate in the public interest and consistent with the protection of investors, may permit by rule, regulation, or order; and

(iv) the company does not purchase any security issued by an investment company or by any company that would be an investment company except for the exclusions from the definition of the term "investment company" under paragraph (1) or (7) of section 3(c), other than—

(I) any debt security that meets such standards of creditworthiness as the Commission shall adopt; or

(II) any security issued by a registered open-end investment company that is required by its investment policies to invest not less than 65 percent of its total assets in securities described in subclause (I) or securities that are determined by such registered open-end investment company to be comparable in quality to securities described in subclause (I).

(B) Notwithstanding the exemption provided by this paragraph, section 9 (and, to the extent necessary to enforce section 9, sections 37 through 50) shall apply to a company described in this paragraph as if the company were an investment company registered under this Act.

(C) Any company proposing to rely on the exemption provided by this paragraph shall file with the Commission a notification stating that the company intends to do so, in such form and manner as the Commission may prescribe by rule.

(D) Any company meeting the requirements of this paragraph may rely on the exemption provided by this paragraph upon filing with the Commission the notification required by subparagraph (C), until such time as the Commission determines by order that such reliance is not in the public interest or is not consistent with the protection of investors.

(E) The exemption provided by this paragraph may be subject to such additional terms and conditions as the Commission may by rule, regulation, or order determine are necessary or appropriate in the public interest or for the protection of investors.

(b) Exemption of employees' security company upon application; matters considered.—

Upon application by any employees' security company, the Commission shall by order exempt such company from the provisions of this Act and of the rules and regulations hereunder, if and to the extent that such exemption is consistent with the protection of investors. In determining the provisions to which such an order of exemption shall apply, the Commission shall give due weight, among other things, to the form of organization and the capital structure of such company, the persons by whom its voting securities, evidences of indebtedness, and other securities are owned and controlled, the prices at which securities issued by such company are sold and the sales load thereon, the disposition of the proceeds of such sales, the character of the securities in which such proceeds are invested, and any relationship between such company and the issuer of any such security.

(c) Exemption of persons, securities or any class or classes of persons as necessary and appropriate in public interest.—

The Commission, by rules and regulations upon its own motion, or by order upon application, may conditionally or unconditionally exempt any person, security, or transaction, or any class or classes of persons, securities, or transactions, from any provision or provisions of this Act or of any rule or regulation thereunder, if and to the extent that such exemption is necessary or appropriate in the public interest and consistent with the protection of investors and the purposes fairly intended by the policy and provisions of this Act.

(d) Exemption of closed-end investment companies.—

The Commission, by rules and regulations or order, shall exempt a closed-end investment company from any or all provisions of this Act, but subject to such terms and conditions as may be necessary or appropriate in the public interest or for the protection of investors, if—

    (1) the aggregate sums received by such company from the sale of all its outstanding securities, plus the aggregate offering price of all securities of which such company is the issuer and which it proposes to offer for sale, do not exceed $10,000,000, or such other amount as the Commission may set by rule, regulation or order;

    (2) no security of which such company is the issuer has been or is proposed to be sold by such company or any underwriter therefor, in connection with a public offering, to any person who is not a resident of the State under the laws of which such company is organized or otherwise created; and

    (3) such exemption is not contrary to the public interest or inconsistent with the protection of investors.

(e) Application of certain specified provisions of subchapter or otherwise exempt companies.—

If, in connection with any rule, regulation, or order under this section exempting any investment company from any provision of section 7, the Commission deems it necessary or appropriate in the public interest or for the protection of investors that certain specified provisions of this Act pertaining to registered investment companies shall be applicable in respect of such company, the provisions so specified shall apply to such company, and to other persons in their transactions and relations with such company, as though such company were a registered investment company.

(f) Exemption of closed-end company treated as business development company.—

Any closed-end company which—

    (1) elects to be treated as a business development company pursuant to section 53; or

    (2) would be excluded from the definition of an investment company by section 3(c)(1), except that it presently proposes to make a public offering of its securities as a business development company, and has notified the Commission, in a form and manner which the Commission may, by rule, prescribe, that it intends in good faith to file, within 90 days, a notification of election to become subject to the provisions of sections 54 through 64,

shall be exempt from sections 1 through 52, except to the extent provided in sections 58 through 64.

Transactions by Unregistered Investment Companies

Sec. 7.   (a) Prohibition of transactions in interstate commerce by companies.—

No investment company organized or otherwise created under the laws of the United States or of a State and having a board of directors, unless registered under section 8, shall directly or indirectly—

    (1) offer for sale, sell, or deliver after sale, by the use of the mails or any means or instrumentality of interstate commerce, any security or any interest in a security, whether the issuer of such security is such investment company or another person; or offer for sale, sell, or deliver after sale any such security or interest, having reason to believe that such security or interest will be made

the subject of a public offering by use of the mails or any means or instrumentality of interstate commerce;

(2) purchase, redeem, retire, or otherwise acquire or attempt to acquire, by use of the mails or any means or instrumentality of interstate commerce, any security or any interest in a security, whether the issuer of such security is such investment company or another person;

(3) control any investment company which does any of the acts enumerated in paragraphs (1) and (2);

(4) engage in any business in interstate commerce; or

(5) control any company which is engaged in any business in interstate commerce.

The provisions of this subsection (a) shall not apply to transactions of an investment company which are merely incidental to its dissolution.

(b) Prohibition of transactions in interstate commerce by depositors or trustees of companies.—

No depositor or trustee of or underwriter for any investment company, organized or otherwise created under the laws of the United States or of a State and not having a board of directors, unless such company is registered under section 8 or exempt under section 6, shall directly or indirectly—

(1) offer for sale, sell, or deliver after sale, by use of the mails or any means or instrumentality of interstate commerce, any security or any interest in a security of which such company is the issuer; or offer for sale, sell, or deliver after sale any such security or interest, having reason to believe that such security or interest will be made the subject of a public offering by use of the mails or any means or instrumentality of interstate commerce;

(2) purchase, redeem, or otherwise acquire or attempt to acquire, by use of the mails or any means or instrumentality of interstate commerce, any security or any interest in a security of which such company is the issuer; or

(3) sell or purchase for the account of such company, by use of the mails or any means or instrumentality of interstate commerce, any security or interest in a security, by whomever issued.

The provisions of this subsection (b) shall not apply to transactions which are merely incidental to the dissolution of an investment company.

(c) Prohibition of transactions in interstate commerce by promoters of proposed investment companies.—

No promoter of a proposed investment company, and no underwriter for such a promoter, shall make use of the mails or any means or instrumentality of interstate commerce, directly or indirectly, to offer for sale, sell, or deliver after sale, in connection with a public offering, any preorganization certificate or subscription for such a company.

(d) Prohibition of transactions in interstate commerce by companies not organized under laws of the United States or a State; exceptions.—

No investment company, unless organized or otherwise created under the laws of the United States or of a State, and no depositor or trustee of or underwriter for such a company not so organized or created, shall make use of the mails or any means or instrumentality of interstate commerce, directly or indirectly, to offer for sale, sell, or deliver after sale, in connection with a public offering, any security of which such company is the issuer. Notwithstanding the provisions of this subsection and of section 8(a), the Commission is authorized, upon application by an investment company organized or otherwise created under the laws of a foreign country, to issue a conditional or unconditional order permitting such company to register under this Act and to make a public offering of its securities by use of the mails and means or instrumentalities of interstate commerce, if the Commission finds that, by reason of special circumstances or arrangements, it is both legally and practically feasible effectively to enforce the provisions of this Act against such company and that the issuance of such order is otherwise consistent with the public interest and the protection of investors.

(e) Disclosure by exempt charitable organizations.—

Each fund that is excluded from the definition of an investment company under section 3(c)(10)(B) of this Act shall provide, to each donor to such fund, at the time of the donation or within 90 days after the date of enactment of this subsection, whichever is later, written information describing the material terms of the operation of such fund.

Registration of Investment Companies

Sec. 8.   (a)   Notification of registration; effective date of registration.—

Any investment company organized or otherwise created under the laws of the United States or of a State may register for the purposes of this Act by filing with the Commission a notification of registration in such form as the Commission shall by rules and regulations prescribe as necessary or appropriate in the public interest or for the protection of investors. An investment company shall be deemed to be registered upon receipt by the Commission of such notification of registration.

(b)   Registration statement; contents.—

Every registered investment company shall file with the Commission, within such reasonable time after registration as the Commission shall fix by rules and regulations, an original and such copies of a registration statement, in such form and containing such of the following information and documents as the Commission shall by rules and regulations prescribe as necessary or appropriate in the public interest or for the protection of investors:

(1)   a recital of the policy of the registrant in respect of each of the following types of activities, such recital consisting in each case of a statement whether the registrant reserves freedom of action to engage in activities of such type, and if such freedom of action is reserved, a statement briefly indicating, insofar as is practicable, the extent to which the registrant intends to engage therein:

(A)   the classification and subclassification, as defined in sections 4 and 5, within which the registrant proposes to operate;

(B)   borrowing money;

(C)   the issuance of senior securities;

(D)   engaging in the business of underwriting securities issued by other persons;

(E)   concentrating investments in a particular industry or group of industries;

(F)   the purchase and sale of real estate and commodities, or either of them;

(G)   making loans to other persons; and

(H)   portfolio turn-over (including a statement showing the aggregate dollar amount of purchases and sales of portfolio securities, other than Government securities, in each of the last three full fiscal years preceding the filing of such registration statement);

(2)   a recital of all investment policies of the registrant, not enumerated in paragraph (1), which are changeable only if authorized by shareholder vote;

(3)   a recital of all policies of the registrant, not enumerated in paragraphs (1) and (2), in respect of matters which the registrant deems matters of fundamental policy;

(4)   the name and address of each affiliated person of the registrant; the name and principal address of every company, other than the registrant, of which each such person is an officer, director, or partner; a brief statement of the business experience for the preceding five years of each officer and director of the registrant; and

(5)   the information and documents which would be required to be filed in order to register under the Securities Act of 1933 and the Securities Exchange Act of 1934 all securities (other than short-term paper) which the registrant has outstanding or proposes to issue.

(c)   Alternative information.—

The Commission shall make provision, by permissive rules and regulations or order, for the filing of the following, or so much of the following as the Commission may designate, in lieu of the information and documents required pursuant to subsection (b):

(1)   copies of the most recent registration statement filed by the registrant under the Securities Act of 1933 and currently effective under such Act, or if the registrant has not filed such a statement, copies of a registration statement filed by the registrant under the Securities Exchange Act of 1934 and currently effective under such Act;

(2)   copies of any reports filed by the registrant pursuant to section 13 or 15(d) of the Securities Exchange Act of 1934; and

(3)   a report containing reasonably current information regarding the matters included in copies filed pursuant to paragraphs (1) and (2), and such further information regarding matters not included in such copies as the Commission is authorized to require under subsection (b).

(d)   Registration of unit investment trusts.—

If the registrant is a unit investment trust substantially all of the assets of which are securities issued by another registered investment company, the Commission is authorized to prescribe for the registrant, by rules and regulations or order, a registration statement which eliminates inappropriate duplication of information contained in the registration statement filed under this section by such other investment company.

(e)   Failure to file registration statement or omissions of material fact.—

If it appears to the Commission that a registered investment company has failed to file the registration statement required by this section or a report required pursuant to section 29(a) or (b), or has filed such a registration statement or report but omitted therefrom material facts required to be stated therein, or has filed such a registration statement or report in violation of section 33(b), the Commission shall notify such company by registered mail or certified mail of the failure to file such registration statement or report, or of the respects in which such registration statement or report appears to be materially incomplete or misleading, as the case may be, and shall fix a date (in no event earlier than thirty days after the mailing of such notice) prior to which such company may file such registration statement or report or correct the same. If such registration statement or report is not filed or corrected within the time so fixed by the Commission or any extension thereof, the Commission, after appropriate notice and opportunity for hearing, and upon such conditions and with such exemptions as it deems appropriate for the protection of investors, may by order suspend the registration of such company until such statement or report is filed or corrected, or may by order revoke such registration, if the evidence establishes—

(1)   that such company has failed to file a registration statement required by this section or a report required pursuant to section 29(a) or (b), or has filed such a registration statement or report but omitted therefrom material facts required to be stated therein, or has filed such a registration statement or report in violation of section 33(b); and

(2)   that such suspension or revocation is in the public interest.

(f)   Cessation of existence as investment company.—

Whenever the Commission, on its own motion or upon application, finds that a registered investment company has ceased to be an investment company, it shall so declare by order and upon the taking effect of such order the registration of such company shall cease to be in effect. If necessary for the protection of investors, an order under this subsection may be made upon appropriate conditions. The Commission's denial of any application under this subsection shall be by order.

Ineligibility of Certain Affiliated Persons and Underwriters

Sec. 9.   (a)   Persons deemed ineligible for service with investment companies, etc.; investment adviser.—

It shall be unlawful for any of the following persons to serve or act in the capacity of employee, officer, director, member of an advisory board, investment adviser, or depositor of any registered investment company, or principal underwriter for any registered open-end company, registered unit investment trust, or registered face-amount certificate company:

(1)   any person who within 10 years has been convicted of any felony or misdemeanor involving the purchase or sale of any security or arising out of such person's conduct as an underwriter, broker,

dealer, investment adviser, municipal securities dealer, government securities broker, government securities dealer, bank, transfer agent, credit rating agency, or entity or person required to be registered under the Commodity Exchange Act, or as an affiliated person, salesman, or employee of any investment company, bank, insurance company, or entity or person required to be registered under the Commodity Exchange Act;

(2)   any person who, by reason of any misconduct, is permanently or temporarily enjoined by order, judgment, or decree of any court of competent jurisdiction from acting as an underwriter, broker, dealer, investment adviser, municipal securities dealer, government securities broker, government securities dealer, bank, transfer agent, credit rating agency, or entity or person required to be registered under the Commodity Exchange Act, or as an affiliated person, salesman, or employee of any investment company, bank, insurance company, or entity or person required to be registered under the Commodity Exchange Act, or from engaging in or continuing any conduct or practice in connection with any such activity or in connection with the purchase or sale of any security; or

(3)   a company any affiliated person of which is ineligible, by reason of paragraph (1) or (2), to serve or act in the foregoing capacities.

For the purposes of paragraphs (1), (2), and (3) of this subsection, the term "investment adviser" shall include an investment adviser as defined in the Investment Advisers Act.

(b)   Certain persons serving investment companies; administrative action of Commission.—

The Commission may, after notice and opportunity for hearing, by order prohibit, conditionally or unconditionally, either permanently or for such period of time as it in its discretion shall deem appropriate in the public interest, any person from serving or acting as an employee, officer, director, member of an advisory board, investment adviser or depositor of, or principal underwriter for, a registered investment company or affiliated person of such investment adviser, depositor, or principal underwriter, if such person—

(1)   has willfully made or caused to be made in any registration statement, application or report filed with the Commission under this Act any statement which was at the time and in the light of the circumstances under which it was made false or misleading with respect to any material fact, or has omitted to state in any such registration statement, application, or report any material fact which was required to be stated therein;

(2)   has willfully violated any provision of the Securities Act of 1933, or of the Securities Exchange Act of 1934, or of the Investment Advisers Act, or of this Act, or of the Commodity Exchange Act, or of any rule or regulation under any of such statutes;

(3)   has willfully aided, abetted, counseled, commanded, induced, or procured the violation by any other person of the Securities Act of 1933, or of the Securities Exchange Act of 1934, or of The Investment Advisers Act, or of this Act, or of the Commodity Exchange Act, or of any rule or regulation under any of such statutes;

(4)   has been found by a foreign financial regulatory authority to have—

(A)   made or caused to be made in any application for registration or report required to be filed with a foreign securities authority, or in any proceeding before a foreign securities authority with respect to registration, any statement that was at the time and in light of the circumstances under which it was made false or misleading with respect to any material fact, or has omitted to state in any application or report to a foreign securities authority any material fact that is required to be stated therein;

(B)   violated any foreign statute or regulation regarding transactions in securities or contracts of sale of a commodity for future delivery traded on or subject to the rules of a contract market or any board of trade; or

(C)   aided, abetted, counseled, commanded, induced, or procured the violation by any other person of any foreign statute or regulation regarding transactions in securities or contracts of sale of a commodity for future delivery traded on or subject to the rules of a contract market or any board of trade;

(5)   within 10 years has been convicted by a foreign court of competent jurisdiction of a crime, however denominated by the laws of the relevant foreign government, that is substantially equivalent to an offense set forth in paragraph (1) of subsection (a); or

(6)   by reason of any misconduct, is temporarily or permanently enjoined by any foreign court of competent jurisdiction from acting in any of the capacities, set forth in paragraph (2) of subsection (a), or a substantially equivalent foreign capacity, or from engaging in or continuing any conduct or practice in connection with any such activity or in connection with the purchase or sale of any security.

(c)   Application of ineligible person for exemption.—

Any person who is ineligible, by reason of subsection (a), to serve or act in the capacities enumerated in that subsection, may file with the Commission an application for an exemption from the provisions of that subsection. The Commission shall by order grant such application, either unconditionally or on an appropriate temporary or other conditional basis, if it is established that the prohibitions of subsection (a), as applied to such person, are unduly or disproportionately severe or that the conduct of such person has been such as not to make it against the public interest or protection of investors to grant such application.

(d)   Money penalties in administrative proceedings.—

(1)   Authority of Commission.—

(A)   In general.—In any proceeding instituted pursuant to subsection (b) against any person, the Commission may impose a civil penalty if it finds, on the record after notice and opportunity for hearing, that such penalty is in the public interest, and that such person—

(i)   has willfully violated any provision of the Securities Act of 1933, the Securities Exchange Act of 1934, the Investment Advisers Act of 1940, or this Act or the rules or regulations thereunder;

(ii)   has willfully aided, abetted, counseled, commanded, induced, or procured such a violation by any other person; or

(iii)   has willfully made or caused to be made in any registration statement, application, or report required to be filed with the Commission under this Act, any statement which was, at the time and in the light of the circumstances under which it was made, false or misleading with respect to any material fact, or has omitted to state in any such registration statement, application, or report any material fact which was required to be stated therein;

(B)   Cease-and-desist proceedings.—In any proceeding instituted pursuant to subsection (f) against any person, the Commission may impose a civil penalty if the Commission finds, on the record, after notice and opportunity for hearing, that such person—

(i)   is violating or has violated any provision of this title, or any rule or regulation issued under this title; or

(ii)   is or was a cause of the violation of any provision of this title, or any rule or regulation issued under this title.

(2)   Maximum amount of penalty.—

(A)   First tier.—

The maximum amount of penalty for each act or omission described in paragraph (1) shall be $5,000 for a natural person or $50,000 for any other person.

(B)   Second tier.—

Notwithstanding subparagraph (A), the maximum amount of penalty for each such act or omission shall be $50,000 for a natural person or $250,000 for any other person if the act or omission described in paragraph (1) involved fraud, deceit, manipulation, or deliberate or reckless disregard of a regulatory requirement.

(C)   Third tier.—

Notwithstanding subparagraphs (A) and (B), the maximum amount of penalty for each such act or omission shall be $100,000 for a natural person or $500,000 for any other person if—

(i) the act or omission described in paragraph (1) involved fraud, deceit, manipulation, or deliberate or reckless disregard of a regulatory requirement; and

(ii) such act or omission directly or indirectly resulted in substantial losses or created a significant risk of substantial losses to other persons or resulted in substantial pecuniary gain to the person who committed the act or omission.

(3) Determination of public interest.—

In considering under this section whether a penalty is in the public interest, the Commission may consider—

(A) whether the act or omission for which such penalty is assessed involved fraud, deceit, manipulation, or deliberate or reckless disregard of a regulatory requirement;

(B) the harm to other persons resulting either directly or indirectly from such act or omission;

(C) the extent to which any person was unjustly enriched, taking into account any restitution made to persons injured by such behavior;

(D) whether such person previously has been found by the Commission, another appropriate regulatory agency, or a self-regulatory organization to have violated the Federal securities laws, State securities laws, or the rules of a self-regulatory organization, has been enjoined by a court of competent jurisdiction from violations of such laws or rules, or has been convicted by a court of competent jurisdiction of violations of such laws or of any felony or misdemeanor described in section 203(e)(2) of the Investment Advisers Act of 1940;

(E) the need to deter such person and other persons from committing such acts or omissions; and

(F) such other matters as justice may require.

(4) Evidence concerning ability to pay.—

In any proceeding in which the Commission may impose a penalty under this section, a respondent may present evidence of the respondent's ability to pay such penalty. The Commission may, in its discretion, consider such evidence in determining whether such penalty is in the public interest. Such evidence may relate to the extent of such person's ability to continue in business and the collectability of a penalty, taking into account any other claims of the United States or third parties upon such person's assets and the amount of such person's assets.

(e) Authority to enter an order requiring an accounting and disgorgement.—

In any proceeding in which the Commission may impose a penalty under this section, the Commission may enter an order requiring accounting and disgorgement, including reasonable interest. The Commission is authorized to adopt rules, regulations, and orders concerning payments to investors, rates of interest, periods of accrual, and such other matters as it deems appropriate to implement this subsection.

(f) Cease-and-desist proceedings.—

(1) Authority of Commission.—

If the Commission finds, after notice and opportunity for hearing, that any person is violating, has violated, or is about to violate any provision of this Act, or any rule or regulation thereunder, the Commission may publish its findings and enter an order requiring such person, and any other person that is, was, or would be a cause of the violation, due to an act or omission the person knew or should have known would contribute to such violation, to cease and desist from committing or causing such violation and any future violation of the same provision, rule, or regulation. Such order may, in addition to requiring a person to cease and desist from committing or causing a violation, require such person to comply, or to take steps to effect compliance, with such provision, rule, or regulation, upon such terms and conditions and within such time as the Commission may specify in such order. Any such order may, as the Commission deems appropriate, require future compliance or steps to effect future compliance, either permanently or for such period of time as the Commission may specify, with such provision, rule, or regulation with respect to any security, any issuer, or any other person.

(2) Hearing.—

The notice instituting proceedings pursuant to paragraph (1) shall fix a hearing date not earlier than 30 days not later than 60 days after service of the notice unless an earlier or a later date is set by the Commission with the consent of any respondent so served.

(3) Temporary order.—

(A) In general.—

Whenever the Commission determines that the alleged violation or threatened violation specified in the notice instituting proceedings pursuant to paragraph (1), or the continuation thereof, is likely to result in significant dissipation or conversion of assets, significant harm to investors, or substantial harm to the public interest, including, but not limited to, losses to the Securities Investor Protection Corporation, prior to the completion of the proceeding, the Commission may enter a temporary order requiring the respondent to cease and desist from the violation or threatened violation and to take such action to prevent the violation or threatened violation and to prevent dissipation or conversion of assets, significant harm to investors, or substantial harm to the public interest as the Commission deems appropriate pending completion of such proceedings. Such an order shall be entered only after notice and opportunity for a hearing, unless the Commission, notwithstanding section 39(a) of this title, determines that notice and hearing prior to entry would be impracticable or contrary to the public interest. A temporary order shall become effective upon service upon the respondent and, unless set aside, limited, or suspended by the Commission or a court of competent jurisdiction, shall remain effective and enforceable pending the completion of the proceedings.

(B) Applicability.—

This paragraph shall apply only to a respondent that acts, or, at the time of the alleged misconduct acted, as a broker, dealer, investment adviser, investment company, municipal securities dealer, government securities broker, government securities dealer, or transfer agent, or is, or was at the time of the alleged misconduct, an associated person of, or a person seeking to become associated with, any of the foregoing.

(4) Review of temporary orders.—

(A) Commission review.—

At any time after the respondent has been served with a temporary cease-and-desist order pursuant to paragraph (3), the respondent may apply to the Commission to have the order set aside, limited, or suspended. If the respondent has been served with a temporary cease-and-desist order entered without a prior Commission hearing, the respondent may, within 10 days after the date on which the order was served, request a hearing on such application and the Commission shall hold a hearing and render a decision on such application at the earliest possible time.

(B) Judicial review.—

(i) 10 days after the date the respondent was served with a temporary cease-and-desist order entered with a prior Commission hearing, or

(ii) 10 days after the Commission renders a decision on an application and hearing under subparagraph (A), with respect to any temporary cease-and-desist order entered without a prior Commission hearing,

the respondent may apply to the United States district court for the district in which the respondent resides or has its principal place of business, or for the District of Columbia, for an order setting aside, limiting, or suspending the effectiveness or enforcement of the order, and the court shall have jurisdiction to enter such an order. A respondent served with a temporary cease-and-desist order entered without a prior Commission hearing may not apply to the court except after hearing and decision by the Commission on the respondent's application under subparagraph (A) of this paragraph.

(C)   No automatic stay of temporary order.—

The commencement of proceedings under subparagraph (B) of this paragraph shall not, unless specifically ordered by the court, operate as a stay of the Commission's order.

(D)   Exclusive review.—

Section 42 of this Act shall not apply to a temporary order entered pursuant to this section.

(5)   Authority to enter an order requiring an accounting and disgorgement.—

In any cease-and-desist proceeding under subsection (f)(1), the Commission may enter an order requiring accounting and disgorgement, including reasonable interest. The Commission is authorized to adopt rules, regulations, and orders concerning payments to investors, rates of interest, periods of accrual, and such other matters as it deems appropriate to implement this subsection.

(g)   Corporate or other trustees performing functions of investment advisors.—

For the purposes of this section, the term "investment adviser" includes a corporate or other trustee performing the functions of an investment adviser.

Affiliations of Directors

Sec. 10.   (a)   Interested persons of company who may serve on board of directors.—

No registered investment company shall have a board of directors more than 60 percentum of the members of which are persons who are interested persons of such registered company.

(b)   Employment and use of directors, officers, etc., as regular broker, principal underwriter, or investment banker.—

No registered investment company shall—

(1)   employ as regular broker any director, officer, or employee of such registered company, or any person of which any such director, officer, or employee is an affiliated person, unless a majority of the board of directors of such registered company shall be persons who are not such brokers or affiliated persons of any of such brokers;

(2)   use as a principal underwriter of securities issued by it any director, officer, or employee of such registered company or any person of which any such director, officer, or employee is an interested person, unless a majority of the board of directors of such registered company shall be persons who are not such principal underwriters or interested persons of any of such principal underwriters; or

(3)   have as director, officer, or employee any investment banker, or any affiliated person of an investment banker, unless a majority of the board of directors of such registered company shall be persons who are not investment bankers or affiliated persons of any investment banker. For the purposes of this paragraph, a person shall not be deemed an affiliated person of an investment banker solely by reason of the fact that he is an affiliated person of a company of the character described in section 12(d)(3)(A) and (B).

(c)   Officers, directors, or employees of one bank as majority of board of directors of company; exceptions.—

No registered investment company shall have a majority of its board of directors consisting of persons who are officers, directors, or employees of any one bank (together with its affiliates and subsidiaries) or any one bank holding company (together with its affiliates and subsidiaries) (as such terms is defined in section 2 of the Bank Holding Company Act of 1956) or any one savings and loan holding company, together with its affiliates and subsidiaries (as such terms are defined in section 10 of the Home Owners' Loan Act), except that, if on March 15, 1940, any registered investment company had a majority of its directors consisting of persons who are directors, officers, or employees of any one bank, such company may continue to have the same percentage of its board of directors consisting of persons who are directors, officers, or employees of such bank.

(d)   Exception to limitation of number of interested persons who may serve on board of directors.—

Notwithstanding subsections (a) and (b)(2) of this section, a registered investment company may have a board of directors all the members of which, except one, are interested persons of the investment adviser of such company, or are officers or employees of such company, if—

(1)   such investment company is an open-end company;

(2)   such investment adviser is registered under the Investment Advisers Act and is engaged principally in the business of rendering investment supervisory services as defined in title II;

(3)   no sales load is charged on securities issued by such investment company;

(4)   any premium over net asset value charged by such company upon the issuance of any such security, plus any discount from net asset value charged on redemption thereof, shall not in the aggregate exceed 2 per centum;

(5)   no sales or promotion expenses are incurred by such registered company; but expenses incurred in complying with laws regulating the issue or sale of securities shall not be deemed sales or promotion expenses;

(6)   such investment adviser is the only investment adviser to such investment company, and such investment adviser does not receive a management fee exceeding 1 per centum per annum of the value of such company's net assets averaged over the year or taken as of a definite date or dates within the year;

(7)   all executive salaries and executive expenses and office rent of such investment company are paid by such investment adviser; and

(8)   such investment company has only one class of securities outstanding, each unit of which has equal voting rights with every other unit.

(e)   Death, disqualification, or resignation of directors as suspension of limitation provisions.—

If by reason of the death, disqualification, or bona fide resignation of any director or directors, the requirements of the foregoing provisions of this section or of section 15(f)(1) in respect of directors shall not be met by a registered investment company, the operation of such provisions shall be suspended as to such registered company—

(1)   for a period of thirty days if the vacancy or vacancies may be filled by action of the board of directors;

(2)   for a period of sixty days if a vote of stockholders is required to fill the vacancy or vacancies; or

(3)   for such longer period as the Commission may prescribe, by rules and regulations upon its own motion or by order upon application, as not inconsistent with the protection of investors.

(f)   Officer, director, etc., of company acting as principal underwriter of security acquired by company.—

No registered investment company shall knowingly purchase or otherwise acquire, during the existence of any underwriting or selling syndicate, any security (except a security of which such company is the issuer) a principal underwriter of which is an officer, director, member of an advisory board, investment adviser, or employee of such registered company, or is a person (other than a company of the character described in section 12(d)(3)(A) and (B)) of which any such officer, director, member of an advisory board, investment adviser, or employee is an affiliated person, unless in acquiring such security such registered company is itself acting as a principal underwriter for the issuer. The Commission, by rules and regulations upon its own motion or by order upon application, may conditionally or unconditionally exempt any transaction or classes of transactions from any of the provisions of this subsection, if and to the extent that such exemption is consistent with the protection of investors.

(g)   Advisory boards; restrictions on membership.—

In the case of a registered investment company which has an advisory board, such board, as a distinct entity, shall be subject to the same restrictions as to its membership as are imposed upon a board of directors by this section.

(h)   Application of section to unincorporated registered management companies.—

In the case of a registered management company which is an unincorporated company not having a board of directors, the provisions of this section shall apply as follows:

(1)   the provisions of subsection (a), as modified by subsection (e), shall apply to the board of directors of the depositor of such company;

(2)   the provisions of subsections (b) and (c), as modified by subsection (e), shall apply to the board of directors of the depositor and of every investment adviser of such company; and

(3)   the provisions of subsection (f) shall apply to purchases and other acquisitions for the account of such company of securities a principal underwriter of which is the depositor or an investment adviser of such company, or an affiliated person of such depositor or investment adviser.

Offers of Exchange

Sec. 11.   (a)   Approval by Commission for exchanges of securities on basis other than relative net asset value.—

It shall be unlawful for any registered open-end company or any principal underwriter for such a company to make or cause to be made an offer to the holder of a security of such company or of any other open-end investment company to exchange his security for a security in the same or another such company on any basis other than the relative net asset values of the respective securities to be exchanged, unless the terms of the offer have first been submitted to and approved by the Commission or are in accordance with such rules and regulations as the Commission may have prescribed in respect of such offers which are in effect at the time such offer is made. For the purposes of this section,

(A)   an offer by a principal underwriter means an offer communicated to holders of securities of a class or series but does not include an offer made by such principal underwriter to an individual investor in the course of a retail business conducted by such principal underwriter, and

(B)   the net asset value means the net asset value which is in effect for the purpose of determining the price at which the securities, or class or series of securities involved, are offered for sale to the public either (1) at the time of the receipt by the offeror of the acceptance of the offer or (2) at such later times as is specified in the offer.

(b)   Application of section to offers pursuant to plan of reorganization.—

The provisions of this section shall not apply to any offer made pursuant to any plan of reorganization, which is submitted to and requires the approval of the holders of at least a majority of the outstanding shares of the class or series to which the security owned by the offeree belongs.

(c)   Application of section to specific exchange offers.—

The provisions of subsection (a) shall be applicable, irrespective of the basis of exchange,

(1)   to any offer of exchange of any security of a registered open-end company for a security of a registered unit investment trust or registered face-amount certificate company; and

(2)   to any type of offer of exchange of the securities of registered unit investment trusts or registered face-amount certificate companies for the securities of any other investment company.

Functions and Activities of Investment Companies

Sec. 12. (a) Purchase of securities on margin; joint trading accounts; short sales of securities; exceptions.—

It shall be unlawful for any registered investment company, in contravention of such rules and regulations or orders as the Commission may prescribe as necessary or appropriate in the public interest or for the protection of investors—

(1) to purchase any security on margin except such short-term credits as are necessary for the clearance of transactions;

(2) to participate on a joint or a joint and several basis in any trading account in securities, except in connection with an underwriting in which such registered company is a participant; or

(3) to effect a short sale of any security, except in connection with an underwriting in which such registered company is a participant.

(b) Distribution by investment company of securities of which it is issuer.—

It shall be unlawful for any registered open-end company (other than a company complying with the provisions of section 10(d)) to act as a distributor of securities of which it is the issuer, except through an underwriter, in contravention of such rules and regulations as the Commission may prescribe as necessary or appropriate in the public interest or for the protection of investors.

(c) Limitations on commitments as underwriter.—

It shall be unlawful for any registered diversified company to make any commitment as underwriter, if immediately thereafter the amount of its outstanding underwriting commitments, plus the value of its investments in securities of issuers (other than investment companies) of which it owns more than 10 per centum of the outstanding voting securities, exceeds 25 per centum of the value of its total assets.

(d) Limitations on acquisition by investment companies of securities of other specific businesses.—

(1)(A) It shall be unlawful for any registered investment company (the "acquiring company") and any company or companies controlled by such acquiring company to purchase or otherwise acquire any security issued by any other investment company (the "acquired company"), and for any investment company (the "acquiring company") and any company or companies controlled by such acquiring company to purchase or otherwise acquire any security issued by any registered investment company (the "acquired company"), if the acquiring company and any company or companies controlled by it immediately after such purchase or acquisition own in the aggregate—

(i) more than 3 per centum of the total outstanding voting stock of the acquired company;

(ii) securities issued by the acquired company having an aggregate value in excess of 5 per centum of the value of the total assets of the acquiring company; or

(iii) securities issued by the acquired company and all other investment companies (other than treasury stock of the acquiring company) having an aggregate value in excess of 10 per centum of the value of the total assets of the acquiring company.

(B) It shall be unlawful for any registered open-end investment company (the "acquired company"), any principal underwriter therefor, or any broker or dealer registered under the Securities Exchange Act of 1934, knowingly to sell or otherwise dispose of any security issued by the acquired company to any other investment company (the "acquiring company") or any company or companies controlled by the acquiring company, if immediately after such sale or disposition—

(i) more than 3 per centum of the total outstanding voting stock of the acquired company is owned by the acquiring company and any company or companies controlled by it; or

(ii) more than 10 per centum of the total outstanding voting stock of the acquired company is owned by the acquiring company and other investment companies and companies controlled by them.

(C) It shall be unlawful for any investment company (the "acquiring company") and any company or companies controlled by the acquiring company to purchase or otherwise acquire any security issued by a registered closed-end investment company, if immediately after such purchase or acquisition the acquiring company, other investment companies having the same investment adviser, and companies controlled by such investment companies, own more than 10 per centum of the total outstanding voting stock of such closed-end company.

(D) The provisions of this paragraph shall not apply to a security received as a dividend or as a result of an offer of exchange approved pursuant to section 11 or of a plan of reorganization of any company (other than a plan devised for the purpose of evading the foregoing provisions).

(E) The provisions of this paragraph shall not apply to a security (or securities) purchased or acquired by an investment company if—

(i) the depositor of, or principal underwriter for, such investment company is a broker or dealer registered under the Securities Exchange Act of 1934, or a person controlled by such broker or dealer;

(ii) such security is the only investment security held by such investment company (or such securities are the only investment securities held by such investment company, if such investment company is a registered unit investment trust that issues two or more classes or series of securities, each of which provides for the accumulation of shares of a different investment company); and

(iii) the purchase or acquisition is made pursuant to an arrangement with the issuer of, or principal underwriter for the issuer of, the security whereby such investment company is obligated—

(aa) either to seek instructions from its security holders with regard to the voting of all proxies with respect to such security and to vote such proxies only in accordance with such instructions, or to vote the shares held by it in the same proportion as the vote of all other holders of such security, and

(bb) in the event that such investment company is not a registered investment company, to refrain from substituting such security unless the Commission shall have approved such substitution in the manner provided in section 26 of this Act.

(F) The provisions of this paragraph shall not apply to securities purchased or otherwise acquired by a registered investment company if—

(i) immediately after such purchase or acquisition not more than 3 per centum of the total outstanding stock of such issuer is owned by such registered investment company and all affiliated persons of such registered investment company; and

(ii) such registered investment company has not offered or sold after January 1, 1971, and is not proposing to offer or sell any security issued by it through a principal underwriter or otherwise at a public offering price which includes a sales load of more than $1^{1}/_{2}$ per centum.

No issuer of any security purchased or acquired by a registered investment company pursuant to this subparagraph shall be obligated to redeem such security in an amount exceeding 1 per centum of such issuer's total outstanding securities during any period of less than thirty days. Such investment company shall exercise voting rights by proxy or otherwise with respect to any security purchased or acquired pursuant to this subparagraph in the manner prescribed by subparagraph (E) of this subsection.

(G)(i) This paragraph does not apply to securities of a registered open-end investment company or a registered unit investment trust (hereafter in this subparagraph referred to as the "acquired company") purchased or otherwise acquired by a registered open-end investment company or a registered unit investment trust (hereafter in this subparagraph referred to as the "acquiring company") if—

(I)   the acquired company and the acquiring company are part of the same group of investment companies;

(II)   the securities of the acquired company, securities of other registered open-end investment companies and registered unit investment trusts that are part of the same group of investment companies, Government securities, and short-term paper are the only investments held by the acquiring company;

(III)   with respect to—

(aa)   securities of the acquired company, the acquiring company does not pay and is not assessed any charges or fees for distribution-related activities, unless the acquiring company does not charge a sales load or other fees or charges for distribution-related activities; or

(bb)   securities of the acquiring company, any sales loads and other distribution-related fees charged, when aggregated with any sales load and distribution-related fees paid by the acquiring company with respect to securities of the acquired company, are not excessive under rules adopted pursuant to section 22(b) or section 22(c) by a securities association registered under section 15A of the Securities Exchange Act of 1934, or the Commission;

(IV)   the acquired company has a policy that prohibits it from acquiring any securities of registered open-end investment companies or registered unit investment trusts in reliance on this subparagraph or subparagraph (F); and

(V)   such acquisition is not in contravention of such rules and regulations as the Commission may from time to time prescribe with respect to acquisitions in accordance with this subparagraph, as necessary and appropriate for the protection of investors.

(ii)   For purposes of this subparagraph, the term "group of investment companies" means any 2 or more registered investment companies that hold themselves out to investors as related companies for purposes of investment and investor services.

(H)   For the purposes of this paragraph the value of an investment company's total assets shall be computed as of the time of a purchase or acquisition or as closely thereto as is reasonably possible.

(I)   In any action brought to enforce the provisions of this paragraph the Commission may join as a party the issuer of any security purchased or otherwise acquired in violation of this paragraph, and the court may issue any order with respect to such issuer as may be necessary or appropriate for the enforcement of the provisions of this paragraph.

(J)   The Commission, by rule or regulation, upon its own motion or by order upon application, may conditionally or unconditionally exempt any person, security, or transaction, or any class or classes of persons, securities, or transactions from any provision of this paragraph, if and to the extent that such exemption is consistent with the public interest and the protection of investors.

(2)   It shall be unlawful for any registered investment company and any company or companies controlled by such registered investment company to purchase or otherwise acquire any security (except a security received as a dividend or as a result of a plan of reorganization of any company, other than a plan devised for the purpose of evading the provisions of this paragraph) issued by any insurance company of which such registered investment company and any company or companies controlled by such registered company do not, at the time of such purchase or acquisition, own in the aggregate at least 25 per centum of the total outstanding voting stock, if such registered company and any company or companies controlled by it own in the aggregate, or as a result of such purchase or acquisition will own in the aggregate, more than 10 per centum of the total outstanding voting stock of such insurance company.

(3)   It shall be unlawful for any registered investment company and any company or companies controlled by such registered investment company to purchase or otherwise acquire any security issued by or any other interest in the business of any person who is a broker, a dealer, is engaged in the business of underwriting, or is either an investment adviser of an investment company or an investment adviser registered under the Investment Advisers Act, unless

(A)   such person is a corporation all of the outstanding securities of which (other than short-term paper, securities representing bank loans, and directors' qualifying shares) are, or after such acquisition will be, owned by one or more registered investment companies; and

(B)   such person is primarily engaged in the business of underwriting and distributing securities issued by other persons, selling securities to customers, or any one or more of such or related activities, and the gross income of such person normally is derived principally from such business or related activities.

(e)   Acquisition of securities issued by corporations in business of underwriting, furnishing capital to industry, etc.—

Notwithstanding any provisions of this Act, any registered investment company may hereafter purchase or otherwise acquire any security issued by any one corporation engaged or proposing to engage in the business of underwriting, furnishing capital to industry, financing promotional enterprises, purchasing securities of issuers for which no ready market is in existence, and reorganizing companies or similar activities; provided—

(1)   That the securities issued by such corporation (other than short-term paper and securities representing bank loans) shall consist solely of one class of common stock and shall have been originally issued or sold for investment to registered investment companies only;

(2)   That the aggregate cost of the securities of such corporation purchased by such registered investment company does not exceed 5 per centum of the value of the total assets of such registered company at the time of any purchase or acquisition of such securities; and

(3)   That the aggregate paid-in capital and surplus of such corporation does not exceed $100,000,000.

For the purpose of paragraph (1) of section 5(b) any investment in any such corporation shall be deemed to be an investment in an investment company.

(f)   Organization and ownership by one registered face-amount certificate company of all or part of capital stock of not more than two other face-amount certificate companies; limitations.—

Notwithstanding any provisions of this Act, any registered face-amount certificate company may organize not more than two face-amount certificate companies and acquire and own all or any part of the capital stock thereof only if such stock is acquired and held for investment: *Provided,* That the aggregate cost to such registered company of all such stock so acquired shall not exceed six times the amount of the minimum capital stock requirement provided in subdivision (1) of subsection (a) of section 28 for a face-amount company organized on or after March 15, 1940: *And provided further,* That the aggregate cost to such registered company of all such capital stock issued by face-amount certificate companies organized or otherwise created under laws other than the laws of the United States or any State thereof shall not exceed twice the amount of the minimum capital stock requirement provided in subdivision (1) of subsection (a) of section 28 for a company organized on or after March 15, 1940. Nothing contained in this subsection shall be deemed to prevent the sale of any such stock to any other person if the original purchase was made by such registered face-amount certificate company in good faith for investment and not for resale.

(g)   Exceptions to limitation on ownership by investment company of securities of insurance company.—

Notwithstanding the provisions of this section any registered investment company and any company or companies controlled by such registered company may purchase or otherwise acquire from another investment company or any company or companies controlled by such registered company more than 10 per centum of the total outstanding voting stock of any insurance company owned by any such company or companies, or may acquire the securities of any insurance company if the Commission by order determines that such acquisition is in the public interest because the financial condition of such insurance company will be improved as a result of such acquisition or any plan contemplated as a result thereof. This section shall not be deemed to prohibit the promotion of a new insurance company or the acquisition of the securities of any newly created insurance company by a registered investment company, alone or with other persons. Nothing contained in this section shall in any way affect or derogate from the powers of any insurance commissioner or similar official or agency of the United States or any State, or to affect the right under State law of any insurance company to acquire securities of any other insurance company or insurance companies.

Changes in Investment Policy

Sec. 13.   (a)   No registered investment company shall, unless authorized by the vote of a majority of its outstanding voting securities—

(1)   change its subclassification as defined in section 5(a)(1) and (2) of this Act or its subclassification from a diversified to a non-diversified company;

(2)   borrow money, issue senior securities, underwrite securities issued by other persons, purchase or sell real estate or commodities or make loans to other persons, except in each case in accordance with the recitals of policy contained in its registration statement in respect thereto;

(3)   deviate from its policy in respect of concentration of investments in any particular industry or group of industries as recited in its registration statement, deviate from any investment policy which is changeable only if authorized by shareholder vote, or deviate from any policy recited in its registration statement pursuant to section 8(b)(3);

(4)   change the nature of its business so as to cease to be an investment company.

(b)   In the case of a common-law trust of the character described in section 16(c), either written approval by holders of a majority of the outstanding shares of beneficial interest or the vote of a majority of such outstanding shares cast in person or by proxy at a meeting called for the purpose shall for the purposes of subsection (a) be deemed the equivalent of the vote of a majority of the outstanding voting securities, and the provisions of paragraph (42) of section 2(a) as to a majority shall be applicable to the votes cast at such a meeting.

(c)   Limitations on actions.—

(1)   In general.—

Notwithstanding any other provision of Federal or State law, no person may bring any civil, criminal, or administrative action against any registered investment company, or any employee, officer, director, or investment adviser thereof, based solely upon the investment company divesting from, or avoiding interest in, securities issued by persons that the investment company determines, using credible information available to the public—

(A)   conduct or have direct investments in business operations in Sudan described in section 3(d) of the Sudan Accountability and Divestment Act of 2007 (50 U.S.C. § 1701 note); or

(B)   engage in investment activities in Iran described in § 8532(c) of Title 22.

(2)   Applicability.—

(A)   Rule of construction.—

Paragraph (1) does not prevent a person from bringing an action based on a breach of a fiduciary duty owed to that person with respect to a divestment or non-investment decision, other than as described in paragraph (1).

(B)   Disclosures.—

Paragraph (1) shall not apply to a registered investment company, or any employee, officer, director, or investment advisor thereof, unless the investment company makes disclosures in accordance with regulations prescribed by the Commission.

(3)   Person defined.—

For purposes of this subsection, the term "person" includes the Federal Government and any State or political subdivision of a State.

Size of Investment Companies

Sec. 14.   (a)   Public offerings.—

No registered investment company organized after the date of enactment of this Act, and no principal underwriter for such a company, shall make a public offering of securities of which such company is the issuer, unless—

     (1)   such company has a net worth of at least $100,000;

     (2)   such company has previously made a public offering of its securities, and at the time of such offering had a net worth of at least $100,000; or

     (3)   provision is made in connection with and as a condition of the registration of such securities under the Securities Act of 1933 which in the opinion of the Commission adequately insures

        (A)   that after the effective date of such registration statement such company will not issue any security or receive any proceeds of any subscription for any security until firm agreements have been made with such company by not more than twenty-five responsible persons to purchase from it securities to be issued by it for an aggregate net amount which plus the then net worth of the company, if any, will equal at least $100,000;

        (B)   that said aggregate net amount will be paid in to such company before any subscriptions for such securities will be accepted from any persons in excess of twenty-five;

        (C)   that arrangements will be made whereby any proceeds so paid in, as well as any sales load, will be refunded to any subscriber on demand without any deduction, in the event that the net proceeds so received by the company do not result in the company having a net worth of at least $100,000 within ninety days after such registration statement becomes effective.

At any time after the occurrence of the event specified in clause (C) of paragraph (3) of this subsection the Commission may issue a stop order suspending the effectiveness of the registration statement of such securities under the Securities Act of 1933 and may suspend or revoke the registration of such company under this Act.

     (b)   Study on effects of size.—

The Commission is authorized, at such times as it deems that any substantial further increase in size of investment companies creates any problem involving the protection of investors or the public interest, to make a study and investigation of the effects of size on the investment policy of investment companies and on security markets, on concentration of control of wealth and industry, and on companies in which investment companies are interested, and from time to time to report the results of its studies and investigations and its recommendations to the Congress.

Investment Advisory and Underwriting Contracts

Sec. 15.   (a)   Written contract to serve or act as investment adviser; contents.—

It shall be unlawful for any person to serve or act as investment adviser of a registered investment company, except pursuant to a written contract, which contract, whether with such registered company or with an investment adviser of such registered company, has been approved by the vote of a majority of the outstanding voting securities of such registered company, and—

     (1)   precisely describes all compensation to be paid thereunder;

     (2)   shall continue in effect for a period more than two years from the date of its execution, only so long as such continuance is specifically approved at least annually by the board of directors or by vote of a majority of the outstanding voting securities of such company;

     (3)   provides, in substance, that it may be terminated at any time, without the payment of any penalty, by the board of directors of such registered company or by vote of a majority of the outstanding voting securities of such company on not more than sixty days' written notice to the investment adviser; and

(4) provides, in substance, for its automatic termination in the event of its assignment.

(b) Written contract with company for sale by principal underwriter of security of which company is issuer; contents.—

It shall be unlawful for any principal underwriter for a registered open-end company to offer for sale, sell, or deliver after sale any security of which such company is the issuer, except pursuant to a written contract with such company, which contract—

(1) shall continue in effect for a period more than two years from the date of its execution, only so long as such continuance is specifically approved at least annually by the board of directors or by vote of a majority of the outstanding voting securities of such company; and

(2) provides, in substance, for its automatic termination in the event of its assignment.

(c) Approval of contract to undertake service as investment adviser or principal underwriter by majority of noninterested directors.—

In addition to the requirements of subsection (a) and (b) of this section, it shall be unlawful for any registered investment company having a board of directors to enter into, renew, or perform any contract or agreement, written or oral, whereby a person undertakes regularly to serve or act as investment adviser of or principal underwriter for such company unless the terms of such contract or agreement and any renewal thereof have been approved by the vote of a majority of directors, who are not parties to such contact or agreement or interested persons of any such party, cast in person at a meeting called for the purpose of voting on such approval. It shall be the duty of the directors of a registered investment company to request and evaluate, and the duty of an investment adviser to such company to furnish, such information as may reasonably be necessary to evaluate the terms of any contract whereby a person undertakes regularly to serve or act as investment adviser of such company. It shall be unlawful for the directors of a registered investment company, in connection with their evaluation of the terms of any contract whereby a person undertakes regularly to serve or act as investment adviser of such company, to take into account the purchase price or other consideration any person may have paid in connection with a transaction of the type referred to in paragraph (1), (3), or (4) of subsection (f).

(d) Equivalent of vote of majority of outstanding voting securities in case of common-law trust.—

In the case of a common-law trust of the character described in section 16(c), either written approval by holders of a majority of the outstanding shares of beneficial interest or the vote of a majority of such outstanding shares cast in person or by proxy at a meeting called for the purpose shall for the purposes of this section be deemed the equivalent of the vote of a majority of the outstanding voting securities, and the provisions of paragraph (42) of section 2(a) as to a majority shall be applicable to the vote cast at such a meeting.

(e) Exemption of advisory boards or members from provisions of this section.—

Nothing contained in this section shall be deemed to require or contemplate any action by an advisory board of any registered company or by any of the members of such a board.

(f) Receipt of benefits by investment adviser from sale of securities or other interest in such investment adviser resulting in assignment of investment advisory contract.—

(1) An investment adviser, or a corporate trustee performing the functions of an investment adviser, of a registered investment company or an affiliated person of such investment adviser or corporate trustee may receive any amount or benefit in connection with a sale of securities of, or a sale of any other interest in, such investment adviser or corporate trustee which results in an assignment of an investment advisory contract with such company or the change in control of or identity of such corporate trustee, if—

(A) for a period of three years after the time of such action, at least 75 percentum of the members of the board of directors of such registered company or such corporate trustee (or successor thereto, by reorganization or otherwise) are not

(i) interested persons of the investment adviser of such company or such corporate trustee, or

(ii)   interested persons of the predecessor investment adviser or such corporate trustee; and

(B)   there is not imposed an unfair burden on such company as a result of such transactions or any express or implied terms, conditions, or understandings applicable thereto.

(2)(A)   For the purpose of paragraph (1)(A) of this subsection, interested persons of a corporate trustee shall be determined in accordance with section 2(a)(19)(B): *Provided,* That no person shall be deemed to be an interested person of a corporate trustee solely by reason of

(i)   his being a member of its board of directors or advisory board or

(ii)   his membership in the immediate family of any person specified in clause (i) of this subparagraph.

(B)   For the purpose of paragraph (1)(B) of this subsection, an unfair burden on a registered investment company includes any arrangement, during the two-year period after the date on which any such transaction occurs, whereby the investment adviser or corporate trustee or predecessor or successor investment advisers or corporate trustee or any interested person of any such adviser or any such corporate trustee receives or is entitled to receive any compensation directly or indirectly

(i)   from any person in connection with the purchase or sale of securities or other property to, from, or on behalf of such company, other than bona fide ordinary compensation as principal underwriter for such company, or

(ii)   from such company or its security holders for other than bona fide investment advisory or other services.

(3)   If—

(A)   an assignment of an investment advisory contract with a registered investment company results in a successor investment adviser to such company, or if there is a change in control of or identity of a corporate trustee of a registered investment company, and such adviser or trustee is then an investment adviser or corporate trustee with respect to other assets substantially greater in amount than the amount of assets of such company, or

(B)   as a result of a merger of, or a sale of substantially all the assets by, a registered investment company with or to another registered investment company with assets substantially greater in amount, a transaction occurs which would be subject to paragraph (1)(A) of this subsection,

such discrepancy in size of assets shall be considered by the Commission in determining whether or to what extent an application under section 6(c) for exemption from the provisions of paragraph (1)(A) should be granted.

(4)   Paragraph (1)(A) of this subsection shall not apply to a transaction in which a controlling block of outstanding voting securities of an investment adviser to a registered investment company or of a corporate trustee performing the functions of an investment adviser to a registered investment company is—

(A)   distributed to the public and in which there is, in fact, no change in the identity of the persons who control such investment adviser or corporate trustee, or

(B)   transferred to the investment adviser or the corporate trustee, or an affiliated person or persons of such investment adviser or corporate trustee, or is transferred from the investment adviser or corporate trustee to an affiliated person or persons of the investment adviser or corporate trustee: *Provided,* That (i) each transferee (other than such adviser or trustee) is a natural person and (ii) the transferees (other than such adviser or trustee) owned in the aggregate more than 25 per centum of such voting securities for a period of at least six months prior to such transfer.

Changes in Board of Directors; Provisions Relative to Strict Trusts

Sec. 16. (a)   Election of directors.—

No person shall serve as a director of a registered investment company unless elected to that office by the holders of the outstanding voting securities of such company, at an annual or a special meeting duly called for that purpose; except that vacancies occurring between such meetings may be filled in any otherwise legal manner if immediately after filling any such vacancy at least two-thirds of the directors then holding office shall have been elected to such office by the holders of the outstanding voting securities of the company at such an annual or special meeting. In the event that at any time less than a majority of the directors of such company holding office at that time were so elected by the holders of the outstanding voting securities, the board of directors or proper officer of such company shall forthwith cause to be held as promptly as possible and in any event within sixty days a meeting of such holders for the purpose of electing directors to fill any existing vacancies in the board of directors unless the Commission shall by order extend such period. The foregoing provisions of this subsection shall not apply to members of an advisory board.

Nothing herein shall, however, preclude a registered investment company from dividing its directors into classes if its charter, certificate of incorporation, articles of association, by-laws, trust indenture, or other instrument or the law under which it is organized, so provides and prescribes the tenure of office of the several classes: *Provided,* That no class shall be elected for a shorter period than one year or for a longer period than five years and the term of office of at least one class shall expire each year.

(b)   Term vacancies.—

Any vacancy on the board of directors of a registered investment company which occurs in connection with compliance with section 15(f)(1)(A) and which must be filled by a person who is not an interested person of either party to a transaction subject to section 15(f)(1)(A) shall be filled only by a person

(1)   who has been selected and proposed for election by a majority of the directors of such company who are not such interested persons, and

(2)   who has been elected by the holders of the outstanding voting securities of such company, except that in the case of the death, disqualification, or bona fide resignation of a director selected and elected pursuant to clauses (1) and (2) of this subsection (b), the vacancy created thereby may be filled as provided in subsection (a).

(c)   Trustees of common-law trusts.—

The foregoing provisions of this section shall not apply to a common-law trust existing on the date of enactment of this title under an indenture of trust which does not provide for the election of trustees by the shareholders. No natural person shall serve as trustee of such a trust, which is registered as an investment company, after the holders of record of not less than two-thirds of the outstanding shares of beneficial interest in such trust have declared that he be removed from that office either by declaration in writing filed with the custodian of the securities of the trust or by votes cast in person or by proxy at a meeting called for the purpose. Solicitation of such a declaration shall be deemed a solicitation of a proxy within the meaning of section 20(a).

The trustees of such a trust shall promptly call a meeting of shareholders for the purpose of voting upon the question of removal of any such trustee or trustees when requested in writing so to do by the record holders of not less than 10 per centum of the outstanding shares.

Whenever ten or more shareholders of record who have been such for at least six months preceding the date of application, and who hold in the aggregate either shares having a net asset value of at least $25,000 or at least 1 per centum of the outstanding shares, whichever is less, shall apply to the trustees in writing, stating that they wish to communicate with other shareholders with a view to obtaining signatures to a request for a meeting pursuant to this subsection (c) and accompanied by a form of communication and request which they wish to transmit, the trustees shall within five business days after receipt of such application either—

(1)   afford to such applicants access to a list of the names and addresses of all shareholders as recorded on the books of the trust; or

(2)   inform such applicants as to the approximate number of shareholders of record, and the approximate cost of mailing to them the proposed communication and form of request.

If the trustees elect to follow the course specified in paragraph (2) of this subsection (b) the trustees, upon the written request of such applicants, accompanied by a tender of the material to be mailed and of the reasonable expenses of mailing, shall, with reasonable promptness, mail such material to all shareholders of record at their addresses as recorded on the books, unless within five business days after such tender the trustees shall mail to such applicants and file with the Commission, together with a copy of the material to be mailed, a written statement signed by at least a majority of the trustees to the effect that in their opinion either such material contains untrue statements of fact or omits to state facts necessary to make the statements contained therein not misleading, or would be in violation of applicable law, and specifying the basis of such opinion.

After opportunity for hearing upon the objections specified in the written statement so filed, the Commission may, and if demanded by the trustees or by such applicants shall, enter an order either sustaining one or more of such objections or refusing to sustain any of them. If the Commission shall enter an order refusing to sustain any of such objections, or if, after the entry of an order sustaining one or more of such objections, the Commission shall find, after notice and opportunity for hearing, that all objections so sustained have been met, and shall enter an order so declaring, the trustees shall mail copies of such material to all shareholders with reasonable promptness after the entry of such order and the renewal of such tender.

Transactions of Certain Affiliated Persons and Underwriters

Sec. 17. (a) Prohibited transactions.—

It shall be unlawful for any affiliated person or promoter of or principal underwriter for a registered investment company (other than a company of the character described in sections 12(d)(3)(A) and (B)), or any affiliated person of such a person, promoter, or principal underwriter, acting as principal—

(1) knowingly to sell any security or other property to such registered company or to any company controlled by such registered company, unless such sale involves solely

(A) securities of which the buyer is the issuer,

(B) securities of which the seller is the issuer and which are part of a general offering to the holders of a class of its securities, or

(C) securities deposited with the trustee of a unit investment trust or periodic payment plan by the depositor thereof;

(2) knowingly to purchase from such registered company, or from any company controlled by such registered company, any security or other property (except securities of which the seller is the issuer);

(3) to borrow money or other property from such registered company or from any company controlled by such registered company (unless the borrower is controlled by the lender) except as permitted in section 21(b); or

(4) to loan money or other property to such registered company, or to any company controlled by such registered company, in contravention of such rules, regulations, or orders as the Commission may, after consultation with and taking into consideration the views of the Federal banking agencies (as defined in section 3 of the Federal Deposit Insurance Act), prescribe or issue consistent with the protection of investors.

(b) Application for exemption of proposed transaction from certain restrictions.—

Notwithstanding subsection (a), any person may file with the Commission an application for an order exempting a proposed transaction of the applicant from one or more provisions of that subsection. The Commission shall grant such application and issue such order of exemption if evidence establishes that—

(1) the terms of the proposed transaction, including the consideration to be paid or received, are reasonable and fair and do not involve overreaching on the part of any person concerned;

(2) the proposed transaction is consistent with the policy of each registered investment company concerned, as recited in its registration statement and reports filed under this Act; and

(3) the proposed transaction is consistent with the general purposes of this Act.

(c) Sale or purchase of merchandise from any company or furnishing of services incident to lessor-lessee relationship.—

Notwithstanding subsection (a), a person may, in the ordinary course of business, sell to or purchase from any company merchandise or may enter into a lessor-lessee relationship with any person and furnish the services incident thereto.

(d) Joint or joint and several participation with company in transactions.—

It shall be unlawful for any affiliated person of or principal underwriter for a registered investment company (other than a company of the character described in section 12(d)(3)(A) and (B)), or any affiliated person of such a person or principal underwriter, acting as principal, to effect any transaction in which such registered company, or a company controlled by such registered company, is a joint or a joint and several participant with such person, principal underwriter, or affiliated person, in contravention of such rules and regulations as the Commission may prescribe for the purpose of limiting or preventing participation by such registered or controlled company on a basis different from or less advantageous than that of such other participant. Nothing contained in this subsection shall be deemed to preclude any affiliated person from acting as manager of any underwriting syndicate or other group in which such registered or controlled company is a participant and receiving compensation therefor.

(e) Acceptance of compensation, commissions, fees, etc.—

It shall be unlawful for any affiliated person of a registered investment company, or any affiliated person of such person—

(1) acting as agent, to accept from any source any compensation (other than a regular salary or wages from such registered company) for the purchase or sale of any property to or for such registered company or any controlled company thereof, except in the course of such person's business as an underwriter or broker; or

(2) acting as broker, in connection with the sale of securities to or by such registered company or any controlled company thereof, to receive from any source a commission, fee, or other remuneration for effecting such transaction which exceeds

(A) the usual and customary broker's commission if the sale is effected on a securities exchange, or

(B) 2 per centum of the sales price if the sale is effected in connection with a secondary distribution of such securities, or

(C) 1 per centum of the purchase or sale price of such securities if the sale is otherwise effected unless the Commission shall, by rules and regulations or order in the public interest and consistent with the protection of investors, permit a larger commission.

(f) Custody of securities.—

(1) Every registered management company shall place and maintain its securities and similar investments in custody of

(A) a bank or banks having the qualification prescribed in paragraph (1) of section 26(a) of this Act for the trustees of unit investment trusts; or

(B) a company which is a member of a national securities exchange as defined in the Securities Exchange Act of 1934, subject to such rules and regulations as the Commission may from time to time prescribe for the protection of investors; or

(C) such registered company, but only in accordance with such rules and regulations or orders as the Commission may from time to time prescribe for the protection of investors.

(2) Subject to such rules, regulations, and orders as the Commission may adopt as necessary or appropriate for the protection of investors, a registered management company or any such custodian with the consent of the registered management company for which it acts as custodian, may deposit all or any part of the securities owned by such registered management company in a system for the

central handling of securities established by a national securities exchange or national securities association registered with the Commission under the Securities Exchange Act of 1934, or such other person as may be permitted by the Commission, pursuant to which system all securities of any particular class or series of any issuer deposited within the system are treated as fungible and may be transferred or pledged by bookkeeping entry without physical delivery of such securities.

(3) Rules, regulations, and orders of the Commission under this subsection, among other things, may make appropriate provision with respect to such matters as the earmarking, segregation, and hypothecation of such securities and investments, and may provide for or require periodic or other inspections by any or all of the following: Independent public accountants, employees and agents of the Commission, and such other persons as the Commission may designate.

(4) No member of a national securities exchange which trades in securities for its own account may act as custodian except in accordance with rules and regulations prescribed by the Commission for the protection of investors.

(5) If a registered company maintains its securities and similar investments in the custody of a qualified bank or banks, the cash proceeds from the sale of such securities and similar investments and other cash assets of the company shall likewise be kept in the custody of such a bank or banks, or in accordance with such rules and regulations or orders as the Commission may from time to time prescribe for the protection of investors, except that such a registered company may maintain a checking account in a bank or banks having the qualifications prescribed in paragraph (1) or section 26(a) of this Act for trustees of unit investment trusts with the balance of such account or the aggregate balances of such accounts at no time in excess of the amount of the fidelity bond, maintained pursuant to section 17(g) of this Act, covering the officers or employees authorized to draw on such account or accounts.

(6) The Commission may, after consultation with and taking into consideration the views of the Federal banking agencies (as defined in section 3 of the Federal Deposit Insurance Act), adopt rules and regulations, and issue orders, consistent with the protection of investors, prescribing the conditions under which a bank, or an affiliated person of a bank, either of which is an affiliated person, promoter, organizer, or sponsor of, or principal underwriter for, a registered management company, may serve as custodian of that registered management company.

(g) Bonding of officers and employees having access to securities or funds.—

The Commission is authorized to require by rules and regulations or orders for the protection of investors that any officer or employee of a registered management investment company who may singly, or jointly with others, have access to securities or funds of any registered company, either directly or through authority to draw upon such funds or to direct generally the disposition of such securities (unless the officer or employee has such access solely through his position as an officer or employee of a bank) be bonded by a reputable fidelity insurance company against larceny and embezzlement in such reasonable minimum amounts as the Commission may prescribe.

(h) Provisions in charter, by-laws, etc., protecting against liability for willful misfeasance, etc.—

After one year from the effective date of this Act neither the charter, certificate of incorporation, articles of association, indenture of trust, nor the by-laws of any registered investment company, nor any other instrument pursuant to which such a company is organized or administered, shall contain any provision which protects or purports to protect any director or officer of such company against any liability to the company or to its security holders to which he would otherwise be subject by reason of willful misfeasance, bad faith, gross negligence or reckless disregard of the duties involved in the conduct of his office.

(i) Provisions in contracts protecting against willful misfeasance, etc.—

After one year from the effective date of this Act no contract or agreement under which any person undertakes to act as investment adviser of, or principal underwriter for, a registered investment company shall contain any provision which protects or purports to protect such person against any liability to such company or its security holders to which he would otherwise be subject by reason of willful misfeasance, bad faith, or gross negligence, in the performance of his duties, or by reason of his reckless disregard of his obligations and duties under such contract or agreement.

(j)   Rules and regulations prohibiting fraudulent, deceptive or manipulative courses of conduct.—

It shall be unlawful for any affiliated person of or principal underwriter for a registered investment company or any affiliated person of an investment adviser of or principal underwriter for a registered investment company, to engage in any act, practice, or course of business in connection with the purchase or sale, directly or indirectly, by such person of any security held or to be acquired by such registered investment company in contravention of such rules and regulations as the Commission may adopt to define, and prescribe means reasonably necessary to prevent, such acts, practices, or courses of business as are fraudulent, deceptive or manipulative. Such rules and regulations may include requirements for the adoption of codes of ethics by registered investment companies and investment advisers of, and principal underwriters for, such investment companies establishing such standards as are reasonably necessary to prevent such acts, practices, or courses of business.

Capital Structure

Sec. 18.   (a)   Qualifications on issuance of senior securities.—

It shall be unlawful for any registered closed-end company to issue any class of senior security, or to sell any such security of which it is the issuer, unless—

(1)   if such class of senior security represents an indebtedness—

(A)   immediately after such issuance or sale, it will have an asset coverage of at least 300 per centum;

(B)   provision is made to prohibit the declaration of any dividend (except a dividend payable in stock of the issuer), or the declaration of any other distribution, upon any class of the capital stock of such investment company, or the purchase of any such capital stock, unless, in every such case, such class of senior securities has at the time of the declaration of any such dividend or distribution or at the time of any such purchase an asset coverage of at least 300 per centum after deducting the amount of such dividend, distribution, or purchase price, as the case may be, except that dividends may be declared upon any preferred stock if such senior security representing indebtedness has an asset coverage of at least 200 per centum at the time of declaration thereof after deducting the amount of such dividend; and

(C)   provision is made either—

(i)   that, if on the last business day of each of twelve consecutive calendar months such class of senior securities shall have an asset coverage of less than 100 per centum, the holders of such securities voting as a class shall be entitled to elect at least a majority of the members of the board of directors of such registered company, such voting right to continue until such class of senior security shall have an asset coverage of 110 per centum or more on the last business day of each of three consecutive calendar months, or

(ii)   that, if on the last business day of each of twenty-four consecutive calendar months such class of senior securities shall have an asset coverage of less than 100 per centum, an event of default shall be deemed to have occurred;

(2)   if such class of senior security is a stock—

(A)   immediately after such issuance or sale it will have an asset coverage of at least 200 per centum;

(B)   provision is made to prohibit the declaration of any dividend (except a dividend payable in common stock of the issuer), or the declaration of any other distribution, upon the common stock of such investment company, or the purchase of any such common stock, unless in every such case such class of senior security has at the time of the declaration of any such dividend or distribution or at the time of any such purchase an asset coverage of at least 200 per centum after deducting the amount of such dividend, distribution or purchase price, as the case may be;

(C)   provision is made to entitle the holders of such senior securities, voting as a class, to elect at least two directors at all times, and, subject to the prior rights, if any, of the holders of any other class of senior securities outstanding, to elect a majority of the directors if at any time dividends on such class of securities shall be unpaid in an amount equal to two full years' dividends on such securities, and to continue to be so represented until all dividends in arrears shall have been paid or otherwise provided for;

(D)　provision is made requiring approval by the vote of a majority of such securities, voting as a class, of any plan of reorganization adversely affecting such securities or of any action requiring a vote of security holders as in section 13(a) provided; and

(E)　such class of stock shall have complete priority over any other class as to distribution of assets and payment of dividends, which dividends shall be cumulative.

(b)　Asset coverage in respect of senior securities.—

The asset coverage in respect of a senior security provided for in subsection (a) may be determined on the basis of values calculated as of a time within forty-eight hours (not including Sundays or holidays) next preceding the time of such determination. The time of issue or sale shall, in the case of an offering of such securities to existing stockholders of the issuer, be deemed to be the first date on which such offering is made, and in all other cases shall be deemed to be the time as of which a firm commitment to issue or sell and to take or purchase such securities shall be made.

(c)　Prohibitions relating to issuance of senior securities.—

Notwithstanding the provisions of subsection (a) it shall be unlawful for any registered closed-end investment company to issue or sell any senior security representing indebtedness if immediately thereafter such company will have outstanding more than one class of senior security representing indebtedness, or to issue or sell any senior security which is a stock if immediately thereafter such company will have outstanding more than one class of senior security which is a stock, except that

(1)　any such class of indebtedness or stock may be issued in one or more series: *Provided,* That no such series shall have a preference or priority over any other series upon the distribution of the assets of such registered closed-end company or in respect of the payment of interest or dividends, and

(2)　promissory notes or other evidences of indebtedness issued in consideration of any loan, extension, or renewal thereof, made by a bank or other person and privately arranged, and not intended to be publicly distributed, shall not be deemed to be a separate class of senior securities representing indebtedness within the meaning of this subsection (c).

(d)　Warrants and rights to subscription.—

It shall be unlawful for any registered management company to issue any warrant or right to subscribe to or purchase a security of which such company is the issuer, except in the form of warrants or rights to subscribe expiring not later than one hundred and twenty days after their issuance and issued exclusively and ratably to a class or classes of such company's security holders; except that any warrant may be issued in exchange for outstanding warrants in connection with a plan of reorganization.

(e)　Application of section to specific senior securities.—

The provisions of this section 18 shall not apply to any senior securities issued or sold by any registered closed-end company—

(1)　for the purpose of refunding through payment, purchase, redemption, retirement, or exchange, any senior security of such registered investment company except that no senior security representing indebtedness shall be so issued or sold for the purpose of refunding any senior security which is a stock; or

(2)　pursuant to any plan of reorganization (other than for refunding as referred to in paragraph (1) of this subsection), provided—

(A)　that such senior securities are issued or sold for the purpose of substituting or exchanging such senior securities for outstanding senior securities, and if such senior securities represent indebtedness they are issued or sold for the purpose of substituting or exchanging such senior securities for outstanding senior securities representing indebtedness, of any registered investment company which is a party to such plan of reorganization; or

(B)　that the total amount of such senior securities so issued or sold pursuant to such plan does not exceed the total amount of senior securities of all the companies which are parties to such plan, and the total amount of senior securities representing indebtedness so issued or sold pursuant to such plan does not exceed the total amount of senior securities representing indebtedness of all such companies, or, alternatively, the total amount of such senior securities so issued or sold pursuant to such plan does not have the effect of increasing the ratio of senior securities representing indebtedness to the securities representing stock or the ratio of senior securities representing stock to securities junior thereto when compared with such ratios as they existed before such reorganization.

(f)   Senior securities securing loans from bank; securities not included in "senior security".—

(1)   It shall be unlawful for any registered open-end company to issue any class of senior security or to sell any senior security of which it is the issuer, except that any such registered company shall be permitted to borrow from any bank: *Provided,* That immediately after any such borrowing there is an asset coverage of at least 300 per centum for all borrowings of such registered company: *And provided further,* That in the event that such asset coverage shall at any time fall below 300 per centum such registered company shall, within three days thereafter (not including Sundays and holidays) or such longer period as the Commission may prescribe by rules and regulations, reduce the amount of its borrowings to an extent that the asset coverage of such borrowings shall be at least 300 per centum.

(2)   "Senior security" shall not, in the case of a registered open-end company, include a class or classes or a number of series of preferred or special stock each of which is preferred over all other classes or series in respect of assets specifically allocated to that class or series: *Provided,* That

(A)   such company has outstanding no class or series of stock which is not so preferred over all other classes or series, or

(B)   the only other outstanding class of the issuer's stock consists of a common stock upon which no dividend (other than a liquidating dividend) is permitted to be paid and which in the aggregate represents not more than one-half of 1 per centum of the issuer's outstanding voting securities. For the purpose of insuring fair and equitable treatment of the holders of the outstanding voting securities of each class or series of stock of such company, the Commission may by rule, regulation, or order direct that any matter required to be submitted to the holders of the outstanding voting securities of such company shall not be deemed to have been effectively acted upon unless approved by the holders of such percentage (not exceeding a majority) of the outstanding voting securities of each class or series of stock affected by such matter as shall be prescribed in such rule, regulation, or order.

(g)   "Senior security" defined.—

Unless otherwise provided: "Senior security" means any bond, debenture, note, or similar obligation or instrument constituting a security and evidencing indebtedness, and any stock of a class having priority over any other class as to distribution of assets or payment of dividends; and "senior security representing indebtedness" means any senior security other than stock.

The term "senior security", when used in subparagraphs (B) and (C) of paragraph (1) of subsection (a), shall not include any promissory note or other evidence of indebtedness issued in consideration of any loan, extension, or renewal thereof, made by a bank or other person and privately arranged, and not intended to be publicly distributed; nor shall such term, when used in this section 18, include any such promissory note or other evidence of indebtedness in any case where such a loan is for temporary purposes only and in an amount not exceeding 5 per centum of the value of the total assets of the issuer at the time when the loan is made. A loan shall be presumed to be for temporary purposes if it is repaid within sixty days and is not extended or renewed; otherwise it shall be presumed not to be for temporary purposes. Any such presumption may be rebutted by evidence.

(h)   "Asset coverage" defined.—

"Asset coverage" of a class of senior security representing an indebtedness of an issuer means the ratio which the value of the total assets of such issuer, less all liabilities and indebtedness not represented by senior securities, bears to the aggregate amount of senior securities representing indebtedness of such issuer. "Asset coverage" of a class of senior security of an issuer which is a stock means the ratio which the value of the total assets of such issuer, less all liabilities and indebtedness not represented by senior securities, bears to the aggregate amount of senior securities representing indebtedness of such issuer plus the aggregate of the involuntary liquidation preference of such class of senior security which is a stock. The involuntary liquidation preference of a class of senior security which is a stock shall be deemed to mean the amount to which such class of senior security would be entitled on involuntary liquidation of the issuer in preference to a security junior to it.

(i)   Future issuance of stock as voting stock; exceptions.—

Except as provided in subsection (a) of this section, or as otherwise required by law, every share of stock hereafter issued by a registered management company (except a common-law trust of the character described in section 16(c)) shall be a voting stock and have equal voting rights with every other outstanding voting stock: *Provided,* That this subsection shall not apply to shares issued pursuant to the terms of any warrant or subscription right outstanding on March 15, 1940, or any firm contract entered into before March 15, 1940, to purchase such securities from such company nor to shares issued in accordance with any rules, regulations, or orders which the Commission may make permitting such issue.

(j)   Securities issued by registered face-amount certificate of company.—

Notwithstanding any provision of this Act, it shall be unlawful, after the date of enactment of this Act, for any registered face-amount certificate company—

(1)   to issue, except in accordance with such rules, regulations, or orders as the Commission may prescribe in the public interest or as necessary or appropriate for the protection of investors, any security other than

(A)   a face-amount certificate;

(B)   a common stock having a par value and being without preference as to dividends or distributions and having at least equal voting rights with any outstanding security of such company; or

(C)   short-term payment or promissory notes or other indebtedness issued in consideration of any loan, extension, or renewal thereof, made by a bank or other person and privately arranged and not intended to be publicly offered;

(2)   if such company has outstanding any security, other than such face-amount certificates, common stock, promissory notes, or other evidence of indebtedness, to make any distribution or declare or pay any dividend on any capital security in contravention of such rules and regulations or orders as the Commission may prescribe in the public interest or as necessary or appropriate for the protection of investors or to insure the financial integrity of such company, to prevent the impairment of the company's ability to meet its obligations upon its face-amount certificates; or

(3)   to issue any of its securities except for cash or securities including securities of which such company is the issuer.

(k)   Application of section to companies operating under Small Business Investment Act provisions.—

The provisions of subparagraphs (A) and (B) of paragraph (1) of subsection (a) of this section shall not apply to investment companies operating under the Small Business Investment Act of 1958, and the provisions of paragraph (2) of said subsection shall not apply to such companies so long as such class of senior security shall be held or guaranteed by the Small Business Administration.

Dividends

Sec. 19.   (a)   Dividends; restriction; exception.—

It shall be unlawful for any registered investment company to pay any dividend, or to make any distribution in the nature of a dividend payment, wholly or partly from any source other than—

(1)   such company's accumulated undistributed net income, determined in accordance with good accounting practice and not including profits or losses realized upon the sale of securities or other properties; or

(2)   such company's net income so determined for the current or preceding fiscal year;

unless such payment is accompanied by a written statement which adequately discloses the source or sources of such payment. The Commission may prescribe the form of such statement by rules and regulations in the public interest and for the protection of investors.

(b)   Long-term capital gains; limitation.—

It shall be unlawful in contravention of such rules, regulations, or orders as the Commission may prescribe as necessary or appropriate in the public interest or for the protection of investors for any registered investment company to distribute long-term capital gains, as defined in the Internal Revenue Code of 1954, more often than once every twelve months.

Proxies; Voting Trusts; Circular Ownership

Sec. 20.   (a)   Prohibition on use of means of interstate commerce for solicitation of proxies.—

It shall be unlawful for any person, by use of the mails or any means or instrumentality of interstate commerce or otherwise, to solicit or to permit the use of his name to solicit any proxy or consent or authorization in respect of any security of which a registered investment company is the issuer in contravention of such rules and regulations as the Commission may prescribe as necessary or appropriate in the public interest or for the protection of investors.

(b)   Prohibition on use of means of interstate commerce for sale of voting-trust certificates.—

It shall be unlawful for any registered investment company or affiliated person thereof, any issuer of a voting-trust certificate relating to any security of a registered investment company, or any underwriter of such a certificate, by use of the mails or any means or instrumentality of interstate commerce, or otherwise, to offer for sale, sell, or deliver after sale, in connection with a public offering, any such voting-trust certificate.

(c)   Prohibition on purchase of securities knowingly resulting in cross-ownership or circular ownership.—

No registered investment company shall purchase any voting security if, to the knowledge of such registered company, cross-ownership or circular ownership exists, or after such acquisition will exist, between such registered company and the issuer of such security. Cross-ownership shall be deemed to exist between two companies when each of such companies beneficially owns more than 3 per centum of the outstanding voting securities of the other company. Circular ownership shall be deemed to exist between two companies if such companies are included within a group of three or more companies, each of which—

(1)   beneficially owns more than 3 per centum of the outstanding voting securities of one or more other companies of the group; and

(2)   has more than 3 per centum of its own outstanding voting securities beneficially owned by another company, or by each of two or more other companies, of the group.

(d)   Duty to eliminate existing cross-ownership or circular ownership.—

If cross-ownership or circular ownership between a registered investment company and any other company or companies comes into existence upon the purchase by a registered investment company of the securities of another company, it shall be the duty of such registered company, within one year after it first knows of the existence of such cross-ownership or circular ownership, to eliminate the same.

Loans

Sec. 21.   It shall be unlawful for any registered management company to lend money or property to any person, directly or indirectly if—

(a)   the investment policies of such registered company, as recited in its registration statement and reports filed under this Act, do not permit such a loan; or

(b)   such person controls or is under common control with such registered company; except that the provisions of this paragraph shall not apply to any loan from a registered company to a company which owns all of the outstanding securities of such registered company, except directors' qualifying shares.

Distribution, Redemption, and Repurchase of Redeemable Securities

Sec. 22. (a) Rules relating to minimum and maximum prices for purchase and sale of securities from investment company; time for resale and redemption.—

A securities association registered under section 15A of the Securities Exchange Act of 1934 may prescribe, by rules adopted and in effect in accordance with said section and subject to all provisions of said section applicable to the rules of such an association—

(1) a method or methods for computing the minimum price at which a member thereof may purchase from any investment company any redeemable security issued by such company and the maximum price at which a member may sell to such company any redeemable security issued by it or which he may receive for such security upon redemption, so that the price in each case will bear such relation to the current net asset value of such security computed as of such time as the rules may prescribe; and

(2) a minimum period of time which must elapse after the sale or issue of such security before any resale to such company by a member or its redemption upon surrender by a member;

in each case for the purpose of eliminating or reducing so far as reasonably practicable any dilution of the value of other outstanding securities of such company or any other result of such purchase, redemption, or sale which is unfair to holders of such other outstanding securities; and said rules may prohibit the members of the association from purchasing, selling, or surrendering for redemption any such redeemable securities in contravention of said rules.

(b) Rules relating to purchase of securities by members from issuer investment company.—

(1) Such a securities association may also, by rules adopted and in effect in accordance with said section 15A, and notwithstanding the provisions of subsection (b)(6) thereof but subject to all other provisions of said section applicable to the rules of such an association, prohibit its members from purchasing, in connection with a primary distribution of redeemable securities of which any registered investment company is the issuer, any such security from the issuer or from any principal underwriter except at a price equal to the price at which such security is then offered to the public less a commission, discount, or spread which is computed in conformity with a method or methods, and within such limitations as to the relation thereof to said public offering price, as such rules may prescribe in order that the price at which such security is offered or sold to the public shall not include an excessive sales load but shall allow for reasonable compensation for sales personnel, broker-dealers, and underwriters, and for reasonable sales loads to investors. The Commission shall on application or otherwise, if it appears that smaller companies are subject to relatively higher operating costs, make due allowance therefor by granting any such company or class of companies appropriate qualified exemptions from the provisions of this section.

(2) At any time after the expiration of eighteen months from the date of enactment of the Investment Company Amendments Act of 1970 (or, if earlier, after a securities association has adopted for purposes of paragraph (1) any rule respecting excessive sales loads), the Commission may alter or supplement the rules of any securities association as may be necessary to effectuate the purposes of this subsection in the manner provided by section 19(c) of the Securities Exchange Act of 1934.

(3) If any provision of this subsection is in conflict with any provision of any law of the United States in effect on the date this subsection takes effect, the provisions of this subsection shall prevail.

(c) Conflicting rules of Commission and associations.—

The Commission may make rules and regulations applicable to registered investment companies and to principal underwriters of, and dealers in, the redeemable securities of any registered investment company, whether or not members of any securities association, to the same extent, covering the same subject matter, and for the accomplishment of the same ends as are prescribed in subsection (a) of this section in respect of the rules which may be made by a registered securities association governing its members. Any rules and regulations so made by the Commission, to the extent that they may be inconsistent with the rules of any such association, shall so long as they remain in force supersede the rules of the association and be binding upon its members as well as all other underwriters and dealers to whom they may be applicable.

(d)   Sale of securities except to or through principal underwriter; price of securities.—

No registered investment company shall sell any redeemable security issued by it to any person except either to or through a principal underwriter for distribution or at a current public offering price described in the prospectus, and, if such class of security is being currently offered to the public by or through an underwriter, no principal underwriter of such security and no dealer shall sell any such security to any person except a dealer, a principal underwriter, or the issuer, except at a current public offering price described in the prospectus. Nothing in this subsection shall prevent a sale made

    (i)   pursuant to an offer of exchange permitted by section 11 including any offer made pursuant to section 11(b);

    (ii)   pursuant to an offer made solely to all registered holders of the securities, or of a particular class or series of securities issued by the company proportionate to their holdings or proportionate to any cash distribution made to them by the company (subject to appropriate qualifications designed solely to avoid issuance of fractional securities); or

    (iii)   in accordance with rules and regulations of the Commission made pursuant to subsection (b) of section 12.

(e)   Suspension of right of redemption or postponement of date of payment.—

No registered investment company shall suspend the right of redemption, or postpone the date of payment or satisfaction upon redemption of any redeemable security in accordance with its terms for more than seven days after the tender of such security to the company or its agent designated for that purpose for redemption, except—

    (1)   for any period (A) during which the New York Stock Exchange is closed other than customary week-end and holiday closings or (B) during which trading on the New York Stock Exchange is restricted;

    (2)   for any period during which an emergency exists as a result of which (A) disposal by the company of securities owned by it is not reasonably practicable or (B) it is not reasonably practicable for such company fairly to determine the value of its net assets; or

    (3)   for such other periods as the Commission may by order permit for the protection of security holders of the company.

The Commission shall by rules and regulations determine the conditions under which (i) trading shall be deemed to be restricted and (ii) an emergency shall be deemed to exist within the meaning of this subsection.

(f)   Restrictions on transferability or negotiability of securities.—

No registered open-end company shall restrict the transferability or negotiability of any security of which it is the issuer except in conformity with the statements with respect thereto contained in its registration statement nor in contravention of such rules and regulations as the Commission may prescribe in the interests of the holders of all of the outstanding securities of such investment company.

(g)   Issuance of securities for services or property other than cash.—

No registered open-end company shall issue any of its securities

    (1)   for services; or

    (2)   for property other than cash or securities (including securities of which such registered company is the issuer), except as a dividend or distribution to its security holders or in connection with a reorganization.

Distribution and Repurchase of Securities; Closed-End Companies

Sec. 23.   (a)   Issuance of securities.—

No registered closed-end company shall issue any of its securities

    (1)   for services; or

(2)   for property other than cash or securities (including securities of which such registered company is the issuer), except as a dividend or distribution to its security holders or in connection with a reorganization.

(b)   Sale of common stock at price below current net asset value.—

No registered closed-end company shall sell any common stock of which it is the issuer at a price below the current net asset value of such stock, exclusive of any distributing commission or discount (which net asset value shall be determined as of a time within forty-eight hours, excluding Sundays and holidays, next preceding the time of such determination), except

(1)   in connection with an offering to the holders of one or more classes of its capital stock;

(2)   with consent of a majority of its common stockholders;

(3)   upon conversion of a convertible security in accordance with its terms;

(4)   upon the exercise of any warrant outstanding on the date of enactment of this Act or issued in accordance with the provisions of section 18(d); or

(5)   under such other circumstances as the Commission may permit by rules and regulations or orders for the protection of investors.

(c)   Purchase of securities of which it is issuer; exceptions.—

No registered closed-end company shall purchase any securities of any class of which it is the issuer except—

(1)   on a securities exchange or such other open market as the Commission may designate by rules and regulations or orders: *Provided,* That if such securities are stock, such registered company shall, within the preceding six months, have informed stockholders of its intention to purchase stock of such class by letter or report addressed to stockholders of such class; or

(2)   pursuant to tenders, after reasonable opportunity to submit tenders given to all holders of securities of the class to be purchased; or

(3)   under such other circumstances as the Commission may permit by rules and regulations or orders for the protection of investors in order to insure that such purchases are made in a manner or on a basis which does not unfairly discriminate against any holders of the class or classes of securities to be purchased.

Registration of Securities Under Securities Act of 1933

Sec. 24.   (a)   Registration statement; contents.—

In registering under the Securities Act of 1933 any security of which it is the issuer, a registered investment company, in lieu of furnishing a registration statement containing the information and documents specified in schedule A of said Act, may file a registration statement containing the following information and documents:

(1)   such copies of the registration statement filed by such company under this Act, and of such reports filed by such company pursuant to section 29 or such copies of portions of such registration statement and reports, as the Commission shall designate by rules and regulations; and

(2)   such additional information and documents (including a prospectus) as the Commission shall prescribe by rules and regulations as necessary or appropriate in the public interest or for the protection of investors.

(b)   Filing of three copies of advertisement, pamphlet, etc. in connection with public offering; time of filing.—

It shall be unlawful for any of the following companies, or for any underwriter for such a company, in connection with a public offering of any security of which such company is the issuer, to make use of the mails or any means or instrumentalities of interstate commerce to transmit any advertisement, pamphlet, circular, form letter, or other sales literature addressed to or intended for distribution to prospective investors unless three copies of the full text thereof have been filed with the Commission or are filed with the Commission within ten days thereafter:

(1)   any registered open-end company;

(2)   any registered unit investment trust; or

(3)   any registered face-amount certificate company.

(c)   Additional requirement for prospectuses relating to periodic payment plan certificates or face-amount certificate.—

In addition to the powers relative to prospectuses granted the Commission by section 10 of the Securities Act of 1933, the Commission is authorized to require, by rules and regulations or order, that the information contained in any prospectus relating to any periodic payment plan certificate or face-amount certificate registered under the Securities Act of 1933 on or after the effective date of this title be presented in such form and order of items, and such prospectus contain such summaries of any portion of such information, as are necessary or appropriate in the public interest or for the protection of investors.

(d)   Application of other provisions to securities of investment companies, face-amount certificate companies, and open-end companies or unit investment trust.—

The exemption provided by paragraph (8) of section 3(a) of the Securities Act of 1933 shall not apply to any security of which an investment company is the issuer. The exemption provided by paragraph (11) of said section 3(a) shall not apply to any security of which a registered investment company is the issuer. The exemption provided by section 4(3) of the Securities Act of 1933, as amended, shall not apply to any transaction in a security issued by a face-amount certificate company or in a redeemable security issued by an open-end management company or unit investment trust, if any other security of the same class is currently being offered or sold by the issuer or by or through an underwriter in a distribution which is not exempted from section 5 of said Act, except to such extent and subject to such terms and conditions as the Commission, having due regard for the public interest and the protection of investors, may prescribe by rules or regulations with respect to any class of persons, securities, or transactions.

(e)   Amendment of registration statements relating to securities issued by face-amount certificate companies, open-end management companies or unit investment trusts.—

For the purposes of section 11 of the Securities Act of 1933, as amended, the effective date of the latest amendment filed shall be deemed the effective date of the registration statement with respect to securities sold after such amendment shall have become effective. For the purposes of section 13 of the Securities Act of 1933, as amended, no such security shall be deemed to have been bona fide offered to the public prior to the effective date of the latest amendment filed pursuant to this subsection. Except to the extent the Commission otherwise provides by rules or regulations as appropriate in the public interest or for the protection of investors, no prospectus relating to a security issued by a face-amount certificate company or a redeemable security issued by an open-end management company or unit investment trust which varies for the purposes of subsection (a)(3) of section 10 of the Securities Act of 1933 from the latest prospectus filed as a part of the registration statement shall be deemed to meet the requirements of said section 10 unless filed as part of an amendment to the registration statement under said Act and such amendment has become effective.

(f)   Registration of indefinite amount of securities.—

(1)   Registration of securities.—

Upon the effective date of its registration statement, as provided by section 8 of the Securities Act of 1933, a face-amount certificate company, open-end management company, or unit investment trust, shall be deemed to have registered an indefinite amount of securities.

(2)   Payment of registration fees.—

Not later than 90 days after the end of the fiscal year of a company or trust referred to in paragraph (1), the company or trust, as applicable, shall pay a registration fee to the Commission, calculated in the manner specified in section 6(b) of the Securities Act of 1933, based on the aggregate sales price for which its securities (including, for purposes of this paragraph, all securities issued pursuant to a dividend reinvestment plan) were sold pursuant to a registration of an indefinite amount of securities under this subsection during the previous fiscal year of the company or trust, reduced by—

(A) the aggregate redemption or repurchase price of the securities of the company or trust during that year; and

(B) the aggregate redemption or repurchase price of the securities of the company or trust during any prior fiscal year ending not more than 1 year before the date of enactment of the Investment Company Act Amendments of 1996, that were not used previously by the company or trust to reduce fees payable under this section.

(3)   Interest due on late payment.—

A company or trust paying the fee required by this subsection or any portion thereof more than 90 days after the end of the fiscal year of the company or trust shall pay to the Commission interest on unpaid amounts, at the average investment rate for Treasury tax and loan accounts published by the Secretary of the Treasury pursuant to section 3717(a) of Title 31, United States Code. The payment of interest pursuant to this paragraph shall not preclude the Commission from bringing an action to enforce the requirements of paragraph (2).

(4)   Rulemaking authority.—

The Commission may adopt rules and regulations to implement this subsection.

(g)   Additional prospectuses.—

In addition to any prospectus permitted or required by section 10(a) of the Securities Act of 1933, the Commission shall permit, by rules or regulations deemed necessary or appropriate in the public interest or for the protection of investors, the use of a prospectus for purposes of section 5(b)(1) of that Act with respect to securities issued by a registered investment company. Such a prospectus, which may include information the substance of which is not included in the prospectus specified in section 10(a) of the Securities Act of 1933, shall be deemed to be permitted by section 10(b) of that Act.

Plans of Reorganization

Sec. 25. (a)   Filing of reorganization plan and other information with Commission.—

Any person who, by use of the mails or any means or instrumentality of interstate commerce or otherwise, solicits or permits the use of his name to solicit any proxy, consent, authorization, power of attorney, ratification, deposit, or dissent in respect of any plan of reorganization of any registered investment company shall file with, or mail to, the Commission for its information, within twenty-four hours after the commencement of any such solicitation, a copy of such plan and any deposit agreement relating thereto and of any proxy, consent, authorization, power of attorney, ratification, instrument of deposit, or instrument of dissent in respect thereto, if or to the extent that such documents shall not already have been filed with the Commission.

(b)   Advisory report by Commission at request of shareholders.—

The Commission is authorized, if so requested, prior to any solicitation of security holders with respect to any plan of reorganization, by any registered investment company which is, or any of the securities of which are, the subject of or is a participant in any such plan, or if so requested by the holders of 25 per centum of any class of its outstanding securities, to render an advisory report in respect of the fairness of any such plan and its effect upon any class or classes of security holders. In such event any registered investment company, in respect of which the Commission shall have rendered any such advisory report, shall mail promptly a copy of such advisory report to all its security holders affected by any such plan: *Provided,* That such advisory report shall have been received by it at least forty-eight hours (not including Sundays and holidays) before final action is taken in relation to such plan at any meeting of security holders called to act in relation thereto, or any adjournment of any such meeting, or if no meeting be called, then prior to the final date of acceptance of such plan by security holders. In respect of securities not registered as to ownership, in lieu of mailing a copy of such advisory report, such registered company shall publish promptly a statement of the existence of such advisory report in a newspaper of general circulation in its principal place of business and shall make available copies of such advisory report upon request. Notwithstanding the provision of this section the Commission shall not render such advisory report although so requested by any such investment company or such security holders if the fairness or feasibility of said plan is in issue in any proceeding pending in any court of competent jurisdiction unless such plan is submitted to the Commission for that purpose by such court.

(c)   Enjoinder of plan of reorganization.—

Any district court of the United States in the State of incorporation of a registered investment company, or any such court for the district in which such company maintains its principal place of business, is authorized to enjoin the consummation of any plan of reorganization of such registered investment company upon proceedings instituted by the Commission (which is authorized so to proceed upon behalf of security holders of such registered company, or any class thereof), if such court shall determine that any such plan is not fair and equitable to all security holders.

(d)   Application of section to reorganizations under Title 11.—

Nothing contained in this section shall in any way affect or derogate from the powers of the courts of the United States and the Commission with reference to reorganizations contained in Title 11 of the United States Code.

Unit Investment Trusts

Sec. 26.   (a)   Custody and sale of securities.—

No principal underwriter for or depositor of a registered unit investment trust shall sell, except by surrender to the trustee for redemption, any security of which such trust is the issuer (other than short-term paper), unless the trust indenture, agreement of custodianship, or other instrument pursuant to which such security is issued—

     (1)   designates one or more trustees or custodians, each of which is a bank, and provides that each such trustee or custodian shall have at all times an aggregate capital, surplus, and undivided profits of a specified minimum amount, which shall not be less than $500,000 (but may also provide, if such trustee or custodian publishes reports of condition at least annually, pursuant to law or to the requirements of its supervising or examining authority, that for the purposes of this paragraph the aggregate capital, surplus, and undivided profits of such trustee or custodian shall be deemed to be its aggregate capital, surplus, and undivided profits as set forth in its most recent report of condition so published);

     (2)   provides, in substance,

         (A)   that during the life of the trust the trustee or custodian, if not otherwise remunerated, may charge against and collect from the income of the trust, and from the corpus thereof if no income is available, such fees for its services and such reimbursement for its expenses as are provided for in such instrument;

         (B)   that no such charge or collection shall be made except for services theretofore performed or expenses theretofore incurred;

         (C)   that no payment to the depositor of or a principal underwriter for such trust, or to any affiliated person or agent of such depositor or underwriter, shall be allowed the trustee or custodian as an expense (except that provision may be made for the payment to any such person of a fee, not exceeding such reasonable amount as the Commission may prescribe as compensation for performing bookkeeping and other administrative services, of a character normally performed by the trustee or custodian itself); and

         (D)   that the trustee or custodian shall have possession of all securities and other property in which the funds of the trust are invested, all funds held for such investment, all equalization, redemption, and other special funds of the trust, and all income upon, accretions to, and proceeds of such property and funds, and shall segregate and hold the same in trust (subject only to the charges and collections allowed under clauses (A), (B), and (C)) until distribution thereof to the security holders of the trust;

     (3)   provides, in substance, that the trustee or custodian shall not resign until either

         (A)   the trust has been completely liquidated and the proceeds of the liquidation distributed to the security holders of the trust, or

(B)   a successor trustee or custodian, having the qualifications prescribed in paragraph (1), has been designated and has accepted such trusteeship or custodianship; and

(4)   provides, in substance,

(A)   that a record will be kept by the depositor or an agent of the depositor of the name and address of, and the shares issued by the trust and held by, every holder of any security issued pursuant to such instrument, insofar as such information is known to the depositor or agent; and

(B)   that whenever a security is deposited with the trustee in substitution for any security in which such security holder has an undivided interest, the depositor or the agent of the depositor will, within five days after such substitution, either deliver or mail to such security holder a notice of substitution, including an identification of the securities eliminated and the securities substituted, and a specification of the shares of such security holder affected by the substitution.

(b)   Bank or affiliated person of bank as trustee or custodian.—

The Commission may, after consultation with and taking into consideration the views of the Federal banking agencies (as defined in section 3 of the Federal Deposit Insurance Act), adopt rules and regulations, and issue orders, consistent with the protection of investors, prescribing the conditions under which a bank, or an affiliated person of a bank, either of which is an affiliated person of a principal underwriter for, or depositor of, a registered unit investment trust, may serve as trustee or custodian under subsection (a)(1).

(c)   Substitution of securities.—

It shall be unlawful for any depositor or trustee of a registered unit investment trust holding the security of a single issuer to substitute another security for such security unless the Commission shall have approved such substitution. The Commission shall issue an order approving such substitution if the evidence establishes that it is consistent with the protection of investors and the purposes fairly intended by the policy and provisions of this Act.

(d)   Binding contract or agreement embodying applicable provisions deemed to qualify non-complying instrument by which securities were issued.—

In the event that a trust indenture, agreement of custodianship, or other instrument pursuant to which securities of a registered unit investment trust are issued does not comply with the requirements of subsection (a) of this section, such instrument will be deemed to meet such requirements if a written contract or agreement binding on the parties and embodying such requirements has been executed by the depositor on the one part and the trustee or custodian on the other part, and three copies of such contract of agreement have been filed with the Commission.

(e)   Liquidation of unit investment trust.—

Whenever the Commission has reason to believe that a unit investment trust is inactive and that its liquidation is in the interest of the security holders of such trust, the Commission may file a complaint seeking the liquidation of such trust in the district court of the United States in any district wherein any trustee of such trust resides or has its principal place of business. A copy of such complaint shall be served on every trustee of such trust, and notice of the proceeding shall be given such other interested persons in such manner and at such times as the court may direct. If the court determines that such liquidation is in the interest of the security holders of such trust, the court shall order such liquidation and, after payment of necessary expenses, the distribution of the proceeds to the security holders of the trust in such manner and on such terms as may to the court appear equitable.

(f)   Exemption.—

(1)   In general.—

Subsection (a) does not apply to any registered separate account funding variable insurance contracts, or to the sponsoring insurance company and principal underwriter of such account.

(2)   Limitation on sales.—

It shall be unlawful for any registered separate account funding variable insurance contracts, or for the sponsoring insurance company of such account, to sell any such contract—

(A) unless the fees and charges deducted under the contract, in the aggregate, are reasonable in relation to the services rendered, the expenses expected to be incurred, and the risks assumed by the insurance company, and, beginning on the earlier of August 1, 1997, or the earliest effective date of any registration statement or amendment thereto for such contract following the date of enactment of this subsection, the insurance company so represents in the registration statement for the contract; and

(B) unless the insurance company—

(i) complies with all other applicable provisions of this section, as if it were a trustee or custodian of the registered separate account;

(ii) files with the insurance regulatory authority of the State which is the domiciliary State of the insurance company, an annual statement of its financial condition, which most recent statement indicates that the insurance company has a combined capital and surplus, if a stock company, or an unassigned surplus, if a mutual company, of not less than $1,000,000, or such other amount as the Commission may from time to time prescribe by rule, as necessary or appropriate in the public interest or for the protection of investors; and

(iii) together with its registered separate accounts, is supervised and examined periodically by the insurance authority of such State.

(3) Fees and charges.—

For purposes of paragraph (2), the fees and charges deducted under the contract shall include all fees and charges imposed for any purpose and in any manner.

(4) Regulatory authority.—

The Commission may issue such rules and regulations to carry out paragraph (2)(A) as it determines are necessary or appropriate in the public interest or for the protection of investors.

Periodic Payment Plans

Sec. 27. (a) Sale of certificates; restrictions.—

It shall be unlawful for any registered investment company issuing periodic payment plan certificates, or for any depositor of or underwriter for such company, to sell any such certificate, if—

(1) the sales load on such certificate exceeds 9 per centum of the total payments to be made thereon;

(2) more than one-half of any of the first twelve monthly payments thereon, or their equivalent, is deducted for sales load;

(3) the amount of sales load deducted from any one of such first payments exceeds proportionately the amount deducted from any other such payment, or the amount deducted from any subsequent payment exceeds proportionately the amount deducted from any other subsequent payment;

(4) the first payment on such certificate is less than $20, or any subsequent payment is less than $10;

(5) if such registered company is a management company, the proceeds of such certificate or the securities in which such proceeds are invested are subject to management fees (other than fees for administrative services of the character described in clause (C), paragraph (2), of section 26(a) exceeding such reasonable amount as the Commission may prescribe, whether such fees are payable to such company or to investment advisers thereof; or

(6) if such registered company is a unit investment trust the assets of which are securities issued by a management company, the depositor of or principal underwriter for such trust, or any affiliated person of such depositor or underwriter, is to receive from such management company or any affiliated person thereof any fee or payment on account of payments on such certificate exceeding such reasonable amount as the Commission may prescribe.

(b) Exemptions.—

If it appears to the Commission, upon application or otherwise, that smaller companies are subjected to relatively higher operating costs and that in order to make due allowance therefor it is necessary or appropriate in the public interest and consistent with the protection of investors that a provision or provisions of paragraph (1), (2), or (3) of subsection (a) relative to sales load be relaxed in the case of certain registered investment companies issuing periodic payment plan certificates, or certain specified classes of such companies, the Commission is authorized by rules and regulations or order to grant any such company or class of companies appropriate qualified exemptions from the provisions of said paragraphs.

(c)   Sale of certificates; requirements.—

It shall be unlawful for any registered investment company issuing periodic payment plan certificates, or for any depositor of or underwriter for such company, to sell any such certificate, unless—

     (1)   such certificate is a redeemable security; and

     (2)   the proceeds of all payments on such certificate (except such amounts as are deducted for sales load) are deposited with a trustee or custodian having the qualifications prescribed in paragraph (1) of section 26(a) for the trustees of unit investment trusts, and are held by such trustee or custodian under an indenture or agreement containing, in substance, the provisions required by paragraphs (2) and (3) of section 26(a) for the trust indentures of unit investment trusts.

(d)   Surrender of certificates; regulations.—

Notwithstanding subsection (a) of this section, it shall be unlawful for any registered investment company issuing periodic payment plan certificates, or for any depositor of or underwriter for such company, to sell any such certificate unless the certificate provides that the holder thereof may surrender the certificate at any time within the first eighteen months after the issuance of the certificate and receive in payment thereof, in cash, the sum of

     (1)   the value of his account, and

     (2)   an amount, from such underwriter or depositor, equal to that part of the excess paid for sales loading which is over 15 per centum of the gross payments made by the certificate holder. The Commission may make rules and regulations applicable to such underwriters and depositors specifying such reserve requirements as it deems necessary or appropriate in order for such underwriters and depositors to carry out the obligations to refund sales charges required by this subsection.

(e)   Refund privileges; notice; rules.—

With respect to any periodic payment plan certificate sold subject to the provisions of subsection (d) of this section, the registered investment company issuing such periodic payment plan certificate, or any depositor of or underwriter for such company, shall in writing

     (1)   inform each certificate holder who has missed three payments or more, within thirty days following the expiration of fifteen months after the issuance of the certificate, or, if any such holder has missed one payment or more after such period of fifteen months but prior to the expiration of eighteen months after the issuance of the certificate, at any time prior to the expiration of such eighteen-month period, of his right to surrender his certificate as specified in subsection (d) of this section, and

     (2)   inform the certificate holder of

        (A)   the value of the holder's account as of the time the written notice was given to such holder, and

        (B)   the amount to which he is entitled as specified in subsection (d) of this section. The Commission may make rules specifying the method, form, and contents of the notice required by this subsection.

(f)   Charges, statement; rules; surrender of certificates; regulations.—

With respect to any periodic payment plan (other than a plan under which the amount of sales load deducted from any payment thereon does not exceed 9 per centum of such payment), the custodian bank for such plan shall mail to each certificate holder, within sixty days after the issuance of the certificate, a statement of charges to be deducted from the projected payments on the certificate and a notice of his right of withdrawal as specified in this section. The Commission may make rules specifying the method, form, and contents of the notice required by this subsection. The certificate holder may within forty-five days of the mailing of the notice specified in this subsection surrender his certificate and receive in payment thereof, in cash, the sum of

    (1)   the value of his account, and

    (2)   an amount, from the underwriter or depositor, equal to the difference between the gross payments made and the net amount invested. The Commission may make rules and regulations applicable to underwriters and depositors of companies issuing any such certificate specifying such reserve requirements as it deems necessary or appropriate in order for such underwriters and depositors to carry out the obligations to refund sales charges required by this subsection.

(g)   Governing provisions; election.—

Notwithstanding the provisions of subsections (a) and (d), a registered investment company issuing periodic payment plan certificates may elect, by written notice to the Commission, to be governed by the provisions of subsection (h) rather than the provisions of subsections (a) and (d) of this section.

(h)   Sale of certificates; restrictions.—

Upon making the election specified in subsection (g), it shall be unlawful for any such electing registered investment company issuing periodic payment plan certificates, or for any depositor of or underwriter for such company, to sell any such certificate, if—

    (1)   the sales load on such certificate exceeds 9 per centum of the total payments to be made thereon;

    (2)   more than 20 per centum of any payment thereon is deducted for sales load, or an average of more than 16 per centum is deducted for sales load from the first forty-eight monthly payments thereon, or their equivalent;

    (3)   the amount of sales load deducted from any one of the first twelve monthly payments, and thirteenth through twenty-fourth monthly payments, the twenty-fifth through thirty-sixth monthly payments, or the thirty-seventh through forty-eighth monthly payments, or their equivalents, respectively, exceeds proportionately the amount deducted from any other such payment, or the amount deducted from any subsequent payment exceeds proportionately the amount deducted from any other subsequent payment;

    (4)   the deduction for sales load on the excess of the payment or payments in any month over the minimum monthly payment, or its equivalent, to be made on the certificate exceeds the sales load applicable to payments subsequent to the first forty-eight monthly payments or their equivalent;

    (5)   the first payment on such certificate is less than $20, or any subsequent payment is less than $10;

    (6)   if such registered company is a management company, the proceeds of such certificate or the securities in which such proceeds are invested are subject to management fees (other than fees for administrative services of the character described in clause (C) of paragraph (2) of section 26(a)) exceeding such reasonable amount as the Commission may prescribe, whether such fees are payable to such company or to investment advisers thereof; or

    (7)   if such registered company is a unit investment trust the assets of which are securities issued by a management company, the depositor of or principal underwriter for such trust, or any affiliated person of such depositor or underwriter, is to receive from such management company or any affiliated person thereof any fee or payment on account of payments on such certificate exceeding such reasonable amount as the Commission may prescribe.

(i)   Applicability to registered separate account funding variable insurance contracts.—

    (1)   This section does not apply to any registered separate account funding variable insurance contracts, or to the sponsoring insurance company and principal underwriter of such account, except as provided in paragraph (2).

(2)   It shall be unlawful for any registered separate account funding variable insurance contracts, or for the sponsoring insurance company of such account, to sell any such contract unless—

(A)   such contract is a redeemable security; and

(B)   the insurance company complies with section 26(f) and any rules or regulations issued by the Commission under section 26(f).

(j)   Termination of sales.—

(1)   Termination.—

Effective 30 days after the date of enactment of the Military Personnel Financial Services Protection Act, it shall be unlawful, subject to subsection (i)—

(A)   for any registered investment company to issue any periodic payment plan certificate; or

(B)   for such company, or any depositor of or underwriter for any such company, or any other person, to sell such a certificate.

(2)   No invalidation of existing certificates.—Paragraph (1) shall not be construed to alter, invalidate, or otherwise affect any rights or obligations, including rights of redemption, under any periodic payment plan certificate issued and sold before 30 days after such date of enactment.

Face-Amount Certificate Companies

Sec. 28.   (a)   Issuance or sale of certificates.—

It shall be unlawful for any registered face-amount certificate company to issue or sell any face-amount certificate, or to collect or accept any payment on any such certificate issued by such company on or after the effective date of this Act, unless—

(1)   such company, if organized before March 15, 1940, was actively and continuously engaged in selling face-amount certificates on and before that date, and has outstanding capital stock worth upon a fair valuation of assets not less than $50,000; or if organized on or after March 15, 1940, has capital stock in an amount not less than $250,000 which has been bona fide subscribed and paid for in cash; and

(2)   such company maintains at all times minimum certificate reserves on all its outstanding face-amount certificates in an aggregate amount calculated and adjusted as follows:

(A)   the reserves for each certificate of the installment type shall be based on assumed annual, semi-annual, quarterly, or monthly reserve payments according to the manner in which gross payments for any certificate year are made by the holder, which reserve payments shall be sufficient in amount, as and when accumulated at a rate not to exceed $3\frac{1}{2}$ per centum per annum compounded annually, to provide the minimum maturity or face amount of the certificate when due. Such reserve payments may be graduated according to certificate years so that the reserve payment or payments for the first certificate year shall amount to at least 50 per centum of the required gross annual payment for such year and the reserve payment or payments for each of the second to fifth certificate years inclusive shall amount to at least 93 per centum of each such year's required gross annual payment and for the sixth and each subsequent certificate year the reserve payment or payments shall amount to at least 96 per centum of each such year's required gross annual payment: *Provided,* That such aggregate reserve payments shall amount to at least 93 per centum of the aggregate gross annual payments required to be made by the holder to obtain the maturity of the certificate. The company may at its option take as loading from the gross payment or payments for a certificate year, as and when made by the certificate holder, an amount or amounts equal in the aggregate for such year to not more than the excess, if any, of the gross payment or payments required to be made by the holder for such year, over and above the percentage of the gross annual payment required herein for such year for reserve purposes. Such loading may be taken by the company prior to or after the setting up of the reserve payment or payments for such year and the reserve payment or payments for such year may be graduated and adjusted to correspond with the amount of the gross payment or payments made by the certificate holder for such year less the loading so taken;

(B)   if the foregoing minimum percentages of the gross annual payments required under the provisions of such certificate should produce reserve payments larger than are necessary at $3\frac{1}{2}$ per centum per annum compounded annually to provide the minimum maturity or face amount of the certificate when due, the reserve shall be based upon reserve payments accumulated as provided under preceding subparagraph (A) of this paragraph except that in lieu of the $3\frac{1}{2}$ per centum rate specified therein, such rate shall be lowered to the minimum rate, expressed in multiples of one-eighth of 1 per centum, which will accumulate such reserve payments to the maturity value when due;

(C)   if the actual annual gross payment to be made by the certificate holder on any certificate issued prior to or after the effective date of this Act is less than the amount of any assumed reserve payment or payments for a certificate year, such company shall maintain as a part of such minimum certificate reserves a deficiency reserve equal to the total present value of future deficiencies in the gross payments, calculated at a rate not to exceed $3\frac{1}{2}$ per centum per annum compounded annually;

(D)   for each certificate of the installment type the amount of the reserve shall at any time be at least equal to

(1)   the then amount of the reserve payments set up under section 28(a)(2)(A) or (B);

(2)   the accumulations on such reserve payments as computed under subparagraphs (A) or (B) of this paragraph (2);

(3)   the amount of any deficiency reserve required under subparagraph (C) hereof; and

(4)   such amount as shall have been credited to the account of each certificate holder in the form of any credit, or any dividend, or any interest in addition to the minimum maturity amount specified in such certificate, plus any accumulations on any amount or amounts so credited, at a rate not exceeding $3\frac{1}{2}$ per centum per annum compounded annually;

(E)   for each certificate which is fully paid, including any fully paid obligations resulting from or effected upon the maturity of the previously issued certificate, and for each paid-up certificate issued as provided in subsection (f) of this section prior to maturity, the amount of the reserve shall at any time be at least equal to

(1)   such amount as and when accumulated at a rate not to exceed $3\frac{1}{2}$ per centum per annum compounded annually, will provide the amount or amounts payable when due and

(2)   such amount as shall have been credited to the account of each such certificate holder in the form of any credit, or any dividend, or any interest in addition to the minimum maturity amount specified in the certificate, plus any accumulations on any amount or amounts so credited, at a rate not exceeding $3\frac{1}{2}$ per centum per annum compounded annually;

(F)   for each certificate of the installment type under which gross payments have been made by or credited to the holder thereof covering a payment period or periods or any part thereof beyond the then current payment period as defined by the terms of such certificate, and for which period or periods no reserve has been set up under subparagraph (A) or (B) hereof, an advance payment reserve shall be set up and maintained in the amount of the present value of any such unapplied advance gross payments, computed at a rate not to exceed $3\frac{1}{2}$ per centum per annum compounded annually;

(G)   such appropriate contingency reserves for death and disability benefits and for reinstatement rights on any such certificate providing for such benefits or rights as the Commission shall prescribe by rule, regulation, or order based upon the experience of face-amount companies in relation to such contingencies.

At no time shall the aggregate certificate reserves herein required by subparagraphs (A) to (F), inclusive, be less than the aggregate surrender values and other amounts to which all certificate holders may be then entitled.

For the purpose of this subsection (a), no certificate of the installment type shall be deemed to be outstanding if before a surrender value has been attained the holder thereof has been in continuous default in making his payments thereon for a period of one year.

(b)   Asset requirements prior to sale of certificates.—

It shall be unlawful for any registered face-amount certificate company to issue or sell any face-amount certificate, or to collect or accept any payment on any such certificate issued by such company on or after the effective date of this Act, unless such company has, in cash or qualified investments, assets having a value not less than the aggregate amount of the capital stock requirement and certificate reserves as computed under the provisions of subsection (a) hereof. As used in this subsection, "qualified investments" means investments of a kind which life-insurance companies are permitted to invest in or hold under the provisions of the Code of the District of Columbia as heretofore or hereafter amended, and such other investments as the Commission shall by rule, regulation, or order authorize as qualified investments. Such investments shall be valued in accordance with the provisions of said Code where such provisions are applicable. Investments to which such provisions do not apply shall be valued in accordance with such rules, regulations, or orders as the Commission shall prescribe for the protection of investors.

(c)   Certificate reserve requirements.—

The Commission shall by rule, regulation, or order, in the public interest or for the protection of investors, require a registered face-amount certificate company to deposit and maintain, upon such terms and conditions as the Commission shall prescribe and as are appropriate for the protection of investors, with one or more institutions having the qualifications required by paragraph (1) of section 26(a) for a trustee of a unit investment trust, all or any part of the investments maintained by such company as certificate reserve requirements under the provisions of subsection (b) hereof: *Provided, however,* That where qualified investments are maintained on deposit by such company in respect of its liabilities under certificates issued to or held by residents of any State as required by the statute of such State or by any order, regulation, or requirement of such State or any official or agency thereof, the amount so on deposit, but not to exceed the amount of reserves required by subsection (a) hereof for the certificates so issued or held, shall be deducted from the amount of qualified investments that may be required to be deposited hereunder.

Assets which are qualified investments under subsection (b) and which are deposited under or as permitted by this subsection (c), may be used and shall be considered as a part of the assets required to be maintained under the provision of said subsection (b).

(d)   Provisions required in certificate.—

It shall be unlawful for any registered face-amount certificate company to issue or sell any face-amount certificate, or to collect or accept any payment on any such certificate issued by such company on or after the effective date of this Act, unless such certificate contains a provision or provisions to the effect—

(1)   that, in respect of any certificate of the installment type, during the first certificate year the holder of the certificate, upon surrender thereof, shall be entitled to a value payable in cash not less than the reserve payments as specified in subparagraph (A) or (B) of paragraph (2) of subsection (a) and at the end of such certificate year, a value payable in cash at least equal to 50 per centum of the amount of the gross annual payment required thereby for such year;

(2)   that, in respect of any certificate of the installment type, at any time after the expiration of the first certificate year and prior to maturity, the holder of the certificate, upon surrender thereof, shall be entitled to a value payable in cash not less than the then amount of the reserve for such certificate required by numbered items (1) and (2) of subparagraph (D) of paragraph (2) of subsection (a) hereof, less a surrender charge that shall not exceed 2 per centum of the face or maturity amount of the certificate, or 15 per centum of the amount of such reserve, whichever is the lesser, but in no event shall such value be less than 50 per centum of the amount of such reserve. The amount of the surrender value for the end of each certificate year shall be set out in the certificate;

(3)   that, in respect of any certificate of the installment type, the holder of the certificate, upon surrender thereof for cash or upon receipt of a paid-up certificate as provided in subsection (f) hereof,

shall be entitled to a value payable in cash equal to the then amount of any advance payment reserve under such certificate required by subparagraph (F) of paragraph (2) of subsection (a) hereof in addition to any other amounts due the holder hereunder;

(4) that any time prior to maturity, in respect of any certificate which is fully paid, the holder of the certificate, upon surrender thereof, shall be entitled to a value payable in cash not less than the then amount of the reserve for such certificate required by item (1) of subparagraph (E) of paragraph (2) of subsection (a) hereof, less a surrender charge that shall not exceed 2 per centum of the face or maturity amount of the certificate, or 15 per centum of the amount of such reserve, whichever is the lesser: *Provided, however,* That such surrender charge shall not apply as to any obligations of a fully paid type resulting from the maturity of a previously issued certificate. The amount of the surrender value for the end of each certificate year shall be set out in the certificate;

(5) that in respect of any certificate, the holder of the certificate, upon maturity, upon surrender thereof for cash or upon receipt of a paid-up certificate as provided in subsection (f) hereof, shall be entitled to a value payable in cash equal to the then amount of the reserve, if any, for such certificate required by item (4) of subparagraph (D) of paragraph (2) of subsection (a) hereof or item (2) of subparagraph (E) of paragraph (2) of subsection (a) hereof in addition to any other amounts due the holder hereunder.

The term "certificate year" as used in this section in respect of any certificate of the installment type means a period or periods for which one year's payment or payments as provided by the certificate have been made thereon by the holder and the certificate maintained in force by such payments for the time for which the same have been made, and in respect of any certificate which is fully paid or paid-up means any year ending on the anniversary of the date of issuance of the certificate.

Any certificate may provide for loans or advances by the company to the certificate holder on the security of such certificate upon terms prescribed therein but at an interest rate not exceeding 6 per centum per annum. The amount of the required reserves, deposits, and the surrender values thereof available to the holder may be adjusted to take into account any unpaid balance on such loans or advances and interest thereon, for the purposes of this subsection and subsections (b) and (c) hereof.

Any certificate may provide that the company at its option may, prior to the maturity thereof, defer any payment or payments to the certificate holder to which he may be entitled under this subsection (d), for a period of not more than thirty days: *Provided,* That in the event such option is exercised by the company, interest shall accrue on any payment or payments due to the holder, for the period of such deferment at a rate equal to that used in accumulating the reserves for such certificate: *And provided further,* That the Commission may, by rules and regulations or orders in the public interest or for the protection of investors, make provision for any other deferment upon such terms and conditions as it shall prescribe.

(e) Liability of holder to legal action for unpaid amount of certificate.—

It shall be unlawful for any registered face-amount certificate company to issue or sell any face-amount certificate, or to collect or accept any payment on any such certificate issued by such company on or after the effective date of this Act, which certificate makes the holder liable to any legal action or proceeding for any unpaid amount on such certificate.

(f) Optional right to paid up certificate in lieu of cash surrender value.—

It shall be unlawful for any registered face-amount certificate company to issue or sell any face-amount certificate, or to collect or accept any payment on any such certificate issued by such company on or after the effective date of this Act,

(1) unless such face-amount certificate contains a provision or provisions to the effect that the holder shall have an optional right to receive a paid-up certificate in lieu of the then attained cash surrender value provided therein and in the amount of such value plus accumulations thereon at a rate to be specified in the paid-up certificate equal to that used in computing the reserve on the original certificate under subparagraph (A) or (B) of paragraph (2) of subsection (a) of this section, such paid-up certificate to become due and payable at the end of a period equal to the balance of the term of such original certificate before maturity; and during the period prior to maturity such paid-up certificate shall have a cash value upon surrender thereof equal to the then amount of the reserve therefor; and

(2)   unless such face-amount certificate contains a further provision or provisions to the effect that if the holder be in continuous default in his payments on such certificate for a period of six months without having exercised his option to receive a paid-up certificate, as herein provided, the company at the expiration of such six months shall pay the surrender value in cash if such value is less than $100 or if such value is $100 or more shall issue such paid-up certificate to such holder and such payment or issuance, plus the payment of all other amounts to which he may be then entitled under the original certificate, shall operate to cancel his original certificate: *Provided,* That in lieu of the issuance of a new paid-up certificate the original certificate may be converted into a paid-up certificate with the same effect; and

(3)   unless, where such certificate provides, in the event of default, for the deferment of payments thereon by the holder or of the due dates of such payments or of the maturity date of the certificate, it shall also provide in effect for the right of reinstatement by the holder of the certificate after default and for an option in the holder, at the time of reinstatement, to make up the payment or payments for the default period next preceding such reinstatement with interest thereon not exceeding 6 per centum per annum, with the same effect as if no such default in making such payments had occurred.

The term "default" as used in this subsection (f) shall, without restricting its usual meaning, include a failure to make a payment or payments as and when provided by the certificate.

(g)   Application of section to company issuing certificates only to holders of previously issued certificates.—

The foregoing provisions of this section shall not apply to a face-amount certificate company which on or before the effective date of this Act has discontinued the offering of face-amount certificates to the public and issues face-amount certificates only to the holders of certificates previously issued pursuant to an obligation expressed or implied in such certificates.

(h)   Declaration or payment of dividends.—

It shall be unlawful for any registered face-amount certificate company which does not maintain the minimum certificate reserve on all its outstanding face-amount certificates issued prior to the effective date of this Act, in an aggregate amount calculated and adjusted as provided in section 28, to declare or pay any dividends on the shares of such company for or during any calendar year which shall exceed one-third of the net earnings for the next preceding calendar year or which shall exceed 10 per centum of the aggregate net earnings for the next preceding five calendar years, whichever is the lesser amount, or any dividend which shall have been forbidden by the Commission pursuant to the provision of the next sentence of this paragraph. At least thirty days before such company shall declare, pay, or distribute any dividend, it shall give the Commission written notice of its intention to declare, pay, or distribute the same; and if at any time it shall appear to the Commission that the declaration, payment or distribution of any dividend for or during any calendar year might impair the financial integrity of such company or its ability to meet its liabilities under its outstanding face-amount certificates, it may by order forbid the declaration, distribution, or payment of any such dividend.

(i)   Application of section to certificates issued prior to effective date of section.—

The foregoing provisions of this section shall apply to all face-amount certificates issued prior to the effective date of this subsection; to the collection or acceptance of any payment on such certificates; to the issuance of face-amount certificates to the holders of such certificates pursuant to an obligation expressed or implied in such certificates; to the provisions of such certificates; to the minimum certificate reserves and deposits maintained with respect thereto; and to the assets that the issuer of such certificate was and is required to have with respect to such certificates. With respect to all face-amount certificates issued after the effective date of this subsection, the provisions of this section shall apply except as hereinafter provided.

(1)   Notwithstanding subparagraph (A) of paragraph (2) of subsection (a), the reserves for each certificate of the installment type shall be based on assumed annual, semi-annual, quarterly, or monthly reserve payments according to the manner in which gross payments for any certificate year are made by the holder, which reserve payments shall be sufficient in amount, as and when accumulated at a rate not to exceed $3\frac{1}{2}$ per centum per annum compounded annually, to provide the minimum maturity or face amount of the certificate when due. Such reserve payments may be

graduated according to certificate years so that the reserve payment or payments for the first three certificate years shall amount to at least 80 per centum of the required gross annual payment for such years; the reserve payment or payments for the fourth certificate year shall amount to at least 90 per centum of such year's required gross annual payment; the reserve payment or payments for the fifth certificate year shall amount to at least 93 per centum of such year's gross annual payment; and for the sixth and each subsequent certificate year the reserve payment or payments shall amount to at least 96 per centum of each such year's required gross annual payment: *Provided,* That such aggregate reserve payments shall amount to at least 93 per centum of the aggregate gross annual payments required to be made by the holder to obtain the maturity of the certificate. The company may at its option take as loading from the gross payment or payments for a certificate year, as and when made by the certificate holder, an amount or amounts equal in the aggregate for such year to not more than the excess, if any, of the gross payment or payments required to be made by the holder for such year, over and above the percentage of the gross annual payment required herein for such year for reserve purposes. Such loading may be taken by the company prior to or after the setting up of the reserve payment or payments for such year and the reserve payment or payments for such year may be graduated and adjusted to correspond with the amount of the gross payment or payments made by the certificate holder for such year less the loading so taken.

(2) Notwithstanding paragraphs (1) and (2) of subsection (d),

(A) in respect of any certificate of the installment type, during the first certificate year, the holder of the certificate, upon surrender thereof, shall be entitled to a value payable in cash not less than 80 per centum of the amount of the gross payments made on the certificate; and

(B) in respect of any certificate of the installment type, at any time after the expiration of the first certificate year and prior to maturity, the holder of the certificate, upon surrender thereof, shall be entitled to a value payable in cash not less than the then amount of the reserve for such certificate required by clauses (1) and (2) of subparagraph (D) of paragraph (2) of subsection (a), less a surrender charge that shall not exceed 2 per centum of the face or maturity amount of the certificate, or 15 per centum of the amount of such reserve, whichever is lesser, but in no event shall such value be less than 80 per centum of the gross payments made on the certificate. The amount of the surrender value for the end of each certificate year shall be set out in the certificate.

Periodic and Other Reports of Affiliated Persons

Sec. 29.   (a)   Annual report by company.—

Every registered investment company shall file annually with the Commission such information, documents, and reports as investment companies having securities registered on a national securities exchange are required to file annually pursuant to section 13(a) of the Securities Exchange Act of 1934 and the rules and regulations issued thereunder.

(b) Semi-annual or quarterly filing of information; copies of periodic or interim reports sent to security holders.—

Every registered investment company shall file with the Commission—

(1) such information, documents, and reports (other than financial statements), as the Commission may require to keep reasonably current the information and documents contained in the registration statement of such company filed under this title; and

(2) copies of every periodic or interim report or similar communication containing financial statements and transmitted to any class of such company's security holders, such copies to be filed not later than ten days after such transmission.

Any information or documents contained in a report or other communication to security holders filed pursuant to paragraph (2) may be incorporated by reference in any report subsequently or concurrently filed pursuant to paragraph (1).

(c) Minimizing reporting burdens.—

(1) The Commission shall take such action as it deems necessary or appropriate, consistent with the public interest and the protection of investors, to avoid unnecessary reporting by, and minimize

the compliance burdens on, registered investment companies and their affiliated persons in exercising its authority—

    (A)   under subsection (f); and

    (B)   under subsection (b)(1), if the Commission requires the filing of information, documents, and reports under that subsection on a basis more frequently than semiannually.

    (2)   Action taken by the Commission under paragraph (1) shall include considering, and requesting public comment on—

    (A)   feasible alternatives that minimize the reporting burdens on registered investment companies; and

    (B)   the utility of such information, documents, and reports to the Commission in relation to the costs to registered investment companies and their affiliated persons of providing such information, documents, and reports.

(d)   Reports under this section in lieu of reports under other provisions of law.—

The Commission shall issue rules and regulations permitting the filing with the Commission, and with any national securities exchange concerned, of copies of periodic reports, or of extracts therefrom, filed by any registered investment company pursuant to subsections (a) and (b), in lieu of any reports and documents required of such company under section 13 or 15(d) of the Securities Exchange Act of 1934.

(e)   Semi-annual reports to stockholders.—

Every registered investment company shall transmit to its stockholders, at least semiannually, reports containing such of the following information and financial statements or their equivalent, as of a reasonably current date, as the Commission may prescribe by rules and regulations for the protection of investors, which reports shall not be misleading in any material respect in the light of the reports required to be filed pursuant to subsections (a) and (b):

    (1)   a balance sheet accompanied by a statement of the aggregate value of investments on the date of such balance sheet;

    (2)   a list showing the amounts and values of securities owned on the date of such balance sheet;

    (3)   a statement of income, for the period covered by the report, which shall be itemized at least with respect to each category of income and expense representing more than 5 per centum of total income or expense;

    (4)   a statement of surplus, which shall be itemized at least with respect to each charge or credit to the surplus account which represents more than 5 per centum of the total charges or credits during the period covered by the report;

    (5)   a statement of the aggregate remuneration paid by the company during the period covered by the report

    (A)   to all directors and to all members of any advisory board for regular compensation;

    (B)   to each director and to each member of an advisory board for special compensation;

    (C)   to all officers; and

    (D)   to each person of whom any officer or director of the company is an affiliated person; and

    (6)   a statement of the aggregate dollar amount of purchases and sales of investment securities, other than Government securities made during the period covered by the report:

Provided, That if in the judgment of the Commission any item required under this subsection is inapplicable or inappropriate to any specified type or types of investment company, the Commission may by rules and regulations permit in lieu thereof the inclusion of such item of a comparable character as it may deem applicable or appropriate to such type or types of investment company.

(f)   Additional information.—

The Commission may, by rule, require that semi-annual reports containing the information set forth in subsection (e) include such other information as the Commission deems necessary or appropriate in the public interest or for the protection of investors.

(g)   Certificate of independent public accountants.—

Financial statements contained in annual reports required pursuant to subsections (a) and (e), if required by the rules and regulations of the Commission, shall be accompanied by a certificate of independent public accountants. The certificate of such independent public accountants shall be based upon an audit not less in scope or procedures followed than that which independent public accountants would ordinarily make for the purpose of presenting comprehensive and dependable financial statements, and shall contain such information as the Commission may prescribe, by rules and regulations in the public interest or for the protection of investors, as to the nature and scope of the audit and the findings and opinion of the accountants. Each such report shall state that such independent public accountants have verified securities owned, either by actual examination, or by receipt of a certificate from the custodian, as the Commission may prescribe by rules and regulations.

(h)   Duties and liabilities of affiliated persons.—

Every person who is directly or indirectly the beneficial owner of more than 10 per centum of any class of outstanding securities (other than short-term paper) of which a registered closed-end company is the issuer or who is an officer, director, member of an advisory board, investment adviser, or affiliated person of an investment adviser of such a company shall in respect of his transactions in any securities of such company (other than short-term paper) be subject to the same duties and liabilities as those imposed by section 16 of the Securities Exchange Act of 1934 upon certain beneficial owners, directors, and officers in respect of their transactions in certain equity securities.

(i)   Disclosure of church plan participants.—

A person that maintains a church plan that is excluded from the definition of an investment company solely by reason of section 3(c)(14) shall provide disclosure to plan participants, in writing, and not less frequently than annually, and for new participants joining such a plan after May 31, 1996, as soon as is practicable after joining such plan, that—

    (1)   the plan, or any company or account maintained to manage or hold plan assets and interests in such plan, company, or account, are not subject to registration, regulation, or reporting under this title, the Securities Act of 1933, the Securities Exchange Act of 1934, or State securities laws; and

    (2)   plan participants and beneficiaries therefore will not be afforded the protections of those provisions.

(j)   Notice to Commission.—

The Commission may issue rules and regulations to require any person that maintains a church plan that is excluded from the definition of an investment company solely by reason of section 3(c)(14) to file a notice with the Commission containing such information and in such form as the Commission may prescribe as necessary or appropriate in the public interest or consistent with the protection of investors.

Accounts and Records

Sec. 30.   (a)   Maintenance of records.—

    (1)   In general.—

Each registered investment company, and each underwriter, broker, dealer, or investment adviser that is a majority-owned subsidiary of such a company, shall maintain and preserve such records (as defined in section 3(a)(37) of the Securities Exchange Act of 1934) for such period or periods as the Commission, by rules and regulations, may prescribe as necessary or appropriate in the public interest or for the protection of investors. Each investment adviser that is not a majority-owned subsidiary of, and each depositor of any registered investment company, and each principal underwriter for any registered investment company other than a closed-end company, shall maintain and preserve for such period or periods as the Commission shall prescribe by rules and regulations, such records as are necessary or appropriate to record such person's transactions with such registered company. Each person having custody or use of the securities, deposits, or credits of a registered investment company shall maintain and preserve all records that relate to the custody or use by such person of the securities, deposits, or credits of the registered investment company for such period or periods as the Commission, by rule or regulation, may prescribe, as necessary or appropriate in the public interest or for the protection of investors.

(2)   Minimizing compliance burden.—

In exercising its authority under this subsection, the Commission shall take such steps as it deems necessary or appropriate, consistent with the public interest and for the protection of investors, to avoid unnecessary recordkeeping by, and minimize the compliance burden on, persons required to maintain records under this subsection (hereafter in this section referred to as "subject persons"). Such steps shall include considering, and requesting public comment on—

(A)   feasible alternatives that minimize the recordkeeping burdens on subject persons;

(B)   the necessity of such records in view of the public benefits derived from the independent scrutiny of such records through Commission examination;

(C)   the costs associated with maintaining the information that would be required to be reflected in such records; and

(D)   the effects that a proposed recordkeeping requirement would have on internal compliance policies and procedures.

(b)   Examinations of records.—

(1)   In general.—

All records required to be maintained and preserved in accordance with subsection (a) shall be subject at any time and from time to time to such reasonable periodic, special, and other examinations by the Commission, or any member or representative thereof, as the Commission may prescribe.

(2)   Availability.—

For purposes of examinations referred to in paragraph (1), any subject person shall make available to the Commission or its representatives any copies or extracts from such records as may be prepared without undue effort, expense, or delay as the Commission or its representatives may reasonably request.

(3)   Commission action.—

The Commission shall exercise its authority under this subsection with due regard for the benefits of internal compliance policies and procedures and the effective implementation and operation thereof.

(4)   Records of persons with custody or use.—

(A)   In general.—

Records of persons having custody or use of the securities, deposits, or credits of a registered investment company that relate to such custody or use, are subject at any time, or from time to time, to such reasonable periodic, special, or other examinations and other information and document requests by representatives of the Commission, as the Commission deems necessary or appropriate in the public interest or for the protection of investors.

(B)   Certain persons subject to other regulation.—

Any person that is subject to regulation and examination by a Federal financial institution regulatory agency (as such term is defined under section 212(c)(2) of title 18, United States Code) may satisfy any examination request, information request, or document request described under subparagraph (A), by providing to the Commission a detailed listing, in writing, of the securities, deposits, or credits of the registered investment company within the custody or use of such person.

(c)   Regulatory authority.—

The Commission may, in the public interest or for the protection of investors, issue rules and regulations providing for a reasonable degree of uniformity in the accounting policies and principles to be followed by registered investment companies in maintaining their accounting records and in preparing financial statements required pursuant to this Act.

(d) Exemption authority.—

The Commission, upon application made by any registered investment company, may by order exempt a specific transaction or transactions from the provisions of any rule or regulation made pursuant to subsection (e), if the Commission finds that such rule or regulation should not reasonably be applied to such transaction.

Accountants and Auditors

Sec. 31. (a) Selection of accountant.—

It shall be unlawful for any registered management company or registered face-amount certificate company to file with the Commission any financial statement signed or certified by an independent public accountant, unless—

    (1) such accountant shall have been selected at a meeting held within thirty days before or after the beginning of the fiscal year or before the annual meeting of stockholders in that year by the vote, cast in person, of a majority of those members of the board of directors who are not interested persons of such registered company;

    (2) such selection shall have been submitted for ratification or rejection at the next succeeding annual meeting of stockholders if such meeting be held, except that any vacancy occurring between annual meetings, due to the death or resignation of the accountant, may be filled by the vote of a majority of those members of the board of directors who are not interested persons of such registered company, cast in person at a meeting called for the purpose of voting on such action;

    (3) the employment of such accountant shall have been conditioned upon the right of the company by vote of a majority of the outstanding voting securities at any meeting called for the purpose to terminate such employment forthwith without any penalty; and

    (4) such certificate or report of such accountant shall be addressed both to the board of directors of such registered company and to the security holders thereof.

If the selection of an accountant has been rejected pursuant to paragraph (2) or his employment terminated pursuant to paragraph (3), the vacancy so occurring may be filled by a vote of a majority of the outstanding voting securities, either at the meeting at which the rejection or termination occurred or, if not so filled, at a subsequent meeting which shall be called for the purpose. In the case of a common-law trust of the character described in section 16(c), no ratification of the employment of such accountant shall be required but such employment may be terminated and such accountant removed by action of the holders of record of a majority of the outstanding shares of beneficial interest in such trust in the same manner as is provided in section 16(c) in respect of the removal of a trustee, and all the provisions therein contained as to the calling of a meeting shall be applicable. In the event of such termination and removal, the vacancy so occurring may be filled by action of the holders of record of a majority of the shares of beneficial interest either at the meeting, if any, at which such termination and removal occurs, or by instruments in writing filed with the custodian, or if not so filed within a reasonable time then at a subsequent meeting which shall be called by the trustees for the purpose. The provisions of paragraph (42) of section 2(a) as to a majority shall be applicable to the vote cast at any meeting of the shareholders of such a trust held pursuant to this subsection.

    (b) Selection of controller or other principal accounting officer.—

No registered management company or registered face-amount certificate company shall file with the Commission any financial statement in the preparation of which the controller or other principal accounting officer or employee of such company participated, unless such controller, officer or employee was selected, either by vote of the holders of such company's voting securities at the last annual meeting of such security holders, or by the board of directors of such company.

    (c) Reports of accountants and auditors.—

The Commission is authorized, by rules and regulations or order in the public interest or for the protection of investors, to require accountants and auditors to keep reports, work sheets, and other documents and papers relating to registered investment companies for such period or periods as the Commission may prescribe, and to make the same available for inspection by the Commission or any member or representative thereof.

Filing of Documents With Commission in Civil Actions

Sec. 32. Every registered investment company which is a party and every affiliated person of such company who is a party defendant to any action or claim by a registered investment company or a security holder thereof in a derivative or representative capacity against an officer, director, investment adviser, trustee, or depositor of such company, shall file with the Commission, unless already so filed,

    (1) a copy of all pleadings, verdicts, or judgments filed with the court or served in connection with such action or claim,

    (2) a copy of any proposed settlement, compromise, or discontinuance of such action, and

    (3) a copy of such motions, transcripts, or other documents filed in or issued by the court or served in connection with such action or claim as may be requested in writing by the Commission. If any document referred to in clause (1) or (2)—

    (A) is delivered to such company or party defendant, such document shall be filed with the Commission not later than ten days after the receipt thereof; or

    (B) is filed in such court or delivered by such company or party defendant, such document shall be filed with the Commission not later than five days after such filing or delivery.

Destruction and Falsification of Reports and Records

Sec. 33. (a) Willful destruction.—

It shall be unlawful for any person, except as permitted by rule, regulation, or order of the Commission, willfully to destroy, mutilate, or alter any account, book, or other document the preservation of which has been required pursuant to section 30(a) or 31(c).

(b) Untrue statements or omissions.—

It shall be unlawful for any person to make any untrue statement of a material fact in any registration statement, application, report, account, record, or other document filed or transmitted pursuant to this Act or the keeping of which is required pursuant to section 30(a). It shall be unlawful for any person so filing, transmitting, or keeping any such document to omit to state therein any fact necessary in order to prevent the statements made therein, in the light of the circumstances under which they were made, from being materially misleading. For the purposes of this subsection, any part of any such document which is signed or certified by an accountant or auditor in his capacity as such shall be deemed to be made, filed, transmitted, or kept by such accountant or auditor, as well as by the person filing, transmitting, or keeping the complete document.

Unlawful Representations and Names

Sec. 34. (a) Misrepresentation of guarantees.—

(1) In general.—

It shall be unlawful for any person, issuing or selling any security of which a registered investment company is the issuer, to represent or imply in any manner whatsoever that such security or company—

    (A) has been guaranteed, sponsored, recommended, or approved by the United States, or any agency, instrumentality or officer of the United States;

    (B) has been insured by the Federal Deposit Insurance Corporation; or

    (C) is guaranteed by or is otherwise an obligation of any bank or insured depository institution.

(2) Disclosures.—

Any person issuing or selling the securities of a registered investment company that is advised by, or sold through, a bank shall prominently disclose that an investment in the company is not insured by the Federal Deposit Insurance Corporation or any other government agency. The Commission may, after consultation with and taking into consideration the views of the Federal banking agencies (as defined in section 3 of the Federal Deposit Insurance Act), adopt rules and regulations, and issue orders, consistent with the protection of investors, prescribing the manner in which the disclosure under this paragraph shall be provided.

    (3)   Definitions.—

The terms "insurance depository institution" and "appropriate Federal banking agency" have the same meaning as given in section 3 of the Federal Deposit Insurance Act.

    (b)   Unlawful representation of sponsorship by United states or agency thereof.—

It shall be unlawful for any person registered under any section of this Act to represent or imply in any manner whatsoever that such person has been sponsored, recommended, or approved, or that his abilities or qualifications have in any respect been passed upon by the United States or any agency or officer thereof.

    (c)   Statement of registration under securities provisions.—

No provision of subsection (a) or (b) shall be construed to prohibit a statement that a person or security is registered under this Act, the Securities Act of 1933, or the Securities Exchange Act of 1934, if such statement is true in fact and if the effect of such registration is not misrepresented.

    (d)   Deceptive or misleading names.—

It shall be unlawful for any registered investment company to adopt as a part of the name or title of such company, or of any securities of which it is the issuer, any word or words that the Commission finds are materially deceptive or misleading. The Commission is authorized, by rule, regulation, or order, to define such names or titles as are materially deceptive or misleading.

Breach of Fiduciary Duty

Sec. 35.   (a)   Civil actions by Commission; jurisdiction; allegations; injunctive or other relief.—

The Commission is authorized to bring an action in the proper district court of the United States, or in the United States court of any territory or other place subject to the jurisdiction of the United States, alleging that a person who is, or at the time of the alleged misconduct was, serving or acting in one or more of the following capacities has engaged within five years of the commencement of the action or is about to engage in any act or practice constituting a breach of fiduciary duty involving personal misconduct in respect of any registered investment company for which such person so serves or acts, or at the time of the alleged misconduct, so served or acted—

    (1)   as officer, director, member of any advisory board, investment adviser, or depositor; or

    (2)   as principal underwriter, if such registered company is an open-end company, unit investment trust, or face-amount certificate company.

If such allegations are established, the court may enjoin such persons from acting in any or all such capacities either permanently or temporarily and award such injunctive or other relief against such person as may be reasonable and appropriate in the circumstances, having due regard to the protection of investors and to the effectuation of the policies declared in section 1(b) of this Act.

    (b)   Compensation or payments as basis of fiduciary duty; civil actions by Commission or security holder; burden of proof; judicial consideration of director or shareholder approval; persons liable; extent of liability; exempted transactions; jurisdiction; finding restriction.—

For the purposes of this subsection, the investment adviser of a registered investment company shall be deemed to have a fiduciary duty with respect to the receipt of compensation for services, or of payments of a material nature, paid by such registered investment company, or by the security holders thereof, to such investment adviser or any affiliated person of such investment adviser. An action may be brought under this subsection by the Commission, or by a security holder of such registered investment company on behalf of such company, against such investment adviser, or any affiliated person of such investment adviser, or any other person enumerated in subsection (a) of this section who has a fiduciary duty concerning such compensation or payments, for breach of fiduciary duty in respect of such compensation or payments paid by such registered investment company or by the security holders thereof to such investment adviser or person. With respect to any such action the following provisions shall apply:

(1) It shall not be necessary to allege or prove that any defendant engaged in personal misconduct, and the plaintiff shall have the burden of proving a breach of fiduciary duty.

(2) In any such action approval by the board of directors of such investment company of such compensation or payments, or of contracts or other arrangements providing for such compensation or payments, and ratification or approval of such compensation or payments, or of contracts or other arrangements providing for such compensation or payments, by the shareholders of such investment company, shall be given such consideration by the court as is deemed appropriate under all the circumstances.

(3) No such action shall be brought or maintained against any person other than the recipient of such compensation or payments, and no damages or other relief shall be granted against any person other than the recipient of such compensation or payments. No award of damages shall be recoverable for any period prior to one year before the action was instituted. Any award of damages against such recipient shall be limited to the actual damages resulting from the breach of fiduciary duty and shall in no event exceed the amount of compensation or payments received from such investment company, or the security holders thereof, by such recipient.

(4) This subsection shall not apply to compensation or payments made in connection with transactions subject to section 17 of this Act, or rules, regulations, or orders thereunder, or to sales loads for the acquisition of any security issued by a registered investment company.

(5) Any action pursuant to this subsection may be brought only in an appropriate district court of the United States.

(6) No finding by a court with respect to a breach of fiduciary duty under this subsection shall be made a basis

(A) for a finding of a violation of this title for the purposes of sections 9 and 48 of this Act, section 15 of the Securities Exchange Act of 1934, or section 203 of the Investment Advisers Act, or

(B) for an injunction to prohibit any person from serving in any of the capacities enumerated in subsection (a) of this section.

(c) Corporate or other trustees performing functions of investment advisers.—

For the purposes of subsections (a) and (b), the term "investment adviser" includes a corporate or other trustee performing the functions of an investment adviser.

Larceny and Embezzlement

Sec. 36. Whoever steals, unlawfully abstracts, unlawfully and willfully converts to his own use or to the use of another, or embezzles any of the moneys, funds, securities, credits, property, or assets of any registered investment company shall be deemed guilty of a crime, and upon conviction thereof shall be subject to the penalties provided in section 48. A judgment of conviction or acquittal on the merits under the laws of any State shall be a bar to any prosecution under this section for the same act or acts.

Rules, Regulations, and Orders; General Powers of Commission

Sec. 37. (a) Powers of Commission.—

The Commission shall have authority from time to time to make, issue, amend, and rescind such rules and regulations and such orders as are necessary or appropriate to the exercise of the powers conferred upon the Commission elsewhere in this title, including rules and regulations defining accounting, technical, and trade terms used in this Act, and prescribing the form or forms in which information required in registration statements, applications, and reports to the Commission shall be set forth. For the purposes of its rules or regulations the Commission may classify persons, securities, and other matters within its jurisdiction and prescribe different requirements for different classes of persons, securities, or matters.

(b)   Filing of information and documents.—

The Commission, by such rules and regulations or order as it deems necessary or appropriate in the public interest or for the protection of investors, may authorize the filing of any information or documents required to be filed with the Commission under this Act, the Investment Advisers Act, the Securities Act of 1933, the Securities Exchange Act of 1934, or the Trust Indenture Act of 1939, by incorporating by reference any information or documents theretofore or concurrently filed with the Commission under this Act or any of such Acts.

(c)   Good faith conformance with rules, regulations, and orders.—

No provision of this Act imposing any liability shall apply to any act done or omitted in good faith in conformity with any rule, regulation, or order of the Commission, notwithstanding that such rule, regulation, or order may, after such act or omission, be amended or rescinded or be determined by judicial or other authority to be invalid for any reason.

Procedure for Issuance of Rules and Regulations

Sec. 38.   Subject to the provisions of the Federal Register Act and regulations prescribed under the authority thereof, the rules and regulations of the Commission under this Act, and amendments thereof, shall be effective upon publication in the manner which the Commission shall prescribe, or upon such later date as may be provided in such rules and regulations.

Procedure for Issuance of Orders

Sec. 39.   (a)   Notice and hearing.—

Orders of the Commission under this Act shall be issued only after appropriate notice and opportunity for hearing. Notice to the parties to a proceeding before the Commission shall be given by personal service upon each party or by registered mail or certified mail or confirmed telegraphic notice to the party's last known business address. Notice to interested persons, if any, other than parties may be given in the same manner or by publication in the Federal Register.

(b)   Application verified under oath admissible as evidence.—

The Commission may provide, by appropriate rules or regulations, that an application verified under oath may be admissible in evidence in a proceeding before the Commission and that the record in such a proceeding may consist, in whole or in part, of such application.

(c)   Parties.—

In any proceeding before the Commission, the Commission, in accordance with such rules and regulations as it may prescribe, shall admit as a party any interested State or State agency, and may admit as a party any representative of interested security holders, or any other person whose participation in the proceeding may be in the public interest or for the protection of investors.

Hearings by Commission

Sec. 40.   Hearings may be public and may be held before the Commission, any member or members thereof, or any officer or officers of the Commission designated by it, and appropriate records thereof shall be kept.

Enforcement of Act

Sec. 41.   (a)   Investigation.—

The Commission may make such investigations as it deems necessary to determine whether any person has violated or is about to violate any provision of this Act or of any rule, regulation, or order hereunder, or to determine whether any action in any court or any proceeding before the Commission shall be instituted under this title against a particular person or persons, or with respect to a particular transaction or transactions. The Commission shall permit any person to file with it a statement in writing, under oath or otherwise as the Commission shall determine, as to all the facts and circumstances concerning the matter to be investigated.

(b)   Administration of oaths and affirmations, subpoena of witnesses, etc.—

For the purpose of any investigation or any other proceeding under this Act, any member of the Commission, or any officer thereof designated by it, is empowered to administer oaths and affirmations, subpena witnesses, compel their attendance, take evidence, and require the production of any books, papers, correspondence, memoranda, contracts, agreements, or other records which are relevant or material to the inquiry. Such attendance of witnesses and the production of any such records may be required from any place in any State or in any Territory or other place subject to the jurisdiction of the United States at any designated place of hearing.

(c)   Jurisdiction of courts of United States.—

In case of contumacy by, or refusal to obey a subpena issued to, any person, the Commission may invoke the aid of any court of the United States within the jurisdiction of which such investigation or proceeding is carried on, or where such person resides or carries on business, in requiring the attendance and testimony of witnesses and the production of books, papers, correspondence, memoranda, contracts, agreements, and other records. And such court may issue an order requiring such person to appear before the Commission or member or officer designated by the Commission, there to produce records, if so ordered, or to give testimony touching the matter under investigation or in question; any failure to obey such order of the court may be punished by such court as a contempt thereof. All process in any such case may be served in the judicial district whereof such person is an inhabitant or wherever he may be found. Any person who without just cause shall fail or refuse to attend and testify or to answer any lawful inquiry or to produce books, papers, correspondence, memoranda, contracts, agreements, or other records, if in his or its power so to do, in obedience to the subpena of the Commission, shall be guilty of a misdemeanor, and upon conviction shall be subject to a fine of not more than $1,000 or to imprisonment for a term of not more than one year, or both.

(d)   Action for injunction.—

Whenever it shall appear to the Commission that any person has engaged or is about to engage in any act or practice constituting a violation of any provision of this Act, or of any rule, regulation, or order hereunder, it may in its discretion bring an action in the proper district court of the United States, or the proper United States court of any Territory or other place subject to the jurisdiction of the United States, to enjoin such acts or practices and to enforce compliance with this Act or any rule, regulation, or order hereunder. Upon a showing that such person has engaged or is about to engage in any such act or practice, a permanent or temporary injunction or decree or restraining order shall be granted without bond. In any proceeding under this subsection to enforce compliance with section 7, the court as a court of equity may, to the extent it deems necessary or appropriate, take exclusive jurisdiction and possession of the investment company or companies involved and the books, records, and assets thereof, wherever located; and the court shall have jurisdiction to appoint a trustee, who with the approval of the court shall have power to dispose of any or all of such assets, subject to such terms and conditions as the court may prescribe. The Commission may transmit such evidence as may be available concerning any violation of the provisions of this Act, or of any rule, regulation, or order thereunder, to the Attorney General, who, in his discretion, may institute the appropriate criminal proceedings under this Act.

(e)   Money penalties in civil actions.—

(1)   Authority of Commission.—

Whenever it shall appear to the Commission that any person has violated any provision of this Act, the rules or regulations thereunder, or a cease-and-desist order entered by the Commission pursuant to section 9(f) of this Act, the Commission may bring an action in a United States district court to seek, and the court shall have jurisdiction to impose, upon a proper showing, a civil penalty to be paid by the person who committed such violation.

(2)   Amount of penalty.—

(A)   First tier.—

The amount of the penalty shall be determined by the court in light of the facts and circumstances. For each violation, the amount of the penalty shall not exceed the greater of

(i) $5,000 for a natural person or $50,000 for any other person, or (ii) the gross amount of pecuniary gain to such defendant as a result of the violation.

(B) Second tier.—

Notwithstanding subparagraph (A), the amount of penalty for each such violation shall not exceed the greater of

    (i) $50,000 for a natural person or $250,000 for any other person, or

    (ii)   the gross amount of pecuniary gain to such defendant as a result of the violation, if the violation described in paragraph (1) involved fraud, deceit, manipulation, or deliberate or reckless disregard of a regulatory requirement.

(C) Third tier.—

Notwithstanding subparagraphs (A) and (B), the amount of penalty for each such violation shall not exceed the greater of (i) $100,000 for a natural person or $500,000 for any other person, or (ii) the gross amount of pecuniary gain to such defendant as a result of the violation, if—

    (I)   the violation described in paragraph (1) involved fraud, deceit, manipulation, or deliberate or reckless disregard of a regulatory requirement; and

    (II)   such violation directly or indirectly resulted in substantial losses or created a significant risk of substantial losses to other persons.

(3)   Procedures for collection.—

(A)   Payment of penalty to Treasury.—

A penalty imposed under this section shall be payable into the Treasury of the United States, except as otherwise provided in section 308 of the Sarbanes-Oxley Act of 2002 and Section 21F of the Securities Exchange Act of 1934.

(B)   Collection of penalties.—

If a person upon whom such a penalty is imposed shall fail to pay such penalty within the time prescribed in the court's order, the Commission may refer the matter to the Attorney General who shall recover such penalty by action in the appropriate United States district court.

(C)   Remedy not exclusive.—

The actions authorized by this subsection may be brought in addition to any other action that the Commission or the Attorney General is entitled to bring.

(D)   Jurisdiction and venue.—

For purposes of section 43 of this Act, actions under this paragraph shall be actions to enforce a liability or a duty created by this title.

(4)   Special provisions relating to a violation of a cease-and-desist order.—

In an action to enforce a cease-and-desist order entered by the Commission pursuant to section 9(f), each separate violation of such order shall be a separate offense, except that in the case of a violation through a continuing failure to comply with the order, each day of the failure to comply shall be deemed a separate offense.

Court Review of Orders

Sec. 42.   (a)   Any person or party aggrieved by an order issued by the Commission under this Act may obtain a review of such order in the court of appeals of the United States within any circuit wherein such person resides or has his principal place of business, or in the United States Court of Appeals for the District of Columbia, by filing in such court, within sixty days after the entry of such order, a written petition praying that the order of the Commission be modified or set aside in whole or in part. A copy of such petition shall be forthwith transmitted by the clerk of the court to any member of the Commission, or any officer thereof designated by the Commission for that purpose, and thereupon the Commission shall file in the court the record upon which the order complained of was entered, as provided in section 2112 of title 28, United States Code. Upon the filing of such petition such court shall have jurisdiction, which upon the filing of the record shall be exclusive, to affirm, modify, or set aside such order, in whole or in part. No objection to the order of the Commission shall be considered by the court unless such objection shall have been urged before the Commission or unless there were reasonable grounds for failure so to do. The findings of the Commission as to the facts, if supported by substantial evidence, shall be conclusive. If application is made to the court for leave to adduce additional evidence, and it is shown to the satisfaction of the court that such additional evidence is material and that there were reasonable grounds for failure to adduce such evidence in the proceeding before the Commission, the court may order such additional evidence to be taken before the Commission and to be adduced upon the hearing in such manner and upon such terms and conditions as to the court may seem proper. The Commission may modify its findings as to the facts by reason of the additional evidence so taken, and it shall file with the court such modified or new findings, which, if supported by substantial evidence, shall be conclusive, and its recommendation, if any, for the modification or setting aside of the original order. The judgment and decree of the court affirming, modifying, or setting aside, in whole or in part, any such order of the Commission shall be final, subject to review by the Supreme Court of the United States upon certiorari or certification as provided in section 1254 of Title 28, United States Code.

(b)   The commencement of proceedings under subsection (a) to review an order of the Commission issued under section 8(e) shall operate as a stay of the Commission's order unless the court otherwise orders. The commencement of proceedings under subsection (a) to review an order of the Commission issued under any provision of this Act other than section 8(e) shall not operate as a stay of the Commission's order unless the court specifically so orders.

Jurisdiction of Offenses and Suits

Sec. 43.   The district courts of the United States and the United States courts of any Territory or other place subject to the jurisdiction of the United States shall have jurisdiction of violations of this Act or the rules, regulations, or orders thereunder, and, concurrently with State and Territorial courts, of all suits in equity and actions at law brought to enforce any liability or duty created by, or to enjoin any violation of, this Act or the rules, regulations, or orders thereunder. Any criminal proceeding may be brought in the district wherein any act or transaction constituting the violation occurred. A criminal proceeding based upon a violation of section 33, or upon a failure to file a report or other document required to be filed under this Act, may be brought in the district wherein the defendant is an inhabitant or maintains his principal office or place of business. Any suit or action to enforce any liability or duty created by, or to enjoin any violation of, this Act or rules, regulations, or orders thereunder, may be brought in any such district or in the district wherein the defendant is an inhabitant or transacts business, and process in such cases may be served in any district of which the defendant is an inhabitant or transacts business or wherever the defendant may be found. In any action or proceeding instituted by the Commission under this title in a United States district court for any judicial district, a subpoena issued to compel the attendance of a witness or the production of documents or tangible things (or both) at a hearing or trial may be served at any place within the United States. Rule 45(c)(3)(A)(ii) of the Federal Rules of Civil Procedure shall not apply to a subpoena issued under the preceding sentence. Judgments and decrees so rendered shall be subject to review as provided in sections 1254, 1291, 1292, and 1294 of Title 28, United States Code. No costs shall be assessed for or against the Commission in any proceeding under this Act brought by or against the Commission in any court. The Commission may intervene as a party in any action or suit to enforce any liability or duty created by, or to enjoin any noncompliance with, section 35(b) of this Act at any stage of such action or suit prior to final judgment therein.

Information Filed With Commission

Sec. 44.   (a)   The information contained in any registration statement, application, report, or other document filed with the Commission pursuant to any provision of this Act or of any rule or regulation thereunder (as distinguished from any information or document transmitted to the Commission) shall be made available to the public, unless and except insofar as the Commission, by rules and regulations upon its own motion, or by order upon application, finds that public disclosure is neither necessary nor appropriate in the public interest or for the protection of investors. Except as provided in section 24(c) of the Securities Exchange Act of 1934, it shall be unlawful for any member, officer, or employee of the Commission to use for personal benefit, or to disclose to any person other than an official or employee of the United States or of a State, for official use, or for any such official or employee to use for personal benefit, any information contained in any document so filed or transmitted, if such information is not available to the public.

(b) Photostatic or other copies of information contained in documents filed with the Commission under this Act and made available to the public shall be furnished any person at such reasonable charge and under such reasonable limitations as the Commission shall prescribe.

Annual Reports of Commission; Employees of the Commission

Sec. 45. (a) Omitted.

(b) Hiring and leasing authority.—

The provisions of section 4(b) of the Securities Exchange Act of 1934 shall be applicable with respect to the power of the Commission—

(1) to appoint and fix the compensation of such employees as may be necessary for carrying out its functions under this Act, and

(2) to lease and allocate such real property as may be necessary for carrying out its functions under this Act.

Validity of Contracts

Sec. 46. (a) Waiver of compliance as void.—

Any condition, stipulation, or provision binding any person to waive compliance with any provision of this Act or with any rule, regulation, or order thereunder shall be void.

(b) Equitable results; rescission; severance.—

(1) A contract that is made, or whose performance involves, a violation of this Act, or of any rule, regulation, or order thereunder, is unenforceable by either party (or by a nonparty to the contract who acquired a right under the contract with knowledge of the facts by reason of which the making or performance violated or would violate any provision of this Act or of any rule, regulation, or order thereunder) unless a court finds that under the circumstances enforcement would produce a more equitable result than nonenforcement and would not be inconsistent with the purposes of this Act.

(2) To the extent that a contract described in paragraph (1) has been performed, a court may not deny rescission at the instance of any party unless such court finds that under the circumstances the denial of rescission would produce a more equitable result than its grant and would not be inconsistent with the purposes of this Act.

(3) This subsection shall not apply

(A) to the lawful portion of a contract to the extent that it may be severed from the unlawful portion of the contract, or

(B) to preclude recovery against any person for unjust enrichment.

Liability of Controlling Persons; Preventing Compliance With Act

Sec. 47. (a) Procurement.—

It shall be unlawful for any person, directly or indirectly, to cause to be done any act or thing through or by means of any other person which it would be unlawful for such person to do under the provisions of this Act or any rule, regulation, or order thereunder.

(b) For purposes of any action brought by the Commission under subsection (d) or (e) of section 41, any person that knowingly or recklessly provides substantial assistance to another person in violation of a provision of this Act, or of any rule or regulation issued under this Act, shall be deemed to be in violation of such provision to the same extent as the person to whom such assistance is provided.

(c) Obstructing compliance.—

It shall be unlawful for any person without just cause to hinder, delay, or obstruct the making, filing, or keeping of any information, document, report, record, or account required to be made, filed, or kept under any provision of this Act or any rule, regulation, or order thereunder.

INVESTMENT COMPANY ACT OF 1940

Penalties

Sec. 48. Any person who willfully violates any provision of this Act or of any rule, regulation, or order hereunder, or any person who willfully in any registration statement, application, report, account, record, or other document filed or transmitted pursuant to this Act or the keeping of which is required pursuant to section 30(a) makes any untrue statement of a material fact or omits to state any material fact necessary in order to prevent the statements made therein from being materially misleading in the light of the circumstances under which they were made, shall upon conviction be fined not more than $10,000 or imprisoned not more than five years, or both; but no person shall be convicted under this section for the violation of any rule, regulation, or order if he proves that he had no actual knowledge of such rule, regulation, or order.

Effect on Existing Law

Sec. 49. Except where specific provision is made to the contrary, nothing in this Act shall affect

(1) the jurisdiction of the Commission under the Securities Act of 1933, the Securities Exchange Act of 1934, the Trust Indenture Act of 1939, or title II of this Act, over any person, security, or transaction, or

(2) the rights, obligations, duties, or liabilities of any person under such Acts; nor shall anything in this Act affect the jurisdiction of any other commission, board, agency, or officer of the United States or of any State or political subdivision of any State, over any person, security, or transaction, insofar as such jurisdiction does not conflict with any provision of this Act or of any rule, regulation, or order hereunder.

Separability of Provisions

Sec. 50. If any provision of this Act or any provision incorporated in this Act by reference, or the application of any such provision to any person or circumstances, shall be held invalid, the remainder of this Act and the application of any such provision to person or circumstances other than those as to which it is held invalid shall not be affected thereby.

Short Title

Sec. 51. This Act may be cited as the "Investment Company Act of 1940."

Effective Date

Sec. 52. The effective date of the provisions of this Act, so far as the same relate to face-amount certificates or to face-amount certificate companies, is January 1, 1941. The effective date of provisions hereof, insofar as the same do not apply to face-amount certificates or face-amount certificate companies is November 1, 1940. Except as herein otherwise provided, every provision of this subchapter shall take effect on November 1, 1940.

Election to Be Regulated as a Business Development Company

Sec. 53. (a) Eligibility.—

Any company defined in section 2(a)(48)(A) and (B) may elect to be subject to the provisions of sections 54 through 64 by filing with the Commission a notification of election, if such company—

(1) has a class of its equity securities registered under section 12 of the Securities Exchange Act of 1934; or

(2) has filed a registration statement pursuant to section 12 of the Securities Exchange Act of 1934 for a class of its equity securities.

(b) Form and manner of notification; effect.—

The Commission may, by rule, prescribe the form and manner in which notification of election under this section shall be given. A business development company shall be deemed to be subject to sections 54 through 64 upon receipt by the Commission of such notification of election.

(c) Revocation or withdrawal of election.—

Whenever the Commission finds, on its own motion or upon application, that a business development company which has filed a notification of election pursuant to subsection (a) of this section has ceased to engage in business, the Commission shall so declare by order revoking such company's election. Any business development company may voluntarily withdraw its election under subsection (a) by filing a notice of withdrawal of election with the Commission, in a form and manner which the Commission may, by rule, prescribe. Such withdrawal shall be effective immediately upon receipt by the Commission.

Functions and Activities of Business Development Companies

Sec. 54. (a) Permissible assets; percentage.—

It shall be unlawful for a business development company to acquire any assets (other than those described in paragraphs (1) through (7) of this subsection) unless, at the time the acquisition is made, assets described in paragraphs (1) through (6) below represent at least 70 per centum of the value of its total assets (other than assets described in paragraph (7) below):

(1) securities purchased, in transactions not involving any public offering or in such other transactions as the Commission may, by rule, prescribe if it finds that enforcement of this Act and of the Securities Act of 1933 with respect to such transactions is not necessary in the public interest or for the protection of investors by reason of the small amount, or the limited nature of the public offering, involved in such transactions—

(A) from the issuer of such securities, which issuer is an eligible portfolio company, from any person who is, or who within the preceding thirteen months has been, an affiliated person of such eligible portfolio company, or from any other person, subject to such rules and regulations as the Commission may prescribe as necessary or appropriate in the public interest or for the protection of investors; or

(B) from the issuer of such securities, which issuer is described in section 2(a)(46)(A) and (B) but is not an eligible portfolio company, because it has issued a class of securities with respect to which a member of a national securities exchange, broker, or dealer may extend or maintain credit to or for a customer pursuant to rules or regulations adopted by the Board of Governors of the Federal Reserve System under section 7 of the Securities Exchange Act of 1934, or from any person who is an officer or employee of such issuer, if—

(i) at the time of the purchase, the business development company owns at least 50 per centum of—

(I) the greatest number of equity securities of such issuer and securities convertible into or exchangeable for such securities; and

(II) the greatest amount of debt securities of such issuer,

held by such business development company at any point in time during the period when such issuer was an eligible portfolio company, except that options, warrants, and similar securities which have by their terms expired and debt securities which have been converted, or repaid or prepaid in the ordinary course of business or incident to a public offering of securities of such issuer, shall not be considered to have been held by such business development company for purposes of this requirement; and

(ii) the business development company is one of the 20 largest holders of record of such issuer's outstanding voting securities;

(2) securities of any eligible portfolio company with respect to which the business development company satisfies the requirements of section 2(a)(46)(C)(ii);

(3) securities purchased in transactions not involving any public offering from an issuer described in sections 2(a)(46)(A) and (B) or from a person who is, or who within the preceding thirteen months has been, an affiliated person of such issuer, or from any person in transactions incident thereto, if such securities were—

(A) issued by an issuer that is, or was immediately prior to the purchase of its securities by the business development company, in bankruptcy proceedings, subject to reorganization under the supervision of a court of competent jurisdiction, or subject to a plan or arrangement resulting from such bankruptcy proceedings or reorganization;

(B)   issued by an issuer pursuant to or in consummation of such a plan or arrangement; or

(C)   issued by an issuer that, immediately prior to the purchase of such issuer's securities by the business development company, was not in bankruptcy proceedings but was unable to meet its obligations as they came due without material assistance other than conventional lending or financing arrangements;

(4)   securities of eligible portfolio companies purchased from any person in transactions not involving any public offering, if there is no ready market for such securities and if immediately prior to such purchase the business development company owns at least 60 per centum of the outstanding equity securities of such issuer (giving effect to all securities presently convertible into or exchangeable for equity securities of such issuer as if such securities were so converted or exchanged);

(5)   securities received in exchange for or distributed on or with respect to securities described in paragraphs (1) through (4) of this subsection, or pursuant to the exercise of options, warrants, or rights relating to securities described in such paragraphs;

(6)   cash, cash items, Government securities, or high quality debt securities maturing in one year or less from the time of investment in such high quality debt securities; and

(7)   office furniture and equipment, interests in real estate and leasehold improvements and facilities maintained to conduct the business operations of the business development company, deferred organization and operating expenses, and other noninvestment assets necessary and appropriate to its operations as a business development company, including notes of indebtedness of directors, officers, employees, and general partners held by a business development company as payment for securities of such company issued in connection with an executive compensation plan described in section 57(j).

(b)   Valuation of assets.—

For purposes of this section, the value of a business development company's assets shall be determined as of the date of the most recent financial statements filed by such company with the Commission pursuant to section 13 of the Securities Exchange Act of 1934, and shall be determined no less frequently than annually.

Qualifications of Directors

Sec. 55.   (a)   Non-interested persons.—

A majority of a business development company's directors or general partners shall be persons who are not interested persons of such company.

(b)   Vacancies; suspension of provisions.—

If, by reason of the death, disqualification, or bona fide resignation of any director or general partner, a business development company does not meet the requirements of subsection (a) of this section, or the requirements of section 15(f)(1) of this Act with respect to directors, the operation of such provisions shall be suspended for a period of 90 days or for such longer period as the Commission may prescribe, upon its own motion or by order upon application, as not inconsistent with the protection of investors.

Transactions With Certain Affiliates

Sec. 56.   (a)   Transactions involving controlling or closely affiliated persons.—

It shall be unlawful for any person who is related to a business development company in a manner described in subsection (b) of this section, acting as principal—

(1)   knowingly to sell any security or other property to such business development company or to any company controlled by such business development company, unless such sale involves solely

(A)   securities of which the buyer is the issuer, or

(B)   the securities of which the seller is the issuer and which are part of a general offering to the holders of a class of its securities;

(2) knowingly to purchase from such business development company or from any company controlled by such business development company, any security or other property (except securities of which the seller is the issuer);

(3) knowingly to borrow money or other property from such business development company or from any company controlled by such business development company (unless the borrower is controlled by the lender), except as permitted in section 21(b) or section 61; or

(4) knowingly to effect any transaction in which such business development company or a company controlled by such business development company is a joint or a joint and several participant with such person in contravention of such rules and regulations as the Commission may prescribe for the purpose of limiting or preventing participation by such business development company or controlled company on a basis less advantageous than that of such person, except that nothing contained in this paragraph shall be deemed to preclude any person from acting as manager of any underwriting syndicate or other group in which such business development company or controlled company is a participant and receiving compensation therefor.

(b) Controlling or closely affiliated persons.—

The provisions of subsection (a) of this section shall apply to the following persons:

(1) Any director, officer, employee, or member of an advisory board of a business development company or any person (other than the business development company itself) who is, within the meaning of section 2(a)(3)(C) of this Act, an affiliated person of any such person specified in this paragraph.

(2) Any investment adviser or promoter of, general partner in, principal underwriter for, or person directly or indirectly either controlling, controlled by, or under common control with, a business development company (except the business development company itself and any person who, if it were not directly or indirectly controlled by the business development company, would not be directly or indirectly under the control of a person who controls the business development company), or any person who is, within the meaning of section 2(a)(3)(C) or (D), an affiliated person of any such person specified in this paragraph.

(c) Exemption orders.—

Notwithstanding paragraphs (1), (2), and (3) of subsection (a), any person may file with the Commission an application for an order exempting a proposed transaction of the applicant from one or more provisions of such paragraphs. The Commission shall grant such application and issue such order of exemption if evidence establishes that—

(1) the terms of the proposed transaction, including the consideration to be paid or received, are reasonable and fair and do not involve overreaching of the business development company or its shareholders or partners on the part of any person concerned;

(2) the proposed transaction is consistent with the policy of the business development company as recited in the filings made by such company with the Commission under the Securities Act of 1933, its registration statement and reports filed under the Securities Exchange Act of 1934, and its reports to shareholders or partners; and

(3) the proposed transaction is consistent with the general purposes of this Act.

(d) Transactions involving noncontrolling shareholders or affiliated persons.—

It shall be unlawful for any person who is related to a business development company in the manner described in subsection (e) of this section and who is not subject to the prohibitions of subsection (a) of this section, acting as principal—

(1) knowingly to sell any security or other property to such business development company or to any company controlled by such business development company, unless such sale involves solely

(A) securities of which the buyer is the issuer, or

(B) securities of which the seller is the issuer and which are part of a general offering to the holders of a class of its securities;

(2) knowingly to purchase from such business development company or from any company controlled by such business development company, any security or other property (except securities of which the seller is the issuer);

(3) knowingly to borrow money or other property from such business development company or from any company controlled by such business development company (unless the borrower is controlled by the lender), except as permitted in section 21(b); or

(4) knowingly to effect any transaction in which such business development company or a company controlled by such business development company is a joint or a joint and several participant with such affiliated person in contravention of such rules and regulations as the Commission may prescribe for the purpose of limiting or preventing participation by such business development company or controlled company on a basis less advantageous than that of such affiliated person, except that nothing contained in this paragraph shall be deemed to preclude any person from acting as manager of any underwriting syndicate or other group in which such business development company or controlled company is a participant and receiving compensation therefor.

(e) Noncontrolling shareholders or affiliated persons; executive officer.—

The provisions of subsection (d) of this section shall apply to the following persons:

(1) Any person

(A) who is, within the meaning of section 2(a)(3)(A), an affiliated person of a business development company,

(B) who is an executive officer or a director of, or general partner in, any such affiliated person, or

(C) who directly or indirectly either controls, is controlled by, or is under common control with, such affiliated person.

(2) Any person who is an affiliated person of a director, officer, employee, investment adviser, member of an advisory board or promoter of, principal underwriter for, general partner in, or an affiliated person of any person directly or indirectly either controlling or under common control with a business development company (except the business development company itself and any person who, if it were not directly or indirectly controlled by the business development company, would not be directly or indirectly under the control of a person who controls the business development company).

For purposes of this subsection, the term "executive officer" means the president, secretary, treasurer, any vice president in charge of a principal business function, and any other person who performs similar policymaking functions.

(f) Approval of proposed transactions.—

Notwithstanding subsection (d) of this section, a person described in subsection (e) may engage in a proposed transaction described in subsection (d) if such proposed transaction is approved by the required majority (as defined in subsection (o)) of the directors of or general partners in the business development company on the basis that—

(1) the terms thereof, including the consideration to be paid or received, are reasonable and fair to the shareholders or partners of the business development company and do not involve overreaching of such company or its shareholders or partners on the part of any person concerned;

(2) the proposed transaction is consistent with the interests of the shareholders or partners of the business development company and is consistent with the policy of such company as recited in filings made by such company with the Commission under the Securities Act of 1933, its registration statement and reports filed under the Securities Exchange Act of 1934, and its reports to shareholders or partners; and

(3) the directors or general partners record in their minutes and preserve in their records, for such periods as if such records were required to be maintained pursuant to section 30(a), a description of such transaction, their findings, the information or materials upon which their findings were based, and the basis therefor.

(g)   Transactions in the ordinary course of business.—

Notwithstanding subsection (a) or (d), a person may, in the ordinary course of business, sell to or purchase from any company merchandise or may enter into a lessor-lessee relationship with any person and furnish the services incident thereto.

(h)   Inquiry procedures.—

The directors of or general partners in any business development company shall adopt, and periodically review and update as appropriate, procedures reasonably designed to ensure that reasonable inquiry is made, prior to the consummation of any transaction in which such business development company or a company controlled by such business development company proposes to participate, with respect to the possible involvement in the transaction of persons described in subsections (b) and (e) of this section.

(i)   Rules and regulations of Commission.—

Until the adoption by the Commission of rules or regulations under subsections (a) and (d) of this section, the rules and regulations of the Commission under subsections (a) and (d) of section 17 applicable to registered closed-end investment companies shall be deemed to apply to transactions subject to subsections (a) and (d) of this section. Any rules or regulations adopted by the Commission to implement this section shall be no more restrictive than the rules or regulations adopted by the Commission under subsections (a) and (d) of section 17 that are applicable to all registered closed-end investment companies.

(j)   Warrants, options, and rights to purchase voting securities; loans to facilitate executive compensation plans.—

Notwithstanding subsections (a) and (d) of this section, any director, officer, or employee of, or general partner in, a business development company may—

(1)   acquire warrants, options, and rights to purchase voting securities of such business development company, and securities issued upon the exercise or conversion thereof, pursuant to an executive compensation plan offered by such company which meets the requirements of section 80a–60(a)(4)(B); and

(2)   borrow money from such business development company for the purpose of purchasing securities issued by such company pursuant to an executive compensation plan, if each such loan—

(A)   has a term of not more than ten years;

(B)   becomes due within a reasonable time, not to exceed sixty days, after the termination of such person's employment or service;

(C)   bears interest at no less than the prevailing rate applicable to 90-day United States Treasury bills at the time the loan is made;

(D)   at all times is fully collateralized (such collateral may include any securities issued by such business development company); and

(E)(i)   in the case of a loan to any officer or employee of such business development company (including any officer or employee who is also a director of such company), is approved by the required majority (as defined in subsection (o)) of the directors of or general partners in such company on the basis that the loan is in the best interests of such company and its shareholders or partners; or

(ii)   in the case of a loan to any director of such business development company who is not also an officer or employee of such company, or to any general partner in such company, is approved by order of the Commission, upon application, on the basis that the terms of the loan are fair and reasonable and do not involve overreaching of such company or its shareholders or partners.

(k)   Restriction on brokerage commissions.—

It shall be unlawful for any person described in subsection (l)—

(1)   acting as agent, to accept from any source any compensation (other than a regular salary or wages from the business development company) for the purchase or sale of any property to or for such business development company or any controlled company thereof, except in the course of such person's business as an underwriter or broker; or

(2)   acting as broker, in connection with the sale of securities to or by the business development company or any controlled company thereof, to receive from any source a commission, fee, or other remuneration for effecting such transaction which exceeds—

(A)   the usual and customary broker's commission if the sale is effected on a securities exchange;

(B)   2 per centum of the sales price if the sale is effected in connection with a secondary distribution of such securities; or

(C)   1 per centum of the purchase or sale price of such securities if the sale is otherwise effected,

unless the Commission, by rules and regulations or order in the public interest and consistent with the protection of investors, permits a larger commission.

(*l*)   Persons subject to brokerage commission restrictions.—

The provisions of subsection (k) of this section shall apply to the following persons:

(1)   Any affiliated person of a business development company.

(2)(A)   Any person who is, within the meaning of section 2(a)(3)(B), (C), or (D), an affiliated person of any director, officer, employee, or member of an advisory board of the business development company.

(B)   Any person who is, within the meaning of section 2(a)(3)(A), (B), (C), or (D), an affiliated person of any investment adviser of, general partner in, or person directly or indirectly either controlling, controlled by, or under common control with, the business development company.

(C)   Any person who is, within the meaning of section 2(a)(3)(C), an affiliated person of any person who is an affiliated person of the business development company within the meaning of section 2(a)(3)(A).

(m)   Receipt of fee or salary from transaction participant.—

For purposes of subsections (a) and (d), a person who is a director, officer, or employee of a party to a transaction and who receives his usual and ordinary fee or salary for usual and customary services as a director, officer, or employee from such party shall not be deemed to have a financial interest or to participate in the transaction solely by reason of his receipt of such fee or salary.

(n)   Profit-sharing plans.—

(1)   Notwithstanding subsection (a)(4) of this section, a business development company may establish and maintain a profit-sharing plan for its directors, officers, employees, and general partners and such directors, officers, employees, and general partners may participate in such profit-sharing plan, if—

(A)(i) in the case of a profit-sharing plan for officers and employees of the business development company (including any officer or employee who is also a director of such company), such profit-sharing plan is approved by the required majority (as defined in subsection (*o*)) of the directors of or general partners in such company on the basis that such plan is reasonable and fair to the shareholders or partners of such company, does not involve overreaching of such company or its shareholders or partners on the part of any person concerned, and is consistent with the interests of the shareholders or partners of such company; or

(ii)   in the case of a profit-sharing plan which includes one or more directors of the business development company who are not also officers or employees of such company, or one or more general partners in such company, such profit-sharing plan is approved by order of the Commission, upon application, on the basis that such plan is reasonable and fair to the shareholders or partners of such company, does not involve overreaching of such company or its shareholders or partners on the part of any person concerned, and is consistent with the interests of the shareholders or partners of such company; and

(B) the aggregate amount of benefits which would be paid or accrued under such plan shall not exceed 20 per centum of the business development company's net income after taxes in any fiscal year.

(2) This subsection may not be used where the business development company has outstanding any stock option, warrant, or right issued as part of an executive compensation plan, including a plan pursuant to section 80a–60(a)(4)(B), or has an investment adviser registered or required to be registered under the Investment Advisers Act.

(o) Required majority for approval of proposed transactions.—

The term "required majority", when used with respect to the approval of a proposed transaction, plan or arrangement, means both a majority of a business development company's directors or general partners who have no financial interest in such transaction, plan, or arrangement and a majority of such directors or general partners who are not interested persons of such company.

Changes in Investment Policy

Sec. 57. No business development company shall, unless authorized by the vote of a majority of its outstanding voting securities or partnership interests, change the nature of its business so as to cease to be, or to withdraw its election as, a business development company.

Incorporation of Provisions

Sec. 58. Notwithstanding the exemption set forth in section 6(f), sections 1, 2, 3, 4, 5, 6, 9, 10(f), 15(a), (c), and (f), 16(b), 17(f) through (j), 19(a), 20(b), 321a) and (c), 32 through 46, and 48 through 52 of this Act shall apply to a business development company to the same extent as if it were a registered closed-end investment company.

Functions and Activities of Business Development Companies

Sec. 59. Notwithstanding the exemption set forth in section 6(f), section 12 shall apply to a business development company to the same extent as if it were a registered closed-end investment company, except that the Commission shall not prescribe any rule, regulation, or order pursuant to section 12(a)(1) governing the circumstances in which a business development company may borrow from a bank in order to purchase any security.

Capital Structure

Sec. 60. (a) Exceptions for business development company.—

Notwithstanding the exemption set forth in section 6(f), section 18 shall apply to a business development company to the same extent as if it were a registered closed-end investment company, except as follows:

(1) Except as provided in paragraph (2), the asset coverage requirements of subparagraphs (A) and (B) of section 18(a)(1) (and any related rule promulgated under this Act) applicable to business development companies shall be 200 percent.

(2) The asset coverage requirements of subparagraphs (A) and (B) of section 18(a)(1) and of subparagraphs (A) and (B) of section 18(a)(2) (and any related rule promulgated under this Act) applicable to business development companies shall be 150 percent if—

(A) not later than 5 business days after the date on which those asset coverage requirements are approved under subparagraph (D) of this paragraph, the business development company discloses that the requirements were approved, and the effective date of the approval, in—

(i) any filing submitted to the Commission under section 78m(a) or 78o(d) of the Securities Exchange Act of 1934; and

(ii) a notice on the website of the business development company;

(B)   The business development company discloses, in each periodic filing required under section 78m(a) of the Securities Exchange Act of 1934—

(i)   the aggregate outside principle amount or liquidation preference, as applicable, of the senior securities issued by the business development company and the asset coverage percentage as of the date of the business development company's most recent financial statements included in that filing;

(ii)   that the business development company, under subparagraph (D), has approved the asset coverage requirements under this paragraph; and

(iii)   the effective date of the approval described in clause (ii);

(C)   with respect to a business development company that is an issuer of common equity securities, each periodic filing of the company required under section 78m(a) of the Securities Exchange Act of 1934 includes disclosures that are reasonably designed to ensure that shareholders are informed of—

(i)   the amount of senior securities (and the associated asset coverage rations) of the company, determined as of the date of the most recent financial statements of the company included in that filing; and

(ii)   the principle risk factors associated with the senior securities described in clause (i), to the extent that risk is incurred by the company; and

(D)   the company—

(i)(I) through a vote of the required majority (as defined in section 57(o)), approves the application of this paragraph to the company, to become effective on the date that is 1 year after the date of approval; or

(II)   obtains, at a special or annual meeting of shareholders or partners at which a quorum is present, the approval of more than 50 percent of the votes cast for the application of this paragraph to the company, to become effective on the first day after the date of the approval; and

(ii)   if the company is not an issuer of common equity securities that are listed on a national securities exchange, extends, to each person that is a shareholder as of the date of an approval described in subclause (I) or (II) of clause (i), as applicable, the opportunity (which may include a tender offer) to sell the securities held by that shareholder as of that applicable approval date, with 25 percent of those securities to be repurchased in each of the 4 calendar quarters following the calendar quarter in which that applicable approval date takes place

(3)   Notwithstanding section 18(c), a business development company may issue more than one class of senior security representing indebtedness—

(4)   Notwithstanding section 18(d)—

(A)   a business development company may issue warrants, options, or rights to subscribe or convert to voting securities of such company, accompanied by securities, if—

(i)   such warrants, options, or rights expire by their terms within ten years;

(ii)   such warrants, options, or rights are not separately transferable unless no class of such warrants, options, or rights and the securities accompanying them has been publicly distributed;

(iii)   the exercise or conversion price is not less than the current market value at the date of issuance, or if no such market value exists, the current net asset value of such voting securities; and

(iv)   the proposal to issue such securities is authorized by the shareholders or partners of such business development company, and such issuance is approved by the required majority (as defined in section 56(o)) of the directors of or general partners in such company on the basis that such issuance is in the best interests of such company and its shareholders or partners;

(B) a business development company may issue, to its directors, officers, employees, and general partners, warrants, options, and rights to purchase voting securities of such company pursuant to an executive compensation plan, if—

(i)(I) in the case of warrants, options, or rights issued to any officer or employee of such business development company (including any officer or employee who is also a director of such company), such securities satisfy the conditions in clauses (i), (iii), and (iv) of subparagraph (A); or

(II) in the case of warrants, options, or rights issued to any director of such business development company who is not also an officer or employee of such company, or to any general partner in such company, the proposal to issue such securities satisfies the conditions in clauses (i) and (iii) of subparagraph (A), is authorized by the shareholders or partners of such company, and is approved by order of the Commission, upon application, on the basis that the terms of the proposal are fair and reasonable and do not involve overreaching of such company or its shareholders or partners;

(ii) such securities are not transferable except for disposition by gift, will, or intestacy;

(iii) no investment adviser of such business development company receives any compensation described in section 205(a)(1) of the Investment Advisers Act, except to the extent permitted by paragraph (1) or (2) of section 205(b); and

(iv) such business development company does not have a profit-sharing plan described in section 56(n);

(C) a business development company may issue warrants, options, or rights to subscribe to, convert to, or purchase voting securities not accompanied by securities, if—

(i) such warrants, options, or rights satisfy the conditions in clauses (i) and (iii) of subparagraph (A); and

(ii) the proposal to issue such warrants, options, or rights is authorized by the shareholders or partners of such business development company, and such issuance is approved by the required majority (as defined in section 56(o)) of the directors of or general partners in such company on the basis that such issuance is in the best interests of the company and its shareholders or partners.

Notwithstanding this paragraph, the amount of voting securities that would result from the exercise of all outstanding warrants, options, and rights at the time of issuance shall not exceed 25 per centum of the outstanding voting securities of the business development company, except that if the amount of voting securities that would result from the exercise of all outstanding warrants, options, and rights issued to such company's directors, officers, employees, and general partners pursuant to any executive compensation plan meeting the requirements of subparagraph (B) of this paragraph would exceed 15 per centum of the outstanding voting securities of such company, then the total amount of voting securities that would result from the exercise of all outstanding warrants, options, and rights at the time of issuance shall not exceed 20 per centum of the outstanding voting securities of such company.

(5) For purposes of measuring the asset coverage requirements of section 18(a), a senior security created by the guarantee by a business development company of indebtedness issued by another company shall be the amount of the maximum potential liability less the fair market value of the net unencumbered assets (plus the indebtedness which has been guaranteed) available in the borrowing company whose debts have been guaranteed, except that a guarantee issued by a business development company of indebtedness issued by a company which is a wholly-owned subsidiary of the business development company and is licensed as a small business investment company under the Small Business Investment Act of 1958 shall not be deemed to be a senior security of such business development company for purposes of section 18(a) if the amount of the indebtedness at the time of its issuance by the borrowing company is itself taken fully into account as a liability by such business development company, as if it were issued by such business development company, in determining whether such business development company, at that time, satisfies the asset coverage requirements of section 18(a).

(b) Compliance.—

A business development company shall comply with the provisions of this section at the time it becomes subject to sections 55 through 65, as if it were issuing a security of each class which it has outstanding at such time.

Loans

Sec. 61. Notwithstanding the exemption set forth in section 6(f), section 21 shall apply to a business development company to the same extent as if it were a registered closed-end investment company, except that nothing in that section shall be deemed to prohibit—

(1)   any loan to a director, officer, or employee of, or general partner in, a business development company for the purpose of purchasing securities for such company as part of an executive compensation plan, if such loan meets the requirements of section 56(j); or

(2)   any loan to a company controlled by a business development company, which companies could be deemed to be under common control solely because a third person controls such business development company.

Distribution and Repurchase of Securities

Sec. 62. Notwithstanding the exemption set forth in section 6(f), section 23 shall apply to a business development company to the same extent as if it were a registered closed-end investment company, except as follows:

(1)   The prohibitions of section 23(a)(2) shall not apply to any company which

(A)   is a wholly-owned subsidiary of, or directly or indirectly controlled by, a business development company, and

(B)   immediately after the issuance of any of its securities for property other than cash or securities, will not be an investment company within the meaning of section 3(a).

(2)   Notwithstanding the provisions of section 23(b), a business development company may sell any common stock of which it is the issuer at a price below the current net asset value of such stock, and may sell warrants, options, or rights to acquire any such common stock at a price below the current net asset value of such stock, if—

(A)   the holders of a majority of such business development company's outstanding voting securities, and the holders of a majority of such company's outstanding voting securities that are not affiliated persons of such company, approved such company's policy and practice of making such sales of securities at the last annual meeting of shareholders or partners within one year immediately prior to any such sale, except that the shareholder approval requirements of this subparagraph shall not apply to the initial public offering by a business development company of its securities;

(B)   a required majority (as defined in section 56(o)) of the directors of or general partners in such business development company have determined that any such sale would be in the best interests of such company and its shareholders or partners; and

(C)   a required majority (as defined in section 56(o)) of the directors of or general partners in such business development company, in consultation with the underwriter or underwriters of the offering if it is to be underwritten, have determined in good faith, and as of a time immediately prior to the first solicitation by or on behalf of such company of firm commitments to purchase such securities or immediately prior to the issuance of such securities, that the price at which such securities are to be sold is not less than a price which closely approximates the market value of those securities, less any distributing commission or discount.

(3)   A business development company may sell any common stock of which it is the issuer at a price below the current net asset value of such stock upon the exercise of any warrant, option, or right issued in accordance with section 80a–60(a)(4).

Accounts and Records

Sec. 63. (a) Exception for business development company.—

Notwithstanding the exemption set forth in section 6(f), section 30 shall apply to a business development company to the same extent as if it were a registered closed-end investment company, except that the reference to the financial statements required to be filed pursuant to section 29 shall be construed to refer to the financial statements required to be filed by such business development company pursuant to section 13 of the Securities Exchange Act of 1934.

(b) Risk factors statement; availability.—

(1) In addition to the requirements of subsection (a), a business development company shall file with the Commission and supply annually to its shareholders a written statement, in such form and manner as the Commission may, by rule, prescribe, describing the risk factors involved in an investment in the securities of a business development company due to the nature of such company's investment portfolio and capital structure, and shall supply copies of such statement to any registered broker or dealer upon request.

(2) If the Commission finds it is necessary or appropriate in the public interest and consistent with the protection of investors and the purposes fairly intended by the policy and provisions of this Act, the Commission may also require, by rule, any person who, acting as principal or agent, sells a security of a business development company to inform the purchaser of such securities, at or before the time of sale, of the existence of the risk statement prepared by such business development company pursuant to this subsection, and make such risk statement available on request. The Commission, in making such rules and regulations, shall consider, among other matters, whether any such rule or regulation would impose any unreasonable burdens on such brokers or dealers or unreasonably impair the maintenance of fair and orderly markets.

Liability of Controlling Persons; Preventing Compliance With Act

Sec. 64. Notwithstanding the exemption set forth in section 6(f), section 47 shall apply to a business development company to the same extent as if it were a registered closed-end investment company, except that the provisions of section 47(a) shall not be construed to require any company which is not an investment company within the meaning of section 3(a) to comply with the provisions of this Act which are applicable to a business development company solely because such company is a wholly-owned subsidiary of, or directly or indirectly controlled by, a business development company.

SELECTED RULES AND REGULATIONS UNDER INVESTMENT COMPANY ACT OF 1940

17 C.F.R. § 270.___

Rule 0–1.   Definition of Terms Used in This Part

(a)   As used in the rules and regulations prescribed by the Commission pursuant to the Investment Company Act of 1940, unless the context otherwise requires:

(1)   The term Commission means the Securities and Exchange Commission.

(2)   The term act means the Investment Company Act of 1940.

(3) The term section refers to a section of the Act.

(4) The terms rule and regulations refer to the rules and regulations adopted by the Commission pursuant to the Act, including the forms for registration and reports and the accompanying instructions thereto.

(5) The term administrator means any person who provides significant administrative or business affairs management services to an investment company.

(6)(i) A person is an independent legal counsel with respect to the directors who are not interested persons of an investment company ('disinterested directors') if:

(A) A majority of the disinterested directors reasonably determine in the exercise of their judgment (and record the basis for that determination in the minutes of their meeting) that any representation by the person of the company's investment adviser, principal underwriter, administrator ('management organizations'), or any of their control persons, since the beginning of the fund's last two completed fiscal years, is or was sufficiently limited that it is unlikely to adversely affect the professional judgment of the person in providing legal representation to the disinterested directors; and

(B) The disinterested directors have obtained an undertaking from such person to provide them with information necessary to make their determination and to update promptly that information when the person begins to represent, or materially increases his representation of, a management organization or control person.

(ii) The disinterested directors are entitled to rely on the information obtained from the person, unless they know or have reason to believe that the information is materially false or incomplete. The disinterested directors must re-evaluate their determination no less frequently than annually (and record the basis accordingly), except as provided in paragraph (iii) of this rule.

(iii) After the disinterested directors obtain information that the person has begun to represent, or has materially increased his representation of, a management organization (or any of its control persons), the person may continue to be an independent legal counsel, for purposes of paragraph (a)(6)(i) of this rule, for no longer than three months unless during that period the disinterested directors make a new determination under that paragraph.

(iv) For purposes of paragraphs (a)(6)(i)–(iii) of this rule:

(A) The term person has the same meaning as in section 2(a)(28) of the Act and, in addition, includes a partner, co-member, or employee of any person; and

(B) The term control person means any person (other than an investment company) directly or indirectly controlling, controlled by, or under common control with any of the investment company's management organizations.

(7) Fund governance standards. The board of directors of an investment company ("fund") satisfies the fund governance standards if:

(i) At least seventy-five percent of the directors of the fund are not interested persons of the fund ('disinterested directors') or, if the fund has three directors, all but one are disinterested directors;

(ii) The disinterested directors of the fund select and nominate any other disinterested director of the fund;

(iii) Any person who acts as legal counsel for the disinterested directors of the fund is an independent legal counsel as defined in paragraph (a)(6) of this rule;

(iv) A disinterested director serves as chairman of the board of directors of the fund, presides over meetings of the board of directors and has substantially the same responsibilities as would a chairman of a board of directors;

(v) The board of directors evaluates at least once annually the performance of the board of directors and the committees of the board of directors, which evaluation must include a consideration of the effectiveness of the committee structure of the fund board and the number of funds on whose boards each director serves;

(vi) The disinterested directors meet at least once quarterly in a session at which no directors who are interested persons of the fund are present; and

(vii) The disinterested directors have been authorized to hire employees and to retain advisers and experts necessary to carry out their duties.

(b) Unless otherwise specifically provided, the terms used in the rules and regulations in this part shall have the meaning defined in the Act. The terms "EDGAR," "EDGAR Filer Manual," "electronic filer," "electronic filing," "electronic format," "electronic submission," "paper format," and "signature" shall have the meanings assigned to such terms in Regulation S–T—General Rules for Electronic Filings.

(c) A rule or regulation which defines a term without express reference to the act or to the rules and regulations, or to a portion thereof, defines such terms for all purposes as used both in the act and in the rules and regulations in this part, unless the context otherwise requires.

(d) Unless otherwise specified or the context otherwise requires, the term "prospectus" means a prospectus meeting the requirements of section 10(a) of the Securities Act of 1933 as amended.

(e) [Omitted].

Rule 0–11. Customer Identification Programs

Each registered open-end company is subject to the requirements of 31 U.S.C. 5318(*l*) and the implementing regulation at 31 CFR 103.131, which requires a customer identification program to be implemented as part of the anti-money laundering program required under subchapter II of chapter 53 of title 31, United States Code and the implementing regulations issued by the Department of the Treasury at 31 CFR part 103. Where 31 CFR 103.131 and this chapter use different definitions for the same term, the definition in 31 CFR 103.131 shall be used for the purpose of compliance with 31 CFR 103.131. Where 31 CFR 103.131 and this chapter require the same records to be preserved for different periods of time, such records shall be preserved for the longer period of time.

Rule 2a–4. Definition of "Current Net Asset Value" for Use in Computing Periodically the Current Price of Redeemable Security

(a) The current net asset value of any redeemable security issued by a registered investment company used in computing periodically the current price for the purpose of distribution, redemption, and repurchase means an amount which reflects calculations, whether or not recorded in the books of account, made substantially in accordance with the following, with estimates used where necessary or appropriate:

(1) Portfolio securities with respect to which market quotations are readily available shall be valued at current market value, and other securities and assets shall be valued at fair value as determined in good faith by the board of directors of the registered company.

(2) Changes in holdings of portfolio securities shall be reflected no later than in the first calculation on the first business day following the trade date.

(3) Changes in the number of outstanding shares of the registered company resulting from distributions, redemptions, and repurchases shall be reflected no later than in the first calculation on the first business day following such change.

(4) Expenses, including any investment advisory fees, shall be included to date of calculation. Appropriate provision shall be made for Federal income taxes if required. Investment companies which retain realized capital gains designated as a distribution to shareholders shall comply with paragraph (h) of Item 6–03 of Regulation S–X.

(5) Dividends receivable shall be included to date of calculation either at ex-dividend dates or record dates, as appropriate.

(6) Interest income and other income shall be included to date of calculation.

(b)   The items which would otherwise be required to be reflected by paragraph (a)(4) and (6) of this rule need not be so reflected if cumulatively, when netted, they do not amount to as much as one cent per outstanding share.

(c)   Notwithstanding the requirements of paragraph (a) of this rule, any interim determination of current net asset value between calculations made as of the close of the New York Stock Exchange on the preceding business day and the current business day may be estimated so as to reflect any change in current net asset value since the closing calculation on the preceding business day.

* * *

Rule 2a19-3. Certain Investment Company Directors Not Considered Interested Persons Because of Ownership of Index Fund Securities

If a director of a registered investment company ("Fund") owns shares of a registered investment company (including the Fund) with an investment objective to replicate the performance of one or more broad-based securities indices ("Index Fund"), ownership of the Index Fund shares will not cause the director to be considered an "interested person" of the Fund or of the Fund's investment adviser or principal underwriter (as defined by section 2(a)(19)(A)(iii) and (B)(iii) of the Act).

Rule 2a51-1. Definition of Investments for Purposes of Section 2(a)(51) (Definition of "Qualified Purchaser"); Certain Calculations

(a)   *Definitions.* As used in this rule:

(1)   The term "Commodity Interests" means commodity futures contracts, options on commodity futures contracts, and options on physical commodities traded on or subject to the rules of:

(i)   Any contract market designated for trading such transactions under the Commodity Exchange Act and the rules thereunder; or

(ii)   Any board of trade or exchange outside the United States, as contemplated in Part 30 of the rules under the Commodity Exchange Act.

(2)   The term "Family Company" means a company described in paragraph (A)(ii) of section 2(a)(51) of the Act.

(3)   The term *Investment Vehicle* means an investment company, a company that would be an investment company but for the exclusions provided by sections 3(c)(1) through 3(c)(9) of the Act or the exemptions provided by rules 3a-6 or 3a-7, or a commodity pool.

(4)   The term "Investments" has the meaning set forth in paragraph (b) of this rule.

(5)   The term "Physical Commodity" means any physical commodity with respect to which a Commodity Interest is traded on a market specified in paragraph (a)(1) of this rule.

(6)   The term "Prospective Qualified Purchaser" means a person seeking to purchase a security of a Section 3(c)(7) Company.

(7)   The term "Public Company" means a company that:

(i)   Files reports pursuant to section 13 or 15(d) of the Securities Exchange Act of 1934; or

(ii)   Has a class of securities that are listed on a "designated offshore securities market" as such term is defined by Regulation S under the Securities Act of 1933.

(8)   The term "Related Person" means a person who is related to a Prospective Qualified Purchaser as a sibling, spouse or former spouse, or is a direct lineal descendant or ancestor by birth or adoption of the Prospective Qualified Purchaser, or is a spouse of such descendant or ancestor, *provided that,* in the case of a Family Company, a Related Person includes any owner of the Family Company and any person who is a Related Person of such owner.

(9)   The term "Relying Person" means a Section 3(c)(7) Company or a person acting on its behalf.

(10) The term "Section 3(c)(7) Company" means a company that would be an investment company but for the exclusion provided by section 3(c)(7) of the Act.

(b)   *Types of Investments.* For purposes of section 2(a)(51) of the Act, the term "Investments" means:

(1)   Securities (as defined by section 2(a)(1) of the Securities Act of 1933), other than securities of an issuer that controls, is controlled by, or is under common control with, the Prospective Qualified Purchaser that owns such securities, unless the issuer of such securities is:

(i)   An Investment Vehicle;

(ii)   A Public Company; or

(iii)   A company with shareholders' equity of not less than $50 million (determined in accordance with generally accepted accounting principles) as reflected on the company's most recent financial statements, *provided that* such financial statements present the information as of a date within 16 months preceding the date on which the Prospective Qualified Purchaser acquires the securities of a Section 3(c)(7) Company;

(2)   Real estate held for investment purposes;

(3)   Commodity Interests held for investment purposes;

(4)   Physical Commodities held for investment purposes;

(5)   To the extent not securities, financial contracts (as such term is defined in section 3(c)(2)(B)(ii)) of the Act entered into for investment purposes;

(6)   In the case of a Prospective Qualified Purchaser that is a Section 3(c)(7) Company, a company that would be an investment company but for the exclusion provided by section 3(c)(1) of the Act, or a commodity pool, any amounts payable to such Prospective Qualified Purchaser pursuant to a firm agreement or similar binding commitment pursuant to which a person has agreed to acquire an interest in, or make capital contributions to, the Prospective Qualified Purchaser upon the demand of the Prospective Qualified Purchaser; and

(7)   Cash and cash equivalents (including foreign currencies) held for investment purposes. For purposes of this rule, cash and cash equivalents include:

(i)   Bank deposits, certificates of deposit, bankers acceptances and similar bank instruments held for investment purposes; and

(ii)   The net cash surrender value of an insurance policy.

(c)   *Investment Purposes.* For purposes of this rule:

(1)   Real estate shall not be considered to be held for investment purposes by a Prospective Qualified Purchaser if it is used by the Prospective Qualified Purchaser or a Related Person for personal purposes or as a place of business, or in connection with the conduct of the trade or business of the Prospective Qualified Purchaser or a Related Person, *provided that* real estate owned by a Prospective Qualified Purchaser who is engaged primarily in the business of investing, trading or developing real estate in connection with such business may be deemed to be held for investment purposes. Residential real estate shall not be deemed to be used for personal purposes if deductions with respect to such real estate are not disallowed by section 280A of the Internal Revenue Code.

(2)   A Commodity Interest or Physical Commodity owned, or a financial contract entered into, by the Prospective Qualified Purchaser who is engaged primarily in the business of investing, reinvesting, or trading in Commodity Interests, Physical Commodities or financial contracts in connection with such business may be deemed to be held for investment purposes.

(d)   *Valuation.* For purposes of determining whether a Prospective Qualified Purchaser is a qualified purchaser, the aggregate amount of Investments owned and invested on a discretionary basis by the Prospective Qualified Purchaser shall be the Investments' fair market value on the most recent practicable date or their cost, *provided that:*

(1)   In the case of Commodity Interests, the amount of Investments shall be the value of the initial margin or option premium deposited in connection with such Commodity Interests; and

(2) In each case, there shall be deducted from the amount of Investments owned by the Prospective Qualified Purchaser the amounts specified in paragraphs (e) and (f) of this rule, as applicable.

(e) *Deductions.* In determining whether any person is a qualified purchaser there shall be deducted from the amount of such person's Investments the amount of any outstanding indebtedness incurred to acquire or for the purpose of acquiring the Investments owned by such person.

(f) *Deductions: Family Companies.* In determining whether a Family Company is a qualified purchaser, in addition to the amounts specified in paragraph (e) of this rule, there shall be deducted from the value of such Family Company's Investments any outstanding indebtedness incurred by an owner of the Family Company to acquire such Investments.

(g) *Special Rules for Certain Prospective Qualified Purchasers.*

(1) *Qualified Institutional Buyers.* Any Prospective Qualified Purchaser who is, or who a Relying Person reasonably believes is, a qualified institutional buyer as defined in paragraph (a) of rule 144A of this chapter, acting for its own account, the account of another qualified institutional buyer, or the account of a qualified purchaser, shall be deemed to be a qualified purchaser *provided:*

(i) That a dealer described in paragraph (a)(1)(ii) of rule 144A of this chapter shall own and invest on a discretionary basis at least $25 million in securities of issuers that are not affiliated persons of the dealer; and

(ii) That a plan referred to in paragraph (a)(1)(i)(D) or (a)(1)(i)(E) of rule 144A of this chapter, or a trust fund referred to in paragraph (a)(1)(i)(F) of rule 144A of this chapter that holds the assets of such a plan, will not be deemed to be acting for its own account if investment decisions with respect to the plan are made by the beneficiaries of the plan, except with respect to investment decisions made solely by the fiduciary, trustee or sponsor of such plan.

(2) *Joint Investments.* In determining whether a natural person is a qualified purchaser, there may be included in the amount of such person's Investments any Investments held jointly with such person's spouse, or Investments in which such person shares with such person's spouse a community property or similar shared ownership interest. In determining whether spouses who are making a joint investment in a Section 3(c)(7) Company are qualified purchasers, there may be included in the amount of each spouse's Investments any Investments owned by the other spouse (whether or not such Investments are held jointly). In each case, there shall be deducted from the amount of any such Investments the amounts specified in paragraph (e) of this rule incurred by each spouse.

(3) *Investments by Subsidiaries.* For purposes of determining the amount of Investments owned by a company under section 2(a)(51)(A)(iv) of the Act there may be included Investments owned by majority-owned subsidiaries of the company and Investments owned by a company ("Parent Company") of which the company is a majority-owned subsidiary, or by a majority-owned subsidiary of the company and other majority-owned subsidiaries of the Parent Company.

(4) *Certain Retirement Plans and Trusts.* In determining whether a natural person is a qualified purchaser, there may be included in the amount of such person's Investments any Investments held in an individual retirement account or similar account the Investments of which are directed by and held for the benefit of such person.

(h) *Reasonable Belief.* The term "qualified purchaser" as used in section 3(c)(7) of the Act means any person that meets the definition of qualified purchaser in section 2(a)(51)(A) of the Act and the rules thereunder, or that a Relying Person reasonably believes meets such definition.

Rule 2a51–2. Definitions of Beneficial Owner for Certain Purposes Under Sections 2(a)(51) and 3(c)(7) and Determining Indirect Ownership Interests

(a) *Beneficial Ownership: General.* Except as set forth in this rule, for purposes of sections 2(a)(51)(C) and 3(c)(7)(B)(ii) of the Act, the beneficial owners of securities of an excepted investment company (as defined in section 2(a)(51)(C) of the Act) shall be determined in accordance with section 3(c)(1) of the Act.

(b) *Beneficial Ownership: Grandfather Provision.* For purposes of section 3(c)(7)(B)(ii) of the Act, securities of an issuer beneficially owned by a company (without giving effect to section 3(c)(1)(A) of the Act) ("owning company") shall be deemed to be beneficially owned by one person unless:

(1)   The owning company is an investment company or an excepted investment company;

(2)   The owning company, directly or indirectly, controls, is controlled by, or is under common control with, the issuer; and

(3)   On October 11, 1996, under section 3(c)(1)(A) of the Act as then in effect, the voting securities of the issuer were deemed to be beneficially owned by the holders of the owning company's outstanding securities (other than short-term paper), in which case, such holders shall be deemed to be beneficial owners of the issuer's outstanding voting securities.

(c)   *Beneficial Ownership: Consent Provision.* For purposes of section 2(a)(51)(C) of the Act, securities of an excepted investment company beneficially owned by a company without giving effect to section 3(c)(1)(A) of the Act ("owning company") shall be deemed to be beneficially owned by one person unless:

(1)   The owning company is an excepted investment company;

(2)   The owning company directly or indirectly controls, is controlled by, or is under common control with, the excepted investment company or the company with respect to which the excepted investment company is, or will be, a qualified purchaser; and

(3)   On April 30, 1996, under section 3(c)(1)(A) of the Act as then in effect, the voting securities of the excepted investment company were deemed to be beneficially owned by the holders of the owning company's outstanding securities (other than short-term paper), in which case the holders of such excepted company's securities shall be deemed to be beneficial owners of the excepted investment company's outstanding voting securities.

(d)   *Indirect Ownership: Consent Provision.* For purposes of section 2(a)(51)(C) of the Act an excepted investment company shall not be deemed to indirectly own the securities of an excepted investment company seeking a consent to be treated as a qualified purchaser ("qualified purchaser company") unless such excepted investment company, directly or indirectly, controls, is controlled by, or is under common control with, the qualified purchaser company or a company with respect to which the qualified purchaser company is or will be a qualified purchaser.

(e)   *Required Consent: Consent Provision.* For purposes of section 2(a)(51)(C) of the Act, the consent of the beneficial owners of an excepted investment company ("owning company") that beneficially owns securities of an excepted investment company that is seeking the consents required by section 2(a)(51)(C) ("consent company") shall not be required unless the owning company directly or indirectly controls, is controlled by, or is under common control with, the consent company or the company with respect to which the consent company is, or will be, a qualified purchaser.

NOTES to Rule 2a51–2:

1.   On both April 30, 1996 and October 11, 1996, section 3(c)(1)(A) of the Act as then in effect provided that: (A) Beneficial ownership by a company shall be deemed to be beneficial ownership by one person, except that, if the company owns 10 per centum or more of the outstanding voting securities of the issuer, the beneficial ownership shall be deemed to be that of the holders of such company's outstanding securities (other than short-term paper) unless, as of the date of the most recent acquisition by such company of securities of that issuer, the value of all securities owned by such company of all issuers which are or would, but for the exception set forth in this subparagraph, be excluded from the definition of investment company solely by this paragraph, does not exceed 10 per centum of the value of the company's total assets. Such issuer nonetheless is deemed to be an investment company for purposes of section 12(d)(1).

2.   Issuers seeking the consent required by section 2(a)(51)(C) of the Act should note that section 2(a)(51)(C) requires an issuer to obtain the consent of the beneficial owners of its securities and the beneficial owners of securities of any "excepted investment company" that directly or indirectly owns the securities of the issuer. Except as set forth in paragraphs (d) (with respect to indirect owners) and (e) (with respect to direct owners) of this rule, nothing in this rule is designed to limit this consent requirement.

Rule 2a51–3. Certain Companies as Qualified Purchasers

(a)   For purposes of section 2(a)(51)(A)(ii) and (iv) of the Act, a company shall not be deemed to be a qualified purchaser if it was formed for the specific purpose of acquiring the securities offered by a company excluded from the definition of investment company by section 3(c)(7) of the Act unless each beneficial owner of the company's securities is a qualified purchaser.

(b)   For purposes of section 2(a)(51) of the Act, a company may be deemed to be a qualified purchaser if each beneficial owner of the company's securities is a qualified purchaser.

Rule 3a–1.   Certain *Prima Facie* Investment Companies

Notwithstanding section 3(a)(3) of the Act, an issuer will be deemed not to be an investment company under the Act; *Provided,* That:

(a)   No more than 45 percent of the value (as defined in section 2(a)(41) of the Act) of such issuer's total assets (exclusive of Government securities and cash items) consists of, and no more than 45 percent of such issuer's net income after taxes (for the last four fiscal quarters combined) is derived from, securities other than:

(1)   Government securities;

(2)   Securities issued by employees' securities companies;

(3)   Securities issued by majority-owned subsidiaries of the issuer (other than subsidiaries relying on the exclusion from the definition of investment company in section 3(b)(3) or section 3(c)(1) of the Act) which are not investment companies; and

(4)   Securities issued by companies;

(i)   Which are controlled primarily by such issuer;

(ii)   Through which such issuer engages in a business other than that of investing, reinvesting, owning, holding or trading in securities; and

(iii)   Which are not investment companies;

(b)   The issuer is not an investment company as defined in section 3(a)(1)(A) or section 3(a)(1)(B) of the Act and is not a special situation investment company; and

(c)   The percentages described in paragraph (a) of this rule are determined on an unconsolidated basis, except that the issuer shall consolidate its financial statements with the financial statements of any wholly-owned subsidiaries.

Rule 3a–2.   Transient Investment Companies

(a)   For purposes of sections 3(a)(1)(A) and 3(a)(1)(C) of the Act, an issuer is deemed not to be engaged in the business of investing, reinvesting, owning, holding or trading in securities during a period of time not to exceed one year; *Provided,* That the issuer has a *bona fide* intent to be engaged primarily, as soon as is reasonably possible (in any event by the termination of such period of time), in a business other than that of investing, reinvesting, owning, holding or trading in securities, such intent to be evidenced by:

(1)   The issuer's business activities; and

(2)   An appropriate resolution of the issuer's board of directors, or by an appropriate action of the person or persons performing similar functions for any issuer not having a board of directors, which resolution or action has been recorded contemporaneously in its minute books or comparable documents.

(b)   For purposes of this rule, the period of time described in paragraph (a) shall commence on the earlier of:

(1)   The date on which an issuer owns securities and/or cash having a value exceeding 50 percent of the value of such issuer's total assets on either a consolidated or unconsolidated basis; or

(2) The date on which an issuer owns or proposes to acquire investment securities (as defined in section 3(a) of the Act) having a value exceeding 40 per centum of the value of such issuer's total assets (exclusive of Government securities and cash items) on an unconsolidated basis.

(c) No issuer may rely on this rule more frequently than once during any three-year period.

Rule 3a–3. Certain Investment Companies Owned by Companies Which Are Not Investment Companies

Notwithstanding section 3(a)(1)(A) or section 3(a)(1)(C) of the Act, an issuer will be deemed not to be an investment company for purposes of the Act; *Provided,* That all of the outstanding securities of the issuer (other than short-term paper, directors' qualifying shares, and debt securities owned by the Small Business Administration) are directly or indirectly owned by a company which satisfies the conditions of paragraph (a) of rule 3a–1 under the Act and which is:

(a) A company that is not an investment company as defined in section 3(a) of the Act;

(b) A company that is an investment company as defined in section 3(a)(1)(C) of the Act, but which is excluded from the definition of the term "investment company" by section 3(b)(1) or 3(b)(2) of the Act; or

(c) A company that is deemed not to be an investment company for purposes of the Act by Rule 3a–1.

Rule 3a–4. Status of Investment Advisory Programs

NOTE:

This rule is a nonexclusive safe harbor from the definition of investment company for programs that provide discretionary investment advisory services to clients. There is no registration requirement under section 5 of the Securities Act of 1933 with respect to programs that are organized and operated in the manner described in Rule 3a–4. The rule is not intended, however, to create any presumption about a program that is not organized and operated in the manner contemplated by the rule.

(a) Any program under which discretionary investment advisory services are provided to clients that has the following characteristics will not be deemed to be an investment company within the meaning of the Act:

(1) Each client's account in the program is managed on the basis of the client's financial situation and investment objectives and in accordance with any reasonable restrictions imposed by the client on the management of the account.

(2)(i) At the opening of the account, the sponsor or another person designated by the sponsor obtains information from the client regarding the client's financial situation and investment objectives, and gives the client the opportunity to impose reasonable restrictions on the management of the account;

(ii) At least annually, the sponsor or another person designated by the sponsor contacts the client to determine whether there have been any changes in the client's financial situation or investment objectives, and whether the client wishes to impose any reasonable restrictions on the management of the account or reasonably modify existing restrictions;

(iii) At least quarterly, the sponsor or another person designated by the sponsor notifies the client in writing to contact the sponsor or such other person if there have been any changes in the client's financial situation or investment objectives, or if the client wishes to impose any reasonable restrictions on the management of the client's account or reasonably modify existing restrictions, and provides the client with a means through which such contact may be made; and

(iv) The sponsor and personnel of the manager of the client's account who are knowledgeable about the account and its management are reasonably available to the client for consultation.

(3) Each client has the ability to impose reasonable restrictions on the management of the client's account, including the designation of particular securities or types of securities that should not

be purchased for the account, or that should be sold if held in the account; *Provided, however,* that nothing in this rule requires that a client have the ability to require that particular securities or types of securities be purchased for the account.

(4)   The sponsor or person designated by the sponsor provides each client with a statement, at least quarterly, containing a description of all activity in the client's account during the preceding period, including all transactions made on behalf of the account, all contributions and withdrawals made by the client, all fees and expenses charged to the account, and the value of the account at the beginning and end of the period.

(5)   Each client retains, with respect to all securities and funds in the account, to the same extent as if the client held the securities and funds outside the program, the right to:

    (i)   Withdraw securities or cash;

    (ii)   Vote securities, or delegate the authority to vote securities to another person;

    (iii)   Be provided in a timely manner with a written confirmation or other notification of each securities transaction, and all other documents required by law to be provided to security holders; and

    (iv)   Proceed directly as a security holder against the issuer of any security in the client's account and not be obligated to join any person involved in the operation of the program, or any other client of the program, as a condition precedent to initiating such proceeding.

(b)   As used in this rule, the term sponsor refers to any person who receives compensation for sponsoring, organizing or administering the program, or for selecting, or providing advice to clients regarding the selection of, persons responsible for managing the client's account in the program. If a program has more than one sponsor, one person shall be designated the principal sponsor, and such person shall be considered the sponsor of the program under this rule.

Rule 3a–5.   Exemption for Subsidiaries Organized to Finance the Operations of Domestic or Foreign Companies

(a)   A finance subsidiary will not be considered an investment company under section 3(a) of the Act and securities of a finance subsidiary held by the parent company or a company controlled by the parent company will not be considered "investment securities" under section 3(a)(1)(C) of the Act; *Provided that:*

(1)   Any debt securities of the finance subsidiary issued to or held by the public are unconditionally guaranteed by the parent company as to the payment of principal, interest, and premium, if any (except that the guarantee may be subordinated in right of payment to other debt of the parent company);

(2)   Any non-voting preferred stock of the finance subsidiary issued to or held by the public is unconditionally guaranteed by the parent company as to payment of dividends, payment of the liquidation preference in the event of liquidation, and payments to be made under a sinking fund, if a sinking fund is to be provided (except that the guarantee may be subordinated in right of payment to other debt of the parent company);

(3)   The parent company's guarantee provides that in the event of a default in payment of principal, interest, premium, dividends, liquidation preference or payments made under a sinking fund on any debt securities or non-voting preferred stock issued by the finance subsidiary, the holders of those securities may institute legal proceedings directly against the parent company (or, in the case of a partnership or joint venture, against the partners or participants in the joint venture) to enforce the guarantee without first proceeding against the finance subsidiary;

(4)   Any securities issued by the finance subsidiary which are convertible or exchangeable are convertible or exchangeable only for securities issued by the parent company (and, in the case of a partnership or joint venture, for securities issued by the partners or participants in the joint venture) or for debt securities or non-voting preferred stock issued by the finance subsidiary meeting the applicable requirements of paragraphs (a)(1) through (a)(3) of this rule;

(5)   The finance subsidiary invests in or loans to its parent company or a company controlled by its parent company at least 85% of any cash or cash equivalents raised by the finance subsidiary

through an offering of its debt securities or non-voting preferred stock or through other borrowings as soon as practicable, but in no event later than six months after the finance subsidiary's receipt of such cash or cash equivalents;

(6)   The finance subsidiary does not invest in, reinvest in, own, hold or trade in securities other than Government securities, securities of its parent company or a company controlled by its parent company (or in the case of a partnership or joint venture, the securities of the partners or participants in the joint venture) or debt securities (including repurchase agreements) which are exempted from the provisions of the Securities Act of 1933 by section 3(a)(3) of that Act; and

(7)   Where the parent company is a foreign bank as the term is used in rule 3a–6, the parent company may, in lieu of the guaranty required by paragraph (a)(1) or (a)(2) of this rule, issue, in favor of the holders of the finance subsidiary's debt securities or non-voting preferred stock, as the case may be, an irrevocable letter of credit in an amount sufficient to fund all of the amounts required to be guaranteed by paragraphs (a)(1) and (a)(2) of this rule, *provided that:*

(i)   Payment on such letter of credit shall be conditional only upon the presentation of customary documentation, and

(ii)   The beneficiary of such letter of credit is not required by either the letter of credit or applicable law to institute proceedings against the finance subsidiary before enforcing its remedies under the letter of credit.

(b)   For purposes of this rule,

(1)   A "finance subsidiary" shall mean any corporation

(i)   All of whose securities other than debt securities or non-voting preferred stock meeting the applicable requirements of paragraphs (a)(1) through (a)(3) or directors' qualifying shares are owned by its parent company or a company controlled by its parent company; and

(ii)   The primary purpose of which is to finance the business operations of its parent company or companies controlled by its parent company;

(2)   A "parent company" shall mean any corporation, partnership or joint venture

(i)   That is not considered an investment company under section 3(a) or that is excepted or exempted by order from the definition of investment company by section 3(b) or by the rules or regulations under section 3(a);

(ii)   That is organized or formed under the laws of the United States or of a state or that is a foreign private issuer, or that is a foreign insurance company as those terms are used in rule 3a–6; and

(iii)   In the case of a partnership or joint venture, each partner or participant in the joint venture meets the requirements of paragraphs (b)(2)(i) and (ii).

(3)   A "company controlled by the parent company" shall mean any corporation, partnership or joint venture

(i)   That is not considered an investment company under section 3(a) or that is excepted or exempted by order from the definition of investment company by section 3(b) or by the rules or regulations under section 3(a);

(ii)   That is either organized or formed under the laws of the United States or of a state or that is a foreign private issuer or that is a foreign bank or foreign insurance company as those terms are used in Rule 3a–6; and

(iii)   In the case of a corporation, more than 25 percent of whose outstanding voting securities are beneficially owned directly or indirectly by the parent company; or

(iv)   In the case of a partnership or joint venture, each partner or participant in the joint venture meets the requirements of paragraphs (b)(3)(i) and (ii), and the parent company has the power to exercise a controlling influence over the management or policies of the partnership or joint venture.

(4)   A "foreign private issuer" shall mean any issuer which is incorporated or organized under the laws of a foreign country, but not a foreign government or political subdivision of a foreign government.

Rule 3a–6.   Foreign Banks and Foreign Insurance Companies

(a)   Notwithstanding section 3(a)(1)(A) or section 3(a)(1)(C) of the Act, a foreign bank or foreign insurance company shall not be considered an investment company for purposes of the Act.

(b)   For purposes of this rule:

(1)(i)   "Foreign bank" means a banking institution incorporated or organized under the laws of a country other than the United States, or a political subdivision of a country other than the United States, that is:

(A)   Regulated as such by that country's or subdivision's government or any agency thereof;

(B)   Engaged substantially in commercial banking activity; and

(C)   Not operated for the purpose of evading the provisions of the Act;

(ii)   The term "foreign bank" shall also include:

(A)   A trust company or loan company that is:

(1)   Organized or incorporated under the laws of Canada or a political subdivision thereof;

(2)   Regulated as a trust company or a loan company by that country's or subdivision's government or any agency thereof; and

(3)   Not operated for the purpose of evading the provisions of the Act; and

(B)   A building society that is:

(1)   Organized under the laws of the United Kingdom or a political subdivision thereof;

(2)   Regulated as a building society by that country's or subdivision's government or any agency thereof; and

(3)   Not operated for the purpose of evading the provisions of the Act.

(iii)   Nothing in this rule shall be construed to include within the definition of "foreign bank" a common or collective trust or other separate pool of assets organized in the form of a trust or otherwise in which interest are separately offered.

(2)   "Engaged substantially in commercial banking activity" means engaged regularly in, and deriving a substantial portion of its business from, extending commercial and other types of credit, and accepting demand and other types of deposits, that are customary for commercial banks in the country in which the head office of the banking institution is located.

(3)   "Foreign insurance company" means an insurance company incorporated or organized under the laws of a country other than the United States, or a political subdivision of a country other than the United States, that is:

(i)   Regulated as such by that country's or subdivision's government or any agency thereof;

(ii)   Engaged primarily and predominantly in:

(A)   the writing of insurance agreements of the type specified in section 3(a)(8) of the Securities Act of 1933, except for the substitution of supervision by foreign government insurance regulators for the regulators referred to in that section; or

(B)   the reinsurance of risks on such agreements underwritten by insurance companies; and

(iii)   Not operated for the purpose of evading the provisions of the Act. Nothing in this rule shall be construed to include within the definition of "foreign insurance company" a separate account or other pool of assets organized in the form of a trust or otherwise in which interests are separately offered.

NOTE: Foreign banks and foreign insurance companies (and certain of their finance subsidiaries and holding companies) relying on rule 3a–6 for exemption from the Act may be required by rule 489 under the Securities Act of 1933 to file Form F–N with the Commission in connection with the filing of a registration statement under the Securities Act of 1933.

* * *

Rule 3a–7.   Issuers of Asset-Backed Securities

Notwithstanding section 3(a) of the Investment Company Act, any issuer who is engaged in the business of purchasing, or otherwise acquiring, and holding eligible assets (and in activities related or incidental thereto), and who does not issue redeemable securities will not be deemed to be an investment company; *Provided That:*

(1)   The issuer issues fixed-income securities or other securities which entitle their holders to receive payments that depend primarily on the cash flow from eligible assets;

(2)   Securities sold by the issuer or any underwriter thereof are fixed-income securities rated, at the time of initial sale, in one of the four highest categories assigned long-term debt or in an equivalent short-term category (within either of which there may be sub-categories or gradations indicating relative standing) by at least one nationally recognized statistical rating organization that is not an affiliated person of the issuer or of any person involved in the organization or operation of the issuer, except that:

(i)   Any fixed-income securities may be sold to accredited investors as defined in paragraphs (1), (2), (3), and (7) of Rule 501(a) under the Securities Act of 1933 and any entity in which all of the equity owners come within such paragraphs; and

(ii)   Any securities may be sold to qualified institutional buyers as defined in Rule 144A under the Securities Act and to persons (other than any rating organization rating the issuer's securities) involved in the organization or operation of the issuer or an affiliate, as defined in Rule 405 under the Securities Act, of such a person;

Provided, That the issuer or any underwriter thereof effecting such sale exercises reasonable care to ensure that such securities are sold and will be resold to persons specified in paragraphs (a)(2) (i) and (ii) of this rule;

(3)   The issuer acquires additional eligible assets, or disposes of eligible assets, only if:

(i)   The assets are acquired or disposed of in accordance with the terms and conditions set forth in the agreements, indentures, or other instruments pursuant to which the issuer's securities are issued;

(ii)   The acquisition or disposition of the assets does not result in a downgrading in the rating of the issuer's outstanding fixed-income securities; and

(iii)   The assets are not acquired or disposed of for the primary purpose of recognizing gains or decreasing losses resulting from market value changes; and

(4)   If the issuer issues any securities other than securities exempted from the Securities Act by section 3(a)(3) thereof, the issuer:

(i)   Appoints a trustee that meets the requirements of section 26(a)(1) of the Act and that is not affiliated, as that term is defined in Rule 405 under the Securities Act, with the issuer or with any person involved in the organization or operation of the issuer, which does not offer or provide credit or credit enhancement to the issuer, and that executes an agreement or instrument concerning the issuer's securities containing provisions to the effect set forth in section 26(a)(3) of the Act;

(ii)   Takes reasonable steps to cause the trustee to have a perfected security interest or ownership interest valid against third parties in those eligible assets that principally generate the cash flow needed to pay the fixed-income security holders, provided that such assets otherwise required to be held by the trustee may be released to the extent needed at the time for the operation of the issuer; and

(iii) Takes actions necessary for the cash flows derived from eligible assets for the benefit of the holders of fixed-income securities to be deposited periodically in a segregated account that is maintained or controlled by the trustee consistent with the rating of the outstanding fixed-income securities.

(b) For purposes of this rule:

(1) Eligible assets means financial assets, either fixed or revolving, that by their terms convert into cash within a finite time period plus any rights or other assets designed to assure the servicing or timely distribution of proceeds to security holders.

(2) Fixed-income securities means any securities that entitle the holder to receive:

(i) A stated principal amount; or

(ii) Interest on a principal amount (which may be a notional principal amount) calculated by reference to a fixed rate or to a standard or formula which does not reference any change in the market value or fair value of eligible assets; or

(iii) Interest on a principal amount (which may be a notional principal amount) calculated by reference to auctions among holders and prospective holders, or through remarketing of the security; or

(iv) An amount equal to specified fixed or variable portions of the interest received on the assets held by the issuer; or

(v) Any combination of amounts described in paragraphs (b)(2)(i), (ii), (iii), and (iv) of this rule;

Provided, That substantially all of the payments to which the holders of such securities are entitled consist of the foregoing amounts.

Rule 3a–8.   Certain Research and Development Companies

(a) Notwithstanding Rules 3(a)(1)(A) and 3(a)(1)(C) of the Act, an issuer will be deemed not to be an investment company if:

(1) Its research and development expenses, for the last four fiscal quarters combined, are a substantial percentage of its total expense for the same period;

(2) Its net income derived from investments in securities, for the last four fiscal quarters combined, does not exceed twice the amount of its research and development expenses for the same period;

(3) Its expenses for investment advisory and management activities, investment research and custody, for the last four fiscal quarters, combined, do not exceed five percent of its total expenses for the same period;

(4) Its investments in securities are capital preservation investments, except that:

(i) No more than 10 percent of the issuer's total assets may consist of other investments, or

(ii) No more than 25 percent of the issuer's total assets may consist of other investments, provided that at least 75 percent of such other investments are investments made pursuant to a collaborative research and development arrangement;

(5) It does not hold itself out as being engaged in the business of investing, reinvesting or trading in securities, and it is not a special situation investment company;

(6) It is primarily engaged, directly, through majority-owned subsidiaries, or through companies which it controls primarily, in a business or businesses other than that of investing, reinvesting, owning, holding, or trading in securities, as evidenced by:

    (i)   The activities of its officers, directors and employees;

    (ii)   Its public representations of policies;

    (iii)   Its historical development; and

    (iv)   An appropriate resolution of its board of directors, which resolution or action has been recorded contemporaneously in its minute books or comparable documents; and

    (7)   Its board of directors has adopted a written investment policy with respect to the issuer's capital preservation investments.

(b)   For purposes of this rule:

    (1)   All assets shall be valued in accordance with section 2(a)(41)(A) of the Act;

    (2)   The percentages described in this rule are determined on an unconsolidated basis, except that the issuer shall consolidate its financial statements with the financial statements of any wholly-owned subsidiaries;

    (3)   Board of directors means the issuer's board of directors or an appropriate person or persons performing similar functions for any issuer not having a board of directors;

    (4)   Capital preservation investment means an investment that is made to conserve capital and liquidity until the funds are used in the issuer's primary business or businesses;

    (5)   Controlled primarily means controlled within the meaning of section 2(a)(9) of the Act with a degree of control that is greater than that of any other person;

    (6)   Investment made pursuant to a collaborative research and development arrangement means an investment in an investee made pursuant to a business relationship which:

    (i)   Is designed to achieve narrowly focused goals that are directly related to, and an integral part of, the issue's research and development activities;

    (ii)   Calls for the issuer to conduct joint research and development activities with the investee or a company controlled primarily by, or which controls primarily, the investee; and

    (iii)   Is not entered into for the purpose of avoiding regulation under the Act;

    (7)   Investments in securities means all securities other than securities issued by majority-owned subsidiaries and companies controlled primarily by the issuer that conduct similar types of businesses, through which the issuer is engaged primarily in a business other than that of investing, reinvesting, owning, holding, or trading in securities;

    (8)   Other investment means an investment in securities that is not a capital preservation investment; and

    (9)   Research and development expenses means research and development costs as defined in FASB ASC Topic 730, *Research and Development*, as currently in effect or as it may be subsequently revised.

Rule 3c–1.   Definition of Beneficial Ownership for Certain Rule 3(c)(1) Funds

(a)   As used in this rule:

    (1)   The term "Covered Company" means a company that is an investment company, a Section 3(c)(1) Company or a Section 3(c)(7) Company.

    (2)   The term "Section 3(c)(1) Company" means a company that would be an investment company but for the exclusion provided by section 3(c)(1) of the Act.

    (3)   The term "Section 3(c)(7) Company" means a company that would be an investment company but for the exclusion provided by section 3(c)(7) of the Act.

(b)   For purposes of section 3(c)(1)(A) of the Act, beneficial ownership by a Covered Company owning 10 percent or more of the outstanding voting securities of a Section 3(c)(1) Company shall be deemed to be beneficial ownership by one person, *provided that:*

(1)   On April 1, 1997, the Covered Company owned 10 percent or more of the outstanding voting securities of the Section 3(c)(1) Company or non-voting securities that, on such date and in accordance with the terms of such securities, were convertible into or exchangeable for voting securities that, if converted or exchanged on or after such date, would have constituted 10 percent or more of the outstanding voting securities of the Section 3(c)(1) Company; and

(2)   On the date of any acquisition of securities of the Section 3(c)(1) Company by the Covered Company, the value of all securities owned by the Covered Company of all issuers that are Section 3(c)(1) or Section 3(c)(7) Companies does not exceed 10 percent of the value of the Covered Company's total assets.

* * *

Rule 3c–4.   Definition of "Common Trust Fund" as Used in Section 3(c)(3) of the Act

The term "common trust fund" as used in section 3(c)(3) of the Act shall include a common trust fund which is maintained by a bank which is a member of an affiliated group, as defined in section 1504(a) of the Internal Revenue Code of 1954, and which is maintained exclusively for the collective investment and reinvestment of monies contributed thereto by one or more bank members of such affiliated group in the capacity of trustee, executor, administrator, or guardian, provided that:

(a)   The common trust fund is operated in compliance with the same state and federal regulatory requirements as would apply if the bank maintaining such fund and any other contributing banks were the same entity; and

(b)   The rights of persons for whose benefit a contributing bank acts as trustee, executor, administrator, or guardian would not be diminished by reason of the maintenance of such common trust fund by another bank member of the affiliated group.

* * *

Rule 3c–6.   Certain Transfers of Interests in Section 3(c)(1) and Section 3(c)(7) Funds

(a)   As used in this rule:

(1)   The term Donee means a person who acquires a security of a Covered Company (or a security or other interest in a company referred to in paragraph (b)(3) of this rule) as a gift or bequest or pursuant to an agreement relating to a legal separation or divorce.

(2)   The term Section 3(c)(1) Company means a company that would be an investment company but for the exclusion provided by section 3(c)(1) of the Act.

(3)   The term Section 3(c)(7) Company means a company that would be an investment company but for the exclusion provided by section 3(c)(7) of the Act.

(4)   The term Transferee means a Section 3(c)(1) Transferee or a Qualified Purchaser Transferee, in each case as defined in paragraph (b) of this rule.

(5)   The term Transferor means a Section 3(c)(1) Transferor or a Qualified Purchaser Transferor, in each case as defined in paragraph (b) of this rule.

(b)   Beneficial ownership by any person ("Section 3(c)(1) Transferee") who acquires securities or interests in securities of a Section 3(c)(1) Company from a person other than the Section 3(c)(1) Company shall be deemed to be beneficial ownership by the person from whom such transfer was made ("Section 3(c)(1) Transferor"), and securities of a Section 3(c)(7) Company that are owned by persons who received the securities from a qualified purchaser other than the Section 3(c)(7) Company ("Qualified Purchaser Transferor") or a person deemed to be a qualified purchaser by this rule shall be deemed to be acquired by a qualified purchaser ("Qualified Purchaser Transferee"), provided that the Transferee is:

(1)   The estate of the Transferor;

(2)   A Donee; or

(3)   A company established by the Transferor exclusively for the benefit of (or owned exclusively by) the Transferor and the persons specified in paragraphs (b)(1) and (b)(2) of this rule.

Rule 6b–1. Exemption of Employees' Securities Company Pending Determination of Application

Any employees' securities company which files an application for an order of exemption under section 6(b) of the Act shall be exempt, pending final determination of such application by the Commission, from all provisions of the act applicable to investment companies as such.

* * *

Rule 6c–11. Exchange-Traded Funds.

    (a)   Definitions.

        (1)   For purposes of this rule:

Authorized participant means a member or participant of a clearing agency registered with the Commission, which has a written agreement with the exchange-traded fund or one of its service providers that allows the authorized participant to place orders for the purchase and redemption of creation units.

Basket means the securities, assets or other positions in exchange for which an exchange-traded fund issues (or in return for which it redeems) creation units.

Business day means any day the exchange-traded fund is open for business, including any day when it satisfies redemption requests as required by section 22(e) of the Act (15 U.S.C. 80a–22(e)).

Cash balancing amount means an amount of cash to account for any difference between the value of the basket and the net asset value of a creation unit.

Creation unit means a specified number of exchange-traded fund shares that the exchange-traded fund will issue to (or redeem from) an authorized participant in exchange for the deposit (or delivery) of a basket and a cash balancing amount if any.

Custom basket means:

        (i)   A basket that is composed of a non-representative selection of the exchange-traded fund's portfolio holdings; or

        (ii)   A representative basket that is different from the initial basket used in transactions on the same business day.

Exchange-traded fund means a registered open-end management company:

        (i)   That issues (and redeems) creation units to (and from) authorized participants in exchange for a basket and a cash balancing amount if any; and

        (ii)   Whose shares are listed on a national securities exchange and traded at market-determined prices.

Exchange-traded fund share means a share of stock issued by an exchange-traded fund.

Foreign investment means any security, asset or other position of the ETF issued by a foreign issuer as that term is defined in § 240.3b–4 of this title, and that is traded on a trading market outside of the United States.

Market price means:

        (i)   The official closing price of an exchange-traded fund share; or

        (ii)   If it more accurately reflects the market value of an exchange-traded fund share at the time as of which the exchange-traded fund calculates current net asset value per share, the price that is the midpoint between the national best bid and national best offer as of that time.

National securities exchange means an exchange that is registered with the Commission under section 6 of the Securities Exchange Act of 1934 (15 U.S.C. 78f).

Portfolio holdings means the securities, assets or other positions held by the exchange-traded fund.

Premium or discount means the positive or negative difference between the market price of an exchange-traded fund share at the time as of which the current net asset value is calculated and the exchange-traded fund's current net asset value per share, expressed as a percentage of the exchange-traded fund share's current net asset value per share.

(2) Notwithstanding the definition of exchange-traded fund in paragraph (a)(1) of this rule, an exchange-traded fund is not prohibited from selling (or redeeming) individual shares on the day of consummation of a reorganization, merger, conversion or liquidation, and is not limited to transactions with authorized participants under these circumstances.

(b) *Application of the Act to Exchange-Traded Funds.* If the conditions of paragraph (c) of this rule are satisfied:

(1) *Redeemable security.* An exchange-traded fund share is considered a "redeemable security" within the meaning of section 2(a)(32) of the Act (15 U.S.C. 80a–2(a)(32)).

(2) *Pricing.* A dealer in exchange-traded fund shares is exempt from section 22(d) of the Act (15 U.S.C. 80a–22(d)) and § 270.22c–1(a) with regard to purchases, sales and repurchases of exchange-traded fund shares at market-determined prices.

(3) *Affiliated transactions.*

(i) A person who is an affiliated person of an exchange-traded fund (or who is an affiliated person of such a person) solely by reason of the circumstances described in paragraphs (b)(3)(i)(A) and (B) of this rule is exempt from sections 17(a)(1) and 17(a)(2) of the Act (15 U.S.C. 80a–17(a)(1) and (a)(2)) with regard to the deposit and receipt of baskets:

(A) Holding with the power to vote 5% or more of the exchange-traded fund's shares; or

(B) Holding with the power to vote 5% or more of any investment company that is an affiliated person of the exchange-traded fund.

(4) *Postponement of redemptions.* If an exchange-traded fund includes a foreign investment in its basket, and if a local market holiday, or series of consecutive holidays, or the extended delivery cycles for transferring foreign investments to redeeming authorized participants prevents timely delivery of the foreign investment in response to a redemption request, the exchange-traded fund is exempt, with respect to the delivery of the foreign investment, from the prohibition in section 22(e) of the Act (15 U.S.C. 80a–22(e)) against postponing the date of satisfaction upon redemption for more than seven days after the tender of a redeemable security if the exchange-traded fund delivers the foreign investment as soon as practicable, but in no event later than 15 days after the tender of the exchange-traded fund shares.

(c) *Conditions.*

(1) Each business day, an exchange-traded fund must disclose prominently on its website, which is publicly available and free of charge:

(i) Before the opening of regular trading on the primary listing exchange of the exchange-traded fund shares, the estimated cash balancing amount (if any) and the following information (as applicable) for each portfolio holding that will form the basis of the next calculation of current net asset value per share:

(A) Ticker symbol;

(B) CUSIP or other identifier;

(C) Description of holding;

(D) Quantity of each security or other asset held; and

(E) Percentage weight of the holding in the portfolio;

(ii) The exchange-traded fund's current net asset value per share, market price, and premium or discount, each as of the end of the prior business day;

(iii) A table showing the number of days the exchange-traded fund's shares traded at a premium or discount during the most recently completed calendar year and the most recently completed calendar quarters since that year (or the life of the exchange-traded fund, if shorter);

(iv) A line graph showing exchange-traded fund share premiums or discounts for the most recently completed calendar year and the most recently completed calendar quarters since that year (or the life of the exchange-traded fund, if shorter);

(v) The exchange-traded fund's median bid-ask spread, expressed as a percentage rounded to the nearest hundredth, computed by:

(A) Identifying the exchange-traded fund's national best bid and national best offer as of the end of each 10 second interval during each trading day of the last 30 calendar days;

(B) Dividing the difference between each such bid and offer by the midpoint of the national best bid and national best offer; and

(C) Identifying the median of those values.

(vi) If the exchange-traded fund's premium or discount is greater than 2% for more than seven consecutive trading days, a statement that the exchange-traded fund's premium or discount, as applicable, was greater than 2% and a discussion of the factors that are reasonably believed to have materially contributed to the premium or discount, which must be maintained on the website for at least one year thereafter.

(2) The portfolio holdings that form the basis for the exchange-traded fund's next calculation of current net asset value per share must be the ETF's portfolio holdings as of the close of business on the prior business day.

(3) An exchange-traded fund must adopt and implement written policies and procedures that govern the construction of baskets and the process that will be used for the acceptance of baskets; *provided, however*, if the exchange-traded fund utilizes a custom basket, these written policies and procedures also must:

(i) Set forth detailed parameters for the construction and acceptance of custom baskets that are in the best interests of the exchange-traded fund and its shareholders, including the process for any revisions to, or deviations from, those parameters; and

(ii) Specify the titles or roles of the employees of the exchange-traded fund's investment adviser who are required to review each custom basket for compliance with those parameters.

(4) An exchange-traded fund that seeks, directly or indirectly, to provide investmentreturns that correspond to the performance of a market index by a specified multiple, or to provide investment returns that have an inverse relationship to the performance of a marketindex, over a predetermined period of time, must comply with all applicable provisions of Rule 18f–4.

(d) *Recordkeeping.* The exchange-traded fund must maintain and preserve for a period of not less than five years, the first two years in an easily accessible place:

(1) All written agreements (or copies thereof) between an authorized participant and the exchange-traded fund or one of its service providers that allows the authorized participant to place orders for the purchase or redemption of creation units;

(2) For each basket exchanged with an authorized participant, records setting forth:

(i) The ticker symbol, CUSIP or other identifier, description of holding, quantity of each holding, and percentage weight of each holding composing the basket exchanged for creation units;

(ii) If applicable, identification of the basket as a custom basket and a record stating that the custom basket complies with policies and procedures that the exchange-traded fund adopted pursuant to paragraph (c)(3) of this rule;

(iii) Cash balancing amount (if any); and

(iv) Identity of authorized participant transacting with the exchange-traded fund.

* * *

Rule 8f–1. Deregistration of Certain Registered Investment Companies

A registered investment company that seeks a commission order declaring that it is no longer an investment company may file an application with the Commission on Form N–8f if the investment company:

(a) Has sold substantially all of its assets to another registered investment company or merged into or consolidated with another registered investment company;

(b) Has distributed substantially all of its assets to its shareholders and has completed, or is in the process of, winding up its affairs;

(c) Qualifies for an exclusion from the definition of "investment company" under section 3(c)(1) or section 3(c)(7) of the Act; or

(d) Has become a business development company.

NOTE to Rule 8f–1: Applicants who are not eligible to use Form N–8F to file an application to deregister may follow the general guidance for filing applications under Rule 0–2 under the Exchange Act.

Rule 10b–1. Definition of Regular Broker or Dealer

The term "regular broker or dealer" of an investment company shall mean:

(a) One of the ten brokers or dealers that received the greatest dollar amount of brokerage commissions by virtue of direct or indirect participation in the company's portfolio transactions during the company's most recent fiscal year;

(b) One of the ten brokers or dealers that engaged as principal in the largest dollar amount of portfolio transactions of the investment company during the company's most recent fiscal year; or

(c) One of the ten brokers or dealers that sold the largest dollar amount of securities of the investment company during the company's most recent fiscal year.

Rule 10f–1. Conditional Exemption of Certain Underwriting Transactions

Any purchase or other acquisition by a registered management company acting, pursuant to a written agreement, as an underwriter of securities of an issuer which is not an investment company shall be exempt from the provisions of section 10(f) upon the following conditions:

(a) The party to such agreement other than such registered company is a principal underwriter of such securities, which principal underwriter

(1) Is a person primarily engaged in the business of underwriting and distributing securities issued by other persons, selling securities to customers, or related activities, whose gross income normally is derived principally from such business or related activities, and

(2) Does not control or is not under common control with such registered company.

(b) No public offering of the securities underwritten by such agreement has been made prior to the execution thereof.

(c) Such securities have been effectively registered pursuant to the Securities Act of 1933 prior to the execution of such agreement.

(d) In regard to any securities underwritten, whether or not purchased, by the registered company pursuant to such agreement, such company shall be allowed a rate of gross commission, spread, concession or other profit not less than the amount allowed to such principal underwriter, exclusive of any amounts received by such principal underwriter as a management fee from other principal underwriters.

(e)   Such agreement is authorized by resolution adopted by a vote of not less than a majority of the board of directors of such registered company, none of which majority is an affiliated person of such principal underwriter, of the issuer of the securities underwritten pursuant to such agreement or of any person engaged in a business described in paragraph (a)(1) of this rule.

(f)   The resolution required in paragraph (e) of this rule shall state that it has been adopted pursuant to this rule, and shall incorporate the terms of the proposed agreement by attaching a copy thereof as an exhibit or otherwise.

(g)   A copy of the resolution required in paragraph (e) of this rule, signed by each member of the board of directors of the registered company who voted in favor of its adoption, shall be transmitted to the Commission not later than the fifth day succeeding the date on which such agreement is executed.

Rule 10f–2.   Exercise of Warrants or Rights Received on Portfolio Securities

Any purchase or other acquisition of securities by a registered investment company pursuant to the exercise of warrants or rights to subscribe to or to purchase securities shall be exempt from the provisions of section 10(f) of the act, *Provided,* That the warrants or rights so exercised

(a)   Were offered or issued to such company as a security holder on the same basis as all other holders of the class or classes of securities to whom such warrants or rights were offered or issued, and

(b)   Do not exceed 5 percent of the total amount of such warrants or rights so issued.

Rule 10f–3.   Exemption for the Acquisition of Securities During the Existence of an Underwriting or Selling Syndicate

(a)   *Definitions.—*

(1)   "Domestic Issuer" means any issuer other than a foreign government, a national of any foreign country, or a corporation or other organization incorporated or organized under the laws of any foreign country.

(2)   "Eligible Foreign Offering" means a public offering of securities, conducted under the laws of a country other than the United States, that meets the following conditions:

(i)   The offering is subject to regulation by a "foreign financial regulatory authority," as defined in section 2(a)(50) of the Act, in such country;

(ii)   The securities are offered at a fixed price to all purchasers in the offering (except for any rights to purchase securities that are required by law to be granted to existing security holders of the issuer);

(iii)   Financial statements, prepared and audited in accordance with standards required or permitted by the appropriate foreign financial regulatory authority in such country, for the two years prior to the offering, are made available to the public and prospective purchasers in connection with the offering; and

(iv)   If the issuer is a Domestic Issuer, it meets the following conditions:

(A)   It has a class of securities registered pursuant to section 12(b) or 12(g) of the Securities Exchange Act of 1934 or is required to file reports pursuant to section 15(d) of the Securities Exchange Act of 1934; and

(B)   It has filed all the material required to be filed pursuant to section 13(a) or 15(d) of the Securities Exchange Act of 1934 for a period of at least twelve months immediately preceding the sale of securities made in reliance upon this (or for such shorter period that the issuer was required to file such material).

(3)   *Eligible Municipal Securities* means "municipal securities," as defined in section 3(a)(29) of the Securities Exchange Act of 1934 (15 U.S.C. 78c(a)(29)), that are sufficiently liquid that they can be sold at or near their carrying value within a reasonably short period of time and either:

(i)   Are subject to no greater than moderate credit risk; or (ii)　If the issuer of the municipal securities, or the entity supplying the revenues or other payments from which the issue is to be paid, has been in continuous operation for less than three years, including the operation of any predecessors, the securities are subject to a minimal or low amount of credit risk.

(4)　"Eligible Rule 144A Offering" means an offering of securities that meets the following conditions:

(i)　The securities are offered or sold in transactions exempt from registration under section 4(2) of the Securities Act of 1933, Rule 144A thereunder, or Rules 501–508 thereunder;

(ii)　The securities are sold to persons that the seller and any person acting on behalf of the seller reasonably believe to include qualified institutional buyers, as defined in Rule 144A(a)(1) of this chapter; and

(iii)　The seller and any person acting on behalf of the seller reasonably believe that the securities are eligible for resale to other qualified institutional buyers pursuant to Rule 144A of this chapter.

(5)　(Managed portion of a portfolio of a registered investment company) means a discrete portion of a portfolio of a registered investment company for which a subadviser is responsible for providing investment advice, provided that:

(i)　The subadviser is not an affiliated person of any investment adviser, promoter, underwriter, officer, director, member of an advisory board, or employee of the registered investment company; and

(ii)　The subadviser's advisory contract:

(A)　Prohibits it from consulting with any subadviser of the investment company that is a principal underwriter or an affiliated person of a principal underwriter concerning transactions of the investment company in securities or other assets; and

(B)　Limits its responsibility in providing advice to providing advice with respect to such portion.

(6)　(Series of a series company) means any class or series of a registered investment company that issues two or more classes or series of preferred or special stock, each of which is preferred over all other classes or series with respect to assets specifically allocated to that class or series.

(7)　(Subadviser) means an investment adviser as defined in section 2(a)(20)(B) of the Act.

(b)　*Exemption for Purchases by Series Companies and Investment Companies with Managed Portions.* For purposes of this rule and section 10(f) of the Act, each Series of a Series Company, and each Managed Portion of a registered investment company, is deemed to be a separate investment company. Therefore, a purchase or acquisition of a security by a registered investment company is exempt from the prohibitions of section 10(f) of the Act if section 10(f) of the Act would not prohibit such purchase if each Series and each Managed Portion of the company were a separately registered investment company.

(c)　*Exemption for Other Purchases.* Any purchase of securities by a registered investment company prohibited by section 10(f) of the Act will be exempt from the provisions of that section if the following conditions are met:

(1)　*Type of Security.* The securities to be purchased are:

(i)　Part of an issue registered under the Securities Act of 1933 that is being offered to the public;

(ii)　Part of an issue of government securities, as defined in Section 2(a)(16) of the Act;

(iii)　Eligible Municipal Securities;

(iv)　Securities sold in an Eligible Foreign Offering; or

(v)　Securities sold in an Eligible Rule 144A Offering.

(2)　*Timing and Price.*

(i)   The securities are purchased prior to the end of the first day on which any sales are made, at a price that is not more than the price paid by each other purchaser of securities in that offering or in any concurrent offering of the securities (except, in the case of an Eligible Foreign Offering, for any rights to purchase that are required by law to be granted to existing security holders of the issuer); and

(ii)   If the securities are offered for subscription upon exercise of rights, the securities shall be purchased on or before the fourth day preceding the day on which the rights offering terminates.

(3)   *Reasonable Reliance.* For purposes of determining compliance with paragraphs (c)(1)(v) and (c)(2)(i) of this rule, an investment company may reasonably rely upon written statements made by the issuer or a syndicate manager, or by an underwriter or seller of the securities through which such investment company purchases the securities.

(4)   *Continuous Operation.* If the securities to be purchased are part of an issue registered under the Securities Act of 1933 that is being offered to the public, are government securities (as defined in Section 2(a)(16) of the Act), or are purchased pursuant to an Eligible Foreign Offering or an Eligible Rule 144A Offering, the issuer of the securities must have been in continuous operation for not less than three years, including the operations of any predecessors.

(5)   *Firm Commitment Underwriting.* The securities are offered pursuant to an underwriting or similar agreement under which the underwriters are committed to purchase all of the securities being offered, except those purchased by others pursuant to a rights offering, if the underwriters purchase any of the securities.

(6)   *Reasonable Commission.* The commission, spread or profit received or to be received by the principal underwriters is reasonable and fair compared to the commission, spread or profit received by other such persons in connection with the underwriting of similar securities being sold during a comparable period of time.

(7)   *Percentage Limit.*

(i)   *Generally.* The amount of securities of any class of such issue to be purchased by the investment company, aggregated with purchases by any other investment company advised by the investment company's investment adviser, and any purchases by another account with respect to which the investment adviser has investment discretion if the investment adviser exercised such investment discretion with respect to the purchase, does not exceed the following limits:

(A)   If purchased in an offering other than an Eligible Rule 144A Offering, 25 percent of the principal amount of the offering of such class; or

(B)   If purchased in an Eligible Rule 144A Offering, 25 percent of the total of:

(1)   The principal amount of the offering of such class sold by underwriters or members of the selling syndicate to qualified institutional buyers, as defined in Rule 144A(a)(1) under the Securities Act; plus

(2)   The principal amount of the offering of such class in any concurrent public offering.

(ii)   *Exemption from Percentage Limit.* The requirement in paragraph (c)(7)(i) of this rule applies only if the investment adviser of the investment company is, or is an affiliated person of, a principal underwriter of the security; and

(iii)   *Separate Aggregation.* The requirement in paragraph (c)(7)(i) of this rule applies independently with respect to each investment adviser of the investment company that is, or is an affiliated person of, a principal underwriter of the security.

(8)   *Prohibition of Certain Affiliate Transactions.* Such investment company does not purchase the securities being offered directly or indirectly from an officer, director, member of an advisory board, investment adviser or employee of such investment company or from a person of which any such officer, director, member of an advisory board, investment adviser or employee is an affiliated person;

provided, that a purchase from a syndicate manager shall not be deemed to be a purchase from a specific underwriter if:

(i)   Such underwriter does not benefit directly or indirectly from the transaction; or

(ii)   In respect to the purchase of Eligible Municipal Securities, such purchase is not designated as a group sale or otherwise allocated to the account of any person from whom this paragraph prohibits the purchase.

(9)   [Removed and Reserved]

(10)   *Board Review.* The board of directors of the investment company, including a majority of the directors who are not interested persons of the investment company:

(i)   Has approved procedures, pursuant to which such purchases may be effected for the company, that are reasonably designed to provide that the purchases comply with all the conditions of this rule;

(ii)   Approves such changes to the procedures as the board deems necessary; and

(iii)   Determines no less frequently than quarterly that all purchases made during the preceding quarter were effected in compliance with such procedures.

(11)   *Board Composition.* The board of directors of the investment company satisfies the fund governance standards defined in Rule 0–1(a)(7).

(12)   Maintenance of Records. The investment company:

(i)   Shall maintain and preserve permanently in an easily accessible place a written copy of the procedures, and any modification thereto, described in paragraphs (c)(10)(i) and (c)(10)(ii) of this rule; and

(ii)   Shall maintain and preserve for a period not less than six years from the end of the fiscal year in which any transactions occurred, the first two years in an easily accessible place, a written record of each such transaction, setting forth from whom the securities were acquired, the identity of the underwriting syndicate's members, the terms of the transaction, and the information or materials upon which the determination described in paragraph (c)(10)(iii) of this rule was made.

Rule 11a–1. Definition of "Exchange" for Purposes of Section 11 of the Act

(a)   For the purposes of section 11 of the Act, the term "exchange" as used therein shall include the issuance of any security by a registered investment company in an amount equal to the proceeds, or any portion of the proceeds, paid or payable—

(1)   Upon the repurchase, by or at the instance of such issuer, of an outstanding security the terms of which provide for its termination, retirement or cancellation, or

(2)   Upon the termination, retirement or cancellation of an outstanding security of such issuer in accordance with the terms thereof.

(b)   A security shall not be deemed to have been repurchased by or at the instance of the issuer, or terminated, retired or canceled in accordance with the terms of the security if—

(1)   The security was redeemed or repurchased at the instance of the holder; or

(2)   A security holder's account was closed for failure to make payments as prescribed in the security or instruments pursuant to which the security was issued, and notice of intention to close the account was mailed to the security holder, and he had a reasonable time in which to meet the deficiency; or

(3)   Sale of the security was restricted to a specified, limited group of persons and, in accordance with the terms of the security or the instruments pursuant to which the security was issued, upon its being transferred by the holder to a person not a member of the group eligible to purchase the security, the issuer required the surrender of the security and paid the redemption price thereof.

(c) The provisions of paragraph (a) of this rule shall not apply if, following the repurchase of an outstanding security by or at the instance of the issuer or the termination, retirement or cancellation of an outstanding security in accordance with the terms thereof—

(1) The proceeds are actually paid to the security holder by or on behalf of the issuer within 7 days, and

(2) No sale and no offer (other than by way of exchange) of any security of the issuer is made by or on behalf of the issuer to the person to whom such proceeds were paid, within 60 days after such payment.

(d) The provisions of paragraph (a) of this rule shall not apply to the repurchase, termination, retirement, or cancellation of a security outstanding on the effective date of this rule or issued pursuant to a subscription agreement or other plan of acquisition in effect on such date.

* * *

Rule 12b–1. Distribution of Shares by Registered Open-End Management Investment Company

(a)(1) Except as provided in this rule, it shall be unlawful for any registered open-end management investment company (other than a company complying with the provisions of section 10(d) of the Act) to act as a distributor of securities of which it is the issuer, except through an underwriter;

(2) For purposes of this rule, such a company will be deemed to be acting as a distributor of securities of which it is the issuer, other than through an underwriter, if it engages directly or indirectly in financing any activity which is primarily intended to result in the sale of shares issued by such company, including, but not necessarily limited to, advertising, compensation of underwriters, dealers, and sales personnel, the printing and mailing of prospectuses to other than current shareholders, and the printing and mailing of sales literature;

(b) A registered, open-end management investment company ("company") may act as a distributor of securities of which it is the issuer, *Provided,* That any payments made by such company in connection with such distribution are made pursuant to a written plan describing all material aspects of the proposed financing of distribution and that all agreements with any person relating to implementation of the plan are in writing, *and further provided,* That:

(1) Such plan has been approved by a vote of at least a majority of the outstanding voting securities of such company, if adopted after any public offering of the company's voting securities or the sale of such securities to persons who are not affiliated persons of the company, affiliated persons of such persons, promoters of the company or affiliated persons of such promoters;

(2) Such plan, together with any related agreements, has been approved by a vote of the board of directors of such company, and of the directors who are not interested persons of the company and have no direct or indirect financial interest in the operation of the plan or in any agreements related to the plan, cast in person at a meeting called for the purpose of voting on such plan or agreements;

(3) Such plan or agreement provides, in substance:

(i) That it shall continue in effect for a period of more than one year from the date of its execution or adoption only so long as such continuance is specifically approved at least annually in the manner described in paragraph (b)(2);

(ii) That any person authorized to direct the disposition of monies paid or payable by such company pursuant to the plan or any related agreement shall provide to the company's board of directors, and the directors shall review, at least quarterly, a written report of the amounts so expended and the purposes for which such expenditures were made; and

(iii) In the case of a plan, that it may be terminated at any time by vote of a majority of the members of the board of directors of the company who are not interested persons of the company and have no direct or indirect financial interest in the operation of the plan or in any agreements related to the plan or by vote of a majority of the outstanding voting securities of such company; and

(iv)   In the case of an agreement related to a plan:

(A)   That it may be terminated at any time, without the payment of any penalty, by vote of a majority of the members of the board of directors of such company who are not interested persons of the company and have no direct or indirect financial interest in the operation of the plan or in any agreements related to the plan or by vote of a majority of the outstanding voting securities of such company on not more than sixty days' written notice to any other party to the agreement, and

(B)   For its automatic termination in the event of its assignment;

(4)   Such plan provides that it may not be amended to increase materially the amount to be spent for distribution without shareholder approval and that all material amendments of the plan must be approved in the manner described in paragraph (b)(2); and

(5)   Such plan is implemented and continued in a manner consistent with the provisions of paragraphs (c), (d), and (e) of this rule;

(c)   A registered open-end management investment company may rely on the provisions of paragraph (b) of this rule only if its board of directors satisfies the fund governance standards as defined in Rule 0–1(a)(7).

(d)   In considering whether a registered open-end management investment company should implement or continue a plan in reliance on paragraph (b) of this rule, the directors of such company shall have a duty to request and evaluate, and any person who is a party to any agreement with such company relating to such plan shall have a duty to furnish, such information as may reasonably be necessary to an informed determination of whether such plan should be implemented or continued; in fulfilling their duties under this paragraph the directors should consider and give appropriate weight to all pertinent factors, and minutes describing the factors considered and the basis for the decision to use company assets for distribution must be made and preserved in accordance with paragraph (f) of this rule;

NOTE: For a discussion of factors which may be relevant to a decision to use company assets for distribution, see Investment Company Act Releases Nos. 10862, September 7, 1979, and 11414, October 28, 1980.

(e)   A registered open-end management investment company may implement or continue a plan pursuant to paragraph (b) of this rule only if the directors who vote to approve such implementation or continuation conclude, in the exercise of reasonable business judgment and in light of their fiduciary duties under state law and under sections 36(a) and (b) of the Act, that there is a reasonable likelihood that the plan will benefit the company and its shareholders;

(f)   A registered open-end management investment company must preserve copies of any plan, agreement or report made pursuant to this rule for a period of not less than six years from the date of such plan, agreement or report, the first two years in an easily accessible place;

(g)   If a plan covers more than one series or class of shares, the provisions of the plan must be severable for each series or class, and whenever this rule provides for any action to be taken with respect to a plan, that action must be taken separately for each series or class affected by the matter. Nothing in this paragraph (g) shall affect the rights of any purchase class under Rule 18f–3(f)(2)(iii).

(h)   Notwithstanding any other provision of this rule, a company may not:

(1)   Compensate a broker or dealer for any promotion or sale of shares issued by that company by directing to the broker or dealer:

(i)   The company's portfolio securities transactions; or

(ii)   Any remuneration, including but not limited to any commission, mark-up, mark-down, or other fee (or portion thereof) received or to be received from the company's portfolio transactions effected through any other broker (including a government securities broker) or dealer (including a municipal securities dealer or a government securities dealer); and

(2)   Direct its portfolio securities transactions to a broker or dealer that promotes or sells shares issued by the company, unless the company (or its investment adviser):

(i)   Is in compliance with the provisions of paragraph (h)(1) of this rule with respect to that broker or dealer; and

(ii)   Has implemented, and the company's board of directors (including a majority of directors who are not interested persons of the company) has approved, policies and procedures reasonably designed to prevent:

(A)   The persons responsible for selecting brokers and dealers to effect the company's portfolio securities transactions from taking into account the brokers' and dealers' promotion or sale of shares issued by the company or any other registered investment company; and

(B)   The company, and any investment adviser and principal underwriter of the company, from entering into any agreement (whether oral or written) or other understanding under which the company directs, or is expected to direct, portfolio securities transactions, or any remuneration described in paragraph (h)(1)(ii) of this rule, to a broker (including a government securities broker) or dealer (including a municipal securities dealer or a government securities dealer) in consideration for the promotion or sale of shares issued by the company or any other registered investment company.

* * *

Rule 12d1-1. Exemptions for Investments in Money Market Funds

(a)   Exemptions for acquisition of money market fund shares. If the conditions of paragraph (b) of this rule are satisfied, notwithstanding sections 12(d)(1)(A), 12(d)(1)(B), 12(d)(1)(G), 17(a), and 57 of the Act and Rule 17d-1:

(1)   An investment company ("acquiring fund") may purchase and redeem shares issued by a money market fund; and

(2)   A money market fund, any principal underwriter thereof, and a broker or a dealer may sell or otherwise dispose of shares issued by the money market fund to any acquiring fund.

(b)   *Conditions.*

(1)   *Fees.* The acquiring fund pays no sales charge, as defined in rule 2830(b)(8) of the Conduct Rules of the NASD ("sales charge"), or service fee, as defined in rule 2830(b)(9) of the Conduct Rules of the NASD, charged in connection with the purchase, sale, or redemption of securities issued by a money market fund ("service fee"); or the acquiring fund's investment adviser waives its advisory fee in an amount necessary to offset any sales charge or service fee.

(2)   *Unregistered money market funds.* If the money market fund is not an investment company registered under the Act:

(i)   The acquiring fund reasonably believes that the money market fund satisfies the following conditions as if it were a registered open-end investment company:

(A)   Operates in compliance with Rule 2a-7;

(B)   Complies with sections 17(a), (d), (e), 18, and 22(e) of the Act;

(C)   Has adopted procedures designed to ensure that it complies with sections 17(a), (d), (e), 18, and 22(e) of the Act, periodically reviews and updates those procedures, and maintains books and records describing those procedures;

(D)   Maintains the records required by Rules 31a-1(b)(1), 31a-1(b)(2)(ii), 31a-1(b)(2)(iv), and 31a-1(b)(9); and

(E)   Preserves permanently, the first two years in an easily accessible place, all books and records required to be made under paragraphs (b)(2)(i)(C) and (D) of this rule, and makes those records available for examination on request by the Commission or its staff; and

(ii)   The adviser to the money market fund is registered with the Commission as an investment adviser under section 203 of the Investment Advisers Act of 1940.

(c)   *Exemption from certain monitoring and recordkeeping requirements under Rule 17e–1.* Notwithstanding the requirements of Rules 17e–1(b)(3) and 17e–1(d)(2), the payment of a commission, fee, or other remuneration to a broker shall be deemed as not exceeding the usual and customary broker's commission for purposes of section 17(e)(2)(A) of the Act if:

(1)   The commission, fee, or other remuneration is paid in connection with the sale of securities to or by an acquiring fund;

(2)   The broker and the acquiring fund are affiliated persons because each is an affiliated person of the same money market fund; and

(3)   The acquiring fund is an affiliated person of the money market fund solely because the acquiring fund owns, controls, or holds with power to vote five percent or more of the outstanding securities of the money market fund.

(d)   *Definitions.*

(1)   *Investment company* includes a company that would be an investment company under section 3(a) of the Act but for the exceptions to that definition provided for in sections 3(c)(1) and 3(c)(7) of the Act.

(2)   *Money market fund* means:

(i)   An open-end management investment company registered under the Act that is regulated as a money market fund under Rule 2a–7; or

(ii)   A company that would be an investment company under section 3(a) of the Act but for the exceptions to that definition provided for in sections 3(c)(1) and 3(c)(7) of the Act and that:

(A)   Is limited to investing in the types of securities and other investments in which a money market fund may invest under Rule 2a–7; and

(B)   Undertakes to comply with all the other requirements of Rule 2a–7, except that, if the company has no board of directors, the company's investment adviser performs the duties of the board of directors.

Rule 12d1–3. Exemptions for Investment Companies Relying on Section 12(d)(1)(F) of the Act

(a)   *Exemption from sales charge limits.* A registered investment company ("acquiring fund") that relies on section 12(d)(1)(F) of the Act to acquire securities issued by an investment company ("acquired fund") may offer or sell any security it issues through a principal underwriter or otherwise at a public offering price that includes a sales load of more than $1\frac{1}{2}$ percent if any sales charges and service fees charged with respect to the acquiring fund's securities do not exceed the limits set forth in rule 2830 of the Conduct Rules of the NASD applicable to a fund of funds.

(b)   *Definitions.* For purposes of this rule, the terms "fund of funds", "sales charge", and "service fee" have the same meanings as in rule 2830(b) of the Conduct Rules of the NASD.

Rule 12d1–4. Exemptions for Investments in Certain Investment Companies

(a)   Exemptions for acquisition and sale of acquired fund shares. If the conditions of paragraph (b) of this rule are satisfied, notwithstanding sections 12(d)(1)(A), 12(d)(1)(B), 12(d)(1)(C), 17(a), 57(a)(1)–(2), and 57(d)(1)–(2) of the Act:

(1)   A registered investment company (other than a face-amount certificate company) or business development company (an "acquiring fund") may purchase or otherwise acquire the securities issued by another registered investment company (other than a face-amount certificate company) or business development company (an "acquired fund");

(2)   An acquired fund, any principal underwriter thereof, and any broker or dealer registered under the Securities Exchange Act of 1934 may sell or otherwise dispose of the securities issued by the acquired fund to any acquiring fund and any acquired fund may redeem or repurchase any securities issued by the acquired fund from any acquiring fund; and

(3) An acquiring fund that is an affiliated person of an exchange-traded fund (or who is an affiliated person of such a fund) solely by reason of the circumstances described in Rule 6c–11(b)(3)(i) and (ii), may deposit and receive the exchange-traded fund's baskets, provided that the acquired exchange-traded fund is not otherwise an affiliated person (or affiliated person of an affiliated person) of the acquiring fund.

(b)   Conditions.

(1)   Control.

(i)   The acquiring fund and its advisory group will not control (individually or in the aggregate) an acquired fund;

(ii)   If the acquiring fund and its advisory group, in the aggregate, (A) hold more than 25% of the outstanding voting securities of an acquired fund that is a registered open-end management investment company or registered unit investment trust as a result of a decrease in the outstanding voting securities of the acquired fund, or (B) hold more than 10% of the outstanding voting securities of an acquired fund that is a registered closed-end management investment company or business development company, each of those holders will vote its securities in the same proportion as the vote of all other holders of such securities; provided, however, that in circumstances where all holders of the outstanding voting securities of the acquired fund are required by this rule or otherwise under section 12(d)(1) to vote securities of the acquired fund in the same proportion as the vote of all other holders of such securities, the acquiring fund will seek instructions from its security holders with regard to the voting of all proxies with respect to such acquired fund securities and vote such proxies only in accordance with such instructions; and

(iii)   The conditions in paragraphs (b)(1)(i)–(ii) of this rule do not apply if:

(A)   The acquiring fund is in the same group of investment companies as an acquired fund; or

(B)   The acquiring fund's investment sub-adviser or any person controlling, controlled by, or under common control with such investment sub-adviser acts as an acquired fund's investment adviser or depositor.

(2)   Findings and Agreements.

(i)   Management companies.

(A)   If the acquiring fund is a management company, prior to the initial acquisition of an acquired fund in excess of the limits in section 12(d)(1)(A)(i) of the Act, the acquiring fund's investment adviser must evaluate the complexity of the structure and fees and expenses associated with the acquiring fund's investment in the acquired fund, and find that the acquiring fund's fees and expenses do not duplicate the fees and expenses of the acquired fund;

(B)   If the acquired fund is a management company, prior to the initial acquisition of an acquired fund in excess of the limits in section 12(d)(1)(A)(i) of the Act, the acquired fund's investment adviser must find that any undue influence concerns associated with the acquiring fund's investment in the acquired fund are reasonably addressed and, as part of this finding, the investment adviser must consider at a minimum the following items:

(1)   The scale of contemplated investments by the acquiring fund and any maximum investment limits;

(2)   The anticipated timing of redemption requests by the acquiring fund;

(3)   Whether and under what circumstances the acquiring fund will provide advance notification of investments and redemptions; and

(4)   The circumstances under which the acquired fund may elect to satisfy redemption requests in kind rather than in cash and the terms of any such redemptions in kind; and

(C)   The investment adviser to each acquiring or acquired management company must report its evaluation, finding, and the basis for its evaluations or findings required by paragraphs (b)(2)(i)(A) or (B), as applicable, to the fund's board of directors, no later than the next regularly scheduled board of directors meeting.

(ii)   Unit investment trusts. If the acquiring fund is a unit investment trust ("UIT") and the date of initial deposit of portfolio securities into the UIT occurs after the effective date of this rule, the UIT's principal underwriter or depositor must evaluate the complexity of the structure associated with the UIT's investment in acquired funds and, on or before such date of initial deposit, find that the UIT's fees and expenses do not duplicate the fees and expenses of the acquired funds that the UIT holds or will hold at the date of deposit.

(iii)   Separate accounts funding variable insurance contracts. With respect to a separate account funding variable insurance contracts that invests in an acquiring fund, the acquiring fund must obtain a certification from the insurance company offering the separate account that the insurance company has determined that the fees and expenses borne by the separate account, acquiring fund, and acquired fund, in the aggregate, are consistent with the standard set forth in section 26(f)(2)(A) of the Act.

(iv)   Fund of funds investment agreement. Unless the acquiring fund's investment adviser acts as the acquired fund's investment adviser and such adviser is not acting as the sub-adviser to either fund, the acquiring fund must enter into an agreement with the acquired fund effective for the duration of the funds' reliance on this rule, which must include the following:

(A)   Any material terms regarding the acquiring fund's investment in the acquired fund necessary to make the finding required under paragraph (b)(2)(i)–(ii) of this rule;

(B)   A termination provision whereby either the acquiring fund or acquired fund may terminate the agreement subject to advance written notice no longer than 60 days; and

(C)   A requirement that the acquired fund provide the acquiring fund with information on the fees and expenses of the acquired fund reasonably requested by the acquiring fund.

(3)   Complex fund structures.

(i)   No investment company may rely on section 12(d)(1)(G) of the Act or this rule to purchase or otherwise acquire, in excess of the limits in section 12(d)(1)(A) of the Act, the outstanding voting securities of an investment company (a "second-tier fund") that relies on this rule to acquire the securities of an acquired fund, unless the second-tier fund makes investments permitted by paragraph (b)(3)(ii) of this rule; and

(ii)   No acquired fund may purchase or otherwise acquire the securities of an investment company or private fund if immediately after such purchase or acquisition, the securities of investment companies and private funds owned by the acquired fund have an aggregate value in excess of 10 percent of the value of the total assets of the acquired fund; provided, however, that the 10 percent limitation of this paragraph shall not apply to investments by the acquired fund in:

(A)   Reliance on section 12(d)(1)(E) of the Act;

(B)   Reliance on Rule 12d1–1;

(C)   A subsidiary that is wholly-owned and controlled by the acquired fund;

(D)   Securities received as a dividend or as a result of a plan of reorganization of a company; or

(E)   Securities of another investment company received pursuant to exemptive relief from the Commission to engage in interfund borrowing and lending transactions.

(c)   Recordkeeping. The acquiring and acquired funds relying upon this rule must maintain and preserve for a period of not less than five years, the first two years in an easily accessible place, as applicable:

(1)   A copy of each fund of funds investment agreement that is in effect, or at any time within the past five years was in effect, and any amendments thereto;

(2)   A written record of the evaluations and findings required by paragraph (b)(2)(i) of this rule, and the basis therefor within the past five years;

(3)   A written record of the finding required by paragraph (b)(2)(ii) of this rule and the basis for such finding; and

(4)   The certification from each insurance company required by paragraph (b)(2)(iii) of this rule.

(d)   Definitions. For purposes of this rule:

Advisory group means either:

(1)   An acquiring fund's investment adviser or depositor, and any person controlling, controlled by, or under common control with such investment adviser or depositor; or

(2)   An acquiring fund's investment sub-adviser and any person controlling, controlled by, or under common control with such investment sub-adviser.

Baskets has the same meaning as in Rule 6c–11(a)(1).

Exchange-traded fund means a fund or class, the shares of which are listed and traded on a national securities exchange, and that has formed and operates in reliance on Rule 6c–11 or under an exemptive order granted by the Commission.

Group of investment companies means any two or more registered investment companies or business development companies that hold themselves out to investors as related companies for purposes of investment and investor services.

Private fund means an issuer that would be an investment company under section 3(a) of the Act but for the exclusions from that definition provided for in section 3(c)(1) or section 3(c)(7) of the Act.

Rule 12d2–1. Definition of Insurance Company for Purposes of Sections 12(d)(2) and 12(g) of the Act

For purposes of sections 12(d)(2) and 12(g) of the Act, "insurance company" shall include a foreign insurance company as that term is used in rule 3a–6 under the Act.

* * *

Rule 12d3–1. Exemption of Acquisitions of Securities Issued by Persons Engaged in Securities Related Businesses

(a)   Notwithstanding section 12(d)(3) of the Act, a registered investment company, or any company or companies controlled by such registered investment company ("acquiring company") may acquire any security issued by any person that, in its most recent fiscal year, derived 15 percent or less of its gross revenues from securities related activities unless the acquiring company would control such person after the acquisition.

(b)   Notwithstanding section 12(d)(3) of the Act, an acquiring company may acquire any security issued by a person that, in its most recent fiscal year, derived more than 15 percent of its gross revenues from securities related activities, provided that:

(1)   Immediately after the acquisition of any equity security, the acquiring company owns not more than five percent of the outstanding securities of that class of the issuer's equity securities;

(2)   Immediately after the acquisition of any debt security, the acquiring company owns not more than ten percent of the outstanding principal amount of the issuer's debt securities; and

(3)   Immediately after any such acquisition, the acquiring company has invested not more than five percent of the value of its total assets in the securities of the issuer.

(c)   Notwithstanding paragraphs (a) and (b) of this rule, this rule does not exempt the acquisition of:

(1)   A general partnership interest; or

(2)   A security issued by the acquiring company's promoter, principal underwriter, or any affiliated person of such promoter, or principal underwriter; or

(3)   A security issued by the acquiring company's investment adviser, or an affiliated person of the acquiring company's investment adviser, other than a security issued by a subadviser or an affiliated person of a subadviser of the acquiring company provided that:

(i)   Prohibited relationships. The subadviser that is (or whose affiliated person is) the issuer is not, and is not an affiliated person of, an investment adviser responsible for providing advice with respect to the portion of the acquiring company that is acquiring the securities, or of any promoter, underwriter, officer, director, member of an advisory board, or employee of the acquiring company;

(ii)   Advisory contract. The advisory contracts of the Subadviser that is (or whose affiliated person is) the issuer, and any Subadviser that is advising the portion of the acquiring company that is purchasing the securities:

(A)   Prohibit them from consulting with each other concerning transactions of the acquiring company in securities or other assets, other than for purposes of complying with the conditions of paragraphs (a) and (b) of this rule; and

(B)   Limit their responsibility in providing advice to providing advice with respect to a discrete portion of the acquiring company's portfolio.

(d)   For purposes of this rule:

(1)   "Securities related activities" are a person's activities as a broker, a dealer, an underwriter, an investment adviser registered under the Investment Advisers Act of 1940, as amended, or as an investment adviser to a registered investment company.

(2)   An issuer's gross revenues from its own securities related activities and from its ratable share of the securities related activities of enterprises of which it owns 20 percent or more of the voting or equity interest should be considered in determining the degree to which an issuer is engaged in securities related activities. Such information may be obtained from the issuer's annual report to shareholders, the issuer's annual reports or registration statement filed with the Commission, or the issuer's chief financial officer.

(3)   "Equity security" is as defined in Rule 3a-11.

(4)   "Debt security" includes all securities other than equity securities.

(5)   Determination of the percentage of an acquiring company's ownership of any class of outstanding equity securities of an issuer shall be made in accordance with the procedures described in the rules under Rule 16.

(6)   Where an acquiring company is considering acquiring or has acquired options, warrants, rights, or convertible securities of a securities related business, the determination required by paragraph (b) of this rule shall be made as though such options, warrants, rights, or conversion privileges had been exercised.

(7)   The following transactions will not be deemed to be an acquisition of securities of a securities related business:

(i)   Receipt of stock dividends on securities acquired in compliance with this rule;

(ii)   Receipt of securities arising from a stock-for-stock split on securities acquired in compliance with this rule;

(iii)   Exercise of options, warrants, or rights acquired in compliance with this rule;

(iv)   Conversion of convertible securities acquired in compliance with this rule; and

(v)   Acquisition of Demand Features or Guarantees, as these terms are defined in Rules 2(a)-7(a)(9) and 2a-7(a)(16) respectively, provided that, immediately after the acquisition of any Demand Feature or Guarantee, the company will not, with respect to 75 percent of the total value of its assets, have invested more than ten percent of the total value of its assets in securities underlying Demand Features or Guarantees from the same institution. For the purposes of this rule, a Demand Feature or Guarantee will be considered to be from the party to whom the company will look for payment of the exercise price.

(8)   Any class or series of an investment company that issues two or more classes or series of preferred or special stock, each of which is preferred over all other classes or series with respect to assets specifically allocated to that class or series, shall be treated as if it is a registered investment company.

(9)   Subadviser means an investment adviser as defined in section 2(a)(20)(B) of the Act.

Rule 15a–1.   Exemption From Stockholders' Approval of Certain Small Investment Advisory Contracts

An investment adviser of a registered investment company shall be exempt from the requirement of sections 15(a) and 15(e) of the act that the written contract pursuant to which he acts shall have been approved by the vote of a majority of the outstanding voting securities of such company, if the following conditions are met:

(a)   Such investment adviser is not an affiliated person of such company (except as investment adviser) nor of any principal underwriter for such company.

(b)   His compensation as investment adviser of such company in any fiscal year of the company during which any such contract is in effect either

(1)   Is not more than $100 or

(2)   Is not more than $2,500 and not more than %P1/40%P of 1 percent of the value of the company's net assets averaged over the year or taken as of a definite date or dates within the year.

(c)   The aggregate compensation of all investment advisers of such company exempted pursuant to this rule in any fiscal year of the company either

(1)   Is not more than $200 or

(2)   Is not more than 1/20 of 1 percent of the value of the company's net assets averaged over the year or taken as of a definite date or dates within the year.

* * *

Rule 17a–1.   Exemption of Certain Underwriting Transactions Exempted by Rule 10f–1

Any transaction exempted pursuant to Rule 10f–1 shall be exempt from the provisions of section 17(a)(1) of the Act.

Rule 17a–2.   Exemption of Certain Purchase, Sale or Borrowing Transactions

Purchase, sale or borrowing transactions occurring in the usual course of business between affiliated persons of registered investment companies shall be exempt from section 17(a) of the Act provided

(a)   The transactions involve notes, drafts, time payment contracts, bills of exchange, acceptance or other property of a commercial character rather than of an investment character;

(b)   The buyer or lender is a bank; and

(c)   The seller or borrower is a bank or is engaged principally in the business of installment financing.

Rule 17a–3.   Exemption of Transactions With Fully Owned Subsidiaries

(a)   The following transactions shall be exempt from section 17(a) of the act:

(1)   Transactions solely between a registered investment company and one or more of its fully owned subsidiaries or solely between two or more fully owned subsidiaries of such company.

(2) Transactions solely between any subsidiary of a registered investment company and one or more fully owned subsidiaries of such subsidiary or solely between two or more fully owned subsidiaries of such subsidiary.

(b) The term "fully owned subsidiary" as used in this rule, means a subsidiary

(1) All of whose outstanding securities, other than directors' qualifying shares, are owned by its parent and/or the parent's other fully owned subsidiaries, and

(2) Which is not indebted to any person other than its parent and/or the parent's other fully owned subsidiaries in an amount which is material in relation to the particular subsidiary, excepting

(i) Indebtedness incurred in the ordinary course of business which is not overdue and which matures within one year from the date of its creation, whether evidenced by securities or not, and

(ii) Any other indebtedness to one or more banks or insurance companies.

Rule 17a–4. Exemption of Transactions Pursuant to Certain Contracts

Transactions pursuant to a contract shall be exempt from section 17(a) of the Act if at the time of the making of the contract and for a period of at least six months prior thereto no affiliation or other relationship existed which would operate to make such contract or the subsequent performance thereof subject to the provisions of said section 17(a).

Rule 17a–5. Pro Rata Distribution Neither "Sale" Nor "Purchase"

When a company makes a pro rata distribution in cash or in kind among its common stockholders without giving any election to any stockholder as to the specific assets which such stockholders shall receive, such distribution shall not be deemed to involve a sale to or a purchase from such distributing company as those terms are used in section 17(a) of the Act.

Rule 17a–6. Exemption for Transactions With Portfolio Affiliates

(a) *Exemption for Transactions with Portfolio Affiliates.* A transaction to which a fund, or a company controlled by a fund, and a portfolio affiliate of the fund are parties is exempt from the provisions of section 17(a) of the Act, provided that none of the following persons is a party to the transaction, or has a direct or indirect financial interest in a party to the transaction other than the fund:

(1) An officer, director, employee, investment adviser, member of an advisory board, depositor, promoter of or principal underwriter for the fund;

(2) A person directly or indirectly controlling the fund;

(3) A person directly or indirectly owning, controlling or holding with power to vote five percent or more of the outstanding voting securities of the fund;

(4) A person directly or indirectly under common control with the fund, other than:

(i) A portfolio affiliate of the fund; or

(ii) A fund whose sole interest in the transaction or a party to the transaction is an interest in the portfolio affiliate; or

(5) An affiliated person of any of the persons mentioned in paragraphs (a)(1)–(4) of this rule, other than the fund or a portfolio affiliate of the fund.

(b) *Definitions.*

(1) Financial interest.

(i) The term financial interest as used in this rule does not include:

(A) Any interest through ownership of securities issued by the fund;

(B) Any interest of a wholly-owned subsidiary of a fund;

(C)   Usual and ordinary fees for services as a director;

(D)   An interest of a non-executive employee;

(E)   An interest of an insurance company arising from a loan or policy made or issued by it in the ordinary course of business to a natural person;

(F)   An interest of a bank arising from a loan or account made or maintained by it in the ordinary course of business to or with a natural person, unless it arises from a loan to a person who is an officer, director or executive of a company which is a party to the transaction, or from a loan to a person who directly or indirectly owns, controls, or holds with power to vote, five percent or more of the outstanding voting securities of a company which is a party to the transaction;

(G)   An interest acquired in a transaction described in paragraph (d)(3) of Rule 17d–1; or

(H)   Any other interest that the board of directors of the fund, including a majority of the directors who are not interested persons of the fund, finds to be not material, provided that the directors record the basis for that finding in the minutes of their meeting.

(ii)   A person has a financial interest in any party in which it has a financial interest, in which it had a financial interest within six months prior to the transaction, or in which it will acquire a financial interest pursuant to an arrangement in existence at the time of the transaction.

(2)   Fund means a registered investment company or separate series of a registered investment company.

(3)   Portfolio affiliate of a fund means a person that is an affiliated person (or an affiliated person of an affiliated person) of a fund solely because the fund, a fund under common control with the fund, or both:

(i)   Controls such person (or an affiliated person of such person); or

(ii)   Owns, controls, or holds with power to vote five percent or more of the outstanding voting securities of such person (or an affiliated person of such person).

Rule 17a–7.   Exemption of Certain Purchase or Sale Transactions Between an Investment Company and Certain Affiliated Persons Thereof

A purchase or sale transaction between registered investment companies or separate series of registered investment companies, which are affiliated persons, or affiliated persons of affiliated persons, of each other, between separate series of a registered investment company, or between a registered investment company or a separate series of a registered investment company and a person which is an affiliated person of such registered investment company (or affiliated person of such person) solely by reason of having a common investment advisor or investment advisers which are affiliated persons of each other, common directors, and/or common officers, is exempt from section 17(a) of the Act; *Provided,* That:

(a)   The transaction is a purchase or sale, for no consideration other than cash payment against prompt delivery of a security for which market quotations are readily available;

(b)   The transaction is effected at the independent current market price of the security. For purposes of this paragraph the "current market price" shall be:

(1)   If the security is an "NMS stock" as that term is defined in Rule 600 of Regulation NMS, the last sale price with respect to such security reported in the consolidated transaction reporting system ("consolidated system") or the average of the highest current independent bid and lowest current independent offer for such security (reported pursuant to Rule 602 of Regulation NMS) if there are no reported transactions in the consolidated system that day; or

(2)   If the security is not a reported security, and the principal market for such security is an exchange, then the last sale on such exchange or the average of the highest current independent bid and lowest current independent offer on such exchange if there are no reported transactions on such exchange that day; or

(3)   If the security is not a reported security and is quoted in the NASDAQ System, then the average of the highest current independent bid and lowest current independent offer reported on Level 1 of NASDAQ; or

(4)   For all other securities, the average of the highest current independent bid and lowest current independent offer determined on the basis of reasonable inquiry;

(c)   The transaction is consistent with the policy of each registered investment company and separate series of a registered investment company participating in the transaction, as recited in its registration statement and reports filed under the Act;

(d)   No brokerage commission, fee (except for customary transfer fees), or other remuneration is paid in connection with the transaction;

(e)   The board of directors of the investment company, including a majority of the directors who are not interested persons of such investment company

(1)   Adopts procedures pursuant to which such purchase or sale transactions may be effected for the company, which are reasonably designed to provide that all the conditions of this rule in paragraphs (a) through (d) have been complied with,

(2)   Makes and approves such changes as the board deems necessary, and

(3)   Determines no less frequently than quarterly that all such purchases or sales made during the preceding quarter were effected in compliance with such procedures;

(f)   The board of directors of the investment company satisfies the fund governance standards defined in Rule 0–1(a)(7); and

(g)   The investment company

(1)   Maintains and preserves permanently in an easily accessible place a written copy of the procedures (and any modifications thereto) described in paragraph (e) of this rule, and

(2)   Maintains and preserves for a period not less than six years from the end of the fiscal year in which any transactions occurred, the first two years in an easily accessible place, a written record of each such transaction setting forth a description of the security purchased or sold, the identity of the person on the other side of the transaction, the terms of the purchase or sale transaction, and the information or materials upon which the determinations described in paragraph (e)(3) of this rule were made.

Rule 17a–8.   Mergers of Affiliated Companies

(a)   A Merger of a registered investment company (or a series thereof) and one or more other registered investment companies (or series thereof) or Eligible Unregistered Funds is exempt from sections 17(a)(1) and (2) of the Act if:

(1)   The Surviving Company is a registered investment company (or a series thereof).

(2)   As to any registered investment company (or series thereof) participating in the Merger ("Merging Company"):

(i)   The board of directors, including a majority of the directors who are not interested persons of the Merging Company or of any other company or series participating in the Merger, determines that:

(A)   Participation in the Merger is in the best interests of the Merging Company; and

(B)   The interests of the Merging Company's existing shareholders will not be diluted as a result of the Merger.

(ii)   The directors have requested and evaluated such information as may reasonably be necessary to their determinations in paragraph (a)(2)(i) of this rule, and have considered and given appropriate weight to all pertinent factors.

Note to paragraph (a)(2)(i): For a discussion of factors that may be relevant to the determinations in paragraph (a)(2)(i) of this rule, see Investment Company Act Release No. 25666, July 18, 2002.

(iii)   The directors, in making the determination in paragraph (a)(2)(i)(B) of this rule, have approved procedures for the valuation of assets to be conveyed by each Eligible Unregistered Fund participating in the Merger. The approved procedures provide for the preparation of a report by an Independent Evaluator, to be considered in assessing the value of any securities (or other assets) for which market quotations are not readily available, that sets forth the fair value of each such asset as of the date of the Merger.

(iv)   The determinations required in paragraph (a)(2)(i) of this rule and the bases thereof, including the factors considered by the directors pursuant to paragraph (a)(2)(ii) of this rule, are recorded fully in the minute books of the Merging Company.

(3)   Participation in the Merger is approved by the vote of a majority of the outstanding voting securities (as provided in section 2(a)(42) of the Act) of any Merging Company that is not a Surviving Company, unless-

(i)   No policy of the Merging Company that under section 13 of the Act could not be changed without a vote of a majority of its outstanding voting securities, is materially different from a policy of the Surviving Company;

(ii)   No advisory contract between the Merging Company and any investment adviser thereof is materially different from an advisory contract between the Surviving Company and any investment adviser thereof, except for the identity of the investment companies as a party to the contract;

(iii)   Directors of the Merging Company who are not interested persons of the Merging Company and who were elected by its shareholders, will comprise a majority of the directors of the Surviving Company who are not interested persons of the Surviving Company; and

(iv)   Any distribution fees (as a percentage of the fund's average net assets) authorized to be paid by the Surviving Company pursuant to a plan adopted in accordance with Rule 12b-1 are no greater than the distribution fees (as a percentage of the fund's average net assets) authorized to be paid by the Merging Company pursuant to such a plan.

(4)   The board of directors of the Merging Company satisfies the fund governance standards defined in Rule 0–1(a)(7).

(5)   Any Surviving Company preserves written records that describe the Merger and its terms for six years after the Merger (and for the first two years in an easily accessible place).

(b)   For purposes of this rule:

(1)   Merger means the merger, consolidation, or purchase or sale of substantially all of the assets between a registered investment company (or a series thereof) and another company;

(2)   Eligible Unregistered Fund means:

(i)   A collective trust fund, as described in section 3(c)(11) of the Act;

(ii)   A common trust fund or similar fund, as described in section 3(c)(3) of the Act; or

(iii)   A separate account, as described in section 2(a)(37) of the Act, that is neither registered under section 8 of the Act, nor required to be so registered;

(3)   Independent Evaluator means a person who has expertise in the valuation of securities and other financial assets and who is not an interested person, as defined in section 2(a)(19) of the Act, of the Eligible Unregistered Fund or any affiliate thereof except the Merging Company; and

(4)   Surviving Company means a company in which shareholders of a Merging Company will obtain an interest as a result of a Merger.

Rule 17a-9.   Purchase of Certain Securities From a Money Market Fund by an Affiliate, or an Affiliate of an Affiliate

The purchase of a security from the portfolio of an open-end investment company holding itself out as a money market fund by any affiliated person or promoter of or principal underwriter for the money market fund or any affiliated person of such person shall be exempt from section 17(a) of the Act provided that:

(a)   In the case of a portfolio security that has ceased to be an Eligible Security (as defined in Rule 2a–7(a)(12)), or has defaulted (other than an immaterial default unrelated to the financial condition of the issuer):

(1)   The purchase price is paid in cash; and

(2)   The purchase price is equal to the greater of the amortized cost of the security or its market price (in each case, including accrued interest).

(b)   In the case of any other portfolio security:

(1)   The purchase price meets the requirements of paragraph (a)(1) and (2) of this rule; and

(2)   In the event that the purchaser thereafter sells the security for a higher price than the purchase price paid to the money market fund, the purchaser shall promptly pay to the fund the amount by which the subsequent sale price exceeds the purchase price paid to the fund.

* * *

Rule 17a–10. Exemption for Transactions With Certain Subadvisory Affiliates

(a)   *Exemption.* A person that is prohibited by section 17(a) of the Act from entering into a transaction with a fund solely because such person is, or is an affiliated person of, a subadviser of the fund, or a subadviser of a fund that is under common control with the fund, may nonetheless enter into such transaction, if:

(1)   *Prohibited Relationship.* The person is not, and is not an affiliated person of, an investment adviser responsible for providing advice with respect to the portion of the fund for which the transaction is entered into, or of any promoter, underwriter, officer, director, member of an advisory board, or employee of the fund.

(2)   *Prohibited Conduct.* The advisory contracts of the subadviser that is (or whose affiliated person is) entering into the transaction, and any subadviser that is advising the fund (or portion of the fund) entering into the transaction:

(i)   Prohibit them from consulting with each other concerning transactions for the fund in securities or other assets; and

(ii)   If both such subadvisers are responsible for providing investment advice to the fund, limit the subadvisers' responsibility in providing advice with respect to a discrete portion of the fund's portfolio.

(b)   *Definitions.*

(1)   Fund means a registered investment company and includes a separate series of a registered investment company.

(2)   Subadviser means an investment adviser as defined in section 2(a)(20)(B) of the Act.

Rule 17d–1.   Applications Regarding Joint Enterprises or Arrangements and Certain Profit-Sharing Plans

(a)   No affiliated person of or principal underwriter for any registered investment company (other than a company of the character described in section 12(d)(3)(A) and (B) of the Act) and no affiliated person of such a person or principal underwriter, acting as principal, shall participate in, or effect any transaction in connection with, any joint enterprise or other joint arrangement or profit-sharing plan in which any such registered company, or a company controlled by such registered company, is a participant, and which is entered into, adopted or modified subsequent to the effective date of this rule, unless an application regarding such joint enterprise, arrangement or profit-sharing plan has been filed with the Commission and has been granted by an order entered prior to the submission of such plan or modification to security holders for approval, or prior to such adoption or modification if not so submitted, except that the provisions of this rule shall not preclude any affiliated person from acting as manager of any underwriting syndicate or other group in which such registered or controlled company is a participant and receiving compensation therefor.

(b) In passing upon such applications, the Commission will consider whether the participation of such registered or controlled company in such joint enterprise, joint arrangement or profit-sharing plan on the basis proposed is consistent with the provisions, policies and purposes of the Act and the extent to which such participation is on a basis different from or less advantageous than that of other participants.

(c) "Joint enterprise or other joint arrangement or profit-sharing plan" as used in this rule shall mean any written or oral plan, contract, authorization or arrangement, or any practice or understanding concerning an enterprise or undertaking whereby a registered investment company or a controlled company thereof and any affiliated person of or a principal underwriter for such registered investment company, or any affiliated person of such a person or principal underwriter, have a joint or a joint and several participation, or share in the profits of such enterprise or undertaking, including, but not limited to, any stock option or stock purchase plan, but shall not include an investment advisory contract subject to section 15 of the Act.

(d) Notwithstanding the requirements of paragraph (a) of this rule, no application need be filed pursuant to this rule with respect to any of the following:

(1) Any profit-sharing, stock option or stock purchase plan provided by any controlled company which is not an investment company for its officers, directors or employees, or the purchase of stock or the granting, modification or exercise of options pursuant to such a plan, provided:

(i) No individual participates therein who is either: (a) An affiliated person of any investment company which is an affiliated person of such controlled company; or (b) an affiliated person of the investment adviser or principal underwriter of such investment company; and

(ii) No participant has been an affiliated person of such investment company, its investment adviser or principal underwriter during the life of the plan and for six months prior to, as the case may be: (a) Institution of the profit-sharing plan; (b) the purchase of stock pursuant to a stock purchase plan; or (c) the granting of any options pursuant to a stock option plan.

(2) Any plan provided by any registered investment company or any controlled company for its officers or employees if such plan has been qualified under section 401 of the Internal Revenue Code of 1954 and all contributions paid under said plan by the employer qualify as deductible under section 404 of said Code.

(3) Any loan or advance of credit to, or acquisition of securities or other property of, a small business concern, or any agreement to do any of the foregoing ("Investments"), made by a bank and a small business investment company (SBIC) licensed under the Small Business Investment Act of 1958, whether such transactions are contemporaneous or separated in time, where the bank is an affiliated person of either (i) the SBIC or (ii) an affiliated person of the SBIC; but reports containing pertinent details as to Investments and transactions relating thereto shall be made at such time, on such forms and by such persons as the Commission may from time to time prescribe.

(4) The issuance by a registered investment company which is licensed by the Small Business Administration pursuant to the Small Business Investment Act of 1958 of stock options which qualify under section 422 of the Internal Revenue Code, as amended, and which conform to Rule 805(b) of Chapter I of Title 13 of the Code of Federal Regulations.

(5) Any joint enterprise or other joint arrangement or profit-sharing plan ("joint enterprise") in which a registered investment company or a company controlled by such a company, is a participant, and in which a portfolio affiliate (as defined in Rule 17a-6(b)(3)) of such registered investment company is also a participant, provided that:

(i) None of the persons identified in Rule 17a-6(a) is a participant in the joint enterprise, or has a direct or indirect financial interest in a participant in the joint enterprise (other than the registered investment company);

(ii) Financial interest.

(A) The term financial interest as used in this rule does not include:

(1) Any interest through ownership of securities issued by the registered investment company;

(2)   Any interest of a wholly owned subsidiary of the registered investment company;

(3)   Usual and ordinary fees for services as a director;

(4)   An interest of a non-executive employee;

(5)   An interest of an insurance company arising from a loan or policy made or issued by it in the ordinary course of business to a natural person;

(6)   An interest of a bank arising from a loan to a person who is an officer, director, or executive of a company which is a participant in the joint transaction or from a loan to a person who directly or indirectly owns, controls, or holds with power to vote, five percent or more of the outstanding voting securities of a company which is a participant in the joint transaction;

(7)   An interest acquired in a transaction described in paragraph (d)(3) of this rule; or

(8)   Any other interest that the board of directors of the investment company, including a majority of the directors who are not interested persons of the investment company, finds to be not material, provided that the directors record the basis for that finding in the minutes of their meeting.

(B)   A person has a financial interest in any party in which it has a financial interest, in which it had a financial interest within six months prior to the investment company's participation in the enterprise, or in which it will acquire a financial interest pursuant to an arrangement in existence at the time of the investment company's participation in the enterprise.

(6)   The receipt of securities and/or cash by an investment company or a controlled company thereof and an affiliated person of such investment company or an affiliated person of such person pursuant to a plan of reorganization: Provided, That no person identified in Rule 17a–6(a)(1) or any company in which such a person has a direct or indirect financial interest (as defined in paragraph (d)(5)(ii) of this rule):

(i)   Has a direct or indirect financial interest in the corporation under reorganization, except owning securities of each class or classes owned by such investment company or controlled company;

(ii)   Receives pursuant to such plan any securities or other property, except securities of the same class and subject to the same terms as the securities received by such investment company or controlled company, and/or cash in the same proportion as is received by the investment company or controlled company based on securities of the company under reorganization owned by such persons; and

(iii)   Is, or has a direct or indirect financial interest in any person (other than such investment company or controlled company) who is:

(A)   Purchasing assets from the company under reorganization; or

(B)   Exchanging shares with such person in a transaction not in compliance with the standards described in this paragraph (d)(6).

(7)   Any arrangement regarding liability insurance policies (other than a bond required pursuant to Rule 17g–1 under the Act); Provided, That

(i)   The investment company's participation in the joint liability insurance policy is in the best interests of the investment company;

(ii)   The proposed premium for the joint liability insurance policy to be allocated to the investment company, based upon its proportionate share of the sum of the premiums that would have been paid if such insurance coverage were purchased separately by the insured parties, is fair and reasonable to the investment company;

(iii)   The joint liability insurance policy does not exclude coverage for bona fide claims made against any director who is not an interested person of the investment company, or against the investment company if it is a co-defendant in the claim with the disinterested director, by another person insured under the joint liability insurance policy;

(iv)   The board of directors of the investment company, including a majority of the directors who are not interested persons with respect thereto, determine no less frequently than annually that the standards described in paragraphs (d)(7)(i) and (ii) of this rule have been satisfied; and

(v)   The board of directors of the investment company satisfies the fund governance standards defined in Rule 0–1(a)(7).

(8)   An investment adviser's bearing expenses in connection with a merger, consolidation or purchase or sale of substantially all of the assets of a company which involves a registered investment company of which it is an affiliated person.

Rule 17e–1.   Brokerage Transactions on a Securities Exchange

For purposes of section 17(e)(2)(A) of the Act, a commission, fee or other remuneration shall be deemed as not exceeding the usual and customary broker's commission, if:

(a)   The commission fee, or other remuneration received or to be received is reasonable and fair compared to the commission, fee or other remuneration received by other brokers in connection with comparable transactions involving similar securities being purchased or sold on a securities exchange during a comparable period of time;

(b)   The board of directors, including a majority of the directors of the investment company who are not interested persons thereof,

(1)   Has adopted procedures which are reasonably designed to provide that such commission, fee or other remuneration is consistent with the standard described in paragraph (a) of this rule,

(2)   Makes and approves such changes as the board deems necessary, and

(3)   Determines no less frequently than quarterly that all transactions effected pursuant to this rule during the preceding quarter (other than transactions in which the person acting as broker is a person permitted to enter into a transaction with the investment company by Rule 17a–10) were effected in compliance with such procedures; and

(c)   The board of directors of the investment company satisfies the fund governance standards in Rule 0–1(a)(7); and

(d)   The investment company:

(1)   Shall maintain and preserve permanently in an easily accessible place a copy of the procedures (and any modification thereto) described in paragraph (b)(1) of this rule; and

(2)   Shall maintain and preserve for a period not less than six years from the end of the fiscal year in which any transactions occurred, the first two years in an easily accessible place, a record of each such transaction (other than any transaction in which the person acting as broker is a person permitted to enter into a transaction with the investment company by Rule 17a–10) setting forth the amount and source of the commission, fee or other remuneration received or to be received, the identity of the person acting as broker, the terms of the transaction, and the information or materials upon which the findings described in paragraph (b)(3) of this rule were made.

Rule 17f–1.   Custody of Securities With Members of National Securities Exchange

(a)   No registered management investment company shall place or maintain any of its securities or similar investments in the custody of a company which is a member of a national securities exchange as defined in the Securities Exchange Act of 1934 (whether or not such company trades in securities for its own account) except pursuant to a written contract which shall have been approved, or if executed before January 1, 1941, shall have been ratified not later than that date, by a majority of the board of directors of such investment company.

(b)   The contract shall require, and the securities and investments shall be maintained in accordance with the following:

(1)   The securities and similar investments held in such custody shall at all times be individually segregated from the securities and investments of any other person and marked in such manner as to clearly identify them as the property of such registered management company, both upon physical inspection thereof and upon examination of the books of the custodian. The physical segregation and marking of such securities and investments may be accomplished by putting them in separate containers bearing the name of such registered management investment company or by attaching tags or labels to such securities and investments.

(2)   The custodian shall have no power or authority to assign, hypothecate, pledge or otherwise to dispose of any such securities and investments, except pursuant to the direction of such registered management company and only for the account of such registered investment company.

(3)   Such securities and investments shall be subject to no lien or charge of any kind in favor of the custodian or any persons claiming through the custodian.

(4)   Such securities and investment shall be verified by actual examination at the end of each annual and semi-annual fiscal period by an independent public accountant retained by the investment company, and shall be examined by such accountant at least one other time, chosen by the accountant during the fiscal year. A certificate of such accountant stating that an examination of such securities has been made, and describing the nature of the examination, shall be transmitted to the Commission promptly after each examination.

(5)   Such securities and investments shall, at all times, be subject to inspection by the Commission through its employees or agents.

(6)   The provisions of subparagraph (1), (2) and (3) of this paragraph shall not apply to securities and similar investments bought or sold to such investment company by the company which is custodian until the securities have been reduced to the physical possession of the custodian and have been paid for by such investment company: *Provided,* That the company which is custodian shall take possession of such securities at the earliest practicable time. Nothing in this subparagraph shall be construed to relieve any company which is a member of a national securities exchange of any obligation under existing law or under the rules of any national securities exchange.

(c)   A copy of any contract executed or ratified pursuant to paragraph (a) of this rule shall be transmitted to the Commission promptly after execution or ratification unless it has been previously transmitted.

(d)   Any contract executed or ratified pursuant to paragraph (a) of this rule shall be ratified by the board of directors of the registered management investment company at least annually thereafter.

Rule 17f-2.   Custody of Investments by Registered Management Investment Company

(a)   The securities and similar investments of a registered management investment company may be maintained in the custody of such company only in accordance with the provisions of this rule. Investments maintained by such a company with a bank or other company whose functions and physical facilities are supervised by Federal or State authority under any arrangement whereunder the directors, officers, employees or agents of such company are authorized or permitted to withdraw such investments upon their mere receipt are deemed to be in the custody of such company and may be so maintained only upon compliance with the provisions of this rule.

(b)   Except as provided in paragraph (c) of this rule, all such securities and similar investments shall be deposited in the safekeeping of, or in a vault or other depository maintained by, a bank or other company whose functions and physical facilities are supervised by Federal or State authority. Investments so deposited shall be physically segregated at all times from those of any other person and shall be withdrawn only in connection with transactions of the character described in paragraph (c) of this rule.

(c)   The first sentence of paragraph (b) of this rule shall not apply to securities on loan which are collateralized to the extent of their full market value, or to securities hypothecated, pledged, or placed in escrow for the account of such investment company in connection with a loan or other transaction authorized by specific resolution of its board of directors, or to securities in transit in connection with the sale, exchange, redemption, maturity or conversion, the exercise of warrants or rights, assents to changes in terms of the securities, or other transactions necessary or appropriate in the ordinary course of business relating to the management of securities.

(d) Except as otherwise provided by law, no person shall be authorized or permitted to have access to the securities and similar investments deposited in accordance with paragraph (b) of this rule except pursuant to a resolution of the board of directors of such investment company. Each such resolution shall designate not more than five persons who shall be either officers or responsible employees of such company and shall provide that access to such investments shall be had only by two or more such persons jointly, at least one of whom shall be an officer; except that access to such investments shall be permitted (1) to properly authorized officers and employees of the bank or other company in whose safekeeping the investments are placed and (2) for the purpose of paragraph (f) of this rule to the independent public accountant jointly with any two persons so designated or with such officer or employee of such bank or such other company. Such investments shall at all times be subject to inspection by the Commission through its authorized employees or agents accompanied, unless otherwise directed by order of the Commission, by one or more of the persons designated pursuant to this paragraph.

(e) Each person when depositing such securities or similar investments in or withdrawing them from the depository or when ordering their withdrawal and delivery from the safekeeping of the bank or other company, shall sign a notation in respect of such deposit, withdrawal or order which shall show

(1) The date and time of the deposit, withdrawal or order,

(2) The title and amount of the securities or other investments deposited, withdrawn or ordered to be withdrawn, and an identification thereof by certificate numbers or otherwise,

(3) The manner of acquisition of the securities or similar investments deposited or the purpose for which they have been withdrawn, or ordered to be withdrawn, and

(4) If withdrawn and delivered to another person the name of such person. Such notation shall be transmitted promptly to an officer or director of the investment company designated by its board of directors who shall not be a person designated for the purpose of paragraph (d) of this rule. Such notation shall be on serially numbered forms and shall be preserved for at least one year.

(f) Such securities and similar investments shall be verified by actual examination by an independent public accountant retained by the investment company at least three times during each fiscal year, at least two of which shall be chosen by such accountant without prior notice to such company. A certificate of such accountant, stating that an examination of such securities and investments has been made, and describing the nature and extent of the examination, shall be attached to a completed Form N–17f–2 and transmitted to the Commission promptly after each examination.

Rule 17f–3.   Free Cash Accounts for Investment Companies With Bank Custodians

No registered investment company having a bank custodian shall hold free cash except, upon resolution of its board of directors, a petty cash account may be maintained in an amount not to exceed $500: *Provided,* That such account is operated under the imprest system and is maintained subject to adequate controls approved by the board of directors over disbursements and reimbursements including, but not limited to fidelity bond coverage of persons having access to such funds.

Rule 17f–4.   Custody of Investment Company Assets With a Securities Depository

(a) *Custody Arrangement with a Securities Depository.* A fund's custodian may place and maintain financial assets, corresponding to the fund's security entitlements, with a securities depository or intermediary custodian, if the custodian:

(1) Is at a minimum obligated to exercise due care in accordance with reasonable commercial standards in discharging its duty as a securities intermediary to obtain and thereafter maintain such financial assets;

(2) Is required to provide, promptly upon request by the fund, such reports as are available concerning the internal accounting controls and financial strength of the custodian; and

(3) Requires any intermediary custodian at a minimum to exercise due care in accordance with reasonable commercial standards in discharging its duty as a securities intermediary to obtain and

thereafter maintain financial assets corresponding to the security entitlements of its entitlement holders.

(b) *Direct Dealings with Securities Depository.* A fund may place and maintain financial assets, corresponding to the fund's security entitlements, directly with a securities depository, if:

(1)   The fund's contract with the securities depository or the securities depository's written rules for its participants:

(i)   Obligate the securities depository at a minimum to exercise due care in accordance with reasonable commercial standards in discharging its duty as a securities intermediary to obtain and thereafter maintain financial assets corresponding to the fund's security entitlements; and

(ii)   Requires the securities depository to provide, promptly upon request by the fund, such reports as are available concerning the internal accounting controls and financial strength of the securities depository; and

(2)   The fund has implemented internal control systems reasonably designed to prevent unauthorized officer's instructions (by providing at least for the form, content and means of giving, recording and reviewing all officer's instructions).

(c)   *Definitions.* For purposes of this rule the terms:

(1)   Clearing corporation, financial asset, securities intermediary, and security entitlement have the same meanings as is attributed to those terms in § 8–102, § 8–103, and §§ 8–501 through 8–511 of the Uniform Commercial Code, 2002 Official Text and Comments, which are incorporated by reference in this rule pursuant to 5 U.S.C. 552(a) and 1 CFR part 51. The Director of the Federal Register has approved this incorporation by reference in accordance with 5 U.S.C. 552(a) and 1 CFR part 51. You may obtain a copy of the Uniform Commercial Code from the National Conference of Commissioners on Uniform State Laws, 211 East Ontario Street, Suite 1300, Chicago, Il 60611. You may inspect a copy at the following addresses: Louis Loss Library, U.S. Securities and Exchange Commission, 100 F Street, NE., Washington, DC 20549, and Office of the Federal Register, National Archives and Records Administration, 800 North Capitol Street, NW, Suite 700, Washington, DC.

(2)   Custodian means a bank or other person authorized to hold assets for the fund under section 17(f) of the Act or Commission rules in this chapter, but does not include a fund itself, a foreign custodian whose use is governed by Rule 17f–5 or Rule17f–7, or a vault, safe deposit box, or other repository for safekeeping maintained by a bank or other company whose functions and physical facilities are supervised by a federal or state authority if the fund maintains its own assets there in accordance with Rule 17f–2.

(3)   Fund means an investment company registered under the Act and, where the context so requires with respect to a fund that is a unit investment trust or a face-amount certificate company, includes the fund's trustee.

(4)   Intermediary custodian means any subcustodian that is a securities intermediary and is qualified to act as a custodian.

(5)   Officer's instruction means a request or direction to a securities depository or its operator, or to a registered transfer agent, in the name of the fund by one or more persons authorized by the fund's board of directors (or by the fund's trustee, if the fund is a unit investment trust or a face-amount certificate company) to give the request or direction.

(6)   Securities depository means a clearing corporation that is:

(i)   Registered with the Commission as a clearing agency under section 17A of the Securities Exchange Act of 1934; or

(ii)   A Federal Reserve Bank or other person authorized to operate the federal book entry system described in the regulations of the Department of Treasury codified at 31 CFR 357, Subpart B, or book-entry systems operated pursuant to comparable regulations of other federal agencies.

Rule 17f-5. Custody of Investment Company Assets Outside the United States

(a) *Definitions.* For purposes of this rule:

(1) "Eligible Foreign Custodian" means an entity that is incorporated or organized under the laws of a country other than the United States and that is a Qualified Foreign Bank or a majority-owned direct or indirect subsidiary of a U.S. Bank or bank-holding company.

(2) "Foreign Assets" means any investments (including foreign currencies) for which the primary market is outside the United States, and any cash and cash equivalents that are reasonably necessary to effect the Fund's transactions in those investments.

(3) "Foreign Custody Manager" means a Fund's or a Registered Canadian Fund's board of directors or any person serving as the board's delegate under paragraphs (b) or (d) of this rule.

(4) "Fund" means a management investment company registered under the Act and incorporated or organized under the laws of the United States or of a state.

(5) "Qualified Foreign Bank" means a banking institution or trust company, incorporated or organized under the laws of a country other than the United States, that is regulated as such by the country's government or an agency of the country's government.

(6) "Registered Canadian Fund" means a management investment company incorporated or organized under the laws of Canada and registered under the Act pursuant to the conditions of Rule 7d-1.

(7) "U.S. Bank" means an entity that is:

(i) A banking institution organized under the laws of the United States;

(ii) A member bank of the Federal Reserve System;

(iii) Any other banking institution or trust company organized under the laws of any state or of the United States, whether incorporated or not, doing business under the laws of any state or of the United States, a substantial portion of the business of which consists of receiving deposits or exercising fiduciary powers similar to those permitted to national banks under the authority of the Comptroller of the Currency, and which is supervised and examined by state or federal authority having supervision over banks, and which is not operated for the purpose of evading the provisions of this rule; or

(iv) A receiver, conservator, or other liquidating agent of any institution or firm included in paragraphs (a)(7)(i), (ii), or (iii) of this rule.

(b) *Delegation.* A Fund's board of directors may delegate to the Fund's investment adviser or officers or to a U.S. Bank or to a Qualified Foreign Bank the responsibilities set forth in paragraphs (c)(1), (c)(2), or (c)(3) of this rule, *provided that*:

(1) *Reasonable Reliance.* The board determines that it is reasonable to rely on the delegate to perform the delegated responsibilities;

(2) *Reporting.* The board requires the delegate to provide written reports notifying the board of the placement of Foreign Assets with a particular custodian and of any material change in the Fund's foreign custody arrangements, with the reports to be provided to the board at such times as the board deems reasonable and appropriate based on the circumstances of the Fund's arrangements; and

(3) *Exercise of Care.* The delegate agrees to exercise reasonable care, prudence and diligence such as a person having responsibility for the safekeeping of the Fund's Foreign Assets would exercise, or to adhere to a higher standard of care, in performing the delegated responsibilities.

(c) *Maintaining Assets with an Eligible Foreign Custodian.* A Fund or its Foreign Custody Manager may place and maintain the Fund's Foreign Assets in the care of an Eligible Foreign Custodian, *provided that*:

(1) *General Standard.* The Foreign Custody Manager determines that the Foreign Assets will be subject to reasonable care, based on the standards applicable to custodians in the relevant market,

if maintained with the Eligible Foreign Custodian, after considering all factors relevant to the safekeeping of the Foreign Assets, including, without limitation:

(i) The Eligible Foreign Custodian's practices, procedures, and internal controls, including, but not limited to, the physical protections available for certificated securities (if applicable), the method of keeping custodial records, and the security and data protection practices;

(ii) Whether the Eligible Foreign Custodian has the requisite financial strength to provide reasonable care for Foreign Assets;

(iii) The Eligible Foreign Custodian's general reputation and standing; and

(iv) Whether the Fund will have jurisdiction over and be able to enforce judgments against the Eligible Foreign Custodian, such as by virtue of the existence of offices in the United States or consent to service of process in the United States.

(2) *Contract.* The arrangement with the Eligible Foreign Custodian is governed by a written contract that the Foreign Custody Manager has determined will provide reasonable care for Foreign Assets based on the standards specified in paragraph (c)(1) of this rule.

(i) The contract must provide:

(A) For indemnification or insurance arrangements (or any combination) that will adequately protect the Fund against the risk of loss of Foreign Assets held in accordance with the contract;

(B) That the Foreign Assets will not be subject to any right, charge, security interest, lien or claim of any kind in favor of the Eligible Foreign Custodian or its creditors, except a claim of payment for their safe custody or administration or, in the case of cash deposits, liens or rights in favor of creditors of the custodian arising under bankruptcy, insolvency, or similar laws;

(C) That beneficial ownership of the Foreign Assets will be freely transferable without the payment of money or value other than for safe custody or administration;

(D) That adequate records will be maintained identifying the Foreign Assets as belonging to the Fund or as being held by a third party for the benefit of the Fund;

(E) That the Fund's independent public accountants will be given access to those records or confirmation of the contents of those records; and

(F) That the Fund will receive periodic reports with respect to the safekeeping of the Foreign Assets, including, but not limited to, notification of any transfer to or from the Fund's account or a third party account containing assets held for the benefit of the Fund.

(ii) The contract may contain, in lieu of any or all of the provisions specified in paragraph (c)(2)(i) of this rule, other provisions that the Foreign Custody Manager determines will provide, in their entirety, the same or a greater level of care and protection for the Foreign Assets as the specified provisions, in their entirety.

(3)(i) *Monitoring the Foreign Custody Arrangements.* The Foreign Custody Manager has established a system to monitor the appropriateness of maintaining the Foreign Assets with a particular custodian under paragraph (c)(1) of this rule, and to monitor performance of the contract under paragraph (c)(2) of this rule.

(ii) If an arrangement with an Eligible Foreign Custodian no longer meets the requirements of this rule, the Fund must withdraw the Foreign Assets from the Eligible Foreign Custodian as soon as reasonably practicable.

(d) *Registered Canadian Funds.* Any Registered Canadian Fund may place and maintain its Foreign Assets outside the United States in accordance with the requirements of this rule, *provided that:*

(1) The Foreign Assets are placed in the care of an overseas branch of a U.S. Bank that has aggregate capital, surplus, and undivided profits of a specified amount, which must not be less than $500,000; and

(2)   The Foreign Custody Manager is the Fund's board of directors, its investment adviser or officers, or a U.S. Bank.

NOTE to Rule 17f–5: When a Fund's (or its custodian's) custody arrangement with an Eligible Securities Depository (as defined in Rule 17f–7) involves one or more Eligible Foreign custodians through which assets are maintained with the Eligible Securities Depository, Rule 17f–5 will govern the Fund's (or its custodian's) use of every Eligible Foreign custodian, while 17f–7 will govern an Eligible Foreign custodian's use of the Eligible Securities Depository.

Rule 17f–7.   Custody of Investment Company Assets With a Foreign Securities Depository

(a)   *Custody arrangement with an Eligible Securities Depository.* A Fund, including a Registered Canadian Fund, may place and maintain its Foreign Assets with an Eligible Securities Depository, *provided that*:

(1)   *Risk-limiting safeguards.* The custody arrangement provides reasonable safeguards against the custody risk associated with maintaining assets with the Eligible Securities Depository, including:

(i)   *Risk analysis and monitoring.* (A) The fund or its investment adviser has received from the Primary Custodian (or its agent) an analysis of the custody risks associated with maintaining assets with the Eligible Securities Depository; and

(B)   The contract between the Fund and the Prime Custodian requires the Primary Custodian (or its agent) to monitor the custody risks associated with maintaining assets with the Eligible Securities Depository on a continuing basis, and promptly notify the Fund or its investment adviser of any material change in these risks.

(ii)   *Exercise of care.* The contract between the Fund and the Primary Custodian states that the Primary Custodian will agree to exercise reasonable care, prudence, and diligence in performing the requirements of paragraphs (a)(1)(i)(A) and (B) of this rule, or adhere to a higher standard of care.

(2)   *Withdrawal of assets from Eligible Securities Depository.* If a custody arrangement with an Eligible Securities Depository no longer meets the requirements of this rule, the Fund's Foreign Assets must be withdrawn from the depository as soon as reasonably practicable.

(b)   *Definitions.* The terms "Foreign Assets," "Fund," "Qualified Foreign Bank," "Registered Canadian Fund," and "U.S. Bank" have the same meaning as in Rule 17f–5. In addition:

(1)   "Eligible Securities Depository" means a system for the central handling of securities as defined in Rule 17f–4 that:

(i)   Acts as or operates a system for the central handling of securities as or equivalent book-entries in the country where it is incorporated, or a transnational for the central handling of securities or equivalent book-entries;

(ii)   Is regulated by a foreign financial regulatory authority as defined under section 2(a)(50) of the Act;

(iii)   Holds assets for the custodian that participates in the system on behalf of the Fund under safekeeping conditions no less favorable than the conditions that apply to other participants;

(iv)   Maintains records that identify the assets of each participant and segregate the system's own assets from the assets of participants;

(v)   Provides periodic reports to its participants with respect to its safekeeping of assets, including notices of transfers to or from any participant's account; and

(vi)   Is subject to periodic examination by regulatory authorities or independent accountants.

(2)   "Primary custodian" means a U.S. Bank or Qualified Foreign Bank that contracts directly with a Fund to provide custodial services related to maintaining the Fund's assets outside the United States.

NOTE to 17f–7: When a Fund's (or its custodian's) custody arrangement with an Eligible Security Depository involves one or more Eligible Foreign Custodian's (as defined in Rule 17f–5) through which assets are maintained with the Eligible Securities Depository, Rule 17f–5 will govern the Fund's (or its custodian's) use of each Eligible Foreign Custodian, while Rule 17f–7 will govern an Eligible Foreign Custodian's use of the Eligible Securities Depository.

Rule 17g–1. Bonding of Officers and Employees of Registered Management Investment Companies

(a)   Each registered management investment company shall provide and maintain a bond which shall be issued by a reputable fidelity insurance company, authorized to do business in the place where the bond is issued, against larceny and embezzlement, covering each officer and employee of the investment company, who may singly, or jointly with others, have access to securities or funds of the investment company, either directly or through authority to draw upon such funds or to direct generally the disposition of such securities, unless the officer or employee has such access solely through his position as an officer or employee of a bank (hereinafter referred to as "covered persons").

(b)   The bond may be in the form of (1) an individual bond for each covered person or a schedule or blanket bond covering such persons, (2) a blanket bond which names the registered management investment company as the only insured (hereinafter referred to as "single insured bond") or (3) a bond which names the registered management investment company and one or more other parties as insureds (hereinafter referred to as a "joint insured bond"), such other insured parties being limited to (i) persons engaged in the management or distribution of the shares of the registered investment company, (ii) other registered investment companies which are managed and/or whose shares are distributed by the same persons (or affiliates of such persons), (iii) persons who are engaged in the management and/or distribution of shares of companies included in paragraph (b)(3)(i) of this rule, (iv) affiliated persons of any registered management investment company named in the bond or of any person included in paragraph (b)(3)(i) or (b)(3)(iii) of this rule hereinabove who are engaged in the administration of any registered management investment company named as insured in the bond, and (v) any trust, pension, profit-sharing or other benefit plan for officers, directors or employees of persons named in the bond.

(c)   A bond of the type described in paragraphs (b)(1) or (b)(2) of this rule shall provide that it shall not be cancelled, terminated or modified except after written notice shall have been given by the acting party to the affected party and to the Commission not less than sixty days prior to the effective date of cancellation, termination or modification. A joint insured bond described in paragraph (b)(3) of this rule shall provide, that (1) it shall not be cancelled terminated or modified except after written notice shall have been given by the acting party to the affected party, and by the fidelity insurance company to all registered investment companies named as insureds and to the Commission, not less than sixty days prior to the effective date of cancellation, termination, or modification and (2) the fidelity insurance company shall furnish each registered management investment company named as an insured with (i) a copy of the bond and any amendment thereto promptly after the execution thereof, (ii) a copy of each formal filing of a claim under the bond by any other named insured promptly after the receipt thereof, and (iii) notification of the terms of the settlement of each such claim prior to the execution of the settlement.

(d)   The bond shall be in such reasonable form and amount as a majority of the board of directors of the registered management investment company who are not "interested persons" of such investment company as defined by section 2(a)(19) of the Act shall approve as often as their fiduciary duties require, but not less than once every twelve months, with due consideration to all relevant factors including, but not limited to, the value of the aggregate assets of the registered management investment company to which any covered person may have access, the type and terms of the arrangements made for the custody and safekeeping of such assets, and the nature of the securities in the company's portfolio: Provided, however, That

(1)   the amount of a single insured bond shall be at least equal to an amount computed in accordance with the following schedule:

Amount of registered management investment company

Minimum amount of bond (in gross assets—at the end of the most recent dollars)

Fiscal quarter prior to date (in dollars)

Up to 500,000	50,000.
500,000 to 1,000,000	75,000.
1,000,000 to 2,500,000	100,000.
2,500,000 to 5,000,000	125,000.
5,000,000 to 7,500,000	150,000.
7,500,000 to 10,000,000	175,000.
10,000,000 to 15,000,000	200,000.
15,000,000 to 20,000,000	225,000.
20,000,000 to 25,000,000	250,000.
25,000,000 to 35,000,000	300,000.
35,000,000 to 50,000,000	350,000.
50,000,000 to 75,000,000	400,000.
75,000,000 to 100,000,000	450,000.
100,000,000 to 150,000,000	525,000.
150,000,000 to 250,000,000	600,000.
250,000,000 to 500,000,000	750,000.
500,000,000 to 750,000,000	900,000.
750,000,000 to 1,000,000,000	1,000,000.
1,000,000,000 to 1,500,000,000	1,250,000.
1,500,000,000 to 2,000,000,000	1,500,000.
Over 2,000,000,000	1,500,000 plus 200,000 for each 500,000,000 of gross assets up to a maximum bond of 2,500,000.

(2) A joint insured bond shall be in an amount at least equal to the sum of (i) the total amount of coverage which each registered management investment company named as an insured would have been required to provide and maintain individually pursuant to the schedule hereinabove had each such registered management investment company not been named under a joint insured bond, plus (ii) the amount of each bond which each named insured other than a registered management investment company would have been required to provide and maintain pursuant to federal statutes or regulations had it not been named as an insured under a joint insured bond.

(e) No premium may be paid for any joint insured bond or any amendment thereto unless a majority of the board of directors of each registered management investment company named as an insured therein who are not "interested persons" of such company shall approve the portion of the premium to be paid by such company, taking all relevant factors into consideration including, but not limited to, the number of the other parties named as insured, the nature of the business activities of such other parties, the amount of the joint insured bond, and the amount of the premium for such bond, the ratable allocation of the premium among all parties named as insureds, and the extent to which the share of the premium allocated to the investment company is less than the premium such company would have had to pay if it had provided and maintained a single insured bond.

(f) Each registered management investment company named as an insured in a joint insured bond shall enter into an agreement with all of the other named insureds providing that in the event recovery is received under the bond as a result of a loss sustained by the registered management investment company and one or more other named insureds, the registered management investment company shall receive an equitable and proportionate share of the recovery, but at least equal to the amount which it would have received had it provided and maintained a single insured bond with the minimum coverage required by paragraph (d)(1) of this rule.

(g)   Each registered management investment company shall:

(1)   File with the Commission (i) within 10 days after receipt of an executed bond of the type described in paragraphs (b)(1) or (b)(2) of this rule or any amendment thereof, (a) a copy of the bond, (b) a copy of the resolution of a majority of the board of directors who are not "interested persons" of the registered management investment company approving the form and amount of the bond, and (c) a statement as to the period for which premiums have been paid; (ii) within 10 days after receipt of an executed joint insured bond, or any amendment thereof, (a) a copy of the bond, (b) a copy of the resolution of a majority of the board of directors who are not "interested persons" of the registered management investment company approving the amount, type, form and coverage of the bond and the portion of the premium to be paid by such company, (c) a statement showing the amount of the single insured bond which the investment company would have provided and maintained had it not been named as an insured under a joint insured bond, (d) a statement as to the period for which premiums have been paid, and (e) a copy of each agreement between the investment company and all of the other named insureds entered into pursuant to paragraph (f) of this rule; and (iii) a copy of any amendment to the agreement entered into pursuant to paragraph (f) of this rule within 10 days after the execution of such amendment,

(2)   File with the Commission, in writing, within five days after the making of any claim under the bond by the investment company, a statement of the nature and amount of the claim,

(3)   File with the Commission, within five days of the receipt thereof, a copy of the terms of the settlement of any claim made under the bond by the investment company, and

(4)   Notify by registered mail each member of the board of directors of the investment company at his last known residence address of (i) any cancellation, termination or modification of the bond, not less than forty-five days prior to the effective date of the cancellation or termination or modification, (ii) the filing and of the settlement of any claim under the bond by the investment company, at the time the filings required by paragraph (g)(2) and (3) of this rule are made with the Commission, and (iii) the filing and of the proposed terms of settlement of any claim under the bond by any other named insured, within five days of the receipt of a notice from the fidelity insurance company.

(h)   Each registered management investment company shall designate an officer thereof who shall make the filings and give the notices required by paragraph (g) of this rule.

(i)   Where the registered management investment company is an unincorporated company managed by a depositor, trustee or investment adviser, the terms "officer" and "employee" shall include, for the purposes of this rule, the officers and employees of the depositor, trustee, or investment adviser.

(j)   Any joint insured bond provided and maintained by a registered management investment company and one or more other parties shall be a transaction exempt from the provisions of section 17(d) of the Act and the rules thereunder, if:

(1)   The terms and provisions of the bond comply with the provisions of this rule;

(2)   The terms and provisions of any agreement required by paragraph (f) of this rule comply with the provisions of that paragraph; and

(3)   The board of directors of the investment company satisfied the fund governance standards defined in Rule 0–1(a)(7).

(k)   At the next anniversary date of an existing fidelity bond, but not later than one year from the effective date of this rule, arrangements between registered management investment companies and fidelity insurance companies and arrangements between registered management investment companies and other parties named as insureds under joint insured bonds which would not permit compliance with the provisions of this rule shall be modified by the parties so as to effect such compliance.

Rule 17j–1.   Personal Investment Activities of Investment Company Personnel

(a)   *Definitions.* For purposes of this rule:

(1)   "Access Person" means:

(i)   Any Advisory Person of a Fund or of a Fund's investment adviser. If an investment adviser's primary business is advising Funds or other advisory clients, all of the investment adviser's directors, officers, and general partners are presumed to be Access Persons of any Fund advised by the investment adviser. All of a Fund's directors, officers, and general partners are presumed to be Access Persons of the Fund.

(ii)   Any director, officer or general partner of a principal underwriter who, in the ordinary course of business, makes, participates in or obtains information regarding, the purchase or sale of Covered Securities by the Fund for which the principal underwriter acts, or whose functions or duties in the ordinary course of business relate to the making of any recommendation to the Fund regarding the purchase or sale of Covered Securities.

(2)   "Advisory Person" of a Fund or of a Fund's investment adviser means:

(i)   Any director, officer, general partner or employee of the Fund or investment adviser (or of any company in a control relationship to the Fund or investment adviser) who, in connection with his or her regular functions or duties, makes, participates in, or obtains information regarding, the purchase or sale of Covered Securities by a Fund, or whose functions relate to the making of any recommendations with respect to such purchases or sales; and

(ii)   Any natural person in a control relationship to the Fund or investment adviser who obtains information concerning recommendations made to the Fund with regard to the purchase or sale of Covered Securities by the Fund.

(3)   "Control" has the same meaning as in section 2(a)(9) of the Act.

(4)   "Covered Security" means a security as defined in section 2(a)(36) of the Act, except that it does not include:

(i)   Direct obligations of the Government of the United States;

(ii)   Banker's acceptances, bank certificates of deposit, commercial paper and high quality short-term debt instruments, including repurchase agreements; and

(iii)   Shares issued by open-end Funds.

(5)   "Fund" means an investment company registered under the Investment Company Act.

(6)   An "Initial Public Offering" means an offering of securities registered under the Securities Act of 1933, the issuer of which, immediately before the registration, was not subject to the reporting requirements of sections 13 or 15(d) of the Securities Exchange Act of 1934.

(7)   "Investment Personnel" of a Fund or of a Fund's investment adviser means:

(i)   Any employee of the Fund or investment adviser (or of any company in a control relationship to the Fund or investment adviser) who, in connection with his or her regular functions or duties, makes or participates in making recommendations regarding the purchase or sale of securities by the Fund.

(ii)   Any natural person who controls the Fund or investment adviser and who obtains information concerning recommendations made to the Fund regarding the purchase or sale of securities by the Fund.

(8)   A "Limited Offering" means an offering that is exempt from registration under the Securities Act of 1933 pursuant to section 4(a)(2) or section 4(a)(5) or pursuant to Rule 504 or Rule 506 under the Securities Act of 1933.

(9)   "Purchase or sale of a Covered Security" includes, among other things, the writing of an option to purchase or sell a Covered Security.

(10)   "Security Held or to be Acquired" by a Fund means:

(i)   Any Covered Security which, within the most recent 15 days:

(A)   Is or has been held by the Fund; or

(B)   Is being or has been considered by the Fund or its investment adviser for purchase by the Fund; and

(ii)   Any option to purchase or sell, and any security convertible into or exchangeable for, a Covered Security described in paragraph (a)(10)(i) of this rule.

(11) "Automatic Investment Plan" means a program in which regular periodic purchases (or withdrawals) are made automatically in (or from) investment accounts in accordance with a predetermined schedule and allocation. An Automatic Investment Plan includes a dividend reinvestment plan.

(b)   *Unlawful actions.* It is unlawful for any affiliated person of or principal underwriter for a Fund, or any affiliated person of an investment adviser of or principal underwriter for a Fund, in connection with the purchase or sale, directly or indirectly, by the person of a Security Held or to be Acquired by the Fund:

(1)   To employ any device, scheme or artifice to defraud the Fund;

(2)   To make any untrue statement of a material fact to the Fund or omit to state a material fact necessary in order to make the statements made to the Fund, in light of the circumstances under which they are made, not misleading;

(3)   To engage in any act, practice or course of business that operates or would operate as a fraud or deceit on the Fund; or

(4)   To engage in any manipulative practice with respect to the Fund.

(c)   *Code of Ethics.*

(1)   *Adoption and Approval of Code of Ethics.*

(i)   Every Fund (other than a money market fund or a Fund that does not invest in Covered Securities) and each investment adviser of and principal underwriter for the Fund, must adopt a written code of ethics containing provisions reasonably necessary to prevent its Access Persons from engaging in any conduct prohibited by paragraph (b) of this rule.

(ii)   The board of directors of a Fund, including a majority of directors who are not interested persons, must approve the code of ethics of the Fund, the code of ethics of each investment adviser and principal underwriter of the Fund, and any material changes to these codes. The board must base its approval of a code and any material changes to the code on a determination that the code contains provisions reasonably necessary to prevent Access Persons from engaging in any conduct prohibited by paragraph (b) of this rule. Before approving a code of a Fund, investment adviser or principal underwriter or any amendment to the code, the board of directors must receive a certification from the Fund, investment adviser or principal underwriter that it has adopted procedures reasonably necessary to prevent Access Persons from violating the Fund's investment adviser's, or principal underwriter's code of ethics. The Fund's board must approve the code of an investment adviser or principal underwriter before initially retaining the services of the investment adviser or principal underwriter. The Fund's board must approve a material change to a code no later than six months after adoption of the material change.

(iii)   If a Fund is a unit investment trust, the Fund's principal underwriter or depositor must approve the Fund's code of ethics, as required by paragraph (c)(1)(ii) of this rule. If the Fund has more than one principal underwriter or depositor, the principal underwriters and depositors may designate, in writing, which principal underwriter or depositor must conduct the approval required by paragraph (c)(1)(ii) of this rule, if they obtain written consent from the designated principal underwriter or depositor.

(2)   *Administration of Code of Ethics.*

(i)   The Fund, investment adviser and principal underwriter must use reasonable diligence and institute procedures reasonably necessary to prevent violations of its code of ethics.

(ii)   No less frequently than annually, every Fund (other than a unit investment trust) and its investment advisers and principal underwriters must furnish to the Fund's board of directors, and the board of directors must consider, a written report that:

(A) Describes any issue arising under the code of ethics or procedures since the last report to the board of directors, including, but not limited to, information about material violations of the code or procedures and sanctions imposed in response to the material violations; and

(B) Certifies that the Fund, investment adviser or principal underwriter, as applicable, has adopted procedures reasonably necessary to prevent Access Persons from violating the code.

(3) *Exception for principal underwriters.* The requirements of paragraphs (c)(1) and (c)(2) of this rule do not apply to any principal underwriter unless:

(i) The principal underwriter is an affiliated person of the Fund or of the Fund's investment adviser; or

(ii) An officer, director or general partner of the principal underwriter serves as an officer, director or general partner of the Fund or of the Fund's investment adviser.

(d) *Reporting Requirements of Access Persons.*

(1) *Reports required.* Unless excepted by paragraph (d)(2) of this rule, every Access Person of a Fund (other than a money market fund or a Fund that does not invest in Covered Securities) and every Access Person of an investment adviser of or principal underwriter for the Fund, must report to that Fund, investment adviser or principal underwriter:

(i) *Initial Holdings Reports.* No later than 10 days after the person becomes an Access Person (which information must be current as of a date no more than 45 days prior to the date the person becomes an Access Person):

(A) The title, number of shares and principal amount of each Covered Security in which the Access Person had any direct or indirect beneficial ownership when the person became an Access Person;

(B) The name of any broker, dealer or bank with whom the Access Person maintained an account in which any securities were held for the direct or indirect benefit of the Access Person as of the date the person became an Access Person; and

(C) The date that the report is submitted by the Access Person.

(ii) *Quarterly Transaction Reports.* No later than 30 days after the end of a calendar quarter, the following information:

(A) With respect to any transaction during the quarter in a Covered Security in which the Access Person had any direct or indirect beneficial ownership:

(1) The date of the transaction, the title, the interest rate and maturity date (if applicable), the number of shares and the principal amount of each Covered Security involved;

(2) The nature of the transaction (*i.e.*, purchase, sale or any other type of acquisition or disposition);

(3) The price of the Covered Security at which the transaction was effected;

(4) The name of the broker, dealer or bank with or through which the transaction was effected; and

(5) The date that the report is submitted by the Access Person.

(B) With respect to any account established by the Access Person in which any securities were held during the quarter for the direct or indirect benefit of the Access Person:

(1) The name of the broker, dealer or bank with whom the Access Person established the account;

(2) The date the account was established; and

(3) The date that the report is submitted by the Access Person.

(iii) *Annual Holdings Reports.* Annually, the following information (which information must be current as of a date no more than 45 days before the report is submitted):

(A) The title, number of shares and principal amount of each Covered Security in which the Access Person had any direct or indirect beneficial ownership;

(B) The name of any broker, dealer or bank with whom the Access Person maintains an account in which any securities are held for the direct or indirect benefit of the Access Person; and

(C) The date that the report is submitted by the Access Person.

(2) *Exceptions from reporting requirements.*

(i) A person need not make a report under paragraph (d)(1) of this rule with respect to transactions effected for, and Covered Securities held in, any account over which the person has no direct or indirect influence or control.

(ii) A director of a Fund who is not an "interested person" of the Fund within the meaning of section 2(a)(19) of the Act, and who would be required to make a report solely by reason of being a Fund director, need not make:

(A) An initial holdings report under paragraph (d)(1)(i) of this rule and an annual holdings report under paragraph (d)(1)(iii) of this rule; and

(B) A quarterly transaction report under paragraph (d)(1)(ii) of this rule, unless the director knew or, in the ordinary course of fulfilling his or her official duties as a Fund director, should have known that during the 15-day period immediately before or after the director's transaction in a Covered Security, the Fund purchased or sold the Covered Security, or the Fund or its investment adviser considered purchasing or selling the Covered Security.

(iii) An Access Person to a Fund's principal underwriter need not made a report to the principal underwriter under paragraph (d)(1) of this rule if:

(A) The principal underwriter is not an affiliated person of the Fund (unless the Fund is a unit investment trust) or any investment adviser of the Fund; and

(B) The principal underwriter has no officer, director or general partner who serves as an officer, director or general partner of the Fund or of any investment adviser of the Fund.

(iv) An Access Person to an investment adviser need not make a separate report to the investment adviser under paragraph (d)(1) of this rule to the extent the information in the report would duplicate information required to be recorded under Rule 204–2(a)(13) of the Investment Advisers Act of 1940.

(v) An Access Person need not make a quarterly transaction report under paragraph (d)(1)(ii) of this rule if the report would duplicate information contained in broker trade confirmations or account statements received by the Fund, investment adviser or principal underwriter with respect to the Access Person in the time period required by paragraph (d)(1)(ii), if all of the information required by that paragraph is contained in the broker trade confirmations or account statements, or in the records of the Fund, investment adviser or principal underwriter.

(vi) An Access Person need not make a quarterly transaction report under paragraph (d)(1)(ii) of this rule with respect to transactions effected pursuant to an Automatic Investment Plan.

(3) *Review of reports.* Each Fund, investment adviser and principal underwriter to which reports are required to be made by paragraph (d)(1) of this rule must institute procedures by which appropriate management or compliance personnel review these reports.

(4) *Notification of reporting obligation.* Each Fund, investment adviser and principal underwriter to which reports are required to be made by paragraph (d)(1) of this rule must identify all

Access Persons who are required to make these reports and must inform those Access Persons of their reporting obligation.

(5) *Beneficial ownership.* For purposes of this rule, beneficial ownership is interpreted in the same manner as it would be under Rule 16a–1(a)(2) of the Exchange Act in determining whether a person is the beneficial owner of a security for purposes of section 16 of the Securities Exchange Act of 1934 and the rules and regulations thereunder. Any report required by paragraph (d) of this rule may contain a statement that the report will not be construed as an admission that the person making the report has any direct or indirect beneficial ownership in the Covered Security to which the report relates.

(e) *Pre-approval of investments in IPOs and limited offerings.* Investment Personnel of a Fund or its investment adviser must obtain approval from the Fund or the Fund's investment adviser before directly or indirectly acquiring beneficial ownership in any securities in an Initial Public Offering or in a Limited Offering.

(f) *Recordkeeping requirements.*

(1)   Each Fund, investment adviser and principal underwriter that is required to adopt a code of ethics or to which reports are required to be made by Access Persons must, at its principal place of business, maintain records in the manner and to the extent set out in this paragraph (f), and must make these records available to the Commission or any representative of the Commission at any time and from time to time for reasonable periodic, special or other examination:

(A)   A copy of each code of ethics for the organization that is in effect, or at any time within the past five years was in effect, must be maintained in an easily accessible place;

(B)   A record of any violation of the code of ethics, and of any action taken as a result of the violation, must be maintained in an easily accessible place for at least five years after the end of the fiscal year in which the violation occurs;

(C)   A copy of each report made by an Access Person as required by this rule, including any information provided in lieu of the reports under paragraph (d)(2)(v) of this rule, must be maintained for at least five years after the end of the fiscal year in which the report is made or the information is provided, the first two years in an easily accessible place;

(D)   A record of all persons, currently or within the past five years, who are or were required to make reports under paragraph (d) of this rule, or who are or were responsible for reviewing these reports, must be maintained in an easily accessible place; and

(E)   A copy of each report required by paragraph (c)(2)(ii) of this rule must be maintained for at least five years after the end of the fiscal year in which it is made, the first two years in an easily accessible place.

(2)   A Fund or investment adviser must maintain a record of any decision and the reasons supporting the decision, to approve the acquisition by investment personnel of securities under paragraph (e), for at least five years after the end of the fiscal year in which the approval is granted.

Rule 19a–1. Written Statement to Accompany Dividend Payments by Management Companies

(a)   Every written statement made pursuant to section 19 by or on behalf of a management company shall be made on a separate paper and shall clearly indicate what portion of the payment per share is made from the following sources:

(1)   Net income for the current or preceding fiscal year, or accumulated undistributed net income, or both, not including in either case profits or losses from the sale of securities or other properties.

(2)   Accumulated undistributed net profits from the sale of securities or other properties (except that an open-end company may treat as a separate source its net profits from such sales during its current fiscal year).

(3)   Paid-in surplus or other capital source. To the extent that a payment is properly designated as being made from a source specified in subparagraph (1) or (2) of this paragraph, it need not be designated as having been made from a source specified in this subparagraph.

(b)   If the payment is made in whole or in part from a source specified in paragraph (a)(2) of this rule the written statement shall indicate, after giving effect to the part of such payment so specified, the deficit, if any, in the aggregate of

(1)   Accumulated undistributed realized profits less losses on the sale of securities or other properties and

(2)   The net unrealized appreciation or depreciation of portfolio securities, all as of a date reasonably close to the end of the period as of which the dividend is paid. Any statement made pursuant to the preceding sentence shall specify the amount, if any, of such deficit which represents unrealized depreciation of portfolio securities.

(c)   Accumulated undistributed net income and accumulated undistributed net profits from the sale of securities or other properties shall be determined, at the option of the company, either

(1)   From the date of the organization of the company,

(2)   From the date of a reorganization, as defined in clause (A) or (B) of section 2(a)(33) of the Act,

(3)   From the date as of which a write-down of portfolio securities was made in connection with a corporate readjustment, approved by stockholders, of the type known as "quasi-reorganization," or

(4)   From January 1, 1925, to the close of the period as of which the dividend is paid, without giving effect to such payment.

(d)   For the purpose of this rule, open-end companies which upon the sale of their shares allocate to undistributed income or other similar account that portion of the consideration received which represents the approximate per share amount of undistributed net income included in the sales price, and make a corresponding deduction from undistributed net income upon the purchase or redemption of shares need not treat the amounts so allocated as paid-in surplus or other capital source.

(e)   For the purpose of this rule, the source or sources from which a dividend is paid shall be determined (or reasonably estimated) to the close of the period as of which it is paid without giving effect to such payment. If any such estimate is subsequently ascertained to be inaccurate in a significant amount, a correction thereof shall be made by a written statement pursuant to section 19(a) of the Act or in the first report to stockholders following discovery of the inaccuracy.

(f)   Insofar as a written statement made pursuant to section 19(a) of the Act relates to a dividend on preferred stock paid for a period of less than a year, a company may elect to indicate only that portion of the payment which is made from sources specified in paragraph (a)(1) of this rule, and need not specify the sources from which the remainder was paid. Every company which in any fiscal year elects to make a statement pursuant to the preceding sentence shall transmit to the holders of such preferred stock, at a date reasonably near the end of the last dividend period in such fiscal year, a statement meeting the requirements of paragraph (a) of this rule on an annual basis.

(g)   The purpose of this rule, in the light of which it shall be construed, is to afford security holders adequate disclosure of the sources from which dividend payments are made. Nothing in this rule shall be construed to prohibit the inclusion in any written statement of additional information in explanation of the information required by this rule. Nothing in this rule shall be construed to permit a dividend payment in violation of any State law or to prevent compliance with any requirement of State law regarding dividends consistent with this rule.

Rule 19b–1.   Frequency of Distribution of Capital Gains

(a)   No registered investment company which is a "regulated investment company" as defined in section 851 of the Internal Revenue Code of 1986 ("Code") shall distribute more than one capital gain dividend ("distribution"), as defined in section 852(b)(3)(C) of the Code, with respect to any one taxable year of the company, other than a distribution otherwise permitted by this rule or made pursuant to section 855 of the Code which is supplemental to the prior distribution with respect to the same taxable year of the company and which does not exceed 10% of the aggregate amount distributed for such taxable year.

(b)   No registered investment company which is not a "regulated investment company" as defined in section 851 of the Code shall make more than one distribution of long-term capital gains, as defined in the Code, in any one taxable year of the company: *Provided,* That a unit investment trust may distribute capital gain dividends received from a "regulated investment company" within a reasonable time after receipt.

* * *

(e)   If a registered investment company because of unforeseen circumstances in a particular taxable year proposes to make a distribution which would be prohibited by the provisions of this rule, it may file a request with the Commission for authorization to make such a distribution. Such request shall comply with the requirements of Rule O–2, and shall set forth the pertinent facts and explain the circumstances which the company believes justify such distribution. The request shall be deemed granted unless the Commission within 15 days after receipt thereof shall deny such request as not being necessary or appropriate in the public interest or for the protection of investors and notify the company in writing of such denial.

(f)   A registered investment company may make one additional distribution of long-term capital gains, as defined in the Code, with respect to any one taxable year of the company, which distribution is made, in whole or in part, for the purpose of not incurring any tax under section 4982 of the Code. Such additional distribution may be made prior or subsequent to any distribution otherwise permitted by paragraph (a) of this rule.

Rule 20a–1.   Solicitation of Proxies, Consents and Authorizations

(a)   No person shall solicit or permit the use of his or her name to solicit any proxy, consent, or authorization with respect to any security issued by a registered fund, except upon compliance with Regulation 14A, Schedule 14A, and all other rules and regulations adopted pursuant to section 14(a) of the Securities Exchange Act of 1934 that would be applicable to such solicitation if it were made in respect of a security registered pursuant to section 12 of the Securities Exchange Act of 1934. Unless the solicitation is made in respect of a security registered on a national securities exchange, none of the soliciting material need be filed with such exchange.

(b)   If the solicitation is made by or on behalf of the management of the investment company, then the investment adviser or any prospective investment adviser and any affiliated person thereof as to whom information is required in the solicitation shall upon request of the investment company promptly transmit to the investment company all information necessary to enable the management of such company to comply with the rules and regulations applicable to such solicitation. If the solicitation is made by any person other than the management of the investment company, on behalf of and with the consent of the investment adviser or prospective investment adviser, then the investment adviser or prospective investment adviser and any affiliated person thereof as to whom information is required in the solicitation shall upon request of the person making the solicitation promptly transmit to such person all information necessary to enable such person to comply with the rules and regulations applicable to the solicitation.

Instruction.   Registrants that have made a public offering of securities and that hold security holder votes for which proxies, consents, or authorizations are not being solicited pursuant to the requirements of this rule should refer to section 14(c) of the Securities Exchange Act of 1934 and the information statement requirements set forth in the rules thereunder.

* * *

Rule 22c–1.   Pricing of Redeemable Securities for Distribution, Redemption and Repurchase

(a)   No registered investment company issuing any redeemable security, no person designated in such issuer's prospectus as authorized to consummate transactions in any such security, and no principal underwriter of, or dealer in any such security shall sell, redeem, or repurchase any such security except at a price based on the current net asset value of such security which is next computed after receipt of a tender of such security for redemption or of an order to purchase or sell such security; *Provided,* That:

(1)   This paragraph shall not prevent a sponsor of a unit investment trust (hereinafter referred to as the "Trust") engaged exclusively in the business of investing in eligible trust securities (as defined in Rule 14a–3(b)) from selling or repurchasing Trust units in a secondary market at a price based on the offering side evaluation of the eligible trust securities in the Trust's portfolio, determined at any time on the last business day of each week, effective for all sales made during the following week, if on the days that such sales or repurchases are made the sponsor receives a letter from a qualified evaluator stating, in its opinion, that:

(i)   In the case of repurchases, the current bid price is not higher than the offering side evaluation, computed on the last business day of the previous week; and

(ii)   In the case of resales, the offering side evaluation, computed as of the last business day of the previous week, is not more than one-half of one percent ($5.00 on a unit representing $1,000 principal amount of eligible trust securities) greater than the current offering price.

(2)   This paragraph shall not prevent any registered investment company from adjusting the price of its redeemable securities sold pursuant to a merger, consolidation or purchase of substantially all of the assets of a company which meets the conditions specified in Rule 17a–8.

(3)   Notwithstanding this paragraph (a), a registered open-end management investment company (but not a registered open-end management investment company that is regulated as a money market fund under Rule 2a–7 or an exchange-traded fund as defined in paragraph (a)(3)(v)(A) of this rule) (a "fund") may use swing pricing to adjust its current net asset value per share to mitigate dilution of the value of its outstanding redeemable securities as a result of shareholder purchase or redemption activity, provided that it has established and implemented swing pricing policies and procedures in compliance with the paragraphs (a)(3)(i) through (v) of this rule.

(i)   The fund's swing pricing policies and procedures must:

(A)   Provide that the fund must adjust its net asset value per share by a single swing factor or multiple factors that may vary based on the swing threshold(s) crossed once the level of net purchases into or net redemptions from such fund has exceeded the applicable swing threshold for the fund. In determining whether the fund's level of net purchases or net redemptions has exceeded the applicable swing threshold(s), the person(s) responsible for administering swing pricing shall be permitted to make such determination based on receipt of sufficient information about the fund investors' daily purchase and redemption activity ("investor flow") to allow the fund to reasonably estimate whether it has crossed the swing threshold(s) with high confidence, and shall exclude any purchases or redemptions that are made in kind and not in cash. This investor flow information may consist of individual, aggregated, or netted orders, and may include reasonable estimates where necessary.

(B)   Specify the process for how the fund's swing threshold(s) shall be determined, considering:

(1)   The size, frequency, and volatility of historical net purchases or net redemptions of fund shares during normal and stressed periods;

(2)   The fund's investment strategy and the liquidity of the fund's portfolio investments;

(3)   The fund's holdings of cash and cash equivalents, and borrowing arrangements and other funding sources; and

(4)   The costs associated with transactions in the markets in which the fund invests.

(C)   Specify the process for how the swing factor(s) shall be determined, which must include: (1) the establishment of an upper limit on the swing factor(s) used, which may not exceed two percent of net asset value per share; and (2) the determination that the factor(s) used are reasonable in relationship to the costs discussed in this paragraph. In determining the swing factor(s) and the upper limit, the person(s) responsible for administering swing pricing may take into account only the near-term costs expected to be incurred by the fund as a result of net purchases or net redemptions that occur on the day the swing factor(s) is used, including spread costs, transaction fees and charges arising from asset purchases or asset sales resulting from those purchases or redemptions, and borrowing-related costs associated with satisfying redemptions.

(ii)   The fund's board of directors, including a majority of directors who are not interested persons of the fund must:

(A)   Approve the fund's swing pricing policies and procedures;

(B)   Approve the fund's swing threshold(s) and the upper limit on the swing factor(s) used, and any changes to the swing threshold(s) or the upper limit on the swing factor(s) used;

(C)   Designate the fund's investment adviser, officer, or officers responsible for administering the swing pricing policies and procedures ("person(s) responsible for administering swing pricing"). The administration of swing pricing must be reasonably segregated from portfolio management of the fund and may not include portfolio managers; and

(D)   Review, no less frequently than annually, a written report prepared by the person(s) responsible for administering swing pricing that describes:

(1)   its review of the adequacy of the fund's swing pricing policies and procedures and the effectiveness of their implementation, including the impact on mitigating dilution;

(2)   any material changes to the fund's swing pricing policies and procedures since the date of the last report; and

(3)   its review and assessment of the fund's swing threshold(s), swing factor(s), and swing factor upper limit considering the requirements of paragraphs (a)(3)(i)(B) and (C) of this rule, including the information and data supporting the determination of the swing threshold(s), swing factor(s), and swing factor upper limit.

(iii)   The fund shall maintain the policies and procedures adopted by the fund under this paragraph (a)(3) that are in effect, or at any time within the past six years were in effect, in an easily accessible place, and shall maintain a written copy of the report provided to the board under paragraph (a)(3)(ii)(C) for six years, the first two in an easily accessible place.

(iv)   Any fund (a "feeder fund") that invests, pursuant to section 12(d)(1)(E) of the Act, in another fund (a "master fund") may not use swing pricing to adjust the feeder fund's net asset value per share; however, a master fund may use swing pricing to adjust the master fund's net asset value per share, pursuant to the requirements set forth in this paragraph (a)(3).

(v)   For purposes of this paragraph (a)(3):

(A)   *Exchange-traded fund* means an open-end management investment company (or series or class thereof), the shares of which are listed and traded on a national securities exchange, and that has formed and operates under an exemptive order under the Act granted by the Commission or in reliance on an exemptive rule adopted by the Commission.

(B)   *Swing factor* means the amount, expressed as a percentage of the fund's net asset value and determined pursuant to the fund's swing pricing policies and procedures, by which a fund adjusts its net asset value per share once a fund's applicable swing threshold has been exceeded.

(C)   *Swing pricing* means the process of adjusting a fund's current net asset value per share to mitigate dilution of the value of its outstanding redeemable securities as a result of shareholder purchase and redemption activity, pursuant to the requirements set forth in this paragraph (a)(3).

(D)   *Swing threshold* means an amount of net purchases or net redemptions, expressed as a percentage of the fund's net asset value, that triggers the application of swing pricing.

(E) *Transaction fees and charges* means brokerage commissions, custody fees, and any other charges, fees, and taxes associated with portfolio asset purchases and sales.

(b) For the purposes of this rule,

(1) The current net asset value of any such security shall be computed no less frequently than once daily, Monday through Friday, at the specific time or times during the day that the board of directors of the investment company sets, in accordance with paragraph (d) of this rule, except on (i) days on which changes in the value of the investment company's portfolio securities will not materially affect the current net asset value of the investment company's redeemable securities, (ii) days during which no security is tendered for redemption and no order to purchase or sell such security is received by the investment company, or (iii) customary national business holidays described or listed in the prospectus and local and regional business holidays listed in the prospectus; and

(2) A "qualified evaluator" shall mean any evaluator which represents it is in a position to determine, on the basis of an informal evaluation of the eligible trust securities held in the Trust's portfolio, whether—

(i) The current bid price is higher than the offering side evaluation, computed on the last business day of the previous week, and

(ii) The offering side evaluation, computed as of the last business day of the previous week, is more than one-half of one percent ($5.00 on a unit representing $1,000 principal amount of eligible trust securities) greater than the current offering price.

(c) Notwithstanding the provisions above, any registered separate account offering variable annuity contracts, any person designated in such account's prospectus as authorized to consummate transactions in such contracts, and any principal underwriter of or dealer in such contracts shall be permitted to apply the initial purchase payment for any such contract at a price based on the current net asset value of such contract which is next computed:

(1) Not later than two business days after receipt of the order to purchase by the insurance company sponsoring the separate account ("insurer"), if the contract application and other information necessary for processing the order to purchase (collectively, "application") are complete upon receipt; or

(2) Not later than two business days after an application which is incomplete upon receipt by the insurer is made complete, *Provided,* That, if an incomplete application is not made complete within five business days after receipt,

(i) The prospective purchaser shall be informed of the reasons for the delay, and

(ii) The initial purchase payment shall be returned immediately and in full, unless the prospective purchaser specifically consents to the insurer retaining the purchase payment until the application is made complete.

(3) As used in this rule:

(i) "Prospective Purchaser" shall mean either an individual contract-owner or an individual participant in a group contract.

(ii) "Initial Purchase Payment" shall refer to the first purchase payment submitted to the insurer by, or on behalf of, a prospective purchaser.

(d) The board of directors shall initially set the time or times during the day that the current net asset value shall be computed, and shall make and approve such changes as the board deems necessary.

Rule 22c-2. Redemption Fees for Redeemable Securities

(a) *Redemption fee.* It is unlawful for any fund issuing redeemable securities, its principal underwriter, or any dealer in such securities, to redeem a redeemable security issued by the fund within seven calendar days after the security was purchased, unless it complies with the following requirements:

(1) *Board determination.* The fund's board of directors, including a majority of directors who are not interested persons of the fund, must either:

(i)   Approve a redemption fee, in an amount (but no more than two percent of the value of shares redeemed) and on shares redeemed within a time period (but no less than seven calendar days), that in its judgment is necessary or appropriate to recoup for the fund the costs it may incur as a result of those redemptions or to otherwise eliminate or reduce so far as practicable any dilution of the value of the outstanding securities issued by the fund, the proceeds of which fee will be retained by the fund; or

(ii)   Determine that imposition of a redemption fee is either not necessary or not appropriate.

(2)   *Shareholder information.* With respect to each financial intermediary that submits orders, itself or through its agent, to purchase or redeem shares directly to the fund, its principal underwriter or transfer agent, or to a registered clearing agency, the fund (or on the fund's behalf, the principal underwriter or transfer agent) must either:

(i)   Enter into a shareholder information agreement with the financial intermediary (or its agent); or

(ii)   Prohibit the financial intermediary from purchasing in nominee name on behalf of other persons, securities issued by the fund. For purposes of this paragraph, "purchasing" does not include the automatic reinvestment of dividends.

(3)   *Recordkeeping.* The fund must maintain a copy of the written agreement under paragraph (a)(2) that is in effect, or at any time within the past six years was in effect, in an easily accessible place.

(b)   *Excepted funds.* The requirements of paragraph (a) of this rule do not apply to the following funds, unless they elect to impose a redemption fee pursuant to paragraph (a)(1) of this rule:

(1)   Money market funds;

(2)   Any fund that issues securities that are listed on a national securities exchange; and

(3)   Any fund that affirmatively permits short-term trading of its securities, if its prospectus clearly and prominently discloses that the fund permits short-term trading of its securities and that such trading may result in additional costs for the fund.

(c)   *Definitions.* For the purposes of this rule:

(1)   *Financial intermediary* means:

(i)   Any broker, dealer, bank, or other person that holds securities issued by the fund, in nominee name;

(ii)   A unit investment trust or fund that invests in the fund in reliance on section 12(d)(1)(E) of the Act; and

(iii)   In the case of a participant-directed employee benefit plan that owns the securities issued by the fund, a retirement plan's administrator under section 3(16)(A) of the Employee Retirement Income Security Act of 1974 (29 U.S.C. 1002(16)(A)) or any person that maintains the plan's participant records.

(iv)   *Financial intermediary* does not include any person that the fund treats as an individual investor with respect to the fund's policies established for the purpose of eliminating or reducing any dilution of the value of the outstanding securities issued by the fund.

(2)   *Fund* means an open-end management investment company that is registered or required to register under section 8 of the Act, and includes a separate series of such an investment company.

(3)   *Money market fund* means an open-end management investment company that is registered under the Act and is regulated as a money market fund under Rule 2a-7.

(4)   *Shareholder* includes a beneficial owner of securities held in nominee name, a participant in a participant-directed employee benefit plan, and a holder of interests in a fund or unit investment trust that has invested in the fund in reliance on section 12(d)(1)(E) of the Act. A shareholder does not

include a fund investing pursuant to section 12(d)(1)(G) of the Act, a trust established pursuant to section 529 of the Internal Revenue Code (26 U.S.C. 529), or a holder of an interest in such a trust.

(5) *Shareholder information agreement* means a written agreement under which a financial intermediary agrees to:

(i) Provide, promptly upon request by a fund, the Taxpayer Identification Number (or in the case of non U.S. shareholders, if the Taxpayer Identification Number is unavailable, the International Taxpayer Identification Number or other government issued identifier) of all shareholders who have purchased, redeemed, transferred, or exchanged fund shares held through an account with the financial intermediary, and the amount and dates of such shareholder purchases, redemptions, transfers, and exchanges;

(ii) Execute any instructions from the fund to restrict or prohibit further purchases or exchanges of fund shares by a shareholder who has been identified by the fund as having engaged in transactions of fund shares (directly or indirectly through the intermediary's account) that violate policies established by the fund for the purpose of eliminating or reducing any dilution of the value of the outstanding securities issued by the fund; and

(iii) Use best efforts to determine, promptly upon request of the fund, whether any specific person about whom it has received the identification and transaction information set forth in paragraph (c)(5)(i) of this rule, is itself a financial intermediary ("indirect intermediary") and, upon further request by the fund:

(A) Provide (or arrange to have provided) the identification and transaction information set forth in paragraph (c)(5)(i) of this rule regarding shareholders who hold an account with an indirect intermediary; or

(B) Restrict or prohibit the indirect intermediary from purchasing, in nominee name on behalf of other persons, securities issued by the fund.

Rule 22d–1. Exemption From Section 22(d) to Permit Sales of Redeemable Securities at Prices Which Reflect Sales Loads Set Pursuant to a Schedule

A registered investment company that is the issuer of redeemable securities, a principal underwriter of such securities or a dealer therein shall be exempt from the provisions of section 22(d) to the extent necessary to permit the sale of such securities at prices that reflect scheduled variations in, or elimination of, the sales load. These price schedules may offer such variations in or elimination of the sales load to particular classes of investors or transactions, *Provided that:*

(a) The company, the principal underwriter and dealers in the company's shares apply an scheduled variation uniformly to all offerees in the class specified;

(b) The company furnishes to existing shareholders and prospective investors adequate information concerning any scheduled variation, as prescribed in applicable registration statement form requirements;

(c) Before making any new sales load variation available to purchasers of the company's shares, the company revises its prospectus and statement of additional information to describe that new variation; and

(d) The company advises existing shareholders of any new sales load variation within one year of the date when that variation is first made available to purchasers of the company's shares.

* * *

Rule 24b–1. Definitions

(a) The term "form letter" as used in section 24(b) of the Act includes

(1) One of a series of identical sales letters, and

(2)   Any sales letter a substantial portion of which consists of a statement which is in essence identical with similar statements in sales letters sent to 25 or more persons within any period of 90 consecutive days.

(b)   The term "distribution" as used in section 24(b) of the Act includes the distribution or redistribution to prospective investors of the content of any written sales literature, whether such distribution or redistribution is effected by means of written or oral representations or statements.

(c)   The term "rules and regulations" as used in section 24(a) and (c) of the Act shall include the forms for registration of securities under the Securities Act of 1933 and the related instructions thereto.

Rule 24b–2.   Filing Copies of Sales Literature

Copies of material filed with the Commission for the sole purpose of complying with section 24(b) of the Act either shall be accompanied by a letter of transmittal which makes appropriate references to said section or shall make such appropriate reference on the face of the material.

Rule 24b–3.   Sales Literature Deemed Filed

Any advertisement, pamphlet, circular, form letter or other sales literature addressed to or intended for distribution to prospective investors shall be deemed filed with the Commission for purposes of section 24(b) of the Act upon filing with a national securities association registered under section 15A of the Securities Exchange Act of 1934 that has adopted rules providing standards for the investment company advertising practices of its members and has established and implemented procedures to review that advertising.

Rule 24b–4.   Filing Copies of Covered Investment Fund Research Reports

A covered investment fund research report, as defined in paragraph (c)(3) of Rule 139B under the Securities Act of 1933 (15 U.S.C. 77a et seq.), of a covered investment fund registered as an investment company under the Act, shall not be subject to section 24(b) of the Act or the rules and regulations thereunder, except that such report shall be subject to such section and the rules and regulations to the extent that it is otherwise not subject to the content standards in the rules of any self-regulatory organization related to research reports, including those contained in the rules governing communications with the public regarding investment companies or substantially similar standards.

Rule 30a–1.   Annual Report for Registered Investment Companies

Every management company must file an annual report on Form N–CEN at least every twelve months and not more than seventy-five calendar days after the close of each fiscal year. Every unit investment trust must file an annual report on Form N–CEN at least every twelve months and not more than seventy-five calendar days after the close of each calendar year. A registered investment company that has filed a registration statement with the Commission registering its securities for the first time under the Securities Act of 1933 is relieved of this reporting obligation with respect to any reporting period or portion thereof prior to the date on which that registration statement becomes effective or is withdrawn.

Rule 30a–2.   Certification of Form N–CSR

(a)   Each report filed on Form N-CSR (§§ 249.331 and 274.128 of this chapter) by a registered management investment company must include certifications in the form specified in Item 19(a)(3) of Form N–CSR, and such certifications must be filed as an exhibit to such report. Each principal executive and principal financial officer of the investment company, or persons performing similar functions, at the time of filing of the report must sign a certification.

(b)   Each report on Form N-CSR filed by a registered management investment company under Section 13(a) or 15(d) of the Securities Exchange Act of 1934 (15 U.S.C. 78m(a) or 78o(d)) and that contains financial statements must be accompanied by the certifications required by Section 1350 of Chapter 63 of Title 18 of the United States Code (18 U.S.C. 1350) and such certifications must be furnished as an exhibit to such report as specified in Item 19(b) of Form N–CSR. Each principal executive and principal financial officer of the investment company (or equivalent thereof) must sign a certification. This requirement may be satisfied by a single certification signed by an investment company's principal executive and principal financial officers.

(c)   A person required to provide a certification specified in paragraph (a) or (b) of this rule may not have the certification signed on his or her behalf pursuant to a power of attorney or other form of confirming authority.

(d)   The certification requirements of this rule do not apply to XBRL-Related Documents, as defined in Rule 11 of Regulation S–T.

Rule 30a–3.   Controls and Procedures

(a)   Every registered management investment company, other than a small business investment company registered on Form N–5, must maintain disclosure controls and procedures (as defined in paragraph (c) of this rule) and internal control over financial reporting (as defined in paragraph (d) of this rule).

(b)   Each such registered management investment company's management must evaluate, with the participation of the company's principal executive and principal financial officers, or persons performing similar functions, the effectiveness of the company's disclosure controls and procedures, within the 90-day period prior to the filing date of each report on Form N–CSR.

(c)   For purposes of this rule, the term disclosure controls and procedures means controls and other procedures of a registered management investment company that are designed to ensure that information required to be disclosed by the investment company on Form N–CSR is recorded, processed, summarized, and reported within the time periods specified in the Commission's rules and forms. Disclosure controls and procedures include, without limitation, controls and procedures designed to ensure that information required to be disclosed by an investment company in the reports that it files or submits on Form N–CSR is accumulated and communicated to the investment company's management, including its principal executive and principal financial officers, or persons performing similar functions, as appropriate to allow timely decisions regarding required disclosure.

(d)   The term internal control over financial reporting is defined as a process designed by, or under the supervision of, the registered management investment company's principal executive and principal financial officers, or persons performing similar functions, and effected by the company's board of directors, management, and other personnel, to provide reasonable assurance regarding the reliability of financial reporting and the preparation of financial statements for external purposes in accordance with generally accepted accounting principles and includes those policies and procedures that:

(1)   Pertain to the maintenance of records that in reasonable detail accurately and fairly reflect the transactions and dispositions of the assets of the investment company;

(2)   Provide reasonable assurance that transactions are recorded as necessary to permit preparation of financial statements in accordance with generally accepted accounting principles, and that receipts and expenditures of the investment company are being made only in accordance with authorizations of management and directors of the investment company; and

(3)   Provide reasonable assurance regarding prevention or timely detection of unauthorized acquisition, use, or disposition of the investment company's assets that could have a material effect on the financial statements.

Rule 30a–4.   Annual Report for Wholly-Owned Registered Management Investment Company Subsidiary of Registered Management Investment Company

Notwithstanding the provisions of Rule 30a–1, a registered management investment company that is a wholly-owned subsidiary of a registered management investment company need not file an annual report on Form N–CEN if financial information with respect to that subsidiary is reported in the parent's annual report on Form N–CEN.

Rule 30b1–4. Report of Proxy Voting Record

Every registered management investment company, other than a small business investment company registered on Form N–5, shall file an annual report on Form N–PX not later than August 31 of each year, containing the registrant's proxy voting record for the most recent twelve-month period ended June 30.

Rule 30b1–7. Monthly Report for Money Market Funds

Every registered open-end management investment company, or series thereof, that is regulated as a money market fund under Rule 2a–7 must file with the Commission a monthly report of portfolio holdings on Form N–MFP (Rule 201 of this Act), current as of the last business day or any subsequent calendar day of the preceding month, no later than the fifth business day of each month.

Rule 30b1–8. Current Reports for Money Market Funds

Every registered open-end management investment company, or series thereof, that is regulated as a money market fund under Rule 2a–7, that experiences any of the events specified on Form N–CR (Rule 222 of this Act), must file with the Commission a current report on Form N–CR within the period specified in that form.

Rule 30b1–9. Monthly Report

Each registered management investment company or exchange-traded fund organized as a unit investment trust, or series thereof, other than a registered open-end management investment company that is regulated as a money market fund under Rule 2a–7 or a small business investment company registered under form N–5, must file a monthly report of portfolio holdings on form N–PORT, current as of the last business day, or last calendar day, of the month. A registered investment company that has filed a registration statement with the Commission registering its securities for the first time under the Securities Act of 1933 is relieved of this reporting obligation with respect to any reporting period or portion thereof prior to the date on which that registration statement becomes effective or is withdrawn. Reports on Form N–PORT must be filed with the Commission no later than 30 days after the end of each month.

Rule 30b1–10. Current Report for Open-End Management Investment Companies

Every registered open-end management investment company, or series thereof but not a fund that is regulated as a money market fund under this Rule 2a–7, that experiences any event specified on Form N–LIQUID, must file Commission a current report on Form N–LIQUID within the period specified in that form.

Rule 30d–1. Filing of Copies of Reports to Shareholders

A registered management investment company, other than a small business investment company registered on Form N–5, that is required to file annual and quarterly reports pursuant to section 13(a) or 15(d) of the Securities Exchange Act of 1934 shall satisfy its requirement to file such reports by the filing, in accordance with the rules and procedures specified therefor, of reports on Form N–CSR. A registered unit investment trust or a small business investment company registered on Form N–5 that is required to file annual and quarterly reports pursuant to section 13(a) or 15(d) of the Securities Exchange Act of 1934 shall satisfy its requirement to file such reports by the filing, in accordance with the rules and procedures specified therefor, of reports on Form N–CEN.

Rule 32a–4. Independent Audit Committees

A registered management investment company or a registered face-amount certificate company is exempt from the requirement of section 32(a)(2) of the Act that the selection of the company's independent public accountant be submitted for ratification or rejection at the next succeeding annual meeting of shareholders, if:

(a) The company's board of directors has established a committee, composed solely of directors who are not interested persons of the company, that has responsibility for overseeing the fund's accounting and auditing processes ("audit committee");

(b)   The company's board of directors has adopted a charter for the audit committee setting forth the committee's structure, duties, powers, and methods of operation or set forth such provisions in the fund's charter or bylaws; and

(c)   The company maintains and preserves permanently in an easily accessible place a copy of the audit committee's charter and any modification to the charter.

Rule 34b–1.   Sales Literature Deemed to Be Misleading

Any advertisement, pamphlet, circular, form letter, or other sales literature addressed to or intended for distribution to prospective investors that is required to be filed with the Commission by section 24(b) of the Act ("sales literature") shall have omitted to state a fact necessary in order to make the statements made therein not materially misleading unless the sales literature includes the information specified in paragraphs (a) and (b) of this rule.

NOTE to Introductory Text of Rule 34b–1: The fact that the sales literature includes the information specified in paragraphs (a) and (b) of this rule does not relieve the investment company, underwriter, or dealer of any obligations with respect to the sales literature under the antifraud provisions of the federal securities laws. For guidance about factors to be weighed in determining whether statements, representations, illustrations, and descriptions contained in investment company sales literature are misleading, see Rule 156 under the Securities Act of 1933.

(a)   Sales literature for a money market fund shall contain the information required by paragraph (b)(4) of Rule 482 under the Securities Act of 1933, presented in the manner required by paragraph (b)(5) of that rule.

(b)(1)   Except as provided in paragraph (b)(3) of this rule:

(i)   In any sales literature that contains performance data for an investment company, include the disclosure required by paragraph (b)(3) of Rule 482 under the Securities Act of 1933, presented in the manner required by paragraph (b)(5) of that rule.

(ii)   In any sales literature for a money market fund:

(A)   Accompany any quotation of yield or similar quotation purporting to demonstrate the income earned or distributions made by the money market fund with a quotation of current yield specified by paragraph (e)(1)(i) of Rule 482 of the Securities Act;

(B)   Accompany any quotation of the money market fund's tax equivalent yield or tax equivalent effective yield with a quotation of current yield as specified in Rule 482(e)(1)(iii) of the Securities Act; and

(C)   Accompany any quotation of the money market fund's total return with a quotation of the money market fund's current yield specified in paragraph (e)(1)(i) of Rule 482 of the Securities Act. Place the quotations of total return and current yield next to each other, in the same size print, and if there is a material difference between the quoted total return and the quoted current yield, include a statement that the yield quotation more closely reflects the current earnings of the money market fund than the total return quotation.

(iii)   In any sales literature for an investment company other than a money market fund that contains performance data:

(A)   Include the total return information required by paragraph (d)(3) of Rule 482 of the Securities Act;

(B)   Accompany any quotation of performance adjusted to reflect the effect of taxes (not including a quotation of tax equivalent yield or other similar quotation purporting to demonstrate the tax equivalent yield earned or distributions made by the company) with the quotations of total return specified by paragraph (d)(4) of Rule 482 of this chapter;

(C)   If the sales literature (other than sales literature for a company that is permitted under Rule 35d–1(a)(4) to use a name suggesting that the company's distributions are exempt from federal income tax or from both federal and state income tax) represents or implies that the company is managed to limit or control the effect of taxes on company performance, include the quotations of total return specified by paragraph (d)(4) of Rule 482 of this chapter;

(D)   Accompany any quotation of yield or similar quotation purporting to demonstrate the income earned or distributions made by the company with a quotation of current yield specified by paragraph (d)(1) of Rule 482 of the Securities Act; and

(E)   Accompany any quotation of tax equivalent yield or other similar quotation purporting to demonstrate the tax equivalent yield earned or distributions made by the company with a quotation of tax equivalent yield specified in paragraph (d)(2) and current yield specified by paragraph (d)(1) of Rule 482 of the Securities Act.

(2)   Any performance data included in sales literature under paragraphs (b)(1)(ii) or (iii) of this rule must meet the current requirements of paragraph (g) of Rule 482 of the Securities Act.

(3)   The requirements specified in paragraph (b)(1) of this rule shall not apply to any quarterly, semi-annual, or annual report to shareholders under Section 30 of the Act containing performance data for a period commencing no earlier than the first day of the period covered by the report; nor shall the requirements of paragraphs (d)(3)(ii), (d)(4)(ii), and (g) of Rule 482 of this chapter apply to any such periodic report containing any other performance data.

Note: Sales literature (except that of a money market fund) containing a quotation of yield or tax equivalent yield must also contain the total return information. In the case of sales literature, the currentness provisions apply from the date of distribution and not the date of submission for publication.

Rule 35d-1.   Investment Company Names

(a)   For purposes of section 35(d) of the Act, a materially deceptive and misleading name of a Fund includes:

(1)   Names suggesting guarantee or approval by the United States government. A name suggesting that the Fund or the securities issued by it are guaranteed, sponsored, recommended, or approved by the United States government or any United States government agency or instrumentality, including any name that uses the words "guaranteed" or "insured" or similar terms in conjunction with the words "United States" or "U.S. government."

(2)   Names suggesting investment in certain investments or industries. A name suggesting that the Fund focuses its investments in a particular type of investment or investments, or in investments in a particular industry or group of industries, unless:

(i)   The Fund has adopted a policy to invest, under normal circumstances, at least 80% of the value of its Assets in the particular type of investments, or in investments in the particular industry or industries, suggested by the Fund's name; and

(ii)   Either the policy described in paragraph (a)(2)(i) of this rule is a fundamental policy under section 8(b)(3) of the Act, or the Fund has adopted a policy to provide the Fund's shareholders with at least 60 days prior notice of any change in the policy described in paragraph (a)(2)(i) of this rule that meets the requirements of paragraph (c) of this rule.

(3)   Names suggesting investment in certain countries or geographic regions. A name suggesting that the Fund focuses its investments in a particular country or geographic region, unless:

(i)   The Fund has adopted a policy to invest, under normal circumstances, at least 80% of the value of its Assets in investments that are tied economically to the particular country or geographic region suggested by its name;

(ii)   The Fund discloses in its prospectus the specific criteria used by the Fund to select these investments; and

(iii)   Either the policy described in paragraph (a)(3)(i) of this rule is a fundamental policy under section 8(b)(3) of the Act, or the Fund has adopted a policy to provide the Fund's shareholders with at least 60 days prior notice of any change in the policy described in paragraph (a)(3)(i) of this rule that meets the requirements of paragraph (c) of this rule.

(4)   Tax-exempt Funds. A name suggesting that the Fund's distributions are exempt from federal income tax or from both federal and state income tax, unless the Fund has adopted a fundamental policy under section 8(b)(3) of the Act:

(i)   To invest, under normal circumstances, at least 80% of the value of its Assets in investments the income from which is exempt, as applicable, from federal income tax or from both federal and state income tax; or

(ii)   To invest, under normal circumstances, its Assets so that at least 80% of the income that it distributes will be exempt, as applicable, from federal income tax or from both federal and state income tax.

(b)   The requirements of paragraphs (a)(2) through (a)(4) of this rule apply at the time a Fund invests its Assets, except that these requirements shall not apply to any unit investment trust (as defined in section 4(2) of the Act) that has made an initial deposit of securities prior to July 31, 2002. If, subsequent to an investment, these requirements are no longer met, the Fund's future investments must be made in a manner that will bring the Fund into compliance with those paragraphs.

(c)   A policy to provide a Fund's shareholders with notice of a change in a Fund's investment policy as described in paragraphs (a)(2)(ii) and (a)(3)(iii) of this rule must provide that:

(1)   The notice will be provided in plain English in a separate written document;

(2)   The notice will contain the following prominent statement, or similar clear and understandable statement, in bold-face type: "Important Notice Regarding Change in Investment Policy"; and

(3)   The statement contained in paragraph (c)(2) of this rule also will appear on the envelope in which the notice is delivered or, if the notice is delivered separately from other communications to investors, that the statement will appear either on the notice or on the envelope in which the notice is delivered.

(d)   For purposes of this rule:

(1)   Fund means a registered investment company and any series of the investment company.

(2)   Assets means net assets, plus the amount of any borrowings for investment purposes.

Rule 38a–1.   Compliance Procedures and Practices of Certain Investment Companies

(a)   Each registered investment company and business development company ("fund") must:

(1)   *Policies and procedures.* Adopt and implement written policies and procedures reasonably designed to prevent violation of the Federal Securities Laws by the fund, including policies and procedures that provide for the oversight of compliance by each investment adviser, principal underwriter, administrator, and transfer agent of the fund;

(2)   *Board approval.* Obtain the approval of the fund's board of directors, including a majority of directors who are not interested persons of the fund, of the fund's policies and procedures and those of each investment adviser, principal underwriter, administrator, and transfer agent of the fund, which approval must be based on a finding by the board that the policies and procedures are reasonably designed to prevent violation of the Federal Securities Laws by the fund, and by each investment adviser, principal underwriter, administrator, and transfer agent of the fund;

(3)   *Annual review.* Review, no less frequently than annually, the adequacy of the policies and procedures of the fund and of each investment adviser, principal underwriter, administrator, and transfer agent and the effectiveness of their implementation;

(4)   *Chief compliance officer.* Designate one individual responsible for administering the fund's policies and procedures adopted under paragraph (a)(1):

(i)   Whose designation and compensation must be approved by the fund's board of directors, including a majority of the directors who are not interested persons of the fund;

(ii) Who may be removed from his or her responsibilities by action of (and only with the approval of) the fund's board of directors, including a majority of the directors who are not interested persons of the fund;

(iii) Who must, no less frequently than annually, provide a written report to the board that, at a minimum, addresses:

(A) The operation of the policies and procedures of the fund and each investment adviser, principal underwriter, administrator, and transfer agent of the fund, any material changes made to those policies and procedures since the date of the last report, and any material changes to the policies and procedures recommended as a result of the annual review conducted pursuant to paragraph (a)(3) of this rule; and

(B) Each Material Compliance Matter that occurred since the date of the last report; and

(iv) Who must, no less frequently than annually, meet separately with the fund's independent directors.

(b) *Unit investment trusts.* If the fund is a unit investment trust, the fund's principal underwriter or depositor must approve the fund's policies and procedures and chief compliance officer, must receive all annual reports, and must approve the removal of the chief compliance officer from his or her responsibilities.

(c) *Undue influence prohibited.* No officer, director, or employee of the fund, its investment adviser, or principal underwriter, or any person acting under such person's direction may directly or indirectly take any action to coerce, manipulate, mislead, or fraudulently influence the fund's chief compliance officer in the performance of his or her duties under this rule.

(d) *Recordkeeping.* The fund must maintain:

(1) A copy of the policies and procedures adopted by the fund under paragraph (a)(1) that are in effect, or at any time within the past five years were in effect, in an easily accessible place; and

(2) Copies of materials provided to the board of directors in connection with their approval under paragraph (a)(2) of this rule, and written reports provided to the board of directors pursuant to paragraph (a)(4)(iii) of this rule (or, if the fund is a unit investment trust, to the fund's principal underwriter or depositor, pursuant to paragraph (b) of this rule) for at least five years after the end of the fiscal year in which the documents were provided, the first two years in an easily accessible place; and

(3) Any records documenting the fund's annual review pursuant to paragraph (a)(3) of this rule for at least five years after the end of the fiscal year in which the annual review was conducted, the first two years in an easily accessible place.

(e) *Definitions.* For purposes of this rule:

(1) *Federal Securities Laws* means the Securities Act of 1933, the Securities Exchange Act of 1934, the Sarbanes-Oxley Act of 2002, the Investment Company Act of 1940, the Investment Advisers Act of 1940, Title V of the Gramm-Leach-Bliley Act, any rules adopted by the Commission under any of these statutes, the Bank Secrecy Act as it applies to funds, and any rules adopted thereunder by the Commission or the Department of the Treasury.

(2) *A Material Compliance Matter* means any compliance matter about which the fund's board of directors would reasonably need to know to oversee fund compliance, and that involves, without limitation:

(i) A violation of the Federal Securities Laws by the fund, its investment adviser, principal underwriter, administrator or transfer agent (or officers, directors, employees or agents thereof),

(ii) A violation of the policies and procedures of the fund, its investment adviser, principal underwriter, administrator or transfer agent, or

(iii) A weakness in the design or implementation of the policies and procedures of the fund, its investment adviser, principal underwriter, administrator or transfer agent.

H. INVESTMENT ADVISERS ACT OF 1940 AND SELECTED RULES

Findings

Sec. 201. Upon the basis of facts disclosed by the record and report of the Securities and Exchange Commission made pursuant to section 30 of the Public Utility Holding Company Act of 1935, and facts otherwise disclosed and ascertained, it is found that investment advisers are of national concern, in that, among other things—

(1) their advice, counsel, publications, writings, analyses, and reports are furnished and distributed, and their contracts, subscription agreements, and other arrangements with clients are negotiated and performed, by the use of the mails and means and instrumentalities of interstate commerce;

(2) their advice, counsel, publications, writings, analyses, and reports customarily relate to the purchase and sale of securities traded on national securities exchanges and in interstate over-the-counter markets, securities issued by companies engaged in business in interstate commerce, and securities issued by national banks and member banks of the Federal Reserve System; and

(3)   the foregoing transactions occur in such volume as substantially to affect interstate commerce, national securities exchanges, and other securities markets, the national banking system and the national economy.

Definitions

Sec. 202.   (a)   In general.—

When used in this Act, unless the context otherwise requires, the following definitions shall apply:

(1)   "Assignment" includes any direct or indirect transfer or hypothecation of an investment advisory contract by the assignor or of a controlling block of the assignor's outstanding voting securities by a security holder of the assignor; but if the investment adviser is a partnership, no assignment of an investment advisory contract shall be deemed to result from the death or withdrawal of a minority of the members of the investment adviser having only a minority interest in the business of the investment adviser, or from the admission to the investment adviser of one or more members who, after such admission, shall be only a minority of the members and shall have only a minority interest in the business.

(2)   "Bank" means

(A)   a banking institution organized under the laws of the United States or a Federal savings association, as defined in section 2(5) of the Home Owners' Loan Act,

(B)   a member bank of the Federal Reserve System,

(C)   any other banking institution, savings association, as defined in section 2(4) of the Home Owners' Loan Act, or trust company, whether incorporated or not, doing business under the laws of any State or of the United States, a substantial portion of the business of which consists of receiving deposits or exercising fiduciary powers similar to those permitted to national banks under the authority of the Comptroller of the Currency, and which is supervised and examined by State or Federal authority having supervision over banks or savings association, and which is not operated for the purpose of evading the provisions of this Act, and

(D)   a receiver, conservator, or other liquidating agent of any institution or firm included in clauses (A), (B), or (C) of this paragraph.

(3)   The term "broker" has the same meaning as given in section 3(a)(4) of the Securities Act of 1934.

(4)   "Commission" means the Securities and Exchange Commission.

(5)   "Company" means a corporation, a partnership, an association, a joint-stock company, a trust, or any organized group of persons, whether incorporated or not; or any receiver, trustee in a case under Title 11 of the United States Code, or similar official, or any liquidating agent for any of the foregoing, in his capacity as such.

(6)   "Convicted" includes a verdict, judgment, or plea of guilty, or a finding of guilt on a plea of nolo contendere, if such verdict, judgment, plea, or finding has not been reversed, set aside, or withdrawn, whether or not sentence has been imposed.

(7)   The term "dealer" has the same meaning as given in section 3(a)(5) of the Securities Exchange Act of 1934.

(8)   "Director" means any director of a corporation or any person performing similar functions with respect to any organization, whether incorporated or unincorporated.

(9)   "Exchange" means any organization, association, or group of persons, whether incorporated or unincorporated, which constitutes, maintains, or provides a market place or facilities for bringing together purchasers and sellers of securities or for otherwise performing with respect to securities the functions commonly performed by a stock exchange as that term is generally understood, and includes the market place and the market facilities maintained by such exchange.

(10)   "Interstate commerce" means trade, commerce, transportation, or communication among the several States, or between any foreign country and any State, or between any State and any place or ship outside thereof.

(11) "Investment adviser" means any person who, for compensation, engages in the business of advising others, either directly or through publications or writings, as to the value of securities or as to the advisability of investing in, purchasing, or selling securities, or who, for compensation and as part of a regular business, issues or promulgates analyses or reports concerning securities; but does not include

    (A)   a bank, or any bank holding company as defined in the Bank Holding Company Act of 1956 which is not an investment company, except that the term "investment adviser" includes any bank or bank holding company to the extent that such bank or bank holding company serves or acts as an investment adviser to a registered investment company, but if, in the case of a bank, such services or actions are performed through a separately identifiable department or division, the department or division, and not the bank itself, shall be deemed to be the investment adviser.

    (B)   any lawyer, accountant, engineer, or teacher whose performance of such services is solely incidental to the practice of his profession;

    (C)   any broker or dealer whose performance of such services is solely incidental to the conduct of his business as a broker or dealer and who receives no special compensation therefor;

    (D)   the publisher of any bona fide newspaper, news magazine or business or financial publication of general and regular circulation;

    (E)   any person whose advice, analyses, or reports relate to no securities other than securities which are direct obligations of or obligations guaranteed as to principal or interest by the United States, or securities issued or guaranteed by corporations in which the United States has a direct or indirect interest which shall have been designated by the Secretary of the Treasury, pursuant to section 3(a)(12) of the Securities Exchange Act of 1934, as exempted securities for the purposes of that Act;

    (F)   any nationally recognized statistical rating organization, as that term is defined in section 3(a)(62) of the Securities Exchange Act of 1934, unless such organization engages in issuing recommendations as to purchasing, selling, or holding securities or in managing assets, consisting in whole or in part of securities, on behalf of others;

    (G)   any family office, as defined by rule, regulation, or order of the Commission, in accordance with the purposes of this title; or

    (H)   such other persons not within the intent of this paragraph, as the Commission may designate by rules and regulations or order.

(12) "Investment company", affiliated person, and "insurance company" have the same meanings as in the Investment Company Act of 1940. "Control" means the power to exercise a controlling influence over the management or policies of a company, unless such power is solely the result of an official position with such company.

(13) "Investment supervisory services" means the giving of continuous advice as to the investment of funds on the basis of the individual needs of each client.

(14) "Means or instrumentality of interstate commerce" includes any facility of a national securities exchange.

(15) "National securities exchange" means an exchange registered under section 6 of the Securities Exchange Act of 1934.

(16) "Person" means a natural person or a company.

(17) The term "person associated with an investment adviser" means any partner, officer, or director of such investment adviser (or any person performing similar functions), or any person directly or indirectly controlling or controlled by such investment adviser, including any employee of such investment adviser, except that for the purposes of section 203 of this Act (other than subsection (f) thereof), persons associated with an investment adviser whose functions are clerical or ministerial shall not be included in the meaning of such term. The Commission may by rules and regulations classify, for the purposes of any portion or portions of this Act, persons, including employees controlled by an investment adviser.

(18) "Security" means any note, stock, treasury stock, security future, bond, debenture, evidence of indebtedness, certificate of interest or participation in any profit-sharing agreement, collateral-trust certificate, preorganization certificate or subscription, transferable share, investment contract, voting-trust certificate, certificate of deposit for a security, fractional undivided interest in oil, gas, or other mineral rights, any put, call, straddle, option, or privilege on any security (including a certificate of deposit) or on any group or index of securities (including any interest therein or based on the value thereof), or any put, call, straddle, option, or privilege entered into on a national securities exchange relating to foreign currency, or, in general, any interest or instrument commonly known as a "security", or any certificate of interest or participation in, temporary or interim certificate for, receipt for, guarantee of, or warrant or right to subscribe to or purchase any of the foregoing.

(19) "State" means any State of the United States, the District of Columbia, Puerto Rico, the Virgin Islands, or any other possession of the United States.

(20) "Underwriter" means any person who has purchased from an issuer with a view to, or sells for an issuer in connection with, the distribution of any security, or participates or has a direct or indirect participation in any such undertaking, or participates or has a participation in the direct or indirect underwriting of any such undertaking; but such term shall not include a person whose interest is limited to a commission from an underwriter or dealer not in excess of the usual and customary distributor's or seller's commission. As used in this paragraph the term "issuer" shall include in addition to an issuer, any person directly or indirectly controlling or controlled by the issuer, or any person under direct or indirect common control with the issuer.

(21) "Securities Act of 1933", "Securities Exchange Act of 1934", and "Trust Indenture Act of 1939", mean those Acts, respectively, as heretofore or hereafter amended.

(22) "Business development company" means any company which is a business development company as defined in sections 2(a)(48) of the Investment Company Act and which complies with section 54 of the Investment Company Act, except that—

    (A)   the 70 per centum of the value of the total assets condition referred to in sections 2(a)(48) and 54 of the Investment Company Act shall be 60 per centum for purposes of determining compliance therewith;

    (B)   such company need not be a closed-end company and need not elect to be subject to the provisions of sections 54 through 64 of the Investment Company Act; and

    (C)   the securities which may be purchased pursuant to section 54(a) of the Investment Company Act may be purchased from any person.

For purposes of this paragraph, all terms in sections 2(a)(48) and 54 of the Investment Company Act shall have the same meaning set forth in such Act as if such company were a registered closed-end investment company, except that the value of the assets of a business development company which is not subject to the provisions of sections 54 through 64 of the Investment Company Act shall be determined as of the date of the most recent financial statements which it furnished to all holders of its securities, and shall be determined no less frequently than annually.

(23) "Foreign securities authority" means any foreign government, or any governmental body or regulatory organization empowered by a foreign government to administer or enforce its laws as they relate to securities matters.

(24) "Foreign financial regulatory authority" means any

    (A)   foreign securities authority,

    (B)   other governmental body or foreign equivalent of a self-regulatory organization empowered by a foreign government to administer or enforce its laws relating to the regulation of fiduciaries, trusts, commercial lending, insurance, trading in contracts of sale of a commodity for future delivery, or other instruments traded on or subject to the rules of a contract market, board of trade or foreign equivalent, or other financial activities, or

    (C)   membership organization a function of which is to regulate the participation of its members in activities listed above.

(25) "Supervised person" means any partner, officer, director (or other person occupying a similar status or performing similar functions), or employee of an investment adviser, or other person who provides investment advice on behalf of the investment adviser and is subject to the supervision and control of the investment adviser.

(26) The term separately identifiable department or division of a bank means a unit—

(A) that is under the direct supervision of an officer or officers designated by the board of directors of the bank as responsible for the day-to-day conduct of the bank's investment adviser activities for one or more investment companies, including the supervision of all bank employees engaged in the performance of such activities; and

(B) for which all of the records relating to its investment adviser activities are separately maintained in or extractable from such unit's own facilities or the facilities of the bank, and such records are so maintained or otherwise accessible as to permit independent examination and enforcement by the Commission of this Act or the Investment Company Act of 1940 and rules and regulations promulgated under this Act or the Investment Company Act of 1940.

(27) The terms 'security future' and 'narrow-based security index' have the same meanings as provided in section 3(a)(55) of the Securities Exchange Act of 1934.

(28) The term 'credit rating agency' has the same meaning as in section 3 of the Securities Exchange Act of 1934.

(29)[1] The term "private fund" means an issuer that would be an investment company, as defined in section 3 of the Investment Company Act of 1940, but for section 3(c)(1) or 3(c)(7) of that Act.

(30) The term "foreign private adviser" means any investment adviser who—

(A) has no place of business in the United States;

(B) has, in total, fewer than 15 clients and investors in the United States in private funds advised by the investment adviser;

(C) has aggregate assets under management attributable to clients in the United States and investors in the United States in private funds advised by the investment adviser of less than $25,000,000, or such higher amount as the Commission may, by rule, deem appropriate in accordance with the purposes of this subchapter; and

(D) neither—

(i) holds itself out generally to the public in the United States as an investment adviser; nor

(ii) acts as—

(I) an investment adviser to any investment company registered under the Investment Company Act of 1940; or

(II) a company that has elected to be a business development company pursuant to section 53 of the Investment Company Act of 1940, and has not withdrawn its election.

(29)[2] The terms 'commodity pool', 'commodity pool operator', 'commodity trading advisor', 'major swap participant', 'swap', 'swap dealer', and 'swap execution facility' have the same meanings as in section 1a of the Commodity Exchange Act (7 U.S.C. 1a).

(b) Applicability to Federal or State government, agency, or instrumentality, or to officers, agents, or employees thereof.—

No provision in this Act shall apply to, or be deemed to include, the United States, a State, or any political subdivision of a State, or any agency, authority, or instrumentality of any one or more of the foregoing, or any corporation which is wholly owned directly or indirectly by any one or more of the

---

[1] Another par. (29) appears after par. (30).

[2] So in original. Another par. (29) appears after par. (28).

foregoing, or any officer, agent, or employee of any of the foregoing acting as such in the course of his official duty, unless such provision makes specific reference thereto.

(c)   Consideration of promotion of efficiency, competition, and capital formation.—

Whenever pursuant to this Act the Commission is engaged in rulemaking and is required to consider or determine whether an action is necessary or appropriate in the public interest, the Commission shall also consider, in addition to the protection of investors, whether the action will promote efficiency, competition, and capital formation.

Registration of Investment Advisers

Sec. 203.   (a)   Necessity of registration.—

Except as provided in subsection (b) and section 203A of this Act, it shall be unlawful for any investment adviser, unless registered under this section, to make use of the mails or any means or instrumentality of interstate commerce in connection with his or its business as an investment adviser.

(b)   Investment advisers who need not be registered.—

The provisions of subsection (a) of this section shall not apply to—

(1)   any investment adviser, other than an investment advisor who acts as an investment adviser to any private fund, all of whose clients are residents of the State within which such investment adviser maintains his or its principal office and place of business, and who does not furnish advice or issue analyses or reports with respect to securities listed or admitted to unlisted trading privileges on any national securities exchange;

(2)   any investment adviser whose only clients are insurance companies;

(3)   any investment adviser that is a foreign private adviser;

(4)   any investment adviser that is a charitable organization, as defined in section 3(c)(10)(D) of the Investment Company Act of 1940, or is a trustee, director, officer, employee, or volunteer of such a charitable organization acting within the scope of such person's employment or duties with such organization, whose advice, analyses, or reports are provided only to one or more of the following:

(A)   any such charitable organization;

(B)   a fund that is excluded from the definition of an investment company under section 3(c)(10)(B) of the Investment Company Act of 1940; or

(C)   a trust or other donative instrument described in section 3(c)(10)(B) of the Investment Company Act of 1940, or the trustees, administrators, settlors (or potential settlors), or beneficiaries of any such trust or other instrument;

(5)   any plan described in section 414(e) of the Internal Revenue Code of 1986, any person or entity eligible to establish and maintain such a plan under the Internal Revenue Code of 1986, or any trustee, director, officer, or employee of or volunteer for any such plan or person, if such person or entity, acting in such capacity, provides investment advice exclusively to, or with respect to, any plan, person, or entity or any company, account, or fund that is excluded from the definition of an investment company under section 3(c)(14) of the Investment Company Act of 1940;

(6)(A)   any investment adviser that is registered with the Commodity Futures Trading Commission as a commodity trading advisor whose business does not consist primarily of acting as an investment adviser, as defined in section 202(a)(11) of this Act, and that does not act as an investment adviser to—

(i)   an investment company registered under the Investment Company Act of 1940; or

(ii)   a company which has elected to be a business development company pursuant to section 53 of the Commodity Futures Modernization Act of 2000 and has not withdrawn its election; or

(B)   any investment adviser that is registered with the Commodity Futures Trading Commission as a commodity trading advisor and advises a private fund, provided that, if after the date of enactment of the Private Fund Investment Advisers Registration Act of 2010, the business of the advisor should become predominately the provision of securities-related advice, then such adviser shall register with the Commission;

(7) any investment adviser, other than any entity that has elected to be regulated or is regulated as a business development company pursuant to section 54 of the Investment Company Act of 1940 (15 U.S.C. 80a–53), who solely advises—

(A) small business investment companies that are licensees under the Small Business Investment Act of 1958;

(B) entities that have received from the Small Business Administration notice to proceed to qualify for a license as a small business investment company under the Small Business Investment Act of 1958, which notice or license has not been revoked; or

(C) applicants that are affiliated with 1 or more licensed small business investment companies described in subparagraph (A) and that have applied for another license under the Small Business Investment Act of 1958, which application remains pending; or

(8) any investment adviser, other than an entity that has elected to be regulated or is regulated as a business development company pursuant section 53 of the Investment Company Act of 1940, who solely advises—

(A) rural business investment companies; or

(B) companies that have submitted to the Secretary of Agriculture an application in accordance with section 2009cc–3(b) of Title 7 that—

(i) have received from the Secretary of Agriculture a letter of conditions, which has not been revoked; or

(ii) are affiliated with 1 or more rural business investment companies described in subparagraph (A).

(c) Procedure for registration; filing of application; effective date of registration; amendment of registration.—

(1) An investment adviser, or any person who presently contemplates becoming an investment adviser, may be registered by filing with the Commission an application for registration in such form and containing such of the following information and documents as the Commission, by rule, may prescribe as necessary or appropriate in the public interest or for the protection of investors:

(A) the name and form of organization under which the investment adviser engages or intends to engage in business; the name of the State or other sovereign power under which such investment adviser is organized; the location of his or its principal office or place of business and branch offices, if any; the names and addresses of his or its partners, officers, directors, and persons performing similar functions or, if such an investment adviser be an individual, of such individual; and the number of his or its employees;

(B) the education, the business affiliations for the past ten years, and the present business affiliations of such investment adviser and of his or its partners, officers, directors, and persons performing similar functions and of any controlling person thereof;

(C) the nature of the business of such investment adviser, including the manner of giving advice and rendering analyses or reports;

(D) a balance sheet certified by an independent public accountant and other financial statements (which shall, as the Commission specifies, be certified);

(E) the nature and scope of the authority of such investment adviser with respect to clients' funds and accounts;

(F) the basis or bases upon which such investment adviser is compensated;

(G) whether such investment adviser, or any person associated with such investment adviser, is subject to any disqualification which would be a basis for denial, suspension, or revocation of registration of such investment adviser under the provisions of subsection (e) of this section; and

(H) a statement as to whether the principal business of such investment adviser consists or is to consist of acting as investment adviser and a statement as to whether a substantial part of the business of such investment adviser, consists or is to consist of rendering investment supervisory services.

(2) Within forty-five days of the date of the filing of such application (or within such longer period as to which the applicant consents) the Commission shall—

(A) by order grant such registration; or

(B) institute proceedings to determine whether registration should be denied. Such proceedings shall include notice of the grounds for denial under consideration and opportunity for hearing and shall be concluded within one hundred twenty days of the date of the filing of the application for registration. At the conclusion of such proceedings the Commission, by order, shall grant or deny such registration. The Commission may extend the time for conclusion of such proceedings for up to ninety days if it finds good cause for such extension and publishes its reasons for so finding or for such longer period as to which the applicant consents.

The Commission shall grant such registration if the Commission finds that the requirements of this section are satisfied and that the applicant is not prohibited from registering as an investment advisor under section 203A of this Act. The Commission shall deny such registration if it does not make such a finding or if it finds that if the applicant were so registered, its registration would be subject to suspension or revocation under subsection (e) of this section.

(d) Other acts prohibited by subchapter.—

Any provision of this Act (other than subsection (a) of this section) which prohibits any act, practice, or course of business if the mails or any means or instrumentality of interstate commerce are used in connection therewith shall also prohibit any such act, practice, or course of business by any investment adviser registered pursuant to this section or any person acting on behalf of such an investment adviser, irrespective of any use of the mails or any means or instrumentality of interstate commerce in connection therewith.

(e) Censure, denial, or suspension of registration; notice and hearing.—

The Commission, by order, shall censure, place limitations on the activities, functions, or operations of, suspend for a period not exceeding twelve months, or revoke the registration of any investment adviser if it finds, on the record after notice and opportunity for hearing, that such censure, placing of limitations, suspension, or revocation is in the public interest and that such investment adviser, or any person associated with such investment adviser, whether prior to or subsequent to becoming so associated—

(1) has willfully made or caused to be made in any application for registration or report required to be filed with the Commission under this Act, or in any proceeding before the Commission with respect to registration, any statement which was at the time and in the light of the circumstances under which it was made false or misleading with respect to any material fact, or has omitted to state in any such application or report any material fact which is required to be stated therein.

(2) has been convicted within ten years preceding the filing of any application for registration or at any time thereafter of any felony or misdemeanor or of a substantially equivalent crime by a foreign court of competent jurisdiction which the Commission finds—

(A) involves the purchase or sale of any security, the taking of a false oath, the making of a false report, bribery, perjury, burglary, any substantially equivalent activity however denominated by the laws of the relevant foreign government, or conspiracy to commit any such offense;

(B) arises out of the conduct of the business of a broker, dealer, municipal securities dealer, investment adviser, bank, insurance company, government securities broker, government securities dealer, fiduciary, transfer agent, credit rating agency, foreign person performing a function substantially equivalent to any of the above, or entity or person required to be registered under the Commodity Exchange Act or any substantially equivalent statute or regulation;

(C) involves the larceny, theft, robbery, extortion, forgery, counterfeiting, fraudulent concealment, embezzlement, fraudulent conversion, or misappropriation of funds or securities or substantially equivalent activity however denominated by the laws of the relevant foreign government; or

(D) involves the violation of section 152, 1341, 1342, or 1343 or chapter 25 or 47 of Title 18, or a violation of substantially equivalent foreign statute.

(3) has been convicted during the 10-year period preceding the date of filing of any application for registration, or at any time thereafter, of—

(A) any crime that is punishable by imprisonment for 1 or more years, and that is not described in paragraph (2); or

(B) a substantially equivalent crime by a foreign court of competent jurisdiction.

(4) is permanently or temporarily enjoined by order, judgment, or decree of any court of competent jurisdiction, including any foreign court of competent jurisdiction, from acting as an investment adviser, underwriter, broker, dealer, municipal securities dealer, government securities broker, government securities dealer, transfer agent, credit rating agency, foreign person performing a function substantially equivalent to any of the above, or entity or person required to be registered under the Commodity Exchange Act or any substantially equivalent statute or regulation, or as an affiliated person or employee of any investment company, bank, insurance company, foreign entity substantially equivalent to any of the above, or entity or person required to be registered under the Commodity Exchange Act or any substantially equivalent statute or regulation, or from engaging in or continuing any conduct or practice in connection with any such activity, or in connection with the purchase or sale of any security.

(5) has willfully violated any provision of the Securities Act of 1933, the Securities Exchange Act of 1934, the Investment Company Act of 1940, this Act, the Commodity Exchange Act, or the rules or regulations under any such statutes or any rule of the Municipal Securities Rulemaking Board, or is unable to comply with any such provision.

(6) has willfully aided, abetted, counseled, commanded, induced, or procured the violation by any other person of any provision of the Securities Act of 1933, the Securities Exchange Act of 1934, the Investment Company Act of 1940, this Act, the Commodity Exchange Act, the rules or regulations under any of such statutes, or the rules of the Municipal Securities Rulemaking Board, or has failed reasonably to supervise, with a view to preventing violations of the provisions of such statutes, rules, and regulations, another person who commits such a violation, if such other person is subject to his supervision. For the purposes of this paragraph no person shall be deemed to have failed reasonably to supervise any person, if—

(A) there have been established procedures, and a system for applying such procedures, which would reasonably be expected to prevent and detect, insofar as practicable, any such violation by such other person, and

(B) such person has reasonably discharged the duties and obligations incumbent upon him by reason of such procedures and system without reasonable cause to believe that such procedures and system were not being complied with.

(7) is subject to any order of the Commission barring or suspending the right of the person to be associated with an investment adviser;

(8) has been found by a foreign financial regulatory authority to have—

(A) made or caused to be made in any application for registration or report required to be filed with a foreign securities authority, or in any proceeding before a foreign securities authority with respect to registration, any statement that was at the time and in light of the circumstances under which it was made false or misleading with respect to any material fact, or has omitted to state in any application or report to a foreign securities authority any material fact that is required to be stated therein;

    (B) violated any foreign statute or regulation regarding transactions in securities or contracts of sale of a commodity for future delivery traded on or subject to the rules of a contract market or any board of trade; or

    (C) aided, abetted, counseled, commanded, induced, or procured the violation by any other person of any foreign statute or regulation regarding transactions in securities or contracts of sale of a commodity for future delivery traded on or subject to the rules of a contract market or any board of trade, or has been found, by the foreign financial regulatory authority, to have failed reasonably to supervise, with a view to preventing violations of statutory provisions, and rules and regulations promulgated thereunder, another person who commits such a violation, if such other person is subject to his supervision; or

    (9) is subject to any final order of a State securities commission (or any agency or officer performing like functions), State authority that supervises or examines banks, savings associations, or credit unions, State insurance commission (or any agency or office performing like functions), an appropriate Federal banking agency (as defined in section 3 of the Federal Deposit Insurance Act (12 U.S.C. § 1813(q))), or the National Credit Union Administration, that—

    (A) bars such person from association with an entity regulated by such commission, authority, agency, or officer, or from engaging in the business of securities, insurance, banking, savings association activities, or credit union activities; or

    (B) constitutes a final order based on violations of any laws or regulations that prohibit fraudulent, manipulative, or deceptive conduct.

(f)   Bar or suspension from association with investment adviser; notice and hearing.—

The Commission, by order, shall censure or place limitations on the activities of any person associated, seeking to become associated, or, at the time of the alleged misconduct, associated or seeking to become associated with an investment adviser, or suspend for a period not exceeding 12 months or bar any such person from being associated with an investment adviser, broker, dealer, investment adviser, municipal securities dealer, municipal advisor, or nationally recognized statistical rating organization, if the Commission finds, on the record after notice and opportunity for hearing, that such censure, placing of limitations, suspension, or bar is in the public interest and that such person has committed or omitted any act or omission enumerated in paragraph (1), (5), (6), (8) or (9) of subsection (e) of this section or has been convicted of any offense specified in paragraph (2) or (3) of subsection (e) within ten years of the commencement of the proceedings under this subsection, or is enjoined from any action, conduct, or practice specified in paragraph (4) of subsection (e). It shall be unlawful for any person as to whom such an order suspending or barring him from being associated with an investment adviser is in effect willfully to become, or to be, associated with an investment adviser without the consent of the Commission, and it shall be unlawful for any investment adviser to permit such a person to become, or remain, a person associated with him without the consent of the Commission, if such investment adviser knew, or in the exercise of reasonable care, should have known, of such order.

(g)   Registration of successor to business of investment adviser.—

Any successor to the business of an investment adviser registered under this section shall be deemed likewise registered hereunder, if within thirty days from its succession to such business it shall file an application for registration under this section, unless and until the Commission, pursuant to subsection (c) or subsection (e) of this section, shall deny registration to or revoke or suspend the registration of such successor.

(h)   Withdrawal of registration.—

Any person registered under this section may, upon such terms and conditions as the commission finds necessary in the public interest or for the protection of investors, withdraw from registration by filing a written notice of withdrawal with the Commission. If the Commission finds that any person registered under this section, or who has pending an application for registration filed under this section, is no longer in existence, is not engaged in business as an investment adviser or is prohibited from registering as an investment adviser under section 203A of this Act, the Commission shall by order cancel the registration of such person.

(i)   Money penalties in administrative proceedings.—

(1) Authority of commission.—

(A) In general.—

In any proceeding instituted pursuant to subsection (e) or (f) against any person, the Commission may impose a civil penalty if it finds, on the record after notice and opportunity for hearing, that such penalty is in the public interest and that such person—

(i) has willfully violated any provision of the Securities Act of 1933, the Securities Exchange Act of 1934, the Investment Company Act of 1940, or this Act, or the rules or regulations thereunder;

(ii) has willfully aided, abetted, counseled, commanded, induced, or procured such a violation by any other person;

(iii) has willfully made or caused to be made in any application for registration or report required to be filed with the Commission under this Act, or in any proceeding before the Commission with respect to registration, any statement which was, at the time and in the light of the circumstances under which it was made, false or misleading with respect to any material fact, or has omitted to state in any such application or report any material fact which was required to be stated therein; or

(iv) has failed reasonably to supervise, within the meaning of subsection (e)(6), with a view to preventing violations of the provisions of this Act and the rules and regulations thereunder, another person who commits such a violation, if such other person is subject to his supervision; and that such penalty is in the public interest.

(B) Cease-and-desist proceedings.—

In any proceeding instituted pursuant to subsection (k) against any person, the Commission may impose a civil penalty if the Commission finds, on the record, after notice and opportunity for hearing, that such person—

(i) is violating or has violated any provision of this title, or any rule or regulation issued under this title; or

(ii) is or was a cause of the violation of any provision of this title, or any rule or regulation issued under this title.

(2) Maximum amount of penalty.—

(A) First tier.—

The maximum amount of penalty for each act or omission described in paragraph (1) shall be $5,000 for a natural person or $50,000 for any other person.

(B) Second tier.—

Notwithstanding subparagraph (A), the maximum amount of penalty for each such act or omission shall be $50,000 for a natural person or $250,000 for any other person if the act or omission described in paragraph (1) involved fraud, deceit, manipulation, or deliberate or reckless disregard of a regulatory requirement.

(C) Third tier.—

Notwithstanding subparagraphs (A) and (B), the maximum amount of penalty for each such act or omission shall be $100,000 for a natural person or $500,000 for any other person if—

(i) the act or omission described in paragraph (1) involved fraud, deceit, manipulation, or deliberate or reckless disregard of a regulatory requirement; and

(ii) such act or omission directly or indirectly resulted in substantial losses or created a significant risk of substantial losses to other persons or resulted in substantial pecuniary gain to the person who committed the act or omission.

(3) Determination of public interest.—

In considering under this section whether a penalty is in the public interest, the Commission may consider—

    (A) whether the act or omission for which such penalty is assessed involved fraud, deceit, manipulation, or deliberate or reckless disregard of a regulatory requirement;

    (B) the harm to other persons resulting either directly or indirectly from such act or omission;

    (C) the extent to which any person was unjustly enriched, taking into account any restitution made to persons injured by such behavior;

    (D) whether such person previously has been found by the Commission, another appropriate regulatory agency, or a self-regulatory organization to have violated the Federal securities laws, State securities laws, or the rules of a self-regulatory organization, has been enjoined by a court of competent jurisdiction from violations of such laws or rules, or has been convicted by a court of competent jurisdiction of violations of such laws or of any felony or misdemeanor described in subsection (e)(2) of this section;

    (E) the need to deter such person and other persons from committing such acts or omissions; and

    (F) such other matters as justice may require.

    (4) Evidence concerning ability to pay.—

In any proceeding in which the Commission may impose a penalty under this section, a respondent may present evidence of the respondent's ability to pay such penalty. The Commission may, in its discretion, consider such evidence in determining whether such penalty is in the public interest. Such evidence may relate to the extent of such person's ability to continue in business and the collectability of a penalty, taking into account any other claims of the United States or third parties upon such person's assets and the amount of such person's assets.

    (j) Authority to enter order requiring accounting and disgorgement.—

In any proceeding in which the Commission may impose a penalty under this section, the Commission may enter an order requiring accounting and disgorgement, including reasonable interest. The Commission is authorized to adopt rules, regulations, and orders concerning payments to investors, rates of interest, periods of accrual, and such other matters as it deems appropriate to implement this subsection.

    (k) Cease-and-desist proceedings.—

    (1) Authority of Commission.—

If the Commission finds, after notice and opportunity for hearing, that any person is violating, has violated, or is about to violate any provision of this Act, or any rule or regulation thereunder, the Commission may publish its findings and enter an order requiring such person, and any other person that is, was, or would be a cause of the violation, due to an act or omission the person knew or should have known would contribute to such violation, to cease and desist from committing or causing such violation and any future violation of the same provision, rule, or regulation. Such order may, in addition to requiring a person to cease and desist from committing or causing a violation, require such person to comply, or to take steps to effect compliance, with such provision, rule, or regulation, upon such terms and conditions and within such time as the Commission may specify in such order. Any such order may, as the Commission deems appropriate, require future compliance or steps to effect future compliance, either permanently or for such period of time as the Commission may specify, with such provision, rule, or regulation with respect to any security, any issuer, or any other person.

    (2) Hearing.—

The notice instituting proceedings pursuant to paragraph (1) shall fix a hearing date not earlier than 30 days nor later than 60 days after service of the notice unless an earlier or a later date is set by the Commission with the consent of any respondent so served.

(3)   Temporary order.—

(A)   In general.—

Whenever the Commission determines that the alleged violation or threatened violation specified in the notice instituting proceedings pursuant to paragraph (1), or the continuation thereof, is likely to result in significant dissipation or conversion of assets, significant harm to investors, or substantial harm to the public interest, including, but not limited to, losses to the Securities Investor Protection Corporation, prior to the completion of the proceedings, the Commission may enter a temporary order requiring the respondent to cease and desist from the violation or threatened violation and to take such action to prevent the violation or threatened violation and to prevent dissipation or conversion of assets, significant harm to investors, or substantial harm to the public interest as the Commission deems appropriate pending completion of such proceedings. Such an order shall be entered only after notice and opportunity for a hearing, unless the Commission, notwithstanding section 211(c) of this Act, determines that notice and hearing prior to entry would be impracticable or contrary to the public interest. A temporary order shall become effective upon service upon the respondent and, unless set aside, limited, or suspended by the Commission or a court of competent jurisdiction, shall remain effective and enforceable pending the completion of the proceedings.

(B)   Applicability.—

This paragraph shall apply only to a respondent that acts, or, at the time of the alleged misconduct acted, as a broker, dealer, investment adviser, investment company, municipal securities dealer, government securities broker, government securities dealer, or transfer agent, or is, or was at the time of the alleged misconduct, an associated person of, or a person seeking to become associated with, any of the foregoing.

(4)   Review of temporary orders.—

(A)   Commission review.—

At any time after the respondent has been served with a temporary cease-and-desist order pursuant to paragraph (3), the respondent may apply to the Commission to have the order set aside, limited, or suspended. If the respondent has been served with a temporary cease-and-desist order entered without a prior Commission hearing, the respondent may, within 10 days after the date on which the order was served, request a hearing on such application and the Commission shall hold a hearing and render a decision on such application at the earliest possible time.

(B)   Judicial review.—

Within.—

(i)   10 days after the date the respondent was served with a temporary cease-and-desist order entered with a prior Commission hearing, or

(ii)   10 days after the Commission renders a decision on an application and hearing under subparagraph (A), with respect to any temporary cease-and-desist order entered without a prior Commission hearing,

the respondent may apply to the United States district court for the district in which the respondent resides or has its principal place of business, or for the District of Columbia, for an order setting aside, limiting, or suspending the effectiveness or enforcement of the order, and the court shall have jurisdiction to enter such an order. A respondent served with a temporary cease-and-desist order entered without a prior Commission hearing may not apply to the court except after hearing and decision by the Commission on the respondent's application under subparagraph (A) of this paragraph.

(C)   No automatic stay of temporary order.—

The commencement of proceedings under subparagraph (B) of this paragraph shall not, unless specifically ordered by the court, operate as a stay of the Commission's order.

(D) Exclusive review.—

Section 213 of this Act shall not apply to a temporary order entered pursuant to this section.

(5) Authority to enter order requiring accounting and disgorgement.—

In any cease-and-desist proceeding under paragraph (1), the Commission may enter an order requiring accounting and disgorgement, including reasonable interest. The Commission is authorized to adopt rules, regulations, and orders concerning payments to investors, rates of interest, periods of accrual, and such other matters as it deems appropriate to implement this subsection.

(*l*) Exemption of venture capital fund advisers.—

(1) In general

No investment adviser that acts as an investment adviser solely to 1 or more venture capital funds shall be subject to the registration requirements of this title with respect to the provision of investment advice relating to a venture capital fund. Not later than 1 year after the date of enactment of this subsection, the Commission shall issue final rules to define the term 'venture capital fund' for purposes of this subsection. The Commission shall require such advisers to maintain such records and provide to the Commission such annual or other reports as the Commission determines necessary or appropriate in the public interest or for the protection of investors.

(2) Advisers of SBICS.—

For purposes of this subsection, a venture capital fund includes an entity described in subparagraph (A), (B), or (C) of subsection (b)(7) (other than an entity that has elected to be regulated or is regulated as a business development company pursuant to section 53 of the Investment Company Act of 1940).

(3) Advisers of RBICS

For purposes of this subsection, a venture capital fund includes an entity described in subparagraph (A) or (B) of subsection (b)(8) (other than an entity that has elected to be regulated as a business development company pursuant section 53 of the Investment Company Act of 1940).

(m) Exemption of and reporting by certain private fund advisers.—

(1) In general.—

The Commission shall provide an exemption from the registration requirements under this section to any investment adviser of private funds, if each of such investment adviser acts solely as an adviser to private funds and has assets under management in the United States of less than $150,000,000.

(2) Reporting.—

The Commission shall require investment advisers exempted by reason of this subsection to maintain such records and provide to the Commission such annual or other reports as the Commission determines necessary or appropriate in the public interest or for the protection of investors.

(3) Advisers of SBICS.—

For purposes of this subsection, the assets under management of a private fund that is an entity described in subparagraph (A), (B), or (C) of subsection (b)(7) (other than an entity that has elected to be regulated or is regulated as a business development company pursuant to section 53 of the Investment Company Act of 1940) shall be excluded from the limit set forth in paragraph (1).

(4) Advisers of RBICS

For purposes of this subsection, the assets under management of a private fund that is an entity described in subparagraph (A) or (B) of subsection (b)(8) (other than an entity that has elected to be regulated or is regulated as a business development company pursuant to section 53 of the Investment Company Act of 1940) shall be excluded from the limit set forth in paragraph (1).

(n) Registration and examination of mid-sized private fund advisers.—

Registration and Examination of Mid-Sized Private Fund Advisers—In prescribing regulations to carry out the requirements of this section with respect to investment advisers acting as investment advisers to mid-sized private funds, the Commission shall take into account the size, governance, and investment strategy of such funds to determine whether they pose systemic risk, and shall provide for registration and examination procedures with respect to the investment advisers of such funds which reflect the level of systemic risk posed by such funds.

Advisers Subject to State Authorities

Sec. 203A.   (a)   Advisers subject to State authorities.—

(1)   In general.—

No investment adviser that is regulated or required to be regulated as an investment adviser in the State in which it maintains its principal office and place of business shall register under section 203, unless the investment adviser—

(A)   has assets under management of not less than $25,000,000, or such higher amount as the Commission may, by rule, deem appropriate in accordance with the purposes of this title; or

(B)   is an adviser to an investment company registered under the Investment Company Act.

(2)   Treatment of mid-sized investment advisers.—

(A)   In general.—

No investment adviser described in subparagraph (B) shall register under section 203, unless the investment adviser is an adviser to an investment company registered under the Investment Company Act of 1940, or a company which has elected to be a business development company pursuant to section 54 of the Investment Company Act of 1940, and has not withdrawn the election, except that, if by effect of this paragraph an investment adviser would be required to register with 15 or more States, then the adviser may register under section 203.

(B)   Covered persons.—

An investment adviser described in this subparagraph is an investment adviser that—

(i)   is required to be registered as an investment adviser with the securities commissioner (or any agency or office performing like functions) of the State in which it maintains its principal office and place of business and, if registered, would be subject to examination as an investment adviser by any such commissioner, agency, or office; and

(ii)   has assets under management between—

(I)   the amount specified under subparagraph (A) of paragraph (1), as such amount may have been adjusted by the Commission pursuant to that subparagraph; and

(II) $100,000,000, or such higher amount as the Commission may, by rule, deem appropriate in accordance with the purposes of this title.

(3)   Definition.—

For purposes of this subsection, the term "assets under management" means the securities portfolios with respect to which an investment adviser provides continuous and regular supervisory or management services.

(b)   Advisers subject to Commission authority.—

(1)   In general.—

No law of any State or political subdivision thereof requiring the registration, licensing, or qualification as an investment adviser or supervised person of an investment adviser shall apply to any person—

(A)   that is registered under section 203 as an investment adviser, or that is a supervised person of such person, except that a State may license, register, or otherwise qualify any investment adviser representative who has a place of business located within that State;

(B)   that is not registered under section 203 because that person is excepted from the definition of an investment adviser under section 202(a)(11); or

(C)   that is not registered under section 203 because that person is exempt from registration as provided in subsection (b)(7) of such section, or is a supervised person of such person; or

(D)   that is not registered under section 203 of this Act because that person is exempt from registration as provided in subsection (b)(8) of such section, or is a supervised person of such person.

(2)   Limitation.—

Nothing in this subsection shall prohibit the securities commission (or any agency or office performing like functions) of any State from investigating and bringing enforcement actions with respect to fraud or deceit against an investment adviser or person associated with an investment adviser.

(c)   Exemptions.—

Notwithstanding subsection (a), the Commission, by rule or regulation upon its own motion, or by order upon application, may permit the registration with the Commission of any person or class of persons to which the application of subsection (a) would be unfair, a burden on interstate commerce, or otherwise inconsistent with the purposes of this section.

(d)   State assistance.—

Upon request of the securities commissioner (or any agency or officer performing like functions) of any State, the Commission may provide such training, technical assistance, or other reasonable assistance in connection with the regulation of investment advisers by the State.

Reports by Investment Advisers

Sec. 204.   (a)   In general.—

Every investment adviser who makes use of the mails or of any means or instrumentality of interstate commerce in connection with his or its business as an investment adviser (other than one specifically exempted from registration pursuant to section 203(b) of this Act), shall make and keep for prescribed periods such records (as defined in section 3(a)(37) of the Securities Exchange Act of 1934), furnish such copies thereof and make and disseminate such reports as the Commission, by rule, may prescribe as necessary or appropriate in the public interest or for the protection of investors. All records (as so defined) of such investment advisers are subject at any time, or from time to time, to such reasonable periodic, special, or other examinations by representatives of the Commission as the Commission deems necessary or appropriate in the public interest or for the protection of investors.

(b)   Records and reports of private funds.—

(1)   In general.—

The Commission may require any investment adviser registered under this title—

(A)   to maintain such records of, and file with the Commission such reports regarding, private funds advised by the investment adviser, as necessary and appropriate in the public interest and for the protection of investors, or for the assessment of systemic risk by the Financial Stability Oversight Council (in this subsection referred to as the 'Council'); and

(B)   to provide or make available to the Council those reports or records or the information contained therein.

(2)   Treatment of records.—

The records and reports of any private fund to which an investment adviser registered under this title provides investment advice shall be deemed to be the records and reports of the investment adviser.

(3) Required information.—

The records and reports required to be maintained by an investment adviser and subject to inspection by the Commission under this subsection shall include, for each private fund advised by the investment adviser, a description of—

(A) the amount of assets under management and use of leverage, including off-balance-sheet leverage;

(B) counterparty credit risk exposure;

(C) trading and investment positions;

(D) valuation policies and practices of the fund;

(E) types of assets held;

(F) side arrangements or side letters, whereby certain investors in a fund obtain more favorable rights or entitlements than other investors;

(G) trading practices; and

(H) such other information as the Commission, in consultation with the Council, determines is necessary and appropriate in the public interest and for the protection of investors or for the assessment of systemic risk, which may include the establishment of different reporting requirements for different classes of fund advisers, based on the type or size of private fund being advised.

(4) Maintenance of records.—

An investment adviser registered under this title shall maintain such records of private funds advised by the investment adviser for such period or periods as the Commission, by rule, may prescribe as necessary and appropriate in the public interest and for the protection of investors, or for the assessment of systemic risk.

(5) Filing of records.—

The Commission shall issue rules requiring each investment adviser to a private fund to file reports containing such information as the Commission deems necessary and appropriate in the public interest and for the protection of investors or for the assessment of systemic risk.

(6) Examination of records.—

(A) Periodic and special examinations.—

The Commission—

(i) shall conduct periodic inspections of the records of private funds maintained by an investment adviser registered under this title in accordance with a schedule established by the Commission; and

(ii) may conduct at any time and from time to time such additional, special, and other examinations as the Commission may prescribe as necessary and appropriate in the public interest and for the protection of investors, or for the assessment of systemic risk.

(B) Availability of records.—

An investment adviser registered under this title shall make available to the Commission any copies or extracts from such records as may be prepared without undue effort, expense, or delay, as the Commission or its representatives may reasonably request.

(7) Information sharing.—

(A) In general.—

The Commission shall make available to the Council copies of all reports, documents, records, and information filed with or provided to the Commission by an investment adviser under this subsection as the Council may consider necessary for the purpose of assessing the systemic risk posed by a private fund.

(B)   Confidentiality.—

The Council shall maintain the confidentiality of information received under this paragraph in all such reports, documents, records, and information, in a manner consistent with the level of confidentiality established for the Commission pursuant to paragraph (8). The Council shall be exempt from section 552 of title 5, United States Code, with respect to any information in any report, document, record, or information made available, to the Council under this subsection.'.

(8)   Commission confidentiality of reports.—

Notwithstanding any other provision of law, the Commission may not be compelled to disclose any report or information contained therein required to be filed with the Commission under this subsection, except that nothing in this subsection authorizes the Commission—

(A)   to withhold information from Congress, upon an agreement of confidentiality; or

(B)   prevent the Commission from complying with—

(i)   a request for information from any other Federal department or agency or any self-regulatory organization requesting the report or information for purposes within the scope of its jurisdiction; or

(ii)   an order of a court of the United States in an action brought by the United States or the Commission.

(9)   Other recipients confidentiality.—

Any department, agency, or self-regulatory organization that receives reports or information from the Commission under this subsection shall maintain the confidentiality of such reports, documents, records, and information in a manner consistent with the level of confidentiality established for the Commission under paragraph (8).

(10)   Public information exception.—

(A)   In general.—

The Commission, the Council, and any other department, agency, or self-regulatory organization that receives information, reports, documents, records, or information from the Commission under this subsection, shall be exempt from the provisions of section 552 of title 5, United States Code, with respect to any such report, document, record, or information. Any proprietary information of an investment adviser ascertained by the Commission from any report required to be filed with the Commission pursuant to this subsection shall be subject to the same limitations on public disclosure as any facts ascertained during an examination, as provided by section 210(b) of this title.

(B)   Proprietary information.—

For purposes of this paragraph, proprietary information includes sensitive, non-public information regarding—

(i)   the investment or trading strategies of the investment adviser;

(ii)   analytical or research methodologies;

(iii)   trading data;

(iv)   computer hardware or software containing intellectual property; and

(v)   any additional information that the Commission determines to be proprietary.

(11)   Annual report to Congress.—

The Commission shall report annually to Congress on how the Commission has used the data collected pursuant to this subsection to monitor the markets for the protection of investors and the integrity of the markets.

(c)   Filing depositories.—

The Commission may, by rule, require an investment adviser—

(1) to file with the Commission any fee, application, report, or notice required to be filed by this title or the rules issued under this title through any entity designated by the Commission for that purpose; and

(2) to pay the reasonable costs associated with such filing and the establishment and maintenance of the systems required by subsection (c).

(d) Access to disciplinary and other information.—

(1) Maintenance of system to respond to inquiries.—

(A) In general.—

The Commission shall require the entity designated by the Commission under subsection (b)(1) to establish and maintain a toll-free telephone listing, a readily accessible electronic or other process, to receive and promptly respond to inquiries regarding registration information (including disciplinary actions, regulatory, judicial, and arbitration proceedings, and other information required by law or rule to be reported) involving investment advisers and persons associated with investment advisers.

(B) Applicability.—

This subsection shall apply to any investment adviser (and the persons associated with that adviser), whether the investment adviser is registered with the Commission under section 203 or regulated solely by a State, as described in section 203A.

(2) Recovery of costs.—

An entity designated by the Commission under subsection (b)(1) may charge persons making inquiries, other than individual investors, reasonable fees for responses to inquiries described in paragraph (1).

(3) Limitation on liability.—

An entity designated by the Commission under subsection (b)(1) shall not have any liability to any person for any actions taken or omitted in good faith under this subsection.

(e) Records of Persons With Custody or Use—

(1) In general.—

Records of persons having custody or use of the securities, deposits, or credits of a client, that relate to such custody or use, are subject at any time, or from time to time, to such reasonable periodic, special, or other examinations and other information and document requests by representatives of the Commission, as the Commission deems necessary or appropriate in the public interest or for the protection of investors.

(2) Certain persons subject to other regulation.—

Any person that is subject to regulation and examination by a Federal financial institution regulatory agency (as such term is defined under section 212(c)(2) of title 18, United States Code) may satisfy any examination request, information request, or document request described under paragraph (1), by providing the Commission with a detailed listing, in writing, of the securities, deposits, or credits of the client within the custody or use of such person.

Prevention of Misuse of Nonpublic Information

Sec. 204A. Every investment adviser subject to section 204 of this Act shall establish, maintain, and enforce written policies and procedures reasonably designed, taking into consideration the nature of such investment adviser's business, to prevent the misuse in violation of this Act or the Securities Exchange Act of 1934, or the rules or regulations thereunder, of material, nonpublic information by such investment adviser or any person associated with such investment adviser. The Commission, as it deems necessary or appropriate in the public interest or for the protection of investors, shall adopt rules or regulations to require specific policies or procedures reasonably designed to prevent misuse in violation of this Act or the Securities Exchange Act of 1934 (or the rules or regulations thereunder) of material, nonpublic information.

Investment Advisory Contracts

Sec. 205.   (a)   Compensation, assignment, and partnership-membership provisions.—

No investment adviser, registered or required to be registered with the Commission, shall enter into, extend, or renew any investment advisory contract, or in any way perform any investment advisory contract entered into, extended, or renewed on or after the effective date of this Act, if such contract—

(1)   provides for compensation to the investment adviser on the basis of a share of capital gains upon or capital appreciation of the funds or any portion of the funds of the client;

(2)   fails to provide, in substance, that no assignment of such contract shall be made by the investment adviser without the consent of the other party to the contract; or

(3)   fails to provide, in substance, that the investment adviser, if a partnership, will notify the other party to the contract of any change in the membership of such partnership within a reasonable time after such change.

(b)   Compensation prohibition inapplicable to certain compensation computations.—

Paragraph (1) of subsection (a) shall not—

(1)   be construed to prohibit an investment advisory contract which provides for compensation based upon the total value of a fund averaged over a definite period, or as of definite dates, or taken as of a definite date;

(2)   apply to an investment advisory contract with

(A)   an investment company registered under the Investment Company Act, or

(B)   any other person (except a trust, governmental plan, collective trust fund, or separate account referred to in section 3(c)(11) of the Investment Company Act), provided that the contract relates to the investment of assets in excess of $1 million,

if the contract provides for compensation based on the asset value of the company or fund under management averaged over a specified period and increasing and decreasing proportionately with the investment performance of the company or fund over a specified period in relation to the investment record of an appropriate index of securities prices or such other measure of investment performance as the Commission by rule, regulation, or order may specify;

(3)   apply with respect to any investment advisory contract between an investment adviser and a business development company, as defined in this Act, if

(A)   the compensation provided for in such contract does not exceed 20 per centum of the realized capital gains upon the funds of the business development company over a specified period or as of definite dates, computed net of all realized capital losses and unrealized capital depreciation, and the condition of section 80a–60(a)(4)(B)(iii) of the Investment Company Act is satisfied, and

(B)   the business development company does not have outstanding any option, warrant, or right issued pursuant to section 80a–60(a)(4)(B) of the Investment Company Act and does not have a profit-sharing plan described in section 56(n) of the Investment Company Act;

(4)   apply to an investment advisory contract with a company excepted from the definition of an investment company under section 3(c)(7) of the Investment Company Act; or

(5)   apply to an investment advisory contract with a person who is not a resident of the United States.

(c)   Measurement of changes in compensation.—

For purposes of paragraph (2) of subsection (b) of this section, the point from which increases and decreases in compensation are measured shall be the fee which is paid or earned when the investment performance of such company or fund is equivalent to that of the index or other measure of performance, and an index of securities prices shall be deemed appropriate unless the Commission by order shall determine otherwise.

(d)   "Investment advisory contract" defined.—

As used in paragraphs (2) and (3) of subsection (a) of this section, "investment advisory contract" means any contract or agreement whereby a person agrees to act as investment adviser to or to manage any investment or trading account of another person other than an investment company registered under the Investment Company Act.

(e)   Exempt persons and transactions.—

The Commission, by rule or regulation, upon its own motion, or by order upon application, may conditionally or unconditionally exempt any person or transaction, or any class or classes of persons or transactions, from subsection (a)(1) of this section, if and to the extent that the exemption relates to an investment advisory contract with any person that the Commission determines does not need the protections of subsection (a)(1) of this section, on the basis of such factors as financial sophistication, net worth, knowledge of and experience in financial matters, amount of assets under management, relationship with a registered investment adviser, and such other factors as the Commission determines are consistent with this section. With respect to any factor used in any rule or regulation by the Commission in making a determination under this subsection, if the Commission uses a dollar amount test in connection with such factor, such as a net asset threshold, the Commission shall, by order, not later than 1 year after the date of enactment of the Private Fund Investment Advisers Registration Act of 2010, and every 5 years thereafter, adjust for the effects of inflation on such test. Any such adjustment that is not a multiple of $100,000 shall be rounded to the nearest multiple of $100,000.

(f)   Authority to restrict mandatory pre-dispute arbitration.—

Authority to Restrict Mandatory Pre-dispute Arbitration—The Commission, by rule, may prohibit, or impose conditions or limitations on the use of, agreements that require customers or clients of any investment adviser to arbitrate any future dispute between them arising under the Federal securities laws, the rules and regulations thereunder, or the rules of a self-regulatory organization if it finds that such prohibition, imposition of conditions, or limitations are in the public interest and for the protection of investors.

Prohibited Transactions by Investment Advisers

Sec. 206.   It shall be unlawful for any investment adviser, by use of the mails or any means or instrumentality of interstate commerce, directly or indirectly—

(1)   to employ any device, scheme, or artifice to defraud any client or prospective client;

(2)   to engage in any transaction, practice, or course of business which operates as a fraud or deceit upon any client or prospective client;

(3)   acting as principal for his own account, knowingly to sell any security to or purchase any security from a client, or acting as broker for a person other than such client, knowingly to effect any sale or purchase of any security for the account of such client, without disclosing to such client in writing before the completion of such transaction the capacity in which he is acting and obtaining the consent of the client to such transaction. The prohibitions of this paragraph shall not apply to any transaction with a customer of a broker or dealer if such broker or dealer is not acting as an investment adviser in relation to such transaction; or

(4)   to engage in any act, practice, or course of business which is fraudulent, deceptive, or manipulative. The Commission shall, for the purposes of this paragraph (4) by rules and regulations define, and prescribe means reasonably designed to prevent, such acts, practices, and courses of business as are fraudulent, deceptive, or manipulative.

Exemptions

Sec. 206A.   The Commission, by rules and regulations, upon its own motion, or by order upon application, may conditionally or unconditionally exempt any person or transaction, or any class or classes of persons, or transactions, from any provision or provisions of this Act or of any rule or regulation thereunder, if and to the extent that such exemption is necessary or appropriate in the public interest and consistent with the protection of investors and the purposes fairly intended by the policy and provisions of this Act.

Material Misstatements

Sec. 207.   It shall be unlawful for any person willfully to make any untrue statement of a material fact in any registration application or report filed with the Commission under section 203 or 204 of this Act, or willfully to omit to state in any such application or report any material fact which is required to be stated therein.

General Prohibitions

Sec. 208.   (a)   Representations of sponsorship by United States or agency thereof.—

It shall be unlawful for any person registered under section 203 of this Act to represent or imply in any manner whatsoever that such person has been sponsored, recommended, or approved, or that his abilities or qualifications have in any respect been passed upon by the United States or any agency or any officer thereof.

(b)   Statement of registration under Securities Exchange Act of 1934 provisions.—

No provision of subsection (a) shall be construed to prohibit a statement that a person is registered under this Act or under the Securities Exchange Act of 1934, if such statement is true in fact and if the effect of such registration is not misrepresented.

(c)   Use of name "investment counsel" as descriptive of business.—

It shall be unlawful for any person registered under section 203 of this Act to represent that he is an investment counsel or to use the name "investment counsel" as descriptive of his business unless

     (1)   his or its principal business consists of acting as investment adviser, and

     (2)   a substantial part of his or its business consists of rendering investment supervisory services.

(d)   Use of indirect means to do prohibited act.—

It shall be unlawful for any person indirectly, or through or by any other person, to do any act or thing which it would be unlawful for such person to do directly under the provisions of this Act or any rule or regulation thereunder.

Enforcement of Act

Sec. 209.   (a)   Investigation.—

Whenever it shall appear to the Commission, either upon complaint or otherwise, that the provisions of this Act or of any rule or regulation prescribed under the authority thereof, have been or are about to be violated by any person, it may in its discretion require, and in any event shall permit, such person to file with it a statement in writing, under oath or otherwise, as to all the facts and circumstances relevant to such violation, and may otherwise investigate all such facts and circumstances.

(b)   Administration of oaths and affirmations, subpena of witnesses, etc.—

For the purposes of any investigation or any proceeding under this Act, any member of the Commission or any officer thereof designated by it is empowered to administer oaths and affirmations, subpena witnesses, compel their attendance, take evidence, and require the production of any books, papers, correspondence, memoranda, contracts, agreements, or other records which are relevant or material to the inquiry. Such attendance of witnesses and the production of any such records may be required from any place in any State or in any Territory or other place subject to the jurisdiction of the United States at any designated place of hearing.

(c)   Jurisdiction of courts of United States.—

In case of contumacy by, or refusal to obey a subpena issued to, any person, the Commission may invoke the aid of any court of the United States within the jurisdiction of which such investigation or proceeding is carried on, or where such person resides or carries on business, in requiring the attendance and testimony of witnesses and the production of books, papers, correspondence, memoranda, contracts, agreements, and other records. And such court may issue an order requiring such person to appear before the Commission or member or officer designated by the Commission, there to produce records, if so ordered, or to give testimony touching the matter under investigation or in question; and any failure to obey such order of the court may be punished by such court as a contempt thereof. All process in any such case may be served in the judicial district whereof such person is an inhabitant or wherever he may be found. Any person who without just cause shall fail or refuse to attend and testify or to answer any lawful inquiry or to produce books, papers, correspondence, memoranda, contracts, agreements, or other records, if in his or its power so to do, in obedience to the subpena of the Commission, shall be guilty of a misdemeanor, and upon conviction shall be subject to a fine of not more than $1,000 or to imprisonment for a term of not more than one year, or both.

(d) Action for injunction.—

Whenever it shall appear to the Commission that any person has engaged, is engaged, or is about to engage in any act or practice constituting a violation of any provision of this Act, or of any rule, regulation, or order hereunder, or that any person has aided, abetted, counseled, commanded, induced, or procured, is aiding, abetting, counseling, commanding, inducing, or procuring, or is about to aid, abet, counsel, command, induce, or procure such a violation, it may in its discretion bring an action in the proper district court of the United States, or the proper United States court of any Territory or other place subject to the jurisdiction of the United States, to enjoin such acts or practices and to enforce compliance with this title or any rule, regulation, or order hereunder. Upon a showing that such person has engaged, is engaged, or is about to engage in any such act or practice, or in aiding, abetting, counseling, commanding, inducing, or procuring any such act or practice, a permanent or temporary injunction or decree or restraining order shall be granted without bond. The Commission may transmit such evidence as may be available concerning any violation of the provisions of this subchapter, or of any rule, regulation, or order thereunder, to the Attorney General, who, in his discretion, may institute the appropriate criminal proceedings under this Act.

(e) Money penalties in civil actions.—

(1) Authority of Commission.—

Whenever it shall appear to the Commission that any person has violated any provision of this Act, the rules or regulations thereunder, or a cease-and-desist order entered by the Commission pursuant to section 203(k) of this Act, the Commission may bring an action in a United States district court to seek, and the court shall have jurisdiction to impose, upon a proper showing, a civil penalty to be paid by the person who committed such violation.

(2) Amount of penalty.—

(A) First tier.—

The amount of the penalty shall be determined by the court in light of the facts and circumstances. For each violation, the amount of the penalty shall not exceed the greater of

    (i) $5,000 for a natural person or $50,000 for any other person, or

    (ii) the gross amount of pecuniary gain to such defendant as a result of the violation.

(B) Second tier.—

Notwithstanding subparagraph (A), the amount of penalty for each such violation shall not exceed the greater of

    (i) $50,000 for a natural person or $250,000 for any other person, or

    (ii) the gross amount of pecuniary gain to such defendant as a result of the violation, if the violation described in paragraph (1) involved fraud, deceit, manipulation, or deliberate or reckless disregard of a regulatory requirement.

(C) Third tier.—

Notwithstanding subparagraphs (A) and (B), the amount of penalty for each such violation shall not exceed the greater of

     (i) $100,000 for a natural person or $500,000 for any other person, or

     (ii)   the gross amount of pecuniary gain to such defendant as a result of the violation, if—

         (I)   the violation described in paragraph (1) involved fraud, deceit, manipulation, or deliberate or reckless disregard of a regulatory requirement; and

         (II)   such violation directly or indirectly resulted in substantial losses or created a significant risk of substantial losses to other persons.

    (3)   Procedures for collection.—

    (A)   Payment of penalty to treasury.—

A penalty imposed under this section shall be payable into the Treasury of the United States, except as otherwise provided in section 7246 of the Sarbanes-Oxley Act of 2002 and section 21F of the Securities Exchange Act of 1934.

    (B)   Collection of penalties.—

If a person upon whom such a penalty is imposed shall fail to pay such penalty within the time prescribed in the court's order, the Commission may refer the matter to the Attorney General who shall recover such penalty by action in the appropriate United States district court.

    (C)   Remedy not exclusive.—

The actions authorized by this subsection may be brought in addition to any other action that the Commission or the Attorney General is entitled to bring.

    (D)   Jurisdiction and venue.—

For purposes of section 214 of this Act, actions under this paragraph shall be actions to enforce a liability or a duty created by this Act.

    (4)   Special provisions relating to violation of cease-and-desist order.—

In an action to enforce a cease-and-desist order entered by the Commission pursuant to section 203(k) of this Act, each separate violation of such order shall be a separate offense, except that in the case of a violation through a continuing failure to comply with the order, each day of the failure to comply shall be deemed a separate offense.

  (f)   Aiding and abetting.—

Aiding and Abetting—For purposes of any action brought by the Commission under subsection (e), any person that knowingly or recklessly has aided, abetted, counseled, commanded, induced, or procured a violation of any provision of this Act, or of any rule, regulation, or order hereunder, shall be deemed to be in violation of such provision, rule, regulation, or order to the same extent as the person that committed such violation.

Disclosure of Information by Commission

Sec. 210.   (a)   Information available to public.—

The information contained in any registration application or report or amendment thereto filed with the Commission pursuant to any provision of this Act shall be made available to the public, unless and except insofar as the Commission, by rules and regulations upon its own motion, or by order upon application, finds that public disclosure is neither necessary nor appropriate in the public interest or for the protection of investors. Photostatic or other copies of information contained in documents filed with the Commission under this Act and made available to the public shall be furnished to any person at such reasonable charge and under such reasonable limitations as the Commission shall prescribe.

  (b)   Disclosure of fact of examination or investigation; exceptions.—

Subject to the provisions of subsections (c) and (d) of section 209 of this Act, and section 24(c) of the Securities Exchange Act of 1934, the Commission, or any member, officer, or employee thereof, shall not make public the fact that any examination or investigation under this Act is being conducted, or the results of or any facts ascertained during any such examination or investigation; and no member, officer, or employee of the Commission shall disclose to any person other than a member, officer, or employee of the Commission any information obtained as a result of any such examination or investigation except with the approval of the Commission. The provisions of this subsection shall not apply—

(1)   in the case of any hearing which is public under the provisions of section 212 of this Act; or

(2)   in the case of a resolution or request from either House of Congress.

(c)   Disclosure by investment advisor of identity of clients.—

No provision of this Act shall be construed to require, or to authorize the Commission to require any investment adviser engaged in rendering investment supervisory services to disclose the identity, investments, or affairs of any client of such investment adviser, except insofar as such disclosure may be necessary or appropriate in a particular proceeding or investigation having as its object the enforcement of a provision or provisions of this Act or for purposes of assessment of potential systemic risk.

Consultation

Sec. 210A.   (a)   Examination results and other information.—

(1)   The appropriate Federal banking agency shall provide the Commission upon request the results of any examination, reports, records, or other information to which such agency may have access—

(A)   with respect to the investment advisory activities of any

(i)   bank holding company or savings and loan holding company;

(ii)   bank; or

(iii)   separately identifiable department or division of a bank, that is registered under section 203 of this Act; and

(B)   in the case of a bank holding company or savings and loan holding company or bank that has a subsidiary or a separately identifiable department or division registered under that section, with respect to the investment advisory activities of such bank or bank holding company or savings and loan holding company.

(2)   The Commission shall provide to the appropriate Federal banking agency upon request the results of any information with respect to the investment advisory activities of any bank holding company or savings and loan holding company, bank, or separately identifiable department or division of a bank, which is registered under section 203 of this Act.

(3)   Notwithstanding any other provision of law, the Commission and the appropriate Federal banking agencies shall not be compelled to disclose any information provided under paragraph (1) or (2). Nothing in this paragraph shall authorize the Commission or such agencies to withhold information from Congress, or prevent the Commission or such agencies from complying with a request for information from any other Federal department or agency or any self-regulatory organization requesting the information for purposes within the scope of its jurisdiction, or complying with an order of a court of the United States in an action brought by the United States, the Commission, or such agencies. For purposes of section 552 of Title 5, United States Code, this paragraph shall be considered a statute described in subsection (b)(3)(B) of such section 552.

(b)   Effect on authority.—

Nothing in this section shall limit in any respect the authority of the appropriate Federal banking agency with respect to such bank holding company or savings and loan holding company (or affiliates or subsidiaries thereof), bank, or subsidiary, department, or division or a bank under any other provision of law.

(c)   Definition.—

For purposes of this section, the term "appropriate Federal banking agency" shall have the same meaning as given in section 1813 of Title 12, United States Code.

Rules, Regulations, and Orders of Commission

Sec. 211.   (a)   Power of Commission.—

The Commission shall have authority from time to time to make, issue, amend, and rescind such rules and regulations and such orders as are necessary or appropriate to the exercise of the functions and powers conferred upon the Commission elsewhere in this subchapter. For the purposes of its rules or regulations the Commission may classify persons and matters within its jurisdiction and prescribe different requirements for different classes of persons or matters, including rules and regulations defining technical, trade, and other terms used in this title, except that the Commission may not define the term 'client' for purposes of paragraphs (1) and (2) of section 206 to include an investor in a private fund managed by an investment adviser, if such private fund has entered into an advisory contract with such adviser.

(b)   Effective date of regulations.—

Subject to the provisions of chapter 15 of title 44, United States Code, and regulations prescribed under the authority thereof, the rules and regulations of the Commission under this Act, and amendments thereof, shall be effective upon publication in the manner which the Commission shall prescribe, or upon such later date as may be provided in such rules and regulations.

(c)   Orders of Commission after notice and hearing; type of notice.—

Orders of the Commission under this Act shall be issued only after appropriate notice and opportunity for hearing. Notice to the parties to a proceeding before the Commission shall be given by personal service upon each party or by registered mail or certified mail or confirmed telegraphic notice to the party's last known business address. Notice to interested persons, if any, other than parties may be given in the same manner or by publication in the Federal Register.

(d)   Good faith compliance with rules and regulations.—

No provision of this Act imposing any liability shall apply to any act done or omitted in good faith in conformity with any rule, regulation, or order of the Commission, notwithstanding that such rule, regulation, or order may, after such act or omission, be amended or rescinded or be determined by judicial or other authority to be invalid for any reason.

(e)   Disclosure Rules on Private Funds—The Commission and the Commodity Futures Trading Commission shall, after consultation with the Council but not later than 12 months after the date of enactment of the Private Fund Investment Advisers Registration Act of 2010, jointly promulgate rules to establish the form and content of the reports required to be filed with the Commission under subsection 204(b) and with the Commodity Futures Trading Commission by investment advisers that are registered both under this title and the Commodity Exchange Act (7 U.S.C. 1a et seq.).

(g)[15] Standard of conduct.—

(1)   In general.—

The Commission may promulgate rules to provide that the standard of conduct for all brokers, dealers, and investment advisers, when providing personalized investment advice about securities to retail customers (and such other customers as the Commission may by rule provide), shall be to act in the best interest of the customer without regard to the financial or other interest of the broker, dealer, or investment adviser providing the advice. In accordance with such rules, any material conflicts of interest shall be disclosed and may be consented to by the customer. Such rules shall provide that such standard of conduct shall be no less stringent than the standard applicable to investment advisers under section 206(1) and (2) of this title when providing personalized investment advice about securities, except the Commission shall not ascribe a meaning to the term "customer" that would include an investor in a private fund managed by an investment adviser, where such private fund has entered into an advisory contract with such adviser. The receipt of compensation based on commission

---

[15]   So in original. No subsection (f) was enacted.

or fees shall not, in and of itself, be considered a violation of such standard applied to a broker, dealer, or investment adviser.

(2)   Retail customer defined

For purposes of this subsection, the term "retail customer" means a natural person, or the legal representative of such natural person, who—

(A)   receives personalized investment advice about securities from a broker, dealer, or investment adviser; and

(B)   uses such advice primarily for personal, family, or household purposes.

(h)   Other matters.—

The Commission shall—

(1)   facilitate the provision of simple and clear disclosures to investors regarding the terms of their relationships with brokers, dealers, and investment advisers, including any material conflicts of interest; and

(2)   examine and, where appropriate, promulgate rules prohibiting or restricting certain sales practices, conflicts of interest, and compensation schemes for brokers, dealers, and investment advisers that the Commission deems contrary to the public interest and the protection of investors.

(i)   Harmonization of enforcement.—

The enforcement authority of the Commission with respect to violations of the standard of conduct applicable to an investment adviser shall include—

(1)   the enforcement authority of the Commission with respect to such violations provided under this subchapter; and

(2)   the enforcement authority of the Commission with respect to violations of the standard of conduct applicable to a broker or dealer providing personalized investment advice about securities to a retail customer under the Securities Exchange Act of 1934, including the authority to impose sanctions for such violations,

and the Commission shall seek to prosecute and sanction violators of the standard of conduct applicable to an investment adviser under this subchapter to same extent as the Commission prosecutes and sanctions violators of the standard of conduct applicable to a broker or dealer providing personalized investment advice about securities to a retail customer under the Securities Exchange Act of 1934.

Hearings

Sec. 212.   Hearings may be public and may be held before the Commission, any member or members thereof, or any officer or officers of the Commission designated by it, and appropriate records thereof shall be kept.

Court Review of Orders

Sec. 213.   (a)   Petition; jurisdiction; findings of Commission; additional evidence; finality.—

Any person or party aggrieved by an order issued by the Commission under this Act may obtain a review of such order in the United States court of appeals within any circuit wherein such person resides or has his principal office or place of business, or in the United States Court of Appeals for the District of Columbia, by filing in such court, within sixty days after the entry of such order, a written petition praying that the order of the Commission be modified or set aside in whole or in part. A copy of such petition shall be forthwith transmitted by the clerk of the court to any member of the Commission, or any officer thereof designated by the Commission for that purpose, and thereupon the Commission shall file in the court the record upon which the order complained of was entered, as provided in section 2112 of Title 28, United States Code. Upon the filing of such petition such court shall have jurisdiction, which upon the filing of the record shall be exclusive, to affirm, modify, or set aside such order, in whole or in part. No objection to the order of the Commission shall be considered by the court unless such objection shall have been urged before the Commission or unless there were reasonable grounds for failure so to do. The findings of the Commission as to the facts, if supported by substantial evidence, shall be conclusive. If application is made to the court for leave to adduce additional evidence, and it is shown to the satisfaction of the court that such additional evidence is material and that there were reasonable grounds for failure to adduce such evidence in the proceeding before the Commission, the court may order such additional evidence to be taken before the Commission and to be adduced upon the hearing in such manner and upon such terms and conditions as to the court may seem proper. The Commission may modify its findings as to the facts by reason of the additional evidence so taken, and it shall file with the court such modified or new findings, which, if supported by substantial evidence, shall be conclusive, and its recommendation, if any, for the modification or setting aside of the original order. The judgment and decree of the court affirming, modifying, or setting aside, in whole in or in part, any such order of the Commission shall be final, subject to review by the Supreme Court of the United States upon certiorari or certification as provided in section 1254 of title 28, United States Code.

(b)   Stay of Commission's order.—

The commencement of proceedings under subsection (a) of this section shall not, unless specifically ordered by the court, operate as a stay of the Commission's order.

Jurisdiction of Offenses and Suits

Sec. 214.   (a)   In General.—The district courts of the United States and the United States courts of any Territory or other place subject to the jurisdiction of the United States shall have jurisdiction of violations of this Act or the rules, regulations, or orders thereunder, and, concurrently with State and Territorial courts, of all suits in equity and actions at law brought to enforce any liability or duty created by or, to enjoin any violation of this Act or the rules, regulations, or orders thereunder. Any criminal proceeding may be brought in the district wherein any act or transaction constituting the violation occurred. Any suit or action to enforce any liability or duty created by, or to enjoin any violation of this Act or rules, regulations, or orders thereunder, may be brought in any such district or in the district wherein the defendant is an inhabitant or transacts business, and process in such cases may be served in any district of which the defendant is an inhabitant or transacts business or wherever the defendant may be found. In any action or proceeding instituted by the Commission under this title in a United States district court for any judicial district, a subpoena issued to compel the attendance of a witness or the production of documents or tangible things (or both) at a hearing or trial may be served at any place within the United States. Rule 45(c)(3)(A)(ii) of the Federal Rules of Civil Procedure shall not apply to a subpoena issued under the preceding sentence. Judgments and decrees so rendered shall be subject to review as provided in sections 1254, 1291, 1292, and 1294 of Title 28, United States Code. No costs shall be assessed for or against the Commission in any proceeding under this Act brought by or against the Commission in any court.

(b)   Extraterritorial Jurisdiction.—The district courts of the United States and the United States courts of any Territory shall have jurisdiction of an action or proceeding brought or instituted by the Commission or the United States alleging a violation of section 206 involving—

(1)   conduct within the United States that constitutes significant steps in furtherance of the violation, even if the violation is committed by a foreign adviser and involves only foreign investors; or

(2)   conduct occurring outside the United States that has a foreseeable substantial effect within the United States.

Validity of Contracts

Sec. 215.   (a)   Waiver of compliance as void.—

Any condition, stipulation, or provision binding any person to waive compliance with any provision of this Act or with any rule, regulation, or order thereunder shall be void.

(b)   Rights affected by invalidity.—

Every contract made in violation of any provision of this Act and every contract heretofore or hereafter made, the performance of which involves the violation of, or the continuance of any relationship or practice in violation of any provision of this Act, or any rule, regulation, or order thereunder, shall be void

(1)   as regards the rights of any person who, in violation of any such provision, rule, regulation, or order, shall have made or engaged in the performance of any such contract, and

(2) as regards the rights of any person who, not being a party to such contract, shall have acquired any right thereunder with actual knowledge of the facts by reason of which the making or performance of such contract was in violation of any such provision.

Sec. 216.   [Omitted.]

Penalties

Sec. 217.   Any person who willfully violates any provision of this Act, or any rule, regulation, or order promulgated by the Commission under authority thereof, shall, upon conviction, be fined not more than $10,000, imprisoned for not more than five years, or both.

Hiring and Leasing Authority of the Commission

Sec. 218.   The provisions of section 4(b) of the Securities Exchange Act of 1934 shall be applicable with respect to the power of the Commission—

(1) to appoint and fix the compensation of such other employees as may be necessary for carrying out its functions under this Act, and

(2) to lease and allocate such real property as may be necessary for carrying out its functions under this Act.

Separability of Provisions

Sec. 219.   If any provision of this Act or the application of such provision to any person or circumstances shall be held invalid, the remainder of the Act and the application of such provision to persons or circumstances other than those as to which it is held invalid shall not be affected thereby.

Short Title

Sec. 220.   This Act may be cited as the "Investment Advisers Act of 1940".

Effective Date

Sec. 221.   This Act shall become effective on November 1, 1940.

State Regulation of Investment Advisers

Sec. 222.   (a)   Jurisdiction of State regulators.—

Nothing in this Act shall affect the jurisdiction of the securities commissioner (or any agency or officer performing like functions) of any State over any security or any person insofar as it does not conflict with the provisions of this Act or the rules and regulations thereunder.

(b)   Dual compliance purposes.—

No State may enforce any law or regulation that would require an investment adviser to maintain any books or records in addition to those required under the laws of the State in which it maintains its principal office or place of business, if the investment adviser—

(1) is registered or licensed as such in the State in which it maintains its principal office or place of business; and

(2) is in compliance with the applicable books and records requirements of the State in which it maintains its principal office or place of business.

(c)   Limitation on capital and bond requirements.—

No State may enforce any law or regulation that would require an investment adviser to maintain a higher minimum net capital or to post any bond in addition to any that is required under the laws of the State in which it maintains its principal office or place of business, if the investment adviser—

(1) is registered or licensed as such in the State in which it maintains its principal office or place of business; and

(2) is in compliance with the applicable net capital or bonding requirements of the State in which it maintains its principal office or place of business.

(d)   National de minimis standard.—

INVESTMENT ADVISERS ACT OF 1940

No law of any State or political subdivision thereof requiring the registration, licensing, or qualification as an investment adviser shall require an investment adviser to register with the securities commissioner of the State (or any agency or officer performing like functions) or to comply with such law (other than any provision thereof prohibiting fraudulent conduct) if the investment adviser—

    (1)   does not have a place of business located within the State; and

    (2)   during the preceding 12-month period, has had fewer than 6 clients who are residents of that State.

Custody of Client Accounts

Sec. 223.   An investment adviser registered under this title shall take such steps to safeguard client assets over which such adviser has custody, including, without limitation, verification of such assets by an independent public accountant, as the Commission may, by rule, prescribe.

Rule of Construction Relating to the Commodities Exchange Act

Sec. 224.   Nothing in this title shall relieve any person of any obligation or duty, or affect the availability of any right or remedy available to the Commodity Futures Trading Commission or any private party, arising under the Commodity Exchange Act (7 U.S.C. 1 et seq.) governing commodity pools, commodity pool operators, or commodity trading advisors.

SELECTED RULES AND REGULATIONS UNDER INVESTMENT ADVISERS ACT OF 1940

17 C.F.R. § 275.___

Rule 202(a)(1)–1. Certain Transactions Not Deemed Assignments

A transaction which does not result in a change of actual control or management of an investment adviser is not an assignment for purposes of section 205(a)(2) of the Act.

Rule 202(a)(11)(G)–1. Family Offices

(a) *Exclusion*. A family off**Exemption for Limited Offers and Sales Without Regard to Dollar** ice, as defined in this rule, shall not be considered to be an investment adviser for purpose of the Act.

(b) *Family office*. A family office is a company (including its directors, partners, members, managers, trustees, and employees acting within the scope of their position or employment) that:

(1) Has no clients other than family clients; provided that if a person that is not a family client becomes a client of the family office as a result of the death of a family member or key employee or other involuntary transfer from a family member or key employee, that person shall be deemed to be a family client for purposes of this rule for one year following the completion of the transfer of legal title to the assets resulting from the involuntary event;

(2)   Is wholly owned by family clients and is exclusively controlled (directly or indirectly) by one or more family members and/or family entities; and

(3)   Does not hold itself out to the public as an investment adviser.

(c)   *Grandfathering.* A family office as defined in paragraph (a) above shall not exclude any person, who was not registered or required to be registered under the Act on January 1, 2010, solely because such person provides investment advice to, and was engaged before January 1, 2010 in providing investment advice to:

(1)   Natural persons who, at the time of their applicable investment, are officers, directors, or employees of the family office who have invested with the family office before January 1, 2010 and are accredited investors, as defined in Regulation D under the Securities Act of 1933;

(2)   Any company owned exclusively and controlled by one or more family members; or

(3)   Any investment adviser registered under the Act that provides investment advice to the family office and who identifies investment opportunities to the family office, and invests in such transactions on substantially the same terms as the family office invests, but does not invest in other funds advised by the family office, and whose assets as to which the family office directly or indirectly provides investment advice represents, in the aggregate, not more than 5 percent of the value of the total assets as to which the family office provides investment advice; provided that a family office that would not be a family office but for this subsection (c) shall be deemed to be an investment adviser for purposes of paragraphs (1), (2) and (4) of section 206 of the Act.

(d)   *Definitions.* For purposes of this rule:

(1)   *Affiliated Family Office* means a family office wholly owned by family clients of another family office and that is controlled (directly or indirectly) by one or more family members of such other family office and/or family entities affiliated with such other family office and has no clients other than family clients of such other family office.

(2)   *Control* means the power to exercise a controlling influence over the management or policies of a company, unless such power is solely the result of being an officer of such company.

(3)   *Executive officer* means the president, any vice president in charge of a principal business unit, division or function (such as administration or finance), any other officer who performs a policy-making function, or any other person who performs similar policy-making functions, for the family office.

(4)   *Family client* means:

(i)   Any family member;

(ii)   Any former family member;

(iii)   Any key employee;

(iv)   Any former key employee, provided that upon the end of such individual's employment by the family office, the former key employee shall not receive investment advice from the family office (or invest additional assets with a family office-advised trust, foundation or entity) other than with respect to assets advised (directly or indirectly) by the family office immediately prior to the end of such individual's employment, except that a former key employee shall be permitted to receive investment advice from the family office with respect to additional investments that the former key employee was contractually obligated to make, and that relate to a family-office advised investment existing, in each case prior to the time the person became a former key employee.

(v)   Any non-profit organization, charitable foundation, charitable trust (including charitable lead trusts and charitable remainder trusts whose only current beneficiaries are other family clients and charitable or non-profit organizations), or other charitable organization, in each case for which all the funding such foundation, trust or organization holds came exclusively from one or more other family clients;

(vi)   Any estate of a family member, former family member, key employee, or, subject to the condition contained in paragraph (d)(4)(iv) of this rule, former key employee;

(vii)   Any irrevocable trust in which one or more other family clients are the only current beneficiaries;

(viii) Any irrevocable trust funded exclusively by one or more other family clients in which other family clients and non-profit organizations, charitable foundations, charitable trusts, or other charitable organizations are the only current beneficiaries;

(ix)   Any revocable trust of which one or more other family clients are the sole grantor;

(x)   Any trust of which: (A) each trustee or other person authorized to make decisions with respect to the trust is a key employee; and (B) each settlor or other person who has contributed assets to the trust is a key employee or the key employee's current and/or former spouse or spousal equivalent who, at the time of contribution, holds a joint, community property, or other similar shared ownership interest with the key employee; or

(xi)   Any company wholly owned (directly or indirectly) exclusively by, and operated for the sole benefit of, one or more other family clients; provided that if any such entity is a pooled investment vehicle, it is excepted from the definition of "investment company" under the Investment Company Act of 1940.

(5)   *Family entity* means any of the trusts, estates, companies or other entities set forth in paragraphs (v), (vi), (vii), (viii), (ix), or (xi) of subsection (d)(4) of this rule, but excluding key employees and their trusts from the definition of family client solely for purposes of this definition.

(6)   *Family member* means all lineal descendants (including by adoption, stepchildren, foster children, and individuals that were a minor when another family member became a legal guardian of that individual) of a common ancestor (who may be living or deceased), and such lineal descendants' spouses or spousal equivalents; provided that the common ancestor is no more than 10 generations removed from the youngest generation of family members.

(7)   *Former family member* means a spouse, spousal equivalent, or stepchild that was a family member but is no longer a family member due to a divorce or other similar event.

(8)   *Key employee* means any natural person (including any key employee's spouse or spouse equivalent who holds a joint, community property, or other similar shared ownership interest with that key employee) who is an executive officer, director, trustee, general partner, or person serving in a similar capacity of the family office or its affiliated family office or any employee of the family office or its affiliated family office (other than an employee performing solely clerical, secretarial, or administrative functions with regard to the family office) who, in connection with his or her regular functions or duties, participates in the investment activities of the family office or affiliated family office, provided that such employee has been performing such functions and duties for or on behalf of the family office or affiliated family office, or substantially similar functions or duties for or on behalf of another company, for at least 12 months.

(9)   *Spousal equivalent* means a cohabitant occupying a relationship generally equivalent to that of a spouse.

Rule 202(a)(30)–1.   Foreign Private Advisers

(a)   *Client.* You may deem the following to be a single client for purposes of section 202(a)(30) of the Investment Advisers Act of 1940:

(1)   A natural person, and:

(i)   Any minor child of the natural person;

(ii)   Any relative, spouse, spousal equivalent, or relative of the spouse or of the spousal equivalent of the natural person who has the same principal residence;

(iii)   All accounts of which the natural person and/or the persons referred to in this paragraph (a)(1) are the only primary beneficiaries; and

    (iv) All trusts of which the natural person and/or the persons referred to in this paragraph (a)(1) are the only primary beneficiaries;

    (2)(i) A corporation, general partnership, limited partnership, limited liability company, trust (other than a trust referred to in paragraph (a)(1)(iv) of this rule), or other legal organization (any of which are referred to hereinafter as a—legal organization) to which you provide investment advice based on its investment objectives rather than the individual investment objectives of its shareholders, partners, limited partners, members, or beneficiaries (any of which are referred to hereinafter as an—owner); and

    (ii) Two or more legal organizations referred to in paragraph (a)(2)(i) of this rule that have identical owners.

  (b) *Special rules regarding clients.* For purposes of this rule:

    (1) You must count an owner as a client if you provide investment advisory services to the owner separate and apart from the investment advisory services you provide to the legal organization, provided, however, that the determination that an owner is a client will not affect the applicability of this rule with regard to any other owner;

    (2) You are not required to count an owner as a client solely because you, on behalf of the legal organization, offer, promote, or sell interests in the legal organization to the owner, or report periodically to the owners as a group solely with respect to the performance of or plans for the legal organization's assets or similar matters;

    (3) A limited partnership or limited liability company is a client of any general partner, managing member or other person acting as investment adviser to the partnership or limited liability company;

    (4) You are not required to count a private fund as a client if you count any investor, as that term is defined in paragraph (c)(2) of this rule, in that private fund as an investor in the United States in that private fund; and

    (5) You are not required to count a person as an investor, as that term is defined in paragraph (c)(2) of this rule, in a private fund you advise if you count such person as a client in the United States.

Note to paragraphs (a) and (b): These paragraphs are a safe harbor and are not intended to specify the exclusive method for determining who may be deemed a single client for purposes of section 202(a)(30) of the Investment Advisers Act of 1940.

  (c) *Definitions.* For purposes of section 202(a)(30) of the Investment Advisers Act of 1940:

    (1) *Assets under management* means the regulatory assets under management as determined under Item 5.F of Form ADV.

    (2) *Investor* means:

    (i) Any person who would be included in determining the number of beneficial owners of the outstanding securities of a private fund under section 3(c)(1) of the Investment Company Act of 1940, or whether the outstanding securities of a private fund are owned exclusively by qualified purchasers under section 3(c)(7) of that Act; and

    (ii) Any beneficial owner of any outstanding short-term paper, as defined in section 2(a)(38) of the Investment Company Act of 1940, issued by the private fund.

Note to paragraph (c)(2): You may treat as a single investor any person who is an investor in two or more private funds you advise.

    (3) *In the United States* means with respect to:

    (i) Any client or investor, any person who is a U.S. person as defined in Rule 902(k) under the Securities Act of 1933, except that any discretionary account or similar account that is held for the benefit of a person in the United States by a dealer or other professional fiduciary is in the United States if the dealer or professional fiduciary is a related person, as defined in Rule 206(4)–2(d)(7), of the investment adviser relying on this rule and is not organized, incorporated, or (if an individual) resident in the United States.

Note to paragraph (c)(3)(i): A person who is in the United States may be treated as not being in the United States if such person was not in the United States at the time of becoming a client or, in the case of an investor in a private fund, each time the investor acquires securities issued by the fund.

(ii)   Any place of business, *in the United States*, as that term is defined in Rule 902(*l*) under the Securities Act of 1933; and

(iii)   The public, *in the United States*, as that term is defined in Rule 902(*l*) under the Securities Act of 1933.

(4)   *Place of business* has the same meaning as in Rule 222–1(a) under the Investment Advisers Act of 1940.

(5)   *Spousal equivalent* has the same meaning as in Rule 202(a)(11)(G)–1(d)(9) under the Investment Advisers Act of 1940.

(d)   *Holding out.* If you are relying on this rule, you shall not be deemed to be holding yourself out generally to the public in the United States as an investment adviser, within the meaning of section 202(a)(30) of the Investment Advisers Act of 1940, solely because you participate in a non-public offering in the United States of securities issued by a private fund under the Securities Act of 1933.

Rule 203–1.   Application for Investment Adviser Registration

(a)   Form ADV. (1) To apply for registration with the Commission as an investment adviser, you must complete Form ADV (17 CFR 279.1) by following the instructions in the form and you must file Part 1A of Form ADV, the firm brochure(s) required by Part 2A of Form ADV and Form CRS required by Part 3 of Form ADV electronically with the Investment Adviser Registration Depository (IARD) unless you have received a hardship exemption under § 275.203–3. You are not required to file with the Commission the brochure supplements required by Part 2B of Form ADV.

(2)(i)   On or after June 30, 2020, the Commission will not accept any initial application for registration as an investment adviser that does not include a Form CRS that satisfies the requirements of Part 3 of Form ADV.

(ii)   Beginning on May 1, 2020, any initial application for registration as an investment adviser filed prior to June 30, 2020, must include a Form CRS that satisfies the requirements of Part 3 of Form ADV by no later than June 30, 2020.

NOTE TO PARAGRAPH (a)(1): Information on how to file with the IARD is available on the Commission's website at http://www.sec.gov/iard. If you are not required to deliver a brochure or Form CRS to any clients, you are not required to prepare or file a brochure or Form CRS, as applicable, with the Commission. If you are not required to deliver a brochure supplement to any clients for any particular supervised person, you are not required to prepare a brochure supplement for that supervised person.

(b)   When filed. Each Form ADV is considered filed with the Commission upon acceptance by the IARD.

(c)   Filing fees. You must pay FINRA (the operator of the IARD) a filing fee. The Commission has approved the amount of the filing fee. No portion of the filing fee is refundable. Your completed application for registration will not be accepted by FINRA, and thus will not be considered filed with the Commission, until you have paid the filing fee.

* * *

Rule 203(*l*)–1.   Venture Capital Fund Defined

(a)   *Venture capital fund defined.* For purposes of section 203(*l*) of the Act (15 U.S.C. 80b–3(1)), a venture capital fund is any entity described in subparagraph (A), (B), or (C) of rule 203(b)(7) of the Act (15 U.S.C. 80b–3(b)(7)) (other than an entity that has elected to be regulated or is regulated as a business development company pursuant to section 54 of the Investment Company Act of 1940 (15 U.S.C. 80a–53)) or any private fund that:

(1)   Represents to investors and potential investors that it pursues a venture capital strategy;

(2)   Immediately after the acquisition of any asset, other than qualifying investments or short-term holdings, holds no more than 20 percent of the amount of the fund's aggregate capital contributions and uncalled committed capital in assets (other than short-term holdings) that are not qualifying investments, valued at cost or fair value, consistently applied by the fund;

(3)   Does not borrow, issue debt obligations, provide guarantees or otherwise incur leverage, in excess of 15 percent of the private fund's aggregate capital contributions and uncalled committed capital, and any such borrowing, indebtedness, guarantee or leverage is for a non-renewable term of no longer than 120 calendar days, except that any guarantee by the private fund of a qualifying portfolio company's obligations up to the amount of the value of the private fund's investment in the qualifying portfolio company is not subject to the 120 calendar day limit;

(4)   Only issues securities the terms of which do not provide a holder with any right, except in extraordinary circumstances, to withdraw, redeem or require the repurchase of such securities but may entitle holders to receive distributions made to all holders pro rata; and

(5)   Is not registered under section 8 of the Investment Company Act of 1940, and has not elected to be treated as a business development company pursuant to section 54 of that Act.

(b)   *Certain pre-existing venture capital funds.* For purposes of section 203(*l*) of the Investment Advisers Act of 1940 and in addition to any venture capital fund as set forth in paragraph (a) of this rule, a venture capital fund also includes any private fund that:

(1)   Has represented to investors and potential investors at the time of the offering of the private fund's securities that it pursues a venture capital strategy;

(2)   Prior to December 31, 2010, has sold securities to one or more investors that are not related persons, as defined in Rule 206(4)–2(d)(7) under the Investment Advisers Act of 1940, of any investment adviser of the private fund; and

(3)   Does not sell any securities to (including accepting any committed capital from) any person after July 21, 2011.

(c)   *Definitions.* For purposes of this rule:

(1)   *Committed capital* means any commitment pursuant to which a person is obligated to:

(i)   Acquire an interest in the private fund; or

(ii)   Make capital contributions to the private fund.

(2)   *Equity security* has the same meaning as in section 3(a)(11) of the Securities Exchange Act of 1934 and Rule 3a11–1 under the Securities Exchange Act of 1934.

(3)   *Qualifying investment* means:

(i)   An equity security issued by a qualifying portfolio company that has been acquired directly by the private fund from the qualifying portfolio company;

(ii)   Any equity security issued by a qualifying portfolio company in exchange for an equity security issued by the qualifying portfolio company described in paragraph (c)(3)(i) of this rule; or

(iii)   Any equity security issued by a company of which a qualifying portfolio company is a majority-owned subsidiary, as defined in section 2(a)(24) of the Investment Company Act of 1940, or a predecessor, and is acquired by the private fund in exchange for an equity security described in paragraph (c)(3)(i) or (c)(3)(ii) of this rule.

(4)   *Qualifying portfolio company* means any company that:

(i)   At the time of any investment by the private fund, is not reporting or foreign traded and does not control, is not controlled by or under common control with another company, directly or indirectly, that is reporting or foreign traded;

(ii)   Does not borrow or issue debt obligations in connection with the private fund's investment in such company and distribute to the private fund the proceeds of such borrowing or issuance in exchange for the private fund's investment; and

(iii) Is not an investment company, a private fund, an issuer that would be an investment company but for the exemption provided by Rule 3a–7 under the Investment Company Act of 1940, or a commodity pool.

(5) *Reporting or foreign traded* means, with respect to a company, being subject to the reporting requirements under section 13 or 15(d) of the Securities Exchange Act of 1934, or having a security listed or traded on any exchange or organized market operating in a foreign jurisdiction.

(6) *Short-term holdings* means cash and cash equivalents, as defined in Rule 2a51–1(b)(7)(i) under the Investment Company Act of 1940, U.S. Treasuries with a remaining maturity of 60 days or less, and shares of an open-end management investment company registered under section 8 of the Investment Company Act of 1940 that is regulated as a money market fund under Rule 2a–7 under the Investment Company Act of 1940.

Note: For purposes of this rule, an investment adviser may treat as a private fund any issuer formed under the laws of a jurisdiction other than the United States that has not offered or sold its securities in the United States or to U.S. persons in a manner inconsistent with being a private fund, provided that the adviser treats the issuer as a private fund under the Investment Advisers Act of 1940 and the rules thereunder for all purposes.

Rule 203(m)–1. Private Fund Adviser Exemption

(a) *United States investment advisers.* For purposes of section 203(m) of the Investment Advisers Act of 1940, an investment adviser with its principal office and place of business in the United States is exempt from the requirement to register under section 203 of the Act if the investment adviser:

(1) Acts solely as an investment adviser to one or more qualifying private funds; and

(2) Manages private fund assets of less than $150 million.

(b) *Non-United States investment advisers.* For purposes of section 203(m) of the Investment Advisers Act of 1940, an investment adviser with its principal office and place of business outside of the United States is exempt from the requirement to register under section 203 of the Act if:

(1) The investment adviser has no client that is a United States person except for one or more qualifying private funds; and

(2) All assets managed by the investment adviser at a place of business in the United States are solely attributable to private fund assets, the total value of which is less than $150 million.

(c) *Frequency of Calculations.* For purposes of this rule, calculate private fund assets annually, in accordance with General Instruction 15 to Form ADV.

(d) *Definitions.* For purposes of this rule:

(1) *Assets under management* means the regulatory assets under management as determined under Item 5.F of Form ADV (rule 279.1 of this chapter) except that the regulatory assets under management attributable to a private fund that is an entity described in subparagraph (A), (B), or (C) of rule 203(b)(7) of the Act (15 U.S.C. 80b–3(b)(7)) (other than an entity that has elected to be regulated or is regulated as a business development company pursuant to section 54 of the Investment Company Act of 1940 (15 U.S.C. 80a–53)) shall be excluded from the definition of assets under management for purposes of this rule.

(2) *Place of business* has the same meaning as in Rule 222–1(a) under the Investment Advisers Act of 1940.

(3) *Principal office and place of business* of an investment adviser means the executive office of the investment adviser from which the officers, partners, or managers of the investment adviser direct, control, and coordinate the activities of the investment adviser.

(4) *Private fund assets* means the investment adviser's assets under management attributable to a qualifying private fund.

(5) *Qualifying private fund* means any private fund that is not registered under section 8 of the Investment Company Act of 1940 and has not elected to be treated as a business development company pursuant to section 54 of that Act. For purposes of this rule, an investment adviser may treat as a

private fund an issuer that qualifies for an exclusion from the definition of an—investment company, as defined in section 3 of the Investment Company Act of 1940, in addition to those provided by section 3(c)(1) or 3(c)(7) of that Act, provided that the investment adviser treats the issuer as a private fund under the Investment Advisers Act of 1940 and the rules thereunder for all purposes.

(6) *Related person* has the same meaning as in Rule 206(4)–2(d)(7) under the Investment Advisers Act of 1940.

(7) *United States* has the same meaning as in Rule 902(*l*) under the Securities Act of 1933.

(8) *United States person* means any person that is a U.S. person as defined in Rule 902(k) under the Securities Act of 1933, except that any discretionary account or similar account that is held for the benefit of a United States person by a dealer or other professional fiduciary is a United States person if the dealer or professional fiduciary is a related person of the investment adviser relying on this rule and is not organized, incorporated, or (if an individual) resident in the United States.

Note to paragraph (d)(8): A client will not be considered a United States person if the client was not a United States person at the time of becoming a client.

Rule 203A–1.   Eligibility for SEC Registration; Switching to or from SEC Registration

(a) *Eligibility for SEC registration of mid-sized investment advisers*—If you are an investment adviser described in section 203A(a)(2)(B) of the Investment Advisers Act of 1940:

(1) *Threshold for SEC registration and registration buffer.* You may, but are not required to register with the Commission if you have assets under management of at least $100,000,000 but less than $110,000,000, and you need not withdraw your registration unless you have less than $90,000,000 of assets under management.

(2) *Exceptions.* This paragraph (a) does not apply if:

(i) You are an investment adviser to an investment company registered under the Investment Company Act of 1940 or to a company which has elected to be a business development company pursuant to section 54 of the Investment Company Act of 1940, and has not withdrawn the election; or

(ii) You are eligible for an exemption described in Rule 203A–2 of this chapter.

(b) *Switching to or from SEC registration*—

(1) *State-registered advisers—switching to SEC registration.* If you are registered with a state securities authority, you must apply for registration with the Commission within 90 days of filing an annual updating amendment to your Form ADV reporting that you are eligible for SEC registration and are not relying on an exemption from registration under sections 203(*l*) or 203(m) of the Investment Advisers Act of 1940.

(2) *SEC-registered advisers—switching to State registration.* If you are registered with the Commission and file an annual updating amendment to your Form ADV reporting that you are not eligible for SEC registration and are not relying on an exemption from registration under sections 203(*l*) or 203(m) of the Investment Advisers Act of 1940, you must file Form ADV–W (17 CFR 279.2) to withdraw your SEC registration within 180 days of your fiscal year end (unless you then are eligible for SEC registration). During this period while you are registered with both the Commission and one or more state securities authorities, the Act and applicable State law will apply to your advisory activities.

Rule 204–3.   Delivery of Brochures and Brochure Supplements

(a) General requirements. If you are registered under the Act as an investment adviser, you must deliver a brochure and one or more brochure supplements to each client or prospective client that contains all information required by Part 2 of Form ADV (17 CFR 279.1).

(b) Delivery requirements. You (or a supervised person acting on your behalf) must:

(1) Deliver to a client or prospective client your current brochure before or at the time you enter into an investment advisory contract with that client.

(2) Deliver to each client, annually within 120 days after the end of your fiscal year and without charge, if there are material changes in your brochure since your last annual updating amendment:

(i) A current brochure, or

(ii) The summary of material changes to the brochure as required by Item 2 of Form ADV, Part 2A that offers to provide your current brochure without charge, accompanied by the Web site address (if available) and an e-mail address (if available) and telephone number by which a client may obtain the current brochure from you, and the Web site address for obtaining information about you through the Investment Adviser Public Disclosure (IAPD) system.

(3) Deliver to each client or prospective client a current brochure supplement for a supervised person before or at the time that supervised person begins to provide advisory services to the client; provided, however, that if investment advice for a client is provided by a team comprised of more than five supervised persons, a current brochure supplement need only be delivered to that client for the five supervised persons with the most significant responsibility for the day-to-day advice provided to that client. For purposes of this rule, a supervised person will provide advisory services to a client if that supervised person will:

(i) Formulate investment advice for the client and have direct client contact; or

(ii) Make discretionary investment decisions for the client, even if the supervised person will have no direct client contact.

(4) Deliver the following to each client promptly after you create an amended brochure or brochure supplement, as applicable, if the amendment adds disclosure of an event, or materially revises information already disclosed about an event, in response to Item 9 of Part 2A of Form ADV or Item 3 of Part 2B of Form ADV (Disciplinary Information), respectively, (i) the amended brochure or brochure supplement, as applicable, along with a statement describing the material facts relating to the change in disciplinary information, or (ii) a statement describing the material facts relating to the change in disciplinary information.

(c) Exceptions to delivery requirement.

(1) You are not required to deliver a brochure to a client:

(i) That is an investment company registered under the Investment Company Act of 1940 or a business development company as defined in that Act, provided that the advisory contract with that client meets the requirements of section 15(c) of the Investment Company Act of 1940; or

(ii) Who receives only impersonal investment advice for which you charge less than $500 per year.

(2) You are not required to deliver a brochure supplement to a client:

(i) To whom you are not required to deliver a brochure under subparagraph (c)(1) of this rule;

(ii) Who receives only impersonal investment advice; or

(iii) Who is an officer, employee, or other person related to the adviser that would be a "qualified client" of your firm under Rule 205–3(d)(1)(iii).

(d) Wrap fee program brochures.

(1) If you are a sponsor of a wrap fee program, then the brochure that paragraph (b) of this rule requires you to deliver to a client or prospective client of the wrap fee program must be a wrap fee program brochure containing all the information required by Part 2A, Appendix 1 of Form ADV. Any additional information in a wrap fee program brochure must be limited to information applicable to wrap fee programs that you sponsor.

(2) You do not have to deliver a wrap fee program brochure if another sponsor of the wrap fee program delivers, to the client or prospective client of the wrap fee program, a wrap fee program brochure containing all the information required by Part 2A, Appendix 1 of Form ADV.

Note to paragraph (d): A wrap fee program brochure does not take the place of any brochure supplements that you are required to deliver under paragraph (b) of this rule.

(e)   Multiple brochures. If you provide substantially different advisory services to different clients, you may provide them with different brochures, so long as each client receives all information about the services and fees that are applicable to that client. The brochure you deliver to a client may omit any information required by Part 2A of Form ADV if the information does not apply to the advisory services or fees that you will provide or charge, or that you propose to provide or charge, to that client.

(f)   Other disclosure obligations. Delivering a brochure or brochure supplement in compliance with this rule does not relieve you of any other disclosure obligations you have to your advisory clients or prospective clients under any federal or state laws or regulations.

(g)   Definitions. For purposes of this rule:

(1)   Impersonal investment advice means investment advisory services that do not purport to meet the objectives or needs of specific individuals or accounts.

(2)   Current brochure and current brochure supplement mean the most recent revision of the brochure or brochure supplement, including all amendments to date.

(3)   Sponsor of a wrap fee program means an investment adviser that is compensated under a wrap fee program for sponsoring, organizing, or administering the program, or for selecting, or providing advice to clients regarding the selection of, other investment advisers in the program.

(4)   Supervised person means any of your officers, partners or directors (or other persons occupying a similar status or performing similar functions) or employees, or any other person who provides investment advice on your behalf.

(5)   Wrap fee program means an advisory program under which a specified fee or fees not based directly upon transactions in a client's account is charged for investment advisory services (which may include portfolio management or advice concerning the selection of other investment advisers) and the execution of client transactions.

Rule 204-4. Reporting by Exempt Reporting Advisers

(a)   *Exempt reporting advisers.* If you are an investment adviser relying on the exemption from registering with the Commission under section 203(l) or 203(m) of the Investment Advisers Act of 1940, you must complete and file reports on Form ADV (17 CFR 279.1) by following the instructions in the Form, which specify the information that an exempt reporting adviser must provide.

(b)   *Electronic filing.* You must file Form ADV electronically with the Investment Adviser Registration Depository (IARD) unless you have received a hardship exemption under paragraph (e) of this rule.

Note to paragraph (b): Information on how to file with the IARD is available on the Commission's website at http://www.sec.gov/iard.

(c)   *When filed.* Each Form ADV is considered filed with the Commission upon acceptance by the IARD.

(d)   *Filing fees.* You must pay FINRA (the operator of the IARD) a filing fee. The Commission has approved the amount of the filing fee. No portion of the filing fee is refundable. Your completed Form ADV will not be accepted by FINRA, and thus will not be considered filed with the Commission, until you have paid the filing fee.

(e)   *Temporary hardship exemption.*

(1)   *Eligibility for exemption.* If you have unanticipated technical difficulties that prevent submission of a filing to the IARD, you may request a temporary hardship exemption from the requirements of this chapter to file electronically.

(2)   *Application procedures.* To request a temporary hardship exemption, you must:

(i)   File Form ADV-H (17 CFR 279.3) in paper format no later than one business day after the filing that is the subject of the ADV-H was due; and

(ii)   Submit the filing that is the subject of the Form ADV–H in electronic format with the IARD no later than seven business days after the filing was due.

(3)   *Effective date—upon filing.* The temporary hardship exemption will be granted when you file a completed Form ADV–H.

(f)   *Final report.* You must file a final report in accordance with instructions in Form ADV when:

(1)   You cease operation as an investment adviser;

(2)   You no longer meet the definition of exempt reporting adviser under paragraph (a); or

(3)   You apply for registration with the Commission.

Note to paragraph (f): You do not have to pay a filing fee to file a final report on Form ADV through the IARD.

Rule 204A–1. Investment Adviser Codes of Ethics

(a)   *Adoption of code of ethics.* If you are an investment adviser registered or required to be registered under section 203 of the Act, you must establish, maintain and enforce a written code of ethics that, at a minimum, includes:

(1)   A standard (or standards) of business conduct that you require of your supervised persons, which standard must reflect your fiduciary obligations and those of your supervised persons;

(2)   Provisions requiring your supervised persons to comply with applicable Federal securities laws;

(3)   Provisions that require all of your access persons to report, and you to review, their personal securities transactions and holdings periodically as provided below;

(4)   Provisions requiring supervised persons to report any violations of your code of ethics promptly to your chief compliance officer or, provided your chief compliance officer also receives reports of all violations, to other persons you designate in your code of ethics; and

(5)   Provisions requiring you to provide each of your supervised persons with a copy of your code of ethics and any amendments, and requiring your supervised persons to provide you with a written acknowledgment of their receipt of the code and any amendments.

(b)   *Reporting requirements.*

(1)   *Holdings reports.* The code of ethics must require your access persons to submit to your chief compliance officer or other persons you designate in your code of ethics a report of the access person's current securities holdings that meets the following requirements:

(i)   *Content of holdings reports.* Each holdings report must contain, at a minimum:

(A)   The title and type of security, and as applicable the exchange ticker symbol or CUSIP number, number of shares, and principal amount of each reportable security in which the access person has any direct or indirect beneficial ownership;

(B)   The name of any broker, dealer or bank with which the access person maintains an account in which any securities are held for the access person's direct or indirect benefit; and

(C)   The date the access person submits the report.

(ii)   *Timing of holdings reports.* Your access persons must each submit a holdings report:

(A)   No later than 10 days after the person becomes an access person, and the information must be current as of a date no more than 45 days prior to the date the person becomes an access person.

(B)   At least once each 12-month period thereafter on a date you select, and the information must be current as of a date no more than 45 days prior to the date the report was submitted.

(2) *Transaction reports.* The code of ethics must require access persons to submit to your chief compliance officer or other persons you designate in your code of ethics quarterly securities transactions reports that meet the following requirements:

(i) *Content of transaction reports.* Each transaction report must contain, at a minimum, the following information about each transaction involving a reportable security in which the access person had, or as a result of the transaction acquired, any direct or indirect beneficial ownership:

(A) The date of the transaction, the title, and as applicable the exchange ticker symbol or CUSIP number, interest rate and maturity date, number of shares, and principal amount of each reportable security involved;

(B) The nature of the transaction (i.e., purchase, sale or any other type of acquisition or disposition);

(C) The price of the security at which the transaction was effected;

(D) The name of the broker, dealer or bank with or through which the transaction was effected; and

(E) The date the access person submits the report.

(ii) *Timing of transaction reports.* Each access person must submit a transaction report no later than 30 days after the end of each calendar quarter, which report must cover, at a minimum, all transactions during the quarter.

(3) *Exceptions from reporting requirements.* Your code of ethics need not require an access person to submit:

(i) Any report with respect to securities held in accounts over which the access person had no direct or indirect influence or control;

(ii) A transaction report with respect to transactions effected pursuant to an automatic investment plan;

(iii) A transaction report if the report would duplicate information contained in broker trade confirmations or account statements that you hold in your records so long as you receive the confirmations or statements no later than 30 days after the end of the applicable calendar quarter.

(c) *Pre-approval of certain investments.* Your code of ethics must require your access persons to obtain your approval before they directly or indirectly acquire beneficial ownership in any security in an initial public offering or in a limited offering.

(d) *Small advisers.* If you have only one access person (i.e., yourself), you are not required to submit reports to yourself or to obtain your own approval for investments in any security in an initial public offering or in a limited offering, if you maintain records of all of your holdings and transactions that this rule would otherwise require you to report.

(e) *Definitions.* For the purpose of this rule:

(1) *Access person* means:

(i) Any of your supervised persons:

(A) Who has access to nonpublic information regarding any clients' purchase or sale of securities, or nonpublic information regarding the portfolio holdings of any reportable fund, or

(B) Who is involved in making securities recommendations to clients, or who has access to such recommendations that are nonpublic.

(ii) If providing investment advice is your primary business, all of your directors, officers and partners are presumed to be access persons.

(2) *Automatic investment plan* means a program in which regular periodic purchases (or withdrawals) are made automatically in (or from) investment accounts in accordance with a predetermined schedule and allocation. An automatic investment plan includes a dividend reinvestment plan.

(3) *Beneficial ownership* is interpreted in the same manner as it would be under Rule 16a–1(a)(2) of the Securities Exchange Act of 1934 in determining whether a person has beneficial ownership of a security for purposes of section 16 of the Securities Exchange Act of 1934 and the rules and regulations thereunder. Any report required by paragraph (b) of this rule may contain a statement that the report will not be construed as an admission that the person making the report has any direct or indirect beneficial ownership in the security to which the report relates.

(4) *Federal securities laws* means the Securities Act of 1933, the Securities Exchange Act of 1934, the Sarbanes-Oxley Act of 2002, the Investment Company Act of 1940, the Investment Advisers Act of 1940, title V of the Gramm-Leach-Bliley Act, any rules adopted by the Commission under any of these statutes, the Bank Secrecy Act as it applies to funds and investment advisers, and any rules adopted thereunder by the Commission or the Department of the Treasury.

(5) *Fund* means an investment company registered under the Investment Company Act.

(6) *Initial public offering* means an offering of securities registered under the Securities Act of 1933, the issuer of which, immediately before the registration, was not subject to the reporting requirements of sections 13 or 15(d) of the Securities Exchange Act of 1934.

(7) *Limited offering* means an offering that is exempt from registration under the Securities Act of 1933 pursuant to section 4(2) or section 4(5) or pursuant to Rules 504, 505, or 506 under the Securities Act of 1933.

(8) *Purchase or sale of a security* includes, among other things, the writing of an option to purchase or sell a security.

(9) *Reportable fund* means:

(i)   Any fund for which you serve as an investment adviser as defined in section 2(a)(20) of the Investment Company Act of 1940 (i.e., in most cases you must be approved by the fund's board of directors before you can serve); or

(ii)   Any fund whose investment adviser or principal underwriter controls you, is controlled by you, or is under common control with you. For purposes of this rule, control has the same meaning as it does in section 2(a)(9) of the Investment Company Act of 1940.

(10) *Reportable security* means a security as defined in section 202(a)(18) of the Act, except that it does not include:

(i)   Direct obligations of the Government of the United States;

(ii)   Bankers' acceptances, bank certificates of deposit, commercial paper and high quality short-term debt instruments, including repurchase agreements;

(iii)   Shares issued by money market funds;

(iv)   Shares issued by open-end funds other than reportable funds; and

(v)   Shares issued by unit investment trusts that are invested exclusively in one or more open-end funds, none of which are reportable funds.

Rule 205–1. Definition of "Investment Performance" of an Investment Company and "Investment Record" of an Appropriate Index of Securities Prices

(a)   "Investment performance" of an investment company for any period shall mean the sum of:

(1)   The change in its net asset value per share during such period;

(2)   The value of its cash distributions per share accumulated to the end of such period; and

(3)   The value of capital gains taxes per share paid or payable on undistributed realized long-term capital gains accumulated to the end of such period;

expressed as a percentage of its net asset value per share at the beginning of such period. For this purpose, the value of distributions per share of realized capital gains, of dividends per share paid from investment income and of capital gains taxes per share paid or payable on undistributed realized long-term capital gains shall be treated as reinvested in shares of the investment company at the net asset value per share in effect at the close of business on the record date for the payment of such distributions and dividends and the date on which provision is made for such taxes, after giving effect to such distributions, dividends and taxes.

(b) "Investment record" of an appropriate index of securities prices for any period shall mean the sum of:

(1) The change in the level of the index during such period; and

(2) The value, computed consistently with the index, of cash distributions made by companies whose securities comprise the index accumulated to the end of such period;

expressed as a percentage of the index level at the beginning of such period. For this purpose cash distributions on the securities which comprise the index shall be treated as reinvested in the index at least as frequently as the end of each calendar quarter following the payment of the dividend.

Rule 205–2. Definition of "Specified Period" Over Which the Asset Value of the Company or Fund Under Management Is Averaged

(a) For purposes of this rule:

(1) "Fulcrum fee" shall mean the fee which is paid or earned when the investment company's performance is equivalent to that of the index or other measure of performance.

(2) "Rolling period" shall mean a period consisting of a specified number of subperiods of definite length in which the most recent subperiod is substituted for the earliest subperiod as time passes.

(b) The specified period over which the asset value of the company or fund under management is averaged shall mean the period over which the investment performance of the company or fund and the investment record of an appropriate index of securities prices or such other measure of investment performance are computed.

(c) Notwithstanding paragraph (b) of this rule, the specified period over which the asset value of the company or fund is averaged for the purpose of computing the fulcrum fee may differ from the period over which the asset value is averaged for computing the performance related portion of the fee, only if

(1) The performance related portion of the fee is computed over a rolling period and the total fee is payable at the end of each subperiod of the rolling period; and

(2) The fulcrum fee is computed on the basis of the asset value averaged over the most recent subperiod or subperiods of the rolling period.

Rule 205–3. Exemption From the Compensation Prohibition of Section 205(a)(1) for Investment Advisers

(a) *General.* The provisions of section 205(a)(1) of the Act will not be deemed to prohibit an investment adviser from entering into, performing, renewing or extending an investment advisory contract that provides for compensation to the investment adviser on the basis of a share of the capital gains upon, or the capital appreciation of, the funds, or any portion of the funds, of a client, Provided, That the client entering into the contract subject to this rule is a qualified client, as defined in paragraph (d)(1) of this rule.

(b) *Identification of the client.* In the case of a private investment company, as defined in paragraph (d)(3) of this rule, an investment company registered under the Investment Company Act of 1940, or a business development company, as defined in section 202(a)(22) of the Act, each equity owner of any such company (except for the investment adviser entering into the contract and any other equity owners not charged a fee on the basis of a share of capital gains or capital appreciation) will be considered a client for purposes of paragraph (a) of this rule.

(c) *Transition rules.*—

(1) *Registered investment advisers.* If a registered investment adviser entered into a contract and satisfied the conditions of this rule that were in effect when the contract was entered into, the

adviser will be considered to satisfy the conditions of this rule; *Provided,* however, that if a natural person or company who was not a party to the contract becomes a party (including an equity owner of a private investment company advised by the adviser), the conditions of this rule in effect at that time will apply with regard to that person or company.

(2) *Registered investment advisers that were previously not registered.* If an investment adviser was not required to register with the Commission pursuant to section 203 of the Act and was not registered, section 205(a)(1) of the Act will not apply to an advisory contract entered into when the adviser was not required to register and was not registered, or to an account of an equity owner of a private investment company advised by the adviser if the account was established when the adviser was not required to register and was not registered; *provided,* however, that section 205(a)(1) of the Act will apply with regard to a natural person or company who was not a party to the contract and becomes a party (including an equity owner of a private investment company advised by the adviser) when the adviser is required to register.

(3) *Certain transfers of interests.* Solely for purposes of paragraphs (c)(1) and (c)(2) of this rule, a transfer of an equity ownership interest in a private investment company by gift or bequest, or pursuant to an agreement related to a legal separation or divorce, will not cause the transferee to "become a party" to the contract and will not cause section 205(a)(1) of the Act to apply to such transferee.

(d) *Definitions.* For the purposes of this rule:

(1) The term qualified client means:

(i) A natural person who, or a company that, immediately after entering into the contract has, under the management of the investment adviser, at least the applicable dollar amount specified in the most recent order;

(ii) A natural person who, or a company that, the investment adviser entering into the contract (and any person acting on his behalf) reasonably believes, immediately prior to entering into the contract, either:

(A) Has a net worth (together, in the case of a natural person, with assets held jointly with a spouse) of more than the applicable dollar amount specified in the most recent order. For purposes of calculating a natural person's net worth:

(1) The person's primary residence must not be included as an asset;

(2) Indebtedness secured by the person's primary residence, up to the estimated fair market value of the primary residence at the time the investment advisory contract is entered into may not be included as a liability (except that if the amount of such indebtedness outstanding at the time of calculation exceeds the amount outstanding 60 days before such time, other than as a result of the acquisition of the primary residence, the amount of such excess must be included as a liability); and

(3) Indebtedness that is secured by the person's primary residence in excess of the estimated fair market value of the residence must be included as a liability; or

(B) Is a qualified purchaser as defined in section 2(a)(51)(A) of the Investment Company Act of 1940 at the time the contract is entered into; or

(iii) A natural person who immediately prior to entering into the contract is:

(A) An executive officer, director, trustee, general partner, or person serving in a similar capacity, of the investment adviser; or

(B) An employee of the investment adviser (other than an employee performing solely clerical, secretarial or administrative functions with regard to the investment adviser) who, in connection with his or her regular functions or duties, participates in the investment activities of such investment adviser, provided that such employee has been performing such functions and duties for or on behalf of the investment adviser, or substantially similar functions or duties for or on behalf of another company for at least 12 months.

(2)   The term company has the same meaning as in section 202(a)(5) of the Act, but does not include a company that is required to be registered under the Investment Company Act of 1940 but is not registered.

(3)   The term private investment company means a company that would be defined as an investment company under section 3(a) of the Investment Company Act of 1940 but for the exception provided from that definition by section 3(c)(1) of such Act.

(4)   The term executive officer means the president, any vice president in charge of a principal business unit, division or function (such as sales, administration or finance), any other officer who performs a policy-making function, or any other person who performs similar policy-making functions, for the investment adviser.

(5)   The term most recent order means the most recently issued Commission order in accordance with paragraph (e) of this Rule and as published in the Federal Register.

(e)   *Inflation adjustments.* Pursuant to section 205(e) of the Act, the dollar amounts referenced in paragraphs (d)(1)(i) and (d)(1)(ii)(A) of this rule shall be adjusted, by order of the Commission, issued on or about May 1, 2026 and approximately every five years thereafter. The adjusted dollar amounts established in such orders shall be computed by:

(1)   Dividing the year-end value of the Personal Consumption Expenditures Chain-Type Price Index (or any successor index thereto), as published by the United States Department of Commerce, for the calendar year preceding the calendar year in which the order is being issued, by the year-end value of such index (or successor) for the calendar year 1997;

(2)   For the dollar amount in paragraph (d)(1)(i) of this rule, multiplying $750,000 times the quotient obtained in paragraph (e)(1) of this rule and rounding the product to the nearest multiple of $100,000; and

(3)   For the dollar amount in paragraph (d)(1)(ii)(A) of this rule, multiplying $1,500,000 times the quotient obtained in paragraph (e)(1) of this rule and rounding the product to the nearest multiple of $100,000.

Rule 206(3)–1.   Exemption of Investment Advisers Registered as Broker-Dealers in Connection With the Provision of Certain Investment Advisory Services

(a)   An investment adviser which is a broker or dealer registered pursuant to Section 15 of the Securities Exchange Act of 1934 shall be exempt from section 206(3) in connection with any transaction in relation to which such broker or dealer is acting as an investment adviser solely

(1)   By means of publicly distributed written materials or publicly made oral statements;

(2)   By means of written materials or oral statements which do not purport to meet the objectives or needs of specific individuals or accounts;

(3)   Through the issuance of statistical information containing no expressions of opinion as to the investment merits of a particular security; or

(4)   Any combination of the foregoing services: *Provided, however,* That such materials and oral statements include a statement that if the purchaser of the advisory communication uses the services of the adviser in connection with a sale or purchase of a security which is a subject of such communication, the adviser may act as principal for its own account or as agent for another person.

(b)   For the purpose of this rule, publicly distributed written materials are those which are distributed to 35 or more persons who pay for such materials, and publicly made oral statements are those made simultaneously to 35 or more persons who pay for access to such statements.

NOTE: The requirement that the investment adviser disclose that it may act as principal or agent for another person in the sale or purchase of a security that is the subject of investment advice does not relieve the investment adviser of any disclosure obligation which, depending upon the nature of the relationship between the investment adviser and the client, may be imposed by subparagraphs (1) and (2) of Section 206 or the other provisions of the federal securities laws.

Rule 206(3)-2.   Agency Cross Transactions for Advisory Clients

(a)   An investment adviser, or a person registered as a broker-dealer under section 15 of the Securities Exchange Act of 1934 and controlling, controlled by, or under common control with an investment adviser, shall be deemed in compliance with the provisions of section 206(3) of the Act in effecting an agency cross transaction for an advisory client, if:

(1)   The advisory client has executed a written consent prospectively authorizing the investment adviser, or any other person relying on this rule, to effect agency cross transactions for such advisory client, provided that such written consent is obtained after full written disclosure that with respect to agency cross transactions the investment adviser or such other person will act as broker for, receive commissions from, and have a potentially conflicting division of loyalties and responsibilities regarding, both parties to such transaction;

(2)   The investment adviser, or any other person relying on this rule, sends to each such client a written confirmation at or before the completion of each such transaction, which confirmation includes

(i)   A statement of the nature of such transaction,

(ii)   The date such transaction took place,

(iii)   An offer to furnish upon request, the time when such transaction took place, and

(iv)   The source and amount of any other remuneration received or to be received by the investment adviser and any other person relying on this rule in connection with the transaction, *Provided, however,* That if, in the case of a purchase, neither the investment adviser nor any other person relying on this rule was participating in a distribution, or in the case of a sale, neither the investment adviser nor any other person relying on this rule was participating in a tender offer, the written confirmation may state whether any other remuneration has been or will be received and that the source and amount of such other remuneration will be furnished upon written request of such customer;

(3)   The investment adviser, or any other person relying on this rule, sends to each client, at least annually, and with or as part of any written statement or summary of such account from the investment adviser or such other person, a written disclosure statement identifying the total number of such transactions during the period since the date of the last such statement or summary, and the total amount of all commissions or other remuneration received or to be received by the investment adviser or any other person relying on this rule in connection with such transactions during such period;

(4)   Each written disclosure and confirmation required by this rule includes a conspicuous statement that the written consent referred to in paragraph (a)(1) of this rule may be revoked at any time by written notice to the investment adviser, or to any other person relying on this rule, from the advisory client; and

(5)   No such transaction is effected in which the same investment adviser or an investment adviser and any person controlling, controlled by or under common control with such investment adviser recommended the transaction to both any seller and any purchaser.

(b)   For purposes of this rule the term "agency cross transaction for an advisory client" shall mean a transaction in which a person acts as an investment adviser in relation to a transaction in which such investment adviser, or any person controlling, controlled by or under common control with such investment adviser, acts as broker for both such advisory client and for another person on the other side of the transaction.

(c)   This rule shall not be construed as relieving in any way the investment adviser or another person relying on this rule from acting in the best interests of the advisory client, including fulfilling the duty with respect to the best price and execution for the particular transaction for the advisory client; nor shall it relieve such person or persons from any disclosure obligation which may be imposed by subparagraphs (1) or (2) of section 206 of the Act or by other applicable provisions of the federal securities laws.

Rule 206(3)–3T. Temporary Rule for Principal Trades With Certain Advisory Clients

(a)   An investment adviser shall be deemed in compliance with the provisions of section 206(3) of the Advisers Act when the adviser directly or indirectly, acting as principal for its own account, sells to or purchases from an advisory client any security if:

(1)   The investment adviser exercises no "investment discretion" (as such term is defined in section 3(a)(35) of the Securities Exchange Act of 1934 ("Exchange Act")), except investment discretion granted by the advisory client on a temporary or limited basis, with respect to the client's account;

(2)   Neither the investment adviser nor any person controlling, controlled by, or under common control with the investment adviser is the issuer of, or, at the time of the sale, an underwriter (as defined in section 202(a)(20) of the Advisers Act) of, the security; except that the investment adviser or a person controlling, controlled by, or under common control with the investment adviser may be an underwriter of an investment grade debt security (as defined in paragraph (c) of this rule);

(3)   The advisory client has executed a written, revocable consent prospectively authorizing the investment adviser directly or indirectly to act as principal for its own account in selling any security to or purchasing any security from the advisory client, so long as such written consent is obtained after written disclosure to the advisory client explaining:

(i)   The circumstances under which the investment adviser directly or indirectly may engage in principal transactions;

(ii)   The nature and significance of conflicts with its client's interests as a result of the transactions; and

(iii)   How the investment adviser addresses those conflicts;

(4)   The investment adviser, prior to the execution of each principal transaction:

(i)   Informs the advisory client, orally or in writing, of the capacity in which it may act with respect to such transaction; and

(ii)   Obtains consent from the advisory client, orally or in writing, to act as principal for its own account with respect to such transaction;

(5)   The investment adviser sends a written confirmation at or before completion of each such transaction that includes, in addition to the information required by Rule 10b–10 under the Exchange Act, a conspicuous, plain English statement informing the advisory client that the investment adviser:

(i)   Disclosed to the client prior to the execution of the transaction that the adviser may be acting in a principal capacity in connection with the transaction and the client authorized the transaction; and

(ii)   Sold the security to, or bought the security from, the client for its own account;

(6)   The investment adviser sends to the client, no less frequently than annually, written disclosure containing a list of all transactions that were executed in the client's account in reliance upon this rule, and the date and price of such transactions;

(7)   The investment adviser is a broker-dealer registered under section 15 of the Exchange Act and each account for which the investment adviser relies on this rule is a brokerage account subject to the Exchange Act, and the rules thereunder, and the rules of the self-regulatory organization(s) of which it is a member; and

(8)   Each written disclosure required by this rule includes a conspicuous, plain English statement that the client may revoke the written consent referred to in paragraph (a)(3) of this rule without penalty at any time by written notice to the investment adviser.

(b)   This rule shall not be construed as relieving in any way an investment adviser from acting in the best interests of an advisory client, including fulfilling the duty with respect to the best price and execution for the particular transaction for the advisory client; nor shall it relieve such person or persons from any obligation that may be imposed by sections 206(1) or (2) of the Advisers Act or by other applicable provisions of the federal securities laws.

(c)   For purposes of paragraph (a)(2) of this rule, an investment grade debt security means a non-convertible debt security that, at the time of sale, is rated in one of the four highest rating categories of at least two nationally recognized statistical rating organizations (as defined in section 3(a)(62) of the Exchange Act)

(d)   This rule will expire and no longer be effective on December 31, 2016.

Rule 206(4)–1.   Investment Adviser Marketing

As a means reasonably designed to prevent fraudulent, deceptive, or manipulative acts, practices, or courses of business within the meaning of section 206(4) of the Act (15 U.S.C. 80b–6(4)), it is unlawful for any investment adviser registered or required to be registered under section 203 of the Act (15 U.S.C. 80b–3), directly or indirectly, to disseminate any *advertisement* that violates any of paragraphs (a) through (d) of this section.

(a)   *General prohibitions.* An *advertisement* may not:

(1)   Include any untrue statement of a material fact, or omit to state a material fact necessary in order to make the statement made, in the light of the circumstances under which it was made, not misleading;

(2)   Include a material statement of fact that the adviser does not have a reasonable basis for believing it will be able to substantiate upon demand by the Commission;

(3)   Include information that would reasonably be likely to cause an untrue or misleading implication or inference to be drawn concerning a material fact relating to the investment adviser;

(4)   Discuss any potential benefits to clients or investors connected with or resulting from the investment adviser's services or methods of operation without providing fair and balanced treatment of any material risks or material limitations associated with the potential benefits;

(5)   Include a reference to specific investment advice provided by the investment adviser where such investment advice is not presented in a manner that is fair and balanced;

(6)   Include or exclude performance results, or present performance time periods, in a manner that is not fair and balanced; or

(7)   Otherwise be materially misleading.

(b)   *Testimonials and endorsements.* An *advertisement* may not include any *testimonial* or *endorsement*, and an adviser may not provide compensation, directly or indirectly, for a *testimonial* or *endorsement*, unless the investment adviser complies with the conditions in paragraphs (b)(1) through (3) of this section, subject to the exemptions in paragraph (b)(4) of this section.

(1)   *Required disclosures.* The investment adviser discloses, or reasonably believes that the person giving the *testimonial* or *endorsement* discloses, the following at the time the *testimonial* or *endorsement* is disseminated:

(i)   Clearly and prominently:

(A)   That the *testimonial* was given by a current client or investor, and the *endorsement* was given by a person other than a current client or investor, as applicable;

(B)   That cash or non-cash compensation was provided for the *testimonial* or *endorsement*, if applicable; and

(C)   A brief statement of any material conflicts of interest on the part of the person giving the *testimonial* or *endorsement* resulting from the investment adviser's relationship with such person;

(ii)   The material terms of any compensation arrangement, including a description of the compensation provided or to be provided, directly or indirectly, to the person for the *testimonial* or *endorsement*; and

(iii) A description of any material conflicts of interest on the part of the person giving the *testimonial* or *endorsement* resulting from the investment adviser's relationship with such person and/or any compensation arrangement.

(2) *Adviser oversight and compliance.* The investment adviser must have:

(i) A reasonable basis for believing that the *testimonial* or *endorsement* complies with the requirements of this section; and

(ii) A written agreement with any person giving a *testimonial* or *endorsement* that describes the scope of the agreed-upon activities and the terms of compensation for those activities.

(3) *Disqualification.* An investment adviser may not compensate a person, directly or indirectly, for a testimonial or endorsement if the adviser knows, or in the exercise of reasonable care should know, that the person giving the testimonial or endorsement is an ineligible person at the time the testimonial or endorsement is disseminated. This paragraph shall not disqualify any person for any matter(s) that occurred prior to May 4, 2021, if such matter(s) would not have disqualified such person under § 206(4)–3(a)(1)(ii) of this chapter, as in effect prior to May 4, 2021.

(4) *Exemptions.* (i) A *testimonial* or *endorsement* disseminated for no compensation or *de minimis compensation* is not required to comply with paragraphs (b)(2)(ii) and (3) of this section;

(ii) A *testimonial* or *endorsement* by the investment adviser's partners, officers, directors, or employees, or a person that controls, is controlled by, or is under common control with the investment adviser, or is a partner, officer, director or employee of such a person is not required to comply with paragraphs (b)(1) and (2)(ii) of this section, provided that the affiliation between the investment adviser and such person is readily apparent to or is disclosed to the client or investor at the time the *testimonial* or *endorsement* is disseminated and the investment adviser documents such person's status at the time the *testimonial* or *endorsement* is disseminated;

(iii) A *testimonial* or *endorsement* by a broker or dealer registered with the Commission under section 15(b) of the Securities Exchange Act of 1934 (15 U.S.C. 78o(a)) is not required to comply with:

(A) Paragraph (b)(1) of this section if the *testimonial* or *endorsement* is a recommendation subject to § 240.15*l*–1 (Regulation Best Interest) under that Act;

(B) Paragraphs (b)(1)(ii) and (iii) of this section if the testimonial or endorsement is provided to a person that is not a retail customer (as that term is defined in § 240.15*l*–1 (Regulation Best Interest) under the Securities Exchange Act of 1934 (15 U.S.C. 78o(a)); and

(C) Paragraph (b)(3) of this section if the broker or dealer is not subject to statutory disqualification, as defined under section 3(a)(39) of that Act; and

(iv) A *testimonial* or *endorsement* by a person that is covered by rule 506(d) of the Securities Act of 1933 with respect to a rule 506 securities offering and whose involvement would not disqualify the offering under that rule is not required to comply with paragraph (b)(3) of this section.

(c) *Third-party ratings.* An *advertisement* may not include any *third-party rating*, unless the investment adviser:

(1) Has a reasonable basis for believing that any questionnaire or survey used in the preparation of the *third-party rating* is structured to make it equally easy for a participant to provide favorable and unfavorable responses, and is not designed or prepared to produce any predetermined result; and

(2) Clearly and prominently discloses, or the investment adviser reasonably believes that the *third-party rating* clearly and prominently discloses:

(i) The date on which the rating was given and the period of time upon which the rating was based;

(ii) The identity of the third party that created and tabulated the rating; and

(iii) If applicable, that compensation has been provided directly or indirectly by the adviser in connection with obtaining or using the *third-party rating*.

(d) *Performance.* An investment adviser may not include in any *advertisement*:

(1) Any presentation of gross performance, unless the *advertisement* also presents net performance:

(i) With at least equal prominence to, and in a format designed to facilitate comparison with, the gross performance; and

(ii) Calculated over the same time period, and using the same type of return and methodology, as the gross performance.

(2) Any performance results, of any portfolio or any composite aggregation of related portfolios, in each case other than any private fund, unless the advertisement includes performance results of the same portfolio or composite aggregation for one-, five-, and ten-year periods, each presented with equal prominence and ending on a date that is no less recent than the most recent calendar year-end; except that if the relevant portfolio did not exist for a particular prescribed period, then the life of the portfolio must be substituted for that period.

(3) Any statement, express or implied, that the calculation or presentation of performance results in the advertisement has been approved or reviewed by the Commission.

(4) Any related performance, unless it includes all related portfolios; provided that related performance may exclude any related portfolios if:

(i) The advertised performance results are not materially higher than if all related portfolios had been included; and

(ii) The exclusion of any related portfolio does not alter the presentation of any applicable time periods prescribed by paragraph (d)(2) of this section.

(5) Any extracted performance, unless the advertisement provides, or offers to provide promptly, the performance results of the total portfolio from which the performance was extracted.

(6) Any *hypothetical performance* unless the investment adviser:

(i) Adopts and implements policies and procedures reasonably designed to ensure that the *hypothetical performance* is relevant to the likely financial situation and investment objectives of the intended audience of the *advertisement*,

(ii) Provides sufficient information to enable the intended audience to understand the criteria used and assumptions made in calculating such *hypothetical performance*, and

(iii) Provides (or, if the intended audience is an investor in a *private fund* provides, or offers to provide promptly) sufficient information to enable the intended audience to understand the risks and limitations of using such *hypothetical performance* in making investment decisions; Provided that the investment adviser need not comply with the other conditions on performance in paragraphs (d)(2), (4), and (5) of this section.

(7) Any *predecessor performance* unless:

(i) The person or persons who were primarily responsible for achieving the prior performance results manage accounts at the advertising adviser;

(ii) The accounts managed at the predecessor investment adviser are sufficiently similar to the accounts managed at the advertising investment adviser that the performance results would provide relevant information to clients or investors;

(iii) All accounts that were managed in a substantially similar manner are advertised unless the exclusion of any such account would not result in materially higher performance and the exclusion of any account does not alter the presentation of any applicable time periods prescribed in paragraph (d)(2) of this section; and

(iv) The *advertisement* clearly and prominently includes all relevant disclosures, including that the performance results were from accounts managed at another entity.

(e) *Definitions.* For purposes of this section:

(1) *Advertisement* means:

(i) Any direct or indirect communication an investment adviser makes to more than one person, or to one or more persons if the communication includes *hypothetical performance*, that offers the investment adviser's investment advisory services with regard to securities to prospective clients or investors in a *private fund* advised by the investment adviser or offers new investment advisory services with regard to securities to current clients or investors in a *private fund* advised by the investment adviser, but does not include:

(A) Extemporaneous, live, oral communications;

(B) Information contained in a statutory or regulatory notice, filing, or other required communication, provided that such information is reasonably designed to satisfy the requirements of such notice, filing, or other required communication; or

(C) A communication that includes *hypothetical performance* that is provided:

(1) In response to an unsolicited request for such information from a prospective or current client or investor in a *private fund* advised by the investment adviser; or

(2) To a prospective or current investor in a *private fund* advised by the investment adviser in a one-on-one communication; and

(ii) Any *endorsement* or *testimonial* for which an investment adviser provides compensation, directly or indirectly, but does not include any information contained in a statutory or regulatory notice, filing, or other required communication, provided that such information is reasonably designed to satisfy the requirements of such notice, filing, or other required communication.

(2) *De minimis compensation* means compensation paid to a *person* for providing a *testimonial* or *endorsement* of a total of $1,000 or less (or the equivalent value in non-cash compensation) during the preceding 12 months.

(3) A *disqualifying Commission action* means a Commission opinion or order barring, suspending, or prohibiting the person from acting in any capacity under the Federal securities laws.

(4) A *disqualifying event* is any of the following events that occurred within 10 years prior to the person disseminating an *endorsement* or *testimonial*:

(i) A conviction by a court of competent jurisdiction within the United States of any felony or misdemeanor involving conduct described in paragraph (2)(A) through (D) of section 203(e) of the Act;

(ii) A conviction by a court of competent jurisdiction within the United States of engaging in, any of the conduct specified in paragraphs (1), (5), or (6) of section 203(e) of the Act;

(iii) The entry of any final order by any entity described in paragraph (9) of section 203(e) of the Act, or by the U.S. Commodity Futures Trading Commission or a self-regulatory organization (as defined in the Form ADV Glossary of Terms)), of the type described in paragraph (9) of section 203(e) of the Act;

(iv) The entry of an order, judgment or decree described in paragraph (4) of section 203(e) of the Act, and still in effect, by any court of competent jurisdiction within the United States; and

(v) A Commission order that a person cease and desist from committing or causing a violation or future violation of:

(A) Any scienter-based anti-fraud provision of the Federal securities laws, including without limitation section 17(a)(1) of the Securities Act of 1933 (15 U.S.C. 77q(a)(1)), section 10(b) of the Securities Exchange Act of 1934 (15 U.S.C. 78j(b)) and 17 CFR 240.10b–5, section 15(c)(1) of the Securities Exchange Act of 1934 (15 U.S.C. 78o(c)(1)), and section 206(1) of the Investment Advisers Act of 1940 (15 U.S.C. 80b–6(1)), or any other rule or regulation thereunder; or

(B) Section 5 of the Securities Act of 1933 (15 U.S.C. 77e);

(vi) A *disqualifying event* does not include an event described in paragraphs (e)(4)(i) through (v) of this section with respect to a person that is also subject to:

(A) An order pursuant to section 9(c) of the Investment Company Act of 1940 (15 U.S.C. 80a–3) with respect to such event; or

(B) A Commission opinion or order with respect to such event that is not a *disqualifying Commission action*; provided that for each applicable type of order or opinion described in paragraphs (e)(4)(vi)(A) and (B) of this section:

(*1*) The person is in compliance with the terms of the order or opinion, including, but not limited to, the payment of disgorgement, prejudgment interest, civil or administrative penalties, and fines; and

(*2*) For a period of 10 years following the date of each order or opinion, the advertisement containing the *testimonial* or *endorsement* must include a statement that the person providing the testimonial or endorsement is subject to a Commission order or opinion regarding one or more disciplinary action(s), and include the order or opinion or a link to the order or opinion on the Commission's website.

(5) *Endorsement* means any statement by a person other than a current client or investor in a *private fund* advised by the investment adviser that:

(i) Indicates approval, support, or recommendation of the investment adviser or its supervised persons or describes that person's experience with the investment adviser or its supervised persons;

(ii) Directly or indirectly solicits any current or prospective client or investor to be a client of, or an investor in a *private fund* advised by, the investment adviser; or

(iii) Refers any current or prospective client or investor to be a client of, or an investor in a *private fund* advised by, the investment adviser.

(6) *Extracted performance* means the performance results of a subset of investments extracted from a *portfolio*.

(7) *Gross performance* means the performance results of a *portfolio* (or portions of a *portfolio* that are included in *extracted performance*, if applicable) before the deduction of all fees and expenses that a client or investor has paid or would have paid in connection with the investment adviser's investment advisory services to the relevant *portfolio*.

(8) *Hypothetical performance* means performance results that were not actually achieved by any *portfolio* of the investment adviser. *Hypothetical performance* includes, but is not limited to:

(i) Performance derived from model *portfolios*;

(ii) Performance that is backtested by the application of a strategy to data from prior time periods when the strategy was not actually used during those time periods; and

(iii) Targeted or projected performance returns with respect to any *portfolio* or to the investment advisory services with regard to securities offered in the *advertisement*.

(iv) *Hypothetical performance* does not include:

(A) An interactive analysis tool where a client or investor, or prospective client, or investor, uses the tool to produce simulations and statistical analyses that present the likelihood of various investment outcomes if certain investments are made or certain investment strategies or styles are undertaken, thereby serving as an additional resource to investors in the evaluation of the potential risks and returns of investment choices; provided that the investment adviser:

(*1*) Provides a description of the criteria and methodology used, including the investment analysis tool's limitations and key assumptions;

(*2*) Explains that the results may vary with each use and over time;

(3) If applicable, describes the universe of investments considered in the analysis, explains how the tool determines which investments to select, discloses if the tool favors certain investments and, if so, explains the reason for the selectivity, and states that other investments not considered may have characteristics similar or superior to those being analyzed; and

(4) Discloses that the tool generates outcomes that are hypothetical in nature; or

(B) *Predecessor performance* that is displayed in compliance with paragraph (d)(7) of this section.

(9) *Ineligible person* means a person who is subject to a *disqualifying Commission action* or is subject to any *disqualifying event*, and the following persons with respect to the *ineligible person*:

(i) Any employee, officer, or director of the *ineligible person* and any other individuals with similar status or functions within the scope of association with the *ineligible person*;

(ii) If the *ineligible person* is a partnership, all general partners; and

(iii) If the *ineligible person* is a limited liability company managed by elected managers, all elected managers.

(10) *Net performance* means the performance results of a *portfolio* (or portions of a *portfolio* that are included in *extracted performance*, if applicable) after the deduction of all fees and expenses that a client or investor has paid or would have paid in connection with the investment adviser's investment advisory services to the relevant *portfolio*, including, if applicable, advisory fees, advisory fees paid to underlying investment vehicles, and payments by the investment adviser for which the client or investor reimburses the investment adviser. For purposes of this rule, *net performance*:

(i) May reflect the exclusion of custodian fees paid to a bank or other third-party organization for safekeeping funds and securities; and/or

(ii) If using a model fee, must reflect one of the following:

(A) The deduction of a model fee when doing so would result in performance figures that are no higher than if the actual fee had been deducted; or

(B) The deduction of a model fee that is equal to the highest fee charged to the intended audience to whom the *advertisement* is disseminated.

(11) *Portfolio* means a group of investments managed by the investment adviser. A *portfolio* may be an account or a *private fund* and includes, but is not limited to, a *portfolio* for the account of the investment adviser or its *advisory affiliate* (as defined in the Form ADV Glossary of Terms).

(12) *Predecessor performance* means investment performance achieved by a group of investments consisting of an account or a private fund that was not advised at all times during the period shown by the investment adviser advertising the performance.

(13) *Private fund* has the same meaning as in section 2(a)(29) of the Act.

(14) *Related performance* means the performance results of one or more *related portfolios*, either on a *portfolio*-by-*portfolio* basis or as a composite aggregation of all *portfolios* falling within stated criteria.

(15) *Related portfolio* means a *portfolio* with substantially similar investment policies, objectives, and strategies as those of the services being offered in the *advertisement*.

(16) *Supervised person* has the same meaning as in section 2(a)(25) of the Act.

(17) *Testimonial* means any statement by a current client or investor in a *private fund* advised by the investment adviser:

(i) About the client or investor's experience with the investment adviser or its supervised persons;

(ii)   That directly or indirectly solicits any current or prospective client or investor to be a client of, or an investor in a *private fund* advised by, the investment adviser; or

(iii)   That refers any current or prospective client or investor to be a client of, or an investor in a *private fund* advised by, the investment adviser.

(18)   *Third-party rating* means a rating or ranking of an investment adviser provided by a person who is not a *related person* (as defined in the Form ADV Glossary of Terms), and such person provides such ratings or rankings in the ordinary course of its business.

Rule 206(4)–2.   Custody of Funds or Securities of Clients by Investment Advisers

(a)   Safekeeping required. If you are an investment adviser registered or required to be registered under section 203 of the Act, it is a fraudulent, deceptive, or manipulative act, practice or course of business within the meaning of section 206(4) of the Act for you to have custody of client funds or securities unless:

(1)   Qualified custodian. A qualified custodian maintains those funds and securities:

(i)   In a separate account for each client under that client's name; or

(ii)   In accounts that contain only your clients' funds and securities, under your name as agent or trustee for the clients.

(2)   Notice to clients. If you open an account with a qualified custodian on your client's behalf, either under the client's name or under your name as agent, you notify the client in writing of the qualified custodian's name, address, and the manner in which the funds or securities are maintained, promptly when the account is opened and following any changes to this information. If you send account statements to a client to which you are required to provide this notice, include in the notification provided to that client and in any subsequent account statement you send that client a statement urging the client to compare the account statements from the custodian with those from the adviser.

(3)   Account statements to clients. You have a reasonable basis, after due inquiry, for believing that the qualified custodian sends an account statement, at least quarterly, to each of your clients for which it maintains funds or securities, identifying the amount of funds and of each security in the account at the end of the period and setting forth all transactions in the account during that period.

(4)   Independent verification. The client funds and securities of which you have custody are verified by actual examination at least once during each calendar year, except as provided below, by an independent public accountant, pursuant to a written agreement between you and the accountant, at a time that is chosen by the accountant without prior notice or announcement to you and that is irregular from year to year. The written agreement must provide for the first examination to occur within six months of becoming subject to this paragraph, except that, if you maintain client funds or securities pursuant to this rule as a qualified custodian, the agreement must provide for the first examination to occur no later than six months after obtaining the internal control report. The written agreement must require the accountant to:

(i)   File a certificate on Form ADV–E (17 CFR 279.8) with the Commission within 120 days of the time chosen by the accountant in paragraph (a)(4) of this rule, stating that it has examined the funds and securities and describing the nature and extent of the examination;

(ii)   Upon finding any material discrepancies during the course of the examination, notify the Commission within one business day of the finding, by means of a facsimile transmission or electronic mail, followed by first class mail, directed to the attention of the Director of the Office of Compliance Inspections and Examinations; and

(iii)   Upon resignation or dismissal from, or other termination of, the engagement, or upon removing itself or being removed from consideration for being reappointed, file within four business days Form ADV–E accompanied by a statement that includes:

(A)   The date of such resignation, dismissal, removal, or other termination, and the name, address, and contact information of the accountant; and

(B)   An explanation of any problems relating to examination scope or procedure that contributed to such resignation, dismissal, removal, or other termination.

(5)   Special rule for limited partnerships and limited liability companies. If you or a related person is a general partner of a limited partnership (or managing member of a limited liability company, or hold a comparable position for another type of pooled investment vehicle), the account statements required under paragraph (a)(3) of this rule must be sent to each limited partner (or member or other beneficial owner).

(6)   Investment advisers acting as qualified custodians. If you maintain, or if you have custody because a related person maintains, client funds or securities pursuant to this rule as a qualified custodian in connection with advisory services you provide to clients:

(i)   The independent public accountant you retain to perform the independent verification required by paragraph (a)(4) of this rule must be registered with, and subject to regular inspection as of the commencement of the professional engagement period, and as of each calendar year-end, by, the Public Company Accounting Oversight Board in accordance with its rules; and

(ii)   You must obtain, or receive from your related person, within six months of becoming subject to this paragraph and thereafter no less frequently than once each calendar year a written internal control report prepared by an independent public accountant:

(A)   The internal control report must include an opinion of an independent public accountant as to whether controls have been placed in operation as of a specific date, and are suitably designed and are operating effectively to meet control objectives relating to custodial services, including the safeguarding of funds and securities held by either you or a related person on behalf of your advisory clients, during the year;

(B)   The independent public accountant must verify that the funds and securities are reconciled to a custodian other than you or your related person; and

(C)   The independent public accountant must be registered with, and subject to regular inspection as of the commencement of the professional engagement period, and as of each calendar year-end, by, the Public Company Accounting Oversight Board in accordance with its rules.

(7)   Independent representatives. A client may designate an independent representative to receive, on his behalf, notices and account statements as required under paragraphs (a)(2) and (a)(3) of this rule.

(b)   Exceptions. (1) Shares of mutual funds. With respect to shares of an open-end company as defined in section 5(a)(1) of the Investment Company Act of 1940 (15 U.S.C. 80a–5(a)(1)) ("mutual fund"), you may use the mutual fund's transfer agent in lieu of a qualified custodian for purposes of complying with paragraph (a) of this rule.

(2)   Certain privately offered securities. (i) You are not required to comply with paragraph (a)(1) of this rule with respect to securities that are:

(A)   Acquired from the issuer in a transaction or chain of transactions not involving any public offering;

(B)   Uncertificated, and ownership thereof is recorded only on the books of the issuer or its transfer agent in the name of the client; and

(C)   Transferable only with prior consent of the issuer or holders of the outstanding securities of the issuer.

(ii)   Notwithstanding paragraph (b)(2)(i) of this rule, the provisions of this paragraph (b)(2) are available with respect to securities held for the account of a limited partnership (or a limited liability company, or other type of pooled investment vehicle) only if the limited partnership is audited, and the audited financial statements are distributed, as described in paragraph (b)(4) of this rule.

(3)   Fee deduction. Notwithstanding paragraph (a)(4) of this rule, you are not required to obtain an independent verification of client funds and securities maintained by a qualified custodian if:

(i)   you have custody of the funds and securities solely as a consequence of your authority to make withdrawals from client accounts to pay your advisory fee; and

(ii)   if the qualified custodian is a related person, you can rely on paragraph (b)(6) of this rule.

(4)   Limited partnerships subject to annual audit. You are not required to comply with paragraphs (a)(2) and (a)(3) of this rule and you shall be deemed to have complied with paragraph (a)(4) of this rule with respect to the account of a limited partnership (or limited liability company, or another type of pooled investment vehicle) that is subject to audit (as defined in rule 1–02(d) of Regulation S–X (17 CFR 210.1–02(d))):

(i)   At least annually and distributes its audited financial statements prepared in accordance with generally accepted accounting principles to all limited partners (or members or other beneficial owners) within 120 days of the end of its fiscal year;

(ii)   By an independent public accountant that is registered with, and subject to regular inspection as of the commencement of the professional engagement period, and as of each calendar year-end, by, the Public Company Accounting Oversight Board in accordance with its rules; and

(iii) Upon liquidation and distributes its audited financial statements prepared in accordance with generally accepted accounting principles to all limited partners (or members or other beneficial owners) promptly after the completion of such audit.

(5)   Registered investment companies. You are not required to comply with this rule (17 CFR 275.206(4)–2) with respect to the account of an investment company registered under the Investment Company Act of 1940 (15 U.S.C. 80a–1 to 80a–64).

(6)   Certain Related Persons. Notwithstanding paragraph (a)(4) of this rule, you are not required to obtain an independent verification of client funds and securities if: (i) you have custody under this rule solely because a related person holds, directly or indirectly, client funds or securities, or has any authority to obtain possession of them, in connection with advisory services you provide to clients; and

(ii)   your related person is operationally independent of you.

(c)   Delivery to Related Person. Sending an account statement under paragraph (a)(5) of this rule or distributing audited financial statements under paragraph (b)(4) of this rule shall not satisfy the requirements of this rule if such account statements or financial statements are sent solely to limited partners (or members or other beneficial owners) that themselves are limited partnerships (or limited liability companies, or another type of pooled investment vehicle) and are your related persons.

(d)   Definitions. For the purposes of this rule:

(1)   Control means the power, directly or indirectly, to direct the management or policies of a person, whether through ownership of securities, by contract, or otherwise. Control includes:

(i)   Each of your firm's officers, partners, or directors exercising executive responsibility (or persons having similar status or functions) is presumed to control your firm;

(ii)   A person is presumed to control a corporation if the person:

(A)   Directly or indirectly has the right to vote 25 percent or more of a class of the corporation's voting securities; or

(B)   Has the power to sell or direct the sale of 25 percent or more of a class of the corporation's voting securities;

(iii) A person is presumed to control a partnership if the person has the right to receive upon dissolution, or has contributed, 25 percent or more of the capital of the partnership;

(iv)   A person is presumed to control a limited liability company if the person:

(A)   Directly or indirectly has the right to vote 25 percent or more of a class of the interests of the limited liability company;

(B) Has the right to receive upon dissolution, or has contributed, 25 percent or more of the capital of the limited liability company; or

(C) Is an elected manager of the limited liability company; or

(v) A person is presumed to control a trust if the person is a trustee or managing agent of the trust.

(2) Custody means holding, directly or indirectly, client funds or securities, or having any authority to obtain possession of them. You have custody if a related person holds, directly or indirectly, client funds or securities, or has any authority to obtain possession of them, in connection with advisory services you provide to clients. Custody includes:

(i) Possession of client funds or securities (but not of checks drawn by clients and made payable to third parties) unless you receive them inadvertently and you return them to the sender promptly but in any case within three business days of receiving them;

(ii) Any arrangement (including a general power of attorney) under which you are authorized or permitted to withdraw client funds or securities maintained with a custodian upon your instruction to the custodian; and

(iii) Any capacity (such as general partner of a limited partnership, managing member of a limited liability company or a comparable position for another type of pooled investment vehicle, or trustee of a trust) that gives you or your supervised person legal ownership of or access to client funds or securities.

(3) Independent public accountant means a public accountant that meets the standards of independence described in rule 2–01(b) and (c) of Regulation S–X (17 CFR 210.2–01(b) and (c)).

(4) Independent representative means a person that:

(i) Acts as agent for an advisory client, including in the case of a pooled investment vehicle, for limited partners of a limited partnership (or members of a limited liability company, or other beneficial owners of another type of pooled investment vehicle) and by law or contract is obliged to act in the best interest of the advisory client or the limited partners (or members, or other beneficial owners);

(ii) Does not control, is not controlled by, and is not under common control with you; and

(iii) Does not have, and has not had within the past two years, a material business relationship with you.

(5) Operationally independent: for purposes of paragraph (b)(6) of this rule, a related person is presumed not to be operationally independent unless each of the following conditions is met and no other circumstances can reasonably be expected to compromise the operational independence of the related person: (i) client assets in the custody of the related person are not subject to claims of the adviser's creditors; (ii) advisory personnel do not have custody or possession of, or direct or indirect access to client assets of which the related person has custody, or the power to control the disposition of such client assets to third parties for the benefit of the adviser or its related persons, or otherwise have the opportunity to misappropriate such client assets; (iii) advisory personnel and personnel of the related person who have access to advisory client assets are not under common supervision; and (iv) advisory personnel do not hold any position with the related person or share premises with the related person.

(6) Qualified custodian means:

(i) A bank as defined in section 202(a)(2) of the Advisers Act (15 U.S.C. 80b–2(a)(2)) or a savings association as defined in section 3(b)(1) of the Federal Deposit Insurance Act (12 U.S.C. 1813(b)(1)) that has deposits insured by the Federal Deposit Insurance Corporation under the Federal Deposit Insurance Act (12 U.S.C. 1811);

(ii) A broker-dealer registered under section 15(b)(1) of the Securities Exchange Act of 1934 (15 U.S.C. 78o(b)(1)), holding the client assets in customer accounts;

(iii) A futures commission merchant registered under section 4f(a) of the Commodity Exchange Act (7 U.S.C. 6f(a)), holding the client assets in customer accounts, but only with respect to clients' funds and security futures, or other securities incidental to transactions in contracts for the purchase or sale of a commodity for future delivery and options thereon; and

(iv) A foreign financial institution that customarily holds financial assets for its customers, provided that the foreign financial institution keeps the advisory clients' assets in customer accounts segregated from its proprietary assets.

(7) Related person means any person, directly or indirectly, controlling or controlled by you, and any person that is under common control with you.

Rule 206(4)–3. Reserved and Removed

Rule 206(4)–4. Reserved and Removed

Rule 206(4)–5. Political Contributions by Certain Investment Advisers

(a) Prohibitions. As a means reasonably designed to prevent fraudulent, deceptive or manipulative acts, practices, or courses of business within the meaning of section 206(4) of the Act (15 U.S.C. 80b–6(4)), it shall be unlawful:

(1) For any investment adviser registered (or required to be registered) with the Commission, or unregistered in reliance on the exemption available under section 203(b)(3) of the Investment Advisers Act of 1940, or that is an exempt reporting adviser, as defined in Rule 204–4(a) under the Investment Advisers Act of 1940, to provide investment advisory services for compensation to a government entity within two years after a contribution to an official of the government entity is made by the investment adviser or any covered associate of the investment adviser (including a person who becomes a covered associate within two years after the contribution is made); and

(2) For any investment adviser registered (or required to be registered) with the Commission, or unregistered in reliance on the exemption available under section 203(b)(3) of the Investment Advisers Act of 1940, or that is an exempt reporting adviser, or any of the investment adviser's covered associates:

(i) To provide or agree to provide, directly or indirectly, payment to any person to solicit a government entity for investment advisory services on behalf of such investment adviser unless such person is:

(A) A regulated person; or

(B) An executive officer, general partner, managing member (or, in each case, a person with a similar status or function), or employee of the investment adviser; and

(b) Exceptions.

(1) De minimis exception. Paragraph (a)(1) of this rule does not apply to contributions made by a covered associate, if a natural person, to officials for whom the covered associate was entitled to vote at the time of the contributions and which in the aggregate do not exceed $350 to any one official, per election, or to officials for whom the covered associate was not entitled to vote at the time of the contributions and which in the aggregate do not exceed $150 to any one official, per election.

(2) Exception for certain new covered associates. The prohibitions of paragraph (a)(1) of this rule shall not apply to an investment adviser as a result of a contribution made by a natural person more than six months prior to becoming a covered associate of the investment adviser unless such person, after becoming a covered associate, solicits clients on behalf of the investment adviser.

(3) Exception for certain returned contributions.

(i) An investment adviser that is prohibited from providing investment advisory services for compensation pursuant to paragraph (a)(1) of this rule as a result of a contribution made by a covered associate of the investment adviser is excepted from such prohibition, subject to paragraphs (b)(3)(ii) and (b)(3)(iii) of this rule, upon satisfaction of the following requirements:

(A)   The investment adviser must have discovered the contribution which resulted in the prohibition within four months of the date of such contribution;

(B)   Such contribution must not have exceeded $350; and

(C)   The contributor must obtain a return of the contribution within 60 calendar days of the date of discovery of such contribution by the investment adviser.

(ii)   In any calendar year, an investment adviser that has reported on its annual updating amendment to Form ADV (17 CFR 279.1) that it has more than 50 employees is entitled to no more than three exceptions pursuant to paragraph (b)(3)(i) of this rule, and an investment adviser that has reported on its annual updating amendment to Form ADV that it has 50 or fewer employees is entitled to no more than two exceptions pursuant to paragraph (b)(3)(i) of this rule.

(iii)   An investment adviser may not rely on the exception provided in paragraph (b)(3)(i) of this rule more than once with respect to contributions by the same covered associate of the investment adviser regardless of the time period.

(c)   Prohibitions as applied to covered investment pools. For purposes of this rule, an investment adviser to a covered investment pool in which a government entity invests or is solicited to invest shall be treated as though that investment adviser were providing or seeking to provide investment advisory services directly to the government entity.

(d)   Further prohibition. As a means reasonably designed to prevent fraudulent, deceptive or manipulative acts, practices, or courses of business within the meaning of section 206(4) of Advisers Act of 1940, it shall be unlawful for any investment adviser registered (or required to be registered) with the Commission, or unregistered in reliance on the exemption available under section 203(b)(3) of the Investment Advisers Act of 1940, or that is an exempt reporting adviser, or any of the investment adviser's covered associates to do anything indirectly which, if done directly, would result in a violation of this rule.

(e)   Exemptions. The Commission, upon application, may conditionally or unconditionally exempt an investment adviser from the prohibition under paragraph (a)(1) of this rule. In determining whether to grant an exemption, the Commission will consider, among other factors:

(1)   Whether the exemption is necessary or appropriate in the public interest and consistent with the protection of investors and the purposes fairly intended by the policy and provisions of the Advisers Act (15 U.S.C. 80b);

(2)   Whether the investment adviser:

(i)   Before the contribution resulting in the prohibition was made, adopted and implemented policies and procedures reasonably designed to prevent violations of this rule; and

(ii)   Prior to or at the time the contribution which resulted in such prohibition was made, had no actual knowledge of the contribution; and

(iii)   After learning of the contribution:

(A)   Has taken all available steps to cause the contributor involved in making the contribution which resulted in such prohibition to obtain a return of the contribution; and

(B)   Has taken such other remedial or preventive measures as may be appropriate under the circumstances;

(3)   Whether, at the time of the contribution, the contributor was a covered associate or otherwise an employee of the investment adviser, or was seeking such employment;

(4)   The timing and amount of the contribution which resulted in the prohibition; (5) The nature of the election (*e.g.*, federal, state or local); and (6) The contributor's apparent intent or motive in making the contribution which resulted in the prohibition, as evidenced by the facts and circumstances surrounding such contribution.

(f)   Definitions. For purposes of this rule:

(1)   Contribution means any gift, subscription, loan, advance, or deposit of money or anything of value made for:

(i) The purpose of influencing any election for federal, state or local office; (ii) Payment of debt incurred in connection with any such election; or (iii) Transition or inaugural expenses of the successful candidate for state or local office.

(2) Covered associate of an investment adviser means:

(i) Any general partner, managing member or executive officer, or other individual with a similar status or function;

(ii) Any employee who solicits a government entity for the investment adviser and any person who supervises, directly or indirectly, such employee; and

(iii) Any political action committee controlled by the investment adviser or by any person described in paragraphs (f)(2)(i) and (f)(2)(ii) of this rule.

(3) Covered investment pool means:

(i) An investment company registered under the Investment Company Act of 1940 (15 U.S.C. 80a) that is an investment option of a plan or program of a government entity; or

(ii) Any company that would be an investment company under section 3(a) of the Investment Company Act of 1940 (15 U.S.C. 80a–3(a)), but for the exclusion provided from that definition by either section 3(c)(1), section 3(c)(7) or section 3(c)(11) of that Act (15 U.S.C. 80a–3(c)(1), (c)(7) or (c)(11)).

(4) Executive officer of an investment adviser means:

(i) The president;

(ii) Any vice president in charge of a principal business unit, division or function (such as sales, administration or finance);

(iii) Any other officer of the investment adviser who performs a policy-making function; or

(iv) Any other person who performs similar policy-making functions for the investment adviser.

(5) Government entity means any state or political subdivision of a state, including:

(i) Any agency, authority, or instrumentality of the state or political subdivision;

(ii) A pool of assets sponsored or established by the state or political subdivision or any agency, authority or instrumentality thereof, including, but not limited to a "defined benefit plan" as defined in section 414(j) of the Internal Revenue Code (26 U.S.C. 414(j)), or a state general fund;

(iii) A plan or program of a government entity; and

(iv) Officers, agents, or employees of the state or political subdivision or any agency, authority or instrumentality thereof, acting in their official capacity.

(6) Official means any person (including any election committee for the person) who was, at the time of the contribution, an incumbent, candidate or successful candidate for elective office of a government entity, if the office:

(i) Is directly or indirectly responsible for, or can influence the outcome of, the hiring of an investment adviser by a government entity; or

(ii) Has authority to appoint any person who is directly or indirectly responsible for, or can influence the outcome of, the hiring of an investment adviser by a government entity.

(7) Payment means any gift, subscription, loan, advance, or deposit of money or anything of value.

(8) Plan or program of a government entity means any participant-directed investment program or plan sponsored or established by a state or political subdivision or any agency, authority or instrumentality thereof, including, but not limited to, a "qualified tuition plan" authorized by section

529 of the Internal Revenue Code (26 U.S.C. 529), a retirement plan authorized by section 403(b) or 457 of the Internal Revenue Code (26 U.S.C. 403(b) or 457), or any similar program or plan.

(9)   Regulated person means:

(i)   An investment adviser registered with the Commission that has not, and whose covered associates have not, within two years of soliciting a government entity:

(A)   Made a contribution to an official of that government entity, other than as described in paragraph (b)(1) of this rule; and

(B)   Coordinated or solicited any person or political action committee to make any contribution or payment described in paragraphs (a)(2)(ii)(A) and (B) of this rule;

(ii)   A broker, as defined in section 3(a)(4) of the Securities Exchange Act of 1934 or a dealer, as defined in section 3(a)(5) of that Act, that is registered with the Commission, and is a member of a national securities association registered under 15A of that Act, provided that:

(A)   The rules of the association prohibit members from engaging in distribution or solicitation activities if certain political contributions have been made; and

(B)   The Commission, by order, finds that such rules impose substantially equivalent or more stringent restrictions on broker-dealers than this rule imposes on investment advisers and that such rules are consistent with the objectives of this rule; and

(iii)   A—municipal advisor registered with the Commission under section 15B of the Exchange Act and subject to rules of the Municipal Securities Rulemaking Board, provided that:

(A)   Such rules prohibit municipal advisors from engaging in distribution or solicitation activities if certain political contributions have been made; and

(B)   The Commission, by order, finds that such rules impose substantially equivalent or more stringent restrictions on municipal advisors than this rule imposes on investment advisers and that such rules are consistent with the objectives of this rule.

(10)   Solicit means:

(i)   With respect to investment advisory services, to communicate, directly or indirectly, for the purpose of obtaining or retaining a client for, or referring a client to, an investment adviser; and

(ii)   With respect to a contribution or payment, to communicate, directly or indirectly, for the purpose of obtaining or arranging a contribution or payment.

Rule 206(4)–6.   Proxy Voting

If you are an investment adviser registered or required to be registered under section 203 of the Act, it is a fraudulent, deceptive, or manipulative act, practice or course of business within the meaning of section 206(4) of the Act, for you to exercise voting authority with respect to client securities, unless you:

(a)   Adopt and implement written policies and procedures that are reasonably designed to ensure that you vote client securities in the best interest of clients, which procedures must include how you address material conflicts that may arise between your interests and those of your clients;

(b)   Disclose to clients how they may obtain information from you about how you voted with respect to their securities; and

(c)   Describe to clients your proxy voting policies and procedures and, upon request, furnish a copy of the policies and procedures to the requesting client.

Rule 206(4)–7.   Compliance Procedures and Practices

If you are an investment adviser registered or required to be registered under section 203 of the Investment Advisers Act of 1940, it shall be unlawful within the meaning of section 206 of the Act for you to provide investment advice to clients unless you:

(a) *Policies and procedures.* Adopt and implement written policies and procedures reasonably designed to prevent violation, by you and your supervised persons, of the Act and the rules that the Commission has adopted under the Act;

(b) *Annual review.* Review, no less frequently than annually, the adequacy of the policies and procedures established pursuant to this rule and the effectiveness of their implementation; and

(c) *Chief compliance officer.* Designate an individual (who is a supervised person) responsible for administering the policies and procedures that you adopt under paragraph (a) of this rule.

Rule 206(4)–8.   Pooled Investment Vehicles

(a) *Prohibition.* It shall constitute a fraudulent, deceptive, or manipulative act, practice, or course of business within the meaning of section 206(4) of the Act for any investment adviser to a pooled investment vehicle to:

(1)   Make any untrue statement of a material fact or to omit to state a material fact necessary to make the statements made, in the light of the circumstances under which they were made, not misleading, to any investor or prospective investor in the pooled investment vehicle; or

(2)   Otherwise engage in any act, practice, or course of business that is fraudulent, deceptive, or manipulative with respect to any investor or prospective investor in the pooled investment vehicle.

(b) *Definition.* For purposes of this rule "pooled investment vehicle" means any investment company as defined in section 3(a) of the Investment Company Act of 1940 or any company that would be an investment company under section 3(a) of that Act but for the exclusion provided from that definition by either section 3(c)(1) or section 3(c)(7) of that Act.

Rule 222–2.   Definition of "Client" for Purposes of the National De Minimis Standard

For purposes of section 222(d)(2) of the Investment Advisers Act of 1940, an investment adviser may rely upon the definition of—client provided by Rule 202(a)(30)–1, without giving regard to paragraph (b)(4) of that section.

II. RELATED LAWS AND REGULATIONS

MAIL AND WIRE FRAUD STATUTES

18 U.S.C. § ___

Sec. 1341.   Frauds and Swindles

Whoever, having devised or intending to devise any scheme or artifice to defraud, or for obtaining money or property by means of false or fraudulent pretenses, representations, or promises, or to sell, dispose of, loan, exchange, alter, give away, distribute, supply, or furnish or procure for unlawful use any counterfeit or spurious coin, obligation, security, or other article, or anything represented to be or intimated or held out to be such counterfeit or spurious article, for the purpose of executing such scheme or artifice or attempting so to do, places in any post office or authorized depository for mail matter, any matter or thing whatever to be sent or delivered by the Postal Service, or deposits or causes to be deposited any matter or thing whatever to be sent or delivered by any private or commercial interstate carrier, or takes or receives therefrom, any such matter or thing, or knowingly causes to be delivered by mail or such carrier according to the direction thereon, or at the place at which it is directed to be delivered by the person to whom it is addressed, any such matter or thing, shall be fined under this title or imprisoned not more than 20 years, or both. If the violation occurs in relation to, or involving any benefit authorized, transported, transmitted, transferred, disbursed, or paid in connection with, a presidentially declared major disaster or emergency (as those terms are defined in section 102 of the Robert T. Stafford Disaster Relief and Emergency Assistance Act), or affects a financial institution, such person shall be fined not more than $1,000,000 or imprisoned not more than 30 years, or both.

Sec. 1342.   Fictitious Name or Address

Whoever, for the purpose of conducting, promoting, or carrying on by means of the Postal Service, any scheme or device mentioned in section 1341 of this Act or any other unlawful business, uses or assumes, or requests to be addressed by, any fictitious, false, or assumed title, name, or address or name other than his own proper name, or takes or receives from any post office or authorized depository of mail matter, any letter, postal card, package, or other mail matter addressed to any such fictitious, false, or assumed title, name, or address, or name other than his own proper name, shall be fined under this title or imprisoned not more than five years, or both.

Sec. 1343.   Fraud by Wire, Radio, or Television

Whoever, having devised or intending to devise any scheme or artifice to defraud, or for obtaining money or property by means of false or fraudulent pretenses, representations, or promises, transmits or causes to be transmitted by means of wire, radio, or television communication in interstate or foreign commerce, any writings, signs, signals, pictures, or sounds for the purpose of executing such scheme or artifice, shall be fined under this title or imprisoned not more than 20 years, or both. If the violation occurs in relation to, or involving any benefit authorized, transported, transmitted, transferred, disbursed, or paid in connection with, a presidentially declared major disaster or emergency (as those terms are defined in section 102 of the Robert T. Stafford Disaster Relief and Emergency Assistance Act), or affects a financial institution, such person shall be fined not more than $1,000,000 or imprisoned not more than 30 years, or both.

Sec. 1344.   Bank Fraud

Whoever knowingly executes, or attempts to execute, a scheme or artifice—

(1)   to defraud a financial institution; or

(2)   to obtain any of the moneys, funds, credits, assets, securities or other property owned by or under the custody or control of a financial institution, by means of false or fraudulent pretenses, representations, or promises;

shall be fined not more than $1,000,000, or imprisoned not more than 30 years, or both.

Sec. 1345.   Injunctions Against Fraud

(a)(1)   If a person is—

(A)   violating or about to violate this Act or section 287, 371 (insofar as such violation involves a conspiracy to defraud the United States or any agency thereof), or 1001 of this Act;

(B)   committing or about to commit a banking law violation (as defined in section 3322(d) of this Act); or

(C)   committing or about to commit a Federal health care offense;

the Attorney General may commence a civil action in any Federal court to enjoin such violation.

(2)   If a person is alienating or disposing of property, or intends to alienate or dispose of property, obtained as a result of a banking law violation (as defined in section 3322(d) of this Act) or a Federal health care offense or property which is traceable to such violation, the Attorney General may commence a civil action in any Federal court—

(A)   to enjoin such alienation or disposition of property; or

(B)   for a restraining order to—

(i)   prohibit any person from withdrawing, transferring, removing, dissipating, or disposing of any such property or property of equivalent value; and

(ii)   appoint a temporary receiver to administer such restraining order.

(3)   A permanent or temporary injunction or restraining order shall be granted without bond.

(b)   The court shall proceed as soon as practicable to the hearing and determination of such an action, and may, at any time before final determination, enter such a restraining order or prohibition, or take such other action, as is warranted to prevent a continuing and substantial injury to the United States or to any person or class of persons for whose protection the action is brought. A proceeding under this section is governed by the Federal Rules of Civil Procedure, except that, if an indictment has been returned against the respondent, discovery is governed by the Federal Rules of Criminal Procedure.

Sec. 1346.   Definition of "Scheme or Artifice to Defraud"

For the purposes of this Act, the term "scheme or artifice to defraud" includes a scheme or artifice to deprive another of the intangible right of honest services.

Sec. 1348.   Securities and Commodities Fraud

Whoever knowingly executes, or attempts to execute, a scheme or artifice—

(1)   to defraud any person in connection with any commodity for future delivery, or any option on a commodity for future delivery, or any security of an issuer with a class of securities registered under section 12 of the Securities Exchange Act of 1934 or that is required to file reports under section 15(d) of the Securities Exchange Act of 1934; or

(2)   to obtain, by means of false or fraudulent pretenses, representations, or promises, any money or property in connection with the purchase or sale of any commodity for future delivery, or any option on a commodity for future delivery, or any security of an issuer with a class of securities registered under section 12 of the Securities Exchange Act of 1934 or that is required to file reports under section 15(d) of the Securities Exchange Act of 1934;

shall be fined under this title, or imprisoned not more than 25 years, or both.

RACKETEER INFLUENCED AND CORRUPT ORGANIZATIONS ACT

18 U.S.C. § ___

Sec. 1961. Definitions

As used in this chapter—

(1) "racketeering activity" means

(A) any act or threat involving murder, kidnapping, gambling, arson, robbery, bribery, extortion, dealing in obscene matter, or dealing in a controlled substance or listed chemical (as defined in section 102 of the Controlled Substances Act), which is chargeable under State law and punishable by imprisonment for more than one year;

(B) any act which is indictable under any of the following provisions of Title 18, United States Code: Section 201 (relating to bribery), section 224 (relating to sports bribery), sections 471, 472, and 473 (relating to counterfeiting), section 659 (relating to theft from interstate shipment) if the act indictable under section 659 is felonious, section 664 (relating to embezzlement from pension and welfare funds), sections 891–894 (relating to extortionate credit transactions), section 1028 (relating to fraud and related activity in connection with identification documents), section 1029 (relating to fraud and related activity in connection with access devices), section 1084 (relating to the transmission of gambling information), section 1341 (relating to mail fraud), section 1343 (relating to wire fraud), section 1344 (relating to financial institution fraud), section 1351, section 1425 (relating to the procurement of citizenship or nationalization unlawfully), section 1426 (relating to the reproduction of naturalization or citizenship papers), section 1427 (relating to the sale of naturalization or citizenship papers), sections 1461–1465 (relating to obscene matter), section 1503 (relating to obstruction of justice), section 1510 (relating to obstruction of criminal investigations), section 1511 (relating to the obstruction of State or local law enforcement), section 1512 (relating to tampering with a witness, victim, or an informant), section 1513 (relating to retaliating against a witness, victim, or an informant), section 1542 (relating to false statement in application and use of passport), section 1543 (relating to forgery or false use of passport), section 1544 (relating to misuse of passport), section 1546 (relating to fraud and misuse of visas, permits, and other documents), sections 1581–1592 (relating to peonage, slavery, and trafficking in persons), sections 1831 and 1832 (relating to economic espionage and theft of trade secrets), section 1951 (relating to interference with commerce, robbery, or extortion), section 1952 (relating to racketeering), section 1953 (relating to interstate transportation of wagering paraphernalia), section 1954 (relating to unlawful welfare fund payments), section 1955 (relating to the prohibition of illegal gambling businesses), section 1956 (relating to the laundering of monetary instruments), section 1957 (relating to engaging in monetary transactions in property derived from specified unlawful activity), section 1958 (relating to use of interstate commerce facilities in the commission of murder-for-hire), sections 2251, 2251A, 2252, and 2260 (relating to sexual exploitation of children), sections 2312 and 2313 (relating to interstate transportation of stolen motor vehicles), sections 2314 and 2315 (relating to interstate transportation of stolen property), section 2318 (relating to trafficking in counterfeit labels for phonorecords, computer programs or computer program documentation or packaging and copies of motion pictures or other audiovisual works), section 2319 (relating to criminal infringement of a copyright), section 2319A (relating to unauthorized fixation of and trafficking in sound recordings and music videos of live musical performances), section 2320 (relating to trafficking in goods or services bearing counterfeit marks), section 2321 (relating to trafficking in certain motor vehicles or motor vehicle parts), sections 2341–2346 (relating to trafficking in contraband cigarettes), sections 2421–24 (relating to white slave traffic), sections 175–178 (relating to biological weapons), sections 229–229F (relating to chemical weapons), section 831 (relating to nuclear materials),

(C) any act which is indictable under Title 29, United States Code, section 186 (dealing with restrictions on payments and loans to labor organizations) or section 501(c) (relating to embezzlement from union funds),

(D) any offense involving fraud connected with a case under Title 11, (except a case under section 157 of this title), fraud in the sale of securities, or the felonious manufacture, importation, receiving, concealment, buying, selling, or otherwise dealing in a controlled substance or listed chemical (as defined in section 102 of the Controlled Substances Act), punishable under any law of the United States,

(E) any act which is indictable under the Currency and Foreign Transactions Reporting Act,

(F) any act which is indictable under the Immigration and Nationality Act, section 274 (relating to bringing in and harboring certain aliens), section 277 (relating to aiding or assisting certain aliens to enter the United States), or section 278 (relating to importation of alien for immoral purpose) if the act indictable under such section of such Act was committed for the purpose of financial gain, or

(G) any act that is indictable under any provision listed in section 2332b(g)(5)(B);

(2) "State" means any State of the United States, the District of Columbia, the Commonwealth of Puerto Rico, any territory or possession of the United States, any political subdivision, or any department, agency, or instrumentality thereof;

(3) "person" includes any individual or entity capable of holding a legal or beneficial interest in property;

(4) "enterprise" includes any individual, partnership, corporation, association, or other legal entity, and any union or group of individuals associated in fact although not a legal entity;

(5) "pattern of racketeering activity" requires at least two acts of racketeering activity, one of which occurred after the effective date of this chapter and the last of which occurred within ten years (excluding any period of imprisonment) after the commission of a prior act of racketeering activity;

(6) "unlawful debt" means a debt

(A) incurred or contracted in gambling activity which was in violation of the law of the United States, a State or political subdivision thereof, or which is unenforceable under State or Federal law in whole or in part as to principal or interest because of the laws relating to usury, and

(B) which was incurred in connection with the business of gambling in violation of the law of the United States, a State or political subdivision thereof, or the business of lending money or a thing of value at a rate usurious under State or Federal law, where the usurious rate is at least twice the enforceable rate;

(7) "racketeering investigator" means any attorney or investigator so designated by the Attorney General and charged with the duty of enforcing or carrying into effect this chapter;

(8) "racketeering investigation" means any inquiry conducted by any racketeering investigator for the purpose of ascertaining whether any person has been involved in any violation of this chapter

or of any final order, judgment, or decree of any court of the United States, duly entered in any case or proceeding arising under this chapter;

(9) "documentary material" includes any book, paper, document, record, recording, or other material; and

(10) "Attorney General" includes the Attorney General of the United States, the Deputy Attorney General of the United States, the Associate Attorney General of the United States, any Assistant Attorney General of the United States, or any employee of the Department of Justice or any employee of any department or agency of the United States so designated by the Attorney General to carry out the powers conferred on the Attorney General by this Act. Any department or agency so designated may use in investigations authorized by this Act either the investigative provisions of this Act or the investigative power of such department or agency otherwise conferred by law.

Sec. 1962.   Prohibited Activities

(a)   It shall be unlawful for any person who has received any income derived, directly or indirectly, from a pattern of racketeering activity or through collection of an unlawful debt in which such person has participated as a principal within the meaning of section 2, Title 18, United States Code, to use or invest, directly or indirectly, any part of such income, or the proceeds of such income, in acquisition of any interest in, or the establishment or operation of, any enterprise which is engaged in, or the activities of which affect, interstate or foreign commerce. A purchase of securities on the open market for purposes of investment, and without the intention of controlling or participating in the control of the issuer, or of assisting another to do so, shall not be unlawful under this subsection if the securities of the issuer held by the purchaser, the members of his immediate family, and his or their accomplices in any pattern or racketeering activity or the collection of an unlawful debt after such purchase do not amount in the aggregate to one percent of the outstanding securities of any one class, and do not confer, either in law or in fact, the power to elect one or more directors of the issuer.

(b)   It shall be unlawful for any person through a pattern of racketeering activity or through collection of an unlawful debt to acquire or maintain, directly or indirectly, any interest in or control of any enterprise which is engaged in, or the activities of which affect, interstate or foreign commerce.

(c)   It shall be unlawful for any person employed by or associated with any enterprise engaged in, or the activities of which affect, interstate or foreign commerce, to conduct or participate, directly or indirectly, in the conduct of such enterprise's affairs through a pattern of racketeering activity or collection of unlawful debt.

(d)   It shall be unlawful for any person to conspire to violate any of the provisions of subsections (a), (b), or (c) of this section.

Sec. 1963.   Criminal Penalties

(a)   Whoever violates any provision of section 1962 of this Act shall be fined under this Act or imprisoned not more than 20 years (or for life if the violation is based on racketeering activity for which the maximum penalty includes life imprisonment) or both, and shall forfeit to the United States, irrespective of any provision of State law—

(1)   any interest the person has acquired or maintained in violation of section 1962;

(2)   any—

(A)   interest in;

(B)   security of;

(C)   claim against; or

(D)   property or contractual right of any kind affording a source of influence over;

any enterprise which the person has established, operated, controlled, conducted, or participated in the conduct of, in violation of section 1962; and

(3)   any property constituting, or derived from, any proceeds which the person obtained, directly or indirectly, from racketeering activity or unlawful debt collection in violation of section 1962.

The court, in imposing sentence on such person shall order, in addition to any other sentence imposed pursuant to this section, that the person forfeit to the United States all property described in this subsection. In lieu of a fine otherwise authorized by this section, a defendant who derives profits or other proceeds from an offense may be fined not more than twice the gross profits or other proceeds.

(b)   Property subject to criminal forfeiture under this section includes—

(1)   real property, including things growing on, affixed to, and found in land; and

(2)   tangible and intangible personal property, including rights, privileges, interests, claims and securities.

(c)   All right, title, and interest in property described in subsection (a) vests in the United States upon the commission of the act giving rise to forfeiture under this section. Any such property that is subsequently transferred to a person other than the defendant may be the subject of a special verdict of forfeiture and thereafter shall be ordered forfeited to the United States, unless the transferee establishes in a hearing pursuant to subsection (*l*) that he is a bona fide purchaser for value of such property who at the time of purchase was reasonably without cause to believe that the property was subject to forfeiture under this section.

(d)(1)   Upon application of the United States, the court may enter a restraining order or injunction, require the execution of a satisfactory performance bond, or take any other action to preserve the availability of property described in subsection (a) for forfeiture under this section—

(A)   upon the filing of an indictment or information charging a violation of section 1962 of this chapter and alleging that the property with respect to which the order is sought would, in the event of conviction, be subject to forfeiture under this section; or

(B)   prior to the filing of such an indictment or information, if, after notice to persons appearing to have an interest in the property and opportunity for a hearing, the court determines that—

(i)   there is a substantial probability that the United States will prevail on the issue of forfeiture and that failure to enter the order will result in the property being destroyed, removed from the jurisdiction of the court, or otherwise made unavailable for forfeiture; and

(ii)   the need to preserve the availability of the property through the entry of the requested order outweighs the hardship on any party against whom the order is to be entered:

Provided, however, That an order entered pursuant to subparagraph (B) shall be effective for not more than ninety days, unless extended by the court for good cause shown or unless an indictment or information described in subparagraph (A) has been filed.

(2)   A temporary restraining order under this subsection may be entered upon application of the United States without notice or opportunity for a hearing when an information or indictment has not yet been filed with respect to the property, if the United States demonstrates that there is probable cause to believe that the property with respect to which the order is sought would, in the event of conviction, be subject to forfeiture under this section and that provision of notice will jeopardize the availability of the property for forfeiture. Such a temporary order shall expire not more than fourteen days after the date on which it is entered, unless extended for good cause shown or unless the party against whom it is entered consents to an extension for a longer period. A hearing requested concerning an order entered under this paragraph shall be held at the earliest possible time, and prior to the expiration of the temporary order.

(3)   The court may receive and consider, at a hearing held pursuant to this subsection, evidence and information that would be inadmissible under the Federal Rules of Evidence.

(e)   Upon conviction of a person under this section, the court shall enter a judgment of forfeiture of the property to the United States and shall also authorize the Attorney General to seize all property ordered forfeited upon such terms and conditions as the court shall deem proper. Following the entry of an order declaring the property forfeited, the court may, upon application of the United States, enter such appropriate restraining orders or injunctions, require the execution of satisfactory performance bonds, appoint receivers, conservators, appraisers, accountants, or trustees, or take any other action to protect the interest of the United States in the property ordered forfeited. Any income accruing to, or derived from, an enterprise or an interest in an enterprise which has been ordered forfeited under this section may be used to offset ordinary and necessary expenses to the enterprise which are required by law, or which are necessary to protect the interests of the United States or third parties.

(f)   Following the seizure of property ordered forfeited under this section, the Attorney General shall direct the disposition of the property by sale or any other commercially feasible means, making due provision for the rights of any innocent persons. Any property right or interest not exercisable by, or transferable for value to, the United States shall expire and shall not revert to the defendant, nor shall the defendant or any person acting in concert with or on behalf of the defendant be eligible to purchase forfeited property at any sale held by the United States. Upon application of a person, other than the defendant or a person acting in concert with or on behalf of the defendant, the court may restrain or stay the sale or disposition of the property pending the conclusion of any appeal of the criminal case giving rise to the forfeiture, if the applicant demonstrates that proceeding with the sale or disposition of the property will result in irreparable injury, harm or loss to him. Notwithstanding 31 U.S.C. 3302(b), the proceeds of any sale or other disposition of property forfeited under this section and any moneys forfeited shall be used to pay all proper expenses for the forfeiture and the sale, including expenses of seizure, maintenance and custody of the property pending its disposition, advertising and court costs. The Attorney General shall deposit in the Treasury any amounts of such proceeds or moneys remaining after the payment of such expenses.

(g)   With respect to property ordered forfeited under this section, the Attorney General is authorized to—

(1)   grant petitions for mitigation or remission of forfeiture, restore forfeited property to victims of a violation of this Act, or take any other action to protect the rights of innocent persons which is in the interest of justice and which is not inconsistent with the provisions of this chapter;

(2)   compromise claims arising under this section;

(3)   award compensation to persons providing information resulting in a forfeiture under this section;

(4)   direct the disposition by the United States of all property ordered forfeited under this section by public sale or any other commercially feasible means, making due provision for the rights of innocent persons; and

(5)   take appropriate measures necessary to safeguard and maintain property ordered forfeited under this section pending its disposition.

(h)   The Attorney General may promulgate regulations with respect to—

(1)   making reasonable efforts to provide notice to persons who may have an interest in property ordered forfeited under this section;

(2)   granting petitions for remission or mitigation of forfeiture;

(3)   the restitution of property to victims of an offense petitioning for remission or mitigation of forfeiture under this Act;

(4)   the disposition by the United States of forfeited property by public sale or other commercially feasible means;

(5)   the maintenance and safekeeping of any property forfeited under this section pending its disposition; and

(6)   the compromise of claims arising under this Act.

Pending the promulgation of such regulations, all provisions of law relating to the disposition of property, or the proceeds from the sale thereof, or the remission or mitigation of forfeitures for violation of the customs laws, and the compromise of claims and the award of compensation to informers in respect of such forfeitures shall apply to forfeitures incurred, or alleged to have been incurred, under the provisions of this section, insofar as applicable and not inconsistent with the provisions hereof. Such duties as are imposed upon the

Customs Service or any person with respect to the disposition of property under the customs law shall be performed under this Act by the Attorney General.

(i)   Except as provided in subsection (*l*), no party claiming an interest in property subject to forfeiture under this section may—

(1)   intervene in a trial or appeal of a criminal case involving the forfeiture of such property under this section; or

(2)   commence an action at law or equity against the United States concerning the validity of his alleged interest in the property subsequent to the filing of an indictment or information alleging that the property is subject to forfeiture under this section.

(j)   The district courts of the United States shall have jurisdiction to enter orders as provided in this section without regard to the location of any property which may be subject to forfeiture under this section or which has been ordered forfeited under this section.

(k)   In order to facilitate the identification or location of property declared forfeited and to facilitate the disposition of petitions for remission or mitigation of forfeiture, after the entry of an order declaring property forfeited to the United States the court may, upon application of the United States, order that the testimony of any witness relating to the property forfeited be taken by deposition and that any designated book, paper, document, record, recording, or other material not privileged be produced at the same time and place, in the same manner as provided for the taking of depositions under Rule 15 of the Federal Rules of Criminal Procedure.

(*l*)(1)   Following the entry of an order of forfeiture under this section, the United States shall publish notice of the order and of its intent to dispose of the property in such manner as the Attorney General may direct. The Government may also, to the extent practicable, provide direct written notice to any person known to have alleged an interest in the property that is the subject of the order of forfeiture as a substitute for published notice as to those persons so notified.

(2)   Any person, other than the defendant, asserting a legal interest in property which has been ordered forfeited to the United States pursuant to this section may, within thirty days of the final publication of notice or his receipt of notice under paragraph (1), whichever is earlier, petition the court for a hearing to adjudicate the validity of his alleged interest in the property. The hearing shall be held before the court alone, without a jury.

(3)   The petition shall be signed by the petitioner under penalty of perjury and shall set forth the nature and extent of the petitioner's right, title, or interest in the property, the time and circumstances of the petitioner's acquisition of the right, title, or interest in the property, any additional facts supporting the petitioner's claim, and the relief sought.

(4)   The hearing on the petition shall, to the extent practicable and consistent with the interests of justice, be held within thirty days of the filing of the petition. The court may consolidate the hearing on the petition with a hearing on any other petition filed by a person other than the defendant under this subsection.

(5)   At the hearing, the petitioner may testify and present evidence and witnesses on his own behalf, and cross-examine witnesses who appear at the hearing. The United States may present evidence and witnesses in rebuttal and in defense of its claim to the property and cross-examine witnesses who appear at the hearing. In addition to testimony and evidence presented at the hearing, the court shall consider the relevant portions of the record of the criminal case which resulted in the order of forfeiture.

(6)   If, after the hearing, the court determines that the petitioner has established by a preponderance of the evidence that—

(A)   the petitioner has a legal right, title, or interest in the property, and such right, title, or interest renders the order of forfeiture invalid in whole or in part because the right, title, or interest was vested in the petitioner rather than the defendant or was superior to any right, title, or interest of the defendant at the time of the commission of the acts which gave rise to the forfeiture of the property under this section; or

(B) the petitioner is a bona fide purchaser for value of the right, title, or interest in the property and was at the time of purchase reasonably without cause to believe that the property was subject to forfeiture under this section;

the court shall amend the order of forfeiture in accordance with its determination.

(7) Following the court's disposition of all petitions filed under this subsection, or if no such petitions are filed following the expiration of the period provided in paragraph (2) for the filing of such petitions, the United States shall have clear title to property that is the subject of the order of forfeiture and may warrant good title to any subsequent purchaser or transferee.

(m) If any of the property described in subsection (a), as a result of any act or omission of the defendant—

(1) cannot be located upon the exercise of due diligence;

(2) has been transferred or sold to, or deposited with, a third party;

(3) has been placed beyond the jurisdiction of the court;

(4) has been substantially diminished in value; or

(5) has been commingled with other property which cannot be divided without difficulty;

the court shall order the forfeiture of any other property of the defendant up to the value of any property described in paragraphs (1) through (5).

Sec. 1964. Civil Remedies

(a) The district courts of the United States shall have jurisdiction to prevent and restrain violations of section 1962 of this Act by issuing appropriate orders, including, but not limited to: ordering any person to divest himself of any interest, direct or indirect, in any enterprise; imposing reasonable restrictions on the future activities or investments of any person, including, but not limited to, prohibiting any person from engaging in the same type of endeavor as the enterprise engaged in, the activities of which affect interstate or foreign commerce; or ordering dissolution or reorganization of any enterprise, making due provision for the rights of innocent persons.

(b) The Attorney General may institute proceedings under this section. Pending final determination thereof, the court may at any time enter such restraining orders or prohibitions, or take such other actions, including the acceptance of satisfactory performance bonds, as it shall deem proper.

(c) Any person injured in his business or property by reason of a violation of section 1962 of this Act may sue therefor in any appropriate United States district court and shall recover threefold the damages he sustains and the cost of the suit, including a reasonable attorney's fee, except that no person may rely upon any conduct that would have been actionable as fraud in the purchase or sale of securities to establish a violation of section 1962. The exception contained in the preceding sentence does not apply to an action against any person that is criminally convicted in connection with the fraud, in which case the statute of limitations shall start to run on the date on which the conviction becomes final.

(d) A final judgment or decree rendered in favor of the United States in any criminal proceeding brought by the United States under this chapter shall estop the defendant from denying the essential allegations of the criminal offense in any subsequent civil proceeding brought by the United States.

Sec. 1965. Venue and Process

(a) Any civil action or proceeding under this Act against any person may be instituted in the district court of the United States for any district in which such person resides, is found, has an agent, or transacts his affairs.

(b) In any action under section 1964 of this Act in any district court of the United States in which it is shown that the ends of justice require that other parties residing in any other district be brought before the court, the court may cause such parties to be summoned, and process for that purpose may be served in any judicial district of the United States by the marshal thereof.

(c)   In any civil or criminal action or proceeding instituted by the United States under this chapter in the district court of the United States for any judicial district, subpenas issued by such court to compel the attendance of witnesses may be served in any other judicial district, except that in any civil action or proceeding no such subpena shall be issued for service upon any individual who resides in another district at a place more than one hundred miles from the place at which such court is held without approval given by a judge of such court upon a showing of good cause.

(d)   All other process in any action or proceeding under this Act may be served on any person in any judicial district in which such person resides, is found, has an agent, or transacts his affairs.

Sec. 1966.   Expedition of Actions

In any civil action instituted under this chapter by the United States in any district court of the United States, the Attorney General may file with the clerk of such court a certificate stating that in his opinion the case is of general public importance. A copy of that certificate shall be furnished immediately by such clerk to the chief judge or in his absence to the presiding district judge of the district in which such action is pending. Upon receipt of such copy, such judge shall designate immediately a judge of that district to hear and determine action.

Sec. 1967.   Evidence

In any proceeding ancillary to or in any civil action instituted by the United States under this chapter the proceedings may be open or closed to the public at the discretion of the court after consideration of the rights of affected persons.

Sec. 1968.   Civil Investigative Demand

(a)   Whenever the Attorney General has reason to believe that any person or enterprise may be in possession, custody, or control of any documentary materials relevant to a racketeering investigation, he may, prior to the institution of a civil or criminal proceeding thereon, issue in writing, and cause to be served upon such person, a civil investigative demand requiring such person to produce such material for examination.

(b)   Each such demand shall—

(1)   state the nature of the conduct constituting the alleged racketeering violation which is under investigation and the provision of law applicable thereto;

(2)   describe the class or classes of documentary material produced thereunder with such definiteness and certainty as to permit such material to be fairly identified;

(3)   state that the demand is returnable forthwith or prescribe a return date which will provide a reasonable period of time within which the material so demanded may be assembled and made available for inspection and copying or reproduction; and

(4)   identify the custodian to whom such material shall be made available.

(c)   No such demand shall—

(1)   contain any requirement which would be held to be unreasonable if contained in a subpena duces tecum issued by a court of the United States in aid of a grand jury investigation of such alleged racketeering violation; or

(2)   require the production of any documentary evidence which would be privileged from disclosure if demanded by a subpena duces tecum issued by a court of the United States in aid of a grand jury investigation of such alleged racketeering violation.

(d)   Service of any such demand or any petition filed under this section may be made upon a person by—

(1)   delivering a duly executed copy thereof to any partner, executive officer, managing agent, or general agent thereof, or to any agent thereof authorized by appointment or by law to receive service of process on behalf of such person, or upon any individual person;

1884

(2)   delivering a duly executed copy thereof to the principal office or place of business of the person to be served; or

(3)   depositing such copy in the United States mail, by registered or certified mail duly addressed to such person at its principal office or place of business.

(e)   A verified return by the individual serving any such demand or petition setting forth the manner of such service shall be prima facie proof of such service. In the case of service by registered or certified mail, such return shall be accompanied by the return post office receipt of delivery of such demand.

(f)(1)   The Attorney General shall designate a racketeering investigator to serve as racketeer document custodian, and such additional racketeering investigators as he shall determine from time to time to be necessary to serve as deputies to such officer.

(2)   Any person upon whom any demand issued under this section has been duly served shall make such material available for inspection and copying or reproduction to the custodian designated therein at the principal place of business of such person, or at such other place as such custodian and such person thereafter may agree and prescribe in writing or as the court may direct, pursuant to this section on the return date specified in such demand, or on such later date as such custodian may prescribe in writing. Such person may upon written agreement between such person and the custodian substitute for copies of all or any part of such material originals thereof.

(3)   The custodian to whom any documentary material is so delivered shall take physical possession thereof, and shall be responsible for the use made thereof and for the return thereof pursuant to this chapter. The custodian may cause the preparation of such copies of such documentary material as may be required for official use under regulations which shall be promulgated by the Attorney General. While in the possession of the custodian, no material so produced shall be available for examination, without the consent of the person who produced such material, by any individual other than the Attorney General. Under such reasonable terms and conditions as the Attorney General shall prescribe, documentary material while in the possession of the custodian shall be available for examination by the person who produced such material or any duly authorized representatives of such person.

(4)   Whenever any attorney has been designated to appear on behalf of the United States before any court or grand jury in any case or proceeding involving any alleged violation of this chapter, the custodian may deliver to such attorney such documentary material in the possession of the custodian as such attorney determines to be required for use in the presentation of such case or proceeding on behalf of the United States. Upon the conclusion of any such case or proceeding, such attorney shall return to the custodian any documentary material so withdrawn which has not passed into the control of such court or grand jury through the introduction thereof into the record of such case or proceeding.

(5)   Upon the completion of—

(i)   the racketeering investigation for which any documentary material was produced under this Act, and

(ii)   any case or proceeding arising from such investigation,

the custodian shall return to the person who produced such material all such material other than copies thereof made by the Attorney General pursuant to this subsection which has not passed into the control of any court or grand jury through the introduction thereof into the record of such case or proceeding.

(6)   When any documentary material has been produced by any person under this section for use in any racketeering investigation, and no such case or proceeding arising therefrom has been instituted within a reasonable time after completion of the examination and analysis of all evidence assembled in the course of such investigation, such person shall be entitled, upon written demand made upon the Attorney General, to the return of all documentary material other than copies thereof made pursuant to this subsection so produced by such person.

(7)   In the event of the death, disability, or separation from service of the custodian of any documentary material produced under any demand issued under this section or the official relief of

such custodian from responsibility for the custody and control of such material, the Attorney General shall promptly—

        (i)　designate another racketeering investigator to serve as custodian thereof, and

        (ii)　transmit notice in writing to the person who produced such material as to the identity and address of the successor so designated.

Any successor so designated shall have with regard to such materials all duties and responsibilities imposed by this section upon his predecessor in office with regard thereto, except that he shall not be held responsible for any default or dereliction which occurred before his designation as custodian.

    (g)　Whenever any person fails to comply with any civil investigative demand duly served upon him under this section or whenever satisfactory copying or reproduction of any such material cannot be done and such person refuses to surrender such material, the Attorney General may file, in the district court of the United States for any judicial district in which such person resides, is found, or transacts business, and serve upon such person a petition for an order of such court for the enforcement of this section, except that if such person transacts business in more than one such district such petition shall be filed in the district in which such person maintains his principal place of business, or in such other district in which such person transacts business as may be agreed upon by the parties to such petition.

    (h)　Within twenty days after the service of any such demand upon any person, or at any time before the return date specified in the demand, whichever period is shorter, such person may file, in the district court of the United States for the judicial district within which such person resides, is found, or transacts business, and serve upon such custodian a petition for an order of such court modifying or setting aside such demand. The time allowed for compliance with the demand in whole or in part as deemed proper and ordered by the court shall not run during the pendency of such petition in the court. Such petition shall specify each ground upon which the petitioner relies in seeking such relief, and may be based upon any failure of such demand to comply with the provisions of this section or upon any constitutional or other legal right or privilege of such person.

    (i)　At any time during which any custodian is in custody or control of any documentary material delivered by any person in compliance with any such demand, such person may file, in the district court of the United States for the judicial district within which the office of such custodian is situated, and serve upon such custodian a petition for an order of such court requiring the performance by such custodian of any duty imposed upon him by this section.

    (j)　Whenever any petition is filed in any district court of the United States under this section, such court shall have jurisdiction to hear and determine the matter so presented, and to enter such order or orders as may be required to carry into effect the provisions of this section.

BANKRUPTCY ACT

(Excerpts)

Obtaining Credit

Sec. 364. (a) If the trustee is authorized to operate the business of the debtor under section 721, 1108, 1203, 1204, or 1304 of this Act, unless the court orders otherwise, the trustee may obtain unsecured credit and incur unsecured debt in the ordinary course of business allowable under section 503(b)(1) of this Act as an administrative expense.

(b) The court, after notice and a hearing, may authorize the trustee to obtain unsecured credit or to incur unsecured debt other than under subsection (a) of this section, allowable under section 503(b)(1) of this Act as an administrative expense.

(c) If the trustee is unable to obtain unsecured credit allowable under section 503(b)(1) of this Act as an administrative expense, the court, after notice and a hearing, may authorize the obtaining of credit or the incurring of debt—

(1) with priority over any or all administrative expenses of the kind specified in section 503(b) or 507(b) of this Act;

(2) secured by a lien on property of the estate that is not otherwise subject to a lien; or

(3) secured by a junior lien on property of the estate that is subject to a lien.

(d)(1) The court, after notice and a hearing, may authorize the obtaining of credit or the incurring of debt secured by a senior or equal lien on property of the estate that is subject to a lien only if—

(A) the trustee is unable to obtain such credit otherwise; and

(B) there is adequate protection of the interest of the holder of the lien on the property of the estate on which such senior or equal lien is proposed to be granted.

(2) In any hearing under this subsection, the trustee has the burden of proof on the issue of adequate protection.

(e) The reversal or modification on appeal of an authorization under this section to obtain credit or incur debt, or of a grant under this section of a priority or a lien, does not affect the validity of any debt so incurred, or any priority or lien so granted, to an entity that extended such credit in good faith, whether or not such entity knew of the pendency of the appeal, unless such authorization and the incurring of such debt, or the granting of such priority or lien, were stayed pending appeal.

(f) Except with respect to an entity that is an underwriter as defined in section 1145(b) of this Act, section 5 of the Securities Act of 1933, the Trust Indenture Act of 1939, and any State or local law requiring registration for offer or sale of a security or registration or licensing of an issuer of, underwriter of, or broker or dealer in, a security does not apply to the offer or sale under this section of a security that is not an equity security.

Postpetition Disclosure and Solicitation

Sec. 1125. (a) In this section—

(1) "adequate information" means information of a kind, and in sufficient detail, as far as is reasonably practicable in light of the nature and history of the debtor and the condition of the debtor's books and records, including a discussion of the potential material Federal tax consequences of the

plan to the debtor, any successor to the debtor, and such a hypothetical investor in the case, that would enable a hypothetical reasonable investor typical of holders of claims or interests of the relevant class to make an informed judgment about the plan, but adequate information need not include such information about any other possible or proposed plan, and in determining whether a disclosure statement provides adequate information, the court shall consider the complexity of the case, the benefit of additional information to creditors and other parties in interest, and the cost of providing additional information; and

(2)   "investor typical of holders of claims or interests of the relevant class" means investor having—

(A)   a claim or interest of the relevant class;

(B)   such a relationship with the debtor as the holders of other claims or interests of such class generally have; and

(C)   such ability to obtain such information from sources other than the disclosure required by this section as holders of claims or interests in such class generally have.

(b)   An acceptance or rejection of a plan may not be solicited after the commencement of the case under this Act from a holder of a claim or interest with respect to such claim or interest, unless, at the time of or before such solicitation, there is transmitted to such holder the plan or a summary of the plan, and a written disclosure statement approved, after notice and a hearing, by the court as containing adequate information. The court may approve a disclosure statement without a valuation of the debtor or an appraisal of the debtor's assets.

(c)   The same disclosure statement shall be transmitted to each holder of a claim or interest of a particular class, but there may be transmitted different disclosure statements, differing in amount, detail, or kind of information, as between classes.

(d)   Whether a disclosure statement required under subsection (b) of this section contains adequate information is not governed by any otherwise applicable nonbankruptcy law, rule, or regulation, but an agency or official whose duty is to administer or enforce such a law, rule, or regulation may be heard on the issue of whether a disclosure statement contains adequate information. Such an agency or official may not appeal from, or otherwise seek review of, an order approving a disclosure statement.

(e)   A person that solicits acceptance or rejection of a plan, in good faith and in compliance with the applicable provisions of this title, or that participates, in good faith and in compliance with the applicable provisions of this title, in the offer, issuance, sale, or purchase of a security, offered or sold under the plan, of the debtor, of an affiliate participating in a joint plan with the debtor, or of a newly organized successor to the debtor under the plan, is not liable, on account of such solicitation or participation, for violation of any applicable law, rule, or regulation governing solicitation of acceptance or rejection of a plan or the offer, issuance, sale, or purchase of securities.

(f)   Notwithstanding subsection (b), in a small business case—

(1)   the court may determine that the plan itself provides adequate information and that a separate disclosure statement is not necessary;

(2)   the court may approve a disclosure statement submitted on standard forms approved by the court or adopted under section 2075 of title 28; and

(3)(A)   the court may conditionally approve a disclosure statement subject to final approval after notice and a hearing;

(B)   acceptances and rejections of a plan may be solicited based on a conditionally approved disclosure statement if the debtor provides adequate information to each holder of a claim or interest that is solicited, but a conditionally approved disclosure statement shall be mailed not later than 25 days before the date of the hearing on confirmation of the plan; and

(C)   the hearing on the disclosure statement may be combined with the hearing on confirmation of a plan.

(g)   Notwithstanding subsection (b), an acceptance or rejection of the plan may be solicited from a holder of a claim or interest if such solicitation complies with applicable nonbankruptcy law and if such holder was solicited before the commencement of the case in a with applicable nonbankruptcy law.

Exemption From Securities Laws

Sec. 1145.   (a)   Except with respect to an entity that is an underwriter as defined in subsection (b) of this section, section 5 of the Securities Act of 1933 and any State or local law requiring registration for offer or sale of a security or registration or licensing of an issuer of, underwriter of, or broker or dealer in, a security do not apply to—

(1)   the offer or sale under a plan of a security of the debtor, of an affiliate participating in a joint plan with the debtor, or of a successor to the debtor under the plan—

(A)   in exchange for a claim against, an interest in, or a claim for an administrative expense in the case concerning, the debtor or such affiliate; or

(B)   principally in such exchange and partly for cash or property;

(2)   the offer of a security through any warrant, option, right to subscribe, or conversion privilege that was sold in the manner specified in paragraph (1) of this subsection, or the sale of a security upon the exercise of such a warrant, option, right, or privilege;

(3)   the offer or sale, other than under a plan, of a security of an issuer other than the debtor or an affiliate, if—

(A)   such security was owned by the debtor on the date of the filing of the petition;

(B)   the issuer of such security is—

(i)   required to file reports under section 13 or 15(d) of the Securities Exchange Act of 1934; and

(ii)   in compliance with the disclosure and reporting provision of such applicable section; and

(C)   such offer or sale is of securities that do not exceed—

(i)   during the two-year period immediately following the date of the filing of the petition, four percent of the securities of such class outstanding on such date; and

(ii)   during any 180-day period following such two-year period, one percent of the securities outstanding at the beginning of such 180-day period; or

(4)   a transaction by a stockbroker in a security that is executed after a transaction of a kind specified in paragraph (1) or (2) of this subsection in such security and before the expiration of 40 days after the first date on which such security was bona fide offered to the public by the issuer or by or through an underwriter, if such stockbroker provides, at the time of or before such transaction by such a stockbroker, a disclosure statement approved under section 1125 of this Act, and, if the court orders, information supplementing such disclosure statement.

(b)(1)   Except as provided in paragraph (2) of this subsection, and except with respect to ordinary trading transactions of an entity that is not an issuer, an entity is an underwriter under section 2(a)(11) of the Securities Act of 1933, if such entity—

(A)   purchases a claim against, interest in, or claim for an administrative expense in the case concerning the debtor, if such purchase is with a view to distribution of any security received or to be received in exchange for such a claim or interest;

(B)   offers to sell securities offered or sold under the plan for the holders of such securities;

(C)   offers to buy securities offered or sold under the plan from the holders of such securities, if such offer to buy is—

(i)   with a view to distribution of such securities; and

(ii)   under an agreement made in connection with the plan, with the consummation of the plan, or with the offer or sale of securities under the plan; or

(D)   is an issuer, as used in such section 2(a)(11), with respect to such securities.

(2)   An entity is not an underwriter under section 2(a)(11) of the Securities Act of 1933 or under paragraph (1) of this subsection with respect to an agreement that provides only for—

(A)(i)   the matching or combining of fractional interests in securities offered or sold under the plan into whole interests; or

(ii)   the purchase or sale of such fractional interests from or to entities receiving such fractional interests under the plan; or

(B)   the purchase or sale for such entities of such fractional or whole interests as are necessary to adjust for any remaining fractional interests after such matching.

(3)   An entity other than an entity of the kind specified in paragraph (1) of this subsection is not an underwriter under section 2(a)(11) of the Securities Act of 1933 with respect to any securities offered or sold to such entity in the manner specified in subsection (a)(1) of this section.

(c)   An offer or sale of securities of the kind and in the manner specified under subsection (a)(1) of this section is deemed to be a public offering.

(d)   The Trust Indenture Act of 1939 does not apply to a note issued under the plan that matures not later than one year after the effective date of the plan.

INDEX

References are to Section and Rule

NOTE: This Index is not intended to be all-inclusive, rather it is designed to direct the user to the more important provisions of the statutes and rules.

Key

IAA = Investment Advisers Act of 1940

ICA = Investment Company Act of 1940

RICO= Racketeer Influenced and Corrupt Organizations Act

Rules= Securities and Exchange Commission Rules

SA = Securities Act of 1933

SEA = Securities Exchange Act of 1934

ACCELERATION OF EFFECTIVE DATE
Generally, SA § 8(a), SA Rule 461

ACCOUNTANTS
Audit requirements, SEA § 10A
Civil liabilities, SA § 11
Foreign Corrupt Practices Act, SEA § 13(b)(2)
Practice before the SEC, SEC Rules of Practice § 2(e)

ACCREDITED INVESTOR
Defined, SA § 2(a)(15), SA Rules 215, 501(a)
Transactions Involving, SA §§ 4(a)(5), 4(a)(7), SA Rules 505, 506

ADMINISTRATIVE PROCEEDINGS
Bar orders, SEA § 15(c)(4), IAA § 203(e)(6)
Cease and desist, SA § 8A, SEA § 21C, IAA § 203(k)(1), ICA § 9(f)
Civil penalties, SEA § 21B, IAA § 203(1), ICA § 9(d), (e)
Securities and Exchange Commission, SEA §§ 21C, 22, Rules of Practice

AFFILIATE
See, also, Investment Companies, Affiliated persons
Defined, SA Rule 501, SEA Rule 12b–1

ALL-OR-NONE OFFERINGS
Manipulation, SEA Rules 10b–9, 15c2–4

ANALYSTS, RESEARCH
Certification, Regulation AC

ANNUAL REPORT TO SHAREHOLDERS
Generally, SEA Rules 13a–1—13a–2, 14a–3(b), SEA & Form 10K, 10K–5B

ANTI-FRAUD PROVISIONS
Generally, SA §§ 12(a)(2), 17(a), SEA §§ 10(b), 14(e), 18(a), SEA Rules 10b–5, 14a–9

ARBITRAGE
Short-swing profits, SEA § 16(e), SEA Rule 16e–1

AT MARKET OFFERINGS
Stabilization prohibited, Regulation M

ATTORNEYS
Admission to practice before SEC, SEC Rules of Practice 2(e)
Attorneys fees, SA § 11(e)

AUDITORS
Generally, SEA § 10A
Independence, SEA § 10A
Oversight Board, Sarbanes-Oxley Act, § 101

BANKS
Brokerage activities, SEA § 15
Defined, SEA § 3(a)(6), IAA § 202(a)(2), ICA § 2(a)(5)
Exempt securities, SA § 3(a)(2)
Government Securities Dealers, SEA § 15C
Municipal Securities Dealers, SEA § 15B

BAR ORDERS
Generally, SEA §§ 15(c)(4), 21(d)(2)

BENEFICIAL OWNERSHIP
Five-percent ownership reporting requirements, SEA § 13(d), SEA Rules 13d–1—13d–7, Schedule 13D
Insider reporting requirements, SEA § 16(a), SEA Rules 16a–1—16a–11
Ten-percent beneficial ownership.
  Liability for short-swing profits, SEA § 16(b), SEA Rules 16b–1 et seq.
  Reporting requirements, SEA § 16(a), SEA Rules 16a–1 et seq.

BESPEAKS CAUTION
Generally SA § 27A, SEA § 21E(d)

BROKER-DEALERS
Associate Persons, defined, SEA Rule 3a4–1
Broker, defined, SEA § 3(a)(4), IAA § 202(a)(3), ICA § 2(a)(6)
Confirmation of sales of securities, SEA Rule 10b–10
Dealer, defined, SA § 2(a)(12), SEA § 3(a)(5), IAA § 202(a)(7), ICA § 2(a)(11)
Exempt transactions (Securities Act of 1933), SA §§ 4(a)(3), 4(a)(4)
Exemptions from registration as, SEA § 15
Government securities dealers, SEA § 15C
Manipulation, SEA §§ 9, 15(c)
Margin Requirements, SEA § 7, Federal Reserve Regulations G, T, U, X
Municipal securities dealers, SEA § 15B
Net capital rule, SEA Rule 15c3–1
Penny stocks, SEA §§ 3(a)(51), 15(b)(6), 15(g), 17B, SEA Rules 15g–1 et seq.
Price quotations, SEA Rules 15c2–7, 15c2–11
Prospectus delivery requirements, SA § 5, SA Rules 153–153b, 174

INDEX

INDEX